Universal Technological Dictionary: Or, Familiar Explanations of the Terms Used in All Arts and Sciences

George Crabb

Nabu Public Domain Reprints:

You are holding a reproduction of an original work published before 1923 that is in the public domain in the United States of America, and possibly other countries. You may freely copy and distribute this work as no entity (individual or corporate) has a copyright on the body of the work. This book may contain prior copyright references, and library stamps (as most of these works were scanned from library copies). These have been scanned and retained as part of the historical artifact.

This book may have occasional imperfections such as missing or blurred pages, poor pictures, errant marks, etc. that were either part of the original artifact, or were introduced by the scanning process. We believe this work is culturally important, and despite the imperfections, have elected to bring it back into print as part of our continuing commitment to the preservation of printed works worldwide. We appreciate your understanding of the imperfections in the preservation process, and hope you enjoy this valuable book.

UNIVERSAL
TECHNOLOGICAL DICTIONARY

OR

FAMILIAR EXPLANATION

OF THE TERMS

USED IN

ALL ARTS AND SCIENCES,

CONTAINING

DEFINITIONS DRAWN FROM THE ORIGINAL WRITERS,

AND ILLUSTRATED BY PLATES, DIAGRAMS, CUTS, &C.

BY GEORGE CRABB, AM.

AUTHOR OF ENGLISH SYNONYMES EXPLAINED.

IN TWO VOLUMES.

VOL. I.

LONDON:
PRINTED FOR BALDWIN, CRADOCK, AND JOY, PATERNOSTER-ROW,
BY C. BALDWIN, NEW BRIDGE-STREET.

1823.

Crabb, (Geo.) *Well-known Author of English Synonymes Explained*, UNIVERSAL TECHNOLOGICAL DICTIONARY, or familiar explanation of the terms used in all arts and sciences, with definitions drawn from the original writers, 2 vols, 4to, calf, a sound copy, 1.75, London, 1823. 209

IN ADDITION TO HUNDREDS OF ILLUSTRATIONS in the text, THIS EXCELLENT WORK has 60 engraved plates including illustrations of heraldry, ichthyology, ornithology and natural history generally, architecture, anatomy, botany, conchology, entomology, coins, etc.

PREFACE.

As this work differs in many material points from anything which has hitherto been offered to the public, a few observations may be deemed necessary to explain the views of the Compiler with regard to his plan, and the execution of it.

To present the curious reader with a clue for understanding every subject which may incidentally come before his notice was one of his primary objects; and, next to this, he proposed to himself to furnish the inquirer with the means of extending his knowledge as far as he pleased. For the attainment of the first object, he has made his selection of words as copious as possible; and, at the same time, by consulting brevity in his definitions, has endeavoured to keep the work within a convenient size. In the catalogue of words there may possibly be some so obsolete, or grown out of use, and others so modern, or come so little into use, that they may rarely, if ever, be called for by any class of readers: but, as they occur in the writings of those who have acquired an authority or a name, the Compiler did not feel himself justified in rejecting such words, according to his own private opinion. But, in regard to the extent of the definitions and explanations to be given under each head, he had no other rule to follow than his own judgment. Considering himself in the character of a general reader, he looked upon every thing that was necessary to illustrate the meaning and application of technical terms as essential to be admitted into this work; and, on the other hand, whatever did not immediately answer this end, he regarded as irrelevant. The only deviation from this plan will be found under the Synopses of the Sciences, where, to preserve a connection between the different parts of any science, something more than the simple terminology has been occasionally introduced.

As this work is compiled for the use of readers of all descriptions, it is very natural to expect that many will be disappointed at not finding their favourite study more largely discanted upon, and will be apt to charge this omission upon the inadvertence of the compiler; but a moment's reflection will convince every candid reader, that to make a consistent work, suited to the object proposed, it was essential for him to pursue one uniform rule throughout. To have given copious details on any particular science would have justly subjected him to the charge of having capriciously deviated from his plan; but to have entered equally at large into all the sciences, would have been to make a work totally different from the one proposed. Nothing remained, therefore, but, by following one uniform plan, to comprehend whatever would be most generally useful. It was presumed that no one would refer to a work of this kind for information on a subject in which he was a proficient; but, as few persons are perfectly versed in more than one art or science, they will of course find it serviceable to refer to on subjects with which they are less familiar; and those who wish for more information than what it immediately affords, may gratify their curiosity by consulting the original authors referred to in the body, and at the end, of the Dictionary; by the insertion of which, the Compiler's second principal object has been attained.

It would have been very agreeable to him, if, in every instance, he could have rendered his definitions and explanations correct and distinct; but, owing to the scanty information to be derived from ancient sources, and the vague, fluctuating, and often contradictory representations of modern writers, he has not been enabled always to succeed to the extent of his wishes. In some sciences, as Chemistry, both the nomenclature of the science, and the science itself, are subject to such changes, as to render the most general statements necessary in order to guard against falling into contradictions: in Botany, and other branches of Natural History, writers have made so free with the nomenclature, by coining terms of their own, that they have involved the whole in a labyrinth of words, from which no one could extricate himself, but by adopting some such course as that which has been pursued throughout this work,— of translating all the synonymous appellations of different writers into one language, like that of Linnæus, which has justly acquired a higher degree of authority than that of any other writer of the same date. The Compiler feels it, however, necessary to add, that he has made these remarks less with a view of casting a censure on others, than of pointing out the difficulties to which he himself has been exposed.

There is one more particular, in respect to the plan of this work, which may demand some explanation in order to guard against disappointment; namely, that, although this work professes to embrace the whole circle of the Arts and Sciences, yet the proper names of particular persons and places are excluded from the number, on the ground that they admit of description rather than definition, and are, therefore, more fitted for an Historical than a Technological Dictionary. But the names of communities, sects, &c. were not considered of this sort; because, being given on the ground of some general principle, or common property, they admitted of a precise explanation like other common names.

PREFACE.

vii

Although the Compiler has thought proper to say thus much by way of explanation, he is far from supposing that, in a work of this magnitude and multifarious nature, there are not oversights and inaccuracies which will call for the indulgence of the reader; but he trusts that no error has been suffered to escape the press which can materially affect the sense, or diminish the usefulness, of the work.

For the purpose of preserving an orderly arrangement, and assisting the reader in finding the particular application of any word, each definition has been headed by the name of the science to which it belongs, put in an abbreviated form; of which the following is an explanation:—

LIST OF ABBREVIATIONS.

AGRIC.	Agriculture.	DIAL.	Dialling.	MECH.	Mechanics, or Mechanic Arts.
ALCH.	Alchemy.	DIOPT.	Dioptrics.		
ALGEB.	Algebra.	ECC.	Ecclesiastical History.	MED.	Medicine.
ANAT.	Anatomy.	ELEC.	Electricity.	MET.	Metaphysics.
ANT.	Antiquities.	ENT.	Entomology.	METAL.	Metallurgy.
ARCHÆOL.	Archæology, or Antiquities of the Middle Ages.	ETH.	Ethics.	MIL.	Military Affairs.
		FALCON.	Falconry.	MIN.	Mineralogy.
		FLUX.	Fluxions.	MUS.	Music.
ARCHER.	Archery.	FORT.	Fortification.	MYTH.	Mythology.
ARCHIT.	Architecture.	GEOG.	Geography.	NAT.	Natural History.
ARITH.	Arithmetic.	GEOM.	Geometry.	NUMIS.	Numismatics.
ASTROL.	Astrology.	GRAM.	Grammar.	OPT.	Optics.
ASTRON.	Astronomy.	HER.	Heraldry.	ORN.	Ornithology.
BIBL.	Biblical Subjects.	HORT.	Horticulture.	PALM.	Palmistry.
BOT.	Botany.	HUSBAND.	Husbandry.	PER.	Perspective.
CARP.	Carpentry.	HYD.	Hydrostatics.	PHY.	Physics.
CATOP.	Catoptrics.	ICH.	Ichthyology.	POET.	Poetics.
CHEM.	Chemistry.	LAW	Law.	POLIT.	Political Concerns.
CHRON.	Chronology.	LOG.	Logic.	PRINT.	Printing.
COM.	Commerce.	MAG.	Magic Arts.	RHET.	Rhetoric.
CON.	Conchology.	MAN.	Manege.	SPORT.	Sports.
CONIC.	Conic Sections.	MAR.	Marine Affairs.	THEOL.	Theology.
COOK.	Cookery.	MASON.	Masonry.	VET.	Veterinary Art.
CUS.	Customs.	MATH.	Mathematics.	ZOOL.	Zoology.

ERRATA.

ANATOMY, Plate No. I. (9),   *read*   No. I. (7).
Ditto ...... Ditto No. II. (10) —— No. II. (8).
In the reference to the Plate of Printing (56), fig. 5, referring to the *Press*, should be 6.
ASTRONOMY; the Satellites of Saturn are five in number, &c... } *read* the Satellites of Saturn are seven in number.
AURUM, Gold, the heaviest of all metals .... } —— the heaviest of all the metals *except Platina*.
BELUEDERE .... —— BELVEDERE.

There are also some inaccuracies in the Greek accentuation in the former part of the work, which unfortunately escaped the press; but, being of a nature not the least calculated to mislead any who take an interest in this part of the subject, it has not been deemed necessary to notice them as Errata.

N.B. *The Binder will place Plates 1 to 36 inclusive at the end of the first volume, in their numerical order, and Plates 37 to 60 at the end of the second in like manner.*

UNIVERSAL

TECHNOLOGICAL DICTIONARY.

A.

A, the first letter of the alphabet, is used either as a word, an abbreviation, or a sign.

A (*Bibl.*) for α, *alpha*, is used in the Revelations of St. John, for the beginning or first; and ω, *omega*, for the end or last.

A (*Ant.*) as a preposition, was employed to signify an office or situation; as,

A *libellis*, he who received all the petitions addressed to the prince: "Epaphroditum *a libellis*, capitali poena condemnavit." *Suet. Domit.* c. 14. Also on an inscription by Gruterus. D. M. QUADRATO. SCRINIANO. A. LIBELLIS. CLAUDIA. TRYPHERA. FECIT. *Divino Monitu Quadrato Scriniano a libellis Claudia Tryphera fecit.*

A *manu*, i. e. *servus a manu*; a scribe or amanuensis. "Thallo *a manu*, crura effregit." *Suet. Aug.* c. 67. Also on an inscription. QUINTAE. GAM. MARTIAE. N. L. F. AN. VI. ATTICUS. A. MANU. SPONSUS. LOC. D. EX. D. D. *Quintæ Gamiæ Martiæ Numerii Lucii filiæ anno VI Atticus a manu sponsus Locus datus ex decreto Decurionis.*

A *memoriâ*, he who dictated the answers of the emperor to petitions, &c. as Festus did for Antoninus, according to Herodian: "Ὁ τῆς δὴ βασιλέως μνήμης προϊσὼς, qui erat imperatori à memoriâ." *Herod.* l. 4, c. 14.

A *pedibus*, a running footman, who attended his master wherever he went: "Pollucem servum *a pedibus* mecum Romam misi." *Cic. ad Atticum*, lib. 8, ep. 5.

A *rationibus*, he who acted as house steward, by keeping the private accounts, &c. "Ante omnes Pallantem *a rationibus* suspexit." *Suet. Claud.* c. 28.

A *studiis*, he who managed the literary pursuits of his master: "Super hos Polybium *a studiis* suspexit." *Suet. Claud.* c. 28. Also on an inscription. TI. CLAUDIUS. LEMNUS. DIVI. CLAUDII. AUGUSTI. LIB. A. STUDIIS. *Titus Claudius Lemnus divi Claudii Augusti libertus a studiis.*

A *voluptatibus*, he who catered for the pleasures of the prince: an office first appointed by Tiberius, according to Suetonius. [For similar examples, vide *Mari. Smet. Inscription.; Gruter. Inscription. Vet.; Goltz. Thesaur.; Spon. Miscell. Antiq.*]

A, as an abbreviation [vide *Abbreviation*] was employed by the Romans on different occasions. 1. By the judges, who, in passing sentence, threw tablets into a box or urn containing the letter A, for *absolvo*, I acquit, if they aquitted the accused: hence this letter is called by Cicero, *litera salutaris*, a salutary or saving letter: but if they condemned the person, they employed the letter C, for *condemno*, I condemn, hence styled *litera tristis*, the sad letter: and in dubious cases they used the letters N.L. *non liquet*, it does not appear plain. 2. By the people in repealing of laws, when they used the letter A, for *antiquo*, I reject. 3. On inscriptions, coins, &c.; if Greek, A stood for *Argos, Athens*, &c.; if Roman, for *Augustus, Aulus, Atticus*, &c.: when double it signified *Augusti*: when treble, A. A. A. *auro, argento, ære*; as A. A. A. F. F. *auro, argento, ære, flando, feriundo*. 4. In marking the day, A stood for *ante*, as A.D. *ante diem kalendarum*, before the calends. *Val. Prob. Pet. Diacon. et alii Grammat. Veter.; Goltz. Fasti., Græc., et Thesaurus; Smet. Inscript. Vet.; Vaillant. Numismat. Græc., Numismat. Imperat. Roman. Roman. Famil., et Seleucidarum, &c.; Grut. Thesaur. Inscript. Antiq.; Spanheim. Dissert.; Patin. Imperat. Roman. et Roman. Famil.; Morel. Thesaur.; Gesner. Numis. &c.*

A (*Numis.*) as a sign, stands on Greek coins and inscriptions for πρῶτα, πρῶτος, πρῶτον, denoting propriety and dignity. *Vaill. Numism. Græc.*

A (*Archæol.*) as a sign, was sometimes used for the number of 500; and with a superscription, thus, Ā, for 5000.

A (*Lit.*) stands as an abbreviation for *artium*, in marking University degrees; as, A.M. *artium magister*, master of arts; A.B. *artium baccalaureus*, bachelor of arts.

A (*Chron.*) as an abbreviation, stands commonly for *anno* or *ante*; as, A.C. *ante Christum*, before Christ; A.D. *anno Domini*, the year of our Lord; A.M. *anno mundi*, the year of the world. [vide *Abbreviation*] As a sign, it is used in the Gregorian and Julian calendars for the first of the dominical letters. [vide *Chronology*]

A (*Astron.*) as an abbreviation, stands for *ante*, to mark the time of day; as, A.M. *ante meridiem*, before noon or midday, in distinction from P.M. *post meridiem*, afternoon.

A (*Com.*) is employed by merchants as an abbreviation for *accepté*, accepted, on bills of exchange; as, A.S.P. *accepté sous protest*. As a sign in a merchant's accounts, A denoting the first set of books, B the second, &c.

A (*Mus.*) as a preposition, French and Italian, is used in music books. 1. To denote the number of voices, answering to the English *for* before any figure; as à 2, for 2 voices; à 4, for 4 voices, &c. 2. To denote the style of composition and performance; as, *à ballata*, after the manner of a ballad; *à la Grec*, in the Greek style; *à cembalo*, for the harp; &c.

A, as a sign, is used in music books by itself, for the sixth note in the gamut, answering to the monosyllable *la*, contrived by Guido Aretino.

A *above G gamut* signifies the note one tone higher than G gamut.

A *above the bass cliff*, the note a third higher than the bass cliff.

A *above the treble cliff*, the next note higher than the treble cliff.

A (*Algeb.*) as a sign, stands for the known quantity; as, *a, b, c*, in distinction from the unknown quantities *x, y, z*. [vide *Algebra*]

A (*Her.*) as a sign, stands for the *dexter chief*, or chief point in an escutcheon. [vide *Heraldry*]

A (*Chem.*) when treble, as A.A.A. denotes *amalgama*, or amalgamation.

A (*Log.*) is employed as a sign to denote an universal affirmative proposition, according to the verse,

Asserit A, negat E, verum generaliter ambæ.

Thus in the first mood, a syllogism consisting of three universal propositions, is said to be in *bArbArA*, the A thrice repeated denoting three universal propositions. [vide *Logic*]

A (*Gram.*) in words of Greek derivation, as a preposition in composition, has a privative or negative sense; as *acatalectic*, &c.; in Saxon words it is equivalent to *on* or *in*, as *ashore, abed*, &c.

A (*Med.*) marked thus, Ā, is used in prescriptions for the Greek preposition ἀνὰ, each, as Ā, or Ā.Æ.P. of each, i. e. of each ingredient, equal parts.

A (*Alch.*) i. e. *α, alpha*, stands for the restitution of a long life, *ω, omega*, for the end.

AABA'N (*Chem.*) lead.

AA'M (*Com.*) a liquid measure at Amsterdam, containing about sixty-three pounds Avoirdupois weight.

AA'NES (*Mus.*) the modes and tones of the modern Greeks.

AAVO'RA (*Bot.*) a species of palm.

AB (*Ant.*), as a preposition, is employed with nouns to denote a relation, office, &c. after the same manner as *a* ; as, *ab epistolis*, a scribe or secretary, to be found on inscriptions and elsewhere. SEX. POMPEIUS. SEX. F. FELIX. SEX. POMPEII. AB. EPISTOLIS. *Sextus Pompeius Sexti filius, Felix Sexti Pompeii ab epistolis*. [vide *A*.]

AB (*Archæol.*) as an abbreviation, stands for abbot or abbey, and when affixed to the names of places, it shows, probably, that they belonged to some abbey. *Blount*.

AB (*Chron.*) the fifth month of the Jewish sacred year, and the eleventh of the civil year.

A'BAB (*Mil.*) a sort of militia among the Turks.

ABA'BILO (*My.*) or *Abibil* ; an unknown or fabulous bird, mentioned in the Koran. Said Ben Giabin asserts that it had the beak of a bird and the foot of a dog. *Boch. Hieroz.* l. 6, c. 14.

A'BACA (*Com.*) a sort of hemp or flax, prepared from an Indian plantain.

ABACINA'RE (*Archæol.*) to deprive of one's eyes, particularly by red hot irons, which the Italians call *bacini*.

ABACI'STA (*Archæol.*) λογιστικός, *ratiocinator*, in the East *algorista*, in Italian, *abbachiere*, and *abbachista*; an arithmetician, or one who addicted himself to the study of the abacus. "Abacum certè primus Gebertus a Saracenis capiens regulas dedit, quæ a sudantibus Abacistis vix intelliguntur." *Will. Malmesb. Hist. Angl.* l. 2, c. 10.

ABA'CK (*Mar.*) the situation of the sails of a ship when they are pressed against the masts by the force of the wind; so the sails are said to be *taken aback* when by a change of wind or otherwise they are put into that situation, or *laid aback* to effect an immediate retreat.

A'BACOT (*Archæol.*) a cap of state in the form of a double crown, worn by the ancient kings of England. *Chron. An.* 1463.

ABA'CTOR (*Archæol.*) from *abigo*, to drive away: a stealer of cattle in herds or large numbers, in distinction from the *fur*, or thief, who took one or two. *Isidor. Etymol.* l. 12.

A'BACUS (*Ant.*) from ἄβαξ, ἀβακος, i. e. *α*, priv. and βάσις, not having a basis or stand: 1. A cup-board or board fixed against the wall, on which were placed the cups and vessels for supper. *Juv. Sat.* 3, v. 203.

*Lectus erat Codro Proculâ minor, urceoli sex
Ornamentum abaci.*

Cic. in Verr. l. 4. c. 16 ; *Liv.* l. 39, c. 7 ; *Plin.* l. 37, c. 2 ; *Buleng. de Imperat. Rom.* l. 2, c. 34 ; *Salmas. ad Jus. Attic et Rom.* c. 23. 2. A draught or dice-board, on which the ancients used to play with dice or small stones. *Macrob. Saturn.* l. 5 ; *Stuck. Ant. Conviv.* l. 11, c. 16 ; *Buleng. de Lud. Vet.* c. 58.

ABACUS (*Math.*) Heb. פאב, *abak*. "Mensula hyalini pulveris respersione colorata, in qua calculatores numeros et figuras delineant." *Mart. Capell. de Septem. Lib. Art.* l. 6. *Pers. Sat.* 1, v. 131.

*Nec qui abaco numeros et secto in pulvere metas
Scit risisse vafer.*

The *abacus* was an instrument for calculations, used, with some variations, both by the ancients and moderns, consisting of a board of an oblong figure, divided by several lines or wires, and mounted with an equal number of little ivory balls or pegs, by the arrangement of which they expressed units, tens, hundreds, thousands, &c. according to the subjoined figure.

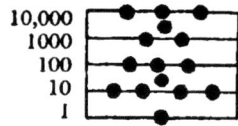

The value of each ball or peg on the lowest line is 1, on the second 10, on the third 100, on the fourth 1000, on the fifth 10,000 ; and the balls in the middle spaces signify half as much as each of those in the lines above them: the amount of all the balls represented in the above figure will, therefore, be 37,391. *Bud. in Pandect.* p. 128 ; *Volaterran. Comm. Urban.* p. 1033 ; *Ferret. Mus. Lapid.* l. 1, *Memor.* 33 ; *Velser. Rer. Vindel.* p. 221 ; *Ful. Ursin. et Ciaccon. in Explic. Inscr. Diullianæ et Lib. de Numm.* ; *Ant. Augustin. Numis. Dial.* 9 ; *Pignor. Comm. de Serv.* p. 339.

ABACUS *Pythagoricus* (*Arith.*) the table of Pythagoras, for the more easy learning of numbers and calculations, similar to our multiplication table.

ABACUS *Logisticus*, a right-angled triangle, whose sides, about the right angle, contain all the numbers from 1 to 60, and its area, the products of each two of the opposite numbers: also called a *canon of sexagesimals*, which is in fact a multiplication table carried to 60 both ways.

ABACUS, also Arithmetic itself, according to Lucas Pacciolus, probably contracted from Arabicus.

ABACUS (*Archit.*) or *Abaciscus*, the upper member of the capital of a column, which serves as a crowning to the whole. The invention is ascribed to Callimachus, a statuary of Athens, who took the idea from an acanthus growing out from a basket covered with a tile, so as to form a kind of scroll after the shape of the tile, whence he made the abacus to be represented by the tile, the acanthus by the volutes, and the basket by the body of the capital. In the Tuscan, Doric, and Ionic orders, the *Abacus* is most commonly square ; but in the Corinthian and Composite orders its figure varies, the four faces being circular, and hollowed inwards, the four corners cut off, as in the annexed figure, where *a b c d* represent a square, equal to the plinth of the base; *a b, b c, c d*, and *a d*, the circular arches, drawn from centres that are the vertices of equilateral triangles: then if the ends of the arches be cut off by the equal lines A B, C D, E F, G H, the figure A B C D E F G H is a section of the abacus. The term abacus is applied to different members by different writers. *Vitruv.* l. 4, c. 1; *Senec. Epist.* 87; *Bald. Lex. Vitruv.*; *Pallad. de Archit.* l. 1, &c.; *Scamoz. dell' Archit. Univ.* Part 2. l. 6, c. 29, &c.

ABACUS (*Mus.*) a key-board or instrument of ancient invention, for dividing the intervals of the octave.

ABACUS *et Palmulæ*, an ancient contrivance, by which the strings of the polyplectra, or many-stringed instruments, were struck with a plectrum made of quills.

ABACUS *Harmonicus*, the structure and disposition of the keys of a musical instrument, either to be touched with the hands or the feet, according to *Kircher*.

ABACUS *Major* (*Min.*) a trough in which the ore is washed. *Agric. de Re. Metal.* l. 8.

A'BADA (*Zool.*) an animal on the coast of Bengal with two horns, one on the forehead, and one on the neck. It is said to be about the size of a fowl, having the tail of an ox, and the mane and head of an horse; but the existence of such an animal is not yet ascertained.

ABA'FT (*Mar.*) the hinder part of a ship; as, *abaft* the main-mast, i. e. nearer to the stern.

ABAFT *the beam*, i. e. the relative situation of an object in some part of the horizon, contained between a line drawn at right angles to the keel, and the point to which the ship's stern is directed.

A'BAGUN (*Or.*) or *the stately abbot*, as its name imports, is an Ethiopian bird, remarkable for its beauty, and for a sort of horn growing on its head, instead of a crest, which has the appearance of a mitre. *Lobo. Relat.* p. 71.

A'BAJOUR (*Archit.*) a sky-light or small sloping aperture, which is made in the walls of prisons and subterraneous buildings for the reception of light.

ABA'ISIR (*Chem.*) another name for Spodium.

ABALIENA'TIO (*Ant.*) *est ejus rei quæ est mancipi, aut traditio alteri nexu*; a sort of alienation, a legal cession or transfer to another of that which one holds in one's own right. The effects called here *res mancipi* were cattle, slaves, and other possessions within the Italian territories. The formula called *traditio nexu* was a formal renunciation either in the presence of a magistrate, or by the ceremony of weights and money in hand. *Cic. Top.* c. 85; *Ulp. Institut.* c. 19; *Augustin. ad Leg.* xii. *Tab.* § 25; *Bud. in Pandect.* p. 26.

ABALIENA'TUS (*Med.*) corrupted; *Membra abalienata*, limbs dead or benumbed. *Celsus*; *Scribonius Largus*.

TO ABA'NDON (*Mil.*) to leave a place to the mercy of an enemy.

ABA'NDONED (*Law*) an epithet for goods knowingly and willingly renounced by the proprietor; also for lands which the sea has retired from and left dry.

ABA'NDONING (*Law*) the voluntary or forcible yielding the possession of goods: if to creditors it is termed *cession*; if in order to be free from the charges to which one is subject by possessing them, it is called *giving up*.

ABA'NDUM (*Archæol.*) *abandonum, res in bannum missa*; in French, *chose abandonnée*: any thing confiscated or proscribed, from the three words *a ban don*, i. e. given to the ban.

A'BANET (*Ant.*) or *Abnet*, אבנט, *αβανιθ*; a girdle that priests wore among the Jews.

ABA'NGA (*Bot.*) or *Palma Ady*; a species of palm-tree in the island of St. Thomas. *C. Bauh.*

ABAPTI'STON (*Surg.*) vel *Abaptista*, *αβάπτιςον*, from *α*, priv. and *βαπτίζω, mergo*, to sink; a kind of trepan made so as not to sink into the brain. *Gal. de Meth. Med.* l. 4, c. 6.

ABA'REA (*Archæol.*) a sort of shoe among the Spaniards.

ABARE'MO *Temo* (*Bot.*) a tree which grows in Brazil, the roots of which are a deep red, and its bark of an ash colour, bitter to the taste, and yielding a decoction fit for the detersion of inveterate ulcers.

A'BARI (*Bot.*) *Abaro* or *Abarum*; a great tree of Ethiopia that bears a fruit like a pompion.

ABARNA'RE (*Archæol.*) to disclose a crime to a magistrate. *Leg. Canut. apud Brompton.*

ABARTA'MEN (*Min.*) another name for lead.

ABARTICULA'TION (*Med.*) a species of articulation of the bones, admitting of a manifest motion called also *diarthrosis* and *dearticulatio*, to distinguish it from another sort of articulation called *synarthrosis*, which admits of a very obscure motion.

A'BAS (*Med.*) the same as Epilepsia.

ABAS (*Com.*) a weight used in Persia for pearls, equal to three grains and a half.

ABAS (*Ent.*) a species of Bombyx.

ABA'SED (*Her.*) an epithet for the vol or wing of an eagle, turned downwards towards the point of the shield, or when the wings are shut, the natural way of bearing them being to be displayed. A bend, chevron, pale, &c. is said to be *abased* when their points terminate in or below the centre of the shield; an ordinary is said to be *abased* when below its due situation.

ABA'SIR (*Chem.*) another name for Spodium.

ABA'SSI (*Com.*) a Persian silver coin nearly equal in value to a shilling. *Fryer's New Account of India and Persia.*

ABA'T-CHAUVEE (*Com.*) a sort of wool of subaltern quality in France.

TO ABA'TE (*Law*) from the Fr. *Abattre*. 1. To destroy or remove, as to *abate* a nuisance. *Vet. Nat. Br.* 45; *Stat. Westm.* l. 1, c. 17. 2. To defeat, as to *abate* a writ by showing some error or exception. *Brit.* c. 48; *Stat.* 34 E. 1; *Stat.* 11 H. 6, c. 2; *Staundf. P. C.* 148. 3. To get possession by intrusion, in contradistinction to disseise: thus an *abator* is one who steps in between the former possessor and his heir. Coke, in his first Institutes, explains the difference between the words *Disseisin, Abatement, Intrusion, Deforciament, Usurpation,* and *Perpresture. Bract.* l. 4, c. 2; *Britt.* c. 51; *Vet. N. B.* 115; 1 *Inst.* 277, a.

TO ABATE (*Man.*) a horse is said to *abate* when, working upon curvets, he puts both his hind legs to the ground at once, and observes the same exactness successively.

ABATE'LEMENT (*Com.*) an interdict of the Consuls, barring all merchants and dealers of the French nation from carrying on any trade, who disavow their bargains or refuse to pay their debts.

ABA'TEMENT (*Law*) 1. The act of abating in the different senses of the verb. [vide *Abate*] 2. *A plea in abatement* is a plea put in by the defendant, praying that the writ or plaint may abate, that is, that the suit of the plaintiff may cease for the time being. The following are the principal pleas in abatement: 1. To the jurisdiction of the court. 2. To the person of the plaintiff in case of—*a*, outlawry; *b*, excommunication; *c*, alienage; *d*, attaint, &c. 3. To the person of the defendant in case of—*a*, privilege; *b*, misnomer; *c*, addition. 4. To the writ and action. 5. To the count or declaration. 6. On account of—*a*, the demise of the king; *b*, the marriage or death of the parties, &c. *Bracton.* l. 4, c. 2; *Britt.* c. 51, &c.; *Vet. N. B.* fol. 114, 115; *Staundf. P. C.* 148, &c.; *Thel. Dig.* l. 10, c. 1, sect. 5; *Co. Lit.* 303, a.

ABATEMENT (*Her.*) a certain mark of disgrace added to the coat-armours of certain persons. *Abatements* are called in Latin *Diminutiones vel Discernula Armorum*, of which Guillim mentions nine different sorts, as follow: 1. The *Delf*, exactly a square in the middle of the coat. 2. An *Escutcheon reversed*, or a small escutcheon turned upside down in the middle of the coat. 3. A *Point parted dexter*, when the upper right corner of the escutcheon is parted from the whole. 4. A *Point in Point*, when the ends of two arched lines are joined in the middle of the escutcheon so as to part off the base from the rest. 5. A *Point Champagne*, or a hollow arched line cutting off the base of the escutcheon. 6. A *Plain Point*, or a straight line parting

B 2

off the base of the escutcheon. 7. A *Gore*, or two hollow lines between the sinister chief and the sinister base. 8. A *Gusset*, or a line sloping a little, and then perpendicular from the upper corner to the bottom or base. These eight *Abatements*, if ever they were used, required to be of a stained colour, *i. e. Sanguine* or *Tenne*; but it is supposed by modern heraldic writers that these distinctions were only imaginary. 9. The ninth and last abatement is when the whole coat is reversed, which was never done but to a traitor. An instance of this kind occurs in the arms of Sir Andrew de Harcla, Knt. who for his treachery towards his master king Edward II, by taking a bribe from the Scots, was first degraded, then drawn, hanged, beheaded, and quartered, in 1322. He beareth *White*, a *Red Cross*, and, in the first quarter, a *Black Martlet*, according to the annexed cut. *Selden. Tit. of Honour*, p. 337, 338; *Guill. Disp. of Herald.*

ABATEMENT (*Com.*) or *Rebate*. 1. A discount in the price of commodities when the buyer advances the sum directly for which he might have taken time. 2. A deduction from the duties paid for goods, when they are found to have been damaged.

A'BATIS (*Archæol.*) he who measures out corn with *batis*, i. e. *mensuris*, an avener or steward of the stables.

ABATIS (*Mil.*) or *Abbatis*, an intrenchment formed by trees felled and laid together.

ABA'TOR (*Law*) one who intrudes into houses or lands that are void by the death of the former possessor, and not yet entered upon by his heir. 1 *Inst.* sect. 475.

A'BATOS (*Ant.*) from α, priv. and βαίω, *eo*, to go, viz. inaccessible, an epithet for a rock or island of the Nile on which none dare set foot but the priests; the same epithet was applied to the inmost recesses of the temple, called by the Latins *Penetralia*. *Lucan.* l. 10, v. 323.

Hinc abaton quam nostra vocat veneranda vetustas
Terra potens, primos sensit percussa tumultus.

Sen. Nat. Quest. l. 4, c. 6; *Fest. de Signif. Verb.*

ABATTU'TA (*Mus.*) an Italian expression employed in music books after a break in the time of any piece, signifying that the time is to be *beaten* as before.

ABATU'DA (*Archæol.*) an epithet for any thing diminished in value, particularly money, as *moneta abatuda*, clipt money.

A'BATURES (*Sport.*) the sprigs or grass that the stag throws down in passing by.

ABA'VI (*Bot.*) a large tree in Æthiopia, bearing fruit like a gourd. *Raii Hist. Plant.*

ABB (*Mech.*) or *Abwool*, the yarn of a weaver's warp.

A'BBACY (*Ecc.*) *Abbatia*, the government of an abbey.

ABBA'ISSEUR (*Anat.*) one of the muscles of the eye. *Winslow.*

A'BBATIS (*Mil.*) vide *Abatis*.

A'BBEY (*Ecc.*) a religious house under the government of an abbot: anciently one third of the benefices in England were, by the Pope's grant, appropriated to the abbeys, and other religious houses, which at their dissolution amounted to the number of 190, that became lay-fees, the revenue of which were from 200*l.* to 3,500*l.* per annum, amounting on an average calculation to 2,853,000*l.* per annum. *Burn. Hist. Ref.*

A'BBOT (*Ecc.*) Abbas, Abbat, from Abba, Father, the head or governor of an abbey, of which there were different descriptions; as,—*Bishop Abbots*, whose abbeys have been erected into bishopricks;—*Cardinal Abbots*, who are also cardinals;—*Commendatory Abbots*, or bishops *in commendam*, who are seculars, performing no spiritual office, and having no spiritual jurisdiction, although they have undergone the tonsure, and are obliged by their bulls to take orders when they come of age;—*Croziered Abbots*, such as bear the crozier or staff;—*Mitred Abbots*, i. e. sovereign or general abbots, who were lords of parliament, and independent of any person but the pope. They were called mitred, from the mitre which they wore;—*Secundary Abbots*, the same as priors;—*Regular Abbots*, real monks, who have taken the vow, and wear the habits.

ABBOT (*Polit.*) or *Abbot of the people*, a chief in the republic of Genoa, who was chosen by the people in the fourteenth century.

ABBRE'VIATED (*Bot.*) *abbreviatus*, an epithet for the perianth; *perianthium abbreviatum*, an abbreviated perianth, when it is shorter than the tube of the corolla, as in *Pulmonaria maritima*. *Linn. Phil. Bot.*

ABBREVIA'TION (*Gram.*) a contracted manner of writing words so as to retain only single letters. Such abbreviations were common among the Greeks and Romans, as they are now among the moderns.

Greek Abbreviations on Coins, Inscriptions, &c.

A.

Α. ἀγαθή, Ἄκτια, Ἀθηνῆ, ἄρχοντος, Ἀσία. Α.ΒΑΣ. Ἀντιπάτρου Βασιλέως. ΑΒ. ΑΒΑ. ΑΒΑΚ. ΑΒΑΚΑΙΝ. Ἀβακαινινῶν. ΑΒ. ΑΒΔ. ΑΒΔΗ. Ἀβδηριτῶν. ΑΒ. ΑΒΥ. ΑΒΥΔΗ. Ἀβυδηνῶν. ΑΒΡ. Ἀβρότονον. ΑΓ. ἀγαθή. ΑΓΑΘΟ. Ἀγαθοκλέους. ΑΓΡ. Ἀγρίππα. ΑΘΗΝΑ. Ἀθηναιῶν. ΑΛΕΞ. Ἀλεξανδρεία. ΑΛΕΞΑΝ. Ἀλεξανδριανή, Ἀλεξάνδρω. ΑΛΕΞΑΝΔΡΟΥ. Ἀλεξανδρουπόλεως. ΑΜΑC. Ἀμασία. ΑΝΑΖ. Ἀναζάρβα. ΑΝΕΘΗ. ἀνέθηκε. ΑΝΘΗΔ. Ἀνθηδῶνος. ΑΝΘΥ. Ἀνθύπατος. *Proconsul*. ΑΝΚΥΡ. Ἀνκύρας. ΑΝΟC. ἀνθύπατος. ΑΝΤ. ΑΝΤΙΟ. Ἀντιοχίων. ΑΝΤΙ. Ἀντιστρατηγὸς. ΑΝΤ. ΑΝΤΩ. Ἀντωνιανῆς. ΑΠΟ. Ἀπολλιναρία. ΑΠΟΛ. Ἀπολλωνιατῶν. ΑΡΓ. Ἀργαίος. ΑΡΙΣ. Ἄριστος. ΑΡΧ. Ἀρχιερέως. ΑΣΚΑΛ. Ἀσκαλωνιτῶν. ΑΣΚΛΗ. Ἀσκληπιῷ. ΑΣΚΛ. Ἀσκληπιάδε. ΑΣΙΑ. Ἀσιάρχω. ΑΣΥ. Ἄσυλος, Ἄσυλμ. ΑΥΡ. Αὐρηλίας. ΑΥΤΟΚ. Αὐτοκράτωρ. ΑΥ. ΑΥΤΟ. ΑΥΤΟΝ. Αὐτόνομος.

Β.

Β. ΒΑΛ. Βαλέριος, *Valerius*. Β. ΒΕΛ. Βελίτον. Β. ΝΕΩ. δὶς Νεωκόρων. ΒΑ. Βάβα. ΒΑ. ΒΑΣ. ΒΑΣΙ. βασιλεὺς, βασιλέα. ΒΟΥΣ. Βουσιριτῶν.

Γ.

Γ. γραμματικὸς, γερουσίας. ΓΟΡΤΥ. Γορτυνίων. ΓΡ. ΓΡΑ. ΓΡΑΜ. γραμματέως.

Δ.

Δ. δίς. ΔΑΚ. Δακικός. ΔΑΜ. δαμασία. ΔΗΜ. δῆμος. ΔΗΜΗΤ. Δημήτηρ. ΔΕΜΟCΤΡ. Δεμοστράτε. ΔΙΑΔΟΥ. διαδωμενιανὸς. ΔΙΚ. δίκαιος. ΔΙΟΝΥ. Διονυσία. ΔΡΟΥC. Δρουσίλλαν, *Drusillam*. ΔΩΡ. δῶρα.

Ε.

Ε. ΕΠ. ἐπί. ΕΛΕΥΘ. ἐλευθέρας. ΕΞΟ. ἐξουσία. ΕΡΜΟ. Ἑρμοπολιτῶν. ΕΡΜΟΚ. Ἑρμοκλέους. ΕΤΟ. ἔτος. ΕΥ. εὐσεβής. ΕΥΓ. εὐγενέως. ΕΦ. ΕΦΕ. Ἐφεσίων. ΕΧ. ἔχοντος.

Η.

ΗΓ. ΗΓΕ. ἡγεμόνος. ΗΡΑΚ. Ἡρακλείδα, Ἡρακλεωπολιτῶν.

Θ.

Θ. Θεῶν. ΘΑ. Θασίων. ΘΥ. Θυγάτηρ.

Ι.

Ι. ΙΟ. ΙΟΥ. Ἰούλιος, *Julius*. Ι. ΙC. ΙCΤ. ΙCΤΡ. Ἱερον, Ἱερῷ. ΙΕ. ἱερᾶς, ἱερά, Ἱεροπολιτῶν. ΙΗΛ. Ἰσραήλ. ΙΛΗΜ. Ἱερουσαλήμ. ΙΛΙ. Ἰλιέων. ΙΟ. Ἰωάννης. ΙΟΝ. Ἰονῶν. ΙΠΠ. ἱππικω, ἵππον. ΙC. Ἰησοῦς. ΙCΘ. ΙCΘΜ. Ἴσμια.

Κ.

Κ. Κιλικία, *Cilicia*. Κοίντος, *Quintus*. Κ. ΚΑΙ. ΚΑΙC. Καῖσαρ. ΚΑΙΑΡ. Καισαρείας, Καίσαρις, Καισαρέων. ΚΑΛ. Καλυ-

ABBREVIATION.

κάδην. ΚΑΝΟ. Κανοβιτῶν. ΚΑΝΟΘ. Κανοθαίων. ΚΑΠΙΤΟ. καπιτολιέων. ΚΑΣ. Κάσσιος, *Cassius*. ΚΑΣΤΑΒ. Κασταβαλέων. ΚΕ. Κίσαρος, *Cæsaris*. ΚΕΛ. Κελσῦ, *Celsi*. ΚΙΛΒ. Κιλβιανῶν. ΚΛ. Κλαύδιος, *Claudius*. ΚΛΑΥΔ. Κλαυδιοπολιτῶν. ΚΛΑΖΟΜ. Κλαζομενίων. ΚΟΙ. Κοινὸν. ΚΟΜ. Κομινία, Κομινίων, Κομμαγενῆς, Κομμόδε. ΚΟΠΤ. ΚΟΠΤΙΤ. Κοπτιτῶν. ΚΣ. Κύριος. ΚΤΙΣ. Κτιστῆς, Κτιστῦ. ΚΥ. ΚΥΙΝ. Κύιντος, *Quintus*. ΚΥ. ΚΥΠ. Κυπρίων. ΚΥΔΩ. Κυδωνιατῶν. ΚΥΖ. ΚΥΖΙ. Κυζικηνῶν. ΚΥΘΟ. Κυθοπόλεως. ΚΥΝΟ. Κυνοπολιτῶν.

Λ.

Λ. ΛΙ. ΛΙΚ. Λικίνιος, *Licinius*. Λ. ΛΟΥ. ΛΟΥΚ. Λεύκιος, *Lucius*. ΛΑΟ. ΛΑΟΔ. ΛΑΟΔΙΚ. Λαοδικέων. ΛΕΠ. Λεπίδα, *Lepidi*. ΛΙΒ. ΛΙΒΑΝ. Λιβάνα, Λιβάνῳ. ΛΟΓΓΕΙ. Λογγείνα, *Longini*. ΛΥΚΟ. Λυκοπολιτῶν.

Μ.

Μ. Μᾶρκος, *Marcus*, Μακριανιανὴ, Μονή. ΜΑ. Μακεδόνων. ΜΑΓΝ. ΜΑΓΝΗ. Μαγνητῶν. ΜΑΙΑΝ. ΜΑΙΑΝΔ. Μαίανδρος, Μαιάνδρον. ΜΑΡ. Μαρσυίας. ΜΕΜΦ. Μεμφιτῶν. ΜΕΝ. Μενοιτῶν. ΜΕΝΕ. Μενελαϊτῶν. ΜΕΝΟΦ. Μενοφλεε. ΜΕΣΣΑΛ. Μεσσαλίνα, *Messalina*. ΜΕ. ΜΕΤ. ΜΕΤΡ. ΜΕΤΡΟΠ. Μητρόπολις, Μητροπόλεως. ΜΕΤΗΛΙ. Μητηλιτῶν. ΜΗΤΡΟΔΩ. Μητροδώρα. ΜΗΡ. μήτηρ. ΜΡΣ. μητρὸς. ΜΥΡ. Μύρωνος. ΜΥΡΙΝΑ. Μυριναίων. ΜΥΤΙ. Μυτιληναίων.

Ν.

Ν. ΝΕ. ΝΕΩ. ΝΕΩΚ. Νεωκόρων. ΝΑΙΒ. Ναιβία, Ναιβιάνα, *Nævio*, &c. ΝΑΚΡΑΣΙ. Νακρασιτῶν. ΝΑΥ. ΝΑΥΑΡ. ναυαρχίδος. ΝΕ. νεωκόρος. ΝΕ. ΝΕΑΠ. Νεαπόλεως, Νεαπολιτῶν. ΝΕ. ΝΕΡ. ΤΡΑΙ. Νερυιανὴ Τραιανὴ, *Nerviana Trajana*. ΝΕΙ. ΝΕΙΚ. ΝΕΙΚΟΜ. ΝΕΙΚΟΜΗΔ. Νεικαίων, Νικαιέων, Νεικομηδέων. ΝΕΟΚΑΙΣ. Νεοκαισαρέων. ΝΕΡ. Νέρυας, *Nervæ*. ΝΕΡΑΤ. Νερατία. ΝΙΓ. Νίγρος, *Niger*. ΝΙΚΟΠΟΛ. Νικοπολιτῶν. ΝΥΣΣ. Νύσσης.

Ο.

Ο. Οτιλιανὴ, Οκταυία, *Octavii*. ΟΛΥΜ. ΟΛΥΜΠ. Ὀλύμπιος, Ὀλύμπια. ΟΜΟ. ΟΜΟΝ. Ὁμόνοια. ΟΝ. ὄντος. ΟΞΥΡ. ΟΞΥΡΙΝΧ. ὀξυρινχυτῶν. ΟΠ. Ὀπήλιος, *Opelius*. OCTI. Ὀτιλιανὸς, *Hostilianus*. ΟΥΑΛ. ΟΥΑΔΕ. Οὐαλεριανὸς, *Valerianus*, Οὐάλης, *Valens*. ΟΥΗΡ. Οὐῆρος, *Verus*. ΟΥΛΠ. Οὐλπίας, *Ulpiæ*. ΟΥΛΠΙΑΝ. Οὐλπιανῦ, *Ulpiani*. ΟΥΝΟϹ. ἐρανὸς.

Π.

Π. ΠΟ. ΠΟΝ. Πόντου, Πυβλίυ, *Publii*. Π. ΠΡ. ΠΡΟ. πρὸς, πρώτη. ΠΑΛ. ΠΑΛΑ. Παλάτυ. ΠΑΛΑΙ. Παλαιστινῆς. ΠΑΝ. Πανίψ. ΠΑΝΗ. Πανηγυριστῦ. ΠΑΝΟ. Πανοπιτῶν. ΠΑΝΟΡ. Πανορμιτᾶν. ΠΑΡΘ. Παρθικὸς. ΠΑΤΡ. Πατρέων. ΠΑΥΛ. Παύλυ. ΠΛΥΣ. Παυσανίας. ΠΑΦΛΑΓ. παφλαγονίας. ΠΕ. ΠΕΣ. Πεσσινεντίων. ΠΕΔΟΥ. Πεδουσίυ. ΠΕΛΟΥ. Πελυσιωτῶν. ΠΕΠΑ. Πιπαρεθίων. ΠΕΡ. ΠΕΡΓ. ΠΕΡΓΑ. Περγαμηνῶν. ΠΕΣΚ. πεσκεύνιος, *Pescennius*, Πεσκινενίων. ΠΗΡ. πατὴρ. ΠΡΣ. πατρὸς. ΠΙΝ. Πιναμυτίων. ΠΟΛΛΙ. Πολλίωνος, *Pollione*. ΠΟΜΠ. Πομπηία, *Pompeii*, Πομπηιανῶν, Πομπωνίων. ΠΟΝΤ. Ποντία. ΠΟΣΙΔ. Ποσιδωνία. ΠΡ. ΠΡΡ. ΠΡΕΣ. ΠΡΕΣΒ. Πρεσβευτύ. ΠΡ. ΠΡΙΣ. ΠΡΙΣΚ. Πρίσκυ, *Prisci*. ΠΡ. ΠΡΟ. Πρόβα, *Probo*, πρὸς, πρώτη, πρώτυ. ΠΡΟΔ. ΠΡΟΔΙ. προδίκυ. ΠΡΟΣΩ. Προσωπιτῶν. ΠΡΥΤ. Πρυτανίδος. ΠΥΘ. Πυθία.

Ρ.

ΡΟΥΦ. Ρούφου, *Rufi*. ΡΥΝΔ. ΡΥΝΔΑ. Ρυνδάκυ.

С.

C. CE. CEB. CEBA. CEBAC. Σεβαστὸς, Σεβαστὴ, Σεβαστῶν, *Augustus, Augusta, Augustorum*. C. CT. CTP. CTPA. CTPAT. CTPATH. ϛρατηγῶ. C. CY. Συρίας. CAB. Σαβείνυ, *Sabini*. CABIN. Σαβινία. CAIT. Σαιττηνῶν. CAΛ. Σαλλίυ, Σαλλουστίυ, *Sallio, Sallustio*. CAΛO. Σαλονινὸς, *Saloninus*. CAMA. Σαμαρείας. CAMO. Σαμοσατέων. CAT. Σατορνεινῦ, *Saturnino*.

CEBEN. Σεβεννυτῶν. CEΛEY. CEΛEYK. Σελευκίων. CEOY. Σευηρὸς, *Severus*. CEΠT. Σεπτιμία, *Septimio*. CEP. Σερυία, *Servio*. CI. CIΠ. CIΠY. Σιπύλυ, *Sipylo*. CIKIN. Σικιννία, *Sicinnio*. CMY. CMYP. Σμυρναίων. CO. COΦ. COΦI. CO
ΦΙC. σοφιστὲ. COYΛ. Σαλπικία, *Sulpicio*. CTPOC. σωτῆρος. CTEΦANH. Στεφανηφόρυ. CTPAB. Στράβωνος. CTPATONI. Στρατονικῦ, Στρατονικεανῦ. CΩT. Σωτῆρι.

Τ.

Τ. Ταύρου, Τίτυ, *Tito*, τῶν. ΤΑ. ΤΑΤ. τατιανῦ. ΤΑΝ. ταναγραίων. ΤΑΝΙ. τανιτῶν. ΤΑΡC. τάρσυ. ΤΕΜ. τεμένει. ΤΕΝΤΥΡ. Τεντυριτῶν. ΤΗ. τὴν. ΤΙΑΝ. Τιανῶν. ΤΙ. ΤΙΒ. ΤΙΒΕΡ. Τιβέριος, Τιβερία, *Tiberius, Tiberio*, Τιβερίεων. ΤΟΥΛ. Τουλλίυ, *Tullio*. ΤΡΟΧ. Τροχμῶν. ΤΥΡ. Τύρυ.

Υ.

ΥΠ. ὑπὸ. ΥΠΑ. Ὕπατος, ὑπατορικήν, *Consul, Consularem*. ΥΠΙ. Ὑπίψ. YC. υἱός.

Φ.

Φ. ΦΑΒ. Φαβίυ, *Fabio*. ΦΑΝ. Φαννία, *Fannio*. ΦΗCΤ. Φηστῦ, *Festo*. ΦΙ. Φιλοπόλι, Φιλοπάτορος. ΦΙΛΟ. Φιλομιλέων. ΦΑ. ΦΛΑ. ΦΛΑΟ. ΦΛΑΟΥ. Φλαυία, *Flavio*, Φλαυίων. ΦΟ. ΦΟΚ. ΦΟΚΑ. Φωκαίων. *Goltz. Græc., et Thesaur.; Vaillant Numismat. Græc.; Montfaucon, Palæograph.*

Greek Abbreviations in Books.

ABBREVIATION.

Roman Abbreviations on Coins, Inscriptions, &c.

A.

A. Augustus, Augustalis, Aulus, absolvo, absolutio, ager, agit, aiunt, aliquando, antiquo, assolet, aut. A.A. Augusti, Augusta. A.A. Aulus Agerius; æs alienum; ante audita; apud agrum; aurum; argentum. A.A.A. Augusti. A.A.A.F.F. ære, argento, auro, flando, feriundo, *vel* flavo feriundo. A.A.A.F.QU.TY. auri, argenti, æris flator, fabricæ Quirinalis Tyborini. A.A.C. ante auditam causam. A.A.S.L.M. apud agrum sibi loco monumenti. A.AV. alter ambove. A.B. alia bona. ABN. Abnepos. ABS. absolutus. A.B.V. à bono viro. AB.U.C. ab urbe condita. AC. actio. A.C. alius civis, acta causa. ACB. actionibus. ACC. accepta, acceptat, acceperat. ACC9. accusatio. AC.D.N. actione Domini nostri. AC.D.Q.P.T. actione dotis, quæ tibi petitur. ACH. Achaiæ. ACIN. actionem. AC.L.AQ. actio legis Aquiliæ. ACM. actionem. ACO. accusatio. ACON. actionem, *vel* actionum. A.COSS.CI. à consulibus civitatum. AC.P. actor provinciæ. AC.P.R. actor Provinciæ Romanæ. A.C.P.VI. ad caput pedes sex. A.CSL. à consulibus. A.C.S.L.E.C. à Consiliariis suæ legionis et civitatis. ACT. actor, *vel* auctoritas. ACT.T. auctoritas tua. ACTI. actionem. A.C.V. à claro viro. A.CUB.AUGG. a cubiculis Augustorum. AD. adest, *vel* adjutor. A.D. ante diem. AD.D. ad discendum, *vel* ad discordiam. AD.E. ad effectorem, *vel* ad exactorem, *vel* ad extorrem. AD.F. ad finem, *vel* ad frontem. ADJ. adjutor. ADIAB. Adiabenicus. ADJ.P. adjutor patriæ, *vel* populi, *vel* provinciæ. AD.L. ad locum. ADLR. adulteravit. ADN. adnepos. ADOP. *vel* ADP. adoptivus. A.D.P. ante diem pridie. AD.P.XII. ad pedes duodecim. AD.QS. ad Quæstores. AD.QSR. ad Quæstorem. AD.QU. ad Quæstorem, *vel* ad quæstionem. ADV. adversum. ÆD. ædes. ÆD.D. ædem dedicavit. ÆDIL. Ædiles. ÆDIL.CUR. Ædilis curulis. ÆDILL. Ædiles. ÆD.IN.M. ædes inscripsit mercede. ÆD.PL. Ædilis plebis. ÆD.S. ædibus sacris. ÆG. æger. ÆQ.P. æqualis persona. ÆR. ærarium, *vel* ærarii, *vel* æreum. ÆR.COL. ære collato. ÆR.P. ære publico. ÆR.ST. ærario Saturni. ÆT. æternitas. AF. affectus. A.F. alit facto. A.F.P.R. Actum fide Publici Rutilii, *vel* ante factum, post relatum, *vel* Æmilus fecit, plectitur Rutilius. AFR. Africæ. AG. agit, *vel* Agrippa, *vel* agro. A.G. Aulus Gellius. AGR. agitur. AGR.F. Agrippæ filius. A.H. alius homo. A.J. à judice. AL. alluit. A.L. ad locum, *vel* aliâ lege. A.L.Æ. arbitrium litis æstimandæ, *vel* liti æstimandum. ALA.LG. aliâ lege, *vel* legione. A.L.E. arbitrium liti examinandæ, *vel* existimandæ, *vel* existimandum. AL.III.L. Alpinæ tertiæ legionis. ALL. allegata, *vel* alligata. ALXA. Alexander. AM. amicus. AM.N. amicus noster. AMN. amantissimus. AM.NT.AMN. amicus noster amantissimus. AM.P. amabilis persona. A.N. annus, anilis. ANG.P. angelus percussit. ANM. anima. AN.M. actionem mandati. AN.N. ante noctem. ANN. annis. ANN.P. annonæ præfectus. ANT. Antonius, *vel* antestatus, ante, *vel* antea. ANT.T.C. ante terminum constitutum. A.O. alii omnes. AO.P. auro puro, *vel* auro posito. AP. apud. A.P. Antonii prætoria. APA. amputatæ. AP.A. apud acta. A.P.CLN. ad pedes columnæ. AP.JUD. apud judicem. AP.N. apud nos. APP. Appius, appellat. APPN. appellantur. AP.P.URB. apud præfectum urbis. A.P.R.C. anno post Romam conditam. A.P.T. ad potestatem tuam. AQUI.S. Aquiliana stipulatio. AQL. Aquileia. AQ.MAR. aqua marcia. ARAB. Arabicus, *vel* Arabia. A.RA.MIL.FRU. à rationibus militaris frumenti. ARC. arca. ARG. argumentum. ARM. Armenia, *vel* Armenicus. ARM.E. arma ejus. ARM.P. arma publica. AR.VV.D.D. Arma votiva dono dedit. A.S. à suis. A.S.L.F. à sua lege fecit. A.S.TT. à supra tectis. A.T. autoritas tua. A.TE. à tergo. A.T.M.D.O. aio te mihi dare oportere. A.TP. annuo tempore. A.TT. ante titulum. ATQ. atque. ATR. autoritas, *vel* autor. AUG. Augustus, *vel* augur. AUC. *aut* AUTR. auctoritas, *vel* autor. AUGG. Augusti, *viz.* de duobus. AUGGG. Augustorum, *viz.* de tribus. AUG.F. Augusti filius. AUG.P. Augusti puer. AUG.N. Augustus noster, *vel* Augusti nepos. AUG.CUR.RP. Augustalis curator reipub. AUG.ET.Q.AUG. Augustalis et Quæstor Augustalium. AUT.PR.R. autoritas provinciæ Romanorum. A.X. annis decem.

B.

B. Balbus, Brutus, bonus, bona, bonæ, benè, Bacchus. B.A. bonam actionem, bonis amabilis, bonis auguriis, bonis avibus, bonis auspiciis. B.C. bonorum concessum. B.D. bonum datum. B.D.S.M. bene de se meriti. B.E. bonorum emptor. B.E.CA. bona ejus caduca. B.E.E. bona ex edicto. B.ER. Bona eorum. B.ER.INT. B.E.I. bona eorum inveniuntur. B.E.IA. bona ejus instituta. BF. benefecit, beneficium. B.F. bonum factum, bona fides, bona filia, bona fortuna. B.F.C. bonâ fide contractum. BF.D. beneficium dedit. B.FL. bonorum filius. B.F.P. bonæ fidei possessor. BF.COS. beneficiarius Consulis. BF.PR. beneficiarius Prætoris. BF.TRIB. beneficiarius Tribuni. B.GR. bona gratia. B.H. bonus homo, *vel* bona hæreditaria, bonorum hæres. B.HTS. bonorum hæreditas. B.H.S.I. bona hic sita invenies. B.J. bonum judicium. B.L. bona lex. B.LB. bonorum liberi. B.M. bonæ memoriæ, bona materia, bona materna, bene merenti, &c. B.MN. bona munera. B.M.F. benè merita fecit. B.M.P. benè merenti posuit. B.MN. bona munera. B.M.F.C. benè merenti faciendum curavit. B.M.P.C. benè merenti ponendum curavit. B.N. bona nostra. BN. benè, bona. BN.H.I. bona hic invenies. B.O. benè optimè. B.P. bonum publicum, bona paterna, bonorum potestas, *vel* possessio. BO.EM. bonorum emptores. B.P. bona possessio, bonorum possessor, *vel* bonum publicum, bona paterna, bonorum potestas. B.PC. bona pecunia. B.PN. bonorum possessionem. B.PO. Bonorum possessio. B.PR. PR. beneficiarium præfecto prætorio. B.PRO. beneficiarius Proconsulis. B.Q. bona quæsita. BR. bonorum. B.R. bonorum rector. B.RP.N. bono Reipubl. natus. BR.SI. bonorum servi. BRT. Britannicus. B.S. bene satisfecit, bona sua. B.T. bonorum tutor. B.V. benè vixit, bonus vir, bonorum venditor, bona vestra, bona vacantia. B.V.A. boni viri arbitratu. B.VT. bona vendita. B.V.V. balnea, vina, Venus.

C.

C. *pro* Caio, *i. e.* viro. C. colonia. Ↄ. *inversa* Caiam et mulierem *sign.* C.C. causa cognita. C.C.C. calumniæ cavendæ causâ. C. centum. C9. Cautio. CIↃ. *vel* CXↃ. mille. ↃↃ. quinque millia. CCCIↃↃↃ. centum millia. CCC.T.P. ter centum terræ pedes. CA.AM. causa amabilis. CÆS.AUG. Cæsar Augustus. CÆSS. AUGG. Cæsares Augusti, *scilicet* de duobus. CÆSSS. AUGGG. Cæsares Augusti, de tribus. CALA. Calumnia. CA.M.V. causa memorati viri. CAP. capitalis. CAR.COJU. carissimæ conjugi. C.E.C. colonis ejus coloniæ. CEL. celeres. CEN.A. censoris arbitratu. CEN.PP. *vel* CENS. censor perpetuus. CENT. centurio, centuria. CENTU. centuriones. CESS. censores. C.F. Caii filius. C.H. custos hæredum. CIC. Cicero. C.J.C. Caius Julius Cæsar. C.IV. causa justa. CIV. civitas, civis. C. iii. INV. cubitos tres invenies. C. ii. INV.P. cubitos duos invenies plumbum. CL. Claudius. CL.V. clarissimi viri. CL.F. clarissima filia, *vel* fœmina. C.L. Caius libertus. C.LARN. comes largitionum. CL. COS.DESIG. Claudius Consul designatus. CLS. clarissimus. CM. comis. C.M. *vel* CA.M. causa mortis. C.M. capitis minutio, *vel* civis malus. C.M.D. centum millia denariorum. C.M.F. clarissimæ memoriæ fœmina. C.

ABBREVIATION.

M.L. centum millia. C.M.T. causa mali tui. C.MT. crementum multum. C.M.V. clarisimæ memoriæ vir. CN. Cneius, *vel* Cnevius. C.N. Caius noster, Cæsar noster, civis noster. C.N.EE.C.C. credimus non esse causam convictam. C9NS. cautiones. CNTO. centenario. CNT. VI. centenaria sex. CO. conjugi, controversia. C9. civitas omnis. COH. cohors. COL. colonia, coloni, collega, collegium. COM. comes. CŌM.OB. Comitia Obriziaca. CON. consularis. CON.SEN.E.OR.PQ.R. consensu Senatus, equestris ordinis Populique Romani. CONS. *vel* CS. consiliarius. COS. Consul. COSS. Consules. COS. QUAR. Consul quartum, *vel* quartò. COS. DES. Consul designatus. COACT.ABD. coactus abdicavit. COM.OR. comes orientis. COMM.CONS. communi consensu. CONJU. conjunxit. CONJU.OBQUÆ. conjugi obsequentissimæ. CONLIB. conlibertus, conliberta. COR. Cornelius. CORP. corpus. CORN. AURS. coronas aureas. CORN. cornibus. COSS.S.S. consulibus supra scriptis. CONT. contubernalis. CQ. R. F. cautumque ratum fore. C.R. civis Romanus. CR. Creticus, Crispus, contractum, contrarium. C.R.C. cujus rei causa. C. REP. causa reipub. CRI. consulari. CS. Cæsar, causa, consiliarius, communis. CS.A. Cæsar Augustus. CSL controversia. C.S.L. comes sacrarum largitionum. C.S FL. cum suis filiis. C.S.H. cum suis hæredibus. C.S.S. cum suis servis. C.S.P.E. cum sua pecunia est. CS.M. Cæsar Maximus. CT. caput, *vel* civitas. C.T. certo tempore. CTR. cæterum. CT.R. civitas Romana. CTR.M. citrà mirum. CT.RO. civitas Romana. CTRIO. centurio. C.V. centum virum, *vel* clarissimus vir, *vel* causa virginum. CUJ. cujus. CUL. cultores. CUR. curionum, curiarum, cursor. CUR.P. cursus publicus. CUR.COL. curator coloniæ. CUR. KAL. curator kalendarii. CUR.P.P. curator pecuniæ publicæ. CUR.RP. curator reipublicæ. CUST. custos.

D.

D. Divus, Decius, Decimus, diebus, devotus, diutius, dedicavit. D.A. Divus Augustus. D.Æ. de ærario. D. AUG. Deo Augusto, *vel* Divo Augusto. D.B.M. de bene merentibus. D.B.J. diu bene juvantibus. D.C.S. de consilii sententià. DD. dedimus, dedicatio. D.D.D. datus decreto decurionum, *vel* dono dedit dicavit. D. D.D.D. dignum Deo donum dedit. DD.NN. Domini nostri. D.D.DQ. dat dicat dedicatque. D.DQ. dedit, donavitque. D.DQ.S. Dis Deabusque sacrum. DE. Decius. DEC. decurio. DECB. December. D.EE. damnatum esse. DEG.A.M. degenerat à majoribus. DEGN. T.O. degenerem te ostendis. DES. *vel* DESIG. designatus. DFTI. defuncti. DICT. dictator. DIG. M. dignus memoria, vel morte. DIL. dilectus, *vel* dilectissimus. D. M. Diis manibus. D.M.Æ. Deo magno æterno. DN. dominus, damnum. DN.N. Dominus noster. D.O. Diis omnibus, *vel* Deo Optimo. D.IM.S. Diis immortalibus sacrum. D.J.S. Decimus Julius Silvanus. D.OPA. data opera. DOCS. Dioclesianus. DOT.R. dotem recuperabit. D.P. Divus pius, Diis penatibus, patriis, *vel* de periculo, dotem petit, *vel* devota persona; *vel* decretum principis. D.PEC.R. de pecuniis repetundis. D.PP. Deo perpetuo. DPC. deprecatio. DPO. deportatio. DPF. de præfecto. D.P.ORT. de parte orientis. DPS. discipulus. DQ. denique. D.Q. Diis Quirinalibus. D.Q.R. de qua re. D.Q.S. die quo supra. DR. Drusus. D.RS. de regibus. D.RM. de Romanis. D.R.P. dare promittit, de republica. DS. Deus. D.S.S.P. de sapientia sua perficet. DT. duntaxat, durat. D.T.G.Q.S. de tuo genio quod sentis, &c. D.V. devotus vir, vester, *vel* Diis volentibus, *vel* dies quintus. D.VS. Deæ virgines, de virtutibus, *vel* de verbis. DUL. dulcissimus. DUS. devotus, &c.

E.

E. est, ens, ejus. E.B. ejus bona. E.C. è comitio, *vel* capitolio. E.D. ejus domus, *vel* dominus. E.E. esse, ex edicto. E.F. ejus filius. E.H. ejus hæres, ex hæredibus, *vel* ex hæreditate est. EIMO. ejusmodi. E.L. edita lex. EM. *vel* EIM. ejusmodi. E.M. ex more. EMP. emptor. E.N. etiam nunc, est noster, *vel* non. EN. enim. EOR. eorum. EP. epistola. E.P. edendum parcè. E.P. è palatio, è publico. EPM. epitaphium. EP.M. epistolam misit. E.PP. et præparat. EPS. episcopus. EQ.P. eques publicus. EQ.R. eques Romanus. EQ.M. equitum magister. EQ.OR. equestris ordinis. ER. erit, *vel* erunt. E.R.A. ea res agitur. E.R.B. ejus regit bona. ERG. ergo. ER.L.M.ÆTN. erit locus memoriæ æternæ. ERP. eripiet. ER.P. erit paratus. E.S. è senatu. E.S.Æ.MR. è sacra æde Martis. ET. etiam. ET.NC. et nunc. EU. ejus. EUR. Europa. E.V.V.N.V.V.E. ede ut vivas, ne vive ut edas. EX. exigitur. EX.A.D. ex ante diem. EX.B.S. ex bonis suis. EX.C. ex consuetudine, concione, conditione, &c. EX.A.D.C.A. ex autoritate divi Cæsaris Augusti. EX.I.Q. ex jure Quiritium. EX.M. ex malitià. EX.M.D. ex memorià dixi. EXPR.T. experientia tua. EX.R. exactis regibus. EX.S.C. ex senatus consulto. EX.V. ex voto.

F.

F. fecit, felix, familia, fuit, fit, figura, fides, filius, Flavius, Februarius, fur. FA. filia. FABR. fabrum, *vel* fabrorum. FAC.B. factum benè. FAC.C. faciendum curavit. FA.F. factum feliciter. FAM. familiaris. FAMA. familia. FB. fabricabant. F.C. fidei commissum, fiducia, *vel* fidei causa, *vel* fraude creditoris, *vel* faciendum curavit. FC. fecit *vel* fecerunt, &c. FD.M. fides mundi. FE. fundamentum, *vel* fortem, *vel* familiæ. FEA. fœmina. FEB. Februarius. F.E. factum est, *vel* filius ejus. F.E.D. factum esse dicitur. F.ED. factum edicto. FER. fecerunt. FER.LAT.C. feriarum latinarum causâ. F.F. fratris filius. F. FA. *vel* FAM. filius familias. F.FBC. fecit fabricatio. F.FE. fabricari fecerunt. F.F.F. ferro, flamma, fama, *vel* fortior, fortuna, fato. F.J. fieri jussit. FI.B. fide bonâ. FI.C. fiscum, *vel* fidei commissum. FIC. RP.C. fiscum reipubl. causæ. FID. fides. FID.D. fide dignus. FIL. filius. FID.IMP. fides imperatoria. FID.INTEMP. fides intemperata. FID.P.S. fides Patrum Scriptorum. FID.P.R. fides Populi Romani. FID.R. fides regia. FID.R.P. fides reipublicæ. FID.SER. fidelis servus. F.JR. fidei jussores. FL. filius, flamen, Flavius. FLAM. Flaminius, flamen, *vel* flamina. FLAM.DIAL. *vel* FL.D. flamen Dialis. FLAM.QI. flamen Quirinalis. FLAM. MART. flamen Martialis. FLAM.P.H.P.H.C. Flamini, provinciæ Hispaniæ, provinciæ Hispaniæ citerioris. FLAV. Flavianus, *vel* Flavia, *scil* tribus. FLA.R. filia regis. FLB. flabrum. FL.P. flamen perpetuus. F.M. fati munus, *vel* fieri mandavit, *vel* ferit memoriam, *vel* factum memoratum. F.M.I. *vel* F.M.1T. fati munus implent, *vel* implevit. F.N. fides nostra. F.N.C. fidei nostræ commisit, *vel* commissum. FN. AGR. fines agrorum. FO. forum. FOR. forte, *vel* fortis, *vel* foràs, *vel* fortuna. F.P. forma publica, fama publica, fidei promissor, *vel* fides promissa. F.PP.R. forum Populi Romani. FR. frontes, fratres, *vel* forem. F.R. forum Romanum, regundorum, *vel* regum. FR.F. fratris filius. FR.COR. forum Cornelii. FR.J. forum Julium. FR.L. forum Livium. FR.S. forum Sempronii. FRS. fortis. FRMS. fortissimus. FU.C. fraudisve causâ. FUNC. functus.

G.

G. gaudium, gens, genius, Gellius, Gaius, gratia, &c. G. AUG. genio Augusti. GAV.V. gravitas vera, *vel* vestra. G.B. gens bona. G.D. gens desolata. GD. gaudium. GEN.CORN. gente Corneliorum, &c. GENS. gentes. GER. Germanicus. G.F. gula filiorum, Germanus frater, Germanæ fidelis. GG. *vel* GS. gesserunt. GL. gloria. GL.N.L. gloria nominis Latini. GL.P. gloria parentum, *vel* patriæ, *vel* populi. GL.P.R. gloria Pop. Romani, &c.

ABBREVIATION.

GL.S. Gallius Sempronius. G.M. gens mala. GN. gens, *vel* genus. GN.R.S. genus Romani Senatus. GOTH. Gothicus. G.R. genus regium, *vel* rarum. GR. gerens, *vel* gerit. GR.D. Graiis dedit, *vel* datum. GR.E. gratia ejus, &c. GRC. Græcus. GR.P. gloriæ parentum. G.S. genio sacro. GS. gravitas, *vel* genus, *vel* gessit, *vel* gesserunt. GT. gentem, *vel* gentes. G.T. gravitas tua. GU. genus. G.V. Gravis Valerius. GX. grex.

H.

H. Hadrianus, honestas, hic, hæc, hoc, hæredes, homo, habet, huic, hora, honor. H.Æ.M. hæredem meum. H.ÆS. PRC. hæredes principis. H.B.F. homo bonæ fidei. H.BV.P. hæreditas, bonorumve possessio. HC.AM.N. hunc amicum nostrum. HC.L. hunc locum. HC.V. hunc virum, huic vitæ. H.D. hic dedicavit, dedicârunt, *vel* dedicaverunt. H.D.D. hoc dono datur. HEL. Helvetia. H.E.M.TBNR. hæc est memoria Tribunorum. HER.F. hæredem facit. HER.S. Herculis sacrum. HER.EX.T. F.C. hæredes ex testamento faciendum curavit. H.HB.P. hic habes pecuniam. H.HON. homo honestus. H.J. hæreditatis jure, *vel* hercle juravit, *vel* hic inveniet. H.INS. hæres institutus. H.L. honesto loco, hic locus. H.L.H. N.S. hic locus hæredes non sequitur. H.L.N. honesto loco natus. H.M. honesta mulier, *vel* hora mala, *vel* hora mortis. H.M.D.A. hoc mandavit dari Augustus. H.M.EXT.N.REC. hoc monumentum exteras non recipit. H.M.P. hic memoriæ posuit, *vel* hoc monumentum posuit. H.M.S.M. hic mater sua mortua, *vel* hora mala sumpsit moram. HO. homo, *vel* honestus. HO.H. homo honestus. HOM. homo. HOR. hora. H.P. hora pessima, honesta persona, hic posuit, honestus puer, *vel* hæreditatis possessio. H.POSS. hæreditatis possessor, *vel* possessores. H.PS. hora pessima. H.R. honesta ratio. HR. hæres. H.RC. honestæ recordationis. H.R.I.P. hic requiescit in pace. H.S. hæc sit, hic sit, hoc satis, hora sacra, *vel* Herculis sacrum, H.S.E. hic situs est, *vel* hic sepultus est. H.S.F. hoc sacellum fecit. H.SPL.M. AUC. hæc sepultura modò aucta. H.S.V.F.M. hoc sibi vivens fieri mandavit. HU. hujus. H.V.B.P. herus verus bonorum possessor.

I.

I. in, inter, interdum, intrà, unum, Junius, Julius. JAD. jamdudum. I.AGL. in angulo. JA.RI. jam respondi. I.B. in brevi. J.C. Juris consultus, Julius Cæsar. J.C.E.V. justa causa esse videtur. JD. Judex, interdum, idus, indicatum. I.D. inferis diis, *vel* in dimidio, *vel* juris dicendi juridicendo, *vel* in domino. J.D.C. juris dicendi causâ. IDQ. idemque. I.D.T.S.P. in diem tertium, *sive* perendinum. ID.E. idem est. I.E. interest, in eum, *vel* judex esto, *vel* in ære. J.F. Julii filius, *vel* in foro, &c. I.FO.C. in foro Cæsaris. I.FO.P. in foro pacis, *vel* Palladis. I.FO. TR. in foro transitorio. IFT. interfuerunt. IG. igitur. I.G. in agro. J.H. justus homo, *vel* in honestatem. J.H.S. Jesus hominum Salvator. III.VIR. Triumviri. II.V.DD. duum viris dedicantibus. I.J. In jure, inibi, jus jurandum. J.J.J. justa judicavit judicia. IIR. integrè restituit. IL. illustris. J.L. jure legis, *vel* in loco, *vel* justa lex. I.L.A. in loco absente. I.L.D. in loco divino, *vel* loco domus. I.L.P. in loco publico, *vel* loco præsente. J.L.R. in loco religioso. IL.S.T. illustris sublimitas tua. IM. hymnus, jam. IMP. Imperator. IMPP. Imperatores, *viz.* de duobus. IMPPP. Imperatores, *viz.* de tribus. I.M.CTT. in media civitate. IMM. immunis. I.MO. in medio. IMPL. Imperialis. I.M.TPL. in medio templo. IN.D. intercisum diem. J.N.EE. Justum non esse, &c. INT. *vel* INC. initio. IN.B.M. in bonâ memoriâ. IN.FR.P.VI. Lat. VII. in fronte pedes sex, latum *vel* in latitudine, eptem. INL. MA.T. illustris magnificentia tua. INTS. introeuntes. IN.H.H. in hoc honore. IN.H.DD. in honorem dedicatum. IN.H.M. in hoc magistratu. IN.H.MM.S.P.S. in hoc monumento sunt pecuniæ sacræ. IN.M.M.E. in magistratu mortuus est. IN.PR.O.E. in prælio occisus est. I.N.R.I. Jesus Nazarenus, rex Judæorum. IN.TUT. in tutelam. IN.ÆR.PP.R. in ærario Pontificum Romanorum. J.O.M.D. Jovi optimo maximo dedicatum. J.O. M.H. Jovi optimo maximo Hammoni. J.P. justa persona, in publico, jus prætoris, *vel* præcepti, justus possessor, *vel* in possessione, *vel* jus pontificum, *vel* intrà provinciam. I.PNA. in piscinâ. I.PS. in possessione. I.PT. in positione. I.PTE. in pariete. J.S. judicium solvi, in senatu *vel* judicio senatûs, *vel* judicium solius, *vel* judicatum solvi. I.S.C. in senatus consulto, *vel* judex sacrarum cognitionum. I.S.S. infrà, *vel* inferiùs scripta sunt. I.T. intra tempus, *vel* jure testamenti. I.T.C. intra tempus constitutum. IT.II.CL. intra duos colles. IT.II.SPL. intra duo sepulchra. IT.LM. intra limen, *vel* limites. IV. *vel* iiii. quatuor. J.V. justus vir. JUC. judicium. J.U.D. Juris utriusque Doctor. JURD. jurisdictio. JUD. judicium. JUDA. judicia. JUL. Julius. JUN. Junius. JUV. juvenis, *vel* juventus. JUVEN.M. juvenum moderator.

K.

K. calendæ, caput, cardo, castra, charissime, Cœlius. KAR. Carthago. K.AUG. calendas Augusti. K.DD. castra dedicavit, *vel* dedicamus, *vel* dedicaverunt. K.FEB. calendis Februarii. KD. calendæ, *vel* calendis. KL.NOV. calendis Novembris. KL.OCT. calendis Octobris. KM. charissimus. K.MA. calendis Maii. K.MART. calendis Martii. K.MR. chara memoria. KO. Carolo. K.P. Carolo positus. K.Q. calendæ Quintiles. KRM. carmen, *viz.* tonus *vel* sonus. KR.AM.N. carus amicus noster. K.R.N. carus rex noster. K.S. calendæ Sextiles.

L.

L. Lucius, Lælius, libertus, locus, lex, lector, quinquaginta. L.A. lex alia. LD. laudandum. L.DD.D. locum Diis dicavit. L.DIV. locus divinus. L.M.D.CQ. libens meritò dicat consecratque. LEG. legio. LEG.E.D. lege ejus damnatus. L.F. Lucius filius, *vel* Lucii filii. LG. legavit, *vel* leges. LG.D. legio decima, *vel* legem dat, *vel* dedit. LG.F.S. legem fecit suam. LG.S.J. legem servare jussit. LG.S.P. legem servare promisit. L.H. locum hunc, *vel* locus hæredum. LIB. libertas, libertus, *vel* liberti, &c. L. J.D.A.C. lex Julia de adulteriis coercendis. L.I.J. locus in jure. L.I.J.Q. locus injuriæ Quiritum. L.IMPL. locus imperialis. L.IT.F. locus inter fines. L.JU.REP. lex Juliæ repetundarum. L.J.Q. locus juri Quiritum. LITR. litoræ. L.M.D. locus mortuis dedicatus. L.M.E. lex mecum est, &c. LL. Lælius, legibus. L.L. Lucii libertus, *vel* Lucius libertus. LL.D. Legum Doctor. L.L.PQ.E. libertis, libertatibus, posterisque eorum. L.LUC.Q.F. Licius Luceius Quinti filius. L.M. locus monumento, *vel* more tuorum, *vel* libens meritò, &c. L.N. Latini nominis. LONG. P.VII.L.P.III. longum pedes septem, latum pedes tres. L.P. locus propitius, *vel* proprius, *vel* lege punitus, *vel* Latini prisci, *vel* locus publicus, *vel* privatus, &c. L.R.J. lex regia justa. L.S. laribus sacrum, *vel* locus sacer. L.SC. locus sacer, &c. LT.PR. Latini patres. L.V. lex verus. L.VAL. Lucius Valerius, &c. LUD. AP. ludi Apollinares. LUD.SEC. ludi seculares.

M.

M. Marcus, Mutius, Martius, monumentum, mulier, miles, meum, *vel* meam, mihi, molestus, mors, modo, munus, merito, M'. Manius. M. *vel* MUL. mulier. M.ÆM. Marcus Æmilius. MAM. Mamercus. MA.F. manifestum fecit. MAF. manifestum. MAG.EQ. magister equitum. MAG. MIL. magister militum. MAG. et DEC. magister, et Decuriones. M.AG. militis ager. MAR.ULT. Mars ultor. MAT. P.FEC.ET.S.ET.S.PQ.E. Mater piissima fecit, et sibi, et suis posterisque eorum. M.AUR. Marcus Aurelius. MAX. CS. Maximus Cæsar. MAX.POT. Maximus Pontifex.

ABBREVIATION.

M.B. mulier bona. M.D. Medicinæ Doctor. M.D.O. mihi dare oportet. M.E.M. manceps ejus mancipii. MENS. menses. MENS.JAN. mensis Januarii. MER.S. Mercurio sacrum. M.F. Marci filius, mala fide, malè fidus, vel malæ fidei. M.F.C. monumentum fieri curavit. MG. magis. M.H. malus homo. M.H.E. mihi hæres erit. MI. mihi. M.J. maximo Jove. MIL.IN.COH. militavit in cohorte. M9.ML. miles, vel maleficus. MIL. milites. MM. militum, &c. MMN. matrimonium. MMT. monumentum. M.N. millia nummus, vel nummorum. MO. modi, modo, mors. M.P. Marcus Pacuvius, maximus princeps, malè posuit, vel malè positus. M.P.D. majorem partem diei. M.POP. Marcus Popilius. M.P.II. millia passuum duo. M.R. miles Romanus, milites Ravennatis. MS. menses, mensibus, molestus. M.S. manu scriptum, memoriæ sacrum. M.S.P. memoriæ suæ posuit. M.T.C. vel M.TUL.CIC. Marcus Tullius Cicero. M.T. martis tempore, &c. MU. Mutius. M.VI. mensibus sex. MUL.B. mulier bona. MUL.M. mulier mala. MUL.P. mulier pessima. MUN.JUL. municipium Julia.

N.

N. num, nec, non, nomen, Nonius, nummorum, nascitur, nisi, numerator. N. vel N̄. noster, nepos, numisma. NAT. natalia, natio, vel natione. NAV. navis, vel navibus. NBL. nobilis. N.C.C. non calumniæ causa. NEG. negotiator. NEP. nepos. N.F.C. nostræ fidei commissum. N.F.N. nobili familia natus. N.H. notus homo. N.L. nominis Latini, vel non longe, non liquet. NN. nostrorum. NO. nostrum, nobis. NOBB. nobilibus. NOB.G. nobilis generatus, seu nobilis genere. NOB.F.N. nobili familia natus. NON. nonarum. NON.APR. nonis Aprilis. NOR. nostrorum. N.P. nihil potest. NQ. nusquam, vel nonque, namque, vel nunquam. NR. noster. N.S.E. non sic est. NT. nominatus, vel Novum Testamentum, vel nostri temporis, &c. NU. nuptias. NU. non vis, vel non vacat, vel non valet.

O.

O. optimo, oportet. OB. Obriziacum, vel obriacum, orbem, obiter, obiit. OB.M.E. ob merita ejus. OB.ME.P.E.C. ob merita pietatis et concordiæ. O.BO. omnia bona. OD. ordo. O.D.M. opera domus munus. O.H.S.S. ossa hic sita sunt. O.L. operas locavit. O.M. optimus maximus. OM. omnium. OMA. omnia. OMIS. omnibus. OM.V.F. omnium vivis fecit. ON. omnino. ONA. omnia. ONT.IMP. ornamentum imperiale. OO. oportebit, oportuit omnino, et aliquando omnes. O.O.TS. ornamenta omnibus sextus. OP. optimo, vel opiter, vel oportere. OP.PRIN. optimo principi. OPP. oppidum. OPT. oportere. OR. ornato, vel ordo. ORB.PAR. orbati parentes. ORD. ordinis. OR.M. ordo militum. ORN.IMP. ornamentum imperiale. OS. omnes. OS.C. omnes conciliant. OST. ostia. OT.FN. ostium fenestræ. O.V.D. omni virtuti dedito. O.V.F. optima viventi fecit.

P.

P. Publius, pes, posuit. PACE.P.R. pace populo Romano. PA.DIG. vel P.D. patriatus dignitas. PAR. parentum. PAT. patritius. P.C. pactum conventum, pecunia constituta, patrono coloniæ, vel ponendum curavit. P.C̄. Post consulatum. P.D. publicè dedit. PEC. peculium, vel pecunia. P.F. pius felix. P.FE. publicè fecit. PFM. paterfamilias. P.H.C. publicus honor curandus. P.H. positus hic. PICEN. Piceni. PIENT. pientissimus. P.IR. populus, vel Publius irrogavit. P.J.R. populum jure rogavi. P.JV. vel J. principi juventutis. P.L. Publii libertus. P.M. principi militiæ, pontifex maximus. POM. Pompeius. PON.M. pontifex maximus. POP. populus. POSTH. posthumius, vel posthumus. POT. potestas. P.P. pater patriæ, pater patratus. PQ. postquam. P.R. populus Romanus. PR. prætor. PR.PR. præfectus prætorii. PRÆ.URB. præfectus urbis. PRÆ.PRÆS. præfectus præsidii. PRIN.JUVENT. princeps juventutis. PROCOS. proconsul. PR.PER. prætor peregrinus. PR.S. prætoris sententia. PRÆF. præfectus. PRÆF.VIGIL. præfectus vigilum. PRID.NON.APR. pridie nonas Aprilis. PRID.KAL. vel K. pridie kalendas. PRON. pronepos, vel pronepris. PRS. præses. PRSS. presides, vel prætores. P.S. posuit sibi, plebiscitum. PSC. plebiscita. P.S.F. publicè sibi fecit, vel publicæ saluti fecit. P.S.F.C. publicæ saluti faciendum curavit, vel publico, vel proprio sumptu faciendum curavit. PU. pupilla. PUB. publicus.

Q.

Q. Quintus, vel Quintius. Q. vel QU. quartus. QUÆS. quæstor. QAM. quemadmodum. Q.B.F. quare bonum factum. Q.B M.V. quæ benè mecum vixit. Q.D.C. Quâ de causâ. Q.D.R. quâ de re. Q E.R.E. quanti ea res erit. Q.F. Quinti filius. QUIR. Quirites. Q.L. Quinti libertus, &c. QM. quomodo. Q.N.A.N.N. quandoque neque ais, neque negas. Q.SS.S. quæ superscripta sunt. QT. quantum. Q̄T. quotiens.

R.

RAV. Ravenna. R.C. Romana civitas. R.D. regis domus. REG. regi. REI.M. rei militaris. RESP. respublica. REST. restituit, restitutor. R.F.E.D. rectè factum esse dicitur. R.F.E.V. rectè factum esse videtur. R.G.C. rei gerundæ causa. RG.F. regis filius. RP.C. reipublicæ constituenda.

S.

S. sacrum, sepulcrum, senatus. S.C. senatus consultum. SC.MM. sanctæ memoriæ. SCS. sanctus. SCIP. Scipio. S.D. salutem dicit. SD̄. secundum. SEMP. Sempronius. SEPT. Septimius. SER. Servius, Sergius. SEX. sextus. SEV. Severus. SF. satisfecit. SFT. satisfactum. SIL. Silius. S.L.J.CQ.O.R.E. satisfecit lex, jus, causaque omnium rerum esto. S.O. sine occasione. SP. Spurius. S.P.D. salutem plurimam dicit. SP.D̄. supra dictum. S.P.Q.R. Senatus Populusque Romanus. S.T. sine testibus. ST. statutum. S.T.D. Sacræ Theologiæ Doctor. STIP. stipendionem vel stipendavit. S.U.LQ. sibi uxori liberisque. SUM.MAG. summus magistratus. SYL. Sylla.

T.

T. Titus, Titius, Tullius. T.A. Titus Annius, vel tutoris authoritate. TAB. tabularius. TAB.P.H.C. tabularius provincia Hispaniæ citerioris. TAR. Tarquinius. T.AUG. tutelæ Augustæ. TB. tibi. TER. Terentius. T.F. Titi filius. T.F.I. testamenta fieri jussit. TI. vel TIB. Tiberius. TI.F. Tiberii filius. TI.L. Tiberii libertus. TI.N. Tiberii nepos. TIB.D.F.M. tibi dulci filio meo. T.J.AV.P.U.D. tempore judicem, arbitrumve postulat, ut dit. TIB.CS. Tiberius Cæsar. TIB.CL. Tiberius Claudius. T.LEG.III. tribunus legionis tertiæ. T.LIV. Titus Livius. TM. tantum, terminus, thermæ. TM.P. terminum posuit, vel terminus positus. TM.DD. terminum dedicavit, vel dedicante, vel thermæ dedicatæ. T.P. titulum posuit. TR. trans. TR.CEL. tribuni celerum. TR.ÆR. tribuni ærarii. TR.LEG.II. tribunus legionis secundæ. TR.M. vel MIL. tribuni militum. TR.PL.DESS. tribuni plebis designati. TR.POT. tribunicia potestate. TRV.CAP. triumviri capitales. TRV.MON. triumviri monetales. TRIB.POT. vel PT. tribunitiâ potestate. TUL. Tullius. TU.H. Tullus Hostilius. TUR. turma. TUT. tutela.

V.

V.A. veterano assignatus. VAL. Valerius, vel Valerianus. VAL.CS. Valerius Cæsar. VAT. vates, vel vatum. VB. verba, vobiscum. V.B. viro bono. V.B.A. viri boni

ABBREVIATION.

arbitratu. V.B.F. vir bonæ fidei. V.C. vir consularis, clarus, *vel* clarissimus, usucapio, urbis conditæ. V.CC. valuerunt consules. V.C.C.F. vale conjunx charissima, feliciter. V.D. vivus dedit. V.D.A. vale dulcis amice. V.DD. voto dedicatur. V.DICT. vir dictatorius. V.D. N.V. vale decus nostræ urbis. V.E. verum etiam, vir egregius, *aut* excellens. V.E.FL.AUG.PP. vir egregius, *aut* excellens, flamen Augusti *vel* Augustalis perpetuus. VESP. Vespasianus. VET. veteranus, *vel* vetaria, *scil.* tribu. VET.AUG.N. veteranus Augusti nostri. VET.LEG.S. veteranus legionis secundæ. UF. usufructus. V.G. verbi gratiâ. V.J. vir justus, *vel* illustris. VIC. victores, victor, *vel* victoria. VIR.VE. virgo vestalis. VIX. vixit. VIX. A.LIIX. vixit annis quinquaginta octo VIX.A.III.M.XI. D.XV. vixit annis tribus, mensibus undecim, diebus quindecim. VL. videlicet. ULPS. Ulpius, *vel* Ulpianus. VM. vestrum. VM.E. verum etiam. V.M.M. votum meritò Minervæ. V.MUN. vias munivit. V.N. quinto nonas. V.N.U. viro nostro urbis. V.S. votum solvit. V.V. virgini Vestali. V.V.E. vobis visum erit.

X.

X.P. decem pondo, decem pedes. XPS. Christus. X.V. decem viri. [For the Greek and Roman numerals, vide *Numeral.*] *Liv. Hist.; Tac. Annal. &c.; Val. Prob. Pet. Diacon. et alii Grammat. Lat. Vet.; Goltz. Fast.; Smet. Inscript. Vet.; Gruter. Thes. Inscript. passim.*

Modern Abbreviations used in Law Books.

A. (a.) B. (b.) A. front, B. back of a lease. Abr.Ca. abridged cases of equity. A. An. anonymous. An.B. Anonymous Benloe, *i. e.* Reports printed at the end of Benloe. Al. Aleyn. And. Anderson. Andr. Andrews. Ass. assize. Ast.Ent. Aston's Entries Atk. Atkyns. Ayl. Ayliffe.

B.

Bac. Abr. Bacon's Abridgement. Banc.Sup. upper bench. Benl.Bendl. Benloe, Bendloe. B.Tr. Bishop's Trial. Bl. Blount. Bla.Com. Blackstone's Commentaries. Bo.R. Act. Booth's Real Actions. Bra. Brady and Bracton. Bridg. Bridgman. Br. Brooke, Browne, Brownlow. Br. Brev. Jud. and Ent. Brownlow Brevia Judicial. &c. Bro.Brow. Ent. Brown's Entries. Bro.V.M. Brown's Vade Mecum. B.N.C. Brook's New Cases. Brownl.Rediv. Brownlow Redivivus. B. or C.B. common bench. B.R. King's Bench. Bulst. Bulstrode. Bur. Burrow.

C.

C. codex (juris civilis). Ca. case or placita. Cal. Callis, Calthrope. Cart. Carter. Carth. Carthew. Cas.BR. Cases temp. W. III. (12. Mod.) Cas.L.Eq. Cases in Law and Equity. C.P. Common Pleas. Ca.P. Cases in Parliament. Cawl. Cawley. Ch.Cas. Cases in Chancery. Ch.Pre. Precedents in Chancery. Ch.R. Reports in Chancery. Clay. Clayton. Cl.Ass. Clerk's Assistant. Clift. Clift's Entries. Cod. or Cod.Jur. Codex by Gibson. Co Cop. Coke's Copyholder. Co.Ent. Coke's Entries. Co.Lit. Coke on Lyttleton (1 Inst.) Co.P.C. Coke's Pleas of the Crown. Co M.C. Coke's Magna Charta (2 Inst.) Co. on Courts. Coke's 4 Inst. Com. Comberbach. Com. Comyn's Reports. Com.Dig. Comyn's Digest. Con. contra. Cot. Cotton. Cro. Croke's Keilway. Cro. (1.2.3.) Croke (Eliz. Jam. Cha.) Cromp. Crompton.

D.

D. dictum, digest. Dal. Dalison. Dalt. Dalton. D'An. D'Anvers. Dav. Davis. Dig. Digest of Writs. Dugd. Dugdale. Di.Dy. dyer. D^r doctor. Dub. dubitatur.

E.

E. Easter Term. Eq.Ca. Equity Cases or Reports. E. of Cov. Earl of Coventry's case.

F.

Far. Farresley. Ff. answering to the Greek π. pandectæ *juris civilis.* Fin. Finch's Reports. F.Fitz. Fitzherbert. F.N.B. Fitzherbert Natura Brevium. Fitz-G. Fitz-Gibbon. Fl. Fleta. Fol. Foley's Poor Laws. Forr. Forrester. Fort. Fortescue. Fost. Forst. Foster, Forster. Fra. Francis. Freem. Freeman's Reports.

G.

Gilb. Gilbert. Godb. Godbolt. Godol. Godolphin. Golds. Goldsborough. Gro. de j. b. Grotius de jure belli.

H.

Han. Hansard. Hard. Hardres. Hawk. Hawkins. H.H. P.C. Hale's Hist. Plac. Cor. H.P.C. Hale's Pleas of the Crown. Her. Herne. Het. Hetley. H.Hil. Hilary Term. Hob. Hobart. Hugh. Hughes. Hut. Hutton.

J.

Jan. Angl. Jani Anglorum. Jenk. Jenkins. 1.2.Inst.C. (1.2.) Coke's Institutes. Just. 1.2.3. Justinian's Instit. lib. 1. tit. 2. sec. 3. Jon. 1.2. Jones, W. and T. Jud. judgments.

K.

Keb. Keble. Kel. Sir John Kelynge. Kel.1.2. Wm. Kelynge's Rep. 2 Parts. K.C.R. Reports temp. King C. Keilw.Kel. Keilway. Ken. Kennet.

L.

Lamb. Lambard. La. Lane. Lat. Latch. Leon. Leonard. Lev. Levinz. Le. Ley. Lib.Ass. Liber Assisarum. Lib. Feud. Liber Feudorum. Lib.Intr. Old Book of Entries. Lib.Pl. Liber Placitandi. Lil.Abr. Lilly's Practical Register, or an Abridgement, &c. Lind. Linwood. Lyt. Lyttleton. Lut. Lutwyche.

M.

Mad. Madox. Mal. Malyne. Man. Manwaring. Mar. March. M.Mich. Michaelmas Term. Mo.Mod.Ca. modern cases. Mod.c.l.&eq. modern cases in law and equity. Mod.Int. 1.2. Modus Intrand. 1.2. Moll. Molloy.

N.

N.Benl. New Benloe. N.L. Nelson's Lutwyche. N.Nov. novellæ (juris civilis). No.N. novæ narrationes.

O.

O.Benl. Old Benloe. Off.Br. officina brevium. Off.Ex. office of executors. Ord.Cla. Clarendon's orders. Ow. Owen.

P.

Pal. Palmer. P.Pas. Easter Term. Pl.Pla.P.p. placita. P.C. pleas of the crown. P.W. Peere Williams. Perk. Perkins. Pig. Pigot. Pl.Com. Plowden's Commentaries. Pol. Pollexfen. Poph. Popham's Reports. 2.Poph. Cases at the end of Poph. Rep. P.R.C.P. Pract. Register in the Common Pleas. P.R.Ch. Pract. Register in Chancery. Pr.Reg.Cha. precedents in Chancery. Priv.Lond. privilegia Londini. Pr.St. private statute.

Q.

Quinti Quinto. Year Book, 5 Hen. V. Q.War. quo warranto.

R.

R. resolved, repealed. R.S.L. readings on the Statute Law. Rast. Rastall. Ld.Raym. Lord Raymond's Reports. Raym.T. Sir Tho. Raymond's Reports. Reg.Brev. Registrum Brevium. Reg.Pl. Regula Placitandi. Reg. Jud. registrum judiciale. Reg.Orig. Registrum omnium Brevium originalium. Rep.(1.2.&c.) 1. 2. &c. Coke's Reports. Rep.Eq. Gilbert's Reports in Equity. Rep.Q.A. Reports *temp.* Q. Anne. Rob. Robinson. Roll. roll of the term. Roll.Ab. Rolle's Abridgement of Cases, &c. Ry.F. Rymer's Fœdera.

ABBREVIATION.

S.

Salk. Salkeld. Sav. Savile. Saund. Saunders. S. §. section. S. B. upper bench. S. C. same case. Sec. section. Sel. Selden. Sel. Ca. select cases. Sem. *semble*, seems. Sess. Ca. sessions cases. Show. shower. Sid. Siderfin. Skin. Skinner. Som. Somner, Somers. Spel. Spelman. St. Ca. Stillingfleet's Cases. S. P. same point. S. C. C. Select Chancery Cases. Stamf. St. P. C. & Pr. Stamforde Pleas and Prerog. Stat. W. statute Westminster. Stra. Strange. Sty. style. St. Tri. State Trials. Swin. Swinburne.

T.

Th. Dig. Theloal's Digest. Th. Thesaurus Brevium. Toth. Tothill. T. R. *teste rege*. T. R. E. or T. E. R. *tempore Regis Edwardi*. Tr. Eq. Treatise of Equity. Trem. Tremaine. Trin. Trinity Term.

V.

Vaug. Vaughan. Vent. Ventris. Vet. Utr. Old B. entries Vet. n. br. *old natura brevium*. Vern. Vernon. Vid. Vidian. Vin. Abr. Viner's Abridgement.

W.

W. 1. W. 2. statutes Westminster. Win. Winch.

Y.

Y. B. Year book. Yelv. Yelverton's Reports.

Abbreviations used in Commerce.

A. *accepté*, accepted. Acct. Account. A. P. *à protester*. A. S. P. *accepté sous protest*. A. S. P. C. *accepté sous protest pour mettre à compte*. C. *compte*, account. C. O. *compte ouvert*, open account. C. C. *compte courant*, account current. M. C. *mon compte*, my account. S. C. *son compte*, his account. L. C. *leur compte*, their account. N. C. *notre compte*. C. Quintal or hundred weight. D. ou d. *deniers tournois*. DAL. D^RE. *daller, daldre*. DEN. *deniers de gros*. D^o. ditto. DUC. D^D. ducat. F. d'or, florins of gold. F. FL. F^S. florins. F^O. folio. Gr. gros. L G. ou L. de G. livres de gros. L. ST. *livres sterling*, pounds sterling. L^V. livres. ℒ. *livres tournois*. M. M^C. marc or marcs. M. L. *marc lubs*. N^o. *numero*. ON. ONC. onces. P. *protesté, payé*. P^R. C^T. per cent. P^R. O/O. *pour cent*. R. *reçû*. Rec^t. received. Rec^t. receipt. R^O. recto. R^S. *remises*. R. R^X. R^LE. *rixdale, richedale, rixdollar*. S. *sols tournois*. T^RE. T^RS. *traité, traités*.

Modern Abbreviations in vulgar Use.

A.

a. acre. a. or adj adjective. A. B. or B. A. *Artium Baccalaureus*, Bachelor of Arts. Abp. archbishop. A. C. *ante Christum*, before Christ. Acct. accompts. A. D. *anno Domini*, in the year of our Lord. ad. or adv. adverb. A. F. or A. fir. firkin of ale. A. M. *ante meridiem*, before noon; or *anno mundi*, in the year of the world. ā *ana*, each. Ank. anker of brandy. A. P. G. Professor of Astronomy in Gresham College. A. U. C. *anno urbis conditæ*, in the year of the city, i. e. the building of Rome.

B.

B. *basso*, bass. B. or bk. book. Bar. barrels or barleycorns. Bart. baronet. B. C. before Christ, or bass continued. B. C. L. Bachelor of Civil Law. B. D. *Baccalaureus Divinitatis*, Bachelor of Divinity. B. F. or B. fir. firkin of beer. B L. *Baccalaureus Legum*, Bachelor of Laws. B. M. *Baccalaureus Medicinæ*, Bachelor of Medicine. Bp. bishop. B V. *beata Virgo*, blessed Virgin. Bu. Bushel.

C.

C. or cap. *caput*, chapter. C. or cent. *centum*, a hundred. C. B. Companion of the Bath. C. C. 200, or Caius College. C. C. C. 300, or Corpus Christi College. CCCC. 400. Cap. captain. Ch. Ch. Christ Church. Chal. chaldron. Chron. Chronicles. Cit. citizen. Co. company. Cochl. *cochleare*, a spoonful. Col. colonel or Colossians. Coll. college. Conj. conjunction. Cor. Corinthians. C. P. S. *Custos Privati Sigilli*, Keeper of the Privy Seal. Cr. creditor. C. S. *Custos Sigilli*, Keeper of the Seal. Ct. count. Cwt. hundred-weight.

D.

D. *denarius*, pence. Dan. Daniel. D. D. *Divinitatis Doctor*, Doctor of Divinity. Dec. December. Deg. degrees. Deut. Deuteronomy. D. F. *Defensor Fidei*, Defender of the Faith. D. G. *Dei gratia*, by the grace of God. Do. *ditto*, the same. Dr. doctor, debtor, or dram. D. T. *Doctor Theologiæ*, Doctor of Divinity. Dwt. pennnyweight.

E.

E. east. Eccl. Ecclesiastes. Eccles. ecclesiastical. E. E. English ells. E. G. *exempli gratiâ*, for example. Ep. epistle. Eph. Ephesians. Esq. esquire. Ex. example. Exon. Exeter. Exr. executor.

F.

F. *fiat*, let it be done; or *forte*, strong. Far. farthing. F. A. S. *Fraternitatis Antiquariorum Socius*. Fellow of the Antiquarian Society. F. E. or Fl. E. Flemish ells. F. E. or Fr. E. French ells. Feb. February. Fig. figure. F. L. S. *Fraternitatis Linneanæ Socius*, Fellow of the Linnæan Society. F. R. S. & A. S. *Fraternitatis Regiæ Socius et Associatus*, Fellow and Associate of the Royal Society. F. S. A. Fellow of the Society of Arts. Ft. feet. Fth. fathom. Fur. furlong.

G.

Gal. gallons or Galatians. G. C. B. Knight Grand Cross of the Bath. Gen. general or Genesis. Gent. gentleman. G. R. *Georgius Rex*, King George. Gr. grains.

H.

H. or hr. hours. Heb. Hebrews. Hhd. hogsheads. H. M. S. His Majesty's ship.

I.

Ib. or ibid. *ibidem*, in the same place. I. e. *id est*, that is. Jer. Jeremiah. J. H. S. *Jesus hominum Salvator*, Jesus the Saviour of men. In. inches. Incog. *incognitò*, unknown, as a stranger. Inst. instant, or of this month. Interj. interjection. Itin. itinerary.

K.

K. A. Knight of St. Andrew, in Russia. K. A. N. Knight of Alexander Neweki, in Russia. K. B. Knight of the Bath. K. B. A. Knight of St. Bento d'Airs, in Portugal. K. B. E. Knight of the Black Eagle, in Russia. K. C. Knight of the Crescent, in Turkey. K. C. B. Knight Commander of the Bath. K. C. S. Knight of Charles III. of Spain. K. F. Knight of Ferdinand, of Spain. K. G. F. Knight of the Golden Fleece, in Spain. K. G. V. Knight of Gustavus Vasa, of Sweden. K. J. Knight of Joachim. K. L. Knight of Leopold, of Austria. K. M. Knight of Malta. K. M. H. Knight of Mont, in Holstein. K. M. J. Knight of Maximilian Joseph, in Bavaria. K. P. Knight of St. Patrick. K. M. T. Knight of St. Maria Theresa, in Austria. K. N. S. Knight of the Royal North Star, in Sweden. K. R. E. Knight of the Red Eagle, in Russia. K. S. Knight of the Sword, in Sweden. K. S. A. Knight of St. Anne, in Russia. K. S. E. Knight of *St. Esprit*, i. e. of the Holy Ghost, in France. K. S. F. Knight of Ferdinand, of Sicily. K. S. G. Knight of St. Georgia, in Russia. K. S. L. Knight of the Sun and Lion, in Persia. K. S. P. Knight of St. Stanislaus, in Poland. K. S. W. Knight of St. Wlademir, in Russia. K. W. Knight of William, in the Netherlands. K. T. Knight of the Thistle. K. T. S. Knight of the Tower and Sword, in Portugal. Kil. kilderkin. Kt. knight.

L.

L. or lib. *libra*, pound. L. or lib. *liber*, book. L. D. Lady Day. Ldp. lordship. Lea. leagues. Lev. Leviticus.

ABBREVIATION.

Lieut. lieutenant. LL.D. *Legum Doctor*, Doctor of Laws. L.S. *locus sigilli*, the place of the seals.

M.

M. *mille*, a thousand; marquis; minutes; miles; in a recipe, *manipulus*, a handful; *misce*, mingle; and *mixtura*, a mixture; as a brand, murder; in astronomical tables, meridional or *meridies*. M.A. *Artium Magister*, Master of Arts. Mal. Malachi. Matt. Matthew. M.B. *Medicinæ Baccalaureus*, Bachelor of Physic; or *Musicæ Baccalaureus*, Bachelor of Music. M.D. *Medicinæ Doctor*, Doctor of Physic. Mast^r. master. Mem. *memento*, remember. Messrs. *Messieurs*, gentlemen. M.P. member of parliament. Mr. mister. Mrs. mistress. MS. *manuscriptum*, manuscript. MSS. *manuscripta*, manuscripts.

N.

N. north, note, noun, or nails. N.B. *nota bene*, observe, take notice. Nem. con. or Nem. diss. *nemine contradicente*, or *nemine dissentiente*, unanimously. No. *numero*, number. Nov. November. N.S. new style. Numb. numbers.

O.

Obt. obedient. Oct. October. O.S. old style. Oxon. Oxford. Oz. ounces.

P.

P. pints, poles, or pugil, the eighth part of a handful. Parl. parliament. Part. participle. Per cent. *per centum*, by the hundred. Pet. Peter. Phil. or Philip. Philippians. Pk. pecks. Pl. plural. P.M. *post meridiem*, afternoon. P.M.G. Professor of Music in Gresham College. Pot. pottles. Prep. preposition. Pres. president. Pret. preterite. Prob. problem. Prof. professor. Prof.Th.Gr. Professor of Divinity in Gresham College. Pron. pronoun. Prop. proposition. Prov. provost. P.S. *postscriptum*, postscript or Psalms. Pt. or pts. part or parts, pint or pints. Pun. puncheon.

Q.

Q. question; and *quasi*, as though. Q.D. *quasi dictum*, as if it were said. Q.E.D. *quod erat demonstrandum*, which was to be demonstrated. Q.E.F. *quod erat faciendum*, which was to be done. Q.PL. *quantum placet*, as much as you please. Qr. or qrs. quarter or quarters. Q.S. *quantum sufficit*, a sufficient quantity, or as much as will do. Q.V. *quantum vis*, as much as you will; or *quod vide*, which see.

R.

R. *rex*, king; or roods. Rec. *recipe*, take. Rec^d. received. Rect. rector. Reg.Prof. regius professor. Rev. revelation. Rev^d. reverend. R.N. royal navy. Rom. Romans. Rt. Hon. right honourable. Rt. Wpful. right worshipful. Run. runlet.

S.

S. south. S. or St. saint. S. or Sec. seconds. Sec. secretary. Sept. September. Sh. shillings. Sol. solution and Solomon. Sr. Sir. S.S. *socius* and *societatis*. St. street.

T.

Theor. theorem. Tim. Timothy. Tit. Titus.

V.

V. verb or verse; or *vide*, see. v.a. verb active. Ult. *ultimo*, last, or of last month. V.n. verb neuter. Viz. *videlicet*, that is to say, namely.

W.

W. or wk. weeks.

X.

Xmas. Christmas. Xn. Christian. Xper. Christopher.

Y.

Ye. the. Ym. them. Yn. then. Yr. your and year. Ys. this. Yt. that.

ABBREVIATION (*Math.*) the reducing of fractions to the lowest terms, which is performed by dividing both the numerator and denominator by any term which will divide them, without leaving a remainder; thus, $\frac{14}{16}$ becomes equal to $\frac{7}{8}$, to $\frac{1}{2}$, and lastly to $\frac{1}{4}$, the lowest terms if divided successively by 2; and in Algebra $\frac{12\,abx^2}{4\,acx}$ becomes equal to $\frac{3\,bx}{c}$ if divided by $4ax$. *Wallis. Math.*

ABBREVIATION (*Print.*) characters or signs are called abbreviations, which stand for any word or syllable, as y^e for *the*, or ē for *em*, *en*, y^t for *that*, &c. These were formerly in use, but are now obsolete.

ABBREVIATION (*Alch.*) a short way of performing a process.

ABBRE'UVOIRS (*Arch.*) vide *Abreuvoir*.

ABBRO'CHEMENT (*Law.*) *Abbrocamentum*, forestalling a market or fair.

ABBUTTALS (*Law*) vide *Abuttals*.

A'BDALS (*Hist.*) from *abda*, a pious man, a hermit; a sect of enthusiasts among the Persians, who pretended to inspiration. An abdal was *furens deo*, like the Sybils of old.

A'BDAR (*Polit.*) an officer of the King of Persia, who acted as his cup-bearer.

ABDELA'RI (*Bot.*) an Egyptian plant, the fruit of which would nearly resemble a melon if it were not so oblong, and its extremities so acute. *Raii Hist. Plant.*

ABDELA'VI (*Bot.*) an Egyptian plant, very like a melon: Melo Ægyptius. *C. Bauh. Pin.*; *Prosp. Alp. Ægypt.*

A'BDEST (*Theol.*) the ablution or washing of the hands, face, and other parts, according to the religious rites of the Mahometans. "I have seen many go out of the mosque in the midst of their devotions to take fresh abdest." *Pitt's faithful Account of the Mahometans.*

ABDE'VENAM (*Astrol.*) the head of the twelfth figure of the heavens.

ABDICA'TIO (*Ant.*) ἀποκήρυξις, a formal renunciation of children by their parents, which was a Grecian custom prohibited by the laws of the Romans. *Lucian in Abdicat.*

A'BDITÆ causæ (*Med.*) hidden or remote causes. *Celsus.*

ABDITO'RIUM (*Archæol.*) a hiding place, as the chest in York Cathedral for preserving valuables. *Mon. Anglic.*

ABDO'MEN (*Anat.*) so called, from *abdo*, to hide, because the viscera are hidden in it, is that cavity which was termed by the ancients, κατακοιλία, *imus venter* or *alvus*, the lower belly, beginning immediately under the thorax, or middle belly, and ending at the pelvis of the ossa innominata. The abdomen is divided into four regions, three of which are anterior and one posterior. The anterior are the *epigastric*, or superior region; the *umbilical*, or middle region; and the *hypogastric*, or lower region. The posterior region is the *regia lumbaris*, or Loins. The *epigastric region* is situated at a small depression, called the Pit of the Stomach, and is divided into three parts; the one middle, named *epigastrium*; and two lateral, named *hypochondria*. The *umbilical region* is divided into one middle, called properly the *regio umbilicalis*, or the Navel; and two lateral, called the *ilia*, or Flanks. The *hypogastric* region is divided into one middle, named the *pubis*; and two lateral, called the *inguina*, or Groins. The cavity of the abdomen is separated from that of the thorax by the muscular diaphragm, or Midriff; and the bottom of the abdomen, which answers to the pelvis of the skeleton, is terminated anteriorly by the Pudenda, and posteriorly by the *clunes* or Buttocks. The space between the *anus* and *pudenda* is called the *perinæum*; and the membrane with which the abdomen is lined, is called the *peritonæum*. Its contents, or viscera, are anteriorly, the *epiphron*, the *ventriculus*, or Stomach; the Intestines, large and small; the Mesentery, the Pancreas, Spleen, Liver and Gall-bladder; posteriorly, the Kidneys, Ureters, and *receptaculum chyli*, Urinary Bladder, and in women the *uterus*, or Womb, &c. *Hippocrat. de Nat. Hom. et Struct. Hom. &c.*; *Aristot. Hist. Anim.* l. 1, c. 13; *Ruff. Ephes. de Appell. Part. Corp. Hum.* l. 1, c. 3, &c.; *Jul. Poll. Anom.* l. 2, segm. 168, &c.; *Gal. de Meth. Med.* l. 6; *Oribas. Med. Coll.*

l. 24, c. 1, &c.; *Fallop. Anat.*; *Eustach*; *Tab. Anatom.*; *Gorr. Def. Med. in Voc.* κοιλία; *Foes. Oeconom. Hippocrat. Meister. Surg.* p. 141, &c.; *Winslow's Anatom.*; *Chesselden's Anat.* &c.

ABDOMEN *of Fishes*, in comparative anatomy, is covered in its lower part with a black thin membrane answering to the human *peritonæum*, and consisting of annular segments. It lies behind the thorax, from which it is separated by a membranous partition, but no muscular diaphragm.

ABDO'MINAL (*Anat.*) an epithet for what belongs to the abdomen, as the *Abdominal* arteries, muscles, nerves, &c.—*Abdominal Ring*, or the *Annulus Abdominis*, an oblong tendinous opening in the groin, through which the spermatic chord passes in men, and the round ligament of the uterus in women. It is through this aperture that the intestines fall in cases of rupture.

ABDOMINA'LES (*Ich.*) the fourth order of fishes having the ventral fins behind the pectoral. [Vide *Pisces.*] It includes the following genera—namely the *Cobitis*, Loche; of the same thickness nearly from head to tail.—*Amia*; head naked, bony, and rough.—*Silurus*; head naked, broad, compressed.—*Teuthis*; head truncate on the forehead.—*Loricaria*; head smooth, depressed.—*Salmo*, Salmon, head smooth, compressed.—*Fistularia*, Tobacco-Pipe-Fish; body round, gently tapering from the jaws to the tail.—*Esox*, Pike; head flattish above, dorsal and anal fins very short.—*Elops*; head smooth, edges of the jaws and palate rough, with teeth.—*Argentina*, Argentine; teeth in the jaws and tongue.—*Atherina*, Atherine; upper jaw a little flat, gill membrane brayed.—*Mugil*, Mullet; lips membranaceous, teeth.—*Exocœtus*, Flying-Fish; head scaly.—*Polynemus*; head compressed and covered with scales.—*Clupea*, Herring; belly carinate and serrate, tail forked.—*Cyprinus*, Carp; mouth small, without teeth. *Linn. Syst. Nat.*

ABDU'CENT (*Anat.*) an epithet for some muscles. vide *Abductor*.

ABDUCE'NTES *Nervi*, part of the sixth pair of nerves, so called because they are lost on the abductores oculi.

ABDU'CTION (*Surg.*) κατάγμα. 1. A fracture of the bones καυλῆδον, after the manner of a stalk, when the extremities of the fractured bone recede from each other. *Gal. Meth. Med.* l. 2, &c. 2. A strain, according to *Cælius Aurelianus de Morb. Chron.* l. 5, c. 1.

ABDUCTION (*Law*) the carrying away any person by force, as the "abduction of an heiress."

ABDUCTION (*Log.*) an argument that leads from the conclusion to the demonstration of a proposition.

ABDU'CTOR (*Anat.*) from *ab* and *duco*, to draw away; an epithet for several muscles which serve the office of drawing away the parts to which they are annexed, as—*Abductor auris*, called by Winslow *Posterior Auris*, by others *Triceps*, pulls the ear backwards.—*Abductor minimi digiti manus vel pedis*, the former of which is called by Winslow *Hypothenar*, and the latter *Parathenar*; they draw the little finger or toe from the rest.—*Abductor pollicis manus vel pedis*, called by Winslow *Thenar*, draws the thumb or great toe from the rest.—*Abductor oculi*, or *indignatorius*, *abducens*, or *musculus exterior*, the scornful muscle is so called, because it expresses scorn, by moving the eye outwards from the great to the little angle.

ABE'LE *Tree* (*Bot.*) the *great white Poplar*, the *Populus alba* of Linnæus.

ABE'LIANS (*Ecc.*) heretics who rejected marriage. This sect arose in the reign of Arcadius, and terminated in that of Theodosius the younger. *August. ad quod vult Deum, et de Hæres.* c. 87.

ABELICE'A (*Bot.*) a small tree in Crete, otherwise called *Pseudo Platanus*. *Raii Hist. Plant.*

ABELMO'LUCH (*Bot.*) a sort of *palma Christi*. *Raii Hist. Plant.*

ABELMO'SCHUS (*Bot.*) the seed of an Egyptian plant which resembles musk in its perfume, and is used by the Arabians, on account of its agreeable flavour, in their coffee. The plant is called musk mallow, and is the *Hibiscus Abelmoschus* of Linnæus. *Raii Hist. Plant.*

A'BELMUSK (*Bot.*) vide *Abelmoschus*.

A'BER (*Geog.*) 1. A Persian word for *on* or *upon*, is used in composition for some places situated on mountains, as Abercobad, &c. 2. Aber, a British word for the fall of one stream or rivulet into another: whence the name of several towns built upon such confluences, as Aberdeen, &c. *Sylv. Gyrald. Itin.* l. 2, c. 1.

ABERDAVI'NE (*Or.*) the *Spinus Fringilla* of Linnæus. *Willough. Ornith.*

A'BEREMURDER (*Law*) plain downright murder in distinction from manslaughter; it is compounded of the Saxon *abere*, notorious, and *mor*, murder. *Leg. Can.* c. 9; *apud Brompt. Chron.*; *Hen. I.* c. 13; *apud Lambard, seu Wylckens.*

ABERRA'TION (*Astron.*) from *ab* and *erro*, to wander, a term applied to the apparent motion of the celestial bodies occasioned by the progressive motion of light and the earth's annual motion in its orbit, which was first discovered by Dr. Bradley, Astronomer Royal, and an account of it was given by himself in the Philosophical Transactions of March, 1728, No. 406.

ABERRATION *of a Star*, an ellipse which appears to be described in the heavens in consequence of the earth's motion in its orbit and the progressive motion of light. The transverse axis of this ellipse is nearly equal, in quantity, for every star, that is, to 40°; the conjugate axis varies for every star, as the sine of the star's latitude, that is, radius is to the sine of the star's latitude, as the transverse axis to the conjugate axis, and consequently a star in the pole of the ecliptic, its latitude being there 90°, will appear to describe a small circle about that pole as a centre, whose radius is equal to 20°.

ABERRATION *of the Planets* is equal to their geocentric motion, or the space through which they appear to move, as seen from the earth during the time that the light is passing from the planet to the earth. *Clair. Acad. Franc.* 1746-7; *Maupert. de la Parall. de la Lune,* § 11; *Simpson's Essays*; *Mem. de Berlin.* tom. ii. p. 14, &c.

ABERRATION (*Opt.*) the deviation of the rays of light when inflected by a lens or speculum, whereby they are prevented from meeting in what is called the geometrical focus. There are two sorts of *aberration*, the one arising from the figure of the lens which produces a geometrical dispersion of the rays when these are perfectly equal in all respects; the second arising from the unequal refrangibility of the rays of light, called after the name of its discoverer, the "Newtonian Aberration."

ABE'SUM (*Chem.*) unslacked or quick lime.

TO ABE'T. (*Law*) Sax. *a* for *ad* or *usque*, and *bedan* or *beteren*, to stir, to encourage, or set on.

ABE'TTOR (*Law*) vide *Accessary*.

ABEVACUA'TIO (*Med.*) a partial evacuation.

ABE'YANCE (*Law*) from the Fr. *beer*, or *bayer*, to gape after in expectance: lands are in *abeyance* which are not actually in the possession, but only in the expectance of him who is next to inherit them. 1 *Inst.*

ABGATO'RIA (*Archæol.*) the alphabets. *Mat. West.*

A'BHAL (*Bot.*) an eastern fruit of a ruddy colour, held to be a powerful emmenagogue.

A'BIB (*Chron.*) אביב, a ripe ear of corn, according to St. Jerom, the name of the first month in the Jewish sacred year, answering to part of March and April, and so called because in Palestine barley was in ear at that time. *Boch. Hieroz. Pars Prior,* l. 2, c. 10.

A'BICUM (*Med.*) a covering.

A'BIES (*Bot.*) ἐλάτη, the fir-tree, which Homer calls ἐλάτη ἐρανομάχη, i. e. the fir stretching itself towards heaven; it is the *Pinus picea*, the *Pinus balsamea*, and the *Pinus abies* of Linnæus. *Theophrast.* l. 1, c. 8, &c.; *Plin.* l. 16, c. 39; *J. Bauh. Hist. Plant.*; *C. Bauh. Enum. Plant.*; *Gerard. Herbal.*; *Park. Theat. Botan.*; *Raii Hist. Plant. &c.*

ABIGA (*Bot.*) from *abigendo partu*, the same as Chamapitys.

ABI'GEVUS (*Law*) or *Abigens*. vide *Abactor*.

AB'ISHERING (*Law*) abishering, or mishering, an exemption from amercements.

A'BIT (*Min.*) or *Aboit*. Ceruss.

ABITE'LLO (*Ecc.*) a sort of ignominious garment, which penitents in the Romish church were obliged to wear by way of penance. *Eymeric. Director Inquisit. Pars.* 3. p. 332.

ABJURA'TIO (*Law*) an oath taken to leave the realm for ever. By the 21 *Jac.* c. 28, this privilege, which had been hitherto granted to some criminals on confession of their crime, was abolished. *Staundf. Offic. Cor.* l. 116, c. 49; 2 *Inst.* 628.

ABJURA'TION (*Ecc.*) or recantation of any doctrines, was enjoined by the Romish church upon all heretics, to be performed publicly before they were admitted to communion. *Eymeric. Direct. Inquisit. Pars.* 3, p. 323; *Simanc. de Cathol. Instit.* c. 1, &c.

A'BLAB (*Bot.*) a shrub of the height of a vine which is said to grow in Egypt.

ABLACTA'TION (*Med.*) from *a*, priv. and *lacto*, to suckle, weaning a child.

ABLACTATION (*Hort.*) a species of ingrafting, by leaving the graft on its proper stock till it be fully incorporated with the new stock.

ABLA'NIA (*Bot.*) a genus of plants, the *Trichocarpus* of Linnæus. *Aublet. Hist. des Plant.*

A'BLAQUE (*Com.*) a fine sort of Persian silk, otherwise called the Ardessine silk.

ABLAQUEA'TION (*Agric.*) the digging about and baring the roots of trees. *Plin.*

ABLA'TION (*Phy.*) *ablatio*, from *ab* and *fero*, to take off or away, a taking away, another name for Abstraction. *Scalig. De Caus. Ling. Lat.*

ABLA'TIO (*Gram.*) the same as Aphæresis. *Scalig. de Caus. Ling. Lat.*

ABLATIO (*Math.*) the same as subtraction.

ABLATIO (*Med.*) 1. An evacuation. 2. A subtraction from the usual diet. 3. An interval between two fevers.

ABLATIO (*Chem.*) the removal of any thing from a process.

A'BLATIVE (*Gram.*) *ablativus*, i. e. taking away, the sixth case in Latin nouns which signifies taking from;—*Ablative absolute*, a noun, with a participle in the ablative case, is said to be absolute when it does not depend upon any other word. This sort of case is mostly used in the Latin language, and answers to the genitive absolute of the Greek. *Charis. Sos. Instit. Gram.* l. 1; *Diomed.* l. 1; *Isid. Orig.* l. 1.

ABLE'CTI (*Ant.*) ἀπολίκτοι, *Selecti*, a chosen band of foreign troops, selected, according to Polybius, from the 'Extraordinarii Sociorum.' *Polyb.* l. 6, c. 31.

ABLE'GMINA (*Ant.*) choice pieces of the sacrifices among the Romans, sprinkled with flour and offered to the gods. *Tertull. Apolog.* c. 13; *Fest. de Signif. Verb.*; *Buleng. de Sortib.* l. 1, c. 6; *Kipping. Ant. Roman,* l. 1, c. 2.

ABLE'PSIA (*Med.*) ablepsy, or blindness, from α priv. and βλέπω, video.

ABLUE'NTIA (*Med.*) from *abluo*, to wash away, *abluents*, or *abluent* medicines, which carry off impurities from any part of the body. *Gal. de Simplic. Med.* l. 1, c. 37.

ABLU'TION (*Ant.*) from *abluo*, to wash off; the purification of the human body, among the Jews and the Heathens, from some religious pollution.

ABLUTION (*Med.*) 1. Cleansing the body externally or internally. 2. The preparing of a medicine in any liquor, so as to cleanse it from its dregs or any ill quality.

ABNEGA'TION (*Theol.*) the renouncing of passions, pleasures, or lusts.

ABNODA'TION (*Hort.*) the cutting away, or pruning off the knots of trees.

ABO'ARD (*Mar.*) i. e. on board, or in the inside of a ship. Thus " to go *aboard* " is to enter a ship, and " to *board* a ship" is to enter it in a hostile manner —" To fall *aboard* of," is to strike against it whilst in motion.—" *Aboard* maintack," an order to draw one of the corners of the main-sail down to the chess tree.

ABO'I-VENTS (*Fort.*) small lodgements constructed in a covered way to protect soldiers from the weather.

A'BOLA (*Ant.*) Ἄβολα, a sort of dice reckoned among the unlucky by Pollux. *Poll. Onom* l. 7, c. 33; *Hesychius.*

ABOLITA (*Numis.*) an epithet signifying cancelled in application to debts, as on a medal of Adrian which represents, as in the annexed figure, the emperor standing in his paludamentum, with a torch in his right hand, ready to set some papers on fire, whereby he would cancel the arrears due from the people to the treasury. The inscription RELIQUA VETERA H. S. NOVIES MILL. ABOLITA i. e *reliqua vetera sestertium novies millies abolita*. *Gessn. Impp. Num. Tab.* 89, fig. 25; *Vaill. Num. Imp. Rom.* vol. i.; *Hard. Select. Oper.* p. 756; *Occon. Num. Imp.* p. 170; *Pemb. Num. Antiq.* part 3, tab. 63.

ABOLI'TIO Criminis (*Ant.*) the extinction of an action at law, by which the defendant gets his discharge. *Suet. in Aug.* c. 32.

ABOLITIO (*Law*) abolition, leave given by the king or the judges for an accuser to desist from farther prosecution. *Stat.* 25, *Hen.* 8.

ABOLITIO (*Met.*) the entire extinction of a thing.

ABO'LLA (*Ant.*) a cloak used by the Greeks and Romans in following the camp. It was generally lined and doubled, and distinct from the toga.

Mart. l. 8, *Epig.* 46, v. 1.

Nescit cui dederit Turiam Crispinus abollum,
Dum mutat cultus, induiturque togam.

The abolla was also worn by judges in the execution of their office, whence *facinora majoris abollæ*, in Juvenal, for crimes of great magnitude. *Varro apud Non.* l. 14, c. 9; *Turneb. Adv.* l. 27, c. 15; *Salmas de Mod. Usur.* c. 3; *Bulenger. de Imp. Rom.* l. 4, c. 39; *Ferrar. de Re Vest.* l. 1, c. 2, &c.

ABOMA'SUM (*Anat.*) from *ab*, dim. and *omasum*, ἤνυστρον, the paunch, the fourth stomach of a ruminating beast. *Aristot. Hist. Animal.* l. 3, c. 14.

ABORI'GINES (*Ant.*) Αὐτόχθονες, the ancient and original inhabitants of Italy supposed to have been conducted into Latium by Saturn, *vel quod ab origine*, according to Servius; *vel Aberrigines errantes aut vagantes*, according to Festus; *vel ὄρει, quod in montibus degerent*, according to Dionysius Halicarnassus. *Dion. Halicarn. Antiq. Rom.* l. 1; *Liv.* l. 1, c. 1; *Justin.* l. 41; *Sigon. de Nomin. Rom.* c. 4; *Cluv. Ital. Antiq.*; *Panvin. Descript. Urb. et Ferrar. de Orig. Rom. apud Græv. Thes. Antiq. Rom.* tom. 1 & 3.

ABO'RTIENS (*Bot.*) *palaceus* according to Ray, and *sterilis* according to Tournefort; an epithet for a flower which falls off without fruit. *Raii Hist. Plant*; *Tournef. Instit.*; *Linn. Phil. Botann.* p. 219.

ABO'RTION (*Hort.*) a term applied to trees when the fruits fall off, or are blasted before they come to maturity.

ABORTI'VA, *Medicamenta*, (*Med.*) ἀμβλωτικά, medicines

calculated to produce abortion. *Hippoc. de Morb. Mul.* l. 5, 6, &c.; *Foes. Oeconom.* &c.

ABORTIVE (*Bot.*) *Abortiens*, an epithet for a flower which does not come to maturity. *Linn. Phil. Bot.*—*Abortive corn*, corn which shows itself by a deformity in the stalk, leaves, ear, and even grain.

ABORTUS (*Surg.*) or *Aborsus*, from *ab* and *orior*, to come before the time; miscarriage, the emission or ejection of an imperfect foetus, called by Hippocrates ἀποφθορά διαφθορά, ἐκτρωσμός; Galen says that among the Attics it was called ἄμβλωσις. *Hippoc. de Morb. Mul.* c. 5, 6; *Gal. comm.* 1, in lib. 6, *Hippoc.*; *Gorr. Defin. Med.*; *Foes. Oeconom. Hippocrat.*; *Castell. Lex. Medic.*

ABOUCOU'CHOU (*Com.*) a sort of woollen cloth manufactured in Languedoc, Provence, and Dauphiné.

A'BOUKELB (*Com.*) or *Abukelb*, a Dutch coin current in Egypt, something inferior in value to a Spanish piastre, 4s. 8d. It bears the impression of a lion which, however, the Arabians have changed to *kelb*, a dog; either to show their contempt for Christians, or on account of its base alloy.

ABO'UT (*Mar.*) the situation of a ship immediately after she has tacked.—*About ship*, an order to the crew to prepare for tacking.

ABOUT (*Mil.*) a term for the movement by which a body of troops changes its front.—*Right about*, when the soldier turns by a semicircular movement to the right —*Left about*, when the soldier makes a semicircular movement to the left.

ABOUT (*Mech.*) Fr. that part of a piece of wood which is between one of the ends of the piece and a mortise.

ABO'UTED (*Hort.*) a term formerly used for budded, in application to trees. It properly signifies a swelling that comes to a head or abscess, and is figuratively applied to buds which rise up in the form of small heads.

ABP. An abbreviation for archbishop.

A'BRA (*Com.*) a Polish coin worth about three half-pence.

A'BRABAX (*Magic*) *Abraxas*, or *Abrasax*, a magical word comprehending the days of the year in numeral letters. Vide *Abrasax*.

A'BRACADABRA (*Magic*) a cabalistical word used as a charm against fevers, and formed of dropping every time the last letter when written in a kind of cone, as

```
א ב ר כ ד א ב ר א
א ב ר כ ד א ב ר
א ב ר כ ד א ב
א ב ר כ ד א
א ב ר כ
א ב ר
א ב
א
```

ABRA'CALAM (*Magic*) a cabalistical word serving as a charm among the Jews. This, as well as the former *Abrabax*, and the following *Abrasax* [Vide *Abrasax*,] express the name of a Syrian idol. *Selden de Diis Syriis*.

ABRA'HAMITES (*Ecc.*) 1. An order of monks exterminated for idolatry by Theophilus. 2. A sect of heretics called after their leader Abraham, who adopted the errors of Paulus.

ABRA'SA (*Med.*) ulcers attended with, or liable to, abrasion. *Castell. Lex. Med.*

ABRASA'X (*My.*) the name given by the heretic Basilides to God and Jesus Christ, whom they worshipped under the figure of Isis. Osiris, and other Ægyptian gods, as also under the figure of animals, with the head of a cock, a lion, a beetle, or a sphinx; the body of a man, as in the annexed cut; and the tail of a serpent, &c. They impiously conceived our Saviour to be the material sun, in imitation of the Egyptians, who worshipped the sun under the name of Osiris, &c. The word ΑΒΡΑΣΑΞ, *Abrasax*, or *Abraxas*, was chosen because the letters, of which it is composed, make up 365, the number of days, according to the Greek computation by letters, in which the sun performs his annual revolution, i. e. as follows:

A	B	P	A	C	A	Ξ
1	2	100	1	200	1	60

This word was employed as a talisman, and the image was worshipped as a magical deity, who was to dispel evils. *S. Iren. adv. Hæres.* l. 1, c. 2; *Tertul. de Præc.* c. 46; *Euseb. Eccl. Hist.* l. 4, c. 7; *Hieron. adv. Lucif. in Amor.* l. 2; *S. Epiphan. Hæres.* 24; *S. August. de Hæres. et ad quod vult Deum*; *Baron. Annal. Ann.* 120; *Montfaucon. Antiq. expliq.* vol. i. p. 369, et seq.

ABRA'SIO, from *ab* and *rado, to pare*; the paring off of superficial ulcerations. *Castell. Lex. Med.*

ABRA'XAS (*Magic*) vide *Abrasax*.

ABRE'AST (*Mar.*) side by side, or opposite to; the situation of two or more ships when standing together, particularly as regards the line of battle at sea.—*Abreast* line, the line abreast is formed by the ships being equally distant from and parallel to each other, so that the length of each ship forms a right angle with the extent of the squadron or line abreast.—*Abreast* of a place, directly opposite to it, as "a fleet abreast of Beechy-Head," i. e. off, or directly opposite to it.—*Abreast* within the ship, implies on a parallel line with the beam.

ABREAST (*Mil.*) a term formerly used for any number of men in front. They are, at present, determined by files.

ABRE'TTE (*Bot.*) vide *Abelmochus*.

ABREUVO'IR (*Mil.*) a French word for a watering place, or any place dug for retaining water, as in the case of encampment.

ABREUVO'IRS (*Archit.*) 1. The interstices between two stones to be filled up with mortar or cement. 2. Small trenches which are made in stone quarries to carry off the water.

A'BRI (*Mil.*) French for shelter, cover; as *être à l'abri*, to be under the cover of a wood, &c.

TO ABRI'DGE (*Law*) *Abbreviare*, from the Fr. *abréger*; to make a count or declaration shorter.

TO ABRIDGE (*Algeb.*) to reduce a compound equation or quantity to a more simple form of expression, as $x^2 + (a+b)x - \frac{ab}{c} = 0$, by putting $p = a+b$ and $g = \frac{ab}{c}$ becomes $x^2 + px - g = 0$.

ABROHA'NI (*Com.*) or *mallemolle*, a certain muslin, or clear white cotton cloth from the East Indies.

ABRO'MA (*Bot.*) from α priv. and βρῶμα, food, i. e. not fit for food; a genus of plants; class 18 *Polyadelphia*, order 2 *Dodecandria*.

Generic Character. CAL. *perianth* nine-leaved. COR. *petals* five; *nectary* five-cleft. STAM. *filaments* five. PIST. *germ* subcylindrical. PER. *capsule* ovate five-winged, five-celled; *seeds* winged.

Species. The two species are the *Abroma Augusta, Theobroma Augusta seu Althæa Luzonis*, maple leaved abroma tree, a native of New South Wales and the Philippines.— *Abroma, Wheleri*, Wheler's abroma, a shrub, native of the East Indies. *Linn. Spec. Plant.*

ABROMIOS (*Ant.*) Ἀβρώμιος, a sort of drinking cup mentioned by Pollux. *Pol. Onomast.* l. 6, c. 16.

ABROTANOIDES (*Nat.*) a kind of coral in the form of the abrotanum. *Raii Hist. Plant.*

ABROTANOIDES (*Bot.*) the *Artemisia Æthiopica*, the *Protea serraria*, and the *Seriphium cinereum*, *plumosum*, and *fuscosum* of Linnæus. *Bauh. Pin.*; *Raii Hist.*

ABROTANUM (*Bot.*) ἀβρότονον, southernwood; a plant so called, διὰ τὸ ἁβρὸν φαίνεσθαι, on account of its delicate appearance. Nicander describes it as a wild plant of the woods. *Nicand. Theriac.*

Ναὶ μὴν ἀβροτόνοιο τοτ' ἄγριον ὄρεσι θάλλει
Αὖρον ὑπὸ βρυσεω.

Abrotanum is the *Artemisia abrotanum*; the *Santolina chamæcyparissus*, *villosa*, and *rosmarifolia*; and the *Tanacetum* of Linnæus. *Theophrast. Hist. Plant.* l. 6, c. 8; *Diosc.* l. 3, c. 29; *Plin.* l. 19, c. 6; *Gal. de Simpl.* l. 6; *J. Bauh. Hist. Plant.*; *Ger. Herb.*; *Park. Theat. Bot.*; *Raii Hist. Plant.*; *Boerhaav. Ind.* &c.; *Tournef. Instit.*

ABROTONITES (*Med.*) ἀβροτονίτης, wine impregnated with abrotanum. *Diosc.* l. 5, c. 62.

ABROTONUM (*Bot.*) vide *Abrotanum*.

ABRUPTE *Pinnatum* (*Bot.*) abruptly pinnated, an epithet for a leaf which has neither leaflet (foliolum), tendril, nor clasper (cirrus) at the end. *Linn. Philosoph. Bot.*

ABRUPTIO (*Med.*) vide *Abductio*.

ABRUPTUS (*Ich.*) abrupt, an epithet for the lateral line in fishes, when divided into two or more parts not contiguous.

ABRUS (*Bot.*) ἁβρός, *mollis*, *delicatus*, from the softness of its leaves; a kind of kidney bean growing in Egypt, "Phaseolus ruber abrus vocatus." Now called Jamaica wild Liquorice, from its resembling the liquorice in taste. *Prosper. Alpin. Ægypt.*

ABRUS in the Linnæan System, a genus of plants, Class 17 *Diadelphia*, Order 4 *Decandria*.

The Generic Character. CAL. *perianth* one leafed. COR. papilionaceus: *wings* oblong; *keel* oblong. STAM. *filaments* 9; *anthers* oblong, erect. PIST. *germ* cylindrical; *style* subulate; *stigma* in form of a head. PER. *legume* like a rhomb; *seeds* solitary.

Species. The only species is the *Abrus precatorius, glycine; Abbrus konni, phaseolus seu orobus Americanus*, Jamaica wild Liquorice; a tree, native of the Indies. *Prosper. Alpin. Ægypt.*; *Raii Hist. Plant.*; *Breyn. Prodrom.*; *Parkins. Theat. Botanic.*; *Herman. Catalog.*; *Plucken. Phytograph.* &c.

ABSCEDENTIA (*Med.*) from *ab* and *cedo*, to go; the diseased or decayed part which abscedes from the body. *Cels.* l. 5, c. 18.

ABSCESSUS (*Med.*) ἀπόστημα, abscess, an inflammatory tumor. *Hippoc.* l. 4, *Aphor.* 31; *Ruff. Ephes. de Ves. Affect.* c. 9; *Cels. de Re Med.* l. 2, c. 9; *Paul. Ægin.* l. 4, c. 18; *Oribas. de Curat. Morb.* l. 3, c. 43, et 9 *Act. Terah.* 4, *Serm.* 2, c. 32, &c.; *Act. de Meth. Med.* l. 1, c. 17.

ABSCISS (*Math.*) *Abscissa*, or *Abscisse*, from *ab* and *scindo*, to cut off, τὸ ἀποκομμένον; the segment of any diameter or axis of a curve, as A C, or C B, cut off by another line

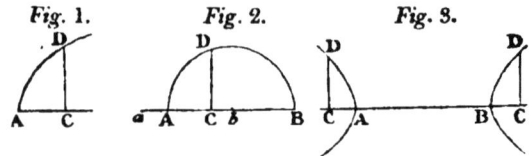

Fig. 1.   Fig. 2.   Fig. 3.

called the ordinate, as D C. The abscisses are understood to commence at the vertex of the curve, as A or B, *fig.* 1, 2, unless expressed otherwise, as in *fig.* 2, where *a* C, A C, C *b*, and C B, are all abscisses. Each ordinate, in a common parabola, has but one abscias, as A C, *fig.* 1; in the circle and ellipse, two lying on opposite sides, as A C, C B, *fig.* 2; and, in the hyperbola, also two lying on the same side, as C A, C B, *fig.* 3. When an abscias and its corresponding ordinate are considered together they are called *coordinates* of the curve, by means of which the equation of a curve is defined. [Vide *Curve.*] *Apollon. Conic.* l. 1, pr. 20, &c.; *Wallis. Mathemat.*; *Wolf. Mathemat. Curs.*

ABSCISSIO (*Med.*) abscission, or cutting off, from *ab* and *scindo*, to cut; 1. cutting away an unsound or luxuriant part. 2. The sudden termination of a disease in death.

ABSCISSIO (*Rhet.*) a figure of speech of cutting short in the discourse after we have begun to speak of any thing. *Cic. ad Heren.* l. 4, c. 54.

ABSCISSION (*Astrol.*) the cutting off the light of the first of three planets when the third comes in conjunction with the middle one.

ABSCONSIO (*Med.*) from *abscondo*, to hide; a sinus or cavity of a bone which receives and conceals the head of another bone.

ABSENT (*Mil.*) a term employed in regimental returns to account for the deficiency of any in a regiment or company.—*Absent with leave*, officers with permission, or non-commissioned officers on furlough excused parade or field duty.—*Absent without leave*, a milder term often used for desertion.

ABSINTHII (*Bot.*) a species of Chrysomela.

ABSINTHITES (*Med.*) ἀψινθίτης, wine impregnated with absinthium or wormwood. *Discor.* l. 5, c. 49.

ABSINTHIUM (*Bot.*) ἀψίνθιον, from ἀ priv. and ψύχω, or τέρψις, *delectatio*, i. e. unpleasant; a plant, so called on account of its bitterness. *Theophrast. Hist. Plant.* l. 9, c. 18; *Dioscor.* l. 3, c. 26; *Plin.* l. 27, c. 7; *Gal. de Simpl.* l. 6. —*Absinthium* is the *Artemisia*; the *Achillea Ægyptiaca, et Clavenæ*; the *Parthenium hysterophorus*; the *Senecio abrotanifoliis*; and the *Tanacetum incanum et annuum* of Linnæus. *J. Bauh. Hist. Plant.*; *C. Bauh. Pin.*; *Ger. Herb.*; *Parkins. Theat. Botan.*; *Raii Hist. Plant.*; *Boerh. Ind.*; *Tournef. Instit.*; *Dale Pharmacop.*

ABSIS (*Math.*) *Abses*, or *Absides*. vide *Apsis*.

ABSOLUTE, *absolutum*, i. e. *ab alio solutum*, dependant on no other thing, as

ABSOLUTE (*Theol.*) free from conditions; so the decrees of God are said to be absolute in regard to man.—*Absolute*, without any cause; thus God is said to be absolute.

ABSOLUTE (*Phy.*) without relation to, or dependance on what is external; as—*Absolute time*, which flows equally in itself without relation to any thing external, as duration.—*Absolute space*, which remains similar and immoveable without relation to any thing exterior.—*Absolute motion*, which is the transfer of any body from one absolute place to another. *Newt. Princ. Math.* def. viii.—*Absolute gravity*, the whole force with which a body is impelled towards the centre, in distinction from specific gravity.

ABSOLUTE (*Gram.*) without regimen or government, as an ablative or genitive *absolute* when the case depends on no other words, as in the Latin *Augusto imperatore*, Augustus being emperor; in the Greek the genitive is employed in place of the ablative.—*Absolute noun*, a noun that needs no other word to be joined to it, as God, reason, horse, &c. *Prisc.* l. 2.—*Absolute degree*, in the comparison of adjectives, the same as the positive.

ABSOLUTE (*Law*) without condition or encumbrance, as an "*absolute* bond," *simplex obligatio*, in distinction from a conditional bond. An "*absolute* estate," one that is free from all manner of condition or encumbrance.

ABSOLUTE *number* (*Algeb.*) the *Homogeneum Comparationis* of Vieta is the term in an equation which is completely known, as in $x^2 + ax = b$, b is the absolute or known quantity. *Viet. Art. Analyt.* c. 8.

ABSOLUTE *equation* (*Astron.*) the sum of the optic and eccentric equation. [vide *Equation*]

ABSOLUTE (*Ecc.*) among the Romanists, in opposition to declaratory. They hold that a priest can forgive sins absolutely; but the protestants say, that the forgiveness is only declaratory.

ABSOLU'TELY (*Log.*) applied to the terms of a proposition, signifies without relation to any thing else.

ABSOLUTELY (*Geom.*) entirely or completely, as a circle is said to be *absolutely* round, in contradistinction to a figure that is partly so, as an oval, &c.

ABSOLU'TIO (*Rhet.*) that perfect division of any cause which embraces all the parts. *Cic. Invent.* l. 1, c. 22.

ABSOLU'TION (*Ecc.*) 1. A judical act in the Romish church whereby a priest, as a judge, by virtue of a power supposed to be delegated to him from Christ, takes upon him to remit the sins of penitents. *Order. Vital.* l. 5. 2. An act, in the reformed as well as in the Romish church, by which a man who stands excommunicated is freed or released from the excommunication.—*Absolutio ad cautelam*, that which is given to an excommunicated person when he wishes to make his appeal against the sentence, and also that which the pope gives to those to whom he grants benefices.

ABSOLUTION (*Law*) a definitive sentence whereby a man accused of any crime is acquitted.

ABSOLUTO'RIUM (*Med.*) an absolute or perfect remedy; also a perfect cure.

ABSOLUTO'RIUS (*Ant.*) from *absolvo*, to acquit; absolvatory, as *tabula absolutoria*, a bill of discharge.

ABSONIA'RE (*Archæol.*) to shun, detest; a term used in the oath of allegiance taken by the Anglo-Saxons.

TO ABSO'RB (*Hort.*) a term applied to all greedy branches that, growing on fruit trees, drink up and rob the other branches of the nutritious juice which is requisite to promote their growth.

ABSORBE'NTIA *Medicamenta* (*Med.*) medicines which have the power of drying up redundant humours.

ABSO'RBENTS (*Chem.*) an epithet for alkaline, or such earthy bases as have the property of absorbing or neutralizing acids; a term used more by the ancients than the moderns.

ABSO'RBENT *vessels* (*Ana.*) *absorbentia vasa*, from *absorbeo*, to absorb or dry up; vessels which carry any fluid into the blood, as the *lacteals*, which absorb the chyle; the *lymphatics*, &c.

A'BSQUE *hoc* (*Law*) i. e. without this; words of exception made use of in a traverse.

ABSTE'MII (*Ecc.*) a name given to persons who could not partake of the sacrament from their natural aversion to wine.

ABSTE'NSIO (*Law*) withholding the heir from taking possession.

ABSTE'NTIO (*Med.*) the retention or suppression of the excrements.

ABSTE'RGENTS (*Med.*) *abstergentia medicamenta*, from *abstergo*, to rinse away; medicines capable of cleansing by the power of dissolving concretions.

ABSTE'RSIVE *Medicines* (*Med.*) vide *Abstergents*.

A'BSTINENCE (*Ecc.*) a ceremony in the Romish church of abstaining from food in a partial manner, by which it is distinguished from fasting, which is almost entire abstinence: hence the terms "Days of abstinence," and "Fastdays."

ABSTINENCE (*Hierog.*) the moral virtue of abstaining from indulgence is represented in painting, by a woman of a healthy constitution holding one hand to her mouth; and in the other a scroll, with the words *Utor, non abutor;* I use, but do not abuse.

ABSTINENCE *from evil* is represented by a woman crowned with laurels, leaning on a pedestal, and looking attentively on a decalogue which lies before her. Under her feet lie serpents, tortoises, and broken arrows; and by her side stands a camel.

ABSTINENCE (*Med.*) from *abstineo*, to abstain. 1. Abstinence from all food, or particular kinds of food. 2. Suppression or compression, as *abstinentia sudoris*, suppression of the sweat; *spiritus ob abstinentiam clausus*, wind shut up by compressure. *Cæl. Aur. de Acut. Morb.* l. 2, c. 82.

A'BSTINENTS (*Ecc.*) heretics professing abstinence from marriage, and particular foods, &c. They appeared in France and Spain about the end of the third century. *Philastr. de Hæres.* c. 26; *Baron Annal. Ann.* 228; *Prateol. de Hæres.*

A'BSTRACT (*Law*) an abridgement or epitome of any original writing.

ABSTRACT (*Log.*) *abstractus*, an epithet applied to whatever is separated from any other thing by an operation of the mind, termed *abstraction;* thus any thing may be said to be considered in the *abstract*.—An *abstract idea* is a simple idea detached and separated from any particular subject or complex idea, as the idea of rationality abstracted or separated from that of corporeal agency.—*Abstract quality*, that quality which is considered as abstracted from the subjects in which it inheres, as whiteness, which is a quality considered abstractedly from a wall, a flower, a man, &c.—*Abstract term*, a term which expresses qualities without regard to the subject, *vox abstracta*, as visibility, rationality, whiteness, &c. in distinction from the concrete.

ABSTRACT *Noun* (*Gram.*) or noun substantive, denotes that which is real, but which subsists only in the understanding; it is distinguished from the *noun adjective*, and answers to the abstract term in logic, as whiteness, coldness, valor, &c.

ABSTRACT (*Math.*) or *pure*, an epithet for that sort of mathematics which treats of the properties of magnitude, figure, and quantity, abstractedly and generally, without regard to any particular object, as arithmetic and geometry, in distinction from mixed mathematics, in which simple and abstract quantities are applied to particular sensible objects, as astronomy, mechanics, optics, &c.—*Abstract numbers* are such as are considered abstractedly, or without regard to any object which they may represent, as 5, 6, 7, &c. in distinction from *concrete* numbers, where the thing is specified with the number, as 5 feet, 6 inches, 7 yards, &c.

ABSTRA'CTIO (*Phy.*) from *abstraho*, to draw asunder; ἀφαίρεσις, τὸ χωρίζειν; a separation of one thing from another, to which it is usually joined. It is of different kinds; namely, *Abstractio realis*, *qui fit ὄντως, re ipsa*, the actual separation of one thing from another, as gold from the earth.—*Abstractio mentalis*, νοητικη, mental abstraction, or the separation of universals from particulars, as the consideration of whiteness in distinction from the wall, the milk, snow, &c. in which it exists; this is taking things in the abstract, and is either—*Abstractio logica*, the abstraction of accidents from their subject, as animal from man or brute.—*Abstractio mathematica*, the abstraction of the form of bodies from the matter *secundum rationem;* or,—*Abstractio metaphysica*, the abstraction of the form of bodies from the matter *secundum rem*, i. e. *Abstractio realis*, real abstraction. *Aristot. Physic.* l. 2, c. 2; *Alex. de Alex. in Met. Aristot.* l. 3; *Albertus Mag. Phy.* l. 1, tr. 1, c. 2; *Fonsec. in Met. Aristot.* l. 5, c. 28, quæst. 6; *Scal. Exercit.* 307, 342.

ABSTRA'CTION (*Chem.*) The process of drawing off by distillation any part of a compound, and returning it again to the residue to be redistilled any number of times; thus arsenic acid may be procured by abstracting arsenic with nitrous acid.

ABSTRACTITIUS (*Chem.*) *vel Abstractivus*, from *abstraho*, to draw away; abstractitious, an epithet for the native spirits of aromatic vegetables, in distinction from those produced by fermentation.

ABSU'RDUM (*Log.*) vide *Reductio ad Absurdum.*

A'BSUS (*Bot.*) a species of the *Cassia* of Linnæus. *Prosp. Alpin.*

ABSY'NTHIUM (*Bot.*) the same as Absinthium.

ABU'NDANCE (*Med.*) *abundantia*, a term employed for an excess of humours.

ABU'NDANT (*Math.*) an epithet for a number, whose aliquot parts, when added together, make a sum greater than the number itself, as 12; the aliquot parts of which 1, 2, 3, 4, 6, are 16; it is opposed to a deficient number.

ABUNDANT *Year* (*Chron.*) a Jewish year when it has a day more than ordinary, in distinction from the defective year. *Scal. Emendat. Temp. l. 2.*

ABUNDA'NTIA (*Numis.*) *Abundantia* was the name of the goddess of plenty on medals, who is called *Copia* by the poets. In the annexed cut, she is represented seated on a chair, like the Roman chairs in general, only that the two sides are wrought into the shape of two Cornucopias, to denote the character of this goddess. The figure of Abundantia is given on medals of *Trajan, Caracalla, Eliogabalus, Alexander Severus, Gordian, Pius, Trajan Decius, Gallienus, Tetricus, Probus, Numerianus, Carinus, Carus, Dioclesian,* and *Valerius Maximianus*; sometimes with the simple inscription ABUNDANTIA, but mostly with the addition of AUG*usti* AUGG. *Augustorum* AUGG. NN. *Augustorum Nostrorum*; sometimes ABUNDANTIA PERPETUA.

ABUNDANTIA *Temporum*, an inscription on a medal of Salonina, the wife of Gallienus the emperor, which bears on the obverse, as on the subjoined cut, her head with a

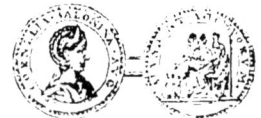

stola or robe over the breast, and the inscription CORNELIA. SALONINA. AUG.; on the reverse, a figure of Salonina, sitting with three boys standing before her, while she pours out coins from the cornucopia which she had in her lap; near her is a female figure standing; and on the right hand, behind the chair, a military figure. *Vaillant. Numism. Imperator. Roman.; Patin. Numis. Imperat. Roman.; Morell. Thesaur. Imp. Roman.; Occo. Numis. Roman. Imperat.; Bandur. Num. Imper. Roman.*

ABUNDANTIA (*Med.*) abundance, or excess of humours.

ABU'SE (*Med.*) *abusus*, from *abutor*, to abuse, an ill use of a thing, applied to nonnaturals in medicines.

ABU'SIO (*Rhet.*) κατάχρησις, a figure of speech by which words are used with some deviation from their proper meaning; thus "worship," which is strictly applied to God only, may also, by *abusio* or misuse, be applied to magistrates, &c.; as in the Scripture, "They worshipped God and the king."

ABU'TILON (*Bot.*) a plant formerly called in English the Yellow Mallow, from its great resemblance to the mallow, both in leaf and flower. Its different species are now known by the names of the *Hibiscus ciliaceus,* the *Melochia pyramidata et tomentosa,* the *Malva caroliniana,* the *Napœa scabra,* and the *Sida spicata,* in the Linnæan system. *J. Bauh. Hist. Plant.; Casp. Bauhin. Pin.; Ger. Herb.; Parkin. Theat. Botan.; Raii Hist. Plant.; Pluk. Almag. Botan.*

ABU'TMENTS (*Arch.*) or *Butments*, the extremities of a bridge, by which it is made to rest upon the banks or sides of rivers, &c.

ABUTMENTS (*Carpent.*) the junctions or meetings of two pieces of timber.

ABU'TTALS (*Law*) from the Fr. *abouter*, to but against, or terminate; the *buttings* or boundings of land. The sides of the lands are properly said to be adjoining, and the ends *abutting* to the thing that is contiguous.

ABY'SS (*Bibl.*) *abyssus*, from α, priv. and βυσσος, Ionice, pro βυθος, a depth, i. e. without a bottom; a depth, an epithet for, 1. Hell. *Luke* viii. 31, &c. 2. The common receptacle for the dead, the grave, or depth of the earth. *Rom.* x. 7. 3. The deepest parts of the sea. *Psalm* xxiv. 29.

ABY'SSUS (*Med.*) the deep, abyss, a proper receptacle for the seminal matter. *Castell. Lex. Med.*

ACA'CALIS (*Bot.*) ἀκακαλις, a shrub bearing a papilionaceous flower, and siliqeous fruit like a tamerisk. *Diosc.* l. 1, c. 118.

ACA'CIA (*Bot.*) ἀκακια, from ἀκάζω, to sharpen; a thorny tree of Egypt, called, by Theophrastus, Ἀκανθη Αἰγυπτικη, by Pliny *acacia,* or the *spina Ægyptiaca,* was supposed by some to be the tree which yielded the *Gummi Arabicum,* or Gum Arabic. *Theophrast. Hist. Plant. l. 9, c. 1; Dioscor. l. 1, c. 130; Plin. l. 24, c. 12.*

ACACIA, in the Linnean system, is the *Mimosa nilotica*; but the Common Acacia, otherwise called *Pseudo-acacia,* or False Acacia, is the *Robinia pseudo-acacia*; and the Rose Acacia, a shrub so called from its rose-coloured flowers, is the *Robinia hispida* of Linnæus. *Prosper. Alpin. de Plant. Ægypt.; J. Bauh. Hist. Plant.; C. Bauh. Enumerat.; Ger. Herb.; Parkin. Theat. Botan.; Raii Hist. Plant.; Tournef. Instit.; Boerhaav. Ind. Plant.*

ACA'CIANS (*Ecc.*) heretics so called after one Acacius, bishop of Cæsarea, who denied the son to be of the same substance as the father. *Baron. Annal. Ann. 359.*

ACADE'MIA (*Ant.*) Cic. Ἀκαδημία, a Gymnasium at Athens, in a grove of the suburbs, where Plato taught. It derived its name from Academus.
Hor. Ep. 22, v. 45.

Atque inter silvas Academi quærere verum.

This school of Plato, in which it was forbidden to laugh, was called *Academia vetus,* in distinction from the *Academia nova,* or *secunda,* founded by Arcesilaus, who departed from the doctrines of Plato; and *Academia tertia,* which was founded by Carneades, or, according to Diogenes Laertius, by Lacydes. Eusebius also makes mention of a fourth *Academia* founded by Antiochus. *Cic. Quæst. Academ. l. 1. c. 4—12; Diog. Laert. Proœm. Segm. 18, 19, &c.; Æl. Var. Hist. l. 3, c. 35; Euseb. Evang. Præparat.* l. 14.

ACADE'MICS (*Ant.*) *academici,* a name for the followers of Plato; a sect of philosophers, so called from the Ἀκαδημία, where he taught.

ACA'DEMY (*Lit.*) from *academia,* a society of learned men instituted and protected by public authority: the first of which, among the moderns, was that founded by Charlemagne at the instance of Alcuin, an English monk; this has been followed by several others, of which the principal are the—*Academia Secretorum Naturæ,* established at Naples in 1560, by Baptista Porta.—*Academia Lyncei,* founded at Rome, among whose early members was Galileo.—*Academia del Limento,* founded at Florence in 1657, by Prince Leopold of Tuscany.—*Academia Degl' Inquieti,* founded at Bologna about the same time.—*Academie Royale,* founded at Paris in 1666.—*Academie Imperiale,* at Petersburg, founded by Peter the Great in 1725.—*Academie Royale des Sciences, &c.* founded, at Berlin, by Frederic I. in 1700, of which Leibnitz was the first president.—*Academie Royale,* at Stockholm, in 1739.

ACADEMY, a collegiate school for the training of youth in the sciences, of which there are three royal foundations in England, two for the military at Woolwich and Midhurst; and one at Portsmouth for the navy.

ACÆ'NA (*Bot.*) a genus of plants, Class 4 *Tetrandria*, Order 1 *Monogynia*.
Generic Characters. CAL. perianth four-leaved; *leaflets* ovate.—COR. none, unless the calyx be termed as such.—STAM. *filaments* equal; *anthers* quadrangular.—PIST. *germ* inferior; *style* very small; *stigma*, a small membrane.—PER. one-celled berry; *seeds* single.
Species.—The *Acæna* is a Mexican plant, having only one species, namely, the *Acæna elongata*. *Linn. Spec. Plant.*

ACA'HI (*Chem.*) alum-water.

ACA'JA (*Bot.*) *Prunus Brasiliensis fructu racemosa*, a tree of Brazil, growing to the size of a tall lime, on the extreme branches of which certain birds build their nests pendulous, that they may be out of the way of serpents. *Marcgrav. Hist. Brasil.; Raii Hist. Plant.*

ACAJA'IBA (*Bot.*) *Acajou*, or *Acajuba*; the *Anacardium occidentale* of Linnæus, and in English the Cashew-tree; the fruit of which is called the Cashew-nut, from which is extracted an oil used by painters to give a black colour, and also a spirit is distilled equal in strength to arrack or rum. *Ger. Herb.; Pis. et Marcgrav. Hist. Bras.; Raii Hist. Plant.*

ACAJOUA'NUM *lignum* (*Bot.*) a sort of wood of a red colour, which is never touched by worms.

A'CALAI (*Chem.*) salt.

ACALE'PHE (*Bot.*) or *Acalypha*, the Ακαληφη of Theophrastus, and Ἀκαλυφη of Dioscorides; a herb so called, παρα το μη εχειν καλην ἁφην, i. e. from its not being pleasant to the touch. *Theophrast. Hist. Plant.* l. 7, c. 7; *Aristoph. Equit.* v. 420; *Diosc.* l. 4, c. 94; *Athen.* l. 3, c. 12.

ACA'LYPHA, in the Linnæan system, the *Rhinocarpus* of Boerhaave or Tickfruit; a genus of plants, Class 21 *Monoecia*, Order 8 *Monodelphia*.
Generic Characters of the Male Flowers. CAL. perianth three or four-leaved; *leaflets* roundish.—COR. none.—STAM. *filaments* eight to sixteen; *anthers* roundish.
Generic Characters of the Female Flowers. CAL. perianth three-leaved; *leaflets* subovate.—COR. none.—PIST. *germ* roundish; *styles* three; *stigmas* simple.—PER. *capsule* roundish; *seeds* solitary.
Species.—Plants of this tribe are either annuals or shrubs, but mostly the latter; and natives of the Indies or America. The principal species are the—*Acalypha Virginiana*, or *Mercurialis tricoccos*.—*Acalypha Zeylanica*, or *Cupameni*; Indian Acalypha.—*Acalypha Australis*, or *Ricinoides*; South American Acalypha.—*Acalypha betulina*, or *Cauda*.—*Acalypha mappa, Ricinus mappa*, or *Folium mappæ*; a shrub, native of the Malaccas.—*Acalypha lanceolata*, or *Ricinocarpus Indica*, &c. *Raii Hist. Plant.; Herm. Catal.; Sloan. Hist. Jamaic.; Linn. Spec. Plant.*

ACA'MATOS (*Med.*) from α, priv. and κάμνω, to labour; a position of the limbs longest to be borne without weariness.

ACA'MPTE (*Opt.*) an epithet applied by Leibnitz to a figure which is opaque and polished, and consequently possesses properties necessary for reflecting light, yet does not reflect it. *Leib. Epist.* tom. iii. p. 263.

ACA'NGA (*Bot.*) a species of the *Bromelia* of Linnæus.

ACA'NOR (*Chem.*) a sort of chemical furnace.

ACA'NOS (*Bot.*) Ἀκανος, a herb, the *Onopordium Acanthium* of Linnæus. *Theoph. Hist. Plant.* l. 1, c. 16; *Diosc.* l. 6, c. 3.

ACA'NTHA (*Bot.*) vide *Acanthus*.

ACANTHA (*Anat.*) the acute processes of the vertebræ, the spine of the tibia, or the *Spina Dorsi*. *Gorr. Defin. Med.*

ACANTHA (*Ich.*) the fins of fishes.

ACANTHA'BOLUS (*Surg.*) from ἄκανθα, a thorn, and βαλλω, to throw; a chirurgical instrument for extracting thorns, pieces of bone, &c. *Paul. Æginet.*

ACATHA'CEOUS (*Bot.*) ακανθώδης, from ἄκανθα, *aculeum*; prickly as plants of the thistle kind. *Diosc.* l. 3, c. 14.

ACA'NTHALEUCE (*Bot.*) ἀκανθαλευκη, *Alba spina*, white thorn.

ACA'NTHE (*Bot.*) another name for the *Cinara* of Linnæus.

ACA'NTHIA (*Ent.*) a division of the genus *Cimex*.

ACA'NTHICE (*Bot.*) ἀκανθικη μαστιχη, the liquid which the head of the Helxines (ἕλξινη) contains, used by females for mastick. *Theoph.* l. 6, c. 4.

ACA'NTHINUM (*Chem.*) gum.

ACA'NTHIS (*Or.*) ἀκανθις, ἀκανθοφαγος, an eater of thorns; a bird of mean colour, but agreeable voice, of which *Virg.* Georg. 3, v. 338, says

Litoraque halcyonem resonant, et Acanthida dumi.

It is supposed to be what we call the linnet. *Aristot. Hist. Anim.* l. 8, c. 3; *Aldrov. Arnithol. in voc. Carduelis.*

ACA'NTHIUM (*Bot.*) the *Onopordium acanthium, Illyricum et Arabicum* of Linnæus. *Raii Hist. Plant.*

ACANTHE'IDES (*Zo.*) the same as echinos.

ACANTHEIDES (*Bot.*) prickliest Thistle, a species of the *Carduus* of Linnæus.

ACA'NTHUS (*Arch.*) an ornament in the capital of a Corinthian pillar, invented, according to Vitruvius, by Callimachus, who took the idea from observing an Acanthus grow over a tile that had been placed on a tomb. *Vitruv.* l. 4, c. 2; *Bald. Lex. Vitruv.*

ACANTHUS (*Bot.*) the ἄκανθος of Theophrastus, and *Acanthus* of Virgil, called by Herodotus ἄκανθα, by Strabo ἄκανθα, by Dioscorides ἄκανια, and by Pliny *Spina Ægyptiaca*; is a shrub answering to the *Acacia* of Bauhine, and the *Mimosa nilotica* of Linnæus. Its fruit in the pod (ἴλλοβος) is termed, by Virgil, a berry.
Georg. 2, v. 119.

Et quid odorato referam sudantia ligno
Balsamaque et baccas semper frondentis Acanthi?

ACANTHUS, the herb, called by Dioscorides ἄκανθα, is distinguished by the epithet *mollis*, smooth, because it is provided with spines so soft that it might be used for garlands. *Theoc. Idyl.* l. 1, v. 55.

Παντᾷ δ' ἀμφὶ δέπας περιπέπταται ὑγρὸς ἄκανθος.

Virg. Eclog. 3, v. 45.

Et molli circùm est ansas amplexus acantha.

This, as well as the former, is called *Acanthus*, because it is thorny, which was also a general name for many thorny plants. It is called *Branca ursina* by Bauhine, Brank ursine by Dale, and Bears-breech, vulgarly. *Herod.* l. 2, c. 96; *Theophrast. Hist. Plant.* l. 4; *Steph. Byz. de Urb.; Dioscor.* l. 3; *Plin.* l. 22; *Ovid. Metam.* l. 13; *Vitruv.* l. 4; *Athen. Deipnos.* l. 15; *Gal. de Simpl.* l. 6; *Aet.* l. 1; *Marcell. Empiric.* l. 6; *Salmas. Exercitat. Plin.; &c.*

ACANTHUS, in the Linnæan system, a genus of plants, Class 14 *Didynamia*, Order 2 *Angiospermia*.
Generic Characters. CAL. perianth unequal, permanent.—COR. one-petalled, unequal; *tube* very short; *upper-lip* none; *under-lip* very large.—STAM. *filaments* four; *anthers* oblong.—PIST. *germ* conical; *style* filiform; *stigmas* two.—PER. *capsule* subovate, with a point; *claws* alternate; *seeds* ovate.
Species. The species are mostly shrubs, as the *Acanthus mollis sativus*, seu *Mollis Virgilii Carduus*, seu *Branca Ursi* vel *Ursina*, Brank ursine, a native of Italy, where it is

used medicinally.—*Acanthus carduifolius*, Thistle-leaved Acanthus, native of the Cape of Good Hope.—*Acanthus spinosus aculeatus* seu *sylvestris*, Prickly Acanthus, a native of Italy.—*Acanthus Dioscoridis vel sativus*, native of Lebanon, and supposed by Linnæus to be the genuine species of Dioscorides.—*Acanthus ilicafolius*, the *Paina-Schulli* of Rheed, native of the Indies, &c. *J. Bauh. Hist. Plant.*; *C. Bauh. Pin. Theat. Botan.*; *Ger. Herb.*; *Park. Theat. Botan.*; *Raii Hist. Plant.*; *Tourn. Inst. Herb.*; *Boerh. Ind. Plant.*; *Linn. Spec. Plant.*

ACANTHY'LLIS (*Or.*) another name for Acanthis.

ACA'NTICONE (*Min.*) a species of the *Epidote* family.

ACA'NUS (*Bot.*) vide Acanos.

ACA'NZII (*Mil.*) Turkish light-horse, the Avant-guard of the Grand Seignor's army.

ACAPA'TLI (*Bot.*) another name for the *Piper Longum* of Linnæus. *Raii Hist. Plant.*

ACA'PNON (*Bot.*) another name for the *Sampsuchum* of Linnæus.

ACAPNON (*Nat.*) ἀκάπνιςω, from α, priv. and καπνός, smoke; honey taken from the hive without smoking the bees. *Strabo.* l. 9; *Plin.* l. 11, c. 16.

ACA'RNA (*Bot.*) Ἀκαρνα, Fish-Thistle, a species of the *Atractilis*, the *Carlina*, and the *Ericus* of Linnæus. *Theoph.* l. 6, c. 3.

ACA'RNAN (*Ich.*) a sea-fish, mentioned by Athenæus and Aldrovandus. *Castel.*

A'CARON (*Bot.*) the Wild Myrtle; the *Myrtus Brabantia* of Linnæus.

ACA'RTUM (*Chem.*) red-lead.

A'CARUS (*Ent.*) Ἄκαρι, Tick, a genus of animals of the Class *Insecta*, Order *Aptera*.

Generic Characters. Mouth without proboscis.—Feelers two as long as the sucker.—Eyes two placed on each side of the head.—Legs eight.

Species. The most remarkable species are the *Acarus sciro*, the Cheese Mite, found in cheese and meal.—*Acarus ricinus*, Dog-Tick, which infests dogs.—*Acarus exulcerans*, the Itch-Mite, found on the hands and joints of persons infected with the itch.—*Acarus autumnalis*, the Harvest Bug, which attaches itself to plants and animals in autumn.—*Acarus telarius*, spins its web on the bark of trees, which, being dispersed by the winds, covers the fields with innumerable threads.—*Acarus coleoptratorum*, which is found on the bodies of several coleopterous insects.—*Acarus vegetans*, Vegetating Mite, an insect so called from the singular manner in which it is affixed to the limbs or wing-shells of the insect it infests.

ACATALE'CTIC (*Gram.*) Ἀκατάληκτος, i. e. *acatalecticus versus cui in fine nihil deest*, from α, priv. and καταληγω, to end; a perfect or acatalectic verse, not having a syllable too much or too little. *Diomed.* l. 3.

ACATALE'PSIA (*Phy.*) Ἀκαταληψία, incomprehensibility, uncertainty in science.

ACATALIS (*Bot.*) another name for the Juniperus.

ACATASTA'TÆ (*Med.*) from α, priv. and καθίσταμαι, to determine; an epithet for fevers that are irregular and variable in their appearances; or urines that are turbid. *Hippocrat. de Rat. Vict. in Acut. Morb.* & *Gal. Com.*

ACATE'RA (*Bot.*) Juniperus niger.

ACATERY (*Hist.*) a sort of check between the clerks of the king's kitchen, and the purveyors.

ACATHA'RSIA (*Med.*) Ἀκαθαρσία, from α, priv. and καθαίρω, to purge; impurity of the humours.

ACATHI'STUS (*Mus.*) Ἀκάθιςος, a solemn hymn, anciently sung in the Greek church, in the fourth week of Lent. *Curopalat. de Off. Constantin.* c. 12.

ACA'TIUM (*Ant.*) ἀκάτιον, the largest sail placed in the middle of the ship. *Poll. Onon.* l. 2, c. 81; *Isidor. Orig.* l. 19, c. 3.

ACA'TO (*Chem.*) or *Araxos*, soot.

ACA'ULIS (*Bot.*) from α, priv. καυλός, a stem, i. e. *sine caule*, stemless; an epithet for a plant; *Planta acaulis*, a plant wanting a stem, as the *Viola odorata*; also for the cap of the fungi, as *Pileus acaulis*, or *sessilis*, when the cap is not supported by a stalk. *Linn. Phil. Botan.*

ACA'ULOS (*Bot.*) the Carlina Acaulis of Linnæus. *Bauh. Hist. Plant.*

ACCAPITA'RE (*Law*) to pay relief to lords of manors. *Flet.* l. 2, c. 50.

ACCA'PITUM (*Law*) i. e. *Relevium*, a relief to lords of manors.

ACCE'DAS ad Curiam (*Law*) a writ issuing from Chancery to a sheriff, where a man has received false judgment. *F.N.B.* 18; *Reg. Orig.* 9, 56.—*Accedas ad Vice-Comitem*, a writ to a coroner, commanding him to deliver a writ to a sheriff, who having a writ, called a *pone*, suppresses it. *Reg. Orig.* 83.

ACCELERATED (*Phy.*) an epithet for motion when it increases by continual accessions of velocity, which may be either equably or unequably accelerated, as the *accelerated* motion of pendulums, projectiles, compressed bodies, &c. The term is opposed to *retarded*, which expresses a diminution of velocity.

ACCE'LERATING, or *Accelerative* (*Mech.*) *acceleratrix*, an epithet for that force which causes an increased velocity of motion. *Newt. Princip.* def. 8.

ACCELERA'TION (*Phy.*) *acceleratio*, from *ac*, or *ad*, and *celero*, to quicken; increased velocity of motion, which is principally applied to falling bodies tending towards the centre of the earth by the force of gravity. Acceleration is either equable or variable.—*Equable acceleration* is that in which the accessions of velocity are always equal in equal times.—*Variable acceleration* is when the accessions in equal times either increase or decrease. *Galil. Dial.* 2.

ACCELERATION (*Astron.*) is applied to the fixed stars, the planets, and the moon.—*Acceleration of the fixed stars*, is the time which the stars, in one diurnal revolution, anticipate the mean diurnal revolution of the sun.—*Acceleration of a planet*, when its real diurnal motion exceeds its mean diurnal motion.—*Acceleration of the moon*, the increase of the moon's mean motion from the sun, compared with the diurnal motion of the earth.

ACCE'LERATIVE (*Phy.*) vide *Accelerating*.

ACCELERATO'RES *urinæ* (*Anat.*) muscles so called because they serve to expedite the passage of the urine.

ACCE'NDONES (*Ant.*) a kind of gladiators or supernumeraries, whose office was to excite and animate the combatants. *Salmas. in Tertull. de Pall.* c. 6.

ACCE'NSOR (*Ant.*) vide *Acolythus*.

ACCE'NSUS (*Ant.*) an officer who attended on the consuls and prætors acting as a clerk of the assizes, or crier of the court to summon the witnesses, &c.; so called *quod alios ad prætorem acciret*. Before the introduction of clocks he used also to cry the hour at the third hour at noon, and at the ninth hour. *Varr. de Ling. Lat.* l. 5, c. 9; *Cic. de Leg.* l. 2, c. 24; *Ad. Frat.* l. 1, ep. 1; *Plin.* l. 7, c. 60; *Var. de Vit. Pop. Rom. Apud. Non. Marcell.* l. 12, c. 8; *Suet. in Jul.* c. 20; *August. Ad. Leg.* xii. *Tab.* § 44; *Sigon. de Antiq. Jur. Civ. Roman.*; *Manut. de Civit. Rom. apud Thesaur. Græc.* tom. 1, p. 36; *Salmas. de Mil. Rom.* c. 14; *Buleng. de Imp. Rom.* l. 6, c. 16. This officer seems also to have acted as a scribe, according to Cicero, and some inscriptions T. TITIENUS FELIX, AUGUSTALIS SCRIBA LIBR. ÆDIL. CURUL. VIATOR ÆDILIS. PLEBIS. ACCENSUS. *Cic. in Verr.* l. 3, c. 66; *Buleng. de Imp. Rom.* l. 6; *Pollet. For. Rom.* l. 5, c. 13.

ACCENSUS, a kind of adjutant appointed by the tribunes to assist the centurion or decurion; or, according to Festus, a supernumerary soldier who was ready to supply the place of any one that died. *Varr. de Vit. Pop. Rom.* l. 3 apud *Non.* l. 12, c. 8; *Liv.* l. 1, c. 43; *Fest. de Verb. Signif.*; *Salmas. de Re Mil.* c. 14; *Rosin. Antiq. Rom.*

A'CCENT (*Gram.*) *Accentus*, from *ac*, or *ad*, and *cantus*, a song; an inflection of tone which is either *acute*, *grave*, or *circumflex*: the—*Acute accent* (´) sharpens or raises the syllable.—*Grave accent* (`) depresses the syllable.—*Circumflex accent* (ˆ) both elevates and depresses, i.e. *per arsin et thesin*; as in the word *natura*; when I say, *natu*, the voice is elevated, and it is called *arsis*; but when I say *ra*, the voice is depressed, and it is called *thesis*. *Varro. de Lat. Lin.*; *Quint. Inst.* l. 12, c. 10; *Diomed.* l. 2; *Prisc. de Accent. apud Vet. Grammat.*; *Isid. Orig.* l. 1, c. 17.

ACCENTS *Greek*, the Greek accents are now known but little, except by the marks over the vowels; they are three, namely, acute (´), grave (`), and circumflex (ˆ); words are denominated differently according to the position of the accent, as—*Proparoxytons*, with the acute on the antepenultimate, as πώδημος.—*Paroxytons*, having the acute on the penultimate, as λύχνος.—*Oxytons*, having the grave or acute accent on the last syllable, as ισθμός, διά.—*Barytons*, with the grave accent, or no accent, on the last syllable, as τιμή, σῶμα.—*Circumflex*, those with the circumflex on the last syllable, as πῶ.—*Ante-circumflex*, with the circumflex on the penultimate, as βοᾶτι.—To these may be added the breathings, which are two; viz. the lenis or mild (᾿), as ἄξω, and the asper or aspirate (῾), as ἵκατο, which is pronounced Hικατο. Every word beginning with a vowel has either the *lenis* or the *asper*, and when two ρ's come together, the first has the *lenis*, and the second the *asper*, as πόρρα.

ACCENTS *Hebrew*, the Hebrew accents consisted either of points which served as vowel points, which will be noticed under the head of points, or of accents, properly so called, which are either tonic, distinctive, or servile.—*Tonic accents* stand for notes to sing by.—*Distinctive accents* distinguish the sense.—*Servile accents*, *accentus ministri*, or *serviles*, serve to show the construction and connexion of words.

ACCENTS are moreover distinguished as they stand over or under the letters.

Hebrew Accents under the Letters.

Name.	Figure, Place, and Power.
Silluk	א Punctum.
Atnack	א Colon.
Tiphcha	א Semicomma primum.
Tebir	א Ditto.
Jethif	א Semicolon.
Munach	א Semicomma.
Merca simplex	א Ditto.
Merca duplex	א Ditto.
Mahpach	א Ditto.
Darga	א Ditto.
Jerach ben jomo	א Ditto.

Hebrew Accents above the Letters.

Paser minor	א Semicomma quartum.
Paser major	א Ditto.
Karne para	א Ditto.
Schalscheleth	א Semicolon.
Pesik, or Legarme	א Ditto.

Name.	Figure, Place, and Power.
Telischa ketanna	א Semicomma.
Sarka	א Semicomma primum.
Pasta	א Ditto.
Geresch	א Semicomma secundum.
Geraschajim	א Ditto.
Telischa Gedola	א Semicomma tertium.
Segol, or Segolta	א Strong colon.
Sakeph katon	א Comma.
Sakeph gadol	א Ditto.
Refia, or Rebhia	א Ditto.

The Greek and Roman accentual marks are placed over the vowels, as follow:

Greek Accents and Breathings.

´ Acute, as	ά έ ή ί ό ύ ώ ὔ
` Grave, as	ὰ ὲ ὴ ὶ ὸ ὺ ὼ ὒ
˜ Circumflex, as	ᾶ ῆ ῖ ῶ ῦ ῷ ὖ
᾿ Lenis, as	ἀ ἐ ἠ ἰ ὀ ὐ ὠ ὒ
῾ Asper, as	ἁ ἑ ἡ ἱ ὁ ὑ ὡ ὕ
᾿´ Acute lenis, as	ἄ ἔ ἤ ἴ ὄ ὔ ὤ ὔ
᾿` Grave lenis, as	ἂ ἒ ἢ ἲ ὂ ὒ ὢ ὒ
῾´ Acute asper, as	ἅ ἕ ἥ ἵ ὅ ὕ ὥ ὕ
῾` Grave asper, as	ἃ ἓ ἣ ἳ ὃ ὓ ὣ ὓ
᾿˜ Circumflex lenis, as	ἆ ἦ ἶ ὦ ὖ ὦ ὖ
῾˜ Circumflex asper, as	ἇ ἧ ἷ ὧ ὗ ὧ ὗ

Roman Accents.

´ Acute, as   á é í ó ú.
` Grave, as   à è ì ò ù.
ˆ Circumflex, as â ê î ô û.
¸ Cedilla used only under the French c, as ç.
˜ over the Spanish n, thus ñ.

ACCENT (*Mus.*) the modulation of the voice in singing.

ACCENTED (*Mus.*) an epithet for those notes or bars on which the emphasis naturally falls.

ACCENTS (*Mus.*) *accentus*; a verse or song.

ACCE'NTOR (*Mus.*) he that sings the highest part, or treble in a choir.

ACCE'PTANCE (*Law*) *Acceptatio*, from *accipio*, to accept; an accepting of a thing, or a tacit agreement, as if *husband* and *wife*, seised of lands in right of the wife, join and make a lease reserving rent; and after the death of the husband the wife receives or accepts the rent, by this acceptance the lease is confirmed, and it shall bind her. 1 *Inst.* 273.

ACCEPTANCE of a bill (*Com.*) the signing, subscribing, and making a person debtor for the contents.

ACCEPTA'TIO (*Ant.*) a discharge from the creditor to the debtor, which is in civil law, what an acquittance is in common law. *Bud. in Pandect.* p. 178.

ACCE'PTOR (*Ant.*) vide *Accipiter*.

ACCEPTOR (*Com.*) the person who accepts a bill of exchange by signing it, and obliging himself to pay the contents.

ACCEPTO'RIUS *modiolus* (*Ant.*) a vessel employed in the aqueducts for holding water, in distinction from the *erogatorius*, by which it was dealt out. *Keuchen. in Frontin. de Aqueduct.* l. 1 apud *Thes. Græv. Antiq. Rom.* vol. 4, p. 1638.

ACCERSITO'RES (*Ant.*) Runners who went before to announce the arrival of any one. *Pignor. de Serv.* p. 255.

ACCE'SSA (*Archæol.*) *Accessio, Accessus*; the access of the sea, i. e. the tide in distinction from the recessus or ebb.

A'CCESSARY (*Law*) or *Accessory, accessorius*, from *ac* and *cedo*, to come; one guilty of an offence not principally, but by a direct participation, as of command, &c.; if simply by advice or abetting he is an *abettor*; if by act and deed, as a principal, he is an *accomplice*. Accessories are either so before the fact or after.—*Accessories before the fact*, are those who being absent, yet procure or command another to commit a crime.—*Accessories after the fact*, those who receive and relieve the felon, knowing the felony to have been committed. 3 *Inst.* 138; 1 *Hale. Pleas of the Crown*, 613, &c.; *Hawk. P. C.* l. 2, c. 37, &c.

ACCE'SSIBLE (*Math.*) an epithet for any height or depth which can be approached so as to be measured by applying a proper instrument.

ACCESSIBLE (*Mil.*) an epithet for any place that may be approached by a hostile force. A fortress may be accessible both by sea or land.

ACCE'SSION (*Med.*) *accessio*, from *accedo*, to approach, πρόσθεσις, the beginning of a paroxysm, or a fit of an intermitting fever.

ACCESSION (*Pol.*) from *accedo*, to approach; an approach or coming to; as of a king who takes possession of his throne, or of any person who comes into possession of property.

ACCESSION (*Ecc.*) a term used in the election of a pope, when one or more cardinals accede or go over to a particular side so as to give it the majority, which is one mode of election in distinction from acclamation, or scrutiny. Vide *Accessus*.

ACCESSO'RIUS *Musculus* (*Anat.*) another name for the *flexor digitorum* and *sacro lumbaris*.—*Accessorius Nervus*, a name given, by Willis, to the eighth pair of nerves which arise by several filaments, from both sides of the *medulla spinalis*.

A'CCESSORY (*Law*) vide *Accessary*.

ACCE'SSUS (*Ant.*) from *accedo*, to approach; a climbing machine used for ascending the walls of besieged towns. *Vitruv.* l. 10, c. 19.

ACCESSUS (*Ecc.*) *vel per accessum*, a mode of electing the pope, when all the cardinals, with one consent, approach him and salute him by the title of *Papa*. This is called, in English, "An election by acclamation." *Ceremonial Rom.* l. 1, § 1.

ACCIACATU'RA (*Mus.*) Italian, for a sweeping of the chords of the harpsichord, and dropping sprinkled notes usual in accompaniments.

A'CCIDENS (*Phy.*) or *per Accidens*, κατὰ συμβιβηκός; a term applied to the operations of natural bodies, in distinction from *per se*; thus fire is said to burn *per se*, but a hot iron *per accidens*. *Aristot. Analyt. Post.* l. 1, c. 3.

A'CCIDENT (*Log.*) *Accidens*, from *accido*, to befal or happen to a thing, τὸ συμβιβηκός; that which belongs incidentally to substances. Accidents are of different kinds, namely:—*Accidens particulare*, a particular accident, that which is in a subject, but attributed to no subject; as a garment that belongs to a man, but forms no part of a man.—*Accidens prædicabile*, a predicable accident, which is in a subject, and predicated of, or attributed to, a subject; but belongs incidentally to it, in distinction from the essence, as white, black. This is, as Porphyry defines it, what comes to, or goes from, a thing, χωρὶς τῆς τοῦ ὑποκειμένου φθορᾶς, i. e. without destroying the subject. It is divided into common and proper.—*Accidens commune*, κοινόν, a common accident, belongs to several subjects; as animality, which is common to man and beast.—*Accidens proprium*, ἴδιον, a proper accident, which is peculiar to one subject; as risibility to man.—*Accidens separabile*, χωριστόν, a separable accident, which may be separated from a subject; as sleeping from a man.—*Accidens inseparabile*, ἀχώριστον, an inseparable accident, which cannot be separated from the subject; as blackness from the skin of an Ethiopian.—*Accidens prædicamentale*, a predicamental accident, which includes the last nine of the predicaments; as quantity, quality, action, passion, &c. in distinction from the οὐσία, or substance, which is the first predicament. *Porphyr. Isagog.*; *Aristot. Analyt.*

ACCIDE'NTAL *Colours* (*Opt.*) those which depend on the eye, in distinction from those which are produced by the light.

ACCIDENTAL *Point* (*Perspect.*) that point in which a right line drawn from the eye, parallel to another given right line, cuts the picture or plane. Thus, suppose A B to be

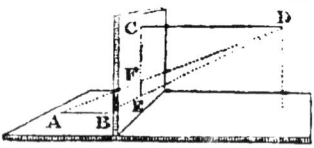

the line given in perspective, C F E the perspective plane, D the eye, C D the line parellel to A B; then is C the *accidental point*.

ACCI'DENTS (*Logic*) vide *Accident*.

ACCIDENTS (*Metaph.*) are distinguished into primary and secondary.—*Primary accidents* are such as are absolute; as quantity and quality.—*Secondary accidents* are *quando*, when; *ubi*, where; *situs*, situation; *habitus*, habit, &c.

ACCIDENTS (*Gram.*) the inflexions of words, or the accents in letters and syllables.

ACCIDENTS (*Her.*) the tincture and differences in blasoning, or the points and abatements in an escutcheon.

ACCIPE'NSER (*Ich.*) vide *Acipenser*.

ACCI'PITER (*Or.*) the hawk, a well-known bird of prey, so called on account of its rapacity, from *accipio*, to seize, i. e. to seize or take birds. The Hebrew name יֵץ is derived from נֵץ, to fly; because it is a bird of swift flight, as the Greek ἱέραξ, from τὸ ῥᾷον ἵεσθαι, to go freely. This bird was made emblematical of the winds, on account of the swiftness of its flight, which, together with its rapacity, has been celebrated by the poets. *Hom. Iliad.* l. 15, v. 237, speaking of Apollo,

Βῆ δὲ κατ' Ἰδαίων ὀρέων Ἴρηκι ἐοικὼς
Ὠκέϊ φασσοφόνῳ ὅστ' ὤκιστος πετεηνῶν.

Odyss. l. 15, v. 525.

Κίρκος Ἀπόλλωνος ταχὺς ἄγγελος.

Hom. Il. l. 16, v. 582.

Ἴθυσεν δὲ διὰ προμάχων Ἴρηκι ἐοικὼς
Ὠκέϊ, ὅστ' ἐφόβησε κολοιούς τε ψῆράς τε
Ὡς ἰθὺς Λυκίων Πατρόκλεις ἱπποκέλευθε.

Hesiod. Oper. l. 1, v. 210.

Ὡς ἔφατ' ὠκυπέτης ἴρηξ, τανυσίπτερος.

Ovid Metam. l. 11, v. 664.

—*Accipiter nulli satis æquus in omnes
Sævit aves, aliisque dolens fit causa dolendi.*

Ovid. de Arte Amand. l. 2, v. 147.

Odimus accipitrem quia vivit semper in armis.

Martial l. 14, ep. 216.

*Prædo fuit volucrum, famulus nunc aucupis, idem
Decipit et captas non sibi mæret aves.*

Claud. Eidyll. 1, v. 81.

*Non ferus accipiter, non armiger ipse tonantis
Bella movent.*

For the sharpness of its sight, it was made emblematical of the sun, to which it was held sacred by the Egyptians;

and on this account is called by Aristophanes κατ' ὀφθαλμώς, and by Virgil *ales sacer*. Callimachus mentions six species of the hawk, and Pliny sixteen; but Aristotle gives the names of only ten, viz. Τρίορχης, αἰσάλων, κίρκος, ἀστρίας, Φασσοφόνος, πέρκης, ἁλιος, πύρνος, σπιζίας, Φρυνολόχος. *Buteo, asalo, circus, asterias, palumbarius, pernes, lævis, pernes, spizia, rubetarius*. The two species principally known are the—*Accipiter palumbarius*, or Goss-hawk, so called because it takes doves. It is the ἱέραξ Φασσοφόνος of Aristotle; the *Accipiter palumbarius* of Aldrovandus; and the *Falco palumbarius* of Linnæus.—*Accipiter fringillarius*, or the Sparrow-hawk, so called because it catches sparrows, is the ἱέραξ σπιζίας of Aristotle; the *Accipiter fringillarius vulgo Nisus sparviero dictus* of Aldrovandus; and the *Falco nisus* of Linnæus. *Herodot.* l. 2, c. 65, &c.; *Aristot. Hist. Animal.* l. 9; *Diodor.* l. 2; *Cic. de Nat. Deor.* l. 3, c. 14; *Virg. Æn.* l. 11, v. 721; *Apul. Apolog.* l. 1; *Plin.* l. 10, c. 8; *Plut. de Isid. et Osir.*; *Ælian. Hist. Anim.* l. 2, c. 42; *Horopol. de Hierogl.* l. 2, c. 14; *Oppian. Ixeut.* l. 1; *Eustath in Odyss.* l. 15; *Gregor. Nazianz.* l. 10, c. 16; *August. contra Manat.*; *Jul. Firm. Mathes.* l. 5, c. 7; *Sidon. Apollinar. Paneg. ad Avit.*; *Oros. Hist.* l. 2, c. 14; *Demet. Præf. ad Hierocosoph*; *Isidor. Orig.* l. 12; *Gesner de Avib*; *Aldrov. Ornith.* l. 1; *Bellon. de Avibus*; *Alex. ab Alexand. Gen. D.* l. 5, c. 13; *Boch. Hieroz.* l. 1, &c.; *Thuan. de Re Accipiter*, l. 1; *Will. Ornith.*; *Raii Hist.*; *Linn. Syst. Nat.*

ACCIPITER (*Numis.*) this bird [vide *Accipiter* under *Ornithology*], was worshipped in Egypt for Osiris, on account of its fierceness and violence, which attributes it was supposed to possess in common with Osiris or the sun. The subjoined figure represents a medal of Adrian, bearing, on

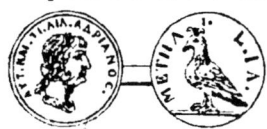

the obverse, the head of the emperor, crowned with laurel. The inscription, ΑΥΤοκράτωρ ΚΑΙσαρ ΤΙβέριος ΑΙΛιος ΑΔΡΙΑΝΟC; on the reverse, the *accipiter* with the flower of the *lotus* on its head, standing on a small staff: the inscription ΜΕΤΗΛΙτῶν L. IA. i. e. *Metelitarum anno undecimo*. *Vaillant Numis. Ptolem.*

ACCIPITER (*Surg.*) the name of a bandage which was put over the nose; so called from its resemblance to the claw of a hawk.

ACCI'PITRES (*Or.*) the first order in the Linnean system, in the class *Aves*, or Birds, having an angular toothlike process on the upper mandible, including the following genera, namely,—*Vultur*, the Vulture, having the bill hooked, and the head naked.—*Falco*, the Eagle, Falcon, Kite, Hawk, &c. having the bill hooked, and covered at the base with a cere.—*Strix*, the Owl, having the bill hooked, with a frontlet of covered bristles.—*Lanius*, the Shrike, having the bill straightish and notched.

ACCIPITRI'NA (*Bot.*) another name for the hawkweed.

ACCI'SE (*Com.*) a duty in Holland on different sorts of commodities, as wheat, coals, &c.

ACCLAMA'TIO (*Ant.*) acclamation, or shouting, which among the Romans was performed by a certain tune or modulation of the voices in accordance, and was employed either for the purpose of praise or dispraise. *Acclamations* were adopted on most public occasions, as in the case of marriages, congratulations of emperors or generals, in the theatre, the senate, and other places. The form of the acclamation varied with the occasion; on saluting a newly elected general, they cried out *Dii te servent, Imperator*; on applauding the performances of any declaimer or orator, they would cry out *Bene et præclare*; *Belle et festive, non potest melius*, &c. Sometimes, however, the acclamation was employed to express a contrary feeling, as on the death of Commodus. *Cic. de Orat.* l. 3, c. 26; *Hor. de Art. Poet.* v. 428; *Mart.* l. 2, epig. 27; *Pers. Sat.* 1, v. 49; *Senec. Octav.* act 4, scen. 1, v. 704, and epist. 59; *Plin.* l. 2, epist. 14, &c.; *Quintil. Instit. Orat.* l. 8, c. 3; *Suet in Ner.* c. 20, and in *Domit.* c. 23; *Dio.* l. 43, &c.; *Arrian in Epict.* l. 2, c. 23; *Vopisc. in Prob.* c. 10; *Lamprid. in Commod.* c. 18, and in *Anton. Diadum*, c. 1; *Bud in Pandect.* p. 74; *Sigon de Ant. Jur. Provin.* l. 2, c. 7; *Ferrar. de Acclamat.* l. 1, c. 2, &c.; *Buleng. de Cir.* c. 49; *Laz. Comm. Reip. Rom.* l. 9, c. 2.

ACCLAMA'TION (*Ecc.*) a mode of electing the Pope, when the cardinals, with one consent, address him by the title of "Papa," as soon as he makes his appearance among them.

ACCLI'VIS (*Anat.*) another name for the muscle called *obliquus ascendens abdominis*.

ACCLI'VITY (*Math.*) the steepness, or slope, of any place inclined to the horizon reckoned upwards.

A'CCOLA (*Ant.*) a husbandman who came from other parts to till the ground: *Eo quod perveniens terram colat*, In distinction from the *incola qui propriam terram colit*: i. e. who tills his native soil. *Isid. Orig.* l. 12, c. 1.

ACCOLA'DE (*Archæol.*) from *ac* or *ad* and *collum*, the neck; a ceremony used in knighting, when the king puts his hand round the neck of the knight, *Wilhelm Malmsbur. de Gest. Reg. Angl.*

ACCOLADE (*Mus.*) the brace which includes all the parts of a score.

A'CCOLER (*Com.*) the making of a bracket in the margin of an account book in France, so as to comprehend several sums in one.

A'CCOLLE (*Her.*) collared or wearing a collar.

ACCOMMODA'TION bill (*Com.*) a bill given as an accommodation instead of a loan of money, which is commonly taken up by the drawer.

ACCOMPAGNE'E (*Her.*) between.

ACCO'MPANIMENT (*Mus.*) An instrumental part added to a composition by way of embellishment.—*Accompaniment ad libitum*, when the piece may be performed with or without the accompaniment at pleasure.—*Accompaniment-obligato*, when the accompaniment is indispensable to the piece.

ACCO'MPANIMENTS (*Mus.*) instrumental parts added incidentally to any piece.

ACCOMPANIMENTS (*Her.*) such things as are usually applied about the shield, as the belt, mantlings, &c.

ACCO'MPANIST (*Mus.*) the performer of the accompaniment.

ACCO'MPLICE (*Law*) vide *Accessary*.

ACCO'MPT (*Com.*) vide *Account*.

ACCO'NTUM (*Ant.*) a Grecian dart or javelin, somewhat similar to the Roman *pilum*.

ACCO'RD (*Mus.*) an agreement in pitch and tone, as applied to the voice, or to instruments. Rousseau defines it a union of two or more sounds made at the same time, so as to form an harmonic whole. Accords are divided by Rousseau into—*Accords consonans*, or *consonances*, when the intervals formed by two sounds are agreeable to the ear.—*Accords dissonans*, or *dissonances*, those which contain some *dissonance*, or discordant sound, which is disagreeable to the ear.—*Accords parfaits*, which consist of three different sounds, having the grave sound as the fundamental.—*Accords imparfaits*, which have not the grave sound.

ACCORD (*Law.*) an agreement between two or more persons, when any one is injured by a trespass or offence, to satisfy him with some recompence.

ACCORDATU'RA (*Mus.*) an Italian word for the tuning of an instrument.

ACCO'STED (*Her.*) from the Latin *ac* and *costa*, a rib or side; side by side, as in the annexed figure. " Chevron between six rams accosted." The family of Harman bear this coat of arms on a field azure.

ACCO'TEMENT (*Mech.*) an upsetting among paviours; a space of ground which is between the border of the road and the ditch.

ACCO'UCHEMENT (*Med.*) Fr. delivery, or lying-in; hence the practitioners have been styled *accoucheurs*.

ACCO'UNT (*Com.*) or *accounts*, in general all computations.—*Books of accounts*, or *Merchants' Accounts*; the books in which all the transactions of a merchant are entered and digested in proper order. [Vide *Book-keeping*.] Whence the different phrases.—*To open an account*, or to enter it for the first time in a ledger.—*To keep open an account*; when merchants agree to honour each other's bills of exchange reciprocally.—*To affirm an account*; to declare and make oath that it is true.—*To dispute*, or *note an account*; to make remarks or objections on the several items of an account.—*To settle an account*; to cast it up and balance it.—*To post a sum to an account*; to enter into the ledger the articles for which any persons become either debtors or creditors.—*Account paper*; a fine large paper in France on which accounts were written.—*Account of sales*; an account given by one merchant to another of the disposal, charges, commission, and net produce from the sale of certain goods.

ACCOUNT *personal* (*Mil.*) or *pay-account*; an account which is kept by army agents of monies received and disbursed for subsistence and allowance.—*Clothing account*; an account kept by the army-agent of monies received and disbursed for the clothing of the regiment.

ACCOUNT (*Chron.*) the same as style, ' the old or new account,' i. e. the old or new style.

ACCOUNT (*Law*) *computus*; a writ or action against a bailiff or receiver, who refuses to render an account. *Stat. of Westm.* 2 c. 1; *F. N. B.* 13, 116.

ACCO'UNTANT (*Law*) one obliged to render an account to another.—*Accountant-general*; an officer in the court of chancery, to receive all money lodged in court.

ACCO'UTREMENTS (*Mil.*) the habits, equipage, and furniture of a soldier, such as belts, pouches, cartridge-boxes, &c.

ACCRE'SSIMENTS (*Mus.*) or *Accress*, the same as augmentation.

ACCRE'TIO (*Phy.*) from *ac* or *ad* and *cresco*, to grow; accretion, or the increase of a body by growth.

ACCRETIO (*Med.*) a growing together, as the fingers or toes to one another.

ACCRO'CHE (*Law*) from the French *accrocher*, to hook to; to encroach. *Stat.* 25, *Ed.* 3. Among the French, to delay; as *accrocher un process*, to stay proceedings in a court.

ACCRU'ED (*Her.*) an epithet for a tree full grown.

ACCUBA'TIO (*Hist.*) accubation, or a mode of reclining on couches side by side at meals, customary among the Romans. *Cic. in Ver.* l. 5, c. 31; *Petron. Arb.* c. 36; *Isidor Origen.* l. 20, c. 2; *Lips. Ant. Lect.* vol. 2, p. 144; *Stuck. de Ant. Conv.* l. 2, c. 34; *Philand. in Vitruv.* l. 6, c. 2; *Buleng. de Conviv.* l. 1, c. 32; *Ciaccon de Triclin.* p. 252.

ACCU'BITA (*Ant.*) the couches on which the ancients used to recline. *Spartian in Æl. Ver.* c. 5; *Lamprid. in Heliogab.* c. 19, &c.; *Buleng. de Conviv.* l. 1, c. 30; *Salmas in Tertull. de Pall.* p. 174.

ACCU'LER (*Mil.*) to come to close action, or to drive an army into such a situation as to compel it to action.

ACCUSA'TIO (*Med.*) Vide *Indicatio*.

ACCUSATIO (*Ant.*) accusation, among the Romans, consisted of three parts: namely,—*Postulatio*, or a petition to produce the charge.—*Delatio*, the bringing before the court; and *accusatio*, in the strict sense, or the substantiating the charge. *Ascon in Cic.* p. 65, &c.; *Senec. Controvers.* l. 4; *Ulpian. de Accusat.*; *Sigon de Iudic.* l. 2, c. 8, &c.; *Manut de Leg.* c. 828, &c.; *Rosin Ant. Rom.* l. 9, c. 29.

ACCU'SATIVE (*Gram.*) *Accusativus*, κατηγορικός, the fourth case of nouns, because we accuse *accusamus*, commend, or predicate something of some one. *Varr. de Ling. Lat.* l. 7; *Sosip. Charis. Instit. Grammat.* l. 5; *Diomed.* l. 1; *Priscian. Gramm.* l. 5; *Cledon. de Art. Gram. apud Putsch. Grammat. Lat. Auctor Ant.*; *Isidor. Orig.* l. 1, c. 16.

ACE (*Games*) that side of a die on which the number one is expressed: also the card on which there is but one figure.

ACE'DIA (*Med.*) ἀκηδία, from α pro αγω, a particle of excess, and κῆδος, care; a term used by Hippocrates for fatigue. *Hippoc.* περὶ ἀδιν.

ACE'PHALI (*Ecc.*) ἀκέφαλοι, from α, priv. and κεφαλή, a head; heretics, so called because they admitted no lawful superior, either layman or ecclesiastic. They were similar to the levellers in the time of Henry I. There were also priests of this name, who submitted to no bishop. *Leontius de Sectis*, act. 5; *Baron. Annal. Ann.* 433; *Prateol. de Hæret. Doct. Omn.*

ACEPHALI *versus* (*Rhet.*) *mutili in principio*; verses that begin with a short syllable instead of a long one. *Macrob. Saturnal.* l. 5, c. 15.

ACEPHALI (*Zool.*) ἀκέφαλοι, from α, priv. and κεφαλή, a head; headless, an epithet for crabs, and other such animals as have their senses about the breasts or hearts. *Gal. de Usu. Part.* l. 8, c. 4.

A'CER (*Bot.*) or *Aceris*, according to Solinus; the Maple-tree, a tree so called from *acer* hard, as Vossius thinks, because of the great hardness of its wood, answering to the σφενδάμνος of the Greeks, from σφοδρός, *durus*, hard; or, as Perotius thinks, from *acer*, sharp, because it exercises the wit of man in the liberal arts, according to the words of Pliny, " *Acer operum elegantiâ et subtilitate cedro secundum.*" The root is used in physic, and a juice is extracted from it in the spring, which serves as a sweet drink. There are three species of it mentioned by the ancients, viz. *Acer album, acer venis distinctum, et acer zygia vel carpinum*; but, according to Pliny, there were ten species. *Columel.* l. 5, c. 7; *Plin.* l. 16, c. 26; *Hesychius.*; *Salmas Exercit. Plin.* p. 507.

ACER, in the Linnæan system, a genus of plants, Class 23 *Polygamia*, Order 1, *Monœcia*.

Generic Characters.—CAL. perianth one-leafed.—COR. petals five.—STAM. filaments eight; anthers simple; pollen cruciform.—PIST. germ compressed; style filiform; stigmas two (or three) pointed.—PER. capsules, the number of the stigmas coalescent at the base; seeds solitary.

Species. The principal species of the *Acer* are as follow: *Acer sempervirens*, Evergreen Maple, a shrub.—*Acer pseudo-platanus*, Great Maple; a British plant, but not indigenous.—*Acer saccharinum*, American Sugar Maple, from which the inhabitants make sugar.—*Acer palmatum*, or *Kevan Mokf*, Hand-leaved Maple, native of Japan.—*Acer campestre*, or *minus*, Common or Small Maple, a British plant, but not indigenous.—*Acer negundo*, or *maximum*, Virginian, Ash-leaved Maple.—*Acer dasycarpum*, *eriocarpum*, or *rubrum*, a native of Pennsylvania. *Parkin. Theat. Botan.*; *J. Bauh. Hist. Plant.*; *C. Bauh. Pin.*; *Ger. Herb*; *Raii Hist. Plant. et Synop*; *Tournef. Inst.*; *Boerhaav. Ind.*; *Dillen. Catalog.*

ACER is also a name for the *Bannisteria laurifolia* and the *Triopteris critrifolia* of Linnæus. *Plum. Spec. Sloan. Jam.*

ACE'RATOS (*Med.*) ἀκέρατος from α, priv. and κεράννυμι, to mix; unmingled, uncorrupted; an epithet for the humours. *Hippocrat de Affect*; *Foes. Oeconom. Hippocrat.*

ACE'RBUS (*Med.*) sour, harsh, or astringent; as unripe fruit.

ACE'RIC (*Chem.*) an epithet for a vegetable acid from the *acer campestre*.

ACE'RIDES (*Med.*) ἀκηρίδες, from α, priv. and κηρός, wax; plasters without wax. *Gal. de Med. Compos. per gen.* l. 4, c. 14.

ACERO'SÆ arbores (*Bot.*) the pine tribe, a sort of ligneous plants. *Linn. Phil. Bot.*

ACERO'SUS (*Med.*) ἀχυρώδης, from ἄχυρον, chaff; an epithet employed by Hippocrates for the coarsest bread made of flour not separated from the chaff. *Hippoc.* περὶ ὑγριῶν χρώσιος. *Foes. Oeconom. Hippocrat.*

ACEROSUS (*Bot.*) linear, persistent; an epithet for a leaf.—*Folium acerosum*, a leaf, needle-shaped, and inserted at the base into the branch by articulation, as in the pine, fir, and juniper. *Linn. Phil. Bot.*

ACE'RRA (*Ant.*) an altar erected near the bed of a deceased person on which incense was burnt; it was so called because perfumes were, *accensi*, burnt upon them to prevent unpleasant smell. The *Acerra* was also a little pot which contained the perfumes. *Horat.* l. 3, od. 8, v. 2.

> *Quid velint flores et acerra thuris*
> *Plena, miraris.*

Ovid de Pont. l. 4, epist. 8, v. 39.

> *Nec quæ de parva pauper diis libat acerra,*
> *Thura minus grandi quam data lance valent.*

The *Acerra* was very similar in form to what is now used in the church of Rome. *Cic. de Leg.* l. 2, c. 24; *Fest. de Sign. Verb*; *Ferret Mus. Lapid.* l. 4, Memor. 9; *August. in Leg.* xii. Tab. § 43; *Hotman. Antiq. Rom.* l. 3, c. 1; *Meurs. de Funer.* c. 6; *La Chaussé Insign. Pontif. Max.* tab. 8.

ACE'SCENT (*Chem.*) an epithet for substances which readily run into the acid fermentation.—*Acescent liquids*, those liquids in which the acid fermentation has commenced.

ACE'STIDES (*Chem.*) from ἀκή, acies, a point; chimneys of furnaces, narrow at the top, for melting brass.

ACE'STORIS (*Med.*) ἀκεστωρίς, from ἄκος, healing; a term used by Hippocrates for a female physician, or a midwife. *Hippoc.* περὶ φυσῶν, &c.; *Foes. Oeconom. Hippocrat.*

ACETA'BULUM (*Ant.*) ὀξύβαφον; a vessel for vinegar. 2. A measure equal to the one eighth of a modern pint. *Athen.* l. 2, c. 26. *Gal. de Mensur*, &c. c. 2.

ACETABULUM (*Med.*) κοτύλη, *cavitas*, or ὀξύβαφον, the cup, from its resemblance to that vessel: 1. A cavity, or socket in the *os coxendix*, or hip-bone, to receive the head of the *femur*, or thigh-bone. *Ruff. Ephes.* l. 1, c. 9; *Gal. Comm. in Hippoc. de Fract.* &c.; *Foes. Oeconom. Hippocrat.* 2. A glandular substance found in the *placenta* of some animals. *Gal. de Usu Part.* l. 15, c. 53.

ACETABULUM (*Bot.*) another name for the Cotyledon.

ACETA'RIA (*Med.*) from *acetum*, vinegar. Acetars, 1. Salads. *Plin.* l. 19, c. 4. 2. Pickles, as the *acetarium scorbuticum* of Bates.

A'CETATE (*Chem.*) any salt formed by the union of acetic acid with a salifiable base, as the acetate of potash, of soda, of lead, &c. in distinction from the acetite. [vide *Acetite*]

AC *ttiam billæ* (*Law.*) i. e. and also to a bill to be exhibited for 20*l*. debt, &c. words in a writ where the action requires bail.

ACE'TIC acid (*Chem.*) radical vinegar, or vinegar in a particularly concentrated state. [vide *Acetum*]

A'CETITE (*Chem.*) any salt formed by the union of acetous acid with an alcaline or earthy base. [vide *Acetate* and *Chemistry*]

ACETO'SA (*Bot.*) ὀξαλίς, *herba acida*, so called from ὀξύς, acid; sorrel, from the Anglo-Saxon ᚱᚢᚾ, sour, the *Rumex* of Linnæus. *Gal. de Alim. Fac.* l. 2; *J. Bauh. Hist. Plant.*; *C. Bauh. Pin.*; *Raii Hist. Plant.*; *Tournef. Inst. Herb.*; *Dillen. Catalog. Plant.*; *Boërh. Ind.*

ACETOSE'LLA (*Bot.*) *herba acida*, from *ab* and *sapore acetosa*, an acid taste; Wood-sorrel, a species of the *oxalis*, and of the *Rumex* of Linnæus. *J. Bauhin. Hist.* &c. [vide *Acetosa*]

ACE'TOUS acid (*Chem.*) distilled vinegar. [vide *Acetum*]

ACE'TUM (*Nat.*) ἀκητόν, an epithet for honey that is liquid, which is reckoned the best sort. *Plin.* l. 11, c. 15; *Hesychius*.

ACETUM (*Chem.*) from *aceo*, to sharpen; Vinegar or any acid liquor made from potulent juices, particularly wine and beer.—*Acetum distillatum*, distilled vinegar, or vinegar purified by distillation, is now called Acetous Acid, because it is a strong acid of an agreeable odour, somewhat differing from simple vinegar.—*Acetum radicatum*, or radical vinegar, the strongest acid of vinegar, is still more concentrated than the former. Its phlegm being abstracted it is now termed Acetic Acid.—*Acetum philosophicum*, an acid distilled from honey.—*Acetum esurinum*, distilled vinegar, so called because it creates an appetite.

ACHÆ'MENIS (*Bot.*) a herb which, according to Pliny, when thrown into an army, was wont to cause a general panic. *Plin.* l. 26, c. 8.

ACHA'NIA (*Bot.*) Ἀχανής, *non hians*, because the corolla does not open: a genus of plants, Class 16 *Monodelphia*, Order 6 *Polyandria*.

Generic Characters. CAL. *perianth* double.—COR. subclavate; *petals* erect.—STAM. *filaments* numerous; *anthers* oblong.—PIST. *germ* subglobular; *style* filiform; *stigmas* capitate.—PER. *berry* subglobular; *seeds* solitary.

Species. The principal species are the—*Achania malvaviscus*, otherwise called *Malvaviscus arboreus, arborescens*; *Malva arborea*; *Hibiscus malvaviscus, seu frutescens*; or *Alcea indica*, Bastard Achania, or Malvaviscus; a shrub, native of Jamaica and Mexico.—*Achania mollis*, Woolly Achania, a shrub, native of America.—*Achania pilosa*, Hairy Achania, a shrub, native of Jamaica. *Pluken. Almag. Bot.*; *Dillen. Hort. Elth.*; *Brown. Hist. Jamaic.*; *Linn. Spec. Plant.*

ACHA'OVA (*Med.*) an Egyptian herb, like chamomile. *Prosp. Alpin. de Med. Ægypt.*

ACHARI'STON (*Med.*) ἀχάριστον, from α, priv. and χάρις, thanks; thankless, an epithet for an excellent medicine, so called because many who were cured by it never feed their physician. *Gal. de Comp. Med. sec. loc.* l. 4, c. 6; *Aet. Tetrab.* 2. serm. 4, c. 110.

A'CHAT (*Law.*) from *acheter*, to buy; a contract or bargain.

ACHA'TES (*Min.*) Ἀχάτης, agate; a precious stone representing different objects, from which it derives the different names of phassachates, cerachates, dendrachates, &c. according as it represents a dove, wax, a tree, &c. It was said to be generated in the river Achate. *Sil. Ital.* l. 14, v. 228.

> *Et pellucentem splendenti gurgite Achaten.*

and had medicinal virtues ascribed to it. *Theophrast. de Lapid.*; *Plin.* l. 37, c. 10; *Solin.* c. 11; *Isid. Orig.* l. 16, c. 11; *Marbod. de Lapid.*

ACHA'TORS (*Law.*) Purveyors, so called from their frequent bargaining. 36 E. 3.

ACHE'IR (*Med.*) Ἄχειρ, from α, priv. and χείρ, hand, handless.

ACHEIROPOE'TA (*Ecc.*) An image of the blessed virgin, to whom the popes used to pay particular reverence at Easter. It was so called to signify that it was made without hands.

ACHE'RNER (*Ast.*) or *Acher-Nahr*, called, by Ptolemy, ἔσχατος τοῦ ποταμοῦ; the name of a star of the first magnitude in the southern extremity of Eridanus, marked (*a*) by Bayer. Its longitude for 1761 was ♓ 11° 55′ 1″, and latitude south 59° 22′ 4″.

ACHE'TA (*Ent.*) a division in the genus of insects called *Gryllus* in the Linnean system.

A'CHIA (*Nat.*) a kind of cane in the East Indies which is pickled green.

A'CHIAR (*Nat.*) a Malayan word for all sorts of pickled fruits and roots.

ACHI'COLUM (*Ant.*) a sweating bath. *Cæl. Aurel. de Acut.* l. 3, c. 17.

ACHILLE'A (*Bot.*) ἀχιλλεία, or *Achilleon*, ἀχίλλειον; a plant so called because Achilles, who was the disciple of Chiron, is said to have used it in the healing of wounds. *Plin.* l. 25, c. 4; *Athen. Deipnos.* l. 3, c. 30.

ACHILLEA, *in the Linnean system*, a genus of plants; Class 19 *Syngenesia*, Order 2 *Polygamia superflua*. It is classed, by Tournefort and others, under the genera *Millefolium* and *Ptarmica*, and is called in English Milfoil or Maudlin.
Generic Character. CAL. common, ovate; *scales* ovate.—COR. compound radiate; *corollets* tubular.—STAM. *filaments* five; *anther* cylindrical.—PIST. *germ* small; *style* filiform; *stigma* obtuse.—PER. none; *receptacle* filiform; *seeds* solitary.
Species. The species are mostly perennials and natives of Europe; the principal are the *Achillea ageratum*, Sweet Milfoil or Maudlin.—*Achillea falcata*, Sickle-leaved Milfoil.—*Achillea tomentosa*, Woolly Milfoil.—*Achillea pubescens*, Downy Milfoil.—*Achillea impatiens*, Impatient Milfoil.—*Achillea atrata*, or *Chamamælum alpinum*, Camomile-leaved Milfoil.—*Achillea moschata*, Genipe Iva moschata, Tanacetum alpinum, or Dracunculus alpinus, Musk Milfoil, or Swiss Genipe.—*Achillea nana*, Dwarf Milfoil.—*Achillea magna*, or *Millefolium maximum*, Great Milfoil or Yarrow.—*Achillea millefolium*, Common Milfoil, a native of Britain, &c. *Dodon. Stirp. Hist. Pemptad.; Bauh. Pin.; Ger. Herb.; Park. Theat. Botan.; Raii Hist. Plant.; Linn. Spec. Plant.*

ACHILLEA is also the name of the *Athanasia annua*; the *Senecio abrotanifolius*; and the *Chrysanthemum millefolium* of Linnæus. *Lob. Adv. Stirp. et Plant. Icon.*

ACHILLE'ION (*Med.*) ἀχίλλειον, from *Achilles*; a sort of spunge proper for making tents.

ACHILLE'IOS (*Med.*) ἀχίλλειος, a sort of maze made of Achillean barley. *Foes. Oeconom. Hippocrat.*

ACHILLE'IS (*Med.*) ἀχιλληίς, a sort of barley used medicinally for making barley-water, so called, according to Galen, from a certain husbandman named Achilles. *Gal. de Med. Simpl. Fac.* l. 8.

ACHI'LLES (*Log.*) an epithet for an argument (λόγος) invented by Zeno against motion, founded on the assumption that the swifter animal can never overtake the slower. It takes its name from Achilles, either because it was supposed to be insuperable like him, or because he was compared in the argument with a tortoise. Can Achilles overtake a tortoise in running? Certainly: but if there were motion he could not overtake it, therefore, there is not motion. As the assumption or premise is here false, of course, the conclusion is false. *Aristot.* l. 6, c. 14; *Simplic. et Themist. in Aristot. ad locum.*

ACHI'LLIS *Tendo* (*Anat.*) vide *Tendo Achillis*.

ACHIMBA'SSI (*Med.*) chief physician at Grand Cairo. *Prosp. Alp.*

ACHI'MENES (*Bot.*) the *Columnea longifolia et hirsuta* of Linnæus. *Brown. Hist. Jam.*

ACHIMENIS (*Bot.*) vide *Achæmenis*.

ACHIO'TE (*Med.*) lozenges made of achiote. *Raii Hist. Plant.*

A'CHIOTL (*Bot.*) the *Bixa Orleana* of Linnæus. *C. Bauh. Pin.; Hermand. Nov. Plant. Mex. Hist.; Raii Hist. Plant.*

A'CHITH (*Bot.*) a sort of vine in Madagascar.

A'CHLYS (*Med.*) ἀχλύς, cloudiness; 1. dimness of sight. *Hippocrat. Prædict.* l. 1. 2. The pupil of the eye. *Prædict.* l. 2. 3. Condensed air in the uterus. *Hippocrat. de Morb. Mul.* l. 2; *Gorr. Defin. Med.; Foes. Oeconom. Hippocrat.*

ACHMA'DIUM (*Chem.*) antimony.

A'CHNE (*Med.*) ἄχνη, literally, chaff, or froth of the sea, signifies medicinally, 1. A whitish mucilage in the eyes of persons having fevers. *Hippocrat. Epidem.* sect. 1. 2. Lint recommended by Hippocrates in a fracture of the nose. *Hippocrat. de Art.; Gorr. Def. Med.; Foes. Oeconom. Hippocrat.*

ACHOA'VAN (*Bot.*) a sort of chamomile.

A'CHOR (*Med.*) ἀχώρ, probably from ἰχώρ, a watery discharge, Scald-Head: an ulcer in the head which, swelling and breaking into holes, discharges an honey-like humour; when the perforations are large it is called *favus*, a Honeycomb, and *tinea*, from the similitude of the holes to those made in cloth by moths; when this disorder affects the face it is called *crusta lactea*, Milk-Scab. *Gal. de Tum. præt. Nat. c.* 5; *Heister. Chirurg.* l. 5, c. 10.

ACHORI'STOS (*Med.*) ἀχώριστος, from *a*, priv. and χωρίς, without, inseparable; an epithet for a symptom; thus a pungent pain in the side is an inseparable symptom of a pleurisy.

A'CHRAS (*Bot.*) ἀχράς, a sort of wild pear-tree, ἄπιος ἀγρίος, according to Dioscorides, the *Pyrus sylvatica* of Varro, and *Pyrus sylvestris* of Pliny, on which, according to Aristotle, swine fattened: it was called by Brown the Bully-tree, or Nisberry Bully-tree, and now more generally the Sapota-tree. *Diosc.* l. 1, c. 148; *Brown. Hist. Jam.*

ACHRAS, *in the Linnean system*, is a genus of plants; Class 6 *Hexandria*, Order 1 *Monogynia*.
Generic Characters. CAL. *perianth* six-leaved; *leaflets* ovate.—COR. one petalled; *border* cut into six subovate flat divisions; *scales* at the jaws of the corolla.—STAM. *filaments* short; *anthers* sharp.—PIST. *Germ* roundish; *style* awl-shaped; *stigma* obtuse.—PER. *pome* globose; *seeds* solitary.
Species. The species of this tribe are mostly natives of America; the principal of which are the *Achras mammosa*, Sapota mammosa, Zapota major, Malus Persica maxima, or Arbor Americana pomifera, Mammee Sapota; a tree.—*Achras sapota* or *zapota*, Common Sapota; a tree.—*Achras dissecta*, Ballata, or Manil-kara, Cloven-flowered Sapota; a native of the Philippine islands.—*Achras salicifolia*, or *Brumelia salicifolia*, Willow-leaved Sapota.—*Achras argentea*, a tree, &c. *Raii Hist. Plant.; Pluk. Almag. Botan.; Plum. Plant. Amer.; Sloan. Jamaic.; Brown. Hist. Jamaic.; Jacq. Amer. Hist.; Linn. Spec. Plant.*

A'CHROI (*Med.*) ἄχροοι, from *a*, priv. and χρόα, colour, colourless; from a deficiency of blood.

ACHROMA'TIC (*Opt.*) an epithet for a sort of telescopes used first by Dr. Bevis to remedy aberrations and colours.

ACHROMATIC *Telescope*, a species of refracting telescope, invented by Mr. Dolland to refract the light in contrary directions.

ACHRO'NICAL (*Ast.*) vide *Acronical*.

A'CHTELING (*Com.*) a liquid measure in Germany.

ACHTENDE'ELEN (*Com.*) a corn measure used in some parts of Germany equal to 536 pounds avoirdupoise weight.

A'CHY (*Bot.*) a species of Cacia, in Arabia.

ACHYRACA'NTHA (*Bot.*) the *Achyranthes* of Linnæus. *Dillen. Hort.*

ACHYRA'NTHES (*Bot.*) from Ἄχυρον, chaff, and ἄνθος, a flower, formed after the manner of Ananthes, Dianthes, and similar words in Theophrastus; a genus of plants; Class 5 *Pentandria*, Order 1 *Monogynia*.

Generic Characters. Cal. *perianth* outer three-leaved.—Cor. none; *nectary* of five valves.—Stam. *filaments* filiform; *anthers* ovate.—Pist. *germ* superior; *style* filiform; *stigma* bifid.—Per. *capsule* roundish; *seed* single.

Species. The species of this genus are mostly shrubs or perennials; as the *Achyranthes aspera, Amaranthus zeylanicus, Auricula canis* or *cadeli,* Rough Achyranthes.—*Achyranthes muricata,* or *Blitum frutescens,* Prickly Achyranthes.—*Achyranthes prostrata, Auris canina,* or *Verbena indica,* Prostrate Achyranthes, &c. Bont. Hist. Nat. Ind. Orient.; Pluk. Phytog.; Pluk. Almag. Sloan, &c.

A'CHYRON (*Med.*) ἄχυρον, chaff, *Hipp.*; bran or straw.

A'CIA (*Med.*) a kind of thread for sowing wounds. *Gal. comm. in Hippoc.; Cels. de Re. Med.* l. 5, c. 26.

Acia (*Bot.*) in Guiana *Aciona,* according to Jussieu, *Acioa*; a genus of plants; Class 16 *Monodelphia,* Order 6 *Dodecandria.*

Generic Characters. Cal. *perianth* one-leafed; *border* five-parted; *parts* roundish.—Cor. *petals* five—Stam. *filaments* twelve; *anthers* roundish.—Pist. *germ* ovate; *style* filiform; *stigma* acute.—Per. *drupe* ovate; *seed* a nut ovate.

Species. The principal species are the *Acia dulcis amara,* &c.

ACICO'SA (*Bot.*) a herb similar to Paraguay.

ACI'CULA (*Ich.*) diminutive, from *acus,* a fish, called also *acus, ϛαλδιξ. Prisc.*

Acicula (*Bot.*) another name for *chervil,* or shepherd's needle.

ACICULA'RIS (*Bot.*) from *Acus,* a needle. 1. Acicular, or needle-shaped, an epithet for the *pili,* or hairs of plants. 2. A species of *Scirpus. Linn. Philos. Botan.*

A'CID (*Chem.*) vide *Acids.*

Acid *Holder,* a part of the chemical apparatus, consisting of a glass phial, so constructed that any acid or liquor may be dropped from it into a retort without admitting the external air.

ACIDIFI'ABLE *base* (*Chem.*) a base or substance which, without decomposition, can unite with oxygen in such quantities as to acquire the properties of an acid.

ACI'DIFYING *base* (*Chem.*) that principle in any substance which generates acids: oxygen is the chief acidifying base.

ACIDO'TON (*Bot.*) *Plin.*; a genus of plants: Class 21 *Monoecia,* Order 7 *Polyandria.*

Generic Characters. Cal. *perianth* five-leaved; *leaflets* ovate lanceolate.—Cor. none.—Stam. *filaments* numerous; *anther* cordate-ovate.

Species. The only species is the *Acidoton urens,* seu *Urtica urens arborea,* a shrub, native of Jamaica. *Sloan. Hist. Jamaic.*

Acidoton is also the *Adelia Acidoton* of Linnæus. *Brown. Hist. Jamaic.*

A'CIDS (*Chem.*) substances which impress the taste with a sour sharp sensation, change vegetable blue colours to red, and combine with alkalines so as to form salts. They were divided by chemists originally into—*Natural Acids,* such as have a sharpness of taste of their own from their nature, as the juice of lemons, &c.—*Artificial Acids,* which are generated from substances, not properly acids, by means of fire, as from vegetables, minerals, &c.—*Dulcified Acids,* those which are now called Æthers.—*Vegetable Acids,* which are especially prepared from vegetable substances, as citric acid, acetic acid, &c.—*Animal Acids,* which are generated from animal substances, as lactic acid, saccolactic, phosphoric, &c. acids.—*Mineral Acids,* those generated from mineral substances.—*Manifest* or *Perfect Acids,* such as affect the tongue sensibly with the taste of sharpness, or, in the language of modern chemistry, those which have their base saturated with oxygen, and are distinguished by the termination *ic,* as Nitric Acid.—*Dubious latent* or *imperfect Acids,* those which have not a sufficient degree of acidity to affect the taste, but have the other properties that distinguish the perfect acids, or those acids whose base predominates over the oxygen, which are distinguished by the termination *ous,* as Nitrous Acid.—*Acids* are now distinguished into incombustible and combustible.—*Incombustible Acids* are those which are formed by the combination of oxygen, the *acidifying principle* with one combustible, which is considered as the *acidifiable base* or *radical.*—*Combustible Acids* are those which contain two or more combustibles. The following table, taken from Thomson's Chemistry, exhibits a view of the modern distribution of acids.

CONSTITUENTS.

Acids.	Base.		Oxygen.
Nitric	Azote	100	285·8
Nitrous	—	100	228·57
Hyponitrous	—	100	171·43
Carbonic	Carbon	100	266·66
Boracic	Boron	100	228·57
Silica	Silicon	100	100·
Phosphoric	Phosphorus	100	200·
Phosphorous	—	100	133·3
Hypophosphorous	—	100	66·6
Sulphuric	Sulphur	100	150·
Sulphurous	—	100	100·
Hyposulphurous	—	100	50·
Arsenic	Arsenic	100	52·631
Arsenious	—	100	31·6
Antimonic	Antimony	100	35·556
Antimonious	—	100	23·7
Chromic	Chromium	100	87·72
Molybdic	Molybdenum	110	50·
Molybdous	—	100	33·3
Tungstic	Tungsten	100	25·
Columbic	Columbium	100	5·5

The termination *ic,* in the above acids, expresses the higher state of oxygenation, and that of *ous* the lower.

Combustible Acids containing two or more simple combustible Substances as a Base.

ATOMS OF

Acids.	Hydrogen.	Carbon.	Oxygen.
Acetic	3	4	3
Benzoic	6	15	3
Succinic	2	4	3
Moroxylic	—	—	—
Camphoric	—	—	—
Boletic	—	—	—
Suberic	—	—	—
Pyrotartaric	—	—	—
Oxalic	1	2	3
Mellitic	1	4	3
Tartaric	3	4	5
Citric	3	4	4
Rheumic	—	—	—
Kinic	—	—	—
Saclactic	5	6	8
Uric	—	—	—
Laccic	—	—	—
Malic	—	—	—
Sorbic	—	—	—
Formic	—	—	—
Lactic	—	—	—
Zumic	—	—	—
Gallic	3	6	3
Tannin	9	18	12

To these may be added acids containing supporters as well as combustibles:

Acids	Compounded of	
Chloric }	Chlorine	Oxygen
Perchloric		
Muriatic	Chlorine	Hydrogen
Chlorocarbonic	Chlorine gas	Carbonic oxide gas
Iodic	Iodine	Oxygen
Chloriodic	Chlorine	Iodine
Hydriodic	Iodine	Hydrogen
Fluoric	Fluorine	Hydrogen
Fluoboric	Fluorine	Boron
Fluosilic	Fluorine	Silicon
Chlorocyanic	Chlorine	Cyanogen
Hydrocyanic	Hydrogen	Cyanogen
Sulphocyanic	Sulphur	Cyanogen
Ferrocyanic	Iron	Cyanogen

ACI'DULÆ (*Min.*) from *acidus*, acid; mineral waters in general, but particularly those of the brisk cold kind. *Plin.* l. 31, c. 2.

ACI'DULOUS (*Chem.*) an epithet expressing either in general a slight degree of acid, or in particular an excess of acid in a compound salt; thus acidulous sulphat of potash is the sulphat of potash with an excess of acid.

ACI'DULUM (*Chem.*) a genus of native vegetable salts, consisting of potash saturated with an excess of acid, consisting of two species, tartareous acidulum, or the acidulous tartrite of potash, and the oxalic acidulum, or the acidulous oxulat of potash.

A'CIES (*Chem.*) the same as Chalybs.

ACI'NACES (*Ant.*) ἀκινάκης, from ἀκὴ, an edge; the name of a Persian scimitar.

ACINACIFO'RMIS (*Bot.*) from ἀκινάκης, a scimitar; scimitar-shaped, an epithet for a leaf: *Folium acinaciforme*, a leaf which has one edge convex and sharp, the other straight and thick, as in the *Mysembryanthemum*. *Linn. Phil. Bot.*

ACINE'SIA (*Med.*) ἀκινησία, from α, priv. and κινέω, to move; a term employed by Galen to express the interval of rest which takes place between the contraction and dilatation of the pulse. *Gal. de Diff. Puls.* l. 1, c. 7.

A'CINI (*Bot.*) granulations.

ACINIFO'RMIS (*Anat.*) or *Acina Tunica*, a coat of the eye. [vide *Uvea Tunica*]

A'CINOS (*Bot.*) ἄκινος, a species of the *Thymus* of Linnæus. *Dioscor.* l. 3, c. 50; *J. Bauh. Hist. Plant.*; *C. Bauh. Pin.*; *Raii Hist. Plant.*

ACKNO'WLEDGEMENT money (*Law.*) Money paid by tenants on the death of their landlords.

ACMA'STICA *febris* (*Med.*) ἀκμαστικὸς πυρετὸς, from ἀκμάζω, to flourish; a fever which, during the whole course, maintains itself in the same vigour without either increasing or diminishing in its violence. *Gal. de Diff. Feb.* l. 2, c. 2; *Act. de Meth. Med.* l. 2, c. 1.

A'CME (*Med.*) ἀκμὴ signifies literally a point, but is taken figuratively for the height of a disorder. Physicians commonly reckon three stages in disorders; namely, the ἀρχὴ, or commencement, i. e. the first attack; the ἀνάβασις, or growth; and the ἀκμὴ when it is at the highest pitch of violence. It also implies the highest pitch of exercise. *Hippocrat.* l. 1, *Aphor.* 1; *Gal. de Differ. Feb.* l. 2, c. 2.

ACME'LLA (*Chem.*) a plant of Ceylon, which is well known as a lithontriptic and diuretic; it is the *Verbesina acmella* of Linnæus. *Herman. Catalog. Plant.*

A'CMO (*Bot.*) red coral.

A'CNE (*Med.*) from ἄχνη, chaff; a tubercle on the face which Aetius calls ἀχμὴν. *Gorr. Def. Med.*

ACNE'STES (*Med.*) from α, priv. and κνάω, to scratch; a part of the spine in quadrupeds, so called because it cannot to be reached to be scratched.

ACNE'STIS (*Bot.*) the same as Urtica.

A'CNIDA (*Bot.*) from α, priv. and κνίδη, a nettle, to which it bears some resemblance without having its pruriency; a genus of plants; Class 22 *Dioecia*, Order 5 *Pentandria*.
Generic Characters. CAL. perianth five-leaved; *leaflets* ovate; COR. none.—STAM. *filaments* five; *anthers* versatile.
Species. The principal species is the *Acnida cannabina*, otherwise called *Cannabis*, Virginian hemp, an annual. *C. Bauh. Pin.*; *Linn. Spec. Plant.*

A'CO (*Ich.*) a sort of fish in the lake Como.

ACOE'LIOS (*Med.*) ἀκοίλιος, from α, priv. and κοιλία, *venter*, without a belly, or seeming to be so as one wasted away.

ACOEME'TI (*Ecc.*) ἀκοίμητοι, a set of monks, who kept up their devotions by turns incessantly day and night; and they were so called, on account of their continued watchfulness, from α, priv. and κοιμάω, to sleep. *Evagr. Eccles. Hist.* l. 3, c. 19; *Theodor. Lect.* l. 1; *Niceph. Calist.* l. 15, c. 23.

ACO'ETON (*Nat.*) vide *Acetum*.

ACOLUTHI (*Ecc.*) from ἀκόλυθος, *sequitor pedissequus*; attendants or under deacons, who wait upon the priests, in their office, to carry the wax lights, &c. *S. Cyprian.* ep. 7; *Euseb.* l. 6, c. 43; *Augustin.* ep. 62. 100; *S. Gregor.* l. 7, indict. 1, ep. 1; *Hesychius.*; *Isidor. Orig.* l. 7, c. 12; *L'Ordre Roman.*; *Les Anciens Rituels.*

A'COMAS (*Bot.*) a tree in America used for ship-building.

A'CON (*Ant.*) a sort of Discus.

ACO'NION (*Med.*) ἀκόνιον, a medicine prepared by levigation on a stone. *Dioscor.* l. 1, c. 129.

A'CONITE (*Bot.*) Wolf's-bane, or Monk's-hood. [vide *Aconitum*]

ACONITIFO'LIA (*Bot.*) the *Podophyllum peltatum* of Linnæus. *Boerhaav. Ind. Plant.*

ACONI'TON (*Med.*) ἀκόνιτον, from α, priv. and κονία, plaister; vessels not plaistered or lined within. *Dioscor.* l. 4, c. 65.

ACONI'TUM (*Bot.*) ἀκόνιτον, a poisonous plant, which the poets fable to have been produced from the foam of the dog Acheron, when he was dragged by Hercules from Hell. *Nicand. in Alexand.*

'Αλλ' ἤτοι χυλοῖσι μὲν ἰδὶ σομίοισι δυσαλθὲς
Πιθοίης ἀκόνιτον, ὃ δή ῥα' ἀχιρονίδις ὄχθαι
Φύωσιν.

Dionys. Perieges. v. 789.

'Ουδαίω προνίδιμω μύγας κόνα χαλκεόφωτον
Χιρσὶν ἀπειλκόμενον μεγαλόφρωτος 'Ηρακλῆος
Δεινὸν ἀπὸ σομάτων βαλίων σιαλώδεα χυλὸν
Τὸν μιν ἰδέξατο γαῖα καὶ ἀνδρώσι πῆμ' ἐφύτευσεν.

Others ascribe its origin to the gall, from the liver of Prometheus, which was eaten by the vulture.
Auson. in Monosyllab.

Unde Prometheo de corpore sanguineus ros
Aspergit cautes et dura aconita creat eos.

The *aconitum* is so called from *aconæ*, i. e. the naked rocks on which it grows.
Nicand. in Alexipharm.

——— ἐν δ' ἀκονκίοις
Τῆλε λίαν ἀκόνιτον κιαβλάςησιν ὀρόγκοις.

Ovid. Met. l. 7, v. 416.

Quæ quia nascuntur dura vivacia caute
Agrestes aconita vocant.

Others derive it, and with equal reason, from α, priv. and κονίς, dust, because it grows without much earth; or from ἀκὴ, a dart, because savages used to poison their darts with it. *Theoph.* l. 9, c. 16; *Dioscor.* l. 4, c. 77; *Plin.* l. 6, c. 1, l. 27, c. 3; *Gal. de Simplic. Med. Fac.* l. 6.

ACONITUM, in the Linnean system, a genus of plants; Class 13 *Polyandria*, Order 3 *Trigynia*.
Generic Character. COL. none.—COR. *petals* five; *nectaries* two.—STAM. *filaments* subulate; *anthers* erect.—PIST.

Germ three; *stigmas* simple.—PER. *Capsules* ovate, subulate; *seeds* very many.

Species. The species of this genus are all perennials; the principal of which are the *Aconitum lycoctorum*, or the *Napellus magnus*, Great yellow Monk's-hood, or Wolf's-bane.—*Aconitum napellus*, or the *Napellus verus*, common Monk's-hood, or Wolf'sbane.—*Aconitum anthora*, *Aconitum salutiferum*, *Anthora vulgaris*, or *Antithora*, Salutary Monk's-hood.—*Aconitum variegatum*, *Napellus minor*, or *Lycoctonum cœruleum*, Variegated or small blue Monk's-hood, &c. *J. Bauh. Hist. Plant.*; *C. Bauh. Pin.*; *Ger. Herb.*; *Park. Theat. Botan.*; *Tournef. Instit.*; *Boerh. Ind.*

ACONITUM is also the name of the *Helleborus hyemalis* of Linnæus. *C. Bauh. Pin.*

ACO'NTIAS (*Zo.*) a very poisonous serpent.

ACONTIAS (*Ast.*) a blazing star shooting like an arrow. *Plin.* l. 2, c. 24.

A'COPA (*Med.*) ἄκοπα, from ἀ, priv. and κόπος, labour; medicines against weariness. *Hippocrat. Aphor.* l. 2; *Cels.* l. 5, c. 24; *Plin.* l. 37, c. 10; *Gal. de Comp. Med. per Gen.* l. 7, c. 11, &c.; *Oribas. Synops.* l. 3, c. 10; *Paul. Æginet.* l. 7, c. 19.

A'COPIS (*Nat.*) ἄκοπις, from ἀ, priv. and κόπος, labour: a precious stone, good against weariness. *Plin.* l. 37, c. 10.

A'COPOS (*Bot.*) Bean-trefoil.

A'COR (*Med.*) acrimony in the stomach.

ACORDI'NA (*Chem.*) Indian Tutty.

A'CORI (*Min.*) Blue Coral on the coast of Africa.

ACO'RIA (*Med.*) ἀκορία, insatiability, or, according to Hippocrates, a sharp appetite. *Hippoc. Epid.* l. 6, c. 4, *Aphor.* 20.

ACORI'TES *Vinum* (*Nat.*) 'Ἀκορίτης οἶνος, a wine made of the Acorus and liquorice roots. *Dios.* l. 5, c. 73.

A'CORN (*Med.*) the seed of the oak used as an astringent.

ACORN (*Mar.*) a little ornamental piece of wood fashioned like a cone, and fixed above the vane on the mast head.

ACORN *shell* (*Con.*) the name of a genus of shells classed in the Linnean system under the Lepas. [vide *Lepas*]

ACO'RNA (*Bot.*) ἄκορνα, from ἀ, i. e. ἄγαν, very, and κόρνος, a spine, i. e. very thorny; a herb similar to the *Atractylis*.

A'CORNED (*Her.*) a tree with acorns on it. "He beareth *argent* an oak *acorn'd* proper, over all on a fesse gules three royal crowns." This coat was given by Charles II. to Colonel Carloss, a Staffordshire gentleman, for the signal service he performed in preserving his Majesty in the oak after the battle of Worcester.

A'CORUS (*Bot.*) ἄκορος, Sweet Rush, a plant so called because it was useful for disorders in the κόραι, or pupils of the eye. *Theoph.* l. 1, c. 22; *Diosc.* l. 1, c. 2; *Gal. de Simplic. Pliny*, l. 25, c. 13.

ACORUS, *in the Linnean system*, is a genus of plants; Class 6 *Hexandria*, Order 1 *Monogynia*.

Generic Characters. CAL. *spadix* cylindric; *spathe* none; *perianth* none.—COR. *petals* six.—STAM. *filaments* thickish; *anthers* thickish.—PIST. *Germ* gibbous; *style* none; *stigma* a prominent point.—PER. *capsule* short; *seeds* many.

Species. The principal species is the *Acorus calamus*, Common Sweet Rush; a perennial, native of Britain. *C. Bauh. Pin.*; *Park. Theat. Botan.*; *Raii Hist. Plant.*; *Merr. Pin. Britt.*; *Pluk. Almag. Botan.*; *Tourn. Inst. Herb.*; *Boerh. Ind. Plant.*

ACO'SMIA (*Med.*) ἀκοσμία, irregularity in fevers. *Hippoc. Progn.* l. 3, c. 7; *Castel. Lex Med.*

ACO'SMOI (*Ant.*) ἄκοσμοι, from ἀ, priv. and κόσμος, an ornament; an epithet for bald people, because they have lost their greatest ornament. *Poll. Onomast.* l. 2, c. 26.

ACOTYLE'DONES (*Bot.*) from ἀ, priv. and κοτύληδων, acotyledonous, or lobeless. 1. An epithet for a description of plants whose seeds have no lobes or cotyledons, and of course when they vegetate they produce no seminal leaves, as in the *Cryptogamia*. 2. One of Jussieu's natural order of plants. *Linn. Phil. Bot.*

ACO'USIA (*Med.*) ἀκουσία, involuntary, an epithet applied by Hippocrates to tears.

ACO'USTIC (*Anat.*) the same as auditory, an epithet for the nerve of the ear, ἀκυστικὸν νεῦρον, which assists the sense of hearing. *Gorr. Def. Med.*

ACO'USTICA (*Med.*) from ἀκούω, audio; remedies against deafness.

ACOUSTICA (*Phy.*) from ἀκούω, audio; acoustics, or the doctrine of hearing and sound.

ACQUI'ESCENCE (*Com.*) consent, in French *commerce*, to any judgment or sentence, judicial or by arbitration.

ACQUIETA'NDIS *plegiis* (*Law*) a writ of justicies lying for surety against a creditor, who refuses to acquit him after the debt is satisfied. *Regis. of Writs.*

ACQUIETA'NTIA de *Shiris et Hundredis* (*Law*) freedom from suits and services in shires and hundreds.

ACQUIETA'RE (*Law*) to acquit, or pay. *Mon. Angl.*

ACQU'IT (*Com.*) a discharge or receipt.—*Acquit, à caution*, a certificate to exempt goods that are exported or transported from a visitation on the road.—*Acquit, à caution de transit*, a certificate to exempt goods from the payment of duties in their passage through a particular place.—*Acquit de franchise*, a certificate exempting merchandize from paying duties on exportation.—*Acquit de payment*, a certificate, in which the quantity of goods, amount of duties paid, names of the persons sending, &c. are mentioned.

ACQUI'TTAL (*Law*) from the Latin *acquietare*. 1. A discharge from the claims of a superior lord. 2. A discharge from the suspicion of guilt: *acquietatus de felonia*, acquitted of felony. Acquittal is of two kinds, namely—*Acquittal, in deed*, when a person is cleared by a verdict.—*Acquittal, in law*, when, if two persons be indicted for felony, the one as principal, and the other as accessory, and the jury acquits the principal, in this case, by law, the accessory is also acquitted. 2 *Inst.* 384.

ACQUI'TTANCE (*Law*) the same as receipt.

ACRA'IPALA (*Med.*) ἀκραίπαλα, remedies for surfeits, &c. *Gorr. Def. Med.*

A'CRAS (*Bot.*) vide *Achras*.

ACRASI'A (*Ant.*) ἀκρασία, from ἀ, priv. and κεράννυμι, drinking unmixed wine, which was synonymous with intemperance among the Greeks.

ACRA'TIA (*Med.*) ἀκράτεια, from ἀ, priv. and κράτος, strength; imbecility, or incapacity to move. *Hippocrat.* l. 7, *Aphor.* 40; *Gal. Comm.*; *Gorr. Def. Med.*; *Foes. Oeconom. Hippocrat.*

ACRATI'SMA (*Ant.*) ἀκράτισμα, from ἀ, priv. and κεράννυμι, to mix, a breakfast consisting of bread steeped in wine not mixed with water. *Gal. de Loc. Affect.* c. 5, &c.; *Plut. Sympos.* l. 8, prob. 6; *Athen.* l. 1; *Schol. in Theocrit.*; *Gorr. Def. Med.*

ACRATOME'LI (*Med.*) wine mixed with honey.

A'CRE (*Agr.*) from *ager*, a field. 1. A measure of land equal to forty perches in length, and four in breadth. 24 Hen. 8, c. 14; 33 Ed. 1, st. 6. 2. An open unmeasured field, as *Castle Acre*, *West Acre*, &c.

A'CREA (*Anat.*) ἄκρεα, from ἄκρη, *summa*; the *extremities* according to Hippocrates. *Foes. Oecon. Hippocrat.*

A'CRE-FIGHT (*Law*) a sort of duel fought by single combatants, English and Scotch, on the frontiers of their kingdoms.

ACRE'ME (*Archæol.*) ten acres of land.

ACRIBE'A (*Med.*) ἀκρίβεια, from ἀκριβής, correct; an exact description of diseases.

ACRI'MONY (*Med.*) from *acer*, sharp; sharpness or pungency in the humours of the body; also, in chemical substances, as alkalies, &c.

A'CRIS (*Med.*) ἄκρις, the extremities of fractured bones. *Hippocrat. de Art.*

ACRIS (*Ent.*) the locust, which was so called because it fed on τὰς ἄκρας τῶν φυτῶν, i. e. the tops of plants.

ACRI'SIA (*Med.*) ἀκρισία, from α, priv. and κρίνω, to judge, want of a crisis, or discriminating state in a disorder which is very fluctuating. *Gal. Comm. 2. in Hippocrat. Epid.* l. 1.

ACRI'VIOLA (*Bot.*) the *Tropæolum majus* of Linnæus. *Boerharv. Ind. Herb.*

A'CROAMA (*Ant.*) ἀκρόαμα, *res aliqua audita*, from ἀκροάομαι, to hear, i. e. any thing heard or listened to with attention. 1. A philosophical lecture of the higher sort. 2. A ludicrous recitation. 3. Symphony, or vocal concert. *Manut. in Cic. Sex. c. 54*; *Plin. Epist.* l. 6, ep. 31; *Suet. in August. c. 74*; *Plut. Sympos.* l. 7, c. 8; *Gell.* l. 20, c. 5; *Salmas. in Lamprid. Alex. Sever. c. 32.*

ACROAMA'TICA (*Ant.*) ἀκροαματικά, the subtle parts of Aristotle's philosophy, which he taught only to his constant followers, in distinction from the ἐξωτερικά, consisting of more familiar subjects. *Aul. Gell.* l. 20, c. 5.

ACROBA'TICHON (*Archit.*) from ἄκρος, and βαίνω, going aloft; a climbing machine. *Vitruv.* l. 10, c. 1; *Gyrald. de Poet. Dial.* 6; *Bald. Lex Vitruv.*

ACROBOLI'STÆ (*Ant.*) ἀκροβολισταί, soldiers of Tarentum, who were expert in the use of the javelin, which they threw to a great distance while on horseback; so called from ἄκρος and βάλλω. *Ælian. Tact. c. 45.*

ACROBY'STIA (*Anat.*) vide *Acroposthia*.

ACROCHEI'RIA (*Ant.*) or *Acrocheirismos*, ἀκροχειρία, a species of wrestling in which only the hands are employed. *Poll. Onom.* l. 2, § 153.

ACROCO'LIA (*Ant.*) ἀκροκώλια, from ἄκρος, extreme, and κῶλον, a limb; the extremities of animals, and also the internal parts, the giblets. It was particularly applied to Pensile-Wart. *Poll. Onom.* l. 4, § 195; *Cels.* l. 5, c. 28; *Gal. Defin. Med. &c. Actuar. in voc. μυωκηλία.*

ACRO'DRYA (*Bot.*) ἀκρόδρυα, from ἄκρος and δρῦς, an oak; all fruits having hard rinds or shells. *Theophrast.* l. 2, c. 7.

ACROLE'NIA (*Anat.*) ἀκρωλένια, the great processes of the ulna. *Poll. Onomast.* l. 2, § 140; *Gorr. Def. Med.*

ACROMA'LLOS (*Ant.*) ἀκρόμαλλος, short wool, of which the Belgæ made their garments, in distinction from the βαθύμαλλος, or long wool. *Strab.* l. 4; *Ferrar. de Re Vest.* l. 2, c. 2, &c.

ACRO'MION (*Anat.*) ἀκρώμιον, or ἐπωμίς, from ὦμος, the shoulder; *Scapula, Humeri summitas sive Humeri Mucro*; the superior process of the shoulder, the shoulder-blade. *Ruff. Ephes. de Appell. Part. Corp. Hum.* l. 1, c. 9; *Oribas. Med. Collect.* l. 25, c. 3.

ACRO'MPHALIUM (*Anat.*) ἀκρομφάλιον, from ἄκρος, the extreme, and ὀμφαλός, the navel; the tip of the navel. *Poll. Onom.* l. 2, segm. 169.

A'CRON (*Med.*) ἄκρον, from ἄκρος, the highest; an epithet, signifying the best of its kind, as ἄκρον ἴρινον, the best sort of the *unguentum irinum*. *Hippocrat. de Morb. Mul.*

A'CRON (*Bot.*) the top of the thistle.

ACRONY'CHIA (*Bot.*) an epithet for a plant; the *Lawsonia Acronychia* of Linnæus.

ACRO'NYCHAL (*Astron.*) ἀπὸ τῆ ἄκρας, from the first point, νυκτός, of night; an epithet for the rising of a star when the sun sets, or the setting of a star when the sun rises. *Ptol. Almag.* l. 8, c. 4. [vide *Astronomy*]

ACRONY'CTÆ (*Astron.*) ἀκρόνυκται, stars rising in the twilight about sun-setting, for ἀκρόνυξ is the evening twilight.

ACROPA'THOS (*Med.*) ἀκρόπαθος, from ἄκρος, extreme, and πάθος, affection; an affection or disease on the surface of the body, such as the καρκίνοι ἀκροπαθοί, open cancers, in distinction from the κρυπτοί, occult or internal. *Hippocrat. Prorrhet.* l. 2.

A'CROPIS (*Med.*) ἄκροπις, an epithet for the tongue, which, by reason of dryness or any muscular imperfection, is incapable of articulation. *Hippocrat. Epidem.* l. 7; *Gal. Exeges. Hippocrat. Vocab.*

ACROPO'STHIA (*Anat.*) ἀκροποσθία, the extremity of the prepuce. *Hippocrat.* l. 2, *Aph.* 48; *Poll. Onomast.* l. 2, segm. 171; *Ruff. Ephes. de Appell. Part. Corp. Hum.* l. 1, c. 12.

A'CROS (*Med.*) ἄκρος, extreme; an epithet for a disease at its height.

ACROS (*Anat.*) an epithet for the prominence of a bone.

ACROS (*Bot.*) an epithet for the top of herbs.

A'CROSPIRE (*Bot.*) the sprout at the ends of barley when it is malted, whence the epithet acrospired for barley in that condition.

ACRO'STICHUM (*Bot.*) a genus of plants, Class 24 *Cryptogamia*, Order 1 *Filices*.

Generic Character. *Fructifications* cover the whole undersurface of the frond.

Species. The species are mostly perennials, the principal of which are—*Acrostichum citrifolium*, *Hemionitis parasitica*, or *Lingua cervina*, native of America.—*Acrostichum crinitum*, *Lingua cervina*, or *Phyllitis crinita*, native of the East Indies.—*Acrostichum aureum*, *Phyllitis ramosa*, *Lonchitis palustris maxima*, *Lingua cervina aurea*, or *Filix palustris*, native of Jamaica.—*Acrostichum biforme*, or *Osmunda coronaria*, native of the East Indies.—*Acrostichum serrulatum*, or *Polypodium fuscum*, native of Spain, &c. &c. *Raii Hist. Plant.*; *Pluk. Almag. Botan.*; *Plum. Plant. Amer.*; *Linn. Spec. Plant.*

ACRO'STICK (*Lit.*) ἀκροστιχίς, i. e. ἄκρον τῦ στιχῦ, the beginning; a set of verses, the first letters of which contain some name or sentence, such as the famous verses of the Sibyl of Erythræa, which contain the words ΙΗΣΟΥΣ ΧΡΙΣΤΟΣ ΘΕΟΥ ΥΙΟΣ ΣΩΤΗΡ ΣΤΑΥΡΟΣ, which are given at large by Lylius Giraldus. *Cic. de Divin.* l. 2, c. 54; *Euseb. de Vit. Constantin.* l. 4; *Ludovic. Vives ad August. de Civit. Dei*, l. 18, c 23; *Lyl. Gyrald. de Poet. Histor. Dialog.* 2.

ACROSTO'LIUM (*Ant.*) ἀκροστόλιον, the extreme part of the ornament on the prow of the ship. *Poll. Onom.* l. 1, segm. 86.

ACROTE'RIA (*Anat.*) ἀκρωτήρια, from ἄκρος, extreme; the extremities of the human body, as the fingers' ends, &c. *Hippocrat.* l. 7, *Aphor.* 1, et *Gal. Comm.*; *Gorr. Def. Med.*; *Foes. Oeconom. Hippocrat.*

A'CROTERS (*Archit.*) ἀκρωτήρια, from ἄκρος, extreme. 1. Small pedestals placed on the pediments which serve to support statues. 2. The sharp pinnacles, or spiry battlements, standing in ranges on flat buildings, with rails and balusters. 3. The figures made, either of stone or metal, which are placed as ornaments or crownings on the tops of temples. *Vitruv.* l. 3, c. 2; *Bald. Lex Vitruvian. Rhodig. Antiq. Lect.* l. 21, c. 33; *Salmas. ad Spartian. in Nig.* c. 12.

ACROTERIA'SMUS (*Med.*) ἀκρωτηριασμός, a term used by Hippocrates for an amputation of the ἀκρωτήρια, or extremities. *Hippocrat.* l. 7, *Aphor.* 26.

ACROTHY'MION (*Med.*) ἀκροθύμιον, a species of wart, which is hard, rough, broad at the base, and narrow at the top. *Cels.* l. 5, c. 28.

ACRY'DIUM (*Ent.*) a name given by Fabricius to a division of the genus of insects, called by Linnæus *Gryllus*.

ACT (*Phy.*) the effective application of some power or faculty.

ACT of Faith (*Ecc.*) in Spanish *Auto da Fe*; a solemn act of the inquisition, by which they bring to punishment those who are declared to be heretics.

ACT (*Polit.*) any public act, or proceeding of the government, as an—*Act of Parliament*, a deed or decree of the high court of Parliament.—*Act of grace*, an Act of Parliament, which grants a general and free pardon; it is sometimes passed at the commencement of a new reign.—*Act of curatory*, in the Scotch law, an act to be extracted by the clerk upon any one's acceptation of being curator.—*Act before answer*, when the lords ordain probation to be led before they determine the revelancy, and then take both at once under their consideration.

ACT (*Lit.*) the close of the session at Oxford, when degrees are regularly taken; whence the *Act Term*, or that term in which the act falls.

ACT is also an abbreviation for *Acta*, as—Act. S. R. for *Acta Societatis Regiæ*, or Philosophical Transactions of the Royal Society.—Act. Med. for *Acta Medica*, Medical Transactions, &c.

A'CTA (*Ant.*) the acts or proceedings of the government, which were either public or private.—*Acta publica* were edicts, decrees of the senate, laws, &c.; hence the public measures of Gracchus and Cæsar are termed *Acta*. Cicero refers particularly to the *Acta Cæsaris* in his seventh Philippic.—*Acta privata* were whatever was transacted in private, or in respect to private individuals; whence Cicero says, *In publicis actis nihil est lege gravius, in privatis firmissimum est testamentum*.

ACTA, *Tabulæ* or *Commentarii*, were also the registers or books in which affairs of state, &c. were enrolled. These were *Acta publica* and *Acta diurna* or *urbana*.—*Acta publica* contained an account of the proceedings of the senate and the people.—*Acta diurna* were chronicles of the city, or whatever was of daily occurrence; whence Tacitus says, *Ex dignitate populi Romani repertum est inlustres res annalibus, talia (nempe de ædificiis) diurnis urbis actis mandare*. These *acta* were similar to our gazettes. Cic. ad Fam. l. 12, ep. 8; Tacit. Annal. l. 5, c. 14, et l. 13, c. 31; Plin. Epist. l. 5, ep. 14.

ACTA (*Lit.*) transactions. [vide *Act*]

A'CTÆA (*Bot.*) ἀκταία, a diminutive of ἀκτή, a plant, recommended by Pliny for its medicinal virtues. Ray supposes it to be the *Aconitum racemosum*, which is a very poisonous plant. Plin. l. 27, c. 7; Paul. Æginet. l. 3, c. 48.

ACTÆA, *in the Linnæan system*, a genus of plants, Class 13 *Polyandria*, Order 1 *Monogynia*. It is called by Tournefort *Christophoriana*; in English, Herb Christopher, or Bane-Berry.
Generic Character. CAL. *perianth* four-leaved; *leaflets* roundish.—COR. *petals* four.—STAM. *filaments* capillary; *anthers* roundish.—PIST. *germ* superior; *style* none.—PER. *berry* oval, globose; *seeds* numerous.
Species. The principal species are the—*Actæa spicata*, a perennial, native of Britain.—*Actæa racemosa, seu Christophoriana*, American black or wild Snakeroot, a perennial, native of Florida.—*Actæa Japonica*, Japanese Herb Christopher, a shrub, native of Japan, &c.

A'CTE (*Bot.*) ἀκτή, the elder, called in Latin *Sambucus*, and classed as a genus under that name by Linnæus.

A'CTIA (*Ant.*) ἄκτια, scilicet, ἀγῶνα, *Ludi Actiaci*, Actian games, quinquennial games sacred to Apollo, instituted, or, as some will have it, revived, by Augustus, in commemoration of his victory over M. Anthony at Actium.
Virg. Æn. l. 3, v. 280.

Actiaque Iliacis celebramus littora ludis.

Stephanus says, they were celebrated every third year, and consisted in gymnastic, equestrian, and naval contests. Strab. l. 7; Plut. in Anton.; Steph. Byz. de Urb.; Serv. in Virg.; Suid.

ACTIA (*Numis*) the celebration of the Actian games is commemorated on several medals, as in the annexed figure, which represents a woman standing with a small temple in one hand, and a cornucopia with a small temple resting on it in the other; and at her feet two urns filled with the rewards for the games. The inscription ΠΕΡΙΝΘΙΩΝ. ΙΩΝΩ. ΝΒ. ΝΕΩΚΟΡΩΝ ΑΚΤΙΑ ΠΥΘΙΑ, i. e. *Perinthiorum Ionium, Iterum Œdituorum, Actia Pythia*. The Perinthians were descendants of the Ionians. Froehl. Not. Element. Numis.

A'CTIAN (*Ant.*) *actiacus*, an epithet for any thing appertaining to Actium, as the *Actian games*. [vide *Actia*] The *Actian Æra*, which was dated from the victory at Actium, U. C. 714, B. C. 37.

ACTIAN Æra (*Num.*) this æra is marked on coins with the inscription ΕΤΟΥΣ ΝΙΚΗ, i. e. the year of victory. Vaillant. Numis. Græc.

ACTI'LIA (*Mil.*) military utensils.

A'CTINE (*Bot.*) the *Brassica napus* of Linnæus.

A'CTING (*Log.*) τὸ ποιεῖν, the fifth predicament, or category; the subject of which is called the agent.

ACTI'NIA (*Ent.*) a genus of animals, Class *Vermes*, Order *Mollusca*.
Generic Character. Body oblong, contractile; *mouth* surrounded with numerous cirri.
Species. These marine animals are viviparous, and have no aperture, except the mouth. They assume various forms; and when the *tentacula* are all expanded, they have the appearance of full-blown flowers. The principal species are—*Actinia bellis*, the Sea-Daisy.—*Actinia dianthus*, the Sea-Carnation.—*Actinia calendula*, the Sea-Marigold, &c.

ACTINOBOLI'SMUS (*Med.*) ἀκτινοβολισμός, irradiation, or the instantaneous action of the animal spirits, by which they convey the inclinations of the mind to the organs of voluntary motion.

ACTINOBOLISMUS (*Phy.*) the diffusion or diradiation of light and sound.

ACTI'NOLITE glassy (*Min.*) from ἀκτίς, *radius*, and λίθος, *lapis*; a species of minerals, the *Actinotus vitreus* of Linnæus.

ACTINO'TUS (*Min.*) a genus of minerals, Class *Earths*, Order *Talcose*, consisting of carbonate of magnesia, oxide of iron, and silica: harsh to the touch, shining, breaking into indeterminate fragments, and melting in the fire with ebullition. The principal species are the—*Actinotus vulgaris asbestoid*.—*Actinotus vitreus*, Glassy Actinote, &c.

A'CTIO (*Ant.*) 1. The act of the magistrates and senates, the same as *acta*. 2. The management of a cause, consisting either of accusation or defence; where there were several pleadings in the same cause, they were divided into first, second, &c. thence the *actio prima, secunda, tertia*, &c. of Cicero *in Verrem*. 3. A suit at law, an action against any one, by which a person sought redress, either *accusando*, by accusing; or *petendo*, by suit. Of these actions there were several kinds, as—*Actio in rem*, real action, for obtaining that to which one had a real right, *jus in re*, but which was possessed by another. These actions were either—*Actio civilis*, according to the laws by which the citizens were governed one with another, which was called *Vindicatio*.—*Actio prætoria*, according to the decrees of the prætor who governed the city.—*Actio socialis*, according to the laws of their allies. —*Actio in personam*, personal action against a person for doing or omitting to do that which he was bound either to do, or to abstain from. Of these actions there are several kinds, as—*Actio empti, venditi, locati*, &c. for contracts and obligations, in buying, selling, &c.—*Actio adjectitia qualitatis*, against a person on account of the contracts of others.—*Actio institoria*, against him who carried on trade for the benefit of another.—*Actio exercitoria*, against him who sent a ship to sea on any trading concern.—*Actio de peculio*, against the master of a family, for contracts made either by his son or slave.—*Actio jussu*, if the contract was made by the master's order.—*Actio tributoria*, against a master for not distributing the goods of his slave among his creditors.—*Actio redhibitoria*, against the seller for selling a bad article, which he was compelled to take back, and to restore the money.—*Actio ex furto*, for theft, *ex rapina*, for robbery, *ex damno*, for loss or damage, *ex injuria*, for personal injury, comprehending the personal wrongs, and their several punishments.—*Actio noxalis*, against a person for injuries done by those under his power.—*Actio mixta*, which lies against any one, both for the recovery of the thing, and the punishment of the person. *Ulpian. Instit.* 1; *Justin. Pandect. et Instit*; *Sigon. de Judic*. l. 1, &c.; *Pollet. For. Rom*. l. 5; *Ursat. de Not. Rom.*

ACTIO (*Law*) vide Action.

A'CTION (*Ant.*) vide Actio.

ACTION (*Phy.*) actio, τὸ ποιεῖν, the application of the agent to the patient, by which some change is produced, as boiling, which is the action of fire on the water to which it is communicated; it is either physical or habitual.—*Physical action*, arising from the exercise of the physical power, as generally in generation, corruption, &c. or particularly in seeing, hearing, local motion, &c.—*Habitual* or *acquired action*, arising from habit or experience, which consists in speculation, θεωρία, as the contemplation of the heavens, of physical or mathematical objects; practice, πρᾶξις, which is either moral, political, or ecclesiastical; doing or making, ποίησις, which includes the arts liberal and mechanical. *Arist. Physic.*; *Melancth. Metaph.*

ACTION (*Log.*) τὸ ποιεῖν, the fifth predicament or category, into which all things have been divided. It is opposed to passion, and is divided into—*Action imminent*, that action which remains in the agent so as not to pass over to any other thing without itself, as going, walking, running, &c.—*Action transient*, that which passes from the agent to the patient, as burning, striking, breaking, &c. *Arist. Categ.*; *Boeth. de Categor.*; *Wall. Instit. Log.*

ACTION (*Mech.*) a force impressed upon a body so as to change its state of rest, or uniform motion. It arises from *percussion, pressure*, or *centripetal force*. *Newton Princ.* def. 4.—*Quantity of action*, the continual product of the mass of a body by the space which it runs through, and by its celerity. *Maupert. Acad. des Sciences, Paris*, 1744, *Berlin*, 1746.

ACTION (*Med.*) function of the body, which is divided into vital, natural, animal, or voluntary.—*Vital action*, which is immediately essential for the preservation of life, as the motion of the heart and lungs.—*Natural action*, which is remotely necessary for the continuance of the animal, as the digestion of the aliments, &c.—*Animal* or *voluntary actions*, which depend upon the will, as walking, running, &c.

ACTION (*Eth.*) or *moral action*, a voluntary action of any creature capable of distinguishing between good and evil, or whatever a rational agent thinks, does, or even omits to do, with respect to the end he ought to aim at, and the rule he is to be guided by. A *morally good action* is that which is agreeable to the law of God; in distinction from a *morally evil action*, which is disagreeable to the Divine law, as revealed in Scripture.

ACTION (*Law*) the process or form of a suit at law to recover a right. Actions are generally divided into criminal or civil.—*Criminal actions* are to have judgment for damage to the party injured.—*Civil actions* for the recovery of a debt, &c.

Criminal actions consist of—*Actions, penal*, for some penalty or punishment.—*Actions upon statute*, for the breach of a statute, whereby the injured party has his action.—*Actions, popular*, for the breach of some penal statute where every one has his action: it is otherwise called *a qui tam action*, from the form of words used in this action; namely, *qui tam pro domino rege sequitur quam pro se ipso*, &c.

Civil actions consist of different kinds, as—*Actions, real*, whereby a man claims title to lands, &c which are called *possessory*, if of his own possessions; *auncestral*, if of an ancestor.—*Actions, personal*, claiming a debt, goods, damages, &c.—*Actions, mixed*, which lie both for the thing demanded, and against the person having it.

Actions are also distinguished into

Actions, local, when confined to a particular county.—*Actions, transitory*, which may be laid in any county.—*Actions, perpetual*, which may not be determined by time.—*Actions, temporary*, that are expressly limited.—*Actions, joint*, where several persons conjointly sue or are sued.—*Actions, several*, where persons are severally charged.—*Actions on assumpsit*, or promises, for a breach of promise, &c.—*Actions on covenant*, for a breach of covenant.—*Actions on debt*, to compel the payment of a debt.—*Actions of detinue*, to compel the redelivery of goods (or their value) which have been delivered in charge.—*Actions of trespass*, for any injury denominated a trespass.—*Actions of trover*, for goods which have come into the possession of another by finding, or otherwise, which he refuses to restore to the owner.—*Actions on the case*, that is, an action on a man's own particular case, in distinction from those on any of the above-mentioned cases.—*Actions, prejudicial*, otherwise called *preparatory* or *principal*, arising from some doubt in the principal, as in case a man sues his younger brother for lands descended from his father; and it is objected to him, that he is a bastard, which question must be tried before the cause can proceed further: it is, therefore, termed *prejudicialis quia prius judicanda*. *Bract.* lib. 8, c. 4.—*Action of a writ*, when one pleads some matter by which he shows the plaintiff had no cause to have the writ.—*Action of abstracted multures*, i. e. an action for multures, in the Scotch law, against those who are thirled to a mill, and come not, or an action to compel persons to grind at a mill according to their tenure.—*Action for poynding of the ground*, i. e. an action, in the Scotch law, for poynding or distraining the land, founded on some infeofment for an annuity. *Bract. de Leg.* l. 3; *Fleta.* l. 1; *Glanville.* l. 1; *Mirror.* c. 21, &c.; *F. N. B.* 92; *Co. in Lytt.* 1 *Instit.* sect. 285, 2 *Inst.* sect. 40; *Hawk. P. C.* 244, &c.; *Comyn. Digest.*

ACTION (*Paint.*) the posture of the figure, or that which is expressed by the disposition of its parts, or the passion that appears in the face of it.

ACTION (*Poet.*) an event or series of occurrences mutually connected with, or dependent upon, each other, either real or imaginary, that makes the subject of a dramatic or epic poem, &c.

ACTION (*Rhet.*) an accommodating the person to the subject, or the management of the voice and gesture suitably to the matter delivered.

ACTION *of the mouth* (*Man.*) the agitation of the tongue and mandible of a horse in champing the bit.

ACTION (*Com.*) moveable effects; a creditor seizes on a merchant's actions, that is, his actual debts.—*Action, re-*

hibitory, by which the buyer may oblige the seller to take back damaged goods.—*Action of a company*, 1. The equal portion of their joint stock. 2. The bonds, contracts, or stock in general, which the directors of trading companies deliver to those who have made themselves proprietors.

French actions, or stocks, are—*Actions simples*, which have a share in all the company's profits and losses, with no security but in their funds.—*Actions Rentieres*, which have a profit of two per cent. with the King's security. —*Actions Interessées*, or bearing interest, which have the above profit, and the King's security, besides a share in the overplus of the dividends; whence the phrase " To feed an *action*," i. e. to pay exactly when they become due the several sums subscribed to the stock of the company. *A fed action*, one on which all payments have been made, and is capable of sharing in the company's dividends.

ACTIONA'RE (*Law*) i. e. *in jus vocare*, to prosecute.

A'CTIONARY (*Fr. Com.*) or *Actionist*, a proprietor of actions.

AC'TIVE (*Phy.*) capable of communicating motion or action, as the cause of gravity or fermentation, which are active principles. *Newt. Princip.*

ACTIVE *verb* (*Gram.*) a sort of verb which denotes action, as I love, in distinction from the passive or neuter.

ACTIVITY (*Phy.*) faculty of acting, as the activity derived from attraction. *Newt. Princip.*—*Sphere of Activity*, the space within which the efficacy of a body extends, as the sphere of activity of a loadstone.

ACTON *Burnel* (*Law*) the statute of 11 *Ed.* I. ordaining the *statute merchant*, amended by 13 *Ed.* I. It was so termed from a place named Acton Burnel, where it was made.

A'CTOR (*Ant.*) 1. in the forensic sense, Plaintiff, he who brings an action against any one, whether as *accusator vel petitor*; but, in a dramatic sense, an actor or player. *Oratores sunt veritatis ipsius actores; imitatores veritatis histriones. Cic. Orat.* l. 3, c. 56. 2. One who pleads or manages the cause of another; a Counsellor or Proctor. 3. A slave to whom the management of any concern is entrusted.

ACTOR *ecclesiæ* (*Archæol.*) he who administered the possessions, &c. of the church.—*Actor advocatus*, vel *defensor Ecclesiæ*, the pleading patron of the church.—*Actor dominicus, qui res domini agit*; a Lord's-bailiff or Attorney. —*Actor villarum, villicus qui prædiorum curam agit*; Head-bailiff of a village.

ACTS *of the Apostles* (*Bibl.*) a canonical book of the New Testament written by St. Luke, and containing a considerable part of the history of St. Peter and St. Paul. *Tertull. contra Marcion.* l. 5, c. 1, &c.; *Chrysos. in Acta. Homil.; Epiphan. Hæres.* 30; *August. de Utilit. Cred.* c. 3, &c.; *Hieron. Epist.* 103, *de Script. Eccles.; Oecumen. in Act. Apost.* p. 20; *Grab. Spiceleg.* &c.

Spurious acts of the apostles were supposed to be written by Abdias the impostor.—*Acts of St. Peter*, otherwise called *Periodi Petri*, a book full of visions and fables. *Fab. Apocr. N. T.* p. 759.—*Acts of St. Paul*, a continuation of St. Paul's narrative to the end of his life, which Eusebius calls spurious. *Euseb. Hist. Eccles.* l. 3. c. 3.—*Acts of St. John the Evangelist*, mentioned by Epiphanius and St. Augustin, contain incredible stories of that apostle; and are supposed to be the acts of St. John published by Abdias the impostor. *Epiphan. Hæres.* 42. 47; *Aug. de Fide.* cap. 4 and 405, *contra Adversar. Leg. et Proph.* l. 1, c. 20.—*Acts of St. Andrew* were used by the Manichees, according to St. Augustin and Epiphanius. *Epiphan. Hæres.* 61; *St. August. contra Adversar. Leg. et Prophet.* c. 20.—*Acts of St. Thomas* were used by the Manichees, according to St. Augustin. *Aug. contra Adimant.* c. 17; *contra Faust.* l. 29, c. 79; *De Serm. Domini in Monte.* c. 20.— *Acts of St. Philip* was a book used by the Gnostics. *Cotel. Monum. Eccles.* t. 3. 428.—*Acts of St. Matthias*; the work which bears this title is not admitted by the critics to contain the genuine acts of the apostle, whose name it bears. *Tillemont. Eccles. Hist.* tom. 1.

ACTS (*Ant.*) vide *Acta*.

ACTS, *clerk of the* (*Mar.*) an officer who receives and enters the Lord Admiral's commissions and warrants, and registers the acts and orders of the commissioners of the navy.

A'CTUAL (*Phy.*) in act or done, as distinguished from the Potential.

ACTUA'LIS (*Med.*) acting by an immediate inherent power, as fire, which is actual, in distinction from a cautery, which is virtual, and acts by an indirect or borrowed power.

ACTUA'RIA (*Ant.*) a sort of small swift sailing vessel plied with oars, so called because they are *cito agantur*. *Non.*

ACTUA'RII (*Ant.*) 1. Notaries or short-hand writers who took down the *acta* or public proceedings. *Suet. Jul.* c. 55; *Pollet. For. Rom.* l. 5, c. 12. 2. Those who took account of the military concerns. *Ammian.* l. 20, c. 5; *Aurel. Victor. de Cæsar.*

A'CTUARY (*Law*) a clerk that registers the acts of the convocation.

ACTUA'TION (*Med.*) the change wrought on any thing taken into the body by vital heat, which is necessary to make it act.

A'CTUS (*Ant.*) 1. The forms used in making bargains, &c. as *actus legitimi*, &c.—2. A certain portion of a play, an act. *Fest. de Verb. Signif.*—3. A measure of land either 4 feet wide and 120 long, as between neighbours' fields, or 120 feet square. *Varr. de Re Rust.* l. 1, c. 10; *Columel.* l. 5, c. 1; *Frontin. Expos. Form.* p. 30; *Alex. Gen. Dier.* l. 2.

ACTUS (*Phy.*) ἐνέργεια, energy, or the active principle, which is called *Actus purus*, having nothing in common with matter, as God, in distinction from the *Actus impurus*, which communicates with the power of matter, such as physical forms. *Aristot. Metaph.* l. 9, c. 1, &c.

A'CUANITES (*Ecc.*) another name for the Manichæans.

A'CUBENE (*Astron.*) a star of the third magnitude in the southern claw, *chela* or *brachium* of Cancer, marked (α) by Bayer. It is called by Ovid *Labia*, by others *Acetabulum*. Its longitude, for 1761, was ♌ 10° 18' 9", South Latitude 5° 5' 56".

ACUI'TION (*Med.*) from *acuo*, to sharpen: the sharpening of medicines to increase their effect, as vegetable acids may be sharpened by mineral acids.

ACUI'TZCHUARIA (*Bot.*) a plant of Mechoachan, in South America, from which a water was distilled called *the enemy of poisons*.

ACU'LEATED (*Bot.*) *aculeatus*, prickly; an epithet applied to different parts of plants.—*Caudex aculeatus*, an aculeated stem, when the remains of the leaf are set with prickles, as in *Coccus aculeatus, Polypodeum asperum*, &c.— *Caulis aculeatus*, prickly stalk, when along the stem there are pointed protuberances.—*Folium aculeatum*, prickly leaf, when the surface of the leaf is covered with prickles.

ACULEO'SA (*Bot.*) the *Gortneria cibaris* of Linnæus.

A'CULER (*Man.*) the motion of a horse when in working upon volts he does not go far enough forward at every time, or movement.

ACU'LEUS (*Bot.*) a Prickle that is a persistent production issuing from the bark, as in *Rosa centifolia*, the Rose, or, in the words of Linnæus, *Mucro pungens cortici tantum affixus*. The *Aculeus* is distinguished into the— *Rectus*, straight, when the prickle is not bent.—*Incurvus*, incurved, when it is curved inwards.—*Recurvus*, recurved, when it is curved upwards.—*Cincinnatus*, rolled up, when rolled up with its apex inwards.

ACUPU'NCTURE (*Surg.*) from *acus*, a needle, and *pungo*,

to prick; a method of bleeding by making many small punctures.

A'CURON (*Bot.*) ἄκυρον, the *Alisma* of Linnæus. *Diosc.* l. 3, c. 169.

A'CUS (*Surg.*) a Needle or instrument for confining the lips of wounds.

Acus *Pastoris* (*Bot.*) Shepherd's Needle, the *Scandix anthriscus*, the *Acus moschata*, and the *Geranium* of Linnæus.

ACU'STICUS (*Med.*) the same as acoustic.

ACU'TE (*Geom.*) from *acuo*, to sharpen, an epithet for several things.—*Acute angle* ὀξεῖα γωνία, that which is less than a right angle, or the measure of 90 degrees, the quadrant of a circle, as A B C, *fig.* 1, which is less than the

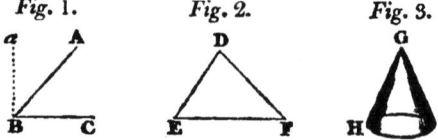

Fig. 1. Fig. 2. Fig. 3.

angle *a* B C.—*Acute-angled Triangle*, one whose angles are all three acute, as D E F, *fig.* 2.—*Acute-angled Cone*, one whose opposite sides make an acute angle at the vertex, as G H I, *fig.* 3.—*Acute-angled section of a cone*, an ellipsis made by a plane cutting both sides of an acute-angled cone. *Euclid. Elem.* defin. l. 1; *Apollon. Conic.* l. 1, prob. 20, &c.; *Papp. Math. Collect.*

ACUTE (*Bot.*) an epithet for different parts of a flower ending in a sharp point, as *Folium acutum*, an acute leaf; *Ligulum acutum*, an acute strap; *Stigma acutum*, a pointed stigma.

ACUTE (*Mus.*) an epithet for a sound which is sharp or elevated, in distinction from a grave sound. *Euclid. Introduct. Harmon.*

ACUTE *Accent* (*Gram.*) that elevation of the voice with which any syllable or word is pronounced, marked thus [´]. *Priscian. de Accent.*

ACUTE (*Med.*) an epithet for a disease which is violent and comes quickly to a crisis. *Hippocrat. de Rat. Vict. in Acut.* &c. and *Gal. Comm.*; *Aret. de Caus. et Sign. Acut. Morb.*; *Cels.* l. 3, c. 1; *Aet. Tetrab.* l. 2, serm. 1; *Paul Æginet. de Re Med.* l. 2.

ACUTE (*Chem.*) an epithet for a liquor which is made more piercing by a stronger.

ACUTENA'CULUM (*Surg.*) a handle for a needle now called Portaiguille.

ACUTIA'TOR (*Archæol.*) one who whets or grinds cutting instruments.

A'CYLOS (*Bot.*) ἄκυλος, the fruit of the *Ilex*, distinguished by Homer from the βάλανος, or acorn, the fruit of the *Quercus*. *Odyss.* l. 10, v. 242.

Περρίκυλον, βάλανον τ' ἔβαλε.

Theocrit. Idyl. 5, v. 94; *Theophrast. Hist. Plant.* l. 3, c. 16; *Plin.* l. 6, c. 6; *Gal. de Alim.*

ACYRO'LOGY (*Gram.*) ἀκυρολογία, from ἄκυρος, careless, and λόγος, speech; improper diction, as "one who fears may hope," for fear is the contrary of hope. *Isidor.* l. 1, c. 33.

A.D. (*Chron.*) an abbreviation for *Anno Domini*. [vide *Abbreviations*]

AD (*Ant.*) this preposition forms a part of several peculiar phrases among the Latin writers, as—*Ad bestias*, a punishment among the Romans of exposing criminals to wild beasts. *Ulpian.*; *Tertull. Apol.* c. 40; *Bud. in Pandect.* vol. i. p. 240; *Holman. Antiq. Roman.*—*Ad ludos*, a similar punishment of being obliged to fight with either man or beast at the public games.—*Ad metalla*, another Roman punishment borrowed from the Egyptians of condemning criminals to work at the mines.

AD *scalum* (*Archæol.*) by the scale, that is, by weighing in the scale, a mode of counting money at the mint, when a certain portion having been told out the remainder is weighed by it. This is distinguished from a mode of weighing called *ad Pensum*, which was employed for money that was diminished in quantity by clipping, wearing, &c.

AD *absurdum* (*Logic*) vide *Reductio*.

AD *valorem* (*Com.*) i. e. according to the value, a term applied to the duties or customs when rated according to the value of the commodities.

AD *libitum* (*Mus.*) or *Con ad lib*, at pleasure; a term signifying that the performer may introduce into the composition any thing extemporaneous according to his own fancy; hence an *ad libitum pause*, or an *ad libitum cadenza*.—*Ad longum*, old compositions so termed, consisting of notes of equal duration and generally the longest in use.—*Ad omnem tonum*, a term in such old compositions as preserved their harmony from whatever tone or note the *cantus* started.

AD *inquirendum* (*Law*) a judicial writ commanding inquiry to be made of any thing relating to a cause depending in the king's courts. *Reg. Judic.*—*Ad jura regis*, a writ brought by the King's clerk presented to a living against him who sought to eject him. *Reg. of Writs*, 61.—*Ad largum*, at large, as title *at large*, assize *at large*.—*Ad quod damnum*, a writ to inquire when a grant intended to be made by the King will be to the damage of him or others. *F. N. B.* 221.—*Ad terminum qui præteriit*, a writ of entry, where a man having leased lands, &c. for a term of life or years, is kept from them by the tenant or possessor after the term is expired.—*Ad ventrem inspiciendum*, vide *Ventre inspiciendo*.—*Ad vitam aut culpam*, an office to be so held as to determine only by the death or delinquency of the possessor; in other words, it is held *quamdiu se bene gesserit*.

ADA'CTED (*Mil.*) driven into the earth with large malls applied to stakes, or piles, used in securing ramparts or pontoons.

ADA'GIO (*Mus.*) a term in music books denoting the slowest time, except the grave, especially if repeated *adagio, adagio*.

A'DAL (*Med.*) a term used by Paracelsus for that part of plants in which their virtue consists.

ADA'LIDES (*Polit.*) the name of certain military officers in Spain, who are spoken of in the laws of King Alphonsus.

A'DAMANT (*Min.*) *Adamas*, so called from α, priv. and δαμάω, to conquer, because of its hardness: it is a sort of diamond, and the hardest, most brilliant, and most valuable of the precious stones. *Adamas* is classed by Linnæus under the Silicious earths. [vide *Adamas*]

ADAMA'NTINE *Earth* (*Min.*) or *Adamantine Spar*, a sort of hard and ponderous earth which, under the name of *Adamantinus*, forms the sixth order of earths in the Linnean system.

ADAMA'NTIS (*Bot.*) a species of plant so called from its resemblance to Adamant. *Plin.* l. 24, c. 16.

A'DAMAS (*Min.*) Adamant, or Diamond, a genus of Silicious Earths, consisting of silica and carbon. It is slightly ponderous, extremely hard, shines in the dark after having been exposed to the rays of the sun, and consumes altogether like an inflammable substance. It is found, in Golcondo and Brazil, enclosed generally in loose earth or sand. *Linn. System. Nat.*

ADA'MI *pomum* (*Bot.*) the *Citrus aurantium* of Linnæus.

ADAMI *pomum* (*Anat.*) the convex part of the Thyrsia cartilage.

ADA'MIANI (*Ecc.*) vide *Adamites*.

ADA'MICA *terra* (*Geol.*) an oily slimy substance of the sea-waters.

ADA'MITA (*Med.*) the stone in the bladder, so called by Paracelsus. *De Tartar.* l. 1.

ADAMI'TES (*Ecc.*) or, according to Epiphanius, *Adamiani*, Ἀδαμιάνοι; heretics of the second century, who assumed that name from Adam, whose innocence they affected to imitate, and whose nudity they actually put in practice at their meetings. *Clemen. Alexand.* l. 3, &c.; *S. Epiphan.*

Hæres. 52; *S. August. Hæres.* 31; *Theodoret. de Fab. Hæret,* l. 1.

ADAMI′TUM (*Med.*) the same as Athiasis.

ADAM'S *Needle* (*Bot.*) an Indian plant of which the inhabitants made coarse bread in times of scarcity. It is the *Yucca gloriosa* of Linnæus.

ADA′MUS (*Alch.*) the Philosopher's Stone. *Theat. Chem.* vol. i.

ADANSO′NIA (*Bot.*) a genus of plants; Class 16 *Monadelphia,* Order 7 *Polyandria,* so named from M. Adanson, the French Naturalist.

Generic Character. CAL. *perianth* one-leaved.—COR. *petals* five.—STAM. *filaments* united at bottom into a tube; *anthers* kidney-shaped.—PIST. *Germ* ovate; *style* very long; *stigmas* many, prismatic.—PER. *capsule* ovate; *seeds* numerous.

Species. The only species is the *Adansonia digitata,* Baobab, *Abavi, Abavo Arbor,* or *Guanabanus,* Ethiopian Sour Gourd, or Monkeys' Bread. *J. Bauh. Hist. Plant.; C. Bauh. Pin; Raii Hist. Plant.; Vesl. Plant. Ægypt.; Linn. Spec. Plant.*

ADA′RCES (*Nat.*) ἀδάρκης, a kind of salt concretion adhering to herbs and canes in the fens and marshes of Galatia. It is said to clear the skin of freckles, &c.; and was so called from α, priv. and δέρκω, to see, because it was not to be seen among the rushes. *Diosc.* l. 5, c. 137.

ADA′RCONIM (*Bibl.*) אדרכונים, a sort of money mentioned, 1 *Chron.* xxix. 7, and *Ezra* viii. 27, called, in the Septuagint, χρυσοί, and, in the Vulgate, *aurei*; they are the same as δαρεικοί, the Daricks of the Greeks, a gold coin valued at twenty drachmas. *Gronov. de Pecun. Vet.* l. 3, c. 7.

ADA′RME (*Com.*) a small Spanish weight, the sixteenth of our ounce Troy weight.

ADA′RNECK (*Chem.*) *Auripigmentum,* or orpiment.

ADARTICULA′TION (*Anat.*) a species of articulation the same as Arthrodia.

A′DATAIS (*Com.*) a clear fine Bengal muslin.

ADCE′NSI (*Ant.*) vide *Accensi.*

A′DCHER (*Bot.*) the *Andropogon schoenanthus* of Linnæus.

ADCORDA′BILES *Denarii* (*Archæol.*) money paid by the vassal to his lord upon the selling or exchanging of a feud.

ADCORPORA′TION (*Med.*) vide *Incorporation.*

ADCREDULITA′RE (*Archæol.*) to purge oneself of an offence by oath.

ADCRESCE′NTES (*Ant.*) a sort of soldiers, the same as Accensi.

A′DDAD (*Bot.*) a poisonous plant in Numidia.

ADDEPHA′GIA (*Med.*) ἀδδηφαγία, from ἄδην, excessively, and φάγω, to eat; voracity.

A′DDER (*Zo.*) the name of a small poisonous serpent, with plates on the belly, and scales under the tail, greatly resembling the viper *Coluber verus* of Linnæus, which inhabits Europe, and is not rare in our own country. It is called in Saxon Æðder, Ætter, Ætter, Naððre; in low German and Dutch, adder and natter, from eitter, poison.

ADDER (*Her.*) the poisonous serpent has been made a charge in coats of arms, of which Guillim gives two examples, as follow:

ADDER, *nowed or knotted,* as in fig. 1. "The field is *gules,* an adder nowed, *or,* by the name of Nathiley."

Fig. 1. Fig. 2.

 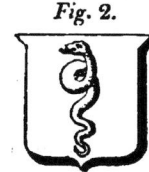

ADDER, *curling erected,* as in fig. 2. "*Or,* an adder curling erected upon its tail, in *pale sable.*" This coat was allowed or assigned by patent, dated January 2, 1606, by William Camden, Clarencieux, to Sir Thomas Coach, of the city of London.

ADDER'S *grass* (*Bot.*) a herb so called, as Skinner supposes, because it serves as a lurking place for adders.—*Adder's tongue,* the *Ophioglossum* of Linnæus, a herb so called because it has a single leaf that puts forth a spike in the shape of an adder's tongue.—*Adder's wort,* a herb so called because it is imagined to cure the bite of a serpent.

ADDER *stung* (*Med.*) stung by adders and venemous creatures, as in the case of cattle.

ADDI′CTI (*Ant.*) those who, according to the laws of the twelve tables, were delivered over to their creditors to be made slaves until they discharged their debts. *Cic. Rosc. Com.* c. 14; *Flacc,* c. 20, &c.; *Liv.* l. 6, c. 14, &c.; *Alex. Gen. Dier.* l. 5, c. 4.

ADDI′TAMENT (*Med.*) any thing added to the ordinary ingredients.

ADDITAMENTS (*Her.*) what is added to coat armour to distinguish the bearer. *Guill.*

ADDITAMENTS (*Chem.*) things added to a menstruum, to render it more efficacious in dissolving any mixed body.

ADDITAME′NTUM (*Anat.*) the same as *Epiphysis necatum*; the Epiphysis of the Ulna.—*Additamentum coli,* the *Appendicula cæci vermiformis.*

ADDITION (*Law*) whatever is added to a man's name by way of title, as additions of degree, estate, mystery, place. —*Additions of degree,* are Knight, Lord, Earl, Marquis, and Duke.—*Additions of an estate or quality,* are Yeoman, Esquire, Gentleman, and the like.—*Additions of mystery,* are such as Scrivener, Painter, Mason, and the like.— *Additions of place* are of London, York, &c.

ADDITION (*Nat.*) a name given by distillers to whatever is added to a liquor to improve its spirit, which includes ferments and every thing else which is not expressly of the same nature as the liquor.

ADDITION (*Arithm.*) the uniting or joining together several numbers into one sum.—*Addition of integers,* the first of the four fundamental rules of arithmetical operation, which is either performed by placing the figures under one another in columns, or by means of the sign plus [+], which is called the sign of addition, as 6 + 3 = 9, that 6 plus, or added to 3, is equal to 9. This operation is either simple or compound.—*Simple addition,* the method of collecting several numbers into one sum, as 4, 5, 9, which, added together, make 18.—*Compound Addition,* the method of collecting quantities of different denominations into one sum, as pounds, shillings, pence, yards, feet, and inches, &c.— *Addition of Vulgar Fractions* is the adding together the numerators into one sum, when the fractions have, by the rules of reduction, been brought to a common denomination, as in the adding of $\frac{1}{2}$, $\frac{1}{3}$, and $\frac{1}{4}$ together, they are first reduced [vide *Reduction*], to $\frac{6}{12}$, $\frac{4}{12}$, and $\frac{3}{12}$, then $\frac{6}{12} + \frac{4}{12} + \frac{3}{12} = \frac{13}{12}$.—*Addition of decimals* is performed in the same manner as that of whole numbers, only having regard to the decimal points, that they should range under one another, as

```
 34· 17
 19· 143
167· 13
————————
220· 443
```

—*Addition of circulating decimals* is performed by changing each of them into its equivalent vulgar fraction, and finding the sum of such fractions.

ADDITION (*Algeb.*) the finding the sum of several algebraical

ADDITION *of surds* is performed by reducing the surds to the same denomination or radical, as far as it can be done: then add the rational parts, and subjoin the common surd, as $\sqrt{8} + \sqrt{18} = \sqrt{(4 \times 2)} + \sqrt{(9 \times 2)} = 2\sqrt{2} + 3\sqrt{2} = 5\sqrt{2} = \sqrt{50}$.

ADDITION *of ratios*, vide *Composition*.

ADDITION (*Mus.*) a dot marked on the right side of a note.

ADDITIONA'LES (*Law*) additional terms, or propositions, to be added to a former agreement.

A'DDITIVE (*Math.*) a term employed to denote something to be added in distinction from something to be subtracted, as *additive* equations, *additive* ratios, &c.

ADDI'XIT (*Ant.*) the word which the Augurs used to signify that the birds foretold a joyful event. " Fabio auspicanti priusquam egrederetur de Tarento aves semel et iterum addixerunt." *Liv.* l. 27, c. 16; *Fest. in Voc. Prætor.*

ADDO'RSED (*Her.*) Back to Back, as two Lions rampant, or, addorsed, which Guillim calls endorsed. Leigh says this coat was borne by Achilles at the siege of Troy, and he takes it to represent two champions who have met in the field of battle, but being prevented by the interposition of the prince from engaging in combat, turn back to back, and so go off the field.

ADDO'SSER (*Mil.*) Fr. to place one thing behind another, as a tent, &c. *Addosser une Compagnie*, to post one company in the rear of the other.

ADDRE'SS (*Com.*) whatever directs to the person or the place, as, ' My address is at Lyons, to the house of N. N.' i. e. where goods may be sent me. A bill of exchange payable to the address of N. N. points out the place of payment. ' This bill is to the address of Mr. N.' signifying that it is drawn upon him.

ADDU'CENT (*Anat.*) an epithet for certain muscles. [vide *Adductor.*]

ADDUCTO'RES (*Anat.*) or *Adducentes*, from *ad* and *duco*, to draw to, or towards; an epithet for some muscles which draw those parts of the body to each other in which they are inserted, in distinction from the *Abductores*, as the—*Adductor minimi digiti et pedis*, which draws the third and fourth lesser toes to the others.—*Adductor oculi*, which draws the eye to the nose, also called *hibitorius*, because it directs the eye of the person drinking towards the cup. —*Adductor femoris primus, secundus, &c.* otherwise called Triceps, which serves to draw the thigh inwards.—*Adductor pollicis*, which brings the thumb nearer to the forefinger.—*Adductor pollicis pedis*, the Antithenar of Winslow, which brings the great toe nearer to the rest.

A'DEB (*Com.*) a large Egyptian weight, used principally for rice, somewhat less than an English pound. *Pocock. Trav. in Egypt.*

A'DEC (*Chem.*) sour Milk.

ADECA'TIST (*Ecc.*) one not decimated, or who is against paying tithes, from α, priv. and δικατιω, to decimate.

A'DECH (*Alch.*) the internal or invisible part of man, that impresses the forms or images of external material objects on the mind. *Paracel. Chirurg. Tract.* 2.

ADE'CTA (*Med.*) from α, priv. and δακω, to bite; an epithet for medicines which relieve pain, as lenitives, &c. *Cels. apud Gorr. Def. Med.*

ADELANTA'DO (*Polit.*) a governor of a Spanish province.

ADE'LIA (*Bot.*) from ἄδηλος, obscure, or indistinct; a genus of plants, Class 22 *Dioecia*, Order 12 *Monadelphia*, the Bernardia of Brown.

Generic Character. CAL. perianth one-leaved; *leaflets* oblong.—COR. none.—STAM. *filaments*, many; *anthers* roundish.

Species. The species are the *Adelia Bernardia, ricinella*, and *acidotum*, which are shrubs, and natives of Jamaica. *Linn. Spec.*

A'DELING (*Polit.*) in Saxon, Ethling; a title of honour among the Saxons.

ADE'LPHÆ (*Numis.*) Ἀδιλφαι, sisters; an epithet on a medal of Caracalla for two cities, inscribed ΠΛΩΤΕΙΝΟΠΟΛΙΣ ΔΟΜΝΟΠΟΛΙΣ ΑΔΕΛΦΑΙ.

ADE'LPHI (*Numis.*) Ἀδιλφοι, brothers, an epithet on a medal of the brothers, Drusus and Germanicus, represents them on the obverse, with the inscription ΔΡΟΤΣΟΣ ΚΑΙΣΑΡ

ΓΕΡΜΑΝΙΚΟΣ ΚΑΙΣΑΡ ΑΔΕΛΦΟΙ, i. e. *Drusus Cæsar Germanicus Cæsar, fratres:* on the reverse, a crown, with the words circumscribed ΕΠΙ ΑΛΕΞΑΝΔΡΟΥ ΚΛΕΩΝΟΣ ΣΑΡΔΙΑΝΩΝ. i. e. *sub Alexandro Cleone Sardianorum Prætore*, and inscribed within the crown ΚΟΙΝΟΥ. ΑCΙΑC. by which latter words is to be understood, that this crown of laurel was decreed to them by the universal consent of all the cities of Asia. *Seguin. Numissel Antiq.*

ADE'LPHIA (*Med.*) or *Adelphixis*, a term used by Hippocrates for analogy, as applied to diseases.

ADELPHIA'NI (*Ecc.*) a sect of heretics who fasted always on Sundays. *Theodoret. Hist. Eccles.* l. 4, c. 10; *Cedren. Compend. Hist.* p. 242.

ADE'LPHIDES (*Bot.*) Ἀδιλφιδκ, a kind of palm-tree, whose fruit has the taste of figs.

ADE'LPHON (*Numis.*) αδιλφῶν, i. e. *fratris sororisque*, brother and sister, an inscription on a medal of Ptolemy Philadelphus and Arsinoe, both his sister and wife.

ADEMO'NIA (*Med.*) αδημωνία, from δαιμων, *fortuna*, restlessness and anxiety in diseases. *Hippoc. de Epidem.* l. 1; *Gorr. Defin. Med.; Foes. Oeconom. Hippoc.*

ADE'MPTION (*Law*) taking away a legacy, or revoking a grant, &c.

A'DEN (*Med.*) *glandula*, a gland.

ADENANTHE'RA (*Bot.*) from ἀδην, a gland, and ανθυρα, an anther; a genus of plants, Class 10 *Decandria*, Order 1 *Monogynia*.

Generic Characters. CAL. *perianth*, one-leaved.—COR. five-petaled; *petals* lanceolate.—STAM. *filaments* subulate; *anthers* roundish.—PIST. *germ* oblong; *style* subulate; *stigma* simple.—PER. a *legume* long; *seeds* very many.

Species. The principal species are the—*Adenanthera pavonina*, a shrub, native of India.—*Adenanthera scandens*, a shrub, native of Mallicollo, an island in the South Seas, &c. *Raii Hist. Plant.; Rheed. Hort. Ind. labar.*

ADENDE'NTES (*Med.*) from ἀδην, and *edo*, to eat; ulcers which eat and destroy the glands.

ADE'NIA (*Bot.*) a genus of plants, Class *Hexandria*, Order *Monogynia*, given by Forskal in his *Flora Ægyptiaca Arabica.*

ADENO'IDES (*Anat.*) glandiform; an epithet for the *Glandulæ prostatæ. Ruff. Ephes. de Appell. Part. Corp. Human.* l. 1, c. 29; *Gal. de Usu Part.* l. 14, c. 11; *Gorr. Def. Med.*

A'DENOS (*Com.*) marine Cotton from Aleppo.

ADENO'SUS *abscessus* (*Med.*) a crude tubercle, resembling a gland, which proceeds from obstructed viscidities.

ADEPHA'GIA (*Ant.*) ἀδηφαγία, gluttony, which was worshipped as a goddess among the Greeks, and had a temple in Sicily, according to Athenæus. *Deipnosph. l. 10, c. 4.*

A'DEPS (*Anat.*) fat; an animal oil in the *membrana adiposa*, which differs from the *Pinguedo*, by being a thicker, harder, and more earthy substance. *Ruff. Ephes. de Appell. Part. Hum. Corp. l. 1, c. 35; Gal. de Usu Part.*

ADE'PT *philosophy* (*Alch.*) the science which professes to teach the transmutation of metals, and finding the philosopher's stone. The *Adepti*, or Adepts, were such as were initiated into the adept philosophy.—*Adept medicine*, that which treats of diseases contracted by celestial operations. *Paracel. Peragran.*

ADER'AIMIN (*Astron.*) or *alderaimin*, a star of the third magnitude in the left shoulder of Cepheus, marked α, by Bayer. Its longitude for 1761 was ♈ 9° 30′ 8″, latitude North 68° 56′ 20″. *Ulug. Beigh. apud Hyde; Bayer Uranomet.*

ADESSENA'RIANS (*Ecc.*) a branch of the sacramentarians who derived their name from the Latin *adesse*, to be present; because they believed the presence of Christ's body in the eucharist, though in a manner different from the Romish church. *Prateol. de Vit. Sect. et Dogm. Hæret. Omn.*

ADFE'CTED (*Algeb.*) vide *Affected*.

A'DHA (*My.*) or *adcha*, i. e. sacrifices, a festival which the Mahometans celebrate on the 12th day of the month Dhoulhegiat, which is the 12th and last month of their year. This month, being particularly destined for the ceremonies which the pilgrims observe at Mecca, takes its name from that circumstance: the word signifying the *month of pilgrimage*.

ADHATO'DA (*Bot.*) the Malabar Nut; a species of the *Justicia* of Linnæus.

ADHERENCE, *Action of* (*Law*) an action in the Scotch Law, competent to a husband or a wife, to compel either party to adhere in case of desertion.

ADHE'SION (*Phy.*) from *ad* and *hæreo*, the union of two substances, similar or dissimilar; as of mercury to gold, in distinction from cohesion, which retains together component particles of the same mass. *Adhesion* arises either from the compression of external bodies, or from a principle of attraction between particular bodies. James Bournelli considered the pressure of the external air as the proximate cause; but later experiments have led to the conclusion, that it arises from the natural tendency to adhesion in the bodies themselves.

ADHESION (*Med.*) the junction of parts that ought to be separated, as the adhesion of the lungs to the Pleura.

ADHE'SIVE *inflammation* (*Surg.*) a modern term in surgery for that species of inflammation which terminates by an adhesion of the inflamed parts.

ADHESIVE *plaster*, a plaster made of common litharge plaster and resin, which is so called for its adhesive properties.

A'DHIL (*Astron.*) a star of the sixth magnitude in the garment σύρμα of Andromeda, marked (β) by Bayer. *Ptol. Almag. l. 7, c. 5; Bayer. Uranomet.*

A'DHO (*Chem.*) or *Ado*; Buttermilk.

ADJA'CENT (*Math.*) from *ad* and *jacio*, to lie, lying near; an epithet applied to angles when they lie so as to have but one common side, and the other two sides form one continued right line, as in the annexed diagram, where the adjacent angles C B A and C B D have the legs A B and D B in one straight line.

ADIA'CHYTOS (*Med.*) from α, priv. and διαχύω, to be profuse, or to scatter; an epithet used by Hippocrates to imply not foppish or extravagant. *Hippocrat. de Decent. Habit.*

ADIA'NTHUM (*Bot.*) vide *Adiantum*.

ADIA'NTUM (*Bot.*) ἀδίαντον, a plant; so called from α, priv. and διαίνω, to moisten or become wet, because its leaves throw off the wet. *Nicand. Theriac.*

Ἀχραὶς τ᾽ ἀδίαντον ὅ ἐκ ὀμβροιο ῥαγέντος
Λιπταλίη πίπτουσα ἰοτὶς πετάλοισιν ἐφίζει.

Hippocrates calls it καλλίφυλλον, beautiful-leaved; Theocritus χλωρὸν ἀδίαντον, the green *adiantum*. *Hippocrat. de Nat. Mul.; Theophrast. Hist. Plant. l. 7, c. 13; Dioscor. l. 4, c. 136; Plin. l. 22, c. 21; Schol. in Theocrit. Idyl. 13, v. 14; Schol. in Nicand. Theriac.*

ADIANTUM, *in the Linnæan system*, a genus of plants, Class *Cryptogamia*, Order *Filices*, in English Maidenhair.

Generic Character. Fructifications assembled in oval spots, at the end of the fronds.

Species. The species of this tribe are perennials, and mostly natives of the East and West Indies. The principal are the—*Adiantum reniforme* or *monophyllum*, *Hemionitis* or *Felix Hemionitis*, Kidney-leaved Maidenhair.—*Adiantum radiatum*, *Lonchitis radiata*, or *Trichomanes Americanum radiatum*, rayed Maidenhair.—*Adiantum fragrans* or *Polypodium fragrans*, sweet-scented Maidenhair.—*Adiantum denticulatum* or *Lonchitis serrata*, toothleaved Maidenhair.—*Adiantum lunulatum* or *Pteris lunulata*.—*Adiantum varium*, or *Asplenium varium*, &c. *J. Bauh. Hist. Plant.; C. Bauh. Pin.; Ger. Herb.; Park. Theat. Botan.; Raii Hist. Plant.; Pluk. Phytograph.; Tournef. Instit.; Bœrh. Ind. Plant.*

ADIANTUM is also the name for the *Asplenium obtusifolium* and *nigrum* of Linnæus. *Raii Hist. Plant.*

ADIA'PHORISTS (*Ecc.*) from ἀδιάφορος, indifferent; the name of those moderate reformers who, according to the sentiments of Melancthon, declared that in matters of an indifferent nature, compliance with the edicts of the Emperor was a duty, in consequence of which they adhered to the Interim of Charles V. *Spondan. Continuat. Baron. Annal. Ann. 1525; Prateol. de Vit. &c. Hæret. Omn.*

ADIA'PHOROUS (*Chem.*) from α, priv. and διαφέρω, *differo*, without difference; a spirit distilled from tartar, neither acid, vinous, nor urinous.

ADIA'PNEUSTIA (*Med.*) ἀδιαπνευστία, to breathe, from α, priv. and διαπνέω, difficult or impeded respiration. *Gal. Meth. Med. l. 11, c. 4.*

ADIAPTO'TOS (*Med.*) ἀδιάπτωτος, from α, priv. and διαπίπτω, to fall through; a remedy for the colic. *Gal. de Comp. Med. sec. Loc.; Gorr. Def. Med.*

ADIARRHO'EA (*Med.*) ἀδιάρροια, from α, priv. and διαρρέω, to flow through; an entire suppression of all evacuations. *Erotian. Lex. Hippocrat.; Foes. Oeconom. Hippocrat.*

ADIATHORO'SUS (*Chem.*) a spirit distilled from tartar.

A'DIBAT (*Alch.*) mercury.

A'DICE (*Bot.*) the same as *Urtica*.

ADJECTI'TIOUS (*Archit.*) an epithet for any thing added to a building.

A'DJECTIVE (*Gram.*) or *noun adjective*, from *adjicio*, to adjoin; a part of speech which is added to a noun in order to qualify its signification; as a *good* man, a *large* house.

ADJICIA'LIS *cœna* (*Ant.*) a particular festival among the Romans, so called because it seems that something *adjiciebatur* was added to the ordinary entertainment. *Senec. Epist. 95; Plin. l. 10, c. 20; Tacit. Annal. l. 2, c. 65; Scalig. Conject. in Varr. p. 118; Lips. de Mag. Rom. l. 4, c. 9; Ursin. Append. ad Ciaccon. de Triclin. p. 175; Buleng. de Imper. Roman. l. 2, c. 32.*

AD INQUIRE'NDUM (*Law*) a judicial writ commanding inquiry.

ADJO'URNMENT (*Law*) *Adjournamentum*, a putting off until another time or place, as the Adjournment of Parliament, or a Writ of Adjournment for a court of justice to be held at some other time or place.

ADIPO'CERE (*Chem.*) from *adeps*, fat, and *cera*, wax; fatty wax, a concretion or substance resembling ammonial soap. It forms a class of biliary calculi, like spermaceti.

ADIPO'SUS (*Anat.*) adipous, or fat; an epithet for certain membranes, veins, &c.—*Adiposa membrana*, a membrane which encloses the *cellulæ adiposæ*, but more particularly that in which the kidneys are wrapt up.—*Adiposæ cellulæ*, a number of cells or holes full of fat.—*Adiposa vena*, a vein arising from the descending trunk of the cava, which spreads itself on the coat and fat of the kidneys.—*Adiposi ductus*, certain vessels of the animal body which convey the adeps or fat into the interstices of the muscles or parts that are between the flesh and skin.

ADI'PSA (*Med.*) vide *Adipson*.

ADIPSA'THEON (*Bot.*) a thorny shrub in the island of Rhodes.

ADI'PSIA (*Med.*) from α, priv. and δίψα, thirst; want of thirst, a genus of diseases, Class *Locales*, Order *Dysorexiæ*, in Cullen's Nosology.

ADI'PSON (*Med.*) from α, priv. and δίψα, thirst; any drink that quenches or prevents the thirst. Hippocrates applies the term to the ptissana. *Hippocrat. de Rat. Vict. in Acut. Morb.*; *Gal. de Comp. Med. sec. Loc.*

ADI'PSOS (*Bot.*) ἄδιψος, from α, priv. and δίψα, thirst; an epithet for the *Glycorrhiza*, or Liquorice-Tree, from its property of assuaging thirst. According to Solinus, the Ægyptian palm was also so called. *Hippocrat. de Rat. Vict. in Acut. Morb*; *Theophrast. Hist. Plant.* l. 9, c. 13; *Dioscor.* l. 3, c. 7; *Plin.* l. 22, c. 9; *Gal. de Simpl.* l. 6; *Foes. Oeconom. Hippocrat.*

ADIPSOS (*Med.*) a catapotium or pill, made by Asclepiades. *Gal. de Comp. Med. sec. Loc.* c. 8; *Trallian.* l. 7.

ADIRA'TUS (*Law*) strayed or lost.

A'DIT (*Min.*) the shaft or entrance into a mine.

ADIT (*Mil.*) a passage under ground, by which the miners approach the part they intend to sap.

A'DITUS (*Ant.*) a passage to the seats of a theatre. *Vitruv.* l. 5, c. 3. The *Aditus* in a ship is that space where it is broadest. *Ovid. Metam.* l. 3, v. 722; *Scheff. de Re Nav.* l. 1, c. 6.

ADJUDICA'TION (*Law*) the adjudging or determining a cause in favour of some person.—*Adjudication*, in the Scotch Law, is an action by which a creditor attaches the heritable estate of his debtor's heir in payment of his debt; also that by which the holder of an heritable right, labouring under any defect in point of form, may supply that defect.

A'DJUNCTS (*Log.*) whatever is joined to a thing, as to its subject; as knowledge to the soul, or greenness to grass, &c. These are more commonly termed the accidents of the subject. [vide *Accident*]

ADJUNCTS (*Rhet.*) certain words or things added to others to amplify the discourse, or augment its force.

ADJUNCTS (*Med.*) qualities, dispositions, and symptoms.

ADJUNCTS (*Eth.*) vulgarly called circumstances, are comprehended in this verse.—

Quis, quid, ubi, quibus auxiliis, cur, quomodo, quando.

Quis, to denote the person; *quid*, the matter; *ubi*, the place; *quibus auxiliis*, the instruments; *cur*, the efficient cause and end; *quomodo*, the manner; and *quando*, the time.

ADJUNCTS (*Mus.*) the intervals which constitute the relation and connexion between the principal mode, and the modes of its two fifths.

ADJUNCTS (*Lit.*) a class of members in the Royal Academy at Paris, attached to the pursuit of particular sciences, who were twelve in number, namely, two for geometry, two for anatomy, two for mechanics, two for astronomy, two for chemistry, and two for botany. They were elected in 1716 in lieu of the *elevés*.

ADJUNCTS (*Polit.*) colleagues or fellow officers associated with any other to assist him in his office, or inspect his proceedings.

AD JU'RA regis (*Law*) vide *Ad*.

A'DJUTANT (*Mil.*) from *adjuvo*, to help; one who assists a superior officer in a regiment, distributing the pay to the men, exercising them when they are assembled, and presiding over the punishments of delinquents. The *Adjutant-General* is an officer of distinction, who assists the general with his council and personal service.

ADJU'TOR (*Ant.*) an assistant or deputy, who was named after his office, as—*Adjutor actoris*, an assistant to the steward.—*Adjutor admissionum*, an assistant to the master of the ceremonies.—*Adjutor aruspicum*, an assistant to the aruspices or soothsayers on public occasions.—*Adjutor prætoris*, a deputy-prætor.—*Adjutor principis*, a king's commissioner, who acted in the name of the prince.—*Adjutor provinciæ*, a deputy-lieutenant, of whom frequent mention is made in inscriptions. *Cassiodor Var.*; *Pancirol Notit. Dig. Imp. Orient.*; *Pignor. de Serv.*; *Buleng. de Imp. Rom.*; *Ursat. de Not. Roman.*; *Salmas. in Lamprid.*; *Græv. Thesaur. Antiq. Roman.* vol. ii. p. 533, &c.

ADJUTO'RIUM (*Anat.*) a bone between the cubit and the scapula, so called because it is of use in raising the arm.

ADJUTORIUM (*Med.*) a topical or external application to assist an internal medicine.

ADJU'TRIX (*Numis.*) the good genius of the emperor Victorinus is so called, as in the annexed cut, which represents the head of a female figure half naked, with a bow; the inscription ADJUTRIX AUG. On the obverse of this medal is the head of the emperor himself. *Occo. Numis Imper. Roman.*; *Pembroch. Numis. Antiq.*

ADJUVA'NTIA (*Med.*) from *adjuvo*, to help, aiding; an epithet applied to medicines that help nature.

AD LA'RGUM (*Law*) at large, as "a title *at large*."

A'DLE (*Nat.*) the state of an egg which is putrid from long keeping.

ADLE'CTI (*Ant.*) 1. Inferior Deities enrolled from among men into the number of the gods. *Cæl. Rhodig. Antiq. Lect.* l. 22, c. 2; *Bud. Pandect.* p. 53. 2. Soldiers who were enrolled into any particular class, or raised to a particular rank. *Ursat. de Not. Roman. apud Græv. Thes. Antiq. Roman.* tom. xi. p. 531. 3. Senators who, on account of their poverty, were enrolled from the equestrian into the senatorial order. *Suet. in Jul.* c. 80; *Fest. de Signif. Verb*; *Alex. ab Alex. Gen. Dier.* l. 4, c. 2; *Bud. in Pandect.* p. 53. 4. Adjuncts, or assistants to the actors on the stage, according to an inscription on a stone.

ADLEGA'TION (*Polit.*) a right claimed by the German States of adjoining plenipotentiaries to those of the emperor for the transaction of affairs relating to the empire in general. It is distinguished from legation, which is the sending ambassadors on one's own account.

ADLEGIA'RE (*Law*) in French *alier*, to purge oneself of a crime by oath. *LL. Aelfred apud Brompton.*

ADLOCU'TIO (*Ant.*) from *adloquor*, to speak to or address; an address or harangue of the emperor to his soldiers.

ADLOCUTIO (*Numis.*) many medals of the emperors represent them in the act of haranguing their soldiers, as those of Nero, Caligula, Galba, Vespasian, Adrian, Domitian, Nerva, M. Aurelius, L. Verus, Severus, Macrinus, Alex. Severus, Julia Mammæa, Gordian, Phillip Sen., Valerian, Tacitus, Probus, and Numerian, with the following inscriptions.

ADLOCUTIO
ADLOCUTIO S. C.
ADLOCUTIO AUG.
ADLOCUTIO AUGG.
ADLOCUTIO AUGUSTOR.
ADLOCUTIO BRITANNICA
ADLOCUTIO COH.
ADLOCUTIO COHORT
ADLOCUTIO COH. PRÆTOR
ADLOCUTIO MILITUM.

The subjoined cut, *fig.* 1, represents Nero addressing the

Fig. 1.   *Fig.* 2.   *Fig.* 3.

soldiers from an elevation, while they stand, near the *prætorium*, with their military standards. He is robed in the *toga*, and another figure near him also robed. *Fig.* 2, represents the emperor Galba, in his military robe, haranguing the soldiers as they stand with their legionary ensigns. *Fig.* 3, represents Vespasian, crowned with laurel, in the same act. *Vaillant. Num. Imp. &c.*; *Patin. Num. Imp.*

AD LONGUM (*Mus.*) at full length. [vide *Ad*]

ADMANUE'NSIS (*Archæol.*) the same as *amanuensis*.

ADME'ASUREMENT (*Law*) *admensuratio*, a writ against those usurping more than their own share, as in the Admeasurement of Pasture, and the Admeasurement of Dower. The *Admeasurement of pasture* is a writ against those having common pasturage, who surcharge the pasture. *Admeasurement of dower* is a writ against a widow holding more from the heir, as dower, than she is entitled to. *Britt.* c. 58, &c.; *Flet.* l. 4, c. 23; *Reg. Orig.* 156.

ADMEASUREMENT *of a ship* (*Mar.*) a measurement made to ascertain its tonnage.

ADMI'NICLE (*Ant.*) a term applied to the attributes or ornaments wherewith Juno is represented on medals.

ADMINICLE (*Law*) 1. A term, in the Scotch Law, for any writing or deed referred to by a party, in an action at law, for proving his allegations. 2. An ancient term for aid or support. 3. A term in Civil Law for imperfect proof.

ADMINICULATOR (*Ecc.*) an ancient officer of the church, who defended the cause of widows and orphans.

ADMINISTRATION (*Law*) the disposing, in Civil Law, of the estate or effects of a man who dies intestate.

ADMINISTRATION (*Com.*) a staple magazine or warehouse established by the Spaniards in Callao, a port of Lima, where vessels must unload.

ADMINISTRATOR (*Polit.*) he who administers or manages the public concerns in the place of a sovereign prince.

ADMINISTRATOR (*Law*) he to whom the estate and effects of an intestate person are committed by the ordinary, for which he is accountable as an executor.

ADMINISTRATO'RES (*Ant.*) *ipsius Patrisfamilias ministri in mensa.* *Alfen. de Verb. Signif.*

ADMINISTRATRIX (*Law*) she that hath the goods and chattels of an intestate person committed to her charge as an administrator.

ADMIRA'BILIS *Sal* (*Chem.*) another name for Glauber's salt.

ADMIRAL (*Mar.*) *admiralius, admirallus, admirallis, Capitaneus custos maris*, from the Saxon, aen-mepeal, all over the sea, or, as some say, from the Arabic, *amer* or *emir*, a governor, and ἄλς, the sea; an officer of the first rank and command in a fleet.—*Lord High Admiral*, an officer that used to have the government of the king's navy by the king's patent. The term seems to have been first used in the time of Edward I.; and the first Admiral of England was Richard Fitz-Alan, Earl of Arundel. 10 *Ric.* 2. The office is now vested in the Lords commissioners of the Admiralty, who have the same power and authority.—*Admiral of the fleet*, the highest officer under the Admiralty of Great Britain, is distinguished when he embarks on any expedition by the union flag at the main-top gallant-mast-head.—*Vice Admiral*, 1. The officer next in rank and command to the Admiral, has his flag displayed at the fore-top gallant-mast-head. 2. A civil officer appointed by the Lords commissioners of the Admiralty, of whom there are upwards of twenty in different parts of Great Britain, with judges and marshals under them for exercising jurisdiction in maritime affairs. Their decisions, however, are not final, an appeal lying to the court of Admiralty in London.—*Rear Admiral*, the officer next in rank and command to the Vice Admiral, carries his flag at the mizen-top gallant-mast-head.—*Admiral of the red, white*, &c. that is, of the red squadron, the white squadron, &c. so denominated from the colour of the flag. [vide *Flag*] —*Admiral of the Cinque Ports*, the warden of the Cinque Ports has the jurisdiction of Admiral within these ports, exempt from the jurisdiction of the Admiralty of England.

ADMIRAL, a name given also to the most considerable ship of a fleet of merchantmen, or of the vessels employed in the cod fishery of Newfoundland. This ship directs the movements of the rest.

A'DMIRALTY (*Mar.*) in French, *amirauté*, the office of Lord High Admiral, whether discharged by one or many.—*Lords commissioners of Admiralty*, those who execute the office of Lord High Admiral by the *Stat.* 2 W. & M. They are seven in number.—*Admiralty court*, the supreme court held by the Lord High Admiral or Lords commissioners for the trial of maritime causes, established in the reign of Edward III. The jurisdiction of this court is confined to the main sea, or coasts of the sea not being in any county. —*Admiralty office*, an office near Whitehall, wherein are transacted all maritime affairs belonging to the jurisdiction of the Lord High Admiral, where the Lords commissioners at present meet on certain days for the management of the navy; and where formerly the Lord High Admiral determined all causes, civil and criminal, committed at sea, which are now decided at Doctors' Commons, or the Old Bailey. *Stowe's Survey.*

ADMIRATION (*Gram.*) the note or mark [!] expressing admiration.

ADMI'SSIO (*Ant.*) an appellation for certain parts of the *atrium*, or audience-chamber, divided off by hangings, into which persons were admitted to the prince according to their different degrees of favour; thence termed *amici admissionis primæ, secundæ, vel tertiæ.* *Senec. de Benef.* l. 6, c. 33, 34; *Lamprid. Alex. Sev.* c. 20; *Lips. in Tac. Annal.* l. 6, c. 29; *Salmas. in Spartian Adrian.* c. 18.

ADMI'SSION (*Law*) the ordinary's declaration, that he approves the parson who is presented to the cure of the church. When the patron has presented to a church, the bishop on examination admits the clerk by saying, *admitto te habilem.* *Co. Lit.* 344. *a.*

ADMISSION'ALES (*Ant.*) gentlemen ushers, or those who admitted persons into the presence of the prince. *Lamprid. in Alex. Sev.* c. 4; *Ammian.* l. 15, c. 5; *Lips. in Tacit. Annal.* l. 6, c. 29.

ADMISSIO'NUM *Magister* (*Ant.*) another name for *Admissionalis.*

ADMI'TTANCE (*Law*) the admittance of a tenant to a copyhold estate, which may be either by voluntary grant when the lord is proprietor, by the surrender of the prior tenant, or by descent.

ADMITT'ENDO *clerico* (*Law*) a writ granted to one that has recovered the right of presentation against the bishop.

Reg. Orig. 31, 33; *New Nat. Brev.* 84.—*Admittendo in socium*, a writ for associating certain persons to justices of assize. *Reg. Orig.* 206.

ADMONI'TIO (*Ant.*) *edicto admonere, rescripto admonere*, &c. an injunction or proclamation.—*Admonitio fustium*, a beating with sticks, which was a military punishment.

ADMONITIO (*Archæol.*) a summons, particularly of debtors.

ADMORTIG'ATION (*Archæol.*) the reduction of the property of lands or tenements to mortmain.

ADNA'TA (*Nat.*) or *Adnascentia*, προσφυῆς, from *adnascor*, to grow to adnate, or adherent; an epithet for what grows upon animal or vegetable bodies inseparably, as hair, &c. or accidentally, as fungus, &c. *Plin.* l. 16, c. 93.

ADNATA (*Anat.*) or *adnascentia*; branches that sprout out of the main stock, as the veins and arteries.—*Adnata tunica*, the coat of the eye which makes what is called the White. *Winslow.*

ADNA'TUS (*Bot.*) adnate, growing or fixed to, as applied to off-sets, or small bulbs produced from the main bulb and closely adjoining to it, as in Narcissus, Lily, Hyacinth, &c.—*Adnatus* is also applied to different parts of plants, as the leaf, stipule, &c. as *Folium adnatum*, a leaf adhering to the stem.—*Stipula adnata*, a stipule adhering to the petiole.—*Anthera adnata*, an anther closely attached to both sides of the filaments.—*Stylus adnatus*, a style adhering to the corolla, as in the *Canna*. *Linn. Phil. Botan.*

ADNI'CHELLED (*Law*) the same as annulled.

ADN'OMEN (*Ant.*) vide *Agnomen*.

A'DNOUN (*Gram.*) the same as substantive.

ADOLE'SCENCE (*Ant.*) *Adolescentia*; the period of youth among the ancients from twelve to twenty-five.

AD O'MNEM *tonum* (*Mus.*) vide *Ad*.

ADONI'A (*Ant.*) Ἀδώνια; festivals in Sicily, in honor of Adonis, at which lamentations formed a part of the ceremony, whence ἀδώνια ἄγειν signified, according to Suidas, Ἄδωνιν κλαίζειν, to mourn over Adonis. *Plut. in Nic.*; *Ammian Marcell.* l. 22, c. 9; *Macrob. Saturnal,* l. 1, c. 21; *Natal Com.* l. 5, c. 16; *Meurs. Græc. Fest.*; *Selden de Diis Syr.*

ADO'NIC *verse* (*Poet.*) *Metrum Adonicum*; a short kind of verse used first in bewailing the death of Adonis. It consists of a dactylic dimeter catalectic; or, more properly, of a dactyle and a spondee; as, ὦ τὸν Ἄδωνιν, or "*Fundĭtĕ flētūs.*" *Serv. Centrimet.*; *Plot. de Met.*

ADO'NIDIS *horti* (*Hort.*) or *Adonis Horti*, i. e. the gardens of Adonis; plants, flowers, &c. in pots or boxes set on the outside of windows, &c. *Plin.* l. 19, c. 19.

ADO'NIS (*Bot.*) Pheasant's-Eye, or Bird's-Eye; a genus of plants, Class 13 *Polyandria*, Order 7 *Polygynia*.
Generic Character. CAL. *perianth* five-leaved; *leaflets* obtuse.—COR. *petals* from five to fifteen.—STAM. *filaments* very short; *anthers* oblong.—PIST. *germs* numerous; *styles* none; *receptacle* oblong; *seeds* numerous.
Species. The principal species are the *Adonis æstivalis*, or *sylvestris*, tall Adonis, an annual.—*Adonis autumnalis*, common Adonis, or Bird's-Eye, an annual.—*Adonis vernalis*, or *Flos Adonis*, perennial or spring Adonis, a perennial.—*Adonis appennina*, or *Helleborus niger*, appennine Adonis, a perennial.—*Adonis capensis, Actæa trifoliata, Christophoriana Africana, Ranunculus Æthiopicus,* cape Adonis, a perennial.—*Adonis vesicatoria* or *Imperatoria*. *Dod. Stirp. Hist. Pemptad.*; *Ger. Herb.*; *Raii Hist. Plant.*; *Pluk. Almag. Botan.*

A'DONISTS (*Lit.*) those who contend against the Hebrew points; in distinction from the Ichorists, who maintain their use.

ADO'PTER (*Chem.*) a chemical vessel, with two necks interposed between the retort and receiver.

ADOPTIA'NI (*Eccl.*) adoptianists; a sect of heretics in the 8th century, who denied that Christ was the proper or natural, but only the adopted, son of God. Their heresy was condemned in a synod at Frankfort, held by Charlemagne in 794. *Hor. Hist. Eccles.* per. 2, art. 2.

ADO'PTIO (*Ant.*) Adoption; a solemn act among the Greeks and Romans, whereby a man made another his son, investing him with all the rights and privileges of that relationship. It was distinguished from *arrogatio*, in as much as the former was done by means of the Prætor, and the latter by means of the people. *Aul. Gell.* l. 5, c. 19.

ADOPTIO (*Numis.*) the form of adoption is painted on the medals of Adrian and Trajan, as in the subjoined cut,

which represents on the obverse, the head of Trajan crowned, and the inscription NERVA TRAIAN CAES*ar* GERM*anici* NER*væ* AUG*usti Filius Potestate* TR*ibunitia*; on the reverse, Nerva, in a military habit, with a spear in his left hand, offering his right hand to Trajan, with the legend ADOPTIO. *Vaillant. Numis. Imp. Roman. Tristan. Commentaires Historiques,* vol. 1, p. 378.

ADO'PTION (*Hier.*) is represented by the figure of an elderly woman embracing a youth with her right arm, and holding in her left the eagle called *ossifraga*, which is said to reject her young for a time, and afterwards to take them again.

ADOR (*Bot.*) ἀδώρ, another name for *Spelta*.

A'DORAT (*Chem.*) a chemical weight of four pounds.

ADORA'TIO *purpuræ* (*Ant.*) a mode of saluting the emperors among the Romans, by lifting up their purple with the right hand and applying it to the lips, in imitation of the worship or adoration which they offered to the gods. *Ammian Marcel.* l. 15, c. 5; *Cassiodor.* l. 11. ep. 20; *Pancirol Notit. Dig. Imper. Occid.* c. 30; *Buleng. de Imp. Roman.* l. 1, c. 11.

ADORA'TION (*Ant.*) *adoratio*, from *ad* and *os*, i. e. to apply the hand to the mouth; a mode of reverence anciently shown to the gods, by raising the right hand to the mouth and applying it gently to the lips. "*In adorando dextram ad osculum referimus.*" *Plin.* l. 28, c. 2. This kiss was called *osculum libatum*. The Romans performed the ceremony of *adoration* veiled, to all the gods except Saturn, whom they worshipped as the god of truth, from whom nothing should be concealed. *Apul. Apol.*; *Spartian in Adrian,* c. 26; *Turneb. Adversar.* l. 18, c. 6; *Stuck. de Sacrif.* p. 5; *Kipping. Antiq. Roman.* l. 1, c. 9, s. 5.

A'DOS (*Chem.*) water wherein iron has been extinguished.

ADOS (*Mil.*) a French term for a bank of earth raised against a wall.

A *double* (*Mus.*) or, double A, i. e. A below G gamut.

ADOSCULA'TION (*Bot.*) joining or inserting one part of a plant into another. *Grew. Anat. of Plants.*

ADO'XA (*Bot.*) Fumitory, or Hollow Root; a genus of plants, Class 8 *Octandria*, Order 4 *Pentagynia*.
Generic Characters. CAL. *perianth* inferior.—COR. monopetalous.—*Clefts* ovate.—STAM. *filaments* subulate; *anthers* roundish.—PIST. *germ* below the receptacle of the corolla; *styles* simple; *stigmas* simple.—PER. a globose berry; *seeds* solitary.
Species. The only species is the *Adoxa moschatellina, Moschatellina moschatella, Ranunculus, Fumaria bulbosa,* Bulbous Fumitory, Hollow Root, Tuberous Moschatell; a perennial, native of Britain. *Ger. Herb.*; *Park. Theat. Botan.*; *Raii. Hist. Plant.*; *Mer. Hist. Plant.*

AD *pondus omnium* (*Med.*) signifying that the last prescribed medicine ought to weigh as much as all the medicines mentioned before.

ADPRE'SSUS (*Bot.*) appressed, or squeezed close to; an epithet applied to different parts of a plant, as—*Folium adpressum*, a leaf that turns up and lays its upper surface to the stem, as if pressed to it by violence.—*Calyx adpressus*, a calyx that is close to the peduncle.—*Pedunculus adpressus*, one that is close to the branch or stem.

AD *quod damnum* (*Law*) a writ to inquire whether a grant to be made by the king, as a market, fair, &c. will be to his damage. *F. N. B.* 221, &c.

ADRA'CHNE (*Bot.*) ἀδράχνη; a tree which is found in great abundance in Crete, on the hills of Leuce, and in stony places; and is called by the modern Greeks, ἀδραχλα. *Theoph.* l. 1, c. 8; *Clus. Hist.* l. 1, c. 31. According to Pliny, it must be distinguished from Ἀνδράχνη, which is a herb. "*Adrachnen omnes fere Græci portulacæ nomine interpretantur, cum illa sit herba et andrachne vocetur.*" *Plin.* l. 13, c. 22.

A'DRAGANTH (*Bot.*) the name of a herb, which is the *Astragalus Tragacanthus* of Linnæus.

ADRECT'ARE (*Law*) to set right.

A'DRIANISTS (*Ecc.*) two different sects of heretics of this name. 1. A sect mentioned by Theodoretus, which he says was a branch sprung from Simon Magus; but of this sect no mention is made by any other writer. *Theodoret. Hæret. Fab.* l. 1. 2. A sect of anabaptists, in the 16th century, who, after their leader, one Adrian, held many errors, particularly respecting our Saviour. *Prateol. Dogm. omn. Hæret.*; *Spondan continuat Baron. Annal.*

ADRI'FT (*Mar.*) from *a* or *ab*, and *drift* driven; an epithet for a vessel broken loose from her moorings and driven about by the waves.

ADRO'BOLON (*Chem.*) Indian Bdellium. *Gorr. Def. Med.*

ADROGA'TION (*Ant.*) the adoption of persons grown to an age to dispose of themselves. [vide *Adoption*]

A'DROS (*Med.*) ἀδρός, plump and full; applied to the habit of the body, and also to the pulse; ἀδρὸς σφυγμὸς, a full pulse. *Hippocrat. de Genit. &c.*; *Gal. de Meth. Med.* l. 14; *Gorr. Def. Med.*; *Foes. Oeconom. Hippocrat.*

ADRO'TERON (*Bot.*) a plentiful grain.

ADSCE'NDENS (*Bot.*) vide *Ascendens.*

ADSCRI'PTI (*Math.*) an epithet for the tangents of arcs.

ADSCRIPTI'TII (*Ant.*) vide *Ascriptitii.*

ADSE'RTOR (*Ant.*) the asserter and supporter of another's liberty; from *adserere manu in libertatem*, to maintain the freedom of another; to bail him and advocate his cause. *Fest. de Signif. Verb.*

ADSESSO'RES (*Ant.*) vide *Assessores.*

ADSTRI'CTION (*Med.*) from *ad* and *stringo*, to bind. 1. The styptic quality of medicines. 2. The retention of the natural evacuations, particularly those of the bowels.

AD *terminum qui preterit.* (*Law*) a writ for the lessor, or his heirs, against a tenant who holds lands or tenements after the expiration of the lease. *F. N. B.* 201.

ADVA'NCE (*Com.*) anticipation of time; as when money is paid in advance before goods are delivered. " To be in advance with a merchant:" to lend him money. Advance for the drawer of a bill; when the person who negotiates it receives more than the contents. Advance for the payer and loss for the drawer; when he to whom the bill belongs does not receive the full value of it.

ADVANCE upon *seamen's wages* (*Mar.*) wages paid before they are due. Every volunteer is entitled to an advance of two months' wages before he proceeds to sea.

TO ADVANCE *money* (*Com.*) to be at the expense of an undertaking before the time of being reimbursed.

ADVANCE (*Mil.*) or *advanced*, an epithet for any part of an army which is in front of the rest; as, the advance guard, the first line or division of the army ranged or marching in battle array; it is also said of a battalion, or of guns, when brought in front and before the first line. It is figuratively applied to the promotion of the officers and soldiers.

ADVANCE *fosse* (*Fort.*) a ditch thrown round the esplanade or glacis of a place.

ADVA'NCER (*Hunt.*) one of the starts or branches of a buck's attire, between the back antler and the palm.

ADVA'NCEMENTS *of money in the bank* (*Com.*) monies advanced by the Bank, on Government and other good securities.

ADVA'NTAGE *ground* (*Mil.*) the ground that gives superiority or an opportunity for annoyance and resistance.

A'DUAR (*Polit.*) a name for the moveable villages erected of tents, among the Arabians.

A *Due* or *A 2* (*Mus.*) for two voices.

A'DVENT (*Ecc.*) *adventus*. 1. The coming of our Saviour. 2. The feast commemorative of the Advent, which falls about a month before Christmas.—*Advent Sundays*, the four Sundays preceding Christmas Day, the first commencing either with that Sunday which falls on St. Andrew's day, namely, the 30th of November, or the nearest Sunday to it, before or after.

ADVENTI'TIOUS (*Law*) *Adventitius*, from *advenio*; what comes incidentally; as, *adventitia bona*, goods that fall to a man otherwise than by inheritance; or, *adventitia dos*, a dowry given by some other friend beside the parent.

ADVENTITIOUS *glandules* (*Anat.*) kernels which sometimes make their appearance in the neck, holes under the arms, &c.

ADVENTITIOUS *matter* (*Phy.*) matter which does not properly belong to any body or substance, either natural or mixed, but comes to it from some other place, as in the freezing of water, when some frigorific particles adventitious to the water are added, either from the air or the freezing mixture.

AD *ventrem inspiciendum* (*Law*) Vide *Ventre inspiciendo.*

ADVE'NTURE (*Com.*) i. e. *at a venture*; goods sent out at a venture.

ADVENTURE, *bill of*, a writing signed by a merchant, to testify that the goods shipped on board a certain vessel are at the venture of another person, he himself being answerable only for the produce.

ADVE'NTURER (*Com.*) 1. A person not known or established in public business; a trickster. 2. A merchant's ship that goes to traffic within the limits of a company's grant without licence.

ADVE'NTURERS (*Com.*) those who by the name of proprietors undertake the settlements of distant colonies.

ADVENTURERS, a name also applied to the enterprizing pirates who joined together against the Spaniards in the West Indies, otherwise known by the name of Buccaneers.

ADVENTURERS (*Her.*) or *Merchant Adventurers*, the name of an ancient company of merchants or traders, erected for the discovery of lands, territories, trading places, &c. hitherto unknown. This society had its rise in Burgundy, under John, Duke of Brabant, in 1428; and, being translated into England, was successively confirmed by Edward III., and IV., Richard III., Henry IV., V., VI., and VII., who gave it its present name. They bear for arms, *Nebule* of six pieces, *argent* and *azure*, on a chief quarterly *or* and *gules*; in the first and fourth two red roses, and in the second and third a lion of England.

ADVENTURERS *Merchant* (*Com.*) those who adventure their goods to sea, in distinction from inland traders.

ADVE'NTURINE (*Com.*) a precious stone of a yellowish brown colour.

ADVE'NTUS (*Numis.*) the arrival of the emperors at Rome and other places was commemorated by medals struck in commemoration of the event. The inscriptions employed on such occasions were as follow: ADVENTUS AUGUSTI, seu AUG. IMP. on the coming of Trajan to Rome after the death of Nerva, U.C. 852, A.D. 99. ADVENTUS AUG. S.C. on Adrian's first arrival at Rome as emperor, U.C. 871, A.D. 118. ADVENTUS AFRICÆ, on his arrival in Africa, U.C. 876, A.D. 123. ADVENTUS GALLIÆ, on his arrival in Gaul.—ADVENTUS ITALIÆ, on his arrival in Italy. ADVENTUS JUDEÆ, on his arrival in Judea. ADVENTUS MAURITANIÆ, on his arrival in Mauritania. ADVENTUS ASIÆ, on his arrival in Asia. ADVENTUS BITHYNIÆ, on his arrival in Bithynia. ADVENTUS CILICIÆ, on his arrival in Cilicia. ADVENTUS HISPANIÆ, on his arrival in Spain. ADVENTUS PHRYGIÆ, on his arrival in Phrygia. ADVENTUS SICILIÆ, on his arrival in Sicily. ADVENTUS AUG. COS. III. P.P. on Adrian's return to Rome, U.C. 887, A.D. 134. ADVENTUS AUG. S.C., on the arrival of M. Aurelius from Germany, U.C. 927, A.D. 174. ADVENTUS AUG., on the return of Commodus from the conquest of Germany, U.C. 933, A.D. 180. ADVENTUS AUG. IMP., on the return of Severus from Asia, U.C. 949, A.D. 196. ADVENTUS AUG. FELICISSIMO, S.C., on the triumphant return of Severus from Gaul, U.C. 954, A.D. 201. ADVENT. AUGG., on the triumphant return of Severus from Parthia, U.C. 955, A.D. 202. ADVENT. AUG., on the triumphant return of Antoninus Caracalla from the East with his father, U.C. 955, A.D. 202. ADVENTUS AUGG., on Caracalla's return with his brother, and with the ashes of his father, U.C. 964, A.D. 211. ADVENTUS AUGG., on the return of Philip with his son to Rome, U.C. 998, A.D. 245. ADVENTUS AUGG., on the arrival of Trajan Decius at Rome after having conquered Marinus, U.C. 1002, A.D. 249. ADVENTUS AUG., on the return of Q. Hostilianus to his father, with his brother Decius. This medal is supposed by Vaillant to belong properly to Decius, as history gives no account of the arrival of Hostilianus at Rome from any place. ADVENTUS AUG. S.C. on the return of Trebonianus Gallus to Rome after his victory, U.C. 1004, A.D. 251. ADVENTUS AUGG. S.C. on the triumphant arrival of Gallienus from Germany, U.C. 1007, A.D. 254. ADVENTUS AUG., on his return from his victory over Regillianus, U.C. 1012, A.D. 259. ADVENTUS AUG., on the triumphant return of Gallienus from Thrace and Macedonia, U.C. 1016, A.D. 263. ADVENTUS AUG., on the return of M. Aurelius Claudius from his victory over Aureolus, U.C. 1021, A.D. 268. ADVENTUS AUG. IMP., on the coming of Tacitus to the army, U.C. 1029, A.D. 276. ADVENTUS PROBI. AUG. XXI., on the arrival of Probus after his conquest of the Germans, U.C. 1029, A.D. 276. ADVENTUS AUG. H.S. on the return of Probus to Rome after his conquests in Gaul, U.C. 1024, A.D. 281. ADVENTUS AUG. R.X.Z., on the first arrival of Dioclesian at Rome, U.C. 1037, A.D. 284. FELIX ADVENTUS AUGG. N.N., on the triumphant return of Dioclesian and Maximianus, U.C. 1055, A.D. 302. ADVENTUS AUG. on the return of Carusius into Britain, U.C. 1044, A.D. 291. FELIX ADVENTUS AUG. N. CON. on the arrival of Constantine at Constantinople after the Gothic war, A.D. 334. ADVENTUS AUGUSTI ROM. IMP., on the arrival of Jovianus at Rome, after the conquest of the Persians, A.D. 364. The manner of representing the adventus was either in the form of a religious or military ceremony, as in fig. 1, where the emperor Adrian, on his arrival in Sicily, is represented standing near a tripod; opposite to him the goddess Ceres crowned with ears of corn, and offering other ears. In fig. 2, Trabinianus Gallus and Volusianus are represented

Fig. 1.   *Fig.* 2.

on horseback, preceded by a figure of victory, and emblematical of their successes over the Goths.

ADVENTUS *jocundus* (*Archæol.*) a tribute paid to the lord on coming to any dignity.

A'DVERB (*Gram.*) *adverbium*, i. e. *verbo adjectum*, a part of speech added to a verb to complete its signification.

ADVERSA'RIA (*Ant.*) *quia scriberentur in adversâ tantum et non in aversâ paginâ*. A memorandum book, to note down whatever occurs, particularly in courts of Law; or a day-book for pecuniary purposes. *Cic. Rosc. Com.* c. 4; *Salmas. de Usur.* p. 147.

ADVE'RSATIVE *particle* (*Gram.*) that which denotes some contrariety; as but, however, &c.

ADVE'RSITOR (*Ant.*) *qui in adversum it*; a servant among the Romans who went to meet his master on the road.

ADVE'RSUS (*Bot.*) an epithet for a leaf, as *folium adversum*, a vertical leaf; so called when its margin is turned towards the stem. *Linn. Phil. Bot.*

TO ADVERTI'SE (*Com.*) from *adverto*, to warn or give notice, to send notice to all merchants or traders when a bill or any thing else is lost, giving an exact description of the same.

ADVE'RTISEMENT (*Com.*) a name for any printed publication of circumstances, either of public or private interest.

ADVI'CE (*Com.*) the communicating to another by letter what passes: as a letter of *advice*, informing a correspondent that one has drawn upon him, or concerning the sending of goods, with the invoice annexed.—*Advice to the Bank*, notice to the proper clerks of bills payable, with an exact description of the contents and parties.

ADVICE *boat* (*Mar.*) a small boat employed for carrying despatches and orders.

AD *vitam aut culpam* (*Law*) an office held for the term of a person's life, or during his good conduct.

ADULA'RIA (*Min.*) a subspecies of the Feldspar family.

ADU'LT (*Law*) a term applied by civilians between fourteen and twenty-five years of age.

ADULTERA'TIS *judicii* (*Ant.*) bribing the judges.

ADULTERA'TION (*Law*) a general term for rendering the coin of the realm of less value than it ought to be: which comprehends *debasing* the coin, by the admixture of impure metals, or the use of an undue alloy, &c.; and *counterfeiting* the coin, which is forging a stamp upon a baser metal. The former is sometimes from state-necessity an act of authority; but the latter is always the fraudulent act of individuals for purposes of private gain.

ADULTERATION (*Med.*) the debasing and corrupting of medicines.

ADU'LTERINE (*Law*) a term in the Civil Law for the issue of an adulterous intercourse.

ADULTE'RIUM (*Ecc.*) the intruding into, or invading a bishopric during the lifetime of the bishop, who was supposed to be allied to his church by a spiritual marriage.

ADULTERIUM (*Nat.*) a term for ingrafting of trees.

ADU'LTERY (*Law*) from *ad* and *alter*, another person; a criminal conversation between two married persons, or a married and an unmarried person.

ADULTERY (*Med.*) an overloading of the body with aliment at the instigation of the appetite. *Paracel.*

ADU'MBRATED (*Her.*) an epithet for any figure in coat armour which is borne so shadowed or obscured that nothing is visible but the bare purfile, or, as the painters call it, the outline.

ADUMBRA'TIO (*Bot.*) the whole history of a plant, comprehending the name, etymology, class, character, difference, variety, synonyms, description, figure, place, and time. *Linn. Phil. Bot.*

ADUMBRATION (*Her.*) the shadow or outlines only of the arms borne by a family in decay.

A'DVOCATE (*Law*) 1. A pleader in the civil or ecclesiastical law, who maintains or defends the right of his client in the same manner as the counsellor does in the common law.—*Lord Advocate*, an officer of state in Scotland appointed by the king to advise about the making and executing law, to defend his right and interest in all public assemblies, to prosecute capital crimes, &c.—*College* or *faculty of advocates*, a college consisting of 180 appointed to plead in all actions before the lords of session.—*Church* or *ecclesiastical advocates*, pleaders appointed by the church to maintain its rights. 2. A patron who has the advowson or presentation to a church. *Glan.* l. 13, c. 19, l. 4, c. 7; *LL. Longobard.* l. 2.

ADVOCA'TIO (*Ant.*) 1. A calling or assembling together a multitude of friends with cries and clamour to one's assistance: *Virginius filiam suam obsoleta veste, comitantibus aliquot matronis, cum ingente advocatione in forum deducit. Liv.* l. 3, c. 47; *Pollet. For. Rom.* l. 2, c. 1. 2. The office of an advocate or pleader, pleading either for or against a person: *In fine sententiæ adjecit, quod ego et Tacitus injunctâ advocatione diligenter, fortiter functi essemus. Plin.* l. 2, ep. 10; *Pollet. For. Rom.* l. 2, c. 1. 3. A delay of judgment granted at the request of either party wishing for further time to prepare an answer and to take advice. *Cic. in Verr.* l. 1, c. 49, *et ad Fam.* l. 7, ep. 2; *Senec. de Consol. ad Marc.* c. 10, *et de Ira.* l. 1, c. 16.

ADVOCA'TION (*Law*) a writing in the Scotch Law drawn up in the form of a petition, called a *bill of advocation*, whereby a party in an action applies to the supreme court to advocate its cause, and to call the action out of an inferior court before itself.—*Letters of advocation* are the decree or warrant of the Supreme Court, or court of Session, discharging the inferior tribunal from all farther proceedings in the matter, and advocating the action to itself.

ADVOCA'TIONE *decimarum* (*Law*) a writ that lies for tithes demanding the fourth part or upwards that belong to any church. *Reg. Orig.* 29.

ADVOCA'TUS (*Ant.*) *amicus quem litigator ad eum vocat;* advocate, or one who was called to assist another man in his cause by his presence, his counsel, his testimony or otherwise: *Armatos homines, quos in Senatum induxerat, Antonius consul advocatos vocat, vellem adesset sine advocatis.* When the advocate was employed to plead the cause of the defendant, in a court of law, he was styled *patronus. Cic. Philipp.* 1, c. 7, *et Ascon. in Cic.* p. 20.

ADVO'W (*Law*) or *Avow*, from *advocare*, to justify; an act formerly done, as, in the case of things stolen, he in whose possession they were found was obliged *advocare* i. e. to produce the seller in order to justify the sale. *Fleta.*

ADVO'WEE (*Ecc.*) an advocate of a church or religious house. [vide *Adascatus*]

ADVOW'SON (*Law*) from advow or *advocare*, a right of presentation to a church or benefice. He who possesses this right is called the patron; when there is no patron, or he neglects to exercise his right within six months, it is called a *Lapse*, i. e. a title given to the ordinary to collate to a church; when a presentation is made by one who has no right it is termed a *usurpation*.—*Advowsons* are of different kinds, as—*Advowson appendant*, when it depends upon a manor, &c.—*Advowson in gross*, when it belongs to a person and not to a manor.—*Advowson presentative*, when the patron presents to the Bishop.—*Advowson collative*, when it is lodged in the Bishop.—*Advowson donative*, when the king or patron puts the clerk into possession without presentation.—*Advowson of the moiety of the church*, where there are two several patrons, and two incumbents in the same church.—*A Moiety of Advowson*, where two must join in the presentation of one incumbent.—*Advowson of religious houses*, that which is vested in any persons who founded such a house.

ADU'STION (*Med.*) an inflammation of the parts about the brain and its members. *Oribas. Synopsis*, l. 5, c. 13.

ADU'STUS (*Med.*) from *aduro*, to burn; *adust*, or adusted, i. e. scorched, burnt, as applied to the fluids of the body when they are rendered acrid by the heat.

A'DY (*Bot.*) a name for the Palm-tree, in the island of St. Thomas. *Raii Hist. Plant.*

ADYNA'MIA (*Med.*) ἀδυναμία, from α, priv. and δύναμις, *potentia*, impotence or weakness. *Hippoc. Coac. Prænot.* l. 1, &c.; *Gal. Comm. et Different. Morb.* c. 5, *et Defin. Med.* &c.; *Goor. Defin. Med.*; *Foes. Oeconom. Hippocrat.* It is formed into an order of diseases under the class *Neuroses. Cullen's Nosology.*

ADY'NAMON (*Med.*) ἀδύναμον, from ἀδυναμία, *impotentia;* a fictitious wine allayed with water, and boiled away so as to make it of a suitable strength for weak patients. *Dioscor.* l. 5, c. 13; *Plin.* l. 14, c. 16.

A'DYTUM (*Ant.*) ἄδυτον, that part of the temple to which there is no *aditus* or admission, except for the priests, from α, priv. and δύω, to enter. *Cæs. de Bell. Civil.* l. 3, c. 105; *Paus.* l. 10.

ADZ (*Carp.*) or *addice*, a tool similar to an axe, but having its blade athwart the handle.

ÆACE'A (*Ant.*) games in honour of Æacus. *Isocrat. in Evagor.*; *Hesychius.*; *Meurs. Græc. Fer. apud Gronov. Antiq. Græc.* tom. vii. p. 710.

ÆA'CIDES (*Ant.*) Αἰακίδης, a patronymic for Achilles, Peleus, and other descendants of Æacus. *Hom. Il.* l. 9, v. 184, &c.; *Virg. Æn.* l. 1, v. 99, &c.; *Paus.* l. 1, c. 10.

ÆANTI'A (*Ant.*) Αἰάντια, a festival in honour of Ajax at Salamis. *Isocrat. in Evagor.*; *Plut. in Demosth.*; *Pausan.* l. 2, c. 29; *Schol. in Pind. Olymp.* od. 7; *Meur. Græc. Fer. apud Gronov. Antiq. Græc.* tom. vii. 710.

ÆBU'TIA *Lex* (*Ant.*) a law, so called from one of the Æbutian family in Rome, by whom it was made, prohibiting the proposer of a law from bestowing any office on himself or his colleagues. *Cic. Agrar.* orat. 2, c. 8.

ÆCHMO'LOTARCH (*Ecc.*) a title given by the Jews to the principal leader or governor of the Jews during their captivity; a head of their religion like the *Episcopus Judæorum* now in England. [vide *Aichmolotarch*]

Æ'DEPOL (*Ant.*) an oath by Pollux which, at first, could be taken by the women only, but in time became common among the men as well as the women. *Aul. Gell.* l. 11, c. 6.

Æ'DES *sacræ* (*Ant.*) sacred edifices which were temples in every respect, except the want of consecration.

Æ'DES (*Numis.*) a temple was dedicated to Faustina, the wife of Antoninus Pius, who died in the third year of his reign, and was deified by the senate. The annexed cut represents this temple as it is given on a medal of Faustina, with the inscription AEDes DIVæ FAVSTINÆ. *Vaillant. Numis. Imperat. Roman.*; *Mediob. Occo. Numis. Imperat. Roman.*

ÆDI'CULA (*Ant.*) a small *ædes* or temple, which was in every village or parish, answering to the parish church of the present day.

ÆDI'LES (*Ant.*) Roman magistrates so called, *a cura ædium*, i. e. from the care of the temples, which were particularly entrusted to their charge. They had moreover to see that all public buildings, streets, and highways were kept clean, and in good repair; to make provision for public games, funerals, and other spectacles; to take care of weights and measures; and to inspect the markets, &c. At first two ædiles were chosen from among the plebeians, to which others were afterwards added from the patricians. *Ascon. in Cic. Sigon.; de Jur. Civ. Roman.; Hotoman de Majis. Rom.; Manutius, Bulengerus, Pighius, Ursatus, &c. apud Græc. Thesaur. Antiq. Roman.*

The *Ædiles* were distinguished into the—*Ædiles plebeii*, who were chosen from the plebeians in the *Comitia curiata* as assistants to the tribunes. *Dionys. Hcl.* l. 6; *Liv.* l. 2, c. 56.—*Ædiles curules*, so called from the curule chair in which they sat, were created, U. C. 388, from the patricians, to provide for certain public games. *Liv.* l. 6, c. 42.—*Ædiles cereales* were created by Cæsar for keeping the records in the temple of Ceres. *Dio.* l. 43.—*Ædiles alimentarii*, known by that name from the abbreviation ÆDIL. ALIM., were especially charged with the care of the public granaries. *Turneb. Adv.* l. 11, c. 10.

ÆDILI'TIUM *Edictum* (*Ant.*) the sentence of the Ædile allowing redress to the purchaser of a beast.

ÆDI'TUUS (*Ant.*) or *æditumnus*, according to Gellius, an officer who had the charge of the temples, so called from *Ædes tueri*, i. e. to protect the temples. *Varro de Lat. Lin.* l. 6, c. 2; *Festus de Verb. Sign.; Aul. Gell.* l. 12, c. 10; *Ursatus de Not. Roman.; Dempster. Paralip. ad Rosin. Antiq., et Guther. de Jur. Man. apud Græv. Thesaur. Antiq. Roman.* vol. ii. p. 536, &c.

ÆDŒ'IA (*Anat.*) vide *Pudenda*.

Æ'DOR (*Or.*) a sort of bird of the genus *Muscicapa*, or Fly Catchers.

ÆDOSO'PHIA (*Med.*) from αἰδοῖα, *pudenda*, and ψοφέω, to send forth; a flatus passing from the uterus, or urinary-bladder, through the vagina, or urethra.

ÆGAGRO'PHILA (*Med.*) from αἴγαγρος, the rock goat, and πῖλος, the hair; little balls composed of hairs in the stomach of the goat, which have been employed medicinally.

Æ'GIAS (*Med.*) vide *Ægis*.

ÆGI'CERAS (*Bot.*) from αἴξ, a goat, and κέρας, a horn; a genus of plants, Class 5 *Pentandria*, Order 1 *Monogynia*.
Generic Character. CAL. *perianth* one-leaved.—COR. *petals* five.—STAM. *filaments* five.—PIST. *germ* oblong.—PER. *capsule* bowed; *seed* single.
Species. The principal species are the—*Ægiceras majus, Rhizofera corniculata*, or *Mammosa fruticosum*, &c.; a shrub, native of the Moluccas.—*Ægiceras minus, Umbraculum maris*, a shrub, &c. *Rumph. Herb. Amb.; Linn. Spec. Plant.*

ÆGI'DIUM (*Med.*) αἰγίδιον, a collyrium for inflamed eyes.

Æ'GILOPS (*Med.*) an abscess in the canthus, or corner of the eye near the nose; a disorder so called from αἴξ, a goat, and ὤψ, the eye, either because goats were peculiarly subject to it, or because those suffering from it had a cast in the eye like the goats, which Virgil describes to be *transversa tuentibus hircis*. Paulus Ægineta calls this abscess *Anchilops*, before it has broken, and *Ægilops* afterwards; Fallopius and others give it the name of *Fistula lachrymalis*. [vide *Anchilops*, &c.] *Gal. Def. Med.; Cels.* l. 7, c. 7; *Oribas de Loc. Affect. Curat.* l. 4, c. 32; *Aet. Tetrab.* 2, serm. 3, c. 85, &c.; *Paul. Æginet.* l. 3, c. 22; *Aet. de Meth. Med.* l. 2, c. 7; *Fallop. Obs. Anatom.* c. 6; *Wiseman. Chirurg. Essay; Heist. Chirurg.* part 2, sect. 2, c. 54.

ÆGILOPS (*Bot.*) αἰγίλωψ, from αἴξ, a goat, and ὤψ, a face; received its name, according to Dioscorides, from its power to cure the disease in the eye, called the Ægilops. *Theoph.* l. 8, c. 4; *Diosc.* l. 4, c. 12.

ÆGILOPS, *in the Linnean system*, a genus of plants; Class 23 *Polygamia*, Order 1 *Monoecia*, in English, Great Wild-Oat-Grass or Drank.
Generic Characters. CAL. *valves* ovate.—COR. *glume* bivalvular; *nectary* two-leaved; *leaflets* ovate.—STAM. *filaments* three; *anthers* oblong.—PIST. *Germ* turbinate; *styles* two; *stigmas* hairy.—PER. none; *seeds* oblong.
Species. The principal species are the *Ægilops ovata, caudata, triuncialis*, and *squarrosa*, which are mostly annuals, and of the Natural Order of Grasses.

ÆGILOPS is also the name of the *Andropogon contortium*, and the *Avena fatua* of Linnæus. *Raii Hist. Plant.*

ÆGINE'TIA (*Bot.*) a species of the *Orobanche* of Linnæus.

ÆGINE'TICUM *æs* (*Ant.*) the money of Ægina, which was the first that was coined. *Æl. Var. Hist.* l. 12, c. 20.

ÆGINE'TON (*Ant.*) Αἰγινητῶν ἑορτή, a festival, celebrated at Ægina by the free denizens only, in honour of Neptune, which lasted sixteen days. *Plut. Græc. Quæst.*

ÆGI'PHILA (*Bot.*) from αἴξ, a goat, and φιλέω, to like, because goats are fond of it; a genus of plant, Class 4 *Tetandria*, Order 1 *Monogynia*.
Generic Characters. CAL. *perianth* one-leaved.—COR. *petals* one; *tube* cylindrical; *clefts* oblong.—STAM. *filaments* capillary; *anthers* roundish.—PIST. *germ* roundish; *style* capillary; *stigmas* simple.—PER. *berry* roundish; *seed* either in pairs or solitary.
Species. The species are mostly shrubs, the principal of which are the—*Ægiphila Martiniensis*, native of Martinique.—*Ægiphila elata*, or *Knoxia scandens*, native of the West Indies.—*Ægiphila villosa*, or *Manabea villosa*, a native of Cayenne. *Brown. Hist. Jamaic.; Linn. Spec. Plant.*

ÆGI'RINON (*Med.*) αἰγείρινον, a medicine; so called because the αἴγειρος, i. e. the poplar, is the chief ingredient in it.

ÆGI'ROS (*Bot.*) αἴγειρος κρητική, the black poplar, which is used medicinally. *Hippocrat. de Mul.; Foes. Oeconom. Hippocrat.*

Æ'GIS (*My.*) Αἰγίς, a shield, particularly Jupiter's shield, so called because it was supposed to be covered with the skin of the goat αἴξ, named Amalthea. Jupiter afterwards gave it to Minerva, who placed upon it a Medusa's head, as represented on a medal of Syracuse, according to the annexed figure. *Goltz. Græc. mag.* tab. 4, numm. 6.

ÆGIS (*Med.*) an affection of the eye when it has small αἰγίδες, i. e. *cicatrices*. which cause a dimness of sight. *Hippocrat. Prædict.* l. 2; *Foes. Oeconom. Hippocrat.*

ÆGITHUS (*Or.*) αἴγιθος, a very little bird, said by Aristotle to be at variance with the ass. *Aristot. de Hist. Anim.* l. 9, c. 6.

ÆGLEFI'NUS (*Ich.*) a name for the Hadock, a species of the *Gasamundus* of Linnæus. *Will. Ichth.*

Æ'GLEUS (*Bot.*) another name for the Chamæleon.

ÆGOCE'PHALA (*Or.*) a name for the common Godwit; a species of the *Scolopax* of Linnæus. *Will. Ornith.*

ÆGO'CERAS (*Bot.*) αἰγόκερας, the Greek name for the herb called Foenugreek. *Gorr. Def. Med.*

ÆGOCE'RATOS (*Bot.*) the *Hugonia mystax* of Linnæus. *Raii Hist. Plant.*

ÆGO'CEROS (*Astron.*) the same as *Capricornus*.

ÆGOLE'THRON (*Bot.*) from αἴξ, and ὄλεθρος, pernicious; a plant answering to the *Azalea portica* of Linnæus, or the *Chamærodendron* of Tournefort. *Plin.* l. 21, c. 13; *Tournef. Instit.*

ÆGO'NYCHON (*Bot.*) αἰγώνυχον, the Greek name for the *Lithospermum* of Linnæus. *Dioscor.* l. 2, c. 158.

ÆGOPHTHA'LMOS (*Min.*) from αἴξ, and ὀφθαλμὸς, an eye; a precious stone resembling a goat's eye. *Plin.* l. 37, c. 11; *Salmas. ad Solin.* p. 706.

ÆGOPO'DIUM (*Bot.*) from αἴξ, a goat, and πῦς, foot, Goatweed: 1. a genus of plants, Class 5 *Pentandria*, Order 2 *Digynia*.
Generic Characters. CAL. umbel universal manifold, partial similar; *involucre* none; *proper perianth* scarcely observable.—COR. *universal* uniform; *particular* obovate.—STAM. *filaments* simple; *anthers* roundish.—PIST. *germ* inferior; *styles* simple; *stigmas* headed.—PER. none; *fruit* ovate-oblong; *seeds* two.
Species. The only species is the *Ægopodium podagraria*, *Ligusticum podagraria*, *Seseli ægopodium*, *Angelica sylvestris*, &c. a native of Britain, and a perennial. *Ger. Herb.*; *Park. Theat. Botan.*; *Rivin. Ord. Plant.*; *Mor. Hist. Plant.*; *Pet. Herb. Britan.*; *Linn. Spec. Plant.*
ÆGOPODIUM is also a name for the *Cicuta maculata* and the *Smyrnium aureum* of Linnæus. *Gron.*

ÆGO'PRICON (*Bot.*) a genus of plants, Class 21 *Monoecia*, Order 1 *Monandria*.
Generic characters. CAL. one-leaved.—COR. none.—STAM. *filaments* one; *anther* ovate.
Species. The only species is the *Agopricon betulinum* seu *Maprounea Guianensis*, a shrub, native of Guiana. *Linn. Spec. Plant.*

ÆGOPROSO'PHRON (*Med.*) Ægidion.

ÆGYLOPS (*Bot.*) vide *Ægilops*.

ÆGY'PTIA (*Med.*) αἰγυπτία, an epithet for several medicines mentioned by Galen, Paulus Ægineta, and Mirepsus. *Gal. de Med. Com. sec. Gen.* l. 6, c. 8, &c.; *Paul. Æginet.* l. 7, c. 24; *Mirep. de Antidot.* sect. 1, c. 228, &c.—*Ægyptia stypteria*, αἰγυπτία στυπτηρία, Egyptian alum, recommended by Hippocrates. *Epidem.* l. 1, &c.—*Ægyptia ulcera*, Syrian Ulcers in the fauces. *Aret. de Acut. Morb.* l. 1, c. 9.

ÆGYPTIA *Moschata* (*Bot.*) the same as *Abelmoschus*.

ÆGYPTI'ACUM *Unguentum* (*Med.*) a detersive ointment.

ÆGYPTIACUM *Balsaman* (*Bot.*) vide *Balsamum*.

ÆGYPTI'LLA (*Nat.*) a precious stone; said to have the remarkable quality of giving water the colour and taste of wine. *Plin.* l. 37, c. 10.

ÆGY'PTIUM (*Med.*) Αἰγύπτιον, a topic in uterine disorders, of which there were four sorts, namely, αἰγύπτιον ἔλαιον, and αἰγύπτιον ἐλαιόλευκον, Egyptian oil of two sorts; αἰγύπτιον μύρον λευκόν, white Egyptian ointment; and the fourth, μύρον αἰγύπτιον, Egyptian ointment simply. *Hippocrat.* περὶ γυναικ. l. 2, &c.; *Dioscor.* l. 1, c. 62, &c.; *Gal. Comm. in Hippocrat.*; *Erotian Lex. Hippocrat.*; *Paul. Æginet.* l. 7, c. 20; *Gorr. Defin. Med.*; *Foes. Oeconom. Hippocrat.*—*Ægyptium pharmacum*, a detergent for the eyes.—*Ægyptium linum*, αἰγύπτιον λίνον, a kind of tow for the polypus in the nose, mentioned by Hippocrates. *Hippoc. de Morb.* l. 2; *Foes. Oeconom. Hippocrat.*

ÆICHRY'SON (*Bot.*) the same as *Sedum*.

ÆI'GLUCES (*Nat.*) αειγλυκὴς, from ἀεὶ, always, and γλυκὺς, sweet; a name for a sweet wine.

ÆI'THALES (*Bot.*) from ἀεὶ, always, and θάλλω, to be green; another name for the *Sedum*.

ÆI'ZOON (*Bot.*) from ἀεὶ, always, and ζωόω, to live; another name for the *Sedum*.

AE'L (*Gram.*) *al* or *eal*, like πᾶν in Greek, a Saxon particle, signifying *all*; is used in compound names, as *Ælpin*, i. e. all conqueror; *Ælbend*, all industrious, &c. to which the Greek names, Pammachius, Pancratus, &c. in some measure answer.

AEL, or *Ælf*, a Saxon particle, signifying *help*, otherwise written *ulf*, *wulf*, *hulf*, *hilf*, or *helf*, and used in compound names; as *Alewin*, victorious help; *Aelwold*, an auxiliary governor; *Aelgiva*, a giver of aid, &c.; to which Boetius, Symmachus, and Epicurus, bear an evident analogy.

Æ'LIA (*Ant.*) *Aelia lex*, a name given to certain laws; so called from the *Ælii*, by whom they were made. 1. A law made by Quintus Ælius Tubero, A. U. 55, for sending two colonies into the country of the Bruttii. *Liv.* l. 34, c. 53. 2. A law made by Q. Ælius Pætus, A. U. 586, ordaining, that, in public affairs, the Augurs, *de cælo servarent*, i. e. should observe the skies. *Cic. pro Sext.* c. 15, 53; *Post. Red. in Sen.* c. 5, &c. &c. 3. *Ælia Sexta lex*, a law made, A. U. 756, by Augustus, in the consulship of Ælius Sextus, respecting the manumission of slaves. *Suet. Aug.* c. 40; *Dio.* l. 65, in Aug.

AELU'ROPO (*Med.*) from αἴλυρος, a cat, and πῦς, a foot, i. e. a cat's foot; a syrup from the plant cat's-foot, or the *Gnathalium* of Linnæus.

AEM (*Com.*) *Am*, or *Awme*, a liquid measure in Germany, differing in size in different parts.

ÆMI'LIA *Lex* (*Ant.*) the name given to two laws enacted by the Æmilii, namely, one by Æmilius the dictator, U.C. 309, to limit the censorship to a year and a half, and a sumptuary law, in 675, by M. Æmilius Lepidus, or, according to Pliny, of M. Æmilius Scaurus, in 638. *Liv.* l. 4, c. 24, &c.; *Plin.* l. 8, c. 57; *Aurel. Vict. de Vir. illust.* c. 72; *Aul. Gel.* l. 2, c. 24; *Macrob. Saturn.* l. 2, c. 13; *August. de Leg. in Æmilia*; *Hotman. Antiq. Rom.*; *Pigh. Annal. Roman*; *Panvin Fastor. Rosin. Antiq. apud Roman. Græv. Thes. Antiq. Roman.* vol. viii, &c.

ÆNEATO'RES (*Ant.*) trumpeters; so called from Æneus.

ÆNITTOLO'GIUS *versus* (*Poet.*) a sort of verse having two dactyles and three trochees; as

Pretia dira placent truci juventæ.

Scal. Poet. p. 2, c. 24.

Æ'OLIAN *mode* (*Mus.*) Αἰολὶς ἁρμονία, one of the five principal modes of ancient music, the fundamental chord of which was immediately above that of the Phrygian. It derived its name from Æolia, not from the Æolian islands, and was of a grave character, according to Lasus, who is quoted by Athenæus. Pratinas, on the same authority, calls it the medium between the quick and the slow.

Μὴ σύντονον δίωκιμὴ τ' ἀνειμέναν
Ἰαστὶ μυσαν, ἀλλὰ τὰν μέσαν νέων
Ἄρουραν αἰολίζε τῷ μέλει.

Athen. Deipnos. l. 14, c. 5; *Apul. Platon. Florid.*; *Cæl. Rhodig.* l. 9, c. 3.

ÆO'LIC (*Gram.*) an epithet for what belongs to the Æolians, as—*Ælic dialect*, Αἰολὶς διάλεκτος, that mode of writing the Greek which was adopted by the writers of the Æolian nation, which most resembled the Doric. *Joann. Char. Technicon. Eustath.* περὶ διαλέκ.—*Æolic digamma*, a name given to the letter F, which the Æolians used to prefix to words beginning with vowels, as Ϝοινος, for οἶνος, and also to insert in the middle of words, between vowels, as οϜις, for οἶς.—*Æolic verse*, or *carmen æolicum*, a kind of measure, consisting, first, of an iambic or spondee, then of two anapests, divided by a syllable; and, lastly, a syllable common. It is otherwise called Archilochian and Pindaric, from the poets by whom it was used. *Prisc. de Met.* l. 1; *Terent. Maur. de Met.*; *Mar. Victor. Ars. Grammat.* l. 3; *Scalig. Poet.*

ÆOLO'PILE (*Ant.*) from αἰόλου πύλαι, i. e. Gates of the Wind; a device for remedying smoky chimneys. *Vitruv.* l. 1, c. 6.

ÆOLOPILE (*Hydraul.*) a hollow ball of metal, with a very small hole or opening, used to show the convertibility of water into steam.

ÆOLOPILE (*Pneumat.*) the above-mentioned instrument also serves to show the cause and production of the wind. *Descart.*

Æ'OLUS (*Mech.*) a machine invented by Mr. Tidd for ventilating rooms.

ÆQU

ÆOLUS *Harp.* (*Mus.*) or Æolian Harp; a musical instrument, producing melody by the wind.

Æ'ON (*Med.*) αἰών. 1. The natural age or life of man from his birth to his death. *Gal. Exeges. Hippocrat. Vocab.; Hesychius.* 2. The spinal marrow. *Erot. Lex Hippocrat.; Hesychius; Foes. Oeconom. Hippocrat.*

ÆONE'SIS (*Med.*) αἰόνησις; the moistening external parts by perfusion or fomentation. *Grot. Lex Hippocrat.; Foes. Oeconom. Hippocrat.*

Æ'ONION (*Bot.*) αἰόνιον; a Greek name for a sort of sedum. *Gorr. Def. Med.*

Æ'ORA (*Ant.*) αἰώρα; a festival in honour of Erigone. *Hygin. Fab.* 116; *Hesych. in Voc.* αἰώρα; *Voss. de Orig. & Progress. Idol.* l. 1, c. 13; *Meurs. Græc. Fer.* l. 1.

ÆORA (*Med.*) a species of exercise by gestation, as swinging, riding, &c. adapted for weak persons; so called from αἰωρέω, to lift up. *Cels.* l. 7, c. 26; *Erotian Lex Hippocrat.; Aet. Tetrab.* 1. serm. 3, c. 6; *Gorr. Def. Med.; Foes. Oeconom. Hippocrat.*

ÆQUA'BILIS (*Phy.*) equable; an epithet applied to motion, celerity, &c. [vide *Equable*]

Ex ÆQUA'LI, sc. *distantia* (*Math.*) or *ex æquo*, at equal distance: a term applied to any number of magnitudes more than two, and as many others, so that they are proportional when taken two and two of each rank, in such wise that the first is to the last of the first rank of magnitudes as the first is to the last of the second, &c.—*Ex Æquali, ex æqualitate*, or *ex æquo ratio*, διὰ ἴσου λόγος, is when the first magnitude is to the second of the first rank as the first to the second of the other rank; and as the second is to the third of the first rank, so is the second to the third of the other; and so on in order: whence this is called ordinate proportion: thus, suppose there be three magnitudes, *a, b, c*, and as many others, *d, e, f*, which taken two and two have the same ratio, that is, such that as *a* is to *b* so is *d* to *e*; and as *b* is to *c* so is *e* to *f*; then *a* shall be to *c* as *d* is to *f*.—*Ex Æquali, in proportione perturbata, seu inordinata*, i. e. from equality in perturbate or disorderly proportion, is when the first magnitude is to the second of the first rank as the last but one is to the last of the second rank, and so on; as, suppose there be four magnitudes, *a, b, c, d*, and other four, *e, f, g, h*, which taken two and two, in cross order, have the same ratio, that is, *a* to *b* as *g* to *h*; *b* to *c* as *f* to *g*; and *c* to *d* as *e* to *f*; then *a* will be to *d* as *e* to *h*. *Euclid. Def Elem.* l. 5.

ÆQUA'LIS (*Bot.*) equal; an epithet applied to the gills, anthodium, and filaments.—*Lamellæ æquales*, when all the gills reach from the stalk to the margin.—*Anthodium æquale*, when the leaves of the anthodium are all of equal length.—*Filamenta æqualia*, when the filaments are of equal length.

ÆQUALIS *Polygamia*, the name of the first order in the Class *Syngenesia*, of Linnæus, containing those compound flowers which have all the florets hermaphrodite and alike. It includes the following genera.—

The Genera of Æqualis Polygamia.

Scolymus, Golden Thistle
Cichorium, Succory
Catananche
Seriola
Hypochæris, Cat's-ear
Geropogon, Old Man's beard
Rothia
Andryala
Triptilion
Tragopodon, Goat's beard
Helmintia
Picris, Ox-tongue
Apargia
Scorzonera, Viper's-grass
Leontodon, Dandelion
Crepis, Hawk's-beard
Chondrilla, Gum Succory
Prenanthes
Lactuca, Lettuce
Heracium, Hawk's-weed
Sonchus, Sow-thistle
Lacintha
Lapsana, Nipple-wort
Rhagadiolus
Krigia
Hyoseris, Swine's Succory
Hedypnois, Hawkbit
Thrineia
Tolpis
Atractylis
Acarna
Serratula, Saw-wort
Carthamus, Bastard Saffron
Carlina, Carline Thistle
Aretium, Burdock
Pteronia
Stobæa
Lachnospermum
Barnadesia
Cynara, Artichoke
Johannia
Cnicus
Carduus, Thistle
Onoseris
Stokesia
Leatris
Vernonia
Onopordon, Cotton Thistle
Stehælina
Haynea
Calea, Halbert-weed
Bidens, Bur Marygold
Spilanthes
Athanasia
Santolina, Lavender-cotton
Cæsulia
Tarchonanthus, African Flea-bane
Kuhnia
Eupatorium, Hemp Agrimony
Chrysocoma, Goldilocks
Mikania
Kleinia
Cacalia
Lavenia
Ageratum
Stevia
Hymenopappus
Cephalophora
Pentzia
Ethulia
Piqueria
Balsamita

ÆQUALIS (*Math.*) vide *Equal*.

ÆQUALIS (*Med.*) consistent with itself, or always the same; as an *equal* pulse, that keeps the same tenor; an *equal* temperament, or constitution, that is, not subject to altercations or excesses.

ÆQUA'LITAS (*Math.*) vide *Equality*.

Æ'QUANS (*Math.*) a particular circle. [vide *Equant*]

ÆQUA'TIO (*Alg.*) vide *Equation*.

ÆQUA'TOR (*Astron.*) vide *Equator*.

ÆQUA'TUS (*Astron.*) vide *Equated*.

ÆQUIANGULA'TUS (*Math.*) vide *Equiangular*.

ÆQUI'DICI *versus* (*Poet.*) ἰσόλεκτοι; verses, different members of which have an opposite diction, as, *alba ligustra cadunt; vaccinia nigra leguntur.* *Virg. E.* 2, 18.

ÆQUILA'TERUS (*Math.*) vide *Equilateral*.

ÆQUILI'BRIUM (*Math.*) vide *Equilibrium*.

ÆQUIMU'LTIPLEX (*Math.*) vide *Equimultiple*.

ÆQUINOCTIA'LES (*Bot.*) equinoctial solar flowers; i. e. flowers so called by Linnæus, which open and usually shut at certain determinate hours of the day, observing, therefore, equal or European hours, as some species of the *Alyssum, Anagallis, Convolvulus, Hieracium, &c.*

ÆQUINOCTIALIS (*Math.*) vide *Equinoctial*.

ÆQUINOCTIALIS (*Ent.*) an epithet for a species of *Scarabæus*.

ÆQUINO'CTIUM (*Astron.*) vide *Equinox*.

ÆQUIPO'LLENS (*Math.*) vide *Equipollent*.

ÆQUIPOLLE'NTIA *nominum* (*Log.*) the equivalence in the sense of two propositions differing in certain syncatagoremata, as "Not every man is learned," or "Some man is not learned."

Æ'QUITAS (*Numis.*) Equity, according to Cicero, is threefold, as regards *superos*, the gods above, which is *piety*; the *manes*, or gods below, which is *sanctity*; and as regards men, which is *justice*. Equity is mostly represented on medals under the figure of a female, as in fig. 1, holding a pair of scales in her right hand, and a lance or cornucopia

Fig. 1.   *Fig.* 2.

in the left; sometimes as in fig. 2, under the triple figure of goddess Moneta, holding the scales in the right and a cornucopia in the left, as on the medals of *Galba, Vitellius, Vespasianus, Titus, Domitianus, Nerva, Adrian, Antoninus, Pertinax, Severus, Julia Pia, Geta, Macrinus, Elagabulus, Julia Soemias, Alexander Severus, Julia Mamæa, Maximilian, Gordianus Pius, Philippus* (Sen. and Jun.), *Decentius, Gallienus, Salonina, Lic Valerianus, Claudius Gothicus, Tacitus, Florianus, Probus Carinus,* and *Allectus,* bearing the inscriptions—AEQUITAS and AEQUITAS AUG*usti.*—AEQUITAS AUGG. *Augustorum.*—AEQUITAS AUGUST*i.*—AEQUITAS AUG*usti* COS. *Consulis, &c.*—AEQUITAS AUGusti *Nostri.*— AEQUITAS AUGUSTI TR*ibunitiâ Potestate, &c.*—AEQUITAS PUBLICA.—AEQUITATI AUGG. *Augustorum.*—AEQUITATI PUBLICAE. *Vaillant. Numis. Imp. Roman.; Mediobarb. Oxon. Numis.*

ÆQUIVALENTIA *nominum* (*Log.*) the same as *Æquipollentia.*

ÆQUIVALENTIA (*Phy.*) equivalence is three-fold—*Æquivalentia moralis,* when one thing is of equal value with another in the estimation of men; as he by whose contrivance another is killed is equivalent to the murderer.—*Æquivalentia physica,* when a physical body contains within itself those perfections conjointly which are found separate in other bodies; as when a man contains the strength of two, he is equivalent to two men in matters of strength.—*Æquivalentia statica,* when a less weight is equal or equivalent to a greater, by reason of distance or some other circumstance.

ÆQUI'VOCA *æquivocata* (*Log.*) equivocation, or things equivocal in their name, which may be so either *casu,* i. e. an accidental equivocation, as *taurus,* which signifies either an animal or a sign in the heavens; or *consilio,* an intentional equivocation, as *acute,* which is applicable either to instruments or pains; such terms are otherwise called analogous.

ÆQUIVOCA *æquivocantia* (*Log.*) the same as *vox æquivoca*; an equivocal term.

ÆQUI'VOCUS (*Log.*) *quod una vox plurimis rebus ex æquo serviat,* ὁμώνυμος, equivocal; an epithet applied to the *vox,* or word, when it admits of a double signification, as *Gallus,* which is the name either for a cock or a Frenchman.

ÆQUIVOCUS (*Nat.*) equivocal; an epithet applied to a supposed mode of generation of plants and animals, from the combination of solids and fluids.

Ex ÆQUO (*Math.*) vide *Ex Æquali.*

ÆR (*Nat.*) vide Air.

A'ER (*Med.*) air is defined by Hippocrates to be the circumambient breath, which is the author of every thing that happens to the bodies of men, either good or evil. *Hippocrat.* περὶ φυσῶν. *Erotian. Lex Hippocrat.; Foes. Oeconom. Hippocrat.*

Æ'RA (*Ant.*) the plural of *æs,* money; was used in accounts for our vulgar word *item.*—*Æra militaria,* or *æs militare*; military pay, or the money assigned to the *Tribuni Ærarii,* out of the treasury, for the pay of the army, according to the inscription AERA. STIPENDIAQUE; and another MIL*es* AER*um* XII. i. e. *stipendiorum duodenûm. Varr. de Lat. Ling.* l. 4; *Liv.* l. 5, c. 10; *Gruter. Thes. Inscript. Vet.* p. 508, &c.—*Æra auxiliaria,* brazen vessels, by the noise of which, as by a sort of charm, the ancients thought to prevent an eclipse of the moon.

Ovid. Met. l. 4, v. 333.

Cum frustra resonant æra auxiliaria lunæ.

Rhodig. Antiq. Lect. l. 19, c. 10; *Turneb. Adv.* l. 22, c. 24.

ÆRA (*Chron.*) the name of any date, period, or event, from which a calculation of years is made to commence. It is now substituted in chronology for the word *epocha,* which was in use among the Greeks. [vide *Epocha*] The term was first employed on the occasion of a tribute imposed by the emperor Augustus on the Spaniards, and is, on that account, supposed to have been formed from the initials A. E. R. A. i. e. *annus erat regni Augusti*; others derive it from *æra*; the plural of *æs,* signifying coin stamped with particular dates; also the items in an account. Since its introduction it has been applied to any important period from which a reckoning has commenced, of which the following are the principal—*Æra of the creation,* computed by Usher to have happened 4004 B. C. and 710 of the Julian period; chronologers, however, differ in their accounts of this æra.—*Æra of the Olympiads* began from the new moon in the summer solstice Jul. Per. 3938, A. M. 3228, B. C. 776.—*Roman Æra* is dated from the foundation of the city, in the 7th Olympiad, xii. Kal. Mai, i. e. April 21. Jul. Per. 3966, A. M. 3256, B. C. 748.—*Æra of Nabonasser* is dated from Jul. Per. 3967, Feb. 26, A. M. 3257, B. C. 747.—*Æra Phillipic,* or the year of Alexander's death, commenced Jul. Per. 4390, A. M. 3680, B. C. 324. —*Æra of the Seleucidæ,* or *Æra of the Kingdom of the Greeks,* called by the Jews the *Æra of Contracts,* because they were obliged to use this æra in all their civil contracts, commenced Jul. Per. 4403, A. M. 3693, B. C. 311. —*Spanish Æra* was dated from the publication of the edicts at Rome, for imposing the tax before mentioned. Jul. Per. 4677, A. M. 3947, B. C. 39.—*Æra Actian* is dated from the conquest of Egypt by Augustus, i. e. in the 187th Olympiad, U. C. 724, Jul. Per. 4684, A. M. 3974, B. C. 30.—*Christian Æra* is dated from the birth of our Saviour, respecting the true time of which authors have differed variously: some place it two, some four, and some five, or more years before the vulgar æra, which is computed at the year of the world 4004 by Usher, and most modern chronologers after him, who suppose the birth of Christ to have happened in the year of the world 4000, and of the Julian period 4714.—*Æra of Diocletian* is dated from the first year of Diocletian. Jul. Per. 4997, A. M. 4267, A. D. 284.—*Æra of Martyrs,* the same as that of Diocletian, so called on account of the persecution of the Christians, which happened in his reign.—*Æra,* Turkish or Arabian, or the æra of the Hegira, is dated from the flight of Mahomed, which is said to have happened A. D. 610. *Ruf. Fest. Brev.; Julian. Toletan. Episcop. contra Jud.* l. 3; *Papias. in Voc. Æra; Luitprand. in Legat.; Scalig. de Emendat. Tempor.* l. 5; *Vas. Chron. Hispan.* c. 22; *Baron. Not. in Martyrol.* 22 Octob.; *Petav. de Doctrin. Temp.* l. 10, c. 68, &c.; *Ricciol. Chronol. &c.*

ÆRA (*Bot.*) αἶρα, the Greek name for cockle or darnel.

ÆRA'RII *præfectus* (*Ant.*) the officer who had charge of the exchequer, the treasurer of the exchequer. This charge was given first to the quæstors, afterwards to the prætors.— *Ærarii Quæstores,* the quæstors so called because they had charge of the treasury or exchequer.—*Ærarii Prætores,* the prætors so called because they were also treasurers of the exchequer.—*Ærarii Fusores,* coiners of the æs, or money, at the mint; likewise all workmen in brass or copper. *Tacit. Annal.* l. 13, c. 28; *Hist.* l. 4, c. 9; *Sueton.; Aug.* c. 36; *Dio.* l. 33; *Alex. Gen. Dier.* l. 2, c. 2; *Laz. Comm. Reip. Rom.* l. 2, c. 14; *Pancirol. de Corp. Artific.* § 17.

ÆRA'RIUM (*Ant.*) the treasury, a public place so called because there the citizens deposited the æra, or copper money, before the gold and silver were coined.—*Ærarium Saturni,* at the bottom of the Capitoline hill, was so called because it was the temple of Saturn employed as the treasury; whence the ancient inscription given by Gruterus, VIII. VIR. III. AERARI SATURNI, i. e. "octumvir tertium, Ærarii Saturni." *Aurel. Vict. de Orig. Gen. Rom.* c. 3; *Fabric. Descript. Urb. Rom.; Grut. Thes. Inscript. Vet.*—*Ærarium sanctius,* contained the tribute money, and other moneys destined for particular purposes.

as also the public accounts; it was so called because it was situated in the interior of the temple, where it was more retired and secure. *Cic. ad Attic.* l. 7, c. 21; *Cæs. de Bello, Civ.* l. 1, c. 14; *Plin.* l. 33, c. 3; *Appian. de Civ. Bell.* l. 2; *Flor. Epit.* l. 4, c. 2; *Oros.* l. 6, c. 15.—*Ærarium privatum* contained the emperor's privy purse.—*Ærarium Ilithyæ*, or *Junonis Lucinæ*, so called because it received the moneys paid on the birth of a child. *Dionys.* l. 4; *P. C.*—*Ærarium militare*, a military chest, or a particular treasury in which the money was kept that was destined for the pay of the soldiers, according to an inscription, PRÆF. MILIT. AERARI. *Tacit. Annal.* l. 1, c. 78; *Suet. in Aug.* c. 49; *Dio.* l. 55; *Grut. Thes. Inscript. Vet.*—*Ærarium vicesimarum*, the treasury which contained the money raised by way of tribute from foreign countries, which was so called because they paid the twentieth of inheritances, &c.—*Ærarium imperatorum*, the same as the *fiscus imperatoris*; the exchequer. *Blond. Triumph. Rom.*; *Bud. in Pandect.*; *Calcagni de Verb. Signif.*; *Alex. ab Alex. Gen. Dier.*; *Gyrald. Synt. Deor.*; *Laz. Comm. Reip. Rom.*; *Marlian. Top. Urb. Rom.*; *Panv. Descript. Urb. Rom.*; *Fabric. Descript. Urb. Rom.*; *Hotman. Ant. Rom.*; *Manut. in Cic. ad Attic.*; *Camerar. de Re Numm.*; *Pancirol. Descript. Urb. Rom.*; *Demster. Paral. ad Rosin. Antiq.*; *Buleng. de Imp. Rom.*; *Donat. de Urb.*; *Sperling. de Numm. non cus.*; *Ursin. in Marlianum*; *Kipping. Antiq. Rom.*; *Ois. in Gell.*; *Franckens de Ærar.*; *Ursat. de Not. Rom.*; *Gothofr. Burman de Vectig. Dissert. apud Græv. Thes. Antiq. Roman.* vol. i. ii. iii. &c.

ÆRARIUS (*Ant.*) 1. A citizen of the lowest class, who paid few or no taxes, and had no votes. He was so called because *Æra tributi loco pendebat*; wherefore in *Ærarios referre* signified to degrade a citizen, which the Censors used to do in cases of immorality. Thus senators were expelled from the senate, and knights deprived of their horses, by which they were reduced to the condition of *Ærarii*, or the meanest citizens. *Ascon. in Cic. Div.* l. 2, c. 66; *Liv.* l. 24, c. 18; *Sigon. de Antiq. Jur. Rom.* l. 1, c. 17; *Manut. in Cic. Or.*; *Gronov. de Pecunia.* 2. An officer appointed by the emperor Severus to distribute the bounty of the prince from the treasury or exchequer. *Lamprid. in Sever.*; *Pancirol. Notit. Dignit. Imp. Orient.* c. 79. 3. The last on the list of candidates who offered to contend in the public games. *Panvin. de Lud. Circens.* l. 1, c. 14; *Laz. Comm. Reip. Rom.* l. 10, c. 5.

ÆRARIUS, an epithet for what belongs to, or is connected with, the treasury or exchequer.—*Ærarius Tribunus*, a paymaster to the army, so called *a tribuendo ære*. *Cic. Planc.* c. 8; *Varro de Lat. Ling.* l. 5; *Plin.* l. 34, c. 1; *Ascon. ad Cic. in Verr.* 3; *Fest. de Signif. Verb.*; *Grut. Thes. Inscript. Vet.*—*Ærarius miles*, a mercenary soldier, or one who received pay. *Varro de Lat. Ling.* l. 4; *Plin.* l. 34, c. 1; *Grut. Thes. Inscript. Vet.*

ÆRATED (*Chem.*) an epithet for water having brass in it.

ÆRDA'DI (*Alchem.*) spirits supposed by Paracelsus to inhabit the air. *Parac. de Vit.*

ÆRE *diruti milites* (*Ant.*) soldiers whose pay, *æs*, was, *dirutus*, stopped or taken from them for some misdemeanor. *Varro. apud Non.* l. 12, c. 53; *Fest. de Verb. Signif.*

ÆRE'OLUM (*Ant.*) the thirty-sixth part of a dram.

AE'RIAL *acid* (*Chem.*) the same as *Carbonic acid*.

AERIAL *perspective* (*Per.*) that which represents bodies diminished and weakened in proportion to their distance from the eye.

AE'RIANS (*Ecc.*) Αιριανοι, *aeriani*, a sect of heretics in the fourth century, called after their leader Aerius, who maintained, among other things, that there was no difference between priests and bishops. *Epiphan. Hæres.* l. 3, c. 75; *August. Her.* 53; *Inuph-Chron. Ann.* 349.

AE'RIE (*Falc.*) or *Airy*, from the German *ey*, an egg; a receptacle for eggs, a hawk's nest. "*Unusquisque liber homo habeat in boscis oerias accipitrum.*" *Fleta.*

AERIFICA'TIO (*Chem.*) the producing air from other bodies, or rather converting them into air.

AE'RIS *flos* (*Med.*) χαλκȣ ἄνθος, *flowers of copper*, or copper reduced to small grains, when in a state of fusion. *Dioscor.* l. 5, c. 88; *Oribas. Synop.* l. 2, c. 6; *Med. Collect.* l. 13; *Aet. Tetrab.* l. serm. 2, c. 81; *Paul. Æginet. de Re Med.* l. 7, c. 3, *apud Med. Art. Princip.*—*Aeris squamæ*, χαλκȣ λεπτίς, flakes of copper, which fly off by hammering the metal when heated. *Dioscor.* l. 5, c. 89; *Oribas. Med. Collect.* l. 13; *Aet. Tetrab.* 1, serm. 2, c. 59, *apud Med. Art. Princip.*

AERI'TIS (*Bot.*) another name for *Anagallis*.

AE'ROGRAPHY (*Nat.*) from ἀηρ, air, and γράφω, to describe; a description of the air and its properties.

AE'ROLITHS (*Nat.*) or *Ærolites*, from ἀηρ, air, and λίθος, a stone; air stones, or meteoric stones, falling from the atmosphere.

AERO'LOGY (*Med.*) from ἀηρ, air, and λόγος, doctrine; the study of the air, as connected with the animal economy.

AE'ROMANCY (*Ant.*) ἀερομαντεία, aeromancy; a mode of divination from certain spectres and appearances in the air. They sometimes wrapped their head in a cloth, and having placed a bowl full of water in the open air, proposed their question in a whisper; at which time, if the water boiled or bubbled, they supposed what they said was approved. [vide *Hydromancy*]

AE'ROMETRY (*Nat.*) *Aerometria*, the art of measuring the air, so as to ascertain its pressure or weight, its elasticity, rarefaction, &c. *Wolf. Math. cur.*

A'ERONAUT (*Nat.*) one who sails or floats in the air in a balloon.

AEROPHO'BIA (*Med.*) from ἀηρ, air. and φοβέω, to fear; a species of frensy with which some that are affected are afraid of a lucid air, and others of that which is obscure. *Cæl. Aurelian. de Acut. Morb.* l. 3, c. 12.

AEROPHYLA'CEA (*Nat.*) a name employed by Kircher for caverns or reservoirs of air supposed to exist in the bowels of the earth.

AEROSCO'PIA (*Pneu.*) ἀεροσκοπία, from ἀηρ, air, and σκοπέω, to observe; aeroscopy, or observations on the air.

AERO'SIS (*Med.*) an imaginary resolution of the blood into vapour, brought about by ventilation.

AEROSTA'TICA (*Nat.*) from ἀηρ, air, and στατική, the doctrine of weights; the science of weights suspended in the air.

AEROSTA'TION (*Nat.*) from ἀηρ, air, and στατική, the doctrine of weights: i. e. the modern art of navigating the air in air balloons or aerostatic machines.

AE'ROSTATS (*Nat.*) or *Aerostatic machines*; another name for air balloons.

ÆRO'SUS *lapis* (*Min.*) cadmia.

ÆRUGINO'SUS (*Med.*) ἰώδης, from *ærugo*, verdigrease; æruginous, or verdigrease colour, as the bile discharged from the stomach. *Ruff. Ephes.* l. 1, c. 36.

ÆRUGINOSUS (*Orn.*) an epithet for a species of *falco*.

ÆRUGO (*Met.*) ἰος, from *æris rubigo*, verdigrease, or the rust of any metal, particularly copper. *Oribas. Synop.* l. 2, c. 61; *Aet. Tetrab.* 1, serm. 2, c. 56.—*Ærugo rasa*, or *rasilis*, ἰος ξυστὸς, rust scraped from a copper plate hung over the strongest vinegar. *Dioscor.* l. 5, c. 92; *Aet. Tetrab.* serm. 2, c. 55.

ÆRUSCATO'RES (*Ant.*) beggars, or vagabonds, who went about collecting *æs*, money, by various arts.

ÆS (*Ant.*) χαλκος, brass or copper, a durable and sonorous metal; so called from *aër*, the air, without which it will not emit sound, or more probably from αἴθω, to shine. Its use was first discovered by the Telchines, who were expert artists in Crete. *Cassiod.; Var.* l. 3, c. 31; *Gyrald. Synt. Deor.* i. p. 24; *Jun. Catal. Archit.* p. 101; *Rhodig. Ant. Lex.* l. 19, c. 10; *Turneb. Ant. Adv.* l. 6, c. 10; *Pancirol. Notit. Dignit. Imp. Orient.* c. 137.—*Æs alienum*, money that is borrowed, or that which is not our own, but is owing to others. *Senec. de Benef.* l. 5, c. 14; *Ulpian. de Verb. Signif.* i. 219.—*Æs caldarium*, copper, of which cauldrons were made; it is both malleable and fusible. *Plin.* l. 34, c. 8; *Salmas. Exerc. Plin.* p. 758.—*Æs candidum*, white brass, a vein of which is found under a vein of silver. *Savot. de Numm. Ant.* l. 12, c. 16.—*Æs circumforaneum*, money taken in the haymarket. *Cic. ad Attic.* l. 2, ep. 1.—*Æs confessum*, a debt that is owned. *Cic. de Orat.* l. 2, c. 63; *Aul. Gell.* l. 15, c. 13; l. 20, c. 1.—*Æs Corinthium* was made from three metals, gold, silver, and copper; and, according to Pliny, it received its name from the taking and burning of Corinth, U.C. 608, by Mummius, when the gold and silver and copper from the statues mixed together. *Cic. Tusc. Quæst.* l. 4, c. 32; *Plin.* l. 34, c. 2.—*Æs coronarium*, a ductile sort of brass, of which crowns were made for actors. *Plin.* l. 33, c. 9.—*Æs corybantium*, is so called because the priests of Cybele used it for the sacred timbrels.—*Æs curionum*, money so called because it was given to the Curio for the discharge of his office.—*Æs cyprium*, copper; a ductile kind of brass first found in Cyprus, from which it took its name. It was made from an ore, called Cadmia, and answers to what is now called Pinchbeck. *Isidor.* l. 16, c. 19.—*Æs dodonæum*, so called because the sacred cauldrons of Apollo were made of it. *Erasm. Adag.* p. 276. —*Æs factum*, factitious brass used in vases.—*Æs flavum*, so called from its colour. It is drawn from a mineral, which the Latins call *cadmia*, and the Gauls *calamin*.— *Æs grave*, so called from its weight which was fixed by law. *Liv.* l. 4, c. 60.—*Æs hæreditarium*, so called from the law of the twelve tables, which obliges heirs to divide a portion among the creditors. *August. in Leg.* xii.—*Æs hepatizon*, so called because it approaches to the colour of the liver, now called Bronze.—*Æs hordearium*, public money; so called because it was given in payment for the food of the horses.—*Æs Indicum*, a kind of brass, so bright, pure, and void of rust, that it was not distinguishable by the colour from gold.—*Æs infectum*, unwrought brass.—*Æs manuarium*, money collected from different quarters. *Aul. Gell.* l. 18, c. 13.—*Æs militare*, the money set apart for the pay of the soldiers. *Varro. de Lat. Ling.* l. 4; *Tacit. Annal.* l. 1, c. 78; *Dio.* l. 55, p. 565.—*Æs ollarium*, called *patin* by the Gauls, a kind of brass which could not be gilded, on account of the lead which was mixed with it. *Plin.* l. 34, c. 9.—*Æs Persicum*, vide *Æs Indicum*.—*Æs pyropum*, brass which, in its brightness, resembled fire. *Diodor.* l. 1; *Plin.* l. 34, c. 8.—*Æs regulare*, brass that is both fusible and malleable. *Plin.* l. 34, c. 8.—*Æs resignatum*, a soldier's pay, of which he was mulcted for any misdemeanour. *Fest. de Signif. Verb.*—*Æs rude*, unwrought brass, or bullion.—*Æs Saturnium*, coin kept in *ærarium Saturni*, the treasury of Saturn. —*Æs signatum*, brass that is coined. *Plin.* l. 33, c. 3.—*Æs uxorium*, money paid as a tax by those who remained unmarried.—*Per Æs et libram*, a formula among the Romans of ratifying their purchases and sales. *Fest. de Signif. Verb.*; *Isidor. Orig.*; *Rhodig. Ant. Lect.*; *Aug. in Leg.* xii. tab.; *Stuch. de Sacrif.*; *Erasm. Adag.*; *Phil. Bochart. Hieroz.*; *Fabric. Descript. Urb. Rom.*; *Salmas. Exercit. Plin.*; *Gronov. de Pecun. Vet.*; *Savot. de Re Numm.*; *Græv. Thes. Antiq. Roman.* tom. 2, &c.

Æs ustum (*Met.*) χαλχὸς καυκωμένος, burnt brass, is made of red copper, cut into plates, and put into a crucible, with sulphur, and a little common salt, *stratum super stratum*, and set over a fierce charcoal fire. *Dioscor.* l. 5, c. 87; *Oribas.* l. 13; *Paul. Æginet de Re Med.* l. 7, c. 3.

Æ'SCHYNES (*Ecc.*) the name of three sects of heretics that sprang from the Montanists, who, among other strange notions, affirmed Christ to be both father and son. *Epiphan. Hæres.*

ÆSCHYNO'MENE (*Bot.*) from αἰσχύνομαι, to be ashamed; an epithet for a plant vulgarly called the "Sensitive Plant," on account of its property of retreating from the touch.

ÆSCHYNOMENE, *in the Linnæan System*, a genus of plants, Class 17 *Diadelphia*, Order 4 *Decandria*.

Generic Characters. CAL. *perianth* one-leaved.—COR. papilionaceous; *banner* subcordate; *wings* subovate; *keel* lunate.—STAM. *filaments* ten; *anthers* small.—PIST. *germ* oblong; *style* subulate; *stigmas* simple. PER. *legume* long; *seeds* solitary.

Species. The species are shrubs and annuals, the principal of which are the—*Æschynomene grandiflora*, Great-flowered Æschynomene, a shrub, native of the East Indies.—*Æschynomene coccinea*, Scarlet-flowered Æschynomene, a shrub.—*Æschynomene aspera*, seu *Mimosa*, Rough-stalked Æschynomene, an annual, native of the East Indies.—*Æschynomene Americana*, seu *Hedysarum*, Hairy Æschynomene, an annual, native of Jamaica.—*Æschynomene pumila*, *Hedysarum*, seu *Malam-Toddavaddi*, &c. Dwarf Æschynomene, an annual, native of India.—*Æschynomene sensitiva*, seu *Hedysarum arborescens*, a shrub, native of Jamaica, &c. *Raii Hist. Plant.*; *Plum. Plant. Amer.*; *Linn. Spec. Plant.*

ÆSCHYNO'MENOUS (*Bot.*) from αἰσχύνομαι, to be bashful; sensitive, an epithet for such plants as move upon being touched.

Æ'SCULUS (*Bot.*) from *esca*, food, because it was first used for food; a kind of glandiferous tree, which, according to Virgil, was sacred to Jupiter.

Georg. l. 2, v. 16.
— *nemorumque Jovi quæ maxima frondet,*
Æsculus atque habitæ Graiis oracula quercus.

It is supposed to answer to the αἰγίλωψ of Theophrastus. *Hist. Plant.* l. 3, c. 9.

ÆSCULUS, *in the Linnean system*, a genus of plants, Class 7 *Heptandria*, Order 1 *Monogynia*. It is called by Tournefort *Hippocastanum*.

Generic Characters. CAL. *perianth* one-leaved.—COR. *petals* five.—STAM. *filaments* subulate; *anthers* ascending.—PIST. *germ* roundish; *style* subulate; *stigma* acuminate.—PER. *capsule* leathery; *seeds* two.

Species. The principal species are the—*Æsculus Hippocastanum*, Common Horse-chesnut, a tree, native of Asia.—*Æsculus flava*, Yellow-flowered Horse-chesnut, a tree, native of North Carolina.—*Æsculus pavia*, Scarlet Horse-chesnut, a tree, native of Carolina.—*Æsculus variegata*, a tree, native of South Carolina.—*Æsculus parviflora*, a tree. *Ger. Herb.*; *Park. Theat. Botan.*; *Raii Hist. Plant.*; *Pluk. Almag. Botan.*

ÆS'HNA (*Ent.*) a division of the genus *Libellula*, comprehending those insects which, according to Fabricius, have the portions of the lip equal.

ÆSTA'TES (*Med.*) from *æstas*, summer; freckles in the skin.

ÆSTIMA'TIO (*Ant.*) an estimate of damages.

ÆSTIMATIO *Capitis* (*Archæol.*) an estimate of the head, or a valuation of a person's estate and rank, according to which, on the commission of any crimes towards those persons, King Athelstane ordained certain fines to be paid. The fine for any offence towards the king was 30,000 thrymsas.

Æ'STIVA (*Ant.*) *æstiva loca* vel *castra æstiva*. 1. Summer encampments for the soldiers, in distinction from the hibernia or winter quarters. *Tac. Annal.* l. 1, c. 31. 2. Shady places for the cattle. *Serv. in Virg. Georg.* l. 2; *Lact. in Stat. Theb.* l. 1.

H

ÆSTIVA'LIA (*Archæol.*) a species of greaves or buskins worn in summer.

ÆSTIVA'LIS (*Astron.*) from *Æstas*, summer; Æstival, an epithet for the summer solstice.

ÆSTIVA'LIS (*Bot.*) or *æstivus*, an epithet for flowers that blossom in the summer, i. e. summer flowers.

ÆSTIVA'TIO (*Bot.*) estivation, the time when flowers arrive at their perfection, or, as Martin defines it, the disposition of the petals within the floral gem or bud, of which Linnæus speaks more at large under the head of the sleep of plants. [vide *Somnus*]

ÆSTPHA'RA (*Med.*) incineratio.

ÆSTUA'RIUM (*Med.*) estuary.

ÆSTUA'TIO (*Chem.*) the fermenting of liquor when mixed.

Æ'STUS *marinus* (*Phy.*) seu *reciprocatio maris*, the tide, or flux and reflux, which is triple according to the difference in the times.—*Æstus diurnus*, what happens within the space of twenty-four hours.—*Æstus menstruus*, what happens twice in the month at new and full moon.—*Æstus annuus*, what happens twice in the year at the equinoxes.

ÆSYMNE'TÆ (*Ant.*) αἰσυμνῆται, a name for rulers whose authority equalled that of kings, to which the dignity of dictator, among the Romans, is supposed to have owed its origin. *Aristot. Polit.* l. 3, c. 15; *Hesychius*; *Alexand. ab Alexand.* l. 4, c. 13.

Æ'TAS *Mundi* (*My.*) the poets divide the age of the world into four periods according to the manners of the age.— *Ætas aurea*, the golden age in the reign of Saturn, when men lived in innocence and simplicity. *Ovid. Met.* l. 1, v. 89.

Aurea prima sata est ætas quæ, vindice nullo
Sponte suâ, sine lege, fidem rectumque colebat.

Ætas argentea, the silver age at the beginning of Jupiter's reign, when they showed propensities to evil. *Ovid. Met.* l. 1, v. 114.

Sub Jove mundus erat: subiit argentea proles
Auro deterior, fulvo pretiosior are.

Ætas ærea, the brazen age followed soon after, when they commenced war and rapine. *Ovid. Met.* l. 1, v. 126.

Sævior ingeniis, et ad horrida promptior arma.

Ætas ferrea, the iron age, when vice became prevalent. *Ovid. Met.* l. 1, v. 127.

Nec scelerata tamen. De duro est ultima ferro
Protinus irrumpit venæ pejoris in ævum
Omne nefas.

Ætas hominis (*Ant.*) *dimensio vitæ*, according to Scaliger, i. e. properly human life, or that space of life on which the frame of the body begins to undergo a notable change, as—*Ætas augmenti*, αὔξησις, while it is increasing after the birth.—*Ætas consistentiæ*, ἀκμή, the middle state, while it is neither increasing nor decreasing.—*Ætas decrementi*, μαράνσεως, while it is on the decline.

Ætas, human life was likewise divided into the following stages; namely—*Ætas infans*, *quod adhuc fari nescit*, the time from the birth to the seventh year.—*Ætas pueritiæ*, *a puritate*, from the seventh to the fourteenth year.—*Ætas adolescentiæ*, *quod sit ad gignendum adductus*, from the age of puberty to the twenty-eighth year.—*Ætas Juventutis quod juvare posse incipiat*, from the prime of life to the age of fifty.—*Ætas Senectutis*, *a sensus diminutione*, old age to the end of life. *Aristot. de Vit. et Mort.*; *Isid. Orig.* l. 11, c. 2.

Ætas, the age, or period of life, was also distinguished among the Romans according to their offices, as— *Ætas Ædilitia*, the age to be elected to the ædileship is supposed to have been not before thirty-seven, although the time is not precisely fixed by any law.—*Ætas consularis*, the age for the consulship was forty-three.—

Ætas urbani magistratus, the age for a civic magistrate was twenty-seven. *Polyb.* l. 6, c. 17.—*Ætas judicum*, the age for being appointed judges was not to be under thirty nor above sixty by the law of Augustus *Sueton. in August* c. 32.—*Ætas Prætoria*, the age for the prætorship was forty, for it preceded the consulship by two years, and followed the ædileship after an interval of two years. *Cic. ad Fam.* l. 10, ep. 25.—*Ætas militaris*, the age to be enlisted was seventeen, to be discharged forty-five. *Polyb.* l. 4, c. 17; *Dionys.* l. 4, p. 221; *Aul. Gell.* l. 10, c. 28.—*Ætas Quæstoria*, &c. the age for serving the office of quæstor, tribune, &c. is supposed to have been twenty-seven, or at least not earlier. *Vel. Pater.* l. 2, c. 94; *Tac. Annal.* l. 3, c. 29; *Sueton. in Cal.* c. 1; *Dio.* l. 53; *Spartian. in Did. Julian.* c. 1.— *Ætas Senatoria*, the age for admission into the senate is not defined by ancient writers, but is supposed to have succeeded the quæstorship. *Gruch. de Comit.*; *Manut. de Leg. Roman.*; *Sigon. de Antiq. Jur. Civ. Roman.*; *Alex. Gen. Dier.*; *August. de Leg. in Vill. Annal.*; *Hotman. de Rit. Nupt.*; *Lips. de Magistrat. Rom.*; *Demster. Paralip. ad Ant Ros.*; *Græv. Thes. Ant. Rom.* tom. 1, &c.

ÆTAS *mundi* (*Chron.*) vide *Age*.

ÆTA'TE *probanda* (*Law*) a writ of inquiry, whether the heir of a tenant that held of the king in chief by chivalry be of full age. *Reg. Orig.* 294.

ÆTE'RNA (*Num.*) vide *Æternitas*.

ÆTERNA'LES (*Ecc.*) a sect of heretics that maintained the eternity of the world *a parte post*, i e. that after the resurrection it should continue the same as it now is.

ÆTE'RNITAS (*My.*) Eternity was worshipped as a god by the ancients, of which the Pythagoreans, Plato and Hermes Trismegistus made time to be the image. *Gyrald. Synt. Deor.* l. 1, p. 59.

ÆTERNITAS (*Numis.*) Eternity was represented in various forms on medals, sometimes under the figure of the sun and moon for their durability; sometimes by the elephant for its length of years, as on a medal of Faustina, *fig.* 1,

Fig. 1. Fig. 2. Fig. 3.

where a chariot is drawn by two elephants; sometimes by a phœnix and a globe, the one for its long life, and the other for its supposed eternity, as on a medal of Faustina, where a female figure is holding a phœnix and a globe, *fig.* 2. There were besides several other representations, as of a serpent winding itself round a globe, or with its tail brought down to its mouth, or of a figure veiled to imply that eternity is inscrutable, or of a head with two faces, implying that it can see backwards and forwards. On a medal of Faustina, *fig.* 3, eternity is represented as carrying this empress to heaven, and holding a lighted flambeau in her hand. The medals of the emperors representing eternity refer most commonly to the perpetuity of the government in their own family. The emperors, whose medals had the figure of eternity, were *Augustus*, *Vespasian*, *Titus*, *Domitian*, *Severus*, *Caracalla*, *Geta*, *Alexander Severus*, *Gordianus Philippus*, *Gallienus*, *Claudius Gotthicus*, *Quintilian*, and *Maximian*. The inscriptions on the medals were as follow:

AETERNITAS.—AETERNITAS. AUG. or AUGG.— AETERNITAS. FLAVIORUM. — AETERNITAS. IMP. or IMPERII.—AETERNITATI AUGUSTI

AUGUS. or AUGG. — AETERNITATIBUS. — AETERNIT. AUG. and AUGG &c.—AETERNIT. IMP. and IMPERIT. &c.—AFTER. AUG. P. M. &c. —AET. AUG. COS. &c.—AETERNA. FELICITAS. MEMORIA, &c.—AETERNI. IMPERII.

ÆTHER (*My.*) *αίθη*, that subtle part of the air which was taken by the heathens for Jupiter, and which, being easily inflammable, is the fittest for producing the thunder and lightning ascribed to him; whence the word was supposed to come from *αίθω*, to burn.

ÆTHER (*Nat.*) Ether was supposed by Aristotle to come from *άπὸ τȣ̃ αίπι θεῖν*, i. e. always running, because of its constantly fluctuating nature. The word is taken to signify, 1. The firmament which is above the region of the air. 2. A subtle fluid supposed to be the cause of gravitation, and other phenomena otherwise inexplicable. *Aristot. de Mund.* c. 2.

ÆTHER (*Chem.*) a very light volatile inflammable liquor distilled from a mixture of Alcohol and acid in equal proportions.

ÆTHE'REA (*Bot.*) a herb mentioned by Cælius Aurelianus; the *Eryngium* of Linnæus.

ÆTHE'REAL *matter* (*Nat.*) the same as Æther.

ÆTHEREAL *world* (*Nat.*) all that space above the upper element; viz fire, which the ancients imagined to be perfectly homogeneous, incorruptible, and unchangeable.

ÆTHEREAL *oil* (*Chem.*) an animal or vegetable oil highly rectified.

ÆTHE'REUS *spiritus* (*Chem.*) an epithet for Æther.

ÆTHIO'PICÆ (*Med.*) an epithet applied to many medicines of a black colour.

ÆTHIO'PICUS *lapis* (*Min.*) Ethiopian stone, a stone of great medicinal virtue, according to Oribasius. *Med. Collect.* l. 15, c. 7.

ÆTHIO'PIS (*Bot.*) 'Αιθιωπίς, the *Salvia Æthiopis* of Linnæus; a herb which grows in Illyria and Greece, and much resembles the common clary, whereon it is called, by Dale, the *Ethiopian Clary*. It has the stinking smell of Archangel, and the root, which is fibrous, is made into a decoction. *Dioscor.* l. 4, c. 105; *Plin.* l. 26, c. 4; *Paul. Ægin.* l. 7, c. 3; *Myrep.* sect. 8, c. 54; *C. Bauh. Pin. Plant.*; *Raii Hist. Plant.*

ÆTHIOPS (*Med.*) a medicine so called from its black colour: there are different kinds, as *Æthiops' mineral*, an incorporation of sulphur and mercury —*Antimonial Æthiops*, an incorporation of antimony and mercury.—*Vegetable Æthiops*, reduced to powder in the open air.—*Æthiops Jovialis*, a mixture of tin, mercury, and sulphur.

ÆTHNA (*Nat.*) subterraneous fire.

ÆTHO'LICES (*Med.*) *αίθολικες*, from *αίθω*, uro; pustules raised in the skin by heat. *Erotian Lex. Hippocrat.*; *Galen in Exiges. voc. Hippocrat.*; *Foes. Oeconom. Hippocrat.*

ÆTHU'SA (*Bot.*) Fools' Parsley; a genus of plants, Class 5 *Pentandria*, Order 2 *Digynia*.

Generic Characters. CAL. *umbel universal* spreading, *partial* also spreading; *involucre universal* none; *partial* linear; *proper perianth* scarcely observable.—COR. *universal* nearly uniform, *partial* unequal.—STAM. *filaments* simple; *anthers* roundish.—PIST. *germ* inferior; *styles* reflex; *stigmas* obtuse. PER. none; *fruit* roundish; *seeds* two.

Species.—The principal species are *Æthusa Cynapium, Coriandrum Cynapium, Cinapium seu Cicutaria, &c.* Common Fools' parsley; an annual, native of Britain.—*Æthusa Bunius, Carum Bunius, Daucus Pyrenaicus, &c. Bunius seu Saxifraga montana, &c.* Coriander-leaved Fools' Parsley; a biennial, native of the Pyrenees.—*Æthusa Meum, Athamanta Meum, Ligusticum Meum, Seseli Meum, seu Meum Spignel,* Meu or Bawd-money; a perennial, native of Europe.—*Æthusa Fatua,* Fine-leaved Fools' Parsley; a perennial. *I. Bauhin. Hist. Plant.*; *C. Bauhin. Pin. Theat. Bot.*; *Ger. Herb.*; *Park. Theat. Botan.*; *Linn. Spec. Plant.*

ÆTHYA (*Orn.*) *αίθυα*, a sea fowl, answering to the Fulica or Coot.

ÆTIANS (*Ecc.*) *Ætiani*; a sect of heretics, from one Ætius, of Antioch, who maintained doctrines respecting the Trinity, &c. differing somewhat from the Arians. *St Athanas. de Synod.*; *S. Gregor. Nyssen. contra Eunom.*; *Philostrat.* l. 3, &c.; *Epiphan. Hæres.* 76; *August. Hæres.* 74; *Socrat. Hist. Eccles.* l. 1, c. 28; *Sozomen.* l. 3, &c.: *Theodoret.* l. 2, &c.; *Baron Annal Ann,* 356, &c. *Tillemont Hist Eccles.* tom. 6; *Du Pin, &c.*

ÆTIO'LOGY (*Rhet.*) *αίτιολογία*, from *αίτια*, cause or reason, and *λογος*, an account; a showing the reasons for a thing, called by Quintilian " *Causarum relatio*;" by Cicero " Ad propositum subjecto ratio." *Cic. de Orat.* l. 3, c. 52; *Quintilian,* l. 6, c. 3; *Alex. πιρίσχημ*; *Ald. Rhet.* vol. 1, p. 577; *Rutil. Lup.* l. 2. c. 19.

ÆTIOLOGY (*Med.*) the theory of physic, and the causes of diseases.

ÆTITES (*Min.*) *αίτιτης*, eagle stone; a species of ore of a kidney form, imbedded in iron shot clay. Pliny says it was found in eagles' nests. *Dioscor.* l. 5, c. 161; *Plin.* l. 36, c 21; *Aet. Tetrab.* l. serm. 2, c. 32.

A'ETOMA (*Med.*) *αίτωμα*, the roof of a house. *Gal. Exeges.*

AETO'NYCHON (*Bot.*) another name for the *Lithospermum.*

A'FFA (*Com.*) an ounce weight of gold on the coast of Guinea.

TO AFFE'AR (*Archæol.*) to confirm, ratify. *Shakspeare.*

TO AFFE'CT (*Law*) to make over, pawn, or mortgage any thing to assure the payment of a sum of money, or discharge any other duty.

AFFE'CTED (*Algeb.*) *affectus* or *adfectus*: an epithet, the first use of which is attributed to Vieta, by whom it was applied to a quantity having coefficients, as $4a$, in which a is affected by the coefficient 4; or having the sign $+$ or $-$, as $-4a$. An equation is said to be affected when the unknown quantity rises to two or more powers, as $x^3 - x^2 + 9x = r$. *Vieta in Art. Analyt. et Isagog.* c. 8.

AFFE'CTION (*Phy.*) *πάθος, affectio ab afficiendo eò quod subjectum, dum de illo prædicatur, afficint;* any thing peculiarly attributed to a body and resulting from its essence. As respects the subject, affections are divided into—*Affections of the mind,* which are any commotions of the mind.—*Affections of the body,* which are certain modifications of matter introduced by motion in this or that way: these are divided into—*Affections primary,* which either arise out of the idea of matter, as magnitude, quantity; or out of the form, as quality and power; or out of both, as motion, place, and time.—*Affections secondary* or *derivative* such as arise out of primary ones, as divisibility, continuity, contiguity; or out of quantity, as equality, inequality, &c.; or out of figure, as a circle, square, &c.; out of qualities, as strength, health, &c.

AFFECTION (*Met.*) is said of being, in its abstract form, and is divided into—*Affections united,* which are predicated of being singly and solely, and are convertible without a conjunction, as ' every being is good,' and ' all good is a being.'—*Affections disunited,* are predicated of being with a disjunctive term, and, by taking in both parts of the sentence, are convertible with it, as ' being is either necessary or contingent,' and ' whatever is necessary or contingent is being.'

AFFECTION (*Law*) the making over, pawning, or mortgaging a thing to assure the payment of a sum of money, or the discharge of some other duty or service.

AFFECTION (*Paint.*) a lively representation of any passion in a figure.

H 2

AFFECTION (*Med.*) a general term to denote any disorder with which the whole body or any part of it is affected, or under which it suffers. It is commonly defined by some epithet, as the—*Affectio colica*, the colic affection, or simply the colic.—*Affectio melancholica*, melancholy.—*Affectus implicatus*, a complicated affection or disorder, is one in which many parts are affected with different disorders. *Hippocrat. de Epidem.* l. 3. and *Gal. Comm.* 2.

AFFE'ERERS (*Law*) *Afferatores*; those who in Courts-Leet, upon oath, settle and moderate the fines. *Hawkins P. C.* l. 2, c. 112.

TO AFFE'RE (*Law*) signifies either "to affere an amercement," i. e. to mitigate the rigour of a fine; or "to affere an account," i. e. to confirm it upon oath in the Exchequer.

A'FFERI (*Archæol.*) cattle fit for husbandry, according to our old law writers. *Fleta.* l. 2, c. 73, § 6, &c.

AFFETTUO'SO (*Mus.*) or *Affetto*, Italian, signifying, in an affecting style; a term employed in music-books at the beginning of a movement.

AFFI'ANCE (*Theol.*) that acquiescence of the mind, under all circumstances, grounded on a perfect confidence in the wisdom and goodness of the supreme disposer of all things.

AFFIANCE (*Law*) from *affidare*, or *dare fidem*, to give a pledge; a plighting of troth between a man and a woman. *Lit.* sect. 39.

AFFI'CHE (*Com.*) a posting-bill or any advertisement pasted up in public places to make things known.

AFFIDA'RE (*Law*) i. e. *dare fidem*; to plight one's faith or swear fealty.

AFFIDA'RI (*Law*) to be mustered or enrolled for a soldier. *MS. Dom. de Farendon*, 22. 25.

AFFIDA'TI (*Lit.*) the name which the academicians of Pavia assume.

AFFIDA'TIO *Dominorum* (*Law*) an oath taken by the Lords in parliament. *Hen. VI. Rot. Parl.*

AFFIDA'TUS (*Law*) a tenant by fealty.

AFFIDA'VIT (*Law*) an oath in writing, sworn before some one duly authorized to administer it.

AFFI'DRA (*Chem.*) Ceruss.

AFFILIA'TIO (*Archæol.*) or *adfiliatio*, an adoption into a son's place.

A'FFINAGE (*Com.*) an action by which any thing is refined, so as to make it purer and better; more particularly applied to the refining of metals.

AFFI'NIS (*Law*) from *affinis*, or *ad finis*, i. e. appertaining to the boundary; προσηκων κατ' επιγαμιαν, a cousin or kinsman by marriage; *uxoris cognati sunt, affines mariti.*

AFFI'NITY, degrees of (*Bible*) There are several degrees of affinity, or relationship by marriage, mentioned in Leviticus xviii., which were regarded as impediments to marriage.

AFFINITY, degrees of (*Law*) The prohibited degrees of affinity specified in God's law, were particularized by two different statutes of Henry VIII. that is, 18 Hen. VIII. c. 7; 25 Hen. VIII. c. 22: at present the prohibited degrees are all those which are under the 4th degree; but between collaterals, those in the 4th degree and upwards, as first cousins, are permitted to marry. *Gibs. Cod.* 413.

AFFINITY (*Phy.*) the tendency which the particles of matter have to be attracted to each other at insensible distances, in distinction from *attraction*, properly so called. This *Affinity* is of different kinds, as—*Chemical affinity*, or *Elective attraction*, distinguished from all other kinds of attraction, as the affinity of sulphuric acid for potash and lime.—*Compound affinity*, the union of different bodies in one homogeneous mass.—*Compound elective affinity*, or *double elective attraction*, when there are more than four substances; as, if nitric acid be added to the sulphat of ammonia, no decomposition takes place; but if nitrat of potash be added, then two new bodies are formed, that is, the potash attracts the sulphuric acid, and the nitric acid the ammonia.—*Intermediate affinity*, a union by the help of a medium; as azote with fixed alkalies, by the help of nitric acid.—*Quiescent* and *dwellent affinity*: the former of these terms, according to Mr. Kirwan, expresses the force exerted to preserve the old combination; and the latter, that which tends to destroy it.—*Reciprocal affinity*, when a separation is caused between two substances by a third, with which one of them is united, but afterwards separated again by the influence of the separated principle.

AFFI'ON (*Chem.*) an Arabic name for opium.

AFFI'OUME (*Com.*) or *Fiume*; a kind of flax which comes from Egypt, by way of Marseilles and Leghorn.

AFFI'RMANCE (*Law*) from *affirmare*: the confirming a former law. 8 *Hen. VI.*

AFFI'RMANT (*Law*) the same when applied to Quakers, as deponent when applied to others.

AFFIRMA'TION (*Law*) a simple asseveration, which, according to a set form of words, is allowed to the Quakers in the lieu of an oath. 7 *Will. III.*

AFFI'RMATIVE (*Log.*) an epithet for a species of proposition wherein any predicate is affirmed of its subject, or it is predicated affirmatively of the subject; as, 'a horse is an animal:' here 'animal' is affirmed of a *horse*. This is opposed to the negative.

AFFIRMATIVE (*Algeb.*) an epithet either for a sign or a quantity. This term was first used by Vieta.—*Affirmative* or *positive quantity*, any quantity that is absolutely to be added, in distinction from the negative quantity to be subtracted.—*Affirmative* or *positive sign*, marked thus (+) signifies *plus*, and more, or added to, and is annexed to the affirmative quantity, as $a + b$, signifies that b must be added to a. *Viet. ad Logist. Spec. Not. prior.*

AFFIRMATIVE (*Ecc.*) an epithet for those who being charged with heresy before the Inquisition, do affirm the same when called upon to answer. *Emeric. Director. Inquisit.* pars 2, quæst. 34.

AFFI'X (*Gram.*) any letter or syllable affixed or placed at the end of words, as ment, in the word amendment.

AFFLA'TUS *Divinus* (*Ant.*) an inspiration of some deity. *Cic. de Nat. Deor.* l. 2, c. 66.

AFFLATUS (*Med.*) from *af* or *ad* and *flo*, to blow; a blast or vapour that affects the body with some sudden distemper.

AFFLU'X (*Med.*) a flowing of humours to any part.

AFFO'DIUS (*Zool.*) a sort of serpent, the same as the Hæmorrhous.

AFFO'RAGE (*Com.*) a duty paid in France to the lord of the district, for permission to sell wine or other liquors within his district.

AFFORA'RE (*Archæol.*) to set a price on any thing.

AFFORA'TUS (*Archæol.*) appraised or valued.

AFFORCIAME'NTUM (*Law*) a strong hold.—*Afforciamentum curiæ*, the calling of a court on any extraordinary occasion.

AFFORCIA'RE (*Law*) to increase, as in the case of increasing a jury: *Cum in veritate dicenda sunt sibi contrarii*; i. e. when they are not agreed on their verdict. *Bract.* l. 4, c. 19.

AFFO'REST (*Law*) to turn ground into a forest. *Chart. de Forest.*

TO AFFRA'NCHISE (*Law*) to set a person free from bondage.

AFFRA'Y (*Law*) from the Fr. *affrayer*, to frighten, signified, originally, the appearing in armour not usually worn, to the terror of others; but now implies a skirmishing or

4

fighting between two or more persons, to the terror of the king's subjects. *Stat. 2 Ed. III.; 3 Inst. 158, &c.*

AFFREIGHTMENT (*Law*) *affretamentum*; the freight of a ship. *Stat. 11 Hen. IV.*

AFFRE'NGI (*Chem.*) red lead.

A'FFRI (*Archæol.*) 1. vide *Afferi*. 2. *Affri* or *Afri* bullocks, horses, or beasts of the plough. *Mon. Angl.* par. 2, f. 291.

AFFRODYNE, or *Affrodite* (*Chem.*) vide *Venus*.

AFFRO'NTE (*Her.*) an epithet for a savage's head that on a charge is fullfaced, as on the annexed cut.

AFFU'SIO (*Med.*) affusion. 1. Pouring a liquor on something. 2. The same as *suffusio*.

AFFU'T (*Mil.*) French for a gun-carriage.

A *flat* (*Mus.*) that which is the seventh of B flat.

AFLO'AT (*Mar.*) floating; as a ship is *afloat* when the water is deep enough to buoy her up from the ground.

A'FORA (*Bot.*) without valves; an epithet for the pericarps of some plants, according to Camellus' system. [vide *Botany*]

AFO'RE (*Mar.*) that part of a ship which lies forward or near the stem; so likewise, adverbially, the manger stands *afore* the foremast; that is, further forward, or nearer the stem.

A *fortiori* (*Log.*) a term employed in a chain of reasoning, to imply that what follows is a more powerful argument than what has been already adduced.

A'FRAGAN (*Chem.*) verdigrease.

A'FRICAN *company,* (*Com.*) or the Royal African company, was incorporated in the 14th of Charles II. and was empowered to trade from Barbary to the Cape of Good Hope. The arms of this company are—" *Or,* an elephant with a castle on his back; *sable*, ensigned with a flag; *gules*, on a canton quarterly *azure* and *gules*; on the first and last a fleur de lis of France, and in the second and third a lion of England."

AFRICAN *Bladder Nut* (*Bot.*) the *Royena* of Linnæus, a shrub.—*African flea-bane,* the *Tarchonanthes* of Linnæus, a shrub.—*African Marigold,* the *Tagetes erecta* of Linnæus, an annual.—*African Ragwort,* the *Othonna* of Linnæus, a shrub.

A'FRICUS (*Ant.*) a south-west wind, so called because it blew from Africa. Horace calls it *protervus*. *Hor. Epod.* od. 16, v. 22.

A'FSLAGERS (*Com.*) those appointed by the Burgomasters of Amsterdam to preside over sales, after the manner of our auctioneers.

AFT (*Mar.*) *abaft* or *behind*, near the stern of the ship, as " To run out the guns *afore* and *aft*," i. e. from one end to the other.—" Right *aft*," i. e. in a direct line with the stern when applied to any distant object.—" To haul *aft* the fore sheet or main sheet," i. e. to pull the sails more towards the stern.

AFTER (*Mar.*) the hinder part of the ship, as the *after*-hatchway, the *after*-capstan, *after*-sails, &c.—*After-guard,* a name for the seamen who are stationed on the poop and quarter-deck of vessels, to attend and work the aftersails, &c.

AFTER-MATH (*Agric.*) or *after-grass,* the second grass which springs up after mowing.

AFTERBIRTH (*Med.*) the placenta. [vide *Placenta*]

A'GA (*Polit.*) an officer at the court or in the armies of the grand seignor, as *Buguk Imrakor Aga,* the grand equerry.—*Spahilar Agassi,* general of the cavalry.—*Capi Agassi,* governor of the pages.—*Janissar Agassi,* general of the janissaries, &c. The particle *si* is here added because the words Spahilar, Capi, &c. are in the genitive. *Ricaut. Ottom. Emp.*

AGALA'CTIA (*Med.*) ἀγαλακτία, from *a,* priv. and γάλα, milk, Agalaxy, or want of milk; whence the epithet, in Hippocrates, of ἀγάλακτος, applied to a woman wanting milk at the time of lying-in; and ἀγάλακτος, applied by Galen and others to the pastures which are unfavourable to the generation of milk in the animals who feed upon them. *Hippocrat. de Mul. & Gal. Com; Gorr. Def. Med.; Foes. Oeconom. Hippocrat.*

AGA'LLIS (*Bot.*) vide *Anagallis*.

AGA'LLOCHA (*Bot.*) a species of the *excæcaria* of Linnæus.

AGA'LLOCHUM (*Bot.*) Ἀγάλλοχον, the *Indian Aloe*, or the *Excæcaria Agallocha* of Linnæus, is so called from ἀγάλλομαι, to exult, because it seems to exult in sending forth its odours. It is a sort of sweetscented wood, which is exported from India, and is used in suffumigations instead of frankincense. Dioscorides speaks of its medicinal virtues. *Dios.* l. 1, c. 21; *Oribas. Medec. Collect.* l. 11; *Paul. Æginet. de Re Med.* l. 7, c. 3; *C. Bauhin. Pin.*

AGA'LLUGI (*Bot.*) or *Agallugun,* vide *Agallochum*.

AGA'LMA (*Law*) the impression or image of any thing on a seal. *Chart. Edg. Reg. pro Westmonast. Eccles. anno 698.*

AGALMA'TOLITE (*Min.*) bildstein, or figure-stone; a species of the soapstone family.

AGAPA'NTHUS (*Bot.*) a genus of plants, Class 6 *Hexandria,* Order 1 *Monogynia*.

Generic Character. CAL. *spathe* common, gaping at the side.—COR. one-petalled; *tube* cornered; *border* sixparted.—STAM. *filaments* six; *anthers* kidney-shaped.—PIST. *germ* superior; *style* filiform; *stigma* simple.—PER. *capsule* oblong; *valves* navicular; *dissepiment* contrary; *seeds* numerous.

The Species are—*Agapanthus umbellatus,* African Blue Lily, a perennial, native of the Cape of Good Hope.—*Agapanthus ensifolius,* a perennial, native of the Cape of Good Hope. *Pluk. Phytogr.; Comm. Hort. Medi.; Breyn. Icon. Rar. et Exot. Plant.; Linn. Spec. Plant.*

AGAPETÆ (*Ecc.*) ἀγαπηταί. 1. A society of unmarried women who professed to lead a holy and recluse life; but, on account of their immoralities, their house was broken up by order of a general council, under Pope Innocent II. 2. The priests who acted as father confessors to these women, and who were also called Agapetæ. *Epiphan. Hæres.* c. 63; *Hieron. ad Occan. de Vit. Cleric.; Pallad. in Vit. S. Chrysostom; Concil. Laodic. Ann. 364; Concil. Constantin.* 5, 6; *Gregor.* ii. epist. 54; *Baron. Annal. Ann.* 57; *Prateol. Elench. Hæret.; Sander. Hæres.* c. 68 and 79.

AGA'RIC (*Bot.*) ἀγαρικόν, another name for the Mushroom, the *Agaricus* of Linnæus, which grows on oaks, or the roots, and is either male or female. The former is used in dyeing, and the latter in medicine. [vide *Agaricum* and *Agaricus*]

AGARICO'IDES (*Bot.*) a sort of Fungus like the Agaric.

AGA'RICUM (*Bot.*) ἀγαρικόν, Agaric; a plant, so called from the town of Agaria, in Sarmatia. It is reckoned of a warm and astringent quality, good for the gripes, crudities, fractures, and the like. *Dioscor.* l. 3, c. 1; *Plin.* l. 25, c. 9; *Gal. de Simpl. Med. Fac.* l. 6, c. 5; *Oribas. Med. Collect.* l. 15, c. 1; *Act. Tetrab.* 4, serm. 1, c. 81; *Paul Æginet.* l. 5, c. 64; *Act. de Meth. Med.* l. 5, c. 12; *J. Bauh. Hist. Plant.; C. Bauh. Pin.; Ræii Hist. Plant. &c.*

AGA'RICUS (*Bot.*) a genus of plants, Class 24 *Cryptogamia,* Order *Fungi. Linn. Spec. Plant.*

Generic Character. PILEUS. *gills* underneath, composed of *lamina,* differing in substance from the rest of the plant; *seeds* numerous between the two lamina.

Species. The genus Agaricus may be divided into, 1. Those

whose stem is surrounded with a ring and curtain. [vide *Fungi*] 2. Those having a stem with a curtain, but no ring. 3. Those whose stem is annulate without a wrapper. 4. Those without stem or wrapper. 5. Those with a funnel form, or oblique cap. 6. Those with a cap halved, and stem lateral. 7. Those with a coriaceous cap and gills. 8. Those with a cap striate and plaited. 9. Those with the cap opake and conic.

AGAS'YLLIS (*Bot.*) ἀγάσυλλις, a shrub, which, according to Dioscorides, produces the Gum Ammoniac. *Dioscor.* l. 3, c. 98.

A'GATE (*Min.*) ἀχάτης, a precious stone, first found in Sicily, which is variegated with veins and clouds that form different figures, from which it derived different names. [vide *Achates*] It is composed of chrystal debased by earth, and formed, not by repeated incrustations round a nucleus, but by a simple concretion.

AGATE (*Mech.*) a stone of the agate kind engraven by art, which, among antiquarians, constitutes a species of antique gems.

AGATHOPHY'LLUM (*Bot.*) a genus of plants, Class 11 *Dodecandria*, Order 1 *Monogynia*.
Generic Characters. CAL. perianth very small.—COR. petals six.—STAM. filaments twelve; anthers roundish.—PIST. germ superior; style very short; stigma pubescent.—PER. drupe somewhat globose; seed a nut, somewhat globose; the kernel convex.
Species. The only species is the *Agathophyllum aromaticum.* Linn. Spec. Plant.

AGA'VE (*Bot.*) from ἀγαυός, admirable; a genus of plants, Class 6 *Hexandria*, Order 1 *Monogynia*.
Generic Character. CAL. none.—COR. one-petalled; border six-parted; parts lanceolate.—STAM. filaments filiform; anthers linear.—PIST. germ oblong; style filiform; stigma headed.—PER. capsule oblong; seeds numerous.
Species. Plants of this tribe are mostly shrubs, the principal of which are the—*Agave Americana*, aloe, &c. American Agave.—*Agave Virginica*, seu subcaulescens, Virginian Agave, native of Cuba, &c. *J. Bauh. Hist. Plant.; Ger. Herb.; Park. Theat. Bot.; Raii Hist. Plant.; Linn. Spec. Plant.*

AGE (*My.*) vide *Ætas*.

AGE (*Ant.*) vide *Ætas*.

AGE (*Chron.*) any period or limit of time which, for the convenience of chronology and history, is distinguished by events that have happened in the world. The generality of chronologers agree in making seven ages, or periods, that is, six ages before Christ, and one after; but they differ as to the division of these periods. The following is the division according to Usher.

Ages of the World.

1. From the creation of the world until the deluge, 1656, which contains 1656 years.—2. From the deluge till the time of the departure of Abraham to the land of Canaan, 2083, which contains 427 years. *Gen.* xi. 31, 32.—3. From the time of Abraham to the departure of the children of Israel from Egypt, 2153, which contains 430 years. *Exod.* xii. 29, 30, 31. 37. 41. 51.; *Num.* xxxiii. 3.—4. From the departure of the children of Israel from Egypt to the fourth year and second month of the reign of Solomon, 2992, containing 479 years. 1 *Kings* vi. 1. 37; 2 *Chron.* iii. 2.—5. From the reign of Solomon to the captivity, 3416, which contains 424 years.—6. From the captivity to the birth of Christ, 4000, which contains 584 years.—7. From the birth of Christ to the present period.

AGE (*Law*) that special time when men or women are enabled to do what, for want of years, they are prohibited doing: thus, twelve is the age for taking the oath of allegiance in a leet; fourteen, or for a woman twelve, the age of discretion, for consenting to a marriage, or choosing a guardian; twenty-one the full age. A person under the age of twenty-one may make a purchase; but, at his full age, he may agree or disagree to it. Fourteen is the age by law to be a witness, although a child of nine years of age has, in some cases, been admitted to give evidence. No one can be chosen member of parliament under the age of twenty-one; ordained as a priest before the age of twenty-four; nor be a bishop before thirty. 1 *Inst.* 78.—*Age prier*, in Latin *ætatis precatio*, when an action being brought against a person under age for lands which he hath by descent, he, by petition or motion, shows the matter to the court, and prays that the motion may be staid till he is of full age.

AGE *of the Moon* (*Astron.*) the number of days elapsed since the last new moon.

AGE *of a Horse* (*Vet.*) is known by his teeth, hoof, coat, tail, and ears.

AGE *of a Hart* (*Hunt.*) is judged by the furniture of his head.

AGE *of Trees* (*Bot.*) is commonly judged by the number of circles which appear on the trunk or stock of a tree cut perpendicularly.

A'GELA (*Ant.*) assemblies of boys in Crete so called. *Cæl. Rhodig.* l. 18, c. 26.

AGE'LÆUS (*Med.*) ἀγιλαῖος, an epithet for the coarsest sort of bread.

AGE'MA (*Ant.*) ἄγημα, a choice band of soldiers, mostly cavalry, among the Macedonians, answering to the Roman legion, of which Livy makes mention, in speaking of the army of Antiochus, " Addita his ala mille ferme equitum, agema eam vocabant," l. 37, c. 40; and in another place, " Delecta deinde et viribus, et robore ætatis ex omni cætratorum numero duo erant agemata; hanc ipsi legionem vocabant," l. 42, c. 51. It is also spoken of by other authors. *Diodor.* l. 19, c. 28; *Arrian. Alexand. Exped.* l. 3, &c ; *Quint. Curt.* l. 4, c. 13; *Suidas.; Cæl. Rhodig. Ant. Lect.* l. 21, c. 31, &c.

AGEMO'GLANS (*Pol.*) vide *Agiamoglans*.

AGE'NDA (*Ecc.*) the office or service of the church.—*Agenda matutina et vespertina*, morning and evening prayers.—*Agenda Dei*, the office of the day.—*Agenda Mortuorum*, the service for the dead, i. e. offices or masses for the dead.

AGENDA is also the name of the book which contains the ritual or church service of the Romish church.

AGENDA (*Com.*) 1. A pocket or memorandum book, in which a merchant sets down what is to be done in the day. 2. A pocket almanack which a merchant carries with him for ascertaining dates.

AGENE'SIA (*Med.*) vide *Anaphrodisia*.

AGENFRI'DA (*Law*) the true Lord or owner of any thing. *Leg. Inæ. apud Brompton.*

A'GENHINE (*Archæol.*) *familiaris seu famulus domesticus:* he who lay a third night at an inn, and was called a third night awnhide, for whom his host was answerable if he committed any offence. " Item secundum antiquam consuetudinem dici poterit de familia cujus qui hospitatus fuerit cum alio per tres noctes: quia prima nocte dici poterit UNEATH, i. e. incognitus; secunda vero GUST, i. e. hospes; tertia nocte hogen hyne, i. e. familiaris." *Leg. Ed. Confess. apud Brompton.*

AGENO'RIDES (*Ant.*) a patronymic for the descendants of Agenor, particularly Cadmus. *Ovid. Met.* l. 3, v. 8.

A'GENT (*Phy.*) *Agens*, τὸ ποιοῦν; any thing having the power to act on another object, as cold.—*Agent univocal* is that which produces an effect of the same kind and denomination as itself.—*Agent equivocal* is that which produces an effect of a different kind from itself.

5

AGENT, *natural* or *physical* (*Met.*) that which is determined by the author of nature to produce a univocal, or one sort of effect, with an incapacity to produce the contrary thereto, as the fire, which only heats, but does not cool.—*Agent, free* or *voluntary*, that which may equally do one thing, or the contrary to that, not acting from any predeter ination, but from choice, such as man, or the rational part of him, the soul.

AGENT (*Com.*) one who is commissioned to take care of the business of another, as *agent* to the several regiments of the army, *agents* for taxes, &c.—*Agents of the Bank and Exchange*, officers in France for transacting the business of Exchange between the Bankers and Merchants.

AGENT (*Pol.*) a person in the service of Government, who, in a foreign country, superintends the concerns of the nation that are entrusted to him.

AGENT, army (*Mil.*) a person in the civil department of the army between the paymaster general and the paymaster of the regiment, through whom every regimental concern of a pecuniary nature is transacted. He is obliged to give securities to government.—*Half-pay agent*, a person named or appointed by an officer on half-pay to receive his allowance.—*Agent*, among the French, is the person who is entrusted with the interior economy of a regiment, troop, or company.

AGENT, Navy (*Mar.*) a person on shore employed by officers and seamen to manage their concerns in regard to their pay, prize-money, &c.—*Agent victualler*, an officer stationed at a royal port to regulate the victualling of the king's ships.

AGENT *and Patient* (*Law*) when one person is both the doer of the thing, and the party to whom it is done, as when a woman endows herself with the best part of her husband's possessions.

AGE'NTES *in rebus* (*Polit.*) officers at the court of Constantinople, who had the direction of all the public carriages, of the couriers, of the journeys of the emperor and his household, &c. *Aurel. Vict. de Cæsar.* c. 39; *Hieron. in Abdiam.*; *Pancirol. Notit. Dig. Imp. Orient.* c. 65.

A'GER (*Ant.*) a field, land, lands, or country, so called, according to Varro, from *ago*, to act, because work is done in fields. The Augurs distinguished the country round Rome into the—*Ager Romanus*, so called from the city of Rome.—*Ager Gabinius*, from the town Gabinium.—*Ager peregrinus*, from *pergo*, or *progredior*, because they went out of the *Ager Romanus* into it.—*Ager hosticus*, from *hostis*, an enemy.—*Ager incertus*, because it was doubtful to which of the four above-mentioned it belonged. To these may be added other distinctions, as the —*Ager arcifinus* or *arcifinalis*, from *arceo*, to keep off, because it was fitted to keep off an enemy.—*Ager occupatorius*, from *occupo*, to seize, because it was taken possession of by force of arms.—*Ager assignatus*, land portioned out.—*Ager compascuus*, common for the cattle, also called *ager scripturarius*, because it was entered in the books of the Roman publicans or tax-gatherers.—*Ager decumanus*, glebe or tithe land, so called because a tenth of the produce was paid to the Censors.—*Ager solutus*, fields not hedged or walled in.—*Ager vectigalis*, lands taken from an enemy that paid a certain annual tribute; they were also called *Ager publicus* when occupied by Roman colonists. *Cato de Re Rust.* c. 142; *Varro de Lingua Lat.* l. 4, c. 4; *Cic. Top.* c. 3; *de Offic.* l. 1, c. 7, &c.; *Hygin. de Limit. Constit.* p. 203, &c.; *Tacit. German.* c 29; *Frontin. de Agror. Qualitat.*; *Fest. de Verb. Signif.*; *Isid. Orig.* l. 15, c. 13; *Turneb. Adver.* l. 1, c. 6; *Manut. Robertellus, &c. apud Græv. Thes. Antiq.* vol. iii. &c.

AGE'RASY (*Med.*) ἀγηρασία, from α, priv. and γῆρας, old age; a vigorous old age.

AGERATO'IDES (*Bot.*) from *ageratum*, a species of the *Eupatorium* of Linnæus.

AGERA'TUM (*Bot.*) ἀγήρατος, i. e. μὴ γηρῶν, *non senescens*, not growing old, Sweet Maudlin; a plant so called, according to Pliny, because its flower does not decay soon. *Diosc.* l. 4, c. 59; *Plin.* l. 27, c. 4.

AGERATUM, in the Linnean system, a genus of plants; Class 19 *Syngenesia*, Order 1 *Polygamia Æqualis*.
Generic Character. CAL. common oblong.—COR. compound uniform; *corollets* hermaphrodite; *proper* monopetalous.—STAM. *filaments* capillary; *anther* cylindric. —PIST. *germ* oblong; *style* filiform; *stigmas* two.—PER. none; *calyx* unchanged; *seeds* solitary; *receptacle* naked.
Species. The species are—*Ageratum conyzoides*, *Eupatorium humile Africanum*, seu *Americanum*, &c. seu *Conyza*, &c. Hairy Ageratum; an annual, native of America.—*Ageratum ciliare*, seu *Centaurium ciliare*, &c. native of the East Indies—*Ageratum latifolium*, an annual, native of Peru. *J. Bauhin. Hist. Plant.*; *C. Bauhin. Pin. Theat. Bot.*; *Ger. Herb.*; *Park. Theat.*; *Raii Hist. Plant.*; *Tourn. Inst. Herb.*; *Boerh. Ind. Plant.*

AGERATUM is also a name for the *Achillea ageratum*; the *Athanasia annua*; the *Conyza lin'fo'ia*; the *Eupatorium ageratoides*; and the *Senecio abrotonifoliis* of Linnæus. *Ger. Herb.*; *Raii Hist. Plant.*; *Camer. de Plant. Epit.*; *Tournef. Instit.*

AGE'RATUS *lapis* (*Min.*) Ἀγήρατος λίθος, a stone used by cobblers to polish women's shoes. It is esteemed discussive and astringent. *Gal. de Med. facil. Parab.* c. 18; *Oribas. Med. Collect.* l. 15, c. 1; *Paul. Æginet. de Re Med.* l. 7, c. 3.

AGETORI'ON (*Ant.*) ἀγητόριον, a Grecian festival mentioned by Hesychius.

A'GE *vitæ* (*Med.*) an antidote used for procuring longevity. *Myrep. de Antidot.* c. 500.

AGE'USTIA (*Med.*) from α, priv. and γνώμαι, to taste; a term used for fasting.

A'GGER (*Ant.*) 1. The middle and more elevated part of a military way, formed by the *coaggeratio*, or heaping of the stones and strata. 2. The mound of earth raised for a rampart to a town. *Varro de Ling. Lat.* l. 4, c. 32, *et Scal. in Varr.*

AGGE'STUM *Terræ* (*Ant.*) χῶμα, a grave made of earth, which served formerly instead of a tomb. *Solin. apud Salmas.* p. 1219.

AGGISU'ED-BUND (*Com.*) vide *Aggoued-bund*.

AGGLUTINA'NTIA (*Med.*) agglutinants or agglutinating, medicines that tend to the healing or reunion of parts that are separated. *Paul. Æginet. de Re Med.* l. 3, c. 22. &c.

AGGLUTINA'TIO *Pilorum* (*Med.*) reducing the hairs of the eyelids that grow inwards to their natural order. *Aet. Tetrab* 2, serm. 3, c. 681.

AGGLUTINA'TION (*Med*) from *ad* and *glutino*; the reunion of any separated parts of the body. [vide *Prosthesis*]

AGGLUTINATION (*Astron.*) the meeting of two or more stars in the same part of the zodiac, or, as it is more commonly understood, the seeming coalition of several stars so as to form a nebulous star.

AGGO'UED-BUND (*Com.*) the best of the six sorts of silks that are gathered in the great Mogul's dominions.

AGGREGA'TÆ (*Bot.*) from *aggrego*, aggregates or collectives; an epithet for the forty-eighth order in Linnæus' natural arrangement, including the aggregate flowers properly so called.

AGGREGATÆ *glandulæ* (*Med.*) small glands supposed to be lodged in the cellular coat of the intestines.

A'GGREGATE (*Phy.*) *aggregatum*, from *aggrego*, to assemble together; the whole sum or mass resulting from the collection of several small things into one body.

AGGREGATE (*Bot.*) *aggregatus*, from *aggrego*, to collect or assemble; an epithet applied to the flower which has some part of the fructification common to several florets: the part which serves as a bond to the rest is either the receptacle or the calyx; and the partial or component flower is called the *floscule* or floret of Aggregate flowers. There are seven kinds; namely, 1. The Umbellate; 2. The Cymose; 3. The Compound; 4. The Aggregate, properly so called, having a dilated receptacle, and the florets on peduncles, as *Scabiosa, Knautia, Cephalanthus, Globularia,* &c.; 5. The Amentaceous; 6. The Glumose, as the grasses; 7. The Spadiceous, as the palms, also *Calla, Dracontium, Pothos, Arum, Zostera,* &c.

AGGREGATE is also an epithet for the bud, *gemma*; bristle, *seta*; root, *radix*: a bud is aggregate when many stand close together, as in *Zanthoxylum fraxineum*; a bristle is aggregate when many are joined together; a root is aggregate when several bulbs are connected together at the base.

AGGREGA'TION (*Phy.*) a species of union by which several things that have no natural dependance or connection one with another are collected together so as to form one mass.

AGGRE'SSES (*Her.*) vide *Pellet.*

AGGRE'STEIN (*Falcon.*) a disease in hawks proceeding from a sharp humour.

AGHE'USTIA (*Med.*) from *a*, priv. and γινόμαι, to taste; defect or loss of taste, a genus of diseases, Class *Locales,* Order *Dysesthiæ,* in Cullen's Nosology.

AGIAMO'GLANS (*Polit.*) untaught Christian children, who, being taken while young, are instructed by the Turkish officers in the Mahometan religion, and made janizaries. *Ricaut. Turk. Emp.* l. 1, c. 10.

AGI'LD (*Law*) exempt from the customary fine or penalty.

A'GILER (*Archæol.*) an observer or informer.

AGILLA'RIUS (*Archæol.*) an heyward, herdsward, or keeper of cattle in a common field, who is sworn at the Lords' court by solemn oath.

A'GIO (*Com.*) a Venetian word for assistance, signifies also, the Exchange or difference between the Bank-money and Current-money or Cash, as when a merchant stipulates to receive for his goods 100 livres bank-money, or 105 cash or current-money; the Agio is said to be 5 per cent. *Agios* vary in every place, and at different times in the same place: at Venice it is of two kinds; namely—*Agio constant,* or *Bank-Agio,* which is 20 per cent.—*Fluctuating Agio,* which is from 120 to 128, and is also called *sopragio,* because it is calculated on the Bank-money after the first *agio* is added.

AGIOSYMA'NDRUM (*Ecc.*) from ἅγιος, holy, and σημαίνω, to signify; a wooden instrument used by the Greek churches, and others, under the dominion of the Turks, for calling together assemblies of the people.

A'GIOTAGE (*Com.*) a French word for usury.

AGI'ST (*Law*) from the Saxon ᵹiꞅte, a bed or biding place; taking in the cattle of strangers to feed in the King's forest. *Chart. de Foresta.* 9 *Hen. III.*; *Manw. For. Laws,* c. 11, &c.

AGI'STER (*Law*) *Gist-Taker,* or *Agistator,* the officer appointed to take cattle into the King's forest. *Manw. For. Laws,* c. 11, &c.

AGI'STAGE (*Law*) or *agistment, Agistamentum,* from the French *geyser, gister,* in Latin, *jacere,* to lie; because the cattle are *levant* and *couchant* while they are on the land. 1. The taking other men's cattle on one's own ground at a certain rate per week. 2 *Inst.* 643. 2. The profit from such feeding or pasturage. 3. The *agistment* of sea-banks is where lands are charged with a tribute to keep out the sea.

AGITA'TION (*Phy.*) a brisk intestine motion excited among the particles of a body; thus fire agitates the subtlest particles of bodies.

AGITATION (*Med.*) the exercise of the body, as from riding, which agitates the whole system in a salutary manner.

AGITATION (*Law*) *agitatio animalium in Foresta;* the drift of beasts in the Forest. *Leg. Forest.*

AGITA'TO (*Mus.*) Italian, signifying in a rapid manner, i. e. a rapid and broken style of performing.

AGITATO'RES (*Ant.*) ἐλατῆρες; charioteers, particularly those who drove the chariots at the games. *Cic. ad Attic.* l. 13, ep. 21; *Buleng. de Circ.*

AGITATORES (*Archæol.*) a name given to players in the middle ages, who were forbidden church communion: " De agitatoribus qui fideles sunt, placuit quamdiu agitant a communione separari." *Conc. Arel. Sub. Sylv.*

A'GITATORS (*Polit.*) 1. Persons chosen, in the time of the rebellion, out of every regiment, to sit in council, and manage the affairs of the parliament army. 2. Confidential persons employed to mix with their fellow subjects or comrades for the purpose of discovering their views and turning informers.

AGLA'SPIDES (*Ant.*) a regiment of soldiers among the Romans, so called from ἀγλαΐα, splendid, and ἀσπίς, a shield; i. e. from the splendour of their shields. *Liv.* l. 44, c. 41.

A'GLETS (*Bot.*) or *Agleeds,* pendants which hang on the tip end of chives and threads, as tulips, roses, &c. *Grew. Anat. of Plants.*

A'GLITHES (*Bot.*) ἀγλίθις; the divisions or segments of a head of garlic, which are usually called the cloves. *Hippocrat. de Morb. Mul.* l. 2.

AGLUTI'TION (*Med.*) from *a,* priv. and *glutio,* to swallow; a difficulty or impediment in swallowing.

A'GME (*Surg.*) ἀγμή, from ἄγω, to break; the Greek name for a fracture.

A'GMEN (*Ant.*) a Roman army in march; so called from *ago,* to act, in distinction from the *acies,* or army drawn up in battle array. The Agmen was divided into the—*Agmen primum,* the troops in the front, answering to our van-guard, which were the *Hastati,* or spearsmen.—*Agmen medium,* the troops in the centre, or the main-guard, which were the *Principes.*—*Agmen postremum,* the troops in the rear, or the rear-guard, which consisted of the *Triarii,* or veterans.—*Agmen longum,* an army marching in single files.—*Agmen pilatum,* an army in close ranks and files, having a narrow front; so called either from its form, or because the front ranks consisted of javelin men. *Virg. Æn.* l. 12, v. 121.

—————— Pilataque plenis
Agmina se fundunt portis.

—*Agmen quadratum,* a squadron or battalion; so called from its form approaching to the figure of a square. *Polyb.* l. 6, c. 38; *Frontin. Stratag.* l. 1, c. 6; *Isid. Orig.* l. 9, c. 3; *Veget. de Re Mil.* l. 3, c. 21; *Salmas de Re Mil.* c. 7; *Ramus. de Milit. Cæsar apud Græv. Thesaur. Antiq. Roman.* vol. 10, &c.

A'GNACAT (*Bot.*) a tree growing about the Isthmus of Darien, resembling a pear tree. *Raii Hist. Plant.*

A'GNAIL (*Med.*) a sore slip of skin at the root of the nail.

AGNA'NTHUS (*Bot.*) the *Cornutia pyramidata* of Linnæus. *Plum. Nov. Gen. Plant.*

AGNA'TA (*Bot.*) vide *Adnata.*

AGNA'TI (*Ant.*) kindred; so called because, *agnoscuntur,* i. e. they are reckoned the first in the line of relationship, and stand in the son's stead in default of male issue. The *Agnati* are on the father's side, in distinction from the *Cognati* on the mother's side, the *Affines* who are allied by marriage, and the *Propinqui* or relations in general. *August. de Leg.; Sigon. de Nom. Roman.* &c. *apud Græv. Thes. Antiq. Roman.* vol 2, 8, &c.

AGNA'TION (*Law*) that relation by blood which is between such males as are descended from the same father; in distinction from cognation, or consanguinity, which includes the descendants from females.

A'GNIL (*Bot.*) the *Indigofera tinctoria* of Linnæus.

AGNI'NA *membrana* (*Anat.*) or *Pellicula*; a membrane which involves the fœtus.

AGNI'TION (*Poet.*) ἐπίγνωσις, recognition; a part of the fable in an epic poem, as the agnition of Ulysses in the Odyssey. *Aristot. de Poet.* c. 16.

AGNO'IA (*Med.*) ἄγνοια, from *a*, priv. and γινώσκω, to know; privation of knowledge, or losing the recollection of our friends, in consequence of a fever. *Hippocrat. Prædict.* l. 1, & *Gal. Comm.* 2.; *Foes. Oeconom. Hippocrat.*

AGNOIETÆ (*Ecc.*) ἀγνοῆται, from ἀγνοέω, to be ignorant of; a name for two different sects of heretics. 1. A sect of the fourth century, who called in question the omniscience of God. *Socrat. Eccles. Hist.* l. 5, c. 24: *Sozom. Hist.* l. 6, c. 26; *Nicephor.* l. 12, c. 30; *Prateol. Elench. Hæret.* 2. A sect of the sixth century, who denied that Christ knew the day of judgment. They are probably but one and the same sect, avowing different doctrines at different times. *Johann. Damascen. de Hæres.*; *Nicephor. Eccles.* l. 18, c. 45.

AGNO'MEN (*Ant.*) from *ad*, and *Nomen*, *quasi accedens nomen*; a name or title affixed to a name by way of distinction; as, Africanus, the agnomen of Scipio, who conquered Africa. It is the last of the three among the Roman names. [vide *Nomen*]

A'GNUS *castus* (*Bot.*) a tree so called, from ἄγνος, chaste because the chaste matrons used to sleep upon it during the Thesmophoria, or feast of Ceres. It is more commonly called λύγος, οἶσος, osier, from the toughness of its rods. *Hippocrat. de Morb. Mul.* l. 1; *Nicand. Theriac.* v. 71; *Dioscor.* l. 1, c. 135; *Plin.* l. 24, c. 19; *Gal. de Simpl. Med. Fac.* l. 16; *Eustath. ad Il.* l. 11; *Aet. Tetrab.* 1. serm. 1.

Agnus *castus*, in the Linnæan System, the *Vitex Agnus castus*, or the Chaste Tree. *Ger. Herb.*; *Park. Theat. Bot.*— *Agnus Scythicus*, the Scythian Lamb, described by Kircher and others as a plant betwixt the vegetable and the animal, has been discovered to be a fern cut into the shape of a lamb, for the purposes of deception. *Kirch. Ars Magna*; *Kaemf. Amoenit. Exot.*

Agnus *Dei* (*Ecc.*) the figure of the Holy Lamb holding the cross, stamped upon a piece of white wax of an oval form, and consecrated by the pope. *Alcuin. de Divin. Offic.*; *Cerem. Rom.* l. 1, sect. 7; *Baron. Annal. ann.* 58.

AGO'GE (*Mus.*) ἀγωγή, one of the subdivisions of the Melopeia. *Eucl. lib. de Mus. Art.*

Agoge (*Med.*) 1. The order and tenor of a thing, as the procedure of a distemper, or the course of a man's life. *Hippocrat. Epidem.* l. 7; *Gal. ad Glauc.* l. 2. 2. The state and disposition of the surrounding atmosphere. *Hippocrat. Epidem.* l. 1, &c. and *Gal. Com.*; *Gorr. Def. Med.*; *Foes. Oeconom. Hippocrat.*; *Castell Lex Med.*

Agoge (*Min.*) or *Agogæ*, little channels through which the water runs from gold ore that has been washed in it, and in which the gold is deposited. *Plin.* l. 33, c. 4.

AGOMPHI'ASIS (*Med.*) from *a*, priv. and γόμφος, a socket; a disorder in the teeth, by being loose in the sockets. *Gorr. Def. Med.*

A'GON (*Ant.*) ἀγών, a Greek name for any contest, but particularly applied to the public games in which the principal contests took place.

AGONA'LES (*Ant.*) priests so called, which were added by Tullus Hostilius to the number of the Salii.

AGONA'LIA (*Ant.*) festivals in Rome, celebrated in honor of Janus, or Agonius, on the 11th of January, the 21st of May, and 13th of December, ἀπὸ τῶν ἀγώνων, i. e. from the games and contests usually celebrated at that time, wherefore called, likewise, *Agonia*, according to *Ovid. Fast.* l. v. 331.

Et prius antiquus dicebat Agonia sermo.

Varr. de L. L. l. 5; *Macrob. Saturn.* l. 1, c. 4.

AGONA'LIS *dies* (*Ant.*) the fourth day after the Nones and ninth day of the month, on which day, when the feast of Agonalia was celebrated, a ram was sacrificed to Janus according to *Ovid. Fast.* l. 1.

*Quatuor adde dies, ductus ex ordine Nonis
Janus Agonali luce piandus erit.*

A'GONE (*Bot.*) another name for the *Hyoscemus niger* of Linnæus.

A'GONES (*Ant.*) the priests who struck the victims so called from the ancient custom among the Romans for the priest to inquire *agone?* i. e. shall I strike? *Fest. de Signif. Verb.*—*Agones Capitolini*, games celebrated every fifth year on the Capitoline hill, where artists of every description used to contend. It was instituted by Domitian, who assigned a crown of oak to the victors. *Juven. sat.* 6, v. 386.

*An Capitolinum deberet Pollio quercum
Sperare.*

Mart. l. 4, epig. 44.

O cui Tarpeias licuit contigere quercus.

Sueton. in Domit. c. 4; *Schol. in Sueton. Scalig. de Emendat. Temp.* l. 5; *Panvin. Fast.* l. 2; *Rosin. Antiq. Roman.*

AGO'NIA (*Ant.*) the same as *Agonalia*.

Agonia (*Med.*) ἀγονία, from *a*, priv. and γόνος, an offspring; a term used by Hippocrates for sterility. *Hippoc. Epidem.* l. 2.

Agonia (*Med.*) ἀγωνία, agony; a struggle, as between life and death. *Gal. de Symptom. Caus.* l. 2, c. 5; *Gorr. Def. Med.*

AGONICLI'TÆ (*Ecc.*) vide *Agonyclitæ*.

AGONI'STARCH (*Ant.*) he who took charge of the combatants, that they might be exercised previous to the contests. This office is mentioned in an ancient inscription quoted by Ligorius, APOLLINI. INVICTO SACRUM Marcus AURELIUS. Marci AUGusti LIBertus APOLLONIUS. AGONISTARCHA. COMMODIANUS. *Mercur. de Arte Gymnast.* l. 1, c. 12.

AGONI'STICI (*Ecc.*) a name given by the Donatists to those whom they sent about in the country to seize the Catholics.

AGONI'STICUM (*Med.*) ἀγωνιστικόν, an application of excessively cold water in case of fever. *Gal.* περὶ μαρασμοῦ; *Paul. Æginet de Re Med.* l. 2, c. 30.

AGO'NIZANTS (*Ecc.*) certain friars in Italy who assisted those that were in their last agonies.

A'GONOS (*Med.*) from *a*, priv. and γόνος, an offspring; barren. 1. An epithet applied by Hippocrates to women who, though capable of breeding, had never had children. *Hippocrat. Epidem.* l. 2. 2. To signify equal, as applied to days, ἄγονοι ἡμέραι, equal days, as the fourth and sixth, on which a crisis is not to be expected, in distinction from the γόνιμοι ἡμέραι, the unequal days, as the third or seventh, when the crisis commonly happens, *Hippocrat. Epidem.* l. 2. sect. 6; *Gorr. Defin. Med.*; *Foes. Oeconom. Hippocrat.*

AGONOTHETA (*Ant.*) ἀγωνοθέτης, from ἀγών, and τίθημι, i. e. *Agonis dispositor*; the judge at the games, who distributed the prizes. *Poll. Onomast.* l. 3. c. 30; *Phavorinus*; *Hesychius*; *Suidas*.

AGONYCLI'TÆ (*Ecc.*) Ἀγονυκλῖται, from *a*, priv. γόνυ, the knee, and κλίνω, to bend, Agonyclites, or not benders of the knee, a sect of the 7th century, who objected to kneeling at prayer. *Johann. Damasc. Hæres.* c. 91.

AGORÆ'US (*Med.*) ἀγοραῖος, an epithet for bread that is very coarse.

AGORA'NOMI (*Ant.*) ἀγορανόμοι, Athenian magistrates who presided over the market, so called because they administered justice in the ἀγορά, or forum. They answered to the Ædiles or Æditui of the Romans, and were chosen by lot. To these men a certain toll was paid by all the market folks, whence Decæpolis is introduced by Aristophanes, demanding an eel of the Bæotian for the τελες της αγοςας, i. e. the toll of the market. *Acharn.* act 1, sc. 4.

Α'γοςᾶς τέλος ταύτῳ γίκε δώσεις ἐμοι.

They were ten in number, five for the city and five for the Piræus, and had, according to Theophrastus, in his book *De Legibus,* to see that no one was wronged in the market. *Plat. de Leg.* l. 6; *Lysias.Orat. cont. Dardan; Artemidor. Oneirocrit.* l. 2, c. 31; *Harpocration Lex; Meurs. de Pir.* c. 4.

A'GRA *Caramba* (*Bot.*) an odoriferous wood that comes from the isle of Hayman, in China.

AGRA'RIA *Lex* (*Ant.*) from *ager*, land; a law for distributing among the soldiers the land gotten by conquest. This law was proposed four several times, i. e. by Spurius Cassius, Licinus Stolo, Tiberius Gracchus, and lastly by Julius Cæsar, who prevailed, by his intrigues, in carrying a measure that proved fatal to the republic. U. C. 695. B. C. 59. *Dionys.* l. 8, c. 69; *Cic. de Leg.* and *Agrar. contra Rull.*; *Liv.* l. 2, c. 41, &c.: *Flor.* l. 3, c. 3, &c.

AGRA'RIÆ *Stationes* (*Ant.*) a kind of advance guard among the Romans, that was posted in the fields. *Veget. de Re Mil.* l. 3, c. 8; *Ammian Marcell.* l. 31, c. 8; *Turneb. Adver.* l. 4, c. 7.

AGREA'GE (*Com.*) a name among the merchants of Bourdeaux for courtage or brokerage.

AGREE'MENT (*Law.*) a joining together two or more minds in any thing done or to be done.

AGRE'STA (*Med.*) the juice of unripe grapes.

AGRE'STEN (*Chem.*) Acid-stone Tartar.

A'GRI (*Law*) arable lands in the common fields.

A'GRIA (*Bot.*) Holly, the *Ilex aquifolium* of Linnæus.

AGRIA (*Med.*) a pustule on the skin; so called on account of its malignity, from the Greek ἄγριος, fierce. *Cels.* l. 5, c. 28.

AGRIA'MPELOS (*Bot.*) from ἄγριος, wild, and ἄμπελος, a vine; the wild vine or Black Briony, the *Brionia alba* of Linnæus.

A'GRICULTURE, from *ager*, a field, and *colo*, to till, may be defined the cultivating of land, for the benefit of man and beast, in distinction from Horticulture, which is the cultivation of gardens, or particular portions of ground for the benefit of man only. Agriculture is divided into *Theoretical,* which is Agriculture properly so called; and *Practical,* which is called Husbandry. He who follows agriculture as a science is termed an *Agriculturist;* and he who practices husbandry is a *Husbandman.*

Agriculture, or the Theory of Agriculture.

The theory of agriculture comprehends the nature and properties of lands, the different sorts of plants fitted for it, and the rotation of crops.

Different kinds of Lands.

Land is distinguished by the name of *soil* when its qualities are considered as a light soil, heavy soil, stiff soil, rich soil, or poor soil.

As to its application. Land is denominated—*Meadow* or *grass lands,* where grass is allowed to grow.—*Pasture land,* that on which cattle is fed.—*Arable land,* land fit for ploughing.—*Fallow land,* which is left to lie fallow, or without a crop for a certain time.—*Wood-lands,* or lands covered with wood, which are either *woods* having trees and underwood; or *groves* having only timber.—*Pastures* are either *up-lands* which are never overflowed by rivers, *marsh lands* which lie near water, or *fenny lands* which receive and retain the water from the up-land.—*Fore-land* is that piece of land which lies to seaward in marsh-land, a—*Garden* is cultivated for domestic use and pleasure.—*Orchard* is a species of garden destined for fruit-trees.—*Vineyard* is a place set apart for the growth of vines.—*Hop-grounds,* or *Hop-plantations,* for the growth of hops.—*Plantations* are small patches of trees to serve for ornament, and—*Nurseries* are the grounds where young trees are reared.—*Lay* is any piece of land laid down with grass: this grass is called the *sward,* and the land therefore is named also *sward-land.*—A *Field* is any portion of land parted off for the purposes of agriculture: when enclosed by a hedge or wall, it is a *close* or *enclosure,* otherwise it is an *open-field.* The *fences* of fields are either *ditches,* with or without an embankment; *ha-has,* or sunk fences; *palings,* or timber fences, in different forms; *hedges,* with or without a ditch, consisting of *dead-hedges* formed of stakes: *live-hedges,* or *quickset-hedges,* planted with the quick of Whitethorn, Blackthorn, Holly, &c.

Land is moreover differently denominated according to the tenure by which it is held; namely,—*Freehold,* if free of all legal incumbrances; and the person holding such land is a *Freeholder* or *Land-Proprietor.*—*Copyhold,* if held under a copy or contract with the Lord of the Manor; and the person so holding is a *Copy-holder.*—*Farm,* if it be held by a lease or contract with the proprietor: the person letting the farm is called the *Landlord,* and the person hiring is the *Farmer* or *Tenant.*

Plants of different Kinds.

Plants which are used in agriculture serve either for food or commerce, and are distinguished into Culmiferous and Leguminous. The fruit or seed of Culmiferous plants is *corn* or *grain;* the leaves and roots of Leguminous plants, which serve as food for man, are *vegetables.*

Culmiferous Plants are of different kinds, namely—Wheat, *triticum,* which grows best on a stiff or clay-soil, and is sown in October. [vide *Wheat*]—Rye, *secale,* which grows best in a chalky soil.—Barley, *hordeum,* which requires a mellow soil, rather light than stiff, and is sown in April. [vide *Barley*]—Oats, *avena,* which succeeds in most soils, even the poorest, and is sown in March.

Leguminous Plants are as follow:—Potatoes, *Solanum tuberosum,* which are planted in April.—Turnips, *Brassica rapa,* which are sown in June.—Pease, *pisum,* sown in February.—Beans, *Vicia faba,* sown in February.—Carrots, *daucus,* sown in March or April.—Parsnips, *pastinaca,* in Autumn.—Cabbages, *Brassica oleracea,* in March or April.—Burnet, *poterium,* recommended as food for cattle, on account of its being an evergreen, is adapted to a poor soil, and is sown in March.—Beet, *beta,* is sown in March.

Plants which are cultivated, particularly for commerce, serve various purposes besides that of food. They are either *herbaceous* or *woody.*

Herbaceous Plants of this sort, are—Flax, *linum,* used for the making of linen, and extracting an oil, grows on a deep sandy loam.—Hemp, *cannabis,* the same.—Rape or Cole-seed, *Brassica napus,* which is cultivated for its oil, grows any where.—Woad, *isatis,* which is used in dyeing, is cultivated in a blackish heavy mould.—Hops, *humulus,* used in malt liquor, grow in a black loose moor-soil.

The woody kinds of plants are either Fruit-Trees, or Timber-Trees. The two most important sorts of fruit-trees are the Apple, from which Cyder is made; and the Pear, which yields Perry. Among the timber-trees are the Oak, Elm, Ash, Larch, &c. which are each spoken of in their proper places.

Plants which grow spontaneously, and are therefore hurt-

AGRICULTURE.

ful, are called *weeds*, such as the—Thistle, *carduus*, which grows on strong land, and burns the corn.—Twitch-Grass, *ophyris*, which keeps the land loose and hollow.—May-Weed, *anthemis*, which infests barley.—Goose-Grass, or Wild-Tansy, *tanacetum*, which grows mostly on strong clays.—Cockle, *Agrostemma githago*, which infests barley.—Fern, *filix*, and Furze or Brake, *Pteris aquilina*, which grow mostly in a sandy brown soil.—Rushes or Flags, *juncus*, aquatic weeds, which grow in marsh-lands.

Plants in agriculture are exposed to particular diseases, as the—*Blight* in wheat, supposed to be caused by an insect.—*Mildew*, a more frequent disease, consists of a powder that attaches to the grain in the ear. It is either black or red, the former of which is called *smut*. Washing the grain, that is, to be sown in a lie, has been found to be an efficacious remedy.—*Grub* is a kind of worm which feeds upon the roots of the corn.—Turnips and Hops are both subject to a particular *fly*, called after the plants they infect.—Potatoes are exposed to the *curl*, which attacks the leaves of the plants.

Rotation of Crops.

A *crop* is that which is produced by a single act of cultivating a field, and supplying it with grain or seed. A field is said to be *cropped* when it is occupied with any vegetation. An *etch crop* is that which is second in rotation.—*Rotation of crops*, or the manner in which they succeed each other in the same field, varies with the circumstance of the soil; but, as a general rule, wheat may follow fallow on a clay soil, then peas, barley, hay, and oats; on a light soil barley may follow turnips, then hay, oats, fallow, and wheat.

Husbandry, or Practical Agriculture.

Under this part of Agriculture are comprehended the labours of Husbandry, with the implements and animals appertaining thereto.

Labours of Husbandry.

The labours of husbandry are those which belong to the field, and those of the farm-yard.

The labours of the field consist of preparing the land for the reception of the grain, committing the grain to the earth, and gathering in the fruits.

Preparing the Land.

The preparation of the land requires both general and particular labours. The general labours are—*Breaking up* the ground, i. e. opening it for the first time.—*Hedging*, or the enclosing land with a hedge. The person who does this work is the *Hedger*, and the ways of doing it are various, as, *Plashing a hedge*, i. e. bending down the shoots of an old hedge.—*Riddering a hedge*, cutting away the superfluous shoots.—*Eddowing a hedge*, &c. [vide *Hedge*]—*Land-draining*, another important labour is the carrying off stagnant water from the surface of the soil, by means of *drains* or channels made in the earth. *Drains* are either open or hollow. *Open drains* are those which run along the surface of the earth. *Hollow drains* are placed under the earth. [vide *Drain*]

The particular preparatory labours are—*Ploughing*, or turning up the earth with a plough. Lands are ploughed so as to make furrows and ridges. *Furrows* are the tracks of the plough. *Ridges* are made up of a certain number of furrows between the *henting* or *water-furrows*. Lands ploughed with ridges of two bouts or rounds, are called *two bouted lands*; those which are ploughed with broad ridges are *broad-lands*; and those parts of ploughed fields that run along the hedges are *head-lands*, or *hedge-lands*. When the furrow is turned towards the unploughed ground, this is termed *Rice-balking*.—*Fallowing land* is the ploughing up a fallow; *twifallowing* is ploughing it a second time; and *trifallowing* is the third ploughing.—*Rolling* is the operation by which the clods of earth are broken with a roller, and—*Harrowing* is the loosening the earth with the harrow after it has been ploughed.—*Burn-beating*, otherwise called *Denshiring*, i. e. *Devonshiring*, probably from the county where it commenced, is the burning of land, or rather the weeds, as heath, furze, &c. as it lies in heaps on the land.—Land is said to be *brought to a season* when it is made fine, by ploughing, &c.—*To Lay up land*, is to plough it the first time for any particular occasion.—*Manuring land* is the supplying it with any sort of manure; and *dressing* land is the mixing any other soil with the earth to alter its texture and properties.

Seed Time. When the land is prepared, the next step is the sowing the seeds or grain. Whatever is raised by seed is *sown*, *set*, or *drilled*.—*Sowing* is done with the hand, and when scattered over the ground, it is called *sowing broadcast*.—*Setting* is dropping the grain from the hand into holes made with the *dibble*, as in the case of wheat, peas, beans, &c.—*Drilling* is the sowing of seeds in *drills*, or rows, which is done by a machine, called the *drill-plough*. When the earth is supplied with grain, then it is necessary to *weed*, i. e. to clear it of the weeds which grow, and, in some cases, as that of turnips, it is necessary to *hoe*, i. e. to loosen the earth with the hoe, and remove some of the plants.—*Planting* is the raising of plants by means of others, or parts of others. Hops are planted by means of *sets*. Trees are raised by *layers* from the mother plant; or by *suckers* from the mother root, as the Elm, Elder, &c.; or by *slips*, *cuttings*, or *sets*, as Willows, Sallow, Ozier, and the like. Some are raised from seed, as the Oak, Chesnut, Ash, &c.; and the young plants, after they first come up, are termed *seedlings*.

Harvest. The seed time is succeeded by the *harvest*, or the gathering in of the fruits. The time for cutting grass and making hay is the *haysel*. That of cutting the corn is properly the harvest. Hay is mowed, i. e. cut with a scythe; and the grass so cut is called the *swath*. —*Strewing* the grass, is scattering it evenly over the ground, which is done either with a fork, or the hand.—*Winrowing* is the gathering into small rows the grass so strewed.—*Cocking* is the raising it into heaps.—Hay is carted on waggons by one who *pitches* with a pitchfork; and afterwards *stacked*, i. e. put upon a stack, which, if the hay be not properly made will *heat*, and sometimes be set on fire.—If the same meadow be mowed a second time, this mowing is called the *Aftermath*.—When hay is to be sold it is taken to the market in certain quantities, called a *load* or *truss*.—Wheat is ripe when the ear is yellow and hangs down. It is *reaped*, i. e. cut with a sickle, and made up into *sheaves*, i. e. bundles tied up with a *wisp* or band of straw. When several sheaves are set up in a slanting direction against each other, it is termed a *shock*, which is afterwards *carted* and placed in a barn. The heap thus raised in the barn is termed the *goff*. When a field is cleared of the shocks, the gleaners are let in to gather the scattered ears of corn, which is called *leasing* or *gleaning*. The straw of wheat or rye which is left after cutting, is the *stubble*. —Barley is ripe when the red *roan* or reddish colour is gone off, when it is mowed, and left to lie on the *swath*. If it be *inned* or *housed* wet, it will *mowburn*, which renders it unfit for *malting*, or the making of malt. If the weather be wet after it is reaped, it is apt to *must*, i. e. to spire or sprout, unless it be turned and shaken.

AGRICULTURE.

Corn is *thrashed* by the help of a flail; and *winnowed*, or cleansed, of the *chaff* or husk by means of a fan. The *Offal* is the defective grain that remains after winnowing and cleansing. When grain is thrashed, it is laid up in *granaries* until it goes to market; and, for the better preservation of it, is turned and *screened*, i. e. run through a screen. Wheat is ground either in a wind or or watermill, and yields *flour*, which is the finest part of the grain, and *meal* and *pollard*, which have different portions of the *bran* or husk mixed with it.—*Peas* are commonly reaped with a hook at the end of a long stick, and left to lie in small heaps till the *haum*, i. e. the stalks, and the *cods*, are dry.—*Hops* are ripe when they begin to colour; and are gathered by picking the hops from the *haum*, or *bind*, which is round the pole, after which they are dried to a certain *gage of draught*, in a *kiln* covered with hair, over a *staddle*, in which is a charcoal fire. *Hack dried hops* are those which are imperfectly dried. After drying, the hops are *bagged*, or put into bags called *pockets*, in which manner they are carried to market.—*Hemp* and *flax*, which are ripe when they begin to grow brown, are gathered by *pulling* and *tying* up in handfuls.—*Madder*, which is three years in coming to maturity, consists of three different sorts when it is gathered, namely, *mill-madder*, the first, is the outer rind or husk, which, when pared off, is the inferior; the second, or middle rind, is termed Number O: *crop-madder*, the third and best sort, is the heart and pith.—*Trees* are transplanted, which are removed from the spot where they were reared or have been growing. They are *pruned*, i. e. cleared of their dead woods or superfluous branches with a pruning knife: they are *lopped* when the larger branches that form the top are cut off. When trees have been often lopped, and are grown old, they are called *pollards*. Timber is *felled* when the trunk is cut down, so as to leave only a stump. It is *barked*, when it is stripped of its bark. To *stadle* a wood, is to leave young trees at certain distances.

Labours of the Yard House.

Under this head are to be reckoned the management of animals, malting, brewing, baking, management of the dairy, &c.

The animals on a farm are termed the *live stock*, and consist of either beasts called *cattle*, or birds called *poultry*. Beasts are either beasts of burden, as horses, &c.; or grazing beasts, as oxen, sheep, &c.—*Horses* are distinguished into *draught-horses*, *riding-horses*, &c. [vide *Horse*] A *team* of horses is any number that go together either in a waggon or plough. The young of a horse is termed a *foal* while it sucks, and a *colt* before it is broken in for use. The *stable* is the place set apart for the horses; the *stall* is a partition in the stable for a single horse; the *litter* is his bed of straw; the *rack* is the place railed off for his hay; the *manger* is a trough for his corn; and the *bin* is the chest to hold the chaff or the corn. Of grazing beasts there is the—*Ox*, of which the male is called the *bull*, and the female the *cow*. The young of a cow, while it sucks, is a *calf*, afterwards a *steer* if male, a *heifer* if female, and a *bud* as soon as it has budding horns. Oxen of the black kind are called *black cattle*, and cows which are kept for their milk are called *milch-cows*.—*Sheep* are bred for their flesh and their wool. The male of the sheep is the *ram*, which, when cut, is a *weather*; the female the *ewe*, which, when it is old, is a *crone*. *Polled sheep* are those without horns, which are reckoned the best breeders. The young of sheep are termed *lambs*, and the bringing forth is *yeaning* or *lambing*.

Shearing of sheep is taking off their wool with shears; whence, as shearing takes place annually, their age is reckoned thereby, as *one-shear sheep*, *two-shear sheep*, &c. Sheep are penned or folded, that is, they are fastened within a narrow space called a *pen*, by means of *hurdles* or moveable gates, which are fixed into the ground, and tied together with ozier-twigs.—*Swine* are kept for breeding and fatting, of which the male is the *boar*, and, after it is cut, is a *hog*; the female is the *sow*, and, after it is cut, the *spayed gelt*. The young of the sow is the *pig*, and the bringing forth is *farrowing*; while a pig sucks it is a *sucking pig*; when fit for roasting, it is a *roaster*; and, when it is three quarters of a year old, it is a *young shoot*. Swine *shackle* in corn fields or on mash, i. e. the acorns that are under the tree; their flesh is called *pork*, but that of the boar is *brawn*.—*Poultry* are the domestic *fowls* or birds kept for their flesh, and their eggs. The male bird is generally the *cock*, the female the *hen*; but of geese the male is the *gander*, the female the *goose*; and of ducks the male is the *drake*, and the female the *duck*. Poultry *hatch* their young by sitting upon their eggs a certain time; a hen brings forth *chickens* after twenty days' sitting; a duck brings forth *ducklings* after thirty days; a goose, *goslings*; a Turkey, *turkey-pouts*; and a swan, *cygnets*. *Green geese* are the young geese fatted in spring, *stubble geese*, those which are fatted in the stubble. *Barn door fowls* are full grown chickens which are fatted by the barn-door.—*Bees* are kept for their honey and wax. An *apiary* is a bee-garden, or the place where bees are kept; the *hives* or wicker baskets are their houses, which are placed on stools or benches in a sheltered spot. The *swarming* of bees is the collection of the young bees in the open air, which light on some place, and form themselves into a compact body. The honey and wax is collected into a solid substance called the *comb*. The *virgin honey* is that which flows of itself out of the comb when taken out of the hive, and also that which comes from the first year's swarm.

Malting is the making of malt out of barley, which is done by a particular process, and the person who causes it to be done is the *malster*. Barley is first steeped, that is, left in water for three nights till it be drenched; it is afterwards laid on the floor, and the quantity laid down, at a given time, is called a *couch*. In this state it sends forth a sprout, which is called the *spire* or *come*, and the second *spire*, which succeeds the first, and comes at the end of the barley, is called the *acrospire*. This determines the state of the grain, whether it be fit for the next process, which is *kiln-drying*, i. e. drying it by the fire of the kiln, after which it becomes *malt*. This is then *cleansed* in order to clear it of the sprout or come before it goes to the mill to be ground.—*Brewing* is the making of malt, with the assistance of hops, into beer; *wort* is the essence of the malt before the hop is put to it. *Strong-beer* is made of the first wort, which is drawn from the malt; *ale* is a middle sort of beer; *small-beer*, otherwise called *table-beer*, is the weakest kind of the three; *homebrewed beer* is that which is brewed in private families, in distinction from that which is made in the public breweries. *Mashing* is the putting of the malt to the hot water in the mash-tub; *grains* are the malt after it has been worked off the usual number of times; *yeast* is the frothy ferment which rises from the working of the beer in the cask.—*Baking* is the process of making bread out of flour with the assistance of yeast; *white-bread* is the finest sort made of the flour; *Brown-bread* is that which is made of meal; *Rye-bread* is that which is made of rye, which, on account of its colour, is called *black-bread*, and for its worthlessness

Pumpernickel, i. e. *bon pour Nickel*, or good for nothing; *slackbaked bread* is that which is not properly baked.

The *dairy* comprehends all that is made from milk. The *cream* is the essence of the milk which settles on the top, and is *skimmed*, or taken off with a *skimmer*. *Flet-milk* is that from which the cream has been taken. *Butter* is made from the cream by the process of *churning*: the liquid which remains after it has been made is called *butter-milk*. *Cheese* is made by means of the *runnet*, which turns the milk to *curd*; this is hardened in a *vat*. The liquid which remains from the curd is *whey*.

To the above may be added the following catalogue of agricultural labours through the year, beginning with the first month in order.—*January*. Ploughing lands for beans and pease. Breaking up lays. Cattle tended with turnips, and well-fenced against the frost. Fences tended. Trees lopped of dead boughs. Cows calve, and sows farrow. Lands to be cleared of bushes.—*February*. Lands to be dunged. Grey Peas and Beans to be sown and harrowed. Fences repaired and planted. Vines planted. Meadows cleared of the moles. The pastures drained for the young lambs to be dry. Barley thrashed for malting.—*March*. Marsh-grounds to be ditched. Hop-grounds set. Land ploughed for barley. Barleys sown and harrowed. Wheats rolled.—*April*. Barley, seed-time. Summer-fallowing. Fodder to be provided for the cattle, particularly the cows. Hop-yards provided with poles. Timber felled and pealed. The dairy to be well tended.—*May*. Lambs and sheep to be washed. Thrashing of corn. Barley or wheat fed as occasion may serve. Corn-fields weeded. Buck-wheat, Flax, and Hemp sown. Hops tended on the poles, and weeded. Quicksets weeded. Bees tended. Land twi-fallowed.—*June*. Sheep shorne. Summer fallowing carried on. Bushes, thorns, &c. cleared away. Haysel begun.—*July*. Haysel finished. Try-fallowing. Hemp and flax plucked.—*August*. Reaping, mowing, and all sorts of harvest going on. Managing pastures, hop-picking and kiln-drying hops.—*September*. Farmers enter on fresh farms. Seeds thrashed. Fruits and honey gathered. Ditches, &c. made. Hemp plucked and dressed. Brakes gathered for firing.—*October*. Wheat and Rye-sowing. Laying up barley-land. Acorns, hawes, &c. sown. Quickset planted.—*November*. Swine fatted and killed. Rearing of poultry and ploughing finished.—*December*. Cattle provided with fodder and housing. Dung carted, &c.

Implements of Husbandry.

The most important of all agricultural implements is the *plough*; the parts of which are the *head*, which is designed to go into the ground; the *heel*, which is the hinder end; the *base* or bottom, otherwise called the *sole*; the *sock*, a hollow shoeing of iron fixed to the end of the head; the *stilt*, or handle for the driver; the *beam*, or long piece of wood, in which is fixed the *coulter*, or sharp iron that cuts the ground; the *bridle* or *muzzle* at the end of the beam, by which the horses are put to; the *cross-tree*, to which the traces are fixed. The back of a plough is usually called the *land-side*, and that board which receives the turf or sod is the *mould-board*, *earth-board*, or *broad-board*. A plough is said to *be in trim*, or to *swim fair* when it goes on steadily in the ground. Ploughs are named differently according to their make or use, as the *chain plough*, the *wheeled-plough*, the *sward-cutter*, the *drill-plough*, the *paring-plough*, &c.—The implements for fencing and ditching are the *bill*, or curved hatchet; *skavel*, a sort of ditching spade; *skuppat*, a scooper or hollow shovel used in marsh-lands; *didall*, a short spade for ditching.—Those used in draining are the *waterlevel*, for measuring the level of the land at a distance; *forks* and *crooks* for clearing away sedges; *wheel* and *hand-barrows*; short *scythes* for mowing down grass; and *strong water-boats* fitted to resist the water.—Those used in other labours of the field are the *waggon*, which is the largest kind of carriage; the *cart*, which is the smallest; and the *tunbril*, which is the heaviest and stoutest made. The parts of a carriage are the *axle-tree*, which supports the *body*, or the whole machine; the *wheel*, which consists of the *nave*, into which the *spokes* are fixed; the *felloes*, which form the *orb* of the wheel, and the *tire*, or *iron-band*, which goes round the orb. *Clombing* a wheel is arming the axle-tree with iron plates. *Shoeing* a wheel is arming the felloes with iron stakes. To these may be added *cromes*, or dung-forks, scythes, sickles, &c.

AGRIELÆ'A (*Bot.*) ἀγριελαία, from ἄγριος, wild, and ἐλαία, an olive, in Latin *oleaster*; the tree called the Wild Olive, or the *Olea sylvestris* of Linnæus. *Dioscor.* l. 1, c. 122; *Gorr. Def. Med.*

AGRIFO'LIUM (*Bot.*) the *Ilex aquifolium* of Linnæus.

AGRIMO'NIA (*Bot.*) Agrimony, a plant of the spriggy kind, φυγαιώδις, answers to the *Eupatorium* of Dioscorides, which is a cleanser of the blood, and a strengthener of the liver. *Diosc.* l. 4, c. 4.

AGRIMONIA, *in the Linnean system*, is a genus of plants; Class 11 *Dodecandria*, Order 2 *Digynia*.

Generic Character. CAL. *perianth* one-leaved.—COR. *petals* five; *claws* narrow.—STAM. *filaments* capillary; *anthers* small.—PIST. *germ* inferior; *styles* simple; *stigmas* obtuse.—PER. none; *calyx* contracted at the neck; *seeds* two.

Species. The principal species are the—*Agrimonia eupatoria*, seu *Eupatorium*, Common Agrimony; a perennial, native of Britain.—*Agrimonia repens*, Creeping Agrimony; a perennial, native of America.—*Agrimonia*, *Agrimonoides*, seu *Agrimoniæ similis*, &c. Three-leaved Agrimony; a perennial, native of Italy. *J. Bauhin. Hist. Plant.*; *C. Bauhin. Pin. Theat. Botan.*; *Ger. Herb.*; *Park. Theat. Botan.*; *Raii Hist. Plant.*; *Tourn. Inst. Herb.*; *Boerh. Ind. Plant.*; *Linn. Spec. Plant.*

AGRIMONIA is also the name for several species of the *Bidens* and the *Triumphetta* of Linnæus. *Raii Hist. Plant.*

A'GRIMONY (*Bot.*) the name of four different sorts of plants in the Linnean system, i. e. the *Agrimonia*; the *Ageratum*, or Bastard Hemp; the *Eupatorium*, or Hemp; and the *Bidens*, or Water-Hemp.

AGRIOCA'RDAMUM (*Bot.*) Ἀγριοκάρδαμον, from ἄγριος, wild, and κάρδαμον, Nasturtium; the *Iberis* of Linnæus. *Paul. Æginet. de Re Med.* l. 3, c. 77.

AGRIOCA'STANUM (*Bot.*) Earth-nut, or Pig-nut, the *Bunium Bulbocastanum* of Linnæus.

AGRIOCINA'RIA (*Bot.*) Wild Artichoke, the *Cynara scolymus* of Linnæus.

AGRIOCOCCIME'LA (*Bot.*) the *Prunus spinosa* of Linnæus.

AGRIOME'LA (*Bot.*) the *Pyrus malus* of Linnæus. *J. Bauh. Hist. Plant.*; *Raii Hist. Plant.*

A'GRION (*Ent.*) a division of the genus *Libellula*, according to Fabricius, consisting of those insects, of this tribe, which have their wings erect when at rest.

AGRIO'NIA (*Ant.*) Ἀγριώνια, or, according to Hesychius, Ἀγριάνια; an annual festival in honour of Bacchus, which was celebrated generally in the night. It is so called, according to Plutarch, from ἄγριος, rustic and rude, because of the rudeness and intemperance with which the celebration of this festival was attended, or from ἀγριεύς, the surname of Bacchus for his cruelty. *Plut. Sympos.* l. 8, quest. 1; & *in Anton.*; *Meurs. de Græc. Fer.*

AGRIOPA'LMA (*Bot.*) Archangel, or dead nettle.

AGRIOPASTINA'CA (*Bot.*) the wild parsnip or carrot.

AGRIOPHY'LLON (*Bot.*) the *Peucedanum officinale* of Linnæus.

AGRIORI'GANUM (*Bot.*) the *Heracleëticum* of Linnæus.

AGRIOSELI'NUM (*Bot.*) the *Smyrnium olusatrum* of Linnæus.

A'GRIOT (*Bot.*) a sour or tart cherry.

AGRIPA'LMA (*Bot.*) the *Leonurus cardiaca* of Linnæus.

AGRI'PPÆ (*Surg.*) a name for children born with their feet foremost. The name is supposed by some to be derived from *ægro partu*; by others, from Agrippa, the Roman, who came into the world in this manner. *Plin.* 1. 7, c. 8; *Gell.* l. 16, c. 16; *Non. Marcell.* c. 19; *Salmas. Exercit. Plinian.* p. 31.

A'GRIUM (*Chem.*) an impure fossil alkali.

A'GROM (*Med.*) a disease of the tongue frequent in India.

AGROSTE'MMA (*Bot.*) from ἀγρυ στεμμα, *Agri corona*, Campion; a genus of plants, Class 10 *Decandria*, Order 4 *Pentagynia*.
Generic Characters. CAL. perianth one-leaved.—COR. petals five; *claws* length of the tube of the calyx; *border* spreading.—STAM. *filaments* awlshaped; *anthers* simple.—PIST. *germ* ovate; *styles* filiform; *stigmas* simple.—PER. *capsule* oblong ovate; *seeds* very many; *receptacles* free.
Species. The species are—*Agrostemma githago*, *Lolium lychnis seu gigatho*, an annual, native of Britain.—*Agrostemma coronaria*, Rose Campion, a biennial, native of Italy.—*Agrostemma flos Jovis*, Umbellate Rose Campion, a perennial, native of Switzerland. *Ger. Herb.*; *Park. Theat. Botan.*; *Raii. Hist. Plant.*; *Mor. Hist. Plant.*; *Herm. Cat. Lugd. Batav.*; *Mild. Linn. Spec. Plant.*

AGRO'STIS (*Bot.*) ἀγρωστις, Bent Grass, a herb, so called because it grows in the fields, is a tall grass, the leaves of which, according to Dioscorides, are pointed, hard, and broad, like those of a reed. The root bruised and applied agglutinates wounds. It is called by Theocritus the πιλίτης ἀγρωστις. *Theoc. Idyl.* 13, v. 43; *Theoph. Hist. Plant.* l. 1, c. 10; *Diosc.* l. 4, c. 30; *Oribas. Med. Coll.* l. 15, c. 1; *Aet. Tetrab.* l. serm. 1.

AGROSTIS, in the Linnean system, a genus of plants, Class 3 *Triandria*, Order 2 *Digynia*.
Generic Characters. CAL. glume one-flowered—COR. bivalve.—STAM. *filaments* longer than the corolla; *anthers* forked.—PIST. *germ* roundish; *styles* reflex; *stigmas* longitudinally hispid.—PER. *corolla* growing to the seed, not gaping; *seed* roundish, pointed at both ends.
Species.—The principal species are the—*Agrostis monantha*, seu *Gramen segetum*, silky Bent Grass, an annual, native of Britain.—*Agrostis arundinacea*, Arundo agrostis, Calamagrostis arundinacea seu Gramen miliaceum, reedy Bent Grass, a perennial, native of Britain.—*Agrostis sylvatica* seu *pannicula*, &c. wood Bent Grass, a perennial, native of Britain.—*Agrostis pungens* seu *Phalaris disticha*, &c. prickly Bent Grass, a perennial, native of Spain.—*Agrostis rupestris*, *Avena monantha* seu *Gramen paniculatum*, &c. an annual, native of Switzerland, &c. *J. Bauh. Hist. Plant.*; *C. Bauh. Pin.*; *Ger. Herb.*; *Park. Theat. Botan.*; *Raii Hist. Plant.*; *Tournef. Inst.*; *Boerhaav. Ind. Plant.*; *Linn. Spec. Plant.*

AGROSTIS is also a name for the *Cenchra racemosus* and the *Milium lendigerum* and *paradoxum* of Linnæus. *Bauh. Hist. Plant.*; *Ger. Herb.*; *Raii Hist. Plant.* &c.

AGRO'TERA (*Ant.*) an annual sacrifice at Athens, in honour of Diana ἀγροτέρα, i. e. the huntress; also a temple dedicated to Diana. *Xenoph. Exped. Cyr.*

AGRO'UND (*Mar.*) i. e. on the ground; a term applied to a ship when any part of it rests on the ground so as to render it immoveable.

AGRY'PNIA (*Med.*) ἀγρυπνία, from α, priv. and ὕπνος, sleep; sleeplessness, called by Celsus, on the authority of Hippocrates, *nocturnæ vigiliæ*, or wakefulness in the night season, which he reckons among the bad symptoms. *Hippocrat.* l. 3, aphor. 24, and *Gal. Comm.* 1, *in Hippocrat. Prædict.* l. 6; *Cels.* l. 2, c. 1; *Gorr. Def. Med.*; *Foes. Oeconom. Hippocrat.*

AGRY'PNIS (*Med.*) ἀγρυπνίς; a festival in honour of Bacchus, at Arbela, in Sicily. *Hesychius.*

AGUE (*Med.*) from the French *aigue*, sharp or acute; an intermitting fever, with hot and cold fits alternately. In the vulgar sense, the ague is a fever attended with cold shiverings.—*Ague Cake*, a tumor in the spleen which often follows agues.—*Ague Drops*, a medicine consisting of the solution of arsenic in water, for the cure of the ague.

AGUE Tree (*Bot.*) the Sassafras, or *Laurus sassafras* of Linnæus; a tree so called from the medicinal virtue in its wood for curing agues.

A GUI-l'an-neuf (*Archæol.*) i. e. new year to the misletoe; a name for a ceremony among the Gauls, who, on the first day of the new year, went about gathering misletoe, and repeating *a-gui-l'an-neuf*, in which they were joined by the multitude. A similar practice prevailed in some parts of France, under the shape of begging for tapers to light the churches, until the 17th century, when it was abolished by the interference of the church.

A'GUL (*Bot.*) a little prickly shrub growing in Persia and Arabia, the *Hedysarum alhagi* of Linnæus.

A'GURAH (*Ant.*) אגורה, a Hebrew coin, which Buxtorf explains by *Nummulus*, a small coin.

AGUSADU'RA (*Archæol.*) a fee paid by vassals to their lords, for the sharpening their ploughshares, &c.

AGU'STINE (*Chem.*) a name given to a supposed new earth, so called from its forming insipid salts with acids.

A'GUTI (*Zool.*) or Long-eared Cavy, the name of an American animal resembling a guinea-pig, the *Cavia aguti* of Linnæus, which lives in hollow trees or burrows, is very voracious, and uses its fore paws like hands.

AGUITEPA (*Bot.*) a Brazilian plant, the root of which is medicinal. It is the *Thalia geniculata* of Linnæus. *Maregrav. Hist. Bras.*

AGYNE'IA (*Bot.*) from α, priv. and γυνή, wife; a genus of plants, Class 21 *Monoecia*, Order 11 *Monadelphia*.
Generic Characters.—CAL. six-leaved, *leaflets* oblong.—COR. none.—STAM. *filaments* none; *anthers* three or four in the male.—PIST. *germ* of the size of the calyx; neither *style* nor *stigma*.—PER. supposed to be a tricoccous *capsule*.
Species. The species are mostly shrubs, and natives of the East Indies and China.

AGY'NEI (*Ecc.*) a set of heretics who sprung up in 694, and said that God forbad marriage and eating of flesh. *Prateol Dogmat. Hæret.*

A'HALOTH (*Bot.*) the Hebrew name for the *Lignum Aloes.*

AHAME'LLA (*Bot.*) the *Verbesina acmella* of Linnæus.

AHE'AD (*Mar.*) further on than the ship, in opposition to astern, or behind the ship. "To run *ahead* of one's reckoning," i. e. to sail beyond the place erroneously estimated in the dead reckoning as the ship's station.—*Line ahead.* [vide *Line*]

AHME'LLA (*Bot.*) the *verbesina acmella* of Linnæus. [vide *Acmella*]

AHOU'AI (*Bot.*) or *ahovai*, a tree of Brazil, growing to the size of a pear-tree, and bearing fruit the size of a chesnut. *C. Bauh. Pin.*; *Raii Hist. Plant.*

A-HU'LL (*Mar.*) a term for a ship when all her sails are furled and her helm lashed on the lee-side.

AHU'SAL (*Chem.*) the sulphur of arsenic.

AICHMA'LOTARCH (*Theol.*) or *Æchmalotarch*, Ἀχμαλωτιχνς, which signifies, literally, prince or chief of the captives, was the title which the Jews pretend to have belonged to him who governed that people during their captivity at Babylon. They believe him to have been constantly of the tribe of Judah, although there is no proof of the existence of such a character before the end of the second century, when Huna was invested with it, after which the office continued till the eleventh century. *Prid. Connect.* part 2, book 4.

AI'D (*Hist.*) an Arabic term for a festival, so named because it returns every year.

AID (*Law*) in French *aide;* a subsidy granted to the crown, or to any lord, as in the case of knighting a son or marrying a daughter.—*Aids customary* or *common*, are those which were given by the right of custom, such as those above-mentioned.—*Aids reasonable*, are those which were given in an emergency.—*Aids gracious* or *noble*, are those which were given voluntarily.—*Aid prier*, a petition in court, to call in the help of another person who has an interest in the thing contested, as a servant having done any thing lawfully in right of his master shall have aid of him. *F. N. B.* 50.—*Aid of the king*, where the king's tenant prays aid of the king on account of rent demanded of him by others. *Stat.* 4 *Ed. I.* c. 1, &c. 14 *Ed. III.* st. 1. c. 14, &c. and 1 *H. IV.* c. 8.

AID de camp (*Mil.*) an officer that always attends on each of the generals in his camp, to receive and carry orders.—*Aid de camp major*, an officer who assists the major-general, and supplies his place in his absence.

AID (*Man.*) the assistance given to the movements of a horse by the rider, with his bridle and accoutrements; thus, a horse is said to know his aids, or take his aids with vigour. The aids are of two sorts—*Aid inner*, as the inner heel, inner leg or inner rein, &c.—*Aid outer*, as the outer heel, leg, rein, &c.

AIDE du Parc des Vivres (*Mil.*) an officer in France acting immediately under the commissary of stores and provisions.

A'IGHENDALE (*Com.*) a liquid measure in Lancashire, containing seven quarts.

A'IGLETT (*Her.*) an eaglet or young eagle.

A'GREMORE (*Mech.*) a term used by the artificers in a laboratory to signify the charcoal in a state fitted for the making of powder.

AI'GRIS (*Com.*) a stone which serves as current coin among the Issinois, a tribe of Africans, where it is looked upon as a precious stone, although it possesses no real value. It is of a greenish blue colour, without any lustre. It is hard in its texture, but does not admit of any great polish.

AIGUEMARI'NE (*Min.*) or *Aquamarine*, another name for the emerald.

AIGUI'LLE (*Mil.*) an instrument used by engineers to pierce a rock for the lodgement of powder, as in a mine: or to mine a rock so as to excavate it and make roads.—*Aiguille de Chariot*, French for the draught-tree of a chariot.

AIGUI'LLES (*Mech.*) French for the short upright pieces of wood used in the roofs of houses.

AIGUILLES (*Hyd.*) round or square pieces of wood which serve to go up and down by way of a flood-gate.

AIGUILE'TTES (*Mil.*) French for the tagged points which hang from the soldiers' uniforms, particularly among the Russians and Prussians.

AIGUI'SCE (*Her.*) or *Eguisce*, an epithet for a cross: a cross *aiguisce* is that which has the two angles at the ends cut off so as to terminate in two points, in distinction from the cross *fitchee*, which goes tapering to a sharp point.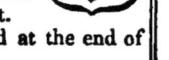

AI'GULET (*Mech.*) a point of gold placed at the end of fringes.

AIL (*Law*) or *Aiel*, from the French *aieul*, an ancestor, or a grandfather; a writ which lies where a man's grandfather being seized of lands and tenements in fee simple the day that he died, and a stranger abateth or entereth the same day and dispossesses the heir of his inheritance. *F. N. B.* 222.

AIL'ANTHUS (*Bot.*) from the Amboyna word *Aylanto*, i. e. the tree of heaven; a genus of plants, Class 23 *Polygamia*, Order 1 *Monoecia*.
  Generic Characters. CAL. *perianth* one-leaved.—COR. *petals* five.—STAM. *filaments* ten; *anthers* oblong.—PIST. *germs* from three to five; *styles* lateral; *stigmas* capitate.—PER. *capsules* compressed; *seeds* solitary.
  Species.—The species are—*Ailanthus glandulosa*, Tall Ailanthus, a tree, native of China.—*Ailanthus excelsa*, a tree, native of the East Indies. *Linn. Spec. Plant.*

AI'LERONS (*Mech.*) 1. The short boards which are set into the outside of the wheel of a watermill, which are called, in English, *ladles* or *aveboards*. 2. The buttresses or tarlings laid along the sides of rivers or water-coarses, in order to prevent them from undermining any building.

AIM of a bow or gun (*Sport.*) the button or mark to take aim by.

AIM *frontlet* (*Mil.*) a piece of wood hollowed out to fit the muzzle of a gun, so as to make it level with the breech, formerly in use among gunners.

A in alt. (*Mus.*) the second note in Alt, the ninth above G or treble cliff-note.—*A in Altissimo*, the second note in altissimo, or the octave above A in Alt.

AJOURE' (*Her.*) from the French *jour*, a day, or light; an epithet for that part of the field which, by the removal of an ordinary or part of it, is exposed to the view.

AIR (*Nat.*) *aer*, ἀηρ, one of the four elements, so called because, ἀιρω, it lifts things up from the earth, or because αιι ρι, it is always flowing; a rare invisible and extremely elastic fluid, not condensible by cold, or any other means, into a solid state. *Plat. in Cratin.; Arist. de Anim.* l. 1, c. 2; and *Met.* l. 1, c. 3.

AIR (*Chem.*) was expressed in ancient chemistry by the character of a triangle, thus [△].

AIR, in modern Chemistry, is distinguished into atmospheric, factitious, fixed, vital, &c.—*Air, atmospheric* or *common*, an invisible, insipid, inodorous, ponderous, and elastic fluid, consisting of two parts, vital air or oxygen gas, and mephitic air or azotic gas.—*Air factitious*, that particular sort of air which has been discovered and distinguished by means of chemical experiments. Such sorts of air are commonly known by the name of *gases*, of which the following are the principal.—*Air, fixed* or *fixable*, called by Van Helmont, *Gas sylvestre*, an inodorous and elastic fluid like the former, but of superior gravity. It is called *fixed air*, because it is found in a fixed state in lime, alkalies, &c. It is also called *carbonic acid gas*, from its acid properties. —*Air, vital* or *oxygen gas*, is the union of oxygen with caloric, and forms a constituent part of the common air. It is absolutely essential for the respiration of every animal, and on that account termed vital.—*Air inflammable*, or *Hydrogen gas*, an extremely inflammable substance, which is ten or even twelve times lighter than common air, and, by its mixture with oxygen gas, will produce the most intense heat that is known. It is fatal to animals that are obliged to breathe it; but for its lightness is generally used in the construction of air balloons.—*Air mephitic*, so called from its impurity, has also the name of *Azotic gas*, because it is destructive to life; and of *nitrogen gas*, because it is a union of nitrogen with caloric. It is the second principal ingredient in atmospheric air, being, in fact, atmospheric air deprived of its oxygen. Its principal properties are that of extinguishing flame and life, as in mines, where it is called *fire damp*, that is, *fire quencher*.—

AIR

Airs acid, those acids which assume the form of airs or gases, and in consequence receive the name of air, as—*Air phlogisticated*, the same as *mephitic air* or *vital gas*. [vide *Air mephitic*]—*Air Empyreal*, or *dephlogisticated*, the same as *vital air*. [vide *Air vital*]—*Air alkaline*, another name for *Ammonia*.—*Air dephlogisticated nitrous*, another name for the acid called *nitrous oxyd*.—*Air dephlogisticated marine*, another name for *oxymuriatic acid*. In this manner other acids are denominated.

AIR (*Anat.*) the fine aerial substance supposed to be enclosed in the labyrinth of the inward ear, and to minister to the due conveyance of the sounds in the sensory.

AIR *Bladder* (*Ich.*) the vesicles in fishes, by the contraction or dilation of which they raise or sink themselves in the water.

AIR-*vessel* (*Bot.*) or *Air-bag*, the name given by Withering to the *Folliculus* of Linnæus. [vide *Folliculus*]

AIR-*threads* (*Nat.*) a name given to the long filaments so frequently observed in the autumn season, floating in the air. These are formed by the long legged field spider, which supports itself upon them to a considerable height when it is in quest of prey.

AIR *Balloon* (*Pneum.*) a machine so constructed as to be able to float in the air and carry weight. It is filled with a species of air called hydrogen gas, or air inflammable.—*Air cane*, an air gun converted into a walking stick.—*Air gun*, an instrument for propelling bullets solely by means of condensed air.—*Air holder*, a part of the chemical apparatus, otherwise called a gazometer.—*Air hole*, a hole in a furnace just under the hearth to admit air, for increasing the force of the fire.—*Air-jacket*, a leathern jacket made with bags or bladders, communicating with each other, by the help of which when filled with air, and placed under the breast, a person may be supported in the water.—*Air lamp*, a pneumatic machine, formed by the combination of inflammable air and electricity to produce a flame, which, by means of a stop-cock, may be repressed or continued at pleasure.—*Air pipes*, pipes which are adapted to the holds of vessels, or other close places, for the purpose of clearing them of the foul air.—*Air pump*, a machine for exhausting the air out of vessels, so as to obtain a vacuum as far as possible. [vide *Pneumatics*]—*Air shaft*, a passage for the conveyance of air into mines, or other subterraneous places.—*Air trunk*, a contrivance for the clearing of rooms of the foul air, in which a number of persons are assembled.

AIR *vessel* (*Hyd.*) 1. A vessel of air, contained in water engines, which force the water out in a stream as fast as it is admitted. 2. A metallic cylinder in the improved fire engines, which is constructed so as to retain the air which is requisite for forcing out the water in an equable stream.

AIR (*Mus.*) or *Airia*, an air: 1. Any melody that comes within the reach of vocal expression. 2. In a stricter sense, any composition for a single voice.—*Air, with variations*, a melody varied, *ad libitum*, by the compiler.—*Air tendre*, an air, so denominated for the tenderness of its style.

AIR (*Man.*) a cadence and liberty of motion accommodated to the natural disposition of a horse, which makes him rise with obedience, measure, and time. [vide *Airs*]

AI'RA (*Bot.*) αἶρα, the Greek name for Lolium or Darnel, has been given by Linnæus to a genus of plants, Class 3 *Triandria*, Order 2 *Digynia*, called in English Aira Grass.
Generic Character. CAL. glume two flowered; *valves* ovate-lanceolate.—COR. bivalve; Nectary two-leaved; *leaflets* acute.—STAM. *filaments* capillary; *anthers* oblong.—PIST. *germ* ovate; *styles* cetaceous; *stigmas* pubescent.—PER. none; *seeds* subovate.
Species. The species mostly consist of different species of the *Avena* or *Gramina* of other writers. *J. Bauh in Hist. Plant.*; *C. Bauh Pin.*; *Ger. Herb.*; *Park. Theat.*

AJU

Botan.; *Raii Hist. Plant.*; *Tournef. Inst. Herb.*; *Boerh. Ind. Plant.*; *Linn. Spec. Plant.*

AIRA, as a species, answers to the *Cynosurus cæruleus* and the *Melica cærulea* and *lanatus* of Linnæus. *Jacqu. Stirp. in Vindel.*

AIR-BAG (*Bot.*) *folliculus*. [vide *Folliculus*]

AI'RE (*Falc.*) or *Airy*, a nest of hawks, or other birds of prey, especially the nest used by falcons for hatching their young in.

AIRE (*Math.*) French for, 1. The area, or inside of any geometrical figure. 2. The space between the walls of a building. 3. A smooth and even spot of ground on which one treads.

AI'R-GUN (*Pneum.*) vide *Air*.

AI'R-HOLE (*Pneum.*) vide *Air*.

AI'RING (*Vet.*) the exercise given to horses in the open air.

AI'R-PIPES, *Air-pump* (*Pneum.*) vide *Air*.

AI'R-SHAFT (*Pneum.*) vide *Air*.

AI'RS, *high* or *low* (*Man.*) the motions of a horse that rise higher than *terra a terra*, and works at curvets, &c.

AI'RY (*Falc.*) vide *Aerie* and *Aire*.

AIRY *Meteors* (*Astron.*) such as are bred from flatulous and spirituous exhalations.

AIRY *Triplicity* (*Astrol.*) the signs *Gemini*, *Libra*, and *Aquarius*.

AIS *d'entrevoux* (*Mech.*) French for boards or planks which cover the space between the rafters or beams in a building.

AISCE'AU (*Mech.*) French for a chipaxe, or one-handed plane axe, used for hewing timber smooth.

AISCE'TTE (*Mech.*) French for a small plane axe.

AISIME'NTA (*Law*) easements or conveniences, including any liberty of passage, open way, water-course, &c. for the ease and convenience of any tenant of either house or land.

AI'SLE (*Her.*) winged; an epithet for a bird in a charge having wings.

AI'SLES (*Archæol.*) the wings or side passages belonging to a church; so called from the French *les aisles*.

AI'SSE (*Mech.*) French for a linch pin.

AISSI'EU (*Mech.*) French for the axle-tree or axis, otherwise called a tympan or tambour, round which a rope may be wound for the purpose of drawing it up, after the manner of a crane.

AISTHETE'RIUM (*Med.*) *sensorium commune*, the Common Sensory.

AITO'NIA (*Bot.*) a genus of plants, Class 16 *Monadelphia*, Order 4 *Octandria*.
Generic Character. CAL. *perianth* one-leaved; *segments* sharp.—COR. *petals* four.—STAM. *filaments* awlshaped; *anthers* ovate.—PIST. *germ* superior; *style* one; *stigma* obtuse.—PER. *berry* ovate; *seeds* many.
Species. The only species is *Aitonia Capensis*, seu *Cotyledon*, a shrub, native of the Cape of Good Hope. *Linn. Spec. Plant.*

AJUBATI'PITA *Brasiliensium* (*Bot.*) a Brasilian shrub, five or six palms high, from the almond-like fruit of which is extracted an oil that is used by the savages in anointing themselves. *Raii Hist. Plant.*

AJU'GA (*Bot.*) another name for the *Abiga*, is, *in the Linnean system*, a genus of plants, Class 14 *Didynamia*, Order 1 *Gymnospermia*, called by Tournefort *Bugula*, in English Bugle.
Generic Characters. CAL. *perianth* one-leaved; *segments* nearly equal.—COR. monopetalous; *tube* cylindric; *upper lip* very small; *lower* large; *middle division* very large; *side ones* small.—STAM. *filaments* subulate; *anthers* twin.—PIST. *germ* four parted; *style* filiform; *stigmas* two.—PER. none; *seeds* somewhat oblong.
Species. The species are either perennials, as—*Ajuga alpina*, Alpine Bugle.—*Ajuga reptans*, common Bugle,

&c.; or else annuals, as the—*Ajuga chamæpitys, chia, salicifolia*, &c. They are taken mostly from the genus *Chamæpitys* of other authors. *Ger. Herb.; Park. Theat. Botan.; Raii Hist. Plant; Tournef. Instit.; Boerhaav. Ind.*

A'JUTAGE (*Hyd.*) a kind of tube or spout filled to the cistern or pipe of the *jet d' eau.*

AIZOON (*Bot.*) ἀεὶ ζῶον, i. e. always living, a genus of plants, Class 12 *Icosandria*, Order 4 *Pentagynia*.

Generic Characters. CAL. perianth one-leaved.—COR. none.—STAM. filaments very many, capillary; anthers simple.—PIST. germ five-cornered; styles five; stigmas simple.—PER. capsule five-celled; seeds kidney-shaped.

Species. The species are either annuals, as the—*Aizoon canariense, hispanicum*, &c.; or biennials, as the—*Aizoon lanceolatum, sarmentosum*, &c.; or shrubs, as the—*Aizoon fruticosum, rigidum*, &c. all which are natives of the Cape of Good Hope.

AIZOON is also the name of several species of the *Sedum* of Linnæus. *J. Bauh. Hist. Plant.; C. Bauh. Pin.; Boerhaav. Ind.*, &c.

A'KER-STAFF (*Agric.*) an instrument for clearing the coulter of the plough.

A'KETON (*Mil.*) vide *Aqueton*.

A'KOND (*Polit.*) the third pontifex in Persia, who is also an officer of justice.

AL (*Gram.*) 1. An Arabian particle, answering to the English *the*, and employed in the same manner to mark any thing distinctly, as Alcoran, from *coran*, to read; the Reading, or Book, in distinction from all others. 2. *Al*, or *ald*, from the Saxon Ælb, old, is affixed to old towns, as Aldborough, &c.

A-LA (*Gram.*) French for *in the*, used adverbially, as *à la François*, in the French fashion: *à la mode*, in the fashion.

A-LA Grec (*Mus.*) in the Greek style, as applied to chorusses.—*A la Polacca*, in the Polish style.

ALA (*Ant.*) or *Alæ*, the wings of an army, or the horse on each side flanking the foot. They were so called because they stood on the right and left, as the wings on the body of a bird. According to Vegetius, they were also called *vexillationes*. *Aul. Gell.* l. 16, c. 4; *Veget. de Re Mil.* l. 2, c. 1; *Serv. in Æn.* l. 9, v. 604; *Laz. Comm. Reip. Roman.* l. 6, c. 2; *Panvin. Imper. Roman.* c. 16; *Pancirol. Notit. Dignit. Imp. Orient.* c. 33, apud *Græv. Thes. Antiq. Roman.* vol. 10, &c.; *Salmas. de Re Milit. Roman.* c. 8.

ALA, or *Alæ* (*Bot.*) 1. The same as *Axilla*. 2. A wing or membrane on the sides of a petiole or footstalk, or attached to a seed or seed-vessel; which last is distinguished by the names of *Monopterygia* or *alatæ*, *Dipterygia* or *bialatæ*, *Tripterygia* or *trialata*, &c. according as there is one, two, three, or more wings. 3. The two side petals of a papilionaceous flower. *Linn. Phil. Botan.*

ALA, or *Alæ* (*Anat.*) μασχάλη, the arm-pit. *Hippocrat. de Art.; Gorr. Defin. Med.*—*Alæ aurium*, πτερυγώματα τῶν ὤτων, the superior parts of the external ear. *Gal. Introd.* c. 10, &c.—*Ala*, or *Alæ Nasi*, πτερυγία ῥινός, the cartilages which are joined to the extremities of the bones of the nose, and form the moveable part. *Gal. de Usu. Part.* l. 11.—*Alæ ossis Sphenoides*, the two apophyses of the os sphenoides.—*Ala*, or *Alæ Pudendi*, the same as *Nymphæ*.

ALA (*Ecc.*) vide *Alæ*.

ALABA'NDICA Rosa (*Bot.*) so called from Alabanda in Asia; a sort of damask rose with whitish leaves.

ALABA'NDICUM Opus (*Ant.*) a proverb for any bad workmanship, for which the Alabandenses were famous.

ALABA'NDICUS Lapis (*Min.*) a blackish sort of stone, the powder of which makes grey hairs black. *Æt. Tetrab.* l. serm. 2, c. 33.

ALABA'RCHES (*Ant.*) a tribute paid for the feeding of cattle; also, the gatherer of the tribute, and a nickname of Pompey, on account of his having raised taxes in Syria. *Cic. ad Attic.* l. 2, ep. 17; *Joseph. Antiq. Ind.* l. 20, c. 5; *Euseb. Hist. Eccles.* l. 2, c. 5.

ALABA'RI (*Min.*) lead.

ALABA'STER (*Ant.*) an alabaster box, or a box made of the alabaster stone.

ALABASTER (*Min.*) *Alabastrites* so called from Alabastrum, a town of Egypt; a soft kind of marble. Being easily cut, it was converted by the ancients into boxes for perfumes. It was of various colours, and streaked with veins. The burnt stone, with rosin or pitch, is a discutient. *Dioscr.* l. 5, c. 153; *Plin.* l. 37, c. 10; *P. Æginet.* l. 7, c. 3.

ALABASTRI'TES (*Min.*) 1. The Alabaster-stone, [vide *Alabaster*]. 2. A species of the *Inolithus* of Linnæus.

ALABA'STRON (*Med.*) ἀλάβαστρον, an ointment mentioned by Myrepsus. Sect. 3, c. 61.

ALABA'STRUM (*Ant.*) the box made of the alabaster-stone. *Plin.* l. 9, c. 35.

ALABASTRUM (*Min.*) or *Alabastrites*, the name among the ancients for the Alabaster-stone, which is classed by Linnæus under the species of *Gypsum*, or Plaster of Paris. *Aldrov. Mus. Metall.; Linn. System. Nat.*

ALABA'STRUS (*Bot.*) the herbaceous leaves of a plant which encompass the flower, particularly the rose. *Plin.* l. 21, c. 4.

A'LACAB (*Chem.*) Sal Ammoniac.

ALA'DINISTS (*Theol.*) a sect of Mahometans answering to free-thinkers among the Christians.

A'LÆ (*Anat.*) [vide *Ala*]

ALÆ (*Ant.*) the prominent parts of the prow of a vessel. *Poll. Onomast.* l. 1, c. 9.

ALÆ the corners of a garment, the lappets.

ALÆ Ecclesiæ (*Ecc.*) *les ailes de l'eglise*, the wings or aisles of a church.

ALÆ'A (*Ant.*) ἀλαία, a festival in Peloponnesus called after Alæa, the surname of Minerva. *Paus.* l. 8, c. 47.

A'LAFI (*Chem.*) Alkali.

ALA'IA phthisis (*Med.*) ἀλαία φθίσις, from ἀλαίος, blind; a consumption caused by a fluxion of humours in the head. *Gal. Exeges Vocab. Hippoc.*

A'LALITE (*Min.*) a stone of the Chrysolite family.

A'LAMACH (*Astron.*) Almak called Cothurnus, by Hyde; a star of the third magnitude in the southern foot of Andromeda, marked (γ) by Bayer.

A-LA-MI'RE (*Mus.*) the lowest note but one in the three septenaries of the gamut or scale of music.

ALAMO'DE (*Com.*) a thin light glossy black silk, not quilted or crossed, chiefly for women's hoods.

ALA'NA terra (*Min.*) English Oker, now called Red Ochre, the *Ochra ferri* of Linnæus, supposed to be what the ancients called *Samius lapis*, the Samian stone; a light white stone, inclining to red, which was procured principally in France. It is detersive and desiccative.

ALANA'BOLUS (*Min.*) a sort of earth mentioned by Paulus Æginetes, which is supposed to be the same as the *Alana terra*.

ALA'NDAHAL (*Bot.*) the *Colocynthis* of Linnæus.

ALANEA'RIUS (*Falcon.*) a falconer, or a keeper of dogs for hawking.

ALANFU'TA (*Anat.*) a vein between the chin and under lip.

A'LANT (*Her.*) a mastiff dog with short ears; one of the supporters to the arms of Lord Dacres.

A'LA pouli (*Bot.*) another name for the *Bilimbi* or *Averrhoe bilimbi* of Linnæus.

ALAQUE'CA (*Med.*) a stone found in little polished fragments in the East Indies, and much used to stop bleeding.

AL A'RAF (*Theol.*) the party-wall that separates heaven from hell, according to the creed of the Mahometans.

ALA′RES (*Ant.*) *Alarii milites*, the soldiers in the Roman army who formed the *alæ* or flanks, which were mostly cavalry. *Cæs. de Bell. Gall.* l. 1, c. 51; *Liv.* l. 35, c. 5.

ALA′RIS (*Med.*) alar or wing-shaped; an epithet for a vein in the bend of the arm.

ALARIS (*Bot.*) alar or wing-shaped; an epithet for the peduncle and the head.—*Pedunculus alaris*, an alar peduncle, or one that stands in the axillæ of the branches, as *Linum radiola*.—*Capitulum alare*, an alar head, or one that sits in the axillæ of the branches.

ALA′RM (*Mil.*) any notice given either by the beat of the drum or the firing of cannon, &c. which shall cause the men to run to their arms.—*Alarm post*, in the field, is the spot fixed upon by the quarter-master-general for each regiment to march to in case of an alarm: in the garrison, a similar place is marked out by the governor.—*Alarm-bell*, a bell which is made for the purpose of ringing an alarm.—*False alarms*, stratagems of war, which are employed either by an enemy for the purpose of harrassing, or by commanders for the purpose of trying the vigilance of the men.

ALARM (*Fenc.*) another name for an appeal or challenge.

ALA′TAN (*Chem.*) Lithargyrum.

A′LATUR (*Chem.*) Æs ustum.

ALATERNOI′DES (*Bot.*) another name for the *Phylica cricoides*; the *Clutea alaternoides*; the *Creanthus Africanus*; the *Ilex cassine* and the *Mirica cordifolia* of Linnæus. *Raii Hist. Plant.*

ALATE′RNUS (*Bot.*) a name formerly for a genus of plants, the species of which are now the *Rhamnus alaternus* and *phylica*; the *Celastrus*; and the *Ilex cassine*, *Paragua* and *vomitoria* of Linnæus. *Clus. Rar. Plant. Hist.*; *J. Bauh. Hist. Plant.*; *C. Bauh. Pin.*; *Ger. Herb.*; *Parkins. Theat. Botan.*; *Raii Hist. Plant.*; *Boerhaav. Ind. Botan.*

ALA′TI (*Anat.*) an epithet for such as have their scapulæ or shoulder-blade very prominent, who are supposed to be subject to consumptions.

ALATI *processus*, the processess of the Os sphenoides.

ALA′TUS (*Bot.*) winged, or provided with a membrane like a wing.

ALAU′DA (*Or.*) Lark, a genus of animals, Class *Aves*, Order *Passeres*.
Generic Characters. Bill cylindrical.—Mandibles equal.—Tongue bifid.—Hind claw straight.
Species. The principal species are the—*Alauda arvensis*, in French *l' Alouette*, the Sky Lark.—*Alauda cristatella*, in French *le Lulu*, Lesser crested Lark.—*Alauda arborea*, in French *l' Alouette de bois ou le Cujulier*, Wood-Lark.—*Alauda Italica*, in French *Giarola*, Italian Lark.—*Alauda capensis*, in French *Cravate jaune*, Cape Lark.—*Alauda mosellana*, in French *le Rousseline*, Marsh Lark.—*Alauda Senegalensis*, in French *Grisette*, Senegal Lark.—*Alauda minor seu Agrestis*, Field Lark.—*Alauda Ludoviciana*, in French *la Farlouzanne*, Louisana Lark.—*Alauda alpestris*, in French *le Haupecol*, Shore Lark.—*Alauda Africana*, in French *le Sioli*, African Lark.—*Alauda undata*, in French *la Coquillade*, Undated Lark.—*Alauda pratensis*, in French *l' Alouette de près*, Tit-Lark.—*Alauda sepiaria*, in French *Alouette pipi*, Pipit-Lark, &c.

ALAU′DÆ (*Mil.*) a legion of Transalpine Gauls who were in Cæsar's army. Suetonius says they were so called in the Gallic tongue. *Sueton. in Jul. Cæs.* c. 24.

ALA′USA (*Ich.*) vide *Alosa*.

ALA′Y (*Polit.*) a Turkish word signifying triumph, is taken for a ceremony of proclaiming war in Turkey, which is a sort of masquerade.

ALAY (*Sport.*) a term used for fresh dogs when they are sent into the cry.

A′LBA (*Ant.*) a sort of tunic, so called from its whiteness, of which mention is made in the letter of the emperor Valerian. *Trebell. Poll. in Claud.*

ALBA (*Archæol.*) the Alb. 1. A surplice anciently used by officiating priests, so called because it was made of white linen. *Con. Carthag.* IV. can. 4; *Alcuin de Offic. Divin.*; *Amalar. Eccles. Offic.* l. 2. 2. A vestment worn by persons newly baptized, as an emblem of purity; whence they were called *Albati*. *St. Ambrosius de his qui Myster. in.*; *Dionys. Areop. de Hier. Eccl.* c. 1, 2, &c.; *St. August.* epist. 168, &c.; *Alcuin. de Divin. Offic.* &c.

ALBA *firma* (*Law*) or *Album*, a yearly rent payable to the chief lord of a hundred, paid in white money or silver, in distinction from that paid in grain, &c. which was called *reditus nigri*. *2 Inst.* 19, &c.

ALBA (*Min.*) a sort of pearl of peculiar excellence. *Lamprid. in Heliogab.*; *Suidas*.

ALBA *terra* (*Alch.*) a name for the philosopher's stone, which was a composition of quicksilver and sulphur.

ALBA *spina* (*Bot.*) vide *Acacia*.

ALBA *vitiligo* (*Med.*) vide *Vitiligo*.

ALBA *pituita* (*Med.*) vide *Leucophlegmatia*.

ALBADA′RA (*Anat.*) an Arabic term for the sesamoide bone of the first joint of the great toe.

ALBAGIA′ZI (*Anat.*) Arabic for the *os sacrum*.

ALBAHU′RIM (*Astrol.*) a figure consisting of sixteen sides, on which astrological physicians built their prognostics.

ALBAME′NTUM (*Nat.*) vide *Album ovi*.

ALBA′RA (*Med.*) the same as *Alphus*.

ALBARA (*Bot.*) the *Canna angustifolia* of Linnæus. *Pis. Braz. Plant.*

ALBA′RII (*Ant.*) those who whitened earthen vessels, in distinction from the *Dealbatores* who whitened walls.

ALBA′RUS (*Chem.*) arsenic.

ALBARUS *alba* (*Med.*) the same as *Leuce*.—*Albarus nigra*, the same as *Lepra Græcorum*.

ALBA′TI (*Ant.*) clothed with the Alba [vide *Alba*]; an epithet for soldiers who were employed for parade on public occasions: "Jamprimum inter Togatos Patres et Equestrem ordinem, albatos milites et omni populo præunte." *Trebel. Poll. in Gall.*

ALBATI (*Ecc.*) an epithet, 1. For ecclesiastics in their clerical robes, who *Albas gerunt seu in Albis sunt*. 2. For those who, on receiving baptism, were clothed in the Alba. [vide *Alba*]

ALBA′TIO (*Chem.*) *Albificatio*, from *albeo*, to whiten; blanching metals.

A′LBATROSS (*Or.*) or Man of War Bird, the *Diomedea* of Linnæus; a water bird which inhabits most seas, particularly within the Tropics, between three and four feet long, and lays eggs as large as a goose, the white of which cannot be hardened by boiling.

A′LBE (*Com.*) a small coin in Germany equal to a penny.

ALBE′DO (*Med.*) whiteness, particularly as applied to urines, which are of four kinds, chrystalline, snowy, limey, and limpid. *Theophil de Urin.* c. 5; *Actuar. de Urin.* c. 8.

AL′BERAS (*Bot.*) the *Stophisagria* of Linnæus.

A′LBERGE (*Bot.*) a small forward pear of a yellow colour.

ALBERGE′LIUM (*Mil.*) an habergeon, a defence for the neck. *Hovedon.*

ALBE′RNUS (*Com.*) a stuff resembling camblet, which is manufactured in the Levant.

ALBE′RTUS (*Numis.*) a gold coin worth about fourteen livres, which was coined during the administration of Albertus, Archduke of Austria.

ALBE′STON (*Chem.*) Quick-Lime.

A′LBETAD (*Chem.*) Galbanum.

A′LBI (*Chem.*) Sublimate.

ALBICA′NTIA *Corpora* (*Anat.*) glands behind the infundibulum of the pelvis of the cerebrum.

ALB

ALBIGE'NSES (*Ecc.*) a sect of heretics in the twelfth century, who opposed the doctrine and discipline of the Romish church. They derive their name from the city of Albi where they established themselves, but they were also known by the different names of Henricians, Petrobusians, Publicans or Poplicians, Bon-hommes or Puritans, &c. according to their different tenets, which were mostly after the Manichean scheme. *Prateol. Vit. et Dogm. Hæret. omn.*; *Sander. Hæres.*; *Baron. Annal.* and *Bzov. Hist. Eccles.*

ALBI'GO (*Bot.*) mildew, a whitish mucilaginous coating of the leaves of plants, produced either by small plants or insects.

A'LBIMEC (*Chem.*) Orpiment. [vide *Auripigmentum*]

A'LBINOS (*Nat.*) the name given by the Portuguese to the white Moors, who are looked upon as monsters by the negroes.

ALBI'NUM (*Bot.*) the *Gnaphalium Diorcum* of Linnæus; a species of plant, so called from the whiteness of its blossoms.

A'LBIS (*Nat.*) pitch from the bark of the yew-tree.

ALBITROSSE (*Or.*) vide *Albatross*.

ALBO *marginatum* (*Bot.*) having white on the margin; an epithet for a leaf.—*Albo variegatum*, having white in the centre; an epithet for a leaf.

A'LBOR *Ovi* (*Nat.*) Albumen Ovi.

A'LBORA (*Med.*) a species of itch consisting of the Morphew, Serpigo and Leprosy. *Paracel. de Apostem.* c. 42.

ALBO'REA (*Chem.*) Mercury.

A'LBORO (*Ich.*) a common name, in the markets of Rome and Venice, for the small red fish called the *Erethymus*.

A'LBOT (*Chem.*) a crucible.

A'LBOTAT (*Chem.*) Ceruss.

A'LBOTIM (*Chem.*) Turpentine.

A'LBOTIS (*Med.*) Terminthus.

ALBU'CA (*Bot.*) a genus of plants; Class 6 *Hexandria*, Order 1 *Monogynia*.
 Generic Characters. CAL. none.—COR. petals six.—STAM. *filaments* shorter than the corolla.—PIST. *germ* oblong; *style* three-sided; *stigma* a triangular pyramid.—PER. *capsule* oblong; *seeds* numerous.
 Species. The species are mostly perennials, and natives of the Cape of Good Hope. *Raii Hist. Plant.*; *Mor. Hist. Plant.*; *Linn. Spec. Plant.*

ALBUGI'NEA (*Anat.*) from *albus*; an epithet for the *tunica adnata oculorum*, as also for the coat of the testicles, so called from its colour which is white.

ALBUGI'NEUS humour (*Anat.*) the aqueous humour of the eye. [vide *Aqueous Humour*]

ALBU'GO *oculorum* (*Anat.*) a disease in the eye, which consists of a pearl or white speck. *Plin.* l. 20, c. 5, &c.; *Oribas. de Loc. Affect.* l. 4, c. 24; *Aet. Tetrab.* 2, serm. 3, c. 37, &c.; *Paul. Æginet. de Re Med.* l. 3, c. 22; *Actuar. de Meth. Med.* l. 6, c. 5.

ALBUGO *Coralli* (*Nat.*) the magistery of Coral.—*Albugo Ovi*, the white of an egg. [vide *Albumen*]

A'LBULÆ *Aquæ* (*Med.*) Ἀλβυλαι, the mineral waters of Albula, in Italy, by which wounds were healed, according to Pliny. *Hist. Nat.* l. 31, c. 2; *Gal. de Meth. Med.* l. 8, c. 2; *Aet. Tetrab.* 3, serm. 3, c. 30.

A'LBUM (*Ant.*) a white table wherein the prætors had their decrees written, also a muster-roll, or list of names, as the *Album Judicum*, *Album senatorium*, &c. *Cic. Orat.* l. 2, c. 12; *Senec. de Benef.* l. 3, c. 7; *Plin. Præfat.*; *Tacit. Annal.* l. 4, c. 118; *Sueton. in Claud.* c. 16; *Dio. in August.*; *Bud. in Pandect.*; *Salmas de Med. Usur.* p. 678.

ALBUM *balsamum* (*Med.*) Capivi Balsamum.—*Album Hispanicum*, Spanish White; a cosmetic.—*Album Græcum* or *Canis*, Dog's-dung applied to Ulcers, &c. *Dale. Phar-*

ALC

macop.—*Album Jus*, a broth made from fish for sick people. *Oribas.*

ALBUM *Oculi* (*Anat.*) the White of the eye.—*Album Ovi*, the white of an egg. [vide *Albumen*]

ALBUM *Olus* (*Bot.*) Corn Salad.

ALBUM *Nigrum* (*Nat.*) Mouse-dung.

ALBUM (*Law*) vide *Alba Firma*.

ALBU'MEN (*Nat.*) the White of an egg, called by Aristotle λευκων, by Celsus *Ovi candidum*, by Pliny *Ovi Albus liquor*, by Palladius *Ovi Albor*, *Ovi Album*, or *Albumentum*. *Aristot. de Gen. Animal.* l. 3, c. 2; *Dioscor.* l. 2, c. 155; *Plin.* l. 10, c. 53; *Gal. de Simplic.* l. 11; *Harv. de Gen. Animal. Exercit.* 60.

ALBUMEN (*Bot.*) the substance of the lobes of seeds corresponding to the white of an egg. *Grew. Anat. of Plants.*

ALBU'MOR (*Nat.*) vide *Albumen*.

ALBU'RNUM (*Bot.*) the soft white substance in trees next to the *liber*, or inner bark, which gradually acquires solidity, until it becomes wood. It is, according to Linnæus, *Intermedia substantia libri et ligni*, and is vulgarly called Sap, to distinguish it from the heart, which is harder, and of a deeper colour. It derives its name *albo colore* from its white colour. *Plin.* l. 16, c. 38; *Linn. Phil. Botan.*

ALBU'RNUS (*Ich.*) the Bleak, the *Cyprinus alburnus* of Linnæus; a little fish mentioned by Ausonius, the catching of which was an amusement for children. *Auson. Mosel.* v. 126.

 Alburnos prædam puerilibus hamis.

A'LBUS *Liquor* (*Nat.*) vide *Albumen*.

ALBUS *Spinus* (*Bot.*) White Thorn.

ALBUS *Romanus Pulvis* (*Med.*) magnesia.—*Albus fluor*, vide *Fluor Albus*.

ALBUS (*Com.*) a small coin current in Cologne, a halfpenny in value.

A'LCA (*Or.*) the Auk, a genus of birds of the Order *anseres*.
 Generic Character. Bill strong, thick, compressed.—Nostrils linear.—Tongue almost as long as the bill.—Toes no back toe.
 Species. The principal species are as follow; namely—*Alca impennis*, in French *le grand Pingoin*, Penguin, or Great Auk. From the smallness of its wings it is unable to fly, and is observed by mariners never to go beyond soundings.—*Alca torda*, in French *le Pingoin*, the Razor-bill Auk or Murre, so called from the sharp edges of the bill.—*Alca arctica*, in French *le Macareux*; the *Pica marina* of Aldrovandus, and the Puffin or Coulterneb of Willoughby.—*Alca alle*, in French *la petit Guillemot*; the Little Black and White Diver of Willoughby, the *Mergulus melanoleucos* of Ray, is now more commonly known by the name of the Little Auk. —*Alca pygmæa*, an American and Asiatic bird, is still smaller than the preceding, being not more than seven inches long.

A'LCADE (*Polit.*) an inferior minister of justice in Spain.

A'LCAHEST (*Chem.*) vide *Alkahest*.

A'LCAHOL (*Chem.*) Alcohol.

ALCA'IC *Dactylic* (*Poet.*) an alcaic verse, in which the dactyl is the principal foot.—*Alcaic Strophe*, a strophe in which the Alcaic verse prevails.—*Alcaic Verse*. [vide *Alcaics*]

ALCA'ICS (*Poet*) *Carmen Alcaicum*, i. e. Alcaic Verse; a sort of verse so called from the poet Alcæus, by whom it was first used. Alcaics are of three sorts; namely— The *lesser Alcaic*, which consists of two dactyles and two trochees, as

 Hor. Carm. l. 2, od. 3, v. 28.

 Exili | um impŏsi | tūrā | cȳmbæ.

The *greater Alcaic*, which consists of five feet; the first a spondee, or iambic; the second an iambic; the third a cæsura, or long syllable; the fourth and fifth dactyles, as *Hor. Carm.* l. 1, od. 3, v. 25.

Omnēs | ĕŏ | dēm | cŏgĭmŭr | ōmnĭŭm
Versă | tūr ūr | nā, &c.

These two are called Alcaic Dactylics.—The third and last sort consists of four feet, the first an epitrite, the second and third choriambuses, and the fourth a bacchius, as
Hor. l. 1, od. 8.

Tĕ Dĕŏs ō | rō Sўbărĭn | cūr prŏpĕrēs | ămāndo.

A'LCALI (*Chem.*) vide *Alkali*.
ALCALE'SCENT, &c. (*Chem.*) vide *Alkalescent, &c.*
ALCA'NCALI (*Med.*) an antidote used in burning fevers. *Myrep.* sect. 1, c. 24.
ALCA'NNA (*Bot.*) the *Anchusa* of Linnæus, more commonly called Alkanet.
ALCAVA'LA (*Com.*) a custom-house duty paid in Spain, on imported goods, at the rate of five per cent. on the price of the commodity.
A'LCEA (*Bot.*) ἀλκία, a sort of wild mallows which was employed in medicine as an emollient. *Dioscor.* l. 3, c. 164; *Plin.* l. 27, c. 4; *Paul. Æginet. de Re Med.* l. 7, c. 3.
ALCEA, *in the Linnean system*, a genus of plants; Class 16 *Monodelphia*, Order 7 *Polyandria*, in English the Vervain Mallow.
  Generic Characters. CAL. double.—COR. petals five.—STAM. *filaments* uniting into a sort of five-angled cylinder at bottom; *anthers* almost kidney-shaped.—PIST. *germ* orbiculate; *style* cylindric; *stigmas* setaceous.—PER. *arils* many-jointed; *seed* one.
  Species. The Species are the—*Alcea rosea*, Common Holly-hock, a native of China.—*Alcea ficifolia*, Fig-leaved Holly-hock.—*Alcea Africana*, African Holly-hock, native of Africa. *J. Bauh. Hist. Plant.; C. Bauh. Pin.; Ger. Herb.; Park. Theat. Botan.; Raii Hist. Plant.; Tournef. Inst.; Boerhaav. Ind. Plant.; Linn. Spec. Plant.*
ALCEA is also the name for different species of the *Hibiscus* and *Malva* of Linnæus. *Bauh. Raii, &c.*
ALCE'BRIS *vivum* (*Chem.*) the same as *Sulphur vivum*.
ALCE'DO (*Or.*) a genus of animals; Class *Aves*, Order *Picæ*.
  Generic Characters. Bill triangular.—Tongue Fleshy.—Feet (in most) gressorial.
  Species The principal species are—*Alcedo gigantea*, in French *le plus grand Martin Pecheur*, Giant King-fisher, inhabits New Holland.—*Alcedo torquata*, in French *l' Alatli*, Cinereous King-fisher, inhabits Martinique.—*Alcedo atracapilla*, in French *le Martin-pêcheur à coiffe noir*, Blackcapped King-fisher.—*Alcedo cancrophaga*, in French *le Crabièr*, Crab-eating King-fisher.—*Alcedo flavescens*, in French *Tenrou-joulon*, Flavescent King-fisher. *Alcedo Brasiliensis*, in French *le Gip-Gip*.—*Alcedo cristata*, in French, *le Vintsi*, Crested King-fisher, inhabits Amboyne and the Philippine islands.
A'LCHAHIL (*Chem.*) Rosemary.
ALCHA'MIA (*Chem.*) vide *Alchemy*.
ALCHEMI'LLA (*Bot.*) or *Alchimella*, from having been celebrated by the Alchymists, Ladies Mantle; a genus of plants, Class 4 *Tetandria*, Order 1 *Monogynia*.
  Generic Characters. CAL. *perianth* one-leaved; *edge* flat.—COR. none.—STAM. *filaments* erect; *anthers* roundish. PIST. *germ* ovate; *style* filiform; *stigma* globular.—PER. none; *seed* solitary.
  Species. The species are—*Alchemilla vulgaris*, seu *Pes Leonis*, Common Ladies Mantle, or Bearsfoot. A perennial, native of Britain.—*Alchemilla Alpina, Stellarea argentia*, seu *Heptaphillon Cinquefoit*, or Alpine Ladies Mantle; a perennial, native of Britain.—*Alchemilla pentaphyllea*, seu *alpina, &c.* Five-leaved Ladies Mantle; a perennial, native of the Alps.—*Alchemilla Capensis*, native of the Cape of Good Hope.—*Alchemilla Aphanes, hirsuta, monandra, annuus*, seu *minima montana, Aphanes*, or *Scandix minor*, an annual.—*Alchemilla Arvenis*, an annual, native of Britain *J. Bauh. Hist. Plant.; C. Bauh. Pin. That. Botan.; Ger. Herb.; Park. Theat. Botan.; Raii Hist. Plant.; Tourn. Inst. Herb.; Boerh. Ind. Plant.; Wild. Linn. Spec. Plant.*
ALCHEMI'STOR (*Alch.*) Alchymist, a studier of Alchymy.
AL'CHEMY (*Chem.*) vide *Alchymy*.
ALCHIME'LLA (*Bot.*) vide *Alchemilla*.
ALCHI'TRAN (*Chem.*) the oil of Juniper.
ALCHOCO'RDEN (*Astrol.*) a planet that bears rule in the principal places of astrological figures at a person's nativity.
ALCHO'LLEA (*Mech.*) a sort of meat pickled, dried, and potted.
ALCHO'RNEA (*Bot.*) from Mr. Alchorne, of London; a genus of plants, Class 22 *Dioecia*, Order 13 *Monadelphia*.
  Generic Characters. CAL. *perianth* three or five leaved; *leaflets* ovate.—COR. none.—STAM. *filaments* eight; *anthers* ovate.—PIST. a rudiment.
  Species. The only species is the *Alchornea latifolia*, a shrub, native of Jamaica. *Linn. Spec. Plant.*
A'LCHYMY (*Chem.*) that branch of chemistry which more particularly treats of the transmutation of metals. It is compounded of the Arabic particle *al*, the, and the Greek χημία, preparing of metals, i. e. 'The chemistry,' by distinction from every other branch of the art.
ALCHYMY is also the name of a composition of copper and arsenic, which is used for Kitchen utensils.
ALCI'BION (*Bot.*) from ἀλκη, strength, and βίος, life; a herb that is good against the stinging of serpents.
ALCMA'NIC *verse* (*Poet.*) so called from the lyric poet, Alcmann, its inventor, consists of three dactyls and a long syllable.
A'LCOB (*Chem.*) Sal Ammoniac.
ALCOCHO'RDON (*Astrol.*) vide *Alchocorden*.
ALCODE'TA (*Chem.*) the tartareous sediment of urine.
A'LCOHOL (*Chem.*) Alcahol or *Alkohol*. 1. The powder of lead ore, a fine unpalpable powder with which the Eastern ladies tinged their hair. 2. Any powder reduced to the highest state of purity. 3. Spirits of wine, or any other fermented liquor, rectified to the highest state of perfection. *Paracel. de Tartar.*
ALCOHOLIZA'TION (*Chem.*) the reducing of bodies to a fine and unpalpable powder; or in liquids, the depriving liquid spirits of their phlegm or watery quality, so as to rectify them highly.
A'LCOL (*Chem.*) vinegar.
A'LCOLA (*Med.*) the same as aphtha.
ALCOLA (*Alch.*) the tartar or excrement of wine. *Paracel. de Urin.* c. 2.
ALCOLI'SMUS (*Chem.*) Alcolizing or reducing any substance to fine particles.
ALCOLI'TA *Urina* (*Med.*) a urine so called from the Alcola which it contains. *Paracel. de Urin.* c. 2.
A'LCORAD (*Astrol.*) a contrariety of light in the planets.
A'LCORAN (*My.*) i. e. the Koran or reading, from the Arabic *al*, the, and *Koran*, to read; a collection of fables and impostures, invented by Mahomet, which is held sacred by the Musselmen, as their Bible, or rule of faith.
ALCORAN (*Lit.*) a name given to some extravagant productions of the monks in former times, as the "Alcoran of the

Cordeliers," in which St. Francis is preposterously extolled, and put on a level with our Saviour.

A'LCORANISTS (*Theol.*) strict adherents to the letter or text of the Koran.

ALCORA'NES (*Archæol.*) high slender towers, generally built by the Mahometans near their mosques.

A'LCYON (*Or.*) vide *Halcyon*.

ALCYO'NIUM (*Con.*) a genus of animals, Class *Vermes*, Order *Zoophyta*.
Generic Characters. Animal in the form of a plant.—Stem fixed, fleshy, gelatinous, spongy, or coriaceous.
Species. The principal species are the—*Alcyonium digitatum*, Dead-man's hand.—*Alcyonium bursa*, Sea-purse.—*Alcyonium ficus*, Sea-fig, &c.

ALDABA'RAN (*Astron.*) or the Bull's Eye, a star of the first magnitude in the southern eye of the constellation Taurus, which Ptolemy calls ὁ λαμπρὸς τῶν ὑαδῶν, i. e. the bright star of the Hyades. The Right Ascension for 1812 was 66° 17′ 4″: Declination, 16° 7′ 31″ N.: Annual Variation in Right Ascension 51″ 31:. in Declination 8″ 16. *Ptolem. Almagest.* l. 7, c. 5, &c.; *Ulug. Beigh. apud Hyde Relig. Vet. Persar.*; *Bayer. Uranomet.*

A'LDER (*Bot.*) the *Betula Alnus* of Linnæus, a well-known tree which thrives particularly in moist places. It is called in Greek κλήθρα, in Latin *Alnus*, in German *Eller*, in Danish *Ell*, in Swedish *All*, *Ahl*, &c. The principal sorts of alder are three, namely, the *round-leaved*, or *common alder*, the *long-leaved*, and the *dwarf alder*. It is propagated by layers or truncheons, which are planted in February or March, and is of great use for making fences. The wood is valuable for piles and pumps, and all other works which remain under water, and is also much used by turners. The bark is employed in tanning.—*Black alder*, the *Rhamnus frangula* of Linnæus.

ALDERA'IMEN (*Astron.*) vide *Aderaimin*.

A'LDERMAN (*Polit.*) Ealdenman, formerly one of the three degrees of Nobility among the Saxons. Atheling was the first, Thane the lowest, and Alderman the same as Earl among the Danes. Now Aldermen are associates to the chief civil magistrates of a city or town corporate.

ALDERMA'NNUS totius Angliæ (*Law*) an officer answering to the Lord Chief Justice.—*Aldermannus Hundredi*, an office first appointed in the reign of Henry I.

ALDROVA'NDA (*Bot.*) a genus of plants, so called after Aldrovandus, the naturalist, Class 5 *Pentandria*, Order 5 *Pentagynia*.
Generic Characters. CAL. *perianth* five-parted.—COR. *petals* five.—STAM. *filaments* length of the flowers; *anthers* simple.—PIST. *germ* globose; *styles* very short; *stigmas* obtuse.—PER. *capsule* globose; *seeds* ten.
Species. The only species is the *Aldrovanda vesiculosa*, seu *Lenticula palustris*, &c. native of Italy. *Pluk. Almag. Botan.*; *Linn. Spec. Plant.*

ALE (*Husband.*) a species of beer, which is distinguished by having less of the hop.—*Pale Ale* is brewed from malt slightly dried.—*Brown Ale* is brewed from malt high dried.—*Ale-House*, a house that is licensed to sell ale. Stat. 5 & 6 Ed. VI.—*Ale Shot*, a reckoning to be paid at an Ale-house.

ALE-*silver* (*Law*) a rent or tribute annually paid to the Lord of the Manor by those that sell ale within the liberties of the city.—*Ale-taster*, an officer for inspecting the quality of the beer sold in Ale-houses in the city. *Kitch.* 46.—*Ale-Conner*, an officer in the city of London to inspect the measures of Ale-house Keepers.

ALE *cost* (*Bot.*) or *ale-coast*, from its being put into Ale; an old name for the *Tanacetum Balsamita* of Linnæus.—*Ale-Hoof*, Ground Ivy, so called because it serves to clear ale or beer.

ALE *Gill* (*Med.*) or *Gill-ale*, a kind of medicated liquor from the infusion of ground-ivy in malt liquor. *Quinc. Med. Dispens.*

ALECENA'RIUM (*Falcon.*) a sort of hawk called the Lanner-Hawk.

ALE-CONNER (*Archæol.*) vide *Ale*.

ALECTO'RIA (*Min.*) or *Lapis Alectorius*, from ἀλέκτωρ, a cock; a gem so called because it is found in the stomach of cocks.

ALECTORO'LOPHUS (*Bot.*) a plant so called from ἀλέκτωρ, a cock, and λόφος, a crest, because its leaves resemble the crest of a cock. By the earlier botanists, it is called either by this name, or by that of *Gallæ Crista* and *Pedicularis*. In the Linnæan system it is classed under the *Bartsia*, *Pedicularis*, and *Rhinanthus*. *Plin.* l. 21, c. 5; *Dodon. Stirp. Hist.*; *Clus. Rar. Plant. Hist.*; *J. Bauh. Hist. Plant.*; *C. Bauh. Pin.*; *Raii Hist. Plant.*; *Linn. Spec. Plant.*

ALE'CTRA (*Bot.*) a genus of plants, Class 14 *Didynamia*, Order 2 *Angiospermia*.
Generic Characters. CAL. *perianth* one-leaved; *clefts* ovate. COR. one-petalled; *tube* by degrees widened a little; *border* expanding.—STAM. *filaments* four; *anthers* twin.—PIST. *germ* ovate; *style* filiform; *stigma* incurved.—PER. *capsule* ovate; *seeds* solitary.
Species. The only species is the *Alectra Capensis*, an annual, native of the Cape of Good Hope. *Linn. Spec. Plant.*

ALECTRYOMA'NCY (*Ant.*) *Alectryomanteia*, from ἀλέκτωρ, and μαντεία, a prophecy or divination by means of cocks. It was performed by writing the twenty-four letters of the alphabet in the dust, on each of which a grain of corn was laid: then a cock magically prepared was let loose among them, and those letters, out of which he picked the corns, being joined together into words, were supposed to declare what they purposed to know. In this manner Jamblicus, the master of Proclus, is said to have divined that a person, named Theodosius, Theodotus, Theodorus, or Theodectes, was to succeed the emperor Valens, which coming to the emperor's ears, he put to death several persons whose names began with those letters, and obliged Jamblicus to poison himself, in order to escape his fury. *Zonar. Annal.*

ALE'CTRYONON *Agon* (*Ant.*) ἀλεκτρυόνων ἀγών, i. e. the contest of cocks, an annual festival, which was celebrated by cock-fighting. It was instituted by Themistocles, in commemoration of his victory over the Persians, which had been presaged by the crowing of cocks. *Plutarch. in Themistoc.*

A'LE-DRAPER (*Archæol.*) a humourous name for an Ale-house keeper.

A-LE'E (*Mar.*) i. e. *A lee*, the situation of the helm when pushed close down to the lee side of the ship, in order to put the ship about.

ALEFA'NTES (*Chem.*) flower of salts.

A'LEGAR (*Chem.*) sour ale used by the Dyers.

A'LE-HOOF (*Bot.*) a plant, the *Glycome hederacea* of Linnæus, so called from its use to clear ale or beer.

ALEI'PHA (*Med.*) Ἄλειφα, the oil of vegetables. *Gal. Exeg. apud Hippocrat.*

ALEIPTE'RIUM (*Ant.*) ἀλειπτήριον, the place in the Gymnasium at Athens where the combatants used to anoint themselves, so called from ἀλείφω, to anoint.

ALELAI'ON (*Med.*) Ἁλέλαιον, oil beat up with salt to apply to tumours. *Galen. de Remed. Parab.*; *Foes. Oeconom. Hippocrat.*

ALE'MA (*Chem.*) ἄλημα, boiled meal.

ALE'MBIC (*Chem.*) *Alembicus*, compounded of the Arabic particle *al*, and the Greek ἄμβιξ, a cup; is the cap or head to a distilling vessel, which was called the body. The whole apparatus is now called by the name of Alembic, and is of two sorts, beaked and blind.—*Alembicus rostratus*, a beaked Alembric, has a canal or pipe from the head into the receiver.—*Alembicus cœcus*, a blind Alembic, is one without a pipe. *Paracel. Archidox.* l. 3.

ALE'MBOR (*Chem.*) vide *Alembroth*.

ALE'MBROTH (*Chem.*) the philosopher's salt, in the language of Paracelsus; a fixed alkaline salt. *Paracel. Diction.*

ALEOPHA'NGINÆ *pilulæ* (*Med.*) aromatic pills.

ALEO'RE (*Med.*) ἄλεωρη, ease from the abatement of a distemper. *Hippocrat. Prognost.* sect. 1; *Foes. Oeconom. Hippocrat.*

A'LEOS (*Med.*) ἄλεος, as an epithet, signifies heaped, condensed; as a substantive, heat or warmth. *Hippocrat. de Morb. Mul.*, l. 1; *Hesychius.*

A'LER *sans jour* (*Law*) to be finally dismissed the court, because there is no further day assigned for appearance. *Kitch.* 146.

A'LES (*Med.*) ἄλες, condensed; an epithet applied by Hippocrates to the excrements. *Hippocrat. de Morb. Mul.* l. 1.

ALES (*Chem.*) a compound salt.—*Ales crudum*, crude ales drops which often fall in the night time in June.

A'LESCH (*Chem.*) alumen.

A'LE-SHOT (*Archæol.*) a reckoning to be paid at an ale-house.

A'LE-SILVER (*Archæol.*) a rent annually paid to the lord mayor by those who sell ale within the city.

A'LE-STAKE (*Archæol.*) a maypole; so called because ale was sold there.

A'LET (*Falcon.*) the true falcon of Peru, that never lets her prey escape.

A'LE-TASTER (*Archæol.*) the same as Ale-Conner.

ALE'TIDES (*Ant.*) festivals at Athens, in commemoration of Erigone, who wandered with a dog in search of her father Icarus, so called from ἀλάομαι, to wander. *Athen.* l. 14, c. 3.

ALE'TON (*Med.*) ἄλετον, from ἀλέω, to grind; the meal of any sort of corn ground, as it is explained by Erotian and Hesychius *Erot. Lex*; *Hesych. Lex*; *Foes. Oeconom. Hippocrat.*

A'LETRIS (*Bot.*) a genus of plants, Class 6 *Hexandria*, Order 1 *Monogynia*.
Generic Characters. CAL. none.—COR. one-petalled.—STAM. *filaments* awlshaped; *anthers* oblong.—PIST. *germ* ovate; *style* subulate; *stigma* trifid.—PER. *capsule* ovate; *seeds* very many.
Species. The principal are the—*Aletris farinosa*, seu *acaulis*, seu *Hyacinthus floritanus*, &c. American Aletus, a perennial, native of America.—*Aletris Capensis*, seu *veltheimia*, Waved-leaved Aletris, native of the Cape of Good Hope.—*Aletris uvaria*, seu *Aloe uvaria*, Great Orange-flowered Aletris, native of the Cape of Good Hope.—*Aletris fragrans*, Sweetscented Aletris, a shrub, native of Africa. *Pluk. Almag. Botan.*; *Jacqu. Hort. Botan.*; *Linn. Spec. Plant.*

ALEURI'TES (*Bot.*) ἀλευρίτης, from ἄλευρον, meal which is scattered over different parts of the tree; a genus of plants, Class 21 *Monoecia*, Order 8 *Monadelphia*.
Generic Characters. CAL. *perianth* three-cleft; *clefts* ovate.—COR. *petals* five; *nectary* five scales.—STAM. *filaments* numerous; *anthers* roundish.—PIST. *germ* conic superior; *style* none; *stigmas* two.—PER. *berry* large; *seeds* two.
Species. The principal are the—*Aleurites triloba*, a shrub, native of the Society Islands.—*Aleurites Moluccana*, *Jatropha Moluccana*, seu *Nux Moluccana*, a shrub, native of the Moluccas.—*Aleurites laccifera*, *Croton lacciferum*, *Ricinoides aromatica arbor*, *Ricinus aromati-*

cus spicatus, seu *Halicus terrestris*, a shrub, native of the East Indies, &c. *Linn. Spec. Plant.*

ALEU'RON (*Med.*) Ἄλευρον, from ἀλέω, to grind, properly signifies the meal of corn; but is used by Hippocrates for the meal of lentils. *Hippocrat. de Morb. Mul.* l. 2; *Erotian. Lex Hippocrat.*; *Foes. Œconom. Hippocrat.*

ALEXA'NDRI *antidotus aurea* (*Med.*) an antidote for defluxions from the head. *Myrep. de Antidot.* sect. 1, c. 1.—*Alexandri collyrium*, an ointment for the eyes. *Aet. Tetrab.* 2. serm. 3, c. 39.

ALEXA'NDRIAN *library* (*Lit.*) an immense collection of books, formed at a vast expense by the Ptolemies, and afterwards burnt by order of the caliph Omar, A.D. 624. It is said that the volumes of this library supplied fuel for the 4000 baths in the city during the space of six months.

ALEXANDRI'NA *aqua* (*Ant.*) baths in Rome built by the emperor Severus.

ALEXANDRINA *laurus* (*Bot.*) the *Ruscus epiglossum* of Linnæus.

ALEXA'NDRINE (*Poet.*) or Alexandrian, the name of a particular verse in modern poetry, consisting of ten, twelve, or even thirteen syllables, and so called from a certain French poem on the life of Alexander the Great.

ALEXANDRI'NUM *emplastrum* (*Med.*) a plaster of wax, alum, &c. *Cels. de Re Med.* l. 5, c. 19.

ALEXA'NTHUS (*Chem.*) or *Altingas*, flowers of copper.

ALEXETE'RIA (*Med.*) vide *Alexipharmica*.

ALEXIPHA'RMICA (*Med.*) ἀλεξιφάρμακα, from ἀλέξω, to drive away, and φάρμακον, a poison; alexipharmics, or remedies against poisons; otherwise called *Alexiteria*. *Gal. de Simplic. Med. fac.* l. 5, c. 18; *Gorr. Defin. Med.*

ALEXIPYRE'TICUM (*Med.*) from ἀλέξω, arceo, and πυρετός, a fever; a remedy for a fever.

ALEXITE'RIA (*Med.*) vide *Alexipharmica*.

ALFA'CTA (*Chem.*) distillation.

ALFA'DIDAM (*Chem.*) the scoria of gold, iron, &c.

ALFA'NDIGA (*Com.*) the custom-house at Lisbon.

ALFA'TIDA (*Chem.*) burnt copper.

ALFA'TIDE (*Chem.*) sal ammoniac.

A'LFDOUGH (*Cook.*) a name given by the Moors to a sort of vermicelli, which they make of flour and water, and use much at their entertainments.

ALFE'CCA (*Astron.*) or Alphecca, an Arabic name for the star which Ptolemy calls ὁ λαμπρὸς ἀςὴρ ἐν τῷ ςεφάνῳ, i. e. the bright star in the crown; called by Manilius *Lucida corona*. *Ptol. Almagest.* l. 7, c. 5; *Manil. Astronom.* l. 1; *Ul. Beigh. apud Hyde. Relig. vet. Persar.*; *Bayer. Uranomet.*

ALFE'SERA (*Med.*) a confect, good for spasmodic affections. *Mesue.*

ALFE'TUM (*Archæol.*) of ælan, *accendere*, to make to burn, and fæt, *vas*, a vessel; a cauldron in which boiling water being put the accused person was to hold his hand and arm up to the elbow, and if it came out unhurt he was judged innocent. *Leg. Adelst. Reg. apud Brompton.*

A'LFIDAS (*Chem.*) Plumbum.

A'LGÆ (*Bot.*) a sea weed; so called from the *algor* or coldness of water in which it grows.

ALGÆ (*Bot.*) the second of the seven families, and the eighth of the nine tribes or nations, into which Linnæus divides all vegetables, comprehending such as have the root, leaves, and stem, all in one; as *Lichens* or Liverworts, *Fuci*, Sea-weeds, &c.

ALGÆ, *in the artificial system of Linnæus*, is the third order of the Class *Cryptogamia*, and comprehends the following genera—*Lichen*, Liverwort, having its fructifications on a smooth shining receptacle.—*Tremella*, fructification in a gelatinous substance.—*Ulva*, fructification in a membrana-

ALGEBRA.

ceous substance.—*Fucus*, Sea-weed, substance coriaceous, seeds in a gelatinous bladder.—*Conferva*, substance capillary, or fibres continuous.—*Byssus*, substance lanuginous nor nearly fibrous.

A'LGALI (*Chem.*) Nitre.

A'LGALY (*Med.*) an hollow leaden probe invented by Dr. Hale for extracting the stone.

A'LGAMET (*Chem.*) Coals.

A'LGARAB (*Med.*) the Arabic name for the disease called the Anchylops.

A'LGARES (*Med.*) a strong emetic and cathartic powder prepared from butter of antimony.

A'LGAROTH (*Med.*) *Algeroth*, a preparation of antimony and sublimate, so called from its inventor Algerothos, a physician at Verona. *Castell. Lex. Med.*

ALGA'TIA (*Chem.*) Civet.

ALGA'TRANE (*Chem.*) a sort of pitch or bituminous matter found in the isle of Plata.

A'LGEBRA, the science of computing abstract quantities by means of symbols or signs. It is so called from the Arabic word *Alghebra*, according to Lucas de Burgo, who makes *Alghebra e Almucabala*, to signify the art of restitution and comparison, opposition and restoration, or resolution and equation, which all denote different parts in the operation of equations. Others derive it from the particle *al*, the, and *Geber*, the inventor of the science; or from *geber*, to reduce fractions to integers. By Lucas de Burgo himself, the first writer on Algebra in Europe, it was called, in Italian, *L'Arte Magiore*, to distinguish it from Arithmetic, or *L'Arte Minore*, although it had been long known in Italy by the name of *Regola de la Cosa*, or Rule of the Thing. It was called *Specious Arithmetic* by Vieta, and *Universal Arithmetic* by Newton.

Algebraic Quantities.

Quantities are of different kinds; namely—*Known quantities*, the values of which are known; these are commonly represented by the first letters of the alphabet, as a, b, c, d, &c.—*Unknown quantities*, the values of which are unknown, which are represented by the letters x, y, z.—*Simple quantities* are those which consist of one term, as $a, 2b$, &c.—*Compound quantities* consist of several terms; if the quantity consist of two terms only it is called a *binomial*, as $a + b$; when of three terms a *trinomial*, as $a + b + c$; and if of four terms a *quadrinomial*, &c.—*Similar quantities* are those which are expressed by the same letter, as $a + 3a$.—*Dissimilar* or *unlike quantities* are expressed by different letters, as $a + b$.—*Positive quantities* are those which are to be added, having the sign $+$ prefixed to them, as $+b$ or $+c$.—*Negative quantities* are those which are to be subtracted, having the sign $-$ prefixed to them, as $-a$ or $-b$, &c. When no sign is prefixed to a quantity it is understood to be positive, as $a - b$, where a is a positive.—*Co-efficient of a quantity* is any number prefixed to a letter, as in $5a$, $4b$, the 5 and 4 are co-efficients. When no number is prefixed it is understood to be unity, as a for $1a$.—*Residual quantities* are binomials, having one negative quantity, as $c - d$.—*Affected quantities* are those which have some number or sign joined to them, as $5b$ or $-a$.—*Multiple of a quantity* is that which contains it a certain number of times; thus $16a$ is the multiple of $4a$.—*Measure of a quantity* is that which is contained in another a certain number of times, as $4a$, the measure of $16a$.—*Common measure* is that quantity which measures or divides two quantities without leaving a remainder, as $2a$, which is the common measure of $6a$ and $10a$.—*Rational quantities* are those which have some common measure, as $6a$ and $10a$, both of which may be measured or divided by $2a$, so as to make $3a$ and $5a$ without any remainder.—*Irrational quantities*, otherwise called *surds* or *incommensurable quantities*, are those which cannot be measured by any other quantity without a remainder, and have the radical sign $\sqrt{}$ prefixed to them, as $\sqrt{a}$ or $\sqrt{b^3}$, i. e. the square root of a, or of b cube.—*Quantities* that have no common measure but unity are said to be *prime* to one another.—*Reciprocal of a quantity* is that quantity inverted, or unity divided by it; thus $\frac{b}{a}$ is the reciprocal of $\frac{a}{b}$, and $\frac{1}{b}$ is the reciprocal of b.—*Power of a quantity* is its square, cube, &c. as a^2, the square of a; a^3, the cube; a^4, the biquadrate, or fourth power of a, &c.: these different degrees are also called *dimensions*.—*Indices*, or exponents, are the figures which are placed above the letters to denote the powers, as the 2 in a^2, the 3 in a^3, &c.

Algebraic Signs.

Signs express the relations of quantities; they are of different kinds, as follow:——$+$, the *sign of addition*, which is called *plus*, signifies that the quantity, to which it is prefixed, is to be added, as $a + b$, i. e. a plus b or a added to b.——$-$, the *sign of subtraction*, which is called *minus*, signifies that the quantity must be subtracted, as $a - b$, i. e. a minus b, or a subtracted from b. The first of these is called the *positive* or *affirmative* sign, the second the *negative* sign. When several of these signs are prefixed to different quantities they are called *like signs*, when they are all affirmative, or all negative; and *unlike signs* when they are some affirmative, and some negative; thus in $a + 2b + 3c$, or $a - 2c - 4d$, the signs are like, but in $a + 3c - 4d$ they are unlike.——$\times$, the *sign of multiplication*, as $a \times b$ signifies that a is to be multiplied by b. Multiplication may be expressed also by a note, or full-point $(\,.\,)$, and by the word *into*, as $\overline{a+b} \cdot \overline{c+d}$, or $a+b$ into $c+d$.
——$\div$, the *sign of division*, as $a \div b$ signifies that a is to be divided by b; this may be expressed also in the form of a fraction, as $\frac{a}{b}$.——$: :: :$ the *sign of proportion*, as $a : b :: c : d$, signifies that a bears the same proportion to b that c bears to d.——$\sqrt{}$, the *radical sign*, denotes the square root of the quantity before which it is placed, as $\sqrt{a^2}$, the square root of a^2, i. e. a; the same sign may be used with figures to express the root of the cube, biquadrate, &c. as $\sqrt[3]{a^3}$, $\sqrt[4]{a^4}$, &c.: these roots may likewise be expressed by fractions, $\frac{1}{2}$, $\frac{1}{3}$, $\frac{1}{4}$, &c. as $a^{\frac{1}{2}}$, $a^{\frac{1}{3}}$, $a^{\frac{1}{4}}$, $a^{\frac{1}{n}}$, which represents the square, cube, biquadrate, and nth root of a respectively.——a^{-1}, a^{-2}, a^{-3}, &c. denote the negative powers of a, and are equivalent to $\frac{1}{a^1}$, $\frac{1}{a^2}$, $\frac{1}{a^3}$, &c.——$=$, the *sign of equality*, as $a + b = x$, which signifies that a added to b is equal to x.——∞, the *sign of difference*, when it is not known, which is the greater, as $a \infty x$, which signifies either $a - x$ or $x - a$.——$\sqsubset$ or $>$ is put between two quantities to express that the former is greater than the latter, as $a \sqsubset b$ or $a > b$, i. e. a greater than b.——$\sqsupset$ or $<$ signifies the reverse of the preceding, as $a \sqsupset b$ or $a < b$, i. e. a less than b.—*Vinculum*, a line drawn over several quantities signifies that they are taken collectively, as $\overline{a - b + c} \times \overline{d - e}$, signifies that the quantity represented by $a - b + c$ is to be multiplied by $d - e$; thus suppose a to stand for 6,

ALGEBRA.

b for 5, c for 4, d for 3, and e for 1; then $a - b + c$ is $6 - 5 + 4 = 5$, and $d - e$ is $3 - 1 = 2$, therefore $\overline{a - b + c} \times \overline{d - e}$ is $5 \times 2 = 10$. In like manner are expressed the powers and the roots of quantities; thus $\overline{a + b}|^2$ denotes the square, or second power of $a + b$ considered as one quantity, and $\overline{a + b}|^3$ the third power; so that, suppose $a = 4$, $b = 2$, then $a + b = 4 + 2 = 6$, and $\overline{a + b}|^2 = \overline{4 + 2}|^2 = 6^2 = 6 \times 6 = 36$, the square of 6, or of $a + b$, also $\overline{a + b}|^3 = \overline{4 + 2}|^3 = 6^3 = 6 \times 6 \times 6 = 216$, the cube of 6, or $a + b$; and so in regard to the roots of quantities, $\sqrt{a + b}$ denotes the square root of $a + b$; suppose $a = 100$, $b = 44$, then $\sqrt{a + b} = \sqrt{100 + 44} = \sqrt{144} = 12$.——∴ or ∵ is used in operations to signify *ergo*, therefore.

Operations in Algebra.

The operations in Algebra are Addition, Subtraction, Multiplication, Division, Fractions, Involution, Evolution, Irrational Quantities, Infinite Series, Proportion, and Equations.

Addition.

Addition consists of three cases; namely, 1. To add quantities that are like, and have like signs, which is done by adding the co-efficients and prefixing the sign, as

To	$+5a$	To	$-6b$	To	$3a - 4x$
Add	$+4a$	Add	$-2b$	Add	$5a - 8x$
Sum	$+9a$		$-8b$		$8a - 12x$

2. To add quantities that are alike, but have unlike signs, which is done by subtracting the lesser co-efficient from the greater, and prefixing the sign of the greater to the remainder, as

To	$-4a$	$5b - 6c$	$a + 6x - 5y + 8$
Add	$+7a$	$-3b + 8c$	$-5a - 4x + 4y - 3$
Sum	$+3a$	$2b + 2c$	$-4a + 2x - y + 5$

3. To add quantities that are unlike, which is done by setting the quantities down one after another, with their proper signs, as

To	$+2a$	$3a$	$4a - 4b + 3c$
Add	$+3b$	$-4x$	$-4x - 4y + 3z$
Sum	$+2a + 3b$	$3a - 4x$	$4a - 4b + 3c - 4x - 4y + 3z$

Subtraction.

Subtraction is performed by simply changing the signs of the quantity to be subtracted, and then proceeding as in the last case of addition, as

From	$+5a$	$8a - 7b$	$2a - 3x + 5y - 6$
Sub.	$+3a$	$3a + 4b$	$6a + 4x + 5y + 4$
Rem.	$5a - 3a$ or $2a$	$5a - 11b$	$-4a - 7x \quad 0 - 10$

Multiplication.

Multiplication is performed by multiplying the co-efficients together, and affixing the letters after one another to the product, in which case like signs produce $+$, and unlike signs $-$, as

Mult.	$+a$	$-12a$	$-2a$	$-6x$
By	$+b$	$-4b$	$+4b$	$-5a$
Product	$+ab$	$+48ab$	$-8ab$	$+30ax$

When the quantities are compound, multiply every part of the multiplicand by all the parts of the multiplier, and add the product as in common multiplication, as

Mult.	$a + b$		$2a - 3b$
By	$a + b$		$4a + 5b$
	$aa + ab$		$8aa - 12ab$
	$+ab + bb$		$+10ab - 15bb$
Prod.	$aa + 2ab + bb$		$8aa - 2ab - 15bb$

Mult.	$2a - 4b$		$xx - ax$
By	$2a - 4b$		$x + a$
	$4aa - 8ab$		$xxx - axx$
	$+8ab - 16bb$		$+axx - aax$
	$4aa \ldots 0 - 16bb$		$xxx \ldots 0 - aax$

Powers of the same root are multiplied by adding their indices or exponents; thus if you multiply a^3 by a^2 the product is $a^{3+2} = a^5$; b^4 multiplied by b makes $b^{4+1} = b^5$; and x^n into x is x^{n+1}, x^n into x^2 is x^{n+2}, &c.

Division.

Division is performed by expunging the letters that are common to the dividend and divisor when placed in the form of a fraction, and dividing the coefficient by any term that will divide them without any remainder. Like signs produce $+$, and unlike signs $-$; thus

$$8bc \div 2b = \frac{8bc}{2b} = 4c; \quad -12ab \div +3a = \frac{-12ab}{+3a} = -4b; \quad -6bc \div -2c = \frac{-6bc}{-2c} = +3b; \quad 10ab + 15ac \div +20ad = \frac{10ab + 15ac}{+20ad} + 5a = \frac{2b + 3c}{4d}.$$

When the quantities are compound the letters must be arranged according to the dimensions of some one letter, both in the dividend and divisor, and then proceed to work each term as in long division of numbers; thus

$$a + b\,)\,aa + 2ab + bb\,(\,a + b$$
$$aa + ab$$
$$+\ ab + bb$$
$$ab + bb$$

Here the quantities are arranged according to the dimensions of the letter a, then aa divided by a gives a the quotient, which, multiplied into the divisor, gives $aa + ab$, and this subtracted gives $+ab + bb$; ab divided by a gives $+b$, and makes, by multiplication, $ab + bb$.

The powers of the same root are divided by subtracting their indices; thus $a^5 \div a^2 = a^{5-2} = a^3$; $b^6 \div b^2 = b^{6-2} = b^4$; $a^7 b^2 \div a^2 b = a^{7-2} b^{2-1} = a^5 b$.

Fractions.

Fractions consist, as in whole numbers, of a *numerator*, which is placed above the line, and a *denominator* below it, as $\frac{a}{b}$. If the numerator a be greater than the denominator b, then it is an *improper fraction*; if the quantity consist of an integer and a fraction it is a *mixed fraction*, as $a + \frac{a^2}{b}$. A mixed fraction is reduced to an improper one by multiplying the integral part into the denominator, adding the numerator to the product, and placing the denominator under the sum, as

$2\frac{3}{5} = \frac{2 \times 5 + 3}{5} = \frac{13}{5}$; $a + \frac{a^2}{b} = \frac{a \times b + a^2}{b} = \frac{ab + a^2}{b}$; $a - x + \frac{a^2 - ax}{x}$; first $a - x \times x = ax - x^2$, then $ax - x^2$ added to $a^2 - ax = a^2 - x^2 = \frac{a^2 - x^2}{x}$.

An improper fraction is reduced to a mixed one by dividing the numerator of the fraction by the denominator; the quotient is then the integral part, and the remainder set over the denominator gives the fraction, as $\frac{ab + a^2}{b} = a + \frac{a^2}{b}$; $\frac{ax + 2xx}{a+x} = x + \frac{xx}{a+x}$; $\frac{aa + xx}{a-x} = a + x + \frac{2xx}{a-x}$.

To reduce fractions to a common denominator, multiply each numerator into all the denominators but its own for new numerators; and all the denominators together for a new denominator; thus $\frac{a}{b}$, $\frac{b}{c}$, and $\frac{c}{d}$, are reduced to the fractions $\frac{acd}{bcd}$, $\frac{bbd}{bcd}$, $\frac{ccb}{bcd}$, having the common denominator bcd.

To reduce fractions to their lowest terms, divide the numerator and denominator by their common measure, i. e. some number which divides them both without a remainder; thus $\frac{2ab}{4bc} \div 2b = \frac{a}{2c}$; $\frac{a^2 b^2 c}{a^3 b} \div a^2 b = \frac{bc}{a}$; and $\frac{6a^2 b - 12ax}{ba^2 x} \div 6a = \frac{ab - 2x}{6a^2 x}$. When the common measure is not found by inspection, then divide the greater number by the less, and, if there be a remainder, divide the last divisor by it, and so on until no remainder is left; then the last divisor is the common measure, thus, to find the common measure of $a^2 - b^2$, and $a^2 - 2ab + b^2$,

$a^2 - b^2) a^2 - 2ab + b^2 (1$
$\quad\quad a^2 - b^2$
$\quad\quad \overline{\quad\quad\quad\quad\quad\quad}$
$\quad\quad\quad - 2ab + 2b^2$ remainder.

This divided by $-2b$ is reduced to $a - b$; then
$a - b) a^2 - b^2 (a$
$\quad\quad a^2 - b^2$
$\quad\quad \overline{\quad\quad\quad}$

therefore $a - b$ is the greatest common measure to the fraction $\frac{a^2 - 2ab + b^2}{a^2 - b^2}$, then $\frac{a^2 - 2ab + b^2}{a^2 - b^2} \div a - b = \frac{a+b}{a-b}$. Fractions are added, subtracted, and multiplied, after preparing the quantities by reduction, as in whole numbers; thus add $\frac{a}{c}$ to $\frac{b}{x}$, then $\frac{ax}{cx} + \frac{bc}{cx} = \frac{ax + bc}{cx}$ the sum; from $\frac{a}{c}$ take $\frac{b}{x}$, then $\frac{ax}{cx} - \frac{bc}{cx} = \frac{ax - bc}{cx}$; $\frac{a}{c} \times \frac{b}{x} = \frac{ab}{cx}$; but, in dividing fractions, invert the divisor, and then proceed as in multiplication; thus $\frac{2a}{b} \div \frac{4c}{d} = \frac{2a}{b} \times \frac{d}{4c} = \frac{2ad}{4bc} = \frac{ad}{2bc}$, the quotient required.

Involution.

Involution is the continual multiplication of a quantity into itself; the products arising thence are called the *powers* of the quantity, and the quantity itself is called the *root*, as $a \times a = aa$ or a^2; $a \times a \times a = aaa$ or a^3. When the sign of the root is $+$, all the powers of it will be $+$; but, if it be $-$, then the even powers will be $+$, and the odd powers $-$; thus, the second power of $-a$ is $-a \times -a = +a^2$, but the third power of a is $+a^2 \times -a = -a^3$. The powers of quantities are multiplied by adding, and divided by subtracting, their exponents. When a lesser power is divided by a greater, the exponent must be negative; thus $\frac{a^4}{a^6} = a^4 \div a^6 = a^{4-6} = a^{-2}$, or, as it is otherwise expressed, $\frac{1}{a^2}$. These negative powers are also multiplied by adding, and divided by subtracting, their exponents; thus $a^{-2} \times a^{-3} = a^{-2-3} = a^{-5}$.

Binomial Theorem.

To remove the trouble and entanglement of raising compound quantities, Sir Isaac Newton formed a general theorem, the principles of which, as illustrated by Maclaurin, are as follow:

1st, That, in the first term of any power of $a \mp b$, the quantity a has the exponent of the power required, which decreases gradually in the following terms, and is never found in the last. The powers of b are in the contrary order; for it is never found in the first term; and its exponent in the second term is unit, in the third 2, and so on till the last, which becomes equal to the exponent required. As the exponents of a thus decrease, and, at the same time, those of b increase, the sum of their exponents is always the same, and is equal to the exponent of the power required; thus in the sixth power of $a + b$, viz. $a^6 + 6a^5 b + 15 a^4 b^2 + 20 a^3 b^3 + 15 a^2 b^4 + 6 a b^5 + b^6$, the exponents of a decrease in this order; namely, 6, 5, 4, 3, 2, 1, 0, and those of b increase in the contrary order, 0, 1, 2, 3, 4, 5, 6, &c.; the sum of their exponents is always the same, and equal to the exponent of the power required.

2dly, To find the co-efficient of any term, the co-efficient of the preceding term being known, " divide the co-efficient of the preceding term by the exponent of b in the given term, and multiply the quotient by the exponent of a, in the same term, increased by unit." Thus to find the co-efficients of the terms of the sixth power of $a + b$ you find the terms are

$a^6, a^5 b, a^4 b^2, a^3 b^3, a^2 b^4, a b^5, b^6$;

and you know the co-efficient of the first term is unity; therefore, by the rule, the co-efficient of the second term will be $\frac{1}{1} \times \overline{5+1} = 6$; that of the third term will be $\frac{6}{2} \times \overline{4+1} = 3 \times 5 = 15$; that of the fourth term will be $\frac{15}{3} \times \overline{3+1} = 5 \times 4 = 20$; those of the following terms will be 15, 6, 1.

According to these rules, if, in general, $a + b$ be raised to any power m, the terms without their co-efficients will be $a^m, a^{m-1} b, a^{m-2} b^2, a^{m-3} b^3, a^{m-4} b^4, a^{m-5} b^5$, &c. continued till the exponent of b becomes equal to m; the co-efficients of the respective terms will be, 1 m, $m \times \frac{m-1}{2}$, $m \times \frac{m-1}{2} \times \frac{m-2}{3}$, $m \times \frac{m-1}{2} \times \frac{m-2}{3} \times \frac{m-3}{4}$, $m \times \frac{m-1}{2} \times \frac{m-2}{3} \times \frac{m-3}{4} \times \frac{m-4}{5}$, &c. continued until you have one co-efficient

ALGEBRA.

more than there are units in m; hence the whole theorem will be $\overline{a+b}^m = a^m + m a^{m-1} b + m \times \frac{m-1}{2}$
$\times a^{m-2} b^2 + m \times \frac{m-1}{2} \times \frac{m-2}{3} \times a^{m-3} b^3 + m \times \frac{m-1}{2} \times \frac{m-2}{3} \times \frac{m-3}{4} \times a^{m-4} b^4 +$, &c.

To illustrate this still further, let it be required to raise $a + b$ to the third power: here, the exponent of the proposed power being 3, the first term a^m of the theorem will be a^3, the second term $m\, a^{m-1} b$ will be $3\, a^{3-1} b$ or $3\, a^2 b$; the third term $m \times \frac{m-1}{2} a^{m-2} b^2$ will be $3 \times \frac{3-1}{2} a^{3-2} b^2$, or $3 \times \frac{2}{2} \times a^1 b^2$, that is, $3\, a\, b^2$; the fourth term $m \times \frac{m-1}{2} \times \frac{m-2}{3} a^{m-3} b^3$ will become $3 \times \frac{3-1}{2} \times \frac{3-2}{3} a^{3-3} b^3 = 3 \times \frac{2}{2} \times \frac{1}{3} \times a^0 b^3 = \frac{1}{1} a^0 b^3 = b^3$. Hence the third power of $a + b$ is found to be $a^3 + 3 a^2 b + 3 a b^2 + b^3$.

If a quantity consisting of three or more terms is to be involved, you may distinguish it into two parts, considering it as a binomial, and raise it to any power by the preceding rules; and then, by the same rules, you may substitute, instead of the powers of these compound parts, their values: thus, $\overline{a+b+c}^2 = \overline{a+b+c}^2 = \overline{a+b}^2 + 2 c \times \overline{a+b} + c^2 = a^2 + 2 a b + b^2 + 2 a c + 2 b c + c^2$, and $\overline{a+b+c}^3 = \overline{a+b}^3 + 3 c \times \overline{a+b}^2 + 3 c^2 \times \overline{a+b} + c^3 = a^3 + 3 a^2 b + 3 a b^2 + b^3 + 3 a^2 c + 6 a b c + 3 b^2 c + 3 a c^2 + 3 b c^2 + c^3$. In these examples $a + b + c$ is considered as composed of the compound part $a + b$ and the simple part c; and then the powers of $a + b$ are formed by the preceding rules, and substituted for $\overline{a+b}^2$ and $\overline{a+b}^3$.

Evolution.

Evolution, the reverse of Involution, is the resolving of powers into their roots. The roots of simple quantities are extracted by dividing their exponents by the number that denominates the root required; thus the square root of $a^8 = a^{\frac{8}{2}} = a^4$, the cube root of $6 x^3 = 2 x^{\frac{3}{3}} = 2 x$. The extraction of compound quantities is performed, as in common arithmetic, by extracting the root of each part, thus: let the square root of $a^2 + 2 a b + b^2$ be found, then

$$a^2 + 2 a b + b^2\; (a + b$$
$$a^2$$
$$2 a + b)\; 2 a b + b^2$$
$$+ b\; \; 2 a b + b^2$$

When the number denoting the root is not a divisor of the exponent of the given power, then the root required will have a fractional exponent; thus the square root of a^3 is $a^{\frac{3}{2}}$, and the square root of a is $a^{\frac{1}{2}}$. Powers that have fractional exponents are called *Surds*, or *Imperfect Powers*.

Surds.

Surds are quantities which have no exact root, and are expressed either by fractional indices, or by means of the radical sign $\sqrt{}$, as before observed; thus $a^{\frac{1}{2}} = \sqrt[2]{a^3}$, $a^{\frac{5}{3}} = \sqrt[3]{a^5}$, and $a^{\frac{m}{n}} = \sqrt[n]{a^m}$.

Surds are multiplied and divided by adding and subtracting their exponents like rational quantities, thus $a^{\frac{1}{3}} \times a^{\frac{4}{3}} = a^{\frac{5}{3}} = a^3$, $a^{\frac{3}{4}} \times a^{\frac{5}{4}} = a^{\frac{3}{4} + \frac{5}{4}} = a^{\frac{17}{12}} = \sqrt[12]{a^{17}}$, and $\dfrac{a^{\frac{7}{3}}}{a^{\frac{2}{3}}} = \dfrac{7-3}{a^2} = a^{\frac{4}{3}} = a^2$.

If the surds are of different rational quantities, multiply or divide them together, and set the common radical sign over their product or quotient; thus $\sqrt[3]{a^2} \times \sqrt[3]{b^3} = \sqrt[3]{a^2 b^3}$; $\dfrac{\sqrt[3]{9}}{\sqrt[3]{24}} = \sqrt[3]{\dfrac{9}{24}} = \sqrt[3]{\dfrac{3}{8}}$.

Surds may also be involved and evolved after the same manner as perfect powers; thus the square of $a^{\frac{3}{2}}$ is $a^{2 \times \frac{3}{2}} = a^3$, the cube of $a^{\frac{2}{3}}$ is $a^{3 \times \frac{2}{3}} = a^2$; the square root of $a^{\frac{3}{2}}$ is $a^{\frac{1}{2} \times \frac{3}{2}} = a^{\frac{3}{4}}$; the cube root of $a^{\frac{3}{4}}$ is $a^{\frac{1}{4}}$. Rational Quantities may be reduced to the form of surds by raising the quantity to the power that is denominated by the name of the surd, and then setting the radical sign over it, thus $a = \sqrt[2]{a^2} = \sqrt[3]{a^3} = \sqrt[4]{a^4} = \sqrt[n]{a^n}$; and the cube root of $2 x^2 = 2 x^2 \times 2 x^2 \times 2 x^2 = \sqrt[3]{8 x^6}$, or $(8 x^6)^{\frac{1}{3}}$.

To reduce surds to their most simple terms find the greatest power in the given surd, and set its root before the remaining quantity with the radical sign prefixed; thus, $\sqrt{12} = \sqrt{4} \times \sqrt{3} = 2 \sqrt{3}$; $\sqrt{a^2 x^3} = \sqrt{a^2 x^2} \times \sqrt{x} = a x \sqrt{x}$.

Surds are reduced to others of the same value that shall have the same radical sign by reducing the fractional exponents to fractions having the same value and a common denominator; thus, to reduce $\sqrt[3]{3}$ and $\sqrt[2]{2}$ to the same denominator, consider $\sqrt[3]{3}$ as equal to $3^{\frac{1}{3}}$ and $\sqrt[2]{2} = 2^{\frac{1}{2}}$, then $3^{\frac{1}{3}} = 3^{\frac{2}{6}}$ and $2^{\frac{1}{2}} = 2^{\frac{3}{6}}$, consequently $\sqrt[3]{3} = \sqrt[6]{3^2} = \sqrt[6]{27}$, and $\sqrt[2]{2} = \sqrt[6]{2^3} = \sqrt[6]{4}$; so that the proposed surds are reduced to other equal surds, $\sqrt[6]{27}$ and $\sqrt[6]{4}$ having a common radical sign.

Infinite Series.

Infinite Series is an infinite series of terms to which a division may be extended when the divisor is not contained in the dividend; as if it were required to divide 1 by $1 - x$, then

$$1 - x\,)\; 1\; (1 + x + x^2 + x^3 + x^4 + x^5, \&c.$$
$$\underline{1 - x}$$
$$+ x$$
$$\underline{+ x - x^2}$$
$$+ x^2$$
$$\underline{+ x^2 - x^3}$$
$$+ x^3$$
$$\underline{+ x^3 - x^4}$$
$$+ x^4$$
$$\underline{+ x^4 - x^5}$$
$$+ x^5, \&c.$$

Proportion.

Proportion is of two sorts, namely, arithmetical and geometrical.—*Arithmetical Proportion* denotes the relation of two quantities as respects their difference. Four

ALGEBRA.

quantities are said to be in arithmetical proportion when the difference between the first and second is equal to the difference betwixt the third and fourth, as 3, 7, 12, 16, and the quantities $a, a + b, e, e + b$. But quantities form a series in arithmetical proportion when they increase or decrease by the same constant difference; as $a, a + b, a + 2b, a + 3b, a + 4b$, &c.; $x, x - b, x - 2b$, &c. This is called *Arithmetical Progression*. In arithmetical proportion the sum of the extremes is equal to the sum of the means, thus $3 + 16 = 7 + 12 = 19$; and $a + e + b = a + b + e$.—*Geometrical Proportion* denotes that relation between two quantities, which consists in one being contained in the other a certain number of times. If of four quantities the quotient of the first and second be equal to the quotient of the third and fourth, then those quantities are said to be in Geometrical Proportion, as 2, 6, 4, 12, or the quantities a, ar, b, br, which are expressed in this manner:

$$2 : 6 :: 4 : 12 \qquad a : ar :: b : br$$

i. e. as 2 is to 6 so is 4 to 12, or as a is to ar so is b to br. In these quantities the first and third terms are called the *antecedents*, the second and fourth the *consequents*. A series is said to be in Geometrical Proportion when it increases by one common multiplier, or decreases by one common divisor, as

$$a, ar, ar^2, ar^3, ar^4, \&c. \text{ or } a, \frac{a}{r}, \frac{a}{r^2}, \frac{a}{r^3}, \&c.$$

This is called *Geometrical Progression*, and the common multiplier or divisor is called their *Common Ratio*. In Geometrical Proportion the product of the extremes is equal to the product of the means, as $2 \times 12 = 6 \times 4 = 24$; and $a \times br = ar \times b$. This sort of Proportion is moreover distinguished into the *direct*; thus, $a : b :: c : d$; *inverse*, $b : a :: d : c$; *alternate*, $a : c :: b : d$; *compound*, $a : a + b :: c : c + d$; *divided*, $a : a - b :: c : c - d$; *mixed*, $b + a : b - a :: d + c : d - c$; by multiplication, $ra : rb :: c : d$; by division, $a \div r : b \div r :: c : d$; *harmonical*, $a : d :: a \smile b : c \smile d$.

Equations.

An *Equation* is the ratio of Equality between two quantities differently denominated, expressed by the sign of equality (=) as $2 + 3 = 7 - 5$, or $a + b = c$. The quantities are called the *terms* of the Equation, as a, b, c, &c.; their places before or after the sign, the *sides* of the Equation; thus, $a + b$ is one side and c the other. The *root* of an Equation is the value of the unknown quantity contained in it, as in $3x + 18 = 24$, 2 is the root; for if you substitute 2 in the place of x you have $3 \times 2 + 18 = 6 + 18 = 24$.

Roots are either positive or negative, real or imaginary.—*Positive roots* are those that have a positive sign expressed or understood, as $x = 3$ or $x = + a$.—*Negative roots* have a negative sign prefixed to them, as $x = -5$. *Real roots* are those which contain some real or possible quantity, as those before mentioned.—*Imaginary roots* are those to which no absolute value can be attached, which, nevertheless, may be substituted for the unknown quantity so as to answer the condition of the equation. The square root of a negative quantity is always imaginary, as $\sqrt{-1}$. Every equation has as many roots, real or imaginary, as there are units in the highest power of the unknown quantity; thus, an equation of the second degree has two roots, one of the third degree three, of the fourth four, &c. as $x^3 - 8 = 0$, which has three roots, namely, one real, as $x = 2$, and two imaginary, as $x = -1 + \sqrt{-3}$, and $x = 1 - \sqrt{-3}$.

Different kinds of Equations.

Equations are of different kinds according to their powers.—*Simple Equations*, called by Vieta *pure Equations*, are those which have the unknown quantity of the first dimension only, as $7x = 35$.—*Affected*, called by Vieta *adfected*, and by Harriot *compound* Equations, are those which have the unknown quantity rising to two or more powers, as $x^2 + ax = b$, or $3x - 4x^2 + x^3 = 25$. Affected Equations are denominated after the highest power contained in them, as—*Quadratic Equations*, which rise to two powers, as $ax^2 = b$; this is called a *simple quadratic*, in distinction from the *affected quadratic*, into which the unknown quantity enters in the first as well as the second degree, as $ax^2 + bx = c$, or $x^2 + a = bx$.—*Cubic Equations* are those in which the unknown quantity is of three dimensions, as $x^3 = 25$, or $y^3 = a^3 - b^3$.—*Biquadratic Equations*, in which the unknown quantity rises to the fourth degree, as $x^4 = 25$, or $y^4 + aby^2 + a^2cy = a^3d$. Equations are moreover distinguished, according to their form, into—*Literal Equations*, in which all the quantities, both known and unknown, are expressed by letters, as $ax^2 + bx = c$.—*Numeral Equations*, those in which the co-efficients of the quantities are given in numbers, as $5x^2 + 7x = 16$.—*Binomial Equations*, such as have only two terms, as $x^5 = a, x^6 = b$, &c.—*Fluxional Equations*, equations of fluxions.—*Fluential Equations*, equations of fluents.—*Exponential Equations*, those in which the exponent is a variable or unknown quantity, as $a^x = b, x^x = a$, &c.—*Eminential Equations*, a sort of assumed equation that contains another equation eminently.—*Differential Equations*, such as involve or contain differential quantities, as the equation of $3x^2 dx - 2, axdx + aydx + axdy = 0$.—*Reciprocal Equations* are those in which the co-efficients of each pair of terms equally distant from the extremes are equal to each other, as $ax^7 + bx^6 + cx^5 = 0$; and $cx^2 + bx + a = 0$; $x^3 + 3x^2 + 3x + 1 = 0$; and $x^4 + ax^3 + bx^2 + ax + 1 = 0$.—*Determinate Equations*, those equations in which only one unknown quantity enters, in distinction from—*Indeterminate Equations*, in which there are more unknown quantities than there are independent equations, as $16p - 419 = 1$.—*Transcendental Equations* are either such as contain transcendental quantities, or such fluxional equations as do not admit of finite algebraical fluents,

thus, $y = \dfrac{\ddot{x}}{\sqrt{(a^2 - x^2)}}$ and $y =$ fluent of $\dfrac{\dot{x}}{\sqrt{(ax - x)^2}}$ are transcendant equations.—*Equation of a Curve*, an equation showing the nature of a curve by expressing the relation between the absciss and its corresponding ordinate, or else the relation of their fluxions; thus the equation of the circle is $ax - x^2 = y^2$, where a is its diameter, x any absciss or part of that diameter, and y the ordinate at that point of the diameter; so that whatever absciss is denoted by x, the square of the corresponding ordinate will be $ax - x^2$; in like manner the

equation of the ellipse is $\dfrac{p}{a}(ax - x^2) = y^2$; of the

hyperbola $\dfrac{p}{a}(ax + x^2) = y^2$; of the parabola, $px = y^2$;

where a is an axis, and p the parameter.

Operations with Equations.

Equations undergo various operations, as Generation, Reduction, Solution or Resolution, Depression, Extermination, Elimination, Transformation, Construction.

Generation of Equations is the multiplying of certain as-

L 2

ALGEBRA.

sumed simple equations together to produce compound ones; thus, suppose $x = a$, $x = b$, $x = c$, &c. or $x - a = 0$, $x - b = 0$, $x - c = 0$, then these last multiplied together become

$x - a = 0$
$x - b = 0$
───────────
$x^2 - \begin{Bmatrix} a \\ b \end{Bmatrix} x + ab = 0$
$x - c \qquad\qquad = 0$
───────────
$x^3 - \begin{Bmatrix} a \\ b \\ c \end{Bmatrix} x^2 + \begin{matrix} ab \\ ac \\ bc \end{matrix} x + abc = 0$
$x - d \qquad\qquad\qquad\qquad = 0$
───────────
$x^4 - \begin{Bmatrix} a \\ b \\ c \\ d \end{Bmatrix} x^3 - \begin{Bmatrix} ab \\ ac \\ bc \\ ad \\ bc \\ cd \end{Bmatrix} x^2 \begin{Bmatrix} abc \\ abd \\ acd \\ dbc \end{Bmatrix} x + abcd = 0$

This method was invented by Harriot, in order to show the nature of compound equations.

Reduction of Equations.

Reduction of Equations is the reducing them to the simplest form that is most commodious for their resolution: this consists of certain general rules, namely—1. Any quantity may be transposed from one side of the equation to the other by changing its sign; thus if $5x + 50 = 4x + 56$, then by transposition $5x - 4x = 56 - 50$ and $x = 6$; so likewise if $2x + a = x + b$, then $2x - x = b - a$, or $x = b - a$; for to take a quantity from one side and to place it with a contrary sign on the other, is to subtract it from both sides, and consequently if from equals you take equals the remainders will be equal. 2. If each side of an equation be divided by the same quantity, the results will be equal; for if equals be divided by equals the quotients will be equal; thus, if $ax = b$, then $x = \dfrac{b}{a}$; and if $3x + 12 = 27$, then, by Rule the first, $3x = 27 - 12 = 15$; and by this rule $x = \dfrac{15}{3} = 5$; also if $ax + 2ba = 3cc$, then, by Rule 1, $ax = 3cc - 2ba$; and, by this rule, $x = \dfrac{3cc}{a} - 2b$. 3. If every term on each side be multiplied by the same quantity the results will be equal, for if equals be multiplied by equals the products will be equal. In this manner an equation may be cleared of fractions, as if $\dfrac{x}{b} = b + 5$, then multiplying both sides by b you have $x = bb + 5b$; if $\dfrac{x}{5} + 4 = 10$, then multiplied by 5 it becomes $x + 20 = 50$, and, by Rule the first, $x = 50 - 20 = 30$; if $\dfrac{4x}{3} + 72 = 2x + 6$, then $4x + 72 = 6x + 18$; by Rule the first, $72 - 18 = 6x - 4x$, or $54 = 2x$; and, by Rule the second, $x = \dfrac{54}{2} = 27$. If there are more fractions than one in the given equation, you may, by reducing them to a common denominator, and then multiplying all the other terms by that denominator, abridge the operation thus; if $\dfrac{x}{5} + \dfrac{x}{3} = x - 7$,

then $\dfrac{3x + 5x}{15} = x - 7$; and, by this rule, $3x + 5x = 15x - 105$; and, by Rules 1 and 2, $x = \dfrac{105}{7} = 15$. 4. If the unknown quantity involve a surd root, let all the other terms be transposed to the contrary side, and involve both sides to the power denominated by the surd, of which the equation will thus become free: if there are more surds than one the operation must be repeated; thus, if $\sqrt{4x + 16} = 12$, then $4x + 16 = 144$, and $4x = 144 - 16 = 128$, and $x = \dfrac{128}{4} = 32$; if $\sqrt{ax + b^2} = 3b$, then $ax + b^2 = 9b^2$; by transposition, $ax = 9b^2 - b^2 = 8b^2$; and by division, $x = \dfrac{8b^2}{a}$; if $\sqrt{x + a} = c - \sqrt{x + b}$, then $x + a = c^2 - 2c\sqrt{x + b} + x + b$; and by transposition, $c - x + 2c\sqrt{x + b} = c^2 + b - a$, or $2c\sqrt{x + b} = c^2 + b - a$, and dividing by $2c$ we get $\sqrt{x + b} = \dfrac{c}{2} + \dfrac{b - a}{2c}$; then squaring again we have $x + b = \overline{\dfrac{c}{2} + \dfrac{b - a}{2c}}^2$; therefore $x = \overline{\dfrac{c}{2} + \dfrac{b - a}{2c}}^2 - b$. 5. If the roots be extracted from each side of an equation the results will be equal; if $x^2 = 25$, then $x = \sqrt{25} = 5$; if $x^2 + 6x + 9 = 20$, then $x + 3 = \pm\sqrt{20}$ and $x = \pm\sqrt{20} - 3$. 6. A proportion may be converted into an equation by multiplying extremes and means together; if $x : 16 - x :: 3 : 5$; then $5x (x \times 5) = 48 - 3x (16 - x \times 3)$, and by transposition $5x + 3 = 48$, or $8x = 48$; hence $x = \dfrac{48}{8} = 6$. 7. If any quantities be found with the same sign, and multiplied or divided by the same quantity on both sides of the equation, they may be struck out thus: if $3x + b = a + b$, then $3x = a$, and $x = \dfrac{a}{3}$; if $3ax + 5ab = 8ac$, then $3x + 5b = 8c$, and $x = \dfrac{8c - 5b}{3}$; if $\dfrac{2x}{3} + \dfrac{8}{3} = \dfrac{16}{3}$, then $2x + 8 = 16$, and $x = 4$. 8. Any quantity may be substituted for another which is its equal; thus, if $3x + y = 24$, and $y = 9$, then $3x + 9 = 24$, $x = \dfrac{24 - 9}{3} = 5$; if $3y + 5x = 120$, and $y = 5x$, then $15x + 5x (= 20x) = 120$, and $x = \dfrac{120}{20} = 6$. 9. In quadratic equations extract the square root on both sides, and proceed according to the preceding rules: thus, let $5x^2 - 45 = 0$, then by transposition $5x^2 = 45$, $x^2 = 9$; therefore $x = \sqrt{9} = \pm 3$. But if both the first and second powers of the unknown quantity be found in an equation, arrange the terms according to the dimensions of the unknown quantity, beginning with the highest, and transpose the known quantities to the other side; then if the square of the unknown quantity be affected with a co-efficient, divide all the terms by this co-efficient; add to both sides the square of half the co-efficients, and extract the square root on both sides; thus, suppose $y^2 + ay = b$, by adding the square of $\frac{a}{2}$ to both sides, $y^2 + ay + \frac{a^2}{4} = b + \frac{a^2}{4}$; by extracting the root $y + \frac{a}{2} = \pm\sqrt{b + \frac{a^2}{4}}$; by transposition, $y = \pm\sqrt{b + \frac{a^2}{4}} - \frac{a}{2}$. The signs $+$ and $-$ are prefixed to both the preceding roots, because the square root of any quantity may be either positive or negative; consequently quadratic equations admit of two solutions.

Resolution or Solution of Equations.

Resolution of Equations is the determination of the values of the unknown letters or quantities of which the equation is composed. 1st, If the equation consist of only one unknown quantity, bring it by the rules of reduction to stand alone on one side, and its value will then stand on the other, thus:

Example I.

A person being asked what was his age, answered that $\frac{3}{4}$ of his age, multiplied by $\frac{1}{12}$ of his age, gives a product equal to his age; quere, what was his age?

Let his age be x; then $\frac{3x}{4} \times \frac{x}{12} = x$, that is, $\frac{3x^2}{48} = x$; by Rule 3, $3x^2 = 48x$; by Rule 7, $3x = 48$; whence, by Rule 2, $x = 16$.

Example II.

If A can perform a piece of work in 8 days, and B in 10 days, in what time will they finish it together.

Let x be the time required; then since A in one day performs $\frac{1}{8}$ part of the work, in x days he performs $\frac{x}{8}$ parts of it; and in the same time B performs $\frac{x}{10}$ parts of it; and calling the work 1, $\frac{x}{8} + \frac{x}{10} = 1$, $10x + 8x = 80$, $18x = 80$, $x = \frac{80}{18} = 4\frac{8}{18} = 4\frac{4}{9}$ days.

Example III.

What quantity is that which, being divided by 4, and having 9 subtracted from the quotient, the remainder shall be 20.

Put x for the number required, then dividing x by 4, and subtracting 9 from the quotient $\frac{x}{4}$, the remainder is $\frac{x}{4} - 9$, equal by the question to 20; whence $\frac{x}{4} - 9 = 20$, $\frac{x}{4} = 29$, and $x = 116$.

2dly. If there are two unknown quantities, then there must be two equations arising from the conditions of the question; and if the values of these two quantities in each equation be found, then, by putting these values equal to each other, there will arise a new equation involving one unknown quantity, thus:

Example I.

Let $x + y = 9$, and $3x + 5y = 37$, be given to find x and y; then $y = 9 - x$, and $5y = 37 - 3x$, $y = \frac{37 - 3x}{5}$; now these two quantities, $9 - x$, and $\frac{37 - 3x}{5}$, are both equal to y, and things that are equal to one and the same thing are equal to each other; therefore $\frac{37 - 3x}{5} = 9 - x$, $37 - 3x = 45 - 5x$, $2x = 8$ $x = 4$, and $y = 9 - x = 5$.

Example II.

Let the sum of two quantities s, and their difference d, be given to find the quantities themselves.

Let x and y be the quantities; then by the question, $x + y = s$, and $x - y = d$; whence $x = s - y$, and $x = d + y$, and $d + y = s - y$ $\therefore 2y = s - d$, $y = \frac{s-d}{2}$, and $x = \frac{s+d}{2}$.

Example III.

A privateer running at the rate of 10 miles an hour, discovers a ship 18 miles off, making way at the rate of 8 miles an hour, how many miles can she run before she be overtaken.

Let x be the number of miles she can run, and y the number that the privateer must run to overtake her: then, by the question, $y = x + 18$, and $x : y :: 8 : 10$; whence $10x = 8y$, $x = \frac{4y}{5}$, and $x = y - 18$; therefore $y - 18 = \frac{4y}{5}$, $5y - 90 = 4y$, and $y = 90$, $x = y - 18 = 72$.

Sometimes the value of one quantity being found is substituted for that quantity in the equation, as, let $x + 3y = 9$, and $2x + 7y = 20$, be given to find x and y; then $x = 9 - 3y$, and by substituting this expression of x, $2 \times \overline{9 - 3y} + 7y = 20$, or $18 - 6y + 7y = 20$, and $y = 20 - 18 = 2$; therefore $x = 9 - 3y = 9 - 6 = 3$.

Sometimes the co-efficients, if they are the same in both equations, may be added or subtracted, as occasion requires. Thus let $x + y = 15$, and $x - y = 7$, be given to find x and y; then, by subtraction, $2y = 8$, and $y = 4$; by addition, $2x = 22$, and $x = 11$. If the co-efficients are different, the terms of the first equation may be multiplied by the coefficient of the unknown quantity in the second, and those of the second equation by the co-efficient of the same unknown in the first, and then add or subtract as before: thus,

Example I.

Let $x + 3y = 35$, $5x - y = 105$, be given to find x and y; from five times the first equation take the second, and you will have $14y = 70$; hence $y = \frac{70}{14} = 5$; and from three times the second equation take the first, and there will remain $14x = 280$; whence $x = \frac{280}{14} = 20$.

Example II.

Given $ax + by = c$, and $dx + ey = f$, to find x and y. From e times the first equation take b times the second, and there will remain $aex - bdx = ce - bf$; hence $x = \frac{ce - bf}{ae - bd}$. Again, from a times the second equation take d times the first, and you will have $aey - dby = af - dc$; whence $y = \frac{af - dc}{ae - db}$.

Example III.

Suppose $x + y = s$, and $x : y :: a : b$; hence $bx = ay$;

ALGEBRA.

then the second equation being taken from b times the first leaves $by = bs - ay$; hence $ay + by = bs$; therefore $y = \dfrac{bs}{a+b}$. Now write $\dfrac{bs}{a+b}$ instead of y in the second equation, namely, in $bx = ay$, and you will have $bx = \dfrac{abs}{a+b}$, or $x = \dfrac{as}{a+b}$.

When you have two equations of different dimensions, if you cannot reduce the higher to the same dimension with the lower, raise the lower to the same dimension with the higher. Thus let the sum of two quantities, s, and the difference of their squares, d, be given, to find the quantities. Put x and y for the two quantities; then by the question, $x + y = s$, and $x^2 - y^2 = d$; $x = s - y$, $x^2 = s^2 - 2sy + y^2$, and $x^2 = d + y^2$; $d + y^2 = s^2 - 2sy + y^2$, $d = s^2 - 2sy$; whence $2sy = s^2 - d$, $y = \dfrac{s^2 - d}{2s}$, and $x = \dfrac{s^2 + d}{2s}$.

3dly. If there are three unknown quantities, and consequently three equations, find two equations involving two unknown quantities, and then proceed as before: thus,

Example I.

Suppose $x + y + z = 12$, $x + 2y + 3z = 20$, and $\dfrac{x}{3} + \dfrac{y}{2} + z = 6$; then $x = 12 - y - z$, $x = 20 - 2y - 3z$, and $x = 18 - \dfrac{3y}{2} - 3z$; and $12 - y - z = 20 - 2y - 3z$, $12 - y - z = 18 - \dfrac{3y}{2} - 3z$. As these two last equations involve only y and z, they are to be resolved by the preceding rules, as follows; $2y - y + 3z - z = 20 - 12 = 8$, $y + 2z = 8$, and $36 - 3y - 6z = 24 - 2y - 2z$, $12 = y + 4z$; whence $y = 8 - 2z$, and $y = 12 - 4z$; consequently $8 - 2z = 12 - 4z$, $2z = 12 - 8 = 4$, and $z = 2$; $y = 8 - 2z = 4$; $x = 12 - y - z = 6$.

Questions of this kind may also be resolved by multiplication, addition, and subtraction, as the case requires; thus,

Example II.

Suppose $2x + y + 2z = 40$, $3x + 3y - z = 48$, $x + z = 2y$. Take twice the third equation from the first, and there will remain $y = 40 - 4y$, or $5y = 40$; therefore $y = \dfrac{40}{5} = 8$, by substituting 8 for y in the sum of the second and third equations, there will arise $4x + 3 \times 8 = 48 + 2 \times 8$, or $4x = 40$, and $x = \dfrac{40}{4} = 10$; and by writing 10 for x, and 8 for y, in the third given equation, you will have $10 + z = 2 \times 8$; hence $z = 16 - 10 = 6$.

Example III.

Suppose $x + y = a$, $x + z = b$, $y + z = c$; from the sum of the first and second equations take the third, and there will remain $2x = a + b - c$; therefore $x = \dfrac{a + b - c}{2}$. Again, from the sum of the first and third equations take the second, and you will have $2y = a + c - b$, and $y = \dfrac{a + c - b}{2}$. Lastly, from the sum of the second and third equations subtract the first, and there will remain $2z = b + c - a$; hence $z = \dfrac{b + c - a}{2}$.

Depression of Equations is the reducing them to lower degrees; as, from biquadratics to cubics, or from cubics to quadratics. Thus, if the equation be $x^3 - 6x^2 + 11x - 6 = 0$, and it be discovered that x is equal to 2, then $x - 2$ will be a divisor, by which, if the given equation be divided, it will be depressed to the quadratic $x^2 - 4x + 3 = 0$.

Transformation of Equations is the changing their form, in order to prepare them for a more ready solution. This is effected by changing the signs of the terms alternately, beginning with the second. Thus, the roots of the equation $x^4 - x^3 - 19x^2 + 49x - 30 = 0$, are $+1 + 2 + 3 - 5$; these, by changing the signs of the second and fourth terms in the same equation, namely, $x^4 + x^3 - 19x^2 - 49x - 30 = 0$, become $-1 - 2 - 3 + 5$. Equations may also be transformed into others that shall have roots greater or less than the roots of the proposed equation by some given difference. Thus, suppose the equation to be the cubic $x^3 - px^2 + qx - r = 0$; then let it be transformed into another whose roots shall be less than the roots of this equation by some given difference, e; that is, suppose $y = x - e$, and consequently $x = y + e$; then, instead of x and its powers, substitute $y + e$ and its powers, and there will arise this new equation.

$$\left.\begin{array}{l} x^3 = y^3 + 3ey^2 + 3e^2y + e^3 \\ -px^2 = - py^2 - 2pey - pe^2 \\ +qx = + qy + qe \\ -r = - r \end{array}\right\} = 0$$

Whose roots are less than the roots of the preceding equation by the difference (e).

Extermination, or *Elimination*, is the taking away any unknown quantities in a given equation, so as to facilitate the solution of the question, of which many examples may be found under the head of the Resolution of Equations.

Extermination is one mode of transforming equations by taking away the second, or any other intermediate term out of an equation; or, in other words, to put the equation into such a form that the new equation may want the second, third, or fourth, &c. term. This is only to divide the co-efficient of the second term of the proposed equation by the number of dimensions of the equation; and, assuming a new unknown quantity, y, add to it the quotient having its sign changed, and then substitute this aggregate for the unknown quantity: thus, suppose it be required to exterminate the second term out of this equation, $x^3 - 9x^2 + 26x - 34 = 0$, then let $x - 3 = y$, or $y + 3 = x$, which, being substituted, will make the new equations.

$$\left.\begin{array}{l} x^3 = y^3 + 9y^2 + 27y + 27 \\ -9x^2 = - 9y^2 - 54y - 81 \\ +26x = + 26y + 78 \\ -34 = - 34 \end{array}\right\} = 0$$

$$\overline{y^3 * - y - 10 = 0}$$

In this example the (*) denotes that the second dimension of y is wanting. If the proposed equation is a biquadratic, as $x^4 - px^3 + qx^2 - rx + s = 0$, then, by supposing $x - \frac{1}{4}p = y$, or $x = y + \frac{1}{4}p$, an equation will arise having no second term, and so on, with higher dimensions, of which more may be seen in Maclaurin's Algebra, as also on the extermination of the third and other terms.

ALGEBRA.

Finding the Limits of Equations, is that process by means of which the solution of equations is sometimes much facilitated, particularly in those cases where it is necessary to proceed by approximation; for since it is evident that a root must lie between certain limits, that is, that it must be greater than one known quantity, and less than another; we are led to a near proximate value by an easy process. Thus, suppose it were required to find a number greater than the greatest root of the equation $x^3 - 5x^2 + 7x - 1 = 0$; then, assuming $x = y + e$, we have this new equation,

$$\left.\begin{array}{l} x^3 = y^3 + 3ey^2 + 3e^2y + e^3 \\ -5x^2 = \quad\quad -5y^2 - 10ey - 5e^2 \\ +7x = \quad\quad\quad\quad\quad +7y + 7e \\ -1 = \quad\quad\quad\quad\quad\quad\quad -1 \end{array}\right\} = 0$$

Then, if 3 be substituted for e, each of the quantities $e^3 - 5e^2 + 7e - 1$, $3e^2 - 10e + 7$, $3e - 5$, is positive, or all the values of 7 are negative; therefore 3 is greater than the greatest value of x. In the same manner you may find a limit less than the least root of an equation, as $x^3 - 3x + 72 = 0$, assuming $x = y + e$; then

$$\left.\begin{array}{l} x^3 = y^3 + 3ey^2 + 3e^2y + e^3 \\ -3x = \quad\quad\quad\quad -3y - 3e \\ 72 = \quad\quad\quad\quad\quad\quad -72 \end{array}\right\} = 0$$

and here, if 5 be substituted for e, every term becomes positive; consequently, 5 is greater than the greatest root of the equation $x^3 - 3x - 72 = 0$, and 5 less than the least root of the equation $x^3 - 3x + 72 = 0$; of which more may be seen in Maclaurin's and Wood's Algebra.

Approximations of Equations is a method of coming nearer and nearer to the roots of equation, which is very similar to the method in arithmetic called Double Position, or Trial and Error. Various modes of Approximation have been devised by different authors; but that proposed by Newton, and somewhat varied by Raphson, is considered to be the most simple and practical. Of these varieties a farther account may be found in the writings of Newton, Wallis, Raphson, &c.

Construction of Equations is the finding the roots of equations by means of geometrical figures, which is effected by the intersection of lines or curves with each other, according to the rank of the equation; for the roots of equations are the ordinates of the curves at the points of intersection, with a right line. A simple equation is constructed by the intersection of one right line with another; a quadratic, by the intersection of a right line with a circle or any conic section; a cubic and biquadratic equation, by the intersection of one conic section with another. Thus, suppose the simple equation $ax = b^2 + c^2$, and the right-angled triangle, A B C, to be constructed having its base b and its perpendicular c, then the square of the hypothenuse $= b^2 + c^2$, which call h^2; then the equation is $ax = h^2$, and $x = \dfrac{h^2}{a}$ a third proportional to a and h^2.

If it be a simple quadratic, as $x^2 = ab$, then $a : x :: x : b$, or $x = \sqrt{ab}$, a mean proportional between a and b; thus, upon a straight line take A B $= a$, and B C $= b$, describe the semi-circle A D C, and raise the perpendicular to meet in D; so shall B D be $= x$, the mean proportional between A B and B C, or a and b.

If the quadratic be affected as $x^2 + 2ax = b^2$, then draw the right-angled triangle A B C, having the base A B $= a$, perpendicular, B C $= b$; from the point A at the distance of A C describe the semicircle D C E; so shall D B and B E be the two roots of the given equation $x^2 + 2ax = b^2$. [vide *Construction*]

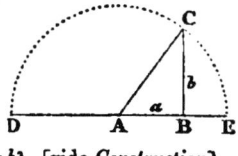

Principal writers on Algebra in chronological succession.

Diophanti "Quæstiones Arithmeticæ;" *Lucæ Paccioli* "Summa Arithmeticæ et Geometriæ," &c.; *Rudolphus* "De Algebra seu Cossa;" *Stifelii* "Arithmetica integra;" *Cardani* "Ars Magna," &c.; *Tartaleæ* "Quesiti et Inventioni diverse;" *Scheubelii* "Algebræ compendiosa facilisque Descriptio," &c.; *Recorde's* "Cossic Art," "Whetstone of Art," &c.; *Peletarii* "Cenomani de occulta Parte Numerorum," &c.; *Bombelli's* "Algebra;" *Gossalini* "De Arte magna," &c.; *Clavii* "Geometria practica, Arithmetica practica, Algebra," &c.; *Stevini* "Arithmetica et Algebra;" *Vietæ* "Opera Mathematica," Schooten's Edit.; *Girarde's* "Invention nouvelle en l'Algebre," &c.; *Harriot's* "Artis Analyticæ Praxis," &c.; *Oughtred's* "Clavis," &c.; *Descartes* "De Problematibus, quæ construi possunt adhibendo tantum Lineas et Circulos;" *Francisci a Schooten* "Commentarii in Cartesii Geometriam et Exercitationes Mathematicæ," &c.; *Gregorii* "Geometricæ Exercitationes;" *Kersey's* "Elements of Algebra; *Barrow's* "Optical and Geometrical Lectures;" *Leibnitii* "Methodus Differentialis," &c.; *Baker's* "Geometrical Key, or Gate of Equations unlocked;" *Wallisii* "Mathesis Universalis, seu Arithmeticum Opus integrum," &c.; *Raphson's* "Analysis Æquationum universalis;" *Dechale's* "Cursus, seu Mundus mathematicus;" *Ward's* "Compendium of Algebra;" *Marquis de l' Hopital's* "Analyse des infiniment Petits," &c.; *Newton's* "Arithmetica Universalis," &c.; *Maclaurin's* "Treatise on Algebra;" *Simpson's* "Algebra;" *Saunderson's* "Elements of Algebra," &c. &c.

ALGEBRA'IC (*Algeb.*) or *Algebraical*, any epithet for what belongs to Algebra; thus, an *Algebraic Curve* is one in which the relation between the absciss and ordinates can be expressed by an algebraic equation, as $dx - x^2 = y^2$ for the circle, supposing d to express the diameter, x the absciss, and y the ordinate.

ALGEBRA'IST (*Math.*) one skilled in the science of Algebra.

ALGE'DO (*Med.*) suppressed Gonorrhea, or the suppression of the discharge from the gonorrhea. *Cockb. on Gonorrh.*

ALGE'MA (*Med.*) ἄλγημα, the disease whence the pain proceeds, in which sense the term is frequently used by Hippocrates. *Gorr. Def. Med.*

A'LGENEB (*Astron.*) an Arabic name for a star of the second magnitude in Pegasus. Its longitude is 27° 46′ 12″ of Taurus, its latitude 30° 50′ 28″ North, according to Flamstead. *Bayer. Uranomet.*

ALGI'RA (*Zo.*) a Moorish Lizard, and a species of the *Lacerta* of Linnæus.

ALGO'IDES (*Bot.*) an aquatic plant, so called from its resemblance to the Alga, having imperfect hermaphrodite flowers. *C. Bauh. Pin.; Raii Hist. Plant.; Pluken. Phytograph.*

A'LGOL (*Astron.*) an Arabic name for a star, called by Ulug Beigh, *Ras Algali*, i. e. the Head of a demon; by Ptolemy ὁ λαμπρὸς ἐν τῷ Γοργονίῳ, i. e. the bright star in the Gorgons Head. It is now known by the name of Algol, or Medusa's Head, and is a star of the second magnitude, according to Ptolemy; marked (β) by Bayer; but by others it is reckoned to be of the third magnitude. Its longitude was 21° 50′ 42″ of Taurus, and its latitude 23° 23′ 47″ North, according to Flamstead. *Ptol. Almagest.* l. 7, c. 5; *Ul. Beigh. apud Hyde. Relig. Vet. Per.*; *Bayer. Uranomet.*; *Ricciol. Almagest. nov.* l. 6, c. 4, &c.; *Flamstead. Catal.*

A'LGORAB (*Ast.*) an Arabic name for a fixed star of the third magnitude, ἐν δεξιᾷ πτέρυγι, i. e. in the right wing of the constellation Corvus, marked (δ) by Bayer. *Ptol. Almag.* l. 7, c. 5; *Bayer. Uranomet.*; *Ricciol. Almag. nov.* l. 6, c. 5.

A'LGORITHM (*Math.*) from the Arabic *al*, the, and the Greek ἀριθμός, *Algorism* or *Algorithm*; the art of computation by numeral figures, as in Arithmetic.

ALGOSA'REL (*Bot.*) the *Daucus carrota* of Linnæus.

A'LGUAZIL (*Polit.*) an officer of justice in Spain.

ALHA'BAR (*Astron.*) a star in the Great Dog.

ALHA'GI (*Bot.*) a species of the *Hedysarum* of Linnæus. *Raii Hist. Plant.*

ALHA'NDEL (*Bot.*) the *Cucumis colocynthis* of Linnæus.

ALHANDEL (*Med*) a species of troche as old as Mesue, but not now used. *Quin. Dispen.*

ALHA'NNA (*Min.*) vide *Alana Terra.*

ALHA'SEF (*Med.*) a kind of pustule, otherwise called *Hydroa.*

ALHE'NNA (*Bot.*) another name for the *Lausonia inermis* of Linnæus.

ALHIDA'DE (*Mech.*) Alidade, the label index or ruler, moveable about the centre of an Astrolabe.

ALHO'LLAND tide (*Ecc*) another name for *All-Saints' Day.*

A'LIAS (*Law*) a second or further writ after a capias, &c. which has been issued without effect —*Alias Dictus*, a description of the defendant by an addition to his real name of that whereby he is bound in the writing.

ALIBA'NIES (*Com.*) cotton cloth imported into Holland from the East Indies.

ALIBA'NTES (*Ant.*) ἀλιβάντες, a term among the Greeks for those who, on account of their poverty, were deprived of sepulture.

A'LICA (*Nat.*) from *alo*, to nourish; a nourishing kind of farinaceous food, a sort of Frumenty; also a kind of wheat, χόνδρος, which was used medicinally. *Hippocrat. Aphor.*; *Aret. de Caus. et Sig. Morb. Acut.* l. 1, c. 10; *Dioscor.* l. 2, c. 18; *Plin.* l. 18, c. 7; *Cels. de Re Med.* l. 3, c. 6; *Oribas. Med. Collect.* l. 4, c. 1; *Raii Hist. Plant.*; *Gorr. Med. Def. in Voc.* χόνδρος.

A'LICANDE (*Bot.*) vide *Aliconde.*

A'LICES (*Med.*) the little red spots in the skin, which precede the eruption of pustules in the small-pox.

A'LICONDE (*Bot.*) an Ethiopian tree, from the bark of which flax is spun.

A'LICORNU (*Zol.*) vide *Unicornu.*

A'LIDADE (*Mech.*) vide *Alhidade.*

A'LIEN (*Law*) one born in a foreign country out of the allegiance of the King. 1 *Inst.*—*Alien priories*, those cells of monks formerly established in England, which belonged to foreign ministers.—*Alien office*, the office at Gravesend, where all aliens are examined before they are permitted to proceed further into the country.

ALIEN duty (*Com.*) an impost laid on all goods imported by aliens over and above the customs paid on goods imported by British subjects.—*Alien's duty*, otherwise called *petty customs*, or *navigation duties*, a custom paid on fish not caught in British vessels.

ALIENA'TIO Mentis (*Med.*) a wandering or derangement.

ALIENA'TION (*Law.*) vide *Aliene.*—*Alienation office*, an office to which all writs of covenants and entries are carried for the recovery of fines levied thereon.

TO ALI'ENE (*Law*) from *alieno*; to convey the property of a thing to another.—*To aliene in fee*, to sell the fee simple thereof.—*To aliene in mortmain*, to make over lands or tenements to a religious house, or body politic.

ALIFO'RMES Processus (*Anat.*) the prominences of the Os cuneiforme, which are otherwise called Pterogoides.—*Aliformes musculi*, muscles in the form of a wing which rise from the Ossa Pterogoidea.

ALI'GNMENT (*Mar.*) a supposed line drawn to preserve a fleet, or part thereof, in its just direction.

A'LIMENT (*Med.*) *alimentum*, from *alo*, to nourish; the food which serves to nourish the body, or that which, by the heat and ferment of the stomach, may be dissolved and converted into the juice called Chyle.

ALIME'NTARIES (*Ant.*) *alimentarii pueri*, or *alimentariæ puellæ*, children who were educated at the public expense, who were sometimes called after the name of the founder, as the Faustinæ, a community of females instituted by Antoninus Pius, and called after the name of his wife Faustina. *Jul. Capitolin. in Anton. et Sever.*

ALIME'NTARY canal (*Anat.*) the whole tract of intestines, including the stomach.—*Alimentary duct*, the same as the Thoracic duct.

A'LIMONY (*Law*) from *alo*, to feed; the allowance made to a married woman upon a separation from her husband.

A'LIMOS (*Bot.*) ἄλιμος, from ἀ, priv. and λιμός, hunger; a plant so called because it is said to drive away hunger and thirst. *Theophrast. Hist. Plant.* l. 4, c. 20; *Dioscor.* l. 1, c. 120; *Plin.* l. 17, c. 24; *Salmas. in Solin.* c. 16.

ALINDE'SIS (*Med.*) ἀλίνδησις, a species of exercise mentioned by Hippocrates, which consisted of rolling in the dust after being anointed with oil. *Hippocrat. de Vict. Rat.* l. 2; *Foes. Oeconom. Hippocrat.*

ALINTHI'SAR (*Anat.*) the same as Hypostaphyle.

A'LIOCAB (*Chem.*) the same as Sal Ammoniac.

A'LIO Die (*Ant.*) the words used by the Augur in dissolving the Comitia, on religious grounds: "Quid gravius quam rem susceptam dirimi si Augur alio die dixerit." *Cic. de Leg.* c. 50.

ALIPÆ'NA (*Med.*) vide *Alipe.*

ALIPA'SMA (*Med.*) from ἀλείφω, to anoint; an anointment rubbed over the body to prevent sweat. *Gorr. Def. Med.*

A'LIPE (*Med.*) ἄλιπα, applications to wounds in the cheek to prevent inflammation; they were so called from ἀ, priv. and λιπαίνω, to anoint, because they had no fat in them. They were otherwise called by the Greeks ἔναιμα. *Gal. de Compos. Med.* l. 1, c. 15; *Cels. de Re Med.* l. 5, c. 19; *Gorr. Def. Med.*

ALI'PILUS (*Ant.*) the name of the slave who plucked the hairs from the armpits of those who bathed. *Senec. Epist.* 56; *Cœl. Rhodig. Ant. Lect.* l. 30, c. 19; *Turneb. Adv.* l. 27, c. 10; *Mercur. de Art. Gymnast.* l. 1, c. 12; *Salmas. in Tertull. de Pall.*; *Stuck. Ant. Conviv.* l. 2, c. 25.

ALIPTA (*Ant.*) Aliptes, ἀλείπτης, ἀπὸ τοῦ ἀλείφω, i. e. from anointing; slaves who anointed those who went to the bath. *Cic. Famil.* l. 1, ep. 9; *Cels. de Re Med.* l. 1, c. 1; *Juven. Sat.* 3, v. 76; *Rhodig. Ant. Lect.* l. 3, c. 19; *Turneb. Adv.* l. 16, c. 15; *Mercur. de Arte Gymnast.* l. 1, c. 12, &c.

A'LIQUANT Part (*Arith.*) *aliquanta pars;* an indeterminate part of a number which will not measure it without a remainder, as the aliquant part of 10.

A'LIQUOT Part (*Ant.*) *aliquota pars;* a determinate part of a greater number which will measure or divide it without a remainder, as 3, the aliquot part of 12.

ALI'SANUS (*Bot.*) the *Rhexia virginica* of Linnæus. *Pluken. Phytog.*

ALI'SMA (*Bot.*) ἄλισμα, a plant so called from its supposed virtue in curing the bite of a sea-hare. It was also supposed to have the power of breaking the stone in the kidneys, &c. *Dioscor.* l. 3, c. 169; *Plin.* l. 25, c. 10; *Oribas. Med. Coll.* l. 11.

ALISMA, *in the Linnean system*, is a genus of plants; Class 6 *Hexandria*, Order 5 *Polygynia*.
   Generic Characters. CAL. *perianth* three-leaved.—COR. three-petalled; *petals* roundish.—STAM. *filaments* awl-shaped; *anthers* roundish.—PIST. *germs* more than five; *styles* simple; *stigmas* obtuse.—PER. *capsules* compressed; *seeds* solitary.
   Species. Plants of this kind are perennials, as—*Alisma Plantago, Damasonium*, seu *Plantago aquatica*, Great Water Plantain, a native of Great Britain.—*Alisma damasonium*, seu *Damasonium stellatum*, Star-headed Water-Plantain, a native of England.—*Alisma natans, Damasonium repens*, seu *Ranunculus palustris*, native of France, &c. *J. Bauh. Hist. Plant.*; *C. Bauh. Pin.*; *Ger. Herb.*; *Park. Theat. Botan.*; *Raii Hist. Plant.*; *Tournef. Inst.*; *Boerhaav. Ind.*; *Linn. Spec. Plant.*

ALISMA is also the name of different species of the *Primula* and *Senecio* of Linnæus.

ALI'STELES (*Chem.*) Sal Ammoniac.

ALKADA'RII (*Theol.*) a sect of Mahometans, who assert the doctrine of free-will, and deny the absolute decrees of the Almighty.

A'LKAHEST (*Chem.*) or *alcahest*, a name first used by Paracelsus, by whom it was probably coined to signify a universal menstruum. It is explained by Van Helmont to signify a salt of the highest sort, that had attained to the highest state of purity and subtlety. It was supposed to possess the virtue of pervading every substance; and while it acted on every thing else, it remained itself immutable. *Paracel. de Vir. Memb.* l. 2, c. 6; *Van Helmon. Arcan. Paracels.*

A'LKALE (*Chem.*) the fat of a hen.

A'LKALI (*Chem.*) or *alcali*, a perfectly pure salt, altogether without any acidity, caustic in taste, and volatalized by heat. It combines with acids, so as to produce an ebullition and effervescence. Alkalies are distinguished according to the substances from which they are extracted, namely, the—*Animal alkalies*, procured from Hartshorn, and other animal substances.—*Vegetable alkalies*, procured from the ashes of Wormwood, and other plants.—*Fossile and mineral alkali*, procured from different parts of the earth, especially in Egypt, from sea-salt, &c.
   Alkalies are moreover distinguished, according to their volatility, into—*Volatile alkalies*, which are gaseous, as Ammonia; and—*Fixed alkalies*, which remain fixed even in the fire, as Potash and Soda. The word *alkali* is derived from *kali*, an Arabic name for a certain herb on the coast of Egypt, the ashes of which yield a remarkably salt and acrid taste. This salt, which now goes by the name of Alkali, or Alkaline salt, was originally called *Lixivius Cinis, Lixivium Cineris*, lixivious salts, *Rochetta*, or Soda. *Plin.* l. 14, c. 2; *Paracel. Archedox.* l. 4; *Var. Helm. Comp. et Mist. Elam.* sect. 12; *Theat. Chem.* vol. 2, p. 470.

A'LKANET, Dyer's (*Bot.*) or *alcanna*, a plant, the *Anchusa tinctoria* of Linnæus, the root of which yields a fine deep red, that is used much by the dyers. It is cultivated in the South of France, and much resembles Bugloss.

ALKEKE'NGI (*Bot.*) a plant called Winter Cherry by Dale. It is the *Atropa physaloides*, and different species of the *Physalis* of Linnæus. Its medicinal virtues are that of an aperient and diuretic. *C. Bauh. Pin.*; *Parkins. Theat. Botan.*; *Boerhaav. Ind. Botan.*

ALKE'RMES (*Med.*) a confect mentioned in Quincy's Dispensatory, of which Kermes is the principal ingredient.

A'LKIAN (*Chem.*) that spirit which nourishes a man. *Theat. Chem.* vol. 5, p. 155.

ALKI'BRIC (*Chem.*) Sulphur vivum.

AL'KIN (*Chem.*) pot-ash.

A'LKIR (*Chem.*) smoke of coal.

ALL'-GOOD (*Bot.*) the *Chenopodium*, or *Bonus Henricus*, of Linnæus; a plant so called because it is applied by the common people to the healing of slight wounds.—*All-Heal*, or *Clown's All-Heal*, the *Stachys* of Linnæus, otherwise called Wound-Wort.—*All-Seed* [vide *All-Seed*]—*All-Spice* [vide *All-Spice*]

ALL-H'ALLOWTIDE (*Ecc.*) the name for All-Saints' day.—*All-Saints*, a festival observed in the Christian church on the first day of November, in commemoration of all the saints.—*All-Souls*, a festival observed in the Romish on the second of November, when prayers are offered up for all departed souls.

A'LKOHOL (*Chem.*) vide Alcohol.

A'LLA (*Mus.*) Italian, for in the, is used adverbially as follows:—*Alla*, or *All antica*, in the old style applied to compositions after the manner of the last age.—*Alla breve*, quick; that is, a species of quick time.—*Alla caccia*, in the hunting style, applied to music imitative of the chace.—*Alla capella*, in the church style, or after the manner of sacred music.—*Alla Zoppa*, or *alzop*, in an affected style, or *all' improvista*, extemporaneous.—*Alla*, or *al' loco*, in its place, denoting, in violin music, that the hand, having been shifted, must return to its place.—*Alla moderna*, in the modern style, applied to compositions since the time of Handel.—*Alla*, or *All' ottavo*, in the octave, applied to voices or instruments when the parts lie note for note, an octave above or below.—*Alla*, or *All' reverso*, the reverse, applied to parts in a contrary direction.—*Alla segno*, or *Al' Seg*, marked thus, : 𝒮 : i. e. to the mark, denoting that the performer must return to the mark.—*Alla Russe, Scozzese, Siciliana, Italianne*, &c., in the Russian, Scotch, &c. style.

ALLAGO'STEMON (*Bot.*) a class of plants, according to Monk's system.

ALLAMA'NDA (*Bot.*) from Mr. Allamand, a Dutch surgeon, a genus of plants, Class 5 *Pentandria*. Order 1 *Monogynia*.
   Generic Characters. CAL. *perianth* one-leaved.—COR. one-petalled; *tube* cylindric; *border* semiquinquefid; *divisions* spreading.—STAM. *filaments* scarcely any; *anthers* five.—PIST. *germ* oval; *style* filiform; *stigma* headed.—PER. *capsule* orbicular; *seeds* very many.
   Species. The only species is the *Allamanda Cathartica, Orelia grandiflora Galarips, Echinus scandens*, &c. seu *Apocynum scandens*, a shrub, native of Guiana. *Barrel. Plant. Gall. Hispan. et Ital.*; *Aubl. Hist. Plant. Guian.*; *Linn. Spec. Plant.*

A'LLANITE (*Min.*) a species of the ores of Uranium, being a silicate of cerium and iron.

ALL *antica* (*Mus.*) Italian, for in the old style, applied to compositions of the old school.

ALLANTO'IDES (*Anat.*) Ἀλλαντοειδὴς, *Allantois* Ἀλλαντοεις, from ἀλλᾶς, a sausage, or hog's-pudding : the urinary membrane, so called from its resemblance to a pudding. This membrane reaches from one corner of the uterus to the other. *Galen. de Sem.* l. 1, c. 7. In brutes it is called the *Sarciminalis Punica*, or Gut Pudding.

A'LLEGER (*Chem.*) or *alegar, ale aigue*, vinegar made of ale, now in common use.

ALLE'GIANCE (*Law*) from *ab* or *ad*, and *ligo*, i. e. *ligamen fidei*, a bond of fidelity; the natural, lawful, and faithful obedience which every subject owes to his prince. 1 *Inst.* 129, &c.—*Oath of Allegiance*, the oath which all persons are required to take before they enter upon any office, and on other occasions, specified in different statutes. *Eliz.* c. 1, 5; 3 *Jac.* 1.

ALLEGIA'RE (*Law*) to justify or defend in due course of law. *Leg. Alured. apud Brompton.*

ALLEGO'RICUS methodus (*Rhet.*) ἀλληγορικὸς μέθοδος, an allegorical mode of speech when the authority of others *allegatur*, that is, is quoted in confirmation of what is adduced. *Hermog. περὶ ιδ.*

A'LLEGORY (*Rhet.*) ἀλληγορία, a figurative sort of discourse, by which something else is meant than what is expressed by the literal words, so called from ἄλλο, another thing, and ἀγορεύω, to speak, *i. e.* to speak differently from what one means. According to Cicero, it answers to the Latin *Immutatio*; but Quintillian renders it by *Inversio*. The allegory is a continued metaphor, of which Horace's Ode to the *Navis*, or ship, is a happy illustration; where by the ship is meant the republic; by the waves, the civil wars; by the port, peace and concord; by the oars, the soldiers; by the mariners, the magistrates, &c. *Heraclid. Pont. in Alleg. Hom.* c. 5; *Demet. Elocut.*; *Cicer. Orat.* c. 27; *Quintil.* l. 9, c. 6; *Sosepat. Charis. Inst. Gramm.* l. 4.

ALLEGRAME'NTE (*Mus.*) Italian, for rather quick.

ALLEGRE'SSIMO (*Mus.*) Italian, for very quick [vide *Allegro*]

ALLEGRE'TTO (*Mus.*) Italian, for a time not so quick as *Allegro* of which it is a diminutive.

A'LLEGRO *allo* (*Mus.*) Italian, for the third degree of quickness.—*Allegro agitato*, quick and agitated.—*Allegro furioso*, vehemently quick.—*Allegro assai*, more quick.—*Allegro di molto*, very quick.—*Allegro non molto*, not very quick.—*Allegro ma non preste*, quick, but not in the extreme.

ALLELE'NGYON (*Pol.*) ἀλληλέγγυον, a sort of tribute or rate paid by the rich for the support of the poor when they entered the army. *Zonar.* vol. 3; *Constit. Niceph. Jur. Orient. Roman.* l. 1; *Buleng. de Vectig.* c. 79.

ALLELU'JA (*Ecc.*) הללויה, from הלל, praise ye, and יה, the Lord; that part of sacred music which was formerly employed by religious assemblies as a call on each other to praise the Lord.

ALLELUJA (*Bot.*) the *Acetosa* of Linnæus.

ALLEMA'NDE (*Mus.*) a French word, signifying German, because it is supposed to be of German origin; an epithet for a slow air, or melody in common.

A'LLENCE (*Min.*) another name for *Stannum*.

ALLER (*Ant.*) vide *Alder*.

ALLER *sans jour* (*Law*) see *Aler*.

ALLE'RION (*Her.*) a small bird painted without beak or feet, like the martlet, or martinet; or, according to some, like an eagle without beak or feet, so called because they have nothing perfect but the wings. They differ from martlets therein, that their wings are expanded, whilst those of the martlet are close.

ALLEVE'URE (*Com.*) a brass coin struck in Sweden, worth about 2½d. English money.

ALLEVIA'RE (*Law*) to levy or pay an accustomed fine.

A'LLEY (*Horticul.*) a walk in a garden-bed which separates the squares of a parterre. This is of different sorts, as a—*Counter alley*, an alley by the side of another that is greater—*Diagonal alley*, that cuts a parterre from angle to angle—*Front alley*, that runs straight from the front of a building—*Transverse alley*, which cuts a front alley at right angles.

ALLEY (*Perspect.*) that which is larger at the entrance than at the issue, in order to make the length appear greater.

ALL-FO'URS (*Sport.*) a game of cards played by two, which is so called from the four sorts of cards, called High and Low, Jack of Trumps, and the Game, which, when joined in the hand of either party, constitutes him the winner.

A'LL-GOOD (*Bot.*) vide *All*.

ALL-HA'LLOW-TIDE (*Ecc.*) vide *All*.

A'LL-HEAL (*Bot.*) vide *All*.

A'LLIAR *æris* (*Alch.*) philosophical copper for preparing the philosopher's stone.

ALLIA'RIA (*Bot.*) a plant which was formerly reckoned an excellent anti-scorbutic. It is the *Erisymum alliaria* of Linnæus. *Bauh. Hist. Plant.*; *Raii. Hist. Plant.* &c.

ALLIBA'LLIES (*Com.*) a fine clear muslin, of which the piece contains twenty-one yards, and is one yard wide.

A'LLICA (*Ent.*) a species of Papilio.

A'LLICAR (*Chem.*) the same as Acetum.

ALLIE'NSIS *dies* (*Ant.*) an ominous day among the Romans, which was the anniversary of their defeat by the Gauls near the Allia. *Cic. ad Attic.* l. 9, ep. 5; *Liv.* l. 6, c. 1; *Siccam in Fast. Kalend. Roman.* c. 5.

ALLIGA'TI (*Ant.*) those slaves among the Romans who were obliged to work in chains. *Columel.* l. 1, c. 9.

ALLIGA'TION (*Arit.*) a rule in Arithmetic by which questions relating to the compounding of different simples are resolved; so called from *alligare*, to bind or connect. Alligation is of two kinds, medial and alternate.—*Alligation medial*, a rule for finding the mean rate of a mixture compounded out of certain quantities.—*Alligation alternate*, a rule to find out such quantities as are necessary to make a mixture to bear a rate proposed, the rates of the simples being given. *Luc. de Burg. Sum. Arith.*

A'LLIGATOR (*Zool.*) an amphibious animal in the West Indies, the *La carta alligator*, so nearly resembling the crocodile of the Nile, both in form and habits, as to be considered merely a variety which difference of climate produces. It is but little inferior to the crocodile in size, and will sometimes grow to the length of eighteen or twenty feet. The opinion of Aristotle, and other ancient naturalists, that animals of this description move their upper jaw only, appears, upon closer inspection, to be incorrect.

ALLIGATOR *pear* (*Bot.*) the *Laurus persea* of Linnæus.

ALLIGATU'RA (*Sur.*) the same as ligature.

ALL' *improvista* (*Mus.*) Italian for extemporaneous, applied to the performance.

ALLIO'NIA (*Bot.*) a genus of plants so called from Professor Allioni, Class 4 *Tetrandria*, Order 1 *Monogynia*.
Generic Characters. CAL. *perianth* common; *proper* obsolete.—COR. *proper* one-petalled.—STAM. *filaments* setaceous; *anthers* roundish.—PIST. *germ* inferior; *style* setaceous; *stigma* multifid.—PER. none; *seeds* solitary; *receptacle* naked.
Species. There are two species, namely, the *Allionia violacea*, a native of South America; and *Allionia incarnata seu Wedelia*, an annual native of Peru.

A'LLIOTH (*Astron.*) an Arabic name for a star in the tail of the great bear, which signifies, literally, a horse. It is marked ε by Bayer. *Ulug. Beigh apud Hyd. de Relig. Vet. Persar.*; *Bay. Uranomet.*

ALLIO'TICUM (*Med.*) from ἀλλοιόω, to change; an alterative medicine, composed of antiscorbutics.

ALLITERA'TION (*Gram.*) a repeating and playing upon the same letter.

A'LLIUM (*Bot.*) in Greek σκόροδον, the herb Garlic, which was held in reverence by the Egyptians, and in abhorrence by the Greeks, so that no one dare approach the temple of Ceres, the mother of the Gods, after having eaten of it. It was, however, esteemed good food for soldiers, to animate them before they went to battle, to which Aristophanes alludes,
Aristoph. Equit.

ἱν' ἄμεινον ἐπὶ τὰς ἰσκοροδισμένος μάχῃ.

It was reckoned of no less efficacy for the rowers on board a ship, according to *Plautus*. *Plaut. Poen.* act. 5, scen. 5, v. 34.

———— Tam autem plenior
Allii ulpicique quam Romani remiges.

Hence the vulgar proverbs of *allium ne comedas*, for lead a quiet life, and *allium in retibus*, in reference to the quantity of garlic which the Athenian mariners took with them. Horace makes frequent allusions to its offensive smell and coarseness for food, particularly in his ode to Mæcenas. *Horat. Epod.* 3, v. 1.

> *Parentis olim si quis impid manu*
> *Senila guttur fregerit*
> *Edat cicutis allium nocentius, &c.*

Its medicinal virtues are much commended by the ancient physicians, particularly for its efficacy against the bite of the viper. *Hippocrat. de Rat. Vict. in Acut. Morb.* l. 2; *Theophrast.* l. 7, c. 4; *Dioscor.* l. 2, c. 182; *Plin.* l. 19, c. 6; *Columel.* l. 2, c. 3; *Gal. de Simpl. Med. Fac.* l. 8; *Orobas. Med. Collect.* l. 11; *Aet. Tetrab.* l. serm. 1; *Paul Æginet.* l. 7, c. 3.

ALLIUM, *in the Linnean system*, is a genus of plants, Class 6 *Hexandria*, Order 1 *Monogynia*.

Generic Characters. CAL. *spathe* common.—COR. *petals* six.—STAM. *filaments* six; *anthers* oblong.—PIST. *germ* superior; *style* simple; *stigma* sharp.—PER. *capsule* very short; *seeds* few.

Species. The species are mostly perennials, as—*Allium ampeloprasum, seu Porrum ampeloprasum, seu Scorodoprasum latifolium, &c.* Great Round-headed Garlick, a native of Britain.—*Allium sub-hirsutum, Moly angustifolium seu Dioscoridis*, Hairy Garlick, native of Africa.—*Allium roseum seu Moly minus*, Rose Garlick, native of Montpellier.—*Allium sativum*, Common Garlick.—*Allium scorodoprasum, sativum alterum, Allioprassum seu Porrum*, Rocambole, native of Sweden.—*Allium moschatum seu Moly moschatum*, Musk-smelling Garlick.—*Allium ascalonicum seu Cepa ascalonica*, Shallot, or Eschallote, a native of Palestine.—*Allium odorum*, sweet-smelling Garlick, native of Europe.—*Allium fistulosum, seu Cepa oblonga*, Welsh onion, or Ciboule, native of Siberia.—*Allium Schænoprasum, seu Cepa palustris*, Chives, native of Siberia; but—*Allium porrum, seu Porrum, &c.* the Common Leek, is a biennial. *J. Bauh. Hist. Plant.; C. Bauh. Pin.; Ger. Herb.; Park. Theatr. Botanicum; Raii Hist. Plant.; Journal Instit.; Boerhaav. Ind.*

ALLIUM is also the name of some species, as the *Hypoxis fascicularis*, and the *Tradescentia Virginica* of Linnæus. *C. Bauh. Pin.*

ALLOBRO'GICUM *vinum* (*Med.*) a sort of harsh wine of Savoy and Dauphiny. *Cels. de Re Med.* l. 4, c. 6.

ALLOCA'TION (*Law*) an allowance made on account in the Exchequer.—*Allocatione facienda*, a writ for an accountant to receive such sums from the treasurer as he has expended. *Reg. Orig.* 206.

ALLOCA'TO *comitatu* (*Law*) a new writ of exigent allowed before any county court holden, on the former not being fully served or complied with. *Fitzh. Exig.* 14.

ALLOCA'TUR (*Law*) i. e. it is allowed; a term applied to the certificate of allowance by the master on taxation of costs.

ALLO'CHOI (*Med.*) ἀλληχόοι, those talking deliriously, as it is commonly read in Hippocrates; but Galen reads it σιαλοχόοι, those who spit much, which reading is approved by Erotian. *Hippocrat. de Epidem.* l. 2; *Gal. Exeges.; Hippocrat. Vocab.; Erotian. Lex. Hippocrat.; Foes. Œconom. Hippocrat.*

ALLO'CHROITE (*Min.*) a sort of stone of the garnet kind.

ALLO'CO (*Mus.*) vide *Alla*.

ALLOCO'TON (*Med.*) ἀλλόκοτον, absurd or unnatural, as applied by Hippocrates. *Hippocrat. de Morb. Med.; Gal. Exeges. Vocab. Hippocrat.; Erot. Lex. Med. Hippocrat.; Gorr. Def. Med.; Foes. Œconom. Hippocrat.*

ALLOEO'THETA (*Gram.*) ἀλλοιόθετα, from ἀλλοῖος, various, and θέσις, disposed; a figure of grammar varying from the ordinary rules of Syntax, as a noun in the singular with a verb plural, *Pars abiere*. Priscian calls this *varietas*.

ALLODE'MIA (*Med.*) ἀλλοδημία, a term used by Hippocrates for travelling into a foreign country. *Hippocrat. de Intern. Affect.; Foes. Œconom. Hippocrat.*

ALLO'DIAL (*Law*) *Allodialis*, exempt from rent or services, as allodial lands, which pay not fine, rent, or services. *Domesday Book*.

ALLO'GNOON (*Med.*) ἀλλογνοῶν, delirious, i. e. ἀλλαγινώσκων παρὰ τὰ ὄντα, i. e. one knowing things different from what they really are. *Gal. Exeges. Vocab. Hippocrat.; Erotian. Lex. Med. Hippocrat.; Foes. Œconom. Hippocrat.*

ALLO'NGE (*Fenc.*) a thrust or pass at the adversary.

ALLO'PHASIS (*Med.*) Ἀλλόφασις, i. e. speaking things different from what they really are; delirium, as it is applied by Hippocrates. *Gal. Comm. in Prognost.; Erot. Lex. Med. Hippocrat.; Hesych. Lex.; Gorr. Def. Med.; Foes. Œconom. Hippocrat.*

ALLO'PHYLI (*Bibl.*) ἀλλόφυλοι, signifies literally strangers; but is commonly employed in Scripture for the Philistines.

ALLO'PHYLUS (*Bot.*) ἀλλόφυλος, literally a stranger, i. e. an exotic, a genus of plants, Class 8 *Octandria*, Order 1 *Monogynia*.

Generic Characters. CAL. *Perianth* four-leaved; *leaflets* orbiculate.—COR. *petals* four; *claws* broad.—STAM. *filaments* filiform; *anthers* roundish.—PIST. *germ* superior; *style* filiform; *stigma* bifid.

Species. The Species are *Allophylus Zeylanicus*, a shrub, native of Ceylon.—*Allophylus rigidus*, native of Hispaniola.—*Allophylus racemosus*, native of Hispaniola.—*Allophylus cominia, Rhus cominia, Cominia, seu Toxicodendron arboreum*, native of Jamaica.—*Allophylus ternatus*, a shrub, native of Cochin China. *Raii Hist. Plant.; Sloan. Hist. Jamaic.; Brown. Hist. Jamaic.; Wild. Linn. Spec. Plant.*

ALLO'TMENT (*Mar.*) allowing half the pay of the private and non-commissioned officers of the royal navy to be paid monthly to the wife, children, or mother of the parties.

ALLOTMENT *of goods* (*Com.*) when any cargo is divided into several parcels, to be bought by different persons, whose names being written upon as many pieces of paper, are indifferently applied to the respective parcels.

ALL *ottave* (*Mus.*) Italian, for in the octave; an expression applied to the instruments or voices, when their parts lie an octave above or below some other part.

ALLO'WANCE (*Mar.*) the ratio or quantum of provisions served out to the seamen on board.—*Short allowance*, when necessity obliges a curtailment of the usual quantity.—*Two thirds allowance*, when two thirds only of the usual quantity is allowed.—*To stop the allowance*, a last resource when the provisions are nearly exhausted.

ALLO'Y (*Com.*) a mixture of other metals with silver or gold. *Stat.* 9, *Hen. V.* A pound weight of standard gold in the mint is 22 carats fine, and 2 carats allay or alloy. Of standard silver 11 ozs. 2 dwts. of fine, and 18 dwts. of allay.

ALL'-SAINTS (*Ecc.*) a festival. [vide *All*]

A'LL-SEED (*Bot.*) the *Chemopodium polyspermum* and *Linum radiola* of Linnæus.

ALL *segno* (*Mus.*) *Al Seg*, or the character : 𝄋 : Italian for the words, to the sign. [vide *Alla*]

A'LL-SOULS (*Ecc.*) a festival. [vide *All*]

A'LL-SPICE (*Bot.*) the *Myrtus Pimento* of Linnæus.

A'LLUM (*Min.*) vide *Alum*.

ALLU'MINOR (*Archæol.*) one whose business it is to allumine or paint upon paper, parchment, &c. *Stat.* 1, R. 3, c. 9.

ALLU'VIAL (*Law*) belonging to a deluge or alluvion; as *alluvial soil*, i. e. soil that has been brought to other lands by means of floods.

ALLU'VION (*Law*) from *alluo*, to wash to; an accession of land washed to the shore by inundations.

A'LMA (*Med.*) or *Halma*, ἅλμα, the first motion made by the fœtus in the womb to free itself from confinement. *Hippocrat. apud Hesychium*.

ALMA-MA'TER (*Lit.*) a title given to Oxford or Cambridge by such as have received their education in either university.

ALMACA'NTAR (*Astron.*) *Almincatarath*, from the Arabic *Almocantharat*; a name for the Parallels of altitude on the celestial globe whose zenith is the pole or vertical point.

ALMACA'NTER'S *staff* (*Mech.*) an instrument for observing at sea the sun's amplitude rising and setting.

A'LMADY (*Com.*) 1. A vessel in the East Indies, made in the form of a weaver's shuttle. 2. An African canoe made of the bark of trees.

A'LMAGESTUM (*Lit.*) the title of Ptolemy's celebrated work on Astronomy, so called by the Arabians, who adding the particle *al* to the μέγιστη of the Greek title συνταξις μεγίστη, thus formed the word *Almagist*. Riccioli has given a similar title, *Almagistum Novum*, the New Almagest, to his work on astronomy.

A'LMAGRA (*Min.*) a kind of ochre.

A'LMAIN *rivets* (*Mil.*) a certain light kind of armour worn by the Germans.

ALMAKA'NDA (*Chem.*) litharge.

A'LMAN (*Metal.*) a furnace used by refiners for separating metals.

A'LMANAC (*Chron.*) a calendar or table, containing an account of the months, weeks, and days of the year, with the festivals, changes of weather, &c. It is in French *Almanac*, in Italian *Almanacco*, in Spanish *Almanaque*, in German *Almanach*; and is derived by Golius from the Arabic particle *al*, and *Mana*, a measure or reckoning; by Scaliger, from the same particle, *al*, and the Greek μὲν, a month; by Verstigan, from the compound Saxon word Al-mon-aht, i. e. All-Moon-Heed, or an account of every moon, which the Saxons are said to have kept very carefully. The latter seems to be the immediate derivation, and the former that which is more remote.

ALMANAC *Nautical* (*Astron.*) or *Astronomical Ephemeris*, is published under the direction of the board of Longitude, for the use of mariners, containing an account of the longitude, latitude, ascension, declination, &c. of the heavenly bodies.

A'LMAND *cathartica* (*Bot.*) a plant of Surinam, supposed by the inhabitants to be good for the colic.

ALMA'NDINE (*Min.*) a coarse sort of ruby, approaching in colour nearer to the granate than the ruby.

ALMA'RCAB (*Chem.*) litharge of silver.

ALMA'RGAN (*Min.*) coral.

ALMELILE'TU (*Med.*) a preternatural heat, less than a fever.

A'LMENE (*Chem.*) Sal Gemma.

ALMENE (*Com.*) an Indian weight of about two pounds.

A'LMISA (*Chem.*) Musk.

ALMISA'DAR (*Chem.*) Sal Ammoniac.

A'LMOIN (*Law*) vide *Frank Almoin*.

ALMONA'RIUM (*Archæol.*) a safe or cupboard in which broken victuals were kept that were to be given to the poor.

A'LMOND (*Metal.*) vide *Alman*.

ALMOND (*Bot.*) the nut or fruit of the almond tree, whether sweet or bitter, called in French *Amande*, in German *Mandel*, in Latin *Amygdala*, and in Greek ἀμυγδαλή.

ALMOND-*tree* the *Amygdalus communis* of Linnæus; a pretty tall tree, resembling a peach tree, which is one of the first trees that blossoms. It is a native of the Holy Land. There are different sorts of trees so called, as the—Common Dwarf Almond, or *Amygdalis nana* of Linnæus.—African Almond, the *Brabeium stellafolium*.—Hoary Dwarf Almond, the *Amygdalis incana*.—Silvery-leaved Almond, the *Amygdalis orientalis* of Linnæus.

ALMOND (*Com.*) a Portuguese measure of oil, equal to four gallons two quarts.

ALMOND (*Anat.*) a name for the glandular substances on each side the uvula at the root of the tongue, otherwise called *tonsillæ*.

ALMOND-*stone* (*Min.*) the *amygdalites* of Linnæus, a sort of stones consisting of glandules that resemble the almond in shape.

A'LMONER (*Archæol.*) or almner *eleemosynarius*; an officer in the king's house who distributed the king's alms every day. *Fleta*, l. 2, c. 22.

A'LMONRY (*Archæol.*) *Eleemosyna*; the office or dwelling of the almoner.

ALMOXARIFA'RGO (*Com.*) a duty of two and a half per cent. on bulls' hides in Spain.

ALMS *feoh* (*Archæol.*) Saxon for alms-money, given first by Ina, king of the West Saxons.—*Alms-basket*, the basket in which the provisions are put that are to be given away.—*Alms-house*, a house endowed with a revenue for the maintenance of a certain number of poor aged persons.—*Alms-man*, a man who is supported by alms or charity.

ALMU'CIUM (*Archæol.*) vide *Almutium*.

ALMUGAVA'RI (*Archæol.*) a name for the Spanish soldiers who distinguished themselves against the Saracens. *Roder. Tolit. de Reb. Hispan.* l. 9, c. 16; *Pachymer*. l. 2, c. 13.

ALMU'GIA (*Astrol.*) the planets facing one another in the zodiac.

ALMU'GIM (*Bibl.*) a sort of wood mentioned 1 Kings x. 2. It is called by the Septuagint ξύλα πεύκινα, by the Vulgate *ligna pinea*.

ALMU'NIA (*Archæol.*) a sort of tenure among the Spaniards.

ALMU'TEN (*Astrol.*) the lord of a figure, or strongest planet in a nativity.

ALMU'TRIUM (*Archæol.*) a cap made with lambs or goats' skins. *Dugd. Mon. Angl.*

ALNABA'TI (*Med.*) a gentle laxative.

A'LNAGE (*Com.*) the measure of an ell. 17 *stat Ed.* 4.

ALNAGE (*Law*) 1. A measure by the ell. 2. An officer to inspect the alnage or measuring. 25 *Ed.* 3.

A'LNEC (*Min.*) Tin.

ALNE'RIC (*Chem.*) Sulphur vivum.

ALNE'TUM (*Archæol.*) a grove of alder trees. *Domesday-book*.

ALNI *effigie* (*Bot.*) the *Cratægus aria* of Linnæus. *Bauh Hist. Plant.*

ALNIFO'LIA (*Bot.*) the *Clethra alnifolia* of Linnæus *Pluken. Phytograph.*

A'LNUS (*Bot.*) alder; a tree so called, either because, *alatur amne*, it thrives by the river side, or from the Hebrew אלון, *alon*, an oak. It is called in the Greek κλήθρα, and its bark was reckoned drying and astringent. The wood is celebrated by the poets on account of its fitness for the building of ships.

Virg. Georg. l. 2, v. 451.

Nec non et torrentem undam levis innatat alnus.

Lucan. l. 3, v. 441.

Et fluctibus aptior alnus.

Claudian.

Qui dubiis ausus committere fluctibus alnum.

Theophrast. Hist. Plant. l. 3, c. 14; *De Caus Plant.* l. 3, c. 17; *Dioscor.* l. 3, c. 25; *Plin.* l. 16, c. 26; *Vitruv. de Architect.* l. 2, c. 9; *Ovid. Met.* l. 13.

ALNUS, *in the Linnean system*, is the *Bætula alnus*, the

Conocarpus erecta, and the *Rhamnus frangula* of Linnæus. *Lob. Plant.* seu *Stirp. Hist.*; *J. Bauh. Hist. Plant.*; *C. Bauh. Pin.*; *Raii Hist. Plant.*; *Tournef. Instit.*; *Boerhaav. Ind.*

A'LOA (*Ant.*) Ἀλῶα, festivals at Athens in honour of Bacchus and Ceres, celebrated by an offering from the fruits of the earth in the time of harvest, from ἅλως, a barn, whence Ceres is called Ἁλωΐς, *aloas*, that is, a filler of barns. *Demosthen. in Neær.*; *Harpocrat. Lex*; *Hesychius*; *Eustath.* in Il. 9, v. 588; *Meurs. Eleus. apud Gronov.* vol. 7.

A'LOE (*Bot.*) ἀλόη, the name of a plant, comes in all probability from the Hebrew אהל, which signifies the same thing. The aloe, which comes from India, resembles the squill, only that it is bigger and provided with fatter leaves. The juice, which is found sticking to the plant like a tear, is exceedingly bitter, but of great use in medicine, particularly as a purgative. *Dioscor.* l. 3, c. 25; *Plin.* l. 27, c. 4; *Ruff. Ephes. Fragment. de Med. Purg.*; *Gal. Comm. 2 in Hippocrat. de Art.* c. 49; *Cels. de Re Med.* l. 2, c. 12; *Oribas. Med. Coll.* l. 7, c. 27; *Aet. Tetrab.* 1. serm. 3, c. 24; *Actuar. de Meth. Med.* l. 5, c. 8; *Salmas. Exercitat. Plin.* 1053.

ALOE, in the Linnæan system, a genus of plants, Class 6 Hexandria, Order 1 Monogynia.
  Generic Character. CAL. none.—COR. one-petalled; *tube* gibbous; *border* spreading.—STAM. *filaments* awlshaped, *anthers* oblong.—PIST. *germ* ovate, *style* simple, *stigma* obtuse.—PER. *capsule* oblong, *seeds* several.
  Species. The species are mostly shrubs, and natives of the Cape of Good Hope. *J. Bauh. Hist. Plant.*; *C. Bauh. Pin.*; *Ger. Herb.*; *Park. Theat. Botan.*; *Raii Hist. Plant.*
  ALOE is also the name of some species, as the—*Crapula perfoliata*; the *Agave Americana*; the *Dacæna marginata*; the *Aletris uvaria*; and the *Yucca aloifolia* of Linnæus. *J. Bauh. Hist. Plant.*; *Raii Hist. Plant.*; *Pluk. Phytograph.*

ALOEDA'RIA (*Med.*) aloetics, medicines consisting chiefly of aloes. *Aet. Tetrab.* 1, serm. 3, c. 105.

A'LOES (*Med.*) the inspissated juice of the aloe, which is of different sorts, namely, the—*Common Aloes*, or the juice of the officinal aloe.—*Hepatic Aloes*, the juice of the Guinea aloe, so called from its liver-like colour.—*Caballine* or *Horse Aloes*, from the same plant, but of a coarser sort, which is commonly given to horses.—*Saccotrine Aloes*, from the juice of the aloe of Sacotra.

ALOE'TICS (*Med.*) vide *Aloedaria*.

ALOE'XYLUM (*Bot.*) the *aquilaria* of Linnæus.

ALO'FT (*Mar.*) at the mast-head, or in the top of the rigging.

ALO'GIA (*Ecc.*) ἀλογία; silent feasts, or where there was no discourse held; from α, priv. and λογός, a discourse. *August. epist.* 86.

ALOGIA'NI (*Ecc.*) or Alogi, ἄλογοι, a sect of heretics so called, from α, priv. and λογός the word, because they rejected the λόγος, or Word of St. John. *Epiphan. Hæres.* c. 51; *August. ad quod vult Deum.* c. 30.

A'LOGOS (*Rhet.*) ἄλογος, disproportionate; an epithet for the first long syllable, because it does not bear a due λόγος or proportion to the rest of the foot. *Dionys. Hal. de Comp.* c. 16.

A'LOGOS (*Med.*) ἄλογος, without due cause; a term employed by Hippocrates in speaking of disorders, as when a fever disappears without any critical evacuation, he says it is resolved ἀλόγως, i. e. without an adequate cause, and is consequently subject to a relapse. *Gal. Comm. 2 in Hippocrat.*

ALOGOTROPHY (*Med.*) ἀλογοτροφία, from τρέφω, to nourish, and ἄλογος, without proportion; disproportionate nutrition in different parts of the body.

ALO'NG-side (*Mar.*) parallel to a ship, a wharf; "To lay along-side," to place a ship by the side of another.—*Along-shore*, along the coast, applied to coasting navigation.—*Along-shore-owner*, one who sends his ship to sea in want of stores and provisions.—*Along-lying*, the state of being pressed down sideways by a weight of sail in a fresh wind.

ALOO'F (*Mar.*) at a distance; a term employed in sea phrases, as "To keep aloof," commonly called "To keep the luff," a command given by the pilot or the officer to the helmsman, to direct the ship's course nearer the wind.

ALO'PECES (*Anat.*) ἀλώπεκες, from ἀλώπηξ, a fox; psoa muscles; so called because they are very strong in foxes. *Ruff. Ephes. Appell.* l. 1, c. 30.

ALOPE'CIA (*Med.*) ἀλωπεκία, a falling off of the hair; a distemper so called from ἀλώπηξ, a fox, and πίπτω, to fall; because foxes are very liable to such a defluxion of the hair. Celsus calls it a kind of area. *Cels.* l. 6, c. 4; *Plin.* l. 20, c. 5; *Gal. de Comp. Med. secund. Loc.* l. 1, c. 2; *Oribas. de Loc. Affec.* l. 4. c. 5; *Aet. Tetrab.* 2, serm. 3, c. 55; *Alex. Trallian.* l. 1, c. 1; *Paul. Æginet.* l. 3, c. 1; *Actuar. de Meth. Med.* l. 2. c. 5.

ALO'PECURO *veronica* (*Bot.*) the *Mentha auricularia* of Linnæus.

ALOPECU'ROS (*Bot.*) the *Betonica alopecuros* of Linnæus. *J. Bauh. Hist. Plant.*; *Ger. Herb.*; *Raii Hist. Plant.*

ALOPECU'RUS (*Bot.*) from ἀλώπηξ, οὐρά, i. e. a fox's tail; the Fox-tail or Fox-tailed Grass; a genus of plants, Class 3 Triandria, Order 2 Digynia.
  Generic Characters. CAL. *glume* one-flowered; *valves* ovate.—COR. one-valved; *valve* ovate; *awn* twice as long.—STAM. *filaments* three: *anthers* forked at each end.—PIST. *germ* roundish; *styles* two; *stigmas* villous. PER. none, the corolla investing the seed; *seed* ovate.
  Species. The species are mostly perennials, as the—*Alopecurus bulbosus*, seu *Gramen typhoides*, &c. Bulbous Fox-tail Grass.—*Alopecurus pratensis* seu *Gramen phaleroides*, &c. Meadow Fox-tail Grass, &c.; but some are said to be annuals, as the *Alopecurus monspeliensis*, Bearded Fox-tail Grass, and *Alopecurus paniceus*, Hairy Fox-tail Grass. *J. Bauh. Hist. Plant.*; *C. Bauh. Pin.*; *Ger. Herb.*; *Park. Theat Botan.*; *Linn. Spec. Plant.*

A'LOPEX (*Zool.*) Brant Fox, a species of the *Canis* of Linnæus.

A'LOSA (*Ich.*) the shad, a species of the *Clupea* of Linnæus.

A'LOSAT (*Chem.*) argentum vivum.

ALO'TIA (*Ant.*) festivals in Arcadia in commemoration of a victory obtained over the Lacedæmonians, many of whom were taken prisoners that were called in Greek ἀλῶται.

ALOVE'RIUM (*Archæol.*) a purse.

A'LP (*Or.*) a Bullfinch.

A'LPHA (*Gram.*) ἄλφα, from the Hebrew אלף; the first letter in the Greek alphabet, so called by the ancient Syrians because this word signified an ox in the Phœnician tongue, which was reckoned by Cadmus the first of the three necessaries of life. *Plut. Synops.* l. 2, quæst. c. 3; *Hesychius*; *Scal. Animadvers. in Euseb. Chron.*

A'LPHABET (*Gram.*) *alphabetum*, the whole order of letters which are used in any language, so called from *alpha* and *beta*, the first and second letters of the Greek alphabet. The following are the principal alphabets which have been or are in use among different nations.

The Alphabets of different nations, in alphabetical order.

Alphabet of Abraham, a Chaldean alphabet, ascribed by the Rabbis to Abraham, but without any authority.

Abyssinian the same as the *Æthiopian*.

Alphabet of Adam, a Chaldean alphabet ascribed to Adam.

Æolian, a variation of the ancient Greek, attributed to the Æolians by Theseus Ambrosius.

ALPHABET.

African, a sort of Arabic alphabet.

Anglo-Norman, a sort of Gothic character. [vide *Gothic*]

Arabic consists of different characters. The most ancient Arabic is called the Kufic, so named from the city of Kufa, on the Euphrates, which does not appear to be now in use. The specimen given in Tab. IV, No. 18, [Pl. 4] was communicated to Dr. Morton of the British Museum, by Dr. Hunt, Arabic professor at Oxford, from MSS. in the Bodleian Library. It consists of *initials* or letters used at the beginning, *medials* or letters in the middle, and *finals* or letters used at the end. The modern Arabic is supposed by some to have been invented by the vizier Molach, A.D. 933, with which he wrote the Koran three times, and in a manner so fair and correct as to make it a perfect model of writing. This alphabet consists also of four sorts of characters, namely, single, initial, medial, and final, which is the common character of the Arabians, Turks, and Persians; but the two latter nations have added four more letters, namely, ܝ *p*, ܝ *ch*, ܝ *zh*, ܝ *g*, and given a different power to others. There are two other variations of the Arabic, namely, the African and Mauritanian, which are said to be used in different parts of Africa.

Arcadian, a variation of the Latin, taken from the Eugubian tables, and so called because it is supposed to have been brought by Evander from Arcadia into Latium. [vide *Latin*]

Armenian is used not only in Armenia but in Asia Minor, Syria, Tartary, &c. It differs in its character according to the use which is made of it, but approaches, in some respects, very near to the Chaldee or Syriac, and to the Greek in others. The characters given in Tab. V, No. 31, [Pl. 5] are the common printing character of the Armenian, capitals and small letter. There is also an ornamental kind of character, which is termed blooming or flowery, because it is used for the titles of books; and Duret likewise mentions an ancient Armenian character, which he says was taken from an inscription over an entrance into the castle of Curcho. *Choron. Hist. Armen.* l. 2, c. 2, &c.; *Schroeder. Thesaur. Ling. Armen.*; *Duret. Tresor. des Lang.* p. 725.

Attic, a variation of the ancient Greek. [vide *Greek*]

Bali, an alphabet of a dialect in Bali, an island north of Java.

Barman, an alphabet used in the kingdom of Ava, which, in the order, power, and general form of its letters, resembles the Sanscrit.

Bastard or *Mongrel*, first made by a German named Heilman in 1490, was in common use, in France, in the fifteenth century; so called because it was derived from the *Lettres de Forme*, or Gothic character, but it has most of its angles cut off or diminished. Fournier gives four varieties of this bastard character. The specimens given in Tab. VI, No. 45, [Pl. 6] are of the ancient and the round Bastard.

Batta, an alphabet of one of the principal languages in Sumatra.

Bengallee, an alphabet now used in the extensive country of Bengal, which is under the dominion of the East, very similar to the Sanscrit.

Black Letter, a sort of English alphabet, as in Tab. VI, No. 48. [Pl. 6.]

Bulgarian, a character similar to that of the Illyrian.

Bullantic or *Imperial*, an alphabet of ornamented capitals, which was so called because it was employed in writing the papal bulls.

Cadeaux, flourishing capitals that were used in French writing of the fifth century.

Cadmean, the original Greek alphabet, which is supposed to have been first introduced into Greece by Cadmus. [vide *Greek*]

Chaldee, many alphabets have been given under this name which more properly belong to the Phenician or Syriac, and several have been ascribed by the Rabbis to Adam, Enoch, Noah, Abraham, and Moses, but without any authority that entitles them to credit. The character of the Chaldee is the same at present as that of the Hebrew.

Chancery, a sort of English law alphabet, as in Tab. VI, No. 49, [Pl. 6.]

Of Charlemagne, the name of three alphabets which are attributed to the emperor Charlemagne, by whom they are said to have been introduced, at the commencement of the ninth century, for the purpose of improving the letters used in his dominions, of which a specimen is given in Tab. VI, No. 47, [Pl. 6.]

Chinese, this language has no proper alphabet, but consists of 214 Key-words, or radical characters, that serve to form 80,000 characters of which it is composed, of which a specimen is given in Tab. I, No 6, [Pl. 1.]

Church Text, a sort of English, as in Tab. VI, No. 51, [Pl. 6.]

Coptic, an alphabet so called from Coptos, a city of Egypt, where it was used, is a mixture of Greek and Egyptian. There are two characters under this name, one of which is the ancient, and the other the modern Coptic, as given in Tab. V, No. 30, [Pl. 5.] The latter, which consists of thirty-two letters, is only to be met with in the books of the Christians of Egypt, by whom it was used in the translation of the Sacred Writings. *Kircher. Oedip. Ægypt. et Copt.*; *Pocock. in Not. ad Spec. Hist. Arab.*; *Montfauc. Palæograp.* l. 4, c. 7; *Univ. Anc. Hist.* vol. i, p. 512; *Wilkins. Dissert. de Ling. Copt.*

Court Text, a sort of handwriting among the English lawyers. [vide *English*]

Croatian has the same characters as the Illyrian.

Dalmatian, Tab. V, No. 33, [Pl. 5] is said to have been invented by St. Jerom. It has been used for the translation of the Sacred Writings, besides missals and breviaries. *Duret. Tresor. des Lang.* &c. p. 738.

Doric, a variety of the ancient Greek. [vide *Greek*]

Egyptian, the characters of the ancient Egyptians were of three kinds; namely ἐπιςολογραφικὸς, or vulgar; ἱερατικὸς, or sacred; and ἱερογλυφικὸς, hyeroglyphick. Many vestiges remain of their hieroglyphic writing, of which only conjectural explanations can be offered; of this sort is the one given in Tab. I, No. 5, [Pl. 1]. Their letters are in all probability lost, notwithstanding many characters have been given under this name, particularly one by Theseus Ambrosius, which is, however, unsupported by any authority. The Coptic is the only Egyptian character that remains. *Herod.* l. 2, c. 36; *Diodor. Sic.* l. 3; *Heliodor. Æthiop.* l. 4; *Clem. Alexandrin. Strom.* l. 5; *Eustath. on Hom. Il.* l. 6, v. 168; *Athanas. Kirch. Oedip. Theat. Hieroglyphic.* p. 12, &c.; *Marsham. Canon. Chronol.*

English, the characters bearing this name are the Old English, or Black Letter, Tab. VI, No. 48, [Pl. 6] called by the French *Lettres de Forme*. It was first used by Guttemberg and Faust at Mentz, and was by them denominated *Lettres Burgeoises*; Round Chancery and Running Chancery, as in No. 49, used in the enrollments of letters patent; Court or Exchequer Text, as No. 50, which were invented by the English lawyers about 1550; Church Text, as in No. 51, which was invented about the same time for the use of the church; Secretary, which is the modern style of writing among the lawyers, in engrossing their conveyances and legal instruments.

Ethiopic, otherwise called *Amharic* or *Abyssinian*, is evi-

ALPHABET.

dently derived from the Samaritan or Phenician, as will appear from the specimen given in Tab. IV, No. 21 [Pl. 4]; but, contrary to the custom of the Orientals, it is written from the right to the left. According to Diodorus and Heliodorus the Ethiopians as well as the Egyptians used the hieroglyphical mode of writing. *Diodor. Sic.* l. 3; *Heliodor. Æthiop.* l. 4: *Eustath. in Il.* l. 6, v. 168; *Marian. Victor. Instit. Ling. Æthiop.*; *Walton. in Introd. ad Lect. Ling. Oriental.*; *Ludolf. Hist. Æthiop.* l. 1, c. 15; and *Gram. Æthiop.*; *Loescher. de Caus. Ling. Herb.* p. 201.

Etruscan, Tab. III, No. 15, [Pl. 3] the first alphabet used in Italy, so called from the Etrusci, the most ancient inhabitants of that country; is a sort of Pelasgian or Arcadian characters, which were disposed after the Greek fashion, βυςροφηδὸν, i. e. alternately from left to right, and from right to left. There are two other alphabets attributed to the Etruscans, which Theseus Ambrosius says were used as secret characters by their priests, but without stating any authority. The Etruscan characters are to be found on many coins, as in No. 16, which represents, on the obverse, the head of Janus covered with a helmet, and, on the reverse, a club of Hercules, with the inscription FELAΘPI, i. e. Felathri, a town of Latium, now called Velletri. *Tab. Eugub. apud Dempster. de Etrusc. Regal.* tom. i. p. 91; *Marian de Etrusc. Metrop.*; *Gori. Mus. Etrusc.* p. 401; *Swinton. de Primev. Etrusc. Dissert.*

Flemish is the proper character of the Austrian and French Netherlands, used in their common printing, which much resembles the old English, as Tab. VI, No. 41, [Pl. 6.]

Franco Gallic, so called from its being a mixture of French and Gaulish characters, was used under the first race of the kings of France in their public acts.

Franks, an alphabet which was used by the earliest inhabitants of the Low Countries, and afterwards transferred to Gaul. It was a variety of the Latin alphabets used at that time. There is also another alphabet under this name belonging to the *Lingua Franca*, a kind of jargon spoken on the Mediterranean; the characters of which are like the language composed of French, vulgar Greek, Spanish, and Italian, Tab. VI, No. 42, [Pl. 6.]

French, or *ancient French*, an alphabet distinguished by this name, and of which a specimen, also of the current hand, is given in Tab. VI, No. 43, [Pl. 6] was used in the fifth century under the first race of the French kings.

Georgian, an alphabet which consists of four different characters; namely, the ancient Georgian, immediately derived from, and nearly allied to, the Greek; two consisting of capitals and small letters, called *sacred*, because they are used in transcribing their Holy Books; the fourth is the running-hand of the Georgians. The specimen given in Tab. V, No. 32, [Pl. 5] is of the ordinary printing character.

German consists of two characters, capitals and small letter, which are used for general printing, and two also for writing, or the current-hand, as in Tab. VI, No. 40.

Gothic, the most ancient characters under this name are attributed to Ulphilas, bishop of the Goths in 388, although, according to others, the Goths had the use of letters from the earliest period. The first specimen of this alphabet, in Tab. VI, No. 35, bears a strong affinity to the Runic; the second is formed from the Greek and Latin; a third alphabet, which is attributed to Albert Durer in the sixteenth century, is very similar to the German. To the above may be added the Mœso-Gothic, as given in No. 35, which is also attributed to Ulphilas, and was used in the translation of the Holy Scriptures; and an old English or Norman character, which is called in French *les Lettres Tourneures*, and by Astle modern Gothic. It was formerly much used in adorning Roman missals.

Greek. Under this name is comprehended a greater variety of Alphabets than that of any other language, for the Greek characters were employed by very many countries that did not speak the Greek; and, in Greece itself, it underwent many changes, according to the diversity of dialects, or the different periods in which it was used. It is generally admitted, on the authority of Herodotus, Pliny, Plutarch, and others, that Cadmus, the Phenician, introduced the first Greek alphabet into Bœotia, where he settled, B. C. 1500, although Diodorus is of opinion that the Pelasgian letters were prior to the Cadmean. It is evident, however, from comparing the specimens of the Cadmean and Pelasgic alphabets given in Tab. II, No. 7. [Pl. 2] with the Phenician, Tab. I, No. 3, [Pl.1] that they sprung from one and the same origin; but the former appears, from many of its letters, to be made by the inversion of the Phenician character. The Cadmean, or, as it is otherwise called, the Attic or Ionic alphabet, is drawn from coins and medals, the Pelasgian from the Eugubian tables; the former consisted originally, as is supposed, of only sixteen letters, to which eight others were afterwards added; the number of the latter varies according to the account of different writers, Dr. Swinton making it to consist of thirteen, Father Gori of twelve, and others of twenty. The next in succession is the Sigean alphabet, so called because the letters of which it is composed are taken from the Sigean inscription engraven on a marble pillar near the promontory and town of Sigeum, near Troy; the reading of which, in the common Greek characters, is as follows:

Φανοδικο ειμι τυ ιερμοκρατος το προ
κονισιο καγο κρατιρα κακιςατοι και
ηθμοι ις πρυτανιιον ιδεκα μνιμα
Σιγιυιυσι ις και μ' εποιισιι ι αισοτες και ι αδιλφοι.
Εαι διτι πασχο μιλε δαινει ιε σιγιι.

A specimen of the letters with the deficiencies, as supplied by Chishull, are given in No. 8, and a *facsimile* of the inscription itself in Tab. III, Plate 3, No. 11. The antiquity of this alphabet is evinced by its being read alternately from left to right, and from right to left, which manner of writing was called βυςρο-φηδὸν, because it resembled the turning of oxen at both ends of a furrow. It is besides observable that the H for the long E, and the Ω for the long O were not then in use, which were afterwards introduced by Simonides. Other Greek characters are also drawn from medals and inscriptions; namely, the Nemean, B. C. 430, engraven on marbles, as is supposed, before the Peloponnesian war; the Delian from inscriptions on the remains of a stately building on Mount Cynthus, in the island of Delos; the Athenian; and the Teian. About 500 years before the Christian Æra Simonides completed the Greek alphabet called the Ionic, which is given in No. 9, to which is annexed other Greek alphabets of different ages; namely, one used in the time of Alexander the Great, B. C. 330, No. 10; the alphabet drawn from the coins of the Antiochi, Kings of Syria, &c. B. C. 240 to 187; that of Constantine the Great, A. D. 306; of Justinian the Great, A. D. 527; of Heraclius, A. D. 610; of Leo Jaurus, A. D. 716; a specimen of small Greek letters, and another of capitals, in the eighth century: it is observable, in the first, that the *sigma* obtains the sixth place, according to the ancient alphabets, that *iota* has the form of *eta* inverted, and that *upsilon* follows the *omicron* as well as the *tau*; an alphabet used in the time of Charlemagne in the ninth century; the Greek of

Fac Similes, Tab. III, No. 12, 13, [Plate 3]; namely, of Bazil and Constantine, A.D. 900. To these may be added a MS. of the New Testament in the British Museum, presented to King Charles I, in 1628, by Cyrillus Lucario, patriarch of Alexandria, and supposed to have been written upwards of 1400 years; and a specimen of small Greek writing, as practised in the ninth century. This specimen is taken from a copy of Chrysostom's Homilies on the Psalms, in the French King's library, which Montfauçon has inserted in his Palæographia; also two Greek coins, No. 14; the first of which contains, on the reverse, the Θ for ΘΕΒΑΙΩΝ, as is supposed; the head, on the obverse, being ascribed to Cadmus: the second contains, on the obverse, the head of a lion, with the inscription REGION, i. e. Regiorum, a town in Italy, on the reverse, the head of an ox. *Herodot.* l. 1, c. 49; *Diodor.* l. 1; *Dionys.* l. 1; *Plin.* l. 7, c. 56; *Plut. Sympos.* l. 9, probl. 3; *Pausan.* l. 5, c. 17; *Euseb. in Chron.*; *Victorin. de Gramm.* l. 1; *Isidor. Orig.* l. c. 3; *Harpocration*; *Suidas.* in Κάδμος; *Eustath. in Il.* l. 18; *Tzelz. Chil.* sect. 398; *Scal. Animadvers. in Euseb.*; *Bochart. de Col. Phœnic.* l. 1, c. 21; *Voss. de Art. Grammat.* l. 1; *Spanheim. Dissert.* 1. *de Usu et Præstant. Num.*; *Salmas. ad Inscript. Herod.* p. 31; *Dr. Barnard's Tables*; *Montfauçon. Palæograph. Græc.*; *Chishul. Antiquit. Asiat.*; *Dr. Morton's Tables.*

Hebrew, under this name two fanciful alphabets are given by Theseus Ambrosius and Duret, which are attributed, on the authority of the Rabbis, to Solomon. Those most worthy of note are the ancient and modern Hebrew, Tab. I, No. 1, [Pl. 1]; the former of which is supposed to have been invented by Esdras after the Captivity, and to have given rise to the latter. A question has, however, here arisen respecting the original Hebrew character, which has undergone much discussion among the learned, both Jews and Christians. The more prevailing opinion is, that the character known by the name of Samaritan, or Phenician, was the original Hebrew character; and that the present alphabet was invented after the captivity, although the two Buxtorfs and others contend that the Hebrew letters, now in use, are the same as those in which the Law and Prophets were written by Moses: the former of these two opinions principally rests on the authority of Samaritan inscriptions on coins, which are admitted to have been struck before the Captivity. Of these, three specimens are given at the bottom of Tab. I, [Pl. 1] which represent the censor on the obverse, and, on the reverse, Aaron's rod budding; the inscriptions, the "Shekel of Israel" and "Jerusalem the Holy." These three coins are all of less value than the full shekel, the first of which has א over the censor, being called *a half shekel*; the second having ר, *the third of a shekel*; and the third also having ר *the fourth of a shekel*. To the above alphabets may be added the Rabbinical Hebrew, which is the current-hand in use among the Jews at present. *Euseb. in Chron. et Scalig. in Euseb.*; *Hieron. de Esd. et in Ezech.* c. 9; *Waser. de Antiq. Ebræor. Numm.*; *Villalpand. de Appar. Urb. et Templ.* part 2, l. 2, disp. 4, c. 21; *Walton. Prolegom. II, &c. de Ling. Heb.*; *Schickard. de Num.*; *Baron. Annal.* ann. 180; *Reland de Num. Ebræor.*; *Morin. Exercit. de Ling.* part 2, c. 6, &c.

Huns, an alphabet so called because it was used by the Huns, who settled in Pannonia, or Hungary, in 370.

Jacobite, an alphabet formed from the Greek, and used by the Jacobites, an heretical sect, in their religious service.

Japonese consists of three characters; namely, two that are in common use, and one that is used only at court. The specimen given in Tab. IV, No. 26, [Pl. 4] is of the common character, which, like the Chinese, is written from top to bottom.

Icelandic is the same as the Runic.

Illyrian. There were two alphabets of this name, according to John Baptist Palatin; one said to have been invented by St. Cyril, and the other by St. Jerom, or, according to Aventinus, in his Annals, by one Methodius, a bishop of Illyrium, who used it in the translation of the Scriptures; the former bears a great affinity to the Russian; the latter is most like the Dalmatian. *Duret. Tres. des Lang.* p. 741.

Indian, the same as the Ethiopian. Duret also mentions another Indian alphabet, which is generally used among the Easterns. *Duret. Tres. des Lang.* p. 383.

Irish. This alphabet, Tab. V, No. 29, [Pl. 5.] bears, in the opinion of Vallancy, the greatest affinity to the Phenician, from which he supposes it to be derived. But the Irish used other mysterious alphabets in their incantations, after the manner of those given under the name of Ogums, from *Oga*, and *Ogma*, an augury. The three principal Ogums used by the Irish were the *Ogum Beath*, when *bt* or *beath* was placed always for the letter *a*; *Ogum Coll*, when, for vowels, dipthongs, and tripthongs in the *Ogum*, the letter *c* was variously repeated; *Ogum Croabh*, or the *virgular Ogum*, having a line or stem called the Croabh, through which, and on each side, are drawn perpendicular strokes. *Wurm. de Lit. Run.*; *O'Mulloy. Irish. Gramm.*; *Raban. Maur. de Usu Lit.*; *O'Flahrt. Ogyg.*; *Oconner's Dissert. seu Hibern. Rer. Chronolog.*; *Ware. Antiq. of Ireland.*; *Ledwig. Antiq.*

Italic, a well known alphabet formed from the Roman, which was called likewise Venetian, because it was first cut at Venice, and afterwards *Lettres Aldines*, from Aldus Minutius, by whom it was invented about 1512.

Kufic, the ancient Arabic. [vide *Arabic*]

Latin, the most ancient alphabet of the inhabitants of Italy, was the Etruscan, [vide *Etruscan*] which underwent successive changes, as are noted in Tab. III, No. 15, [Pl. 3] until it arrived at its present state, in which it is more generally known by the name of Roman. *Dionys. Halic.* l. 1; *Hygin. Fab.* 277; *Plin.* l. 7, c. 63; *Tacit. Annal.* l. 11; *Quintil. Instit.* l. 1, c. 4; *Diomed. Gramm. Instit.* l. 1; *Marius Victorinus, Priscian. &c. apud Gramm. Vet. Putsche's Edit.*; *Cyprian. de Varietat. Idol.*; *Auson. Idyll.* 12; *Isidor. Orig.* l. 1, c. 4; *Voss. de Art Grammat.*; *Lips. de Pronunt. Ling. Lat.* c. 8; *Spanheim. de Usu et Præstant. Numis. Antiq. Dissert.* 1, p. 114; *Montfauçon. Palæograph. Græc.*; *Dr. Morton's Tables*; *Massey. Orig. et Prog. of Letters.*

Lombard, a variety of the Latin character, as Tab. VI, No. 46, [Pl. 6.]

Malabaric, an alphabet consisting of sixteen vowels, and thirty-five simple consonants or radicals, as in Tab. IV. No. 23, [Pl. 4.] *Alphabet. Var. Congregat. de Propagand. Fide.* vol. ii.

Malayan, the character of this alphabet is the same as the Arabic.

Mantchon, a sort of Tartaric. [vide *Tartaric*]

Mendean, an alphabet used by the Mendes, a people of Egypt, A. D. 277, which was formed from the Syriac.

Monk's, a mode of writing among the ancient Britons by cutting letters upon sticks, either in a square or triangular form, very similar to that which is given as a specimen of the Welch or Bardic alphabet.

Norman, there are two alphabets given under this name on the authority of the venerable Bede, one of which was a variety of the Greek, and the other, as in Tab. VI, No. 44, [Pl. 6.]

ALPHABET.

Palmyrian, which was first decyphered by the Abbe Barthelemé, is read from right to left. It bears a strong affinity to the Hebrew.

Pelasgian, a name given to the alphabet which the Greeks derived from the Phenicians, whom they called Πελασγοί, *Pelasgii quasi Pelagi*, from πέλαγος, the sea, because they traversed the ocean, and carried on commerce with other nations. A specimen of the Pelasgian is to be found in Tab. II, No. 8, [Pl. 2.]

Persian, the modern alphabet of the Persian is nearly the same as the Arabic, except the addition of four letters, and a few slight differences in the powers given to the letters. An ancient character is given by Hyde, that is, called *Zend* or *Pazend*, and is supposed to have been used by Zoroastre. *Hyde de Relig. Vet. Persar.*

Phœnician. Under this name is comprehended a great variety of characters, which are drawn from coins and inscriptions, and are generally supposed to have been in use among the Phenicians, who had alphabetical characters as early as any people in the world. The specimen in Tab. I, No. 3, [Pl. 1] is given on the authority of Scaliger, who supposes this to have been the original Hebrew character, otherwise called the Samaritan.

Roman, the modern name for the Latin.

Runic, a character derived from the Mæso-Gothic, was used by several nations of the North, as in Tab. VI, No. 36, [Pl. 6].

Russian is evidently derived from the Greek, as may be seen in Tab. V, No. 34, [Pl. 5.]

Samaritan is the name given to the Phenician character, which is most generally supposed to be that which was used by the Jews from the time of Moses to the Captivity, although this has been a subject of dispute among the learned. [vide *Hebrew*] The name was given to this character because the Samaritans continued to use it, after the captivity, in writing the Pentateuch. The ancient Samaritan has been collected, by Walton, from coins and inscriptions, of which specimens are given at the bottom of Tab. I, [Pl. 1]: the modern Samaritan differs somewhat from the ancient, as may be seen by comparing them in Tab. I, No. 2. Duret has given two other alphabets under this name, the characters of which are said to be formed according to the course and movements of nature.

Sanscrit. The alphabet of the Sanskrita, i. e. the perfect or polished language of the Hindu class, is called the Devanagari, which is given in Tab. IV, No. 25, [Pl. 4] according to the form and order in which it is drawn out in Wilkins' Grammar.

Saracen. Theseus Ambrosius gives one Saracen alphabet, which he says was used at the time of their conquests. It bears some affinity to the Phenician, as in Tab. IV, No. 20, [Pl. 4.] Another alphabet under this name is quoted by Dr. Morton on the authority of Kircher, which is very similar to the Arabic. *Duret. Tres. des Lang.* p. 475; *Dr. Morton's Tables.*

Saxon consists of two characters, the ancient and modern, Tab. VI, No. 38, [Pl. 6.]

Sclavonian, the alphabet used by the ancient inhabitants of Sclavonia, bore some resemblance to the Illyrian.

Secretary, a sort of writing among English lawyers, which is used in engrossing.

Servian, an alphabet bearing some affinity to the Greek, is attributed to St. Cyril, A. D. 700. There are other characters under this name, which are ascribed to St. Jerom.

Siamic, an alphabet much resembling the Chinese.

Stranghelo, a name for the ancient Syriac, from the Greek ςρογγυλὴ, round, or rather rude and rough. [vide *Syriac*]

Syriac consists of two characters; the ancient, called the Stranghelo, which is said to have been in use, B. C. 300; and the modern Syriac, which consists of Initials, Medials, and Finals, like the Arabic, as in Tab. I, No. 4, [Pl. 1.] From this character two others were formed, called Nestorian, because they were used by the Nestorians of Syria, but differing only in some few particulars. A fifth and sixth sort of Syriac have been given under the names of Syro-Galilean and Syro-Hebraic, but without sufficient authority.

Sumatran. The dialects of Sumatra have each its peculiar alphabet, of which Marsden, in his Comparative Vocabulary, has taken notice, as the Batta, Lampoor, Rejang, &c. A specimen of the latter is given in Tab. IV, No. 28, [Pl. 4.]

Talenga, an alphabet, used in the kingdom of Decan, very similar to the Malabaric.

Tamoulic, an alphabet much used in India in letter-press printing.

Tartaric is the same as the Arabic, but the Mantchou Tartar is a different character, as in Tab. IV, No. 24, [Pl. 4.]

Teutonic. Under this name is given the specimen, as in Tab. VI, No. 39, [Pl. 6] which is said to have been taken from an ancient MS. in the cathedral of Wurzburg.

Thibetan, the alphabet used by the Lamas; the specimen of which, in Tab. IV, No. 27, [Pl. 4] has been copied from the second volume of the "Alphabeta Varia Typis sacræ Congregationis de Propaganda Fide."

Turkish is the same as the Arabic, except the addition of five letters.

Welsh, or, as it is called in Wales, *Coelbren y Beirz*, i. e. the Bardic alphabet; consisted of sixteen primitive or radical characters, and twenty-four secondary ones. It was formed by cutting the letters on a stick in a triangular or square form, as in Tab. VI, No. 37.

Tables of Alphabets according to their Derivation and Affinity.

These Tables are given in six plates in the following order; namely,

Table I, Plate 1.—Oriental Alphabets.

1. Hebrew, ancient, modern, and rabbinical. 2. Samaritan, ancient and modern. 3. Phenician. 4. Syriac, ancient and modern. 5. Egyptian Hieroglyphic. 6. Chinese Characters. At the bottom, Samaritan Coins.

Table II, Plate 2 and 3.—Greek Alphabets.

7. Cadmean. 8. Pelasgian, Sigean, Nemean, Delian, Athenian, and Teian. 9. Ionic, or alphabet of Simonides. 10. Greek alphabets of different ages, from 330 B. C. to 900 A. D.

Table III, Plate 3.—Latin Alphabets.

11. Sigean Inscription. 12, 13. Fac Similes of Greek MSS. in the second and ninth centuries. 14. Greek coins. 15. Latin characters of different ages. 16. An Etruscan coin.

Table IV, Plate 4.—Alphabets derived from, or allied to, the Oriental Alphabets.

17. Cufic. 18. Arabic. 19. Persian. 20. Saracen. 21. Ethiopic. 22. Mendean. 23. Malabaric. 24. Mantchou Tartar. 25. Sanscrit. 26. Japonese. 27. Thibetan. 28. Rejang.

Table V, Plate 5.—Alphabets derived from the Oriental or Greek Alphabets.

29. Ancient Irish, Bobeloth and Bethluisnon; Ogums, namely, Croabh and O'Sullivan's. 30. Coptic. 31. Armenian. 32. Georgian. 33. Dalmatian. 34. Russian.

Table VI, Plate 6.—Alphabets derived from the Greek or Latin.

Northern Alphabets. 35. Gothic, ancient, modern, and Mæso-Gothic. 36. Runic. 37. Welsh. 38. Saxon, ancient and modern. 39. Teutonic. 40. German, printing and current. 41. Flemish.—*French Alphabets.* 42. Franks. 43. French, ancient and current. 44. Norman and Anglo-Norman. 45. Bastard, ancient and round. 46. Lombard. 47. Charlemagne.—*English Alphabets.* 48. Black Letter. 49. Chancery, Round and Running. 50. Court Text. 51. Church Text.

ALPHE'TI (*Astron.*) another name for the star *Lucida Corona.*

ALPHITE'DON (*Med.*) ἀλφιτηδον, from ἄλφιτον, bran; a fracture of a bone into small fragments like bran.

A'LPHITON (*Med.*) ἄλφιτον, or in the plural ἄλφιτα, a term used by Hippocrates for a sort of hasty pudding. *Hippocrat. de Mul.* 1. 2, &c.; *Gal. de Alim.* l. 1; *Gorr. Def. Med.*; *Foes. Œconom. Hippocrat.*

ALPHO'NSINE *tables* (*Astron.*) astronomical tables made by Alphonsus, king of Arragon.

A'LPHUS (*Med.*) ἄλφος, from αλφαίνω, to whiten; because it turns the skin white; the white leprosy, a species of vitiligo, i. e. the *Vitiligo alba*, in which, according to Celsus, the skin is of a white colour, with a kind of roughness. The *Alphus* is less virulent than another species called the *Leuce. Cels.* l. 5, c. 18; *Gal. Introd.* c. 17; *Oribas. de Morb. Curat.* l. 3, c. 58; *Aet. Tetrab.* 4, serm. 1. c. 132; *Actuar. de Meth. Med.* l. 2, c. 11.

ALPI'NIA (*Bot.*) a genus of plants called after Prosper Alpinus, Class 1 *Monandria*, Order 1 *Monogynia.*
Generic Character. CAL. *perianth* one-leaved; *leaflets* equal.—COR. monopetalous; *tube* cylindrical; *border* three-parted; *nectary* two-parted.—STAM. *filament* proper none; *anther* large.—PIST. *germ* inferior; *style* filiform; *stigma* obtuse.—PER. *capsule* ovate.
Species. The species are perennials, as—*Alpinia racemosa, Amomum pyramidale* seu *Zingiber sylvestre.*—*Alpinia galanga, Maranta galanga* seu *Amomum galanga*, &c.

A'LQUIFOU (*Com.*) or *Arquifou,* a sort of mineral lead ore used by potters.

ALRA'MECA (*Astron.*) *Alrumech,* an Arabic name for the star *Arcturus.*

ALRA'TICA (*Anat.*) an imperforation of the vagina.

A'LSADAF (*Conchol.*) the *unguis odoratus* and the *murex,* of the shell of which it was supposed to be a part.

A'LSAMECH (*Anat.*) the great foramen in the *Os petrosum.*

ALSI'MBEL (*Bot.*) or *Simbala,* the Spikenard of India.

A'LSINA (*Bot.*) the *Thelygonum* of Linnæus.

ALSINA'STRUM (*Bot.*) the *Elatine* of Linnæus.

A'LSINE (*Bot.*) ἀλσίνη, a plant so called, from ἄλσος, a grove, because it delights in the shade, *in lucis nascitur.* It is sometimes called, in English, Mouse-ear, from the resemblance which its leaves bear to the ears of a mouse; but its general name is Chickweed. This plant is of an astringent and refrigerating quality. *Dioscor.* l. 4, c. 87; *Plin.* l. 27, c. 4; *Oribas. Med. Coll.* l. 11; *Aet Tetrab.* 1, serm. 1; *Paul. Æginet.* l. 7, c. 3; *Lem. des Drog. Dale Pharmacop.*

ALSINE, *in the Linnean system,* a genus of plants, Class 5 *Pentandria,* Order 3 *Trigynia.*
Generic Characters. CAL. *perianth* five-leaved.—COR. *petals* five.—STAM. *filaments* capillary; *anthers* roundish. —PIST. *germ* subovate; *styles* filiform; *stigmas* obtuse. PER. *capsule* none; *seeds* very many.
Species. The species are annuals, as the—*Alsine media* seu *Holosteum alsine,* Common Chickweed, native of Britain.—*Alsine segetalis* seu *Spergala.*—*Alsine mucronata* seu *Arenaria,* &c.

ALSINE is also the name of different species of the *Arenaria, Callitricha, Draba, Glinus, Holosteum, Campanula, Cerasteum,* &c. *Bauh. Hist. Plant.*; *Raii Hist. Plant.*; &c.

ALSINEFO'RMIS (*Bot.*) the *Montia fontana* of Linnæus.

ALSINE'LLA (*Bot.*) the *Sagina procumbens* of Linnæus.

A'LSINES *facie* (*Bot.*) the *Thelygonum cynocrambe* of Linnæus.

ALSTO'NIA (*Bot.*) a genus of plants called after Mr. Alston, professor at Edinburgh, Class 13 *Polyandria,* Order 1 *Monogynia.*
Generic Characters. CAL. *perianth* inferior; *scales* ovate. COR. one-petalled.—STAM. *filaments* very many; *anthers* orbiculate.—PIST. *germ* superior; *style* simple; *stigma* capitate-obovate.
Species. The only species is the *Alstonia theæformis* seu *Symplocos Alstonia,* a shrub, native of South America.

ALSTROME'RIA (*Bot.*) a genus of plants called after Mr. Alstromer, a Swedish naturalist, Class 6 *Hexandria,* Order 1 *Monogynia.*
Generic Characters. CAL. none.—COR. six.—STAM. *filaments* awlshaped; *anthers* oblong.—PIST. *germ* inferior; *style* filiform; *stigmas* three.—PER. *capsule* roundish; *seeds* very many.
Species. The species are mostly perennials, as the *Alstroemeria pelegrina, ligtu, salsilla,* &c.

ALT (*Mus.*) Italian for that portion of the great scale between F above the treble cliff and G in *altissimo.*

A'LTA (*Mus.*) or *Alt,* Italian for high or higher; as 8vo. *alta,* an octave higher.

ALTA *tenura* (*Law*) the high tenure, or tenure in chief by military service.

ALTA'IR (*Astron.*) a star of the first magnitude in the constellation Aquila.

A'LTAR (*Bibl.*) in Latin *altare,* from *altus,* high, because altars were set up by the heathens in high places; or, in all probability, because it was raised above the ground; a table or raised place on which any offering was made to the Almighty. The first altar mentioned is that built by Noah after the flood, on which he offered burnt-offerings. *Genes.* viii. 20. The altars which Moses raised by the command of God were made of earth or rough stones. *Exod.* xx. 24; but that built by Solomon was of brass. 2 *Chron.* iv. 1, 2, 3. The two principal altars of the Jews were, the Altar of Burnt-Offerings, the Altar of Incense: there was also the Altar, or rather Table, of Shew Bread.

The *Altar of Burnt-Offerings* was a kind of coffer of shittim wood, covered with brass, which in the time of Moses, was five cubits, or two yards and a half square, and three cubits, or a yard and a half high; but that made by Solomon was much larger. 2 *Chron.* iv. 1, &c. To this altar, as in fig. 1, belonged—1. The *Horns,* or four spires, one at each corner. 2. The *Grate* of brass, on which the fire was made. 3. The *Pan* which received the ashes. 4. The *Rings* and *Chains* by which it was fixed to the four horns of the altar. 5. The *Kibbish,* or ascent to the altar. *Exod.* x. 26, &c.; 2 *Chron.* iv. 1, &c.

The *Altar of Incense,* a small table of shittim-wood covered with gold, one cubit in length, one in width, and two in height. To this, as in fig. 2, belongs—1. The *Horns,* as

Fig. 1.   *Fig.* 2.

in the first. 2. The *Crown*, which was made of pure gold. 3. The *Rings* under the crown. 4. The *Censor*, which was placed upon it. *Exod.* xxx. 1, &c. This was the altar hidden by Jeremiah before the captivity. *2 Maccab.* ii. 5, &c.

The *Altar*, or *Table of Shew Bread*. vide *Table*.

An *altar* at Athens is spoken of by St. Paul as bearing the inscription ἀγνώστῳ Θεῷ, i. e. to the unknown God, to which a something similar is mentioned by Pausanias and Lucian. Hereupon St. Jerom, and some other of the Fathers, raised a question as to what this altar was; but St. Chrysostom naturally solves the difficulty by supposing that the Athenians, a superstitious people, being fearful least they should have forgotten any divinity in their religious worship, set up an altar " To the unknown God," whoever that might be; whence St. Paul takes occasion to preach the true God, who was to them an unknown God, whom they ignorantly worshipped. *Luc. in Philostrat. ad Fin.*

ALTAR *Ant.*) in Greek Βωμός, was called in Latin either *altare* or *ara*: the *altare*, according to Servius, was dedicated *Diis superis*, i. e. to the Gods above; and the *Ara Diis inferis*, or gods below: this distinction, however, is not made by either of the Plinys or by Tacitus. The altars of the Greeks were called Βωμοὶ ἔμπυροι, when designed for sacrifices by fire; ἄπυροι, if without fire; and ἀναίμακτοι, if without blood; on which two latter sort of altars only cakes, fruits, and inanimate things could be offered, according to the doctrine of Pythagoras. *Orph. de Achat.*

Πρῶτα μὲν ἐν σκιώδεντας ἀναιμάκτων ἐπὶ Βωμῶν.

The form of the altars was generally similar to the altar of incense among the Jews. [vide *Consecratio* and *Pietas*] *Plin.* l. 15, c. 30; *Tacit. Annal.* l. 16, c. 30; *Plin. Panag.* c. 1, § 5; *Diog. Laert. in Pythag.*; *Serv. in Eccl.* l. 5, v. 65; *Prudent.* περὶ στφ, l. 10, v. 49; *Berthold. de Ara,* c. 2.

ALTAR (*Ecc.*) the table in churches where the communion is administered.—*Altar of Prothesis*, a kind of small preparatory altar, in which the priests of the Greek church bless the bread before they carry it to the Altar or Communion Table.

ALTERA'TA (*Mus.*) Italian, things altered, or innovations; a term applied by old musicians to the deviations from the diatonic scale.

ALTE'RATIVES (*Med.*) *Alterantia medicamenta*, such medicines as induce a change in the blood and juices for the better, without any manifest operation or evacuation, as sea-water in the case of scrophula. *Gal. de Nat. Facultat.* l. 3.

ALTERA'TRIX (*Med.*) alterative, an epithet for such things as have the power of inducing a desirable change in the system.

ALTE'RCUM (*Bot.*) or *Altercangenon*, a herb among the Arabians, which is called by the Greeks ὑοσκύαμος. [vide *Hyoscyomus*]

A'LTERN Base (*Trig.*) in oblique triangles, is that which is distinguished from the true base: supposing this to be the sum of the two sides, then the difference of the sides is the altern base; or if the difference of the sides be the true base, then their sum is the altern base.

ALTE'RNATE angles (*Geom.*) angles formed by a line cutting two parallel lines which are on opposite sides of the cutting line; thus. the internal angles A and B, or *a* and *b*, formed by the line C D cutting the parallel lines E F and G H are alternate.—*Alternate ratio*, is the comparing of

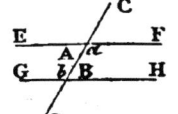

the antecedent with the antecedent, and the consequent with the consequent: supposing there be four quantities proportional, namely A B C D, whereof A is to B as C is to D, then the ratio is alternate, if it be said that A is to C as B to D.

ALTERNATE (*Her.*) the position of quarterings, partitions, and other figures that succeed one another by turns.

ALTERNATE (*Bot.*) *alternus*, an epithet for the leaf, (*folium*); the flower, (*flos*); and the peduncle, (*pedunculus*); when they come out one after or above another in succession or gradation.

ALTERNATE (*Med.*) different medicines employed by turns.

ALTE'RNATELY pinnate (*Bot.*) *alternatim pinnatum*, an epithet applied to a leaf (*folium*) when the leaflets (*foliola*), or a pinnated leaf, stand alternately.

ALTERNATION (*Math.*) *alternatio*, changing the order or position of any proposed number of things, as *a* and *b*, which admit of two changes, *a b* and *b a*; or *a*, *b* and *c*, which admit of six changes, &c.

ALTERNATION (*Mus.*) changes rung on bells.

ALTHÆ'A (*Bot.*) ἀλθαία; a plant so called, from ἄλθος, a remedy, on account of its great efficacy in medicine. It was much used as an emollient, particularly in application to wounds. *Theoph. Hist. Plant.* l. 9, c. 19; *Dioscor.* l. 3, c. 163; *Plin.* l. 20, c. 21; *Gal. de Meth. Med.* l. 14, c. 5; *Suidas*.

ALTHÆA, in the Linnean system, a genus of plants, Class 16 *Monadelphia*, Order 5 *Polyandria*, in English, Marshmallow.

Generic Character. CAL. *perianth* double.—COR. fivepetalled.—STAM. *filaments* many; *anthers* subreniform.—PIST. *germ* orbiculate; *style* cylindrical; *stigmas* many.—PER. *arils* not jointed; *seed* one.

Species. The species are some annuals, as *Althæa acaulis* seu *Malva rosea, &c.*; some perennials, as *Althæa officinalis*, Common Marsh-mallow; *Althæa cannibina* seu *Alcea cannabina*, Hemp-leaved Marsh-mallow, &c.; some biennials, as *Althæa rosea, pallida, ficifolia, &c. J. Bauh. Hist. Plant.; C. Bauh. Pin.; Ger. Herb.; Park. Theat. Botan.; Raii Hist. Plant.; Tournef. Inst.; Boerhaav. Ind. Plant.; Linn. Spec. Plant.*

ALTHA'NACA (*Chem.*) orpiment.

ALTHEBE'GIUM (*Med.*) a swelling as in a cachexy.

A'LTICA (*Ent.*) a division of the genus *Cantharis*, according to Fabricius, consisting of the insects of this tribe, which are of an oblong shape, and have the lip bifid.

A'LTIMAR (*Min.*) burnt copper.

A'LTIMETRY (*Math.*) the art of taking and measuring heights.

A'LTIN (*Com.*) a small coin in Muscovy.

ALTI'NEAR (*Min.*) a factitious kind of salt used in separating metals.

ALTI'NGAT (*Min.*) rust of copper.

ALTINU'RAUM (*Chem.*) vitriol.

ALTI'SSIMO (*Mus.*) or, abbreviated, *altiss.* an Italian epithet for notes above F in alt.

ALTI'STA (*Mus.*) an Italian name for the vocal performer who takes the *alto primo* part.

ALTITO'NANS (*Mus.*) highsounding; an epithet applied to the counter-tenor of anthems, &c. signifying the highest of the parts intended for the adult male voice.

A'LTITUDE (*Geom.*) the height of an object, or its elevation above that plane to which the base is referred.—*Altitude of a figure*, the perpendicular or nearest distance of its vertex from the base, as the right line B D drawn from the vertex B of the triangle A B C perpendicular to the line A C which is the altitude of the

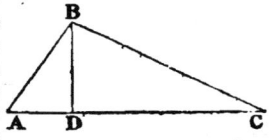

triangle.—*Altitude of an object*, is an elevation of an object above the plane of the horizon, or a perpendicular let fall to that plane; as A B, the perpendicular, let fall from a tower, as in the annexed diagram. Altitudes are either accessible or inaccessible. *Accessible altitudes* 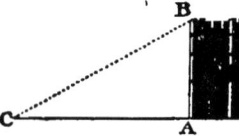 are those whose base may be approached so as to measure the distance between it and the station from which the measure is to be taken.—*Inaccessible altitudes* are when no access is to be had to the base of the object. The altitudes of the pyramids, according to Plutarch, were measured by means of their shadows and that of a pole set up beside them, making the altitude of the pole and the pyramid proportional to their shadows. *Euclid. Elem. Def.* l. 6; *Wolf. Elem. Math.* tom. 1, § 115, &c.

ALTITUDE *of the Eye* (*Perspect.*) a right line let fall from the eye perpendicular to the geometrical plane, being the the point from which the principal ray proceeds.

ALTITUDE (*Astron.*) the arc of a vertical circle measuring the height of the sun, moon, or any other celestial object above the horizon. Altitudes are distinguished into—*Apparent altitude*, that which appears by sensible observation made at any place on the surface of the earth.—*True altitude*, that which results from the correction of the apparent altitude on account of refraction and altitude. Let C D be the true horizon, H O the sensible horizon, D Q a vertical circle whose centre C is the centre of the earth, L any point in the heavens, H the place of observation, and L M an 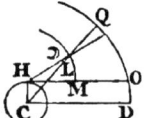 arc of a circle drawn through L about the centre H, then is L M the *apparent altitude* of the point L, which is always less than the *true altitude* which is D Q. The true altitudes of the sun, fixed stars, and planets, differ but very little from their apparent altitudes: the difference of the moon, however, is about 52 minutes.—*Meridian altitude*, an arc of the meridian intercepted between the horizon and the centre of the object on the meridian, as in the annexed diagram, where H Z R N represents the meridian, H R the horizon, S the star; then is R S the meridian altitude.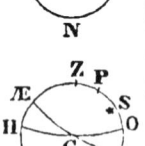
—*Altitude* or *Elevation of the Pole*, an arc of the meridian P O intercepted between the horizon H O and P the pole of the world; this is equal to the latitude of the place.—*Altitude of the Equator*, an arc of the meridian H Æ, intercepted between the horizon H O and the equator, Æ Q being always equal to the complement of the latitude of the place.— *Altitude of the Tropics*, otherwise called the *Solstitial altitude of the Sun*, is his meridian altitude when in the solstitial points.—*Altitude of the Horizon*, or of the stars, &c. seen in it, is the quantity by which it is raised by refraction.— *Altitude of the Nonagesimal*, is the altitude of the 90th degree of the Ecliptic, counted upon it from the point where it cuts the horizon. It is equal to the angle made by the ecliptic and horizon where they intersect at that time.—*Altitude of the Cone of the Earth's or Moon's Shadow*, the height of the shadow of the body made by the sun, and measured from the centre of the body. This is found when the sun is at a mean distance, by saying, as the apparent semidiameter of the sun, i. e. about 16, is to Radius, so is the same diameter of the earth to a fourth proportional 214.8 semidiameters of the earth, which is the altitude. The greatest altitude of the earth's shadow is 217 semidiameters of the earth; and the altitudes of the earth's and moon's shadows are nearly as 11 to 3, the proportion of their diameters.—*Circles of Altitude* [vide *Circle*].—*Parallax of Altitude* [vide *Parallax*].—*Parallels of Altitude* [vide *Parallel*].—*Quadrant of Altitude* [vide *Quadrant*].—*Refraction of Altitude* [vide *Refraction*]. *Ricciol. Almag.* l. 1, c. 12, l. 3, c. 10, &c.; *Keil. Lect. ad ver. Astronom.* l. 19, &c.; *Wolf. Elem. Math.* tom. 3, § 73, &c.

ALTITUDE *of Motion* (*Mech.*) a term employed by Dr. Wallis, to signify the measure of any motion estimated in the line of direction of the moving force. *Wall. de Mechan.*—*Equal altitude Instrument*, an instrument used to observe a celestial object when it has the same or an equal altitude on both sides of the meridian. It is very useful in adjusting clocks, &c.

A'LTO *tenore* (*Mus.*) Italian for the upper or counter-tenor part in music of several parts. *Alto cliff*, the Cliff when placed on the third line of the stave.—*Alto concertante*, the tenor of the little chorus which sings throughout.— *Alto primo*, the first or upper alto, in distinction from the —*Alto secondo*, or lower alto.—*Alto ripieno*, the tenor of the great chorus which performs in the full parts.—*Alto viola*, the small tenor of the violin.

ALTO *et Basso* (*Law*) *ponere se in arbitrio in alto et basso*, the absolute submission of all differences, high and low, to an arbiter.

A'LTOM (*Com.*) the Turkish name for a sequin.

A'LVARISTS (*Ecc.*) a branch of the Thomists, so called from their leader Alvarez, who maintained the efficacy of divine grace, in distinction from the former, who maintained its sufficiency.

ALUCI'TA (*Ent.*) a division of the genus *Phalæna*, according to Gmelin.

A'LUD (*Bot.*) the same as Agallochum.

ALU'DEL (*Chem.*) an earthen tube or vessel without a bottom, used in sublimations. Such vessels are without a bottom, and are fitted into one another as occasion may require. At the bottom of the furnace there is a pot, holding the matter that is to be sublimed, and at the top there is a head, to receive the flowers that sublime up thither.

ALVEA'RE (*Nat.*) Alveary, a bee-hive.

ALVEA'RIUM (*Anat.*) the bottom of the concha, or the external ear.

ALVEOLA'RIS *processus* (*Anat.*) the same as *Maxillaria superiora ossa*.

A'LVEOLATE (*Bot.*) *alveolatus*, Honey-combed, an epithet applied to the receptacle when it is divided into open cells, like a honey-comb, with a seed lodged in each, as in *Onopordum*. *Linn. Philos. Botan.*

A'LVEOLI (*Anat.*) from Alveus, the sockets in the jaws for the teeth.

A'LVEOLUS (*Nat.*) a name for the waxen cells of which the comb in a bee-hive consists.

ALVEOLUS (*Min.*) a marine body so called, which is frequently found in a fossil state. It is of a conic shape, and composed of several hemispheric cells, like those which form the comb of a bee-hive, having a pipe of communication similar to that in the thick nautilus.

A'LVEUS (*Ant.*) 1. a boat formed from the trunk of a tree hollowed out, which was in use among the ancients. According to Ovid, Romulus and Remus were exposed in a bark of this kind.
Ovid. Fast. l. 2, v. 407.

Sustinet impositos summâ cavus alveus undâ,
Heu quantum fati parva tabella tulit,
Alveus in limo sylvis appulsus opacis,
Paullatim fluvio deficientis sedet.

Liv. l. 1, c. 4; *Patercul.* l. 2, c. 107; *Gyrald. de Navig.* c. 8; *Schaef. de Milit. Nav.* l. 1, c. 3. 2. A chess-board, or any table for gaming, the furrows of which resembled the beds, *alvei*, of a river. *Plin.* l. 37, c. 2; *Dolet. de Re Nav. apud Gronov. Thes. Antiq. Græc.* vol. 11, p. 657.

ALVEUS (*Anat.*) a canal or duct through which some fluid passes.—*Alveus communis*, the common duct or communication of the ampullæ of the membranaceous semicircular canals in the internal ear.—*Alveus ampullescens*, part of the duct conveying the chyle to the subclavian vein.

ALVI'DUCA (*Med.*) Purgatives.

ALVIFLU'XUS (*Med.*) a diarrhœa, or purging.

A'LUM (*Min.*) vide *Alumen*.

ALUM (*Chem.*) Alumen, so called from ἅλς, the sea; a saline humour of the earth, *Salsugo terræ*, of an astringent, hardening, and corroding quality; whence called in Greek συντρψια, from σύστω, to bind. Alum is either natural or factitious.—*Natural Alum*, which was well known to the ancients, is a kind of whitish friable stone, formerly found in the island of Melos, Macedonia, Egypt, &c. of which there were different kinds, namely, the *scissile*, σχιςη, sometimes called τριχίτις, because when pulled asunder it runs into hairs; and also *plumose*, because it was composed of featherlike fibres; the round, ςρογγυλη; and the liquid, which, to be good, must have a milky property. When alum is melted, so as to become a white porous substance, it is called *burnt Alum*.—*Factitious alum*, which is the modern alum, is composed of other ingredients besides the concreted juice. It is commonly made of a stone, of seaweed, and of urine, and known by the names of *rock*, or *English Alum*, which is colourless, and *Roch*, or *Roman Alum*, which is of a reddish colour.—*Saccharine Alum* is a composition of common alum with rose-water and the white of eggs, which serves as a cosmetic. *Hippocrat. Dioscor.* l. 5, c. 123; *Plin.* l. 25, c. 15; *Gal. de Simplic.* l. 9, &c.; *Oribas Med. Coll.* l. 15, c. 1; *Aet. Tetrab.* 4, serm. 2, c. 25.

ALUM-WATER (*Paint.*) a preparation used by painters in water-colours, prepared by dissolving common alum in water.

ALUM *Stone* (*Surg.*) a stone or calx used in surgery, which is probably alum calcined so as to become corrosive.

ALUM *Earth* (*Min.*) the earth from which alum is extracted, that is, pure clay.—*Alum Ores*, the ores or stone from which alum is prepared.—*Alum-Works*, where alum is manufactured, in distinction from alum mines, where the natural alum is found. In these mines are found the stones or ores of which the alum is made, called *doggers*, i. e. a sort of coal snake-stones, and also a brown alum-slate, a sort of clay-slate, so called from its aluminous taste. Besides these stones is found likewise the water, or liquid, which, when it first appears, is called the *virgin water*. To these ingredients are added urine and the sea-weed called *kelp*. When the alum is made, the *mothers*, or liquor, that remains is put into a boiler, where, by the help of kelp-lees, it ferments, and is then put into a *settler* of lead, where the nitre and *slam* sink to the bottom; after which it is scooped out into a *cooler*, made of deal boards, when, by the addition of fresh urine, the alum is made to *strike*, or *shoot*, that is, to harden about the sides and at the bottom of the cooler.

ALU'MEN (*Min.*) Alum, a genus of Salts *in the Linnean system*, formed by the combination of the earth called Alumine, or pure clay, with sulphuric acid, potash, and ammonia. The principal species of alumen are, the—*Alumen nativum*, seu *nudum*, natural Alum.—*Alumen commune*, seu *factitium*, the rock Alum.—*Alumen butyraceum*, Stone-Butter, or Mountain-Butter.—*Alumen romanum*, Roche Alum.—*Alumen Schisti Alumina*, or Aluminous Earth.

ALU'MINA (*Min.*) Alumine, or the Earth of Alum, an argillaceous, soft, and insipid sort of earth, which is the base of alum, being the principal part of clay. When obtained in a small quantity of water, it is very light, friable, and spongy, and on that account is called the *spongy Alumina*, in distinction from the gelatinous Alumina, which is obtained in a large quantity of water. Alumina is the base of several salts when combined with acids, as the Nitrate of Alumina, the Sulphate of Alumina, &c. formed by the combination of Alumina with nitric, sulphuric, &c. acids.

ALUMINA'RIS (*Min.*) another name for the Alumina.

ALU'MINITE (*Min.*) a species of alum, which is a subsulphate of Alumina.

ALU'MINOUS *Earth* (*Min.*) Alumina, or Alum Earth, the earth from which alum is procured. [vide *Alum*, *Alumina*]—*Aluminous Waters*, waters impregnated with particles of alum.

ALU'RNUS (*Ent.*) a genus of animals, Class *Insecta*, Order *Coleoptera*.
Generic Character. *Antennæ* filiform, short.—*Feelers* from 4 to 6, very short.—*Jaw* horny, arched.
Species. The species are—*Alurnus grossus*, having a scarlet thorax.—*Alurnus femoratus*, having the thighs and hind shanks toothed.—*Alurnus dentipes*, of a black colour, &c.

ALU'SAR (*Chem.*) Manna.

ALU'TA (*Med.*) soft thin leather used to spread plasters on.

A'LVUS (*Anat.*) the Belly, comprehending the stomach and entrails. *Ruf. Ephes. de Appel. Part. Corp. human.* l. 1, c. 11.

ALVUS (*Med.*) the belly, in relation to stools or the condition of the bowels, as it is used by Celsus, answering to the κοιλίη of Hippocrates, and other Greek writers. *Hippocrat.* l. 2, aphor. 20, &c.; *Cels. de Re Med.* l. 2, c. 12, &c.; *Gal. Comm. in Hippocrat.*; *Aet. Tetrab.* 1, serm. 2, c. 184; *Trallian.* l. 1, c. 11; *Actuar. de Meth. Med.* l. 4, c. 6.

A'LYCE (*Med.*) ἀλύκη, the same as *Alysmos*.

A'LYPUM (*Bot.*) ἄλυπον, a herb so called from α, privative, and λύπη, pain, because it relieves pain. It is called, in English, Herb Terrible, from its violently purging quality, and *in the Linnean system* is the *Globularia alypum*, a spriggy plant, of an acrid viscous taste, and a very strong cathartic, which purges phlegm, bile, &c. It has been doubted by some whether the *Alypum* of Dioscorides is the same as that of more modern Botanists; but their descriptions correspond so considerably as to leave little room for doubt. *Dioscor.* l. 4, c. 180; *Plin.* l. 27, c. 4; *P. Æginet. de Re Med.* l. 7, c. 3; *Actuar. de Meth. Med.* l. 5, c. 8; *Clus. Rar. Plant. Hist.*; *J. Bauh. Hist. Plant.*; *C. Bauh. Pin.*; *Raii Hist. Plant.*; *Parkins. Theat. Botan.*; *Tournef. Inst.* &c.

ALY'SMOS (*Med.*) ἀλυσμός, anxiety, or the restless uneasiness attendant on sickness; a term used frequently in this sense by Hippocrates. *Gal. Exeg. Vocab. Hippocrat.*; *Erotian Lex. Hippocrat.*; *Gorr. Defn. Med.*; *Foes. Œconom. Hippocrat.*

ALYSSOI'DES (*Bot.*) different species of the *Alyssum* of Linnæus, Bauhin, Tournefort, &c.

ALY'SSON (*Bot.*) different species of the *Alyssum*, the *Clypeola*, the *Draba*, and the *Marrubrium* of Linnæus, Bauhin, Raii, &c.

ALY'SSUM (*Bot.*) ἄλυσσον, Madwort, from α, privative, and λύσσα, madness; a plant so called because it was supposed to cure the bite of a mad dog. *Dioscor.* l. 3, c. 105; *Plin.* l. 24, c. 12; *Gal. de Simplic.* l. 2, c. 11, &c.; *Oribas Med. Coll.* l. 15, c. 1; *Paul. Æginet. de Re Med.* l. 7, c. 3.

ALYSSUM, *in the Linnean system*, a genus of plants, Class 15 *Tetradynamia*, Order 1 *Siliculosa*.
Generic Character. CAL. *perianth* four-leaved; *leaflets* ovate, oblong.—COR. four-petalled; *petals* flat.—STAM. *filaments* six; *anthers* spreading.—PIST. *germ* subovate; *style* simple; *stigma* obtuse.—PER. *silicle* subglobose; *seeds* few.
Species. The species are some shrubs, as the—*Alyssum halimifolium*, *Thlaspi fruticosum*, seu *Leucorium spinosum*, sweet Madwort.—*Alyssum saxatile Lunaria*, seu *Thlaspi*,

&c. Yellow Madwort, &c. Some species are perennials, as—*Alyssum incanum*, *Mœnchia incana*, &c. Hoary Madwort.—*Alyssum montanum*, *Clypeola montana*, *Adyseton montanum*, &c. Mountain Madwort, &c. Some are annuals, as—*Alyssum minimum*, *lunaria annua*, &c. Least Madwort. — *Alyssum clypeatum*, *Leucorum alyssoides*, *Alysson Dioscoridis*, &c. Bucklerpodded Madwort, &c. *J. Bauhin. Hist. Plant.*; *C. Bauh. Pin. Boerhaav. Ind.*; *Linn. Spec. Plant.*

ALYSSUM is also the name of different species of the *Clypeola*, the *Draba*, the *Myagrum*, and the *Veronica* of Linnæus. *C. Bauh. Pin.*; *Ger. Herb.*; *Tournef. Inst.*

ALYTA'RCHUS (*Ant.*) ἀλυτάρχης, the name of the chief officer among the Eleans, who was appointed to keep good order at the games. He was called by the rest of the Greeks ῥαβδοφόρος, or μαστιγοφόρος, answering to the Lictor of the Romans. Those who were under the Alytarches were called Alytæ.

A'LZEGI (*Chem.*) Ink.

ALZEMA'FOR (*Chem.*) Cinnabar.

A'LZILAT (*Med.*) a weight of three grains.

A'LZOFAR (*Chem.*) Burnt Copper.

A'LZUM (*Bot.*) the tree that produces the gum Bdellium.

A. M. (*Gram.*) an abbreviation for Anno Mundi, &c. [vide *Abbreviations*]

A'MA (*Ant.*) or Ames, ἄμης, a sort of cake made with milk. *Aret. de Curat. Morb. Acut.* l. 1, c. 3; *Suidas.*

AMA'BYR (*Archæol.*) a custom in the honour of Clun, belonging to the Earls of Arundel. "Pretium virginitatis domino solvendum."

AMA'ENDAVA (*Or.*) a species of finch, the *Fringilla Amaduvada* of Linnæus.

AMA'IN (*Mar.*) from *a*, or *ab*, and *main*, the hand, i. e. offhand, at once, applied to any movement of the tackle, as "To lower *amain*," to lower at once, or let go the fall of the tackle: "To strike *amain*," to lower the topsail: "To wave *amain*," to make a sign to another vessel, by waving a bright sword, that it should strike its topsails.

AMA'LGAMA (*Chem.*) from ἅμα, together, and γαμέω, to marry; a soft paste produced by the incorporation of mercury with a metal, as the amalgama of mercury with lead, &c. *Shaw's Boerhaav. Pract. Operat. Chem. Proc.* 203.

AMALGAMA is expressed by chemical writers by the character ⚭ or ⧻

AMALGAMA'TION (*Chem.*) the process of mixing mercury with gold, silver, and other metals, so as to reduce them to an impalpable powder. This operation is marked by the three letters A A A. All metals may be amalgamated with mercury except iron, but gold amalgamates more readily than silver, and this than lead, copper, or tin, which is the least fitted for amalgamation.

AMANDI'NUS *lapis* (*Min.*) a gem of various colours, which is said to resist poisons. *Albert. Mag. De Lapid. Pret.*

AMANI'TÆ (*Bot.*) ἀμανῖται, Truffles, a sort of fungi or mushrooms, which, according to Oribasius, were the least hurtful of all the sorts. They are so called, from *α*, priv. and μανία, madness, i. e. not poisonous. *Oribas. Med. Coll.* l. 2, c. 25; *Aet. Tetrab.* 1, serm. 1; *Paul. Æginet.* l. 1, c. 77; *Myrep.* sect. 38, c. 371; *Actuar. de Spir. Anim.* c. 6; *J. Bauh. Hist. Plant.*; *C. Bauh. Pin.*; *Tournef. Instit.*

AMA'NNIA (*Bot.*) vide *Ammania*.

AMANUE'NSIS (*Ant.*) from *a manu*, i. e. by the hand, or one serving by the hand; a slave who used to be employed in writing; a transcriber.

AMA'RA (*Ant.*) ἀμάρα, a furrow or channel through which water flows.

AMARA (*Med.*) bitters, the essence of any bitter substance; or the whole substance itself, of which great use is made in medicine, particularly for bracing the relaxed fibres of the organs of digestion. *Ruf. Ephes. de Appel. Part. hum. Corp.* l. 1. c. 23; *Oribas.* l. 13, c. 5; *Aet. Tetrab.* 1, serm. 1; *Paul. Æginet. de Re Med.* l. 7, c. 3.

AMARA *dulcis* (*Bot.*) vide *Dulcamara*.—*Amara Indica*, the *Momordica charantia* of Linnæus.

AMA'RACUS (*Bot.*) ἀμάρακος, a plant spoken much of by the ancients, particularly for its medicinal virtues, being a principal ingredient in *Acopas* and *Malagmas*, on account of its warming quality. Nicander celebrates the Amaracus as a garden flower.
Nicand. Ther.

——— μάλα δ' ἂν ἀμάρακος ὕλη
Χραισμήεις πρασιῆς τε καὶ ἀνδράσιοισι κλοάζοι.

According to Catullus it was used as a nuptial garland.
Catull. Carm. 60, v. 7.

Cinge tempora floribus
Suavolentis amaraci.

Virgil speaks of its fragrance.
Virg. Æn. l. 1, v. 693.

——— ubi mollis amaracus illum
Floribus et dulci adspirans complectitur umbra.

Theophrast. Hist. Plant. l. 6, c. 7; *Ruf. Ephes. Fragm. apud Med. Princip.* p. 127; *Dioscor.* l. 1, c. 58; *Plin.* l. 21, c. 2; *Gal. de Antidot.* l. 1, c. 9; *Athen.* l. 15, c. 5; *Myrep. de Antidot.* sect. 1, c. 21.

AMARACUS, in the Linnean system, is the *Origanum marjorana*, or Sweet Marjoram. *C. Bauh. Pin.*; *Salmas. de Homonym. Hyl. Iatr.* c. 13; *Raii Hist. Plant.*; *Tournef. Instit.*; *Boerhaav. Ind. Botan.*

AMARA *dulcis* (*Bot.*) vide *Dulcamara*.

A'MARANTH (*Bot.*) the *Amaranthus* of Linnæus, an annual, which produces a beautiful flower.—*Globe Amaranth*, an annual, the *Gomphrena globosa* of Linnæus.

AMARA'NTHI *Spica* (*Bot.*) a species of the *Phryma* of Linnæus.

AMARA'NTHO *affinis* (*Bot.*) the *Gomphrena globosa* and *Illecebrum sessile* of Linnæus.

AMARANTHOI'DES (*Bot.*) the *Celosia mexsoniæ*, the *Gomphrena perennis*, and *Illecebrum sessile* of Linnæus. *Pluken. Almag.*, &c.

AMARA'NTHUS (*Bot.*) or *Amarantus*, ἀμάραντος, a plant, so called from *α*, priv. and μαραίνομαι, to fade, i. e. never fading, because it retains its freshness a long time. According to Dioscorides, it was a remedy against the bites of serpents. *Dioscor.* l. 4, c. 57; *Plin.* l. 21, c. 8; *Oribas. Med. Coll.* l. 11; *Paul. Æginet. de Re Med.* l. 7, c. 3.

AMARANTHUS Amaranth, *in the Linnean system*, a genus of plants, Class 21 *Monoecia*, Order 5 *Pentandria*.

Generic Character. CAL. *perianth*, five or three-leaved; *leaflets* lanceolate.—COR. none.—STAM. *filaments* five, or three capillary; *anthers* oblong.—PIST. *germ* ovate; *styles* three; *stigmas* simple permanent.—PER. *capsule* ovate; *seed* single.

Species. Plants of this tribe are annuals, of which the principal are the—*Amaranthus albus*, White Amaranth.—*Amaranthus polygonoides*, *Blitum polygonoides*, *Chenopodium humile*, &c. Spotted-leaved Amaranth.—*Amaranthus polygamus*, Hermaphrodite Amaranth.—*Amaranthus oleraceus*, Eatable Amaranth.—*Amaranthus tricolor*, Three-coloured Amaranth.—*Amaranthus blitum*, Least Amaranth.—*Amaranthus hypochondriacus*, Prince's-feather Amaranth, &c. *J. Bauh. Hist. Plant.*; *C. Bauh. Pin. Theat. Botan.*; *Ger. Herb.*; *Park. Theat. Botan.*; *Raii Hist. Plant.*; *Pluk. Almag. Botan.*; *Tournef. Inst.*; *Boerhaav. Ind.*; *Linn. Spec. Plant.*

AMARANTHUS is also the name of the *Achyranthes corymbosa*, different species of the *Celosia*, the *Illecebrum sessile*, the *Iresine celessoides*, and the *Rivina humilis* of Linnæus. *Bauh. Hist.*; *Pluk. Almag.*—*Amaranthus luteus*, the *Gnaphalium arena* of Linnæus.—*Amaranthus capensis*, the *Hypoxis stellata* of Linnæus, &c.

AMARI'LLA (*Bot.*) a species of the *Gentiana* and the *Polygala amara* of Linnæus.

AMA'RUM (*Min.*) Sulphate of Magnesia, or Epsom Salt; a genus of mineral substances, Class *Salts*, a bitter taste, easily soluble in water, and melting in heat.

AMA'RUS *dulcis Orientalis* (*Bot.*) the same as *Costus*.

AMARUS (*Min.*) a genus of earths, of the Class *Silices*, consisting of silica, with a small quantity of magnesia, alumina, and carbonate of lime.

AMARY'LLIS (*Bot.*) or Lily, a genus of plants, Class 6 *Hexandria*, Order 1 *Monogynia*.
  Generic Characters. CAL. spathe oblong.—COR. petals six; nectary six.—STAM. filaments six; anthers rising.—PIST. germ roundish; style filiform; stigma trifid.—PER. capsule subovate; seeds several.
  Species. The species are perennials, and mostly inhabit the East and West Indies. The principal are the—*Amaryllis atamasco*, the Atamasco Lily.—*Amaryllis pumilis*, the Dwarf Amaryllis.—*Amaryllis formosissima*, *Lilio-Narcissus*, &c. the Jacobea Lily.—*Amaryllis lutea*, *Narcissus autumnalis*, Yellow Amaryllis or Autumnal Lily.—*Amaryllis sarniensis*, *Narcissus japonicus*, the Guernsey Lily, &c. *J. Bauh. Hist. Plant.*; *Linn. Spec. Plant.*

AMARY'NTHIA (*Ant.*) ἀμαρυνθία, festivals celebrated in honour of Diana at Amarynthusa, a village of Eubœa. *Paus. l. 1, c. 31.*

AMASO'NIA (*Bot.*) a genus of plants, called after Mr. Amason, a traveller, Class 14 *Didynamia*, Order 2 *Angiospermia*.
  Generic Character. CAL. perianth one-leaved.—COR. one-petalled; border quinquefid.—STAM. filaments four; anthers oval.—PIST. germ ovate; style in the situation and form of the stamens; stigmas two.—PER. none; seeds a nut ovate.
  Species. The species are the *Amasonia erecta* and *pumicea*. *Linn. Spec. Plant.*

AMATO'RIA *Febris* (*Med.*) the same as *Chlorosis*.—*Amatoria Veneficia*, the same as *Philtra*. *Castell. Lex. Med.*

AMATO'RIUS (*Anat.*) another name for the muscles called *obliquus superior* and *inferior Oculi*, because they are used in ogling.

AMA'TYQUIL (*Bot.*) the *Arbutus unedo* of Linnæus.

AMAURO'SIS (*Med.*) ἀμαύρωσις, the Gutta serena. [vide *Gutta serena*]

AMA'ZONUM *Pistillum* (*Med.*) Ἀμαζόνων τροχίσκος, the Amazonian trochee; a medicine given to chlorotic maids. *Galen. de Comp. Med. sec. Loc. l. 8.*

A'MBA (*Bot.*) the same as the *Manga* or Mango tree.

AMBA'IBA (*Bot.*) a beautiful tree of Brazil, the *Cecropia peltata* of Linnæus, the outer bark of which resembles that of the fig-tree. *Marcgrav. Pison. Med. Bras.*; *Raii Hist. Plant.*

AMBAITI'NGA (*Bot.*) an Indian tree, the oily juice of which, like that of the *Ambaiba*, is of a cooling and astringent nature. *Marcgrav. Pison. Med. Brasil.*; *Raii Hist. Plant.*

A'MBALAM (*Bot.*) an Indian tree, the fruit of which is a kind of kernel that is good to assuage pains in the ears; of the root is made a pessary that promotes the menstrual discharge. The bark converted into a powder is beneficial in dysenteries, and a decoction of its wood is given with success in gonorrhœas. *Raii Hist. Plant.*

AMBAPA'IA (*Bot.*) an Indian tree; the *Carica Papaya* of Linnæus. *C. Bauh. Pin.*; *Raii Hist. Plant.*

A'MBAR (*Chem.*) vide *Ambra*.

AMBA'RE (*Bot.*) an Indian tree, the leaves of which are as large as those of the walnut. The pulp of the ripe fruit when seasoned with vinegar and salt creates an appetite. *C. Bauh. Pin.*; *Lem. de Drug.*

AMBARVA'LES *fratres* (*Ant.*) the priests who offered the sacrifices at the ambarvalia. *Vet. Grammat.*

AMBARVA'LIA (*Ant.*) feasts among the Romans in honour of Ceres, *ut arva fruges ferrent*. They are so named from going round the fields, *Ambiendis arvis*, which was a part of their ceremony. Servius says that the victim was taken round the fields, according to Virgil.
Georg. l. 1, v. 345.

Terque novas circum felix eat hostia fruges.

The festival was celebrated twice a year, in April and July. *Cato de Re Rust. c. 142*; *Fest. de Signif. Verb.*; *Macrob. l. 3, c. 5*; *Gyrald. Syntag. Dior. l. 17, p. 488*; *Turneb. Adv. l. 18, c. 17*; *Alex. Gen. Dier. l. 3, c. 12*; *Rosin. Kipping, &c. apud Græv. Antiq. Roman.*

AMBARVA'LIÆ *Hostiæ* (*Ant.*) the victims sacrificed at the Ambarvalia, which were a sow, a sheep, and a bull. [vide *Ambarvalia*]

AMBARVA'LIS *Flos* (*Bot.*) the *Polygala vulgaris* of Linnæus. *Dodon. Stirp. Hist.*

A'MBE (*Surg.*) ἄμβη, a lip or edge, because its extremity runs out like the edge or brim of a pot; a chirurgical instrument used in restoring a luxation of the shoulder. *Hippocrat. de Artic. l. 6*; *Gal. Exeges. Vocab. Hippocrat.*; *Heist. Chirurg. p. 1, l. 3, c. 7.*

AMBE'GNIS (*Ant.*) an epithet for the weather sheep which was led to be sacrificed between two lambs; so called from *ambo*, both, i. e. both sides, and *agnus*, a lamb. *Fest. de Verb. Signif.*

A'MBELA (*Bot.*) the *Nymphæa lotus* of Linnæus.

AMBELA'NIA *acida* (*Bot.*) the *Willaughbeia acida* of Linnæus.

A'MBER (*Min.*) the *Succinum* of Linnæus, a brittle hard resinous substance, which in Greek is called ἅρπαξ, i. e. the Snatcher, because, according to Pliny, it snatches straws, leaves, &c. to itself. The Arabic name, Kerabe, signifies the same thing, namely, an "Attractor of Straw." By the Greeks of later ages, as Nicetas Chroniates relates, amber is called ἄμπαρ: but what may be the origin of this word, which is neither Greek nor Arabic, it is difficult to conjecture, unless we are to suppose that it comes from *Hambara*, which, according to Leo Africanus, signifies a whale. Amber is usually transparent, of a yellow and a deep colour, but sometimes it is colourless. It is highly electric; and if a piece be kindled it burns to the end with pungent white vapours, without melting. It takes a good polish, and is made into beads, necklaces, and other ornaments; specific gravity from 1·078 to 1·085. Many virtues are ascribed to amber, particularly when taken inwardly, in a cold state of the brain, in catarrhs, &c. Ancient authors affirm that amber works out of springs like bitumen, which is warranted by the discoveries of modern writers, who assure us that it is got out of the German sea, where it rises in a bituminous form. *Plin. l. 37, c. 2*; *Salmas. de Homonym. c. 101*; *Boerhaav. Chem.*—*Liquid Amber*, or *Liquid Ambar*, a fat resinous substance, of the consistence of Venice Turpentine, of an acrimonious taste, but an aromatic and fragrant smell. It distils from a tree in New Spain, and is used in medicine as an emollient.

AMBER, *Oil of* (*Chem.*) an acid liquor drawn from amber, which is supposed to be the liquid storax, sold by druggists.

AMBE'RBOI (*Bot.*) different species of the *Centaurea* of Linnæus.

A'MBERGRIS (*Min.*) the *Ambra grisea* of Aldrovandus, and the *Ambra* of Linnæus, a solid sebaceous or fat substance, not ponderous, of an ash colour, variegated like marble, and often marked with white specks. It is supposed to be the excrement of the spermatic whale, having frequently been met with in the intestines of that fish. It is found floating on the waters, or on the shores of the Moluccas, and other islands in the Indian Ocean. It breaks easily, but cannot be reduced to powder; melts like wax, and is somewhat soluble in spirits of wine, with the assistance of heat. Specific gravity 0·926.

A'MBER Tree (*Bot.*) the *Anthospermum* of Linnæus, a shrub, the beauty of which lies in its small evergreen leaves, which grow as close as heath, and which being bruised between the fingers, emits a very fragrant odour. —*Amber-seed*, a seed brought from Martinico and Egypt, of a bitterish taste, and resembling millet-seed.

A'MBIDEXTER (*Med.*) ἀμφιδέξιος, a man who can play equally with both hands. *Hippocrat.* l. 7, aphor. 43; *Gal. Exeges. Vocab. Hippocrat.*; *Foes. Œconom. Hippocrat.*

AMBIDEXTER (*Law*) one who plays on both sides, as a juror who takes money for giving his verdict.

AMBIE'GNA bos (*Ant.*) an ox; so named by the augurs, because it had the other victims around it. *Varro de Ling. Lat.* l. 6, c. 3; *Buleng. de Sort.* c. 6.

A'MBIENT (*Phy.*) or *circumambient*, an epithet for whatever encompasses other things; thus, bodies are called ambient or circumambient which surround other bodies, and the air which immediately encompasses or surrounds all bodies on the earth is called the *ambient air*.

AMBI'GENAL (*Math.*) an epithet given by Sir Isaac Newton, in his *Enumeratio Linearium tertii Ordinis*, to one of the triple hyperbolas of the second order, E G F having one of its infinite legs, G E, falling within the angle A C D, formed by the asymptotes A C C D, and the other leg, G F, falling without the angle.

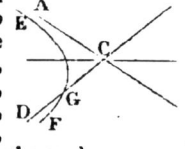

A'MBIT *of a Figure* (*Math.*) the same as the *Perimeter*, i. e. the line, or the sum of the lines by which the figure is bounded.

AMBI'TION (*Hierog.*) was represented as a young man clad in green, and crowned with ivy, and going to climb up a steep ascent, at the top of which appeared crowns and sceptres. He had a lion by his side to denote fortitude, which is the companion of ambition.

A'MBITUS (*Ant.*) from *ambire*, to go about; a going round, or canvassing for a place: whence comes the word ambition, to signify an immoderate thirst for honours, because the *ambitus* was commonly attended with bribery and corruption, notwithstanding the severity with which it was punished. *Cic. in Sallust.*; *Fest. de Verb. Signif.*; *Bud. in Pandect.* p. 195.—*Ambitus Urbis*, the circuit of the city, which, in the time of Vespasian, A. U. C. 828, was estimated at 13 miles. *Plin.* l. 3, c. 5; *Panciroll. Descript. Urb.*; *Panvin. Descript. Urb. et Nardin. Rom. Vet.*; *apud Græv. Thes. Antiq. Roman.* tom. iii. p. 377.—*Ambitus Ædium*, a vacant space which was left between houses for going round. *Fest. de Verb. Signif.*

A'MBLE (*Man.*) the peculiar pace of a horse, when two legs of the same side move at the same time.

AMBLIGO'NAL (*Geom.*) ἀμβλυγώνιος, an epithet for a figure that contains an obtuse angle.

AMBLO'SIS (*Med.*) the same as *Abortus*.

AMBLO'TICA *Medicamenta* (*Med.*) Medicines which produce abortion.

AMBLYO'GMOS (*Med.*) ἀμβλυωγμὸς, a word frequently used by Hippocrates for dimness of sight. *Hippocrat. Predict.* l. 1, c. 18, &c.; *Gal. Exeges. Vocab. Hippocrat.*; *Foes. Œconom. Hippocrat.*

AMBLYO'PIA (*Med.*) ἀμβλυωπία, a word used by Hippocrates for debility of sight; but by Paulus Æginata and Actuarius, for the *gutta serena*. *Hippocrat.* sect. 3, aphor. 31; *Act. de Meth. Med.* l. 2, c. 7; *Gorr. Def. Med.*; *Foes. Œconom. Hippocrat.*

A'MBON (*Anat.*) ἄμβων, the edge of the sockets in which bones are inserted, as the *femur* in the *acetabulum*. *Castell. Lex. Med.*

A'MBORA (*Bot.*) the *Mithradatea* of Linnæus.

A'MBRA (*Min.*) the *Ambra grisea* of Aldrovandus, the *Ambra maritima* of Linnæus, and the *Ambergrise* of Dale; a fragrant fat resinous substance, the excrement of the Spermacetti Whale, Class *Inflammabilia*. [vide *Amber*]

AMBRA (*Mid.*) a vessel among the Saxons, containing a measure of salt, &c. *Brompt.*

A'MBRAM (*Min.*) the same as *Succinum*.

AMBRA'RIA (*Bot.*) the *Anthospermum Æthiopicum* of Linnæus.

AMBRO'MA (*Bot.*) the same as *Abroma*.

AMBRO'SIA (*My.*) ἀμβροσία, a name given to the food of the gods, from α, priv. and βροτὸς, mortal, i. e. food which makes immortal, or the food of immortals. Homer uses this word very frequently. *Il. passim.*

AMBROSIA (*Ant.*) 1. A libation which consisted of water, honey, and all sorts of fruits, which was used according to Athenæus in the consecration of Jupiter Ctesias' statue. 2. A festival celebrated in honour of Bacchus. *Scholiast. in Hes. Oper. et Dies.* l. 2.

AMBROSIA (*Bot.*) a small shrub, called by some *Botrys*, which has a grateful smell, and a very astringent taste. Dioscorides ranks it among the coronary plants, ςιφανωματικὰ; but, according to Nicander, the appellation of *Coronary Ambrosia* was bestowed by some on the lily. *Nicand. in Ther.*

Ἀ κρίνα λίμμα δ᾽ ἄλλοι επιφθέγγονται ἀοιδών
Οἱ δὲ ἀμβροσίῳ.

Dioscor. l. 3, c. 129; *Plin.* l. 17, c. 4, &c.; *Athen.* l. 15; *Oribas. Med. Collect.* l. 11; *Aet. Tetrab.* 1, serm. 1; *Paul. Ægin. de Re Med.* l. 7, c. 3; *Salmas. de Homonym.* c. 62.

AMBROSIA, in the Linnean system, a genus of plants, Class 21 *Monoecia*, Order 5 *Pentandria*, in English, Oak of Jerusalem.
Generic Characters. CAL. *perianth* common.—COR. *compound* uniform; *proper* one-petalled.—STAM. *filaments* very small; *anthers* erect.—PIST. *style* filiform; *stigma* orbiculate.—REC. common.—PER. *nut* subovate; *seed* single.
Species. The species are mostly annuals, as the—*Ambrosia elatior*, Tall Ambrosia.—*Ambrosia artemisifolia*, Mugwort-leaved Ambrosia, &c. *J. Bauh. Hist. Plant.*; *C. Bauh. Pin.*; *Ger. Herb.*; *Park. Theat. Botan.*; *Raii Hist. Plant.*; *Tournef. Inst.*

AMBRO'SIAN *Office* (*Ecc.*) a formula of worship used in the church of Milan; so called from St. Ambrose, bishop of Milan.

AMBROSI'NIA (*Bot.*) a genus of plants, so called from the Ambrosini, brothers and professors of botany at Bologne fifty-two years, Class 21 *Monoecia*, Order 1 *Monandria*.
Generic Character. CAL. *spathe* one-leaved; *partition* membranaceous.—COR. none.—STAM. *filaments* none; *anthers* very many; *nectaries* two.—PIST. *germ* solitary; *style* cylindrical; *stigma* obtuse.—PER. *capsule* roundish; *seeds* many.
Species. The species are the *Ambrosinia Bassii, seu Arisarum*, and the *Ambrosinia maculata*, both perennials. *Raii Hist. Plant.*

A'MBRY (*Med.*) or *Aumery*, from *Eleemosynaria*; a place where vessels and domestic utensils were kept.

AMBUBA'LÆ (*Ant.*) loose women, who went about as min-

strels, probably so called from *ambu*, i. e. *circum*, around, and *Baiæ*, a place of pleasure in Italy which they much frequented.
Horat. l. 1, sat. 2, v. 1.

Ambubaiarum Collegia Pharmacopolæ.

Sueton. in Neron. c. 27; *Scalig. Conject. in Varr.* p. 54; *Turneb. Adv.* l. 1, c. 27.

AMBUBE'IA (*Bot.*) the common Cichory.

AM'BULANTS (*Com.*) Brokers or Exchange Agents in Amsterdam who are not sworn before the magistrates.

AMBULATI'VA (*Med.*) the same as *Herpes*.

AMBULA'TOR (*Archæol.*) Ambler, a sort of horse which went an ambling pace.

AMBULATO'RIA *turris* (*Ant.*) an engine or battery on wheels for taking towns. *Vitruv. de Architect*, l. 10, c. 19.

AMBULATORIA *voluntas* (*Law*) a man's will or testament as long as he lives and has the power of changing it.

AM'BULO (*Med.*) a disease arising from inflation.

AM'BULON (*Bot.*) a tree, the fruit of which resembles sugar in its taste, and in bulk a coriander seed. *Raii Hist. Plant.*

AMBU'RBIA (*Ant.*) a festival, which consisted in going round the walls of the city in solemn procession, from *ambiendo urbe*, i. e. going round the city.
Lucan. l. 1, v. 592.

*Mox jubet et totam pavidis a civibus urbem
Ambiri, et festo purgantes mœnia lustro
Longa per extremos pomœria cingere fines.*

Fest. de Verb. Signif; *Vopisc. in Aurel.* c. 20; *Serv. in Virg.* l. 3; *Eccl.* 3, v. 77; *Gyrald. Syntag. Deor.* l. 17; *Jos. Scalig. Castig. in Fest.*; *Turneb. Adver.* l. 18, c. 17.

AMBURBIA'LES *hostiæ* (*Ant.*) victims which were carried round the city in celebrating the Amburbia. *Fest. de Verb. Signif.*

AMBU'STA (*Med.*) burns or scalds, for the cure of which the ancient physicians gave many prescriptions. *Aet. Tetrab.* 4, serm. 2, c. 64; *Paul. Ægin. de Re Med.* l. 4, c. 2.

AMBU'STION (*Med.*) burning, or any solution of continuity produced by fire, or bodies heated by fire. *Heist. Chirurg.* l. 4, c. 15.

AMBU'TUA (*Bot.*) the *Cisampelos Pareira* of Linnæus.

AM'EA (*Bot.*) a plant used in Africa against bleeding at the nose.

AME'DIANS (*Ecc.*) a congregation of religious in Italy; so called from their professing themselves to be *amantes Deum*, lovers of God, or *amati Dei*, beloved of God. They wore a grey habit and wooden shoes, but no breeches.

AMEDA'NA (*Bot.*) the *Alnus vulgaris* of Linnæus.

AMELA'NCHIER (*Bot.*) the *Chionanthus Virginica* and *Mespelus Amelanchia* of Linnæus. *Raii Hist. Plant.*

A'MEL *corn* (*Com.*) French rice, by which starch is made.

A'MELI (*Bot.*) a Malabar plant, from the leaves of which a decoction is made that is good for colics.

AMELLOI'DES (*Bot.*) a species of the *Cineraria* of Linnæus.

AME'LLUS (*Bot.*) one of those herbs which Virgil reckons to be agreeable to bees.
Virg. Georg. l. 4, v. 271.

*Est etiam flos in pratis, cui nomen amello,
Fecere agricolæ, facilis quærentibus herba.*

AMELLUS, in the Linnean system, a genus of plants, Class 19 Syngenesia, Order 2 *Polygamia superflua*.
Generic Characters. CAL. common imbricate.—COR. compound radiate; *corollets* hermaphrodite, very many in the disc; *females* very many in the ray; *proper* of the hermaphrodite tubulous; *female* ligulate—STAM. *filaments* five; *anther* cylindrical—PIST. *germ* obovate; *style* filiform; *stigmas* two.—PER. none; *calyx* unchanged; *seeds* solitary; *down* capillary; *receptacle* chaffy.

Species. Plants of this tribe are shrubs, as the—Amellus, lychnitis, buphthalmum, verbesina, seu chrysanthemum, trailing Amellus, &c.

AMELLUS is also the name of the *Calea Amellus*, the *Erigeron acre*, and the *Aster Amellus* of Linnæus. *Raii Hist. Plant.*

AME'LPODI (*Bot.*) an Indian tree, used as an antidote against the bites of serpents. *Raii Hist. Plant.*

A'MEN (*Bibl.*) from אמן, true, certain; a term employed either in affirmation, as by our Saviour, Amen, amen, verily, verily, or in confirmation, as Numb. v. 22. Deut. xxvii. 15.

AME'NABLE (*Law*) tractable, or governable, as applied to a woman who submits to her husband; also to be responsible in a court of justice.

AME'NDE (*Archæol.*) a mulct or pecuniary punishment formerly imposed in France by the sentence of the judge for any crime, as false prosecution, a groundless appeal, and the like.

AMENDE *Honourable* (*Law*) that which was imposed upon a person by way of disgrace or infamy, as a punishment for any offence, or for the purpose of making reparation for any injury done to another, as the walking into church in a white sheet, with a rope about the neck, and a torch in the hand, and begging pardon either of God or the King, or any private individual, for some delinquency.

AME'NDMENT (*Law*) *emendatio*, the correction of an error in any process, which may be amended either before or after judgment. Errors are now effectually obviated by the statutes of amendment and jeofails. 14 *Ed.* 3, c. 6; 8 *Hen.* 6, c. 15.

AME'NE (*Chem.*) Common Salt.

AMENE'NOS (*Med.*) from α, priv. and μένος, strength, a term used by Hippocrates for weak.

A'MENT (*Bot.*) *Amentum*, otherwise called *Julus*, *Nucamentum*, and *Catulus*, in English, Catkin, from the French *châton*, a cat's-tail, to which it bears a resemblance; a long and simple stem, which is thickly covered with scales, under which are the flowers, or their essential parts, as in the annexed figure, which represents the catkin of a hazel. It is either Cylindrical, *Cylindricum*, i. e. equally thick above and below—Attenuated, *Attenuatum*, growing thinner and thinner, to a point—Slender, *Gracile*, i. e. in proportion to its length—Ovate, *Ovatum*, i. e. thick below, and round above. Examples of the Catkin, are found in the Willows, *Salices*, Hazel, *Corylus Avellana*, Hornbeam, *Carpinus*, &c. The Ament of the Willow, in vulgar language, is called the Palm.

AMENTA'CEÆ (*Bot.*) one of Linnæus' Natural Orders of plants, comprehending those plants whose fruit is a catkin. *Linn. Philos. Botan.* &c. This is also the name of a class in the system of Tournefort and others.

AMENTA'CEOUS *Flowers* (*Bot.*) one species of the *Aggregate Flowers*, borne or growing in an ament or catkin.

AME'NTIA (*Med.*) Madness, a genus of diseases, Class *Neuroses*, Order *Vesaniæ*.

AME'NTUM (*Ant.*) from ἅμμα, a chain; the thong with which the spear was drawn back after it had been darted. *Virg. Æn.* l. 9, v. 665.

Intendunt acres arcus, amentaque torquent.

Fest. de Verb. Signif.; *Turneb. Adver.* l. 28, c. 5, &c.; *Lips. Poliorc.* l. 4, dial. 5.

AMENTUM *Sessile* (*Chem.*) Alum.

AME'RCIAMENT (*Law*) or *Amercement*, a pecuniary punishment arbitrarily imposed by some lord or count, in distinction from a fine, which is expressed according to statute. *Kitch.* 78.—*Amerciament royal*, when the Amerciament is made by the sheriff, or any other officer of the King.

A'MERI (*Bot.*) the *Indigofera tinctoria* of Linnæus. *Rheed.*

AME'RICAN *Earthnut* (*Bot.*) a plant, so called from its nut-like fruit, which is used for chocolate in South Carolina. From this nut is extracted an oil, which is used for lamps in the Eastern countries. The Earth or Ground Nut is the *Arachis hypogea* of Linnæus.

AMERI'MNUM (*Bot.*) a genus of plants, Class 17 *Diadelphia*, Order 4 *Decandria*.
Generic Characters. CAL. *Perianth* one-leaved; *teeth* sharp. COR. papilionaceous; *standard* expanding; *wings* lanceolate; *keel* short.—STAM. *filaments* ten; *anthers* roundish.—PIST. *germ* pedicelled—PER. *cells* disposed longitudinally within; *seeds* solitary.
Species. The species are shrubs, as the—*Amerimnum Brownei*, a shrub, native of Jamaica.—*Amerimnum ebenus, Pterocarpus, Aspalathus, Pseudo-Ebenus,* seu *Brya*, &c. Prickly Amerimnum, &c. *Sloan. Hist. Jam.*; *Linn. Spec. Plant.*

A'METHYST (*Bibl.*) in the Hebrew אחלמה, achalma, which signifies sleep; the precious stone [vide *Amethyst*] which is the ninth in order in the high priest's breast-plate, on which was engraven the name of Issachar. *Exod.* xxviii. 19, &c.

AMETHYST (*Min.*) ἀμέθυσος, a sort of precious stone, so called from α, privative, and μεθύσκω, to inebriate, because it resists or drives away inebriation. It is a hard, beautiful, shining, transparent stone, of different colours, but mostly purple or violet. It comes from the Indies, and is used in medicine as an astringent. The amethyst is now reckoned among the Quartz Family of stones, and is the *Quartzum Amethystus* in the Linnean system. *Plin.* l. 37, c. 9; *Epiphan. de 12 Gem.* p. 229; *Isid. Orig.* l. 16, c. 9; *Albert Mag. de Min.* l. 2; *Aldrov. Mus. Matall.*; *Geoff. Prælect.*

AMETHYST (*Her.*) the colour of the precious stone called the amethyst was formerly used in blazoning instead of purple.

AMETHY'STA (*Med.*) ἀμέθυσα, medicines which remove the inebriating effects of wine. *Gal. de Comp. Med. sec Loc.* l. 2.

AMETHY'STEA (*Bot.*) a genus of plants, so called from its resemblance in colour to the Amethyst, Class 2 *Diandria*, Order 1 *Monogynia*.
Generic Character. CAL. *perianth* one-leaved tube; *tube* bell-shaped.—COR. one-petalled; *border* five-parted; *upper lip* erect; *lower* three-parted.—STAM. *filaments* filiform; *anthers* simple.—PIST. *germ* quadrifid; *style* size of the stamina; *stigmas* two.—PER. none; *seeds* four.
Species. The only species is the *Amethystea cœrulea,* an annual, native of Siberia.

AMETHY'STINA (*Ant.*) Purple garments, which were of the colour of the Amethyst. *Salmas in Vopisc. Aurel.* c. 46.

AMETHYSTINA (*Bot.*) another name for the *Amethystea*.

AMETHYSTIZO'NTES (*Min.*) the best sort of Carbuncle. *Plin.* l. 37, c. 9.

AMETHY'STUS (*Min.*) Amethyst; the *Quartzum amethystus* of Linnæus

AME'TRIA (*Med.*) ἀμετρία, receding from a due temperament.

TO AME'UBLE (*Hort.*) a French term for turning up or loosening the earth which is grown hard, or incrusted over by means of rains, heat, &c.

A ME'ZZA *aria* (*Mus.*) Italian for the notes which keep the middle compass of the voice, for which they are composed—*A mezza di voce,* a soft tone, or gradual diminution of the voice.

A'MIA (*Ich.*) A'μια, from α, priv. and μία, alone, or from its going in company, ἅμα, with other of its kind. A fish, the growth of which, according to Pliny, is so rapid that it might be perceived every day. Aetius says that its flesh is very hard. *Aristot. Nat. Hist.* l. 1, c. 1; *Plin.* l. 9, c. 15; *Aet. Tetrab.* 1, serm. 2.

AMIA, *in the Linnean system,* a genus of fishes, having its head flattened and naked, numerous sharp teeth, two cirri, and a gill membrane, 12 rays. The single species is called *Amia calva,* which inhabits the waters of Carolina.

A'MIANTH (*Min.*) *Amiantus lapis*, or *Amiant*, Earth-Flax, λίθος ἀμίαντος, a sort of stone-like scissile alum, generated in Cyprus. It was said to be efficacious against sorceries, to resist poisons, and to cure the itch. As it may be drawn into threads fit for work, it was wrought, according to Dioscorides, into a cloth, which, if thrown into the fire, did not consume, but came out the brighter and purer. *Dioscor.* l. 5, c. 156; *Plin.* l. 36, c. 18; *Paul Æginet. de Re Med.* l. 7, c. 3.

AMIA'NTUS, *in the Linnean system,* is classed under *Asbestus,* but by former mineralogists it constituted a genus of stones. *Gessn. de Lapid.*; *Aldrov. Mus. Metall.*

A'MICABLE *Numbers* (*Arith.*) such as are mutually equal to the sum of one another's aliquot parts, as 284 and 220 for all the aliquot parts of 220, namely, 1, 2, 4, 5, 10, 11, 20, 22, 44, 55, 110, added together, are equal to 284; and all the aliquot parts of 284, namely, 1, 2, 4, 71, 142, added together, are equal to 220. The only pairs of *amicable* numbers besides this, which have been hitherto discovered, are, 6232 and 6368; 17296 and 18416; 9363584 and 9437056. The name of *amicable* was first given to these numbers by Van Schooten, but their property had been already treated of by Rudolphus, Descartes, and others. *V. Schoot. Exercitat. Geometr. Miscellan.* sect. 11.

AMI'CE (*Ecc.*) an ecclesiastical vestment, [vide *Amictus*] common to bishops and presbyters, which was tied round the neck, and covered the breast and heart.

AMI'CTUS (*Ecc.*) Amice, the undermost of the six garments worn by priests. These were the *Amictus, Alba, Cingulum, Stola, Munipulus. Innocent.* III. *de Myst.* l. 1, c. 10; *Amalar. de Eccles. Offic.* l. 2, c. 17.

AMICTUS (*Ant.*) a name for every sort of external garment. *Ferrar. de Re Vest.* l. 2, c. 1.

AMI'CULUM (*Ant.*) from *amicio,* to wrap; an upper garment worn by females; a sort of cloak.
Plaut. Cist. act 1, scen. 1, v. 117.

Amiculum hoc sustolle saltem Sil. *Sine trahi dum egomet trahor.*

It seems also to have been used by men occasionally, according to Quintus Curtius. *Liv.* l. 27, c. 4; *Val. Max.* l. 5, c. 2; *Q. Curt.* l. 5, c. 1; *Ferrar. de Re Vest.* l. 1, c. 3.

AMICULUM (*Anat.*) the same as *Amnios.*

AMI'CUS *Curiæ* (*Law*) a friend of the court, who, as a stander by, when a judge is doubtful, or mistaken in a matter of law, may inform the court. 2 *Inst.* 178.

AMI'D-SHIPS (*Mar.*) i. e. in the middle of the ship; a term applied either to her length or her breadth, as "The enemy boarded us *amid-ships*," i. e. between the stem and stern. "Put the helm *amid-ships*," i. e. between the two sides.

A'MIENS (*Com.*) a gold coin, value 17s. 1¼d.

AMI'NEUM *vinum* (*Ant.*) or *Ammineum vinum,* Ἀμιναῖος οἶνος, Aminean wine, a particular sort of wine, which was highly esteemed for imbecilities in the stomach. Macrobius makes the Falernian and Aminean wines to be the same; but Virgil distinguishes them from each other.
Virg. Georg. l. 2, v. 96.

———*Nec cellis ideo contende Falernis.*
Sunt etiam Amineæ vites, firmissima vina.

It is supposed to have derived its name from the vines of the Aminei, a people of Thessaly, which were planted in different parts of Italy. *Plin.* l. 14, c. 2; *Gal. de Antidot.* l. 1; *Macrob. Saturn.* l. 2, c. 16; *Aet. Tetrab.* 1, serm. 1.

AMINEUM *Acetum* (*Chem.*) Vinegar made of the Aminean wine.

AMI'NIA (*Bot.*) a sort of Cotton-tree in Brazil. *Maregrav. Pis.*

AMI'TTERE *legem terræ* (*Law*) or *liberam legem* to lose the liberty of swearing in any court. *Glanvil.* l. 2.

AMMANI'TÆ (*Bot.*) vide *Amanitæ*.

AMMA'NNIA (*Bot.*) a genus of plants, called after Professor Ammann, of Petersburgh, Class 4 *Tetrandria*, Order 1 *Monogynia*.
 Generic Character. CAL. *perianth* bell-shaped.—COR. none.—STAM. *filaments* bristly; *anthers* twin.—PIST. *germ* subovate; *style* simple; *stigma* headed.—PER. *capsule* roundish; *seeds* numerous.
 Species. The species of this genus are annuals, as the—*Ammannia latifolia Isnardia*, seu *Aparines*, &c. Broad-leaved Ammannia.—*Ammannia ramosior*, seu *Ludwegia aquatica*, Branching Ammannia.—*Ammannia baccifera*, seu *Cornelia verticillata*, Berrybearing Ammannia, &c.

AM'MI (*Bot.*) ἄμμι, or *Amium*, a plant, the seed of which was reckoned strongly diuretic. *Dioscor.* l. 3, c. 70; *Plin.* l. 20, c. 15.

AMMI, *in the Linnean system*, a genus of plants, Class 5 *Pentandria*, Order 2 *Digynia*, in English Bishop's-weed.
 Generic Characters. CAL. *universal umbel* manifold; *partial* short; *universal involucre* of many acute leaflets; *partial* many-leaved; *leaflets* linear; *proper perianth* scarcely apparent.—COR. *universal* uniform; *proper* of five petals.—STAM. *filaments* capillary; *anthers* roundish.—PIST. *germ* inferior; *styles* reflex; *stigmas* obtuse.—PER. none; *seeds* two.
 Species. The species are, the—*Ammi majus*, seu *Vulgare*, seu *Ammioselinon*, Common Bishop's-weed, an annual, native of the South of Europe.—*Ammi Copticum*, an annual, native of Egypt.—*Ammi glaucifolium*, seu *petræum*, seu *Daucus petræus*, &c. a perennial, native of France.—*Ammi daucifolium*, seu *majus*, &c. *Crithmum pyrenaicum*, seu *Apium Pyrenaicum*, a perennial, native of the Pyrenees. *J. Bauhin Hist. Plant.; C. Bauhin Pin. Theat.; Ger. Herb.; Park Theat. Botan.; Raii Hist. Plant.; Tourn. Inst. Herb.; Rivin. Ord. Plant.; Boerh. Ind. Plant.; Linn. Spec. Plant.*

AMMI is also the name of the *Sison Ammi*, the *Cicuta bulbifera*, the *Seseli ammoides*, and the *Sium falcaria* of Linnæus. *Bauh. Tournef.* &c.

A'MMION (*Chem.*) the same as *Cinnabaris*.

AMMIOSELI'NON (*Bot.*) the *Ammi majus* of Linnæus. *Dodon. Stirp. Histor.*

AMMOBRA'GIUM (*Archæol.*) a service, the same as *Chevage*, according to Spelman.

AMMOCHO'ZIAL (*Med.*) a remedy for drying the body, by covering it with hot sand. *Cels. de Re Med.* l. 3, c. 1; *Dioscor.* l. 5, c. 167; *Gal. de Præcog.*; *Oribas. Med. Coll.* l. 10, c. 8.

AMMOCHRY'SUS (*Min.*) 1. A sort of stone found in Bohemia, which is sometimes yellow, and sometimes of a gold colour. It will crumble into sand, and is used for strewing on paper. *Lem. des Drogues.* 2. A sort of mud, of a gold colour, which is found in mineral waters in Friseland. *Castell. Lex. Med.*

AMMODYTES (*Zool.*) a venomous serpent, of a sandy colour, and a cubit in length; the bite of which, according to Aetius, is generally followed by speedy death. *Aet. Tetrab.* 4, serm. 1, c. 25.

AMMODYTES is also the name of a species of the *Coluber* of Linnæus.

AMMODYTES (*Ich.*) the Launce; a genus of fishes of the *Apodal* Order, having the *head* compressed, and narrower than the body, the *teeth* very sharp, the *lower jaw* narrow and pointed, the *body* long and square, and the *caudal fin* distinct. The only species is the *Ammodytes gobianus*, or Sand Launce, which inhabits the sandy shores of the Northern Seas, buries itself, on the recess of the tides, a foot deep in the sand, with its nose out, and is a prey to other rapacious fish.

AMMO'NIA (*Chem.*) a gaseous substance in modern chemistry, formed from the combination of hydrogen with azote. It is commonly prepared by the mixture of Sal Ammoniac with twice its weight of quick lime. It is transparent and colourless, like air, acrid and caustic to the taste, like fixed alkalies, is used as a stimulant in fainting, but is fatal to animals when they breathe it. Its specific gravity is 0·590 that of common air being 1. Ammonia was not known to the ancients, but the alchemists were acquainted with it in an impure state, by whom it was called Volatile Alkali, or Hartshorn, because it was often distilled from the hart of the horn, Spirit of Urine, and Spirit of Sal Ammoniac; from both of which substances it may be obtained by a similar process. It is one of the salifiable bases by the help of which the salts are produced, as the acetate of Ammonia, &c.

AMMO'NIAC (*Chem.*) or Gum Ammoniac, ἀμμωνιακὸν, *Ammoniacum*; a fat resinous substance brought from the East Indies, which is agglutinated together in small pieces of a yellowish white colour, a smell more pleasant than that of Galbanum, and of a nauseous sweet taste, mixed with bitter. The tree which yields it is called in the Greek *Agasyllis*, and in the Arabic *Altarthub*; but nothing certain is known respecting it at present. Nicander, in his Alexipharmics, puts Ammonion for Ammoniacum:

——ἐν δὲ ἱκαμὶς
Θάλπε βαλὼν χύτρῳ Ἀμμώνιον.

It is supposed to derive its name from Ammonia, in Lybia, where it was found.

Ammoniac, according to modern chemists, is composed of the following ingredients, in nearly the following proportions:—

Resin	70·0
Gum	18·4
Glutinous matter	4·4
Water	6·0
Loss	1·2
	100·0

AMMONIAC (*Min.*) or Sal Ammoniac, ἅλας Ἀμμωνιακὸν, *Sal Ammoniacus*; a fossile salt which was said to be dug out of the sands of Ammonia, from which it took its name. [vide Gum Ammoniac] *Sal Ammoniac*, as a native salt, is not known to the moderns; but a factitious kind, of the same name, is a neutral salt, composed of a volatile alkaline and the acid of sea-salt, and is therefore called *Muriate of Ammonia*.

AMMO'NIS *Cornu* (*Min.*) a fossile, of an ash-colour, found in the shape of a ram's horn.

AMMONI'TÆ (*Min.*) Snake-Stones; a sort of fossils which abound in the alum works in Yorkshire, and other parts of England. They are made up of circles, like the rings of a snake rolled up.

AMMONI'TRUM (*Chem.*) the lixivious salt of a burnt vegetable, now called Frit. *Plin.* l. 36, c. 26.

AMMO'NIUM (*Chem.*) vide *Ammoniac*.

AMMO'PHILA (*Ent.*) Sand Wasp; a genus of animals, Class *Insectæ*, Order *Hymenoptera*.
 Generic Character. Snout inflected; *jaws* forcipated; *antennæ* filiform; *eyes* oval; *wings* planed; *sting* concealed in the abdomen.
 Species. The species of this genus resemble the sphex in economy as well as in form.

AMMUNI'TION (*Mil.*) Military stores, including not only

cannon, powder, balls, &c. but all sorts of weapons, offensive and defensive.—*Ammunition bread*, that which is served to the soldiers of a garrison or army.

AM'NA *alchalizata* (*Chem.*) water run through limestone, and impregnated with its particles. *Paracel. Lexic.*

AMNE'STIA (*Ant.*) ἀμνηστία, from α, priv. and μνάομαι, to remember; amnesty, or oblivion of the past, an act of princes to their subjects, or states one to another, which had its origin in a law enacted by Thrasybulus after the expulsion of the thirty tyrants, by which it was decreed to bury all past injuries in oblivion, for the speedier conciliation of all parties. *Val. Max. l. 4, c. 1.*

AM'NION (*Ana.*) ἀμνίον, the internal membrane which surrounds the fœtus. It is very thin and pellucid in the early stage of pregnancy, but increases in thickness and strength in the latter months. *Ruf. Ephes. Appell. Part. human. Corp. l. 1, c. 37; Gal. de Dissect. Vulvæ, c. 10; Gorr. Def. Med.; Foes. Œconom. Hippocrat.*

AMNION (*Bot.*) the liquor in the *Succulus colliquamenti*, or vesicle of the seed, from which the cotyledons are formed.

AMNIO'TIC *Acid* (*Chem.*) an acid found in the amnion of a cow.

AMOEBÆ'UM *Carmen* (*Ant.*) verse, in which one answereth another by course, as in some of Virgil's eclogues. *Fest. de Signif. Verb.*

AMOLY'NTON (*Med.*) ἀμόλυντον, from α, priv. and μολύνω, to make dirty; a topical application, which, if handled, will not soil the fingers. *Cæl. Aurelian. de Acut. Morb. l. 2, c. 27.*

AMO'MI (*Bot.*) Jamaica pepper, so called by the Dutch.

AMO'MIS (*Bot.*) Pseudo Amomum.

AMO'MUM (*Bot.*) ἄμωμον, a plant, so called from its fragrant odour, the Greek word signifying what is pure and blameless. It was one of the aromatic herbs which was used for the preservation of dead bodies, whence is derived the word *mummy*. The poets take it for any ointment or perfume.

Juv. sat. 4, v. 108.

Et matutino sudans Crispinus amomo,
Quantum vix redolent duo funera ——.

Ovid. Trist. l. 3, eleg. 3, v. 69.

Atque ea cum foliis et amomi pulvere misce:
Inque suburbano condita pone solo.

According to Dioscorides it is of a healing, drying, astringent, hyptotic, and anodyne quality. *Dioscor. l. 1, c. 14; Plin. l. 13, c. 1, &c.; Oribas. Med. Coll. l. 11; Aet. Tetrab. 1, serm. 1; Paul. Æginet. de Re Med. l. 7, c. 3; Salmas. de Homonym.*

AMOMUM, in the Linnean system, a genus of plants, Class 1 *Monandria*, Order 1 *Monogynia*.
Generic Characters. CAL. perianth one-leaved.—COR. monopetalous; tube cylindraceous; border three-parted; nectary two-leaved.—STAM. filaments none; anther oblong.—PIST. germ inferior; style filiform; stigma turbinate.—PER. capsule fleshy; seeds several.
Species. The species are mostly perennials, as the—*Amomum zinziber*, seu *Ilschi*, Narrow-leaved Ginger.—*Amomum cardamomum*, seu *Cardamomum minus*, Cardamom. —*Amomum granum paradisi*, Grains of Paradise.—*Amomum galanga*, seu *Maranta galanga*, Galangale, &c. *J. Bauh. Hist. Plant.; C. Bauh. Pin. Theat.; Ger. Herb.; Park. Theat. Botan.; Raii. Hist. Plant.; Tournef. Inst. Herb.*

AMOMUM is also a name for the *Solanum pseudo-capsicum*, the *Curcuma longa*, and a species of the *Sison* of Linnæus. *J. Bauh. Hist. Plant.; C. Bauh. Pin.; Park. Theat. Botan.; Raii Hist. Plant.*

AMONGEA'BA (*Bot.*) a kind of grass good for a fomentation in a tenesmus.

AMO'RGE (*Nat.*) ἀμόργη. 1. The fæces of the expressed oil. [vide *Amurca*] 2. The purple dye made in the island of Amorgos. *Poll. Onom. l. 7, c. 16; Suidas.; Harpocration, &c.*

AMO'RGINON (*Ant.*) Ἀμόργινον, or, in the feminine, Ἀμοργίνη; a vestment, made of the Amorgis or flax in the island of Amorgus.

AMO'RGIS (*Nat.*) Ἀμοργίς, the flax, not unlike byssus, from which the ἀμόργινα are made in the island of Amorgus.

AMO'RIS *Pomum* (*Bot.*) the *Solanum lycopersicum* of Linnæus.

AMORI'SCO (*Mus.*) in a Moorish style; an expression applied to old English ballads, signifying that the air is to resemble a Moorish dance.

AMO'RPHA (*Bot.*) from α, priv. and μορφή, the form; a genus of plants, Class 17 *Diadelphia*, Order 3 *Decandria*.
Generic Characters. CAL. perianth one-leaved.—COR. petal one.—STAM. filaments erect; anthers simple.—PIST. germ roundish; style subulate; stigma simple.—PER. legume lunulate; seeds two.
Species. The species are shrubs, as the *Amorpha fruticosa*, seu *Barba Jovis*, &c. Bastard Indigo, &c. *Linn. Spec. Plant.*

AMO'RPHOUS (*Nat.*) from α, priv. and μορφή, the form; shapeless, of no determinate shape when broken.

AMORTIZA'TION (*Law*) an alienation of lands or tenements in mortmain. *2 Stat. Ed. 1.*

AMO'RTISE (*Law*) from the French *Amortir*, to alien lands in mortmain.

AMPA'NA (*Bot.*) the *Borassus flabelliformis* of Linnæus.

AMPE'LION (*Med.*) vine leaves, which are good for making pessaries. *Hippocrat. de Nat. Mulieb.; Foes. Œconom. Hippocrat.*

A'MPELIS (*Or.*) Chatterer; a genus of birds, of the Order *Passeres*.
Generic Character. Bill straight and convex.—*Nostrils* covered with bristles.—*Tongue* sharp and bifid.—*Feet* simple, with three toes before, and one behind.
Species. All the species but one are natives of America, as—*Ampelis Cristata*, Crested Chatterer.—*Ampelis Carnifer*, seu *Cotinga rubra*, Red bird from Surinam, or Red Chatterer.—*Ampelis Cuprea*, seu *Coccinea*, Cupreous Chatterer.—*Ampelis cinerea*, seu *Lanius Neugeta*, in French, *Cotinga gris de Cayenne*, Grey Shrike.— *Ampelis luteus*, Yellow Chatterer.—*Ampelis Cotinga Cayanensis*, seu *Cayana*, in French *Cotinga de Cayenne*, le *Quereiva*, Purple-throated Chatterer.—*Ampelis Cotinga*, in French *le Cordon bleu*, Purple-breasted Manakin, or Purple-breasted Chatterer.—*Ampelis Pompadoura*, seu *Cotinga purpurea*, le *Pacapacon Pompadour*, Grey Chatterer, or Pompadour Chatterer.—*Ampelis Phœnicia*, Red-winged Chatterer.—*Ampelis tersa*, la *Tersine*, Blue-breasted Chatterer.—*Ampelis Maynana*, seu *Cotinga Maynanensis*, in French *le Cotinga à plumes soyenses*, Silky Chatterer.—*Ampelis variegata*, seu *Cotinga nævia*, in French *l'averano*, Variegated Chatterer. —*Ampelis carunculata*, seu *Cotinga alba*, in French *le Cotinga blanc*, Carunculated Chatterer.—*Ampelis superba*, Superb Chatterer.—*Ampelis umbellata*, seu *cephalopterus ornatus*, Umbrellad Chatterer.—*Ampelus garrulea*, Waxen Chatterer.

AMPELITES *terra* (*Min.*) ἀμπελίτης, from ἄμπελος, a vine, because it kills the worms at the roots of the vines; Canal Coal, a species of black earth, which is more medicinal than other earths. It has a discussive and refrigerating virtue, and is used as an ingredient in cosmetics for the eyelids, καλλιβλέφαρα, and for dyeing the hair. *Dioscor. l. 5, c. 181; Oribas. Med. Coll. l. 13; Aet. Tetrab. 1,* serm. 2, c. 9; *Marcel. Empir.* c. 7; *Lemer. des Drogues.*; *Dale Parmacop.*

AMPELODE'SMOS (*Bot.*) from ἄμπελος, a vine, and δισ-μός, a band; a kind of herb with which the vines in Sicily used to be tied.

AMPE'LOLEUCE (*Bot.*) the name of a white sort of vine mentioned by Pliny. *Nat. Hist.* l. 23, c. 1.

AMPELOPRA'SUM (*Bot.*) from ἄμπελος, a vine, and πράσον, a leek; a herb growing among vines, called leek-vine, a species of the *Allium* of Linnæus.

AMPE'LOS *Agria* (*Bot.*) Briony, or Wild-Vine.

AMPHEMERI'NOS (*Med.*) an epithet for a quotidian fever, or a fever which brings on a paroxysm or fit every day, from ἀμφί, signifying a revolution, and ἡμέρα, a day.

AMPHIARTHRO'SIS (*Anat.*) from ἀμφί, *circum*, on both sides, and ἀρθρωσις, articulation; a mixed sort of articulation, between the diarthrosis and the synarthrosis. [vide *Articulation*]

AMPHI'BIA (*Zo.*) from ἀμφί, *utrinque*, and βία, *vita*, that is, both ways of life, because the animals live as well on land, or in the air, as in the water. The third class into which the animal world is divided, consisting of two orders, *Reptilia*, Reptiles, with feet, and *Serpentes*, Serpents, without feet, having plates, scales, or rings on the belly.

Reptilia comprehend *Testudo*, the Tortoise, covered with a shell—*Draco*, the Dragon, having wings and a tail—*Rana*, the Frog or Toad—*Lacerta*, the Crocodile, Alligator, Lizard, Newt, Salamander, Chameleon, Eft, Siren, which is two-footed, tailed, and naked.

Serpentes comprehend *Crotalus*, the Rattle Snake.—*Boa*, without a rattle.—*Coluber*, the Viper, having plates on the belly, and scales on the tail.—*Anguis*, the Snake, having scales under the tail.—*Amphisbæna*, having rings on the body.—*Cæcilia*, having wrinkles on the body and tail.—*Acrochordus*, having tubercles. A more particular account of this class will be found under each genus.

AMPHIBIALITHUS (*Foss.*) so called from being the part of an amphibious animal; a genus of petrefactions in the Linnæan system.

AMPHIBLESTROI'DES (*Med.*) from ἀμφίβληστρον, a net, and εἶδος, the form, i. e. Net-formed; the Retina, or Net-like coat of the eye. *Ruf. Ephes. Appell. Part. Corp. human.* l. 1, c. 23.

A'MPHIBOLE (*Min.*) a species of Hornblende.

AMPHIBO'LIA (*Rhet.*) ἀμφιβολία, from ἀμφί, on both sides, and βάλλω, to throw; Amphibology, or Ambiguity of expression when a sentence carries a double sense, as "Aio te, Æacide, Romanos vincere posse." It is distinguished from an equivocation, which lies in a single word, as Captare "lepores," where *lepores* signifies either hares or jests. *Aristot. Rhet.* l. 3, c. 5; *Cic. de Invent.* l. 2, c. 40; *Quint. Instit.* l. 7, c. 9; *Hermog. περὶ διννοτ*; *Voss. Instit. Rhet.* p. 167.

AMPHIBRA'CHYS (*Gram.*) ἀμφίβραχυς, from ἀμφί, *utrinque*, and βραχύς, *brevis*, i. e. short on both sides; a foot, having a long syllable between two short ones, as ὁμήρος. *Hæphest.* ἐγχειρίδ.

AMPHIBRA'NCHIA (*Nat.*) from ἀμφί and βράγχια, *branchiæ*; the parts about the tonsils.

AMPHICAU'STIS (*Bot.*) a sort of wild barley.

AMPHI'CTYONES (*Ant.*) Ἀμφικτύονες, the judges who constituted the Amphictyonic council. [vide *Amphictyonium*]

AMPHICTYO'NIA (*Ant.*) Ἀμφικτυονία, a general name for any assembly of the Grecian cities, who met to consult about the common good. [vide *Amphictyonium*]

AMPHICTYO'NIUM *concilium* (*Ant.*) the Council of the Amphictyones, founded, as is generally supposed, by a king of Athens of the same name. It consisted at first of deputies from only seven cities, which were afterwards increased to twelve, namely, from the Ionians, Dorians, Bœotians, Magnesians, Phthians, Locrians, Malians, Phocians, Thessalians, Dolopians, Perhebians, and Ætians. *Diodor.* l. 16, c. 16; *Plin.* l. 36, c. 19.

AMPHI'DEON (*Med.*) the orifice of the uterus.

AMPHIDIARTHRO'SIS (*Anat.*) an articulation of the lower jaw, partly by a ginglymus, and partly by an arthrodia.

AMPHIDRO'MIA (*Ant.*) Ἀμφιδρομία, from ἀμφί, around, and δρόμος, a course; a festival at Athens celebrated on the fifth day after the birth of a child, when it was carried round the fire and presented to the Lares, or household gods, on which occasion an entertainment was given, and presents made to the attendants. A description of the whole ceremony is to be found in the verses of Ephippus, as quoted by Athenæus. *Plat. in Thæatet.*; *Lysias in Orat. apud Harpocrat.*; *Schol. in Aristoph. Lysistrat.*; *Poll. Onom.* l. 2, segm. 8; *Athen.* l. 2, c. 24, and l. 9, c. 2; *Harpocration*; *Hesychius*; *Suidas.*; *Cæl. Rhodig.* l. 22, c. 12; *Meurs. Hist. Miscel.*; *Turneb. Adv.* l. 3, c. 6.

AMPHIJE'NE (*Min.*) a species of garnet.

AMPHI'MACER (*Gram.*) Ἀμφίμακρος, from ἀμφί, on both sides, and μακρός, long, i. e. a foot, having a short syllable in the middle, and a long one on each side, as ὑγιῶν *Hæphest.* ἐγχειρίδ.

AMPHIMA'SCHALI (*Ant.*) ἀμφιμάσχαλοι, an epithet for coats with two sleeves, which were worn by freemen only, in distinction from the ἑτερομάσχαλοι, or coats with one sleeve, which was the peculiar dress of slaves. To this Aristophanes alludes.

Equit. act 2, scen. 4, v. 47.

Οὐ πώποτ' ἀμφιμάσχαλε τὸν δῆμον ἠξίωσας.

Alexand. Gen. Dier. l. 5, c. 18; *Cæl. Rhodig. Antiq. Lect.* l. 16, c. 10.

AMPHIMERI'NA *Febris* (*Med.*) a tertian remittent fever.

A'MPHIPLEX (*Anat.*) the part betwixt the scrotum and anus. *Ruf. Ephes. de Appell. Part. Corp. human.* l. 1, c. 12.

AMPHIPNEU'MA (*Med.*) the same as *Dyspnœa*.

AMPHI'POLI (*Ant.*) Ἀμφίπολοι, magistrates appointed by Timoleon at Syracuse, after the expulsion of Dionysius the Tyrant, who derive their name from their being supposed to be ministers to Jupiter. *Diod.* l. 16.

AMPHI'PPI (*Ant.*) ἀμφίπποι, *desultores*; horse soldiers who used to charge with two horses, so that they might leap from one to the other; to which Homer alludes.

Hom. Il. l. 15, v. 684.

Θρώσκων ἄλλοτ' ἐπ' ἄλλον ἀμείβεται.

Suidas in Verb. ἵππικά. *Cæl. Rhodig. Antiq. Lect.* l. 21, c. 30.

AMPHIPRO'STYLOS (*Ant.*) ἀμφιπρόστυλος, from ἀμφί, on both sides, and πρόστυλος, a prostyle or column; a house with pillars, or piazzas, on both sides. *Vitruv.* l. 3, c. 1; *Salmas. in Solin.* p. 1217.

AMPHISBÆ'NA (*Zool.*) ἀμφισβαίνα, from ἀμφί, both ways, and βαίνω, to go; a venomous serpent in Lybia with two heads, and moving forward with either end. *Lucan.* l. 9, v. 719.

Et gravis in geminum surgens caput Amphisbæna.

Nicander, in his Theriacæ, calls it ἀμφίκαρπον, i. e. having a head at both ends. This notion of the ancients arose from the shape of the animal; the body of which is of equal thickness throughout its whole length, so that it is not easy to distinguish the head from the tail. The bites of these serpents resemble the stings of wasps. *Plin.* l. 8, c. 23; *Solin. Polyhist.* c. 27; *Act. Tetrab.* 1, serm. 1; *Paul. Æginet. de Re Med.* l. 5, c. 13; *Actuar. de Meth. Med.* l. 6, c. 11.

AMPHISBÆNA, *in the Linnean system*, a genus of animals; Class *Amphibia*, Order *Serpentes*.
Generic Character. Rings on the body and the tail.—*Scales* none.—*Tail* hardly to be distinguished from the body.
Species. The species are the *Amphisbæna fuliginosa, flava, varia, alba, magnifica,* &c.

AMPHI'SCII (*Astron.*) from ἀμφὶ, on both sides, and σκία, a shadow; the inhabitants of the Torrid Zone, who have their shadow turned to the north one part of the year, and to the south the other. When the sun is in the zenith they have no shadow, wherefore Pliny calls them *Ascii*; and to this Lucan alludes, when speaking of Syene, that was placed under the tropic of Cancer; he says, " Umbras nusquam flectente Syene." *Luc.* l. 2, v. 587; *Cleomed. de Mund.* l. 1; *Plin.* l. 2, c. 74.

AMPHI'SMILA (*Anat.*) ἀμφισμίλη, from ἀμφὶ, on both sides, and σμίλη, a knife; a dissecting knife with an edge on both sides. *Galen apud Castell.*

AMPHI'SCIEN cockatrice (*Her.*) vide *Basilisk*.

AMPHI'TANE (*Chem.*) Tincal.

AMPHI'TAPÆ (*Ant.*) garments having hair on both sides, on which persons slept.
Lucill. l. 1.

Psilæ, atque amphitapæ, villis ingentibus molles.

Ulpian. de Aur. et Argent. Leg.; Hesychius; Non. l. 14, c. 24; *Cæl. Rhodig. Antiq. Lect.* l. 16, c. 2; *Ferrar. de Re Vest.* l. 2, c. 1, &c.

AMPHITHA'LAMUS (*Ant.*) from ἀμφὶ, on both sides, and θάλαμος, the marriage bed; the maid's room on both sides that of her mistress's. *Vitruv.* l. 6, c. 10.

AMPHITHE'ATRE (*Ant.*) *Amphitheatrum*, ἀμφιθέατρον, from ἀμφὶ, on both sides, and θέατρον, i. e. a theatre on both sides; a circular building so constructed as to appear to be composed of two theatres, or one entire theatre all round;
Ovid. Met. l. 11, v. 25.

——————— *structo utrimque theatro*
Ceu matutinâ cervus periturus arenâ.

The form of which was either round or oval, as in the annexed figure, which represents an amphitheatre adorned with columns, and, in the interior, the emperor sitting in the midst of the spectators; in the area a bull, and a man seated on an elephant engaged in battle; on the left an obelisk; and on the right a colossal statue; the inscription MUNIFICENTIA GORDIANI AUGusti. The principal parts of the amphitheatre were the—*Arena*, or place where the gladiators fought.—*Cavea*, or hollow part where the beasts were kept—*Podium*, or projection at the top of the wall, which surrounded the arena, and was assigned to the senators, &c. for their use—*Gradus*, or benches rising all round above the Podium—*Aditus*, or entrances; and the—*Vomitoriæ*, or gates which terminated the Aditus. *Vitruv.* l. 5, c. 7; *Liv.* l. 41, c. 31; *Senec. de Ira,* l. 2, c. 12; *Plin.* l. 36, c. 15; *Sueton. in Cal.* c. 30; *Dio.* l. 61; *Tertull. de Spectac.* c. 12; *Vopisc. in Prob.* c. 19; *Treb. Poll. in Gallien.* c. 12; *Cassidor. Var.* l. 5, c. 4; *Isidor. Orig.* l. 18, c. 52; *Lips. de Amphitheat.* c. 8; *Panciroll. Descript. Urb. apud Græv. Thes. Rom. Antiq.* tom. iii. p. 322.

AMPHITRI'TE (*Con.*) a genus of animals of the Class *Vermes*, Order *Mollusca*.
Generic Character. Body annulate.—*Peduncles* small.—*Feelers* two.—*Eyes* none.
Species. The principal species are the—*Amphitrite infundibulum*, found near King's-bridge, in Devonshire.—*Amphitrite convolutus*, found on the southern coast of Devonshire.—*Amphitrite ventilabrum*, found on different parts of the English coast.—*Amphitrite rosea*, having the feelers beautifully spotted with crimson.—*Amphitrite campanulata*, &c.

AMPHODO'NTA (*Zo.*) ἀμφόδοντα, from ἀμφὶ, on both sides, and ὀδοὺς, a tooth; animals having teeth in both jaws. *Erot. Lex. Hippocrat.*; *Foes. Œconom. Hippocrat.*

A'MPHORA (*Ant.*) ἀμφορεὺς, per Sync. pro ἀμφιφορεὺς, from ἀμφὶ, on both sides, and φέρω, to bear, because it has two handles for holding by; a vessel and liquid measure, among the ancients, containing above seven gallons. The *Amphora* is represented on the coins of Athens, and is supposed to be symbolical of this city, where earthen-ware was first made, as in the annexed figure, which represents *Jupiter Fulgurator,* i. e. the darter of lightning; the inscription ΑΘΕ, i. e. Ἀθηναίων, *Atheniensium*. *Cato de Re Rust.* c. 114; *Cic. in Verr.* 2, c. 74; *Colum.* l. 12, c. 28; *Pæt. de Rom. Pond. &c. apud Græv. Thes. Antiq. Rom.* vol. ii. p. 1627; *Beger. Thes. Brandenburgh.*

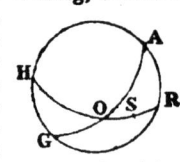

AMPHORA (*Com.*) the largest measure used at Venice, equal to four English gallons.

AMPHORA'ICUM (*Ant.*) the name for the wine which was kept in the amphora.

AMPHORA'RIUS (*Ant.*) from ἀμφορεὺς, a tankard bearer.

AMPHORI'TES (*Ant.*) a sort of literary contest in the island of Ægina, where an ox was the reward bestowed upon the poet, who made the best dithyrambic verses in honour of Bacchus.

AMPLEXA'TIO (*Alchem.*) a term among the alchymists for a matrimonial union between their mercury called the white female, and gold, called the red husband.

AMPLEXICA'ULE (*Bot.*) stem-clasping; an epithet for a leaf.

AMPLIA'TION (*Law*) *ampliatio*, a deferring of judgment till the cause is further examined. In this case the judges pronounced the word *amplius*, or by writing the letters N. L. for *non liquet*, signifying that the cause was not clear. *Manut. ad Cic. in Verr.* 1, c. 29; *Sigon. de Jud.* l. 2, c. 22; *Turneb. Adv.* l. 1, c. 3; *Pollet. For. Rom.* l. 4, c. 15.

AMPLIA'TIO (*Com.*) the duplicate of a receipt account, and the like. " To sign a copy by ampliation" is to sign a duplicate of it.

AMPLIFICA'TION (*Rhet.*) *amplificatio*, a figure of speech which consists of enlarging on an argument so as to make it appear either better or worse in the minds of the audience, and thus excite their approbation, or the contrary emotion towards the subject of discourse; it is called by the Greeks αὔξησις. *Aristot. Rhet.* l. 2, c. 26; *Cic. Orat.* l. 3, c. 27; *Quintil. Instit.* l. 3, c. 7; *Sulpic. Vict. Instit. Rhet.* p. 249.

A'MPLITUDE (*Ast.*) *amplitudo*, an arc of the horizon intercepted between its east and west points, and the centre of the sun or stars at their rising and setting. *Amplitude* is called *ortive*, or *Eastern*, when the star is rising, and *occiduous*, or *Western*, when it is setting. Each of these amplitudes is likewise termed *Northern* or *Southern*, as the point of rising or setting is in the northern or southern hemisphere; thus let H R be the horizon, A G the Equinoctial, O the true East or West point of the horizon, S the centre of the sun or star at its rising or setting, then the arc O S is the amplitude.—*Complements of the Amplitude*, vide *Azimuth*.

AMPLITUDE, *Magnetical* (*Mar.*) an arc of the horizon between the sun or star at its rising, and the magnetic East or West point indicated by the compass.

AMPLITUDE, *complement of the* (*Gun.*) the range of shot, or the horizontal right line drawn from the mouth of the cannon to the spot where the shot finally rests.

AMPLU'STRIA (*Ant.*) ornaments for ships. [vide *Aplustria*]

AMPO'TIS (*Med.*) ἄμπωτις, from ἀναπίνω, to regurgitate; the recess of the humours from the circumference of the body to the internal parts.

AMPU'LLA (*Ant.*) a flagon for oil, or a jug for beer, which was set on the table. It was sometimes made of glass, as *Mart.* l. 6, epig. 28, v. 3.

*At tu multa diu dicis, vitreisque tepentem
Ampullis potus semisupinus aquam.*

Sometimes of skins, as
Plaut. Rud. act 3, scen. 4, v. 51.

*Nisi erit tam sincerum, ut quivis dicit ampullarius
Optimum esse opere faciundo corium, et sincerissimum.*

The form of the ampulla is as in the annexed figure. *Cic. de Fin.* l. 14, c. 12; *Apul. Flor.* l. 2; *Plin. Epist.* l. 4, ep. 30; *Suet. in Domit.* c. 21; *Stuck. Antiq. Conviv.* l. 2, c. 25; *Fabric. Descript. Urb. Rom.* c. 18.

AMPULLA (*Chem.*) any vessel having a belly, as cucurbits, bolt-heads, receivers, &c.

AMPULLA (*Anat.*) the first appearance of the heart, liver, &c. in a fœtus after conception. *Hildanus*.

AMPULLA (*Bot.*) the bladder; a round, hollow, closed body that is found at the roots of some plants, as in the sub-

joined figure, which represents the root of the *Utricularia Aldrovanda*.

AMPULLA'SCENS *alvus* (*Anat.*) the most tumid part of Pecquet's duct.

AMPUTA'TION (*Surg.*) from *am* and *puto*, i. e. *scindo*, to cut; the cutting off a limb, which operation is described by Celsus, l. 7, c. 23, &c.

AMPUTATION is also used, by Cælius Aurelianus, to signify deprivation of speech, and, in regard to the nerves, to take away the strength. *Cæl. Aurel. de Acut. Morb.* l. 2, c. 6; *Chronic.* l. 4, c. 7.

AMPUTATU'RA (*Med.*) a wound from amputation.

AMSE'GETES (*Ant.*) those whose lands lay against the high road. *Fest. de Verb. Signif.*

AMU'CTICA (*Med.*) ἀμυκτικά, from ἀμύσσω, to vellicate; medicines serving to vellicate the bronchia, and produce coughing. *Cæl. Aurel. Chron.* l. 2, c. 6.

AMVE'TTI (*Bot.*) an Indian tree.

AMULE'TUM (*Ant.*) *Amunetum*, from ἀμύνω, to keep off; Amulet, the name of a particular form of words or of medicines, which, tied about the neck, were supposed to expel disease. *Le Clerc Hist. de la Medic.*

AMU'RCA (*Nat.*) the Mother of the lees of the pressed olive, which is of use for hydropical persons. It is called by Dioscorides ἀμόργη. *Cat. de Re Rust.* c. 100; *Dioscor.* l. 1, c. 138; *Plin.* l. 15, c. 11; *Columel.* l. 2, c. 20; *Oribas. Med. Coll.* l. 14, c. 1; *Aet Tetrab.* 1, serm. 1; *Paul. Æginet. de Re Med.* l. 7, c. 3.

AMU'SSIS (*Ant.*) or *Amussium*, a Carpenter's Rule.

A'MY (*Law*) from the French *ami*; the friend or guardian to whom an infant is entrusted: *prochain amy*, the next friend; *alien amy*, a foreigner subject to some prince who is on friendly terms.

A'MYCHE (*Med.*) ἀμυχή, from ἀμύσσω, to scratch; a superficial exulceration or scarification, according to Hippocrates.

AMYE'TICA (*Med.*) stimulating and vellicating medicines. *Cæl. Aurel. de Acut. Morb.* l. 2, c. 6.

AMY'GDALA (*Bot.*) ἀμυγδάλη, so called because it has many furrows; the almond or fruit of the almond tree. The sweet and esculent almond is much inferior in virtue to the bitter, which, among other medicinal qualities, attenuates and provokes urine. *Theophrast. Hist. Plant.* l. 2, c. 1; *Dioscor.* l. 1, c. 176; *Plin.* l. 15; *Paul. Æginet.* l. 7, c. 12.

AMY'GDALÆ *faucium* (*Anat.*) the almonds or kernels of the throat, otherwise called *Tonsillæ*.

AMYGDALA'TUM (*Med.*) an amygdalate or emulsion of almonds.

AMYGDA'LEA (*Ant.*) the same as *Amygdale*.

AMYGDALI'NUM *oleum* (*Phar.*) oil of almonds.

AMY'GDALIS *similis* (*Bot.*) the *Theobroma* of Linnæus.

AMYGDALI'TES (*Bot.*) a herb of the spurge kind, having the leaf of the almond. *Plin.* l. 26, c. 8.

AMYGDALA'D (*Min.*) the *Amygdalites vulgaris* of Linnæus.

AMYGDALOI'DES (*Bot.*) the *Euphorbia palustris* of Linnæus.

AMYGDALOPE'RZICUM (*Bot.*) the Almond Peach.

AMYGDA'LUM (*Bot.*) ἀμύγδαλον, the fruit of the Amygdalus.

AMY'GDALUS (*Bot.*) *Amygdala*, ἀμυγδαλῆ, Almond-tree; a tree so called, from ἀμύσσω, to tear with the nails; because the stone of the fruit is furrowed as if torn with the nails. [vide *Amygdala*]

AMYGDALUS, *in the Linnean system*, a genus of plants, Class 12 *Icosandria*, Order 1 *Monogynia*.

Generic Characters. CAL. *perianth* one-leaved, tubulous; divisions spreading.—COR. of five petals, oblong-ovate.—STAM. *filaments* shorter by half than the corolla; *anthers* simple.—PIST. *germ* roundish; *style* simple; *stigma* headed.—PER. *a drupe* roundish, villose; *seed* a nut ovate compressed.

Species. The principal species are the—*Amygdalus Persica*, the Peach or Nectarine Tree.—*Amygdalus communis*, the common Almond Tree.—*Amygdalus nana*, Common Dwarf Almond.—*Amygdalus pumila*, Double-flowered Dwarf Almond.

AMYGDALUS is also the name of the *Brabeium stelluli-folium*, and the *Catappa terminalis* of Linnæus. *Raii Hist. Plant.*

AMYGDALY'TES (*Min.*) almond-stone, a genus of earths of the *aggregate* order.

Generic Character. The amygdalytes consists of various elliptical stones imbedded together, so as form an irregular mass.

Species. The species of this genus may be divided into those which have a talcose base, those with a calcareous base, those with an argillaceous base, and those with a siliceous base.

A'MYLA (*Chem.*) any sort of chemical fæcula. *Castell. Lex Med.*

A'MYLON (*Nat.*) or *Amylum*, ἄμυλον, from α, priv. and μύλη, a mill; because it is made without a mill; starch, or the fæcula of wheat, which is good for rheum in the eyes. *Dioscor.* l. 2, c. 123; *Plin.* l. 18, c. 7; *Oribas. Med. Coll.* l. 1, c. 17; *Aet. Tetrab.* 1, serm. 1; *P. Ægin. de Re Med.* l. 1, c. 78; *Myrep. de Antid.* l. 1, c. 425.

A'MYON (*Anat.*) an epithet for a limb so emaciated as for the muscles to disappear.

A'MYRIS (*Bot.*) ἄμυρις, a genus of plants, Class 8 *Octandria*, Order 1 *Monogynia*.

Generic Character. CAL. *perianth* one-leaved.—COR. *petals* spreading.—STAM. *filaments* awlshaped; *anthers* oblong.—Pist. *germ* superior; *style* thickish; *stigma* four-cornered.—Per. *berry* roundish; *seed* nut round.

Species. The species are mostly shrubs, as the—*Amyris Gileadensis,* the Balsam of Gilead-tree.—*Amyris elemifera,* Gum Elemi-tree.—*Amyris opobalsamum, Opobalsamum, &c.* Balsam of Mecca tree.—*Amyris balsamifera,* Sweet Amyris, White Candle-wood or Rose-wood.—*Amyris toxifera, Toxicodendron, &c.* Poison-ash, &c. *Raii Hist. Plant.; Pluk. Almag.*

A'NA (*Med.*) ἀνά, a term in prescriptions for each, which is commonly written A or A A.

Ana (*Com.*) an Indian coin equal to a shilling and 1/4 of a penny.

ANABA'PTISTS (*Ecc.*) an heretical sect who admit none to the ordinance of baptism but such as can give an account of their faith. They are called Anabaptists, that is " Rebaptizers," from ἀναβαπτίζω, to baptize again, because they rebaptize all before they join their community, that have already received baptism. *Geneb. in Clemens.* viii; *Prateol. Doctrin. Hæret Omn.; Sander. de Origin et Progress Schismat. Anglican.; Spondan. Contin. Baron. Annal. Ann.* 1522.

ANABA'SII (*Ant.*) expeditious couriers or messengers mentioned by St. Jerom. *Adver. Ruffin.*

ANA'BASIS (*Ant.*) ἀνάβασις, from ἀναβαίνω, to ascend; the title of Xenophon's description of the younger Cyrus' expedition against his brother.

Anabasis (*Med.*) an increase of fever in general. *Gal. de Morb. Temp.* c. 2; *Gorr. Defin. Med.*

Anabasis (*Bot.*) a plant mentioned by Pliny, which was otherwise called *equisetum,* or Horse-hair. *Plin.* l. 26, c. 7.

Anabasis, *in the Linnean system,* a genus of plants, Class 5 *Pentandria,* Order 2 *Digynia.*

Generic Character. Cal. *perianth* three-leaved leaflets, roundish—Cor. five-petalled.—Stam. *filaments* filiform; *anthers* roundish.—Pist. *germ* roundish; *styles* acuminate; *stigmas* obtuse.—Per. *berry* roundish; *seed* single.

Species. The species are—*Anabasis aphylla, Salsola baccifera* seu *Kali bacciferum,* Leafless Anabasis, a shrub, native of the South-east of Europe—*Anabasis foliosa, Salsola clavifolia,* Leafy Anabasis, an annual, native of the South-east of Europe—*Anabasis tamariscifolia* seu *Kali fruticosum,* Tamarisk-leaved Anabasis, a shrub, native of Spain—*Anabasis spinosissima,* seu *Salsola echinus,* Thorny Anabasis, a shrub, native of Alexandria—*Anabasis Cretacea,* a perennial, native of Siberia. *Linn. Spec. Plant.*

ANABA'TICA (*Med.*) ἀναβατικὰ, a continued fever increasing in malignity. *Gal. de Differ. Puls.* l. 2, c. 1; *Gorr. Defin. Med.*

ANABATHRA (*Ant.*) from ἀναβαίνω, *ascendo;* 1. Stepping stones or blocks placed by the way side for mounting or dismounting. 2. Ranges of seats in the theatres. 3. A throne in the palace at Constantinople where the emperor used to sit.

Juven. sat. 7, v. 46.

Et quæ conducto pendent anabathra tigillo.

Bergier. de Viis. Milit. l. 4, sect. 39; *Lips. ad Belg.* l. 2, ep. 48.

ANABIBA'ZON (*Astron.*) the dragon's head or Northern node of the moon.

ANA'BOLE (*Med.*) from ἀναβάλλω, to cast up; throwing any thing off the stomach.

ANA'BOLEUS (*Ant.*) Ἀναβολεὺς, in the Latin *strator;* an equerry or groom of the stables; so called from his assisting his master to mount his horse. *Plutarch in Crass.; Suidas; Eustath. in Odyss.* l. 1, v. 155.

ANABROCHI'SMOS (*Med.*) ἀναβροχισμὸς, from ἀνὰ, upwards, and βρόχος, a cord; an operation for fastening the hairs of the eyelids when offensive to the eyes. *Cels. de Re Med.* l. 7, c. 7; *Gall. Comm.* 4, in *Hippocrat. de Rat. Vict.; Paul Æginet. de Re Med.* l. 6, c. 13; *Gorr. Defin. Med.; Foes. Œconom. Hippocrat.*

ANABRO'SIS (*Med.*) ἀνάβρωσις, from ἀναβιβρώσκω, to consume; a corrosion of the solid parts by acrid humours.

ANA'BULA (*Zool.*) a kind of beast in Ethiopia, having a head like a camel, a neck like a horse, legs like an ox, and reddish all over, with white spots.

ANACALYPTE'RIA (*Ant.*) Ἀνακαλυπτήρια, from ἀνακαλύπτω, to unveil; festivals among the Greeks on the third day after marriage, when the bride was allowed to take off her veil which she had hitherto always worn. The presents made at that time to the bride had also that name, and, according to Hesychius, the day was called ἀνακαλυπτήριον. *Jul. Pollux.* l. 3, segm. 36; *Harpocration; Hesychius; Suidas; Cæl. Rhodig. Antiq. Lect.* l. 1, c. 26.

ANACA'MPSEROS (*Bot.*) Orpine, or Live Long; a plant that grows to the height of a foot and more. It is of a detersive and vulnerary quality, fit for ruptures. The leaves of the anacampseros have a glutinous acidity, and give a strong red tincture to blue paper. *Plin.* l. 24, c. 17; *J. Bauh. Hist. Plant.; C. Bauh. Pin.; J. Tournef. Instit.; Lem. des Drogues.*

ANACA'MPTICS (*Opt.*) a species of optics, otherwise called catoptrics.

ANACA'RDIOS *antidotus Theodotus* (*Med.*) a confect of warm ingredients, good for epilepsies and apoplexies. *Myrep. de Antidot.* sect. 1, c. 219; *Trallian,* l. 7, c. 10; *Gorr. Def. Med.*

ANACA'RDINA *confectio* (*Med.*) a confect of anacardiums. *Mes.*

ANACA'RDIUM (*Bot.*) Cassa, Cajou, or Cashew tree, from ἀνὰ, upward, and καρδία, the heart; because the pulp of the fruit has a nut growing out at the end of it instead of its enclosing the seed. This is said to be hot, dry, and comforting to the vitals. *Paul. Æginet. de Re Med.* l. 7, c. 11; *Gorr. Defin. Med.*

Anacardium, *in the Linnean system,* a genus of plants, Class 9 *Enneandria,* Order 1 *Monogynia.*

Generic Characters. Cal. *perianth* five-leaved; *leaflets* ovate.—Cor. *petals* five.—Stam. *filaments* ten; *anthers* roundish.—Pist. *germ* kidney-shaped; *style* subulate; *stigma* small—Per. none; *receptacle* fleshy; *seed* a nut kidney-shaped.

Species. The only species are the *Anacardium occidentale, Pomifera* seu *potius Prumifera Indica, Acajou, Cassuvium, Caschou* seu *Kapa-mava,* Cashew Nut, Cassu or Acajou, a shrub, native of the Indies. *Brown. Hist. Jamaic.; Jacqu. Hist. Americ.; Linn. Spec. Plant.*

Anacardium, a name, a species of the *Semicarpus* and the *Avicenna tomentosa* of Linnæus. *J. Bauhin. Hist. Plant. C. Bauhin. Pin.; Ger. Herbal; Raii Hist. Plant.; Pluk. Almag. Botan.*

Anacardium *orientale* (*Bot.*) Malacca Bean Tree; a plant from which an oil like that of almonds is extracted, which is of medicinal virtue. *Lem. des Drog.*

ANACATHA'RSIS (*Med.*) ἀνακάθαρσις, from ἀνακαθαίρομαι, to purge upwards; a purgation of the lungs by expectoration. *Gal. Com. in Hippocrat.* l. 5, aphor. 8.

ANACATHA'RTICA (*Med.*) from ἀνακαθαίρομαι, to purge upwards; a species of purgatives that promote expectoration.

ANACE'IA (*Ant.*) Ἀνάκεια, a festival in honour of Castor and Pollux, who were called *Anaces,* ἄνακες ἢ ἄνακτες, and their temple *Anaceum,* ἀνάκειον. *Jul. Poll.* l. 1, c. 1; *Paus.* l. 10, c. ult.

ANACEPHALÆO'SIS (*Rhet.*) ἀνακεφαλαίωσις, from ἀνὰ, again, and κεφαλαία, to rehearse; recapitulation, or summing up of the heads of a discourse. This is called, in

Latin, *collectio*; and Cicero also speaks of a species of recapitulation which he calls *enumeratio*. *Cic. Brut.* c. 88, *et de Inven.* l. 1, c. 52; *Quintil. Instit.* l. 6, c. 1; *Hermog.* περὶ δινότ, p. 26; *Apsin. Art Rhet. Ald. Edit.* p. 706.

ANACHI'TES (*Min.*) the name of the gem *adamas*, or Adamant, which is so called because it serves as an antidote, and expels all vain fears from the mind. *Plin.* l. 37, c. 4.

ANACHORE'TA (*Ecc.*) ἀναχωρητής, from ἀναχωρέω, *recedo*, an anchoret; a hermit, or one who secludes himself altogether from the society of man. The first monks were of this description, as St. Paul, the hermit, who, to avoid the persecution, fled into the desert, and passed his days in religious contemplation. This mode of life was frequently followed until the foundation of the monastery of the Cenobites. *Hier. Vit. St. Paul. Eremit. &c.; Allatius de Consensu Eccl. Orient. et Occident.; Du Pin. Bibl. des Aut. Eccles.*

ANACHRE'MPSIS (*Med.*) ἀναχρέμψις, from ἀνά, up, and χρέμπτομαι, to hawk; a purgation of the lungs by means of hawking. It is otherwise called *apochrempsis*. *Gal. in Hippocrat.* l. 4, aphor. 47; *Foes. Œconom. Hippocrat.*

ANA'CHRONISM (*Chron.*) *anachronismus*, ἀναχρονισμός, from χρόνος, time; an error in time by placing an event earlier or later than it really happened.

ANACINE'MATA (*Ant.*) ἀνακινήματα, gesticulations and motions used by the combatants before they entered the lists. *Foes. Œconom. Hippocrat.*

ANA'CLASIS (*Anat.*) the elevation of the arm so that the humerus with the arm should appear to be one bone. *Hippocrat. de Fract.* sect. 3; *Foes. Œconom. Hippocrat.*; *Gorr. Defin. Med.*

ANACLASIS (*Rhet.*) Ἀνάκλασις, reflection; a figure of speech which is understood by the auditor in a contrary sense to what was intended to be conveyed. Quintilian calls this " antanaclasis." *Quint.* l. 9, c. 3; *Rutil. Lup.* l. 1, c. 5.

ANACLA'STICS (*Phy.*) from ἀνακλάω, to refract; a species of optics which treats of the refraction of light.

ANACLETE'RIA (*Ant.*) Ἀνακλητηρία, from ἀνακαλέω, to proclaim; festivals observed in all the regal states of Greece when their princes came of age to take the government upon themselves. *Polyb. Hist.* l. 18, c. 38.

ANACLINO'PALE (*Ant.*) Ἀνακλινοπάλη, wrestling and struggling while the combatants are on the ground; a sort of combat to which Martial alludes. *Mart.* l. 14, ep. 201.

Non amo qui vincit, sed qui succumbere novit
Et dicit melius τὴν ἀνακλινοπάλην.

ANACLI'NTERIA (*Ant.*) ἀνακλιντήρια, pillows among the Greeks, on which they rested their heads. This sort of pillow is called by Aristophanes ἐπικλιντηρία.

ANA'CLISIS (*Med.*) ἀνάκλισις, the reclining of a sick person. *Gal. Com.* 1, in *Hippocrat. de Art.*; *Foes. Œconom. Hippocrat.*; *Gorr. Defin. Med.*

ANACLI'SMOS (*Med.*) ἀνακλισμός, that part of a chair on which the back of a sick person leans. *Hippocrat.* περὶ ἄρθρων.

ANACOLLE'MA (*Med.*) ἀνακόλλημα, from ἀνακολλάω, to agglutinate; topics to prevent defluxions of humours upon the eyes. *Gal. de Comp. Med. Gen.* l. 6, c. 8; *Paul. Æginet.* l. 7, c. 16; *Myreps.* sect. 10, c. 3.

ANACOLU'PPA (*Bot.*) an Indian plant, the juice of which is a preservative against the effects of the bite of the Cobra Capella. *Raii Hist. Plant.*

ANACOLU'THON (*Rhet.*) ἀνακόλουθον, *inconsequentia*, inconsequence; in speech, when that which answers to the preceding is not expressed.

ANACOMI'DE (*Med.*) ἀνακομιδή, a word frequently used by Hippocrates, to denote restoration of strength to a patient after an illness. *Hippocrat. de Morb.* l. 2, &c.; *Gorr. Def. Med.*; *Foes. Œconom. Hippocrat.*

ANACO'NDO (*Zool.*) the name of a large and terrible snake in the island of Ceylon, supposed to be the same as the *Boa constrictor* of Linnæus.

ANACOUPHI'SMATA (*Ant.*) a sort of exercise or gestation among the ancients, mentioned by Hippocrates, which consisted, according to Madame Dacier, in leaping. *Hippocrat.* περὶ δίαιτης, l. 2.

ANACO'STE (*Com.*) a sort of woollen diaper made in Flanders and Holland, after the manner of the serges of Caen.

ANACREO'NTIC *verse* (*Gram.*) a sort of verse so called after Anacreon, by whom it was first used. It consisted of three feet, generally spondees and iambics, sometimes anapæsts.

ANA'CRISIS (*Ant.*) ἀνάκρισις, examination of witnesses.

ANACRO'SIS (*Poet.*) the name of a Parthian song, in which the combat of Apollo and the Pythian serpent is described.

ANA'CTES (*Hist.*) the title assumed by the sons and brothers of the kings of Cyprus, who administered the government while the latter took their pleasure. *Aristot. apud Harpocrat.*

ANACTO'RION (*Bot.*) the same as *Gladiolus*.

ANACY'CLUS (*Bot.*) from ἀνακυκλέω, to encircle; a genus of plants, Class 19 *Syngenesia*, Order 2 *Polygamia superflua*. Generic Characters. CAL. common, *scales* sharp.—COR. compound.—STAM. *filaments* five; *anther* cylindric.—PIST. *germ* flatted; *style* filiform; *stigmas* in the floscules.—PER. none; *seed* solitary; *receptacle* chaffy; *chaffs* obtuse.

Species. The species are—*Anacyclus Creticus*, *Cotula Cretica* &c. seu *Santolinoides annua*, &c. Trailing Anacyclus, an annual, native of Crete.—*Anacyclus Orientalis* seu *Chamæmelum Orientale*, Eastern Anacyclus, native of the East.—*Anacyclus aureus*, *Chamæmelum luteum* seu *aureum*, &c. seu *Anthemis chrysanthemum*, Golden-flowered Anacyclus, an annual or perennial, native of the South or East of Europe.—*Anacyclus valentinus*, *Chrysanthemum valentinum*, *Buphthalmum lanuginosum*, &c. seu *Chamæmelum tenuifolium*, Fine-leaved Anacyclus, an annual, native of Valentine.—*Anacyclus Alexandrinus*, an annual, native of Egypt. *J. Bauhin. Hist. Plant.*; *C. Bauhin. Pin. Theat.*; *Linn. Spec. Plant.*

ANADE'MA (*Ant.*) ἀνάδημα, a kind of ornament worn by Grecian women about their heads. *Jul. Poll. Onomast.* l. 5, c. 16, segm. 96.

ANADENDRO'MALACHE (*Bot.*) the same as *Althæa*.

ANADE'NDRON (*Bot.*) the same as *Althæa*.

ANADE'SMA (*Med.*) a bandage for wounds.

ANADIPLO'SIS (*Med.*) ἀναδίπλωσις, a reduplication of the paroxysm of a semitertian fever. *Gal. de Typis*, c. 4; *Trallian.* l. 12, c. 2; *Gorr. Defin. Med.*

ANADIPLO'SIS (*Rhet.*) a repetition at the commencement of a verse of the last word in the preceding; as,
Virg. ecl. 8, v. 55.

―――――― *Sit Tityrus Orpheus,*
Orpheus in Sylvis ――――

or of any word by way of emphasis, as in Cicero's orations, " *Dic, dic planius.*" This is called ἐπανάληψις by Alexander, in his book, περὶ σχημάτων. *Demet. de Elocut.*; *Cic. in Verr.* 3; *Quintil. Instit.* l. 9, c. 3; *Alexand.* περὶ σχημ. *apud. Ald.* 582.

ANA'DOSIS (*Med.*) ἀνάδοσις, a distribution of aliment over the whole body. *Gal. in Tim. Plat.* c. 16.

ANADRO'ME (*Med.*) ἀναδρομή, a recess of pains from the inferior to the superior part of the body. *Hippocrat. de Prædict. &c.*; *Foes. Œconom. Hippocrat.*

ANADRO'MOS (*Nat.*) an epithet for fish which at certain seasons ascend from the sea into the rivers. *Trallian.* l. 1, c. 15.

ANADYO'MENE (*Ant.*) a painting, by Apelles, of Venus coming out of the sea, and wringing her wet hair, which Augustus bought of the Coans, and placed in the temple of Julius Cæsar. It was a little defaced in one place, but no painter could be found at Rome to repair the damage.

ANÆSTHE'SIA (*Med.*) ἀναισθησία, from α, priv. and αἴσθησις, sensation; an insensibility to the touch, the consequence of disease, particularly the palsy. *Aret. de Sign. et Caus. Chron.* l. 1, c. 7.

ANAGALLIDA'STRUM (*Bot.*) the *Centunculus minimus* of Linnæus.

ANAGA'LLIS (*Bot.*) ἀναγαλλίς, a plant so called, ἀπὸ τοῦ ἀναγαγεῖν, i. e. from its reviving the spirits. It was reckoned a lenitive that was very efficacious in curing inflammations. *Dioscor.* l. 2, c. 209; *Plin.* l. 25, c. 13; *Gal. de Simpl.* l. 6; *Oribas. Med. Coll.* l. 11; *Act. Tetrab.* 1, serm. 1; *Paul. Æginet. de Re Med.* l. 7, c. 3; *Marcellin. de Med.* c. 1.

ANAGALLIS, *in the Linnean system*, a genus of plants, Class 5 *Pentandria*, Order 1 *Monogynia*.
  Generic Characters. CAL. *perianth* five-parted; *divisions* keeled.—COR. wheel-shaped; *border* five-parted; *divisions* ovate.—STAM. *filaments* erect; *anthers* simple.—PIST. *germ* globose; *style* filiform; *stigma* capitate.—PER. *capsule* globose; *seeds* very many; *receptacle* globose.
  Species. The species are either annuals, as the *Anagallis arvensis*, Common Pimpernel.—*Anagallis latifolia*, Broad-leaved Pimpernel; or perennials, as *Anagallis monelli*, Upright Pimpernel.—*Anagallis tenella*, Bog-Pimpernel, Loose-Strife, or Money-Wort, &c. *J. Bauhin. Hist. Plant.; C. Bauhin. Pin. Theat.; Ger. Herb.; Park. Theat. Botan.; Raii Hist. Plant.; Tourn. Inst. Herb.; Dill. Plant. Cat. Giss.; Boerh. Ind. Plant.; Linn. Spec. Plant.*

ANAGALLIS is also a name for the *Centunculus minimus evolvulus et absinoides*; the *Lysimachia nemorum* and *nummularia*, and the *Veronica Anagallis* of Linnæus. *Raii, Tourn. &c.*—*Anagallis aquatica*, the *Veronica Betabunga* and *Veronica Anagallis*, the *Montia fontana, Pepis portula*, and *Samolus erandi* of Linnæus. *Bauh. Ger. Raii, &c.*—*Anagallis cærulea*, the *Gratiola monnicra* of Linnæus. *Sloane.*

ANAGARGALI'CTA (*Med.*) Ἀναγαργάλικτα, Gargarisms, with which the fauces are washed. *Hippocrat. de Affect.; Gorr. Defin. Med.; Foes. Œconom. Hippocrat.*

ANAGLY'PHA (*Ant.*) ἀνάγλυφα, from ἀνὰ and γλύφω, to carve out; vessels or plate, *in asperitatem excisa*, chased, embossed, or wrought with the hammer, not engraved. *Plin.* l. 33, c. 11; or *opera signi*, as Virgil calls them. *Æn.* l. 5, v. 267.

ANAGLYPHA is also the art of embossing.

ANAGLYPHA (*Anat.*) the same as *Calamus scriptorius*.

ANAGNO'STES (*Ant.*) ἀναγνώστης, a reader, or a person in families of distinction, whose office it was to read at their meals. *Cic. ad Attic.* l. 1, ep. 12, &c.; *Fam.* l. 5, ep. 9.

ANAGO'GE (*Bibl.*) ἀναγωγή, the mystical interpretation of Scripture; one of the four ordinary modes of interpretation, in distinction from the *literal, allegorical*, and *tropological*.

ANAGOGE (*Anat.*) an efflux of the blood from the inferior parts of the body, as from the breast, &c. according to Aretaus; but, as Gorræus thinks, Hippocrates takes it, in his aphorisms, for an expulsion of the blood from the lungs. *Aret. de Caus. et Sign. Acut. Morb.* l. 2, c. 2; *Gorr. Defin. Med.*

ANAGO'GIA (*Ant.*) Ἀναγωγία, an annual festival in Sicily, celebrated by the Inhabitants of Mount Eryx in honour of Venus, who was said to retire with all the doves from her usual abode. Her return nine days after with the doves was celebrated by another festival, entitled καταγωγία Catagogia. *Æl. Var. Hist.* l. 1, c. 15; *Hist. An.* l. 4, c. 2.

ANAGO'GICAL (*Bibl.*) or *mystical*, an epithet applied to a mode of interpreting Scripture. [vide *Anagoge*]

A'NAGRAM (*Ant.*) ἀνάγραμμα, *anagramma*; the change of one word into another by the transposition of its letters, as Amor into Roma. As also of several words, as from the question of Pilate to our Saviour, *Quid est veritas* is made the appropriate answer *Est vir qui adest*.

ANAGRA'PHE (*Ant.*) ἀναγραφή, from ἀναγράφω, *describo*; an inventory or commentary.

A'NAGROS (*Com.*) a measure for grain at Seville, equal to about 10¼ quarters English measure.

ANAGY'RIS (*Bot.*) ἀνάγυρις, or ἀνάγυρος, a plant, resembling the vine in leaf and branch, which has a very fœtid odour, whence the proverb κινεῖς τὸν ἀνάγυρον, Anagyrum moves, for one who brings himself into trouble. The juice of the root is diaphoretic and digestive: the seed is taken as an emetic. *Diosc.* l. 5, c. 147; *Plin.* l. 27, c. 4; *Suidas.; Oribas. Med. Coll.* l. 11; *Paul. Æginet.* l. 7, c. 3.

ANAGYRIS, *in the Linnean system*, a genus of plants, Class 10 *Decandria*, Order 1 *Monogynia*.
  Generic Characters. CAL. *perianth* bell-shaped; *mouth* five-toothed.—COR. papilianaceous; *standard* obcordate; *wings* ovate oblong; *keel* straight.—STAM. *filaments* parallel; *anthers* simple.—PIST. *germ* oblong; *style* simple; *stigma* villose.—PER. *legume* oblong; *seeds* six or more.
  Species. The species are the—*Anagyris fœtida*, Stinking Bean-Trefoil, a shrub, native of Italy.—*Anagyris Cretica*, a shrub, native of Candia.—*Anagyris inodora*, a shrub, native of Cochin China. *J. Bauhin. Hist. Plant.; C. Bauhin. Pin. Theat.; Ger. Herb.; Park. Theat. Botan.; Raii Hist. Plant.; Tourn. Inst. Herb.; Boerh. Ind. Plant.; Linn. Spec. Plant.*

ANAGYRIS *non fœtida* (*Bot.*) the *Cytisus laburnum* of Linnæus. *Bauh. Hist. Plant.*

A'NAL *fin* (*Ich.*) the fin placed between the vent and tail, which expands perpendicularly.

ANA'LCIME (*Min.*) a species of Zeolite.

ANALE'CTA (*Ant.*) ἀνάλεκτα, *collectanea*, from ἀναλέγομαι, to gather, or collect; fragments or crumbs falling from the table, which were picked up, and not swept away, as the pavements of the Roman floors were too finely inlaid to admit of sweeping. *Mart.* l. 7, ep. 20, v. 16.

*Colligere longa turpe nec putat dextrâ
Analecta, quicquid et canes reliquerunt.*

Rhodig. Antiq. Lect. l. 13, c. 31; *Turneb. Adver.* l. 24, c. 33; *Ursin. Append. ad Ciacon. Triclin.; Alex. Gen. Dier.* l. 4, c. 21.

ANALECTA (*Lit.*) a name of modern invention for collections out of authors.

ANALE'CTÆ (*Ant.*) ἀπὸ τοῦ ἀναλέγεσθαι, *à colligendo*, i. e. from collecting; slaves among the Romans, who picked up the crumbs that fell after meals. [vide *Analecta*]

ANALECTI'DES (*Ant.*) ἀπὸ τοῦ ἀναλέγεσθαι, *à colligendo*, i. e. from collecting; stuffed cushions to lay on the shoulders, in order to make a crooked body straight.

ANALE'MMA (*Ant.*) ἀνάλημμα, from ἀναλαμβάνω, to resume; a planisphere, or projection of the sphere, on the plane of the meridian.

ANALE'NTIA (*Med.*) a species of Epilepsy, proceeding from affections of the stomach. *Paracel. Generat. Caduc.* tab. 5; *Johann. Anglic. Ros. Anglic. de Epilep.*

ANALE'PSIA (*Med.*) vide *Analentia*.

ANALE'PSIS (*Med.*) ἀνάληψις, from ἀναλαμβάνω, to recover. 1. The regaining of strength. 2. The suspension of any member, as of the arm when hung in a sling. *Gal. Comm.*

2, in *Hippocrat. de Med. Offic.*; *Gorr. Def. Med.*; *Foes. Œconom. Hippocrat.*

ANALE'PTICS (*Med.*) ἀναληπτικα, from ἀναλαμβάνω, to restore; a species of restoratives which serve to repair the strength, and to raise the depressed spirits. *Gal. de Sanitat. tuend.* l. 1, &c.

ANA'LOGY (*Log.*) ἀναλογια, from ἀνά, equally, and λόγος, called by Quintilian *ratio*, seu *proportio*, by Aulus Gellius *Convenientia*, seu *Ratio proportionis*, the relation which things bear, or are supposed to bear, to one another, from their resemblance or proportion to one another, as in regard to words that bear an analogy to each other in declension, conjugation, &c.; as if the nominative be *malus dolus*, the oblique cases be *mali* and *doli*, *malo* and *dolo*; but, if in the nominative, they are alike, and in the oblique cases different, then it is not *Analogy*, but *Anomaly*, as *lupus* and *lepus*, which, in the oblique cases make *lupi* and *leporis*. *Cic. ad Attic.* l. 6, ep. 2; *Varr. de Lat. Lin.* l. 9; *Quint. Instit.* l. 1, c. 4.

ANALOGY (*Math.*) the comparison or proportion of numbers or magnitudes one to another, thus, as 4 is to 2, so is 8 to 4.

ANA'LOGISM (*Log.*) ἀναλογισμός, from ἀναλογία, Ratiocination, or investigation of things by the analogy they bear to one another, as the judging of diseases, by the likeness of their appearance, or of their causes.

ANA'LOGOUS Term (*Log.*) *Vox analoga*, seu *Analogicum*; a term applied to two different objects, from some certain analogy or resemblance which they bear to one another, as, in speaking of pictures, they may be called the King, Queen, &c. meaning the picture of the King. Such words are in Rhetoric said to be metaphorical.

ANA'LYSIS (*Log.*) ἀνάλυσις, *resolutio*, from ἀναλύω, to resolve; the unfolding any matter, so as to discover its composition, as when one proceeds from universals to particulars, by the help of certain media or premises, in distinction from the Synthesis or composition adopted in Grammar, which proceeds from particulars, as letters, syllables, &c. up to generals, which are sentences: whence the logical treatise of Aristotle is termed *Analytica*.

ANALYSIS (*Math.*) the resolution of problems, which is of two kinds, Ancient and Modern.—*Ancient Analysis* is the proceeding from the thing sought, as taken for granted, through all its consequences, to something really known, which is opposed to the *Synthesis*, or composition, which takes for granted that which is found in the last step of the analysis; and, proceeding by a backward course of deduction, arrives at what was taken for granted, or the first step of the Analysis. Euclid's *Data* afford the best examples of the Ancient Analysis.—*Modern Analysis* is the resolution of problems by reducing them to equations by the help of symbolical characters. This is divided, with respect to its object, into—*Analysis of Finites*, which is otherwise called Algebra.—*Analysis of Infinites*, of which fluxions and the differential calculus form the principal parts.—*Analysis of Powers*, which is the same as Evolution.—*Analysis of Curve lines*, which shows their constitution, properties, &c.

ANALYSIS (*Chem.*) the decomposition of bodies, as vegetables, minerals, &c. so as to discover their component parts, which is effected either by fire, as in general cases, or by menstrua, as in the case of bodies compounded of several substances, which may be soluble in spirits of wine, water, and the like.

ANALYSIS (*Anat.*) the dissection of the human body, which is so called in lieu of the more familar term *anatomy*.

A'NALYST (*Math.*) one who adopts the Analytical method; also the title of a treatise, by Bishop Berkeley, on the doctrine of Fluxions.

ANALY'TICS (*Log.*) ἀναλυτικά, the books of Aristotle for the resolving of arguments. [vide *Analysis*]

ANA-MA'LLA (*Bot.*) a species of Brasilian-tree, from the leaves of which a decoction may be made.

ANAMNE'SIS (*Rhet.*) ἀνάμνησις, an enumeration of the things treated of, before which is a sort of recapitulation. *Aristot.* l. 3, c. 19.

ANAMNE'STICA (*Med.*) from ἀναμνάομαι, to remind; medicines to improve the memory.—*Anamnestica Signa*, commemorative signs which discover the preceding state of the body.

ANAMORPHO'SIS (*Per.*) the representation of some image, either on a plane or a curve surface, deformed or distorted; but which, in another point of view, shall appear regular, and drawn in just proportion. Thus, suppose the square A B C D to be drawn, divided into a number of small squares or areolas, as in the annexed diagram, *fig.* 1, within which may be drawn the image to be distorted. This is called the *craticular prototype*. Then to produce an anamorphosis let *a b*, as in *fig.* 2, be drawn equal to A B, and divided into the same number of equal parts as the prototype A B, and erect at the middle point E, the perpendicular E V, as also V S, perpendicular to E V making E *b*, so much longer and V S so much shorter, as it is intended that the image shall be so much the more distorted. From each of the points of division draw right lines to the point V, also the right line *a* S, and, lastly, through the points *c, e, f, g*, &c. parallel lines to *a b*, then will *a b c d* be the space called the *craticular ectype*, in which the monstrous projection is to be drawn.

Fig. 1.

Fig. 2.

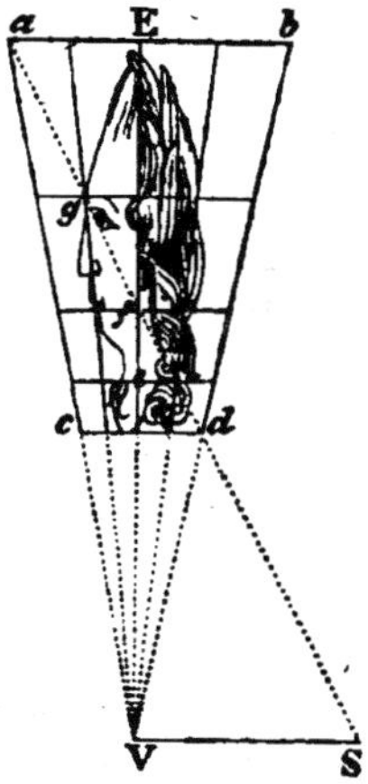

ANA'NAS (*Bot.*) a plant called the Brazil Yayanna or Pine apple; the fruit of which is reckoned astringent. This plant is classed by Linnæus under the *Bromelia*.

ANANCÆ'ON (*Rhet.*) ἀναγκαῖον, *necessarium*; a figure in rhetoric by which only necessary things are expressed to the rejection of all ornaments; it is properly the dry style as opposed to the τὸ σιπττὸν, the 'Flowery style.' *Aristot. Rhet.* l. 3, c. 13; *Dionys. Jud. Thucyd.* c. 22; *Cic. de Orat.* c. 21; *Plut. in Cat.*; *Quintil. Instit.* l. 9, c. 3; *Rutil. Lup.* l. 1, c. 20; *Ulp. Prologem. ad Demosth. Aristid.* πολ. λογ. *Ald.* p. 658.

ANANCHI'TIS (*Min.*) a sort of gem by which the images or visions of the gods are said to be worked in hydromancy. *Plin.* l. 37, c. 11.

ANA'NES (*Mus.*) a term for the modes and tones in the Greek church.

ANA'NDRIA (*Bot.*) a species of the *Tussilago* of Linnæus.

ANANTAPO'DOTON (*Rhet.*) ἀνανταπόδοτον, a figure of speech in which some part, as the apodosis, for example, is understoood, ἢν μὲν συμβῇ ἡ πεῖρα, 'Sin conatus ille recte successerit,' *scilicet*, 'bene est, which is the apodosis here understood. *Schol. in Thucid.* l. 3.

ANA'PALIN (*Med.*) ἀνάπαλιν, on the contrary side, opposed to Cataxin, κατάξιν, on the same side; applied frequently, by Hippocrates, to the transmutation and fluxes of the humours. *Gorr. Def. Med.*; *Foes. Œconom. Hippocrat.*

ANAPÆ'STUS (*Gram.*) ἀνάπαιστος, Anapæst; a metrical foot, having the two first short and last long (˘ ˘ ¯), the contrary of a Dactyle, as πολεμῶν. It is derived from ἀναπαίω, to reverberate, because it reverberates the dactyle with its own sound. *Quintil. Instit.* l. 9, c. 4; *Hæphest. Enchyrid.*; *Isid.* l. 1, c. 16.

ANAPÆ'STIC *verse* (*Gram.*) what consists mostly of Anapæsts.

ANAPHONE'SIS (*Med.*) ἀναφώνησις, a species of exercise strongly recommended by the ancient physicians.

ANA'PHORA (*Gram.*) ἀναφορά, a figure in rhetoric when the same word is repeated at the beginning of every verse, or member of a sentence, as
Virg. Eclog. l. 4, v. 58.

Pan etiam Arcadiâ mecum si judice certet
Pan etiam Arcadiâ dicat se judice victum.

According to Demetrius it comprehends the Epanaphoran, the Asyndeton, and the Homoestuleuton. *Demet. de Elocut.* § 141; *Hermogen.* περὶ ἰδίων; *Long. de Sub.* l. 20, c. 1.

ANAPHORA (*Astron.*) an ascension or rising of the twelve signs of the zodiac from the East to the West by the daily course of the heavens. *Firmic.*

ANAPHRODI'SIA (*Med.*) ἀναφροδισία, from α, priv. and ἀφροδίσιος, *venereus*; *impotentia venerea*.

ANAPHRO'MELI (*Med.*) from ἀνὰ, ἀφρὸς, froth, and μέλι, honey; despumated honey, which will no longer froth when boiled.

ANA'PLASIS (*Surg.*) ἀνάπλασις, reformation; the replacing a fractured bone as it was before it was broken.

ANAPLERO'SIS (*Surg.*) Ἀναπλήρωσις, the restoring of deficiencies. *Gal. de Dynam. lib. ascript.*

ANAPLERO'TICS (*Surg.*) from ἀναπληρόω, to fill up; a species of medicines which tend to encourage the growth of flesh in wounds. *Gal. de Dynam. lib. ascript.*

ANAPLEU'SIS (*Med.*) ἀνάπλευσις, the exfoliation or rotting away of the bones from a redundance of humours. *Hippocrat. de Fract. &c.*; *Erot. Lex. Hippocrat.*; *Paul. Æginet. de Re Med.* l. 6, c. 107; *Gorr. Def. Med.*; *Foes. Œconom. Hippocrat.*

ANAPNEU'SIS (*Med.*) ἀνάπνευσις, from ἀναπνέω, to respire; a respite from pain. *Aret. de Cur. Acut. Morb.* l. 2, c. 1; *Foes. Œconom. Hippocrat.*

ANAPODOPHY'LLUM (*Bot.*) the *Podophyllum peltatum* of Linnæus.

ANA'RAPHE (*Surg.*) ἀναρραφή, retraction of the upper eyelid when relaxed. *Aet. Tetrab.* 2, serm. 3, c. 69.

ANA'RCHI (*Ant.*) ἄναρχοι; an epithet applied by the Athenians to the four supernumerary days in their year, in which they had no magistrates.

A'NARCHY (*Polit.*) Ἀναρχία, *ubi nullus imperat*, i. e. the condition of a city, commonwealth, or state without a head or sovereign, as "In those days there was no king in Israel, but every man did that which was right in his own eyes."

ANA'RHICAS (*Ich.*) Wolf-fish; a genus of animals; Class *Pisces*, Order *Apodal*.
Generic Characters. Head blunt.—*Gill-membrane* seven-rayed.—*Body* roundish.—*Caudal fin* distinct.
Species. The species are—*Anarhicas lupus*, Ravenous Wolf-fish.—*Anarhicas minor*, Lesser Wolf-fish.—*Anarhicas pantherinus*, Panther Wolf-fish.

ANARRHEGNI'MIA (*Med.*) or *Anarrhexis*, from ἀνὰ, again, and ῥήγνυμι, to break; a fresh fracture or opening of a wound.

ANARRHI'NON (*Bot.*) vide *Antirrhinum*.

ANARRHŒ'A (*Med.*) ἀνάρροια, a flux of humours from the inferior parts upwards. *Castell. Lex. Med.*

ANARRHO'PIA (*Med.*) ἀναρροπία, from ἀνὰ, and ῥέπω, to move or creep; a tendency of the humours to verge upwards. *Hippocrat. de Humor.*; *Gorr. Defin. Med.*; *Foes. Œconom. Hippocrat.*

ANA'RTHROI (*Med.*) an epithet used by Hippocrates for a people of Scythia, so fat and bloated that they were ἄναρθροι, i. e. their joints were not discernible. *Hippocrat. de Aer.*

A'NAS (*Or.*) a genus of animals; Class *Aves*, Order *Anseres*.
Generic Characters. Bill convex, obtuse.—*Tongue* fringed. *Three fore-toes* connected.
Species. This genus consists of three divisions, which are distinguished, in English, by the names of the Swan, the Goose, and the Duck. The most remarkable species under each of these divisions are the following; namely— *Anas cygnus*, the Wild Swan.—*Anas olor*, in French *le Cygne*, the Tame Swan.—*Anas anser*, in French *l'Oye privée*, the Grey Lag Goose, or Common Wild Goose.—*Anas segetum*, the Bean Goose.—*Anas erythropus*, the Bernacle Goose.—*Anas bernicla*, in French *le Cravant* or *les Canes de Mer*, Brent Goose.—*Anas mollissima*, the Eider Duck.—*Anas spectabilis*, in French *le Canard à tête grise*, the King Duck.—*Anas nigra*, in French *la Macreuse*, the Black Diver or Scoter.— *Anas marila*, in French *le petit Morillon rayé*, the Scaup. —*Anas tadoma*, in French *la tadome*, the Shield-drake, or Borough Duck.—*Anas boschas*, in French *le Canard domestique*, the Mallard or Common Wild Duck.— *Anas clypeata*, in French *le Souchet*, the Shoveler.— *Anas acuta*, in French *le Canard à longue queue*, the Sea-Pheasant, Cracker, or Pintail.—*Anas penelope*, the Wigeon.—*Anas strepera*, in French *le Chipeau*, the Gadwall or Gray.—*Anas querquedula*, in French *la Sarcelle*, the Garganey.—*Anas crecca*, in French *la petite Sarcelle*, the Teal. *Belon. Hist. des Ors.*; *Gessn. de Av. Nat.*; *Willough. Ornith.*; *Raii Synop.*; *Brisson. Ornith.*; *Linn. System. Nat.*

ANASA'RCA (*Med.*) ἀνασάρκα, from ἀνὰ, and σὰρξ, flesh; a species of dropsy, in which the flesh is puffed up. This is called ὑποσάρκα by Hippocrates, and κατασάρκα by Heracles Tarentinus, according to Cœlius Aurelianus. *Gal. Comm.* 3. *in Hippocrat. de Acut. Morb.*; *Aret. de Sig. et Caus. Acut. Morb.* l. 2, c. 1; *Cæl. Aurelian. de Acut. Morb.* l. 3, c. 8; *Trallian.* l. 9, c. 2; *Act. de Meth. Med.* l. 5, c. 6. This disease is placed as a genus by Cullen, under the Class *Cacheciæ*, Order *Intumescentiæ*.

ANASARCA (*Bot.*) the dropsy in plants, from an excess of water or rain.

ANASCHONA'DI (*Bot.*) the *Elaphantopus scaber* of Linnæus.

ANA'SPASIS (*Med.*) ἀνάσπασις; a contraction of the stomach. *Hippocrat. de Prisc. Medicin.*

ANA'SSA (*Bot.*) the *Bromelia ananas* of Linnæus.

ANASTA'LTICS (*Med.*) from ἀναστέλλω, to contract; restringent or styptic medicines.

ANA'STASIS (*Med.*) ἀνάστασις, from ἀνίστημι, to rise up; used by Hippocrates to signify a migration of humours, when expelled from one part they are obliged to go to another. *Hippocr. de Epidem*, sect 7; *Gorr. Defin. Med.*; *Foes. Œconom. Hippocrat.*

ANASTA'TICA (*Bot.*) ἀναστατικα, from ἀνίστημι, to rise up, or revive; a plant so called from its quality of reviving in water.

ANASTATICA, *in the Linnean system*, is a genus of plants, Class 15 *Tetradynamia*, Order 1 *Siliculosa*, in English, the Rose of Jericho.
Generic Characters. CAL. *perianth* four-leaved; *leaflets* ovate, oblong.—COR. *tetrapetalous*; *petals* roundish.— STAM. *filaments* six; *anthers* roundish.—PIST. *germ* bifid; *style* subulate; *stigma* capitate.—PER. *silicle* very short; *seeds* solitary.
Species. The species are, *Anastatica hierochuntica*, *Thlaspi Rosa de Hiericho dictum*, seu *Rosa Hierochuntea*, Common Anastatica, or Rose of Jericho, an annual, native of the coast of the Red Sea.—*Anastatica syriaca*, *Bunias syriaca*, *Myagrum rostratum*, *Thlaspi*, &c. seu *Rosa*

hierocontea, &c. Syrian Anastatica, native of Syria. *C. Bauhin Pin. Theat.; Raii Hist. Plant.; Mor. Hist. Plant.; Linn. Spec. Plant.*

ANASTOICHEIO'SIS (*Chem.*) ἀναστοιχίωσις, from ἀνὰ and στοιχίω, an element; re-elementation, or the resolution of the solids and fluids into their first elements. *Gal. de Sympt. Caus.* l. 3, c. 2; *Gorr. Def. Med.; Castell. Lex. Med.*

ANASTOMO'SIS (*Med.*) ἀναστόμωσις, from ἀνὰ and στόμων, to close the mouth; 1. An opening of the mouths of the vessels for the discharge of any fluid, as the menses, which are discharged by *Anastomosis* into the uterus. 2. The inosculation of the arteries and veins, i. e. their running into one another. *Hippocrat. de Mul.* l. 1; *Cels. de Re Med.* l. 4, c. 4; *Gal. de Meth. Med.* l. 5; *Cæl. Aurel. de Pard. Passion.* l. 3, c. 10; *Gorr. Defin. Med.; Foes. Œconom. Hippocrat.*

ANASTOMOSIS (*Bot.*) a similar process of the juices in vegetable as of the fluids in animal bodies. [vide *Anastomosis*]

ANASTOMO'TICA (*Med.*) ἀναστομωτικὰ; a species of aperitive medicines. [vide *Anastomosis*]

ANA'STROPHE (*Rhet.*) ἀναστροφὴ, from ἀνὰ and στρέφω, to turn a figure of speech by the inversion of words, as *Italiam contra*, which, according to Quintilian, is reckoned a species of solecism. *Quintil. G. Instit. Orator.* l. 1, c. 5; *Aristid.* πολλὶ λόγ. *Ald.* p. 658.

ANA'STROUS *signs* (*Astron.*) a name given to the *duodecatomoria*, or the twelve portions of the ecliptic, which the signs anciently possessed, but which they have since deserted by the precession of the equinoxes.

ANA'TA (*Com.*) or *Anotto*, a sort of red dye brought from the West Indies, which is used in England for colouring cheese.

ANATA'SE (*Min.*) the *Titanum ruthila* of Linnæus.

ANATA'SIS (*Med.*) ἀνάτασις, from ἀνατείνω, an extension of the body upwards. *Galen. Quid fit Med.*

ANA'TES (*Med.*) a disease of the anus.

ANATHE'MA (*Ant.*) ἀνάθημα, from ἀνατιθῦναι, to set apart, dedicate, or devote to a sacred purpose; an offering made to any God, and laid up in the temple. *Poll. Onomast.* l. 1, c. 1, segm. 27.

ANA'THEMA (*Ecc.*) ἀνάθεμα, from ἀνατίθεσθαι, to remove from others, as something set apart and devoted; a sentence of excommunication, by which a person was either cut off from all communion with the faithful, as was the practice among the Hebrews, and after them of the Christians; or else of being devoted to death and utter destruction, as was frequently practised among the Hebrews, in the case of the Canaanitish cities, of Achan and others; and in some instances, as of Codrus and Curtius, among the heathens, who made a voluntary devotion of themselves, which was the same as anathematizing themselves, that is, setting themselves apart for some exclusive object.

ANATHRON (*Min.*) a fossil which vegetates on rocks, in the form of a white stony moss.

ANATHYMIA'SIS (*Med.*) from ἀναθυμιάω, to fumigate, signifies evaporation.

ANATOCISM (*Com.*) ἀνατοκισμὸς, usurious interest, or compound interest for monies lent.

ANATOMY.

ANATOMY, ἀνατομία, from ἀνατέμνω, to dissect, or cut asunder; is the separation of the parts of an animal body, so as to come at the knowledge of the component parts. The word anatomy is commonly applied to the dissection of a human subject in a healthy state, in distinction from *morbid anatomy*, or the anatomy of diseased subjects, and *comparative anatomy*, or the dissection of animals. The body is composed of solids and fluids, and is generally divided into the Head, Trunk, and Extremities.

The Solids.

The solids consist of fibres, or small filaments, which differ in their degree of hardness or elasticity. They are divided into *integumenta*, the Integuments; *ossa*, the Bones; *cartilagines*, Cartilages; *ligamenta*, Ligaments; *membranæ*, the Membranes; *vasa*, the Vessels; *musculi*, the Muscles; *nervi*, the Nerves; and *glandulæ*, the Glands.

Integuments are the coverings of the whole body, comprehending the—*Epidermis*, Cuticle or Skarfskin, which is the outermost.—*Rete mucosum*, a net-work immediately under the epidermis.—*Cutis vera*, the real Skin, which retains and carries off all the humours of the body.—*Corpus adiposum, seu Membrana adiposa*, the Fat, a cellular substance, containing an unctuous juice. To the above may be added—*Capillus*, the Hair, which consists of cellular filaments, and is denominated the Beard, Eyelashes, &c. according to the place in which it grows. [vide *Hair*]—*Unguis*, the Nails, which are horny substances.

Bones are hard and brittle substances, composed of *lamellæ*, or plates, lying upon one another, and joined together by transverse fibres. They are covered with an exquisitely sensible vascular membrane, called the *periosteum*, which on the cranium, or skull, is called the *pericranium*. On the surface of the bones are both eminences and cavities. The eminences are called Processes, which are of two sorts, namely, the *epiphysis* and the *apophysis*. The *epiphyses*, or *appendices*, are, as it were, parts added to the bone; the *apophyses* are set upon or growing to a large bone, so as to make one, as the nasal apophysis.

Processes have different names, according to their figure. A process like a ball is called *caput*, the Head; when flattened, *condyle*; the narrow part of the process *cervix*, the Neck. A rough process is a Tuberosity; and one terminating with a sharp point *corona* which, from its resemblance to other substances, is termed mastoid, styloid, anchoroid, spinal, &c. Long ridges are called *spinæ*, the sides of which are *labia*, Lips. Processes which form the brims are *supercilia*.

The cavities and depressions of bones are of two sorts, namely—*Glenæ*, which are narrow and shallow, and—*Cotylæ*, which are deep and wide. These are subdivided into—*Pits*, or small roundish holes—*Furrows*, or long narrow channels—*Nitches*, or *Notches*, small branches in the bones—*Sinuosities*, broad but superficial depressions—*Fossæ*, large deep cavities—*Sinuses*, still larger cavities, within the substance of the bone itself—*Foramina*, Holes through the body of the bone. The internal structure of the bones consists of cells, filled with a fluid fat, called Marrow, that is contained in Follicles.

The juncture of the bones with each other is called Articulation, from the *articulus*, or Joint, at the ends of the bones. This is of two kinds, namely—Articulation, properly so called, and *symphysis*, Connection. Articulation is either *diarthrosis*, or Separated Articulation, and *synarthrosis*, or Conjoined Articulation. Diarthrosis is subdivided into *enarthrosis*, or the Ball and Socket, when a large head is received into a deep cavity; *arthrodia*, when a round head is received into a small cavity; *gynglimus*, when a bone receives, and is received into another bone.—*Synarthrosis* is the fixing of two bones together without motion, which is of two kinds, namely—by ingrailing, or, as the joiners call it, dovetailing, which is termed *sutura*, a Suture, and by a junction on a more extended surface, which was termed *harmonia*.—*Symphysis*, or Connection, is that species of articulation which takes place through the medium of another body;

ANATOMY.

this is either *synchrondrosis*, a Cartilaginous Connection; *syneurosis*, a Ligamentary Connection; or *syssarcosis*, a fleshy Muscular Connection. [vide Pl. 7, fig. 1, 2, and the article *Bone*]

Cartilages are smooth white substances, which are harder than all the other solid parts of the body, except the bones. They are covered with a membrane called the *perichondium*.

Ligaments are close compacted fibrous substances. The ligaments at the joint are called Capsular, because they retain in *capsulæ*, or bags, the mucilaginous liquor called *synovia*, with which the joints are kept moist.

The *Muscle* is a bundle of fleshy or tendinous fibres, consisting of the Belly or Body, which is the fleshy part; the Head and the Tail, which are the tendinous parts; these are otherwise called *aponeuroses* or tendons. The head is fixed on the immoveable joint called the Origin, and the tail on the part to be moved, called the Insertion. The membranes, in which the muscles are enclosed, are called *vaginæ* or sheaths. As the motions of the human body are performed by means of the muscles, they derive their names mostly from their office; as the *abductor, elevator, flexor, extensor*, &c. [vide *Muscle*] When muscles act in opposite directions they are called Antagonists; but when several concur in the same motion they are termed *congeneres*. [vide Pl. 7, fig. 4, 5, 6]

Membranes are expanded substances of a pliable texture, and fitted to serve as coverings for other parts of the body, as the *skin, peritoneum, pleura, dura mater*, &c.

The *vessels* are ducts or canals, composed of membranes, the strata of which are called *tunicæ* or Coats. They may be divided generally into Blood Vessels and Absorbents. Blood-Vessels, so called because they serve to circulate the blood through the body, are either *arteriæ*, Arteries, or *venæ*, Veins; the former of which convey the blood from the heart, and the latter return it to the heart. [vide *Artery* and *Vein*] The arteries have a beating motion, called the Pulse, which the veins have not. This pulsation arises from what is termed the *systole* and *diastole*, i. e. the dilatation and contraction of the heart. [vide Pl. 7, fig. 3]

Absorbents, so called from their absorbing any fluid and carrying it to the blood, are the *vasa lactea*, the Lacteals; *vasa lymphatica*, the Lymphatics; together with their common trunk, the Lacteal Sac and Duct. The Lacteals absorb the chyle and the Lymphatics the lymph. The Lacteal Sac, or *receptaculum chyli*, serves, as its name denotes, to retain the chyle, and sends it by the Thoracic Duct through the whole body. The lymphatics, with the lacteals of the intestines, form what is called the Absorbent System. Most vessels are parted off into branches, which are again split into smaller branches or ramifications, the last or smallest extremities of which are termed *capillary*.

Nerves are long white medullary cords, springing from the *cerebrum* or Brain and Spinal Marrow, whence they are generally distinguished into the *cerebral* and *spinal* nerves. The cerebral are subdivided into the *olfactory, optic, auditory*, &c. nerves, according to their use. [vide *Nerve*] They go out in *bundles* or *pairs*, and are afterwards distributed by *branches, ramifications*, and *filaments*, over every part that is endowed with sensibility. In several places the nerves communicate with each other, which communication is called a *plexus*; in other places they unite into Knots, called *ganglions*. [vide Pl. 8, fig. 2]

Glands are secretory vessels, composed of all the different sorts of vessels, enclosed in a membrane, and serving to secrete some fluid. As to their fabric, they are *conglobate or simple, conglomerate or compound*. As to their contents, *mucous, sebaceous, lymphatic, salival, lachrymal*, &c.

Fluids.

The fluids of the body are those humours or juices which serve either to sustain life or preserve the frame in a healthy state. The principal of these are *sanguis*, the Blood; *chylus*, the Chyle; *lympha*, the lymph; and *bilis*, the Bile.

Blood is a red homogeneous fluid, of a saltish taste, a somewhat urinous smell and glutinous consistence, which circulates in the heart, arteries, and veins.

Chyle, a milk-like liquor, secreted in the lacteal vessels, by digestion, from the chyme or indigested mass of food that passes from the stomach into the duodenum. The chyle is that fluid substance from which the blood is formed.

Lymph, a liquid contained in the lymphatic vessels, has a fatuous smell, no taste, and a crystalline colour: its use is to return the superfluous nutritious jelly from every part, and to mix it with the chyle in the thoracic duct, for the purpose of furnishing nutriment to the animal.

Bile, a bitter fluid, secreted in the glandular substance of the liver. In a healthy state it is a yellow-green colour, and of the consistency of thin oil. Its principal use is to separate the chyle from the chyme, with which it mixes in the duodenum.

To the above might be added *pituita*, Phlegm; *saliva*, Spittle; *mucus; lachrymæ*, Tears; *sudor*, Perspiration; *urina*, Urine; *menses; lac*, Milk; and *semen;* which are all excretions from the blood, and, in a healthy state, pass off from the body at particular periods, of which more may be found under their respective heads.

Of these component parts, in different proportions, are formed the three principal divisions of the body before mentioned, namely, the Head, the Trunk, and the Extremities.

THE HEAD.

The *head* consists of *caput*, the Head, properly so called, and *cervix*, the Neck. The parts of the head are external or internal.

External Parts of the Head.

The external parts of the head are, the Hairy Scalp and the Face. The Hairy Scalp is composed of the common integuments; its uppermost part is called the *vertex seu fontenella*, the Crown; the forepart, the *sinciput;* the hind part, *occiput*, or Back of the Head; and the lateral parts, *tempora*, the Temples. The Face comprehends *frons*, the Forehead; *oculus*, the Eye; *auris*, the Ear; *nasus*, the Nose; and *os*, the mouth.

The *eye* is composed, externally, of *supercilia*, the Eyebrows; *cilia*, the Eyelashes; *palpebræ*, the Eyelids, the angles of which are called *canthi*, the margin *tarsus; glandulæ lachrymalis*, the Lachrymal Glands; *puncta lachrymalia; canales lachrymales*, Lachrymal Ducts; *saccus lachrymalis*, the Lachrymal Sac; *ductus nasalis*, the Nasal Duct; *membrana conjunctiva seu albuginea*, the White.

The *internal* parts of the eye compose what is called the Ball or Globe. These are *tunicæ*, the Coats; *cameræ*, the Chambers; and *humores*, the Humours; besides the Muscles, Fat, Nerves, and Glands. The principal coats of the eye are *tunica sclerotica*, or the Cornea, which is the external and thickest coat; *tunica choroidea*, or the Choroides, which is the middle. The perforated septum of the choroides has the name of *uvea;* the anterior lamina of the septum is termed the *iris;* the radiated plicæ of the posterior lamina *processus ciliares*; and the hole near the centre of the *septum pupilla*, the Pupil, which is capable of contraction or dilatation. The third and innermost of the coats is the *retina*.—*Cameræ*, the Chambers of the eye, are the *camera anterior* and *posterior*, situated between the *cornea lucida*, or the anterior portion of the sclerotica and the uvea.— *Humores*, the humours of the eye, are three, namely, the *Aqueous Humour*, which is contained in the two chambers; *Crystalline Lens* or Humour; and the *Vitreous Humour*: these two last are enclosed in capsular tunicæ, called *crystallina* and *vitrea*. All these soft parts are enclosed in a funnel-shaped cavity, called an Orbit, which is formed by seven bones, namely, the *os frontis*, *os sphenoidale*, *os ethmoides*, *os maxillare*, *os malæ*, *os unguis*, and *os palati*. [vide *Eye*]

The *Ear* is divided into the external and internal.

Auricula, the External Ear, consists of a large cartilage that is divided into two portions, namely, the *pinna*, which is large and solid, and the *lobus*, or Lobe, which is soft and small, and forms the lower part. The external ear contains besides several eminences, namely, the *helix*, *anthelix*, *tragus*, and *antitragus*; and, also, some depressions, as the *fossa navicularis* or *scapha*, the *concha*, and the *meatus*.

The *Internal Ear* consists of, *meatus auditorius internus*, the Internal Auditory Passage; *membrana tympani*, the membrane which separates the external from the internal parts of the ear; *tympanum*, the Drum or Barrel of the ear; and the Labyrinth, which consists of three portions, namely, *cochlea*, the anterior; *vestibulum*, the middle; and the semicircular canals. [vide *Ear*]

The *nose* consists, *externally*, of the Root; the Arch; Back or Spine, called the *spina nasi*; the Sides of the arch; the Tip of the nose; the *alæ* or *pinnæ*, which are the Sides of the nostrils; the *nares*, or External Nostrils.

The *internal parts of the nose* are, the Internal Nares, which consist of the *septum narium*; the *subseptum*, or pillar of fat under the *septum narium*; the Convolutions; the *conchæ superiores* and *inferiores*; the *sinus maxillares*, and *sinus sphenoidales*; the *ductus lachrymalis*; the *ductus palatini*, and the *membrana pituitaria*, which lines the whole cavity of the nostrils. [vide *Nose*]

The *mouth* consists, *externally*, of *labia*, the Lips, which are upper and lower, and composed of a border or edge, and of commissures or angles; *fossula*, the depression which runs from the *septum narium* to the edge of the upper lip; *Cheeks*, the upper prominent part of which is called the *mala*; *Chin*, the anterior protuberance by which the lower part of the face is terminated.

The *internal parts of the mouth* are *palatum*, the Palate, or roof of the mouth; *septum palati*, or *velum palati*, the soft part of the palate, which forms two arches; *uvula*, the conical fleshy substance at the root of the tongue; *amygdalæ* or *tonsillæ*, the Tonsils, two glandular substances, one on each side the basis of the tongue; *gingivæ*, the Gums, which contain the teeth; *maxillæ*, the Jaws, which are composed of bones, and are either upper or lower; the *fræna*, of the lips; *lingua*, the Tongue, which consists of an Apex, a Root or Basis, and a Frænum. [vide *Mouth*]

Internal Parts of the Head.

The internal parts of the head are contained within an oval cavity, called the *cranium* or Skull, which is formed of eight bones. [vide *Bones*, and Pl. 8, fig. 1] The contents of the Skull are comprehended under the general name of *cerebrum*, the Brain, which is immediately surrounded by two membranes, called by the Greeks μήνιγγες, or, by others, *matres*, i. e. the *pia mater* and the *dura mater*, between which lies a third membrane, called the *tunica arachnoidea*. The duplicatures or circumvolutions of these membranes are called *septa*, the upper of which has the name of the *falx*. The cerebrum consists of three portions, namely, the *cerebrum*, or Brain, properly so called; the *cerebellum*, or Little Brain; and the *medulla oblongata*; to which is added sometimes a fourth, namely, the *medulla spinalis*, which fills the great canal of the *spina dorsi*.

The *cerebrum* is divided into two lateral portions, called *hemispheres*, the extremities of which are termed *lobes*. Its substance is of two kinds, namely, the outer, that is cortical, and is called the *cortex*; and the inner, which is called the *substantia medullaris* or *substantia alba*.

The cavities of the brain, called *ventricles*, are four in number, and separated by a membrane called the *septum lucidum*. In each of these is the *choroid plexus*, formed of blood-vessels. There is also another small cavity or *fossula*, called the *infundibulum*, the superior opening of which is called the *foramen commune anterius*. The principal prominences are the *corpus callosum*, the lower side of which forms a sort of vault called the *fornix*; the *corpora striata*, two striated prominences; *thalami nervorum opticorum*; *corpora quadragemina*, four medullary projections, originally called *nates* and *testes*; the *pineal gland*, a cerebrine tubercle on the nates, and the *crura cerebri*, two medullary columns proceeding from the basis of the brain to the medulla oblongata. To these may be added the *glandula pituitaria*, a small spongy body in the sella sphenoidalis.

On the *cerebellum* are observed four eminences, called *appendices vermiformes*; a fourth ventricle; a valve, called the *valvula magna cerebri*; lamina or ramifications, called *arbor vitæ*, the trunks of which are termed *pedunculi cerebelli*.

The *medulla oblongata* is a medullary continuation of the cerebrum and cerebellum, having anterior branches, called *brachia*, and posterior, called *crura medullæ*. Its transverse process is called *processus annularis*. The extremity of the medulla is called the *cauda*; its tubercles, *corpora olivaria et pyramidalia*; to which may be added the *medullary papillæ* that are productions of the *infundibulum*.

The lower part of the *medulla spinalis* is called *caudina equina*; but, in other particulars, it resembles the parts before described. From the cerebrum, and the other parts of the brain, arise the nerves which are dispersed through the body. [vide *Nerves*, and Pl. 8, fig. 2]

THE NECK.

The neck may be added either to the head, to the thorax, or to both. The fore part is called the Throat, and the hind part the Nape. The parts of the throat are the *fauces*, a cavity behind the tongue; *larynx*, which consists of five cartilages, a part of the *trachea*; *pharynx*, a muscular bag, which receives the masticated food; *œsophagus*, or *gula*, the Throat, a membranous and muscular tube.

The salival glands, which are three pair, namely, the *glandulæ parotides*, *maxillares*, and *sublinguales*, so called from their situation. [vide *Neck*]

THE TRUNK.

The Trunk consists of *spina*, the Spine; *thorax*, the Chest; and *abdomen*, the Belly.

The Spine.

The spine is a bony column, consisting of a chain of *bones*, called *vertebræ*, which are divided into true or false. [vide *Vertebræ*, *Bones*, and Pl. 7, fig. 1 and 2]

ANATOMY.

The Thorax.

The fore part of the thorax is the Breast, the hind part the Back; the lateral part the Sides. These are severally formed by *sternum*, the Breast-Bone; *vertebræ dorsi*, the Dorsal Vertebræ; and *costæ*, the Ribs. [vide *Bones*, &c.] The thorax has externally the *mammæ*, or Breasts, in the middle of which is the *papilla*, or Nipple, surrounded by a disc, called the *areola;* within are the *tubuli lactiferi*, or Lactiferous Ducts. The cavity of the thorax contains the *pleura*, a membrane with which it is lined; *mediastinum*, a membranous septum; *pulmones* the lungs; *cor*, the Heart, and *pericardium*, the Heartpurse, a membranous bag, within which it is enclosed. The largest part of the heart is called the Base, the narrower extremity the Apex. It is divided by a membrane called the *septum medium* or *septum cordis*, into two cavities, called *ventriculi*, ventricles, having several eminences or inequalities, called *fossulæ, thymus gland, ductus thoracicus*, and the *ductus lacteus*. [vide *Thorax*]

The Abdomen.

The abdomen is divided into four regions, three of which are anterior, and one posterior.—The *anterior regions*, are the *epigastric*, or upper region, which is divided into the *epigastrium*, or middle, and the *hypochondria*, or lateral parts; the *umbilical*, or middle region, consisting of the *regio umbilicalis*, or Navel, in the middle, and the *ilia*, or Flanks, on the sides; the *hypogastric*, or lower region, which is divided into the *pubis*, or middle part, and the *inguina*, or Groins, on each side.—The posterior region is the *regio lumbaris*, or Loins.

The cavity of the abdomen is separated from that of the thorax by the muscular diaphragm, called the Midriff. Its *viscera*, or contents, are enclosed in a membrane, called the *peritonæum*, and are as follow: namely, the —*Ventriculus*, the Stomach which has two orifices, namely, the *cardia*, which is the upper; and the *pylorus*, which is the lower. It is composed of three coats, namely, the outermost, which is *membranous;* the middle, which is *muscular;* and the inner, which is *nervous*, and covered with vessels. To these has been added a fourth, called *villous*. The stomach performs the office of *digestion*, which is now generally supposed to be effected by the *saccus gastricus*, or Gastric Juice, which flows from the *tunica nervosa*, aided by the continual contraction and relaxation of the muscular tunic, which is called the *peristaltic motion*.—The *intestines* are a long pipe or canal, which, by its convolutions, forms six portions, three small and three large, namely, the *duodenum, jejunum, ileum, cæcum, colon,* and *rectum*. The small intestines have valves, or folds, called *valvulæ conniventes;* the large intestines have fatty appendages, called *appendiculæ epiploicæ*. The membranes belonging to the intestines are the Mesentery, Mesocolon, and the *omentum*, or *epiploon*, by which they are kept in their places and preserved from injuries, whilst by their peristaltic motion they expel the *fæces* collected in them. —*Hepar*, the liver, is divided into two lobes, and is suspended in the body by means of ligaments, which connect it with the diaphragm, &c. It is composed of small vessels, or the ramifications of vessels, called *folliculi*, or *pori biliarii*, because in them is secreted the humour called the Bile. The ducts of the liver are the *ductus hepaticus;* the *ductus cysticus;* and the *ductus chelodochus*, which is composed of the two former. On the hollow side of the liver lies the *vesicula fellis*, or the Gall-Bladder.—*Pancreas*, a glandular viscus, consists of innumerable small glands that form one duct, called *ductus pancreaticus*, the Pancreatic Duct; its office is to secrete a juice distinguished by the name of the *succus pancreaticus*, the Pancreatic Juice.—*Lien*, the Spleen, is connected with the stomach by its blood vessels, called *vasa brevia*.—*Renes*, the Kidneys, are composed of three substances, namely, the external, which is cortical; the middle, which is tubular; and an inner substance, which is medullary. They have also a peculiar membrane, called the *membrana propria*, and an excretory duct, called the *ureter*, the origin of which, expanded into the form of a funnel, is called the *pelvis*.—*Urinaria vesica*, the Urinary Bladder, a fleshy membranous pouch, is divided into the Body, the Fundus, or upper part, and the Neck, which is the lower part, that is, contracted by the *sphincter* muscle.

The lower part of the Abdomen is, in the skeleton, called the *pelvis*, which is formed by the *ossa ilia* and *ischia*, the *os sacrum*, the *os coccygis*, and the *ossa pubis*, and is terminated anteriorly by the *pudenda*, and posteriorly by the *clunes*, or Buttocks. [vide *Bones* and Pl. 8, fig. 3] The space between the *anus* and *pudenda* is called the *perinæum*.

The *pudenda*, or organs of generation, are distinguished into the male and female. The male organs are the *testes, vesiculæ seminales, prostatæ,* and *penis*.—The *testes* are composed of many minute vessels, convoluted into different heaps, by means of which is formed a body called the *epididymis*. They are enclosed in three integuments, or coats, namely, the *scrotum*, common to both, the *tunica vaginalis*, and the *tunica albuginea;* besides a muscular lining of the *scrotum*, called the *dartos*, by which it is corrugated. The principal vessels are the *vasa præparantia*, commonly called the spermatic Chord, and the *vasa deferentia*. The most important muscle is the *cremaster*.—*Vesiculæ seminales* are two in number, on each side the bladder, which serve as receptacles for the seed.—*Prostatæ*, or *corpus glandulosum*, a conglomerate gland, situated at the neck of the bladder.—The *penis* is composed of two spongy substances, called *corpora cavernosa*, and covered with a particular integument, called the *præputium*. The extremity of the penis is the *glans*, or *balanus*, and the ligament by which it is tied to the glans is the *frænum*. The canal or urinary passage of the penis is the *urethra*, in which is a longitudinal orifice, called the *meatus urinarius*.

The female organs of generation are external or internal. The external are the *vulva, mons veneris, labia, nymphæ*, and *clytoris*, the branches of which are called the *crura*. —The internal parts are the *vagina*, or neck of the womb, the *hymen*, and the *carunculæ myrtiformes*, formed from the hymen and the *uterus* or Womb.

The *uterus* is divided into three parts, namely, the *fundus*, or upper part; the Body, and the *cervix*, or lower part, the entrance into which is called the *os uteri*. It is tied by two sorts of ligaments, called *ligamenta lata* and *ligamenta rotunda*, i. e. two broad and two round. To one end of the *ligamenta lata* are tied the *ovaria* or *testes* in females: along the other end run the *tubæ Fallopianæ*. The vessels of the uterus are subject to a periodical discharge, which is called *menstruation*, and that which is discharged the *menses*. The formation of the parts of an animal in the womb constitutes a *gravid uterus*. The commencement of this process is called *conception* or *impregnation;* and that which follows is *gestation* till the time of delivery, when the young is brought forth. The first rudiments of the animal are called the *embryo*, which, with the *umbilical chord* and *membranes*, constitute the *ovum*. When the parts of the embryo are to be distinguished from one another, it is termed the *fœtus*. The membranes of the ovum and fœtus are the *amnios*, which is true or false, and the *chorion*. These mem-

ANATOMY.

branes contain a fluid, called the *liquor amnii*, in which the embryo floats; and from the flocculent vessels of the amnion is formed the vascular substance called the *placenta*. The placenta and membranes which come away after the birth of the child are known by the name of *secundines*, or *after-birth*.

The Extremities.

The extremities are superior and inferior. The superior extremities consist of *summitas humeri*, the Shoulder; *brachium*, the Arm; and *manus*, the Hand.—The *shoulder* is composed of *clavicula*, the Collar Bone; *scapula*, the Shoulder Blade; and *axilla*, the Armpit.—The arm is composed of the *os humeri*, *ulna*, and *radius*, the two last of which make what is called the Fore-arm, in which anteriorly is the bend of the arm; and posteriorly, *angulus cubiti*, the elbow.—The hand consists of the *carpus*, or the Wrist; *metacarpus* and *digiti manus*, or Fingers; *dorsum manus*, the Back of the hand; and *vola*, the Palm.

The inferior extremities consist of *coxa* or *regio ischiadica*, the Hip; *femur*, the Thigh; *tibia*, the Leg; and *pes*, the Foot. The thigh is composed of the *os femoris*, the Thigh Bone.—The leg is composed of the *genu*, the knee; *tibia*, *fibula*, *pate'la*, or Knee-Pan; *poples*, the Ham; *cavum poplitis*, the Hollow of the Thigh; *sura*, the Calf; and *malleolus*, the Ankle.—The foot consists of *tarsus*, the Instep; *metatarsus*, or *dorsum*, the Back; *digiti pedis*, the Toes; and *planta*, the Sole. [vide *Bones* and Plate I.]

Explanation of the Plates.

Plate No. I. (9)

Fig. 1.—1. Os Frontis. 2. Sutura coronalis. 3. Os Verticis. 4. Sutura squamosa. 5. Os Temporis. 6. Processus mamillaris. 7. Os Mala. 8. Ossa Nasi. 9. Ossa Maxillaris superiora. 10. Os Maxillæ inferioris. 11. Vertebræ Colli. 12. Vertebræ Lumborum. 13. Os Sacrum. 14. Sternum. 15. Scapula. 16. Costæ veræ. 17. Costæ nothæ. 18. Claviculæ. 19. Processus coracoideus. 20. Os Humeri. 21. Ulna. 22. Radius. 23. Os Ilium. 24. Crista Ossis Ilii. 25. Ischium. 26. Os Pubis. 27. Foramen magnum. 28. Os Femoris. 29. Trochanter major. 30. Trochanter minor. 31. Patella. 32. Tibia. 33. Fibula. 34. Talus. 35. Os Calcaneum. 36. Ossa Tarsi.

Fig. 2.—1. Os parietale. 2. Sutura sagittalis. 3. Sutura lambdoidalis. 4. Os occipitis. 5. Sutura squamosa. 6. Maxilla inferior. 7. Vertebræ Colli. 8. Vertebræ Dorsi. 9. Vertebræ Lumborum. 10. Os Sacrum. 11. Os Occygis. 12. Clavicula. 13. Scapula. 14. Spina Scapulæ. 15. Acromion. 16. Os Humeri. 17. Ulna. 18. Radius. 19. Ossa Carpi. 20. Ossa Metacarpi. 21. Ossa Digitorum. 22. Ilium. 23. Ischium. 24. Os Femoris. 25. Collum Ossis Femoris. 26. Trochanter major. 27. Trochanter minor. 28. Condylus exterior Ossis Femoris. 29. Condylus interior Ossis Femoris. 30. Tibia. 31. Fibula. 32. Os Calcaneum. 33. Ossa Tarsi. 34. Ossa Metatarsi.

Fig. 3.—1. Aorta A. Valvulæ semilunares. 2. Arteria coronaria magna. 3. Ligamentum arteriosum. 4. Arteriæ subclaviæ. 5. Arteriæ carotides. 6. Arteriæ vertebrales. 7. Arteriæ temporales. 8. Arteriæ occipitales. 9. Contorsiones Carotidis; C, Glandula pituitaria; D, Arteriæ ophthalmicæ. 10. Contorsiones vertebrales. 11. Ramificationes arteriæ. 12. Arteriæ mammariæ. 13. Arteriæ cubitales. 14. Arteria Aorta descendens. 15. Arteria bronchialis. 16. Arteriæ intercostales. 17. Arteria cæliaca. 18. Arteriæ hepaticæ. 19. Arteria cystica. 20. Arteria coronaria inferioris stomachi. 21. Arteria pylorica. 22. Arteria epiploica. 23. Arteria coronaria superioris stomachi. 24. Arteriæ phrenicæ. 25. Arteria splenica. 26. Arteria mesenterica superior. 27. Arteria mesenterica inferior. 28. Arteriæ emulgentes. 29. Arteriæ vertebrales lumborum. 30. Arteriæ spermaticæ. 31. Arteria sacra. 32. Arteriæ iliacæ. 33. Arteriæ externæ. 34. Arteriæ internæ. 35. Arteriæ umbilicales. 36. Arteriæ epigastricæ. 37. Arteriæ Penis. 38. Arteriæ crurales.

Fig. 4.—1. Frontales. 2. Orbicularis Palpebræ. 3. Zygomaticus major. 4. Nasales Labri superioris. 5. Depressor Labri inferioris. 6. Depressor anguli Oris. 7. Platisma myoides. 8. Pectoralis. 9. Latissimus Dorsi. 10. Serratus magnus. 11. Externus obliquus abdominis. 12. Rectus abdominis. 13. Pyramidales. 14. Linea alba. 15. Gracilis. 16. Adductor longus tricipitis Femoris. 17. Pectineus. 18. Psoas magnus. 19. Iliacus internus. 20. Sartorius. 21. Glutæus medius. 22. Fascialis. 23. Vastus externus. 24. Rectus Femoris. 25. Vastus internus. 26. Pars bicipitis. 27. Pars Gastrocnemii. 28. Soleus. 29. Peroneus longus. 30. Extensor longus digiti Pedis. 31. Tibialis anticus. 32. Deltoides. 33. Triceps. 34. Biceps. 35. Brachiæus externus. 36. Supinator longus. 37. Pronator rotundi Radii. 38. Radialis internus. 39. Palmaris longus. 40. Sublimis. 41. Ulnaris internus. 42. Abductor longus Pollicis. 43. Radialis externus longus.

Fig. 5.—1. Occipitalis. 2. Attollens Auricularis. 3. Orbiculares Palpebrarum. 4. Latissimus Colli. 5. Mastoidæus. 6. Trapezius. 7. Deltoides. 8. Biceps. 9. Brachialis internus. 10. Triceps. 11. Supinator longus. 12. Radialis internus. 13. Radialis externus longior. 14. Radialis externus brevior. 15. Ulnaris externus. 16. Abductor Pollicis longus Manus. 17. Infraspinatus. 18. Teres minor. 19. Teres major. 20. Latissimus Dorsi. 21. Pectoralis. 22. Serratus magnus. 23. Obliquus externus Abdominis. 24. Tensor vaginæ Femoris. 25. Glutæus medius. 26. Glutæus magnus. 27. Semitendinosus. 28. Biceps Cruris. 29. Vastus externus. 30. Rectus Cruris. 31. Gastrocnemius. 32. Soleus. 33. Tendo Achilles. 34. Peroneus longus. 35. Peroneus brevis. 36. Extensor longus digiti Pedis. 37. Tibialis anticus. 38. Ligamentum a patella ad libram pertinens. 39. Vastus internus. 40. Sartorius. 41. Triceps pars quæ longus vocatur. 42. Triceps pars quæ brachialis vocatur. 43. Brachialis externus. 44. Biceps Brachii. 45. Pronator teres. 46. Palmaris longus. 47. Sublimis. 48. Ulnaris internus. 49. Ulnaris externus.

Fig. 6.—1. Temporalis. 2. Mastoidæus. 3. Trapezius. 4. Deltoides. 5. Brachiæus. 6. Gemellus. 7. Palmaris longus. 8. Sublimis. 9. Ulnaris externus. 10. Radialis externus longior. 11. Extensor communis digitorum. 12. Infra spinatus. 13. Latissimus Dorsi. 14. Obliquus externus Abdominis. 15. Glutæus medius. 16. Glutæus major. 17. Gracilis. 18. Adductor magnus Femoris. 19. Semitendinosus. 20. Biceps Cruris. 21. Vastus externus. 22. Gastrocnemius. 23. Soleus. 24. Tendo Achillis.

Plate No. II. (10)

Fig. 1.—1. Sutura coronalis. 2. Sutura sagittalis. 3. Sutura lambdoidalis. 4. Sutura squamosa. 5. Sutura transversalis. 6. Os Frontis. 7. Os Bregmatis. 8. Os Occipitis. 9. Os Temporis. 10. Processus mastoideus. 11. Meatus auditorius. 12. Processus styliformis. 13. Processus jugalis. 14. Os sphenoides. 15. Os Malæ. 16. Os Nasi. 17. Os Unguis. 18. Os plenum.

19. Ductus ad nasum. 20. Maxilla superior. 21. Foramen maxillæ superiori. 22. Maxilla inferior. 23. Processus coronalis. 24. Processus condyloides. 25. Foramen. 26. Dentes incisorii. 27. Dentes canini. 28. Dentes molares. 29. Os Triquetium. 30. Foramen.

Fig. 2.—1. Cerebrum. 2. Cerebellum. 3. Corpus pyramidale. 4. Annular Protuberance. 5. Processus mamillaris. 6. Optic Nerves. 7. Motores Oculorum. 8. The fourth pair of Nerves. 9. The fifth pair spreading into three branches. 10. The sixth pair. 11. The seventh pair. 12. The eighth pair. 13. The recurrent nerves joined with the eighth pair. 14. The recurrent nerves after leaving the eighth pair. 15. The trunks of the eighth pair. 16. Intercostal nerves. 17. Phrenic nerves. 18. Branches of nerves going to the spermatic vessels, &c. 19. Branches of the ninth pair. 20. The sciatic and crural nerves. 21. The brachial nerves; a communication between the dorsal and intercostal nerves.

Fig. 3.—1. The Larynx. 2. The internal jugular vein. 3. The subclavian vein. 4. The vena cava descendens. 5. The right auricle of the heart. 6. The right ventricle. 7. Part of the left ventricle. 8. The Aorta descendens. 9. The Arteria pulmonalis. 10. The right lobe of the Lungs, part of which is cut off to show the Gall-bladder and vessels. 11. The left lobe of the lungs. 12. The Diaphragm. 13. The Liver. 14. The ligamentum rotundum. 15. The Gall-bladder. 16. The Stomach pressed by the liver towards the left side. 17. The small intestines. 18. The Spleen.

Fig. 4.—1. The right ventricle of the Fœtus distended by wax. 2. The right auricle. 3. The left ventricle. 4. Branches of the pulmonary veins of the right lobe of the lungs. 5. Arteries of the left lobe of the lungs. 6. The vena cava descendens. 7. The Aorta ascendens. 8. The Arteria pulmonalis. 9. The Ductus arteriosus.

Fig. 5.—1. The parenchymous substance of the Pancreas laid open. 2. The Pancreatic Duct. 3. Branches of the Pancreatic Duct. 4. The Bile Duct joining the Pancreatic Duct. 5. The Duodenum opened. 6. The orifices of the Bile and Pancreatic Ducts.

Fig. 6.—1. The Kidney divested of its external coat. 2. A kidney in its natural state. 3. The Vena Cava. 4. The Aorta. 5. The Renal Glands with their vessels. 6. The Emulgent vessels. 7. The Ureters. 8. The Urinary Bladder. 9. The neck of the Bladder. 10. The Testes. 11. The process of the Peritonæum. 12. The Cremaster muscle cut off. 13. The Spermatic vessels. 14. The Epididymis. 15. The Vasa Deferentia. 16. The corpus glandosum. 17. The two bodies which compose the Penis. 18. The Prepuce. 19. The Glans Penis. 20. The insertion of the spermatic veins into the emulgent. 21. Vesiculæ seminales. 22. The insertion of the ureters. 23. Veins which run into the back of the Penis. 24. Arteries which arise on each side.

Fig. 7.—The Pulmonary Artery.

Fig. 8.—1. The upper orifice of the Stomach. 2. The Stomach. 3. The Pylorus. 4. Arteries. 5. Veins which accompany the arteries. 6. The Duodenum. 7. The Small Intestines. 8. The valve in the Colon. 9. The Appendiculum of the Cæcum. 10. The Colon. 11. The Rectum. 12. The Constrictor of the Anus. 13. The Elevatores Ani. 14. The Anus.

The principal Writers on Anatomy in chronological Succession.

Hippocratis " Opera;" *Aristoteles* " De Partibus Animalium," &c.; *Aretæus* " De Causis et Signis Morborum acutorum," &c.; *Rufus Ephesius* " De Appellationibus Partium humani Corporis;" *Galen* " De Administratione Anatomiæ," " De Usu Partium," &c.; *Oribasii* " Medicæ Collectiones;" *Berengarii Carpensis* " Isagoge," &c.; *Vassæi Catalaunensis* " In Anatomen Corporis humani Tabulæ quatuor;" *Vesalius* " De Re Anatomica," &c.; *Fallopii* " Observationes Anatomicæ," &c.; *Eustachii* " Opuscula Anatomica," " Tabulæ Anatomicæ," &c.; *Caspari Bauhini* " Institutiones Anatomicæ," &c.; *Fabricii* " De Aqua pendente," " Opera Anatomica," &c.; *Riolani* " Schola Anatomica," &c.; *Harvey* " Exercitatio Anatomica de Motu Cordis et Sanguinis in Animalibus," &c.; *Albini* " Tabulæ Anatomicæ," &c.; *Chesselden's* " Anatomy of the Human Body;" *Heister's* " Compendium Anatomicum," &c.; *Highmore's* " Corporis humani Disquisitio Anatomica," &c.; *Hoffmanni* " Dissertationes Anatomico-physiologicæ," &c.; *Keil's* " Anatomy of the human Body abridged;" *Malpighii* " Observationes Anatomicæ," &c.; *Munro's* " Osteology;" *Piquet's* " Experimenta nova Anatomica," &c.; *Swammerdam's* " Miraculum Naturæ," &c.; *Winslow's* " Anatomique de la Structure du Corps humain," &c.

A'NATON (*Min.*) the same as Anatron.

ANATRE'SIS (*Anat.*) ἀνάτρησις, from ἀνὰ, and τρέω, *perforo;* trepanning.

ANA'TRIS (*Chem.*) mercury.

ANA'TRON (*Min.*) 1. The same as Natron. 2. The spume or gall of glass, which bubbles on the surface while in the furnace. 3. The same as *Terra Saracenica.* 4. The same as Anathron.

ANATRO'PE (*Med.*) ἀνατροπὴ, from ἀνατρέπω, to subvert; a relaxation of the stomach.

ANA'TTO (*Chem.*) vide *Anata.*

ANA'TUM (*Nat.*) *ovorum testa.*

ANA'UDIA (*Med.*) the same as *Catalepsis.*

ANA'UDOS (*Med.*) ἄναυδος, from α, priv. and αὐδὴ, voice, speechless; an epithet for one who has lost his speech, in distinction from ἄφωνος, who has lost his voice. *Gal. Exeg. Vocab. Hippocrat.; Cels. de Re Med.* l. 5; *Cœl. Aurelian de Morb. Chron.* l. 2, c. 1; *Alex. Trall.* l. 1, c. 2; *Gorr. Defin. Med.*

ANAVI'NGA (*Bot.*) An evergreen that grows in Malabar, and in Cochin China.

ANAXAGO'RIA (*Ant.*) Ἀναξαγόρια, a festival observed at Lampsacus in honour of Anaxagoras. *Diogen. Laert. in Anax.*

ANAXY'RIDES (*Ant.*) ἀναξυρίδες, a sort of breeches or drawers worn by the Scythians, according to Hippocrates, from ἀνασύρω, to draw up. *Hippocrat. de Aer.; Poll. Onomast.* l. 7, c. 13, segm. 59, &c.

A'NBAR (*Min.*) vide *Ambra.*

ANBLA'TUM (*Bot.*) the name for a species of plant; the *Lathrea anblatum* of Linnæus.

A'NCEPS (*Med.*) doubtful as to the nature of the disease or effects of the medicine.

ANCEPS (*Bot.*) an epithet for a stem and a leaf which has both its edges sharp.

A'NCESTOR (*Law*) *antecessor*, a natural person, who has gone before in a family, in distinction from a predecessor, who belongs to a body politic. *Co. Lit.* 78, b.

ANCE'STREL (*Law.*) relating or belonging to one's ancestors, as ancestral homage.

A'NCHOR (*Ant.*) vide *Anchora.*

ANCHOR (*Mar.*) the instrument which holds a ship in its place, consists of four principal parts; namely, the Ring, the Stock, the Shank, and the Arms.—The *ring* (*a*) is the upper part, to which the cable is attached; and the square part (*b*), through which a hole is punched to receive the ring, is called the *square*.—The *stock* (*c*) is the large beam, which is fixed to the square.—The *shank* or *beam* (*d*) is the longest part of the anchor.—The two *arms* (*ff*) branch from the shank, and run into the ground;

they consist of *palms* or *flooks* (g g), which are broad plates of a triangular form at nearly the extremity of the arm; the broad part is called the *blade*, and the extreme sharp point the *bill*.—The *throat* of the arm (h h) is the angular point near the shank.—The *trend* (e) is a distance marked on the shank, which is equal to that between the throat of one arm and its bill.—The *crown* is that part where the arms are joined to the shank. The flatted surface at the lower extremity of the shank is called the *Scarf*, which is formed with a *shoulder* on each side for the purpose of *shutting on*, i. e. joining the arms to the shanks. The *small round* is the diameter of the shank where it is the smallest, which is near the stock.

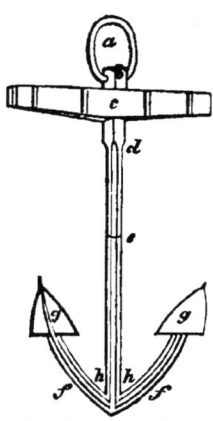

The different sorts of anchors are the—*Sheet anchor*, in French *maitresse ancre*, the largest and strongest sort, which is never used but in the last extremity.—*Best bower anchor*, in French *la seconde ancre*, and *small bower*, in French *ancre d'affourche*. These two last are smaller than the rest, and carried on the bows, whence they take their name.—*Stream anchor*, less than the preceding, and the *kedge anchor*, the smallest of all.—*Pilot's anchor*, betwixt the two last in size, and used by the pilots for dropping a vessel in a stream.—*Flood anchor*, for a ship riding during flood tide.—*Ebb anchor*, for a ship riding during the ebb tide.—*Sea anchor*, in French *ancre du large*, which lies towards the offing.—*Shore anchor*, in French *ancre de terre*, which is between the ship and the shore.—*Floating anchor*, in French *ancre flottante*, which is sunk below the swell of the sea where there is no other anchorage.

The movements and situations of the *anchor* are as follow: "*Anchor* comes home," when it is dislodged from its bed.—"*Anchor* drags," when it makes an effort to come home.—"*Anchor* is foul," when it gets entangled with another anchor, and the like.—"*Anchor* is a cock-bill," when suspended from the cat-head ready to let go.—"*Anchor* is a-peek," when drawn so tight as to bring the ship over it.—"*Anchor* is a-trip, or a-weigh," when just drawn out of the ground.—"To lie at *anchor*," the situation of a ship which rides by her anchor.—"To back the *anchor*," in French *empenneller l'ancre*, to lay down a small anchor a-head of the large one, by which the ship rides.—"To cat the *anchor*," in French *caponer l'ancre*, to draw the anchor perpendicularly up to the cat-head by a tackle called a cat.—"To fish the *anchor*," in French *traverser l'ancre*, to draw up the flooks of a ship's anchor towards the top of the bow by a machine called a fish.—"To steer the ship to her *anchor*," in French *gouverner l'ancre*, to steer the ship's-head to the place where the anchor lies when they are heaving the cable into the ship.—"To sweep the *anchor*," in French *draguer l'ancre*, to drag for an anchor that has been lost.—"To shoe the *anchor*," in French *couvrir les pattes de l'ancre*, to cover the flooks with a broad triangular piece of plank.—"To weigh the *anchor*," in French *lever l'ancre*, to heave the anchor out of the ground by its cable; sometimes it is performed by mechanical powers fixed in the long boat.

ANCHOR (*Her.*) an emblem of hope, was borne in coat armour, most commonly in pale, as in the annexed figure. He beareth "*gules*, an anchor in pale *argent*, the timber or cross piece thereof *or*; name Goodrood."

ANCHOR (*Com.*) a measure of brandy containing ten gallons; the same as *anker*.

ANCHOR (*Archit.*) a carving somewhat resembling an anchor.

A'NCHORA (*Ant.*) ἄγχυρα, from ἀγκύλος, crooked anchor; a naval instrument, so called from its curved form. Its invention is of such antiquity as to be attributed to Midas, and, according to some, to Anacharsis. At first they were made of stone or wood, with lead affixed to them, but afterwards of iron, and in shape very similar to what is now in use, except that it wanted the stock, as may be seen from the annexed figure, taken from a marble. The anchor is most frequently to be found on the coins of the Seleucidæ, by whom it was used, in consequence of a prediction, to Seleucus, that he should reign in that place where he dug up an anchor, which happened in Babylon. The arms of the anchors were called ὀδόντες, *dentes*, teeth, whence the name of ὀδές, *dens*, was substituted for an anchor among the Greek and Latin poets. Some anchors which had but one arm were called ἑτερόστομοι, and those with two ἀμφίστομοι. The anchor which was the biggest, and used only on particular occasions, was called ἄγκυρα ἱερά, *anchora sacra*, whence the proverb *sacram anchoram solvere*, i. e. to be driven to one's last shifts. *Diodor.* l. 5; *Strab.* l. 10; *Plin.* l. 8, c. 56; *Poll. Onom.* l. 1, c. 9; *Polyæn.* l. 3, c. 9; *Athen.* l. 5; *Arrian. in Perip.*; *Suidas. in Voc.* ζεύγμα.; *Leo. Tact.* c. 20, § 140; *Gyrald. de Navigat.* c. 12; *Sheff. de Re Naval*, &c.

A'NCHORAGE (*Mar.*) 1. The ground fit to hold the Anchor. 2. A duty taken of ships for the use of the haven, where they cast anchor. 3. The ground in port and haven belonging to the king; no person can let an anchor fall thereon without paying therefor to the king's officers. 4. The set of anchors belonging to a ship.

ANCHORA'LIS *processus* (*Anat.*) the same as the *Processus coracoides*.

A'NCHORED (*Her.*) or *Ancred*, a cross, the four extremities of which resemble the flooks of an anchor.

A'NCHORET (*Ecc.*) a hermit. [vide *Anachoreta*.]

A'NCHOR-GROUND (*Mar.*) ground fit for holding the anchor.

A'NCHORING (*Mar.*) the process of fixing a ship by her anchor.

A'NCHOR-STOCK (*Mar.*) a method of working planks so that they should appear in the shape of an anchor stock.

A'NCHOVY (*Ich.*) the ἐγκρασίχολος of Aristotle, *Clupea encrasicolus* of Linnæus; a small fish, caught in great quantities in the Mediterranean, having a slender body, but thicker in proportion than the herring. It is brought over pickled, and used in sauces. *Aristot. Hist. Anim.* l. 6, c. 15; *Athen.* l. 7, c. 8; *Rondelet. & Gessn. de Piscib.*; *Will. Ichthiol.*

ANCHOVY *pear* (*Bot.*) the fruit of a tree in the West Indies, called by Linnæus the *Grias cauliflora*. It is about the size of an alligator's egg, and very similar in shape, of a brown colour, and commonly used as a pickle.

ANCHU'SA (*Bot.*) Alkanet, in Greek ἄγχουσα; a plant so called from its power of producing suffocation, according to Nicander, Dioscorides, Pliny, and Galen. The root was reckoned astringent, and good for ambustions and the bites of venomous serpents. According to Galen, it was used as a cosmetic, and is at present employed in dying, being covered with a red bark, which gives a red dye or tincture to any infusion. *Theophrast. Hist. Plant.* l. 7, c. 9; *Dioscor.* l. 4, c. 23; *Plin.* l. 22, c. 21, &c.; *Gal. de Simpl.* l. 6; *Orib. Med. Coll.* l. 15; *Aet. Tetrab.* 1, serm. 1; *Paul Æginet.* l. 7, c. 3; *Act. de Meth. Med.* l. 6, c. 8.

ANCHUSA, *in the Linnean system*, a genus of plants, Class

5 *Pentandria*, Order 1 *Monogynia*, in English Alkanet, or Bugloss.

Generic Characters. CAL. *perianth* five-parted.—COR. monopetalous; *tube* cylindrical; *limb* semiquinquefid.—STAM. *filaments* very short; *anthers* oblong.—PIST. *germs* four; *style* filiform; *stigma* obtuse.—PER. none; *seeds* four.

Species. The species are perennials, as the—*Anchusa officinalis*, seu *Buglossum sylvestre*, officinal or garden Alkanet, or Bugloss, a native of Britain.—*Anchusa tinctoria*, *Buglossum tinctorium*, seu *Lithospermum villosum*, dyer's Alkanet, native of Montpellier.—*Anchusa sempervivens*, evergreen Alkanet, native of Britain, &c. *J. Bauh. Hist. Plant.*; *C. Bauh. Pin. Theat.*; *Ger. Herb.*; *Park. Theat. Botan.*; *Raii Hist. Plant.*; *Tourn. Inst. Herb.*; *Boerh. Ind. Plant.*; *Linn. Spec. Plant.*

ANCHUSA, a name for several species, as the—*Barleria longifolia*; the *Borago Indica* and *Zeylanica*; the *Lithospermum Orientale*, *purpureum et cœruleum*; the *Myosotis lappilla* and *spinocarpos*; the *Onosma cinioides*, and the *Pulmonaria Sibirica* of Linnæus. Bauhin, Gerard, Rai, &c.

A'NCHYLE (*Med.*) the same as *Anchylosis.*

ANCHYLO'MERIS (*Med.*) a concretion of the soft parts.

A'NCHYLOPS (*Med.*) the same as *Ægilops.*

ANCHYLO'SIS (*Med.*) from ἀγκύλος, crooked; a stiff joint, a species of contraction.

ANCHY'NOPES (*Bot.*) the same as *Phœnix.*

ANCHYROI'DES (*Anat.*) the same as *Caracoides.*

A'NCI (*Med.*) vide *Galiancon.*

A'NCIENT (*Mil.*) a term used formerly to express the grand ensign or standard of an army; also the standard bearer.

ANCIENT *demesne* (*Law*) a tenure by which all the manors belonging to the crown in the days of St. Edward and William the Conqueror were held. The latter caused the number and names of all manors, after a survey of them, to be enrolled in the book called the Doomsday-Book; and all lands found therein belonging to the crown, under the title of *Terra Regis*, are called *Ancient Demesne*. 9 *H.* 4, c. 5; 8 *H.* 6, c. 26; *F. N. B.* 14, 228, &c.; *Kitch.* 98, &c.; 4 *Inst.* 269; *New Nat. Brev.* 32, 35.

A'NCIENTS (*Law*) a term for gentlemen in the Inns of Court who are of a certain standing. In the Middle Temple all who have passed their readings are termed *ancients*: in Gray's Inn the ancients are the oldest barristers; besides which the society consists of *benchers*, barristers, and students. In the inns of Chancery it consists of ancients and students, or clerks.

A'NCIENTY (*Law*) a term for eldership or seniority used in the stat. of Ireland. 14 *Hen.* 8.

ANCI'LE (*Ant.*) *Ancyle*, a sacred shield among the Romans, which was said to have fallen from heaven in the reign of Numa, who ordered eleven others to be made in imitation of it, and appointed an order of priests, called the Salii, to watch over their safety in the temple. It was so called, according to Ovid, because it was rounded, or had all its angles cut off.

Ovid. Fast. l. 3, v. 377.

Idque ancila vocat; quod ab omni parte recisum est.
Quaque notes oculis, angulus omnis abest.

The ancile was generally supposed to have fallen on the calends, or first of March, on which day the feast of Mars and Juno was celebrated, which were called, on that account, the Ancilia, or feast of the Ancilia, when the priests carried the Ancilia in solemn procession round the city, dancing, and singing praises in honour of the god Mars. Virg. Æn. l. 8, v. 664.

Hic exultantes Salios, nudosque Lupercos,
Lanigerosque apices, et lapsa ancilia cælo
Extuderat.

Juven. sat. 2, v. 125.

Arcano qui sacra ferens nutantia loro
Sudavit clypeis ancilibus.

Ovid. Fast. l. 3, v. 259.

Quis mihi nunc dicet, quare cœlestia Martio
Arma ferant Salii.

During the celebration of this festival all public or important business was suspended; and it was deemed unfortunate to undertake an expedition on those days to be married on those days. *Dionys. Hal.* l. 2; *Val. Max.* l. 1, c. 1; *Liv.* l. 1, c. 20; *Tacit. Hist.* l. 1, c. 89; *Suet. in Otho.* c. 8; *Plut. in Num.*; *Obseq. de Prod.* c. 104; *Schol. in Horat. Carm.* l. 3, od. 5, v. 10; *Serv. in Æn.* l. 7, v. 188; *Fest. de Signif. Verb.*

ANCILE (*Numis.*) the form of the ancile, or sacred shield [vide *Ancile*] is mostly compared to the Thracian *pelta*, which it resembled in its circular or crescent-like form, as may be observed in the annexed figure, the reverse of a monetal coin of the Licinian family, representing the ancilia on each side the apex, or priest's cap. This is supposed by Vaillant to have been struck by Publius Licinius Stolo, in honour of Augustus, on his triumphant return from Syria; the inscription *Publius STOLO III. VIR.* *Vaill. Numis. Imper. Rom.*; *Patin. Num. Imp. Rom.*; *Beg. Brand. Thes.* tom. 2; *Morell. Thesaur. Numis.*

ANCI'STRUM (*Bot.*) a genus of plants, Class 2 *Diandria*, Order 1 *Monogynia*.

Generic Characters. CAL. *perianth* one-leaved.—COR. superior.—STAM. *filaments* capillary; *anthers* roundish.—PIST. *germ* oblong; *style* filiform; *stigma* pencil-shaped.—PER. none; *seed* single.

Species. The species are perennials, as—*Ancistrum decumbens*, *latebrosum*, &c. *Linn. Spec. Plant.*

ANCLA'BRA (*Ant.*) brazen vessels which the priests used in their sacrifices. *Fest. de Signif. Verb.*

A'NCLE (*Anat.*) the malleolus, which is either outer, *externus*, or inner, *internus*. [vide *Malleolus*]

A'NCON (*Anat.*) ἀγκών, the elbow; the gibbous eminence, or flexure of the cubit, on which we lean, being the greatest of the two apophyses of the Ulna, and the same as the *olecranon*. *Ruf. Ephes. de Appel. Part. Corp. human.* l. 1, c. 10; *Orib.* l. 25, c. 1; *Castell. Lex. Med.*

ANCONÆ'US (*Anat.*) the same as *Cubitalis musculus.*

ANCO'NES (*Archit.*) from ἀγκών, the elbow; the consoles or ornaments cut on the corners of arches. *Vitruv. de Archit.* l. 4, c. 6.

ANCO'NY (*Mech.*) a bloom or mass of iron wrought into the figure of a flat bar.

A'NCORA (*Ant.*) vide *Anchora.*

ANCORA (*Min.*) Calx.

ANCORA'LIA (*Ant.*) or *ancorarii funes*; the ropes to which the anchors were fixed. The Venetians, according to Cæsar, used chains instead of ropes. *Cæs. de Bell. Gall.* l. 3, c. 15; *Liv.* l. 22, c. 19.

ANCORA'LIS (*Anat.*) the same as *Coracoides Processus.*

A'NCRED (*Her.*) vide *Anchored.*

A'NCTER (*Surg.*) ἀγκτήρ, from ἄγκω, to constrict. 1. The fibula or button by which the lips of wounds are held together. 2. That part of the neck which is subject to choaking. *Cels.* l. 5, c. 26; *Gal. de Meth. Med.* l. 1; *Gorr. Def. Med.*

ANCU'BITUS (*Med.*) that affection of the eyes in which they seem to contain sand.

ANCUMULE'NTÆ (*Ant.*) women in the time of their menstruation who are supposed to have contracted an inquinamentum. *Fest. de Verb. Signif.*

ANCY'LE (*Ant.*) vide *Ancile.*

ANCYLE (*Med.*) a fixation of the joints from a settlement of the humours. *Hippocrat. de Art.; Cels. l. 5, c. 18, &c.; Gal. Defin. Med.; Act. Tetrab. 2, serm. 4, c. 36; Paul. Æginet. de Re Med. l. 4, c. 55; Scribon. Larg. de Compos. Med. c. 104; Gorr. Defin. Med.; Foes. Œconom. Hippocrat.*

ANCY'LIA (*Ant.*) vide Ancile.

ANCYLOBLE'PHARON (*Med.*) ἀγκυλοβλέφαρον, from ἀγκύλος, curved or closed, and βλέφαρον, the eyelid; a disease of the eye which closes the eyelids. *Cels. de Re Med. l. 7, c. 7; Paul Æginet. de Re Med. l. 6, c. 15; Gorr. Def. Med.*

ANCY'LOGLOSSUM (*Med.*) ἀγκυλόγλωσσον, from ἀγκύλος, crooked, and γλῶττα, the tongue, tongue-tied; a contraction of the ligaments of the tongue so as to hinder the speech. *Act. Tetrab. 2, serm. 4, c. 36; Paul. Æginet. de Re Med. l. 6, c. 39; Gorr. Defin. Med.*

ANCYLOME'LE (*Surg.*) ἀγκύλος, crooked, and μήλη, a knife; a surgeon's probe. *Gorr. Defin. Med.*

ANCYLO'SIS (*Med.*) the same as Ancyle.

ANCYLO'TOMOS (*Surg.*) ἀγκυλοτόμος, from ἀγκύλος, crooked, and τέμνω, to cut; any crooked surgical knife. *Paul. Æginet. apud Gorr. Def. Med.*

A'NCYRA (*Surg.*) from ἄγκυρα, an anchor; a surgical hook. Epicharmus gives the same name to the *membrum virile*. *Gorr. Def. Med.*

ANCYRO'IDES (*Anat.*) or coracoides; the name of a process from the upper part of the neck of the Scapula, or shoulder-blade, resembling an anchor, from which it takes its name. *Ruf. Ephes. de Appell. Part. Human. Corp. l. 2, c. 2; Oribas. Med. Coll. l. 25, c. 1.*

A'NDA (*Bot.*) a tree; the wood of which is spongy and light. The fruit is said to be purgative.

ANDA'BATÆ (*Ant.*) gladiators who fought blindfolded; whence the proverb *Andabatarum more*, denoting rash and inconsiderate measures. *Cic. ad. Fam. l. 7; Hieron. contra Jovian.; Rhodig. Antiq. Lect. l. 11, c. 11; Turneb. Adv. l. 19, c. 8; Alex. Gen. Dier. l. 6, c. 22.*

ANDA'NTE (*Mus.*) Italian for exact and just time in playing, so as to keep the notes distinct from each other, chiefly in respect to the thorough bass.—*Andante largo* signifies that the music must be slow, the time exactly observed, and each note distinct.

ANDANTI'NO (*Mus.*) an Italian word for gentle, tender; somewhat slower than Andante.

A'NDARAC (*Chem.*) red orpiment.

A'NDAS (*Chem.*) a solution of salt.

A'NDERA (*Archæol.*) 1. A swath in mowing. 2. As much ground as a man can stride over at once.

ANDI'RA (*Bot.*) a tree of Brazil, the bark, wood, and fruit of which are as bitter as aloes. *G. Pison. Med. Bras.*

ANDIRA *guacu* (*Zool.*) a kind of bat, in Brazil, the tongue and heart of which are reckoned poisons.

A'NDIRONS (*Mech.*) or Hand-irons, according to Skinner; irons placed before the grate of a kitchen chimney for the spits to turn in, or for the chimney of a chamber where wood may be laid. They are so called because they may be taken up by the hand.

ANDRA'CHNE (*Bot.*) ἀνδράχνη, or *atticè*, ἀνδράχλη; the name of a tree like a strawberry-tree, which, according to Pliny, answered most to the Portulaca or Purslain of the Latins. This name has, however, been given to many other plants. *Theophrast. Hist. Plant. l. 7, c. 4; Dioscor. l. 2, c. 15; Plin. l. 13, c. 22; Gal. de Simpl. l. 6; Oribas. Med. Coll. l. 15; Hellod. apud. Phot. Bibliothek; Phavorin. Lex.; Act. Tetrab. 1, serm. 1; Gorr. Defin. Med.*

ANDRACHNE, in the Linnean system, a genus of plants, Class 21 *Monoecia*, Order 11 *Gynandria*.

Generic Characters. CAL. perianth five-leaved.—COR. petals five; nectary leaflets five.—STAM. filaments five; anthers simple.—PIST. germ superior; styles three; stigmas globose.—PER. capsule globose-trilobate; seeds in pairs.

Species. There are but few species of this genus, which are shrubs. *Linn. Spec. Plant.*

ANDRACHNE Theophrasti (*Bot.*) the Arbutus andrachne of Linnæus.

ANDRANOTO'MIA (*Anat.*) from ἀνὴρ, vir, and ἀνατομή; the dissection of a male subject. *Castell. Lex. Med.*

A'NDRAPHAX (*Bot.*) ἀνδράφαξ, stinking orache; the Chenopodium vulgare of Linnæus. *Hippocrat. de Mul.*

ANDRAPODOCAPE'LOI (*Ant.*) ἀνδραποδοκάπηλοι, from ἀνδράποδον, a slave, and κάπηλος, a seller; a slave merchant or dealer, who attended the slave market at Athens to dispose of their slaves. *Galen.*

ANDRAPODI'STES (*Ant.*) ἀνδραποδιστής, slave-mongers who were mostly kidnappers that stole children to sell them, for which the Thessalians were noted, according to Aristophanes. *Aristoph. Plut. act 2, scen. 5.*

κερδαίνειν βουλομένος τις
Ἔμπορος, ἥκων ἐκ Θετταλίας παρὰ πλείων ἀνδραποδισταῖς.

ANDRE'NA (*Ent.*) a division of the genus *apis*, according to Fabricius, consisting of those insects of this tribe having the tongue three-cleft.

ANDRE'OLITE (*Min.*) cross-stone; a species of stone of the zeolite family.

A'NDREW, ST. Knights of (*Her.*) an order instituted by Peter the Great, in 1698. The badge of this order is a gold medal, on one side whereof is represented St. Andrew's Cross, with these words: "*Cazar Pierre Monarque de toute la Russie.*"—*St. Andrew's Cross* was in the form of the letter X.

ANDREW'S day, St. (*Ecc.*) a festival celebrated in the Christian church on the 30th of November, in honour of the apostle St. Andrew.

A'NDRIA (*Ant.*) Ἀνδρία, a name given to the public entertainments in Crete, which were called by the Spartans φιδίτια. *Plut. in Lycurg.*

ANDRIA (*Lit.*) the title of one of Terence's plays.

ANDRIA (*Med.*) an hermaphrodite.

ANDRO'CHIA (*Archæol.*) a name given, by Fleta, to a milk-maid. *Flet. l. 2, c. 87.*

ANDROGENI'A (*Med.*) ἀνδρογενία, from ἀνὴρ, homo, and γίνομαι, gigno; a propagation of the male sex.

ANDROGEO'NIA (*Ant.*) ἀνδρογεώνια, annual games celebrated in the Ceramicus at Athens, by the command of Minos, in memory of his son Androgeos, who was murdered by the Athenians. *Plut. in Thes.; Hesych. Lex.*

ANDRO'GYNA dichogamia (*Bot.*) the same as Dichogamia.

ANDRO'GYNE (*Med.*) ἀνδρογύνη, from ἀνὴρ, a man, and γυνὴ, a woman; hermaphrodites, or effeminate men. *Hippocrat. de Vict. in Acut. Morb.*

ANDRO'GYNOUS (*Bot.*) androgynus, from ἀνὴρ, a man, and γυνὴ, a woman; an epithet for plants bearing male and female flowers on the same root, without any mixture of hermaphrodites: androgynous plants are found mostly in the Class Monoecia.

ANDROGYNOUS is also an epithet for flowers having stamens or pistils only.

ANDROGYNOUS (*Astrol.*) an epithet for a planet that is sometimes hot and sometimes cold.

ANDRO'IDES (*Mech.*) the name given to an automaton in the form of a man, who, by means of springs, walks, talks, handles, &c. like a man.

A'NDROLEPSY (*Ant.*) ἀνδροληψία, from ἀνὴρ, a man, and λαμβάνω, to seize; an action, according to the laws of Athens, against such as protected murderers, by which the relations of the deceased were empowered to seize three men in the city or house where the malefactor had fled, till he either surrendered or satisfaction was made in some other way for the murder. *Demosthen. contra Aristocrat.; Poll. Onomast. l. 8, c. 6.*

ANDRO'MACHI *theriaca* (*Med.*) the treacle of Andromachus, the physician; or Venice treacle, consisting of more than sixty ingredients. *Gal. de Antidot. l. 2; Aet. Tetrab. 13, serm. 3, c. 13; Act. de Meth. Med. l. 5, c. 6; Myrep. de Pil. sec. 32.*

ANDRO'MEDA (*Astron.*) ἀνδρομίδα, a constellation of the Northern hemisphere, containing 23 stars according to Ptolemy, and 27 stars according to Kepler and Bayer, of which the three principal are of the second magnitude, although Ptolemy reckons them to be of the third; namely, the first, in the head, which is called ὀμφαλὸς ἵππου; the second, in the girdle, called by the Arabians *mirach*; and the third, in the Southern foot, called *alamak*. This constellation is called by the Arabians *marah musalseleth*, or the woman chained; because Andromeda is represented as a female bound to a rock, according to the fable of the Greeks, who say that Andromeda, the daughter of Cassiopeia, was bound to a rock by the Nereids, and afterwards released by Perseus.
Manil. Astronom. l. 1, v. 355.

*Andromedam vastos metuentem piscis hiatus
Expositam ponto deflet, scopulis que revinctam
Ne veteran Perseus cœlo quoque servet amorem
Auxilioque juvet.*

Arat. de Apparent. v. 197; *Hipparch. in Arat.; Hygin. Astronom. Poet.; Eratosthen Asterism; Ptol. Almagest. l. 7, c. 5.*

ANDROMEDA (*Bot.*) a genus of plants, Class 10 *Decandria*, Order 1 *Monogynia*.
Generic Characters. CAL. *perianth* five-parted.—COR. monopetalous.—STAM. *filaments* subulate; *anthers* two-horned.—PIST. *germ* roundish; *style* cylindric; *stigma* obtuse.—PER. *capsule* roundish; *partitions* contrary; *seeds* very many.
Species. The species are mostly shrubs, and natives of Lapland, North America, and Russia, as the *Andromeda tetragona, paniculata, calyculata, &c.*; but the *Andromeda palifolia, Erica humilis seu Rhododendron*, Marsh Andromeda, is a native of Britain. *Raii Hist. Plant.; Pluk. Almagest. Botan.; Linn. Spec. Plant.*

ANDRO'NION, i. e. *Andronis pistelli* (*Med.*) trochees of Andron.

ANDROPO'GON (*Bot.*) from ἀνήρ, a man, and πώγων, a beard; a genus of grasses, Class 23 *Polygamia*, Order 1 *Monoecia*.
eneric Characters. CAL. a glume.—COR. a glume; *nectary* two-leaved.—STAM. *filaments* three; *anthers* oblong.—PIST. *germ* oblong; *styles* two; *stigmas* obtuse.—PER. none; *seed* solitary.
Species. The species are very numerous in the Linnean system, and are some of them called, by other writers, *Lagurus*, as the *Andropogon divaricatum, nardus*, &c. some *Festuca*, as *Andropogon distachium, hartum*, &c. some *Chloris*, as the *Andropogon pubescens, fasciculatum, polydactylon*, &c. *J. Bauh. Hist. Plant.; Raii Hist. Plant.; Pluk. Almag. Botan.; Linn. Spec. Plant.*

A'NDROSACE (*Bot.*) a genus of plants, Class 5 *Pentandria*, Order 1 *Monogynia*.
Generic Character. CAL. *involucre* many-leaved; *perianth* one-leaved.—COR. monopetalous; *tube* ovate; *border* flat; *divisions* ovate-oblong; *throat* beset with glands.—STAM. *filaments* very short; *anthers* oblong.—PIST. *germ* globose; *style* filiform; *stigma* globose.—PER. *capsule* globose; *seeds* very many; *receptacle* erect.
Species. Some of the species are annuals, as—*Androsace maxima seu Alsini affinis*, Oval-leaved Androsace.—*Androsace septentrionalis, Aretia seu Alsine verna*, Tooth-leaved Androsace, &c.; but some are perennials, as the —*Androsace lactea, Aretia seu Sedum Alpinum*, Grass-leaved Androsace.—*Androsace odoratissima seu orientalis.*—*Androsace chamæjasme seu Sedum minus*, &c. *J. Bauh. Hist. Plant.; C. Bauh. Pin.; Ger. Herb.; Park. Theat. Botan.; Raii Hist. Plant.; Tournef. Inst.; Boerharv. Index Plant.; Linn. Spec. Plant.*

ANDROSA'CHE (*Nat.*) Sea Navel-wort; a submarine production found on the rocks and shells of fishes. Its powder is diuretic

ANDROSACHE *diapeusia* (*Bot.*) the *Aretia Helvetica* of Linnæus.—*Androsache caulescens*, the *Aretia Alpina* of Linnæus.

ANDROSÆ'MUM (*Bot.*) ἀνδρόσαιμον, Tutsan or Park-leaves; a sort of hypericum, the flower of which yields juice like man's blood, whence it is called ἀνδρόσαιμον, *androsæmon*, ἀνδρός αἷμα, i. e. man's blood. The leaves, when bruised, yield a resinous smell: the seed pounded and drunk in a decoction, was reckoned good for the bile. *Dioscor. l. 2, c. 172; Plin. l. 27, c. 4; Gal. de Simpl. l. 4; Oribas. Med. Coll. l. 15; Aet. Tetrab. 1, serm. 1; Paul. Æginet. de Re Med. l. 7, c. 3; Lem. des Drog.*

ANDROSÆMON, in the Linnean system, the name of several species of the *Hypericum*.

A'NDRUM (*Med.*) an epidemic disease on the coast of Malabar, the same as the *Hydrocele*.

ANDRY'ALE (*Bot.*) from ἀνδρὸς ἄλη, i. e. the wandering of a man; a genus of plants, Class 19 *Syngenesia*, Order 1 *Polygamia Æqualis*.
Generic Characters. CAL. common.—COR. *compound* umbricate; *corrullules* hermaphrodite.—STAM. *filaments* five; *anthers* cylindrical.—PIST. *germ* ovate; *style* filiform; *stigmas* two.—PER. none; *seeds* solitary; *down* capillary; *receptacle* villose.
Species. The species are mostly perennials, as the *Andryale cheiranthifolia, pinnatifida seu Hieracium incanum, &c.*; but the *Andryale integrifolia seu Sonchus villosus*, Hairy Androsace, is an annual. *J. Bauh. Hist. Plant.; C. Bauh. Pin.; Park. Theat. Botan.; Raii Hist. Plant.; Linn. Spec. Plant.*

TO AN'EAL (*Mech.*) to bake or harden glass, tiles, &c. in the fire.

A'NEE (*Com.*) a corn measure in France, containing six gallons.

ANEE (*Com.*) a French measure for grain, equal to as much as an ass can carry.

A'NEGRAS (*Com.*) a measure of corn used in Seville, above half a peck English.

ANEILE'MA (*Med.*) Ἀνείλημα, an involution of the parts occasioned by the gripes. *Hippocrat. de Vet. Med.*

ANE'MIUS *furnus* (*Alch.*) a wind furnace, used for making strong fires.

ANEMO'METER (*Aer.*) from ἄνεμος, the wind, and μέτρον, a measure; an instrument for measuring the force of the wind, which was invented by Wolfius.

ANE'MONE (*Bot.*) ἀνεμώνη, a plant so called, ἀπὸ τοῦ ἀνέμου, from the wind, because it is easily destroyed by the wind, to which Ovid refers.
Ovid. Met. l. 10, v. 737.

————————*brevis est tamen usus in illo.
Namque malè hærentem, et nimiâ levitate caducum
Excutiunt idem, qui præstant nomina, venti.*

It is fabled to have sprung from the tears of Venus, on the death of Adonis, according to
Bion. Idyl. 1.

Αἰ αἰ τὰν Κυθέρειαν, ἀπώλετο καλὸς Ἄδωνις
Δάκρυον ἁ Παφία τόσον ἐκχέει, ὅσον Ἄδωνις
Αἷμα χέει, τὰ δὲ πάντα ποτὶ χθονὶ γίγνεται ἄνθη
Αἷμα ῥόδον τίκτει, τὰ δὲ δάκρυα τὰν ἀνεμώναν.

others, according to the Scholiast on Theocrites, make it to have sprung from the blood of Adonis. It is reckoned to be detersive and aperient. *Theophrast.* l. 6, c. 7; *Dioscor.* l. 2, c. 207; *Plin.* l. 21, c. 23; *Oribas. Med. Coll.* l. 15; *Aet. Tetrab.* 4, serm. 3, c. 12; *Paul. Æginet. de Re Med.* l. 7, c. 3.

ANEMONE, *in the Linnean system,* a genus of plants, Class 13 *Polyandria,* Order 7 *Polygynia.*

Generic Characters. CAL. none.—COR. petals in two or three rows.—STAM. filaments numerous; anthers twin.—PIST. germs numerous; styles acuminate; stigmas obtuse.—PER. none; receptacle globular or oblong; seeds very many.

Species. The species are perennials, as—*Anemone Hepatica, Hepatica* seu *Trifolium hepaticum,* Hepatica.—*Anemone patens* seu *Pulsatilla patens,* Woolly-leaved Anemone.—*Anemone Alpina* seu *Burseriana,* Alpine Anemone, &c. &c. *J. Bauh. Hist. Plant.; C. Bauh. Pin.; Ger. Herb.; Park. Theat. Botan.; Raii Hist. Plant.; Tournef. Inst.; Boerhav. Ind. Plant.; Linn. Spec. Plant.*

ANEMONOSPE'RMOS (*Bot.*) the *Arctotis aspera* and *Gorteria rigens* of Linnæus.

ANEMO'SCOPE (*Mech.*) from ἄνεμος, the wind, and σκοπέω, to behold; an instrument for foretelling the changes of the wind and weather. Such an instrument was invented by Otto Guerick, consisting of a little man in a glass tube, which rose and fell according to the changes of the weather. *Acta Erud.* 1664.

AN E'ND (*Mar.*) perpendicular, as applied to any mast or boom. The top mast is *an end* when hoisted up to its usual station at the head of the lower masts.

A'NEOS (*Med.*) ἄνεως, deprived of voice and reason.

ANETHINUM *vinum aut oleum* (*Med.*) ἀνήθινος οἶνος, a preparation of wine or oil with Anethum. *Dioscor.* l. 5, c. 75.

ANETHO'XULA (*Bot.*) the woody root of Dill. *Myrep.* sect. 8, c. 52.

ANE'THUM (*Bot.*) ἄνηθον, probably changed from ἀνίκητον, or ἀνίκητος, unconquered, to denote its power; Dill, a plant so called because it sharpens the appetite. It was used for garlands by the ancients.

Theocrit. idyl. 7.

Κἠγὼ τῆνο καθ' ἅμας, ἀνήθινον, ἢ ῥοδόεντα
Ἢ καὶ λευκοΐων στέφανον περὶ κρατὶ φυλάσσων
Τὸν στιλισιτικὸν οἶνον ἀπὸ κρητῆρος ἀφυξῶ
Πὰρ πυρὶ κεκλιμένος.

Virg. Eclog. 2, v. 48.
Narcissum et florem jungit bene olentis anethi.

and formed, according to Plinius Valerius, a principal ingredient in the food given to the athletæ, on account of its nutritious quality. *Dioscor.* l. 3, c. 67; *Plin.* l. 20, c. 18; *Oribas. Synop.* l. 1, c. 22; *Plin. Valer.* l. 4, c. 27.

ANETHUM, in the *Linnean system,* a genus of plants, Class 5 *Pentandria,* Order 2 *Digynia.*

Generic Characters. CAL. umbel, universal and partial, manifold; involucre neither universal nor partial; perianth proper, obsolete.—COR. universal uniform; flosculi all fertile; proper petals five.—STAM. filaments capillary; anthers roundish.—PIST. germ inferior; styles approximating; stigmas obtuse.—PER. none; fruit subovate; seeds two.

Species. The species are—*Anethum graveolens* seu *hortense,* Common Dill, an annual, native of Portugal.—*Anethum segetum* seu *sylvestre, &c.* seu *Fœniculum Lusitanicum, &c.* an annual, native of Portugal.—*Anethum fœniculum, Fœniculum dulce* seu *Ligusticum fœniculum,* Fennel or Finckle, a perennial, native of Britain. *J. Bauhin. Hist. Plant.; C. Bauhin. Pin. Theat.; Ger. Herb.; Park. Theat. Botan.; Raii Hist. Plant.;* *Tourn. Inst. Herb.; Boerh. Ind. Plant.; Linn. Spec. Plant.*

ANETICUS (*Med.*) ἀνετικός, from ἀνίημι, to remit; assuaging pain, an epithet applied to remedies. *Castell. Lex. Medic.*

A'NEURISM (*Med.*) ἀνεύρισμος, from ἀνευρύνω, to dilate; a tumour in the arteries from excessive dilatation. *Gal. Definit. Med.; Aet. Tetrab.* 7, serm. 3, c. 10; *Paul. Æginet. de Re Med.* l. 6, c. 37.

ANFE'LTYHDE (*Archæol.*) Anfealtihle, a simple accusation from which, according to the Saxon law, a man might be discharged upon his own oath and that of two men, in distinction from the *Accusatio triplex,* which required the oaths of five more. *Leges Adelstani apud Brompton.*

A'NGARI (*Ant.*) a Persian word for post-boys or couriers, who were employed to carry letters, and go on different errands. *Joseph. Antiq.* l. 11, c. 6; *Hesychius et Suidas; Rhodig. Antiq. Lect.* l. 18.

ANGA'RIA (*Ant.*) the post-office or post-houses where the angari or post-boys stopped. [vide *Angari*]

ANGEIO'TOMY (*Anat.*) ἀγγειοτομία, from ἀγγεῖον, a vessel, and τέμνω, to cut; a dissection of the blood vessels, consisting of arteriotomy, and phlebotomy.

A'NGEL (*Numis.*) an English gold coin, equal to 6s. 8d.; so called from its having the impression of an angel on it, as in the subjoined figure of a coin of Edward the Fourth, which represents the archangel Michael standing with one

foot on the dragon, which he is piercing with his spear, the upper end of which terminates in a cross, the inscription EDWARD DEI GRA. REX ANGL. Z. FRANC.; on the reverse, a ship, with a large cross for the mast, the letter E on the right side, and a rose on the left; on the side of the ship the arms of England quartered with those of France, the inscription PER CRUCEM TUA SALUA NOS XPE REDEMPT.

ANGEL *shot* (*Gun.*) a cannon bullet cut in two, and the halves linked together with a chain.

ANGEL *bed* (*Mech.*) an open bed without bed posts.

ANGEL *fish* (*Ich.*) the ῥίνη of Aristotle, the *Squatina* of Pliny, the *Ange* or *Angelot* of Belonius, the *Monk* or *Angel-fish* of Ray, the *Squalus squatina* of Linnæus, a fish, which connects the genus of Rays and Sharks. It differs from both in the situation of its mouth, which is placed at the extremity of the head. It is extremely voracious and fierce, and, like the Rays, feeds on flounders and flat-fish. The aspect of this fish is extremely malignant, and its skin very rough. *Aristot. Hist. Anim.* l. 5, c. 5; *Plin.* l. 9, c. 12; *Athen.* l. 7, c. 19; *Oppian. Halicut.* l. 1; *Rondel. Gessn. de Pis. Will. Ichth.; Raii Synop. Pisc.*

A'NGELET (*Numis.*) a gold coin equal to half an angel. [vide *Angel*]

ANGE'LIC *Habit* (*Ecc.*) angelica vestis, ἀγγελικὸν σχῆμα; a monkish garment which laymen put on a little before their death, that they might have the benefit of the prayers of the monks. *Allat. de Cons. Eccl. Occid. et Orient.* l. 3, c. 8; *Euchalog. Græcor.* p. 499.

ANGE'LICA (*Bot.*) from the angelic virtue ascribed to it, a genus of plants, Class 5 *Pentandria,* Order 2 *Digynia.*

Generic Characters. CAL. universal umbel manifold.—COR. universal uniform; partial petals five.—STAM. filaments simple; anthers simple.—PIST. germ inferior; styles reflex; stigmas obtuse.—PER. none; fruit roundish; seeds two.

Species. The species are biennials, as the *Angelica arc-angelica* and *lucida*; or perennials, as the *Angelica sylvestris, verticillaris*, &c. *J. Bauhin. Hist. Plant.; C. Bauhin. Pin. Theat.; Ger. Herb.; Park. Theat. Botan.; Raii Hist. Plant.; Tourn. Inst. Herb.; Boerh. Ind. Plant.; Linn. Spec. Plant.*

ANGELICA is also the name of several species, as the *Chærophyllum aromaticum*, the *Cicuta maculata*, the *Laserpitium latifolium Smyrnium*, and *Aman* of Linnæus. *C. Bauhin. Pin.*, &c.—*Angelica-tree*, the *Arabia spinosa* of Linnæus.

ANGE'LICÆ (*Ecc.*) an order of nuns who had two houses in Italy, at Milan, and Cremona. It was founded by Louisa Torelli, countess of Guastalli, by permission of Pope Paul III. in 1534. *Hellot. Hist. des Ord. Mon.* tom. iv. c. 16.

ANGE'LICI (*Ecc.*) Ἀγγελικοι, heretics of the third century, so called, as Epiphanius thinks, because they believed that the world was made by angels; and Augustin adds that they also worshipped angels. *Epiphan. Hæres.* 6; *Augustin. Hæres.* 39; *Baron. Annal. Ann.* 360.

ANGELICI (*Her.*) an order of knighthood, instituted in 1191, by Angelus Flavius Comnenus, emperor of Constantinople.

ANGE'LICUS *pulvis* (*Chem.*) mercury.

ANGERONA'LIA (*Ant.*) a festival celebrated at Rome on the 12th Kal. Jan. i. e. the 21st of December, in honour of the goddess Angerona, to whom sacrifices were offered in the curia or senate-house. *Varro de Lat. Ling.* l. 5; *Gyrald. Syntag. Deor.* 1, p. 57; *Vaill. Numism. Imperat.* vol. 2; *Ursat. de Not. Roman. apud Græv. Thes. Antiq. Roman.* tom. ii, p. 675.

A'NGI (*Med.*) buboes or tumours in the groin.

ANGIGLO'SSI (*Med.*) Stammerers.

A'NGILD (*Law*) a single fine for an offence, in distinction from the *two-gild* and *tri-gild*, the double and treble fine. *Laws of Ina.*

A'NGINA (*Med.*) κυνάγχη, from ἄγχω, to strangle, or suffocate; the Quinsey [vide *Cynanche*], a disease in the throat, of which three species are mentioned by the ancients, namely, *Angina aquosa, Angina gangrænosa*, and *Angina stridula*, the Croup. *Hippocrat. de Prognost.; Aret. de Curat. Morb. Acut.* l. 1, c. 7; *Cels. de Re Med.* l. 4, c. 4; *Gal. de Loc. Affect.* l. 4; *Aet. Tetrab.* 2, serm. 4, c. 47; *Alex. Trallian.* l. 4, c. 1; *Act. de Meth. Med.* l. 2, c. 10; *Gorr. Defin. Med.; Foes. Œconom. Hippocrat.*—*Angina pectoris*, a disease described by Dr. Heberdeen, consisting of an acute constrictory pain at the lower end of the *sternum*.

ANGIOLO'GIA (*Med.*) from ἀγγεῖον, a vessel, and λόγος, a speech; Angiology, the doctrine of the arteries, nerves, and other vessels. *Gal. Introduc.*

ANGIOPTERIS (*Bot.*) the *Onoclea* of Linnæus.

ANGIOSPE'RMIA (*Bot.*) from ἀγγεῖον, a vessel, and σπέρμα, seed, i. e. Seed included in a vessel or capsule; an epithet for the second Order of the 14th Class *Didynamia*, including the genera, having the Calyces undivided: as—*Æginetia, Tanaecium*. Those having the Calyces bifid, as—*Orobanche*, Broomrape; *Crescentia*, Calabash-tree; *Obolaria; Hebenstreitia; Torenia; Castilleia; Acanthus; Premna.* Those having the Calyces trifid, as—*Halleria.* Those having the Calyces quadrifid, as—*Lathræa; Euphrasia*, Eye-bright; *Rhinanthus*, Yellow Rattle; *Melampyrum*, Cow Wheat; *Lippia; Bartsia; Schwalbea; Barleria; Laeselia; Gmelina; Lantana.* Those having the Calyces five cleft, as—*Limosella; Avicennia; Tozzia; Phaylopsis; Browallia; Brunsfelsia; Holmskioldia; Lindernia; Conobea; Columnea; Vandellia; Russelia; Scrophularia; Digitalis*, Fox Glove; *Antirrhinum*, Snap Dragon; *Fluellin*, Toad Flax; *Pedicularis*, Louse Wort; *Mimulus*, Monkey Flower; *Sesamum*, Oily Grain; *Alectra; Ges-*

neria; Cyrilla; Stemodia; Achimenes; Celsia; Hemimeris; Sibthorpia; Capraria; Bignonia; Incarvillea; Ruellia; Bucknera; Erinus; Petrea; Mamilea; Anarrhinum; Gerardia; Dodartia; Chelone; Pentstemon; Gloxinia; Tourretia; Martynia; Maurandia; Millingtonia; Tartula; Pedalium; Linnea; Cornutia; Ovieda; Amasonia; Besleria; Bantia; Spielmannia; Vitex, Chaste-Tree; *Myoporum; Citharexylon; Volkameria; Clerodendron; Duranta.* Calyces many cleft, as—*Hyobanche; Lepidagathis; Cymbaria; Thunbergia; Melianthus*, Honey-Flower.

ANGIOSPE'RMOS (*Bot.*) an epithet for any flower having its seed included in a capsule, in distinction from those that are Gymnospermos, or naked seeded; hence also plants are likewise denominated *Angiospermia*, of which description is the second order in the Class *Didynamia*. [vide *Angiospermia*]

AN'GLE (*Math.*) from the Greek ἀγκύλος, bent, denotes the inclination of two lines, or planes, to each other, which meet together in a point called the *vertex* or angular point. The lines are called the legs or sides of the angle, which is named either by one letter, as A, or by three letters, as B A C, the middle of which always stands for the angle to be described. Angles are measured by an arc of a circle, drawn from the vertex with any radius at pleasure, as the arc D E, drawn from A, which is a measure of the angle B A C, i. e. the angle B A C is said to be as many degrees as the arc D E, a circle being always supposed to be divided into 360 degrees.

Fig. 1.

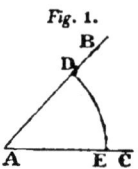

Angles in Geometry.

Angles, as to their magnitude, are right, oblique, or equal. A *right angle* is formed by one perpendicular right line falling upon another, as B A C, which is subtended by the quadrant of a circle, is consequently equal to 90 degrees.—*Oblique angle* is formed by lines not perpendicular, which are either acute or obtuse.—An *Acute angle* is less than a right angle, and consequently less than 90 degrees, as D A B.—*Obtuse angle* is greater than a right angle, and consequently more than 90 degrees, as E A B.—*Equal angles* are those whose arcs or measures *k m* and *m o* are proportionate to the radii.

Fig. 2.

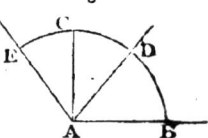

Fig. 3.

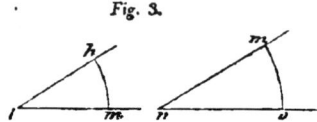

As to their construction; *angles* are rectilinear, curvilinear, mixed, plane, spherical, solid, &c.—*Rectilinear angle* is formed by two legs, which are right lines, as in the preceding figures.—*Curvilinear angle* has two curved lines for its legs, as A C B, in *fig.* 4, formed by the arcs B C and A C.—*Mixed angle* has one of its legs a right line, and the other as the angles B C D, in *fig.* 4, and B C E formed by arc B C, and the right lines D C or C E, so also A C D or A C E curved.—*Plane angle* is the inclination of two lines in the same plane, and meeting in a point. The above-mentioned angles are all of this description.—*Spherical angle* is an angle formed on the surface of the sphere by the intersection of two great circles, or the inclination of the planes of those circles, as

Fig. 4.

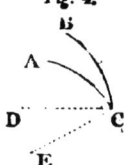

ANGLE.

A D C, in *fig. 5*, or B D E.—*Solid angle* is the inclination of more than two right lines that touch one another, and are not in the same superficies, as where two walls and the ceiling meet, in which case a solid angle is formed by three lines. To these may be added others less usual, as a—*Horned angle*, made by a right line, whether secant or tangent, with the circumference of a circle.—*Lunular angle*, formed by the intersection of two circular lines, one convex, and the other concave.—*Cissoid angle*, an inner angle made by two spherical convex lines intersecting each other.—*Sistroid angle*, in the form of a sistrum.—*Pelecoid angle*, in the form of a hatchet.

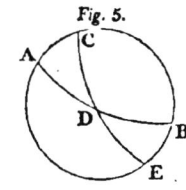

Fig. 5.

As to their situation; *angles* are contiguous, adjacent, vertical, alternate, external, internal, &c. — *Contiguous angles* have the same vertex, and one leg common to both, as A B C E B A.—*Adjacent angles* are those of which the leg of the one produced forms the leg of the other, as E B C, *fig. 6*, and E B D.—

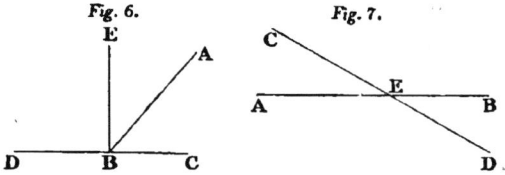

Fig. 6.   Fig. 7.

Vertical, or *opposite angles*, are those which are made by lines cutting or intersecting each other, which are consequently opposite to each other, as the angles C E A, *fig. 7*, D E B. An angle in a triangle is also said to be opposed to the side that subtends it, as the angle B, *fig. 8*, to the line A C.—*Internal angles* are those which are made within any right lined figure, in distinction from the *external angles*, which are placed without the figure.—*Internal and opposite angles* are formed by a line cutting two parallel lines, as B G H, *fig. 9*, and G H D, in distinction from the *external angles*, E G B, and D H F.—*Alternate angles* are those which lie in the opposite sides of two parallel lines, as A G H, and G H D.—*Homologous*, or *like angles*, are those which in two separate figures preserve the same order in both.—*Angles at the centre* are those whose vertex is in the centre of a circle, as H, *fig. 10*, in distinction from the *angle at the circumference*, whose vertex is in the circumference, as D.—The *angle in a segment* is that

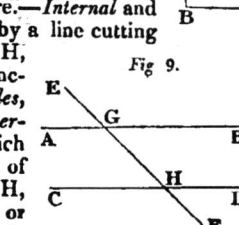

Fig. 8.

Fig. 9.

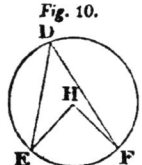 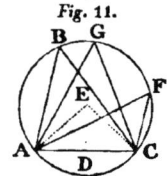

Fig. 10.   Fig. 11.

which two chords of a circle make with each other at the perephery; thus the two chords A B, *fig. 11*, and C B make the angle B, which is an angle in the segment. This angle is said to *insist* or *stand* on the circumference, which is included by the base of the segment, as A D C.—If the angle at the circumference stand on a semicircle, or has the diameter for its base, it is a right angle, and is called an *angle in a semicircle*, as A B C, *fig. 12*; if it stand on a segment greater than a semicircle it is acute, and is called an *angle in the greater segment*, as A D C, *fig. 13*; if on a less it is obtuse, and called an *angle in the less segment*, as A G C, *fig. 14*. Moreover all angles, as A B C,

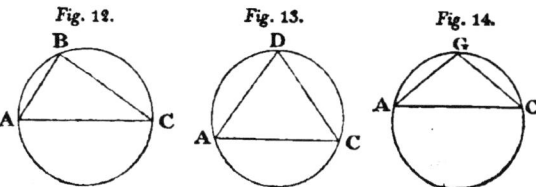

Fig. 12.   Fig. 13.   Fig. 14.

A G C, and A D C in a segment, or which stand on the same arc, are equal to one another.—*An angle of a segment* is, according to Euclid, that which is contained by a chord, and the circumference of a circle, or otherwise that which is made by a chord with a tangent at the point of contact, as A C D, *fig. 15*, which is formed by the line A B touching the circle, and the chord D C. This is also called the *angle of the less segment*, in distinction from D C B, which is the *angle of the greater segment*.—*An angle of contact* is that which is formed by a tangent to a curve, as A C D.

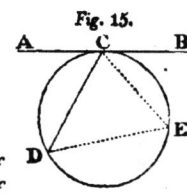

Fig. 15.

ANGLE (*Astron.*) is made either by the circles of the sphere, which are spherical angles, or of right lines supposed to be drawn from the celestial bodies in given positions, which are right-lined angles.

Angles in Astronomy.

Spherical angles in astronomy are as follow; namely, the—*Angle of the ecliptic and meridian*, made by an arch of the ecliptic and meridian, which is a right angle at the solstitial points, and otherwise oblique.—*Angle of the ecliptic and the horizon*, otherwise called the *angle of the ascendant*, or *the angle of the East*, the angle which the portion of the ecliptic above the horizon makes with the horizon.—*Angle of the ecliptic and equator* is the inclination of the axis of the earth to the axis of the ecliptic, which is 23° 28'.—*Angle of the equator and meridian*, which is always a right angle.—*Angle of the equator and the horizon*, which, in a right sphere, is a right angle, in an oblique sphere, oblique.—*Angle of the ecliptic and a verticle circle*, which is always a right angle.—*Angle of longitude* is the angle which the circle of a star's longitude makes with the meridian at the pole of the ecliptic.—*Angle of right ascension* is the angle which the circle of the star's right ascension makes with the meridian at the pole of the equator.—*Angle of the same position* is an angle made by the meeting an arc of the meridian with an arc of the azimuth, or any other great circle passing through the body of the sun. [vide *Astronomy*]

The right-lined angles are as follow; namely, the—*Angle of commutation*, or the *angle at the sun*, which is the difference between the true place of the sun when seen from the earth, and the place of a planet reduced to the ecliptic, as T S B, in the annexed figure, supposing T B to be the orbit of the earth,

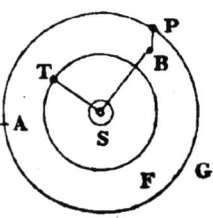

R

ANGLE.

A P G the orbit of the planet, S the sun, and P the planet.—*Angle of elongation*, or *angle at the earth*, is the distance of any planet from the sun with respect to the earth; the greatest elongation is the greatest distance which the planet recedes from the sun, as the angle S T D, which supposes A B C to represent the orbit of the earth, F D V that of Venus, T the earth, V Venus, and S the sun. This angle is $47\frac{1}{2}$, but the greatest elongation made by Mercury is not more than $27\frac{1}{2}$.—*Paralactic angle*, or *angle at the planet*, is the difference between the two angles, under which the true and apparent distances of a planet from the zenith are seen. [vide *Parallax*] *Kepler. Epit.* l. 6; *Ricciol. Almag.* l. 1, c. 22; *Keil. Introd. ad Ver. Astron.*

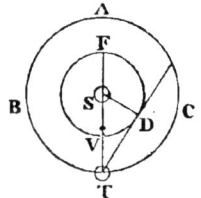

ANGLE *of the rhumb* (*Mar.*) the angle which the rhumb line makes with the meridian.

ANGLE (*Fort.*) the inclination of two lines, which are used in fortifying, or the erection of a fortification. These are divided into two general sorts, real and imaginary, or occult. The *real angles* appear actually in the work itself, as the *flanked angle*, the *angle of the epaule*, &c. The *occult*, or *imaginary angles*, are those which only serve the purpose of the construction, and no longer exist after the work is completed, as the *angle at the centre*, the *angle of the polygon*, &c.

Angles in Fortification.

The angles in fortification are as follow; namely, the—*Angle of the exterior figure*, or *angle of the polygon*, is the angle intercepted between the two outermost sides, or bases of the polygon, as *a b d*, in the subjoined figure,

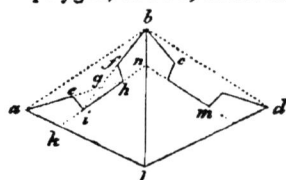

formed by the sides *a b* and *b d*.—*Angle of*, or *at the centre*, is the angle formed at the centre of the polygon, as *a l d*.—*Angle of the bastion*, or the *flanked angle*, is the angle formed by the two faces of the bastion, as *f b c*, formed by *f b* and *b c*. It is the outermost part of the bastion most exposed to the fire of the enemy.—*Angle of the interior figure*, the angle formed in the centre of the bastion by the meeting of the innermost sides of the figure *k n* and *n m*.—*Angle of the triangle*, half the angle of the polygon, as *l b a* or *l b d*.—*Angle of the flank* or *curtin*, the angle contained between the curtin and the flank, as *f h i*.—*Angle of the epaule*, the angle formed by the flank and face of the bastion, *b f h*.—*Diminished angle*, the angle *b a e* formed by the meeting of the exterior sides of the polygon, *b a*, *a e*.—*Angle of the tenaille*, or *exterior flanking angle*, the angle formed by the two rasant lines of defence, i. e. the two faces of the bastion prolonged, as *a g b*.—*Angle flanking inwards* or *upwards*, an angle formed by the flanking line with the curtin, as *k n b*.—*Re-entering angle*, *angle re-entrant*, an angle whose vertex turns inwards towards the place, as *h* or *i*.—*Saliant*, or *sortant angle*, the angle advancing its point towards the field or country, as *e* or *f*.—*Angle of the circumference*, the angle made by the arch, which is drawn from one gorge to another.—*Angle of the counterscarp*, the angle formed by the two sides of the counterscarp meeting before the middle of the curtin.—*Angle forming the flank*, the angle consisting of one flank and one demigorge.—*Angle forming the face*, the angle made by one flank and one face.—*Angle of the gorge*, the angle formed by the prolongation of the curtins intersecting each other.—*Angle of the complement of the line of defence*, the angle formed by the intersection of the two complements with each other.—*Angle of the line of defence*, the angle made by the flank and the line of defence.—*Angle of the moat*, the angle made before the curtin where it is intersected.—*Dead angle*, a re-entering angle not flanked or defended.

ANGLE (*Opt.*) the inclination of any two lines formed by the rays of light.

Angles in Optics.

The angles in optics, and its branches, catoptrics, and dioptrics are as follow; namely, the—*Optic angle*, the angle included or contained between the two rays of light drawn from the extreme points of an object, as A B C, which is comprehended between the rays A B and B C.—*Angle of the interval* is the angle subtended by two lines drawn from the eye to those objects.—*Angle of incidence* is the angle which a ray of light forms with a perpendicular at the point where it falls or first touches, as A B F, supposing A B to be the

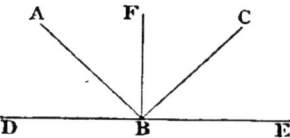

line representing the incident ray of light, B the point at which it falls, and F B the perpendicular. According to Dr. Barrow and some others, the angle of incidence is the angle formed by the incident line A B and the plane D B E, which is acted upon.—*Angle of reflection* is the angle formed by a reflected ray of light with a perpendicular at the point of contact, from which it rebounds, as F B C. Upon the equality of these two angles is founded the whole science of catoptrics.—*Angle of refraction* is the angle which a ray of light refracted makes with the ray of incidence, as F N H, supposing D N E to be the plane, M N the ray of incidence, N H the ray continued, and N F the refracted ray.—*Refracted angle* is the angle which a refracted ray makes with a perpendicular to

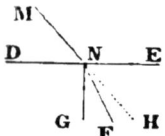

the refracting surface; thus let G N be perpendicular to the refracting surface D E, then is G N F the refracted angle.—*Angle of inclination* is the angle made by a ray of incidence and an axis of incidence. *Alhazen. de Opt.*; *Vitell. de Optic.*; *Kepler. Paralop. Prop.* 5, &c.; *Cartes. Dioptric.* c. 2, § 2; *Huygen. Dioptric.*; *Kircher. Ars. Mag. Luc. et Umb.* l. 8, c. 2; *Newt. Opt.* c. 8, § 10, &c.; *Voss. de Nat. et Prop. Luc.* p. 36.

ANGLE *of Emergence* (*Nat.*) the angle which any body, projected from one fluid or medium into another, makes at its going out, or emerging from, the latter, with a perpendicular to those planes, as the angle K G H; thus, suppose A B and C D to be parallel planes bounding water or glass, and a body as a ray of light, for example, to be projected into them at E in the

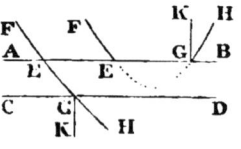

direction of F E, and going out at G in the direction of G H; then G K being made perpendicular to A B and C D, the angle G H K is the angle of emergence.

ANGLE (*Mech.*) the inclination of any two lines supposed to be formed by the bodies impelled towards each other.

Angles in Mechanics.

The angles in mechanics are—the angle of incidence, the angle of reflection, the angle of elevation, and the angle of direction.—*Angle of incidence*, an angle which a line of direction of an impinging body makes at the point of contact.—*Angle of reflection*, the angle which a line of direction of a body rebounding after it has struck another body makes at the point of impact. The equality of these two lines is a fundamental principle in mechanics as in optics.—*Angle of elevation*, the angle comprehended between a line of direction of a projectile and an horizontal line.—*Angle of direction*, an angle comprehended between the lines of direction of two conspiring forces.

ANGLE *of a battalion* (*Mil.*) the angle made by the last men at the extremity of the ranks and files.—*Front angles*, the two last men of the front rank.—*Rear angles*, the two last men of the rear rank.

ANGLE *of a wall* (*Archit.*) the angle formed by the meeting of the two sides or faces of a wall.

ANGLE (*Diall.*) the angle that is made by a right line proceeding from the sun to the dial plate.

ANGLE-*bar* (*Carpent.*) the upright bar at the meeting of any of the two sides of the window.—*Angle-braces*, timbers opposite to each angle in a quadrangular frame, which serve as a brace or tie, the two sides forming the angle opposite to which they are fixed.—*Angle-rafter* [vide *Hipped roof*]—*Angle-rib*, a curved piece of timber in a ceiling or vault, fixed between two parts which form the angle.—*Angle-staff*, or *staff-beads*, beads fixed to the exterior angles of any wall, as a protection against accidents.

ANGLE (*Astrol.*) vide *Angles.*

A'NGLER (*Ich.*) the βάτραχος ἁλιεύς of Aristotle, the *Rana piscatrix* of Pliny, *la Grenouille de mer, le Diable de mer*, of Belonius, the Toad-Fish, Frog-fish, or Sea Devil, of Willoughby, the *Lophius piscatorius* of Linnæus, a singular fish, which is also known at present by the name of the Fishing Frog, from the resemblance which it bears to that animal in the state of a tadpole. Pliny tells us that " It puts forth the slender horns which it has beneath its eyes, enticing by that means the little fish to play round till they come within reach, when it springs on them;" from which characteristic it has acquired its modern name. Its head is much bigger than its whole body, and the mouth of a prodigious width. The fishermen on the coast of Scarborough have a great regard for it, and always set it at liberty when it is caught, from a supposition that it is a great enemy to the dog-fish, the bodies of which have been found in its stomach. *Aristot.* l. 9, c. 37; *Plin.* l. 9, c. 24; *Gessn. de Pis.*; *Rondelet de Pisc. Marin.*; *Will. Ichth.*

ANGLES (*Astrol.*) certain houses in the scheme of the heavens: the first house is called the *angle* of the East, the seventh the *angle* of the West, the fourth house is the *angle* of the North, the tenth the *angle* of the South.

A'NGLICISM (*Gram.*) an idiom or manner of speech peculiar to the English.

A'NGLICUS *Sudor* (*Med.*) vide *Sudor Anglicus.*

A'NGOLAM (*Bot.*) a very tall and beautiful tree of Malabar; the expressed juice from whose root kills worms. *Raii Hist. Plant.*

ANGO'NES (*Ant.*) ἄγγων, a kind of spear used by the Franks. *Suidas.*

A'NGOR (*Med.*) ἄγχω, a concentration of the natural heat of the body, causing a palpitation of the heart. *Hippocrat. Epid.* l. 1.

A'NGRACUM (*Bot.*) the *Epidendrum ovatum et scriptum* of Linnæus.

ANGSA'NA (*Bot.*) or *Angsava*, an Indian tree, from which, when wounded, issues a liquor of a gummy consistence, sold for the *sanguis draconis.* It is astringent, and good for the aphthæ. *Raii Hist. Plant.*; *Commel. Hort.*; *Med. Anstel.*

A'NGUELLES (*Falcon.*) small worms cast up by sick hawks.

A'NGUIFER (*Astron.*) vide *Serpentarius.*

A'NGUILLA (*Numis.*) the eel, was a symbol in the coins of Agrigentum, Adranum, and other cities of Sicily, as in the subjoined cut, which represents on the obverse the

Cancer marinus, with a shell above and an eel below; and on the reverse an eagle tearing a hare; the inscription, ΑΔΡΑΝΙΩΝ. *Goltz. Sicil.*; *Haverkamp. Parut. Sicil. Descritt.*

ANGUILLA (*Ich.*) the eel, a fish named by Aristotle ἐγχέλυς, and classed by Linnæus under the *Muræna.* *Aristot. Hist. An.* l. 2, c. 13, &c.

ANGUILLA'RIA (*Bot.*) the *Ardicia excelsa* and *Zeylanica* of Linnæus.

ANGUILLA'RIS (*Ich.*) a species of the *Silurus* of Linnæus.

A'NGUINA (*Bot.*) the *Calla* and the *Tricosanthes Anguina* of Linnæus.

ANGUI'NEAL (*Geom.*) a sort of hyperbola of a serpentine figure; a species of the second order of curves, according to Newton.

A'NGUINUM (*Zool.*) a bed or knot of snakes. *Plin.* l. 29, c. 3.

A'NGUIS (*Numis.*) the snake, an emblem of Æsculapius, is mostly represented on coins twining round a staff, which is in the hands of an old man; but in the annexed figure it represents Æsculapius himself, who is said to have appeared under this form when the vessel which was sent to fetch his image from Epidaurus arrived in the Tiber. The old man rising out of the water is supposed to be the river-god Tiber, before whom he is rearing himself. *Valer. Maxim.* l. 1, c. 8; *Aur. Victor. de Illust.* c. 22.

ANGUIS (*Zool.*) ἰνώδρις, Snake, a genus of animals, Class *Amphibia*, Order *Serpentes.*

Generic Characters. Scales on the belly, and under the tail.

Species. Animals of this genus mostly inhabit the Indies. The species which are natives of Europe are—*Anguis fragilis*, the Blind-Worm, and *Anguis Eryx*, Aberdeen Snake.

ANGUIS *vulgaris* (*Zool.*) the *Coluber natrix* of Linnæus.—*Anguis Æsculapii*, a perfectly harmless species of serpent, which is good against the plague, and resists poison. *Lem. des Drog.*

A'NGUIUM *senectæ* (*Nat.*) the *Exuviæ* Slough, or cast-off skins of serpents or snakes, a decoction of which is good for pains in the ear, &c. *Dioscor.* l. 2, c. 19; *Aet. Tetrab.* 2, serm. 4, c. 33.

A'NGULAR *motion* (*Mech.*) the motion of any body which moves circularly about a point, as the angular motion of a pendulum, which moves about its centre of motion.

ANGULAR *motion* (*Astron.*) the motion of the planets round the sun as their centre, or the increasing angle made by two lines drawn from a central body, as the sun or earth, to the apparent places of two planets in motion.

ANGULAR (*Bot.*) *angulatus*, an epithet for a stem; *angulatus caulis*, an angular stem, i. e. a stem grooved longitudinally, with more than two hollow angles. It may be triangular, *triangularis*, quadrangular, *quadrangularis*, &c. or obtuse-angled, *obtuse-angulatus*, acute-angled, *acute-angularis*, &c. according to the number and measure of the angles. Anthers are also angular, *angulatæ*, when they have several deep furrows that form four or more angles. The Stigma is angular, *angulosum*, when its close deep furrows occasion projecting angles and leaves; and pericarps are likewise so named, according to the number of their angles.

ANGULAR *capital* (*Archit.*) any capital which has two or more fronts alike, so as to return at the angles of the building.—*Angular modillons*, those which are placed at the return, i. e. at the turning of a cornice.

ANGULA'RIS *Arteria* (*Anat.*) the same as *Maxillaria*.—*Angularis Musculus*, the same as the *Levator Scapulæ*.

ANGULA'TED (*Bot.*) vide *Angular*.

ANGULA'TUS (*Bot.*) angular, or angled. [vide *Angular*]

A'NGULI *oculi* (*Anat.*) vide *Canthi*.

ANGULO'SUS (*Bot.*) vide *Angular*.

A'NGULUS *oculi* (*Anat.*) vide *Canthus*.

ANGU'RIA (*Bot.*) Water Melon, a genus of plants, Class 21 *Monoecia*, Order 2 *Diandria*.

Generic Characters. CAL. monophyllous; *divisions* lanceolate.—COR. pentapetalous.—STAM. *filaments* two; *anther* creeping up and down.—PIST. *germ* inferior, oblong; *style* semibifid; *stigmas* bifid.—PER. *pome* oblong; *seeds* very many.

Species. The species are, the—*Anguria trilobata*, a perennial, native of Carthagena.—*Anguria pedata*, seu *polyphyllos*, a perennial, native of St. Domingo.—*Anguria trifoliata*, seu *Cucumis triphyllus*, native of St. Domingo. *Plum. Plant. Americ.; Linn. Spec. Plant.*

ANGURIA *Citrullus*, the *Cucurbita Citrullus* of Linnæus.

ANGU'STIA (*Anat.*) narrowness of the vessels.

ANGUSTIFO'LIA (*Bot.*) narrow-leaved; an epithet for many plants.

ANGUSTU'RA *cortex* (*Bot.*) a bark which comes from the Spanish main, and is a powerful bitter.

ANHALDI'NUM (*Med.*) a corrosive described by Hartman.

ANHALTI'NA (*Med.*) medicines promoting perspiration.—*Anhaltina aqua*, a cordial distilled from aromatic ingredients.

ANHELA'TIO (*Med.*) *Anhelitus*; panting or shortness of breath. Plin. l. 22, c. 23; Aet. Tetrab. 2, serm. 4, c. 7; Paul. Æginet. de Re Med. l. 3, c. 29.

ANHELI'TUS (*Chem.*) smoke; also horse-dung.

ANHI'MA (*Orn.*) an aquatic bird of prey of Brasil, bigger than a swan: on its head is a horn, the powder of which is an antidote against poison. *Lem. des Drog.*

A'NHLOTE (*Law*) a term used to signify that every one should pay his respective share, as *Scot and Lot*, according to the custom of the country.

ANHUI'BA (*Bot.*) an Indian plant; the same as Sassafras.

ANHY'DRITE (*Min.*) a species of Sulphate.

A'NI (*Orn.*) a species of the *Crotophagos* of Linnæus.

ANI *procidentia* (*Med.*) vide *Procidentia Ani*.

ANIA'DA (*Alch.*) the Astral and Celestial powers.

ANIA'DON (*Alch.*) the celestial body implanted in Christians by the Holy Spirit, by means of the sacraments.

A'NIBA (*Bot.*) the *Cedrota* of Linnæus.

ANICETON (*Med.*) ἀνίκητον; 1. An epithet for a plaster described by Galen and Aetius. *Gal. de Comp. Pharm. Sec. Loc.* l. 1, c. 8; *Aet. Tetrab.* 4, serm. 3, c. 16.—2. The same as *Anisum*.—3. An epithet for the *Anethum*.

A'NIL (*Bot.*) the *Indigofera tinctoria* of Linnæus.

A'NIMA (*Phys.*) from ἄνεμος, the wind, and πνέω, to breathe; the principle of life which the Author of our being breathes into us.—*Anima mundi*, or the ψυχὴ τοῦ κόσμου, the soul of the world; a certain pure ethereal substance or spirit which is diffused through the mass of the world, organizing and actuating the whole and the different parts. *Plat. Tim.*

ANIMA (*Chem.*) a concentration of the virtues of bodies by means of solution, distillation, or any other processes which can develop their powers. Of this description is—*Anima Jaspidis, Anima Aloes*, &c.—*Anima Hepatis*, the same as *Sal Martis.*—*Anima pulmonum*, a name for Saffron, from its supposed use in Asthmas.—*Anima Saturni*, a white powder, obtained by pouring distilled vinegar on litharge, and much used in enamelling.

ANIMA *orticulorum* (*Bot.*) the name for *Hermodactylus*.

A'NIMÆ (*Nat.*) the vesicles of herrings, because they are light, and full of wind. They are supposed to be diuretic.

A'NIMAL (*Phy.*) a living body, endued with sensation and spontaneous motion.—*Animal faculty* is that faculty by which man exercises his senses, and all the other animal functions.—*Animal functions*, those functions or offices which are performed by the different members of the body, as seeing, hearing, voluntary motion, and the like.—*Animal frame*, or animal part of man; the bodily part, in distinction from the rational part.

ANIMAL *secretion* (*Anat.*) the process whereby the divers juices of the body are secreted or separated from the common mass of the blood by means of the glands.—*Animal motion*; the same as muscular motion.—*Animal spirits*, a fine subtle juice or humour in animal bodies, supposed to be the great instrument of muscular motion, sensation, &c. as distinguished from natural and vital. *Gal. de Caus. Puls.*

ANIMAL *kingdom* (*Zool.*) *Animale Regnum*; one of the three principal divisions into which Linnæus divided all organized bodies, consisting of classes, orders, genera, and species.

Animals were by him divided into six classes, namely, the —*Mammalia*, or such as suckle their young, mostly quadrupeds.—*Aves*, Birds, which are oviparous.—*Amphibia*, Amphibious Creatures, living either on land or in the water.—*Pisces*, Fishes, which live only in the water, and are covered with scales.—*Insecta*, Insects, which have few or no organs of sense, and a bony coat of mail.—*Vermes*, Worms, which have mostly no feet.

First Class.

The *Mammalia* consist of seven orders, namely, the—*Primates, Bruta, Feræ, Glires, Pecora, Belluinæ*, and *Cete*.

First order.

The *Primates* are divided into 4 genera, namely—*Homo*, Man.—*Simia*, the Ape, the Baboon, and the Monkey.—*Lemur*, the Lemur.—*Vespertilio*, the Bat.

Second order.

Bruta, the second order, comprehends the following genera, namely—*Bradypus*, the Sloth.—*Myrmecophaga*, the Ant-Eater.—*Dasypus*, the Armadillo.—*Rhinoceros*, the Rhinoceros.—*Sokotyro.*—*Elephas*, the Elephant.—*Trichechus*, the Morse, Walrus.—*Manis*.

Third order.

Feræ, the third order, comprehends ten genera, namely—*Phoca*, the Seal.—*Canis*, the Dog, the Wolf, the Fox, and the Hyæna.—*Felis*, the Lion, the Tyger, the Leopard, the Tyger-Cat, the Lynx, and the Cat.—*Viverra*, the Weasel, the Shunk, the Civet, the Genet, and the Fitchet.—*Mustela*, the Otter, the Martin, the Ferret, the Polecat, the Ermine, and the Stoat.—*Ursus*, the Bear, the Badger, the Racoon, and the Glutton.—*Didalphis*, the Opossum, Marmose, Phalanger, and the Kangaroo.—*Talpa*, the Mole.—*Sorex*, the Shrew.—*Erinaceus*, the Hedge-Hog.

Fourth order.

Glires, the fourth order, comprehends the following genera, namely—*Histrix*, the Porcupine.—*Cavia*, the Cavy.—*Castor*, the Beaver.—*Mus*, the Rat, the Musk-Rat, and the Mouse.—*Arctomys*, the Marmot.—*Sciurus*, the Squirrel.—*Myoxus*, the Dormouse.—*Dipus*, the Jerboa.—*Lepus*, the Hare, and the Rabbit.—*Hyrax*.

Fifth order.

Pecora, the fifth order, comprehends the following genera, namely—*Camelus*, the Camel, the Lama.—*Moschus*, the Musk.—*Cervus*, the Stag, the Deer, the Moose, or Elk.—*Camelopardalis*, the Camelopard, or Giraffe.—*Antilopus*, the Antelope.—*Capra*, the Goat.—*Ovis*, the Sheep.—*Bos*, the Ox.

Sixth order.

Belluinæ, the sixth order, comprehends the following genera, namely—*Equus*, the Horse, the Ass, and the Mule.—*Hippopotamus*, the River-Horse.—*Tapir*, the Tapir.—*Sus*, the Hog.

Seventh order.

Cete, the seventh order, comprehends the following genera, namely—*Monodon*, the Monodon.—*Balæna*, the Whale.—*Physeter*, the Cachelot.—*Delphinus*, the Porpoise, the Dolphin, and the Grampus.

Second Class.

Aves, Birds, the second class, is divided into six orders, namely—*Accipitres*, *Picæ*, *Anseres*, *Grallæ*, *Gallinæ*, *Passeres*.

First order.

Accipitres, the first order, comprehends four genera, namely—*Vultur*, the Vulture and the Condur.—*Falco*, the Eagle, the Kite, the Buzzard, the Falcon, and the Hawk.—*Strix*, the Owl.—*Lanius*, the Shrike, the Butcher Bird, and the Woodchat.

Second order.

Picæ, the second order, comprehends the following genera, namely—*Ramphastos*, the Toucan.—*Momotus*, the Motmot.—*Psittacus*, the Parrot, the Maccaw, the Parrokeet, the Cockatoo, and the Lory.—*Scythrops*.—*Buceros*, the Horn-Bill.—*Crotophaga*, the Ani.—*Glaucopis*, the Wattle Bird.—*Corvus*, the Crow, the Rook, the Raven, the Jack-Daw, and the Jay.—*Coracias*, the Roller.—*Oriolus*, the Oriole.—*Gracula*, the Grackle.—*Paradisea*, the Bird of Paradise.—*Bucco*, the Barbet.—*Trogon*, the Curucui.—*Cuculus*, the Cockoo.—*Yunx*, the Wryneck.—*Picus*, the Woodpecker.—*Sitta*, the Nuthatch.—*Todus*, the Toddy.—*Alcedo*, the Kingsfisher.—*Galbula*, the Jacama.—*Merops*, the Bee-Eater.—*Upupa*, the Hoop or Hoopo.—*Certhia*, the Creeper.—*Trochilus*, the Humming-Bird.—*Buphuga*.

Third order.

Anseres, the third order, comprehends the following genera, namely—*Anas*, the Swan, the Goose, the Duck, the Shoveler, and the Teal.—*Mergus*, the Merganser, the Goosander, the Dunn-Diver, and the Smew.—*Alca*, the Auk or Razorbill.—*Aptenodytes*, the Penguin.—*Procellaria*, the Petrel.—*Diomedea*, the Albatross or Man-of-War Bird.—*Pelicanus*, the Pelican, the Corvorant, the Shag, the Crane, the Gannet, and the Booby.—*Plotus*, the Darter.—*Phæton*, the Tropic Bird.—*Colymbus*, the Guillemot, the Diver, and the Grebe.—*Larus*, the Gull, and the Tarrock or Kittiwake.—*Sterna*, the Tern.—*Rynchops*, the Skimmer.

Fourth order.

Grallæ, the fourth order, comprehends the following genera, namely—*Phœnicopteros*, the Flamingo.—*Platalea*, the Spoonbill.—*Palamedea*, the Screamer.—*Mycteria*, the Jabiru.—*Cancroma*, the Boatbill.—*Scopus*, the Umbre.—*Ardea*, the Heron, the Crane, the Stork, and the Bittern.—*Tantalus*, the Ibis.—*Corrira*, the Courier.—*Scolopax*, the Curlew, the Whintrel, the Snipe, the Woodcock, the Godwit, and the Red Shank.—*Tringa*, the Sandpiper, the Phalarope, and the Purre.—*Charadrius*, the Plover and the Dotterel.—*Recurvirostra*, the Avocet.—*Hæmatopus*, the Sea-Pie or Pied Oyster, and the Catcher.—*Glareola*, the Pratincole.—*Fulica*, the Gallinule, the Moor-Hen, and the Coot.—*Vaginalis*, the Sheathbill.—*Parra*, the Jacana.—*Rallus*, the Rail, the Crake or Sand-Rail, the Brook-Ouzel or Water-Rail, and the Soree.—*Psophia*, the Trumpeter.

Fifth order.

Gallinæ, the fifth order, includes the following genera, namely—*Otis*, the Bustard.—*Struthio*, the Ostrich, and the Cassowary or Emu.—*Didus*, the Dodo.—*Pavo*, the Peacock.—*Meleagris*, the Turkey.—*Penelope*, the Guam and the Yacou.—*Crax*, the Curassow.—*Phasianus*, the Pheasant.—*Numidia*, the Pintado or Guinea Hen.—*Tetrao*, the Grous, the Moorcock, the Partridge, the Quail, and the Tinamou.

Sixth order.

Passeres, the sixth order, includes the following genera, namely—*Columba*, the Pigeon, the Ring-Dove, the Turtle-Dove, &c.—*Alauda*, the Lark.—*Sturnus*, the Stare or Starling, and the Crake or Water-Ouzel.—*Turdus*, the Thrush, the Field-Fare, the Blackbird, and the Ring-Ouzel.—*Ampelis*, the Chatterer.—*Colius*, the Coly.—*Loxia*, the Grossbeak, the Crossbill, and the Haw-Finch.—*Emberiza*, the Bunting.—*Tanagra*, the Tanajer.—*Fringilla*, the Finch, the Chaffinch, the Siskin, the Redpole, the Linnet, the Twite, and the Sparrow.—*Phytotoma*, the Phytotoma.—*Muscicapa*, the Fly-Catcher.—*Motacilla*, the Wagtail or Warbler, the Nightingale, the Hedge Sparrow, the Wren, the White-Throat, the Wheat-Ear, and the Red-Start.—*Pipra*, the Minnakin.—*Parus*, the Titmouse.—*Hirundo*, the Swallow and the Swift.—*Caprimulgus*, the Goatsucker.

Third Class.

Amphibia, Amphibious animals, the third class, is divided into two orders, namely—*Reptilia*, Reptiles, and *Serpentes*, Serpents.

First order.

Reptilia, Reptiles, the first order, comprehends the following genera, namely—*Testudo*, the Tortoise and the Turtle.—*Rana*, the Toad, the Frog, and the Natter-Jack.—*Draco*, the Flying Dragon.—*Lacerta*, the Crocodile, the Alligator, the Lizard, the Guana, the Newt, the Salamander, the Chameleon, the Eft.—*Siren*.

Second order.

Serpentes, Serpents, the second order, includes the following genera, namely—*Crotalus*, the Rattle-Snake.—*Boa*.—*Coluber*, the Viper and the Asp.—*Anguis*, the Snake and the Blind-Worm.—*Amphisbæna*.—*Cæcilia*.—*Achrocordus*, the Warted Snake.

Fourth Class.

Pisces, Fishes, the fourth class, is divided into six orders, namely—*Apodal*, *Jugular*, *Thoracic*, *Abdominal*, *Branchiostegous*, *Chondropterigious*.

First order.

Apodal, the first order, contains the following genera, namely—*Muræna*, the Eel.—*Gymnotus*.—*Trichiuris*.—

ANIMAL.

Anarhicas, the Wolf Fish.—*Ammodytes*, the Launce.—*Stromateus*.—*Xiphias*, the Sword-Fish.—*Sternopfyx*.—*Leptocephalus*, the Morris.—*Stylephorus*.—*Ophidium*.—*Gymnothorax*.

Second order.

Jugular, the second order, contains the following genera, namely—*Callionymus*, the Dragonet.—*Uranoscopus*.—*Trachinus*, the Sting-Bull or Weaver,—*Gadus*, the Cod-Fish, the Bib, the Whiting, the Coal-Fish, the Hake, the Barbot, and the Rockling.—*Blennius*, the Blenny.—*Kurtus*.

Third order.

Thoracic, the third Order, contains the following genera, namely—*Cepola*.—*Echineis*, the Sucking-Fish.—*Coryphœna*.—*Gobius*, the Goby.—*Cottus*, the Bull-Head, the Father Lasher, and the Miller's Thumb.—*Scorpœna*.—*Zeus*, the John Doree.—*Pleuronectes*, the Hollibut, the Flounder, the Plaise, the Dab, the Sole, the Smeardab, the Pearl, and the Turbot.—*Chætodon*.—*Sparus*, the Gilthead, the Pudding-Fish.—*Scarus*.—*Labrus*, the Wrasse, the Goldfinny, the Camber, and the Cook.—*Sciæna*.—*Perca*, the Perch, the Basse, the Luffe, the Black Fish, and the Squirrel-Fish,—*Trachychthys*.—*Gasterosteus*, the Stickleback.—*Scomber*, the Mackerel, the Thunny, the Scad, and the Yellow-Tail.—*Centrogaster*.—*Mullus*, the Surmullet—*Trigla*, the Gurnard, the Piper, and the Tub-Fish.—*Lonchiurus*.

Fourth order.

Abdominal, the fourth order, comprehends the following genera, namely—*Cobitis*, the Loche and the Mud-Fish.—*Amia*.—*Silurus*.—*Teuthis*.—*Salmo*, the Salmon, the Trout, the Salmon-Trout or Bull-Trout, the Charr, the Smelt, the Gurniad, and the Lavaret.—*Fistularia*, the Tobacco-Pipe-Fish.—*Esox*, the Pike and the Garfish.—*Elops*.—*Argentina*, the Argentine.—*Atherina*, the Atherine or Silver-Fish.—*Mugil*, the Mullet.—*Excocoetus*, the Flying Fish.—*Polynemus*.—*Clupea*, the Herring, the Pilchard, the Sprat, the Shad, and the Anchovy.—*Cyprinus*, the Carp, the Barbel, the Gudgeon, the Tench, the Crucian, the Gold-Fish, the Dace, the Roach, the Finscale or Rud, the Red Eye, the Bleak, the Bream, the Minnow, and the Graining.—*Loncaria*.

Fifth order.

Branchiostegous, the fifth order, comprehends the following genera, namely—*Mormyrus*.—*Ostracion*.—*Tetrodon*, the Sun-Fish.—*Diodon*.—*Singnathus*, the Pipe-Fish and the Needle-Fish.—*Pegasus*.—*Centriscus*.—*Balistes*.—*Cyclopterus*, the Sucker.—*Lophius*, the Fishing-Frog, and the Angler or Frog-Fish.

Sixth order.

Chondropterigious, the sixth order, contains the following genera, namely—*Acipenser*, the Sturgeon.—*Chimæra*, the Sea-Monster.—*Squalus*, the Shark, the Dog-Fish, the Tope, the Sea-Fox, and the Angel-Fish.—*Pristis*, the Saw-Fish.—*Raia*, the Ray, the Skate, the Thornback.—*Petromyzon*, the Lamprey, and the Pride.—*Gastrobranchus*, the Hag or Hag-Fish.

Fifth Class.

Insecta, Insects, the fifth class, is divided into seven orders, namely—*Coleoptera, Hemiptera, Lepidoptera, Neuroptera, Hymenoptera, Diptera,* and *Aptera*.

First order.

Coleoptera, the first order, contains the following genera, namely—*Scarabæus*, the Beetle,—*Lucanus*.—*Dermestes*, the Leather-Eater.—*Synodendron*.—*Bostrichus*.—*Melyris*.—*Ptinus*, the Death-Watch.—*Hister*.—*Gyrinus*, the Water-Flea.—*Byrrhus*.—*Anthrenus*.—*Silpha*, the Carrion Beetle.—*Nitidula*.—*Opatrum*.—*Titroma*.—*Tetratoma*.—*Cassida*.—*Coccinella*.—*Chrysomela*.—*Cryptocephalus*.—*Hispa*.—*Bruchus*.—*Pausus*.—*Zygia*.—*Zonitis*.—*Apalus*.—*Brentus*.—*Curculio*.—*Rhinomacer*.—*Attelabus*.—*Notoxus*.—*Cerambyx*.—*Calopus*.—*Leptura*.—*Necydalis*.—*Lampyris*, the Fire-Fly.—*Horia*.—*Cucujus*.—*Cantharis*.—*Serropalpus*.—*Elater*.—*Cucindela*.—*Bupestris*.—*Hydrophilus*, the Water-Clock.—*Dytiscus*.—*Carabus*.—*Tenebrio*.—*Pimelia*.—*Lytta*.—*Meloe*.—*Mordella*.—*Staphylinus*.—*Forficula*, the Earwig.—*Erodius*.—*Manticora*.—*Alurnus*.

Second order.

Hemiptera, the second order, contains the following genera, namely—*Blatta*, the Cockroach.—*Pneumora*.—*Mantis*.—*Gryllus*, the Locust, the Grasshopper, and the Cricket.—*Fulgora*, the Lanthorn Fly.—*Cicada*.—*Notonecta*, the Boat Fly.—*Nepa*, the Water Scorpion.—*Cimex*, the Bug.—*Macrocephalus*.—*Aphis*, the Plant-Louse.—*Chermes*.—*Coccus*, the Cochineal.—*Thrips*.

Third order.

Lepidoptera, the third order, contains the following genera, namely—*Papilio*, the Butterfly.—*Sphinx*, the Hawk-moth.—*Phalæna*, the Moth.

Fourth order.

Neuroptera, the fourth order, contains the following genera, namely—*Libellula*, the Dragon-Fly.—*Ephemera*, the Day-Fly.—*Phryganea*.—*Hemerobius*.—*Myrmeleon*, the Lion-Ant.—*Panorpa*.—*Raphidia*.

Fifth order.

Hymenoptera, the fifth order, contains the following genera, namely—*Cynips*, the Gall-Fly.—*Tenthredo*, the Saw-Fly.—*Sirex*, the Tailed Wasp.—*Ichneumon*, the Ichneumon.—*Sphex*.—*Ammophila*.—*Scolia*.—*Thynnus*.—*Lucopsis*.—*Tiphia*.—*Chalcis*.—*Chrysis*, the Golden Fly.—*Vespa*, the Wasp.—*Apis*, the Bee.—*Formica*, the Ant or Emmet.—*Mutilla*.

Sixth order.

Diptera, the sixth order, contains the following genera, namely—*Oestrus*, the Gad-Fly and the Breeze.—*Tipula*, the Crane-Fly.—*Diopsis*.—*Musca*, the Fly.—*Tabanus*.—*Culex*, the Gnat.—*Empis*.—*Stomoxys*.—*Conops*.—*Asilus*.—*Bombylius*, the Humble-Bee.—*Hippobosca*.

Seventh order.

Aptera, the seventh order, contains the following genera, namely—*Lepisma*.—*Podura*, the Spring-Tail.—*Termes*, the White Ant.—*Pediculus*, the Louse and Crab-Louse.—*Acarus*, the Tick, the Harvest-Bug, and the Itch-Mite—*Phalangium*.—*Aranea*, the Spider.—*Scorpio*, the Scorpion.—*Cancer*, the Crab, the Lobster, the Prawn, the Shrimp, and the Squill.—*Monoculus*.—*Oniscus*.—*Scolopendra*.—*Julus*.—*Pulex*, the Flea.—*Hydrachna*.

Sixth Class.—Vermes.

The sixth class is divided into five orders, namely—*Intestina, Mollusca, Testacea, Zoophyta,* and *Infusoria*.

First order.

Intestina, the first order, contains the following genera, namely—*Ascaris*.—*Trichocephalus*.—*Filaria*.—*Scolex*.—*Ligula*.—*Strongylus*.—*Echinorynchus*.—*Cucullanus*.—*Caryophyllæus*.—*Linguatula*.—*Fasciola*, the Gourd-Worm or Fluke.—*Tænia*, the Tape-Worm.—*Furia*.—*Godius*, the Hair-Worm.—*Lumbricus*, the Earth-Worm, the Dew-Worm, and the Lug.—*Planaria.*—*Sipunculus,* the Tube-Worm.—*Hirudo,* the Leech.—*Uncinaria.*—*Hænica.*

Second order.

Mollusca, the second order, contains the following genera, namely—*Limax,* the Slug or Snail.—*Onchidium.*—*Laplisia,* the Sea Hare.—*Doris,* the Sea Lemon.—*Aphrodita.*—*Spio.*—*Amphitrite.*—*Terebella.*—*Nereis.*—*Nais.*—*Ascidia.*—*Salpa.*—*Dagysa.*—*Clava.*—*Actinia,* the Sea Daisy, the Sea Marigold, and the Sea Carnation.—*Mammaria.*—*Pedicillaria.*—*Tethys.*—*Plerotrachea.*—*Derris.*—*Holothuria.*—*Lobaria.*—*Triton.*—*Lernæa.*—*Scyllæa.*—*Clio.*—*Sepia,* the Cuttle-Fish.—*Lucernaria.*—*Medusa,* the Sea-Nettle.—*Physsophora.*—*Asterias,* the Star-Fish and the Sea-Star.—*Echinus,* the Sea Urchin.

Third order.

Testacea, Shells, the third order, comprehends the following genera, namely—*Chiton.*—*Lepas,* the Acorn Shell.—*Phloas.*—*Mya.*—*Solen,* the Razor-Sheath.—*Tellina.*—*Cardium,* the Cockle.—*Mactra.*—*Donax.*—*Venus.*—*Spondylus.*—*Chama.*—*Arca,* the Ark.—*Ostrea,* the Oyster.—*Anomia.*—*Mytilus,* the Mussel.—*Pinna.*—*Argonauta.*—*Nautilus.*—*Conus,* the Cone.—*Cypræa,* the Cowrie or Gourie.—*Bulla.*—*Voluta,* the Mitre or Volute.—*Buccinum,* the Whelk.—*Strombus.*—*Murex.*—*Trochus.*—*Turbo,* the Wreath.—*Helix,* the Snail.—*Nerita,* the Nerite.—*Haliotis,* the Sea-Ear.—*Patella,* the Limpet.—*Dentalium,* the Tooth-Shell.—*Serpula.*—*Teredo.*—*Sabella.*

Fourth order.

Zoophyta, the fourth order, contains the following genera, namely—*Tubipora,* the Tubipore.—*Madrepora,* the Madripore.—*Millepora,* the Millepore.—*Cellepora,* the Cellepore.—*Isis,* the Coral.—*Antipathes.*—*Gorgonia,* the Red Coral.—*Alcyonium.*—*Spongia,* the Sponge.—*Flustra,* the Hornwrack.—*Tubularia.*—*Corallina,* the Coralline.—*Sertularia.*—*Pennatula,* the Sea-Pen.—*Hydra,* the Polype.

Fifth order.

Infusoria, the fifth order, contains the following genera, namely—*Branchionus.*—*Vorticella.*—*Trichoda.*—*Cercaria.*—*Bursaria.*—*Gonium.*—*Colpoda.*—*Paramecium.*—*Cyclidium.*—*Vibrio.*—*Bacillaria.*—*Enchelis.*—*Volvox.*—*Monas.*—*Leucopera.*

ANIMA'LCULÆ (*Zool.*) very small animals, scarcely discoverable by the naked eye, which, by the help of microscopes, are found in fluids, and also in solids.

ANIMA'TE *power* (*Mech.*) a power in animal beings, in distinction from that which exists in inanimate bodies, as springs, &c.

ANIMA'TED *mercury* (*Chem.*) quicksilver impregnated with some subtle and spirituous particles, so as to render it capable of growing hot when mixed with gold. *Libav. Apoc. Hermet.* part 1, c. 10.—*Animated needle,* a needle touched with a stone.

ANIMA'TION (*Alch.*) the fermentation produced by the conjunction of mercury with any metal. *Libav. Apoc. Hermet.* part 1, c. 10; *Castell. Lex Med.*

A'NIME *gummi* (*Chem.*) a gum or white resin, brought from America, which flows, by an incision, from a tree, the *Hymenea courbaril* of Linnæus. Dioscorides and Serapio call it *Aminea,* which has been corrupted into *Animé.* The former says that it is an inferior kind of myrrh. The best Gum Animé is white, dry, friable, clean, of a good smell, that soon consumes when thrown into the fire, and contains a great deal of oil and essential salt. It is discussive, good for the head-ache, and a strengthener of the brain.

There are two sorts principally spoken of, namely, the Oriental and the Western; but Bauhine reckons five sorts. *Dioscor.* l. 1, c. 77; *Clus. Ray. Plant. Hist.*; *J. Bauh. Hist. Plant.*; *Raii Hist. Lem. des Drog.*

ANIME (*Her.*) an epithet implying that the eyes of any rapacious creature are borne of a different tincture from that of the creature itself.

ANIME'LLÆ (*Anat.*) the Glandules under the ears and the lower jaws.

A'NIMUS (*Met.*) the mind, or reasoning faculty, in distinction from *anima,* the being or substance in which the faculty exists.

ANI'NGA *ibis* (*Bot.*) an Indian aquatic plant that grows five or six feet high, with leaves similar to the water-lily. From the bulbous root of the aningas is expressed an oil of great medicinal use for fomentation. *Pis. Marc. Hist. Braz.*; *Raii Hist. Plant.*

AN *jour et wast.* (*Law*) a forfeiture when a man has committed petty treason and felony, and has lands held of some common person, which shall be seized for the king, and remain in his hands a year and a day next after the attainder, and then the trees shall be pulled up; except he to whom the lands should come by escheat or forfeiture, redeem it of the king.

ANISA'TUM (*Med.*) from ἄνισον, Anise-seed; a wine in which Anise seeds are infused.

ANISATUM (*Bot.*) a species of the *Illicium* of Linnæus.

ANISCA'LPTOR (*Anat.*) the same as *Latissimus Dorsi.*

A'NISE (*Bot.*) a small oblong seed, produced from the *Anisum,* or the *Pimpinella anisum* of Linnæus. [vide *Anisum*]

ANISE (*Com.*) a sort of greyish wood that is brought from the Indies in logs, and has a scent similar to that of the plant.

A'NISEED-TREE (*Bot.*) the *Illicium* of Linnæus.

ANI'SIFOLIUM (*Bot.*) the *Limonia acidissima* of Linnæus.

ANISOCY'CLA (*Archæol.*) a machine constructed of many unequal circles, by the help of which the ancients discharged arrows or stones from their scorpions or crossbows. *Vitruv. de Architect.* l. 10, c. 1; *Turneb. Adver.* l. 9, c. 20; *Bald. Lec. Vitruvian.*

ANISOMARA'THRUM (*Bot.*) the *Scandix australis* of Linnæus.

A'NISUM (*Bot.*) ἄνισον, Anise, probably from ἀνίκητον, invictum, invincible, to denote its superior power above other medicines; a plant, the seed of which is an anodyne, diaphoretic, diuretic, and discutient. It is the *Pimpinella anisum* of Linnæus. *Theoph. Hist. Plant.* l. 7, c. 3; *Dioscor.* l. 3, c. 65; *Plin.* l. 20, c. 17; *Gal. de Simplic.* l. 6; *Oribas Med. Coll.* l. 11; *Aet. Tetrab.* 1, serm. 1; *Paul. Æginet. de Re Med.* l. 7, c. 3; *Myrep. de Antidot.* sect. 1, c. 23; *J. Bauh. Hist. Plant.*; *Parkin. Theat. Botan.*; *Raii Hist. Plant.*—*Anisum Africanum,* the *Bubon galbinatum* of Linnæus.

A'NKER (*Com.*) a liquid measure at Amsterdam, containing thirty-two gallons wine measure in England.

A'NLÆ (*Archæol.*) a falchion or sword shaped like a scythe.

A'NN (*Com.*) abbreviated for *annum,* as *per annum,* yearly.

ANN (*Law*) or *Annat,* half a year's stipend, in the Scotch Law, over and above what is owing for the incumbency, due to the minister's relict, children, or near akin.

ANNABA'SSES (*Com.*) a coarse blanketting made in France for the Guinea trade.

ANNA'LES (*Ant.*) Annals, from *annus,* a year, signifying an account of what was done within the year; small books in which were registered the names of the magistrates, together with the names of the persons, places, and things connected with their magistracy. Whence Cicero makes

ANN

the distinction between Annals and History. " *Historia nihil aliud nisi Annalium confectio.*" *De Orat.* l. 2, c. 12; *Aul. Gell.* l. 1, c. 1; *Ferrar. de Origin. Roman. apud Græv. Thesaur. Antiq. Rom.* tom. 1, &c.—*Annales maximi* was also the name given to the annals of the state, because they were consecrated and confirmed by the *Pontifex maximus*, or High-Priest; they were also called *Commentarii. Cic. de Orat.* l. 2, c. 12; *Liv.* l. 4, c. 3; *Fest. de Verb. Signif.*; *Turneb. in Cic. de Leg.*; *Alex. Gen. Dier.* l. 2, c. 8, &c.

ANNALES (*Archæol.*) 1. Public acts registered every year. *Leg. Cod. Theod.* 2. a sort of annual census.

ANNALES (*Law*) yearlings, or cattle a year old.

ANNA'LIS *lex* (*Ant.*) a law for regulating the age at which offices might be enjoyed. It was proposed U. C. 573, by L. Vilius or Julius, who, on that account, was surnamed *Annalis*. What the precise age fixed for each magistracy was is not ascertained. [vide *Ætas*] *Cic. de Or.* l. 2, c. 65; *Liv.* l. 4, c. 44; *Manut. de Leg.* c. 6.—*Annalis clavus*, the nail was so called which was driven into the wall of the temple every year, to mark the succession and number of years. [vide *Clavus*]

ANNA'TES (*Law*) Annats, or first fruits paid out of spiritual benefices to the Pope, being the value of one year's profit. *Stat.* 25, *Hen.* 8.

A'NNE'S *Day, St.* (*Ecc.*) a festival kept in the Romish church on the 26th of June, and in the Greek church on the 9th of December, in honour of Anna, the mother of the Virgin Mary.

ANNE'AL (*Bot.*) the same as *Anil.*

ANNEA'LING *of tile* (*Mech.*) from the Saxon *ælan*, to set on fire; the burning of tiles, so as to harden them.

ANNEXA'TION (*Law*) uniting lands or rents to the crown.

ANNIE'NTED (*Law*) in French *aneantie*; abrogated or made null.

A'NNI *Tempora constantia* (*Med.*) καθιςῶτις καιροὶ, Consistent seasons, which keep their usual and expected temperature, in distinction from the inconsistent seasons, καιροὶ ἀκατάςατοι, which are unstable, and not to be relied upon. *Hippoc. Aph.*; *Foes Œconom. Hip.*

ANNI *nubiles* (*Law*) the age at which a girl becomes by law fit for marriage, which is twelve.

ANNIVE'RSARY (*Ecc.*) the yearly obit or service performed in the Romish church once every year for a person deceased, i. e. properly on the anniversary of his or her decease.

ANNIVERSARY *days* (*Law*) Days so called because they returned at the revolution of every year, *quovis anno vertente*. These days were kept solemn every year, in commemoration of the death or martyrdom of any saint. *Alcuin. de Divin. Offic.*; 1 *Ed.* 6.

A'NNO *Domini* (*Chron.*) abbreviated A. D. the computation of time from the incarnation of our Saviour, which is used as the date for all public deeds and writings in England, on which account it is called the 'Vulgar Æra.' This computation is supposed to be three years later than the real time of our Saviour's Incarnation. [vide *Æra*]

ANNOI'SANCE (*Law*) the same as *Nuisance*.

ANNO'MŒANS (*Ecc.*) vide *Anomœans*.

ANNO'NA (*Ant.*) from *annus*, a year, signified properly a year's produce from one's land; but it is also taken for the provision of corn, and whatever else was necessary for the sustenance of man, whence *annonæ caritas* signifies dearness of provisions, or a dear market. *Cic. in Verr.* l. 3, c. 92.—*Annona militaris*, the public allowance of bread, fodder, &c.—*Annonæ*, in the plural, the loaves themselves. *Lamprid. in Sever.* c. 41; *Cod. Theodos. de Erag. Mil. Annon.*

ANNONA (*Numis.*) is commonly represented on coins by ears of corn, and a cornucopeia, as in the annexed figure, on a coin of the emperor Claudius, bearing the inscription ANNONA. AUG. The female, which is the figure of the goddess Ceres, is sometimes represented holding a spear, a lance, and sometimes a measure, with ears of corn, &c. To the inscription is frequently added the words PROVIDENT*ia*, FELICITAS, FELICISSIMI SAECULI. AETERN*a* CERES, &c.

ANNONA (*Bot.*) a genus of plants in the hot climates; so called because its fruit is grateful to the natives, Class 13 *Polyandria*, Order 7 *Polygynia*.

  Generic Characters. CAL. *perianth* three-leaved; *leaflets* cordate.—COR. *petals* six.—STAM. *filaments* scarcely any; *anthers* very numerous.—PIST. *germ* roundish; *styles* none; *stigmas* obtuse.—PER. *berry* very large; *seeds* very many.

  Species. The plants of this tribe are all shrubs, and mostly natives of America or India, as—*Annona tripetala*, *Cherimolia*, seu *Guanabanus*, Broad-leaved Custard-Apple. —*Annona squamosa*, seu *Atamaran*, Undulated Custard-Apple.—*Annona reticulata*, Netted Custard-Apple. —*Annona Asiatica*, seu *Keschta*, Asiatic Custard-Apple, &c.

ANNONA'RII (*Ant.*) forestallers of the market, who bought up all the provisions before hand in order to raise the market.

A'NNORA (*Chem.*) calcined egg-shells, or quick-lime.

ANNOTA'TIO (*Med.*) the beginning of a febrile paroxysm.

A'NNUA *pensione* (*Law*) a writ from the king to an abbot, or a prior, demanding of him an annual pension due to him for one of his chaplains, &c. *Reg. Orig.* 165, 307.

A'NNUAL (*Bot.*) an epithet for any plant or root which perishes within the compass of a year, in distinction from *Biennials* or *Perennials*. The stem of herbaceous plants is annual, but the root is perennial, which distinguishes them from trees and shrubs.

ANNUAL (*Astron.*) an epithet employed frequently to denote what is done in the space of a year, or returns every year.—*Annual motion of the earth*. [vide *Earth*]—*Annual argument of longitude*. [vide *Argument*]—*Annual epacts.* [vide *Epact*]—*Annual equation*, the equation of the mean motion of the sun and moon, and of the moon's apogee and nodes.

ANNUAL *Pension* (*Law*) vide *Annua pensione*.—*Annual rent*, in the Scotch Law, a yearly profit due to a creditor by way of interest for a given sum of money.—*Right of annual rent*, the original right of burdening land with a yearly payment for the loan of money.

ANNUA'LIA (*Law*) a yearly stipend assigned to a priest for celebrating an anniversary for the soul of a deceased person, &c.

ANNUALIA (*Archæol.*) oblations made by the relations of deceased persons on the anniversary of their death, which was called the Year's Day or the year's Mind.

ANNUE'NTES *musculi* (*Anat.*) muscles of the back or head; so called because they perform the office of nodding or bending the head downward.

ANNU'ITY (*Law*) a yearly rent to be paid for term of life or years, or in fee. *Reg. Orig.* 158. — *Writ of Annuity*, the writ that lies against a man for the recovery of such a rent, if not satisfied every year according to the grant. *Co. Lit.* 144.—*Annuity of teinds or tithes*, in the Scotch law, what is allowed yearly to the king out of the teinds not paid to the bishop.

ANNUITY (*Com.*) what is payable at any stated period within a year. Annuities are yearly, half-yearly, or quarterly, that is, payable by the year, half-year, or quarter.—*Certain annuity*, one that is in perpetuity.—*Contingent Annuity*, one depending on some contingency, as a life annuity.—*Annuity in possession*, when it has already commenced.—*Annuity in reversion*, when it will commence at some given future period.—*Annuity in arrears*, what is forborne for any number of years.

A'NNULAR *bone* (*Anat.*) *Circulus osseus*, a ring-like bone placed before the cavity of the tympanum in the fœtus.—*Annular cartilage*, the second cartilage at the head of the larynx or Windpipe.—*Annular ligament*, a strong ligament encompassing the carpus or wrist after the manner of a bracelet.

ANNULARIS *digitus*, the ring-finger next to the little one.—*Annularis vena*, the vein next to the ring-finger. *Aet. Tetrab.* 1, serm. 3, c. 12.—*Annularis musculus*, the *Sphincter Ani*.—*Annularis processus*, a protuberance of the medulla. *Ruf. Ephes. de Appell. Part. hum. Corp.* l. 1, c. 10.

AN'NULATE (*Bot.*) *annulatus*, an epithet for a capsule, stem, and root.—*Capsula annulata*, an annulate capsule, is encircled by an articulated ring.—*Radix annulata*, an annulate root, is furnished on its upper surface with alternately raised and depressed bands.—*Caudex annulatus*, an annulate stem, is that which has the remains of the leaves at regular distances resembling annular elevations, as in the *Corypha rotundifolia*.

AN'NULET (*Archæol.*) a little square moulding to accompany a larger, or to separate the flutings of a column; also, a narrow flat moulding that encompasses other parts of a column, which is called by the different names of *Fillet, Listel Cincture, List Tænia, Square, Rabit*, and *Supercilium*.

ANNULET (*Her.*) a little ring [O] borne in the coats of arms, supposed to be taken for rings of mail, which was an armour of defence. The annulet is the charge which distinguishes the fifth son of any family. It is supposed to remind him that he should achieve great actions, according to the old motto, *Jus aureorum Annulorum*.

A'NNULUS (*Geol.*) a ring; a species of Volutæ.

ANNULUS (*Bot.*) a membranaceous part of the fungi, of which there are different kinds, namely—*Annulus erectus*, fixed below and free above.—*Annulus invertus*, fixed above and free below.—*Annulus sessilis*, attached by one side.—*Annulus mobilis*, to be moved up and down.—*Annulus persistens*, lasting as long as the fungus.—*Annulus fugax*, disappearing when the fungus develops itself.—*Annulus arachnoides*, composed of a white web.

ANNUNCI'ADE (*Her.*) the name of several orders; so called in honour of the Annunciation to the Blessed Virgin. The most distinguished order of this name was that instituted by Amadeo, the sixth Earl of Savoy, in commemoration of the victory obtained by the first Earl over the Turks, whom he drove from the Isle of Rhodes. The collar belonging to this order is of gold, on which these letters are engraven, F.E.R.T. *Fortitudo ejus Rhodum tenuit*. To this collar is appended a tablet, wherein is the figure of the Annunciation.

ANNUNCIA'TION (*Ecc.*) *annunciatio*, from *ad* and *nuncio*, to tell; the delivery of a message, particularly the Angel's message to the Virgin Mary, concerning the birth of our Saviour.—*Annunciation of our Lady*, a festival in the Christian Church commemorative of the Annunciation to the Blessed Virgin, which is celebrated on the 25th of March.

ANNUNCIATION (*Theol.*) a name given by the Jews to a part of their ceremonial of the Passover.

ANNUNCIATOR (*Ecc.*) an officer in the church of Constantinople, whose office it was to announce to the people the festivals that were to be celebrated.

A'NO (*Med.*) ἄνω, upwards, opposed to κάτω, downwards, in respect to purgatives, which operate upwards or downwards.

ANO'BIUM (*Ent.*) a division of the genus *Ptinus*, according to Fabricius, comprehending the insects of this tribe, which have the feelers clavate.

ANOCATHA'RTICA (*Med.*) Emetics.

ANOCHEI'LON (*Anat.*) ἀνωχειλον, from ἄνω, upper, and χειλος, the lip; the upper lip. *Castell. Lex. Med.*

A'NOCHUS (*Med.*) from ἀνέχω, to retain; a stoppage of the intestinal discharge.

A'NODA (*Bot.*) the *Sida* of Linnæus.

A'NODINA (*Med.*) vide Anodynes.

ANOD'MON (*Med.*) without smell, as applied to pus. *Hippoc. in Coac.*; *Foes. Hippocrat. Œconom.*

A'NODUS (*Chem.*) what is separated from the nourishment by the kidneys.

A'NODYNES (*Med.*) ἀνώδυνα, anodyna, from α, priv. and ὀδύνη, pain; medicines so called because they ease pain and procure sleep, such as the medicinal preparations of the poppy. *Cels. de Re Med.* l. 5, c. 25, &c.; *Gal. de Simpl. Med.* l. 5, c. 11; *Cels. Aurel. de Tard. Pass.* l. 3, c. 4; *Trallian.* l. 10; *Myreps. de Antidot.* sect. 1, c. 178; *Marcell. de Med.* c. 25; *Gorr. Def. Med.*; *Foes. Œconom. Hippocrat.*

ANODY'NUM (*Med.*) Anodyne Balsam.—*Anodynum minerale*, the same as *Nitrum*.

ANODY'NUS *fotus* (*Med.*) Anodyne fomentation.

ANO'EA (*Med.*) ἄνοια, from α, priv. and νοέω, to think; privation of understanding, madness.

ANOI'NTERS (*Ecc.*) a name given to a particular sect, who were so called because they anointed all whom they admitted into their society.

ANOMÆ'ANS (*Ecc.*) ἀνόμοιοι, an heretical sect, which held most of the doctrines of the Arians, particularly that the essence of the Son was unlike that of the Father. *Socrat. Hist. Eccles.* l. 2, c. 45, l. 3, c. 25, &c.; *Sozom. Hist.* l. 4, c. 14; *Theodoret.* l. 4; *S. Hilar. in Constant.*

ANOMÆ'OS (*Med.*) ἀνόμοιος, dissimular, as applied to vicious humours.

ANO'MALÆ *plantæ* (*Bot.*) from *anomalus*, irregular; the twenty-sixth class of plants in the system of Ray.

ANOMA'LIA (*Med.*) ἀνωμαλία, from α, priv. and ὁμαλός, equal, inequality, or irregularity, as applied to the pulse. *Galen. Defin. Med.*; *Actuar.* περὶ διαγνώσεως παθῶν, l. 1, c. 1; *Gorr. Defin. Med.*

ANOMALIA (*Astron.*) vide Anomaly.

ANOMALI'STIC Year (*Astron.*) or periodical year; that space of time in which the earth, or a plane, passes through its orbit, which is 365 d. 6 h. 15 m. 10 sec.

ANO'MALOUS (*Gram.*) ἀνώμαλος, from α, priv. and ὁμαλός, equal, i. e. without rule; an epithet applied to verbs that are irregularly formed, of which the Greek affords many examples.

ANO'MALY (*Astron.*) ἀνωμαλία, irregularity; the irregularity in the motion of a planet, whereby it deviates from the aphelion or apogee, or it is the distance from the aphelion or apogee. It is sometimes taken for the argument of anomaly, which is the arc between the line of the apsides and the line of mean motion. Kepler distinguished anomaly into mean or simple, eccentric, and true, or equated.—*Mean* or *simple anomaly*, the distance of the mean place of a planet from the apogee; thus, suppose E S D to be the sun's orbit, A M N B the ecliptic, the earth at T, the sun at S, and A B the line of the apses, then is the angle A T M, or the arc A M, the sun's mean anomaly; in the modern astronomy the mean anomaly is the time in which a planet moves from its aphelion to the mean place or point in its orbit; thus, suppose a planet P to describe an ellipse, A P B, about the sun, S, in one focus, let A B be the line of the apses, A

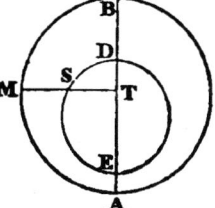

the aphelion, and B the perihelion, then the mean anomaly is the time in which the planet moves from the aphelion to its mean place, P; and since the elliptic area A S P is proportional to the time in which the planet describes the arc A P, that area may represent the mean anomaly.—*Eccentric anomaly*, or the angle at the centre, is the arc A D of the eccentric circle A D B, intercepted between the aphelion and the point D, determined by the perpendicular D P E to the line of the apses A B; or it is the angle A E D at the centre of the circle.—*True* or *equated* anomaly, otherwise called *the angle at the sun*, is the angle A S P at the sun, which the planet's distance, A P, from the aphelion appears under.

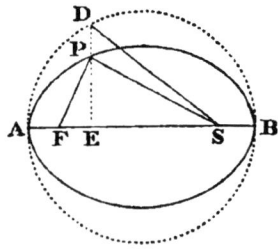

ANO'MIA (*Con.*) Bowl-shell, a genus of animals, Class *Vermes*, Order *Testacea*.
Generic Characters. Shell inequivalve.—*Valve* one, perforated near the hinge; affixed by that perforation to some other body.
Species. The principal species of this genus, which mostly inhabit the Mediterranean, and adhere to oyster-shells, are, the—*Anomia ephippium*, the Wrinkled Bowl-Shell.—*Anomia electra*, the Amber Bowl-Shell.—*Anomia squamula*, the Scaly Bowl-Shell, &c.

ANOMO'EOS (*Med.*) ἀνόμοιος, heterogeneous; applied to the humours which are preternatural and vicious. *Foes. Œconom. Hippocrat.*

ANOMORHOMBOI'DEA (*Min.*) a sort of crystals; so called because their plates are composed of irregular arrangements of short and thick rhomboidal concretions.

ANO'MPHALOS (*Anat.*) ἀνόμφαλος, without a navel, as our first parents were supposed to be.

ANO'NA (*Bot.*) the genus Annona, as also the *Achras mammosa et sapota*, the *Chrysophyllum cainito*, and the *Cratæva gynandra et tapia* of Linnæus. *Raii Hist. Plant.*

ANO'NIS (*Bot.*) or *Ononis*, ἀνωνὶς, ὀνωνίς, or ὀνωνίς, from α, priv. and ὀνίμι, to be of use; a plant so called, because it seems to be worthless. In English it is called Restharrow; and in the Linnean system is the *Glycine-tomentosa*, the *Hedysarum hamatum*, and several species of the *Ononis*. The root is heating and attenuating; the bark, drank in wine, provokes urine; the root, boiled in oxycras, eases the toothache. *Theoph. Hist. Plant.* l. 6, c. 5; *Dioscor.* l. 3, c. 21; *Plin.* l. 21, c. 16; *Gal. de Simplic.* l. 6; *Oribas. Med. Coll.* l. 15; *Paul. Æginet. de Re Med.* l. 7, c. 3.

ANONYMOUS (*Com.*) ἀνώνυμος, anonymous; from α, priv. and ὄνομα, a name, nameless; an epithet applied to partnerships in France, which are not acknowledged openly as partnerships, but are known only to the parties themselves.

ANONYMOUS *spirit* (*Chem.*) a sort of spirit that may be separated from tartar, and several sorts of wood.

ANONYMOUS (*Lit.*) an epithet applied to books or writings the author of which is not named.

ANO'NYMUS (*Bot.*) ἀνώνυμος, from α, priv. and ὄνομα, a name; anonymous; an epithet for many exotics.

ANONYMUS (*Anat.*) the second cartilage of the throat. [vide *Cricoides*]

A'NORA (*Chem.*) Ovorum Testæ.

ANORCHI'DES (*Anat.*) such as are born without testicles.

ANORE'XIA (*Med.*) ἀνορεξία, from α, priv. and ὄρεξις, *appetitus*; loathing of food. *Gorr. Def. Med.*; *Foes. Œconom. Hippocrat.*

ANOREXIA, in Cullen's Nosology, is a genus of diseases.

ANO'SIA (*Med.*) ἀνοσία; from α, priv. and νόσος, disease; absence of disease.

ANO'SMIA (*Med.*) from α, priv. and ὀσμή, smell, i. e. without smell; a disease attended with a diminution or loss of smell.

ANO'TTA (*Bot.*) the *Bixa orellana* of Linnæus.

A'NSÆ (*Ast.*) the various positions of the rings of Saturn, which appear like *Ansæ*, or handles.

A'NSEL (*Com.*) a weight. [vide *Aunsel*]

A'NSER (*Astron.*) a small star, of the 5th or 6th magnitude, in the Milky Way. *Hevel. Prodrom. Astron.*

A'NSERES (*Or.*) the third order of birds, Aves, having the bill somewhat obtuse, and covered with a skin, gibbous at the base; the mouth toothed; the tongue fleshy; feet palmate, formed for swimming. It includes the following genera, namely: 1. Those having a bill with teeth, as—*Anas*, Goose, Swan, Duck, &c.; bill convex, obtuse.—Three fore toes connected.—*Mergus*, Merganser; bill hooked at the point; feet four-toed; the outer toe longest.—*Phaeton*, Tropic-Bird; bill sharp edged; hind toe turned forwards.—*Plotus*, Darter; bill pointed; feet, all the toes connected. 2. Those having a bill without teeth, as—*Rynchops*; bill, the upper mandible much shorter, lower truncate.—*Diomedea*, Albatross; bill, upper mandible hooked, lower truncate; feet four-toed, all placed forward.—*Aptenodyta*, Penguin; bill sharp edged; feet fettered, four-toed.—*Alca*, Auk; bill short, compressed; feet mostly three-toed.—*Procellaria*, Petrel; bill hooked at the point, mandibles equal; feet, the back toe pointing downwards.—*Pelicanus*, Pelican; bill furnished with a nail; feet, all the fore toes palmate.—*Larus*, Gull; bill sharp edged; feet, back toe small.—*Sterna*, Tern; bill pointed; feet, back toe small.—*Colymbus*; bill subulate; feet fettered.

ANSERI'NA (*Bot.*) the *Potentilla Anserina* of Linnæus.

ANSPESA'DE (*Mil.*) a subaltern in the French army, below a corporal, but above a sentinel.

A'NSWER (*Law*) a form of defence.

A'NT (*Ent.*) a gregarious and proverbially industrious tribe of insects, which on that account is made the emblem of industry. They are divided, like the Bees and Wasps, into males, females, and neutrals, which last constitute the great mass of this tribe, and appear to conduct the business of the nest. Ants feed both on animal and vegetable substances, and if left at liberty will pick the bones of any dead animal until they have rendered it a naked skeleton. By this means good skeletons of frogs, snakes, &c. have been obtained.

ANT (*Chem.*) This insect yields a very grateful acid by distillation, which resembles vinegar, except that it forms crystals with magnesia, iron, and zinc.

A'NTBEAR (*Zool.*) a name which Ray gives to two species of the bear that devour Ants.

ANT *Eater* (*Zool.*) the English name for an American quadruped, classed by Linnæus as a genus of Mammalia, under the name of *Myrmecophaga*.

ANTACHA'TES (*Min.*) a precious stone of the agate kind, which on being burnt yields a perfume of myrrh. *Plin.* l. 37, c. 19.

ANT-A'CIDA (*Med.*) acids that correct or destroy the acidity of the humours.

A'NTÆ (*Archit.*) Jaumbs or square pillars on each side the doors of the temples. The capitals of the Antæ seldom corresponded with those of the column; but in the temples of Minerva Pollias, and Apollo Didymæus, in Ionia, they bear a strong resemblance, having also volutes, though not in the same proportion, nor hanging in the same manner. *Vitruv.* l. 3, c. 1; *Fest. de Verb. Signif.*; *Serv. in Virg. Eclog.* l. 2; *Salmas. in Solin.* p. 1216.

ANTAGONI'STA (*Anat.*) ἀνταγωνιστής, from ἀντί and ἀγωνίζομαι, to contend; i. e. one thing acting against another; an epithet applied to muscles acting contrary ways, as the

Abductor of the cubitus, which serves to stretch the arm out, and the *Adductor*, which pulls it back.

ANTA'LGICS (*Med.*) medicines which assuage pain.

ANTA'LIUM (*Con.*) *Antale*, or *tubulus marinus*, a little shell, the size of a pipe, which contains small sea-worms.

ANTA'LKALINA (*Med.*) Medicines which possess the power of neutralizing alcalies, such as the antacids, &c.

ANTANACLA'SIS (*Rhet.*) ἀντανάκλασις, from ἀντανακλάω, to refract; a figure in rhetorick, when that which is spoken in one sense is turned to another or contrary sense. *Quint. Instit.* l. 9, c. 3; *Rutil. Lup.* l. 1, c. 5.

ANTANAGO'GE (*Rhet.*) ἀνταναγωγη, from ἀντάγω, to set forth in opposition; recrimination; a figure of speech when one answers a charge by a counter charge of the same kind.

ANTANISOPHY'LLUM scandens (*Bot.*) the *Boerhavia scandens* of Linnæus.

ANTAPHRODISI'ACOS (*Med.*) ἀνταφροδισιακὸς, from ἀντι, and Ἀφροδίτη, Venus; anti-venereals, or medicines tending to extinguish venereal appetite.

ANTAPHRODI'TICA (*Med.*) the same as Antiphrodisiacos.

ANTAPODO'SIS (*Med.*) ἀνταπόδοσις, from ἀνταποδίδωμι, to reciprocate; periodical returns of the paroxysms of fevers. *Hippocrat. Aphor.* sect. 12; *Gorr. Def. Med.*; *Foes. Oeconom. Hippocrat.*

ANTAPODOSIS (*Rhet.*) ἀνταπόδοσις, the counter part or latter clause of a similitude, answering to the former called by Quintilian "Redditio." *Quint. Instit.* l. 8, c. 3.

ANTA'RCTIC (*Astron.*) ἀνταρκτικὸς from ἀντι, opposite, and ἄρκτος, the Northern Bear; an epithet for one of the Poles and one of the Circles.—*Antarctic Pole*, the South Pole, or the pole opposite to the Northern.—*Antarctic Circle*, one of the lesser circles, drawn on the globe at the distance of 23 degrees and a half from the Antarctic, or South Pole. *Gem. Elem. Astron.* c. 2; *Cleom. de Mund.* l. 1; *Procl. de Sphaer.*

ANTARTHRI'TICS (*Med.*) ἀνταρθριτικὰ, from ἀντι, and ἀρθρίτις, the gout; medicines against the gout.

ANTA'RES (*Ast.*) the Scorpion's heart; a star of the first magnitude in the Scorpion. Its longitude for 1700, according to Hevelius, was in ♐ 5° 32' 43", and S. Lat. 4° 27' 19".

ANTASTHMA'TICS (*Med.*) ἀντασθματικὰ, from ἀντι and ἄσθμα, asthma; medicines against the Asthma.

ANTEAMBULO'NES (*Ant.*) from *ante*, and *ambulo*, to walk; clients who walked before their patrons. *Mart.* l. 2, epig. 18, v. 5.

Sum comes ipse tuus, tumidique anteambulo regis.

Sueton. in Vesp. c. 2; *Bud. in Pandect.* p. 137; *Salmas. ad Trebell. in Claud.* c. 14.

ANTECA'NIS (*Astron.*) the same as *Canis major*.

ANTECE'DENCE (*Astron.*) vide Antecedentia.

ANTECE'DENT (*Log.*) *Antecedens*, from *ante*, and *cedo*, to go; the premises of a syllogism, in distinction from the consequent conclusion. 2. *Locus proprius dialecticorum*, a conclusion.

ANTECEDENT *of a ratio* (*Geom.*) ἡγούμενος τε λόγε; the first of the two terms of a ratio, in distinction from the consequent or last term; as, if *a* be to *b* as *c* to *d*, then *a* and *c* are the antecedents, *b* and *d* consequents. *Def. Euc. Elem.* l. 5.

ANTECEDENT (*Gram.*) that word to which the relative refers.

ANTECEDENT (*Phy.*) the cause that is first observed.

ANTECEDENT *Decree* (*Theol.*) a decree preceding some other decree, or some action of the creature, or the provision of the action.

ANTECEDE'NTAL *method* (*Geom.*) a mode of Geometrical proportion, derived from the examination of the antecedents and consequents of ratios, invented by Mr. James Glennie, and illustrated in 1789, in a treatise on "General Proportion."

ANTECEDE'NTIA (*Astron.*) an epithet applied to the motion of the planets when they appear to move εἰς τὰ προηγούμενα westward, or contrary to the usual order of the signs, in distinction from the eastward motion, when they are said to move εἰς τὰ ἑπόμενα i.e. "in consequentia." *Ptol. Almag.* l. 8, &c.

ANTECEDENTIA *Signa* (*Med.*) signs of diseases; such as the bad disposition of the blood, which are first observed.

ANTECESSO'RES (*Ant.*) men who for their skill were held in high esteem, and took the lead on all occasions. Justinian gave this name to professors of the law. *Turneb. Adv.* l. 8, c. 19.—*Antecessores equites*, parties of dragoons sent out on the scout; called by Cæsar "ante cursores." *Cæs. de Bell. Gall. Cic.* l. 5, c. 45; *Hist. de Bell. Afric.* c. 12; *Turneb. Adver.* l. 24, c. 16.

ANTE'CIANS (*Astron.*) vide Antoeci.

ANTECŒ'NIUM (*Ant.*) from *ante*, and *cœnum*, supper; πρόδειπνον, a collation before supper, or the first course at supper, consisting of eggs, herbs, &c. customary among the Greeks and Romans. *Macrob. Saturn.* l. 3, c. 12; *Turneb. Adv.* l. 17, c. 10; *Lips. Antiq. Lect.* vol. 3, p. 147.

ANTECURSO'RES (*Ant.*) vide Antecessores.

A'NTEDATE (*Com.*) a date that precedes the real one, as the antedate of a bill, that which is earlier than the time when it is drawn.

ANTEDILU'VIANS (*Ant.*) from *ante* and *diluvium*, the deluge; persons living before the deluge.

ANTEJURAME'NTUM (*Law*) an oath taken both by the accuser and accused, before any trial or purgation.

ANTELA'BIA (*Anat.*) προχείλα, from *ante*, before, and *labia*, the lips; the extremities of the lips. *Ruf. Ephes. Appell. Part. Human. Corp.* l. 1, c. 6.

A'NTELIX (*Ant.*) or Antihelix, fron *anti*, opposite to, and *helix*; in the Greek ἀνθέλιξ; that part of the ear which is opposite to the helix. *Ruf. Ephes. de Appell. Part. human. Corp.* l. 1, c. 6.

A'NTELOPE (*Zool.*) the *Antilopus* of Linnæus; an African beast, like a deer, which is remarkable for its swiftness. The hoofs and horns are used in medicine, and are esteemed good against the epilepsy and hysterics. *Gessn. de Quad.*; *Aldrov. de Quad.*

ANTELUCA'NÆ *cœnæ* (*Ant.*) suppers early in the morning.

ANTEMBALLO'MENOS (*Med.*) ἀντεμβαλλόμενος, from ἀντι, for, and ἐμβάλλω, to throw or put in, substituted; an epithet applied to any medicine substituted for another.

ANTE'MBASIS (*Anat.*) ἀντέμβασις, from ἀντι, and ἐμβαίνω, to enter; a mutual insertion of the bones.

ANTEMERI'DIAN (*Astron.*) abbreviated A. M. from *ante*, and *meridies*, the noon; the time before noon.

ANTEME'TICS (*Med.*) ἀντεμετικὰ, from ἀντι, against, and ἐμετικὸς, vomiting; remedies against præternatural vomiting.

ANTEMURA'LE (*Ant.*) the name among the ancients for what is now called the counterscarp, or outwork in fortification.

ANTENCLE'MA (*Rhet.*) ἀντέγκλημα, a figure of speech, in which the accused draws his defence out of the accusation itself, as when Orestes says, "It is true I killed my mother, and I did rightly, for she killed my father." *Cic. de Invent.* l. 2, c. 26; *Hermogenes in Partit.*; *Quintil.* l. 7, c. 4; *Sopat. διαιρ. Ald. Ed.* p. 289.

ANTENDEI'XIS (*Med.*) ἀντένδειξις, a contra indication; when any thing happens contrary to the primary indication, as an inflammatory pleurisy indicates phlebotomy, but the weakness of the patient is a contrary indication. *Gal. de Meth. Med.* l. 9, c. 7; *Gorr. Def. Med.*

ANTE'NNA (*Ant.*) the *sail-yard*, or the beam which crosses the mast for the purpose of extending the sails. It is called in the Greek κέρας, a horn; in which sense Virgil, and after him Silius Italicus, uses the Latin *cornu.* The parts of the Antennæ are: ἄμβολα and σύμβολα, junctures in the middle, by which it could be bent; ἀγκύλαι, the arms, inclining to an orbicular figure; and ἀκρώπαια, the extremities. *Cæs. de Bell. Gall.* l. 3, c. 14; *Poll. Onomast.* l. 1, c. 9; *Tertull. cont. Marcion.* l. 3; *Artemidor. de Interpret. Somn.* l. 1; *Schol. in Hom. Il.* l. 18; *Macrob. Saturn.* l. 5, c. 21; *Jun. Catal.; Gyrald. de Nav.* c. 12; *Scheff. de Re Nav.* l. 2, c. 5.

A'NTE *Nicene (Ecc.)* an epithet for what preceded the council of Nice.

ANTE'NNÆ *(Ent.)* the Horns, or hornlike processes, projecting from the head of insects.

ANTEPENU'LTIMATE *(Gram.)* from *ante,* before, *pene,* almost, and *ultimus,* the last; the syllable before the two last.

ANTEPA'GMENTA *(Archit.)* ornaments to the doors, so called because *ante pangantur* they are fixed before the porches or doors wrought in timber or stone, according to an ancient inscription—TACITO ANTEPAGMENTA ABIEGNA LATA S═─. *Vitruv. de Architect.* l. 4, c. 6; *Bald. Lex. Vitruv.*

ANTEPHIA'LTICS *(Med.)* from ἀντι, and ἐφιάλτης; remedies against the night-mare.

ANTEPA'NNI *(Ant.)* or *antipana,* from the modern Greek ἀντιπανία; the band with which the anterior part of the garment was fastened. *Salmas. de Re Mil. Roman.*

ANTEPILE'PTICS *(Med.)* ἀντιπληπτικά, from ἀντι, and ἐπιληψία, *epilepsis;* remedies against the epilepsy.

A'NTERA *(Bot.)* the same as *Anthera.*

ANTE'RIDES *(Arch.)* in the Greek ἀντηρίδες, or ἐρείσματα; props or buttresses which served to support a wall. *Vitruv.* l. 6, c. 2; l. 10, c. 1, & *Philand. in Vitruv.; Hesychius; Bald. Lex Vitruv.; Salmas. Plin. Exercitat.* p. 856.

ANTE'RIOR *(Anat.)* before in position; an epithet applied to the muscles and other parts of the body.

A'NTES *(Arch.)* vide *Antæ.*

ANTES *(Agr.)* the outermost rows of vines in the vineyards, so called because they stand *ante* foremost. *Fest. de Verb. Signif.*

ANTESIGNA'NI *(Ant.)* soldiers, so called because they marched *ante signa* immediately before the standards, so as to form the van or front of the army. The *hastati* and *principes* used to occupy this post. *Cæs. de Bell. Civ.* l. 1, c. 57; *Liv.* l. 2, c. 20, &c.; *Leps de Mil. Roman.* l. 4, dial. 3; *Salmas. de Re Mil.* c. 1, &c. *Schel. in Hygin. apud Græv. Thes. Antiq. Roman.* tom 10, p. 1055, &c.

ANTESTA'RI *(Ant.)* from *ante, before,* and *testari,* to call to witness; to call any one as a witness, or to subpœna a person, which was done among the Romans by touching the right ear, to which custom Plautus and Horace alludes. *Plaut. Pers.* act 4, scen. 9, v. 10.

———— *Tuane ego causa carnifex*
Cuiquam mortali libero aures alteram.

Horat. l. 1, sat. 9, v. 75.

Casu venit obvius illi?
Adversarius; et, Quò tu, turpissime? magna
Exclamat voce; et, licet antestari? Ego vero
Oppono auriculam; rapit in jus; clamor utrimque
Undique concursus. Sic me servavit Apollo.

Plin. l. 11, c. 45; *Ursat. de Not. Roman. apud Græv. Thes. Antiq. Roman.* tom. 11, p. 549, &c. &c.

ANTE'STATURE *(Fort.)* a traverse or small entrenchment made of palisadoes, or of sacks filled with earth.

ANTEUPHO'RBIUM *(Bot.)* the *Cacalia Antephorbium* of Linnæus.

ANTHA'LIUM *(Bot.)* the μαλακόβολλα of Theophrastus, a plant which is said to grow freely on the banks of rivers. *Theophrast. Hist. Plant.* l. 4, c. 10; *Plin.* l. 21, c. 15.

A'NTHEA *(Med.)* from ἄνθος, redness, like the top of a carbuncle.

A'NTHELIX *(Anat.)* vide *Antelix.*

ANTHE'LMIA *(Bot.)* a species of the *Spigelia* of Linnæus.

ANTHELMI'NTICA *(Med.)* from ἀντι, and ὅλμινς, *vermes;* vermifuges, or remedies against worms.

A'NTHEMIS *(Bot.)* ἀνθεμίς, a plant called by some λευκάνθεμος, ἡρώθεμος, and χαμαίμηλος, which was reckoned efficacious against the stone. *Dioscor.* l. 3, c. 153; *Plin.* l. 21, c. 16, &c.; *Oribas. Med. Coll.* l. 11, 15, &c.; *Aet. Tetrab.* 1, serm. 1; *Paul. Æginet. de Re Med.* l. 7, c. 3.

ANTHEMIS, in the Linnean system, a genus of plants, Class 19 *Syngenesia,* Order 2 *Polygamia Superflua.*

Generic Characters. CAL. common hemispherical; *scales* linear—COR. compound radiate—STAM. *filaments* five; *anther* cylindrical.—PIST. *germ* oblong; *style* filiform; *stigmas* two—PER. none; *calyx* unchanged; *seeds* solitary; *down* margined or none; *receptacle* chaffy.

Species. The species are either annuals or perennials. Among the annuals are the—*Anthemis cota, Chamæmelum annuum* seu *Bellis montana,* native of Italy.—*Anthemis cotula* seu *Chamæmelum fœtidum,* Stinking Chamomile. —*Anthemis Chia* seu *Chamæmelum Chium,* Cut-leaved Chamomile, native of Chios, &c. Among the perennials are the—*Anthemis nobilis, Chamæmelum nobile* seu *odoratum, Leucanthemum* seu *Matricaria,* Common or Sweet Chamomile, a native of Britain.—*Anthemis pyrethrum, Chamæmelum* seu *Pyrethrum,* Spanish Chamomile or Pellitory, &c. *J. Bauhin. Hist. Plant.; C. Bauhin. Pin. Theat.; Ger. Herb.; Park. Theat. Botan.; Raii Hist. Plant.; Pluk. Almag. Botan.; Mor. Hist. Plant.; Linn. Spec. Plant.*

A'NTHER *(Bot.)* from the Greek ἀνθηρός, florid, and ἄνθος, a flower; a part of the stamen of the flower which is placed on the filament. It is called, by Ray, the *apex,* or Chive; by Malpigi, *capsula staminis;* by Grew, the Summit, Pendent, or Tip. It is defined by Linnæus *Pars floris gravida polline, quod natura dimittit;* i. e. a part of the flower big with pollen or farina, which it emits or explodes when ripe; or it may be defined to be a vessel destined to retain and emit, in its proper season, a dust, which serves to impregnate the germ.

Anthers differ as to their figure, number, situation, manner of bursting, and number of their cells.

As to its figure, the anther is—Oblong, as in *Lilium,* and Grasses.—Arrow-shaped *sagittata,* as in the *Crocus,* fig. 1; so also in *Linum, Bromelia, &c.*—Angular, *angulata,* i. e. having deep furrows that form angles, as in the Tulip.—Horned, *cornuta,* as in *Asarum,* fig. 2.; so in *Hamamelis, Vaccinium, Pyrola.*—Forked, *bifurcata,* i. e. bifid, or cleft above and below, as in *Festuca,* fig. 3, and in most Grasses.—Two-horned, *bicornis,* having two subulate prolongations at the apex, as in *Vaccinium.*—Subulate or awlshaped, as in *Corus, Roella,* fig. 2.—Awned, *aristata,* having two bristle-shaped appendages at the base, as in *Erica, Arborea,* fig. 4.—Heartshaped *Cordata,* as in *Turnera frutescens,* fig. 5; so in *Thea, Crapraria, Bucida, Malpigia,* &c.—Crested, *cristata,* having two cartilaginous points at the sides or the base, as in *Erica,* fig. 6.—Dentated, having indentations on the margin, as in the Yew.—Hastate, or shaped like the head of a halbert, as in *Jacquinea.*—Spiral, or turned like a screw, as in *Chironia.*

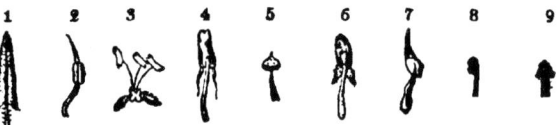

As to its situation, the anther is mostly—Erect, *erecta,* i. e. standing with its base straight on the point of the filament.—Incumbent, *incumbens*, i. e. obliquely or horizontally attached to the filaments, as in fig. 7.—Lateral, *lateralis*, i. e. attached by its side to the point of the filament, as in fig. 8.—Adnate, *adnata*, when it is closely attached to both sides of the filament, as in fig. 6 and 9. Connate, *connata*, when several grow together, forming a tube.—Sitting, *sessilis*, that has no filament.

As to their number, there is generally one anther to each filament, but in *Cucurbita* there is one to three filaments; in the Class *Syngenesia*, one to five. On the other hand there are in *Mercurialis* two, and in *Tumaria* three anthers to a filament: in *Bryonia* five to three filaments; in *Theobroma* five to each. In some flowers anthers are regularly wanting on one or more of the filaments, as in *Chelone*, *Curcuma*, &c. which are called Barren filaments.

As to their manner of bursting: anthers burst at the side in most plants; at the point, as in *Galanthus*; from the base, upwards, as in *Epimedium* and *Leontice*.

As to their number of cells, anthers are unilocular, having but one cell or cavity, as in *Mercurialis*; bilocular, as in *Epimedium*, *Asclepias*, *Daphne*, and *Helleborus*; multilocular, as in *Fritillaria*, *Tropæolum*.

ANTHE'RA (*Med.*) medicines so called from their florid red colour. *Cel. de Re Med.* l. 6, c. 2; *Gal. de Meth. Med.* l. 5; *Paul. Æginet. de Re Med.* l. 3, c. 66.

ANTHE'REON (*Anat.*) ἀνθερεών, the chin, or that part of the face where the beard grows, according to Hippocrates and most writers; but Suidas and Cælius Aurelianus explain it by the beginning of the neck and throat. *Hippocrat. Epid.* l. 5; *Suidas*; *Cal Aurel. de Tard.* l. 1, c. 3.

ANTHE'RICUM (*Bot.*) ἀνθέρικος, is called, by Theophrastus, the stem, and by Dioscorides, the flower of the Asphodel. *Theophrast.* l. 1, c. 7; l. 7, c. 12; *Dioscor.* l. 1, c. 199; *Plin.* l. 21, c. 17; *Scholiast. in Theocrit.* idyl. 1; *Suidas*; *Hesychius*.

ANTHERICUM, a genus of plants, Class 6 *Hexandria*, Order 1 *Monogynia*.

Generic Character. CAL. none.——COR. petals six—STAM. *filaments* subulate; *anthers* small—PIST. *germ* obscurely three-cornered; *style* simple; *stigma* obtuse.—*capsule* ovate; *seeds* numerous.

Species. The species of this genus are mostly perennials, and natives of the Cape of Good Hope, India, &c. as—*Anthericum ramosum*, Branching Anthericum.—*Anthericum liliago*, seu *Phalangium liliago*, Grass-leaved Anthericum, &c. But the *Anthericum liliastrum*, Savoy Anthericum or Spider-Wort, is a native of the Alps; and the *Anthericum ossifragum*, Lancashire Anthericum or Asphodel, a native of Europe, &c.

ANTHE'SIS (*Bot.*) ἄνθησις, *efflorescentia*, efflorescence; that state of vegetation in which the flower is completely developed.

ANTHESPHO'RIA (*Ant.*) Ἀνθέφορα, from ἄνθος, a flower, and φέρω, to carry; a festival celebrated in Sicily, in which flowers were strewed in the temple, in honour of Proserpine, who was carried away by Pluto while gathering flowers. It is called by Plutarch Φερεφαττία, and in the Latin *Florilegium*. It was observed, according to Pausanias, in honour of Juno, to whom a temple was dedicated under the name of ἀνθία. *Poll. Onomast.* l. 1, c. 1, segm. 37; *Pausan.* l. 2.

ANTHESTE'RIA (*Ant.*) Ἀνθεστηρία, festivals in honour of Bacchus, among the Greeks, celebrated on the 11th, 12th, and 13th days of the month Anthesterion. These days were distinguished by the names of the πιθοιγία, χοαί, and χύτροι, during which the slaves were allowed to make themselves merry, and at the end of the festivals were dispersed with the command Θύραζε Κᾶρες, οὐκ ἔτ᾽ Ἀνθεστήρια, i. e. "Be gone, o Carian slaves, the Anthesteria are over." *Ælian. Var. Hist.* l. 2, c. 41; *Schol. in Aristoph.*; *Harpocration*;

Suidas. cent. vii. prov. 90; *Etymolog. Magnum*; *Zenob.* cent, iv. prov. 32; *Meurs. Græc. Fer.* l. 1.

ANTHESTE'RION (*Chron.*) Ἀνθεστηρίων the sixth month of the Athenian year, consisting of twenty-nine days, and answering to the latter part of our November and the beginning of December. This month was so called from the feast Anthesteria, which was celebrated at that time. *Macrob. Saturnal.* l. 1, c. 14; *Gaza de Mens. Attic.*; *Scalig. de Emendat. Tempor.*

A'NTHIA (*Ich.*) ἀνθία, a kind of fish, the fat of which is good against humours. *Aristot. Hist. Animal.* l. 9, c. 37.

A'NTHINES (*Med.*) ἀνθίνης, from ἄνθος, a flower; medicated wines and oils infused in flowers. *Gal. Exeg. in Vocab. Hippocrat.*; *Foes. Œconom. Hippocrat.*; *Gorr. Defin. Med.*

ANTHISTI'RIA (*Bot.*) from Ἀνθεστηρία [vide *Anthesteria*] a genus of plants, Class 23 *Polygamia*, Order 1 *Monoecia*.

Generic Characters. CAL. glume four-valved; *valves* equal.—COR. glume two-valved; *valves* lanceolate.—STAM. *filaments* three; *anther* oblong.—PIST. *germ* oblong; *styles* two; *stigmas* hairy.—PER. none, except the closed calyx; *seed* oblong.

Species. The species of this genus are perennials, and mostly natives of India, as—*Anthesteria imberbis* seu *Stipa paleacea*—*Anthistiria glauca* seu *Stipa arguens*, &c.—*Anthistiria Japonica* seu *Andropogon Cilialum*, &c.—but the *Anthistiria ciliata* is an annual. *Linn. Spec. Plant*.

ANTHO'CEROS (*Bot.*) a genus of Algæ, Class *Cryptogamia*.

Generic Characters. Male flowers within the substance the leaf. CAL. *leaf* one; *blossom* none.—STAM. *filaments* hardly any; *anthers* from three to eight. Female flowers on the same plant. CAL. *leaf* one; *blossom veil* fibrous.—PIST. *germ.* short, conical; *style* very short; *summit* simple.—PER. *capsule* very long, awlshaped; *seeds* many.

ANTHO'DIUM (*Bot.*) the *Calyx communis* of Linnæus, and the Common Perianth or Calyx which contains a great number of flowers that appear but as one, as in *Leontodon taraxacum*, Blue-bottle; *Centaurea cyanus*, Sunflower, &c.

ANTHOLO'GION (*Ecc.*) a church book, mass book, or missal in the Greek church, which contained a collection of devotional pieces.

ANTHOLY'ZA (*Bot.*) from ἄνθος, a flower, and λύσσα, madness; a genus of plants; Class 3 *Triandria*, Order 1 *Monogynia*.

Generic Characters. CAL. spathes two valved.—COR. *petal* one.—STAM. *filaments* long; *anthers* acute.—PIST. *germ* inferior; *style* filiform; *stigma* trifid.—PER. *capsule* roundish; *seeds* many.

Species. The species are mostly perennials, and natives of the Cape of Good Hope. *Linn. Spec. Plant*.

A'NTHONY, *Knights of St.* (*Her.*) a military order instituted by Albert, Duke of Bavaria, when he designed to make war against the Turks in 1382. The knights wore a collar of gold made in the form of a hermit's girdle, from which hung a stick cut like a crutch, with a little bell, as they are represented in the pictures of St. Anthony. There was another order of this name instituted as early as 370 by John, emperor of Ethiopia.

ANTHONY's *fire*, *St.* (*Med.*) a name given to the disorder called the Erysipelas, which is said to have been cured by St. Anthony.

ANTHOPHY'LLUS (*Bot.*) vide *Carophylli*.

ANTHROPO'LOGY (*Theol.*) an ascription of human passions to the divine being.

ANTHROPOMA'NCY (*Ant.*) from ἄνθρωπος and μαντεία, a species of divination by inspecting human entrails.

ANTHROPOSCO'PIA (*Eth.*) from ἄνθρωπος, a man, and σκοπέομαι, to behold; a judging of human characters.

A'NTHORA (*Bot.*) seu *Antithora*, Salutary Monk's Hood; the *Aconitum Anthora* of Linnæus. *J. Bauh. Hist. Plant.*; *Ger. Herb.*; *Park. Parad.*; *Raii Hist. Plant.*

A'NTHOS (*Bot.*) ἄνθος, 1. Flowers in general; 2. Rosemary in particular.

ANTHOSPE'RMUM (*Bot.*) from ἄνθος and σπέρμα, flower-seed; a genus of plants; Class 23 *Dioecia*, Order 4 *Tetrandria*.
  Generic Characters. CAL. *perianth* one-leaved.—COR. none.—STAM. *filaments* four; *anthers* twin.—PIST. *germ* inferior; *styles* two; *stigmas* simple.
  Species. The species are mostly shrubs, and natives of the Cape of Good Hope, as *Anthospermum cancellatum*, *Æthiopicum*, &c. *Pluk. Phytog.*; *Linn. Spec. Plant.*

ANTHOXA'NTHON (*Bot.*) the *Rumex maritimus* of Linnæus.

ANTHOXA'NTHUM (*Bot.*) from ἄνθος and ξανθός, Yellow-flower; a genus of plants; Class 2 *Diandria*, Order 2 *Digynia*.
  Generic Characters. CAL. *glume* one-flowered; *valves* ovate.—COR. *glume* one-flowered; *nectary* two-leaved.—STAM. *filaments* two; *anthers* oblong.—PIST. *germ* oblong; *styles* two; *stigmas* simple.—PER. *glume* of the corolla grows to the seed; *seed* one.
  Species. The plants of this tribe are grasses and perennials, as the *Anthoxanthum odoratum*, Sweet Vernal-Grass, &c. *J. Bauhin. Hist. Plant.*; *C. Bauhin. Pin. Theat.*; *Raii Hist. Plant.*; *Pluk. Almag. Botan.*; *Linn. Spec. Plant.*

ANTHOXANTHUM is also the name of the *Rumex maritimus*; the *Cripsis aculeata*; the *Festuca spadicea* of Linnæus. *Bauh. Hist. Plant. &c.*

ANTHRA'CIA (*Med.*) a burning swelling. [vide *Carbuncle*]

ANTHRACI'TES (*Min.*) vide *Schistos*.

ANTHRACO'SIS *oculi* (*Med.*) a scaly corrosive ulcer in the eye.

A'NTHRAX (*Ent.*) a division of the genus *Bombylius*, according to Fabricius, comprehending the insects of this tribe, which have the antennæ distant, and the last joint setaceous.

ANTHRE'NUS (*Ent.*) a genus of animals; Class *Insecta*, Order *Coleoptera*.
  Generic Character. *Antennæ* clavate.—*Feelers* unequal.—*Jaws* membranaceous.—*Lip* entire.—*Head* hid under the thorax.
  Species. The principal species are the—*Anthrenus denticornis*, which inhabits Santa Cruz.—*Anthrenus histrio*, which inhabits Germany, &c.

ANTHRI'BOS (*Ent.*) a division of the genus *Curculio*, comprehending those species of insects which have the lip bifid, jaw bifid, and snout short.

ANTHRI'SCUS (*Bot.*) the *Chærophyllum tumulum* and *Scandix anthriscus* of Linnæus.

ANTHROPO'GRAPHUS (*Ant.*) from ἀνθρώπος, a man, and γράφω, to paint, i. e. a painter of man; a surname of Dionysius, the painter who painted men only. *Plin.* l. 35, c. 10.

ANTHROPOLI'THUS (*Foss.*) from ἀνθρώπος, a man, and λίθος, a stone; a genus of petrefactions of the human body and its parts.

ANTHROPO'LOGY (*Anat.*) from ἀνθρώπος, a man, and λόγω, to discourse upon the study of man anatomically.

ANTHROPOMORPHI'TES (*Ecc.*) from ἀνθρώπος, man, and μορφή, the form; heretics in the fourth century, who maintained that God had bodily shape. *S. Epiphan. Hæres.* 70; *S. August. Hæres.* 50.

ANTHROPOMO'RPHOS (*Nat.*) another name for the mandrake.

ANTHROPOPHA'GI (*Ant.*) another name for cannibals, or men eaters.

ANTHROPOSO'PHIA (*Anat.*) the knowledge of the nature of man.

AN'THUMON (*Bot.*) the Epithymon, or dodder growing on thyme.

ANTHY'LLIS (*Bot.*) ἀνθυλλις, Kidney-Vetch; a plant which was reckoned very good for diseases in the kidneys. *Diosc.* l. 3, c. 153; *Gal. de Simpl. Med.* l. 6; *Oribas. Med. Coll.* l. 11; *Aet. Tetrab.* 1, serm. 1; *Paul. Æginet.* l. 7, c. 3.

ANTHYLLIS, in the Linnean system, a genus of plants; Class 17 *Diadelphia*, Order 4 *Decandria*.
  Generic Characters. CAL. *perianth* one-leafed.—COR. papilionaceous.—STAM. *filaments* connate; *anthers* simple.—PIST. *germ* oblong; *style* simple; *stigma* obtuse.—PER. *Legume* roundish; *seeds* one or two.
  Species. The species are either perennials or shrubs. Among the perennials are the—*Anthyllis vulneraria*, Common Ladies' Fingers or Kidney-Vetch, native of Britain.—*Anthyllis montana* seu *Astragalus purpurea*, Mountain Ladies' Fingers or Kidney-Vetch.—*Anthyllis polycephala*, &c. Among the shrubs are the—*Anthyllis barba Jovis*, Silvery Anthyllis or Jupiter's Beard.—*Anthyllis cytasoides* seu *Cytisus incanus*, Downey-leaved Anthyllis, &c. There are also a few annuals and biennials among the species. *J. Bauhin. Hist. Plant.*; *C. Bauhin. Pin. Theat.*; *Ger. Herb.*; *Park. Theat. Botan.*; *Raii Hist. Plant.*; *Tourn. Inst. Herb.*; *Boerh. Ind. Plant.*; *Linn. Spec. Plant.*

ANTHYLLIS is also the name for several species, as the *Arenaria peploides*; the *Aspalathus anthylloides*; the *Camphorosma acuta*; the *Cressa polycarpon et tetraphyllum*; the *Salsola fruticosa*; the *Teucrium iva*; and the *Frankenia pulverulenta* of Linnæus. *Clus.*; *Bauh.*; *Ger.*; *Raii*; *Park*, &c.

ANTHYLLO'IDES (*Bot.*) the *Salsola polyclonos* of Linnæus; also an epithet for the *Aspalathus* of Linnæus.

ANTHYPNO'TICA (*Med.*) from ἀντί and ὕπνος, sleep; remedies against excessive sleep.

ANTHYPA'LLAGE (*Rhet.*) ἀνθυπαλλαγή, a commutation in cases, as when Homer says, Οἱ δὲ δύω σκόπελοι, ὁμὲν οὐρανὸν εὐρὺν ἱκάνει; instead of the more common form, τῶν δὲ δύω σκοπέλων, &c. *Hom. Odyss.* l. 13, v. 75; *Demet. de Eloc.* § 60.

ANTHYPO'PHORA (*Rhet.*) Ἀνθυποφορά, from ἀντί, contra, ὑπό, under, and φέρω, to carry, a figure of speech, wherein the objections of an adversary are brought forward in order to be answered. *Ulpin. ad Demost. Orat. Olynth.* 1, p. 5; *Hermog. de Invent.* l. 3.

ANTHYPOCHO'NDRIACUM *sal* (*Chem.*) the residuum remaining after the distillation of the water and sublimation of the Sal Ammoniac.

ANTHY'STERICA (*Med.*) from ἀντί, and ὑστέρα, the womb; medicines against hysterical affections.

A'NTIA *Lex* (*Ant.*) a law made by Antius Restro against luxury. Seeing the inefficacy of his measure, he never after supped abroad, that he might not be a witness to the extravagance which he could not suppress. *Aul. Gel.* l. 2, c. 24; *Macrob.* l. 2, c. 13.

ANTI'ADES (*Anat.*) ἀντιάδες. 1. *Tonsillæ*, the tonsils. 2. The tonsils in an inflamed state. *Hippocrat. de Morb.* l. 2; *Ruff. Ephes. de Appel. Part. Corp. human.* l. 1, c. 6, l. 2, c. 4; *Cel. de Re Med.* l. 7, c. 12; *Gal. de Symp. Caus.* c. 4, &c.; *Oribas. de Loc. Affect. Curat.* l. 3, c. 68; *Aet. Tetrab.* 2, serm. 4, c. 51; *Paul. Æginet. de Re Med.* l. 3, c. 26; *Gorr. Def. Med.*; *Foes. Œconom. Hippocrat.*

ANTIA'GRI (*Med.*) from ἀντιάδες, and ἄγρα, a prey; tumours of the tonsils.

ANTIARTHRI'TICA *Antiasthmatica* (*Med.*) vide *Antarthritics*, &c.

ANTIBA'CCHIUS (*Gram.*) παλιμβάκχιος, a foot; in verse having the two first long, and the last short, as *νάτυρά*;

pes bacchio contrarius. Terentian. Maur. de Met.; Hæphest. Enchyrid. Mar. Vict. Centimet.

ANTICACHE'CTICS (*Med.*) from ἀντί and καχεξία, *cachexia*; remedies against the cachexy.

ANTICA'DMIA (*Min.*) a substitute for the real cadmia.

A'NTICAR (*Chem.*) Borax.

ANTICA'RDIUM (*Anat.*) from ἀντί, opposite to, and καρδία, os ventriculi, the pit of the stomach.

ANTICATARRHA'LIS (*Med.*) from ἀντί, against, and κατάῤῥους catarrh; a remedy against the catarrh.

ANTICAU'STIC (*Med.*) from ἀντί and καυσός, a burning fever; a remedy against a burning fever.

A'NTICHAMBER (*Archæol.*) any outer chamber next to the principal chambers or room, where persons wait who are in attendance on the great.

A'NTICHEIR (*Anat.*) ἀντίχειρ, the Greek name for the *pollex*, or thumb. *Gal. de Mus. Dissert.* c. 22; *Gorr. Def. Med.*

ANTICHOLE'RICA (*Bot.*) the *Sophora heptaphylla* of Linnæus.

ANTI'CHORUS (*Bot.*) if from χορός, and *Antichorus*, if from χωρίς, a genus of plants, Class 8, Octandria, Order 1 Monogynia.
  Generic Characters. CAL. perianth four-leaved; *leaflets* lanceolate.—COR. *petals* four.—STAM. *filaments* setaceous; *anthers* roundish.—PIST. *germ* superior; *style* cylindric; *stigma* obtuse.—PER. *capsule* subulate: *seeds* very many.
  Species. The only species is the *Antichorus depressus*, seu *Justicia edulis*, an annual, native of Arabia. *Linn. Spec. Plant.*

ANTICHRE'SIS (*Ant.*) a mortgage, or pawn, left for the creditor to use till the debt be paid. *Hotoman.*

A'NTICHRIST (*Ecc.*) the great adversary of Christ who is described in the Bible.

ANTICHTHO'NES (*Geog.*) another name for the Antipodes.

ANTI'CIPANS (*Med.*) from *ante* and *capio*, to take before the time, anticipating; an epithet for a fever, the paroxysms of which anticipate the time of the preceding paroxysm.

ANTICIPA'TIO (*Rhet.*) vide *Prolepsis*.

ANTICNE'MION (*Med.*) ἀντικνήμιον, from ἀντί, opposite to, and κνήμη, the leg; the fore part of the tibia which is bare of flesh. *Poll. Onom.* l. 2, segm. 190.

ANTICO'LICA (*Med.*) from ἀντί and κωλική, the colic; remedies against the colic.

ANTICONTO'SIS (*Med.*) ἀντικόντωσις, from ἀντί and κόντος, a staff; supporting with a staff or crutch.

A'NTICOR (*Vet.*) from *ante*, before, and *cor*, the heart; a dangerous disease near the heart of horses.

ANTI'CUM (*Ant.*) scilicet *ostium*, from *ante*, before, that is, a porch before a door or a fore-door. *Fest. de Signif. Verb.*

ANTIDA'CTYLUS (*Gram.*) a foot, opposite to *a dactyle*; the same as the *Anapest*.

ANTIDE'SMA (*Bot.*) from ἀντί, instead of, and δεσμός, a chain; so called because it is good for making ropes, a genus of plants, Class 22 Dioecia, Order 5 Pentandria.
  Generic Characters. CAL. *perianth* five-leaved; *leaflets* oblongish.—COR. none.—STAM. *filaments* five; *anthers* roundish.—PIST. *germ* superior; *style* none; *stigmas* five.—PER. *drupe* roundish; *seed* none.
  Species. The species are mostly shrubs and natives of the East Indies. *Linn. Spec. Plant.*

ANTIDIA'PHORISTS (*Ecc.*) those who opposed the adiaphorists.

ANTIDIA'STOLE (*Med.*) ἀντιδιαστολή, from ἀντί, in distinction from, and διαστέλλω, to discriminate; a discrimination of one disease or symptom from another.

ANTIDICOMARIA'NITES (*Ecc.*) the followers of Helvidius, who denied the perpetual virginity of the Virgin Mary, A. D. 373. *Epiphan. Hæres.* 78; *St. August. Hæres.* 84; *St. Hieron. cont. Helvid.*; *Baron. Annal. Ann.* 373.

ANTIDI'NICA (*Med.*) from ἀντί, and δῖνος, vortex; remedies against a vertigo.

ANTIDOTA'RIUM (*Med.*) a book in which Antidotes are described.

A'NTIDOTE (*Med.*) ἀντίδοτος, *Antidotus*, from ἀντί, against, and δοτός, given; a counter poison, or counteracting medicine in general. *Cel. de Re Med.* l. 5, c. 22; *Gal. de Antidot.*; *Oribas. Synop.* l. 3; *Aet. Tetrab.* 4, serm. 1; *Trallian.* l. 4, &c.; *Paul. Æginet. de Re Med.* l. 7, c. 3; *Myreps. de Antidot.*; *Gorr. Defin. Med.*

ANTIDO'TUS (*Chem.*) the philosopher's stone.

ANTIDYSENTE'RICA (*Med.*) from ἀντί, against, and δυσεντερία, dysenteria; remedies against the dysentery.

ANTIELMI'NTHICKS, *Antiemetica*, &c. (*Med.*) vide *Anthelminthicks*, &c.

A'NTIENT (*Law*) vide *Ancient*.

ANTIEPILE'PTIC *elixir* (*Chem.*) the spirit of a human head, mixed with an equal quantity of spirit of wine, in which opium has been dissolved.

ANTIFE'BRILE (*Med.*) a remedy against a fever.

ANTIGONI'A (*Ant.*) Ἀντιγόνεια, sacrifices in honour of Antigonus. *Plut. in Ag.*

A'NTIGRAPHE (*Ant.*) ἀντιγραφή, a name for the oath which the defendant was obliged to take before a lawsuit was commenced in Greece.

ANTIGRAPHE is also an action against any one laying claim to a vacant inheritance, i. e. the inheritance of a person who dies childless. *Jul. Poll.* l. 8, c. 6; *Harpocration.*

ANTIGRA'PHEUS (*Ant.*) ἀντιγραφεύς, a Receiver-general among the Greeks.

ANTIHE'CTICA (*Med.*) from ἀντί, against, and ἑκτικός, the hectic; remedies against a hectic fever.

ANTIHE'LIX (*Anat.*) the same as *Antelix*.

ANTILE'NA (*Ant.*) a poitrel, or breast-leather for horses.

ANTILE'PSIS (*Surg.*) ἀντίληψις, the hold for a bandage to keep it from slipping. *Hippoc. de Med.*; *Gorr. Defin. Med.*; *Foes. Œconom.*

ANTILO'BIUM (*Med.*) ἀντιλόβιον, from ἀντί, contra, and λοβός, *lobus*; that part of the ear opposite to the lobe. *Ruf. Ephes. Appellat. Part. human. Corp.* l. 1, c. 6; *Poll. Onom.* l. 2, segm. 86.

ANTILO'GARITHM (*Math.*) the complement of the logarithm of any sine, tangent, or secant to 90 degrees.

ANTILOI'MICA (*Med.*) from ἀντί, against, and λοιμός, the plague; remedies against the plague.

ANTILO'PUS (*Zool.*) Antelope, a genus of animals, Class Mammalia, Order Pecora.
  Generic Characters. Horns hollow, persistent, annulate.—Foreteeth lower, eight.—Canine teeth or tusks none.
  Species. The species are distinguished into the Antelopes, with straight or nearly straight horns, those with curved horns, and those with hooked horns.
  Of the first kind are the—*Antilopus oryx*, or *Capra gazella*, in French, *le Pasan*, Ægyptian Antelope.—*Antilopus gazella*, *Hircus bezoardicus*, *Capra bezoartica*, Algazel Antelope, a species in India and Persia, which affords the Bezoar.—*Antilopus oreotragus*, in French, *Sauteur des Rochers*, Klipspringer.—*Antilopus grimmia*, the Guinea Antelope, &c. &c.
  Those of the second kind are the—*Antilopus Nyl-ghau*, the Nilgau, or White-footed Antelope.—*Antilopus stripciseros*; *Bos strepticeros*, in French, *le Condoma*, Striped Antelope, native of the Cape of Good Hope.—*Antilopus cervicapra*, Common Antelope.—*Antilopus euchore*, Spring-Bock, the Springer Antelope, a native of the Cape of Good Hope, so called from the prodigious

leaps it takes on the sight of any body.—*Antilopus arundinacea*, Retbock, a species so called from its frequenting reedy places.—*Antilopus Dorcas*, Barbary Antelope, &c. &c. supposed to be the Dorcas of Ælian.

Those of the third kind are the—*Antilopus Gnu*, the Gnow or Ox-headed Antelope.—*Antilopus Rupicapra*, in French, *le Chamois*, the Chamois Antelope, a native of Switzerland.

ANTILY'SSUS (*Med.*) from ἀντί, and λύσσα, madness; a remedy against madness.

ANTIME'RIA (*Rhet.*) a figure in which one part of speech is put for another.

ANTIMETA'BOLE (*Rhet.*) ἀντιμεταβολὴ, from ἀντί, and μεταβάλλω; a figure, wherein words are repeated in the same sentence in a different case or person, as " Non ut edam vive sed ut vivam edo," or " Qui stultis videri eruditi volunt, stulti eruditis videntur." *Quintil. Instit.* l. 9, c. 3, l. 10, c. 7; *Longin.* l. 23, c. 1; *Voss. Instit. Rhet.* l. 5, p. 404.

ANTIMETA'THESIS (*Rhet.*) ἀντιμετάθεσις, a figure of speech, by which the hearer is, as it were, transported to the scene of action, τὴν ψυχὴν διὰ τῶν τόπων ἄγει, τὴν ἀκοὴν ὄψιν ποιῶν. *Longin. de Sublimit.* sect. 26; *Alexand. περὶ σχημ. Ald.* p. 586.

ANTIMO'NIAL *silver ore* (*Min.*) an alloy of silver.—*Antimonial red ore*, the *Stibium rubrum* of Linnæus.—*Antimonial sulphuret*, or *brittle silver ore*; an ore and a sulphuret of silver.—*Antimonial ochre*, the *Stibium stibigo* of Linnæus.

ANTIMO'NIATE (*Chem.*) a salt, formed by the combination of antimonic acid with a salifiable base, as the *antimoniate* of Ammonia, of Potash, &c.

ANTIMO'NIC *acid* (*Chem.*) a particular kind of acid prepared from antimony, in the form of a white powder, insoluble in water, but capable of reddening vegetable blues.

ANTIMO'NIOUS *acid* (*Chem.*) Antimonic acid deprived of some of its oxygen. It is otherwise called the *oxide of antimony*.

ANTIMO'NITE (*Chem.*) a salt, formed by the combination of antimonious acid, with a salifiable base.

A'NTIMONY (*Min.*) the στίμμι of Dioscorides, probably the τετράγωνον of Hippocrates, the *lapis spumæ candidæ nitentisque, non tamen translucentis* of Pliny, and the *Antimonium* of Basil Valentine; a metallic, solid, heavy brittle substance, probably so called from ἀντί, against, and μόνος, alone, i. e. an enemy to solitude, because it is very seldom found pure, but mostly mixed with some other metals. It is sometimes found in the state of an oxyde, called *antimonial ochre*; but the most abundant ore of antimony is that in which it is combined with sulphur, called the *sulphuret of antimony*.—*Oxides of antimony* are formed by the combination of antimony with oxygen. The three oxides of antimony which are best known are distinguished by the names of the protoxide, the deutoxide, and the peroxide. The *protoxide* is grey; the *deutoxide*, formerly called *Argentine flowers of antimony*, or *calx of antimony*, now called *antimonious acid*, is white; and the *peroxide*, or antimonic acid, is straw yellow.—*Salts of antimony* are formed by the combination of antimonial acids, with a salifiable base. Those which are formed by antimonic acid are called *antimoniates*; those formed by antimonious acid are *antimonites*, as the *antimoniate* of copper, or the *antimonite* of copper, &c. To these may be added a third sort of salts, which contain the protoxide of antimony, as the *tartrate of potash and antimony*, otherwise called *tartar emetic*, so the *acetate, succinate, benzoate*, &c. of antimony.—*Alloys of Antimony* are formed by combining antimony with arsenic, potassium, &c. The alloy of antimony with iron was formerly called the *martial regulus*; that of antimony with copper the *regulus of Venus*.—*Chloride of Antimony* is formed by the combination of antimony with chlorine: this, as a medicinal preparation, was formerly called *butter of antimony*.—*Ores of Antimony* are mostly found in veins, either as an alloy, a sulphuret, or an oxide.—*Native Antimony* is an ore, and an alloy of antimony, silver, and iron; but it is seldom found pure.—*Crude antimony* is the native mineral antimony melted down and cast into stones, otherwise called *antimony in substance.*—*Prepared antimony* is that which has passed through some process, by which its powers are altered, as the sulphur of antimony, formerly called *golden sulphur, mineral kermes*, or *Carthusian powder*, which was reckoned a grand panacea; *glass of antimony; liver of antimony; magistory of antimony*, and the like.

ANTINEPHRI'TICA (*Med.*) ἀντινεφριτικὰ, from ἀντί, against, and νεφρῖτις, a pain in the kidneys; remedies against the disorders in the kidneys.

ANTINOI'A (*Ant.*) ἀντινοΐα, annual sacrifices and quinquennial games instituted by Adrian in honour of Antinous, at Mantinea in Arcadia, where he was worshipped as a god. *Paus.* l. 8, c. 9.

ANTINO'MIA (*Rhet.*) 'Αντινομία, i. e. a state of contrary laws; a double statement composed of a double description, and a double judgment, since laws are explained both ways according to contrary opinions. *Cic. de Invent.* l. 2, c. 49; *Hermog. de Partit.*

ANTINO'MIANS (*Ecc.*) a sect of heretics, who, according to Pontanus, sprung up in the sixteenth century, having John Agricola as their leader. They maintained that faith alone without good works was sufficient for salvation.

ANTI'NOUS (*Ast.*) a part of the constellation Aquila.

ANTIO'CHIAN *sect* (*Ant.*) *Antiochianæ Partés*, a name given to the fifth academy, or branch of Academics, so called from one Antioch, a cotemporary with Cicero. *Cic. Academ.* l. 1, c. 3.

Antiochian *Epocha* (*Numis.*) was the same as the Augustan and Julian Epocha.

ANTIPÆDOBA'PTISTS (*Ecc.*) those who are against infant baptism.

ANTIPAGMENTA (*Ant.*) vide *Antepagmenta*.

ANTIPA'RALLELS (*Geom.*) lines which make equal angles with two other lines, but in a contrary order; thus, suppose A B and A C be any two lines, and F C, F E two

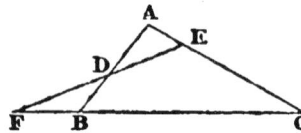

others cutting them so as to make the angle B equal to the angle E, and the angle C equal to the angle D, then B C and D E are antiparallels, with respect to A B and A C.

ANTIPARALY'TICA (*Med.*) from ἀντί and παράλυσις, paralysis; remedies against the palsy.

ANTIPARA'STASIS (*Rhet.*) ἀντιπαράστασις, from ἀντί, against, and παρίστημι, to compare, i. e. to set up one thing against another; a figure of speech by which one grants what the adversary says, but denies his inference. *Hermog. περὶ ευρ.*; *Apsin. Rhet.*

ANTIPA'THES *Min.*) ἀντιπαθὴς, a mineral which answers to what is now called Black Coral. *Dioscor.* l. 5, c. 140.

Antipathes (*Ent.*) a genus of animals; Class *Vermes*, Order *Zoophyta*.

Generic Characters. Animal growing in the form of a plant.—*Stem* expanded at the base.

Species. The principal species which inhabit the Indian seas are the *Antipathes spiralis*, with a spiral rough stem. —*Antipathes apex*, &c.

ANTI'PATHY (*Med.*) *Antipathia*, ἀντιπάθεια, from ἀντί and

πίδες; an occult quality of repulsion in certain things to one another, as in the case of burnt leather, which Galen says was supposed to cure galls by a sort of antipathy. *Gal. de Simpl. l. 11; Castel. Lex.*

ANTIPELA'RGIA (*Ant.*) a law among the ancients whereby children were obliged to furnish necessaries to their parents in imitation of the stork, whence it is sometimes called *Lex ciconaria,* or the Stork's Law.

ANTIPERI'STASIS (*Med.*) ἀντιπερίστασις, from ἀντί, against, and πίστημι, to stand around; a cohibition or straightening all around, as by the circumambient air or water; thus, on account of the antiperistasis, or being beset with the opposite quality, springs are hottest in the winter, or in cold weather. *Theophrast. de Ign.*

ANTIPHA'RMACUM (*Med.*) the same as Antidote, a remedy against poison.

ANTIPHE'RNA (*Ant.*) ἀντίφερνα, from ἀντί and φερνή, dower; presents made by the bridegroom to the bride in lieu of her portion.

ANTIPHLOGI'STICA (*Med.*) from ἀντί, and φλέγω, to burn; remedies for inflammation.

ANTIPHO'NA (*Mus.*) ἀντιφωνα, from ἀντί, against, and φωνή, a voice; when each side of a quire alternately sings a verse.

ANTIPHRA'SIS (*Gram.*) ἀντίφρασις, from ἀντί, opposite to, and φράζω, to speak, i. e. to speak what is contrary to the meaning; a figure in grammar when a word has a meaning contrary to the original sense, as ' Parcæ,' the fates, " quia minime parcant." *Rutil. Lup.*

ANTIPHTHI'SICA (*Med.*) from ἀντί, against, and φθίσις, consumption; remedies against a consumption.

ANTI'PHTHORA (*Bot.*) ἀντιφθορά, from ἀντί, against, and φθορά, corruption; a species of Wolf's-bane, which resists corruption.

ANTI'PHYSICA (*Med.*) ἀντιφυσικά, from ἀντί, against, and φυσάω, to inflate; remedies against flatulence.

ANTI'PHYSON (*Nat.*) from ἀντί, against, and φύσις, nature; an epithet for the loadstone, because it seemed to act against nature.

ANTIPLEURI'TICUM (*Med.*) from ἀ. τ., against, and πλευρῖτις; a remedy against the pleurisy.

ANTIPODA'GRICA (*Med.*) the same as Antarthritica.

ANTI'PODES (*Ast.*) ἀντίποδες, from ἀντί, opposite to, and πούς the foot; people dwelling on the opposite side of the earth with their feet to our feet. The Antipodes are 180 degrees distant from each other every way, having equal latitudes, the one North and the other South, but opposite longitudes. [vide *Astronomy*] Consequently, when it is day to the one, it is night to the other, and when summer to the one, winter to the other, &c. Plato first conceived the idea, and gave the name of Antipodes to inhabitants of the world thus relatively situated; the existence of which was disputed by the ancient fathers. Manilius has given a description of them in verse. *Astron. l. 1, v. 236.*

> *Pars ejus ad Arctos*
> *Eminet, Austrinis pars est habitabilis oris*
> *Sub pedibusque jacet nostris, supraque videtur*
> *Ipsa sibi; fallente solo declivia longa*
> *Et pariter surgente viâ, pariterque cadente.*

Cicero and Pliny call them Ἀντίχθονες, *Antichthones;* Albertus Magnus *Antigenæ. Cic. Tuscul. l. 1, c. 28; Cleom. de Mund. l. 1; Strab. l. 1; Pompon. Mel. l. 1; Plin. l. 2, c. 66; Solin. c. 66; Lactant. Instit. Divin. l. 3, c. 24; August. de Civ. Dei, l. 6, c. 9; Macrob. de Somn. Scip; Mart. Capell. l. 6; Stœflin. Procl. de Sphær.*

ANTIPO'DIA (*Gram.*) a figure by which one foot is changed for another, if both be of equal measure.

A'NTIPOPE (*Ecc.*) a false pope set up by a faction.

ANTIPRA'XIA (*Med.*) from ἀντί, against, and πράσσω, to do; a contrariety of functions and temperaments in different parts of the body, as a cold stomach joined with a hot liver. *Castel. Lex. Med.*

ANTIPTO'SIS (*Gram.*) from ἀντί, instead of, and πτῶσις, case; a figure by which one case is put for another.

ANTIPYRE'TICON (*Med.*) from ἀντί, against, and πυρετός, a fever; a febrifuge.

ANTIQUA'RII (*Lit.*) 1. The monks who were employed in making new copies of old books. 2. The copies themselves of the old books.

ANTIQUARTANA'RIUM (*Med.*) or *antiquartium,* a remedy for a quartan fever.

ANTI'QUI *morbi* (*Med.*) old and inveterate diseases lengthened out to many years.

ANTIRRHI'NUM (*Bot.*) or *Anarrhinum,* ἀντίρρινον, ἀνάρρινον, Snap Dragon or Calves-Snout; a plant, so called because the figure of its flower resembles the snout of a calf, from ἀντί, instead of, and ῥίν, a snout. It is seldom used in medicines, but has been employed as a charm against spectres and the like. *Theophrast. Hist. Plant. l. 9, c. 21; Dioscor. l. 4, c. 133; Plin. l. 25, c. 10; Apul. c. 86; Gal. de Simpl. l. 6; Paul. Æginet. de Re Med. l. 7, c. 3.*

Antirrhinum, *in the Linnean system,* a genus of plants; Class 14 *Didynamia,* Order 2 *Angiospermia.*

Generic Characters. CAL. *perianth* five parted; *divisions* oblong.—COR. monopetalous; *tube* oblong; *nectary* prominent.—STAM. *filaments* four; *anthers* converging.—PIST. *germ* roundish; *style* simple; *stigma* obtuse.—PER. *capsule* roundish; *seeds* very many; *receptacles* reniform.

Species. The species are mostly annuals or perennials. Among the former are the—*Antirrhinum versicolor,* Spike-flowered Toad-flax.—*Antirrhinum procumbens,* seu *Linaria pumila,* Procumbent Toad-flax.—*Antirrhinum arvense* seu *Linaria arvensis,* Yellow Corn Toad-flax, &c.—*Antirrhinum elatine,* Sharp-pointed Toad-flax or Fluellin. Among the perennials are the—*Antirrhinum cymbalaria* seu *Linaria cymbalaria,* Ivy-leaved Toad-flax.—*Antirrhinum repens,* Creeping Toad-flax.—*Antirrhinum sparteum,* Branching Toad-flax.—*Antirrhinum saxatile,* Rock Toad-flax, &c. *J. Bauh. Hist. Plant.; C. Bauh. Pin. Theat.; Ger. Herb.; Park. Theat. Botan.; Raii Hist. Plant.; Tourn. Inst. Herb.; Boerh. Ind. Plant.; Linn. Spec. Plant.*

ANTI'SCIANS (*Ast.*) from ἀντί, opposite to, and σκία, a shadow; the people who, dwelling in the opposite hemispheres of North and South, have their shadows at noon fall directly opposite to each other; consequently, those living in the Southern Frigid and Temperate Zones are Antiscians to those living in the North Frigid and Temperate Zones. Lucan alludes to the surprize which the Arabians, going into Italy, expressed on seeing the shadows turning to the right, which they had always seen turn to the left.
Lucan. l. 3, v. 247.

> *Ignotum vobis, Arabes, venistis in orbem,*
> *Umbras mirati nemorum non ire sinistras.*

Amm. Marcell. l. 22, c. 15; Schol. in Luc. 4, c. 16; Ricciol. Almag. l. 1, c. 20.

ANT'ISCION *signs* (*Astrol.*) certain signs in the Zodiack, which, with reference to each other, are equally distant from the tropical signs, Cancer and Capricorn; so that, when a planet is in such a station, it is said to cast its *antiscion,* i. e. to give a virtue or influence to another star or planet that is in the opposite sign.

ANTISCO'LICA (*Med.*) vide *Anthelmintica.*

ANTISCORBU'TIC (*Med.*) remedies against the scurvy.

ANTISE'PTICS (*Med.*) from ἀντί, against, and σηπτικός, putrefying; resisters of putrefaction.

ANTISI'GMA (*Gram.*) a mark ⊃ in ancient writings where the order of the verses is to be changed. *Isid. Orig.* l. 1, c. 20.

ANTI'SPASIS (*Med.*) ἀντίσπασις, from ἀντί, against, and σπάω, to draw back; a revulsion or drawing away of humours while in actual motion. *Gal. de Meth. Med.* l. 5, c. 9; *Gorr. Defin. Med.*; *Foes. Œconom. Hippocrat.*

ANTISPASMO'DICS (*Med.*) from ἀντί, against, and σπασμός, convulsions; remedies against spasms.

ANTISPA'STIC verse (*Poet.*) ἀντισπαστικὸν μέτρον; verse consisting principally of antispasts, or antispastic feet.

ANTISPA'STICON (*Med.*) ἀντισπαστικὸν; a medicine acting by Antispasis. [vide *Antispasis*]

ANTISPA'STUS (*Gram.*) Ἀντίσπαστος, from ἀντισπάω, to draw contrary ways; a foot of four syllables in verse, having the first syllable short, then two long, and the last short, as Ălēxăndĕr. *Diomed.* l. 3; *Hephest. Enchyrid.*; *Victorin. de Carm.*

ANTI'SPODA (*Nat.*) or antispodia, ἀντίσποδα, from ἀντί, instead of, and σποδός, spodium; a kind of medicinal ashes made of herbs, which may be used as a substitute for spodium. *Dioscor.* l. 5, c. 186; *Plin.* l. 34, c. 13; *Gal. de Simpl.* l. 9; *Oribas Med. Coll.* l. 13; *Gorr. Defin. Med.*

ANTI'STASIS (*Rhet.*) ἀντίστασις, a sort of anticlema, or figure of speech, in which a person justifies himself for having done what is laid to his charge, by showing its expediency. *Hermog.* διαίρεσις et *Sopatr. Schol. in Hermog. Ald. Ed.* p. 256; *Syrian. Ald.* p. 95; *Mar. Victorin. in Cic. Rhet.*

ANTISTERI'GMA (*Med.*) ἀντιστήριγμα, a word used by Hippocrates for a crutch or support. *Hippocrat. de Artic.*; *Gorr. Defin. Med.*; *Foes. Œconom. Hippocrat.*

ANTISTE'RNON (*Anat.*) ἀντίστερνον, from ἀντί, and στέρνον, pectus; the back, which is opposite to the breast. *Ruf. Ephes. Appell. Part. Human. Corp.* l. 2, c. 4.

ANTI'STES sacrorum (*Ant.*) the High-Priest among the Romans. *Plin.* l. 7, c. 3; *Bud. in Pandect.* p. 6; *Pollet. For. Rom.* l. 2, c. 1.

ANTISTI'TIUM (*Archæol.*) a Monastery.

ANTISTOI'CHON (*Gram.*) ἀντίστοιχον, from ἀντί, instead of, and στοιχεῖον, an element; a figure in which one letter is put for another, as *promuscis* for *proboscis*.

ANTI'STROPHA (*Rhet.*) ἀντιστροφά; arguments so called from ἀντί, against, and τρέπω, to turn, because they may be turned against him by whom they are advanced. *Dionys. Hal. Art. Rhet.* c. 9; *Aul. Gell.* l. 5, c. 10; *Sopat. ad Hermog. Ald. tom.* 2, p. 54.

ANTI'STROPHE (*Rhet.*) ἀντιστροφή, from ἀντί, against, and τρέφω, verto. 1. An alternate conversion of the same words in different sentences, as "Servus domine," and "Domine servus." *Eustat. ad Hom. Il.* l. 13; *Hermog. περὶ σχημ. Ald. Edit. tom.* 1, p. 176; *Alexand. περὶ σχημ. Ald. Edit.* p. 583. 2. A sort of dancing performed by the chorus, who by the strophe turned to the one hand, and by the antistrophe to the other; whence the ancient poetry was divided into the στροφή, strophe, when the chorus turned from the right to the left; the ἀντιστροφή, antistrophe, when they turned from the left to the right; and ἐπωδός, when they rehearsed their part standing still.

ANTITA'SIS (*Surg.*) from ἀντί, and τείνω, to extend; the contra extension of dislocated bones.

ANTITA'CTES (*Ecc.*) a sect of heretics, who taught that sin deserved rather reward than punishment. *Clem. Alexand. Strom.* 3; *Baron. Annal. Ann.* 120; *Du Pin. Bibl. Eccles.* prem. siec.

ANTI'THENAR (*Anat.*) from ἀντί, and θέναρ, the hollow of the hand or foot; the *Abductor pollicis.*

ANTI'THESIS (*Rhet.*) ἀντίθεσις, from ἀντί, in opposition, and τίθημι, to place; a figure in which contraries are opposed to contraries. *Hermog. περὶ ἰδ. Ald. Ed. tom.* 1, p. 48; *Alexand. περὶ σχημ.*; *Apsius Art. Rhet.* p. 695; *Schol. ad Hermog. tom.* 2; *Rhet. Ald.* p. 271; *Suidas in voc. ἀντίθεσις.*

ANTITHETA'RIUS (*Law*) the name given to a man who endeavours to discharge himself of the crime of which he is accused by retorting the charge on the accuser. *Leg. Canuti apud Brompton.*

ANTI'THETON (*Gram.*) ἀντίθετον, contraries opposed to each other; as "Vicit pudorem libido, timorem audacia, rationem amentia." *Cic. pro Cluent. et de Orat.* c. 50.

ANTITRA'GUS (*Anat.*) the part of the ear opposite to the Tragus, according to Rufus Ephesius, on the authority of Oribasius. *Ruf. Ephes. apud Oribas. Med. Coll.* l. 25, c. 1.

ANTITRAGUS (*Bot.*) the *Crypsis aculeata* of Linnæus.

ANTITRI'NITARIANS (*Ecc.*) such as deny the holy Trinity.

A'NTITYPE (*Theol.*) from ἀντί, instead of, and τύπος, a type; what answers to or is prefigured by a type; as the Paschal lamb was a type to which our Saviour, the Lamb of God, was the Antitype.

ANTIVENE'REA (*Med.*) Medicines against the *Lues venerea.*

A'NTLER (*Sport.*) the starts or branches of a deer's attire, properly the first branches. There is the Bes-Antler, the Sur-Antler, and the Brow-Antler.—The Bes-Antler is the start or branch next above the Brow-Antler.—The Sur-Antler is the topmost start or branch; and—the Brow-Antler is that next the head.

A'NTOCOW (*Vet.*) vide *Anticor.*

ANTOE'CI (*Astron.*) ἀντοικοι, from ἀντί, against, and οἶκος, a house; inhabitants of the earth who live under the same meridian East or West, but under opposite parallels of latitude North and South. They have their noon or midnight at the same hour, but their seasons are contrary, i. e. when it is spring with the one, it is autumn with the other, and when winter with the one, it is summer with the other. The length of the night and day is equal in both. *Cleom. de Mund.* l. 1; *Ricciol. Almag.* l. 1. c. 20.

ANTO'NIA Lex (*Ant.*) a law so called from Mark Anthony, the proposer, by which it was prohibited to make a dictator; and no one, under pain of death, dare accept the office when offered. *Appian. de Bell. Civil.* l. 3, p. 542; *Hotmann. Roman. Antiq.* l. 1, p. 196.

ANTO'NIAN (*Min.*) a mineral water of Germany, containing carbonated soda, common salt, and calcareous earth.

ANTO'NII Sancti ignis (*Med.*) St. Anthony's Fire, because it was supposed to be miraculously cured by that Saint.

ANTONOMA'SIA (*Rhet.*) ἀντονομασία, from ἀντί, instead of, and ὄνομα, a name, i. e. one name instead of another; a figure by which one name is put for another, as an appellative for a proper name, as the Poet for Homer or Virgil, the Apostle for St. Paul. *Dionys. Hal. de Hom. Poes.*; *Quint. Instit.* l. 6, c. 29; *Tryph. de Trop.*; *Voss. Instit. Rhet.* l. 4, p. 165.

ANTONOMA'STICA (*Con.*) the same as *Cochlea cælata.*

ANTOPHY'LLON (*Bot.*) *Antophyllus*, ἀντοφύλλον, from ἀντί, against, and φύλλον, a leaf; because its leaves stand opposite to one another; the Male Caryophyllus, or, according to Ray, a name given by the chemists to the full grown Caryophyllus. *Myrep. de Antid.*; *Raii Hist. Plant.*

ANTRI'SCUS (*Bot.*) a plant, the leaves of which resemble Hemlock. *Bauh.*

A'NTRUM buccinosum (*Anat.*) the same as *Cochlea.—Antrum genæ*, maxillary sinus.—*Antrum Pylori*, the great concavity of the stomach near the Pylorus.

ANTY'LLION (*Med.*) a very astringent malagma.

A'NVIL (*Mech.*) the tool on which smiths hammer their work.

ANVIL (*Her.*) a charge, as party per chevron, *argent and sable*, three anvils, counter charge, name Smith, of Abingdon, Berks.

A'NUS (*Anat.*) the orifice of the *intestinum rectum*, through which the *fæces* are discharged. *Gal. de Usu. Part.* l. 5, c. 18.—*Anus Cerebri*, that cavity in the brain which arises from the contract of the four trunks of the *Medulla spinalis*.

ANUS (*Bot.*) the posterior opening of a monopetalous flower.

ANYPEUTHYNA (*Med.*) ἀνυπεύθυνα, from α, priv. ὑπεύθυνος, obnoxious; things for which one is not accountable; in which sense Hippocrates uses it for those circumstances which are above the ordinary controul of a physician, and for which he is not accountable. *Hippocrat.* παραγγελ.

A'ORIST (*Gram.*) ἀόριστος, from α, priv. and ὁρίζω, to define, i. e. indefinite; the name of a Greek tense, denoting great uncertainty of time.

A'ORTA (*Anat.*) ἀορτὴ, from ἀείρω, to lift up, is the name of a little chest, and was applied to the great artery of the heart in the days of Aristotle; it was called by Aretæus ἀρτηρία παχεῖα, the great artery proceeding from the left ventricle of the heart, from which all the other arteries mediately or immediately proceed. It is distinguished into the ascending and descending, from the manner in which it runs; the *Aorta ascendens* distributing its branches to the upper part of the Thorax, the head, and upper extremities; the *Aorta descendens* supplying the rest of the Thorax, the Diaphragm, &c. *Aristot. Hist. Anim.* l. 3, c. 3, &c.; *Gal. de Dissect. Ven.* The annexed cut represents a part of the trunk of the Aorta turned inside out; *a a* the glandulous membrane; *b b* the vascular membrane; *c* the internal tunic.

AOVO'RA (*Bot.*) an Indian plant, the fruit of which is as large as a hen's egg, and is astringent. *Lem. des Drog.*

APA'CTUS (*Bot.*) a genus of plants; Class 11 *Dodecandria*, Order 1 *Monogynia*.
Generic Characters. CAL. none.—COR. four-petalled; petals roundish.—STAM. filaments from sixteen to twenty.—PIST. germ superior; style none.
Species. The only species is *Apactis Japonica*, a shrub, native of Japan. *Linn. Spec. Plant.*

APÆDEU'SIA (*Lit.*) ἀπαιδευσία, ignorance, or a want of information in general; whence those who were so deficient were termed *Apædeutæ*.

APÆDEU'TÆ (*Lit.*) vide *Apædeusia*.

APA'GMA (*Surg.*) the same as *Abductio*.

APAGO'GE (*Ant.*) ἀπαγωγή; the carrying a criminal taken in the fact before a magistrate. *Poll. Onom.* l. 6, segm. 154.

APAGOGE (*Log.*) the same as *Reductio*.

APAGO'GICAL *demonstration* (*Log.*) the same as *Reductio ad Absurdum*.

APA'LLAGE (*Med.*) ἀπαλλαγή, from ἀπαλλάσσω, to change; any alteration in general, but in particular by a deliverance from a disease. *Hippocrat.* l. 2, Aph. 45; *Foes. Œconom. Hippocrat.*

A'PALUS (*Ent.*) a genus of animals, Class *Insecta*, Order *Coleoptera*.
Generic Character. Antennæ filiform.—Feelers equal, filiform.—Jaw horny.—Lip membranaceous, truncate.
Species. There are only two species, the *Apalus bimaculatus* and *Amaculatus*.

A'PANAGE (*Law*) or *Appennage*, among the French, was the assignment of lands by the king to the younger sons, which revert to the crown upon the failure of male issue.

APA'NTHISMUS (*Anat.*) ἀπάνθισμος, signifies literally a very fine and almost imperceptible line in painting, but is applied, by a figure, to the small capillary veins, from their resemblance to these lines. *Gal. de Ven. et Art.* c. 8.

APANTHROPIA (*Med.*) ἀπανθρωπία, from α, priv. and ἄνθρωπος, a man; a term used by Hippocrates for an aversion to company, or a love of solitude. *Hippocrat. Coac. Præd.*

APARACHYTUM *vinum* (*Med.*) ἀπαράχυτον οἶνος, wine unmixed with sea water. *Gal. de Comp. Med. Sec. Gen. et Meth. Med.*

APARA'GUA (*Bot.*) a species of Briony growing in Brasil.

APA'RGIA (*Bot.*) ἀπαργία; the name of an herbaceous plant mentioned by Theophrastus, who only distinguishes it by the epithet of ἐπιγειόφυλλον, i. e. having the leaf issue from the root instead of from the stem, after the manner of the Dandelion. *Theophrast.* l. 7, c. 9.

APARGIA, *in the Linnean system*, a genus of plants, Class 19, Order 1 *Polygamia Æqualis*.
Generic Characters. CAL. common imbricate; scales several.—COR. compound imbricate; corollets hermaphrodite; proper monopetalous.—STAM. filaments five; anthers cylindric.—PIST. germ subovate; styles filiform; stigmas two.—PER. none; calyx oblong; seeds solitary; down sessile; receptacle naked.
Species. The plants of this tribe are mostly perennials, and are called *Leontodon*, or *Hieracium*, by the ancient botanists. *Dodon. Hist. Stirp.; Lobel. Plant.* seu *Stirp. Plant.; J. Bauh. Hist. Plant.; C. Bauh. Pin.; Ger. Herb; Park. Theat. Botan.; Raii Hist. Plant.; Linn. Spec. Plant.*

APARI'NE (*Bot.*) ἀπαρίνη, a plant, the expressed juice of which was said to cure the bites of serpents. *Theophrast. Hist. Plant.* l. 7, c. 14; *Dioscor.* l. 3, c. 14; *Plin.* l. 27, c. 5.

APARINE, *in the Linnean system*, is a species of the *Galium*.

A'PARINES (*Bot.*) the *Ammannia latifolia* of Linnæus.

APARITHME'SIS (*Rhet.*) ἀπαρίθμησις, a figure of speech, which consists in enumerating or distinguishing several particulars by means of the particles firstly, then, or moreover, finally, &c. *Hermog. ɩδ. Ald. Ed.* tom. i, p. 48; *Aristid.* περὶ λογισμῶν. p. 650.

A'PATE (*Ent.*) a division of the genus Dermestes, according to Fabricius, comprehending those insects of this tribe which have the jaw one-toothed.

APA'THES (*Ant.*) ἀπαθεῖς, from α, priv. and πάθος, affection; a sort of philosophers who pretended to have no affections. *Plin.* l. 7, c. 19.

APATISA'TIO (*Law*) an agreement or compact made with another. *Upton.* l. 2, c. 12.

APATI'TES (*Min.*) a genus of calcareous and brittle earths; consisting of carbonate of lime and phosphoric acid.

APATU'RIA (*Ant.*) Ἀπατούρια, a festival at Athens, from ἀπάτη, deceit, because it was instituted in commemoration of a stratagem by which Xanthus, king of Bœotia, was killed by Melanthus, king of Athens. It was celebrated for three days, the first of which was called Δόρπια or Δορπεῖα; the second, Ἀναῤῥύσις; and the third, κουρεῶτις. *Herod.* l. 1, c. 147; *Plat. in Tim. & Procl. in Plat.; Xenoph. Hellen.* l. 1, c. 7; *Aristoph. in Nub. & Schol. in Aristoph.; Poll. Onom.* l. 6, segm. 102; *Harpocration; Etymol. Magn.; Suidas; Simplic. ad Aristot. Phys.* l. 4.

APAULETE'RIA (*Ant.*) ἀπαυλητήρια, the garment presented by the bridegroom on the day called the *Apaulia*. [vide *Apaulia*]

APA'ULIA (*Ant.*) ἀπαύλια, the second day of the marriage festival, when the bride's departure from her father's house was celebrated. *Poll. Onomast.* l. 3, c. 3; *Hesychius; Suidas; Etymologic. Magn. Phavorinus.*

APA'UME (*Her.*) a hand opened, with the full palm appearing, and the thumb and fingers extended, as may be seen in the arms of a baronet. [vide *Canton*]

A'PE (*Zool.*) a name for different species of the Simia which are without tails. They are imitative, full of gesticulations, chatter with their teeth, and macerate their food in their cheeks before they swallow it. This tribe of animals is also remarkable for being lascivious, thievish, and gregarious.—*Sea Ape*, a marine animal on the coast of America.

APECHE'MA (*Med.*) ἀπήχημα, from ἀπὸ, and χῆος, sound; i. e. repercussion of sound; but in a medical sense, a contra fissure.

APEA'K (*Mar.*) when the cable is drawn so tight as to bring the vessel directly over the anchor, the ship is said to be *apeak*.

APE'BA (*Bot.*) the *Aubletia* of Linnæus. *Marc. Hist. Bras.*

APELLI'TÆ (*Ecc.*) hereticks in the second century, so called from their leader Apelles, who, among other heresies, denied the spirituality of Christ and the resurrection of the dead. *Tertul. de Præsc.* c. 30, &c.; *Euseb. Hist.* l. 3, c. 13; *S. Epiphan. Hæres.* 44; *S. August. Hæres.* 23; *Baron. Annal. Ann.* 146.

APE'PSIA (*Med.*) the same as *Dyspepsia*.

A'PER (*Nat.*) the boar, which is a symbol of several cities, is supposed to refer to the Erymanthian boar which was killed by Hercules; it is represented, as in the annexed figure, on a coin of Abacænum, in Sicily, with an acorn

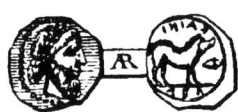

lying before it.—The legend ABAKAINI. *Parut. Sicil. Descritt.*; *D'Orville Sicul.*; *Pemb. Numismat. Antiq.*

APE'RIENS *palpebram rectus* (*Anat.*) the same as *Elevator palpebræ superioris*.

APE'RIENTS (*Med.*) *aperientia*, from *aperio*, to open; opening medicines. *Cels. de Re Med.* l. 5, c. 18; *Gal. de Simpl.* l. 5.

APERI'TTOS (*Med.*) ἀπέριττος, from α, priv. and περιττός, redundant; an epithet for aliment not generating much excrement. *Gorr. Defin. Med.*

APE'RTIS *portarum* (*Astrol.*) some great and manifest change of the air upon certain configurations.

APERTU'RA *tabularum* (*Law*) the breaking open a last will and testament.—*Apertura feudi*, the loss of a feudal tenure by default of issue to him, to whom the feud or fee was granted.

A'PERTURE (*Opt.*) a hole next to the object-glass of a telescope, through which the light and image of the object is conveyed from the tube into the eye. *Huygen. Diopt.* prop. 53, 56.

APERTURE (*Archit.*) an opening in any building, as doors, windows, &c.

APERTURE (*Geom.*) the opening or angle formed by the meeting of two right lines.

APE'RTUS (*Med.*) an epithet in Scribonius Largus, answering to the *ulceratus* of Pliny; as, *Strumæ aperta*, ulcerated humours. *Plin.* l. 30, c. 5; *Reod. in Scribon. Larg.*

A'PES (*Zool.*) vide *Apis*.

APE'TALÆ (*Bot.*) the fourth class of plants, according to Haller's system.

APE'TALOUS (*Bot.*) from α, priv. and πέταλον, a petal, a flower-leaf; an epithet for plants that have no petals.

A'PEX (*Ant.*) from *apiendo*, i. e. *ligando*, binding. 1. A little woollen tuft on the flamens or high priest's cap. 2. The cap itself, of which a representation is given under *Ancilia*. 3. A hat, or any thing capped. 4. The crest of a helmet.
Virg. Æn. l. 12, v. 492.

———— *Apicem tamen incita summum*
  Hasta tulit.

Plin. l. 22, c. 23; *Val. Max.* l. 1, c. 1; *Lucan.* l. 1, v. 604; *Serv. in Virg. Æn.* l. 10, v. 270; *Scalig. Conj. ad Varr.* p. 37; *Turneb. Adv.* l. 29, c. 31.

APEX (*Zool.*) the crest or crown of birds. *Plin.* l. 11, c. 37.

APEX (*Geom.*) the angular point of a cone or conic section.

APEX (*Con.*) the beak, tip, or extremity of a shell. The *apices* are *Auriformes*, auriform or ear-shaped, having an incurvated arch between the beaks.—*Corniformes*, horn-shaped, i. e. long and mucronated or pointed.—*Inflexi*, inflex, or bending towards each other.—*Reflexi*, reflex, turned towards the *areola*.—*Spirales*, spiral, i. e. twisted spirally.

APEX (*Bot.*) the upper extremity of a leaf, farthest from the base or insertion.

APEX *literarum* (*Gram.*) the mark which serves as an accent.

APEX *legis* (*Law*) a quirk.

A'PHACA (*Bot.*) Ἀφάκα, the Wild Vetch, a small shrub that grows in ploughed lands, the seeds of which are of an astringent quality; it is the *Lathyris aphaca* of Linnæus. *Theophrast. Hist. Plant.*; *Dioscor.* l. 2, c. 78; *Plin.* l. 21, c. 17; *Oribas. Med. Coll.* l. 11; *Paul. Æginet.* l. 7, c. 3; *Geopon. Auct.* l. 12, c. 1; *Ger. Herb.*; *Park. Theat. Bot.*; *C. Bauh. Pin.*; *Raii Hist. Plant.*

APHÆ'RESIS (*Gram.*) ἀφαίρεσις, from ἀφαιρέω, to take away; a figure which takes away a letter or syllable from the beginning of a word, as *ruit* for *iruit*.

APHÆRESIS (*Med.*) a taking away of any superfluous part medicinally or chirurgically. *Hipp. Coac. Prænot. &c.*; *Foes. Œconom. Hippocrat.*

A'PHANES (*Bot.*) ἀφανής, obscure; a genus of plants so called from its diminutive size, Class 4 *Tetandria*, Order 2 *Digynia*.
Generic Characters. CAL. perianth one-leaved.—COR. none—STAM. filaments four; anthers roundish—PIST. germ ovate; style filiform; stigma headed.—PER. none; Calyx containing the seeds in the bottom; seeds ovate.
Species. The only species is the *Aphanes arvensis*, *Alchimilla aphanes*, *Percepier Anglorum*, seu *Polygonum selinoides*, an annual, native of Europe. *Ger. Herb.*; *J. Bauhin. Hist. Plant.*; *C. Bauhin. Pin. Theat.*; *Park. Theat. Botan.*; *Raii Hist. Plant.*; *Mor. Hist. Plant.*; *Linn. Spec. Plant.*

APHASSO'MENOS (*Med.*) ἀφασσόμενος, from ἀφάσσω, to stroke; rubbed with the fingers, or gently felt, to discover any disorder in the part. *Gal. Exeges. in Vocab. Hippocrat.*; *Foes. Œconom. Hippocrat.*

APHE'BRIOC (*Chem.*) Sulphur.

APHELICE'STEROS (*Med.*) ἀφηλικέστερος, from ἀπὸ, away from, and ἡλικία, youth; past the flower of youth. *Hippocrat. Epid.* l. 7.

APHE'LION (*Ast.*) or *Aphelium*, from ἀπὸ, from, and ἥλιος, the sun; that point at which the earth or any planet is most distant from the sun. In the Copernican system it is that end of the greater axis of an elliptical orbit of the planet most remote from the focus wherein the sun is, as A in the figure under the head *Anomaly*. In the Ptolemaic system, the Apogee supplies the place of the Aphelion. [vide *Astronomy* and *Anomaly*]

APHE'LLAN (*Ast.*) the name of a bright star in the constellation Gemini.

A'PHESIS (*Med.*) ἄφεσις, from ἀφίημι, to remit; the remission of a disorder. *Gal. Exeges. Vocab. Hippoc.*; *Gorr. Defin. Med.*; *Foes. Œconom. Hippocrat.*

APHE'TA (*Astrol.*) a planet, taken to be the giver of life in a nativity.

APHILANTHRO'PIA (*Med.*) ἀφιλανθρωπία, from α, priv. and φιλανθρωπία; the first degree of melancholy which produces an aversion to society. *Castell. Lex. Med.*

A'PHIS (*Ent.*) Plant-Louse, a genus of animals, Class *Insecta*, Order *Hemiptera*.
Generic Characters. Snout inflected; antennæ longer than thorax; wings either four upright or none; feet formed for walking; abdomen generally furnished with two horns or processes.

The numerous species of this tribe of insects are remarkable for infesting plants, the leaves of which they cause to crumple up, and consume their juices. They are sometimes winged and sometimes apterous, and are supposed to possess the extraordinary faculty of continued impregnation, one single act of which in a female is sufficient for many successive generations. The species are principally distinguished by the names of the plants which they infest, as the—*Aphis salicis*, one of the largest kind of Aphides that infest the willows.—*Aphis rosæ*, of a bright colour, which is found in great numbers on the leaves, stalks, and buds of roses.—*Aphis tiliæ*, the Lime-tree Aphis, one of the most beautiful of the genus.—*Aphis millefolii*, the Yarrow Aphis.—The Common Green Aphis is called the Fly, when it infests hop-yards.

APHLEGMA'NTON (*Med.*) ἀφλέγμαντος, from α, priv. and φλέγμα, *phlegma*, void of phlegm; an epithet for pus which marks it to be laudable. *Hippocrat. Prædict.* l. 2; *Gorr. Defin. Med.*; *Foes. Œconom. Hippocrat.*

A'PHODOS (*Med.*) ἄφοδος, the recrements of the aliment which pass off by stool. *Gal. com.* 5, *in Epid.* l. 6; *Foes. Œconom. Hippocrat.*

APHO'NI (*Med.*) ἄφωνοι, from α, priv. and φωνή, voice; those who labour under a deprivation of voice from an apoplectic affection, or any other cause. *Gorr. Def. Med.*; *Foes. Œconom. Hippocrat.*

APHO'NIA (*Med.*) ἀφωνία, from α, priv. and φωνή, the voice; a deprivation of voice, or palsy of the tongue. *Gal. in Hippocrat.* l. 6, aphor. 51; *Gorr. Defin. Med.*; *Foes. Œconom. Hippocrat.*

APHONIA now constitutes a genus of diseases, Class *Locales*, Order *Dysunesiæ*, in Cullen's Nosology.

A'PHORISM (*Phi.*) ἀφορισμός, from ἀφορίζω, to define, or separate; a sentence comprehending, within a few words, all the properties of a thing, as the Aphorisms of Hippocrates, Boerhaave, &c.

APHO'RME (*Med.*) ἀφορμή, from ἀπὸ, and ὁρμὴ, impetus; the exciting cause of a disease. *Gal. comm.* 3, *in Hippocrat. Epidem.* l. 6; *Gorr. Defin. Med.*; *Foes. Œconom. Hippocrat.*

APHORME (*Ant.*) ἀφορμή, money placed as a deposit in the banker's hands, otherwise called Εισθήκη; Ἀφορμῆς δίκη is a suit about a deposit. *Poll.* l. 3, c. 9; *Harpocration*; *Hesychius*; *Suidas*.

APHRA'CTA (*Ant.*) open vessels which were used in naval engagements. *Cic. ad Attic.* l. 6, ep. 8; *Scheff. de Mil. Nav.* l. 2, c. 2.

APHRI'TE (*Min.*) from ἀφρὸς, spume, or froth; Silvery Chalk, a species of stone of the carbonate family, so called from its frothy appearance.

APHRO'DES (*Med.*) ἀφρώδης, from ἀφρὸς, spume; frothy in application to the blood and excrements.

APHRODI'SIA (*Ant.*) Ἀφροδίσια, festivals in honour of Ἀφροδίτη, Venus, in different parts of Greece, as at Cyprus, Paphos, Corinth. At the latter place it was celebrated by harlots, according to Athenæus. *Strab.* l. 14; *Athen.* l. 13, c. 4; *Clemen. Protreptric.*; *Firm. de Error. Profess. Relig.*

APHRODISIA (*Med.*) ἀφροδίσια, from ἀφροδίτη; venereal commerce. *Gal. de Top.* l. 7; *Gorr. Defin. Med.*

APHRODISICIA'STICON (*Med.*) ἀφροδισιαστικον, a troche so called, by Galen, because the stools which it produced were frothy. He recommends it in dysenteries.

APHRODI'SIUS *morbus* (*Med.*) the *Lues venerea*.

APHRODISIUS (*Chron.*) the eleventh month of the Bithynian year, commencing on the 25th of July.

APHRODI'TA (*Ent.*) a genus of animals, Class *Vermes*, Order *Molusca*.
Generic Characters. Body creeping, oblong, with fasciculate feet, each side; *mouth* cylindrical, retractile; *feelers* two, setaceous; *eyes* four.
Species. The principal species are the—*Aphrodita aculeata*, the Sea-Mouse, four or five inches long, often found in the belly of the cod-fish.—*Aphrodita squamosa*, covered with two rows of large scales, about an inch long.—*Aphrodita minuta*, not an inch long, &c.

APHRODITA'RIUM (*Med.*) ἀφροδιτάριον. 1. A sort of collyrium. 2. A sort of powder. *Paul. Ægin. de Re Med.* l. 4, c. 40; l. 7, c. 13.

APHROGA'LA (*Med.*) ἀφρόγαλα, from ἀφρὸς, spume, or froth, and γάλα, *lac*; the froth of milk, good for an habitual heat in the stomach. *Gal. de Meth. Med.* l. 7, c. 4.

APHROLI'TRUM (*Min.*) or Aphronitrum, ἀφρόλιτρον, ἀφρόνιτρον, the spume of nitre. *Plin.* l. 31, c. 10; *Gorr. Defin. Med.*

A'PHRON (*Bot.*) from α, priv. and φρήν, the mind, from its inebriating quality; a wild kind of poppy. *Plin.* l. 20, c. 19.

APHRON (*Med.*) a cephalic plaster. *Aet. Tetrab.* 4, serm. 3, c. 13.

APHRONI'TRUM (*Min.*) ἀφρόνιτρον, the spume or flower of nitre; natron. *Plin.* l. 31, c. 10.

APHROSELE'NOS (*Min.*) ἀφροσέληνος, a stone; so called from its representing the moon as it were in a glass. *Paul. Æginet. de Re Med.* l. 7, c. 3; *Gorr. Defin Med.*

APHROSY'NE (*Med.*) from ἄφρων, simple; dotage.

A'PHTHÆ (*Med.*) ἄφθαι, the thrush; a disease consisting of ulcers in the mouth, to which children are very subject. *Hippocrat.* l. 3, aphor. 24; *Aret. de Caus. et Sign. Acut. Morb.* l. 1, c. 9; *Cels. de Re Med.* l. 2, c. 1, &c.; *Gal. de Comp. Med. Sec. Loc. &c.*; *Oribas. de Loc. Affect.* l. 4, c. 68; *Aet. Tetrab.* 2, serm. 4; *Paul. Æginet.* l. 1, c. 10; *Actuar. de Meth. Med.* l. 6; *Gorr. Defin. Med.*; *Foes. Œconom. Hippocrat.*

APHTHÆ constitutes now a genus of diseases in Cullen's Nosology, Class *Pyrexiæ*, Order *Exanthemata*.—*Aphthæ Serpentes*, vide *Cancrum Oris*.

APHTHA'RDOCITES (*Ecc.*) a sect of heretics which branched off from the Eutichians in the sixth century. They denied the passion of our Saviour, maintaining that his body was immortal from the moment of his conception. They are so called from ἄφθαρτος, incorruptible, and δοκεῖν, to think. *Sander. Hæres. Ann.* 585.

A'PHYA (*Ich.*) ἀφύα, from α, priv. and φύω, to beget; a small fish of a pale white colour; so called because it is supposed not to be generated in the ordinary way; but, according to Aristotle, from the froth of the sea. It is a species of the *Cyprinus* of Linnæus. *Aristot. Hist. Anim.* l. 6, c. 15; *Athen.* l. 8, c. 14; *Gal. Exeges. Vocab. Hippocrat.*

APHYLLA'NTES *Anguillaræ* (*Bot.*) the *Globularia vulgaris* of Linnæus.

APHYLLA'NTHES (*Bot.*) from α priv. φύλλον, leaf, and ἄνθος, a flower, i. e. an apetalous flower; a genus of plants, Class 6 *Hexandria*, Order 1 *Monogynia*.
Generic Characters. CAL. *glumes* univalve—COR. *petals* six; *claws* slender.—STAM. *filaments* setaceous; *anthers* oblong—PIST. *germ* superior; *style* filiform; *stigmas* three.—PER. *capsule* turbinate; *seeds* ovate.
Species. The only species is the *Aphyllanthes monspeliensis*, seu *Monspeliensum*, seu *Caryophyllus cæruleus*, &c. a perennial, native of the South of France. *Lob. Adv. Stirp.*; *J. Bauhin. Hist. Plant.*; *C.Bauhin. Pin. Theat.*; *Mor. Hist. Plant.*; *Wild. Linn. Spec. Plant.*

APHYLLA'NTI *affinis* (*Bot.*) the *Globularia cordifolia* of Linnæus.

APHY'LLON (*Bot.*) the *Oribanche* of Linnæus.

APHY'LLOUS (*Bot.*) from α, priv. and φύλλον, a leaf; leafless; an epithet applied to the stem, leaf, or whirl; as *aphyllus caulis*, a leafless stem; *aphyllus flos*, a flower having no calyx; *aphyllus verticellus*, a whirl having no leaves about it.

APHYTA'GORAS (*Bot.*) an Indian tree, which is said by Clusius to bear amber.

APHYTEI'A (*Bot.*) from α, priv. and φυτον, a plant, plantless; a genus of plants, Class 16 *Monadelphia*, Order 1 *Triandria*, having neither root, stem, nor leaves, parasitical-terrestrial, and consisting of a fructification only.
Generic Characters. CAL. perianth monophyllous.—COR. rudiments of three petals.—STAM. filaments short; *anthert* convex.—PIST. germ inferior; *style* thickish; *stigma* three-cornered.—PER. berry one-celled; *seeds* numerous.
Species. The only species is the *Aphyteia hydnora*, seu *Hydnora africana*, native of the Cape of Good Hope. *Linn. Spec. Plant.*

A'PIARY (*Zool.*) a place in which bees are kept.

APIA'RIUS (*Zool.*) a bee-merchant.

APIA'STRA (*Or.*) Bee-Eater, a sort of bird mentioned by Servius.

APIA'STRUM (*Bot.*) from *apes*, the bees; the herb which bees delight in, Balm-gentle or Mint. *Plin. l. 20, c. 11.*

A'PICA *ovis* (*Zool.*) a small-bodied sheep, bearing little wool, a pilled ewe. *Fest. de Verb. Signif.*

A'PINEL (*Bot.*) a root met with in the American islands, remarkable for its destructive quality to serpents, who shun it, and every thing rubbed with it. The plant is the *Aristolochia anguicida* of Linnæus.

A'PIOS (*Bot.*) απιος, round knob-rooted spurge, the root of which is like an onion, and the juice purgative. It is a species of the *Glycine*, and of the *Euphorbia* of Linnæus. *Dioscor. l. 4, c. 177; Plin. l. 26, c. 8; Oribas. Med. Coll. L 11; Aet. Tetrab. 1, serm. 1.*

APIOSCO'RODON (*Bot.*) the *Cratæva gynandra* of Linnæus. *Pluk. Almag.*

A'PIS (*Ent.*) the bee, a well known insect; so called because, according to Virgil—
Virg. Georg. l. 4, v. 257,
————— *pedibus connexæ ad limina pendent;*
or from απυς, i. e. without feet, because they are born without feet; a genus of animals, Class *Insecta*, Order *Himenoptera*.
Generic Character. Mouth horny.—Feelers four, unequal.—Antennæ short.—Wings flat.—Sting of the females and neutrals concealed in the abdomen.
Species. The species of this genus are divided by Linnæus into two assortments, namely, those whose body is slightly covered with a fine hair or down, and those whose body is very villose or hairy. The principal species in the first division is the—*Apis mellificus*, the Honey-Bee.—*Apis centuncularis*, the Carpenter-Bee. Those in the second division, which are commonly known by the name of Humble-Bee, are the—*Apis lapidarius*, so called because its nest is situated in gravelly places. It is one of the largest insects of the tribe.—*Apis terrestris*, of the same size as the former, of a black colour, with the thorax marked by a yellow bar.—*Apis Hortorum*, with the thorax and abdomen yellow.

APIS (*Astron.*) or *Musca*, the Bee or Fly, a southern constellation, consisting of four stars.

APIS (*Numis.*) the Bee was represented on the coins of many cities, because it was chosen as the symbol of new colonies. It is most frequently to be met with on the coins of Athens and Ephesus, as in the annexed figure of a coin

belonging to the latter city, where the stag and the palm on the obverse are emblematical of Diana, the tutelary goddess of the place; and, on the reverse, the inscription ΕΦ, with the figure of a bee, denotes the city. *Beg. Brand. Thes.* vol. i. 503.

A'PIUM (*Bot.*) σιλινον, smallage or parsley, a garden herb, which, according to Homer, was the food of the war horses.
Hom. Il. l. 2, v. 775.

————ἵπποι δὲ παρ' ἅρμασιν οἶσιν ἕκαστος,
Λωτὸν ἐρεπτόμενοι ἐλεόθρεπτόν τε σίλινον
Ἕστασαν.

It is likewise celebrated by the poets as a coronary plant. *Pind. Olymp. od. 13.*

Δύο δ' αὐτὸν ἐρέψαι πλόκοι σιλί
Νωι ἐν ἰσθμιάδεσσιν.

Anacreon. Fragm. 17.

Ἐπὶ δ' ὄφρυσι σιλίνων στεφανίσκος
Θέμενοι θαλίαις ἑορτὴν ἀγάγωμεν Διονύσῳ.

Hor. l. 2, od. 7, v. 24.

————Quis udo
Deproperare apio coronas
Curatve myrto?

Diodor. l. 16; Callimach. apud Plut. Sympos. l. 5; Plin. l. 19, c. 8, &c.; Polyæn. Stratag. l. 5, c. 12; Arnob. l. 5; Alex. Gen. Dier. l. 5, c. 26; Suidas.; Stuck. Ant. Conviv. l. 1, c. 26.

APIUM, in the Linnean system, a genus of plants, Class 5 *Pentandria*, Order 2 *Digynia*.
Generic Characters. CAL. umbel universal of fewer rays; partial of more; involucre universal small; partial similar; proper perianth obsolete.—COR. universal uniform; proper petals roundish.—STAM. filaments simple; anthers roundish.—PIST. germ inferior; styles reflex; stigmas obtuse.—PER. none; fruit ovate; seeds two.
Species. The two species are the *Apium petroselinum*, Parsley, a biennial, native of Sardinia; and *Apium graveolens*, Smallage, a biennial, native of Britain. *J. Bauhin. Hist. Plant.; C. Bauhin. Pin. Theat.; Ger. Herb.; Park. Theat. Botan.; Raii Hist. Plant.; Tourn. Inst. Herb.; Boerh. Ind. Plant; Wild. Linn. Spec. Plant.*

A'PLOME (*Min.*) a species of garnet.

APLU'DA (*Bot.*) the chaff or bran of any corn; so called, according to Festus, because, *applodatur*, it is flapped off from the grain. *Plin. l. 18, c. 10; Aul. Gell. l. 11, c. 7; Fest. de Verb. Signif.*

APLUDA, in the Linnean system, a genus of plants, Class 23 *Polygamia*, Order 1 *Monoecia*.
Generic Characters. CAL. involucre common unvalve; valve ovate.—COR. glume bivalve; valve exterior navicular, interior lanceolate; nectary very small.—STAM. filaments three; anthers linear.—PIST. germ oblong; styles two; stigmas oblong.—PER. none; corolla cherishes the seed; seed ovate-oblong.
Species. The species are perennials, as the—*Apluda mutica, zeujites*, and *aristata*. *Linn. Spec. Plant.; Brown. Hist. Jamaic.; Wild. Linn. Spec. Plant.*

APLU'STRIA (*Ant.*) ἄφλαστα, ornaments at the stern, answering to the acrostolia at the prow, to which the poets frequently refer.
Hom. Il. l. 15, v. 717.

Ἕκτωρ δὲ πρύμνηθεν ἐπεὶ λάβεν οὐχὶ μεθίει
Ἄφλαστον μετὰ χερσὶν ἔχων.

Luc. l. 3, v. 671.

*Invenit arma furor: remum contorsit in hostem
Alter; at hi totum validis aplustre lacertis,
Avulsumque rotant excusso remige sedes.*

Juv. sat. 10, v. 135.

> *Et curtum temonis jugum, victæque triremis*
> *Aplustre, et summo tristis captivus in arcu,*
> *Humanis majora bonis creduntur.*

Poll. Onom. l. 1, c. 9; *Fest. de Verb. Signif.*; *Eustath. in Hom.*; *Hesychius.*

APLY′SIA (*Con.*) a genus of animals, Class *Vermes*, Order *Mollusca.*

Generic Character. Body covered with reflexible membranes.—*Shield* horny on the back, guarding the lungs.—*Aperture* on the right side.—*Vent* on the extremity of the back.—*Feelers* four, resembling ears.

Species. The two species are the—*Aplysia depilans,* depilatory Sea-Hare.—*Aplysia mustelina,* the tawny Sea-Hare.

APLY′TOS (*Med.*) from *α*, priv. and *πλύω*, to wash; an epithet for wool, as ἱμίον ἄπλυτον, unwashed wool, called in Latin *Lana succida.*

APNŒ′A (*Med.*) ἄπνοια, from *α*, priv. and *πνέω*, *spiro;* a difficulty of respiration, or suppression of breathing. *Gal. de Diffic. Spir.* l. 1.

APOBA′MMA (*Nat.*) ἀπόβαμμα, from ἀποβάπτω, to tinge; a slight tincture applied to liquors in which gold coins or red hot irons have been quenched. *Castell. Lex. Med.*

APOBATE′RIA (*Ant.*) a valedictory poem or speech made by a person on his leaving his country.

APOBRA′SMA (*Nat.*) ἀπόβρασμα, the bran of wheat, or the froth of the sea. *Hippocrat. de Nat. Puer.*; *Foes. Œconom. Hippocrat.*; *Castell. Lex. Med.*

APO′CALYPSE (*Bibl.*) ἀποκάλυψις, from ἀποκαλύπτω, to reveal; the Greek name for the book of Revelations.

APOCAPNI′SMUS (*Nat.*) from καπνός, smoke; suffumigation.

APOCA′RSAMUM (*Med.*) a poisonous drug growing in Abyssinia.

APOCA′RTEREON (*Med.*) ἀποκαρτέριον, starving oneself to death. *Hippocrat. de Rat. Vict. in Morb. Acut.*

APOCATA′STASIS (*Med.*) ἀποκατάστασις, from ἀποκαθίστημι, to restore; an amendment, recovery, or cessation of a disorder, in which sense Hippocrates uses the verb in many places, and Aretæus the noun. *Aret.* l. 1, c. 10; *Foes. Œconom. Hippocrat.*

APOCATHA′RSIS (*Med.*) ἀποκάθαρσις, an expurgation or evacuation of any kind, as of pus from the breast by spitting, according to Hippocrates, and the vomitings mentioned by Thucydides, which affected the patients during the memorable plague at Athens. *Thucyd.* l. 2; *Foes. Œconom. Hippocrat.*

APO′CECAULISMENON (*Surg.*) a fracture after the manner of a stalk.

APO′CENOS (*Med.*) the same as *Abevacuatio.*

APOCERU′GMA (*Med.*) ἀποκήρυγμα, a declaration made to a patient respecting his case. *Foes. Œconom. Hippocrat.*

APO′CHA (*Law*) a discharge for money that has been paid. *Ulp.*

APOCHRE′MMA (*Med.*) ἀπόχρεμμα, sputum discharged by apochrempsis, or hawking. *Hippoc. Coac. et de Loc. in Homine;* *Gorr. Def. Med.*; *Foes. Œconom. Hippocrat.*

APOCHYLI′SMA (*Med.*) the same as *Sapa.*

APO′CHYMA (*Med.*) a kind of Zopissa, made of the resin and wax scraped from ships, or from the pitch-tree. *Aet. Tetrab.* 4, serm. 3, c. 20; *Paul. Æginet. de Re Med.* l. 7, c. 3; *Gorr. Defin. Med.*

APOCLA′SMA (*Surg.*) the same as *Abductio.*

APOCLE′TI (*Ant.*) a select council of the Etolians mentioned by Livy. *Hist.* l. 35, c. 34, &c.

APO′COPE (*Gram.*) ἀποκοπή, from ἀπό and κόπτω, *scindo;* a figure by which the last letter or syllable of a word is cut off, as *viden'* for *videsne.*

APOCOPE (*Med.*) the same as *Abscissio.*

APOCRISIA′RIUS (*Ecc.*) ἀποκρισιάριος, from ἀποκρίνομαι, to answer; the surrogate, commissary, or chancellor to a bishop.

APO′CRISIS (*Med.*) the same as *Eccrisis.*

APOCROU′STION (*Med.*) from ἀποκρούω, to repel; a repellant, or a remedy of a repelling or astringent nature. *Gorr. Def. Med.*

APO′CRYPHA (*Theol.*) from ἀποκρύπτω, to hide; *occulta scripta,* certain books of doubtful authority which are not received into the canon of holy writ. Of this description is the book of the Maccabees, although it is admitted to contain a true history.

APOCYE′SIS (*Med.*) ἀποκύησις, bringing forth young; a birth.

APO′CYNON (*Ant.*) ἀπόκυνον, from ἀπό and κύων, a dog; because it was supposed to restrain the fury of dogs; a bone in the left side of a frog which served to keep dogs off from a person; and also a shrub, Dog's Bane, that kills dogs which eat of it. *Diosc.* l. 4, c. 81; *Pliny* l. 24, c. 11, l. 32, c. 5.

APO′CYNUM (*Bot.*) ἀπόκυνον, the name of a plant [vide *Apocynon*], and *in the Linnean system,* a genus of plants, Class 5 *Pentandria,* Order 2 *Digynia.*

Generic Characters. CAL. *perianth* one-leaved.—COR. monopetalous; *nectary* of five glandular corpuscles surrounding the germ.—STAM. *filaments* very short; *anthers* oblong.—PIST. *germs* two; *styles* short; *stigma* roundish.—PER. *follicles* two; *seeds* numerous; *receptacle* subulate.

Species. The species are mostly perennials. *J. Bauhin. Hist. Plant.*; *C. Bauh. Pin. Theat.*; *Ger. Herb.*; *Park. Theat. Botan.*; *Raii Hist. Plant.*; *Pluk. Almag. Botan.*; *Tourn. Hist. Herb.*; *Wild. Linn. Spec. Plant.*

APOCYNUM is also the name of several species, as the—*Asclepias amœna purpurescens,* &c. the *Ceropegia tenuifolia,* the *Cynanchum virginale et acutum,* the *Echites biflora, suberecta,* &c. of Linnæus. *Bauh., Ray, Pluk., &c.*

APOCYRTE′MENA (*Med.*) ἀποκυρτώματα, gathering to a sharp head, as applied to suppurations.

APODACRYTICA (*Med.*) ἀποδακρυτικά, from ἀπό and δάκρυ, a tear, Apodacrytics; medicines provoking tears, and carrying off superfluous humours at the eyes.

A′PODAL (*Ich.*) the first order of fishes having no ventral fins. It includes the following genera:—*Murœna,* Eel, caudal, dorsal, and anal fins united.—*Gymnotus,* Gymnote, dorsal fins none.—*Gymnothorax,* pectoral fin none.—*Trichiurus,* body ensiform, tail subulate, without fin.—*Anarhichas,* Wolf-fish, body roundish, caudal fin distinct.—*Ammodytes,* Launce; body long, square.—*Ophidium,* teeth both in the jaws and palate, body ensiform.—*Stomateus,* body oval, broad.—*Xyphias,* Sword-fish, head furnished with a sword-shaped upper jaw.—*Sternoptyx,* gill membrane none.—*Leptocephalus,* head small, narrow, pectoral fins none.—*Stylephorus,* pectoral fins small, dorsal as long as the back, caudal short.

APODE′CTÆ (*Ant.*) ἀποδέκται, receivers general among the Athenians, to whom all the revenues of the state were paid. They were ten in number, and had to decide all controversies, except those which were of the greatest importance. *Aristot. Polit.* l. 6, c. 8; *Poll. Onom.* l. 8, segm. 97; *Sigon. de Rep. Athen.* l. 4, c. 8.

APODECTÆ′I (*Ant.*) ἀποδέκται, Athenian officers who measured the corn, whence they were also called σιτομέτραι. [vide *Sitometræ*]

A′PODES (*Or.*) *Plin.* ἄποδες, from *α*, priv. and πούς, *pes;* a species of bird, having very short feet, or, according to Pliny, wanting the use of their feet. *Aristot. Hist. Anim.* l. 9, c. 30; *Plin.* l. 10, c. 39.

APODI′CTICA (*Rhet.*) ἀποδεικτικά, from ἀποδείκνυμι, to demonstrate; an epithet for arguments which are fitted for

4

proving the truth of any point, in distinction from τὰ πανηγυρικά. *Hermog. de Invent.* l. 3, Ald. edit. p. 140.

APODIDRASCI'NDA (*Ant.*) ἀποδιδρασκίνδα, from ἀποδιδράσκω, to run away; a game now known by the name of Hide and Seek.

APODIO'XIS (*Rhet.*) ἀποδίωξις, a figure of speech by which one rejects certain particulars as unworthy of notice. This is also called ἀποπλάνησις, or, as it is interpreted by Cicero, *erroris inductio*, because it is much used by orators to mislead or carry away from the subject. *Cic. de Orat.* l. 3, c. 52; *Jul. Rufin. Fig.* 12.

APODI'XIS (*Rhet.*) ἀπόδιξις, from ἀποδίκνυμι, to demonstrate; an evident demonstration, called by Cicero *Argumenti conclusio*. *Cic. Acad.* l. 2, c. 8.

APO'DOSIS (*Rhet.*) ἀπόδοσις, *reditio*, from ἀποδίδωμι, to restore; a figure consisting of the latter part, or application of a similitude. *Hermog. περὶ ἰδέας*; Ald. Ed. vol. 1, p. 6.

APODYTE'RIUM (*Ant.*) ἀποδυτήριον, from ἀποδύω, to strip: the place where those undressed who frequented the bath; it was also used as the dressing-room. *Varr. de Vit. Rom.* l. 2, c. 1; *Cic. ad Q. Fra.* l. 3, ep. 1; *Poll. Onom.* l. 3, c. 30; *Plin.* l. 5, ep. 6.

APŒ'UM (*Med.*) ἄποιον, from α, priv. and ποῖον, *quale*; insipid, or having no quality of astringency, acrimony, &c.

APOGÆ'I (*Nat.*) ἀπόγαιοι, from ἀπὸ and γῆ, *terra*; winds blowing from land.

APOGE'E (*Ast.*) ἀπόγαιον, from ἀπὸ, *ab*, and γαῖα, *terra*; or that point of the orbit at which the sun, moon, or any planet is, ἀπογαιότατος, most distant from the earth. The ancients, considering the earth as the centre of the universe, had most regard to the apogee and perigee, which the moderns, who make the sun to be centre, have exchanged for the aphelion and perihelion. This point is called by the Arabians the *Aux*, and by the Greeks the ἀψίς, the apsis.— *Line of the apogee*, which is also called the line of the Apsides, a right line drawn from the highest to the lowest apsis through the centre of the world. [vide *Anomaly*]

APOGEU'SIA (*Med.*) vide *Ageustia*.

APO'GRAPHE (*Ant.*) ἀπογραφή, a rendering up of one's accounts in order to clear oneself from the charge of owing money to the state. *Suidas.*

APOLE'CTI (*Ant.*) ἀπόλεκτοι, chosen senators in the council of the Ætolians. *Liv.* l. 25, c. 4.

APOLE'PSIS (*Med.*) ἀπόληψις, *suppressio arteriarum*, &c.; tying a vein or artery to stop an hæmorrhage. *Hippocrat. Epid.* l. 6; *Gal. Comm.* 2 in *Hippocrat.*; *Erot. Lex. Hippocrat.*

APOLE'XIS (*Med.*) ἀπόληξις, the decay of life.

APOLI'DES (*Ant.*) those who were banished to some remote part, and condemned to hard labour, with the loss of the Roman citizenship. *Marcian. de Pœn.* l. 17; *Spanheim de Constitut.*; *Antonin. Imperat. Exercitat.* 1; apud *Græv. Thesaur. Antiq. Rom.* tom. 11, p. 14.

APOLINO'SIS (*Med.*) vide *Amolinon*.

APOLLINA'RES *ludi* (*Ant.*) games celebrated in honour of Apollo, which were appointed by a decree of the senate, U. C. 542, in consequence of the prediction of the prophet Marcius relative to the battle of Cannæ. *Liv.* l. 25; *Macrob.* l. 1, c. 17; *Laz. Comm. Reip. Rom.* l. 10, c. 8; *Ursat. de Not. &c.*; apud *Græv. Thesaur. Ant. Roman.* tom. 11, &c.

APOLLINA'RIANS (*Ecc.*) Ἀπολλινάριοι, the followers of one Apollinarius, a bishop of Laodicea, who held heretical notions respecting the Holy Trinity. *S. Athanas. Epist. ad Antioch.*; *S. Basil. Epist.*; *S. Hieronom. in Chron. ad Ann.* 366, &c.; *S. Epiphan. in Panar.*; *Socrat. Hist. Eccles.* l. 2, c. 46; *Sosom. Hist. Eccles.* L 6, c. 27.

APOLLO'NIA (*Ant.*) ἀπολλώνια, a festival celebrated at Ægialea to commemorate the return of Apollo and Diana, who had fled from that place into Crete. *Pausan.* l. 2, c. 8.

APO'LLYON (*Bibl.*) ἀπολλύων, from ἀπὸ and ὀλλύμι, to destroy; the destroyer, a name in Scripture given to the Devil.

APO'LYSIS (*Med.*) ἀπόλυσις, 1. Exclusion, as of the fœtus, or the secundines. 2. The solution of a disease, or the untying a bandage. *Hippocrat. Epid.* l. 5, *de Coac. Prænot.* &c.; *Gal. περὶ τῆς μητ. ἀπατ.*; *Foes. Œconom. Hippocrat.*

APOMA'GMA (*Med.*) ἀπόμαγμα, from ἀπομάττω, to wipe away; any thing that serves for abstersion or cleansing, as a linen handkerchief, or a sponge. *Foes. Œconom. Hippocrat.*

APOMATHE'MA (*Med.*) Ἀπομάθημα, from ἀπο, priv. and μανθάνω, to learn; unlearning, or forgetting what has been learned.

APOMECO'METRY (*Mech.*) from ἀπὸ μῆκος, at a distance, μετρίω, to measure; the art of measuring things afar off, in order to ascertain their distance.

APOME'LI (*Med.*) ἀπόμελι, from ἀπο and μέλι, honey; a sweet drink made of honey-combs diluted. *Gal. Comm.* 3, in *Hippocrat. περὶ ἀγμῶν*; *Aet. Tetrab.* 2, serm. 1, c. 137; *Paul. Æginet.* l. 7, c. 15; *Myreps. sect.* 5; *Foes. Œconom. Hippocrat.*

APO'MPÆA (*Ant.*) ἀπομπαῖα, certain days on which sacrifices were offered up to the gods, called πομπεῖα. *Hesychius.*

APOMYLLE'NE (*Med.*) ἀπομυλλήνη, a distortion and convulsion, particularly of the cheek, occasioned by a blow. *Erot. Lex. Hippocrat.*

APONENSE'MENOS (*Med.*) ἀπονενεμμένος, from ἀπόνω, to be averse; disgusted with, or loathing. *Gal.* l. in *Hippocrat. Epid.* l. 5.

APONEURO'SIS (*Med.*) ἀπονεύρωσις, from ἀπὸ and νεῦρον, a nerve; the extension of a nerve, a tendon, or chord. *Gorr. Defin. Med.*; *Foes. Œconom. Hippocrat.*

APONOGE'TON (*Bot.*) a genus of plants; Class 11 *Dodecandria*, Order 4 *Tetragynia*.
Generic Characters. CAL. none.—COR. none.—STAM. *filaments* eleven to nineteen.—PIST. *germs* usually four; *styles* none; *stigmas* subulate.—PER. *capsules* four; *seeds* in each capsule three.
Species. The species are perennials, as *Aponogeton monastachyon, distachyon*, &c. *Linn. Spec. Plant.*

APO'PHASIS (*Ant.*) ἀπόφασις, a disclosure, from ἀποφαίνω, to unfold; the disclosure or discovery which the Liturgi used to make on oath of their estates. *Suidas.*

APOPHASIS (*Rhet.*) ἀπόφασις, a figure of speech in which the orator seems to decline stating that which he wishes to insinuate, as if he should say, " I will not attempt to show you in how many particulars he has failed to prove his point." *Poll. Onom.* l. 2, segm. 129; *Hermog. περὶ δεινοτ.*; *Gregor. in Hermog.* c. 37; *Ruf. in Fig.* 7; *Ulpian. ad Demosth. Olynth.* 1.

APOPHASIS *bonorum* (*Ant.*) an inventory, or properly an account taken of estates when they were exchanged, in order to avoid public employments; for it was a custom among the Greeks, when any man would excuse himself from a troublesome office by casting it upon another richer than himself, that the person selected should have the power of challenging him to make an exchange of estates, and thereby compel him to fill the office he wished to get rid of.

APOPHLE'GMATISM (*Med.*) ἀποφλεγματισμός, from ἀπὸ and φλέγμα, phlegm; a medicine to promote the carrying off phlegmatic humours. *Gal. de Simplic.* l. 5; *Oribas. de Loc. Affect.* l. 4, c. 40; *Aet. Tetrab.* 1, serm. 4, c. 96; *Trallian.* l. 3, c. 6; *Actuar. de Meth. Med.* l. 5, c. 11; *Gorr. Defin. Med.*; *Foes. Œconom. Hippocrat.*

APOPHORE'TA (*Ant.*) from ἀποφορέω, to take away; a

Greek name in use among the Romans for presents made in the Saturnalia to the guests, which they were to take with them, of which Martial gives a copious account in his fourteenth book of Epigrams, bearing this title. *Mart. in Apoph.; Sueton. in Cal.* c. 55; *Ambros. Exhort. ad Virgin.; Symmach.* l. 2, ep. 80; *Turneb. Adv.* l. 9, c. 29; *Stuck. Antiq. Conviv.* l. 4, c. 5.

APO'PHRADES (*Med.*) from ἀποφράς, inauspicious; an epithet for the day in which a disorder comes to a crisis or no crisis at all. *Castell. Lex. Med.*

APO'PHROGISM (*Ant.*) the impression of any images on a seal, such as that of the gods or heroes, which the ancients used to put upon their seals.

A'POPHTHEGM (*Rhet.*) ἀπόφθεγμα, from ἀποφθέγγομαι, to speak; a brief and pithy saying, especially of some worthy person.

APOPHTHA'RMA (*Med.*) the same as Apophthora.

APO'PHTHORA (*Med.*) ἀποφθορά, from φθείρω, to destroy; the term mostly employed by Hippocrates for Abortion.

APO'PHYAS (*Med.*) ἀποφυάς, from ἀπό and φύω, to grow, i. e. excrescence; the ramification of the veins.

A'POPHYGE (*Arch.*) ἀποφυγή, a concave part, or ring of a column lying above or below a flat member. *Vitruv.* l. 4, c. 7.

APO'PHYLITE (*Min.*) a species of Zeolite.

APO'PHYSIS (*Anat.*) ἀπόφυσις, from ἀπό and φύω, to grow, i. e. an excrescence; that kind of eminence of a bone which is contiguous, and makes it one piece with itself. *Ruf. Ephes. Appell. Part. hum. Corp.* l. 1, c. 10; *Gal. de Ossib.; Oribas. Med. Coll.* l. 25; *Gorr. Defin. Med.; Foes. Œconom. Hippocrat.*

Apophysis (*Bot.*) an excrescence from the theca of the musci.

APOPLE'CTA (*Anat.*) the internal jugular vein. *Castell. Lex. Med.*

APOPLE'CTICA (*Med.*) 1. Medicines against the apoplexy. 2. A fever succeeding an apoplexy.

Apoplectica vena (*Anat.*) the jugular vein.

A'POPLEXY (*Med.*) ἀποπληξία, from ἀπό and πλήττω, to strike; that disorder which suddenly surprises the brain, and takes away all sense and motion. *Hippocrat.* l. 7, *Aphor.* 4; *Aret.* l. 1, c. 7; *Cels. de Re Med.* l. 3, c. 1; *Gal. in Hippocrat. Aphor.; Cœl. Aurelian. de Acut. Morb.* l. 3, c. 5; *Oribas. Med. Coll.* l. 8, c. 6; *Aet. Tetrab.* 2, serm. 2, c. 27; *P. Æginet. de Re Med.* l. 3, c. 18.

Apoplexy now constitutes a genus of diseases in Cullen's Nosology; Class *Neuroses*, Order *comata*.

APOPO'MPÆ (*Anat.*) ἀποπομπαῖ, an epithet for certain days, on which sacrifices were offered to the gods, called πομπαῖοι. *Hesychius, Phavorinus.*

APO'RIA (*Rhet.*) ἀπορία, addubitatio; a figure, when one is in doubt or perplexity what to do. *Rutil. Lup.* l. 2, c. 10.

Aporia (*Med.*) from α, priv. and πόρος, a duct; 1. A doubtful disease. 2. The same as Alysmus.

APORIA'RE (*Law*) to bring to poverty.

APORRHA'IDES (*Con.*) a sort of shell-fish.

APORRHI'PSIS (*Med.*) ἀπόρριψις, abjection; a precipitate throwing off the clothes, as in a state of delirium. *Hippocrat. de Rat. Vict. in Morb. acut.*

APORRHŒ'A (*Med.*) ἀπόρροια, a defluxion of humours, vapours, and sulphurous effluvia passing off from the body.

Aporrhœa (*Astrol.*) when the moon separates from one planet and applies to another.

A'POS (*Or.*) the same as Apus.

APOSCEPARNI'SMUS (*Sur.*) from σκέπαρνον, an axe; a fracture of a bone like a chip cut by an axe.

APOSCHA'SIS (*Med.*) ἀπόσχασις, scarification.

APOSIOPE'SIS (*Rhet.*) ἀποσιώπησις, called by Cicero *reticentia;* taciturnitas, by Celsus; *obticentia*, by Macrobius; from ἀποσιωπάω, taceo: a figure of speech by which one, through anger or earnestness, leaves out some word, or part of a sentence, to be understood, as *Virg. Æn.* l. 1, v. 135.

Quos ego — Sed motos præstat componere fluctus.

Where may be understood the word *puniam. Demet. de Elocut.* § 264; *Cic. Orat.* l. 3, c. 25; *Quintil.* l. 9, c. 22; *Tiber. Rhet.* c. 10; *Alex. περὶ σχημ. Ald. Edit.* p. 579; *Gregor. ad Hermog.* c. 7; *Macrob. sat.* 4, c. 6.

APOSI'TIA (*Med.*) ἀποσιτία, the same as Anorexia.

APOSI'TICA (*Med.*) ἀποσιτικά, what causes Apositia. *Gal. Exeg. Vocab. Hippocrat.*

APOSPA'SMA (*Surg.*) ἀπόσπασμα, from ἀπό and σπάω, to pluck; the rending asunder a ligament, &c. *Gal. Comm.* 3, *in Hippocrat. κατ' ἰατρ.*

APOSPHACE'LISIS (*Surg.*) ἀποσφακέλισις, from σφάκελος, a mortification; a mortification caused by too tight a bandage.

APOSPHA'GMA (*Ant.*) ἀπόσφαγμα, from ἀποσφάττω, to slay; the blood flowing from the slaughtered beast into the vessel which was variously prepared for food.

Aposphagma (*Med.*) fæculent strainings. *Gal. Exeges. Vocab. Hippocrat.*

APOSPHI'NXIS (*Surg.*) ἀπόσφιγξις, from ἀπό, priv. and σφίγγω, to bind; easing a bandage.

APOSPONGI'SMUS (*Med.*) ἀποσπογγισμός, wiping off with a spung.

APOSTALA'GMA (*Med.*) or Apostagma, ἀποστάλαγμα, from ἀποσταλάζω, to distil; the sweet juice which distils from the grapes before they are trodden. *Castell. Lex. Med.*

APOSTA'RE (*Law*) wilfully to violate the laws. *Leg. Edw. Conf. apud Brompton.*

APO'STASIS (*Med.*) ἀπόστασις, from ἀφίστημι, to separate from; 1. The same as Abscessus. 2. When the fragment of a bone comes away by a fracture it is called an apostasis. 3. The passing off of a distemper by excretion, or by a settlement in one particular part. 4. The transition from one distemper into another. *Gal. Comm. in Hippocrat. Epidem.*

APOSTA'TA *capiendo* (*Law*) a writ for the apprehension of one who, having entered into some orders of religion, departs from them, and wanders about the country. *Reg. Orig.* 71. 267.

APOSTA'XIS (*Med.*) ἀπόσταξις, from ἀποστάζω, to distil; any defluxion, but particularly of blood from the nose, as it is generally used by Hippocrates.

APOSTE'MA (*Med.*) ἀπόστημα, from ἀφίστημι, to depart from, *suppuratio;* an imposthume, or unnatural swelling of any corrupt matter.

APOSTEMA'TIÆ (*Med.*) ἀποστηματίαι, those who void pus downwards.

APOSTERI'GMATA (*Med.*) ἀποστηρίγματα, from ἀποστηρίζω; 1. Supports for a weak part, as pillows, bolsters, &c. *Gal. Comm.* 3, *in Hippocrat. κατ' ἰατρ.* 2. Deeprooted disorders in the intestines. *Hippocrat. de Flat.*

A POSTERIO'RI (*Log*) a term employed in demonstrating a truth, whether mathematical or philosophical, as when a cause is proved from an effect.

APO'STLE (*Bibl.*) ἀπόστολος, from ἀποστέλλω, to send; signifies literally a messenger or ambassador, but is now particularly applied to those disciples of our Saviour, who were commissioned to preach the gospel.

APO'STOLATE (*Ecc.*) the office and dignity of an apostle. It was also employed formerly as a title for a bishop.

APO'STOLE (*Ant.*) a tribute which was sent to the emperor by the Jews. *Jul. Epist. ad Jud.; Buleng. de Vectigal.*

APO'STOLI (*Ant.*) a name for letters demissory, which were sent from one court of justice to another to certify an appeal.—*Apostoli*, magistrates at Athens who had the charge of equipping the fleet.

APOSTO'LIC (*Ecc.*) or *Apostolical*, an epithet for what belonged to the Apostles, as the Apostolical age, doctrine, &c.—*Apostolical churches*, those churches which were founded immediately by the Apostles, particularly the churches of Rome, of Alexandria, of Antioch, and of Jerusalem. It is now applied by the catholics to the Romish church only, as when they speak of the *apostolic see*, an *apostolic* nuncio, an *apostolic* brief, and the like.—*Apostolic Fathers*, the Christian converts of the first century. *Sozom. Hist. Eccles.* l. 1, c. 16.

APOSTO'LICI (*Ecc.*) Apostolians, heretics of the third century, who affected to despise marriage, and to abstain from wine, and every indulgence. Baronius speaks also of another sect of the same name, who sprung up, in Perigord, in the twelfth century, who held similar principles. *S. Epiphan. Hæres.* c. 61; *Augustin. Hæres.* c. 40; *Baron. Annal. Ann.* 260 & 1147; *Sander. Hæres.* c. 144.

APOSTO'LICUM (*Ecc.*) a particular song or hymn anciently used in the churches.

APOSTOLO'RUM *unguentum* (*Med.*) an ointment composed of twelve ingredients.

APO'STRACOS (*Anat.*) ἀπόστρακος, an epithet for a bone which is dried so as to become a mere skeleton. *Gorr. Def. Med.*

APO'STROPHE (*Med.*) ἀποστροφή, from ἀποστρέφω, verto, to turn from; a turning away from or loathing to food. *Paul. Æginit.* l. 3, c. 7.

APOSTROPHE (*Rhet.*) ἀποστροφή, aversio; a figure when we turn our speech from the judge or auditor to one that is absent. *Hermog. περὶ ἰδ.; Quintil.* l. 9, c. 2; *Long.* l. 16, c. 2; *Sopat. διαιρ.; Jul. Rufin. de Figur.*

APOSTROPHE (*Gram.*) a mark (') showing that a vowel is cut off, as *Ain'* for Aisne.

APOSY'RMA (*Med.*) the same as Abrasum.

APOTEICHI'SMOS (*Ant.*) the work of circumvallation, or the act of surrounding a town that was to be besieged with a line of circumvallation. *Poll. Onom.* l. 7, segm. 120.

APOTELE'SMA (*Med.*) the event of a disease. *Cæl. Aur.*

APOTELESMA'TICI (*Ant.*) those who tell fortunes and calculate nativities, holding all things subject to the power of the planets.

APOTHE'CA (*Ant.*) ἀποθήκη, *repositorium*; signifies properly a cellar or warehouse, but particularly a medicine shop, or a gally-pot.

APOTHE'CARY (*Med.*) from ἀποθήκη, a medicine-shop; signifies properly the keeper of a medicine-shop, but more generally any compounder of medicines, who also, in some countries, practises the art of medicine.

APOTHECA'RY'S *Company* (*Her.*) obtained a charter of incorporation in the fifteenth year of King James I. Their arms are argent, Apollo, armed with a bow and arrow, bestriding a Python; their supporters two unicorns, and the crest a rhinoceros surmounting a torce and helmet. The motto " Opifer per Orbem dicor."

APOTHEO'SIS (*Ant.*) deification, or placing among the number; an honour conferred on several of the Roman emperors at their decease. The ceremony of the apotheosis is described at length by Herodian.

APOTHERAPŒ'IA (*Med.*) ἀποθεραπεία; 1. The completion of a cure. 2. The exercise of friction and bathing, employed for the final removal of lassitude. *Gal. de San. tuend.* l. 2, c. 4; *Gorr. Def. Med.; Foes. Œconom. Hippocrat.*

APOTHE'RNUM (*Med.*) ἀπόθερνον, a pickle made of mustard, oil, and vinegar. *Gal. de Atten. Diæt.* c. 11.

APO'THESIS (*Surg.*) ἀπόθεσις, from ἀποτίθημι, to place; the placing of a fractured limb in the position in which it ought to remain.

APOTHRA'USIS (*Surg.*) the removal of a fragment of fractured bone. *Gorr. Defin. Med.*

APO'TOCOS (*Med.*) Abortive.

APO'TOME (*Math.*) ἀποτομή, from ἀποτέμνω, to cut off; the rational remainder or residual between two lines or quantities which are commensurable only in power, as in

A———B———C, A B is the difference, or Apotome, between A C and C B. Euclid distinguishes Apotomes into six sorts.—The *first* Apotome is, when the greater is rational, and the difference between their squares is a square number, as in the numbers $6 + \sqrt{20}, 6 - \sqrt{20}$ is the Apotome.—The *second* Apotome is when the less number is irrational, as $\sqrt{18} - 4$, the difference between the squares 18 and 16, is 2 and the $\sqrt{2}$ is as 1 to 3.—The *third* Apotome is when both the numbers are irrational, as $\sqrt{24} - \sqrt{18}$, for the difference of their squares 24 and 8 is 6, and $\sqrt{6}$ is to $\sqrt{24}$ as 1 to 2.—The *fourth* Apotome is when the greatest number is rational, and the square root of the difference of the squares has no ratio to it, such is $4 - \sqrt{3}$, where the difference of the squares 16 and 3 is 13, and $\sqrt{13}$ has no ratio in numbers to 4.—The *fifth* Apotome is when the least number is rational, and the square root of the difference of the squares of the two numbers has not a ratio in numbers to the greatest, as $\sqrt{6} - 2$, where the difference of the squares 6 and 4 is 2, and $\sqrt{2}$ to $\sqrt{6}$ has not a ratio in numbers.—The *sixth* Apotome is when both the numbers are irrationals, and the square root of the difference of their squares has not a ratio in numbers to the greatest, as $\sqrt{6} - \sqrt{2}$, where the difference of the squares 6 and 2 is 4, and $\sqrt{4}$ to $\sqrt{6}$ is not a rational ratio. *Euclid. Elem.* b. 10, prop. 80, et seq.; *Papp. Math. Coll. Introd.* l. 7; *Luc. de Burg.; Stifel. Arith. Integ.* l. 2, c. 13, &c.; *Oughtred. Clav. Mathemat.*

APOTOME (*Mus.*) the difference between the greater and less semitone, being expressed by the ratio of 128 to 125.

APOTROPÆ'A (*Ant.*) ἀποτρόπαια, from ἀποτρέπω, to avert; sacrifices offered to the Apotropæi Dii, ἀλεξίκακοι, *Averruncatores vel malorum depulsores*, i. e. the gods who delivered them from all hurtful things.

APOTROPAI'A (*Med.*) the same as *Amulets*.

APOZE'MA (*Med.*) a decoction.

APPARA'TOR (*Ant.*) the same as *Apparitor*.

APPARA'TUS (*Surg.*) the collection and right disposition of the instruments of surgery, &c.

APPARATUS is also a term among Lithotomists for the particular operation with its apparatus, which is employed in the extraction of the stone. There are two sorts, the *Apparatus major*, or High Operation, and the *Apparatus minor*, or Low Operation.—*Apparatus major* is that which is performed immediately above the Pubes, in that part of the bladder which is not covered with the Peritonæum.—*Apparatus minor* is performed in the perinæum, by laying open the neck and lateral part of the bladder, so as to allow the extraction of the stone.

APPARATUS (*Chem.*) the machinery for performing experiments, as the vessels, and other utensils belonging to a laboratory.

APPARATUS (*Pneum.*) comprehends those peculiar instruments by which the aeriform fluids may in distillations, solutions, &c. be caught and collected. The principal of these machines is the pneumismatic trough.

APPA'RENT (*Astron.*) an epithet applied to things as they appear to the eye, in distinction from what they really are, as in regard to conjunction, diameter, distance, &c. of the heavenly bodies.—*Apparent conjunction of the planets* is when they appear to be placed in the same right line with the eye of the spectator.—*Apparent diameter* is the angle under which we see the sun, moon, and stars, as when we see the sun, S, under the angle D O E. This angle is the sun's apparent diameter, which is the least when he is in ♋, and the greatest when in ♓. *Ptol: Almag.* l. 5, c. 14; *Kepl. Tab. Rudolph.* p. 92, &c. and *Astron. Optic.* c. 10; *Cassin. apud Ricciol. Almag. Nov.* l. 3, c. 10, &c.; *Tych. Brah. Progymnas,* l. 1, c. 1; *De la Hire Tab. Astron.; Hevel. in Tractat. de Mer.* p. 101; *Huygen. System. Saturn.* p. 77.—*Apparent horizon.* [vide *Horizon*]—*Apparent place of a planet,* that point in the sphere of the world at which you see the centre of the sun, moon, or stars, from the surface of the earth.—*Apparent station,* the position or appearance of a planet or comet in the same point of the zodiac for several days successively.—*Apparent time.* [vide *Equation* and *Time*]

APPARENT *distance* (*Opt.*) that distance which we judge an object to be from us when seen from a far off, which may be very different from the real distance; for the heavenly bodies appear to be at the same distance, although there is the difference of many thousand miles between their distances.—*Apparent motion,* that motion which we perceive in a distant body that is moving whilst the eye is either at rest or in motion; or that motion which an object at rest seems to have whilst the eye itself only is in motion; thus very swift motions, as those of the luminaries, may not appear to be any motions; and on the other hand, supposing the eye to move forwards in one direction, any remote object at rest will appear to move in a parallel line the contrary way. The more oblique the eye is to the line or plane which a distant body moves in, the more will the apparent motion differ from the true one. Suppose a body to revolve equably in the circumference of a circle, A B F C E D, describing equal arcs in equal times, and the eye be at O in the plane of that circle, when at the point A it seems for some time to stand still, and constantly afterwards to move faster till it gets to the point F, where the motion appears to become the greatest; after which it appears to decrease till the body comes to C, when it will again seem to stand still; and then its apparent motion will increase backwards till the body arrives at E, where it will seem again to move fastest.—*Apparent magnitude of an object,* the magnitude as it appears to the eye, the measure of which is the quantity of the optic angle; as suppose D to be an

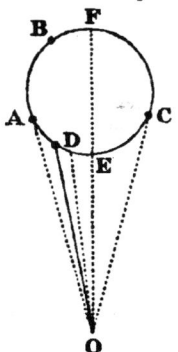

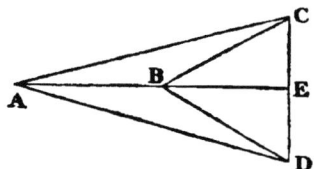

object viewed by the eye at A B, then C A D is the apparent magnitude of the object when viewed at A, and C B D the apparent magnitude of that object viewed at B.—*Apparent figure,* the figure or shape under which an object appears when seen at a distance.—*Apparent place of an object,* that in which it appears when seen through or in glass, water, or other refracting substances. When an object is seen in a convex glass, its apparent place will be more remote than the true place, and the reverse when it is seen through a plane or concave glass.—*Apparent place of the image of an object,* that in which the image of an object appears to be which is made by the reflection of a speculum. This, according to Euclid and others, is when the reflected rays meet the perpendicular drawn from the object to the speculum. *Eucl. Catop.* prop. 16, &c.; *Kepl. in Vitell.* prop. 18.

APPARENT (*Law*) an epithet for an heir, as the heir *apparent,* or immediate heir to the crown, in distinction from the *presumptive heir.*

APPARITION (*Astron.*) the becoming visible, as applied to the heavenly bodies which appear above the horizon.—*Circle of apparition,* that circle or imaginary line within which the stars are always visible in any given latitude, in distinction from the *circle of occultation.*

APPARITO'RES (*Ant.*) from *appareo,* to appear, or be at hand; public officers so called because they were always at hand to wait upon the magistrates. Under this general name were included the Scribes, Accensi, Præcones, &c. They also acted as lictors to the priests, according to an inscription in the Appian way, APPARITORI PONTIFICUM PARMULARIO. *Cic. in Verr.* act. 3, c. 78; *Serv. in Virg. Æn.* l. 12, v. 850; *Bud. in Pandect.* p. 244; *Sigon. de Ant. Jur. Civ. Rom.* l. 2, c. 15; *Guther. de Vet. Jur. Pontif.* l. 2, c. 13.

APPA'RITORS (*Law*) or messengers who serve the process of the spiritual court. *Stat.* 21, *Hen.* 8.—*Apparitors comitatus,* Sheriffs' officers. *Hale's Sheriff's Acco.* 104.

APPA'RLEMENT (*Law*) a French term corrupted from *pareillement,* signifying in like manner, as *apparlement* of wars, i. e. after the manner of wars. *Stat.* 2, *R.* 2.

APPARU'RA (*Archæol.*) furniture implements, as *Carrucarum apparura,* plough tackle.

APPE'AL (*Law*) from *appello,* to appeal. 1. The removal of a cause from an inferior to a superior judge. [vide *Audita Querela,* &c.] 2. An accusation by a private subject for any heinous offence, as appeals of *Mayhem, de pace, de plagio, de imprisimento,* which are not capital; or appeals of Murder, Larceny, or Robbery, Rape, and Arson, which are capital. *Glanv. de Leg.* &c. l. 2, c. 1; *Bract.* l. 3, tract 2, c. 19; *Britt.* c. 22, &c.; *Horn. Mir. of Just.* c. 2, sect. 11; *Staundf. Plac. Coron.* l. 2, c. 5, &c.; 1 *Inst.* 288, &c.

APPE'ARANCE (*Per.*) the representation or projection of a figure, &c. on the perspective plane.

APPEARANCE *direct* (*Opt.*) the view or sight of any object by direct rays, without refraction or reflection.

APPEARANCE (*Law*) the defendant's engaging to answer an action entered against him.

APPEARANCE (*Astron.*) the same as *Phænomenon* or *Phasis.*

APPE'ARAND (*Law*) vide *Heir-apparent.*

APPE'L (*Mil.*) French for a roll-call.

APPEL (*Fenc.*) a smart blow with the sword-blade on that of the antagonist on the contrary side to that which has been engaged. It is generally accompanied with a stamp of the foot, and serves the purpose of procuring an opening.

APPE'LLANT (*Law*) he who makes the appeal.

APPELLA'TIO (*Law*) vide *Appeal.*

APPE'LLATIVE (*Gram.*) the common name, as opposed to the proper. *Prisc. Inst. Gramm.* l. 1.

APPELLEE' (*Law*) he of whom the appeal or accusation is made.

APPE'LLOR (*Law*) the same as *Appellant.*

APPE'NDENS (*Law*) *appendant,* or belonging to something else; as an advowson *appendant* to a manor, &c. *Co. Lit.* 121, &c.

APPENDI'CULA *vermiformis* (*Anat.*) a worm-formed appendage to the *intestinum cæcum.*

APPENDI'CULATE (*Bot.*) *appendiculatus;* appendicled, or appended, at the extremity; an epithet applied to the petiole; *Petiolus appendiculatus,* a petiole that has a small leaf or leaves at the base.

APPENDICULATE (*Med.*) connected in any way.

APPENDICULATE (*Ich.*) an epithet for the Botany Bay *Squalus* of Linnæus.

APPENDI'TIA (*Law*) from *appendo*, to hang at or on; the appurtenances to a dwelling, &c. thus pent-houses are the *appenditia domus*, &c.

APPE'NDIX (*Lit.*) from *appendo*, to hang at or on; a supplement to any work by way of addition or illustration.

APPENDIX (*Med.*) the same as *Apophysis*; parts connected with the whole: the Fallopian tubes are appended to the *uterus*.

APPENDIX (*Bot.*) a thorn having red berries; also the berries themselves hanging on are appendices.

A'PPENNAGE (*Law*) *apanage*, from *appendage*; a child's portion; properly the portion of the king's younger children in France.

APPE'NSA (*Med.*) a species of amulet.

APPE'NSIO (*Med.*) from *appendo*, to hang up; the suspension of a broken limb, principally the arm in a scarf. *Castell.*

APPENSU'RA (*Law*) the payment of money at the scale, or by weight.

APPETE'NTIA *cibi*, an appetite.—*Appetentia gloria*, ambition.

APPETI'TUS *caninus* (*Med.*) the same as *Bulima*.

A'PPLE (*Bot.*) the well-known fruit of a tree of the same name, the *Pyrus malus* of Linnæus, which, in its cultivated state, is called the *Malus sativa*, or Common Apple-Tree; and in its wild state, *Malus sylvestris*, the Wilding or Crab. The most esteemed sorts of apples, in England, are, according to the order of their ripening, the—Codlin, which comes first to the market; the Margaret Apple, not so long as the Codlin; the Pearmain; the Quince; the Golden Renette, which ripens in October; the Hertfordshire Pearmain, fit for use in November; the Russet, a good kitchen apple from October to April; Nonpareil, one of the most esteemed fruits, which is not ripe before Christmas; and Golden Pippin, an apple almost peculiar to England. The sorts best fitted for cyder are the Red-Streak, the Devonshire Royal Wilding, the Whitsour, the Herefordshire Under Leaf; John-Apple or Deux-annes, Everlasting Hanger, and Gennet Moyle.

There are other plants which have also the name of Apple, as follows—Custard apple, the *Annona*; Love apple, the *Solanum*; Mad apple, the *Solanum*; Pine apple, the *Bromelia*; Purple apple, the *Annona*; Sour apple, the *Annona*; Thorn apple, the *Datura*; Water apple, the *Annona* of Linnæus.

A'PPLICATE (*Geom.*) another name for the ordinate or right line that is drawn to a curve and bisected by its diameter. [vide *Ordinate*]—*Applicate number.* [vide *Concrete*]

APPLICA'TION (*Med.*) *applicatio*, any communication to the body, externally or internally, by way of a remedy.

APPLICATION (*Math.*) the bringing one thing near to another for the purpose of measuring it. Thus a longer space is measured by the continual application of a less, as a yard by a foot or inch. The number 24 is measured or divided by the application of 6; or the rectangle ab applied to the line c gives $\frac{ab}{c}$.—*Application*, παραβολὴ, a term to express the fitting of two quantities whose areas are equal but figures different, as when Euclid shows how on a given line παραβαλλεῖν, to apply a parallelogram, equal to a right-lined figure given. *Euclid Elem.* l. 6, prop. 28, &c. —*Application of one science to another*, is the employing the rules and principles of the one for perfecting the other; as of Algebra to Geometry, when geometrical theorems are solved by algebraical investigations.—*Application of Mechanics to Geometry*, consists chiefly in employing the centre of gravity of figures for determining the contents of solids described by those figures.—*Application of Geometry and Astronomy to Geography*, consists in determining the longitudes and latitudes of places, the figure of the globe, &c. by geometrical and astronomical operations and principles.—*Application of Geometry and Algebra to Physics and Natural Philosophy*, the reduction of any physical principles or operations to a comparison of angles and lines, &c. as in the science of Catoptrics for example, which rests on the datum, " That the angle of incidence is equal to the angle of reflection." This species of application was first introduced by Newton.

APPLICATION (*Astrol.*) the approaching of any two planets to each other.

APPODIA'RE (*Archæol.*) to lean upon.

APPOGIATU'RA (*Mus.*) an Italian word for a note of embellishment.

APPOINTEE' (*Mil.*) a foot soldier in France, who, for long service and great bravery, received pay above a private centinel.

APPOI'NTMENT *of a ship* (*Mar.*) its equipment, furniture, &c.

APPO'LLON (*Astron.*) a name given to the star Castor.

APPO'NERE (*Law*) to pledge or pawn. *Neubrigensis.*

APPO'RTIONMENT (*Law*) a dividing of rents.

APPO'RTUM (*Ant.*) the revenue or profit which a thing brings in to its owner. *Stat.* 1, 35 *Ed.* 1, *De Apportis Rel.*

APPO'SAL *of Sheriffs* (*Law*) the charging them with money received upon the account in the Exchequer. *Stat* 22 *Car.* 2.

APPO'SER (*Law*) an examiner; an officer in the court of Exchequer, called the foreign apposer.

APPOSI'TIO (*Med.*) the same as *Additio*.

APPOSI'TION (*Gram.*) the situation of two nouns standing in the same case, as Cicero, the orator.

APPRAI'SER (*Com.*) one sworn to value goods, &c.

APPREHE'NSION (*Log.*) *apprehensio*, the first power of the mind, by which it simply contemplates things without pronouncing any thing about them.

APPREHENSION (*Law*) the capture of the person.

APPRE'NDRE (*Law*) a fee or profit to be taken or received. *Stat.* 2 *Ed.* 6.

APPRE'NTICE (*Law*) a young person bound by indentures or articles of agreement, to a tradesman or artificer, to learn his trade or mystery.

APPRE'SSED (*Bot.*) *appressus*, pressed or squeezed close; an epithet for a leaf, calyx, and peduncle. *Folium appressum*, a leaf, the disk of which approaches so near to the stem as to seem as if it had been pressed to it by violence. *Calyx appressus*, a calyx that presses close on the peduncle. *Pedunculus appressus*, a peduncle that is close to the branch or stem.

APPRI'ZING (*Law*) a name for an action in the Scotch law, by which a creditor formerly carried off the estates of the debtor in payment of the debts due to him, in lieu of which adjudications are now resorted to.

APPRO'ACH (*Math.*) or *the Curve of equable Approach*, a problem, first proposed by Leibnitz, to find a curve down which a body descending by the force of gravity shall make equal approaches in equal times. This curve has been found, by Bernouilli and others, to be the second cubical parabola, placed with its vertex uppermost.—*Method of Approaches*, a method of resolving certain problems in Algebra, by assigning certain limits to the quantity, and then approaching nearer and nearer until the point is reached. *Wall. Oper. Math.*

APPRO'ACHES (*Fort.*) the works whereby the besiegers approach the besieged place, such as the first, second, and third Parallels, Trenches, &c.—*Counter Approaches*, are those which are carried on by the besieged against those of the besiegers.

APPROACHING (*Hort.*) the inoculating or ingrafting the sprig of one tree into another without cutting it off from the parent stock. It is also called *Inarching*.

APPROACHING (*Sport.*) a term for the devices employed by the sportsman to get near shy birds.

APPROPIARE (*Med.*) to appropriate or adapt medicines to a particular part of the body.—*Appropiare communiam*, to discommon or inclose any piece of land which was before common.—*Appropiare ad honorem*, to bring a manour within the extent and liberty of such an honour.

APPROPRIATION (*Law*) the annexation of an ecclesiastical benefice to the proper and perpetual use of some religious body. If to the use of lay persons it is termed Impropriation. 27 Hen. 8, c. 13; Co. Lit. 46.

APPROPRIATION (*Med.*) that action of the natural heat by which the humours and animal spirits are so united with the body as to enable them to perform their proper function.

TO APPROVE (*Law*) *approbare*, to increase the profit upon a thing; as to approve land by increasing the rent. 2 Inst. 784.

APPROVEMENT (*Law*) *approbatio*. 1. The inclosing the common land within the lord's waste, so as to leave egress and regress to the tenant who is a commoner. *Reg. Jud.* 8, 9. 2. The augmentation of the profits of lands. Stat. of Mert. 20 Hen. 8; F. N. B. 71; Crompt. Just. 250.

APPROVER (*Law*) *approbator*, one confessing himself guilty of felony, and appealing others of the same crime to save himself. (*Bract.*) l. 3, tract. 2, c. 33; *Standf. Plac. Coron.* 52; *Crompt. Just.* 250.

APPROVERS (*Law*) *approbatores*. 1. Bailiffs or lords in their franchises; such persons in the marshes of Wales as had licence *de vendre et acheter* beasts. 2. Those who were sent to increase the farms of hundreds, &c. Stat. 2, Edw. 3.—*Approvers of the King*. 1. Such as have the letting of the king's demesne. Stat. 51 Hen. 3. 2. Sheriffs. Edw. 3, stat. 1.

APPROXIMATE (*Bot.*) *approximatus*; an epithet for a leaf; *approximatum folium*, a leaf that stands close to the stem.

APPROXIMATION (*Math.*) a continual approach to a root or quantity sought, but not expected to be found.

APPROXIMATION (*Med.*) a method of cure by transplanting a disease into an animal or vegetable subject by way of immediate contact. *Castell. Lex. Med.*

APPRUARE (*Law*) to take to one's own use or profit. *Stat. Will.* 2.

APPRYSING (*Law*) vide *Apprising*.

APPUI (*Men.*) a stay upon the hand; that is, the reciprocal sense between the horse's mouth and the bridle hand.—*True* or *right appui* is the nice bearing or stay of the bridle.—*Dull* or *deaf appui* is when the tongue is so thick, that the bit cannot work or bear upon the bars.—*Too much appui*, when the horse throws himself too much upon the bit.—*Full appui*, a firm stay without resting heavy.

APPUI (*Mil.*) a French term for any particular given point or body upon which troops are formed, or by which they are marched in line or column.—*Aller à l'appui* is to go to the assistance of any body of men.

APPULSE (*Astron.*) the approach of two luminaries to one another, so as to be seen as it were together in the same telescope.

APPULSUS (*Law*) from *appello*, to drive; the driving or coming of cattle to the water.

APPURTENANCE (*Law*) in Latin *pertinentia*, in French *appartinir*; whatever thing corporal or incorporal appertains to another thing as the principal, as hamlets to a chief manor, &c.; or right of common, &c. *Co. Lit.* 121.

APRE (*Her.*) a figure like a bull, except that the tail is short, and without the testes; the sinister supporter of the Russia merchants' company.

APRICOT (*Bot.*) or *apricock*, a sort of wall-fruit, which requires much sun to ripen it. It was reckoned by the ancients to be allied both to the Apple, *malum*, and to the Plum, *prunus*; and is called by Dioscorides μῆλα Ἀρμενιακά, σιρικοκκία, or βιρικοκκια; by Pliny, *Præcocia*; and is now, in the Linnean system, the *Prunus Armeniaca*. The principal sorts of this fruit are the Masculine, the Orange, the Algier, the Roman, the Turkey, the Breda, and the Brussells, which last is ripe the latest of all the Apricots. *Dioscor.* l. 1, c. 163; *Plin.* l. 15, c. 12; *Columel. in Hort.*; *Paul. Æginet.* l. 1, c. 81.

APRIL (*Chron.*) *Aprilis*, i. e. *Aperilis*, because the spring, *aperit*, opens or commences with this month.
Virg. Georg. l. 1, v. 217.

Candidus auratis aperit cum cornubus annum
Taurus.

The second month of Romulus' year and the fourth of Numa's year, which began in January. Romulus consecrated this month to Venus, the mother of Æneas.
Ovid. Fast. l. 1, v. 39.

Martis erat primus mensis, Venerisque secundus:
Hæc generis princeps, ipsius ille pater.

Hor. l. 4, od. 11, v. 14.

Idus tibi sunt agendæ;
Qui dies mensem Veneris marinæ
Findit Aprilem.

APRON (*Gunn.*) a piece of thin or sheet lead, used to cover the vent or touch-hole of a cannon.—*Apron of a dock*, a flooring raised at the entrance of the dock, a little higher than the bottom.—*Apron of a ship*, a piece of curved timber fixed behind the stern.

APRON (*Carpent.*) a platform, or flooring of plank, raised at the entrance of a dock, against which the gates are shut.—*Apron piece*, or pitching piece, in double-flighted stairs, for supporting the carriage piece or rough strings.

APRONIA (*Bot.*) a name for the *Nigra vitis*, or Black Briony.

APROXIS (*Bot.*) the name given by Pythagoras to a herb, whose root takes fire at a distance like Naphtha. *Plin.* l. 24, c. 17.

APSIDES (*Astron.*) or Apses, from *apsis*, ἀψίς, *connexio*; two points in the orbits of the planets at the greatest and least distance from the sun or the earth, as A and B in the article *Anomaly*. [vide *Anomaly*]

APSINTHATUM (*Med.*) from ἀψίνθιον, *apsinthium*; a sort of drink accommodated to the stomach made of wormwood. *Aet. Tetrab.* 1, serm. 3, c. 69.

APSINTHIUM (*Bot.*) the same as *Absinthium*.

APSIS (*Ecc.*) a place in ancient churches where the clergy used to sit; so called from ἀψίς, an arch, because it was arched. *August.* ep. 23; *Greg. Turon.* l. 10, c. 31, &c.; *Cœl. Rhodig. Antiq. Lect.* l. 28, c. 10.

APSIS (*Math.*) vide *Apsides*.

APSYCHIA (*Med.*) the same as *Lipocthymia*.

APSYRTOS (*Bot.*) a name for common horehound.

TO APTATE *a planet* (*Astrol.*) to strengthen it in the position of a house and dignities, to its greatest advantage.

APTENADYTES (*Or.*) Penguin, a genus of animals, of the Class *Aves*, Order *Anseres*.
Generic Characters. Bill straight.—Tongue with reflected prickles.—Wings fin-shaped, without quill-feathers, covered with a strong, broad membrane.—Tail, short, wedged.

APTERA (*Ent.*) ἄπτερος, i. e. without wings, from *a*, priv. and πτερόν, a wing; the seventh order having no wings. It includes the following

Podura, Spring-Tail; *Termes*; *Pediculus*, Louse; *Pulex*, Flea; *Acarus*, Tick; *Hydrachna*, Head; *Phalangium*; *Aranea*, Spider; *Scorpio*, Scorpion; *Cancer*, Crab, Lobster; *Monoculus*; *Oniscus*; *Scolopendra*; *Julus*, Lip.

A'PTOTE (*Gram.*) ἄπτωτον, from α, priv. and πτῶσις, case; a noun without cases, as Nequam. *Sosipat. Char. Inst. Gram.* l. 1; *Priscian. de Art. Gram.* l. 5.

A'PUA (*Ich.*) ἀφύη, a worthless little fish; called by some the Loach. The same name is given to the *Clupea Encrasicholus* of Linnæus, now called the Anchovy. *Arist. Hist. Animal.* l. 6, c. 15; *Plin.* l. 31; *Gesn. de Aquat. Rai. Ichth.; Aldrov. de Pisc.*, &c.

A'PUS (*Or.*) ἄπυς, without feet, the Martinet; so called because it does not use its feet; a kind of Swallow; the *hirundo apus* of Linnæus. *Plin.* l. 11, c. 47.

Apus (*Astron.*) or *Apous*, a constellation near the south pole, having eleven stars, according to Bayer. *Uranomet.*

APU'TASY (*Bot.*) a tree found on the coast of Guinea, used by the natives as an antiscorbutic.

APY'CNI (*Mus.*) ἀπυκνοί, a name given by the Greeks to the three notes *proslambanomenos, nete symnemenon*, and *nete hyperbolæon*, which are so called because they contain a perfect sound, and do not press on either side upon the compact intervals.

APY'RA (*Min.*) a species of the *Argilla* of Linnæus.

APYRE'XIA (*Med.*) ἀπυρεξία, from α, priv. and πυρετός, fever; the abatement of a fever.

APY'RINA (*Med.*) Current-wine.

APYROME'LE (*Surg.*) ἀπυρομήλη, from α, priv. πυρὴν, nucleus, and μήλη a probe; a probe without a button. *Gal. Exeges Vocab. Hippoc.*

A'PYRON (*Min.*) from α, priv. and πυρ, fire: 1. Sulphur vivum. *Diosc.* l. 5, c. 124. 2. A chemical preparation, otherwise called Æthiops.

APYRO'THIUM (*Min.*) Sulphur vivum.

A'QUA (*Chem.*) i. e. *a quâ vivimus*, by which we live; as *unda* comes from *unde sunt omnia*, i. e. whence all things are; Water, an insipid, ponderous, transparent, colourless, uninflammable, and fluid body, formed by the union of oxygen and hydrogen. The substances contained in water are held either in suspension or solution; by the first are meant clay, silex, calcareous earth, and magnesia; by the latter, air of different kinds, carbonic acid, simple or compound alkalies, lime, the sulphates, muriates, hepatic gas, &c.—*Aqua pura*, Pure or common water is distinguished into—*Aqua pluvia*, called by Ovid *aqua pluvialis*, by Pliny *aqua imbrium*, by Horace *aqua cælestis*; Rain Water, which is the purest or freest from the impregnation of foreign bodies.—*Aqua fontana*, Spring Water; the next in purity, often contains common salt and carbonate of lime. It is unfit for the dressing of food, or the dissolving of soap, owing to the quantity of earthy salts which it holds in solution.—*Aqua puteana*, called by Columella *putealis*, Well-Water, known by the name of hard-water, which is the most liable to be impregnated with the soil.—*Aqua fluvialis*, River-Water, is generally as pure if not purer than spring water, if the motion be rapid and the bed silicious sand.—*Aqua nivalis*, Snow-Water, which, when melted, is destitute of all gaseous bodies.—*Aqua palustris*, Marsh-Water, which is stagnant and impregnated with many animal and vegetable substances.—*Aqua marina*, Sea-Water, which, in addition to common salt, contains sulphate of magnesia, of soda, and of lime, muriate of magnesia, and of lime, in different proportions.—*Aqua mineralis*, Mineral-Water, whatever is impregnated in a sensible manner with any mineral. The substances which these waters are found to contain are thirty-eight in number, consisting of air, and gases, acids, alkalies, earth, and salts, according to the predominance of which they are distinguished into the classes. 1. The Acidulous, in which carbonic acid prevails. 2. The Chalybeate, in which iron is discovered. 3. The hepatic, or sulphureous, which contain sulphurated hydrogen gas. 4. The saline, which contains only salts in solution without iron, or carbonic acid in excess.—*Aqua distillata*, Distilled-Water, which is drawn from vegetables or any other substance, and is either simple when drawn by simple water; but compound, spirituous, or medicated, as lavender water, peppermint water, &c. when drawn by means of any other liquid substance.—*Aqua fortis*, made of a mixture of saltpetre, vitriol, and potter's-earth, in equal parts.—*Aqua extincta*, aquafortis, on which river water has been poured to qualify its corrosive quality.—*Aqua omnium florum*, made of cow-dung when the cows go to grass.—*Aqua regulus* or *regia*, made by the dissolution of sal ammoniac in the spirit of nitre.—*Aqua secunda*, made of water and the precipitate of silver.—*Aqua cælestis*, rectified spirits of wine.—*Aqua vitæ*, a cordial water made of beer, strongly hopped, and well fermented.—*Aqua tophania*, a noted Italian poison, called after the name of the woman who employed it.—*Aqua epidemica*, Plague Water, made of rosemary, angelica, French brandy, &c.—*Aqua odorifera*, Honey-Water, made of honey, coriander seeds, spirits of wine, &c.—*Aqua vulnerata*, Arquebusade-Water, made of various aromatics.

Aqua *intercus* (*Med.*) the same as *Anasarca*.—*Aqua periandri*, that humour which is collected in the bag of the heart.

Aqua *marina* (*Min.*) seu *Beryllus*, a species of *Gemma* of Linnæus.

Aqua *Benedicta* (*Ecc.*) Holy Water, otherwise called *Aqua aspersionis*, because both persons and things are sprinkled with it among the Roman Catholics.

AQUÆDU'CTA *Fallopia* (*Anat.*) a bony canal in the os petrosum.

AQUÆDU'CTUS (*Ant.*) from *aqua ducenda*, Aqueduct, a Conduit for water by pipes, of which, in the time of the Emperor Nerva, there were nine that emptied themselves through 13,594 pipes of an inch diameter. *Plin.* l. 31, c. 6; *Frontin. de Aquæduct. apud Græv. Thesaur. Antiq. Roman.* tom. 4, &c.

AQUA'GIUM (*Law*) i. e. *aquæ agium*: 1. A watercourse. 2. A toll for water.

AQUALI'CULUS (*Anat.*) ἦτρον, properly signifies that part of the belly which reaches from the navel to the pubes; but it is sometimes used to express the stomach or intestinal tube. *Ruf. Ephes. Appellat. Part. human. Corp.* l. 1, c. 11; *Oribas. Med. Coll.* l. 25, c. 1.

AQUA'RIA *libra* (*Mech.*) an instrument for measuring the height of water. *Vitruv. de Architect.* l. 8, c. 5.

AQUA'RIANS (*Ecc.*) Heretics; so called because they used only water at the Lord's Supper; a practice which was condemned by S. Cyprian in 252. *S. Cyp.* epist. 63.

AQUA'RIUS (*Ant.*) ὑδροφύλαξ, *Aquaductuum Curator*, the name of the person who had charge of the conduits or aqueducts, of whom mention is made in an ancient inscription. NYMPHSANC. SAC. EPICTETUS AQUARIUS. AUGUSTI. *N. Nic. ad Fam.* l. 8, ep. 6; *Manut. in Cic. ad loc. Turneb. Adver.* l. 14, c. 13.

Aquarius (*Ast.*) ὑδροχόος, the water bearer, a constellation in the heavens; so called, as is supposed, because at its rising there is much rain. It is the eleventh sign in the zodiac, reckoned from Aries, and is commonly marked [♒]. It rises in January, and sets in February, and is supposed by the Poets to be Ganymede or Deucalion. *Virg. Georg.* l. 3, v. 303.

——— *cum frigidus olim*
Jam cadit, extremoque irrorat Aquarius anno.

This constellation contains 45 stars according to Ptolemy, 45 according to Kepler, 41 Tycho, 47 Hevelius, 108

Flamstead; among which is one of the first magnitude, called *Fomahaut* or *Fomelhaut*, and one of the third, called *Scheat*. *Arat. in Apparent. et Hipparch. in Arat. Manil. Astronom.* l. 4; *Hygin. Poet. Astronom.*; *Vitruv.* l. 9, c. 6.

AQUA'RTIA (*Bot.*) a plant; so named by Jacquin in honour of his friend and assistant Benoit Acquart.

AQUARTIA, in the *Linnæan* system, is a genus of plants, Class 4 *Tetrandria*, Order 1 *Monogynia*.

Generic Characters. CAL. *perianth* monophyllous; *tube* bell-shaped.—COR. *monopetalous*; *tube* very short.—STAM. *filaments* short; *anthers* erect.—PIST. *germ* ovate; *style* filiform; *stigma* simple.—PER. *berry* globular; *seeds* very many.

Species. The two species are *Aquartia aculeata*, a shrub, native of South America.—*Aquartia microphylla*, a shrub. *Linn. Spec. Plant.*

AQUA'TIC (*Nat.*) ἐνυδρος, Aquatic; belonging to, or living in, the water; an epithet applied to different sorts of birds, plants, or flowers. Also, an epithet in natural history for different species of animals and plants.

AQUA'TICS (*Bot.*) trees that grow on the banks of rivers, in marshes, and watery places.

AQUA-TI'NTE (*Paint.*) a method lately invented of etching on copper, by which a soft colour is produced resembling a fine drawing in water colours. It is effected by means of a powder.

AQUA'TUM *aquæum* (*Nat.*) the chalaza of an egg.

A'QUEDUCT (*Anat.*) vide *Aquæductus*.

A'QUEOUS (*Anat.*) vide *Aqueus*.

AQUE'TTA (*Chem.*) the same as *Aqua Tophania*.

A'QUEUS *humor occuli* (*Anat.*) the aqueous or watery humour of the eye; the first, or outermost, and thinnest of the three.

AQUIFO'LIUM (*Bot.*) the *Ilex cassine* of Linnæus.

A'QUILA (*Ant.*) the Eagle was reckoned by the ancients, not only the king of the birds, but the minister of Jupiter, who is said to have carried Ganymede up into heaven in the form of an eagle; whence he is styled by the poets *ales Jovis, armiger*, and the like.

Pind. Olymp. od. 2.

——— λάβοες
παγγλωσσία κοράκες ὡς
ἄκραντα γαρύετον
Διὸς πρὸς ὄρνιχα θεῖον.

Theocrit. idyl. 17, v. 72.

Διὸς, αἴτιος ὄρνις Ζηρὸς πῦ τόδε σῆμα.

Virg. Æn. l. 5, v. 254.

——— quem præpes ab Ida
Sublimem pedibus rapuit Jovis armiger uncis.

Hor. Carm. l. 4, od. 4, v. 1.

Qualem ministrum fulminis alitem.

Stat. Theb. l. 7, v. 674.

——— nec segnius ardens
Accurrit, niveo quam flammiger ales olori
Imminet.

This bird is particularly distinguished for his fierceness, loftiness of flight, rapidity, and quickness of sight; whence Homer designates him commonly by the epithets ὑψιπέτης, or simply πετῖηνὸς, i. e. by distinction; thus, when describing the combat between Achilles and Hector, he says,

Il. l. 22, v. 308.

——— ὥς τ' αὐτὸς ὑψιπετήεις
Ὅς, τ' ἴησι πεδίον δὲ διὰ νεφέων ἐρεβεννῶν
Ἁρπάξων ἢ ἄρν' ἀμαλὴν, ἢ πτῶκα λαγωόν.

Virg. Æn. l. 11, v. 758.

Utque volans alta, raptum cum fulva draconem
Fert aquila.

Hor. l. 1, sat. 3, v. 26.

Cur in amicorum vitiis tam cernis acutum,
Quam aut aquila, aut serpens Epidaurius?

As a bird of omen it was reckoned lucky when it appeared on the right hand, as we learn from Homer.—

Hom. Odyss. l. 15, v. 115.

Ὡς ἄρα οἱ εἰπόντι ἐπέπτατο δεξιὸς ὄρνις
Αἰετὸς ἀργὴν χῆνα φέρων ὀνύχεσσι πέλωρος.

Aquila legionaria, the figure of the eagle, with expanded wings, made either of gold or silver, was chosen by the Romans as their ensign, one of which belonged to each legion, wherefore the term *aquila* is sometimes used for a legion.

Lucan. l. 1, v. 244.

Ut notæ fulsere aquilæ, Romanaque signa.

[vide *Aquila*, under *Numismatics*]

AQUILA (*Num.*) the eagle was chosen, as the symbol of empire, first by the Persians, and afterwards by the Romans, in consequence of which he is represented on coins in a variety of forms, sometimes standing on thunder, as *fig.* 1, or on a crown, as in *fig.* 2; the first of which is the reverse of a coin of Ptolemy Soter, the inscription ΠΤΟΛΕΜΑΙΟΥ ΣΩΤΗΡΟΣ, in the area AB, i. e. Ἀβυδηνῶν, *Abydenorum*; the second a coin of Achæus, the son of Seleucus, the inscription ΑΧΑΙΟΥ ΒΑΣΙΛΕΩΣ. On the coins of Sicily

Fig. 1. Fig. 2. Fig. 3. Fig. 4.

the eagle was a frequent symbol, as in *fig.* 3, the reverse of a coin of Agrigentum, where two eagles are standing over a hare, which is supposed to be emblematical of the victory obtained by Gelo, King of Syracuse, and his father-in-law, Theron, King of Agrigentum, over the Carthaginians, the inscription ΑΚΡΑΓΑΝΤΙ·ῶν, i. e. *Agrigentinorum*. On another coin of the same city one eagle is tearing another, as in *fig.* 4, which was emblematical of the civil wars between Cæsar and Pompey. The consecration of the emperors was some times depicted by an eagle with a man on its back, supposed to be the soul of the deceased emperor which it was bearing to heaven. [vide *Consecratio*] But the most frequent representation of the eagle was that of the *Aquila legionaria*, as in the subjoined figure of the coin of Augustus, struck by the town of

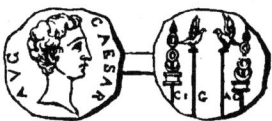

Acci, in Spain. On the obverse, is the head of Augustus, with the inscription AUG*ustus* CAESAR; on the reverse two legionary eagles between two military standards, the common symbol of this town, the inscription *Colonia Julia Gemella Acci*. *Xenophon. Cyrop.* l. 7, c. 1, and *Anab.* l. 1, c. 10; *Sallust. de Bell. Cat.*; *Hist. de Bell. Civ.* l. 3, c. 99; *Diodor.* l. 1; *Joseph. de Bell. Jud.* l. 3, c. 5; *Plin.* l. 10, c. 4; *Tacit. Annal.* l. 15, c. 29; *Flor.* l. 11, c. 12; *Quint. Curt.* l. 3, c. 3; *Sueton. in Aug.*; *Dio.* l. 40; *Lactant.* l. 1, c. 2; *Herod.* l. 4, c. 3; *Veget.* l. 2, c. 8; *Serv. in Æn.* l. 9, c. 161; *Fulgent. Mythol.* l. 2, c. 25; *Vaillant. Numis. Præst. Imperat.*; *Haverkamp. Parut. Sicil. Discrit.*; *Florez. Med. de Espan.*; *Spanh. Dissert. de Præst. et Usu Num.*; *Harduin.*; *Num. A-t. Illust.*; *Beg. Thes. Brand.*; *Froeh. Not. Elem.*;

AQUILA (*Astron.*) the Eagle, in the Arabic *Al*

the Persian tables, the Flying Vulture, one of the forty-eight old constellations, which, according to the fables of the Greeks, represented Ganymede, who was transported to heaven, and made cup-bearer to Jupiter. Ptolemy reckons nine stars in this constellation, Kepler twelve, Bayer thirty-two, Tycho and Flamstead seventy-one, among which was one in the shoulder of the first magnitude called *Altair*. *Arat. Apparent., et Hipparch. in Arat.; Eratosth. Characterism.; Ptol. Almag. l. 7, c. 5; Hygin. Astron. Poet.; Man. Astron. l. 1.*

AQUILA (*Zool.*) the Eagle is classed, *in the Linnean system*, under the genus *Falco*. [vide *Falco*]

AQUILA *alba* (*Chem.*) the same as *Mercurius dulcis*.—*Aquila philosophorum* is the name given by the alchymists to the process of reducing metals to their first matter.

A'QUILÆ (*Anat.*) ἀετοί, the veins which pass through the temples into the head. *Ruf. Ephes. Appell. Part. Corp. hum.*

AQUILÆ *lignum* (*Bot.*) Eagle wood, generally sold for Agallochum, is that part which is nearest the bark.

AQUILA'RIA (*Bot.*) from *aquila*, an eagle, eagle wood; a genus of plants, Class 10 *Decandria*, Order 1 *Monogynia*.
Generic Characters. CAL. *perianth* one-leaved; *tube* bell-shaped; *border* five-cleft; *clefts* ovate.—COR. none; *nectary* one-leaved; *clefts* bifid.—STAM. *filaments* ten; *anthers* oblong.—PIST. *germ* ovate; *style* none; *stigma* simple.—PER. *capsule* obovate; *seeds* solitary.
Species. The only species is the *Aquilaria ovata*, a shrub, native of Malacca. *Linn. Spec. Plant.*

AQUILE'GIA (*Bot.*) *Columbina*, a plant so called, from *aquila*, an eagle, because of the resemblance its nectaries are supposed to bear to the eagle's claws; a genus of plants, Class 13 *Polyandria*, Order 5 *Pentagynia*.
Generic Characters. CAL. none.—COR. *petals* five; *nectaries* five.—STAM. *filaments* thirty to forty; *anthers* oblong.—PIST. *germs* five; *styles* longer than the stamens; *stigmas* erect; *chaffs* ten.—PER. *capsules* five; *seeds* very many.
Species. The species are perennials, as the *Aquilegia vulgaris, viscosa*, &c. *J. Bauhin. Hist. Plant.; C. Bauhin. Pin. Theat.; Ger. Herb.; Park. Theat. Botan.; Raii Hist. Plant.; Tourn. Inst. Herb.; Linn. Spec. Plant.*

AQUILI'CEA *sambucina* (*Bot.*) the *Leea sambucina* of Linnæus.

AQUILI'CIUM (*Ant.*) particular sacrifices performed among the Romans during a period of great drought. *Fest. de Verb. Signif.*

AQUI'LIFER (*Ant.*) from *aquila* and *fero*, to bear; the standard bearer among the Romans, who had in his ensign the picture of an eagle. *Suet. in Jul. c. 62; Sigon. de antiq. Jur. Provinc. l. 2, c. 2; Ursat. de Nat. Rom. apud Græv. Thes. Antiq. Rom. tom. 11, p. 960.*

A'QUILINE (*Nat.*) an epithet for any thing connected with or belonging to an eagle, as an *aquiline nose*, i. e. a nose crooked like an eagle's beak.

A'QUILO (*Nat.*) the North-West wind; so called from its rapidity and vehemence resembling the flight of the eagle. Horace gives it the epithet of *impotens*, i. e. *valde potens*, very powerful.
Hor. l. 3, od. 30, v. 3.

*Quod non imber edax, non Aquilo impotens
Possit diruere.*

It is named by the Greeks *Boreas*. *Plin. l. 2, c. 47; Fest. de Verb. Sig.*

A'RA (*Ant.*) from *ardore*, heat or burning; because the victime *ardent*, burn upon it: a place reared for offering sacrifices *diis inferis et superis*, i. e. to the gods above and below; in distinction from the *altare*. [vide *Altare*] In the phrase, *Certare pro aris et focis*, *ara* is put for the altar in the impluvium or middle of the house, in which the Penates were worshipped. The *ara* was a place of refuge or asylum for slaves who fled from their masters, and criminals who wanted to escape justice, as we learn from the poets. *Plaut. Rud. act 3.*

LA. *Mihi non liceat meas ancillas Veneris de ard abducere?*
DAE. *Non licet; ita est lex apud nos.*

Terent. Heaut. act. 5, scen. 2, v. 22.

―――― *nemo accusat, Syre, te; nec tu aram tibi
Nec precatorem pararis.*

Ovid. Trist. l. 5, eleg. 2, v. 43.

―――― *Sacram, quamvis invinus, ad aram
Confugiam: nullas summovet ara manus.*

Tibull. l. 4, carm. 13, v. 23.

*Sed Veneris sanctæ considam vinctus ad aras
Hæc notat injustos, supplicibusque favet.*

Altars were erected not only in honour of particular deities, but also on particular occasions; as votive *altars*, *altars* of apotheosis, or consecration of the emperors; *altars* of peace; *altars* of adoption, and the like. [vide *Consecratio, Pietas*, &c.] Herodotus makes the Egyptians to have been the first who erected altars to the gods, in which they probably imitated the example of the patriarchs, who set up altars to the true God. *Herodot. l. 2, c. 4; Cic. pro Dom. c. 40, et de Nat. Deor. l. 3, c. 10; Varro. de Ling. Lat. l. 4, c. 4; Tacit. Ann. l. 1, c. 14; Dio. 55; Isid. Orig. l. 15, c. 4; Berthold. de Ara.*

ARA (*Astron.*) one of the old constellations in the southern hemisphere, which was fabled to have been that at which the giants entered into their conspiracy against the gods; wherefore Jupiter, in commemoration of the event, transplanted the altar into the heavens.
Manil. Astron. l. 1, v. 421.

―――― *Tunc Jupiter aræ
Sidera constituit, quæ nunc quoque maxima fulgent.*

It contains seven stars according to Ptolemy, and nine according to Flamstead. *Hygin. Astron. Poet.; Ptol. Almag. l. 7, c. 5; Flamstead. Cælest. Machin.*

ARA *parva* (*Surg.*) βωμὸς μικρὸς, a neat kind of bandage or filleting; so called because, when fixed, its four corners represented an altar. *Gal. de Fascic.*

A'RABESQUE (*Paint.*) or *Moresque*; a style of ornament in painting and sculpture, so called from the Arabians and Moors, who rejected the representation of animals.

A'RABIC *Figures* (*Math.*) or Arabic characters, the numeral characters 0, 1, 2, 3, 4, 5, 6, &c. now in common use, which are so called because they were borrowed from the Arabs on the revival of learning in the eleventh century.

ARABIC (*Nat.*) an epithet for a transparent sort of gum, called "Gum Arabic," which exudes from the Egyptian Acacia. It is brought from Turkey in small irregular masses, of a pale yellow colour. Being glutinous and demulcent, it is good for coughs, diarrhœas, &c.

ARA'BICI (*Ecc.*) heretics of the third century, who had their rise in Arabia, and who maintained the belief that the soul died or slept till the day of judgment, and then had its resurrection without the body. *August. de Hær. 83; Niceph. l. 5, c. 23.*

ARA'BICA *antidotus* (*Med.*) a preparation of myrrh and Indian spices for the liver. *Myrep.*

ARA'BICUM *Gummi* (*Chem.*) Gum Arabic. [vide *Gummi*]

ARA'BICUS *lapis* (*Min.*) a stone like ivory blemished with spots.

A'RABIS (*Bot.*) ἀραβίς, Wall-Cress, a genus of plants, Class 15 *Tetradynamia*, Order 2 *Siliquosa*.
Generic Characters. CAL. *perianth* four-leaved; *leaflets* ovate.—COR. four-petalled; *petals* spreading.—STAM. *filaments* subulate; *anthers* cordate.—PIST. *germ* columnar; *style* none; *stigma* obtuse.—PER. *silique* compressed; *seeds* very many.

Species. Some of the species are annuals, as—*Arabis thaliana*, Common Wall-Cress.—*Arabis hispida*, seu *Cardamine pumila*, Rough Wall-Cress, &c. Some are perennials, as—*Arabis grandiflora*, Great-flowered Wall-Cress.— *Arabis bellidifolia*, seu *Sinapi*, Daisy-leaved Wall-Cress, &c. *J. Bauhin Hist. Plant.; Ger. Herb.; Park. Theat. Botan.; Raii Synop. Meth. Stirp.; Pluk. Almag. Botan.; Mor. Hist. Plant.; Wild. Linn. Spec. Plant.*

ARABIS is also the name of the *Cardamine bellidifolia* of Linnæus.

ARABIS *Malagma* (*Med.*) the Arabians malagma for strumous swellings. *Cel.* l. 5, c. 18.

A'RABLE *land* (*Agric.*) land fit to be ploughed.

ARABO-TEDE'SCO (*Archit.*) a style of architecture, in which the Moorish and the modern Gothic are combined.

A'RAC (*Cook.*) an Indian spirituous liquor, prepared from rice, or sugar fermented with the juice of Cocoa.

ARACA-PU'DA (*Bot.*) a species of the *Drosera* of Linnæus. —*Araca guam*, a species of the Goava tree.—*Araca miro*, a shrub growing in Brasil, the fruit of which has a sweetish musky taste, and somewhat the savour of mulberries. *Pis. Marcgr. Med. Braz.*

A'RACE (*Law*) in French *arracher*; to rase or pluck up.

A'RACH (*Bot.*) vide *Orache*.

ARACHI'DNA (*Bot.*) or *Arachidnoides*. 1. Another name for the *Arachis*. 2. The *Glycine subterranea*, and the *Lathyrus amphicarpos* of Linnæus. *Bauh. Hist. Plant.; Plum. Descript. des Plant. de l' Amer.*

A'RACHIS (*Bot.*) ἄραχος, ἄραχις, ἀραχίδα, and ἀραχίδνα, a plant called by Dale Wild Vetch, or Strangle Tare, the medicinal virtues of which are the same as those of the vetch tribe. *Theophrast. Hist. Plant.* l. 1, c. 1.

ARACHIS, in the Linnean system, a genus of plants, Class 17 *Diadelphia*, Order 4 *Decandria*.
Generic Characters. CAL. *perianth* two-parted; *upper lip* ovate: *under lip* lanceolate.—COR. papilionaceous.—STAM. *filaments* ten; *anthers* alternately roundish and oblong.—PIST. *germ* oblong; *style* subulate; *stigma* simple.—PER. *Legume* ovate-oblong; *seeds* two.
Species. The species are—*Arachis hypogæa*, Common Earth or Ground Nut, a perennial, native of Peru.—*Arachis fruticosa*, Shrubby Earth or Ground Nut, native of the East Indies. *Raii Hist. Plant.; Pluk. Almag. Botan.; Plum. Nov. Plant. Amer.; Brown. Hist. Jamaic.; Linn. Spec. Plant.*

ARACHIS, the *Glycine Africana* of Linnæus. *Burm. Prodr.*

ARACHNOI'DES (*Anat.*) ἀραχνοειδής, from ἀράχνη, a spider, i. e. spider-formed. 1. The name of the coat between the *Pia* and the *Dura Mater*. 2. The crystalline humour of the eye, which, according to Celsus and others, immediately invests the vitreous humour. *Ruf. Ephes.* l. 1, c. 2, 3; *Cels.* l. 7, c. 7; *Gal. de Meth. Med.* l. 1, c. 3. 3. An epithet for a pulse that was small, and moved like a spider's web by every breeze. Also for urine resembling a spider's web. *Gal. Def. Med; Gorr. Def. Med.*

ARACHNOI'DEUS (*Bot.*) Cobwebbed; an epithet for the ring of the fungi, which is composed of a very white web, also of a leaf, a peduncle, and a calyx, when they are covered with a thick interwoven pubescence, resembling a cobweb.

A'RACHUS (*Bot.*) vide *Aracus*.

A'RACON (*Min.*) Brass.

A'RACUS (*Bot.*) Strangle Tare, or Wild Vetch; the *Orabus canescens* of Linnæus.

A'RADOS (*Med.*) ἄραδος, perturbation in the stomach from the concoction of discordant food. *Hip. de Rat. Vict. in Acut. Morb.*

ARÆO'METER (*Mech.*) or Water-Poise, from ἀραιός, thin, and μέτρον, a measure, an instrument for measuring the density and gravity of fluids.

ARÆO'STYLOS (*Archit.*) from ἀραιός, thin, and στύλος, a pillar; a sort of intercolumniation, in which the columns are at a distance from each other. *Vitruv.* l. 3, c. 2.

ARÆO'TICS (*Med.*) ἀραιωτικά, from ἀραιόω, to rarify; medicines which rarify the humours, so that they may pass off more freely.

A'RAHO (*Law*) i. e. *in araho conjurare*; to make oath in the church, or some holy place.

ARAI'NS (*Com.*) striped or checked armorines, or taffeties, which come from the Indies.

ARA'LIA (*Bot.*) a genus of plants, Class 5 *Pentandria*, Order 5 *Pentagynia*.
Generic Characters. CAL. *involucre* very small; *perianth* five-toothed.—COR. *petals* five.—STAM. *filaments* five; *anthers* roundish.—PIST. *germ* roundish; *styles* very short; *stigmas* simple.—PER. *berry* roundish; *seeds* solitary.
Species. The species are mostly shrubs, as the—*Aralia spinosa*, the Thorny Aralia, or Angelica-Tree, &c. *Park. Theat. Botan.; Raii Hist. Plant.; Pluk. Almag. Botan. et Phytogr.; Mor. Hist. Plant.; Linn. Spec. Plant.*

ARALIA *capitata*, the *Hedera capitata* of Linnæus. *Jacqn. Hist. Americ.*

ARALIA'STRUM (*Bot.*) another name for the *Panax* of Linnæus.

ARA'NEA (*Ent.*) Spider; a well-known genus of animals, Class *Insecta*, Order *Aptera*.
Generic Characters. Mouth with short horny jaws.—*Feelers* two, jointed.—*Eyes* eight, sometimes six.—*Legs* eight. —*Abdomen* terminated by papillæ, or teats, through which the insect draws its thread.
Species. The principal species are—*Aranea diadema*, one of the largest of the common spiders, of a deep chesnut brown, which is seen during the autumnal season in gardens, &c.—*Aranea Tarantula*, the Tarantula spider, the bite of which it was formerly supposed could be cured only by music.—*Aranea nobilis*, a very beautiful species, with an orange-coloured thorax.—*Aranea scenica*, a small species, seen on the walls of gardens: this is one of those species which darts suddenly on its prey.—*Aranea extensa*, a smallish species, of a fine green colour.—*Aranea lævipes*, of a grey colour, with legs beautifully crossed by numerous alternate black and white bars.—*Aranea palustris*, of a lengthened form, and brown colour, found in damp places.—*Aranea aquatica*, a middle-sized species, of a deep chesnut colour, residing entirely under water.—*Aranea avicularia*, or Bird-catching Spider, a gigantic species, not uncommon in the East Indies, where it is of sufficient size to seize on small birds, which it destroys by wounding with its fangs.

ARANEA (*Anat.*) vide *Tunica Arachnoides*.

ARANEA (*Com.*) a silver ore, found only in the mines of Potosi, so called from its resemblance to a cobweb.

ARANEO'SA *urina* (*Med.*) ἀραχνοειδής οὖρον, Urine containing something like spiders' webs, with a fatness at the top, indicating something like a colliquation. *Hippocrat. in Coac. Prænotat. Cels.* l. 8, c. 2; *Foes. Œconom. Hippocrat.*

ARANEO'SUS *pulsus* (*Med.*) A small pulse that moves as if it were shaken by short puffs of air. *Gal. de Differ. Puls.*

ARA'NEUS *niger* (*Ent.*) the Black Spider; from which a water is distilled that is an excellent cure for wounds. *Dale.*

ARAPABA'CA (*Bot.*) the *Spigelia anthelmia* of Linnæus.

ARA'RA (*Bot.*) a tree of the Juniper kind.

A'RATE (*Com.*) vide *Arobe*.

ARATIA (*Law*) Arable grounds.

ARA'TICU (*Bot.*) the *Annona muricata* of Linnæus.

ARA'TRUM (*Ant.*) the Plough; the invention of

ARB

ascribed by some to Ceres, by others to Bacchus, or to Triptolemus. *Orph. Hymn. ad Cer.*; *Diodor.* l. 3; *Virg. Georg.* l. 1, v. 147; *Ovid. Met.* l. 5, v. 341.

ARATRUM *terræ* (*Law*) as much land as could be ploughed with one plough.

ARATU'RA *terræ* (*Law*) the service which the tenant is to do for his lord by ploughing his land.

AR'BALET (*Mil.*) a kind of weapon, vulgarly called a cross-bow.

A'RBALIST (*Mil.*) a cross-bow.

AR'BITER (*Ant.*) a sort of judge appointed by the Prætor to decide by equity rather than by the strict letter of the law, who is called *Judex honorarius* by Cicero. *Tusc.* l. 5, c. 41; *Offic.* l. 3, c. 16, &c.; *Senec. de Benef.* l. 3, c. 7; *Fest. de Verb. Signif.*—*Arbiter bibendi* was the master of the feast, or the toast-master, who was chosen by the *Tali*, or *Tesseræ*, and prescribed rules for the company. *Hor.* l. 2, od. 7, v. 25.

> *Quem Venus arbitrum*
> *Dicet bibendi?*

He was called by the Greeks συμποσιαρχος, βασιλευς, ϛρατηγος. *Rhodig. Ant. Lect.* 7, c. 26; *Putean. Relig. Cons. Prisc. apud Græv. Thes. Antiq. Rom.* tom. 12, p. 248, &c.

ARBITER (*Law*) any one to whom a reference is made for the decision of any disputes in law.

A'RBITRARY *punishments* (*Law*) those which are left to the decision of the judge, in distinction from those which are defined by a statute.

ARBITRA'TION *of Exchange* (*Com.*) is the method of remitting to and drawing upon foreign places in such a manner as shall turn out the most profitable. *Arbitration* is either simple or compound.—*Simple arbitration* respects three places only, where, by comparing the par of arbitration between a first and second place, and that between a first and third, the rate between the second and third is discovered.—The *compound Arbitration* comprehends cases of exchange between three, four, or more places.

ARBI'TRII (*Mus.*) certain extemporaneous preludes.

AR'BOR *Americana fraxinifolus* (*Bot.*) the *Swietenia Mahagoni* of Linnæus.

ARBOR *Aquatica Brasiliensis*. [vide *Aninga*]—*Arbor Aromatica Magellanica*, Winter's Bark, or Wild Cinnamon-tree; the *Wintera Aromatica* of Linnæus.—*Arbor Camphorifica Japonica*, the *Laurus Camphora* of Linnæus.—*Arbor crepitans*, the *Hura crepitans* of Linnæus.—*Arbor in aqua nascens*, the *Nyssa denticulata* of Linnæus.—*Arbor Judæ*, the *Cercis* of Linnæus.—*Arbor laurifolia venenata*, the Poison Tree.—*Arbor Saponaria*, the *Sapindus saponaria* of Linnæus.—*Arbor Virginiana Benzoinum fundens*, the *Laurus Benzoin* of Linnæus.—*Arbor Vitæ*, the *Thuja* of Linnæus.—*Arbor Zeylonica*, the *Chionanthus Zeylonica* of Linnæus.

ARBOR *Dianæ* (*Chem.*) a particular crystallization, from the solution of Mercury in salts.—*Arbor Hermetis*, a process of the revification of Mercury.

ARBOR *Martis*, Coral, it being supposed to grow like a tree or plant, under the water of the sea.

ARBOR *Porphyriana* (*Log.*) otherwise called *scala prædicamentalis*; a scale of beings, or a figure formed by three rows or columns of words, the middle of which contained the genus or species, bearing some analogy to the trunk and branches of a tree, as

SUBSTANCE.

Thinking		Extended
	BODY.	
Inanimate		Animate
	ANIMAL.	
Irrational		Rational
	MAN.	
This		That
	PLATO.	

ARC

ARBOR (*Mech.*) 1. The principal part of a machine, which serves to support the rest. 2. The spindle or axis on which the instrument or machine turns.

ARBOR *vitæ* (*Med.*) a medicine drawn from the *Arbor vitæ*.

ARBO'REOUS (*Bot.*) an epithet for mosses, &c. growing on trees, in distinction from such as grow on the ground.

A'RBORES (*Bot.*) Trees; the name of one of the Natural Families of plants, consisting of a durable stem and branches.—*Arbores caducæ*, Trees that have been cut and sprout up again.

ARBORE'SCENT (*Bot.*) *Arborescens*, an epithet for a stem which becomes woody.

ARBU'SCULA (*Bot.*) a little tree or shrub.—*Arbuscula Africana repens*, an African trailing shrub, with leaves something like the *Orache*.

ARBU'STIVA (*Bot.*) the 39th order in Linnæus' fragments of a natural arrangement. *Phil. Bot.*

ARBU'STUM (*Bot.*) an orchard, hopyard, or vineyard.

A'RBUTUS (*Bot.*) κομαρος, Strawberry tree; a tree, the leaves of which resemble those of the laurel, and its fruit is that of the strawberry plant. It is very sharp and austere, and when eaten, according to Dioscorides, it occasions head-aches, and pains in the stomach. Virgil speaks of it as grateful food for kids.
Virg. Ecl. 3, v. 82.

> *Dulce satis humor, depulsis arbutus hædis.*

Horace commends it for the shade which it affords. *Hor.* l. 1, od. 1, v. 21.

> ———— *nunc viridi membra sub arbuto*
> *Stratus.*

Dioscor. l. 1, c. 175; *Plin.* l. 15, c. 24; *Oribas. Med. Coll.* l. 11; *Aet. Tetrab.* 1, serm. 1; *Paul. Æginet. de Re Med.* l. 7, c. 3.

ARBUTUS, *in the Linnean system*, a genus of plants, Class 10 Decandria, Order 1 Monogynia.
Generic Characters. CAL. *perianth* five-parted.—COR. monopetalous.—STAM. *filaments* ten.—PIST. *germ* subglobular; *style* cylindric; *stigma* obtuse.—PER. berry roundish; *seeds* small.
Species. The species are mostly shrubs, as—*Arbutus unedo*, the Common Strawberry-Tree.—*Arbutus pumila*, the Dwarf Strawberry-Tree.—*Arbutus laurifolia*, the Laurel-leaved Strawberry-Tree, &c.

A'RC (*Math.*) or arch, any part of a curve line, as a circle ellipse, &c. as A F, F B, or B G, of the circle A B G D. The right line joining the extremes of any arc is the *chord*, as A G is the chord of the arc A B G, and K M the chord of the arc K D M.—*Circular Arcs* are the measures of angles; thus suppose the arc F B to contain 29° 25′, then the angle F C B contains also 29° 25′; and as the arc B G is the quadrant of the circle A B G D, then the angle B C G is 90°, i. e. the fourth part of 360°, into which the whole circumference of every circle is supposed to be divided. Arcs are equal, similar, and concentric.—*Equal arcs* are the arcs of the same or equal circles, which contain the same number of degrees.—*Similar arcs* are the arcs of unequal circles that have the same number of degrees, or that are the like parts of their respective circles, as the arcs A B and M N. Similar arcs are proportionate to their radii, i. e. A B is to M N as C A is to C M.—*Concentric arcs* are those that have the same centre drawn from different radii, as the arcs A B and M N having the same centre, C.

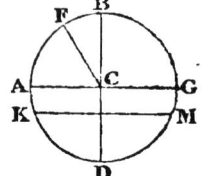

ARC (*Astron.*) is differently named, according to the circle to which it is applied, as an arc of the meridian, by which the latitude, &c. is measured, an arc of a parallel, circle, &c.—*Diurnal arc*, that part of a circle parallel to the equator, described by the sun in his course from his rising to his setting, in distinction from his *nocturnal arc*, which is described from his setting to his rising.—*Arc of progression or direction*, an arc of the ecliptic, which a planet seems to describe when its motion is direct, or according to the order of the signs.—*Arc of retrogradation*, an arc of the ecliptic, described by a planet while it is retrograde, or moving contrary to the order of the signs.—*Arc between the centres*, in eclipses, is an arc passing from the centre of the earth's shadow perpendicular to the moon's orbit, meeting her centre at the middle of an eclipse.—*Arc of vision*, that which measures the sun's depth below the horizon, when a star, before hid by his rays, begins to appear again. This arc varies for different planets, as, for Mercury 10°, for Venus 5, Mars 11¼, Jupiter 10, Saturn 11; for a star of the first magnitude 12°, for one of the second, 13, &c. It will sometimes also vary for the same planet. *Ptol. Almag.* l. 13, c. 7; *Magin. Theor. Planet.* l. 2, c. 15; *Kepler. Epit.* p 369; *Ricciol.* l. 1, c. 32.

A'RCA (*Con.*) Ark-Shell; a genus of animals, Class *Vermes*, Order *Testacea*.

Generic Character. Animal a tethys; *shell* bivalve equivalve; *hinge* with numerous sharp teeth, alternately inserted between each other.

Species. The species are divided into—Those which have their margin entire, beaks recurved, as *Arca tortuosa*, &c.—Those which have their beaks inflected, as *Arca Noæ*, Noah's Ark, &c.—Those which have their margin crenate, beaks recurved, as *Arca lactea*, &c.—Those which have their margin crenate and beaks inflected, as *Arca undata*.

ARCA *arcanorum* (*Alch.*) *Mercurius philosophorum*.

ARCA *cyrographica* (*Archæol.*) a common chest, with three locks and keys, kept by certain Christians and Jews, wherein all mortgages, &c. belonging to the latter were kept to prevent fraud, by order of Richard I. *Hoved. Annal.*

ARCA'DE (*Archit.*) an opening in the wall of a building, formed by an arch.

ARCA'NNE (*Min.*) Ochre.

ARCA'NUM (*Alch.*) from *arca in qua, quæ clausa sunt, tuta manent*; a name for chemical preparations kept secret by the authors. Paracelsus describes it as a principal medium which ought to be investigated by experience.—*Arcanum materiale*, a specific extract more nearly allied to the matter of the body.—*Arcanum specificum*, an extract of the interior nature.—*Arcanum coralinum*, the red precipitate of mercury.—*Arcanum duplex*, or *duplicatum*, a sort of salt from the distillation of double Aqua fortis, the Sulphate of Pot-ash in modern chemistry.—*Arcanum Jovis*, an amalgama of tin and quicksilver digested in nitre.—*Arcanum tartari*, Acetate of Pot-ash.

ARCA'TA (*Mus.*) or *Arcote*, when placed at a particular part, signifies it must be played with the *arco*.

ARC-BOUTA'NT (*Archit.*) an arched buttress.

ARCEUTHOS (*Bot.*) the same as *Juniperus*.

A'RCH (*Geom.*) vide Arc.

ARCH (*Archit.*) that part of a building which derives its name from its curved figure. The parts of an arch are the *reins* or *springing walls* by which it is supported.—The *drift* or *push* of an arch is that force which the arch exerts in the whole length of the building.—*Keystone* is the middle of the voussoir immediately over the centre of the arch.—*Voussoirs*, the archstones, or stones which immediately form the arch.—*Pitch*, the perpendicular height from the spring or impost to the keystone.—*Intrados*, the under sides of the voussoir, in distinction from the—*Extrados*, or upper surface.—*Springing lines*, the bounding lines of the intrados.—*Chord* or *Span*, that line which extends from the springing line on one side of the arch to that on the opposite side.—*Vertex* or *Crown*, that part of the intrados most remote from the span.—*Section*, that vertical plane figure contained by the span and the intrados.—*Haunches* or *Flanks*, the curved parts on the top of the section, between the crown and each extremity of the spanning line. [vide *Bridge*]

Arches are variously named, according to the figure of the section, as *circular, elliptical, cycloidal*, &c.—*Circular arches* are distinguished into perfect and imperfect.—*Perfect arches* form an exact semicircle: they are called by the French *arcs en plein centre*.—*Imperfect* or diminished arches do not form an exact semicircle. They are, moreover, distinguished into—*Scheme* or *Skene arches*, which are flat arches.—*Pointed* arches, otherwise called *Gothic*, or by the Italians *arches di terzo et di quarto acuto*, i. e. of the third and fourth point; because they consist of two arcs of a circle meeting in an angle at the top, and drawn from the division of a chord into three or more points at pleasure.—*Strait arches*, those which have their upper and under edges parallel strait lines instead of a curve.—*Arch of Equilibrium*, is that which is in equilibrium in all its parts, having no tendency to break in one part more than another. [vide *Bridge*]

ARCH (*Gram.*) in composition, signifies *chief*, from ἀρχός, *princeps*, as Archbishop, Archduke, &c.

ARCH (*Mus.*) a curve formerly placed over a bass note, to signify that it was accompanied with the imperfect fifth.

ARCH (*Bot.*) *fornix*, a small elongation of the corolla, which commonly covers the stamina, or is situated at the aperture of the corolla, as in *Symphytum officinale*, or Gomfrey.

ARCH (*Her.*) arches are borne in coat armour, as in the annexed figure. "He beareth *gules* three single arches, their capitals and pedestals *or*, by the name of *Arches*." These are supposed to be arches of a bridge.

ARCHÆO'LOGY, from ἀρχαῖος, ancient, and λόγος, doctrine; the science which treats of antiquities in general. The term is now particularly applied to the antiquities of the Middle Ages.

ARCHÆRE'SII (*Chron.*) the same as *Anarchi*.

ARCHA'LTES (*Alch.*) the pillars of the earth, supported by the power of God only.

ARCHA'NGEL (*Bibl.*) *Archangelus*, ἀρχάγγελος, *princeps angelorum*, the prince of angels, as Michael is called.

ARCHANGEL (*Bot.*) the *Archangelica* and *Lamium* of Linnæus.—Baum-leaved Archangel, the *Melittis melissophylum*, of Linnæus.—Yellow-leaved Archangel, the *Galeopsis galeobdolon*.

ARCHBI'SHOP (*Ecc.*) *archiepiscopus*, ἀρχιεπίσκοπος, *princeps episcoporum*; the chief prelate, having an authority over other bishops.

ARCHBU'TLER (*Polit.*) one of the great officers at the court of the German emperor, who presents the cup to him on solemn occasions.

ARCHDA'PIFER (*Ant.*) the chief sewer; one of the principal officers of the Germanic empire belonging to the Count Palatine.

ARCHDEA'CON (*Ecc.*) *archdeaconus*, ἀρχιδιάκονος, a substitute for the bishop, who has a superintendant power over the clergy within his district.—*Archdeacon's Court*, an inferior court within the jurisdiction of the archdeacon.

ARCHDU'KE (*Polit.*) one having a pre-eminence over other dukes.

ARCHDUKE'S *crown* (*Her.*) closed at the top by a scarlet cap, and encompassed with a circle of gold.

A'RCHE (*Med.*) ἀρχή, *initium*, the first attack of a disorder.

A'RCHED *buttresses* (*Archit.*) or Arch-butments, otherwise called *flying buttresses*; props, in the form of an arch, which are employed in sacred edifices, of the pointed style, for sustaining the vaults of the nave.

ARCHED *legs* (*Vet.*) the defect of a horse who has his knees bent archwise. This relates to the fore quarters, and happens to such horses as are spoiled by travelling.

ARCHED (*Bot.*) the same as *Vaulted*.

ARCHEGO'NOS *morbus* (*Med.*) the same as *Acutus morbus*.

ARCHE'ION (*Ant.*) ἀρχεῖον, which is rendered in the Latin *summum templum*, a particular part of the temple, which served as a repository or treasury for any thing that was valuable, whether of public or private property; whence also the epithets given to it by Pollux, μεγαλόπλουτον πολύχρυσον ἀρχιπλούτων. This place, according to Suidas, was likewise employed as a judgment hall. *Poll. Onom.* l. 1, c. 23; *Suidas*; *Bud. in Pandect.* p. 245.

ARCHE'NDA (*Med.*) a powder prepared from the *Alcanna*.

A'RCHER (*Ast.*) the constellation named Sagittarius.

A'RCHERY (*Law*) an ancient service of keeping a bow for the use of the lord to defend his castle. *Co. Lit.* sect. 157.

ARCHERY, the art of shooting with the bow. This art was learnt by means of *pricking*, i. e. shooting at a *mark* or *butt*, called a popinmoye or popinjay, because it was made in the shape of a parrot.

Bows were called, as to their shape, *long-bows* or *cross-bows*; as to their quality and materials, *steel-bows*, *yew-bows*, and *livery-bows*, a coarse sort of bow.—Cross-bows were of two kinds, called *latches* and *prodds*.—Those who used the long-bow were called *archers*, in distinction from the *cross-bowmen*, who were so denominated from their use of the cross-bow; both of whom were employed in the English army long after the introduction of fire arms.

The *bow* consisted of the *stave*, or straight wooden part; the *arch* which was to be bent; the *string* by which it was bent; and the *nook*, or *nut*, in which the string was fixed. Bow-staves were made either of steel or wood; the latter either of yew, ash, or elm, of which the first was reckoned the best. The smaller bows were bent by means of an instrument called a *goat's foot*, and the long bows either by the help of a *stirrup*, or a machine called a *moulinet*. Cross-bows discharged not only arrows but also darts, called *quarreaux* or *quarrels*, stones, leaden-balls, &c.

Arrows were reckoned in *garbs*, *sheaves*, or *bundles*, each sheaf consisting of twenty-four arrows. Their heads were made of the best iron pointed with steel, which were mostly *barbed* and *feathered*; some were likewise *acerata*, that is, sharpened, or *non acerata*, that is, blunt. The arrows were carried in a *quiver* or case, and those who used them were obliged to have a *bracer* or piece of leather, on which the bow-string rested; *shooting gloves*, to protect the fingers; and *sharp-pointed stakes* which served as a defence against the cavalry in the day of battle. Those who manufactured the bows were called *bowyers*; those who made the arrows and quarrels were *fletchers*; and those who made the arrow-heads were termed *arrow-head-makers*.

A'RCHES (*Archit.*) vide *Arch*.

ARCHES (*Her.*) a sort of canting or allusive arms; as *three arches* for a person named Arches. [vide *Arch*]

ARCHES, Court of (*Law*) the most ancient consistory belonging to the Archbishop of Canterbury, for the determination of ecclesiastical matters. It was so called from the church of St. Mary-le-Bow, i. e. *de Arcubus*.—*Dean of Arches*, the chief judge of this court, who has also a peculiar jurisdiction over thirteen parishes in London. 4 *Inst.* 337, &c.

A'RCHET (*Mus.*) the same as *Arco*.

A'RCHETYPE (*Paint.*) *Archetypum*, ἀρχέτυπον, from ἀρχὴ, *principium*, and τύπος, *figura*, a figure; the original of a picture or drawing.

ARCHETYPE (*Com.*) the original standard for the weights kept at the mint.

ARCHE'US (*Alch.*) the power or principle in nature, which, according to Paracelsus, disposes and orders all matter according to its form. This Archæus, or *primum mobile*, in animal bodies is in the stomach.

ARCHEZO'STIS (*Bot.*) the same as *Bryonia alba*.

ARCHIACO'LUTHUS (*Ecc.*) the chief of the acolythi or ministers in cathedral churches.

ARCHIA'TER (*Med.*) ἀρχίατρος, from ἀρχὴ, chief, and ἰατρὸς, physician; a physician to the prince, according to Mercurialis, Casaubon, and Vossius; or the prince of physicians; or, which is more probable, it signifies both.

ARCHIEPI'SCOPAL (*Ecc.*) belonging to an archbishop.

ARCHIGERO'NTES (*Ant.*) ἀρχιγέροντες, *principes seniorum*, the overseers of the king's household. *Hottom.*

ARCHIGRA'MMATEUS (*Ant.*) ἀρχιγραμματεὺς, *scribarum præfectus*, the principal secretary.

ARCHIGUBE'RNUS (*Ant.*) or *Archigubernator*, i. e. *gubernatorum princeps*, sive *classis præfectus*, the admiral of a squadron. *Diodor.* l. 20.

A'RCHIL (*Com.*) a dye made of the *Lichen roccella*.

ARCHILO'CHIAN *verse* (*Poet.*) *Archilochium Carmen*, a verse so called from the poet Archilochus, of which there were different kinds, as the *Iambic trimeter catalectic*, which consists of five feet; the *Iambic dimeter hypermeter*, i. e. Iambic dimeter, with an additional syllable at the end, &c.

A'RCHIMAGIA (*Alch.*) Chemistry; or the art of making gold and silver.

A'RCHIMAGIRUS (*Ant.*) head cook.

ARCHI'MANDRITE (*Ecc.*) another name for *Abbot*.

ARCHI'MIA (*Alch.*) the art of changing imperfect metals into those that are perfect.

ARCHISTRATE'GUS (*Ant.*) from ἀρχὸς, chief, and στρατηγὸς, a leader; the chief leader or generalissimo of an army.

A'RCHITECT (*Ant.*) ἀρχιτέκτων, from ἀρχὸς, the chief, and τέκτων, a workman, Architect; a master builder, or a person skilled in architecture.

ARCHITECTO'NICE, vide *Architecture*.

ARCHITECTO'NIC *nature* (*Nat.*) the same as *Palastic Nature*.

A'RCHITECTURE, *Architectura*, ἀρχιτεκτονικὴ, from ἀρχὸς, the chief, and τεκτονία, building; the art of building any edifice. It is divided into civil, military, and naval architecture. *Civil architecture* is applied to the erection of buildings for the purposes of civil life. *Military architecture* is the art of erecting places for the purposes of security against the attacks of an enemy. *Naval architecture* is the art of constructing ships. The two last branches of architecture are treated of under the heads of *Fortification* and *Ship-building*. Civil Architecture is again divided into theoretical and practical architecture. *Theoretical architecture* comprehends those rules of science, the application of which gives stability and beauty to every edifice. It is therefore mostly employed about the exterior and decorative parts of buildings. *Practical architecture* is mostly concerned with the operative part of erecting an edifice; and is consequently more employed about the interior economy. The theory of architecture is properly *architecture* so called: the practical part is mostly called *Building*, and may be found treated of under that head.

Architecture, according to Vitruvius, comprehends, *ordinatio*, in Greek, τάξις, Order; *dispositio*, διάθεσις; *eurithymia*, Proportion; *symmetria*, Symmetry; *decor*, Propriety; *distributio*, Distribution; which four are comprehended under the Greek name οἰκονομία.—*Ordination* is the modification of all the members, or parts, to the

ARCHITECTURE.

whole work.—*Disposition* is the adaptation, or apt collocation, of things for producing a suitable composition or combination. The different kinds of disposition are *ichnography*, or the drawing of geometrical plans; *orthography*, or the taking of elevations; and *scenography*, or the drawing of those plans in perspective.—*Eurithmy* is the harmonious correspondence of the parts with one another, in length, breadth, and thickness.—*Symmetry* is the proportion of one member to another, or to the whole.—*Propriety* is the suitableness of the building to the purpose for which it is intended, and all other relative circumstances.—*Distribution* is the arrangement of the work according to the nature of the situation, the materials, and the like.

The principal parts of a building on which the skill of an architect is displayed, are beginning from the foundation upwards, as follows: namely, the pedestal, column, architrave, arches, pediments, mouldings, and ornaments.

Pedestal.

The pedestal, called by Vitruvius, *stylobates*, serves as a foot to the column which rests upon it. The principal parts of the pedestal are three, namely—*Basis*, the Base, which is the foot of the pedestal.—*Die*, a square trunk, which forms the body.—*Corona*, the cornice, which serves for the head. The different sorts of pedestals are as follow: namely, the—*Tuscan, Doric, Ionic, Corinthian*, and *Composite pedestals*, which belong to the five orders. [vide Plate 9 and 10.]—*Square pedestal*, one whose height and width are equal.—*Double pedestal*, that which supports two columns.—*Continued pedestal*, that which supports a row of columns.

Columns.

The Column, *columna*, in Greek, συλὸς, the cylindrical body, which serves as the chief support and ornament of a building. The column consists of three principal parts, namely, the—*Basis*, which is the lowest part.—*Frustum*, the Fust or Shaft, which is the body; and—*Capitula*, the Capital.

Columns are of different kinds, according to their proportions, as the *Doric, Ionic, Corinthian, Tuscan*, and *Composite columns*, of which more may be seen under the head of *Orders*.—According to their materials, as *moulded, fusible, transparent, scagliola*, and *masonic columns*.—According to their construction or formation, as *columns in bands*, or *tambours; columns in trencheons*, or *banded columns; attic, conical, conoidal, cylindridal, cylindroidal, polygonal columns*.—According to the decoration of their shafts, as *bark-formed, cabled, carolytic, fluted, twisted columns*.—According to their disposition, as *angular, cantoned, coupled, doubled*, &c. [vide Column]

A *pillar* is an irregular kind of column, which deviates from the just proportions of the latter.—A *pilaster* is a small kind of column which is square instead of being round: otherwise it consists of the same parts and proportions. Pilasters are mostly employed in interior decorations, because they occupy less space.—*Attics* are a sort of pilasters with their cornices, which are ememployed at the upper extremity of a building. They derive their name from the Athenians, by whom they were first used for the purpose of concealing the roofs of their houses.

Columns are either *insulated*, i. e. stand singly, at a distance from any wall; or else they are *engaged* and stand near a wall. When several columns stand together in one building, their distance from each other is called the *intercolumniation*, which is of different kinds, as it was distinguished among the ancients into *pycnostyle*, when the columns stood thickly together; *areostyle*, when they were at a considerable distance; *diastyle*, when three diameters distant; *eustyle*, when two diameters and a quarter, which was reckoned a happy medium between the picnostyle and the areostyle; *systyle*, when the columns stood thick, but not so thick as the pycnostyle. When a range of columns support an entablature, this is termed a *colonnade*; which is distinguished according to the number of its columns, into *tetrastyle, hexastyle, octostyle*, &c.

Entablature.

The entablature, otherwise called *trabeation*, is comprehended by Vitruvius under the general name of ornament. The word is immediately derived from the French, which is formed from the Latin, *tabulatum*, a stage or story. The entablature is supported by the column, and consists of three principal divisions, namely—the *Architrave*, in Greek, ἐπιςυλιον, in Latin, *epistylium*, the epistyle or beam, which rests upon the capitals of the columns.—*Frize*, in Greek, ζωοφόρος, in Latin, *zoophyrus*, which is formed by the cross beams that support the roof.—*Cornice*, in Latin, *corona*, which is formed by the ends of the timbers of the roof.

Arches.

An arch is a concave structure, raised on a mould, called the *centering*, and in a curved form, serving as the inward prop of some superstructure. The supports of an arch are the *springing walls* or *reins*; the under surface is the *intrados*; the upper surface the *extrados*; the line extending from one rein to the other is the *chord* or *span*; the most remote part from the span is the *vertex* or *crown*; the curved parts on each side the vertex are *haunches*, or *flanks*. To these parts may be added the—*Archivault*, or contour of the arch, an assemblage of mouldings on the face of the arch.—*Impost*, a capital or plinth which sustains the arch.—*Piers*, the walls which support the arches of a bridge, and from which they spring, as bases to stand upon.—*Voussoirs*, or *arch-stones*, the stones which immediately form the arch of a bridge, &c. That which is in the middle is called the *Key-stone*.

Arches are employed in different parts of large buildings, and are of various kinds, according to the figure of the section; as *semicircular, elliptical, scheme, pointed, rampant, extradossed, perfect, imperfect, surbassed, diminished, horse shoe, surmounted*, &c. When employed as props to buildings, they are called *arc-boutants*, or *flying buttresses*; when in the interior of buildings to form the ceiling, they are termed *vaults*. When several arches stand together, they form a range which is called an *arcade*. [vide Arch and Building]

Pediments.

A Pediment is a kind of low pinnacle, called, in French, *fronton*, and, in Latin, *fastigium*, which serves as a crowning to porticoes, or to finish a frontispiece. Its area is called the *tympan*; and its figure is commonly triangular, but sometimes circular; in the former case it is termed a *pointed pediment*.

Mouldings.

A moulding is any projection from the naked part of a wall, column, &c. which serves as a decoration, either singly, or when brought together into an assemblage. Mouldings are of different kinds, as follows: namely,—*Fillet*, a small square moulding that separates the larger mouldings. The fillets in a Doric architrave are each called a *regula.—Annulet*, a narrow flat moulding in different parts of a column.—*Plinth*, a flat square member, resembling a brick or tile, which serves as a support to the base of the column or pedestal.—*Cavetto*, a concave moulding in the pedestal and entablature, which is *recta*, when in its natural position, and *reversa* when turned upside down.—*Ovolo*, or *quarter round*, a convex moulding, the reverse of the cavetto.—*Cyma*, or *ogee*, a wavelike moulding, which is either *recta* or *reversa*.—*Torus*, a large round moulding in the bases of the columns.—*Astragal*, a small round moulding, like the *torus*, encompassing the shaft of a column.—*Bead*, a small round moulding, like a bead in different parts of the column.—*Scotia*, a hollow obscure moulding of the base.—*Apophyge*, or *scape*, a moulding, partly concave and partly straight, which joins the bottom of the shaft to the base; also the top of the shaft to the fillet under the astragal.—*Frize*, or *hypotrachelion*, a flat member on the capital of a column.—*Volute*, a spiral or scroll of the capital.—*Bell of a capital*, that part under the abacus which contains the caulicles, leaves, scrolls, &c.—*Abacus*, a square table on the upper part of the capital of a column.—*Facia*, or *fascia*, Face or Platband, a flat member of the architrave.—*Guttæ*, an ornament in the shape of drops under the triglyphs of the frize.—*Tænia*, a small square fillet above the guttæ.—*Triglyphs*, ornamental tablets in the frize of the entablature.—*Metops*, the square interval between the triglyphs.—*Consoles*, or brackets, with scrolled ends for the support of the cornice.—*Soffit*, or *larmier*, the eaves or drip of the cornice.—*Modillions*, or *mutules*, projecting bodies under the soffits, resembling inverted consoles.—*Dentils*, ornaments in the cornice shaped like teeth, and placed in a square moulding, called *denticle*. [vide Plate 9 and 11]

The proportions of these several parts to each other are regulated by a given rule or measure, called a *module*, for which the diameter or semidiameter of the bottom of the column is commonly taken, which is subdivided into sixty parts, called *minutes*.

Ornaments.

Ornaments comprehend all the sculpture, or carved work, with which any piece of architecture is decorated, and derive their names from the figure which they are intended to represent, as *foliage, roses, egg, egg* and *anchor, festoons, fretwork*, and the like. [vide Plate 11] The disposition of the several members in a column constitutes what is termed an *order*, which, as far as respects the use of the arch in modern times, has been termed *a style of Architecture*.

Orders and Styles.

There are five principal orders among the ancients, three of which are Grecian, and two Roman; namely, the Doric, Ionic, Corinthian, Tuscan, and Composite.

The *Doric Order*, the most ancient of all, is said to have been invented by Dorus after the proportions of a man's body, making the thickness of the shaft, at the base of the column, equal to the sixth part of the height, including the capital. This order is now distinguished by the name of *Grecian* and *Roman Doric*; the former of which is the original model of that style of architecture drawn from specimens which are extant in different parts of Greece; the latter, which is but an imperfect imitation of the Doric, taken principally from the theatre of Marcellinus, at Rome, is the style which is now most commonly known by that name. [vide Plate 10]

The *Ionic Order*, so called from Ionia, where it had its origin, copied the gracefulness of women, making the thickness of the column, and the volutes to represent the tresses of hair falling to the right and left. [vide Plate 9 and 10]

The *Corinthian Order*, called, by Scamozzi, the *Virginal Order*, derived its name from a Corinthian maid, whose tomb gave rise to the ornament in the capital of this column, which represents the flower *Acanthus*. The height of the Corinthian capital is also much greater than that in the Ionic Order, so as to give the whole the appearance of slender delicacy. [vide Plate 10]

The *Tuscan Order* derives its origin and name from Tuscany, in Italy. The shaft of this column is six times the diameter, the base and capital each half a diameter, and, consequently, the whole height seven times the diameter. [vide Plate 9 and 10]

The *Composite Order*, so called because it is composed of the Ionic and Corinthian Orders, is of Roman extraction, and, on that account, called likewise the *Roman*, or *Italian Order*. It is more slender than the Corinthian, the column, including its base and capital, being ten diameters in height. [vide Plate 9 and 10]

There were other styles among the ancients which have also been distinguished by the name of *Orders*; namely, the—*Attic Order*, a name sometimes given to the Attic pilasters which are frequently placed at the top of edifices over the other orders.—*Persian*, or *Persic Order*, is applied to the statues of men, which serve to support the entablature in the place of columns. It is so called because the figures of the Persian captives, taken by the Lacedemonians in their war with the Persians, were employed in this manner. The figures themselves were called *Persians*, or *Atlantides*, and by the Romans *Telamones*.—The *Cariatic Order* differs from the preceding only in as much as the statues represented women instead of men, being the figures of the Caryatides, or Carian women, who were taken captives by the Athenians when they destroyed the city of the Carians after the Persian war. Besides the Caryatides and the Persians, figures were sometimes used by the Romans for the support of entablatures, the upper part of which represented the head and breast of a human body, and the lower the inverted frustum of a square pyramid. They were called *Termini*, because they were used by the ancients as boundaries, and were made to represent the god *Terminus*. Persian figures are generally charged with a Doric entablature; the Caryatides with an Ionic, or Corinthian architrave cornice; and the Termini with an entablature of any of the three Grecian orders.

Styles of architecture are distinguished by the different forms of the arch, as orders are by that of the column. The two principal styles which are now in use are the Saxon and the Gothic.—The *Saxon Style* is characterized by its semicircular arches, and massive columns.—The *Gothic Style* is otherwise called the *Pointed Arch*, in Italian *di terzo* and *quarto acuto*, because the arch which is used in this style meets in a sharp point. The Gothic has been, moreover, divided into the *simple* and the *florid*, according as the workmanship was more or less decorated. The florid Gothic, which surpasses the Grecian architecture in grandeur and elegance, is particularly chosen for sacred edifices.

Principal Authors on Architecture.

Vitruvius "De Architectura;" *Philandri, Barbari*, and *Salmasii* "Commentarii in Vitruvium;" *Sir Henry Wotton's* "Elements of Architecture;" *Leo Baptista de Albertis* "De Re ædificatoriâ libri decem;" *Palladio* "De Architectura libri quatuor," and "De Templis Romanis;" *Philibertis de Lorme* "De Architectura libri novem;" *Vignola* "Cour d'Architecture," &c.; *Scamozzi*

ARCHITECTURE.

"Œuvres d'Architecture;" *Blondel* "Cursus Architecturæ;" *Perrault* "Architecture generale de Vitruve reduite en Abregé," and "Ordonnance de cinq espèces de Colomnes," &c.; *Goldmanni* "Tractatus de Stylometris," &c.

Explanation of the Plates.

Plate No. I. (9)—Members of the Pedestal, Column, and Entablature, in the five Orders.

Tuscan Order.

Pedestal.—*Base.* a, Plinth. b, List, or Fillet. c, Cavetto reversa.—*Die*, or *Body.*—*Cornice.* d, Cavetto, i. e. Cavetto recta; Fillet. e, Band.
Column.— *Base.* f, Plinth. g, Torus; Fillet.—*Shaft.* h, Apophyge, or Cincture, and Body, or Diameter below the break; Apophyge and Body above; Fillet. i, Astragal.—*Capital.* k, Gorge, Freeze, or Neck of the Capital; Fillet. l, Ovolo, or Echinus. m, Abacus.
Entablature.—*Architrave.* n, First, or small Fascia. o, Second, or large Fascia; List, or Band.—*Frize*, or *Zophyrus.*—*Cornice.* Cavetto; Fillet; Ovolo, p, Corona; Fillet. q, Cima recta, Cymatium, or ogee; Fillet.

Doric Order.

Pedestal.—*Base*; Plinth. A, Cima reversa; Cavetto reversa.—*Die*, or *Body.*—Cornice; Cavetto; Ovolo; Corona.
Column.—*Base*; lower Torus. B, Scotia; upper Torus.—*Shaft*, Apophyge and Body below the break; Apophyge and Body above; Astragal.—*Capital*; Frize, or Neck. C, Anulets; Ovolo; Abacus; Cyma recta.
Entablature.—*Architrave*; first Fascia; second Fascia. D, Guttæ. E, Tænia.—*Frize.* F, Metops. G. Triglyphs. H, Cap of Triglyphs; Cavetto; Ovolo. I, Mutule. K, Cap of Mutule; Corona; Cima reversa; Cima recta.

Ionic Order.

Pedestal.—*Base*; Plinth; Cima reversa. L, Bead; Cavetto.—*Die.*—Cornice; Cavetto; Ovolo and Bead; Corona.
Column.—*Base*; Plinth; lower Torus; Scotia; upper Torus.—*Shaft*; Body below; Body above, with Fluting. —*Capital*; Astragal; Ovolo. M, Volute; Abacus.
Entablature.—*Architrave*; first, second, and third Fascia; Cima reversa. — *Frize.* — *Cornice*; Cavetto; Ovolo. N, Modillions; Caps; Corona; Cima reversa.

Corinthian Order.

Pedestal.—*Base*; Plinth; Torus; Cima reversa; Cima recta.—*Die.*—*Cornice*; Cima recta; Ovolo; Corona; Cima reversa.
Column.—*Base*; Plinth; lower Torus; Scotia; upper Torus; Bead.—*Shaft*; Body below, above with Apophyges; Astragal.—*Capital.* O, Bell adorned with the leaves of the Acanthus; Abacus.
Entablature.—*Architrave*; first, second, and third Fascia; Cima reversa. — *Frize.*— *Cornice*; Cima reversa. P, Dentils; Ovolo; Modillions in the form of Consoles; Corona; Cima reversa; Cima recta.

Composite Order.

Pedestal.—*Base*; Plinth; Torus; Cima reversa; Bead.— *Die.*—*Cornice*; Bead; Cima recta; Corona; Cima reversa.
Column.—*Base*; Plinth; lower Torus; Scotia; double Astragal; Scotia; upper Torus; Bead.—*Shaft*; Body below and above, with Apophyges. — *Capital*; Bell adorned with the leaves of the Acanthus; Astragal; Ovolo; Volute; Abacus.
Entablature.—*Architrave*; first and second Fascia; Cima reversa; Cavetto.—*Frize.*—*Cornice*; Cima reversa; Modillions; Corona; Cima reversa; Cima recta.

Plate No. II. (10.)—The five Orders in General.

These five orders are collected from the foregoing proportions, allowing their several heights to be as follow: namely, *Tuscan*, 10 modules, 45 minutes. — *Roman Doric*, 12 modules, 20 minutes, the proportions of which may be compared with the *Grecian Doric*, both being of the same altitude.—*Ionic*, 13 modules, 31 minutes. —*Corinthian*, 14 modules, 12 minutes. — *Composite*, 14 modules. The module in this plate is marked by the figures 15, 14, 13, &c. which may be easily reduced to minutes by the scale laid down.

Plate No. III. (11.)

Ornaments. A, Eggs. B, Channels. C, Foliage. D, Rose. E, Festoon. F, Fretwork.—*Mouldings.* G, Torus. H, Astragal. I, Cavetto. K, Ovolo. L, Scotia. M, Cima Recta. N, Cima reversa. O, Apophyge.— P, Doric Intercolumniation.— Q, Corinthian Capital. R, Composite Capital.

ARCHITECTURE (*Perspect.*) a sort of building, the members of which are of different measures and modules, and diminish in proportion to their distance so as to make the building appear longer and larger to the view than it really is.

ARCHI'TRAVE (*Archit.*) a French term, from ἀρχὴ, chief, and *trabs*, a beam; signifying that division of the entablature, which rests upon the column, and is supposed to represent the principal beam in the building; whence it has the name, in English, of the Reason-Piece, or Master-Piece in porticoes, &c.; the Mantle-Piece in chimneys; and the Hyperthyron over doors, &c. It is called in Greek ἐπιςύλιον, by Vitruvius *epistylium*, the Epistyle, i. e. ἐπὶ τοῦ ςυλου, upon the column, because it rests upon the column. *Vitruv.* l. 3, c. 3; *Plut. in Peric.*; *Bald. Lex. Vitruv.*—*Architrave Cornice*, an architrave crowned with a cornice.—*Architrave doors*, those which have an architrave on the jaunbs, or over the door windows; on the cappiece if straight; and on the arch if the top be curved.— *Architrave windows* are usually an ogee raised out of the solid timber with a list over it; but sometimes the mouldings are struck and laid on; sometimes cut in brick.

ARCHI'TRICLINUS (*Ant.*) *qui præest triclinio*, the major domo, or steward of the household. *Stuck. de Ant. Conviv.* l. 2, c. 7.

ARCHI'VAULT (*Arch.*) or *Archivolt*, the contour of an arch or a frame set off with mouldings running upon the faces of the arch-stones, and bearing upon the imposts.

ARCHI'VES (*Archæol.*) from *arca*, a chest, or more probably from ἀρχεῖον, the treasury in the Greek temples [vide *Archeion*]; a place where the records, &c. belonging to the crown and kingdom are kept; the office of the rolls, &c.; also the rolls themselves.

A'RCH-LUTE (*Mus.*) a theorbe, or large lute. [vide *Arcileuto*]

A'RCHON (*Hist.*) the chief magistrate of Athens; the office was at first perpetual, and afterwards annual. *Vel. Pat.* l. 1, c. 2. 8; *August. de Civ. Dei.* l. 18, c. 20.

ARCHO'NTICKS (*Ecc.*) heretics who held that Archangels created the world, &c. They were a branch of the Valentinians. *Epiphan. Hæres.* 40; *August. Hæres.* 20; *Baron. Annal. Ann.* 195.

ARCHOPTO'MA (*Med.*) a bearing down of the rectum.

A'RCILEUTO (*Mus.*) Italian for an archlute, or very long lute used by the Italians for playing a thorough base.

A'RCION (*Bot.*) or *Arcium*. [vide *Arctium*]

ARCITE'NENS (*Ast.*) another name for Sagittarius. *Prisc.*

A'RCO (*Mus.*) an Italian word signifying the Arc or Bow, with which the violin and other string instruments are played. In violin music it denotes that the bow must be used instead of the fingers.

A'RCOS (*Chem.*) Burnt Copper.

ARCTA'TA *pars* (*Med.*) the part compressed or closed by a fibula.

ARCTA'TIO (*Med.*) a constipation of the intestines from inflammation, or a præternatural streightness of the *pudendum muliebre*.

A'RCTIC (*Astrol.*) ἀρκτικός, from ἄρκτος, the bear; an epithet for what lies towards the North, as the Arctic circle, and the Arctic Pole.—*Arctic circle*, one of the lesser circles of the sphere, which is twenty-three degrees and a half distant from the North Pole.—*Arctic Pole*, the same as the North Pole. *Procl. de Sphær. Cleom. l. 1.*

A'RCTIZITE (*Min.*) a sort of stone of the *Feldspar* family.

A'RCTOMYS (*Zool.*) Marmot, a genus of animals; Class *Mammalia*, Order *Glires*.
Generic Characters. Fore-teeth wedged, two in each jaw. Grinders upper five each jaw; lower four; clavicles perfect.
Species. The *Arctomys* is so similar to the mouse that it scarcely deserves to be reckoned a distinct genus. The principal species are—*Arctomys Marmota*, the Marmot.—*Arctomys Bobac*, le Boback, the Bobac.—*Arctomys citellus*, le Zizel, the Varigated Marmot, &c.

ARCHTO'PHYLAX (*Astron.*) the Bear-Ward, a name for Bootes. *Arat. de Phænom. Cic. in Arat.*

A'RCTOPUS (*Bot.*) ἀρκτόπους, Bear's-Foot; a genus of plants; Class 23 *Polygamia*. Order 3 *Dioecia*.
Generic Characters. CAL. umbel universal long, partial shorter; perianth five parted.—COR. universal uniform; proper petals five.—STAM. filaments five; anthers simple.—PIST. germ none; styles two; stigmas simple.—PER. abortive; seeds solitary.
Species. The only species is the *Arctopus echinatus*, Prickly leaved Arctopus, a perennial, native of the Cape of Good Hope. *Linn. Spec. Plant.*

A'RCTOS (*Astron.*) ἄρκτος ursa, a name for the two Northern constellations, namely, the *Ursa major* and *minor*, which were also known by the names of *Helice* and *Cynosura*, which were carefully observed by the sailors.
Arat. de Apparent.

Οἱ τὴν μὲν, κυνόσυραν ἐπίκλησιν καλέουσι
Τὴν δ' ἑτέρην Ἑλίκην.

These stars never set to us, to which Virgil and others allude.
Virg. Georg. l. 1, v. 246.

Arctos, Oceani metuentes æquore tingi.

Ovid. Fast. l. 4.

Esse duas Arctos, quarum Cynosura petatur
Sidonius, Helicen Graia carina notet.

Homer speaks of Arctos in the singular.
Odyss. l. 5, v. 273.

Ἄρκτον θ' ἣν καὶ Ἄμαξαν, ἐπίκλησιν καλέουσιν
Ἥτ' αὐτοῦ στρέφεται καί τ' Ὠρίωνα δοκεύει
Οἴη δ' ἄμμορός ἐστι λοετρῶν Ὠκεανοῖο.

ARCTOSCO'RDON (*Bot.*) Bear's Garlic.

ARCTOSTA'PHYLOS (*Bot.*) from ἄρκτος, and σταφυλὴ, uva; because it is eaten by bears; a species of the *vaccinium* of Linnæus.

ARCTOTHE'CA (*Bot.*) the *Gorteria rigens* and the *Arctotis* of Linnæus. *Raii Hist. Plant.*

ARCTO'TIS (*Bot.*) from ἄρκτος, ursa, the bear; because of its shagginess. 1. A genus of plants, Class 19 *Syngenesia*, Order 4 *Polygamia Necessaria*.
Generic Characters. CAL. common roundish.—COR. compound radiate.—STAM. filaments five; anthers cylindric.—PIST. germ scarcely visible; style cylindric; stigma simple.—PER. none; calyx unchanged; seeds, in the hermaphrodites, none—in the females, solitary; receptacle villose or chaffy.
Species. The species are annuals, as the *Arctotis calendulacea serrata*, &c.; biennials, as the *Arctotis grandifolia*, &c.; perennials, as *Arctotis tenuifolia*, *argentea*, &c.; shrubs, as *Arctotis angustifolia aspera*, &c. *Linn. Spec. Plant.*

ARCTOTIS is also the *Gorteria rigens* of Linnæus.

ARCTU'RA (*Med.*) inflammation of the finger or the toe, from the curvature of the nail. *Linn.*

ARCTU'RUS (*Astron.*) ἀρκτοῦρος, a star of the first magnitude in the tail of the bear, which Erotian makes to signify the same as *Archtophylax*, i. e. the keeper of the bear, because keepers were called οὖροι; but others derive it from ἄρκτος, the bear, and οὐρά, a tail. This star is called by Homer ὀψιδύων; by Pliny *gladius aut pugio Bootis*; by Isidore *arctuzona*; in the Arabic *alkameluz*. Aratus distinguishes it for its brightness.
Phænom. v. 93.

Καὶ μάλα πᾶς ἀρίδηλος· ὑπὸ ζώνῃ δὲ οἱ αὐτὸς
Ἐξ ἄλλων Ἀρκτοῦρος ἑλίσσεται ἀμφαδὸν ἀστήρ·

which is rendered by Cicero,

Huic autem subter præcordia fixa videtur
Stella micans radiis arcturus nomine clara.

So Manilius *Astron. l. 5, v. 351.*

Nunc subit Arcitenens, cujus pars quinta nitentem
Arcturum ostendit ponto.

It was the portender of storms, according to Plautus and others.
Plaut. in Rudent.

Arcturus signum sum omnium quam acerrimum
Vehemens sum cum exorior, cum occido vehementior.

Virg. Æn. l. 1, v. 743.

———— Unde imber et ignes,
Arcturum pluviasque Hyades, geminosque Triones.

Hor. Carm. l. 3, od. 1, v. 27.

Nec sævus Arcturi cadentis
Impetus.

Virgil recommends ploughing barren lands at the rising of Arcturus.
Virg. Geor. l. 1, v. 67.

At si non fuerit tellus fœcunda sub ipsum
Arcturum tenui sat erit suspendere sulco.

According to Pliny it rose on the 12th, and according to Columella on the 5th of September; but now it rises as late as October. *Hippocrat. Epidem. l. 1; Hipparch. in Arat.; Plin. l. 6, c. 23; Ptolem. de Apparent; Erotian. Lex Hippocrat.; Hesychius; Suidas.*

ARCTURUS *verbascum* (*Bot.*) a species of the *Celsia* of Linnæus.

ARCUA'LIA *ossa* (*Anat.*) the bones of the Sinciput, or the temple bones.

ARCUA'LIS *sutura* (*Anat.*) another name for the *Sutura coronalis*, from its bow-like shape.

ARCUA'TIO (*Med.*) Arcuation; a gibbosity of the fore parts, with a curvation of the bone of the sternum of the tibia, or dorsal vertebræ.

ARCUA'TION (*Hort.*) the raising of plants by layers.

ARCUA'TUS *morbus* (*Med.*) the same as *Icterus*.

ARCUATUS (*Bot.*) bent like a bow.

ARCUBALI'STA (*Ant.*) from *arcus*, a bow, and βάλλω, to cast; a cross bow, which has been contracted into *arbalist*.

ARCU'LÆ (*Anat.*) κοιλίδες, the caverns or orbits of the eyes. *Ruf. Ephes. Appell. Part. human. Corp. l. 3, c. 1.*

A'RCUS (*Numis.*) the Bow; was the symbol of many cities, in honour of Diana, as on the annexed figure, which represents the reverse of a medal of Agrippina, struck by the Acmonians: the inscription ΕΠΙ ΣΕΡΟΤΙΝΙΟΥ ΚΑΠΙΤΩΝΟΣ ΚΑΙ ΙΟΥΛΙΑΣ ΣΕΟΥΡΑΣ ΑΚΜΟΝΕΩΝ, i. e. *sub Serotinio Capitone et Juliâ Severâ Acmoniensium*. Sometimes Apollo is also represented with his bow bent ready to shoot the serpent, Python, as in the annexed figure, which represents a coin of Ægina, bearing the inscription ΑΙΓΙΝΗ, *Ægina*. *Vaillant. Numis. Græc. Peller. Rec. de Med.*—*Arcus triumphalis*, the Triumphal Arch, is represented on the coins of several emperors, commemorative of their victories, as in the annexed figure, representing a coin of Augustus Cæsar, on which an equestrian statue, by the side of the triumphal arch, the inscription S. P. Q. R. IMP. CAES. Triumphal arches are represented on the coins of Drusus, Claudius, Nero, Galba, Titus, Domitian, Trajan, Antoninus, M. Aurelius, L. Verus, Gallienus, and Postumus, sen. *Goltz. Num. Aug. Cæs.*; *Vaillant. Num. Imp. Rom.*; *Tristan. Comment. Histor.* vol. i.; *Morell. Famil. Pompeian.*; *Beg. Thes. Brand.* tom. ii.

A'RDABAR (*Chem.*) a sort of arum.

A'RDAS (*Chem.*) sordes or filth.

ARDA'SSINE (*Com.*) a sort of Persian silk of the finer kind.

ARDE'A (*Or.*) a sort of water-fowl of the heron tribe: so called from the loftiness of its flight, to which Virgil alludes. *Virg. Georg.* l. 1, v. 363.

> *In sicco ludunt fulicæ; notasque paludes*
> *Deserit, atque altam supra volat Ardea nubem.*

ARDEA, in the Linnean system, a genus of birds, in the Order *Grallæ*.
Generic Characters. *Bill* straight, long, pointed.—*Nostrils* linear.—*Tongue* sharp.—*Feet* four-toed cleft.
Species. The species are distinguished by the English names of the Crane, the Stork, the Heron, and the Bittern, as—*Ardea grus*, in French, *le Grue*, the *Gru* or *Grua* of Aldrovandus, the Common Crane, having its head bald.—*Ardea ciconia*, in French, *le Cicogne*, the Stork, having its orbits naked.—*Ardea major*, or *cinerea*, the *Heron cendre* of Belon, and *Heron hupé* of Brisson, the Heronshaw or Common Heron.—*Ardea alba*, in French, *le Heron blanc*, the White Heron.—*Ardea Garzetta*, in French, *l'Aigrette*, the Egret, or Dwarf Heron.—*Ardea nyctocorax*, or *grisea*, in French, *le Heron gris*, or *Bithreau*, the Night Heron.—*Ardea comata*, the *Cancrofagus luteus* of Brisson, in French, *Crabier de Mahon*, the Squacco of Ray, the Squacco Heron.—*Ardea stellaris*, or *Botaurus*, in French, *le Butor*, the *Trombone*, or *Terrabuso* of Aldrovandus, the Bittour, Miredrum, or Bittern.—*Ardea minuta*, or *Ardeola*, in French, *le Blongios*, the Little Bittern Heron.

A'RDENS *febris* (*Med.*) καῦσις, an ardent or burning fever; a species of tertian remittent.

A'RDENT *spirits* (*Chem.*) distilled spirits, which will take fire, and burn as spirits of wine, &c.

ARDE'NTES *papulæ* (*Med.*) the same as *Ecbrasmata*.

ARDE'NTIA (*Med.*) things unfit to be eaten and drank, being subject to combustion, as amber, turpentine, and the like.

A'RDEOLA (*Or.*) dim. of *ardea*, a little heron; the *Ardea minuta* of Linnæus.

A'RDERS (*Agric.*) the fallowings or ploughings of grounds, &c.

ARDE'SIA (*Min.*) a genus of *Argillaceous* earths, consisting of alumina and silica, with some oxyde of iron and carbonate of lime, magnesia, and petroleum.
Species. The principal species are—*Ardesia novacula*, or *Schistus scriptura alba*, Novaculite, Turkey Hone, or Whetstone.—*Ardesia tabularis*, *Schistus tabularis*, or *Schistus subtilior niger*.—*Ardesia tegularis*, *Schistus Ardesia*, or *Schistus durus*, Argillite, Argillaceous Schistus, Slate, &c.

ARDI'SIA (*Bot.*) a genus of plants, Class 5 *Pentandria*, Order 1 *Monogynia*.
Generic Characters. CAL. *perianth* one-leaved.—COR. one-petalled.—STAM. *filaments* five; *anthers* acute.—PIST. *germ* superior; *style* subulate; *stigma* simple.—PER. *berry* roundish; *seed* single.
Species. The species are mostly shrubs, and natives of the Indies, as *Ardisia excelsa*, *zeylanica*, &c.

A'RDOR (*Med.*) an intense heat in the body.—*Ardor urinæ*, vide *Dysuria*.—*Ardor ventriculi*, vide *Cardialgia*.

ARDUI'NA (*Bot.*) from *Pietro Ardium* of Padua; a genus of plants, Class 5 *Pentandria*, Order 1 *Monogynia*.
Generic Characters. CAL. *perianth* five-parted.—COR. one-petalled.—STAM. *filaments* five; *anthers* oblong.—PIST. *germ* superior; *style* filiform; *stigma* bifid.—PER. *berry* globular oval; *seeds* solitary.
Species. The only species is *Arduina bispinosa*, Two-spined Arduina, a shrub, native of the Cape of Good Hope. *Linn. Spec. Plant.*

ARE' (*Mus.*) *ala mire*, one of the eight notes in the scale.

A'REA (*Ant.*) from *areo*, to grow dry, because the fruits, *arescunt*, grow dry; a threshing floor, which, among the Romans, was placed near the house, on high ground, open on all sides, and elevated in the middle. *Varr. de Lat. Ling.* l. 4, c. 4; *Aul. Gell.* l. 11, c. 10, &c.

AREA (*Archit.*) the site or space of ground on which any building is erected.

AREA (*Geom.*) the superficial content of any figure, as a triangle, quadrangle, &c. which is estimated by small squares or parts of squares. Suppose A B C D to be a rectangle, consisting of twelve inches, twelve feet, or twelve yards; then each of the little squares, as *a* or *b*, will be one inch, one foot, or one yard square.

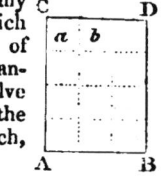

AREA (*Opt.*) vide *Field*.

AREA (*Min.*) the mass dug from the mines, or the place where it is dug.

AREA (*Med.*) the same as *Alopecia*.

AREA'LU (*Bot.*) the *Ficus religiosa* of Linnæus.

A'REB (*Com.*) a nominal money used in accounts in the dominions of the Great Mogul.

ARE'CA (*Bot.*) the Indian nut, the fruit of a kind of palm-tree which the Indians chew, and roll up in a betel leaf to help digestion. *Kæmpf. Amœnitat.*

ARECA, in the Linnean system, a genus of plants, Class 21 *Monoecia*, Order 8 *Monadelphia*.
Generic Characters. CAL. *spathe* bivalve.—COR. *petals* three.—STAM. *filaments* nine.—PER. *berry* subovate; *seed* ovate.
Species. The species are mostly shrubs, and natives of the Indies, as the *Areca oleracea*, the Cabbage-Tree.—*Areca catechu*, &c. *Linn. Spec. Plant.*

ARE'FACTIO (*Med.*) Arefaction, or the drying of medicines, so as to reduce them to a powder.

AREI'RA (*Bot.*) a species of *Selimus* of Linnæus.

ARE'LI (*Bot.*) the *Nerium oleander* of Linnæus.

AREMA'ROS (*Bot.*) vide *Cinnabaris*.

ARE'NA (*Ant.*) the amphitheatre, and that part of it in particular where the gladiators contended; so called from the sand with which it was strewed. *Plin.* l. 8, c. 7.

ARENA (*Min.*) a genus of earths of the *Siliceous* order.
  Generic Characters. The *Arena* consists of comminuted Siliceous stones, not fusible, *per se*, but melting with soda into glass.
  Species. The principal species are—*Arena silicea*, Flint Stones.—*Arena saxosa*, Gravel.—*Arena quartzosa*, Common Sand.—*Arena farinacea*, Dust or Grit.—*Arena mobilis*, Quick Sand.

ARENA'MEN (*Chem.*) Bole Armoniac.

ARENA'RIA (*Bot.*) from *Arena*, sand, its native soil Sandwort; a genus of plants, Class 10 *Decandria*, Order 3 *Trigynia*.
  Generic Characters. CAL. perianth five-leaved; *leaflets* oblong.—COR. *petals* five.—STAM. *filaments* ten; *anthers* roundish.—PIST. *germ* ovate; *styles* from erect reflex; *stigmas* thickish.—PER. *capsule* ovate; *seeds* very many.
  Species. The species are mostly perennials, as—*Arenaria peploides*, Sea Sandwort or Chickweed.—*Arenaria multicaulis*, many stalked Sandwort.—*Arenaria montana*, Mountain Sandwort, &c. Some few are annuals, as—*Arenaria trinerva*, Plantain-leaved Chickweed.—*Arenaria serpyllifolia*, Least Chickweed, or Thyme-leaved Sandwort.—*Arenaria media*, Middle or Downy Sandwort, &c. These annuals are all natives of Britain.

ARENA'RII (*Ant.*) those who fought with beasts in the amphitheatre. *Symmach. Epist.* l. 5, ep. 57; *Lips. de Amphith.* c. 3.

ARENA'TIO (*Med.*) Besprinkling or bathing patients with hot sand. *Castell. Lex. Med.*

ARE'NDATE (*Min.*) another name for *Epidote*.

ARE'NTES (*Med.*) a sort of cupping glasses.

A'REOLA (*Anat.*) a diminutive of *area*; a circle which surrounds the nipple of the breast.

AREO'METER (*Mech.*) from ἀήρ, the air, and μετρέω, to measure; an instrument for measuring the weight of liquors.

AREO'PAGITÆ (*Ant.*) Ἀρεοπαγῖται, a sort of judges at Athens; so called from the court of the Areopagus where they presided. *Cic. de Offic.* l. 1, ad *Attic.* l. 1, ep. 14.

AREO'PAGUS (*Ant.*) from ἄρειος πάγος, i. e. Mars-hill; so called, as some say, because Mars was first tried there for the murder of Halerrhotius. A village or hill in the neighbourhood of Athens, where the first capital sentence is said to have passed; whence it became a court or judgment-hall for life and death. *Isocrat. Areopagitic. Licurg. in Leocrat.; Demosth. in Aristocrat.; Dimarch. in ristcgit.; Poll. Onomast.* l. 8, c. 9; *Harpocration, Suidas, Etymologicon*, &c.

AREO'STYLE (*Archit.*) a species of intercolumniation mentioned by Vitruvius, in which the columns are placed at considerable intervals between each other, from ἀραιός, a few, and στύλος, a column. *Vitruv. de Architect.* l. 3, c. 2.

A'RES (*Alch.*) the last of the three disposers of nature, which distributes the species into individuals. *Paracel. de Vit. Long.* l. 3, c. 12, &c.

ARE'STA Bovis (*Bot.*) vide *Anonnis*.

ARETÆNO'IDES (*Anat.*) vide *Arytænoides*.

ARETHU'SA (*Bot.*) a genus of plants, Class 20 *Gynandria*, Order 1 *Diandria*.
  Generic Characters. CAL. *spathe* leafy; *perianth* none.—COR. ringent; *petals* five; *nectary* one-leaved.—STAM. *filaments* two; *anthers* ovate.—PIST. *germ* oblong; *style* oblong; *stigma* funnel shaped.—PER. *capsule* oblong ovate; *seeds* numerous.
  Species. The species are mostly perennials and natives of America, the Cape of Good Hope, &c. as *Arethusa bulbosa, ophioglossoides, divaricata*, &c. *Linn. Spec. Plant.*

ARE'TIA (*Bot.*) from *Aretius*, a Botanist at Berne; a genus of plants, Class *Pentandria*, Order 1 *Monogynia*.
  Generic Characters. CAL. *perianth* one-leaved.—COR. monopetalous.—STAM. *filaments* five; *anthers* erect.—PIST. *germ* roundish; *style* filiform; *stigma* flat-headed. PER. *capsule* one-celled; *seeds* five.
  Species. The species are perennials, as—*Aretia helvetica, Alpina*, &c. *Linn. Spec. Plant.*

A'REUS (*Med.*) a pessary, mentioned by Paulus Ægineta. *De Re Med.* l. 7, c. 3.

A'RFAR (*Chem.*) Arsenic.

ARGA'GANON (*Med.*) Medicines against the leprosy.

A'RGAL (*Nat.*) Hard lees sticking to the sides of wine glasses; another name for *Tartar*.

A'RGAN (*Bot.*) A species of *Elæodendrum*.

A'RGEMA (*Med.*) ἄργεμα, *Albugo*; an ulceration of the Cornea. [vide *Albugo*]

ARGEMO'NE (*Bot.*) ἀργεμώνη, or *Argemonia*; a plant like wild poppy, so called because it cures the disease in the eyes called the ἄργεμα, or *Albugo oculi*. *Dioscor.* l. 2, c. 208; *Plin.* l. 25, c. 9.

ARGEMONE, in the *Linnean system*, a genus of plants; Class 13 *Polyandria*, Order 1 *Monogynia*.
  Generic Characters. CAL. *perianth* three-leaved; *leaflets* roundish, with a point.—COR. *petals* six.—STAM. *filaments* numerous; *anthers* oblong.—PIST. *germ* ovate; *style* none; *stigma* thickish.—PER. *capsule* ovate; *seeds* numerous; *receptacles* linear.
  Species. The Species are annuals, as *Argemone Mexicana, Armeniaca, Pyrenaica*, &c. *Linn. Spec. Plant.*

ARGEMONE is also the *Papaver argemone, hybridum, Alpinum, et dubium* of Linnæus. *Bauh.; Park. &c.*

A'RGENT (*Her.*) a French word for silver, is used to denote the white colour marked in the coats of arms of baronets, knights, and gentlemen; the white colour in the coat of a sovereign prince is called *Luna*, that in the arms of the nobility *Pearl*. It is marked in painting by leaving the field blank, or without any dot and line, as in the annexed figure.

ARGENTANGI'NA (*Law*) from *argentum*, silver, and *angina*, the quinsey, in Greek ἀργυράγχη, silver quinsy; when a pleader being bribed feigns himself sick, and not able to speak.

ARGE'NTEA (*Bot.*) the *Protea potentilla* of Linnæus.

ARGENTEO-MARGINATUM (*Bot.*) Silver-bordered, an epithet for leaves, &c.

ARGENTEUM (*Bot.*) the *Potentilla anserina* of Linnæus. *Bauh.*

ARGENTI'NA (*Ich.*) *Argentine*, a genus of animals; Class *Pisces*, Order *Abdominales*.
  Generic Characters. Teeth in the jaws and tongue.—Rays branchiostegous eight.—Vent near the tail.—Fins ventral composed of many rays.
  Species. The species are *Argentina sphyræna*, European Argentine.—*Argentina glossodonta*, &c.

ARGENTINA (*Bot.*) the *Potentilla anserina* of Linnæus.

ARGE'NTINE (*Ich.*) vide *Argntina*.

ARGENTINE (*Min.*) Slate-spar, a calcareous salt of the Carbonate family.

ARGENTINE (*Chem.*) flowers of Antimony, a preparation of Antimony with acid.

ARGE'NTUM *factum* (*Anat.*) called by Valerius Maximus *argentea vasa*, i. e. Plate or silver wrought into vessels of different kinds. *Val. Max.* l. 2, c. 9; *Aul. Gell.* l. 4, c. 8.—*Argentum infectum*, unwrought silver, or silver in the lump. *Liv.* l. 34, c. 52; *Isidor. Orig.* l. 16, c. 17.—*Argentum escarium*, the plate or silver vessels at table. *Ulp.* l. 19, § 12; *ff. de Aur. Donat. in Virg. Æn.* l. 1, v. 644.—*Argentum signatum*, silver coin, or silver stamped.—*Argentum pustulatum* or *granulatum*, silver chased or embossed, which was of the purest kind. *Mart.* l. 7,

epig. 69; *Sueton. in Ner.* c. 44.—*Argentum viatorium*, money for travelling. *Scævol. Leg.* 40; *ff. de Aur. &c.*—*Argentum purum*, plain silver, in distinction from the *cælatum* that was carved.
Juv. sat. 9, v. 141.

———— *argenti vascula puri.*

Plin. l. 3, ep. 1; *Paull. Leg.* 6, *ff. de Aur. et Arg. Legat.*
ARGENTUM *album* (*Archæol.*) silver coin. *Domesday Book.*
ARGENTUM *Dei* (*Law*) money given as earnest at the making of a bargain.
ARGENTUM (*Min.*) ἄργυρος, from ἀργός, white, silver; a genus of metals.
  Generic Characters. Of a white colour, hard, tenacious, sonorous, exceedingly malleable, and ductile; specific gravity before hammering 10,478, melting in a perfect red heat, and soluble in nitric acid.
  Species. The species are *Argentum nativum*, seu *Argentum nudum*, Native Silver. [vide *Silver*]—*Argentum nigrum*, *Argentum fuliginosum*, seu *Argentum mineralisatum*, Black-silver, Black-silver-ore.—*Argentum corneum*, *Argentum diaphanum*, seu *Argentum acidum sale mineralisatum*, Corneous Silver Ore or Muriate of silver.—*Argentum electrum*, Auriferous Native Silver. — *Argentum stibiatum*, Antimoniated Native Silver, Antimoniated Silver Ore.—*Argentum arseniacum*, Arsenicated Silver, Arsenicated Native Silver, or Arsenical Silver.—*Argentum molybdænatum*, Molybdenic Silver Ore.—*Argentum vitreum*, *Argentum mineralisatum*, seu *Argentum sulphuratum mineralisatum*, Sulphurated Silver Ore, Vitreous Silver, or Sulphuret of Silver.—*Argentum fragile*, Antimoniated Silver Ore, Brittle Silver Ore, or Antimoniated Sulphuret.—*Argentum nitens*, Cupriferous sulphurated Silver or Cupriferous Sulphuret.—*Argentum rubrum*, *Argentum rubescens*, *Argentum sulphure*, &c. seu *Argentum arsenico-minerale*, Light red Silver Ore.—*Argentum album*, Plumbiferous Silver Ore or Grey Silver Ore.
ARGENTUM *vivum*, Quick Silver, the *Hydrargyrum* of Linnæus.
ARGETE'NAR (*Astron.*) a star of the fourth magnitude in Eridanus.
A'RGIL (*Min.*) *Argilla*, White Clay; a fat soft kind of earth, of which potters' vessels are made. [vide *Argilla*]
ARGI'LLA (*Min.*) from ἀργίλλα, or ἀργή, white, i. e. Whiteearth; a genus of argillaceous earths.
  Generic Character. Alumina and Silica, with some oxyde of iron and inflammable matter; opake, soft to the touch, earthy, contracting, and becoming harder in the fire.
  Species. The species are *Argilla porcella*, *Terra porcellana*, seu *Argilla apyra*, Porcelain Clay.—*Argilla leucargilla*, Potters' Clay, Pipe Clay, or Common Clay.—*Argilla lithomarga*, *Talcum subfriabile*, seu *Lithomarga*, Lithomarge or Potters' Clay.—*Argilla fullonica*, seu *Argilla vitrescens*, Fuller's Earth.—*Argilla crustacea*, *Argilla fullonica*, seu *Argilla vitrescens*.—*Argilla Lemnia*, *Argilla incarnata*, *Terra Lemnia*, seu *Argilla crustacea*, Lemnian earth.—*Argilla communis*, Common Clay.—*Argilla bolus*, *Argilla ore liquescens*, seu *Argilla vitrescens*, Bole.—*Argilla cimolia*, Cimolite.—*Argilla sinensis*, seu *Argilla flavescens*, Poliershiefer—*Argilla rubrica*, seu *Talcum*.—*Argilla subfissile*, Reddle.—*Argilla lutea*, Yellow Ochre.—*Argilla viridis*, *Bolus viridis*, Terra verde.—*Argilla Tripolitana*, seu *Argilla scabra*, Tripolis.
ARGILLA'CEUS (*Min.*) Argillaceous, the fourth order of earths, according to Gmelin, which are mostly soft and plastic. They are as follow : — *Aluminaris*, consisting almost entirely of alumina; meagre to the touch.—*Argilla*, consisting of alumina and silica.—*Puteolana*, of alumina, silica, and iron.—*Cæmentum*, as the former, but hardish, lightish, porous, of an earthy texture.—*Cariosus*, Rottenstone, consisting of alumina, &c. but light, soft, porous, falling to powder in water.—*Ardesia*, of alumina and silica, with some oxide of iron and carbonate of lime, magnesia, and petroleum.—*Basaltes*, Basalt, consisting of more silica, and less of alumina and oxyde of iron.—*Lava*, consisting of alumina,[r]&c. but generally of a dull colour.—*Mica*, of alumina, &c. but lightish and parasitical.—*Opalus*, of alumina, &c. but melting with the greatest difficulty.—*Zeolithus*, of a little alumina, and a large proportion of silica, &c.—*Schorlus*, of alumina, &c. but easily melting into a glass.
ARGI'LLITE (*Min.*) a species of clay-slate.
A'RGO *Navis* (*Astron.*) Ἀργὼ ναῦς, the ship; a constellation called after the ship of Jason and his companions, which was said to be translated into the heavens, which is situated near to the *Canis Major.*
Arat. Phænom. v. 342.

———————— Ἀργὼ
Ἡδ̓ι κυνὸς μεγάλοιο κατ᾽ οὐρὴν ἕλκεται
Πρυμνόθεν.

Manill. Astronom. l. 1, v. 401.

*Tum Procyon, velozque lepus. Tum nobilis Argo
In cælum subducta, mari quod prima cucurrit.*

It contained, according to Ptolemy, forty-five stars, according to Kepler fifty-three, to Bayer sixty-three, and to Hevelius sixty-four; of these, one in the rudder, called by Proclus κάνωβος, i. e. Canopus, and in the Arabic *Suhel*, is of the first magnitude. This constellation is called by Catullus *currus volans*. *Ptol. Almag.* l. 7, c. 5; *Hygin. Astron. Poet.*; *Hipparch. in Arat.*; *Eratosth. Characteris.*
ARGONA'UTA (*Con.*) a genus of animals; Class *Vermes*, Order *Testacea.*
  Generic Characters. Animal a Sepia or Clio.—Shell univalve, one-celled.
  Species. The most remarkable of the species is the *Argonauta Argo*, or the famous Nautilus, which was supposed by the ancients to have first taught men the use of sails. When it means to sail it discharges a quantity of water, by which it was made heavier than the seawater, and, rising to the surface, erects its arms and throws out a membrane between them, by which means it is driven forwards like a vessel under sail; two of the arms it hangs over the shell to serve as oars or as a rudder. The keel or ridge of the shell is slightly toothed on each side.
ARGONAUTICA (*Lit.*) the account of the expedition of the Argonauts, as that of Valerius Flaccus, Orpheus, &c.
ARGOPHY'LLUM (*Bot.*) from ἀργός, white, and φύλλον, a leaf, Whiteleaf; a genus of plants, Class 5 *Pentandria*, Order 1 *Monogynia.*
  Generic Characters. CAL. *perianth* short.—COR. *petals* five; *nectary* five-angled.—STAM. *filaments* five; *anthers* ovate.—PIST. *germ.* turbinate; *style* filiform; *stigma* globular.—PER. *capsule* hemispherical; *seeds* very many.
  Species. The only species is *Argophyllum nitidum*, a shrub, a native of New Caledonia.
A'RGUMENT (*Astron.*) any quantity or equation on which depends another quantity relating to the motion of the planets; or, in other words, it is an arc whereby another arc is to be sought, bearing a certain proportion to the first arc. The argument is of different kinds, namely—*Argument of inclination*, or *Argument of latitude*, the arc of a planet's orbit intercepted between the ascending node and the place of the planet from the sun, numbered according to the succession of the signs.—*Menstrual argument of latitude* is the distance of the moon's true place from the sun's true place, by which is found the quantity of the real obscuration in eclipses.—*Annual argument of the moon's apogee*, the distance of the sun's place from the

moon's apogee, i. e. an arc of the ecliptic comprised between these two places.—*Argument of the parallax*, denotes the effect it produces on the observation, which serves for determining the true quantity of the horizontal parallax.—*Argument of the equation of the centre*, is the same as the anomaly.

ARGUMENT (*Log.*) whatever is added or offers itself to the mind, so as to create belief in regard to any subject or matter laid down.

ARGUMENT (*Lit.*) the summary of the contents of any book or chapter in a work.

ARGUMENT (*Paint.*) the persons represented in a landscape, in contradistinction to the country or prospect.

ARGUMENTA'TION (*Log.*) an operation of the intellect, by which any proposition is proved by the help of other propositions. The proposition to be proved is called the *assumption*, and when it is proved, or drawn to a conclusion, it is termed the *conclusion*.

ARGYRA'SPIDES (*Ant.*) from ἄργυρος, and ἄσπις, a shield; a company in Alexander's army, who were so called because they wore silver shields.

ARGYRI'TÆ (*Ant.*) ἀργυρίται, from ἄργυρος, money; games upon wagers for money, &c. as horse-races for plates, &c.

ARGYRI'TIS terra (*Min.*) ἀργυρῖτις γῆ. 1. The sort of earth taken from silver mines. 2. *Spuma argenti*, the scum or froth arising from the silver, or the lead that is mixed with the silver on trial. *Dioscor.* l. 5, c. 102; *Plin.* l. 33, c. 6; *Oribas.* l. 13.

ARGYRO'COME (*Bot.*) ἀργυροκόμη, from ἄργυρος, silver, and κόμη, hair; the *Baccharis halimifolia*, the *Gnaphaleum margaritaceum*, the *Peranthemum vestilum* and *speciocissimum* of Linnæus. *Park. Theat. Bot.*

ARGYRO'DAMAS (*Min.*) 1. ἀργυροδάμας, from ἄργυρος, silver, and ἀδάμας, Adamant, a silver diamond; a sort of precious stone. *Plin.* l. 37, c. 10. 2. A kind of talc of a silver colour that will not yield to fire. *Castell. Lex. Med.*

ARGYRODE'NDROS (*Bot.*) the *Portea argentea* of Linnæus. *Raii Hist. Plant.*

ARGYROGO'NIA (*Chem.*) ἀργυρογονία, from ἄργυρος, silver, and γίνομαι, to produce; an argentific seed, perfectly digested from the solution of silver. *Castell. Lex Med.*

ARGYROLI'BANUM (*Bot.*) the White Olibanum.

ARGYROPHO'RA (*Med.*) a costly antidote. *Myrep. Antidot.* c. 320.

ARGYROPŒ'IA (*Alch.*) ἀργυροποιΐα, from ἄργυρος, silver, and ποιέω, to make; the art of making silver out of more imperfect metals, by means of the philosopher's stone.

ARGYROTHROPHE'MA (*Med.*) from ἀργυροτροφή, nourishment; a cooling food made with milk. *Gal. de Suc.*

ARGYTHA'MNIA (*Bot.*) from ἀργός, albus, and θαμνίον, shrub; White-Shrub, a genus of plants, Class 21 *Monoecia*, Order 4 *Tetrandria*.
    Generic Characters. CAL. perianth four-leaved; *leaflets* lanceolate.—COR. *petals* four; *nectary* roundish.—STAM. *filaments* four; *anthers* simple.—PIST. *rudiment* of a style.—PER. *capsule* tricoccous; *seed* solitary.
    Species. The only species is the *Argythamnia candicans*, a shrub, native of Jamaica. *Linn. Spec. Plant.*

ARHEUMATI'STOS (*Med.*) ἀρευματιστός, from α, priv. and ῥεῦμα, rheum; without rheumatism: applied to the joints in particular. *Castell. Lex. Med.*

A'RIA (*Mus.*) Italian for an air.—*Aria Buffo*, a comic air.

ARIA (*Bot.*) ἀρία, a plant, the fruit of which mitigates coughs. It is a species of the *Cratægus* of Linnæus.—*Aria Bepou*, the *Melia azederachta* of Linnæus.—*Aria vecla*, the *Cleome viscosa* of Linnæus.

A'RIANISM (*Ecc.*) the heresy of Arius, who, in the fourth century, denied that the Son was of the same substance with the Father. *Athanas.* orat. 1, *ad Serap; Epiphan. Hæres.* 68; *Socrat. Hist. Eccles.* l. 1, c. 6; *Sozom.* l. 2, c. 32, &c.

A'RIDA *medicamenta* (*Med.*) dry medicines, such as powders.

ARI'DITAS (*Med.*) dryness, from disease, as in a fever.

ARIDU'RA (*Med.*) a total consumption or withering away of the body or its members.

ARI'E *aggiunte* (*Mus.*) Italian for supplementary airs to an oratorio, &c.

ARI'ERBAN (*Law*) vide *Arrierban*.

A'RIES (*Ant.*) κριός, a battering ram; a formidable warlike machine, invented, as is mostly supposed, by the Carthaginians. It was constructed with a head of iron, called in Greek κεφαλή, or ἐμβολή, resembling a ram's head, which was sometimes enclosed or covered with a shroud to protect the soldiers, which was called χελώνη, *aretaria testudo*. The use of this machine in levelling the walls of towns is spoken of by the poets.
Luc. l. 1. v. 383.
> *Tu quocunque voles in planum ducere muros*
> *His Aries actus disperget saxa lacertis.*

Claud.
> *Tum, tua murali libretur machina fulsu*
> *Saxa rotet præceps Aries, protectaque portus*
> *Testudo feriat, ruat emensura juventus.*

Cic. de Offic. l. 1, c. 11; *Cæs. de Bell. Gall.* l. 2; *Liv.* l. 38, c. 5; *Plin.* l. 7, c. 56; *Athen. apud Turneb. Adv.* l. 23, c. 31; *Vitruv.* l. 10, c. 19; *Appian. in Bell. Mithridat.; Joseph. de Bell. Jud.* l. 3, c. 9; *Aul. Gel.* l. 1, c. 13; *Tertull. de Pall.* c. 1; *Veget. de Re Mil.* l. 4, c. 14.

ARIES (*Astron.*) the first sign marked (♈) in the Zodiac, into which when the sun enters, the days and nights are equal. Ptolemy reckoned 18 stars in this constellation, Tycho Brahe 21, Bayer 18, Hevelius 27, and Flamstead 66; of which one only is of the second magnitude, two of the third, and the rest smaller. *Ptol. Almag.* l. 7, c. 5; *Tych. Brah. Mech. Astron.; Bayer Uranomet.; Hevel. Machin. cælest.; Flamst. Hist. cælest. Britan.*

ARIES (*Zool.*) the ram; the male of the first and common species of the *Ovis* of Linnæus.

ARIES (*Ich.*) a great sea fish with horns like a ram, much of the nature of the Shark. *Plin.*

ARIE'TTA (*Mus.*) an Italian diminutive of *Aria*, signifying a short air.—*Arietta alla Veneziana*, little airs in the Venetian style.

ARIETTI'NA (*Mus.*) Italian for the same as *Arietta*.

ARIE'TUM *levatio* (*Archæol.*) a sort of tournament or tilting.

ARI'LLA (*Bot.*) a grape stone.

ARILLA'TUS (*Bot.*) provided with an aril.

ARI'LLUS (*Bot.*) aril, the outer coat of a seed falling off spontaneously, or inclosing the seed partially. It is called *succulentus*, succulent, when it is thick and fleshy, as in *Euonymus Europæus*; *cartilagineus*, cartilaginous, when the membrane is thick; *membranaceus*, membranaceous, when consisting of a thin tunicle; *dimidiatus*, halved, when covering half the seed; *lacerus*, torn, i. e. irregularly laciniated; *calyptratus*, capped, when covering the top of the seed, as the calyptra encircles the top of the theca of mosses; *reticulatus*, netlike, when it embraces the seed like a fine web, as in some species of the *Orchis*.

ARIO'SE *cantate* (*Mus.*) Italian for a kind of speaking airs.

ARIO'SO (*Mus.*) Italian for the movement or time of a common air in musical composition.

A'RIS (*Surg.*) the name of an instrument, according to Galen. *Exiges. Vocab. Hippocrat.*

ARIS (*Bot.*) the same as the *Arisarum*.

ARISA'RUM (*Bot.*) ἀρίσαρον, Friar's Cowl; a small plant with a root like that of the olive, but more acrimonious than the Arum. *Dioscor.* l. 2, c. 198; *Plin.* l. 24, c. 16.

ARISARUM, *in the Linnean system*, is classed under the *Ambrosinia* and the *Arum*. *C. Bauh. Pin.; Ger. Herb.; Park. Theat. Bot.; Raii Hist. Plant.; Tournef. Instit.*

A'RISH (*Com.*) a Persian measure of length equal to 3197 feet.

ARI'STA (*Bot.*) the beard of corn, or the ear of corn; so called from *areo*, to grow dry, because it dries.
Virg. Æn. l. 7, v. 720.

Vel quam sole novo densæ torrentur aristæ.

Arista, in modern Botany, the Awn is the pointed beard that sits on the flower of grasses, which is called—*Nuda*, naked, when not hairy.—*Plumosa*, feathered, when beset with fine hairs, as in the *Stipa pennata*.—*Recta*, when it is straight.—*Geniculata*, geniculated, when it has a joint in the middle by which it is bent, as in the common oat *Avena sativa*.—*Recurvata*, bent, when bent in the form of a bow.—*Tortilis*, twisted, when it is bent in a serpentine form.—*Terminalis*, when situated on the point of the glume.—*Dorsalis*, when situated behind the apex, or on the back of the glume.

ARISTA (*Num.*) is an emblem of plenty on medals, as in the annexed figure, which represents the head of Agrippina, the mother of Nero; the inscription ΑΓΡΙΠ-ΠΙΝΑΝ ΣΕΒΑΣΤΗΝ, i. e. *Agrippinam Augustam*. *Vaillant. Num. Græc.*

ARISTA'TUS (*Bot.*) awned.

ARISTE'A (*Bot.*) a genus of plants; Class 3 *Triandria*, Order 1 *Monogynia*.
Generic Characters. CAL. *spathes* bivalve.—COR. *petals* six.—STAM. *filaments* three; *anthers* oblong.—PIST. *germ* inferior; *style* filiform; *stigma* funnel-form.—PER. *capsule* oblong; *seeds* very many.
Species. The species are all perennials. *Linn. Spec. Plant.*

ARISTELLA (*Bot.*) a species of the *Stipa* of Linnæus.

ARISTIO'NIS *machinamentum* (*Surg.*) a machine for restoring luxations. *Oribas. de Machin.*

ARISTO'CRACY (*Polit.*) ἀριστοκρατία, that form of government where the supreme power is lodged in the hands of the chiefs or nobles, from ἄριστος, the chief or best, and κράτος, power. *Aristot. de Politic.* l. 4, c. 7.

ARISTOLO'CHIA (*Bot.*) Birthwort, a plant so called from its efficacy in promoting the *Lochia*, or evacuations of child-bed-women, after the *fœtus* and *secundines* are expelled. *Hippocrat. de Mul.; Theophrast. Hist. Plant.* l. 9, c. 13; *Nicand. in Theriac.; Cic. de Div.* l. 1, c. 10; *Dioscor.* l. 3, c. 4, &c.; *Gal. de Simplic.* l. 6; *Oribas. Med. Coll.* l. 1; *Aet. Tetrab.* 1, serm. 1; *Paul. Æginet.* l. 7, c. 3; *Salmas. ad Solin.* p. 504.

ARISTOLOCHIA, *in the Linnean system*, a genus of plants; Class 19 *Gynandria*, Order 4 *Hexandria*.
Generic Characters. CAL. none.—COR. monopetalous.—STAM. *filaments* none; *anthers* six.—PIST. *germ* oblong; *style* scarcely any; *stigma* subglobular.—PER. *capsule* large; *seeds* several.
Species. The species are either shrubs or perennials; among the former are—*Aristolochia bilobata*, Two lobed Birthwort, native of Dominica.—*Aristolochia peltata*, Peltated Birthwort, native of St. Domingo.—*Aristolochia erecta*, Upright Birthwort, native of New Spain.—*Aristolochia odoratissima*, Sweet scented Birthwort, native of Jamaica.—*Aristolochia anguicida*, Snake-killing Birthwort, native of Carthagena.—*Aristolochia sempervirens*, Evergreen Birthwort, &c. Among the perennials are—*Aristolochia serpentaria*, Virginia Birthwort or Snake-root.—*Aristolochia clematitis*, Common Birthwort, a native of Britain, &c. *Linn. Spec. Plant.*

ARISTOTE'LIA (*Bot.*) a genus of plants, so called from the philosopher Aristotle, Class 11 *Dodecandria*, Order 1 *Monogynia*.

Generic Characters. CAL. *perianth* one-leaved.—COR. *petals* five.—STAM. *filaments* fifteen; *anthers* linear.—PIST. *germ* superior; *style* filiform; *stigmas* three.—PER. *berry* subglobular; *seeds* two.
Species. The only species is the *Aristotelia Macqui*, Shining leaved Aristotelia, a shrub, native of Chili. *Linn. Spec. Plant.*

ARITHMETIC is the science of computation, or estimating quantities, from the Greek ἀριθμέω, to number, or calculate. It is of different kinds, namely—*Theoretical Arithmetic*, which considers the abstract properties and relations of numbers.—*Practical Arithmetic*, the art or practice of computing numbers, or finding from them certain other numbers whose relation to the former is known.—*Instrumental Arithmetic* is a mode of computing numbers by means of some instrument, as the ten fingers, the abacus, Napier's Bones, &c.—*Logarithmetical Arithmetic* is performed by tables of Logarithms.—*Political Arithmetic* is the application of arithmetic to political subjects.—*Numeral Arithmetic* teaches the calculus of determinate quantities by the numeral characters, 1, 2, 3, &c.—*Specious, literal, or universal Arithmetic*, is the computation of abstract quantities by means of letters, which is otherwise called Algebra.—*Binary Arithmetic* is performed by means of two figures, as 1 and 0.—*Tetractical Arithmetic* by means of four figures, as 1, 2, 3, 0.—*Decadal Arithmetic* by a series of ten characters, as 1, 2, 3, 4, 5, 6, 7, 8, 9, 10, such as are now in common use.—*Duodenary Arithmetic* by a series of twelve figures instead of ten.—*Integral Arithmetic* treats of whole numbers.—*Fractional Arithmetic* of fractional numbers.—*Decimal Arithmetic* is the working with decimal fractions.—*Sexagesimal Arithmetic* treats of the doctrine of sexagesimal fractions.—*Arithmetic of Infinites* is the summing up a series of numbers, of which the number of terms is infinite.—*Harmonical Arithmetic* is the doctrine of numbers, as it relates to the comparison and reduction of numbers.—*Vulgar Arithmetic* is the computation of numbers in the ordinary concerns of life according to certain rules, called *Operations*; these are, Numeration, Addition, Subtraction, Multiplication, Division, Reduction, Rule of Three, Practice, Tare and Tret, Interest, Exchange, Barter, Profit and Loss, Position, Progression, Permutation, Fractions, Decimals, Square and Cube Root, &c.; all which will be considered in their respective places.

Numbers, which are the foundation of Arithmetic, are of different kinds.—*Whole numbers*, either a unit or units, as a pound, a yard, &c. or 1, 2, 3, &c.—*Fractions*, or *broken numbers*, which are less than unity, as $\frac{1}{3}$, that is, one third of a unit.—*Mixed numbers* consist of a whole number and a fraction, as $1\frac{1}{4}$.—*Even numbers* may be divided into two equal whole numbers, as 4, which may be divided into 2 and 2.—*Odd numbers* cannot be equally divided.—*Prime numbers* can only be divided by themselves or by unity, as 5, which may be divided by 5 or 1.—*Compound numbers* are produced by multiplying two or more numbers together.—*Square number*, or *square*, the product of any number multiplied by itself, as 4 the product of 2 multiplied by 2.—*Cube number*, or *cube*, the product of any number multiplied by its square, as 8 the product of 2 multiplied by 4.—*Aliquot part* is that which is contained a precise number of times in an integer, as 2 the aliquot part of 10, because it is contained in it five times.—*Aliquant part* is that which is not contained in an integer a certain number of times without a remainder, as 5, which is the aliquant part of 7, 11, &c.—*Rational number* is that which is commensurable to unity.—*Irrational number*, or *surd*, is that which is incommensurable to unity.—*Abstract number* is any number considered independently of or abstracted from all things.—*Concrete number* is any number connected with some thing or things; thus, 5, 7, 8, &c. are abstract numbers, but 5 pounds, 7 ounces, &c. are concrete.

The characters employed in Arithmetic are either numeral letters, such as were used by the Phœnicians, Greeks, &c. [vide Plate 13 and Notation] figures called *digits*, [vide Plate 13 and Notation] letters, used as symbols, and signs, or arbitrary characters, which serve to shorten the different operations. [vide *Algebra*] Those used in Vulgar Arithmetic are the sign of addition, marked thus, + ; the sign of subtraction, thus, — ; the sign of multiplication, thus, × ; and the sign of division, ÷ . the remaining signs will be found under the head of Algebra.

Writers on Arithmetic.

Nicomachi, " Arithmetica;" Boetii " Arithmetica;" Pselli, " Compendium Arithmeticæ veterum;" Lucas de Burgo " De Arithmetica," &c.; Stifelii, " Arithmetica integra;" Tartagliæ, " Arithmetica practica;" Henischii, " Arithmetica perfecta;" Recorde, Clavius, Leotaude, Wallis, &c. &c. &c. [vide *Algebra*]

Explanation of the Plate.

Plate 12.

This plate contains the numerical characters in the order of derivation, or chronological succession, beginning with A. Phœnician, drawn from the coins of Sidon, by Dr. Swinton. B. Greek, derived from the Phœnician. C. Irish, also derived from the Phœnician, and taken from MS.; and another Irish, derived from the Arabian. D. Palmyrene. E. Ægyptian. F. Indian, ancient and modern. G. Arabian. H. Figures of Planudes. I. Figures of Boetius. K. Arabian and Persian figures in 800, from Moreton's Tables. L. Spanish numerals in 1000, from Moreton's Tables. M. Figures of John Sacro de Bosco, from Dr. Wallis. N. Coins of Sidon, having on the obverse a turreted head with a branch of palm, emblematical of the country, and on the reverse three Phœnician letters, that form the word Sidon, over the prow of a ship, the usual symbol of the city where it was struck. The characters in the exergue form, according to Dr. Swinton, the inscription " In the year of Sidon 120. 127. 130;" i. e. the proper æra of Sidon.

ARITHME'TICAL (*Math.*) an epithet for any thing relating to arithmetic, as—*Arithmetical complement of a logarithm.* [vide *Complement*]—*Arithmetical instruments,* contrivances by which calculations are made, as the Abacus, Napier's Bones, &c.—*Arithmetical mean,* the middle term of three quantities in arithmetical progression, or half the sum of two proposed quantities, as in 2, 4, 6, 4 is the arithmetical mean.—*Arithmetical progression or proportion.* [vide *Progression* and *Proportion*]—*Arithmetical ratio,* the difference between any two adjacent terms in arithmetical progression.—*Arithmetical scale,* the scale of rotation by which arithmetical operations are performed, as the binary, denary, &c. [vide *Notation*]—*Arithmetical triangle,* a table of numbers in the form of a triangle.

ARI'THMOS (*Med.*) ἀριθμός, *numerus;* the numeral differences of diseases, by which they were distinguished.

A'RK (*Geom.*) vide *Arc.*

ARK (*Astron.*) vide *Arc.*

ARLESPE'NNY (*Cus.*) Earnest given to servants when they were hired.

A'RLES *crudum* (*Alch.*) Drops falling in June, especially by night. *Paracel. de Grad. et Comp.*

ARM (*Anat.*) vide *Brachium.*

ARM, *fore,* that part lying between the elbow and the wrist.

ARM *presentation* (*Mid.*) when the arm of the child comes foremost.

ARM *of a horse* (*Men.*) the fore thigh.

ARM (*Mar.*) each extremity of a bibb or bracket.—*Arm of an anchor,* that part of an anchor on which the palm is shut. [vide *Anchor*]

ARM *of the sea* (*Geog.*) when the sea runs any way into the land.

ARM (*Her.*) the human arm is borne in coat armour, either erect or cubit, i. e. couped at the elbow, or embowed in armour, that is, couped at the shoulder, bent, grasping a military standard, and the like, as in the annexed figure. " Field argent, a fess embattled; base a chevron indented; *gules* between three boars' heads, erased *azure;* out of the embattlements in chief issuant a dexter arm embowed in armour, encircled by a wreath of laurel, and the hand grasping a stand of military colours, representing the invincible standard of the French taken in Egypt." These are the arms of the distinguished general Sir Ralph Abercrombie.

TO ARM (*Men.*) the action of a horse when he endeavours to defend himself against the bit, to prevent being checked thereby.

TO ARM *a shot* (*Gun.*) to roll rope, yarn, &c. about the end of the iron bar which passes through the shot.

A'RMA (*Ant.*) vide *Militia.*

ARMA (*Archæol.*) vide *Arms* and *Armour.*

ARMA *dare* (*Law*) to dub a knight.—*Arma capere vel suscipere,* to be made a knight.—*Arma deponere,* a punishment enjoined when a man had committed an offence against the king. *Walsing.* p. 507; *Orderic. Vit.* l. 8, *de Hen.* &c.—*Arma libera,* a sword and a lance usually given to a servant when he was made free. *Leg. Wil. apud Brompt.*—*Arma moluta,* sharp weapons, that cut instead of bruising, called by Fleta *arma emolita. Brac.* l. 3; *Flet.* l. 1, c. 38, &c.—*Arma reversata,* a punishment inflicted on one convicted of treason or felony, as in the case of Hugh Spenser, mentioned by our historian Knighton. " Primo vestierunt eum uno vestimento cum armis suis reversatis." *Knight,* l. 3, p. 2546.

ARMA (*Bot.*) arms, weapons of defence, as thorns, stings, &c.

ARMA'DA (*Mar.*) a Spanish name for a fleet of men of war, and applied in particular to that of the Spaniards destined for the invasion of England in the reign of Elizabeth.

ARMADI'LLA (*Mar.*) a small squadron in Span'sh America.

ARMADI'LLO (*Zool.*) a creature of the amphibious kind in the West Indies, whose body is covered with a bony shell-like armour; the *Dasypus* of Linnæus.

A'RMALA (*Bot.*) Wild Rue.

ARMA'LGOL (*Chem.*) the same as *Corallium.*

ARMAME'NTA (*Ant.*) all kinds of tools for husbandry.—*Armamenta navium,* the tackling of the ship. *Tac. Hist.* l. 5, c. 23.

ARMAMENTA'RIUM (*Ant.*) an armoury, or a storehouse for ordnance and shipping; " Aperire armamentarium jussit, rapta statim arma, &c." *Tac. Hist.* l. 1, c. 38.

ARMAND (*Vet.*) a confection to prevent or cure the loss of appetite in horses.

ARMA'RIUM (*Ant.*) from *arma;* a storehouse for all sorts of arms or utensils.

ARMATU'RA (*Ant.*) from *armo,* to arm; the military exercise in use among the Romans which consisted either in throwing the spear or javelin, shooting with the bow, &c.

ARMATURA, also a denomination given to the soldiers in the emperor's retinue.

ARMATU'RE (*Archit.*) a French word comprehending the bars, iron pins, stirrups, and all the iron holdfasts used in carpentry.

A'RME (*Mil.*) a French term for any distinct body of armed men.—*Arme blanche* signifies a sword or bayonet; *arme à feu*, fire-arms, *arme de trait*, a bow or cross-bow.

ARME (*Anat.*) ἁρμός, from ἅρω, to fit, *apto*; a joining of the parts of the body; a coalition of wounds in general; the joining of the sutures of the head. *Gal. in Exeg.; Erot. Lex. Hippocrat.; Hesychius.*

A'RMED (*Mil.*) an epithet signifying generally provided with or carrying arms, as an armed body of men, *i. e.* a military detachment provided with arms and ammunition for an engagement.

ARMED (*Mar.*) an epithet for a bar-shot, &c. when rope-yarn is rolled about the end of the iron-bar which runs through the shot.—*Armed ship*, that which is fitted out and provided in all respects for a man of war.

ARMED (*Her.*) an epithet in blazoning for lions, eagles, cocks, &c. painted with their respective arms, as claws, talons, spurs, &c. of different tincture from that of their bodies.

ARMED *loadstone* (*Nat.*) when it is capped, cased, or set in iron to make it take up a greater weight.

A'RMENA (*Surg.*) τὰ ἁρμενα, a whole surgical apparatus, or the whole apparatus for bathing, &c. *Hippocrat. de Rat. Vict. in Morb. acut.; Hesychius.*

ARMENI'ACA *malus* (*Bot.*) the Apricot-tree, the *Prunus Armeniaca* of Linnæus. *Ger. Herb.; J. Bauh. Hist. Plant.; Raii Hist. Plant. &c.*

ARMENI'ACUM (*Bot.*) ἀρμενιακόν, *Armeniaca malus*, the Prunus Armeniaca of Linnæus. *Dioscor.* l. 1, c. 165; *Plin.* l. 15, c. 12; *Oribas Med. Collect.* l. 2, c. 48; *Paul. Æginet. de Re Med.* l. 1, c. 82; *Act. de Spir. Anim. Nat.* c. 6.

ARME'NIAN *stone* (*Min.*) Ἀρμένιον, *Armenus lapis*, an opake sort of stone of a greenish blue colour like the *lapis lazuli*. It is used as a purgative. *Dioscor.* l. 5, c. 105; *Aet. Tetrab.* serm. 2, c. 12; *Act. de Urin. Differ.* c. 9.—*Armenian Bole*, a native bole or earth brought from Armenia commonly called Bole Armoniac. It is a fat kind of earth of considerable use as an absorbent, astringent, and vulnerary.

ARME'NIANS (*Eccl.*) a denomination of professing Christians in Armenia who formed two sects; one which adhered to the catholic church, and another which rejected the episcopacy.

ARME'RIA (*Bot.*) Meadow pink; a plant, the flowers of which are good as an alexipharmic. In the Linnæan system it is the *Dianthus barbatus*.

ARME'RIUS *flos* (*Bot.*) The Silene armeria of Linnæus. *Dodon. Stirp. Hist.*

A'RMES *à l'épreuve* (*Mil.*) a French phrase for armour of polished steel.—*Armes à la légère*, light-armed troops.—*Armes au pied!* ground arms!

ARMIGER (*Ant.*) ὁπλοφόρος, ὁπλίτης, an Armour-bearer.

ARMIGER (*Law*) Knight or Esquire; a title of dignity to such gentlemen as bear arms; they are of two kinds.—*Armiger by courtesy*, as sons of noblemen, eldest sons of knights, &c.—*Armiger by creation*, such as the king's servants, &c.

ARMIGER (*Cus.*) the higher servants in convents.

ARMI'LLA (*Ant.*) a bracelet or ornament for the wrist presented as a badge of distinction to soldiers. *Liv.* l. 1, c. 2; l. 10, c. 44; *Plin.* l. 10, c. 15; *Fest. de Verb. Signif.; Isidor. Orig.* l. 19, c. 31.

ARMILLA (*Polit.*) one of the coronation garments.

ARMILLA (*Mech.*) an iron ring, hoop, or brace, wherein the gudgeons of a wheel move. *Vitruv.* l. 10, c. 6.

ARMILLA (*Anat.*) a circular ligament comprehending the manifold tendons of the whole hand as it were in a circle. *Castell Lex Med.*

ARMI'LLARY *sphere* (*Astron.*) an artificial sphere so called from *armilla*, a bracelet, or ring, because it is composed of a number of circles of metal, wood, or paper, representing the several circles of the sphere of the world put together in their natural order. [vide *Astronomy*] *Armillary trigonometer*, an instrument invented by Mr. Munro Murray, and improved by Mr. Ferguson, consisting of five semicircles divided and graduated so as to serve for the expeditious resolution of many problems in astronomy.

ARMILLA'TI *cursores* (*Ant.*) runners, or posts, wearing bracelets by way of a badge.

ARMI'LLUM (*Ant.*) *vas quod armo*, i. e. *humero deportetur*, a wine vessel, carried in sacrifices on the shoulders.

ARMILU'STRUM (*Ant.*) *ab armis lustrandis*, a solemn feast at Rome, in which all the people being armed went to the sacrifices at the sound of the trumpet. *Varr. de Lat. Ling.* l. 4, c. 32; *Fest. de Verb. Signif.*

A'RMING-*Buckle* (*Her.*) a buckle in the shape of a lozenge.

ARMI'NIANISM (*Ecc.*) the doctrines of one Arminius, a professor of Leyden, who maintained certain tenets respecting free-will, the atonement, &c. in 1603, which were condemned by the synod of Dort.

ARMI'SCARA (*Law*) a sort of punishment imposed upon an offender by the judge. *Malmsb.* l. 3; *Walsingh.* p. 430.

ARMI'STICE (*Mil.*) *armistitilum*, i.e. *sistere ab armis*, a temporary cessation of arms.

A'RMLET (*Geog.*) a small arm or branch of a sea, river, &c.

ARMLET (*Mil.*) a piece of armour for the arm.

ARMO'NIAC (*Chem.*) the same as *Ammoniac*.

A'RMOR (*Law*) or *arms*; any thing that a man either wears for his defence, or takes into his hand in his anger, to strike or throw at another. *Comp. Inst.* 65.

A'RMORER (*Mar.*) an officer who takes charge of the arms in a vessel.

A'RMORINGS (*Mar.*) the same as waste clothes.

ARMO'RIAL (*Her.*) an epithet for what belongs to coat armour, as armorial bearings, armorial ensigns, &c.

ARMO'RUM *pugna* (*Ant.*) a sort of gymnastics used formerly by the Romans as a military exercise. *Orib. Med. Coll.* l. 6, c. 36.

A'RMORY (*Her.*) the art of blazoning and marking all coats of arms.

ARMORY (*Mil.*) the place where armour and arms are kept.

A'RMOUR (*Mil.*) a name for all such habiliments as serve to defend the body from wounds, as helmets, cuirasses. A suit of armour formerly consisted of a helmet, a shield, a cuirasse, a coat of mail, a gantlet, &c.—*Armour-bearer*, the person who was formerly employed to carry the armour of another.

A'RMOURER (*Mil.*) the person who makes and deals in arms.

A'RMOURERS' *Company* (*Her.*) a company in the city of London which was incorporated in the beginning of the reign of Henry VI; the king himself being pleased to be free of their company. Their arms are *argent* on a chevron *gules*, a gauntlet between four swords in saltire on a chief *sable*, a buckler *argent*, charged with a cross gules betwixt two helmets of the first. Their crest is a man demi-armed at all points surmounting a torce and helmet. Their motto " Make all sure."

A'RMOURY (*Mil.*) a storehouse for arms.

A'RMS (*Mil.*) any kind of weapon that is used either for offence or defence.—*Arms of offence* include *fire-arms*, or those which are discharged by fire, *swords, bayonets*, &c.—*Arms of defence* consist of shields, helmets, coats of mail, and every species of repulsive or impenetrable covering.—*Bells of arms*, or *Bell-tents*, a kind of tents in the shape of a cone where the company's arms are lodged in the field.—*Arms of parade* or *courtesy*, those used in ancient justs and tournaments, as unshod lances, swords without edge, wooden swords, &c.—*Pass of arms*, a kind of combat in which ancient cavaliers undertook to defend a pass against all attacks.—*Stand of arms*, a complete set of

ARM

arms for one soldier.—*Place of arms*, a part of the covert way opposite to the re-entering angle of the counterscarp projecting outward in an angle.

ARMS (*Mech.*) the two ends of an axle-tree in a carriage.

ARMS (*Her.*) or coats of arms; any signs of arms, or armour, painted on shields, targets, banners, &c. and denoting some act or quality of the bearer.

Arms are of various kinds, as—*Arms of dominion*, borne by kings and emperors.—*Arms of pretension*, borne by sovereigns who are not in possession of the dominions they represent, as the arms of France formerly quartered in those of England.—*Arms assumptive*, such as a man may of right assume with the approbation of his sovereign, as in the annexed figure. " The field is *argent*, on a bend *gules* between three pellets, as many swans proper, rewarded with a canton sinister azure, thereupon a demi-ram mounting *argent* armed, *or* between two fleurs de lis of the last, over all a baton dexterwise, as the second in the canton." This is the arms of Sir John Clarke; the canton was the arms of the Duke of Longueville, which being granted to Sir John Clarke as a reward for taking prisoner Lewis de Orleans, Duke of Longueville, are what is called *Arms assumptive*.—*Arms of patronage*, such as governors of provinces, &c. add to their arms.—*Arms of alliance*, such as are taken by the issues of heiresses to show their descent, paternal and maternal.—*Arms of succession*, taken by those who inherit certain fiefs or manors.—*Arms of adoption*, those taken from another family to be quartered with the paternal one.—*Arms paternal and hereditary*, such as are transmitted from the first obtainer to his son, grandson, great grandson, &c.—*Arms of concession*, augmentations granted by sovereigns.—*Arms canting* or *allusive*, whose figures allude to the names, professions, &c. as a *trevet* for a person named Trevet, three covered cups for one named Butler, &c.

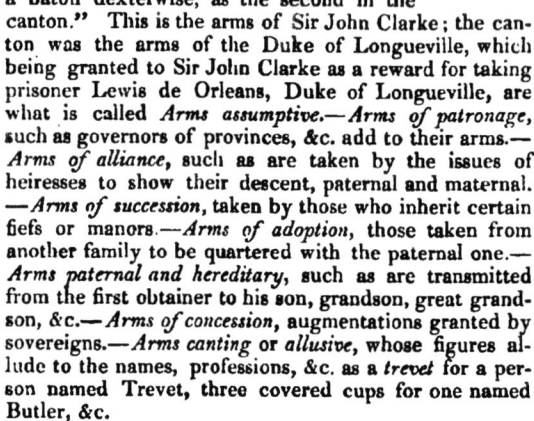

Arms vary also according to the mode of marshalling, as the arms of a husband and wife, &c. of which farther account may be seen under the head of *Heraldry* or *Marshalling*.

ARMS (*Falcon.*) the legs of a bird of prey from the thighs to the feet.

A'RMY (*Ant.*) vide *Militia*.

ARMY (*Mil.*) is a term used either in a general or a particular sense. *Army*, in a general sense, is taken for the whole armed force raised for the defence of the country by land. The English army consists of the—*Militia*, which is raised for home service and by ballot.—*Volunteers*, those who volunteer their services to government on particular occasions.—*Fencibles*, raised by enlisting for a limited time and a particular service.—*Regulars*, enlisted without any limitation of time or place. They are so called because they are better disciplined, and consequently rank higher than any other force. They are also termed the *line*, because they act in a more compact body. Formerly there were foreign troops called *mercenaries*, because they served for hire; otherwise named *routers* or *ryters*, i.e. horsemen, Brabançons, Provençales, Colerelli, and Flemings.

Army, in a limited sense, signifies a body of troops completely equipped and disciplined for service, whence it is mostly confined in its application to the Regulars. An army is generally divided into three corps, each consisting of *Brigades*, *Regiments*, *Battalions*, and *Squadrons*. The first corps is called the *front line*, a part of which forms the *vanguard*, the second the *main body*, and the third the *rear-guard*, or corps of reserve. The whole is under the command of one general, who is styled, by distinction, the *Commander in Chief*. The officers under him are *general-officers*, *field-officers*, *staff-officers*, and *subalterns*. The soldiers are called *privates*, common men, or *rank and file*, in distinction from the officers. They are moreover distinguished, according to the nature of their service or their equipment, into *horse* or *foot*, otherwise called *infantry* or *cavalry*. The cavalry consists of *hussars*, or *light horse*, and *heavy horse*.—*Dragoons* are soldiers serving either on foot or on horseback.—*Marines* are soldiers trained up to serve at sea.—*Artillerymen* serve the artillery.—*Guards* are those who protect the king's person, and consist of the *life-guards*, the *horse-guards*, and the *foot-guards*, which are collectively called *household troops*.—*Grenadiers*, so called because they were formerly trained in the art of throwing hand grenades, are a picked body of men, distinguished by their size and dress.—*Riflemen*, or *sharp-shooters*, those who are exercised particularly in the use of the rifle, and in sharp-shooting.—*Fusileers*, are so called from the fusil which they carry, and *musketeers* from the *musket*: the latter term is no longer in use.—*Men at arms* were those formerly who were equipped in a complete suit of armour.—*Pioneers*, those who are employed during the march in mending the roads, cutting down hedges, &c.

The exercising of soldiers in military movements and discipline is called *drilling*; those who are so trained are called *recruits*; the person training is the *drill serjeant*; the exercise in which they are trained is either manual or platoon. The *manual exercise* teaches the use of the firelock, and the movements of the body; the *platoon exercise* is that which is performed in companies. When soldiers are brought to act together in large bodies, they go through a variety of manœuvres. The duties of a soldier are various, according as he is in camp, in garrison, or in quarters, in the field of battle, or at a siege. In all cases they move by certain signals, either from the beat of the drum, or the sound of the trumpet, the former of which is called the *beat*, and the latter the *sounding*. The beats of the drum are differently named, according to the purpose for which it is beaten; as, the *general*, for a general march; the *reveillé*, at break of day for the soldiers to rise; the *assembly*, or *troop*, for the troops to assemble, &c. [vide *Beat*] The soundings are also differently named: as *butte sella*, put on your saddles; *monte caballo*, mount on horseback, &c.

The *materiel* of an army, as the French term it, consists of the horses, cannon, stores, provisions, and every thing necessary for service.

Armies are moreover distinguished, according to their service, into the—*Covering army*, which is used to cover and protect every place.—*Blockading army*, which is employed to invest a town, so as to reduce it by assault or famine.—*Army of observation*, an army employed in watching the movements of an enemy.—*Army of reserve*, an army which is reserved, or kept apart, for any particular exigency, as to renew an engagement in case of defeat, to secure a victory, and the like.—*Flying army*, a strong body of horse and foot, always in motion to protect its own army.

ARNA'LDIA (*Med.*) from ἄρς, a lamb, because lambs were subject to it, a malignant disease, attended with an Alopecia; a kind of Lues venerea.

ARNA'LIA (*Archæol.*) Arable lands. *Dooms-day book.*

A'RNAUTS (*Mil.*) Turkish light cavalry, whose only weapon was a sabre.

A'RNICA (*Bot.*) a genus of plants, Class 19 *Syngenesia*, Order 2 *Polygamia*, *Superflua*, called *Doronicum* by Bauhin.

Generic Characters. CAL. common imbricate; *leaflets* lanceolate.—COR. compound radiate.—STAM. *filaments* very short; *anthers* cylindric.—Pist. *germ* oblong; *style* simple; *stigma* bifid.—Per. none; *calyx* unchanged; *seeds* solitary; *down* simple; *receptacle* naked.

Species. The species are mostly perennials or shrubs, as—*Arnica montana Doronicum*, or *Caltha alpina*, the Mountain Arnica.—*Arnica scorpioides*, or *Aster scorpioides*, Alternate-leaved Arnica.—*Arnica maritima*, *Aster* or *Helenium maritimum*, Sea Arnica. &c. *Clus. Pann.; Dod. Pempt.; C. Bauh. Pin.; Raii Hist. Plant.*

ARNOGLO'SSUM (*Bot.*) ἀρνόγλωσσον, from ἀρήν, a lamb, and γλῶσσα, a tongue; a species of the *Plantago* of Linnæus. *Theophrast.* l. 7, c. 10.

ARNO'LDISTS (*Ecc.*) the followers of one Arnold of Brescia, who set themselves up against the Roman pontiff.

ARNO'TTO (*Bot.*) or Anata, the *Bixa orihlana* of Linnæus. [vide *Anata*]

A'RNOTTS (*Bot.*) the roots of a plant frequently turned up in ploughing, resembling a chesnut when roasted. They seem to be the roots of a species of *Bunium*.

A'ROBE (*Com.*) a Portuguese measure for sugar, equal to twenty-five bushels.

ARO'MA (*Bot.*) ἄρωμα, from ἀρόω, aro; all sweet spices, but particularly myrrh.

Aroma (*Alch.*) another name for *Aroph*.

AROMATA'RIUS (*Archæol.*) a Grocer.

AROMA'TICA (*Bot.*) from ἄρωμα, all fragrant things, as spices, herbs, seeds, &c.; also confects or pills, made of aromatic herbs.

AROMATI'TES (*Nat.*) ἀρωματίτης: 1. *vinum aromate consitum*, Hippocras, or wine brewed with spices. *Dioscor.* l. 5, c. 64—5; *Plin.* l. 14, c. 16. 2. A precious stone, in colour and smell resembling myrrh. *Plin.* l. 37, c. 10.

A'RON (*Bot.*) vide *Arum*.

ARO'NIA (*Bot.*) a species of the *Mespilus* of Linnæus.

A'ROPH (*Alch.*) 1. A Lithontriptic medicine prepared by distillation. *Parac. de Vir. Memb.* l. 2, c. 10. 2. The flowers raised by sublimation of equal portions of Lapis Hæmatitis and Sal Ammoniac. *Parac.* 3. A distillation of saffron and bread. *Van. Helm. de Lithias.* c. 7.

ARO'TUS (*Theol.*) and *Marotus*, two Angels; so called by the Mahometans, whom they believe to have been sent from heaven to teach men their duty.

A'ROUGHCAIN (*Zool.*) an animal in Virginia resembling the beaver.

A'RPA (*Mus.*) Italian for a harp.—*Arpa dopper*, a double harp.

ARPA'GIUS (*Med.*) a name for one who died in his cradle.

ARPE'GGIO (*Mus.*) or *Argo*, Italian for a mark in Music, signifying that the movement of the several notes must be heard not together, but one after another in the style of harp music.—*Arpeggio accompaniment* consists chiefly of the notes of the several chords taken in returning successions.

A'RPEX (*Law*) or *Arpente*, an acre or furlong of ground equal to 100 perches. *Doomsday Book*.

ARPENTA'TOR (*Law*) a measurer or surveyor of land.

ARQUA'TUS *morbus* (*Med.*) the jaundice; so named from its resembling the colour of the rainbow.

ARQUEBUSA'DE (*Med.*) Aqua Sclopetaria.

A'RQUEBUSE (*Mil.*) in French *Arquebuse*, a large hand gun, somewhat bigger than our musket.

ARQUEBU'SIER (*Mil.*) a soldier that bears an arquebuse.

A'RRAC (*Com.*) a spirituous liquor distilled in India from the Cocoa-tree, rice, or sugar Mort; also, in Tartary, from Mares' milk; this liquor is very strong, and intoxicates more than rum or brandy.

Arrac (*Bot.*) another name for the *Oryza* and *Palma* of Linnæus.

A'RRACH (*Bot.*) vide *Arach*.

ARRA'CHE (*Her.*) erased or torn up by the roots.

A'RRAGONITE (*Min.*) a species of calcareous salt.

ARRAIA'TIO *peditum* (*Law*) arraying the foot soldiers.

ARRA'IERS (*Law*) *arraitores*, officers who had the charge of the soldiers' armour.

To ARRA'IGN *a writ of assize* (*Law*) to cause the demandant to be called to make the plaint, and to set the cause in such order as the tenant may be forced to answer thereunto.—*To arraign a prisoner*, to bring him forth to trial, read the indictment to him, and put the question of guilty or not guilty. *Co. Lit.* 262, &c.

A'RRAPHON (*Anat.*) ἄρραφον, from α, priv. and ῥάπτω, to knit together; an epithet signifying without a suture, applied to the cranium when it is so disposed, whether naturally or apparently.

A'RRAS *Hangings* (*Com.*) Tapestry made at Arras, in the county of Artois, in Flanders.

ARRA'Y (*Mil.*) the drawing up, or ranging of soldiers in order of battle.

Array (*Law*) the setting forth a jury impanelled upon a cause F. N. B. 157.—*To challenge an array*, to except at once against all the persons arrayed or impanelled. If the sheriff be of affinity to either of the parties, or for any other partiality, the *array* shall be *quashed*. *Co. Lit.* 156, &c.

ARRA'YERS (*Mil.*) vide *Arraiers*.

ARREA'RAGE (*Law*) arrears; money unpaid at the due time: as rent, moneys in hand, or arrears of an account, pensions, and the like.

ARRECTA'TUS (*Law*) suspected of any crime. *Offic. Coronat.*

ARRE'CTED (*Law*) reckoned, considered. *Inst.* 173.

ARRENA'TUS (*Law*) Arraigned. *Rot. Parl.* 21. *Ed.* 1.

ARRENTA'TION (*Law*) *ad certum reditum dimittere*; licencing the owner of lands in the forest to enclose them with a hedge and a little ditch, under a yearly rent.—*Saving the arrentation*, saving the power to give such licences. *Ord. Forest.* 34 *Ed.* 1. st. 5.

ARREPHO'RIA (*Ant.*) ἀρρηφόρια, a festival in honour of Minerva, celebrated at Athens in the month Scirrophorion. It is so called ἀπὸ τῶ ἄρρητα φέρειν, i. e. because certain mysterious things were carried about by four noble virgins. *Harpocration.; Suidas.; Etymologicon. Magnum.*

ARRE'ST (*Law*) *arrestum*, in French *arrêter*. 1. The restraint of a man's person by the lawful warrant of some court of record, or officer of justice. 2. The decree of a court, by which a man is arrested. An arrest in a civil case must be by virtue of a precept; but, in a criminal case, it may be done without a warrant. *Wood's Inst.* 575.—*Arrest of judgment*, a staying of judgment. To move an *arrest* of judgment, is to show cause why judgment should be stayed, notwithstanding verdict given. 2 *Inst.* 210.—*Arrest of inquest*, is to plead in arrest of taking the inquest upon a former issue, and to show cause why an inquest should not be taken.

ARRESTA'NDIS *bonis ne dissipentur* (*Law*) a writ for him whose cattle or goods, being taken during a controversy, are likely to be wasted and consumed. *Reg. Orig.* 126.

ARRESTA'NDO *ipsum qui pecuniam recipit, &c.* (*Law*) a writ for the apprehension of him who hath taken the king's prest money to serve in the wars, and hides himself when he should go. *Reg. Orig.* 24.

ARRE'STMENT (*Law*) the command of a judge in the Scotch law, discharging any person in whose hands the debtor's moveables are, to pay or deliver up the same, till the creditor who hath procured the arrestment to be laid on be satisfied.—*Arrestment jurisdictionis fundandæ causâ*, an arrestment which is used to bring a foreigner under the jurisdiction of the courts of Scotland.

ARRE'STO (*Law*) *facto super bonis mercatorum alienigenorum*, a writ which lies for a denizen against the goods of aliens found in this kingdom, in recompence for goods

ARRE'STS (*Vet.*) mangy humours upon a horse's hinder legs, between the ham and the pastern.

ARRETTED (*Law*) arrectatus, i. e. *ad rectum vocatus*; convened before a judge, and charged with a crime.—*Ad rectum habere malefactorem*, is, according to Bracton, to have a malefactor forthcoming to be put to his trial. Sometimes it is used for imputed or laid to his charge; as no folly may be *arreted* to any one under age. *Bract.* l. 3, tract 2, c. 10; *Staundf. Plac. cor.* 45; *Lyt. Cap. Rom. remitter.*

A'RRHÆ (*Law*) earnest-money given in evidence of a bargain.

ARRHÆ'A (*Med.*) ἄρροια, from α, priv. and ῥέω, to flow; a retention or obstruction of the menstrual discharge. *Gal. in Exeges. Vocab. Hippocrat.*

ARRHOBONA'RII (*Ecc.*) heretics of the 16th century, who denied that the eucharist was the sign of the real flesh and blood, but only a pledge of them. *Præteol. Doct. Omn. Hæret.*

ARRHO'STIA (*Med.*) ἀῤῥωστία, infirmity or debility. *Hipp.*

ARRI'ERE-BAN (*Archæol.*) the edict of the old French and German kings, commanding all their tenants to come into the army, and in case of their refusal to be deprived of their estates.

ARRIE'RE-GUARD (*Mil.*) that part of an army which marches in the rear.

A'RRIS (*Archit.*) the intersection or line formed by the meeting of the exterior surfaces of two bodies, as the *arris of a stone*: it answers to what is vulgarly called the *edge*, which latter term in building is confined to the two surfaces of rectangular bodies, as boards, planks, &c.—*Arris fillet*, a small piece of timber, of a triangular section, used in raising the slates against chimney-shafts, or against a wall that cuts obliquely across the roof.

ARRO'NDIE (*Her.*) rounded or circular; an epithet for a tierce, as a tierce in *gyrons arrondie*.

A'RROW (*Arch.*) the well-known missile which is discharged from a bow, the pointed part of which is called the Arrow-Head. Bundles of arrows are called sheaves. [vide *Archery*]

ARROW (*Her.*) this weapon, when borne in coats of arms, is commonly said to be *barbed and feathered*, as in the subjoined *fig.* 1. The field is azure, three broad arrows; *or*, barbed and feathered *argent*; name, Hales. The arrow-head is also borne as a charge, as in *fig.* 2. The field is

Fig. 1. Fig. 2.

vert on a chevron, *argent*; three barbed arrow-heads, *sable*, by the name of Keymis, of Gloucestershire.

A'RROW-GRASS (*Bot.*) the *Triglochin* of Linnæus.—*Arrow-head*, the *Sagittaria* of Linnæus, a plant so called because its leaves resemble the head of an arrow.—*Arrow-root*, an Indian root of which starch was made. It is also employed medicinally, and is esteemed a warm alexipharmic. It is the root of the plant which by Linnæus is classed under the genus *Maranta*.—*Arrow-headed*, or Arrow-shaped, [vide *Sagittate*]

ARRU'RA (*Law*) one day's work at the plough, which the tenant was obliged to give his lord.

ARS *notoria* (*Alch.*) a pretended way of acquiring sciences by means of infusion.—*Ars transcendens*, the transcendant art, called also *Raimond Lully's art*, by which a man can dispute upon subjects in a style altogether unintelligible.

A'RSENAL (*Mil.*) a public storehouse for arms and all sorts of ammunition.

ARSE'NIATE (*Chem.*) the name of a sort of salts formed by the combination of arsenic acid with different bases, as the *arseniate* of ammonia, of potash, &c.

A'RSENIC (*Min.*) a ponderous mineral body. [vide *Arsenicum*]

ARSENIC (*Chem.*) was distinguished formerly by the character o–o ○|○

Arsenic is now distinguished into yellow, white, and red.— *Yellow arsenic* is the native arsenic dug out of the mines, which is otherwise called Arsenic ore, or the *Arsenicum nativum* of Linnæus.—*White arsenic*, or the oxyde of arsenic, is arsenic reduced to powder by the mixture of oxygen, or by exposure to the air; of this there are two sorts, namely, the *protoxide of arsenic*, or *arsenious acid*, which, when exposed to a moderate heat in contact with air, sublimes in a white powder; and the *peroxide*, or *arsenic acid*, which is formed by an additional dose of oxygen. —*Red arsenic*, otherwise called *sulphuret of arsenic*, or *realgal*, is formed by heating arsenious acid, or arsenic acid with sulphur.—*Butter of arsenic*, a composition formed of arsenic and corrosive sublimate; it is otherwise called *chloride of arsenic*, because it may be prepared of arsenic and chlorine gas.—*Arsenic bloom*, another name for an arseniate, or arsenic salt, which is a sort of stone dug out of the mines in Germany.

ARSENIC acid (*Chem.*) an acid formed by the combination of arsenic with a dose of oxygen, in distinction from *arsenious acid*, which contains a less dose.

ARSE'NICAL (*Min.*) an epithet for what contains or belongs to arsenic, as *arsenical pyrites*, &c.—*Arsenical magnet*, a preparation of antimony with sulphur and white arsenic.—*Arsenical caustic*, a preparation of antimony with white arsenic.—*Arsenical solution*, a solution of arsenic with sub-carbonate of potash in distilled water.

ARSE'NICUM (*Min.*) ἀρσενικόν, arsenic; a well-known mineral, called by Aristotle σανδαράχη, by Theophrastus ἀῤῥενικόν, by the Romans *orpimentum* and *arsenicum*; it is a reddish-coloured ponderous, caustic, corrosive, and highly poisonous substance; which was used by the ancients in medicine and painting. *Aristot. de Hist. Anim.* l. 8, c. 24; *Theophrast.; Dioscor.* l. 5, c. 121; *Plin.* l. 34, c. 18; *Cels. de Re Med.* l. 5, c. 5; *Gal. de Comp. Med. sec. Loc.* l. 4; *Oribas. Med. Collect.* l. 2; *Gorr. Def. Med.*

ARSENICUM, in the Linnean system, a genus of metals.
Generic Characters. Blueish white, soon becoming black, and falling to powder in the air; soft and extremely brittle; specific gravity 8·310.
Species. The principal species are—*Arsenicum nativum*, Native Arsenic.—*Arsenicum californa*, White Arsenic. —*Arsenicum auripigmentum, Arsenicum flavum, seu Pyrites nudus*, Orpiment, or Yellow Sulphurized Arsenic.— *Arsenicum sandaraca, Arsenicum rubrum*, Red Arsenic, or Realgar.—*Arsenicum sulphuratum*, White Mundic, or Arsenical Pyrites.—*Arsenicum albicans*, Misspickel.

A'RSENITE (*Chem.*) the name for a sort of salts formed by the combination of arsenious acid with different bases.

A'RSIS (*Gram*) ἄρσις, from αἴρω, to elevate, signifies the elevation of the voice, in distinction from the thesis or depression of the voice, corresponding to the motion of lifting up and setting down again of the foot, which the Greeks call ἄρσις and θέσις.

ARSIS (*Mus.*) and Thesis, the raising and falling of the hand as applied to the beating of time. *Schol. Anon. in*

Hermog. τις, *id.* l. 1; *Meibom. in Quintil.* l. 9, c. 4; *Prisc. de Accent.*; *Eustath. in Hom. Il.* v. 566.

A'RSMART (*Bot.*) the *Polygonum* of Linnæus.

A'RSON (*Law*) from *ardeo*, to burn; setting houses, &c. on fire, which is felony by common law. 3 *Inst.* 66.

A'RSURA (*Law*) 1. Trial of money by fire after it has been coined. 2. The diminution and loss of metal occasioned by this trial. 3. The dust and sweepings of metals that are melted down by silversmiths.

ART, the contrivance and disposal of things by the help of thought and experience, and according to prescribed rules, so as to make them serve the purposes for which they were designed.—*Liberal arts*, those which are noble and worthy to be cultivated, without regard to the lucre which they may bring; such as architecture, grammar, the military art, music, navigation, painting, poetry, &c. These are commonly distinguished by the name of the seven liberal arts.—*Mechanic arts*, those wherein the hand and body are more concerned than the mind; which are followed for the sake of the gain that accrues from them; as weaving, turnery, &c.—*A term of art*, a word used in the sense of any particular art or profession.—*Transcendant art*, otherwise called *Raymond Lully's art*, a method of descanting upon subjects in a manner so mysterious and abstruse as to be totally unintelligible.—*St. Anselm's art*, a superstitious or pretended method of curing wounds by touching the linen with which the wounds have been covered.—*The black art*, the same as magic.—*Angelic art*, a pretended method of coming at the knowledge of any thing that is desired by means of spirits or dæmons.

ART [vide *Arts*]

ART, *Terms of* (*Gram.*) any term used in the particular sense of an art or profession.

ART *and Part* (*Scotch Law*) when, in the commission of a crime, the same person was both a contriver and actor.

ARTE'DIA (*Bot.*) from Mr. Artedi, a Swedish botanist, a genus of plants, Class 5 *Pentandria*, Order 2 *Digynia*.
Generic Characters. CAL. *umbel* universal, spreading.—COR. *universal* difform.—STAM. *filaments* five; *anthers* simple.—PIST. *germ* small; *styles* reflex; *stigmas* simple.—PER. none; *fruit* roundish; *seeds* two.
Species. The only species is the—*Artedia squamata*, an annual, native of Mount Lebanus.

ARTEMI'SIA (*Ant.*) Ἀρτεμισία, a festival celebrated in different parts of Greece, particularly at Delphi, where they offered a mullet to the goddess Diana, for its supposed chastity. *Liv.* l. 25, c. 23; *Athen.* l. 7, c. 21; *Hesychius.*

ARTEMISIA (*Bot.*) Ἀρτεμισία. Mother-Herb, a plant, which was reckoned of great efficacy in promoting the uterine evacuations. It is called by Apuleius *Parthenium*, and is supposed to derive its name from Ἄρτεμις, Diana, who presided over women in child-bed. *Dioscor.* l. 3, c. 127; *Plin.* l. 26, c. 5, &c.; *Apul. de Herb.* l. 10; *Oribas. Med. Coll.* l. 11; *Paul. Æginet.* l. 7, c. 3; *Kirch. Œdip. Ægyptac.* vol. 3, p. 72.

ARTEMISIA, in the Linnean system, a genus of plants, Class 19 *Syngenesia*, Order 1 *Polygamia Æqualis*, answering to the *Abrotanum* and *Absinthium* of Tournefort.
Generic Characters. CAL. *common* roundish.—COR. *compound.*—STAM. *filaments* capillary; *anthers* cylindric.—PIST. *germ* small; *style* filiform; *stigma* bifid.—PER. none; *calyx* scarcely changed; *seeds* solitary; *receptacle* flat.
Species. The plants of this genus are either undershrubs or herbs, as—*Artemisia abrotanum*, *Abrotanum vulgare*, Common Southernwood.—*Artemisia campestris*, seu *Abrotanum campestre*, Field Southernwood.—*Artemisia absinthium*, *Absinthium vulgare*, Common Wormwood.—*Artemisia pontica*, *Absinthium ponticum*, Roman Wormwood.—*Artemisia rupestris*, Creeping Wormwood.—*Artemisia vulgaris*, Mugwort.—*Artemisia dracunculus*, seu *Draco herba*, Tarragon, &c. *Dodon. Pempt.*; *J. Bauh. Hist. Plant.*; *Ger. Herb.*; *Park. Parad.*; *Raii Hist. Plant.*; *Tournef. Inst.*; *Boerh. Lugdb.*

ARTEMI'SION (*Chron.*) Ἀρτεμισίων; a month among the Macedonians when the vernal equinox commenced. *Gal. Com.* 1, *in Hippocrat. Epid.* l. 1.

ARTEMO'NIUM (*Med.*) *Abollyrium.* *Gal.*

ARTE'NNA (*Or.*) an aquatic web-footed bird, called also *Diomedea Castell. Lex. Med.*

ARTE'RIA (*Anat.*) ἀρτηρία, the Greek for Artery, was used by Hippocrates to signify what is now called the *Arteria aspera*, or Windpipe, and is derived from τηρέω, to keep, and ἀήρ, the air, because it serves as a channel for the air. The term is now applied to the conical tubes which convey the blood from the heart to all parts of the body. The arteries consist of three coats, the *external* containing blood-vessels; the *middle* consisting of elastic fibres, that contract and dilate; and the *internal*, which is a fine dense membrane that supports the fibres. By the circulation of the blood through the arteries is produced the particular motion called the pulse, which arises from the alternate dilatation of the arteries, called the *diastole*, and their contraction, called the *systole*. The time which the fibres of the arteries take in performing their systole, i. e. returning to their natural state, is the distance between two pulses. The heart discharges the blood into two great blood-vessels, called the *Arteria pulmonalis* and the *Aorta*.

The *arteria pulmonalis*, or Pulmonary Artery, rises from the right ventricle of the heart, and dividing itself to the right and left, carries the blood by innumerable ramifications through the lungs. [vide *Pulmonary Artery*]

The *Aorta* goes from the left ventricle of the heart, and is divided into the *Aorta ascendens* and the *Aorta descendens*. The *Aorta* is called *ascendens* from the point where it leaves the heart to its great curvature or arch, from which it is principally distributed to the thorax, the head, and the upper extremities. The *Aorta descendens* is the remaining part of this trunk from the arch to the *Os Sacrum*, or the Bifurcation. It is distributed to the diaphragm, abdomen, and lower extremities. From each of these divisions arise what are called original or capital branches, from which smaller branches and ramifications proceed.

Branches of the Aorta ascendens.

The capital branches from the *Aorta ascendens* are—*Arteriæ subclaviæ*, the Subclavian Arteries, which run under the clavicle, or collar-bone.—*Carotides*, the Carotids, which go from the arch of the aorta directly to the head.—*Arteriæ coronariæ*, Coronary Arteries of the heart, so called because they form a sort of crown on the basis of the heart.

The principal subordinate branches from these are from the Subclavian Arteries, the—*Mammaria interna*, the *Mediastana*, the *Pericardia*, the *Diaphragmatica minor sive superior*, *Thymica*, *Trachealis*, *Vertebrales*, *Cervicales*, and *Intercostales*. The Axillary Artillery, which is only a continuation of the Subclavian from where it goes out of the thorax to the axilla, detaches chiefly the *Mammaria externa*, *Thoracica superior et inferior*, *Scapularis externa*, *Scapularis interna*, *Humeralis*, *Musculalis*, &c.—The *Carotids* are divided into external and internal; the external sends out the *Maxillaris interna*, *Occipitalis*, *Temporalis*, *Lingualis*, &c. The internal sends out the *Ophthalmic* and middle *Cerebral Arteries*.

Branches of the Aorta descendens.

The capital branches from the *Aorta descendens* are—

In the breast, the *Bronchial, Œsophageal, Intercostal,* and *Inferior Diaphragmatic.*—Within the abdomen, the *Cœliac,* which divides into the *Hepatic,* the *Coronaria ventriculi,* and the *Splenic;* the *Mesenteric Superior* and *Inferior,* the *Emulgents,* the *Spermatics,* the *Lumbar arteries,* &c.—At the bifurcation the *Aorta* divides into the *Iliacs,* which are divided into internal and external. The internal gives off the *Sacral, Gluteal, Ischiatic,* &c; the external sends forth the *Epigastric, Femoral, Tibial,* &c. [vide *Anatomy*] Hippocrat. de Cord. &c.; Ruf. Ephes. Appell. Part. Corp. Hum. l. 2, c. 17; Gal. de Anat. Administ. l. 7, &c.; Aul. Gell. l. 18, c. 10; Philaret. de Puls. l.1, c.3,4; Oribas. Med. Coll. l.23, c.11, &c.

ARTERI'ACA (*Med.*) ἀρτηριακά, medicines against disorders in the *Anteria aspera.*

ARTERIO'TOMY (*Surg.*) ἀρτηριοτομία, the opening of an artery with a view of taking away blood. Gal. apud Oribas. Med. Coll. l. 7, c. 13; Paul. Æginet. l. 6, c. 4.

ARTETI'SCIUS (*Surg.*) one who suffers the loss of any member.

ARTHANI'TA (*Bot.*) from ἄρτος, bread; Sow Bread, a plant so called because it is the food of swine. It is of a very forcing nature, and is the *Cyclamen Europæum* of Linnæus.

A'RTHEL (*Law*) or *Ardhel,* a Welsh word for a vouchee allowed to one who was taken with stolen goods in his hand, by whom he was allowed to clear himself of the charge. This privilege occasioning a delay in the administration of justice, provision was made against it by stat. 28 Hen. 8.

ARTHE'TICA (*Med.*) or *Arthretica,* from ἄρθρον, a joint; Ground-Pine, a plant so called because it is good for the gout, and disorders in the joints.

ARTHRO'ICUM (*Med.*) an oil extracted from roots and bread digested in dung.

ARTHRE'MBOLUS (*Surg.*) ἀρθρέμβολος, from ἄρθρον, a joint, and ἐμβάλλω, to impel; an instrument for reducing luxated bones. Castell. Lex. Med.

ARTHRI'TIC (*Med.*) an epithet for what belongs to the gout.

ARTHRI'TIS (*Med.*) ἀρθρῖτις, morbis articularis, i. e. joint evil; the gout, a disorder in the joints, which, if it lie in the feet, is called *podogra;* if in the hips, *sciatica;* if in the hands, *chiragra.* Hippocrat. l. 3, aph. 6; Aret. de Caus. et Sympt. Acut. Morb. l. 2, c. 12; Cœl. Aurelian. Chron. l. 5, c. 3; Gal. de Fin. Med.

ARTHROCA'CE (*Med.*) from ἄρθρον, a joint, and κακόν, an evil; a disease in the cavity of the bone.

ARTHRO'DIA (*Anat.*) from ἄρθρον, a joint, and δέχομαι, to receive; a species of articulation, when the flat head of one bone is received into the shallow socket of another. *Winslow. Anat.*

ARTHRODY'NIA (*Med.*) vide *Rheumatism.*

A'RTHRON (*Anat.*) ἄρθρον, articulus, a joint.

ARTHROPYO'SIS (*Med.*) from ἄρθρον, a joint, and πύον, pus; an abscess or inflammation in a joint.

ARTHROPYOSIS is a genus of diseases, Class *Pyrexiæ,* Order *Phlegmasiæ,* in Cullen's Nosology.

ARTHRO'SIS (*Med.*) vide *Articulation.*

A'RTICHOKE (*Bot.*) a plant very like a thistle, with scaly heads, like the cone of a pine tree. It is the *Cynara* of Linnæus.—*Jerusalem artichoke,* a plant, the root of which resembles a potatoe, and has the taste of the artichoke. It is the *Helianthus tuberosus* of Linnæus.

A'RTICLE (*Law*) the clause or condition in a covenant.—*Lords of articles,* a committee of the Scotch Parliament, which was abolished in 1689, because it was supposed to increase too much the power of the crown.—*Articles of Roup,* the conditions under which property is exposed to sale in Scotland.

ARTICLE (*Gram.*) a part of speech which commonly serves to distinguish the gender of nouns. In modern languages it also serves to distinguish things, and is divided into the Definite and Indefinite.—*Definite article,* which in English is "The," defines and specifies some particular thing pointed out.—*Indefinite article,* which is "A," is applied in the indefinite sense to any thing.

ARTICLES (*Ecc.*) or *the thirty-nine Articles,* a name for thirty-nine points of faith which have been adopted by the "Church of England," and to which all persons must subscribe before they are admitted into Holy Orders.—*Articles of the Clergy,* statutes containing certain articles relating to the church, the clergy, and other ecclesiastical matters.

ARTICO'CCA (*Bot.*) Artichoke.

ARTICULA'RIS morbus (*Med.*) the swelling, &c. from the gout, or the gout itself.

ARTI'CULATE adjudication (*Law*) a term used in the Scotch law in cases where there is more than the debt due to the adjudging creditor, when it is usual to accumulate each debt by itself, so that any error which may arise in ascertaining one of the debts need not reach to all the rest.

ARTICULA'TED (*Bot.*) articulatus, jointed; an epithet for different parts of a plant, as—*Radix articulata,* a root which has one knob growing out of another, so that the whole seems to consist of connected members.—*Folium articulatum,* a cylindrical hollow leaf, having its cavities divided by horizontal partitions, as the *Juncus articulatus.*—*Filamentum articulatum,* a filament having a moveable joint, as in *Salvia officinalis,* the Sage.—*Lomentum articulatum,* a loment, having its transverse partitions visible on the outside, so that they may be easily divided into joints, as in *Hedysarum.*—*Pili articulati,* hairs divided into distinct members or joints, like the antennæ of some insects.

ARTICULA'TION (*Anat.*) ἄρθρωσις; the fit adjustment of the bones together, which is articulation, properly so called, in distinction from *symphisis,* the connection or keeping them together, which is another sort of articulation. Articulation is of three kinds, namely—*Diarthrosis,* when the bones are allowed a certain degree of motion—*Synarthrosis,* when the bones remain fixed in their situation; and—*Amphiarthrosis,* which is a species composed of the two preceding.

ARTICULATION (*Bot.*) 1. The springing or shooting of plants from joint to joint. 2. *Articulatio arborum,* the hurting or bruising of young vine shoots, &c. Plin. l. 17, c. 21.

ARTICULATION (*Gram.*) the articulate or distinct utterance of each syllable or sound, so as to render oneself intelligible.

ARTICULATION (*Mus.*) that distinctness and accuracy of expression which gives every sound with truth and perspicuity.

ARTICULA'TUS (*Bot.*) vide *Articulated.*

ARTI'CULI Clerici (*Ecc.*) vide *Articles.*

ARTI'CULUS (*Ecc.*) an article or complaint exhibited by way of libel in a court Christian. Sometimes the religious bound themselves to obey the ordinary without this formal process.

ARTICULUS (*Anat.*) ἄρθρον, dim. of *artus,* a limb; a joint or connexion of bones adapted for motion.

ARTICULUS *mortis* (*Med.*) the instant of death or expiration.

ARTICULUS (*Bot.*) joint; that part of a culm between two knots. Linn. Phil. Bot.

ARTICULUS (*Gram.*) vide *Article.*

ARTICULUS (*Law*) vide *Article.*

A'RTIFEX (*Med.*) the Physician who practises the art of medicine from rational principles, confirmed by experience. *Castell.*

ARTIFI'CIAL Argument (*Rhet.*) a name for those proofs or considerations that proceed from the genius, industry, or invention of the orator; such are definitions, causes, effects, &c.

ARTIFICIAL *Lines* (*Geom.*) lines so contrived on a sector as to represent the logarithmal lines and tangents.—*Artificial numbers*, logarithmical numbers relating to sines, tangents, and secants.

ARTIFICIAL *Day* (*Astron.*) that space of time which intervenes between the rising and setting of the sun, in distinction from the night, when he is under the horizon.

ARTIFICIAL (*Chem.*) a name for whatever is prepared from cinnabar, &c.

ARTILLERY (*Mil.*) in a general sense, implies all sorts of great guns, mortars, howitzers, petards, &c., together with all the apparatus and stores which are requisite for service in the field, at sieges, &c.; but in a particular sense it implies the science of artillery and gunnery.—*Train of artillery*, a train formed of the attendants and carriages which follow the artillery into the field.—*Park of artillery*, the place set apart by the general for the depot of guns, ammunition, and stores, to be in readiness, as occasion may require.—*Honourable Artillery Company*, a band of infantry, consisting of 600 men, of which the Prince of Wales for the time being is always colonel. This corps forms part of the militia, or city guard, of London.

ARTISCOCCUS *lævis* (*Bot.*) the same as the *Cinara* of Linnæus.

ARTISCUS (*Med.*) ἀρτίσκος, from ἄρτος, bread; a troche made in the form of a loaf; but particularly that which is made of viper's flesh. *Castell. Lex. Med.*

ARTIST, a proficient in the liberal arts, in distinction from *artisan*, or one who follows one of the mechanic arts.

ARTIST (*Chem.*) a term used by Paracelsus and others for a chemist and an alchymist.

ARTOCARPUS (*Bot.*) from ἄρτος, bread, and καρπός, fruit, Bread-fruit Tree; a genus of plants; Class 21 *Monoecia*, Order 1 *Monandria*.
Generic Characters. CAL. none.—COR. to each two petals.—STAM. filament filiform; anther oblong.—PIST. germs very many; *style* to each filiform; *stigma* single.—PER. fruit ovate-globular; seeds oblong.
Species. The species are—*Artocarpus incisa*, *Sitodium incisum*, *Radermachia incisa*, *Soccus lanosus*, seu *granosus*, in French *Le Rima ou Fruit à Pain*, Bread-fruit Tree, Native of the Molucca Islands.—*Artocarpus integrifolia*, *Sitodium macrocarpon*, seu *cauliflorum*, *Radermachia integra*, *Soccus arboreus*, seu *Tojacca-maram Indica*, Indian Jaca Tree, a shrub, native of the East Indies.—*Artocarpus Philippensis*, a shrub, native of the Phillippine Islands.—*Artocarpus pubescens*, *Ansjeli*, seu *Castanea Malabarica*, a shrub, native of Malabar. *Linn. Spec. Plant.*

ARTOCREAS (*Med.*) from ἄρτος, bread, and κρέας, flesh; a pasty.

ARTOMELI (*Med.*) a Cataplasm, from ἄρτος, bread, and μέλι, honey.

ARTOPTA (*Med.*) from ἄρτος, bread, and ὀπτάω, to bake; a vessel for baking a pye or pudding; applied metaphorically to women who have easy labours. *Castell.*

ARTOS (*Med.*) ἄρτος, bread; the different sorts of which, mentioned by Hippocrates and Galen, are as follow:—ἄρτος ἄζυμος, unleavened bread, most nourishing.—Ἄρτος δίπυρος, bread twice baked, prescribed in the dropsy.—Ἄρτος ἔξοπτος, toasted bread prescribed in a dysentery.—Ἄρτος ἐσχαρίτης, bread baked on a hearth, a very bad sort.—Ἄρτος ζυμίτης, leavened bread, light but not nutritive.—Ἄρτος καθαρός, bread made of fine flour.—Ἄρτος κλιβανίτης, testaceous bread, so called from κλίβανος, a moveable oven, the vessel in which it was baked; it was very dry but not nourishing.—Ἄρτος ἐγκρυφίης, subcinericious bread baked under the embers, which was the worst sort.—Ἄρτος ὀβελίας, bread spitted and roasted, which was rather nutritious.—Ἄρτος σιμιδαλίτης, bread made of fine flour, mentioned by Hippocrates, Galen, and Athenæus, as very nutritious.—Ἄρτος ἐκ χόνδρου, bread made of alica, which was extremely nourishing.—Ἄρτος σιλιγνίτης, bread made of *siligo*, the purest and finest flour; this was a Roman bread, and the most nutritive of all.—Ἄρτος αὐτοπυρίτης, bread of the wheat itself, or unsifted meal, which was reckoned the least nutritive of all. *Hippocrat. de Vict. in acut. Morb.* l. 2, &c.; *Gal. Exeges. et de Alim. Fac.* l. 1; *Athen. Deipnos.* l. 3; *Gorr. Def. Med.*; *Foes. Œconom. Hippocrat.*

ARTOTYRITÆ (*Ecc.*) *panem et caseum offerentes*, heretics in the second century offering bread and cheese at the communion. *Epiphan. Hæres.* 49; *S. Augustin. Hæres.* 27; *Baron. Annal. Ann.* 173; *Du Pin. Bibl. des Aut. des premiéres Siécles.*

ARTUS (*Anat.*) *quod membra membris artentur*, 1. A limb. τὰ κῶλα, the extreme and most compacted parts of the body. *Fest. de Verb. Signific.*; *Castell. Lex. Med.* 2. A joint, the members of which extend themselves from the trunk, and are divided into joints. *Castell.*

ARVALES (*Ant.*) the twelve priests appointed by Romulus to celebrate the festival of the Ambarvalia. *Plin.* l. 18, c. 2; *Aul. Gell.* l. 6, c. 7; *Fulgent. de Prisc. Sermon.*

ARVIL (*Archæol.*) *Arval*, or *Arfal*, funeral rites.—*Arvil supper*, a funeral entertainment formerly made in the northern parts of England.—*Arvil bread*, bread given to the poor at a funeral.

ARUM (*Bot.*) ἄρον, Cuckow-Pint; a plant probably so called from ἱερόν, sacred. It has leaves like the *Dracunculus*, which it resembles also in its medicinal virtues. *Diosc.* l. 2, c. 197; *Plin.* l. 24, c. 16.

ARUM, *in the Linnean system*, a genus of plants, Class 21 *Monoecia*, Order 9 *Polyandria*.
Generic Characters. CAL. spathe one-leaved.—COR. none.—STAM. filaments none; anthers sessile.—PIST. germ each obvate; style none; stigma bearded with villose hairs.—PER. berry globular; seeds several.
Species. The species are mostly perennials, as—*Arum crenitum*, seu *muscivorum*, seu *dracunculus*, Hairy-sheathed Arum.—*Arum dracunculus*, *Dracontium*, seu *Dracunculus polyphyllus*, Long-sheathed Arum, or Common Dragon.—*Arum Dracontium*, Short-sheathed Arum or Green Dragon.—*Arum esculentum*, seu *Caladium aquatile*, Esculent Arum, or Indian Kale.—*Arum maculatum*, Common Arum.—*Arum arisarum*, seu *Arisarum latifolium*, Broad-leaved hooded Arum, or Friar's Cowl, &c. *J. Bauh. Hist. Plant.*; *C. Bauh. Pin.*; *Ger. Herb.*; *Park. Theat. Bot.*; *Raii Hist. Plant.*; *Tournef. Inst.*; *Boerhaav. Ind.* &c.

ARUM is also the *Calla Æthiopica et orientalis* of Linnæus.

ARUNCO (*Zool.*) the Chili toad.

ARUNCUS (*Bot.*) from ἤρυγγος, hair hanging from the chin of goats, Goat's-beard; a species of *Spirœa* of Linnæus. *Aristot. Hist. Anim.* l. 9, c. 4; *Plin.* l. 8, c. 50.

ARUNDELIAN *marbles* (*Ant.*) ancient marbles illustrative of the history and mythology of the ancients, so called from the Earl of Arundel, by whom they were transported from the island of Paros into England. They contain the principal epochas in the Athenian history, from the first year of Cecrops, 1582 years B. C. to 354 years B. C. *Selden. Marmor. Arundel.*; *Prid. Marmor. Oxoniens.*

ARUNDINACEA (*Bot.*) reedy, an epithet for some plants.

ARUNDINETUM (*Bot.*) a place where reeds grow.

ARUNDINEUS (*Bot.*) Arundineous, abounding in reeds.

ARUNDINOSUS (*Bot.*) Arundinose, or full of reeds.

ARUNDO (*Bot.*) from *areo*, to dry; a plant so called because, *arescit*, it dries quickly. It has some medicinal virtues, particularly if applied as a powder to wounds; it attracts any matter that is lodged in them. *Plin.* l. 16, c. 35; *Oribas. de Morb. Curat.* l. 3, c. 32; *Aet. Tetrab.* l.

ARUNDO, *in the Linnean system*, a genus of plants, Class 3 *Triandria*, Order 2 *Digynia*.
Generic Characters. CAL. two-valved; *valves* oblung.—

ASA

Cor. two-valved; *valves* oblong; *nectary* two-leaved.—Stam. *filaments* three; *anthers* forked at both ends.—Pist. *germ* oblong; *styles* two; *stigmas* simple.—Per. none; *seed* single.

Species. The species are perennials, as the—*Arundo bambu*, Bambu, Mambu, *Bambos arundinacea*, Tabacir, seu *Mambu arbor*, seu *Canna*, &c. Bamboo Cane.—*Arundo donax*, seu *sativa*, Cultivated Reed.—*Arundo phragmites*, Common Reed.—*Arundo epizegos*, seu *Calamagrostis minor*, Small Reed-Grass.—*Arundo calamagrostis*, *Calamagrostis*, seu *Gramen arundinaceum*, Wood Reed-grass.—*Arundo arenaria*, seu *Spartum spicatum*, Sea Reed-grass. *J. Bauh. Hist. Plant.*; *C. Bauh. Pin.*; *Ger. Herb.*; *Park. Theat. Botan.*; *Raii Hist. Plant.*; *Tournef. Instit.*; *Boerhaav. Ind.*

Arundo is also the *Canna Indica*, the *Saccharum officinarum*, and the *Calamus rotany* of Linnæus.

Arundo (*Mech.*) the reed or instrument which separated the threads of the warp.

ARU'RA (*Law*) vide *Arrura*.

ARU'SPEX (*Ant.*) i. e. *Avispex*, because *inspexit*, he inspected the entrails of birds; a soothsayer or diviner who examined the birds, in distinction from the *augurs*, who examined the entrails, &c. of victims at the sacrifices for the purpose of divination; but the aruspex used also to examine the entrails. The college of the Aruspices grew into an order, as we learn from an inscription dug up, at Rome, in 1605; L. FONTEIUS. FLAVIANUS HARUSPEX. AUGG. CC. PONTIFEX. DICTATOR. ALBANUS. MAG. PUBLICUS HARUSPICUM ORDINI HARUSPICUM. LX. D. D. *Cic. de Div.* l. 1, c. 41; *Dionys. Hal.* l. 2; *Plin.* l. 7, c. 3; *Val. Max.* l. 1, c. 1; *Q. Curt.* l. 7, c. 7; *Herodian.* l. 4, c. 12; *Jul. Obseq. de Prodig.*; *Firmic. Astron.* l. 2; *Isid. Orig.* l. 8, c. 9; *Buleng. de Sort.*; *Ursat. de Not. Roman. apud Græv. Thes. Antiq.* vol. xi.

ARYTÆNO-EPIGLOTTI (*Anat.*) fleshy *fasciculæ* fixed to the Arytænoides and the Epiglottis.

ARYTÆNOIDES (*Anat.*) ἀρυταινοειδής, from ἀρύταινα, a cup, and εἶδος, a figure funnel shaped; Arytenoides two cartilages constituting the head of the Larynx. *Oribas. Med. Coll.* l. 24, c. 9.

ARYTÆNOIDÆI (*Anat.*) a name for some muscles of the Larynx.

ARY'THMUS (*Med.*) ἄρυθμος, from α, priv. and ῥυθμός, rhythm, signifies, properly, a modulation of time in music, but is taken also for order and harmony in other things. The word is used by Galen for the pulse not modulated according to nature, in opposition to the εὔρυθμος, or just modulation. *Gal. de Diff. Puls.* l. 1, c. 9.

A'S (*Ant.*) from *æs*, brass, because money was first coined from brass; 1. a Roman pound weight containing 12 ounces. 2. Any thing divided into equal parts, as an inheritance, land, &c. whence *ex asse hæredem facere*, to make one heir to the whole fortune.
Mart. l. vii. epig. 65.

Hæredem Fabius Labienum ex asse reliquit.

3. The smallest brass coin, as a farthing, 12 of which made a denier, equal to ¾ English money. *Var. de Lat. Ling.* l. 5; *De Vit. Pop. Roman.* l. 1, *apud Non.* l. 12, c. 50; *Plin.* l. 33, c. 3; *Columel.* l. 5, c. 3; *Vitruv. de Architect.* l. 3, c. 1; *Suet. in August.* c. 91; *Gal. de Pond.*; *Macrob. Saturn.* l. 2, c. 4; *Gronov. de Pec. Vet.*; *Salmas. in Vopisc.*; *Pætus de Vet. Ponder. &c. &c. apud Græv. Thes. Antiq.* vol. v. xi.

A'SA *dulcis* seu *odorata* (*Chem.*) vide *Benzoicum*.—*Asa fœtida*, a gum resin of a very fetid smell; which is an excellent remedy in hysterical disorders, a good sudorific and strengthener of the stomach. It is extracted from a plant

ASB

of the same name, a native of Persia. *Kempf. Amœnitat.*

Asa *fœtida* (*Bot.*) a plant from which asa fœtida is extracted. It is the *Ferula assa fœtida* of Linnæus.

ASAPHATUM (*Med.*) a sort of serpigo, or intercutaneous itch, generated in the pores like worms.

A'SAPHEIS (*Med.*) ἀσαφεῖς, obscure; applied to patients who do not utter their words distinctly. *Hipp. Prorrhet.* l. 1.

A'SAPPI (*Mil.*) vide *Azapes*.

A'SAR (*Com.*) a gold coin at Ormuz, in the Persian Gulf, worth 6s. 8d. sterling.

ASARABA'CCA (*Bot.*) the *Asarum* of Linnæus.

ASA'RCON (*Nat.*) ἄσαρκον, fleshless; applied by Aristotle to the head, in distinction from the fleshy parts.

A'SARI *pulvis compositus* (*Med.*) a powder made of the leaves of Asarum, Marjoram, Marum, and Lavender.

ASARI'NA (*Bot.*) the *Antirrhinum* of Linnæus.—*Asarina erecta*, the *Chelone penstemon* of Linnæus.

ASARI'TES (*Med.*) ἀσαρίτης, from ἄσαρον, a diuretic wine made of Asarum. *Diosc.* l. 5, c. 68.

ASARO'TA (*Ant.*) ἀσάρωτα, from α, priv. and σαρόω, to sweep; a fine pavement laid in dining-rooms of such small tiles that it appears never to be swept. They were artificially inlaid in different colours.
Stat. Sylv. l. 3, v. 85.

— varias ubi picta per artes
Gaudet humus, suberantque novis assarota figuris.

Plin. l. 36, c. 25; *Vitruv. de Architect.* l. 6, c. 5, et *Philand. ad Loc.*; *Salmas in Solin.* p. 1214; *Gyrald. Oper.* tom. 2, p. 643; *Rhodig. Antiq. Lect.* l. 21, c. 32.

A'SARUM (*Bot.*) ἄσαρον, from α, priv. and σαίρω, to adorn, Asarabacca, or Wild Spikenard; a plant so called, according to Pliny, because it was not inserted in garlands. It has leaves like ivy, and its roots are heating and diuretic. *Dioscor.* l. 1, c. 9; *Plin.* l. 12, c. 13; *Oribas. Med. Coll.* l. 11; *Aet. Tetrab.*, serm. 1; *Paul. Æginet. de Re Med.* l. 7, c. 3; *Myrep. de Antidot.*

Asarum, *in the Linnean system*, a genus of plants, Class 11 *Dodecandria*, Order 1 *Monogynia*.

Generic Characters. Cal. *perianth* one-leaved.—Cor. none.—Stam. *filaments* twelve; *anthers* oblong.—Pist. *germ* inferior; *style* cylindric; *stigma* stellate.—Per. *capsule* coriaceous; *seeds* several.

Species. The species are perennials, as the—*Asarum Europœum*, *Canadense*, and *Virginicum*. *J. Bauh. Hist. Plant.*; *C. Bauh. Pin.*; *Ger. Herb. &c.*; *Park. Theat. Botan.*; *Raii Hist. Plant.*; *Tournef. Instit.*; *Boerhaav. Ind.*

Asarum is also a species of the *Cytisus* of Linnæus. *Bauh. &c.*

ASA'SI (*Bot.*) a tree growing on the coast of Guinea, the infusion of whose leaves cures the tooth-ache.

ASBE'STINUM (*Nat.*) or *Asbestos*, ἄσβεστον, inextinguishable, from α, priv. and σβεννύμι, to extinguish; a kind of flax of which cloth was made that was cleansed by fire, as tobacco pipes are, but was not consumed. *Plin.* l. 19, c. 1; *Ferrar. de Vet. Lucern. &c. apud Græv. Thes. Antiq. Roman.* tom. 12, &c.

Asbestinum (*Mech.*) the cloth or paper which was made of the Abestinum.

ASBE'STUS (*Min.*) ἀσβεστος, inextinguishable; a kind of stone which being set on fire cannot be quenched. *Plin.* l. 37, c. 10; *Solin.* p. 7; *Isid. Orig.* l. 16, c. 4.

Asbestus, *in the Linnean system*, a genus of minerals, Class *Talcose Earths*, consisting of carbonate of magnesia, silica, and generally alumina.

Species. The species consist of such as have all their fibres parallel, as—*Asbestus amiantus*, seu *Amiantus fibrus*, Amiant, or Flexible Asbestus.—*Asbestus vulgaris*, or *Amiantus immaturus*, Common Asbestus, or Asbest; and of such as have the fibres interwoven and breaking into obtuse-angled fragments, as—*Asbestus suber, Amiantus corticosus, Asbestus fibrus flexibilibus*, seu *Suber montanum*, Elastic Asbestus, or Mountain Cork.—*Asbestus lignum*, Ligniform Asbestus.—*Asbestus caro*, seu *Amiantus corticosus flexilis*, Mountain Leather.

ASCALABO'TES (*Zool.*) ἀσκαλαβώτης, a kind of lizard. *Gal. de Simpl.* l. 2.

ASCA'LAPHUS (*Ent.*) a division of the genus Myrmeleon, according to Fabricius, comprehending those insects of this tribe having the feelers nearly equal, jaw ciliate, lip horny, rounded.

ASCA'LIA (*Bot.*) ἀσκαλία, an artichoke bottom. *Theophrast. Hist. Plant.* l. 6, c. 4; *Plin.* l. 21, c. 16.

ASCALO'NIA (*Bot.*) a kind of onion, so called from the town of Ascalon.

ASCALONI'TIDES (*Bot.*) Eschalots, or barren onions.

ASCARDAMY'CTES (*Med.*) ἀσκαρδαμύκτης, one who keeps his eyes fixed without twinkling. *Hippocrat. de Epidem.* l. 2.

ASCA'RIDES (*Ent.*) ἀσκαρίδες, from ἀσκίω, to move; small worms bred in the *intestinum rectum*, which cause by their motion a continual irritation and titillation. *Gal. Exeges. Vocab. Hippocrat.*; *Aet. Tetrab.* 1, serm. 2, c. 41; *Paul. Æginet. de Re Med.* l. 4, c. 58; *Actuar. de Meth. Med.* l. 1, c. 21.

ASCARIDES, *in the Linnean system*, a genus of insects, Class *Vermes*, Order *Intestina*.
Generic Characters. Body round, elastic; head with three vesicles; tail obtuse; intestines spiral and milk-white.
Species. The species are distinguished according to the animal which they infest, namely—Those infesting the Mammalia, *Ascaris vermicularis*, in the intestines of children; *Ascaris canis*, in the intestines of the dog, &c.; those found in birds, as *Ascaris aquilæ, cornicis*, &c. in the intestines of an eagle, crow, &c.—Those infesting reptiles, as *Ascaris testudinis lacertæ*, &c. in the intestines of the tortoise, lizard, &c.—Those infesting fishes and those infesting worms.

ASCARI'NA (*Bot.*) from *ascaris*, to which the shape of the anther is like; a genus of plants, Class 22 *Dioecia*, Order 1 *Monandria*.
Generic Character. CAL. Ament filiform.—COR. none.—STAM. filaments single.—PIST. germ globose; style none; stigma flat.—PER. drupe; seed single.
The only species is *Ascarina polystachia*, a shrub, native of the Society Isles. *Linn. Spec. Plant*.

ASCA'RIS (*Ent.*) vide *Ascarides*.

ASCAU'LES (*Ant.*) ἀσκαύλης, a bagpipe.

ASCE'NDANT (*Law*) such relations as have gone before in families reckoned upwards.

ASCENDANT (*Archit.*) an ornament in masonry and joiner's work which borders the three sides of doors, windows, and chimneys; it is otherwise called *chambranle*.

ASCENDANT (*Astrol.*) that degree of the ecliptic which rises at a person's nativity, and is supposed to have an influence on his future life. This is otherwise called the *First House*, the *Angle of the East*, the *Oriental Angle*, or the Significator of life. Hence the expression, "This or that planet ruled in his Ascendant."

ASCE'NDING (*Astron.*) an epithet applied to any star, degree, or point in the heavens, which is rising above the horizon.—*Ascending Latitude*, the latitude of a planet when going towards the North.—*Ascending Node*, that point of a planet's orbit where it crosses the ecliptic whilst proceeding northward. It is otherwise called the *Northern Node*, and is marked by the character ☊ representing a node or knot, in distinction from the descending node.—*Ascending signs*, those which are upon the ascent, or rising, from the nadir to the zenith.

ASCENDING *stem* (*Bot.*) *caulis ascendens*, that part of a plant which rises above the ground in the form of wood and leaf, in distinction from the *caulis descendens*, the descending stem or root.

ASCENDING (*Anat.*) an epithet for that part of the *aorta* from where it leaves the heart to its great curvature or arch.

ASCE'NSION *Day* (*Ecc.*) a festival observed in the Christian church ten days before Whitsuntide, in commemoration of our Saviour's ascension into Heaven. It is otherwise called *Holy Thursday*.

ASCENSION (*Astron.*) that degree of the equator reckoned from the first of Aries eastward, which rises with a star, or any point in the Ecliptic.—*Ascension* is right or oblique.—*Right ascension*, that degree of the equinoctial reckoned from Aries which rises with the sun, or a star, in a right sphere.—*Right ascension of the mid-heaven* is the right ascension of that point of the equator which is in the meridian.—*Oblique ascension*, that degree of the equinoctial reckoned from Aries which rises with the sun or a star in an oblique sphere.—*Arc of oblique ascension*, an arc of the horizon intercepted between the beginning of Aries and the point of the Equator, which rises with a star or planet in an oblique sphere. This varies with the latitude of the place.—*Refraction of ascension* [vide *Refraction* and *Astronomy*]

ASCENSIONAL *Difference* (*Astron.*) is the difference between the right and oblique ascension of the same point in the sphere; or it is the space of time the sun rises or sets before or after six o'clock.

ASCE'NSUS *morbi* (*Med.*) the ascent or increase of a disease.

ASCE'NT (*Nat.*) *Ascensus*, from *ad* and *scando*, to climb; the motion of a body tending upward.—*Ascent of fluids*, the ascent or rising of fluids in a glass tube, or any vessel, above the surface of their own level.

ASCENT (*Log.*) a sort of reasoning by which one ascends from particulars to universals.

ASCENT (*Chem.*) a sort of sublimation and *distillation*.

ASCESTE'RICUM (*Ecc.*) a Monastery.

ASCETÆ (*Ant.*) the same as *Athletæ*.

ASCETE'RIA (*Ecc.*) ἀσκητήρια, from ἀσκέω, to exercise; cloisters or places where people gave themselves up to meditation and prayers. *Theodoret.* l. 6, &c.

A'SCHIA *Thymallus* (*Ich.*) the Grayling or Umber; a sort of fish, the fat of which is used in medicine to take away specks from the eyes.

A'SCIA (*Med.*) from ἀξίνη, an axe or hatchet; a bandage in the form of the axe. *Gal. Com.* 2 in *Hippocrat. de Art*.

ASCI'DIA (*Ent.*) a genus of animals, Class *Vermes*, Order *Mollusca*, found in the sea, and adhering by their base to the rocks.
Generic Characters. Body fixed roundish.—Apertures two, one on the summit, the other lower.
Species. The species of this genus are principally found in the sea, and adhere by their base to rocks, shells, and other submarine substances. They are more or less gelatinous, and have the power of squirting out the water they take in, and alternately contracting and dilating themselves; some of them are esculent, most of them sessile, though a few are furnished with a long stalk or tubular stem.

ASCIDIFO'RMIS (*Bot.*) bottle-shaped; an epithet for the *bracteæ* in the *Ascium* and *Ruyschia*.

ASC'IDIUM (*Bot.*) the Bottle, a species of *fulcrum*, which is a foliaceous body, cylindrical, and hollow, having its mouth furnished with a complete cover that opens occasionally. It is either *sessile*, sitting, i. e. supported on a foot stalk, or *petiolatum* pedicelled, i. e. situated at the extremity of a leaf, as in the *Nepenthes distillatoria*. This body generally contains pure water.

A'SCIA (*Astron.*) ἄσκιοι, from ἀ, priv. and σκιά, shade; inhabitants of the globe having no shadow, such as those in the torrid zone, who twice a year have their sun at noon in the zenith. *Plin.* l. 2, c. 75.

ASCI'TES (*Med.*) ἀσκίτης, from ἀσκός, a bottle; a species of dropsy, distending the belly in the shape of a bottle. *Aret. de Sign. et Caus. Morb. Acut.* l. 2, c. 1; *Cels. de Re Med.* l. 3, c. 21; *Oribas. Synops.* l. 9, c. 23; *Aet. Tetrab.* 3, serm. 2, c. 21; *Paul. Æginet.* l. 3, c. 48.

Ascites has been classed by Cullen as a genus of diseases, Class *Cachexiæ*, Order *Intumescentiæ*.

ASCI'TICUS (*Med.*) ascitick; an epithet which signifies labouring under an *ascites*.

ASCI'UM (*Bot.*) a genus of plants, Class 13 *Polyandria*, Order 1 *Monogynia*.
Generic Characters. Cal. *perianth* five-leaved; *leaflets* roundish.—Cor. *petals* five.—Stam. *filaments* very many; *anthers* oblong.—Pist. *germ* ovate; *style* very short; *stigma* headed.—Per. *berry* one-celled; *seeds* very many.
Species. The species are *Ascium morantea*, a shrub, native of Guiana.—*Ascium violaceum*, a shrub, native of Guiana. *Linn. Spec. Plant.*

ASCLEPI'A (*Ant.*) Ἀσκληπιία, a festival in honour of Æsculapius, celebrated all over Greece, but with the greatest solemnity, by the Epidaurians. It was also called ἱερὸς ἀγών, the sacred contest, because poets and musicians contended for victory at this festival. *Plat. in Ion.*

ASCLEPI'ADÆ (*Biog.*) the descendants of Æsculapias, of whom Hippocrates was one in the eighteenth degree.

ASCLEPIADÆ'AN *verse* (*Poet.*) a sort of verse; so called from Asclepias, the inventor, consisting of four feet, a spondee, choriambus, and two dactyls; or a spondee, two choriambus, and a pyrrhicius.
Hor. l. 1, od. 1, v. 1.

Mæcē | nās ătăvīs | ēdĭtĕ | rēgĭbŭs.

Or, according to the second form,

Mæcē | nās ătăvīs | edĭtĕ re | gibus.

Plotin. & Mar. Vict. de Met.; *Serv. de Cent.*

ASCLE'PIAS (*Bot.*) a genus of plants, Class 5 *Pentandria*, Order 2 *Digynia*.
Generic Characters. Cal. *perianth* five-cleft.—Cor. monopetalous; *divisions* ovate-acuminate; *nectaries* five, fleshy or cowled.—Stam. *filaments* five; *anthers* oblong; *pollen* collected into ten corpuscles.—Pist. *germs* two oblong; *styles* two subulate; *stigma* common to both.—Per. *follicles*, two large oblong; *seeds* numerous; *receptacle* membranaceous.
Species. The species are mostly perennials and shrubs. Of the former kinds are the—*Asclepias Syriaca*, *Apocynum Syriacum*, seu *Beidessar*, Syrion Swallow-Wort.—*Asclepias incarnata*, seu *Apocynum Canadense*, Flesh-coloured Swallow-Wort, &c. Of the latter kind are the —*Asclepias undulata*, seu *Apocynum Africanum*, Wave-leaved Swallow-Wort.—*Asclepias gigantea*, seu *Ericu*, Curl-flowered gigantic Swallow-Wort.—*Asclepias curassaoica*, seu *Curassoa*, Swallow-Wort or Bastard Ipecacuanha, &c. *J. Bauhin. Hist. Plant.*; *C. Bauh. Pin.*; *Ger. Herb.*; *Park. Theat. Botan.*; *Raii Hist. Plant.*; *Tourn. Inst.*; *Boerh. Ind.*; *Linn. Spec. Plant.*

ASCLE'PIOS (*Med.*) 1. A dry Smegma. *Paul. Ægin.* l. 7, c. 13. 2. A troche. *Aet. Tetrab.* 4, serm. 2, c. 50. 3. A Collyrium. *Gal. Ex. Scribon.*

ASCODROGI'TES (*Ecc.*) Heretics in the second century, who, under the pretence of inspiration, introduced bacchanals into their worship. *August. Her.* 62; *Philast. de Har. Baron. Annal. Ann.* 173.

ASCO'LIA (*Ant.*) Ἀσκωλία, from ἀσκός, a bottle; a festival among the rustic Athenians in honour of Bacchus, at which they leaped upon a bladder filled with oil and wine. *Virg. Georg.* l. 2, v. 384.

——————— atque inter pocula læti
Mollibus in pratis unctos saliere per utres.

Schol. in Aristoph. Plut. act 5, scen. 1; *Phurnut. de Bacch.*

ASCOLIA'SMUS (*Ant.*) ἀσκωλιασμός, from ἀσκός, a leathern bottle; a game among boys of beating one another with thongs.

ASCO'MA (*Med.*) ἄσκωμα, the eminence in the pubes at years of maturity, particularly in the female. *Ruf. Ephes. Appell. Part. Corp. human.* l. 1, c. 11.

ASCRIPTI'TII (*Ant.*) *Ascriptivi*, or *Adscriptivi*, supernumerary soldiers, who served to supply the losses in the legions. *Varr. de Lat. Ling.* l. 6, *et de Vit. Pop. Rom.* l. 3; *Lamprid. in Alex. Sever.*; *Trebell. Poll. de Balist. Tyrann.*

ASCRIPTITII (*Archæol.*) 1. A kind of villeins who attach themselves to some new lord, and become his vassals. 2. Foreigners, or aliens, who are newly admitted to the freedom of a city.

ASCYRO'IDES (*Bot.*) the same as *Ascyrum*.

A'SCYRUM (*Bot.*) ἄσκυρον, from α, priv. and σκύρος, rough, St. John's Wort; a plant very similar to the *Hypericum*, but the leaves larger and thicker; the seeds in hydromel are good for the sciatica and the bile. *Diosc.* l. 3, c. 172; *Plin.* l. 27, c. 5; *Oribas. Med. Coll.* l. 11.

Ascyrum, a genus of plants, Class 18 *Polyadelphia*, Order 4 *Polyandria*.
Generic Characters. Cal. *perianth* four-leaved.—Cor. *petals* four-ovate.—Stam. *filaments* numerous; *anthers* roundish.—Pist. *germ* oblong; *style* scarcely any; *stigma* simple.—Per. *capsule* oblong; *seeds* numerous.
Species. The species are—*Ascyrum*, *Crux Andrea*, seu *Hypericoides*, Common Ascyrum, or St. Andrew's Cross, native of Virginia.—*Ascyrum*, *Hypericoides*, seu *Hypericum pumilum*, seu *sempervirens*, a shrub, native of Virginia.—*Ascyrum villosum*, *Hypericum pilosum*, seu *Virginianum*, a shrub, native of Virginia.—*Ascyrum stans*, seu *Hypericum tetrapetalum*, a shrub, native of North America. *Ger. Herb.*; *J. Bauh. Hist. Plant.*; *C. Bauh. Pin.*; *Park. Theat. Botan.*; *Raii Hist. Plant.*; *Tourn. Instit.*; *Boerhaav. Ind.*

ASDE'NIGI (*Min.*) Blood-stone.

A'SE (*Med.*) ἄση, loathing of food from a conflux of humours to the stomach. *Hipp.* l. 5, aphor. 61, &c.

A'SEB (*Min.*) the same as *Alumen*.

Aseb (*Med.*) the same as *Hydroa*.

A'SEGEN (*Bot.*) vide *Sanguis Draconis*.

A'SEKI (*Polit.*) or *Asekai*, a Turkish name for the favourite sultanas who have brought forth sons.

ASE'LLI (*Astron.*) two stars of the fourth magnitude, which, according to Pliny, portend storms. *Plin.* l. 18, c. 35.

ASE'LLUS (*Ich.*) Cod-fish, or Keeling, was formerly reckoned a genus of fishes by Willoughby, but is classed in the Linnean system under the Gadus. *Plin.* l. 9, c. 16; *Wil. Ichth.*; *Raii Synop.*

ASE'MOS (*Med.*) ἄσημος, from α, priv. and σῆμα, a sign; an epithet, signifying without the ordinary signs or reasons, applied to diseases and their changes. *Hipp. Epid.* l. 2.

ASGA'NDES (*Ant.*) ἀσκάνδης, a Persian messenger or courier. *Plut. in Alex.*

ASH (*Bot.*) a well known tree, the timber of which is next to the oak in value, being of service in every sort of handicraft. The tree is raised best by the keys gathered, when they are about to fall, in October; they are sown in January, and best transplanted in October or November; they are felled when the sap is at rest, from October to November, but the lopping of pollards is better done in the spring. When the young plants are cut down they throw up straight shoots called *ground-ash*. The principal sorts

3

of ash are the Common, Flowering, and Manna Ash, the *Fraxina*; Mountain Ash, the *Sorbus*; Poison Ash, the *Rhus* in the Linnean system.—*Ash-weed*, the *Ægopodium* of Linnæus.

ASHA'RIANS (*Theol.*) a sect of Mahometans opposed to the Motazales, or orthodox sect.

A'SHES (*Ant.*) a mode of punishment, in use among the Persians, of throwing criminals from a great height into ashes, with which they were suffocated to death.

ASHES (*Chem.*) the residue of combustion, in general containing earth and fixed salts.—*Vegetable ashes* are produced from the burning of vegetable substances, as fuel.—*Animal ashes*, produced from animal substances, as the *cornu cervi calcinatum*.—*Mineral ashes*, the calces of minerals.

ASHES (*Mech.*) the skimmings of metal among the letter-founders, and the sweepings of their house, from which refiners afterwards draw the remainder of the metal by the fierceness of their fires.—*Fat ashes*, those which are heavy and contain much metal.—*Lean ashes* are light, containing little metal.

A'SH-FIRE (*Chem.*) when the vessel, containing the substance to be heated, is covered with ashes.

A'SH-HOLE (*Mech.*) the hole in the earth of a furnace, which receives the ashes to be taken away.

A'SHLAR (*Mason.*) free stone as it comes from the quarry.

A'SHLERING (*Carpent.*) quartering to tack to in garrets perpendicular to the floor.

ASHO'RE (*Mar.*) on the shore or land, as opposed to aboard; but a ship is said to be *ashore* when she has run aground, or on the sea coast.

ASH-WE'DNESDAY (*Ecc.*) the first day in Lent, so called from the ancient custom of fasting in sack-cloth and ashes.

ASIA'RCHES (*Ant.*) ἀσιάρχης, a governor of the provinces, who used to preside over the public games.

ASI'DE (*Lit.*) a term in plays for what is to be said on the stage without being heard by the other performers.

A'SILUS (*Ent.*) an insect so called, either from its infesting *asellos*, young asses, or from ἄση and ἰλύς, both which signify mud. It was used, according to Pliny, as an amulet, and was called *oestron* by the Greeks. *Plin.* l. 11, c. 28; *Aldrov. Ichth.*—*Asilus marinus*, οἶστρος θαλάσσιος, the sea breeze, which gets under the fins of the Thunny, and stings them so that they leap out of the water. *Plin.* l. 11, c. 29.

ASILUS, *in the Linnean system*, a genus of insects, of the order *Diptera*.
Generic Characters. Mouth with a horny sucker.—Antennæ filiform.—Body conic.
Species. The principal species of this genus are the—*Asilus crabroniformis*, nearly equalling a hornet in length.—*Asilus gibbosus*, larger than the former, a native of Lapland.—*Asilus flavus*, the size of a wasp, and of a black colour, with a yellow abdomen.—*Asilus forcipatus*, of a blackish brown colour, and considerably smaller than the former.—*Asilus tipuloides*, one of the smallest species.

ASINA'RIA (*Ent.*) Ἀσιναρία, a festival, in Sicily, in commemoration of the victory obtained over the Athenians, when Demosthenes and Nicias were taken prisoners; it was so called from the river Asinarius, near which the battle was fought. *Demosthen. in Nic.*

A'SINUS (*Zool.*) the Ass is classed, *in the Linnean system*, as a species of the *Equus*, or Horse.

A'SIO (*Or.*) horned owl, a species of the *Strix* of Linnæus; a bird, so called because it has ears like an ass.

ASI'RACUS (*Ent.*) ἀσίρακος, a species of locusts.

A'SITI (*Med.*) ἄσιτοι, from α, priv. and σιτίον, food; an epithet for those abstaining from food.

A'SJOGAM (*Bot.*) an Indian tree, the juice of whose leaves is good for the colic. *Raii Hist. Plant.*

A'SIUS (*Min.*) vel *Assius Lapis*, ἄσιος ἢ ἄσσιος λίθος; a stone, so called from Ἄσσος, a city of Troas. It is a soft, friable, and tophous substance, having a fine powder growing upon it called the *Flower of the Asian Rock*, which is colliquative, digestive, and preservative like salt. *Cel.* l. 4, c. 24; *Dioscor.* l. 5, c. 142; *Gal. de Simpl.* l. 9; *Oribas. Synop.* l. 2, c. 12; *Aet. Tetrabib.* 2, serm. 3, c. 38; *Paul. Æginet. de Re Med.* l. 7, c. 3; *Actuar. de Meth. Med.* l. 6, c. 5.

ASLA'NI (*Com.*) the Turkish name for a Dutch dollar.

A'SMAGA (*Chem.*) mixing certain metals together.

ASP (*Zool.*) a very small kind of serpent, the *Coluber aspis* of Linnæus, peculiar to Lybia and Egypt, the bite of which is deadly: its poison is so quick in the operation that it kills without the possibility of applying a remedy. Those who are bitten by it die within three hours, and their death, which comes on by sleep, is attended with no pain; circumstances which induced Cleopatra to adopt this mode of dispatching herself.

ASP (*Bot.*) or *Aspen-tree*, a kind of poplar, the *Populus tremula* of Linnæus, the leaves of which are remarkable for their perpetually tremulous motion.

ASPADIA'LIS *Ischuria* (*Med.*) suppression of the urine from the Urethra being imperforated.

ASPA'LATHUS (*Bot.*) ἀσπάλαθος, a plant which, according to Theocritus, grows on the mountains.
Theocrit. Idyl.

Ἐν γὰρ ὄρει ῥάμνοι τε καὶ ἀσπάλαθοι κομόωνται.

The scholiast, on this verse, makes the Aspalathus to be a sort of Acanthus, so called because its thorns cannot be easily, ἀποσπᾶσθαι, plucked out of the bodies of those who are beaten with it; wherefore, according to Plato, tyrants were scourged with it, in Tartarus. It is of a heating, astringent, and abstersive quality, good as a decoction for aphthæ and removing impurities. *Plat. de Repub.* l. 10; *Dioscor.* l. 1, c. 19; *Plin.* l. 24, c. 13; *Oribas. Med. Coll.* l. 11; *Aet. Tetrab.* 1, serm. 2, c. 196; *Paul. Æginet. de Re Med.* l. 7, c. 3.

ASPALATHUS, *in the Linnean system*, a genus of plants; Class 17 *Diadelphia*, Order 4 *Decandria*, in English Rhodium or Rose-Wood.
Generic Characters. CAL. *perianth* one-leaved.—COR. *papilionaceus.*—STAM. *filaments* ten; *anthers* oblong.—PIST. *germ* ovate; *style* simple; *stigma* sharp.—PER. *legume* ovate; *seeds* generally two.
Species. The species are mostly shrubs and natives of the Cape of Good Hope, as—*Aspalathus spinosa*, seu *Genistella spinosa Africana*, Thorny Aspalathus, or Rosewood.—*Aspalathus chenopoda*, *Genista Africana*, *Chemælarix*, seu *Chenopoda monomatopensis*, &c.

ASPALATHUS is also the *Robinia spinosa* and *pygmea*, the *Spartium spinosum*, and the *Amerimnum ebenus* of Linnæus. *Bauh. Hist. Plant.* &c.

A'SPALAX (*Bot.*) ἀσπάλαξ, a plant which, according to the description of Theophrastus, resembles the crocus in having more root than leaf. *Theophrast. Hist. Plant.* l. 1, c. 11; *Plin.* l. 19, c. 6.

ASPA'RAGIN (*Chem.*) the juice extracted from Asparagus.

ASPA'RAGUS (*Bot.*) ἀσπάραγος, a well known plant, so called, according to Varro, because it springs up from rough twigs. The root of this plant is one of the five opening roots, and it is also of singular efficacy in disorders of the eye. *Theophrast.* l. 6, c. 3; *Cato de Re Rust.* c. 6; *Varr. de Lat. Ling.* l. 4; *Colum. de Re Rust.* l. 2, c. 3; *Dioscor.* l. 2, c. 152; *Plin.* l. 19, c. 8, &c.; *Athen.* l. 2, c. 22; *Gal. de Simp.* l. 6; *Oribas. Synop.* l. 2, c. 1; *Aet. Tetrab.* 1, serm. 1; *Paul. Æginet.* l. 7, c. 3.

ASPARAGUS, a genus of plants; Class 6 *Hexandria*, Order 1 *Monogynia*.
Generic Characters. CAL. none.—COR. *petals* six.—STAM.

filaments six filiform; *anthers* roundish.—Pist. *germ* turbinate; *style* very short; *stigma* a prominent point.—Per. *berry* globular; *seeds* two.

Species. The species are either perennial or shrubs, but mostly the latter, as—*Asparagus officinalis*, Common Asparagus.—*Asparagus frutescens*, *Africanus*, seu *tenuifolius*, Larch-leaved Asparagus.—*Asparagus horridus*, seu *Hispanicus*, Thorny Asparagus.—*Asparagus aphyllus*, seu *Corruda altera*, Prickly Asparagus.—*Asparagus Capensis*, seu *Corruda Africana*, Cape Asparagus, &c. *J. Bauh. Hist. Plant.*; *C. Bauh. Pin.*; *Ger. Herb.*; *Park. Theat. Botan.*; *Raii Hist. Plant.*; *Tournef. Instit.*; *Boerhaav. Ind.*

ASPA′SIA (*Med.*) a constrictive medicine for the Pudenda Muliebria. *Castell. Lex. Med.*

A′SPECT (*Astron.*) the situation of the stars and planets in respect to each other. These configurations of the planets were regarded by astrologers as having an influence over sublunary affairs, wherefore they were much noticed in the study of astrology. Aspect is an angle formed with the earth by the luminous rays of two planets so situated as to be capable of acting upon sublunary natures, according to Kepher, or perhaps more correctly, according to Wolfius, the meeting of luminous rays emitted from two planets to the earth according to their situation with respect to each other. The ancient astronomers reckoned five different aspects; namely, *Conjunction, Sextile, Quartile, Trine, Opposition*; the signs and distances of which are as follows:

Name.	Character.	Distance.
Conjunction	☌	0° = 0′ sign
Sextile	✱	60 = 2 signs
Quartile	□	90 = 3 signs
Trine	△	120 = 4 signs
Opposition	☍	180 = 6 signs

To these Kepler added eight new aspects, as the Demisextile of 30°, Decile of 36°, Octile of 43°, Quintile of 72°, &c. [vide *Astronomy*] *Vitruv. de Architect.* l. 9, c. 4; *Jovian. Pontan. de Cel. Reb.* l. 1; *Kepler. Epitom. &c.*

Aspect *double* (*Paint.*) when a single figure represents two or more different objects.

A′SPEN-TREE (*Bot.*) the *Populus tremula* of Linnæus, or Trembling Poplar, a sort of popular which is much more tender of its branches than the common kind. [vide *Asp*]

A′SPER (*Com.*) a Turkish coin equal to ⅔d, also a money of account at Constantinople.

A′SPERA *Arteria* (*Anat.*) the windpipe, so called from the inequality of its cartileges. [vide *Trachea*] *Aret. de Sign. et Caus. acut. Morb.* l. 1, c. 7; *Aet. Tetrab.* 2, serm. 3, c. 5.

ASPE′RGINES (*Med.*) from *aspergo*, to sprinkle; medicines administered by way of sprinkling.

ASPE′RIFOLIÆ (*Bot.*) Rough leaved, the name of a class in Ray's and Herman's systems, and of the forty-third order in Linnæus' Fragments of a natural Method.

ASPE′RSED (*Her.*) strewed or powdered.

ASPERU′GO (*Bot.*) from *asperita*, or roughness, which this plant has in common with several genera of the natural order of *Asperifoliæ*. *Plin.* l. 24, c. 17.

Asperugo, *in the Linnean system*, a genus of plants, Class 5 *Pentandria*, Order 1 *Monogynia*.

Generic Characters. Cal. *perianth* one leaved.—Cor. one-petalled—Stam. *filaments* five; *anthers* oblongish.—Pist *germs* four; *style* filiform; *stigma* obtuse.—Per. none; *calyx* very large; *seeds* four.

Species. The two species are the *Asperugo procumbens*, *Buglossum sylvestre*, seu *Aparine major Plinii*, Procumbent Asperugo, an annual, native of Britain; *Asperugo Ægyptica*, *Lycopsis Ægyptiaca*, *Anchusa verrucosa*, seu *flava*, Egyptian Asperugo, an Annual, native of Egypt.

ASPE′RULA (*Bot.*) a diminutive of *asper*, rough because the seeds are roughish; a genus of plants, Class 4 *Tetrandria*, Order 1 *Monogynia*.

Generic Characters. Cal. *perianth* small.—Cor. one-petalled.—Stam. *filaments* four at the top of the tube; *anthers* simple.—Pist. *germ* twin; *style* filiform; *stigmas* headed.—Per. two dry united *berries*; *seed* solitary.

Species. The species are mostly perennials, as—*Asperula odorata*, *Galium odorata*, *Rubeola montana odorata*, seu *Hepatica stellaria*, Sweet-scented Woodroof.—*Asperula cynanchica*, *Galium cynanchicum*, seu *Rubia cynanchica*. Squinancy-Wort, &c.; but the—*Asperula arvensis*, *Rubia asperula*, seu *Rubeola cærulea*, Blue or Field Woodroof, a native of Britain, is an annual; and the—*Asperula Calabrica*, *Oleander Creticus*, *Thymelæ*, *Sherardia*, *Pavetta fœtidissima*, *Rubeola valeriana*, seu *Nerum*, Calabrian Woodroof, a native of Calabria, is a shrub. *Ger. Herb.*; *J. Bauh. Hist. Plant.*; *Park. Theat. Bot.*; *Raii Hist. Plant.*; *Tournef. Inst. Rei Herb.*; *Boérhaav. Ind.*

ASPHA′LATHUS (*Bot.*) the same as *Aspalathus*.

ASPHALTI′TIS (*Bot.*) ἀσφαλτίτις, a kind of trefoil, which Dioscorides calls ἀσφάλτιον. *Dioscor.* l. 3, c. 123.

Asphaltitis (*Anat.*) the last vertebræ of the loins. *Gorr. Defin. Med.*

ASPHA′LTOS (*Min.*) or *Asphaltum*, ἄσφαλτος, *asphaltos*; Jews' Pitch: a solid, brittle, ponderous substance; of a discutient, emollient, and agglutinant quality. It is the *Bitumen Asphaltum* of Linnæus.

ASPHENDA′MNOS (*Bot.*) Mountain Maple.

A′SPHODEL (*Bot.*) a plant. [vide *Asphodelus*]

ASPHO′DELUS (*Bot.*) ἀσφόδελος, Asphodel, or King's Spear; a well-known plant, so called from the ashes, σποδὸς, of the dead bodies that were burnt; because the ancients used to put the asphodel into the tombs, that there might be food in the regions below for the departed spirits. This plant bears on the top of its smooth stalk a small flower, called Anthericus.

Nicand. Theriac.

'Αγριοὶ ἀσφοδέλοιο διανθέος ἄλλοτε ῥίζαν
Ἄλλοτε καυλεῖον ὑπέρτερον ἀνθερίκοιο
Πολλάκι δ' αὖ καὶ σπέρμα. ὅτε λοβὸς ἀμφὶς ἀέξει.

Hippocrat. de Intern. Affect.; *Theophrast. Hist. Plant.* l. 1, c. 16; l. 7, c. 12; *Dioscor.* l. 2, c. 199; *Plin.* l. 22, c. 22; *Schol. in Nicand. Gal. de Simplic.* l. 4; *Oribas. Med. Coll.* l. 11; *Aet. Tetrab.* 1, serm. 1; *Paul. Æginet. de Re Med.* l. 7, c. 3.

Asphodelus, a genus of plants, Class 6 *Hexandria*, Order 1 *Monogynia*.

Generic Characters. Cal. none.—Cor. one-petalled.—Stam. *filaments* six; *anthers* oblong.—Pist. *germ* roundish; *style* subulate; *stigma* truncate.—Per. *capsule* globular; *seeds* several.

Species. The species are mostly perennials; but the *Asphodelus luteus*, Yellow Asphodel, or King's-spear, is a biennial. *J. Bauh. Hist. Plant.*; *C. Bauh. Pin.*; *Ger. Herb.*; *Park. Theat. Botan.*; *Raii Hist. Plant.*; *Tournef. Instit. Rei Herb.*; *Boerhaav. Ind.*

ASPHURELA′TÆ (*Min.*) semi-metallic fossils, fusible by fire, and not malleable when in their purest state. They are intimately connected with sulphur and metallic ores.

ASPHY′XIA (*Med.*) ἀσφυξία, from α priv. and σφύζω, to beat like the pulse; an apparent privation of pulse; or according to Cælius Aurelianus, a smallness and amputation of the pulse. *Cæl. Aurel. de Tard. Pass.* l. 4, c. 3; *Gal. de Diff. Puls.* l. 4, c. 3.

A′SPIC (*Bot.*) another name for the *Lavandula Stoechas* of Linnæus.—*Oil of aspic*, an extraction from the root of a plant called Aspic. *Geoff. Mem. de l' Academ.* 1715.

ASPI'DION (*Bot.*) a name for the *Alysson* of Dioscorides.

ASPIDI'SCI (*Ant.*) ἀσπιδίσκοι, dim. of ἀσπίς; short shields or ornaments in the fashion of shields.

ASPIDI'SCOS (*Anat.*) ἀσπιδίσκος, a buckler, is metaphorically applied to the *Sphincter ani*. *Cœl. Aurelian. Tard. Pass.* l. 3, c. 3.

ASPILA'TES (*Min.*) ἀσπιλάτης, from α, priv. and σπίλος, a spot. 1. A precious stone, of a silver colour, good against lunacy. 2. A sparkling gem in Arabia. *Plin.* l. 37, c. 10.

A'SPIRATE (*Gram.*) the character in the Greek (marked thus, ʽ) to denote that the vowel must be sounded with a breathing, as ὑ, which is sounded with an *h* instead of *e*. The letter *h*, in modern languages, is called aspirate when it is sounded, in distinction from *h* mute, which is not sounded.

A'SPIS (*Ant.*) ἀσπίς, in Latin *clypeus*, and in English *shield*, was a defence for the whole body, according to the manner in which it was anciently made. It was composed either of wickers, or light wood, or hides doubled into several folds, and fortified with several plates of metals, to which Homer frequently alludes. They were mostly made of ox-hides, and therefore commonly called ἀσπίδες βόειαι. The principal parts of the shield were the ἄντυξ ἴτυς, περιφέρεια, or κύκλος, the outermost round, circle, or circumference; ὀμφαλός, in Latin *umbo*, the Boss, jutting out in the middle of the buckler; τελαμών, a thong of leather, whereby they hung over the shoulder. The shields were of different kinds, varying both in size and form. The general form was round, whence ἀσπίδες εὔκυκλοι; but the γέρρον was squared, the θυρεός was oblong, the λαισήϊον was composed of hides with the hair, and the πέλτη was a small light buckler. [vide *Militia*] *Poll. Onom.* l. 1, c. 10; *Eustath. in Hom.*

Aspis (*Zool.*) ἀσπίς, Asp, the most venomous of all serpents; is classed by Linnæus under the *Coluber*. Galen makes three species of the Aspis, namely, χερσαῖα, χελιδονία, and πτυάς, which is the most pernicious of all. [vide *Asp*] *Gal. de Theriac. ad Pison.* l. 1, c. 8; *Act. Tetrab.* 4, serm. 3, c. 15; *Paul. Æginet.* l. 5, c. 18.

ASPLE'NIUM (*Bot.*) ἀσπλήνιον, or Spleenwort; a plant so called from its efficacy in curing disorders of the spleen. It is a small plant, consisting of leaves only, and is one of the five capillary plants. *Theophrast. Hist. Plant.* l. 9, c. 19; *Dioscor.* l. 3, c. 151; *Plin.* l. 27, c. 5; *Oribas. Med. Coll.* l. 11; *Paul. Æginet. de Re Med.* l. 7, c. 3.

ASPLENIUM, *in the Linnean system*, a genus of plants, Class 24 *Cryptogamia*, Order 1 *Filices*, the *Trichomanes* and *Lingua cervina* of Tournefort.

Generic Character. FRUCTIFICATIONS disposed in right lines under the disk of the frond.

Species. The species are mostly perennials, as—*Asplenium rhizophyllum*, seu *Phyllitis*, Rootleaved Spleenwort.—*Asplenium hemionitis*, seu *Hemionitis*, Mule's-tongue Spleenwort.—*Asplenium nidus*, seu *Scolopendria*, Bird's-nest Spleenwort.—*Asplenium ceterach*, Common Spleenwort, or Miltwaste.—*Asplenium trichomanes*, *Polytrichum* seu *Adiantum*, Common Maidenhair.—*Asplenium septentrionale*, *Achrostichum*, *Holosteum*, *Filicula*, seu *Filix*, Forked Fern, &c. &c. *Dodon. Stirp. Hist.*; *Clus. rar. Plant. Hist.*; *J. Bauh. Hist. Plant.*; *C. Bauh. Pin.*; *Park. Theat. Botan.*; *Raii Hist. Plant.*; *Tournef. Inst.*; *Boerhaav. Ind.*

ASPLENIUM is also the *Acrostichum rufum* and the *Meniscum* of Linnæus.

ASPORTA'TION (*Law*) a felonious carrying away.

ASPRE'DO *cernua* (*Ichth.*) the name of a fish answering to the *Perca cernua* of Linnæus. In the head of this fish is a bone good for the stone, &c. *Gesn. de Aquat.*; *Raii Ichth. Aldrov. de Pis.*

ASPRE'LLA (*Bot.*) the *Equisetum majus* of Linnæus.

A'SPRIS (*Bot.*) the same as *Ægilops*.

ASS (*Zool.*) the well-known animal which is nearly allied to the horse, and is the *Equus asinus* of Linnæus.

Ass (*Her.*) was a charge in coats of arms, where it was the emblem of patience, as "Argent, a fess between three asses passant; in the arms of the Ascough family."

A'SSABA (*Bot.*) an Indian plant used medicinally.

A'SSAC (*Chem.*) the same as *Gummi ammoniacum*.

A'SSACH (*Law*) a mode of purgation used in Wales, of clearing oneself from a criminal charge by the oath o 300 men. It was abolished in the reign of Henry the Fifth. 1 Hen. 5.

ASSA-FŒTIDA (*Chem.*) vide *Asa*.

ASSA'I (*Mus.*) Italian for an augmentative expression which in any composition indicates that the time must be accelerated or retarded, as *allegro*, quick; *allegro assai*, still quicker; *adagio*, slow; *adagio assai*, still slower.

A'SSALA (*Bot.*) Nutmeg.

ASSA'LIÆ (*Ent.*) worms that breed among planks.

ASSANE'GI (*Min.*) the powder that falls off from the wall of salt in the salt mines.

A'SSANUS (*Com.*) a weight among the ancients, consisting of two drams. *Gal. de Ponder. et Mensur.*

ASSARABA'CCA (*Bot.*) vide *Asarum*.

ASSA'RON (*Ant.*) another name for the measure called in the Scriptures *omer*.

ASSA'RTUM (*Law*) or *assertum*, from *exertum*, pulled up by the roots; assart, an offence of plucking up trees by the roots in the forests. *Charta Forest. Anno* 9 H. 3, c. 4; *Flet.* l. 4, c. 22; *Crompt. Jur.* 177; *Manw. For. Laws*, part 1, p. 171.

ASSA'SSIN (*Law*) one who kills another unlawfully and by surprize. The word is supposed to be derived from a certain prince of the family of the Arsacidæ, called the "Old Man of the Mountain," who was wont to fall on defenceless persons that came in his way.

ASSA'TIO (*Med.*) ὄπτησις and τηγάνισις, roasting and frying. *Gal. Alim. Fac.* l. 3, c. 2.

ASSATU'RA (*Med.*) the piece of meat just removed from the fire after roasting, which, when wrapped up in a cloth, was reckoned among poisons.

ASSA'ULT (*Law*) an attempt or offer, with violence, to do bodily hurt to another. *Lil. Assis.* pl. 60; *Lamb. Errenarch.* l. 1, c. 3.—*Assault and battery*, an assault with actual blows.

ASSA'Y (*Law*) from *essayer*, to try; a mode of trying metals, or separating them from all foreign bodies inherent in them; thus gold and silver are assayed by the refiner, to obtain them in their finest or purest state. It was formerly called the *touch*, and those who had the care of it were called the *officers of the touch*.—*Assay Master*, the master of the mint, who weighs the bullion, and takes care that it be according to the standard.—*Assay of weights and measures*, an examination of them by the questmen in the city, &c. *Reg. Orig.* 279.

ASSAY-BALANCE (*Mech.*) a particular kind of balance or scales employed by Assayers.

ASSA'YER *of the king* (*Law*) an officer of the king's mint for the trial of silver: he is indifferently appointed between the master of the mint and the merchants that carry silver thither for exchange.

ASSA'YING (*Mus.*) a flourishing previous to the performance.

ASSAYSI'ARE (*Law*) to associate or take as fellow judges. *Cart. Abbat. Glast. M. S.*

ASSECURA'RE (*Archæol.*) to make secure by pledges, or any solemn interposition of faith. *Hoveden, Anno* 1174.

ASSEDA'TION (*Law*) possession, in the Scotch law, by a tack or lease, &c.

ASSE'MBLY (*Ecc.*) or General Assembly of the Church of Scotland, the highest ecclesiastical court in Scotland, composed of a representation of the ministers and elders of the Kirk.

ASSEMBLY *unlawful* (*Law*) the meeting of three or more persons to do an unlawful act, although they may not carry their purpose into effect.

ASSEMBLY (*Mil.*) the second beat of the drum before the march.

ASSE'NT *royal* (*Law*) the assent of the king to the bills that have passed the two Houses of Parliament, the form of which, when given to a public bill, is " Le Roy le veut ;" but to a private bill, " Soit fait comme il est desiré." The royal assent may be given either in person, through the medium of the clerk, by commission to certain lords, or by writing.

A'SSERS (*Archit.*) *asseres*, laths which support the tiles of the roof, in imitation of which the dentils were made. *Vitruv.* l. 4, c. 2 ; *Fest. de Verb. Signif.* ; *Bald. Lex. Vitruv.*

ASSERVA'TIO (*Med.*) the same as *Conservatio.*

TO ASSE'SS (*Law*) to rate, or to fix the proportion which every person has to pay of any particular taxes.

ASSE'SSOR (*Ant.*) *Cujus officium est assidere præsidi ;* an assistant in council.

ASSESSOR (*Anat.*) vide *Prostatæ.*

ASSESSOR (*Law*) those that assess the public taxes, of which there were two in every parish, to rate every person according to the value of his estate. *Stat.* 16 *and* 17 *Car.* II.

ASSE'TS (*Law*) from *assez*, enough ; goods and chattels sufficient for an heir or executor to discharge the debts and legacies of the testator or ancestor. *Assets* are either real or personal, assets per descent, or assets entre maines. — *Real assets* are lands in fee simple whereof a man dies seized. — *Personal assets*, any personal estate. — *Assets per descent*, where a person is bound in an obligation, and dies seized of lands, that land shall be *assets*, and the heir shall be charged as far as the land descended to him shall extend. — *Assets entre maines*, when sufficient is left to discharge all debts and legacies ; or where some commodity or profit ariseth to them in right of the testator : these are *assets entre maines*, or in hand.

ASSERVIA'RE (*Law*) to draw or drain water from marshgrounds. *Mon. Anglican.*

ASSIDE'ANS (*Theol.*) ἀσιδαῖοι, a sect of the Jews who are mentioned in the Maccabees, 1 Macc. ii. 42, as a people who were devoted to the law. They are supposed to derive their name from חסידים, merciful, holy, because they professed particular holiness of life. From them sprung the Pharisees. *Reland. Antiq. Sac. Pars.* 2, c. 11; *Prid. Connect.* part 2, book 3, &c.

A'SSIDENS *signum* (*Med.*) συνιδρύων, a sign or symptom usually attendant on a disorder, but not inseparable from it, in distinction from the *pathognomonic*, which is inseparable. *Gal. Com.* 3, *in Hippocrat. Epid.* l. 3.

ASSIDE'RE (*Law*) to assess or tax equally. *Math. Par.*

ASSI'DUUS (*Med.*) the same as *Continuus.*

ASSIE'NTO (*Com.*) a contract between the king of Spain and the South-Sea company for furnishing the Spanish settlements with slaves.

TO ASSI'GN (*Law*) 1. To make a right over to another ; as to assign an estate, an annuity, bond, &c. over to another. 2. To appoint, as to appoint a deputy, &c. Justices are also said to be assigned to take assizes. *Stat.* 11 *H.* 6, c. 2, 3. 3. To set forth or point out, as " *to assign* errors," to show where the error is committed, or to *assign* false judgment ; to show wherein it was unjust. *F. N. B.* 19, &c. ; *Reg. Orig.* 72.

ASSIGN. vide *Assignee.*

ASSI'GNABLE *magnitude* (*Math.*) any finite magnitude that can be expressed or specified.

ASSIGNA'TIO *agrorum* (*Ant.*) the assignment of land to soldiers, either as debentures or for reward of services. *Cic. ad Fam.* l. 8, ep. 13, &c.

ASSIGNA'TION (*Law*) the ceding or yielding a thing to another in the Scotch law, of which intimation must be made.

ASSIGNE'E (*Law*) or assign, he to whom any thing is assigned, as an assignee to a Bankrupt's estate. — *Assignee, or assign by deed*, is one appointed, as when a lessee of a term assigns the same to another, in distinction from an *Assignee, or assign in law*, whom the law makes so without any appointment, as an executor, who is *assignee* in law to a testator.

ASSI'GNMENT (*Law*) 1. The making over the interest a man hath in a concern to another, as the assignment of an estate freehold, or for term of years, by a deed in writing. *Co. Lit.* 2. The deed itself ; thus in assignments the words *grant, assign*, and *set over*, are required. *Inst.* 30. — *Assignment of a dower*, the setting out a woman's marriage portion by the heir.

ASSIMILA'TION (*Phy.*) a sort of motion, by which some bodies are changed into other bodies, aptly disposed into a nature homogeneous to their own ; as the assimilation of the food with the body.

ASSIMILATION (*Med.*) ἐξομοίωσις, an action by which the nourishment assimilates with the thing nourished, which requires πρόσθεσις, apposition, and πρόσφυσις, agglutinatio, or adherence. It differs only in name from nutrition. *Gal. de Fac. Nat.* l. 3, c. 1, *et de Caus. Sympt.* l. 3, c. 2.

ASSIMULA'RE (*Law*) to put highways together. *Leg. Hen.* 1, c. 8, *apud Brompton.*

ASSIMULA'TIO (*Archæol.*) counterfeiting.

ASSI'S (*Med.*) an Egyptian bolus, consisting of a powder prepared from hemp leaves. *Prosp. Alp.*

ASSIS (*Her.*) *sejant*, or sitting, as a lion *assis affronté*, or *sejant gardant affronté*. [vide *Sejant*]

ASSISTE'NTES (*Anat.*) or *astites glandulosi*, the prostate glands; so called because they lie near the bladder. [vide *Parastatæ*]

ASSI'SA (*Law*) from *assideo*. [vide *Assize*] — *Assisa cadere*, to be nonsuited when the complainant, from defect of legal evidence, can proceed no farther. *Bract.* l. 2, c. 7 ; *Flet.* l. 4, c. 15. — *Assisa cadit in juratum*, is where a thing in controversy is so doubtful that it must necessarily be tried by a jury. *Flet.* l. 4, c. 15. — *Assisa continuanda vel prorogenda.* [vide *Assize*] — *Assisa panis et cerevisæ.* [vide *Assize*] — *Assisa de utrum*, a writ. [vide *Juris utrum*] — *Assisa Nocumenti.* [vide *Nuisance*] — *Assisa capi in modum assisæ* — *Assisa judicium*, a judgment of the court given either against the plaintiff or the defendant.

ASSI'SE (*Law*) vide *Assize.*

ASSI'SUS (*Law*) rented or farmed out for such an assize or assessment. *Terra assisa* was opposed to *Terra dominica*, the latter being held in domain, and the former let out to smaller tenants.

ASSI'THMENT (*Law*) a weregeld or compensation by a pecuniary mulct for any offence, from *ad* and the Saxon *ριthe*, in lieu of, because it was paid in lieu of any other punishment.

A'SSIUS *lapis* (*Min.*) vide *Asius.*

ASSI'ZE (*Law*) *assisa*, from *assidere*, to sit together ; signifies, in its proper sense, an assembly of knights, and other substantial men, with the justice, at a certain time, and in a certain place, for the due administration of justice. In this sense assizes are general when the justices go their circuits with commission to take all assizes ; or they are special when special commissions are granted to try particular causes. The commissions for general assizes are five in number ; namely, — Commission of *oyer* and *terminer* for the trial of felonies, treasons, &c.—Of *gaol delivery*, for the trial of all persons committed to gaol for any offence.—Of *assize*, for trials upon writs of assize.—Of *nisi prius*, for the trial of civil causes, in the vacation, that have been brought to issue in the courts above by a jury of twelve men of the county where the cause of action arises, with this proviso, *nisi prius*, i. e. unless, before the day prefixed, the judges of assize come into the county in question, which they are sure to do in the preceding vacation.—*A commission of the peace* in every county of the circuits where all justices of the peace are bound to attend. *Bract.* l. 2, &c.; *Flet.* l. 4; 4 *Inst.* 265.— *Clerk of assize*, an officer of the court who sets down all things judicially done by the justices of assize in court. *Assize* signifies also, 1. A writ of assize for the recovery of things immoveable, of which one has been disseized. This was of different kinds; namely,—*Assize of novel disseisin*, a remedy, *maxime festinum*, for the recovery of lands or tenements.—*Assize of mort d'ancestor*, when a man's ancestors died seized of lands, and, after their death, a stranger abated.—*Assize of darrein presentment*, where a man's ancestors have presented a clerk to a church, and, afterwards the church being void, a stranger presents his clerk to the church, whereby the right of the proprietor is disturbed. *Stat.* 20, *H.* 3, *c.* 3; *Westm.* 2, c. 13, &c.; *Bract.* l. 4; *F. N. B.* 105. 190, &c.; *Co. Lit.* 154, &c.; *Reg. Orig.* 208, &c.; *New. Nat. Brev.* 417, &c.— *Assize at large*, a writ brought by an infant to inquire whether his ancestors were of full good memory when he made the deed whereby he claims his right.—*Assize in point of assize*, when the defendant pleads directly to the writ, no wrong.—*Assize out of the point of assize*, when the defendant pleads something by way of exception.—*Assize of right of damages*, when the tenant confesseth an ouster.— *Assisa continuanda*, a writ directed to justices of assize for the continuation of a cause when certain records alleged cannot be produced in time by the party that has occasion to use them.—*Assisa proroganda*, a writ for the stay of proceedings by reason of the parties being employed in the King's business. 2. *Assize* is sometimes taken for a statute, as — *Assiza panis et cerevisæ*, assize of Bread and Beer, a statute for regulating their weight and quantity.—*Assize of the forest*, touching orders to be observed in the King's forest.— *Assize of the King*, the same as the statute of view of Frankpledge. 51 *H.* 3; *Manw. For. Laws*, 35. 3. *Assize* is likewise sometimes taken for a jury where *assizes of novel disseisin* are tried. 6 *Hen.* 6, c. 2.

ASSI'ZER *of weights and measures* (*Law*) an officer who has the care and oversight of those matters.

ASSI'ZORS (*Law*) in the Scotch Law answer to the jurors in the English Law.

ASSOCIA'TION (*Law*) a writ directed to justices of assize to have others associated unto them as colleagues in assize. *F. N. B.* 185; *Reg. Orig.* 201, &c.; *New. Nat. Brev.* 416, &c.—*Association of Parliament*, the solemn association which Parliament entered into, in the reign of William III, to defend his Majesty's person and government. 7 & 8 *Will. III*, cap 2, made void by 1 *Ann. Stat.* 1, cap. 22, § 2.

ASSOCIATION *of Ideas* (*Phil.*) that connexion between certain ideas which causes them to succeed each other involuntarily in the mind.

ASSO'DES (*Med.*) from *assáre*, to burn; a continual fever with excessive heat inwardly, though not so great externally. It is arranged by Cullen under the Tertian Remittents.

ASSOI'LE (*Law*) to deliver from excommunication. *Staundf. Plac. Cor.* 72.

A'SSONANCE (*Gram.*) a jingling of words which have the same sound, but are not intended to rhyme.

A'SSONANT *rhymes* (*Poet.*) a sort of verses common among the Spaniards which rhyme but imperfectly.

ASSO'NIA (*Bot.*) from *asso*, a Spanish botanist; a genus of plants, Class 16 *Monadelphia*, Order 5 *Dodecandria*.
Generic Characters. CAL. *perianth* double.—COR. *petals* five.—STAM. *filaments* fifteen; *anthers* oblong.—PIST. *germ* roundish; *style* simple; *stigmas* five.—PER. *capsule* subglobose; *seeds* solitary.
Species. The species are perennials, as *Assonia palmata*, *angulata*, &c.

ASSU'MINA (*Bot.*) a shrub on the coast of Guinea, which destroys the *vena medinensis*.

ASSU'MPSIT (*Law.*) from *assumo*, a voluntary promise, by which a man takes upon himself to perform or pay any thing to another.—*Action of assumpsit*. [vide *Action*]

ASSU'MPTION (*Log.*) the postulate or thing supposed, which is the minor or second proposition in a syllogism. [vide *Syllogism*]

ASSUMPTION (*Med.*) the receiving of any thing into the body through the mouth, as an aliment, &c. *Castell. Lex. Med.*

ASSUMPTION (*Ecc.*) 1. A feast, celebrated on the 15th of August, in the Romish church, in commemoration of the miraculous ascent of the Holy Virgin. 2. The day of the death of a Saint.

ASSU'MPTIVE *Arms* (*Her.*) such arms as a man hath a right to assume to himself by virtue of some action; as if a man, being no gentleman by blood, shall take prisoner any nobleman and gentleman, he may bear the shield of that prisoner, and enjoy it to him and his heirs for ever, as in the case of Sir John Clark, who, in the reign of Henry VIII, took the arms of his prisoner the Duke de Longueville. [vide *Arms*]

ASSU'RANCE (*Com.*) vide *Insurance*.

ASSURANCE *of lands* (*Law*) where lands are conveyed by a deed.

ASSU'RGENS (*Bot.*) rising in a curve to an erect position, an epithet for a *petiole* and for leaves.—*Petiolus assurgens*, a rising *petiole*.—*Folia assurgentia*, rising leaves.

ASSY'ZERS (*Law*) jurors, or those who serve on an inquest in the Scotch Law.

ASSY'THMENT (*Law*) Reparation for mutilation and slaughter in the Scotch Law.

A'STACUS (*Icht.*) the lobster, which, in the Linnean system, forms a division of the Cancer or Crab. *Plin.* l. 9, c. 31; *Gesn. de Aquat.*; *Rondelet. de Aquat.*; *Aldrov. Ichth.*

ASTA'NDÆ (*Ant.*) vide *Asgandæ*.

ASTA'THIANS (*Ecc.*) heretics and followers of one Sergius in the ninth century, who renewed the Manichean impostures. *Baron. Annal. Ann.* 810.

A'STAZOF (*Med.*) 1. An ointment of litharge, spernisla, and houseleek. 2. A mixture of rosewater and camphor. *Paracel. de Apostem.* c. 38.

ASTCHA'CHILOS (*Med.*) a gangrenous ulcer at the juncture of the feet. *Paracel. de Apostem.* c. 18,

A'STEISM (*Rhet.*) ἀστεϊσμός, from ἀστεῖος, *urbanus*; a pleasant trope, or kind of irony, as
Virg. Eclog. 3, v. 90.

Qui Bavium non odit, amet tua carmina, Mævi.

Demet. Eloc. 128; *Longin. de Sublin.* l. 34, c. 2; *Philostrat. Vit. Sophist.* tom. i. p. 540.

A'STER *Samius* (*Min.*) from ἀστὴρ, a star; a kind of bright earth dug in the island of Samos, so called from its resembling a star. It is efficacious against spitting of blood. *Diosc.* l. 15, c. 172; *Plin.* l. 35, c. 16; *Gal. de Camp. Med. sec. gen.* l. 4; *Oribas. Med. Collec.* l. 13;

Aet. Tetrab. 1, serm. 1; *Paul. Æginet. de Re Med.* l. 7, c. 3.

ASTER Atticus (*Bot.*) ἀςὴρ ἀττικὸς, a plant, so called from the figure of its flower, which resembles that of a star. It was also called *Bubonium* from its efficacy in curing a bubo. *Dioscor.* l. 4, c. 120; *Plin.* l. 27, c. 5; *Gal. de Simpl.* l. 6; *Oribas. Med. Coll.* l. 11; *Aet. Tetrab.* 1, serm. 1; *Paul. Æginet. de Re Med.* l. 7, c. 3.

ASTER, *in the Linnean system*, a genus of plants, Class 19 *Syngenesia*, Order 2 *Polygamia Superflua*, in English Starwort.
 Generic Characters. CAL. common imbricate.—COR. compound radiate.—STAM. filaments five; anthers cylindric.—PIST. germ oblong; style filiform; stigma bifid.—PER. none; calyx scarcely changed; seeds solitary; receptacle naked.
 Species. The species are perennials, as—*Aster tripolium*, seu *Tripolium*, the Sea-Starwort.—*Aster Amellus*, seu *Amellus*, Italian Starwort, &c. Ger. Herb.; C. Bauh. Pin.; Raii Hist. Plant.; Tournef. Inst. Rei Herb.; Boerhaav. Ind.

ASTER (*Law*) or *homo aster*, a man that is resident. *Britt.* 151.

ASTERA'NTIUM (*Bot.*) the herb called *imperatoria*, masterwort, or pellitory of Spain. *Dodon. Stirp. Hist.*

ASTE'RIA (*Min.*) the Bastard Opal, a sort of gem.

ASTE'RIAS (*Or.*) ἀςερίας, a kind of heron or egret, the *Accipiter palumbarius* of Pliny, the *Falco palumbarius* of Linnæus, and the Gosshawk of Willoughby *Aristot. Hist. Anim.* l. 9, c. 36; *Plin.* l. 10, c. 60.

ASTERIAS (*Bot.*) the *Gentiana lutea* of Linnæus.

ASTERIAS (*Con.*) Star-fish or Sea-star, a genus of animals, Class *Vermes*, Order *Mollusca*.
 Generic Characters. Body depressed, covered with a coriaceous coat, furnished with five or more rays, and numerous retractile tentacula.—Mouth in the centre.
 Species. These animals are all inhabitants of the sea, and feed on oysters, to whose beds they are very destructive. They easily renew any parts which are lost by violence, and fix themselves to the bottom by swimming on the back, and bending the rays. The species are distinguished into the *lunate, stellate*, &c.

ASTE'RICUM (*Bot.*) ἀςερικὸν, *muralis herba*; pellitory of the wall. *Plin.* l. 22, c. 17.

ASTERISCOI'DES (*Bot.*) a species of the *Osmites* of Linnæus.

ASTERI'SCUS (*Bot.*) the *Buphthalmium* and the *Silphium asteriscus* of Linnæus. *Tournef.; Dillen. &c.*

A'STERISK (*Gram.*) ἀςερίσκος, a diminutive of ἀςὴρ, a star; a little mark in the form of a star (*) shewing something to be noted. *Isid. Orig.* l. 1, c. 20.

A'STERI Similis (*Bot.*) the *Erigeron alpinum* of Linnæus.

ASTERI'SMUS (*Ast.*) ἀςερισμὸς, an asterism or constellation of fixed stars.

ASTE'RN (*Mar.*) behind a ship, as opposed to *ahead*, which is before.

ASTEROCE'PHALUS (*Bot.*) the *Scabiosa* of Linnæus.

ASTEROI'DES (*Bot.*) Bastard Star-wort. 1. The *Buphthalmium* of Linnæus. *Tournef.* 2. A species of the *Conyza* of Linnæus.

ASTEROPLATYCA'RPOS (*Bot.*) the *Orthonna pectinata* of Linnæus.

ASTERO'PTEROS (*Bot.*) the *Leysera* of Linnæus.

ASTEROPO'DIUM (*Min.*) a gem, very similar to the Asteria.

A'STHMA (*Med.*) ἄσθμα, from ἄω, to breath; signifies, according to Hippocrates, a quick and difficult respiration, such as people experience after running, and is the highest degree of dyspne. *Hippocrat.* aph. 46; *Aret. de Sign. de Caus. Morb. Acut.* l. 1, c. 11; *Gal. Comm. in Hippocrat. ad loc. Oribas. de Loc. Affec.* l. 3, c. 79; *Paul. Æginet. de Re Med.* l. 3, c. 29.

ASTHMA is a disorder which consists in a chronical and sometimes periodical difficulty of breathing, with a sense of stricture across the breast, and is classed by Cullen as a genus of diseases in the Class *Neurosis*, Order *Spasmi*. The species are—*Asthma spontaneum*, when without any manifest cause.—*Asthma plethoricum*, when arising from plethora.—*Asthma exanthematicum*, originating in the repulsion of some acid humour.

A'STOMOS (*Anat.*) ἄςομος, from ἀ, priv. and ςόμος, without mouths. Pliny speaks of a people in India without mouths, who live *anhelatu et odore*.

ASTRA'BA (*Lit.*) 1. The Pack-saddle or Sumpter-mule; a title of one of Plautus' plays. 2. A stepping-stone on which to mount horses. *Suidas; Hesychius, &c.*

A'STRAGAL (*Archit.*) ἀςράγαλος, the ancle-bone; a small round moulding, encompassing the fut or shaft of a column, which was made to imitate the form of those bones which are placed at the juncture of the neck of the foot, as in the annexed figure ⊂⊃ *Vitruv. de Archit.* l. 3, c. 3; *Philand. Bald. Lex Vitruv.*

ASTRAGAL (*Gun.*) the corner ring of a piece of ordnance.

ASTRAGALOI'DES (*Bot.*) the *Phaca* of Tournefort.

ASTRAGALOMA'NCY (*Ant.*) ἀςραγαλομαντεία, a species of divination, by throwing small pieces marked with the letters of the alphabet, from the accidental disposition of which the answer was sought.

ASTRA'GALUS (*Anat.*) the ancle-bone, or sling-bone, the superior and first bone of the foot, so called from ἀςράγαλος, a die, because it resembled a die in shape. It is divided into two portions; one posterior, which is large, and as it were the body; and one anterior, which is an apophysis. *Ruf. Ephes. Appell. Part Corp. Human.* l. 3, c. 5; *Oribas.* l. 25, c. 3.

ASTRAGALUS (*Bot.*) Liquorice-Vetch, a plant so called from the ancle-bone, which its seed resembles in shape. Its root is sweetish, astringent, and gives a tincture of red to blue paper. *Dioscor.* l. 4, c. 62; *Plin.* l. 26, c. 8; *Cal. de Simpl.* l. 6.

ASTRAGALUS (*Bot.*) a genus of plants, Class 17 *Diadelphia*, Order 4 *Decandria*.
 Generic Characters. CAL. perianth one-leaved.—COR. papelionaceous.—STAM. filaments diadelphous; anthers roundish.—PIST. germ nearly columnar; style subulate; stigma obtuse.—PER. legume two-celled; seeds kidney-shaped.
 Species. The species are perennials, as—*Astragalus onobrychis*, Purple-spiked Milk-Vetch.—*Astragalus cicer*, *Cicer silvestre*, seu *Glaux*, Blad Milk-Vetch, &c.—*Astragalus hypoglottis*, seu *Glaux montana purpurea*, Purple Mountain Milk-Vetch, &c. *Clus. Hist. rar. Plant.; J. Bauh. Hist. Plant.; C. Bauh. Pin.; Ger. Herb.; Park. Theat. Botan.; Raii Hist. Plant.*

ASTRAGALUS is also the *Anthyllis montana*; the *Bisurrula*; the *Hedysarum argentatum*; the *Indigofera hirsuta*; the *Orobus vernus* and *tuberosus*; and the *Phaca* of Linnæus. *Bauh.; Park.; &c.*

A'STRAL (*Astron.*) belonging to the stars.

ASTRA'LISH (*Min.*) that ore of gold which lies as yet in its first state.

ASTRA'NTIA (*Bot.*) Master Wort, a genus of plants, Class 5 *Pentandria*, Order 2 *Digynia*.
 Generic Characters. CAL. umbel universal rays very few; partial very numerous.—COR. universal uniform.—STAM. filaments five; anthers simple.—PIST. germ oblong; styles two; stigmas simple.—PER. fruit ovate; seeds two.
 Species. The species are perennials, as—*Astrantia major*,

Helleborus, seu *Veratrum,* Great Master-Wort.—*Astrantia minor,* seu *Helleborus,* Little or Alpine Master-Wort.—*Astrantia ciliaris,* seu *jassione, &c.* Dodon. Stirp. Hist.; Ger. Herb.; J. Bauh. Hist. Plant.; C. Bauh. Pin.; Park. Theat. Botan.; Raii Hist. Plant.; Tournef. Instit. Rei Herb.; Boerhaav. Ind.

ASTRA'RIUS *hæres* (*Law*) from *astre,* the hearth of a chimney, where the ancestor, by conveyance, hath set his heir apparent and his family in a house in his lifetime. *Co. Lit.*

ASTRI'CTA (*Med.*) an epithet applied to the belly, in opposition to the *soluta,* or relaxed.

ASTRICTO'RIA (*Med.*) the same as *Astringentia.*

ASTRI'NGENIS (*Med.*) *astringentia,* those things which have a binding quality, as Peruvian Bark, &c.

A'STRIOS (*Min.*) from ἄστρον, a kind of gem found in India, resembling chrystal. *Plin. l.* 37, c. 9; *Isid. Orig. l.* 16, c. 13.

ASTRO'BOLOS (*Min.*) from ἄστρον and βάλλω, to dart; a gem like a fish's eye. *Plin. l.* 37, c. 9.

ASTROBOLI'SMOS (*Med.*) ἀστροβολισμός, from ἄστρον, a star, and βάλλω, to strike; with regard to plants, denotes planet stricken; with regard to man, it signifies apoplexy. *Theoph. de Caus. Plant. l.* 5, c. 2; *Gorr. Defin. Med.*

ASTRODI'CTICUM (*Astron.*) an instrument for several persons to view the stars at the same time, invented by Mr. Weighel.

ASTROGNO'SIA (*Astron.*) a knowledge of the fixed stars, from γινώσκω, to know, and ἄστρον.

ASTRO'IDES (*Her.*) a star consisting of six points or more, in distinctiom from a mullet, consisting only of five. [vide *Mullet* and *Star*]

ASTRO'ITES (*Min.*) a stone having the figure of a star upon it. It is a species of the *Helmintholithus* of Linnæus. *Plin. l.* 37, c. 9.

ASTROLA'BIUM (*Astron.*) ἀστρολάβιον, from ἄστρον, a star, and λαμβάνω, to take; Astrolabe, an instrument described by Ptolemy, which was chiefly used by navigators to take the height of the pole, &c. at sea. It is now superseded by Hadley's quadrant. *Ptol. Almag. l.* 5, c. 1.

A'STROLABE, *Sea,* an instrument for taking altitudes by sea.

ASTRO'LOGY, an art of judging or predicting human events by the influence of the stars, which is now generally exploded.

ASTRO'NIUM (*Bot.*) a genus of plants, Class 22 *Pentandria,* Order 5 *Dioecia.*

Generic Characters. For the male. CAL. *perianth* five-leaved; *leaflets* ovate.—COR. *petals* five ovate; *nectary* five.—STAM. *filaments* five; *anthers* oblong. For the female. CAL. *perianth* five-leaved; *leaflets* oblong.—COR. *petals* five.—PIST. *germ* ovate; *styles* three; *stigmas* sub-capitate.—PER. none; *calyx* coloured; *seed* one oval.

Species. The only species is, *Astronium graveolens,* a shrub, native of Carthagena. *Linn. Spec. Plant.*

ASTRONO'MICAL (*Astron.*) an epithet for any thing relating to astronomy, as *astronomical* Day, Hour, Year, in distinction from the *civil* Day, Hour, Year. [vide *Day, &c.*]—*Astronomical Characters,* those used in astronomy. [vide *Characters*]—*Astronomical Horizon,* in distinction from the *Sensible Horizon.* [vide *Horizon*]—*Astronomical Place of a Star or Planet,* the longitude of a star or place in the ecliptic, reckoned from the beginning of Aries.—*Astronomical Hours,* such as are reckoned from the noon or mid-day of one day to the noon or midnight of another.—*Astronomical observations,* such observations as are made with suitable instruments by astronomers on the heavenly bodies to ascertain their forms, appearances, motions, &c. The observations of Hipparchus, which are the earliest handed down to us from the Greeks, are given in Ptolemy's Almagest.—*Astronomical Tables,* are computations of the motions, places, and other phenomena of the planets, both primary and secondary. Tables of this description are to be found in Ptolemy's Almagest, which have, however, been superseded by more modern and correct calculations.

ASTRONOMICAL *Calendar,* an instrument consisting of a board on which is pasted an engraven and printed paper, with a brass slider, which carries a hair, and shows upon sight the meridian altitude and declination of the sun.—*Astronomical Quadrant,* a mathematical instrument for taking observations of the sun. [vide *Astronomy*] *Astronomical Telescope,* so called because it is only used in astronomical observation, consists of an object-glass, and an eye-glass, both convex.—*Astronomical Sector,* an instrument for finding the difference in right ascension and declination between two objects whose distance is too great to be seen through a fixed telescope.

ASTRONO'MICALS (*Math.*) i. e. *Astronomical Numbers,* a name for sexagesimal fractions, because they were formerly used in astronomical calculations.

ASTRO'NOMY, so called from ἄστρον, a star, and νόμος, a law, is a science which teaches the measures and motions of the heavenly bodies, or, in other words, it comprehends the whole docrine of the sphere. It consists of two parts, theoretical and practical.

Theoretical Astronomy.

The theory of astronomy comprehends a knowledge of the circles of the sphere, and of the affections of the sphere.

The Circles of the Sphere.

The *sphere* is the concave orb, or expanse, which invests the celestial bodies.—The *circles of the sphere* are those which cut the sphere, or have their circumference either in the immoveable or moveable superficies of the sphere.—To every circle of the sphere belongs a centre, an axis, and two poles.—The *centre* is the middle point round which the sphere revolves.—The *axis* is a right line drawn through the centre, on which the body revolves.—The *poles* are the extreme points of the axis.

Every circle is divided into 360 parts called *degrees,* each degree into 60 *minutes,* and each minute into 60 *seconds.* Circles are divided into great and small.—*Great circles* are such as cut the sphere into two equal parts, the centres of which are the centres of the sphere.—The *small circles of the sphere* are those which divide it unequally, and consequently do not pass through its centre.

Great Circles of the Sphere.

The great circles of the sphere are—the Horizon, Meridian, Equator, Ecliptic with the Zodiac, the Colures, the Vertical Circles, Circles of Declination, Circles of Latitude, Horary Circles, and Circles of Position.

Horizon. The Horizon is a great circle which divides the sphere into two hemispheres, upper and lower.—The *upper hemisphere* is that above the head of the spectator, and the *lower hemisphere* that under his feet. The horizon is divided into the rational and sensible. The *rational,* which is the Horizon properly so called, belongs to all the spheres; but the *sensible Horizon* has respect to different parts of the same sphere. The poles of the Horizon are the two vertical points called the Zenith and the Nadir, as in fig. 1, plate 13, where C represents the centre of the mundane sphere, B A E N the globe of the earth, H V R K the heavens, or celestial meridian, H C R the Horizon, H V R the upper hemisphere of the universe, B A E of the earth; H R K and B N E the lower hemispheres, V K the axis, V and K the poles,

ASTRONOMY.

or the Zenith and Nadir. The sensible horizon is *h r*, which is a small circle of the sphere.

Meridian. The Meridian is a vertical circle drawn through the poles of the world P Q, as A Z B N in fig. 2.

Equator. The *Equator*, so called in the terrestrial sphere; but, in the celestial sphere, the *Equinoctial*, is a circle drawn from the East to the West, by which it divides the sphere into the Northern and Southern hemisphere, as A H Q G, fig. 3.

Ecliptic. The Ecliptic is that circle in the heavens which the sun seems to describe in its course. It cuts the Equator at two points, called the Equinoctial points, where the Ecliptic is at the greatest distance from the Equator, and makes with it an angle of inclination of nearly 23½ degrees, called the *obliquity of the Ecliptic*, as in fig. 3, where E G L H represents the Ecliptic, A H Q G the Equator; the arc A E, or the angle A G E, formed by the intersection of A Q, and E L the obliquity of the Ecliptic. E and L the *Equinoctial Points*, the former of which is called the *vernal equinox*, and the latter the *autumnal equinox*. The Zodiac is a girdle, or belt, in the celestial sphere, which extends about eight degrees on each side the Ecliptic, as C P, fig. 7. It is divided into the *Dodecamatoria*, or twelve portions, called the *signs of the Zodiac*.

Colures. The Colures are circles which circumscribe the globe from North to South, and pass through the poles of the world; the first, called the *Equinoctial colure*, passes through the beginning of Aries and Libra; the second, called the *Solstitial Colure*, passes through the beginning of Cancer and Capricorn.

Vertical or *Azimuth circles.* A Vertical or Azimuth circle is a great circle passing through the Zenith and Nadir, cutting the horizon at right angles; it is also called a circle of altitude, because the altitudes of the heavenly bodies are measured upon it, as A Z B N, fig. 2, passing through the points Z N. The *prime* or *primary vertical circle*, is that which passes through the East and West points, and is always at right angles to the meridian, which is also a vertical circle passing through the North and South points. The points in which this prime circle Z D N E cuts the Horizon A D B E are called *Cardinal Points*, which are A North, B South, E East, and D West.

Circles of Declination. A circle of declination is a circle passing through the poles of the world, and having its poles in the Equator, as in fig. 4, where H O R represents the horizon, A Q the Equator, Z N the vertical circle, and P G D K the circle of declination passing through the poles of the Equator and the poles of the world P K. These circles are so called because the declination of the heavenly bodies is marked upon them.

Circles of Latitude. A Circle of Latitude is drawn through the poles of the Ecliptic, as in fig. 6, where H Z R Q represents the Meridian, Z C the Ecliptic, E Q the Equator, G P the poles of the Ecliptic, then the circle G I P L G will be the Circle of Latitude, so called because the latitude of the stars is reckoned upon it.

Horary Circles. Horary Circles are those circles whose poles are in the Equator, through whose poles they are drawn at the distance of fifteen degrees from one another, which is equal to an hour in time, as in fig. 5, where H Q B R A represents the Meridian, H R the horizon, E Q the Equator, A B the poles of the Equator, and the figures the twelve hours of the day and of the night.

Circles of Position. A circle of position is a circle drawn through the intersections of the Horizon and the Meridian, and through a star, or any point in the sphere, as in fig. 10, where H V R represents the Meridian, H A R the horizon, then H P R the Circle of Position passing through H and R, where the meridian and horizon mutually intersect each other; and, supposing the arc of a vertical circle to be drawn as V P A, then H P V or R P V is the angle of position.

Circles of Longitude and Right Ascension. The Circle of Longitude, which is the same as the Ecliptic, and the Circle of Right Ascension, which is the same as the Equator, are both so called from their use.

Small Circles of the Sphere.

The small circles of the sphere are the Tropics, Polar Circles, Almacantar Circles, Parallels of Latitude, and Circles of Apparition and Occultation.

Tropics. The Tropics are drawn parallel to the equator at the distance of twenty-three degrees and a half from it on each side; that on the North side is the Tropic of Cancer, as C R, fig. 7; that on the South side is the Tropic of Capricorn, as K P.

Polar Circles. The Polar Circles are drawn parallel to the Equator at the distance of twenty-three degrees and a half from the Poles; that at the North Pole is called the Arctic Circle, as T M, fig. 7; and that at the South Pole the Antarctic Circle.

Almacantar Circles. Almacantars, or Circles of Altitude, are parallel to the Horizon, and drawn from its Poles, as in fig. 8, where H V R represents the Meridian, H O R the Horizon, A S L an Almacantar circle drawn parallel to the Horizon; they are so called because the altitude of celestial objects is marked by them.

Parallels of Latitude. Parallels of Latitude are circles drawn parallel to the Equator on the terrestrial sphere, as in fig. 9, where E N Q S represents the terrestrial sphere, E Q the Equator, L M and O P parallels, N E S and N G S Meridians.

Circles of Apparition and *Occultation* are drawn parallel to the Equator, and are so called because within these circles the stars are perpetually visible or otherwise to the inhabitants of any sphere, as in any given latitude in the terrestrial sphere. By means of these circles other divisions are formed, both of the earth itself and its inhabitants, as zones, climates, antipodes, antoeci, perioeci, &c. of which more may be seen under the practical part.

The most important of the above-mentioned circles are to be seen in fig. 7, where G represents the centre of the mundane sphere, A E B Q the Meridian, and, at the same time, the Solstitial Colure, A G B its diameter, which also represents the horizon and the axis of the Equator, E G the Equator or Equinoctial, of which A B are the Poles, which are also the poles of the world, A the South Pole, and B the North, C P the Zodiac with the Ecliptic, C R the Tropic of Cancer, and K P the Tropic of Capricorn, T M and N O the Polar Circles, i. e. T M the Arctic, and N O the Antarctic.

Affections of the Sphere.

The affections of the sphere are either general or particular, i. e. such as belong equally to the sphere in general, or are applied in different ways to particular celestial bodies.

General Affections of the Sphere.

The general affections are as follow; namely, the Order or System of the Sphere, Positions of the Sphere, Longitude, Latitude, Altitude, Declination, Ascension, Descension, Azimuth, Amplitude, Zenith Distance, and Polar Distance.

System of the Sphere. The order or system of the sphere is the order in which the different celestial bodies are supposed to be placed in regard to each other, on which a variety of hypotheses have been formed that have been denominated systems; the principal of these are the Ptolemaic, Copernican, Tychonic, &c.

Ptolemaic System. The Ptolemaic System, so called from Ptolemy, a distinguished astronomer, whose system was that of the ancients in general. According to this system, which is represented in fig. 11, the Earth is supposed to be the immoveable centre of the universe, round which all the heavenly bodies revolved as crystalline spheres, one included in the other; thus the Moon (☾) occupies the place nearest to the earth, and the six other planets in their order; namely, Mercury (☿), Venus (♀), the Sun (☉), Mars (♂), Jupiter (♃), Saturn (♄): these are succeeded by the sphere of the fixed stars, otherwise called the *firmament*, or the *eighth sphere*, and two other spheres called crystalline, all which were put in motion by the outermost sphere, called the Primum Mobile, or prime mover.

Copernican System. The Copernican system, as represented in plate 14, fig. 13, places the Sun in the centre of the world, round which the Earth and all the planets move in their orbits; each of which is singly treated of under the Solar System. This system, though called Copernican, because Copernicus was the reviver of it, is as old as Pythagoras, from whom it was called the Pythagorean System.

Tychonic System. The Tychonic System, or the system of Tycho Brahe, a Danish astronomer, supposes the Earth to be fixed in the centre of the world, as in plate 13, fig. 12, round which the sun, stars, and planets revolved in twenty-four hours; but it differs from the Ptolemaic System by allowing the Sun to be the centre of the planetary motions, which the planets performed in their respective years, as the sun revolves round the earth in a solar year. This system was afterwards altered by Longimontanus, who allowed the motion of the earth on its own axis, but denied its annual motion round the sun.

To the above systems might be added the Egyptian, and others, which, as they have not obtained any considerable number of followers, are not entitled to any particular consideration in this place.

Positions of the Sphere. The Positions of the Sphere respect the relative situation of the Equator and the Horizon, and are three-fold; namely, right, oblique, and parallel.—*A right sphere* is that in which the Equator cuts the horizon at right angles, as in plate 15, fig. 14, where the Equator E Q cuts the Horizon H O. In this case the poles of the world are in the Horizon; namely, at H and O.—*An oblique sphere* is that in which the Equator cuts the Horizon obliquely, as in fig. 15; the poles of the world P and S are then obliquely situated above and below the horizon.—*A parallel sphere* is that in which the Equator is parallel with the horizon H O, as in fig. 16, and the poles of the world are the poles of the Horizon.

Longitude. Longitude, in the celestial sphere, is the distance of a star, or any other heavenly body from the first point of Aries, or from East to West, measured on the Equinoctial, as in plate 13, fig. 6. Suppose the star to be in K, the beginning of Aries to be Z, and through K a circle of latitude P K I G L be drawn, cutting the ecliptic in I, the longitude of the star K will be Z I. The longitude of the Sun is what is called the *Sun's place* in the ecliptic.—*Longitude*, in the terrestrial sphere, is the distance of the meridian of any place from the first meridian, which is either eastward or westward, and reckoned on the Equator.

Latitude. Latitude, in the celestial sphere, is the distance of a star or any celestial object from the ecliptic, northward or southward, measured on a circle of latitude; or it is an arc of that circle intercepted between the Ecliptic and the centre of the star, as in fig. 6, where A Z H Q represents the Meridian and Solstitial Colure; Z C the Ecliptic, E Q the Equinoctial; G the South Pole, and N the North Pole of the Ecliptic; P K I G L a circle of latitude; then if a star be in I it will have no latitude; if in K its North latitude will be the arc I K; if in F its Southern latitude F I. The greatest latitude a star can have is 90 degrees, and the greatest latitude of a planet nearly 8 degrees. The Sun being always in the ecliptic has no latitude.—*Latitude*, in the terrestrial sphere, is the distance of any place from the equator, reckoned in degrees, minutes, or geographical miles, &c. Latitude is either North or South.

Altitude. Altitude of a star, or any point in the heavens, is its height above the Horizon, as in plate 13, fig. 8, where V R N represents the Meridian, V the Zenith, N the Nadir, H O R the Horizon, S the Star, and Z S the altitude or arc of the vertical circle V Z N M. Altitudes may be either true or apparent.—*Apparent Altitude* is that which appears by sensible observation.—*True Altitude* is that which results from correcting the apparent, on account of refraction and parallax.—*Meridian Altitude* is the greatest altitude when the object is upon the Meridian.—*Altitude or Elevation of the Pole*, the arc R P (in fig. 4) of the Meridian, intercepted between the Horizon R and the Pole P; this is always equal to the latitude of the place.—*Altitude or Elevation of the Equator*, the arc H A of the Meridian, intercepted between the Horizon H R and the Equator A Q. The elevation of the Equator is equal to Z P, the co-latitude of the place; therefore the elevation of the Pole and the Equator make up the quadrant of a circle.—*Altitude of the Nonagesimal* is the altitude of the 90th degree of the Ecliptic, counted from the point where it cuts the Horizon, i. e. from its rising point; this is equal to the angle K M I, in plate 15, fig. 18, which is formed by the intersection of E L the Ecliptic and H R the Horizon, and is called the *angle* of the East, or of the *Ascendant*.

Declination. Declination of a star, or any celestial object, is its distance from the Equator, measured on an arc of a great circle, as in plate 15, fig. 19, where H E R Q represents the Meridian, E O Q the Equator, A the South Pole, B the North Pole, A O B I A a circle of Declination; then, if a star be in O or I it has no declination; if in S, or the parallel C N, its Northern Declination will be the arc O S; but if the star be in M, or on the parallel K P, the Southern Declination will be M O; so, in like manner, if the star be in the Horizon, as G or F, the Northern Declination will be F I, and the Southern, G O.

Ascension. Ascension of any star or point in the heavens, is an arc of the Equinoctial, intercepted between the beginning of Aries eastward, and that point of the Equinoctial which rises with the star. This is either right or oblique.—*Right ascension* is an arc of the equinoctial which rises with a star in a right sphere.—*Oblique ascension* is that which arises with a star in an oblique sphere.—*Ascension of the mid-heaven* is the right ascension of that point of the Equinoctial which is in the meridian.

Descension. Descension of any star or point in the heavens, is an arc of the Equinoctial, intercepted between the beginning of Aries and that point which sets with any celestial object. This is either right or oblique, as it sets in a right or oblique sphere. Ascension and Descension, with respect to the stars, are otherwise called their astronomical rising and setting, in distinction from their poetical rising and setting.

Ascensional Difference. Ascensional Difference is the difference between the right and oblique ascensions; thus,

2 B

ASTRONOMY.

suppose, as in plate 15, fig. 19, a star to be in F, the rising point of the horizon, and a circle of declination be drawn through it, B F I A, the arc of the Equinoctial D I will be the ascensional difference of the star F; but the point rising with it will be the point of the Equinoctial D.

Azimuth. Azimuth is the distance of a star or any celestial object from the North or South points, reckoned upon an arc of the horizon towards the East or West points, when the object is above the horizon; thus, suppose a star to be in Z or S, the point of a vertical circle passing through Z, as in plate 13, fig. 8, the azimuth of that star will be the arc H Z, and the complement of the azimuth is Z O.

Amplitude. Amplitude is the distance of a star or any heavenly body from due East or West at the time of its rising or setting.

Zenith Distance. Zenith Distance is the number of degrees that any star or heavenly body wants of 90 degrees when it is upon the meridian or at its greatest height.

Polar Distance. Polar Distance of a star or any celestial object, is an arc of the meridian contained between the centre of that object and the Pole of the Equinoctial.

Rising and Setting. Rising of any celestial object is the becoming visible, or ascending above the horizon, in distinction from *setting*, or the becoming invisible by descending below the horizon. The faint light which we perceive before the sun rises, and after he is set, is called the *Crepusculum*, or Twilight. The arc described by the heavenly bodies from their rising to their setting, is called the *diurnal arc*, in distinction from that which they describe from their setting to their rising, which is the *nocturnal arc*. The rising and setting of the stars is either astronomical or poetical.—The *astronomical rising or setting* are the same as Ascension or Descension.—The *poetical rising* and *setting*, so called because they are spoken of by the poets, are of three kinds, namely, cosmical, achronical, and heliacal.—The *cosmical* rising or setting of a star is when it rises with the sun, or sets when the sun rises, as in plate 15, fig. 20, where the sun is rising in E and the stars I, L are rising with it, or the stars F, R, G are setting with it.—*Achronical* rising or setting is when a star rises at sun-set, or sets with the sun, as in fig. 21, where E, the sun, is setting; F G, the stars, are setting, and I K L rising.—*Heliacal* rising is when a star first becomes visible in the morning, after having been so near the sun as to be hidden by the splendour of his rays; and the *heliacal* setting is when a star first becomes invisible in the evening, by reason of its nearness to the sun: thus, for the heliacal rising, suppose, as in fig. 22, the rising sun to be in E and the star to be in F, which has just emerged from his rays and is become visible; on the following days he will appear more distant, as at G: for the setting, suppose a star L, which one day is seen in the Horizon A I C after the setting of the sun, and the next day becomes invisible when it reaches to the point of setting, on account of its near approach to the sun.

Culminating. Culminating, or Southing, is when a star or any other heavenly body comes to the Meridian of any place; for then its altitude at that place is the greatest.

Occultation. Occultation is the obscuration or hiding from our sight any star or planet by the interposition of any celestial body.

Place. The Place of a star, or any other celestial object, simply denotes the sign and degree of the Zodiac which the luminary is in; but, in respect to the eye of the observer, it is distinguished into physical or optical.—The *physical place* of a star is that point in which the centre of the body lies, as S in plate 15, fig. 23.—The *optical place* is that point on the surface of the mundane sphere where the spectator sees the centre of the star, &c. The optical place is either true or apparent.—The *true*, or *real optic place*, is that point where a spectator, at the centre of the earth, would see the object, as B in fig. 23.—The *apparent* or *visible place* is that point where a spectator, situated on the surface of the earth, at E, would see the object as the point C.

Parallax. Parallax, or Parallax of Altitude, is the difference between the true and apparent optical place of a star or any other celestial object, as in plate 15, fig. 24. Suppose C to be the centre, A the place of the spectator on the surface, S any object, Z H the sphere of the fixed stars to which the places of all the bodies in our system are referred, Z the Zenith, H the Horizon; then, if C S *m*, A S *n*, be drawn, *m* is the place seen from the centre, and *n* from the surface; *m n* is the arc of parallax, and the angle made by lines drawn through the centre of the object from these several points is called the parallactic angle, as *m* S *n*, or its equal A S C. Parallax from the zenith to the horizon affects the altitude of an object, which, when it is in the zenith, has no parallax; and when in the horizon has the greatest, as at *s*; wherefore the *horizontal parallax* is distinguished from the rest. The Moon's greatest horizontal parallax is 1° 1′ 25″, and the least 54′ 5″. The fixed stars, owing to their immense distance, have no parallax. There are other sorts of parallax, as the—*Parallax of right ascension and descension*, which is an arc of the Equinoctial, D *d*, as in plate 15, fig. 17, by which the parallax of altitude increases the ascension and diminishes the descension.—*Parallax of declination* is an arc of a circle of declination, *s* I, by which the parallax of altitude increases or diminishes the declination of a star.—*Parallax of latitude* is an arc of a circle of latitude, S I, by which the parallax of altitude increases or diminishes the latitude.—*Menstrual parallax of the Sun*, an angle formed by two right lines, one drawn from the earth to the sun, and another from the sun to the moon, at either of their quadratures.—*Parallax of the annual orbit of a planet* is the difference between the heliocentric and geocentric place of a planet, or the angle at any planet subtended by the distance between the earth and sun, as the S R T in plate 18, fig. 29, which is explained under the *eccentric place of planets*.

Refraction. Refraction is an inflection of the rays of the stars, &c. in passing through our atmosphere, the effects of which are directly the opposite to those of parallax, for the parallax diminishes the altitude of objects, and the refraction increases it. There are as many kinds of refraction as of parallax, namely—*Refraction of altitude*, which is the principal sort, as in plate 15, fig. 25, where C O G represents the quadrant of a vertical circle, A the centre of the earth, T B the quadrant of a great circle described from A as the centre, D R E a quadrant of the spherical superficies described by the vapours round the earth, A B G the rational horizon, T R O the sensible horizon, S the true place of the star, of which S R is the radius, which by refraction is inflected from the straight line S R L towards the perpendicular R A, and from that line to T; wherefore the star will appear in the line T R O, and at the point O in the horizon, though it be really below the horizon.—*Refraction of declination* is an arc of a circle of declination, by which the declination is decreased or diminished.—*Refraction of ascension and descension* is an arc of the Equinoctial, by which ascension or descension is increased or diminished. [vide *Refraction*]

Aberration. Aberration, an apparent motion of the heavenly bodies, occasioned by the earth's annual motion in its orbit combined with the progressive motion of light,

ASTRONOMY.

as in plate 15, fig. 26. Suppose S to represent a fixed star, V F the direction of the earth's motion, S F the direction of a particle of light entering the axis ac of a telescope at a, and moving through a F while the earth moves from c to F; then, if the telescope keep parallel to itself, the light will descend in the axis, and as the place measured at F by the telescope is s, the angle S F s is the aberration, or the difference between the true place of the star and the place measured by the instrument.

Particular affections of the sphere.

The particular affections of the sphere are such as belong to some particular spheres, or which belong to all the spheres in different measures. The spheres, or celestial bodies, are divided in respect to motion and rest, into *fixed stars* and *planets*.

Fixed Stars.

The fixed stars are so called because they preserve nearly the same relative distance with respect to each other; but they are subject to an increase of longitude of about 50¼ seconds in a year, as also to a small variation in their latitudes, declinations, and right ascensions, which was ascribed by the ancients to a motion called the *trepidation*, or *libration*, of the eighth sphere; but by the moderns this motion is supposed to be apparent, and occasioned by the retrograde motion of the Equinoxes, called the *precession of the Equinoxes*.

The fixed stars are distinguished, as to their magnitudes and distribution.

Magnitudes of the stars. The magnitudes of the stars are commonly estimated as at the bottom of the planisphere [plate 16], from those of the first to those of the seventh magnitude, according to the magnitude and splendour of their light: besides which, they are, moreover, distinguished, according to the arrangement of Bayer, in his Uranometria, by the letters of the Greek alphabet, α being affixed to those of the first magnitude, β to those of the second, and γ to those of the third, and so on.

Distribution. The distribution of the stars is generally into formed, unformed, and nebulous.—*Formed stars* are those which are arranged under certain figures called *Constellations.*—*Unformed stars* such as are brought under no positive form, but are scattered about.—*Nebulous stars*, or *Nebulæ*, are such as are smaller than the seventh magnitude, and present only a dim hazy light, like little specks or clouds. Of these nebulæ is formed a whitish luminous tract, which seems to encompass the heavens like a girdle of a considerable though unequal breadth, varying from about 4 to 20 degrees, as may be seen in the planisphere, beginning at Cygnus; this is well known by the name of the *galaxy*, *via lactea*, or Milky Way.

Constellations. The constellations are divided into Northern, Southern, and Zodiacal; and in the following Catalogue they are arranged according to their proximity to the Poles within the parallels of latitude, by which they may be more easily traced by the reader.

The Northern Constellations are those which are north of the Equinoctial; the Southern, those which are south; the Zodiacal, those which are contained within the zodiac: the latter are, moreover, distinguished into *ascending*, through which the planets ascend northerly, as Capricorn, Aquarius, Pisces, &c.; the *descending* through which the planets descend towards the South, as Cancer, Leo, Virgo, &c. These are called Signs of the Zodiac, because they are marked with particular characters, as may be seen in the planisphere.

Northern Constellations.

Names.	Ptol.	Tycho.	Hevel.	Brit. Cat.	Principal Stars.	
Ursa major	18	21	27	66		
Draco	31	32	40	80	Rastaber	3
Lyra	10	11	17	22	Vega	1
*Camelopardalus	—	—	—	—		
Cepheus	13	4	51	35	Alderaimin	3
Lacerta	—	—	—	16		
Cygnus	19	18	47	81	Deneb Adige	1
Vulpeculus et Anser	—	—	27	37		
Cerberus	—	—	—	—		
Ramus	—	—	—	—		
Hercules	29	28	45	113	Ras Algatha	13
Corona borealis, seu septentrionalis	8	8	8	21		
Asterion et Chara	—	—	23	25		
Cassiopeia	13	26	37	55		
Perseus	29	29	46	59	Algeneb	2
Andromeda	23	23	47	66	Almak	2
Sagitta	5	5	5	18		
Serpentarius	29	15	40	74	Ras Alhagi	3
Bootes	23	18	52	54	Arcturus	1
Cor Caroli	—	—	—	3		
Lynx	—	—	19	44		
Pegasus	20	19	38	89	Markab	2
Equulus	4	4	6	10		
Delphinus	10	10	14	18		
Aquila et Antinous	{ —	12	28	} 71	Altair	1
	{ —	315	19			
Serpens	13	13	22	64		
Scutum Sobieski	—	—	7	8		
Mons Menelaus	—	—	—	11		
Coma Berenices	—	14	21	43		
Leo Minor	—	—	—	53		
Auriga	14	9	40	66	Capella	
Caput Medusæ, vide *Perseus*.						
Triangulum	4	4	12	16		
Musca	—	—	—	6		
Triangulum minus	—	—	—	10		
Cetus	22	21	45	97	Menkar	2

Zodiacal Constellations.

Names.	Ptol.	Tycho.	Hevel.	Brit. Cat.	Principal Stars.	
Aries ♈	18	21	27	66		
Taurus ♉	44	43	51	141	Aldebaran	1
Gemini ♊	25	25	38	85	Castor & Pollux	1 & 2
Cancer ♋	13	15	29	83		
Leo ♌	35	30	49	95	Regulus	1
Virgo ♍	32	33	50	110	Spica Virginis	1
Libra ♎	17	10	20	51	Zubenich Meli.	2
Scorpio ♏	24	10	20	44	Antares	1
Sagittarius ♐	31	14	22	69		
Capricornus ♑	28	28	29	51		
Aquarius ♒	45	41	47	108	Scheat	3
Pisces ♓	38	36	39	113		

Southern Constellations.

Names.	Ptol.	Tycho.	Hevel.	Brit. Cat.	Principal Stars.	
Xiphias	—	—	—	7		
Hydrus	—	—	—	10		
Chamæleon	—	—	—	10		
Argo navis	45	3	4	64	Canopus	1
Robur Caroli	—	—	—	12		
Crozier or *Crux*	—	—	—	4		
Apus, seu *Avis Indica*	—	—	—	11		
Toucan	—	—	—	9		
Columba Noachi	—	—	—	10		
Pavo	—	—	—	14		
Eridanus	34	10	27	84	Achernar	1

* Those in Italics are modern constellations.

ASTRONOMY.

Names.	Ptol.	Tycho.	Hevel.	Brit. Cat.	Principal Stars.	
Lepus	12	13	16	19		
Canis Major	29	13	21	31	Sirius	1
Centaurus	37	—	—	35		
Triangulum australe	—	—	—	5		
Indus	—	—	—	12		
Phœnix	—	—	—	13		
Ara	7	—	—	9		
Grus	—	—	—	14		
Hydra	—	—	—	—		
Canis minor	2	2	13	14		
Orion	38	42	62	78	Betelgeuse	1
Monoceros	—	—	19	31		
Sextans Uraniæ	—	—	11	41		
Crater	7	3	10	31	Alkes	3
Corvus	7	4	—	9	Algorab	3
Lupus	19	—	—	24		
Piscis australis	18	—	4	24	Fomelhant	1
Corona australis	13	—	—	12		

Since the construction of this planisphere, other constellations have been formed, which are of minor importance, as *Taurus Poniatowski, Pyxis nautica, Fornax chemica,* &c. &c.

Planets.

A planet is a heavenly body which either moves, or appears to move, perpetually within a certain limit, called his *orbit* or *path;* or supposing the sun, according to the Copernican System, to be immoveable in the centre of the sphere, then the planets are defined to be celestial bodies moving round the sun, or some other body, in elliptical orbs, having a focus for a centre. In this sense they are distinguished into primary or secondary.—*Primary planets* are those which move about the sun.—*Secondary planets,* otherwise called *satellites,* move about some other planet, as the moon about the earth. The primary planets hitherto discovered are 11 in number, which are distinguished by the following names and characters, as Mercury ☿, Venus ♀, the Earth ⊕, Mars ♂, Vesta ⚶, Juno ⚵, Ceres ⚳, Pallas ⚴, Jupiter ♃, Saturn ♄, and the Georgium Sidus ♅. The satellites hitherto discovered are 18 in number, the Earth having the Moon for one satellite, Jupiter four, Saturn seven, and the Georgium Sidus six.

The sun and planets, together with the comets, comprehend what is now commonly called the *Solar System,* in which the sun is supposed to be the centre of motion round which the other celestial bodies revolve at different distances, and in different periods of time. The affections of the solar system are either general or particular.

General Affections of the Solar System.

The general affections of the Solar System are mostly the affections of motion.

Motion. The motion of the planets is of different kinds, as mean, true, direct, retrograde, &c.—*Mean motion* is that by which a planet is supposed to move equably in its own orbit.—*True motion* is that which the planet actually performs in the heavens, as seen from the earth.—*Direct motion* is when a planet appears to a spectator on earth to move in *signa consequentia,* i. e. according to the order of the signs, as *aries, taurus, gemini,* &c. from east to west.—*Retrograde motion* is when the planet appears to move in *signa antecedentia,* i. e. in a contrary order of the signs, as *gemini, taurus, aries,* &c. Planets are said to be stationary when they seem to remain fixed in one point of the heavens for some time.—*Diurnal motion* is the number of degrees and minutes which the planet passes over within twenty-four hours.

Aphelion. Aphelion is a point in the orbit of a planet which is at the greatest distance from the sun, as in plate 18, fig. 27, where S represents the sun in the focus, round which, as its centre, the planet P describes the ellipse A P B, then A is the point of the orbit, which is the aphelion, or at the greatest distance from the sun. In the motion of the sun about the earth, this point is called the *apogee,* or the greatest distance from the earth.

Perihelion. Perihelion is the point of the planet's orbit, which is at the least distance from the sun, as the point B. This, according to the Ptolemaic system, is the *perigee,* or the point nearest the earth.

Apsis. Apsis of an orbit is its aphelion or perihelion, its apogee or perigee.—*Line of the Apsides,* or *Apses,* is a right line, as A B, drawn from the aphelion to the perihelion.

Eccentricity. Eccentricity is the distance of the centre of the orbit C from the sun S. In the ancient astronomy this was called the distance of the centre of the orbit from the earth.—*Eccentric* circle is the circle B D A E, described from the centre of the orbit C, with half the axis C A for a radius. In the old astronomy this eccentric circle was the orbit of the planet itself.

Anomaly. Anomaly is the distance of the planet from its aphelion or apogee.—*Mean* or *simple Anomaly* is, in modern astronomy, the time in which a planet moves from the aphelion A, to its mean place or point in the orbit P, and, as the area A S P, is proportional to the time in which the planet describes the arch A P; that area may be the measure of mean anomaly. In ancient astronomy the mean anomaly was the distance of the mean place of a planet from the apogee.—*Eccentric anomaly,* or anomaly of the centre, is the arc A K of the eccentric circle, intercepted between the aphelion A and the perpendicular K L, drawn through the centre of the planet P.—*True* or *equated anomaly,* otherwise called *the angle at the sun,* is the angle A S P, under which the planet's distance from the aphelion A P, appears. In the motion of the sun this will be the distance of the true place of the sun from the apogee, as seen by a spectator on the earth, or, which is the same thing, the distance of the true place of the earth from the apogee, as seen from the sun.

Equation. Equation is an arc of the Ecliptic to be added to, or subtracted from, the mean motion or place, that it may be reduced to the true, or from the true, that it may be reduced to the mean.—*Equation of the centre,* or *prosthaphæresis,* the difference between the true and mean motion, or between true and mean place of a planet; or, which is the same thing, the difference between the true and equated anomaly.

Thus, suppose ♈ ♋ ♎ ♑, plate 18, fig. 28, to be the Ecliptic, S the sun, M P N A the orbit of the Earth, its centre C, A P the line of the apsides, A the aphelion, then if the Earth be in L, the arc A L, or the angle A C L is the mean anomaly, and the arc of the ecliptic ♑ ♒, or the angle A S L is the true anomaly; which, if taken from the true anomaly, leaves the angle C L S, which is the equation or prosthaphæresis. It is so called because it is sometimes to be added to, and sometimes subtracted from, the mean anomaly, to give the true one. Thus, suppose the earth to be in R, the mean anomaly to be P C R, and then, if C R S be added to it, the true anomaly will be P S R and the place of the Earth in the Ecliptic will be found, consequently C R S is the Equation.—*Annual equation,* an equation either of the mean motion of the sun and moon, or of the moon's apogee and nodes, &c. [vide *Equation*]

Eccentric place of a planet. Eccentric place of a planet,

4

in its orbit, is the place in which it appears when seen from the sun, as represented by the line S P, plate 18, fig. 29, where N E O R is put for the Ecliptic, N P O Q for the orbit of the planet, S for the Sun, T for the Earth, and P for the planet.—*Eccentric place in the Ecliptic*, or the *place of the planet reduced to the Ecliptic*, is a point of the Ecliptic to which the planet, as seen from the sun is referred, as R S. This coincides with the *heliocentric longitude*, or the longitude of the planet viewed from the sun, and is therefore called the *heliocentric place*.—*Geocentric place of a planet*, as T R, is the point of the Ecliptic to which the planet viewed from the earth is referred.—*Angle of Commutation*, E S R, is the difference between the true place of the sun, E, when seen from the earth, and the place of the planet reduced to the Ecliptic.

Nodes. Nodes are the two points of N and O in fig. 29, where the planet intersects the Ecliptic. They are ascending and descending.—*Ascending node*, otherwise called the *Dragon's head* in the Moon, and marked (☊), is that point N, where the planet ascends from the South to the North side of the Ecliptic.—*Descending node*, or *Dragon's tail*, marked (☋), is that point O, where the planet descends from the North to the South side of the Ecliptic.

Inclination. Inclination is the angle at the sun R S P, in fig. 29, under which the distance of the planet P from the Ecliptic, P R, appears when viewed from the sun. The greatest inclination or declination is called the inclination of the orbit of a planet, which varies for different planets, as may be seen hereafter.

Argument. Argument, an arc given, by which another arc is found, as—*Argument of inclination*, or *argument of latitude*, an arc of a planet's orbit, as N P, in fig. 29, intercepted between the Ascending Node and the planet's place, numbered according to the succession of signs.—*Menstrual argument of latitude*, the distance of the moon's true place from the sun's true place.—*Annual argument of the moon's apogee*, or simply *annual argument*, the distance of the sun's place from the place of the moon's apogee, or an arc of the Ecliptic, comprised between these two places.

Reduction to the Ecliptic. Reduction to the Ecliptic is the difference between the argument of latitude N P, fig. 29, and the arc of the Ecliptic N R, intercepted between the place of the planet R, brought back to the Ecliptic, and the ascending node N.

Curtate Distance. Curtate distance, the distance from the sun of the place of a planet reduced to the Ecliptic.

Curtation, the difference between the distance of a planet from the sun, as P S, and the curtate distance S R.

Aspect. Aspect is the situation of the planets, (and also of the stars), with respect to each other. The aspects are five in number, namely, Conjunction, Sextile, Quartile, Trine, and Opposition.—*Conjunction*, marked (☌), when they are in the same sign and degree.—*Sextile* (✶), when they are two signs distant, as Cancer (♋), and Virgo (♍), Scorpio (♏), and Capricornus (♑), Pisces (♓), and Taurus (♉), are each in sextile aspect, i. e. at the distance of 60 degrees, or the sixth part of a circle from each other.—*Quartile* (□), when they are three signs, 90 degrees, or the fourth part of a circle distant from each other, as Cancer (♋), and Libra (♎), Capricornus (♑), and Aries (♈).—*Trine* (△), when they are four signs, 120 degrees, or the third part of a circle from each other, as Cancer (♋), Scorpio (♏), and Pisces (♓).—*Opposition*, when they are six signs, 180 degrees, or half a circle from each other. The Conjunction and Opposition are called *Syzygies;* the quartile aspect, the *quadrature;* and the trine, *triplicity.*

—Other aspects have since been added to these, as *decile, tridecile,* &c. [vide *Aspect*]

Transit. Transit is the apparent passage of any planet over the *disc* or face of the sun, or any planet. Mercury and Venus, in their transits over the sun's disc, appear like specks.

Eclipses. An Eclipse is a species of occultation, particularly applied to the sun and the planets.—*Duration of an eclipse* is the time of its continuance, or the time of the immersion and emersion.—*Immersion*, or *Incidence* of an Eclipse, is the moment when the eclipse begins, or when part of the planet is obscure.—*Emersion* or *expurgation* of an Eclipse, is the time when the eclipsed body begins to re-appear, or emerge out of the shadow. Quantity of an eclipse, is the portion of the luminary that is eclipsed. This is usually measured by dividing the diameter of the luminary into twelve equal parts, called *digits*.—*Annular eclipse*, is when the whole body is eclipsed, except a ring or annulus, which appears round its limb or edge. Eclipses are also distinguished into *partial*, when only a part of the luminary is eclipsed; *total*, when the whole is eclipsed; and *central*, when the centre of the three bodies is in the same right line. [vide *Eclipse*]—*Penumbra* is a faint or partial shadow in an eclipse, observed between the perfect shadow and the full light. The penumbra arises principally from the magnitude of the sun's body: thus, suppose S to be the sun, as in plate 18, fig. 31, T the moon, the shadow of the moon to be G H, then the penumbra, or imperfect shadow, will be H L and G E.—*Scruples of incidence*, an arc of the moon's orbit, described by her from the beginning of the eclipse, to the time when her centre falls into the shadow. [vide *Eclipse* and *Scruple*]—*Eclipse of the Moon*, the privation of the light of the Moon, occasioned by the interposition of the earth, as in fig. 32, where A B represents the Sun, F C D the conical shadow of the Earth, H, G the Moon partially eclipsed, I the same totally eclipsed, and K its situation when not at all eclipsed. Lunar eclipses happen only at the time of the full moon, because it is only at that time that the earth is between the sun and the moon. They do not, however, happen every full moon, only when the moon's latitude, or distance between the centres of the earth and moon is less than the sum of the apparent semidiameters of the moon and the earth's shadow. This happens mostly at the moon's nodes.—*Eclipse of the sun*, is an occultation of the sun's body, occasioned by the interposition of the moon between the sun and the earth This is represented in fig. 33, where S is the sun, *m* the moon, *c d* the earth, *m n o p* the moon's conical shadow extended over that track of the earth, C O D to which only the eclipse is complete, then D e *n p* is the faint shadow, called the *penumbra.*

Phases. Phases are the forms under which the illuminated parts of a planet are seen, and are particularly applied to the Moon, Mercury, or Venus; thus, suppose S to represent the sun in plate 18, fig. 34, T the earth, and A B C D, &c. the moon's orbit. When the moon is at A, in conjunction with the sun, S, her dark side, being turned towards the earth, she will be invisible as at *a*, and is then called the *new moon:* when she comes to her first octant, as at B, and a quarter of her enlightened side is turned towards the earth, she will then appear to be *cusped* or horned, as at *b*. When she has run through her first quarter, as at C, she is said to be a *half moon*, as at *c*. At D she is in her second octant, and shows more than half her enlightened side, wherefore she is said to be *gibbous*, as at *d*. Her whole enlightened side being turned to the earth, in her opposition at E, she is called a *full moon*, as at *e*. In the same manner she decreases

ASTRONOMY.

from E to A, being gibbous at *f*, a half moon at *g*, and horned at *h*, until the change at A.

Revolution. Revolution is the course of a celestial body from any point of its orbit to the same point again. This is twofold, namely, diurnal and sidereal.—*Diurnal revolution* is the revolution which any celestial body performs on its own axis, which is called diurnal, because the space of time in which this is performed is called *a day*.—*Sidereal revolution* is the revolution which the body performs round another body: the space of time in which this is performed is called a *year*. Sometimes this is called a tropical revolution, if the body be supposed to move from either of the tropics, and to return to the same point again: wherefore the year, in that case, is called a *tropical year*.

Time. Time is that portion of duration which is measured by the motion of the heavenly bodies.—Time is true or apparent, and mean.—*True* or *apparent time* is the unequal time which is measured by the motion of the sun in the ecliptic.—*Mean time* is the equal time which is measured by the mean motion of the sun.—The *equation* of time is the difference between the mean and true time.

Particular affections of the Solar System.

The particular affections of the Solar System are magnitudes, relative distances, peculiar motions, &c. which belong in various proportions and measures to the bodies that compose this system.

The Sun ☉.

The Sun, plate 14, is an immense body of fire, situated near the centre of the orbits of the planets. He is discovered by the *maculæ*, or spots, on his disc to have a motion on his own axis, which he performs in $25\frac{1}{2}$ days, or in 25 days 10 hours; besides which, he is supposed to be agitated by a small motion caused by the attractions of the various surrounding planets. But the apparent annual motion of the sun is explained, according to the Copernican System, on the supposition of the earth's real motion round the sun. The figure of the sun is spheroidal, like that of the planets; his diameter is equal to a hundred diameters of the earth, and therefore the body of the sun must be one million times greater than that of the earth. His mean apparent diameter, according to Newton, is 32' 12", and his horizontal parallax is now fixed at $8"\frac{1}{10}$. The proportional magnitudes of the sun as seen from the different planets are given in plate 19, fig. 38.

Mercury ☿.

Mercury is the least of all planets, as in plate 14 and 19, and performs his periodical revolution round the sun in 87 days, 23 ho. 15 min. 43 sec.; his greatest elongation is 28° 20' distance from the sun, nearly 37 millions of miles, and eccentricity of his orbit is estimated at one-fifth of his mean distance from the sun; his apparent diameter is 11"; hence his real diameter is 3108 miles, and his magnitude $\frac{1}{14}$ the magnitude of the earth.

To illustrate the apparent paths of the planets in general, that of Mercury and Venus is given in plate 19, fig. 36, where the dotted line represents the sun's path in the ecliptic, the looped circles the motion of Mercury for seven years, and that of Venus for eight years, in which time Mercury makes 23 loops, crossing itself so many times, but Venus makes only five. The dotted lines from the earth to the ecliptic shows Mercury's apparent or geocentric motion therein for one year; in which time his path makes three loops; he has three inferior and as many superior conjunctions with the sun; is six times stationary, and three times retrograde. For the better understanding of this plate, let us suppose Mercury to set out from A towards B with a direct motion; when he comes to B he appears to stand still in the 24° of ♐ at F, as shown by the line B F; whilst going from B to C the line B F is supposed to move with him, and goes backward from F to E, or contrary to the order of the signs; when he is at C he appears stationary at E, having gone back $11\frac{1}{4}$. Now supposing him to be stationary at C on the 1st of January, on the 10th he will appear in the heavens, as at 20 near F; on the 20th he will be seen at G; on the 31st at H; on the 10th of February at I; on the 20th at K, and on the 28th at L; on the 10th of March he appears at M; on the 20th at N; on the 31st at O; on the 10th of April stationary at P; on the 20th he seems to have gone back to O, and on the 30th to be stationary at Q; from the 30th of April to the 10th of May he seems to move from Q to R, and on the 20th he is seen at S, thus going forward or backward according to the order of the letters by which his path may be easily traced.

Venus ♀.

Venus, the brightest of all the planets, is also to appearance the largest; but her real magnitude, as may be seen in plate 19, fig. 37, is somewhat less than the earth. Her apparent diameter is stated to be 58" 79", consequently her real diameter is 7498 miles. The eccentricity of her orbit is nearly 500,000 miles, her greatest elongation 47° 48'; her revolution round the sun is performed in 224 d. 16 h. 49 m. 10 sec. and her distance from the sun is nearly 69 millions of miles. When Venus appears west of the sun she is a morning star, and when eastward of the sun she is an evening star.

The Earth ⊕.

The earth is a globe 95 millions of miles distant from the sun, 7964 miles in diameter, of a spherical figure, but generally supposed to be somewhat flatter at the poles than at the equator. According to the Copernican System the earth revolves on its own axis every 24 hours from West to East, which causes an apparent diurnal motion of all the heavenly bodies from East to West, and performs her annual revolution round the sun in 365 d. 5 h. 49 m. from either of the equinoxes or solstices to the same again; but from any fixed star to the same again, as seen from the sun in 365 d. 6 h. and 9 m. the former being the length of the tropical year, and the latter the length of the sidereal.

The earth's axis makes an angle of $23\frac{1}{2}$ with the axis of its orbit, which keeps always the same oblique direction towards the same fixed stars throughout its annual course, which causes the vicissitudes of the seasons, and the difference in the length of the days and nights, as may be seen in plate 20, fig. 46, where *a, b, c, d, e, f, g, h*, represents the earth in eight different parts of its orbit equi-distant from one another. N *s* its axis, N its North Pole, *s* its South Pole, and S the sun, nearly in the centre of the earth's orbit. As the earth goes round the sun according to the order of the letters *a, b, c, d*, &c. its axis N *s* keeps the same obliquity, and is still parallel to M N *s*. When the earth is at *a*, its North Pole inclines towards the sun S, and brings all the northern places more into the light than at any other time of the year; but when the earth is at *e*, the North Pole declines from the sun, which occasions the northern places to be more in the dark than in the light, and the reverse at the southern places. When the earth is at *e* or *g*, its axis inclines neither to nor from the sun, wherefore the poles are in the boundary of light and darkness,

ized and the sun being directly over the equator makes equal day and night at all places. When the earth is at *b* it is halfway between the summer solstice and harvest equinox; at *d* it is between the harvest equinox and the winter solstice; at *f* halfway between the winter solstice and the spring equinox; and *h* halfway between the spring equinox and the summer solstice. The axis of the earth is subject to a libratory motion, called *the nutation of the earth's axis*, which is about 19″ in 9 years, and in returning to the same spot the same period of time, making about eighteen years and seven months, the period in which the moon performs the motion of her nodes.

The Moon ☽.

The Moon, though considered as a primary planet, is only a satellite to the earth, which she attends in its revolution round the sun every year. The moon's orbit is inclined to the ecliptic in an angle which is at medium 5° 9′, her mean horizontal parallax is 57′ 48″, her mean distance from the earth is upwards of two hundred thousand miles; her mean apparent diameter is stated to be 31′ 7″, consequently her real diameter is 2144 miles, and her magnitude $\frac{1}{50}$ of that of the earth. The principal motions peculiar to the moon are as follow, namely, —*Periodical* or *sidereal motion* of the moon on her own axis, when she returns to the point of the zodiac from which she set out; which revolution she performs in 27 d. 7 h. 43 m. 11 sec. called the *periodical month*. — *Synodical motion*, or her motion in her orbit round the earth, which she performs in 29 d. 12 h. 44 m. 12 sec. called the *synodical month*.—*Motion of libration*, a wavering motion of the moon about her own axis, by which she seems to turn one time towards the East, and the other towards the West.—*The motion of the moon's anomaly*, or *apogee*, which she has in common with the other planets, is performed at the rate of 6° 41″ for the diurnal motion, in the period of 8 y. 311 d. 8 h. 34 m. 57 sec. called the *anomalistic month*; her motion of the nodes, or her revolution from the ascending node to the same point again, she performs at the rate of 3° 10′ for the diurnal motion, in the period of 18 y. 223 d. 7 h. 13 m. 17 sec. which is called the *dracontic month*.

The disc or face of the moon is greatly diversified with inequalities, which, through a telescope, have the appearance of hills and vallies. These spots have been delineated on a map, as in plate 18, fig. 35, to each of which different names of astronomers and philosophers have been given by different writers.

Mars ♂.

Mars is a planet well known by his dusky red colour. He revolves on his axis in 24 h. 39 m. 22 s. and performs his revolution round the sun in 1 y. 321 d. 23 h. 15 m. 44 s. His apparent semidiameter at his nearest distance is .25″, consequently his mean distance from the sun is 144907630 miles, his diameter 4218 miles, and his magnitude rather more than $\frac{1}{4}$ of that of the earth. (Plate 19, fig. 37.) The apparent motion of Mars, like that of Venus, is sometimes direct, sometimes retrograde, and sometimes stationary; sometimes he rises before the sun, and at other times he sets after the sun. The inclination of his orbit to the plane of the ecliptic is 1° 51′, the place of his ascending node about 18° in Taurus, and his horizontal parallax is said to be 23″ 6.

Vesta ⚶.

This planet was discovered by Dr. Olbers, of Bremen, on the 29th of March, 1807. It has the appearance of a star of the fifth magnitude, (as in plate 14, fig. 13) and performs its revolution in about 3 y. 66 d. 4 h.; its mean distance is 2,163, the inclination of its orbit 7° 8′ 20″, and the place of its perihelion in 13° of the eighth sign, the place of its ascending node in 14° 38′ of the third sign. The orbits of this planet, as also of Ceres, Pallas, and Juno, are given in fig. 13, together with their eccentricities and the intersections of their orbits one with another, which latter affection is peculiar to them in distinction from the other planets. The points of intersection however necessarily vary with the changes which the planets experience in their aphelia.

Juno ⚵.

Juno was discovered by Mr. Harding, of Libienthal, near Bremen, on the 1st of September, 1804, having the appearance of a star of the eighth magnitude, as in plate 14, fig. 13. It is distinguished from the rest of the planets by the eccentricity of its orbit, as may be seen in fig. 13. It performs its revolution in 4 y. 128 d.; its apparent mean diameter, as seen from the earth, is 3″ .057; its diameter is 1425 miles; mean distance from the sun 280 millions of miles; inclination of its orbit 13° 3′ 37″ .29.

Ceres ⚳.

Ceres was discovered by M. Piazzi, astronomer royal at Palermo, in Sicily, on the 1st of January, 1801. She is of a ruddy colour, appears like a star of the eighth magnitude, as in plate 14, fig. 13, and performs her revolution round the sun in 4 y. 7 m. 10 d. Her mean distance from the sun is 260 millions of miles; her apparent mean diameter, as seen from the earth, 2″ 5; and the eccentricity of her orbit is little less than that of Mercury.

Pallas ⚴.

Pallas was discovered by Dr. Olbers, in March, 1802. It is nearly of the same magnitude with Ceres, but of a less ruddy colour. It performs its revolution round the sun in 4 y. 7 m. 11 d., its annual motion being 2° 18′ 11″, and its mean distance from the sun 266 millions of miles.

Jupiter ♃ and his satellites.

Jupiter, the biggest of all the planets, as may be seen in plate 19, fig. 37, is above 1000 times as big as our earth, his diameter being 81,000 miles. He is upwards of 400 millions of miles distant from the sun, round which he performs his annual revolution in 11 y. 315 d. 14 h. 27 m. 11 s., while he revolves on his own axis in 9 h. 56 m. Jupiter is surrounded with faint substances, called *belts*, which, owing to their variable appearance, are supposed to be clouds, and he is attended with four satellites, as in plate 14, fig. 13, which revolve round him as the moon does round the earth, and supply him with light, wherefore they are called *moons*. Their periodical revolutions are, for the first, 1 d. 18 h. 27 m. 33 s.; for the second, 3 d. 13 h. 13 m. 42 s.; for the third, 7 d. 3 h. 42 m. 33 s.; for the fourth, 16 d. 16 h. 32 m. 8 s. Jupiter's orbit is 1° 20′ inclined to the ecliptic; his North node is in about the 7th degree of Cancer, and his South node in nearly the same degree of Capricorn. As his axis is so nearly perpendicular to his orbit, he has no sensible change of seasons. The eccentricity of his orbit is $\frac{1}{4}$ his mean distance from the sun.

Saturn ♄, his satellites, and his ring.

Saturn shines with a pale feeble light, being the farthest of any of the planets that can be seen without a telescope. It is upwards of 700 millions of miles distant from the sun, round which it performs its annual revolution in 29 y. 167 d. 5 h., travelling at the rate of 18,000 miles

ASTRONOMY.

every hour. His diameter is above 67,000 miles, and consequently he is more than 600 times as big as our earth. The inclination of his orbit is said to be 2° 29′ 50″, and he revolves, according to Herschel, on his axis from West to East in 10 h. 16 m. 2 s. The most remarkable features in the appearance of Saturn, when seen through a telescope, are his satellites and his ring, both of which are to be seen in plate 14, and the latter also in plate 20, fig. 40. The disc of Saturn is likewise crossed by obscure zones, or belts, like those of Jupiter. The satellites, which are five in number, as marked by the round points in their orbits, revolve round the planet in different periods, namely, for the first, or nearest, 0 d. 22 h. 37 m. 23 s.; the second in 1 d. 8 h. 53 m. 9 s.; the third, 1 d. 21 h. 18 m. 27 s.; the fourth, 2 d. 17 h. 44 m. 51 s.; the fifth in 4 d. 12 h. 25 m. 11 s.; the sixth, 15 d. 22 h. 41 m. 16 s.; the seventh in 79 d. 7 h. 53 m. 43 s. The ring of Saturn encircles him much in the same manner as the horizon encircles the artificial globe; and when seen through the telescope it appears to be double, being divided into an interior and exterior, as he is represented in fig. 40.

The Georgium Sidus ♅ and his satellites.

The Georgium Sidus (Plate 14) was discovered by Dr. Herschel in 1781, by whom it obtained its name, although on the continent it is better known by the name of Uranus, or Herschel. It is the most distant of all the planets hitherto discovered, its revolution round the sun completing, as is supposed, a period of not less than 83 of our years. The revolutions of its six satellites, according to Herschel, are as follow—for the first, or nearest, 5 d. 21 h. 25 m.; for the second, 8 d. 17 h. 1 m. 19 s.; for the third, 10 d. 23 h. 4 m.; for the fourth, 13 d. 11 h. 5 m. 1¼ s.; for the fifth, 38 d. 1 h. 49 m.; for the sixth, 107 d. 16 h. 40 m.

The Comets.

The Comets are solid opaque bodies, which, according to Newton, are a kind of planets moving in exceedingly oblique and eccentric orbits, similar to what is represented in plate 14. The train of light which is frequently observable in them is called its *tail*; which light is emitted by its *nucleus*, or Head, that is ignited by the sun. Comets have the appearance of being *tailed* when they are westward of the sun, and set after him. Others are called *bearded*, because they emit a light resembling a beard in appearance when they are eastward of the sun; and others are termed *hairy*, when their light resembles hair, as when the sun and comet are diametrically opposite.

Practical Astronomy.

Practical astronomy comprehends that part of the science which may be learned by the means of machines or instruments, of which the principal are the Globes, the Orrery, and the Astronomical Quadrant.

The Use of the Globes.

A Globe is an artificial representation of any sphere, and is of two kinds, namely, *terrestrial*, which gives a representation of the earth, and *celestial*, that which represents the heavens, as may be seen in plate 20, fig. 43. The parts of the globes, and their several uses, are as follow:—

Axis. The axis is a brass wire, as A, on which the body of the globe is made to turn, so as to represent the motion of the earth or the heavens on their own axis, the two extremities of which, N and S, are the North and South poles.

The *brazen Meridian*, M, is a strong brass ring which encompasses the globe from North to South. The use of the Meridian is as follows:—1. It divides the globe into two hemispheres, East and West, in the former of which all bodies rise, and in the latter they set; by which both the diurnal and nocturnal arcs are divided into two equal portions, making forenoon, noon, afternoon, and midnight. Each of these four quadrants of the circle consists of 90 degrees, namely, two numbered from the equator to the poles, and the other two from the poles to the equator, as in plate 20, fig. 42. 2. It measures the greatest altitude of the heavenly bodies; on that account called their Meridian altitude. 3. It measures the elevation of the pole in an oblique and parallel sphere. 4. In a right sphere, being in the place of the horizon, it determines the right ascension of the celestial bodies. 5. It measures the declination of the heavenly bodies when they are brought to its graduated edge. The declination of the sun is thus measured by means of his place in the ecliptic, i. e. the sign and degree he is in on any given day, as marked on the horizon. 6. It measures the latitude of all places on the terrestrial globe by means of the degrees and minutes thereon marked, and also the longitude of places as marked on the equator, by showing the point where the latter is intersected by it. 7. It serves for the solution of all problems where the globe requires to be *rectified* for the latitude of the place, or for the sun's place. When the pole, North or South, is elevated above the horizon any number of degrees, equal to the latitude of the place, or the declination of the sun, the globe is said to be *rectified* for the latitude and sun's place; but in the latter case the index, or hour circle, must be turned to twelve, or noon. 8. It answers as a general meridian for all the meridian circles which are drawn on the globe at the distance of fifteen degrees from each other; and by it also parallels of latitude may be drawn on the globe at the smallest possible distance from each other.

Horizon. The Horizon, or rational Horizon, H, is the frame which supports the globe, and is divided into several concentric spaces, containing a calender of the months and days, corresponding to the 12 zodiacal constellations, each divided into 30 parts. In most globes the circle of bearings follows, marked with the cardinal and collateral points of the compass, also the circle of azemuths and amplitudes. The use of the Horizon is as follows:—1. It divides the globe into two hemispheres, upper and lower, i. e. northern and southern, and cuts the meridian at right angles. 2. It is the circle from which the altitudes of the poles and of the heavenly bodies are reckoned. 3. It determines the true rising and setting of the celestial bodies, as also their course above and below itself, which is called the *artificial day* and *night*. 4. Not only the four cardinal points, North, South, East, and West, but also four other points are marked upon it namely, the rising and setting points in the two solstices. 5. It measures the amplitude of the heavenly bodies, which is an arc of the horizon intercepted between the true East or West points and the centre of the sun or stars at their rising or setting, according to their different declinations and latitudes. 6. It is the circle in which are marked the regions or points in the sphere, from which the winds derive their names; whence these points are called the points of the compass. 7. It measures the ascensions and descensions of the heavenly bodies, &c.

Horary Circle. The Horary, or Hour Circle, is a small circle of brass, as in fig. 43, which is usually divided into twice 12 hours, the upper of which represents noon, and the lower midnight. This circle is divided so that the hours should correspond to the *meridian circles*, otherwise called *horary circles*, drawn on the globe, as M m m, &c., plate 20, fig. 41, reckoning an hour of time equal to fifteen degrees of longitude.

Quadrant of Altitude. The Quadrant of Altitude is a thin flexible piece of brass, so formed at one end, with the assistance of a screw, as to fix on any part of the horizon: it is so called because it measures the altitudes of celestial bodies, and serves the purpose of the vertical circles which are not drawn on the globe. It is divided upwards from 0 to 90 degrees, and downwards from 0 to 18 degrees. The upper divisions are used to determine the distances of places on the terrestrial globe, or the distances, altitudes, &c. of the celestial bodies on the celestial globe: for this purpose the quadrant must be screwed upon the brass meridian over the latitude of any given place, which is called *rectifying for the zenith ;* for supposing the pole to be elevated so many degrees above the horizon as are equal to the latitude of the place, then the same degree on the meridian, reckoned from the equator, is the zenith point. The lower division serves to measure the beginning, end, and duration of twilight.

Equator. The Equator on the terrestrial globe, or Equinoctial on the celestial, has the degrees and minutes marked upon it (as E in fig. 42), 180 degrees each way, i. e. Eastward and Westward, or 360 degrees quite round, numbered from a given point, called the *first meridian*, for which that which passes through the capital of the country is generally chosen. The use of the Equator is as follows:—1. It divides the globe into two equal parts, called the Northern and Southern hemispheres, every part of which is 90 degrees distant from the poles. 2. It intersects the ecliptic at two points, called the *equinoctial points*, namely, Aries and Libra. Whenever the sun comes to these points, the days and nights are equal all over the world; wherefore these periods are called the Equinoxes. 3. From this circle the declination of the sun or stars on the celestial globe, or the latitude of places on the terrestrial, are reckoned on the meridian. 4. On this circle are reckoned the right and oblique ascensions on the celestial globe, and the longitude of places on the terrestrial.

Ecliptic. The Ecliptic, e in fig. 41, and C P in plate 19, fig. 7, is the circle so called because eclipses of the sun and moon happen only within that circle. The use of the ecliptic is as follows:—1. It cuts the equator at two opposite points, making an angle of 23½, called the obliquity of the ecliptic. 2. By this obliquity of the ecliptic is determined the greatest declination of the sun, as well as the distance of the tropics from the equator, and the poles of the ecliptic from the poles of the equator. 3. It is divided into the twelve portions of thirty degrees, corresponding to the days of the month, which are distinguished by the signs of the zodiac. 4. In this circle the sun advances one degree every 24 hours, and thirty degrees every month, passing through the whole 360 degrees in a year; whence it is called the *sun's path*. 5. From this circle is measured the latitude of the stars.

Zodiac. The Zodiac is the broad belt or circle drawn on the celestial globe at the distance of about eight degrees on each side the ecliptic, E, which marks the boundary within which the planets perform their revolutions.

Colures. The Colures divide the ecliptic into four equal parts, and mark the four seasons of the year. The meridian, A E B Q, in pl. 19, fig. 7, represents the solstitial colure.

By the help of the lesser circles the terrestrial globe is divided into different portions called *Zones*, which are large, and *Climates*, which are small portions. The zones are five in number; namely, two frigid, two temperate, and one torrid. The *North frigid zone* lies within the arctic circle, T M, in fig. 7 ; and *South frigid zone* within the antarctic circle. The *North temperate zone* extends from the arctic circle to the tropic of Cancer, C R ; the *South temperate zone* from the antarctic circle to the tropic of Capricorn, K P. The *torrid zone* lies between the tropics. *Climates* are portions of the earth, contained between two small circles parallel to the equator, of such a breadth that the longest day in the parallel nearest the pole exceeds the longest day in the parallel of latitude nearest the equator, by half an hour, in the torrid and temperate zones, and by a month in the frigid zones; so that there are twenty-four climates between the equator and each polar circle, and six climates between each polar circle and its poles.

The inhabitants of the earth are likewise distinguished, by their relative situations with regard to each other, into Antoeci, Perioeci, and Antipodes. The *Antoeci* are those who live in the same degree of longitude, and in equal degrees of latitude, but the one North and the other South: they have noon at the same time, but contrary seasons of the year; consequently, the length of the days to the one is equal to the length of the nights to the other. *Perioeci* are those who live in the same latitude, but in opposite longitudes; consequently, when it is noon with the one it is midnight with the other: they have the same seasons of the year, and the same lengths of days. *Antipodes* are those who live diametrically opposite to each other; their latitudes, longitudes, seasons of the year, days, nights, being all contrary. There are other distinctions of the inhabitants into Amphiscii, Heteroscii, and Periscii, according to the manner in which their shadows fall. [vide *Amphiscii*, &c.]

The Orrery.

The Orrery is a machine which has been contrived to display the solar system with the order, motions, excentricities, and other affections of the sun and the planets. It has been constructed in a variety of forms more or less complete, but the one which is given in plate 20, fig. 45, affords the best representation of the planets that can be given on paper.

Astronomical Quadrant.

This instrument is so called because it is constructed for the purpose of taking observations of the heavenly bodies. It is usually made of brass or iron bars, having its limb A B, pl. 19, fig. 39, divided into degrees and minutes, and furnished either with two pair of plain sights, or two telescopes, one on each side of the quadrant, as C D and E F, moveable about the centre by means of the screw G; the dented wheels H and I serve to direct the instrument to any object of which the observer wishes to take the altitude, &c. This quadrant is sometimes provided with only one telescope, and a plummet to direct its movements.

Principal Writers on Astronomy in Chronological Succession.

Plato " Dialogi de Astronomia ;" *Aristoteles* " De Cœlo ;" *Eratosthenes* " De Characterismis Astrorum ;" *Aratus* " De Apparentiis ;" *Hipparchi Bithyni* " Enarrationum in Arati et Eudoxi Phænomena tres libri ;" *Gemini* " Isagoge in Arati Phenomena seu Elementa Astronomica ;" *Theodosius* " De Sphærâ ;" *Cleomedes* " De Sphærâ ;" *Manilii* " Astronomicon Poeticon ;" *Dionysius Areopagita* " De Eclipsi in Morte Christi ;" *Hygini*

"Astronomicon Poeticon;" *Plinii* "Historiæ naturalis, l. 1," &c.; *Procli* "Commentarii in Euclidem;" Ptolemæi "Almagestum," &c.; *Theonis patris Hypatice* "Commentarii in Ptolemæum;" *Martianus Capella* "De Nuptiis Mercuriæ et Philologiæ," &c.; *Achillis Tatii* "Isagoge in Arati Phænomena;" *Albategnus* "De Scientiâ Stellarum;" *Alfragani* "Elementa Astronomica,;" *Johannes de Sacrobosco* "De Sphærâ;" *Alphonsi X. Regis* "Tabulæ;" *Purbachii* "Epitome Ptolomæi Almagesti," &c.; *Regiomantanus* "De Cometis," &c.; *Pontanus* "De Rebus Cœlestibus;" *Stoefleri* "Commentarii in Proclum;" *Copernicus* "De Revolutionibus;" *Tycho Brahe* "De Mechanica Astronomiæ," &c.; *Clavii* "Kalendarii Reformatio," &c.; *Josephus Scaliger* "De Cyclometriæ," &c.; *Kepleri* "Rudolphinæ Tabulæ, Epitome Astronomiæ Copernici," &c.; *Bayeri* "Uranometria;" *Riccioli* "Almagestum novum;" *Hevelii* "Machina cælestis," &c.; *Newtonis* "Principia," &c.; *Flamstead's* "Historia cœlestis Britannica;" *Cassini* "Recueil d'Observations," &c.; *Gregorii* "Elementa Astronomiæ," &c.

ASTRO'SCOPE (*Astron.*) a kind of astronomical instrument composed of telescopes for the observation of the stars, invented and described by William Shukhard, of Tubingen, in 1698.

ASTROSCO'PIA (*Astron.*) from ἄστρον and σκέπτομαι, *speculor*; observation and contemplation of the stars.

ASTROTHE'SIA (*Astron.*) the same as Astrum.

A'STRUM (*Astron.*) or *Astron*, a constellation or assemblage of stars, in distinction from *aster*, a single star.

ASTRUM (*Chem.*) the virtue and power which accrues to things from their preparation, as the *astrum* of salt, its resolution with water or oil. *Dict. Paracelsic.*

ASTRUM (*Med.*) troches in the form of an asterisk. *Gal. de Comp. Med. sec loc.* l. 8, c. 3.

ASTRUM (*Law*) a house or place of habitation. *Placit. Hilar.* 18 Ed. 1.

A'SYLA (*Bot.*) a herb with which cattle cure themselves when they have eaten pimpernel. *Plin.* l. 27, c. 13.

ASY'LUM (*Ant.*) ἄσυλον, from α, priv. and συλάω, to violate, i. e. an inviolable place, or a place of refuge for offenders, where they were screened from the hands of justice. The *asyla*, among the Jews, were the temple, the altar of burnt offering, and the cities of refuge mentioned in Exodus xxi. 33, and Numbers xxxi. 11. A similar custom prevailed both among the Greeks and the Romans, where temples, altars, and statues, were places of refuge for criminals of every description, as Tacitus informs us, to the violation of public justice. It is said that the first asylum was erected, at Athens, by the Heraclidæ, for the protection of those who dreaded the resentment of such as had suffered from the oppression and tyranny of their grandfather Hercules. The tomb of Theseus was an asylum for slaves; the temple of Diana, at Ephesus, an asylum for debtors. At the building of Rome, Romulus left a space as a place of refuge for all sorts of persons, slaves or free-born, who wished to settle under his government: to which Virgil and Juvenal allude.
Virg. Æn. l. 8, v. 342.

Hinc lucum ingentem, quem Romulus acer asylum Rettulit.

Juven. sat. 8, v. 272.

Et tamen, ut longe repetas, longeque revolvas Nomen, ab infami gentem deducis asylo.

According to Suetonius this custom was abolished by Tiberius, at Rome; but it continued in the Græcian provinces, as we learn from the coins of Claudius, Vespasian, Domitian, Trajan, M. Aurelius, Macrinus, Elegabulus, and Decius, which were struck by the cities of Seleucia, Damascus, Heraclea, Laodicea, Antioch, Samosata, &c. bearing the inscription ΙΕΡΑ ΚΑΙ ΑϹΥΛΟϹ, i. e. sacred and inviolable. *Dionys. Hal.* l. 2; *Liv.* l. 35, c. 51; *Tacit. Annal.* l. 3, c. 60; *Plut. de Superstit. et de Vitand. Usur.*; *Sueton. in Tib.* c. 37; *Non. Marcell.* l. 1, c. 209; *Serv. in Æn.*; *Vaillant. Numis. Græc.*; *Spanheim. de Præst. et Us. Numm. Dissert.* 9, p. 778, &c.

ASYM'METRY (*Math.*) ἀσυμμετρία, a relation between two quantities, having no common measure, as between 1 and the $\sqrt{2}$.

ASY'MPTOTE (*Meth.*) ἀσύμπτωτος, a name for lines continually approaching each other, but which, if infinitely produced, can never meet, so called from α, priv. and συμπίπτω, to meet; or, in other words, a tangent to the curve when conceived to be at an infinite distance, which is best illustrated by the asymptote of the conchoid, as in the subjoined figure: suppose A B C to be part of a

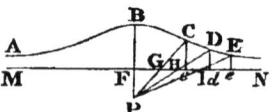

conchoid, and the line M N be so drawn that the parts F B, G C, H D, I E, &c. of right lines drawn from the pole P to the curve B C D, be equal to each other, then will the line M N be the asymptote of the curve, because the perpendicular C c is shorter than F B, and D d than C c, &c. so that two lines continually approach, yet the points E e, &c. can never coincide.—*Of curves* of the first kind, that is, the Conic Sections, only the hyperbola has more than one asymptote; all curves of the second kind have one at least, and may have three; and all curves of the fourth kind may have four. The conchoid, cissoid, and logarithmic curve have each one.—*Asymptotes of the hyperbola* are thus described; suppose, as in the annexed figure, C P to be a diameter of an hyperbola, R A S and C D the semiconjugate to it; then, if F E be a tangent at the point A, A E = F A = C D, and the lines C G, C G, be drawn from the centre C through the points E and F, these lines C G, C G, will be the asymptotes of the hyperbola R A S. *Apollon. Perg. Con. Sect.* l. 2, prop. 1, &c.

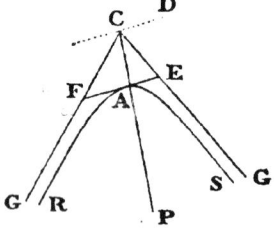

ASYMPTO'TON (*Med.*) ἀσύμπτωτον, i. e. not meeting, not compressed or brought into contact. *Hippocrat.* περὶ χυμῶν; *Gal. ad Glauc.* l. 1.

ASY'NDETON (*Rhet.*) ἀσύνδετον, from α, priv. and σύνδεω, to bind; a figure in which many words are joined without a conjunction, as *veni, vidi, vici.* *Dionys. Hal. in Jud. Lys.* c. 9; *Sophron. apud Phot. Cod.* 5; *Philostrat. in Vit. Antiph.*; *Schol. in Aphthon. Progymn. de Ethopoeia.*

A'TABAL (*Mus.*) a kind of tabor used among the Moors, which is probably a word of Moorish extraction.

ATAMA'RAM (*Bot.*) the *Annona squamosa* of Linnæus.

ATAMA'SCO (*Bot.*) a species of the *Amaryllis* of Linnæus.

ATARA'XIA (*Ant.*) another name for stoical apathy, from α, priv. ταράσσω, to disturb.

ATA'XIA (*Med.*) ἀταξία, from α, priv. and τάσσω, to dispose, irregularity; a term applied to the pulse or to fevers. *Hipp. Epidem.* l. 1 & 3.

A'TCHE (*Com.*) the smallest coin in the Grand Seignor's dominions equal to $\frac{2}{3}$ of a farthing.

ATCHIE'VEMENT (*Her.*) vulgarly called hatchment, the arms of any family, with all the ornaments belonging to their several degrees, as crest, helmet, mantle, &c. or of any person deceased, painted on canvass, and fixed against the wall of his late dwelling-house to denote his death. The atchievement marks not only the degree of the person, but also, whether a bachelor, married man, or widower, a maid, married woman, or widow. [vide *Heraldry*]

ATE'BRAS (*Chem.*) a subliming vessel.

ATE'CHNIA (*Med.*) ἀτιχνία, from α, priv. and τιχνη, art; a want of art.

ATEGAR (*Cus.*) a weapon among the Saxons, which from aeton, to throw, and gapa, weapon, seems to have been a hand weapon.

ATELLA'NÆ (*Ant.*) comic and satirical pieces among the Romans, so called from Atella, a town of the Osci or Tuscany, where they were first represented; they were something similar to our farces. *Cic. ad Fam.* l. 9, ep. 16; *Val. Maxim.* l. 3, c. 4; *Diomed. de Elocut.* l. 3; *Macrob. Saturn.* l. 3, c. 7; *Gyrald. de Sat. Roman.*; *Salmas. Exercitat. Plin.* p. 77.

A-TE'MPO (*Mus.*) Italian for *in time*, an expression employed only when the regular measure has been interrupted.

ATHAMA'NTA (*Bot.*) a genus of plants, Class 5 *Pentandria*, Order 2 *Digynia*, the *Oreoselinum* of Tournefort.
   Generic Characters. CAL. *umbel universal* manifold; *involucre universal*, many leaved.—COR. *universal* uniform.—STAM. *filaments* five; *anthers* roundish.—PIST. *germ* inferior; *styles* two, distant; *stigmas* obtuse.—PER. none; *fruit* ovate oblong; *seeds* two.
   Species. The species are perennials, as—*Athamanta libanotis, Lygusticum, Apium libanotis,* seu *Daucus,* Mountain Spignel, or Stone Parsley.—*Athamanta cervaria, Selinum libanotis, Daucus,* seu *Cervaria,* Broad-leaved Spignel, or Black-Heart Root.—*Athamanta oreoselinum,* seu *Oreoselinum,* Divaricated Spignel, or Mountain Parsley.—*Athamanta Cretensis, Libanotis,* seu *Daucus,* Cretan Spignel, or Candy Carrot. *Clus. Hist. var. Plant.; J. Bauh. Hist. Plant.; C. Bauh. Pin.; Ger. Herb.; Park. Theat. Botan.; Raii Hist. Plant.; Tournef. Inst.*

ATHANA'SIA (*Med.*) from α, priv. and θάνατος, mors; a medicine for infirmities of the liver, &c.

ATHANASIA (*Bot.*) a genus of plants, Class 19 *Syngenesia*, Order 1 *Polygamia Æqualis,* the *Baccharis* of Vaillant.
   Generic Characters. CAL. common umbricate.—COR. compound uniform.—STAM. *filaments* five; *anther* cylindric. —PIST. *germ* oblongish; *style* filiform; *stigma* bifid.
   Species. The species are either shrubs or perennials, as— *Athanasia capitata, Chrysanthemum,* seu *Tanacetum,* Hairy Athanasia.—*Athanasia maritima, Filago maritima, Santolina maritima, Gnaphalium maritimum,* seu *Chrysanthemum,* Sea Athanasia Cudweed, or Cottonweed.—*Athanasia erithmifolia Santolina, Jacobæa,* seu *Coma aurea,* Sampire-leaved Athanasia.—*Athanasia parviflora, Tanicetum erithmifolium, Santolina, Coma aurea, Elichrysum,* seu *Ageratum,* Small-flowered Athanasia, &c. There are a few annuals, namely,—*Athanasia annua, Elichrysum inodorum, Chrysanthemum erymbiferum, Bellis polyclonos.—Achillea inodora,* seu *Ageratum,* the Annual Athenasia. *J. Bauh. Hist. Plant.; C. Bauh. Pin.; Ger. Herb.; Park. Theat. Botan.; Raii Hist. Plant., &c.*

ATHANA'SIAN *creed* (*Ecc.*) a formula of faith which has been adopted into the Liturgy of the Church of England; so called because it is said to have been drawn up by St. Athanasius: a point upon which ecclesiastical writers are not agreed. *Du Pin. Bib. des Aut. de* iv. *Siec.; Waterland. Hist. Athanas. Creed.*

ATHA'NATI (*Ant.*) ἀθάνατοι, immortal; the name of a squadron of ten thousand horse among the Macedonians, which was always kept complete, by filling up the vacancies of every one when he died.

ATHA'NOR (*Chem.*) from the Arabic *Athan*; a digesting furnace which retained the heat for so long a time as a month; and was so contrived that it might be increased or diminished at pleasure.

ATHA'REN (*Astrol.*) a term applied to the moon when she is in the same day and minute as the sun.

A'THE (*Law*) a privilege of administering an oath; such as was granted to the monks of Glastonbury by Hen. II.

A'THELING (*Polit.*) atheling, athel, or abel, Saxon for noble; was the title given to the king's eldest son, as the Prince of Wales is in our time.

ATHE'NA (*Med.*) ἀθηνα, a plaister, recommended by Asclepiades, and mentioned by Orobasius, Actius, and Paulus. *Æginet.*

ATHE'NÆ (*Lit.*) the title of Anthony Wood's History of Oxford.

ATHENÆ'A (*Bot.*) a genus of plants, Class 8 *Octandria*, Order 1 *Monogynia*.
   Generic Characters. CAL. *perianth* one-leaved.—COR. none.—STAM. *filaments* eight; *anthers* sagittate.—PIST. *germ* superior; *style* setaceous; *stigma* depressed.—PER *capsule* globose; *seeds* three to five.
   Species. The only species is the—*Athenæa Guianensis,* seu *Iroucana,* a shrub, native of Guiana.

ATHENÆ'UM (*Ant.*) ἀθηναιον, a public school erected at Athens, which was frequented by philosophers, poets, and rhetoricians, for the purpose of arguing, reciting, declaiming, and other exercises of a scholastic or philosophic kind. There were several buildings of this name at Athens, and one at Rome, erected by the emperor Adrian. *Dio.* l. 73; *Aurel. Vict. de Cæsar.; Lamprid. in Alex.* c. 35; *Capitolin. in Pertinax.* c. 11.

ATHENATO'RIUM (*Chem.*) a thick glass cover, to be luted to a cucurbit when the alumbic is taken off. *Theat. Chem.* vol. iii. p. 33.

ATHENIO'NIS *catapotium* (*Med*) a cough pill mentioned by Celsus, consisting of myrrh, pepper, castor, and apium.

ATHENI'PPON (*Med.*) a collyrium for the eyes, mentioned by Galen, and another by Scribonius Largus.

A'THER (*Nat.*) ἀθηρ, the prickly part, or beard of barley. *Hipp. de Epidem.* l. 5.

ATHE'RA (*Med.*) ἀθηρα, a kind of pap for children; also a kind of liniment. *Dioscor.* l. 2, c. 114; *Plin.* l. 22, c. 25.

ATHE'RINA (*Ich.*) Atherine; a fish very full of bones, but good food and easy of digestion. *Gesn. de Aquat.; Aldrov. Ichth.*

ATHERINA, *in the Linnean system,* a genus of fishes of the Abdominal Order.
   Generic Characters. Upper Jaw a little flat; Gill-membrane brayed; Sides with a silvery stripe.
   Species. The species are the *Atherina hispetus, menidia, schama,* and *Japonica.*

ATHERO'MA (*Med.*) ἀθηρωμα, a kind of tumor in the neck or arm-holes, containing a matter like ἀθηρα, a pap. *Cels. de Re Med.* l. 7, c. 6; *Aet. Tetrab.* 2, serm. 3, c. 83; *Paul. Æginet.* l. 4, c. 33; *Act. Meth. Med.* l. 2, c. 12; *Gorr. Def. Med.*

ATHLE'TÆ (*Ant.*) ἀθληται, from ἀθλέω, to contend; a combatant, champion, or any one who is engaged in the contests usually exhibited at the games, as wrestlers, runners, pugilists, &c. *Vitruv. Præf. in lib.* 9, *Architect.*

ATHLE'TICUS (*Med.*) ἀθλητικός, athletic; an epithet, signifying full, or robust, when applied by Hippocrates to the ἕξις, or habit of the body; full and strong when applied to the *victus*, or food. *Foes. Œconom. Hippocrat.*

ATHLOTHE'TÆ (*Ant.*) ἀθλοθέται, the judges who presided at the Athletic games, in distinction, according to Phavorinus; sometimes from the ἀγωνοθέται, who presided at musical contests.

ATHWA'RT (*Mar.*) an epithet, used in several phrases to signify a cross, the line of the ship's course, as 'We discovered a fleet standing *athwart* us.' "*Athwart* the forefoot" is applied to the flight of a cannon ball, fired from one ship across the line of another's course, but a-head of her to bring her to. "*Athwart hawse*" expresses the situation of a ship when she is driven by wind or tide across the stern of another vessel, whether in contact, or at a small distance from each other. "*Athwart* ships," reaching across the ship from one side to the other.

ATHY'MIA (*Med.*) from α, priv. and θυμὸς, the mind; dejection of spirits attendant upon some diseases.

A'TIA (*Law*) a writ of inquiry, whether a person be committed to prison on just cause of suspicion. [vide *Odio et Atia*]

ATIBAR (*Com.*) Gold dust on the coast of Africa.

ATI'LIA *Lex* (*Ant.*) the name of several laws enacted by members of the Atilian family, as 1, by Atilius, a tribune, concerning the towns which surrendered themselves, U. C. 543. *Liv.* l. 26, c. 33. 2. Concerning the guardians, U. C. 567. *Ulp. in Fragm.* 3. Concerning the military tribunes, passed by L. Atilius and C. Marcius, tribunes of the people. *Liv.* l. 9, c. 30.

ATILIA (*Archæol.*) Utensils or country implements.

ATI'NIA (*Bot.*) a sort of Elm. *Plin.* l. 16, c. 17.

ATINIA *lex* (*Ant.*) a law which gave the tribunes the privilege of a senator. *Aul. Gell.* l. 45, c. 8.

ATI'ZOES (*Min.*) a precious stone, shining like silver, three fingers in size. *Plin.* l. 37, c. 10.

ATLA'NTES (*Archæol.*) ἄτλαντες, from ἀτλάω, to bear; images of men bearing up pillars, or supporting the building; as Atlas bore the heavens on his shoulders. *Vitruv.* l. 6, c. 10.

ATLA'NTIDES (*Astron.*) another name for the *Pleiades*.

ATLA'NTIUS *nodus* (*Bot.*) the first or bottom joint of the thorn which bears up the rest. *Plin.* l. 28, c. 8.

A'TLAS (*Geog.*) the name of a book, containing maps of the whole world; so called from Atlas, who was fabled to have borne the world on his shoulders.

A'TLAS (*Anat.*) the first vertebra of the neck which supports the head.

ATLAS (*Com.*) a satin manufactured in the Indies. *Mort.*

ATMOSPHERE (*Nat.*) from ἀτμὸς, vapour, and σφαῖρα, a sphere or region; signifies properly that region of the air next to the earth, which receives the vapours and exhalations, and is terminated by the refraction of the sun's light. In this sense, it is most commonly understood by natural philosophers; although sometimes it is made to signify the whole mass of ambient air.—*Atmosphere of consistent bodies*, according to Mr. Boyle, is a kind of sphere, formed by the effluvia emitted from them.

ATMOSPHERE (*Elect.*) that sphere which surrounds the surface of electrified bodies, and is formed by the effluvia issuing from them.—*Magnetic atmosphere*, that sphere within which the virtue of the magnet acts.

ATMOSPHE'RIC *Stones* (*Nat.*) vide *Aeroliths*.—*Atmospheric Tides*, certain periodical changes in the atmosphere, similar to those of the ocean, and produced from nearly the same causes; of this description are the Equinoctial winds.

ATMOSPHE'RICAL *clock* (*Mech.*) a machine for measuring the mean temperature of the air, which was proposed by Dr. Brewster.

ATA'CIUM (*Bot.*) a name for *Antirrhinum*.

ATO'CIUM (*Med.*) ἀτόκιον, a medicine which prevents conception.

ATO'LLI (*Med.*) a sort of Indian pap, made of maize.

A'TOM (*Nat.*) ἄτομος, sc., οὐσία, *individua substantia quæ secari non potest*; a thing so small that it cannot be divided.

A'TONY (*Med.*) ἀτονία, from α, priv. and τίνω, to extend; a want of due tension, or a relaxation of the system.

A'TRA *bilis* (*Med.*) Black-Bile, or Melancholy, properly signifies that humour of the body which is rendered, by adustion, preternaturally mordacious, harsh, and malignant. *Aret. de Sign. et Caus. Acut. Morb.* l. 1, c. 5; *Ruf. Ephes.* l. 1, c. 3; *Gal. Comm. in Hippoc. Epidem.* l. 1, &c.

ATRA'CTYLIS (*Bot.*) ἀτρακτυλὶς, distaff-thistle, a plant; so called from ἄτρακτος, a spindle, because the spindle was formerly made of it. Its leaves, when taken by decoction, are aperitive, sudorific, and an antidote against poisons. *Theoph. Hist. Plant.* l. 6, c. 4; *Dioscor.* l. 3, c. 107; *Plin.* l. 21, c. 15, &c.; *Gal. de Simpl.* l. 6; *Oribas. Med. Collect.* l. 15; *Aet. Tetrab.* 1, serm. 1; *Paul. Æginet.* l. 7, c. 3.

ATRACTYLIS, *in the Linnean system*, a genus of plants, Class 19 *Syngenesia*, Order 1 *Polygamia Æqualis*.
Generic Characters. CAL. outer many-leaved.—COR. compound radiate.—STAM. filaments five; anther cylindric.—PIST. germ very short; style filiform; stigma bifid.—PER. none; seeds turbinate; receptacle villose.
Species. The species are some annuals, as—*Atractylis cancellata, Acarna, Eryngium*, seu *Carduus*, Netted Atractylis. Some biennials, as—*Atractylis humilis, Centaurea, Cnicus*, seu *crocodeloides*, Dwarf Atractylis. Some perennials, as—*Atractylis gummifera, Cnicus, Carlina, Carduus*, seu *Chameleon*, Gummy-rooted Atractylis, &c. *Dodon. Stirp. Hist.*; *Clus. Hist. rar. Plant.*; *J. Bauh. Hist. Plant.*; *C. Bauh. Pin.*; *Park. Theat. Botan.*; *Raii Hist. Plant.*; *Tournef. Inst.*

ATRAG'ENE (*Bot.*) Traveller's joy, a plant, the flowers, bark, seeds, and root of which are of a caustic quality.

ATRAGENE, *in the Linnean system*, a genus of plants, Class 13 *Polyandria*, Order 7 *Polygynia*.
Generic Characters. CAL. perianth four-leaved.—COR. petals twelve.—STAM. filaments very many; anthers oblong.—PIST. germs very many; styles villose; stigma simple.—PER. none; seeds very many.
Species. The species are shrubs, as—*Atragene Japonica, Atragene Alpina, Clematis, Capensis*, seu *Pulsatilla, Zeylanica*. *Clus. Hist. rar. Plant.*; *J. Bauh. Hist.*; *C. Bauh. Pin.*; *Ger. Herb.*; *Park. Theat. Bot.*; *Raii Hist. Plant.*

ATRAMENTUM (*Nat.*) the blood of the Cuttle-fish.

ATRAMENTUM *sutorium* (*Chem.*) χάλκανθος, Copperas or Vitriol. *Cic. de Nat. Deor.* l. 2, c. 50; *Plin.* l. 34, c. 12; *Oribas. Med. Collect.* l. 13.

ATRAPHA'XIS (*Bot.*) the Greek name for the *Atriplex*.

ATRAPHAXIS, *in the Linnean system*, a genus of plants, Class 6 *Hexandria*, Order 2 *Digynia*.
Generic Characters. CAL. perianth two-leaved.—COR. petals two.—STAM. filaments six; anthers roundish.—PIST. germ compressed; style none; stigmas two capitate.—PER. none; seed one.
Species. The two species are—*Atraphaxis spinosa*, seu *Atriplex*, Prickly branched Atraphaxis, a shrub, native of Siberia.—*Atraphaxis undulata, Polygonum*, seu *Arbuscula*, Waved-leaved Atraphaxis, a shrub, native of the Cape of Good Hope. *Tournef. Inst. Re. Herb*; *Boerhaav. Ind.*

ATREBA'TICÆ *Vestes* (*Ant.*) χιτῶνες ἀτρεβατικαὶ, a sort of cloths made at Arras, in Flanders. *Suidas.*; *Cæl. Rhodig. Ant. Lect.* l. 16, c. 10.

ATRI'CES (*Med.*) Small tubercles about the anus.

A'TRICI (*Med.*) small sinuses in the intestinum rectum.

ATRIE'NSIS (*Ant.*) *custodes Atrii*; servants of special trust, who had the charge of the images, plate, and pedigree of the family which were kept in the porch, or hall. *Plaut. Asin.* act. 2, scen. 2, v. 84.

*Ex templo facio faciewm me, atque magnificum virum
Dico me esse atriensem.*

Cic. Parad. l. 5; Columel. l. 12, c. 3; Ursin. Append. ad Cratccon. in Triclin.; Nardin. Rom. Vet. l. 6, c. 13.

A-TRI'P (*Mar.*) an epithet applied to the anchor and sails: "The anchor is *a-trip*" when it is just drawn out of the ground in a perpendicular direction. "The top-sails are *a-trip*" when they are just started from the cap.

ATRI'PLEX (*Bot.*) ORACHE, a plant called in the Greek ἀνδραφάξις, or ἀτράφαξις. because, ἄδρως αἴξει, it grows immediately to its full height. The seeds of this plant are purgative, and often act as an emetic. *Theophrast. Hist. Plant.* l. 7, c. 2; *Dioscor.* l. 2, c. 145; *Plin.* l. 20, c. 20; *Cæl. Aurelian. Chron.* l. 5, c. 11; *Oribas. Med. Coll.* l. 15; *Aet. Tetrab.* l, serm. 1; *Paul. Æginet de Re Med.* l. 7, c. 3.

ATRIPLEX, in the Linnean system, a genus of plants, Class 23 *Polygamia*, Order 1 *Monoecia*.

Generic Characters. CAL. *perianth* five-leaved.—COR. none. STAM. *filaments* five; *anthers* twin.—PIST. *germ* orbiculate; *style* short; *stigmas* reflex.—PER. none; *seed* one.

Species. The species are partly annuals, as—*Atriplex marina*, Serrated Sea-Orache.—*Atriplex hastata*, Broad-leaved Wild Orache, vulgarly called Fat-Hen, &c.; and partly shrubs, as—*Atriplex portulacoides, Halimus*, seu *Portulaca marina*, Dwarf Shrubby Orache, or Common Sea Purslane. *Matthiol. Kraeut; Lobel Observat. Sylvest.; J. Bauh. Hist.; C.Bauh.Pin.; Ger.Herb.; Park. Theat. Botan.; Raii Hist. Plant.*

ATRI'PLICIS (*Ent.*) a species of Scarabæus.

A'TRIUM (*Ant.*) a court before the house, and sometimes a churchyard.

ATRO'PA (*Bot.*) from Atropos, one of the Fates, who was supposed to cut the thread of life; a genus of plants, Class 5 *Pentandria*, Order 1 *Monogynia*.

Generic Characters. CAL. *perianth* one-leaved.—COR. *petals* one.—STAM. *filaments* five.—PIST. *germ* semi-ovate; *style* filiform; *stigma* headed.—PER. *berry* globular; *seeds* very many.

Species. The species are mostly perennials, as *Atropa Belladonna*, seu *Solanum*, Deadly Nightshade, or Dwale. —*Atropa mandragora*, Mandrake; but the—*Atropa physaloides*, seu *Alkengi*, Peruvian Deadly Nightshade, is an annual, and some others are shrubs, as *Atropa frutescens, Physalis*, seu *Belladonna*, Shrubby Atropa, &c. *Fuchs. Hist. Stirp. &c. Lobel. Plant. Hist. et Adver.; Clus. Hist. Plant. Rar.; J. Bauh. Hist. Plant.; C. Bauh. Pin.; Ger. Herb.; Park. Theat. Botan.; Raii Hist. Plant.*

ATROPHUS (*Med.*) one labouring under the disease of atrophy.

A'TROPHY (*Med.*) ἀτροφία, from ἀ, priv. and τρέφω, to nourish, atrophy; a sort of consumption by means of a defective nourishment. *Cels.* l. 3, c. 22.

ATROPHY, in Cullen's Nosology, is a genus of diseases, Class *Cachexia*, Order *Marcores*.

ATTA (*Ant.*) ἄττα, or πάτερ, a Thessalian; a term of respect given by young people to their elders. *Fest.*

ATTA (*Med.*) a limper, or one who from some defect in his feet walks on the fore part instead of the tread. *Fest. de Verb. Signif.*

ATTACHIA'RE (*Law*) from *attacher*, to attach, or apprehend by force of a writ, or precept. *Lamb. Eiren.* l. 2, c. 26.

ATTACHIAME'NTA *bonorum* (*Law*) a distress taken upon goods or chattels.—*Attachiamenta de spinis et bosco*, a privilege granted to the officers of a forest, to take to their own use thorns, bushes, &c. of the forest.

ATTA'CHMENT (*Law*) a laying on of hands, or apprehending by virtue of a precept; it differs from an arrest, inasmuch as it lays hold of the goods, as well as the person. It differs from a *capias*, inasmuch as the latter belongs to real and the former to personal actions. *Bract.* l. 4; *Britt.* c. 26; *Flet.* l. 2, c. 1, &c.; *Horn. Mir. of Just.* c. 2, sect. 6; *F. N. B.* 40, &c.; *Kitch*, 79, &c.; *Lamb Eiren.* l. 2, c. 26; *New Nat. Brev.* 6, &c.—*Attachment of privilege*, a power to apprehend a man in a privileged state. *Kitch.* 79.—*Foreign Attachment*, an attachment of the goods of a *foreigner*, to satisfy his creditors.—*Attachment of the forest*, the lower of the three courts held there, of which the Sweynmote is the middle, and the Justice in Eyre's seat the highest. It is so called because attachments against offenders are there received and enrolled. *F. N. B.* 105; *Crompt. Court.* 164; *Manw. For. Laws*, c. 3, &c.

ATTA'CK (*Mil.*) a general assault, or onset, made to gain a post, or any particular point.—*Attack of a siege*, are the works which the besiegers carry on, as trenches, galleries, mines, &c. in order to take the place by storm.—*Regular attack*, an attack made in due form, according to the rules of art, called also right, or *droit*; so also, "To gain a place by right attack," is to gain the place by formal attack and regular works without a general storm.—*False attack*, is an effort of the besiegers to make themselves masters of the place, but made with less vigour than a real attack, in order to divert the attention of the besieged from the point really aimed at.—*Attack in front or flank* i. e. an attack of the salient angle, or both sides of the bastion, which the French call *en Front et sur les Flancs*.—*Attack and Defence*, a part of the drill exercise for recruits learning the sword exercise.

ATTAGEN (*Orn.*) ἀτταγᾶς, called by the Greeks, λαγώπυς, "Harefoot," on account of its downy feet; an Asiatic partridge, native of Ionia in Asia Minor, the flesh of which Aristophanes, in Athenæus, calls "The sweetest that is dressed at public feasts;" also

Hor. Epod. od. 2, v. 53.

*Non Afra avis descendat in ventrem meum,
Non attagen Ionicus.*

Mart. l. 13, ep. 61.

*Inter sapores fertur alitum primus
Ionicarum gustus attagenarum.*

This bird, or one supposed to be like it, is called by the same name by Gessner, Aldrovandus, and Ray, and by Willoughby the GOR-COCK, MOOR-COCK, or RED-GAME. *Plin.* l. 10, c. 48. *Athen.* l. 9, c. 9. *Oribas. Med. Coll.* l. 2, c. 42.

ATTA'INDER (*Law*) *attinctura*; the stain or corruption of blood which arises from being condemned for any crime. —*Attainder on appearance*, is by battle, confession, or verdict.—*Attainder by battle*, is when the party appealed by another chooses to try the truth by battle rather than by jury.—*Attainder by confession*, is either by pleading guilty at the bar before the judges, and not putting oneself on one's trial by a jury; or before the coroner in sanctuary, when, in ancient times, the offender was obliged to abjure the realm. —*Attainder by verdict*, is when the prisoner at the bar pleads not guilty to the indictment, and is pronounced guilty by the verdict of the jury.—*Attainder by process*, or *outlawry*, is when the party fleeth. *Staundf. Plac. Cor.* 44, &c.; *Co. Lit.* 391, &c.—*Bill of attainder*, a bill brought into parliament for attainting persons condemned of high treason, which have been passed into acts occasionally from the reign of Charles II. to the present time.

ATTA'INT (*Law*) 1. *attinctus*, attainted, stained, or blackened. 2. A writ that lieth to inquiry, whether a jury of twelve men gave a false verdict. A verdict cannot be attainted by less than twelve men. *Bract.* l. 4, tr. 1, c. 34; *Flet.* l. 5, c. 22, § 2, &c.; *Co. Ent.* 61.

ATTAINT (*Vet.*) a knock, or hurt, in a horse's leg.

ATTAL-SA'RASIN (*Archæol.*) a name among the ancient miners of Cornwall for an old deserted mine.

ATTE'LABUS (*Ent.*) ἀττέλαβος, ἀττέλιβος, or according to Theophrastus ἀττέλιβος; the smallest kind of locust without wings. *Theophrast. Hist. Plant.* l. 2, c. 4; *Plin.* l. 29, c. 4.

ATTELABUS, in the Linnean system, a genus of animals, Class *Insecta*, Order *Coleoptera*.
  Generic Characters. *Antennæ* moniliform; *head* pointed behind.
  Species. The species are distinguished into those which have their jaws bifid, those which have the jaw one-toothed, hind-feelers hatchet-shaped, and those which have the feelers clavate. Of the first kind are the—*Attelabus coryli*, a small insect found chiefly on hazel-trees, &c.—*Attelabus Betulæ*, which is found on the birch.—Of the second sort is the *Attelabus apiarius*, a species so called from the mischief which it commits among bee-hives.

ATTELA'NÆ (*Ant.*) vide *Attellanæ*.

To ATTE'MPT (*Mar.*) in French *tenter un passage*, to attempt a passage with a vessel.

To ATTE'ND (*Mar.*) in French *veiller aux signaux*, to attend the signals.

ATTE'NDANT (*Law*) one that owes duty or service to another, or is otherwise dependant upon him, as a wife when endowed of lands by a guardian, &c. is attendant on that guardian.

ATTE'NTION! (*Mil.*) the word of command which is given in the British army preparatory to any particular exercise or direction.

ATTENUA'NTIA (*Med.*) attenuants; attenuating medicines, which tend to promote excretion and secretion.

ATTE'NUATED (*Bot.*) tapered, or tapering; an epithet for a leaf, peduncle, scape, &c. as *attenuatum folium*, a leaf tapering towards one or both extremities.

ATTE'RMINING (*Law*) from *Atterminer*, the granting a time or term for the payment.

ATTESTA'TION (*Law*) the act of bearing witness in a court of law; also the evidence given.

A'TTIC (*Ant.*) an epithet denoting purity, as an *Attic* witness.

ATTIC (*Lit.*) an epithet signifying delicate or fine, as the *Attic* muse, and *Attic* salt, i. e. wit which was peculiar to the Athenians.

ATTIC Order (*Archit.*) a little order which is usually placed upon a greater. Instead of pillars, this order has only pilasters, with a cornice and architrave for an entablature, as that, for instance, in the castle of Versailles above the Ionic, on the side of the garden.—*Attic*, or *Athenian base*, a particular kind of base, attached by modern architects to the Doric pillar.—*Attic* signifies also a kind of building in which there is no roof or covering to be seen, as was usual in the houses of the Athenians.—*Attic of a roof*, a sort of platform or parapet, which is of two kinds, namely, the —*Attic continued*, which encompasses the whole pourtour of a building without any interruption.—*Attic interposed*, that which is situated between two tall stories, and sometimes adorned with columns and pilasters.—*Attic story*, the upper story of a house.

ATTIC *dialect* (*Gram.*) a dialect of the Greek; so called because it was used by the Athenians.

A'TTICISM (*Ant.*) ἀττικισμός, an elegancy of speech, after the manner of the Attic dialect.

A'TTICKI (*Vet.*) a breed of Arabian horses.

A'TTICUM (*Med.*) a plaister described by Hippocrates. *Epidem.* l. 4.

ATTICU'RGES (*Ant.*) ἀττικουργής, *attico opere factus*; made after the Athenian fashion.

ATTILA'TUS *equus* (*Ant.*) a horse dressed in his geers or harness. *Flet.* l. 1, c. 23.

ATTI'LTUM (*Ant.*) *attilamentum*; the rigging of a ship. *Flet.* l. 1, c. 25.

ATTI'RE (*Sport.*) the branching horns of a stag.

ATTIRE (*Her.*) the term which designates the horns of stags and similar animals in blazoning coats of arms. The attires of a stag are both the horns affixed to the scalp.

ATTIRE (*Bot.*) a term formerly used to denote one of the three parts belonging to the flower, of which the former are the Empalement and the Foliation. It was either *Florid Attire*, otherwise called *Thrums*, as in the flowers of the Marigold, Tansey, &c.; or it was *Semiform Attire*, consisting of two parts, i. e. the *Chives*, otherwise called *Stamina*; and the *Semets*, or *Apices* in each attire. *Grew. Anat. Plant.*

ATTI'RED (*Her.*) an epithet used in blazoning, in application to such animals as stags, harts, &c. which are provided with horns.

A'TTITUDE (*Paint.*) the posture of a figure or statue, or the disposition of its parts, by which we discover the action it is supposed to be engaged in, and the very sentiment of mind which the artist wishes to delineate.

ATTO'LLENS (*Anat.*) lifting up; an epithet applied to some muscles, as—*Attollens aurem*, a muscle of the ear, whose office it is to draw the ear upwards.—*Attollens oculum*, the same as the Elevator oculi.—*Attollentes*, a pair of muscles which together draw the upper lip upward and outward.

ATTO'NITUS *morbus* (*Med.*) or *attonitus stupor*, Epilepsy; so called because the person affected falls down as it were in a perfect stupor.

ATTORNA'RE *rem* (*Law*) to atturn or turn over money and goods, i. e. to assign them to some particular use and service.

ATTORNA'TO *faciendo vel recipiendo* (*Law*) a writ to command a sheriff, &c. to admit an attorney to appear for the person that owes suit of that court. *F. N. B.* 156.

ATTO'RNEY (*Law*) *attornatus*, from *ad* and *tour*; one that is appointed by another man to do a thing in his absence. *Reg. Orig.* 20, &c.—*Public attorney*, is in the courts of record, king's bench, &c.—*Private attorney* acts upon particular occasions, who is made by letter of attorney.—*Letter of attorney*, an instrument which gives full power to act for another.—*Attorney at law*, any one taking upon him the business of other men by whom he is retained.—*Attorney of the Duchy court of Lancaster*, the second officer in that court, and assessor to the court.—*Attorney General*, a great law-officer under the king, made by letters patent.

ATTO'RNMENT (*Law*) the consent of the tenant to the grant of the seignory, whereby he agreed to become the tenant to the new lord. *Bract.* l. 11, c. 99; *Old Nat. Brev.* 170, &c.; *F. N. B.* 147; *Kitch.* 260; *Reg. Orig.* 170, &c.

ATTRA'CTION (*Nat.*) that universal tendency that all bodies have towards one another, by which the whole system of the universe is supposed to preserve its coherence, and all the several bodies be made to move within their several spheres of activity by mutual attraction to their proper centre. This principle is termed by Copernicus, " An appetence, *appetentia*, which the Creator has impressed upon all the parts of matter, in order to their uniting and coalescing into a globular form, &c." Kepler also speaks of gravity, as " A corporeal and mutual affection between similar bodies in order to their union." This principle has since been applied to the motion of the heavenly bodies by Sir Isaac Newton, in his Principia, for the illustration of the Copernican system. Attraction is of different kinds, as applied to particular bodies, as Magnetism and Electricity.—*Centre of Attraction* [vide *Centre*] *Copernic. de Rev. Orb. Cælest.* l. 1, c. 9; *Kepler. Introduc. Ast. Nov.*; *Gilbert. de Mag.* l. 2, aphor. 86, &c.; *et de Motiv.* &c.; *Newt. Principia Defin.* 8, &c.

ATTRACTION *chemical* (*Chem.*) another name for Affinity. [vide *Affinity*]

ATTRA'CTIVE *force*, any force by which bodies, and the particles of all bodies, are made to tend towards each other without any sensible impulse. Sir Isaac Newton calls this force centripetal; and on it he builds the whole theory of his Principia; but he does not profess to define by what cause or particular mode it acts in and upon all bodies.

ATTRACTI'VUM (*Med.*) a specific which draws out every thing from the body that is hurtful to it. *Parac. de Archidox.* l. 7.

ATTRAHE'NTIA (*Med.*) drawing medicines, such as by their minute particles open the pores of the body, so as to disperse the humours, cause the parts to swell, and draw blisters in the skin.

A'TTRIBUTE (*Theol.*) those properties or excellencies which are attributed to the Divine Being only, as his Self-existence, Immutability, Eternity, Infinite Wisdom, and the like. These attributes have been divided into communicable and incommunicable: the—*Communicable Attributes* of God are power, justice, knowledge; the—*Incommunicable Attributes* of God, which are properly his attributes, are his Self-existence, &c.

ATTRIBUTE (*Log.*) the predicate of any subject, or whatever is affirmed or denied of any thing. Attributes are *positive, negative, common,* and *proper.*—*Positive attribute,* what is affirmed of any thing, as, " That it is animate."—*Negative attribute,* that which is denied of a thing, as, " That it is inanimate."—*Common attribute,* that which is common to several different things, as "Animality."—*Proper attribute,* what is peculiar to one kind only, as " Rationality " to man.

ATTRIBUTES (*Paint.*) symbols added to figures, to intimate their quality and character; as an eagle to Jupiter, to denote his power; a club to Hercules, to denote his prowess, &c.

ATTRIBU'TUM (*Ant.*) ἀποτεταγμένα χρήματα; money assigned for the payment of the soldiers. *Varr. de Lat. Ling.* l. 4, c. 36.

ATTRI'BUTIVES (*Gram.*) words denoting attributes; the same as adjectives.

ATTRI'TION (*Med.*) a superficial galling or fretting from friction.

ATTRITION (*Nat.*) the striking or rubbing of bodies against each other, so as to throw off some of their superficial particles, as amber and other electric bodies are rubbed.

ATTRITION (*Theol.*) the lowest or faintest degree of repentance for sin, as it may affect ourselves; in distinction from contrition, which is the highest degree of repentance.

A'TYPUS (*Med.*) ἄτυπος, from α, priv. and τύπος, a type or form. 1. An epithet for one that is tongue-tied, or that does not speak articulately. 2. An epithet for a disease which has no regularity in its periods.

ATZOZA'TL (*Bot.*) an Indian name for the *Mirabilis Mexicana* of Ray, or the *Mirabilis longiflora* of Linnæus. *Raii Hist. Plant.*

AVA A'VA (*Bot.*) the name of a plant in the Otaheitan language, which is of an intoxicating quality.

AVA'CCARI (*Bot.*) a little Indian tree very similar to the myrtle, but a great deal more astringent.

AVADRA'TES (*Theol.*) a sect of Bramins in India, who exceeded all the rest in austerity.

A'VAGE (*Law*) or *Avisage*, a rent or payment by tenants of the manor of Writtle, in Essex, for the privilege of pennage in the Lord's woods.

AVA'IL *of marriage* (*Law*) that casualty in wardholding by which the superior was entitled to a certain sum from his vassal on his attaining the age of puberty.

AVALA'NCHE (*Nat.*) a French term for the masses of snow which break off from the mountains and rocks of Switzerland, and fall down into the vallies below.

AUA'NSIS (*Bot.*) ἀύανσις, from αύω, to dry; an epithet denoting exsiccation in general, but particularly that of plants, which is caused by age.

AVA'NT (*Mil.*) a French word for foremost, or advanced towards the enemy, as *Avant-Garde,* the van of the army, the next to which is the *Battail,* and the last the *Arriere-garde,* or the rear.—*Avant-train,* the limbers of a field piece, on which are placed two boxes containing ammunition enough for immediate service.

AVANT-*bec* (*Archit.*) the starling of a stone bridge.—*Avant-bec d'amont,* the name of those starlings which are always pointed towards the current of the water, in distinction from the others which are called the *Avant-bec-d'aval.*

AVANT-*chemin-couvert* (*Fort.*) the advanced covered-way which is made at the foot of the glacis to oppose the approaches of an enemy.—*Avant-duc,* the pilework which is formed by a number of trees on the edge or entrance of a river.—*Avant-fosse,* the ditch of the counterscarp next to the country. It is dug at the foot of the glacis.

AVANT *main* (*Man.*) French for the fore-hand of a horse.

AUA'NTE (*Med.*) ἀυαντή, from αύω, to dry; the dry disease in which the patient can neither bear eating or fasting. *Hippocrat. de Morb.* l. 2; *Foes. Œconom. Hippocrat.*

AVA'NTURINE (*Min.*) a reddish-yellow stone covered all over with sparkles which resemble gold; it is used by enamellers.

AVARA'MO-TEMO (*Bot.*) a siliquose tree growing in the Brazils of a very astringent quality. *Raii Hist.*

AVA'ST (*Mar.*) a term of command given at sea signifying hold, stop, stay.

AVA'UNCERS (*Sport.*) the second branch of a hart's-horn.

AU'BIER (*Bot.*) the same as *Albernum.*

AU'BIN (*Man.*) the awkward or imperfect gait of a horse between a trot and an amble.

AUBLE'TIA (*Bot.*) a genus of plants, so called after M. Aublet, a botanist; Class 713 *Polyandria,* Order 1 *Monogynia.*

Generic Characters. CAL. perianth five-leaved.—COR. petals five.—STAM. filaments very many; anthers ovate oblong.—PIST. germ roundish; style long; stigma spreading.—PER. capsule large; seeds very many.

Species. The species are shrubs and natives of Guiana.

AUCTA'RIUM (*Ant.*) from the supine *auctum,* augmented; surplisage, or what is more than just weight or measure. *Fest. de Verb. Signif.*

AU'CTIO (*Ant.*) *publica venditio cum res traditur plus offerenti,* auction, or setting things to a public or open sale.—*Auctio hastæ,* setting to sale under a spear as the custom was by the proclamation of the cryer.—*Auctio regia,* sale of the King's goods.

AU'CTION (*Com.*) a public sale conducted by persons called *auctioneers,* who are licensed to dispose of goods to the highest bidder, according to certain conditions called the *conditions of sale.*—*Mock Auction,* a similar public sale conducted by unlicensed persons for fraudulent purposes.

AU'CTOR *legis* (*Ant.*) *suasor, laudator,* the proposer of a law, or speaker in its favour; but, in regard to senators, it always implies proposer or mover. *Cic. in Dom.* c. 30; *Agr.* orat. 2, c. 5.—*Auctor sententiæ,* the maker of a motion, or the principal defender of it. *Cic. Academ.* l. 4, c. 2, &c.—*Auctor comitiorum,* he who assembled the comitia and presided at the meeting.

AUCTORAME'NTUM (*Ant.*) an indenture or obligation whereby one is bound to serve out a hire.

AUCTO'RES *in senatu* (*Ant.*) the principal senators, or those who, like the consuls, had the power of decreeing or determining. *Cic. Brut.* c. 34, &c.

AUCTUS (*Bot.*) increased, doubled, or calyculated; an epithet for the *Anthodium.* [vide *Calyculate*]

AU'CUBA (*Bot.*) a genus of plants; Class 21 *Monoecia*, Order 4 *Tetrandria.*
Generic Characters. CAL. perianth one-leaved.—COR. four-petalled.—STAM. filaments four; anthers ovate.
Species. The only species is the *Aucuba Japonica*, a shrub, native of Japan. *Linn. Spec. Plant.*

AUCUPA'TION (*Sport.*) fowling, or the art of bird-catching.

AUDFA'RAND (*Cus.*) a term in the North country for children grave and witty above their years.

AU'DIENCE (*Polit.*) 1. A ceremony by which ambassadors or ministers at any court are admitted to a hearing from the sovereign. 2. A Spanish Court of Justice in the West Indies which had several provinces within its jurisdiction. 3. A commission to quell any insurrection which had commenced at any given place.

AUDIENCE *court* (*Law*) a court belonging to the Archbishop of Canterbury, having the same authority with the court of arches. 4 *Inst.* 337.

AUDIE'NDO (*Law*) *et terminando*, a writ, or rather a commission, directed to certain persons for the trying and punishing such persons as have been concerned in a riotous assembly, insurrection, or other heinous misdemeanour.

AUDIE'NTES (*Ecc.*) vide *Auditores.*

AU'DIT (*Com.*) a regular examination of accounts by a proper officer.—*Audit Office*, an office at Somerset House where accounts are audited.

AUDI'TA *querela* (*Law*) a writ whereby a defendant against whom judgment is recovered, is therefore in danger of execution, and may be relieved upon some good matter of discharge. *F. N. B.* 102; *Reg. Orig.* 114.

AU'DITOR (*Law*) an officer of the king, or of any corporate body, appointed annually to examine accounts.—*Auditor of the receipts*, an officer of the exchequer that files the teller's bills, and gives in a weekly account of the receipts, &c. 4 *Inst.* 106.—*Auditors of the mint*, those who make up the accounts of the imprest. These officers formerly had the charge of auditing the king's accounts, &c. 4 *Inst.* 107.

AUDITO'RES (*Ecc.*) or *Audientes*, Catachumens instructed in the mysteries of the christian religion previous to their admission to baptism.

AUDITO'RIUM (*Ecc.*) the auditory, or place in the church for the auditors, now called the *nave.*

AU'DITORY (*Archæol.*) the bench on which magistrates used to sit and hear causes.

AUDITORY *passage* (*Anat.*) *Auditorius meatus*, the passage or entrance into the ear. *Ruf. Ephes. Appel. Part. Corp. Human.* l. 1.—*Auditory nerves*, a pair of nerves arising from the medulla oblongata, and distributed, the one to the ear, the other to the nose, lips, &c. *Gal. Introd.*

AVELLA'NA (*Bot.*) *nux Pontica*, Filbert, a sort of nut so called from Avellanum, a town of Campania, where they abounded. It is the *Corylus avellana* of Linnæus. *Plin.* l. 25, c. 23.; *Ger. Herb.* &c. [vide *Corylus*]

AVELLA'NE (*Her.*) a cross so called because the quarters of it resemble a filbert-nut, as in the annexed figure. According to Morgan, it is the cross which ensigns the mound of authority on the sovereign's globe.

A'VE-MARI'A (*Ecc.*) a prayer so called because it consists of the first words used in the salutation of the Virgin Mary.

AVE'NA (*Bot.*) Oats, in the Greek βρώμος, a plant, the grain of which is astringent and drying. *Dioscor.* l. 2, c. 116; *Plin.* l. 18, c. 17; *Gal. de Aliment.* l. 1, c. 14; *Oribas. Synop.* l. 3, c. 35; *Paul. Æginet.* l. 7, c. 3.

AVENA, Oats, *in the Linnean system*, a genus of plants, Class 3 *Triandria*, Order 2 *Digynia.*
Generic Characters. CAL. glume generally many flowered.—COR. valves two.—STAM. filaments three; anthers oblong.—PIST. germ obtuse; styles two; stigmas simple.—PER. none; seed one.
Species. The species are mostly annuals, as—*Avena fatua, Festuca, Gramen avenaceum*, seu *Ægilops*, Bearded Wild Oat, or Haver.—*Avena sativa*, cultivated Oats.—*Avena nuda*, Pillis, or Pillcorn, &c. except—*Avena clatior, Holcus avenaceus*, seu *Gramen nodosum*, Tall Oat Grass, Quick or Couch Grass, which is a perennial. *J. Bauh. Hist. Plant.*; *C. Bauh. Pin.*; *Ger. Herb.*; *Park. Theat. Botan.*; *Raii Hist. Plant.*; *Tournef. Instit.*

A'VENAGE (*Law*) from *avena*, Oats, i. e. oats paid to a landlord instead of rent or other dues.

AVENA'RIA *cicada* (*Zool.*) a kind of grasshopper that does not appear till the corn is ripe. *Plin.* 11, c. 27.

AVENA'RIUS (*Archæol.*) an officer belonging to the king's stables that provided oats for his horses. *Stat.* 13, *cap.* 8.

AVE'NIUS (*Bot.*) Veinless; an epithet for a leaf.—*Folium avenium*, a leaf without any perceptible veins.

AVE'NQUA (*Bot.*) a Brasilian name for Maiden-hair.

AVENTU'RÆ (*Archæol.*) adventures or trials of skill, military exercises on horseback.

AVE'NTURE (*Law*) for adventure; a mischance, causing the death of a man, as when a person is drowned, or otherwise killed, without any felonious intent. *Co. Lit.* 391.

A'VENUE (*Hort.*) *quo licet venire ad;* i. e. a passage open to a place; a walk or row of trees leading to a house, garden, or some distant object.

AVENUE (*Mil.*) a space left for a passage into a camp, garrison, &c.; an opening or inlet into any fortress.

A'VER (*Archæol.*) vide *Aver-Corn, Aver-Penny*, &c.

A'VERA (*Archæol.*) i. e. *overa*, from *ouvrer*, to work, and in Latin *opera*, a day's work at ploughing, valued at 8*d.* *Doomsday Bk.*; 4 *Inst.* 269.

A'VERAGE (*Law*) *averagium*, the service which a tenant owes to his lord.

AVERAGE *of corn fields* (*Agr.*) the stubble or remainder of straw-grass left in corn fields after the harvest is carried away. In Kent it is called the *Gratten*, in other parts the *roughings*, &c.

AVERAGE (*Com.*) 1. The damage which the vessel, the goods, or the loading sustains from the time of its departure to its return. 2. The charges or contribution towards defraying such damages or the losses of such as have their goods cast overboard for the safety of the ship and the crew. 3. The quota or proportion which each merchant or proprietor in the ship or lading is adjudged, upon a reasonable estimate, to contribute to a common average. This contribution seems to be so called because it is proportioned after the rate of every man's average or goods carried. 4. A small duty joined to primage, which is the master's perquisite. This is called *petty average.*

A'VER-CORN (*Law*) a reserved rent in corn paid to religious houses.

AVE'RIA (*Archæol.*) from *ouvrage*, work; cattle, principally working cattle.

AVE'RIIS *captis in Withernam* (*Law*) a writ for the taking of cattle to his use, who hath cattle unlawfully distrained by another, and driven out of the county where they were taken, so that they cannot be replevied by the sheriff. *Reg. Orig.* 82.

A'VER-LAND (*Law*) Lands ploughed by the tenant, *cum averiis suis*, for the use of the lord. *Mon. Angl.*

AVE'RMENT (*Law*) an offer of the defendant to make good or justify an exception pleaded in abatement, or bar of a plaintiff's action. Averments are either general or particular. *Co. Lit.* 362.

A'VER-PENNY (*Law*) Money paid towards the king's averages or carriages.

AVERRA'RE (*Archæol.*) to carry goods in a waggon, &c. a duty required of some tenants.

AVERRHO'A (*Bot.*) a genus of plants, called after *Averrhoes* of Corduba, Class 10 *Decandria*, Order 4 *Pentagynia*.
  Generic Characters. CAL. *perianth* five-leaved.—COR. *petals* five.—STAM. *filaments* ten; *anthers* roundish.—PIST. *germ* oblong; *styles* five; *stigmas* simple.—PER. *pome* turbinate; *seeds* angular.
  Species. The species are—*Averrhoa Bilimbi, Bilimbing teres*, seu *Bilimbi*, a shrub, native of India.—*Averrhoa carambola, foliolis, &c. Mala goensia, &c. Prunum stellatum, Tamara Conga*, seu *carambolas*, native of India. *C. Bauh. Pin.; Raii Hist. Plant.; Linn. Spec. Plant.*

AVERRUNCA'TIO (*Ant.*) from *averrunco*, to avert; a pruning of vines, and cutting away any thing hurtful; also the averting of evils, hence *Dii averruncent*, God forbid, or forefend; and *averruncus deus* the god whom they supplicated to avert evils.

A'VER-SILVER (*Archæol.*) A custom of rent.

AVE'RSIO (*Med.*) the diverting a flux of humours from one part to another.

AVE'RT (*Man.*) Regular, or enjoined; an epithet in lessons of horsemanship applied to the step or motions of the horse: as *pas averti*, or *pas écouté*, i. e. a step regulated or enjoined.

A'VERY (*Archæol.*) a place where the oats are kept for the king's horses.

A'VES (*Or.*) Birds, the second Class of animals in the Linnean system, comprehending those which are oviparous. [vide *Animal kingdom*]

A'UGE (*Astron.*) vide *Aux*.

AUGE'A (*Archæol.*) a cistern for water.

A'UGER (*Mech.*) a wimble or tool for boring.

AU'GELOT (*Hort.*) or *à l'augelot*, French, for a mode of planting vines, i. e. to dig small trenches in the form of a little trough, for laying in the slips or shoots, which are afterwards covered with earth.

AUGI'TES (*Min.*) from αυγη, splendour; Augite, a precious stone; a stone of the Chrysolite family.

AU'GMENT (*Gram.*) vide *Augmentation*.

AUGMENTA'TION (*Law*) a court erected by Henry VIII. for augmenting the revenues, by suppressing religious houses. 27 Hen. 8.

AUGMENTATION (*Her.*) a particular mark of honour, borne either on an escutcheon, or a canton, as *argent*, a hand, *gules*, borne by every baronet not being of higher dignity, as in the annexed example. "Or, a cross flory sable, with a mullet for difference." These are the arms of the Ainslie family.

AUGMENTATION (*Mus.*) doubling the length of the notes in a fuge or canon.

AUGME'NTUM (*Gram.*) augment, a letter or syllable added or changed in the tenses of Greek verbs. The augment is either syllabic or temporal.—*Augmentum Syllabicum*, the syllabic augment, is the addition of a letter or syllable, as from τύπτω, comes, πτύπτον ιτύψα, &c.—*Augmentum Temporale*, the temporal augment, is the change of a short vowel into a long one, or a diphthong into one still longer, as ἀνύω, ἤνυον.

AUGMENTUM (*Med.*) the increase of a disease from its attack to its utmost violence.

A'UGRE (*Mech.*) vide *Auger*.

A'UGURES (*Ant.*) from *garritus*, the noise of birds; certain officers appointed by Romulus to draw omens from the flight and singing of birds. *Cic. de Divin.* l. 1, c. 17; *Plin.* l. 7, c. 56; *Liv.* l. 1, c. 18; *Sueton. in Aug.* c. 95; *Fest. de Verb. Signif.*

AU'GUST (*Chron.*) the eighth month of the year, called after the emperor Augustus, who entered his second consulship in that month, after the Actian victory. It was before called Sextilis. *Dio.* l. 55; *Macrob. Saturn.* l. 1, c. 12; *C. Gassend. Calend. Roman.* c. 3; *Viol. de Vet. et Nov. Roman.; Temp. Rat. apud Græv. Thes. Antiq. Roman.* tom. viii. p. 194.

AUGU'STA (*Med.*) an epithet for several compound medicines.

AUGUSTA'LES (*Ant.*) priests appointed by Tiberius to perform the sacred rites, instituted in honour of Augustus and the Augustan family. They were twenty-five in number, and chosen by lot from the principal people of the city. Ancient inscriptions make frequent mention of the Augustalis Flamen, and also the Augustalis Sodalis, as NERONI. CAESARI GERMANICI. F. TI. AUGUSTI. N. DIVI AUG. PRON. FLAMINI. AUGUSTALI SODALI AUGUSTALI.—*Augustales*, soldiers whom Augustus had added to the *Ordinarii*, and who commonly formed the van-guard. *Veget. de Re Mil.* l. 2.—*Augustales ludi*, games instituted in honour of Augustus, U. C. 735, and celebrated on the 4. Id. October, i. e. the twelfth of October.

AUGUSTA'LIA (*Ant.*) plays instituted in honour of Augustus. *Tac. Annal.* l. 1, c. 100; *Dio.* l. 54.

AUGUSTA'LIS (*Num.*) a gold coin of the emperors of the East, first struck by Frederic II. in 1231. *Chron. Richard.*

AUGU'STAN *confession* (*Ecc.*) a confession of Christian faith made by the Protestants of Augusta, or Augsburg, in Germany, A.D. 1550.

AUGU'STINS (*Ecc.*) or *Augustin Friars*, black friars, who were of the order of St. Augustin.—*Barefooted Augustins*, a distinct branch of the Augustins, who were founded in Portugal.

AUGUSTI'NIANS (*Ecc.*) heretics of the sixteenth century, who maintained that the gates of heaven were not opened till the general resurrection.

AVICE'NNIA (*Bot.*) a genus of plants, called after Avicenna, the physician, Class 14 *Didynamia*, Order 2 *Angiospermia*.
  Generic Characters. CAL. *perianth* five-parted.—COR. *monopetalous*.—STAM. *filaments* four; *anthers* roundish.—PIST. *germ* ovate; *style* subulate; *stigma* bifid.—PER. *capsule* coriaceous; *seed* one.
  Species. The species are shrubs, as the—*Avicennia tomentosa, Bontia germinans, Donatia, Mangel laurocerasi, &c. Anacardium*, seu *Œpata, &c.* a native of the Indies. *J. Bauh. Hist. Plant.; C. Bauh. Pin.; Raii Hist. Plant.; Pluk. Almagest. Botan.; Linn. Spec. Plant.*

AVICULA'RIA *Sylvii* (*Bot.*) Venus Looking glass.

A'VILA (*Bot.*) a species of apple in the Indies larger than an orange, including nuts, that are an excellent medicine against poisons, &c. *Lemer. des Drog.*

AVISAME'NTUM (*Law*) advice or counsel; *de avisamento et consensu consilii nostri concessimus, &c.* was the common form of our ancient kings' grants.

AUK (*Orn.*) a bird, otherwise called Penguin, or Razorbill, and by Linnæus *Alca*: is an inhabitant of the Arctic seas. This bird is observed by seamen never to wander beyond soundings, and accordingly they conclude, on its appearance, that land is not very remote. The species best known are the Great Auk, *Alca impennis*; the Little Auk, *Alca alle*; and the Puffin Auk, *Alca arctica*.

AU'LA (*Law*) a Court baron.—*Aula regia*, the King's Bench.—*Aula ecclesiæ*, the same as *Navis ecclesiæ*.

AU'LAX (*Bot.*) the *Protea* of Linnæus.

AU'LNAGE (*Com.*) vide *Alnage*.

AU'LOS (*Med.*) the foramen of the exterior vagina. *Hipp. de Mul.* l. 2.

AULULA'RIA (*Ant.*) the name of one of Plautus' comedies.

AUME (*Com.*) vide *Awm*.

AUMO'NE (*Cus.*) Alms.—*Tenure in Aumone*, where lands

are given in alms to a religious house, on condition of prayers being offered up at certain times. *Brit.* 164.

AU'NCEL (*Com.*) or *Auncel weight*, i. e. hand sale weight, from *ansa*, a handle; an ancient kind of hand-weighing, by the hanging of the scales at each end of a beam, and lifting it up with the finger to find the weight of the thing weighed. *Stat.* 5, 25 *Ed.* 2.

AUNCE'STRAL (*Law*) vide *Action*.

AUNCIA'TUS (*Archæol.*) Antiquated.

AVOCA'DO (*Bot.*) a tree that grows in the Spanish West Indies, and in Jamaica, the fruit of which, though very insipid, is much eaten by the natives.

AVOCATO'RIA (*Polit.*) a mandate of the emperor of Germany to a prince of the empire, to stop his unlawful proceedings.

AVOI'DANCE (*Law*) when a benefice is void of an incumbent, which is either in fact or by law.—*Avoidance in fact*, by the death of an incumbent.—*Avoidance in law*, by cession, deprivation, resignation, &c.

AVOIR-DU-POI'SE (*Com.*) i. e. *habere pondus aut justi esse ponderis*; a weight having sixteen ounces to the pound, in distinction from Troy weight, which has only twelve.

AVOLA'TION (*Chem.*) a flying off of the particles, as by evaporation.

A'VOSET (*Orn.*) a bird otherwise called the Scooper or Crooked Bill, is distinguished by its bill, which is three and a half inches long, slender, thin, and turned up nearly half its length. It is the *Recurvirostra* of Gesner; the *Avosetta*, seu *Spinzago d' Acqua* of Aldrovandus; and the *Recurvirostra Avosetta* of Linnæus. *Gesn. Av.*; *Will. Orn.*; *Raii Syn.*; *Aldrov. Ornith.*

AVO'W (*Law*) vide *Advow*.

AVO'WANT (*Law*) one making an avowry.

AVOWEE' (*Law*) an advocate of a church benefice. [vide *Advocate*]

AVO'WRY (*Law*) the plea which the maker of a distress for rent, &c. must put in when the party distrained sues for a replevin.

AVOWTERER (*Ant.*) an adulterer.

AU'RA (*Orn.*) or *Gallinassa*, a species of Indian raven, approaching the eagle in size, the flesh of which is good for the small pox. *Lemery*.

AURA (*Med.*) a vapour, as if from mephitic caves.—*Aura epileptica*, a gradual sensation like air ascending from some determined part of the extremities upwards occasioning an epileptic attack.—*Aura vitalis*, vital heat.

AU'RÆ (*Mech.*) clouts or plates of iron set upon the axletree to save it from fretting.

AURAME'NTUM (*Ant.*) an instrument for taking gold out of the mine; also leaf gold.

AURA'NTIA (*Bot.*) the *Citrus* of Linnæus.

AURANTI'ACUS (*Bot.*) orange, the colour of some flowers.

AURA'NTIUM (*Bot.*) orange, the *Citrus aurantium* of Linnæus.

AURA'TUS *eques* (*Archæol.*) a knight with gilt spurs.

AURE'LIA (*Nat.*) the first apparent change of the eruca or maggot of any insect.

AURELIA'NA (*Bot.*) the *Pinax quinquefolia* of Linnæus.

AURE'OLA (*Paint.*) a crown of glory with which saints, martyrs, and confessors, are adorned, as a mark of their having obtained the victory.

AU'RES (*Archæol.*) an ancient punishment among the Saxons, of cutting off the ears of church robbers and other offenders.

AURE'US (*Num.*) the name of a gold coin current among the Romans, which was equivalent to 25 denarii, or 100 sesterces, and a crown sterling. It was customary to give this piece to the charioteers.

Juven. sat. 7, v. 243.

Accipe, victori populus quod postulat, aurum.

Sueton. in Claud. c. 21; *Dio.* l. 55; *Turneb. Adv.* l. 5, c. 1; *Gron. de Vet. Pecun.* l. 3, c. 15.

AURICHA'LCUM (*Met.*) *quasi orichalchum*, ὀρείχαλκον, mountain brass, from ὄρος, a mountain, and χαλκός, brass; the metal now called brass, being a mixture of copper and lapis calaminaris. It is called Aurichalcum by Plautus, and Orichalcum by Virgil and Horace.

Plaut. Mil. act 3, scen. 1, v. 64.

Cedo mihi tres homines aurichalco contra cum istis moribus.

Virg. Æn. l. 12, v. 87.

——— *auro squallentem, alboque orichalco..*
Circumdat loricam humeris.

Horat. Ars Poet. v. 202.

Tibia non ut nunc orichalco vincta, tubæque
Æmula.

Plat. in Crit.; *Senec.* ep. 90; *Suet. in Vet.* c. 5; *Fest. de Signif. Verb.*

AU'RICLE (*Anat.*) *auricula*. 1. The external ear, or that part of it which is prominent from the head. 2. *Auriculæ cordis*, two appendages of the heart, being muscular caps or bags covering the two ventricles, and seated at its basis. They move regularly like the heart, only in an inverted order, their systole corresponding to the diastole of the heart.

AURICLE (*Bot.*) vide *Auricula*.

AURICO'LLA (*Met.*) the glue or cement of gold. *Oribas. Med. Coll.* l. 13; *Aet. Tetrab.* 1, serm. 1; *Paul. Æginet.* l. 7, c. 3.

AURI'CULA (*Anat.*) vide *Auricle*.

AURICULA *Leporis* (*Bot.*) Hare's Ear, the *Bupleurum falcatum, odonitis, ranunculoides, et tenuissimum*, of Linnæus. *Bauh. Hist.*—*Auricula muris*, Mouse Ear, the *Hieracium auricula et aurantiacum, &c.*—*Auricula Ursi*, the *Primula, &c.* of Linnæus. *Bauh., Tournef.*, &c.

AURICULA'RIA (*Bot.*) Ear-wort, the *Hedyotis auricularia* of Linnæus.

AURICULA'RIUS (*Med.*) an epithet for what belongs to the ears, as *auricularius medicus*, an aurist.

AURICULA'TUS (*Bot.*) Earshaped, an epithet for a leaf; *folium auriculatum*, a leaf having two small lobes bent outwards.

AURI'CULAR *confession*, a mode of confessing sins practised by the Roman Catholics; so called because the penitents whisper their sins into the ears of their confessors.

AURICULA'RIS *Digitus* (*Anat.*) the little finger with which one is most apt to pick the ear.

AURI'FEROUS *silver* (*Min.*) an alloy of silver, of a yellowish colour.

AURIFLA'MMA (*Mil.*) a flag or standard belonging to the abbey of St. Dennis, which the monks used in honour of that saint whenever they were compelled to defend themselves.

AURI'GA (*Ant.*) *quasi curriga*, because, *currum agat*, he drives the chariot; a charioteer at the races, of whom there were different *greges*, or factions, as the *alba vel albata, russata, vaneta, prasina, aurata, et purpurea*, so called from their dress. *Sueton. in Calig.* c. 19, &c.; *Tertull. de Spect.* c. 9; *Rosin. Antiq. Rom.* l. 5, c. 5, &c.

AURIGA (*Astron.*) ἡνίοχος, the Waggoner, called by Manilius and others *Heniochus*, which Ptolemy makes to consist of 14 stars; Kepler and Tycho, of 27; Bayer, of 33; Hevelius, of 40; the British Catalogue, of 66, among which is *Capella*, a star of the first magnitude, which was otherwise call *Olenia*, or *Capra Jovis*, i. e. Amalthea, the nurse of Jupiter.

Arat. v. 16.

Αἲξ ἱερὴ, τὴν μέν τε λόγος Διὶ μαζὸν ἐπισχεῖν
Ὠλενίη δὲ μιν αἶγα Διὸς καλέουσ' ὑποφῆται.

Capella was called *pluvialis*, because it brought rain with it when it rose.

Ovid. Fast. l. 5, v. 111.

Ab Jove surgat opus ; prima mihi nocte videnda
Stella est in cunis officiosa Jovis,
Nascitur Oleniæ sidus pluviale Capellæ
Illa dati cœlum præmia lactis habet.

This constellation is represented by the figure of an old man, with a goat and her kids in his left hand, who is said to have been transported to heaven by Jupiter, on the invention of carriages. *Hipparch. in Arat. ; Eratosth. Characterism. ; Plin.* l. 18, c. 26, &c. ; *Manil. Astron.* l. 1, v. 361 ; *Hygin. Astron. Poet.*

AURIGA (*Med.*) a sort of bandage for the side, made like the traces of a waggon-horse.

AURIGA (*Anat.*) the fourth lobe of the liver. *Castell. Lex. Med.*

AURIGA'RIUS (*Ant.*) a person who kept chariots for use.

AURI'GO (*Med.*) the jaundice.

AURIPIGME'NTUM (*Min.*) Orpiment, the arsenic ore [vide *Arsenic*] which was formerly much used by painters, and is of two kinds, namely, the yellow and red, which is otherwise called Realgar. *Plin.* l. 33, c. 4.

AURI'PLICES (*Ant.*) leaves of gold wrapped together in the shape of a man or woman.

A'URIS (*Anat.*) vide *Ear*.

AURISCA'LPRUM (*Mech.*) an ear-picker.

AU'RIST (*Med.*) an ear-doctor.

AURO'RA (*Astron.*) the morning twilight.—*Aurora borealis*, Northern light, or Streamers, a meteor appearing in the northern part of the heavens, mostly in the winter season and in frosty weather. It appears often in the form of an arch, which is partly bright and partly dark, of a reddish colour inclining to yellow. The matter of which it is composed is not found to have any effect on the rays of light which pass freely through it. In the Shetland Isles these phænomena are the constant attendants on bright evenings, and have obtained the name of the *merry dancers* among the inhabitants, to whom they afford relief amidst the gloom of long winter nights.

AU'RUM *factum* (*Ant.*) Wrought Gold.—*Aurum signatum*, coined gold. [vide *Argentum*]

AURUM (*Min.*) Gold, the heaviest of all metals, the specific gravity being 19·300. It is of a reddish-yellow colour, soft texture, not sonorous, but exceedingly ductile and malleable.

AURUM *potabile* (*Med.*) Tincture of Gold, a rich cordial liquor, with leaf gold in it.—*Aurum fulminans*, Thundering Gold, a powder of gold and aqua regia, so called because of the explosion which it makes by a gentle attrition.—*Aurum horizontale*, a mercurial medicine of a red colour.

AURUM *mosaicum* (*Paint.*) or *musivum*, a composition to lay on a colour like brass or copper. It is known to be a per-sulphuret of tin.

AURUM *Reginæ* (*Law*) the queen's gold; a royal revenue belonging to every queen-consort during her marriage, drawn from fines to the king upon grants.

AU'SPEX (*Ant.*) a diviner by birds, who, when he wished to perform any divination, mounted a tower, his head being covered with a gown peculiar to his office; he then turned his face to the east, marked out the heavens with his *lituus* (a rod which he held in his hand), and afterwards waited for the omen from the quarter to which the bird should fly.

AUSPI'CIUM (*Ant.*) *quasi avispicium*, a divination from the inspection of birds, which, by Pliny, is distinguished from *augurium*, the former being confined to observations on birds, and the latter extending itself to divination from objects in general. The auspice was, however, more minute and particular in its observations on birds than the *augury*. The *Auspicia* were taken either from the noise or the flight of birds, or from the movements of chickens in a coop, &c. *Cic. de Divin.* l. 2, c. 36 ; *Liv.* l. 6, c. 41 ; *Plin.* l. 7, c. 56.

AU'STER (*Ant.*) the South wind.

Virg. eclog. 2, v. 58.

―――― *Floribus Austrum*
Perditus, et liquidis immisi fontibus apros.

AUSCULTA'RE (*Archæol.*) a custom of hearing the monks read the service, by persons appointed to correct them, so that they may officiate in a graceful and impressive manner.

A'USTRAL *signs* (*Astron.*) the six last signs in the zodiac, so called because they are on the south side of the Equinoctial.

AUSTRA'LIS *corona* (*Astron.*) vide *Corona*.—*Australis Piscis*. [vide *Piscis*]

AUSTRI'ACA *sidera* (*Astron.*) spots in the sun, resembling small stars.

AUSTU'RCUS (*Fal.*) a Goshawk.

AUTER-DROIT (*Law*) an expression used when persons sue or are sued in another's right.—*Auterfoits acquit*, a plea by a criminal that he was heretofore acquitted of the same felony or treason; so, in like manner, *Auterfoits convict* or *attaint*, viz. convicted or attainted before of the same crime, &c.

AUTHE'MERON (*Med.*) αὐθήμερον, from αὐτὸς, the same, and ἡμέρα, day; a medicine, so called because it gives relief the same day as it is taken. *Gal. de Comp. Med. sec. Loc.* l. 9, c. 2.

AUTHE'NTICS (*Law*) the title of the third volume of the Roman law; so called because it has its authority from itself; proceeding immediately from the mouth of the emperor. This was a volume of new constitutions, appointed by the emperor Justinian, and introduced into the body of the law under one book, called the Novellæ of Justinian.

AUTHE'PSA (*Ant.*) from αὐτὸς, of itself, and ἕψω, to boil; a kind of brass pot that boils any thing with little or no fire under it. *Cic. pro Rosc.* ; *Lamprid. in Heliogab.* c. 19.

AUTOCHTHO'NES (*Ant.*) αὐτόχθονες, in Latin *indigenæ*, the original inhabitants of a country. The Athenians gave themselves this epithet because they boasted to be as old as χθών, the earth, αὐτή, itself. *Cic. de Orat.* l. 3, c. 83 ; *Paus.* l. 1, c. 14.

AUTO'CRASY (*Polit.*) αὐτοκρατία, from αὐτὸς, oneself, and κράτος, power; government by oneself, or self-supremacy.

AUTO'GENES (*Bot.*) αὐτογενὴς, from αὐτὸς, oneself, and γίνομαι, to be made; self-begotten, applied to the Narcissus, the bulb of which seems to produce its leaves of itself before it is put into the earth.

AUTOGRAPH (*Ant.*) αὐτόγραφος, from αὐτὸς, itself, and γράφω, to write; one's own hand-writing, as *autographa epistola*, a letter of one's own writing, or writing with one's own hand.

AUTOMA'RIA (*Mech.*) the art of making clocks, &c.

AUTO'MATON (*Mech.*) any machine moving by itself, as a spring.

AUTO'MATOS (*Med.*) αὐτόματος, from αὐτὸς, itself, and μάτος, easy; whatever is done more by an effort of nature than by any external action or application. *Hippocrat.* l. 1, aph. 2.

AUTO'MELITE (*Min.*) a mineral of the ruby family.

AUTONO'MIA (*Polit.*) αὐτονομία, independent government, or a government according to one's own laws and customs, in distinction from those towns or countries that were subject to foreign laws. Many cities and places are distinguished by the title of αὐτόνομος, as in the annexed figure of the town of Ægea, representing the head of a goat, with the inscription ΑΙΓΕΑΙΩΝ ΤΗΣ ΙΕΡΑΣ ΚΑΙ ΑΥΤΟΝΟΜΟΥ. *Hard. Numm. Urb.*

AUTOPHO′RAS (*Ant.*) αὐτόφωρος from αὐτός, *ipse*, oneself, and φώρ, a thief, i. e. the very thief; a thief taken in the very fact.

AUTO′PSIA (*Med.*) αὐτοψία, from αὐτός, oneself, and ὄπτομαι, to see; ocular evidence, or the memory of what one sees with one's own eyes; a point strongly insisted upon by the empiric sect.

AUTOPY′ROS (*Med.*) vide *Artos.*

AUTOU′R (*Med.*) a bark much resembling cinnamon.

A′UTUMN (*Astron.*) the third season of the year, which begins at the descending equinox, i. e. in the Northern Hemisphere, when the sun enters Libra, on the 22d day of September; it terminates about the same day of December, when winter commences.

AUTU′MNAL *Equinox* (*Astron.*) the time when the sun enters Libra. [vide *Autumn*]—*Autumnal point*, that point at which the autumnal equinox commences.—*Autumnal signs*, the three signs, Libra, Scorpio, and Sagittarius, through which the sun passes during the autumn season.

AUXE′SIS (*Rhet.*) αὔξησις, a figure of rhetorick when, by hyperbole, a thing is too much magnified. Longin. sect. 12; Schol. in Hermog. Ald. Edit. p. 353.

AUXI′LIARIES (*Mil.*) or *auxiliary forces*, that are employed only on particular occasions, or that come to assist.

AUXI′LIARY *verbs* (*Gram.*) verbs that are principally used in forming the tenses of other verbs, as " To Have " and " To Be."

AUXI′LIUM *ad filium militem faciendum et filiam maritandam* (*Law*) a writ for levying an aid towards the knighting the king's son, or marrying a daughter. F. N. B. 82.—*Auxilium curiæ*, a precept or order for the citing one party at the suit of another.—*Auxilium facere alieni in curia regis*, to be another's friend or solicitor in the king's courts.—*Auxilium regis*, the king's aid, or money levied for the king's use or the public service.—*Auxilium vicecomiti*, a customary aid, or duty payable to sheriffs out of certain manors.

TO AWA′IT (*Law*) to lay in wait, or way-lay.

AWA′ME (*Com.*) the same as Awm.

AWA′RD (*Law*) from the French *agard*, because it is a dictum imposed upon the parties to be observed by them; a judgment given by an arbitrator between two parties on a matter of dispute.

A-WE′ATHER (*Mar.*) the situation of the helm when pushed to the weather side of the ship.

A-WE′IGH (*Mar.*) the state of the anchor when it is drawn out of the ground in a perpendicular direction.

AWL (*Mech.*) a sharp pointed tool.

AW′L-WORT (*Bot.*) the *Subularia* of Linnæus; an annual, so called from the shape of its leaves.—*Awl-shaped*, or *subulate, subulatus.* [vide *Subulate*]

AWM (*Com.*) a measure of Rhenish wine containing forty gallons, mentioned in Stat. 1, Jac. I, now equivalent to a ton.

AWN (*Bot.*) *arista*, the Beard; a slender sharp process issuing from the glume, or chaff in corn and grasses. [vide *Arista*]

A′WNED (*Bot.*) *aristatus*, having an awn; an epithet for the glume and anther.

AW′NLESS (*Bot.*) *muticus*, having no awn, opposed to the awned; an epithet for the glume, as in *Agrostis* and *Aira*, for the calyx of *Serratula*; for the seeds, as in *Adonis*, &c.

AW′NING (*Mar.*) a canopy extending over the deck.

AX (*Mech.*) or *Axe*, a carpenter's tool.

AXAYACA′TL (*Ent.*) a species of fly in Mexico, the eggs of which are gathered from the rushes where they are deposited, and are called *caveare*.

AXE′A *commissura* (*Anat.*) a sort of articulation.

AXE′DO (*Alch.*) a spell to render a person impotent. *Marc. Emp.*

AXE′-FORMED (*Bot.*) vide *Dolabriformed*.

AXE′-STONE (*Min.*) a subspecies of the Nephrite.

AXI′CULUS (*Mech.*) a roller or cylinder.

AXI′LLA (*Anat.*) diminutive of *axis*, the arm-pit, or cavity of the arm.

AXILLA (*Bot.*) the Axil, the angle formed by a branch with a stem, or by a leaf with a branch, resembling the arm-pit in form.

AXILLA′RIS (*Anat.*) belonging to the *axilla*, axillary, or subclavian; an epithet for the vein that passes under the arm-pit, or the arteries which are the continuations of the subclavian, or of the nerve which is a branch of the brachial plexus.

AXI′LLARY (*Bot.*) *axillaris*, an epithet for leaves, the peduncle, and the scape and cirrus: axillary leaves are those growing at the angles formed by the branches with the stem.

A′XINITE (*Min.*) a species of stone of the Epidote family.

AXI′NOMANCY (*Ant.*) ἀξινομαντεία, from ἀξίνη, a hatchet; a sort of divination by means of a hatchet or ax which was fixed on a stake so as to be poised; when the names of the suspected persons being repeated, he, at whose name the hatchet moved, was pronounced guilty.

A′XIOM (*Phi.*) ἀξίωμα, from ἄξιος, worthy, i. e. ἀξιόπιστος, worthy of credit; a self evident proposition, or one requiring no proof, as ' the whole is greater than the part.'

AXI′RNACH (*Med.*) superfluous fat sometimes growing on the tunics of the eyelids, particularly of children.

A′XIS (*Ant.*) ἄξων, from ἄγω, the axle-tree of a wheel; so called because the wheel is driven about it. It is also the name of the board, or tablet, on which the laws of Solon and others were engraven. Vitruv. l. 4, c. 2; Aul. Gell. l. 2, c. 12; Fest. de Verb. Signif.

Axis (*Geom.*) a right line conceived to be drawn from the vertex of a figure to the middle of the base; it is so called because the figure, by revolving round this line, is conceived to generate a solid.—*Axis of a circle*, the same as the diameter. [vide *Circle*]—*Axis of a cone*, the line drawn from the vertex to the centre of the base.—*Axis of a cylinder*, the line drawn from the centre of the one end to that of the other. [vide *Cylinder*]—*Axis of a conic section*, a line going through the middle of the figure, and cutting all the ordinates at right angles. Upon this the figure is supposed to be turned, so as to form the section. The *axes* are of different kinds, namely, transverse, conjugate, determinate, and indeterminate.—*Transverse axis* of an ellipse hyperbole, or parabola, otherwise called the principal axis, is that diameter which passes through the two foci, and the two vertices, as A P, which cuts the ordi-

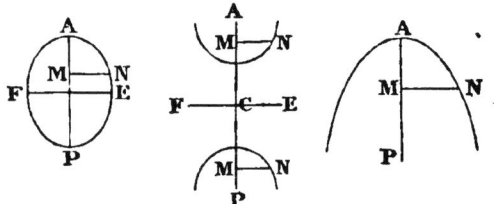

nate M N at right angles.—*Conjugate axis of an ellipse hyperbola, &c.* is the diameter F E passing through the centre and perpendicular to the transverse axis; it is the shortest of the diameters, as the transverse is the longest.—*Determinate axis of an hyperbola*, is a right line drawn between the vertices, or tops of the opposite sections.—*Indeterminate axis of an hyperbola*, the axis which cuts an infinite number of lines at right angles; in this manner A P is determinate if it lies only between the vertices of the opposite sections; but it is indeterminate if it cut the lines M N, C E, M N, &c. at right angles.

Axis (*Astron.*) or *axis of the sphere*, an imaginary right line conceived to pass through the centre of the earth, and terminating in each end at the surface of the mundane sphere. In the Ptolemaic system the sphere was supposed to revolve about this line as an axis in performing its diurnal motion.—*Axis of the earth*, the line connecting its two poles, and about which the earth performs its diurnal rotation from west to east. This is represented in the terrestrial globe by the piece of wood, or iron, on which the globe turns.—*Axis of a planet*, the line passing through its centre, and about which the planet revolves, as the axis of the Sun, Earth, Moon, Jupiter, Mars, and Venus, round which they are known, by observation, to perform their several motions.—*Axis of the Horizon, Equator, Ecliptic, &c.* the right lines passing through the centres of those circles perpendicular to their planes. (vide *Astronomy*)

Axis (*Mech.*) a certain line about which a body may revolve, as the axis of a balance, &c.; so also—*Axis of rotation*, the line about which a body revolves when it is put in motion.—*Axis of oscillation*, a line parallel to the horizon passing through the centre, about which a pendulum vibrates, and perpendicular to the plane in which it oscillates.—*Axis in Peritrochio*, or *Wheel and Axle*, one of the five mechanical powers, or simple machines, which is principally used in the raising of water, as in the annexed figure,

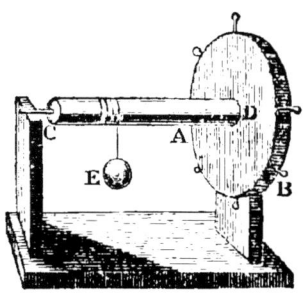

where the circle A B represents that part of the machine which is called the *peritrochium*, and the cylinder C A the *axis*. In the peritrochium are the radii, or spokes, called the *scytalae*, by which it is turned round, and in the cylinder is the rope to which the weight E is fixed that is to be raised. Of this description are capstans, cranes, and the like.—*Axis of a vessel*, the quiescent right line through the middle of it perpendicular to its base, and equally distant from its sides.

Axis *of a magnet* (*Nat.*) a line supposed to pass through the middle of a magnet in such a manner, that, however the magnet is divided, if the division be made according to a plane in which such line is found, the magnet will be cut or separated into two loadstones. The extremes of such lines are called *the poles* of the magnet.

Axis (*Archit.*) is otherwise called *cathetus*. The axis of an Ionic capital is a line passing perpendicularly through the eye of the volute.—*Spiral axis*, is the axis of a twisted column drawn spirally, in order to trace the circumvolutions without.

Axis *of any glass* (*Opt.*) a right line drawn perpendicularly through the centre of a glass, and if it be a convex glass through the thickest part; if it be a concave glass through the thinnest part; which in each of them is termed the *pole* of the glass.—*Axis of a lens*, a right line passing along the axis of that whereof the lens is a segment.—*Optic*, or *visual axis*, a ray passing through the centre of the eye, or falling perpendicularly on the eye.—*Axis of incidence*, in dioptrics, is the line passing through the point of incidence, particularly to the refracting surface.—*Axis of refraction*, is the line continued from the point of incidence, or refraction, perpendicularly to the refracting surface along the further medium.

Axis (*Bot.*) The smooth part in the centre of some fruits about which the other parts are disposed.

Axis (*Anat.*) a name for the second vertebra of the neck, which has a toothlike fixture into the first vertebra. This tooth is sometimes called the *axis*.

A'XLE-TREE (*Mech.*) a piece of wood under a cart, &c. on which the wheel turns.—*Axle-tree pins*, the irons holding the axle-tree to the cart.

AXU'NGIA (*Nat.*) ἀξύγγια, hog's lard. *Paul. Æginet.* l. 7, c. 3.—*Axungia de mumia*, Marrow.—*Axungia vitri*, Sandiver, or Salt of glass.

A'XYRIS (*Bot.*) a genus of plants, Class 21 *Monoecia*, Order 3 *Triandria*.
Generic Characters. CAL. *perianth* three-parted.—COR. none.—STAM. *filaments* three; *anthers* roundish.—PIST. *germ* roundish; *styles* two; *stigmas* acuminate.—PER. none; *seed* one.
Species. The species are annuals, as—*Axyris amaranthoides*, seu *Atriplex montana, &c.* Simple spiked Axyris, &c.—*Axyris hybrida*, native of Siberia.—*Axyris prostrata foliis, &c.* seu *herbacea, &c.* an annual, native of Siberia. *Linn. Spect. Plant.*

AYE'NIA (*Bot.*) from the Duc d'Ayen, a genus of plants, Class 5 *Pentandria*, Order 1 *Monogynia*.
Generic Characters. CAL. *perianth* one-leaved.—COR. pentapetalous.—STAM. *filaments* five; *anthers* roundish.—PIST. *germ* roundish; *style* cylindric; *stigma* obtuse.—PER. *capsule* five-grained; *seeds* solitary.
Species. The species are—*Ayenia pusilla foliis, &c.* Smooth Ayenia, an annual, native of Jamaica.—*Ayenia tomentosa*, native of South America.—*Ayenia magna*, a perennial, native of South America.—*Ayenia laevigata*, a shrub, native of Jamaica. *Linn. Spect. Plant.*

A'YLETS (*Her.*) or *sea-swallows*, a charge in coats of arms represented sable, beaked and legged gules. They are otherwise called Cornish choughs.

A'ZAC (*Chem.*) *Sal ammoniacum*.
AZADARI'CHTA (*Bot.*) The *Melia azaderichta* of Linnæus.
A'ZAGOR (*Chem.*) veridigrease.
AZA'LEA (*Bot.*) from ἀζαλέος, dry, because it grows in dry places; a genus of plants, Class 5 *Pentandria*, Order 1 *Monogynia*.
Generic Characters. CAL. *perianth* five-parted.—COR. monopetalous.—STAM. *filaments* five; *anthers* simple.—PIST. *germ* roundish; *style* filiform; *stigma* obtuse.—PER. *capsule* roundish; *seeds* many.
Species. The species are mostly shrubs, as—*Azalea pontica*, or *Chamaerhodendron ponticum*, Pontic azalea.—*Azalea Indica*, *Chamaerhodendron exoticum*, *Cistus Indicus*, seu *Tsutshusi, &c.* *Linn. Spec. Plant.*

AZA'LDUS (*Archæol.*) a jade or poor horse.
AZAMO'GLANS (*Theol.*) vide *Agamoglans*.
AZANI'TÆ *Acopon* (*Med.*) an ointment. *Paul. Æginet.* l. 7, c. 19.—*Azanitæ ceratum*, a cerate. *Oribas. Med. Coll.* l. 13.
AZA'PPES (*Mil.*) The name by which the Turks distinguish their newly-raised soldiers.
A'ZEG (*Chem.*) vitriol.
AZEMA'SOR (*Chem.*) native cinnabar.

AZE'NSALI (*Bot.*) a sort of moss that grows on rocks; also a sort of black stone found among gold.

A'ZEC (*Chem.*) ink.

A'ZED (*Med.*) an inferior kind of camphor used by the Arabians.

AZE'DARACH (*Bot.*) a species of the *Melia* of Linnæus.

AZE'DEGRIN (*Min.*) the *Lapis hæmatites*.

A'ZEFF (*Chem.*) scissile alum.

A'ZEM (*Polit.*) the name which the Turks give to their grand vizier.

A'ZEROLE (*Bot.*) a kind of medlar-trees, the leaves of which are like parsley.

A'ZIMAR (*Chem.*) Burnt Copper.

A'ZIMEN degrees (*Astrol.*) Degrees of the Zodiac, so called because persons born when any of them are ascending are commonly afflicted with lameness, or some other natural imperfection.

A'ZIMUTH *of the sun, stars, &c.* (*Astron.*) an arc of the horizon, comprehended between the meridian of the place and the azimuth circle, passing through the sun, &c.—*Azimuth circles*, or *vertical circles*. i. e. great circles of the spheres, intersecting each other in the zenith and nadir.—*Magnetical Azimuth*, an arc of the horizon contained between the magnetical meridian and the azimuth or vertical circle of the object.—*Azimuth compass*, an instrument for finding either the magnetical azimuth or amplitude of a circle at sea.—*Azimuth dial*, a dial whose stile or gnomon is perpendicular to the plane of the horizon.

A'ZIMUTHS (*Astron.*) vide *Azimuth Circles*.

AZO'GA *ships* (*Com.*) Spanish ships commonly carrying quicksilver for the use of the miners in extracting the silver.

AZO'T (*Chem.*) another name for *nitrogen*. [vide *Nitrogen*]

AZO'TH (*Alch.*) the Mercurius Philosophorum, or universal remedy. *Paracel. de Philos. Occult.*

A'ZOTITE (*Chem.*) a kind of salt formed from the combination of the protoxide of azote with alcalies.

A'ZUR (*Min.*) Red Coral.

A'ZURE (*Min.*) vide *Copper*.

AZURE (*Her.*) the blue colour in the coats of arms of all persons under the degree of Barons. In engraving, the azure is represented by horizontal lines across the shield from side to side. Azure is the emblem of justice, humility, and loyalty.

A'ZURITE (*Min.*) a species of azure stone.

AZU'RIUM (*Chem.*) a preparation of mercury, sulphur, and sal ammoniac, recommended by Albertus Magnus.

AZY'GES (*Anat.*) ἀζυγής, a name for the *Os Sphenoides*.

A'ZYGUS (*Anat.*) ἄζυγος, from ἀ, priv. and ζυγὸς, a pair, i. e. unpaired, the name of a vein situated within the thorax, on the right side, having no fellow on the left.

A'ZYMA (*Theol.*) ἄζυμα, the feast of unleavened bread among the Jews; from ἄζυμος, unleavened, or unfermented.

B.

B. (*Ant.*) stands as an abbreviation for Balbus, Brutus, &c.; as a numeral for 300, and with a dash over it, as B̄, for 3,000. [vide *Abbreviations*]

B. (*Lit.*) stands for Bachelor. [vide *Abbreviations*]

B. (*Chron.*) stands for one of the Dominical letters. [vide *Dominical Letter* and *Chronology*]

B (*Mus.*) the name of the seventh note in the gamut, to which De Nevers, a French physician, is said to have applied the syllable *si*, Guido having attached syllables only to the other six. [vide *Gamut* and *Music*]

B. (*Her.*) stands for the middle chief in the Escutcheon. [vide *Escutcheon* and *Heraldry*]

BA'ANITES (*Ecc.*) Heretics so called from their leader, one Baanes, who taught the errors of the Manachites in the 9th century.

BA'ARD (*Mar.*) a sort of sea vessel or transport ship.

BA'AS (*Zool.*) the *Bos barbatus* of Linnæus.

BA'AT (*Com.*) a weight in Siam and China equal to half an ounce, also current as a small coin of different values.

BABOO'N (*Zo.*) a sort of monkey with a short tail, which forms one division of the genus *Simia* in the Linnæan system.

BABUZICA'RIUS (*Med.*) vide *Incubus*.

BAC (*Mar.*) a kind of praam or ferry-boat.

BAC (*Mech.*) another name for a tub or cooler.

BAC (*Chem.*) the vessel into which the liquors are poured.

BA'CANON (*Nat.*) βάκανον, the seeds of cabbages.

BACANON (*Med.*) a sort of antidote, which, according to Myrepsus, is a good hepatic medicine.

BACA'NTIBI (*Ecc.*) strolling clerks, who wandered from church to church.

BA'CAR (*Ant.*) *Vas vinarium*, a beaker, or drinking vessel.

BACAR (*Com.*) a weight.

BA'CCA (*Bot.*) from בכה, he wept, on account of the juice or fluid which it contains; a berry, or round soft succulent fruit, containing seeds in a pulpy substance. It is a species of pericarp. Its different kinds are, the—*Bacca succosa*, very succulent, as the Gooseberry, Currant, &c.—*Bacca corticosa*, corticated, or covered with a hard rind, as the *Garcinia Mangostana*, &c.—*Bacca exsucca*, dry, when the skin is coriaceous or coloured, as in the *hedera*.—*Bacca Mono-bi-tri-poly-sperma*, one-two-three, many seeded, according to the number of seeds.—*Bacca Uni-bi-tri-multilocularis*, one-two-three, many celled, according to the number of cells into which the berry is divided.—*Bacca di-tri-pyrena*, one-two, or three, many pyrenous, when the seeds have a hard shell attached to their skin.—*Bacca Bermudensis*, the fruit of *Arbor Saponaria*, the kernel of which, steeped in water, raises a froth, like soap.

BACCALAU'REUS (*Lit.*) Batchelor. [vide *Batchelor*]

BACCA'LIA (*Bot.*) the Bay-tree.

BACCA'TUS (*Bot.*) berried, or soft, like a berry; an epithet for a capsule, a drupe, a silique, and an aril.—*Baccata capsula*, a capsule with a fleshy coat.—*Baccata drupa*, a drupe with a succulent coat, &c.

BACCHANA'LIA (*Ant.*) *Bacchi festa*, Διονύσια. [vide *Dionysia*] Bacchanals, festivals at Rome, in honour of Bacchus, which for their licentiousness were suppressed by a solemn decree of the senate. *Liv.* l. 29, c. 14; *Fest. de Verb. Signif.*; *Lax. Comment. Reip. Roman.* l. 10, c. 9; *Stuck. Antiq. Conviv.* l. 1, c. 33; *Castellan de Fest. Græc. apud Gronov. Thes. Antiq.* tom. 8, p. 637.

BACCHANA'LIANS (*Ant.*) those who performed rites in honour of Bacchus.

BA'CCHANALS (*Ant.*) vide *Bacchanalia*.

BACCHARIO'IDES (*Bot.*) the *Conyza Anthelmintica* of Linnæus.

BA'CCHARIS (*Bot.*) βάκχαρις, a sweet-scented shrubby

plant, which was formerly esteemed a vulnerary, and of which an ointment is supposed to have been made that bore the same name. *Hippocrat. de Mul.; Dioscor.* l. 3, c. 51; *Plin.* l. 21, c. 6; *Athen.* l. 15.

BACCHARIS, in the Linnean system, a genus of plants, Class 19 *Syngenesia*, Order 2 *Polygamia superflua*.
Generic Characters. CAL. common cylindric; scales linear.—COR. compound equal; proper funnel-formed.—STAM. filaments five; anthers tubular.—PIST. germ ovate; style filiform; stigma bifid.—PER. none; calyx unchanged; seeds solitary; receptacle naked.
Species. The species are shrubs.—*Baccharis ivæfolia, Conyza frutescens, Eupatorium Africanum,* Peruvian Ploughman's Spikenard, native of America.—*Baccharis nervifolia,* Oleander Ploughman's Spikenard.—*Baccharis halimifolia, Senecio Virginica, pseudo Helichrysum,* Sea Purslane-leaved Ploughman's Spikenard.—*Baccharis Dioscoridis,* seu *Conyza Major altera indica,* native of Ceylon.—*Baccharis Brasiliana,* native of Brasil.—*Baccharis fœtida,* seu *Conyza Americana,* native of Carolina.—*Baccharis Chinensis,* an undershrub, native of Canton, in China. *Ger. Herb.; J. Bauh. Hist.; C. Bauh. Pin.; Park. Theat. Botan.; Raii Hist. Plant.; Tournef. Inst. de Re Herb.*

BACCHARIS, the species is the *Conyza squarrosa* of Linnæus.

BACCHAROI'DES, the *Conyza athelmintica* of Linnæus.

BACCHI'A (*Ant.*) βάχχια, a festival. [vide *Dionysia*]

BACCHIA (*Med.*) the same as *Gutta rosacea.*

BA'CCHICA (*Bot.*) the same as *Hedera.*

BA'CCHIUS (*Gram.*) βαχχεῖος, a sort of foot so called because it was frequently used in hymns to Bacchus; it consists of three syllables, the first short and two last long, as lĕgēbānt.

BACCI'FERÆ (*Bot.*) Berry-bearing plants; one of the eighteen classes in Morrison's system.

BACHELA'RIA (*Polit.*) the Yeomanry, as distinguished from the Baronage.

BA'CHELOR (*Lit.*) the first degree in the arts and sciences, as Bachelor of arts, B. A.; Bachelor of Divinity, B. D.; Bachelor of Medicine, B. M., &c. It is called in Latin *Baccalaureus,* from *baculus,* a staff, because it was supposed that a staff was given, by way of distinction, into the hands of those who had completed their studies. Some have, however, derived the word from *bas chevaliers,* i. e. knights of a lower order.

BACHELOR, *arms of* (*Her.*) a bachelor, while he remains such, may quarter his paternal coat with other coats, but he may not impale it till he is married. [vide *Heraldry*]

BACHELOR, a title formerly given to knights who had made their first campaign; also to young military men, because they exercised themselves with staves and bucklers.

BACHELOR *of Arms,* a title given to those who for the first time came off victorious in the combat.

BA'CHELORS (*Polit.*) those members belonging to the companies of London who are not yet admitted to the livery.

BACILLA'RIA (*Ent.*) a genus of animals, Class *Vermes,* Order *Infusiora.*
Generic Character. Body consisting of cylindrical straw-like filaments.
Species. The only species is the—*Bacillaria Paradoxa,* seu *Vibrio pazilifer.*

BACI'LLUM (*Med.*) dim. of *baculum,* a troche in the form of a stick.

BACILLUM (*Chem.*) iron instruments in the shape of a *baculum,* or staff.

BACI'NIUM (*Cus.*) a Wash-hand bason; the holding of which at the king's coronation is one kind of service. *Lib. Rub. Seacar. Mon. Angl.*

BACK (*Carp.*) the upper side of a piece of timber when it is fixed in a level or inclined position, in distinction from the lower side, which is called the *Breast*. The same is to be understood with regard to the curved ribs of ceilings, and the rafters of a roof; their upper edges are always called the backs.—*Back of a Window,* in joinery, is the board or wainscotting between the sash frame and the floor, forming a part of the finish of the room in which it is placed.—*Back or hip-moulding,* the backward hips or valley-rafter in the way of an angle for the back part of a building.—*Back-stairs,* stairs leading to an apartment backwards.—*Back-house,* the buildings behind the house, the office houses.

BACK *of the stern-post* (*Mar.*) an additional piece behind the stern-post.—*Back-board,* a board placed in the after part of the ship to lean against, as the back of a chair.—*Back-frame-wheel,* a wheel for laying cordage.—*Back-staff,* an instrument for taking the sun's altitude; so called because the back of the observer is towards the sun. It consists of two concentric arcs and three vanes: the arc of the longer radius, as G F, is 30 degrees, that of the shorter 60 degrees, as D E, making altogether 90 degrees, or a quadrant. The vane A, at the centre, is called the *horizon vane,* because through it the observer must see the horizon; that at B the *shade vane,* because it produces a shadow that directs his eye; that at C the *sight vane,* because through it he looks to make his observation.—*Back-stays,* ropes that stay back or keep up the masts from pitching forward.—*Back-stay-stool,* a piece of plank fitted for the dead eyes and chains for the *back-stays.*

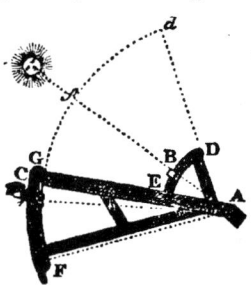

BACK-BERI'NDE (*Law*) or *back bear,* bearing upon the back a sign or circumstance of what the civilians call *furtum manifestum,* theft apparent, which was one of the four cases or circumstances wherein, according to Manwood, a forester may arrest the body of an offender against vert or venison; the three other cases being *stable-stand,* i. e. with the bow bent; *dog-draw,* i. e. drawing a dog or hound after him, to recover the deer that is shot; and *bloody-hand,* i. e. having the hands suspiciously besmeared with blood. *Bract.* l. 3, tract 2, c. 32; *Manw. For. Laws,* pt. 2, c. 18.—*Back-tack,* in the Scotch law, when a wadsetter, instead of occupying the wadset lands, grants a tack thereof to the reverser for payment of a certain sum, under the name of the *tacking duty,* that tack is called a *back-tack.*

BACK-GA'MMON (*Sport.*) a particular game played by two persons, with the help of dice, on a board or table divided into two parts, whereon are 24 black and white spaces, called *points.*

BA'CK-PAINTING (*Paint.*) the method of painting mezzotinto prints pasted on glass, with oil colours.

TO BACK (*Mar.*) is used in several nautical phrases, as—" To *back* an anchor," to carry out a small anchor to support the larger one.—" To *back* a-stern," to manage the oars in rowing in a direction contrary to the usual method.—" To *back* and fill," an operation generally performed in a river when a ship has the tide in her favour and the wind against her.—" To *back* the sails," to arrange them for the ship to retreat or move astern, in consequence of the tide favouring her.—" *Back* the starboard oars!" the command to confine the management to the oars on the right hand side of the boat or ship.—" *Back* the main top-sail!" the command to brace that sail, so that the wind may act on the forepart, and thus retard the ship's course.

BA'CKING *of a wall* (*Carpent.*) the building which forms the inner face of a wall, or the act of building the inner face.

BACKS (*Com.*) the thickest and best tanned hides, used chiefly for soles of shoes.

BA'COPA (*Bot.*) a genus of plants, Class 5 *Pentandria*, Order 1 *Monogynia*.
Generic Characters. CAL. *perianth* one-leaved.—COR. one-petalled.—STAM. *filaments* five; *anthers* sagittate.—PIST. *germ* ovate; *style* short; *stigma* headed.—PER. *capsule* one-celled; *seeds* very many.
Species. The only species is the—*Bacopa aquatica*, native of Cayenne. *Linn. Spec. Plant.*

BA'CTILE (*Archæol.*) a candlestick, properly so called when made *e baculo*, of a stick.

BA'CTRIS (*Bot.*) a genus of plants, Class 21 *Monoecia*, Order 6 *Hexandria*.
Generic Characters. CAL. *spathe* universal one-leaved.—COR. one-petalled.—STAM. *filaments* six; *anthers* oblong.—PIST. *germ* ovate; *style* very short; *stigma* headed.—PER. *drupe* coriaceous; *seed nut* roundish.
Species. The species are—*Bactris minor fructibus*, &c. seu *Cocos (quincensis) aculeata*, &c. a shrub, native of S. America.—*Bactris major fructu*, &c. seu *Fructus exoticus*, a shrub, native of S. America. *Linn. Spec. Plant.*

BA'CULE (*Fort.*) a kind of portcullis, or gate, made like a pitfall, with a counterpoise, and supported by two great stakes.

BACULOME'TRIA (*Math.*) a measuring of lines by means of baculi, or staves.

BADGE (*Her.*) an exterior ornament of a coat of arms, originally worn by the servants, &c. of the nobility. They were much used from the reign of king Edward the First until that of queen Elizabeth, when they grew into disuse.

BADGE (*Mar.*) an ornament placed on the outside of small ships, and commonly decorated with marine figures.

BA'DGER (*Law*) from *baggage*, and *bagagier*, a carrier of bundles; one that buys corn or victuals in one place and sells them in another. *Stat.* 5 and 6 *Ed.* 6; 3 *Eliz.* c. 12.

BADGER (*Nat.*) the *Ursus meles* of Linnæus, an animal which lives in woods and clefts of rocks. It feeds on insects, &c. burrows during winter, hunts by night, and lies concealed by day. It is easily tamed; gravid 7 weeks, and brings 3 to 5 young.

BADGER (*Her.*) has been occasionally used as a charge in coats of arms.

BADIA'GA (*Med.*) a kind of sponge in Russia, the powder of which, according to Bauxbaum, takes away the livid marks from bruises.

BA'DIAN *Semen* (*Bot.*) the same as *Anisum Indicum*.

BADI'GEON (*Mech.*) a mixture of plaster and free-stone ground and sifted together, which is used by statuaries to fill up the little holes and repair the defects in stones. The same name is given by joiners to a composition of sawdust and glue, with which any cavities in their work are filled up.

BADI'TES (*Bot.*) the name for the *Nymphæa*, or *Clava Herculis*; the root of which, according to Marcellus Empiricus, bruised and eaten with vinegar for ten days by a boy, makes him a eunuch without excision.

BA'DIUS (*Bot.*) chesnut or liver brown, an epithet for plants.

BA'ECKIA (*Bot.*) from Abraham Baecka, a friend of Linnæus', a genus of plants. Class 8 *Octandria*, Order 1 *Monogynia*.
Generic Characters. CAL. *perianth* one-leaved.—COR. *petals* five.—STAM. *filaments* eight; *anthers* subovate. PIST. *germ* roundish; *style* filiform; *stigma* capitate.—PER. *capsule* globular; *seeds* a few.
Species. The species are mostly shrubs, as the—*Baeckia frutescens foliis*, &c. seu *Chinensis*, native of China.—*Baeckia densifolia*, seu *foliis*, &c. native of New Holland.—*Baeckia virgata*, native of New Holland. *Linn. Spec. Plant.*

BÆOBO'TRYS (*Bot.*) from βαιος, *parvus*, and βότρυς, *racemus*, the fructifications being in their racemes; a genus of plants, Class 5 *Pentandria*, Order 1 *Monogynia*.
Generic Characters. CAL. *perianth* double.—COR. one-petalled.—STAM. *filaments* five; *anthers* heart-shaped. PIST. *germ* globose; *style* cylindric; *stigma* obtuse.—PER. *berry* globose; *seeds* several.
Species. The species are the—*Bæobotrys nemoralis*, seu *foliis*, &c. a shrub, native of the Isle of Janna, in the South Seas.—*Bæobotrys lanceolata foliis*, &c. seu *Maesa*, a shrub, native of Arabia Felix. *Linn. Spec. Plant.*

BÆ'OS (*Med.*) a malagma. *Paul. Ægin.*

BA'ETAS (*Com.*) a sort of woollen stuff in Spain and Portugal which is not crossed.

BAFFE'TAS (*Com.*) a kind of calico manufactured in India.

BA'FFLING-WINDS (*Mar.*) those winds which wave and shift continually.

BAG (*Com.*) a determinate quantity of goods contained in a bag, varying according to the article, or the place, in size, from three to four hundred weight.

BAG *of madder* (*Her.*) a charge in the Dyer's arms. [vide *Dyer's Company*]

BAGA'VEL (*Archæol.*) a tribute upon all goods brought to the city of Exeter, the collection of which was granted to the citizens by charter, from King Edward I. for repairing the walls, &c.

BAGA'UZ (*Com.*) the sugar canes in the Antilles, after they have passed through the mills.

BAGE'DIA (*Com.*) a pound of twelve ounces.

BAGNIGGE-WE'LLS (*Med.*) Wells, near Islington, containing water slightly brackish, three half-pints of which are purgative.

BA'GNIO (*Med.*) from *bagno*, Italian for a bathing-house, with conveniences for bathing, sweating, and otherwise cleansing the body. It is now most commonly understood to be a brothel.

BAGNOLE'NSES (*Ecc.*) Heretics in the eighth century, who rejected the Old Testament and part of the New. They were a branch of the Manichæans. *Antonin. Sum. Hist.* part iv, sect. 11, c. 7; *Prateol. Doct. Oni. Hæret.*

BA'GPIPE (*Mus.*) a favourite wind instrument among the Highlanders.

TO BAGPIPE *the mizen* (*Mar.*) to lay it back, by bringing the sheet to the mizen shrouds.

BA'G-REEF (*Mar.*) a fourth or lower reef, sometimes used in the royal navy.

BAGUE'TTE (*Archit.*) a small round moulding, less than an astragal, sometimes carved and enriched with foliages, ribbands, laurels, &c.

BAGEL-COYO'LLI (*Bot.*) the same as *Areca*.—*Bagel-Schulli*, an Indian tree, from the roots of which a decoction is made that is diuretic. *Raii Hist. Plant.*

BA'HIR (*Theol.*) a term signifying literally excellent, but applied particularly to the cabbala of the Rabbis, or their book of mysteries.

BAIL (*Law*) from the French *bailler*, Latin *ballium*, and Greek βαλλω, to deliver. 1. The freeing one arrested, or imprisoned upon any action, on surety taken for his appearance on a certain day, and at a certain place. This is what Bracton and the statute of Westminster (made the 3 Ed. I.) calls *replegiari*, and letting out by a sufficient *replegium*; what Britton and the Register express by finding of *Mainprize*; the statute 5 Ed. III. c. 8, by letting to Baile; that of Marlbridge, c. 27 (made 52 Hen. III.), by *tradere in ballium vel replegium*; the statute 2 Ed. III. c. 9, *de homine replegiando*, declareth the effect thereof to be, that he should replevy the prisoner by good Mainprize;

the statute 23 Hen. VIII. calls it *letting to bail*, or *mainprize*; and the statute of 2 P. & M. seems to make all the words synonymous: but according to the modern distinction, to *replevie*, is to redeem a thing by giving pledges, particularly applied to cattle or goods that are distrained; *bailment* signifies delivering a person, who is a prisoner, into the hands of his friends, who are sureties for his appearance; *mainprize* signifies also literally taking a prisoner in hand from *manu captio*, but with this difference, that he who is bailed is always a prisoner to his friends; but he who is mainprized, is said always to be at large.— Bail is either common or special.—*Common bail* is in common concernment, where any sureties may be taken; but —*Special bail* is in matters of greater weight, where special surety of two or more persons must be taken, according to the value of the cause. *Horne's Mir. of Just.* c. 2; *Britt.* c. 2, &c.; *Bract.* l. 3, tract 2, c. 8; *Old. Nat. Brev.* 42; *F. N. B.* 249; *Reg. Orig.* 123; *Lamb. Eiren.* l. 3, c. 2; 4 *Inst.* 179.

BAIL signifies also a limit or bound within a forest.

TO BAIL (*Law*) to be bail or surety for one arrested, &c.; also to hold to bail.

BAILE'E (*Law*) the person to whom the goods of the one that is bailed are delivered.

BA'ILIFF (*Law*) *Balivus*, from βάλλειν, to commit or entrust; Magistrates in France who administered justice in the parliaments or courts, answering to sheriffs or to the bailiffs of hundreds, mentioned by Bracton. There are still *bailiffs* of particular towns in England, as the *bailiff* of Dover Castle, &c.; otherwise *bailiffs* are now only officers or stewards, &c.; as—*Bailiffs of liberties*, appointed by every lord within his liberty, to serve writs, &c.—*Bailiff, errant or itinerant*, appointed to go about the county for the same purpose.—*Sheriff's bailiffs*, sheriff's officers to execute writs. These are also called *bound bailiffs*, because they are usually bound in bond to the sheriff for the due execution of their office.—*Bailiff of courts baron*, to summon the court, &c.—*Bailiffs of husbandry*, appointed by private persons to collect their rents, and manage their estates.—*Water-Bailiffs*, officers in all port towns, for searching ships, gathering toll, &c.

BA'ILIWICK (*Law*) from *balliva*, either the county itself, or any liberty over which the lord appointeth a bailiff, as the bailiff of Westminster. *Wood's Instit.* 206.

BAILLO'NE (*Her.*) a charge in coats of arms, representing a lion rampant, holding a staff in his mouth.

BA'ILLOR (*Law*) the party who delivers the goods of a person that is bailed.

BA'ILMENT (*Law*) from the French *bailler*, to deliver; a delivery of goods in trust upon a contract expressed or implied. Of these there are six sorts, as—1. *Depositum*, a bare and naked bailment, to keep for the use of the bailor. 2. *Accommodatum*, a lending gratis, or delivery of goods, to be returned again in specie. 3. *Locatio*, or *conductio*, a delivery of goods for hire. 4. *Vadium*, a delivery by way of pledge. 5. A delivery of goods to be carried for a reward. 6. *Mandatum*, as it is called by Bracton, a commission or delivery of goods to do something about them, as to carry them, &c. without a reward. 1 *Inst.* 89.

BAI'LO (*Polit.*) the title given at Constantinople to the ambassador of the Republic of Venice, who acts also as consul.

BAILO'QUE (*Com.*) or *Balloque*, a French name for the ostrich feathers that are used as ornaments without dying.

BAIO'CO (*Com.*) a small coin in the Roman state, a hundred of which make a Roman crown.

BAI'RAM (*Theol.*) a festival among the Turks, celebrated after the fast of Ramazan for three days together, in which no work is done; but presents are sent from one to another with manifestations of joy.

BAI'R-MAN (*Law*) a poor insolvent debtor left bare and naked. *Stat. Will. Reg. Scot.*

BAIRN'S *part* (*Law*) Children's part; a third part of the defunct's free moveables, debts deducted, if the wife survive; and a half if there be no relict.

TO BAIT (*Falc.*) the action of a hawk when she claps her wings, or stoops to catch her prey.

BA'JULUS (*Archæol.*) a Bailiff.

BAIZE (*Com.*) or *bays*, in the singular, Bay; a coarse woollen stuff, having a long nap. The name and the thing was introduced into England by the Flemish refugees.

TO BAKE (*Print.*) the letters are said by compositors to *bake* which stick together, in a composed state, from the drying of the ink.

BA'KERS' *Company* (*Her.*) there are two companies of this name, the White and the Brown Bakers.

The *White Bakers* are of great antiquity, having been a company as early as Edward II. Their arms are, as in fig. 1, "*gules*, three garbs, *or*, on a chief; an arm issuing out of a cloud, *proper*, holding a pair of scales, *or*, between three garbs of the first."

Fig. 1.   Fig. 2.

The *Brown Bakers* were incorporated the 19th of James I. Their arms, as in fig. 2, are "*gules*, a hand issuing out of the clouds, *proper*, holding a pair of scales; an anchor in a chief, barry wavy, *or* and *azure*, on a chevron, *gules* between three garbes.

BALÆ'NA (*Zool.*) Whale, the μυςίκητος of Aristotle, the *Musculus* of Pliny; is, *in the Linnean system*, a genus of animals, Class *Mammalia*, Order *Cete*.

Generic Characters. Horny laminæ in the upper jaw in place of teeth.—*Spiracle* with a double external orifice on the top of the head.

Species. The principal species are the—*Balæna Mysticetus*, seu *Groenlands Wallfisch*, the Common Whale.— *Balæna physalus, tripinnis*, &c. *Physalus bellua, Physeter*, seu *Finnfisch*, Fin-Fish, or Finn-backed Mysticete. *Balæna boops, tripinnis, musculus*, &c. seu *Jupiterfisch*, Pike-headed Whale, or Mysticete.—*Balæna gibbosa*, seu *Knotenfisch, Knobbelfisch*, Bunched Mysticete Whale.

BA'LANCE (*Mech.*) an instrument formed by the application of the lever, in order to determine the weight of bodies; of which there are different kinds, named according to their construction, as the *common balance*, the *Roman balance*, or *steelyard*, the *compound balance*, *Danish balance*, *deceitful* or *false balance*, &c.; and also according to their use, as *assay balance*, *hydrostatical balance*, and the like. The Common Balance consists of a lever, called the *beam*, the two halves of which, on each side the axis, are called the *arms*; the line which divides the beam in two is called the *axis*, which, if considered as a point, is called the *centre of motion*; and the extremities, where the weights are applied, are called the *points of suspension*.—*Balance of a clock* or *watch*, that part which by its motion regulates and determines the beat. The circular part of it is called the *rim*, and its spindle the *verge*; besides which it has two *pallets*, or nuts, that play in the fangs of the crown wheel; and in pocket watches the strong stud in which the lower part of the crown wheel lies, is called the *potans*

2 E

or *potance*. The wrought piece which covers the balance and by which the upper pivot plays, is the *lock*, and the small spring in watches is the *regulator*. [vide *Mechanics*]

BALANCE (*Astron.*) a constellation. [vide *Libra*]

BALANCE (*Com.*) is so called in Merchants' Accounts when the debtor and creditor sides are even. The act of so doing is termed "Drawing a *balance*."—*Balance* also signifies the difference between two accounts, which, when added to the one that is deficient, makes them even.—*Balance in trade*, the difference between the value of commodities bought of foreigners, and that of our own products exported.

BALANCE (*Ent.*) a style or oblong body under each wing of the two-winged flies, which is supposed to serve as a balance or poise for them in their flight.

BALANI'NUM *oleum* (*Bot.*) the oil of the *Balanus Myrepsica. Plin.* l. 13, c. 1.

BALANOCA'STANUM (*Bot.*) the same as *Balbocastanum*.

BALANO'PHORA (*Bot.*) the *Lynomorium* of Linnæus.

BA'LANOS (*Bot.*) βαλανος, an acorn; an oak, or any glandiferous tree. *Hippocrat. de Affect.*; *Theoph. Hist. Plant.* l. 1, c. 8.

BALANOS (*Med.*) a suppository or pessary made in form like an acorn.

BALANOS (*Anat.*) the Glans Penis.

BALANUS *Myrepsica* (*Bot.*) the Oily Acorn, the fruit of the *Lignum Nephriticum*.

BALA'RUC, Waters of (*Med.*) saline and purgative waters in France.

BALA'SIUS (*Min.*) a sort of Carbuncle.

BA'LASS-RUBY (*Min.*) a species of stone, of the ruby kind, with crystals of a regular octahedron form.

BALA'STRI (*Com.*) the finest gold cloth of Venice.

BALATRO'NES (*Archæol.*) a profligate set of men; so called from one Servilius Balatro, a noted libertine. *Hor.* l. 1, sat. 2, v. 2, &c.

BALA'USTIUM (*Bot.*) βαλαυστιον, Balaustines; the flowers of the wild Pomegranate; the *Punica granatum* of Linnæus. These flowers were reckoned of an astringent quality. *Diosc.* l. 1, c. 154; *Plin.* l. 13, c. 19.

BALA'ZOES (*Com.*) or white cotton cloths of Mogul.

BA'LBIS (*Med.*) βαλβις, an oblong cavity. *Gal. Exeges. Vocab. Hippocrat.*

BALBITO'DES (*Anat.*) βαλβιτωδις, the cavity at the extremity of the *humerus* to which the *ulna* is articulated. *Hip. de Artic.*

BALBU'TIES (*Med.*) from βαλβαζω, a stammering and precipitate speech.

BALCA'NIFER (*Archæol.*) a standard-bearer.

BALCO'NY (*Arch.*) a projection in the front of a building surrounded with balustrades, and serving the purpose of a small gallery.

BA'LDACHIN (*Archit.*) from the Italian *baldachino*, signifying a sort of canopy erected over an altar as a covering.

BA'LE (*Com.*) a pack, or certain quantity of goods.—*Bale-goods*, such goods as are exported or imported in bales.

TO BALE (*Mar.*) to lade water out of a ship's hold with buckets.

BALE'NGER (*Archæol.*) a kind of barge or water-vessel, *Stat.* 28 H. 6; also a man of war. *Walsing. in R.* 2.

BALRU'GA (*Archæol.*) a territory, or precinct. *Chart. Hen.* 2.

BALI'STA (*Ant.*) vide *Ballista*.

BALISTA (*Her.*) vide *Sweep*.

BALISTRA'RIUS (*Archæol.*) a cross-bowman. 28, 29 Hen. 2.

BALI'STES (*Ich.*) a genus of animals, Class *Pisces*, Order *Branchiostegous*.

Generic Character. Head compressed; *Mouth* narrow; *Teeth* in each jaw 8; *Gills* narrow in the aperture; *Body* rough, with very minute prickles, the scales joined together by the skin.

Species. None of these fishes inhabit the seas of Europe; they feed on other fish, grow to a vast size, and are most of them suspected to be poisonous, particularly the *Balistes monocerus, Sinensis, &c.*

BALISTI'QUE (*Mil.*) a French word signifying the art of projecting heavy substances, as cannon-balls, &c.

BA'LIVA (*Law*) a bailiwick or jurisdiction.

BALIVO AMOVE'NDO (*Law*) a writ to remove a bailiff out of his office. *Reg. Orig.*

BA'LK (*Arch.*) a large piece of timber used as a main beam for a house, a scaffolding, or any other building.

BALK (*Agr.*) a ridge, or bank, between two furrows.

BALK *staff* (*Mar.*) a quarter-staff.

BA'LKERS (*Archæol.*) from the word *Balk*, because they stand higher than others. Persons who from a high place on the coast show the passage of the shoals of herrings to fishermen, or give notice of any thing to others.

BA'LL (*Ent.*) the little case, or cone, of silk in which silk-worms and spiders deposit their eggs.

BALL (*Nat.*) a mass of hair covered with a smooth shining coat, or shell, found in the stomach of goats, &c. and otherwise called Bezoar.

BALL (*Min.*) a term among the Cornish miners for a tin-mine.—*Ball-vein* a sort of iron ore common in the mines of Switzerland.

BALL *of fire* (*Meteor.*) vide *Fire-ball*.

BALL (*Mil.*) any round substance of lead, iron, &c. which is discharged from fire-arms, as musket-balls, cannon-balls, &c.—*Fire-balls*, or *light-balls*, are such as are composed of meal, powder, saltpetre, sulphur, &c. and put into shells which are discharged from mortars for the purpose of setting fire to particular places.—*Smoke-balls*, those which have a larger proportion of pitch, rosin, and sawdust.—*Stink-balls*, those in which horses' hoofs, asa-fœtida, &c. form the principal ingredients.—*Red-hot balls*, such as are sent out in a perfect state of ignition.—*Chain-balls*, two balls linked together by a chain, that do much damage to the rigging of vessels.—*Stang-balls*, commonly called *bar-shot*, are balls of two heads, or two half-balls joined together by a bar of iron.—*Anchor-balls* are composed of the same materials as *fire-balls*, but are made with an iron-bar, one-half of which is fixed within the ball.—*Message-balls*, [vide *Shells*]—*Sky-balls*, those which burst from rockets.—*Water-balls*, those which burn while swimming on the water.—*Sand-balls*, those which burst on the ground.

BALL *martial* (*Med.*) a mixture of iron filings and cream of tartar formed into the consistence of a ball for impregnating water and other liquids.—*Mercurial ball*, an amalgam of mercury and tin moulded into the shape of a ball.

BALL (*Vet.*) the medicines given to a horse in the shape of a ball, and distinguished by the name of a *horse-ball*.

BALL *of a pendulum* (*Mech.*) The weight at the bottom, which, in short pendulums, is called the *bob*.—*Ball and socket*, an instrument made of brass, with a perpetual screw, so as to move in different directions, for the purpose of managing astronomical and surveying instruments.

BALL (*Elect.*) a name for two pieces of cork, or pith of elder-tree, nicely turned in a lathe to the size of a small pea, and suspended by very delicate threads, which serve to discover small degrees of electricity.

BA'LLAST (*Mar.*) from the Teutonic, Ballast; gravel, sand, or any weighty matter, put into a ship's hold to poise her, and bring her sufficiently low in the water. Ships are said to be in *ballast* when they have no other lading.—"*To trench ballast*," is to divide or dispose it.—*Shot-ballast*, when the ballast runs from one side to the other.—*Pea-ballast*, a peculiar kind of fresh-water sand dried by the sun, and used for stowing teas with.—*Shingle-ballast*, coarse gravel used for ballast.—*Stiff ballast*, when the ballast is so heavy as to retard the ship's motion.—*Crank bal-*

last, when the ballast is so light as to endanger the ship upsetting.

BALLA'TA (*Mus.*) Italian for any song, the melody of which is calculated to regulate the measure of a dance.

BALLATOO'NS (*Mar.*) large, heavy barks, or baggage-boats, for carrying wood from Astracan to Moscow.

BA'LLEL (*Bot.*) the *Convolvulus repens* of Linnæus.

BA'LLET (*Mus.*) French for a theatrical representation composed of music and dancing.—*Ballet-master*, the artist who regulates the performance and representation of the ballet.

BALLE'TYS (*Ant.*) βαλλητυς, a festival at Eleusis, in Attica, in honour of Demophoon, the son of Celeus. *Athen.* l. 9; *Hesychius*.

BA'LLI (*Mus.*) Italian for dances between the acts of the operas.

BA'LLIAGE (*Com.*) a duty payable to the City of London, for all the goods and merchandises of aliens, according to the charter of the 16th *Car.* 2.

BA'LLIN (*Com.*) the name for Emballage, or packing, in the South of France and Bayonne.

BALLI'STA (*Ant.*) a machine for war, by which stones and other missile weapons were projected to a distance. *Sil. Ital.* l. 1, v. 334.

> ——— *Adductis stridula nervis*
> *Phocais effundit vastos ballista molares.*

Lucan. l. 3, v. 464.

> *Neque enim solis excussa lacertis*
> *Lancea, sed tenso ballistæ turbine rapta*
> *Haud unum contenta latus transire, quiescit:*
> *Sed pandens perque arma viam, perque ossa, relicta*
> *Morte fugit; superest telo post vulnera cursus;*
> *At saxum quoties ingenti ponderis ictu*
> *Excutitur, qualis rupes, quam vertice montis*
> *Abscidit impulsu ventorum adjuta vetustas,*
> *Frangit cuncta ruens:*

It is so called from the Greek βάλλω, to cast, but the Greeks distinguish this machine by the names πετροβόλος and λιθοβόλος, [vide *Militia*] *Cic. Tuscul.* l. 2, c. 24; *Vitruv.* l. 10, c. 16; *Joseph. de Bell. Jud.* l. 6; *Plin.* l. 7, c. 56; *Appian. in Mithrid. Hegesip.* l. 3, c. 12; *Ammian.* l. 3, c. 24; *Isidor.* l. 18, c. 10; *Lips. Poliorc.* l. 3; dial. 3.

BALLISTA'RII (*Ant.*) a sort of light-armed soldiers. *Veget.* l. 2, c. 2.

BA'LLISTER (*Arch.*) vide *Baluster*.

BALLISTEUM (*Ant.*) βαλλίσιον, a sort of song and dance combined, which was in use among the Romans, so called from βαλλίζω, to dance, or throw about the hands. The French word *ballet*, which is taken in a similar sense, is derived, in all probability, from this word. *Vopisc. in Aurel.*; *Suidas*.

BALLI'STIC *pendulum* (*Mech.*) a machine for ascertaining the velocity of military projectiles, invented by Mr. Benjamin Robins.

BALLI'STICS (*Mil.*) the art of using projectiles.

BA'LLIUM (*Archæol.*) a fortress, or bulwark. *Matth. West. An.* 1265.

BA'LLON (*Ant.*) from the French *ballon* and *balle*, a large ball which princes used in the sports.

BALLON (*Chem.*) or *balloon*; a round, short-necked vessel, used as a receiver in distillation.

BALLON (*Archit.*) a ball, or globe, on the top of a pillar.

BALLON (*Mech.*) a kind of bomb made of pasteboard, and played off in fireworks.

BALLON (*Mar.*) a sort of brigantine in Siam made out of a single trunk not less than a hundred, or a hundred and twenty feet long.

BALLON (*Com.*) or *ballot*, a name in Lorraine for a certain quantity of glass-plates, smaller or larger, according to the quality.

BALLON, a determinate quantity of particular commodities; as a *ballon* of glass, consisting of twelve bundles and a half; a *ballon* of paper, containing fourteen reams.

BALLON (*Pneum.*) *balloon*, or *air-balloon*, the machine invented by Mr. Montgolfier, for navigating the air. [vide *Pneumatics*]

BALLOO'N (*Chem.*) a large glass receiver in the form of a hollow globe, which forms a part of the chemical apparatus.

BA'LLOT (*Polit.*) a diminutive of ball, *i. e.* a little ball used in giving votes: or the act itself of giving votes.

BALLO'TA (*Bot.*) βαλλωτη, Stinking or Black Horehound; a plant so called, from βάλλω, to dart, because it was supposed to open obstructions in the ears, in the same manner that a dart penetrates the body. A cataplasm made of its leaves are, according to Dioscorides, efficacious against the bite of a mad dog. *Dioscorides*, l. 3, c. 117; *Plin.* l. 27, c. 8.

BALLOTA, *in the Linnean system*, a genus of plants, Class 14 *Didynamia*, Order 1 *Gymnospermia*. This plant is, by the earlier botanists, mostly called Marrubium, of which it was reckoned to be a species; Tournefort, however, calls it Ballote.

Generic Characters. CAL. *perianth* one-leaved.—COR. *monopetalous.*—STAM. *filaments* four; *anthers* oblong.—PIST. *germ* quadrifid; *style* filiform; *stigma* slender.—PER. none; *seeds* four.

Species. The species are mostly perennials, as—*Ballota nigra*, Marrubium nigrum, seu Marrubiastrum, Stinking or Black Horehound, a native of Britain.—*Ballota alba*, White Horehound.—But the *Ballota suaveolens*, Bystropogon, Mesosphærum, Mentastrum, seu Melissa, Sweet-smelling Horehound, is an annual.

BALLOTA'DE (*Man.*) the leap of a horse between two pillars made with justness of time.

BALLUSTER (*Arch.*) a small kind of column or pillar.

BALLUSTRA'DE (*Arch.*) a series or rows of ballusters serving as a guard or fence to balconies, staircases, &c. It is so called from *Balustrum*, a space in the ancient baths that was railed in.

BALM (*Bot.*) a contraction of balsam, as the Balm of Gilead, a liquid resin of a whitish or yellow colour, of a fragrant smell, and of a penetrating aromatic taste. The balm flows from the Balsam-Tree. [vide *Balsam*]

BALM *of Gilead* is also a perennial, so called from the fine perfume which it emits when rubbed. It is the *Dracocephalum canariense* of Linnæus.—Balm *of fir-tree*, the *Pinus balsamea* of Linnæus.—Balm, or Balm mint, the *Melissa* of Linnæus; a perennial, so called from the fragrance of its smell which resembles that of the balsam: the sort of balm most known is the garden balm, which is of medicinal and culinary use.

BA'LNEÆ (*Ant.*) public baths or bains for bathing two together, one for the men, and the other for the women. *Vitruv.* l. 5, c. 10.

BALNEA'RIUS (*Ant.*) a name of the thief who stole the clothes of those that were bathing. *Tertull. de Persecut.* c. 13.

BALNEA'TOR (*Ant.*) *qui balneis præest;* the bath keeper, or he who had the charge of the bath.

BA'LNEUM (*Ant.*) βαλνιον, a private bath or bathing place, in distinction from the *Balneæ* or *Balineæ*, which were public baths. *Varr. de Ling. Lat.* l. 8, c. 41.—*Balneum Frigidarium*, the cold-bath.—*Balneum Caldarium*, the hot-bath.—*Balneum Tepidarium*, the warm or tepid-bath.

BALNEUM *arenæ, vel siccum* (*Chem.*) a sand heat for the purification of mercury.—*Balneum mariæ, seu maris*, boiling water, into which the vessel that contains the ingredients to be digested or acted upon is placed.—*Balneum vaporis,*

Vapour-bath, when the vessel is exposed only to the steam of boiling water.

BALOTI'DES (*Man.*) vide *Ballotade*.

BA'LSAM (*Bot.*) the resinous juice which proceeds from the bark of the Balsam-tree. The first sort of Balsam that was known bore the name of Opobalsam, Balm of Gilead, or the Balsam of Mecca, and was produced from a tree, growing in Arabia and Egypt, called, in the Linnean system, the *Amyris Gileadensis*, et *Opobalsamum*. [vide *Balsamum*] This balsam is much in use, among the females of Turkey, as a cosmetic.

BALSAM (*Med.*) a name also given to several medicinal preparations, as the—*Balsam of Sulphur*, or the oily parts of common brimstone dissolved in oil of turpentine.—*Balsam of Saturn*, a solution of the *Saccharum Saturni*, or sugar of lead, made with spirit or oil of turpentine, and digested, &c.

BALSAM *Tree* (*Bot.*) the tree from which the Balm or Balsam of Gilead flows; it is the *Amyris Gileadensis* of Linnæus.

BALSA'MEA (*Bot.*) from *balsamum*, a species of *Pinus*, which see.

BALSAMELÆ'ON (*Bot.*) the same as *Balsamum*.

BALSAME'LLA (*Bot.*) the same as *Balsamina*.

BALSA'MICS (*Med.*) from *balsamum*; balsamic medicines, which Hoffman describes as hot and acrid. Under this description are comprehended Aloe's-wood, Yellow Sanders, Ambergrise, which are very efficacious in all diseases of the head, nerves, spinal marrow, &c.

BALSA'MINA (*Bot.*) a species of *Momordica* of Linnæus.—*Balsamina lutea*, seu *noli me tangere*, a species of *Impatiens* of Linnæus.

BALSA'MINUS (*Bot.*) βαλσάμινος, *oleum balsaminum*, Oil of Balm. *Plin.* l. 23, c. 4.

BALSAMI'TA *major* (*Bot.*) a species of the *Tanacetum* of Linnæus.—*Balsamita minor*, the *Achillea ageratum* of Linnæus.—*Balsamita agerati*, the *Chrysanthemum flosculosum* of Linnæus.

BA'LSAMUM (*Bot.*) βάλσαμον, a tree growing in the valleys of Syria which yields the most precious aromatic, known by the name of Balsam; it is so called from *belsamin*, which, among the Easterns, signifies the chief of aromatics. In the Linnean system it is the *Amyris Gileadensis*. *Theophrast. Hist. Plant.* l. 9, c. 6; *Dioscor.* l. 1, c. 18; *Plin.* l. 12, c. 25; *Oribas. Med. Coll.* l. 11; *Aet. Tetrab.* 1, serm. 1; *Paul. Æginet.* l. 7, c. 3.

BA'LTHEI (*Archit.*) bands or girdles belonging to the Ionic volute, according to Vitruvius. They are supposed to be the bolsters of the volute, and are so called from their resembling the girdles of the soldiers. *Vitruv.* l. 3, c. 3; *Tertull. de Spectac.* 3; *Salmas. in Solin.* p. 919.

BALTIMO'RA (*Bot.*) from Lord Baltimore, a genus of plants, Class 19 *Syngenesia*, Order 4 *Polygamia Necessaria*.
Generic Characters. CAL. common cylindric.—COR. compound radiate.—STAM. *filaments* five; *anthers* cylindric.—PIST. *germ* obscure; *style* short; *stigma* none.—PER. none; *seeds* none; *receptacle* chaffy.
Species. The only species is *Baltimora recta*, seu *Chrysanthemum Americanum*, &c. an annual, native of North America.

BALU'STER (*Archit.*) corruptly written Bannister, a small column or pilaster of different dimensions, from an inch and three quarters to four inches square.

BALUSTRA'DE (*Archit.*) vide *Ballustrade*.—*Feinte balustrade*, French for small pillars or balusters which are fixed half their usual height upon any ground.

BAMBO'O (*Bot.*) or *bambu*, an Indian reed with larger knots than the common reed; the *Arundo bambos* of Linnæus, a plant of which the poorer inhabitants in the East Indies build their houses; paper is also made of the same material, by bruising it, and steeping it in water till it be reduced to a paste. The Turks make their pens of a variety of this cane.—*Bamboo habit*, a Chinese contrivance for one to keep himself above water who does not know how to swim.

BAMBU'SA (*Bot.*) a genus of plants, Class 6 *Hexandria*, Order 1 *Monogynia*.
Generic Characters. CAL. none, except glume like bractes scattered.—COR. glume two-valved; *nectary* two-leaved.—STAM. *filaments* six; *anthers* parellalopiped.—PIST. *germ* oblong; *style* capillary; *stigmas* feathery.—PER. none; *seed* single.
Species. The species are—*Bambusa arundinacea, panicula, &c. Bambos arundinacea, Nastus, Arundo Bambos, &c. Arundo arbor, Arundarbor vasaria, Tabaxir*, seu *Mombu arbor* seu *Illy*, a shrub, native of the Indies.—*Bambusa verticilata, spica, &c. Arundo multiplex, &c. Arundo arbor, &c.* a shrub, native of India.

BA'MIER (*Bot.*) an Egyptian plant, the husk of which is dressed with their meat to give it an agreeable flavour.

BA'MMA (*Med.*) the same as *Embamma*.

BAN (*Law*) in the Latin of the Middle age, *bannum*, Teutonic *bann*, from *binden*, to bind; 1. An outlawry, or banishment by edict or proclamation at the sound of the trumpet. 2. An *arrier ban*, or *reer ban*, an edict by which all vassals were summoned to attend their lord on the field with horses and arms, in pain of being outlawed. *Hottom*. 3. An edict interdicting all intercourse with an enemy. 4. *Banna matrimonialia*, bans which are published in the church previous to the marriage of any couple, who have not obtained a *licence*.

BAN (*Com.*) a sort of fine India cotton.

BAN (*Bot.*) an Egyptian plant called *calaf*.

BANA'NA (*Bot.*) Banana or Plantain-tree, the *Musa sapientum* of Linnæus; an American plant, diuretic, heating and nutritious. *Raii Hist. Plant.*

BANANI'ERA (*Bot.*) the *Ficus Indica* of Linnæus.

BANA'RA (*Bot.*) a genus of plants, Class 12 *Icosandria*, Order 1 *Monogynia*.
Generic Characters. CAL. *perianth* one-leaved.—COR. *petals* six.—STAM. *filaments* fifteen and more; *anthers* roundish.—PIST. *germ* somewhat globose.—PER. *berry* globose; *seeds* very many.
Species. The species are the *Banara quianensis*, et *Banara fagifolia*, shrubs of Cayenne.

BANC *de cit* (*Archit.*) a bed or layer of the upper stones, which is supported by pillars at intermediate distances.

BA'NCAL (*Com.*) an Indian weight of 16 oz. and above.

BANCA'LE (*Archæol.*) a covering for ease or ornament belonging to the seats or benches formerly used.

BA'NCI *jus* (*Law*) vide *Jus*.

BA'NCO (*Com.*) Italian for bank, a term particularly applied to that of Venice.

BA'NCUS (*Archæol.*) bench, a term particularly used in Law, as—*Bancus Regius*, the King's Bench.—*Bancus Communis*, the Common Pleas.

BAND *of Pensioners* (*Polit.*) a particular company of gentlemen bearing halberds, and attending the person of the King upon solemn occasions.

BAND (*Her.*) a military order instituted by Alphonso XI, king of Castile, for the younger sons of the nobility, who are obliged to serve ten years, either by land or sea, before their admission, and are bound to take up arms in defence of the Catholic faith against the infidels.

BAND (*Archit.*) any flat low member or moulding that is broad, but not very deep. It is otherwise called "Face," and by Vitruvius *fascia*. *Vitruv.* l. 3, c. 3.

BAND (*Com.*) a weight of two ounces on the Gold coast.

BAND (*Mil.*) vide *Bands*.

BAND (*Mus.*) a fixed and select body of musicians, particularly such as are attached to every regiment in the English army.

BA'ND Fish (*Ich.*) the *Cepola rubescens* of Linnæus, a fish remarkable for the shortness of its head.

BA'NDAGE (*Surg.*) *deligatio*, seu *fascia*, an apparatus consisting of one or more pieces of linen or flannel, and fitted for the binding up of wounds, &c. Bandages are either simple or compound.—*Simple Bandages*, made of one entire piece of linen, are, as to their form, *circular*, or *annular*, *spiral*, or *obtuse*, &c.; as to their use, *uniting*, *retaining*, *expellent*, &c.—*Compound bandages*, made of several pieces, or of one piece cut into several heads, are the *T. bandages*, the *suspensory*, the *capistrum*, the *eighteen-tail bandage*, or *ascialis*, &c.

BANDA'NNOIS (*Com.*) a species of Indian calicoe.

BANDÉ (*Her.*) vide *Bend*.

BA'NDED (*Her.*) any thing as a garb or wheatsheaf, &c. tied with a band of a different tincture, as "A garb, *or*, banded, *gules*, by the name of Grosvenor." [vide *Garb*]

BANDED *Column* (*Archit.*) any column encircled with bands or annular rustics.

BANDELET (*Archit.*) an ornament encompassing a pillar quite round about like a ring.

BANDELIE'RS (*Mil.*) vide *Bandoleer*.

BANDERE'T (*Mil.*) a name in history for the commander in chief of the Swiss troops in the Canton of Berne.

BA'NDES (*Mil.*) a French name anciently for the infantry of France. It is now used in application to the *Prévôt des Bandes*, i. e. the judge, or Provost Marshal, who tried the men belonging to the *Gardes*.—*Bandes* is also a name for the troops or bands to a mortar carriage.

BANDIE'RE (*Mil.*) an epithet for a particular disposition of the army, as *une armée rangée en front de bandière*, i. e. an army in battle array; *une armée campée en front de bandière*, an army encamped with the regular stand of colours; hence also *la ligne bandière*, the camp colour line.

BANDI'TTI (*Polit.*) *banniti qui carebant jure togæ; quibus aquâ et igne interdictum erat.* Outlaws originally in Italy; robbers in particular.

BA'NDLE (*Com.*) an Irish measure of two feet.

BANDOLEER (*Mil.*) or *bandolier*, a large leathern belt, formerly worn over the right shoulder and hanging under the left arm, to carry some kind of warlike weapon.—*Bandoliers* were also wooden cases to hold the charges of powder, of which each musketeer used to carry twelve hanging on his belt.

BANDO'RE (*Mus.*) *bandusa*, an ancient stringed instrument resembling a lute.

BA'NDROL (*Mil.*) a little flag or streamer, particularly that at the end of a flag.

BA'NDROLLS (*Mil.*) vide *Camp-Colours*.

BANDS (*Mil.*) *train-bands*, or *trained-bands*, i. e. particular regiments composed of the citizens of London, who used to be trained and exercised after the manner of the militia.

BANDS *nave* (*Gun.*) the bands or iron hoops that bind the nave of a gun-carriage at both ends.

BANDS (*Mar.*) slips of canvass strongly sewed across a canvass to strengthen it, as the *reef bands*, &c.

BANDS *of a saddle* (*Mech.*) two flat pieces of iron nailed on each side the bows of the saddle, to keep its form.

BA'NDSUM (*Ant.*) *signum militare*, a banner or standard of the general.

BANDU'RA (*Bot.*) a plant of Columbo, the root of which is astringent. Its seeds and seed-vessels resemble those of gentian. It is the *Nepenthes distillatoria* of Linnæus. *Raii Hist. Plant.*

BA'NDY (*Mech.*) a crooked club or stick to play with.

BANE (*Law*) from the Saxon *bana*, a murderer; the author of mischief to another. *Bract.* l. 2, tract 8, c. 1.

BA'NE-BERRY (*Bot.*) the *Actæa spicata* of Linnæus.

BA'NERET (*Her.*) *banerettus*, a knight made in the field, whose standard was converted into a banner, which he could display in the king's army as barons do. They are next to the baron in dignity; but those banerets who have been created *sub vexillis regiis, in aperto bello, &c.* take place of all baronets. *Smith de Repub. Anglican. c. 18.*

BA'NGLE-EARED (*Man.*) flap-eared, an imperfection in the sit of a horse's ears.

BANGUE (*Bot.*) an Indian plant, with leaves like hemp, of a heating and intoxicating nature. It is the *Acosta* of Ray, and the *Cannabis Indica* of Linnæus.

BA'NIAN (*Archæol.*) vide *Bannians*.

BANIAN *days* (*Mar.*) a cant term among the seamen for days on which no meat is served out to them.

BA'NICA (*Bot.*) the *Pastinica sylvestris* of Linnæus.

BANI'LIA (*Bot.*) the same as *Vanilla*.

BA'NISHMENT (*Law*) from *ban* [vide *Ban*] signifies quitting the realm in consequence of some offence. It is of two kinds, namely, voluntary, i. e. upon oath, or by abjuration; and compulsory, i. e. by transportation. *Staundf. Plac. Coron.* 117.

BANISTE'RIA (*Bot.*) a genus of plants, called after the Rev. John Banister, of Virginia, who lost his life in the search after plants. Class 10 *Decandria*, Order 3 *Trigynia*.
Generic Characters. CAL. *perianth* five-parted.—COR. *petals* five.—STAM. *filaments* ten; *anthers* simple.—PIST. *germs* three; *styles* three; *stigmas* obtuse.—PER. *capsules* three; *seeds* solitary.
Species. The species are all shrubs, and natives of hot climates, particularly of America and Brazil.

BANK (*Law*) was formerly taken for a bench or seat of judgment, as *Bank le Roy*, the King's Bench; *Bank le Common Pleas*, the Common Pleas: so also in Latin *Bancus Regis, &c. Cromp. Just.* 67, 91.—*Days in bank*, stated days of appearance in the Court of Common Pleas in each of the terms, called, in Latin, *dies in banco*. They are generally at the distance of about a week from each other.

BANK (*Com.*) a public office for keeping and circulating money, to be employed in exchanges, discounts, government-loans, &c. of which description is the Bank of England, which was established by charter in the reign of William and Mary, into a corporate body, by the title of The Governor and Company of the Bank of England.—The word *bank* in this sense owes its origin to the Italian *banco*, because the money-changers of this nation, who were the first bankers, used to sit on benches in their courses or exchanges.—*Bank-note*, or *bank-post-bill*, names for the paper currency issued by the Bank of England: the former payable to *bearer on demand*; the latter *to order* seven days after sight.

BA'NKER (*Com.*) one who carries on the trade of private banking.

BANKER (*Mar.*) a vessel employed in the cod fishery on the banks of Newfoundland.

BA'NKING (*Com.*) that particular kind of trade carried on in England, which consists in exchanging and receiving the current cash of individuals, free of interest, and negotiating with it, either in the discount of bills or the advance of money on sufficient securities. This is one of the principal branches of business carried on by the Bank of England, and the peculiar trade of private bankers.—*Banking-House*, any mercantile house which carries on the banking-business, in distinction from the Bank, by which is understood the Bank of England.

BANKING (*Agric.*) the making of banks to oppose the force of the sea.

BA'NKRUPT (*Com.*) a trader who fails, or breaks, so as to be unable to pay his debts. It is compounded of *bancum*, the bench, and *rumpere*, to break, i. e. to break the bench, because the bench of the Italian banker or money-changer is said to have been broken, by way of infamy, when he failed.

BA'NKRUPTCY (*Com.*) from *bankrupt*, the condition of a bankrupt, or becoming a bankrupt.—*Act of bankruptcy*, any act such as that of secreting oneself, &c. which makes a man legally a bankrupt.—*Commission of bankruptcy*, a warrant granted by the Lord Chancellor, on the petition of one or more creditors, against any trader who is charged with an act of bankruptcy.

BA'NKSEA (*Bot.*) a genus of plants, so called from Sir Joseph Banks, the discoverer, Class 4 *Tetrandria*, Order 1 *Monogynia*.
  Generic Characters. CAL. *perianth* one-leaved.—COR. one-petalled.—STAM. *filaments* none; *anthers* four.—PIST. *germ* superior; *style* filiform; *stigma* acute.—PER. *capsule* ovate or globose; *seeds* two.
  Species. The species are shrubs, and natives of New Holland, as *Banksea serrata, integrifolia, ericæfolia, &c.*

BANN (*Law*) vide *Ban.*

BANNA'LIS *mola* (*Archæol.*) the lord of the manor's mill, where his tenants were obliged to grind their corn.—*Bannalia flumina*, rivers whose royalties belong to particular lords of manors.

BA'NNER (*Mil.*) a flag or standard at the end of a lance. The ordnance flag is affixed to the carriage of the right-hand gun of the park. The banner for the kettle-drums and trumpets in the horse equipage must be of the colour and facing of the regiment, that of the kettle-drums bearing in the centre the badge of the regiment, or its rank; and that of the trumpets, the king's cypher and crown. &c.

BANNER (*Her.*) such a flag is borne as a charge in coats of arms, and when open and flying is called "The Banner disveloped," as "The field is *Jupiter*, three banners disveloped, in bend *Sol*," which are said to have been the arms of the kingdom of Baldachia.

BANNERE'T (*Ant.*) vide *Baneret.*

BA'NNIANS (*Theol.*) a religious sect among the Indians, who believe in the transmigration of souls, and therefore abstain from the flesh of all animals, whom they carefully preserve.

BANNI'MUS (*Archæol.*) the first word in the sentence of expulsion of any member from the University of Oxford, which was formerly posted up in some public place.

BA'NNISTER (*Archit.*) vide *Ballister.*

BANNI'TUS (*Law*) an outlaw.

B'ANNOCK (*Cook.*) a sort of oaten cake, in the North of England, baked in the embers or on a hot stone.

BA'NNUM (*Archæol.*) the utmost bounds of a manor or town.

BAPTI'STERY (*Ecc.*) either the place or the vessel in which persons are baptized.

BA'NQUET (*Man.*) a part of the branch of a bridle under the eye, which is rounded like a small rod, and joins the extremities of a bit to the branch.—*Banquet-line*, an imaginary line drawn along the banquet, to adjust the designed force or weakness of the branch.

BANQUE'TTE (*Fort.*) a small foot-place, in form of a step, at the bottom of a parapet.

BA'NTAM-COCK (*Orn.*) a species of the *Gallus*, having the shanks feathered and long feathers behind.

BA'OBAL (*Bot.*) an African fruit, as large as a lemon, resembling a gourd, grateful to the taste, a cooler and quencher of thirst. Prosper Alp Baobal is the *Adansonia digitata* of Linnæus.

BAOBAL *lapidium* (*Min.*) a particular stone resembling the fruit in form.

BA'PHIA (*Ant.*) βαΦια, dye-houses.

BA'PTÆ (*Ant.*) 1. The priests of Cotytto, the goddess of lasciviousness, so called, ἀπὸ τῦ βαπτιν, i. e. from washing, because bathing was a particular rite among them. *Juv. sat.* 2, v. 91.

Talia secretâ coluerunt Orgia tedâ
Cecropiam soliti Baptæ lassare Cotytto.

2. The title of a play of Eupolis, who ridiculed their effeminacy and licentiousness.

BA'PTES (*Min.*) βαπτη, a soft precious stone, of a fragrant smell. *Plin.* l. 37, c. 10.

BA'PTISM (*Theol.*) βαπτισμα, from βαπτιν, to wash; a sacrament of the Christian church, administered, by means of water, to all persons previous to their admission into the number of the faithful. It is performed either by immersion, i. e. dipping, or by sprinkling.

BA'PTIST (*Bibl.*) βαπτιστις, one who performs the office of baptizing, an epithet applied, by way of distinction, to John the Baptist.

BAPTISTE'RIUM (*Ant.*) a tub of wood or stone, used in the bath, by those who went to bathe. *Plin.* l. 2, ep. 16.

BAPTISTERIUM (*Ecc.*) the baptistery or fount used in baptism. *Sidon. Apoll.* l. 2, ep. 1.

BAPTISTUM (*Bot.*) a species of wild mustard, so called from its reddish colour.

BAR (*Mech.*) a long piece of iron or wood, which serves as a fastening to doors and windows, and also as an inclosure. In carriages bars are of different denominations, as cross-bars, shaft-bars, &c.

BAR (*Com.*) a solid mass of metal, as gold, silver, or iron, wrought into a shape somewhat resembling a bar.

BAR (*Mar.*) a rock lying before the harbour in such a manner that ships cannot sail over it but upon the flood.

BAR (*Law*) is taken in different senses. 1. The place parted off by a bar or railing, where serjeants and counsellors at law stand to plead, on one side of which stand also prisoners to plead to the indictment. 2. The profession of a barrister: "To be called to the *bar*," is to be admitted a member of the profession of barristers. 3. A sort of plea, or such a peremptory exception of a defendant as destroys the plaintiff's action. Bars are of different kinds, namely—*Perpetual bar*, which for ever overthrows the action of the plaintiff. *Temporary bar*, which is good for the present.
  Ordinary or *general bar*, or *bar to a common intendment*, usually a bar to the declaration of the plaintiff.—*Special bar*, one which falls out on some special circumstance of the fact.—*Bar at large*, is when the defendant does not traverse the plaintiff's title by pleading, nor confess nor avoid it, but only makes to himself a title in his bar.—*Bar material*, a sort of special bar, which is a plea in stay of the plaintiff's action on some particular matter, as a descent from him that was owner of the land. *Kitch.* 68, &c. &c.—*Bar fee*, a fee of twenty-pence which prisoners acquitted of felony paid to the gaoler.

BAR (*Her.*) one of the honourable ordinaries, consisting of two horizontal lines drawn across the escutcheon, as in fig. 1. The *bar* differs from the *fesse* in three particulars, namely, that it occupies a fifth part of the field instead of a third; it is not limited to any part of the escutcheon, and is never borne single. It has two diminutives, namely, the *closet* (fig. 2), which is half the bar, and the *barrule* (fig. 3),

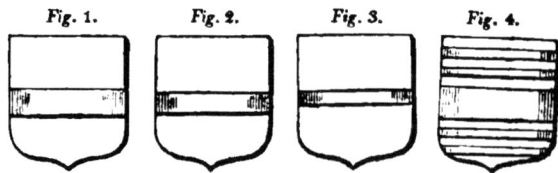

Fig. 1.   Fig. 2.   Fig. 3.   Fig. 4.

which is half the closet. Of the closet there may be five

4

in one field; but the barrulet can be borne only in couples. —*Bars gemelles* are so called when they stand in couples, as in fig. 4. "The field is *argent*, a fesse between two bars, gemelles *gules*, by the name of *Badlemere*."

BAR (*Mus.*) is employed to divide the notes into equal portions in respect to their duration, (as fig. 1.)—*Double bar*, (fig. 2) is introduced at the end of a strain, or a change in the measure or time.—*Dotted bar*, (fig. 3) signifies that the preceding and following strains are to be repeated.—*Half-dotted bar*, (fig. 4) shows that the strain is on the same side of the bar with the dots.

Fig. 1. Fig. 2. Fig. 3. Fig. 4.

BAR (*Man.*) a horse is said "To fall foul of the *bar*" who gets himself entangled in the partition bar that separates two horses in the stable.

TO BAR *a vein* (*Vet.*) to tie it above and below, after the skin has been opened, and then strike it between the ligatures.

BAR-SHOT (*Mil.*) the same as Stang-balls. [vide *Ball*]

BARALI'PTON (*Log.*) an indirect mode of syllogisms, or an imperfect syllogism, consisting of two universals and one particular affirmative proposition, as,
b A   Every animal is endued with sense;
2 A   Every man is an animal; therefore
l I *pton* Something endued with sense is man.

BARA'LLOTS (*Ecc.*) heretics of Bologna, in Italy, who had their wives, children, and every thing in common. From their base spirit they were called Obedientes. *Ferdin. Cordubens. de 8 exig. annon.*

BARA-MARE'KA (*Bot.*) a species of the *Dolichos* of Linnæus.

BARA'NGI (*Polit.*) βαραγγοι, officers in the Greek empire, who had the keys of the city in charge where the emperor resided. This word is of English extraction, according to Curupulates, from *bar*, to fasten, or shut close, because their office was to keep the gates locked; and they were of the English nation to whom this office was entrusted.

BA'RAS (*Med.*) vide *Alphus*.

BARATHRUM (*Ant.*) βαραθρον, a deep pit into which condemned persons were cast headlong, at Athens. It was a dark and noisome hole, having sharp spikes at the top and others at the bottom, to pierce such as were cast in. *Aristoph. in Plut.* act 2, scen.; *Plut in Mar.; Diomed. de Art. Gram.*

BA'RATOR (*Law*) vide *Barrator*.

BARA'TRON (*Ant.*) βαρατρον, games in Threspotia, at which the strongest obtained the victory. *Hesychius.*

BA'RATRY (*Com.*) when the master or mariners cheat the owners by embezzling their goods or running away with the vessel.

BARA'TTA (*Nat.*) a sort of balsam brought from the West Indies.

BARATZ (*Polit.*) a Turkish name for the letters patent granted by the sultan to the grand patriarch, the bishops, &c. for the exercise of their clerical functions.

BARB (*Arch.*) the reflected points of the head of an arrow.

BARB (*Bot.*) γλωχις, glochis, a straight process armed with several teeth pointing backwards like the sting of a bee. It is one sort of pubescence in plants, in distinction from the Hook, *hamus*, which is not bent.

BARB (*Zool.*) a horse of the Barbary breed, much esteemed for its swiftness. Barbs are so much valued by the owners in Barbary, that they preserve their genealogies with as much care as the nobility do of their families in Europe. They are said to be able to outstrip an ostrich in the race, and some will fetch as high a price as 200 or 300 pounds sterling.

TO BARB *a lobster* (*Cook.*) to cut it up.

BA'RBA (*Bot.*) the beard. [vide *Beard*]—*Barba-capra*, the *Spiræa Aruncus* and *Ulmaria* of Linnæus.—*Barba Hirci*, the *Tragopogon* of Linnæus.—*Barba Jovis*, the *Anthyllis barba Jovis*, the *Ebenus Cretica*, and the *Psorella*, of Linnæus.

BA'RBACAN (*Archæol.*) vide *Barbican*.

BARBA'DOES (*Bot.*) or Bastard Cedar, the *Cedrela* of Linnæus.—Barbadoes Cherry, the *Malpighia* of Linnæus.—Barbadoes Gooseberry, the *Cactus Pereskia* of Linnæus.—Barbadoes Wild Olive, the *Bontia* of Linnæus.

BA'RBARA (*Log.*) an arbitrary name for the first mode of the first figures of sylogisms, consisting of three universal propositions, as—
b A r   All animals are endued with sense.
b A   All men are animals; ergo,
r A   All men are endued with sense.

BARBA'REA (*Bot.*) a species of the *Erysimum* and *Sisymbuum* of Linnæus.

BA'RBARISM (*Gram.*) βαρβαρισμος, from βαρβαριζω, to speak a strange tongue; a barbarous kind of speech, used only by the rude and unlettered.

BARBARO'SSA (*Med.*) mercurial medicine.

BA'RBARUM (*Med.*) a plaster for green wounds. *Scrib. Larg.*

BA'RBARY *Falcons* (*Falc.*) a kind of hawks commonly taken in Barbary, which are less than the *tiercel*; they are gentle, but very bold; are plumed with red under the wings, and armed with long talons and stretchers.

BARBE (*Mil.*) the armour of the horses of the ancient knights and soldiers, which covered the neck, breast, and crupper.

BARBE (*Fort.*) or, *to fire en barbe;* to discharge a cannon over the breast-work instead of putting it through the loop-holes.

BARBE *Robert* (*Cook.*) a particular way of dressing hogs' ears.

BA'RBED (*Mech.*) bearded like a fish-hook, set with barbs.

BARBED (*Her.*) 1. An epithet for the full-blown rose, provided with its barbs, or green leaves, which appear on the outside. 2. For the arrow, whose head is pointed and jagged. 3. *Barbed and Crested*, an epithet for the cock, wattled and crested, particularly if of a different tincture.

BARBED (*Bot.*) furnished with a barb, or glochis.

BARBEE (*Her.*) or *barbed*, as *croix barbee*, a cross, the extremities of which are like a barbed fish-hook.

BARBEL (*Ich.*) the *Cyprinus Barbus*, a fish of the carp kind, which lies in holes near the banks, and feeds on testaceous animals, worms, lesser fish, and carcases. It is so very tame as to be often taken by the hand, grows fast, and is long lived. It has the name of *Barbel* from the beards or wattles under its nose.

BARBELICOTÆ (*Ecc.*) an abominable sect of heretics mentioned by Theodoret.

BA'RBER *Chirurgeons* (*Her.*) were incorporated by king Edward IV., but the barbers were separated from the surgeons by 18 Geo. 2, c. 15. Their arms are, " A St. George's cross; *gules* thereon a lion passant; gardant *or* quarterly; the first and fourth a chevron between three fleams; the second and third per *pale argent* and *vert*, a rose, *gules* crowned, and seeded *or.*

BA'RBERRY (*Bot.*) a tart berry, the fruit of the barberry-tree.—*Barberry-tree*, the *Barberis* of Linnæus, a prickly shrub, bearing a tart fruit.

BARBES (*Vet.*) or *barbles*, a disease in horses and black cattle, when they have two small excrescences under the tongue.

BA'RBET (*Zool.*) a species of *Canis familiaris*, with a tail truncate, the hair long and coarse.
BARBET (*Orn.*) the *Bucco* of Linnæus, a bird, living chiefly in warm countries, which is almost covered with bristles, and is very stupid.
BA'RBICAN (*Archæol.*) Barbicanum, a watch-tower of a fortress, or any outwork to a great building.
BA'RBICANAGE (*Archæol.*) money given for the maintenance of a fortress or watch-tower.
BA'RBITON (*Ant.*) βαρβίτον, a musical instrument of three or more strings, of which Horace makes Anacreon to be the inventor. *Poll. Onom.* l. 4, c. 9.
BARBO'TA (*Ich.*) the barbut, a small river fish, the liver of which is remarkable for its size and delicacy.
BA'RBOTINE (*Bot.*) a grain, otherwise called wormseed.
BARCA'LAO (*Com.*) a kind of cod on the coast of Chili.
BARCALO'NGA (*Mar.*) a large Spanish coasting vessel.
BARCA'RIA (*Archæol.*) a sheepcote, or sheepwalk. *M. S. Placit.* Ed. 3.
BARCARO'LLES (*Mus.*) Italian for songs composed by the Venetian Gondoliers.
BARD (*Archæol.*) Bardus, a sort of poets among the Gauls, whose business it was to set forth the deeds of their heroes and great men. *Ammian. Marcell.* l. 15, c. 9; *Buling. de Theat.* l. 2, c. 39.
BARDA'NA (*Bot.*) the *Arctium Lappa* of Linnæus.
BARDE (*Man.*) French for a long saddle for an ass or mule, made only of coarse canvass stuffed with flocks.—*Javelin de Barde*, a barbed javelin for a horseman.
BARDEE'S d'eau (*Com.*) French for a measure used in the making of saltpetre, containing three half-hogsheads of water, which are poured into tubs for the purpose of refining it.
BARDE'LLE (*Man.*) *bardello*, the quilted or canvass saddle with which colts are backed.
BARDE'SENISTS (*Ecc.*) the heretical followers of one Bardesenes, who maintained the Valentinian heresy. *Euseb. Hist. Eccles.* l. 4, c. ult.; *S. Epiphan. de Hær.* c. 56; *St. August. de Hær.* c. 35; *Hieron. in Cat.* c. 38; *Baron. Annal. Ann.* 175; *Tillem. Biblioth. des Aut Eccl. des* 3 prem. siec.
BARDS (*Cook.*) thin broad slices of bacon, with which capons, pullets, &c. are covered, in order to be roasted, baked, &c.
BA'RD-WOOL (*Com.*) when the head and neck is cut off from the fleece. [vide *To Clack*]
BA'RE-PUMP (*Mar.*) a pump for drawing liquor out of a cask.—*Bare-poles*, an epithet for any ship lying to without any sails set. A ship is said to be under *bare-poles*, when having no sails set out at sea.
BA'RGAIN (*Com.*) a contract in buying and selling.
BARGAIN and sale (*Law*) a real contract upon a valuable consideration for passing lands, tenements, &c. 2 Inst. 672.
BARGE (*Mar.*) from *barca*; a very large boat used on rivers, either for pleasure and state, as the royal barge, &c. or for trade, as the coal barge, &c.
BARGE couples (*Arch.*) a beam or piece of wood mortised into another to strengthen the building.—*Barge-course*, part of the tiling of a house that projects over the principal rafter when there is a gable or a gerkin head.
BAR-GEME'L (*Her.*) from the Latin *Gemelli*, twins; a double bar, or two bars placed near each other. [vide *Bar*]
BA'RGH-MASTER (*Min.*) from the Teutonic *berge*, a mine; a master of the mines.—*Bargh-mote*, a court held concerning the mines.
BARI'LLAR (*Polit.*) French for an officer who was formerly employed among the gallies, to superintend the distribution of bread and water.

BARI'LLET (*Mech.*) French for the barrel of a watch; also for the funnel of a sucking-pump.
BA'RING of trees (*Husband.*) laying the roots bare in the winter season, that they may receive the snow water.
BARIPI'CNI (*Mus.*) a name among the Greeks for low sounds in general.
BARITO'NO (*Mus.*) from βαρύτονος, gravitonus, a low pitch of the voice, between bass and tenor.—*Baritono cliff*, the F cliff, so called because it was suited to the baritono voice.
BA'RIUM (*Min.*) a metal of barytes, produced by its chemical decomposition.
BARK (*Bot.*) the skin or covering of a ligneous plant, consisting of three parts, namely—1. The cuticle, or *Epidermis*. 2. The outer bark, *Cortex*. 3. The inner bark, *Liber*.
BARK (*Med.*) *Cortex*, a name given by way of eminence to the Peruvian or Jesuit's bark, which is of such well-known efficacy.
BARK binding (*Hort.*) a distemper in trees cured by slitting the bark.—*Bark galling*, when trees are galled by being bound to stakes.
BARK (*Com.*) a stuff manufactured in the East Indies with bark, which is spun like hemp.
BARK (*Mar.*) in French *barque*, from the Latin *barca*; any small ship, but particularly one carrying three masts.—*Armed bark*, a fireship filled with soldiers for attacking batteries, &c.—*Long bark*, one that has no deck, and is built like a sloop.—*Water bark*, a small kind of vessel for carrying fresh water in Holland.
BA'RKARY (*Archæol.*) a tan-house, or place to keep bark in.
BA'RKING of trees (*Husband.*) peeling the bark off the trees, which must be done in the month of May, because at that time the sap parts the bark from the wood.
BARLE'RIA (*Bot.*) a genus of plants so called by Plumier, after the Rev. J. Barrelier, a Dominican botanist, and M. D. of Paris, Class 14 *Didynamia*, Order 2 *Angiospermia*.
Generic Characters. CAL. perianth four-parted.—COR. monopetalous.—STAM. filaments four; anthers, the upper oblong, the lower withered.—PIST. germ ovate; style filiform; stigma bifid.—PER. capsule acute; seeds two.
Species. The species are mostly shrubs, and natives of America or India.
BARLEY (*Agric.*) a sort of corn or grain botanically named *Hordeum*, which is sown in March, April, and May, succeeds best in light dry soils, and is ripe when the red roan, as it is called, is off. The sorts of barley most used in agriculture are, the Common Spring Barley, the Sprat, or Battle-dore Barley, Common, or Long-eared Barley, &c.—*Barley-mow*, the place where reaped barley is laid up.—*Pearl-barley*, barley stripped of its first coat, and sold at Paris by the druggists, to be used as a diet drink.
BARLEY-CORN (*Arith.*) the smallest measure in England, equal to one-third of an inch.
BA'RLEY-BIRD (*Orn.*) the siskin; so called in Essex because it goes there in barley seed time.
BA'RLEY-WATER (*Med.*) a decoction of pearl-barley, which, for its lubricity and cooling quality, is much used in slow fevers.
BARM (*Nat.*) Yeast; the head or working out of beer, which is used as a ferment to lighten bread.
BA'RNABITES (*Ecc.*) an order of regular priests, of the congregation of St. Paul.
BARNACLE (*Con.*) the *Lepas balanus* of Linnæus, a species of shell-fish which sticks to the bottom of ships, rocks, &c. The *tentacula* from this animal are feathered, for which reason the origin of the Bernacle-goose is ascribed, as we learn from Gerard, in his Herbal, p. 1587, &c.
BARNACLE Goose (*Or.*) or *Bernacle*, a large water-fowl, called by the Scotch a *cleg goose*, has a flat broad bill, with

a hooked point, the forepart of its head white, and the rest of its body mostly black. It is the *Anus erythropus* of Linnæus'

BA'RNACLES (*Vet.*) from the Saxon *bearan*, to carry, or hold up, and *necca*, the neck; irons put on the noses of horses, to make them stand still.

BARNADE'SIA (*Bot.*) a genus of plants named after Barnades, a Spanish botanist, Class 19 *Syngenesia*, Order 1 *Polygamia Æqualis*.
Generic Characters. CAL. common somewhat ventricose.—COR. compound rayed.—STAM. *filaments* five; *anther* cylindric.—PIST. *germ* ovate; *style* filiform; *stigma* bifid.—PER. none; *seeds* very many; *receptacle* flat.
Species. The only species is, the—*Barnadesia spinosa*, a shrub, native of America. *Linn. Spec. Plant*.

BARO'CO (*Log.*) a technical term for the fourth mode of the second figure of syllogisms, containing an universal affirmative and two particular negative propositions, as—
    b A   All believers will be saved.
    r O c Some men will not be saved; ergo,
    c O   Some men are not believers.

BA'ROLITE (*Min.*) the *Barytes Witheringii* of Linnæus, a stone of the *Ponderous Order*, called also the Carbonite of Barytes.

BARO'METER (*Pneum.*) from βαρὺς, heavy, and μέτρα, to measure; an instrument for weighing the gravity of the air, invented by Torricelli. Barometers are variously named, according to their construction, as *horizontal*, *portable*, *wheel*, and *reduced barometer*. [vide *Pneumatics*]

BA'RON (*Law*) in Latin *baro*, from βαρὺς, i. e. having weight or influence; a degree of nobility next to a viscount. Barons are of different kinds, as—*Barons major*, or *by writ*, those who were summoned by writ in the reign of King John to attend Parliament, now termed *Barons by prescription*, for that he and his ancestors have continued barons beyond the memory of man.—*Barons by letters patent*, or *by creation*, those who were made barons by the king's letters patent, whose posterity are now called Lords of Parliament.—*Barons by tenure*, those who are barons by virtue of the barony annexed to their lands or office, as in the case of some ancient barons and bishops.—*Barons by office*, as the barons of Exchequer, of the Cinque Ports, &c.—*Bract*. l. 1; *Glanvil*. c. 8, &c.; *Cambd. Brit*. p. 109; 2 *Inst*. 48, &c.; *Selden's Titles of Honour*, l. 4, c. 13.—*Court Baron*. [vide *Court*]—*Baron and femme*, husband and wife, because *baro* in law, signified a husband.

BARON and *femme* (*Her.*) in blazoning, when the arms of a man and his wife are marshalled together side by side.

BA'RONS' *coronet* (*Her.*) on a gold circle, six pearls, which were assigned to barons by King Charles the Second after the restoration. Previously to this time, the barons wore scarlet caps, turned up with ermine, and on the top a tassel of gold. The pearls on the coronet, though called pearls, are always made of silver.

BA'RONAGE (*Law*) a tax to be raised for the king's use out of the precincts of baronies.

BARO'NES (*Ent.*) small worms.

BA'RONET (*Her.*) the lowest degree of honour, hereditary, created by letters patent, and founded by James I. in 1604. A baronet takes precedence of all knights except Bannerets.—*Baronets' mark*, the arms of the Province of Ulster, viz. *argent*, a hand *gules*, in a canton, or in escutcheon, are borne by every baronet, as in the annexed example. "He beareth, *or*, between two chevronels, three trefoils, slipped, *sable*." These are the arms of the Abdy family.

BA'RONY (*Law*) *baronia*, from *baro*; the honour and territory which gives titles to a Baron, including the fees and lands of Lords, both temporal and spiritual.

BARONY'CHIA (*Bot.*) the *Asplenium* and *Ruta muraria* of Linnæus.

BARO'QUE (*Mus.*) an epithet applied to a composition where the harmony is false and overcharged.

BA'ROS (*Med.*) from βαρὺς, heavy; an epithet expressing an uneasy weight in any part.

BA'ROSCOPE (*Nat.*) from βαρὺς, heavy, and σκοπέω, to view; a sort of barometer.

BAROSSE'LENITE (*Min.*) the *Barytes vulgaris* of Linnæus, a stone, otherwise called the Sulphate of Barytes.—*Compact Barosselenite*, the *Barytes compacta* of Linnæus.

BARO'TE (*Min.*) a name for the *Barytes*.

BARR (*Her.*) vide *Bar*.

BA'RRA (*Com.*) a Portuguese measure, equal to the English ell.

BA'RRACAN (*Com.*) a French woollen stuff resembling the English *barrage*.

BA'RRACKS (*Mil.*) from the Spanish *baracca*, a small cabin; the places erected for the accommodation of both men and horses in the English army. Formerly those used by the cavalry were so called, in distinction from the *huts* built for the use of the infantry.—*Barrack allowance*, a specific allowance of bread, beer, and coals, &c. to the regiments stationed in barracks.—*Barrack-guard*, the name given to the principal guard of a regiment that is in barracks.—*Barrack-Master-General*, a staff officer that is at the head of the barrack department.

BA'RRAGE (*Com.*) a linen, interwoven with worsted flowers in Normandy.

BA'RRAS (*Chem.*) a substance, consisting of rosin and oil, which exudes from the wounds of fir-trees in winter.

BA'RRASTER (*Law*) Barrister.

BA'RRATOR (*Law*) from the French *Barrateur*, a deceiver; a common mover of suits and quarrels, either in courts or elsewhere.

BA'RRATRY (*Com.*) vide *Baratry*.

BA'RREL (*Com.*) 1. A cask or vessel for holding liquor, viz. 31½ gallons of wine, &c.; 32 gallons of ale, and 36 gallons of beer. 2. A cask for other commodities of different measures.

BARREL *of the ear* (*Anat.*) *tympanum*, otherwise called the Drum, is the cavity in which are lodged the bones of the ear.

BARREL *of a watch* (*Mech.*) the cylinder about which the spring is wrapped.

BARRELS (*Mil.*) are of different kinds, as—*Fire-barrels*, that are filled with combustibles, grenades, handspikes, &c.—*Budge-barrels*, that are made in the form of half powder barrels, having at one end a leathern bag with brass nails.—*Water-tight barrels*, such as have six copper hoops, without any hazle hoops.—*Barrels of earth*, a sort of half hogsheads filled with earth, which are used as breastworks for covering the soldiery.

BARREN *Signs* (*Astrol.*) the signs, Gemini, Leo, and Virgo; so called because when the question is asked, whether any particular person shall have children or not; if one of those signs be on the cusp, or first point of the first house, it is taken for granted that the person inquiring shall have none.

BARRE'RIA (*Bot.*) a genus of plants, named after Barrere, a Professor of Perpignan, Class 19 *Syngenesia*, Order 1 *Monogynia*.
Generic Characters. CAL. *perianth* one-leaved.—COR. one-petalled.—STAM. *filaments* five; *anthers* erect.—PIST. *germ* roundish; *style* short; *stigma* trifid.
Species. The species are shrubs and natives of Guiana.

BA'RRETOR (*Law*) vide *Barrator*.

BA'RRETRY (*Com.*) vide *Baratry*.

BARRICA'DE (*Mil.*) or *barricado*, in French *barricade*, in

2 F

Spanish *barricada,* from *barre,* a spar; is a fence hastily raised with stakes, earth, &c. to protect an army from a sudden assault.

BA'RRICADE (*Mar.*) a strong wooden rail, supported by stauncheons, extending across the foremost part of the quarter-deck, employed with a netting as a defence against the grape-shot.

BA'RRIERS (*Fort.*) in French *barrières,* a kind of fence, composed of great stakes, planted ten feet from one another, and erected to defend the entrance of a passage, &c.—*Barrier towns,* fortified places on the frontiers of any country, as were formerly Ypres, Tournay, Mons, Namur, &c. in Flanders.

BARRIERS (*Mil.*) *barrières,* or *jeu de barres,* a martial exercise of men fighting with swords within bars or rails, separating them from the spectators.

BARRINGTO'NIA (*Bot.*) a genus of plants; named by Forster after the Hon. Daines Barrington, Class 16 *Monadelphia,* Order 7 *Polyandria.*
Generic Characters. CAL. *perianth* two-leaved.—COR. *petals* four; *nectary* conic.—STAM. *filaments* very many; *anthers* small.—PIST. *germ* inferior; *style* filiform; *stigma* simple.—PER. *drupe* large; *seed* nut long.
Species. The only species is the *Barringtonia speciosa, Butonica speciosa, Commersonia,* seu *Mammea Asiatica,* &c. Laurel-leaved Barringtonia, a tree, native of the East Indies.

BA'RRISTER (*Law*) a counsellor admitted to plead at the bar. —*Outer barrister* is one who pleads ouster, or without the bar.—*Inner barrister,* a serjeant or king's counsel who pleads within the bar.—*Vacation barrister,* a counsellor newly called to the bar, who is obliged to attend for the six or four next long vacations the exercise of the house.

BA'RROW (*Archæol.*) a large hillock or mount raised in many parts of England, supposed to be the tumuli of the Romans for their dead.

BARROW *hog* (*Husband.*) a boar-hog that has been cut.

BA'RRULET (*Her.*) a diminutive of bar; the fourth part of a bar and twentieth of the field. [vide *Bar*]

BA'RRULY (*Her.*) vide *Barry.*

BA'RRY (*Her.*) or *barways,* from *bar,* a field, divided by horizontal lines into four or more parts. The number of divisions, which must always be specified, as in fig. 1.

" Barry of eight, *or* and *azure,* name Constable."—*Barry, Bendy,* is when the lines run from dexter chief to sinister base, &c. interchangeably varying their tinctures, as in fig. 2; likewise—*Barry pily,* is another particular manner of dividing the field into six or more pieces, as in fig. 3.

BARS (*Mus.*) vide *Bar.*

BARS (*Archæol.*) slender pieces of wood or iron, affixed at certain distances, to make fast and secure.

BARS *hatch* (*Mar.*) bars which lock over the hatches — *Capstan bars,* those which are fitted to the drum head of the capstan.

BARS (*Man.*) or *binders.* 1. Those portions of the hoof of a horse that form the arches, situated between the heels and the frog. 2. The fleshy row that runs across the upper part of the mouth, and reaches almost to the palate.

BA'RTER (*Arith.*) from the Italian *barratare.* 1. Exchanging one commodity for another. 2. The rule by which the proportionate value of the commodities is found. *Luc. de Borg.*

BA'RTON (*Law*) or *Berton,* the demesne lands of a manor; a farm distinct from the mansion.

BARTONA'RII (*Law*) husbandmen who held bartons at the will of the lord.

BARTRA'MIA (*Bot.*) a species of the *Triumfetta* of Linnæus.

BA'RTSIA (*Bot.*) a genus of plants, named after Linnæus' unfortunate friend, John Bartsch, MD. Class 14 *Didynamia,* Order 2 *Angiospermia.*
Generic Characters. CAL. *perianth* one-leaved. — COR. monopetalous.—STAM. *filaments* four; *anthers* oblong. —PIST. *germ* ovate; *style* filiform; *stigma* obtuse.—PER. *capsule* ovate; *seeds* numerous.
Species. The species are mostly perennials, as—*Bartsia coccinea, Pedicularis,* seu *Crista galli,* &c. seu *Horminum,* &c. Red Bartsia, native of Virginia.—*Bartsia pallida foliis alternis,* &c. seu *foliis lanceolatis,* &c. Pale-flowered Bartsia, native of Siberia.—*Bartsia alpina foliis oppositis,* &c. *Staehelinia foliis,* &c. *Staehelinia alpina, Euphrasia caule,* &c. *Euphrasia rubra,* &c. *Chamædry vulgare,* &c. *Clinopodium alpinum,* &c. *Teucrium alpinum, Cratæogonon,* seu *Pedicularis,* Alpine Bartsia, native of Britain; but the—*Bartsia viscosa, Euphrasia latifolia,* seu *Alectorophos,* &c. Viscid Bartsia, or Yellow Marsh Eyebright, native of Britain, is an annual. *Raii Hist. Plant.*

BARU'LES (*Ecc.*) a sect of heretics, who held that our Saviour had only a phantom of a body. *Sander. Hær.* 149.

BA'RUTH (*Com.*) an Indian measure, equal to 54 or 58 pounds, of pepper.

BARUT'INE *silks* (*Com.*) silks manufactured in Persia.

BARYO'CCATON (*Bot.*) the *Stramonium* of Linnæus.

BARYPHO'NIA (*Med.*) from βαρύς, difficult, and φωνη, voice; a difficulty of speech.

BARYPI'CRON (*Bot.*) vide *Absinthium.*

BARYPY'CNI (*Mus.*) βαρυπυκνοι, a name among the Greeks for five of their eight sounds, or principal chords, namely, the *hypate-hypaton,* the *hypate-meson,* the *mese,* the *paramese,* and the *nete diazeugmenon. Euclid. Introd. Harmon.*

BARYTES (*Min.*) a genus of the *Terræ ponderosæ.*
Generic Characters. Ponderous, parasitic, very brittle, entirely soluble in boiling sulphuric acid.
Species. The species are — *Barytes Witheringii,* Barolite, or Carbonate of Barytes.—*Barytes lamellosa,* Carbonate of Barytes. — *Barytes terrestris Baroselenite,* Ponderous Earth-cawk, Earthy sulphate of Barytes.— *Barytes compacta,* Compact Baroselenite, Heavy Spar, or Sulphate of Barytes.—*Barytes bononiensis, Muriaphosphorea,* seu *Gypsum spathosum,* Bononien, or Bologna-stone.—*Barytes lamellata,* Lamellated heavy Spar. —*Barytes vulgaris,* Chrystallized Sulphate of Barytes, Baroselenite, Sulphate of Barytes, Common ponderous Spar, or Cawk.

BAS-CHEVALIE'RS (*Her.*) inferior knights by a bare tenure of military fee, in distinction from bannerets.

BASA'AL (*Bot.*) an Indian tree: a decoction from the leaves of which is used as a gargle. *Raii Hist. Plant.*

BASA'LTES (*Min.*) Basalt, a genus of earths of the Argillaceous order.
Generic Characters. Consisting of more silica and less alumina and oxyde of iron, lime, magnesia, oxyde of manganese and soda; opake, and breaking into indeterminate fragments.
Species. The principal species are—*Basaltes columnaris,* Figurate trap, Basalt.—*Basaltes Trapezum,* seu *saxum impalpabile,* Trap, consisting of the three varieties— 1. Toadstone; 2. Rowley ragg; 3. Whin-stone.

BASA'RACO (*Com.*) a small Indian coin.

BASCA'NIA (*Ant.*) βασκανια, little trifles that smiths were wont to hang at their shop-windows as amulets and charms.

BA'SE, or *basis*, in Greek βάσις, from βαίω, to go; signifies that on which one treads, that is, the lowermost part or foundation of any body.

BASE (*Archit.*) the foot of a pillar, by which it is sustained, or that part that is under the body, or lies upon the pedestal, or zocle, when there is any. [vide *Architecture*] — *Base of a room*, the lower projecting part, which consists of a plinth, and one or more mouldings, called *base-mouldings*.

BASE *of a solid figure* (*Math.*) is its lowermost plain side, or that on which it stands; and if the solid has two opposite parallel plain sides, and one of them is the base, then the other is also called the base. — *Base of a triangle*, or any other plain figure, is usually that which lies the lowest; but any side may be the base, according to the position in which it may be conceived to be lying, or standing.

BASE (*Fort.*) the external side of the polygon in the imaginary line which is drawn from the flanked angle of a bastion to the angle opposite to it. — *Base* also signifies the level line on which any work stands that is even with the ground; thus the base of a parapet is the rampart.

BASE (*Gun.*) is the least sort of ordnance, the diameter of whose base is $1\frac{1}{4}$, weighing 200 pounds, and carrying a ball $1\frac{1}{12}$ inch in diameter. — *Base ring of a cannon*, the great ring next behind the touch-hole.

BASE *line* (*Mil.*) the line on which troops in column move; the first division that marches into the alignment forms the base line which each successive division prolongs. — *Base line* signifies also the line on which all the magazines and means of supply of an army are established.

BASE *line* (*Perspect.*) the common section of a picture, and the geometrical plane.

BASE *distinct* (*Opt.*) that precise distance from the pole of a convex-glass, in which the objects seen through it appear distinct: it is the same as focus.

BASE (*Bot.*) that part on which the whole flower stands, and the fruit too when the flower has faded. There are two kinds of bases, namely, the receptacle and the fruit-bed. [vide *Botany, &c.*]

BASE (*Con.*) the broad extremity of a shell, in distinction from the apex.

BASE *tenure* (*Law*) holding by villeinage, or other customary service, in distinction from the higher tenure *in capite*, or by military service.

BASE (*Chem.*) a term employed by chemists formerly to designate substances of a fixed and inert nature, which combined with and were acted on by more volatile and active menstrua. Of this description were reckoned the alkalies, earths, and metallic oxides, which form compound salts. The modern chemists apply this term, *base*, to the same substances, because, although they do not admit their character, yet they reckon them principal ingredients in the formation of salts, which serve as a convenient mark of distinction between the several sorts of salts that differ in regard to their acid; as salts with an alkaline base, in distinction from salts with a metallic or earthy base. [vide *Chemistry*, or *Salts*]

BA'SELARD (*Ant.*) or Basillard; a weapon mentioned in *Stat.* 12, *Rich.*2, which signifies, according to Mr. Speight, on Chaucer, *pugio vel sicca*, a poignard.

BASE'LLA (*Bot.*) Climbing Nightshade; a genus of plants, Class 5 *Pentandria*, Order 3, *Trigynia*.
Generic Characters. CAL. none. — COR. seven-cleft. — STAM. *filaments* five; *anthers* roundish. — PIST. *germ* superior; *styles* three; *stigmas* oblong. — PER. *corolla* permanent; *seed* single.
Species. The species are annuals, or biennials, and natives of India, &c. as the — *Basella rubra, Cuscutata*, seu *Gandola rubra*, Red Malabar Nightshade. — *Basella alba, Gandola Mirab.* seu *Matasackki*, White Malabar Nightshade, &c.

BASE'LS (*Archæol.*) Baselli; a coin abolished by Henry II.

BA'SEMENT (*Archit.*) a continued base extended along any building, as the basement, or lower story of a house, &c.

BASHA'NAN (*Theol.*) a sect of Mahometans who carried the notion of man's free agency to its utmost length.

BASHA'W (*Polit.*) or Pasha, a title given to the grand officers of the Porte, as the Capudan-Bashaw, the commander at sea, or admiral; Bostangi-Bashaw, the chief officer of the gardens, &c.

BA'SIL (*Bot.*) a perennial, the *Clinopodium* of Linnæus. The principal sorts are the Common Basil and the Bush-Basil, which has an aromatic smell.

BASIL (*Carpent.*) the sloping edge of a chisel, or of the iron of a plane, the angle of which is ground away.

BASIL (*Mech.*) the skin of a sheep tanned.

BASILA'RIS (*Anat.*) from βασιλεύς, a king; royal, an epithet applied by way of distinction to some bones, as the sphenoid and occipital bones. — *Basilaris arteria*, basilary artery, an artery of the brain so called, because it lies upon the basilary process of the occipital bone.

BA'SILEION (*Med.*) a collyrium.

BA'SILEUS (*Ant.*) βασιλεύς, the second in rank among the Athenian archons, who presided over their religious ceremonies, &c. *Lys. dix. αριβ; Demosth. in Næar; Poll. Onomast.* l. 8, c. 9; *Harpocration; Suidas; Sigon de Rep. Athen.* l. 4.

BASILEUS (*Polit.*) βασιλεύς, *rex*, from βασίς λαω, i. e. λᾶς, *fundamentum populi*; a title anciently adopted by our English kings, as *Ego Edgar totius Angliæ basileus confirmavi*.

BASILI'A (*Ant.*) βασιλεία, a festival at Lebadæa in Bœotia. *Schol. in Pind. Olymp.* 9.

BASILIA'RIS *apophisis* (*Anat.*) the great apophysis of the occiput.

BA'SILIC *Constitutions* (*Law*) an abridgement and reform of the emperor Justinian's laws made under Basilius and Leo, whence they were named.

BASI'LICA (*Anat.*) the middle vein of the arm, so named by way of pre-eminence.

BASI'LICÆ (*Ant.*) halls, or spacious buildings, adorned with stately columns, which were employed as courts of justice, and, on the establishment of Christianity, were many of them converted into churches. Suetonius calls the basilic a palace, and Zosimus βασιλικὴ ςοά. *Cic. ad Att.* l. 4, ep. 16; *et Verr.* 4, c. 3; *Vitruv.* l. 5, c. 1; *Senec. de Ira*, l. 3, c. 33; *Joseph. Antiq.* l. 15, c. 11; *Plin.* l. 6, ep. 33; *Zosim.* l. 5, c. 2; *Isidor. Orig.* l. 5; *Marlian Topogr. Urb. Rom.* l. 3, c. 6; *Panciroll Descr. Urb. Rom. apud Grœv. Thes. Antiq. Rom.* vol. 3, p. 360.

BASI'LICON (*Med.*) βασιλικὸν, royal, from βασιλεύς, a king; an ointment consisting of rosin, pitch, oil, wax, &c.; also a sovereign kind of plaster, and an epithet for many compositions. *Cels. de Re Med.* l. 5, c. 19; *Oribas. Synop.* l. 3; *Aet. Tetrab.* 4, serm. 3, c. 21.

BASI'LICUM (*Bot.*) the *Ocimum basilicum* and *tenuifolium*, and the *Basilicum agreste* of Linnæus.

BASI'LICUS (*Astron.*) or basilica, the same as *Regulus*.

BASILICUS *pulvis* (*Med.*) Royal powder; an epithet for several purging powders containing cream of tartar.

BASILI'DIANS (*Ecc.*) a sect of heretics in the second century, who held the errors of Simon Magus. They maintained, among other things, that angels created the world. *Justin. Mart. Dial. cum Tryphon; S. Iren.* l. 22, c. 2; *Tertull. de Præscent. Clem. Aleria, et Strom.* 3; *Epiphan. Hæres.* 23; *St. Augustin. Hæres.*

BASILI'DION (*Med.*) a particular cerate for the itch, described by Galen.

BASILI'NDA (*Ant.*) βασιλίνδα, a sort of game similar to

the choosing of king and queen on Twelfth-night. *Poll. Onomast.* l. 9, c. 7.

BA'SILISK (*Zool.*) βασιλίσκος, *basiliscus*, a poisonous serpent, so called from βασιλεύς, a king, because, according to Nicander, he was ιμυςῶν βασιλευς, the king of the reptiles. *Luc.* l. 9, v. 725.

—— *Late sibi submovet omne*
Vulgus, ac in vacua regnat basiliscus arenâ.

It is also called in English a cockatrice, because it was fabled to be produced from the egg of a cock. This serpent, which is the *Lacerta basiliscus* of Linnæus, is not above three palms long, and distinguished from others of its tribe, by having a white spot on its head resembling a diamond. *Plin.* l. 8, c. 21; *Solin.* c. 27; *Ælian. de Hist. Anim.* l. 3, c. 21; *Gal. ad Pison.* c. 8; *Hor. Hieroz.* l. 1, c. 1, &c.; *Boch. Hieroz. Part. Post.* l. 3, c. 9; *Salmas Plin. Exercitat.* p. 372.

BASILISK (*Mil.*) the name of a large piece of ordnance.

BA'SIN *of a dock* (*Mar.*) a place for water confined by double floodgates, to prevent it running out at ebb tide. It contains vessels before they enter or after they come out of dock.—*Basin of a haven*, that part which opens from a narrow channel into a spacious receptacle.

BASIN (*Anat.*) a round cavity in the form of a tunnel, situate betwixt the anterior ventricles of the brain, and ending at the *glandula pituitaria*.

BASINS *of a balance*, (*Mech.*) the two concave pieces of brass, or other metal, hanging by strings at the extremity of the beam; the one to hold the weights, and the other the things to be weighed.—*Basins, among glass-grinders*, the dishes in which are formed or ground the convex glasses, which are different as the focusses of the glass are at a greater or less distance.—*Basins, with hatters*, the iron moulds in which they form their wool or fur into hats.

BA'SIO-CERA'TO-CHONDRO-GLOSSUS (*Anat.*) vide *Hyoglossus.*

BASIO-GLOSSUM, vide *Hyoglossus.*

BASIO-PHARYNGÆUS, vide *Constrictor pharyngis medius.*

BA'SIS (*Anat.*) βασις, the sole of the foot, according to Hippocrates. *De Artic.*—*Basis cordis*, the superior part of the heart, to distinguish it from its apex, or small point.—*Basis Cerebri*, the lower and posterior part of the brain. *Ruf. Ephes.* l. 1, c. 22.

BASIS (*Med.*) the principal ingredient in a composition.

BA'SKET (*Her.*) vide *Winnowing Basket.*

BASKET *Tenure of Lands* (*Law*) vide *Canes-Tellus.*

BA'SKING SHARK (*Ich.*) a species of the shark, the *Squalus maximus* of Linnæus, so called from its lying much in the sun on the surface of the water. This fish inhabits the Arctic and European seas, feeds on the smaller cetaceous animals, and grows to a prodigious size, but is not very fierce. The liver is very large, and produces much oil.

BASNE'TUM (*Archæol.*) a basnet.

BA'SON (*Anat.*) vide *Basin.*

BA'SS (*Mech.*) a sort of cushion made of straw or rushes; also a collar for horses.

BASS (*Mus.*) in Italian *basso*, the lowest or deepest part of any composition, which is regarded as the foundation of harmony. Bass is of different kinds, as—*Thorough bass*, which includes the fundamental rules of composition.—*Fundamental bass*, which forms the tone, or natural foundation of harmony.—*Ground bass*, is that which commences with some subject of its own, that is continually repeated throughout the movement, whilst the *upper parts* pursue a separate air.—*Figured bass* is that which, while a certain chord or harmony is continued by the parts above, moves in notes of the same harmony.—*Bass cliff*, or F *cliff*, the character marked thus 𝄢, and placed at the beginning of a stave, in which the base, or lower notes of a composition, are placed.—*Bass cliff note*, that note in the bass stave which is placed on the same line with the bass cliff. [vide *Music*]—*Bass voice*, the gravest and deepest of the male voices.—*Bass viol*, a well-known stringed instrument of the same form but larger than a violin.

BASS RELIEF (*Archit.*) vide *Basso Relievo.*

BASSE (*Ich.*) a species of perch, the λάβραξ of Aristotle, the *Perca Labrax* of Linnæus; a strong, active, voracious fish, which Ovid calls *rapidi lupi*, wherefore they are called *lupus* by Rondeletius. The flesh is esteemed as very delicate.

BASSE COURT (*Archit.*) a court separated from the principal one, and destined for the stables, &c.

BA'SSET (*Sport.*) a game of chance, which was invented by a Venetian nobleman.

BASSE'TTO (*Mus.*) or *basso*, a small bass viol.

BA'SSIA (*Bot.*) a genus of plants named after Ferdinand Bassi, curator of the Botanic-garden at Bologna, Class 11 *Dodecandria*, Order 1 *Monogynia.*

Generic Characters. CAL. *perianth* four-leaved.—COR. monopetalous.—STAM. *filaments* sixteen; *anthers* linear. PIST. *germ.* superior; *style* subulate; *stigma* acute.— PER. *drupe* fleshy; *seeds* nuts five.

Species. The species are shrubs, and natives of India.

BA'SSO-RELIEVO (*Archit.*) in French *bas relief*, in English Bass Relief, a sort of sculpture in which the figures are represented as projecting from the back ground, as a kind of relief in distinction from the *alto relievo* and *mezzo relievo.*

BASSO (*Mus.*) Italian for bass, which in choral scores is generally placed against the stave of the instrumental bass.—*Basso* is of different kinds, as *Basso concertante*, the bass of the little chorus.—*Basso repieno*, the bass of the grand chorus.—*Basso continuo*, that part of a composition which is figured for the organ, &c. &c.

BA'SSOCK (*Mech.*) the same as Bass or Hassock.

BASSOO'N (*Mus.*) a wind instrument, consisting of a very long tube, and a reed for the admission of the wind; it comprehends three octaves.

BASSO'VIA (*Bot.*) a genus of plants, Class 5 *Pentandria*, Order 1, *Monogynia.*

Generic Characters. CAL. *perianth* one-leaved.—COR. one-petalled.—STAM. *filaments* five; *anthers* ovate.—PIST. *germ* ovate; *style* short; *stigma* thickish.—PER. *berry* ovate; *seeds* very many.

Species. The only species is the—*Bassovia sylvatica*, a perennial, native of Guiana.

BASS-VI'OL (*Mus.*) vide *Bass.*—*Bass voice.* [vide *Bass*]

BA'STA (*Mus.*) Italian for *enough, stop!* an expression used by the leader of a band.

BA'STARD (*Gunn.*) a name for those pieces of ordnance which are of an unusual size and make.

BASTARD-SCARLET (*Mech.*) a name given to red dyed with bale-madder, which comes the nearest to new scarlet.

BASTARD (*Law*) one born out of lawful wedlock, according to the civil and canon law; but one begotten as well as born out of wedlock, according to the common. 2 *Inst.* 96.—*Bastard-eigné*, a son born out of wedlock, in distinction from another son born of the same man and woman after their marriage. *Lit.* sect. 399, &c.

BASTARD *Alkanet* (*Bot.*) an annual, the *Lithospermum arvense* of Linnæus.—Bastard balm, a perennial, the *Melittis Melissophyllum.*—Bastard Cabbage-tree, the *Geoffroya.*—Bastard Cedar, the *Bubroma Gauzuma.*—Bastard Cress, a biennial, the *Thlaspi.*—Bastard Feverfew, an annual, the *Parthenium Hysterophorus.*—Bastard Gentian, an annual, the *Sarothra.*—Bastard Gromwell, an annual, the *Lithospermum arvense.*—Bastard Hares' Ear, a shrub, the *Phyllis.*—Bastard Hatchet Vetch, an annual, the *Bisserrula.*—Bastard Hemp, a perennial, the *Datisca.*—Bastard Hibiscus, the

Achania.—Bastard Jesuit's Bark-tree, the *Iva frutescens.*—Bastard Indigo, a shrub, the *Amorplia.*—Bastard Knotgrass, the *Corrigiola.*—Bastard Lupine, a perennial, the *Trifolium Lupinaster.*—Bastard Orpine, the *Andrachne.*—Bastard Pellitory, the *Achillea.*—Bastard Pimpernel, an annual, the *Centunculus.*—Bastard Plantain, a large herbaceous plant, the *Heliconia Bihai* and *Centunculus.*—Bastard Quince, a shrub, the *Mespilus Chamætraespilus.*—Bastard Saffron, an annual, the *Carthamus tinctorius.*—Bastard Toadflax, a perennial, the *Thesium linophyllum.*—Bastard Vetch, a perennial, the *Phaca.*

BASTARD *strangles (Vet.)* the strangles in its most violent state.

BA'STARDY *(Law) bastardia*, the defect of birth objected to one born out of wedlock.—*Rights of bastardy*, a right in the French Law, by virtue of which the effects of bastards dying intestate devolved to the king, or the lord of the manor.

BASTE'RIA *(Bot.)* the *Calycanthus florida* of Linnæus.

BA'TA *(Bot.)* the *Musa paradisia* of Linnæus.

BATA'TA *(Bot.)* an Indian name for the potatoe, or the *Solanum tuberosum* of Linnæus.—*Batata* is also a name for a species of the *Dioscerea* of Linnæus.

BATA'TUS *(Bot.)* a species of the *Convolvulus* of Linnæus.

BASTI'LE *(Polit.)* the name of a noted French prison destroyed during the French Revolution.

BA'STION *(Fort.)* a large mass of earth forming part of the inner inclosure of a fortification, anciently called the bulwark. The bastion consists of two *faces*, and an opening towards the centre called the *gorge*. It is of different kinds; namely—*Full*, or *solid bastion*, that in which the level ground within is even with the rampart.—*Empty*, or *hollow bastion*, where the level ground is much lower than the bastion.—*Composed bastion*, when two sides of the interior polygon are very unequal.—*Deformed bastion*, when the irregularity of the lines and angles causes the bastion to appear deformed—*Cut bastion*, that which makes a re-entering angle at the point, sometimes called *bastion with a tenaille*—*Demi-bastion*, one raised on the plane of another bastion, but much higher.—*Regular bastion*, that which has its due proportion of faces, &c.—*Flat bastion*, one constructed on a right line so that its demigorges do not form an angle. [vide *Fortification*]

BA'STON *(Her.)* vide *Batton*.

BASTON *(Law)* a servant or officer belonging to the warden of the Fleet, who attends the king's courts to take such into custody as are committed by the court.

BASTONA'DO *(Polit.)* a mode of punishment, usual among the Turks, of beating the offender on the soles of the feet.

BA'SUS *(Archæol)* strike, as "Per basum tolnetum capere;" to take toll by strike, in distinction from *in cumulo vel cantello*.

BAT *(Zool.)* the *Vespertilio* of Linnæus, an animal that resembles both a bird and a mouse. It has wings, not of feathers, but of a skin distended; lays no eggs, but brings forth its young alive, and suckles them. It is never to be tamed, feeds on insects, and flies about in the dusk of a summer's evening.

BAT *(Her.)* vide *Rere Mouse*.

BAT-*Fowling (Sport.)* a way of catching birds in the night while they are roosting.

BAT-*Horses (Mil.)* or *Baw-Horses*, baggage horses belonging to the officer when on actual duty.—*Bat-Men*, or *Baw-Men*, originally servants hired in war time to take care of the horses belonging to the artillery, &c. The same name is given now to those who are excused regimental duty for the express purpose of attending to the horses belonging to the officers.

BA'TA *(Bot.)* the *Musa Paradisiaca* of Linnæus.

BA'TABLE *ground (Law)* land lying between England and Scotland heretofore in debate, or debatable to whom it belonged.

BA'TAGE *(Mil.)* or *Battage*, French, for the time employed in reducing gunpowder to its proper consistency.

BATA'ILLE *Cheval de (Mil.)* a war horse, or charger.

BATAILLO'N *quarré (Mil.)* French for a battalion formed into a perfect square, which is equally strong on all sides.

BATA'RDE *(Mil.)* an eight pounder among the French.

BATARDEA'U *(Fort.)* a massive perpendicular pile of masonry, whose length is equal to the breadth of the ditch inundation, or any part of a fortification where the water cannot be kept in by any other means.

BA'TCHELOR *(Her.)* vide *Bachelor*.

TO BATE *(Falc.)* the act of a hawk fluttering her wings, either from fist or perch, as it were striving to get away.

BA'TEMENT *(Carp.)* the wasting of stuff in cutting it for a designed purpose; a board is said "to have so much *batement*" from which any quantity is cut off.

BATH *(Bibl.)* בת, a liquid measure of the largest capacity next to the homer, of which it was the tenth part, *Ezek.* xlv. 11. 14. It was equal to the *Epha*, i. e. seven gallons and a half English.

BATH, *Knights of the (Her.)* a military order of Knighthood of uncertain original, but so called from a part of the ceremony. It was restored, if not instituted, by Henry IV, and revived again in the reign of George I. The Knights wear a red ribbon, and their motto is "Tria juncta in uno," alluding to the three cardinal virtues which every knight ought to posses. [vide *Heraldry*]

BATH *(Med.)* any receptacle for water which is convenient for bathing. This is distinguished into the *hot*, *tepid*, or *cold Bath*, according to the temperature of the water.—*Bath* is also any artificial contrivance which is to supply the place of a bath, which is of different kinds, as—*Shower Bath*, an apparatus for applying water to the body through numerous apertures after the manner of a shower.—*Vapour Bath* conveys moisture or heat to the body through the medium of steam, which may be done to any degree of temperature.—*Medicated Bath*, such as is saturated with various mineral, vegetable, and animal substances.—*Dry Bath*, made of ashes, salt, sand, &c. through which heat is conveyed to the body.

BATH *(Chem.)* a contrivance by which heat is conveyed to any substance, as when a body is heated by the steam or vapour of boiling water, it is said to be done by means of a *vapour Bath*.

BATH *(Metal.)* the fusion of metallic matter for any particular purpose: metals are said to be *in bath* when they are melted for refining; and the purifying of gold by antimony is called the bath of gold.

BA'THYS *(Med.)* the best sort of cheese for food used by the great at Rome. *Gal. de Alim. fac.* l. 3, c. 17.

BA'THMIS *(Anat.)* βαθμις, a *sinus*, or cavity of a bone, which receives the protuberance of another at the joints. *Gorr. Def. Med.; Foes. Œconom. Hippocrat.*

BA'THRON *(Sur.)* βάθρον, or βαθρν, as it is written in Hippocrates's Treatise, *de flatibus*, the *scamnum, Hippocratis;* an instrument invented for the extension of fractured limbs. *Oribas. de Machin.* c. 29.

BATI'LLUS *(Mus.)* an instrument, used in the service of the Armenian churches, formed like a staff, and furnished with rings which yield an harmonious sound.

BA'TIS *(Ich.)* βατις, or βατος; a sort of fish, the *Raia batis* of Linnæus.

BATIS *(Bot.)* a genus of plants, Class 22 *Dioecia*, Order 4 *Tetrandria*.

Generic Characters. CAL. *ament* pyramidal.—COR. none.—STAM. *filaments* four; *anthers* oblong.—PIST. *germ* quadrangular; *style* none; *stigma* obtuse.—Per. berry one-celled; *seeds* four.

Species. The only species is the *Batis maritima, maritima erecta,* &c. seu *Kali fruticosum,* &c.; a shrub, native of Jamaica.

BATI'STE (*Com.*) a fine white linen manufactured in Picardy.

BA'TMAN (*Com.*) a Persian weight of four hundred drams.

BAT'ON *de Commandement* (*Mil.*) literally "A staff of command," which was a symbol of authority given to generals in the French army. Henry III, before his accession, received the bâton on being made *generalissimo* of the forces of his brother Charles IX.

BATOO'N (*Archit.*) a moulding in the base of a column.

Batoon (*Mil.*) a truncheon, or marshal's staff.

BATRACHI'TES (*Min.*) a stone, in colour and shape much resembling a green frog. *Plin.* l. 37, c. 10.

BATRA'CHIUM (*Bot.*) Crow's-foot, a sort of herb. *Plin.* l. 25.

BATRACHO'IDES (*Bot.*) the *Geranium, et Phœum pratense, et sylvaticum* of Linnæus. *Bauh. Hist. Plant.*

BATRACHOMYOMA'CHIA (*Lit.*) the title of one of Homer's smaller poems signifying the battle between the frogs and mice, from βάτραχος, a frog, μῦς, mouse, μαχη, a battle.

BA'TRACHUS (*Ich.*) βάτραχος, a sea fish like the frog, called a sea-devil. *Plin.* l. 32, c. 11.

Batrachus (*Med.*) an inflammatory tumor which rises under the tongue, particularly of children. *Paul. Æginet. de Re Med.* l. 3, c. 26.

BA'TTA (*Mil.*) allowances made to troops in India.—*Dry batta,* money which is given in India to the troops in lieu of ratios.—*Full batta,* an additional allowance which is given by the East India Company to their troops.—*Half batta,* half of the above allowance drawn by the troops in garrison.—*Wet batta,* batta given in kind.

BATTA'LIA (*Mil.*) from the Italian *Battaglia,* order of battle.

BATTA'LION (*Mill.*) in French *bataillon,* a body of foot soldiers of from 600 to 800 men.—"To draw up *battalion,*" is to range the men in order of battle.—*Triangular battalion,* a body of troops ranged in the form of a triangle, as was formerly the practice.

BATTA'RDEA (*Archit.*) coffer-dam, a case of piling fixed in the bed of a river for drawing off the water where the pier of a bridge is to be built.

BATTA'TA (*Bot.*) vide *Batata.*

BA'TTEL (*Law*) in French *bataille,* an ancient mode of trial by single combat called *wager of battel,* where, in appeals of felony, the appellee might fight with the appellant to prove his innocence. It was also used in affairs of chivalry or honour, and in civil cases upon issue joined in a writ of right. *Glanv.* l. 2, c. 7; *Brit.* c. 22; *Co. Lit.* 294.

Battel (*Mil.*) vide *Battle.*

BA'TTELED (*Her.*) or *embatteled,* vide *Crenelle.*

BA'TTELER (*Cus.*) a student in the University that battles.

BA'TTEN (*Carp.*) a scantling or piece of wooden stuff from two to four inches broad and one inch thick.—*Batten-door,* a door, on the surface of which are fixed stiles, rails, and munnions, made of battens, so as to give it the appearance of a framed door.—*Batten-floor,* the same as a *Boarded-floor.*

Batten (*Mech.*) the moveable lath or bar of a loom, which serves to strike in, or close, more or less, the threads of a woof.

BA'TTENING (*Carpen.*) the act of fixing battens to walls for nailing of the lath over which the plaister is laid; or it is the battens that are prepared for this purpose.

BA'TTENS (*Mar.*) thin pieces of oak or fir, nailed to the mast-head.—*Battens of the hatches,* narrow laths which serve to keep the tarpaulin close to the hatchways—*Tracing-battens,* pieces of wood to which the seamen's hammocks are slung.

to Batten (*Archit.*) a term used to signify that a wall, piece of timber, and the like, does not stand upright, but leans from a person; in distinction from *overhanging,* when it leans towards the person.

BATTERI'E *de tambour* (*Mil.*) French for a beat of the drum, called in English, the General.

Batterie is also the name for a Battery, as—*Batterie en rouage,* a battery used to dismount the enemy's canon.—*Batterie par camarade,* the discharge of several pieces of ordnance planted above a parapet that is not sufficiently high to admit of embrasures.—*Batterie de canon,* signifies not only a park of artillery, or the place where the ordnance are planted, but also the pieces themselves, as *batterie directe,* cannon planted right in front of a work, &c. [vide *Battery*]

BA'TTERING (*Mil.*) a cannonade of heavy ordnance from the first and second parallel of entrenchment against any fortress or works.—*To batter in breach,* in French *battre en brèche,* is a heavy cannonade of many pieces directed to one part of the revetement from the third parallel.—*Battering-pieces,* the heavy pieces of ordnance used in battering. —*Battering-train,* a train of artillery used solely for besieging a strong place.

Battering ram (*Mil.*) vide *Aries.*

Battering *ram* (*Her.*) the ancient military machine of this name has been used as a charge in some coats of arms, as *argent three battering rams, barwise proper, headed azure, armed and garnished or,* name *Bertie.*

BA'TTERY (*Law*) French *batterie,* an act that tends to a breach of the peace, by violently striking or beating a man, who may therefore indict the person, or have his action of trespass, or of assault and battery; there may be an assault without battery, but there can be no battery without an assault.

Battery (*Mil.*) any raised place on which cannon are planted. It consists of a—*Breastwork, parapet,* or *epaulement.*—*Embrazures,* or open spaces left to put the muzzles of the guns.—*Merlons,* the solid earth between the embrasures.—*Genouillères,* or parts of the parapet which cover the carriages.—*Platform,* or wooden floor to prevent the carriages from sinking.

Batteries are of different kinds, as—*Gun-batteries,* which are the common sort.—*Open batteries,* in French *batteries en plein champ,* different sorts of batteries, when they are exposed to view.—*Covered* or *masked batteries, batteries enterrées,* when hidden by a breastwork.—*Sunk* or *buried batteries,* when the platform is sunk on which the cannon are planted, so that trenches are cut into the earth for firing through.—*Ricochet batteries,* when the elevation is but small, and the balls are made to roll along the opposite parapet to dismount the enemy's cannon.—*Cross batteries,* two batteries firing athwart each other on the same object. They are otherwise called *murdering batteries.*—*Sweeping* or *enfilading batteries,* in French *batteries d'Enfilade,* when they scour or sweep the whole length of a straight line.—*Direct batteries,* in French *batteries directes,* those situated directly opposite to the place intended to be battered.—*Oblique batteries,* in French *batteries en echarde,* when they play obliquely upon any work.—*Reverse* or *murdering batteries,* in French *batteries de reverse,* which play on the enemy's back.—*Redan batteries,* in French *Batteries en redans,* such as flank each other at the saliant or re-entering angles of a fortification.—*Joint batteries,* or in French *Batteries par camerade,* when several guns play upon the same place at the same time.—*Mortar batteries*, in French *Batteries de mortier*, have the parapet inwards, and no embrazures.—*Glancing batteries*, those whose shot strikes the object at an angle of 20°, after which the ball glances from the object and recoils to some adjacent object.—*Fascine* or *Gabion batteries*, in French *Batteries à fascines*, batteries made of fascines instead of rods, when they cannot be procured.—*Battery planks*, the planks used in making platforms.—*Battery boxes*, square chests or boxes filled with earth or dung, and used instead of sods for the erection of batteries.—*Battery nails*, wooden pins made of the toughest wood, with which the platforms are nailed.—*Battery master*, an officer whose business it was to see to the raising of batteries, which office is now suppressed in England.

BATTERY, *floating* (*Mar.*) a battery erected either on simple rafts, or, according to the latest invention of Sir William Congreve, on the hulls of ships.

BATTERY (*Elect.*) a combination of coated surfaces of glass jars, so connected that they may be charged at once and discharged by a common conductor.—*Battery*, or *Pile*, an apparatus employed for accumulating the electricity of galvanism, consisting of plates of copper and zinc, or of silver and zinc, soldered together, and cemented in such manner as to leave a number of water-tight cells. [vide *Chemistry*]

BATTEU'RS d'*Estrade* (*Mil.*) scouts of horsemen sent to collect intelligence.

BA'TTING-STAFF (*Mech.*) a tool used by laundresses to beat washed linen.

BATTITU'RA (*Met.*) the squama or scales which fly off from the metals while under the hammer.

BATTLE (*Law*) vide *Battel*.

TO BATTLE, to take up provision in the college-book at Oxford.

BATTLE *axe* (*Mil.*) an ancient sort of weapon, having an axe and a point at the end, for cutting or thrusting.

BATTLE *axe* (*Her.*) the weapon of this name was frequently used as a charge in coats of arms, as he beareth " *gules* three battle axes, *or*, name *Hackluit*, of Yetton, in Hertfordshire." From this family was descended Richard Hackluit, prebend of Westminster, and author of a collection of sea voyages.

BATTLED (*Archit.*) or *embattled*, an epithet for a wall which has a double row of embattlements.

BATTLED (*Her.*) or *embattled*, an epithet for a line of partition having one battlement upon another.

BA'TTLEDORE (*Sport.*) an instrument used either with a shuttlecock or tennis ball.

BATTLEDORE-SHAPED (*Bot.*) *Spatulatus*; an epithet for a leaf, when its fore part is circular and it grows smaller towards the base, as in the *Cucubalus otites*.

BA'TTLEMENTS (*Arch.*) from battle; notches or indentures in the top of a wall or building, like embrazures, to look through.

BATTO'LOGY (*Gram.*) βαττολογία, from βάττος, a foolish poet of that name, and λόγος, speech; vain babbling; tautology. *Hesychius*; *Suidas*.

BA'TTON (*Her.*) battune, or *baston*, in French *baton*, a staff truncheon, used as an abatement in coats of arms to denote illegitimacy. It is the fourth part of the bend-sinister, as in the annexed figure.

BATTOO'N, vide *Batton*.

BATTRE (*Mil.*) a French word, signifying literally to beat; is also employed in many military phrases in a particular sense, as—*Battre la campagne*, to scour the country.—*Battre de front*, to throw cannon shot in almost a perpendicular direction against any object.—*Battre en brèche*, to batter in breach.—*Battre en flanc*, to direct shot along the front of an object.—*Battre à dos*, to direct the shot along the back part of an object.—*Battre en sape*, to batter a work at the foot of its revetement.—*Battre en salve*, to make a general discharge of heavy ordnance.—*Battre la caisse*, to beat a drum.—*Battre un ban*, to give notice by sound of drum when an officer is to be received, a punishment inflicted, &c.—*Battre la chamade*, to beat a parley.—*Battre aux champs*, to give notice by beat of drum that a regiment is approaching or marching off, &c.—*Battre la charge*, to beat the charge, or to give notice that a general discharge of musketry is about to take place.—*Battre la Diane*, to beat the reveillé.—*Battre les drapeaux*, to announce, by beat of drum, that the colours are to be lodged.—*Battre la generale*, to beat the General.—*Battre la marche*, to give the signal for advancing or retreating.—*Battre la masse*, to give notice by beat of drum, for the soldiers to go to church.—*Battre la priere*, to give notice, by beat of drum, for prayers.—*Battre la retraite*, to beat the retreat, &c. [vide *To Beat*]—*Se Battre en retraite*, to keep up a running fight.

BATZ (*Com.*) a coin of less value than a farthing, current in different parts of Germany.

BAUDRIER (*Mil.*) French for a cross-belt, and also a sword-belt.

BAVE'TTE (*Mil.*) French for a piece or apron of lead, which is placed in front of a water-pipe, or upon a roof that is slated.

BAUGE (*Mil.*) French for a coarse sort of mortar.

BAUGE (*Com.*) a drugget manufactured in Burgundy, with thread spun thick and coarse wool.

BAUHI'NIA (*Bot.*) a genus of plants, called by Plumier after John and Caspar Bauhin, two famous botanists, Class 10 *Decandria*, Order 1 *Monogynia*.
   Generic Characters. CAL. *perianth* oblong.—COR. *petals* five, oblong.—STAM. *filaments* ten; *anthers* ovate.—PIST. *germ* oblong; *style* filiform; *stigma* obtuse.—PER. *legume* oblong; *seeds* many.
   Species. The species are shrubs and natives of India.

BA'VINS (*Mil.*) small faggots of brushwood having no part of the brush taken off, which serve as fascines.

BAULK (*Archit.*) vide *Balk*.

BA'WLING (*Sport.*) a name given to the noise of dogs who are too busy before they find the scent.

BA'WREL (*Falcon.*) a kind of hawk resembling the linnet in size and shape, but having a longer body and tail.

BAY (*Geog.*) in Saxon byʒe, German *Bucht*, from *biegen*, to bend or curve; an arm of the sea stretching inland.

BAY (*Mar.*) any inlet of the sea between two capes or promontories, where shipping may ride. Smaller bays are denominated gulfs or havens, and creeks, which are the smallest of the kind.—*Bay of a ship*, that part on each side, between the decks of large ships of war, which lies before the bits.

BAY (*Mech.*) or *pen*, a pond head, made very high to keep in water for the supply of a mill. *Stat.* 27, *Eliz.*

BAY (*Bot.*) or *Bay-tree*, the female laurel-tree, a well known shrub, which Linnæus has therefore entitled the *Laurus nobilis*. It is an evergreen which grows wild in Italy and France. The leaves and berries of this shrub have an aromatic and astringent taste, and a fragrant smell, whence it is called the Sweet Bay, of which there are several sorts cultivated in gardens, namely, the Broad-leaved Bay, the Common Bay, and the Narrow-leaved Bay; it is generally supposed to be the *Laurus* of the ancients.

BAY (*Sport.*) when a dog detains a partridge till she be shot, he is said to keep her at *bay*; also when the dogs have earthed any vermin, or brought a deer or boar, or the like, to turn against them; then not only the deer but the dogs are said to *bay*.

4

BAY (*Vet.*) a colour in horses; so called from its resembling the colour of a dried bay leaf. There are various shades of this colour, from the bright bay, which is a very beautiful colour, to the dark bay, which approaches very near to the brown, but is more gay and shining. Bay horses have black manes, which distinguish them from the sorrel which have reddish manes.—*Bay* is also the same as a Bay-Horse.

BAY (*Archit.*) 1. A space left in a wall for a door, &c. 2. That part of a barn where the corn is laid.—*Bay of Joists*, the joisting between two binding joists, or between two girders when there are no binding joists.—*Bay of Roofing*, the small rafters, and their supporting purlins between principal rafters.—*Bay-Window*, another name for a *Bow-window*.

BAY (*Fort.*) a hole in a parapet to receive the mouth of a cannon.

BA'Y-SALT (*Chem.*) a salt, so called from its brown colour, which is made of sea-water in France, particularly on the coast of Bretagne, from the middle of May to the end of August, by letting the sea-water into square pits or basons, where, by the rays of the sun, the water is evaporated, and the residue is converted into crystals of salt.

BA'YONET (*Mil.*) in French *Bayonette*, Italian *Bagonetta*, Spanish *Bayoneta*, a kind of triangular dagger, made to fix on the muzzle of a firelock or musket, so as not to interfere with either charging or firing. It is of great use against a charge of the cavalry.

BAYS (*Com.*) vide *Baize*.

BAZA'R (*Com.*) a place designed for trade among the Eastern nations, particularly the Persians. It is sometimes uncovered like our market places, but mostly covered and fitted up with shops for the sale of every article.

BA'ZOT (*Com.*) or *Baza*, cotton, from Said or Zeyde.

BDE'LLA (*Med.*) a horse-leach.

BDE'LLIUM (*Nat.*) βδἐλλιον, from the Hebrew בדלח, the gum of an Arabian tree about the size of the olive-tree. It resembles wax, is somewhat pellucid, moderately heavy, considerably hard, of a bitterish taste, and a sweet smell. Its medicinal virtues consist in mollifying hard swellings and stiff sinews, and in acting as an antidote against the bites of venomous beasts. *Dioscor.* l. 1, c. 80; *Plin.* l. 12, c. 9; *Cel. de Re Med.* l. 7, c. 4; *Gal. de Simplic.* l. 6; *Oribas. de Virt. Simplic.* l. 2; *Aet. Tetrab.* 1, serm. 1; *Paul Æginet. de Re Med.* l. 7, c. 3.

BDELLIUM (*Chem.*) the constituent parts of this gum have been found to be resin, gum, cerasin, and volatile oil.

BEACH (*Mar.*) the sea shore, or margin of the sea, particularly that part washed by the waves.

BEA'CON (*Archit.*) from the Saxon beacone, to discover or descry; a signal by fire, placed on some eminence to prevent shipwrecks; or to give an alarm on the appearance of an enemy.

BEACON (*Her.*) this signal has been used as a charge in coats of arms, representing high standards, bearing the iron pots, with pitch, hemp, and other combustibles set on fire, as " He beareth *sable* three beacons, fired, *or*, the flames, *proper*, by the name of *Dauntre*."

BEA'CONAGE (*Cus.*) a duty paid towards the maintenance of beacons. *Stat. 5, Hen. 4.*

BEAD (*Ecc.*) in Saxon Bede, a prayer; hence, " To say over *beads*," or " To tell one's *beads*," is to say one's prayers; and " Bidding of *beads*," was a charge from the priest to say so many Pater Nosters over their beads for a soul that was deceased.—*Bead-roll*, a list of such as used to be prayed for in the church.

BEAD (*Archit.*) a round moulding, carved in short embossments, like the bead of a necklace. [vide *Architecture*.]

BEAD (*Carpent.*) a circular moulding stuck on the edge of a piece of stuff by a plane of the same. When the bead is flush, i. e. even with the surface, it is called the *quirk-bead*; but when raised, the *cock-bead*. When the bead is stuck on with one quirk only, it is called *Bead* and *Quirk*; but when it is returned on the other surface, it is then a *Bead* and *Double Quirk*, or a *Return Bead*.—*Bead* and *Butt-Work*, a piece of framing, having the pannels flush with the framing; it is called *Bead-Butt* and *Square*, or *Bead-Butt* and *Flush*, when it is bead and butt; or *Bead* and *Flush* on one side, and square only on the other.

BEAD (*Metal*) the small ball or mass of pure metal separated from the scoria, and seen distinct while in the fire.

BEAD-*proof* (*Chem.*) a term among distillers for that proof of the standard strength of spirituous liquors, which consists in the bubbles called *beads*, that will rise and stand on the surface of the liquid for some time after it has been shaken.

BEAD *Tree* (*Bot.*) the *Melia* of Linnæus, a shrub, so called because the nut which it bears is bored through, and strung as beads by the Roman Catholics in Spain and Portugal, where it commonly grows.

BEA'DLE (*Law*) vide *Bedel*.

BEA'DMAKERS (*Com.*) the manufacturers and makers of beads for the use of the Roman Catholics.

BEA'DSMAN (*Ecc.*) one who says over beads or prayers for his patron, &c.

BEA'GLE (*Sport.*) a sort of hunting dog, of which there are three sorts, the southern, the northern, or cut beagle, and a cross breed of the two, which is reckoned the best of the three.

BEAK (*Or.*) the upper part of the bill of a bird.

BEAK (*Falcon.*) the upper and crooked part of the bill of a hawk.

BEAK (*Vet.*) a little shoe at the toe of a horse's foot, about an inch long, turned up and fastened in upon the fore part of the hoof.

BEAK *of a ship* (*Ant.*) vide *Rostrum*.

BEAK-HEAD (*Mar.*) a small platform at the forepart of the upper deck, either for the planting of a gun, or the conveniency of the men.

BEAK (*Archit.*) a little fillet left on the edge of a larmier, which forms a channel behind, for preventing the water from running down the lower bed of the cornice.—*Chin-Beak*, a moulding, the same as the quarter round, except that it is inverted. It is more commonly called a cavetto. [vide *Moulding*]

BEAK (*Carp.*) the crooked end of the hold-fast in a carpenter's bench.

BEA'KED (*Her.*) an epithet in blazoning for birds whose beaks are of a different tincture from the bodies.

BEAKED (*Bot.*) *rostratus*; an epithet for the fruit when it is terminated by a process in the shape of a bird's beak.

BEA'KER (*Mech.*) in the Teutonic, *becker*, a drinking cup; so called from its having a spout like a bird's beak.

BEA'KING (*Sport.*) the fighting of cocks with their bills.

BEAKING *Joint* (*Carpent.*) a name for the heading joints of the boards of a floor when they fall in the same straight line.

BEAM (*Carpent.*) from the Saxon beam, a tree; the largest piece of wood in a building, which is its main support: the dimensions of beams are regulated by statute, so that a beam 15 feet long must be at least 7 inches on one side its square, or end, and 5 the other.

BEAM-*filling* (*Mason.*) the filling up the space between the raison and the roof with bricks or stones; laid betwixt the rafters or the raison, and plastered on with loom.

BEAM *of a plough* (*Mech.*) the stout wooden part into which the iron-work of the plough-tail is fixed.—*Beam of a loom*, a long thick cylinder running along the back of the loom.

BEAM (*Mar.*) the large main timbers that stretch across a ship to support the decks, &c.—*Beak-head beam*, the broadest beam in the ship.—*Midship beam*, the longest beam lodged in the midship frame.—*Orlop beams*, those which support the orlop deck. This word is also used in many phrases, as " On the *beam*," any distance from the ship, or a line with the beams: thus, when a ship steers northward, any object lying east or west is on her starboard or larboard beam. " On the weather-*beam*," i. e. on the weather-side of the ship. " Before the *beam*," an arc of the horizon between the line of the beam and that point of the compass which she steers. " Abaft the *beam*," an arc of the horizon between the line drawn at right angles to the keel, and the point to which the ship's stern is directed. A ship is said " To be on her *beam ends*," when she inclines very much to one side for her beams to be almost in a vertical position.—*Beam of an anchor*, the main piece. vide *Anchor*.

BEAM (*Nat.*) a sort of fiery meteor in the shape of a pillar.

BEAM *of a stag* (*Sport.*) that part of the head where the antlers, &c. grow, which are so called because they grow out of the head as branches out of a tree.—*Beam antler*, the second start in a stag's head.

BEAM (*Falc.*) the long feathers of a hawk's wing.

BEAM (*Her.*) a term used in blazoning coats of arms, for the main horn of a stag, or buck.

BEAM *of a balance* (*Mech.*) the horizontal piece of wood, or iron, on the extremities of which the scales are suspended.—*Beam compass*, an instrument consisting of a wooden or brass square beam having sliding sockets carrying steel or pencil points.

BEAM-TREE (*Bot.*) the *Crategus aria* of Linnæus, a tree which grows to the height of thirty or forty feet; it is so called, because it is particularly fitted for making axletrees, and the like.

BEAN (*Bot.*) the *Vicia Faba* of Linnæus; an edible pulse, of which there are several sorts, as the Common Garden Bean, the Windsor-Bean, the Horse-Bean, &c.—Kidney or French-Bean, the *Phaseolus*, cultivated in gardens, of which the principal sorts are the small White Dwarf, the Scarlet, and the Black Dwarf, or Negro.—Bean Caper, the *Zygophyllum*, a fleshy succulent shrub.—Bean Trefoil, the *Anagyrus*, a hardy, deciduous shrub.—Bean Trefoil-tree, the *Cytisus Laburnum* of St. Ignatius, the fruit of a tree growing in the Philippine Islands, which is the *Ignatii amara*. This fruit was so named by the Jesuits, on account of its medicinal virtues being a specific remedy against poisons, diseases of the nerves, cramps, &c.

BEAN-COD (*Mar.*) a small fishing-boat, or pilot-boat, on the coasts of Portugal.

BEAN-FLY (*Ent.*) a beautiful fly of a pale purple colour, frequently found on bean-flowers.

BEA'R (*Zool.*) a wild beast covered with shaggy hair of a dark brown colour, and having hooked claws for climbing trees. It feeds on honey, insects, and carcases, lies torpid during the winter season, and is gravid six or seven months. It is also related of the she-bear, that she brings forth her young imperfect and deformed, and licks them into shape and perfection. The Black Bear, *Ursus arctos* of Linnæus, is a native of the North of Europe and Asia; but the Polar Bear, *Ursus maritimus*, lives within the Arctic Pole, and is frequently found on the ice-islands.

BEAR, *to sell a*, (*Com.*) to sell stock on the Stock Exchange which one has not.

BEAR (*Mar.*) a square piece of wood with pigs of iron ballast fastened to it for cleaning a ship's deck.

BEAR-*berry* (*Bot.*) the *Arbutus uva ursi* of Linnæus.

BEAR (*Astron.*) the name of two northern constellations, the one called the Great Bear, *Ursa major*, and the other the Little Bear, *Ursa minor*. [vide *Ursa*]

BEAR (*Her.*) this animal occurs frequently as a charge in coats of arms when it is borne *passant*, as in *fig.* 1. " He beareth, *or*, a bear passant, *sable*; by the name of *Fitzourse*: and *rampant*, as in *fig.* 2. " He beareth, *or*,

Fig. 1.  Fig. 2.  Fig. 3.

a bear rampant, *sable*, muzzled, *or*; by the name of *Barnard*. Also, bears' heads are borne in coat armour mostly erased, as in *fig.* 3. " *Argent*, a chevron between three bears' heads erased, *sable*, muzzled, *or*; by the name of *Pennarth*."—*Order of the Bear*, a military order instituted by Frederic II. in 1213. To the collar was attached a medal, on which was represented a bear raised on an eminence of earth.

BEAR-GARDEN (*Archæol.*) a place formerly set apart for the baiting of bears.

BEAR's *breech* (*Bot.*) or Brank Ursine, the *Acanthus spinosus* of Linnæus; a herb, supposed to be the *Mollis acanthus* of Virgil. From this herb is extracted a mucilage which is highly esteemed.—*Bear's ear*, the *Primula auricula*.—*Bear's foot*, the *Helleborus fœtidus*.

BEAR's HEAD (*Her.*) vide *Bear*.

To BEAR (*Mar.*) a term used to denote the situation or movements of a ship, or the persons in a ship. A place is said " To *bear*," i. e. To be, or be seen from a ship in a certain direction, as " The land's end bore E. N. E." A ship is said " To *bear* down upon the enemy," being to windward so as to approach the enemy by sailing large, or from the wind. " To *bear* in with the land," to steer towards it. " To *bear* in with the harbour," to sail into the harbour before the wind, or with the wind large. " To *bear* off," either to steer from the land, or to keep off from any weight, as a cask, boat, &c. when it is hoisting up from rubbing against the sides of the ship, &c. " To *bear* under another ship's lee," to come under the stern of another ship which was to the windward, and so give her the wind. " To *bear* up or away," to change the course of a ship, in order to make her sail before the wind; so called from the motion of the helm, which is borne up, or to windward. " To *bear* up round," to let the ship go between her two sheets directly before the wind. " The ship *bears*," which sinks too deep on the descent of her heavy burden. " The ship *bears* a good sail," when she sails upright in the water. " To *bear* ordnance," *i. e.* to carry great guns. " Bear a hand!" a command given to make haste, or be quick. " *Bear* up the helm," a command to the steersman to let the ship go more at large before the wind.

To BEAR (*Her.*) to have in one's coat of arms, that is, the respective charges, &c.

To BEAR (*Gunn.*) a piece of ordnance is said *to bear* when it lies right with the mark.

To BEAR (*Mech.*) timber is said to bear at its whole length when neither a wall nor post stands between its extremities; otherwise, it is said to bear according to the distance between the bearer and either end.

BEA'RD (*Bot.*) *barba*, a name for the parallel hairs in the pubescence: also for a tuft of stiff hairs terminating the leaves, as in the *Mesembryanthemum barbatum*; and with some botanists the lower lip of a ringent corolla is so called. Beard is, in common language, the name of the awn.

BEARD *of a horse* (*Vet.*) that part beneath the longer mandible on the outside and above the chin, which bears the curb of the bridle.

BEARD *of a letter* (*Print.*) the outer angle of the square shoulder of the shank, which reaches almost up to the face of the letter, and is commonly scraped off by the founder. —*Beard-gage*, an instrument for measuring this angle.

BEARD *of a comet* (*Astron.*) the rays which it emits in the direction in which it moves, in distinction from the tail, or the rays emitted from behind.

BEA'RDED (*Bot.*) *barbatus*, having parallel hairs, or tufts; an epithet for the leaves: also for the corolla, as in *Dianthus barbatus*; and for the nectary in the Iris, &c.

BEA'RDING (*Carp.*) chipping, planing, or otherwise diminishing any piece of timber from a given line, or curve, as the bearding of clamps, planksheers, &c.

BEA'RDLESS (*Bot.*) *imberbis*, without parallel hairs, or tufts; an epithet applied to the corollas, as in some species of the Iris, Gentiana, &c.

BEA'RER (*Com.*) the person carrying any thing.

BEARER (*Carp.*) the post, or wall, trimmed to a beam, to lessen its bearing.

BEARER (*Law*) a person bearing others down with litigation, &c. Stat. 4, Edw. 3.

BEARER (*Her.*) a person bearing a coat of arms in distinction from others by some colour or difference.

BEARER *of a bill* (*Com.*) the person in whose hands the bill is, and in favour of whom the last indorsement is made.

BEA'RING (*Mar.*) 1. The point of the compass that one place bears, or stands off, from another. 2. The situation of any distant object estimated with regard to the ship's position, that is, whether a-head, a-stern, or a-breast, &c.

BEARING (*Her.*) what fills an escutcheon, vide *Charge*.

BEARING (*Archit.*) the distance between the bearer and each end of the timber, as 12, 15, &c. feet bearing.

BEARING-CLAWS (*Sport.*) the foremost toes of a cock.

BEA'STS *of Chase* (*Law*) *Feræ campestres*, are five in number, namely, the buck, doe, fox, marten, and roe. *Manw. For. Laws*, pt. 1, &c.—*Beasts of the Forest*, otherwise called *Beasts of venery*, are the hart, hind, boar, and wolf. *Manw. For. Laws*, pt. 2, c. 4.—*Beasts and fowls of the warren*, are the hare, coney, pheasant, and partridge. *Reg. Orig.* 95, &c. *Co. Lit.* 233.

BEA'T (*Mil.*) from Lat. *batuo*, and Gr. *ϐατίω*, to tread; beating the drum as a signal. [vide *To beat*]

BEAT (*Mus.*) a grace-note marked thus ", or thus χ.

BEAT (*Cus.*) the walk, or round, which the watchman has to take at stated intervals.

To BEAT (*Mil.*) to give a signal by beat of drum, of which there are different kinds, namely, " To *beat* an alarm," to give notice of danger by beat of drum. " To *beat* a charge," to give notice to charge the enemy. " To *beat* the general," to give notice to the troops to march. " To *beat* the reveille," to give notice for leaving quarters. " To *beat* the tat-too," to give notice for retiring to quarters. " To *beat* the troop," to give notice for repairing to their colours. " To *beat* to arms," to give notice for the soldiers to repair to their arms. " To *beat* a parley," to give a signal for a conference with the enemy.

To BEAT (*Sport.*) or tap, is said of coneys or hares when they make a noise at rutting time.

To BEAT *upon the hand* (*Man.*) is said of a horse when it tosses up its nose, and shakes it all of a sudden, to avoid the subjection of the bridle.—To *beat* the dust, is when a horse, at each time or motion, does not take in way or ground enough with his fore-legs.

BEATASSI (*Theol.*) an order or sect of religions among the Turks, to which all the Janizaries belonged.

BEA'TERS (*Print.*) the ink-balls with which the pressmen beat the letters in the chase, or form.

BEATERS (*Mech.*) is the name of those who beat gold.

BEATING *Time* (*Mus.*) that motion of the hand or foot by which the performers themselves, or some person presiding, mark and regulate the measure of the movements. If the time be common or equal, the *beating* is also equal, two down and two up; but when the time is triple, the beating is two down and one up.

BEATING *in of the flanks* (*Vet.*) a disease which consists of an abscess in the loins, with a little pulsation.

BEATING (*Mech.*) *among Bookbinders*, is the process of beating the quires with a hammer; *among the Paperworks*, it is beating the paper.

BEATING (*Mar.*) the act of making a progress against the wind.

BEATING *the wind* (*Archæol.*) a practice, in former times, at a trial by battle, when one of the parties failed to appear, for the other to flourish his sword in the air, which was called *beating the wind*.

BEA'TINGS (*Mus.*) the regular pulsative heavings or swellings of sound produced in an organ by pipes of the same key, when they are not exactly in unison.

BEA'TS *in a clock* or *watch* (*Mech.*) the strokes made by the pallets or fangs of the spindle, or of the pads in a royal pendulum.

BEA'VER (*Zool.*) the *Castor* of Linnæus; an amphibious fourfooted animal, that lives on the banks of rivers and unfrequented lakes, and is remarkable, like the otter, for its skill in building its house. It walks slow, swims dexterously, is very cleanly, eats sitting on its haunches, and conveys its food to its mouth with the fore-paws. The female has four teats, is gravid four months, and seldom brings forth more than two young. This animal is valued both for the fur on its skin, and for the oil which it yields, called *Castor-oil*.—Beaver Rat, the *Mus Coypus* of Linnæus, which inhabits Chili.

BEAVER (*Her.*) this animal is painted as a charge in a coat of arms in a window of New Inn Hall, London, as " *Argent*, a beaver erected *sable* devouring a fish proper, armed *gules*."

BEAVER (*Mil.*) that part of the helmet which defends the sight, and opens in the front.

BEAVER (*Mech.*) the best sort of hat, which is made of the beaver.

BEAVER, or *Beaver-skin* (*Com.*) the fur and skin of the Beaver, or Castor: they are of two sorts, the *coat beaver*, worn by savages as a garment; and the *parchment beaver*, which is as it is taken from the animal.

BEA'U PLEADER (*Law*) *pulchre placitando*, in French *beau-plaider*, to plead fairly; a writ upon the statute of Marlbridge, whereby it is enacted, that neither in the circuit of justices, nor in counties, hundreds, or courts baron, any fines shall be taken for " Fair-pleading," *i. e.* not pleading fairly.

BECABU'NGA (*Bot.*) the *Veronica becabunga* of Linnæus.

BECA'LMED (*Mar.*) an epithet expressing the state of a ship which lies still for want of wind.

BECA'RRE (*Mus.*) French for a Natural. [vide *Natural*]

BE'CKETS (*Mar.*) large hooks, or such things as are used to confine loose ropes, tackles, oars, or spars.

BED (*Mech.*) in Saxon *bedde*, the place for lying in, which is of various kinds, according to the materials of which it is made; as a feather bed, down bed, flock bed, and straw bed; or according to the make of the bedstead, a pallet bed, canopy bed, truckle bed, couch bed, &c.

BED *mouldings* (*Archit.*) the members of a cornice that is placed below the corona.

BED *of snakes* (*Zool.*) a knot of young snakes.

BED (*Gunn.*) a thick plank which lies under a piece of ordnance on the carriage.—*Bed* or *stool for a mortar*, a thick and strong planking hollowed out to receive a mortar.—*Royal beds*, or *coehorn beds*, carriages for a royal mortar, the diameter of which is from 4·6 to 5·6 inches.

BED *for the cask* (*Mar.*) a flat thick piece of timber lodged under the quarters of casks which are stowed in a ship's hold.—*Bed of a barrel screw*, the main piece, through which the puppets work.—*Bed of a bowsprit*, the place of greatest diameter in the bowsprits.—*Bed of a river*, the bottom of a channel in which the stream or current usually flows.

BED (*Hort.*) the place parted off and disposed for flowers.

BED (*Mason.*) a range or course of stones or bricks. The point of the bed is the mortar between two stones placed over each other.—*Bed of a mill*, the nether stone.

BED (*Min.*) a stratum or layer of any earth or stone. The different strata or layers are disposed one above another.

TO BED (*Hunt.*) to hedge in a particular place, which is said of a roe.

TO BED (*Print.*) to lay or fix the stone of the press either on paper, bran, or plaster of Paris.

BED-CHAMBER, *Lords of the* (*Polit.*) twelve noblemen at the British Court, who attend each a month in rotation, and lie in the bed-chamber of the King.

BEDE'GUA (*Bot.*) a species of thistle.

BEDEGU'AR (*Bot.*) the spongy excrescences of the *Rosa Sylvestris*; also a disease in plants, arising from insects, which deposit their eggs in a heap in the apex of a bud.

BE'DE-HOUSE (*Ecc.*) an hospital or alms-house for bede's people, or poor people, who were to pray for their benefactors.

BE'DEL (*Law*) or Beadle, an officer or cryer of a court, an officer to attend at church, an officer of the university, and an officer of the forest; also an officer belonging to any company or corporate body.

BE'DELARY (*Law*) the jurisdiction of a bedel.

BEDE'NGIAR (*Bot.*) Love apples.

BE'DEREPE (*Archæol.*) a service of certain tenants to reap their landlord's corn.

BE'DMAKER (*Cus.*) a servant in the University, whose office it is to wait upon the students.

BE'DMOULDING (*Archit.*) vide *Bed*.

BE'DRIDDEN (*Med.*) confined to one's bed from age or sickness, so as never to be able to leave it.

BEE (*Ent.*) a well-known insect, the *Apis* of Linnæus [vide *Apis*] which carries on the operations of making wax and honey in baskets made for them, called *hives*, or *beehives*, which, when situated in a particular spot, are called an apiary. Bees begin to *swarm*, i. e. to form new colonies, in May or June, according to the state of the weather. In a mild season they swarm much earlier than usual. The swarm commonly consists of a female, called the *queen*, as in *fig.* 1, who is distinguished by her size; the *drones*, as in *fig.* 2, who are supposed to be males that eat, but do

Fig. 1.   *Fig.* 2.   *Fig.* 3.

not work or contribute to the common stock; and the *mules*, or *common bees*, as in *fig.* 3, who are of neither sex, and do the whole work of the hive. The queen bee lives in a larger cell than the rest, called the *royal cell*, where she deposits her eggs, which, in the process of hatching, change to the state of a maggot, a chrysalis, and a bee, after the manner of other insects. The food of the maggot is supposed to be the pastelike substance found in the hives, which is called *bee-bread*.

BEE (*Her.*) this insect is made the emblem of industry and good government in heraldry, and is represented in coat armour, as in *fig*. 1. " He beareth *azure* three bees *volant*

Fig. 1.   *Fig.* 2.

en arriere, by the name of Bye." The *beehive* is also represented, as in *fig*. 2. " He beareth *argent* a beehive, with bees diversely volant, *sable*, by the name of Rooe of Macclesfield."

BEE-FLOWER (*Bot.*) the *Orchis* of Linnæus.

BEECH (*Bot.*) or beech-tree, in Saxon bece, or boe, the *fagus* of Linnæus, a glandiferous tree, raised from seeds, and mostly managed like the oak. The two principal sorts are the Mountain-Beech and the Campestoul, or Wild Beech, which grow to a considerable stature, though the soil be barren. The fruit of this tree is good for fattening swine.

BEEF *à-la-mode* (*Cook.*) beef well beaten, larded, and stewed with lemon, pepper, &c.

BEE'HIVE (*Mech.*) vide *Bee*.

BEELE (*Mech.*) a pick-axe.

BEE'NEL (*Bot.*) an evergreen tree of Malabar, from the leaves of which a liniment is made for the head-ache. *Raii Hist. Plant.*

BEER (*Cook.*) a drink made of malt and hops, by the process of brewing. It is of three kinds, strong beer, ale, and table beer, or small beer.

BEER (*Mech.*) a name given by weavers to 19 ends of yarn running all together out of the trough its whole length.

BEES (*Archit.*) pieces of elm plank bolted to the end of the bowsprit.

BEE'SHA (*Bot.*) a species of Cambu, a decoction of which is good for obstructions.

BEE'STINGS (*Husband.*) the first milk of a cow after calving.

BEET (*Bot.*) a garden herb which is thick and fleshy, the *Beta* of Linnæus.—*Beetrave*, a *beet raddish*, a sort of red beet.

BEE'TLE (*Ent.*) the *Scarabæus* of Linnæus, a well-known insect, produced from the larvæ or grubs that live under ground; it has six feet, and is annular, and hairy at one end. The beetle lives on dry decayed wood, roots of plants, &c.

BEETLE (*Mech.*) a large wooden hammer for driving palisades.

BE'GGAR (*Com.*) one who follows the trade of a beggar.

BE'GLERBEG (*Polit.*) the chief governor of a Turkish province, who has all the inferior officers under his command. The sultan gives each beglerbeg three ensigns, as a mark of royalty.

BE'GMA (*Med.*) βηγμα, from βηξ, a cough; a cough, with what is brought up by expectoration. *Foes. Œconom. Hippocrat.*

BEGO'NIA (*Bot.*) a genus of plants, named by Plumier after Mons. Begon, Class 21 *Monoecia*, Order 7 *Polyandria*.

Generic Characters. CAL. none.—COR. *petals* four.—STAM. *filaments* numerous; *anthers* oblong.—PIST. *germ* inferior; *styles* bifid; *stigmas* six.—PER. *capsule* in most three-cornered.

Species. The species are mostly shrubs or perennials.

BEGU'E (*Vet.*) an old term for the natural mark in a horse's mouth, by which his age may be known.

BEHA'VING *as heir* (*Law*) the same as *gestio pro hærede*.

BEHA'VIOUR (*Law*) vide *Good Behaviour*.

BE'HEMOTH (*Bibl.*) בהמות, an animal described in Job xl. 15. which Bochart supposes to be the same as the river-horse.

BE'HEN (*Bot.*) or *been*, from the Arabic *behen*, or *albehen*, a plant, the root of which is medicinal. There are three sorts of Behen, namely *Behen album*, the White Behen of the ancients, and the *Centaurea behen* of Linnæus.—*Behen rubrum*, Sea Lavender, the *Statice Lemonium*.—*Behen officinarum*, the *Cucubalus behen*. The roots of these plants are cordial and cephalic. *J. Bauh. Hist. Plant.*; *C. Bauh. Pin.; Park. Theat.; Raii Hist. Plant.; Tournef. Instit.; Boerhaav. Ind.*

BEJA'RIA (*Bot.*) a genus of plants, named by Mutis after Bejar, a Spanish botanist, Class 11 *Dodecandria*, Order 1 *Monogynia*.
  Generic Characters. CAL. *perianth* one-leaved.—COR. *petals* seven.—STAM. *filaments* fourteen; *anthers* oblong.—PIST. *germ* superior; *style* columnar; *stigma* thickish.—PER. *berry* juiceless; *seeds* numerous.
  Species. The species are shrubs, and natives of Grenada, Florida, &c.

BEID-EL-O'SSAR, an Ægyptian plant described by Prosper Alpinus, abounding with a milky juice, in which when leather is macerated the hair falls off.

BEI'GE-SERGE (*Com.*) a serge of Poitou, which is black, grey, or tawny.

BEI'T-OLLAH (*Theol.*) literally signifies in the Arabic the house of God, and is applied by the Mahometans to the temple at Mecca, whither the pilgrims resort.

BEJU'CO (*Bot.*) the *Hippocratea comosa* of Linnæus.

BEJU'IO (*Bot.*) a kind of bean in Carthagena.

BE'KAH (*Ant.*) a Jewish coin, worth about 1s. 1½d. of our money.

BE'LAC (*Med.*) a particular kind of bark of Madagascar, slightly bitter and astringent.

BELA'NDRE (*Mar.*) French for a flat-bottomed vessel with masts, sails, &c. which is used in Flanders for the conveyance of goods.

TO BELA'Y (*Mar.*) to fasten a rope, particularly the running rigging, by winding it several times round the cleats, &c.

BELA'YING-PINS (*Mar.*) wooden-pins on which the ropes are belayed or wound.

TO BELE'AGUER (*Mil.*) to besiege.

BELE'CTION *mouldings* (*Carpent.*) those which surround the pannels, and project without the surface of the framing in doors.

BELELA'IS (*Com.*) a species of Bengal silk resembling taffety.

BELEMNI'TES (*Min.*) from βελος, a dart; a kind of stone resembling an arrow in shape; it is sometimes whitish, and sometimes of a gold colour. *Gess. de Lapid.; Aldrov. Mus. Metall.*

BELEMNOI'DES (*Anat.*) from βελος, a dart, and ιδος, the form; a name for the styloid process of the temporal bone.

BE'LFRY (*Ant.*) *belfredum, berpedum, belfragum, brarfreit*, in French *beffroy*, a warlike machine, in form of a tower, formerly used in sieges, under the shelter of which they could fire upon the enemy. It was also employed as a tower.

BELFRY (*Archit.*) that part of a steeple in which the bells are hung, but more particularly that part of the timber work from which the bells are suspended.

BELFRY (*Mar.*) the shelter under which the ship's bell is suspended.

BE'LI (*Bot.*) a tall fruit-tree, not unlike the quince, the *Crateva marmelos* of Linnæus. *J. Bauh. Hist. Plant.*

BE'LIC (*Her.*) vide *Gules*.

BELI'LIA (*Bot.*) an Indian berry-bearing shrub; the *Mussenda frondosa* of Linnæus, a decoction of which is cooling. *Raii Hist. Plant.*

BELL (*Mus.*) the well-known metallic machine which is ranked among musical instruments; it consists of three parts, the *body*, or *barrel*, the *clapper*, and the *ear*, or *cannon*.—*Bell metal*, the metal employed in the manufacture of bells, which usually consists of three parts of copper and one of tin.—*Bell of a horn*, the wide open part, from which the sound issues.

BELL (*Her.*) vide *Bells*.

BELL (*Mar.*) vide *Bells*.

BELL *of a capital* (*Archit.*) a circular moulding, otherwise called the *cobel*.

BELL, *book, and candle-light* (*Ecc.*) the name of an imprecation practised formerly in the Christian church in the 10th and 11th centuries upon the excommunication of a person. It was so called because the people were summoned by the sound of the bell to attend the ceremony of hearing the curse read out of the book by the minister, standing in a balcony, when he extinguished the candle or lamp that he held by throwing it on the ground, thereby denoting that in this manner the excommunicated person would be extinguished if he did not repent.

BELL (*Man.*) a name for the horse in a team who bears the bell.

BE'LL-FLOWER (*Bot.*) the common name for the *Campanula*.—Bellshaped, *campanulatus*, an epithet for the corolla when it swells or bellies, but without any tube, as in the Campanulas, Canterbury bells, &c. also applied to the calyxes and nectaries.—*Bell Pear*, a pear in the shape of a gourd.

BELLADO'NNA (*Bot.*) Deadly Nightshade; the *Atropa belladonna* of Linnæus.

BELLA'TRIX (*Ant.*) a galley for war.

BELLATRIX (*Astron.*) a glittering star, of the 2d magnitude, in the left shoulder of Orion; so called from *bellum* war, over which it was supposed to preside.

BE'LLED (*Her.*) an epithet in blazoning for a hawk, to whose feet bells are affixed.

BELLES LE'TTRES (*Lit.*) a French term, now generally used to imply polite literature.

BE'LL-FOUNDER (*Mech.*) one who casts bells for churches, &c.

BELLIDIA'STRUM (*Bot.*) a species of the *Dronicum* of Linnæus.

BELLIDIOI'DES (*Bot.*) the *Chrysanthemum balsamita* of Linnæus.

BELLI'GERENT (*Mil.*) an epithet for any country which is in a state of warfare; in which case it is called a *belligerent* power.

BE'LLIS (*Bot.*) from Lat. *Bellus*, pretty; in Fr. *Marguerite*, Daisy, a genus of plants, Class 19 *Syngenesia*, Order 2 *Polygamia Superflua*.
  Generic Characters. CAL. *common* hemispheric.—COR. *compound* radiate.—STAM. *filaments* five; *anther* cylindric.—PIST. *germ* ovate; *style* filiform; *stigmas* two.—PER. none; *seeds* solitary; *receptacle* naked.
  Species. The species are—*Bellis perennis scapo nudo, &c.* seu *sylvestris minor*, Perennial, or Common Daisy, a perennial, native of Britain.—*Bellis annua*, seu *Leucanthemum annuum, &c.* Annual Daisy, an annual, native of Sicily, &c.—*Bellis sylvestris*, seu *scapo nudo*, &c. a perennial, native of Italy.

BELLIS, the species is the—*Anthemis cola*, the *Athanasia annua*, the *Calendula nudiculis*, the *Crysanthemum frutescens, serotinum, abratum, leucanthemum, &c.*; the *Cotula coronifolia*, the *Doronicum Bellidiastrum*, and the *Saponaria Bellidifolia* of Linnæus. *Clus. Hist. Plant. Rar.; J. Bauh. Hist. Plant.; Raii Hist. Plant.; Commel. Hort. Med.; Pluken. Almagest. Botan.*

BE'LLIUM (*Bot.*) a genus of plants, Class 19 *Syngenesia*, Order 2 *Polygamia superflua*.
Generic Characters. CAL. common simple.—COR. compound radiated.—STAM. *filaments* four; *anther* cylindric.—PIST. *germ* turbinate; *style* filiform; *stigma* bifid.—PER. none; *seeds* turbinate; *receptacle* naked.
Species. The species are the—*Bellium bellidioides*, &c. *droseræfolia stolonibus*, &c. *annua minima, maritima minima*, &c. seu *foliis parvis*, &c. an annual, native of Italy.—*Bellium minutum, Pectis minuta*, &c. seu *Bellis cretica*, &c. an annual, native of the East.

BELLO'CULUS (*Min.*) from *bellus*, fair, and *oculus*, the eye; a precious stone resembling the eye, and formerly supposed to be useful in its disorders.

BE'LLON (*Med.*) the Devonshire colic, or *colica Pictonum*.

BELLONA'RIA (*Bot.*) from *Bellona*, the goddess; a herb which, if eaten, makes people mad, and act outrageously.

BELLONA'RII (*My.*) priests of Bellona, who cut and maimed themselves in their mad fits. *Tertull. Apolog.* c. 9; *Lact. ant.* l. 1, c. 21.

BELLO'NIA (*Bot.*) a genus of plants, named by Plumier after Pierre Belon, a naturalist; Class 5 *Pentandria*, Order 1 *Monogynia*.
Generic Characters. CAL. *perianth* one-leaved.—COR. monopetalous.—STAM. *filaments* five; *anthers* erect.—PIST. *germ* inferior; *style* subulate; *stigma* acute.—PER. *capsule* turbinate-ovate; *seeds* numerous.
Species. The two species are—*Bellonia aspera, foliis ovalis*, &c. *frutescens*, &c. a shrub, native of America.—*Bellonia spinosa*, &c. a shrub, native of Hispaniola. *Linn. Spec. Plant.*

BE'LLOWS *of an organ* (*Mus.*) the pneumatic part of the machine, by which it is supplied with wind.

BELLOWS (*Her.*) a machine for blowing, the invention of which is ascribed by Strabo to Anacharsis. It occurs sometimes as a charge in coats of arms, as he beareth, "*Argent*, three pair of bellows, *sable*, by the name of Scipton."

BELLS, *Baptism of* (*Ecc.*) a ceremony, in the Romish church, of consecrating bells by sprinkling them with holy water and blessing them, after which they were supposed capable of dispelling evil spirits by their sound.

BELLS (*Her.*) are denominated church bells in coats of arms where they are used as a charge, as he beareth, "*Sable*, a *fesse, ermine*, between three church bells, *argent*, by the name of Bell of Norfolk." Crest, "A falcon rising, *argent*, *jessed* and *belled*, *or*, on his breast an ermine."

BELLS (*Mar.*) half hours of the watch, which are marked by striking the bell at the end of each.

BE'LLUÆ (*Zool.*) the sixth order of animals, Class *Mammalia*, having their fore-feet obtuse, truncate, and feet hoofed. It contains the following genera:—*Equus*, fore-teeth, upper six, lower six; tusks solitary; teats two, inguinal.—*Hippopotamus*, fore-teeth, each jaw; tusks solitary; feet hoofed.—*Tapir*, fore-teeth, each jaw ten; tusks none; hoofs on the fore-feet four, hind-feet three.—*Sus*, fore-teeth, upper four, lower six; tusks, upper two, lower two; snout prominent; feet mostly cloven.

BELLU'TA (*Bot.*) the *Crinum Asiaticum* of Linnæus.

BE'LLY (*Anat.*) vide *Alvus* and *Venter*.—*Belly of a muscle*, the large fleshy part, in contradistinction to the smaller tendinous extremities.

BELLY (*Archit.*) the hollow part of compass timber, the round part of which is called the *back*.

BELLY-*band* (*Man.*) the girt that goes under the belly of the shaft horse, in a carriage, &c.

BELLY *of an instrument* (*Mus.*) the smooth thin board over which the strings are distended, as the belly of a harpsichord, violin, &c.

BE'LLYING (*Bot.*) or bellied, *ventricosus*, swelling out in the middle; an epithet for the perianth, as in *Æsculus*; for the corolla, as in *Digitalis*; so also for the spike, the stipe, &c.

BEL-META'LO *di voce* (*Mus.*) an Italian expression for a clear and brilliant toned *soprano* voice.

BELOMA'NCY (*Ant.*) βελομαντεία, from βέλος, a dart, and μαντεία, divination; a sort of divination, by means of arrows, which was in practice among the Scythians.

BE'LONE (*Ich.*) from βελόνη, a needle; a kind of fish, with a long slender body like a needle, a species of the *Esox* of Linnæus. *Aristot. Hist. Anim.* l. 6, c. 8; *Plin.* l. 9, c. 51.

BELT (*Mil.*) a girdle to hang a sword, or other weapon in, belð, belt, belte, Sax.; belte, Du.; belte, Sw.; all of which come immediately from the Lat. *balteus*. They are of different sorts, as—*Sword-belt*, a leathern strap in which a sword hangs.—*Shoulder-belt*, a broad leathern belt which goes over the shoulder, and to which the pouch is fixed; it is also called *cross-belt*, and should be made of stout smooth buff.—*Waist-belt*, a leathern strap fixed round the waist, by which a sword or bayonet is suspended.—*Belts* were called, by the ancient writers, by different names, as *Zona cingulum, reminiculum, ringa*, and *baldrellus*.

BELT (*Her.*) a badge, or mark of the knightly order given to a person when he was raised to knighthood.

BELT (*Vet.*) a distemper in sheep.

BELT (*Med.*) a bandage applied round the body; in this manner mercury is sometimes employed.

BELT (*Astron.*) vide *Belts*.

BELT (*Mason.*) a range or course of stones or bricks projecting from the rest, which may be either plain or fluted, &c.

BE'LTEIN (*Cus.*) or *Beltane*, from the Gaelic and Irish *beal-tine*, or *Bel's fire*, that is, the sun, *Bel* being a name of the sun among the Gauls; a festival celebrated, in Ireland, on the 21st of June, the summer solstice, when fires were made on the tops of the hills, and every member of the family was made to pass through the fire to ensure good luck.

BELTS (*Astron.*) *fasciæ*, two zones or girdles round the planet Jupiter, which are observed to be sometimes broader, and sometimes narrower, and not always to occupy the same part of the planet's disc.

BELTS (*Geog.*) straits near the Sound which lead from the Baltic into the German ocean.

BELU'CDERE (*Archit.*) a turret, or some part of an edifice raised above the rest for the purpose of extending the prospect of the country around.

BELU'LCUM (*Surg.*) from βέλος, a dart; an instrument for extracting darts.

BELU'TTA (*Bot.*) vide *Bellutta*.

BELZO'INUM (*Chem.*) vide *Benzoinum*.

BE'MA (*Ecc.*) a sort of festival, observed by the Manichees, in honour of Manes, who was slain. *August. Cont. Faust.* l. 18, c. 4.

BE'MBEX (*Ent.*) a division of the genus *Vespa*, according to Fabricius, comprehending the insects of this tribe, which have the tongue inflected, five-cleft.

BEM-CURI'NI (*Bot.*) the *Justicia adhotoda* of Linnæus.

BE'MOL (*Mus.*) another name for B flat. [vide *B*]

BEN *Tamra* (*Bot.*) the Egyptian bean.

BE'NAR (*Mil.*) French for a four-wheeled carriage, which is used to carry stones in the construction of fortified places.

BE'NATH (*Med.*) Arabic for small pustules produced by sweating in the night.

BENCH (*Law*) a seat of justice, as the King's Bench at

Westminster.—*Bench, King's*, a prison belonging to the court of King's Bench.

BENCH (*Mech.*) a particular tool fitted up with a hook, a screw, &c. for laying and fastening boards to it so that they may be planed, &c.—*Bench of a spinning wheel*, or *the reel*, the stool to which the supporters of the wheel, or reel, are fixed.

BENCHER (*Law*) a lawyer of the first rank in the inns of court.

BEND (*Her.*) an honourable ordinary formed by diagonal lines drawn from the dexter, or right corner at top, to the sinister base, or left corner at bottom, which is supposed to represent a shoulder belt or scarf, and to show the wearer to be valiant in war. The content of the bend when charged is the third part of the field, but uncharged it contains only the fifth. The bend taken absolutely signifies the dexter-bend, as in *fig.* 1. "He beareth, *argent*, a bend, *sable*; name Erderswick, of Staffordshire." Otherwise it is called a *bend sinister*, as in *fig.* 2. "He beareth, *gules*, a bend sinister, by the name of Wildestein." Bends are composed of either plain or crooked lines; those composed of crooked lines are engrailed, wavy, crenelle, flory, &c. [vide *Engrailed, &c.*]

Fig. 1. Fig. 2. Fig. 3. Fig. 4.

The *bend* has four different diminutives; namely, the *bendlet*, the *garter*, the *cost*, or *cottise*, and the *ribbon*. [vide *Bendlet, &c.*] It is also borne in three different forms; namely, in-bend, per-bend, and bendy.—*In-bend* is when a charge is borne sloping from the dexter chief to the sinister base, after the manner of a bend, as in *fig.* 3. "He beareth, *argent*, a wyvern volant in-bend, *sable*; name Raynon."—*Per-bend* is when the charge or field is divided by a line drawn after the manner of a bend, as in *fig.* 4. "He beareth, parted by bend crenelle, *pearl* and *ruby*, i. e. *argent* and *gules*." These were the arms of the Right Honourable Robert Boyle, the philosopher.—*Bendy*, or *Bendwise*, vide *Bendy*.

BEND (*Mar.*) 1. The knot by which one rope is fastened to another, or to an anchor, varying in name according to the bend by which the knot is formed, as the *fisherman's bend*, the *carrick-bend*, the *sheet-bend*, &c. To make a carrick-bend, lay the ends of a rope bend, as *a* and *b* in the annexed figure, then pass it through the bight in *d*, and up through the bight *c*. 2. The small rope used to confine the clench of a cable. 3. The thickest and strongest planks in the ship's side, on which men set their feet in climbing up.

TO BEND (*Mech.*) from the Saxon binban, to be; the reducing a body to a curved or crooked form. The bending of boards, planks, &c. is effected by means of heat, whether by boiling or otherwise.

TO BEND (*Mar.*) to fasten one rope to another.—" To *bend* the cable," to clinch, or tie it to the ring of an anchor. " To *bend* two cables," to tie them together so as to make their own ends fast on themselves. " To *bend* a sail," to fasten it to a yard or stay.

BENDIDI'A (*Ant.*) Βενδίδια, a Thracian festival in honour of Diana, who was called Βενδις, by the Thracians. *Strab.* l. 9; *Procl. in Tim.*; *Hesychius*.

BENDING (*Mech.*) vide *To Bend*.

BE'NDLET (*Her.*) one of the diminutives of the bend, which is in size half the breadth of the bend. Bendlets are sometimes borne in an unusual manner, called *enhanced*, i. e. lifted up to a place in which they are not usually borne, as "He beareth, *argent*, three bendlets, *gules*; name Byron, of Nottinghamshire.

BE'NDY (*Her.*) bendwise, or bendways; an epithet for a thing that is divided four, six, or more parts drawn sloping like a bend, as in the annexed figure. "He beareth bendy wavy of six, *argent* and *azure*; name Playters, of Suffolk." A border is also borne bendy.

BE'NE (*Mus.*) vide *Bene placito*.

BENE'APED (*Mar.*) an epithet expressing the state of a ship when the water does not flow high enough to bring her off the ground, out of a dock, or over a bar.

BENEDI'CTINES (*Ecc.*) an order of monks founded by St. Benedict, whose habit was black. They were divided into several congregations.

BENEDI'CTION *generale* (*Mil.*) an invocation made to God by the chaplain of the French army on the eve of an engagement.—*Benediction de Drapeaux*, a consecration of colours.

BENEDI'CTUS (*Med.*) Blessed; an epithet for several compositions on account of their supposed excellence, as *Benedicta aqua*, for lime-water; and also an infusion of *Crocus metallorum*, &c. *Benedictum laxativum*, for Rhubarb. *Benedictum vinum* for antimonial wine.

BENEDICTUS *lapis* (*Alch.*) the philosopher's stone.

BE'NEFICE (*Law*) *beneficium*; a grant of land from a lord to his followers, held at first *ex mero beneficio*, of the donor, but afterwards converted into a perpetual hereditary tenure. 2. Any ecclesiastical living or promotion, but particularly rectories and vicarages. They are either elective or donative. 13 R. 2, st. 2, c. 2; 3 *Instit.* 155; *Spelm. de Feud.* c. 21; *Blount. Anc. Ten.*

BENEFICIA'RII (*Ant.*) 1. Soldiers who were promoted to a higher rank, at first *beneficio*, i. e. by the favour of the tribunes, afterwards by that of other magistrates; wherefore we read in inscriptions of the *Beneficiarius Consulis, Proconsulis, &c.* Liv. l. 9, c. 30; *Veget.* l. 2, c. 7; *Buleng. de Imp. Roman.* l. 6, c. 80; *Ursat. de Not. Roman. apud Græv. Thes. Antiq.* tom. 11, p. 570, &c. 2. Soldiers who were discharged from military duty with a pension allowed to them. *Cæs. de Bell. Civ.* l. 3, c. 88; *Fest. de Verb. Signif.*

BENEFI'CIO *primo ecclesiastico habendo*, a writ from the king to the chancellor to bestow the benefice that shall fall in the king's gift upon this or that man. *Reg. Orig.* 307.

BE'NEFIT *of Clergy* (*Law*) a privilege formerly peculiar to clerks, but in after times made common to laymen, who were convicted of certain crimes, as manslaughter and the like. The mode of obtaining this privilege was thus: the ordinary, his commissioner, or deputy, gives the prisoner at the bar a Latin book, in a black Gothic character, and puts him to read a verse or two; then, if he say *legit ut clericus*, " he reads like a clergyman or scholar," he is only burnt in the hand and set free, for the first time; otherwise he must suffer death.

BENEFIT *societies*, vide *Friendly Societies*.

BENEFIT (*Com.*) a term used at the theatre for the profit of one or more nights, which is given to an actor or a poet.

BENEOLE'NTIA (*Med.*) sweet-smelling medicines.

BENE PLA'CITO (*Mus.*) Italian for *at pleasure*; a term denoting that the performer is at liberty to exercise his taste.

BE'NERTH (*Law*) an ancient service rendered by the tenant to his lord, with his plough and cart. *Lamb. Itin. Co. Lit.* 86.

BENE'VOLENCE (*Law*) a voluntary contribution from the

4

subject to the king, which grew from the time of Henry the Fourth's days.

BENEVOLE'NTIA *regis habenda* (*Law*) the form of purchasing the king's favour, in ancient fines and submissions, to be restored to estate, title, or place.

BENG (*Med.*) a name among the Mahometans for the leaves of hemp made into pills or a conserve, which possess an exhilarating power.

BENGAL QUI'NCE (*Bot.*) the fruit of the *Crateva marmelos* of Linnæus.

BENGI-EI'RI (*Bot.*) the name of an Indian evergreen.

BE'NJAMIN (*Bot.*) vide *Benzoin*.—Benjamin tree, the *Styrax benzoin* of Linnæus.

BENINGA'NIO (*Bot.*) a fruit growing in the bay of St. Augustine, of the size of a lemon, and grateful to the taste.

BENI'GN *disease* (*Med.*) a favourable disease, unattended with dreadful symptoms.

BENMARCI'TO (*Mus.*) Italian for well-marked; an epithet applied to the performance when it must be clear and pointed.

BE'NNET (*Bot.*) or Herb Bennet, *Benedicta herba*, the *Geum urbanum* of Linnæus, a perennial, so called because of its supposed medicinal virtues.

BE'NT-GRASS (*Bot.*) the *Agrostis* of Linnæus, a perennial.

BENVENU'E (*Print.*) i. e. welcome, from the French *bien* and *venir*, to come; a custom among printers for every new workman to pay a certain sum upon first going to the chapel, i. e. the printing-office.

BE'NZOATE (*Chem.*) a salt formed by the combination of Benzoic acid with alkalies, earths, or metallic oxides.

BE'NZOE (*Chem.*) the same as *Benzoin*.

BENZO'IC A'CID (*Chem.*) the acid produced by subliming Benzoin.

BE'NZOIN (*Bot.*) a species of the *Laurus* and the *Styrax* of Linnæus.

BENZOIN (*Chem.*) *Benzoinum, Benzoe, Belzoe, Asa dulcis*, a gum of an agreeable and fragrant smell, produced by incision, from an Indian tree, the *Styrax Benzoin* of Linnæus. The best is hard, solid, shining, and transparent; being of a warming, drying, discussing, and dissolving nature. The two principal sorts are the true Benzoin, and Benzoin in tears.—True Benzoin is of a yellowish gold colour, a highly aromatic smell, but without any taste.—Benzoin in tears, or *Benzoinum amygdaloides*, is a clear transparent mass, of a reddish colour, mixed with whitish tears, resembling almonds. The tincture of Magistery and flowers of Benzoin are particularly good for the lungs, and also for obstructions.

BENZOI'NI *tinctura* (*Med.*) Tincture of Benzoin, made by digesting Benzoin in spirits of wine, a cosmetic. [vide *Lac virginis*]—*Benzoini flores*, Flowers of Benzoin, or the gum sublimed and purified, which is a fine pectoral, now called Benzoic Acid.—*Benzoini oleum*, Essential oil of Benzoin, the oil which rises after the flowers are mixed with a little acid.—*Benzoini magisterium*, Magistery of Benzoin, the gum deposited on mixing the tincture with water, that is, the resinous without the saline part of the gum.

BER (*Bot.*) an Indian tree, the fruit of which is like jujel.

BE'RAMS (*Com.*) a coarse calico made at Surat.

BE'RBERIS (*Bot.*) Barberry, or Pipperidge bush, a genus of plants, Class 6 *Hexandria*, Order 1 *Monogynia*, the fruit of which is very cooling and restringent.
Generic Characters. CAL. *perianth* six-leaved.—COR. *petals* six; *nectary* two, small.—STAM. *filaments* six; *anthers* two.—PIST. *germ* cylindric; *style* none; *stigma* orbiculate.—PER. *berry* cylindric; *seeds* two.
Species. The species are shrubs—*Berberis vulgaris-racemosis, &c. pedunculis, &c. floribus, &c. spinis, &c. dumetorum, Crespinus*, seu *Oxycantha Galeni*, Common Berberry.—*Berberis Cretica*, seu *Lycium Creticum*, seu *Cretan*, or Box-leaved Berberry.

BE'RBIAGE (*Archæol.*) a sort of tenure mentioned by Blount.

BERBICA'RIA (*Ant.*) a sheep-down, or ground to feed sheep. *Leg. Alfredi. Mon. Angl.*

BE'RCARY (*Archæol.*) *Berquarium*, in French *Berquere*; a fold or inclosure for sheep, probably contracted from *berbicaria*: hence *berbicus*, a ram; *berbica*, a ewe; *caro berbicina*, mutton.

BERCE'AU (*Archit.*) French for a full-arched vault.

BERE'ANS (*Ecc.*) a sect of seceders from the Scotch kirk.

BERE'DRIAS (*Med.*) an ointment described by Aetius. *Tetrab.* 4, serm. 4, c. 113.

BEREFELLA'RII (*Archæol.*) seven churchmen so called, anciently belonging to the church of St. John Beverley.

BEREFRE'TT (*Archæol.*) a large wooden tower.

BERENI'CE (*Chem.*) a name for Amber.

Berenice's *Hair* (*Astron.*) vide *Coma Berenices*.

BERENGE'RIANS (*Ecc.*) a sect of heretics in the eleventh century, the followers of one Berenger, who denied the real presence.

BERENI'CIUM (*Chem.*) a sort of nitre mentioned by Galen and others.

BERETI'NUS *fructus* (*Bot.*) a fruit found by Francis Drake's sailors in the Malaccas.

BE'RGAMO (*Com.*) a coarse tapestry, manufactured from several sorts of spun thread, supposed to derive its name from the town Bergamo, where it was said to be invented.

BE'RGAMOT (*Bot.*) in French *Bergamotte*, Italian *Bergamote*; a species of *Pyrus sativa*, of which there are two kinds, namely, the Summer Bergamot and the Autumn Bergamot.

BERGAMOT (*Chem.*) a certain fragrant and cordial essence, extracted from a kind of lemon in Italy; the fruit of a lemon tree ingrafted on a Bergamot pear tree. The liquor is an æthereal oil, very subtile, and of a charming smell. Medicinally it is a cardiac, stomachic, and cephalic.

BERGE'RA (*Bot.*) a genus of plants, named after Professor Berger, of Kiel, Class 10 *Decandria*, Order 1 *Monogynia*.
Generic Characters. CAL. *perianth* five-parted.—COR. *petals* five.—STAM. *filaments* ten; *anthers* round.—PIST. *germ* roundish; *style* filiform; *stigma* turbinate.—PER. *berry* subglobular; *seeds* two.
Species. The only species is the *Bergera Koenigii*, seu *Papaja sylvestris*, a shrub, native of the East Indies.

BERGH-MASTER (*Min.*) from the Saxon *berg*, mountain or mine; a bailiff or chief officer among the Derbyshire miners. *Esc. de Ann.* 16 Ed. 1.

BE'RGHMOTE (*Min.*) Bergmot, from the Saxon *berg*, mountain or mine, and *zemote*, an assembly; an assembly or court for deciding all controversies among the Derbyshire miners.

BE'RGIA (*Bot.*) a genus of plants, named after Professor Bergius, of Stockholm, Class 10 *Decandria*, Order 5 *Pentagynia*.
Generic Characters. CAL. *perianth* five-parted.—COR. *petals* five.—STAM. *filaments* ten; *anthers* roundish.—PIST. *germ* roundish; *styles* five; *stigmas* simple.—PER. *capsule* simple; *seeds* numerous.
Species. The species are natives of India.

BE'RIA (*Archæol.*) or *berie*, an open place, which Cowel says is not, according to Spelman, to be confounded with bury and borough in the names of towns that end with this word. *Beria Sancti Edmundi* [St. Edmond's Bury] mentioned by Matthew Paris, sub. ann. 1174, is not to be taken for the town, but the plain, according to Du Fresne.

BE'RIBERI (*Med.*) a kind of palsy frequent in the East Indies.

BERILLI'STICA (*Alch.*) a kind of magic art in observing

pretended præternatural visions in *ballisti,* or mirror glasses.

BERLI'N (*Mech.*) a sort of carriages made at Berlin.

BERME (*Fort.*) a small space of ground, 4 or 5 feet wide, left without the rampart, between it and the side of the moat.

BERMU'DAS Juniper (*Bot.*) the *Juniperus Bermudiana* of Linnæus.

BERMUDIA'NA (*Bot.*) 1. A species of the *Juniperus* of Linnæus. 2. The *Juniperus barbadensis.* 3. A species of the *Sisyrinchium*, and of the *Iris*.

BE'RNACLE (*Orn.*) a bird of the goose kind, the *Anas erythropus* of Linnæus, formerly called the *tree goose,* because it was supposed to be generated out of wood, or rather to be a species of shell adhering to the bottoms of ships. These birds appear in vast flocks during winter on the north-west coast of this kingdom. They are very shy and wild; but upon being taken grow as tame as the domestic goose. In February they retire as far as Lapland, to breed.

BE'RNARDINES (*Ecc.*) monks of the order of St. Bernard.

BERNA'VI· (*Med.*) an electuary mentioned by Prosper Alpinus.

BE'RNET (*Law*) *incendium,* from the Saxon býnan, to burn; the crime of arson, or wilfully setting on fire, which, according to the laws of Henry I. was one of those crimes which *non emendari possunt.* It is, however, sometimes taken for any capital crime. *Leg. Canut. et H.* 1, apud *Brompt.*

BERQUA'RIUM (*Archæol.*) vide *Bercaria.*

BE'RRA (*Archæol.*) vide *Beria.*

BE'RRIED (*Bot.*) *baccatus;* an epithet for the capsule, and also for the drupe, which is surrounded by a very succulent coat, as the cherry, that seeds, but never bursts.

BE'RRY (*Bot.*) [vide *Bacca*]—Berry-bearing Alder, the *Rhamnus frangula* of Linnæus.

BERS (*Med.*) an exhilarating sort of electuary made by the Egyptians.

BE'RSA (*Archæol.*) a limit within a park.

BERSA'RE (*Archæol.*) to hunt or shoot: the *bursarii* were properly those who hunted the wolf.

BE'RSELET (*Archæol.*) a hound.

BERTHI'NSECK (*Law*) or *berdinseck,* a law in Scotland, by which a man is not hanged, but only whipped, for taking a sheep or calf that he can carry away on his back.

BERTIE'RA (*Bot.*) a genus of plants named by Aublet after Mons. Bertier, Class 5 *Pentandria,* Order 1 *Monogynia*.
Generic Characters. CAL. *perianth* turbinate.—COR. one-petalled.—STAM. *filaments* five; *anthers* linear.—PIST. *germ* roundish; *style* filiform; *stigmas* two-plated.—PER. *berry* globose; *seeds* very many.
Species. The only species is—*Bertieria quianensis*, a shrub, native of Guinea.

BE'RTON (*Archæol.*) vide *Barton.*

BE'RTYING *a ship* (*Mar.*) raising up a ship's sides.

BE'RULA (*Bot.*) Upright water parsnep, which was esteemed an antiscorbutic. *Gal. de Comp. Med.* l. 7, c. 26.

BERU'LIANS (*Ecc.*) a sect of heretics in the 12th century, who affirmed that all human souls were created in the beginning of the world.

BE'RY (*Archæol.*) or *Bury,* the vill or country seat of a nobleman, from beoŋx, a hill, because the castles of the nobility were erected on hills.

BE'RYL (*Min.*) *beryllus,* βήϱυλλος, a precious stone, which, in its purity, is of a perfectly sea-green colour, and on that account has been called *aqua marina.* Pliny mentions several species of the beryl, as the *chrysoberyllus, chrysoprasus, hyacinthizontes,* and *eroides.* *Plin.* l. 37, c. 5; *Solin.* c. 52; *Dionys. Perieg.* v. 1012; *Epiphan. de 12 Gem.*; *Isid. de Origin.* l. 16, c. 17; *Marbod. de Lapid. pret. eq.* Beryl, among the modern lapidaries, is only a fine sort of cornelian, of a more deep bright red.

BERYL (*Paint.*) the sea-green colour prepared in imitation of the beryl.

BERY'TION (*Med.*) βηϱύτιον, a collyrium for the eyes described by Galen.

BES (*Ant.*) 1. A weight of eight ounces, i. e. two-thirds of the *as,* or pound. *Gal. de Comp.* l. 6; *Fest. de Verb. Signific.* 2. A measure of land making two-thirds of an acre.

BESA'CHER (*Bot.*) a fungus, or sponge.

BESAI'LLE (*Law*) or *besayle,* in Latin *proavus,* in French *besayeul;* a writ that lies where the great grandfather was seized the day that he died of any lands or tenements in fee simple, and after his death a stranger entereth the same day upon them, and keepeth out the heir. *F. N. B.* 222.

BESA'NT (*Com.*) or *Bezant,* a very ancient gold coin stamped at Byzantium.

BESANT (*Her.*) vide *Bezant.*

BE'SCA (*Archæol.*) a spade or shovel, whence *una bescata terra inclusa;* a piece of land turned up with a spade in a day. *Mon. Angl.*

BESIE'GED (*Astrol.*) an epithet for a planet which is placed between others of a malignant cast, as Saturn and Mars.

BESI'STAN (*Com.*) or *Berstan,* large galleries vaulted over in Turkey, where the merchants have shops, and expose their goods to sale.

BESLE'RIA (*Bot.*) a genus of plants named by Plumier after Basil Besler, a botanist of Nuremberg. Class 14 *Didynamia,* Order 2 *Angiospermia.*
Generic Characters. CAL. *perianth* one-leaved.—COR. monopetalous.—STAM. *filaments* four; *anthers* oblong.—PIST. *germ* globular; *style* subulate; *stigma* bifid.—PER. *berry* subglobular; *seeds* numerous.
Species. The species are shrubs or perennials.

BE'SORCH (*Com.*) a tin coin at Ormus, in value much less than a farthing.

BESTIA'LES (*Ant.*) in French *bestayles,* Bestials, all kinds of cattle, but particularly those which were anciently purveyed for the king's provision. *Stat.* 4 *Ed.* 3.

BESTIA'RII (*Ant.*) those among the Romans who fought with beasts at their public games, whether by compulsion, as condemned persons, or voluntarily, as gladiators, who made a trade of it. *Cic. in Vaticin.* c. 17; *Suet. Claud.* c. 34; *Tertull. Apol.* c. 35.

BE'STIAS (*Ant.*) or *ad Bestias.* [vide *Ad*]

BE'TA (*Gram.*) the second letter in the Greek Alphabet. [vide *Alphabet*]

BETA (*Bot.*) a plant so called from the Greek letter β, which it resembles in shape whilst the seed is swelling. *Columel.* l. 10.
> *Nomine tum Graio, ceu littera proxima primæ*
> *Pingitur in cera docti mucrone magistri,*
> *Sic et humo pingui ferratæ cuspidis ictu*
> *Deprimitur folio viridis, pede candida, beta.*

Mart. l. 13, epig. 13.
> *Ut sapiant fatuæ fabrorum prandia betæ,*
> *O quam sæpe petet vina, piperque coquus.*

It is one of the five emollient herbs; and on account of its insipidity, those who languished were said *betizare,* to flag like the beet-root. *Catull.* Carm. 66, v. 21.
> *Languidior tenera cui pendens sicula beta*
> *Numquam se medium sustulit ad tunicam.*

Theoph. Hist. Plant. l. 1, c. 5, &c.; *Dioscor.* l. 2, c. 140; *Plin.* l. 19, c. 8.

BETA, Beet, *in the Linnean system,* a genus of plants, Class 5 *Pentandria,* Order 2 *Digynia.*
Generic Characters. CAL. *perianth* five-leaved.—COR. none.—STAM. *filaments* five; *anthers* roundish.—PIST.

germ in a manner below the receptacle; *styles* two; *stigmas* acute.—Per. *capsule* one-celled; *seed* single.

Species. The species are biennials, as—*Beta vulgaris*, Red Garden Beet.—*Beta cicla*, White Garden Beet.—*Beta maritima*, Sea-Beet.—*Beta patula*, Spreading Beet, &c.

BETA'CHES (*Archæol.*) Laymen using glebe lands.

BETEL (*Bot.*) or *Betle*, a species of pepper plant, the leaf of which is universally chewed by the southern Asiatics, to sweeten the breath and strengthen the stomach. This is the *Piper Betle* of Linnæus.—*Betel-nut*, a name given to the *Areca* when slices of it are enclosed in the leaf of the Betel.

BETELGE'USE (*Ast.*) a star of the first magnitude in the right shoulder of Orion. Its right ascension in 1812 was 86° 14' 52", declination North 7° 21' 34", annual variation in right ascension 48" 6, in declination + 1" 5.

BE'THLEMITES (*Ecc.*) certain friars who wore the figure of a star on their breasts, in memory of the star that appeared to the wise men, and conducted them to Bethlehem.

BETI'LLES (*Com.*) a thick sort of muslin; the finer sort resembling cambric, and the coarser calico.

BETLE (*Bot.*) in German *betel*, a plant of the scandent kind, the leaves of which are chewed by the Indians, for the purpose of sweetening their breath.

BETO'NICA (*Bot.*) a plant so called, according to Pliny, because it was found among the Bettones. This plant was reckoned vulnerary, aperient, and diuretic. *Plin.* l. 25, c. 8; *Gal. de Simpl.* l. 7; *Oribas. Med. Coll.* l. 11; *Aet. Tetrab.* 1, serm. 1; *Paul. Ægin.* l. 7, c. 3.

Betonica, *in the Linnean system*, a genus of plants, Class 14 *Didynamia*, Order 1 *Gymnospermia*.

Generic Characters. Cal. *perianth* one-leaved.—Cor. monopetalous.—Stam. *filaments* four; *anthers* roundish.—Pist. *germ* four-parted; *style* filiform; *stigma* bifid.—Per. none; *seeds* four.

Species. The species are perennials. *Dodon. Stirp. Hist.; J. Bauh. Hist. Plant.; C. Bauh. Pin.; Ger. Herb.; Park. Theat.; Raii Hist. Plant.; Linn. Spec. Plant.*

BE'TULA (*Bot.*) a tree so called, according to some, from the bitumen which is extracted from it. *Plin.* l. 16, c. 8.

Betula, the Birch *in the Linnean system*, a genus of plants, Class 21 *Monoecia*, Order 4 *Tetrandria*.

Generic Characters. Cal. *ament* imbricate on every side.—Cor. none.—Stam. *filaments* to each four; *anthers* twin.—Pist. *germ* proper, ovate, compressed; *styles* two; *stigmas* simple.—Per. none; *seeds* solitary.

Species. The species are either trees or shrubs, as—*Betula alba*, Common Birch-tree.—*Betula nana*, the Dwarf Birch-tree.—*Betula nigra*, Virginian Black Birch-tree.—*Betula incana*, seu *Alnus folio incano*, Hoary Alder-tree.—*Betula oblongata*, seu *Alnus folio oblongo*, Turkey Alder.—*Betula serrulata*, Notch-leaved Alder.—*Betula crispa*, Curled-leaved Alder. &c. *J. Bauh. Hist. Plant.; C. Bauh. Pin.; Park. Theat.; Raii Hist. Plant.; Tournf. Instit.; Boerhaav. Ind.*

Betula (*Ent.*) an insect that feeds on the *Betula alba*, a species of the *Chrysomela*.

BE'TULUS (*Min.*) a precious stone, of the white jasper kind. *Plin.* 37, c. 9.

Betulus (*Bot.*) a species of the *Carpinus*.

BETWE'EN-DECKS (*Mar.*) the space contained between two whole decks of a ship.

BE'VEAU (*Mech.*) French for an instrument that is used to carry a mixlined angle from one angle to another.

BE'VEL (*Carp.*) an instrument with a moveable tongue to strike angles of a greater or less number of degrees. This instrument differs from the square and mitre by being moveable, whilst they are fixed, the first at an angle of 90°, and the second at that of 45°, or a right angle, whether it be obtuse or acute; but if it be exactly half a right angle, i. e. if the angle measure 45°, then it is called a mitre; if the quarter of a right angle, i. e. 27½°, it is a half mitre.—*Bevel-angle*, any angle that is not a square.

Bevel (*Her.*) an epithet for a chief in coats of arms which is broken, or opening like a carpenter's rule, as, he beareth "*Argent* a chief bevilé, *vert*, by the name of *Beverlis*."

BE'VELLING (*Carp.*) hewing timber with a proper or regular curve, according to a mould, so that each side should be a plane. If timber be not hewn square, and a square be applied, there will be wood wanting either on the upper or the lower side. This is called being *within* or *without* square. When the wood is deficient on the under side it is called *Under-bevelling*; when it is on the upper side it is called *Standing-bevelling*.

BE'VER (*Archæol.*) from the Ital. *bevere*, to drink. 1. A small collation between dinner and supper. 2. The visor or sight of a head-piece.

BE'VERAGE *to pay* (*Cus.*) to give a treat on the first wearing a new suit of clothes.

BEVE'RCHES (*Archæol.*) customary services done by the tenants at the will of the lord.

BEVIL'E (*Her.*) vide *Bevel*.

BEURE'RIA (*Bot.*) the *Chalcanthus floridus*, and the *Ehretia beureria*, and *excussa*, of Linnæus.

BEURT-SCHE'EPEN (*Com.*) or *Beurt Schuyten*, Turn-ships, or Turn-boats; vessels or boats at Amsterdam which have the exclusive privilege of taking in goods in the seven provinces; so called because they must sail in their turn, according to specific regulations.

BE'VY (*Sport.*) a certain number of animals of the chace when together, as "A *bevy* of roe-bucks," i. e. a herd; "A *bevy* of partridges," i. e. three in number; "A *bevy* of quails," i. e. a flock, or brood.

BEWA'RED (*Ant.*) i. e. expended, or laid out in wares; a term among the Saxons and Britons, who traded only by an exchange of wares.

BE'WITS (*Falcon.*) pieces of leather with which the bells of hawks are fastened and buttoned to their legs.

BEX (*Med.*) βηξ, *tussis*, a cough.

BEXU'GO (*Bot.*) the root of the *Clematis Peruviana*, which is a purgative. *Bauh. Hist. Plant.*

BEY (*Polit.*) an officer of high rank among the Turks, inferior to none but the Pacha.

BEZA'NT (*Num.*) round flat pieces of bullion without any impression, which are supposed to have been the current coin of Byzantium.

Bezant (*Her.*) this coin was probably introduced into coat armour by those who went to the Holy Wars, as in the annexed figure. "He beareth *ermine* on a fess, *gules* three bezants, by the name of *Milward*." They were always of *metal*, and when blazoned, according to the custom of foreign heralds, should be expressly said to be *or* or *argent*.

BEZA'NTLER (*Sport.*) or *bisantler*, the second branch of a stag's horn.

BEZA'NTY (*Her.*) an epithet for a cross composed of bezants.

BE'ZEL (*Archit.*) or *Bezil*, the upper part of the collet of a ring, which encompasses and fastens the stone in it.

BEZO'AR (*Chem.*) from the Persian *bedzher*, an antidote; a medicinal stone brought from the East and West Indies, which was formerly reckoned a sovereign antidote against poisons. It is found to be a morbid concretion in the stomachs of some animals, which consists partly of bile and partly of resin. The bezoars are distinguished into—*Oriental bezoar*, found in the stomach of an animal of the goat kind in Persia, called *pazan*.—*Occidental bezoar*, found in quadrupeds of the deer kind.—*Bezoar hystricus*, found in the gall bladder of the Indian porcupine.—*Monkey bezoar*, found in certain monkeys of Brazil.—*German bezoar*, found in the stomach of the chamois.

BEZOAR *fossile* (*Min.*) a substance so called because it is formed by strata or beds that resemble bezoar, as the Bezoar minerale, or *Terra Sicula*, found in the clay-pits of Italy.

BEZOAR (*Med.*) is also the name of some medicinal preparations, as the—*Bezoar animale*, made of calcined hartshorn and vitriol.—*Bezoar minerale*, a preparation of antimony, made by adding nitrous acid to antimony.

BEZOA'RDIC acid (*Chem.*) a name given to the acid extracted from the urinary calculi formed in the kidneys or gall-bladder.

BEZOA'RDICA *radix* (*Bot.*) a herb so called for its efficacy as a counterpoison; the *Drostera contrayerva* of Linnæus.

BEZOA'RTIC (*Med.*) an epithet for several compositions, as the—*Bezoarticum Joviale*, bezoar mixed with tin.—*Bezoarticum Lunale*, a preparation of antimony and silver, &c.—*Bezoarticum Martiale*, a composition of nitrous acid and butter of antimony.—*Bezoarticus pulvis*, the powder of the oriental bezoar.

BI'A (*Com.*) a Siamese name for the white shells called *cowries* throughout the East Indies.

BIALA'TUS (*Bot.*) two-winged; an epithet applied to the wings or membranes of a seed.

BIA'RCHUS (*Polit.*) a caterer, or one who took charge of the public provisions; an officer in the Greek empire. *Leon. Imp. Constit. l. 3. de Agent. in Reb.; Hieron. Epist. 61. ad Pammach.*

BI'AS (*Mech.*) from the Fr. *biais*, a weight fixed on one side of a bowl, turning the course of the bowl that way to which the bias looks.

BIB (*Ich.*) a species of Cod fish, the *Gadus luscus* of Linnæus, which inhabits European seas. It grows to a foot in length, has a back of a pale olive colour, sides finely tinged with gold, and a belly white. The flesh of this fish is excellent.

BIBBS (*Mar.*) brackets made of elm plank, and bolted to the hounds of the masts, for the purpose of supporting the tresle-trees.

BI'BEROT (*Cook.*) minced meats made of the breasts of partridges and fat pullets.

BIBINE'LLA (*Bot.*) the same as *Pimpernella*.

BI'BIO (*Ent.*) a division of the genus *Musca*, according to Fabricius, comprehending the insects of this tribe which have a sucker with three bristles, and a single-valved sheath.

BIBITO'RIUS *musculus* (*Anat.*) another name for the *Adductor oculi*. [vide *Adductor*]

BIBLIO'GRAPHER (*Lit*) from βίβλος, a book, and γράφω, to write; a describer of books, or one conversant in books.

BIBLIO'GRAPHY (*Lit.*) from βίβλος, a book, and γράφω, to write; a description of books as respects their general contents, different editions, type, and the like.

BI'BLIOMANCY (*My.*) a kind of divination performed by means of the bible, otherwise called *Sortes Biblicæ*, or *Sortes Sanctorum*, which consists in taking passages of scripture at hazard, and drawing conclusions from them concerning futurity.

BIBLIOMA'NIA (*Lit.*) from βίβλος, a book, and μανία, a mania; a rage for books on account of their scarcity, dearness, print, or some other childish reason.

BIBLIO'POLIST (*Lit.*) βιβλιοπωλης, *venditor librorum*; a bookseller.

BIBLIOTA'PHIST (*Lit.*) βιβλιοταφος, from βίβλος, a book, and ταφω, to bury; a hider or burier of books.

BIBLIOTHE'CA (*Lit.*) βιβλιοθηκη, from βίβλος, a book, and *theca*, a chest; a library or repository of books, also the books themselves.

BICA'PSULAR (*Bot.*) *bicapsularis*; having two capsules containing seeds to each flower, an epithet for the pericarp, as in *Pæonia*.

BICA'UDALIS (*Anat.*) the same as *Abductor Auris*.

BICE (*Paint.*) a blue colour prepared from the *Lapis Armenus*; it bears the best body of all bright blues used in common work, as House-painting, &c., but it is the palest in colour.

BI'CEPS (*Anat.*) *bicapital*, or double-headed; an epithet for several muscles having two heads, as—*Biceps Cubiti*, a muscle of the elbow, the outermost head of which rises from the *Acetabulum scapulæ*.—*Biceps Femoris*, which rises from the protuberance of the *Ischium*, on the back part. Its office is to bend the *Tibia*.—*Biceps Humeri*, or *Biceps flexor*, rising, by one head from the glenoid cavity, by the other from the coracoid process. It acts both as a flexor and a rotator.

BICHE'T (*Com.*) a measure in France equal to from thirteen to nineteen bushels.

BICHI'CHIA (*Med.*) troches made of liquorice, almonds, &c. *Castel. Lex. Med.*

BI'CHOS (*Ent.*) a Portuguese name for the worms found under the toes in the Indies, which are destroyed by the Cashew-nut.

BI'CKERN (*Mech.*) or *beak-iron*, the pointed part of an anvil, with which its face is usually made to end.

BICO'RNES (*Bot.*) two-horned; the eighteenth of Linnæus' natural orders of plants, having the anthers furnished with two long straight points or horns, as in *Vaccinium*, *Erica*, *Pyrola*, &c.

BICO'RNIS (*Bot.*) two-horned; an epithet for the *anthera bicornis*, an anther having two subulate prolongations, as in *Arbutus*, *Pyrolus*, &c.

BICUCULLA'TA (*Bot.*) the *Fumaria cucullaria* of Linnæus.

BICU'SPIDES (*Anat.*) two-pointed; an epithet for the teeth which have double fangs.

BIDA'LE (*Ant.*) or *biddal*, an invitation to friends to drink ale at the house of a poor man, who thereby hopes for a charitable contribution for his relief. *Stat. 26. Hen. 8.*

BI'DDING *of Beads* (*Archæol.*) a charge or warning anciently given by the parish priest to his parishioners, that they should pray for the soul of some deceased friend.

BI'DENS (*Ant.*) a two-yearling sheep, which was reckoned fit to be a victim for sacrifice.

BIDENS (*Bot.*) Water Hemp, a genus of plants so called because the seeds are terminated by two teeth or awns, Class 19 *Syngenesia*, Order 1 *Polygamia Æqualis*.

Generic Characters. CAL. common imbricate.—COR. compound uniform.—STAM. *filaments* five; *anther* cylindric.—PIST. *germ* oblong; *style* simple; *stigmas* two.—PER. none; *seeds* solitary; *receptacle* flat.

Species. The species are mostly annuals, as—*Bidens tripartita*, seu *Cannabina aquatica*, Trifid Water-Hemp, Agrimony, or Bur-Marygold.—*Bidens cernua*, *Cannabina*, seu *Eupatorium*, &c. Drooping Water-Hemp, Agrimony, or Bur-Marygold.—*Bidens Chinensis*, seu *Agrimonia Molucca*, &c.; but some are perennials, as the—*Bidens heterophylla*, *Sambucefolia*, &c.; and the—*Bidens frutescens* is a shrub.

BIDENTA'LES (*Ant.*) priests; so named among the Romans, whose office it was to consecrate any place that had been struck by a thunderbolt, or by lightening: this ceremony was performed by the sacrifice of a sheep *bidens*, i. e. two years old, or having two teeth longer than the rest.

BIDO'N (*Com.*) a liquid measure containing about five pints of Paris, i. e. about five quarts English wine measure. It is seldom used but among ships' crews.

BIDUA'NA (*Archæol.*) a fasting for the space of two days.

BIE'NNIALS (*Bot.*) or Biennial Plants; those plants which endure for two years, and then perish. The roots and leaves of biennials are produced in the first year, and in the second year they flower.

BIE'STINGS (*Nat.*) the first milk taken from a cow after calving, which is thick, and of a yellow colour.

BIFA'RIOUS (*Bot.*) pointing two ways; an epithet for the leaves; *folia bifaria*, leaves coming out only on opposite sides of a branch.—*Bifariously hairy* is also applied to the stem or branch when the hairs between any two joints come out on the front and back.

BI'FEROUS *plants* (*Bot.*) those which bear twice a year, as is common in hot climates.

BI'FID (*Bot.*) *bifidus*, cleft, or cloven into two, an epithet for the leaf; the perianth, as in *Utricularia*; the anther, as in the Grasses; the stigma; the strap; the filament; the tendril; the teeth; and the style.

BIFLO'ROUS (*Bot.*) *biflorus*, two-flowered; an epithet for the ear, the peduncle, and the spathe.

BI'FORA (*Bot.*) the name for a class of plants, according to Camellus, having a pericarp with two valves.

BI'FRONS (*Ant.*) double-headed, or double-faced, an epithet for Janus.

To BIFURCATE (*Anat.*) to divide into branches, as nerves and vessels are said to do; thus the bifurcation of the aorta, &c.

BI'GA (*Ant.*) a cart or chariot drawn with two horses, but properly a cart with two wheels, and in our ancient records any waggon or wain. *Plin.* l. 7, c. 56; *Mon. Angl.*

BI'GAMY (*Law*) or a double marriage; marrying two females one after another, both of which were virgins, or the one a virgin and the other a widow, which incapacitated a man for holy orders, according to a canon at Lyons, A. D. 1247. *Stat. 4. Ed. 1.*—*Bigamy*, in the civil law, is the having a plurality of wives or husbands, which is felony. 3 *Inst. Stat. 1. Jac. 1.*

BIGARE'LLA (*Bot.*) a species of the *Prunus* of Linnæus.

BIGA'RIUS (*Ant.*) the charioteer of a biga, or two-wheeled chariot, as we learn from an inscription at Rome. FLORUS. EGO. HICJACEO. BIGARIUS. INFANS. QUI. CITO. DUM. CUPIO. CURRUS. CITO DECIDI. AD. UMBRAS. JANUARIUS. ALUMNO. DULCIS. S. *Ferret. Mus. Lapid.* l. 4.

BIGA'STER (*Anat.*) from *bis* and γαστηρ, *venter*, double-bellied; an epithet for muscles.

BIGA'TI (*Ant.*) money or coin stamped with the figure of a biga, or two-wheeled chariot. *Liv.* l. 23, c. 15, &c.; *Plin.* l. 33, c. 3; *Tacit. de Germ.* c. 5.

BIGE'MINATE (*Bot.*) *bigeminatus*, or *bigeminus*, twinforked; according to Withering, an epithet for a leaf; *folium bigeminum*, a decompound leaf, having a dichotomous or forked petiole, with several folioles or leaflets at the end of each division.

BIGHT (*Mar.*) from the Sax. *bygan*, to bend; the double part of a rope when it is folded, in contradistinction from the end, as "Her anchor hooked the bight of our cable," i. e. caught any part of it between the ends. "The bight of his cable has swept our anchor;" the double part of another ship's cable, as she ranged about, has entangled itself with our cable.

BIGHT (*Geog.*) a small bay between two points of land.

BIGHT (*Man.*) the inward bent of the chambrel; also the bent of the fore knees.

BIGNO'NIA (*Bot.*) a genus of plants, named by Tournefort after the Abbé Bignon, librarian to Lewis XIV., Class 14 *Didynamia*, Order 2 *Angiospermia*.

Generic Characters. CAL. *perianth* one-leaved.—COR. monopetalous.—STAM. *filaments* four; *anthers* reflex.—PIST. *germ* oblong; *style* filiform; *stigma* capitate.—PER. *silique* two-celled; *seeds* very many.

Species. The species are shrubs, as—*Bignonia tomentosa*, seu *Too*, seu *Kiri*, &c.—*Bignonia sempervirens*, *Gelseminum*, *Lasminum*, seu *Syringo*, &c. Carolina Yellow Jasmine. — *Bignonia clematis*, Four-leaved TrumpetFlower.—*Bignonia pentaphylla*, seu *Guari-paraba*, Hairy five-leaved Trumpet-flower.—*Bignonia Leucoxylon*, *Leacoxylon*, seu *Nerio*, &c. Smooth five-leaved Trumpetflower, White Wood, or Tulip-Flower, &c. &c. *Tournef. Instit.*

BIHAI (*Bot.*) the *Strelitzia regina* of Linnæus.

BIHYDRO'GURET *of carbon* (*Chem.*) a gaseous substance, compounded of hydrogen and carbon.

BIJO'RKNA (*Ich.*) a species of the *Cyprinus* of Linnæus.

BI'IS (*Com.*) a weight and measure in the East Indies.

BIJU'GOUS (*Bot.*) *bijugus*, from *bis* and *jugum*, yoked or coupled side by side: an epithet for a leaf; *folium bijugum*, a pinnate leaf, having two pairs of leaflets. *Linn. Philos. Botan.*

BILA'BIATE (*Bot.*) *bilabiatus*, two lipped; an epithet for the corolla and perianth; *corolla bilabiata*, a corolla, having two segments or lips.

BILA'DEN (*Med.*) steel, or rather iron.

BILA'GINES (*Law*) bye-laws of corporations, &c.

BILAMME'LLATE (*Bot.*) *bilammellatus*; an epithet for the stigma; as *stigma bilamellatum*, a stigma in the form of a flatted sphere longitudinally bifid. *Linn. Philos. Botan.*

BILA'N (*Com.*) French for a book, in which bankers and merchants in France write their active and passive debts.

BILA'NCIIS *deferendis* (*Law*) a writ directed to a corporation for the carrying of weights to a particular haven, there to weigh the wool that was licensed to be exported. *Reg. Orig.* 270.

BILA'NDER (*Mar.*) a small merchant vessel with two masts.

BILA'NUS (*Bot.*) the *Crateva Marmelos* of Linnæus.

BILAW (*Law*) vide *Biscot*.

BI'LBO (*Mil.*) the former name of a rapier or small sword.

BI'LBOES (*Mar.*) long bars or bolts of iron with which the feet of offenders at sea are confined: the irons are more or less ponderous, according to the magnitude of the offence.

BILBOQUE'TS (*Mil.*) a French term for small pieces of stone which have been sawed from the block, and laid up in store.

BILE (*Med.*) *Bilis*, χολη, is supposed to be derived from *bis* and *lis*, double strife, because it is supposed to be the principal cause of disputes; a bitter fluid, secreted in the glandular substance of the liver. There are different sorts, according to the colour and state of the fluid, as Pale or Yellow Bile, which Hippocrates calls simply χολη; Black Bile, χολη μιλαινα, a thick black humour, or bile torrefied beyond measure. *Aret. de Caus. et Sign. Morb. acut.* l. 1, c. 15; *Ruf. Ephes. de Appell. Corp. hum.* l. 1, c. 36; *Gal. Comm. 3 in Hippocrat. de Rat. vict. in acut. Morb.*; *Aet. Tetrab.* 3, serm. 4, c. 28; *Gorr. Defin. Med.*; *Foes. Œconom. Hippocrat.*

Bile is now distinguished by the names of *hepatic* and *cystic Bile*.—*Hepatic bile* is that which flows from the liver into the duodenum. This is thin and of a pale yellow colour. —*Cystic bile*, that which regurgitates from the hepatic duct into the gall-bladder, where it becomes thicker and more acrid.

BILE (*Chem.*) the constituent parts of bile are water, a resinous and albuminous principle, soda in its caustic state, and phosphate of lime.

BILGE (*Mar.*) from the Saxon *bilx*, the belly. 1. That

part of the floor of a ship on which it would rest if laid on the ground. 2. The largest circumference of a cask, or that which extends round by the bung hole.—*Bilge water*, that water which, by reason of a ship's flat bottom, remains in the bilge, instead of going into the well.

BI'LGED (*Mar.*) the state of a vessel which, by reason of its striking on a rock, or otherwise, has its bilge fractured or staved in.

BI'LIARY ducts (*Anat.*) *Ductus biliosi*, small canals which convey the bile out of the liver into the hepatic duct, which is formed of these canals, into one trunk.

BILIA'RIS *calculus* (*Med.*) Gall-stone. [vide *Calculus*]

BILI'MBI (*Bot.*) a tree of Malabar; the *Averrhoa biligubri* of Linnæus.

BI'LIOUS (*Med.*) *biliosus*; an epithet for any disorders arising from too copious a secretion of the bile, a bilious fever, a bilious colic, a bilious habit, &c.

BILIS (*Med.*) vide *Bile.—Bilis atra*, black bile, which was supposed to be the cause of melancholy.

BILL (*Mar.*) the point or extremity of the flook of an anchor; also, the ends of a compass or knee timber.

BILL (*Law*) a declaration in writing, expressing the grievance or wrong the plaintiff has suffered from the defendant. 3 *Inst.* 30.—*Bill in Chancery* is a bill filed in Chancery.—*Bill of review*, a bill for the rehearsal of any cause, an error of judgment appearing on the face of the decree.—*True bill*, or *billa vera*, is a presentment or indictment, which, in a criminal cause, a grand jury finds to be true, and endorses accordingly.—*Bill of debt*, a common engagement for money given by one man to another, which is either a *penal bill* having a penalty attached to it, or it is a *single bill*, without any penalty, which is equivalent to a bond. *West Symbol*, l. 2, sect 1 & 6.—*Bill of exceptions* to evidence, is a sort of appeal put in writing, *sedente curia*, in the presence of the judge who tried the cause, and signed by the counsel on each side. It is then signed by the judge, when there goes out a *scire facias* to the same judge, *ad cognoscendum scriptum*.—*Bill in Parliament*, an instrument drawn up by any member, and presented to Parliament for its approbation or rejection. After it has gone through the two houses, and passed the Royal assent, it has the force of a law.—*Bill of Middlesex*, vide *Process.* —*Bill of rights*, a statute passed in the reign of William and Mary; so called because it declared the true rights of British subjects. W. & M. stat. 2, c. 2.

BILL *of exchange* (*Com.*) a note ordering the payment of a sum of money to a person in a given place, in consideration of value received. This bill, when signed by responsible persons, is negotiable. The person who draws up the bill is called the *drawer*, he to whom it is addressed the *drawee*; and when he undertakes to pay the amount, which he does by writing the word *accepted*, signed with his name, he is then called the *acceptor*. The person to whom it is ordered to be paid is called the *payee*, and when he indorses his name he is the *indorser*; if he appoint another to receive the money, that person is, in respect to himself, the *indorsee*. He who is in possession of the bill is called the *holder*. A bill that is to be paid whenever it is presented is called *payable at sight*; sometimes it is payable at so many days after sight, and sometimes after a certain interval from the given date. *Usance* is the time of one, two, or three months after the day of the date of the bill, according to the custom of the place between which the exchanges run. Usance may be either double, treble, or half. When the time is limited, three days are added to the term specified in the bill, which are called *days of Grace.*

Bills are moreover distinguished into *foreign* and *inland*, the first of which pass from one country to another, and the latter between persons residing in the same country.

A bill when presented for payment, and not *taken up*, i. e. payment refused, is said to be *dishonoured*. This refusal is noted on the back of the bill by the notary, which is called simply *noting*, and afterwards it is *protested*, i. e. a declaration is signed by the notary, signifying the acceptance of the bills and refusal of payment.—*Bill of credit.* [vide *Letter*]

Bill is also the name of several other documents employed in trade, as—*Bill of lading*, or *invoice*, a deed signed by the master of a ship, by which he acknowledges the receipt of the merchant's goods, and obliges himself to deliver the same at the place to which they are consigned.—*Bill of parcels*, a particular account given by the seller to the buyer of the sorts and prices of goods bought.—*Bill of sale*, a deed given by a person borrowing a sum of money, and delivering goods as a security to the lender.—*Bill of stores*, a licence granted at the Custom-House to merchants to carry stores and provisions necessary for their voyage custom free.—*Bill of sufferance*, a licence granted to trade from one English port to another without paying custom.—*Bill of the play*, an account of the performance that is to be exhibited at the theatre at any time; and also of the performers who are to take part in it.—*Bill of fare*, an account of the provisions that are in season, and of the dishes that are prepared for an entertainment.

BI'LLA *vera* (*Law*) i. e. true bill; the words of endorsement used by the Grand Jury who find any bill to be true.

BI'LLAGE (*Mar.*) the breadth of a floor of a ship when she lies aground.

BI'LLARD (*Cook.*) an imperfect or bastard capon.

BI'LLET (*Com.*) a diminutive of *bill*; a log of wood for fuel.—*Billet-wood*, small wood, sold in billets, which, according to *statute* 43 *Eliz.* must be three feet four inches long.—*Billet of gold* is the same as wedge or ingot. Stat. 27, *Eliz.*

BILLET (*Mil.*) a ticket for quartering soldiers.

BILLET (*Her.*) a bearing in form of an oblong square, supposed to represent cloth of gold, as in the annexed figure. " *Argent*, a chevron, between three billets, *gules*, by the name of *Kelly*, of *Devonshire*." Guillim thinks that billets represent *billet-doux*, but, according to Smithurst, they signify one employed in embassies.

TO BILLET (*Mil.*) to quarter soldiers in houses by means of billets.

BILLET-DOU'X (*Lit.*) a short love letter sent to a sweetheart or mistress.

BI'LLETY (*Her.*) or *billette*, an epithet used in blazoning, when the billets exceed the number of ten.

BI'LLIARDS (*Sport.*) a game; so called, from *balyard*, the stick with which the ivory balls are struck. It is played upon a table, covered with baize, and furnished with holes, called *hazards* or *pockets*, into which, according to the rules of the game, each party seeks to drive his antagonist.

BILLINGBI'NG (*Bot.*) the same as *Bilimbi*.

BI'LLION (*Arith.*) i. e. bimillion; a million millions.

BI'LLON (*Com.*) a sort of base metal, either gold or silver, in the mixture of which copper predominates.

BI'LLOT (*Coin.*) or bills, bullion of gold or silver in the mass before it is coined.

BILLS *of mortality* (*Law*) annual registers of the deaths and burials which take place in the different parishes in and near London. These bills were first commenced in 1592, during the period of a great pestilence, when they included 109 parishes. The number has since been increased to 146.

BI'LLUS (*Ant.*) a bill stock or staff, which was the only weapon in use for servants and watchmen.

BILO'BATE (*Bot.*) *bilobus*, two-lobed; an epithet for a leaf; *folium bilobum*, a leaf divided into two lobes.

BILO'CULAR (*Bot.*) *bilocularis*, or two-celled; an epithet applied to the anther, the berry, the capsule, the leaf, the nut, the pumpkin, and the seed.

BIME'DIAL (*Geom.*) δύο μέσαι, the sum of two medials, as when two medials, commensurable only in power, and containing a rational rectangle, be compounded, the whole shall be irrational with respect to either of the two parts. This Euclid calls the *first medial*, in distinction from the second, when that rectangle is a medial. *Eucl.* l. 10, prop. 38, 39.

BI'NARY (*Arith.*) an epithet for what appertains to the number of two.—*Binary arithmetic*, or *binary scale*, is that arithmetic in which two figures only are used; namely, 0 and 1; the cypher multiplying by 2 instead of 10; thus, in the number 1111, the first figure on the right hand, according to the denary scale, means simple unity; the second 10; the third 100, or 10^2; the fourth 1000, or 10^3; but, according to the binary scale, the second figure is 2, or 2^1; the third 2^2, or 4; the fourth 2^3, or 8; consequently,

1111, in the first case, $= 10^3 + 10^2 + 10^1 + 1 = 2345$
1111, in the second case, $= 2^3 + 2^2 + 2^1 + 1 = 15$

BINARY *measure* (*Mus.*) a measure in which you beat equally, i. e. the time of rising is equal to the time of falling.

BI'NATE (*Bot.*) an epithet either for a leaf, or a peduncle; *folium binatum*, a leaf having a simple petiole connecting two leaflets at the top of it, which is a sort of digitate leaf; *binati pedunculi*, peduncles in pairs, as in *Capraria*.

BI'NDING (*Archit.*) an epithet for the joists in a floor, into which the trimmers of staircases and chimney walls are framed.

BINDING (*Mar.*) the iron wrought round the dead eyes.— *Binding strakes*, two strakes of oak in the deck to bind it well together.

BINDING *notes* (*Mus.*) notes held together by ties or curves.

BINDING (*Falc.*) a tiring, or when a hawk seizes.

BINDING *of books* (*Mech.*) the art of doing up books in leather.

BI'ND-WEED (*Bot.*) a flower better known by its botanical name of *Convolvulus*.—Rough Bind-Weed, the *Smilax aspera* of Linnæus.

BI'ND-WITH (*Bot.*) a plant better known by its botanical name of *Clematis*.

BINN (*Husband.*) a large chest to put corn in.

BI'NNACLE (*Mar.*) a wooden case containing the compasses, log-glasses, watch-glasses, and lights to show the compass at night. The binnacle consists of three apartments with sliding shutters; the two side ones, *a*, *b*, have always a compass in each, *d*, to direct the way, while the middle division, *c*, has a lamp, or candle, with a pane of glass on either side to throw a light upon the compass in the night.

BINNARIUM (*Archæol.*) a pond, or stew for keeping fish in.

BINO'CLE *telescope* (*Per.*) from *bini* and *oculi*, or binocular telescope; a double perspective glass to see a distant object with both eyes at once.

BINO'CULUS (*Surg.*) a bandage for retaining the dressings upon both eyes.

BINO'MIAL (*Algeb.*) from *bis*, twice, and *nomen*, a name; a term introduced by Recorde to denote any quantity consisting of two names, or terms connected together by the signs $+$; or $-$, as $a + b$, or $a - c$. This epithet has since been applied to different things, as—*Binomial curve*, a curve whose ordinate is expressed by a binomial quantity, as $y = x^n \sqrt{b + d x^n}$.—*Binominal equation*, an equation consisting of two terms, $x^n - 1 = 0$.—*Imaginary*, or *impossible binomial*, a binomial expression of which one of the branches is imaginary, as $a \pm \sqrt{-b}$, or $-a \pm \sqrt{-b}$.—*Binomial surd*, is the same as *Apotome*. [vide *Apotome*]—*Binomial theorem*, a general algebraic expression or formula, by which any power, or root of a quantity, is expanded into a series; this is called the Newtonian Theorem, from Sir Isaac Newton, its discoverer. By the help of this theorem a binomial quantity is readily raised to any given power without the trouble of continued involution, as, for example, $(a + b)^3 = a^3 + \frac{3}{1} a^2 b + \frac{3.2}{1.2} a b^2 + \frac{3.2.1}{1.2.3} b^3$, or $(a + b)^3 = a^3 + 3 a^2 b + 3 a b^2 + b^3$; and, in its most general form, $(a + b)^n = a^n + \frac{n}{1} a^{n-1} b + \frac{a(n-2)}{1.2} a^{n-2} b^2 + n \frac{(n-1)(n-2)}{1.2.3} a^{n-3} b^3$, &c. [vide *Algebra*] *Record. Whet. of Wit.*; *Newt. Commerc. Epist.*

BI'NSECA (*Med.*) mental sickness, or a disordered imagination.

BINTA'MBARA (*Bot.*) the *Convolvulus pes capræ* of Linnæus.

BIO'GRAPHY (*Lit.*) from βίος, life, and γράφω, to write; the writing the lives of eminent persons.

BIOLY'CHNIUM (*Med.*) βιολύχνιον, from βίος and λυχνίον, a lamp; 1. The vital flame, the lamp of life. 2. A secret preparation of human blood.

BI'OS (*Med.*) a Greek term signifying literally life, is taken sometimes in the sense of *victus*, food. *Castel. Lex. Med.*

BIO'TE (*Med.*) βιότη, the time of continuance of aliment in the body. *Gal. apud Castel. Lex. Med.*

BIOTHA'NATOS (*Ant.*) βιοθάνατος, *mors*, from βία, force, and θάνατος, death; persons dying a violent death, particularly by suicide; hence Ordericus Vitalis, speaking of William Rufus, tells us that the bishops, considering his wicked life and bad exit, adjudged him "ecclesiastica veluti biothanetum absolutione indignum." *Lib.* 10, p. 782.

BIO'TICUM *metrum* (*Ant.*) μέτρον βιωτικόν, a measure whereby we buy and sell whatever is necessary for our use.

BI'OVAC (*Mil.*) *bivouac*, from *bis*, double, and the German *Wache*, a guard; an extraordinary guard kept by the whole army which remain under arms all the night to prevent a surprize; whence "To bivouac" is to remain all night under arms; and "To raise the bivouac," to order the men to return to their tents some time after break of day.

BIPA'RTIENT (*Mat.*) *bipartiens*, from *bis* and *partior*, to divide, dividing into two; an epithet for a number that divides another into two equal parts without a remainder.

BIPA'RTITE (*Bot.*) *bipartitus*, divided into two; an epithet for the corolla, the leaf, and the perianth, when they are divided into two parts at the base.

BI'PES (*Ant.*) a biped, or two footed animal.

BIPI'NNATE (*Bot.*) doubly pinnate, or winged, an epithet for a leaf; *folium bipinnatum*, a common petiole, having pinnate leaves on each side of it, as in *Anemone pulsatilla*.

BIPINNATI'FID (*Bot.*) doubly pinnatifid, an epithet for the leaf and the frons; *folium bipinnatifidum*, a petiole having pinnatifid leaves on each side of it; *frons bipinnatifida*, a bipinnated frond, having the foliola cleft halfway down.

BIPINNE'LLA (*Bot.*) the same as *Pimpinella*.

BIQUA'DRATE (*Algeb.*) or *biquadratic*, i. e. the square squared, or the fourth power of any quantity, as 16, which is the biquadrate of 2, thus $2 \times 2 \times 2 \times 2 = 16$.—*Biquadrate root*, the root of a biquadratic power, as 2, the biquadrate root of 16.—*Biquadratic equation*, an equation of the fourth degree in which the unknown quantity rises to the fourth power, as $x^4 + a x^3 + b x^2 + c x + d = 0$, which is a biquadratic equation having the unknown quantity, x, raised to the fourth degree or power. [vide *Algebra*]

BIQUADRA'TICS (*Algeb.*) that part of an equation in which there are biquadratic powers. [vide *Biquadrate*]

BIQUIQUE'NTILE (*Astron.*) an aspect, formed by Kepler, consisting of two-fifths of a whole circle, or 140 degrees distance.

BIRCH-TREE (*Bot.*) a well-known tree, the *Betula* of Linnæus, which is commonly raised from roots and suckers. The timber, which is of an inferior quality, is used for hop-poles, hoops, and the like.

BIRD (*Orn.*) vide *Aves*, and *Ornithology*.—Bird of Paradise, the *Paradisea* of Linnæus, a bird of New Guinea, the bill of which is covered with a belt of downy feathers.

BI'RD-BOLT (*Ich.*) a delicate kind of codfish, otherwise called Burbot.

BIRD-BOLT (*Her.*) a small arrow with three heads, which was discharged at birds from a cross. This arrow is borne in coat armour as in the annexed figure. "He beareth *argent* three bird-bolts *sable*, by the name of Risden. These were the arms of Tristram Risden, esq. the celebrated antiquary. As bird-bolts are borne with two or more heads, the number of heads must always be specified.

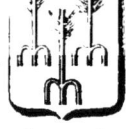

BI'RD-CALL (*Sport.*) a whistle or pipe to decoy birds.—*Bird-lime*, a glutinous matter made of the bark of holly, which being spread upon twigs entangles the feet of birds that light upon it.

BI'RD-CHERRY (*Bot.*) a shrub, the *Prunus padus* of Linnæus.—Bird Pepper, a shrub, the *Capsicum baccatum*.

BI'RDING-PIECE (*Sport.*) a fowling-piece or gun for shooting birds.

BI'RD'S-EYE (*Bot.*) an annual, the *Adonis autumnalis* of Linnæus.—Bird's-Foot, an annual, the *Ornithopus*.—Bird's-foot Trefoil, an herbaceous root, more perennial than otherwise, the *Lotus*.—Bird's-Tongue, a perennial, the *Senecio paludosus*.

BIRE'MIS (*Ant.*) a galley with two benches of oars. *Cic. ad Attic.* l. 16, ep. 4; *Hirt. de Bell. Alex.* c. 47; *Plin.* l. 7, c. 56.

BIRGA'NDER (*Orn.*) a sort of wild goose.

BIRE'THRUS (*Ant.*) the same as *Cucupha*.

BI'RLAW (*Law*) or Bye-law, a law in Scotland, established between neighbours by common consent.—*Birlaw-court*, a court in which cognizance is taken of complaints betwixt neighbours.—*Birlaw-men*, men who are chosen to be judges in the Birlaw court, or arbitrators betwixt neighbours.

BI'RLET (*Archæol.*) a coif or hood.

BI'RSEN (*Med.*) an inflammation in the breast.

BIRT (*Ich.*) a fish of the turbot kind.

BIRTH (*Mar.*) 1. The station in which a ship rides at anchor: "She is in a good *birth*," that is, in a good anchoring-ground. 2. The room where any number of the ship's company mess or reside.

BI'RTH-DAY (*Chron.*) the day on which a person is born, or the anniversary of that day.

BI'RTH-RIGHT (*Law*) honour or estate belonging to a person by right of his birth.

BI'RTH-WORT (*Bot.*) a perennial, the *Aristolochia* of Linnæus.

TO BIRTH *a ship's company* (*Mar.*) to allot to each man the space in which his hammock is to be slung.

BI'RTHING (*Mar.*) the raising the sides of the ship.

BIS (*Com.*) twice; used in accounts to denote duplicates of folios or accounts.

BIS (*Mus.*) in a composition, signifies that the bars included within the same curve is to be sung or played twice successively.

BI'SA (*Com.*) *biza*, or *bize*, a coin of Pegu, equal to half a ducat, or one shilling and eightpence.

BISACU'TUS (*Mil.*) two-edged; an epithet for an iron weapon.

BISA'NTIUM (*Num.*) besant, or besantine, a gold coin of Byzantium current in England, equal to half a ducain silver, or two shillings sterling.

BISCO'CTUS (*Ant.*) an epithet for *panis*, bread, that is, twice baked, whence comes the word biscuit.

BI'-SCOT (*Ant.*) i. e. a double scot, or fine, for every perch of land, in default of not repairing banks, causeways, &c. on a day assigned, the first fine being called bilaw.

BI'SCUIT (*Cook.*) *biscoctus*; twice or much baked bread.—*Sea Biscuit*, a sort of unfermented bread, more baked than any other, and fitted to last good for a year at sea.

BISCUTE'LLA (*Bot.*) from *bis* and *scatella*, diminutive of *scutum*, a shield, the fruit resembling a double shield; Buckler Mustard, a genus of plants, Class 15 *Titradynamia*, Order 1 *Siliquosa*.

  Generic Characters. CAL. *perianth* four-leaved.—COR. four-petalled.—STAM. *filaments* six; *anthers* simple.—PIST. *germ* compressed; *style* simple; *stigma* obtuse.—PER. *silicle* erect; *seeds* solitary.

  Species. The species are either annuals, perennials, or shrubs. Among the annuals are the—*Biscutella auriculata, Thlaspidium, &c. Leuconium, &c.* seu *Jondrabas, &c.* Earpodded Buckler Mustard.—*Biscutella Apula Thlaspidium, &c.; Thlaspi biscutatum, &c. Thlaspi clypeatum,* seu *Jondraba, &c.* Spear-leaved Buckler Mustard, &c. Among the shrubs or perennials are the—*Biscutella sempervirens, Biscutella lævigata, &c. &c.*

BISDIAPA'SON (*Mus.*) a name among the ancients for a double octave.

BISE'CTION (*Math.*) from *bis* and *seco*, to cut; the cutting any quantity, as a line or an angle, into two equal parts.

BISEMA'TUM (*Min.*) Plumbum.

BISERIA'LIS (*Bot.*) two-rowed; an epithet for the *Lamellæ* and *Sorus*.—*Lamellæ biseriales*, gills, which consist of a long and a short gill alternate.—*Sorus biserialis*, the moss which has its seed capsules run in two close lines, as in *Danæa* and *Angiopteris*.

BISERU'LA (*Bot.*) Hatchet Vetch, a genus of plants, Class 17 *Diadelphia*, Order 4 *Decandria*.

  Generic Characters. CAL. *perianth* one-leaved.—COR. papilionaceous.—STAM. *filaments* diadelphous; *anthers* small.—PIST. *germ* oblong; *style* subulate; *stigma* simple.—PER. *legume* large; *seeds* very many.

  Species. The only species is the *Bisserula pelecinus astragalus*, seu *Lunaria, &c.* Bastard Hatchet Vetch, an annual, native of the South of Europe.

BI'SHOP (*Ant.*) vide *Episcopus*.

BISHOP (*Ecc.*) a dignitary in the Christian Church who presides over the clergy within a certain district, called his diocese. The word is derived from the Greek επισκοπος, signifying literally an overseer, and was at first indiscriminately applied to those who presided over a single church, and to those who had many churches: but bishops were from the beginning a superior order of clergy, who became the successors of the apostles both in their office and authority. The bishop is called by Justin Martyr προεςως, by St. Cyprian the *summus sacerdos*, in distinction from *presbyteri et diaconi*, priests and deacons, who might baptize, but not without permission from the bishop, *ob ecclesiæ honorem*. *Clem. Constit. Apostol.* l. 2, c. 1, &c.; *Ignat. in Epist. ad Philadelph.*; *Tertull. de Baptism.* c. 17; *S. Cyprian. Epist.* 66; *S. Chrysostom. Hom.* 10, &c.; *S. Au-*

gust. de Civ. Dei, l. 19, c. 19; *S. Hieron. Epist. ad Evagrium*; *Socrat. Hist. Eccles.*; *D. Gregor. Hom.* 26, in *Evang. &c.*

Bishops are *suffragans* or *assistants* to the archbishop, who is the chief of the clergy in his *Province*. The archbishop is said to be *enthroned*, the bishop to be *installed*; the titles of the archbishop are, *Your Grace* and *Most Reverend Father in God by Divine Providence*; those of a bishop, *My Lord*, or *Right Reverend Father in God by Divine Permission*. An archbishop is *created*, and consecrated by another archbishop, and two bishops: according to a statute in the reign of Henry VIII. a bishop is *elected* by the King's *congé d'élire*, or licence to elect the person named by the King, directed to the Dean and Chapter.—*Suffragan* or *titular bishop*, one who is subordinate or assistant to the bishop or archbishop by whom he is consecrated, to execute such power, jurisdiction, and authority, and to receive such profits, as are specified in his commission.

BI'SHOPPING (*Man.*) a trick among horsedealers of attempting to pass off an old horse for a young one, by operating on his mouth.

BI'SHOPRIC (*Ecc.*) the diocese, or district, over which a bishop presides.

BI'SHOPS-WEED (*Bot.*) an annual, the *Ammi* of Linnæus.

BISI'LIQUOUS (*Bot.*) an epithet for plants contained in two distinct pods.

BI'SK (*Sport.*) in French *bisque*; odds at the play of Tennis, a stroke allowed to the weakest player.

BISK (*Cook.*) a pottage made of quails, capons, &c.

BISLI'NGUA (*Bot.*) the *Hypoglossum* of Linnæus.

BISMA'LVA (*Bot.*) another name for the *Althæa*.

BI'SMIA (*Mus.*) an epithet for piano forte pieces, in which both hands are alternately employed upon the same melody.

BISMI'LLAH (*Theol.*) the term with which the Mahometans begin their Koran, compounded of *bi*, in, *ism*, the name, and *Allah*, God.

BI'SMUTH, *salts of* (*Chem.*) salts formed by the mixture of bismuth, the base, with some acid, as the nitrate of bismuth, the sulphate of bismuth, &c.

BISMU'TUM (*Min.*) *Bismuth*, a genus of metals.
Generic Characters. Reddish-white, soft, brittle, specific gravity 9·822, easily melting, and soluble in acids.
Species. The species are—*Bismutum nativum*, seu *Wismutum nativum*.—*Bismutum ochraceum*, seu *Wismutum pulverulentum*, Flowers of Bismuth, or Bismuth ochre.—*Bismutum sulphuratum*, seu *Wismutum sulphure*, Sulphurated Bismuth, or Sulphuret of Bismuth.—*Bismutum martiale*, seu *Wismutum lamellis cuneatis*, Martial sulphurized Bismuth.

BI'SON (*Zool.*) a variety of the ox, or *Bos taurus* of Linnæus, which has its horns bent forwards, back gibbous, and mane long. *Plin.* l. 8, c. 15; *Gess. de Animal.*; *Aldrov. de Quad.*

BI'SSAC (*Mil.*) French for a wallet, or sack, which opens down the middle.

BISSE'XTILE (*Chron.*) *bissextilis*, or *bissextus*, Leap-Year; a name given by the ancient Romans to that year in which the intercalation of a day took place, by reckoning the sixth of the Calends of March, *i. e.* the 24th of February, twice. This intercalation, which happens every fourth year, was made by Julius Cæsar to compensate for the hours which the sun takes up in his course above 365 days. It is called *intercalaris* by Pliny. *Plin. Nat. Hist.* l. 2, c. 24; *Columel.* l. 3, c. 6; *Ammian.* l. 26, c. 1; *Macrob. Saturnal.* l. 1, c. 14; *Censor de Die Nat.*

BISTA'CIUM (*Bot.*) the same as *Pistacia*.

BI'STER (*Paint.*) a colour made of chimney soot boiled and diluted.

BISTO'RTA (*Bot.*) from *bis* and *torta*, twice twisted, or wreathed; so called from the contortion of its roots, which, medicinally applied, are powerfully astringent, and antiseptic. It is a species of the *Polygonum* of Linnæus.

BISTOU'RY (*Surg.*) a small knife of various forms, according to the purpose for which it is to be used.

BI'SUS (*Archæol.*) or *panis basius*, brown bread.

BIT (*Mar.*) vide *Bitt*.

BIT (*Carpent.*) a boring instrument, so constructed as to be taken out of the handle, which is called the stock, by means of a spring. Bits are of different kinds, as—*Shell-bits*, for boring wood.—*Centre-bits*, which form a cylindrical excavation, by turning on an axis or centre.—*Countersink bits*, for widening the upper part of a hole, &c.

BIT (*Com.*) vide *Bitt*.

TO BIT *the cable*, to put it round the bitts so as to fasten it.

BI'TCHEMARE (*Com.*) a kind of fish on the coast of China, which is salted and dried like cod.

TO BI'TE (*Mar.*) is said of the anchor when it lays hold of the ground.

TO BITE (*Print.*) is said of the frisket of a printing press when it falls upon any of the sides of the pages.

BI'TERNATE (*Bot.*) i. e. doubly ternate, an epithet for a leaf; *folium biternatum*, a petiole having three ternate leaflets, as in Epimedium.

BITHNIMA'LEA (*Med.*) a word coined by Dolæus, to express the active principle presiding over the several functions of the stomach.

BITHY'NICI *tonsoris emplastrum* (*Med.*) a plaster for splenetic people.

BI'THYNUS (*Med.*) the name of a plaster, and a trochee.

BI'TT (*Mech.*) from the verb to bite; any thing that lays hold, or is laid hold of, as—*Bitt of a bridle*, the iron attached to the bridle, which is put into the horse's mouth, called otherwise the *bitt-mouth*.—*Bitt of a poker*, the part which stirs up the fire.—*Bitt of a water-mill on boats*, the piece which fastens the mills to the boats.—*Bitt of a key*, that part in which the wards are cut out.

BITT (*Mar.*) the name for two pieces of timber, in the fore part of the ship, to which the anchor cables are fastened.

BITT (*Com.*) a piece of money value 7½d. current at Barbadoes.

BI'TTACLE (*Mar.*) a frame of timber in the steerage of a ship in which the compass stands. [vide *Binnacle*]

BI'TTEN (*Bot.*) *Præmorsus*, an epithet for a root, a leaf, and a corolla. [vide *Præmorsus*]

BI'TTER (*Mar.*) the turn of the cable round the bitts; thus, a ship stopped by her cable is said to be brought up to a bitter.—*Bitter-end*, that part of the cable which is abaft the bitts, and therefore within boards when the ship rides at anchor.

BITTER *almond* (*Bot.*) a tree, and the fruit of the tree, the *Amygdalus communis* and *Amygdala* of Linnæus.—*Bitter* Cucumber, Gourd, or Apple, an annual, the *Cucumis Colocynthus*, otherwise called *Coloquintida*.—Bitter-Sweet, a perennial, the *Solanum dulcamara*.—Bitter-Vetch, a perennial, the *Orobus*.—Bitter-Wort, another name for Gentian.

BITTER-SALT (*Min.*) the *Amarum geminum* of Linnæus.—Bitter-spar, a species of saline stone, or calcareous salt.

BITTER *principle* (*Chem.*) the bitter parts of vegetable substances, which may be extracted by a chemical principle. —*Artificial bitter*, any bitter formed by the action of nitric acid on vegetable and other substances.

BI'TTERN (*Orn.*) or Bittour, the *Ardea* of Linnæus; a bird of the Heron kind, which is of retired habits, concealing itself in the midst of reeds and rushes in marshes. It has two kinds of notes, the one croaking, when it is disturbed; and the other bellowing, which it commences in the spring, and ends in the autumn. There is a small sort of this bird which is distinguished by the name of the Little Bittern Heron.

BITTERN (*Med.*) a certain very bitter liquor, which drains off in the making of common salt, and is used in the preparation of Epsom salt.

BITU'MEN (*Min.*) a genus of mineral substances of the class *Inflammabilia*.
  Generic Characters. Easily combustible with flame; and emitting, when ignited, a strong odour; greasy to the touch.
  Species. The species are the—*Bitumen Naphtha, seu Bitumen fluidum*, Naphtha, found principally in Persia.—*Bitumen petroleum*, Petrol, or Rock oil, liquid, but of thicker consistence than the former.—*Bitumen Maltha*, Barbadoes Tar, found floating on lakes.—*Bitumen Mumia*, Mineral Mummy, found in the clefts of rocks.—*Bitumen asphaltum*, Asphalt, or Bitumen, which was used by the ancient Egyptians for making mummies.—*Bitumen serum*, Mineral Tallow, found in Finland.—*Bitumen elasticum*, Mineral Cahoutchou, or Elastic Bitumen.—*Bitumen gagas*, jet-black, compact, and glassy.—*Bitumen Ampelites*, Bovey, or Cannel Coal, bituminous wood.—*Bitumen lithanthrax*, common coal.—*Bitumen oxygenatum*, Culm, or Stone Coal, oxygenated carbon.

BI'VALVE (*Bot.*) double-valved; an epithet for the capsule, glume, indusium, and spathe, which is split into two portions, as all the siliques and the glumes in Grasses, &c.

BIVASCULA'RES (*Bot.*) from *bis et vasculum*, a little vessel; bivascular plants, a class in Hermann's system.

BIVE'NTER (*Anat.*) from *bis* and *venter*, the belly biventral; an epithet for a muscle with two bellies, as the *Biventer cervicis*, a muscle of the lower jaw, &c.

BI'XA (*Bot.*) a genus of plants, Class 13 *Polyandria*, Order 1 *Monogynia*.
  Generic Characters. CAL. perianth five-toothed. — COR. double.—STAM. *filaments* numerous; *anthers* erect.— PIST. *germ* ovate; *style* filiform; *stigma* parallelly bifid.—PER. *capsule* ovate-cordate; *seeds* numerous; *receptacle* near.
  Species. The only species is the—*Bixa Orellana, Orleana*, seu *Orellana, Arbor Mexicana, Urucu, Rocu Pigmentaria, Bixa Oviedi*, seu *Achiotl*, Arnotto, Arnotta, or Anata, a shrub, native of America.
  From the red pulp which covers the seeds of this plant is made the drug *Yerra Orellana, Rouco*, or *Arnotto*. [vide *Anata*]

BIZA'RRO (*Mus.*) Italian for strange or fantastical, and applied to the style of movement.

BLA'CCIÆ (*Med.*) the measles.

BLACK (*Phy.*) a colour which is supposed to be produced by the peculiar texture of bodies, which deaden, as it were, the light falling upon them, and reflect none, or very little of it, outwards towards the eye. Sir Isaac Newton considers that, for the production of black colours, the corpuscles must be less than any of those that exhibit other colours.

BLACK (*Paint.*) as a colour or dye, is of different kinds, as follow:—*Lamp black, smoke black*, the smoke of rosin, prepared by melting and purifying the rosin in iron vessels.—*Ivory black*, made of burnt ivory, is used in miniatures.—*Spanish black*, so called because it was first used by the Spaniards, is made of burnt cork.—*Indian ink*, made of burnt horse beans, very commonly used by painters instead of water-colours.—*Earth black*, a kind of coal which is pounded and used in fresco.—*Printer's black*, the same as printer's ink, which is frequently used by painters in washing.—*Bistre*, a colour made of chimney soot, boiled and diluted with water, with which painters wash their designs.—*Dyer's black*, one of the five simple and mother colours used in dying, which is differently made according to the quality of the stuff to be dyed.

BLACK BOOK (*Archæol.*) vide *Liber Niger*.

BLACK BOOK (*Law*) a book kept in the Exchequer, which contains the orders of that court.—*Black maile*, a rent in the Northern counties, either of money, corn, or cattle, and paid to some person in power living on the borders, and allied to the Moss Troopers, to protect them from their robberies.

BLACK-ROD, Usher of the (*Her.*) the Usher of the Order of the Garter, so called because he carries a black rod with a golden lion on the top.

BLACK-HOLE (*Mil.*) a place of confinement to which soldiers are committed at the discretion of the commanding officer.

BLACK-LETTER (*Gram.*) a sort of old English alphabet. [vide *Alphabet*]

BLACK-CATTLE (*Husband.*) a name given to oxen and cows.

BLA'CK-BERRY (*Bot.*) the fruit of the common Bramble, or the *Rubus fruticosus* of Linnæus.

BLA'CKBIRD (*Orn.*) a bird, well known for its fine black colour and beautiful voice. It is the *Turdus merula* of Linnæus, which frequents hedges, sings during spring and summer, and makes its nest of moss, grass, &c.—Black Cap, the *Motacilla atracapilla*, a little bird about five and a half inches in length, which frequents orchards, singing very finely: it is distinguished by the black crown of its head.—Black Cock, or Black Game, a name given to the black sort of grouse.

BLA'CK-FISH (*Ich.*) a fish of the perch kind found in Cornwall; the *Perca nigra* in the Linnean system.

BLA'CK-LEAD (*Min.*) *Plumbago*, or the *Graphites* of Linnæus; a mineral found in lead mines, which is used in making pencils. It is not fusible but by a very violent heat.

BLACKBU'RNIA (*Bot.*) a genus of plants, Class 4 *Tetandria*, Order 1 *Monogynia*.
  Generic Characters. CAL. perianth very short, four-toothed; *teeth* short, acute.—COR. *petals* four, elliptic.— STAM. *filaments* four, rather shorter than the petals.— PIST. *germ* conic; *style* filiform; *stigma* simple.
  Species. The only species is the *Blackburnia pinnata*.

BLACKSTONIA (*Bot.*) the *Chlora perfoliata* of Linnæus.

BLADA'RIUS (*Archæol.*) a corn chandler or mealman, according to old records.

BLADDER, urinary (*Anat.*) vide *Urinary Bladder.—Bladder-Gall*, vide *Gall-Bladder*.

BLADDER, Inflammation of (*Med.*) vide *Cystitis*.

BLADDER (*Bot.*) *utriculus*, a distended membranaceous pericarp, as in the Bladder Senna.—Bladder-Nut, so called from its fruit being contained in a membrane inflated like a bladder. The plant which produces this fruit is a tree, the *Staphylea pinnata* of Linnæus. *Raii Hist. Plant.—*Bladder Senna, a shrub, the *Colutea*. It yields a papilionaceous flower, which is succeeded by pods that resemble the inflated bladder of fishes, in which are contained several kidney-shaped seeds.

BLA'DDERS (*Bot.*) *Vesiculæ*, or *Utriculi*, bags at the root of the *Utricularia*.

BLADE (*Bot.*) the leaf, or first sprout of a plant.

BLADE (*Mech.*) the flat part of a sword or knife, which resembles the blade of grass in shape.

BLA'DE-BONE (*Anat.*) the Shoulder-Bone, called by anatomists the *Scapula*.

BLA'DED (*Her.*) bearing a blade of corn, &c.; an expression in blazonry when the blade is of a different colour from the ear or fruit.

BLA'DHIA (*Bot.*) a genus of plants, named by Thunberg after P. J. Bladh, a Swede, Class 5 *Pentandria*, Order 1 *Monogynia*.

Generic Characters. CAL. *perianth* one-leaved.—COR. one-petalled.—STAM. *filaments* five; *anthers* heart-shaped.—PIST. *germ* superior; *style* filiform; *stigma* simple.—PER. *berry* globose; *seed* single.

Species. The species are shrubs, and natives of Japan, as *Bladhia japonica, foliis,* &c. seu *Sankits,* &c.—*Bladhia crispa, foliis,* &c. seu *Kvakits,* &c.

BLÆ'RIA (*Bot.*) a genus of plants, named after P. Blair, M.D. and a botanist, Class 4 *Tetrandria,* Order 1 *Monogynia.*

Generic Characters. CAL. *perianth* four-parted.—COR. monopetalous.—STAM. *filaments* four; *anthers* oblong.—PIST. *germ* four-cornered; *style* setaceous; *stigma* obtuse.—PER. *capsule* obtuse; *seeds* some roundish.

Species. The principal species are—*Blæria bricoides,* seu *Erica blæria,* &c. Heath-leaved Blæria.—*Blæria ciliaris, articulata,* &c.

BLÆ'SUS (*Med.*) a stammerer.

BLAIR (*Vet.*) a distemper in cattle, being a bladder full of wind and water, rising from the root of the tongue, which grows so large as to stop the breath of the animal.

BLAKE'A (*Bot.*) a genus of plants, named by Brown after Mr. Blake, of Antigua, Class 11 *Dodecandria,* Order 1 *Monogynia.*

Generic Characters. CAL. *perianth of the fruit,* inferior; *of the flower,* superior.—COR. *petals* six.—STAM. *filaments* twelve; *anthers* triangular.—PIST. *germ* inferior; *style* subulate; *stigma* acute.—PER. *capsule* obovate; *seeds* very many.

Species. The species are shrubs, and natives of South America and the West Indies.

BLA'NEA (*Med.*) a purging mixture; so called because it was supposed to evacuate the white phlegmatic humours.

BLANCH *farm* (*Law*) a farm where the rent is paid in silver, not in black cattle.

BLA'NCHING (*Mech.*) the art of making any thing white.

BLANCHING *almonds* (*Cook.*) skinning them by means of hot water.

BLANCHING (*Min.*) annealing, boiling, and cleansing the money that is coined, to give it the necessary lustre and brilliancy.—*Blanching* denotes also the operation of covering iron plates with a thin coat or crust of tin.

BLANCHING (*Hort.*) the method of whitening salads.

BLANK (*Num.*) from *blanc,* white, i. e. empty, or unfilled up; a kind of white money, value 8*d.* coined by Hen. V. in France; but forbidden to be current in England. 2 *Stat.* Hen. 6.

BLANK *bar* (*Law*) the same as common bar, plea in bar. [vide *Bar*]—*Blank bar,* in judicial proceedings, void spaces left by mistake, which may cause an abatement, or demurrer. Stat. 4, Ed. 4; 20 H. 6.—*Blank letter of Attorney,* one in which is a void space left to be filled up by the name of the person who is to act. A *blank* is also a piece of paper at the bottom of which a person has signed his name, the rest being void, commonly entrusted to arbiters or friends for the settlement of a dispute.

BLANK (*Com.*) a void space in a merchant's books, which in a court of law is suspicious.—*Blank endorsement,* when one person writes his name on a bill, leaving an empty space sufficient for writing either an order or a receipt.

BLANK *verse* (*Poet.*) that which has no rhymes.

BLANK (*Archit.*) an epithet for a window or door which is made to appear like a real window or door.

BLA'NKETS (*Mil.*) combustibles made of coarse brown paper, steeped in nitre, dried, and then dipped again in tallow, resin, and sulphur. These blankets are used in fireships.

BLANKETS (*Print.*) woollen cloths to lay between the tympans of a printing press, in order to produce a fair impression of the letter.

BLANKET (*Bot.*) in French *Blanquet,* a large pear, approaching to a round form. *Pyrus sativa fructu æstivo albido majori. Tournef. Instit.*

BLANQUI'LLE (*Num.*) a small coin current in Morocco on the coast of Barbary, equal in value to about three halfpence English.

BLAPS (*Ent.*) a division of the genus *Pimelia,* according to Fabricius, comprehending the insects of this tribe which have the feelers clavate.

BLAPSIGO'NIA (*Nat.*) a disease in bees that do not breed.

BLAPTISE'CULA (*Bot.*) a name for the Cornbottle, because it turns the edge of the mowers.

BLARE (*Com.*) a coin in Berne, a canton of Switzerland, equal to a penny.

BLAS (*Alch.*) the force of motion according to Van Helmont.

BLA'SA (*Bot.*) an Indian tree, the fruit of which is powdered and used to destroy worms.

BLA'SIA (*Bot.*) a genus of plants, Class *Cryptogamia,* Order *Algæ.*

BLAST (*Nat.*) the stroke of a malignant planet, the infection of any thing pestilential, or the blight of corn from a pestilential wind.

TO BLAST (*Min.*) is to blow up mines by the force of gunpowder.

BLASTE'MA (*Med.*) βλάστημα, a bud; is used by Hippocrates for a cutaneous pimple, resembling a bud. *Foes. Œconom. Hippocrat.*

BLA'STINGS (*Nat.*) winds and frosts immediately succeeding rain, which are destructive to the fruits.

BLATTA (*Ant.*) a sort of worm which consumes books and garments.

Martial l. 6, epig. 60.

Quam multi tineas pascunt blattasque diserti.

Horat. l. 2, sat. 3, v. 119.

cui stragula vestis,
Blattarum ac tinearum epulæ, putrescat in arcâ?

Plin. l. 11, c. 8.

BLATTA *Byzantina* (*Nat.*) or *blattea,* θρόμβος αἵματος, concreted blood, particularly that of the purple-fish. *Paul. ex Fest.; Serv. in Æneid.,* &c.

BLATTA (*Ent.*) Cock-Roach; a genus of animals, Class *Insecta,* Order *Hemiptera.*

Generic Characters. Head inflected.—*Antennæ* setaceous; feelers unequal.—*Wing-cases and wings* smooth.—*Thorax* rather flat.—*Legs* formed for running.—*Abdomen* terminating in four spines or bristles.

Species. The principal species which are most known are the—*Blatta gigantea,* the largest of the genus, nearly equal to the egg of an hen in size, native of the warmer parts of Asia, Africa, and South America.—*Blatta orientalis,* the Black Beetle, an insect naturalized in Europe.—*Blatta Americana,* American Cockroach, of a light chesnut colour, common in the warmer parts of America and the West Indies.—*Blatta heteroclita,* shorter and rounder than the rest, and further distinguished by having three spots on one wing-sheath, and four on the other.

BLATTA'RIA (*Bot.*) the *Lysimachia vulgaris* of Linnæus.

BLA'ZON (*Her.*) comes from the German *blasen,* to blow; because a trumpet used to be blown at justs, &c. previous to the herald's recording the achievements of the knights, and signifies the explication of coats of arms in apt and significant terms.

BLA'ZONRY (*Her.*) or blazoning, from *blazon;* that branch of the art of heraldry which consists in expressing in proper terms all that belongs to coats of arms. [vide *Heraldry*]

BLEAK (*Ich.*) a little fish, the *Alburnus* of Ausonius, [vide *Alburnus*] and the *Cyprinus alburnus* of Linnæus, which is very abundant in our rivers. The *bleaks* keep together in great shoals, and at certain seasons are infested with a species of Gordius or hair-worm, which causes them to tumble about on the surface of the waters, apparently in great agonies, and unable to swim any distance. They are then denominated by the sailors *mad bleaks*. The flesh of this fish is very white and good.

BLE'CHNON (*Bot.*) βληχνον, a plant of the fern kind, mentioned by Dioscorides and Pliny. *Dioscor.* l. 4, c. 186; *Plin.* l. 27, c. 9.

BLE'CHNUM, *in the Linnean system*, a genus of plants, Class *Cryptogamia*, Order *Filices*.

BLE'CHON (*Bot.*) Penny-royal.

BLEE'DING (*Med.*) is either an operation of letting blood, which is called *blood-letting*, or it is an involuntary discharge of blood, called an *hæmorrhage*.—*Bleeding* at the nose [vide *Epitaxis*]

BLEIME (*Vet.*) an inflammation arising from bruised blood between the horse's sole and the bone of the foot towards the heels: this may be either accidental or owing to bad shoeing.

BLE'MISH (*Vet.*) any imperfection in a horse which impedes a sound warrant, as broken knees, cracked heels, false quarters, &c.

BLEMISH (*Hunt.*) when the hounds finding where the chace has been, only make a proffer, and return.

BLENCH (*Law*) the same as *Blanche*.

BLENDE (*Min.*) different species of Zincum.

BLE'ND-WATER (*Vet.*) a distemper incident to black cattle, in which their livers are affected.

BLE'NNA (*Med.*) βλιννα, mucus flowing from the brain, through the nostrils. Galen explains it by the word μυξα. *Hippocrat. de Epidem.* l. 2; *Gal. Exeges; Gorr. Def. Med.; Foes. Œconom. Hippocrat.*

BLE'NNIUS (*Ich.*) Blenny, the name of a fish, derived from βλιννα, mucus, because of its slimy nature.

BLENNIUS, *in the Linnean system*, a genus of fishes, Order *Jugulares*.
Generic Characters. Head sloping from the eyes.—*Gill-membrane* with six rays.—*Body* lanceolate.—*Ventral-fins* of two united rays.—*Anal-fin* distinct.
Species. The species consist of such as have a crested head and such as have not.

BLENNY (*Ich.*) vide *Blennius*.

BLENORRHŒ'A (*Med.*) or *Blenorrhagia*, from βλιννα, *mucus*, and ριω, to flow; a gleet, or a discharge of mucus from the urethra.

BLE'PHARA (*Anat.*) βλιφαρα, from βλιπω and Φαρω, a defence for the sight; the eyelids. *Ruf. Ephes. de Appellat. Part Human. Corp.* l. 1, c. 4.

BLEPHA'RIDES (*Anat.*) βλιφαριδις, the hair growing on the eyelids. *Hesychius*.

BLEPHAROPHTHA'LMIA (*Med.*) from βλιφαρα, the eyelids, and οφθαλμια, a disease in the eyes; signifies, literally, a disease in the eyelids.

BLEPHAROPTO'SIS (*Med.*) from βλιφαρα, the eyelids, and πτωσις, a falling; a prolapse or falling of the upper eyelid, so as to cover the cornea.

BLEPHARO'TIS (*Med.*) from βλιφαρα, the eyelids; an inflammation in the eyelids.

BLEPHAROXY'STUM (*Sur.*) βλιφαροξυστρ, from βλιφαρα, the eyelids, and ξιω, to scrape; an instrument, so called by Paulus Æginetta, for scarifying the eyelids. Others give this instrument the name of *asperatum specillum*. *Paul. Æginet. de Re Med.* l. 3, c. 22.

BLESTRI'SMUS (*Med*) βλησμοσμος, from βαλλω, to lie; a restless tossing of the body from one posture to another, as in a phrensy, &c. *Gorr. Def. Med.; Foes. Œconom. Hippocrat.*

BLE'TA (*Archæol.*) peat, or combustible earth, dug up for burning. *Rot. Parl.* 35 Ed. I.

BLETA *white* (*Med.*) milky urine, from diseased kidneys. *Parac. de Tartar.* tract 3, c. 3; *Castell. Lex Med.*

BLE'TE (*Med.*) βλιτοι, from βαλλω, *jacio*; struck or seized with a difficulty of breathing, from an inflammation of the pleura. *Hipp. de Rat. Vict. in Morb. Acut. &c.; Foes. Œconom. Hippocrat.*

BLIGHT (*Bot.*) *ustilago*; a disease incident to plants, particularly the grasses, which affects them seriously, sometimes the whole plants and sometimes only the leaves or blossoms. It consists in a sort of fungus that converts the affected part into a sooty mass, and is commonly produced by dry cold winds which impede the circulation of the vegetable juices.

BLIND (*Surg.*) is an epithet for a blow which is attended with no apparent wound or bruise.

BLIND (*Mech.*) a false light used in shops and warehouses.—*Blinds for windows*, a contrivance to prevent persons from seeing through a window. Blinds are either made of cloth, and are called Canvas Blinds, or of laths, which are Venetian Blinds.

BLINDS (*Mil.*) or, in French, *blindes*, bundles of oziers used at the heads of trenches to protect the men.

BLI'ND-WORM (*Zool.*) or Slow-worm, so called from the smallness of its eyes and the slowness of its motion; a harmless torpid species of serpent, the *Anguis fragilis* of Linnæus.

BLINK *of the ice* (*Mar.*) the dazzling whiteness about the horizon, which is occasioned by the reflection of light from fields of ice.

BLI'NK-BEER (*Husb.*) beer kept unbroached till it is sharp.

BLINKS (*Sport.*) boughs put in the way where deer are likely to pass.

BLI'STER (*Med.*) *vesicatorium emplastrum*, a topical application, which raises small vesicles on the skin filled with a serous fluid.

BLISTERED (*Bot.*) an epithet for a leaf. [vide *Bullate*.]

BLI'TUM (*Bot.*) βλιτον, or βλιτον, a plant, so called from βλητος, struck with a stupor, because of its insipidity; for which reason it was esteemed of no value by the ancients. Nevertheless, the seeds were reckoned good in dysenteries. *Catull. Carm.*

Non assis facis O blitum lacunar.

Hippocrat. de Morb. Mul. l. 2; *Theophrast. Hist. Plant.* l. 7, c. 2; *Dioscor.* l. 2, c. 143; *Plin.* l. 20, c. 22; *Gal. de Alim. Fac.* l. 2, c. 45.

BLITUM, *in the Linnean system*, a genus of plants, Class 1 *Monandria*, Order 2 *Digynia*.
Generic Characters. CAL. *perianth* three-parted; *divisions* ovate.—COR. none.—STAM. *filaments* longer than the calyx; *anthers* twin.—PIST. *germ* ovate; *styles* two erect; *stigmas* simple.—PER. *capsule* ovate; *seed* single.
Species. Plants of this genus are annuals.

BLO'ATED *fish* (*Com.*) a name for herrings half dried.

BLOCK *land* (*Archæol.*) another name for what is now called freehold-land.

BLOCK (*Falcon.*) the perch whereon the hawk is kept.

BLOCK (*Mar.*) a pulley, or system of pulleys, mounted in a frame or shell, which consists of the *shell*, (fig. 1); the *sheave* or *wheel*, (fig. 2) on which the rope runs; the *pin* or *axle*, (fig. 3) on which the sheave turns. To this may be

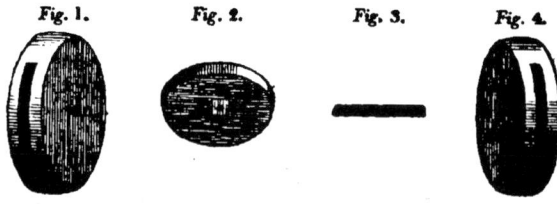

Fig. 1.   Fig. 2.   Fig. 3.   Fig. 4.

added the *strap*, or part by which the block is made fast to any particular station, and is generally made either of rope or iron. The strap terminates with an eye of rope or a hook of iron, by means of which one of the blocks, called the *running block*, is attached to the object on which it acts as a mechanical power, while the other, called the *standing block*, is suspended from some fixed support. In the best blocks those sheaves are called *coaked sheaves*, which have a brass *bush* fitted in the centre, with a round hole through it, to receive the pin. Blocks are of different kinds, as follow:—*Single blocks* are those which have a single sheave, as fig. 4; so, also, *double, treble blocks, &c.* according to the number of blocks.—*Bee-blocks*, those bolted to the bowsprit under the bees.—*Cheek-blocks*, half shells bolted against the mast-head.—*Clew-garnet-blocks*, which are suspended from the yards by a strap with two eyes.—*Clew-line-blocks*, the same as the former, but applied to the topsails.—*Fish-blocks*, which serve to haul up the flooks of the anchor in the ship's bow.—*Bull's-eye*, a kind of wooden thimble, with a hole in the centre and a groove in the circumference.—*Dead-eye*, a large circular piece of wood, having a groove in its circumference.—*Euphroe*, a long piece of wood with a number of holes, through which the crowfoot for the awning is reeved.—*Heart*, a block of wood with a large hole in the centre, and a groove to admit of a rope called a *stay*, &c.

BLOCK (*Sport.*) the small bowl which is used by bowlers to bowl at.

BLOCK-TI'N (*Min.*) the purest kind of tin, which is unmixed, and, as yet, unwrought.

BLOCKA'DE (*Mil.*) the blocking-up the avenues and roads to a place by soldiers, so as to prevent all ingress and egress.

BLOCKADE *of a port or harbour* (*Mar.*) surrounding it with ships so as to prevent ingress and egress.—"To raise a *blockade,*" to force the ships, or troops (if by land), from their stations.

BLODE'UR (*Archæol.*) deep red, whence *blouse*, a red-faced wench.

BLO'MARY (*Mech.*) the first forge in an iron mill.

BLOOD (*Anat.*) in Latin *sanguis*, a red homogeneous fluid, of a saltish taste, a rather urinous smell, and glutinous consistence, which circulates by means of the heart, the arteries, and the veins, through the whole body [vide *Anatomy, Arteries, &c.*]; while it is in motion it is perfectly fluid and red; but, when it is at rest, and grows cool, it separates into two parts; namely, a concrete floating substance of a dark red colour called *cruor crassamentum*, or Cake; and a fluid of a yellow-greenish colour, which is undermost, called the *serum*. By a chemical analysis the blood is found to contain an insipid water which soon becomes putrid, an empyreumatic oil, an ammoniacal spirit, and the remainder carbon, a spongy substance which is with difficulty incinerated.—*Blood vessels*, the vessels by which the blood is distributed to all parts of the body, consisting of arteries and veins. [vide *Anatomy, Artery, Vein*]

BLOOD (*Law*) is regarded in descent of lands; for a person is to be next and most worthy of blood to inherit his ancestor's estate. Co. Lit. 13.—*Princes of the blood*, a name for all princes who are of the blood royal.—*Blood-wit*, or *bloudveit skene*, an amerciament, or fine for bloodshed.

BLOOD *Running-itch* (*Vet.*) a disease in horses similar to the mange.—*Blood-stick*, a stick used in bleeding horses.—*Blood Spavin*, a distemper in horses, which consists in a soft swelling that grows through the hoof, and is usually full of blood.—*Blood-horse*, a particular breed of horses cultivated originally from the Arabian horses; the excellence of which consists in the compactness of his fibre, which increases his strength without adding to his bulk.—*Blood-hounds*, a fierce kind of hunting dogs that are of such quick scent that they can follow the track of the person.

BLOOD, *spitting of* (*Med.*) vide *Hæmotoptysis*.—*Vomiting of blood*, vide *Hæmatemisis*.—*Blood-shot*, a disorder of the eyes, when the blood vessels are distended so as to make the eyes appear red.

BLO'OD-FLOWER (*Bot.*) a bulbous root, the *Hæmanthus* of Linnæus.—Blood-wort, or Blood-dock, a herb, the *Rumex sanguineus*.—Dragon's Blood, vide *Dragon's Blood*.

BLO'OD-LETTING (*Surg.*) an artificial discharge of blood, which is either general, as venesection and arteriotomy, or topical, as by the application of leeches, &c.

BLO'OD-RED *hot* (*Mech.*) the last degree of heat given by smiths to their iron in the forge.

BLO'OD-STONE (*Min.*) a stone, so called because it is effectual in stopping a bleeding. [vide *Hæmatites*]

BLO'OD-SUCKER (*Nat.*) the name of a leach, so called from its sucking the blood of any animal to whom it is applied.

BLOODY *hand* (*Law*) one circumstance by which an offender in killing deer is discovered if he be found with his hands or other parts bloody. [vide *Backberind*]

BLOODY *flux* (*Med.*) vide *Dysentery*.

BLOOM *of iron* (*Com.*) a square piece of two foot long.

BLO'QUER (*Mil.*) a term in French for erecting thick rough walls along the trenches without following the line and the measure, as is usual in other walls; also for filling up the chasms in walls with rubbish and coarse mortar, as is usually done in works constructed under water.

BLO'SSOM (*Bot.*) in common language, answers to the Corolla in the botanical language.

BLOSSOM (*Man.*) an epithet for a horse, whose general colour is white interspersed with sorrel and bay hairs.

BLOT *in Backgammon* (*Sport.*) when a single man is open to be taken up.

BLOW (*Ent.*) or *Fly-Blow*, the ova of flies collected on meat.

BLOW (*Surg.*) vide *Blind*.

BLO'WER (*Zool.*) a kind of whale, so called because it spouts fourth an immense quantity of water.

BLO'WING *of fire-arms* (*Gunn.*) is when the vent or touch-hole is run or gullied, and becomes wide so that the powder will flame out.

BLOWING *glass* (*Mech.*) the process of forming glass into various shapes by means of blowing through a blow-pipe dipped into the melted glass.—*Blowing of tin*, melting the ore of tin after it has been burnt to destroy the mundic.—*Blowing-house*, furnaces where tin ore is melted and cast.

BLOWING-SNAKE (*Zool.*) a kind of snake which swells itself up before it begins to bite.

BLOWN (*Mech.*) a term used in the boiling of sugar when the sides of the copper pan, in which the sugar has been boiled for a considerable time, is beaten with the skimmer, and, a person blowing through the holes of it from one side to the other, certain sparks or small bubbles fly out, which is an indication that the sugar is come to the proper degree of boiling.

BLO'W-PIPE (*Chem.*) an apparatus in chemistry and mineralogy, which consists of a tube ending in a cavity as fine as a wire, through which air may be directed with considerable force against a flame; and, by that means, minute substances may be heated with great rapidity according to the convenience of the operator. In this manner experiments may be made on minerals, and all substances which are exposed to the action of heat.

BLUBBER (*Nat.*) the fat of a whale before it is boiled.

BLUBBER, *sea* (*Con.*) a vulgar name for the *Medusa* of Linnæus.

BLUE (*Phy.*) one of the seven primitive colours, into which they are divided when refracted through a glass prism.

BLUE (*Paint.*) as a colour, is distinguished according to the manner of its preparation, its use, shade, &c. as follows:—*Ultra-marine*, a rich and beautiful blue from an azure stone called the *Lapis lazuli*.—*Blue ashes* are used in limning, fresco, and miniature.—*Turnsole blue*, made of the seed

212

of the turnsole, used in painting on wood.—*Prussian blue*, a colour next to ultra-marine for beauty, if it be used in oil.—*Bice*, or *blue-bice*, is the palest of all the bright blues.—*Smalt* is a sort of blue frequently used instead of bice on common occasions.—*Indigo* is a dark blue extracted from indigo, principally used to shadow upon other blues.—*Blue verditer* is a bright pleasant blue somewhat inclining to a green, which is the easiest to work with in water.

BLUE (*Her.*) is the common name for azure as a tincture in coats of arms. [vide *Azure*]

BLUE-BOTTLE (*Bot.*) the *Cyanus* of Linnæus, an annual having a bell-shaped flower.

BLUE-BOTTLE (*Ent.*) a large kind of fly with a bluish body.

BLUE-BOTTLE (*Her.*) the flower is borne sometimes in coats of arms, as in the annexed figure. "He beareth a chevron, *gules*, between three blue bottles slipped, *proper*; by the name of *Chorley*, of Chorley," an ancient family in the County Palatine, of Lancaster.

BLUEING *of metals* (*Mech.*) the process of heating metals in the fire till they assume a blue colour, which is the practice of gilders before they apply the gold and silver leaf to them.

BLUENESS (*Phy.*) the property of a body which, from the size and texture of the parts that compose its surface, is disposed to reflect the blue or azure rays of light to the eye.

BLUFF (*Mar.*) a high land projecting almost perpendicularly into the sea.—*Bluff bowed*, an epithet for a vessel that has broad and flat bows.—*Bluff-headed*, an epithet for a vessel that has a small rake forward, and her stern too straight up.

BLUNDERBUS (*Mil.*) a short brass gun with a large bore.

BLUNT (*Bot.*) vide *Obtuse*.

B MOLLARE (*Mus.*) or *B molle*, one of the notes of music, otherwise called soft or flat, in opposition to the sharp.

BOA (*Med.*) a pustulous eruption similar to the small pox, which was so called, as is supposed, because oxen were subject to it. *Vet. Gloss.*

Boa (*Zool.*) a huge kind of serpent mentioned by Pliny, in the belly of which was found a young child whole, in the time of the emperor Claudius. It was so called because it used to suck the cows. *Plin.* l. 8, c. 14; *Solin.* c. 2.

Boa, in the Linnean system, a genus of animals, Class *Amphibia*, Order Serpentes.
Generic Characters. Plates on the belly; *plates* under the tail; without a rattle.
Species. The principal species are the—*Boa Constrictor, griseo-flavescens*, &c. *Serpens Ceilonica, &c. excellens*, &c. *blanda*, &c. *Americana arborea*, seu *Le Devin*, Boa Constrictor, or Great Boa, native of Africa, India, &c. This is a serpent of immense size and strength, measuring sometimes twelve yards in length, which, by twisting itself round the bodies of oxen and other animals, breaks their bones and swallows them whole.—*Boa scytale*, seu *cinerea maculis*, &c. Cinereous or Spotted Boa, native of S. America, which is eaten by the natives.—*Boa Cenchris*, seu *Tamacuilla Huilia*, &c. seu *Serpens Oculea*, &c. Ringed or Rufescent Boa, native of South America. —*Boa Enydris*, Water Boa.—*Boa Ophryas*, seu *corpore fusco*, Brown Boa, or Boa with brown body.—*Boa canina, viridis, fasciis*, &c. seu *Serpens Bojobi*, &c. Canine or Green Boa.—*Boa regia, alba, collo*, &c. *Serpens phyticus*, &c. seu *Arabica*, &c. Royal or White Boa.—*Boa phrygia, alba, dorso*, &c. seu *Serpens Phyticus*, &c. Embroidered or White Boa, native of the East Indies. —*Boa Hortulana*, seu *Griseo*, &c. Garden or Yellowish-Grey Boa, native of South America.—*Boa marina, grisea maculis*, &c. seu *Serpens testudinea*, &c. Rat or Grey Boa, native of South America.—*Boa maculis*, &c. seu *Crotalus mutus*, Crotaline Boa, native of Surinam.—*Boa fasciata, flava, corpore*, &c. seu *Bungarum Parnah*, Fasciated or Yellow Boa.

BOA-ATI (*Bot.*) a dry fruit from a tree in the Molucca islands, which is much esteemed as a medicine in the East Indies, and is an article of trade with the Dutch.

BOAR (*Zool.*) the same as swine.

BOAR (*Her.*) a charge in a coat of arms, which betokeneth a man of a bold spirit, and skilful in warlike feats, who will rather die valourously in the field than save himself by ignominious flight; whence no doubt the boar's head is found so frequent in coats of arms. [vide *Boar's Head*]

TO BOAR (*Man.*) the action of a horse when he shoots out his nose as high as his ears, or tosses his nose in the wind.

BOARD (*Polit.*) an office under the control of the executive government, where the business of particular departments is conducted, as the India Board, the Board of Ordnance, the Board of Admiralty, the Board of Works, &c.

BOARD (*Carp.*) all timber sawed to a less thickness than nine inches. All above this thickness are called *planks*; boards that are thinner at one edge than another are called *Feather-edged*. Fir boards are *Deals*, which, if they are one inch and a quarter thick, are called *Whole Deals*; and those half an inch thick, *Split Deals*. [vide *Boards*]

BOARD (*Mech.*) or *pasteboard*, layers of paper so pasted together as to make a substance as hard as a board, of which the coverings of books are made; hence a book is said to be *in boards*, or, abbreviated, *in bds.*, when the boards are only covered with paper, in distinction from a book, *bd.* or *bound*, i. e. when it is put into leather.

BOARD (*Cus.*) the food received at the board or table of another for a certain remuneration.

BOARD (*Mar.*) the space comprehended between any line a ship runs over, between tack and tack, when turning to windward, or against the wind; hence "To make a *board*," "To *board* it up to a place," i. e. to turn to windward. "To make a good *board*," or "To stretch," to sail in a straight line. "To make short *boards*," to tack frequently. "To make a stern *board*," to fall back from the point she has gained on the last tack. "Weather *board*," that side of a ship which is to windward. "A long *board*," to stand a good way off before you tack. "To leave the land on back *board*," to leave it a-stern or behind.
Board is also taken for the ship itself, as "*a-board*," i. e. within a ship. "To go *a-board*," to go into the ship. "To throw *over-board*," to throw out of a ship. "To slip by the *board*," i. e. by the ship's side. "*Board* and *board*," when two ships come so near each other as to touch by the *board* over the ship's side.

TO BOARD (*Mar.*) to enter a ship in battle, or in a forcible manner.

BOARDED *floor* (*Carpent.*) a floor formed of boards, in distinction from a *stone floor*, or a *brick floor*.

BOARDERS (*Mar.*) sailors appointed to make the attack by boarding.

BOARDING (*Carpent.*) the fixing of boards for any purpose, as a floor: also the boards themselves, which are used for the purpose.

BOARDING-HOUSE (*Cus.*) any house in which persons are provided with board and lodging.

BOARDING-PIKE (*Mar.*) a defensive weapon used by sailors in boarding.

BOARDS, *listed* (*Carpent.*) are those reduced in their breadth by taking away the sap wood.—*Lever-boards*, those which are fixed in such a manner as to admit or exclude the air at pleasure.

BOARD-WAGES (*Cus.*) money given to servants in lieu of their diet, which they provide for themselves.

BOARS' HEADS (*Her.*) a charge in coats of arms, as " He beareth *azure* three boars' heads couped within a double tressure, by the name of Gordon, of the illustrious house of Gordon."

BOASTING (*Mech.*) the paring of stones by stone-cutters, with the broad chisel and mallet.—*Boasting*, among carvers, is the rough cutting round the ornaments, so as to reduce them to their contour or outlines.

BOAT (*Mar.*) a small open vessel worked on rivers or small waters, by rowing or sailing. Of the different kinds are—the *long-boat*, which is the largest that accompanies a ship; the *skiff-boat*, or *skiff*; the *ferry-boat, passage-boat*, &c.—*Life-boat*, [vide *Life*]
  Boat is a term used in many sea-phrases, as " To trim the *boat*," to sit in the boat in such a manner as that she shall float upright in the water.—" To moor the *boat*," to fasten the boat with two ropes so as to keep her in a steady position.—" To bale the *boat*," to bale the water out of the boat.—*Boat-rope*, the rope which fastens the boat to the ship.—*Boat-hook*, a long pole with a hook at the end, which is used in boats.—*Train of boats*, small vessels fastened to each other, ascending the Loire in France.—*Boat-skids*, long square pieces of fir extending across the ship, on which the boats, &c. are stowed.—*Boat-swain*, the officer who has the boats, anchors, &c. in his charge.—*Boat-swain's-mate*, an assistant to the boat-swain.

BOAT-BILL (*Orn.*) a bird of South America, the *Cancroma* of Linnæus, which lives upon fish, and darts down upon them as they are swimming. It is so called because its bill resembles a boat in shape.

BOAT-FLY (*Ent.*) an insect with an inflected snout, the *Notonecta* of Linnæus. It lives in stagnant waters, and preys on aquatic animalculæ.

BOAT-SHAPED (*Bot.*) *navicularis*, seu *cymbeformis*, an epithet for a petal, a pericarp valve, &c. hollowed out in the shape of a boat.

BOATING (*Ant.*) a punishment in ancient Persia, of fixing a person between two boats, and leaving him to perish in that condition.

BOAT'S *crew* (*Mar.*) the men appointed to man a boat.

BOATSHAPED (*Bot.*) vide *Boat*.

BOATSWAIN (*Mar.*) vide *Boat*.

BOB *of a pendulum* (*Hor.*) or *Ball of a pendulum*, the metallic weight attached to the lower extremity of a pendulum-rod, by means of an adjusting nut, at such a distance from the point of suspension as the time of a given vibration requires.

BOB *of the Shears* (*Mech.*) that which serves to bring the edges of the shears together.

BOBARTIA (*Bot.*) the *Morea spathacea* of Linnæus.

BOBBINS (*Mech.*) little pins of wood, with a notch, on which thread, &c. is wound.—*Bobbin* is also a sort of tape used in female dress.

BOB STAY (*Mar.*) a rope used to confine the bowsprit to the stem or cut-water.—*Bobstay-holes*, those in the fore-part of the knee.—*Bob of the head*, a rope used for the security of the bob-stay.

BOB-TAIL (*Archer.*) the steel of a shaft or arrow that is small breasted and big towards the head.

BOCARDO (*Log.*) an arbitrary term for a species of syllogism of the fifth mode and third figure, in which the middle proposition is (A) a universal affirmative proposition, the first and last (O) particular negatives, as
  b O   Some animals are not men.
  c A *r* Every animal is endued with sense.
  d O   Therefore something endued with sense is not man.

BOCCA (*Mech.*) the large mouth or opening of a glass-house.

BOCCALE (*Com.*) a liquid measure at Rome, equal to half a gallon.

BOCCARELLA (*Mech.*) a small mouth or opening on each side the *bocca*.

BOCCONIA (*Bot.*) a genus of plants, (named after Paolo Boccone, a physician, Sicilian monk, and botanical writer) Class 11 *Dodecandria*, Order 1 *Monogynia*.
  Generic Characters. CAL. *perianth* two-leaved.—COR. none.—STAM. *filaments* twelve; *anthers* linear.—PIST. *germ* roundish; *style* one; *stigmas* simple.—PER. sub-ovate; *seed* one.
  Species. The species are—*Bocconia frutescens foliis*, &c. *ramosa*, &c, *Chelidonium*, &c. seu *Cocoxihuith*, Shrubby Bocconia, Tree Celandine, or Parrot-weed, a shrub, native of Mexico.—*Bocconia cordata*, seu *foliis*, &c. a shrub, native of China.

BOCHETUM (*Med.*) a second decoction of Lignum Vitæ, &c.

BOCHIA (*Chem.*) a chemical vessel similar to a cucurbit.

BOCIUM (*Med.*) vide *Bronchocele*.

BOCKELET (*Falcon.*) a sort of long-winged hawk.

BOCK-HORD (*Archæol.*) a place where books are kept.

BOCKING (*Com.*) a Dutch word for red-herring.

BOCK-LAND (*Law*) i. e. bookland, deed or charterland; land held by some deed or charter, and not to be made over to another by sale or gift, but left entire to the heir.

BODIANUS (*Ich.*) a genus of fishes of the *Thoracic* Order.
  Generic Character. Gill-cover scaly, serrated, and aculeated.—*Scales* mostly smooth.
  Species. The species are mostly distinguished by their colour, as the—*Bodianus rhodianus*, Rose-coloured Bodian.—*Bodianus maculatus*, &c.

BODICE (*Mech.*) from body; a kind of waistcoat stiffened with whalebone, but not so much as women's stays.

BODKIN (*Mech*) 1. A long sort of pin, on which women used to roll their hair. 2. A long pointed instrument with a handle to it. 3. An instrument with an eye to it, through which thread or ribbon may be drawn.—*Bodkin-work*, a sort of trimming.

BODLEIAN *library* (*Lit.*) a library in Oxford, called after its founder Sir Thomas Bodley, which is noted throughout Europe for its immense collection of valuable books, and manuscripts.

BODY (*Geom.*) or *solid*, that which has three dimensions, length, breadth, and thickness.—*Bodies* are either regular or irregular.—*A regular body* is that which has all its angles, sides, and planes, similar and equal.—An *irregular body* is a solid not bounded with equal and similar surfaces.—*Regular bodies* are also called Platonic, because Plato compared the five elements to them: they are as follow—*Tetraedon*, a body contained under four equilateral triangles, as fig. 1.—*Hexaedron*, containing six squares, as fig. 2.—*Octaedron*, having eight triangles, as fig. 3.—

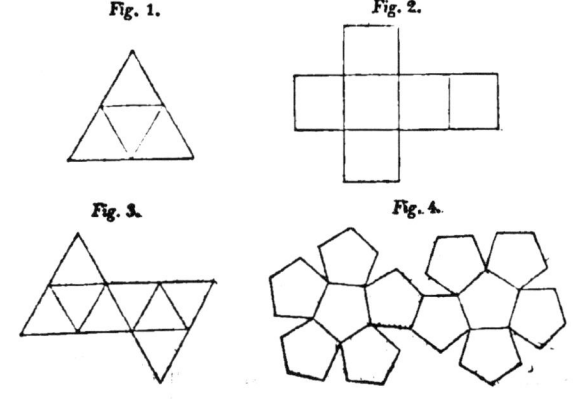

Fig. 1.   Fig. 2.

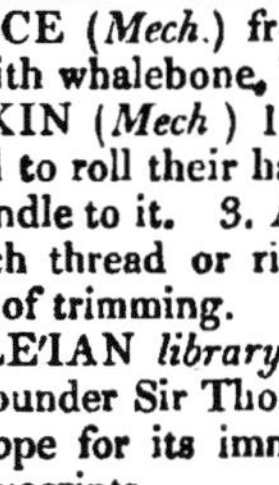

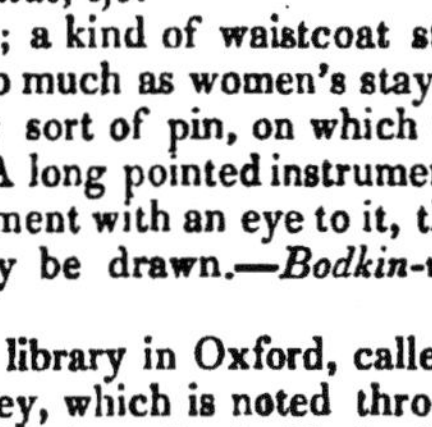

Fig. 3. 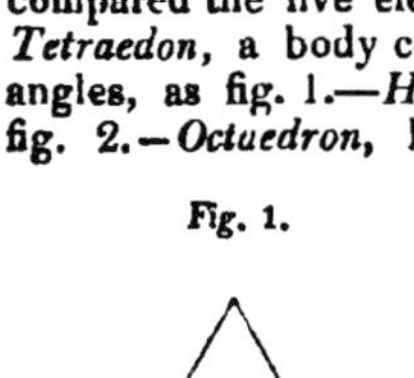   Fig. 4.

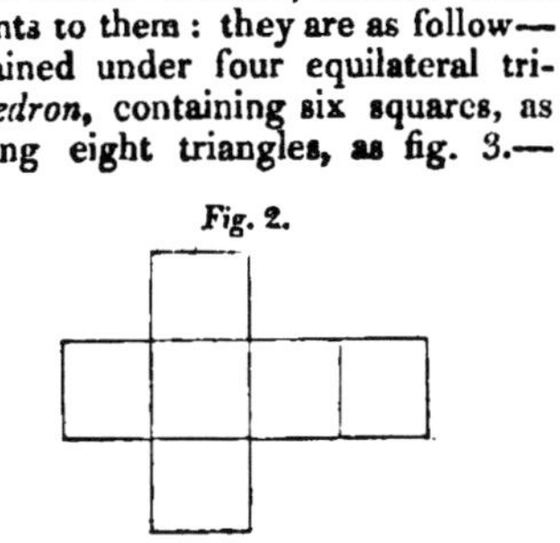

Dodecaedron, containing twelve pentagons, as fig. 4.—*Icosaedron*, containing twenty triangles, as fig. 5.

Fig. 5.

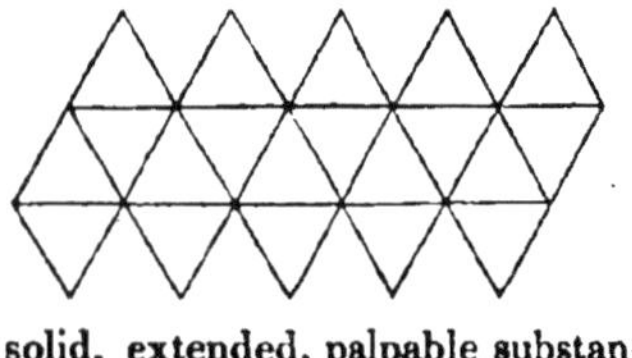

Body (*Phys.*) a solid, extended, palpable substance, which, according to the Newtonian philosophy, consists of massy, hard, impenetrable, moveable particles. Bodies are of different kinds, namely—A *hard body*, whose parts do not yield to any stroke or percussion, but remains unaltered.—A *soft body*, which yields to any stroke, and thereby undergoes a change.—An *elastic body*, that changes its form with every stroke, but recovers it again when the impelling force is removed.

Body (*Hydros.*) is distinguished into solid, fluid, dense, rare, specifically heavy and light.—A *solid body* is that whose particles are kept by a certain continuity which preserves them in the same form.—A *fluid body* is that the particles of which are not so bound together as to preserve a constant cohesion.—A *dense body* is that which within the same space contains a greater mass than another.—A *rare body* is that which contains a less mass within the same space than others.—A *body specifically heavier* is that which with the same volume of matter contains a greater weight.—A *body specifically lighter* is that which with the same volume of matter contains a less weight.

Body (*Opt.*) that which, as the object of sight, is distinguished into luminous or lucid, illuminated, diaphonous or pellucid, and opake.—A *luminous body* is that which diffuses its own light.—An *illuminated body* is that which diffuses a borrowed light.—A *pellucid* or *diaphonous body* is that through which the rays of light easily pass.—An *opake body* intercepts the passage of the rays.

Body (*Anat.*) the animal body is distinguished into Head, Trunk, and Extremities. [vide *Anatomy*]

Body (*Chem.*) is distinguished into imponderable, combustible, or incombustible, inflammable, gaseous, &c. [vide *Chemistry*]

Body (*Mech.*) the solid and more spacious part of many vessels, machines, and the like, as—The *body of a chemical vessel*, that which holds the matter in distillation.—The *body of a pump*, the thickest part of the barrel or pipe.—The *body of a piece of ordnance*, the part contained between the centre of the trunnions and the cascabel.

Body (*Paint.*) or *to bear a body*, a term applied to any colour which is of a nature to be ground so finely, and to mix with the oil so entirely, as to seem only a very thick oil of the same colour; of this nature are white-lead and ceruss, lamp-black, ivory-black, &c.

Body *of a letter* (*Print.*) the space contained between the top and bottom line of a long letter. [vide *Printing*]

Body *of the Place* (*Fort.*) that part inclosed by the bastions, curtains and other works, or the buildings within the inclosure.

Body *of a room* (*Archit.*) the middle open part, in distinction from the recesses or sides.

Body (*Mil.*) any number of forces united under one commander.—The *main body* is that part of an army which occupies the centre between the two wings.—The *body of reserve*, or, simply, the *reserve*, is a select body of troops posted by a general out of the first line of action, to answer some specific or critical purpose.

BOEDRO'MIA (*Ant.*) Βοηδρόμια, an Athenian festival so called, ἀπὸ τῦ βοηδρομεῖν, i. e. from coming to help, because it was instituted in honour of Ion, the son of Ruthus, who went to the assistance of the Athenians, in the reign of king Erichtheus; or, according to Plutarch, to commemorate the victory obtained by Theseus over the Amazons in the month Boedromion. *Plut. in Thes.*; *Harpocration*; *Suidas*, &c.

BOEDRO'MION (*Chron.*) Βοηδρομιών, a month so called by the Greeks, after the festival Boedromia, answering to our March.

BOEHME'RIA (*Bot.*) a genus of plants, named by Jacquin after Professor Boehmer, of Wittenberg, Class 21 *Monoecia*, Order 4 *Tetrandria*.

Generic Characters. CAL. perianth one-leaved.—COR. none; *nectary* none.—STAM. *filaments* four; *anthers* roundish.—PIST. a rudiment, or none.—PER. none; *seed* roundish.

Species. The species are mostly shrubs and natives of America or the West Indies; but the *Boehmeria littoralis* is an annual.

BOERHA'VIA (*Bot.*) Hogweed, a genus of plants, named by Vaillant, after the distinguished physician and botanist, Boerhaave, Class 1 *Monandria*, Order 1 *Monogynia*.

Generic Characters. CAL. perianth oblong.—COR. one-petalled; *nectary* fleshy.—STAM. *filaments* one; *anthers* twin.—PIST. *germ* roundish; *style* filiform; *stigma* capitate.—PER. none; *seed* one.

Species. The species are perennials, as—*Boerhavia erecta*, &c. seu *Solanum bacciferum*, &c. Upright Hogweed.—*Boerhavia diffusa*, *Talu-dama*, seu *Valerianella*, &c. Spreading Hogweed, &c.

BOE'TE (*Gunn.*) an instrument made of brass, to which a steel-tempered blade is attached for diminishing the metal in a cannon and widening the bore.

BOETHEMA'TICA signa (*Med.*) Βοηθηματικὰ σημεῖα, auxiliary signs for observing a curein diseases. *Gal. Def. Med.*

BOE'THI (*Ant.*) Βοηθοί, assistants in any office.

BO'G-RUSH (*Bot.*) a perennial, the *Schoenus* of Linnæus.—Bog-Bean, the *Menanthes trifoliata*.

BOG-IRON-O'RE (*Min.*) a simple mineral, and a kind of sulphuret.

BO'GIA (*Min.*) a sort of gum. [vide *Gamboge*]

BO'GOMILES (*Ecc.*) or *Bongomiles*, heretics of the twelfth century, who, among others, rejected the five books of Moses. *Baron. Annal. Ann.* 1118; *Prateol. Doct. omn. Hæret.*; *Sander. Hæres.* 138.

BOHAD'OCHIA (*Bot.*) the *Peltaria alliacea* of Linnæus.

BOHE'A (*Com.*) one of the superior kinds of tea that comes from China.

BOI'AR (*Polit.*) a great officer of state in Persia.

BOICINI'NGA (*Zool.*) a name in India for the Rattle Snake.

BOIL (*Med.*) *furunculus*, a phlegmonous tumour, which commonly terminates in some sort of pustule.

BOI'LARY (*Mech.*) a salt-house, or place where salt is boiled.

BOILED silk (*Com.*) that which has been boiled in water to facilitate the winding.

BOI'LING (*Phy.*) ebullition, or the bubbling up of any fluid by the application of heat. This consists, in general, in the discharge of some vapour, whether of common air, fixed air, or steam, &c.—*Boiling point*, that point or degree of heat, as marked on the barometer, which is requisite to produce ebullition or boiling in any fluid. This varies in different liquids, and in the same liquid under different pressures of the atmosphere; water begins to boil at 212 degrees of Fahrenheit's scale.

BOJO'BI (*Zool.*) a venomous serpent.

BOIS (*Mil.*) French for wood, is used in some phrases, as *aller au bois*, to go foraging for wood; *bois de remontage* timber for new mounting cannon, &c.; *bois de chauffage* fuel distributed among French troops; *faire haut le bois* is said of pikemen who make a stand advancing their pikes.

BOITIA'PO (*Zool.*) a serpent of Brazil.

BOLBI'DION (*Med.*) βολβιδιον, a small polypus, recommended as a food. *Hipp. de Mul.; Foes. Œconom. Hippocrat.*

BO'LBION (*Med.*) βόλβιον, bulbulus, diminitive of βυλβὸς, *bulbos*, recommended in a pessary. *Hipp. de Mul.; Foes. Œconom. Hippocrat.*

BOLBI'TION (*Med.*) vide *Bolbidion*.

BO'LBITON (*Med.*) βόλβιτος, attic, ξόλιτος, from βολὺ, ejection; cow-dung, recommended as a fomentation. *Hipp. de Mul.; Foes. Œconom. Hippocrat.*

BO'LCHON (*Min.*) the same as *Bdellium*.

BO'LD-SHORE (*Mar.*) a sea coast, so abrupt and steep, that vessels may approach it without danger.

BO'LE (*Min.*) a friable earth of the argillaceous kind, which unites with water so as to form a paste. There are many kinds of boles distinguished either by the name of the place from which they come, as *Armenian, Lemnian, Tuscan* bole, &c.; or from their colour, as *red, white, brown* bole, &c. The principal earth of this kind used in medicine is the *Armenian bole*, or Bole Armenic, a bright red coloured earth, which is often mixed with honey, and applied to the mouth of children having the aphthæ.

BOLE (*Med.*) vide *Bolus*.

BOLE'SIS (*Min.*) Coral.

BOLE'SON (*Chem.*) Balsam.

BOLE'TIC *acid* (*Chem.*) an acid drawn from the juice of the *Boletus pseudo igniarius*.

BOLE'TUS (*Bot.*) a sort of fungus highly esteemed by the ancients, and purchased as a great delicacy for the table. *Mart. l. 13, epig. 47.*

Argentum atque aurum facile est, lanamque togamque Mittere; boletos mittere difficile est.

It was by means of the *boletus* that Claudius was poisoned; to which Juvenal alludes,

Juv. sat. 5, v. 147.

Vilibus ancipites fungi ponentur amicis Boletus domino; sed qualem Claudius edit.

Suet. in Claud. c. 44; Plin. l. 22, c. 22.

BOLETUS, in the Linnean system, a genus of plants, Class *Cryptogamia*, Order *Fungi.*—*Boletus cervi*, the Mushroom. —*Boletus igniarius*, the same as Agaric.

BO'LIS (*Ant.*) 1. The plummet line for sounding. 2. A fiery meteor that darts down. *Plin. l. 2, c. 26.*

BOLI'SMUS (*Med.*) the same as *Bulimus*.

BOLL (*Bot.*) from ball and bowl. 1. The naked trunk of a tree. 2. A poppy head with the seeds.

BOLL *of salt* (*Com.*) a measure of two bushels.

BO'LLARD-TIMBERS (*Mar.*) or Knight-heads, two timbers on each side the bowsprits to secure its inner end.— *Bollards*, large posts set in the ground on each side a dock.

BO'LLERO (*Sport.*) a Spanish dance noted for its voluptuousness.

BO'LLIMONY (*Husband.*) a medley of several sorts of grain.

BO'LLITO (*Paint.*) an Italian name for a sort of sea-green colour in artificial crystal.

BO'LLOCK-BLOCKS (*Mar.*) blocks secured to the topsail yards.

BOLO'GNA *Stone* (*Min.*) a phosphoric stone; the *Barytes bononienses* of Linnæus, which shines in the dark after having been calcined in the fire.

BO'LSTER (*Surg.*) a soft pillow for a broken limb.

BOLSTER (*Man.*) those parts of a saddle which are raised upon the bows to receive the rider's thighs.—*To fit the Bolster*, i. e. to put the cork of the saddle into the bolster to keep it tight.

BOLSTER (*Mar.*) 1. A piece of timber cut and placed for the casement of the cable. 2. The piece bolted to the ship's side on which the stanchions for the linings of the anchors are placed. 3. A small bag of tarred canvass laid between the collars of the stays. 4. A cylindrical piece of iron with a hole through the middle, used when holes are to be punched.

BOLT (*Carpent.*) an iron pin used for strengthening timber. Bolts are distinguished into plate, spring, and round bolts. *Plate* and *spring bolts* are used for doors and windows. *Round bolts* are long iron pins, with a head at one end and a key at the other.—*Bolt-lock* or *nab*, that part of the lock which receives the bolt in shooting it backward and forward.

BOLT (*Mar.*) an iron pin used to fasten parts of a ship; which is distinguished into—*Fend bolts*, bolts with long and thick heads, struck into the uttermost walls or bends of the ship to save the sides from galling.—*Set bolts*, used for forcing the planks together.—*Ring bolts*, which serve to bring the planks together, to which the breeches are fastened.— *Rag-bolts*, which have jags or barbs.—*Clench-bolts*, which are clenched with a rivetting hammer.—*Drive-bolts*, which are used for driving out other bolts.—*Forelock bolts*, which have a forelock of iron at the end driven in, to keep it from starting back.—*Bolt rope*, that to which the edges of the sails are sewed to prevent their rending.—*Bolt-boat*, a strong boat fitted for a rough sea.—*Bolt-sprit.* [vide *Bowsprit*]—*Bolt-augeur*, a large borer or piercer, used by ships' carpenters for boring the holes for bolts.

BOLT (*Gunn.*) the iron pin of a gun carriage, which is of different kinds, namely—*Prize bolts*, large knobs of iron on the cheek of a carriage to prevent the handspike from sliding.—*Traverse bolts*, two short bolts put into each end of an English mortar carriage.—*Transum bolts*, which go between the cheeks of a gun carriage to strengthen the transums.—*Bracket bolts*, which go through the cheeks of a mortar, and by the help of the coins, keep it at any given elevation.

BO'LT-HEAD (*Chem.*) a long straight-necked glass vessel for distillations, which being fitted to the alembic or still, is called a *receiver*; when the neck is well joined to the neck of another, it is called a double-vessel.

BOLT *of silk* (*Com.*) a long narrow piece.—*Bolt of canvass*, a certain quantity, containing twenty-eight ells.

BOLT *and tun* (*Her.*) a charge in coats of arms, consisting of a bird bolt in pale piercing through a tun.

TO BOLT (*Sport.*) a coney is said to be *bolted* when she is first started.

TO BOLT (*Husband.*) to sift flour.

BO'LTER (*Mech.*) the machine for sifting meal.

BO'LTING (*Law*) a legal exercise of arguing cases formerly used in our inns of court.

BO'LTING-CLOTH (*Mech.*) the cloth through which the sifted meal runs, which is of different degrees of fineness.

BOLTO'NIA (*Bot.*) a genus of plants, named after Mr. Bolton, a botanist of Halifax, Class 19 *Syngenesia*, Order 2 *Polygamia Superflua*.

Generic Characters. CAL. common flattish.—COR. compound radiate.—STAM. *filaments* five; *anthers* cylindric. —PIST. *germ* oblong; *style* filiform; *stigmas* two.—PER. none; *seeds* solitary; *receptacle* naked.

Species. The species are the—*Boltonia asteroides, foliis, &c. Matricaria asteroides, &c. foliis, &c. seu Aster americanus, &c.* Star-wort flowered Boltonia.—*Boltonia glastifolia, seu foliis, &c.* Glaucous-leaved Boltonia, a perennial, native of Pennsylvania.

BO'LUS (*Med.*) from βόλος, a clod of earth; a Bolus or Bole, an internal medicine, of a consistency much thicker than honey. [vide *Bole*]

BOMB (*Gunn.*) from βομβὸς, a hollow noise; a shell or hol-

4

low ball of cast iron, which is thrown into towns, when, by bursting, it causes much mischief. They have large vents to receive the fusees or tubes, and are filled with combustible materials of all kinds, nails, old iron, &c. After the bomb has been filled, the fusee is driven into the vent within an inch of the head, and pitched over to preserve it: then they uncase another fusee, put the bomb into the mortar, and cover it with gunpowder dust, which, having taken fire by the flash of the powder in the chamber of the mortar, burns all the time the bomb is in the air, and the composition in the fusee being spent, it fires the powder in the bomb, which, in consequence, bursts, blowing into pieces whatever comes in its way. [vide *Fortification*]—*Bomb-chest*, a wooden chest, filled with bombs, which was formerly buried under ground, in order to blow up those that happened to be on the spot at the time of its bursting.—*Bomb-ketch*, or *bomb-vessel*, a small vessel particularly constructed for carrying and using mortars at sea.—*Bomb-tender*, a small vessel laden with bombs for the use of the bomb-ketch.

BOMBA'RD (*Mil.*) in Latin *bombarda*, in French *bombarde*, a great gun, formerly in use, which carried balls 300 pounds weight, and for the loading of which they employed cranes.

TO BOMBARD (*Mil.*) to shoot bombs into a besieged place.

BOMBARDI'ERS (*Mil.*) non-commissioned officers; so called because they were chiefly employed in mortar and howitzer duty.

BOMBA'RDO (*Mus.*) a wind instrument, resembling a bassoon.

BOMBASI'NE (*Com.*) a sort of slight silken stuff.

BOMBAST (*Com.*) a kind of stuff made of cotton.

BO'MBAX (*Bot.*) Cotton-bush, or Silk-cotton, a genus of plants, Class 16 *Monadelphia*, Order 5 *Polyandria*.
  Generic Characters. CAL. *perianth* one-leaved.—COR. five-parted.—STAM. *filaments* five, or many.—PIST. *germ* roundish; *style* filiform; *stigma* capitate.—PER. *capsule* large; *seeds* very many; *receptacle* columnar.
  Species. The species are shrubs, as the—*Bombax pentandrum, Xylon caule, &c. Gossypium, &c. Eriophoros javana,* seu *Pania Paniala.—Bombax Cuba, Xylon, Gossipium arboreum, &c.* seu *Cuba viticis, &c.—Bombax heptaphyllum floribus, &c. Septenatum, foliis septenatis, &c. Gossypium,* seu *Xylon arbor, &c.* seu *Moul-clauou.—Bombax gossypinum foliis, &c. Ketmia foliis, &c.—Bombax Conga,* seu *Gossipium, &c.—Bombax Erianthos, floribus, &c. caule, &c.—Bombax globosum, floribus, &c.* seu *foliis, &c. Ger. Herb.; J. Bauh. Hist. Plant.; C. Bauh. Pin.; Raii Hist. Plant.; Park. Theat. Botan.; Boerhaav. Ind.; Tournef. Instit.*

BOMBE'LLES (*Mil.*) French for small bombs.

BO'MBIATE (*Chem.*) a salt formed by the combination of bombic acid with different bases, as the bombiate of alumine, &c.

BOMBIC *acid* (*Chem.*) an acid liquor of the silk-worm, contained in a reservoir near the anus. This acid is of a very penetrating nature, and of a yellow amber colour.

BO'MBUS (*Med.*) βόμβος, a reverberating noise, which if in the ears in an acute disorder is a mortal symptom.

BOMBYCI'LLA (*Orn.*) Wax-wing, a genus of birds detached from the Chatterers, of the Order *Passeres*.
  Generic Character. Beak short, and slightly depressed.—*Nostrils* oval, covered with small feathers.—*Feet* four-toed.
  Species. There are two species, namely—*Bombicylla bohemica, Garrulus Bohemicus, le Jaseur de Boheme*, Bohemian Wax-wing, or Chatterer.—*Bombycilla Carolina, Ampelis garrulus,* Carolina Wax-wing.

BOMBY'LIUS (*Ant.*) βομβύλιος, a drinking-cup with a long narrow neck, which is so called from the bubbling noise which it makes in drinking. *Poll. Onomast.* l. 6, c. 46; *Athen.* l. 6, c. 18.

BOMBYLIUS (*Ent.*) the Humble Bee, a sort of bee so called ἀπὸ τῦ βομβυλλιω, that is, from the humming noise which this bee makes; or from βομβυλίος, a drinking-cup with a long neck, which its larva resembles in shape, a genus of animals, Class *Insecta*, Order *Diptera*.
  Generic Characters. Mouth furnished with a long setaceous sucker, formed of two unequal horizontal valves, and containing setaceous stings.
  Species. The species are: 1. Those having two hairy feelers, and antennæ united at the base, as—*Bombylius major,* Humble-bee.—*Bombylius medius.—Bombylius minor.—Bombylius ater.* 2. Those having two suckers, with three incumbent bristles or feelers, and antennæ approximate, as—*Bombylius albifrons, &c.*

BO'MBYX (*Ant.*) βόμβυξ, a sort of pipe made of the reed called βομβυνίας, which was used in the Bacchanalian festival. *Aristot. de Auscult.; Poll.* l. 4, c. 9.

BOMBYX (*Ent.*) the worm mentioned by Aristotle and Pliny, which was supposed to be generated from the flowers of trees in the island of Cos, and spun its threads after the manner of the spider, of which the inhabitants made their garments. The bombyx was so called because it resembled in shape the vessel called the bombylius [vide *Bombylius*] but it is supposed to differ from what is now called the Silk-Worm. *Aristot. Hist. Anim.* l. 5, c. 19; *Plin.* l. 11, c. 22; *Poll.* l. 7, c. 17; *Salmas. in Tertull. de Pall.* c. 3.

BOMO'LOCHUS (*Ant.*) from βωμὸς, an altar, and λοχάω, to lie wait; one who lies wait at the altar to get any thing of the provisions.

BOMPERNI'CKEL (*Med.*) or *Bonpournickel*, good for nothing, i. e. *bon pour* and *nickel*, nothing, corrupted from the Low German *nic*, and the French *nul*, nothing; an epithet applied by a French traveller to the Westphalian black bread, which being made of the unsifted meal, as it comes from the mill, has been reckoned by some of a highly glutinous and nutritious quality.

BON (*Polit.*) French for a written document, by the signature of which a sovereign or a minister confirms some appointment to the person or persons specified.

BON (*Bot.*) the Coffee-tree; the *Caffea Arabica* of Linnæus.

BONA-FI'DE (*Law*) with good faith, i. e. without fraud or subterfuge.—*Bona gestura,* Good Abearing, Good-Behaviour.—*Bona patria,* an assise of twelve men, or good neighbours, otherwise called *juratores*.—*Bona peritura,* perishable commodities, such as, in a wreck, will not last a year and a day, and must therefore be sold by the Sheriff. *Stat. West.* 1, 3 *Ed.* 1.

BO'NACE (*Mar.*) French for calm weather and a smooth sea.

BO'NAROTA (*Bot.*) the *Pæderota bonerota* and *ageria* of Linnæus.

BONA'SIANS (*Ecc.*) or Bonosians, Heretics of the fourth century maintaining that Jesus Christ was the Son of God by adoption only. *Baron. Annal. Ann.* 876.

BONA'SUS (*Zool.*) βίνασος, an animal of the ox kind in Pæonia having the mane of a horse. It is said that when pursued by hunters he emits a noisome odure, for the purpose of deterring them from the pursuit.

BONAVE'NTURE *mizen* (*Mar.*) a second mizen mast added in some large foreign ships, which stands next the poop.

BON *chrétien* (*Bot.*) a sort of summer pear.

BOND (*Carpent.*) from to bind; the binding any two pieces together by tenanting, morticing, &c.; whence the expression " To make good bond," i. e. to fasten them in such manner securely.

BOND (*Mason.*) the disposition of stones or bricks in a building. Stones which have their length placed in the thickness of the wall are called *headers*, and those whose length extends along the face, or exterior of the wall, are

3

called *stretchers*: where this sort of disposition is blended it is called *header* and *stretcher bond*. The stones that are inserted the whole thickness of the wall are called *heading jambs*; and the intermediate stones, having their length placed horizontally in the face, are the *stretching jambs*.—*Heart bond* is when two stones which appear in the front and rear of a wall meet in the centre of it, and when a third stone is placed over the joint, in order to bind the facing and backing together.—*Bond stones* are stretchers used in uncoursed ruble work, which, if they are inserted the whole thickness of the masonry, are called *perpends*, or *perpend stones*.—*English bond* is when to every two courses of headers there is one course of stretchers, the former of which are called *heading-courses*, the latter *stretching-courses*.—*Flemish bond* has one header between every two stretchers.—*Bond-timbers* are the horizontal timbers built in stone or brick walls for strengthening the masonry, &c. Bond-timbers disposed in tires are called *common bond*; those placed in or near the middle of the story are called *chain-timbers*, or *chain-bond*.

BO'NDMAN (*Ant.*) a man who was a slave, in distinction from the bond-maid. They are otherwise called bond-servants.

BOND-SO'COME (*Law*) a custom by which tenants were bound to grind corn at their lord's mill.—*Bond-tenants*, another name for copyholders, or customary tenants.

BO'NDAGE (*Law*) another name for slavery.

BONDS (*Carpent.*) all the timbers disposed in the walls of a house, as bond-timbers, lintels, and wall-plates.

BO'NDSMAN (*Law*) one bound or giving security for another.

BO'NDUC (*Bot.*) the *Guilandina* of Linnæus.

BONDUCE'LLA (*Bot.*) a species of the *Guilandina* of Linnæus.

BONE (*Anat.*) a hard, dry, insensible part of the body, of a whitish colour, composed of a spongy, compact, reticular substance, containing an oily substance, called *marrow*. Bones are covered with an exceedingly sensible membrane, which is generally called *periosteum*, and on the scull the *pericranium*. The processes of bones are distinguished by their figure and situations, into the *head*, the *neck*, the *condyle*, the *tuberosity, crista*, &c. &c. The cavities of bones, which serve for the reception of other bones, &c. are distinguished, according to their magnitude, into *foveæ*, or *pits, foramina*, notches, furrows, &c. &c. The human body is divided, as respects the bones, into the Head, Trunk, and Extremities, which are composed altogether of 238 bones, as in the following table:—

BONES OF THE HEAD.
The Cranium, or Skull.

	No.
Frontal	1
Parietal	2
Occipital	1
Temporal	2
Ethmoid	1
Sphenoid	1

The Face.

Superior maxillary	2
Jugal	2
Nasal	2
Lachrymal	2
Palatine	2
Inferior and spongy	2
Vomer	1
Inferior maxillary	1

The Teeth.

Incisores	8
Cuspidati	4
Molares	20

The Tongue.

	No.
Hyoides Os	1

The Ear.

Malleus	2
Incus	2
Stapes	2
Os Orbiculare	2

BONES OF THE TRUNK.
The Spine.

Vertebræ cervical	7
———— dorsal	12
———— lumbar	5
Os Sacrum	1
Os Coccygis	1

The Thorax.

Sternum, or Breast-bone	1
Costæ, or Ribs	24

BONES OF THE UPPER EXTREMITIES.
The Shoulder.

	No.
Clavicle, or Collar-bone	2
Scapula, or Shoulder-blade	2

The Arm.

Os Humeri	2

The Fore arm.

Ulna	2
Radius	2

The Hand.

Os Naviculare	2
Os Lunare	2

Carpus, or Wrist.

Os Cuneiforme	2
Os Orbiculare	2
Os Trapezium	2
Os Trapezoides	2
Os Magnum	2
Os Unciforme	2
Metacarpus	10
Phalanges	28

BONES OF THE LOWER EXTREMITIES.
The Thigh.

	No.
Femur	2

The Leg.

Patella, or Knee-pan	2
Tibia	2
Fibula	2

The Foot.

Calcaneus	2
Astragalus	2
Os Cuboides	2

Tarsus, or Instep.

Os Naviculare	2
Ossa Cuneiformia	6
Metatarsus	10
Phalanges	28

BONE (*Mar.*) is used in the sea phrase of a ship, "To carry a *bone* in her mouth," when she makes the water foam before her in sailing.

BO'NE-LACE (*Com.*) lace made of bobbins that are formed from bones.

BONES (*Com.*) a sort of bobbins, made of trotter-bones, for weaving bone-lace.

BONES *foul* (*Vet.*) the same as Caries.—*Bone-spavin*, a hard crust in the inside of a horse's heel.

BONES (*Math.*) a name given to Lord Napier's rods for facilitating arithmetical calculations. [vide *Napier's Bones*]

BO'NGOMILES (*Ecc.*) vide *Bogomiles*.

BONGRA'CE (*Archæol.*) a shelter worn on the head to keep the face from tanning.

BONGRACE (*Mar.*) a frame of old ropes, &c. laid in different parts of a ship, to preserve it from the snow.

BO'NIFACE (*Bot.*) the same as the *Laurus Alexandrina*.

BONING (*Mensur.*) a term among surveyors, which signifies laying poles upon the ground in such a manner that all may lie in a straight line, so that the eye can pass them all to the end.

BONIS *non amovendis* (*Law*) a writ to the sheriff of London not to permit one condemned, who brings a writ of error, to remove his goods till the error be tried. *Reg. Orig.* 131.

BO'NNET (*Her.*) a cap of velvet worn without a coronet.

BONNET (*Fort.*) a work of two faces raised before the salient angle of the counterscarp, having a parapet with two rows of palisadoes.—*Bonnet a prêtre*, Priest's-cap; an outwork having three salient angles at the head, and two inward.

BONNET (*Mar.*) an additional part, or a small sail made to fasten with latchings to the foot of the other sails; whence the phrase, "The ship has her course and *bonnet* abroad," when she has the bonnet added to her course.

BONNE'TIA (*Bot.*) a genus of plants named after Mons. Bonnet, of Geneva, Class 13 *Polyandria*, Order 1 *Monogynia*.

Generic Characters. CAL. *perianth* one-leaved.—COR. *petals* five.—STAM. *filaments* very many; *anthers* oblong.—PIST. *germ* oblong; *style* length of the germ; *stigma* three-lobed.—PER. *capsule* oblong; *seeds* very many.

Species. The two species are shrubs, and natives of Cayenne.

BO'NNY (*Min.*) a distinct bed of ore that has no communication with any vein. It is distinguished from a *squat* in shape: the bonny being round, and the *squat* flat.

BONPOURNI'CKEL (*Med.*) vide *Bompournickel*.

BONTA'NS (*Com.*) a kind of stuff of cotton interwoven with worsted at Canton, on the river Gambia.

BO'NTIA (*Bot.*) a genus of plants named after Bontius, a physician of Batavia, Class 14 *Didynamia*, Order 2 *Angiospermia*.
  Generic Characters. CAL. *perianth* one-leaved.—COR. one-petalled.—STAM. *filaments* four; *anthers* simple.—PIST. *germ* ovate; *style* simple; *stigma* bifid.—PER. *drupe* ovate; *seed-nut* oval.
  Species. The only species is—*Bontia daphnoides, foliis alternis*, &c. *arborescens*, &c. *lauricolæ facie, seu Olea sylvestris*, &c. Barbadoes Wild Olive, a shrub, native of the West Indies.

BONUS *Henricus* (*Bot.*) a species of the *Chenopodium* of Linnæus.

BO'NZES (*Theol.*) Indian priests, who wear a charlet of 100 beads round their neck, and carry a staff, at the end of which is a wooden bird.

BOO'BY (*Orn.*) a South American bird of the Pelican tribe.

BOOK (*Lit.*) from the *Ger. buch*, a beech-tree, because the bark of trees was originally used instead of paper: any folded leaves which are or may be written upon.

BOOK *of rates* (*Law*) a book showing the value of goods that pay poundage at the custom house.—*Book of responses*, that which the director of the chancery keeps particularly to note a seizure.

BOOK (*Mil.*) the different books used in the British service are distinguished according to their use, as the—*General order Book*, from which the parole and countersign are taken.—*Regimental order Book*, containing instructions to particular regiments.—*Regimental book*, containing the records of the regiment.—*Black book*, containing the offences, &c. of the non-commissioned officers and soldiers.—*Time book*, a book kept in the war-office, and other offices, to note down the time when the clerks attend.—*Quarter book*, in the ordnance office, containing the names of the officers, their appointments, salaries, &c.—*Practice book*, containing the weight, range, &c. of cannon.

BOOK-KEEPING (*Com.*) the art of keeping a merchant's books or accounts in due order, according to certain rules. To this end merchants always employ two, and sometimes three books, namely, the Waste Book, the Ledger, the Journal, to which may be added the Cash Book and the Bill Book.—*Waste Book* is the book which contains a registry of the common and daily transactions that occur in business, when against every person's name, at the right hand extremity of the same line, D^r. i. e. debtor, or C^r. i. e. creditor, must be written. The act of placing any transaction under a given account is called the entry: if any transaction be entered with the mark D^r. it is called *debiting* the account; if with the mark C^r. it is *crediting*. The accounts of persons are debited under their respective names when they become indebted to the merchant: they are credited when the merchant becomes indebted to them. Accounts of property are debited when they come into the merchant's possession, and credited when they go out of his possession. The goods are either specified particularly, or given under the general name of *sundries*. In the same manner the accounts of profit and loss are kept, which are debited on account of a loss, or credited on account of a gain. Those marked D^r. in the Waste Book are placed on the left hand page, marked D^r. and those marked C^r. on the opposite page, marked *Contra C^r*.—*Ledger* is a book in which the various accounts relating to any individual are arranged in a methodical manner, the act of doing which is called *posting*. The different ledgers which a merchant may want in the course of his transactions are numbered by the letters of the alphabet, A, B, C, &c.; and when a new ledger becomes necessary each account must be balanced by carrying the difference between the two sides to the lighter, and entering it against the words "To *balance*," or "By *balance*," as the entry is to be made on the D^r. or C^r. side: when the difference is carried to the former, it shows the same to be in favour of the person to whose debit it is carried, and when on the C^r. side it is against him.—*Journal* is an intermediate book between the Waste Book and the Ledger, wherein the transactions of the Waste Book are entered in a brief manner, so as to facilitate the posting them into the latter.—*Cash Book* is the book in which the cash-account is kept, by entering moneys due to the merchant on the D^r. side of the person's against whose name it is entered, and those received on the C^r. side. In this book cash is D^r. on the left hand page, and *Contra C^r*. on the right hand.—*Bill Book*, or the book in which all bills payable or receivable are entered, commonly consists of two distinct books, called the *bills receivable book*, and the *bills payable book*. In the former the bills receivable is the only D^r. and accounts credited are entered in the column which shows from whom or on whose account they are received: in the latter the bills payable is the only C^r. and accounts debited are entered in the column which shows by whom or on whose account they are drawn.

Book-keeping is conducted either by double or single entry, which are two different methods of posting the entries of the transactions into the ledger.—*Double Entry* is so called because the same transaction is entered as it were twice, or in two different forms, as in the entry of N. N. D^r. to Cottons, the account of N. N. was debited to Cottons, and the account of Cottons was credited by N. N. each for the same amount. This is called forming the ledger by Double Entry.—*Single Entry*, on the other hand, is that in which the entry is made but once, as in the preceding case, wherein the entry of N. N. D^r. to Cottons, the account of N. N. only is debited to account, with the omission of the Credit Account by N. N.

TO BOOK *a debt* (*Com.*) is to enter a debt against a person's name in account books.

BOOM (*Mar.*) from beam, a long pole to extend the bottoms of particular sails, as the jib-boom, studding sail boom, &c.—*Boom iron*, the iron composed of two rings in which the boom rests.—*Boom of a harbour*, a strong iron chain thrown across a harbour to prevent the entrance of an enemy.—*Fire-boom*, a strong pole thrown out from a ship to prevent the approach of fire-ships, &c.

BOO'MING (*Mar.*) the application of a boom to the sails: also a ship is said *to come booming* when she makes all the sail she can.

BO'OPS (*Ich.*) a fish which is the *Sparus* of Linnæus.

BOOT (*Archæol.*) a species of torture formerly practised in Scotland towards criminals to extort confession. It consisted in fixing a boot of wetted parchment on the leg, which being afterwards dried by the fire, caused exquisite pain by the shrinking.

BOOT was also the name of another punishment, by means of irons so fixed on the legs that when squeezed together they could be broken.—*Boot-haler*, a freebooter or robber.

BOOT *of a coach* (*Mech.*) the space underneath between the coachman and the body of the coach, in which parcels are stowed.—*Boot-tree*, two pieces of wood, the shape of a leg, driven into a boot to stretch it.

BOOT-TO'PPING (*Mar.*) the operation of scraping off the grass, shells, &c. from the ship's bottom.

BOO'TES (*Astron.*) βοώτης, a northern constellation so called from βοῦς, an ox, and ὠθέω, to drive, i. e. the ox-driver, because it seems to follow the great bear as the driver follows his oxen. It was also called by the Greeks *Arctophylax*, ἅμαξα and *Arctos*, and by the Arabians *Aramach*, and in English Charles' Wain.

Hom. Odyss. l. 5, v. 272.

Πληϊάδας τ' ἐσορῶντι, καὶ ὀψὲ δύοντα Βοώτην
Ἄρκτον θ' ἣν καὶ Ἅμαξαν ἐπίκλησιν καλέουσιν.

Arat. Apparent. v. 91.

Ἐξόπιθεν δ' Ἑλίκης φέρεται ἐλάοντι ἐοικὼς
Ἀρκτοφύλαξ, τόν ῥ' ἄνδρες ἐπικλείουσι Βοώτην,
Οὕνεχ' ἁμαξαίης ἐπαφώμενος εἴδεται Ἄρκτου.

Ovid.
  Arctophylax formam terga sequentis habet.

Juv. sat. 5, v. 23.
  Frigida circumagunt pigri sarraca Boötæ.

Manill. Astron. Poet. l. 1. v. 315.
  A tergo nitet Arctophylax, idemque Boötes.

Bootes had, according to Ptolemy, 23 stars, according to Tycho 28, to Bayer 34, to Hevelius 52, to Flamstead 54, one of which, in the skirt of his coat, is Arcturus, a star of the first magnitude. Bootes is represented as a man walking, and grasping a club in his right hand, and is fabled to have been Icarius, who was transported to heaven because he was a great cultivator of the vine; for when Bootes rises the works of ploughing and carting go forward. *Cic. de Nat. Deor.*; *Hygin. Astron. Poet.*; *Plin.* l. 2, c. 41; *Aul. Gell.* l. 2, c. 21; *Gem. Elem. Astron.*; *Hipparch. in Arat.*; *Eratosth. Characteris.*; *Ptol. Almag.* l. 7, c. 5; *Bay. Uranomet. Hevel. Machin. cælest.*

BO'OTING (*Law*) the punishment formerly used in Scotland of putting irons on the legs of offenders.—*Booting corn*, a rent of corn paid by the tenant to his lord by way of compensation for giving him a lease.

BOOTS (*Mil.*) a familiar term in the British army for the youngest officer at a regimental mess.

BOOZE (*Archæol.*) an ox or cow-stall.

BO'RACE (*Min.*) vide *Borax*.

BORA'CHIO (*Archæol.*) a leathern bottle made of swine skin to carry wine in.

BORA'CIC acid (*Chem.*) an acid drawn from borax by combustion.

BORACI'TES (*Min.*) Boracite, a genus of argillaceous earths found at Kahlberg, near Luneberg, situated on a bed of *Gypsum*.

 Generic Characters. Consisting of carbonate of lime, of carbonate of magnesia, and boracic acid, with a little alumina, silica, and oxyde of iron.

 Species. The only species is *Boracites cubicus*, Boracites, Boracite, or Borat of Magnesia.

BO'RAGE (*Bot.*) vide *Borago*.

BORAGINOI'DES (*Bot.*) another name for the Borago.

BORA'GO (*Bot.*) Borage, a plant, the leaves of which are esteemed of a cordial, exhilarating, and refrigerating nature. It answers nearest to the *Buglossum* of the ancients.

BORAGO, *in the Linnean system*, a genus of plants, Class 5 Pentandria, Order 1 Monogynia.

 Generic Characters. CAL. *perianth* five-parted.—COR. *monopetalous.*—STAM. *filaments* five; *anthers* oblong.—PIST. *germs* four; *style* filiform; *stigma* simple.—PER. none; *seeds* four roundish.

 Species. The species are mostly annuals, as *Borago officinalis*, seu *Buglossum*, Common Borage.—*Borago Indica*, Cynoglossoides, seu *Anchusa*, &c. Indian Borage.—*Borago Africana*, Cynoglossoides, seu *Cynoglossum*, African Borage. But the *Borago orientalis* is a perennial; and the *Borago laxiflora* is a biennial. *J. Bauh. Hist. Plant.*; *C. Bauh. Pin.*; *Raii Hist. Plant.*; *Park. Theat. Botan.*; *Tournef. Inst. Re Herb.*; *Boerhaav. Ind.*

BORAGO, the species is the *Cynoglossum Ompholades* of Linnæus. *Park.*

BORAME'TZ (*Bot.*) vide *Agnus Scythicus*.

BORASSUS (*Bot.*) a genus of plants consisting of the *Palmæ* of the largest size, Class 22 *Dioecia*, Order 6 *Hexandria*.

 Generic Characters. CAL. spathe universal.—COR. *perianth proper* three-leaved. — STAM. *filaments* six; *anthers* thicker.—PIST. *germ* roundish; *styles* three; *stigmas* simple.—PER. *berry* (drupe) roundish; *seeds* three.

 Species. The only species is *Borassus flabelliformis, frondibus*, &c. *Palma coccifera, Ampana Carimpara*, seu *Lontarus domestica*, a shrub, native of the East Indies.

BO'RATE (*Chem.*) a salt formed of boracic acid with an earthy, alkaline, or metallic base, as borate of soda, &c.—*Borate of magnesia* is another name for the Boracites.

BORAX (*Min.*) the name of a salt which, by the ancients, was called *chrysocolla*, and is supposed to be derived from the Arabic *Baurac*, which properly signifies nitre. The use of Borax in medicine is to cleanse wounds. *Aristot. de Mirab.*; *Dioscor.* l. 5, c. 104; *Plin.* l. 33, c. 5; *Aet. Tetrab.* 1, serm. 2, c. 81; *Paul. Æginet.* l. 7, c. 3; *Salmas. Homonym. Hyl. Iatr.* c. 121.

BORAX, *in the Linnean system*, a genus of salts, found in Japan, Chili, and Peru, sometimes in the form of solid grains, sometimes in large crystals enclosed in a fatty matter.

 Generic Characters. The generic characters are slightly caustic, rather ponderous, semitransparent, and melting into a transparent glass.

 Species. The species are *Borax sedativa*, seu *Sal naturale*.—*Borax tincal*, *Borax nudus*, seu *Borax crudus*, Borax, Tincal, or Sub-bort of Soda.

BORAX (*Chem.*) was formerly distinguished by this character ⌐⌐.

BORBO'NIA (*Bot.*) a genus of plants named after Gaston Bourbon, Duke of Orleans, Class 17 *Diadelphia*, Order 4 *Decandria*.

 Generic Characters. CAL. *perianth* one-leaved. — COR. *pentapetalous.*—STAM. *filaments* nine; *anthers* small.—PIST. *germ* subulate; *style* very short; *stigma* obtuse.—PER. *legume* roundish; *seed* kidney-form.

 Species. The species are shrubs, and natives of the Cape of Good Hope, as the—*Borbonia ericifolia*, seu *Genista Africana*, &c. a shrub.—*Borbonia trinervia*, seu *Frutex Æthiopicus*, &c.—*Borbonia lanceolata*, *Genista Africana*, &c. *Spartium Africanum*, &c. seu *Frutex Æthiopicus*, &c. Spear leaved Borbonia, &c.

BORBORO'DES (*Med.*) βορβορώδης, earthy, feculent, as βορβορώδης πύον, feculent pus. *Hipp.* l. 7, aphor. 44.

BORBORY'GMUS (*Med.*) βορβορυγμός, from βορβορύζω, to send forth a noise, or murmur. *Gal. Com. in Hippoc.* l. 4, aphor. 73.

BO'RDAGE (*Mar.*) French for the planks of a ship's side.

BORDA'GIUM (*Archæol.*) the same as Bordlode.

BORDA'RIA (*Archæol.*) a cottage, from the Saxon borð, a house.

BORDA'RII (*Archæol.*) or Bordmen, a term frequently used in Domesday book for a sort of boors, who were distinct from the *villani*. They are supposed to have been peasants in a less servile condition, who had a bord or cottage.

BORDA'T (*Com.*) or *bordetti*, a very narrow stuff manufactured in India.

BO'RD-BRIGGH (*Archæol.*) from the Saxon borȝ-bryce, or burȝ-bnych; a pledge, breach, or breach of mutual fidelity.

BO'RDER (*Mil.*) a French term, signifying to line with soldiers, as *border la côte*, to line the coast.

BORDER (*Mech.*) from the Teut. *Bort*, a limit, or a board; the edge of any thing, particularly of a garment, a garden-bed, &c.

BORDER (*Bot.*) the upper or spreading part of a one-petalled corolla. [vide *Limbus*]

BORDER (*Her.*) or *bordure*, in French *bordeure*; is an ordinary, so called because it borders round, and, as it were, hems in the field. They are either plain, as in *fig.* 1, or indented, as in *fig.* 2. "He beareth, *gules,* a bordure indented, *argent.*" Borders are charged with things natural and artificial in the same manner as the field; thus, a border

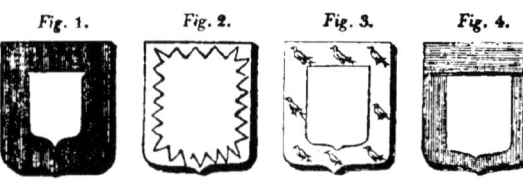

enaluron consists of birds, as in *fig.* 3. He beareth, *argent,* a bordure, *gules,* enaluron of martlets, *or;* so borders *enurey* composed of beasts; *verdoy,* of vegetables; *entoyer,* of inanimate things. Borders always give place to the chief, quarter, and canton, so that in coats charged with a chief, quarter, or canton, the border goes round the field until it reaches them, as in *fig.* 4. "He beareth, *argent,* a border, *gules,* a chief, *azure.*" Borders were anciently used to distinguish one house from another that was descended of one family and the same parents.

BORDEREA′U (*Mil.*) French for a sort of diary, which is kept, for a troop or company, for the purpose of ascertaining what articles have been distributed, and what money paid to the soldiers.

BO′RDERER (*Geog.*) a name for an inhabitant on the extreme borders of a country, and particularly applied, in former times, to those who lived on the borders of England and Scotland.

BORDERERS (*Mil.*) or *King's own borderers,* a name given to the twenty-fifth regiment, because it was originally stationed on the borders of Scotland.

BO′RDER-WARRANT (*Law*) a warrant given by a judge, on either side the borders of England or Scotland, for arresting a person on the opposite side.

BORD-HA′LFPENNY (*Law*) from the Saxon *borb,* a board; a duty paid at fairs and markets for setting up boards, stalls, &c. for vending.—*Bord-lands,* the demesnes, or estate, which lords kept in their hands for the maintenance of their board or table. *Bract.* l. 4, tract. 3, c. 9.—*Bord-lode,* a service required of tenants to carry timber out of the woods of the lord.—*Bord service,* a tenure of bord-lands, by which some lands in the manor of Fulham were held of the bishop of London.

BORDU′RE (*Her.*) vide *Border.*

BORDURE (*Archit.*) French for a profile in relievo, which is either oval or round. When it is square it is called a *cadre,* and serves as a frame for a pannel or a picture.

BORE (*Gun.*) the hollow of a piece of ordnance.

BO′RE COLE (*Bot.*) or Curled Colewort, a hardy species of Kale, which is improved by cold. It is a variety of the *Brassica Oleracea* of Linnæus.

BO′REAL (*Astron.*) an epithet the same as northern, as the boreal signs, Aurora Borealis. [vide *Aurora Borealis*]

BO′REAS (*Ant.*) the North wind, otherwise called *Aquilo;* it derives its name from the Hyperborean mountains, from which it blows, or ἀπὸ τῆ βοᾶν, from the blustering noise which it makes in blowing. It lies, according to Pliny, between Cæcias and Aparctias, answering nearly to that part of the compass which sailors call N.N.E.

Virg. Geog. l. 1, v. 93.

—— *Boreæ penetrabile frigus adurat.*

Ovid makes Boreas say of himself, *Met.* l. 6, v. 691.

Apta mihi vis est, quâ tristia nubila pello :
Et freta concutio, nodosaque robora verto,
Induroque nives, et terras grandine pulso.

Vitruv. l. 1, c. 6; *Plin.* l. 2, c. 47; *Agathem.* l. 1, c. 2.

BOREA′SMI (*Ant.*) Βορεασμοί, an Athenian festival in honour of Boreas, who had an altar at Athens.

BOREL-FOLK (*Archæol.*) country people, from the French *boure,* Flock, because they covered their heads with such stuff.

BO′RER (*Mech.*) an instrument for boring holes.

BORI′DIA (*Med.*) a kind of salt fish eaten raw, which is hard of digestion.

BO′RING (*Vet.*) an operation formerly practised upon horses with wrenched shoulders, by cutting a hole in the part affected, and thrusting in a cold flat iron.

BORNE (*Mason.*) French for a stone stud placed before a wall to secure it against waggons, &c.

BORNO′YER (*Hort.*) a French term signifying to look with one eye through three or more stakes or poles in order to erect a wall, or plant a row of trees.

BOROUGH (*Archæol.*) from the Teut. *Burg,* formerly signified a fenced town, but is now taken for any corporate town which is not a city, and sends burgesses to Parliament. Boroughs in Scotland are divided into *Royal boroughs,* that are held of the King; and *boroughs of barony,* that are held of a subject. The magistrates of royal boroughs have the same jurisdiction within the borough that sheriffs have in the county.—*Borough English,* a custom whereby lands or estates descended to the youngest son.—*Borough-holders,* or *borsholder,* vide *Headborough.—Borough master,* a mayor of a town. *Glanv.* l. 7, c. 8; *Bract.* l. 3, tract. 2, c. 10; *F. N. B.* 150; *Co. Lit.* 33, &c.; *Kitch.* 102; *Lamb. Dut. of Const.*

BO′ROZAIL (*Med.*) a disease in Æthiopia similar to the *lues venerea.*

BORRA′GO (*Bot.*) vide *Borago.*

BORSE′LLA (*Mech.*) an instrument with which glass makers contract or extend their glasses at pleasure.

BORSYCI′TES (*Min.*) a black gem mixed with red and white spots. *Plin.* l. 37, c. 10.

BO′RTMAGAD (*Archæol.*) a housemaid.

BOS (*Zool.*) a genus of animals, Class *Mammalia,* Order *Pecora.*

Generic Characters. Horns hollow.—*Foreteeth* lower eight; tusks none.

Species. The species are *Bos Taurus,* the Ox, including the varieties of the Wild Bull, the Bison, the Bonassus, &c.—*Bos Arnee,* Arnee.—*Bos Bubalus, Bubalus, Bufelus, Le Buffle,* Buffalo.—*Bos Moschatus,* Musk Ox.—*Bos Grunniens, Bubalus cauda, et equina, Le yak,* ou *Buffle à queue de Cheval,* Grunting Ox, or Yak of Tartary.—*Bos Caffer,* Cape Ox.—*Bos Americanus,* American Ox.—*Bos barbatus,* Baas.—*Bos pumilus,* Dwarf Ox.

BO′SA (*Med.*) an inebriating preparation of meal, darnel, &c. *Prosp. Alp.*

BO′SCAGE (*Paint.*) a picture representing much wood, &c.

BOSCAGE (*Archit.*) vide *Bossage.*

BOSCA′GIUM (*Archæol.*) Boscage, the food which woods yield to cattle, as mast, &c. from the Italian *Bosco,* a wood: to be *quit de Boscagio* is to be free of paying a duty for windfalls in the wood. *Manw.*

BOSCA′RIA (*Archæol.*) wood-houses.

BOSCAS (*Or.*) a pigeon, βωσκας from βοσκω.

BOSCAS (*Chem.*) a kind of dry pitch. *Gorr. Med. Def.*

BO′SCUS (*Ant.*) from the Italian *bosco,* wood; all manner of wood. *Stat.* 10, Hen. 6.

BO′SEA (*Bot.*) a genus of plants, (named after Bose, a German senator,) Class 5 *Pentandria,* Order 2 *Digynia.*

Generic Characters. CAL. *perianth* five-leaved.—COR. none.—STAM. *filaments* five; *anthers* simple.—PIST. *germ* ovate-oblong; *style* none; *stigmas* two.—PER. berry globular; *seed* one.

Species. The only species is the *Bosea Yervamora,* Golden-Rod tree, a shrub, native of the Canary Isles.

BOSS (*Mason.*) a vessel in which bricklayers put the mortar used for tiling. It is hung by an iron hook on the laths or the ladder.

Boss *of a bit* (*Her.*) a charge borne in the arms of the loriners or bitmakers' company.

BOSSAGE (*Archit.*) or *Boscage*, a term for any stone having a projecture which is laid rough in a building, in order to be afterwards carved into mouldings, capitals, coats of arms, &c.—*Bossage* is also the name for what is otherwise called *Rustic work*, consisting of stones that seem to project beyond the naked of the building.—*Bossage en liaison*, that which represents squares and stones laid crossways.

BOSSE (*Mil.*) a French term for a glass bottle filled with gunpowder and provided with matches, which, when thrown with force, breaks and explodes to the annoyance of the enemy.

Bosse (*Mason.*) French for a knob or embossment which is left on the dressing of a stone, to show that the dimensions have not been toised. It is afterwards pared off when the work is finished.

BO'STRYCHUS (*Ent.*) a genus of animals, Class *Insecta*, Order *Coleoptera*.

Generic Characters. *Antennæ* clavate.—*Thorax* convex.—*Head* inflected.

Species. Insects of this tribe are very voracious, and make deep irregular channels in the bark of trees.

BOTA (*Archæol.*) a boot, such as the monks used to wear.

BOTANOMA'NCY (*Ant.*) Βοτανομαντεία, divination by means of herbs, especially by those of sage or the fig-tree. The persons who consulted them wrote their own names or their questions on leaves, which they exposed to the wind, and from the scattered letters they collected what they took to be the answer.

BOTANY.

BOTANY is the science which teaches the knowledge of plants. Plants are to be considered as to their Parts, Classification, and Physiology.

Parts of Plants.

The principal Parts of Plants are three; namely, the Stem, *caudex*; the Herb, *herba*; and the Fructification, *fructificatio*.

The Stem.

The Stem is either descending or ascending.—The Descending Stem is the same as the Root, *radix*; the Ascending Stem is the Stem, *caudex*, properly so called.

Root. The root is divided into the *Rhizoma*, the thick fleshy part belonging to biennials and perennials.—*Fibrillæ*, the fibrous prolongations or thread-like parts of the root, which in some plants constitute the only parts of the root.—*Radiculæ*, the fine hair-like prolongations of the roots, which serve as absorbent vessels to nourish the plants.—*Tuber*, the thick fleshy part from which the shoots proceed, as in the *Solanum tuberosum*, the Potatoe.—*Bulbus*, the Bulb, a fleshy body provided with several coats.—*Soboles*, an horizontal prolongation of the root, which produces new plants of its kind, as in the *Triticum repens*, Couch, or Dog's Grass. According to these parts, roots are divided into the *Rhizomatoideæ*, *Fibrillatæ*, *Tuberosæ*, *Bulbosæ*, and *Nothæ*, or spurious roots. The *rhizomatoideæ* are moreover distinguished into the woody, as in trees and shrubs; fleshy, as in *Daucus carota*, the Carrot; hollow, as in *Fumaria bulbosa*; *præmorse*, or bitten-off, as in *Scabiosa succisa*, Devil's-Bit Scabious; *geniculate*, or jointed, as in *Cyclamen*.—The *fibrillatæ* are distinguished into the fibrous, as in *Poa annua*; capillary, or hair-like, as in *Scirpus avicularis*, the Least Club-Rush, &c.—The *tuberosæ* are distinguished into the granulate, or knobbed, as in the *Saxifraga granulata*; testiculated, as in the *Orchis*; digitate or fingered, as in the *Dioscorea alternifolia*, &c.—The *bulbosæ* are distinguished into the imbricated, as in the *Lilium bulbiferum*, or Bulb-bearing Lily; coated, as in the *Allium Cepa*, the Common Onion, &c.—The *nothæ* are distinguished into *divisæ*, the divided; *bissaraceæ*, byssus-like, as in many species of *Agaricus*, &c. [pl. 21]

Stem. The Ascending Stem, *Caudex ascendens*, is the prolongation of the plant above the soil, which is divided into *truncus*, the Trunk; *caulis*, the Stalk; *culmus*, the Straw, or Culm; *scapus*, the Scape; *stipes*, the Stipe; *surculus*, the Shoot; *sarmentum*, the Sarment; *stolo*, the Sucker; *caudex*, the Stem; *petiolus*, the Petiole, or Leaf-Stalk; *pedunculus*, the Peduncle, or Flower-Stalk; and *seta*, the Bristle.—*Truncus*, the Trunk, peculiar to trees and shrubs, the divisions of which are called *Rami*, Branches, and *Ramuli*, Twigs.—*Caulis*, the Stalk, is herbaceous, and belongs only to herbaceous plants. The stalk, in respect to division, is simple, branched, dichotomous, &c.; in respect to the branches, alternate, opposite, distochous, &c.; in respect to position, erect, creeping; or parasitical, as in the *Viscum sarmentosum*, Misletoe; twining from the left to the right, as in *Humulus lupinus*, the Hop; twining from the right to the left, as in *Convolvulus*, the Bindweed; in respect to clothing, as naked, leafless, scaly, prickly, bulb-bearing, &c.; in respect to figure, round, compressed, angled, articulated, &c.; in respect to substance, woody, herbaceous, fleshy, &c.—*Culmus*, the Straw or Culm, proper to Grasses only. The straw is knotted, branched, sheathed, &c.—*Scapus*, the Scape, an herbaceous stem, bearing flowers but not leaves, like the Lilies.—*Caudex*, the Stem, a simple perennial rod, belonging to the Palms and the arboreous Ferns. The Stem is ringed, scaly, tessellated, aculeated, &c.—*Stipes*, the Stipe, is applied only to the Filices, Fungi, &c. The Stipe in the Filices is chaffy, scaly, naked, &c.; in the Fungi, fleshy, leathery, squarrose, &c.—*Surculus*, the Shoot, is a stem of the Mosses; but that sort of stalk which bears the fructification of the *Musci frondosi et Jungermanniæ*, is called *seta*, the Bristle. The Shoot is simple, branched, pinnated, creeping, &c. The Bristle, single, aggregate, axillary, &c.—*Sarmentum*, a filiform stem, that sends forth shoots and produces new plants of the same kind, as *Saxifraga sarmentosa*, the Saxifrage.—*Stolo*, the Sucker, a foliaceous creeping stem, producing leaves, from which comes a new plant, as *Azuga reptans*, Common Bugle, and *Hieracium pilosella*, Mouse-Ear Hawkweed.—*Petiolus*, the Petiole, or Leafstalk, is a stem situated at the base of the leaf. The Petiole is winged, as in the *Citrus aurantium*, the Orange; compressed, as in the *Populus tremula*, the Asp; channelled, as in the *Tussilago petasites*, Common Butter-Burr; inflated, as in the *Trapa natans*, four-awned Caltrops, &c.—*Pedunculus*, the Peduncle, or Flower-Stalk, which is found close under the flower, and may be either a principal stem or a partial stalk, called *Pedicellus*, or Foot-stalk. The Flower-Stalk is one, two, three, flowered, &c., common, partial, axillary, lateral, alar, &c. To the Flower-Stalk belongs *inflorescentia*, the Inflorescence, or the manner in which the flower grows on the stalk. [pl. 21]

Inflorescence. The Inflorescence is of different kinds, namely, *verticillus*, the Whorl; *capitulum*, the Head; *spicula*, the Ear; *spica*, the Spike; *racemus*, the Raceme; *fasciculus*, the Fascicle; *cyma*, the Cyme; *corymbus*, the Corymb; *panicula*, the Panicle; *thyrsus*, the Thyrse; *spadix*, the Spadix; *amentum*, the Catkin; *sorus*, the Moss.—*Verticellus*, the Whorl, or Whirl, which consists of several flowers standing at intervals. It is sessile, as in the *Mentha arvensis*, the Field Mint;

pedicelled, headed, as in *Phlomis tuberosa*; naked, bracteate, &c.—*Capitulum*, the Head, has many flowers, standing thick, so as to form a head. It is spherical, as in the *Gomphrena globosa*; conical, as in the *Trifolium montanum*; leafy, tufted, &c.—*Spicula*, or *Locusta*, the Ear, the flowers of gramineous plants. It is one, two, many flowered, &c.; ovate, oblong, &c.—*Spica*, the Spike, has many flowers without a foot-stalk. It is glomerate, interrupted, verticillated, imbricated, ovate, or ventricose, &c.—*Racemus*, the Raceme, is a peduncle with short lateral branches, as in *Vitis*, the Vine; *Ribes*, the Currant, &c.: this is one-sided, one-rowed, limber, stiff, compound, conjugate, &c.—*Corymbus*, the Corymb, is an erect raceme, the lower peduncles of which are so lengthened as to be of equal height with the upper. These footstalks take their rise from different heights, which distinguish the Corymb from—*Cyma*, the Cyme, where the peduncles take their rise from the same centre; but the subdivisions are irregular, as in *Sambucus nigra*, and from—*Umbella*, the Umbel, where the peduncles take their rise from the same centre, and the whole is disposed in regular order. In an Umbel the flower-stalks are called *Radii*, Rays; and the Umbel is either simple, compound, sitting, peduncled, close, distant, poor, convex, or flat, &c.—*Fasciculus*, the Fascicle, or Bundle, a number of simple peduncles rising at the foot of the stem from several points, as in *Dianthus barbatus*, the Sweet-William.—*Panicula*, the Panicle, is that in which the flowers or fruits are scattered on branches unequally divided, as in *Avena*, Oats, or Oat-Grass, it is either simple, branched, or crowded, &c.—*Thyrsus*, the Thyrse, is a panicle in an ovate form, as in the *Syringa*, *Ligustrum vulgare*, Common Privet, &c.—*Spadix*, an inflorescence, so called from the *vagina*, called Spadix, which contains the flower-stalks, as in the Palms and some plants of the *Arum* genus.—*Amentum*, or *Julus*, the Catkin, is a long stem thickly covered with scales, under which are the flowers, or their essential parts, as in the *Salices*, the Willows; *Corylus avellana*, the Hazel, &c. It is either cylindrical, or attenuated, &c.—*Sorus*, the Mass, the inflorescence peculiar to the Filices, so called from the masses of seed-capsules found on the fronds of these plants. It is either round, lunated, linear, two-rowed, continued, or interrupted, &c. [pl. 21. 22]

Of the Herb.

The Herb consists of *folium*, the Leaf; *frons*, the Frond; and *fulcrum*, the Prop or Fulcre.

Leaf. The Leaf is the production and prolongation of the ascending stem. Leaves are generally divided into simple and compound. The simple Leaf is distinguished, as to its Apex, into acute, or ending in a point; obtuse, or having the point blunt or round; mucronate, præmorse, truncated, &c. As to its Base, into heartshaped, kindeyshaped, earshaped, lunate, arrowshaped, &c. As to its Circumference, spatulate, or in the form of a spatula, rhombic, ovate, lanceolate, lobed, palmated, laciniate, or torn, &c. As respects the Surface, into veined, when the vessels rise from the middle rib; nerved, when the vessels rise from the base to the apex; three-nerved, quintuple-nerved, &c.; channelled, wrinkled, pitted, curled, &c. As to the Margin, toothed, undulated, or bent in and out; crenated, serrated, gnawed, spiny, fringed, &c. As to its Situation, into radical when the leaf springs from the root, as in the *viola odorata*; seminal, when the leaf grows out of the seed, as in Hemp, &c.

Compound Leaves, are those which have several leaves supported by one footstalk. They are of different kinds, as bigeminate, when the divided leafstalk bears two leaves; pinnate, when an undivided leafstalk has leaflets on each side; alternately pinnate, when the leaflets stand alternately on a pinnated leaf, &c.

Frond. The Frond, a kind of leaf proper to the *Palmæ hepaticæ* and *Algæ*, which have the stalk and leaf so intimately connected that they cannot be distinguished. The Frond of the Palms is either fanshaped, as in *Chamærops borassus*; petalled, as in *Corypha*; pinnated, as in *Phœnix*; bipinnated, as in *Caryota*; unfertile, as in *Blechnum*; whirled, as in *Equisetrum*. The Frond of the *Algæ* is in *Lichen saxatilis fraxineus*, &c. gelatinous, as in *Lichen crispus*, *fascicularis*; leathery, as in *Peltidea canina*; imbricated, as in *Lichen saxicola*, *parietinus*, &c.; crustaceous, as in *Lichen saxicola*, *subfuscus*, *Opegrapha pulverulenta*; powdery, as in *Lepra*; threadlike, as in *Lichen jubatus*, *Conferva*, *Geranium*, *Byssus*, &c.; cupbearing, as in *Lichen pyridatus*, *gracilis*, &c. [pl. 29]

Props. The Prop is a sort of leaf which serves to keep the plant erect, and answers several other purposes. It is of different kinds, as—*Stipula*, the stipule, a small leaf that appears on the stem in the place of a footstalk, which are double, solitary, lateral, caducous, deciduous, &c. The stipules also vary in form like the leaves.—*Ramentum*, the Rament, a bristle-shaped leaflet placed in the angle of the petiole, as on the oak.—*Bracteæ*, the Floral Leaves that stand near or between the flowers, which sometimes form *Coma*, a Tuft, as *Fritillarea imperialis*, the Pine Apple,—*Vagina*, the Sheath, the prolongation of a leaf, which rolls itself round the stem, as in the grasses.—*Spatha*, the Spathe, an oblong leaf which surrounds the stem, and serves as a covering for the flower. The spathe is univalve, as in *Arum maculatum*; bivalve, as in *Stratiotes aloides*, the Fresh-water Soldier; one flowered, two-flowered, &c. withering, permanent, &c.—*Ochrea*, the Roll, a leaf-like body, encircling the branches of the Flower-Stalk in some grasses, after the manner of the sheath. The Roll is truncated, oblique, and foliaceous.—*Ascidium*, the Bottle, a foliaceous cylindrical hollow body, which is generally furnished with a cover, and contains water.—*Ampulla*, the Bladder, a round hollow body at the roots of water plants, as in *Utricularia*.—*Ligula*, the Strap, a leaflet at the base of the leaf in grasses only. The strap is entire, bifid, torn, fringed, truncated, &c.—*Involucrum*, the Involucre, consisting of several leaves which surround the flower, particularly of umbelliferous plants before they unfold. The Involucre is common, partial, or halved; one-leaved, as in *Buplerum*; two-leaved, as in *Euphorbia*; three-leaved, as in *Butomus*; tetraphyllous, or four-leaved, as in *Cornus*; pentaphyllous, as in *Daucus*, hexaphyllous, as in *Halmanthus*. Linnæus reckons the involucre as a sort of calyx. [vide *Calyx* and *Involucre*]—*Cirrhus*, the Tendril, a filiform body, which serves for attaching plants to some support, as in the vine, &c. The tendril is either axillary, foliar, petiolar, peduncular, simple, three-branched, &c. [vide *Tendril*]—*Gemma*, the Bud which contains the embryo of leaves. The opening of the bud is called *foliatio*, Foliation; an opening bud cut horizontally presents different appearances, which are distinguished by the names of involute, as in *Humulus lupulus*, the Hop; revolute, as in *Salices*, the Willows; obvolute, as in *Salvia officinalis*, Sage; convolute, as in *Prianus Armenuaca*, the Apricot; riding, as in *Syringa vulgaris*, the Lilac; conduplicate, as in *Fagus sylvatica*, the Beech; plaited, as in *Betula alba*. [vide *Bud*]—*Propago*, the Moss-Bud, is a roundish longish body proceeding from the mother plant, and becoming itself a new one, as in the mosses.

BOTANY.

—*Gongylus*, the knot belonging to the Fuci, which falls off upon the death of the mother plant, and becomes a new one.—*Glandula*, the gland, a round body, situated on the leaves, that serves as an organ of transpiration and secretion.—*Spina*, the Thorn, rises in the interior of the plant, as in *Prunus spinosa*, the Sloe.—*Aculeus*, the Prickle, a persistent production, that issues from the bark, as in the *Rosa centifolia*.—*Arista*, the Awn, a pointed beard on grasses. The Awn is either naked, feathered, straight; geniculated, bent, twisted, terminal, or dorsal. [vide *Arista*]—*Pili*, the Hairs, fine slender bodies, which serve as organs of perspiration. The Hairs are either awl-shaped, as in *Borago officinalis*; bulbous, as in *Centaurea jacea*; hook-shaped, as in *Scabiosa succisa*; articulated, as in *Veronica aphylla*; forked, as in *Apargia hispida*; branched, as in *Ribes grossularia*; the Gooseberry. [vide *Pili*]

Parts of the Fungi, &c. To the above may be added the parts of the Fungi, Filices, and Algæ, which differ so materially, as to admit of little or no comparison with those of other plants, particularly the first, the parts of which are *volva*, the Wrapper; *annulus*, the Ring; *pileus*, the Cap; *peridium*, the Envelope.—*Volva*, the wrapper, is a thick fleshy membrane, as in *Lycoperdon stellata*.—*Annulus*, the Ring, is a thin membrane attached to the stalk, as in *Agaricus conspurcatus*. The Ring is either upright, inverted, sitting, moveable, permanent, fugacious, cobweb-like.—*Pileus*, the Cap, or the top of the Fungus, is distinguished into the flat, round, hollow, bossed, bell-shaped, viscid, scaly, squarrose, halved, stipitate, sitting, &c. The Pileus has also parts peculiar to itself, as *Umbo*, the Boss, which is the centre; *Lamellæ*, the Gills, the thin foliaceous membrane on the underside of the Pileus, which are peculiar to the genus *Agaricus*; *Pori*, the Pores, small holes on the under side of the Pileus, which are peculiar to the *Boleti*; *Aculei*, or *Echini*, the Prickles or projecting points peculiar to the genus *Hydnum*; *Papillæ*, the Warts, small round protuberances on the under surface. [vide *Cap*] —*Peridium*, the Envelope, is a thin membrane, belonging to some Fungi, which cover the seeds, as in *Lycoperdon*, &c. The Envelope is either simple, as in *Physarium*, *Nidularia*, &c.; double, as in *Diderma*; circularly-torn, as in *Arcyria*; dentated, as in *Æcidium*; reticulate, as in *Dictydium*.

The Filices have a tender membrane, called *Indusium*, the Cover which surrounds the *Sorus*. The Cover is either flat, as in *Polypodium*; bottle-shaped, as in *Trichomanes*; bivalve, as in *Hymenophyllum*; continuous, as in *Pteris*; superficial, as in *Scolopendrum*; simple, as in *Pteris*; double, as in *Scolopendrum*, &c.

Some of the Algæ have a peltated concavity, with a raised rim, called *Cyphella*, the Little Cup.

Fructification.

The Fructification consists of the Flower, *Flos*; and the Fruit, *Fructus*.

Flower. The Flower is to be considered as to the parts of which it is composed, and the kinds into which it is divided. The principal parts of the Flower are, *calyx*, the Calyx or Empalement; *corolla*, the Blossom; *stamen*, the Stamen or Chives; *pistillum*, the Pistil or Pointal; and *nectarium*, the Nectary.

Calyx. The Calyx comprehends all the green leaves which serve as an envelope for the flower, of which there are different kinds, as—*Perianthium*, the Perianth, which immediately incloses the flower; and is either abiding, as in *Hyoscyamus niger*, the Henbane; deciduous, as in *Tilia Europæa*, the Lime Tree; withering, *marescens*, as in *Prunus Armeniaca*, the Apricot; caducous, as in *Papaver somniferum*; double, as in *Fragraria vesca*, the Strawberry; labiated, as in *Salvia officinalis*, the Sage; one, two, three-leaved, &c. cleft, bifid, trifid, &c. &c. [vide *Calyx* or *perianth*]—*Anthodium*, the common Perianth, which contains a great number of flowers in one, as in *Leontodon Taraxacum*, the Dandelion; *Centaurea cyanus*, the Blue Bottle; *Helianthus annuus*, the Sunflower, &c. The common Perianth is either one-leaved, many-leaved, simple, equal, scaly, squarrose, fringed, muricated, thorny, turbinated, spherical, cylindrical, flat, doubled, or calyculated. This perianth is called by Linnæus the Common Calyx, and its *foliola* are called *squamæ*. The same name is also given to the *foliola* which cover the Catkin, and serve in place of the Calyx.—*Gluma*, the Glume, or perianth of Grasses.—*Pappus*, a calyx, consisting of hair, which remains till the ripening of the seed.—*Perichætium* is the calyx of the mosses. [vide *Calyx*]

Corolla. The Corolla is the envelope of small leaves, inclosed by the Calyx, and surrounding the interior parts of the flower. The divisions or small leaves of the Corolla are called *Petala*, petals, according to which it is distinguished into *Corolla monopetala*, monopetalous Corolla, when it consists of one piece, or petal; and *Corolla polypetala*, polypetalous Corolla, when it consists of several petals. The monopetalous Corolla is divided into segments, and, as to its form, is either club-shaped, spherical, bell-shaped, cup-shaped, urceolated, funnel-shaped, salver-shaped, wheel-shaped, tongue-shaped, ringent, or bilabiate, &c. The Polypetalous Corolla is either rose-like, mallow-like, cross-like, pink-like, lily-like, papilionaceous, one, two, three, or many-petalled, &c. The other parts of the Corolla are *Tubus*, the hollow underpart of the monopetalous Corolla; *limbus*, the Border or opening of the Corolla; *laciniæ*, the segments or lobes; *galea*, the Helmet, or upper arched *lacinia*; *labia*, the Lips upper and under; *barba*, the Beard, a species of a lip; *rictus*, the Gape between the extremities of the lip; *faux*, the Throat, or opening of the tube; *palatum*, the Palate, or arch of the under lip. The parts of a papilionaceous Corolla are *vexillum*, the Standard; *alæ*, the Wings; *carina*, the Keel. [vide *Corolla*] The Corolla of the Mosses, which differs from that of all other plants, is a pretty hard membrane that closely embraces the pistil, the under part of which perfectly resembles the vagina on the straw of the Grasses, and is called *vaginula*, the little Sheath; the upper part remains attached to the fruit, and is called *calyptra*, the Calyptre, the varieties of which do not appear until the fruit is ripe.

Stamen. The Stamen is one of the essential parts of a flower consisting of—*Filamenta*, Filaments, which support the Anther.—*Anthera*, the Anther, a hollow cellular body.—*Pollen*, a powder, or very fine dust contained in the anther. The Filaments are, as to their figure, capillary, filiform, awl-shaped, dilated, heart-shaped, wedge-shaped, loose, connate, bifid, multifid-jointed, connivant, incurved, declined, hairy, unequal, &c. [vide *Stamen* and *filament*] The Anther is either kidney-shaped, as in *Digitalis purpurea*, the Fox-glove; bifid, as in most Grasses; peltated, as in *Taxus baccata*, the Yew; hairy, as in *Lamium Album*, the Dead-Nettle; crested, as in *Ericæ*, the Heaths; bilocular, unilocular, angulated, &c. [vide *Stamen* and *Anther*]

Pistil. The Pistil, the second essential part of a flower, stands always in the middle, and consists of—*Germen*, the Seed-bud, the undermost part containing the embryo of the fruit.—*Stylus*, the Style or Shaft, a small stalk seated on the Germen.—*Stigma*, the top of the style. The Germen is either sitting, pedicelled, superior, or inferior. The Style is hair-like, bristle-like, thread-like, awl-shaped, club-shaped, dichotomous, bifid, trifid, multifid, &c. terminal, lateral, erect, declined, deciduous, &c. The Stigma is pointed, blunt, oblong, club-shaped, spherical, capitate, emarginated, peltated, angular, three-lobed, cruciform, petal-like, bifid, trifid, multifid, &c.

Nectary. The Nectary is that part of the flower which commonly serves to secrete a sweet juice, called Nectar. Nectaries are of different kinds, as *Glandulæ*, glands which really secrete and exude the sweet juice, and are either sessile, petiolated, spherical, compressed, or flat, &c.—*Squamæ nectariferæ* are small scales that exude honey.—*Pori nectariferi* are small pores that exude honey.—*Cucullus*, the Hood, a hollow body like a hood or bag, as in *Aconitum*, Monkshood.—*Fornix*, the Arch, a small elongation of the Corolla.—*Barba*, the Beard, consisting of soft hairs or bristles.—*Tubus*, the Tube, of the shape of a cylinder, as in *Pelargonium*, Crane's-bill.—*Fovea*, the Pit, a cavity for the reception of honey.—*Plica*, an oblong groove.—*Calcar*, the Spur, a horn-shaped production of the Corolla, in which honey is found, as in *Viola odorata*, March Violet.—*Filum*, the Thread, a long body at the bottom of the flower, as in *Passiflora*, the Passion-Flower.—*Cylindrus*, the Cylinder, a thin cylindrical body surrounding the pistil, as in *Swetenia*.—*Corona*, the Crown, a body much resembling the Corolla.

Fruit. The Fruit proceeds from the Germen, and consists of *pericarpium*, the Pericarp; *semen*, the Seed; and *basis*, the Base.

Pericarp. The Pericarp is the hard hollow body which contains the seed, and is of different kinds; namely, *utriculus*, the Bladder; *samara*, the Winged Fruit; *folliculus*, the Follicle; *capsula*, the Capsule; *nux*, the Nut; *drupa*, the Drupe; *bacca*, the Berry; *pomum*, the Pome; *pepo*, the Pumpkin; *siliqua*, the Silique; *legumen*, the Legume; *lomentum*, the Loment; and *theca*, the Case.—*Utriculus*, the Bladder, a thin skin inclosing a single seed. The Bladder is loose, as in *Adonis*; straight, as in *Galium*; and cut round, as in *Amaranthus*.—*Samara*, the Winged-Fruit, a pericarp containing two seeds at most, as in the fruit of the Elm.—*Folliculus*, the Follicle, an oblong pericarp, filled with seeds.—*Capsula*, the Capsule, is a pericarp, or thin coat divided into cells.

The parts of the capsule are, *dissepimentum*, the partition; *loculamenta*, the cells; *columella*, the Column; *valvulæ*, the Valves; *sutura*, the Suture. The different sorts of capsules are distinguished, as to their figure, into round, long, &c.; as to the number of their cells, into unilocular, or one-celled, bilocular, &c.; as to the number of valves, into one-valved, two, three-valved, &c. as to the number of seeds, into one-seeded, two-seeded, &c.; as to their composition, into berried, corticated, woody, &c.; as to their mode of opening, whether they burst at the top, in the middle, or at the base.—*Nux*, the Nut, a pericarp covered with a hard shell, called the Putamen, the seed of which is called *Nucleus*, the Kernel.—*Drupa*, the Drupe, a nut covered with a fleshy coat, as in the *Prunus cerasus*, the Cherry. The Drupe is berried, as in *Prunus cerasus*, the cherry, *Prunus domestica*, the Plum, *Amygdalus Persica*, the Peach; dry, as in *Amygdalus communis*, the Almond; winged, as in *Halesia*; bursting, as in *Juglans regia*, the Walnut, *Myristica moschata*, the Nutmeg, &c. It is also distinguished as to the number of nuts and cells.—*Bacca*, the Berry, a succulent fruit containing many seeds. The Berry is distinguished, according to the number of the seeds, into one, two, three, or many-seeded, &c.; according to the number of cells, into one, two, three, or many-celled, &c.; and as to its make, succulent, as in *Ribes grossularia*, the Gooseberry; dry, as in *Hedera helix*, the Ivy; corticated, as in *Garcinia mangostana*.—*Pomum*, the Pome, a fleshy fruit, having internally a capsule for the seed.—*Pepo*, Pumpkin, a succulent fruit, having its seeds attached to the inner surface of the rind, as in the *Cucurbita pepo*, the Gourd, &c. The Pumpkin is unilocular, bilocular, multilocular, &c.; halflocular, fleshy, juicy, dry, cortical, &c.—*Siliqua*, the Silique, a dry elongated pericarp, consisting of halves, or valves, as in the *Sinapis alba*, the Mustard: when the Silique is as broad as it is long it is called *silicula*, a Silicle, both of which are distinguished according to the situation of the partition, i. e. whether the valves run parallel with the partition, or whether contrary to the partition.—The *Legume*, a dry elongated pericarp, differing somewhat from the silique. The Legume is membranaceous, coriaceous, fleshy, woody, mealy, ventricose, compressed, channelled, one-seeded, two-seeded, &c.—*Lomentum*, the Loment, an elongated pericarp that bursts differently from the legume. The Loment is cortical, as in *Cassia fistula*; articulated, as in *Hedysarum*; intercepted, as in *Hippocrepis*.—*Theca*, the Case, the fruit of the *frondosi Musci*, which consists of *calyptra*, a calyptre, or tender skin, like a cup; *operculum*, a lid; *fimbria*, the Fringe, a narrow sinuated membrane; *peristoma*, or *peristomium*, the Mouth; *epiphragma*, the Epiphragm, a thin membrane which stretches over the mouth of the Theca; *columella*, or *sporanjidium*, the Column, a slender thread-like body passing through the middle of the Theca, and to which the seed is attached; *apophysis*, a fleshy round or oblong body that appears at the base of the Theca. The calyptre is either entire, as in *Grimmia extinctoria*; half, as in most *Musci*; hairy, as in *Polytrichum*; dentated, as in *Grimmia dentata*. The Lid is distinguished as to its figure into acute, mucronate, convex, &c. The Mouth is either naked or set with membranaceous teeth in different rows and positions.—*Strobile*, a pericarp made of a catkin.—*Apothecium*, a pericarp peculiar to the Lichens.

Seed. The Seed is that part of the plant destined for propagation. It consists of different parts, namely, *cotyledones*, Cotyledons, or Seed-Leaves; *corculum*, the Corcle; *hylum* the Eye; *funiculus umbilicalis*, the Umbilical Chord; *plumula*, the Plumule; and *rostellum*, the Rostel.—*Cotyledons*, are the two lobes, or Seed-Leaves.—*Corculum*, the Corcle, or germ of the new plant.—*Hylum*, the Eye, a deep scar in that part of the seed which has been occupied by the corcle.—*Funiculus umbilicalis*, the Umbilical chord, or the thread by which the seed is attached.—*Plumula*, the Plumule, or that part of the corcle which ascends to form the leaves.—*Rostellum*, the Rostel, the other part of the corcle which descends into the earth, and becomes the root. The seed is, besides, covered with two coats, the one external, called the *tunica externa*, and the other internal, *Membrana interna*. Other parts belonging to the Seed or Pericarp are *arillus*, the Aril; *pappus*, the Down; *desma*, the Tuft; *cauda*, the Tail; *rostrum*, the Beak; *ala*, the Wing; *crista*, the Crest; *costæ*, the Ribs; *verruca*, the Wart; *pruina*, the Hoar; *elater*, the Springer; *capillitium*, the Hair-Net, and the *trichidium*.—*Arillus*, the Aril, is a soft membrane extended over the seed, which is succulent, as in *Enonymus Europæus*, the Spindle-Tree; the Aril, cartilaginous, membranaceous, halved, torn, caped; or netlike, as in the *Orchis*. Sometimes the Aril encloses the pericarp as well as the seed, as in *Myristica moschata*, the Nutmeg.—*Pappus*, or Down, the calyx of each particular floret enclosed in a common perianth. The Down is either sitting, stipitate, abiding, caducous, calycled; or chaffy, as in *Helianthus annuus*, the Sunflower; awned as in *Bidens tripartita*; stellate, hair-like, fringed, setaceous, &c.—*Desma*, or *Coma*, the Tuft, a sort of *pilose pappus*.—*Cauda*, the Tail, a threadlike body that appears on the top of the seed.—*Rostrum*, a persistent style on the seed or pericarp.—*Ala*, the Wing, a cartilaginous membrane on the seed and the pericarp.—*Crista*, the Crest, a cork-like wing on the top of some pericarps.—*Costæ*, the Ribs, prominent ridges on some pericarps.—*Verruca*, the Wart, a protuberance on many seeds.—*Pruina*, the Hoar, a fine white powder that often covers the seeds and the pericarp.—*Elater*, the Springer, a filiform elastic body found on the seeds of the *Musci hepatici*.—*Capillitium*, a Hair-Net that serves to fasten the seeds of some *Fungi*.—*Trichidium*, or *Pecten*, a very tender simple hair which supports the seed in some *Fungi*.

Base. The Base connects all the parts of fructification, and consists of—*Receptaculum*, the Receptacle, or body on which the flower stands. The Receptacle is distinguished as to its form into flat, convex, conical; clubbed as in *Arum*, closed as in *Ficus*; quadrifid as in *Mithridatea quadrifida*; flat as in *Dorstenia*, &c.—*Thalamus*, the Fruit-bed, which encloses the fruit within its substance. This is of different kinds, as *pelta*, the Target, a thin round or oblong fruit-bed, which is chiefly found in the genus *Peltidea*; *scutella*, the Shield, a plate-shaped fruit-bed, proper only to the *Algæ*; *tuberculum*, a convex fruit-bed which has no raised margin; *gyroma*, or *trica*, which has the appearance of a saucer, and is peculiar to the genus *Umbilicaria*; *cistella*, which is in shape like a ball; *orbiculus*, a round fruit-bed flat on both sides, in the substance of some fungi, as *Nidularia*; *linella*, a linear-shaped fruit-bed.

Flowers. Flowers are either simple or compound—The Simple Flower is distinguished into *flos nudus*, the Naked Flower, which has neither calyx nor corolla; *flos apetalus*, the Apetalous Flower, which has no corolla; *flos aphyllus*, or *corallaceus*, the Aphyllous Flower, which has no calyx; *flos hermaphroditus*, the Hermaphrodite Flower, which has no stamina and pistillum; *flos fœmineus*, the Female Flower, having no stamina; *flos masculus*, the Male Flower, having no pistil.—The Compound Flower is that which has several flowers seated close together, so as to have the appearance of but one. It is distinguished according to the form into semifloscular, discoid, radiate, &c. [vide *Flower*]

Classification of Plants.

Plants are classed either according to a natural or an artificial order.

Natural Orders. Plants in their natural order are divided into seven families, namely—*Fungi*, which are fleshy, coriaceous, or woody—*Algæ*, which have neither stem nor leaves.—*Musci*, Mosses, which resemble other plants in nothing, except in their leaves and fruit.—*Filices*, Ferns, that never send forth more than one leaf on a footstalk. Their fructification is either in a spike, whence they are called spiciferæ; or on the back of the leaf *Epiphyllospermæ*; or on the root in the form of a knob, *Rhizospermæ*.—*Gramina*, Grasses, which are distinguished by their stem, which is a culm, or straw.—*Lilia*, Lilies, having a tuberous or bulbous root.—*Palmæ*, Palms, which have an arboreous stem, called *Stipes*, from which rise the leaves, but not the branches.—*Plantæ*, Plants, all those which do not come under the above divisions. These are divided into *Herbæ*, Herbs, which bear flowers and seeds once, and then die. If they die at the end of one year they are called *Annuals*; if they last two years they are called *Biennials*.—*Suffrutices*, Undershrubs, the stem of which perishes annually, but the root remains. These are better known by the name of perennials.—*Frutices*, Shrubs, the stem of which continues many years, and sends forth branches from the bottom.—*Arbores*, Trees, the stem of which sends forth branches from the middle or top.

Artificial System. The artificial system is composed of Classes, Orders, Genera, Species, and Varieties. The Class is the most general division of all, including the greatest number of particular plants that have some common characteristic; the Order is a subdivision of the Class; the Genera are contained in the Order, and the Species in the Genera; when the species differ from each other in any minute particular, it is denominated a Variety. The name of a Genus is called the generic Name: that of a Species or Variety the specific or trivial Name. In this manner different systems have been formed according to the different characters which have been selected as the ground of distinction.

Cæsalpinus, who first systematized Botany, formed fifteen classes from the fruit and the situation of the Corculum. Morison constructed his system according to the flower and the general appearance of the plant, out of which he made eighteen classes, and divided the plants generally into *Lignosæ* and *Herbaceæ*. Hermann made use of the flower, fruit, &c. dividing his plants into *Herbæ gymnospermæ*, *Herbæ angiospermæ*, *Herbæ apetalæ*, and *arbores*. Ray also chose the flower, fruit, and external appearance of the plant, dividing them into, 1. *Herbæ submarinæ*. 2. *Fungi*. 3. *Musci*. 4. *Capillares*. 5. *Apetalæ*. 6. *Planipetalæ*. 7. *Discoideæ*. 8. *Corymbiferæ*. 9. *Capitatæ*. 10. *Solitario Semine*. 11. *Umbelliferæ*. 12. *Stellatæ*. 13. *Asperifoliæ*. 14. *Verticellatæ*. 15. *Polyspermæ*. 16. *Pomiferæ*. 17. *Bacciferæ*. 18. *Multisiliquæ*. 19. *Monopetalæ*. 20. *Di-tripetalæ*. 21. *Siliquosæ*. 22. *Leguminosæ*. 23. *Pentapetalæ*. 24. *Floriferæ*. 25. *Stamineæ*. 26. *Anomalæ*. 27. *Arundinaceæ*. 28. *Arbores apetalæ*. 29. *Fructu umbilicato*. 30. *Fructu non umbilicato*. 31. *Fructu sicco*. 32. *Fructu siliquoso*. 33. *Anomalæ*.

Camellus framed a system from the valves of the capsule, calling his classes *Pericarpia afora*, *unifora*, *bifora*, &c. Rivinus selected the Corolla, dividing the plants into *Flores regulares*, *compositæ*, and *irregulares*, and these again into *Monopetali*, *dipetali*, &c.

Tournefort also made the Corolla the foundation of his system, which was generally adopted until the time of Linnæus. He divided plants into *Herbæ et Suffrutices*, *Arbores et Frutices*, and these again into *Herbæ Floribus monopetalis campaniformibus*, *infundibuliformibus*, &c.

Gleditsch formed his system on the stamina, making the following classes: *Thalastemonis*, *Petalastemonis*, *Calycostemonis*, *Stylostemonis*, and *Cryptostemonis*.

Haller framed a natural system on the Cotyledons, the Calyx, the Corolla, the Stamina, and the sexes of the plants, distinguishing them into—1. *Fungi*. 2. *Musci*. 3. *Epiphyllosperma*. 4. *Apetalæ*. 5. *Gramina*, &c. to the number of fifteen classes.

The system of Linnæus, otherwise called the *sexual system*, because it embraces the sexes of plants in the scheme, consists of classes which are distinguished according to the stamina, and of orders which are mostly taken from the style. From the first to the tenth they are named after the number of the stamina, as—1. *Monandria*, for those having one stamen; 2. *Diandria*, those with two stamina; 3. *Triandria*, those with three stamina; 4. *Tetrandria*, those with four stamina; 5. *Pentandria*, those with five stamina; 6. *Hexandria*, those with six stamina; 7. *Heptandria*, those with seven stamina; 8. *Octandria*, those with eight stamina; 9. *Enneandria*, those with nine stamina; 10. *Decandria*, those

BOTANY.

with ten stamina; 11. *Dodecandria*, including those plants which have from eleven to seventeen stamina; 12. *Icosandria*, those having many stamina inserted in the calyx; 13. *Polyandria*, those having twenty stamina and upwards; 14. *Didynamia*, those having four stamina in one flower, two of which are longer than the rest; 15. *Tetradynamia*, those having six stamina in one flower, two shorter than the rest; 16. *Monodelphia*, those whose filaments are connected in the form of a cylinder or tube; 17. *Diadelphia*, when the filaments form two parcels; 18. *Polyadelphia*, when the filaments form several parcels; 19. *Syngenesia*, when the antheræ are united into one cylinder or tube; this class contains mostly compound flowers; 20. *Gynandria*, when the stamina stand on the style; 21. *Monoecia*, those having flowers male and female in one plant; 22. *Dioecia*, having male and female flowers so divided, that one plant bears only male flowers, and the other only female flowers; 23. *Polygamia*, containing hermaphrodite flowers; 24. *Cryptogamia*, those plants whose flowers are not visible to the naked eye, as the *Filices, Musci*, and *Algæ*.

The Orders are distinguished, 1. According to the number of styles, as *Monogynia*, when there is only one style; so *di—tri—tetra*, &c. *gynia*, two, three, four, &c. styled from the first to the 13th class. 2. According to the manner of producing the seed, as *Gymnospermia*, when the seeds are naked; *Angiospermia*, those which have the seed contained in a pericarp; *Siliculosa* and *Siliquosa*, those which have the seed contained in a silique of different sizes. 3. According to the number of stamina, and connexion of the filament and anthers, from class the 16th to the 23d, with the exception of the 19th. 4. According to the connexion of the flower, which is distinguished in four different forms, namely, 1. *Polygamia æqualis*, when all the florets are hermaphrodites. 2. *Polygamia superflua*, when the disk of the compound flower bears hermaphrodite florets, and the ray fertile florets. 3. *Polygamia frustranea*, when the disk consists of fertile hermaphrodite florets, and the ray of barren female florets. 4. *Polygamia necessaria*, when the disk consists of barren hermaphrodite florets, and the ray of fertile female florets. 5. *Polygamia segregata*, when, besides the common perianth, each floret is provided with its own particular calyx.

The Linnean Orders under each Class.

CLASS I.
Monandria.
2 Orders.
1. Monogynia.
2. Digynia.

CLASS II.
Diandria.
3 Orders.
1. Monogynia.
2. Digynia.
3. Trigynia.

CLASS III.
Triandria.
3 Orders.
1. Monogynia.
2. Digynia.
3. Trigynia.

CLASS IV.
Tetrandria.
3 Orders.
1. Monogynia.
2. Digynia.
3. Tetragynia.

CLASS V.
Pentandria.
7 Orders.
1. Monogynia.
2. Digynia.
3. Trigynia.
4. Tetragynia.
5. Pentagynia.
6. Hexagynia.
7. Polygynia.

CLASS VI.
Hexandria.
6 Orders.
1. Monogynia.
2. Digynia.
3. Trigynia.
4. Tetragynia.
5. Hexagynia.
6. Polygynia.

CLASS VII.
Heptandria.
4 Orders.
1. Monogynia.
2. Digynia.
3. Tetragynia.
4. Heptagynia.

CLASS VIII.
Octandria.
4 Orders.
1. Monogynia.
2. Digynia.
3. Trigynia.
4. Tetragynia.

CLASS IX.
Enneandria.
3 Orders.
1. Monogynia.
2. Trigynia.
3. Hexagynia.

CLASS X.
Decandria.
5 Orders.
1. Monogynia.
2. Digynia.
3. Trigynia.
4. Pentagynia.
5. Decagynia.

CLASS XI.
Dodecandria.
6 Orders.
1. Monogynia.
2. Digynia.
3. Trigynia.
4. Tetragynia.
5. Pentagynia.
6. Dodecagynia.

CLASS XII.
Icosandria.
3 Orders.
1. Monogynia.
2. Pentagynia.
3. Polygynia.

CLASS XIII.
Polyandria.
7 Orders.
1. Monogynia.
2. Digynia.
3. Trigynia.
4. Tetragynia.
5. Pentagynia.
6. Hexagynia.
7. Polygynia.

CLASS XIV.
Didynamia.
2 Orders.
1. Gynospermia.
2. Angiospermia.

CLASS XV.
Tetradynamia.
2 Orders.
1. Siliculosa.
2. Siliquosa.

CLASS XVI.
Monodelphia.
8 Orders.
1. Triandria.
2. Pentandria.
3. Heptandria.
4. Octandria.
5. Decandria.
6. Endecandria.
7. Dodecandria.
8. Polyandria.

CLASS XVII.
Diadelphia.
4 Orders.
1. Pentandria.
2. Hexandria.
3. Octandria.
4. Decandria.

CLASS XVIII.
Polyadelphia.
3 Orders.
1. Dodecandria.
2. Icosandria.
3. Polyandria.

CLASS XIX.
Syngenesia.
5 Orders.
1. Polygamia æqualis.
2. Polygamia superflua.
3. Polygamia frustranea.
4. Polygamia necessaria.
5. Polygamia segregata.

CLASS XX.
Gynandria.
7 Orders.
1. Monandria.
2. Diandria.
3. Triandria.
4. Tetrandria.
5. Pentandria.
6. Hexandria.
7. Octandria.

CLASS XXI.
Monoecia.
8 Orders.
1. Monandria.
2. Diandria.
3. Triandria.
4. Tetrandria.
5. Pentandria.
6. Hexandria.
7. Polyandria.
8. Monodelphia.

CLASS XXII.
Dioecia.
8 Orders.
1. Monandria.
2. Diandria.

3. Triandria.
4. Tetrandria.
5. Pentandria.
6. Hexandria.
7. Polyandria.
8. Monodelphia.

CLASS XXIII.

Polygamia.

3 *Orders.*

1. Monoecia.
2. Dioecia.
3. Trioecia.

CLASS XXIV.

Cryptogamia.

4 *Orders.*

1. Filices.
2. Musci.
3. Algæ.
4. Fungi.

To the above may be added the characters which Linnæus introduced into his system.

1. To mark the duration of plants.
  ♄ a tree or shrub.
  ♃ a perennial.
  ☉ a biennial.
  ♂ an annual.

2. To mark the sex.
  ☿ an hermaphrodite flower.
  ♂ a male flower.
  ♀ a female flower.
  ♂ — ♀ male and female flowers upon one stem.
  ♂ : ♀ male and female flowers on different stems.
  ♄ neuter flowers.
  ☿ | ♀ hermaphrodite and female flowers in one compound flower, as in the class syngenesia.
  ☿ | ♄ hermaphrodite and neuter flowers in one compound flower in the same class.
  ☿ — ♂ hermaphrodite and male flowers on one stem.
  ☿ — ♀ hermaphrodite and female flowers.

Physiology of Plants.

The Physiology of Plants comprehends their vegetation, anatomical structure, chemical composition, and diseases.

Vegetation.—The vegetation of Plants is distinguished according to its different stages or states into—*Germinatio*, Germination, when the seed begins to unfold its tender leaves.—*Vernatio*, or *frondescentia*, Vernation, when the swollen buds of trees, &c. unfold their leaves.—*Somnus*, Sleep, when in the evening, or at night, the leaves of plants hang down.—*Defoliatio*, Defoliation, when in autumn the leaves fall off.—*Virginitas*, Virginity, when the flowers or buds are not yet unfolded.—*Anthesis*, Expansion, when the flowers are perfectly developed.—*Æstivatio*, Estivation, the month or season of the year when the flower is in perfection.—*Fructificatio*, Fructification, when the antheræ communicate the fructifying dust to the neighbouring parts.

Anatomy of Plants.—Plants, as to their Anatomical structure, consist of an—*Epidermis*, or *cutis*, the Cuticle.—*Cortex*, the Outer Bark.—*Liber*, Inner Bark.—*Alburnum*, the Soft Wood.—*Lignum*, Wood.—*Medulla*, the Pith.—*Parenchyma*, a fleshy substance which incloses the pith.—*Vasa pneumataphora*, Air-Vessels, which are the conductors of air.—*Vasa adducentia*, Aducent Vessels, otherwise called spiral Vessels, from their twisted appearance, which proceed either in a straight line with the air-vessels or twine round them.—*Vasa reducentia*, Reducent Vessels, which are supposed to serve the purpose of transpiration. They are more delicate than the preceding.—*Vasa lymphatica*, Lymphatic Vessels, which are very delicate, and reticularly united.—*Tela cellulosa*, Cellular Texture, a delicate membrane which surrounds all the vessels. The juices contained in the cellular texture are lymphatic in all plants, resinous in those of the fir tribe, and gummy in fruit trees.—*Glandulæ*, Glands, round elevated bodies which serve as secretory vessels, and are scattered over different parts of plants.

Chemical Composition of Plants.—Plants are found, on a chemical analysis, to be principally composed of three simple substances, namely, Carbon, Hydrogen, and Oxygen, of which Carbon forms the chief ingredient. There are other simple substances which enter partially into their composition, as Azote, Sulphur, Phosphorus, Muriatic Acid, Silica, Iron, Manganese, Potash, Soda, Lime, Magnesia, and Alumina. The principal compound substances which form the more immediate and sensible ingredients are, the Acids, Mucilage, Sugar, Starch, Albumen, Gluten, Fixed Oil, Wax, Resin, Caoutchouc, Gum Resins, Volatile Oil, Camphor, &c.

Diseases of Plants.—The principal diseases or accidents to which plants are exposed are—*Fissura*, Fissure, the separation of the solid parts into a long cleft, proceeding either from fulness of juice, *Polysarca*, or from frost. In this latter case it degenerates into a chilblain, *pernis*, from which a blackish sharp liquor exudes.—*Defoliatio notha*, Premature Defoliation, when the leaves fall off before the usual period.—*Hæmorrhagia*, Hæmorrhage, which is either spontaneous or occasioned by wounds.—*Albigo*, Mildew, a whitish mucilaginous coating of the leaves of plants, which often causes their decay.—*Melligo*, Honey-Dew, a sweet clear juice found upon the leaves in hot weather.—*Rubigo*, Rust, appears on the leaves and stems of many plants.—*Lepra*, Leprosy, which affects the trunk, especially of young trees.—*Gallæ*, Galls, produced by small flying insects, the *Cynips* of Linnæus. One sort of Gall is called *folliculus carnosus*, found on the leaves of Black Poplar.—*Contorsiones*, Contorsions, produced also by insects on the leaves.—*Verruca*, Wart, a small protuberance found on fruit-trees, particularly the apple.—*Nævi*, or *maculæ*, Moles, which arise from wounds of the cutis.—*Tuber lynosum* is met with on trunks of trees.—*Squamationes*, Spongy Swellings, produced by insects which lay their eggs in the apex of the bud.—*Bedeguar*, a sort of swelling, which occurs in roses only.—*Chlorosis*, an affection of plants which causes the loss of their green colour.—*Icterus* differs from *chlorosis* only in its colour and its cause, which latter is early cold in autumn.—*Anasarca*, Dropsy, which arises from long continued rain.—*Phthiriasis*, a disease in which the whole plant is covered with insects.—*Verminatio*, Worms, a disease in which the larva of insects infest the stem, leaves, and fruit.—*Tabes*, Consumption, which arises from the influence of the abovementioned diseases.—*Debilitas*, Debility, when all the parts of the plant hang down in a relaxed state.—*Suffocatio incrementi*, Stoppage of growth.—*Exulceratio*, Exulceration, the corroded part of a plant, from which proceeds an ichorous water.—*Caranoma*, Cancer, which occurs principally in fruit-trees when they lose much gum.—*Mutilatio*, Mutilation, happens in flowers when single parts do not come to perfection.—*Monstrositas*, Monstrosity, the preternatural form of single parts or a whole plant. One of the most remarkable monstrosities is that called the *Clavus*, in grain, when the seed is swelled three times its usual size and thickness, but has no corcle.—*Sterilitas*, Sterility, is that disease in plants which causes them to yield neither flower nor seed.—*Abortus*, Abortion, when flowering plants provided with perfect female organs of generation do not bear fruit.

Principal Writers on Botany, in Chronological Succession.

Theophrasti " Historia Plantarum;" *Dioscorides* " De Materia Medica;" *Galen* " De Simplicium Medicamentorum Facultatibus," &c.; *Plinii* " Historia Naturalis;" *Oribasii* " Medicæ Collections;" *Paulus Ægineta* " De Re Medica;" *Brunfelsii*, " Historia Plantarum;" *Tragi* " Kraeuterbuch," &c.; *Gesneri*

"Enchiridion historiæ Plantarum;" *Fuchsii* "De Historia Stirpium commentarii insignes;" *Matthioli* "Kræuterbuch;" *Dodonæi* "Stirpium Historiæ;" *Lobelii* "Plantarum, seu Stirpium Historia et Adversaria;" *Clusii* "Rariorum Plantarum Historia," &c.; *Cæsalpini de Plantis,* libri xvi.; *Delechampii* "Historia generalis Plantarum;" *Camerarii* "Hortus medicus philosophicus;" *Prosper Alpinus* "De Plantis Ægypti liber, et de Plantis exoticis libri duo;" *J. Bauhini* "Historia Plantarum;" *Columnæ* "Φυτοβασανος, sive plantarum aliquot Historia;" *C. Bauhini* "Φυτοπιναξ, seu Enumeratio Plantarum ab Herbariis descriptarum," &c.; *Gerarde's* "Herbal, or general History of Plants;" *Parkinson's* "Theatrum Botanicum," &c.; *Raii* "Historia Plantarum," &c.; *Breynii* "Exoticarum et minus cognitarum Stirpium," &c.: *Rheedi* "Hortus Malabaricus Indicus," &c.; *J. Commelini* "Horti medici Amstelodamensis rariorum tam orientalis, quam occidentalis Indiæ Plantarum Descriptio et Icones," *Casp. Commelini* "Flora Malabarica;" *Plukenet* "Phitographia, et Almagestum Botanicum," &c.; *Plumier* "Nova Plantarum Americanarum genera," &c.; *Tournefort* "Institutiones Rei herbariæ;" *Boerhaave* "Index alter plantarum horti Academici Lugdoni-Bativini;" *Vaillant* "Botanicon Parisiense," &c.; *Linnæi* "Systema Plantarum," "Genera Plantarum," "Species Plantarum," "Philosophia Botanica," &c.

Explanation of the Plates.

Plate No. I. (21)

Roots. *Fig.* 1. A creeping scaly root of the *Oxalis laciniata*. 2. A dentated root of the *Ophrys corallorhiza*. 3. A tuberous, pendulous root of the *Spiræa filipendula*. 4. A granulated root of the *Saxifraga granulata*. 5. A palmated root of the *Orchis latifolia*. 6. A root of the *Succisa fuchsii*, which is præmorse, or bitten off. 7. The tunicated bulb of the *Allium cepa*. 8. The scaly bulb of the *Lilium bulbifera*. 9. The horizontal root of the *Gratiola officinalis*, which is jointed and fibrous at the joints. 10. The testiculated or scrotiform root of the *Orchis militaris*: *a*, the old tuber that sent up and nourished the stem of the preceding year; *b*, the new tuber that sent up and nourished the present year's stem.
Stems. *Fig.* 11. A stem bending upwards, *adscendens*. 12. A stem bent downwards, *declinatus*. 13. A sarmentose stem. 14. A flexuose stem of the *Celastrus buxifolius*, which has obovate leaves standing in bundles. 15. A quadrangular stem with stellate leaves, which stand close together. 16. A twining stem which twists itself round its prop from left to right. 17. An articulated stem. 18. A culm, or straw. 19. A naked stipe of the *Boletus bovinus*, a fungus. 20. A surculus, or shoot, of the *Polytrichum commune*, the theca of which is covered with a hairy calyptra. 21. The scape, *a*, of the *Pinguicula vulgaris*, bearing a flower with a horned nectary. 22. A winged petiole or leafstalk, *a*, of the *Citrus aurantium*. 23. The bristle of the *Polytrichum commune* with the *Perichætium*, and the capsule without an operculum.
Inflorescence. *Fig.* 24. A leafy capitulum of the *Gomphrena globosa*. 25. The circinate spike of the *Heliotropium Indicum*. 26. The raceme of the vetch, which has its leaves alternately pinnate and the corolla papilionaceous. 27. A fascicle of the *Rhexia hypericoides*.

Plate No. II. (22)

Inflorescence. *Fig.* 1.—A compound umbel of the *Ammi majus*. 2. The cyme of the *Viburnum opulus*, having large neuter flowers at the extremities. 3. The corymb of the *Achillea crithmifolia*. 4. The panicle of the *Poa trivialis*. 5. A catkin of the *Populus tremula*, bearing female flowers. 6. The univalve spathe of the *Arum maculatum*, in the centre of which stands the spadix. 7. The spadix of the foregoing flower, with female flowers below and male flowers above.
Simple Leaves. *Fig.* 8. A venoso-nerved leaf. 9. A rhombic leaf of *Hibiscus rhombifolius*. 10. An ovate leaf of the *Citrus aurantium*, the Orange. 11. The leaf of the *Lacis fluvialis*, which is laciniate and curled. 12. The lanceolate leaf of the *Nepenthes distillatoria*, which bears a pedicelled ascidium, *a*. 13. A quintuple-nerved leaf. 14. An oval pointed perfoliate leaf of the *Bupleurum rotundifolium*. 15. The leaf of the *Epidendrum præmorsum*, which is, as it were, bitten off at the end. 16. A lyrate leaf. 17. A spatulate leaf. 18. A squarrose laciniate leaf, which is also decurrent, and has a winged footstalk. 19. The imbricated leaves of the *Berkheya ciliaris*, which are ciliated. 20. The singular leaf of the *Sarracenia purpurea*, or Purple Side-saddle Flower. 21. The anomalous leaf of the *Dionæa muscipula*, or Venus's Flytrap.

Plate No. III. (23)

Compound Leaves, Fulcra, &c. *Fig.* 1. A jointedly pinnate leaf of the *Fagara pterota*. 2. A digitato-pinnate leaf of the *Mimosa pudica*. 3. A tripinnate leaf. 4. The alternately pinnate leaf of the *Vicia sativa*, or Common Vetch. 5. The interruptedly pinnate leaf of the *Spiræa filipendula*, the pinnula of which is lanceolate and unequally dentated. 6. A trigeminate leaf of the *Mimosa trigemina*. 7. A triternate leaf. 8. The sinuated leaves of the Common Oak, having the ramenta between them. 9. The frond of the *Polypodium otites* diminished, having a frond with confluent pinnæ, on the back of which are the subrotund sori. 10. The fertile frond of *Osmunda cinnamomea* diminished, which is pinnated; and the unfertile, which is bipinnatifid. 11. The pinnated frond of the *Pteris longifolia*, having linear masses which are marginal and continued. 12. The twining stem of the *Banisteria purpurea*, twining from the right to the left, the leaves of which are opposite and elliptic, and bear a corymbus. 13. Part of a straw with a leaf, and at the base a strap. 14. The *Passiflora tiliæflora*, having, *a*, a round stem; *b*, a heartshaped leaf; *c*, double stipulæ; *d*, an axillary tendril; *e*, a one-flowered peduncle; *ff*, a polypetalous corolla; *gg*, nectaria, which consist of straight threads; and *h*, a pedicelled germen. 15. The *Bupleurum rotundifolium*, with *a*, a perfoliate stem and leaf; *b*, a depauperate umbel; and a pentaphyllous involucrum. 16. The *Sagittaria sagittifolia*, having, *a*, an arrowshaped leaf; *b*, a channelled petiole; *c*, a three-sided scape. The flowers stand in whirls, as at *d d*, and are tripetalous. 17. The *Erythropylon coca* has a veined leaf and lateral peduncles, *a a a*. 18. The two-rowed sori which stand transversely on the frond of the *Danæa nodosa*. 19. The *Agaricus conspurcatus*, a fungus having *a*, an annulated stipe; *b*, the annulus sessile; and *c*, the pileus umbonated and squarrose. 20. The *Geastrum pedicellatum*, a fungus with, *a*, a stellated volva of a spherical figure and *b*, a ciliated orifice. 21. The scape of the *Equisetum arvense*, which is one of the *Filices spiciferæ*. 22. The *Lichen stellaris*, an alga with a stellated frond and scutellæ, or plateshaped fruit-beds in the middle. 23. The *Lichen gracilis*, having a cup-bearing frond.

Plate No. IV. (24)

Fructification. *Fig.* 1. A back view of the Rose, to display the calyx, or cup. *a a a a a*, the segments of the cup. 2. *a*, The flower, in bud, of the *Lilium candidum*, or Common White Lily. *b*. The bellshaped corolla, or blossom, expanding. *ccccc*. The six petals of the corolla quite open. *d*. The pistil, or pointal. *e*. The germ. *f*. The style. *g*. The stigma. *h*. The six stamens. *i*. The filaments. *k*. The anthers. *l*. The germ, advanced into a pericarp, which is here a capsule. *m*. A transverse section of the pericarp, to show the three cells and seeds. 3. A flower of the *Cheiranthus incanus*, or Stock-Gilliflower, showing—*a*. The four petals and the cruciform shape of the corolla. *b*. The calyx of the same, seen from a back view, consisting of four leaflets, and bulging out at the bottom. *c*. A single petal separated, the lower narrow part of which is called the *unguis*, or tail; the upper spreading part, the *lamina*, or border. *d*. A section of the calyx, with the single pistil and six stamens in their proper situation. *e*. The six stamens, two of which are sensibly shorter than the other four. *f*. The pistil separated from the other parts. *g*. A single stamen. *h*. The fruit seed-vessel, or pericarp, called the silique, open from the bottom upwards, and showing the two valves with the seeds ranged along the dissepiment, or partition of the two cells, and the permanent stigma at the top. 4. *a*. The glume, which is the calyx of Grasses. *b*. The anthers on the filaments. *c*. The downy summits of the styles. 5. A flower with the calyx, stamen, and pistils, but the petals taken away. *a*. The calyx or cup. *bbbbbb*. The anthers of the stamens. *c*. The germen. *d*. The style. *e*. The summit. *f*. One of the anthers discharging its pollen. 6. A funnelshaped corolla, or blossom. *a*. The tube. *b*. The border. *c*. The calyx, or cup. 7. A cruciform corolla, with the calyx taken away to show, *a a*, the claws, *ungues*, of the petals. *b b b b*. The limbs, *lamina*, of the petals. *c*. The receptacle. 8. The flower of the *Dimorpha grandiflora*, with its singular corolla. 9. The flower of the *Rupala montana*, the stamina of which stand on the tips of the petals. 10. The flower of the *Sterculia crinita*, which has a pedicelled germen. 11. The flower of the *Fuchsia excorticata*, with a funnelshaped corolla, showing, *a*, its tetraphyllous crown, and, *b*, the three-lobed stigma. 12. The *Aconitum napellus*, or Blue Monk's Hood, showing, *a a*, the two recurved pedunculated nectaries. *b*. A single nectary taken out of the flower. 13. *a*. The nectary of the *Delphinium Ajacis*, or Garden Larkspur, continued backward in the form of a spur. 14. The flower of the *Parnassia palustris*, showing, *a*, the nectareous scales at the base of the stamens. *b*. The five heartshaped nectaries, terminating in hairs, with a little ball on the top of each hair, and placed between the stamens. 15. A petal of the *Ranunculus*, showing, *a a*, the honied gland just above the base on the inside. 16. The nectary of the *Iris*, or Flag, in form of a villous line along the middle of one of the reflex petals. 17. The *Fritellaria Imperialis*, or Crown Imperial, showing an excavation, *a*, at the base of the petal. 18. *a*. The tubular nectaries placed in a ring at the base of the stamens in the *Helleborus fœtidus*, or Stinking Black Hellebore. *b*. A single nectary. 19. *a*. The closed ringent, or personate corolla, of the *Antirrhinum majus*, or Snap-Dragon. *b*. The corolla opened, to show the situation of the stamens. *c*. The capsule, with the permanent style and calyx. 20. *a*. A single flower of the *Digitalis purpurea*, or Purple Fox-glove, showing its open bellshaped corolla. *b*. The inside, exhibiting the situation and structure of the stamens. *c*. The germ, with the style. *d*. The capsule, with the style permanent. 21. *a*. The pericarp of the *Pisum sativum*, or Garden Pea, which is a legume silique, or pod, open, to show, *a b*, the two valves, *dddd*, *ccc*. The seeds, fastened alternately to the sutures of the valves at the back of the legume. *e*. The permanent calyx. 22. Figures of silicles, or small short pods or pouches. *a*. The flat triangular or heartshaped silicle of the Shepherd's Purse. *b*. The oblong silicle of Scurvy-Grass, both shut and open. *c*. The almost spherical silicle of Candy Tuft. 23. A capsule cut open horizontally, to show, *a a a a*, the receptacles and seeds. *b b b b*. The partitions. *c c c c*. The valves to which the partitions are connected. 24. A seed, with its *pappus*, or down. *a*. The hairlike down. *b*. The feathered down. *d*. The pillar, or pedicle, supporting the down. *c*. The seed.

Plate No. V. (25)

Linnean Classes. *Fig.* 1—10 represent the classes *Monandria*, *Diandria*, &c. which are distinguished by the number of the stamens, from one to ten. 11. The class *Dodecandria*, which comprehends plants that have from eleven to nineteen stamens inclusive. 12. *Icosandria*, having about twenty stamens on the Calyx or Corolla. 13. *Polyandria*, having above twenty stamens on the Receptacle, or Base of the Flower. 14. *Didynamia*, having four Stamens, two longer than the other two; one Pistil; and ringent Flowers. 15. *Tetradynamia*, having six Stamens, four longer than the rest; one Pistil; Flowers cruciform. 16. *Monodelphia*, having the filaments united into one body. 17. *Diadelphia*, having the filaments united into two bodies; Corolla papillionaceous. 18. *Polyadelphia*, having the filaments in three or more parcels; Stamens coherent at the top only, or by the Anthers. 19. *Syngenesia*, having the Anthers united, five filaments distinct; one pistil, with Stamens growing out of the Pistil itself. The Flowers are compound. 20. *Gynandria*, having Stamens on the Pistil instead of the Receptacle. All the flowers imperfect, having stamens only, or pistils only. 21. *Monoecia*, having *a*, a male flower, and *b*, a female flower, separate on the same plant. 22. *Dioecia*, having *a*, a plant, with a male flower; *b*, another plant with a female flower. 23. *Polygamia*, having *a*, a plant with a male and hermaphrodite flower; *b*, another plant with a female and hermaphrodite flower. 24. *Cryptogamia*, a felix or Fern, having the fructification upon the back of the leaf.

Plate No. VI. (26)

Linnean Orders. *Fig.* 1—10 represent the Orders according to the number of pistils; namely, 1. *Monogynia*, one Pistil; 2. *Digynia*, two Pistils; 3. *Trigynia*, three Pistils; 4. *Tetragynia*, four Pistils; 5. *Pentagynia*, five Pistils; 6. *Hexagynia*, six Pistils; 7. *Heptagynia*, seven Pistils; 8. *Decagynia*, ten Pistils; 9. *Dodecagynia*, twelve Pistils; 10. *Polygynia*, many Pistils.— *Fig.* 11. *Didynamia Gymnospermia*, having four naked seeds at the bottom of the Perianth; *a*, the four seeds in their natural order; *b*, the Calyx laid open to show them more plainly. 12. *Didynamia Angiospermia*, the Seeds in a Seed vessel which is two-celled, and the seeds, which are many, are fastened to a receptacle in the middle of it. 13. *Tetradynamia siliculosa*, having a Silicle, or short, two-valved Pericarp for the fruit. 14. *Tetradynamia Siliquosa*, having a Silique, or oblong narrow, two-valved Pericarp. 15. *Polygamia Æqualis*, the first of the six Orders belonging to the Class *Syngenesia*, having the whole flower regular, all the Florets alike hermaphrodite, and, consequently, fertile; *a*, a Compound ligulate Flower; *b*, a single Floret; *c*, the germ crowned by its pappus; *d*, the cylinder of anthers with the bifid curled stigma above it. The other Orders are as follow:—16. *Polygamia superflua*, *a*, a radiate

Flower; *b*, a single tubulous and ligulate Floret; *c*, the cylinder of anthers. 17. *Polygamia Frustanea*, *a*, an entire Flower; *b*, a single fertile Floret; *c*, a Floret that is neuter. 18. *Polygamia Necessaria*, *a*, an entire Flower; *b*, a fertile Floret; *c*, a neuter Floret; *d*, a fertile seed; *e*, an abortive Seed. 19. *Polygamia segregata*, *a*, an entire flower; *b*, a single tubulous floret surrounded with its calyx; *c*, one stripped of the calyx. 20. *Monogamia*, *a*, a simple Flower; *b*, the Anthers united. 21. *Trioecia*, the third Order of the Class *Polygamia*, representing *a*, a plant that has male flowers only; *b*, one that has female flowers only; *c*, one that has hermaphrodite flowers only. 22. *Cryptogamia Filices*, a Fern having the fructification on the back of the Leaf. 23. A specimen of the Order *Musci*. 24. A specimen of the Order *Algæ*. 25. A specimen of the Order *Fungi*.

Plates No. VII, VIII. (27, 28)

Linnean Classes and Orders exemplified. *Fig.* 1. *Monandria Monogynia*. *a*. The flower of *Canna Indica*, or Indian Shot, with its monopetalous six-parted Corolla. *b*. The scabrous Germ. *c*. The triphyllous perianth, or calyx on the top of the germ. *d*. The anther growing to one of the Petals, which serves it for a filament. *e*. The Style growing to the petaliform filament. *f*. The scabrous capsule cut open to show the three cells.

Fig. 2. *Diandria Monogynia*. *a*. A Flower of the *Salvia officinalis*, or Garden Sage. *b*. The two Stamens showing the singularity of their structure. *c*. The Pistil separate.

Fig. 3. *Triandria Digynia*, a Branch of the *Dactylis glomerata*, or Hard Grass. *a*. The *Glume*, or Chaff. *b b b*. The three Stamens. *c*. The two reflected Styles with the feathered Stigma.

Fig. 4. *Tetrandria Monogynia*. *a*. An aggregate Flower of the *Scabiosa columbaria*, or Small Scabious consisting of many Flosculus. *b*. A single Floscule with its five-parted Corolla, and the Germ crowned with hairs. *c*. The Calyx with the four stamens, and the Pistil.

Fig. 5. *Pentandria Tetragynia*. *a a a a a*. The veined petals of *Parnassia palustris*. *b b b b b*. The five heart-shaped nectaries. *c c c c c*. The five stamens. *d*. A single anther. *e*. A single nectary. *f*. The germen with the four pistils.

Fig. 6. *Hexandria*. *a*. The flower of the *Trillium erectum*. *b*. The stamens and pistils apart. *c*. A single pistil.

Fig. 7. *Heptandria Heptagynia*, the *Septas Capensis*. *a*. One of the seven Stamens. *b*. One of the seven Pistils.

Fig. 8. *Octandria Tetragynia*, the *Paris quadrifolia*, or Herb Paris. *a*. The four green Petals, 1, 2, 3, 4. *b b b b b b b*. The eight stamens. *c c c c*. The four Pistils.

Fig. 9. *Enneandria Hexagynia*, the *Butonus umbellatus*, or Flowering Rush. *a*. The Flower of six Petals. *b*. The nine Stamens surrounding. *c*. The six Pistils.

Fig. 10. *Decandria Monogynia*, the *Rhododendron chamæcistus*. *a*. One of the ten Stamens. *b*. The Pistil.

Fig. 11. *Dodecandria Dodecagynia*, the *Sempervivum tectorum*, Common Houseleek. *a*. The Peduncle, or Flower-stem, with a reflexed range of flowers. *b*. A flower in front showing the Corolla of twelve Petals. *c*. The Calyx with the Capsules after the flower is past. *d*. A single Capsule. *e*. The twelve Stamens and twelve Styles separated from the flower. *f*. A single Pistil exhibiting the Germ, Style, and Stigma. *g*. Two Stamens.

Fig. 12. *Icosandria Pentagynia*. *a*. A flower of the *Pyrus malus*, or Apple-Tree. *b*. The stamens apart. *c*. The pistils apart.

Fig. 13. *Polyandria Polyginia*, a flower of the *Caltha palustris*, Marsh Marigold, showing *a*, the Corolla with *b*, five Petals.

Fig. 14. *Didynamia Gymnospermia*, the *Glechoma hederacea*, or Ground Ivy. *a*. The kidney-shaped leaves. *b*. The ringent flowers. *c*. A flower opened to show the situation of the Stamens. *d*. A flower exhibiting the cruciform appearance of the anthers. *e*. The Calyxes. *f*. A single Filament. *g*. The Pistil.

Fig. 15. *Tetradynamia Siliquosa*, the *Sisymbrium nasturtium*, or Water Cress. *a a*. The pinnated leaves. *b*. The Corymb of flowers. *d*. A single four-petalled cruciform Flower. *e*. A single Petal. *f*. The Calyx. *g*. The Calyx with the Stamens. *h*. A single Stamen. *i*. The Silique.

Fig. 16. *Monodelphia Polyandria*, the *Althæa officinalis*, or Marsh Mallow. *a*. The Flower showing the five Petals united at bottom; in the centre the column of Stamens with the Pistils in the middle of them. *b*. The column of Stamens and Pistils removed from the Corolla, and showing the rudiment of the fruit underneath. *c*. The Pistil separate. *d*. The Calyx exhibiting the nine divisions of the outer calyx.

Fig. 17. *Diadelphia Decandria*, the *Lathyrus latifolius*, or Everlasting Pea, consisting of a bunch of flowers in their natural size and situation. *a*. The Banner. *b*. One of the Wings. *c*. The keel. *d*. The Stamens and Pistil in their natural situation. *e*. The Stamens showing the simple Filament separate from the compound one.

Fig. 18. *Polyadelphia Polyandria*, the *Hypericum ascyron*, or Garden Tutsan. *a*. The Flower with a Corolla of five petals, and the numerous stamens in the middle. *b*. A single pencil, or parcel of Stamens. *c*. The permanent five-parted Calyx, including the germ terminated by five pistils.

Fig. 19. *Syngenesia*—1. *Polygamia Æqualis*. *a*. The *Eupatorium cannabinum*, Common Hemp Agrimony. *b*. The bunch of Flowers. *c*. A single Flower. *d*. A single bunch.—2. *Polygamia frustanea*. *a*. The compound flower of the *Centaurea montana*, Mountain Blue Bottle, showing the neutral or barren florets on the outside, longer than the fertile ones in the middle, and the ciliated scales of the calyx. *b*. A barren floret. *c*. A fertile floret, with some of the bristles at the base. *d*. The same divested of the Corolla. *e*. The Pistil.

Fig. 20. *Gynandria Monandria*, the *Ophrys muscifera*, or Fly Orchis, showing, *a*, the five Petals, 1, 2, 3, 4, 5. *b*. The lip of the nectary. *c*. The bracte, or floral leaf. *d*. The germen. *e*. The germen and anthers apart. *f*. The germen. *g*. A single anther.

Fig. 21. *Monoecia Syngenesia*. *a*. The male or staminiferous flower of the *Momordica Elaterium*, or Spirting Cucumber. *b*. The female, or pistilliferous flower, with the large germ below the receptacle. *c*. The male flower apart, showing the three filaments with double anthers on two of them, and a simple anther on the third. *d*. The germ, surmounted with the style, divided into three parts, each part sustaining an oblong gibbous stigma. *e*. The divided part of the style, with the stigmas. *f*. Two different views of a single stigma.

Fig. 22. *Dioecia Pentandria*, the *Cannabis sativa*, or Hemp. *a*. The female hemp. *b*. The seed included within the calyx. *c*. The male hemp. *d*. Male flowers, separate.

Fig. 23. *Polygamia Monoecia*. *a a*. The lobed leaves of the *Acer campestre*. *b*. A bunch of flowers. *c*. A perfect flower. *d*. A male flower, with stamens only. *e*. A single perfect flower. *f*. a petal. *g*. A perfect flower, divested of corolla and calyx. *h*. A single stamen. *i*. The pistil, with the two revolute stigmas, and the rudiment of the two capsules, terminating in a wing. *k.* A male or staminiferous flower, and a single petal.

Fig. 24. *Cryptogamia.*—1. *Musci,* the male flower of one of the *Musci frondosi,* with succulent filaments and stamina, some of which are shedding their pollen; others are not so far advanced; and others have already shed their pollen.—2. *Algæ. a a a.* The small or barren flowers of the *Lichen ciliaris,* Ciliated Liverwort. *b b.* The females in a state of ripeness. *c c.* The rooting hairs.—3. *Fungi. a.* The Fungus in its natural state. *b.* The same in its middle state. *c.* Small plants just rising. *d.* A parcel of knotted threads from the fungus, marked *b,* supposed to be the stamens. *e.* The ripe seeds of this fungus much magnified.

BOTA'RGO (*Cook.*) a kind of sausage made of the roes and blood of the sea mullet.

BOTCHING *matrices* (*Print.*) vide *Matrices.*

BOTE (*Law*) in Saxon *bote,* a recompense or amends.—*Bote-house,* an allowance of wood for its repairs.—*Bote-plough,* or *cart,* an allowance of wood for their repairs.—*Bote-hay,* or *hedge,* wood for the repairs of hedges.—*Bote man,* compensation for a man slain.

BOTELLA'RIA (*Archæol.*) a cellar for the butts and bottles.

BO'TEROLL (*Her.*) the tag of a broad sword scabbard, which by the French heraldic writers, is esteemed an honourable bearing. The crampet, which is the badge of the Right Honourable Earl de la War, was meant for the same ornament of the scabbard.

BOTH *sheets aft* (*Mar.*) the situation of a ship that sails right before the wind.

BO'THA (*Law*) a booth or standing in a fair, &c.

BOTHA'GIUM (*Law*) a duty paid to the lord for erecting booths. *Kenn. Par. Ant.*

BOTHE'NA (*Law*) a barony or lordship.

BO'THOR (*Med.*) Arabic for pustules in general, and for particular pustules.

BO'THRION (*Med*) βοθρίον, a tumour in the back of the eye. *Gal. Def. Med.*

BO'TILER *of the king* (*Ant.*) an officer that provides the king's wines, who may choose out of every ship laden with sale wines, one cask before the mast, and one cask behind. 25 Ed. 3, st. 5, c. 21 ; *Flet.* l. 2, c. 21.

BOTIN (*Chem.*) *butino,* turpentine ; also the balsam of turpentine.

BO'TONNY (*Her.*) or *botone,* a cross ; so called because its extremities resemble trefoil. The French call it *Croix trefflee,* as in the annexed figure.

BOTOTHI'NUM (*Med.*) a word which Paracelsus explains to be the *Flower of the Disease. Parac. de Podag. Necromant,* l. 2.

BOTRYI'TIS (*Min.*) βοτρυτις, or *Botritis,* a sort of burnt Cadmia; so called because it resembled a βότρυς, a cluster of grapes. It is collected from the upper part of the furnace, where it is burnt, and is distinguished from the *placitis,* which is collected in the lower part. *Plin.* l. 37, c. 10; *Gorr. Def. Med.*

BOTRYOI'DAL (*Nat.*) clustered like a bunch of grapes ; hence *Botria,* a plant, found in Africa.

BOTRYOI'DES (*Min.*) a species of Suillus.

BO'TRYS (*Bot.*) βοτρυς, Oak of Jerusalem; the Chenopodium ambrosioides et botrys of Linnæus, a herb; so called because its seeds hang down like a βότρυς, a bunch of grapes. It is of a bitter taste, a heating, drying, dissolving, and purgative nature. *Dioscor.* l. 3, c. 130; *Plin.* l. 27, c. 8; *Dodon. Stirp. Hist.*; *Lobel. Plant. et Stirp. Hist. et Advers.*; *C. Bauh. Pin.*

BO'TTINE (*Mil.*) French for the half-boots worn by the dragoons and hussars in foreign armies.

BO'TTLE HEAD (*Ich.*) the name of a sort of whale, called Flounder's Head or Beaked Whale, because its nose resembles the beak of a bird.

BO'TTOM (*Mar.*) the ground or lowest part of any thing; as the bottom of a vessel, or the bottom of the sea: hence a clean or a foul *bottom*; or to go in foreign *bottoms,* when speaking of ships; or a rocky muddy *bottom,* &c. in regard to the water.

BOTTOM *plate* (*Mech.*) a plate of iron belonging to the mould of a printing-press, on which the carriage is fixed.—*Bottom line,* one of the four imaginary lines belonging to the body of a letter in printing.

BO'TTOMRY (*Law*) 1. A contract for borrowing money on the bottom of a ship, which is to be forfeited if the terms of the contract be not fulfilled. 2. Lending money to a merchant on any adventure, the interest to be paid on the return of the ship, but to be lost if she is lost.

BOTTS (*Vet.*) worms that are very troublesome, and even dangerous to horses, breeding in their intestines.

BO'TUS (*Chem.*) a sort of cucurbit.

BOVAR (*Bot.*) Little Lard Pear ; a juicy kind of pear.

BOVA'TA *terræ* (*Law*) as much as an ox can till, i. e. twenty-eight acres, otherwise called an oxgate.

BOUBA'LIOS (*Bot.*) βυβάλιος, the *Cucurnis agrestis* of Linnæus.

BOUBALIOS (*Anat.*) the female pupendum.

BOUBO'N (*Med.*) βυβών, bubo, a tumour in the groin; a term frequently recurring in this sense in Hippocrates, Galen, and Aretæus. *Gorr. Def. Med.* ; *Foes. Œconom. Hippocrat.*

BO'UCERAS (*Bot.*) Fenugreek.

BOUCHE *of court* (*Law*) a certain allowance of provisions to knights and others attending the king upon military expeditions.

BO'UCHERS *d'une armée* (*Mil.*) a French name for those persons who contract to supply the French army with provisions.

BOUCHES *à feu* (*Mil.*) a French name for pieces of ordnance, as cannon and mortars.

BOUCHE'TT (*Bot.*) a sort of pear like the besidery.

BOUCHO'N (*Mil.*) French for the wadding of a cannon.

BOVE'RIUM (*Archæol.*) an ox-stall.

BOVETTUS (*Archæol.*) a young steer or bullock that is cut.

BO'VEY COAL (*Min.*) the *Bitumen amphilites* of Linnæus.

BOUGE' (*Mech.*) the middle or belly of a cask.

BOUGH *of a tree* (*Law*) seisin of land given by it, to be held of the donor *in capite.*

BOUGI'E (*Surg.*) from the French *bougie,* a wax candle; another name for the catheter, which is sometimes made of wax.

BOVI'LLÆ (*Med.*) the measles.

BOUI'LLANS (*Cook.*) little pies made of the breasts of roasted capons, &c.

BOUI'LLON (*Vet.*) a disease in horses when a lump, or excrescence of flesh, grows by or upon the frush.

BOVI'NA *affectio* (*Vet.*) a distemper in black cattle, caused by a worm between the flesh and the skin.—*Bovina fames,* the same as *Bulimus.*

BOUJO'NS (*Cook.*) steaks of veal, with thin slices of bacon rolled up together.

BOVI'STA (*Bot.*) the *Lycoperdon* of Linnæus.

BO'ULDER WALLS (*Archit.*) certain walls built of round flints or pebbles, laid on a strong mortar, particularly near the sea coast.

BOULE'TE (*Man.*) a term used of a horse when the fetlock or pastern-joint bends forward, and out of its natural situation.

BOU'LINS (*Carpent.*) pieces of timber, which are fastened into walls, in order to erect a scaffold.

BOULI'NIS (*Com.*) or *boulynis,* a copper coin, struck at Boulogna, in Italy, which answers to a penny English money.

BO'ULTINE (*Archit.*) a convex moulding, whose convexity is but one fourth of the circle, and is placed next below the plinth in the Tuscan and Doric capital.

BOUND (*Vet.*) from to bind; an epithet applied to any part of an animal that is embraced with an unnatural force, as of a horse *hoof-bound, hide-bound,* &c.

BOUND (*Mar.*) confined to a particular spot or direction, applied to a ship; as *wind-bound, ice-bound,* &c. confined by the wind or ice to a place from which you were sailing homebound, or going homeward, &c.

BO'UNIAS (*Bot.*) vide *Bunias.*

BOUNTY (*Law*) or *Queen Anne's Bounty,* a term applied to the provision made by Queen Anne for the augmentation of poor livings out of the first fruits.

BOUNTY (*Com.*) a premium given by government on the exportation of British manufactures or commodities.

BOUNTY (*Mil.*) a sum of money given by government to men who enlist.—*Fresh bounty,* money given to a soldier when he continues in the service after the expiration of the term for which he enlisted.

BOURGEOI'S (*Polit.*) a French name for the middle order of inhabitants in towns, in distinction from the nobility and gentry.

BOURGEOI'SE (*Cook.*) veal dressed *à la bourgeoise,* after the city fashion, *i.e.* larded, spiced, and stewed with pieces of bacon, &c.

BOURNI'GNOMISTS (*Ecc.*) an enthusiastic sect in the Low Countries, resembling the quakers in England.

BOURRA'DE (*Mil.*) French for a thrust which is made with the barrel end of the musket, instead of the butt.

BOURRELA'T (*Gunn.*) the French for the extremity of a piece of ordnance towards its mouth.

BOURRERIA (*Bot.*) the *Ehretia bourreria* of Linnæus.

BOURRIQUE'T (*Mil.*) French for a basket made use of in mining, to draw up the earth, and to let down whatever may be necessary for the miner.

BOURSEA'U (*Archit.*) French for a round moulding formed by the ridge of lead on the top of a house that is slated.

BOUSSO'LE (*Mar.*) French for the mariner's compass.

BOUSTROPHE'DON (*Gram.*) vide *Bustrophedon.*

BOUTA'DE (*Mus.*) a small kind of ballet.

BOUT (*Man.*) a term used for a horse when he is overdone, and quite spent with fatigue.

BOUTE (*Man.*) an epithet for a horse whose legs are in a straight line from the knee to the coronet.

BOUTE-FE'U (*Archæol.*) an incendiary or wilful firer of houses.

BOUTE-SE'LLE (*Mil.*) French for the signal or word given to the cavalry to saddle their horses.

BOUTO'N (*Gunn.*) French for the sight of a musket.

BOUTON (*Cook.*) a dish of bards of bacon, covered with a farce and ragout, and baked between two fires.

BOUTS-RIME'AUX (*Poet.*) a French term, signifying certain rhymes disposed in order, and given to a poet, together with a subject to be filled up with verses in the same rhymes and the same order.

BO'W (*Mil.*) from the Teut. *bogen,* and *biegen,* to bend; an instrument for the discharge of arrows, bullets, &c. The two principal sorts of bows are the Long Bow and the Cross Bow.—*Long Bow,* the favourite of the English army in former times, is simply a bow with a string fixed at each end, to which the arrow is applied.—*Cross Bow* is a bow strung and set in a shaft of wood, with a trigger, &c.

Bow (*Her.*) a charge in coats of arms, as in the annexed figure, "He beareth three long bows *ermine* bent, in pale *gules,* by the name of Bowes."

Bow (*Math.*) an instrument consisting of an arch of 90 deg. fixed on a staff with vanes, &c. for taking the sun's altitude at sea.—*Bow compasses,* an instrument for drawing arches.

Bow (*Mar.*) the rounding parts of the ship's side on each side its head, distinguished by the starboard and leeboard, or weather and lee bow.—*Lean Bow,* a narrow bow fitted for swift sailing.—*Bluff bow,* a broad bow fitted for a high sea.—*Doubling of the bow,* the thick stuff placed there to prevent the anchor from tearing it.—*On the bow,* an arch of the horizon (not exceeding 45 deg.) between some object and the point of the compass right a head, as a fleet bearing three points on the starboard *bow,* viz. three points from that point of the horizon right a head, or towards the right hand.—*Bow grace,* a frame of old rope, or junk, laid against the bows to defend them from the ice.—*Bow line,* or *Bow ling,* a rope fastened to the bolt rope of a sail by two or three small ropes, called *bridles,* used when the sails must be braced sideways. 'To check the *bow line,*' is to slacken it when the wind becomes more favourable. 'To sharp the main *bowling,* or hale the *bowling,*' to pull it harder.—*Bow-man of the boat,* the man who rows the foremost oar in a boat.—*Bow-piece,* a piece of ordnance lying at the bow.—*Bow-sprit,* a mast projecting over the stem to carry the sail forward.

Bow (*Mech.*) the name of several things so called from their having a curved figure, as the—*Turner's bow,* the pole fixed to the cieling to which the cord is fastened that wheels round the piece to be turned.—*Shipwright's bow,* the beam of wood, or brass, with three long screws that direct a lath of wood, or steel, to any part, particularly used in making the draughts of ships.—*Bow of a key,* the arched part to receive the fingers.—*Bow saw,* a hand saw, having an arched handle.—*Bow of a mold* to a printing-press; a spring wire that is arched conveniently for the purpose.—*Bow of a saddle,* the piece of wood on each side laid archwise to receive the upper part of a horse's back.

Bow *of a violin* (*Mus.*) the round stick furnished with hair with which the performer plays.

BO'W-BEARER (*Law*) an officer in the forest who had charge of the vert, or venison; as also to oversee and make true inquisition of every person, sworn or unsworn, in every bailiwick of the forest. *Crompt. Jur.* 201.

BO'WED (*Bot.*) *arcuatus,* bent like a bow; an epithet for a frond, filament, anther, and legume.

BO'WEL GALLED (*Vet.*) an epithet for a horse when the girth frets his skin between the elbow of his fore-legs and his ribs.

BO'WELS (*Anat.*) the same as *Intestines.*

BO'WEN'S KNOT (*Her.*) a particular sort of knot, so called from the name of the bearer.

BO'WER-ANCHOR (*Mar.*) a name for two anchors which are situated at the bow of a ship.

BO'WET (*Falcon.*) a young hawk, so called when it draws any thing out of the nest and covets to clamber on the boughs.

BOWGE (*Law, Mar.*) vide *Bouche* and *Bow-grace.*

BOW-HAND (*Archer.*) the right-hand, with which the bow is held: hence 'a fine or good *bow-hand.*'

BO'WING (*Mus.*) managing the bow, which constitutes the main art of the performer on the violin.

BOWL (*Mar.*) a round space at the head of the mast for the men to stand in.

BOWL (*Gunn.*) a box to fill with small shot and fire out of a cannon at the enemy when near at sea.

BO'WLDER-STONES (*Min.*) lumps or fragments of stones or marble, broken from the adjacent cliffs, which are so called because they are tumbled backward and forward by the action of the water.

BO'W-LEGGED (*Man.*) a defective conformation of a horse's leg, when the knees come further out than the feet.

BOWLINE (*Mar.*) vide *Bow.*—*Bowline-knot*, a knot so constructed that it should never slip. It is made by laying the end of a rope, *a*, over the standing part, *b*, and turning a bight over the standing part; then leading the end round the standing part through the bight again.—*Bowling-bridle.* [vide *Bow*]

TO BOWLT a coney (*Sport.*) to start it.

TO BOWSE (*Mar.*) to pull upon a body with tackle, or a complication of pulleys, in order to remove any object; hence '*bowse away*' i. e. pull all away; '*bowse, ho!*' pull more upon the tackle.

BO'WSING (*Falc.*) the excessive drinking of a hawk who is always thirsty.

BO'WSPRIT (*Mar.*) vide *Bow*.

BO'WYER (*Mech.*) a bowmaker; one of the City companies, which was incorporated in 1622, but had been a fraternity long before. The arms of this company are "*argent*, on a chevron between three floats, *sable*, as many mullets, *gules*."

BOX (*Bot.*) or Box Tree, the *Buxus* of Linnæus, the wood of which is used by engravers and mathematical instrument-makers. There are two kinds of box, namely, the Dwarf Box, which is used for borders in gardens; and the Tall Box, a shrub or tree, which grows to a considerable height. The box wood is yellow and hard, and bears a good polish.— *Box-thorn*, the *Lycium*, a shrub.

Box (*Mech.*) any case of wood, iron, or leather, which is named according to the use to which it is applied, as—*Cutting-boxes*, chests for keeping cut hay and straw for the use of the cavalry.—*Battery-boxes*. [vide *Battery*]—*Cartridge-boxes*. [vide *Cartridge*.]—*Box-and-needle*, a compass applied to the theodolite, and used for surveying.—*Box of a ribsaw*, two thin iron plates for receiving the saw.—*Box of the pump*, the machine requisite for repairing a pump.—*Nave-boxes*, iron boxes fastened one at each end of the nave, to prevent the arms of the axletree, about which the boxes turn, from causing too much friction.—*Box-dust*, dust for strewing over fresh writing.—*Box-maker*, a maker of boxes, packing-cases, &c.

BO'XHAULING (*Mar.*) a particular method of veering a ship, by keeping the helm hard *a-lee*. It is used when tacking is impracticable.

BOX'ING off (*Mar.*) an operation similar to box-hauling.—*Boxing the compass*, rehearsing the several points of the compass in their proper order.—*Boxing of the stem*, or simply *boxing*, the projection left in the hawse-pieces, in the wake of the hawse-holes.

BO'XUS (*Bot.*) Misletoe.

BO'YAR (*Polit.*) a lord or grandee among the Muscovites.

BOYA'U (*Fort.*) French for a ditch separated from the main trench, covered with a parapet, and serving as a communication from one trench to another.

BRA'BE (*Bot.*) an herb a cubit high, with leaves like dittander, and an umbella like that of elder. *Oribas*.

BRABE'IUM (*Bot.*) a genus of plants, Class 23 *Polygamia*, Order 1 *Monoecia*.
Generic Characters. CAL. ament with ovate scales.—COR. one-petalled.—STAM. filaments four; anthers small.—PIST. germ very small; style filiform; stigma simple.—PER. drupe very dry; seed nut globular.
Species. The only species is the *Brabeum stellulifolium, Amygdalus Æthiopica*, &c. seu *Brabyla Capensis*, African Almond, a shrub, native of the Cape of Good Hope.

BRA'BYLA (*Bot.*) Damescenes.

BRA'CCA (*Archæol.*) 1. A Gaulish name for breeches. 2. A large fleet hound, or hunting dog.

BRACE (*Mech.*) from *brachium*, an arm; any thing which is extended so as to include, lock, or fix other things, as *Braces of a coach*, the thick leather thongs on which it rests; hence also a brace in the sense of a couple, as " a *brace* of partridges," &c.—*Braces of a drum*, the leathers with which the drum head is tightened or relaxed.

BRACE (*Archit.*) the cross beams framed in with bevel joints, which serve to keep the building from swinging either way.

BRACE (*Mar.*) 1. The ropes that are fastened to the yard arms to brace the yard, or bring it to any position. 2. Pieces of iron that serve as supports to different machines in a ship, as the poop lanterns, &c. 3. A security for the rudder, which is fixed to the stern post, and to the bottom of the ship.

BRACE (*Print.*) 1. The stays of the press, which serve to keep it steady in its position. 2. A character (}) designed to hook in, or brace any number of lines.

BRACE (*Com.*) an Italian measure equal to two or three ells, English.

BRACE (*Mus.*) a character similar to that used in printing, which is placed at the beginning of every stave to bind and harmonize the parts.

TO BRACE (*Mar.*) to move the yard by means of braces, as " To *brace* about," to turn the yards round for tacking. " To *brace* the yards sharp up," so that they should make the sharpest angle possible with the keel. " To *brace* to," to ease off the lee braces, and round in the weather braces.

BRACED (*Her.*) the same as *fretted* or *interlaced*. [vide *Interlaced*]

BRA'CELET (*Mil.*) from brace or *brachium*, the arm; a piece of defensive armour for the arm.

BRACELET (*Sport.*) a hound, or rather beagle of the smaller kind. *Rot. Pat. 1 Rich. 2.*

BRACENA'RIUS (*Sport.*) a huntsman or master of the hounds. *Ann. 26 Ed. 1. Rot.*

BRA'CER (*Archer.*) a smooth piece of leather fastened on the outside of the archer's left arm, which serveth to defend his arm from the stripe of the string. *Rog. Asch.*

BRACHE'RIUM (*Med.*) the same as *Amma*.

BRACHE'TUS (*Archæol.*) vide *Braco*.

BRACHIÆ'US (*Anat.*) vide *Brachial*.

BRA'CHIAL (*Anat.*) an epithet for what belongs to the arm, as the brachial artery, &c.

BRACHIA'LIS (*Anat.*) or *brachiæus*, an epithet for two muscles of the arm; namely, the *Brachialis externus*, which is the same as the *Triceps extensor cubiti;* and *Brachialis internus*, a muscle in the forearm.

BRA'CHIATE (*Bot.*) from *brachium*, an arm; an epithet for a stem: *caulis brachiatus*, a stem having branches stretched out like arms in pairs.

BRACHIO-CU'BITAL (*Anat.*) an epithet for an expansion of the lateral ligament fixed in the inner condyle of the *Os Humeri*.—*Brachio-radial*, an expansion of the lateral ligament, on which runs the external condyle.

BRACHI'OLUM (*Math.*) the member of an instrument used upon astrolabes, &c. usually made of brass, with several joints.

BRA'CHIUM (*Anat.*) βραχίων, the arm; that part lying between the cubit and the joint of the shoulder, according to Hippocrates; or the whole arm, from the shoulder to the fingers' ends. *Hippocrat. de Art.; Ruf. Ephes. de Appellat. Part. Corp. hum. l. 1; Gal. de Admin. Anat. l. 8; Gorr. Def. Med.; Foes. Œconom. Hippocrat.*

BRACI'NUM (*Archæol.*) the whole quantity of ale brewed at one time.

BRACI'UM (*Min.*) copper.

BRA'CKET (*Carpent.*) from brace, a kind of stay in the

form of a knee or shoulder for the support of shelves, or a cramp-iron as a stay in timber work.

BRACKET (*Mar.*) 1. A short crooked timber resembling a knee for the support of the gratings, as also of the gallery. 2. Ornaments, as the hair bracket, which is the boundary of the aft-part of the head; and the console-bracket, at the fore-part of the quarter-gallery.

BRA'CKETS (*Gun.*) the cheeks of the travelling carriage of guns or howitzers, which are made of strong wooden planks. This name is also given to that part of a large mortar-bed where the trunnions are placed for the elevation of the mortar.

BRA'CKETTING (*Archit.*) ornamental projections placed in the corners of rooms, called according to the figure of the ceiling which they support, *groin-bracketting, cove-bracketting, dome-bracketting*, &c.

BRA'CHMANS (*Theol.*) or *Brachmins*, a sect of gymnosophists, or philosophers in India, who live only on fruits and herbs, and derive their mission from Confucius.

BRACHYCATALE'CTON (*Poet.*) βραχυκατάληκτον, scil. μέτρον, from βραχύς, short, and καταλήγω, to end; a verse wanting a syllable at the end.

BRACHYCE'PHALI (*Ich.*) a fish of bad juice and rank smell. *Orib. Med. Coll.* l. 2, c. 58.

BRACHY'CERUS (*Ent.*) a division of the genus *Curculio*, consisting of such insects of this tribe as have a horny lip, and feelers very short.

BRACHYCHRO'NIUS (*Med.*) βραχυχρόνιος, from βραχύς, short, and χρόνος, time; an epithet for a disease of short duration. *Gal. Def. Med.*

BRACHYGRA'PHY (*Lit.*) from βραχύς, short, and γράφω, to write; short-hand writing.

BRACHYGLO'TTIS (*Bot.*) the *Cineraria rotundifolia* of Linnæus.

BRACHYLO'GY (*Rhet.*) βραχυλογία, from βραχύς, short, and λόγος, speech; a laconic or concise form of speech similar to the aphorisms of Hippocrates. Tacitus calls it *Imperatoriam brevitatem*, and Plutarch refers to it when speaking of Lycurgus. *Demet. de Elocut.* c. 7; *Quint. Instit.* l. 8, c. 3; *Tacit. Hist.* l. 1, c. 18.

BRACHYPNÆ'A (*Med.*) βραχύπνοια, from βραχύς, short, and πνέω, to breathe; short and small respiration, or a short respiration at small intervals. *Hippoc. de Epid.* l. 1, &c.; *Gal. de Diffic. Resp.* l. 3, c. 8.

BRACHYPO'TÆ (*Med.*) βραχυπόται, from βραχύς, little, and πότος, drinking; little drinkers, like those sometimes who are in a phrensy. *Gal. Comm.* 3 in *Hippocrat. Epid.* l. 3.

BRA'CO (*Archæol.*) a large fleet hound, in distinction from the *brachetus*, the smaller; and *brachete*, the bitch of that breed. *Mon. Angl.*

BRA'CONS (*Carpent.*) French for small stakes of wood which are placed with the cross-beams in the floodgates of large sluices.

BRA'CTEA (*Ant.*) πίταλον ἔλασμα, a thin leaf of gold, or any metal.

BRACTEA (*Bot.*) Bracte, or Floral leaf, one of the seven fulcres or props of plants, as in the Lime, *Tilia Europæa*. It is different from the other leaves in shape and colour, and generally situated on the peduncle. When there are several bractes on one flower they are called a tuft. The bracte is caduceous, *caducea*, when it falls off soon after its evolution; deciduous, *decidua*, when it falls before the leaves; persistant, *persistens*, when it falls with the leaves; coloured, *colorata*, when of any other colour than green.

BRA'CTED (*Bot.*) *bracteatus*, furnished with a bracte; an epithet for the peduncle, the whorl, and the raceme.

BRAD (*Carpent.*) vide *Brads*.

BRADLE'YA (*Bot.*) a genus of plants, named after Professor Bradley, of Cambridge, Class 21 *Monoecia*, Order 1 *Monodelphia*.

Generic Characters. CAL. none.—COR. *petals* six.—STAM. *filaments* three; *anther* cylindric.—PIST. *germ* globose; *style* none; *stigmas* six to eight.—PER. *capsule* depressed; *seed* solitary.

Species. The species are shrubs, and natives of the Indies, &c.

BRADS (*Carpent.*) a kind of nails without heads, which are particularly used in flooring of rooms.

BRADYPE'PSY (*Med.*) βραδυπεψία, from βραδύς, slow, and πέπτω, to boil; weakness of digestion. *Gal. de Diff. Symph.* c. 4.

BRA'DYPUS (*Zool.*) Sloth, a genus of animals, Class *Mammalia*, Order *Bruta*.

Generic Characters. Fore-teeth none; grinders six in each jaw.—Body covered with hair.

Species. The species are *Bradypus Tridactylus, Ignavus*, seu *Ai*, Three-toed Sloth, native of South America.—*Bradypus Didactylus*, seu *Unau*, Two-toed Sloth, native of South America.—*Bradipus Ursinus*, Ursine Bradypus or Ursiform Sloth, or Betre Bear, native of India.—*Bradypus Pentadactylus*, Five-toed Sloth.

BRAG (*Sport.*) a game at cards, in which the knaves and nines are principals.

BR'AGGAT (*Med.*) a name formerly applied to a ptisan of honey and water.

BRAGUE (*Carpent.*) French for a kind of mortise, or joining together.

BRAILS (*Mar.*) ropes for hauling up, or collecting to their yards, the lower extremities of the sails that they may be furled the more conveniently; hence the expression "Brail up," for haul up a sail by the brails.

BRAIN (*Anat.*) the soft contents of the *cranium*, or scull, consisting of the *Cerebrum, Cerebellum*, &c. [vide *Anatomy*, &c.]

BRA'IN-STONE (*Ent.*) the *Madrepora cerebrum* of Linnæus, an insect of the Zoophytes Order.

BRAISES (*Cook.*) meat dressed à la braise, i. e. broiled upon the coals, or else baked in a campaign oven, &c.

BRAIT (*Min.*) a rough diamond.

BRAKE (*Bot.*) a sort of furze.

BRAKE (*Mech.*) 1. An instrument with teeth for dressing flax. 2. A baker's kneading trough. 3. The sharp bit or snafle of a bridle.

BRAKE (*Mar.*) the handle or lever by which a common ship's pump is worked.

BRA'MA (*Ich.*) vide *Bream*.

BRA'MANS (*Theol.*) vide *Brachmans*.

BRA'MBLE (*Bot.*) a shrub which has been classed by Linnæus under the *Rubus*.

BRAMBLE (*Or.*) or *Brambling*, the Mountain Finch, *Fringilla montefringilla*.

BRA'MBLE-NET (*Mech.*) a sort of net for catching birds.

BRAN (*Bot.*) the husk of ground corn, which contains a considerable portion of the glutinous and nutritious quality of the wheat.

BRA'NCA *ursina* (*Bot.*) Bear's Foot. [vide *Acanthus*]

BRA'NCARD (*Mil.*) a sort of hand-barrow.

BRANCH (*Bot.*) *ramus*, a division of the main stem supporting the leaves and fructification.—Branch Leaves, *ramea folia*, leaves growing on the branches.—Branch Peduncle, *rameus pedunculus*, a peduncle springing from a branch.—Fruit branch, that which shoots out of the cut of a preceding year, and is naturally of a considerable thickness.—Half-wood branch, one that is too gross for a fruit branch, and too slender for a wood branch.

BRANCH (*Mech.*) a name for several things, so called from their resemblance in figure, as—Branch of a *candlestick*, or *chandelier*, that which runs off from the main stem.—Branches of the bit of a bridle, the two pieces of bended iron that bear the bit mouth, the chains, and the curb.

BRANCH *of a stag* (*Sport.*) the horns of the head, or the antlers.

BRANCH (*Or.*) a canary bird of the first year brought up by the old one.

TO BRANCH *stand* (*Falc.*) to make a hawk take the branch, or leap from tree to tree, till the dog spring the partridge.

BRANCHE (*Fort.*) a French word applied to the extended sides of the different works which surround a fortified town, as the covert-way, ditch, &c.

BRA'NCHED (*Her.*) a term in blazoning for spread into branches like the horns of a deer.

BRANCHED (*Bot.*) or Branching, *ramosus*; an epithet for a stem, leaf, spine, &c. which, when loaded with many branches, are called *ramosissimus*, very branching.

BRA'NCHER (*Falcon.*) a young hawk, or other bird, that begins to go from branch to branch.

BRA'NCHES (*Carpent.*) the ribs or arches of a Gothic vault, which traverse from one angle to another.

BRA'NCHI (*Med.*) or *Branchæ*, the glandulous tumours of the fauces. *Castell. Lex. Med.*

BRANCHI'Æ (*Ich.*) the gills of a fish.

BRANCHI'ONUS (*Ent.*) a genus of animals, Class *Vermes*, Order *Infusoria*.

Generic Character. *Body* contractile, and covered with a shell.

Species. These animals inhabit the stagnant water, where, from their minuteness, they appear to the naked eye like white specks.

BRANCHIO'STEGOUS (*Ich.*) an Order of fishes, in the Linnean system, comprehending those which have gills without bony rays, and including the following genera: *Mormyrus*; *Ostracion*, *Tetrodon*; *Syngnathus*, Pipe Fish; *Pegasus*; *Centriscus*; *Balistes*; *Cyclopterus*, Sucker; *Lophius*, Frog-fish.

BRA'NCHLET (*Bot.*) *ramulus*, a small branch.

BRA'NCHUS (*Med.*) βράγχος, a hoarseness, or defluxion of humours upon the fauces. *Hippocrat. de Epid.* l. 1; *Cæl. Aurel. Tard. Pass.* l. 2, c. 7; *Foes. Œconom. Hippocrat.*

BRAND (*Archæol.*) a sword.

BRAND (*Or.*) vide *Brant*.

BRANDE'UM (*Ecc.*) the cloth wherewith the bodies of saints and martyrs had been wrapped, cut into small pieces, and distributed as a relic. *Bed. Hist. Angl.* l. 1, c. 3; *Gregor. Turon. de Glor. Confess.* c. 37.

BRA'NDLING (*Sport.*) a worm used in fishing.

BRA'NDRITH (*Mec.*) a fence or rail about a well.

BRA'NDY (*Chem.*) a spirituous and inflammable liquor made from the lees of wine by distillation. Its constituent parts are water, alcohol, and a little oil or resin. It was formerly distinguished by the annexed character, $\triangledown$ and called *Aqua vitæ*.

BRANK (*Bot.*) another name for Buck-Wheat.—Brank Ursine, *Branca ursina*. [vide *Acanthus*]

BRA'NT-FOX (*Zool.*) a sort of black and red fox, the *Canis alopex* of Linnæus.

BRAZIL-WOOD (*Bot.*) an American wood, so called because it was first brought from Brazil.

BRA'SIUM (*Archæol.*) Malt.

BRA'SMA (*Nat.*) βράσμα, a sort of black pepper that is good for nothing; the same as is now observed to corrupt on the plant.

BRASMA'TIAS (*Nat.*) a kind of earthquake, when the earth moves directly upwards.

BRA'SMOS (*Nat.*) βρασμος, fermentation.

BRASS (*Met.*) a factitious metal made of zinc and copper, or copper ore.—*Brass colour*, a colour prepared by braziers to imitate brass, which is red brass or bronze, and yellow or gilt brass.

BRA'SSART (*Her.*) armour for the elbow.

BRASSATE'LLA (*Bot.*) the same as *Ophioglossum*.

BRA'SSES (*Her.*) sepulchral engravings on brass-plates, let into slabs in the pavements of the ancient churches, pourtraying the effigies, &c. of illustrious persons.

BRASSES (*Mech.*) plates let into the heads of spinning wheels, with holes for the spindles to work in.

BRA'SSETS (*Her.*) pieces of armour for the arms.

BRA'SSICA (*Bot.*) in the Greek ράφανος, and in English Cabbage, a well-known vegetable, much used by the ancients and the moderns. *In the Linnean system it is a genus of plants, Class* 15 *Tetradynamia*, Order 2 *Siliquosa*.

Generic Characters. CAL. *perianth* four-leaved; *leaflets* lanceolate.—COR. tetrapetalous; *petals* subovate; *nectareous glands* four ovate.—STAM. *filaments* six, subolate; *anthers* erect.—PIST. *germ* columnar; *style* short; *stigma* capitate.—PER. *silique* long; *partition* with a prominent columnar top; *valves* shorter than the partition.

Species. The principal species are the—*Brassica oleracea*, Common Cabbage.—*Brassica napus*, *Napus sylvestris*, seu *Bunias*, Wild Cabbage, Rape, or Naveu.—*Brassica napus sativa*, Coleseed.—*Brassica rapa*, *Rapa rotunda*, *Rapum majus*, seu *Rapa napus*, Turnep, &c. &c.

BRA'SSICOURT (*Man.*) or *brachicourt*, an epithet for a horse whose legs are naturally bent archwise, in distinction from the bow-legged horse, who is made so by labour.

BRASSIDE'LICA *ars* (*Med.*) a mode of cure by applying the herb brassadella.

BRATHYS (*Bot.*) βράθυς, or βράθυ, a shrub of a habit between the heath and the juniper: it is so called from βραδὺς, slow, because it is of slow growth. According to Pliny it was the name for the herb Savine. *Dioscor.* l. 1, c. 104; *Plin.* l. 24, c. 11.

BRATHYS, *in the Linnean system*, a genus of plants, Class 13 *Polyandria*, Order 5 *Pentagynia*.

Generic Characters. CAL. *perianth* five-leaved.—COR. *petals* five.—STAM. *filaments* many; *anthers* twin.—PIST. *germ* superior; *styles* five; *stigmas* capitate.—PER. *capsule* ovate; *seeds* very many.

Species. The species are all shrubs.

BRA'ULE (*Mus.*) an old French dance performed in a circle.

BRAURO'NIA (*Ant.*) Βραυρωνία, an Athenian festival celebrated every five years in honour of Diana, who was surnamed Brauronia. *Aristoph. Iren.*; *Poll. Onom.* l. 8, c. 9; *Hesychius*.

BRAVU'RA (*Mus.*) Italian for a song of spirit, as also for the execution of the performer.

BRAWN (*Anat.*) the muscular or fleshy part of the body, particularly that of the boar.

BRAY (*Falcon.*) a pannel or piece of leather slit to bind up the legs of a hawk.

BRAY *false* (*Fort.*) a false trench to hide a real one.

BRA'YER (*Print.*) a round wooden rubber used in the ink-block to bray or rub ink.

BRA'ZIER (*Com.*) a maker or seller of brass ware.

BRA'ZING (*Mech.*) the soldering or joining two pieces of iron by means of thin plates of brass melted between the two pieces to be joined.

BREACH (*Fort.*) a gap made in the works of a town by the besiegers. A practicable *breach* is an opening made in a wall by which soldiers may enter. "To repair a *Breach*," to stop or fill up the gap with gabions, fascines, &c. so as to prevent the assault. "To fortify a *Breach*," to render it inaccessible by cheveux de frizes, crowsfeet, &c. "To make a lodgement in the *Breach*" is said of the besiegers who secure themselves in the breach after the besieged have been driven out. "To clear the *Breach*," to remove the rubbish, &c. from the *Breach*.

BREACH *of close* (*Law*) is a sort of trespass by entering on another man's ground without lawful authority.—*Breach of covenant*, the not performing any covenant, &c.—*Breach of duty*, the not executing any office, &c.—*Breach of peace*, offences against the public peace.—*Breach of pound*, breaking any place where cattle are distrained.—*Breach of prison*, an escape by breaking out of prison.

BREAD (*Med.*) vide *Artos*.

BRE'AD-FRUIT-TREE (*Bot.*) the *Artocarpus* of Linnæus, a tree growing in Otaheite, so called because the fruit, which is milky and juicy, supplies the place of bread to the inhabitants. This tree grows to the height of forty feet.—*Bread-nut-tree*, the *Brosimum* of Linnæus.

BREAD (*Law*) or *assize of bread, beer, and ale*. [vide *Assize*]—*Bread of treat*, a name in the statute 51 Hen. 3. of assize of bread and ale for the household bread, as it is now called in distinction from the *wastel*, or *white bread*, and the *cocket*, or *wheaten bread*.

BREA'D ROOM (*Mar.*) that part of the hold in a ship destined to receive the bread and biscuit.

BREAD TURNIP (*Med.*) the expressed juice of turnips mixed with meal.—*Bread-jelly*, bread boiled to a jelly.

BREAK (*Archit.*) the projection in the front of a building carried up more than one story.

BREAK (*Agric.*) a land ploughed the first year after it had lain fallow in sheep-walks.

BREAK *of a deck* (*Mar.*) that part where the descent to the next deck below it commences.—*Break-water*, 1. The hull of a vessel sunk at the entrance of a harbour to break the force of the water. 2. A small buoy fastened to a large one, to show where the latter always is.

BREAK (*Print.*) the short line which ends a paragraph. 2. The piece of metal contiguous to the shank of the letter, so called because it is always broken off.

TO BREAK *in* (*Carpent.*) to cut or break a hole in brickwork with a ripping chissel for the purpose of inserting timber.

BRE'AK-JOINT (*Mason.*) a term for that part of brickwork which consists in laying a third stone over two others that are contiguous, for the purpose of binding them the closer together.

TO BREAK (*Com.*) to become bankrupt.

TO BREAK *off* (*Mil.*) a term in the military movements of the cavalry for diminishing the front, and also for wheeling from the line, as "*Break off* to the left," i. e. wheel to the left.

TO BREAK *ground* (*Fort.*) to open the trenches, or begin the works for a siege.

TO BREAK (*Mar.*) is used in several sea phrases, as "*To break ground*," i. e. to weigh an anchor, and quit a place. "*To break bulk*," to commence unloading a ship. "*To break up*," to rip off the planks of a ship, and take her to pieces, when old and unserviceable. "*To break sheer*," is said of a ship which is driven by the force of the winds out of the position in which she might keep clear of her anchors.

TO BREAK *a horse* (*Man.*) in trotting, is to make him light upon the hand by trotting; to *break* him for hunting, is to supple him, and make him take the habit of running.

TO BREAK *a deer* (*Cook.*) to cut up venison.

BRE'AKERS (*Mar.*) billows breaking over rocks that lie under water.

BREAKING *in* (*Man.*) the discipline of first training a colt to be useful.

BREAKING *of arrestment* (*Law*) an action in the Scotch court, wherein it is narrated, that though arrestment was laid on, payment nevertheless was not made; the pursuer therefore concludes that the breaker should refund him, and besides should be punished according to law.

BREAKING *off* (*Mech.*) breaking the break from the shank of a printing-type.

BREAM (*Ich.*) the *Cyprinus brama* of Linnæus, a fish of the carp kind that grows fast, and has a broad body.—*Sea brenm*, otherwise called Red Gilt Head, the *Sparus pagrus* of Linnæus, a fish of a red colour, with the iris silvery.

BREA'MING (*Mar.*) burning off the filth of grass, sea-weed, &c. from a ship's bottom.

BREA'ST (*Anat.*) the anterior part of the Thorax, the Sternum.—*Breast-bone*, the Sternum. [vide *Anatomy*]—*Breast*, or *Breasts*. vide *Mammæ*.

BREA'STFAST (*Mar.*) the large rope employed to confine a ship sideways to a wharf or quay.—*Breast hooks*, thick pieces of incurvated timber, serving to strengthen the forepart of the ship.—*Breast caskets*, the longest and biggest caskets.—*Breast-rail*, the upper rail of the breast-work.—*Breast-work*, the balustrade of the quarter-deck, &c.

BRE'AST-PAIN (*Vet.*) a disease incident to horses.

BREA'ST-PLATE (*Man.*) a leathern strap running from one side of the saddle, across the horse's breast, to the other, to keep it in its place.—*Breast of a saddle*, that part where the arch or upper part of the bow ends.

BREAST-PLATE (*Mil.*) a piece of defensive armour worn on the breast.

BREA'ST-PLOUGH (*Agric.*) a sort of plough which is driven by the *breast*, and is used in parting turf for denshering the land. [vide *Agriculture*]

BREA'ST-WORK (*Fort.*) works thrown up as high as the breast of the besieged, or those who are defending themselves.

BRE'CCA (*Archæol.*) a breach from the want of repair.

BRE'CCIA (*Min.*) Pudding-stone, a sort of aggregate earths, consisting of fragments of stones conglutinated.

BRE'DWITE (*Archæol.*) a fine, or penalty, imposed for defaults in the assize of bread.

BREE'CH (*Mar.*) the angle of knee-timber in a ship, the inside of which is called the throat.

BREECH *of a gun* (*Gunn.*) the hinder part from the cascabel to the bore.

BRE'ECHING (*Agric.*) the hard and clotted wool cut from the sheep; also long white hairs in wool as stiff as badger's hairs.

BRE'EDING (*Agric.*) a method of improving the race of different animals by crossing or mingling one species or variety with another.

BRE'EZE (*Mar.*) a shifting wind that blows from sea and land alternately.

BREEZE (*Ent.*) or sea-breeze, the *Oestrus* of Linnæus, another name for the Gadfly.

BRE'GMA (*Anat.*) βρεχμὸς, βρέγμα, the middle and forepart of the head. Hippoc. de Vul. Cap.; Cæl. Aurelian. de tard Pass. l. 1, c. 4; Eustath. in Hom. Il. l. 3; Hesychius.

BRE'HON (*Law*) an Irish judge.

BRE'ISMA (*Archæol.*) a weather sheep.

BRE'LISIS (*Nat.*) the caranna, a sort of gum.

BRENA'GRIUM (*Archæol.*) a payment in bran by tenants to their lords.

BRE'NT-GOOSE (*Orn.*) the *Anas Bernicla* of Linnæus. [vide *Bernicle*]

BRE'NTUS (*Ent.*) a genus of insects, Order *Coleoptera*.
Generic Character. *Antennæ* moniliform; *head* projecting into a very long cylindrical snout.
Species. The species are distinguished into those which have the thighs simple, and those that have the thighs toothed.

BRE'SSUMMER (*Carpent.*) a binding inter-tie, or girder, to different parts of a house.

BRE'ST (*Archit.*) another name for the torus.

BRETE'SSE (*Her.*) a charge which is embattled on both sides equal to each other.

BRETO'ISE (*Law*) or *bretoyse*, the law of the Marches of Wales in use among the ancient Britons.

BREVE' (*Law*) a writ so called for its brevity, directed to the Chancellor and Judges, by which a man is summoned or attached to answer an action, &c. Bract. l. 51; Tract. 5, c. 17.—*Breve perquirere*, to purchase a writ or licence of trial in the king's court by the plaintiff.—*Breve de recto*, a writ of right or licence for a person ejected out of an estate to sue for the possession of it.

BREVE (*Mus.*) a note of the third degree of length, marked thus |⊐|; it was formerly marked as a square figure.—*Imperfect breve*, is one that has no dot after it, which is equal to one quarter of a large breve, or to two semibreves.—*Perfect breve* is dotted, and is equal to three semibreves.

BRE'VET (*Mil.*) a term expressive of promotion in the army, from the captain upwards, without additional pay, until it reaches to the rank of Major-General, who is now entitled to a quarterly allowance.—*Brevet-rank*, a rank in the army higher than that for which pay is received.

BRE'VIA TESTATA (*Law*) an ancient term for a deed.

BREVIA *vasa* (*Anat.*) small venous vessels passing from the stomach to the splenetic veins.

BREVIARY (*Ecc.*) a book containing the daily service of the Romish Church.

BRE'VIBUS *et rotulis liberandis* (*Law*) a writ to a sheriff to deliver to his successor the county with the rolls, &c. *Reg. Orig.* 295.

BRE'VIER (*Print.*) a small printing letter, so called, probably, from its having been first used in printing breviaries, or, still more probably, from *brevis*, short, because it is comparatively small. [vide *Printing*]

BRE'VIS *musculus* (*Anat.*) a muscle of the *scapula*.—*Brevis cubiti*, a muscle of the fore-arm.—*Brevis extensor digitum pedis*. [vide *Extensor*]—*Brevis Flexor Pollicis.* [vide *Flexor*]—*Brevis Peroneus*. [vide *Peroneus*] *Brevis Pronator radii*. [vide *Pronator*]

BRE'WERS' *Company* (*Her.*) the brewers were incorporated in 1424, in the 6th year of the reign of Henry VI. Their arms are "Gules on a chevron *argent* between three saltines of garbs *or*, as many tuns *sable*."

BRE'WING (*Mar.*) or a squall brewing; black tempestuous clouds collecting so as to portend a storm.

BREXA'NTES (*Med.*) a small kind of frog, to the blood of which was falsely ascribed, according to Galen, the virtue of restoring the lost hair. *Gal. de San. tuend.* 1. 10.

BRE'YNIA (*Bot.*) a genus of plants named after Breynius, father and son. Class 23, *Polygamia*, Order 2, *Dioecia*.

Generic Characters.—CAL. *perianth* one-leaved.—COR. none.—STAM. *filaments* none; *anthers* five.—PIST. *germ* very small; *style* cylindric; *stigma* blunt.—PER. *berry* dry; *seeds* two.

Species. The only species is *Breynia disticha*, native of New Caledonia and the Isle of Tamia.

BRI'AR (*Bot.*) Wild or Common Briar, the *Rosa canina* of Linnæus.

BRI'BERY (*Law*) when any person in a judicial place takes any fee, gift, reward, or brocage, for doing his office, or by colour of his office, except of the king only. 3 *Inst.* 145.

BRIBO'UR (*Archæol.*) a pilferer.

BRI'CK (*Mech.*) an artificial kind of stone composed of clay, coal-ashes, or sand, &c. dried by the sun, and hardened by fire. Bricks are made in a mould, are dried in a framework called *Hacks*, and burnt in heaps, called *Clamps*, whence the burning itself is also called a *Clamp*. Bricks differ according to their quality.—*Marls* are prepared and tempered with the greatest care; the finest of which are called *firsts*, which are chosen for archways, &c. The next best are called *seconds*.—*Stocks* are a sort of brick next in quality to the seconds of marls. The *grey Stocks* are made of the purest earth: the *red Stocks* are so called from the colour of the earth of which they are made. The finest sort of *Stocks* are called *red Rubbers*.

Bricks are likewise distinguished according to their figure, as—*Compass Bricks*, which are of a circular form. *Concave* or *hollow Bricks*, which are flat on one side and hollowed on the other.—*Feather-edged Bricks*, that are thinner on one edge than the other; also according to their use, as *Caping Bricks*, used for the caping of walls.—*Cogging Bricks*, for the indented work under the caping of walls.—*Dutch* or *Flemish Bricks* used in paving yards, &c.

BRICK (*Chem.*) was formerly distinguished by this character,

BRI'CK-KILN (*Mech.*) a place in which bricks are burnt.

BRI'CKLAYERS' *Company* (*Her.*) was not incorporated before 1586. The Bricklayers' arms are as in the annexed figure. "*Azure* a chevron, *or* between a fleur de Lys, *argent* enters two brick-axes in chief, and a bundle of lathes in base, *or*."

BRICO'LLE (*Archæol.*) an engine for beating down walls.

BRICOLLE (*Sport.*) or bricoil, the rebound of a tennis-ball after a side stroke.

BRI'CUMUM (*Bot.*) a name for Artemisia.

BRI'DEMEN (*Cus.*) and bridemaids, young men and maidens attending the bride on their wedding-day.

BRI'DE-STAKE (*Archæol.*) probably a post set up to dance round like a may-pole.

BRI'DGE (*Archit.*) a structure raised over rivers, &c. commonly formed of some durable materials, as wood, stone, or iron. The principal parts belonging to a bridge are as follow, namely, the *cafferdam*, or *batterdeau*, a case of piling without a bottom fixed in the river water-tight, or nearly so, for the purpose of laying the bottom dry.—*caisson*, a flat-bottomed boat, in which a pier is built; the bottom of which afterwards serves as a foundation for the pier.—*Abutments*, the extremities of the bridge which join to or abut upon the land.—*Piers*, the walls built for the support of the arches.—*Arches*, the circular openings which have different names for their different parts and figure. [vide *Arch*]—*Impost*, that part of the pier on which the feet of the arches stand.—*Piles*, stakes or posts shod with iron, and driven into the bed of the river to serve as a foundation, or to protect the piers.—*Stilts*, a set of piles driven into the space intended for the pier, whose tops being sawed off level above low-water mark, the pier is then raised upon them.—*Jettée*, the border made round the stilts under the pier.—*Starlings*, a kind of case made about a pier of stilts and jettées, &c.—*Pile-driver*, an engine for driving down the piles. [vide Pl. 29, fig. 5]—*Parapet*, the breast-wall made on the top of the bridge to prevent the passengers from falling over.—*Banquet*, the raised footpath at the sides of the bridge next the parapet.

Bridges are of different kinds, according to their materials, construction, or use, namely—*Wooden bridges*, *stone*, or *iron bridges*, according as they are made of wood, stone, or iron.—*Rush bridges*, those which are made of rushes bound fast together, over which planks are laid for passing over marshy places. They are used by soldiers on their march.—*Pendant* or *hanging bridges*, those which are not supported by posts, pillars, or butments, but hang in the air sustained only at the two ends.—*Drawbridge*, that which is fastened with hinges at one end, so that the other may be drawn up, or to one side, so as to admit the passage of a vessel, or in fortifications to prevent the crossing of a ditch.—*Flying bridge*, one composed of two smaller bridges, so constructed one over the other, that by means of ropes and pulleys the upper one may be pushed forward till it reaches the point where it is to be fixed. It is commonly used to surprise works or outposts.—*Bridge of boats*, a number of common boats joined parallel to each other at the distance of six feet, till they reach across a river. They are then covered with planks, so as to serve as a passage for men and horses. This is mostly used in military marches.—

Bridge of communication, a bridge constructed for the purpose of affording a communication between two armies or forts.—*Floating bridge,* a sort of redoubt, consisting of two boats covered with planks, and solidly framed so as to bear either man or horse.—*Ponton bridges,* those which are made of pontons.—*Cask* or *barrel bridges* are a number of casks or barrels, which are made to answer the purpose of pontons.

BRIDGE (*Mus.*) the perpendicular arch in a violin, bass-viol, &c. which stands upon the belly, and serves to support the strings; also the flat ruler laid over the jacks of a harpsichord, or spinnet, to prevent them leaping out of their sockets.

BRIDGE (*Gunn.*) a name for the two pieces of timber which go between the two transoms of a gun-carriage, on which the coins are placed for elevating the piece.

BRIDGE (*Her.*) a charge in coat armour, as in the annexed figure. "He beareth *or* on a bridge of three arches, *gules* masoned *sable*, the streamers transfluent proper, a fane *argent*, name *Trowbridge*."

BRI'DLE (*Man.*) a contrivance made of leather straps and pieces of iron, the parts of which are as follow, namely, the—*Bitt,* or *snafle,* which goes into the horse's mouth.—*Curb,* a chain of iron made fast to the upper part of the branches of the bridle in a hole called the *eye,* and running over the beard of the horse.—*Head-stall,* the leather going from the top of the head to the rings of the bitt.—*Fillet,* which lies over the forehead, and is usually adorned with a rose.—*Throatband,* a leather under the throat.—*Reins,* the thongs for the use of the rider.—*Button and loop,* at the end of the reins.—*Nose-band,* a leather going over the middle of the nose.—*Cavessan,* a false rein.—*Martingale,* a thong of leather, one end of which is fastened under the horse's head, and the other between his legs, to make him hold his head well.

The principal sorts of bridles now in use are the *snafle,* the *curb,* and the *chaff-halter,* which is a lady's bridle with double reins.—*Bridle-hand,* the horseman's left hand; the right hand being the spear, or whip hand.

BRIDLE-ARM *protect* (*Mil.*) a guard used by the cavalry, which consists in having the sword-hilt above the helmet, and the point downwards in advance of the bridle-hand.

BRIDON (*Man.*) or *bridoon,* the snafle and rein of a military bridle, which acts independently of the bit and curb at the pleasure of the rider.

BRIEF (*Law*) an abridgement of the client's case made out for the instruction of counsel on a trial at law.—*Brief al' Evesque,* a writ to the bishop, which, in *Quare impedit,* shall go to remove an incumbent.—*Brief out of the chancery,* a writ to a judge to examine by an inquest whether a man be nearest heir.—*Brief of distress,* a writ out of chancery against a landlord to distress his goods, now obsolete.—*Brief of mort-ancestry,* for entering the heirs of all defuncts.—*Brief,* or *licence,* to make collections for repairing churches, losses by fire, &c.

BRIEF, *Apostolical* (*Ecc.*) a letter which the pope sends to princes and magistrates relative to public affairs. It is so called on account of its brevity, in distinction from the *Bull,* which is drawn up at large, and with all possible form.

BRIEF (*Mus.*) a measure of quantity, which contains two strokes down in beating time, and as many up. It is not now often used.

BRIG (*Mar.*) a small merchantman with two masts.

BRI'GA (*Archæol.*) contention.

BRIGA'DE (*Mil.*) a party of either horse or foot, consisting, in the first case, of eight or ten squadrons; and, in the second, of from four to six battalions.—*Irish Brigade,* were Irish regiments serving in France, Spain, and Naples.—*Brigade Major* is an officer appointed by the brigadier to assist him in the management of his brigade.—*Brigade of a troop of horse,* the third part of it.

TO BRIGADE (*Mil.*) to make any given number of regiments or battalions act together for the purpose of service.

BRIGADI'ER (*Mil.*) the officer who commands a brigade.

BRIGANDI'NE (*Mil.*) a coat of mail, consisting of many jointed and scale-like plates, very pliant and easy for the body. Stat. 45, P. & M.

BRIGANDINE (*Her.*) or *Brigantine.* [vide *Habergeon*]

BRIGANTI'NE (*Mar.*) a small swift sailing vessel.

BRI'GBOTE (*Archæol.*) or *brug bote,* the contribution to the repair of bridges. *Fleta.*

BRIGHT-BAY (*Man.*) the common colour of a horse.

BRIGI'DIANS (*Ecc.*) an order of Swedish nuns, whose founder was named Bridget.

BRILLA'NTE (*Man.*) an epithet for a brisk high mettled stately horse.

BRILLANTE (*Mus.*) Italian for a brisk lively manner.

BRILLS (*Man.*) hairs on a horse's eyelids.

BRI'MSEY (*Her.*) vide *Gad-fly.*

BRI'MSTONE (*Chem.*) the vulgar name for sulphur.

BRINDLED (*Zool.*) spotted; an epithet for cows, &c.

TO BRING (*Mar.*) a term used in several sea phrases, as 'To bring by the lee, to incline rapidly to leeward.—'To bring to, to check the ship's course, to make her lie to, or stationary; also in applying a rope to the capstan, it is said 'Bring to the messenger.'—'To bring up,' a term among the colliers for casting anchor.

TO BRING up (*Mason.*) a chimney foundation, &c. to raise it to any height.

BRI'NGER (*Mil.*) a term employed in the recruiting service, to signify the person who produces a man or a boy within the regulated age that is willing to enlist, for which he is allowed a guinea.—*Bringers up,* a name formerly used in the English army for the whole rear rank of a battalion drawn up.

BRI'NGING to (*Mar.*) checking the course of a ship to wait the approach of another.

BRINGING in (*Man.*) keeping in a horse's nose when he boars.

BRINGING up the rear (*Mil.*) bringing all stragglers to the main body.

BRINS d'est (*Mil.*) French for large stakes or poles, resembling pickets, with iron at each end, which are used to cross ditches.

BRI'ONY (*Bot.*) vide *Bryony.*

BRISE (*Carpent.*) French for a beam in sluices, that is placed swipe fashion, on the top of a large pile.

BRISE (*Agric.*) vide *Brize.*

BRISE (*Her.*) vide *rompu.*

BRI'SKET (*Vet.*) that part of the breast of an animal that lies nearest the ribs.—*Brisket of a horse,* the forepart of the neck at the shoulder down to the forelegs.

BRI'STLE (*Bot.*) *seta,* that sort of stalk which bears only the fructification of the *Musci.* It differs from the flower-stalk, in being always simple, and standing between the fruit and calyx.—*Bristle-shaped, setaceous,* an epithet for a leaf; *folium setaceum,* a leaf in the shape of a bristle, that is, shorter than a capillary leaf.

BRI'STLED (*Her.*) an epithet in blazoning for a boar, having hair on his back and head.

BRI'STLY (*Bot.*) *setosus,* i. e. set with bristles; an epithet for some receptacles that have bristles between the florets.

BRI'STOL *hot waters* (*Chem.*) mineral waters of the lowest temperature of any in England, the constituent parts of which are carbonic acid gas, lime, magnesia, together with muriatic and vitriolic acids. They are used efficaciously in pulmonary disorders.

BRITA'NNICA (*Bot.*) βρετανικα, the *Rumex Britannica* of

Linnæus, a plant; so called, according to Pliny, because it was discovered by the Friezlanders near the British Channel. It is very astringent and efficacious for ulcers in the mouth, &c. *Dioscor.* l. 4, c. 2; *Plin.* l. 25, c. 3.

BRI'ZA (*Bot.*) St. Peter's corn, Spelt Wheat, or Quaking Grass, a genus of plants, Class 3 *Triandria*, Order 2 *Digynia*.
> *Generic Characters.* CAL. glume many-flowered.—COR. bivalve; *nectary* two-leaved.—STAM. *filaments* three; *anthers* oblong.—PIST. *germ* roundish; *styles* two; *stigmas* plumose.—PER. none; *seed* one.
> *Species.* The species are mostly annuals, as—*Briza minor, Poa petiolis*, &c. seu *Gramen tremulum*, &c. small Quaking Grass, an annual, native of Britain.—*Briza virens*, seu *Gramen paniculatum*, Green Quaking-Grass.—*Briza maxima*, &c. Greatest Quaking Grass, &c. But—*Briza medea, Poa petiolis*, &c. *Gramen tremulum*, &c. seu *Phalaris pratensis*, Middle or Common Quaking Grass, Shakers, Ladies' Hair, or Bird's Eyes, is a perennial.

BRIZE (*Agric.*) a sort of ground that has lain long untilled.

BRIZEVE'NT (*Hort.*) shelters on the north side of melon-beds where walls are wanting.

BROACH (*Mech.*) a spit for roasting meat upon.

BROACH (*Mus.*) a wind instrument, the sounds of which are produced by turning round a handle.

BROACH (*Sport.*) the start of the head of a young stag, growing sharp like the end of a spit.

TO BROACH (*Husband.*) to pierce a cask or vessel in order to draw the liquor.

TO BROACH to (*Mar.*) to incline very rapidly to windward, an action differing but in degree from that of *bringing to*.

BROAD-A'RROW (*Her.*) a charge which differs from the pheon only, by having the inside of its barbs plain. [vide *Pheon*]

BROA'D-AXE (*Her.*) a charge occasionally in coats of arms.

BROA'D-SIDE (*Mar.*) 1. A discharge of all the guns on one side of a ship at a time. 2. All that side of the ship above water between the bow and quarter.

BROAD-SIDE (*Print.*) a form of one full page, printed on one side of a whole sheet of paper.

BROAD-SIDE-PI'ECE (*Com.*) a gold coin, worth 23s. or 25s. 6d. G. II.

BRO'ADSWORD (*Mil.*) a sword with a broad blade, chiefly designed for cutting. The principal guards in the broadsword exercise are the—*Inside guard*, which is formed by directing your point in a line about six inches higher than your antagonist's left eye.—*Outside guard* consists in directing your point above your antagonist's right eye.—*Medium guard* is a position between the inside and outside guard.—*Hanging guard* is that in which the hilt of your sword is raised high enough to view your opponent under the shell.—*St. George's guard* protects the head.

BROCA'DE (*Com.*) a kind of stuff, or cloth of gold, silver, or silk, raised and enriched with flowers, &c.

BROCA'GIUM (*Archæol.*) brokery.

BRO'CCOLI (*Bot.*) a variety of the Cauliflower.

BROCH (*Mech.*) vide *Brooch*.

BRO'CHA (*Ant.*) in French *broche*, an awl or large packing needle.

BROCHA (*Archæol.*) *broche*, a spit.

BROCHA (*Her.*) an instrument used by embroiderers, and borne in the arms of the embroiderers' company.

BROCHE'TTE (*Cook.*) a particular way of frying chickens.

BRO'CHIA (*Archæol.*) a great can or pitcher.

BRO'CHITAS (*Vet.*) bending of the teeth, which is a mark of old age in horses, according to Pliny. *Varr. de Re Rust.* l. 2, c. 7; *Plin.* l. 11, c. 38.

BROCHOI'R (*Mech.*) French for a smith's shoeing-hammer.

BRO'CHUS (*Anat.*) one having a prominent upper lip. *Castell. Lex. Med.*

BROCK (*Sport.*) a buck or hart two years old.

BRODERIE'S (*Mus.*) flourishes thrown by performers, *en passant*, into any composition.

BRO'D-HALFPENNY (*Archæol.*) vide *Bord-halfpenny*.

BRO'DIUM (*Med.*) the liquor in which some solid medicine is preserved.

BRO'GGER (*Archæol.*) the same as Broker.—*Brogger of corn*, the same as Badger.

BROKEN-BA'CKED (*Mar.*) an epithet for a vessel so loosened in her frame as to droop at both ends.

BROKEN-LE'TTER (*Print.*) the breaking the orderly succession in which the letter stood in a line or page, and mingling them together.

BROKEN-NU'MBER (*Arith.*) the same as Fraction.

BROKEN-RADIA'TION (*Catop.*) the broken beams of light, as seen through a glass that is cut into several panes or pieces.

BROKEN-RA'Y (*Diop.*) or ray of refraction, a right line, whereby the ray of incident changes its direction, or is broken in traversing the second medium.

BROKEN-WI'ND (*Vet.*) a diseased respiration in horses.—*Broken-knees*, an injury done to the knees of horses.

BRO'KER (*Com.*) *broccator*, from *broca*, a breaking; that is, a broken trader, such being originally the only persons employed in that way. A broker is one who concludes bargains or contracts for merchants, &c. of whom there are several kinds, as—*Exchange Brokers*, such as negotiate in all matters of exchange with foreign countries.—*Ship Brokers*, those who transact business between the owners of vessels, and the merchants who send cargoes.—*Insurance Brokers*, those who manage the concerns, both of the insurers and the insured.—*Stock Brokers*, those who buy and sell stock for other persons.—*Army Brokers*, those who formerly acted between army agents, and individuals wishing to purchase, sell, or exchange commissions.—*Pawn Brokers*, those who lend money upon goods to necessitous people at a certain rate per month.

BRO'ME-GRASS (*Bot.*) the *Bromus* of Linnæus, a sort of grass much resembling the Oat, whence it has also been called Oat-Grass. The species are mostly annuals.

BROME'LIA (*Bot.*) a genus of plants named after Olaus Bromel, a Swede, Class 6 *Hexandria*, Order 1 *Monogynia*.
> *Generic Characters.* CAL. *perianth* three-cornered.—COR. *petals* three.—STAM. *filaments* six; *anthers* erect.—PIST. *germ* inferior; *style* simple; *stigma* obtuse.—PER. *berry* roundish.
> *Species.* The species are shrubs, and natives of South America, Jamaica, &c. as—*Bromelia ananas, Carduus Brasilianus*, &c. *Ananas acostæ ovatæ*, seu *aculeatus*, &c. *Anassa*, seu *Capa-Isiakka*, Ananas, or Pine-Apple.—*Bromelia pinguin, Ananas Americana*, &c. seu *Pinguin*, Pinguin, or Broad-leaved Wild Ananas.—*Bromelia Karatas*, seu *Karatas*, &c. Karatas, or Upright-leaved Wild Ananas.—*Bromelia acanga, Caraguata Mexocotl*, seu *Manguel*, &c. *Park. Theat. Bot.*; *Raii Hist. Plant.*; *Linn. Spec. Plant.*

BRO'MION (*Med.*) a plaister. *Paul Æginet.* l. 7, c. 9.

BRO'MUS (*Bot.*) βρῶμος, a herb described by Dioscorides as very much like the Ægilops in its drying quality. A decoction of this plant is recommended for worms in children. *Dioscor.* l. 4, c. 140; *Plin.* l. 18, c. 10; *Gal. de Simpl.* l. 6; *Oribas Med. Coll.* l. 11; *Aet. Tetrab.* I, serm. 1.

BROMUS, Brome Grass, *in the Linnean system*, a genus of plants, Class 3 *Triandria*, Order 1 *Digynia*.
> *Generic Characters.* CAL. glume many-flowered, bivalve; *valve* ovate.—COR. bivalve; *lower valve* obtuse; *upper valve* lanceolate; *awn* straight; *nectary* two-leaved; *leaflets* ovate.—STAM. *filaments* three, capillary; *anthers*

oblong.—Pist. *germ* turbinate; *styles* two; *stigmas* simple.—Per. *corolla* adhering; *seed* one, oblong.

Species. The species of this genus of Grasses are annuals, and classed by the older botanists under the *festuca.* J. Bauh. Hist. Plant.; C. Bauh. Pin.; Raii Hist. Plant.; Linn. Spec. Plant.

BRO'NCHANT (*Her.*) a French term in blazonry to signify surmounting, as when an escutcheon is strewed with fleurs de lis, and then *bronchant sur le tout,* i. e. over them all, stands a beast, or any thing else, which seems to cover them almost entirely.

BRON'CHIA (*Anat.*) βρόγχια was taken by Hippocrates for the Aorta; but the bronchia, or bronchi, are now the ramifications of the *Arteria aspera,* or Larynx. Hippocrat. de Anatom.; Gal. Exeg. Voc. Hippocrat.; Gorr. Def. Med.; Foes. Œconom. Hippocrat.

BRO'NCHIAL arteries (*Anat.*) branches of the Aorta given off from the chest.—*Bronchial Glands,* glands situated about the *Bronchia* and *Trachea.*

BRONCHOCE'LE (*Med.*) βρογχοκήλη, from βρόγχος, the windpipe, and κήλη, a tumour; a tumour in the neck, principally of women, called a Derby Neck, because the people in Derbyshire are mostly subject to it. It is also frequent in the vallies of the Alps, to which Juvenal alludes.
Juv. sat. 13, v. 162.

Quis tumidum guttur miratur in Alpibus?

Cels. l. 7, c. 13; Paul Æginet. l. 6, c. 38; Gorr. Def. Med.

BRO'NCHOS (*Med.*) the suppression of the voice from a catarrh.

BRONCHO'TOMY (*Surg.*) βρογχοτομία, from βρόγχος, and τέμνω, to cut; an operation of cutting open the windpipe in a membranaceous part, between two rings, for the purpose of preventing suffocation.

BRO'NCHUS (*Anat.*) βρόγχος, the whole *Arteria aspera,* or only the fauces.

BRONTE'UM (*Ant.*) βροντεῖον, from βροντή, thunder; a machine or engine used on the stage to represent thunder. Fest. de Verb. Signif.

BRO'NTIAS (*Min.*) a sort of precious stones supposed to fall with thunder. Plin. l. 37, c. 10.

BRONZE (*Met.*) a compound metal, two-thirds of which consists of copper, and one-third of brass.

BRO'NZITE (*Min.*) a species of stones of the Hornblende family.

BROOCH (*Mech.*) a collar of gold formerly worn about the necks of ladies; also an ornamental pin used in the same manner.

Brooch (*Paint.*) a painting all in one colour.

BROOK-LIME (*Bot.*) a sort of Water Speedwell.

BROOM (*Bot.*) a shrub; the *Genista* and *Spartum* of Linnæus.—African Broom, the *Aspalathus genistoides.*—Butcher's broom. [vide *Butcher*]

BROOM-LANDS (*Agric.*) lands that bear broom.

BROO'MING (*Mar.*) vide *Breaming.*

BRO'SIMUM (*Bot.*) from βρώσιμος, esculentus, a genus of plants, Class 22 *Dioecia,* Order 1 *Monandria.*
Generic Characters. Cal. *ament* common, globular.—Cor. none.—Stam. *filaments* solitary; *anthers* bilamellate.—Pist. *germ* ovate; *style* single; *stigmas* reflex.—Per. *berry* pedicelled; *seeds* solitary.

Species. The species are trees, as the—*Brosimum alicastrum et spurium.*

BROSSÆ'A (*Bot.*) a genus of plants named after Guy de la Brosse, intendant of the royal garden at Paris, Class 5 *Pentandria,* Order 1 *Monogynia.*
Generic Characters. Cal. *perianth* one-leaved.—Cor. monopetalous.—Stam. *Filaments* five.—Pist. *germ* pentacoccous; *style* subulate; *stigma* simple.—Per. *capsule* roundish; *seeds* very many.

Species. The only species is—*Brossæa coccinea,* a shrub, native of South America.

BRO'SSUS (*Archæol.*) bruised, or injured with wounds.

BROTHEL (*Archæol.*) or *bordel,* from the Italian *bordello,* a little house, was at length applied to a house of ill-fame, a stewhouse, of which there were some licensed in the reign of Henry VI, but they were put down in that of Henry VII.

BROUI'LLER (*Man.*) a French term for a horse that plunges, and is in disorder.

BROW (*Anat.*) the *Os Frontis,* or Forehead.

BROW-A'NTLER (*Sport.*) the first start that grows on a stag's head.

BROW-PO'ST (*Carpent.*) an athwart or cross-beam.

BROWA'LLIA (*Bot.*) a genus of plants named after Browallius, Bishop of Aboa, the defender of Linnæus, Class 14 *Didynamia,* Order 2 *Angiospermia.*
Generic Characters. Cal. *perianth* one-leaved.—Cor. monopetalous.—Stam. *filaments* four; *anthers* simple.—Pist. *germ* ovate; *style* filiform; *stigma* thick.—Per. *capsule* ovate; *seeds* numerous; *receptacle* compressed.

Species. The species are annuals, and natives of South America.

BROWN-BILL (*Mil.*) the ancient weapon of the English foot, resembling a battle-axe.

BROWNE'A (*Bot.*) a genus of plants named after Patrick Browne, M. D. and Historian of Jamaica, Class 16 *Monodelphia,* Order 4 *Decandria.*
Generic Characters. Cal. *perianth* one-leaved.—Cor. *outer* monopetalous; *inner* five-petalled.—Stam. *filaments* ten; *anthers* oblong.—Pist. *germ* oblong; *style* subulate; *stigma* obtuse.—Per. *legume* oblong; *seed* solitary.

Species. The species are shrubs.

BRO'WNISTS (*Ecc.*) a sect of independents who rejected both episcopacy and presbyterianism.

BROWZE (*Hort.*) or *browze-wood,* sprouts of trees that shoot forth early in the spring.

BRUCE'A (*Bot.*) a genus of plants named by Sir Jos. Banks after Bruce, the Abyssinian traveller, Class 22 *Dioecia,* Order 4 *Tetrandria.*
Generic Characters. Cal. *perianth* four-parted.—Cor. *petals* four.—Stam. *filaments* four; *anthers* roundish.—Pist. *germs* four; *styles* subulate; *stigmas* acute.—Per. four; *seeds* solitary.

Species. Plants of this genus are shrubs, and natives of the East Indies.

BRUCE'NA (*Archæol.*) briars, or bush-heath.

BRU'CHUS (*Ent.*) βρύχος, from βρύχω, to devour. A kind of locust or caterpillar, a genus of animals, Class *Insecta,* Order *Coleoptera.*
Generic Characters. Antenna filiform.—Feelers equal.—Lip pointed.

Species. The species of this genus are mostly small insects inhabiting the Indies and America. The *Bruchus granarius* is found among beans, vetches, &c.—*Bruchus seminarius* is smaller than the preceding, having the hinder thighs plain.—*Bruchus Bactris,* of a grey colour, is found in the nuts of the Palm of that name.

BRU'GBOTE (*Archæol.*) or *Bruch-bote.* [vide *Brigbote*]

BRUILLE'TUS (*Archæol.*) or *bruillus,* a copse or thicket.

BRUI'SE-WORT (*Bot.*) or *Soap-Wort,* a perennial, the *Saponaria* of Linnæus.

BRUMA'LIA (*Ant.*) a festival celebrated by the Romans in honour of Bacchus twice a year, i. e. on the twelfth of the calends of March, and the eighth of the calends of December. Suidas ascribes the institution of this festival to Romulus. Tertull. de Idol. c. 14; Auctor. Geopon. l. 1, c. 1; Gyrald. Syntag. Deor. l. 8.

BRUNE′LLA (*Bot.*) vide *Prunella*.

BRUNFE′LSIA (*Bot.*) a genus of plants named by Plumier after Brunfelsius, a monk, physician, and botanist of Mentz, Class 14 *Didynamia*, Order 2 *Angiospermia*.
Generic Characters. CAL. perianth one-leaved.—COR. one-petalled.—STAM. *filaments* four, very short; *anthers* oblong.—PIST. *germ* roundish; *style* filiform; *stigma* thickish.—PER. *capsule* one-celled; *seeds* very many.
Species. Plants of this tribe are shrubs, and natives of the East Indies.

BRU′NIA (*Bot.*) a genus of plants named after Cornelius Brun, a traveller, Class 5 *Pentandria*, Order 1 *Monogynia*.
Generic Characters. CAL. perianth common roundish; proper five-leaved.—COR. petals five.—STAM. *filaments* five; *anthers* ovate oblong.—PIST. *germ* very small; *style* simple; *stigma* obtuse.—PER. ....; *seed* .....; *receptacle* common, hairy.
Species. Plants of this genus are shrubs, and natives of Æthiopia, as—*Brunia lanuginosus, seu Tamariscus*, &c. —*Brunia abrotonoides, Levisanus Africanus, seu Erica capitata*, &c. &c.

BRU′NNERS GLANDS (*Anat.*) glands situated between the villous and cellular coat of the intestinal canal.

BRUNSFE′LSIA (*Bot.*) vide *Brunfelsia*.

BRUNSVY′GIA (*Bot.*) the *Amaryllis orientalis*.

BRU′NUS (*Med.*) a sort of *Erysypelas*.

BRU′SCUM (*Bot.*) a bunch or knob in a maple tree.

BRU′XUS (*Bot.*) the *Ruscus aculeatus* of Linnæus.

BRUSH (*Sport.*) the tail of a fox.

BRU′SH-WOOD (*Bot.*) rough, low, and shrubby thickets; also the wood cut from such places for fuel.

BRUSO′LES (*Cook.*) veal and other meats well seasoned and stewed between thin slices of bacon.

BRU′SULA (*Archæol.*) Brushwood.

BRUT (*Mech.*) French for any thing in the rough state, as stones from the quarry.

BRU′TA (*Zool.*) the second order of animals of the Class *Mammalia*, comprehending those animals which have no fore teeth in either jaw; *feet* with strong hoof-like nails, and a slow motion. The genera included in this order are as follow; namely, the—*Rhinoceros*, Brady, having a horn in the middle of its forehead.—*Bradypus*, Sloth—*Myrmecophaga*, Ant-eater.—*Platypus*, having a duck-shaped mouth.—*Manis—Sypus*, Armadillo.—*Sukotyro*, having a horn on each side near the nose.—*Elephas*, Elephant.—*Trichechus*, Morse.

BRUTE-WEIGHT (*Com.*) is when merchandizes are weighed with the cases, &c. in distinction from the *net weight*, when an allowance is made for the packages. This distinction is preserved in the laying on of duties.

BRU′TIA (*Chem.*) the most resinous kind of pitch.

BRUTI′NO (*Chem.*) Turpentine.

BRU′TOBON (*Med.*) a barbarous name for some Greek ointment. *Castell. Lex. Med.*

BRU′TUA (*Bot.*) the *Cissampelos pareira* of Linnæus.

BRUXANE′LLI (*Bot.*) a Malabar tree, the bark of which is diuretic.

BRY′A (*Bot.*) the *Amerymnum ebenus* of Linnæus.

BRYA′NTHA (*Bot.*) or *Bryanthus*, the *Andromeda bryantha* of Linnæus.

BRY′GMUS (*Med.*) βρυγμός, a grating noise made by the gnashing of the teeth.

BRY′ON (*Bot.*) βρύον, a moss growing on the bark of trees, which was used by Hippocrates as a cataplasm, and was reckoned very astringent. *Hippocrat. de Mul. Nat. &c.; Theophrast. Hist. Plant. l. 1, c. 1; Dioscor. l. 1, c. 20; Plin. l. 12, c. 23; Gal. de Meth. Med. l. 3.*—*Bryon thalassium*, Sea Moss. [vide *Alga*]

BRYO′NIA (*Bot.*) βρυωνία, a plant, so called because it bears a flower resembling βρύον, Moss. It is otherwise called *vitis albus*, because its leaves resemble the vine. This plant is of an exulcerating quality, and its root is purgative. *Dioscor. l. 4, c. 185; Plin. l. 23, c. 1; Gal de fac. Simpl. Med. l. 6, c. 34.*

BRYONIA, Bryony, *in the Linnean system*, a genus of plants, Class 21 *Monoecia*, Order 10 *Syngenesia*.
Generic Characters. For the male flower—CAL. *perianth* one-leaved.—COR. five-parted; *divisions* ovate.—STAM. *filaments* three, very short; *anthers* five. For the female flower—CAL. *perianth* as in the males.—COR. the same.—PIST. *germ* inferior; *style* trifid; *stigmas* emarginate.—PER. *berry* subglobular; *seeds* few.
Species. The species of this genus are shrubs, as the—*Bryonia alba*, Black-berried White Briony.—*Bryonia dioica*, Red-berried White Briony.

BRYO′PTERIS (*Bot.*) White Fern of the Oak.

BRY′THION (*Med.*) a malagma. *Paul. Æginet. l. 7, c. 18.*

BRY′TON (*Med.*) a kind of drink made of barley.

BU′BALUS (*Zool.*) βύβαλις, a wild ox or buffalo, native of Africa, the *Bos bubalus* of Linnæus. *Arist. Hist. Anim. l. 3, c. 6; Plin. l. 11, c. 38.*

BUBASTECO′RDIUM (*Bot.*) the *Artemisia angustifolia* of Linnæus.

BU′BBLES (*Phy.*) little round drops or vesicles filled with air, which rise on the surface of any fluid when it is agitated.

BUBBLES (*Com.*) any cheating projects by which the public are defrauded, as the South-Sea speculation, or the Stock-bubbles.

BU′BO (*Med.*) from βουβών, the groin; is the name of any tumor in the lymphatic glands, particularly in the groin or axilla. *Aret. de Caus. et Sign. l. 2, c. 3; Hippocrat. de Natur. Puer.; Gal. de Art. Cur. l. 2, c. 1; Oribas, l. 7, c. 31; Aet. Tetrab. 1, serm. 2, c. 103; Act. l. 2, c. 12; Actuar. de Meth. Med. l. 2, c. 12; Gorr. Def. Med.; Foes. Œconom. Hippocrat.* Buboes are now distinguished into mild, malignant, and venereal. *Heist. Chirur. l. 4, c. 7, 8, 9.*

BU′BON (*Bot.*) contracted from *bubonium*, a genus of plants, Class 5 *Pentandria*, Order 2 *Digynia*.
Generic Characters. CAL. *umbel* universal of ten rays; partial of fifteen; *perianth* five-toothed.—COR. *universal* uniform; *proper* of five petals.—STAM. *filaments* five; *anthers* simple.—PIST. *germ* ovate; *styles* two, setaceous.—PER. none; *fruit* ovate; *seeds* two, ovate.
Species. The species are mostly annuals or perennials, as—*Bubon Macedonicum, Apium Macedonicum, Daucus Macedonicus, seu Petroselinum Macedonicum, &c.* Macedonian Parsley.—*Bubon galbanum, seu Anisum Africanum*, &c. Lovage-leaved Bubon, from which the gum called Galbanum is procured. These are annuals; but the *Bubon rigidum* is a low perennial. *J. Bauh. Hist. Plant.; Park. Theat. Botan.; Raii Hist. Plant.*

BUBO′NIUM (*Bot.*) βουβώνιον, a plant, so called from its supposed efficacy in curing buboes. It is the same as *Aster Atticus*. *Dioscor. l. 4, c. 120; Plin. l. 27, c. 5.*

BUBONOCE′LE (*Med.*) βουβωνοκήλη, from βουβών, the groin, and κήλη, a tumor; the Inguinal Hernia, or rupture of the groin, caused by the descent of the *epiploon*, or intestines; i. e. when the bowels protrude at the abdominal ring. While the intestine continues above the groin it is called Bubonocele, but when it descends into the *scrotum* it is called Enterocele. *Cels. l. 7, c. 19; Gal. de Tum. præt. Nat. c. 19; Paul. Æginet. l. 3, c. 53; Gorr. Def. Med.*

BUBU′LCA (*Ich.*) a small river fish, of a silver colour, the *Sarracenia flava*, of Linnæus.

BUCANEPHY′LLUM (*Bot.*) the *Sarracenia purpurea et flava* of Linnæus.

BUCA′RDIA (*Min.*) a stone shaped like the heart of an ox, from βοῦς, an ox, and καρδία, the heart.

BUCCA (*Anat.*) γναθός, that part which lies under the ball of the cheek. *Gal. Comm. 2 in Hippocrat. de Art.; Gorr. Def. Med.; Foes. Œconom. Hippocrat.*

BUCCACRA'TON (*Ant.*) βυκκάκρατον, a morsel of bread sopped in wine, which served in former times for a breakfast.

BUCCANAL-GLA'NDS (*Anat.*) the small glands of the mouth under the cheek, which assist in secreting the saliva.

BUCCANEE'RS (*Mar.*) a name for the pirates of all nations who used to make war on the Spaniards in their West-India possessions.

BUCCE'A (*Med.*) or *buccella*, a Græco-Latin word for a mouthful; it is used by Paracelsus for a polypus of the nose. *Par. de Apostem.* c. 20.

BUCCELA'TION (*Med.*) from *buccella*, a method of stopping an hæmorrhage by applying pieces of lint to the vein or artery.

BUCCE'LATON (*Med.*) βυκκίλατον, a purging medicine. *Act. Tetrab.* 1, serm. 3, c. 100; *Paul. Æginet.* l. 7, c. 5.

BUCCELLARII (*Archæol.*) the emperor's guards at the court of Byzantium, so called, as is supposed, because they acted as sutlers, and distributed the Buccellatum, or camp-bread, to the soldiers. *Vopisc. in Aurel.*; *Ammian. Marcell.* l. 17, c. 8; *Idac. Chron. Famil.*; *Constantin. Porphyreg.* περὶ Θμ.

BUCCELLA'TUM (*Archæol.*) Biscuit-bread eaten by soldiers and sailors. [vide *Buccellarii*]

BU'CCINA (*Ant.*) a military instrument, called by Festus a crooked horn.

BUCCINA'TOR (*Ant.*) a trumpeter. *Cæs. de Bell. Civ.* l. 2, c. 35.

BUCCINATOR (*Anat.*) a muscle of the cheek, so called from its office of forcing out the breath.

BU'CCINUM (*Con.*) the Whelk, a genus of animals, Class *Vermes*, Order *Testacea*.
Generic Character. Animal a limax or slug.—Shell univalve, spiral.—Aperture ovate, ending in a short canal.
Species. The principal species are the—*Buccinum lapillus*, the Massy Whelk, which yields a fine purple dye.—*Buccinum perdix*, the shell inflated.—*Buccinum bilineatum*, &c.

BUCCO (*Orn.*) Barbet, a genus of birds, of the Order *Picæ*.
Generic Character. Beak strong, pointed.—Nostrils covered with strong bristles.—Feet formed for swimming.
Species. The principal species are the—*Bucco elegans*, in French *le beau Tamatia*, Beautiful Barbet. — *Bucco Philippensis*, in French *le Barbu à gorge jaune*, Yellow-throated Barbet.—*Bucco Africanus*, in French *le bourroudriou*, African Cuckoo, or Barbet.—*Bucco Cayanensis*, in French *le Tamatia à tête et gorge rouges*, Cayenne or Black Barbet, &c.

BU'CCULA (*Ant.*) that part of the helmet which covered the cheeks on each side. *Liv.* l. 44, c. 34; *Turneb. Adv.* l. 9, c. 16.

BUCENTAU'R (*Mar.*) the name of the large vessel which the Venetians formerly used in the ceremony of espousing the sea.

BUCE'PHALON (*Bot.*) the *Trophis Americana* of Linnæus.

BUCEPHALO'PHORUS (*Bot.*) a species of the *Rumex* of Linnæus.

BU'CERAS (*Bot.*) the same as the *Bucida*.

BU'CEROS (*Orn.*) Horn-bill, a genus of birds of the Order *Picæ*.
Generic Character. Bill very large and furnished with a large appendix on the upper mandible.—Eyelids strongly ciliated.—Tongue very short.—Legs short and strong.
Species. The principal species are the—*Buceros rhinoceros*, in French *le Calao rhinoceros*, Rhinoceros Bird, or Rhinoceros Hornbill.—*Buceros monoceros*, in French *le Calao unicorne*, Pied Hornbill.—*Buceros bicornis*, Bifid Casked Hornbill.—*Buceros Abyssinicus*, seu *Abba Gumba*, Abyssinian Hornbill.—*Buceros plicatus*, Indian Raven, or Wreathed Hornbill, &c.

BUCHNE'RA (*Bot.*) a genus of plants, (called after Buchner, a German botanist), Class 14 *Didynamia*, Order 2 *Angiospermia*.
Generic Character. CAL. *perianth* one-leaved. — COR. monopetalous.—STAM. *filaments* four; *anthers* oblong.—PIST. *germ* ovate; *style* filiform; *stigma* obtuse —PER. *capsule* acuminate; *seeds* numerous; *receptacle* fastened to the middle of the partition.
Species. The species are shrubs, and natives of America and the Cape of Good Hope, &c.

BUCI'DA (*Bot.*) a genus of plants, Class 10 *Decandria*, Order 1 *Monogynia*.
Generic Characters. CAL. *perianth* one-leaved.—COR. none.—STAM. *filaments* ten; *anthers* cordate.—PIST. *germ* inferior; *style* filiform; *stigma* obtuse.—PER. *berry* dry ovate; *seed* one.
Species. The single species is the *Bucida buceras*.

BUCK (*Zool.*) signifies either, generally, the same as the Fallow Deer, the *Cervus dama* of Linnæus; or it is the male of this tribe, in distinction from the Doe, or female.

BUCK *of the first head* (*Sport.*) a buck in the fifth year, in distinction from a Great Buck, i. e. one in the sixth year.

BUCK (*Her.*) This animal is represented in coat armour mostly tripping; as, "He beareth *gules* three bucks tripping, *argent*, attired *or*; by the name of *Row*." The buck's head is also a bearing in coats of arms.

BUCK (*Chem.*) a lye made made of ashes and the lather of soap.

TO BUCK (*Min.*) to pound the ore on iron plates to the consistency of gravel.

BU'CK-BASKET (*Mech.*) a basket in which foul clothes used to be carried.

BUCK-BEAN (*Bot.*) a perennial, the *Menyanthes* of Linnæus.—*Buck-thorn*, a shrub, the *Rhamnus* of Linnæus. The principal species is the Purging Buckthorn, *Rhamnus catharticus*, which grows to the height of fourteen feet.—*Buck-Wheat*, otherwise called Brank, or Crap, an annual, the *Polygonum fagopyrum*, which is cultivated as excellent food for swine and poultry.—*Buckmast*, the mast of the beech-tree.

BU'CK-STALL (*Sport.*) a toil for taking deer, which, by the statute 19 H. 7, c. 11, is not to be kept by any person that hath not a park of his own.

BU'CKET (*Mech.*) a kind of pail made of leather, and commonly used for carrying water in quenching fire. Other sorts are made of wood, for drawing water out of a well.

BUCKET (*Her.*) the well-bucket is occasionally used as a bearing in coats of arms.

BUCKET-ROPE (*Mar.*) a rope fastened to the bucket for drawing water up the sides of a ship.

BU'CKLE (*Her.*) the buckle was anciently worn by persons of repute and honour, on their military belts and girdles; wherefore it is an ancient and honourable bearing. It is necessary, however, to describe the shape of the buckle, whether it be round, oval, square, &c. as, "He beareth *sable* a chevron between three oval buckles *argent*, by the name of *Mallet*."

BUCKLE *of beef* (*Cook.*) a piece cut off from the sirloin.

BU'CKLER (*Ant.*) vide *Militia*.

BUCKLER (*Mil.*) an ancient piece of defensive armour made of wicker-work, and worn on the arm. It varied in shape, being round, oval, or square.

BUCKLER-MU'STARD (*Bot.*) an annual, the *Biscutella* of Linnæus.

BU'CKLERS (*Mar.*) two pieces of wood fitted together to stop the hawser-holes, leaving only sufficient space between them for the cable to pass. They serve to prevent the ship taking in much water in a heavy sea.

BU'CKRAM (*Com.*) a sort of cloth stiffened.

BUCK'S HEAD (*Her.*) a bearing occasionally in coats of arms

BUCK'S-HORN PLANTAIN (*Bot.*) an annual, the *Plantago coronopus* of Linnæus.

BUCK-THORN (*Bot.*) vide *Buck*.

BUCO'LICS (*Poet.*) a name for pastoral poems, particularly applied to the pastorals of Virgil.

BUCRA'NION (*Bot.*) Snap Dragon. [vide *Antirrhinum*.]

BUD (*Bot.*) *gemma*, that part of a plant which contains the embryo of the leaves, flowers, &c. for which it is an *hybernaculum*, or Winter Receptacle in cold climates. Buds vary as to their being Leafbearing, *foliaris*, as in Alder; Leaf and Flower bearing, *foliaris et florifera*, as in Poplar, Willow, Ash, &c.: Leaf and Flower bearing together, *communis*, as in most flowers; Leaf, and Male Flower bearing, &c.

Buds, as to their foliation or opening, are—Involute, *involutæ*, when the edges of the leaves are turned in, as in *Humulus lupulus*, the Hop. (fig. 1).—Revolute, *revolutæ*, when the edges of the leaves are rolled outwards, as in the Willows, (fig. 2).—Obvolute, when two simply closed leaves embrace each other, as in *Salvia officinalis*, Sage, (fig. 3)—Convolute, *convolutæ*, when the leaves are rolled up spirally, as in fig. 4.—Riding, *equitantes*, when

several leaves lie parallel and embrace one another, as in *Syringa vulgaris*, the Lilac, (fig. 5).—Conduplicate, *conduplicatæ*, when the sides of the leaves lie parallel to one another, as in *Fagus sylvatica*, the Beech, (fig. 6). —Plaited, *plicatæ*, when the leaves are regularly folded, as in *Betula alba*, the Birch, (fig. 7).—Bent down, *reclinatæ*, when the points of the young leaves hang down. —Circinal, *circinatæ*, when the whole leaf is rolled up, as in the *Filices*.

As to their position they are simple, aggregate, sessile, &c.

BU'DDLE (*Min.*) a frame to receive the ore after it is separated from its coarsest parts.

TO BUDDLE (*Min.*) to wash and cleanse the *Lapis calaminaris*, or stones in general.

BUDDLE'A (*Bot.*) a genus of plants, (called after Adam Buddle, a botanist,) Class 4 *Tetandria*, Order 1 *Monogynia*.
Generic Character. CAL. *perianth* very small.—COR. *monopetalous*, bell-form, four-cleft.—STAM. *filaments* four; *anthers* very short.—PIST. *germ* ovate; *style* simple; *stigma* obtuse.—PER. *capsule* ovate; *seeds* numerous.
Species. The species are shrubs, and natives of Jamaica.

BU'DGE-BARREL (*Mar.*) a small tin barrel to hold gunpowder, having a case or purse made of leather covering the head, to hinder the powder from taking fire.

BUDGE BA'CHELORS (*Polit.*) a company of poor old men clothed in long gowns lined with lamb's fur, who attend on the Lord Mayor at the solemnity of the public show on the first day that he enters upon his office.

BU'DGET (*Polit.*) the statement made by the minister in the House of Commons respecting the finances.

BUFF (*Mech.*) or buffskin: 1. A sort of thick tanned leather, prepared from the skin of the Buffalo. 2. The skin of elks and oxen dressed in oil, and prepared in the same manner as that of the Buffalo.

BU'FFALO (*Zool.*) a wild ox, the *Bos bubalus* of Linnæus, which is a native of Africa, but very abundant in America. It has horns resupinated and flat on the foreside, a tough skin, black hair, small head, and no dewlap.

BUFFE'T (*Mech.*) a repository, or sort of cupboard for plate, glasses, china-ware, &c.

BU'FFLE (*Zool.*) the same as *Buffalo*.

BU'FFO (*Mus.*) Italian for a singer, or actor, when he takes the humorous part in comic operas, &c.

BUFFO'NIA (*Bot.*) a genus of plants called after the naturalist Buffon, Class 4 *Tetandria*, Order 2 *Digynia*.
Generic Character. CAL. *perianth* four-leaved.—COR. *petals* four.—STAM. *filaments* four; *anthers* twin.—PIST. *germ* ovate; *styles* two; *stigmas* simple.—PER. *capsule*; *seeds* two.
Species. The single species, *Buffonia tenuifolia Polygonum*, seu *Alsina polygonoides*, is an annual. *Raii Hist. Plant.*; *Lin. Spec. Plant.*

BU'FO (*Zool.*) the Toad, or *Rana bufo* of Linnæus.

BUFONI'TES (*Min.*) or *Bufonius Lapis*, Toadstone, the *Ichthyolithus bufonites* of Linnæus, is a sort of stone said to have been found in the head of a toad, which is, however, generally supposed to be the grinders of the seawolf.

BUG (*Ent.*) a disgusting insect that infests beds, the *Cimex lectularius* of Linnæus.

BUGA'NTIA (*Med.*) Chilblains.

BU'GGERY (*Law*) an unnatural offence, which was formerly punished with burning alive, but is now felony without benefit of clergy. *Rot. Parl.* 50 *Ed.* 1, 3. No. 58; 25 *H.* 8, *c.* 6; 3 *Inst.* 58.

BU'GLE (*Zool.*) from *bucula*, a young heifer; was formerly the name of a wild ox.

BUGLE (*Mech.*) a sort of glass bead of a shining black colour.

BUGLE (*Bot.*) a vulnerary plant and a biennial, the *Ajuga* of Linnæus.

BUGLE (*Her.*) a frequent bearing in coats of arms, which, when it is provided with a mouth and strings, &c. of a different tincture, is said to be garnished and furnished, as "He beareth *sable* a bugle-horn garnished and furnished *argent*." These were the arms of Bishop Burnet.

BUGLE (*Mil.*) the person who blows the bugle-horn in the British army.

BU'GLE-HORN (*Mus.*) a sort of horn so called, because it was made of the horn of the bugle; it was also called the Hunter's Horn, because it was also used in hunting. The bugle is now used in the British service.

BU'GLES (*Mil.*) *beugles* or *bibles*, engines used formerly for throwing large stones.

BU'GLOSS (*Bot.*) vide *Buglossum* — Viper's Bugloss, a shrub, the *Echium* of Linnæus.

BUGLO'SSUM (*Bot.*) Bugloss, a plant so called from βῦς, an ox, and γλῶσσα, a tongue, on account of the shape and roughness of its leaf. It resembles the Borrage in its qualities, being accounted a cordial, and good for hysterical disorders. The roots are very glutinous, and give a strong tincture of red to blue paper. *Dioscor.* l. 4, c. 128; *Plin.* l. 25, c. 8; *Gal. de Simpl.* l. 6.

Buglossum was reckoned a genus of plants by the earlier botanists, but in the Linnean System is classed under the *Anchusa*, *Asperugo*, *Borago*, *Lithospermum*, and *Lycopsis*. *Lobel Plant.* seu *Stirp. Hist.*; *J. Bauh. Hist. Plant.*; *C. Bauh. Pin. Ger. Herb.*; *Park. Theat. Bot.*; *Raii Hist. Plant.*; *Tournef. Inst.*; *Boerhaav. Ind.*

BUGO'NES (*Zool.*) from βῦς, an ox, and γίνομαι, to be generated; a name given by the ancients to bees, which were supposed to be bred from the putrefaction of an ox.

BU'GULA (*Bot.*) the same as the *Ajuga*.

BU'ILDING is the art of raising buildings according to given designs, which may be called Practical Architecture. [vide *Architecture*] Buildings are distinguished according to their general structure as follow, namely—*Regular building*, one whose plan is square, its opposite sides equal, and disposed with symmetry.—*Irregular building*, that which is not contained within equal and parallel lines, or one whose parts have not a just relation the one to the other in the elevation,—*Insulated building*, one which is not attached to any other, as the Monument.—*Engaged building*, one encompassed having no front towards any street, or public place, nor communication but by a narrow passage.—*Interred* or *sunk building*, the area of which is below the level or surface of the place on which it stands, and of which the lowest courses of stones are hidden.

Buildings as to their particular structure and use are distinguished into Houses, Churches, Theatres, Bridges, Monuments, and the like.

Houses. Houses are places of residence which are distinguished, according to the condition of the inhabitant, into —*Palaces*, which are royal residences.—*Castles*, which are fortified residences, formerly occupied by the nobility.—*Country seats*, or family mansions, the residences of the higher classes.—*Dwelling-houses*, which are occupied by the middle or inferior classes. Houses are divided by walls into distinct rooms, called, according to their use, *parlour, dining-room, chamber,* or *bed-chamber,* &c. The ceiling, or floor, forms other divisions, called *floors*, or *stories*. That which lies the lowest is called the *ground-floor*, or *basement-story;* those which rise above it are called first, second, third floor, or story. All the rooms taken collectively which serve for a residence are called an *apartment*, and when they are on the same floor without a passage between them, they are called *a suite of apartments*.

Churches. A church is an edifice erected for the purpose of public worship, consisting of a *nave* or body, two *aisles* or wings, a *choir, organ-loft,* &c. Churches are distinguished ecclesiastically into *cathedral, metropolitan, parochial, patriarchal,* &c.; and as to their plan, into churches built *in a Greek cross, in a Latin cross, in a Rotunda,* &c.

Theatres. A theatre is an edifice erected for public exhibitions, consisting of a *stage, scenes, orchestra, pit, boxes, galleries,* &c.

Bridges. A bridge is a particular structure raised over a river, canal, or other piece of water, which consists of *piers, arches, imposts, abutments,* &c. [vide *Bridge*, and plate 29, fig. 5]

Monuments. A monument is any structure raised by way of a memorial; this is commonly in the form of a *pillar*, or a *pilaster*, and denominated an *obelisk*. [vide *Architecture* and *Column*]

The two principal arts employed in erecting any building are carpentry and masonry.

Carpentry, and the tools belonging thereto.

Carpentry comprehends all works done in wood, and is either *house-carpentry*, that is, the large rough work, or *joinery*, which is light, ornamental, and more artful. *Timber*, i. e. the wood employed in building, is cut out of the tree into *deals*, which are afterwards broken or cut down into *boards*, or *leaves*, of different thicknesses, so that deals will always have one cut less than there are leaves. When the leaves are thinner than half an inch, the deal will divide into five or more parts, called *five-cut stuff;* and in this manner deals are distinguished according to the number of cuts, and the boards are denominated one inch, one inch and a half, &c. Boards, as to their dimensions in breadth and thickness, are termed *scantlings*. The workman fits the wood for his use by *planing, grooving, rabbetting, mortising,* and *tennanting*. [vide *Planing*, &c.] The making a piece of wood with a straight edge is called *shooting*, and the edge so made is called the *shot*. Boards are joined together by nails and pins, or by the mortise and tennon, or by indenting them together, which is called *dovetailing*. When they are glued together, and a piece of wood called a *clamp* is nailed across, they are said to be *clamped*. The cutting a piece of wood with a bevel, or sloping edge, is called *bevelling*.

When the spot of ground is marked out on which a house is to be built, which is called the *ground-plot*, the carpenters make a frame of the timber-work, which is called a *carcase*. The *carcase*, or *naked flooring*, consists of three tier of beams. Those of the upper tier are called *bridges*, or bridging-joists, those of the lower the ceiling-joists, and those of the middle, which support the other two, the *binding-joists*. Another set of large beams, which shorten the bearings of the others, are called *girders*. [pl. 29, fig. 1, 2] The *carcase roofing* consists also of three tiers of timbers; the first tier, which is inclined to the *pitch* of the roof, is supported by other timbers, which together make vertical frames called *trusses;* the inclined timbers of which, in the upper part of the truss, are called *principal rafters;* these support what are called *purlins*, and by the latter are supported the timbers of the last tier, which are called *bridgings*. The principal rafters rest upon an horizontal piece of timber on the wall-head, called the *raising* or *wall-plate*. *Roofs* are of different forms, the simplest of which is the *shed-roof*, or *lean-to*, otherwise called a *pent-roof*. When the four sides of the roof are formed by inclined planes it is said to be *hipped*, and the inclined ridges springing from the angles of the walls are called the *hips*. There are also curvilineal roofs of different descriptions. [vide *Roof*, and Plate 29, fig. 3] After the chimneys are completed by the bricklayer, then the carpenter proceeds to bring up the stairs and staircases, to hang the doors, &c. *Stairs* are either straight, which ascend in a straight line, or they are *winding*, when they turn round an upright post, called a *newel*, or a circular well-hole. The steps next to the well-hole are narrower than the rest, and are termed *winders*, in distinction from the *flyers*, which continue of the same breadth. A series, or number of flyers connected together, is termed a *flight of steps*. [vide *Stairs*] The joiner's works in the interior are very various, as in the *casements, sashes,* and *sash-frames* to windows, *pannels* to doors, *boxing of windows, nosings* to stairs, *brackets, wainscotting, mouldings* of different kinds, *rails, balusters, centerings* to the arches, &c. of which more may be found in their respective places. The tools used by carpenters and joiners are *planes* of different kinds for smoothing wood. [vide *Plane*] Those used for boring holes are, the *stock*, with *bits* of different sizes, *gimblets*, and *brad-awls*, [vide *Stock*, &c.] Those for parting the wood are *chisels* and *saws* of different kinds. [vide *Chisel* and *Saw*] Those for regulating the form are, the *square* for trying right angles, the *bevel* for oblique angles, which, when it is stationary, is called a *joint-hook;* the *gauge* for reducing a piece of stuff to a parallel breadth; the *straight edge*, a slip of wood straightened at one edge for making straight edges.

Masonry, and the tools belonging thereto.

Masonry comprehends all works done with stones, bricks, and mortar; but, in a particular sense, masonry is confined to the preparing of stones so as to tooth or indent them into each other, in distinction from the bricklayer, who builds with bricks. The walls of a building are raised by either of these artificers, but the chimneys are the particular work of the latter. [vide *Wall* and *Chimney*] The materials of the mason are *stone*, *marble*, and *cement;* those of the bricklayer are *bricks, tiles, mortar, laths, nails,* and *tile-pins;* to which may be added, *plaster* and *slates*. [vide *Stone, Marble,* &c.] The tools belonging to this art are, the *trowel*, the *hammer*, the *plumb-rule*, the *level*, the *raker, hod, rammer, crow, pickaxe, banker, camber-slip, rubbing-stone, scribe, templet, float-stone, lathing-hammer, boss, pantile-strike, scurbage;* besides which the plasterers have *stopping and picking out tools, straight-edges, moulds,* and the like.

Explanation of the Plate (29.)

Fig. 1. *A Floor, with the names of each member.*—1. The Bres-summer. 2. The Summer. 3. Girders framed into the summer. 4. Spaces between the joists. 5. Joists. 6. Trimmers for the chimney way. 7. Trimmers for the staircase, or well-hole.

Fig. 2. *Carcase of a House.*—A A. The breadth of the house, cantilevers, cornices, and eaves. A B. The length of the raftings and furrings, which ought to be three-fourths the breadth of the house. 1. Ground-plate. 2. Girder, or binding interduce. 3. Beam to the roof, or girder to the garret floor. 4. Principal post, and upright brick wall. 5. Braces. 6. Quarters. 7. Interduces. 8. Prick-post, or window-post. 9. Jaumes, or door-posts. 10. King-piece, or joggle-piece. 11. Struts. 12. Collar-beam, strut-beam, wind-beam, or top-beam. 13. Door-head. 14. Principal rafters. 15. Furrings and shreddings. 16. Ends of the lintels and pieces. 17. Bedding, moulding of the cornice over the windows, and space between. 18. Knees of the principal rafters, which are to be of one piece. 19. Purline mortices.

Fig. 3. *A Hip Roof.*—1. The wall. 2. Lintels. 3. Dragon-beam for the hip to stand on. 4. Beam on summer, wherein the dragon-beams are framed. 5. King-piece, or crown-post. 6. Struts, or braces from the crown-post to the hip-rafter. 7. Hips which make the angle equal to the breadth of the house. 8. Hips which make the angle in the diagonal lines from corner to corner.

Fig. 4. *Centering for an arch of a bridge, with the names of the timbers, &c.*—1. Timbers which support the centering. 2, 3. Upper and lower striking plates, cased with copper. 4. Wedge between striking-plates for lowering the centre. 5. Double trussing pieces, to confine braces. 6. Apron-pieces, to strengthen the rib of centre. 7. Bridgings, to keep them at equal distances. 8. Small braces, to confine the ribs tight. 9. Iron straps bolted to trussing pieces and apron pieces. 10. Ends of beams at the feet of truss-pieces. 11. Principal braces.

Fig. 5. *A Bridge, and its several parts.*—C. the Crown. B K. Part of the Extrados. B L. Part of the Intrados. B. The Keystone, or Middle Voussoir. A M. the Span. A. M. The Imposts. E D F G. the Pier. O B. The Pitch, or perpendicular height. H I. The Spandrels.

BUENDE'S (*Mil.*) French for the shield which the Turks and Tartars use when they fight with sabres.

BU'LAFO (*Mus.*) a musical instrument among the Negroes of Guinea, consisting of pipes of wood tied with thongs of leather.

BULA'PATHON (*Bot.*) the herb Patience, or Great Dock.

BULB (*Bot.*) βολβὸς, so called, according to Eustathius, because γῆθεν βάλλεται βια, i. e. is sent out of the ground with force, as it were; an hybernacle or winter receptacle of a plant, composed of the bases of past leaves, and placed immediately upon the root. Bulbs are distinguished into—Scaly, *squamatus*, as in the Lily.—Solid, *solidus*, as in the Tulip.—Coated, *tunicatus*, as in the Onion.—Jointed, as in *Lathræa, Martynia, Adoxa.* [vide *Botany*]

BULB (*Mech.*) the globular part in the tube of a thermometer.

BULBI'FEROUS (*Bot.*) an epithet for plants which are succeeded by bulbs instead of seeds, as the *Allium*, &c.

BU'LBINA (*Bot.*) or *bulbine*, βολβίνη, a bulbous plant having leek blades and a red bulb. Pliny reckons it good for fresh wounds. *Theophrast. Hist. Plant.* l. 7, c. 13; *Plin.* l. 20, c. 9; *Athen.* l. 2.

BU'LBINE (*Bot.*) the same as *Anthericum*.

BULBOCA'STANUM (*Bot.*) the same as *Bunium.*

BULBOCO'DIUM (*Bot.*) a genus of plants, Class 6 *Hexandria*, Order 1 *Monogynia.*

Generic Character. CAL. none.—COR. hexapetalous; *claws* long; *border* erect.—STAM. *filaments* six, subulate; *anthers* incumbent.—PIST. *germ* ovate, subulate; *style* filiform; *stigmas* three.—PER. *capsule* triangular; *seeds* numerous.

Species. The single species is the *Bulbocodium*, seu *Colchicum vernum*, Spring-flowering Bulbocodium.

BULBOCODIUM is also the *Anthericum verotinum, et Græcum.*

BU'LBONACH (*Bot.*) the *Lunaria rediviva* of Linnæus.

BU'LBOUS PLANTS (*Bot.*) *bulbosæ*, plants growing from bulbs; the name of a Class of plants in the systems of Cæsalpinus and Ray.—*Bulbous* is also an epithet for roots that are solid and round, like bulbs, as that of the Turnip, *Ranunculus bulbosus*, &c.

BULBS (*Bot.*) a name formerly given to the round spired beard of flowers.

BU'LBUS *esculentus* (*Bot.*) βολβὸς ἐδώδιμος, the Esculent Bulb, a particular sort so denominated by the ancients, of which nothing certain is known at present, but it is supposed to be the *Cepa ascalonica. Diosc.* l. 2, c. 200; *Cels. de Re Med.* l. 2, c. 18; *Plin.* l. 19, c. 5; *Athen.* l. 2, c. 22; *Gal. de Simplic.* l. 6; *Paul Æginet.* l. 1, c. 76; *Salmas. de Homonym. Hyl. Jatr.* c. 114.—*Bulbus vomitorius*, βολβὸς ἐμετικος, a plant mentioned by Dioscorides to be emetic and diuretic. *Dioscor.* l. 2, c. 201. *Bulbus vomitorius* is called by Ray Musk-Grape-Flower, and in the Linnean system *Hyacinthus Moscari. Raii Hist. Plant.; Linn. Spec. Plant.*

BU'LGA (*Archæol.*) a budget, or coat of mail.

BULGE (*Mar.*) originally written *bilge*, from the Teutonic *Balg*, a bellow; a name for that part of a ship which bulges out at the floor-heads.—*Bulge-way*, a large piece, or large pieces of timber bolted together into one solid piece, which is placed under the bulge of a ship to support her when launching. The support for the bulge-ways to lie on is called the *ways.*

BULGE-WATER-TREE (*Bot.*) the *Geoffroya Jamaicensis* of Linnæus.

BU'LGED (*Mar.*) an epithet for a ship when she has struck off some of her timbers upon a rock or anchor, and when she springs a leak.

BULI'MIA (*Med.*) from βῦ, a particle denoting excess, and λιμός, hunger; voracity of appetite from the diseased state of the stomach. *Gal. Exeges. Vocal. Hip.; Gorr. Def. Med.; Foes. Œconom. Hippocrat.*

BULIMIA is ranked by Cullen as a genus of diseases, under the Class *Locales*, Order *Dysorexiæ.*

BULIMIA'SIS (*Med.*) vide *Bulimia.*

BULI'SMOS (*Med.*) vide *Bulimia.*

BULI'THOS (*Med.*) from βῦς, an ox, and λίθος, a stone; a concretion found in the kidneys and bladder of an ox.

BULK *of a ship* (*Mar.*) the whole cargo stowed in the hold; whence "To break *bulk*," is to take part of the cargo out of the ship's hold.—*Bulk Heads,* partitions built up in several parts of a ship, between two decks, either lengthways or across, to form and separate the other apartments.—*Bulk-head afore,* is the partition between the forecastle and gratings in the head.

BULL (*Zool.*) the male of Black Cattle, the female of which is called the cow: when the male is cut he is called an ox, which is the first species of the Bos, namely, the *Bos taurus* of Linnæus.

BULL (*Astron.*) a constellation. vide *Taurus.*

BULL (*Her.*) as a charge in coats of arms, denotes, according to Guillim, valour and magnanimity. It is mostly borne passant, as "He beareth on a fess *vert* a bull passant, *argent* armed *or*, by the name of Aldrich," father to Dr. Henry Aldrich, canon of Christ Church, Oxford.

BULL (*Ecc.*) *bulla*, a brief or mandate issued by the pope or bishop of Rome, which was so called from the *bulla* or seal of lead or gold which was affixed to it. These bulls are frequently mentioned in our statutes; by one of which, in the reign of Henry 8, they were made void. *Math. Par. Ann.* 1237, 25 *Ed.* 3; 28 *Hen.* 8, c. 16; 2 *P. & M.* c. 8; 18 *Eliz.* c. 2.

BULL *and boar* (*Law*) by the law of some places a parson may be obliged to keep a bull and a boar for the use of the parishioners, in consideration.

BULL *golden* (*Polit.*) a statute or ordnance made by the emperor Charles IV, in 1356, by which he regulated the manner of electing emperors of Germany.

BU'LLA (*Med.*) πομφόλυξ, a bubble, or any vesicle which arises from combustion, or other causes.

BULLA (*Ant.*) an ornament of gold or silver in the shape of a bulla, or bubble of water, which was worn about the neck or breast of the children of the nobility till the age of fourteen.

Propert. l. 4, eleg. 1, v. 132.

Mox ubi bulla rudi demissa est aurea collo.

Pers. sat. 5, v. 31.

Cum primum pavido custos mihi purpura cessit
Bullaque succinctus Laribus donata pependit.

They were sometimes presented on the birth day, according to Plautus.

Plaut. Rud. act 4, scen. 4, v. 127.

Et bulla aurea est, pater quam dedit mihi natali die.

In shape they were either round, as in the annexed figure, heart shaped, or ecliptical. *Ascon. in Cic. Verr.* act 1, c. 58; *Plin.* l. 23, c. 1; *Æl. Var. Hist.* l. 14, c. 34; *Fest. de Verb. Signif.*; *Macrob. Saturn.* l. 1, c. 6; *Schol. in Juven. Sat.*; *Isidor. Orig.* l. 19, c. 31; *Pigh. Annal.* l. 1, p. 44; *Augustin. apud Græv. Thes. Antiq. Roman.* tom. xi.; *Spon. Miscell. Erudit. Act.* sect. 9, p. 299.

BULLA (*Con.*) Dipper, a genus of testaceous animals, Class *Vermes*, Order *Testacea*.

Generic Character. Animal a Liman; *shell* univalve, convolute; *aperture* oblong; *pillar* oblique.

Species. Many of the species are found on the coast of Devonshire, Dorsetshire, &c. as the *Bulla plumula, hydatis, emarginata*, &c.

BULLACE (*Bot.*) a wild sort of plum, the *Prunus insitia* of Linnæus.

BULLARY (*Mech.*) a salt-house, salt-pit, or place where salt is made.

BULLATE (*Bot.*) *bullatus*, an epithet for a leaf; *folium bullatum*, a leaf having protuberances on its surface resembling blisters.

BULL-BEEF (*Cook.*) the flesh of a bull, which is the coarsest kind of beef.

BULL-COMBER (*Ent.*) a sort of beetle, the *Scarabæus tryphæus* of Linnæus.

BU'LL-DOG (*Sport.*) a sort of dog, of English breed, with pendulous lips, of a robust body, and the size of a wolf, so called from its property of attacking the bull; on which account it was formerly used in bull-baiting.—*Bull-feast*, or *Bull-fight*, an entertainment formerly frequent in Spain and Portugal, at which wild bulls are encountered by men on horseback, armed with lances.

BULLEN (*Agric.*) the stalks of hemp pitted.

BULLEN-NAILS (*Carpent.*) a sort of nails with round heads and short shanks, tinned and lacquered, which are used in the hangings of rooms.

BU'LLET (*Mil.*) a name for the leaden balls wherewith all kinds of small fire-arms are loaded. [vide *Ball*]

BULLETI'N (*Polit.*) any official account of public transactions, and the state of health of any members of the royal family, &c.

BULL-FINCH (*Orn.*) a small bird, the *Loxia pyrrhula* of Linnæus, of a cinereous colour, having its head and wings black, and coverts of the tail white. It frequents gardens in the spring, when it is very destructive to the fruit-trees; is easily tamed when young, and may be taught to whistle any tune.

BULL-FROG (*Zool.*) the *Rana catesbeiana*, a remarkable species of the frog in North America; so called because its voice resembles the distant lowing of an ox.

BULL-HEAD (*Ich.*) a sort of fish, the *Cottus* of Linnæus, having its head much broader than its body. It is without teeth, but the edges of its mouth are rough like a file.—Bull Trout, the *Salmo trutta* of Linnæus, a sort of salmon which seldom exceeds two feet in length. This fish inhabits Europe; and, like the rest of its tribe, ascends rivers periodically.

BULLIME'NTA (*Chem.*) chemical vessels such as they appear after scouring, that is, with glittering brightness.

BU'LLIMONY (*Husband.*) a mixture of several sorts of grain together, as peas, oats, vetches, &c.

BULLIO *salis* (*Archæol.*) a measure of salt as much as is made at one wealing or boiling, supposed to be twelve gallons. *Mon. Angl* tom. ii.

BU'LLION (*Min.*) in French *billon*, unwrought gold or silver, i. e. gold or silver in the mass or billet before it is wrought into coin. 9 *Ed.* 3, st. 2, c. 2.

BULLION *of copper* (*Mil.*) was set as an ornament on the breast plates and bridles of horses.

BU'LLOCK-SERGEANT (*Mil.*) a non-commissioned officer in India, who has the care and superintendance of the bullocks on the service.

BULLOSA *febris* (*Med.*) an epithet applied to the vesicular fever, because the skin is covered with little vesicles or blisters.

BULL-RUSH (*Bot.*) the *Scirpus lacustris* of Linnæus.

BULLS-E'YE (*Archer.*) a mark in the shape of a bull's eye, at which archers used to shoot by way of exercise; the centre of a target.

BULLS-EYE (*Mar.*) a sort of small pulley in the form of a ring, having a hole in the middle to admit a rope.—*Bull's eye* is also the name given to the patent reflectors set in to the posts or decks.

BULLS-HE'AD (*Her.*) the bull's head is commonly represented in coats of arms as couped or erased.

BULLS-WO'RT (*Bot.*) or Bishop's Weed, an umbelliferous plant.

BU'LTED (*Husband.*) vide *Bolted*.

BU'LTER (*Husband.*) the bran or refuse of meal after it is dressed.

BULTER (*Husband.*) vide *Bolter*.

BU'LWARK (*Archæol.*) the ancient name for a bastion or rampart.

BUMA'LDA (*Bot.*) a genus of plants, Class 5 *Pentandria*, Order 2 *Digynia*.

Generic Character. CAL. *perianth* one-leafed.—COR. five-petalled.—STAM. *filaments* five; *anthers* twin.—PIST. *germ* superior; *styles* two; *stigmas* simple.—PER. a two-celled capsule.

Species. The only species is the *Bumalda trifolia*, a shrub, native of Japan.

BU'MBOAT (*Mar.*) a sort of wherry used in, and about harbours, to carry provisions, &c. for sale to ships lying at a distance from the shore.

BUME'LIA (*Bot.*) Βυμελία, the Great Ash, so called from the particle βυ, signifying excess, and μελία, an ash. *Theoph.* l. 3, c. 11; *Plin.* l. 6, c. 13; *Plut.* sympos. 8, quæst. 6.

BUMELIA, in the Linnean system, a genus of plants, Class 5 *Pentandria*, Order 1 *Monogynia*.

Generic Character. CAL. *perianth* five-leaved.—COR. one-petalled.—STAM. *filaments* five; *anthers* ovate.—PIST. *germ* superior; *style* thick; *stigma* obtuse.—PER. *drupe* oval; *seed* a single kernel.

Species. The plants of this tribe are all trees or shrubs.

BUMICE'LLI (*Theol.*) a sect of Mahometans, who deal much in sorcery.

BU'MKIN (*Mar.*) or *boomkin*, a short bow, or beam of timber, projecting from each bow of a ship to extend the helm, or lower edge of the foresail.—*Bumkin of a boat*, a small outrigger over the stern usually serving to extend the mizen.

BUNCH (*Bot.*) vide *Racemus*.

BUNCHED (*Bot.*) an epithet for seedpods or roots which stand out in knobs.

BUNDLE (*Com.*) a certain quantity of particular commodities.

BUNDLE (*Bot.*) vide *Fasciculum*.

BUNDLE *pillar* (*Archit.*) a sort of Gothic pillar consisting of several smaller pillars in a cluster.

BUNDLES (*Archæol.*) a sort of records of Chancery lying in the office of the Rolls.

BUNGALOW (*Mech.*) an Indian name for a house with a thatched roof such as is peculiar to the country.

BUNIAS (*Bot.*) βυνιάς, a plant, the seed of which, according to Dioscorides, is an antidote against poisons. *Dioscor.* l. 2, c. 136.

BUNIAS, *in the Linnean system*, a genus of plants, Class 15 Tetradynamia, Order 2 Siliquosa, the *Erucago* of Tournefort.

 Generic Characters. CAL. *perianth* four-leaved — COR. tetrapetalous.—STAM. *filaments* six; *anthers* erect bifid. —PIST. *germ* oblong; *style* none; *stigma* obtuse.—PER. *silicle* irregular; *seeds* few.

 Species. The species are mostly annuals, as the *Bunias cornuta*, seu *Bursa Pastoris*, Horned Bunias.—*Bunias spinosa*, *Brassica spinosa* seu *crambe*, Thorny Bunias.—*Bunias Erucago*, *Myagrum*, *Sinapi*, seu *Eruca*, Prickly-podded Bunias.—*Bunias cakile*, *Cakile*, seu *Raphanus*, Sea Rocket. *J. Bauh. Hist. Plant.*; *Ger. Herb.*; *Park. Theat.*; *Raii Hist. Plant.*; *Linn. Spec. Plant.*

BUNI'TES *Vinum* (*Med.*) βυνίτης οἶνος, a wine made of Bunium, which was reckoned good for disorders in the stomach. *Dioscor.* l. 2, c. 146; *Plin.* l. 20.

BU'NIUM (*Bot.*) βύνιον, a plant which, according to the description of Dioscorides, resembled *Anethum*; but Pliny speaks of it as a sort of Napus. *Dioscorides*, l. 4, c. 124; *Plin.* l. 20, c. 4.

BUNIUM, *in the Linnean system*, a genus of plants, Class 5 Pentandria, Order 2 Digynia.

 Generic Character. CAL. *umbel* both universal and partial; *involucre* both universal and partial.—COR. universal and proper.—STAM. *filaments* five; *anthers* simple.—PIST. *germ* oblong; *stigmas* obtuse.—PER. none; *fruit* ovate; *seeds* two, ovate.

 Species. The only species is the *Bunium bulbocastanum*, seu *Nucula terrestris*.

BUNT (*Mar.*) in French *fonds des voiles*, the middle part, or cavity of the square sails, as the main-sail, fore-sail, &c.—*Bunt-line-cloth*, the linen that is sewed up the sail in the direction of the bunt-lines to prevent the sail from being chafed. —*Bunt-lines*, in French *cargues fonds*, ropes fastened to cringles on the bottoms of the square sails to draw them up to their yards.

BU'NTINE (*Mar.*) or *Bunting*, the thin woollen stuff of which the colours, flags, and signals of a ship are usually made.

BUNTING (*Orn.*) a bird, the *Emberiza* of Linnæus, remarkable for the shape of its bill, the sides of the upper mandible forming a sharp angle bending inwards towards the lower.

BUONO-CA'RDO (*Mus.*) Italian for an instrument resembling a spinnet.—*Buono-mano*, Italian for a good hand, implying a free power of exertion.

BUOY (*Mar.*) a sort of close cask, or block of wood, fastened by a rope to the anchor to point out its situation, that the ship may not come too near it so as to entangle her cables about the stock or flook. The *slings of the buoy* are the ropes fastened about it. " To stream the *buoy*," to let it fall from the ships into the water preparatory to letting go the anchor.—*Buoy-rope*, the rope which fastens the buoy to the anchor. Buoys are of different kinds, as—*Cable-buoys*, common casks employed to buoy up the cables in rocky anchorage.—*Can-buoys*, in the form of a cone, used to point out sand-banks, &c.—*Nun-buoys*, shaped like the middle *frustrum* of two cones. —*Wooden-buoy*, a solid piece of light timber with a hole pierced through the end for the reception of a rope.

BUPE'INA (*Med.*) vide *Bulimia*.

BU'PHAGA (*Or.*) Beef-Eater, a genus of birds, Order Picæ, having the bill straight, and legs fitted for walking. They are a solitary sort of bird, living mostly on the *larvæ* of the gad-fly, which they peck out of the skins of oxen and other animals. The only species is the *Buphaga Africanus*.

BU'PHAGOS (*Med.*) an antidote mentioned by Marcellinus.

BUPHO'NIA (*Ant.*) vide *Diipolea*.

BUPHTHA'LMUM (*Bot.*) βούφθαλμος, Ox-Eye, a plant; so called because its flowers resemble the eye of an ox. It is said to be aperitive and vulnerary. *Dioscor.* l. 3, c. 156; *Oribas. Med. Collect.* l. 15; *Aet. Tetrab.* l, serm. 1; *Paul. Æginet.* l. 7, c. 3.

BUPTHALMUM, *in the Linnean system*, a genus of plants, Class 19 Syngenesia, Order 2 Polygamia superflua.

 Generic Character. CAL. *common* imbricate.—COR. both compound and proper.—STAM. *Of the hermaphrodite.*—*Filaments* five; *anther* tubular.—PIST. *Of the hermaphrodite.*—*Germ* ovate; *style* filiform; *stigmas* thickish. *Of the female.*—*Germ* ancipital; *style* filiform, &c.

 Species. These plants are either annuals or shrubs. Of the first kind are the—*Buphthalmum spinosum*, *Aster lutens*, seu *Aster Alticus*, Prickly Ox-Eye.—*Bupthalmum aquaticum*, Sweet-scented Ox-Eye, &c. Of the latter kind are the—*Buphthalmum frutescens*, *Astericus*, *Corona Solis*, seu *Chrysanthemum*, Shrubby Ox-Eye.—*Buphthalmum salicifolium*, *Asteroides*, seu *Conyza*, Willow-leaved Ox-Eye.—*Buphthalmum grandiflorum*, seu *Chrysanthemum*, Great-flowered Ox-Eye.—*Buphthalmum helianthoides*, *Helianthus*, *Silphium*, &c. Sunflower-leaved Ox-Eye. *Clus. Hist.*; *Prosp. Alpin. de Plant. Exot.*; *J. Bauh. Hist.*; *C. Bauh. Pin.*; *Ger. Herb.*; *Park. Theat.*; *Raii Hist. Plant.*; *Tournef. Inst.*; *Boerhaav. Ind.*; *Linn. Spec. Plant.*

BUPHTHA'LMUS (*Med.*) a diseased enlargement of the eye.

BUPHTHALMUS (*Bot.*) Houseleek.

BUPLEUROI'DES (*Bot.*) an evergreen, in the shape of the Bupleurum.

BUPLEU'RUM (*Bot.*) βούπλευρον, from βοῦς, an ox, and πλευρόν, a side, a plant; so called because it has large rib-like filaments on its leaves. It is reckoned aperitive and discutient. *Nicand. in Ther.*; *Plin.* l. 22, c. 22.

BUPLEURUM, *in the Linnean system*, a genus of plants, Class 5 Pentandria, Order 2 Digynia.

 Generic Characters. CAL. *umbel*, both universal and partial.—COR. both universal and proper.—STAM. *filaments* five; *anthers* roundish.—PIST. *germ* inferior; *styles* two reflected; *stigmas* very small.—PER. none; *fruit* roundish; *seeds* two.

 Species. The species are annuals or perennials. Of the first kind are the—*Bupleurum rotundifolium*, Common Thorough-wax.—*Bupleurum odontites*, Narrow-leaved Hare's Ear, &c. Of the latter kind is the—*Bupleurum stellatum*, Starry Hare's Ear.—*Bupleurum petræum*, seu *Sedum petræum*, Rock Hare's Ear.—*Bupleurum rigidum*, seu *Auricula leporis*, Stiff-leaved Hare's Ear. *Clus. Rar. Plant. Hist.*; *Dodon. Stirp. Pemptad.*; *J. Bauh.*; *C. Bauh. Pin.*; *Ger. Herb.*; *Park. Theat.*; *Raii Hist. Plant.*; *Tournef. Inst.*; *Boerhaav. Ind.*

BUPRE'STIS (*Ent.*) βούπρηστις, the Burn-Cow, an insect; so

BUR

called from βῦ, a particle, signifying excess, and πρήσσω, to burn; because of its very inflammatory quality, which it has in common with the Cantharides. *Dioscor.* l. 2, c. 66; *Plin.* l. 30, c. 4; *Gal. Exeg. Vocab. Hippocrat.*; *Oribas. Med. Coll.* l. 15; *Aet. Tetrab.* 1, serm. 1.

BUPRESTIS, *in the Linnean system*, a genus of insects, Order Coleoptera.
  Generic Character. *Antennæ* filiform.—*Feelers* four.—*Head* partly retracted within the thorax.
  Species. The species of this genus are remarkable for their rich metallic colour, having frequently the appearance of the most highly polished gold or copper. The larvæ are usually found in decayed trees and among timber.

BUPRESTIS (*Bot.*) a large sort of herb mentioned by Hesychius.

BUR (*Min.*) a sort of mineral juice, mentioned by Van Helmont.

BUR (*Mil.*) a broad ring of iron behind the hand, or the place made for the hand on the spears that were used by knights formerly in tilting, which bur was brought to rest when the tilter charged his spear.

BU'RAC (*Chem.*) a general name for all kinds of salts.

BU'RBOT (*Ich.*) a kind of cod, the *Gadus lota* of Linnæus.

BURCA'RDIA (*Bot.*) a genus of plants, called after Henry Burkhard, a botanist and physician, Class 5 Pentandria, Order 5 Pentagynia.
  Generic Characters. CAL. *perianth* five-leaved.—COR. *petals* five.—STAM. *filaments* five; *anthers* ovate.—PIST. *germ* three-cornered; *styles* five; *stigmas* flat.—PER. *capsule* one-celled; *seeds* seven or eight.
  Species. The only species is the—*Burcardia villosa,* seu *Piriqueta villosa,* an annual.

BURCHETA (*Archæol.*) in French *berchi,* a kind of gun used in forests.

BU'RCIFER *regis* (*Law*) or *Pursebearer,* the keeper of the King's privy purse. *Pat.* 17, Hen. 8.

BURDA'RE (*Archæol.*) to jest or trifle. *Matth. Par.*

BU'RDELAY (*Bot.*) a sort of grape.

BURDEN (*Com.*) signifies generally any weight which a man or horse can carry; but when applied to a ship it signifies as much as can be stowed into the hold.—*Beasts of burden,* those beasts which are particularly fitted for carrying burdens, or drawing heavy bodies, as the horse, ox, &c.

BURDEN *of a song* (*Mus.*) that part of a song which is repeated at the end of every stanza; so called from the French *bourdon,* a drone bass, an instrument remarkable for its monotony.

BU'RDO (*Zool.*) a young mule.

BU'RDOCK (*Bot.*) a perennial, the *Aretium* of Linnæus.

BURDU'NCULUS (*Bot.*) a herb mentioned by Marcellus Empiricus.

BUREA'U (*Polit.*) French for an office, or the place where any office is performed.

BURG (*Archæol.*) a walled town or privileged place.—*Burgbote,* from *burg,* a borough, and *bote,* a compensation; a tribute or contribution towards the building, or repairing the walls of a town. *Flet.* l. 1, c. 47.

BU'RGAGE (*Law*) a tenure by which the inhabitants of cities or boroughs held their lands or tenements of the king, or any other lord for an annual rent. *Glanv.* l. 7, c. 3; *Litt.* § 162.

BURGEOIS (*Print.*) a kind of type larger than Brevier.

BU'RGESS (*Law*) *burgarius.* 1. The inhabitant of a walled town. 2. The magistrate of a corporate town, who is also a representative in Parliament.

BU'RGH-BRECHE (*Law*) *fidejussionis violatio,* i. e. a breach of pledge; is used for a fine imposed on the community of a town for a breach of the peace. *Leg. Canut. apud Brompt.*—*Burgh Engloyes,* or *Francoyes,* two particular tenures in the county of Nottingham, the usages of which are that all the tenements, whereof the ancestor dies seized, in *Burgh Engloyes,* descend to the youngest son, and of those in *Burgh Francoyes* to the eldest, as in common law. 1 Ed. III. c. 12.—*Burgh-vote,* vide *Burgbote.*—*Burghmaster,* vide *Burgomaster.*—*Burghmote,* a court of a borough, which is distinct from a Berghmote. [vide *Berg.*]—*Burgh-ware,* vide *Burgess.*

BU'RGLAR (*Law*) from *burg,* a castle, and *latro,* a thief; a breaker into houses by night.

BU'RGLARY (*Law*) *burgi latrocinium,* anciently called *hameseken,* as it still is in Scotland; a breaking in and entering the mansion-house of another in the night to the intent to commit some felony, whether the felonious intent be executed or not. There must be both a breaking and an entering to complete the offence. 3 *Inst.* 64.

BURGOMA'STER (*Polit.*) the chief magistrate in the towns of Germany and Switzerland answering to our mayor.

BURGUNDY (*Husband.*) a French wine which comes from Burgundy.

BURI'N (*Mech.*) an engraver's tool.

BU'RIS (*Med.*) a scirrhous hernia.

TO BURL (*Mech.*) To dress cloth as fullers do; also to pick out the straws or threads of cloth which have not taken the dye.

BURLETTA (*Mus.*) a comic species of musical dance.

BU'RLING-IRONS (*Mech.*) a sort of pincers or nippers.

BURMA'NNIA (*Bot.*) a genus of plants, called after John Burmann, professor of botany, at Amsterdam, Class 6 Hexandria, Order 1 Monogynia.
  Generic Characters. CAL. *perianth* one-leaved.—COR. *petals* three.—STAM. *filaments* five; *anthers* two, always together.—PIST. *germ* cylindric; *style* filiform; *stigmas* three.—PER. *capsule* cylindric; *seeds* numerous.
  Species. These plants, which are perennials, grow in open watery places in Ceylon.

BURN (*Surg.*) vide *Ambustum.*

BURN-BEATING (*Agric.*) a method of manuring lands by cutting off the peat, and burning it in heaps.

BU'RNEC (*Chem.*) pitch.

BU'RNET (*Bot.*) a perennial, the *Poterium* of Linnæus.—Burnet saxifrage, a perennial, the *Pimpernella.*

BURNETA (*Archæol.*) cloth made of dyed wood. The burnet colour, which must be dyed, is distinct from the *brunus,* or *brunet,* which may be made with wool without dying. These are called medleys or russets.

BU'RNING (*Phy.*) the solution of continuity, produced by the action of heat on bodies.

BURNING (*Med.*) or *brenning,* an infectious disease, got by impure commerce.

BURNING *in the hand* (*Law*) a mode of punishment, otherwise called branding.—*Burning of houses,* &c. vide *Arson.*

BURNING-GLASS (*Mech.*) a convex lens which transmits the rays of light by refraction towards a common centre called the *focus.*—*Burning mirrors,* or *specula,* concave reflecting surfaces, which carry the rays of light by reflection to the common centre.

BURNING MOUNTAIN (*Nat.*) the same as *volcano.*

BURNING ZONE (*Geog.*) vide *Torrid Zone.*

BURNT *offering* (*Bibl.*) an offering in which the whole victim was consumed by fire.

BURNT *Brass* (*Chem.*) *Æs ustum,* was formerly distinguished by the annexed character. [vide *Æs ustum*] ♀

BURNT *hartshorn* (*Chem.*) vide *Cornu Ustum.*—*Burnt sponge.* [vide *Spongia usta*]

BURR (*Gunn.*) a round iron ring which serves to rivet the end of the bolt so as to form a round head; also a broad iron ring for a lance.

BURR (*Mil.*) a triangular chisel used to clear the corner of mortices.

BURR (*Sport.*) a round knob of horn next a deer's head; also the lobe or tip of the ear.

BU'RRAS *pipe* (*Mech.*) a utensil for keeping corroding powders, such as vitriol, precipitate, &c.

BU'RREL (*Bot.*) a pear, otherwise called the *red-butter pear*, from its smooth, delicious, and soft pulp.

BU'RREL-SHOT (*Mil.*) small bullets, nails, &c. put into cases to be discharged out of ordnance.

BU'RROCK (*Mech.*) a small wear or dam where wheels are laid in a river to catch fish.

BU'RROW (*Law*) vide *Borough.*—*Burrows*, or *burgh*, a caution, security.

BU'RSA *pastoris* (*Bot.*) the *Bunias cornuta* of Linnæus.

Bursa (*Theol.*) a rich covering of the door of the house at Mecca, which is carried about at the solemn processions of the Mahometans, when those who carry it are made to stop, that the people may touch it.

BU'RSÆ *mucosæ* (*Anat.*) mucous bags which secrete a mucous fat that serves to lubricate tendons, muscles, and bones, in order to render their motion easy.

BURSA'LIS *musculus* (*Anat.*) the *Obturator externus et internus.*

BU'RSAR (*Archæol.*) the treasurer of a monastery or college.

BURSARII (*Archæol.*) stipendiary scholars who lived upon the burse, or joint stock of the college.

BURSA'RIA (*Ent.*) a genus of animals, Class *Vermes*, Order *Infusoria*, consisting of a very simple worm.

BURSE (*Com.*) bursa, or *basilica*, an exchange, or place of meeting for merchants.

BURSE'RA (*Bot.*) a genus of plants, so called after Joachim Burser, the disciple of Casper Bauhin, Class 23 *Polygamia*, Order 2 *Dioecia*.
Generic Character. CAL. perianth one-leaved. — COR. *petals* three.—STAM. *filaments* six; *anthers* ovate.—PIST. *germ* ovate; *style* short, thick.—PER. *capsule* fleshy; *seeds* berried, solitary.
Species. The only species is the *Bursera gummifera* seu *Terebinthus*, the Jamaica Birch-Tree.

BURSERIA (*Bot.*) the *Verbena lappulacea* of Linnæus.

BU'RSHOLDERS (*Law*) vide *Head-borough.*

BUR-SELI'NUM (*Bot.*) a large sort of parsley.

BU'RTON (*Mar.*) a small tackle formed by two blocks.

BUSH (*Mar.*) a circular piece of metal let into the sheaves of such blocks as have iron pins.

BU'SHEL (*Com.*) an English dry measure containing four pecks, or eight gallons.

BUSHELS *of a cart wheel* (*Mech.*) certain irons within the nave to preserve it from wearing.

BUSO'NES *comitatus* (*Law*) a term used by Bracton, which is supposed to signify barons.

BUSS (*Mar.*) bursa, a ship of two masts used by the English and Dutch in their herring fisheries.

BUST (*Sculpt.*) the figure or portrait of a person in relievo, showing only the upper parts of the body.

BUSTROPHE'DON (*Gram.*) from βῦς, an ox, and τρίφω, to turn; a term used by the Greeks to express a manner of writing, which began at the left-hand in one line, and at the right-hand in another, in imitation of the manner in which oxen turn themselves at the end of the furrows.

BUSTUA'RII (*Ant.*) gladiators who fought about the *bustum*, or funeral pile, of any person in the celebration of his obsequies.

BUSTUM (*Ant.*) a funeral pile, on which the dead bodies of the Romans used to be, *combustum*, burnt, from which it derives its name. It was raised of stones.
Propert. l. 4, el. 5, v. 75.

Scabris hoc bustum cædite saxis.

Cic. de Leg. l. 2, c. 26; Fest. de Verb. Signif.; Serv. in Æn. l. 12, v. 201.

BU'STARD (*Or.*) a large bird resembling a turkey, the *Otis* of Linnæus, which runs with great speed, but flies with difficulty. The breed of this bird is almost extirpated in England.

BUTCHER-BIRD (*Or.*) a species of the Shrike, the *Lanius excubitus* of Linnæus. It is remarkable for its ferocity towards the little birds which it kills, tearing them to pieces, and sticking them on thorns.

BUTCHERS, Company of (*Her.*) this fraternity, although very ancient, was not incorporated before the reign of James I. Their arms are, " Azure, two axes saltirewise, *argent*, between three bulls' heads couped, attired, *or*; a boar's head, *gules*, betwixt two garbs, *vert.*"

BUTCHERS'-BROOM (*Bot.*) the *Ruscus* of Linnæus, a shrub, so called because its twigs are used in making besoms for the use of butchers.

BUT-HI'NGES (*Carpent.*) those which are employed in hanging doors, &c.

BUTHSCARLE (*Archæol.*) a mariner.

BUTLER (*Law*) vide *Botiler*.

BUTLERAGE (*Law*) vide *Prisage*.

BUTMENT (*Archit.*) vide *Abutment*.

BUTNE'RIA (*Bot.*) the same as the *Calycanthus*.

BUTOMON (*Bot.*) the *Iris pseudacorus* of Linnæus.

BUTOMUS (*Bot.*) a genus of plants, Class 9 *Enneandria*, Order 3 *Trigynia*.
Generic Character. CAL. involucre simple.—COR. petals six.—STAM. *filaments* nine; *anthers* bilamellate.—PIST. *germs* six; *stigmas* simple.—PER. *capsules* six; *seeds* very many.
Species. The only species is the *Butomus umbellatus*, *Juncus floridus*, seu *Gladiolus aquatilis*, Flowering Rush, or Water Gladiole, a perennial.

BUTO'NICA (*Bot.*) the Barrington.

BUTT (*Gun.*) a solid earthen parapet to fire against in the proving of guns.—*Butt of firelocks*, the thick end which rests against the shoulder when it is fired off.

Butt (*Mar.*) the end of a plank, in a ship's side or bottom, uniting with the end of another plank. " To start, or spring a *butt*," to loosen the end of a plank. " But and butt, the butt ends of two planks that come together. Butt signifies also the lower end of a mast, &c.

Butt (*Agric.*) the end, or short piece of land, in arable ridges or furrows.

Butt (*Com.*) a measure of wine containing 126 gallons.

BUTT-END (*Carpent.*) the largest end of a piece of timber nearest to the root.—*Butt-joint*, a joint in hand railing at right angles to the curve of the rail.

BUTTER-BUR (*Bot.*) a perennial, the *Tussilago alba*, &c. of Linnæus.—Butter-Wort, a perennial, the *Pinguicula* of Linnæus.—Butterflower, the *Ranunculus*.

BU'TTERFLY (*Ent.*) the well-known insect, a species of the *Papilio*, so called because it first appears in the butter season.

Butter of Antimony (*Chem.*) another name for the *muriate of Antimony*.—Butter of bismuth, a chloride of bismuth obtained by heating bismuth with corrosive sublimate.—*Butter of tin*, a compound of one part tin, and three parts corrosive sublimate.—*Butter of wax*, wax when it is of the consistency of butter.

BU'TTERIS (*Vet.*) or *buttrice*, an instrument of steel used in paring the hoof of a horse.

BU'TTERMILK (*Husband.*) the whey separated from the cream after it has been converted into butter.

BU'TTERY (*Archit.*) the store-room for provisions.

BUTTNE'RIA (*Bot.*) a genus of plants, called after August. Buttner, Class 5 *Pentandria*, Order 1 *Monogynia*.
Generic Character. CAL. perianth one-leaved.—COR. petals five.—STAM. *filaments* five; *anthers* twin.—PIST. *germ* roundish; *style* subulate; *stigma* obtuse.—PER. *capsule* roundish; *seeds* solitary.
Species. The species are shrubby perennials.

BU'TTOCK (*Mar.*) that part of a ship which forms its convex breadth a-baft, under the stern.

BUTTON (*Mech.*) any thing in a round form which serves to fasten.

BUTTON *and loop* (*Mar.*) a short piece of rope having, at one end, a walnut knob, and, at the other end, an eye.

BUTTON (*Gunn.*) a part of the cascabel in a gun, or a howitzer, made in the form of a ball.

BUTTON-TREE (*Bot.*) the *Conocarpus erecta* of Linnæus.—Button-Weed, the *Spermacoce*, an annual.—Button-Wood, the *Cephalanthus occidentalis*, a shrub.

BUTTRESS (*Archit.*) a mass of stone-brick work serving to support the sides of walls, which are of two sorts, pillared and arched.—*Pillared buttresses* rise in a perpendicular direction.—*Arched buttresses*, in an arched form.

BUTTRICE (*Vet.*) vide *Butteris*.

BUTTS (*Archer.*) the place where archers meet with their bows and arrows to shoot at a mark, which is called shooting at butts.

BUXBAUMIA (*Bot.*) a kind of moss.

BUXUS (*Bot.*) a genus of plants, Class 21 *Monoecia*, Order 4 *Tetrandria*.
Generic Character. Male flowers prominent from the buds of the plant.—PIST. rudiment of a germ without style or stigma. Female flowers in the same bud with the males. PIST. germ superior; *styles* permanent; *stigmas* obtuse.

BUZONIS (*Archer.*) the shaft of an arrow before it is fledged. *Strab. Ed.* 1.

BUZZARD (*Or.*) a very sluggish bird of the hawk kind, the *Falco buteo* of Linnæus.—*Bald buzzard*, a name given, by Willoughby and Ray, to a bird of the falcon or eagle tribe. Willoughby also gave the name of Honey Buzzard to the *Falco apivorus*, and Moor Buzzard to the *Falco æruginosus* of Linnæus.

BUZZARDET (*Or.*) the *Falco albidus* of Linnæus.

BUZE (*Mech.*) a wooden or leaden pipe to convey the air into mines.

BYARES (*Anat.*) a plexus of blood vessels.

BYE-LAWS (*Law*) from the Saxon bye, a town; the laws of towns, or particular places, or more probably laws made *obiter*, i. e. by the bye; for bye-laws, called in Scotland *birlaws*, are certain orders and constitutions made by corporate bodies, with the consent of those who made them in particular cases, to which the general laws do not extend.

BYRETHRUM (*Med.*) an odoriferous cap filled with cephalic drugs, from the Italian *biretta*, a cap.

BYRSA (*Med.*) βύρσα, a leather skin to spread plasters upon.

BYSAUCHON (*Med.*) from βύω, to stuff up, and αὐχήν, the neck; a morbid stiffness of the neck.

BYSSMA (*Ant.*) garments made of the *byssus*.

BYSSUS (*Ant.*) βύσσος, a fine linen among the ancients, which was obtained from India. *Poll. Onom.* l. 7, segm. 75; *Plin.* l. 19, c. 1; *Tertull. de Cult. Fœmin.* c. 13; *Isid. Orig.* l. 19, c. 27.

Byssus (*Bot.*) a genus of plants, Class *Cryptogamia*, Order *Algæ*.

BYSTROPOGON (*Bot.*) a genus of plants, Class 14 *Didynamia*, Order 1 *Gymnospermia*.
Generic Character. CAL. *perianth* one-leaved.—COR. monopetalous.—STAM. *filaments* four; *anthers* incumbent.—PIST. *germ* superior; *style* subulate; *stigma* bifid.—PER. none; *seeds* four.
Species. Plants of this tribe are shrubby perennials.

BYTHOS (*Anat.*) βυθός, depth; is used by Hippocrates to signify the bottom of the stomach. *Hippocrat. de Nat. Hom.*

BYTTNERIA (*Bot.*) vide *Buttneria*.

C.

C. (*Ant.*) as an abbreviation, stands for *Caius, Cæsar*, &c. As a Numeral, for *Centum*, 100, as CCCC, four hundred. [vide *Abbreviations*]

c. (*Chron.*) stands for *Christi*, as A. C. *Anno Christi*, in the year of Christ. [vide *Abbreviations*]

c. (*Gram.*) stands for *Caius, Corpus Christi*, &c. [vide *Abbreviations*]

c. (*Mus.*) the name of that note in the natural major mode, to which Guido applied the monosyllable, for which the Italians now substitute D·.—*C above G Gamut*, that note which is a fourth higher than G Gamut.—*C above the bass Cliff*, that note which is a fifth higher than the *bass cliff.*—*C above the treble cliff*, a note which is a fourth higher than the treble cliff.

CAA-APIA (*Bot.*) an Indian name for the Brazilian plant, the *Dorstenia Brasiliensis* of Linnæus, with which the inhabitants cure those wounds which are caused by poisoned darts.—*Caa-atega*, a plant of Brazil, the root of which is perfectly cathartic. *Raii Hist. Plant.*

CAABA (*Theol.*) Arabic for the *Beit-Allah*, or the House of God, in Mecca, so called from its cubic form; *caaba* signifying cubic.

CAACICA (*Bot.*) a Brasilian herb, the *Colubrina Lusitana*, which was applied in cataplasms against venomous bites. *Raii Hist. Plant.*

CAACO (*Bot.*) an Indian name for the sensitive plant, the root of which is used by the natives as an antidote.

CAAETIMAY (*Bot.*) the *Senecio Brasiliensis*, a decoction of which is used in the cure of the itch.

CAAGHRYUYS (*Bot.*) *Frutex baccifer Brasiliensis*, a shrub of Brazil, the leaves of which are applied to ulcers.

CAA-OPIA (*Bot.*) the *Hypericum bacciferum*, a tree of Brazil, the bark of which emits a juice which when dried resembles gamboge.

CAAPEBA (*Bot.*) the *Cissampelos Pareira* of Linnæus.

CAAPONGA (*Bot.*) an Indian name for the *Inula arithmoides* of Linnæus, the leaves of which are gently diuretic.

CAAROBA (*Bot.*) an Indian name for a plant, the leaves of which are employed in a decoction for the venereal disease.

CAB (*Ant.*) קב, a Hebrew measure, the sixth part of a Seah, containing three English pints.

CABALA (*Theol.*) קבלה, from קבל, to receive; a traditional or mysterious doctrine, which the ancient Jews say was delivered by word of mouth to Moses.

CABALA (*My.*) an abuse of certain passages of Scripture for magical purposes, as the making of magical words, numbers, &c.

CABALISTIC *Art* (*My.*) the magic art, which teaches the Cabala that was formerly employed in medicine.

CABALLINE (*Vet.*) a coarser sort of aloes used for horses, so called from *caballus*, a horse.

CABALLUS (*Archæol.*) a Keffel or Rosinante, but sometimes taken for a war-horse.

CABANE (*Mar.*) French for a flat-bottomed boat with a deck, which is used for the accommodation of passengers.

CABA'S (*Mil.*) a basket made of rushes, which is used in Languedoc for the purpose of conveying stores and ammunition.

CA'BBAGE (*Bot.*) an edible plant for the pot, the *Brassica* of Linnæus. There are several sorts of cabbage cultivated in gardens, which are varieties of the common Cabbage, or the *Brassica oleracea* of Linnæus: the principal of these are the Kale, or Colewort, the Broccoli, the Cauliflower, and the Broccolo, or Fringed Cabbage, the Turnip Cabbage, &c.—Sea Cabbage, or Wild Colewort, the *Brassica oleracea sylvestris*.—Cabbage-Tree, the *Cacalia Kleinia* of Linnæus, so called from the resemblance its leaves bear to those of the Cabbage.—Cabbage-Bark-Tree, the *Geoffroya Jamaicensis*.

CABBAGE *of a Deer's Head* (*Sport.*) the burr which parts where the horns take their rise.

CABBAGE-WO'RM (*Ent.*) a name for the Caterpillar which particularly infests the Cabbage.

CABBALI'STICAL (*Mag.*) vide *Cabalistic*.

CABE'CA (*Com.*) or *cabesse*, the finest kind of India silks, in distinction from the *bariga*, which is the inferior sort.

CABE'ER (*Com.*) a coin current at Mocha, equal to two shillings and sixpence sterling.

CABELIA'U (*Ich.*) Cod-fish.

CABI'DOS (*Com.*) a Portuguese long-measure, equal to three-fourths of an English yard.

CA'BIN (*Mar.*) the apartment in a vessel for the officers and superior passengers.—*Cabin boy*, the lad who attends on the officers and passengers in the cabin.—*Cabin passengers*, those who pay for accommodations in the cabin, in distinction from the deck passengers, or those who mess with the sailors.

CA'BINET (*Pol.*) Gabinetto, It.; Gavinéte, Sp.; Gabinete, Port. 1. A closet, or private room, in which consultations, particularly on state affairs, are commonly held. 2. The collective body of ministers of state, each of whom may be called a cabinet minister.—*Cabinet council*, a council of cabinet ministers held with particular privacy.

CABINET (*Mech.*) a small or close chest for valuables.—*Cabinet-maker*, a workman who does the finest work.

CA'BLE (*Mar.*) or *Kabel*, a thick rope made of three strands or smaller ropes, and fixed to the anchor to hold a ship fast.—*Cable-tier*, the place on the orlop-deck where the cables are stowed.—*Chief cable*, or *sheet-anchor-cable*, the largest cable in the ship.—*Bower-cable*, a name for either of the two bowers.—*Stream-cable*, a hawser or small rope, smaller than the bower-cable.—*Cable-tire*, the several rolls of cable as they lie one upon another.

In the use of the *cable* there are very many sea phrases, as —" To bend the *cable*," to make it fast to the ring of the anchor. "To unbend the *cable*," to take it away. "To bit the *cable*," to put it round the bits, to fasten or slacken it gradually. "To serve, keckle, or plait the *cable*," to bind it round with ropes, &c. to prevent it from being galled. "To heave in the slack of the *cable*," to draw it into the ship by the capstan or windlass. "To pay out the *cable*, or veer away the *cable*," to slacken it, that it may run out. "To pay the *cable* cheap," is to hand it out apace. "To coil the *cable*," to roll it round in a ring. "To shoot or splice the *cable*," to splice two parts of a cable together by working the several threads of the rope the one into the other. "To slip the *cable*," to let it run quite out when there is no time to weigh anchor.

CABLE is also the name of any large rope which is used for raising weights, as in pullies, cranes, &c.

CABLE (*Archit.*) a moulding of a convex form at the back of the flute, representing a rope or staff laid in a flute.

CABLE (*Mil.*) French for the large rope which is used for dragging the artillery.

CABLE'E (*Her.*) or *cabled*, an epithet for a cross; a cross cablee is made of two ends of a ship's cable.

CA'BLED *flutes* (*Arch.*) flutes filled up with pieces in form of cables.

CABLE'S *length* (*Mar.*) the measure of 120 fathoms.

CA'BLET (*Mar.*) a small cable.

CA'BLING (*Archit.*) the filling of flutes with cables, or the cables themselves so disposed, whether in flutes or without them.

CA'BLISH (*Archæol.*) *cadibulum*, Brushwood, or windfall wood, from *cadere*, to fall.

CABO'CHE (*Carpent.*) French for a long-headed nail.

CABO'SSE (*Her.*) or *cabossed*, from the French *caboche*, Latin *caput*, the head; a term in blazoning when the head of a beast is cut off just under the ears, leaving no neck, as he beareth "*Argent* three Bulls Heads, cabossed *sable*, armed *or*, by the name of *Baynham*, in *Gloucestershire*."

CA'BOTAGE (*Mar.*) the art of navigating so as to avoid all sand-banks, &c.; also the practice of sailing from port to port without stretching out to sea.

CA'BRER (*Man.*) French for to rear as a horse does when improperly checked.

CABRIOLE'T (*Mech.*) a light low chaise.

CABULA'TOR (*Chem.*) Nitre.

CABURE'RBA (*Bot.*) an Indian tree, which, according to Ray, yields the balsam of Peru.

CABU'RNES (*Mar.*) small lines for binding the cable.

CA'CABUS (*Ant.*) a cauldron or kettle so called from the noise which it makes in boiling.

CACA'DE (*Mil.*) a French term for an unlucky enterprize in war, which has been ill-concerted and ill-conducted.

CACAGO'GA (*Med.*) from κακκα, ordure, and αγω, to draw, medicines which, when applied to the fundament, procure stools. *Paul. Æginet.* l. 7, c. 9.

CACA'LIA (*Bot.*) κακαλία, Strange Colts-foot, a plant which, according to Dioscorides, cures coughs when macerated in wine. *Dioscor.* l. 4, c. 123; *Plin.* l. 25, c. 11.

CACALIA, in the Linnean system, a genus of plants, Class 19 *Syngenesia*, Order 1 *Polygamia æqualis*.

Generic Characters. CAL. common simple.—COR. compound tubular.—STAM. *filaments* five; *anther* cylindric. —PIST. germ oblong; *style* filiform; *stigmas* two.—PER. none; *seeds* solitary; *receptacle* naked.

Species. The species are mostly shrubs, and natives of the Cape of Good Hope, as the—*Cacalia papillaris, Kleinia, seu Cacalianthemum*, Rough-stalked Cacalia, a shrub, native of the Cape of Good Hope.—*Cacalia Anteuphorbium, Kleinia, seu Ante-Euphorbium*, Oval-leaved Cacalia.—*Cacalia cuneifolia*, Wedge-leaved Cacalia.—*Cacalia Kleinia, Kleinia, Cacalianthemum Frutex Indica, &c. seu Nec Cacalia, &c*. Oleander-leaved Cacalia, or Cabbage-tree.—*Cacalia repens*, Glaucous-leaved Cacalia.—*Cacalia Ficoides, Kleinia, seu Senecio africanus, &c*. Flat-leaved Cacalia.—*Cacalia carnosa*, Narrow-leaved Cacalia.— *Cacalia articulata, laciniata, seu runcinata*, Jointed-stalked Cacalia.—*Cacalia arbuscula*, native of the Cape of Good Hope.—*Cacalia tomentosa*, woolly-leaved Cacalia, &c. But the following are perennials, as the—*Cacalia sempervirens, carnosa, seu semperviva.* —*Cacalia saracenica, Solidago, &c. Senecio perennis, Virga aurea, seu Conyza montana, &c*. Creeping-rooted Cacalia, native of the South of France.—*Cacalia hastata, seu Senecio, &c*. Spear-leaved Cacalia, native of Siberia.—*Cacalia suaveolens*, sweet-scented Cacalia, native of Virginia.—*Cacalia atriplicafolia, seu virginiana glabra, Porophyllum, seu Nardus americana, &c.*

Orach-leaved Cacalia, a native of Virginia.—*Cacalia alpina, glabra pyrenaica, Allicariæ,* seu *Tussilago Cacalia,* Alpine Cacalia, native of Switzerland.—*Cacalia albifrons, herbacea, hirsuta tomentosa,* seu *Alliaria,* White-leaved Cacalia, a native of Austria, &c.; and the following are annuals, as the—*Cacalia porophyllum, Porophyllum Senecio indicus,* seu *Chrysanthemum americanum, &c.* Perforated Cacalia, native of America.—*Cacalia ruderalis,* seu *Kleinia ruderalis,* an annual, native of St. Domingo.—*Cacalia procumbens,* seu *Sonchus volubilis,* native of China.—*Cacalia Coccinea,* an annual, native of South America, &c.—*Cacalia sonchifolia, Kleinia, Muel Schair, Senecio maderaspatanus, Chondril la Zeylanica, Sonchus amboinensis,* seu *Tagolina lugonum,* Sowthistle-leaved Cacalia, native of China. *Clus. Hist. Plant. Rar. Ger. Herb.; J. Bauh. Hist. Plant.; C. Bauh. Pin.; Park. Theat. Botan.; Raii Hist. Plant.; Tournef. Inst.; Boerhaav. Ind.*

CACALIA'NTHEMUM (*Bot.*) the *Cacalia papillaris et Kleinia* of Linnæus.

CACAMO'TIC *Hanoquiloni* (*Bot.*) the Cathartic potatoe. *Hern. Nov. Plant. Amer. Hist.*

CACANGE'LIA (*Lit.*) κακαγγελια, evil-speaking. *Gal. Exeges.*

CACA'NUM (*Bot.*) a plant mentioned by Paulus Ægineta, and supposed to be the same as the Cacalia of Dioscorides.

CA'CAO-TREE (*Bot.*) the *Theobroma* of Linnæus.

CA'CAO-NUT, the fruit of the Cacao-tree, from which chocolate is made, as also an oil, or butter, which has an anodyne virtue. This oil can be kept a long time without becoming rancid. *J. Bauh. Hist. Plant.; C. Bauh. Pin. Hernand. Plant. Amer. Hist. &c.*

CACA'OTETE (*Min.*) an Indian stone, otherwise called *Lapis corvinus,* which, when heated, cracks like thunder.

CACA'PHONIA (*Med.*) Defective articulation.

CACA'RA (*Bot.*) the *Dolichos bulbosus* of Linnæus.

CACATO'RIA *febris* (*Med.*) An intermittent fever. *Castell. Lex. Med.*

CACA'VA (*Bot.*) Cacavate, or Quahool, the same as Cacao. *Hernand. Hist. Amer.*

CACA'VI (*Nat.*) The same as Cassavi.

CA'CCIA (*Mus.*) an Italian epithet for a sort of composition written in the hunting style.

CACEDO'NIUM *tartarum* (*Med.*) peccant matter in the human body.

CACE'MPHATON (*Gram.*) or *cacephaton,* κακέφατον, from κακός and φήμι, to say; bad diction.

CA'CHALOT (*Ich.*) the *Physeter* of Linnæus, one of the largest of the whale tribe, from the head of which spermaceti is extracted.

CACHE'CTUS (*Med.*) or *cachecticus,* one labouring under a cachexy.

CACHE'POLUS (*Law*) a catchpole, an inferior officer of justice.

CACHE'XIA (*Med.*) κακιξια, from κακός, *malus,* and ἕξις, *habitus;* an ill habit of body. *Aret. de Acut. Morb. l. 1, c.* 16; *Cels. l.* 3, *c.* 22; *Gal. de Meth. Med. l.* 4; *Aet. Tetrab.* 3, serm. 2, *c.* 19; *Actuar. de Meth. Med. l.* 1, *c.* 11.

CACHEXIA, in Cullen's system the third class of diseases, comprehending the three orders, *marcores, intumescentia,* and *impetigines.*

CA'CHLEX (*Med.*) κάχληξ, a pebble to which Galen ascribes an astringent virtue when heated. *Gal. de Simpl. l.* 10.

CACHOLO'NY (*Min.*) the *Chalcedonius Cacholonius* of Linnæus.

CA'CHOS (*Bot.*) the *Solanum pomiferum,* &c. of Linnæus. *Bauh. Pin.*

CA'CHOW (*Bot.*) an aromatic drug. vide *Terra Japonica.*

CA'CHRY (*Bot.*) κάγχρυ, the seed of the *Libanotis,* which, according to Dioscorides, is of a heating and drying quality. *Dioscor. l.* 3. *c.* 88.

CACHRYS (*Bot.*) a genus of plants, Class 5 *Pentandria,* Order 2 *Digynia.*

Generic Character. CAL. *umbel universal* manifold; *partial* similar; *involucre universal* many-leaved; *partial* similar; *perianth* proper, scarcely observable.—COR. *universal* uniform; *flosculus* all uniform; *proper* of five lanceolate petals.—STAM. *filaments* five; *anthers* simple. —PIST. *germ.* turbinate, inferior; *styles* two simple; *stigmas* headed.—PER. *fruit* subovate, angular; *seeds* two, very large.

Species. The species are perennials, as the—*Cachrys libanotis,* seu *Libanotis,* Smooth-seeded Cachrys.— *Cachrys sicula,* seu *Hippomarathrum,* Hairy-seeded Cachrys.—*Cachrys panacifolia,* seu *Panax, &c. Bauh. Hist.; C. Bauh. Pin.; Ger. Herb.; Park. Theat. Botan.; Tournef. Inst.*

CA'CHRYES (*Bot.*) κάχρυς, Maple Chat, or Ash Keys.

CACHU'NDE (*Med.*) a cordial medicine in China and India, composed of amber, cinnamon, juice of roses, &c.

CACHY'MIA (*Met.*) an imperfect metallic body, according to Paracelsus.

CA'CIA *ferrea* (*Archæol.*) an iron spoon.

CACO'A (*Bot.*) the same as *Cacao.*

CACOA-LEXITERIUM (*Med.*) the same as *Alexiterium.*

CACOCHO'LIA (*Med.*) from κακός and χολή, an indisposition of the bile.

CACOCHRO'I (*Med.*) from κακός and χρόα, ill-coloured in the face. *Gal. Com.* 4 *in Hippoc. de Rat. Vict. in Acut. Morb.*

CACOCHY'LIA (*Med.*) from κακός and χυλός, a bad chylification; when the humour called chyle is not duly made. *Cels. l.* 2, *c.* 19.

CACOCHY'MIA (*Med.*) κακοχυμία, from κακός and χυμός, cacochymy, abundance of bad humours in the body, caused by bad nourishment and ill digestion. *Gal. de Sanit. tuend. l.* 5; *Act. de Meth. M. l.* 3, *c.* 9.

CACOCHY'MICAL (*Med.*) or *Cacochymic,* having the humours corrupted, as *cacochymical* blood.

CACODÆMON (*Astrol.*) so called from its dreadful significations, as great losses, &c. The twelfth house scheme, or figure of the heavens.

CACODÆMO'NUM *magia* (*Mag.*) from κακός and δαίμων, diabolical magic. *Castell. Lex. Med.*

CACO'DES (*Med.*) from κακός and ὄζω, ill-scented, fetid.

CACOE'THES (*Med.*) κακοήθης, from κακός and ἦθος, a habit; an epithet applied by Hippocrates to diseases, to denote their malignancy; and by Galen, to symptoms which are dangerous and threatening, or ulcers and tumors which are virulent and malignant. *Gal. Com.* 1, *in Hippocrat. Prædict. l.* 1; *Cels. l.* 5, *c.* 21; *Aet. Tetrab.* 3, serm. 1, *c.* 45; *Foes. Œconom. Hippocrat.; Gorr. Med. Def.*

CACOETHES (*Eth.*) an ill habit or propensity, as the *cacoethes scribendi,* the itch for writing mentioned by Juvenal. *Juv. sat.* 7, *v.* 52.

———— Tenet insanabile multos
Scribendi cacoethes.

CACOPA'THIA (*Med.*) κακοπάθεια, from κακός and πάθος, ill-affection; suffering.

CACO'PHONY (*Med.*) κακοφωνία, from κακός, *malus,* and φωνή, *vox;* a depravation of the voice, of which there are two kinds; aphony, or dumbness; and dysphony, difficulty of speech. *Gal. de diff. Sympt. c.* 3.

CACOPHONY (*Gram.*) a bad tone of the voice, proceeding from the ill disposition of the organs: or, a certain harshness of sound, arising from an improper mixture of the vowels and consonants among themselves. Strabo says, " Theophrastus was first called Tertamus; but Aristotle changed it into Theophrastus, to avoid the cacophony of the former name."

CACOPHONY (*Mus.*) a combination of discordant sounds.

CACOPHRA'STUS (*Med.*) a name given by some to Theophrastus. *Paracelsus*; *Castell. Lex Med.*

CACOPRA'GIA (*Med.*) κακοπραγία, from κακός, ill, and πράσσω, to act; a depraved action of the viscera.

CACORRHEMO'SYNE (*Med.*) the same as *Cacangelia*.

CACORRYTHMUS (*Med.*) the same as *Arythmus*.

CACO'SIS (*Med.*) κάκωσις, from κακός, *malus*; indisposition. *Hippocrat. de Intern. Affect.*

CACOSI'STATA (*Log.*) arguments that will serve as well for one side as the other; as, "You ought to forgive him because he is a child.—No, for that reason I will correct him, that he may be better hereafter."

CACOSI'FIA (*Med.*) the same as *Nausea*.

CACOSPHY'XIA (*Med.*) from κακός and σφίξις, a disorderly beating of the pulse in general. *Gal. de Diff. Sympt.* c. 4.

CACOSTO'MACHUS (*Med.*) κακοστομαχός, from κακός and στόμαχος, unwholesome; a medicinal epithet for food.

CACOSY'NTHETON (*Gram.*) κακοσύνθετον, from κακός, *malus*, and συνθέσις; an ill composition of words in a sentence.

CACOTE'CHNY (*Rhet.*) κακοτεχνία, from κακός, *malus*, and τέχνη, *ars*; a corruption of art. *Quintill.*

CACOTHY'MIA (*Med.*) from κακός and θυμός; an ill disposition of mind.

CACO'TROPHY (*Med.*) κακοτροφία, from κακός, *malus*, and τροφή, nutriment; any sort of vicious nutrition in general. *Gal. de Diff. Symp.* c. 4.

CACOTY'CHE (*Astrol.*) i. e. Bad Fortune; the sixth house of an astrological figure.

CACOZE'LIA (*Rhet.*) from κακός, *malus*, and ζηλόω, *æmulor*; a vicious mode of speech, consisting of an affected or imperfect attempt at the sublime; the bombastic style. *Demet. de Elocut.* § 286; *Quintil. Instit.* l. 8, c, 3; *Suet. Aug.* c. 86; *Longin. de Sublim.* c. 3; *Hermog*: περὶ δεινοτ. *Ald. Edit.*

CA'CTUS (*Bot.*) κάκτος, a prickly plant of Sicily, mentioned by Theophrastus, and also the poet Theocritus, the description of which is copied from the former by Pliny and Athenæus, according to whom it is the same plant which the Romans called *carduus*, and the Greeks κινάρα, the Artichoke. *Theophrast. Hist. Plant.* l. 6, c. 4; *Theocrit. Idyl.* 10; *Plin.* l. 21, c. 16; *Athen.* l. 2.

CACTUS, *in the Linnean system*, a genus of plants, Class 12 Icosandria, Order 1 Monogynia.
Generic Character. CAL. *perianth* one-leaved.—COR. *petals* numerous, rather obtuse.—STAM. *filaments* numerous, subulate; *anthers* oblong, erect.—PIST. *germ* inferior; *style* the length of the stamens, cylindric; *stigma* headed,—PER. *berry* rather oblong; *seeds* numerous, roundish.
Species. This genus consists of succulent plants permanent in duration and singular in structure, which are all natives of the continent of South America. The principal species are as follow: the—*Cactus mammillaris*, *Echinon melocactus*, *Ficoides*, seu *Melocactus*, Smaller Melon Thistle.—*Cactus melocactus*, seu *Melocarduus*, Great Melon Thistle, or Turk's Cap.—*Cactus hexagonus*, seu *Cereus hexagonus*, Six-angled Torch Thistle.—*Cactus grandiflorus*, seu *Cereus grandiflorus*, Great-flowering Creeping Cereus.—*Cactus pendulus*, *Cassyta baccifera*, *Rhipsalia cassutha*, seu *Ibiscum*, Slender Cereus, —*Cactus triangularis*, Triangular Cactus, or Strawberry Pear.—*Cactus opuntia*, *Opuntia vulgaris*, seu *Ficus Indica*, Common Indian Fig, or Prickly Pear.—*Cactus tuna*, seu *Tuna major*, *Opuntia tuna*, Great Indian Fig, or Upright Prickly Pear.—*Cactus cochenillifer*, Cochineal Indian Fig, so called because the insect called the Cochineal feeds upon this plant.—*Cactus phyllanthus*, seu *Phyllanthus Americana*, Spleenwort-leaved Indian Fig.—*Cactus pereskia*, *Malus Americana*, seu *Portulaca Americana*, Barbadoes Gooseberry. *Bauh. Hist. Plant*; *Bauh. Pin.*; *Ger. Herb.*; *Park. Theat. Botan.*; *Raii Hist. Plant*; *Tournef. Inst.*; *Boerh. Ind.*

CACU'BALUM (*Bot.*) a herb which cures tumors, the *Alsine baccifera* of Bauhin, and the Berry-bearing Chickweed of Ray.

CADA'RIANS (*Theol.*) a sect of Mahometans so called, according to Abulpharajius, from the Arabic *cadr*, a decree; not because they maintain, but because they deny, the absolute decrees of the Almighty, in opposition to the generality of Mahometans. *Albufarag. Hist. Dynast. Poc. Edit.*

CADA'VER (*Anat.*) a carcase, corpse, or dead body; so called from *cado*, to fall, because the body falls when stripped of the soul.

CADA'VEROUS (*Nat.*) an epithet signifying like, or appertaining to, a corpse.

CA'DBOTE-FLY (*Ent.*) or Cadworms, the maggot of the insect *Phryganea*, which is a good bait for fish.

CA'DDIS (*Mech.*) a kind of tape or ribbon.

CA'DE (*Com.*) a vessel containing 100 herrings, or 1000 sprats.

CA'DE-LAMB (*Husband.*) a lamb weaned and brought up in the house.

CA'DE-WORM (*Ent.*) vide *Cadbote-fly*.

CADEL-AVA'NACU (*Bot.*) a tree growing in Brazil, the leaves of which are purgative. *Raii Hist. Plant*.

CADE'LSHEER (*Polit.*) a Turkish chief magistrate or governor of a province. There were three who held this rank; namely, one who was set over Natolia; a second over Romania; and a third over Egypt. They had all the cadies under them. *Theven. Voy. de Lev.*

CA'DENCE (*Gram.*) both in verse and prose, is formed by the difference of time in pronouncing.—*Cadence of the voice*, that sound of the voice which falls on the ear at the end, which may be agreeable or otherwise, but is mostly taken for what ends pleasantly to the ear.—*Cadence of a period*, an harmonious fall or termination of a period, or part of a period.

CADENCE (*Mus.*) or *reprize*, in Italian *cadenza*, a pause or suspension at the end of an air, resembling points or virgules in prose. Cadences afford the performer an opportunity of introducing a graceful extempore close. *Cadence* is also taken for the close or embellishment itself, whence the expression "To close the song with a fine *cadence*."—*Cadence* is likewise used in dancing, when the steps follow the notes and measures of the music.

CADENCE (*Mil.*) a regular and uniform method of marching, in which the length of the step, the time, and the distance, are made to accord to a rule.

CADENCE (*Man.*) an equal measure or proportion observed by a horse in all his motions when he is thoroughly managed, and works justly at a gallop, *terrá à terrá*, so that his motions or times have an equal regard to each other.

CA'DENCY (*Her.*) a distinction of houses.

CADE'NE (*Com.*) the smallest Turkey carpets.

CA'DENT (*Astrol.*) an epithet for a planet when it is in a sign opposite to its exaltation.

CADE'NZA (*Mus.*) Italian for the close of an air or song. [vide *Cadence*]

CADET (*Her.*) the younger son of a family.

CADET (*Mil.*) a young gentleman who follows a course of instruction and discipline preparatory to his entering the army; of this description are the cadets, or *gentlemen cadets*, at the military college of Woolwich, &c.—*Cadet* is also a junior officer.—*Cadet* in the French army, is a volunteer serving without pay, for the express purpose of becoming acquainted with military tactics.

CADGE (*Mech.*) a round frame of wood, on which hawks are carried by the cadgers to be sold.

CA'DGER (*Com.*) a huckster; one who brings butter, eggs, and poultry, from the country to market.

CA'DI (*Polit.*) an officer of justice in Turkey, who acts as a judge.

CA'DIA (*Bot.*) from the Arab. *forsk*, a genus of plants, Class 10 *Decandria*, Order 1 *Monogynia*.
Generic Characters. CAL. *perianth* one-leaved.—COR. *petals* five.—STAM. *filaments* ten; *anthers* oblong.—PIST. *germ* linear; *style* bowed; *stigma* acute.—PER. *legume* linear; *seeds* oblong.
Species. The only species is Cadia purpurea Panciatica purpurea, seu *Spændoncea, tamarindifolia*, Purple flowered Cadia, a shrub, native of Arabia Felix.

CADILE'SHER (*Polit.*) vide *Cadelsheer*.

CA'DIS (*Com.*) woollen stuffs of different kinds in France.

CADME'AN *letters* (*Gram.*) the letters composing the Greek alphabet, which are supposed to have been brought out of Phenicia, by Cadmus, 1,500 years before Christ. [vide *Alphabets*, Tab. II, Plate 2.]

CA'DMIA (*Min.*) a mineral; so called from Cadmus, by whom the use of metals is supposed to have been introduced. Cadmia is either natural or artificial.—*Natural cadmia* is of two kinds, namely, *metallic cadmia*, which is otherwise called *cobalt*, and the *fossil cadmia*, otherwise called *Lapis calaminaris*, or the Calamine of the shops, now more commonly known by the name of zinc, from which brass is made.—*Artificial cadmia*, called by Agricola *Cadmia fornacum*, is also of two kinds, namely, that of the ancients, which was only the recrement blown off by the bellows in melting copper; and the *Cadmia officinarum*, the Cadmia of the shops, otherwise called Tutty. The cadmia of the ancients was distinguished by its form into the *bostryitis*, i. e. clustered like a bunch of grapes; *onychitis*, like an onyx stone; *placitis*, crusty; *zonitis*, surrounded with veins like girdles; *ostratitis*, testaceous, &c. This cadmia was much esteemed by physicians for its obstruent and drying virtues. Dioscor. l. 5, c. 84; Plin. l. 34, c. 10; Gal. de Simp. l. 9; Oribus Med. Coll. l. 11; Aet. Tetrab. 1, serm. 1; Paul. Æginet. l. 7, c. 3; Isidor. Orig. l. 16, c. 19; Agricol. de Re Metal. l. 8.

CADMITES (*Min.*) a precious stone having blue specks in it.

CA'DRE (*Mil.*) signifies in French literally a frame; but is used to denote the proposed establishment of a regiment.

CADRI'TES (*Theol.*) a sect among the Mahometans who lead a monastic life.

CADUCA'RIUS (*Ant.*) one made heir to the goods of another who has left no heir, an escheator; whence *caduca bona*, escheats. Isid. Orig. l. 5, c. 25.

CADUCEA'TOR (*Ant.*) a herald among the Romans who went to sue for peace, in distinction from the *feciales*, by whom war was declared. He was so called from the *caduceus* which he carried. [vide *Caduceus*]

CADU'CEUS (*Ant.*) a name for Mercury's rod or sceptre, supposed to be derived from the Greek κηρύκιον. It was furnished with a pair of wings, and two serpents entwine themselves about the top, as in the annexed figure. When found upon medals it is an emblem of peace, and was carried by the Roman heralds who went to proclaim peace, when they were called *caduceatores*. It is said to have been presented by Apollo to Mercury. Liv. l. 8, c. 20; Poll. l. 8, c. 2; Hygin. Astron. Poet.; Plin. l. 29, c. 3.

CADU'COUS (*Bot.*) *caducus*, i. e. falling off before the time; an epithet for different parts of plants, as the stipule bracte, petiole, pappus, &c.—*Bractæ caducæ*, are those which fall off before the end of the summer, as in the *Conglus*, or *vellana*, or Hazel.—*Pappus caducus* is that which falls off upon the ripening of the seed.

CADU'CUS *morbus* (*Med.*) the falling sickness or epilepsy.

CA'DUS (*Ant.*) κάδος, or κάδδος, a Grecian and Roman measure, equal to about ten gallons English. Poll. Onom. l. 9; Plin. l. 14, c. 16.

CÆCA'LISVENA (*Anat.*) the same as *Cæcum intestinum*.

CÆ'CIAS (*Nat.*) καικίας, a northerly wind, which, according to Aristotle, is distinguished from the other winds by its drawing the clouds to itself. Aristot. Prob. sect. 26; Vitruv. l. 1, c. 6; Plin. l. 2, c. 47; Aul. Gell. l. 2, c. 22; Salmas in Solin. p. 1227.

CÆCI'LIA (*Zool.*) a genus of animals, Class *Amphibia*, Order *Serpentes*.
Generic Character. Body and Tail wrinkled.—*Upper lip* with two tentacula.
Species. The species are—*Cæcilia tentaculata*, seu *L'Ibiare*, Eel-shaped Cæcilia, a native of South America.—*Cæcilia Glutinosa*, seu *Serpens cæcilia, ceilonica*, White sided Cæcilia, native of South America.—*Cæcilia Gracilis*, seu *tentaculata*, Slender Cæcilia.

CÆCILIA'NA (*Bot.*) a species of lettuce mentioned by Pliny. Hist. Nat. l. 15, c. 25.

CÆ'CUM *intestinum* (*Anat.*) τὸ τυφλὸν, also called by Ruffus Ephesius, the *Appendicula cæci*, comprehends the first of the three portions into which the large intestines are divided; it is called the *cæcum*, or Blind Gut, because it is perforated at one end only, being a round bag, with the mouth upwards. It has also been called *monomachon*, and by Paracelsus *monocolon*. Ruf. Ephes. l. 1, c. 27; Gal. de Usu. Part. l. 4; Gorr. Def. Med.

CÆ'LUM (*Anat.*) οὐρανὸς, the roof of the mouth. Ruf. Ephes. de Appell. Part. Corp. hum. l. 1, c. 8.

CÆMENTUM (*Min.*) cement. 1. A preparation of brickdust, crocus of Mars, crocus of Venus, alum, vitriol, &c. for the corroding, exalting, and depurating metals; that which is used for the depurating of gold is called *cæmentum regale*. 2. The same thing as lute. [vide *Lute*]—*Cæmentum cupreum*, Cement Copper, or Ziment Copper; copper precipitated from vitriolic waters, by means of iron.

CÆMENTUM, *in the Linnean system*, a genus of earths, Order *Argillaceous*.
Generic Character. It consists of iron, alumina, silica, and carbonate of lime.
Species. The species are—*Cæmentum Tufa*, Tufas or Tuffwacke.—*Cæmentum tarras*, seu *induracum*, Terass, Terras, or Parras.—*Cæmentum columnare*, &c.

CÆNO'PTERIS (*Bot.*) a genus of plants, Class 24 *Cryptogamia*, Order 1 *Filices*.
Generic Character. Fructifications in submarginal lateral lines, covered with a membrane, gaping on the outside.
Species. The only species is *Cænopteris rhizophylla*, native of the island of Dominica.

CÆ'PA (*Bot.*) vide *Cepa*.

CÆRI'TES *tabulæ* (*Ant.*) tables or registers in which the Censors entered the names of those citizens, who for any misdemeanor were deprived of their suffrage or voice at an election; whence the expression *In cæritum tabulas referre*, signifying to lose the right of voting at elections, because the people of Cære, though made denizens of Rome, had, notwithstanding, no voice at elections, wherefore Horace says, *Cærite cerâ digni*, i. e. persons fit to be amerced or degraded. Hor. l. 1, epist. 6, v. 63; Aul. Gell. l. 16, c. 13; Ascon. in Cic.

CÆSALPI'NIA (*Bot.*) a genus of plants, named by Plumier after Cæsalpinus, physician to Clement VIII, of the Class 10 *Decandria*, Order 1 *Monogynia*.
Generic Characters. CAL. *perianth* one-leaved.—COR. *petals* five.—STAM. *filaments* ten; *anthers* oblong.—PIST. *germ* superior; *style* filiform; *stigma* blunt.—PER. *legume* oblong; *seeds* few.
Species. The species are shrubs, as—*Cæsalpinia bijuga, aculeata, vesicaria*, &c. seu *spinosa, Senna spuria*, &c.

Acacia gloriosa, &c. seu *Poinciana bijuga*, native of Jamaica.—*Cæsalpinia pulcherrima*, seu *aculeata*, *Poinciana pulcherrima*, seu *aculeata*, *Senna spuria*, &c. *bristapavonis*, *Frutex pavonius*, *Acacia orientalis*, &c. *Flos pavonis*, seu *Spetti mandaru*, native of the Indies.—*Cæsalpinia elata*, seu *inermis*, seu *Poinciana elata*, &c. native of India.—*Cæsalpinia boviaria*, seu *inermis Poinciana coriaria*, *Siliqua*, seu *Libididi*, native of the island of Caraccas.—*Cæsalpinia brasiliensis*, *inermis*, seu *arborea inermis*, &c. seu *Pseudo Santalum*, &c. Smooth Brassiletto, native of Carolina.—*Cæsalpinia eclimata*, seu *aculeata*, *Pseudo-Santalum*, *Arbor Brasilia*, *Acacia gloriosa*, seu *Iberapitanga*, native of Brasil.—*Cæsalpinia Sappan*, seu *aculeata*, *Lignum Sappan*, seu *Tsiani pangam*, Narrow-leaved Prickly Brasiletto, native of the Indies.—*Cæsalpinia crista*, *aculeata*, seu *polyphylla*, &c. Broad-leaved Prickly Brasiletto, native of Jamaica.—*Cæsalpinia mimosoides*, seu *aculeata*, *Mimosa malabarica*, seu *Kali-lodda-vaddi*, native of the East Indies.—*Cæsalpinia pyramidata*, seu *Robinia pyramidata*, native of the West Indies. *Bauh. Pin.*; *Raii Hist. Plant.*

CÆSALPINIA, as a species, is the *Guilandina Bondu* of Linnæus.

CÆSA'REA *sectio* (*Mid.*) *hysterotomia*, the Cæsarean Section; so called because Cæsar is said to have been born in this manner; the operation of extracting the fœtus from the uterus, by dividing the ligaments of the abdomen. *Plin.* l. 7, c. 9; *Roset. de Hysterot. apud C. Bauh.*; *Heist. Chirurg.* pars. 2, sect. 5, c. 113.

CÆSARIE'NSES (*Ant.*) officers of the treasury at the court of the Greek emperors.

CÆ'SIAS (*Ant.*) vide *Cæcias*.

CÆ'SIUS (*Med.*) grey, like the eyes of a cat; an epithet for urine; as also for the eyes.

CÆ'SO (*Mid.*) one born by means of the Cæsarian operation. *Plin.* l. 7, c. 9.

CÆ'STUS (*Ant.*) μύρμηξ, a kind of club, or rather thong of leather, having plummets of lead fastened to it, which was used by pugilists at the games. *Propert.* l. 3, el. 12.

Nunc ligat ad cæstum gaudentia brachia loris.

Cic. Tusc. Quæst. l. 2, c. 17; *Poll.* l. 3, segm. 150; *Plin.* l. 11, c. 37; *Eustath. in Hom. Il.*; *Serv. in Virg. Æn.* l. 5, v. 457; *Merc. de Arte Gymn.* l. 2, c. 9; *Turneb. Adv.* l. 14, c. 4.

CÆSU'RA (*Poet.*) from *cædo*, to cut; a figure in prosody, by which a division or separation takes place in a foot that is composed of syllables belonging to separate words. It is called in the Greek τομή, or κόμμα, by Cicero and Victorinus *incisio* or *insiscum*. It is divided into four kinds, which take their name from the place where they are found in a verse, as the *Trihemimeris*, when the cæsura is made after the third half foot, as
Virg. Æn. l. 4, v. 64.

Pectori | bus inhians spirantia, consulit exta.

Penthemimeris, when it falls after the fifth half foot, as *Virg. Æn.* l. 5, v. 337.

Emicat | Eurya | lus, et munere victor amici.

Hepthemimeris, when it falls after the seventh half foot, as *Virg. Æn.* l. 1, v. 482.

Per ter | ram et ver | sâ pul | vis inscribitur hastâ.

Ennehemimeris, when it falls after the ninth half foot, as *Virg. Æn.* l. 10, v. 720.

Graius ho | mo, infec | tos lin | quens profu | gus hymenæos.

In all which examples it is observable that the cæsura has the force of converting the short syllables *bus*, *lus*, *vis*, and *gus* into long ones.

CÆ'TERIS *paribus* (*Phil.*) a term frequently used by writers in drawing comparisons between objects, which signifies the rest, or other things, being alike or equal: thus, of a bullet it may be said, *cæteris paribus*, the heavier it is the greater the range, supposing the strength of the powder, the length, and the diameter of the two pieces, &c. to be the same. So in Ethics, *cæteris paribus*, a wealthy man is fitter to be entrusted with power than a poor man, i. e. supposing both to be alike known or esteemed for their moral character.

CA'FFA (*Com.*) painted cloths, manufactured in the East Indies, and sold at Bengal.

CA'FFEIN (*Chem.*) the bitter principle of coffee.

CA'FFILA (*Com.*) a company of travellers, or merchants, who form themselves into a band, for the purpose of passing with greater security through the dominions of the Great Mogul to the East Indies. 2. A fleet of merchant ships, kept by the King of Portugal, which navigate the coast of Guzarat.

CA'FFTAN (*Cus.*) a Persian vest or garment which is now worn by the Turks.

CAG (*Mech.*) a vessel of wood in the form of a barrel, holding about four or five gallons, and sometimes less.

CAGA'STRUM (*Med.*) morbific seed, not innate or hereditary, but adventitious, producing pleurisies, fevers, &c. in distinction from the *Iliastrum*. *Parac. Lex.*

CAGE (*Mech.*) from the Latin *cavea* and *cavus*, hollow; any inclosure for birds or beasts.

CAGE (*Carpent.*) an outer work of timber for the inclosure of other works, as the cage of stairs, which is the same as the wooden case.

CAGE (*Law*) a machine built with lattice-work, which was used as a place of confinement for prisoners. The same name is now given to a temporary place of confinement in each parish for occasional offenders.

CAGE *de la bascule* (*Mil.*) a space into which one part of the drawbridge falls whilst the other part rises and conceals the gate.

CA'GMAG (*Com.*) old geese are so called which are sent up to the London market for sale, when they are become useless in the country. Tough dry meat of any kind is also so called.

CA'HUTE (*Mil.*) French for a small hut, which soldiers make to defend themselves against the inclemencies of the weather.

CA'HYS (*Com.*) a corn measure of Seville, equal to one fourth of a bushel.

CAJA'CIA (*Bot.*) the same as *Cacica*.

CAJAHA'BA (*Bot.*) an Indian plant that entwines itself round trees like ivy.

CA'JAN (*Bot.*) a species of the *Cytisus*.

CAJA'TUS (*Bot.*) a species of the *Æschynomene*.

CAIC (*Mar.*) a galley-boat.

CAIDBEI'A (*Med.*) the *Forskohlea tenacissima* of Linnæus.

CA'JEPUT *oil* (*Med.*) an aromatic oil extracted from an Indian tree; the *Maleleuca leucodendron* of Linnæus.

CAIMA'CAN (*Polit.*) an officer of great dignity in Turkey, of which there are three; one who attends on the Grand Seignor, one attached to the Grand Vizier, and a third, who is governor of Constantinople.

CAI'NITES (*Ecc.*) or *Caineans*, a sect of heretics, branching off from the Gnostics in the second century. They were so called from Cain, whom they professed to honour. They also held Dathan, Abiram, and the other wicked Scripture characters, in veneration.

CAINITO (*Bot.*) a species of the *Chrysophyllum*.

CAJOU' (*Bot.*) the same as *Acajarba*.

CAIRNS (*Archæol.*) or *carnes*, a vulgar name for the heaps to be seen in many parts of Britain, which consist of stones.

CAISSO'N (*Mil.*) a chest filled with bombs and gunpowder,

to be buried under ground till the time for explosion, when it blows up all that is near it.—*Caisson* is also a covered waggon or carriage for the provisions and ammunition belonging to an army.

CAISSON (*Mar.*) a chest in the form of a boat, used in the dock-yards instead of flood-gates, for getting ships in and out.

CAISSON (*Archit.*) the wooden chest, or flat-bottomed boat, sunk in the beds of rivers, &c. to keep off the water while laying the foundation of bridges, &c. It is so contrived that the bottom is made to serve in part for the foundation.

CA'KILE (*Bot.*) a species of *Bunias*.

CAL (*Chem.*) Yellow Arsenic.

CA'LA (*Ant.*) the club or staff carried by slaves who attended their masters to the field of battle.

CA'LABA (*Bot.*) the *Calophyllum* of Linnæus, an Indian tree, from the trunk and branches of which issues a gum like mastich.

CA'LABASH (*Bot.*) a sort of Gourd.—*Calabash Tree*, the *Crescentia* of Linnæus, the fruit of which is enclosed in a shell that serves the natives of the Caribbee islands for a drinking cup, a pot for boiling, a musical instrument, and various other domestic purposes.

CALA'BRA (*Ant.*) a place of meeting for religious matters, as the appointment of festivals, games, sacrifices, &c. *Fest. de Verb. Signif.*

CALABU'RA (*Bot.*) a species of the *Muntingia* of Linnæus.

CALADA'RIS (*Com.*) a coarse calico of Bengal.

CALA'DE (*Man.*) or *casse*, the slope of a manege-ground, down which a horse is ridden several times in a gallop, to make him learn to ply his haunches.

CALA'DIUM (*Bot.*) the *Arum esculentum* of Linnæus.

CALA'C (*Min.*) a kind of Indian tin, from which cerass is made.

CALA'F (*Bot.*) the *Salix Ægyptiaca* of Linnæus.

CALAGUA'BA (*Bot.*) a root brought from America, and used with success in medicine. It is probably a species of the *Polypodium*.

CALAMACO'RUS (*Bot.*) the Indian Reed.

CALAMAGRO'STIS (*Bot.*) Sheer Grass, or Reed Grass, a sort of grass which, according to Dioscorides, is larger than the common sort. *Dioscor.* l. 4, c. 3.

CALAMAGROSTIS is the *Arundo epigejos et calamagrostis* of Linnæus. *Park. Theat. Botan.*; *Raii Hist. Plant.*

CALAMA'NCO (*Com.*) a woollen stuff of Flanders, Brabant, &c. which has a fine gloss upon it, and is chequered in the warp.

CALAMA'RIA (*Bot.*) the *Isoetes lacustris* of Linnæus.

CALAMA'RIÆ (*Bot.*) from *calamus*, the third Order in Linnæus' "Fragments of a Natural Arrangement," comprehending the sedges and other plants nearly allied to the Grasses.

CALAME'DON (*Surg.*) from καλάμος, a reed; a species of fracture which runs along the bone in a right line, but is bent at the extremity.

CALAME'TA (*Ant.*) from *calamus*, a reed; broken pieces of reeds with which the ancients propped their vines in vineyards.

CALAMINARIS *lapis* (*Min.*) the Calamine Stone, the *Zincum calaminaris* of Linnæus, and the Oxyde of zinc of the chymists; a kind of bituminous fossile earth, which when mixed with copper produces brass. [vide *Cadmia*] It is used as an absorbent and drier in outward medicinal applications, but seldom given inwardly. *Gal. de Sanit. tuend.* l. 4; *Oribas Med. Coll.* l. 11; *Aet. Tetrab.* 1. serm. 1; *Paul. Æginet.* l. 7, c. 3.

CA'LAMINE (*Min.*) the *Zincum calaminaris* of Linnæus.

CA'LAMINT (*Bot.*) in Latin *Calamintha*, in Greek καλαμίνθη, a herb; the Mountain Mint.

CALAMI'NTHA (*Bot.*) Calamint, from the two Greek words καλὴ μίνθη, i. e. good mint, is an aromatic herb much used in physic as a cordial, alexipharmic, stomachic, carminative, uterine, and emmenagogue medicine. *Gal. de San. tuend.* l. 4; *Oribas Med. Coll.* l. 11; *Aet. Tetrab.* 1, serm. 1.

CALAMINTHA is the *Melissa Calamintha, grandiflora*, &c. of Linnæus.

CALAMI'STRUM (*Ant.*) a crisping or frizzling iron with which the hair is curled.

CALAMI'TA (*Ant.*) the name for little green frogs living among reeds and shrubs. *Plin.* l. 32, c. 10.

CALAMITA (*Min.*) a dry sort of *Styrax*.

CALAMI'TES (*Min.*) a precious stone which is formed with many joints, after the manner of *calamus*, a reed. *Plin.* l. 37, c. 10.

CALAMI'TIS (*Min.*) 1. A factitious cadmia, which by adhering to iron acquires the form of a reed. 2. A marine stone in the form of a reed.

CA'LAMUS (*Ant.*) κάλαμος. 1. A reed or pipe which was formerly used by rustics as a musical instrument. *Virg. Ecl.* 6, v. 69.

—*Hos tibi dant calamos, en accipe, Musæ*
Ascræo, quos ante seni; quibus ille solebat
Cantando rigidas deducere montibus ornos.

2. A pole or rod to measure with. *Cenal. de Ponder. apud Græv. Thesaur. Antiq. Roman.* tom. 11, p. 148. 3. *Calamus aucupatorius*, a rod which was used in catching hawks.—4. *Calamus scriptorius*, or, according to Apuleius, *chartorius*, a pen, because pens were formerly made of reeds instead of quills. For which purpose the Ægyptian reed was preferred.
Mart. l. 14, v. 38.

Dat chartis habiles calamos Memphitica tellus.

Arundo and *calamus* are sometimes indifferently put for the same thing.
Pers. sat. 3, v. 11.

Inque manus chartæ, nodosaque venit arundo.
Tum queritur, crassus calamo quod pendeat humor,
Nigra quod infusa vanescat sepia lympha:
Dilutas queritur geminet quod fistula guttas.

Cels. l. 5, c. 28; *Apul. Florid.*; *Plin.* l. 6, c. 36; *Voss. de Art. Gram.* l. 1, c. 36; *Hugo de prim. Scrib. Orig.* c. 9; *Salmas. Exercit. Plin.* p. 917, B.

CALAMUS (*Bot.*) Reed, a well known plant, a species of which Dioscorides speaks under the name of the κάλαμος ἀρωματικός, the aromatic reed, and describes it as having a viscous, astringent, and somewhat acrimonious taste. *Theoph. Hist. Plant.* l. 4, c. 12; *Dioscor.* l. 1, c. 17; *Plin.* l. 13, c. 11; *Gal. de Simpl.* l. 7; *Oribas. Med. Coll.* l. 11; *Aet. Tetrab.* 1, serm. 1; *Paul Æginet.* l. 7, c. 3.

CALAMUS, in the Linnean system, a genus of plants, Class 6 *Hexandria*, Order 1 *Monogynia*.

Generic Characters. CAL. *perianth* six-leaved.—COR. none.—STAM. *filaments* six; *anthers* round.—PIST. *germ* roundish; *style* bifid; *stigmas* simple.—PER. membranaceous; *seed* one.

Species. The species are shrubs, and natives of the East Indies, as the—*Calamus Rotang, seu petræus, Arundo Zeylanica, &c. nucifera, &c. seu Rotang Fructus Cannæ, &c. Tsieru Tsierrel, seu Palmijuncus Calapparicus Rattan.*—*Calamus verus, seu Palmijuncus verus*, native of India.—*Calamus Draco, seu Palmijuncus Draco*, native of the East Indies.—*Calamus niger, seu Palmijuncus niger.*—*Calamus viminalis, seu Palmijuncus viminalis*, native of Java.—*Calamus rudentum, seu Palmijuncus albus.*—*Calamus equestris, seu Palmijuncus equestris.*—*Calamus Zalacca, Palmijuncus Zalacca, seu Fructus Baly, &c. Raii Hist. Plant.*

CALAMUS *Scriptorius* (*Anat.*) a canal at the bottom of the fourth ventricle of the brain, so called from its resemblance to the *calamus scriptorius*, or writing pen of the ancients.

CALA'NDO (*Mus.*) or *Caland*, an Italian word, denoting that the time of the passage over which it is written, is to be gradually diminished in quickness.

CALANDRA (*Or.*) a sort of lark.

CALA'NGIUM (*Archæol.*) or *calangre*, a challenge.

CALA'NTICA (*Ant.*) a hurl, or coif, a covering for the female head. *Cic. apud Non.* l. 14, c. 2; *Alex. Gen. Dier.* l. 5, c. 18.

CALA'PPA (*Bot.*) the *Cocos nucifera* of Linnæus.

CALA'SH (*Mech.*) an open travelling chariot.

CALASI'RIS (*Ant.*) καλάσιρις, a linen garment worn by the sacrificers. *Aristoph. in Av.; Herodot.* l. 2, c. 81; *Poll. Onom.* l. 8, c. 16; *Fest. de Verb. Signif.*

CALATA *comitia* (*Ant.*) a name given to the *comitia*, which was held by the appointment of the college of Pontifices, for the purpose of electing the *rex sacrorum*, and other priests, &c. Both the *comitia curiata*, and the *centuriata*, had this name, because they were *calata*, called or summoned by the lictor, or by a trumpeter. *Varro de Ling. Lat.* l. 4, c. 16; *Aul. Gell.* l. 15, c. 27.

CALATHIA'NA (*Bot.*) Calathian Violet, the *Gentiana Pnemonanthe* of Linnæus.

CA'LATHUS (*Ant.*) a basket, or panicle, made of ozier, which was said to be of Grecian origin, and was used for holding flowers.
· *Virg.* ecl. II. v. 45.
—————— *tibi lilia plenis*
Ecce ferunt nymphæ calathis.

Ovid. Fast. l. 4, v. 485, speaking of Proserpine,
Hæc implet lento calathos e vimine nexos.

Vitruv. l. 4, c. 1; *Serv. in Virg. Eclog.; Isidor. Orig.* l. 19, c. 28. 2. A vessel, or pan, for holding cheese.
Virg. Georg. l. 3, v. 400.
Quod surgente die mulsere, horisque diurnis,
Nocte premunt; quod jam tenebris et sole cadente,
Sub lucem exportans calathis, adit oppida pastor.

Columel. l. 7, c. 8. 3. A cup. *Virg. Eclog.* 8, v. 71; *Mart. Apophoret.* 97.

CALA'TOR (*Ant.*) ἀπὸ τῦ καλεῖν, an apparitor, or officer at the call of the magistrates, but more particularly of the priests, whom he attended in the sacrifices, and of whom frequent mention is made in inscriptions, as Q. CÆCILIO FEROCI CALATORI SACERDOTITII TITIALIUM FLAVIALIUM. *Plaut. Rud.* act. 2, scen. 3; *Tacit. Annal.* l. 3, c. 27; *Sueton. Gram.* c. 12; *Popm. Serv.* p. 75; *Pignor. de Serv.* p. 113.

CALATRA'VA *Knights of* (*Her.*) an ancient Spanish military order, so called from a fort of that name, and instituted by Sancho III. Their habit was a black garment with a red cross on the breast.

CA'LBEUS (*Ant.*) a name for the bracelets which were given to soldiers. *Fest. de Verb. Signif.*

CA'LCADIS (*Chem.*) White Vitriol.

CALCA'GIUM (*Ant.*) vide *Calcea*.

CALCA'NEUM (*Anat.*) πτέρνα, the Heel-bone, the largest bone. *Paul. Ægin.* l. 7, c. 14.

CALCA'NTHUS, the same as Vitriol.

CALCAR (*Mech.*) vide *Calcaria Fornax*.

CALCAR (*Bot.*) the Spur, a horned-shaped production of the corolla, in which honey is found. [vide *Spur*]

CALCAR (*Chem.*) a calcining furnace.

CALCAR (*Anat.*) the same as *Calcaneum*.

CALCAR (*Min.*) vide *Calcaria*.

CA'LCARATE (*Bot.*) Calcaratus, from *calcar*, a spur, spurred; an epithet for a calyx, *calcaratus calyx*, a calcarate calyx, as in *Tropæolum*—also for a corolla, *calcarata corolla*, a corolla furnished with a spur, or in the shape of a spur, as in Larkspur, Antirrhinum, &c.

CALCA'REOUS (*Min.*) the third order of the Class Earths, according to Gmelin's system, consisting principally of carbonate of lime.
The *Genera* are as follow, namely—*Creta*, Chalk, calcining in the fire, but not vitrifying.—*Tophus*, precipitated by water under water.—*Spatum*, Spar, crackling in the fire. —*Schistospatum*, a proportion of carbonic acid gas and water.—*Inolithus*, Limestone, entirely soluble in nitric acid with effervescence.—*Stalactites*, Stalactite, formed in the water by the gradual deposition of water.—*Pisolithus*, Carbonate of lime, a very small proportion of sand and oxide of iron, carbonic acid gas and water.— *Marmor*, Marble, burning into quick lime, soluble the greater part in acids.—*Suillus*, Swinestone burning into quick lime.—*Tremolites*, Tremolite, emitting a phosphorescent light in the dark when struck or rubbed.—*Stellaris*, easily melting in the fire.—*Humus*, Mould, consisting of carbonate of lime, a smaller proportion of silica, hydrogen, and carbonic acid gas, and oxyde of iron.—*Marga*, Marl, partly soluble in nitric acid with effervescence; hardening in the fire, and vitrifying in a strong heat.—*Magnesia*, Brown Spar, becoming black in the fire.—*Picrospatum*, Bitterspath; effervescing slowly with acids.—*Gypsum*, not commonly effervescing with nitric acids, and melting with difficulty in the fire.— *Hepaticus*, when rubbed giving out an odour like liver of sulphur, not effervescing with acids.—*Fluor*, not effervescing with acids, but if distilled with the mineral acids, emitting the fluoric acid gas.—*Apatites*, Phosphorite, soluble in nitric acid, melting in the fire with difficulty, emitting a yellowish-green phosphorescent light. —*Boracites*, consisting of carbonate of lime, boracic acid with a little alumina, silica, and oxide of iron, crackling in the fire, and before the blow-pipe contracting and melting into yellowish glass.

CALCARIA FORNAX (*Mech.*) a sort of calcining furnace in glass-houses.

CALCARIS *flos* (*Bot.*) a flower so called because it somewhat resembles *calcaria*, or spurs, in shape, as the Larkspur.

CALCARIS *lapis* (*Min.*) Limestone.

CALCEA (*Ant.*) a causeway, from *calx*, the chalk, or stones, with which it was made; *calcearum operationes*, the work done by the adjoining tenants; and *calcagium*, the tax paid by the neighbourhood for the repair of the causeways.

CALCEARIUM (*Ant.*) an allowance made to the soldiers for their shoes. *Suet. Vespas.* c. 8; *Ulp. Leg.* 21. *ff. de Alim. et Cib. Leg.; Bergier de Viis Milit.* l. 4, c. 2.

CALCEDO'NIUS (*Min.*) Calcedony, vide *Chalcedonius*.

CALCEDONY (*Min.*) *Chalcedonius*.

CALCEDONY (*Lap.*) or *Calcedon*, a defect in some precious stone, either of a foul vein, or a different colour from the rest.

CALCE'NA (*Med.*) a morbous, tartareous matter. *Parac. de Tartar.* l. 2, c. 1.

CALCEOLA'RIA (*Bot.*) from *calceolus*, a slipper, Slipperwort; a genus of plants, Class 2 *Diandria*, Order 1 *Monogynia*.
Generic Characters. CAL. *perianth* one-leaved.—COR. monopetalous.—STAM. *filaments* two; *anthers* incumbent. —PIST. *germ* roundish; *style* very short; *stigma* bluntish. PER. *capsule* subconic; *seeds* numerous.
Species. The species are mostly annuals, as—*Calceolaria pinnata*, seu *Fagelia flavitans*, Pinnated Slipperwort, an annual, native of Peru.—*Calceolaria integrifolia*, seu *serrata*, Whole-leaved Slipper-wort, native of Peru.— *Calceolaria ovata, dichotoma*, seu *integrifolia*, an annual, native of Peru.—*Calceolaria perfoliata*, Perfoliate Slipper-wort, native of Peru.— *Calceolaria crenata*, native of Peru. But—*Calceolaria Fothergillii*, Spatula-leaved Slipper-wort, is a biennial, and native of the Falkland

2 P

isles; and—*Calceolaria plantaginea*, seu *biflora*, Plantain-leaved Slipper-wort.—*Calceolaria nana*, seu *uniflora*, Dwarf Slipper-wort, are perennials.—*Calceolaria* is also the *viola calceolaria* of Linnæus.

CALCE'OLUS (*Bot.*) or *Calciolus*, Our Lady's Slipper, a species of *Alisma*.

CA'LCES *metallic* (*Chem.*) Metals which have undergone the process of calcination, or combustion.

CALCE'TUM (*Ant.*) vide *Calcea*.

CALCE'TUS (*Med.*) impregnated with tartareous particles; an epithet for the blood. *Parac. de Tartar.* l. 2.

CA'LCEUM *equinum* (*Bot.*) the herb Colt's Foot.

CA'LCEUS (*Ant.*) a shoe, or whatever served as a covering for the foot. The *calceus* differed from the *solea*, inasmuch as the former covered the whole foot, and the latter only the sole of the foot. The two sorts of *calcei* spoken of by the ancients are the—*Calcei lunati*, which were worn by the Patricians, so called from an ivory crescent with which they were ornamented, and the—*Calcei mullei*, red shoes, so called from their resemblance to the mullet in colour. They came up to the middle of the leg, but covered only the sole of the foot. They were first worn by the Alban kings, afterwards by the kings of Rome; but on the abolition of the monarchy they were appropriated to those who had borne a curule office. The *calceus lunatus* was otherwise called the *Lunula*. [vide *Lunula*] the *calceus mulleus*, simply *mulleus*. [vide *Mulleus*]

CALCHY'THEOS (*Chem.*) Verdigrease.

CALCHOI'DEA *ossicula* (*Anat.*) the same as *Cuneiformia ossicula*.

CALCI'DICUM (*Med.*) a medicine prepared of arsenic.

CALCIFRA'GA (*Bot.*) Breakstone; an epithet for the *Scolopendrium* of Linnæus. *Scrib. Larg.*

CALCIGRA'DUS (*Med.*) στιροβάτης, one walking, or laying a stress on the heel. *Hipp. de Artic.*; *Foes. Œconom. Hippocrat.*

CALCINA'TION (*Chem.*) the solution of a mixed body by means of heat, or otherwise, into a powder; or, in other words, the dissolution, or corrosion, of compact bodies into their minutest parts, so that they become friable: this was formerly called *Chemical Pulverization*, now more commonly called *Oxidation*. The body so reduced was named a *calx*, in common language a *cinder*, now chemically an *Oxide*. Calcination is performed, or takes place, either by *actual fire*, when the combustible parts of bodies are consumed by exposure to the heat of the fire, or the sun; or by *potential fire*, that is, by the addition of some proper *menstruum*, with or without the aid of fire, which is otherwise called *Corrosion*, as when copper is calcined in spirit of Nitre. Of this description is that sort of *Calcination*, in particular, which is termed *Philosophical*, as when the horns, bones, or hoofs of animals, are suspended over boiling water, or any other liquid, until by the force of the heat they lose their mucilage, and are easily reduced to powder.

That species of Calcination which is performed by means of fire alone, or a dry *menstruum*, is termed a *dry Calcination*, as the calcinations of metallic substances, the deflagration of vegetable substances, the calcination of chalk into lime, &c. in distinction from the *Humid* or *Moist Calcination*, as the calcination of copper and lead by means of vinegar so as to procure verdigrease and ceruss. To this class belongs the calcination by means of the air, as also that of *Amalgamation, Fumigation, Detonation, Granulation, Cementation,* and *Extinction*.

Calcination is also differently denominated according to the objects to which it is applied, as *Ustion*, when applied to hartshorn, alum, and brass.—*Toasting*, when applied to rhubarb and such other substances.—*Decrepitation*, as applicable to common salt.

CALCINA'TORY, a vessel to calcine metals in.

CALCINA'TUM (*Chem.*) a term applied to chemical substances when calcined, as—*Calcinatum majus*, what is dulcified by chemical art and not by nature, as dulcified mercury, &c.—*Calcinatum majus Potterii*, Mercury dissolved in aqua-fortis and precipitated in salt water.—*Calcinatum minus*, what is sweet by nature without edulcoration.

TO CA'LCINE (*Chem.*) to reduce to a powder by means of fire, or of a *menstruum*; a process formerly distinguished by the annexed mark.

CA'LCIS *aqua* (*Min.*) *Calcis liquor*, seu *Calcis vivæ flores*, the solution of lime.

CALCIS *vitriolatæ cataplasma* (*Med.*) a cataplasm of plaster of Paris, which is applied to ulcers.

CALCIS *os* (*Ana.*) vide *Calcaneum*.

CALCITA'RI (*Min.*) the same as *Alcali*.

CALCITE'A (*Min.*) the same as *Vitriol*.

CALCITEO'SA (*Min.*) the same as *Lythargyrum*.

CALCI'THOS (*Min.*) the same as *Ærugo Æris*.

CALCITRA'PA (*Bot.*) the *Centaurea*, &c. and the *Valeriana*, &c. of Linnæus. *Hall.*

CALCITRAPO'IDES (*Bot.*) The *Centaurea Isnardi* of Linnæus.

CALCO'GRAPHIST (*Mech.*) from καλκα, brass, and γράφω, to write; an engraver in brass.

CALCSI'NTER (*Min.*) a subspecies of fibrous limestone.

CA'LCTUFF (*Min.*) a subspecies of fibrous lime.

CA'LCULARY *of a pear* (*Bot.*) a congeries of little hard knots dispersed through the parenchyma of the fruit, which surround the acetary or acid pulpy substance.

CALCULA'TION (*Arith.*) from *calculus*, (the pebble used by the ancients in calculation) the act of computing several sums by means of addition, subtraction, multiplication, division, &c.

CALCULATION (*Mil.*) the art of computing the amplitudes of shells, time of flight, projectile curve, &c.

CALCULA'TOR (*Arith.*) one who makes computations.

CALCULATOR (*Astron.*) a machine invented by Mr. Ferguson in the shape of an orrery, for exhibiting the motions of the earth, moon, &c.

CALCULATO'RES (*Ant.*) accountants or slaves among the Romans, who formerly used to reckon by means of calculi, of whom mention is made in an inscription V. T. P. CÆCILIUS EMPERODIUS VI. VIR. AUG. CALCULATOR. JUSTINÆ. SALENÆ. UXORI. ET SIBI. *Ulpian. Leg.* 7. *ff de Oper. Libert.*; *Modestin. Leg.* 15. *ff. de Excusor. Tutor.*; *Capitolin. de Helv. Pert.*; *Honor. Cod. Theod. de Logogr. et Cons.* l. 5; *Isidor. Orig.* l. 1, c. 3; *Popma. de Operis. Serv.*

CA'LCULUS (*Ant.*) in Greek ψῆφος, signifies, literally, a little stone or pebble, but was afterwards applied to the little balls of ivory or metal, with which computations were made, votes given, and sentences passed by the judges, &c.; whence, among the Romans, *calculus albus* a favourable vote, or a vote of acquittal; and *calculus niger*, or a sentence of condemnation. These calculi were marked with the letters A for *absolvo*, i. e. I acquit; C for *condemno*, I condemn; and N L, *non liquet*, i. e. it is not clear, must be further examined and additional information given.—*Calculi lusorii* were the chess-men, or little balls, which were employed in the game of chess, which the poets allude to, both as to their matter, their colour, and their use. They were made either of ivory, of gold, silver, or glass.

Juv. sat. 11, v. 131.

——— *adeo nulla uncia nobis*
Est eboris, nec tessellæ, nec calculus ex hac
Materia.

Lucan. Ad Pison. v. 180.

Callidiore modo tabula variatur aperta
Calculus, et vitreo peraguntur milite bella.

They were of two colours, black and white.
Lucan. v. 182.

    Ut niveus nigros, nunc et niger alliget albos.

Ovid. Trist. l. 2, v. 477.

    Discolor ut recto grassetur limite miles
    Cum medius gemino calculus hoste perit.

Mart. l. 14, ep. 17.

    Calculus hic gemino discolor hoste perit.

The common men were called *latrunculi*, or latrones. *Mart.* l. 14, ep. 20.

    Insidiosorum si ludis bella latronum
    Gemmeus iste tibi miles et hostis erit.

whence the game was called *ludus latrunculorum*, and was played with thirty calculi, fifteen white and fifteen black, as in the present day. [vide *Chess*] *Poll. Onom.* l. 9, segm. 97; *Senec. de Tranquill. Anim.* c. 14, &c.; *Petron.* c. 33; *Plin.* l. 8, c. 54; *Sidon.* l. 8, ep. 12; *Scholiast. in Theocrit.*; *Gronov. de Vet. Pecun.* l. 3, c. 15.

CALCULUS (*Med.*) the stone or gravel; a disease which consists in the lodgement of a calcareous substance in the bladder or kidneys. The Calculus in the bladder is called *lithiasis*; that in the kidneys *nephritis*. *Aret.* l. 2, c. 3; *Cel.* l. 5, c. 20; *Gal. de San. tuend.* l. 6; *Oribas. de Vist. Simpl.* l. 2, c. 1; *Aet. Tetrab.* 1, serm. 1; *Paul. Æginet.* l. 8, c. 11; *Act. de Meth. Med.* l. 1, c. 22.

CALCULUS (*Chem.*) a name for any calcareous substance formed in the animal body. The ingredients in the different calculi have been found to be not less than twelve, namely, lithic acid, urate of ammonia and soda, phosphate of lime, acid phosphate of lime, ammoniaco-magnesian phosphate, oxalate of lime, carbonate of lime, flint, spermaceti, bezoardic animal resin, and gelatine. The specific gravity of urinary calculi is, in the lightest, 1213,1000; in the heaviest, 1976,1000. The calculus, when single, is usually oval; but when there are several calculi in the bladder the shape is more irregular, and still more so in proportion to their number. They are mostly laminated, and the lamina are of different thickness, and irregular in their direction; in the middle of these a nucleus is commonly seen, of the same mass as the rest. The colour is either white, brown, or resembling that of the mulberry. Those of the latter description, from their resemblance to the mulberry in form as well as colour, are called *mulberry-stones*, which being very rugged, cause the most pain of all. Their smell is partly strong, like that of urine or ammonia, and partly insipid or terreous, especially the white ones, which are like sawed ivory or rasped stone.

CALDA'RIUM (*Ant.*) 1. A sweating room, or a place in the bath heated by means of steam, which Cicero called *Vaporarium*, and Seneca *Sudatorium*, and *Laconicum*. *Cic. ad Quint. Frat.* l. 3, epist. 1; *Vitruv.* l. 5, c. 10; *Senec. epist.* 51: *Plin.* l. 5, epist 6. 2. A vessel or cauldron in which water was heated. *Vitruv.* l. 5, c. 10; *Plin.* l. 5, c. 8; *Bald. Lex. Vitruv.*; *Meurs. de Calid. Pot.* c. 1, § 1; *Græv. Thes. Antiq. Roman.* tom. 12, præfat.

CALDA'RIÆ ITA'LICÆ (*Ant.*) hot baths near Ferrara in Italy, good for retention of urine.

CA'LE (*Mil.*) or *la cale*, a punishment among the French, which is inflicted upon any soldier or sailor that wounds another maliciously. It consists in tying the culprit to the yard-arm, suddenly plunging him into the sea and then drawing him up again, very similar to what is called keel-hauling in the British service.

CA'LEA (*Bot.*) a genus of plants, Class 19 *Syngenesia*, Order 1 *Polygamia Æqualis.*

  Generic Characters. CAL. *common* imbricate.—COR. *compound* uniform.—STAM. *filaments* five; *anthers* cylindric.—PIST. *germ* oblongish; *style* filiform; *stigmas* two. PER. none; *seeds* solitary; *receptacle* chaffy.

  Species. The species are annuals or shrubs. Of the first kind are the—*Calea Jamaicensis, Santolina subhirsuta,* seu *Conyza fruticosa,* native of Jamaica. Of the second kind are the—*Calea oppositifolia, Santolina erecta,* seu *Acmella Jamaicensis, &c.* native of Jamaica.—*Calea amellus, Amellus ramosus,* seu *Santolina scandens, &c.* native of Jamaica.—*Calea lobata, Conyza lobata,* seu *arborescens, &c.* *Santolina erecta, &c.* seu *Virga aurea, &c.*—*Calea scoparia, Chrysocoma arborea, &c.* seu *Sergilus scoparius, &c.*—*Calea aspera,* a native of America, &c.

CALEFA'CIENTS (*Med.*) *calefacientia,* warming medicines; such as have a tendency to stimulate the action of the blood, as anise, carraway, cummin, &c. *Cel.* l. 2, c. 33; *Oribas.* l. 14, c. 19; *Aet. Tetrab.* 1, serm. 2, c. 267; *Paul. Æginet.* l. 3, c. 38, &c.

CALEFA'CTIO (*Chem.*) vide *Calcination.*

CALEFA'CTION (*Phy.*) the exciting or producing heat in a mixt body.

CALEFACTION (*Med.*) a way of preparing simple or compound medicines by a moderate heat of the sun.

CALEFA'CTORY (*Ecc.*) a room in a monastery where the religious persons warm themselves.

CALEFA'GIUM (*Law*) the right to take fuel yearly.

CALENDAR (*Chron.*) an orderly distribution of time into the months, weeks, and days, which constitute the year, together with an account of the festivals, and other such matters as serve for the daily purposes of life. Calendars, of course, vary according to the different forms of the year, and the divisions of time in different countries; the principal of which are the Roman, the Julian, the Gregorian, and the Reformed or Corrected Calendar.—*Roman Calendar,* the first that was formed, owes its origin to Romulus. [vide *Kalendarium*]—*Julian Calendar* is that in which the days of the week are determined by the seven letters, called the *Dominical letters;* namely, A, B, C, D, E, F, G, by means of the solar cycle; and the new and full moons, particularly the paschal full moon, with the feasts of Easter, and the other moveable feasts depending on it, by means of golden numbers, or lunar cycles, rightly disposed through the Julian Year. [vide *Chronology*]—*Gregorian Calendar,* that which, by means of epacts rightly disposed through the several months, determines the new and full moons, the time of Easter, &c. in the Gregorian year. The epacts are here substituted for the golden numbers of the Julian calendar.—*Reformed* or *corrected Calendar* is that which, without the use of either golden numbers or epacts, determines the equinox and the paschal full moon, &c. by computation from astronomical tables. When this calendar was introduced eleven days were omitted in the month of February to make it agree with the Gregorian style. The reformed calendar is ordered to be observed in England by act of Parliament, which fixes that "The Easterday, on which the rest depend, should always fall on the first Sunday after the full moon, which happens upon, or next after, the 21st day of March, so that, if the full moon happens on a Sunday, Easterday is the Sunday after." To the above-mentioned calendars may be added the—*New French Calendar,* which was introduced with the revolution. According to this calendar the year was divided into twelve months, each thirty days, with five supernumerary days to complete the 365; the month was divided into three parts, called *decades;* and the weeks into ten days. This has since fallen into disuse, and been exchanged for the old one on the restoration of the monarchy.—*Calendar months,* the solar months, as they stand in the calendar, as January, thirty-one days, &c.—*Astronomical calendar,* a contrivance by means of a printed paper pasted on board, with a brass slider that carries a hair, to show by inspection the sun's meridian altitude, right ascension, declination, rising, setting, amplitude, &c.

to a greater exactness than can be done by the common globes.

CA'LENDER (*Mech.*) a machine for smoothing linen, so called from *calidus*, hot, because it acts as a species of hot-pressing; also the person who follows the business.

CALENDS (*Chron.*) the first day of the month in the Roman Calendar. [vide *Kalendæ*]

CALE'NDULA (*Bot.*) Marigold, a plant, so called because it flowers every calends or month. The flowers and leaves of this plant are reckoned aperient.

CALENDULA, in the Linnean system, a genus of plants, Class 19 *Syngenesia*, Order 4 *Polygamia Necessaria*.
Generic Characters. CAL. common simple.—COR. compound radiate.—STAM. *filaments* five; *anthers* cylindric. PIST. *germ* oblong; *style* filiform; *stigma* obtuse.—PER. none; *seeds* solitary; *receptacles* naked.
Species. The species are annuals, perennials, or shrubs. Of the first kind are the—*Calendula arvensis*, seu *Caltha officinalis, arvensis*, seu *minima*, Field Marigold, native of Europe.—*Calendula stellata*, Starry Marigold, native of Barbary.—*Calendula sancta*, Palestine Marigold, native of Palestine.—*Calendula officinalis* seu *sativa*, seu *Caltha vulgaris*, Garden Marigold, native of the South of Europe.—*Calendula incana* seu *tomentosa*, seu *Caltha maritima*, native of Portugal.—*Calendula pluvialis, scabra*, seu *humilis Africana*, seu *Caltha Africana*, Small Cape Marigold, native of the Cape of Good Hope.—*Calendula hybrida, Caltha Africana*, seu *Cardispernum, Africanum*, &c. Hybridous or Great Cape Marigold, native of the Cape of Good Hope.—*Calendula nudicaulis* seu *Africana, Bellis*, &c. seu *Caltha Africana*, naked stalked Cape Marigold, native of the Cape of Good Hope. Of the second kind are—*Calendula pumila*, Pigmy Marigold, native of New Zealand.—*Calendula magellanica*, seu *Aster nudicaulis*, &c. native of the straits of Magellan.—*Calendula graminifolia*, seu *Africana*, &c. *Caltha Africana, Dimorphotheca statices*, seu *Bellis Africana*, Grass-leaved Marigold, native of the Cape of Good Hope. Of the third kind are the—*Calendula Tragus* seu *caulescens*, Bending stalked Marigold, native of the Cape of Good Hope.—*Calendula oppositifolia* seu *rosmarinifolia*, Glaucous Marigold, native of the Cape of Good Hope.—*Calendula glabrata*, native of the Cape of Good Hope.—*Calendula fruticosa*, Shrubby Marigold, native of the Cape of Good Hope.—*Calendula arborescens, rigida*, seu *aspera*, native of the Cape of Good Hope. *Trag. Kraeut. von den vier Element. &c.; Cæsalpin. de Plant.; J. Bauh. Hist. Plant.; Ger. Herb.; Park. Theat. Botan.; Raii Hist. Plant.; Tournef. Instit.; Boerhaav. Ind.*

CA'LENTURE (*Med.*) *calentura*, from *caleo*, to grow hot; a burning fever attended with delirium.

CALE'NUM *vinum* (*Ant.*) rich wine of Campania.

CALE'SIUM (*Bot.*) the name of a berry-bearing tree.

CALF (*Sport.*) the male hart or hind of the first year.

CALF, Sea (*Ich.*) a large fish with a velvet spotted skin, the flesh of which is like that of a sucking pig.

CALF-SKIN (*Mech.*) or *calve-skin*, the leather made from the hide of a calf.

CALF'S-SNOUTE (*Bot.*) vide *Calve's-Snout*.

CA'LI (*Chem.*) Pot-Ash.

CA'LIBER (*Gunn.*) *calibre*, or *caliper*, the thickness or diameter of any thing, particularly of the bore of a cannon.—*Caliber campasses*, a sort of compasses made with bowed ends for measuring the diameter of guns, &c.

CALIBERED (*Gunn.*) measured with caliber compasses.

CALIBRE (*Gunn.*) vide *Caliber*.

CALICE (*Ecc.*) vide *Chalice*.

CALICO (*Com.*) a kind of linen made of cotton, principally in the East Indies.

CALIDA'RIUM (*Med.*) vide *Caldarium*.

CA'LIDUCT (*Mech.*) a pipe or canal disposed along the rooms to convey heat to different parts of a building.

CA'LIDUM *innatum* (*Phy.*) innate heat, or that attrition of the parts of the blood which arises from its circulation.

CA'LIGA (*Ant.*) a sort of sandal worn by the Roman soldiers, whence Caligula derived his name. It was put for the condition of a common soldier, of which mention is made in an inscription: C. OPPIO. C. T. VEL OM. NIBUS OFFICIIS IN CALIGA FUNCTO. Whence the soldiers were called *caligati*; and the life of a soldier, by Tertullian, *militia caligata*. They sometimes adorned these *caligæ* with gold and silver nails. *Cic. ad Attic. l. 2, ep. 3; Val. Max. l. 9, c. 1; Senec. de Brev. Vit. c. 17; Tacit. Annal. l. 1, c. 41; Sueton. in Calig. c. 52; Justin. l. 38, c. 10; Dio. l. 57; Tertullian. de Idol. c. 19; Grut. Vet. Inscript. p. 445, and p. 279, &c.*

CALIGA'RIUS (*Ant.*) one who made the sandals for the soldiers called *caligæ*. [vide *Caliga*]

CALIGA'TI (*Ant.*) a name for the Roman soldiers, from the *caliga* which they wore.
Juv. sat. 16, v. 24.

Cum duo crura habeas, offendere tot caligatos.

Of these, mention is made in old inscriptions, as HONORATI. ET. DECURIONES. ET. NUMERUS. MILITUM. CALIGATORUM. [vide *Caliga*]

CALI'GRAPHY (*Mech.*) from καλὸς, fair, and γράφω, to write; the art of fine penmanship, or of writing beautifully.

CALIPER (*Gunn.*) vide *Caliber*.

CALIPH (*Polit.*) in the Arabic *Khalifa*, which signifies a successor; was the title assumed by the successors of Mahomet, which was borne for 656 years, when Bagdad was taken by the Tartars, and Moslaazem, the last of the race of the Abassides, was put to death.

CALIPO'DIUM (*Archæol.*) vide *Calopodium*.

CALI'PPIC *Period* (*Chron.*) a period of seventy-six years, invented by Calippus, an Athenian astronomer, as an improvement on that of Meton, or the cycle of nineteen years. At every recurrence of this period he supposed that the mean, new, and full moons would always return to the same day and hour.

CA'LIVER (*Gunn.*) from *caliber*, a small hand gun used at sea, a harquebuse, or musket formerly in use.

TO CALK (*Mar.*) or *caulk*, from the French *calfater* and *calage*; to drive oakum, spun yarn and wooden pins into all the seams to keep out the water.

CA'LKERS (*Mar.*) the persons employed in calking vessels.

CA'LKING (*Paint.*) a term used when the backside of the design is covered with black lead or red chalk, and the lines traced through on a waxed plate, &c. which leaves an impression of the colour on the plate.

CALKING-IRONS (*Mar.*) the irons employed in calking vessels.

CA'LKINS (*Vet.*) the prominent parts at the extremities of a horse-shoe, bent downwards and forged to a sort of point; they are either single or double, i. e. at one end of the shoe or both.

CALL (*Sport.*) a lesson blown upon the horn to comfort the hounds.

CALL (*Fowl.*) an artificial pipe made to catch quails, &c. by imitating their notes.

CALL (*Mar.*) a whistle, or pipe of silver or brass, for summoning the sailors to their duty.—*Gold call*, with a chain, was formerly the ensign of the office of admiral.

CALL *of the house* (*Polit.*) a Parliamentary term implying an imperative call or summons sent to every member to attend on any particular occasion.

CALL (*Law*) or *calling of the plaintiff*, a form in courts of law of calling upon the plaintiff to appear in cases where, for want of sufficient evidence, he consents to be nonsuited, or to withdraw himself. Accordingly, neither he, nor any for him, appears to answer the summons.

CALL (*Min.*) an English name for the mineral called by the Germans *tungsten*.

CA'LLA (*Bot.*) a genus of plants, Class 20 *Gynandria*, Order 8 *Polyandria*.
 Generic Characters. CAL. spathe one-leaved.—COR. none.—STAM. *filaments* some intermixed with the germs; *anther* simple.—PIST. *germ* to each, obtuse; *style* simple; *stigma* acute.—PER. berries one-celled.
 Species. The species are perennials, as the—Calla Æthiopica, Arum Æthiopicum, seu Americanum, &c. Æthiopian Calla, native of the Cape of Good Hope.—Calla palustris, Dracunculus palustris seu aquatilis, seu Provenzalia palustris, Marsh Calla, native of the North of Europe.—Calla orientalis, Arum minus, &c. seu Carsaami, Oriental Calla, native of Aleppo.—Calla occulta, native of Cochin China. *Dod. Pempt.; C. Bauh. Pin.; Ger. Herb.; Park. Theat.; Raii Hist. Plant.*

CA'LLAF (*Bot.*) a sort of Ægyptian willow mentioned by Prosper Alpinus.

CALLAIS (*Min.*) καλλαΐς, a precious stone of a sea-green colour like a sapphire. *Plin.* l. 37, c. 10.

CALLA'RIAS (*Ich.*) a haddock.

CA'LLIBER (*Gunn.*) vide *Caliper*.

CALLIBER (*Archit.*) the bulk, volume, or diameter of any thing.

CALLIBLE'PHARUM (*Med.*) καλλιβλέφαρον, from κάλλος, beauty, and βλέφαρα, eyelids; a recipe for making the eyelids black, consisting of burnt roseleaves, date-stones, marrow, soot, &c. Terra ampelitis. *Plin.* l. 32, c. 6; *Marcel. de Med.* c. 8.

CALLICA'RPA (*Bot.*) from κάλλος, beauty, and καρπός, fruit, a genus of plants; so named from the beauty of its fruit, Class 4 *Tetrandria*, Order 1 *Monogynia*.
 Generic Characters. CAL. perianth one-leaved.—COR. monopetalous.—STAM. *filaments* four; *anthers* ovate.—PIST. *germ* roundish; *style* filiform; *stigma* thickish.—PER. berry globular; *seeds* four.
 Species. The species are shrubs, as the—Callicarpa americana, Spondylococcas, Burchardia, Johnsonia americana, Anonymus baccifera, &c. seu Frutex baccifer, &c. American Callicarpa, native of Carolina, &c.—Callicarpa cana, tomentosa, seu americana, native of Malabar.—Callicarpa lanata, seu tomentosa, Tomex tomentosa, seu Arbor malabarica, &c. native of India.—Callicarpa macrophylla, native of India.—Callicarpa ferruginea, native of Jamaica.—Callicarpa reticulata, native of Jamaica.—Callicarpa longifolia, native of Malacca.—Callicarpa integrifolia, native of Carthagena.—Callicarpa villosa, native of the East Indies.—Callicarpa japonica, native of Japan.—Callicarpa umbellata, native of Cochin China.—Callicarpa triloba, native of China.—Callicarpa macrophylla, native of India.

CA'LLICO (*Com.*) vide *Calico*.

CALLI'GONUM (*Bot.*) καλλίγονον, a genus of plants, Class 11 *Dodecandria*, Order 4 *Tetragynia*.
 Generic Characters. CAL. perianth one-leaved.—COR. none.—STAM. *filaments* about sixteen; *anthers* roundish. PIST. *germ* superior; *styles* three; *stigmas* capitate.—PER. none; *seed* nut.
 Species. The species are—Calligonum Polygonoides, seu Polygonoides orientale, &c. a shrub, native of the mountain of Ararat.—Calligonum comosum, a shrub, native of Ægypt.—Calligonum Pallasia, seu Polygonoides Pallasia caspica, seu Pteroccus, seu Pteroccus aphyllus, a shrub, native of the coast near the Caspian sea.

CALLI'GRAPHY (*Mech.*) vide *Caligraphy*.

CALLIMA'NCO (*Com.*) vide *Calamanco*.

CA'LLIMUS (*Min.*) κάλλιμος, a stone; found within another, called *Taphiusius*. *Plin.* l. 36, c. 21.

CA'LLION (*Bot.*) a kind of nightshade. *Plin.* l. 23, c. 31.

CALLIO'NYMUS (*Ich.*) καλλιώνυμος, from κάλλος, beauty, and ὄνομα, a name, having a fair name; a sort of fish frequently found in the Mediterranean, which Hippocrates recommends for the dryness of its flesh. Dioscorides also recommends the gall of this fish for disorders in the eyes. *Hippocrat. de Vict. in Acut. Morb.* l. 2; *Dioscor.* l. 2, c. 96; *Plin.* l. 32, c. 7; *Gal. de Simpl.* l. 10, c. 2.

CALLIONYMUS, in the Linnean system, a genus of animals, Class *Pisces*, Order *Jugulares*.
 Generic Characters. *Upper lip* doubled up; *eyes* approximate; *gill-membrane* six rayed.—*Body* naked; *ventral fins* very remote.
 Species. The principal species are the—Callionymus Lyra, Gemmeous Dragonet.—Callionymus Dracunculus, Sordid Dragonet.—Callionymus Indicus, Indian Dragonet.—Callionymus Baikalensis, Baikal Dragonet.—Callionymus Ocellatus, Ocellate Dragonet.—Callionymus Sagitta, Arrow-headed Dragonet.—Callionymus Japonicus, Japan Dragonet.

CALLIPÆ'DES (*Ant.*) old fellows playing the boy. *Fest. de Verb. Signif.*

CA'LLIPER (*Gunn.*) vide *Caliper*.

CALLIPHY'LLUM (*Bot.*) καλλίφυλλον, from κάλλος, beautiful and φύλλον, a leaf; a species of the *Adianthum*.

CALLI'PPII Period (*Chron.*) vide *Calippic*.

CA'LLIS (*Ant.*) called by Livy *deviæ calles*, the name of a path that beasts make in mountains and forests.

CALLIS (*Law*) the king's highway.

CALLI'SIA (*Bot.*) a genus of plants, Class *Triandria*, Order 1 *Monogynia*.
 Generic Characters. CAL. perianth three-leaved.—COR. *petals* three.—STAM. *filaments* three; *anthers* double.—PIST. *germ* superior; *style* capillary; *stigmas* three.—PER. *capsule* ovate; *seeds* two.
 Species. The only species is—Callisia repens, Callisia, seu Hapalanthus repens, creeping Callisia, a perennial, native of America.

CALLISTE'A (*Ant.*) καλλιστεία, a Lesbian festival, at which the women presented themselves in Juno's temple, in order that the prize might be assigned to the fairest. A similar festival was celebrated among the Parrhasians, and the Eleans, at which the prize was assigned to the most beautiful man. *Plat. Euthyd.; Hesychius; Eustath. Il.* l. 9.

CALLISTIANS (*Ecc.*) a set of reformers in Bohemia who obtained permission from the see of Rome to communicate in the sacraments of both kinds. *Spondan. Annal. Ann.* 1421.

CALLISTRU'THIA (*Bot.*) according to Pliny, a sort of fig of an excellent taste. *Plin.* l. 15, c. 18.

CA'LLITHRIX (*Zool.*) a kind of ape in Æthiopia, with a long beard, and a spread tail. *Plin.* l. 8, c. 54.

CALLITRI'CHE (*Bot.*) originally a name for *adianthum*, or Maiden hair; from κάλλος, beauty, and θρίξ, hair, a genus of plants, Class 1 *Monandria*, Order 2 *Digynia*.
 Generic Characters. CAL. none.—COR. *petals* two.—STAM. *filaments* one; *anther* simple.—PIST. *germ* roundish; *styles* two; *stigmas* acute.—PER. *capsule* roundish; *seeds* solitary.
 Species. The species are annuals, as—Callitriche verna, fontana, Stellaria, seu Corispermum, Vernal Star-wort, or Star-headed Water Chickweed, native of Europe.—Callitriche aquatica, Common Water Starwort, native of Britain.—Callitriche autumnalis, seu Stagnalis, Stellaria aquatica, Lenticula palustris, &c. seu Alsine aquatica, &c. Autumnal Star-grass, native of Britain. *C. Bauh. Pin.; Raii Hist. Plant.*

CA'LLONE (*Med.*) καλλονή, a term signifying generally comeliness or decency, but is applied, particularly by Hippocrates, to the decency and gravity of deportment befitting a medical man.

CALLO'SUM *Corpus* (*Anat.*) a medullary prominence in the brain, which is conspicuous in separating the two lateral parts or hemispheres of the Cerebrum.

CA'LLOUS (*Surg.*) a term signifying hardened or indurated, as the callous edges of ulcers.

CA'LLUS (*Med.*) τύλος, πῶρος. 1. Any cutaneous, carneous, and osseous hardness, whether natural or præternatural, but particularly that callosity which is generated about the edges of fractured bones, a sort of gluey substance, that serves to solder them together. 2. *Calli*, πῶροι, nodes of the gout, according to Galen, by whom *callositas* and *callus*, τύλωσις and πῶρος, are also sometimes applied to the eyelids. *Gal. de Comp. Med. sec. Loc.* l. 7, c. 7, &c. 3. The same as *Callosum Corpus*. *Aet. Tetrab.* l, serm. 1; *Paul. Æginet.* l. 4, c. 49; *Act. de Meth. Med.* l. 5, c. 6.

CALMA'RIÆ (*Bot.*) vide *Calamariæ*.

CALOCA'TANOS (*Bot.*) from καλός, beautiful, and κάτανος, a vessel, the wild Poppy; so called from the beauty of its flower.

CALSCHIE'RAI (*Bot.*) a sort of thistle.

CALODE'NDRUM (*Bot.*) from καλός, beautiful, and δένδρον, a tree; a genus of plants, Class 5 *Pentandria*, Order 1 *Monogynia*.
Generic Characters. CAL. perianth one-leaved.—COR. petals five; nectaries five.—STAM. filaments five; anthers ovate cordate.—PIST. germ pedicelled; style filiform; stigma simple.—PER. capsule peduncled; seeds in pairs.
Species. The only species is—*Calodendrum capense, Dictammus capensis*, seu *Pallasia capensis*, a shrub, native of the Cape of Good Hope.

CA'LOMEL (*Chem.*) καλομέλας, from καλός, beautiful, and μέλας, black; so called from its colour and virtues. Mercury well pounded with sulphur, or more properly *Mercurius dulcis* six times sublimed.

CALOME'LANOS *Turqueti* (*Med.*) a purgative composed of *Mercurius dulcis*, Scammony, &c.

CALO'NIA (*Med.*) καλωνία, a sort of myrrh.

CALONNE'A (*Bot.*) the *Galardia* of Linnæus.

CALOPHY'LLUM (*Bot.*) from καλός, fine, and φύλλον, a leaf; a genus of plants, Class 13 *Polyandria*, Order 1 *Monogynia*.
Generic Characters. CAL. perianth four-leaved.—COR. petals four.—STAM. filaments many; anthers erect.—PIST. germ roundish; style filiform; stigma headed.—PER. drupe globular; seed nut globular.
Species. The two species are shrubs, as the *Calophyllum Inophyllum, Arbor Indica, Bintangor maritima, Ponna*, seu *Ponna maram*, native of India.—*Calophyllum Calaba, Inophyllum, Arbor altissima, Tsierou-ponna*, native of the Indies.

CALOPHYLLUM the *Grias* and *Mesua* of Linnæus.

CALOPO'DIUM (*Ant.*) καλοπόδιον, from καλός, wood, and πούς, a foot; a wooden shoe or slipper.—*Calopodium ferratum*, a shoe with an iron plate to slide upon the ice; a skate.

CA'LOPUS (*Ant.*) καλοπούς, from καλός, beautiful, and πούς, a foot; an epithet for persons with pretty feet, particularly slaves. *Schol. Arist.*

CALOPUS (*Ent.*) a genus of animals, Class *Insecta*, Order *Coleoptera*.
Generic Characters. Antenna filiform; feelers four.—Thorax gibbous.—Shells linear.
Species. The species are the—*Calopus serraticornis, Calopus hispicornis*, et *Calopus pygmæus*.

CALO'RIC (*Phy.*) or the Calorific Principle, that principle commonly known by the name of heat, which is supposed to be something independent of the body in which it is found. It was formerly known by the name of the *Igneous Fluid*, or *Igneous Matter*. [vide *Chemistry*]

CALORI'METER (*Mech.*) an instrument by which the quantity of absolute heat existing in a body may be ascertained.

CALO'TE (*Ecc.*) French for a sort of tonsure, which distinguished a person in orders in the Romish church, whence the revolutionary epithet of Calotin for a person having this tonsure.

CALOTE (*Mil.*) a sort of skull-cap worn by the French cavalry under their hats, as a guard against the blows of the sword or sabre. The *Calote* is also a French name for the Lieutenant's Court, at which the first lieutenant of the regiment presided. Like a court of honour, the Calote took cognizance of all affairs in which the laws of honour and good breeding had been violated, answering to the *Regimental Committees* in the British service.

CALOTE *spherique* (*Math.*) the section of a sphere, having a circle for its basis.

CALOTTE (*Archit.*) a concavity or depressure, in the form of a calotte or cap, to diminish the height of a chapel; or that it may not exceed the proportion of the breadth.

CALO'YERS (*Ecc.*) or *Calogers*, Greek monks, of the order of St. Basil, who lead a rigorous and retired life on Mount Athos; so called from καλός, fair, and γῆρας, old age, i. e. men venerable for their years. *Montfauc. Paleograph.*

CA'LPAR (*Ant.*) a sort of earthen vessel which was used: also the wine itself, particularly that which was taken out of the vessel for sacrifice before it might be tasted. *Varr. de Vit. Roman. apud Non.* l. 15, c. 31; *Fest. de Verb. Signif.*

CA'LQUING (*Mar.*) vide *Calking*.

CA'LTHA (*Bot.*) a genus of plants, Class 13 *Polyandria*, Order 7 *Polygynia*.
Generic Characters. CAL. none.—COR. petals five.—STAM. filaments numerous; anthers compressed.—PIST. germ superior; styles none; stigmas simple.—PER. capsules one-celled; seeds very many.
Species. The species are perennials, as—*Caltha palustris, Populago palustris*, seu *major*, Marsh Marigold, *Souci de Marais*, a native of Britain.—*Caltha radicans*, a native of Britain.—*Caltha natans*, seu *Populago*, a native of Siberia. *Clus. Hist. Plant. rar.; Bauh. Hist. Plant.; C. Bauh. Pin.; Ger. Herb.; Park. Theat. Botan.; Raii Hist. Plant.*

CA'LTHULA (*Ant.*) *tunica genus à colore calthæ*; a short cloak, or yellow frock. *Plaut. Epid.* act. 2, scen. 2, v. 47; *Varr. de Vit. Rom. apud Non.* l. 16, c. 1.

CA'LTROPS (*Mil.*) from the Sax. *Coltroepe*, or the French *chauffe-trappas*, and *cheval-trapper*, irons with four spikes, so made that which soever way they fall, one point still lies upward; generally thrown into breaches to annoy the enemy's horse. [vide *Fortification*]

CALTROPS (*Sport.*) an instrument with three iron spikes, used in hunting the wolf.

CALTROPS (*Her.*) is occasionally borne as a charge in coat armour.

CALTROPS (*Bot.*) a herb, the *Tropa natans* of Linnæus, very common in the South of France, where it grows among the corn. It is so called because it resembles the military instrument of the same name, being armed with erect prickles all ways, that greatly annoy the feet of cattle which tread upon them.

CALVA (*Anat.*) and *Calvaria*. The same as *Cranium*.

CA'LVARY *cross* (*Her.*) a charge representing the cross on Mount Calvary, with three steps, supposed to imply the three graces, *Faith, Hope*, and *Charity*; as *gules* a Calvary cross upon three steps *or*; name *Jones*, of Denbighshire.

CA′LVES-SNOUT (*Bot.*) the *Anterrhinum* of Linnæus, a perennial, better known by the name of Snap-Dragon, or Toad-Flax.

CA′LVINISM (*Ecc.*) the doctrines of Calvin and his adherents, who hold that predestination and reprobation depend upon the will of God unconditionally, and without respect to the good or evil works of men. They also maintain that to the predestinated God imparts a grace which they cannot lose, and imputes no sin to the elect, &c. &c.

CALVI′TIES (*Med.*) baldness proceeding from defect of humour, in distinction from *alopecia*, *area*, *ophiasis*, and *tinea*, which proceed from a corruption of the nutritious humours.

CALU′MBA (*Bot.*) a root imported from Columbo, in Ceylon; whence it has also been called Colombo, and Columba. It has an aromatic smell, and a pungent bitter taste, and is a good corrector of putrid bile.

CA′LUMET (*Polit.*) or *Pipe of Peace*, a large tobacco-pipe, as in the annexed figure, made of red, black, or white marble; the head is finely polished, and the quill, which is commonly two feet and a half long, is made of a pretty strong reed or cane, adorned with feathers of all colours, interlaid with locks of women's hair; they tie to it two wings of the most curious birds they can find, which makes the calumet resemble a Mercury's wand. This pipe is a pass and a safe conduct among the allies of the nation who has given it; and in all embassies the ambassador carries it as a symbol of peace, the people who use it being fully persuaded that some great misfortune would befal them if they violated the calumet.

CALUMNIÆ *juramentum* (*Law*) an oath taken by both parties in a cause; the plaintiff, that he did not bring his charge, and the defendant, that he did not deny it, with a design to do each other a wrong, but because they believed their cause to be just and good; also that they would not create unnecessary delays, nor offer the judge or evidence any bribes. If the plaintiff refused this oath, the libel or complaint was dismissed; if the defendant, it was taken *pro confesso*.

CA′LUMNY (*Law*) the crime of accusing another falsely, knowing the accusation to be false.

CALX (*Chem.*) a kind of ashes or fine friable powder which remains of metals, minerals, &c. after they have undergone the violence of fire, and have lost all their humid parts.—*Calx viva*, quick lime, or lime in its most caustic state.—*Calx extincta*, or slacked lime, is lime that has been quenched with water after it has been burnt.—*Calcis aqua*, or *calcis liquor*, lime-water, or a solution of lime in water. [vide *Calcination* and *Lime*]

CALY′BION (*Bot.*) the name of a pericarp adhering closely to the seed.

CALYCA′NTHEMI (*Bot.*) the fortieth Order in Linnæus' Fragments of a Natural Arrangement.

CALYCA′NTHUS (*Bot.*) from κάλυξ and ἄνθος, *flos*, the flower, consisting of calycine folioles without petals; a genus of plants Class 12 *Icosandria*, Order 5 *Polygynia*.
Generic Characters. CAL. *perianth* one-leaved.—COR. none.—STAM. *filaments* numerous; *anthers* oblong.—PIST. *germs* a great many; *stigmas* glandulous.—PER. none; *seeds* very many.
Species. The species are shrubs.—*Calycanthus floridus*, *Buttneria anemones*, &c. *Basteria*, *Beureria*, seu *Frutex corni*, &c. Carolina All-spice, native of Carolina.—*Calycanthus præcox*, *Abai*, seu *Robai*, Japan All-spice, native of Japan.—*Calycanthus Pensylvanicus*, native of North America.—*Calycanthus fertilis*, native of North America.

CALYCI′FLORÆ (*Bot.*) the sixteenth order in Linnæus' fragments of a natural arrangement, comprehending those plants that have only a calyx in which the stamina are inserted, as in *Eleagnus*, *Osyris*, *Hippophæ*, &c.

CALY′CIFORM (*Bot.*) in the form of a calyx, an epithet for the involucrum when it has the appearance of a calyx.

CA′LYCINE (*Bot.*) of, or on, the calyx; an epithet either for the scales or the thorns, as calycine thorns, those which are on the calyx.

CA′LYCLE (*Bot.*) *Calyculus*, a diminutive of calyx, a row of small leaflets placed at the base of the calyx on the outside. The calycle of the seed is the outer proper covering of the seed, which adheres to it to facilitate its dispersion.

CA′LYCLED (*Bot.*) *calyculatus*, calyculated; an epithet either for the perianth or the pappus; *perianthium calyculatum*, a perianth having a calycle at the base, as in Dandelion, *Leontodon taraxacum*, &c.; *pappus calyculatus*, a pappus having a membranaceous calycle that rises over the seed.

CALYCO′STEMON (*Bot.*) *Calycostemones*, a name for a class of plants, according to Gleditsch and Monck, which have their stamina situated on the calyx.

CALYCULUS (*Bot.*) vide *Calycle*.

CALYCULUS *echinorum* (*Zool.*) the prickly cases or skins of sea porcupines. *Apul.*

CALYPTRA (*Bot.*) the Calyptra, a tender skin that loosely covers the top of the theca, like a cup. The calyptra is *villosa*, hairy, when composed of hairs, as in the *Polytrichum commune*; *integra*, entire, when it covers the whole top of the theca, as in the *Grimmia extinctoria*; *dimidiata*, half, when it half covers the theca, as in most of the *Musci*; *dentata*, dentated, when the rim is set with teeth, as in the *Grimmia dentata*.

CALYPTRA′NTHES (*Bot.*) from καλύπτρα, *operculum*, and ἄνθος, flower; a genus of plants, Class 12 *Icosandria*, Order 1 *Monogynia*.
Generic Characters. CAL. *perianth* one-leaved.—COR. none.—STAM. *filaments* very many; *anthers* roundish. PIST. *germ* roundish; *style* simple; *stigma* blunt.—PER. *berry* globular; *seed* single.
Species. The species are shrubs, as *Calyptranthes suzygium*, seu *arborescens*, *Myrtus zuzygium*, *Suzygium*, seu *Zuzygium fruticosum*, native of Jamaica.—*Calyptranthes guineensis*, seu *arborescens*, native of Guinea.—*Calyptranthes caryophillifolia*, seu *arborea*, *Eugenia caryophillifolia*, seu *corticosa*, *Myrtus cumini*, *Jambosa ceramica*, *Arbor Zeylanica*, &c. *Caryophyllus*, seu *Peria Njara*, native of the East Indies.—*Calyptranthes jambolana*, seu *arborea*, *Eugenia jambolana*, *Jambolana*, seu *Jambolifera pedunculata*, native of the East Indies.—*Calyptranthes chytraculia*, seu *arborea*, *Myrtus chytraculia*, seu *Chytraculia arborea*, native of Jamaica. C. Bauh. Pin.; Raii Hist. Plant.

CALYPTRATE (*Bot.*) *calyptratus*, caped; an epithet for the arillus when it covers the seed, as the calyptra surrounds the top of the theca in Mosses.

CA′LYX (*Bot.*) in Greek κάλυξ, a cup; in English, Empalement or Flower-Cup; is defined by Linnæus to be the outer covering of the flower, or the first of the seven parts of fructification, formed of the *cortex*, or Outer Bark. According to this author, the Calyx comprehends *perianthium*, the Perianth; *anthodium*, the Common Perianth, *involucrum*, Involucre; *gluma*, the Glume; *spatha*, the Spathe; *calyptra*, the Calyptre; and *volva*, the Wrapper. —*Perianthium*, the Perianth is that sort of calyx which immediately incloses the flower, as in *fig.* 1, where *a* represents the calyx, and *b* the campanulate corolla. The Perianth is abiding, as in *Hyoscyamus niger*, Henbane; deciduous, as in *Tilia Europæa*; caducous, as in the *Papaver somniferum*, the Poppy; double, as in *fig.* 2, where *a* marks the perianth of the fruit, and *b* the perianth of the flower; one, two, or three-leaved, &c.; labiate, as in *Salvia officinalis*, the Sage, &c.—*Anthodium*, a calyx which contains a great number of flowers in such a manner that these flowers appear to form but one, as in *Leontodon taraxacum*, Dandelion; *Centaurea cyanus*, Blue Bottle, &c.

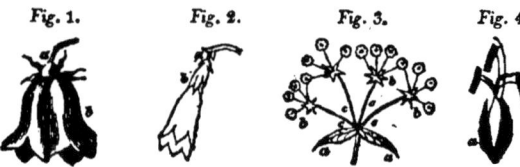

Fig. 1.   Fig. 2.   Fig. 3.   Fig. 4.

The *anthodium* is one or many-leaved, scaly, squarrose, fringed, muricated, thorny, turbinated, doubled or calyculated, &c.—*Involucrum*, the involucre, a calyx peculiar to umbiliferous flowers, which encloses one or several flowers, and is therefore generally distinguished into partial and universal, as in fig. 3, where *a a* represent the universal involucre, *b b b* the partial involucre, *c c c c* the rays of the umbel.—*Gluma*, the glume, a calyx peculiar to the grasses, the leaves of which are called *valvulæ*, Valves, as in fig. 4, where *a* marks one of the valves of a bivalve glume.—*Spatha*, the Spathe, a calyx of the spadix opening or bursting longitudinally in form of a sheath.—*Calyptra*, the calyptre, a calyx of the mosses covering the anther like a hood, according to Linnæus, but it is not generally reckoned among the number of the calyxes.—*Volva*, the Wrapper, a membranaceous calyx of the *fungi*, which, when they are full grown, remains upon the ground.

CAMÆ'A (*Min.*) a gem of the onyx kind.

CAMA'IEU (*Min.*) and *Cameo*, a stone on which are found various figures and representations of landscapes.

CAMAIEU (*Paint.*) a name given to such paintings as have but one colour, where the lights and shades are made on a ground of gold or azure.

CAMA'IL (*Ecc.*) a purple ornament worn by a bishop over his rochet.

CA'MARA (*Anat.*) καμαρα, καμαριον; 1. The *fornix* of the brain. 2. The vaulted part of the auricle leading to the external foramen. *Gal. Def. Med.*; *Oribas. Med. Coll.* l. 24; *Gorr. Def. Med.*

CAMARA (*Bot.*) the Brasilian name for the *Santona* of Linnæus.—*Camara cuba*, a plant with hairy, rough leaves, something like succory; also a species of *Mentastrum*, or Horse-Mint. *Pis. apud Raii Hist. Plant.*—*Camara Mira*, a Brasilian plant, which, according to Piso, opens every day exactly at eleven, and shuts again at two. *Raii Hist. Plant.*—*Camara*, a species of Dwarf-Honey-Suckle.

CAMARAN-BA'YA (*Bot.*) a species of the *Lysimachia* of Linnæus.

CAMARIN-BA'S (*Bot.*) a Brasilian tree, the fruit of which is the size of a plum, but resembles a peach in taste. *Pis. apud Raii Hist. Plant.*

CAMA'RIUM (*Anat.*) καμαριον, the same as *Camara*.

CAMARO'MA (*Surg.*) vide *Camarosis*.

CAMAROSIS (*Archit.*) καμαρωσις, the raising with an arch or vault.

CAMAROSIS (*Surg.*) or, in Latin, *camaroma, cameratio*, a fracture in the cranium, which takes the form of a vault. *Gal. de Fin. Med.*; *Paul. Æginet.* l. 6, c. 89; *Gorr. Def. Med.*

CA'MAX (*Bot.*) from καμαξ, *vitis pedamentum*; a genus of plants in Guiana, Class 5 *Pentandria*, Order 1 *Monogynia*. Generic Characters. CAL. *perianth* one-leaved.—COR. one-petalled.—STAM. *filaments* five.—PIST. *germ* roundish; *style* capillary; *stigmas* three or four.—PER. *berry* ovate; *seeds* very many.

Species. The species are shrubs, as *Camax fraxinea*, seu *Ropourea guianensis*, native of Guiana.—*Camax guianensis*, seu *Ropourea guianensis*, native of Guiana.

CAMBA'YES (*Com.*) cotton cloths made at Bengal, Madras, and other places in India.

CA'MBER (*Mar.*) in general any thing that is round; but chiefly employed for cambering the ways in launching a ship.

CAMBER-BE'AM (*Archit.*) from καμαρα, a vault; a beam cut hollow or archwise in the middle, commonly used in platforms.

CA'MBERED (*Mar.*) an epithet for a deck, the flooring of which is highest in the middle; also when it is irregularly and defectively so, which is otherwise denominated brokenbacked.

CA'MBERING (*Mar.*) the same as cambered.

CA'MBING (*Bot.*) a tree that grows in the Molucca, the bark of which is efficacious in dysenteries.

CA'MBIO (*Com.*) an Italian word for Exchange. [vide *Cambium*]

CAMBIRE'A (*Med.*) the name which Paracelsus gives to a venereal bubo.

CA'MBIS (*Com.*) one trading in notes or bills of exchange.

CA'MBIUM (*Com.*) in Italian *cambio*, from καμπτω, to bend; 1. The exchanging or bartering of commodities, hence *literæ Cambii*, bills of exchange; also *Cambium siccum*, i. e. *pecuniæ permutatio*, αργυρι αλλαγη, exchange of money. 2. The exchange, or place of meeting for merchants.

CAMBIUM (*Med.*) that humour of the body which, *cambitur*, is exchanged into glutinous matter; among the Arabians, a secondary humour, which is immediately converted into aliment, the two others being termed *ros* and *gluten*, according to Avicenna.

CAMBIUM (*Bot.*) a moisture between the cortex and wood, which in the air becomes mucilaginous and tenacious. *Grew. Anat. of Plant.*

CA'MBLET (*Com.*) vide *Camlet*.

CAMBO'GIA (*Bot.*) a genus of plants, named after Cambodia, the province from which it comes, Class 13 *Polyandria*, Order 1 *Monogynia*. This tree produces the gum called *Gamboge*.

Generic Characters. CAL. *perianth* four-leaved.—COR. *petals* four.—STAM. *filaments* very many; *anthers* roundish—PIST. *germ* roundish; *style* none; *stigma* four-cleft. PER. *pome* roundish; *seed* solitary.

Species. The only species is the *Cambogia Gutta, Coddampulli, Carcapuli, Cambogium*, seu *Gambogia*, Gambogetree, a native of the East Indies. *Raii Hist. Plant.*

CAMBOGIUM (*Bot.*) the same as *Cambogia*.

CA'MBRE (*Archit.*) French for the bending a piece of timber, or for the curve of an arch.

CA'MBREL (*Mech.*) or *cambren*, a crooked stick with notches in it, on which butchers hang carcasses of mutton, &c.

CA'MBRER (*Archit.*) to vault, to bend, particularly to fit pannel squares, &c. to any curved dimensions.

CA'MBRIC (*Com.*) a species of very fine white linen made of flax, from *Cambrensis* or *Cambra*, the province where it was first manufactured.

CAMBU'CA (*Med.*) a bubo in the groin. *Castel. Lex. Med.*

CA'MBUI (*Bot.*) the Wild American Myrtle. *Marcgrav. Pis. Bras. Hist.*

CA'MBULU (*Bot.*) a species of the *Bignonia* of Linnæus.

CA'MEL (*Zool.*) a well-known animal of Arabia, remarkable for its swiftness, and its power of subsisting many days without water. It is mild and gentle, unless particularly provoked, patient of hunger, and capable of carrying great weights. The flesh and the milk of this animal constitute the principal food of the inhabitants of Arabia, and the countries where it is a native. [vide *Camelus*]

CAMEL (*Her.*) this animal, in coats of arms, denotes expedition in business; sometimes it is only used as *Canting Arms*, as he beareth, " Argent, a camel passant, by the name of *Camel.*" This coat stands in the church of Bury-Pomeroy, in the county of Devon.

CAMEL (*Mech.*) a machine used for lifting vessels over the Pampus at the mouth of the river Y. A camel is composed of two separate parts, whose outsides are perpendicular, and whose insides are concave, so as to embrace the hull of a ship on both sides.

CAMELA'RIUS (*Ant.*) a camel driver.

CAME'LEON (*Astron.*) one of the southern constellations near the South Pole, which is invisible in our latitude. There are ten stars in this constellation, according to Sharpe's catalogue, which are, however, only of the fifth or sixth magnitude.

CAMELEON (*Zool.*) vide Chamæleon.

CAMELI'NA (*Bot.*) the *Erysimum cheiranthoides* of Linnæus.

CAME'LLIA (*Bot.*) a genus of plants, named after Mr. G. J. Kamel, or Camellus, a botanist in conjunction with Ray, Class 16 *Monadelphia*, Order 5 *Polyandria*.
  Generic Characters. CAL. *perianth* many-leaved.—COR. *petals* five.—STAM. *filaments* numerous; *anthers* simple.—PIST. *germ* roundish; *style* subulate; *stigma* acute.—PER. *capsule* turbinate; *seeds* kernels roundish.
  Species. The species are shrubs, as *Camellia japonica, Thea Chinensis, Tsubakki montanus, sylvestris,* seu *hortensis,* seu *Rosa Chinensis*, Japan Rose, native of Japan.—*Camellia Sasanqua,* seu *Sasankwa*, native of Japan.

CAMELOPA'RDALIS (*Zool.*) or *Camelopardus*, καμηλοπάρδαλις, Camelopard, from κάμηλος and πάρδαλις, a panther; so called, according to Varro, not because it was born of a camel and a panther, but from its figure. It is called in the Arabic *Zurapha*, in the Æthiopian *Nabis*, by the Romans *ovis fera*.
  Horat. l. 2, ep. 1, v. 195.

  Diversum panthera genus confusa camelo.

Varr. de Lat. Ling. l. 5; Plin. l. 8, c. 18; Solin. c. 33; Dion. l. 43.

CAMELOPARDALIS, *in the Linnean system*, a genus of animals, Class *Mammalia*, Order *Pecora*.
  Generic Characters. Horns simple; *fore-teeth* lower eight; *body* whitish mixed with tawny, and sprinkled with numerous rusty spots.
  Species. The only species is *Camelopardalis Giraffa, Cervus Camelopardalis, Camelus Indicus,* seu *Gyraffa*, Camelopard Giraffe, a native of Æthiopia, which is gentle, swift, and elegant; when about to lie down it kneels like the camel.

CAMELOPARDALIS (*Astron.*) a new constellation formed by Hevelius, consisting of thirty-two stars, situated between Cepheus, Cassiopeia, Perseus, the two bears, and Draco.

CAMELOPARDALIS (*Her.*) a charge that is sometimes borne in coats of arms.

CAMELOPO'DIUM (*Bot.*) a sort of Hore-hound.

CAMELS-HA'Y (*Bot.*) a sort of sweet smelling rush growing in Eastern countries; the *Andropogon* of Linnæus.

CAME'LUS (*Zool.*) בָּמָל, κάμηλος, a beast of burden used in Asia, of which the Arabians distinguish three kinds; the first, the *clitellarii*, or, in the Arabic, *hoguin*, i. e. ευγενής, well-born, or of good breed, which have one bunch, and are fitted to carry burdens to the weight of a thousand pounds; second, those with two bunches, called in Arabic *hechti*, by the Greeks βάκτριοι, because they were found originally in Bactria, which are fitted for carrying burdens, or for riding; thirdly, the *graciles*, in Arabic *raguahil*, Greek δρομάδες, dromedaries, so called from their swiftness, were principally used by the nobles. The milk and flesh of the camel were very much esteemed among the ancients, and among the Caspians their finest garments were made of its hair. Herodot. l. 1, c. 80, &c.; Aristot. Hist. Animal. l. 6, c. 26; Diodor. l. 2, &c.; Plin. l. 2, c. 41, l. 8, c. 18; Ælian. l. 17, c. 14; Veget. l. 3, c. 2; Apollon. Mirab. c. 20; Veget. l. 3, c. 23.

CAMELUS, *in the Linnean system*, a genus of animals, Class *Mammalia*, Order *Pecora*.
  Generic Characters. Horns none; *fore-teeth* lower six; *tusks* distant, upper three, lower two; *upper-lip* cleft.
  Species. The principal species are as follow: the *Camelus Dromedarius*, in French *Le Dromadaire*, the Dromedary, or Arabian Camel, a native of Asia and Africa.—*Camelus Bactrianus, Dromedarius*, in French *Le Chameau*, Bactrian Camel, native of India.—*Camelus Glama* seu *Peruvianus, Ovis Peruana*, in French *Le Lama*, the Glama or Llama, native of South America.—*Camelus Vicugna* seu *Laniger, Vicognes* ou *Vicunas*, in French *La Vigogne*, Vicuna or Vicunna.—*Camelus Paco*, Paco or Alpaco, native of Peru.—*Camelus Huanacus, Guanaco-Huanacu, Cervo-Camelus,* seu *Allo-Camelus*, Guanaco, a native of Peru.—*Camelus Arcucanus, Aries moromorus*, in French *Moutons de Perou*, Chilihucque, native of Peru, Camoe, and Chili.

CAMEO (*Paint.*) vide Camaieu.

CA'MERA (*Ant.*) κάμαρα, a vault, or καμπή, a curvature; 1. A kind of ships with close sides, and a wide hold covered at the top, which were used by those who lived near the Black Sea. Tacit. Hist. l. 3, c. 47; Gyrald. de Nairg. c. 18; Alex. Gen. Dier. l. 4, c. 2. 2. A roof. [vide Camara]

CAMERA *terræ* (*Archæol.*) a crooked plot of ground.

CAMERA (*Mus.*) a term in composers' books denoting music for the chamber, or for private concerts.

CAMERA Æolia (*Mech.*) a name given by Kircher to a contrivance for blowing the fire for the fusion of ores without bellows, which is effected by means of water falling through a funnel into a close vessel, which sends from it so much air or vapour as continually blows the fire.—*Camera lucida*, a contrivance of Dr. Hooke's, to make the image of any thing appear on a wall in a light room, either by day or night, which is described in the Philosophical Transactions, vol. ii. No. 38.

CAMERA obscura (*Opt.*) an optical machine or apparatus representing an artificial eye, by which the images of external objects, received through a double convex glass, are shown distinctly, and in their native colours, on a white ground placed within the machine in the focus of the glass. The first invention of this machine is ascribed to John Baptista Porta, by whom it is described at large in his Magia Naturalis. [vide *Optics*]

CAMERA'RIA (*Bot.*) a genus of plants, named by Plumier after J. Camerarius, a physician and botanist, of Nuremberg; it is of the Class 5 *Pentandria*, Order 1 *Monogynia*.
  Generic Characters. CAL. *perianth* five-cleft.—COR. monopetalous.—STAM. *filaments* five; *anthers* converging.—PIST. *germs* two; *styles* hardly any; *stigmas* obscure. PER. *follicles* two; *seeds* numerous.
  Species. The species are shrubs; namely, the *Cameraria latifolia* seu *arborea*, Bastard Mangeneel, native of America.—*Cameraria Zeylanica*, seu *Apocyno Nerium*, native of Ceylon, &c.

CAMERARIA, the *Montia* of Linnæus.

CAMERA'RIUS (*Ant.*) a chamberlain or treasurer.

CAMERA'TIO (*Med.*) vide Camarosis.

CAMERO'NIANS (*Ecc.*) field conventiclers, or a fanatic sort of Scotch Presbyterians, called after one Cameron, their leader, and chaplain of the regiment, to which he also gave his name.

CA'MERY (*Vet.*) a disease in horses, called also the *Frounce*, when small warts or pimples arise in the mouth.

CA'MES (*Min.*) or *camet*, silver.

CAMES (*Mech.*) slender rods of cast lead, of which glaziers make their turned or milled lead for joining the panes or quarrels of glass.

CA'MFERING (*Carpent.*) vide *Chamfering*.

CA'MICA (*Archæol.*) an old word for camlet.

CAMI'LII (*Ant.*) or *Camillæ*, priests instituted by Romulus.

CA'MINUS (*Ant.*) κάμινος, from καίω, to burn; a furnace, or chimney; also a bell.

CA'MION (*Mil.*) a sort of cart or dray with two wheels, drawn by two horses, which serves to convey cannon-balls.

CAMISA'DE (*Mil.*) French for setting upon or surprizing an enemy by night, when the soldiers had their shirts over their clothes, that they might be known to each other.

CA'MISATED (*Ecc.*) clothed in the *camisia*, or surplice.

CAMI'SIA (*Ecc.*) from the Hebrew קמיץ, a long linen vestment of the priests, a surplice.

CAMISIA *fœtus* (*Anat.*) the shirt of the fœtus. [vide *Chorion*]

CAMLET (*Com.*) or *camblet*; in French *camelot*, in Italian *camellato*, a fine stuff, composed of a warp and woof, and manufactured on a loom with two treddles, so called because they were originally made of camel's hair only. Camlets are of different kinds, as follow, namely—*Goat's-hair*, *wool*, or *silk camlets*, according as they are made of those materials.—*Figured camlets*, having figures printed upon them.—*Waved camlets*, having a wave imprinted upon them, as on tabbies.—*Water camlets*, such as undergo a certain preparation with water; but the water camlets of Verona are a kind of tabbies.

CAMLE'TTO (*Com.*) or *Camlettum*, a sort of fine worsted camlets or camelots.

CA'MMARON (*Bot.*) vel *Cammorum*, κάμμαρον, the Aconitum cammarum of Linnæus.

CA'MMOCK (*Bot.*) another name for the herb Rest-harrow.

CAMO'CA (*Ant.*) a garment of silk, or any precious stuff.

CAMOCLA'DIA (*Bot.*) the same as *Comocladea*.

CA'MOMILE (*Bot.*) vide *Chamomile*.

CAMOU'FLET (*Mil.*) French for a stinking kind of combustible blown out of paper cases into the miners' faces while they are working in the galleries of the countermines.—*Camouflet* signifies also the sudden explosion of a pistol when miners encounter one another.

CAMP (*Ant.*) vide *Castrum*, and *Militia*.

CAMP (*Mil.*) the space of ground occupied by an army pitching its tents when in the field, and upon which all its apparatus, baggage, &c. are disposed according to the arrangements of the Quarter-Master-General, by whom the ground is marked out, and to every regiment its portion is allotted.—*Camp colour men*, the men who carry the camp colours.—*Flying camp*, the same as flying army.

CAMP CEI'LING (*Archit.*) a ceiling formed by an inclination of the wall on each side towards the plane surface in the middle, so as to form something like a coved ceiling. It is most frequently used in garrets, where there would otherwise be a deficiency in the height to clear the head.

CA'MP-FIGHT (*Law*) the fighting of two champions or combatants in the field. 3 *Inst.* 221.

CAMP-QUA'RTERS (*Com.*) the quarters which the Siamese and other nations assign to the foreigners with whom they trade.

CAMPA'IGN (*Mil.*) the period within the space of a year that an army continues in the field without going into quarters, which is mostly during the spring and summer seasons.—*Winter campaigns* are so called when military operations are continued through the winter season, which is rarely the case.—*Campaign oven*, a portable oven made of copper, and raised upon feet, so that fire may be made underneath.

CA'MPANA (*Ecc.*) the name of a church bell; so called because the use of it was first introduced into the Christian Church by Paulinus, bishop of Nola, a town of Campania. *Hier*.

CAMPANA'CEÆ (*Bot.*) one of Linnæus's Natural Orders, including the bell-shaped flowers, as the Campanula, Convolvulus, &c.

CAMPA'NIFORM (*Bot.*) the same as *Campanulate*.

CAMPANI'LE (*Archit.*) a tower allotted for the bells in Italy.

CAMPANO'LOGY (*Lit.*) the art of casting and ringing of bells, from *campana*, a bell, and λόγος, a doctrine.

CAMPA'NULA (*Bot.*) a diminutive of *campana*, a bell, a genus of plants, Class 5 *Pentandria*, Order 1 *Monogynia*. Generic characters. CAL. *perianth* five-parted.—COR. monopetalous.—STAM. *filaments* five; *anthers* compressed.—PIST. *germ* angular; *style* filiform; *stigma* three-parted.—PER. *capsule* roundish; *seeds* numerous.

Species. The species are mostly perennials, as—*Campanula rotundifolia*, glabra, seu *Rapunculus sylvestris*, &c. Round-leaved Bell-Flower, a native of Britain.—*Campanula latifolia*, seu *maxima*, *Trachelium anglicum*, &c. seu *majus*, &c. Broad-leaved Bell-Flower, or Giant Throat-wort, a native of Britain.—*Campanula rapunculoides hortensis*, — Rampion-like Bell-Flower, a native of Britain.—*Campanula Trachelium*, *Trachelium majus*, *Cervicaria major*, seu *Rapum sylvestre*, &c. Great bell flower, Great or Nettle-leaved Throat-wort, or Canterbury-Bell, a native of Britain.—*Campanula glomerata*, seu *pratensis Trachelium minus*, seu *Alpinum*, &c. seu *Rapunculus sylvaticus*, &c. Small or Clustered Bell-Flower, or Little Canterbury-Bell, a native of Britain.—*Campanula hederacia*, Ivy-leaved Bell-Flower, a native of Britain.—*Campanula cenisia*, seu *uniflora*, Ciliate Bell-Flower, a native of the Alps of Switzerland.—*Campanula petræa*, seu *Trachelium majus*, &c. Great Stone Throat-Wort. Some are shrubs, as—*Campanula fruticosa*, seu *Prismatocarpus fruticosus*, shrubby Cape Bell-Flower.—*Campanula tenella*, native of the Cape of Good Hope, &c. Some are biennials, as the—*Campanula thyrsoidea*, *Alopecurus Alpinus*, *Cervicaria major*, seu *Trachelium thyrsoides*, Long-spiked Bell-Flower, a native of the Alps.—*Campanula hirsuta*, seu *Rapunculus sylvestris*, Waved-leaved Bell flower, a native of Switzerland.—*Campanula patula*, seu *Rapuntium*, Spreading, or Field Bell-Flower, a native of Britain.—*Campanula rapunculus*, *Rapunculum*, *Rapuntium parvum*, *Rapunculus esculentus*, seu *Erinus Nicandri*, Rampion, a native of Britain. Some are annuals, as the—*Campanula hybrida*, *Speculum Veneris*, *Pentagonium*, *Prismatocarpus*, seu *Onobrychis*, &c. Corn Bell-flower, Corn Violet, or Small Venus' Looking-glass.—*Campanula speculum*, seu *Onobrychis arvensis*, seu *Prismatocarpus speculum*, Venus' Looking-glass.—*Campanula prismatocarpus*, seu *Prismatocarpus nitidus*, Long-capsuled Bell-Flower, a native of the Cape of Good Hope, &c.

CAMPANULA'TA (*Bot.*) the same as *Linnæa*.

CAMPA'NULATE (*Bot.*) *campanulatus*, bell-shaped; an epithet for the corolla, calyx, nectary, &c.; *corolla campanulata*, a corolla that grows wider towards the mouth, so as to resemble a bell, as in the Canterbury Bell; *calyx campanulatus*, a bell-shaped calyx, as in *Chironia*; *nectarium campanulatum*, a bell-shaped nectary, as in Narcissus.

CAMPA'RIUM (*Archæol.*) any portion of a larger field or ground divided off.

CA'MPE (*Zool.*) κάμπη, from κάμπτω, a flexure, because it curls itself when it creeps; a worm or grub with many feet, called a palmer, or caterpillar. It is also an epithet for all large fish, which were so called from their bending their tails.

CAMPE (*Anat.*) a deflexion or bending, as in the perforations of the nostrils; also *the ham*, because it is usually bent; and any articulation. *Gal. de Usu. Parti.* l. 2, c. 2.

CAMPE'CHE-WOOD (*Bot.*) Log-wood; a West Indian wood, from the *Hæmatoxylum campechianum* of Linnæus; the wood is hard, and both the bark and the gum are gentle astringents.

CA'MPHIRE-TREE (*Bot.*) or Camphor-Tree, the *Laurus camphora* of Linnæus; a tree so called because it yields the camphor, which is extracted by distilling the wood with water in pots stuffed with straw, when the camphor sublimes, and concretes upon the straw in the form of a grey powder. [vide *Camphor*]

CA'MPHOR (*Chem.*) *camphura*, and in modern Greek καφορα, is not mentioned by the ancient Greeks, but was introduced by the Arabians. It is a singular substance, dry, friable, of a white colour, an acrid bitter taste, and a penetrating smell. Boerhaave and others looked upon it to be a highly perfect simple and volatile resin, or an oil of a solid form and consistence; but modern chemists have pronounced it to be a substance so peculiar that it cannot be classed with either the oils or the resins. It is altogether volatile and inflammable, soluble in vinous spirits, oils, and mineral acids, but not in water, alcalies, or vegetable acids. Besides the common camphor just described, there is another species, procured from the volatile oils of several plants, as Rosemary, Sage, Lavender, &c.; and an artificial camphor, procured by treating oil of turpentine with muriatic acid.—*Oil of Camphor*, an oil which is procured by the solution of camphor in nitric acid.

CAMPHORA'SMA (*Bot.*) Turkey Balsam; so called from its camphor-like smell.

CAMPHORA'TA (*Bot.*) the *Camphorosma polyemum arvense*, *Selago corymbosa*, of Linnæus. *Bauh.*; *Raii*, &c.

CA'MPHORATE (*Chem.*) camphoric acid combined with alkalies, earths, and metallic oxides, as the *camphorate* of alumine, the *camphorate* of ammonia, &c.

CAMPHORA'TED (*Chem.*) mixed or impregnated with camphire, as saline and camphorated liquors.

CAMPHORA'TUM OLEUM (*Med.*) a mixture of two parts olive oil, with one of camphor.

CA'MPHORIC ACID (*Chem.*) an acid obtained by distilling camphor in nitric acid.

CAMPHORO'SMA (*Bot.*) from *camphora*, and ἰσμη, odor; Camphor-Smell. 1. A genus of plants, Class 4 *Tetrandria*, Order 1 *Monogynia*.

Generic Characters. CAL. perianth pitcher-shaped.—COR. none.—STAM. *filaments* four; *anthers* oval.—PIST. *germ* ovate; *style* filiform; *stigmas* acute. PER. capsule one-celled; *seed* single.

Species. The species are mostly shrubs, as—*Camphorosma paleacea*, seu *fruticosa*, native of the Cape of Good Hope.—*Camphorosma monspeliaca*, *Selago*, seu *Camphorata hirsuta*, seu *monspeliensium*, Hairy Camphorosma, native of Spain, &c. But some are perennials, as—*Camphorosma acuta*, *Camphorata altera*, *Camphorata congener*, seu *Anthyllis altera*, &c. Sharp-leaved Camphorosma, native of Italy.—*Camphorosma glabra*, *Camphorata glabra*, seu *Polyenemon*, Smooth Camphorosma, native of Switzerland, &c. and—*Camphorosma Pteranthus*, *Lonichea cervina*, seu *Pteranthus*, is an annual, and native of Arabia. *Bauh. Pin.*; *Park. Theat. Botan.*; *Raii Hist. Plant.*—*Camphorosma*, is also the *Dracocephalum Canariense* of Linnæus.

CAMPICU'RSIO (*Ant.*) the exercise of training soldiers in marching.

CAMPIDUCTO'RES (*Ant.*) officers who drilled or exercised the young soldiers in their postures and in the use of their arms: they were also called *doctores armorum campigeni*, or in the Greek ὁπλοδιδασκαλοι. *Veget.* l. 1, c. 1; l. 2, c. 23; *Salmas in Lamprid. Alex. Sev.* c. 53; *Vales in Ammian.* l. 15, c. 3.

CAMPI'GENI (*Ant.*) vide *Campiductores*.

CA'MPION (*Bot.*) an annual, the *Agrostemma* of Linnæus. The principal species are as follow; namely—Rose Campion, *Agrostemma coronaria*, a pretty garden flower, having a white tubular or swelling blossom, with red in the middle. When it becomes fixed in a place it grows as freely as a weed.—Corn Campion, or Cockle, a common weed in corn-fields.

CAMPTAU'LA (*Ant.*) a trumpeter. *Vopisc. Carin.* c. 19.

CA'MPUS MARTII (*Archæol.*) or *Maii*, an assembly of the people every year in March or May, where they confederated together to defend the country against all enemies. *Leg. Edw. Confess.*

CA'MPYLON (*Med.*) καμπυλον, from καμπτω, to bend; a distortion of the eye. *Celsus*, l. 1, c. 6.

CAMPYLO'TIS (*Med.*) a preternatural incurvation.

CAMU'NIUM (*Bot.*) the same as *Chalcas paniculata*.

CA'MUS (*Ant.*) 1. κημος, a sort of snaffle or curb, with which spirited horses used to be kept in check. *Hesychius*; *Fest. de Verb. Signif.*; *Isid. Orig.* l. 2, c. 16; *Buleng. de Equit.* c. 17. 2. A sort of vessel made like a funnel, into which the judges used to cast their lots by which they passed sentence on criminals. *Schol. in Aristoph. Eq.* act. 3, scen. 2.

CAN (*Mar.*) the vessel particularly used by seamen in drinking their grog.—*Can-buoy* [vide *Buoy*].—*Canhooks*, an instrument used for slinging a cask by the ends of its staves.

CA'NA (*Archæol.*) a rod or distance in the measure ground.

CA'NABIS (*Bot.*) the same as *Bidens*.

CA'NADA BALSAM (*Bot.*) a balsam which is produced from the *Pinus balsamea*.

CANADE'LLA (*Ich.*) a kind of sea-fish, not unlike the perch.

CANAI'LLE (*Polit.*) a term among the French for the mob or rabble.

CANA'L (*Hydraul.*) an artificial river, provided with locks and sluices, and sustained by banks and mounds. They are sometimes formed for ornament, as the canals of Versailles, Fontainbleau, and St. James's Park; but they are most commonly dug for commercial purposes, to expedite the inland carriage of goods from one place to another.

CANAL (*Archit.*) the same as Flute.—*Canal of the larmier*, the hollow platfond, or the soffit, for preventing the rainwater from reaching the lower part of the cornice.—*Canal of the volute*, the channel on the face of the circumvolutions inclosed by a list in the Ionic capital.

CANAL (*Surg.*) vide *Canalis*.

CANA'L-COAL (*Min.*) otherwise called Bovey-Coal, the *Bitumen ampelites* of Linnæus, a compact jet-black glossy kind of coal, that burns with a bright white flame, like a candle; is easily kindled, and leaves a strong or sooty residuum. It is susceptible of a fine polish, and may, like jet, be made into trinkets. Specific gravity from 1.232 to 1.426.

CANA'LES SEMICIRCULARES (*Anat.*) the three semicircular canals placed in the posterior part of the labyrinth in each ear. They open by five orifices into the *vestibulum*.

CANALICULA'TUS (*Bot.*) channelled; an epithet for a leaf.

CANA'LIS (*Ant.*) from χαυω, to gape; a reed or pipe, so called because it is hollow.

CANALIS (*Anat.*) in the sense of a channel, may be applied to all the vessels of the body; but it is also used in application to particular parts, as—*Canalis arteriosus*, a blood-vessel peculiar to the fœtus, which disappears after the birth. The blood passes through this vessel from the pulmonary artery into the aorta.—*Canalis nasalis*, a canal going from the internal canthus of the eye downwards into the nose: it is situated in the superior maxillary bone, and is lined with the pituitary membrane continued from the nose.—*Canalis Petitianus*, a triangular cavity, (so called from M. Petit, its discoverer,) between the two laminæ of the hyaloid membrane of the eye, in the anterior part, formed by the separation of anterior lamina from the posterior.—*Canalis sempetros*, the half bony canal of the ear.—*Canalis venosus*, another canal peculiar to the fœtus, that conveys the maternal blood from the porta of the liver to the ascending vena, and disappears after the birth.

Canalis is also the name of the middle cavity or perforation in the vertebræ of the neck, through which the spinal marrow reaches from the brain.

CANALIS (*Surg.*) σωλην, a hollow instrument like a reed, made either of wood, or reeds, and linen, which serves for embracing and holding a broken limb. *Hippocrat. de Fract. &c. et Gal. Com. Cel.* l. 8, c. 10; *Paul Æginet.* l. 6, c. 106; *Schultet. Armament.* p. 1, tab. 23.

CA'NAN (*Com.*) a liquid measure of the kingdom of Siam, which the Portuguese call *choup*; it contains a pot, or near two pints, of Paris. One-fourth of the canan is called *loing*, the same as the French *chopine*.

CANARIE'NSIS (*Nat.*) Canary, or belonging to the Canary Islands; an epithet applied to plants and animals; so Canary Birds, &c.

CANARIES (*Mus.*) an old dance.

CANARI'NA (*Bot.*) a genus of plants, so named because it is a native of the Canaries, Class 6 *Hexandria*, Order 1 *Monogynia*.

Generic Characters. CAL. perianth superior.—COR. monopetalous.—STAM. *filaments* six; *anthers* pendulous from the tip.—PIST. *germ* inferior; *style* conical; *stigma* clavated.—PER. *capsule* obtuse; *seeds* numerous.

Species. The species are—*Canarina campanula*, seu *Campanula Canariensis*, &c. Canary Bell-flower, a perennial, native of the Canaries.—*Canarina Zanguebar*, native of Zanguebar.

CANA'RIUM AUGURIUM (*Ant.*) a sacrifice among the Romans, of a red dog, for the purpose of appeasing the fury of the dog-star on the approach of harvest.

Ovid. Fast. l. 4, v. 939.

> Est canis, Icarium dicunt, quo sidere moto
> Tosta sistit tellus, præcipiturque seges
> Pro cane sidereo, canis hic imponitur aræ
> Et, quare pereat, nil nisi nomen habet.

Plin. l. 18, c. 3; *Fest. de Verb. Signif.*; *Alex. Gen. Dier.* l. 3, c. 12; *Salmas.*

CANARIUM (*Bot.*) a genus of plants so named, from *canari*, the vernacular name in the Malay language, Class 22 *Dioecia*, Order 5 *Pentandria*.

Generic Characters. CAL. *perianth* two-leaved.—COR. *petals* three.—STAM. *filaments* five; *anthers* oblong.—PIST. *germ* ovate; *style* scarcely any; *stigma* headed.—PER. *drupe* dry; *seed* nut ovate.

Species. The species are shrubs, as—*Canarium commune*, seu *vulgare*, seu *Mehenbethene*, native of the Moluccas.—*Canarium sylvestre*, a shrub, native of Amboyna.—*Canarium balsamiferum*, seu *odoriferum*, &c. a shrub, native of Amboyna.—*Canarium hirsutum*, seu *odoriferum*, &c. native of the Moluccas.—*Canarium microcarpum*, seu *mirunuum*, native of the Moluccas.—*Canarium decumanum*, native of the Moluccas.

CANA'RY (*Orn.*) or Canary Bird, a well-known singing bird, the *Fringilla Canaria* of Linnæus.

CANA'RY-GRASS (*Bot.*) the *Phalaris* of Linnæus.

CA'NCAMUM (*Nat.*) a kind of gum brought from Arabia, very like myrrh. *Plin.* l. 12, c. 20.

TO CANCEL (*Print.*) to throw aside any portion of a printed work, as single leaves or whole sheets, &c. and print it afresh.

CANCELI'ER (*Falcon.*) is when a light-flown hawk in her stooping turns two or three times upon the wind to recover herself before she seizes her prey.

CANCELLA'RIA CURIA (*Archæol.*) the Court of Chancery.

CANCELLARII (*Ant.*) officers at the emperor's court who attended *ad Cancellos*, i. e. at the bars. *Vopisc. Carin.* c. 16.

CANCELLA'TION (*Law*) expunging the contents of an instrument by means of striking two lines through it in the shape of a cross; so called from *cancellus*, a cross-bar.

CANCELLA'TED (*Bot.*) *cancellatus*, cross-barred or latticed, an epithet for the involucre and capsule. [vide *Latticed*]

CA'NCELLER (*Falcon.*) vide *Cancelier*.

CANCE'LLI (*Archit.*) κιγκλιδες, trellis, or lattice-work, as in latticed windows, &c. made of cross-bars, of wood or iron; also the balusters or rails encompassing the bar of a court of justice; and the chancel of a church. *Schol. Aristoph. in Eq.* act 2, scen. 1; *Spartian. in Caracal*; *Ammian.* l. 30; *Cassiodor.* l. 11, ep. 6; *Anastas. Bibl. in Sixt. Papias. Element.*; *Oder. Vital.* l. 2.

CANCELLI (*Anat.*) the reticular substance in bones.

CANCE'LLUS (*Ent.*) a species of Cancer, under the division *Gammarus*, remarkable for the tenacity with which it keeps hold of whatever it fixes upon.

CA'NCER (*Ent.*) καρκινος, from καρκος, rough; because it has a shell furnished with rough claws; the Crab, an animal frequently spoken of by the ancients. Aristotle mentions three species, namely—Μαια, *mæa*, which is the largest of the kind; —Παγυρος *pagurus*, otherwise called *Cancer marinus*.—*Cancer fluviale*, a variety of which was so much more swift than the rest as to have the name of *equus*. *Aristot. Hist.* l. 4, c. 2; *Plin.* l. 9, c. 31; *Ælian. Hist. Anim.* l. 17, c. 1; *Athen.* l. 3, c. 13.

CANCER, in the Linnean system, a genus of animals, Class *Insecta*, Order *Aptera*.

Generic Character. Legs six or eight, besides chelate claws; *feelers* six, unequal.—*Eyes* two, moveable.—*Mandibles* horny.—*Lip* triple.—*Tail* articulated.

Species. The species are distinguished into the following classes: 1. The Crab, having four filiform antennæ. 2. *Pagurus*, having pedunculate antennæ. 3. *Galathea*, having unequal antennæ. 4. *Astacus*, Lobster, Crawfish, &c. 5. *Squilla*, the Squill, having the shell of the thorax extremely short. 6. *Gammarus*, having very simple antennæ. 7. *Scyllarus*, having two biarticulate plates instead of the hinder antennæ.

CA'NCER (*Numis.*) that species of the cancer known among the ancients by the name of the Pagurus, was the symbol of Agrigentum, and other towns of Sicily, as it is commonly represented on medals. *Goltz. Mag. Græc.*; *Haverkamp. Parut. Sicil. Descrit.*

CANCER (*Astron.*) the fourth sign in the zodiac, marked thus, ♋, which the sun enters on the 21st day of June, thence called the summer solstice. It is called in the Greek ὀκτάπους, i. e. eight-footed, or ἀντίβαμων, i. e. retrograde; in Latin also *Nepa*, *Astacus*, and *Cammarus*; in Arabic *Elsartan*, and consists, according to Ptolemy, of thirteen stars, to Kepler of seventeen, to Bayer of thirty-five, of which two are of the third magnitude, i. e. one in the claws, called by the Arabians *Azubene*, and the other in the southern foot. There are two others of the fourth magnitude, called by the Greeks ὀνοι or ὀνισκοι, *Asini* or *Aselli*, by Manilius *Jugulæ*; and a third of the same magnitude, in the breast of the Cancer, called by the Greeks νεφεληειδης, φατνη, and ευφορβη; and in the Arabic *Mellef*.

According to the fables of the Greeks, the crab was transported to heaven at the request of Juno, because it had been slain by Hercules during his engagement with the serpent Python; but the evident design, both of the figure and the name of this constellation, is, to represent the apparent backward motion of the sun, in which it is said to resemble that animal. *Theophrast. de Vent, &c.; Arat. de Apparent.; Hipparchus ad Phænom. seu Apparent.* l. 3; *Eratosthen. Characteris; Gem. Elem. Astron.* c. 14; *Ptol. Almag.* l. 7, c. 5; *Cleom. de Sphær.; Procl. de Sphær.; Plin.* l. 18, c. 35.—*Tropic of Cancer*, a small circle of the sphere, parallel to the Equator, from which it is 23½° distant, and marks the sun's greatest northern declination. It is so called because it passes through the beginning of the sign Cancer.

CANCER (*Med.*) by this term, as appears from Celsus, the Roman writers understood what the Greeks called *Gangrene* or *Sphacelus*; and the disease, which now passes under the name of cancer, is the same as what the Greeks called καρκίνωμα, from καρκῖνος, a crab; because, as Galen thinks, its puffed veins bore some resemblance to the claws of a crab. It was also called *lupus* by the Romans, because it consumed the body like a wolf. The cancer is an unequal tumour, with very elevated edges, of a livid colour, and extremely painful when it is attended with ulceration; it is called by Hippocrates κρυπτὸν, occult, in distinction from that which is ulcerated, and consequently denominated open. It is generated from black bile, of a corrosive quality, and rises in many parts, but principally infests the *uterus*, the breasts of women, and the glandular parts of the body. *Hippocrat.* l. 6, aphor. 38; *Gal. de Art. Curat. ad Glauc.* l. 2, c. 10; *Cel.* l. 5, c. 28; *Oribas de Morb. Curat.* l. 3, c. 28; *Aet. Tetrab.* 4, serm. 4, c. 43; *Paul. Æginet.* l. 4, c. 26.

Cancer is ranked by Cullen as a genus of diseases, in the Class *Locales*, Order *Tumores*, and has been distinguished into primitive, degenerate, blind, latent, or occult, ulcerated, and confirmed.—*Primitive cancer*, is one that comes of itself, appearing first about the bigness of a pea, causing a continual inward pricking pain.—*Degenerate cancer*, a cancer which succeeds an imposthume, or swelling, that is either obstinate or ill-dressed, and has never been occult.—*Blind, latent*, or *open cancer*, a primitive cancer, before it is grown large, and has been opened, in which state a cancer may remain for several years.—*Ulcerated* or *open cancer*, one that is grown larger than a primitive one, and has been opened.—*Confirmed cancer*, a malignant scirrhous humour, which is accompanied with all the symptoms of a cancerous affection, as burning shooting pains, a livid colour in the skin, &c.—*Cancer of the bone*, a disease in a bone, caused by a sharp humour, and succeeded by an ulcer of the flesh and skin.

CANCRE'NA (*Med.*) the same as *Gangrena*.

CANCRI (*Ant.*) the same as *Cancelli*.

CANCRI'NI *versus* (*Poet.*) a sort of verses, which may be read either backward or forward, as *Roma tibi subito, motibus ibit amor*.

CANCROI'DES (*Ent.*) a species of *Scarabæus, Dermestes*, &c.

CANCRO'MA (*Orn.*) Boat-bill, a genus of animals, Class *Aves*, Order *Grallæ*, having the bill shaped like an inverted boat.
Generic Characters. Bill gibbous.—*Nostrils* small.—*Tongue* small.—*Toes* divided.
Species. The species are—*Cancroma cochlearia*, Crested Boat-bill.—*Cancroma cancrophaga*, White bellied Boat-bill.

CANCRUM *oris* (*Med.*) Canker of the Mouth, a deep, irregular, foul, and fœtid ulcer in the inside of the lips and cheeks.

CA'NDEL (*Bot.*) the *Rhizophora gymnorrhiza* et *candel* of Linnæus.

CANDE'LA (*Bot.*) the *Rhizophora candel* of Linnæus.—*Candela regia*, the same as *Verbascum*.

CANDELA *fumalis* (*Med.*) an oblong mass, consisting of odoriferous powders employed in fumigation.

CANDELA'BRUM (*Ant.*) a candlestick.

CANDELA'RES (*Bot.*) the second Order in Linnæus' fragments of a Natural Arrangement.

CANDELA'RIA (*Bot.*) the same as *Verbascum*.

CA'NDENT (*Chem.*) hot in the highest degree next to fusion.

CA'NDI (*Com.*) or *cando*, a long measure in India, equal to about seven ells.

CANDIDATI (*Ant.*) those who among the Romans offered themselves dressed *candida veste*, in a white robe, as suitors for any office, whence the modern name of *candidate* in the same sense. *Dionys. Hal.* l. 2; *Tertul. de Idol.* c. 18; *Pancirol. Notit. Dig. Imp. Occident.* c. 73; *Ursat. de Not. Roman apud Græv. Thes. Antiq.* tom. xi.—*Candidati Principis*, were the candidates whom the emperor recommended to public favour; also those who read the emperor's speech in the senate. *Quintil. Instit.* l. 6, c. 3; *Suet. in Aug.* c. 56; *Lamprid. in Sever.* c. 43; *Pancirol. Notit. Dig. Imp. Occident.* c. 73.—*Candidati milites*, privileged soldiers, who were clothed in white, and fought near the prince. Of these mention is made in an inscription at Rome. HIC POSITUS EST ANTIOCHUS CANDIDATUS PRIMICER. *Hieron. in Vit. Hilar. Ammian.* l. 15, c. 5; *Veget. de Re Mil.* l. 2, c. 7; *Salmas. in Capitol Gord.*

CA'NDIIL (*Com.*) a measure of capacity in India, by which the burden of a ship is estimated as it is by tons in Europe; 400 candiils being equal to 100 tons.

CANDISA'TIO (*Chem.*) candying or crystallizing sugar after it has been dissolved in water.

CANDITE'ERS (*Fort.*) frames to lay faggots or brushwood on to cover the workmen.

CA'NDLE (*Mech.*) a cylindrical or conical body made of tallow, wax, or spermaceti; whence they are called *tallow, wax*, or *spermaceti* candles. They are called *moulds* when they are made in a mould; and *rush-lights* when the wick is rush instead of cotton.—*Candlestick*, the stand in which candles are fixed.—*Candle-wood*, slips of pine, which are burnt instead of candles by the natives of America.

CANDLE-BERRY-TREE (*Bot.*) the *Myrica* of Linnæus; so called because candles are made of its berries in America.

CA'NDLE-BOMBS (*Chem.*) glass bubbles, with a narrow bore, which, after being filled with water, are stopped up, and passed through the flame of a light, which causes them to explode with a noise.

CA'NDLEMAS-DAY (*Ecc.*) the festival observed in commemoration of the purification of the Virgin Mary, on the second of February; so named from the number of lights used on the occasion, or from the consecration of the candles to be used in the ensuing year, that takes place on this day in the Romish Church.

CA'NDLE-STICK (*Her.*) is borne as a charge in the arms of the founders' company.

CA'NDOCK (*Bot.*) a weed that grows in rivers.

CANDO'U *Purchasii* (*Bot.*) a tree of Brazil, that is very similar to the cork-tree in its wood, and to the walnut-tree in its height.

CA'NDUM (*Chem.*) Candy sugar melted and crystallized.

CANDY-TUFT (*Bot.*) the *Iberis* of Linnæus, of which the Purple Candy-Tuft, *Iberis umbellata*, and the White Candy-Tuft, *Iberis amara*, are annuals; but the other species are perennials.

CANE (*Bot.*) a strong Indian reed; so called from the Hebrew קנה, the Greek κάννα, and the Latin *canna*, of which there are two kinds, namely, the—Bambu, or Bamboo-cane, the *Arundo bamboo*, a woody, hollow, round, knotted reed, growing to the length of forty feet, which serves a very great variety of domestic purposes in India.—Sugar-cane, the *Saccharum*, a perennial, of the reed tribe, remarkable for containing a juice, from which sugar is made. The skin of the sugar-cane is soft, and the spongy matter, or pith, which it contains is very juicy. The sugar-cane will not thrive in England, except in a hot-house, where it is propagated by slips taken from the older plants.

CANE (*Com.*) 1. A long measure of Montpelier, &c. equal to two yards and a half-quarter; that of Spain equal to one yard, and also to one and a half-quarter; that of Naples equal to two yards and a half; that of Marseilles equal to two yards and a half; that of Rome is eight palms; and thirty canes is equal to fifty-five and a half ells. 2. The quantity measured as a cane of cloth, &c. 3. A walking-stick, which consists of a cane. 4. A lance or dart made of a cane.

CANE'LLA (*Bot.*) from *canna*, a reed, because the bark resembled a reed, a genus of plants, Class 11 *Dodecandria*, Order 1 *Monogynia*.
Generic Characters. CAL. *perianth* one-leaved.—COR. *petals* five; *nectary* pitcher-shaped.—STAM. *filaments* none; *anthers* twenty-one.—PIST. *germ* superior; *style* cylindric; *stigmas* two blunt.—PER. *berry* oblong; *seeds* roundish.
Species. The only species is the—*Canella alba, Winterana*, seu *Cubane Winterania Canella, Winteranus cortex, Laurus, Pseudo Cassia*, &c. *Cassia lignea*, &c. seu *cinnamomea*, seu *Cinnamomum Sylvestre*, &c. *Lignum*, seu *Cortex aromaticus, Arbor baccifera*, &c. Laurel-leaved Canella, a shrub, native of the West Indies.

CANE'ON (*Med.*) κανεῖον, the cover of a pot, used in uterine suffumigations. *Foes. Œconom. Hippocrat.*

CANE'PHORÆ (*Ant.*) κανηφόροι, noble virgins of the Athenians; who were so called because they were wont, φέρειν, to carry, κάνα, baskets, at the festival of the Panathenæa of Minerva. *Schol. Aristoph. in Acharn.*; *Harpocration.*; *Hesychius.*

CANEPHO'RIA (*Ant.*) the ceremony of carrying the baskets at the festival of the Panathenæa by the Canephoræ. [vide *Canephoræ*]

CANES operti (*Archæol.*) dogs with whole feet that are not lawed.

CANES *venatici* (*Astron.*) the Grey-Hounds, two northern constellations, otherwise named *Asterion* and *Chara*; in which Hevelius, by whom it was formed, reckoned twenty-five stars; the British Catalogue ten.

CANESTELLUS (*Archæol.*) a basket, or the name of a service by which land was held, that consisted in furnishing baskets. *Lib. Rub. Scacc.*

CA'NFARA (*Archæol.*) a trial by means of hot iron, which was formerly used in this kingdom. It is a sort of ordeal by fire, in which the accused carried hot irons in his hands; and if he came off unhurt, he was judged to be innocent. [vide *Ordeal*]

CA'N-HOOK (*Mar.*) vide *Can*.

CA'NICA (*Com.*) a spice in the island of Cuba; a sort of wild cinnamon, having the taste of the clove.

CA'NICÆ (*Ant.*) brown coarse bread made of bran. *Fest. de Verb. Signif.*

CA'NICEPS (*Ant.*) a name given by Pliny to a sort of wild men, whom he describes as having dog's heads. *Plin.* l. 7, c. 2.

CANICI'DA (*Bot.*) another name for *Aconite*, because it kills dogs.

CANICI'DIUM (*Anat.*) a dissection of living dogs. *Castel. Lex. Med.*

CANI'CULA (*Astron.*) a name given both to *Canis Major* and *Canis Minor*, and also to *Sirius*, particularly by the poets, from which the dog days were called *dies caniculares*. [vide *Canicular*]
Horat. l. 3, od. 13.

Te flagrantis atrox hora Caniculæ.

Pers. sat. 3, v. 5.

En quid agis? Siccas insana Canicula messes
Jamdudum coquit.

Aristot. sect. 1, prob. 1; *Plin.* l. 2, c. 40; l. 18, c. 28.

CANI'CULAR *days* (*Chron.*) *dies caniculares*, the Dog-days; a name given by the ancients to that period of the summer season, between the 15th of July and the 20th of August, when the constellation *Canicula* or *Canis*, and particularly the principal star in that constellation, called *Sirius, Canicula*, or Dog-Star, rises heliacally. For they ascribed the great heat, and the consequent diseases, which generally prevail at this season to the influence of that star [vide *Canicula* and *Canarium*]; but this supposition is now considered to be incorrect.—*Canicular year*, the Egyptian natural year; so called because it was computed from the heliacal rising of the *Canicula, Canis*, or Dog-star. [vide *Canicula* and *Canis*]

CANILI'CULUS (*Anat.*) a little canal.

CANI'NA *appetentia* (*Med.*) the same as *Bulimus*.—*Canina rabies*, the same as *Hydrophobia*.

CANINA (*Bot.*) an epithet for several plants, namely—*Brassica canina*, the *Mercurialis sylvestris* of Linnæus.—*Lingua canina*, the Cynoglossum.—*Malus canina*, the Mandragora.—*Rosa canina*, the Wild Briar.

CANINA'NA (*Zool.*) a species of serpent in America; so called because it may be treated as familiarly as a dog.

CANI'NUS (*Anat.*) canine; an epithet for the teeth, *dentes canini*, the four eye-teeth; so called from their resemblance to the teeth of the dog. They are the *Columellares* or *Comelli* of Varro and Pliny; and are called Eye-teeth, because their fangs extend nearly up to the eye. *Varr. de Re Rust.* l. 2, c. 7; *Plin.* l. 11, c. 38; *Isid. Orig.* l. 11, c. 1.—*Caninus musculus*, the same as the *Levator Anguli oris*.

CANI'PULUS (*Ant.*) a short sword.

CANI'RAM (*Bot.*) a tree of Malabar, the span of which exceeds the grasp of two men, the *Strychnos nux vomica* of Linnæus. *Raii Hist. Plant.*

CANIRU'BUS (*Bot.*) the same as the *Rosa Canina*.

CA'NIS (*Zool.*) a genus of animals, Class *Mammalia*, Order *Feræ*.
Generic Character. Foreteeth, upper 6, lower 6.—Tusks solitary.—Grinders from 6 to 7.
Species. This genus comprehends animals that differ very essentially from each other in their habits, as the Dog, Wolf, Hyæna, Fox, and Jackal. The principal species are as follow, namely—*Canis familiaris*, the Dog, with all its varieties of Spaniel, Hound, Grey-Hound, Pointer, &c. [vide *Dog*]—*Canis lupus*, the Wolf, having its tail bent inward.—*Canis Mexicanus*, the Mexican Wolf, having the tail smooth, and bent downwards.—*Canis Thous*, having a greyish body, the size of a cat, the Surinam Wolf.—*Canis lycaon*, the Black Wolf.—*Canis hyæna*, the Hyæna, of a pale brown colour striped with black.—*Canis cocuta*, the Spotted Hyæna, being of a reddish brown colour spotted with black.—*Canis aureus*, the Jackal, or Lion's Provider, having a straight tail, and a pale tawny body.—*Canis vulpes*, the Fox.—*Canis Alopex*, the Brant Fox, having a straight tail, black at the tip.—*Canis Virginianus*, the Lagopus.—*Canis Lagopus*, the Arctic Fox.—*Canis crucigera*, the Cross Fox.—*Canis australis*, the Wolf Fox.—*Canis Cerdo*, the Fennec, or Zerda, a beautiful African and Asiatic animal, remarkable for the size of its ears, which stand up erect.

CANIS Major (*Astron.*) ὁ κύων, one of the 48 old constellations, called by Homer ἀστὴρ ὀπωρινός, an autumnal constellation, which, according to Ptolemy, contains 18 stars, to Kepler 13, to Tycho 13, to Bayer 19, to Hevelius 21, and to Flamstead 31; the principal of which is Σείριος, Sirius, the Dog-Star. According to the fables of the Greeks, the constellation *canis* was so called from the dog of Orion, the hunter, which was transported to heaven; but Hephæstion and Horus Apollo ascribe the name and figure to the Egyptians, who called it Sothis, and judged of the swelling of the Nile by its rising; wherefore they looked upon it to be the sentinel or watch of the year; and according to their hieroglyphic mode of writing represented it under the figure of a dog.—*Canis Minor*, another of the 48 old constellations, called by the Greeks προκύων, and by the Latins *Antecanis*, because it rises before the *Canis major*. This name is now applied to the principal star in the *Canis minor*, which according to Ptolemy contains two stars, to Kepler 5, to Tycho 5, to Bayer 8, to Hevelius 13, and to Flamstead 14. The Greeks make this also to have been one of Orion's dogs, or, according to another fable, to have been transported to Heaven by Erigone, or the Virgin, daughter of Icarius; but in all probability the Egyptians were the inventors of this as well as the former constellation. The heliacal rising of these two stars being in the hottest season of the year, namely, in the latter part of summer, this period was denominated by the ancients *dies caniculares*, or Dog-days. [vide *Canicula*, and *Canicular Days*] *Arat. de Apparent.*; *Hipparch. ad Arat.*; *Eratosth. Characteris.*; *Cic. ex Arat. de Nat. Deor.* l. 2; *Ptol. Almag.* l. 7, c. 5; *Plin.* l. 18, c. 28; *Gem. Elem. Astron.* c. 14; *Hor. Apoll. Hierog.*; *Petav. Uranolog.*

CA'NISTER (*Ant.*) a canister or panier.

CANI'TIES (*Med.*) hoariness of the hair, grey hairs.

CA'NKER (*Med.*) see *Cancrum oris*.

CANKER (*Bot.*) *carcinoma*, a cancerous affection which occurs frequently in fruit-trees. It shows itself in a large spongy excrescence, which even in the driest weather discharges an acrid corroding ichor. Sometimes it is latent, and spreads far in the bark before it is discovered.

CANKER (*Chem.*) the rust of iron, brass, &c.

CANKER (*Vet.*) a disease in the feet of horses, consisting of a fungous excrescence with fibrous roots. The disease termed the *frush* will, when neglected, often turn to the canker.—*Canker* is also the name of a disease in the ears of dogs, and in the necks of pigeons, which is of a similar nature.

CA'NNA major (*Anat.*) the greater bone of the leg, called also *Focile majus* and *Tibia*.—*Canna minor*, the lesser bone of the leg, called also *Focile minus*.

CANNA (*Bot.*) a genus of plants, Class 1 *Monandria*, Order 1 *Monogynia*.
Generic Characters. CAL. *perianth* three-leaved.—COR. monopetalous; *nectary* petal-like.—STAM. *filaments* none; *anther* linear.—PIST. *germ* roundish; *style* single; *stigma* linear.—PER. *capsule* roundish; *seeds* few.
Species. The species are perennials, as—*Canna indica*, *Carmacorus*, *Gladiolus indicus*, *Arundo indica*, seu *florida*, seu *Kalu Bala*, a native of Asia.—*Canna angustifolia*, *Cannacorus angustifolius*, *Arundo indica*, *Albara*, seu *Pacivira*, Narrow-leaved Indian reed, a native of America.—*Canna glauca*, *Cannoides*, seu *Cannacorus glaucophyllus*, a native of Carolina.—*Canna juncea*, a native of China.—*Canna flaccida*, a native of S. Carolina.—*Canna coccinea*, a native of the Indies.—*Canna lutea*, a native of the East Indies.—*Canna patens*, a native of the Indies.—*Canna gigantea*, native of S. Carolina.

CANNABI'NA (*Bot.*) the *Datisca* of Linnæus. *Tournef. Instit.*

CA'NNABIS (*Bot.*) κάνναβις, hemp, a well-known plant, the seeds of which, in decoctions and emulsions, have been recommended against coughs, &c. *Dioscor.* l. 3, c. 166; *Plin.* l. 19, c. 4; *Oribas. Med. Coll.* l. 11; *Aet. Tetrab.* 1, serm. 1; *Paul. Æginet.* l. 7, c. 3; a genus of plants, Class 22 *Dioecia*, Order 5 *Pentandria*.
Generic Characters. CAL. *perianth* one-leaved.—COR. none.—PIST. *germ* very small.—PER. very small; *seed-nut* globose.
Species. The only species is—*Cannabis sativa*, mas, erratica, seu *semina*, an annual, native of Persia.

CANNACO'RUS (*Bot.*) the *Canna Indica* of Linnæus.

CA'NNEL-COAL (*Min.*) vide *Canal-Coal*.

CA'NNEQUINS (*Com.*) white cotton cloths brought from the East Indies, which are folded square, and are about eight ells long.

CA'NNETS (*Her.*) a charge in which ducks are represented without beak or feet.

CA'NNIONS (*Archæol.*) an old fashioned garment for the leg.

CA'NNISTER (*Mech.*) an instrument used by coopers in racking off wine.

CANNON (*Mil.*) any sort of gun which is too large to be used in the hand. On their first introduction cannons were distinguished by particular names, as, Queen Elizabeth's Pocket Pistol, a 60-pounder, Mounts-Meg, an 80-pounder, in the Tower of London; the Thunderer, an 80-pounder, at Berlin; the Terrible, an 80-pounder, at Malaga, &c. These names were exchanged for others more systematic, and of more general use, namely—

Name.	Pounders.	Cwt.
Cannon Royal, or Carthoun	48	90
Bastard Cannon, or ¾ Carthoun	36	79
Half Carthoun	24	60
Culverin	18	50
Demy-Culverin	9	30
Falcon	6	25
Saker { lowest sort	5	13
ordinary	6	15
largest size	8	18
Basilisk	48	85
Serpentine	4	8
Aspik	2	7
Dragon	6	12
Syren	60	81
Falconet	3, 2, & 1	15, 10, 5

At present cannon, or pieces of ordnance, are distinguished by the weight of the ball they carry; as a 24-pounder, one that discharges a ball of 24 pounds; a 12-pounder, one that carries a ball of 12 pounds. Ship and Garrison-guns consist of 42, 32, 24, 18, 12, 9, 6, and 3-pounders. Battering-guns of 24, 18, and 12-pounders. Field Pieces of 18, 12, 9, 6, 3, 2, 1½, 1, and ½-pounders.

Parts of a Cannon. The parts of a cannon are as follow; namely,—The *reinforce*, that part of a gun next the breech, which is made stronger to resist the force of powder. This is divided into the first and second reinforce, which differ in size.—The *chace*, the whole space from the trunnions to the muzzle.—The *muzzle*, properly so called, is that part comprehended between the muzzle, astragal, and the end.—The *cascable*, the hindermost part of the breech, from the base-ring to the end of the button.—The *cascable-astragal*, the diminishing part between the two breech-mouldings.—The *neck of the cascable*, the narrow space between the breech-moulding and the button.—The *breech* is the solid piece behind, between the vent and the extremity of the base-ring, which terminates the hind part of the gun, exclusive of the cascable.—The *breech-mouldings*, the eminent parts, as squares or rounds, which serve only for ornaments to the piece, &c.—The *base-ring* and *ogee* are ornamental-mouldings; the latter of which is always in the shape of the letter S, after the manner of the ogee in architecture.—The *vent-field* is the part from the vent to the first reinforce-astragal.—The *vent-astragal* and *fillets* are the mouldings and fillets at or near the vent.—The *charging cylinder* is all the space from the chace-astragal to the muzzle-astragal.—The *first reinforce-ring* and *ogee* are the ornaments on the second reinforce.—The *first reinforce-astragal* is the ornament between the first and second reinforce.—The *chase girdle* is the ornament close to the trunnions.—*Trunnions*, two solid cylindrical pieces of metal in every gun, which project from the piece, and by which it is supported upon its carriage.—*Dolphins*, two handles placed on the second reinforce-ring of brass cannons, resembling the fish of that name; they serve for mounting and dismounting the guns.—The *second reinforce-ring* and *ogee* are the two ornaments joining the trunnions.—The *chase-astragal* and *fillets*, the two last-mentioned ornaments jointly.—The *muzzle-astragal* and *fillets*, the joint ornaments nearest the muzzle.—The *muzzle mouldings*, the ornaments at the muzzle of a piece.—The *swelling of the muzzle*, the projected part behind the muzzle mouldings.—The *mouth of a cannon*, the entrance of the bore, or the hollow part which receives the charge.—The *vent*, that which, in small fire-arms, is called the *touch-hole*, a small hole pierced at the end, or near the end, of the bore or chamber, for the purpose of priming the piece with powder, or to introduce the tube in order when lighted to set fire to the charge.—The *chamber* is the place where the powder is lodged which forms the charge.

The tools employed in the use of cannon are as follow:—*Coins*, or *wedges*, to lay under the breech of the gun in order to elevate or depress it.—*Handspikes*, which serve as levers to move and lay the gun.—*Ladles*, which serve to load the gun with loose powder.—*Rammers*, which serve to ram home the wads put upon the powder and shot.—The *sponge* is fixed at the opposite end of the rammer, and serves to clean the gun after it has been fired.—*Screws* are used to field pieces instead of coins, by which the gun is kept to the same elevation.—The *searcher* is an iron hollow, at one end, to receive a wooden handle, and, on the other end, has from four to eight flat springs pointed and turned outwards at the ends.—The *reliever* is an iron flat ring with a wooden handle at right angles to it: it is so called because it serves to relieve or disentangle the searcher, when any one of its springs is caught in a hole on its being introduced into the piece to search it after it is fired.—*Cannon-ball* and *cannon-shot*. [vide *Ball* and *Shot*]

CANNON (*Print.*) one of the largest kinds of type or letter used in a printing office, which by some is supposed to be so called because it was used in the printing of canons, but more probably from its size.

CANNONA'DE (*Mil.*) the firing of several pieces of ordnance against any particular object.

CANNONEE'R (*Mil.*) the person who manages the gun.

CA'NNULA (*Surg.*) a tube of various figures introduced into orifices for the purpose of conveying any fluid, as pus from a wound, &c.

CANO'E (*Mar.*) an Indian boat formed of the trunk of a tree that is hollowed out. The canoes made of the trunk of one tree keep that name as long as they are so small that not above three or four persons can go in them; when they are larger, those of America are called *pirogues*, and those of Guinea *chams*. Among the Greenlanders the man's canoe is called *kaiak*, that of the women *miak*; the latter is a large boat managed by the women for transporting families and effects when they shift their encampments.

CANON *of Scripture* (*Bibl.*) from the Greek κάνων, a rule; signifies that rule by which the genuine books of Scripture are distinguished from those which are either false or doubtful. The Scriptures consist of the Old and New Testament.

Old Testament. The Jews divided the books of the Old Testament into three classes; namely, the Law, the Prophets, and the Hagiography, which by them was called *Chetubim*.

The Law. The First Class comprehended five books; namely, 1. Genesis, so called from the creation of the world. 2. Exodus, from ἔξοδος, the departure of the Israelites out of Egypt. 3. Leviticus, so named from its contents, because it treats of the office and duties of the priest and Levites, and generally called the Levitical Law. 4. Numbers, so named from the numbering of the tribes that came out of Israel. 5. Deuteronomy, i. e. literally, δεύτερος, the second, and νόμος, law, because it contained a repetition, or recapitulation of the Law. These five books, which were written by Moses, are comprehended under the general name of Pentateuch, from πέντε, five, and τεῦχος, a volume.

The Prophets. The Second Class consisted of nine books; namely, 1. Joshua, so called from Joshua, the son of Nun, by whom it was written. 2. Judges, so called because it contained an account of those who immediately succeeded Moses and Joshua as rulers of the people. 3, 4. The two books of Samuel, or the First and Second Books of Kings, so named because they were written by Samuel, and contain an account, not only of himself, but also of the Kings Saul and David. 5, 6. The two books of Kings, or the Third and Fourth Books of Kings, which contain an account of the several Kings of Israel in the order of their succession. 7. Jeremiah, or the book written by Jeremiah. 8. Ezekiel, or the book written by Ezekiel. 9. The twelve minor Prophets, which were all included in one book.

The Hagiography. The third class comprehended nine books; namely, 1. Job, so named from the person whose history it contains. This book is ascribed to Moses. 2. The Psalms, or, as the Hebrew word *Thehelim* implies, the *volume of Hymns*, are ascribed to many different writers, the principal of whom are Moses, David, and Solomon. 3. The Proverbs, also called from the name of their author, the Proverbs of Solomon. 4. Ecclesiastes, or the Preacher, because this book, which was also written by Solomon, was more in the shape of moral discourses than the preceding. 5. The Song of Solomon. 6. Daniel, or the book written by Daniel. 7. Chronicles, called by the Greeks παρα λειπομένα, remaining, because it details more at large the things passed over, or slightly mentioned, in the Books of Kings. 8. Esdras, the book written by Esdras. 9. Esther, which is ascribed to Esdras as the author; to which some added Ruth, and the Lamentations of Jeremiah. These books, amounting in all to twenty-two, constituted the Canon of the Old Testament as received by the Jews; to which the Romish Church have added six other books that were held by the former to be apocryphal; namely, 1. The Wisdom of Solomon. 2. Ecclesiasticus. 3. Tobias. 4. Judith. 5 & 6. Maccabees, which, by the Protestants, are ranked in the same class as they are by the Jews.

New Testament. The New Testament, which consists of twenty-seven books, is divided into four parts; namely, the Gospels, Acts of the Apostles, Epistles, and Revelation.

Gospels. The First Class comprehends the writings of the

CANON.

Evangelists, so called from *εὖ*, well, and *ἀγγελία*, a message; because these books contain the Gospel, or a message of glad tidings to all mankind. They are as follow: 1. Matthew, who wrote in Hebrew, and addressed himself to his own nation. 2. Mark, who wrote in Greek, and for the benefit of the Gentiles. 3. Luke, the most learned of the Evangelists, who wrote also in Greek. 4. John, who was the last, wrote his Gospel in Asia.

The Acts of the Apostles. The Second Class, embraces in one book the Acts of the Apostles, so called from its contents. It is ascribed to the evangelist Luke, and contains the history of the Church at its first commencement after the death of our Saviour.

The Epistles. The Third Class, includes, 1. Fourteen Epistles of St. Paul, nine of which were written to seven churches, and the five others to his disciples Timothy, Titus, and Philemon. 2. Two Epistles of St. Peter, which are called General, because they were addressed not to one church, city, or people, but to all the Gentiles. 3. Three Epistles general of St. John. 4. One Epistle general of St. James. 5. One Epistle general of St. Jude.

The Revelation. The Fourth Class, includes the book called the Revelation, or Apocalypse, which was written by the evangelist St. John, during his banishment to the island of Patmos, and contains an account of the revelation, or manifestation of hidden things, which was made to himself. The spurious or disputed books of the New Testament are still more numerous than those of the Old, being written for the most part by heretics, for the purpose of supporting their own particular opinions. [vide *Acts of the Apostles*]

The following is a list of all the books of the Old and New Testament, together with the number of chapters they contain, according to the order in which they are placed in our authorised version.

Books of the Old Testament.

Books.	Chapters.	Books.	Chapters.
Genesis	50	Ecclesiastes	12
Exodus	40	The Song of Solomon	8
Leviticus	27	Isaiah	66
Numbers	36	Jeremiah	52
Deuteronomy	34	Lamentations	5
Joshua	24	Ezekiel	48
Judges	21	Daniel	12
Ruth	4	Hosea	14
I. Samuel	31	Joel	3
II. Samuel	24	Amos	9
I. Kings	22	Obadiah	1
II. Kings	25	Jonah	4
I. Chronicles	29	Micah	7
II. Chronicles	36	Nahum	3
Ezra	10	Habakkuk	3
Nehemiah	13	Zephaniah	3
Esther	10	Haggai	2
Job	42	Zechariah	14
Psalms	150	Malachi	4
Proverbs	31		

Books of the New Testament.

Books.	Chapters.	Books.	Chapters.
Matthew	28	II. Corinthians	13
Mark	16	Galatians	6
Luke	24	Ephesians	6
John	21	Philippians	4
The Acts	28	Colossians	4
The Epistle to the Romans	16	I. Thessalonians	5
		II. Thessalonians	3
I. Corinthians	16	I. Timothy	6
II. Timothy	4	II. Peter	3
Titus	3	I. John	5
Philemon	1	II. John	1
Epistle to the Hebrews	13	III. John	1
The Epistle of James	5	Jude	1
I. Peter	5	Revelation	22

This body of Scripture is received into the Christian Church as the genuine word of God, on the concurrent testimony not only of Jews and Christians, but of the adversaries of both; to which is sometimes annexed the Apocrypha, as follows:—

Books.	Chapters.	Books.	Chapters.
I. Esdras	9	The Song of the Three Children.	
II. Esdras	16		
Tobit	14	The Story of Susanna	1
Judith	16	Bel and the Dragon	1
The Rest of Esther	6	The Prayer of Manasseh.	
Wisdom	19	I. Maccabees	16
Ecclesiasticus	51	II. Maccabees	15
Baruch, with the Epistle of Jeremiah	3		

Phil. Jud. Oper.; Joseph. Antiq. &c.; 1 Polycarp. Epist.; Just. Mart. Apol. &c.; Iren. adv. Hæres.; St. Clem. Alexand.; Tertull. Apol. &c.; St. Chrysost. Homil. &c.; Orig. Comment. &c.; St. Cyp. Epist.; Arnob. con. Genti.; Lactant. Inst.; Euseb. Hist. Eccles.; Epiphan. Hær. &c.; Hieron. Catal. &c.; August. de Hæres. &c.; Isid. Orig. l. 6, c. 1, 2; Cotel. Pat. Apost. vol. 1; Cave. Hist. Lit.; Tillem. Hist. Eccles. tom. ii. pt. 1; Du Pin. Bibl. Ant. Eccles.; Stillingfleet. Orig. Sac.; Prid. Connect. &c. &c.

CANON (*Ant.*) a customary tribute or impost for tonnage-poundage, and also a payment for corn, &c. *Spart. Sever. c. 8; Lamprid. Heliogab. c. 27.*

CANON (*Ecc.*) a dignitary in the church. [vide *Canons*]

CANON is also applied in the Romish church to any rules, or formulas which serve as rules, as the—*Canon Religiosorum,* the book in convents which contained the rules and institutions of the house.—*Canon of the Mass,* a formula of private prayer used by the priest preparatory to his administering the sacrament.—*Pascal Canon,* a table of the moveable feasts, showing the day on which Easter falls, &c.—*Canon,* lastly, is a list of the saints acknowledged and canonized in the Romish church.

CANON (*Law*) a collection of ecclesiastical rules and constitutions taken from the ancient, general, and provincial councils. It consists of two parts; namely, decrees, called the *Decrees of Gratian*; and the *Decretals,* which contained the decretal epistles or rescripts of the popes.

CANON (*Math.*) a general rule for resolving all cases of a like nature in Geometry, Algebra, &c.: thus the last step of every equation is a *Canon,* which, if turned into words, becomes a rule for resolving all questions similar to the one proposed.—*Canon* is also the name for tables of sines, tangents, &c. whether natural or artificial.

CANON (*Mus.*) a method of determining the intervals of musical notes, which was invented by Ptolemy. *Ptol. Harmon. l. 1, c. 8.*

CANON, in modern music, a vocal composition in one or more parts, in which one takes the lead and the other follows. There are various kinds of Canons, as the simple, double, triple, diminished, reversed, inverted, &c.—*Canone chiuso,* or *Canone in Corpo,* a perpetual figure written upon one line, with certain marks to denote where the imitative parts begin.

CANON (*Surg.*) an instrument used in sewing up wounds.

CANON (*Vet.*) the cylindrical bone in the hinder leg of a horse, which is situated immediately below the hock.

CANON (*Print.*) vide *Cannon*.
CANON (*Mil.*) French for the barrel of any fire-arms, great or small.—*Canon chambré*, a piece not well cast, and on that account unfit for use.—*Canon secret*, pieces of ordnance so disposed on a battery as to be unperceived by the enemy.—*Canon double*, vide *Reveil-matin*.—*Canon rayé*, a rifle gun.
CANONIAI (*Med.*) κανονίαι, those having contracted bellies, as opposed to corpulent persons, according to Hippocrates and Galen. *Hippocrat. de Aer.; Gal. Exeges.*
CANO'NICAL (*Ecc.*) agreeable to the canons of the church, as *Canonical hours*, hours prescribed by the canons for prayers.
CANO'NICI (*Mus.*) the followers of Ptolemy's canon in music, in distinction from *Musici* who followed Aristoxenus and the Pythagorean method.
CANONIZATION (*Ecc.*) the enrolment in the canon of saints.
CANON-MOUTH *of a bitt* (*Man.*) a round but long piece of iron, consisting sometimes of two pieces that couple and bend in the middle. Canon-mouths are designed to keep the horse in subjection.
CANONRY (*Ecc.*) or *Canonship*, an ecclesiastical benefice in some cathedral or collegiate church.
CANONS (*Ecc.*) dignitaries in a cathedral church. They are of several sorts, namely—*Regular Canons*, who still live in community, and to the practice of their rules have added the profession of vows; and—*Secular Canons*, who are lay canons that have been admitted into some chapter of canons. This distinction is principally observed in the Romish church.—*Cardinal Canons*, those who are incardinate, i. e. attached to some church, as priests are to a parish.—*Domicilliary Canons*, young canons who, not being in orders, had no right in any particular chapters. —*Foreign Canons*, those who did not officiate in the canonries to which they belonged.—*Mansionary* or *Residentiary Canons*, who are distinguished from the former by their officiating in their canonries.—*Lay* or *Honorary Canons*, those among the laity who, as a mark of honour and respect, have been admitted into some chapter of canons.—*Expectative Canons*, such as, without having any of the revenue, enjoyed the title and dignity of a canon.—*Minor Canons*, those who perform the duties of the cathedral service in the place of the canons.
CANO'PICON (*Bot.*) a sort of spunge. *Dios.* l. 4, c. 166.
CA'NOPITE (*Med.*) a collyrium for the eyes. *Cel.* l. 6, c. 6.
CANO'PUM (*Bot.*) the flower and bark of the Elder tree.
CANO'PUS (*Ast.*) 1. The name formerly given to a star in the second bend of Eridanus. 2. κανωβος, a bright star, of the first magnitude, in the rudder of the ship Argo, which, according to Pliny and Manilius, was visible at Alexandria in Egypt; but not at Rhodes.
Manil. Astron.. l. 1, v. 215.

Nusquam invenies fulgere Canapum
Donec Niliacas per pontumveneris oras.

Gem. Elem. Astron. c. 2; *Vitruv.* l. 9, c. 7; *Strab.* l. 3; *Plin.* l. 2, c. 70; *Petav. Uranomet.*; *Bay. Uranomet.*
The longitude of Canopus, in 1700, was 10°·52″ in ♋; lat 72° 49′. The right ascension, in 1812, 94° 56′ 46″; declination 52° 35′ 48″; the annual variation in right ascension 20″, in declination 1″ 7.
CA'NOPY (*Archit.*) 1. A covering for a throne or an altar. 2. The label or projecting moulding which surrounds the heads of Gothic arches.
CANSCHI' (*Bot.*) the *Trewia* of Linnæus.
CANT (*Gram.*) a quaint sort of language affected by particular persons, or professions, for sinister purposes, and not authorized by established usage.
CANT (*Com.*) a sale by auction, so called, probably, from *cantare*, to sing or cry aloud; whence, in Scotland, an auction is called an *outcry*.
CANT (*Archit.*) a term expressing the position of any piece of timber not standing square.—*Cant-moulding*, a moulding with a bevelled surface applied, instead of the echinus, to the capitals of columns.
CA'NT-PIECES (*Mar.*) pieces of timber inserted or annexed to the angles.—*Cant-timbers*, in French *couples devoyés*, those timbers which are situated at the two ends of a ship. They are so called because they are canted or raised obliquely from the keel.
CANTABILE (*Mus.*) or *Cantab.* a term implying that the performance must be sung.
CANTA'BRICA (*Bot.*) Lavender-leaved Bindweed, a herb, which, according to Pliny, was first discovered among the Cantabri in Spain, from whom it takes its name. *Plin.* l. 25, c. 8.
CANTABRICA, *in the Linnean system*, a species of Convolvulus.
CA'NTACON (*Bot.*) Garden Saffron.
CANTADOU'RS (*Mus.*) itinerant singers in Provence, who sprung up in the ninth century.
CANTALI'VER (*Archit.*) vide *Cantilever*.
CANTANTE (*Mus.*) a term to denote the vocal part of a composition.
CANTA'O (*Com.*) a wine measure of three gallons in Alicant.
CA'NTAR (*Com.*) the same as *Cantaro*.
CANTA'RA (*Bot.*) the plant which bears St. Ignatius's beam.
CANTARE'LLI (*Ent.*) a species of beetles, which, being macerated in oil, are said to endue it with the virtues of oil of Scorpions. *Castell.*
CANTA'RO (*Com.*) 1. A weight, in Italy, of 150 pounds, or upwards. 2. A measure in Cochin.
CANTA'TA (*Mus.*) a piece of music for one, two, or more voices; and sometimes with one or more instruments, consisting of grave parts and airs intermingled or alternate.
CANTATI'LLA (*Mus.*) a small cantata.
CANTEE'N (*Mil.*) 1. A suttling-house for both officers and men. 2. A leathern or wooden machine for holding different utensils used by the officers. 3. A sort of tin-vessel for holding liquors, which is used by soldiers on their march.
CA'NTEL (*Archæol.*) a lump or mass.
CA'NTER (*Man.*) the well-known pace of a horse, which is a sort of easy gallop. It is however reckoned not to be the natural pace of any horse.
CAN'TERBURY-BELL (*Bot.*) the *Campanula trachelium*, *glomerata, et medium*, of Linnæus, which are all perennials.
CANTARE'LLUS (*Bot.*) the same as the *Chantarellus* of Linnæus.
CA'NTHARI FIGULI'NI (*Chem.*) cucurbits made of potters' ware.
CANTHA'RIAS (*Min.*) a stone having the figure of a beetle upon it. *Plin.* l. 37, c. 10.
CANTHA'RIDES (*Med.*) Spanish flies, a species of shining beetle, of a golden, azure, or greenish colour, and of a fetid smell, which, when powdered and applied to the skin, cause an exulceration, whence they are used in blisters. This insect is classed under the genus *Lytta* in the Linnean system.
CANTHARI'FERA (*Bot.*) the *Nepenthes* of Linnæus.
CANTHARI'NUS (*Ent.*) an epithet for a species of cimex, cerambix, &c.
CA'NTHARIS (*Ent.*) a genus of animals, Class *Insecta*, Order *Coleoptera*.
Generic Characters. *Antennæ* filiform.—*Thorax* mostly margined.—*Shells* flexile.
Species. The species are distinguished into those which have their feelers hatchet-shaped, filiform, or projecting.
CANTHARI'TES (*Nat.*) a kind of outlandish wine, mentioned by Pliny, l. 14, c. 7.
CANTHE'RIUS (*Surg.*) the cross beam between two posts in the machine contrived by Hippocrates for replacing the dislocated bone of the shoulder. *Hippocrat.* περ. αρθ.; *Foes. Œconom. Hippoc.*

CA'NTHARUS (Ant.) a name of several utensils among the Romans, as a jug or tankard, particularly the one sacred to Bacchus. Virgil calls it *gravis*, *Virg.* ecl. 6, v. 17.

Et gravis attrita pendebat cantharus ansa.

and Sidonius makes Bacchus, when he went in triumph, to carry the Cantharus and the Thyrsus:

Cantharus et thyrsus dextroque lævaque feruntur.

and in this manner he is represented on medals, as in the annexed figure of a medal of Antoninus Pius, bearing on the obverse the head of the emperor crowned with laurel, the inscription ΑΥΤοκρατωρ ΚΑΙ Cαις ΑΝΤΩΝΕΙΝΟC CEBαςις ΥCEBης, i. e. *Imperator Cæsar Antoninus Augustus Pius*; on the reverse, a figure of Bacchus, standing with a Cantharus and Thyrsus in his hands, and a tiger at his feet; the incription ΑΒΩΝΟΤΕΙΧΕΙΤΩΝ, i. e. *Abonotitichorum*, the inhabitants of Abonetichus, a town of Paphlagonia. *Plin.* l. 33, c. 2; *Val. Max.* l. 6, c. 3; *Goltz. Thesaur.*; *Vaillant. Numis. Græc.*; *Patin. Numismati. Imperat. Roman.*; *Harduin. Numm. Ant. Illustrat.*; *Spanheim. de Præstan. et Usu Numis.*

CANTHARUS is also the name for a water-spout, and the knocker of a door. *Plaut. Men.* act. 1, scen. 2.

CA'NTHERUS (*Archit.*) or *Cantherius*, a rafter or joist of a house that comes down from the ridge to the eaves. *Vitruv.* l. 4, c. 2.

CANTHERUS (*Carpent.*) a tressel or horse to saw or cut timber on.

CA'NTHUS (*Ant.*) the iron with which the circumference of the cart-wheel is bound. The fello of the wheel, which, according to Quintilian, was a barbarous word first introduced by Persius. *Pers.* sat. 5, v. 70; *Mart.* l. 14, ep. 168: *Quint. Inst.* l. 1, c. 5.

CANTHUS (*Anat.*) κανθός, the corner or angle of the eye. That next the nose is termed the internal or greater *Canthus*; and the farther is the external or lesser *Canthus*. *Ruff. Ephes.* l. 1, c. 4.

CA'NTICÆ (*Ant.*) ancient dramatic soliloquies, supposed to have been introduced as interludes.

CA'NTICI (*Ecc.*) songs so called in the twelfth and thirteenth centuries, which were sung in honour of the Blessed Virgin, and the Saints and Martyrs.

CA'NTICLE (*Theol.*) a sacred hymn or song among the Hebrews, particularly applied to the Song of Solomon.

CANTICLE (*Mus.*) vocal soliloquies in the Greek tragedies.

CANTILE'NA (*Mus.*) the treble melody or upper part of any composition, in distinction from the bass and other inferior parts.—*Cantilena Scotica*, Scottish melody.

CANTILEVER-CO'RNICE (*Archit.*) a cornice formed of modillions or cantilevers.—*Cantilevers*, pieces of wood framed into any side of a house to support the mouldings and eaves over it; a sort of modillions.

CANTIMARO'NS (*Mar.*) or *Catimarons*, a kind of float or raft used by the inhabitants on the coast of Coromandel, in fishing.

CA'NTING (*Archit.*) the act of turning a plank or timber to see the opposite side.

CA'NTING-COINS (*Mar.*) short pieces of wood cut with a sharp ridge, to lie between the casks to prevent them from rolling against each other.

CA'NTION (*Chem.*) the same as *Saccharum*, or Candy.

CA'NTO (*Mus.*) or *Cant*, the melody or highest vocal part. —*Canto concertante*, the treble of the little chorus, or the part which one sings throughout.—*Canto fermo*, the ancient chants of the Romish church.—*Canto figurato*, another name for the *Canto fermo* in its cultivated state.—*Canto plano*, another name for old chanting.—*Canto recitativo*, a speaking song.—*Canto ripieno*, the treble of the grand chorus.

CANTO'N (*Geog.*) a division of a country, as the Cantons of Switzerland.

CANTON (*Her.*) an ordinary, so called because it occupies but a cantel or corner of the escutcheon. It is either dexter or sinister, i. e. on the right or left side of the escutcheon, and is the third of the chief. Dexter in a canton is the sign of a baronet's arms, as in the annexed example. "He beareth *gules* two lions passant, *argent*, between nine crosslets fitchet *or*. These are the arms of the *Acton* family."

TO CANTON (*Mil.*) to disperse troops into summer or winter quarters.

CANTO'NE (*Com.*) a measure in the Moluccas equal to five English pints.

CANTONE (*Archit.*) an epithet for a building, the angles of which are adorned with columns, pilastres, rustic quoins, &c.

CA'NTONED (*Her.*) in French *cantonnée*, a cross between four figures.

CA'NTONMENTS (*Mil.*) distinct situations in towns and villages where the different parts of an army lie encamped.

CA'NTRED (*Archæol.*) or *Kantreff*, from *Centum*, a hundred, and *treff*, a town; a hundred in Wales, i. e. a hundred villages. *Stat.* 28 Hen. 8; *Mon. Anglic.*

CANTUARIE'NSIS AQUA (*Min.*) Canterbury waters in five wells near to each other, which are strongly impregnated with iron, sulphur, and carbonic acid gas.

CA'NTRUM (*Chem.*) or *Cantium*, the same as *Candum*, or Candy.

CA'NTUS (*Mus.*) the mean or counter tenor.—*Cantus Gregorianus*, the Gregorian chant, so called from St. Gregory its inventor, who improved upon that introduced by St. Ambrose.

CA'NVAS (*Paint.*) or *Canvass*, the cloth on which painters usually draw their pictures. It is smoothed over with a slick stone, then sized, and afterwards whited over, when it is called the *primed cloth*, because they take their first sketches on it.

CANVAS (*Mar.*) or *Canvass*, the cloth of which the sails are made, which are distinguished into degrees of fineness by the first eight digits; No. 1 being the coarsest and strongest.

CA'NVASS (*Mus.*) the model or first words whereon an air or piece of music is composed and given to a poet to regulate and finish. The canvass of a song contains certain notes which serve to determine the measure.

CANVASS (*Com.*) from *cannabis*, hemp; a coarse cloth of hemp, unbleached, which is wove regularly in little squares. It is used for working tapestry with the needle, &c.

CANVASS-BAGS (*Fort.*) bags filled with earth for raising a parapet in haste.

CANU'LA (*Surg.*) the same as *Cannula*.

CA'NUM (*Archæol.*) a duty paid to a superior, or lord of the manor.

CA'NUM-CERA'SUM (*Bot.*) the same as *Xylosteum*.

CANZO'NE (*Mus.*) signifies properly an ode or song; but is applied by musicians to a piece of instrumental music, when it signifies sonata: to vocal music, signifying cantata: and to any part of a sonata, to signify the same as allegro.

CANZONE'T (*Mus.*) a diminutive of Canzone, signifying a little air.

CAOPOI'BA (*Bot.*) a Brazilian tree, growing to the height and shape of a beech. *Raii Hist. Plant.*

CAO'UP (*Bot.*) a tree in the island of Maragnam, with leaves not unlike those of the apple tree, and the fruit like that of the orange. *Raii Hist. Plant.*

CAOU'TCHOUC (*Nat.*) the Indian name for *Indian Rubber*, a substance produced from the Syringe tree of Cayenne.

CAP, or *Bonnet* (*Her.*) a bearing in coats of arms.

CAP of Maintenance, or Cap of Dignity, is a cap of state made of crimson velvet, lined and turned up with ermine, as in the annexed figure. It is carried before the king of Great Britain at his coronation and other great solemnities. Such a cap was sent by Pope Julius the second, with a sword, to Henry the eighth, for his writing a book against Martin Luther.

CAP (Mar.) a square piece of timber placed over the head or upper end of a mast, in which is a round hole to receive the top or top-gallant masts, so that by these caps they are kept steady and firm in the tressel-trees.—*Cap of a Block,* a semi-circular projection from the sides and round the end of a block above the pins.—*Cap-Merchant,* the purser of a ship.

CAP of a Gun (Gunn.) vide Apron.

TO CAP (Cus.) to take off the cap, as under-graduates in the university do to their seniors.

TO CAP verses (Lit.) an exercise of the memory among school-boys, who, standing in a row, the first repeats a verse, then the second repeats another, proceeding where he left off, and so on with the rest.

TO CAP a Rope (Mar.) to cover the end of it with tarred canvas.

CAP (Archit.) the uppermost part of any assemblage of principal or subordinate parts. It is applied to the capital of a column, the cornice of a door, the capping or uppermost member of the surbase of a room, &c.

CAP (Bot.) *pileus,* the top of the fungus, in general shaped like a plate or bonnet, as in *fig.* 1, 2, and supported by *a,* the *stipes,* or Stalk, in *fig.* 4. In this body are the organs of generation. The different kinds of the cap are as follow, namely—flat, *planus,* forming a plane expansion, as in *fig.* 3; round, *convexus,* which is convex above, as in *fig.* 1; hollow, *concavus,* where there is a depression on the

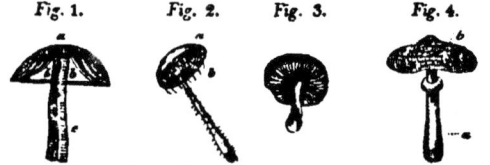

Fig. 1.   Fig. 2.   Fig. 3.   Fig. 4.

upper surface; bossed, *umbonatus,* where there is a prominent point in the centre, as *b* in *fig.* 4; bell shaped, *campanulatus,* when it is very convex above, and spreads wide below, like a bell, as in *Agaricus cimetarius*; viscid, *viscidus,* when the upper surface is covered with a clammy exudation; scaly, *squamosus,* when it is covered with a number of imbricated scales of a different colour from its own, as in *Agaricus muscarius*; squarrose, *squarrosus,* when the scales stand up from the surface, as in *fig.* 4; halved, *dimidiatus,* when it forms only half the figure of a plate, and appears to have one side taken off, as in *Hydnum auriscalpium*; stipitate, *stipitatum,* when supported on a stalk; sessile, *sessilis,* seu *acaulis,* when it is not supported by a stalk. The parts of the cap are as follow, namely—The Boss, *umbo,* the centre of the cap, as *a, fig.* 1 and 2, and *b* in *fig.* 4, which in the latter figure is prominent.—The Gills, *lamellæ,* thin foliaceous membranes on the underside of the mushroom, as in *b b, fig.* 1, and also in *fig.* 2, 3. These contain the capsules of the seed, and are peculiar to the genus *Agaricus.*—The Pores, *pori,* small holes on the underside of the cap, as if made with the point of a needle, peculiar to the *Boleti.*—The Prickles, *echini,* raised projecting points, which, like the pores, contain the organs of generation. They are peculiar to the genus *Hydnum,* as in *fig.* 2.—The Warts, *papillæ,* small round protuberances on the under surface.

CA'P-MERCHANT (Mar.) vide Cap.

CA'P-PAPER (Com.) a large sort of brown paper.

CA'PA viela (Bot.) the *Cleome pentaphylla.*

CAPA-A'GA (Polit.) an old and experienced officer in the seraglio, who has the charge of instructing and superintending the Iconoglans, or Agamoglans.

CAPA'CITY (Law) or *capability,* the right which a body politic has to give or take lands or tenements, &c. or to sue for actions, &c.

CAPACITY (Geom.) the solid content of any body: thence our hollow measures of beer, wine, salt, &c. are called measures of capacity.

CA'PAN (Com.) a coin in Sumatra, equal to about threepence English money.

CAPA'RISON (Man.) or *caparasson,* a horse-cloth, or covering for the trappings or furniture of a horse.

CAPARISON (Mil.) includes the bridle, saddle, and housing of a military horse.

CAPA'RISONED (Her.) applied to a horse completely furnished for the field.

CAPE ASTER (Bot.) the *Cinerea amelloides* of Linnæus.

CA'PE (Law) a judicial writ relative to a plea of lands or tenements, which is so named from the word that denotes its chief end and purpose. It consists of the *Cape magnum* and *Cape parvum.*—*Cape magnum,* or the *grand Cape,* is a writ that lies before appearance, to summon the tenant to answer the default, or according to the Old *Natura Brevium,* where a man hath brought a *Præcipe quod reddat* of a thing touching a plea of land, and the tenant makes default at the day to him given in the original writ, then this writ shall go for the king to take the land into his hands; and if the tenant come not at the day appointed he loseth his lands. *Bract.* l. 3, tract 3, c. 1; *Vet. Nat. Brev.* 161; *Reg. Jud.* fol. 1.—*Cape parvum,* or *petit Cape,* a writ where the tenant is summoned in plea of land, and comes on the summons, and his appearance is recorded: if at the day given him he prays the view, and having it granted, makes default, then this writ shall issue for the king, &c. *Flet.* l. 2, c. 4; *Vet. Nat. Brev.* 162.—*Cape ad Valentiam,* a species of *Cape magnum,* or writ of execution, that lies where one is impleaded of certain lands, and he vouches to warrant another, but the vouchee does not come on the day appointed, then if the demandant recover against the tenant he shall have this writ against the vouchee. *V. N. B.* 616.

CAPE (Geog.) a promontory or head-land which projects into the sea farther than the rest of the coast.

CAPE du Batardeau (Fort.) a roof sloping on both sides, which covers the upper part of the batardeau constructed in the ditch at the salient angle of a bastion.

CA'PELET (Vet.) vide Capellet.

CA'PELINE (Mil.) a kind of iron helmet worn by the French cavalry in the time of John Duke of Britany.

CAPELINE (Surg.) from the French *capeline,* a woman's hat, signifies a double-headed roller for the head.

CAPE'LLA (Archæol.) a chapel or church; also *Capella de Floribus,* a chaplet or garland of flowers.

CAPELLA (Astron.) literally a little goat; the name of a star of the first magnitude in Auriga. Its right ascension for the beginning of 1812 was 75° 42′ 16″, declination 45° 47′ 51″ N., annual variation in right ascension 6″ 21. in declination 5″ 09.

CAPELLA (Chem.) the same as the *Alembic.*

CAPELLA (Mus.) the music and the musicians belonging to a chapel or church.

CAPE'LLET (Vet.) a swelling of a wenny nature, to which horses are subject on the hock, and other parts.

CAPELLETTI (Mil.) the Venetian militia: they were formerly reckoned the best troops in the service.

CAPE'LLUS (Archæol.) a cap or bonnet; whence *Capellus ferreus,* a helmet, or iron head-piece. *Hoved.* p. 61; *Blount. Ten.*

CA'PER (Bot.) the flower or bud of the Caper-Bush, which

is converted into a pickle.—Caper-Beard, a perennial, the *Zygophyllum* of Linnæus.—Caper-Bush, or tree, the *Capparis* of Linnæus.

CAPER (*Mar.*) a privateer or pirate ship.

CAPE'ROLANS (*Ecc.*) a congregation of religious in Italy, founded by Peter Caperole in the 15th century.

CA'PETUS (*Med.*) κάπετος, a hole or notch cut in the *Bathron* or *Scamnum*, which is a machine for restoring luxations. This hole serves for the strengthening or better managing the axis. *Hippocrat. de Art.*; *Gal. Comm.*; *Erot. Lex. Hippocrat.*; *Gorr. Def. Med.*; *Foes. Œconom. Hippocrat.*

CAPHU'RA (*Chem.*) κάφυρα, the same as *Camphora*.

CAPHU'RÆ *oleum* (*Med.*) an aromatic essential oil distilled from the root of the cinnamon-tree.

CAPI-AGA (*Polit.*) vide *Capa-Aga*.

CA'PIAS (*Law*) a writ or process of two kinds; the one called *Capias ad respondendum*, before judgment, where an original is sued out, &c. to take the body of the defendant to answer the plaintiff; and the other a writ of execution, which is of different kinds, as *Capias ad satisfaciendum, utlagatum, &c.—Capias ad satisfaciendum*, a judicial writ of execution that lies where a man recovers for debt, damages, &c. By this writ the sheriff is commanded to take the body of the defendant in execution, and him safely to keep till he satisfy the plaintiff his debt and damages.— *Capias utlagatum*, a writ that lies against a person that is outlawed in any action.—*Capias pro Fine*, a writ formerly against a plaintiff in whose favour judgment was given in the king's courts in cases of assault, &c. that he be arrested till he pay a fine for his wilful delay of justice, considering the offence to be a public misdemeanour as well as a private injury. By Stat. 5 and 6 W. and M. c. 12, no such writ shall issue *for the Fine*, but the plaintiff shall pay 6s. 8d. to the proper officer, and be allowed it against the defendant amongst his other costs.—*Capias in Withernam*, a writ whereby a sheriff is commanded to take other cattle or goods in lieu of those that were formerly unjustly taken and esloined, or otherwise withholden. *Stat. Marlb.* 52 H. 3, c. 23; *Westm.* 2, c. 13; E. 1, c. 11; 19 H. 7, c. 9; *Old Nat. Brev.* 154; *Reg. Orig.* 82, 83.

CAPICATI'NGA (*Bot.*) a species of Acorn, a Brasilian plant. *Pison. de Med. Brasil.*

CAPI'CULY (*Mil.*) another name for the Janizaries.

CAPI'GI (*Polit.*) a porter or door-keeper of the Turkish seraglio.

CAPILA'CTEUM (*Med.*) vide *Aphrogala*.

CAPILLA'CEOUS (*Bot.*) vide *Capillary*.

CAPILLAME'NTA (*Bot.*) another name for the *Stamina* in plants. *Columel. de Re Rust.* l. 4, c. 11.

CAPILLA'RES (*Bot.*) a name given by Ray, Boerhaave, and Morison to a class of Ferns.

CAPI'LLARY (*Nat.*) *capillaris*, from *capilla*, hair; an epithet for any thing like hair.

CAPILLARY (*Anat.*) an epithet for the extreme ramifications of the arteries and veins.

CAPILLARY (*Bot.*) *capillaceus*, or *capillaris*, long and fine, like a hair, an epithet for the leaves, as in *Ranunculus aquatilis*, *Artemisia capillaris*; the filaments, as in *Dipsacus*; the pappus, or down, as in *Sonchus*, *Lactuca*, &c.; the style; and the glands, as in *Ribes*, *Scrophularia*, &c.

CAPILLARY *Tubes* (*Phy.*) small pipes, of the fineness of a hair, by which various natural phænomena are displayed, particularly in regard to fluids.

CAPILLA'TIO (*Surg.*) a capillary fracture of the cranium, so called from its resembling *capillus*, a hair, in fineness.

CAPILLI'TIUM (*Bot.*) 1. Vide *Capillamenta*. 2. *Capillitium*, or Hair-Net, a reticulated collection of hairs that serve to fasten the seeds of some species of Fungi, as in *Cribaria vulgaris*.

CAPILLA'RUM *defluvium* (*Med.*) a falling off of the hair. [vide *Alopecia*]

CAPI'LLUS (*Anat.*) signifies properly the hair of the head, but is made to signify hair in general.

CAPILLUS (*Bot.*) a measure which is the diameter of a hair, or the twelfth part of a line.—*Capillus Veneris*, Maiden-Hair, the *Adianthum* of Linnæus.

CAPIPLE'NIUM (*Med.*) a barbarous word, used to signify a continual heaviness or disorder in the head, called by the Greeks καρηβαρία.

CAPI'SCOLUS (*Ecc.*) an officer who superintended the choir, who is otherwise called the Chanter, or Precentor.

CAPISTRA'TIO (*Med.*) vide *Phimosis*.

CAPI'STRUM (*Ant.*) besides its ordinary meaning of a bridle, was employed to denote, 1. A kind of muzzle or ligature, which was used by ancient trumpeters to secure the cheeks from bursting with the violence of the exertion, and also to modulate the sounds by tempering the inflation of the breath. It is called in Greek φορβειά. *Schol. Aristoph. in Vesp.* p. 470; *Plut. Sym.* l. 7, quest. 8; *Hesychus*; *Suidas*. 2. A band to tie up the vine to the top of the stake. *Columel.* l. 4, c. 20. 3. A cord to hold up the wine-press, and keep it tight. *Cat. de Re Rust.* c. 12; *Turneb. Adv.* l. 8, c. 6; *Voss. Lex. Etymol.*; *Salmas. Exercitat. Plin.* p. 582.

CAPISTRUM (*Surg.*) bandages used about the head, resembling a horse's head-stall. *Castell. Lex. Med.*

CAPITA (*Ant.*) vel *navia*; a game among the Roman youth similar to our Heads and Tails, which consisted in throwing up a coin that had on one side the figure of Janus with his two heads, and on the reverse that of a ship. *Macrob. Sat.* l. 1, c. 7.

CAPITA (*Law*) distribution or succession per capita, i. e. to every one an equal share of the estate, when all the claimants claim in their own right, as kindred in an equal degree, and not *jure representationis*.

CAPITA (*Bot.*) heads in plants, or those globose receptacles of the seed which by their figure represent a head.

CA'PITAL, from *caput*, the head, an epithet for what relates to the head, both in the natural and figurative signification.

CAPITAL *crime* (*Law*) such a crime as subjects the offender to the loss of head or life.

CAPITAL (*Geog.*) the capital or chief city in any country or district.

CAPITAL (*Print.*) or *capital letter*, the larger kind of letter, which is used in the composition of titles, or as initial letters at the commencement of periods, &c.

CAPITAL (*Archit.*) the uppermost part of a column or pilaster, serving for its head or crowning, placed immediately over the shaft, and under the entablature. The capital in all the orders is divided from the shaft by some small member, as an astragal, or a fillet, or a channel; but it varies as to the number and form of the mouldings. The Doric Capital consists of *Trachelion*, a Neck, which is a continuation of the shaft with its fluting, several Fillets, from three to five in number, an Ovolo, and an Abacus.— The Ionic Capital consists of an Ovolo, a Band, or Festoon, with Volutes, and a thin, moulded Abacus.—The Corinthian Capital consists of a Vase, with two rows of leaves attached to the vase, Volutes, and Caulicoli, which spring between each two of the upper row of leaves, the whole of which is crowned with an Abacus.—The *Tuscan Capital* is the simplest and most unadorned of any, consisting mostly of no more than three members, namely, an Abacus, an Ovolo, or Quarter-Round, and under that a Neck, or Collarine.—The *Composite Capital* is so called because it is composed of members taken from the other orders, as an Ovolo from the Doric, an Astragal, together with Scrolls or Volutes, from the Ionic, a double row of leaves from the Corinthian.—*Angular capital*. [vide *Angular*]—*Capital of a baluster* is similar to those of the Doric or Tuscan Orders.—*Capital of a lantern*, the covering by which it is terminated, either in a bell shape or that of a cupola, &c.—*Capital of a triglyph*, the plat-band, or projecting-band, over a triglyph.—*Capital of a niche*, a sort of small canopy over a shallow niche.

CAPITAL (*Com.*) the stock or fund which any trader employs in trade or commerce.—*Capital stock*, the sum of money which the partners of a trading company jointly contribute to be employed in trade, as the capital stock of the Bank of England.

CAPITAL *line* (*Fort.*) an imaginary line dividing any work into similar and equal parts, as a line drawn from the angle of the polygon to the point of the bastion, or from the point of the bastion to the middle of the gorge.

CAPITAL *lees* (*Mech.*) the strong lees made from potashes.

CAPITAL *medicines* (*Med.*) the principal preparations in the shops of apothecaries, as Venice treacle, &c.

CAPITAL *ship* (*Mar.*) a ship of the line.

CAPITA'LE (*Law*) a thing which is stolen, or its value. *Leg. H.* 1, c. 59.—*Capitale vivens*, live stock. *Leg. Athelstan*.

CAPITA'LIA (*Med.*) the same as *Cephalics*.

CAPITA'LIS *Dominus* (*Law*) vide *Capite*.

CAPITA'NEI (*Archæol.*) a denomination formerly given to the nobility in Italy.

CAPITA'TÆ (*Bot.*) the first division of the twenty-first order, i. e. *Compositæ Capitatæ* of Linnæus' Fragments of a Natural Arragement. *Lin. Phil. Bot.* Also the second division of the first order, in the class *Syngenesia*, in his artificial system.

CAPITATÆ is also the name of a class in Ray's system, comprehending the thistles, and such other compound flowers as grow into a head.

CA'PITATE (*Bot.*) *capitatus*, an epithet for a stigma; *stigma capitatum*, the stigma which grows in the form of a hemisphere; and for a whorl, *verticellus capitatus*, a capitated whorl, when the flowers stand so thick as to form a hemisphere, as in *Phlomis tuberosa*.

CAPITATION (*Law*) τευκφάλαιον, a numbering by the head; also a Poll-Tax, called by Appian φορὶς τῶν σωμάτων, a tribute on the body. *Dionys. Halicarn. Antiq.* l. 4; *Plut. de Puer. Instit.*; *Appian in Syriac.*; *Tertull. Apologet.*

CA'PITE *censi* (*Ant.*) οἱ τὸ ἡτικὸν τιλῶντις, the poorer sort of people, who in assessments were valued at nothing, but only named, and reckoned as citizens. *Sallust.*; *Bud. in Pandect.* p. 133; *Sigon. de Ant. Jur. Civ. Roman.* apud *Græv. Thes. Antiq. Roman.* tom. 1, p. 37.

CAPITE (*Law*) or *in Capite tenere*, a sort of ancient tenure, whereby a man held lands of the king immediately, as of the crown, whether by knight's service or in socage. This ancient tenure was of two sorts, one principal and general, which was of the king, as *caput regni et caput generalissimum omnium fœdorum*; the other special or subaltern of a particular subject, who was called *caput feudi seu terræ illius et capitalis Dominus*, because he was the first who granted land in such manner of tenure. Tenures in *Capite* are now abolished; and by stat. 12 Car. 2, c. 24, all tenures are now turned into *free* and *common Socage*. *F. N. B.* 5; *Kitch.* 129; *Dyer*, 44; *Blount Ten.*

CAPITE'LLUM (*Chem.*) the same as *Alembic*; also a lixivium.

CAPITELLUM (*Bot.*) vide *Capitulum*.

CAPITILI'TIUM (*Ant.*) Poll-money.

CAPITILU'VIUM (*Med.*) a bath or lotion for the head.

CA'PITIS *Obliquus Inferior et major* (*Anat.*) vide *Obliquus Inferior*.—*Capitis Par Tertium Fallopii*, vide *Complexus Minor*.—*Capitis Posticus*, vide *Rectus Major*.—*Capitis Rectus*, vide *Rectus Minor*.—*Capitis Vena*, vide *Cephalica Vena*.

CAPITI'TIUM (*Ant.*) a covering for the head. *Stat.* I, *H.* 4.

CA'PITO *Anadromus* (*Ich.*) a fish of the cod kind living both in rivers and seas, so called on account of its great head.

CAPITOLADE (*Cook.*) a particular way of dressing fowls, &c.

CAPITOLI'NI (*Ant.*) those who presided at the Capitoline games, so called from their inhabiting the Capitol at Rome. They were erected into a college by M. Fur. Camillus, the Dictator. *Liv.* l. 5, c. 50.—*Capitolini Ludi*, the Capitoline games instituted by the Romans in commemoration of the deliverance of the Capitol at the time that the city was taken by the Gauls. Poets used to recite their verses at these games. *Liv.* l. 5, c. 50, &c; *Plut. Quæst. Roman.* 52; *Tertull. de Spectac.* c. 5; *Kipping. Antiq. Roman.* l. 2, c. 6.

CAPITO'UL (*Polit.*) or *capitol*, an appellation given to the chief magistrate in Thoulouse.

CAPI'TULA *Ruralia* (*Law*) assemblies or chapters held by rural deans and parochial clergy within the precinct of every distinct deanery.

CAPI'TULAR (*Archæol.*) *Capitulare*, κεφάλων; an epithet for any writing distinguished by capital letters, particularly the books containing the ordinances of the kings, which were called *Capitulares libri*, and the ordinances themselves *Capitularia*, as the "Capitular of Charlemagne."

CAPI'TULARS (*Ecc.*) members of an ecclesiastical chapter.

TO CA'PITULATE (*Mil.*) to surrender any place, or body of troops, on certain conditions.

CAPITULATION (*Mil.*) 1. The conditions on which any place or body of troops is surrendered. 2. The terms which are sometimes made with men on their enlisting.

CAPITULATION (*Polit.*) a contract which the emperor of Germany used to enter into, with the Electors, previous to his election; by this he engaged to defend the church and the empire, and to preserve inviolate the laws, rights, and privileges, not only of the whole empire, but of every particular principality.

CA'PITULI *Agri* (*Archæol.*) headlands, or lands lying at the head or upper end of the furrows. *Kenn. Paroch. Antiq.* p. 137.

CAPITULIFO'RMIS (*Bot.*) an epithet for a flower formed like a *capitulum*, or head.

CAPI'TULUM (*Ant.*) a transverse beam in the military engines of the ancients, wherein were holes for the strings which served to work them up and down.

CAPITULUM (*Ecc.*) signified generally a chapter, but particularly a chapter in the Bible; whence *ire ad capitulum*, to go to a lecture on a chapter of the Bible; also the apartment where the lecture was read.

CAPITULUM (*Bot.*) or Head, a mode of inflorescence, or a manner of flowering, when several flowers form a kind of head or ball. The *capitulum* is of various forms; namely, *globosum* seu *sphæricum*, globose or spherical, as in the annexed figure, which represents the *capitulum* of the *Gomphrena globosa*, Clover; so likewise *foliosum*, leafy, when the head is surrounded with leaves; *comosum*, tufted, having leaves at the point, as in *Bromelia ananas*; *nudum*, naked, when it is devoid of leaves; *terminale*, when it stands on the point of the stem; *axillare*, axillary, or standing in the angles of the leaves.

CAPITULUM (*Anat.*) a small head, or protuberance of a bone received into the concavity of another bone.

CAPI'TZI (*Hist.*) or *capigi*, officers among the Turks who guard the gate of the grand Seignior's palace.

CAPIVA'RD (*Zool.*) an amphibious animal of Brazil, called a Water-Dog, having a body like a hog, a head like a hare, and no tail.

CAPIVI (*Bot.*) or Capevi-Tree, a tree of Brasil, the *Copaifera officinalis* of Linnæus, which yields the balsam of Capivi.

CA'PLAN (*Com.*) a small fish on the coast of Newfoundland, which is used as a bait in fishing for cod.

CAPNELÆ'UM (*Nat.*) καπνέλαιον, a resin which flows spontaneously; Foesius supposes it to be so called from the smoke which it yields when put near the fire. *Gal. de Comp. Med. sec. Loc.* l. 2; *Foes. Œconom. Hippoc.*

CAPNIAS (*Min.*) καπνίας, a kind of jasper, so called from its resembling smoke, καπνὸς, in colour. *Plin.* l. 37, c. 9; *Aet. Tetrab.* 1, serm. 2, c. 56.

CAPNIAS (*Bot.*) a sort of vine producing part white, and part black grapes. *Theoph. de Caus. Plant.* l. 5, c. 3.

CAPNI'STON (*Med.*) a sort of oil prepared of several sorts of spices and oil, the former of which are kindled, and the latter suffumigated.

CAPNITIS (*Min.*) καπνῖτις, a thin sort of cadmia which adheres to the arches and sides of the furnaces. *Plin.* l. 34, v. 10. [vide *Cadmia*]

CAPNITIS (*Min.*) vide *Capnias*.

CAPNO'IDES (*Bot.*) the herb Fumitory.

CA'PNOMANCY (*Ant.*) καπνομαντεία, a sort of divination by the smoke of sacrifices, according to the windings and contortions which they made in ascending.

CAPNO'RCHIS (*Bot.*) a species of Fumitory.

CA'PNOS (*Bot.*) the herb Fumitory.

CA'PO MOLA'GO (*Bot.*) the *Piper Indicum* of Linnæus.

CAPO'LLIN (*Bot.*) a Mexican plant with leaves like those of an almond or a cherry. *Hernand. apud Raii Hist.*

CA'PON (*Nat.*) a castrated cock which is generally fattened for the spit.

CAPONNI'ERE (*Fort.*) a covered lodgement of about four or five feet broad, with a parapet to support planks laden with earth. There is also a *Demi Caponnière*, which is a passage made in a dry ditch, and only defended towards the enemy by a parapet or glacis.

CAPO'T (*Gam.*) a term, at the game of picket, when all the tricks of cards are won.

CAPOTE de Faction (*Mil.*) a large great coat with a hood or cowl, which is worn by sentinels in bad weather.

CAPO'TES (*Bot.*) the *Cratæva marmelos* of Linnæus.

CAPOU'CH (*Ecc.*) a friar's hood.

CA'PPADINE (*Com.*) a sort of silk, with which the shag of some rugs is made.

CAPPA'NUS (*Ent.*) an extremely pernicious worm which adheres to and gnaws the bottoms of ships.

CA'PPARIS (*Bot.*) κάππαρις, Caper-Bush, a shrub, the trunk and fruit of which are pickled for food, and are also used medicinally, particularly in complaints of the spleen. *Hippoc. de Morb.*; *Dioscor.* l. 2, c. 204; *Plin.* l. 20, c. 15; *Gal. de Simpl.* l. 7; *Paul. Ægin.* l. 7, c. 3.

CAPPARIS, in the Linnean system, a genus of plants, Class 12 *Polyandria*, Order 1 *Monogynia*.

Generic Characters. CAL. perianth four leaved; *leaflets* ovate.—COR. petals four.—STAM. *filaments* numerous; *anthers* oblong.—PIST. germ pedicelled; *style* none; *stigma* obtuse.—PER. berry corticose; *seeds* numerous.

Species. The species are shrubs, as *Capparis spinosa*, *pedunculis unifloris*, &c. *aculeata, retuso folio*, seu *spinosa*, &c. Prickly Caper Bush, native of Europe.—*Capparis ovata, pedunculis unifloris*, &c. seu *spinosa, Sicula*, &c. seu *folio acuto*, native of Sicily, Spain, and the north of Africa.—*Capparis Ægyptia*, seu *pedunculis*, &c. native of Egypt.—*Capparis tomentosa*, seu *spinosa, floribus*, &c. native of Senegal.—*Capparis acuminata*, seu *pedunculis unifloris*, &c. native of the East Indies.—*Capparis Zeylanica*, &c. *pedunculis*, &c. seu *spinosa*, &c. native of Ceylon.—*Capparis horrida*, seu *arborea*, &c. native of Coromandel.—*Capparis erythrocarpos, pedunculis*, &c. native of Guinea.—*Capparis sepiaria, pedunculis*, &c. seu *Arbuscula baccifera*, &c. native of India.—*Capparis citrifolia*, seu *spinosa*, &c. native of the Cape of Good Hope.—*Capparis corymbosa*, seu *floribus*, &c. native of Senegal.—*Capparis mariana, pedunculis*, &c. seu *cordifolia*, &c. native of the Marianne Islands.—*Capparis panduriformis*, native of the Mauritius.—*Capparis baducca, inermis*, &c. seu *Baducca*, native of the East Indies.—*Capparis torulosa*, seu *Breynia arborescens*, &c. native of Jamaica.—*Capparis ferruginea*, seu *Cratæva fruticosa*, &c. native of Jamaica.—*Capparis grandis*, seu *arbore*, native of Ceylon.—*Capparis Jamaicensis*, seu *pedunculis, multifloris*, &c. native of Jamaica.—*Capparis verrucosa*, seu *pedunculis multifloris*, &c. native of Carthagena.—*Capparis amplissima, inermis*, &c. seu *pedunculis unifloris*, &c. native of Hispaniola.—*Capparis cynophallophora*, seu *pedunculis*, &c. *flexuosa*, &c. seu *arborescens*, &c. *Morisonia flexuosa, Breynia fruticosa*, &c. *Cynophallophorus*, seu *Penis caninus*, &c. seu *Acaciæ affinis*, &c. native of South America.—*Capparis saligna*, seu *foliis lineari*, &c. native of St. Cruce.—*Capparis linearis*, seu *pedunculis*, &c. native of Carthagena.—*Capparis*, *Breynia pedunculis*, &c. *Cynophallophora*, &c. seu *Breynia foliis*, &c. native of Jamaica. *Prosp. Alpin. Hist. Nat.*; *Ger. Herb.*; *J. Bauh. Hist. Plant.*; *C. Bauh. Pin.*; *Park. Theat. Botan.*; *Raii Hist. Plant.*; *Tournef. Instit. de Re Herb.*; *Boerhaav. Ind.*

CA'PRA (*Ant.*) the goat was an emblem of several towns in Greece, which were called by the name of Ægæa, as in the annexed figure of a medal struck by the town of Ægea, in Cilicia, bearing the inscription ΑΙΓΑΕΩΝ. *Hard. Numm. Ant. illust.*; *Pellerin. Rec. des Med.*

CAPRA (*Zool.*) the Goat, a genus of animals, Class *Mammalia*, Order *Pecora*.

Generic Character. Horns hollow, compressed.—Fore-teeth lower eight.—Tusks none.—Chin bearded.

Species. The principal species are the *Capra ægigrus*, the Common Goat, which includes several varieties.—*Capra ibex*, the Ibex, a wild gregarious species, native of Arabia.—*Capra Caucasica*, the Caucasian Goat, native of Mount Caucasus.

CAPRA (*Astron.*) or the *She-goat*; a name given to the star *Capella*, on the left shoulder of *Auriga*, sometimes to the constellation *Capricorn*, and sometimes to a northern constellation, having three stars.

CA'PRÆ saltantes (*Met.*) fiery meteors or exhalations which sometimes appear in the atmosphere, not in a straight line, but with windings and inflections.

CAPRA'RIA (*Bot.*) a genus of plants, Class 14 *Didynamia*, Order 2 *Angiospermia*.

Generic Characters. CAL. perianth one-leaved; *divisions* linear.—COR. monopetalous; *divisions* oblong.—STAM. *filaments* four; *anthers* cordate.—PIST. germ conical; *style* filiform; *stigma* cordate.—PER. capsule oblong-conical; *seeds* very many.

Species. The species are perennials, biennials, shrubs, &c. as—*Capraria biflora*, seu *foliis alternis*, &c. seu *curassavica*, seu *peruviana*, &c. seu *Gratiolæ affinis*, &c. seu *Lysimachiæ peruvianæ*, &c. Shrubby Goat-weed, or Sweet-weed, a perennial, native of Peru and the West Indies.—*Capraria lucida*, seu *foliis oppositis*, &c. Shining Capraria, a biennial, native of the Cape of Good Hope.—*Capraria lanceolata*, seu *foliis oppositis*, &c. Willow-leaved Capraria, a shrub, native of the Cape of Good Hope.—*Capraria semiserrata*, seu *foliis lanceolatis*, &c. a native of St. Martha.—*Capraria undulata*, seu *foliis oppositis*, Waved-leaved Capraria, a shrub, native of the Cape of Good Hope.—*Capraria humilis*, seu *pubescens*, Dwarf Capraria, an annual, native of the East Indies.—

Capraria durantifolia, seu *Stemodia durantifolia*, seu *Phelypæa erecta*, &c. seu *Veronica caule hexangulari*, &c. native of Jamaica.

CAPRA'RIUS (*Ant.*) the slave who took care of the goats, the goatherd.

CA'PREA (*Zool.*) a roe, roebuck, or deer.

CAPREOLA'RIS (*Med.*) an epithet for such vessels as twine about like the tendrils of vines, as the spermatic vessels, &c.

CAPREOLATA (*Bot.*) a creeping plant of Brazil.

CA'PREOLATE *plants* (*Bot.*) from *Capreolus*, a tendril; plants which have tendrils like the vine, as the cucumber, &c.

CAPREO'LS (*Carpent.*) the struts or braces of a trussed roof.

CAPREO'LUS (*Anat.*) the Helix of the ear; so called on account of its tortuosity.

CAPREOLUS (*Bot.*) the clasp or tendril, by which vines and other creeping plants fasten themselves to those things which are intended for their support. *Varr. de Re Rust.* l. 1, c. 31.

CAPRICA'LEA (*Orn.*) a kind of wild goose, a little bigger than a raven.

CAPRI'CCIO (*Mus.*) Italian for a loose irregular species of composition, in which the composer, without any restraint, continually digresses from his subject.

CAPRICCIO'SO (*Mus.*) an Italian epithet to express that the movement at the beginning of which it is written, is to be played in a fantastic, free style.

CAPRICE'RVA *Occidentalis* (*Zool.*) from *caper*, a goat, and *cervus*, a stag; a West Indian deer, participating both of the nature of the deer and stag, affording the West Indian Bezoar.—*Capricerva Orientalis*, the deer in which the East Indian Bezoar is found.

CAPRICORN (*Astron.*) αἰγόκερως, the goat; a southern constellation, and a sign of the zodiac, which the sun enters about the 21st of December; or the winter solstice, to which the poets allude.

Arat. de Apparent. v. 285.

     — αὐτὰρ ὅγε πρότερος καὶ τοιόθι μᾶλλον
Κέκλιται αἰγόκερως, ἵνα τρέπετ' ἠελίοιο
Μὴ κείνω ἐνὶ μηνὶ περικλύζοιο θαλάσσης
Πεπταμένω ἐνὶ μηνὶ περικλύζοιο θαλάσσης
Πολλαὶ εἰρεσίαι ἐπεὶ ταχινώταταί εἰσιν.

Hor. Carm. l. 2, od. 17.

           seu tyrannus
Hesperiæ Capricornus undæ.

Propert. l. 4, eleg. 1, v. 108.

    Lotus et Hesperid quid Capricornus aquâ.

Manil. Astron. Poet. l. 4, v. 779.

    Tu Capricorne, regis quicquid sub sole cadente
    Est positum ——

This sign, which is marked thus, ♑, to represent the horns of a goat, is fabled to have been Pan, who, in the war of the giants, was transported to heaven in the shape of a goat. Macrobius, who calls *Cancer* and *Capricorn* the gates of the sun, makes the latter sign to represent his ascending motion after the manner of the goat which climbs the rocks. This constellation contains, according to Ptolemy and Tycho, twenty-eight stars; to Bayer and Hevelius, twenty-nine; to Flamstead, fifty-one.—*Tropic of Capricorn*, a small circle of the sphere parallel to the equator, passing through the beginning of *Capricorn*, or the winter solstice, which is the sun's greatest southern declination, namely, 23° 27′ 46″. *Hipparch. ad Arat.*; *Eratosth. Characteris.*; *Cic. de Nat. Deor.* l. 2, c. 44; *Hygin. Astron. Poet.*; *Ptol. Almag.* l. 7, c. 5; *Gemin. Elem. Astron.* c. 4; *Procl. de Sphær.*; *Cleom. de Sphær.*; *Macrob. Sat.* l. 1, c. 21; *Achill. Tat. Isagog.*; *Petav. Uranolog.*; *Bay. Uranomet.*; *Ricciol. Almag. nov.* &c.

CAPRICO'RNUS (*Chem.*) Lead.

CAPRIFICA'TION (*Bot.*) husbanding, or the dressing of wild fig-trees; also the cutting of bark trees that they may grow bigger. *Plin.* l. 15, c. 19.

CAPRIFICIA'LES *Dies* (*Ant.*) the dog-days, in which women used to sacrifice under a fig-tree. *Plin.* l. 11, c. 15.

CAPRI'FICUS (*Bot.*) the same as the *ficus*.

CAPRIFO'LIUM (*Bot.*) the same as *Lonicera*.

CAPRI'GENOUS (*Zool.*) *Caprigenus*; an epithet signifying born of a goat, or the goat kind.

CAPRIMU'LGA (*Zool.*) a large species of viper that is not poisonous; so called from *capra*, a she-goat, and *mulgeo*, to milk; because it was supposed to suck the milk from the goats in the night time. *Castel. Lex. Med.*

CAPRIMU'LGUS (*Orn.*) Goat-sucker, a bird distinguished for its immensely wide gape. It is a genus of the order *Passeres*, in the Linnean system.

Generic Character. *Bill* slightly curved.—*Mouth* extremely wide; *ears* very large.—*Tongue* pointed.—*Tail* not forked.—*Legs* short.

Species. The species are *Caprimulgus Europæus*, in French *l'Engoulevent*, European or Nocturnal Goatsucker.—*Caprimulgus Megacephalus*, Great-headed Goatsucker.—*Caprimulgus grandis*, in French *le grand Tbijau*, Grand Goatsucker.—*Caprimulgus strigoides*, Strigoid Goatsucker.—*Caprimulgus Jamaicensis*, seu *Guirea guerea*, Jamaica Goatsucker.—*Caprimulgus guianensis*, in French *le Montvoyau de la Guiane*, Guiana Goatsucker.—*Caprimulgus carolinensis*, in French *Engoulevent de la Caroline*, Carolina Goatsucker.—*Caprimulgus brachypterus*, in French *l'Engoulevent roux*, Short-winged Goatsucker.—*Caprimulgus villatus*, Banded Goatsucker.—*Caprimulgus incanus*, seu *vociferus*, in French *l'Engoulevent criard*, Virginian Goatsucker.—*Caprimulgus albicollis*, White-throated Goatsucker.—*Caprimulgus Asiaticus*, Bombay Goatsucker.—*Caprimulgus Africanus*, in French *l'Engoulevent à collier*, Bombay Goatsucker.—*Caprimulgus Indicus*, Indian Goatsucker.—*Caprimulgus Cayanus*, in French *l'Engoulevent de Cayenne*, White-necked Goatsucker.—*Caprimulgus semitorquatus*, White-collared Goatsucker.—*Caprimulgus torquatus*, Gold-collared Goatsucker.—*Caprimulgus Popetue*, in French *l'Engoulevent popetue*, Popetue Goatsucker or Night Hawk.—*Caprimulgus forficatus*, in French *l'Engoulevent à queue fourche*, Fork-tailed Goatsucker.—*Caprimulgus novæ Hollandiæ*, New-Holland or Crested Goatsucker.

CA'PRIOLA (*Bot.*) the herb dog's tooth.

CAPRIO'LE (*Mus.*) a caper or leap in dancing like a goat's leap.

CAPRIOLES (*Man.*) leaps of firma, *à firma*, or such as a horse makes in one and the same place, without advancing forwards, and that in such a manner, that when he is in the air, and at the height of his leap, he yerks or strikes out his hind legs even and near. A capriole is the most difficult of all the high manege or raised airs, differing from the croussade in this, that the horse does not show his shoes; and from the balotade in this, that in the latter he does not yerk out.

CA'PRIZANS (*Med.*) δορκαδίζων, a sort of irregular and unequal pulse; so called by Herophilus, because in its motion it resembled the leaping of a goat. *Gal. de Diff. Puls.* l. 1, c. 29.

CAPRI'SANT *pulse* (*Med.*) the same as *Caprizans*.

TO CAPRI'ZATE (*Med.*) to leap like a goat; a term applied to the pulse.

CAPS (*Gunn.*) the coverings made of leather, which serve the same purpose as tompions to preserve the bores of guns and howitzers from the rain.

CA'PSA (*Ant.*) κάψα, κιβωτός. 1. A receptacle for books, cloaths, &c. *Diosc.* l. 3, c. 26. 2. Something whose bottom is a contexture of iron wire.

CAPSA'RIUS (*Ant.*) κιβωτοφόρος καμψύφορος. 1. A servant that waited on noblemen's children to school, and carried their books for them, whom Juvenal calls " *Custos an-*

gustæ verzula capsæ." *Schol. Iuven.* sat. 10, v. 116; *Suet. in Ner.* c. 36; *Ulp.* legg. 13, *ff. de Manum. Vind.* 2. One who was hired to keep people's clothes while they were in the bath. *Paul.* leg. 8, § *ult. de Offic. Præf. Vig.*; *Epiphan. Hæres. de Admitt.*; *Rhodig. Antiq. Lect.* l. 25, c. 20.

CAPSE'LLA (*Bot.*) a name for *Echus*, i. e. *Echium* or Viper's Bugloss. *Marcel. Empir.* c. 20.

CA'PSICUM (*Bot.*) Guinea Pepper, the fruit of which is the strongest kind of Pepper, known better by the name of Cayenne Pepper. The plant is so called from *capsa*, a bag, which it's pods resemble in shape.

CAPSICUM, *is the Linnean system*, a genus of plants, Class 5 *Pentandria*, Order 1 *Monogynia*.

Generic Characters. CAL. *perianth* one-leaved.—COR. monopetalous; *tube* very short; *border* spreading; *divisions* broad.—STAM. *filaments* five; *anthers* oblong.—PIST. *germ* superior; *style* filiform; *stigma* obtuse.—PER. *berry* without pulp; *receptacles* exsuccous; *seeds* very many.

Species. The principal species is an annual; but the rest are shrubs, as—*Capsicum annuum, Piper Indicum,* &c. seu *Vallia-capo-molago*, Annual Capsicum, or Cayenne Pepper, native of South America.—*Capsicum baccatum*, seu *caule fruticoso,* &c. seu *fructu minimo,* &c. seu *minus,* &c. seu *frutescens,* seu *rubrum minimum,* seu *Piper siliquosum,* seu *brasilianum,* &c. Small fruited Capsicum, or Bird Pepper, native of the Indies.—*Capsicum Sinense,* seu *caule fruticoso,* &c. seu *caule floribus,* &c. Chinese Capsicum, native of China.—*Capsicum grossum,* seu *caule suffrutescente,* &c. seu *fructu longo,* &c. seu *Piper Indicum,* &c. Heart-shaped Capsicum, or Bell Pepper, a perennial or shrub, native of India.—*Capsicum frutescens,* seu *caule fruticoso,* &c. seu *brasilianum,* seu *Indicum,* seu *Capo-Malago,* Shrubby Capsicum, a shrub, native of the Indies.—*Capsicum cerasiforme,* seu *caule fruticoso*, a shrub. *J. Bauh. Hist. Plant.*; *C. Bauh. Pin.*; *Ger. Herb.*; *Park. Theat. Botan.*; *Raii Hist. Plant.*; *Tournef. Inst. de Re Herb.*; *Boerhaav.*

CAPSIZE (*Mar.*) to upset or overturn a ship, boat, or any other body.—"*Capsize* the coil of rope," the order to turn it over.

CAPSQUARES (*Gunn.*) a name given to the strong plates of iron which come over the trunnions of a gun, and keep her in her carriage. The capsquare is fastened by a hinge to the prize plate, so that it may lift up and down. It forms the part of an arch in the middle to receive a third part of the trunnions; for two thirds are let into the carriage, and the other end is fastened by two iron wedges, which are called *forelocks* and *keys*.

CAPSTAN (*Mar.*) in French *Cabestan*, a strong massy column of timber in the form of a truncated cone, and having its upper extremity divided into several squares, with holes in them, to receive the bars or levers, as in the annexed figure, where the parts are represented as follow: A, the step in which the spindle works; BB, the beams under the lower and middle decks; CC, the planks of those decks; D, the iron pawl rim; E, the pawl rim; F, the lifter for raising the messenger; GG, the chocks; HH, the whelps; I, the trundleheads; K, the barrel; L, the partners; M, the drumhead; N, the pawls; O, the spindle. There are two capstans in a ship, the fore and the main capstan. The

fore-capstan is placed in the fore part of the ship, abaft the foremast; the *main-capstan* abaft the mainmast. The sea phrases connected with the use of the capstan are as follow: —*To man the capstan,* in French *mettre du monde au cabestan,* to place the sailors at it in readiness to heave.—*To rig the capstan,* in French *armer, ou garnir le cabestan,* to fix the bars in their respective holes, &c.—*To surge the capstan,* in French *choquer au cabestan,* to slacken the rope wound round upon it.—*To heave in at the capstan,* in French *virer au cabestan,* to go round with it, by pushing with the breast against the bars, and drawing in any rope of which the purchase is created.—*To come up the capstan,* in French *devirer,* to turn the capstan the contrary way, thereby letting out some of the rope upon which they had been heaving.—*To pawl the capstan,* in French *mettre les linguets au cabestan,* to fix the pawls to prevent it from recoiling during any pause of heaving.—*Capstan barrel,* the main post of it.—*Capstan bars,* the bars, levers, or pieces of wood put in the capstan holes, in order to wind any thing.—*Jeer capstan,* the machine placed between the mainmast and the foremast, used to heave upon the jeer-rope or upon the viol, and to hold off by, when the anchor is weighing.—*Spindle of a capstan,* the main body of it.—*Whelps of a capstan,* short pieces of wood made fast to it to hinder the cable from coming too high, in turning it about.

CAPSULA (*Anat.*) a diminutive of *capsa*, a chest; a little bag or chest.—*Capsula cordis,* the same as *Pericardium.*—*Capsula communis, Glissonii,* a production of the *Peritonæum,* including the *vena porta* and *biliary duct* in the liver.

CAPSULA (*Chem.*) an earthen vessel in form of a pan, wherein things are put that are to undergo a violent operation by fire.

CAPSULA (*Bot.*) a sort of pericarp, opening in a determinate manner, and containing many seeds. The parts of a capsule are the following, namely,—The Partition, *dissepimentum*, a firm membrane that intersects and divides the inner cavity of a capsule, as *b b b b*, in fig. 1, of a capsule cut transversely.—The Cells, *loculumenta*, the spaces between the partitions, *a a a a*, in fig. 1, and *b*, in fig. 2.—The

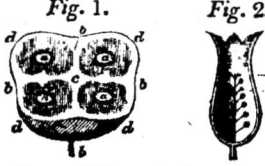

Fig. 1. Fig. 2.

Column, *columella*, a filiform body, that passes through the middle of the capsule, and to which the partitions are attached, as *c*.—The Valves, *valvulæ*, from the outward coat of the capsule, which bursts longitudinally in several parts, as in fig. 1.—The Suture, *sutura*, a deep furrow, which appears on the outside of a coat.

Different sorts of Capsules.

Capsules are distinguished by the number of their cells, valves, and seeds, as follow:—Unilocular, *unilocularis*, when there are no divisions, as in *Trientalis*; bilocular, as in *Hyoscamum*; trilocular, *trilocularis*, as in *Lilium*; quadrilocular, as in *Euonymus*; multilocular, as in *Nymphæa*; bivalved, having two valves, as in *Chelidonium*; trivalved, as in *Viola*, &c.; two seeded, *bisperma*; two, three, or multiseeded. Capsules are moreover distinguished as to their formation into tricoccous, *tricocca*, when a trilocular capsule appears as if three were grown together, as in the *Euphorbia, Ricinus,* &c.; berried, *baccata,* when the coat is fleshy and soft; corticated when the external coat is hard, and the internal soft, as in *Magnolia*, &c.; woody, *lignosa*, when the coat is very hard, but still bursts in valves. As to their mode of bursting, capsules differ materially, some opening at the top, others at the base, and others in the middle. Some are elastic, and open with a spring; others are inflated or puffed up like a bladder.

CAPSULÆ *atrabilariæ* (*Anat.*) *Glandulæ superrenales*, or *Renes succenturiati*, Glandulous bodies lying on the upper part of the kidneys.—*Capsulæ seminales*, the extreme parts of the *Vasa deferentia*, which have their cavities dilated after the manner of capsules.

CAPSULA'RES *arteriæ* (*Anat.*) from *capsulæ*, the arteries of the renal glands; so called because they are enclosed by a capsule.—*Capsulares venæ*, Branches from the emulgents which go into the renal glands.—*Capsulares seminales*, vide *Capsulæ seminales*.

CAPSULA'RIA *ligamenta* (*Anat.*) Capsular ligaments; also called *mucilaginosa ligamenta*, because they contain many glands to separate the Synovia.

CA'PSULATE *pods* (*Bot.*) from *capsa*, a chest; the little short seed vessels of plants.

CAPSULATED (*Bot.*) inclosed in any thing, as a walnut in its green husk.

CA'PTAIN *General* (*Mil.*) the general or commander in chief of an army. By the constitution the King is *captain general* of all the forces of Great Britain.—*Lieutenant Captain*. 1. The commanding officer of a colonel's company or troop in every regiment, who commands as the youngest captain. 2. The Captain's second, or the officer who commands under the captain, and in his absence.—*Captain reformed*, one who, upon a reduction of the forces on the termination of war, loses his company, yet keeps his rank and pay, whether on duty or not,—*Captain on half-pay*, one who loses his company on the reduction of an army, and retires on half pay until seniority puts him into duty and full pay again.—*Captain en Second*, or Second Captain, one whose company having been broken is joined to another to serve under the captain of it.—*Captain of halberts*, or *of black bills*, those who, during the reigns of our ancient kings, had the charge and direction of a body of men called *halberts*, or *black-bills*.

CAPTAIN *of a ship of war* (*Mar.*) or *Post Captain*, in French *Capitaine de haut bord*, an officer qualified to command any ship of war, from a first rate down to a ship rigged sloop.—*Captain of a Merchant ship*, in French *Capitaine marchand*, he who has the direction of the ship's crew and cargo.—*Captains of Port*, in French *Capitaines de Port*, among the French, officers established in some considerable sea-ports where there are arsenals, as at Brest, Toulon, &c.—*Captain's Clerk*, in French *Commis ou Secretaire du capitaine chargé de tenir ses comptes et ses écritures*; a person employed by the captain to take charge of all the books necessary for his accounts.

CAPTAIN *Bashaw* (*Polit.*) or *Capondan Bashaw*, in the polity of the Turks, signifies the Turkish high admiral, who is the third officer in the empire, having the same authority by sea that the vizier has on land.

CA'PTION (*Law*) *captio*, that part of a legal instrument, as a commission, indictment, &c. which shows where, when, and by what authority it is taken, found, or executed.—*Caption*, also another name for an arrest, or the taking a person by a judicial process.—*Caption*, in the Scotch Law, the name of a writ issued by the court of session against the agents of the court to return papers belonging to processes or law-suits, or otherwise to go to prison.

CA'PTIVE (*Mil.*) in French *Captif*, a prisoner of war.

CA'PTURE (*Mar.*) in French *capture*, a prize taken by a ship of war at sea, or by privateers in time of war.

CAPTURE (*Law*) *captura*, the taking of a prey, an arrest, or seizure.

CAPU'CHE (*Ecc.*) in French *capuchon*, Italian *cappuccio*, a monk's hood or cowl.

CAPUCHI'N (*Archæol.*) a cloke with a head to it worn by women, so called because it is made in imitation of the dress of Capuchin monks.

CAPUCHIN *capers* (*Bot.*) called also Nasturces, or Nasturtiums.

CAPUCHI'NS (*Ecc.*) in French *capuchins*, in Italian *cappuccio*; an order of Franciscan friars, so called from their *capuche*, or hood hanging down their back. *Heliot. Hist. des Ord. Mon.* tom. vii. c. 24.

CAPUCHO'N (*Her.*) French for a hood which was sometimes used as a bearing in coat armour; it differed from the chaperon by being closed every way.

CA'PULA (*Ant.*) a wooden utensil with two handles for ladling oil out of one vessel into another; whence the person so doing was called the capulator. *Cat. de Re Rust.* c. 67; *Colum. de R. R.* l. 12, c. 50.

CAPULA'TOR (*Ant.*) an officer belonging to the prefect of the city, who dealt out the oil to the people in the *capula*, or oil-vessel. [vide *Capula*]

CA'PULUM (*Med.*) from κάμπτω, to bend; a contortion of the eyelids, or other parts.

CA'PULUS (*Ant.*) 1. A sword hilt which was often beset with ornaments.

Ovid. Met. l. 7, v. 422.

Cum pater in capulo gladii cognovit eburno
Signa sui generis.

Senec. Hippol. act. 3, scen. 2. v. 897.

Regale parvis asperum signis ebur
Capulo refulget gentis Actææ decus.

2. A bier or carriage on which the dead were carried. *Fest. de Verb. Signif.*

CA'PUR (*Chem.*) the same as Camphora.

CAPU'RA (*Bot.*) a genus of plants, Class 6 *Hexandria*, Order 1 *Monogynia*.

Generic Characters. CAL. none.— COR. monopetalous; *tube* cylindric; *border* six-parted; *divisions* rounded.— STAM. *filaments* hardly any; *anthers* six.—PIST. *germ* superior; *style* cylindrical; *stigma* nearly globose.

Species. The only species is *Capura purpurata*, a shrub, native of India.

CA'PUT (*Anat.*) the superior part of the body, which is divided into the Skull, *Cranium*, and the Face, *facies*. The Skull consists of the Crown, *vertex* or *fontanella*; the posterior part, *Occiput*; the anterior part, *Sinciput*; and the lateral parts, the Temples, *tempora*. The Face consists of the Forehead, Eye-brows, Eye-lids, Eyes, Nose, Mouth, Cheeks, Chin, and Ears. The external integuments of the head are the Hair; the Skin; the *Membrana cellulosa*, an aponeurotic expansion covering the head, neck, and shoulders, like a cap and hood, which Winslow calls a *coif*; and, lastly, the membrane covering the cranium, which is called the *Pericranium*. The other parts of the head, as the brain, bones, muscles, arteries, veins, and nerves, will be found explained under their respective words; as also under the head of Anatomy. [vide Plate 7, fig. 1, 2] *Ruff. Ephes.* l. 1, c. 3; *Cel.* l. 4, c. 1; *Gal. de Ossib. &c.*; *Orib. Med. Coll.* l. 25, c. 3; *Fallop. Exposit. de Ossib.*—*Caput gallaginis*, a kind of *septum*, or spongeous border, at the extremities or apertures of each of the *Vesiculæ seminales*, serving to hinder the semen from going out of its passage.

CAPUT *Obstipum* (*Med.*) a wry neck, which is mostly a spasmodic disorder.—*Caput-purgia*, errhines, medicines, which purge the head.

CAPUT *Gallinacium* (*Bot.*) the *Hedysarum humile* of Linnæus.—*Caput monachi*, the same as *Dens leonis*.—*Caput Medusæ*, the *Elymus caput Medusæ* of Linnæus.

CAPUT *Mortuum* (*Chem.*) the fœces of any body remaining

after all the volatile and humid parts; viz. phlegm, spirit, salt, &c. have been extracted from it by force of fire.

CAPUT *anni* (*Law*) new year's day.—*Caput Baronæ*, the castle, or chief seat of a nobleman.—*Caput Jejunii*, Ash Wednesday, according to our records, being the head, or first day of the beginning of the Lent fast.—*Caput Loci*, the head, or upper end of any place, as *ad Caput villæ*, at the end of the town.—*Caput lupinum*, anciently an outlawed felon was said to have *caput lupinum*, and might be knocked on the head as a wolf: now the wilful killing of such a one would be murder. *Bract.* l. 1; *Hal. P. C.* 497.

CAPUT *Draconis* (*Astron.*) the Dragon's Head; a name given by some to a star of the first magnitude in the constellation Draco.

CAPUT *Argol* (*Astrol.*) a planet of malignant fortune.—*Caput Draconis*, the Dragon's Head, the name of the moon's ascending node.

CAPUTA'GIUM (*Law*) according to some, Head or Poll-money, or the payment of it; but it seems rather to signify what is called *chevagium*.

CAPUT-PU'RGIUM (*Med.*) the same as *Errhinum*.

CAPUUPE'BA *Brasiliensibus* (*Bot.*) *Gramen dactylon plumeum*, a sort of grass in Brasil, the root of which, drank in any convenient liquor, is commmended by the natives against poison. *Raii Hist. Plant.*

CAPYRI'DION (*Med.*) or *capyrion*, a medicated cake much baked.

CAPY'RION (*Med.*) vide *Capyridion*.

CA'PYS (*Ent.*) a species of Sphinx.

CAQUE *de Poudre* (*Mil.*) a tun or barrel of powder.

CAR (*Astron.*) the bear, or Charles's wain.

CAR (*Mil.*) 1. A kind of small carriage used in triumphs, and on other solemn occasions. 2. A carriage with two wheels fitted up with boxes to contain ammunition, and to carry artillery-men that are attached, and formed into brigades, for the purpose of accompanying field ordnance.

CA'R-TAKER *to his Majesty* (*Law*) a sinecure which is enjoyed by the entering clerk at the Pay office, valued 39*l*. per annum, net.

CA'RA (*Bot.*) a species of the *Dioscorea*.—*Cara Brasiliensibus*, a species of *Convolvulus*.

CA'RAB (*Bot.*) another name for the *Silique*.

CARABA'CCIUM *lignum* (*Bot.*) an Indian wood that tastes very much like cloves.

CA'RABE (*Chem.*) Yellow Amber.—*Carabe funerum*, the same as Bitumen.

CA'RABINE (*Mil.*) vide *Carbine*.

CARABINE'ERS (*Mil.*) or *Carbineers*, horsemen armed with carbines, who occasionally act as infantry.

CARABI'NS (*Mil.*) light armed horsemen, who sometimes acted on foot.

CARA'BOLUS (*Bot.*) a kind of wood for making the masts of ships.

CA'RABUS (*Ent.*) κάραβος, from κάρα, the head, i. e. τηχαρα-βαινιν, to walk upon its head; a species of crab much resembling the scorpion. *Aristot. Hist. Animal.* l. 4, c. 3; *Plin.* l. 9, c. 31.

CARABUS, *in the Linnean system*, a genus of insects, of the order Coleoptera.
Generic Character. *Antennæ* filiform.—*Feelers* mostly six.—*Thorax* flat, margined; *shells* margined.
Species. Insects of this genus are nearly allied to the beetle tribe, and live mostly in dry wood where they depose their live. Two species of this insect, namely, the *Carabus chrysocephalus* and *ferrugineus*, are recommended for the tooth ache when pressed between the fingers, and applied to the gum.

CA'RACA (*Bot.*) the *Dolichos bulbosus* of Linnæus.

CARACA'LLA (*Ant.*) a Gaulish kind of vestment introduced into Rome by Aurelius Antonius Bassianus Caracalla, who from thence received his cognomen. *Dio.* l. 78; *Spartian. Anton. Carac.* c. 9; *Aurel. Vict. Epit.* c. 21.

CARACALLA (*Bot.*) the *Phaseolus caracalla* of Linnæus.

CA'RACK (*Mar.*) the name of a large Portuguese ship, a ship of burthen, the same as what are now called *galleons*.

CA'RACOL (*Archit.*) a stair case in the form of a helix, or spiral curve.

CARACOL (*Man.*) in Italian *caracolla*, an oblique pist or tread, traced out in semirounds, changing from one hand to another, without observing a regular ground.

CARACO'LE (*Mil.*) a semicircular motion, or half wheel, used, either by individuals, or squadrons of cavalry, to prevent an enemy from discovering where they intend to make their attack; whence the phrase *caracoler autour d'une troupe d'ennemie*, i. e. to hang on the flanks of an enemy to take him by surprize, or otherwise perplex him.

TO CARACO'LE (*Man.*) in Italian *caracollare*, in Spanish *caracollar*; a term used for a horse to signify that he goes in the form of half-rounds.

CARACO'LI (*Com.*) a kind of metal, of which the Caribbees, or natives of the Lesser Antilles, make a sort of ornament in the form of a crescent, which they call *caracoli*. This metal comes from the main land, and is generally supposed to be a compound of silver, copper, and gold, something like the Corinthian brass of old.

CARACO'RES (*Mar.*) light vessels used by the natives of Borneo, and the islands adjacent, and by the Dutch, as *guarda-costas* in those latitudes.

CARACO'SMOS (*Nat.*) a name for the *Oxygala equinum*, or sour mare's milk, accounted by the Tartars a delicious food.

CA'RACT (*Com.*) vide *Carat*.

CHARA'CTERES (*Ant.*) vide *Phylactery*.

CARAGA'NA (*Bot.*) the *Robinia caragana* of Linnæus.

CARA'GE (*Com.*) a measure of lime equal to sixty-four bushels.

CARA'GI (*Com.*) 1. The duties of importation and exportation, so called in the grand Seignior's dominions. 2. The name of the custom house officers who receive the duties.

CARA'GNA (*Bot.*) the same as *Caranna*.

CA'RAGROUGH (*Com.*) a silver coin of the Turkish empire weighing nine drachms, of which there are four sorts, and all equally current, and of the same value. It goes at Constantinople for one hundred and twenty aspers.

CARAGUA'TA (*Bot.*) the aloe of Brazil, the concreted juice of which is supposed to be ambergrise; it is the *Bromelia acana* of Linnæus.

CA'RAITES (*Ecc.*) from קרא, to read; a sect among the Jews, so called from their strict adherence to the letter of the five books of Moses, rejecting all interpretations, paraphrases, and commentaries of the Rabbis.

CARAMA'NGOE (*Com.*) a drug which comes from China, and is valued much by the Tonquinese for its medicinal virtues.

CARA'MBOLA (*Bot.*) *Malus Indica*, a tree growing in the East Indies which bears fruit three times a year. It is the *Averrhoa carambola* of Linnæus.

CARAMBU (*Bot.*) the *Jussieu repens* of Linnæus.

CARAMEL (*Mech.*) 1. The sixth and last degree of boiling sugar, when if a little be put between the teeth it will break and crackle. 2. A curious sort of sugar work.

CARAME'NO (*Med.*) a name sometimes given to the *Hyboucouhoe Americanus*.

CARAMOU'SEL (*Mar.*) a great ship of burthen.

CARANAI'BA (*Bot.*) a species of palm.

CARANA'SI (*Bot.*) the *Capraria crustacea* of Linnæus.

CARA'NDAS (*Bot.*) the *Carissa carandas* of Linnæus.

CARA'NNA (*Bot.*) *caragna*, or *brelisis*, a tree, supposed to be a species of Palm.

CARANNA (*Com.*) the gum or resin of the Caranna tree,

which is of an aromatic flavour, and is brought from New Spain, and other parts of America.

CARANO'SI (*Bot.*) an Indian shrub; the same as the *Negundo* of Linnæus.

CARA'NTIA (*Bot.*) the *Siliqua dulcis* of Linnæus.

CARAPA'CE (*Com.*) a thick, solid, and firm shell which covers the tortoise or turtle.

CARAPATI'NA (*Bot.*) the same as *Bufonitis*.

CARAPICHE'A (*Bot.*) the same as the *Ipecacuanha*.

CARA'RU Brasiliensibus (*Bot.*) *Blitum Brasilianum Lusitanis*, a species of Blite growing in Brasil; it is the *Amaranthus* of Linnæus.

CARA-SCHULLI (*Bot.*) *Frutex Indicus spinosus*, an Indian shrub like the Caper shrub; the *Barleria luxifolia* of Linnæus, which is used medicinally in various cases.

CA'RAT (*Com.*) *caract*, or *karat*, a weight anciently used by workers in gold to mark the degree of purity that there is in gold, twenty-four of which made a mark. The carat is divided into one-fourth, one-eighth, and one-sixteenth, one-thirty-second, in order to distinguish the greater or less quantity of alloy therein contained; thus twenty-two carats of gold is that which has two parts of silver, or any other metal, and twenty-two of fine gold.

The *carat*, called by the Spaniards *quilate*, is also a certain weight which jewellers and lapidaries use wherewith to weigh precious stones and pearls. This carat weighs four grains, but something lighter than the grains of marc weight. Each of these grains is subdivided into one-second, one-fourth, one-eighth, and one-sixteenth, according to which the price of pearls and precious stones is rated. In Spain the carat or quilate is also of four grains, three carats making a tomin, eight tomins a castellan, six castellans and two tomins one ounce, and eight ounces a marc; but the marc of Spain is about one-seventh lighter than that of France.

CARAVA'N (*Com.*) a company or assembly of travellers or pilgrims, and more particularly of merchants, who for greater security and mutual accommodation travel together through the deserts, and other dangerous places, of Arabia.

CARAVA'NNA (*Law*) a caravan.

CARAVA'NSERA (*Com.*) in the East, a large building or inn for the reception of travellers and the lodging of caravans.

CARAVANSERA Skire (*Com.*) the director, steward, or intendant of a caravansera. The merchants to whom the caravan belongs appoint its officers, and regulate every thing relating to its police or government during the march. There are commonly four principal officers, namely, the *Caravan-Bachi*, or head of the caravan, the *Captain of the march*, the *Captain of stay*, or *rest*, and the *Captain of the distribution*. The first has the uncontrollable command over all the rest, who are each absolute in the several departments which they fill. The caravans are generally distinguished into five sorts, namely—*Heavy caravans*, composed of elephants, camels, and horses.—*Light caravans*, having but few elephants.—*Common caravans*, where there are none of these animals.—*Horse caravans*, in which they use neither dromedaries nor camels.—*Sea caravans*, consisting of a number of merchant ships under the convoy of some men of war.

CARAVA'TA (*Bot.*) the same as *Cacao*.

CARAVE'L (*Mar.*) or *carvel*. 1. A light round old fashioned ship, with a square poop, formerly used in Spain and Portugal. 2. A small vessel used on the coast of France in fishing for herrings on the banks.

CA'RAWAY (*Bot.*) a biennial, the *Carum carui* of Linnæus, which has a taper root like a parsnep, that is also reckoned equal in goodness to the parsnep. The seed, well known by the name of Caraway-seed, is a strong aromatic that abounds in essential oil.

CARA'XEON (*Bot.*) the same as *Gomphrena*.

CA'RBASUS (*Med.*) κάρβασος, ἁρμενον, Lint, thin linen, or soft thread, on which the surgeons spread their ointments; called also *achne, carpia*. *Scrib. Larg.* No. 227.

CA'RBEQUI (*Com.*) or *asper of copper*, a coin current in the province of Georgia, in Asia, forty of which make an abasi, and ten a chasuri.

CA'RBINE (*Mil.*) a sort of fire-arms used by the cavalry, and smaller than the firelock of the infantry.

CARBINE'ERS (*Mil.*) or *carabineers*, men armed with carbines: formerly all light armed horse were called carbineers.

CA'RBO (*Min.*) from the Hebrew חרב, *charab*, to burn: when used without the epithet *fossilis* generally signifies charcoal.—*Carbo fossilis*, or *Lithanthrax*, from *charbah*, burnt Pit coal, or Scotch coal.—*Carbo vegetabilis*, or *Charcoal of Wood*, the coal into which wood is converted by the process of charring.

CA'RBO (*Med.*) the same as *Carbunculus*.

CA'RBON (*Chem.*) or *Carbone*, Charcoal, or more properly the pure basis of charcoal, free from all the hydrogen and earthy or metallic particles which charcoal usually contains. Charcoal is a black, insoluble, inodorous, insipid, and brittle substance, which is an excellent conductor of electricity, but a bad conductor of heat; remains unchanged by air or moisture at common temperatures; is infusible, and easily combustible in oxygen; absorbs gases in various proportions, and destroys the smell and taste of a variety of vegetable and animal substances. Carbon is produced either by the combustion of charcoal or that of the diamond, and other combustible substances, as coals, wood, oil, wax, tallow, &c. By its union with oxygen it produces two gaseous substances; the first of which was formerly called *fixed air*, and now *carbonic acid*; the second, which contains less oxygen than the former, is called either *oxide of carbon*, or *carbonous oxide*, and sometimes *carbonic oxide gas*. [vide *Oxide*] Carbon also combines with hydrogen in two proportions, so as to form two compounds, namely, *olefiant gas*, otherwise called *hydroguret of carbon*, and *carbureted hydrogen*, or *bihydroguret of carbon*; the proportions of which are, one atom of charcoal to two atoms of hydrogen in the former, and an atom of each in the latter. By its combination with azote it forms a gaseous compound, which has been denominated *cyanogen*; and by the combination of phosphorus and sulphur with it, a *phosphuret* and *sulphuret of carbon* are produced. [vide *Chemistry*]

CARBON *humanum* (*Med.*) human ordure, in the language of Paracelsus.

CARBONA'DO (*Cook.*) a steak across, and scotched to be broiled on hot coals.

CA'RBONATE (*Chem.*) a name for salts formed by the union of carbonic acid with different bases; as *carbonate* of copper, of ammonia, of barytes, &c. [vide *Chemistry*]

CARBO'NES *cæli* (*Alch.*) the Stars.

CARBO'NIC *acid* (*Chem.*) or *carbonic acid gas*, a gaseous substance formed by the combination of carbon with oxygen, in the proportion of 27·27 parts carbon to 72·73 oxygen, which is invisible and elastic, like common air, extinguishes flame, is unfit for respiration, has no smell; specific gravity 1·527, that of air being 1·000; is not altered by exposure to heat in close vessels; combines with alkaline, earthy, and metallic bases, so as to produce compound salts, called *carbonates*.

CA'RBONOUS *oxide* (*Chem.*) a composition of carbon and oxygen. [vide *Carbon*]

CA'RBOS (*Min.*) Canal Coal.

CA'RBUNCLE (*Her.*) vide *Escarbuncle*.

CARBUNCLE (*Chem.*) vide *Spinell*.

CARBUNCULATIO (*Med.*) ἀνθράκωσις, a carbuncle incident to the eye. *Gal. Exeg. Vocab.*; *Hippocrat.*; *Gal. de Diff. Morb.*

CARBUNCULATION (*Hort.*) the blasting of the young buds of trees.

CARBUNCULUS (*Min.*) or *rubinus*, the Ruby; a glittering diaphonous gem, of a red colour.

CARBUNCULUS (*Med.*) ἄνθραξ, a carbuncle, from *carbo*, a burning coal, called by Avicenna *Persicus ignis*; an inflammation which for the most part suddenly degenerates into a sphacelus, and corrupts the subjacent parts down to the bones, rendering them as black as a coal. This seems to be the reason why the Latins call such affections *carbunculi*, and the Greeks *anthraces*. *Cel.* l. 5, c. 28; *Gal. de Diff. Morb.* c. 12; *Orib. de Curat. Morb.* l. 3, c. 27; *Act. Tetrab.* 4, serm. 2, c. 12; *Paul. Æginet.* l. 4, c. 25; *Act. de Meth. Med.* l. 2, c. 12.

CARBURET (*Chem.*) a name for the compounds formed by the combination of carbon with metals; the most important of which is the carburet of iron. [vide *Chemistry*]

CARBURETTED hydrogen gas (*Chem.*) a gaseous substance formed by the combination of carbon with hydrogen, in the proportions of one atom of carbon to two atoms of hydrogen; whence it is also called a bihydroguret of carbon. The gas which is known by the name of the *fire-damp* among miners is pure carburetted hydrogen. It possesses the properties of common air, having neither colour, taste, nor smell: specific gravity 0·555.

CARCAMOUSE (*Mil.*) in French *Monton*, *Marmouton*, the battering-ram used by the ancients.

CARCAN (*Law*) in Fr. *Carcan*, an iron collar, sometimes taken for a pillory, and *carcannum* for a prison. *Leg. Caniol. Reg. apud Brompt.*

CARCANET (*Archæol.*) a chain for the neck.

CARCA'PULI (*Bot.*) an Indian tree which affords the Gamboge; the *Cambogia gutta* of Linnæus.

CARCAROS (*Med.*) καρκαρος, from καρκαίρω, to resound; a kind of fever attended with a horror or shivering.

CARCAS (*Bot.*) the same as *Cataputia*.

CARCASS (*Carpent.*) the timber-work of a house before it is either lathed or plastered, or the floors laid.—*Carcass, or Naked flooring*, that which supports the boarding above and the ceiling below. It consists of three tiers of beams, called *joists*; those of the middle tier, called *binding-joists*, support the other two, namely, the *bridgings*, or *bridging-joists*, which form the upper tier, and the *ceiling-joists*, which compose the lower.—*Carcass roofing*, the frame of timber-work which supports the covering of any building. It consists of three tiers of timbers; the first of which compose several vertical frames, called *trusses*; the inclined timbers in each *truss* are called *principal rafters*; the horizontal timbers parallel to each other are *purlins*; the timbers of the third tier are *bridging*, or *common rafters*. The principals rest upon a horizontal piece, called the *raising*, or *wall-plate*.

CARCASS (*Mil.*) in French *carcasse*; an iron case so called because the circles which pass from one plate to another seem to represent the ribs of a human carcass. This case, when filled with combustible materials, is discharged from a mortar, in the same manner as a bomb. There are two sorts of carcasses, namely, the oblong and the round; but the former are entirely out of use in the British service, on account of the uncertainty of their flight.

CARCATUS (*Law*) Loading, a ship freighted. *Pa. R.* 2.

CARCAX (*Bot.*) from κάρα, a head; a species of poppy with a very large head.

CARCELLAGE (*Law*) prison fees.

CARCER (*Med.*) a remedy proper to restrain the loose and disorderly motions both of body and mind. *Parac. de Morb. Amont.* tract 2, c. 3.

CARCERES (*Ant.*) the barriers, made at first of wood or coarse stone, and afterwards of marble, which inclosed the horse-race, particularly that part of it from which the horses started; whence *carcer*, in the singular, for the starting-post. *Virg. Æn.* l. 5, v. 145.

————— *ruuntque effusi carcere currus.*

Varr. de Ling. Lat. l. 4, c. 32; *Dionys.* l. 3; *Suet. in Claud.* c. 21.

CARCHA'RIAS (*Ich.*) καρχαρίας, another name for the *Canis marinus*, or Sea-dog.

CA'RCHEDONY (*Min.*) καρχηδών, *carchedonius lapis*, a sort of precious stone.

CARCHE'SIUM (*Mar.*) καρχήσιον, the top of the mast where the pulley is placed; also a cup described by Athenæus. *Virg. Æn.* l. 5, *et Georg.* l. 4; *Athen.* l. 11.

CARCHE'SIUS *laqueus* (*Surg.*) the name of a bandage, of which there are two sorts, the single and the double. *Gal. Com. in Hippoc. de Artic.*; *Oribas de Laq.* c. 9.

CARCHE'SII (*Ant.*) καρχήσια, the ropes which are extended from the top of the mast, and support the sails. *Gal. Com. in Hippoc. de Artic.*

CA'RCHICHEC *Turcarum* (*Bot.*) Blue Primrose, called Turks Snow Flower. It is reckoned hot, dry, and astringent. *Raii Hist. Plant.*

CARCINA'DÆ (*Ich.*) a name for a very small sort of Sea-fish, resembling Crabs. *Act. Tetrab.* 1, serm. 1.

CARCINE'THRON (*Bot.*) from καρκίνος, a crab; so called from its being jointed like the claws of a crab; a name for the *Polygonum Mas*, or Common Knot Grass, according to Oribasius. *Med. Coll.* l. 11.

CARCINO'DES (*Med.*) καρκινώδης, from καρκίνος, a cancer, and εἶδος, a form; an epithet for a tumour resembling a cancer. *Cel.* l. 6, c. 8; *Orib. de Virtut. Simpl.* l. 2, c. 1.

CARCINO'DEES (*Med.*) *choirades*, καρκινώδεις χοιράδες, strumous swellings of a malignant quality, which are painful to the touch, and exasperated by the application of medicine.

CARCINO'MA (*Med.*) and *carcinos*, from καρκίνος, cancer, and νέμω, to consume; the disease called the Cancer. [vide *Cancer*].

CARCINOMA (*Bot.*) vide *Cancer*.

CA'RCINUS (*Med.*) vide *Cancer*.

CARD (*Sport.*) vide *Cards*.

CARD (*Mech.*) an instrument or comb composed of a great number of small pieces of iron wire, of great use in the manufactories, to comb, disentangle, and range the wool, &c. for the purpose of spinning.

CARD *maker* (*Com.*) one who makes cards for carding wool, &c.

CARD *of a compass* (*Mar.*) in French *rose de vents*, a term applied to the circular paper on which the different points of the compass are projected over the mariner's compass.

CARDAMA'NTICE (*Bot.*) the same as *Cardamine*.

CARDAME'LUM (*Med.*) a sort of medicine mentioned by Galen.

CARDAMI'NDUM (*Bot.*) the same as the *Tropæolum* of Linnæus.

CA'RDAMINE (*Bot.*) Meadow Cress, a plant, so called from its resemblance to the καρδάμου of the Greeks, and the *Nasturtium* of the Latins. *Gal. de Simpl.* l. 8; *Oribas. Med. Coll.* l. 12; *Act. Tetrab.* 1, serm. 3, c. 184; *Ægin.* l. 7, c. 3.

CARDAMINE, *in the Linnean system*, a genus of plants, Class 15 *Tetradynamia*, Order 2 *Siliquosa*.

Generic Characters. CAL. perianth four-leaved; *leaflets* obtuse.—COR. four-petalled; *petals* oblong-obovate.—STAM. *filaments* six; *anthers* small.—PIST. *germ* slender; *style* none; *stigma* entire.—PER. *silique* long; *seeds* very many.

Species. The species are perennials, biennials, and annuals; the perennials are as follow:—*Cardamine bellidifolia, Arabis bellidifolia,* seu *Nasturtium Alpinum, &c.* Daisy-leaved or Alpine Cress, native of Britain.—*Cardamine Alpina,* seu *Nasturtium Alpinum, &c.* native of Switzerland.—*Cardamine asarifolia,* seu *foliis simplicibus, &c.* seu *Nasturtium Alpinum, &c.* seu *montanum, &c.* Asarabacca leaved Cress, native of Italy.—*Cardamine resedifolia,* seu *Nasturtium Alpinum, &c.* Rocket-leaved Cress, native of Switzerland.—*Cardamine pratensis, Turritis,* seu *Flos cuculi,* Common Lady's Smock, or Cuckow-Flower, native of Europe.—*Cardamine amara, Nasturtium,* seu *Sisymbrium aquaticum,* Bitter Cress, native of Britain. The biennials are as follow; namely—*Cardamine thalictroides, Plumieri, foliis ternatis,* seu *Nasturtium montanum,* native of Italy.—*Cardamine impatiens, Sisymbrii cardamines,* seu *Sium minimum, &c.* Impatient Lady's Smock, native of Britain, &c. The annuals are as follow:—*Cardamine parviflora,* seu *Nasturtium pratense, &c.* Little-flowered Lady's Smock.— *Cardamine Græcia,* Greek Cress, &c. *J. Bauh. Hist. Plant.; C. Bauh. Pin.; Ger. Herb.; Park. Theat. Bot.; Raii Hist. Plant.; Tournef. Instit. de Re Herb.; Boerhaav. Ind.*

CARDAMINE is also the *Lepidum Alpinum et petræum.*

CARDAMO'MUM (*Bot.*) from καρδαμον and αμωμον, a plant, so called because it partakes of the nature of both the Cardamum and the Amomum.

CA'RDAMON (*Bot.*) the same as *Cardamine.*

CA'RDAMYLE (*Bot.*) a sort of Maize.

CARDA'SS (*Mech.*) French for a sort of card used in carding silk; also the flocks of silk so carded.

CARDE'GO-INDI (*Bot.*) or *Folium-Indicum,* the leaf of an Indian tree, which, when chewed, renders the saliva slimy.

CA'RDER (*Com.*) one who cards wool.

CA'RDIA (*Anat.*) καρδια. 1. The heart. 2. The left and superior orifice of the stomach; so called on account of its vicinity to the heart. *Ruff. Ephes. l. 1, c. 11; Gal. de Decret. Hippocrat. l. 3.*

CARDIA (*Bot.*) the heart or pith of a tree, called by Pliny *encephalus. Theophrast. Hist. Plant. l. 3, c. 17.*

CA'RDIAC-LINE (*Palmis.*) the line of the heart that encircles the mount of the thumb, which is also called the *line of life.*

CARDI'ACA (*Bot.*) the *Galeopsis galeobdon* of Linnæus.

CARDI'ACA PASSIO (*Med.*) the Cardiac Passion, a disorder frequently mentioned by the ancients, but by the moderns mostly treated under the name of Syncope. It derives its name from the part which was supposed to be affected, and consisted, according to Hippocrates, of a preternatural substance in the stomach and entrance into the belly, with a subsequent biting pain of those parts. *Hippocrat. Epid. l. 1, &c.; Cæl. Aurel. l. 2, c. 33.*

CARDI'ACÆ ARTERIÆ (*Anat.*) another name for the *Coronariæ.*

CARDI'ACE (*Min.*) καρδιακη, a precious stone in the shape of a heart.

CARDI'ACI (*Med.*) καρδιακοι, those affected with the cardialgia.

CA'RDIACS (*Med.*) medicines so called, from καρδια, the heart, because they act upon the heart by their application to the stomach. They are called by Paracelsus *defensiva.*

CARDI'ACUM (*Med.*) a cardiac medicine.

CARDI'ACUS DOLOR (*Med.*) the same as *Cardialgia.*

CARDI'ACUS PLEXUS (*Anat.*) a branch of the *Par vagum,* or eighth pair of nerves which about the first and second rib is sent from its descending trunk, and bestowed upon the heart.

CARDIA'LGIA (*Med.*) καρδαλγια, from καρδια, the heart, or upper orifice of the stomach, and αλγιω, to pain; the heartburn, or pain at the upper orifice of the stomach. *Ruff. Ephes. l. 1, c. 11; Gal. Com. 3 in Hippocrat. Epid.; Trallian. l. 12, c. 4.*—*Cardialgia inflammatoria,* another name for *inflammatio ventriculi.*—*Cardialgia spulatoria.*

CARDI'MELECH (*Med.*) from καρδια, and the Hebrew *melek,* a king; a fictitious term to express a particular sort of active principle in the heart, commonly called the vital function.

CARDIMO'NA (*Med.*) another name for *Cardialgia.*

CA'RDINAL (*Ecc.*) the highest dignitary in the Romish church next to the Pope. The cardinals are 70 in number; namely, six bishops, fifty priests, and fourteen deacons, who are chosen by the pope, and from among whom, when assembled in what is called the *conclave,* the pope in his turn is elected. The name is derived from *cardo,* a hinge; because they serve the Apostolic See as a hinge on which the government of the church turns. For the same reason this term has been employed as an epithet of excellence to many other objects.

CARDINAL *virtues* (*Eth.*) the four virtues of prudence, temperance, justice, and fortitude, on which all others depend.

CARDINAL *points of the compass* (*Mar.*) in French *points cardinaux,* the four principal points or divisions of the horizon, namely, the North, South, East, and West.—*Cardinal winds,* winds blowing from the cardinal points.—*Cardinal signs,* those signs at the four quarters, or the equinoxes and solstices, namely, the signs Aries, Libra, Cancer, and Capricorn.

CARDINAL *numbers* (*Arith.*) such as express the number of things, as one, two, three, &c. in distinction from the ordinal first, second, &c.

CARDINAL *points* (*Astrol.*) the first, fourth, seventh, and tenth houses in a scheme or figure of the heavens.

CARDINAL'S CAP (*Bot.*) or Cardinal Flower, the *Lobelia cardinalis* of Linnæus, a plant, so called because its flower, by the intense redness of its colour, seems to emulate the scarlet robes of a cardinal, especially when the sun shines on it.

CARDINAL'S HAT (*Her.*) a charge in coats of arms, as " The field is *argent,* a Cardinal's Hat, with strings pendant, and platted in true love, the ends meeting in base *gules.*" These are the arms of Sclavonia, on the coast of the Adriatic.

CARDINAME'NTUM (*Anat.*) from *cardo,* a hinge; a hinge-like articulation.

CARDI'NEA (*Ent.*) or *Cardinée,* vide *Foricule.*

CA'RDING (*Com.*) a method of preparing wool, cotton, hair, &c. by passing it between the iron points of two instruments called *cards,* so as to dispose it for spinning.

CARDIOBO'TANON (*Bot.*) καρδιοβοτανον, the name of a herb mentioned by Myrepsus.

CARDIO'GMUS (*Med.*) the same as *Cardialgia.*

CARDIOGNOSTIC (*Med.*) καρδιογνωστικος, of καρδια, the heart, and γνωσκω, to know; knowing the heart. *Ruff. l.*

CARDIO'IDE (*Geom.*) a curve so called by Castelliani, from its resemblance in figure to καρδια, a heart. Its construction is as in the annexed diagram, where through one extremity, A, a circle is drawn, A P B having a diameter A B, and a number of lines A P Q are drawn, cutting the circle in P P: upon these set off P Q equal to the diameter A B; then the curve passing through all the points, P Q will be the cardioide.

CA'RDIOTRO'TUS (*Med.*) καρδιοτρωτος, from καρδια, the heart, and τιτρωσκω, to wound; one who has a wound in his heart. *Gal. Exeg.*

CARDIOSPE'RMUM (*Bot.*) a genus of plants, Class 8 *Octandria,* Order 3 *Trigynia.*

Generic Characters. CAL. *perianth* four-leaved; *leaflets* obtuse.—Cor. petals 4; *nectary* four-petalled; *leaflets* obtuse.—Stam. *filaments* eight; *anthers* small.—Pist. *germ* three-sided; *styles* three; *stigmas* simple.—Per. *capsule* roundish; *seeds* solitary.

Species. The species are annuals or shrubs, as the—*Cardiospermum halicacabum, &c.* seu *Helicacabum,* seu *Pisum vesicarium, &c.* Smooth-leaved Heart-pea, or Heart-seed, an annual, native of the Indies.—*Cardiospermum hirsutum,* seu *Caule petiolis, &c.* native of Guinea, an annual.—*Cardiospermum corindum,* seu *villosum, &c.* Woolly-leaved Heart-pea, or Parsley-leaved Heart-seed, an annual, native of the Brazils.—*Cardiospermum grandiflorum,* seu *foliis pubescentibus, &c.* Great-flowered Heart-seed, a shrub, native of Jamaica.—*Cardiospermum leve,* an annual, native of the Indies. *Tournef. Instit. de Re Herb.*

CARDIR (*Min.*) Tin.

CARDISPE'RMUM (*Bot.*) the same as *Calendula.*

CARDIS MARS (*Min.*) Iron.

CARDI'TIS (*Med.*) vide *Inflammatio cordis.*

CA'RDIUM (*Con.*) Cockle, a genus of insects belonging to the Class Vermes, Order Testacea.

Generic Character. Animal a tethys.—Shell bivalve, nearly equilateral; equivalve ribbed, striate, or grooved.—Hinge with two teeth near the beak.

Species. The species are found in different seas; some in the British channel, as the *Cardium medium, exiguum, aculeatum, spinosum, ciliare, tuberculatum, lævigatum, edule, rubrum, nodosum, arcuatum, discors, elongatum, muricatum, &c.*

CA'RDO (*Anat.*) the articulation, otherwise called *ginglymus,* to which this name has been given on account of its resemblance to a hinge.

CARDONE'T (*Bot.*) the *Carline acaulis* of Linnæus.

CARDO'NIUM (*Med.*) in the language of Paracelsus, wine medicated with herbs.

CARDOO'N (*Bot.*) a plant somewhat resembling an artichoke, the leaves of which are eaten as a sallad. It is the *Cynara cardunculus* of Linnæus.

CARDOPA'TIUM (*Bot.*) thistle, the same as the *Carlina* of Linnæus.

CARDS (*Sport.*) pieces of pasteboard of an oblong figure and different sizes, and marked with four different patterns or *suits,* as the French call them, which were intended to represent the four classes in France, where they were invented about the year 1390, to divert Charles VI. who had fallen into a state of melancholy. By the *cœurs,* Hearts, are meant the *gens de Choeur,* choirmen, or ecclesiastics; for which the Spaniards, who revived the use of cards, have copas or chalices. The nobility were represented by lances or pikes, to which we have given the name of spades, probably from the Spanish word *espadas,* swords, which supply the place of the French pikes. By *carreaux,* diamonds, are designated the order of citizens, including merchants, and the like. *Trefle,* a trefoil-leaf, or clover-grass, was emblematical of the husbandmen or peasantry. This is falsely called clubs in English, because the Spaniards have *bastos,* staves or clubs, on their cards; wherefore we have taken the thing from the French and the name from the Spaniards. The four kings alluded to are David, Alexander, Cæsar, and Charles, who represent the four grand monarchies of the Jews, Greeks, Romans, and Franks, under Charlemagne; the queens are Argine, i. e. *regina,* the queen by descent, Esther, Judith, and Pallas. The knaves represent the servants of the knights, the word knave signifying originally a servant.

CARDUE'LIS (*Orn.*) Gold-finch, Thistle-finch, a species of the *Fringilla* of Linnæus.

CARDUNCE'LLUS (*Bot.*) the *Carthamus mitissimus* and *Carthamus carduncellus* of Linnæus.

CARDU'NCULUS (*Bot.*) the *Carthamus carduncellus* of Linnæus.

CARDUO-CNI'CUS (*Bot.*) another name for the *Atractilis.*

CA'RDUUS (*Bot.*) Thistle, a genus of plants, Class 19 Syngenesia, Order 1 *Polygamia Æquales.*

Generic Characters. Cal. common ventricose.—Cor. compound tubular; *corollules* hermaphrodite.—Stam. *filaments* five; *anthers* cylindrical.——Pist. *germ* ovate; *style* filiform; *stigma* simple.—Per. none; *calyx* converging a little; *seeds* solitary; *receptacle* hairy.

Species. The species are either annuals, biennials, or perennials. Of the first kind are the following—*Carduus leucographus,* seu *Cirsium,* native of Campania.—*Carduus Arabicus,* Arabian Thistle.—*Carduus peregrinus* seu *lacteus, &c.*—*Carduus lanuginosus,* seu *orientalis, &c.* native of Armenia.—*Carduus macrocephalus,* seu *caule tomentoso, &c.*—*Carduus marianus,* seu *Silybum, &c.* Milk or Ladies' Thistle, native of England.—*Carduus crispus,* Curled Thistle, native of Europe. Of the second kind are the following:—*Carduus nutans,* seu *spinosissimus, &c.* Musk Thistle, native of Europe.—*Carduus acanthoides,* seu *polyacanthos,* Prickliest Thistle.—*Carduus palustris,* seu *Cirsium,* Marsh Thistle.—*Carduus candicans,* native of Hungary.—*Carduus personata,* seu *foliis carlinis, &c.* seu *inermis,* seu *mollis, &c.* seu *majus, &c.* seu *Arctium personata, &c.* native of Switzerland.—*Carduus polyanthemus,* seu *pycnocephalus, &c.* seu *Cirsium palustre, &c.* native of Rome. Of the third kind are the following:—*Carduus paniculatus,* native of the Pyrenees.—*Carduus cyanoides,* seu *mollis,* native of Siberia.—*Carduus polyclonos,* seu *inermis, &c.* native of Siberia.—*Carduus defloratus, Cirsium angustifolium,* seu *cirsioides,* Various-leaved Thistle, native of Switzerland.—*Carduus pannonicus,* seu *serratuloides,* seu *Cirsium pannonicum, &c.* native of Austria.—*Carduus cornithoides,* seu *Centaurea nudicaulis, &c.* seu *Jacea, Raponticoides,* &c. native of Italy.—*Carduus canus,* seu *Cirsium montanum, tomentosum, &c.* Hoary Thistle, native of Austria.—*Carduus rivularis,* seu *Cirsium carmolicum,* native of Montpellier.—*Carduus acaulis, Chamæleon exiguus,* seu *Carlina minor,* Dwarf Carline Thistle, native of Europe.—*Carduus pratensis,* seu *heterophyllus,* English Soft or Gentle Thistle, Single Headed or Meadow Thistle, native of the Pyrenees.—*Carduus ochroleucus,* seu *Cirsium ochroleucum.*—*Carduus rigens,* Upright Alpine Thistle, native of Switzerland.—*Carduus Diacantha,* native of Mount Libanus.—*Carduus gnaphaloides,* native of Calabria.—*Carduus horridus,* native of Armenia.—*Carduus benedictus,* the *Centaurea benedicta* of Linnæus.—*Carduus Brassilianus,* the *Bromelia Ananas* of Linnæus—*Carduus fullonum,* the *Dipsacus fullonum* of Linnæus.—*Carduus sphærocephalus,* the *Echinops sphærocephalus* of Linnæus.—*Carduus stellatus,* the *Centaurea Calcitrapa* of Linnæus.—*Carduus Pinea Theophrasti,* the *Atractylis gummifera* of Linnæus. *Lobel. Plant. et Stirp. Hist. et Adver.; Clus. Rar. Plant. Hist.; J. Bauh. Hist. Plant.; C. Bauh. Pin.; Ger. Herb.; Park. Theat. Botan.; Raii Hist. Plant.; Tournef. Instit.; Boerhaav. Ind.; Pluken. Almagest. Botan.*

CAREBA'RIA (*Med.*) καρηβαρια, from καρη, the head, and βαρος heaviness; an uneasy heaviness of the head.

CARE'CTA (*Ant.*) or *carectata,* a cart or cartload-man.

CARECTA'RIUS (*Ant.*) or *caretarius,* a carter.

CARECTATA *plumbi* (*Archæol.*) a pig or mass of lead, weighing 128 stone, or 2100 pounds.

CAREE'NING (*Mar.*) in French *faire à battre, caréner,* heaving the ship down on one side, by applying a strong purchase to her masts, so that it may be cleansed from any filth which adheres to it by breaming.—*A half careen,* when

CAR

it is not possible to come at the bottom of the ship, so that only half of it can be careened.

CAREE′R (*Man.*) the place inclosed with a barrier, wherein the horses run in a ring.

CAREER (*Falcon.*) a flight or tour of the bird, about 120 yards; if she mount more, it is a double career; if less, a semi-career.

CARELE′T (*Mil.*) the same as *Semelle.*

CARE′NA (*Med.*) the twenty-fourth part of a drop.

CARE′NE (*Mil.*) all the parts of a ship under water.

CARE′NUM (*Med.*) κάρηνον, the head.

CA′RET (*Gram.*) Latin for *it wanteth*; is marked by a character in printing or writing in this form (∧), denoting that there is something to be inserted or included.

CARETTI (*Bot.*) a species of the *Guilandia* of Linnæus.

CA′REUM (*Bot.*) or *Cari*, Carraway Seeds; so called from *Caria*, the country whence they are brought.

CAREX (*Bot.*) a genus of plants, Class 21 *Monoecia*, Order 3 *Triandria*.
Generic Characters. CAL. ament oblong; scales acute.—COR. none.—STAM. filaments three; anthers erect.—PIST. germ three-sided; style very short; stigmas two or three.—PER. none; seed single.
Species. The species are perennials:—Carex dioica, *Cyperoides parvum*, &c. seu *Gramen cyperoides*, &c. Small Sedge, native of England, Germany, and Italy.—Carex Davelliana, seu *Gramen cyperoides*, native of Germany. Carex capitata, *Spica andiogyna*, seu *subglobosa*, &c. Round-headed Sedge, native of Lapland.—Carex panciflora, seu *Leucoglochin*, &c. native of Scotland.—Carex microglochin, native of North Lapland.—Carex pulicaris, seu *Gramen*, &c. Flea Sedge, or Flea Grass, native of Europe.—Carex cyperoides, *Scirpus*, seu *Cyperus minor*, &c. native of Bohemia.—Carex fœtida, seu *Gramen alpinum*, &c. native of Switzerland.—Carex curvula, seu *Gramen cyperoides*, native of Switzerland.—Carex maritima, seu *Gramen cyperoides*, &c. Sand or Sea Sedge, native of Europe.—Carex lobata, seu *Cyperoides*, native of the Alps of Switzerland.—Carex leporina, *Lachenalii*, &c. seu *Lagossina*, native of Lapland.—Carex vulpina, seu *Gramen palustre majus*, Great Sedge. *J. Bauh. Hist. Plant.*; *C. Bauh. Pin.*; *Ger. Herb.*; *Park. Theat. Botan.*; *Raii Hist. Plant.*

CAREX Lithosperma, the *Scleria flagellum* of Linnæus.

CA′RFVE (*Husband.*) unbroken or untilled ground.

CA′RGADORS (*Com.*) a name used by the Dutch and Portuguese to signify a kind of brokers, whose only business it is to find freight for ships outward bound, and to give notice to the merchants who have commodities to send by sea of the ships ready to sail, and of the places to which they are bound.

CARGO (*Com.*) *cargaison ou chargement*; the merchandize and effects which are laden on board a ship, exclusive of the crew, ammunition, provision, &c.—Supercargo, a person employed by merchants to go a voyage for the purpose of taking charge of, and disposing of the cargo.

CA′RICA (*Bot.*) καρική, a dried fig; so called from *Caria*, the country from which they were brought.

CARICA, in the Linnean system, a genus of plants, Class 22 *Dioecia*, Order 9 *Decandria*, called by Tournefort *Papaya*.
Generic Characters. CAL. scarce manifest.—COR. monopetalous; tube slender; border five-parted.—STAM. filaments ten; anthers oblong; germ ovate; style none; stigmas broad.—PER. berry very large; seeds numerous.
Species. The species are shrubs, as—Carica Papaya, *Ficus*, seu *Papaya*, &c. Common Papaw Tree, native of the East Indies.—Carica Posoposa, Dwarf Papaw Tree.—Carica pyriformis, seu *Papaya*, &c. native of Peru.—Carica cauliflora, native of the Caraccas.—Carica microcarpa, seu *Ficus*, &c. native of Chili.—Carica spinosa, seu *Jaracatia*, native of Guinea. *J. Bauh. Hist. Plant. Park. Theat. Botan.*; *Raii Hist. Plant.*; *Tournef. Inst. Pluk. Almag. Botan.*

CARICA (*Bot.*) another name for the *Ficus*.

CARICATU′RE (*Paint.*) a way of representing objects distorted and deformed, but still so as to preserve the likeness; from the Italian *caricatura*, which comes from *carica*, a burden, and signifies the same as overcharging.

CA′RICK (*Mar.*) a sort of vessel.

CA′RICOUS tumor (*Surg.*) from *carica*, a swelling resembling the figure of a fig.

CARICUM (*Med.*) or *Carycum*, καρικόν, from *Caricus*, the inventor. 1. A cathartic medicine which deterges sordid ulcers, and eats away proud flesh. *Hipp. de Ulcer.* 2. The name of an oil. *Athen.* l. 2.

CA′RIES (*Med.*) from κείρω, to abrade, a disease of the bones. *Gal. Introd.*; *Aet.* 4, 2, 57; *Aqui.* 4, 20. Class *Locales*.

CARI′LLONS (*Mus.*) small bells, such as are held in the hand, or placed in clocks; a species of chimes frequent in the Low Countries, particularly at Ghent and Antwerp.

CA′RIMA (*Bot.*) the same as *Cassada*.

CARIM-CU′RINI (*Bot.*) the *Justicia ecbolium* of Linnæus.

CARIM-GO′LA (*Bot.*) another name for the *Pontederia* of Linnæus.

CARIMPA′NA (*Bot.*) the *Borassus flabelliformis* of Linnæus.

CARIMTU′MBA (*Bot.*) a species of the *Nepeta* of Linnæus.

CARI′NA (*Ant.*) the keel, or long piece of timber that runs along the bottom of the ship from head to stern. *Ovid. Pont.* l. 4, epist. 3.

Dum mea puppis erat valida fundata carina.

It is frequently taken by the poets for the whole ship. *Virg. Æn.* l. 2, v. 23.

Nunc tantum sinus, et statio malefida carinis.

Ovid. Heroid. ep. 17, v. 103.

Tunc ego te vellem coleri venisse carinâ.

Sallus. de Bell. Jugurth.; *Isid. Orig.* l. 19, c. 1; *Gyrald. de Navigat.* c. 2; *Scheff. de Mil. Naval.* l. 1, c. 6.

CARINA (*Bot.*) the lower petalum or leaf of a papilionaceous flower, which contains the germen and pistillum. It is hollow, and stands underneath the vexillum, to which it is opposite. [vide *Botany*]

CARINA (*Anat.*) the beginning of the entire *vertebræ*, or turning joints.

CARINA (*Nat.*) the first rudiments of the spine of a chicken during incubation.

CARINA (*Archæol.*) a building, near the amphitheatre, in the form of a ship's keel. *Serv. in Virg. Æn.* l. 8, v. 359.

CA′RINATED (*Bot.*) *Carinatus*, from *carina*, the keel, bending or crooked like the keel of a ship; an epithet of a leaf or nectary, *Folium* and *Nectarium carinatum*, a keeled leaf and nectary, i. e. having a longitudinal prominency upon the back like the keel of a vessel.

CARIAPHYLLA′STER (*Bot.*) a species of the *Dodonæa* of Linnæus.

CARIO′SSE (*Bot.*) a Portuguese name for the fruit of the *Ady* or *Palma Ady*, a palm tree in the island of St. Thomas.

CA′RIOUS (*Med.*) rotten, after the manner of the bones.

CA′RIPI (*Mil.*) a kind of cavalry in the Turkish army, 1000 of which are not slaves, nor bred up in the seraglio like the rest, but are generally Moors, or renegado Christians, who have obtained the rank of horse guards to the Grand Seignior.

CARI′SSA (*Bot.*) a genus of plants, Class 5 *Pentandria*, Order 1 *Monogynia*.
Generic Characters. CAL. perianth very small.—COR. mo-

nopetalous; *tube* cylindrical; *border* five-parted.—STAM. *filaments* five; *anthers* oblong.—PIST. *germ* roundish; *style* filiform; *stigma* rather simple.—PER. *berries* two; *seeds* seven.

Species. The species are shrubs, as follow:—*Carissa Carandas, Echites, Carandas,* seu *Lycium,* &c. native of India.—*Carissa spinarum,* native of the East Indies.—*Carissa edulis,* native of Arabia Felix.—*Carissa inermis,* native of the East Indies.

CARI'STIA (*Law*) dearth, scarcity, dearness. *Pat.* 8, *Ed.* 1.

CA'RITAS (*Law*) *Ad caritatem; poculum caritatis,* a grace-cup; or an extraordinary allowance of the best wine, or other liquor, wherein the religious at festivals drank in commemoration of their founders and benefactors. *Cartular. abat. Glaston.*

CA'RIUM *terræ* (*Min.*) lime.

CARK (*Law*) a quantity of wool, whereof thirty make a sarpler. *Stat.* 27, *H.* 6, c. 2.

CA'RKANET (*Archæol.*) vide *Carcan.*

CARL-D'OR (*Com.*) a gold coin of Brunswick, worth five rix-dollars, or about sixteen shillings sterling. These coins at present bear on the obverse the arms of Brunswick, instead of the head of the reigning prince as before: the legend CAROLUS D.G. DUX. BRUNS. ET LUN.; on the reverse, a horse in full speed: legend NUNQUAM RETRORSUM, with the date and value, 10 Thaler, or 5 Thaler, according as it is single or double.

CARLI'NA (*Bot.*) vide *Carline Thistle.*

CARLINA *in the Linnean system,* a genus of plants, Class 19 *Syngenesia,* Order 1 *Polygamia Æqualis.*

Generic Characters. CAL. common ventricose; *scales* numerous.—COR. compound uniform; *corollets* hermaphrodite; *tube* slender; *border* five-cleft.—STAM. *filaments* five; *anthers* cylindric.—PIST. *germ* short; *style* filiform; *stigma* oblong.—PER. none; *calyx* remaining unchanged; *seeds* solitary; *down* plumose; *receptacle* flat; *chaffs* ternate.

Species. The species are mostly perennials, as—*Carlina acaulis,* seu *Chamæleon albus,* Low Carline Thistle, native of Italy, &c.—*Carlina acanthifolia,* Chardousse, &c. seu *Carlinanska,* native of the Pyrenees.—*Carlina adgregata,* seu *caulibus,* native of Croatia.—*Carlina lyrata,* native of the Cape of Good Hope.—*Carlina involucrata,* native of Algiers.—*Carlina corymbosa,* seu *caule,* &c. *Acarina,* &c. seu *Acarus,* &c. Corymbed Carline Thistle, native of Italy. But the—*Carlina vulgaris,* Common Carline Thistle, is a biennial, and native of Europe. The two following are annuals, namely,—*Carlina lanata,* seu *Acarna,* &c. Woolly Carline Thistle, native of Italy.—*Carlina sulphurea,* &c. *Clus. Hist. Plant. rar.* &c.; *J. Bauh. Hist. Plant.*; *C. Bauh. Pin.*; *Ger. Herb.*; *Park. Theat. Botan.*; *Raii Hist. Plant.*; *Tournef. Inst.*

CARLINA is also the *Carduus acaulis,* the *Atractylis gummifera*; the *Arnica crocea,* and the *Cnicus spinosissimus* of Linnæus.

CA'RLINE-THISTLE (*Bot.*) the *Carlina* of Linnæus, a plant of the thistle kind, which is said to have been so called by Charlemagne, because his army was delivered from the plague by the use of its root. It contains an acrid resinous principle, by which it stimulates the solids, dissolves the humours, and promotes perspiration.

CA'RLING-KNEES (*Mar.*) timbers going athwart the ship from the sides to the hatchway, serving to sustain the deck on both sides.

CA'RLINGS (*Mar.*) in French *entremises, ou traversins des baux,* short pieces of timber, ranging fore and aft from one of the deck beams to another, into which their ends are scored. They are used to sustain and fortify the smaller beams of a ship.

CARLI'NO (*Com.*) a small silver coin, current in the kingdom of Naples and in Sicily, worth about threepence three farthings. It is supposed to derive its name from Charles I. king of Naples and Sicily in 1266. The Carlino is also a gold coin of Piedmont, worth five pounds eighteen shillings and eightpence, or threepence according to their present value. The impression on this latter coin is the same as that on the Doppia.

CA'RLOCK (*Chem.*) a sort of Isinglass made with the sturgeon's bladder, which is used for clarifying wine, and also in dyeing.

CARLO SANCTO RADIX (*Bot.*) St. Charles' Root, the bark of which is sudorific, and strengthens the gums and stomach. It is found in Mehoacan, a province of South America.

CARMA'GNOLE (*Mil.*) a name given to the French soldiers who first engaged in the cause of republicanism.

CA'RMAN (*Com.*) one who is employed in carrying goods from the wharfs to the merchants' warehouses, &c. also in timber-yards, &c.

CA'RMEL (*Mil.*) an order of knighthood in France instituted by Henry IV, in 1608, under the title of our Lady of Carmel.

CA'RMELINE-WOOL (*Com.*) the second sort of wool, produced by the animal which the Spaniards call *Vicunna.*

CA'RMELITE (*Bot.*) a sort of pear.

CA'RMELITES (*Ecc.*) an order of monks, founded by Almerius, bishop of Antioch, on mount Carmel in Syria, in 1122. *Baron. Annal. Ann.* 1181.—*Barefooted Carmelites,* a reformed order of Carmelite monks, so called because they went barefoot according to the rules of their order, which was instituted in the 16th century. *Spondan. Contin. Baron. Ann.* 1568; *Hel. Hist. Ord. Mon.*

CA'RMEN (*Ant.*) any set formula of words, whether in prose or verse, used for any specific purpose, of which description was the prayer uttered by the Decii on their devoting themselves to death for the benefit of their country. Moral sentences, incantations, charms, and the like, though written in prose, were called *carmina.* The *carmen,* when written in verse, answered to what is now called a verse, or an ode, as the *carmen seculare,* and the *carmina,* or odes, of Horace. *Cat. Dist. Mor.* n. 1; *Plin.* l. 38, c. 2.

CARMEN (*Med.*) the same as *Incantatio.*

CARMENTA'LIA (*Ant.*) a festival in honour of Carmenta, the mother of Evander, which was celebrated during five days, i. e. from the third of the Ides of January, or the 11th of January, to the 18th of the Calends of February. *Varr. de Lat. Lin.* l. 5, c. 3; *Ovid. Fast.* l. 1, v. 617—631; *Alex. Gen. Dior.* l. 6, c. 8; *Ursat. de Not. Roman. apud Græv. Thes. Antiq. Rom.* tom. 6, p. 2087.

CARMES, Eau de (*Min.*) Carmelite Water, or Magisterial Water of Baumé, which takes its name from being invented by the Carmelites at Paris, and is extremely reviving and good in all sorts of fits.

CA'RMIN (*Nat.*) the same as *Carmine.*

CARMI'NATIVES (*Med.*) *Carminantia,* medicines which promote perspiration, or dilute and relax.

CA'RMINE (*Nat.*) a dross or powder of a very beautiful deep red colour, separated from cochineal by means of a water in which are infused Chouan and Autour. It is used for painting in miniature.

CA'RMOT (*Alch.*) what the philosopher's stone was supposed to consist of. *Castel. Lex Med.*

CARMOUSAL (*Com.*) a Turkish merchant ship.

CARNABA'DIUM (*Med.*) καραβάδιον, καραβάδι, the same as *Cuminum Æthiopicum,* according to Myrepsus.

CARNA'DO (*Com.*) a Spanish coin, six of which make a marvedi.

2 T

CAR

CA'RNAGE (*Mil.*) in French *carnage;* a massacre or great slaughter in consequence of a desperate action between two bodies of armed men.

CARNAGE (*Sport.*) in Italian *carnaggio;* the flesh which is given to the dogs after the chase.

CARNA'LES (*Ant.*) Ædiles, so called because they superintended the markets. *Non. ex Varr.*

CARNA'RIUM (*Archæol.*) a charnel house, or repository for the bones of the dead.

CARNA'TION (*Bot.*) a beautiful sort of Clove-Pink, a variety of the *Dianthus caryophyllus* of Linnæus, the chief excellence of which consists in the brightness of its colours equally marked all over the flowers. It is distinguished by modern florists into four sorts, namely, the—*Flakes*, of two colours only and their stripes large.—*Bizarres*, striped with three or four different colours.—*Piquettes*, having a white ground spotted or pounced with red, purple, and other colours.—*Painted-Ladies*, having the petals of a red or purple colour.

CARNATION (*Paint.*) the flesh colour, which is understood of all the parts of a picture in general which represent flesh, or which are naked without drapery; wherefore, if the flesh be represented to the life, the *carnation* is said to be very good.

CA'RNAVAL (*Ecc.*) vide Carnival.

CA'RNEÆ COLUMNÆ (*Med.*) the fleshy pillars or columns in the cavities of the heart.

CARNE'DDE (*Archæol.*) heaps of stones, supposed to be Druidical remains for confirming and commemorating covenants, &c.

CA'RNEL (*Mar.*) a small Spanish ship which goes with mizzen instead of main sails.—*Carnel-work*, the same as *Carvel-work*.

CARNE'LIAN (*Min.*) or *Cornelian*, a precious stone, of which there are three kinds, distinguished by their colours red, yellow, and white. It is the *Chalcedonius carneolus* of Linnæus.

CA'RNEOL (*Min.*) a sort of precious stone.

CARNEOL (*Bot.*) a kind of herb.

CARNE'OLUS LAPIS (*Min.*) Cornelian, a precious stone, half transparent, which is found in Sardinia.

CA'RNEY (*Vet.*) a disease in horses by which their mouths become so furred and clammy that they cannot feed.

CARNI'CULA (*Med.*) from *caro*, flesh; used by Fallopius instead of *caruncula*, to signify in particular the flesh which surrounds the gums.

CA'RNIFEX (*Ant.*) the public executioner among the Romans, who was forbidden by the laws to have his house in the city. *Cic. pro Rab. c. 5; Sigon. de Ant. Jur. Rom.* l. 2, c. 15; *Fest. de Verb. Signif.*

CARNIFEX (*Alch.*) the spagiric Vulcan, or fire, in the affair of the philosopher's stone.

CARNIFO'RMIS ABSCESSUS (*Med.*) from *caro*, flesh, and *forma*, likeness; an abscess with a hardened orifice, and of a firm substance or hard consistence, like a shell.

CA'RNIVAL (*Ecc.*) in Italian *Carnevale*, is supposed to be derived from the Latin words *carnis intervallum*, i. e. a period for eating flesh, as distinguished from the ensuing period of abstinence during Lent, although others have with equal probability derived it from *carn-a-val*, i. e. flesh to the pot, to denote the time for eating meat. The carnival is a season of festivity among the Italians for the space of twelve days previous to Lent, during which all sorts of games, feasting, entertainments, and diversions of every kind, go forward.

CARNI'VOROUS (*Nat.*) σαρκοφάγος, flesh-devouring; an epithet of the *Assius lapis:* also animals are so called whose food is flesh.

CA'RNO (*Law*) an immunity or privilege. *Cromp. Jurisd.* fol. 191.

CARNE'X CUTIS (*Anat.*) or *panniculus carnosus*, a fleshy membrane that assists the corrugation of the skin.

CARNO'SITY (*Surg.*) a tubercle or fleshy excrescence growing in, and obstructing, any part of the body.

CARNO'SUS (*Bot.*) fleshy; an epithet for roots, &c. [vide *Fleshy*]

CARNO'USE (*Gunn.*) the base ring about the breech of a gun.

CA'RO (*Anat.*) in the general sense, signifies flesh; but in the particular sense, the belly, or red part of a muscle. *Ruff. Ephes. de Appellat. Part. Corp. Human.* l. 1, c. 35; *Gal. de Loc. Affect.* l. 2, c. 2.—*Caro musculosa quadrata*, the *Palmaris brevis*.

CARO *adnata ad testem et ad vasa* (*Surg.*) names given to the sarcocele according to the circumstances in which it takes place.

CARO (*Bot.*) the pulp of the fruit.

CA'ROB (*Com.*) a small weight, the twenty-fourth part of a grain.

CA'ROB-TREE (*Bot.*) a tall-spreading tree, the κεράτιον of the Greeks, and the *Ceratonia siliquosa* of Linnæus, the fruit of which is a pod or bean, resembling a chesnut in taste, and yielding a sort of honey, which serves the Arabians instead of sugar. *Prosper. Alpin de Ægypt. Plant.; J. Bauh. Hist. Plant.*

CARO'BA (*Bot.*) another name for the *Siliqua Dulcis*.

CARŒNUM (*Bot.*) κάροινον, a name for musk when boiled to the consumption of one-third, so as to be reduced to a convenient thickness.

CA'ROL (*Mus.*) from the old Italian *carola;* an old name for a song sung to dancing.

CARO'LA (*Mus.*) Italian; was formerly synonymous with *Ballata*, signifying a song of a plain, simple, popular melody to be sung to a dance.

CAROLA (*Archæol.*) a little pew or closet.

CAROLI'N (*Com.*) or *Carolin d'Or*, a gold coin of Bavaria and Hesse-Darmstadt, worth about one pound sterling. The carolin bears on the obverse the head of the reigning prince Palatinate, with a suitable legend; and, on the reverse, the Virgin and Child supporting the arms of Bavaria. Legend, CLYPEUS OMNIBUS IN TE SPERANTIBUS.—*Carolini* is also the name of an old Swedish coin, now out of circulation.

CAROLINE'A (*Bot.*) a genus of plants, Class 16 *Monadelphia*, Order 7 *Polyandria*.
Generic Characters. CAL. *perianth* one-leaved.—COR. *petals* five.—STAM. monodelphous; *filaments* very numerous; *anthers* oblongish.—PIST. *germ.* inferior; *style* filiform; *stigmas* simple.—PER. *dome* ovate; *seeds* twin.
Species. The species are—*Carolinea princeps*, seu *foliis*, &c. seu *Pachira aquatica*, seu *Sergeant*, &c. seu *Cacao*, &c. a shrub, native of Guinea.—*Carolinea insignis*, seu *foliis*, &c. seu *Bombax*, &c. seu *Xiloxorhitl*, &c. a shrub, native of America.—*Carolinea minor*, a shrub, native of Guiana.

CAROLI'NES (*Ecc.*) the four books composed by the order of Charlemagne, to refute the Second Council of Nice, respecting the worship of images. *Du Pin. Bibl. des Aut. Eccles.* xiii. Siéc.

CAROLI'NGIANS (*Polit.*) a name of the second race of kings in France, of which Pepin was the founder.

CAROLI'TIC COLUMNS (*Archit.*) columns with foliated shafts, decorated with leaves and branches winding spirally around them, or disposed in form of crowns and festoons.

CAROLOSTA'DIANS (*Ecc.*) a branch of the Lutherans, who denied the real presence in the Eucharist; so called from their founder Carolostadius.

CARO'LUS (*Com.*) a broad piece of gold struck in the time of Charles the First, made then for twenty shillings, but since current at twenty-three.

CA'ROMEL (*Chem.*) a name given by the French to the peculiar smell which exhales from sugar when heated.

CARO-MOE'LI (*Bot.*) the *Sideroxylon* of Linnæus.

CARO'PI (*Bot.*) another name for the *Amomum verum*.

CARO'PO (*Ich.*) a species of the *Gymnotus*.

CARO'RA (*Med.*) *Cynnia*, or *Cymia*, the name of a vessel that resembles a urinal.

CA'ROS (*Med.*) καρὸς, from κάρα, the head; because this is the part principally affected; a slight degree of apoplexy. *Dioscor.* l. 4, c. 76; *Plin.* l. 25, c. 13; *Gal. Com. in Hippocrat.* l. 5, aphor. 5; *Aet. Tetrab.* 2, serm. 2, c. 5; *Æginet.* l. 3, c. 9; *Act. de Meth. Med.* l. 4, c. 2.

CAROS (*Bot.*) another name for *Carui*.

CARO'SIS (*Med.*) the same as *Caros*.

CARO'TA (*Bot.*) the *Daucus carota* of Linnæus.

CAROTEE'L (*Com.*) a certain quantity which varied in weight according to the commodity; the caroteel of mace being about three pounds; that of nutmegs from six to seven and a half; that of currants from five to nine pounds weight.

CARO'TIDS (*Anat.*) καρωτίδες, *carotidæ arteriæ*, carotid arteries; two principal arteries which convey the blood to the head: they are so called from κάρα, the *carus*, or sleepiness; because when the current of blood through these vessels is diminished, a stupor ensues. *Ruff. Ephes. de Appell. Part. Hum. Corp.* l. 1, c. 34; *Gal. de Usu. Part.* l. 16; *Gorr. Med. Def.*

CAROU'M (*Bot.*) the same as *Caru*, or *Carum*.

CAROU'SAL (*Mil.*) in French *carroussel*, a magnificent entertainment exhibited by princes or other great personages on some public occasion, consisting of cavalcades of gentlemen richly dressed and equipped, after the manner of the ancient cavaliers, &c.

CAROXYLUM (*Bot.*) a genus of plants, Class 5 *Pentandria*, Order 1 *Monogynia*.

Generic Characters. CAL. perianth two-leaved.—COR. one-petalled; *tube* none; *border* segments obtuse; *nectary* scales five.—STAM. *filaments* five; *anthers* very small.—PIST. *germ* superior; *style* simple; *stigmas* two. —PER. none; *seed* one depressed.

Species. The only species is the *Caroxylon salsola*, seu *Canna bosch*, a perennial, native of Africa.

CARP (*Ich.*) a freshwater fish, the *Cyprinus* of Linnæus, which affords a palatable and nourishing food. Carp sometimes migrate, and spawn about April or May. They are a valuable fish for stocking ponds, being very quick in growth, and spawning three times a year.

CA'RP-STONE (*Min.*) a stone of a triangular form, found in the palate of a carp.

CA'RPASUS (*Bot.*) κάρπασος, so named παρὰ τὸ κάρον ποιεῖν, because it induces sleep upon the person who eats of it; a highly poisonous herb, resembling myrrh, which is spoken of by ancient naturalists.

CARPA'TA (*Bot.*) vide *Cataputia Minor*.

CARPA'THICUM (*Med.*) a name for fine essential oil distilled from the fresh cones of the trees which yield the common turpentine.

CARPÆ'A (*Ant.*) καρπαία, a kind of dance anciently in use among the Athenians and Magnesians, which was performed by two persons, one acting the husbandman, the other the robber. *Athen.* l. 1, c. 13.

CARPEMEALS (*Com.*) a coarse kind of cloth made in the Northern parts of England. 7 Jac. 1, c. 16.

CARPENTA'RIA (*Bot.*) the *Herba Judaica*, a vulnerary plant.

CARPENTA'RIUS (*Ant.*) a maker of *carpenta*; a coachmaker or wheelwright. *Veget.* l. 2, c. 2.

CA'RPENTER *of a ship* (*Mar.*) *maitre charpentier d'un vaisseau*, an officer appointed to examine and keep in order the frame of a ship, with her masts, yards, &c.—Carpenter's mate, in French *aide charpentier*, one appointed to assist the carpenter in his duty.—Carpenter's crew, in French *gens du charpentier*, a set of men employed under the carpenter to make the necessary repairs.

CARPENTERS, *Company of*, (*Her.*) was incorporated in 1476. Their arms are *argent* a cheveron ingrailed between three pairs of compasses pointing towards the base, and a little extended.

CARPENTER'S *rule* (*Carpent.*) a tool generally used in taking dimensions, and in casting up the contents of timber, and of artificer's work.—Carpenter's square, a square, the stock and plate of which consists of one piece of iron plate.

CARPENTER'S *square* (*Her.*) a charge in some coats of arms.

CARPENTRY, one of the arts subservient to architecture. [vide *Building*]

CARPE'NTUM (*Ant.*) 1. A kind of vehicle which is either a chariot for public conveyance, or a cart for agricultural uses. Ovid derives the name from Carmenta, the mother of Evander.

Ovid. Fast. l. 1, v. 619.

Nam prius Ausonias matres carpenta vehebant
Hæc quoque ab Evandri dicta parente reor.

Liv. l. 1, c. 48; *Apul. Met.* l. 10, 11, &c.; *Pallad. de Re Rust.* l. 10, c. 1; *Tacit. Annal.* l. 12, c. 42; *Sueton. in Cal.* c. 15; *Flor.* l. 3, c. 2; *Ammian.* l. 31, c. 2; *Cassiodor.; Var.* l. 6, c. 15; *Isidor. Orig.* l. 20, c. 12; *Scheff. de Re Vehic.* l. 2, c. 17. 2. A tribunal, or the curule chair of the magistrates. *Vopisc. in Aurel.* c. 1; *Cassiodor.* l. 6, c. 3, &c.; *Justin. Novel.* 70.

CARPENTUM (*Astrol.*) the throne or seat of a planet when set where it has most dignities.

CARPERITA'RIA (*Bot.*) the *Erysimum barbaria* of Linnæus.

CARPE'SIUM (*Bot.*) καρπήσιον, a plant resembling cinnamon in its shoots, and a more powerful antidote than the crocus. *Gal. de Antidot.* l. 1.

CARPESIUM, in the Linnean system, a genus of plants, Class 19 *Syngenesia*, Order 2 *Polygamia superflua*.

Generic Character. CAL. common imbricate; *leaflets* larger. —COR. compound equal; *corollets* hermaphrodites in the disk; *border* quinquefid.—STAM. five; *anthers* cylindric. — PIST. *germ* oblong; *style* simple; *stigma* bifid.— PER. none; *calyx* unchanged; *seeds* obovate; *receptacle* naked.

Species. The two species are the—*Carpesium cernuum*, seu *floribus*, &c. seu *Balsamita*, &c. seu *Aster*, &c. seu *Chrysanthemum*, &c. Drooping Carpesium, a shrub, native of Italy.—*Carpesium abrotanoides*, seu *floribus*, a perennial, native of China.

CA'RPET (*Com.*) a covering for the floor, wrought either with the needle or a loom.

CARPET, *to shave the* (*Man.*) is said of a horse when he gallops close, or near the ground.

CARPET-KNIGHTS (*Polit.*) an epithet applied to persons of peaceful professions, who are raised to the dignity of knighthood.

CA'RPHOS (*Bot.*) the herb *Fænugreek*.

CA'RPHUS (*Med.*) a small pustule. *Aet. Tetrab.* 1, serm. 1.

CA'RPIA (*Med.*) Lint.

CARPI'NUS (*Bot.*) a genus of plants, Class 21 *Monoecia*, Order 8 *Polyandria*.

Generic Character. CAL. ament common.—COR. none.— STAM. *filaments* generally ten; *anthers* didymous.—PIST. *germs* two; *stigmas* simple.—PER. none; *ament* very large; *seed* nut-ovate.

Species. The species are—*Carpinus Betulus*, seu *strobi-

lorum, &c. seu *squamis, &c.* seu *vulgaris, &c.* seu *Astrya, &c.* seu *Fagus, &c.* Horn beam, Hard beam, Horse beech, Horn beech, Wych Hasel, a shrub, a native of Europe.—*Carpinus Americana,* seu *strobilorum, &c.* seu *foliis, &c.* a shrub, a native of Canada.—*Carpinus orientalis,* seu *strobilorum, &c.* seu *strobilis, &c.* seu *duinensis, &c.* a shrub, a native of Carniola.—*Carpinus Ostrya,* Hop Horn beam.—*Carpinus virginiana,* Flowering Horn beam.—*Carpinus duinensis.* Dodon. Pemptad.; Lobel. Adversar.; Clus. Rar. Plant. Hist.; Ger. Herb.; Bauh. Hist. Plant.; Park. Theat. Botan.; Raii Hist. Plant.; Tournef. Instit.

CA'RPIO (*Ich.*) the Carp.

CARPI'SCULUS (*Ant.*) a kind of shoe or slipper. Vopis. in Aurel. c. 30.

CARPOBA'LSAMUM (*Bot.*) from καρπός, fruit, and βαλσάμον, balsam, the fruit of the Balsam tree.

CARPO'BOLUS (*Bot.*) the same as *Lycoperdon.*

CARPOCRA'TIANS (*Ecc.*) a sect of heretics named after Carpocrates, their ring-leader, A. D. 120. They owned one sole principal and father of all things; and that the world was created by angels; but denied the divinity of Christ. Iren. l. 1, c. 24; Clem. Alexand. Strom. l. 3; Tertull. de Præsc. c. 48; Epiphan. Hæres. 47; Baron. Annal. Ann. 120.

CARPODE'TUS (*Bot.*) a genus of plants so called from καρπός, fruit, and δέω, to bind, the fruit being surrounded by a fillet; Class 5 *Pentandria,* Order 1 *Monogynia.*

Generic Characters. CAL. *perianth* turbinate: *teeth* subulate.—COR. *petals* five.—STAM. *filaments* five; *anthers* roundish.—PIST. *germ* inferior; *style* filiform; *stigma* flat-headed.—PER. *berry* dry; *seeds* a few.

Species. The only species is the—*Carpodetus serratus,* a native of New Zealand.

CARPOLI'THI (*Min.*) fossils or stony concretions of any kind which have a resemblance to fruit, from καρπός, fruit, and λίθος, a stone.

CARPOLO'GIA (*Med.*) from *carpo,* to pluck or pull gently; a delirious motion of the hands, usually a fatal symptom in fevers.

CARPOPHY'LLUM (*Bot.*) καρποφύλλον, a kind of laurel.

CA'RPOS (*Bot.*) καρπός, a seed or fruit.

CARP-STONE (*Min.*) vide *Carp.*

CA'RPTOR (*Ant.*) or *Carpus,* a carver, or one who served out the meat at meals, who is called *obsonii magister* by Seneca. Senec. de Vit. beat. c. 17; Petron. c. 36; Juv. sat. 9, v. 110.

CA'RPUS (*Anat.*) καρπός, the wrist.

CARR (*Archæol.*) a kind of cart with wheels.

CA'RRACK (*Mar.*) or *carrick, carrucha,* a ship of great burden, so called from the Italian *carico,* or *carco,* a burden or charge. Stat. 2 R. 2, c. 4.

CARRA'GO (*Ant.*) a barricade, sconce, or camp, made by means of carts and waggons, which it was the practice for the Gauls, and other barbarous nations, to put in the way to prevent the progress of the enemy. Cæs. de Bell. Gall. l. 1, c. 2; Polyæn. Strat. l. 3, c. 10; Curt. l. 9, c. 1; Veget. l. 3, c. 10.

CARRA'RA (*Min.*) a sort of white marble, resembling the Parian marble, but harder, and less bright; so called from the town of Carrara where it was found.

CA'RRAT (*Com.*) vide *Carat.*

CARREA'U (*Mil.*) 1. The ground. 2. A very ancient sort of arrow.

CARREAU (*Mason.*) a square piece of stone, which is broader upon the superficies of a wall than it is within.—*Carreau de plancher,* clay made into different shapes and sizes for the pavements of floors, as flat tiles, &c.—*Carreau de Hollande,* Dutch tile.

CARREA'UX (*Mar.*) the bends or wales of a ship.

CARREFOU'R (*Mil.*) a cross-way.

CA'RREL (*Archæol.*) a closet or apartment for privacy and retirement.

CARRELA'GE (*Mil.*) French for all works made of clay, stone, or marble.

CARRELE'R (*Mason.*) French for to cover over or pave with square tiles.

CARRE'TA (*Archæol.*) a carriage, cart, or wain load, as *carreta fœni,* a load of hay.

CA'RRIAGE (*Husband.*) a channel cut for the conveyance of water to overflow ground.

CARRIAGE of a gun (*Mil.*) the machine upon which it is mounted. Carriages are of different kinds, namely—*Block-carriage,* a carriage which is made from a solid piece of timber, hollowed out so as to receive the gun into the cap-squares.—*Garrison-carriage,* that on which garrison pieces are mounted, which are much shorter than others.—*Travelling-carriage,* such as guns are mounted on for sieges, &c.—*Field-carriage,* a lighter sort of carriage than the preceding, which is adapted to the size of the pieces it carries.—*Gallopper-carriage,* which serves for a 1½-pounder.—*Mountain-carriage,* one constructed for mountainous countries.—*Devil-carriage,* a stouter sort of carriage, with four wheels, used for transporting heavy guns.—*Platform-carriage,* one having a platform to carry both the gun and its carriage.—*Truck-carriage,* which serves for conveying guns and other things on a battery.—*Pontoon-carriage,* one constructed with four wheels, for transporting pontoons.

CARRIAGE *of a wooden stair* (*Carpent.*) the frame of timberwork which supports the steps.

CA'RRICK (*Mar.*) vide *Carrack.*—*Carrick bend,* vide *Bend. Carrick-Bits,* the bits which support the windlass.

CA'RRIER (*Falcon.*) a flight or tour of the bird 120 yards; if it mounts higher it is called a *double career.*

CARRIER (*Orn.*) one of the different varieties of pigeons included under the *Columba domestica* of Linnæus, so called from its capacity to be used in conveying letters or intelligence to distant parts.

CARRIE'RE (*Mil.*) a large spot, intended for tournaments, races, and other exercises.—" *Carriere prendre,*" to commence the full speed at which cavalry charge.

CA'RRIERS (*Com.*) all persons carrying goods for hire, as a master and owners of ships, lightermen, stage-coachmen, &c. come under the denomination of *common* carriers.

CA'RRILON (*Mus.*) a short simple air, adapted to the performance of small bells, or clocks.

CA'RRION *crow* (*Orn.*) the *Corvus corone* of Linnæus, so called from the carcasses on which it feeds.

CARROBALISTA (*Ant.*) a carriage for the *balista,* or other warlike engines.

CARRONA'DE (*Mar.*) in French *carronade,* a short piece of ordnance invented by Mr. Gascoine, and originally made at Carron, a river. It differs from ordnance in general, having no trunnions, and being elevated upon a joint and bolt.

CARROO'N (*Law*) a rent paid for the privilege of driving a carr or cart in the city of London.

CA'RROT (*Bot.*) a well-known fleshy root growing in kitchen gardens, the *Daucus* of Linnæus.—*Candy carrot,* the *Athamanta cretensis* of Linnæus, a perennial.

CA'RROUSEL (*Archæol.*) vide *Carousal.*

CA'RROW (*Polit.*) a sort of itinerants in Ireland, who used to wander up and down to gentlemens' houses, living only by cards and dice; who, though they had little or nothing of their own, would nevertheless play for much money.

CARRU'CA (*Ant.*) a splendid kind of carr or chariot, mounted on four wheels, which were made of brass, of ivory, of silver, and even of gold.
Mart. l. 3, ep. 62.

Aurea quod fundi pretio corruca paratur.

Scævol. Leg. 13, *ff. de aur. et arg.*; *Plin.* l. 33, c. 2; *Lamprid. Alex. Sev.* c. 43; *Ammian.* l. 14, c. 6; *Vopisc. Aurel.* c. 46; *Isidor. Orig.* l. 20, c. 12; *Scheff. de Re Vehic.* l. 2, c. 27.

CARRUCA (*Archæol.*) the former name for a plough

CA'RRUCAGE (*Law*) a duty or tax imposed on every plough; also the ploughing of the ground.

CA'RRUCATE (*Archæol.*) ploughed land; or as much arable land as can be tilled in one year.

TO CARRY away (*Mar.*) *emporter*, to break; as "That ship has carried away her fore-topmast;" i. e. has broken it off. "To carry a bone," is said of a ship that makes the water foam before her.

TO CARRY (*Mil.*) to obtain possession of by force, as "To carry the outworks."

TO CARRY on, to prosecute, or continue, as "To carry on the war."

CARRYING power (*Chem.*) that power by which alone fluids acquire heat.

CARRYING (*Falcon.*) a hawk's flying away with the quarry, which is sometimes the consequence of her not being sufficiently broken to the lure.

CARRYING (*Sport.*) is said of a hare who runs on ground where the soil sticks to her feet.

CARRYING (*Man.*) is applied to a horse either in a good or a bad sense. A horse is said to *carry* well that has his neck raised or arched, and "to *carry* ill," or "to *carry* low," when his neck is ill-shaped, so that he lowers his head too much.—*Carrying wind*, an expression applied to a horse that tosses his head above his ears, and does not carry handsomely. It is distinguished from beating on the hand, because in the first case he only tosses his head, without shaking the bridle, but in the latter case he shakes, and resists the bridle. Carrying in the wind is opposed to carrying low.

CART (*Mech.*) a vehicle mounted on two wheels, and drawn by one or more horses.

CART (*Mil.*) this vehicle is much used in the military service, and is denominated variously according to its use, as *ball-cartridge-cart, powder-cart, hand-cart, trench-cart, tumbril-cart*, &c.; the latter is a cart with two wheels, and square bodies, with a canvass painted top, for the conveyance of ammunition.

CARTE (*Mil.*) 1. A thrust with a sword at the inside of the upper part of the body.—*Low carte*, a thrust at the inside of the lower half of the body. 2. A bill of fare, such as is given at a tavern.—*Carte blanche*, a blank paper sent to a person to fill up with such conditions as he pleases.

CARTE *detaillée d'un pays* (*Geog.*) the correct chart or drawing of a country, so that all the places may be seen at once.

CARTE'L (*Mil.*) 1. An agreement between two states at war for the mutual exchange of prisoners. 2. A challenge to a duel.

CARTEL (*Mar.*) in French *cartel, bâtiment parlementaire*, a ship commissioned in time of war to exchange the prisoners of any two hostile powers, or to carry proposals, &c. from one to another.

CARTE'LLI (*Archæol.*) vide *Cartouse*.

CARTE'SIAN *Philosophy* (*Lit.*) or *Cartesianism*, the system of philosophy advanced by Des Cartes, which is founded on two great principles,—the metaphysical and physical. The metaphysical is: I think, therefore I am, or I exist: the physical is, that nothing exists but substance.

CA'RTHAMUS (*Bot.*) Wild or Bastard Saffron, a genus of plants, Class 19 *Syngenesia*, Order 1 *Polygamia Æqualis. Generic Characters.* CAL. common ovate; *scales* numerous. —COR. *compound* uniform; *corollets* equal; *border* five-parted.—STAM. *filaments* five; *anthers* cylindric.—PIST. *germ* very short; *style* filiform; *stigma* simple.—PER. none; *calyx* converging; *seeds* solitary; *receptacle* flat.

Species. The species are annuals, perennials, or shrubs. Among the annuals are the following—*Carthamus tinctorius*, seu *Cnicus*, Officinal Bastard Saffron, a native of Egypt.—*Carthamus flavescens*, seu *Orientalis*, &c. a native of Armenia.—*Carthamus persicus*, a native of Persia. —*Carthamus dentatus*, seu *Cnicus*, &c. a native of Melita. —*Carthamus lanatus*, seu *Atractylis*, &c. Yellow Distaff Thistle, or Woolly Carthamus.—*Carthamus creticus*, seu *Atractylis*, &c. seu *Cnicus*, &c. Cretan Carthamus, a native of Crete. Among the perennials are the following —*Carthamus pectinatus*, a native of Barbary.—*Carthamus multifidus*, seu *caule*, &c. seu *foliis*, &c. a native of Algiers.—*Carthamus tingitanus*, seu *Carduus*, &c. Tangier Carthamus.—*Carthamus cæruleus*, seu *Cnicus*, &c. Blue flowered Carthamus, or Bastard Saffron, a native of Spain.—*Carthamus Pinnatus*, a native of Barbary.—*Carthamus mitissimus*, &c. *Carthamoides*, seu *Carduncellus*, &c. Small Carthamus, a native of Paris.—*Carthamus Carduncellus*, *Cnicus, Carduncellus*, &c. seu *Eryngium*, &c. Mountain Carthamus, &c. Among the shrubs are the following—*Carthamus Arborescens*, seu *Carthamoides, Cnicus*, &c. a native of Spain.—*Carthamus salicifolius*, seu *caule*, &c. seu *fruticosus*, &c. a native of Madeira.—*Carthamus corymbosus*, seu *Chamæleon*, &c. seu *Carduus*, &c. Corymbed Carthamus, a native of Apulia. *Clus. Hist. Plant. rar.*; *Dod. Pempt.*; *C. Bauh. Pin.*; *Ger. Herb.*; *Park. Theat. Bot.*; *Raii Hist. Plant.*

CARTHU'SIANS (*Ecc.*) in French *chatreux*, an order of monks, founded by Bruno, a canon of Rheims, A. D. 1080. *St. Bernard* ep. 11, 12; *Heliot Hist. des Ord. Monast.* tom. vii, c. 53; *Mir. de l'Orig. de Rel.* l. 2, c. 35; *Sainte Marthe Gall. Christ.*

CARTHUSIAN *Powder* (*Med.*) another name for antimony, which owed its introduction to the Carthusians.

CA'RTILAGE (*Anat.*) χόνδρος, from *caro*, flesh; a cartilage or gristle; a whitish or pearl-coloured substance, which is harder than all other parts, except the bones. *Aristot. Hist. Anim.* l. 1, c. 1; *Ruff. Ephes. de Appell. hum. Corp.* l. 1, c. 35; *Oribas. Med. Coll.* l. 25, c. 1.

CARTILA'GINOUS (*Bot.*) *cartilagineus*; an epithet for a leaf and arillus; *folium cartilagineum*, a leaf, having its edge strengthened by a tough rim; *arillus cartilagineus*, an aril of a firm consistence, and thick.

CARTILAGINOUS (*Ich.*) an epithet for all fish whose muscles are supported by cartilages instead of bones.

CARTILA'GO *ensiformis* (*Anat.*) χόνδρος ξιφοειδὴς, the tip or extremity of the *sternum*, which by Hippocrates is called χόνδρος, in the proper sense. *Gal. de Usu. Part.* l. 6.— *Cartilago innominata*, χόνδρος κρικοειδὴς, the second cartilage of the larynx.—*Cartilago scutiformis*, or *peltalis*, from its resemblance to the *scutum*, or *pelta*, the prominences of which are discernible outwardly in the throat. *Gal. de Usu. Part.* l. 6, 7, &c.; *Gorr. Def. Med.*; *Foes. Œconom. Hippocrat.*; *Castell. Lex. Med.*

CARTOO'N (*Paint.*) in French and Spanish *carton*, pasteboard; a design made on strong paper, to be afterwards calked through, and transferred on the fresh plaster of a wall. The most distinguished performances of this kind are the *cartoons* of *Raphael*, seven of which are now preserved in the palace at Hampton Court. The word is derived from the Italian *cartone* and *carta*, paper, signifying several folds of paper.

CARTO'UCH (*Mil.*) a case of wood, bound about with marline, about three inches thick at bottom, holding about 400 musket balls, besides eight or ten iron balls of about a pound each, to be fired out of a howitzer, for the defence of a pass.

CARTOUCHE (*Mil.*) a charge or cartridge.—*Cartouche infamante*, or *Cartouche jaune*, a discharge given to a soldier in the French army, after having been degraded, punished, and rendered unworthy to carry arms.

CARTOUCHE (*Paint.*) a particular mode of sketching out with a crow's quill and Indian ink.

CARTOUCHES (*Archit.*) or *Cartoozes*, Italian *cartoccio*, a kind of blocks or modillions used in the cornices of wainscotted apartments.

CARTOUCHES (*Mil.*) in the artillery services are made of leather to sling over the shoulder of the gunner.—*Cartouches* are also military passes given to soldiers going on furlough.

CARTOU'SE (*Archæol.*) or *Cartouch*, Italian *cartoccio*, an ornament representing a scroll of paper.

CA'RTRIDGE (*Mil.*) a case of paper, parchment, or flannel, fitted to the bore of the piece, and filled with gunpowder, to expedite the discharge of the piece. Cartridges are of two sorts, namely—*Ball-cartridges*, which are used in firing balls.—*Blank-cartridges*, which are used in firing without ball.—*Cartridge-box*, a case of wood, carried by a soldier, which contains several rounds of Ball and Blank Cartridges.

CARTULA'RIES (*Archæol.*) from *charta*, paper; papers wherein the contracts, sales, exchanges, &c. and other acts belonging to churches and monasteries are collected and preserved, and places where papers and records are kept.

CARTWRIGHTS' *timber* (*Com.*) that which is used by cartwrights and coach-makers.

CARVA (*Bot.*) the *Justicia* of Linnæus.

CA'RUAGE (*Ant.*) or *carvage*, two marks of silver, which was taken of every knight's fee, by Henry III., towards the marriage of his sister Isabella to the emperor.

CARU'CA (*Ant.*) in French *charrue*, a plough; from the old Gallic *carr*, which is the present Irish word for any sort of wheeled carriage: hence *churl* and *carlot*, ploughman and rustic.

CARU'CAGE (*Ant.*) *carucagium*, a tribute imposed on every plough for the public service; and as hidage was a taxation by hides, so carucage was by carucates of land. *Mon. Ang.* tom. i. p. 294.

CARUCA'TA *bovum* (*Archæol.*) a team of oxen for ploughing and drawing of land.

CARUCATA *terræ* (*Ant.*) *carucate* or *carue*, a plough of land; which was formerly declared to be 100 acres, by which the subjects have sometimes been taxed. *Bract.* lib. 2, c. 26.

CARUCATA'RIUS (*Ant.*) he who held lands in carvage, or plough-tenure. *Paroch. Antiq.* p. 354.

CARUE (*Archæol.*) the same as *Caruage*.

CA'RVED-WORK (*Mar.*) in French *la sculpture d'un vaisseau*, the ornaments of a ship wrought by a carver.

CA'RVEL (*Mar.*) a small ship or fly boat.—*Carvel-built*, an epithet for a ship that is built in carvel work.—*Carvelwork*, in French *manière ordinaire de border les vaisseaux*, the common method of planking vessels, in contradistinction to clincher work.

CARVE-OF *land* (*Ant.*) vide *Carucate*.

CA'RVER (*Archæol.*) an officer of the table, whose business it was to cut up the meat and distribute it among the guests; he answered to the *carptor* of the Romans.

CARVER (*Com.*) a cutter of wood into various forms and devices, a very ingenious art, divided into several branches, performed by the chair-carver, the frame-carver, the house-carver, and the ship-carver.

CARUI (*Bot.*) or *carvi*, the *Carum carvi* of Linnæus.

CA'RUIFOLIA (*Bot.*) the *Selinum caruifolia* of Linnæus.

CA'RVIST (*Falcon.*) a hawk in the beginning of the year; so called from its being carried on the fist.

CA'RUM (*Bot.*) Caraway, a plant, the seeds of which are remarkably hot, carminative, and stomachic. *Oribas. Synop.* l. 1, c. 5; *Paul. Ægin.* l. 1, c. 72.

CARUM, *in the Linnean system*, a genus of plants, called *Carui* by Tournefort, Class 5 *Pentandria*, Order 2 *Dygynia*.

Generic Character. CAL. umbel universal; *long rays ten*; *umbel partial crowded*.—COR. *universal* uniform; *petals five*.—STAM. *filaments* five; *anthers* roundish.—PIST. *germ* inferior; *styles* two; *stigmas* simple.—PER. none; *fruit* ovate-oblong; *seeds* two.

Species. The species are—*Carum carui*, seu *caule*, &c. seu *Apium*, &c. seu *Seseli*, &c. seu *Ligusticum*, &c. seu *Carum pratense*, &c. Common Caraway, a biennial, native of Europe.—*Carum simplex*, seu *caule*, &c. native of Siberia. *Dod. Hist. Stirp.*; *Lob. Adver.*; *Ger. Herb.*; *J. Bauh. Hist. Plant.*; *C. Bauh. Pin.*; *Park. Theat. Botan.*; *Raii Hist. Plant.*; *Tournef. Instit. de Re Herb.*; *Boerhaav. Ind.*

CARUM is also the *Æthusa bunices* of Linnæus.

CARU'NCULA (*Anat.*) a diminutive of *caro*, flesh; a caruncle, or small piece of flesh, or what has the appearance of flesh: the *Uvula* is sometimes so called.—*Gal. de Comp. Med. sec. Loc.* l. 6, c. 3.—*Carunculæ cuticulares*, the *Nymphæ*.—*Carunculæ lachrymales*, the same as *Carunculæ oculi*.—*Carunculæ mamillares*, the extremities in the tubes of the nipple.—*Carunculæ myrtiformes*; small caruncles at the entrance of the *Vagina*, formed, or rather discovered, by the rupture of the *Hymen*.—*Carunculæ oculi*, long conoidal glands, red externally, situated in the internal *canthi* of the eyes, before the union of the eyelids.—*Carunculæ papillares*, protuberances in the kidneys and the *Urethræ*.

CA'RUS (*Med.*) vide *Caros*.

CA'RYA (*Bot.*) a walnut, or any nut inclosed in a hard shell. *Theoph.* l. 1, c. 18; *Gal. de Alim. Facult.* l. 2; *Athen. Deipnosophist.* l. 2, c. 12; *Oribas. Med. Coll.* l. 15; *Aet. Tetrab.* 1, serm. 1; *Paul. Æginet.* l. 7, c. 3.

CARYA'TES (*Archit.*) or *Caryatides*, a name given to an order of pillars, which consist of female figures, with their arms cut off, and clothed in a robe down to their feet. Vitruvius says they represented the Caryatidæ, the women of Carya, in Asia, who were carried as slaves into Greece, because their town had favoured the Persians. To perpetuate, therefore, the memory of their disgrace, their figures were made to support the entablatures of buildings. *Vitruv.* l. 1, c. 1.

CARYA'TIC *order* (*Archit.*) an order wherein the entablature is supported by female figures instead of columns.

CA'RYCHUS (*Med.*) καρυχος, an ingredient in one of Myrepsus's antidotes, c. 295.

CARYCI'A (*Med.*) or *Caryce*, καρυκια καρυκη, a costly sort of food prepared by the Lydians, according to Galen. Varinus supposes it to be so called because it was black like boiled walnuts. *Aret. de Acut Morb*, l. 1, c. 2; *Gal. Exeges. Vocab. Hippocrat.*; *Erot. Lex. Hippocrat.*

CARYCOI'DEA (*Med.*) καρυκοειδης, from καρυκη, *caryce*, and ειδος, resemblance; an epithet for any thing resembling blood. *Gal. Exeges. Voc. Hippoc.*

CARYE'DON (*Anat.*) the same as *Alphiledon*.

CARYI'TES (*Bot.*) a name for the female Tithymalus. *Diosc.* l. 4, c. 165.

CA'RYL (*Med.*) a confect made of the flowers of the Corallodendron.

CARYO'CAR (*Bot.*) a genus of plants, Class 13 *Polyandria*, Order 4 *Tetragynia*.

Generic Character. CAL. *perianth* quinquepartite; *divisions* obtuse.—COR. *petals* five.—STAM. *filaments* numerous; *anthers* oblong.—PIST. *germ* globose; *styles* four; *stigmas* obtuse.—PER. *drupe* fleshy; *seeds* nuts four.

Species. The species are shrubs, as the—*Caryocar-nuci-*

ferum, native of Berbices.—*Caryocar butyrosum*, seu *Pekea*, &c. seu *Rhizobolus*, seu *Castanea*, &c. native of Guiana.—*Caryocar tomentosum*, seu *foliis*, &c. seu *Pekea*, &c. native of Guiana.

CARYO'CEO (*Bot.*) a Portuguese name for the fruit of the Palm-tree. *Ray.*

CARYOCO'STINUM (*Med.*) from καρυον, caryophyllus, and κοστος, costus, an electuary; so called from its ingredients.

CA'RYON (*Bot.*) καρυον, a nut. It is also applied to all such fruit as inclose something eatable in a hard shell.—*Caryon basilicon*, the same as *Juglans*.—*Caryon Heracleoton*, a small nut, as a hazle nut or filbert, from Heraclea, in Pontus, whence it was brought into Greece.—*Caryon Lepton*, from λιπτος, small, the same as the preceding.

CARYOPHYLLÆ'US (*Conchol.*) a genus of animals, Class *Vermes*, Order *Intestina*, having a round body, and a mouth dilated and fringed.

CARYOPHYLLA'CEOUS (*Bot.*) *Caryophyllaceus, caryophylleus*, Pink-like; an epithet for a corolla, having petals at the base much elongated, as in *Dianthus Caryophyllus*.

CARYOPHYLLA'STER (*Bot.*) the Dodonea of Linnæus.

CARYOPHYLLA'TA (*Bot.*) a species of the *Anemone* of Linnæus.

CARYOPHYLL'ATUM *Alcohol* (*Med.*) medicated alcohol, that cures the caries according to Heister.

CARYOPHY'LLEÆ (*Bot.*) an order of plants in Linnæus' Fragments of a Natural Method, including such as have pink-like flowers.

CARYOPHY'LLI *aromatici* (*Bot.*) aromatic cloves, the fruit of the *Caryophyllus aromaticus*.

CARYOPHY'LLUM (*Bot.*) or caryophyllus, καρυοφυλλον, καρυοφυλλος, Clove-Tree; the name of a tree which literally signifies the leaf of a nut, to which it bears no resemblance whatever. It is called by the Indians *Calafu*; by the inhabitants of the Mollucca Islands *Cangue*; and by the Greeks Cinnamon. Paulus Ægineta is the first who has described this spice under the name of *Caryophyllum*. *Paul. Æginet. de Re Med.* l. 7, c. 3.

CARYOPHYLLUM, in the Linnean system, the *Sarracenia flava et purpurea*.

CARYOPHYLLODE'NDRON (*Bot.*) the same as the *Caryophyllus*.

CARYOPHY'LLUS (*Bot.*) a genus of plants, Class 13 *Polyandria*, Order 1 *Monogynia*.
Generic Characters. CAL. *perianth* of the fruit superior.—COR. *petals* four.—STAM. *filaments* numerous; *anthers* simple.—PIST. *germ* inferior; *style* simple; *stigma* simple.—PER. oval; *seed* single.
Species. The only species is the—*Caryophyllus aromaticus*, Clove-tree, native of the Moluccas, &c.

CARYOPHYLLUS is also the *Aphylanthes Monspiliensis*.

CA'RYOPOS (*Bot.*) the juice of a kind of nut that grows upon a tree resembling cinnamon. *Plin.* l. 12, c. 28.

CARYO'TA (*Bot.*) καρυοτις, one of the three sorts of palms mentioned by Dioscorides and Pliny. The fruit was as big as a walnut, and was sent gilt, according to Martial, as a new year's gift.
Mart. xen. 24.
Aurea porrigitur Jani caryota Kalendis.
Dioscor. l. 1, c. 148; *Plin.* l. 16, c. 28.

CARYOTA, in the Linnean system, a genus of plants, Class *Cryptogamia*, Order *Palmæ*.
Generic Characters. Male Flowers. CAL. *spathe* universal compound; *spadix* ramose.—COR. tripartite; *petals* lanceolate, concave.—STAM. *filaments* very numerous; *anthers* linear. Female Flowers. CAL. common, with the males.—COR. tripartite; *petals* acuminate.—PIST. *germ* roundish; *style* acuminate; *stigma* simple.—PER. *berry* roundish, unilocular; *seeds* two large, roundish.

Species. The two species are the—*Caryota urens*, Palm. *Indica, Schunda-paria*, seu *Segnaster major*.—*Caryotamitis*

CARYO'TI (*Bot.*) καρυοτοι, from καρυον, a nut; a name for the best dates growing in Syria and Palestine. *Gal. de Al. fac.* l. 2, c. 26.

CARY'PTIS (*Bot.*) a kind of Spurge.

CAS (*Com.*) *Caxa, Cayas, Cache, Casses*, and *Casie*; a small coin, made of lead, mixed with the scum of copper. It is current principally at Java, and some of the neighbouring islands.

CAS *Gangythreb* (*Bot.*) another name for the *Verbena*.

CA'SAMUM (*Bot.*) the same as *Arthanita*.

CASA'QUE (*Mil.*) a kind of coat that does not fit so tight as the common coat.

CASA'VA *Gasava*, or *Gazana*, an East Indian silver coin, and one of the roupies current in the dominions of the Great Mogul.

CASBE'QUE (*Com.*) or *Kabesque*, a small copper coin, current in Persia only; worth about six deniers Tournois.

CA'SCABEL (*Mil.*) the pummel or hindermost round knob at the breech of a great gun.

CASCA'DE (*Mil.*) literally a Water-fall, or cataract; in mining it signifies the several ascents or descents which are made.

CASCANS (*Fort.*) in French *Cas-cans*, holes in the form of wells, serving as entrances to galleries, or giving vent to the enemy's mines.

CASCA'RILLA (*Med.*) a diminutive of the Spanish word *Cascara*, bark; was originally employed to signify Peruvian Bark; but is now applied to the bark of the *Croton Cascarilla* of Linnæus, which is a very excellent tonic.

CASCARILLA (*Bot.*) the *Croton Cascarilla* of Linnæus, which affords a medicinal bark of the same name.

CASCHO'U (*Bot.*) the *Anacardium occidentale* of Linnæus.

CASCHU (*Min.*) the same as *Terra Japonica*.

CASE (*Print.*) an oblong frame of wood, divided off into small partitions or compartments, for the reception of the letter, of which there are two kinds, the upper and the lower-case: the upper contains the capitals, and the lower case the small letters. [vide *Printing*]

CASE (*Mech.*) any outside covering or envelope, which serves to enclose a thing entirely. They are mostly made of wood, slightly put together, to serve a temporary purpose, as packing-cases.—*Case-knife*, a large kitchen knife.—*Case-Hardening*, a method of making the surface of iron so hard as to resist the file. This is mostly effected by putting it into a case of loam, mixed with dried hoofs, salt, vinegar, &c.—*Case of a door*, the wooden frame, in which a door is hung.—*Case Bays*, the joists framed between a pair of girders, in naked flooring.—*Case of a Stair*, the wall by which a stair-case is surrounded.

CASE, action on the (*Law*) an action; so called because the whole cause or case, as much as is in the declaration (except time and place), is set down in the writ.

CASE of Glass (*Com.*) in Normandy, consists of 120 feet.

CASE (*Gram.*) *casus*, an accident of nouns, which consists in a variety of declension, to express the different relations of things. In Latin there are six cases, the Nominative, so called from *nomino*, to name, because we name every thing by it.—*Genitive*, because we thereby express the gender, kind, or description of things to which any thing belongs.—*Dative*, from *do*, to give, because it expresses the giving of one thing to another.—*Accusative*, from *accuso*, because we thereby accuse, or call upon a person or thing.—*Vocative*, from *voco*, to call, because we address any object by it.—*Ablative*, from *ablatus*, taken away, because it denotes taking away from a thing. Cases are moreover divided into direct and oblique; of the former kind is the nominative; and, under the latter, are included the other cases.

TO CASE *a hare* (*Cook.*) to skin it, and take out the bowels.
CASE-SHOT (*Mil.*) or *Canister-Shot*, in French *charge à mitraille*; a species of shell containing a number of small balls enclosed in a round tin case, so prepared as to be shot out of great guns.
CASEAI'CA (*Bot.*) the *Samyda* of Linnæus.
CASED (*Mason.*) an epithet for a wall which is covered with finer materials than what are in the inside; thus, brick walls may be cased with stone, or a finer kind of bricks.
CASED (*Carpent.*) an epithet for sash-frames hollowed to receive and conceal the pulley-weights.
CASEMA'TE (*Fort.*) a vault, or arch of mason-work, in that part of the flank of a bastion, which is next the curtain, made to defend the ditch and the face of the opposite bastion.—*Casemates nouvelles*, arched batteries constructed under all the openings of revetments or ramparts.
CA'SEMENT (*Archit.*) in Italian *casamento*, a part of a window that opens on hinges to let in air. Casements are either single or double. The single consist of only one aperture; the double of two apertures, otherwise called *folding-casements*, or French sashes.
CASE'RNER *une troupe* (*Mil.*) to put a troop into barracks.
CASE'RNES (*Fort.*) 1. Large buildings generally erected between the houses of fortified towns and the rampart for the soldiers of the garrison to live in. 2. Barracks.
CASES or *Reports* (*Law*) are the reports of such cases or causes as have been already determined in courts of law, which are carefully preserved.
CASE-SHOT (*Mil.*) vide *Case*.
CASEUS (*Husband.*) from the Arabic *casah*, milk cheese; the curd of milk separated from the whey, and hardened by a slow heat; said to have been first discovered by Aristæus, a pupil of Chiron.
CASH (*Com.*) the stock of ready money which a merchant, &c. has at his disposal.—*Cash-book*, the book in which an account is kept of the disbursements and receipts of money.
CASHEE'RING (*Mil.*) or *cashiering*, from the French *Casser*, to break; a dishonourable dismissal of an officer or soldier. In extreme cases the dismissal is attended with circumstances of infamy.
CASHE'W (*Bot.*) the name of a tree, called, in the Linnean system, the *Anacardium Occidentale*. The fruit of this tree is a nut called the *Cashew-Nut*, the expressed juice of which is made into a pleasant wine, and the spirit distilled from it is stronger than rum or arrack.
CASHI'ER (*Com.*) one who keeps the cash or the money, which it is his business to receive and pay.—*Cashiers of the bank* are officers who sign the notes that are issued out, and examine and mark them when they are returned for payment.
CASHLITE (*Archæol.*) a mulct or fine.
CA'SHOO (*Bot.*) the gum or juice of the East Indian tree, called the Cashew tree; or the *Anacardium* of Linnæus.
CA'SHOW (*Min.*) the same as *Terra Japonica*.
CA'SIA (*Bot.*) the *Nitraria scoberi* of Linnæus.
CASIBOU (*Bot.*) *Cyprus*, a species of exotic privet.
CA'SING *of timber work* (*Mason.*) the plastering a house over with mortar, and striking it while wet with a corner of a trowel by a ruler to make it resemble the joints of free-stone.
CASINGS (*Husband.*) cow-dung dried for fuel.
CASK (*Com.*) a common name for vessels of divers kinds, in contradistinction to the liquor, or other matter it contains. A cask of sugar contains from eight to eleven hundred weight; a cask of almonds about three hundred weight.
CASK (*Mil.*) or *Casket*, in French *Casque*; the ancient helmet or armour for the head.

CA'SKET (*Mar.*) small strings of sinnet that, in furling, make fast the sails to the yard.
CASLEU (*Chron.*) the tenth month of the Jewish year, answering to part of November and December.
CASMINA'RIS (*Bot.*) or *Casmunar*, the same as *Cassummuniar*.
CASQUE (*Her.*) vide *Helmet*.
CA'SSA (*Anat.*) the same as *Thorax*.
CASSA'DA (*Bot.*) or *Cassava*, the root of the plant called, in the Linnean system, *Jatropha Manihot*, from which Tapioca; and also a sort of bread is made in India. The juice of this root, in its unfermented state, is of a highly deleterious quality.
CASSA'LE *vulnus* (*Med.*) from the Arabic *cassa*, a breast; a wound in the breast.
CA'SSAMUM (*Bot.*) the fruit of the Balsam-tree.
CASSAMUNA'IR (*Bot.*) vide *Cassumuniar*.
CASSA'TA (*Law*) or *cassatum*, called by the Saxons hiбe, by Bede, *familia*; a house with land sufficient to maintain one family.
CASSA'TUM (*Med.*) an epithet for weak, spiritless, and grumous blood in the veins, hindering the passage and motion of good blood. *Parac. Archid*. l. 7; *Sect. de Spec. Diaph.*
CASSA'VA (*Bot.*) the same as *Cassada*.
CASSAWA'RE (*Orn.*) vide *Cassowary*.
CASSE *eau de* (*Chem.*) or *Eau de casse-lunetti*, snow water distilled from the flowers of the Cyanus.
CASSER'OLE (*Cook.*) a loaf stuffed with a farce of pullets, and stewed.
CASSETTE (*Mil.*) a casket; also a privy purse.
CASSI-ASCHER (*Mil.*) the provost-marshal in the Turkish army.
CA'SSIA (*Bot.*) κασσία, or κασία, is frequently mentioned by the ancients among the aromatics, but is not described with any particularity. The cassia used in medicine was the κασσία σύριγξ, *cassia fistula*, answering to our cinnamon; and the κασσία μέλαινα κασία κινα θαρνυνη, the purging cassia. *Theophrast. Hist. Plant*. l. 9, c. 5; *Dioscor*. l. 9, c. 5; *Plin*. l. 12, c. 19; *Gal. de Antidot*. &c.; *Actuar. de Meth. Med.* l. 5, c. 2.
CASSIA, a genus of plants, Class 10 *Decandria*, Order 1 *Monogynia*.
  Generic Characters. CAL. *perianth* pentaphyllous.—COR. *petals* five.—STAM. *filaments* ten; *anthers* sterile.—PIST. *germ* long; *style* very short; *stigma* obtuse; PER. *legume* oblong; *seeds* many.
  Species. The species are annuals, shrubs, or perennials. Among the annuals are the following:—*Cassia diphylla*, Two-leaved Cassia, native of India.—*Cassia absus*, *Senna*, &c. seu *Loto*, Four-leaved Cassia, native of India.—*Cassia Tagera*, seu *Tagera*, native of India.—*Cassia obtusifolia*, seu *Gallinania*, &c. Round-leaved Cassia, native of Cuba.—*Cassia sericea*, *sensitiva*, seu *Paiominoba*, native of Jamaica.—*Cassia calcata*, native of America.—*Cassia Senna*, the Egyptian Cassia or Senna, from which is produced the Senna used in medicine.—*Cassia procumbens*, seu *Chæmacrista*, native of the Indies.—*Cassia flexuosa*, native of Brazil.—*Cassia minima*, &c.; but the—*Cassia dimidiata*, Fine-leaved Cassia, is a biennial. Among the shrubs or perennials are the following:—*Cassia tora*, seu *Galega*, Oval-leaved Cassia, or Wild Senna.—*Cassia sennoides*, native of the East Indies.—*Cassia acuminata*, seu *Apoucouira*, &c. native of Guiana.—*Cassia corymbosa*, native of Bonaria.—*Cassia longisiliqua*, native of America.—*Cassia occidentalis*, seu *Senna*, &c. native of Jamaica.—*Cassia planisiliqua*, native of America.—*Cassia Fistula*, seu *Conna*, Alexandria purging Cassia, Cassia-Stick Tree, or Pudding Pipe Tree, native of India. [vide *Cassia*]—*Cassia patula*, native of the West Indies.—*Cassia lineata*,

a perennial, native of Jamaica.—*Cassia arborescens* seu *foliis*, &c. seu *Wellia Tagera*, a shrub, native of the East Indies.—*Cassia ruseifolia* seu *foliis*, &c. a shrub, native of Madeira.—*Cassia biflora*, &c. Two-flowered Cassia, a shrub, native of America.—*Cassia Chinensis*, a shrub, native of Pekin.—*Cassia multiglandulosa*, a shrub, native of Teneriffe.—*Cassia tomentosa*, native of America.—*Cassia liquestrina*, &c. seu *Vahamensis*, a shrub, native of Virginia.—*Cassia florida*, native of the East Indies.—*Cassia stipulacea*, seu *Pseudo Acacia*, &c. native of Chili.—*Cassia alata*, *Faba*, &c. seu *Hernetica*, &c. native of America.—*Cassia Marilandica*, seu *Narilandica*, &c. a perennial native of Virginia.—*Cassia fastigiata*, a shrub, native of the East Indies.—*Cassia frondosa*, a shrub, native of the West Indies.—*Cassia tenuissima*, seu *Senna*, a shrub, native of Havannah.—*Cassia virgata*, a shrub, native of Jamaica.—*Cassia sophora* seu *foliis*, &c. seu *Senna*, &c. seu *Galegæ*, &c. seu *Gallinaria*, &c. seu *Ponnam Tagera*, native of India.—*Cassia mollis*, seu *Fistula*, &c. a shrub, native of South America.—*Cassia javanica*, a shrub, native of the East Indies.—*Cassia grandis*, seu *Arbor*, &c. a shrub, native of Surinam.—*Cassia nigricans*, a shrub, native of Arabia Felix.—*Cassia polyphylla*, &c. a shrub, native of Porto Rico. *Dod. Pempt.*; *Bauh. Hist. Plant.*; *Prosp. Alpin. Ægypt.*; *Raii Hist. Plant.*

CASSIA-FLOWERS (*Med.*) an officinal name for the flowers of the true cinnamon, the *Laurus cinnamon* of Linnæus. They are aromatic, astringent, and useful in decoctions.

CASSIA'NA (*Bot.*) the same as *Cassine*.

CASSI-A'SCHER (*Mil.*) the provost-marshal in a Turkish army.

CA'SSIBOR (*Bot.*) the same as *Coriandrum*.

CA'SSIDA (*Bot.*) the same as the *Scutellaria* of Linnæus.

CASSIDA (*Ent.*) a genus of animals, Class *Insecta*, Order *Coleoptera*.
Generic Character. *Antennæ* moniliform.—*Thorax* and *Shell* margined.—*Head* concealed under the shield.—*Body* above gibbous.
Species. The species are principally distinguished by their colour.

CASSI'DILL (*Archæol.*) a little sack, purse, or pocket. *Mat. Westm.*

CASSIDO'NA (*Bot.*) or *Strickadore*, a plant called Cast-me-down, or Lavender.

CASSIDO'NY (*Min.*) a mineral, and precious stone, with veins of various colours, of which vases are made.

CASSI'NE (*Archæol.*) a farm house surrounded by a ditch, where a number of soldiers have posted themselves to make a stand against the approaches of an enemy.

CASSINE (*Bot.*) a genus of plants, Class 5 *Pentandria*, Order 3 *Trigynia*.
Generic Characters. CAL. *perianth* quinquepartite.—COR. quinquepartite; *divisions* subovate.—STAM. *filaments* five; *anthers* simple.—PIST. *germ* superior; *style* none; *stigmas* three.—PER. *berry* roundish; *seeds* solitary.
Species. The species are shrubs, as the—*Cassine capensis*, *Celastrus*, *Phillyrea*, seu *Frutex*, &c. Cape Cassine, or Phillyrea, native of the Cape of Good Hope.—*Cassine Colpoon*, seu *Evonymus*, &c. native of the Cape of Good Hope.—*Cassine barbara*, native of the Cape of Good Hope.—*Cassine Maurocenia*, &c. *Maurocenia*, &c. *Frangula*, &c. seu *Cerasus*, &c. native of Æthiopia.—*Cassine Peragua* seu *corymbosa*, &c.

CASSINE is also the *Ilex cassine* of Linnæus.

CASSIOBERRY-BUSH (*Bot.*) the *Viburnum cassionoides*.

CASSIOPEIA (*Astron.*) one of the forty-eight old constellations, near Cepheus, not far from the north pole. The number of stars in this constellation are, according to Ptolemy, thirteen; to Hevelius, thirty-seven; to Tycho, forty-six; and to Flamstead, fifty-five. According to the fables of the Greeks, Cassiopeia, with her husband Cepheus, was placed among the constellations to witness the punishment inflicted on their daughter Andromeda.
Arat. de Apparent. v. 653.

Ἡ δὲ καὶ αὐτὴ παιδὸς ἐπιψύεται εἰδώλοιο
Διιλη Κασσιέπεια.

Manil. Astron. Poet. l. 1, v. 353.

Cepheusque Cassiopeia
In pœnas signata suas.

Cassiopeia was also called, among the Greeks, καθίδρα or θρόνος, a throne, because she is represented as sitting in a chair. *Hipparch. ad Arat.*; *Eratosth. Character.*; *Hygin. Astron. Poet.*; *Ptol. Almag.* l. 7, c. 5; *Bayer. Uranomet.*; *Ricciol. Almagest. nov.* &c. Cassiopeia was distinguished in the year 1572, by the appearance of a new star, which exceeded Jupiter in magnitude, and excited very great attention among astronomers; but it diminished by degrees, and, after the lapse of eighteen months, entirely disappeared.

CASSI'QUE (*Polit.*) or *Cacique*, a chief governor, or sovereign lord of a particular district or country in some parts of America.

CA'SSIS (*Mil.*) a casque or helmet.

CASSITE'RIA (*Min.*) a sort of crystal having an admixture of tin.

CASSI'TERON (*Min.*) tin, or white-lead. *Plin.* l. 34, c. 16.

CA'SSITHA (*Bot.*) the *Cuscuta Europæa* of Linnæus.

CA'SSIUS, *Powder of* (*Chem.*) a beautiful precipitate formed by immersing tin in a solution of gold, or by mixing the nitro-muriates of each metal. It gives the finest ruby colour to gold.

CA'SSOB (*Chem.*) the same as *Alcali*.

CA'SSOCK (*Ecc.*) in French *casaque*, in Latin *casula*, a diminutive of *casa*, a covering of any kind; signified originally a cloak, but is now applied to the vestment worn by clergymen under their gowns.

CASSOLE'TA (*Med.*) a kind of humid suffumigation described by *Marcellus de Præs. Remed.* Form.

CASSONA'DE (*Com.*) *Cassonada*, or *Castonade*, cask sugar, or sugar put into casks or chests after the first purification, but which has not been refined.

CASSOURA'RIUS (*Orn.*) or *Cossoway*, the *Struthio Cassuarius* of Linnæus; an exotic bird of the stork kind, which Dr. Grew, in his Comparative Anatomy, affirms to be without a craw. Like the stork it cannot fly far, but it can run with great swiftness.

CASSOWA'RY (*Orn.*) vide *Cassouarius*.

CA'SSU (*Bot.*) the same as *Acajaiba*.

CA'SSULA (*Ecc.*) the cassock.

CASSUMU'NIAR (*Bot.*) a root which comes from the East Indies. It is moderately heating and astringent, and is recommended as an excellent medicine in nervous and other disorders.

CASSU'THA (*Bot.*) or *Cassuta*, the *Cuscuta Europæa* of Linnæus.

CASSU'VIUM (*Bot.*) the *Anacardium occidentale*.

CA'SSYTA (*Bot.*) a genus of plants, Class 9 *Enneandria*, Order 1 *Monogynia*.
Generic Characters. CAL. *perianth* triphyllous; *leaflets* semiovate.—COR. *petals* three; *nectary* oblong.—STAM. *filaments* nine; *anthers* adjoined to the filaments below the lip.—PIST. *germ* ovate; *style* thickish; *stigma* obtuse.—PER. *receptacle* growing out into a depressed globular drupe; *seed* nut globular.
Species. The species are shrubs, as the—*Cassyta filiformis*, *Volutella*, *Cuscuta*, &c. seu *Acatsia-Valli*, native of India.—*Cassyta corniculata*, seu *Cassutha*, &c. native of the island of Celebes.

CAST (*Mech.*) a term particularly applied to figures, or small statues of bronze.—*Cast*, among founders, is applied to tubes of wax fitted in different parts of a mould of the same matter, which when removed leave room for the admission of the melted metal.—*Cast* also signifies a cylindrical piece of brass used by founders in sand to form a canal, or conduit in their moulds.—*Cast*, among plumbers, is a little brazen funnel at the end of a mould for casting pipes without soldering.

CAST (*Polit.*) or *caste*, a tribe or number of families in India, which are of the same rank or profession; the principal of which are the *Bramins*, the first and most noble; the *Cagas*, or princes, who derive their origin from divers royal families: the *Choutres*, who comprehend all artificers; and the *Paria*, who are the lowest and most contemptible of all, with whom it is disgraceful to have any dealings.

CAST (*Falcon.*) a flight, couple, or set of hawks dismissed from the fist.

TO CAST (*Mar.*) a term used in several sea phrases, as "*Cast* off the lead," the act of once heaving the lead into the sea to ascertain what depth of water there is. "To *cast a point in traverse*," to prick down on a chart the point of the compass that any land bears from you. "To be *cast away*," in French *faire naufrage*, the state of a ship which is lost or wrecked on a lee-shore, bank, rock, &c. "To *cast off*, or to *cast* loose the guns," in French *demarrer les cannons*, to untie them.

TO CAST OFF (*Sport.*) *Let go* or *set loose*, as "to *cast off* the dogs in a chase."

TO CAST *a hawk to the perch* (*Falcon.*) to put her upon it.

CAST IRON (*Chem.*) or *Pig-iron*, Iron when first extracted from its ores.—*White Cast Iron* is extremely hard and brittle, as if composed of a congeries of small crystals.—*Grey* or *Mottled Cast Iron* is softer and less brittle than the last.—*Black Cast Iron*, the most fusible and least cohesive of the three.

CASTANEA (*Bot.*) κάστανα, κάστανα, κάστανα; in the singular κάστανον; the chesnut, or the fruit of the Chesnut-tree, called by Theophrastus *Διὸς βάλανος*, and by others κάστανα τυβοινα, σιωπτινα, and ἄμωτα, from Castanea, a town of Thessaly. *Theophrast. Hist. Plant.* l. 2, c. 18; *Nicand. in Alex.*; *Dioscor.* l. 1, c. 145; *Plin.* l. 15, c. 23; *Gal. de Alim. Fac.* l. 2, c. 38; *Athen.* l. 2; *Orib. Eupor.* l. 1, c. 19; *Aet. Tetrab.* 1, serm. 1; *Ægin.* l. 1, c. 83.

CASTANEA is the *Fagus castanea* and the *Æsculus hippocastanum* of Linnæus.

CASTANETS (*Mus.*) in French *castagnettes*, a sort of snappers which dancers of sarabands tie about their fingers to keep time with when they dance.

CASTELLA (*Ant.*) water-houses in the fields built over conduit heads. *Vitruv.* l. 8, c. 7; *Frontin. de Aqueduct.* c. 2.

CASTELLAIN (*Law*) *castellanus*; the lord, owner, or captain of a castle, and sometimes the constable of a fortified house. *Bract.* l. 5. tract. 2, c. 16; 3 *Ed.* 1, c. 7.

CASTELLAMENT (*Cook.*) a march-pane castle, or the imitation of a castle in confectionery.

CASTELLANO (*Com.*) a piece of money in the West Indies, in value something more than a ducat.

CASTELLANY (*Archæol.*) in French *chatellenie*, the manor appertaining to a castle; the extent of its land and jurisdiction.

CASTELLARIUM (*Law*) or *Castellarii*, the precinct or jurisdiction of a castle. *Mon. Angl.* tom. 2, p. 402.

CASTELLARIUS (*Ant.*) one who had charge of the conduits or water-works, of which mention is made in an epitaph: D. M. CLEMENTI CÆSARUM N. SERVV. CASTELLARIO AQUÆ CLAUDIÆ FECIT CLAUDIA SABBATHIS ET SIBI SUIS. *Reines. Inscript.* class 9; *Spon. Miscel. Erud. Antiq.* sect. 6, p. 233, &c.

CASTELLATED (*Mil.*) in French *entouré*; enclosed within a building of stone, &c.

CASTELLATIO (*Archæol.*) the building a castle.

CASTELLORUM OPERATIO (*Law*) castle-work; or service and labour done by inferior tenants for the building and upholding castles of defence.

CASTERIA (*Ant.*) a house wherein oars and other tackling of ships are laid up.
Plaut. Asin. act. 3, scen. 1, v. 16.

Quin Pol si reposivi remum, sola ego in casteria
Ubi quiesco, omnis familiæ causa consistit tibi.

Non. l. 2, c. 128.

CASTIGATORY (*Law*) an engine of correction, on which a woman, who is indicted for being a common scold, shall be sentenced to be placed. 3 *Inst.* 219.

CASTILLANE (*Com.*) or *Castellan*. 1. A gold coin, current in Spain, worth fourteen rials and sixteen deniers, or three livres and ten sols French money. 2. A weight used in Spain for weighing gold; the hundredth part of a pound Spanish weight.

CASTILLEIA (*Bot.*) a genus of plants, Class 14 *Didynamia*, Order 2 *Angiospermia*.
Generic Characters. CAL. one-leaved; *upper lip* bifid; *lower* none.—COR. monopetalous; *upper lip* very long; *lower* very short.—STAM. *filaments* four; *anthers* twin.—PIST. *germ* superior; *style* filiform; *stigma* simple.—PER. *capsule* ovate; *seeds* numerous, small.
Species. The two species are perennials, as—*Castilleia integrifolia*, native of New Granada.—*Castilleia fissifolia*, native of New Granada.

CASTILLE (*Mil.*) formerly the attack of a tower or castle; also a species of military amusement, in which the combatants threw snow-balls at one another.

CASTING (*Mar.*) in French *abatre*, the motion of falling off, so as to bring the direction of the wind on one side of the ship, which before was right a head.

CASTING (*Metall.*) the operation of running any sort of metal into a mould prepared for that purpose, as the casting of letters, bells, &c.

CASTING is also, among sculptors, the taking of casts or impressions of figures in wax, metal, plaster, and the like.

CASTING *of drapery* (*Paint.*) a free, easy, negligent way of clothing any figures.

CASTING *of timber-work* (*Carpent.*) the same as casing of timber.—*Casting of wood*, the same as warping, when the wood shrinks by reason of moisture, air, drought, &c.

CASTING (*Falcon.*) any thing given to a hawk to purge and cleanse his gorge.

CASTING (*Nat.*) a name for that process in nature by which some animals throw off their skins, horns, or other parts of their body which serve either for ornament or use: thus snakes are said to cast their skins, and deer their horns, when the old fall off to make room for the new.

CASTLE (*Law*) or *Castel*, *Castellum*, a fortress in a town; a principal mansion of a nobleman.—*Castle-ward*, *castle-wardum vel wardum castri*: an imposition laid upon such persons as dwell within a certain compass of any castle, towards the maintenance of such as watch and ward the castle. *Magna Charta*, c. 15. 20; 32 *Hen.* 6, c. 48.—*Castle guard rents* were paid by persons dwelling within the liberty of any castle, for the maintaining of watch and ward within the same. *Stat.* 22 and 23 *Car.* 2, c. 24.

CASTLE (*Mil.*) a close head-piece, so called from its protecting the head as a castle does a town.

CASTLE, *fore* (*Mar.*) in French *gaillard d'avant*, a short deck placed in the fore part of the ship, above the upper deck. It is usually terminated, both before and behind, by a breastwork in vessels of war, the foremost part forming the top of the *beak head*, and the hinder part reaching to the after part of the fore chains.—*Prow-castle*, the rise or elevation of the prow over the uppermost deck towards the mizen.—*Stern-castle*, the whole elevation that ranges on the stern over the last deck, where the officers have their cabins and places of assembly.

CASTLE-LE'OD WATERS (*Chem.*) a mineral water found at Castle-Leod in Ross-shire.

CA'STLES (*Her.*) emblems of grandeur and magnificence, denoting likewise a sanctuary and safety. Castles are commonly represented as treble towered, as " The field is *gules*, three castles triple towered within a double tressure, counterflowry *argent*."

CA'STLING (*Nat.*) the young of any animal brought forth or cast before its time.

CA'STOR (*Zool.*) Beaver, a genus of animals, Class *Mammalia*, Order *Glires*.
Generic Character. Fore-teeth upper truncate.—Grinders four each jaw.—Tail long, depressed.—Clavicles perfect.
Species. The two species of the *Castor*, or Beaver, are the *Castor Fiber*, or Common Beaver, and the *Castor huidobrius*, or the Chilese Beaver.

CASTOR (*Astron.*) 1. One of the twins in the constellation better known by the name of Gemini. [vide *Gemini*] 2. A bright star in this constellation, of the first magnitude, whose latitude for the year 1700 was, according to Hevelius, 10° 4′ 20″ N. and its longitude ♋ 16° 4′ 14″. Its right ascension for 1812 was 110° 38′ 45″; declination 32° 17′ 22″ N. Annual variation in right ascension 57″.83; in declination 7″.1.

CASTOR AND POLLUX (*Met.*) a fiery meteor, which at sea appears sometimes adhering to a part of a ship, in the form of a ball, or even several balls. When one is seen alone it is properly called Helena; but two are called Castor and Pollux, and sometimes Tyndaridæ.

CASTOR (*Med.*) vide *Castoreum*.

CA'STOR-OIL (*Chem.*) the oil extracted from the seed of the *Ricinus communis* of Linnæus.

CASTO'REA (*Nat.*) the Beaver's testicles, from which castor is procured. *Plin.* l. 32, c. 3.

CASTO'REUM (*Med.*) καστόριον, or Castor, a medicine made of the liquor contained in little bags near the beaver's groin, good for convulsions; and used to fortify the head and nervous parts. *Aret. de Curat. acut. Morb.* l. 1, c. 6; *Oribas. Med. Collect.* l. 15; *Aet. Tetrab.* 1, serm. 1; *Trall.* l. 1, c. 13.

CASTOREUM (*Zool.*) a Castor.

CA'STRA (*Ant.*) besides the common signification of camp, also signifies quarters, as *castra hyberna*, winter quarters.

CASTRAMETA'TION (*Mil.*) the art of measuring or tracing out the form of a camp on the ground. [vide *Militia*]

CASTRA'NGULA (*Bot.*) the herb Brown-Wort or Water-Betony.

CASTRA'TION (*Surg.*) the cutting or removing away the testes of any animal.

CASTRATION *of a book* (*Lit.*) the cutting out a leaf or sheet of a book, so as to render it imperfect.

CASTRATUS (*Bot.*) from *castro*, to castrate; an epithet signifying the filament without the anther.

CA'STREL (*Falcon.*) or *Kastrel*, in French *Cesterelle*, a kind of hawk, in shape resembling the Lanner, but in size the Hobby.

CASTRE'NSIS (*Ant.*) an epithet for several things belonging to military service, as—*Castrensis corona*, a garland given to him who first enters the enemy's camp.—*Peculium castrense*, goods in war.—*Comes castrensis*, an officer in the emperor's train during war. *Fest. de Reb. Signif.*; *Tertull. de Coron. Mil.* c. 12; *Ammian.* l. 21, c. 9.

CASTRENSIS (*Med.*) an epithet for some contagious epidemic diseases, especially fevers.

CASTRIA'NI (*Ant.*) soldiers that kept the forts on the Roman frontiers.

CA'SUAL EJECTOR (*Law*) a nominal defendant in cases of ejectment, who continues such until appearance by or for the tenant in possession.

CA'SUALS (*Mil.*) or *Casualties*, a term applied to men that are either dead since they were enlisted, have been discharged, or have deserted.

CA'SUALTY *of wards* (*Law*) the mails and duties due to the superiors in ward-holdings.

CASUALTY (*Min.*) a term among tinners for a strong matter separated from the ore by washing.

CASUARI'NA (*Bot.*) a genus of plants, Class 21 *Monoecia*, Order 1 *Monandria*.
Generic Characters. CAL. common; *ament* loosely imbricate.—COR. *scales* two-parted.—STAM. *filament* capillary; *anthers* twin.—PIST. *germ* minute; *style* filiform; *stigmas* two.—PER. *strobile* of bivalve scales gaping perpendicularly.
Species. The species are shrubs, as the—*Casuarina equisetifolia*, Horsetail Casuarina, native of India.—*Casuarina nodiflora*, native of New Caledonia.—*Casuarina stricta*, Upright Casuarina, native of New Holland.—*Casuarina distyla*, seu *dioica*, &c. native of New Holland.—*Casuarina torulosa*, seu *dioica*, Cork-barked Casuarina, native of New Holland.—*Casuarina Africana*, native of Africa.

CA'SU CONSI'MILI (*Law*) a writ of entry granted where a tenant in courtesy, or a tenant for life, or for the life of another, makes over land in fee or in tail, or for the term of another's life. F. N. B. 206.—*Casu matrimonii prolocuti*, a writ which lies against a man who within a reasonable time refuses to marry a woman.—*Casu proviso*, a writ of entry given by the statute of Gloucester, where a tenant in dower aliens in fee or for life, and it lies for him in reversion against the alienee. *Stat. Gloucest.* c. 7; F. N. B. 205.

CASU'LE (*Ecc.*) vide *Cassock*.

CA'SUS (*Med.*) from *cado*, to fall or happen. 1. The same as *Symptoma*. 2. Any thing fortuitous or spontaneous. 3. A fall from an eminence. 4. According to Paracelsus, a present distemper, as also an entire history of a disease.

CASUS OMISSUS (*Law*) where any particular thing is omitted, and not provided for by the statute.

CAT (*Mar.*) in French *chat*. 1. A ship usually employed in the coal trade, formed after the Norwegian model. 2. Cat, in French *capon*, a sort of strong tackle, used to draw the anchor perpendicularly up to the cat head.—*Cat-block*, in French *poulie de capon*, a block with an iron strap and large hook to it, which serves to draw the anchor up to the cat head.—*Cat-fall*, in French *garant de capon*, the rope that forms the tackle for heaving up the anchor from the water's edge to the bow.—*Cat-harpings*, in French *trélingage des haubans sous la hune*, small ropes serving to brace in the shrouds of the lower masts behind their respective yards.—*Cat-heads*, in French *bossoirs*, two strong beams of timber projecting almost horizontally over the ship's bows on each side the bowsprit.—*Cat-holes*, the holes that are directly over the capstan, which are employed in heaving the ship astern by a cable, or a hawse, called sternfast.—*Cat-hook*, the strong hook fitted to the cat-block.—*Cat-o'-nine-tails*, an instrument of punishment used both in the army and navy, so called because it consists of nine cords knotted at intervals, whence the expression " To comb the cat," to arrange the cords so that they should lie uniform.—*Thieves' cat-o'nine-tails*, knotted harder than the rest, used only in cases of flagrant offence.

CAT

CAT (*Mil.*) *cattus, gattus*, or *cat-house*, a shed used for covering soldiers employed in filling up the ditch, mining the walls, &c.: so called because soldiers lay in wait under it as a cat for its prey.—*Castellated cat*, a cat with crenelles or loop-holes whence the archers could discharge their arrows.

CAT (*Her.*) this animal is borne in coat armour as a symbol of liberty, vigilance, forecast, and courage. The Mountain or Wild Cat is always borne gardant; but the Common Cat is always borne passant, as in the annexed example. "He beareth *argent* three cats passant gardant in pale bar-ways."

CAT-GUT (*Mech.*) vide Catgut.

CAT-MINT (*Bot.*) a plant so called because cats like to eat it. It is the *Nepeta* of Linnæus—*Cat-Pear*, a pear in shape like a hen's egg.—*Cat-Thyme*, a shrub, the stalks of which have a grateful but very powerful scent. It is the *Teucrium marum*.

CAT-SALT (*Min.*) a beautiful granulated kind of common salt, formed out of bittern or leach brine.—*Cat-Salve*, vide *Mica*.—*Cat's-Eye*, a sort of gem found in Siberia, having rings like the onyx, and variable colours like the opal.

CATABA'LAM (*Bot.*) the same as *Ambalam*.

CATABA'PTIST (*Ecc.*) one against, or averse to, baptism.

CATABIBA'SIS (*Med.*) from καταβιβαζω, to cause to descend; an exclusion or expulsion of the humours downwards.

CATABIBA'ZON (*Astron.*) καταβιβαζων, i. e. descending; the south node, or dragon's tail; so called because it goes down exactly against the dragon's tail.

CATABLE'MA (*Med.*) καταβλημα, from καταβαλλω, to place around; the outermost fillet which secures the rest of the bandage. *Hipp. Lib. de Artic. & Gal. Com.*

CATABOLE'NSES (*Ant.*) or *Catabulenses*, a sort of postillions in the time of the Roman and Greek emperors, who acted also as public carriers, and sometimes as sutlers to the army. *Cassiod. Var. l. 3, ep. 10.*

CATABO'LICI SPI'RITUS (*Theol.*) καταβολικοι, evil spirits which throw down the persons they possess, or that come at certain times upon appointment and bargain. *Tertull. de Anim. c. 28.*

CATABULE'NSES (*Ant.*) vide *Catabolenses*.

CATACATHA'RTICS (*Med.*) from κατα and καθαρτικα, medicines which purge downwards.

CATACAU'STIC CURVE (*Catop.*) a curve or crooked line found by joining the points of concourse of several reflected rays: suppose an infinite number of rays A B, A C, A D, &c. proceeding from the radiating point A, and reflected at any given curve B D H, so that the angles of incidence should be equal to those of reflection, then the curve B E G, to which the reflected rays B I, C E, D F, &c. are tangents continually, as in the points I, E, F, &c. is called the *catacaustic*, or *caustic by reflection*; and if the reflected ray I B be produced to K, so that A B = B K, and the curve K L be the evolute of the caustic B E G, beginning at the point K, then the portion of the caustic B E = A C − A B + C E − B I continually.

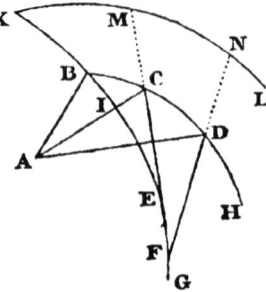

CATACERA'MENUS (*Surg.*) from κατακεραννυμι, splintered or broken into fragments; an epithet for a fracture.

CATACERA'STICOS (*Med.*) κατακεραστικος, the same as *Epicrasticos*.

CATACHLO'OS (*Med.*) καταχλοος, from κατα and χλοα, to make green, a very green colour; an epithet applied to stools, with which *catachola*, very bilious, is synonymous. *Gal. Exeg.*

CATACHRE'SIS (*Rhet.*) καταχρησις, abuse; the same as *Abusio*.

CATACHRE'STICAL (*Rhet.*) καταχρηστικος, abusive; contrary to proper use; far fetched; strained.

CATACHRI'STON (*Med.*) from καταχριω, to anoint; any medicine applied by way of unction.

CATACHY'SIS (*Med.*) καταχυσις, from καταχυω, to pour upon; an affusion.

CATACLA'SIS (*Med.*) κατακλασις, from κατακλαω, to break or distort; breaking, or distortion in general; but particularly that of the eye. *Gal. Exeg. Vocat. Hippoc.*

CATACLE'IS (*Med.*) κατακλεις, from κατα, below, and κλεις, the clavicle, *subclavicle*; the first small rib of the thorax. *Gal. de Ossib. c. 14.*

CATACLI'DA (*Anat.*) another name for the rib called subclavian.

CATACLI'NES (*Med.*) the same as *Clinicus*.

CATACLY'SMA (*Med.*) κατακλυσμα, from κατακλυζω, to wash; the same as Clyster.

CATACLY'SMI (*Med.*) κατακλυσμοι, Embrocations.

CATA'COMBS (*Ant.*) 1. Grottoes, or subterraneous places for the burial of the dead. 2. Divisions in a cellar to stow wine, &c. in

CATACONE'NSIS (*Med.*) from κατακοναω, to irrigate; irrigation by a plentiful affusion of liquor on some part of the body.

CATACO'RES (*Med.*) κατακορης, from κατακεραννυμι, to supersaturate, i. e. full or abundant; an epithet signifying purely or intensely bilious, when applied to stools. *Gal. in Hippocrat. de Rat. Vict. in Morb. Acut.*

CATACOU'STICS (*Mat.*) or *Cataphonics*, the science of reflected sounds; or that part of acoustics which treats of the properties of echoes.

CATACOUSTICS (*Mil.*) are *écoutes*, or small galleries, which communicate with a gallery parallel to the covert way.

CATADIO'PTRICAL Telescope (*Opt.*) the same as *Reflecting Telescope*.

CATADRO'MUS (*Ant.*) καταδρομος. 1. The stadium or place where races were run. *Suet. in Ner. c. 11.* 2. A sort of tight rope on which dancers used to perform their feats. *Suet. in Galba. c. 6; Dio. l. 61; Bud. in Pandect. p. 165.* 3. An engine like a crane, used by builders in lifting up and letting down any great weights.

CATADU'PA (*Nat.*) a sort of cataract in the Nile. *Cic. Som. Scip. c. 5.*

CATÆGIZA'SIS (*Med.*) from καταιγιζω, to repel; a revulsion or rushing back of humours or wind in the intestines.

CATÆONE'NSIS (*Med.*) the same as *Cataconensis*.

CATAFA'LCO (*Archit.*) a decoration on a scaffold of timber for supporting the coffin of a deceased hero, during the funeral solemnity.

CATAGE'MU (*Bot.*) another name for *Gambogia*.

CATAGLY'PHE (*Mech.*) καταγλυφη, from γλυφω, to cut in wood or metal; an excavation, hole, or pit. *Hipp. de Art. et Morb.*

CATA'GMA (*Med.*) καταγμα, from κατα, and αγω, to break, a fracture; the breaking of the bones, or a separation of the continuity of the flesh. *Hippoc. de Art.; Gal. Com.*

CATAGMA'TICA (*Med.*) καταγματικα, from καταγμα, a fracture; remedies for the cure of fractures.

CATAGO'GE (*Med.*) καταγωγη, from καταγω, to bring down; the seat or region of any disease, and the circumjacent part. *Hipp. de Epid. l. 7.*

CATAGRAPH (*Paint.*) καταγραφη, the first draught of a picture. *Plin. l. 35, c. 8.*

CATALE'CTIC verse (*Rhet.*) from καταληγω, to stop or

1

cease; an epithet for a Greek or Latin verse wanting one syllable.

CATALE'NTIA (*Med.*) a kind of Epilepsy, according to Paracelsus. *Paracel. de Morb. Caduc.* l. 1, c. 1, par. 1.

CATALE'PSIS (*Med.*) κατάληψις, from καταλαμβανω, to seize or interrupt; Catalepsy, a species of apoplexy; called by Hippocrates *aphonia*, by Antigenes *anandia*, by Cælius Aurelianus *oppressio* and *apprehensio*. *Hippocrat.* l. 2, aphor. 3; *Gal. de Caus. Puls.* l. 4, c. 16; *Cæl. Aurelian de Acut. Morb.* l. 2, c. 9; *Aet. Tetrab.* 2, serm. 2, c. 4; *Gorr. Def. Med.*; *Foes. Œconom. Hippocrat.*; *Castel. Lex. Med.*

CATA'LLA (*Law*) vide *Catals*.

CATALLIS *captis nomine districtionis* (*Law*) anciently a writ that lay where a house was within a borough, for rent going out of the same; and which warranted the taking of doors, windows, &c. by way of distress of rent. *Vet. Nat. Brev.* 66.—*Catallis reddendis*, an ancient writ which lay where goods, being delivered to any man to keep till a certain day, are not, upon demand, delivered at the day. *Reg. Orig.* 139, *et Vet. Nat. Brev.* 63.

CATALOGUE *raisonné* (*Lit.*) a catalogue or list of works, arranged according to the order of the sciences, in distinction from the common or booksellers' catalogue, which is formed according to the alphabetical arrangement of the authors.

CATALOGUE *of the stars* (*Astron.*) a list of the fixed stars, disposed according to some order, in their several constellations; with the longitudes, latitudes, and right ascensions, &c. of each.

CATALO'NGAY (*Bot.*) the plant which bears the *Faba Sancti Ignatii*.

CATALO'TICA (*Med.*) the same as *Cicatrizantia*.

CATA'LPA (*Bot.*) the *Bignonia catalpa* of Linnæus.

CA'TALS (*Law*) *Catalla*; Goods and Chattels.

CATA'LYSIS (*Med.*) κατάλυσις, from καταλύω, to dissolve or destroy; a paralysis, or such resolution as happens before the death of a patient; also that dissolution which constitutes death.

CATAMARA'N (*Mar.*) in French *radeau servant de bac*, a sort of floating raft, originally used in China, and among the Portuguese, as a fishing boat; small pieces of wood lashed together, one of which serves as a keel, the other two as sides. It is now used at Coromandel, particularly at Madras.

CATAME'NIA (*Med.*) the same as *Menses*.

CA'TAMITE (*Ant.*) *catamitus*, from κατα, for, and μισθος, hire, a boy kept for unnatural practices.

CATANA'NCE (*Bot.*) Candy-lion's-foot.

CATANANCE (*Bot.*) καταναγχη, a plant, mentioned by Dioscorides, which was said to be of an inflammatory nature, and to be used by the Thessalian women in incantations. *Dioscor.* l. 4, c. 133.

CATANANCHE, in the Linnean system, a genus of plants, Class 19 *Syngenesia*, Order 1 *Polygamia Æqualis*.
  Generic Characters. CAL. common imbricate; *leaflets* very many; *squamule* concave.—COR. compound generally imbricate; *corollets* very many; *proper* monopetalous.—STAM. *filaments* five; *anthers* tubular.—PIST. *germ* oblong; *style* filiform; *stigma* bifid.—PER. none; *calyx* unchanged; *seeds* solitary; *receptacle* chaffy.
  Species. The species are perennials, as—*Catananche cærulea, seu squamis, &c. seu Chondrilla, &c.* native of Barbary.—*Catananche exspitosa,* a perennial, native of Atlas. But the—*Catananche lutea, seu Chondrilla, &c. seu Stoebe, &c.* is an annual, native of Crete. *C. Bauh. Pin.*; *Raii Hist. Plant.*; *Tournef. Instit.*

CATA'NTIA (*Med.*) καταντια, the declivity of the members, as of the arms and legs. *Foes. Œconom. Hippocrat.*

CATANTLE'MA (*Med.*) κατανλημα, from καταντλάω, to draw or pour water upon; a kind of lotion by infusion of water.

CATANTLE'SIS (*Med.*) κατάντλησις, from καταντλάω, a lotion with hot water expressed out of sponges, for hot running ulcers of the head. *Marc. Empir.* c. 1.

CATAPA'SMA (*Med.*) or *Catapastum*, from καταπάσσω, to sprinkle upon; a term applied to any dry medicine, reduced to powder, which was fit for inspersion on the human body. *Paul. Æginet.* l. 7, c. 13.

CATAPA'SMUS (*Med.*) καταπασμός, a rubbing of the posterior part of the shoulders and neck downwards, according to Cælius Aurelianus.

CATAPE'LTES (*Med.*) from κατα, against, and πέλτη, a shield; signifies literally a grenado or battery; and is applied to medicines which heal the wounds and bruises made by means of the grenado.

CATAPHI'SMA (*Med.*) a thick poultice of meal and herbs.

CATAPHO'NICS (*Math.*) vide *Catacoustics*.

CATA'PHORA (*Med.*) the same as *Coma*.

CA'TAPHRACT (*Archæol*) a horseman in complete armour.

CATAPHRA'CTA (*Ant.*) a piece of heavy defensive armour with which sometimes only the breast, sometimes the whole body, and the horse also, were covered. *Tacit. Hist.* l. 1, c. 59; *Tertull. de Pall.* c. 4; *Julian.* orat. 1; *Veget.* l. 1, c. 20.

CATAPHRACTA (*Med.*) καταφράκτα, the same as *Quadriga*.

CATAPHRA'CTÆ (*Ant.*) covered ships. [vide *Catastroma*]

CATAPHRACTA'RII (*Ant.*) horsemen in the Roman army armed with the *cataphractæ*. [vide *Cataphracta*] *Lamprid. in Sever.*; *Vopisc. in Aurelian*, &c.

CATAPHRACTI (*Ant.*) καταφρακτοι, an epithet for men armed at all points from top to toe. *Liv.* l. 35, c. 48; *Serv. in Virg. Æn.* l. 11, v. 771; *Propert.* l. 3, eleg. 10; *Lamprid. Alex. Sev.* c. 56; *Amm.* l. 16, c. 10.

CATAPHRA'CTICS (*Med.*) Breast Swaddle; a bandage or ligature for the breast.

CATAPHRA'GMENA (*Ant.*) vide *Catastroma*.

CATAPHRY'GIANS (*Ecc.*) heretics of the second century, and followers of Montanus; so called from their leader who came from Phrygia. *Euseb. Hist. Eccles.* l. 4, c. 27; *Epiphan. Hær.* 47.

CATAPLA'SMA (*Med.*) κατάπλασμα, from καταπλάσσω, to spread like a plaster; a cataplasm or poultice; a soft kind of medicine of which there are different sorts. *Gal. ad Glaucon.* l. 2; *Gorr. Def. Med.*

CATAPLE'XIS (*Med.*) κατάπληξις, from καταπλήσσω, to strike; any sudden stupefaction or deprivation in any of the members or organs. *Hippoc. de Epid.* l. 5, 7, &c.; *Gal. Exeg. Vocab. Hipp.*; *Gorr. Def. Med.*; *Foes. Œconom. Hippocrat.*

CATA'POSIS (*Med.*) κατάποσις, from καταπίνω, to swallow down; deglutition. Hence also

CATAPO'TIUM (*Med.*) a pill. *Hipp. de Epid.* l. 5, &c.

CATA'PPA (*Bot.*) the *Terminalia catappa* of Linnæus.

CATAPSYX'IS (*Med.*) κατάψυξις, from καταψύχω, to refrigerate; a coldness without shivering.

CATAPTO'SIS (*Med.*) κατάπτωσις, from καταπίπτω, to fall down. 1. A falling down, the symptom of apoplexy and epilepsy. 2. The spontaneous falling down of a paralytic limb. *Gal. de tot. Morb. Tempor.* c. 4; *Gorr. Def. Med.*

CATAPU'LTA (*Ant.*) ἀπὸ τῆς πέλτης, i. e. from the pelta, Catapult; a military engine much used by the ancients for throwing huge stones at the enemy. [vide *Militia*] *Plaut. Curc.* act. 5, scen. 3, v. 12,

Te nervo torqueo, itidem ut catapultæ solent.

Diodor. l. 14; *Vitruv.* l. 10, c. 15; *Plin.* l. 7, c. 56; *Ælian. Var. Hist.* l. 6, v. 12; *Plut. Apoth.*; *Lyps. Poliorcet.* l. 3, c. 2.

CATAPU'TIA (*Bot.*) the *Ricinus communis* of Linnæus.

CATARACT (*Geog.*) the fall of water down a rocky precipice in the bed of a river, from κατάρράσσω, to throw down.

CATARACT (*Med.*) from καταρράσσω, to mingle together or put out of order; a disease in the eye; so called because the sense of vision is confounded if not destroyed. It was called by the Greeks ὑπόχυμα and ὑπόχυσις, γλαυκωμα and γλαυκωσις; and was defined a flux of humour about the pupil, which concretes and either wholly intercepts the sight, or renders it dim and obscure; or the concretion of an aqueous humour, which is more or less an impediment to the sight. *Hippocrat.* l. 13, aph. 31; *Gal. Def. Med.*; *Cel.* l. 6, c. 6; *Paul. Æginet.* l. 6, c. 21.

Cataract is now defined to be an affection of the crystalline humour, or its capsule, which becomes so opake, as to prevent the rays of light from passing to the optic nerve. When the opaque lens is much indurated it is termed a *hard cataract*; when the substance of the lens seems to be converted into a whitish, or other kind of fluid, lodged in the capsule, it is denominated a *milky* or *fluid cataract*; when the substance is of a mean consistence neither hard nor soft, but approaching to the consistence of curds, it is named a *soft* or *caseous cataract*. The cataract is moreover divided into incipient and confirmed.—*Incipient cataract* is only suffusion of sight when little clouds, like motes or flies, seem to hover before the eyes.—*Confirmed cataract*, is when the apple of the eye is either wholly, or in part covered, and overspread with a skin, so that the rays of light cannot have admittance to the *retina*.

CATARACT (*Falcon.*) the name of a disease in the eyes of hawks similar to that which affects the human eye.

CATA'RIA (*Bot.*) Cat-mint; the *Hysopus lopanthus* of Linnæus.

CATA'RRH (*Med.*) vide *Catarrhus*.

CATARRHA'LIS *febris amphemerina* (*Med.*) from *catarrhus*, an epithet for a fever which is accompanied with, or proceeds from, a catarrh.

CATARRHE'CTICUS (*Med.*) καταρρηκτικὸς, from ῥήγνυμι, to break; an epithet applied by Hippocrates to substances of a penetrating and dissolving nature, as wine, oxymel, &c. *Hipp. de Rat. Vict. in Acut. Morb.*

CATARRHE'UMA (*Med.*) the same as *Catarrhus*.

CATARRHE'XIS (*Med.*) καταρρηξις, from ῥήγνυμι, to break; a violent and copious eruption and effusion. *Hipp. de Epid.* l. 4, &c. *Catarrhexis*, in Vogel's Nosology, is defined a discharge of pure blood from the intestines, such as takes place in a dysentery.

CATARRHŒ'CUS (*Med.*) καταρροικὸς, from ῥέω, to flow; a word applied to diseases proceeding from distillation of an acrid fluid. *Hippoc.* l. 5, aphor. 24.

CATARRHO'PIA (*Med.*) καταρροπια, from ῥοπα, an inclination; a propensity or inclination downwards, in distinction from *anarrhopia*, or a tendency upwards. *Hippoc. de Humor.*—*Catarrhopia Phymata*, tubercles tending downwards, or, according to Galen, those that have their apex on a depending part. *Gal. Comm. in Hippocrat. de Epid.* l. 6, sect. 1, aph. 12.

CATARRHO'POS *splen* (*Med.*) the spleen verging downwards. *Gal. in Hippocrat. Epid.* l. 6.

CATA'RRHUS (*Med.*) from κάτω and ῥέω, to flow down; signifies, according to Hippocrates and Galen, a distillation or defluxion from the head upon the mouth and *Aspera Arteria*, and through them upon the lungs. *Hippocrat.* l. 7, aph. 38; *Gal. Comm.* 23 *in Prognost.*; *Cels.* l. 2, c. 1; *Cæl. Aurelian de tard Pass.* l. 2, c. 7; *Aet. Tetrab.* l. 2, serm. 3, c. 3; *Marcell. de Medic.* c. 5; *Gorr. Def. Med.*; *Foes. Œconom. Hippocrat.*

Catarrhus, Catarrh, among the moderns, is defined to be a morbid secretion from the mucous membrane of the nose, eyes, throat, mouth, or lungs. It is of two kinds, namely, *catarrhus a frigore*, a common cold in the head; and *catarrhus epidemicus*, or the contagious catarrh, which is better known by the name of the Influenza. It is placed by Cullen as a genus of diseases, under the Class *Pyrexia*, Order *Profluvia*.—*Catarrhus belinsulanus*, seu *Cynanche parotidæa*, the Mumps.—*Catarrhus suffocativus*, seu *Cynanche trachealis*, the Croup.—*Catarrhus spinalis medullæ*, seu *vesicæ*, the Stranguary.

CATASA'RCA (*Med.*) the same as *Anasarca*.

CATASCE'UE (*Ant.*) κατασκευή, a training of the *athletæ*, or wrestlers, preparatory to their entering the lists. *Gal. de San. tuend.* l. 3, c. 2.

CATASCHA'SMOS (*Med.*) κατασχασμός, from σχάζω, to scarify and open a vein; scarification. *Gorr. Def. Med.*; *Foes. Œconom. Hippocrat.*

CATA'SCOPUS (*Ecc.*) an arch-deacon.

CATASI'SIS (*Med.*) κατάσισις, from σιω, to shake; a distention or extension. *Gorr. Def. Med.*; *Foes. Œconom. Hippocrat.*

CATA'STA (*Ant.*) 1. A cage or stall, in which slaves were exposed to sale in the Forum at Rome. *Pers.* sat. 6, v. 76.

—— *ne sit præstantior alter*
Cappadocas rigidâ pingues plausisse catastâ.

Plin. l. 35, c. 18; *Suet. in Grammat.* c. 13; *Schol. in Pers.* 2. A strappado, or some such machine, on which the martyrs used to be tortured. *Prudent. Peristeph.* l. 2, v. 397; *Gest. Mart. S. Marian. et Jacob.*

CATASTA'GMOS (*Med.*) or *Catalagmos*, καταστάγμος, from στάζω, to distil; a name formerly used among the Greeks for a distillation. *Cels.* l. 4, c. 4.

CATASTA'LTICUM (*Med.*) καταςαλτικὸς, from καταςέλλω, to restrain; an epithet signifying styptic, astringent, repressing. *Aet. Tetrab.* 1, serm. 2, c. 230.

CATA'STASIS (*Med.*) κατάστασις, from καθίστημι, to constitute; the constitution of the air or seasons, or the nature of a disease, according to Hippocrates. *Foes. Œconom. Hippocrat.*

CATASTASIS (*Poet.*) the third part of the ancient drama, according to the Greek and Roman models. The catastatis supports, carries on, and heightens the intrigue or action set forth in the Epitasis, till it be ripe for the catastrophe.

CATASTASIS (*Rhet.*) the narration or the narrative part of the orator's speech in which he unfolds the matter in question; and which generally forms the exordium. *Hermog.* περὶ ἰδε. p. 34; *Sopat. Schol. ad Hermog.* p. 19, Ald. tom. ii.; *Apsin. Art. Rhet.* p. 692; *Syrian. ad Hermog.* p. 247.

CATASTE'MA (*Med.*) κατάστημα, the clothing air, motion, and external habit of the body; but by Galen, in his Exegesis, it is explained to signify a leaning or resting upon.

CATA'STOLE (*Med.*) καταςολὴ, is explained by Hippocrates to signify decent dress. *Hippocrat. de Decent. Hab.*; *Foes. Œconom. Hippocrat.*

CATASTRO'MA (*Ant.*) κατάςρωμα, a name for the hatches or decks of a ship on which the men stood to fight. It is sometimes called καταφράγμα; whence the ships were called νῆες πεφραγμέναι ἢ κατάφρακτοι, or covered ships of war, in distinction from the ἄφρακτοι, or the uncovered ships. *Schol. in Thucyd.* l. 7, c. 40; *Gyrald. de Nav.* c. 16; *Scheff. de Mil. Nav.* l. 2. c. 7.

CATA'STROPHE (*Poet.*) καταςροφὴ, the third and last part in the ancient drama, which is called by Aristotle the ἔξοδος. *Aristot. de Poet.* c. 12.

CATATA'SIS (*Med.*) κατάτασις, from κατατείνω, to extend or to place. According to Hippocrates, 1. The extension of a fractured or dislocated limb. 2. The actual replacing it in a proper situation.

CATATO'NUM (*Archæol.*) an epithet for a chapter or capital of a pillar, when it is not of a height proportionate to its breadth.

CATATRI'PSIS (*Med.*) κατάτριψις, from τρίβω, to rub; the attrition or friction of machines, applied by Hippocrates to the organs of the human body.

CATAUDESIS (*Med.*) καταυδησις, vociferation.

CATA'XA (*Mech.*) κατάξα, raw silk, or silk before it is dyed; is so called by Aetius and Actuarius.

CAT-CALL (*Mus.*) or *Cat-pipe*, a harsh sort of pipe that imitates the noise of a cat.

CATCH (*Mar.*) a sort of swift sailing vessel, less than a hoy, that will ride on any sea whatever.

CATCH (*Mus.*) a humourous vocal composition, in which the singers catch up each others' sentences, and give to the words a different sense from that of the original reading.—*Catch-club*, a musical society, who meet together for the purpose of singing catches and glees.

CATCHES (*Mech.*) those parts of a clock, &c. which hold by hooking and catching hold of.

CATCH-FLY (*Bot.*) the *Lychnis visceria* of Linnæus; a plant, having grass-like leaves, and a long stalk, terminated by a cluster of purple flowers. A glutinous liquor exudes from under the leaves that is almost as clammy as birdlime, so that ants and other insects which happen to light upon these places, are fastened to the stalk; whence this plant has the name of Catch-Fly.

CATCHLAND (*Law*) grounds of which it is not known to what parish they belong.—*Catch-pole*, a sheriff's officer.

CATCH-WORD (*Print.*) the last word at the end of a page, and which commences the next.

CATE (*Min.*) a name sometimes given to the *Terra Japonnica* or *Catechu*.

CATECHE'SIS (*Med.*) κατήχησις, from κατηχέω, to instruct by word of mouth; a term used by Hippocrates to signify instruction or directing by word or mouth; whence the terms to catechize and catechetical.

CATECHIST (*Ecc.*) one who, in the early ages of Christianity, was appointed to instruct those who were intended for baptism in the principles of the Christian faith. [vide *Catechumen*]

CATECHU' (*Bot.*) the *Areca catechu* of Linnæus.

CATECHU (*Chem.*) or *Terra Japonica*, a substance obtained, by decoction and evaporation, from a species of Mimosa, which abounds in India. It is of a reddish-brown colour, uniform in texture, brittle and friable, and without smell. There are two kinds of *catechu*: one from Bombay, which has the lightest colour, and a specific gravity of 1·39; and one from Bengal of the colour of chocolate, and the specific gravity 1·28.—*Extractive of catechu*, the catechu washed repeatedly in powder with water till the fluids cease to precipitate gelatine.

CATECHU'MEN (*Ecc.*) κατηχούμενος, one newly instructed and prepared to receive the ordinance of baptism, but not baptized; a novitiate in Christianity. *S. August. Serm. de Tempor.* 116, &c.; *Morin. de Pœnitent.*

CATE'E (*Bot.*) the same as *Acajaiba*.

CATEGORE'MATA (*Log.*) κατηγορήματα, predicables, or predicable terms, which answer to appellatives in grammar. *Porphyr. Isagog.*

CATEGOREMA'TICA *vox* (*Log.*) a categorematical word, or a word which may be predicated, or be the subject of a proposition by itself, as a man, a horse; in distinction from the *Syncategorematica vox*, or part of the subject, as all, every, none.

CATEGO'RICAL (*Log.*) an epithet signifying affirmative or positive, as a categorical proposition, or a categorical syllogism, where all the propositions are affirmatives.

CA'TEGORY (*Log.*) κατηγορια, from κατηγορείν, to predicate; a term signifying predicament, rank, or class, into which Aristotle divides all things logically considered, making ten of these in number; namely, substance, quantity, quality, relation, action, passion, where, when, situation, and habit. *Aristot. de Categ.*

CATEI'A (*Ant.*) a barbed dart, or spear used by the ancient Gauls.

Virg. Æn. l. 7, v. 741.

Teutonico ritu soliti torquere cateiis.

Serv. in Virg.; *Isidor. Orig.* l. 18, c. 7; *Lips. Poliorcet.* l. 4, c. 4.

CATEIA'DION (*Surg.*) κατειάδιον, from κατὰ and ἰά, a blade of grass; a very long instrument which was introduced into the nostrils, in order to provoke an hæmorrhage, in the cure of the *cephalalgia*, or head-ach. *Aret. De curat. Morb. diutum.* l. 1, c. 2.

CATE'LÆ-VEGON (*Bot.*) the *Aristolochia* of Linnæus.

CATELLO'RUM *olium* (*Med.*) from *catulus*, a whelp; olive oil in which young whelps have been boiled until their flesh separates from the bones; to which is added thyme, marjoram, &c.

CATE'LLUS *cinereus* (*Chem.*) a cupel or test, so called from its head resembling that of a dog in shape.

CATE'NA (*Anat.*) a muscle, otherwise called *tibialis anticus*.

CA'TENARY (*Geom.*) from *catena*, a chain; a curve on a crooked line formed by a rope when hanging, between two points of suspension. Suppose a line fixed at the points A and B, then its weight will bend it into the curve, A C B, called the catenary, and if D B 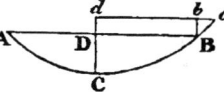 to A B, B *b* parallel to C D, the points, D and *d*, infinitely and *d c* be parallel to the horizon, C D perpendicular near to one another, and *a* be any given quantity, the property of this curve will be as follow; namely, $bc : Bb :: a : CB$.

CATE'NULA (*Bot.*) or *Elator*, vide *Springer*.

CA'TER (*Gam.*) four on cards or dice.—*Cater-point*, the number four.—*Cater-foil*, vide *Quatrefoil*.

CATERER (*Polit.*) from the French *acheter*, to buy; a purveyor, or provider of victuals and other necessaries, in the king's household.

CATE'RGI (*Polit.*) public carriers in the grand seignior's dominions.

CATERPI'LLAR (*Ent.*) the *larva* produced from the egg, and an insect of a moist soft substance without wings, slow in motion, often with numerous feet, sometimes with none, and very voracious of its food; from the *larva* it passes by a *metamorphosis*, or transformation, into the *pupa*, chrysalis, or nymph; and, lastly, it becomes the perfect active insect furnished with *antennæ*.

CATERPILLAR (*Bot.*) a kind of plant resembling caterpillars, which is esteemed for its seed vessels.

CATESBÆ'A (*Bot.*) a genus of plants, Class 4 *Tetrandria*, Order 1 *Monogynia*.

Generic Characters. CAL. *perianth* superior.—COR. monopetalous; *tube* straight; *border* broad.—STAM. *filaments* four; *anthers* oblong.—PIST. *germ* roundish; *style* filiform; *stigma* simple.—PER. berry oval; *seeds* many.

Species. The two species are shrubs, as the—*Catesbæa spinosa*, seu *Frutex spinosus*, Lily-Thorn, native of Providence Island.—*Catesbæa parviflora*, seu *Rhamnus*, &c. native of Jamaica.

CATE-VA'LA (*Bot.*) Common Aloe, or the *Aloe perfoliata* of Linnæus.

CAT-FALL (*Mar.*) vide *Cat*.

CA'T-FISH (*Ich.*) a sea fish in the West Indies, so called from its round head and large glaring eyes.

CA'T-GUT (*Mech.*) a name given to the small strings which are used by different artificers, but particularly musical instrument makers for violins, &c. It is made of the intestines of sheep or lambs.

CATHÆRESIS (*Med.*) καθαίρεσις, from αἱρέω, to take away;

the detraction or subtraction of a part of the body by any evacuation whatever.

CATHÆRETICA (*Med.*) καθαιρετικα, from αιρέω; caustics or remedies which consume superfluous flesh.

CATHA′RIANS (*Ecc.*) or *Cathari*, καθαροι, pure; a title assumed by the Novatians, who pretended to a stricter church discipline than other Christians.

CA′THARISTS (*Ecc.*) a sect of heretics, who were a branch of the Manichees. *August. Hæres.*

CATHA′RMA (*Med.*) καθαρμα, from καθαιρω, to purge; the excrements purged off from any part of the body.

CATHA′RMATA (*Ant.*) καθαρματα, sacrifices to the gods to turn away a pestilence; a victim, or one devoted to be a victim for the purpose of expiation. *Harpocration; Hesychius.*

CATHA′RMOS (*Med.*) καθαρμός, from καθαιρω; purgation by medicines, or the cure of a disorder by superstitious ceremonies or sacrifices.

CA′THAROS (*Med.*) pure or unmixed, as applied to the excrements. *Foes. Œconom. Hippocrat.*

CAT-HARPINGS (*Mar.*) vide *Cat*.

CATHA′RSIS (*Med.*) καθαρσις, a purgation of the excrements either natural or artificial.

CATHA′RTICA (*Med.*) καθαρτικα, from καθαιρω, cathartics; purgative, or purging medicines, which are distinguished, according to their properties, into stimulating, refrigerating, astringent, emollient, and narcotic. *Gal. Com.* 3 *in Hippoc. de Tract.*; *Gorr. Def. Med.*; *Foes. Œconom. Hippocrat.*

CATHA′RTICUS *Sal* (*Med.*) a name for the *Epsom Salts*. — *Catharticus Hispanicus Sal*, a purging salt procured from some springs near Madrid.

CAT-HEAD (*Min.*) a kind of fossil containing nodules with leaves called catheads, which seem to consist of ironstone not unlike that found in the rocks near Whitehaven.

CAT-HEAD (*Mar.*) vide *Cat*.

CATHEAUTO′NPERAS (*Chron.*) καθ' ἑαυτὸν τινας, the month in the beginning of which the winter solstice falls; it is so called by the Macedonians. *Gal. Com. in Hippoc. Epid.* l. 1.

CATHE′DRA (*Archæol.*) a term introduced to denote the pulpit, or the professor's chair; it originally signified any chair.

CATHEDRA (*Med.*) καθέδρη, from καθιζομαι, to sit; the *anus*.

CATHEDRAL (*Ecc.*) the church of the bishop, and head of the diocese.

CATHEDRAL-DU′TY (*Mus.*) a term applied to the duty or service performed by the organist of a cathedral.

CATHEDRA′LITII (*Ant.*) Sedan-men that carry their masters in chairs.

CATHEDRA′TIC *medicines* (*Med.*) from καθαιρω, to destroy; medicines which consume carnosities arising in wounds, as proud flesh, &c.

CATHEDRA′TICUM (*Law*) cathedratic, a sum of two shillings paid by the inferior clergy to the bishop.

CATHEMERI′NA (*Med.*) the same as *Quotidiana Febris*.

CATHEMERI′NOS (*Med.*) the same as *Amphemerinos*.

CATHERE′TICS (*Med.*) the same as *Cathartica*.

CA′THERINE *pear* (*Bot.*) a well-known species of pear.

CATHERINE *wheel* (*Her.*) a sort of wheel, so called from St. Catherine, who suffered martyrdom on such a wheel. It has been occasionally borne in coat armour, and is to be found in the arms of the Turners' Company.

CATHERINE *wheel* (*Archit.*) a large circular ornament in the upper compartment of Gothic windows, filled with a rosette, or radiating divisions.

CATHERINE, *St. Order of* (*Her.*) an order instituted by Catherine, wife of Peter the Great, for ladies of the first quality in the Russian court. The emblems of this order are a red cross supported by a figure of St. Catherine, and the motto *Pro fide et patria*.

CATHERPLUGS (*Mar.*) the same as *Cat-harpings*.

CATHESTE′COS (*Med.*) καθιστικὸς, from καθιστημι, to establish or settle; applied by Hippocrates, in his Aphorisms, to the age of man, and the season of the year; also an epithet for a strict and regular diet, according to Plutarch in his Precepts of Health.

CA′THETER (*Med.*) καθιτηρ, from καθιημι, to introduce; an oblong hollow crooked instrument or tube used in disorders incident to the bladder, called by Celsus *Fistula*. *Cels.* l. 27, c. 6; *Gal. de Meth. Med.* l. 5, c. 5; *Paul. Æginet.* l. 6, c. 59.

CATHETERISMUS (*Med.*) catheterism, the introduction of the catheter into the bladder. *Paul. Æginet.* l. 6, c. 59.

CATHETE′RUS (*Med.*) vide *Catheter*.

CATHE′TI (*Math.*) the two legs of a right angled triangle, including the right angle.

CATHE′TUS (*Geo.*) καθετος, a side, also a perpendicular; a line of a triangle that falls perpendicularly, the bottom being called the base, the other leg the hypothenuse.

CATHETUS *of incidence* (*Catop.*) a right line drawn from a point of the object perpendicular to the reflecting line.—*Cathetus of reflection*, or *of the eye*, a right line drawn from the eye perpendicular to the reflecting line.—*Cathetus of obliquation*, a right line drawn perpendicular to the speculum in the point of incidence or reflection.

CATHETUS (*Archit.*) a line supposed directly to traverse the middle of a cylindrical body, as of a balluster or pillar. *Vitruv.* l. 3, c. 3.—*Cathetus of an Ionic capital*, a line falling perpendicularly and passing through the centre of the volute.

CATHI′DRYSIS (*Med.*) καθιδρυσις, from καθιδρύω, to place together; the reducing of a thing to its proper place.

CATHI′MIA (*Min.*) in the Spagirical language, signifies, 1. A subterraneous mineral vein, whence gold and silver are dug. 2. Concretions in the furnaces of gold and silver. 3. Gold. 4. *Spuma Argenti*. 5. Soot that adheres to the walls in burning of brass.

CA′THMIA *affidia* (*Min.*) 1. The cathimia of silver, which is of the colour of Litharge, i. e. burnt lead. 2. The *spuma auri, æris, et argenti*. There is also the *Cathimia Ferri*.

CA′THODOS (*Med.*) καθοδος, from κατα, downwards; signifies literally descent, and is applied by Hippocrates to the blood which forms the menses. *Foes. Œconom. Hippocrat.*

CATHOLCEUS (*Surg.*) καθολκευς, from κατα and ἑλκιω, to draw over; an oblong fillet which came over the whole bandage of the head, called *periscepastrum*, which it held firm. *Gal. de Fasc.*

CAT-HOLES (*Mar.*) vide *Cat*.

CATHOLIC (*Ecc.*) καθολικὸς, an epithet signifying universal, and applied spiritually to the universal church, which Christ has promised to establish on earth. The Romish church assumes this title to itself as the church which is to be universally established in time. *Euseb.* l. 4; *August. de Ver. Relig.* c. 5, 6.—*Catholic faith*, the fundamental principles of Christianity which are universally admitted by all bearing the name of Christians.

CATHOLIC *fire* (*Chem.*) a little furnace used for all operations, except such as are done by a violent fire.

CATHOLIC *King* (*Polit.*) a title belonging to the King of Spain.

CATHOLICI (*Polit.*) καθολικοι, magistrates with consular dignity, who had charge of the revenues in the provinces under Constantine and his successors. *Euseb.* l. 8, c. 23; *Cajuc. de Jur. Fisc.* l. 5.

CATHO′LICON (*Med.*) or *catholicus*, καθολικος, from κατα and ὅλος, the whole; a general or universal medicine formerly supposed to purge off all bad humours.

CA′THOLICS (*Ecc.*) the prelates patriarchate of Antioch were formerly so called in the time of Justinian.

CATHO′LICUS (*Med.*) the same as *Catholicon*.

CAT-HOOK (*Mar.*) vide *Cat*.

CA′THYGROS (*Med.*) καθυγρος, from κατα and ὑγρὸς, humid,

excessively humid; an epithet applied to the Uterus. Hipp. sect. 6, aph. 62.

CATHY'PNIA (*Med.*) from ὕπνος, sleep; a profound sleep.

CATI (*Com.*) or Cath, 1. A Chinese weight equal to one pound four ounces. It is the only weight at Japan, and is used also at Batavia and other parts of India. 2. A small weight of three grains used by the Eastern lapidaries for weighing emeralds.

CA'TIANG (*Bot.*) the *Dolichos catiang* of Linnæus.

CA'TIAS (*Bot.*) the same as *Ament*.

CATIAS (*Surg.*) κατίας, from καθίημι, to introduce; an incision knife used in extracting a dead fœtus; also in opening an abscess in the uterus. *Paul. l. 6, c. 74.*

CATI'LLIA (*Com.*) a weight of nine ounces.

CATI-MA'RUS (*Bot.*) the *Kleinhora hospita* of Linnæus.

CATI'MIA (*Min.*) the same as *Cadmia*.

CATI'NUM-ALU'MEN (*Chem.*) Pot-ash.

CATI'NUS (*Med.*) the same as *Cupella*.—*Catinus fusorius*, the same as *Crucibulum*.

CATI'SCHON (*Med.*) from κατίσχω, to retain; one who is costive, or not easily purged. *Hippoc. de Epid. l. 6, aph. 8.*

CA'TKIN (*Bot.*) or Catling, the same as *Ament*; so called from its resemblance to a cat's tail. [vide *Ament*]

CA'TLING (*Surg.*) a sort of dismembering knife used in the cutting off any corrupted member or part of the body.

CATLING (*Bot.*) the same as *Catkin*.

CA'TLINGS (*Bot.*) the down or moss growing about walnut-trees resembling the hair of a cat.

CATLINGS (*Mus.*) small cat-gut strings for musical instruments.

CA'TMA (*Min.*) filings of gold.

CA'T-MINT (*Bot.*) vide *Cat*.

CA'T-PURGA'RE (*Med.*) to purge downward.

CATOBLE'CTA (*Zool.*) animals furnished with civet.

CATOBLE'PAS (*Zool.*) or Catoblepon, κατωβλέπων, a wild beast found in Æthiopia, which is fabled to kill like the basilisk, by its look. *Plin. l. 8, c. 21.*

CATOCATHA'RTICA (*Med.*) from κατα, downwards, and καθαίρω, to purge: medicines which operate by stool, in distinction from *anocathartica*, which purge upwards, i. e. emetics.

CATO'CHE (*Med.*) *Catochus*, the same as *Carus*.

CATOCHI'TES (*Min.*) from κατίσχω, to retain; a stone found in Corsica, said to attract and retain the hand when laid upon it. *Plin. l. 37, c. 10.*

CA'TOCHUS (*Med.*) from κατίσχω, to retain; a tetanus or spasmodic affection, in which the body is rigidly held in an upright posture.

CATO'DON (*Zool.*) from κατα, below, and ὀδούς, a tooth; the Spermaceti-Whale, so called because it has teeth only in the lower jaw. It is the *Physeter Catodon* of Linnæus.

CATOECI'DIOS (*Med.*) κατοικίδιος, an epithet signifying domestic, familiar, easy to be made or procured; but applied by Hippocrates to extensions necessary for replacing luxated limbs. *Hipp. de Articul.*; *Foes. Œconom. Hippoc.*

CATŒ'NA DI TRILLI (*Mus.*) a chain or succession of short syllables.

CATOMI'SMOS (*Surg.*) κατωμισμός, from κατα, under, and ὦμος, the shoulder; a method of reducing a luxated humerus. *Æginet. l. 6, c. 114.*

CAT-O'-NINE-TAILS (*Mar.*) vide *Cat*.

CATO'PSIS (*Med.*) from κατόπτομαι, to see with quickness, or acuteness; an acute and quick perception, particularly that acuteness of the faculties which accompanies the latter stages of a consumption.

CATOPSIS (*Opt.*) vide *Catoptrics*.

CATO'PTER (*Med.*) κατοπτήρ, from κατα, through, and ὄπτομαι, to see; the same as *Speculum*.

CATO'PTRICAL CISTULA (*Catop.*) a machine or apparatus by which small things are represented as large; near ones, extremely wide; with other phænomena. It may be made in a variety of different ways to represent different scenes.—*Catoptric dial*, exhibits objects by reflected rays. —*Catoptric telescope*, a telescope which exhibits objects by reflection.

CATO'PTRICS, a branch of the science of optics, which breaks off vision by reflection. [vide *Optics*]

CATO'PTROMANCY (*Ant.*) of κάτοπτρον, a speculum, and μαντεία, divination; a sort of divination among the Greeks, by looking in a mirror which was let down by a thread into a fountain before the temple of Ceres in Achaia. If they saw a ghastly figure in the glass, it was looked upon as a sure sign that the sick person on whose account the ceremony was performed would not recover; but if the image looked fresh, they concluded favourably. *Apul. Met.*

CATO'PTRON (*Catop.*) κάτοπτρον, a kind of optic glass.

CATOPYRI'TES (*Min.*) a kind of precious stone from Cappadocia. *Plin. l. 37, c. 10.*

CATORCHI'TES (*Med.*) κατορχίτης, a sort of wine in which orchis has been infused. *Dioscor. l. 5, c. 41.*

CATORE'TICA (*Med.*) or *catoteretica*, the same as *Purgantia*.

CAT-PEAR (*Bot.*) vide *Cat*.

CAT-PIPE (*Mus.*) the same as *Cat-call*.

CATRICO'NDA (*Bot.*) the *Coix lacryma* of Linnæus.

CAT'S-ROPE (*Mar.*) a rope for hauling up the anchor to the cat-head.

CAT-SILVER (*Min.*) a kind of fossil composed of plates, generally plain and parallel, flexible and elastic. It is of three sorts, the yellow or golden, white or silvery, and the black.

CATS (*Mar.*) vide *Cat-heads*.—*Castellated Cats*, vide *Cat*.

CAT'S-EYE (*Min.*) a stone of a glistening grey with a tinge of green, yellow, or white. It is the *Feldspatum ouelus cati* of Linnæus.

CAT'S-FOOT (*Bot.*) the same as *Ale hoof*, or *Ground Ivy*. —*Cat's-head*, a large sort of apple.—*Cat's-tail*. 1. That which grows in the winter on nut-trees, pine-trees, &c. 2. A kind of reed bearing a spike like the tail of a cat.— *Cat's-tail grass*, a perennial, the *Phleum* of Linnæus.

CAT'S-PAW (*Mar.*) in French *fraicheur*, ou *petit vent sur l'eau*. 1. A light air of wind perceived at a distance in a calm, by the impression made on the surface of the sea. 2. A name for a particular turn made in the bight of a rope, in order to hook a tackle on it.

CA'TTA of Bantam (*Com.*) thin plates of lead on a string, 200 of which make a sata, value 3s. 4d.

CA'T-TAIL (*Bot.*) the same as *Catkin*.

CATTA'RIA (*Bot.*) the same as *Catarea*.

CATTE'E (*Com.*) a weight in Bantam, equal to 1200¼ oz. avoirdupoise; in China, to 16 tail, about 20¼ oz. avoirdupoise; in Japan, to about 2½ oz. avoirdupoise; in Siam, to 26 tail, or 1½ oz. Lisbon; in Sumatra, to 29 oz. avoirdupoise.

CA'TTLE (*Com.*) from *chattel* and *capital*, signifies those quadrupeds which constitute the personal property of a man, and serve for his domestic use. They are distinguished into black cattle, as horses, cows, &c.; horned cattle, as oxen, sheep, &c.; draught cattle, as horses, oxen, &c.

CA'T-THYME (*Bot.*) the *Teucrium marum* of Linnæus. [vide *Cat*]

CATTU-GASTU'RI (*Bot.*) the same as the *Hibiscus*.— *Cattu-shiragam*, a shrub, the seeds of which kill worms. It is the *Conyza* of Linnæus.—*Cattu-tirpali*, the *Piper longum*.

CA'TTY (*Com.*) vide *Cati*.

CATU'LLI-POLA (*Bot.*) the *Pancrateum zeylanicum* of Linnæus.

CATULOTICA (*Med.*) κατυλωτικα, from κατυλόω, to cicatrize; medicines that cicatrize wounds.

CATULUS (*Bot.*) the same as *Julus*.

CATU'RUS (*Bot.*) a genus of plants, Class 22 *Dioecia*, Order 3 *Triandria*.
Generic Characters. CAL. none.—COR. monopetalous; divisions ovate.—STAM. filaments three; anthers roundish.—PIST. germ villose; styles three; stigmas acute.—PER. capsule roundish; seed solitary.
Species. The two species are the—*Caturus spiciflorus*, seu *Acalypha, Watta-Taly*, seu *Cauda, &c.* a shrub, native of the East Indies.—*Caturus scandens*, native of Cochin-China.

CATURUS is also the name of the *Boetsmeria* of Linnæus.

CATUS (*Zool.*) the *Felis catus* of Linnæus.

CATU-TZIE'RU (*Bot.*) the *Limonia* of Linnæus.

CATZU'RUS (*Archæol.*) a hunting horse.

CAVA-VE'NA (*Anat.*) i. e. hollow vein; the largest vein in the body, descending from the heart. It is so named from its large cavity; into which, as into a common channel, all the lesser veins, except the pulmonaris, empty themselves.

CAVÆ'DIUM (*Archit.*) or *cava ædium*, the hall in the midst of a house; or the quadrangle in a college or public building. *Vitruv.* l. 6, c. 3.

CAVA'LAM (*Bot.*) a Malabaric plant, the *Sterculia balangas* of Linnæus.

CAVALCA'DE (*Mil.*) a pompous procession of horses, carriages, &c.

TO CAVALCADE, to skirmish, as horsemen when they march and fire one at another by way of diversion.

CAVALCADOU'R (*Mil.*) a name for the equerry or master of the horse at the court of France.

CAVALI'ER (*Mil.*) a horseman so called, from καβάλλης, and *caballus*, a horse.

CAVALIER (*Man.*) one expert in all the arts of horsemanship.

CAVALIER (*For.*) a work raised within the body of a place ten or twelve feet above the other works. But a French Cavalier, *cavalier de tranchee*, in the attacks, is an elevation which the besiegers make, by means of earth, to enfilade the covert-way.

CAVALI'ERS (*Polit.*) a name for the royalists in the time of Charles I. in distinction from the rebels, contemptuously denominated Round-heads.

CAVA'LLO (*Com.*) a small brass coin in Italy, worth only the 24th part of a penny.

CA'VALRY (*Mil.*) a body of horse.

CAVA'N (*Bot.*) the same as *Cajan*.

CAVAN (*Com.*) a measure, containing fifty Spanish pounds, used in some of the Phillipine islands, especially for measuring rice.

CAVA'TICUS (*Zool.*) an epithet for cockles, or shell-fish that breed in holes.

CAVATI'NA (*Mus.*) a short air without a second part.

CAVA'TION (*Archit.*) digging away the earth for the foundation of a building.

CAVATO'RES (*Ant.*) sculptors of gems.

CAVA'ZION (*Archit.*) vide *Cavation*.

CAUCA'LIS (*Bot.*) καυκαλίς, Bastard Parsley, a plant, so called from the shape of its flower, which resembles καυκίον, a cup; is eaten as a vegetable, and, according to Dioscorides, provokes urine. *Theophrast. Hist. Plant.* l. 7, c. 7; *Dioscor.* l. 2, c. 169; *Plin.* l. 21, c. 15.

CAUCALIS, in the Linnean system, a genus of plants, Class 5 *Pentandria*, Order 2 *Digynia*.
Generic Characters. CAL. umbel universal unequal; umbel partial unequal; involucre universal undivided; involucre partial often five; perianth proper five-toothed.—COR. universal radiate; florets of the disc abortive; proper, one of the disc, male, small; petals unequal.—STAM. in all the flowers; filaments five; anthers small.—PIST. germ, of the ray, oblong; styles two; stigmas two.—PER. fruit ovate oblong; seeds two.
Species. The species are all annuals except the last.—*Caucalis grandiflora*, seu *Echinophora*, &c. Great-flowered Bastard Parsley, native of Europe.—*Caucalis daucoides*, seu *Conium*, &c. seu *Echinophora*, &c. Carrot-leaved Bastard Parsley, native of Germany.—*Caucalis latifolia*, *Tordylium*, *Caucalis arvensis*, *Lappula*, &c. Broad-leaved Bastard Parsley, native of Germany.—*Caucalis Mauritanica*, Barbary Bastard Parsley, native of Mauritania.—*Caucalis pumila*, &c. *Daucus*, *Lappula*, &c. seu *Daucalus*, &c. native of Europe—*Caucalis Africana*, native of the Cape of Good Hope.—*Caucalis leptophylla*, seu *Lappula*, Fine-leaved Bastard Parsley, native of Germany.—*Caucalis platycarpos*, *Lappula*, &c. seu *Echinophora*, native of Gaul.—*Caucalis arvensis*, &c. Corn Bastard Parsley, native of Germany.—*Caucalis anthriscus*, seu *Tordylium*, &c. Hedge Bastard Parsley, native of Europe.—*Caucalis Japonica*, &c. native of Japan.—*Caucalis nodosa*, &c. *Tordylium*, seu *Torilis nodosa*, &c. Knotted Bastard Parsley, native of Carniola.—*Caucalis macrocarpos*, native of Morocco.—*Caucalis Orientalis*, Eastern Bastard Parsley, a biennial. *J. Bauh. Hist. Plant.*; *C. Bauh. Pin.*; *Ger. Herb.*; *Park. Theat. Botan.*; *Raii Hist. Plant.*; *Tournef. Instit.*; *Linn. Spec. Plant.*; &c.

CAUCALIS is also the *Conium Africanum* of Linnæus.

CAUCALO'IDES (*Med.*) καυκαλοειδής, the patella, so called from its supposed similitude to the flower of the Caucus.

CAUCANBARDI'TES (*Ecc.*) a sect of heretics in the sixth century, followers of Severus. *Nicephor.* l. 18, c. 49; *Baron. Annal. Ann.* 535.

CAU'CA (*Ant.*) caucon, or *caucium*, καυκίον, a drinking goblet of wood. *Hieron. in Jovin.* l. 2; *Spart. in Piscen.* c. 10.

CAU'CON (*Bot.*) the herb Horse-tail.

CA'UDA (*Astron.*) the Latin name for tail, is affixed to the names of several constellations, to denote certain stars in their tails, as—*Cauda Capricorni*, a star in the tail of Capricorn, marked γ by Bayer.—*Cauda Ceti*, in the tail of Cetus, marked β.—*Cauda Cygni*, marked α.—*Cauda Delphini*, marked ι.—*Cauda Draconis* [vide *Dragon's tail*].—*Cauda Leonis*, the same as β Leo.—*Cauda Ursæ Majoris*, marked η.—*Cauda Ursæ Minoris*, marked α.

CAUDA (*Bot.*) vide *Tail*.—*Cauda equina*, the same as *Equisetum*.—*Cauda muris*, a species of Ranunculus.—*Cauda porcina*, the same as *Peucedanum*.

CAUDA *Vulpis rubicundi* (*Min.*) Red-Lead.

CAUDA *Terra* (*Law*) a land's end, or the bottom of a ridge in arable land.

CA'UDAL (*Ich.*) an epithet for the fin of a fish which forms its tail. [vide *Ichthyology*]

CAUDA'TIO (*Med.*) from *cauda*, a tail; an elongation of the clitoris.

CAU'DEBEC (*Com.*) a sort of hats (so called from Caudebec, a town in Normandy, where they are principally manufactured) made of lambs' wool, the hair or down of ostriches, or camel's hair.

CAU'DEX (*Bot.*) the trunk or stem of a tree, that part of a tree or shrub between the root and branches. *Theophrast. Hist. Plant.* l. 1, c. 2.
According to Linnæus, the stem is either descending, *caudex descendens*, which terminates in roots; or ascending, *caudex ascendens*, which rises into branches and leaves. *Linn. Phil. Botan.*

CAUDIVE'RBERA (*Zool.*) a species of *Lacerta*.

CAU'DLE (*Med.*) a drink made of milk, ale, wine, eggs, sugar, and spice.

CA'VEA (*Ant.*) the place in the amphitheatre where the wild beasts were kept; frequently, however, the word is applied to the middle, or arena; and sometimes to the whole interior. *Plin.* l. 8, c. 17; *Vopisc. in Prob.* c. 19; *Tertull. contra Mare.* l. 1, c. 27; *Ammian.* l. 29; *Claud. in Cons. Stilich.* l. 2, v. 322; *Salmas. in Vopisc.*

CAVEA (*Palm.*) a hollow in the palm of the hand, in which is a triangle formed by three principal lines—the Cardiac, Cephalic, and Hepatic.

CA'VEAT (*Law*) a kind of process to stop the institution of a clerk to a benefice, or the probate of a will.

CA'VEATING (*Fenc.*) a motion whereby a person, in an instant, brings his sword which was presented to one side of his adversary to the opposite side.

CA'VEDOC (*Com.*) two Persian measures, the first of which is one inch longer than an English yard; the other, which is the shortest, is three-fourths of the longest.

CAVE'RNA (*Anat.*) a cavern; applied to the female *pudenda*.

CAVERNO'SA CORPORA (*Anat.*) two cavernous bodies which principally compose the *penis.*—*Cavernosa clitoris*, two nervous or spongy bodies, like those of the *penis.*—*Cavernosum corpus urethræ*, a third spongeous body of the penis.

CA'VERS (*Min.*) a name among miners for those who steal ore from the mines.

CAVE'SON (*Man.*) a sort of nose-band, either of iron, leather, or wood, fastened round the nose of a horse, to forward the suppling and breaking of the horse.

CAVE'TTO (*Arch.*) an Italian word, from the Latin *cavus*, hollow; signifying a concave moulding, the curvature of whose section does not exceed the quadrant of a circle, as A B in the annexed figure. It is the reverse of the *ovolo*, or quarter-round, and is sometimes used in cornices, pedestals, and the like.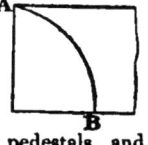

CAUF (*Com.*) a chest with holes at the top, to keep fish alive in the water.

CA'VIA (*Zool.*) a genus of animals, Class *Mammalia*, Order Glires.
Generic Character. Foreteeth two-wedged.—Grinders eight.—Tail short or none.—Clavicles none.
Species. The principal species are the—*Cavia Paca*, Spotted Cavy.—*Cavia aguti*, Long-nosed Cavy.—*Cavia Cobaga*, Guinea Pig.—*Cavia Magellanica*, Patagonian Cavy.—*Cavia Capybari*, River Cavy.

CA'VIÆ (*Ant.*) the part of the sacrifice next the tail. *Fest. de Verb. Signif.*

CAVIA'R (*Com.*) Caveer, or Caviary, the spawn or hard roes of Sturgeon, made into small cakes an inch thick and of a hand's breadth. These are salted and dried in the sun, and in that state are sold as an eatable in Italy and Russia, where they are held in great esteem.

CAVIA'RES HOSTIÆ (*Ant.*) parts of beasts next the tail, to be offered every year for the college of priests.

CAVI'CULA (*Anat.*) or *Cavilla*, the ancle.

CA'VIL (*Rhet.*) vide *Cavillation.*

CAVILLA'TION (*Rhet.*) or *Cavilling*, the advancing a false argument, knowing it to be fallacious, merely for the sake of obtaining a victory; whence *cavil*, the false argument itself.

CA'VIN (*Mil.*) a natural hollow sufficiently capacious to lodge a body of troops and facilitate their approach to a place.

CAVIN (*Fort.*) French for a hollow way which runs round the works of a fortified place and answers the purpose of a trench.

CA'VITAS INNOMINATA (*Anat.*) from *cavus*, a hollow cavity at the anterior or upper part of the anti-helex.

CA'VITAS (*Anat.*) any large hollow places in the body which form or contain some essential part. They are either—*Great Cavities*, as the head, chest, &c.; or *less*, as the ventricles of the heart, brain, &c.

CAUK (*Min.*) a coarse talcy spar, the *Barytes vulgaris* of Linnæus.

CA'UKER (*Vet.*) the bending or turning up of the heels of the shoes of horses, which serves to prevent them from slipping.

CA'UKING (*Archit.*) the art of dovetailing across.

CAUL (*Anat.*) the vulgar name for the *omentum*.

CAULCEIS (*Law*) ways cased with flints, &c. *Stat.* 6. *H.* 6.

CAU'LDRON (*Mech.*) a large kind of boiling vessel.

CAULE'DON (*Surg.*) from καυλός, a stalk, because it is in the shape of a stalk; a species of fracture when the bone is broken transversely, so as not to cohere.

CAULE'SCENT (*Bot.*) an epithet for a plant, *planta caulescens*, having a stem different from that which produces the flower. It is opposed to *acaulis*, or stemless. *Linn. Phil. Botan.*

CA'ULIAS (*Bot.*) καυλίας, an epithet for that juice of the Silphium which flows from the stalk, in distinction from that which flows from the root, and is called ῥιζίας.

CAULI'COLE (*Archit.*) *cauticula*, from *caulis*, a stalk; a name for the eight small stalks between each of the two rows of leaves in the Corinthian capital. *Vitruv.* l. 4, c. 1.

CAULI'FEROUS PLANTS (*Bot.*) from *caulis*, a stalk, and *fero*, to bear; an epithet for plants which have a true caulis or stalk.

CA'ULIFLOWER (*Bot.*) the finest sort of cabbage; a variety of the *Brassica oleracea* of Linnæus.

CAULIFO'RMIS (*Bot.*) stemlike, an epithet for that part of plants which penetrates under the soil.

CA'ULINE (*Bot.*) an epithet for a leaf: *folium caulinum*, a leaf which is attached immediately to the stem.

CA'ULIS (*Bot.*) from the Greek καυλός, which signifies the stem of a tree, is called in Latin *truncus*, and in English *trunk*; but it is now commonly applied to the stalk or herbaceous stem which lasts but one or two years. [vide *Stalk, Stem*]

CAULK (*Mar.*) vide *Calk*.

CAULO'DES (*Bot.*) καυλώδης, a kind of broad-leaved Colewort.

CAULO'TON (*Bot.*) an epithet for the *Beta*, Beet.

CA'ULPES (*Law*) vide *Caupes*.

CA'UMA (*Med.*) καῦμα, from καίω, to burn; any violent heat.

CA'UNGA (*Bot.*) another name for the *Areca*.

CA'UNIÆ (*Bot.*) a kind of figs, so called because they were brought from Caunus, a sea-town of Caria. *Plin* l. 15, c. 19.

CA'UPES (*Law*) or *Capes*, any gift given by a man to his patrons during his own lifetime.

CA'UPONATE (*Archæol.*) from *caupo*, to keep; a victualling house.

CAURCI'NES (*Com.*) Caursini, Italians who came into England about the year 1235, calling themselves Pope's merchants. They derive their name, according to Cowel, from Cavisum Cavisi, a town in Lombardy, where they first practised the arts of usury and extortion. *Mat. Paris.* 403.

CAU'SA *matrimonii prælocuti* (*Law*) a writ wherein a woman gives lands in fee simple to a man that he should marry her, and he refuses so to do within a reasonable time.

CAU'SAL *propositions* (*Log.*) propositions connected together by a causal conjunction, as *because, as, since*, &c.

CAU'SALTY (*Min.*) the earth or stony matter separated from the tin ore in the stamping mill.

CA'USAM *nobis significes* (*Law*) a writ directed to a mayor of a town on delay of the performance of his duty, requiring him to show cause why he so delays it.

CAUSA'RII *milites* (*Mil.*) invalids, or soldiers who were dismissed because they were sick or maimed. *Liv.* l. 6, c. 6.

CAUSE (*Phy.*) whatever produces an effect, or that by which any thing is caused to happen. Causes are distinguished into—*Efficient cause*, the only true and proper cause of any thing, in distinction from a secondary cause, or that which is subservient to another cause. In this sense God is the only efficient cause, or the *first cause*, to which all other causes are secondary.—*Necessary cause*, that which is concerned in producing an effect, not by the will of any agent, but by a necessary law of nature, as the sun emitting its rays, or a spring its waters. This may be otherwise termed a *natural cause*.—*Equivocal cause*, that which is of a different kind and denomination from its effect.—*Accidental cause*, that which produces effects incidentally; as, for the sun to kill any person by the force of its rays.

CAUSE (*Log.*) the end for which a thing is. The *Final cause* is that which is the direct end or motive for an action, &c.

CAUSE (*Med.*) that by which any disease is produced: this is called either remote or proximate; the—*Remote, predisponent*, or *antecedent cause*, called by the Greeks προηγυμίνη, is that which changes the body in such a manner as to dispose it for the reception of disease upon the accession of another cause: this consists principally in temperament, plethora, and cacochymy.—*Proximate cause*, otherwise called the *procatarctic cause*, and by the Greeks the προφασίς, is that cause the accession of which to the remote cause excites, and in conjunction with it forms, the disease. Proximate causes are either external or internal, and by Boerhaave are reduced to four classes; namely, the *ingesta*, or things entering the body; *gesta*, things done, as affections of the mind, exercise, &c.; things retained or excreted; and lastly, things applied to the body, as air, vapour, &c.

CA'USEWAY (*Mech.*) or causey, in French *chaussée*, from the Latin *calcetum*, a pathway made of stones and rubbish, signifies any path raised above the level of the ground that is near it, and paved with stones or gravel.

CA'USIA (*Ant.*) καυσία, a hat worn by the kings of Macedonia. *Poll.* l. 10, c. 31; *Plut. in Demet.*; *Plaut. Mil. Glor.* act 4, scen. 2, v. 4.

Facito ut venias huc ornatus ornatu nauclerico,
Causiam habeas ferrugineam.

CAUSI'DICI (*Law*) causides, lawyers, or pleaders of causes.

CA'USIS (*Med.*) καῦσις, from καίω, to burn; another name for *Ambusta*.

CAUSO'DES *febris* (*Med.*) a burning fever.

CAUSO'MA (*Med.*) from καίω, to burn; a burning heat and inflammation. *Gorr. Def. Med.*

CA'USTIC (*Chem.*) an epithet for potash, from its corrosive quality.

CAUSTIC *stone* (*Surg.*) a caustic composition.

CAUSTIC *curve* (*Geom.*) a curve formed by the concourse or coincidence of the rays of light reflected or refracted from some other curve. The former is called the catacaustic curve, and the latter the diacaustic. [vide *Catacaustic, &c.*]

CAUSTIC *Barley* (*Bot.*) the seeds of the *Cevadilla Hispanorum*; so called from their caustic quality.

CA'USTICA (*Med.*) from καίω, to burn; caustics, so called because when applied to any live part of the body they burn it to a hard crust, or eschar: for this reason they are also called escharotic medicines.

CAU'STICUM *Americanum* (*Med.*) the same as *Cevadilla*.—*Causticum commune fortius*, is made by adding five pounds four ounces of quick lime to water of pure kali sixteen pounds.—*Causticum lunare*, the nitrate of silver, is used by surgeons when melted and cast into cylindrical pieces about the size of common slate pencils.—*Causticum opiatum*, opiated caustic.

CA'USUS (*Med.*) καῦσος, from καίω, to burn; a burning fever, one of the continual kind, attended with a burning heat, and most intense thirst.

CAUTE'LA (*Archæol.*) a cautel, caution, or security.

CA'UTER (*Surg.*) καυτήρ, from καίω, to burn; a seering iron to burn a sore with. *Veget.* l. 2, c. 6.

CAUTERISA'TIO (*Med.*) from καυτηριάζω, cauterising.

CAUTE'RIUM (*Med.*) from καίω, to burn; a cautery, or whatever is applied to any live part of the body for the purpose of burning it to a crust. Cauteries are *actual*, as actual fire, and *potential*, i. e. those which have the power of consuming gradually, as Quick-lime, Butter of Antimony, Oil of Vitriol, &c.—*Silver Cautery*, a cautery made of silver, which is accounted the best of the potential kind.

CA'UTING *iron* (*Vet.*) an iron used to sear or burn the parts of a horse that require it.

CA'UTION (*Cus.*) a sum of money paid on matriculation at the university, by way of caution, or security.

CAUTION (*Mil.*) an explanatory address to the soldiers previous to giving the word of command, that they may the better execute the movement required of them.

CAUTIO'NE *admittenda* (*Law*) a writ lying against a bishop who holds an excommunicated person in prison for contempt.

CA'UTIONER (*Law*) a person in the Scotch law who becomes bound for another to the performance of any deed or obligation.

CA'VY (*Com.*) vide *Caviar*.

CA'WK-STONE (*Min.*) a kind of mineral, akin to the white milky mineral juice of lead-mines.

CA'WKING *time* (*Falcon.*) the pairing time of hawks.

CA'XA (*Com.*) another name for *Cash*.

CA'YA (*Law*) a key or water-lock.

CAYA'GIUM (*Law*) a toll or duty paid at keys or wharfs upon the landing of goods.

CAY'ENNITES (*Ecc.*) vide *Cainites*.

CAY'ENNE (*Bot.*) or *Cayenne Pepper*, a powder prepared from several species of the *capsicum*, but particularly the *capsicum minimum*, or Bird Pepper, which is the hottest of all. In this state it was originally imported from Cayenne, a town on the coast of Guayana, from which it took its names. It is now brought from both the Indies, and sometimes the pods are imported in an unprepared state.

CAYMA'RES (*Zool.*) the West Indian crocodile or alligator.

CAYUTA'NA *luzonis* (*Bot.*) another name for the *Fagara Major*.

CAZA'BI (*Bot.*) the same as *Cassada*.

CA'ZEMATE (*Fort.*) vide *Casemate*.

CA'ZERN (*Fort.*) vide *Casern*.

CA'ZIMI (*Astrol.*) the centre of the sun. A planet is said to be in *cazimi* when it is not above 70 degrees distant from the body of the sun.

CEANOTHOS (*Bot.*) the same as the *Carduus*.

CEANO'THUS (*Bot.*) a genus of plants, Class 5 *Pentandria*, Order 1 *Monogynia*.

Generic Characters. CAL. *perianth* one-leaved; *border* five-parted.—COR. *petals* five.—STAM. *filaments* five; *anthers* roundish.—PIST. *germ* superior; *style* cylindric; *stigma* obtuse.—PER. *berry* dry; *seeds* solitary.

Species. The species are shrubs, as—*Ceanothus americanus*, *Celastrus, seu Evonymus*, &c. American Ceanothus, or New Jersey tea, native of Virginia.—*Ceanothus macrocarpus*, native of New Spain.—*Ceanothus asiaticus, seu Grossularia*, Asiatic Ceanothus, a shrub, native of Ceylon.—*Ceanothus africanus, seu Celastrus, seu Ricindes*, &c. native of Æthiopia.—*Ceanothus capsularis*, native of Otaheite.—*Ceanothus microphyllus*, small-leaved Ceanothus, native of North America.—*Ceanothus laniger*, woolly Ceanothus, native of New Holland.—*Ceanothus nitidus*, glossy Ceanothus, native of New Holland.—*Ceanothus globulosus*, Round-headed Ceanothus, native of New Holland.—*Ceanothus reclinatus*, seu *Rhamnus*, native of Jamaica.—*Ceanothus circumscissus*, seu *Rhamnus circumscissus*, native of the East Indies.

CEA'PEGILDE (*Archæol.*) from the Saxon ceap, cattle, and ʒilb, a yielding; a yielding of cattle.

CE'BELL (*Mus.*) a species of air which was frequent in the time of Charles II.

CEBI *Gallinæ* (*Cook.*) the broiled liver of a hen. *Castell. Lex Med.*

CEBIPI'RA *Brasiliensibus* (*Bot.*) a tree growing in Brazil, the bark of which is bitter and astringent.

CE'BRIS (*Ent.*) a division of the genus *Cryptocephalus* of Linnæus, having the lip entire, and palpigerous at the tip.

CE'BUS (*Zool.*) a sort of monkey.

CE'CIS (*Bot.*) κηκίς, from κηκίω, to spring, because it springs suddenly from the oak. A gall of the oak.

C. CLIFF (*Mus.*) is so called because it gives to the two notes on the same line with itself, the letter C standing for their local name.

CECRO'PIA (*Bot.*) a genus of plants, Class 22 *Dioecia*, Order 2 *Diandria*.
  Generic Characters. CAL. *spathe* ovate.—COR. none, unless the scales be called nectaries.—STAM. *filaments* two; *anthers* oblong.—PIST. *germs* many; *styles* solitary; *stigmas* lacerated.—PER. *berry* one-celled; *seed* oblong.
  Species. The species are shrubs, as the—*Cecropia peltata*, seu *Coilotapalus, Ficus, Yaruma*, &c. seu *Ambaiba*, &c. Trumpet-tree, or Snake-wood, native of Jamaica.—*Cecropia palmata*, seu *Ambayba*, native of Brazil.—*Cecropia concolor*, native of Brazil.

CECRY'PHALOS (*Anat.*) κικρυφαλος, from κρύπτω, to hide, signifies properly a net in which women confined their hair; but it is applied to one of the stomachs of ruminating animals.

CE'DAR (*Bot.*) a well-known evergreen of Mount Libanus, the *Pinus cedrus* of Linnæus. It is very like the juniper in its appearance, as also in its heating and astringent quality. The timber of the cedar is said never to decay; for which reason it is used in the building of ships and roofs. It also produces an oil or juice, with which books were anointed to preserve them from being worm-eaten; whence the *Carmina cedro linenda* of Horace, and *cedro digna* of Persius, for things worthy of immortality. There are other trees bearing this name, as—Barbadoes Cedar, the *Cedrela odorata*.—Bermudas Cedar, the *Juniperus Bermudiana*.—Carolina Cedar, the *Juniperus Virginiana*.—Jamaica Cedar, the *Abroma*.—Lycian and Phœnician Cedar, the *Juniperus Lycia et Phœnicia*.—White Cedar, the *Cupressus thyoides*.

CEDI'LLA (*Gram.*) a mark thus (¸) which is put under the French ç, to give it the sound of s.

CE'DMA (*Med.*) from κεδάω, to disperse; the same as *Pudendagra*.

CE'DMATA (*Med.*) κιδματα, inveterate defluxions of humours on the joints, especially that at the hip.

CE'DRA *essentia de* (*Nat.*) the same as *Bergamotte*.

CEDRA'TUS (*Ant.*) cedrated; i. e. anointed with the oil of cedar trees.

CEDRE'LA (*Bot.*) a genus of plants, Class 5 *Pentandria*, Order 1 *Monogynia*.
  Generic Characters. CAL. *perianth* monophyllous.—COR. funnel-form; *tube* bellied below; *petals* obtuse.—STAM. *filaments* five; *anthers* oblong.—PIST. *receptacle* proper, five-cornered; *germ* globular; *style* cylindric; *stigma* headed.—PER. *capsule* superior; *seeds* numerous; *receptacle* woody.
  Species. The only species is—*Cedrela odorata*, seu *Barbadensium*, Barbadoes Bastard Cedar, a shrub, native of South America.

CEDRELA is also the *Sweetenia* of Linnæus.

CEDRELA'TE (*Bot.*) according to Bellonius, from κίδρος, the Cedar, and ἐλάτη, the Fir-Tree; a species of cedar which is said to exceed all other trees in size. *Plin.* l. 24, c. 5.

CE'DRIA (*Bot.*) κιδρία, from κίδρος, the pitch and resin of the great cedar tree. *Dioscor.* l. 1, c. 105; *Plin.* l. 24, c. 5; *Schol. in Nicand. Theriac.*

CEDRI'NUM (*Chem.*) a name for the composition of wax and resin used for ships.

CEDRINUM *vinum* (*Med.*) κίδρινος οἶνος, Cedar wine. It is heating, diuretic, and gently astringent. *Dioscor.* l. 5, c. 45.

CE'DRIS (*Bot.*) κίδρις, the fruit of the great cedar, which, according to Dioscorides, is heating and prejudicial to the stomach. *Dioscor.* l. 2, c. 105; *Plin.* l. 24, c. 5.

CEDRI'TES (*Bot.*) κιδρίτης, a wine in which the resin, distilled from cedar trees, has been steeped. *Dioscor.* l. 5, c. 47.

CE'DRIUM (*Bot.*) κίδριον, the pitch and resin of the great cedar tree with which books and other things were anointed, to preserve them from moths, worms, and rottenness. Bodies were also embalmed in Egypt with this juice. *Theoph. Hist. Plant.* l. 4, c. 2; *Vitruv.* l. 2, c. 9; *Plin.* l. 16, c. 11.

CE'DRO (*Bot.*) the Citron-tree.

CEDRO'MELA (*Bot.*) the fruit of the Citron-tree.

CEDRONE'LLA (*Bot.*) the *Dracocephalum Canariense* of Linnæus.

CEDRO'STIS (*Bot.*) from κίδρος, because it smells like cedar; the *Bigonia alba* of Linnæus. *Plin.* l. 23, c. 1.

CEDRO'TA (*Bot.*) a genus of plants, Class 8 *Octandria*, Order 1 *Monogynia*.
  Generic Characters. CAL. *perianth* one-leaved; *parts* ovate.—COR. none.—STAM. *filaments* eight; *anthers* roundish.—PIST. *germ* superior; *style* short; *stigma* obtuse.
  Species. The two species are the—*Cedrota longifolia*, seu *Aniba*, &c. a shrub, native of Guiana.—*Cedrota guianensis*, seu *Aniba*, &c. a tree, native of Guiana.

CE'DRUS (*Bot.*) κίδρος, the Cedar-tree; so called from *Kedron*, a valley, where it grew in great abundance. It is the *Pinus cedrus* of Linnæus. This tree is remarkable for the durability of its wood, and the oil or resin which it yields, called *cedria* or *cedrium*. [vide Cedar, Cedria, and Cedrium] It is also the *Cedrela odorata*.—*Cedrus cupressus*, the *Juniperus Lycia*.—*Cedrus Americana*, the same as *Tha.*—*Cedrus baccifera Sabina*, the *Juniperus Sabina*.

CE'DUE (*Chem.*) the air.

CE'DUOUS (*Bot.*) from *cædo*, to cut or lop trees; an epithet applied to trees which used to be cut or lopped.

CEGI'NUS (*Astron.*) a name sometimes given to a star, in the left shoulder of Boötes, which is marked γ by Bayer.

CE'IBA (*Bot.*) the same as the *Bombax*.

CE'ILING (*Mar.*) in French *vaigres* or *vaigrage*, the inside planks of ships.

CEILING (*Archit.*) from *cælum*, the sky; the inside of the roof or top of an apartment, in distinction from the surface of a floor. Ceilings are either flat or coved.—*Flat ceilings* are adorned with large compartments, folinges, or figures, which are formed by raising mouldings on the surface, or by depressing the panels within a moulded inclosure. The compartments in octagon ceilings are called *coffers*, and the mode of making such compartments is called *coffering*.—*Coved ceilings* are sometimes concave round the margin, and flat in the middle, or otherwise they are vaulted. When a ceiling is made on the under side of the rafters of a roof, it is said to be *camp-ceiled*.

CEILING (*Carpent.*) a term denoting the lath and plaster at the top of a room, or on the under side of common or ceiling joists; also the joisting, ribbing, or bracketting, for supporting the lath and plaster of the upper surface or ceiling of a room.—*Ceiling-floor*, the joisting and ceiling supported by the beams of the roof.—*Ceiling-joists*, small beams, which are either mortised into the sides of the binding joists, with pulley mortises, or notched upon, and nailed up to, the under sides of the joists.

CEI'NTRE (*Archit.*) French for a wooden arch to build vaults on.

CEI'NTURE (*Archit.*) French for the ring or circle which goes round the top or base of a column.

CEINTURE *militaire* (*Mil.*) French for a broad leathern belt worn round the waist.

CEI'RIÆ (*Med.*) κειρία, flat worms.

CELANDINE (*Bot.*) a perennial, the *Cheledonum* of Linnæus.

CELA'RENT (*Log.*) a syllogism, in the first figure, having the second proposition a universal affirmative, and the other two universal negatives, as

C e   No animals are devoid of sense.
L a   All men are animals : *ergo*
R e NT   No men are devoid of sense.

CELA'STRUS (*Bot.*) a genus of plants, Class 5 *Pentandria*, Order 1 *Monogynia*.
Generic Characters. CAL. *perianth* one-leafed; *divisions* obtuse.—COR. *petals* five.—STAM. *filaments* five; *anthers* very small.—PIST. *germ* very small; *style* subulate; *stigma* obtuse.—PER. *capsule* coloured; *seeds* few.
Species. The species are shrubs, as the—*Celastrus filiformis*, seu *inermis*, &c. Filiform Branch Staff Tree, native of the Cape of Good Hope.—*Celastrus scandens*, seu *inermis*, &c. seu *punctatus*, &c. seu *Evonymoides*, &c. seu *Frutex*, Climbing Staff Tree, native of Canada. *Celastrus paniculatus*, seu *inermis*, &c. native of the East Indies.—*Celastrus procumbens*, &c. Procumbent Staff Tree, a shrub, native of the Cape of Good Hope.—*Celastrus acuminatus*, &c. Acuminate-leaved Staff Tree, native of the Cape of Good Hope.—*Celastrus cassinoides*, &c. Crenated Staff Tree, native of the Canaries.—*Celastrus striatus*, native of Japan.—*Celastrus cernuus*, native of the Cape of Good Hope.—*Celastrus undatus*, native of the Cape of Good Hope.—*Celastrus edulis*, seu *Catha edulis*, native of Arabia Felix.—*Celastrus crenatus*, &c. Notch-leaved Staff Tree, native of the Marqueses islands.—*Celastrus dilatatus*, seu *Envonymoides*, &c. native of Japan.—*Celastrus myrtifoliis*, &c. Myrtle-leaved Staff Tree, native of Virginia.—*Celastrus Maytenus*, seu *Maytenus*, &c. native of Chili.—*Celastrus alatus*, Wing-branched Staff Tree, native of Japan.—*Celastrus linearis*, seu *spinosus*, &c. Linear-leaved Staff Tree, native of the Cape of Good Hope.—*Celastrus integrifolius*, seu *spinosus*, &c. Entire-leaved Staff Tree, native of the Cape of Good Hope.—*Celastrus emarginatus*, seu *Kattanchi Mullu*, native of the East Indies.—*Celastrus phyllacanthus*, &c. native of Senegal.—*Celastrus buxifolius*, seu *Lycium*, Box-leaved Staff Tree, native of Æthiopia.—*Celastrus pyracanthus*, seu *Lycium*, &c. native of Æthiopia.—*Celastrus lucidus*, seu *Euonymus*, Shining Staff Tree, or Small Hottentot Cherry. — *Celastrus angustifolius*, Narrow-leaved Staff Tree, native of the Isle of Bourbon.
CELASTRUS is also the *Cassine Capensis*.

CE'LATURE (*Mech.*) the art of engraving or cutting in metals.

CELA'TUS *aër* (*Chem.*) air stagnating in wells or close buildings, neither warmed by the sun, nor agitated by the wind.

CELDRA (*Com.*) a measure among the Scotch, called by them a chalder; whence our chaldron of Scotch or Newcastle coals.

CE'LE (*Med.*) κήλη, from κηλέω, to swell out; a hernia or rupture of any kind.

CE'LERES (*Ant.*) a body of 300 men, chosen by Romulus to defend him and execute his commands; they were so called from their quickness of dispatch, from κίλης, a horseman, or from *Celer*, the slayer of Remus. *Dionys. Antiq.* l. 2; *Fest. de Verb. Signif.*; *Serv. in Æn.* l. 9, v. 870; *Sigon. de Antiq. Jur. Civ. Roman.* l. 2, c. 3; *Panvin. de Civit. Roman.* c. 3; *Ursat. de Not. Rom. apud Græv. Thesaur. Antiq.* tom. xi, p. 601.

CE'LERI (*Bot.*) or *celery*, the *Æpium dulce*.

CELE'RIAC (*Bot.*) or *turnip rooted celery*, a species of parsley.

CELERRIMI *descensus linea* (*Math.*) the curve of swiftest descent of a natural body.

CELE'RITY (*Phy.*) an affection of motion by which any moveable body runs through a given space in a given time.

CELE'STIAL (*Astron.*) an epithet for what appertains to the heavens, as the *celestial* sphere, the *celestial* globe, and the like.

CELE'STINE (*Min.*) a species of the Strontian salts.

CELE'STINES (*Ecc.*) an order of monks, founded by one Peter, a Samnite, who was afterwards pope, by the name of Celestin V.

CELEUS'MA (*Ant.*) κέλευσμα, a shout of encouragement, which mariners make to one another whilst they are engaged in any work, similar to " Ho up," and such like words, used among sailors in modern times.
Mart. l. 4, ep. 64, v. 21.

Quem nec rumpere nauticum celeusma.

Serv. in Æn. l. 8; *Gloss. Cyrill.*; *Gyrald. de Navig.* c. 16; *Bud. in Pandect.* p. 106; *Scheff. de Mil. Nav.* l. 3, c. 1.

CELE'USTES (*Ant.*) he who shouted the celeusma to the mariners. [vide *Celeusma*]

CE'LIA (*Ant.*) a kind of ale formerly made in Spain. *Plin.* l. 22, c. 25.

CE'LIAC (*Med.*) vide *Cœliac*.

CELIBA'RIS *hasta* (*Ant.*) a spear with which new married women had their hair trussed up. *Fest. de Verb. Signific.*

CELI'COLI (*Ecc.*) vagabonds condemned by the Emperor Honorius, as heathens and heretics, A. D. 408. *Baron. Annal. Ann.* 408.

CELIDO'GRAPHY (*Astron.*) a description of the spots in the sun.

CELI'FOLI (*Bot.*) the same as *Cœlifolium*.

CE'LIS (*Med.*) κηλίς, a spot or any mark upon the skin.

CE'LL (*Archit.*) in Latin *cella*, from *celo*, to conceal; signifies generally any place in which things, *celantur*, may be concealed or kept apart. It is particularly applied to the smaller and more private apartments of a prison, or those of a monastery.

CE'LLA (*Ant.*) 1. A cellar or storehouse in which things were laid up; as *cella vinaria*, a wine-vault or cellar; *cella pomaria*, an apple loft; *cella promptuaria*, a pantry; *cella penuaria*, a garner or storehouse. *Plaut. Amph.* act 1, scen. 1; *Cato de Re Rust.* c. 13; *Vitruv.* l. 1, c. 4; *Columel.* l. 1, c. 6; *Pallad.* l. 1, c. 2; *Tertull. de Resurrect.* c. 27. 2. The chamber underground where the slaves or domestics slept. *Cicer. Anton.* 2, c. 27; *Varr. de Re Rustic.* l. 1, c. 13; *Vitruv.* l. 6, c. 10; *Senec. de Tranquill.* c. 8; *Plin.* l. 36, c. 2; *Suet. in Cal.* c. 57, &c. 3. A private chapel in a temple, or what is now called the chancel of a church, as the *cella Jovis. Liv.* l. 36, c. 41; *Val. Max.* l. 8, c. 15; *Aul. Gell.* l. 7, c. 1. 4. A private apartment in a bath, which was distinguished as the balneum, into *caldaria*, *frigidaria*, and *tepidaria*. 5. A stew or brothel, the doors of which were marked with the name of the prostitutes, whence it is called by Martial *inscripta cella. Juven.* sat. 6, v. 121; *Mart.* l. 11, ep. 46.

CELLS (*Bot.*) *Loculamenta*, the partitions or hollow places in the pericarp, i. e. in the husk or pod of plants, in which the seeds are lodged. According to the number of these cells perianths are called *one-celled, two-celled*, &c.

CELLS (*Anat.*) little bags or bladders, where fat and fluids of different sorts are lodged.

CELLS (*Nat.*) the little compartments in honeycombs, where the young bees and honey are disposed.

CELLA'RIUS (*Ant.*) a slave who acted as butler.

CELLARIUS (*Archæol.*) the butler or cellarman in a monastery.

CELLEPO'RA (*Con.*) a genus of animals, Class *Vermes*, Order *Zoophyl*.
Generic Characters. Animal an hydra or polype.—Coral somewhat membranaceous, composed of cells.
Species. The principal species are the—*Cellepora pumicosa, annulata spongites*, &c.

CELLERA'RIUS (*Archæol.*) the butler in a monastery.

CE'LLULÆ *adiposæ* (*Anat.*) the *loculi*, or little cells, which contain the fat of bodies in good habit.—*Cellulæ intestini coli*, cavities in the intestines.—*Cellulæ mastoideæ*, very irregular cavities in the substance of the mastoid apophysis, which communicate with each other, and have a common opening towards the inside.

CELLULO'SA *membrana* (*Anat.*) the cellular membrane; a membrane of the greatest extent, and of the utmost importance in the human structure, since it connects and penetrates into almost every part. It is of a vascular contexture, and forms innumerable cells, in which the fat is lodged.—*Cellulosa tunica Ruyschii*, the external or the first coat of the intestines.

CELO'SIA (*Bot.*) a genus of plants, Class 5 *Pentandria*, Order 1 *Monogynia*.
Generic Characters. CAL. *perianth* three-leaved; *leaflets* lanceolate.—COR. *petals* five; *nectary* very small.—STAM. *filaments* five; *anthers* versatile.—PIST. *germ* globular; *style* subulate; *stigma* simple.—PER. *capsule* globular; *seeds* few.
Species. The species are mostly annuals, as the—*Celosia argentea, Amaranthus*, seu *Sfiera*, Silvery-spiked Celosia, native of China.—*Celosia albida, &c.* seu *pyramidalis*, native of the East Indies.—*Celosia margaritacea, &c. Amaranthus, &c.* seu *Belutta, &c.* native of Malabar.—*Celosia cristata*, seu *Amaranthus, &c.* Crested Amaranth, or Cock's-comb, native of Asia.—*Celosia nitida*, seu *Amaranthus, &c.* native of the West Indies.—*Celosia coccinea*, seu *Amaranthus, &c.* Scarlet Celosia, or Chinese Cock's-comb, native of India.—*Celosia castrensis*, seu *Amaranthus, &c.* Branched Celosia, or Cock's-comb, native of India.—*Celosia honsoniæ, Illecebrum*, seu *Amaranthoides, &c.* Downy Celosia, native of the East Indies. But the following are perennials or shrubs:—*Celosia corymbosa, &c.* seu *Paronychia, &c.* native of the East Indies.—*Celosia caudata*, seu *Achyranthes, &c.* native of Arabia Felix.—*Celosia virgata*, seu *fruticosa*, a shrub.—*Celosia polygonoides, &c.* a perennial, native of Malabar.

CELOTO'MIA (*Bot.*) from κηλη, a rupture, and τίμνω, to cut; the operation for a hernia.

CE'LSA (*Alch.*) the beating of the life, or the life's blood.

CE'LSIA (*Bot.*) a genus of plants, Class 14 *Didynamia*, Order 2 *Angiospermia*.
Generic Characters. CAL. *perianth* five-parted; *divisions* lanceolate.—COR. monopetalous; *tube* extremely short; *border* flat; *divisions* roundish.—STAM. *filaments* four; *anthers* roundish.—PIST. *germ* roundish; *style* filiform; *stigma* obtuse.—PER. *capsule* roundish; *seeds* very many; *receptacles* solitary.
Species. The species are as follow; namely—*Celsia orientalis, Verbascum*, seu *Blattaria, &c.* Oriental Celsia, an annual, native of Cappadocia.—*Celsia Arcturus*, seu *Verbascum, &c.* Scollop-leaved Celsia, a biennial, native of Crete.—*Celsia coromandelina*, an annual, native of the East Indies.—*Celsia cretica*, seu *Blattaria, &c.* Great-flowered Celsia, a biennial, native of Crete.—*Celsia betonicifolia*, seu *Blattaria, &c.* a biennial, native of Algiers.—*Celsia capensis*, Cape Celsia, a biennial, native of the Cape of Good Hope.

CE'LTIS (*Bot.*) a tall African tree, resembling a lotus, and bearing a fruit the size of a bean. *Plin.* l. 13, c. 17.

CELTIS, *in the Linnean system*, a genus of plants, Class 23 *Polygamia*, Order 1 *Monoecia*.
Generic Characters. CAL. *perianth* one-leaved; *divisions* ovate.—COR. none.—STAM. *filaments* five; *anthers* oblong.—PIST. *germ* ovate; *styles* two; *stigmas* simple.——PER. *drupe* globular; *seed* nut roundish.
Species. The species are shrubs, as—*Celtis australis*, seu *lotus, &c.* European Nettle Tree, native of Europe.—*Celtis Tournefortii*, seu *orientalis, &c.* native of Armenia.—*Celtis occidentalis, &c.* seu *Lotus, &c.* American Nettle Tree.—*Celtis orientalis, Ulmus, Salvifolia, Mallam*, seu *Papyrus, &c.* Oriental Nettle Tree, native of the East Indies.—*Celtis micrantha, Rhamnus, &c.* seu *Muntingia*, Jamaica Nettle, native of Jamaica.—*Celtis Lima*, seu *Muntingia, &c.* native of the West Indies.

CE'MBALO (*Mus.*) or Cemb, Italian for a harpsichord.

CE'MBRA (*Bot.*) the *Pinus cembra* of Linnæus.

CEME'NT (*Mech.*) *cementum*, a compound of pitch, brickdust, plaster of Paris, &c. used by chasers and other artificers, to be laid under their work, to make it lie firm for receiving the impressions of their punches.—*Royal cement*, a particular manner of purifying gold, by laying over it beds of hard paste, consisting of sal ammoniac, common salt, potters' earth, and brickdust, well moistened with urine.—*Calcareous cement*, any kind of mortar made of lime, sand, fresh water, &c. which is used in buildings. When this is made so as to be impervious to the water, it is called a *water cement*.

CEMENT *Copper* (*Chem.*) the copper procured from the sulphate by precipitation with iron.

CEMENTA'TION (*Chem.*) a mode of making steel. [vide *Chemistry*]

CEMENTS (*Chem.*) or *lutes*, are substances or compositions prepared in various manners, to repair flaws and cracks in vessels.

CE'METERY (*Ecc.*) a repository for the dead.

CE'MOS (*Bot.*) κημος, a kind of herb; the same as the *Leontopodium*. *Plin.* l. 27, c. 8.

CENCHRA'MIDES (*Bot.*) a tree, the fruit of which resembles millet. *Plin.* l. 15, c. 19.

CENCHRA'MIS (*Bot.*) κεγχραμις, a grain or seed of the millet.

CE'NCHRIAS (*Zool.*) κεγχριας, cenchris or cenchrites, from κεγχρος, millet, which it resembles; an animal of the serpent kind: according to Ælian it is at the most a cubit in length, and the bite of it is instant death. *Plin.* l. 20, c. 2; *Act. Tetrab.* 4, serm. 1, c. 25, &c.; *Paul. Æginet.* l. 5, c. 16.

CENCHRIAS (*Med.*) κεγχρος, millet; a spreading inflammation, resembling millet; also called shingles or wild fire.

CE'NCHRIS (*Orn.*) a kastrel or stannel; a kind of speckled hawk. *Plin.* l. 10, c. 52.

CENCHRIS (*Zool.*) a green snake; the *Boa cenchris* of Linnæus.

CENCHRITES (*Zool.*) or *Acontius*, vide *Cenchrias*.

CENCHRITIS (*Min.*) a precious stone with specks, resembling millet seeds.

CE'NCHRUS (*Bot.*) a genus of plants, Class 23 *Polygamia*, Order 1 *Monoecia*.
Generic Characters. CAL. *involucres* many; *perianth* a bivalve glume.—COR. one male, the other hermaphrodite; *proper* each bivalve.—STAM. to each three filaments; *anthers* sagittate.—PIST. *germ* roundish; *style* filiform; *stigmas* two.—PER. none; *seed* roundish.
Species. The species are mostly annuals; namely, the—

Cenchrus lappaceus, Bur Cenchrus, native of India.—*Cenchrus capitatus*, seu *Gramen*, &c. Oval-spiked Cenchrus, native of Gaul.—*Cenchrus echinatus*, *Elymus*, seu *Panicastrella*, &c. seu *Gramen*, &c. Rough-spiked Cenchrus, native of Jamaica.—*Cenchrus tribuloides*, *Panicastrella*, &c. seu *Gramen*, native of Virginia.—*Cenchrus ciliaris*, Ciliated Cenchrus, native of the Cape of Good Hope.—*Cenchrus hordeiformis*, seu *Alopecurus*, &c. native of the Cape of Good Hope.—*Cenchrus purpurascens*, seu *Panicum*, &c. native of Japan. But the —*Cenchrus frutescens*, &c. *Arundo*, &c. seu *Gramen*, &c. is a shrub, and native of Armenia.

CE'NDULÆ (*Archæol.*) small pieces of wood laid in the form of tiles, to cover the roof of a house. *Pat.* 4, *Hen.* 3, p. 210.

CENEA'NGIA (*Med.*) κενεαγγία, from κενός, empty, and ἄγγος, a vessel; any evacuation or inanition of the vessels, from whatever cause, open or occult.

CENE'BRIA (*Med.*) κενέβρια, Carrion; an epithet for the flesh of animals which die of themselves.

CE'NEGILD (*Archæol.*) an expiatory mulct paid to the kindred of the deceased.

CE'NELLA (*Ant.*) acorns from the oak.

CENE'ONES (*Anat.*) κενεῶνες, from κενός, empty the flanks.

CENEFICA'TUM (*Chem.*) or Cinificatum, Calcined.

CENI'GDAM (*Surg.*) *Ceniplam*, *Cenigotam*, and *Cenipolam*; an instrument anciently used for opening the head in epilepsies.

CENI'GOTAM (*Surg.*) vide *Cenigdam*.

CENIOTE'MIUM (*Med.*) a purging medicine affecting the venereal disorder, which is supposed to be mercurial.

CENI'PLAM (*Surg.*) vide *Cenigdam*.

CENI'POLAM (*Surg.*) vide *Cenigdam*.

CENNI'NGA (*Archæol.*) notice given by the buyer to the seller that the thing sold was claimed by another, that he might appear and justify the sale. *Athelst. apud Brompt.* c. 4.

CENO'MUNI (*Hist.*) an ancient people of the Celtic Gaul.

CENO'SIS (*Med.*) from κενός, empty, a general evacuation; in distinction from κάθαρσις, or the evacuation of some particular humour.

CENOTA'PHIUM (*Ant.*) κενοτάφιον, from κενός, empty, and τάφος, sepulchre, a cenotaph; an empty tomb, erected in honour of the dead: called by Ovid "Tumulus sine corpore;" by Suetonius, "Funus imaginarium."
Ovid. Met. l. 11, v. 429.

Et sæpe in tumulis sine corpore nomina legi.

Virgil calls it *tumulus inanis.* *Æn.* l. 3, v. 304.

Hectoreum ad tumulum, viridi quem cespite inanem,
Et geminas causam lacrimis sacraverat aras.

Callimachus calls it κενὸν σᾶμα, epig. 2.

—— Εἰν ἁλί πη φέρεται νέκυς, ἀντὶ δ᾽ ἐκείνου
Οὔνομα καὶ κενὸν σᾶμα παρερχόμεθα.

Suetonius also calls it *tumulus honorarius*, and Lycophron κενήρια.
Lyc. Cassand.

—————— ὡς φθιτῶν θέμις,
Ἀλλ᾽ ἄνομ᾽ οἰκτρὸν καὶ κενήριον γράφας.

Xenophon. *Exped. Cyr.* l. 6; Sueton. *in Claud.* c. 1; *Val. Flacc.* l. 5; *Pausan. in Corinth.*; *Stat. Thebaid.* l. 12, v. 160; *Isidor. Orig.* l. 15, c. 11; *Meurs. ad Lycophron.*; *Kirchmann. de Funer.* l. 3, c. 27; *Diogen. Laert.* l. 1; *Sym.* 97; *Suidas*.

CE'NSAL (*Com.*) on the coast of Provence, and in the ports of the Levant, signifies the same as a broker.

CENSA'RIA (*Archæol.*) from the French *cense*, a farm; a farm, or house and land, let, *ad censum*, at a standing rent.

CENSA'RII (*Archæol.*) Farmers.

CENSE (*Archæol.*) public rates.

CE'NSER (*Ecc.*) a vessel to burn incense in.

CE'NSIO (*Ant.*) a censure or punishment by the censor.

CE'NSITOR (*Ant.*) an assessor or surveyor of lands.

CENSO'RES (*Ant.*) Roman magistrates, of whom there were two, whose office it was to take account of families, to rate men's estate, and to punish misdemeanors and acts of immorality. This they did by turning senators out of the senate, and degrading knights and citizens, which was called "Senatu et Tribu movere." Censors were created U. C. 310, at first from the patricians only, afterwards from both patricians and plebeians. *Dionys. Antiq.* l. 4; *Cic. de Leg.* l. 3, c. 3, &c. and *Ascon. Ped. in Cic.*; *Varr. de Lat. Lin.* l. 5, c. 7; *Liv.* l. 4, c. 8; *Aul. Gell.* l. 4, c. 20; *Zonar. Annal.* l. 7, c. 19.

CENSO'RIÆ *Tabulæ* (*Ant.*) registers or records kept by the censors.

CENSU'RA (*Ant.*) the censorship, or office of censor; likewise a censure, or the exercise of the authority of a censor.

CE'NSURAL *book* (*Archæol.*) a register of taxations.

CE'NSURE (*Law*) from Lat. *census*, a custom observed in divers manors in Cornwall and Devon, where all persons residing therein, above the age of sixteen, are cited to swear fealty to the lord, and to pay 11*d.* per poll, and 1*d.* per ann. ever after. Those thus sworn are called *Censers*.

CENSURE (*Ecc.*) a spiritual punishment inflicted by some ecclesiastical judge in former times, particularly on heretics and schismatics.

CE'NSUS (*Ant.*) a declaration made before and registered by the Censors, containing an enumeration in writing, given by the several subjects of the Roman empire, of their respective names, places of abode, estates, quality, wives, children, domestics, tenants, slaves, &c. It was instituted and performed by Servius Tullius, and was held every five years by the censors after that office was appointed. The *Census* of the people at large was called simply *Census*; that of the *equites*, knights, *census, recensio, recognitio*; and that of *senatores*, senators, *lectio*, and *relectio*. The qualification of a knight was 400,000 sesterces, that of a senator 800,000. The people at large were divided into six classes; namely—The First Class comprehended those who were worth 100,000 sesterces, and consisted of eighty centuries, forty seniors, and as many juniors. The seniors included those who were fifty and upwards, who were appointed to guard the city; the juniors those from the age of seventeen to forty-five, who were employed in war. To these were assigned, as weapons of defence, the *galea*, helmet, *clypeus*, the shield, *ocrea*, the greave, *lorica*, the coat of mail, and every thing which was made of brass: their offensive arms were, *tela*, the javelin, *hasta*, the spear, and *gladius*, the sword. The Second Class comprehended those possessed of 75,000 sesterces, making twenty centuries, ten seniors, and ten juniors. They wore the *scutum* instead of the *clypeus*, but had every thing else the same except the *lorica*. The Third Class included those possessed of 50,000 sesterces, making also twenty centuries, ten seniors, and ten juniors, and having the same arms, except the greaves. The Fourth Class included those possessed of 25,000 sesterces, making twenty centuries, and having the same arms. The Fifth Class consisted of thirty centuries, who were assessed at 11,000 sesterces. They consisted of *accensi, tibicines*, and *cornices*, and carried slings for their arms. The Sixth Class comprehended all who were assessed below 11,000, and consequently exempt from taxation and military service. *Dionys.* l. 4; *Cic. pro Flacc.* c. 32; *Liv.* l. 1, c. 44, &c.; *Aul. Gell.* l. 7, c. 11; *Flor.* l. 1, c. 6; *Isidor. Orig.* l. 5, c. 36; *Sigon. de Antiq. Jur. Civ. Rom.* l. 1, c. 14; *Manut. de Civit. Roman. apud Græv. Thes. Antiq. Roman.* tom. 1, p. 37.

CENT (*Com.*) an abbreviation for *centum*, a hundred. 1. The profit or loss of so much on the hundred in the sale of any commodity; thus the expression "Ten per cent. gain or loss" signifies that the seller has gained or lost ten pounds on every hundred of the price at which he first bought the merchandise, which is one-tenth of profit or one-tenth of loss upon the total of the sale. To gain one hundred per cent. or *cent. per cent.* is the doubling of one's capital; to lose fifty per cent. is to lose one half of it. 2. *Cent.* is the benefit, profit, or interest, on any sum of money which is laid out for improvement: thus we say money is worth four or five per cent. upon exchange; that is, it brings four or five pounds profit for every hundred pounds laid or lent out. 3. *Cent.* is also used with regard to the draughts or remittances of money made from one place to another; thus we say, it will cost 2½ per cent. to remit money to such a city. 4. *Cent.* or *centime*, the hundredth part of any thing, particularly applied to the coin or money of account in America, which is the hundredth part of a dollar; and to the coins, weights, and measures which were introduced into France during the Revolution.

CE'NTAUR (*Astron.*) vide *Centaurus*.

CENTAURE'A (*Bot.*) κενταυρία, κενταύριον, κενταύριον, Centaury; a herb so called from Chiron, the centaur, who was healed by it, is used externally in fomentations against swellings and inflammations. The juice, extract, or infusion of the leaves and roots, of some species are also said to cure intermittents. *Theoph. Hist.* l. 10, c. 1; *Dioscor.* l. 3, c. 8; *Plin.* l. 25, c. 6.

Centaurea, in the Linnean system, a genus of plants, Class 19 *Syngenesia*, Order 3 *Polygamia Frustanea*.

Generic Characters. CAL. common imbricate; *scales* often variously terminated.—COR. *compound* flosculous; *corollules* hermaphrodite; *proper* monopetalous; *tube* filiform; *border* ventricose.—STAM. *filaments* five; *anthers* cylindric.—PIST. *germ* small; *style* filiform; *stigma* very obtuse.—PER. none; *calyx* unchanged; *seeds* solitary; *receptacle* bristly.

Species. The species are mostly annuals or perennials: of the first kind are the following—*Centaurea Crupina, Serratula*, &c. *Chondrilla*, &c. *Senecio*, &c. *Jacea*, seu *Cyanus*, Black seeded Centaury, Bearded Creeper, native of Switzerland, &c.—*Centaurea moschata*, seu *Cyanus*, &c. Purple Sweet Centaury, or Sweet Sultan, native of Greece.—*Centaurea suaveolens, Amberboi*, seu *Cyanus*, native of the East.—*Centaurea lippii*, Egyptian Centaury.—*Centaurea coronopifolia*, seu *Jacea*, a native of Ireland.—*Centaurea cyanus*, seu *Stoebe*, &c. Austrian Centaury, native of Switzerland.—*Centaurea benedicta, Cnicus*, seu *Carduus*, Blessed Thistle, native of Chios. —*Centaurea eriophora*, seu *Calcitrapa*, native of Portugal.—*Centaurea calcitrapa*, seu *Calcitrapa*, native of Switzerland.—*Centaurea crocodylium*, seu *Crocodylium*, native of Syria.—*Centaurea galactites*, native of the South of Europe.—*Centaurea napifolia*, Turnip-leaved Centaury, native of Archipelago. Of the second kind are the following, namely—*Centaurea crucifolia, Jacea, Amberboi*, seu *Stoebe*, &c. — *Centaurea centaurium*, seu *Centaurium*, &c. Great Centaury, native of Italy. —*Centaurea phrygia, Cyanus*, seu *Jacea*, &c. Austrian Centaury, native of Switzerland.—*Centaurea nigrescens*, &c. native of Hungary.—*Centaurea triumfetti*, seu *Cyanus*.—*Centaurea ochroleuca, Caucasica*, seu *Cyanus*,&c. native of Caucasus.—*Centaurea orientalis*, &c. seu *Theiantha*, Oriental Centaury, native of Siberia.—*Centaurea Behen, Rhaponticoides, Serratulæ*, seu *Behen*, &c. native of Asia Minor.—*Centaurea alba, Rhaponticum, Jacea*, seu *Stoebe*, &c. native of Spain.—*Centaurea Rhapontica, Centaureum*, seu *Rhaponticum*, &c. native of Switzerland.—*Centaurea babylonica, Serratula*, &c. seu *Raponticoides*, native of the East.—*Centaurea conifera, Jacea*, seu *Chamæleon*, &c. native of France.—*Centaurea sonchifolia*, native of the Mediterranean.—*Centaurea Isnardi*, seu *Calcitrapoides*, native of Europe.—*Centaurea sempervirens*, seu *Jacea*, &c. Evergreen Centaury, native of Spain.—*Centaurea scabiosa, Cyanus, Scabiosa*, &c. *Jacea*, &c.—Scabious Centaury, or Great Knapweed. But some are biennials, as—*Centaurea nigra*, Black Centaury, or Knapweed, native of England.— *Centaurea peregrina, Nicæensis*, &c.; and some shrubs, as—*Centaurea spinosa*, Prickly-branched Centaury, native of Crete.—*Centaurea hyssopifolia*, native of Spain, &c. *Clus. Hist. Plant. rar.; Bauh. Hist. Plant.; C. Bauh. Pin.; Ger. Herb.; Park. Theat. Bot.; Raii Hist.; Tournef. Inst.; Boerhaav. Ind.; Linn. Spec. Plant.*

CENTAUREA is also the *Cnicus uniflorus* of Linnæus.

CENTAU'REUM (*Bot.*) or *Centaurium*, the *Chlora perfoliata*, and the *Chironia baccifera et frutescens* of Linnæus.

CENTAUROI'DES (*Bot.*) the same as *Gratiola*.

CENTA'URUS (*Astron.*) *Centaur*, one of the 48 old constellations in the southern hemisphere, represented in the form of half man and half horse, who was fabled by the Greeks to have been Chiron the tutor of Achilles. Ptolemy reckons in this constellation 37 stars, Kepler 52, Tycho 4, Bayer 40, and the Britannic Catalogue, &c. 35. *Ptol.* l. 7, c. 5; *Ricciol. Almag. Nov.* l. 6.

CENTELLA (*Bot.*) the *Hydrocotyle villosa* of Linnæus.

CENTE'NAR (*Com.*) a foreign weight of 100, 112, 125, 128, 132, and 140 pounds weight.

CENTENA'RII (*Ant.*) centurions, who had the charge of single centuries. *Veget.* l. 2, c. 8.

CENTENARII (*Law*) petty judges, and under sheriffs of counties, that had rule of an hundred, and judged small matters.

CENTENARIUS (*Chron.*) centenary; an epithet for what belongs to a century or 100 years.

CE'NTER (*Math.*) vide *Centre*.

CENTE'SIMA (*Ant.*) a term signifying the 100th part of an integer, particularly interest of one in the hundred every month. *Cic. in Verr.* 3. c. 70; *Gronov. de Centes.*

CENTE'SIMALS (*Arith.*) the same as *Cents.* [vide *Centigrade*]

CENTICI'PITOUS (*My.*) centiceps, from *centum*, a hundred, and *caput*, a head, an epithet for an animal having 100 heads.

CENTI'FIDOUS (*Math.*) centifidus, from *centum* and *findo*, to split, an epithet for any thing divided into an 100 parts.

CENTIFO'LIA (*Bot.*) a kind of rose in Campania having a hundred or many leaves. *Plin.* l. 21, c. 4.

CE'NTIGRADE (*Arith.*) the division of any thing into a hundred grades, or degrees, called *Centesimals, Centimes*, or *Cents*; thus money, weights, and measures, have been divided into cents, or hundredth parts; and the French have a centigrade thermometer, in which they divide the distance between the freezing and boiling points into 100.

CENTIGRA'NUM (*Bot.*) a kind of wheat having in every ear a hundred grains.

CENTIMO'RBIA (*Med.*) or *Centum-morbia*, from *centum*, a hundred, and *morbus*, a disease, an epithet for a medicine supposed capable of curing a great number of diseases. It is the same as the *Nummularia*.

CE'NTINEL (*Mil.*) vide *Sentinel*.

CENTINE'RVIA (*Bot.*) from *centum*, and *nervia*, a string, an epithet for a plant having many nerves or ribs on its leaves: it is the *Plantago* of Linnæus.

CENTINO'DIA (*Bot.*) *Centum-nodia*, or *Centinodium, Centinody*, from *centum*, a hundred, and *nodus*, a knot; a herb so called from its having many knots and joints; the same as the *Polygonum* of Linnæus.

2 Y

CENTIPE'DA (*Ent.*) Centipede, a worm with many feet; a name given to the wood-louse. *Plin.* l. 18, c. 10.

CENTI'PEDE (*Ent.*) from *centum*, and *pes*, a foot; the name of a well known insect with many feet that infests wood. It is vulgarly called a sow, from its resemblance in shape to the hog.

CENTIPE'LLIO (*Nat.*) the paunch of a stag.

CE'NTIPES (*Ich.*) a fish, otherwise called *scolopendra*, which when it has devoured a hook vomits it up again with its entrails, which it afterwards draws back again into its stomach. *Plin.* l. 9, c. 43.

CE'NTNAR (*Com.*) a weight at Lubeck, consisting of 8 lispards, or 28 pounds.

CE'NTO (*Ant.*) 1. A coverlet or rug made of various shreds. *Macrob. Sat.* 1, 5, c. 2. 2. Patched clothes, such as country fellows wore. *Colum. de Re Rust.* 3. A shroud or tarpaulin to keep off stones or darts from the soldiers in a siege. *Cæs. de Bell. Civ.* l. 2, c. 9. 4. A cover cast over ships, steeped first in vinegar, to keep them from taking fire. *Sisenn. Hist. apud Non.* l. 2, c. 177; *Veget.* l. 4, c. 15. 5. A mop, which was also steeped in vinegar, for the extinguishing of fire. *Ulp. leg.* 12; *Alex. Gen.* l. 5, c. 24.

CENTO (*Poet.*) a poem composed of several pieces selected from other authors.

CENTONA'RII (*Ant.*) Roman officers appointed to provide tents, and other military furniture, called *centones*, or to quench the fire kindled in the camp by the enemy. *Turneb. Adver.* l. 29, c. 16.

CE'NTRAL, an epithet for what belongs to the centre.

CENTRAL *forces* (*Phy.*) are forces which cause a moving body to tend towards or recede from the centre of motion, which are accordingly distinguished into two kinds; namely, centripetal and centrifugal.—*Centripetal force* is that by which a moving body is perpetually urged towards a centre, and made to revolve in a curve instead of a right line.—*Centrifugal force* is that force by which a body revolving about a centre, or about another body, endeavours to recede from it.

CENTRAL *rule* (*Geom.*) a rule for finding the centre of a circle.

CENTRAL *fire* (*Chem.*) that fire which chemists formerly imagined to be in the centre of the earth, the fumes and vapours of which made, as they supposed, the metals and minerals, and brought them to perfection.

CENTRA'LIS *radix* (*Bot.*) central root; that species of root where the shoot proceeds from the middle, as in *Galanthus nivalis*.

CENTRA'TIO (*Med.*) from *centrum*, a centre; the degenerating of a saline principle, contracting a corrosive and ulcerating quality.

CE'NTRE (*Geom.*) κέντρον, a point, from κεντέω, to prick; a point equally remote from the extremes of a line, surface, or solid.—*Centre of a circle*, or *sphere*, that point in the figure from which all lines drawn to the circumference are equal. [vide *Circle*]—*Centre of a conic section*, that point which bisects any diameter, or that point in which all the diameters intersect each other. This point in an ellipse is within the figure, but in the hyperbola without, and in the parabola at an infinite distance.—*Centre of a curve*, of the higher kind, is the point where two diameters concur; and when all the diameters concur in the same point it is called by Sir Isaac Newton *the general centre*.

CENTRE (*Physic.*) is of different kinds; namely—*Centre of attraction*, or *gravitation*, that point into which if all the matter of a body were collected, its action upon any remote particle would still be the same as it is while the body retains its own particular form. The *common centre of attraction* of two or more bodies is that point in which, if a particle of matter were placed, the action of each body upon it would be equal, and consequently it would remain there in *equilibrio*.—*Centre of gravity* of any body, or system of bodies, is that point upon which the parts of the body or bodies do in any situation exactly balance each other. Hence, by means of this property, if the body be supported or suspended by this point, it will rest in any position in which it is put. The centre of gravity of a body is not always within the body itself: thus the centre of gravity of a ring is not in the substance of a ring, but in the axis of its circumscribing cylinder; and the centre of gravity of a hollow staff, or of a bone, is not in the matter of which it is constituted, but somewhere in its imaginary axis. All bodies, however, and systems of bodies, have a centre of gravity, in which the whole gravity, or the whole matter of each body, is conceived to be united. Through the centre of gravity passes a right line, called the *diameter* of gravity; and the intersection of two such diameters determines the centre of gravity. In homogeneous bodies, which may be divided lengthwise into similar and equal parts, the centre of gravity is the same as the *centre of magnitude*; hence, therefore, the centre of gravity of a line is that point which bisects the line; the centre of gravity of a parallelogram, cylinder, &c. is in the middle point of the axis. The position, distance, and motion of the centre of gravity of any body is a medium of the positions and distances of all the particles of the body; which property of this centre has induced some authors to give it the name of the *centre of mean distance*; others, that of the *centre of position*, *centre of inertia*, &c. This point is of the greatest use in mechanics, and in many of the ordinary concerns of life, because the place of the centre of gravity is to be considered as the place of the body itself in computing all mechanical effects.—*Common centre of gravity* of two or more bodies, or of the different parts of the same body, is that point which if it be suspended or supported, the parts of the body, or the bodies, will equiponderate, or rest in any position; thus the point of suspension in a common balance-beam, or steel-yard, is the common centre of gravity for the two parts into which it may be divided.—*Centre of equilibrium* is the same with respect to bodies immersed in a fluid as the centre of gravity is to bodies in free space, being a certain point, upon which if the body or bodies be suspended they will rest in any position.

CENTRE *of motion* (*Mech.*) is that point which remains at rest while all the points of a body move about it, which is the same as the centre of gravity in homogeneous bodies. The centre of motion of a ship is the point upon which a vessel *oscillates*, or rolls, when put in motion. The *velic centre*, or the *velic point*, is the centre of gravity of an equivalent sail, or that single sail whose position and magnitude are such as cause it to be acted upon by the wind when the vessel is sailing, so that the motion shall be the same as that which takes place while the sails have the same position.—*Centre of gyration*, that point in which if the whole mass be collected the same angular velocity will be generated in the same time by a given force acting at any place as in the body or system itself.—*Centre of oscillation*, that point in the axis, or line of suspension, of a vibrating body, or system of bodies, in which if the whole matter or weight be collected, the vibrations will still be performed in the same time, and with the same angular velocity, as before. This point differs from that of gyration, inasmuch as in this case the motion of the body is produced by the gravity of its own particles; but in the case of centre of gyration the body is put in motion by some other force acting at one place only.—*Centre of percussion*, that point where the percussion or stroke is the greatest, in which the whole percutient force of the body is supposed to be collected.—*Centre of pressure* of a fluid against a plane is that point against which a force, equal to the whole pressure, but in a contrary direction to it, will keep the surface at rest; thus, on a plane parallel to the horizon, or on any plane where the pressure is uniform, the centre of pressure coincides with the centre of gravity of the plane.—*Centre of rotation*, that point about which a body, otherwise at liberty, revolves, or tends to revolve, when it is acted upon unequally at different points, or by a force the direction of which does not pass through its centre of gravity.—*Centre of spontaneous rotation* is that point which remains at rest the instant a body is struck, or about which the body begins to move: it was employed first by John Bernouilli to distinguish this centre from the centre of forced rotation.—*Centre of friction*, that point in the base of a body on which it revolves, into which, if the whole surface of the base and the mass of the body were collected and made to revolve about the centre of the base of the given body, the angular velocity destroyed by its friction would be equal to the angular velocity destroyed in the given body by its friction in the same time.—*Centre of conversion*, a term used, by Mr. Parent, in respect to a stick laid on stagnant waters, and then drawn by a thread fastened to it, so that the thread always makes the same angle with it; and, consequently, the stick will be found to turn about a certain point, which point is called the centre of conversion.—*Phonic centre* is a term sometimes used in acoustics for the place where the speaker stands in polysyllabical and articulate echoes.

CENTRE *of equant* (*Astron.*) a term, in the Old Astronomy, for a point in the line of the aphelion supposed to be as far distant from the centre of the eccentric, towards the aphelion, as the sun is from the centre of the eccentric towards the perihelion.

CENTRE (*Dial.*) that point where the gnomon or style, which is placed parallel to the axis of the earth, intersects the plane of the dial.

CENTRE (*Archit.*) a term used to denote a frame of timber constructed for the purpose of supporting the stones or bricks forming an arch or vault, during the erection.

CENTRE *of a bastion* (*Fort.*) a point in the middle of the gorge where the capital line commences, and which is usually at the angle of the inner polygon of the figure. This may otherwise be defined the point where the two adjacent curtains produced intersect each other.

CENTRE *of a battalion* (*Mil.*) in parade is the middle where an interval is left for the colours: in an encampment it is the main street; and on a march it is an interval for the baggage—*Centre of an attack*, the middle point in the front, which is taken before a besieged place, which is one of the three capitals upon which the lines of attack are carried.

CENTRE *of a fleet* (*Mar.*) in French *Centre, ou corps de bataille, d'une armée navale*, the station of the admiral or commander of a fleet.

CENTRE *Phrenique* (*Anat.*) the name of the fibres of the large muscles of the diaphragm.

CENTRIFUGAL (*Phy.*) vide *Central*.

CENTRIFUGAL *machine* (*Mech.*) a machine, so called because it is contrived so as to raise water by means of a centrifugal force combined with the pressure of the atmosphere.

CENTRIGRADE (*Arith.*) vide *Centigrade*.

CENTRINA (*Ich.*) a species of squalus.

CENTRING (*Carpent.*) or *centering*, the frame of timber by which the brick or stone work of arched vaulting is supported during its erection, and from which it receives its curved form.

CENTRING *of an optic glass* (*Mech.*) the grinding it so as that the thickest part be exactly in the middle.

CENTRION (*Med.*) κεντρον, from κεντεω, to prick; an epithet for a plaster used by Galen against stitches in the side.

CENTRIPETAL (*Phy.*) an epithet for a sort of central force. [vide *Central*]

CENTRISCUS (*Ich.*) a genus of animals, Class *Pisces*, Order *Branchiostegosa*.
Generic Character. Head lengthened into a very narrow snout.—*Mouth* without teeth.—*Gills* broad flat.—*Body* compressed.—*Belly* carinate.—*Ventral-fins* united.
Species. The species are, *Centriscus scutatus, colopax, et valitarius.*

CENTRIUM (*Med.*) vide *Centrion*.

CENTROBARIC *method* (*Mech.*) a method of measuring or determining the quantity of any surface or solid by considering it as generated by motion, and multiplying the generating line or surface into the path of its centre of gravity, i. e. "Every figure, whether superficial or solid, generated by the motion of a line or surface, is equal to the product of the generating magnitude into the path of its centre of gravity." The word is derived from *centro-baryco*, i. e. the centre of weight or gravity. [vide *Centro-baryco*]

CENTRO-BARYCO (*Mech.*) from κεντρον, a centre, and βαρυς, another name for the centre of gravity.

CENTROGASTER (*Ich.*) a genus of animals, Class *Pisces*, Order *Thoracica*.
Generic Character. Head compressed, smooth.—*Gill-membrane* mostly seven rayed.—*Body* depressed, smooth.—*Fins* spinous.—*Ventral-fin* connected by a membrane.
Species. The principal species are the *Centrogaster fuscescens, argentatus, equula,* &c.

CENTROPHAGIA (*Bot.*) Penny-royal.

CENTRUM (*Math.*) vide *Centre*.

CENTRUM (*Chem.*) the principal residuum formed, or source of any thing.

CENTRUM (*Bot.*) the herb Clary.

CENTRUM (*Med.*) that part of a medicine in which the greatest virtue resides.

CENTRUM (*Anat.*) the middle point in some parts of the body.—*Centrum nerveum*, the tendinous part of the diaphragm, which has a triangular appearance.—*Centrum ovale*, a part of the *corpus callosum*.

CENTRY (*Mar.*) or *Sentinel*, in French *Centinelle*, a private marine posted in some responsible part of the ship to prevent any surprize.

CENTRY (*Archit.*) a mould for an arch.

CENTRY-BOX (*Mil.*) a wooden hutch erected as a shelter for the centinel.

CENTUM *Capita* (*Bot.*) the same as *Eryngium*.

CENTUMVIRALIS (*Ant.*) an epithet for what belongs to the *Centumviri*; *Centumvirale Judicium*, a sentence in the court of the *Centumviri*; *Centumvirales causæ*, causes heard in the court of the *Centumviri*. *Cic. de Orat.* l. 1, c. 38; *Plin.* l. 6, ep. 33.

CENTUMVIRI (*Ant.*) judges chosen to hear certain causes among the people, three of whom were chosen out of every tribe. *Quintil.* l. 5, c. 10; *Flor. Epitom.* l. 18; *Fest. de Verb. Signif.*; *Hotoman. de Magistrat. Rom. apud Græv. Thes. Antiq. Rom.* tom. ii. p. 1816.

CENTUNCULARIS (*Bot.*) the same as *Centunculus*.

CENTUNCULUS (*Ant.*) 1. A patched coverlet or quilt to sleep on. 2. A horse-cloth laid under the dorsers. *Liv.* l. 7, c. 14.

CENTUNCULUS (*Bot.*) a genus of plants, Class 4 *Tetrandria*, Order 1 *Monogynia*.
Generic Characters. CAL. *perianth* four-cleft.—COR. Monopetalous; *tube* subglobular; *border* flat.—STAM. *filaments* four; *anthers* simple.—PIST. *germ* roundish; *style* filiform; *stigma* simple.—PER. *capsule* globular; *seeds* very many.
Species. The only species is the *Centunculus minimus, Anagallidiastrum, Anagallis,* &c. seu *Alsine,* &c. Bastard Pimpernel, an annual, native of Italy, &c.

CENTU'RIA (*Ant.*) a division of a hundred men, which constituted a part of the classes into which Servius disposed all the Roman citizens according to their property. [vide *Census*] The first class contained eighty centuries; the second, third, and fourth, twenty centuries; the fifth, thirty centuries; and the sixth, or last, but one century. At the election of Consuls, Censors, and Prætors, the people gave their votes by centuries; whence the assembly was called *comitia centuriata*; and that century which had the privilege of giving their votes before the rest was called the *centuria prærogativa*. By the first institution of Servius this privilege was attached to the *classici*, or those of the first class, but afterwards it was determined by lot to whom it should belong. *Cic. Brut.* c. 67, &c.; *Dionys.* l. 2; *Liv.* l. 1, c. 36; *Manut. de Comit. Rom.* c. 4. *Centuria* signifies also, 1. A band of a hundred men commanded by ἑκατόνταρχος, a centurion. It was called τάγμα by Polybius, and, among the Roman writers, *ordo*. The *centuria* was the half of a manipulus, the sixth part of a cohort, and the sixtieth part of a legion, and consisted, according to Vegetius, of 110 men. *Polyb.* l. 6, c. 22; *Varr. de Ling. Lat.* l. 4, c. 16; *Dionys.* l. 10; *Liv.* l. 7; *Aul. Gell.* l. 16, c. 4; *Veget.* l. 2, c. 8. 13, 14, &c. 2. A measure of land consisting of a hundred acres. *Varr. de Re Rust.* l. 1. c. 10; *Colum.* l. 5, c. 1; *Pæt. de Roman. et Græc. Mens.* l. 1; *apud Græv. Thes. Antiq. Roman.* l. 11, &c.

CENTU'RIO (*Ant.*) a captain of a band, or a hundred soldiers. The centurions stood each at the head of his century to lead them up, and the common soldiers were placed at his discretion. The badge of the centurion's office was the *vitis*, or rod of the vine, which he carried in his hand. The centurion, who was chosen from among the Triarii or Pilani, was the most honourable of all, and was denominated *centurio primipili* or *primipulus*. He had the command of four hundred men, and the charge of the standards. *Cæs. de Bell. Gall.* l. 6, c. 39; *Dionys.* l. 9; *Liv.* l. 7, c. 4; *Tacit. Annal.* l. 1, &c.; *Veget.* l. 2, 3; *Sigon. de Jur. Civ. Rom.* l. 1.

CE'NTURY (*Ant.*) vide *Centuria* & *Census*.

CENTURY (*Chron.*) a hundred years.

CENTU'SSIS (*Ant.*) a rate of Roman money containing forty Sesterces, ten Denarii, i. e. about ten groats sterling, or a noble. *Varr. de Lat. Lin.* l. 5, c. 36; *Pers. sat.* 5, v. 191.

CEO'LA (*Archæol.*) a large ship.

CE'PA (*Bot.*) from κεπος, a wool-card, from the likeness of its roots; the Onion.

CEPA'CA (*Bot.*) a species of onion which used to be esteemed for salads in spring, but is now disregarded.

CEPA'STRUM (*Bot.*) another name for the *Allium sylvestre*, Cow-garlick; the *Cepa Ascalonica*, Eschalots, and the *Schœnopressum*, Chives.

CEPHALÆ'A (*Med.*) vide *Cephalalgia*.

CEPHALA'LGIA (*Med.*) or *Cephalæa*, κεφαλαλγία, from κεφαλη, the head, and ἄλγος, pain; a head-ach: when mild, it is called *cephalalgia*; when inveterate, *cephalæa*. *Aret. de Caus. et Sign. Morb. Acut.* l. 1, c. 2.—*Cephalalgia catarrhalis*, another name for a species of catarrh.—*Cephalalgia spasmodica*, the Sick Head-Ach.—*Cephalalgia inflammatoria*, the same as *Phrenitis*.

CEPHALALGIA *herba* (*Bot.*) the same as *Verbena*.

CEPHALA'LGICA (*Med.*) κεφαλαλγικά, medicines for the head-ach.

CEPHALA'NTHUS (*Bot.*) a genus of plants, Class 4 *Tetrandria*, Order 1 *Monogynia*.
 Generic Characters. CAL. *perianth* common none; *perianth* proper one-leaved; *border* quadrifid.—COR. *universal* equal; *proper* monopetalous.—STAM. *filaments* four; *anthers* globose.—PIST. *germ* inferior; *style* longer than the corolla; *stigma* globose.—PER. none; *seeds* solitary; *receptacles* common globular.
 Species. The species are shrubs, as follow; namely, the *Cephalanthus occidentalis*, seu *Scabiosa*, &c. American Button Wood, native of North America.—*Cephalanthus montanus*, *stellatus*, &c.

CEPHALANTHUS is also the *Nauclea orientalis* of Linnæus.

CEPHALA'RTICA (*Med.*) from κεφαλη, the head, and ἀρτίζω, to make clear; medicines which purge the head.

CEPHA'LEA *juvenum* (*Med.*) the head-ach that often attends youth at the approach of puberty, and affects the whole head. *Plin.* l. 20, c. 13.

CEPHALA'TIO (*Ant.*) a capitation, or poll-tax.

CEPHA'LIC (*Med.*) from κεφαλη, the head; an epithet for what appertains to the head.

CEPHALIC *tincture* (*Med.*) a nervous antispasmodic medicine, so called because it relieves the head.

CEPHALIC *vein* (*Anat.*) *vena cephalica*, the anterior vein of the arm, so called because the head was supposed to be relieved by opening it.—*Cephalic of the thumb*, vide *Cephalica*.

CEPHALIC *line*, the line of the head or brain in palmistry.

CEPHALIC *powder* (*Med.*) a powder prepared from the head.

CEPHA'LICA *Pollicis* (*Anat.*) a branch of the cephalic vein running along the lower extremity of the radius between the thumb and the metacarpus.

CEPHA'LICAS (*Mus.*) the name for a character of notation used in the middle ages.

CEPHALICS (*Med.*) cephalic medicines, or such as serve to relieve disorders in the head, of which description is snuff.

CEPHALO'IDES (*Bot.*) κεφαλοειδής, from κεφαλη and εἶδος, likeness; applied to plants that are shaped like a head.

CE'PHALON (*Bot.*) the Date-Tree.

CEPHALONO'SOS (*Med.*) κεφαλόνοσος, from κεφαλη, the head, and νόσος, a disease; a malignant epidemical fever frequent in Hungary.

CE'PHALO-PHARYNGÆUS (*Anat.*) from κεφαλη and φάρυγξ, the throat; a muscle of the Pharynx.

CEPHALOPO'NIA (*Med.*) κεφαλοπονία, from κεφαλη and πόνος, pain, a head-ach.

CEPHALO'TOS (*Bot.*) Capitate, an epithet for plants.

CEPHALOTUS (*Bot.*) the *Thymus cephalotus* of Linnæus.

CEPHALOTRO'TOS (*Surg.*) from κεφαλη, and τιτρώσκω, to wound; wounded in the head.

CE'PHALINE (*Med.*) κεφαλίνη, that part of the tongue which is next the root and nearest the fauces.

CEPHALI'TIS (*Med.*) the same as *Phrenitis*.

CEPHALONOMA'NCY (*Ant.*) κεφαλονομαντεία, from κεφαλη, the head, ὄνος, an ass, and μαντεία, divination; a mode of divination, by means of an ass's head broiled on coals, in order to convict a person of a crime. If the jaws moved, or the teeth chattered, they thought they had detected the offender. *Gyrald. Syntag. Deor.* l. 17.

CE'PHALUS (*Ich.*) κέφαλος, mullet, a fish with a large head; the *Mugi Cephalus* of Linnæus.

CE'PHEUS (*Astron.*) κηφεύς, a constellation in the northern hemisphere, and one of the 48 old asterisms, which is fabled by the Greeks to represent the husband of Cassiopeia and father of Andromeda. [vide *Cassiopeia*] Ptolemy reckons in this constellation 13, Kepler 11, Bayer 17, Hevelius 51, and the British Catalogue 35.

CEPHEUS (*Zool.*) an animal in Æthiopia, with hands and feet like a man. This is doubtless the ape from the Hebrew קוף. *Plin.* l. 8, c. 19.

CEPI *corpus* (*Law*) the return made by the sheriff upon a *capias*, or process to the like purpose, that he "hath taken the body." *F.N.B.* 26.

CEPI'NA (*Bot.*) a bed of onions.

CEPI'NI (*Chem.*) vinegar.

CEPIO'NIDES (*Min.*) precious stones as clear as crystal.

CE'PITES (*Min.*) a species of agate.

CE'POLA (*Ich.*) a genus of animals, Class *Pisces*, Order *Thoracica*.
  Generic Character. Head roundish, compressed.—*Teeth* curved.—*Gill membrane* with six rays.—*Body* ensiform, naked.
  Species. The principal species are the—*Cepola tænia, rubescens, trachyptera, &c.*

CEPPA'GIUM (*Archæol.*) the stumps or roots remaining in the ground, after trees are felled. *Fleta,* l. 2, c. 41.

CE'PPHUS (*Orn.*) a sea-mew; a bird so light that it is carried away with every puff of wind.

CEPS *de Cesar* (*Mil.*) Cæsar's trap; a stratagem which Cæsar adopted to draw the enemy into a forest, where the passage was blocked up.

CE'PULA (*Bot.*) κέπυλα, a name for large Myrobans. *Nic. Myre.* sec. 9, c. 83.

CE'RA (*Med.*) κηρός, from the Arabic *Kira,* or the Chaldean *Kerah,* wax, Bees-wax; a concrete substance, collected from vegetables by bees, and extracted from their combs after the honey is separated from them.—*Cera alba,* white wax; the yellow wax artificially deprived of its colour, by reducing it into thin flakes, by exposing it to the sun and air, and by occasionally sprinkling it with water.—*Cera cinnamomi,* a white sebaceous matter obtained from the fruit of the Cinnamon tree.—*Cera di cardo,* a viscous milky juice, resembling wax, gathered from the *Carduus pinea Theophrasti,* or Pine thistle.—*Cera oleum,* oil of wax, is used as an emollient for healing chaps, roughness of the skin, &c.

CERACHATES (*Min.*) an agate stone of wax colour.

CERÆ'A (*Anat.*) κεραία, from κέρας, a horn; the horns of the uterus. *Ruff. Ephes. de Appellat. Corp. hum.* l. 1, c. 31.

CERA'GIUM (*Archæol.*) cerage, a tribute or payment made for finding candles in the church.

CERA'GO (*Nat.*) the aliment of bees, now called *bee-bread*.

CERA'MBYX (*Ent.*) a genus of animals, Class *Insecta,* Order *Coleoptera*.
  Generic Character. Antennæ setaceous.—*Feelers* four.—*Thorax* spinous or gibbous.—*Shells* linear.
  Species. The species are distinguished into, 1. *Prionus,* or those who have the feelers equal and filiform. 2. *Rhagium,* or those that have the feelers equal and capitate, and the thorax spinous. 3. *Callidium,* or those having the feelers equal and elevated, the thorax unarmed. 4. *Stenocorus,* or those having the feelers unequal, the two fore ones filiform, the hinder ones clavate.

CERA'MICE (*Min.*) or *Cerameta,* κεραμική, or κεραμίτις, joined with γη, earth, signifies Potter's-clay.

CERAMITES (*Min.*) a precious stone, of the colour of a tile.

CERA'MIUM (*Ant.*) a Greek measure of nine gallons.

CERANITES (*Med.*) κεραίτης, from κεράννυμι, to temper together; the name of a troche.

CERA'MIUM (*Ant.*) the same as *Cadus*.

CERA'NTHEMUS (*Bot.*) κεράνθεμος, or κερά:θιμον, from κηρός, wax, and ἄνθεμος, a flower; Bee-glue or Bee-bread.

CERANTHUS (*Bot.*) the *Chionanthus* of Linnæus.

CERARE (*Chem.*) to incorporate or mix.

CERA'RIUM (*Ant.*) Wax-money; a tax which was paid for the seal in wax. *Cic. in Verr.* orat. 3, c. 78.

CERAS (*Bot.*) κέρας, a horn.

CERA'SA (*Bot.*) the *Prunus cerasus* of Linnæus.

CERASIA'TUM (*Med.*) from *cerasus,* a cherry, a purging medicine; so called because the juice of cherries is the principal ingredient.

CERA'SION (*Bot.*) κεράσιον, a cherry.

CERA'SIOS (*Med.*) the name of two ointments in medicine.

CERA'SIN (*Chem.*) a vegetable principle, possessing the appearance of gum, and of a similar taste. It is usually harder, and not so easily reduced to powder as gum.

CERA'SMA (*Med.*) κέρασμα, from κεράννυμι, to mix; a mixture of cold and warm water, when the warm is poured on the cold.

CERA'STES (*Zool.*) κεράστης, κεραστής, from κέρας, a horn; a serpent, a cubit in length, or at the longest two cubits, having two prominences on its head resembling horns. *Nicand. Ther.* p. 19; *Plin.* l. 8, c. 23; *Solin.* c. 27; *Act. Tetrab.* 4, serm. 1, c. 28.

CERASTES is the *Coluber Cerastes* of Linnæus.

CERASTES (*Ent.*) a worm that breeds in figs. *Theoph. Hist. Plant.* l. 9, c. 16; *Plin.* l. 16, c. 41.

CERA'STIUM (*Bot.*) a genus of plants, Class 10 *Decandria,* Order 5 *Pentagynia*.
  Generic Characters. CAL. perianth five-leaved; *leaflets* acute.—COR. petals five.—STAM. *filaments* ten: *anthers* roundish.—PIST. germ ovate; *styles* five: *stigmas* obtuse.—PER. capsule obtuse; *seeds* very many.
  Species. The species are annuals and perennials. The annuals are as follow; namely—*Cerastium perfoliatum, seu Myosotis, &c.* Mouse-ear, native of Greece.—*Cerastium vulgatum, Myosotis, Alsine, seu Auricula,* Common or Narrow-leaved Mouse-ear, native of Europe.—*Cerastium anomalum, &c.* native of Hungary.—*Cerastium viscosum, Myosotis, Alsine, &c.* native of Europe.—*Celastrum semidecandrum, Myosotis, seu Centunculus,* Least Mouse-ear, native of Europe.—*Cerastium pentandrum,* native of Spain.—*Cerastium arvense, seu Myosotis, &c. Centunculus, &c. Caryophyllus, &c. seu Holosteum, &c.* Corn Mouse-ear. The perennials are as follow; namely—*Cerastium tineare,* native of Mount Cenisius.—*Cerastium dichotomum, Lychnis, seu Alsine,* Forked Mouse-ear.—*Cerastium alpinum, Myosotis, Centunculus, seu Centunculus, seu Alsine,* Alpine Mouse-ear, native of Europe.—*Cerastium repens, seu perenne, &c. Stellaria, Myosotis, Ocymoides, seu Lychnis, &c.* Creeping Mouse-ear, or Sea-pink, native of Gaul.—*Cerastium strictum, Myosotis, Alsine, Caryophyllus, &c.* native of Austria.—*Cerastium aquaticum, Alsine, Stellaria, &c.* native of Europe.—*Cerastium latifolium, Myosotis, seu Caryophyllus, &c. seu Herbate,* Broad-leaved Mouse-ear, native of Switzerland.—*Cerastium tomentosum,* native of Granada.—*Cerastium refractum, seu trigynum, seu Myosotis,* native of Mount St. Barnard. *Clus. Hist. Plant. rar.; C. Bauh. Pin.; Ger. Herb.; Park. Theat. Botan.; Raii Hist. Plant.; Tournef. Instit.*

CERASTIUM is also the *Holosteum umbella* of Linnæus.

CE'RASUS (*Bot.*) κέρασος, the Cherry-tree; it received its name from Cerasus, a city of Pontus, whence it was imported to Rome by Lucullus Lucilius, and thence propagated into Britain, according to Pliny. *Theophrast. Hist. Plant.* l. 3, c. 13; *Plin.* l. 15, c. 25; *Athen.* l. 2, &c.

CERASUS is the *Prunus cerasus* of Linnæus.

CERATACHA'TES (*Min.*) from κέρας, a horn, and ἀχάτης, an agate; a species of agate stone, the veins of which resemble the shape of a horn.

CERATAMA'LGAMA (*Med.*) or *Ceratomalgama,* from κηρός, wax, and *amalgama,* a mollifying composition of wax and other ingredients.

CE'RATE (*Med.*) *Ceratum,* a composition of wax, oil, or lard, with or without other ingredients. It is used for plasters; and takes its name from the wax, *cera,* which is the principal ingredient.

CERA'TIA (*Bot.*) κερατία, the Carob-tree; the *Cercis Canadensis* of Linnæus.

CERATIAS (*Astron.*) κερατίας, a blazing star like a horn. *Plin.* l. 2, c. 25.

CERA'TION (*Med.*) the smearing any thing over with wax.

CERATI'TES (*Min.*) the Fossil Unicorn; a stone in the shape of a horn.

CERATI'TIS (*Bot.*) κερατῖτις from κέρας, a horn; the sea violet, according to Marcellus Empiricus; but according to Pliny the *Papaver Corniculatum*. Plin. l. 20, c. 19.

CERA'TIUM (*Bot.*) κεράτιον, the fruit of the Carob-tree.

CERATIUM (*Com.*) a carat.

CERATOCA'RPUS (*Bot.*) a genus of plants, Class 21 *Monoecia*, Order 1 *Monandria*.
  Generic Characters. CAL. perianth one-leaved.—COR. none.—STAM. filament single; anther twin.—PIST. germ oblong; styles two; stigmas simple.—PER. none; seed oblong.
  Species. The only species is the—*Ceratocarpus arenarius*, an annual, native of Tartary.

CERATOCEPHALOI'DES (*Bot.*) the same as the *Bidens*.

CERATOCE'PHALUS (*Bot.*) from κέρας, horn, and κεφαλὴ, the head; from the horn-like appearance of its top. It is the same as the *Bidens*.

CERATO-GLO'SSUS (*Anat.*) from κέρας a horn, and γλῶσσα, a tongue; a muscle so named from its shape and insertion into the tongue.

CERATO-HYOIDÆ'US (*Anat.*) the same as *Stylo-hyoides*.

CERATO'IDES (*Anat.*) κερατοειδὴς, a name for the *Tunica Cornea* of the eye.

CERATOMALA'GMA (*Chem.*) κερατομαλαγμα. [vide *Ceratamalgama*]

CERATO'NIA (*Bot.*) a genus of plants, Class 23 *Polygamia*, Order 3 *Trioecia*.
  Generic Characters. CAL. perianth five-parted.—COR. none.—STAM. filaments five; anthers twin.—PIST. germ lying concealed within a fleshy receptacle; style long; stigma headed.—PER. legume very large; seed solitary.
  Species. The only species is the—*Ceratonia Siliqua*, seu *Siliqua*, &c. the Carob-tree, a shrub, native of Apulia.

CERATONIA is also the *Mimosa ceratonia* of Linnæus.

CERATO-PHARY'NGUS Major et Minor (*Anat.*) the names of two pair of the muscles inserted into the *Os hyoides*.

CERATOPHY'LLUM (*Bot.*) a genus of plants, Class 21 *Monoecia*, Order 8 *Polyandria*.
  Generic Characters. CAL. perianth many-parted; divisions equal.—COR. none.—STAM. filaments from sixteen to twenty; anthers oblong.—PIST. germ ovate; style none; stigma obtuse.—PER. none; seed nut-ovate.
  Species. The species are perennials; namely—*Ceratophyllum demersum*, *Hydroceratophyllum*, *Dichotophyllon*, *Millefolium*, &c. seu *Equisetum*, &c. Prickly-seeded Hornwort, native of Europe.—*Ceratophyllum submersum*, Smooth-seeded Hornwort, native of Europe.

CERA'TUM (*Med.*) from *cera*, wax; cerate, or wax, combined by the assistance of heat, with fixed oils.

CERAU'NIA (*Min.*) κεραυνία, from κεραυνὸς, thunder; thunder-stones, always found near some place blasted with lightning. Ceraunia is a variety of the *Helenintholithus Nautilites* of Linnæus.

CERAU'NIUM (*Bot.*) a kind of puff or mushroom, in Thrace, which grows plentifully after thunder. Plin. l. 19, c. 3.

CERAUNO-CHRY'SOS (*Chem.*) from κεραυνὸς, thunder, and χρυσὸς, gold; a powder so called from the violence of its explosion when heated. In the Latin it is called *aurum fulminaris*.

CE'RBERA (*Bot.*) a genus of plants, Class 5 *Pentandria*, Order 1 *Monogynia*.
  Generic Characters. CAL. perianth five-leaved; leaflets ovate-lanceolate.—COR. monopetalous; tube clavated; border large; divisions oblique.—STAM. filaments five; anthers erect.—PIST. germ roundish; style filiform; stigma headed.—PER. drupe very large; seed nut two-celled.
  Species. The species are shrubs; as the—*Cerbera Ahouai*, *Thevetia*, seu *Ahouai*, Oval-leaved Cerbera, native of Brazil.—*Cerbera ovata*, a native of New Spain.—*Cerbera parviflora*, native of the Friendly Isles.—*Cerbera Manghas, Manghas*, seu *Odollam*, native of the Indies.—*Cerbera maculata*, seu *Ochrosia*, &c. a shrub, native of Bourbon.—*Cerbera Thevetica, Plumeria, Nerio*, seu *Ycotli*, &c. native of Cuba.—*Cerbera salutaris*, seu *Laetaria*, &c. native of Cochin-China.—*Cerbera laurifolia*, native of the West Indies.

CE'RBERUS TRICEPS (*Chem.*) the *Pulvis cornachini*, or a triple mercury, composed of salt, quicksilver, and vitriol.

CERCA'RIA (*Conch.*) a genus of animals, Class *Vermes*, Order *Infusoria*.
  Generic Character. A worm invisible to the naked eye, pellucid, and furnished with a tail.
  Species. The principal species are, the *Cercaria gyrinus, inquieta, lemna*.

CERCELEE (*Her.*) or *Recercelée*, a cross circling or curling at the end, like a ram's horn, as in the annexed figure.

CERCHNA'LEOS (*Med.*) κερχναλέος, any thing which causes wheezing or hoarseness.

CE'RCHNOS (*Med.*) κέρχνος, a wheezing or hoarse noise made in respiration, on account of some disorder in the *larynx*, or *aspera arteria*, or both.

CERCHO'DES (*Med.*) those who suffer from a contracted breathing.

CE'RCIO (*Orn.*) an Indian bird as large as a starling.

CE'RCIS (*Anat.*) κερκὶς, signifies literally a pestle, or an instrument to pound any thing with; but is applied to the bone in the arm called the *radius*.

CERCIS (*Bot.*) a genus of plants, Class 10 *Decandria*, Order 1 *Monogynia*.
  Generic Characters. CAL. perianth one-leaved.—COR. pentapetalous; wings petals two; standard petal one; keel petals two; nectary a style-shaped gland below the germ.—STAM. filaments ten; anthers oblong.—PIST. germ linear-lanceolate; style of the length and situation of the stamens; stigma obtuse.—PER. legume oblong; seeds some roundish.
  Species. The species are shrubs; namely—*Cercis siliquastrum, Arbor Judæ, Siliqua*, seu *Siliquastrum*, Common Judas tree, native of Italy.—*Cercis Canadensis, Siliquastrum*, seu *Ceratia*, &c. Canada Judas tree, Red-Bud tree, native of Virginia.

CE'RCIUS (*Nat.*) vide *Circius*.

CE'RCLE (*Mil.*) or grand circle, a ring formed every evening by the sergeants and corporals of a brigade in the old French military service, to receive orders.—*Cercle meurtrier*, a large flat piece of iron made red hot and thrown at the enemy.

CERCLE' (*Her.*) within a circle or diadem.

CERCLES-GOUDRONNE'S (*Mil.*) pitched hoops, i.e. pieces of old cordage dipped in pitch and tar and placed in a circle on chafing dishes, to light the garrison of a besieged town at post.—*Cercles à feux*, hoops bound round with grenades, loaded pistol-barrels, &c. covered with tow and fireworks, which are driven across the works of the besiegers.

CERCO'DEA (*Bot.*) the same as the *Haloragis*.

CERCOLIPS (*Zool.*) an ape without a tail.

CERCO'PIS (*Ent.*) a division of the genus *Cicada*, having the antennæ filiform, and the lip abbreviated truncate.

CERCO'SIS (*Med.*) κέρκωσις, a disease of the *clitoris*, which consists in a preternatural enlargement.

CE'RDAC (*Chem.*) mercury.

CE'RDONISTS (*Ecc.*) or *Cerdonians*, a sect of heretics, named after their leader Cerdo, who maintained most of the errors of Simon Magus and other gnostics. *Iren. cont. Hæres.* l. 1, 3; *Tertull. de Præs.* c. 51; *St. August. Hær.* 21; *St. Epiphan. Hær.* 51; *Euseb. Ecc. Hist.* l. 4, c. 11; *Baron. Annal. Ann.* 146.

σ CERE (*Mech.*) to rub with wax.

CEREA'LIA (*Ant.*) from *ceres*, corn; all sorts of corn of which bread is made: and *Cerealia arma*, implements of husbandry.

CEREALIA (*Ant.*) or *Cereales Ludi*, solemn games in honour of Ceres, when her votaries ran about with lighted torches, in commemoration of her going about in search of her daughter Proserpine.

Ovid. Fast. l. 4, v. 391.

> *Circus erit pompa celeber, numeroque deorum.*
> *Primaque ventosis palma petetur equis.*
> *Hinc Cereris ludi.*

Tacit. Annal. l. 15, c. 53; *Dio.* l. 48; *Tertull. de Spectac.* c. 7; *Ursat. de Not. Roman. apud. Græv. Thes. Antiq.* tom. ii. p. 603.

CEREBE'LLUM (*Anat.*) and *Cerebellum*, dim. of *Cerebrum*, the posterior part of the brain. [vide *Brain*]

CE'REBRI AFFECTIO SPASMO'DICA (*Med.*) the same as *Apoplexia compressio et concussio*, compression of the brain.—*Cerebri basis*, the same as *Palatum*, which see.—*Cerebri galea*, the same as *Cranium*, which see.

CEREBRUM (*Anat.*) vide *Brain*.—*Cerebrum elongatum*, the same as *Medulla spinalis*.

CEREBRUM *Jovis* (*Chem.*) Burnt Tartar.

CEREFA'CTIO (*Nat.*) the same as *Ceratio*.

CEREFO'LIUM (*Bot.*) the *Chærophyllum sylvestre, tremulum, hirsutum, et aureum* of Linnæus.

CEREI'BA (*Bot.*) a small tree which grows in Brazil, like a willow.

CEREIBU'NA-MANGUE (*Bot.*) another species of the preceding plant.

CERELÆ'UM (*Med.*) κηρέλαιον, from κηρός, wax, and ἔλαιον, oil; the same as *Ceratum*.

CEREMO'NIAL (*Ecc.*) a book containing the ceremonies of the Romish church.

CE'REMONIES, *Master of* (*Polit.*) an officer instituted by James I. for the more honourable reception of ambassadors, &c. He wears a chain of gold about his neck, with a medal, under the crown of Great Britain, having on one side an emblem of peace and the motto *beati pacifici*; on the other, an emblem of war and the motto *Dieu et mon droit*.—*Assistant Master of the Ceremonies*, one who acts in his stead when he is absent.—*Marshal of the Ceremonies*, an officer subordinate to them both.

CERE'TIA (*Bot.*) the *Hymænia corbaril* of Linnæus.

CEREVI'SIA (*Archæol.*) a drink made of any sort of corn.

CEREUS (*Bot.*) or Creeping Cereus, a plant remarkable for the beauty and sweetness of its flowers, which is classed in the Linnean system, under the genus *Cactus*. The most distinguished kinds are the—Great Night-flowering Creeping Cereus, the *Cactus grandiflorus*; the Pink-flowered Creeping Cereus, the *Cactus flagelliformis*; and the Parasitical Creeping Cereus, the *Cactus parasiticus*.

CE'RIA (*Ent.*) a division of the genus of *Musca*, having a single bristle and univalve sheath; *antennæ* seated on a common petiole.

CERIFICA'TIO, the same as *Ceratio*.

CE'RIGON (*Nat.*) a wild American animal, having a skin under the belly, in which it carries its young ones.

CE'RILLA (*Gram.*) vide *Cedilla*.

CE'RIN (*Chem.*) a substance of the consistence of wax, and soluble in fixed and volatile oils.

CERI'NTHE (*Bot.*) a herb which Virgil calls *gramen ignobile*, but nevertheless recommends it as food for bees.

Virg. Georg. l. 4, v. 62.

> ——— *hue tu jussos asperge sapores,*
> *Trita melisphylla, et cerinthæ ignobile gramen.*

Aristotle also recommends it for bees. *Aristot. Hist. Anim.* l. 9, c. 40; *Theophrast.* l. 6, c. 7; *Plin.* l. 21, c. 12.

CERINTHE, in the Linnean system a genus of plants, Class 5 *Pentandria*, Order 1 *Monogynia*.

Generic Characters. CAL. *perianth* five-parted; *divisions* oblong.—COR. *monopetalous; tube* short; *border* tube-bellied; *mouth* five-cleft; *throat* naked.—STAM. *filaments* five; *anthers* acute.—PIST. *germ* four-parted; *style* filiform; *stigma* obtuse.—PER. none; *calyx* unchanged; *seeds* two.

Species. The species are as follow; namely—*Cerinthe major*, Great Honey wort, an annual, native of Siberia.—*Cerinthe aspera*, an annual, native of Europe.—*Cerinthe quarta*, Small Honey wort, a biennial, native of Austria.—*Cerinthe maculata*, a perennial. *Bauh. Pin.; Ger. Herb.; Park. Theat. Botan.*

CERI'NTHIANS (*Ecc.*) a sect of heretics who took their name from one Cerinthus, cotemporary with St. John, who, among other blasphemies, denied that the world was made by God. *S. Iren. Cont. Hæres.* l. 1, c. 25, &c.; *St. Epiphan. Hær.* 28; *Euseb. Ecc. Hist.* l. 4, c. 14; *Baron. Annal. Ann.* 35.

CERINTHO'IDES (*Bot.*) the same as *Pulmonaria*.

CE'RIO (*Med.*) the same as *Achor*.

CE'RION (*Nat.*) κηρίον, a honeycomb, from κηρός, wax; the same as *Achor*.

CERI'TE (*Min.*) an opake and brittle ore, specific gravity 4·660; a species of oxide formed of silica, oxide of cerium, iron, lime-water, and carbonic acid.

CE'RITUS (*Med.*) or *Cerritus*, from Ceres; the disease arising from malt-liquors.

CE'RIUM (*Chem.*) a metal which has been obtained from a Swedish mineral called cerite, which was formerly supposed to be an ore of tungsten. When this mineral is dissolved in nitro-muriatic acid, the solution, after being neutralized by potash, is precipitated by the tartrite of potash. This precipitate, when calcined, is the oxide of cerium, which is white, very hard, brittle, and volatile. It combines with another dose of oxygen, and forms the peroxide of cerium, which is red. Cerium combines with several acids and forms salts, as the *nitrate of cerium*, the *carbonate of cerium*, the *phosphate of cerium*, the *sulphate of cerium*, the *arseniate of cerium*, &c. formed by the combination of cerium with nitric, carbonic, phosphoric, sulphuric, arsenic, &c. acids. The solutions of the oxides in the acids are either yellow or red, and give precipitates of different shades of these colours.

CE'RNUA (*Ich.*) a kind of fish mentioned by Galen.

CERNU'LIA (*Ant.*) a festival in honour of Bacchus.

CE'RNUUS (*Bot.*) from *cernuo*, to fall with the face downwards; an epithet for plants that droop or bend downwards, or hang down their head.

CEROCO'MA (*Ent.*) a division of the genus *Lytta*, in the Linnean system of insects, having the jaw linear, entire.

CERO'GRAPHY (*Ant.*) a writing or painting in wax.

CERO'MA (*Ant.*) or *Ceronium*, κήρωμα, an oil tempered with wax, with which wrestlers were anointed; also the place where they were anointed. *Dioscor.* l. 1, c. 35; *Plin.* l. 28, c. 4.

CE'ROMANCY (*Ant.*) κηρομαντεία, from κηρός, wax, and μαντεία, divination; a divination by means of wax melted over a vessel of water. They let it drop in three distinct spaces, and observed the figure, situation, distance, and concretion of the drops. *Gyrald. Syntagm. Deor.* l. 17.

CERONE'UM (*Ant.*) a cerate; vide *Ceroma*.

CER

CEROPE'GIA (*Bot.*) a genus of plants, Class 5 *Pentandria*, Order 2 *Digynia*.
Generic Characters. CAL. perianth very small.—COR. monopetalous; border very small.—STAM. filaments five; anthers small.—PIST. germ very small; style scarce any; stigmas two.—PER. follicles two; seeds numerous.
Species. The species are perennials; as the—*Ceropegia Candelabrum*, seu *Niota*, &c. a native of Malabar.—*Ceropegia tuberosa*, a native of India.—*Ceropegia bulbosa*, a native of India.—*Ceropegia acuminata*, a native of India.—*Ceropegia sagittata*, seu *Cynanchum*, &c. native of the Cape of Good Hope.—*Ceropegia tenuiflora*, *Cynanchium*, &c. seu *Apocyrium*, native of the Cape of Good Hope.—*Ceropegia obtusa*, native of Cochin China.—*Ceropegia cordata*, native of Cochin China; but the—*Ceropegia dichotoma* is a shrub, and native of the East Indies.

CEROPI'SSUS (*Med.*) κηρόπισσος, from κηρός, wax, and πίσσα, pitch; a plaster made of pitch and wax.

CEROSTRO'TUM (*Ant.*) the inlaying of pieces of ivory, &c. of different colours, in cabinets, chess-boards, &c. *Plin.* l. 11, c. 37.

CEROTUM (*Ant.*) the same as *Ceratum*.

CE'RRI *glans* (*Bot.*) the *Quercus ægilops* of Linnæus.

CE'RRIS (*Bot.*) the same as *Cerrus*.

CE'RRO (*Bot.*) from κέρας, a horn, because its wood is hard like horn; the same as the *Phellodrys*.

CE'RRUS (*Bot.*) or *Cerris*, a kind of *quercus*, or oak, that bears mast-like chesnuts prickly about the cup; the holmtree. *Plin.* l. 16, c. 6.

CE'RTHIA (*Orn.*) Creeper, a genus of animals, Class *Aves*, Order *Picæ*.
Generic Character. Bill arched, pointed.—Tongue generally pointed.—Feet formed for walking.
Species. The species are distinguished by their colour; as the—*Certhia familiaris*, which is grey.—*Certhia viridis*, the green Creeper.—*Certhia aurantia*, the orange-breasted Creeper. Also by the form of the bill; as—*Certhia falcata*, the sickle-billed Creeper.—*Certhia pacifica*, great hook-billed Creeper, &c.

CERTIFICA'NDO *de Recognitione Stapulæ* (*Law*) 1. a writ commanding the mayor of the staple to certify to the Lord Chancellor a statute staple taken before him, where the party himself detains it, and refuses to bring in the same. 2. A like writ to certify a statute merchant, and in other cases. *Reg. Orig.* 148, 151, 152.

CERTIFICATE (*Law*) generally signifies a testimony given in writing of the truth of any thing.—*Certificate*, a writ in any court giving notice to another court of any thing done therein, which is usually by transcript. *Stat.* 34, 35 *Hen.* 8, c. 14; 3 *W. & M.* c. 9.—*Trial by Certificate* is allowed in such case where the evidence of the person certifying is the only proper criterion of the point in dispute. *Litt.* § 102; 1 *Inst.* 74.—*Certificate*, or *Certification of assise*, *Certificatio assisæ novæ disseisinæ*; a writ anciently granted for the re-examining or re-trial of a matter passed by assise before justices. *Bract.* l. 4, c. 19; *Horne's Mirror of Just.* l. 3; *F. N. B.* 181; *Reg. Orig.* 200.—*Bankrupt's certificate*, the paper granted to a bankrupt by the consent of his creditors, certifying that he has surrendered and made a full disclosure of all his property.

CERTI'FICATES (*Mil.*) are of many different kinds in the army; as the certificate from a field-officer to the commander, affirming the eligibility of a person to hold a commission in his Majesty's service.—*Certificate* of the officer upon honour that he does not exceed the regulation in the purchase of his commission.—*Certificate* from a general officer to affirm and prove the losses which officers may sustain in the field.—*Certificate* from regimental surgeons, certifying that men who offer themselves for enlistment are fit to be taken; and in like manner in case of their discharge, &c.

CERTIFICATION (*Law*) Assurance when the judge ascertains the party called, and not appearing, what he will do in such a case.

CERTIORA'RI (*Law*) an original writ issuing out of the Court of Chancery, or King's Bench, directed to an inferior court, and commanding them to certify, or to return the records of a cause depending before them. *F. N. B.* 145, 242; 2 *Hawks. P. C.* c. 27, § 22.

CE'RT-MONEY (*Law*) Head-money paid yearly by tenants of several manors to the lords thereof, for the certain keeping of the leet, and sometime of the hundred.

CERVA'RIA (*Bot.*) the *Athamanta cervaria* of Linnæus.

CERVA'RIO (*Ant.*) a sheep so called, which was sacrificed to Diana instead of a deer, when a deer was not to be had. *Fest. de Verb. Signif.*

CERVA'RIUS *Lupus* (*Zool.*) a beast engendered of a hind and a wolf. *Plin.* l. 27, c. 11.

CERUCHI (*Ant.*) the cords or ropes by which the two horns of the sail-yards were held and managed. Homer called them καλῶας, the Romans sometimes *rudentes*. *Lucan.* l. 10, v. 495.

Transtraque nautarum, summique arsere ceruchi.

Val. Flacc. l. 1, v. 469.

Temperat ut tremulos Zethes fraterque ceruchos.

Scheff. de Mil. Nav. l. 2, c. 25; *Phil. in Vitruv.* l. 10, c. 6.

CE'RUCHIS (*Bot.*) a species of the *Spilanthus* of Linnæus.

CERVE'LLE (*Mil.*) a French word, denoting that earth which, in digging a ditch, or well, is not sufficiently firm to support itself.

CE'RVELAS (*Cook.*) a large kind of Bologna sausage.

CE'RVELAT (*Mus.*) a short kind of bassoon which was blown through a reed like a hautboy.

CERVIANA (*Bot.*) the *Pharnacum cervaniana* of Linnæus.

CERVICA'LIS (*Anat.*) or *Cervicales*, from *cervix*, the neck; an epithet applied to the veins and arteries of the fore-part of the neck, as—*Cervicales arteriæ*, the arteries of the neck.—*Cervicales venæ*, the Cervical veins.—*Cervicalis descendens dorsi*, the same as the *Sacrolumbaris accessorius*.

CERVICA'RIA (*Bot.*) the *Campanula cervicaria* of Linnæus.

CERVI'CULÆ *spiritus* (*Med.*) the spirit of the bone of the stag's heart.

CERVI'NUM *cornu* (*Bot.*) the same as *Coronapus*.

CERVISA'RII (*Law*) a name in Domesday book for such tenants as paid the drinclean duty on ale, from *cervisia*, which signifies ale.

CERVISPI'NA (*Bot.*) the same as the *Rhamnus* of Linnæus.

CE'RVIX (*Anat.*) the neck; that part of the body situated between the head and breast. The neck is divided generally into the anterior part or throat, and the posterior part or nape. Cervix is applied also to other parts of the body, as *cervix uteri*, or that part immediately above the *Os Tincæ*, *cervix vesicæ*, *cervix ossis*, &c.

CERU'MEN (*Chem.*) Ear-wax; a secretion formed in the canal of the external ear, is found, by a chemical analysis, to be very combustible and largely soluble in alcohol, and composed of a fat oil, resembling that of the bile; of an albuminous mucilage, in which the principal bitterness seems to reside, and of a peculiar colouring matter.

CERU'MINA (*Chem.*) the same as *Cerumen*.

CERU'RA (*Law*) a mound, fence, or inclosure.

CE'RUSE (*Chem.*) vide *Cerussa*.

CERUSIA'NA (*Med.*) a compound medicine, mentioned and described by Galen. *Gal. de Compos. Med. sec. Loc.* l. 7, c. 5.

1

CERU'SSA (*Chem.*) Ceruse, White-lead; a carbonate of lead, prepared by exposing thin plates of lead to the hot vapours of vinegar, or other acetic acids.—*Cerussa Antimonii*, Ceruse of Antimony; a perfect oxide of antimony prepared by nitre.

CERUSSE'A *urina* (*Med.*) White urine, which looks as if Ceruse had been mixed with it.

CE'RVUS (*Ant.*) a forked stake or palisado driven into the ground to annoy the enemy; so called from its resembling the horn of a stag in shape. *Tibull.* l. 4, carm. 1, v. 82.

Jam te non alius belli tenet aptius artes:
Qua decuit tutam castris producere fossam;
Qualiter adversos hosti defigere cervos.

Cervus (*Numis.*) is a common symbol of Diana on coins. [vide *Arcus*]

Cervus (*Zool.*) the stag or deer, the female of which was called *cerva*, in the Greek, for both genders, ἔλαφος, is designated by Virgil *æripes*, to denote that it was surefooted. *Virg. Æn.* l. 6, v. 803.

Fixerit æripedem cervam licet.

And by Catullus it is distinguished for its fleetness, when speaking of Achilles. *Catull. Epithal. Pel. et Thes.* v. 342.

Flammea prævertet celeris vestigia cervæ.

The poets Pindar, Anacreon, and Sophocles, have also described the cerva, or hind, as having horns; but in this they are contradicted by Aristotle, Pliny, and other naturalists.

The principal kinds of deer noticed by the ancients, as well as moderns, are—*Tarandus*, τάρανδος, the *Cervus tarandus* of Linnæus, the Rein Deer.—*Cervus*, ἔλαφος, *Cervus elaphus*, the Stag.—*Platyceros*, πλατυκέρως, the *Cervus platyceros*, or Fallow Deer.—*Caprea*, δορκάς, the *Cervus capreolus*, or Roe-Buck.—*Axis*, the *Cervus axis*, or the Spotted Axis. [vide *Cervus*] The cervus is distinguished according to its age, in Greek, into ἐμβρύοις, the young fawns just after they are brought forth; νεβροί, the fawns when they begin to feed; ματτυλίαι, subulones, spitters, whose horns begin to bud forth; κέρασται, those which are furnished with full branching horns. *Aristot. Hist. Anim.* l. 6, 9, &c.; *Plin.* l. 8, 11, &c.; *Ælian. Hist. Anim.* l. 7, &c.

Cervus, in the Linnean system, a genus of animals, Class *Mammalia*, Order *Pecora*.

Generic Character. Horns solid, branched annually, deciduous.—*Fore-teeth*, lower eight.—*Tusks*, upper solitary.

Species. The species differ both in the size of their horns and in their general make. They are as follow, namely—*Cervus alces*, in French *l'Elan*, the Elk, or Moose Deer, the largest of the tribe.—*Cervus tarandus*, the *Rangifer* of Gessner, the *Cervus rangifer* of Ray; in French *le Renne*, the Rein Deer, an inhabitant of Lapland.—*Cervus elaphus*, in French *le Cerf*, the Stag, or Red Deer, the female of which is called the hind. This animal is distinguished by its branching horns.—*Cervus dama*, the *Dama vulgaris* of Gessner, the *Cervus platyceros* of Ray; in French *le Daim et la Daine*, the Fallow Deer, the Common Buck and Doe, having branching horns palmated at the top.—*Cervus Virginiana*, the *Dama Virginiana* of Ray, the Virginian Deer.—*Cervus axis*, in French *l'Axis*, the Spotted Axis, one of the most beautiful animals of this tribe.—*Cervus pygargus*, seu *Cervus aha*, Tailless Deer.—*Cervus Mexicanus*, the *Teutlal maçane* of Hernandez; in French *Chevreuil d'Amerique*, Mexican Deer.—*Cervus porcinus*, in French *Cerf-cochon*, Porcine Deer.—*Cervus capreolus*, the *Capreolus* of Gessner; in French *le Chevreuil*, the Roe.—*Cervus muntjac*, in French *le Chevreuil des Indes*, Rib-faced Deer.—*Cervus Guineensis*, the Grey Deer.

CE'SARE (*Log.*) a syllogism of the second figure, consisting of a universal affirmative proposition between two universal negatives; as,

C e No animal is incorporeal;
S a All angels are incorporeal; therefore,
R e No angel is an animal.

CESA'RIAN SECTION (*Med.*) vide *Cæsarean Section*.

CE'SSAT EXECUTIO (*Law*) an abatement of a writ towards one of two defendants who has been tried and convicted of a trespass, until the same has been tried against the other defendant.

CESSA'TION OF ARMS (*Mil.*) an armistice or occasional truce, particularly in the case of a siege, when, if the governor find that he must either surrender or sacrifice himself and the garrison to the enemy, he plants a white flag on the breach, or beats the *chamade* to capitulate, when both parties cease firing.

CESSA'VIT (*Law*) a writ lying against a man who holds lands by rent or other services, and neglects or ceases to perform his services for two years together; or where a religious house hath lands given it on condition of performing certain offices, as reading prayers, or giving alms, and neglects it. *F. N. B.* 208.

CE'SSE (*Law*) an assessment or tax. *Stat.* 22 Hen. 8, c. 3. Also, an exacting of provisions at a certain rate for the deputy's family and garrison soldiers.

CE'SSIO (*Law*) cession; a ceasing, yielding up, or giving over; as when an ecclesiastical person is created bishop, or a parson of a parish takes another benefice without dispensation, or being otherwise not qualified, they are said to be void by *cession*.

CE'SSION (*Law*) vide *Cessio*.—*Cession*, an act whereby a person surrenders up to another person a right which belonged to himself.—*Cession of effects*, the act of delivering up all effects real and personal by a merchant to his creditors, in order to free himself from all actions and prosecutions; and is either voluntary, which frees the debtor from all the demands of his creditors upon any future estates or effects he may acquire; or *forced*, when his creditors are authorized to seize any effects that may come into his hands in payment of his debts.

CE'SSIONARY BANKRUPT (*Law*) one who has yielded up his estates to be divided amongst his creditors.

CE'SSOR (*Law*) one who ceases or neglects to perform a duty so long as to incur the danger of the law. *F. N. B.* 136.

CE'SSURE (*Law*) or *Cesser*, ceasing; giving over; or departing from. *Stat. West.* 2, c. 1.

CE'SSUS (*Law*) assessments or taxes.

CESTICI'LLUS (*Ant.*) a wisp of straw which women laid upon their heads who carried pails. *Fest. de Verb. Signif.*

CESTREUS (*Ich.*) κεστρεύς, the mullet.

CESTRI'TES *oinum* (*Med.*) κεστρίτης οἶνος, from κέστρον, betony; wine impregnated with betony.

CE'STRON (*Bot.*) the herb Betony.

CESTROSPHE'NDONE (*Ant.*) a sort of sling or engine of war for casting darts. *Liv.* l. 42, c. 65.

CESTRO'TA (*Ant.*) κεστρωτά, pieces of ivory or horn wrought with the tool called the *cestrum*. *Plin.* l. 11, c. 37; *Hesychius*.

CE'STRUM (*Ant.*) κέστρον, a graving tool; and also a borer, awl, or wimble. *Plin.* l. 35, c. 11.

Cestrum (*Bot.*) a genus of plants, Class 5 *Pentandria*, Order 1 *Monogynia*.

Generic Characters. CAL. *perianth* one-leaved; *mouth* five-cleft.—COR. monopetalous; *tube* cylindric; *divisions* ovate.—STAM. *filaments* five; *anthers* roundish.—PIST. *germ* cylindric-ovate; *style* filiform; *stigma* thickish.—PER. *berry* ovate; *seeds* very many.

Species. The species are shrubs.—*Cestrum nocturnum, Jasminoides, Syringa,* seu *Parxu,* Night-smelling Cestrum, native of Jamaica.—*Cestrum laurifolium,* seu *Laureola,* &c. Laurel-leaved Cestrum, native of America.—*Cestrum parqui,* seu *Parqui,* native of Chili.—*Cestrum auriculatum,* seu *Hediunda,* &c. Ear-leaved Cestrum, native of Lima.—*Cestrum scandens,* seu *filamentis,* &c. native of St. Martha.—*Cestrum vespertinum, Ixora,* &c. seu *Jasminum,* &c. Cluster-flowered Cestrum, native of America.—*Cestrum diurnum,* seu *Jasminoides,* &c. Day-smelling Cestrum, native of Chili.—*Cestrum venenatum,* native of the Cape of Good Hope.—*Cestrum tomentosum,* &c. native of America.—*Cestrum hirtum,* &c. native of Jamaica.—*Cestrum latifolium,* native of Trinity Island.—*Cestrum nervosum,* seu *Jasminoides,* &c. native of Carthagena.—*Cestrum macrophyllum,* Large-leaved Cestrum, native of the West Indies.—*Cestrum oleifolium,* Olive-leaved Cestrum, native of the West Indies.—*Cestrum odontospernum,* Tooth-seeded Cestrum, native of the West Indies.

CE'STUI QUE TRUST (*Law*) or *Cestui à que trust,* one in whose trust, or for whose use or benefit, another man is enfeoffed or seised of lands or tenements. *Stat.* 29 *Car.* 2. c. 3.—*Cestui que use,* or *à que use,* one to whose use any other man is enfeoffed of lands or tenements. *Stat.* 27 *Hen.* 8, c. 10.—*Cestui à que vie,* one to whom any lands or tenements are granted for life.

CE'STUS (*Ant.*) a boxing-glove. [vide *Cæstus*]

CESTUS, κιρος, was also a marriage girdle full of studs, wherewith the husband girded his wife at the wedding, and which he loosed again the first night.

CETA'CEOUS (*Zool.*) from *cete,* a whale. Cetaceous, an epithet for a very large sort of fishes which bring forth perfect animals instead of spawn.

CETA'RIA (*Ant.*) places near the sea side where large fish are taken and salted.

CE'TE (*Zool.*) an order of animals under the Class *Mammalia,* of the whale tribe, which have pectoral fins instead of feet, live upon smaller fish, and dwell in the waters. They consist of the following genera—*Monodon,* the Narval, having two teeth in the upper jaw, a spiracle on the fore part of the head, and a white skin spotted on the back with black.—*Balæna,* the Whale, the head of which is about a third part of the body, having a tubercle in which is the spiracle.—*Physeter,* the Cachalot, having teeth in the lower jaw and none in the upper.—*Delphinus,* the Porpoise, the Dolphin, and the Grampus, having teeth in each jaw.

CETERACH (*Bot.*) the *Asplenium ceterach* of Linnæus.

CE'TIC ACID (*Chem.*) a white solid substance, destitute of taste and smell, formed from spermaceti saponified.

CETO'LOGY (*Zool.*) a knowledge of those animals which in the Linnean system are comprehended under the *Cete,* or Whale.

CE'TRA (*Mil.*) a short square target or buckler, used by the Spaniards and Moors, which was made of the skin of the ounce or of the buffalo's hide.

Virg. Æn. l. 7. v. 732.

Lævas cetra tegit.

Liv. l. 28, c. 5; *Plin.* l. 11, c. 39; *Serv. in Virg.; Voss. Lex Etymol.* 34.

CETRO'NIA (*Ent.*) a division of the genus *Scarabæus,* comprehending those insects of that tribe which have their mandibles straight.

CETUS (*Astron.*) κῆτος, in the Arabic *Elkeitos,* the Whale; a southern constellation, and one of the 48 old asterisms. It is fabled to have been the sea monster sent by Neptune to devour Andromeda, which was killed by Perseus. Ptolemy reckons in this constellation 22 stars; Kepler 21; Bayer 27; Hevelius 45; Britannic Catalogue 97, two of which are of the second magnitude, namely, one in the snout of the whale called *Menkar,* and another in the tail called *Deneb. Arat. de Apparent. & Hipparc. ad Arat.; Eratosth. Character; Vitruv.* l. 9, c. 7; *Hygin. Astron. Poet.; Maril. Astron. Poet.; Ptol. Almag.* l. 7, c. 5; *Proc. de Sphær.; Petav. Uranolog.; Bay. Uranomet.; Ricciol. Almag. nov.*

CETUS (*Zool.*) the Whale. [vide *Cete*]

CEVADI'LLA (*Bot.*) Indian Caustic Barley, the seeds of which are extremely burning and caustic.

CEVA'DO (*Com.*) or *Cobit,* a measure in India for silk and linen, which is 27 inches in length.—The lesser *cevado* of Agra and Delli is 32 inches; at Cambaia and at Surate, 35 inches.

CEVI'LLUS (*Min.*) or *Ludus,* a stone mentioned by Paracelsus and Helmont.

CE'YLANITE (*Min.*) a species of stone of the argillaceous kind, found in the island of Ceylon, the *Scorbus genuinus* of Linnæus.

CEYX (*Zool.*) κινξ, the King-fisher, a bird breeding in the halcyon's nest. *Plin.* l. 32, c. 8.

C *fa ut* (*Mus.*) a note in the scale.

CHAA (*Bot.*) the *Thea Bohea* of Linnæus.

CHA'BASITE (*Min.*) a precious stone of the Zeolite family, of a white and sometimes transparent colour.

CHABLE'AU (*Mech.*) a middle-sized rope used to draw craft up a river.

CHACE (*Law*) *chacea,* a station in a forest for game, larger than a park, which may be possessed by a subject though a forest cannot. *Bract.* l. 4, c. 44.

CHACE (*Mar.*) a term used in many sea phrases: a ship is said " To have a good *chace,*" when she is so formed at the stern as to carry many guns. She is said to lie with her foot *in chace* when she lies in the nearest course to meet another ship.—" To give *chace* to a ship," to pursue it.—*Chace-guns,* or *chace-pieces,* guns lying at the head, to fire on a vessel that is pursued, in distinction from the *stern chasers,* which fire on the pursuer.

CHACE (*Mech.*) vide *Chase.*

TO CHACE (*Sport.*) a term used at the game of tennis, when the ball falls in a part of the court beyond which the opposite party must strike it the next time to gain the stroke.

CHA'CEA (*Law*) vide *Chace.*

CHACE'ARE (*Archæol.*) to hunt a hare or fox.

CHA'CEF (*Mech.*) an earthen pot.

TO CHACK (*Man.*) or, *to beat upon the hand,* a term for a horse that is not steady, but tosses up his nose and shakes his head to avoid the subjection of the bridle.

CHACOO'N (*Mus.*) *Chacone,* or *Chaconde,* an air resembling the saraband.

CHACU'RUS (*Law*) in French *Chasseur,* a horse for the chase; a hound or dog; a courser.

CHAD (*Ich.*) or *Shad,* a sort of round fish, the *Clupea alosa* of Linnæus.

CHÆROPHY'LLO *similis* (*Bot.*) the *Aphanes arvensis* of Linnæus.

CHÆROPHY'LLUM (*Bot.*) a genus of plants, Class 5 *Pentandria,* Order 2 *Digynia.*

Generic Characters. CAL. *umbel universal* spreading; *partial* nearly equal as to the number of rays; *involucre universal* none; *partial* subpentaphyllous; *leaflets* lanceolate; *perianth* proper, obscure.—COR. *universal* nearly uniform; *florets of the disk,* abortive; *proper* of five petals.—STAM. *filaments* five; *anthers* roundish.—PIST. *germ* inferior; *styles* two; *stigmas* obtuse.—PER. none; *fruit* oblong; *seeds* two.

Species. The species are perennials and biennials. Of the first kind are the following; namely—*Chærophyllum sylvestre, Cerefolium, Myrrhis,* seu *Cicutaria,* &c. Wild Cicely, Cow-weed, or Common Cow Parsley, native of Europe.—*Chærophyllum aromaticum, Cerefolium, Scandix,* &c. seu *Angelica,* Aromatic Chærophyllum, native of Lusatia.—*Chærophyllum coloratum,* seu *Myrrhis,* native of Illyria.—*Chærophyllum aureum, Cerefolium, Scandix,* seu *Myrrhis,* &c. Golden Chærophyllum, native of Germany.—*Chærophyllum hirsutum,* seu *Seseli, Cerefolium,* &c. native of Switzerland. Of the second kind are the following—*Chærophyllum bulbosum, Myrrhis, Scandix, Bulbocastanum,* seu *Cicutaria,* &c. Tuberous Chervil, native of Germany.—*Chærophyllum aristatum,* &c. native of Japan.—*Chærophyllum temulum,* seu *sylvestre,* &c. seu *Myrrhis, Scandix, Cerefolium,* &c. Wild Chervil, Rough Cow Parsley, native of Europe.—*Chærophyllum Capense,* native of the Cape of Good Hope.—*Chærophyllum scabrum,* seu *Jamma,* native of Jeddo.

CHÆROPHYLLUM is also the *Scandix* of Linnæus.

CHÆTO'DON (*Ich.*) a genus of animals, Class *Pisces,* Order *Thoracica.*

Generic Character. Head small; *mouth* small; *teeth* setaceous.—*Body* broad, compressed.—*Dorsal and anal fins* rigid, fleshy, and coated with scales.

Species. The principal species are the *Chætodon canescens, alepidotus, accuminatus, cornutus,* &c.

CHA'FAR *Alpini* (*Bot.*) a sort of Egyptian melon.

To CHAFE (*Mar.*) in French *brailler, raguer,* to rub or fret the surface of a cable, mast, yard, &c. by the motion of the ship, or otherwise.

CHA'FER (*Ent.*) a name used in composition for three sorts of insects, namely, the Cockchafer, [vide *Cockchafer*] the Stag-chafer, [vide *Stag-chafer*] and the Glimmerchafer. [vide *Glimmer-chafer*]

CHA'FERY *of an iron mill* (*Mech.*) a sort of forge, wherein the iron is wrought, and brought to perfection.

CHAFE-WAX (*Law*) an officer in chancery who prepares the wax for sealing of writs and commissions to be issued out.

CHAFF (*Bot.*) *palea,* a vulgar term for the dry calyx of corn and grass, which is called *gluma* by Linnæus. Chaff is also a dry membranaceous body interposed between two florets in some plants of the class *Syngenesia.*

CHAFF-CUTTER (*Mech.*) a machine for cutting chaff.

CHA'FFEIN (*Archæol.*) a vessel to heat water in.

CHA'FFERS (*Law*) wares or merchandise. *Stat.* 3.

CHA'FFINCH (*Orn.*) a bird so called because it delights in eating chaff; the *Fringilla Cœlebs* of Linnæus.

CHAFF-WEED (*Bot.*) the *Filago Germanica* of Linnæus, an annual.

CHA'FFY (*Bot.*) *paleaceus,* an epithet for a root, receptacle, pappus, stipe, &c.; *radix paleacea,* a chaffy root, having membranaceous scales as many of the filices; *receptaculum paleaceum,* a receptacle with palea chaff or scales, as in *Dipsacus scabiosa; pappus paleaceus,* a chaffy pappus, or one having small leaves, as in the *Helianthus; stipes paleaceus,* a stipe covered with scales.

CHAFING-DISH (*Mech.*) a utensil for warming meat.

CHAGREEN (*Mech.*) a rough-grained leather.

CHAIARXAMBAR (*Bot.*) the *Cassia fistularis* of Linnæus.

CHAIN-BOAT (*Mar.*) a large boat fitted for getting up mooring-chains, anchors, &c.—*Chain-bolts,* bolts driven through the upper end of the preventer plates, and then fastened to a link of the chains.—*Chain-plates,* iron plates bolted to the ship's side, and to which the chains and deadeyes that support the masts by the shrouds are connected.—*Chain-pump,* a sort of pump provided with a chain for pumping water out of the ship's hold. [vide *Pump*]—*Chain-shot,* two shots linked together. [vide *Shot*]—*Chain-wales,* broad timbers jutting out of its sides, serving to spread the shrouds, that they may the better support the masts.

CHAINS (*Mar.*) in French *chaînes de haubans,* strong iron plates fastened through the ship's side to the timbers.—*Top-chains,* in French *chaînes des basses vergues,* are those which preserve the lower yards from falling when in time of battle the ropes are by any means rendered incapable of service.

CHAINS (*Her.*) as badges of dignity, frequently occur in coats of arms, as he beareth " *azure* a chain pendant in pale *or,* a label *gules,*" name Chaindore.

CHA'IN-SHOT (*Mar.*) vide *Chain-Boat.*

CHAIN-SHOT (*Her.*) this weapon is termed, in blazoning, murdering chain-shot, as in the annexed figure, " He beareth *azure* three murdering chain-shots *or.*" This coat was borne by the Earl of Cumberland next to his paternal coat.

CHAIN-TIMBER (*Carpent.*) a timber of larger dimensions than the common timbers, which is placed in the middle of a building to give it ~~strength~~.

CHAIR-CARVER (*Mech.*) one employed in carving chairs, bed-posts, and other furniture which passes through the hands of the cabinet-maker or upholsterer.—*Chair-maker,* one who makes the frames of chairs.

CHA'IR-MAN (*Polit.*) one who takes the chair, and presides at any meeting.

CHAIR-MAN (*Cus.*) a sedan-man, or one who bears a sedan.

CHAISE (*Mech.*) a light open two-wheeled conveyance.

CHA'ITA (*Nat.*) χαίτα, signifies properly the mane of a quadruped, but is used by Ruffus Ephesius to express the hair of the head.

CHA'LAMEAU (*Mus.*) or *Chalmey,* from *calamus,* a reed; a wind instrument blown through a reed.

CHALA'PA (*Med.*) the same as *Jalap.*

CHALA'SSIS (*Ant.*) a sort of garment so called from its looseness; also the knot wherewith a woman's scarf is tied about her neck.

CHALA'STICS (*Med.*) χαλαστικα, from χαλάω, to relax; such medicines as by their temperate heat have the faculty of softening or relaxing the parts which, on account of their extraordinary tension or swelling, occasion pains.

CHALA'STRICUM (*Min.*) pure salt-petre, so called from the town Calastra. *Plin.* l. 31, c. 10.

CHALATO'RII *funes* (*Ant.*) from χαλάω, to let down; ropes to let down the sail-yards. *Veget.* l. 4, c. 23; *Turneb. Adv.* l. 24, c. 25.

CHALA'ZA (*Med.*) χάλαζα, or χαλάζιον, a disorder in the eyelids, which consists in a tubercle, like χάλαζα, hailstones, and is well known by the name of a *stye* or *stia.* It is white, hard, and encysted, and differs from the *crithe,* another species, only in being moveable. The *chalazion* has also been distinguished into scirrhous, cancrous, cystic, and earthy.

CHALAZA (*Vet.*) a disorder to which swine are much exposed, which causes the flesh to be full of tubercles.

CHALAZA (*Nat.*) the treadle of an egg, or the knotty kind of string at each end, whereby the yolk and white are connected together.

CHALAZ'IAS (*Min.*) a stone like hail, and so cold that no fire can heat it. *Plin.* l. 37, c. 11.

CHALA'ZION (*Med.*) vide *Chalaza.*

CHALAZOPHY'LACES (*Ant.*) from χάλαζα, hail, and

2 z 2

CHA

φυλάσσω, to preserve; Grecian priests who pretended to avert hail and tempests by cutting themselves with knives.

CHA'LBANE (*Chem.*) χαλβάνη, Galbanum.

CHALBOT (*Her.*) or *chabot*, a name given in heraldic bearings to the fish called the Bull-Head, or Miller's Thumb, as in the annexed figure. He beareth "Or three chalbots hauriant *gules*, name *Chalbot*."

CHALCA'NTHUM (*Chem.*) or *chalcanthon*, from χαλκος, brass, and ἄνθος, flower, flowers of brass, or vitriol. *Plin.* l. 34, c. 12.—*Chalcanthum rubefactum*, vitriol calcined to redness.

CHA'LCAS paniculata (*Bot.*) the *Murraya exotica* of Linnæus.

CHALCEDO'NIUS (*Min.*) Chalcedony; a genus of earths of the *Siliceous* order, consisting of silica, lime, and oxyde of iron. It is hard, light, and shining within, not mouldering in the air, and admitting of a high polish.
Species. The principal species are as follow—*Chalcedonius genuinus*, seu *Achates*, Chalcedony found in the islands of Scotland, &c.—*Chalcedonius cacholonius*, Kachelony, or Cacholony, found in the Ferroe islands. The Calmucks make their idols of this stone.—*Chalcedonius carneolus*, *Silex ruber*, seu *Carneolus*, Cornelian, or Carnelian, found in layers of agate in Arabia and Hindostan.—*Chalcedonius sardus*, *Silex vagus*, seu *Carneolus albescens*, Sardoine.—*Chalcedonius fasciatus*, Sardonyx, found in Ceylon, Feroe, Iceland, &c. It is grey and pellucid, with milk-white diaphonous bands.—*Chalcedonius onyx*, seu *Achates*, the Onyx, found in the East Indies; it is the hardest of all the species.—*Chalcedonius chrysoprasus*, Chrysoprasium, Achates prasius, seu *Nitrum fluor*, or Chrysoprase, found in Germany, &c.—*Chalcedonius helsotropius*, *Jaspii heliotropius*, seu *Heliotropium*, Heliotrope, or Blood-stone.

CHALCEDONIUS (*Med.*) an epithet for a medicine which Galen directs to be used for disorders in the ears. *Gal. de Comp. Med. sec. Loc.* l. 3, c. 1.

CHA'LCEOS (*Bot.*) a kind of thistle. *Plin.* l. 21, c. 18.

CHALCEI'OS (*Bot.*) the *Echinops sphærocephalus* of Linnæus.

CHALCETUM (*Bot.*) a place where thistles grow. *Plin.* 26. c. 7.

CHALCI'DICE (*Zool.*) χαλκιδικη, a sort of serpent so called from its resembling chalcedony. *Dioscor.* l. 2, c. 70; *Plin.* l. 29, c. 17; *Gal. de Simpl.* l. 11, c. 1.

CHALCI'DICUM (*Archæol.*) Chalcidic, a large stately hall belonging to a court of justice.

CHA'LCIS (*Ich.*) χαλκις, a fish of the turbot kind. *Arist. Hist. Animal.* l. 8, c. 25; *Plin.* l. 9, c. 47; *Colum.* l. 8, c. 17.

CHALCIS (*Ent.*) a genus of animals, Class *Insecta*, Order *Hymenoptera*.
Generic Character. Mouth with a horny compressed jaw; *thorax* gibbous; *abdomen* rounded.
Species. The principal species are, the—*Chalcis clavipes, apiformis.*

CHALCI'TES (*Min.*) a precious stone of the colour of brass. *Plin.* l. 37, c. 11.

CHALCITIS (*Min.*) from χαλκος, brass; a vitriolic mineral containing copper and iron, of a copperish colour. *Plin.* l. 34, c. 12.

CHALCO'GRAPHER (*Mech.*) chalcographus, Gr. χαλκόγραφος, from χαλκος, brass, and γραφω, an engraver; an engraver on brass or copper.

CHALCOI'DES (*Ich.*) a species of *Cyprinus.*

CHALCOLI'BANUM (*Min.*) χαλκολίβανον, a sort of fine brass.

CHA'LCOLITE (*Min.*) a species of ore of the genus of

CHA

oxides, of a glass green colour, translucent, soft, and easily frangible; the *Uranium chalcolithus* of Linnæus.

CHALCOPHO'NOS (*Min.*) χαλκοφανος, from χαλκος, brass, and φωνη, a voice; a black stone that sounds like brass. *Plin.* l. 37, c. 10.

CHA'LCOS (*Min.*) vide *Æs*.

CHALCOSMARA'GDOS (*Min.*) χαλκοσμάραγδος, the bastard emerald. *Plin.* l. 37, c. 5.

CHA'LCUS (*Ant.*) χαλκους, a weight, the 36th part of a dram, 2 gr. the same as *æreolum*; also a coin of seven mites in value. According to Pliny, ten *chalci*, or according to Pollux eight, go to an *obolus*. *Poll. Onom.* l. 9, c. 6; *Plin.* l. 21, c. 34; *Gronov. de Pec. Vet.* l. 3, c. 10; *Cenall. de Pond. apud Græv. Thes. Antiq.* tom. 11, p. 1522.

CHA'LCUTE (*Chem.*) burnt brass.

CHALDE'E (*Gram.*) a dialect of the Hebrew.

CHALDEE paraphrase (*Theol.*) another name for the *Targum*, of which there are three kinds mentioned by Walton, namely, that of Onkelos, that of Jonathan, son of Uzziel, and that of Jerusalem.

CHA'LDRON (*Com.*) or *chalder*, of coals, a measure of 36 bushels.

CHA'LICE (*Ant.*) vide *Simpulum*.

CHALICE (*Ecc.*) from *calyx*, the communion cup used at the sacrament of the eucharist in general.

CHALICRATON (*Med.*) from the old word χαλις, pure wine, and κεραννυμι, to mix; a mixture of wine and water.

CHALI'NOS (*Med.*) from χαλινος, a bridle; that part of the cheeks which on each side is contiguous to the angles of the mouth.

CHALK (*Min.*) a kind of white fossil, the *Creta scriptoria* of Linnæus, consisting principally of the carbonate of lime, and from which lime is made. It is of two sorts; hard, dry, and strong, which is best for lime; and the soft, unctuous chalk, which is best for lands.

CHALK-CUTTER (*Husband.*) a man that digs chalk.—*Chalk-pit*, a pit in which chalk is dug.

CHALK-STONES (*Med.*) a common name for the calcareous concretions in the hands and feet of people violently afflicted with the gout.

CHA'LLENGE (*Law*) *calumnia*, Fr. *chalenger*; an exception taken either against persons, as jurors, or against things, as a declaration, &c. of which there are two kinds, namely, challenge to the array, and challenge to the polls. *Challenge to the array*, is that which is made to the whole jury as it stands arranged in the panel, or little square panel of parchment, on which the jurors' names are written.—*Challenge to the polls*, i.e. to the several particular persons, or heads, in the array. Challenges likewise are distinguished into principal or peremptory, and challenges purcause.—*Peremptory or principal challenge* is that which the law allows without cause alleged, or further examination. Between the peremptory and principal challenge there is this difference, that the former is used only in criminal matters, and the latter in civil actions.—*Challenge purcause* is a challenge upon some cause or reason alleged.—*Challenge to the favour* is a species of challenge purcause where the plaintiff or defendant is tenant to the sheriff, or if the tenant's son hath married the plaintiff's daughter, with many other such like causes. *Staundf. P. C.* 124, 157; *Lamb. Eiren.* l. 4, c. 14; 1 *Inst.* 156, &c.—*Challenge to fight*, is a provocation to another, either by word or letter, to fight a duel, which is now regarded in law as a breach of the peace. *Hawk. P. C.* c. 63, § 3.

CHALLENGE (*Sport.*) a term applied to hounds who begin to cry at the first scent of their game.

CHA'LLENGED (*Sport.*) a term in cockfighting when ten staves of cocks are engaged to fight twenty-one battles, and the odd battle is to have the mastery.

CHAMÆ'PUS (*Ant.*) the bride was so called who went to the bridegroom's house on foot to be wedded.

CHALY'BEATE *chrystals of tartar* (*Chem.*) vide *Cream of Tartar.*

CHALYBEATE *waters*, mineral waters in which iron abounds, as the waters of Tunbridge, the Spa, Cheltenham, &c.

CHALYBEATES (*Med.*) medicinal preparations in which iron forms the principal ingredient.

CHALY'BIS *Rubigo et Sal* (*Chem.*) Salt of Steel. The same as *Sal Martis.*

CHALYBS (*Med.*) properly Steel, but in medicine is taken for iron.—*Chalybs tartarizatus.* vide *Ferrum tartari.*

CHAM (*Polit.*) or *Khan*, a title of the emperor or sovereign prince of Tartary.

CHA'MA (*Zool.*) a sort of Æthiopian wolf spotted like the panther, which was exhibited first at the games given by Pompey. *Plin.* l. 8, c. 19.

CHAMA (*Conch.*) a genus of animals, Class *Vermes*, Order *Testacea.*
Generic Character. Animal a Tethys.—Shell bivalve.—Hinge with a callous gibbosity.
Species. The principal species are the *Chama cor, gigas, hippopus,* &c.

CHAMA'DE (*Mil.*) a beat of drum or sound of trumpet, given as a kind of signal to the enemy to come to a parley.

CHAMÆ (*Com.*) χῆμαι, a sort of cockle-fish, of which Pliny mentions several varieties. *Plin.* l. 32, c. 10.

CHAMÆA'CTE (*Bot.*) from χαμαί, upon the ground, and ἀκτή, the Elder; Dwarf Elder, or Dane wort. *Plin.* l. 24, c. 8.

CHAMÆBA'LANUS (*Bot.*) the *Arachis hypogea* of Linnæus.

CHAMÆ'BATUS (*Bot.*) from χαμαί, on the ground, and βαίνω, to go; an epithet for a plant that creeps along the ground; the same as the *Rubus vulgaris* of Linnæus.

CHAMÆBU'XUS (*Bot.*) the same as *Polygala.*

CHAMÆCE'DRYS (*Bot.*) the same as *Abrotanum fœmina.*

CHAMÆCE'RASUS (*Bot.*) Dwarf cherry-tree. *Plin.* l. 15, c. 25.

CHAMÆCERASUS is a species of the *Prunus* of Linnæus.

CHAMÆCISSUS (*Bot.*) Ground-ivy. *Plin.* l. 16, c. 34.

CHAMÆCISSUS is the *Glechoma hederacea* of Linnæus.

CHAMÆCI'STUS (*Bot.*) the *Andromeda droseroides* of Linnæus.

CHAMÆCLA'MA (*Bot.*) the *Glechoma hederacea* of Linnæus.

CHAMÆCHRYSO'COME (*Bot.*) a species of the *Stahelina* of Linnæus.

CHAMÆCRI'STA (*Bot.*) the *Cassia chamæcrista, procumbens,* &c. of Linnæus.

CHAMÆCYPARI'SSUS (*Bot.*) the Dwarf-cypress. *Plin.* l. 24, c. 15.

CHAMÆDA'PHNE (*Bot.*) χαμαιδάφνη, the herb Periwinkle, a sort of laurel. *Dioscor.* l. 4, c. 149; *Plin.* l. 25, c. 30.

CHAMÆDAPHNE is the same as the *Andromeda* of Linnæus.

CHAMÆDRIFOLIA (*Bot.*) the *Forskoelia tenuissima* of Linnæus.

CHAMÆ'DROPS (*Bot.*) the same as *Chamædrys*, which see.

CHAMÆDRY'TES *vinum* (*Med.*) χαμαιδρύτης οἶνος; wine which has had chamædrys infused in it. *Dioscor.* l. 5, c. 51.

CHAMÆ'DRYS (*Bot.*) χαμαίδρυς, the herb Germander, or English treacle, which is reckoned efficacious against the bites of serpents. *Theoph.* l. 10, c. 10; *Dioscor.* l. 3, c. 112; *Plin.* 24, c. 14.

CHAMÆDRYS, in the *Linnean System*, the *Dryas octopetala.*

CHAMÆFI'CUS (*Bot.*) the *Ficus humilis* of Linnæus.

CHAMÆFI'LIX (*Bot.*) a species of the *Asplenium* of Linnæus.

CHAMÆ-GENI'STA (*Bot.*) the *Genista sagitalis* of Linnæus.

CHAMÆI'AIME (*Bot.*) the same as *Stellaria.*

CHAMÆI'RIS (*Bot.*) the *Iris pumila* of Linnæus.

CHAMÆI'TEA (*Bot.*) the straight dwarf willow with narrow leaves.

CHAMÆLA'ITES *vinum* (*Med.*) χαμαιλαίτης οἶνος, wine impregnated with the *Chamælea.* *Dioscor.* l. 5, c. 70.

CHAMÆLA'RIX (*Bot.*) the *Aspalathus Chenopoda* of Linnæus.

CHAMÆLÆ'A (*Bot.*) the same as the *Cneorum.*

CHAMÆLEA'GNUS (*Bot.*) the same as the *Myrtus Brabantica.*

CHAMÆ'LEON (*Zool.*) vide *Chameleon.*

CHAMÆLEU'CE (*Bot.*) χαμαιλεύκη, the Sussilage, or Coltsfoot, reckoned good for pains in the loins. *Plin.* l. 24, c. 15; *Gal. de Simpl.* l. 6; *Dodon. Pemptad.*

CHAMÆLI'NUM (*Bot.*) the *Linum catharticum*, or purging Flax of Linnæus.

CHAMÆ'MALUS (*Bot.*) a kind of dwarf apple-tree, called *Paradise apple.*

CHAMÆME'LUM (*Bot.*) χαμαίμηλον, the herb Camomile, so well known for its many medicinal virtues, being stomachic, hepatic, emollient, and carminative. It derives its name from χαμαί, dwarf, and μῆλον, apple, because its flower resembles the apple in smell. *Dioscor.* l. 3, c. 154; *Plin.* l. 22, c. 21; *Gal. Exeges. Vocab. Hippocrat.*; *Oribas. Med. Coll.* l. 11.

CHAMÆMÆLUM (*Bot.*) was reckoned as a genus among Botanists formerly, but is classed as a species in the Linnean system under the genus *Achillea, Anthemis, Arctotis, Chrysanthemum, Cotula,* and *Matricaria. Ger. Herb.*; *C. Bauh. Pin.*; *Park. Theat. Bot.*; *Raii Hist. Plant.* &c.; *Tournef. Instit.*; *Boerhaav. Ind.*

CHAMÆME'SPILUS (*Bot.*) the *Mespilus chamæmespilus* of Linnæus.

CHAMÆ-MO'LY (*Bot.*) the *Allium chamæmoly* of Linnæus.

CHAMÆMO'RUS (*Bot.*) the *Rubus chamæmorus.*

CHAMÆMY'RSINE (*Bot.*) a sort of rush, or Butcher's broom. *Plin.* l. 15, c. 7.

CHAMÆNE'RION (*Bot.*) the same as the *Epilobium.*

CHAMÆO'RCHIS (*Bot.*) the *Ophrys Alpina.*

CHAMÆPERICLYME'NUM (*Bot.*) the *Cornus Suecica* of Linnæus.

CHAMÆPEU'CE (*Bot.*) a herb good against a pain in the back. *Dioscor.* l. 4, c. 126; *Plin.* l. 24, c. 15.

CHAMÆPEUCETUINUM *vinum* (*Med.*) χαμαιπιτύινος οἶνος, wine in which bruised leaves of the Chamæpitys have been infused. *Diosc.* l. 5, c. 180.

CHAMÆPI'TYS (*Bot.*) χαμαιπίτυς, the herb Ground-pine, is a strong diuretic, opens obstructions, and powerfully promotes the menstrual discharge. *Dioscor.* l. 3, c. 175; *Plin.* l. 24, c. 6.

CHAMÆPITYS, in *the Linnean system*, the *Cressa Cretica.*

CHAMÆPLA'TANUS (*Bot.*) the dwarf Rose-bag. *Plin.* l. 12, c. 2.

CHAMÆ'PLION (*Bot.*) a name in Oribasius for the *Erysimum.*

CHAMÆPY'XOS (*Bot.*) the same as the *Pseudo-chamæbuxus.*

CHAMÆRA'PHANUM (*Bot.*) the upper part of the root of the *Apium. Paul. Æginet.* l. 7; c. 10.

CHAMÆRHODODE'NDRON (*Bot.*) or *Chamærhododendros*, the *Azalea procumbens,* &c. of Linnæus.

CHAMÆ'RIPHES (*Bot.*) χαμαιριφεῖς, trees growing in Crete and Sicily that resemble the palm. *Theoph. Hist. Plant.* l. 2, c. 8; *Plin.* l. 13, c. 4; *Hesychius.*

CHAMÆROPS (*Bot.*) a sort of palm which, when drunk in wine, is good for pains in the sides. *Plin. l. 26, c. 8.*

CHAMÆROPS (*Bot.*) a genus of plants, Class 23 *Polygamia*, Order 2 *Dioecia*.
Generic Characters. CAL. *spathe* universal; *spadix* branching.—PER. proper tripartite.—COR. tripartite; *petals* ovate.—STAM. *filaments* six; *anthers* linear.—PIST. *germs* three; *styles* permanent; *stigmas* acute; *perdrupes* three; *seeds* solitary.
Species. The species are shrubs, as the—*Chamærops humilis*, *Phoenix humilis*, *Palma minor*, seu *Chamæriphes*, &c. Dwarf Fan palm, native of Sicily.—*Chamærops serrulata*, native of Georgia.—*Chamærops Palmetto*, seu *Corypha*, &c. native of Carolina.—*Chamærops Cochinchinensis*, native of Cochin-china.—*Chamærops excelsa*, seu *Spiro et Sodio*.

CHAMÆRUBUS (*Bot.*) the *Rubus cæsius saxitilis*, &c. of Linnæus.

CHAMÆSPARTIUM (*Bot.*) from χαμαί and σπαρτίον, Spanish broom; the same as the *Genista tinctoria* of Linnæus.

CHAMÆSYCE (*Bot.*) a sort of fig good for all sorts of disorders in the womb. *Theoph. Hist. Plant. l. 9, c. 12; Dioscor. l. 4, c. 170; Plin. l. 24, c. 15.*

CHAMÆTERÆ (*Ant.*) or *Chamæterides*, χαμαιτρίδες, little images resembling handmaids, or waiting women, sitting on the ground.

CHAMÆTRACHEA (*Ent.*) a kind of sea-crab.

CHAMÆZELON (*Bot.*) χαμαίζηλον, a herb, the leaves of which are used in stuffing bed-ticks, &c.

CHAMÆZELOS (*Med.*) χαμαίζηλες, low, depressed.

CHAMBAR (*Med.*) the same as *Magnesia*.

CHAMBELECH (*Med.*) an Elixir.

CHAMBER of a mortar (*Mil.*) a cavity at the bottom of the bore to receive the charge.—*Bottled chamber*, that part where the powder lies.—*Chamber of a mine*, the place where the charge-powder is lodged that is to be used for blowing up the works.—*Chamber of a battery*, a place sunk under ground to hold the powder, bombs, &c. and to preserve them.

CHAMBER (*Her.*) the cylindrical part of ordnance is so denominated, and is sometimes borne in coats of arms without a carriage, as he beareth " Argent a chevron, *sable* surmounted of another *ermine*, between the chambers placed transverse the escutcheon of the second, fired proper;" the name *Chambers*.

CHAMBER of a Lock (*Mech.*) the space between the gates of a lock in a canal, in which the barge rises and sinks so as to pass the lock.

CHAMBERDEKIN (*Law*) or *chamberdeacon*, a name for poor Irish scholars cloathed meanly, and having no rule; or rather Beggars who were banished from England. *Stat. 1. Hen. 5, c. 7, 8.*

CHAMBERLAIN (*Law*) *Camerarius*, a term used variously in our laws and statutes for officers of state, as the *Lord Great Chamberlain of England*, to whom belongs the government of the palace of Westminster.—*Lord Chamberlain of the King's household*, who has the oversight and government of all the officers belonging to the king's chamber, and also of the Wardrobe. Chamberlains are also receivers of rents, as the—*Chamberlain of the Exchequer*, who keeps a controlment of the Pells of receipts, and *exitus*, &c.—*Chamberlain of Chester*, who receives the rents and revenues of that city.—*Chamberlain of London*, who is commonly the receiver of the city rents, payable into the chamber.

CHAMBERLARIA (*Law*) or *Chamberlangeria*, the office of a chamberlain.

CHAMBERS of the king (*Law*) *Regiæ Cameræ*, the havens or ports of the kingdom were anciently so called. *Marc. Claus. p. 242.*—*Chambers at Inns of court*, rooms or apartments belonging to the several inns of court, which are occupied by members of the legal profession; whence the term *chamber-practice* for that branch of the practice which can be followed by barristers or pleaders in their chambers, as distinguished from managing or pleading causes in open court.—*Chambers of commerce*, an assembly of merchants and traders who hear and determine all causes relative to commerce, and inspect the bills of entry and exports.

CHAMBERS (*Anat.*) two spaces between the crystalline lens and the cornea of the eye, divided off by the iris; that before the iris is termed the *anterior chamber*; and that behind it the *posterior chamber*. They are filled with an aqueous fluid.

CHAMBRANLE (*Archit.*) called by Vitruvius *Antepagmenta*, an ornament of brick or wood, which borders the three sides of doors, windows, and chimneys, varying in the different orders of architecture. It is composed of three parts: the top called the *traverse*, and the two sides called the *ascendants*. When the Chambranle is quite plain, it is only a case or frame, as in a door-case and a window frame.

CHAMBRE *depeinte* (*Law*) the painted chamber, anciently called St. Edward's chamber.

CHAMBRE *des comptes* (*Law*) a court established by royal authority for examining the accounts of those who received the royal money.

CHAMBRE (*Mil.*) in French signifies, besides its ordinary meaning, a hollow space or flaw in pieces of ordnance, for which they are invariably condemned.

CHAMBREE (*Mil.*) a term among the French to signify several soldiers lodged in the same room, in barracks, &c.

CHAMBREL (*Vet.*) the joint of the upper part of the hinder leg of a horse.

CHAMBRELECH (*Med.*) an elixir.

CHAMBROCH (*Bot.*) Trefoil.

CHAMEGAOME (*Bot.*) the *Houstonia cærulea* of Linnæus.

CHAMELÆA (*Bot.*) the *Daphne myzereum* of Linnæus.

CHAMELEON (*Bot.*) χαμαιλέων, a thistle so called, according to Dioscorides, from its many colours. It is of two sorts, the one white, which is the Sow-thistle, or Carline; and the other black, which is the *Fuller's Teazle*. *Theoph. Hist. Plant. l. 10, c. 13; Dioscor. l. 3, c. 11; Plin. l. 22, c. 18.*

CHAMELEON, *in the Linnean System*, the *Atractylis gummifera* of Linnæus.

CHAMELEON (*Zool.*) *Chamæleon*, χαμαιλέων, a quadruped of the Lizard tribe in India and New Spain, the *Lacerta Chamæleon* of Linnæus, is said to assume the colour of the objects nearest to it. The ancients supposed it to subsist upon the air; but by later discoveries it has been ascertained that it lives upon flies, which it catches dexterously with its long tongue while it hangs on the branches of the trees. *Aristot. Animal. l. 4, c. 11; Plin. l. 8, c. 33; Ael. Hist. Animal. l. 2, c. 14.*

CHAMELEOS (*Ichn.*) a kind of crab-fish.

CHAMELOT (*Com.*) vide *Camlet*.

CHAMEUNIA (*Med.*) χαμευνία, from χαμαί, on the ground, and ἰυν, a bed; a lying on the ground, or on any hard place.

TO **CHAMFER** (*Archit.*) to channel or make hollow.

CHAMFER (*Archit.*) or *Chamfret*, a smaller channel or furrow on a pillar.

CHAMFERED (*Bot.*) is applied to the stalks of plants which have impressions on them like furrows.

CHAMFERET (*Archit.*) *strix*, or *stria*, a kind of channel or gutter on a column. *Vitruv. l. 3, c. 3.*

CHAMFERING (*Carpent.*) or *Chameraining*, cutting the edge or end of any thing aslope or bevelling.

CHAMFRAIN (*Mil.*) an ancient piece of armour among the French to protect the horse.

CHAMI'RA (*Bot.*) the *Heliophila circæcioides* of Linnæus.

CHA'MOIS (*Zool.*) or Wild Goat, which inhabits the Alpine mountains, having horns erect, round, and smooth. It is classed by Linnæus under the Antelope tribe, of which it is made a species with the name of the *Antilope rupicapra*.

CHA'MOMILE (*Bot.*) a well known odoriferous plant, the *Anthemis* of Linnæus, which is possessed of a very bitter taste, but many medicinal virtues. [vide *Chamæmelum*]

CHAMOMI'LLA (*Bot.*) the *Matricaria suaveolens et Chamomilla* of Linnæus.

CHA'MOS (*My.*) or *Chemosh*, כמוש, an idol of the Moabites.

CHAMOYS (*Mech.*) or *chamois*, leather, vulgarly called *shammy*, the leather which is made of the skin of the wild goat.

CHAMPA'CA (*Bot.*) or *Champacam*, a large tall tree growing in the East Indies, the *Mechelia Champaca* of Linnæus, which bears very fragrant flowers twice a year, but no fruit till far advanced in age. The flowers boiled in oil make an ointment for the head ache.

CHAMPAIGN (*Her.*) an epithet for a sort of abatement, a *Point champaign*, or a mark of dishonour in the coat of one who kills a prisoner of war, in field, after he has craved quarter.

CHAMPAIN *Lychnis* (*Bot.*) a kind of rose, either red or white.

CHAMPAIN *Line* (*Archit.*) a conjunction of straight lines, formerly called indentations, the sides of which are parallel and similar to each other.

CHA'MPANS (*Mar.*) small flat bottomed vessels with one sail, used in China and Japan.

CHAMPA'RTY (*Law*) or *Champerty*, *campi partitio*, because the parties agree to divide the lands, &c. in question; a bargain with the plaintiff or defendant in any suit for part of the land, debt, &c. sued for, if the party who undertake it prevails therein.

CHAMPE'RTORS (*Law*) those who move pleas or suits, or cause them to be moved, either by their own procurement or others, and sue them at their proper cost, upon condition of having part of the land in variance, or part of the gain. 33 *Ed.* I. stat. 2.

CHAMPI'GNON (*Bot.*) a red-gilled edible mushroom, the *Agaricus campestris* of Linnæus, an annual.

CHA'MPION (*Law*) *Campio*; he who fights not only in his own cause, but also in defence of another. *Bract.* l. 3, tract. 2, c. 21.—*Champion of the king*, *Campio regis*, an ancient officer, who at the coronation of our kings, whilst the king is at dinner, rides armed *cap-à-pee* into Westminster-hall, and by the proclamation of a herald, makes a challenge in defence of the king's title to the crown, for which he receives a gilt cup, with a cover, full of wine, as his fee.

CHANCE (*Math.*) vide *Chances*.

CHANCE-ME'DLEY (*Law*) in French *Chance meler*, and Latin *lapsus miscere*, the accidental killing of a man in self defence on a sudden quarrel, without any evil design. *Stamf. P. C.* c. 16; 3 *Inst.* 55-7; 1 *Hawk. P. C.* c. 30, § 1.

CHANCEL (*Archit.*) *Cancelli*, an enclosed space railed off in courts of judicature.—*Chancel of a church*, part of the choir between the altar and the communion table, and the rails or ballustrade that inclose the place where the minister stands at the celebration of the communion. The chancel is also the eastern part of the church, where the altar is placed.

CHA'NCELLOR (*Polit.*) *Cancellarius*, the chief administrator of justice, and next to the sovereign.—*Chancellor of a bishop*, or *of a diocese*, one who is appointed to hold the bishop's courts, and to assist him in matters of ecclesiastical law. Stat. 37 H. 8, c. 1.—*Chancellor of the Duchy of Lancaster*, an officer before whom, or his deputy, the court of the Dutchy chamber of Lancaster is held.—*Chancellor of the Exchequer*, a great officer of state, who used to sit with the judges in court, and in the Exchequer chamber, for the ordering of things to the king's best benefit. He had also great authority in the management of the king's revenue which seems of late to be his chief business, being commonly the first commissioner of the treasury. He is mentioned in stat. 25 *H.* 8, c. 16; 33 *H.* 8, c. 39.—*Chancellor of a University*, one who seals the diplomas, or letters of degrees, &c. given in the university. The Chancellor of the University of Oxford is elected by the masters in convocation, and holds his office *durante vita*.—The *Vice-Chancellor*, who officiates for the chancellor, is nominated by the chancellor, and annually elected by the university in convocation.—The *Pro-vice-chancellors*, of which there are four, are chosen by the vice-chancellor from the heads of colleges, to one of whom he deputes the power of acting in his absence. The Chancellor of the University of Cambridge is the same as that of Oxford, except that he does not hold his office *durante vitâ*, but may be elected every three years.—The *Vice-chancellor* is chosen annually by the senate out of two persons nominated by the heads of colleges and halls.—*Chancellor of the Order of the Garter*, and also of other military orders; an officer who seals the commissions of a chapter and assembly of knights, keeps the register, and delivers the acts under the seal of the order.

CHANCELLOR *of a Cathedral* (*Ecc.*) one who superintends the regular exercise of the cathedral service.

CHA'NCERY (*Law*) *Cancellaria*, the highest court of judicature in this kingdom next to the parliament, was instituted by William the Conqueror. The Lord Chancellor presides over this court, having under him the following officers:—A *Vice-chancellor*, a newly-created officer who sits for the chancellor, or has a separate court if needful. —*Master of the Rolls*, who has the keeping of all the rolls, patents, grants, records, &c. belonging to the court of chancery. He used formerly to act as an assistant to the chancellor—*Twelve Masters in Chancery*, some of whom sit in court, and take notice of such references as are made to them, to be reported to the court.—*Six Clerks in Chancery*, who transact and file all proceedings by bill and answer.—*The Cursitors of the court*, four-and-twenty in number, who make out all original writs in chancery.—The *Register*, or *Registrar*, an officer of great importance, having several deputies under him, to take cognizance of all orders and decrees, enter, and draw them up, &c.—The *Master of the Subpœna office* issues out all writs of subpœna.—The *Examiners* are officers who take the depositions of witnesses, and make out copies of them, &c.—*The Clerks of the Affidavits* file all affidavits used in court, without which they will not be admitted.— *The Clerk of the Rolls* attends constantly at the chapel of the rolls to make search for deeds, &c.—*The Clerks of the Petty-bag-office* who make out writs of summons to Parliament, *congé d'elires*, for bishops, patents for customers; liberates, upon extent of staple; with a variety of other offices.—*The Usher of the Chancery*, formerly had the receiving and custody of all money ordered to be deposited in court, and paid it back by order. This office is now discharged by a new officer, called the *Accountant-General*.— *Serjeant at Arms*, he to whom persons standing in contempt are brought up by his substitute as prisoners.—*Warden of the Fleet* receives such prisoners as stand committed by the court, &c. To the above may be added other officers, as—the *Clerk of the Crown*, the *Clerk and Controller of the Hanaper*, the *Clerk of the Faculties* for dispensations, and the *Clerk of Appeals* on appeals from the court, &c.

The jurisdiction of this court is ordinary or extraordinary. —The *Ordinary Court* is that wherein the Lord Chancellor, Lord Keeper, &c. in his proceedings and judgments is bound to observe the order of the common law acknowledged in Chancery. This court holds plea of recognizances, writs of *scire facias* for repeal of letters patent, &c.— The *Extraordinary Court*, or *Court of Equity*, proceeds by the rules of Equity.

A suit to the extraordinary court of Chancery is commenced, on the part of a subject, by preferring or filing a *bill* in the nature of a petition to the Lord Chancellor, Lord Keeper, &c.; if, on the part of the crown, the matter of the complaint is offered by way of *information*. In the case of exhibiting a bill against a peer in Parliament, the Lord Chancellor writes a letter called a *letter missive*, to which, if no answer be put in, a *subpœna* follows; then an *order* to show cause why a *sequestration* should not issue; and, if he still stands out, a *sequestration* is granted. The same process is followed for a member of the House of Commons, except the letter missive. The form of defence varies according to the foundation on which it is made; if it rest on the matter of the bill therein apparent, it is termed a *demurrer*; if on the foundation of new matter offered, it is a *plea*; if it submits to answer the charges generally, it is an *answer*; if it disclaims all interest in the matters in dispute, it is a *disclaimer*.

CHANCES (*Math.*) a branch of modern analysis, which treats of the probability of certain events taking place by contemplating the different ways in which they may happen or follow. The laws or rules to which this science are to be reduced, are very few or general; and, consequently, leave much to the skill of the analyst. The *probability of an event* is the ratio of the chance for its happening, to all the chances, both for its happening and failing. The *expectation of an event* is the present value of any sum or thing which depends either on the happening or the failing of such an event. Events are *independent* when the happening of any one of them neither increases nor lessens the probability of the rest. Hence, if an event may take place n ways, and each of these be equally likely to happen, the *probability* that it will take place in a specified way is properly represented by $\frac{1}{n}$; certainty being represented by unity; or, which is the same thing, if the value of certainty be unity, the value of the expectation that the event will happen in a specified way is $\frac{1}{n}$. For the sum of all the probabilities is certainty or unity, because the event must take place in some one of the ways, and the probabilities are equal, therefore each of them is $\frac{1}{n}$.

If the certainty be a the value of the expectation will be $\frac{a}{n}$.

If an event happen in a ways, and fail in b ways, all being equally probable, the chance of its happening is $\frac{a}{a+b}$, and the chance of its failing is $\frac{b}{a+b}$.

Examples.

Example 1. The probability of throwing an ace with a single die in one trial is $\frac{1}{6}$; the probability of not throwing an ace is $\frac{5}{6}$; the probability of throwing either an ace or a duce is $\frac{1}{3}$.

Example 2. Let there be n balls, a, b, c, d, &c. thrown promiscuously into a bag, and let it be required to find the probability of any specified number; then, if a person draw out one of them, the probability that it will be a is $\frac{1}{n}$; the probability that it will be either a or b is $\frac{2}{n}$. If two balls be drawn out the probability that these will be a and b is $\frac{2}{n \cdot n-1}$, for there are $n \cdot \frac{n-1}{2}$ combinations of n things taken together, two and two together, and each of these is equally likely to be taken; therefore the probability that a and b will be taken is $\frac{1}{n \cdot \frac{n-1}{2}}$, or $\frac{2}{n \cdot n-1}$.

Example 3. It is required to determine the probability of drawing out of the fifty-two cards in a pack the four aces in four draws, here $m=4$, and $n=52$; whence the probability is $\frac{1 \cdot 2 \cdot 3 \cdot 4}{52 \cdot 51 \cdot 50 \cdot 49}$.

Example 4. To find the probability that an individual of a given age will live one year. In Dr. Halley's tables, out of 586 of the age of 22, 579 arrived at the age of 23; hence the probability that an individual aged 22 will live one year is $\frac{579}{586}$, or $\frac{84}{85}$ nearly; and $\frac{7}{586}$, or $\frac{1}{85}$ nearly is the probability that he will die.

Example 5. To find the probability that an individual of a given age will live any number of years. Let a be the number in the forementioned tables of the given age, $b, c, d \ldots x$ the number left at the end of $1, 2, 3, \ldots t$ years; then $\frac{b}{a}$ is the probability that the individual will live one year; $\frac{c}{a}$ the probability that he will live two years; $\frac{x}{a}$ the probability that he will live t years; also $\frac{a-b}{a}, \frac{a-c}{a}, \frac{a-x}{a}$, are the probabilities that he will die in 1, 2, t years.

If two events be independent of each other, and the probability that one will happen be $\frac{1}{m}$, and the probability that the other will happen be $\frac{1}{n}$, then the probability that both will happen is $\frac{1}{mn}$. For each of the m ways, in which the first can happen or fail, may be combined with each of the n ways in which the other can happen or fail, and there is only one in which both can happen; therefore the probability that this will be the case is $\frac{1}{mn}$. The probability that both do not happen is $1 - \frac{1}{mn}$, or $\frac{mn-1}{mn}$. The probability that they will both fail is $\frac{m-1 \cdot n-1}{m\,n}$. The probability that one will happen and the other fail is $\frac{m+n-2}{m\,n}$; and the probability that the first will fail and the second happen is $\frac{m-1}{m} \times \frac{1}{n}$; and the sum of these, or $\frac{m+n-2}{m\,n}$, is the probability that one will happen, and the other fail. If there be any number of independent events, and the probabilities of their happening be $\frac{1}{m}, \frac{1}{n}, \frac{1}{r}$, &c. respectively, the probability that they will all happen is $\frac{1}{m\,n\,r}$, &c.

Examples.

Example 1. Required the probability of throwing an ace, and then a deuce with one die. The chance of throwing an ace is ⅙, and the chance of throwing a deuce in the second trial is ⅙; therefore the chance of both happening is 1/36.

Example 2. If six white and five black balls be thrown promiscuously into a bag, what is the probability that a person will draw out first a white, and then a black ball? The probability of drawing a white ball first is 6/11, and, this being done, the probability of drawing a black is 5/10, or ½, because there are five white and five black balls left; therefore the probability required is 6/11 × ½ = 3/11.

This subject was partially considered by Huygens, Dr. Halley, and Bernouilli, but much at large by Du Moivre.

CHANCRES (*Med.*) or cankers, ulcers arising from a venereal taint, of which they are frequently the first symptom. They appear in general upon the glans and penis, but sometimes in the adjacent parts that are affected.

CHANDELIER (*Mech.*) a branch for candles.

CHANDELIERS (*Fort.*) a kind of moveable parapet consisting of wooden frames, on which fascines are laid as a cover for the workmen while they are at work in the trenches. [vide *Fortification*]

CHANDIROBA (*Bot.*) a species of the *Feuillia*.

CHANDLER (*Com.*) literally signifies a maker and seller of candles, as a tallow chandler; but is also now used for a dealer in small wares, whence a chandler's shop, a ship chandler, and a corn chandler.

CHANDRY (*Archæol.*) an apartment in the house of a King or nobleman for candles.

CHANFRAIN *blanc* (*Man.*) a white mark on the forehead of a horse.

CHANFREIN (*Man.*) French for the shaffroon or black noddy, on the forehead of a horse.—*Chanfrein de cheval d'armes*, the front-stall, head-piece of, or forehead-piece of, a barbed horse.

CHANFRIN (*Man.*) the fore part of a horse's head extending from under the ears along the interval between the eye-brows down to the nose.

CHANGE (*Mil.*) a word of command given to the man while on the march to shift the firelock from one shoulder to the other.

CHANGE (*Com.*) small coin in exchange for one of larger value, as shillings are the change for a guinea or pound.

CHANGE (*Com.*) vide *Exchange*.

CHANGE (*Hunt.*) when a stag met by chance is taken for the one dislodged and pursued sometime before.

CHANGE *the mizzen* (*Mar.*) in French *Change l'artimon*, an order to bring the mizzen-yard over the other side of the mast.

CHANGEABLE ROSE (*Bot.*) the *Hibiscus mutabilis* of Linnæus; a plant, so called because the flowers change their colour at certain periods: at their first opening they are white, they then change to a blush-rose colour, and as they decay they turn to a purple. This is otherwise called the Martinico Rose.

CHANGER (*Law*) an officer of the mint who exchanges coin for bullion. *Stat.* 2, *Hen.* 6, c. 16.

CHANGER, *Money* (*Com.*) a banker.

CHANGES (*Math.*) the permutations or variations which any number of things may undergo in regard to position or order, &c.; as how many changes may be rung on a given number of bells, or how many different ways any number of letters may be disposed so as to form words, &c. thus, suppose three things, as *a*, *b*, *c*, are to be disposed in a certain order, they will undergo six different changes, as in the margin; since each of the three may be combined three different ways with each combination of the other two, i. e. *a* may be combined with *b c* and *c b*, *b* with *a c* and *c a*, *c* with *a b* and *b a*.

    a, b, c
    b, a, c
    b, c, a
    a, c, b
    c, a, b
    c, b, a

CHANGES (*Mus.*) alternate or variegated peals rung on bells.

CHANNA (*Ich.*) χάννος, χάννη, a sort of sea fish not unlike the perch, but the flesh is somewhat harder. *Plin.* l. 9, c. 25; *Castell. Lex. Med.*

CHANNEL (*Med.*) vide *Canalis*.

CHANNEL (*Geog.*) an arm of the sea running into the land, or a narrow sea between two islands, &c.

CHANNEL *of a horse* (*Vet.*) the hollow between the two nether jaw bones where the tongue is lodged.

CHANNEL (*Archit.*) a gutter or furrow of a pillar. But the *Channel in an Ionic chapiter* is that part which lies somewhat hollow under the *abacus*, and open upon the *echinus*.—*Channel of the Larmier* is the soffit of a cornice.—*Channel of the volute*, the face of its circumvolution.

CHANNELLED (*Bot.*) *caniculatus*, an epithet signifying hollowed above with a deep longitudinal groove, and convex underneath. It is applied to the stem, leaf, and petiole.

CHANNELS (*Mar.*) or *Chain-Wales*, *porte-haubans*; broad thick planks projecting horizontally from the ship's outside, used to extend the shrouds from each other, and from the axis, or middle line of the ship, as a greater security and support to the masts, and to prevent the shrouds from rubbing against the gun-wale.

CHANOS (*Ich.*) vide *Channa*.

CHANSCHENA-POW (*Bot.*) the *Bauhinia tomentosa* of Linnæus.

CHANSON (*Mus.*) French for a song.

CHANSONETTE (*Mus.*) the diminutive of *chanson*, signifying a little song.

CHANSONS *de geste* (*Mus.*) the historical and heroical romances sung from town to town by itinerant minstrels in the thirteenth century.

CHANT (*Mus.*) a species of melody used in cathedrals between an air and recitative, to which the psalms of the day are repeated.—*Chant en Ison*, a name formerly for a species of chant or psalmody consisting of only two sounds.—*Chant sur le Livre*, a part composed from only seeing that on which it is founded.

CHANTANT (*Mus.*) instrumental music which is performed in a smooth, melodious, and singing style.

CHANTE-PLEURE (*Archit.*) French for an outlet made in the wall of a building, which stands near a running stream, in order to let the water that overflows pass freely in and out of the place.

CHANTANELLE (*Bot.*) a species of the *Agaricus*.

CHANTER (*Mus.*) a male singer, or the leader of the choir.

CHANTERELLA (*Bot.*) vide *Chantanelle*.

CHANTERELLE (*Mus.*) the highest or most acute of the

four strings of a violin tuned to E above the treble cliff note.
CHANTERRES (*Mus.*) certain provençal singers of songs and ballads.
CHANTICLEE'R (*Zool.*) a name sometimes given to a cock from his clear loud crow.
CHA'NTIER (*Mech.*) French for a square piece of wood which is used for raising things, particularly in disposing barrels of gunpowder.
CHA'NTLATE (*Archit.*) a piece of wood projecting beyond the wall for supporting two or three rows of tiles to prevent the rain water from trickling down the sides of the wall.
CHA'NTOR (*Mus.*) formerly an appellation given to the master of the choir, which is one of the first dignities of the chapter.
CHANTRESS (*Mus.*) a female singer.
CHA'NTRY (*Ecc.*) a chapel anciently joined to a cathedral or parish church, and endowed with an annual revenue for the maintenance of one or more priests to sing masses for the souls of the founders.—*Chantry priests*, those appointed to sing the mass in the chantries.
CHANTS RO'YAL (*Mus.*) Lyrics on lofty subjects, formerly much used.
CHAO'LOGY (*Lit.*) from χάος, and λόγος, a doctrine; the history and description of chaos.
CHA'OMANCY (*Ant.*) the art of making presages from observations on the air, which was practised by Paracelsus and his followers, who called the air by the name of chaos.
CHA'OS (*Nat.*) from the old word χάω, and χαίνω, to gape; the air, according to Paracelsus.
CHAO'SDA (*Med.*) an epithet for the plague, in the language of Paracelsus.
CHAO'SA (*Bot.*) the Egyptian name for coffee.
CHAP (*Anat.*) the upper or lower parts of a beast's mouth.
CHAPE (*Mil.*) in French *chappe*, and Spanish *chapa*, the little thin plate of silver or iron at the point of a scabbard or sword.
CHAPE, French for a barrel containing another barrel that holds gunpowder; also for a composition of earth, horse-dung, and wadding, to cover the mouth of a cannon or mortar.
CHAPE (*Hunt.*) the tip end of a fox's tail.
CHAPEAU (*Her.*) a cap of state worn by dukes, of scarlet velvet, lined with ermine, on which a nobleman's coat of arms is borne as on a wreath. [vide *Cap*]
CHA'PEL (*Ecc.*) *capella*, in French *chapelle*, commonly called a *chapel of ease*, being built for the convenience of parishioners who dwell far from the parochial church wherein divine service is performed. *A free chapel* is a chapel of ease with a settled revenue for the perpetual maintenance of the curate.
CHAPEL (*Print.*) a printing-office; so called because printing in England was first carried on in a chapel at Westminster Abbey.
CHA'PELET (*Mil.*) French for a piece of flat iron with three tenons, or ends of timber, which is fixed to the end of a cannon.
CHA'PELETS (*Man.*) a couple of stirrup leathers made fast to the saddle, each mounted with a stirrup, and joined at top in a sort of buckle, called the head of the chapelet.
CHAPELLA'NY (*Ecc.*) that which does not subsist by itself, but is built and founded within the precincts of another church, on which it is dependant.
CHA'PELLING a ship (*Mar.*) in French *coiffer faire chapelle*; the act of turning the ship round when close hauled in a light breeze of wind, in order to bring it to its former position.
CHAPELO'NIANS (*Print.*) the members or workmen of a printing-office who have paid a certain fine on admittance.

CHA'PELRY (*Ecc.*) *capellaria*, is to a chapel what a parish is to a church; the precincts and limits thereof.
CHAPERO'N (*Her.*) a hood or cap, particularly that worn by the knights of the garter as a part of their habit.
CHAPERON *of a bit mouth* (*Man.*) a name applied to scatch-mouths, and all others, except anon-mouths, signifying the end of the bit that joins to the branch just by the banquet.
CHAPERONS (*Polit.*) seditious parties who sprung up in France during the reign of King John, in 1358.
CHAPITEAU'X (*Mil.*) two small boards which are joined together obliquely, and serve to cover the touch-hole of a piece of ordnance.
CHA'PITER (*Archit.*) the head or upper part of the pillar. [vide *Capital*]—*Chapiters with mouldings*, those without ornaments, as the Tuscan and Doric.—*Chapiters with sculptures*, those that are set off with leaves, and carved work.
CHA'PITRES (*Law*) *capitula*, signifying in common law a summary of such matters as are to be inquired of or presented before justices in eyre, justices of assize, or of peace. *Britt.* c. 3. *Chapitres* are now commonly articles delivered by the mouth of the justice in his charge to the jury.
CHA'PLAIN (*Ecc.*) *capellanus*, a clergyman who performs divine service in a chapel; particularly one who officiates in the domestic worship of the Royal Family, or any of the nobility, who have a private chapel.
CHAPLAIN, *naval* (*Mar.*) in French *aumonier*, a clergyman of the established church appointed to perform divine service on board a ship.
CHAPLAIN *General* (*Mil.*) an officer appointed for the government of brigade and regimental chaplains, who are recommended by him, and for whose good conduct he is responsible to head-quarters.
CHA'PLET (*Archit.*) a kind of ornamental moulding; a fillet or little round moulding carved into beads or lines, &c.
CHAPLETS (*Ecc.*) are used by both the Roman Catholics and Mahometans; those used by the Roman Catholics are a certain number of beads threaded like a bracelet, by which they count their Pater Nosters and Ave Marias.
CHAPLETS (*Her.*) garlands, or head-bands of leaves, were called by the Romans *coronæ militum*, because they were given to soldiers as rewards of valour. They have since been borne in coats of arms as trophies or ensigns of military prowess, and success, as the field is—" *Or* on a chief *gules*, three chaplets of the first; the name Morrison, of Hartfordshire." A chaplet of roses in heraldry is composed of more than four roses.
CHA'PMAN (*Com.*) a merchant, or one who cheapens or offers to purchase any commodity.
CHAPOURNE'T (*Her.*) a little hood which is occasionally borne in coat-armour.
CHAPPE' (*Her.*) another name for cloaked, which is now more commonly a chief party *per bend dexter* or *sinister*, or both.
CHAPPERONNE' (*Her.*) hooded, or provided with a hood like a friar's cowl.
CHAPPERO'NS (*Cust.*) or *shafferoons*, a name for the little shields, containing deaths' heads, and other funeral devices, placed on the foreheads of horses that draw hearses at funerals.
CHA'PTER (*Ecc.*) *capitulum*, a congregation of clergymen. They are so called in a cathedral church under the dean, because they consist of prebendaries and canons, who are *capita ecclesiæ*, chiefs of the church. 25 *Hen.* 8, c. 21; *Co. Lit.* 103.—*Chapter-house*, a building near a cathedral or collegiate church, where the chapter is held.

4

CHA

CHA'PTRELS (*Archit.*) another name for imposts, or those parts on which the feet of pillars stand.

CHAR (*Ich.*) vide *Charr*.

CHARA (*Bot.*) a genus of plants, Class 21 *Monoecia*, Order 1 *Monandria*.
Generic Character. CAL. perianth four-leaved; *leaflets subulate*—COR. none.—STAM. *filaments* none; *anther* globose.—PIST. *germ* turbinate; *style* none; *stigma* oblong.—PER. *crust* ovate; *seed* single.
Species. The species are perennials or annuals: of the first kind are—*Chara vulgaris*, *Hippuris*, seu *Equisetum*, &c. Common or Stinking Chara, or Stone-wort, native of Europe.—*Chara setosa*, native of the East Indies.—*Chara foliolosa*, native of Pensylvania.—*Chara leglanica*, native of Malabar.—*Chara hispida*, *Hippuris*, seu *Equisetum*, &c. Prickly Chara, or Stone-wort, native of Europe.—*Chara tomentosa*, *Equisetum*, &c. seu *Hippusis*, &c. Brittle Chara, or Stone-wort, native of Europe.—*Chara squamosa*, native of Barbary.—*Chara corallina*, native of Malabar.—*Chara flexilis*, seu *Hippuris*, &c. Smooth Chara, or Stone-wort, native of Europe. Of the second kind are the following—*Chara translucens*, native of Britain.—*Chara nidifica*, native of Britain.—*Chara gracilis*, native of Britain. Ger. Herb.; Raii Hist. Plant.

CHA'RABE (*Med.*) or *Carabe*, Amber.

CHARA'CIA (*Bot.*) a kind of spurge. Plin. l. 26, c. 8.

CHARA'CIAS (*Bot.*) the *Euphorbia Characias* of Linnæus.

CHARACTER (*Lit.*) χαρακτηρ, an impression, from χαρασσω, to engrave; any mark which serves as a sign to denote some particular object. Characters are abbreviations, or characters properly so called. *Abbreviations* are the initials, or other letters, which are substituted for the words of which they form a part. [vide *Abbreviations*]
Characters, properly so called, are distinguished according to the subject, into literal, astronomical, mathematical, chemical, botanical, grammatical, musical, chronological, heraldic, and assayers' characters.

Literal Characters.

Literal characters are either such as serve to express the names of things, which are properly called letters; or they are such as express the things themselves by the representation of their image, or similitude, which are called *hieroglyphics*. Literal characters are, according to their use, *particular* or *universal*. Particular *Characters* are the letters which have been framed by different nations for their own use, and which constitute their alphabets. [vide *Alphabet*]—Universal, or *real Characters*, are fictitious alphabets, which have been invented by different persons as the basis of a universal language. Of this description is the "Real Character of Bishop Wilkins."

Astronomical Characters.

Characters.	Planets.	Characters.	Planets.
☉	The Sun.	♄	Saturn.
☽	The Moon.	♅	Herschel, or the
⊕	The Earth.		Georgium Sidus.
☿	Mercury.	⚳	Ceres.
♀	Venus.	⚴	Pallas.
♂	Mars.	⚵	Juno.
♃	Jupiter.	⚶	Vesta.

Signs of the Zodiac.

Characters.	Signs.	Characters.	Signs.
♈	Aries.	♋	Cancer.
♉	Taurus.	♌	Leo.
♊	Gemini.	♍	Virgo.

CHARACTER.

Characters.	Signs.	Characters.	Signs.
♎	Libra.	♑	Capricorn.
♏	Scorpio.	♒	Aquarius.
♐	Sagittarius.	♓	Pisces.

Phases of the Moon, Aspects, &c.

●	New Moon.	☊	Dragon's Head, or ascending Node.
☽	First Quarter.	☋	Dragon's Trail, or descending Node.
○	Full Moon.	°	Degrees.
☾	Last Quarter.	′	Minutes.
☌	Conjunction.	″	Seconds.
☍	Opposition.	A.M.	ante meridiem, &c.
✻	Sextile.		[vide *Abbreviations*]
▯	Quartile.		
△	Trine.		

Mathematical Characters.

Mathematical characters are distinguished into the arithmetical, algebraical, and geometrical. *Arithmetical characters* comprehend numerals [vide *Arithmetic* and *Notation*] and characters for weights and measures, of which the ancient may be found under *Pondera* and *Mensuræ*, the modern under *Measure* and *Weight*.—The algebraical and geometrical characters are as follow:

Algebraical Characters.

A, B, C, &c.	used first by Stifelius for the unknown or required quantities.
A, E, I, O, U, Y.	used by Vieta for the unknown quantities.
B, C, D, &c.	by Vieta for the known quantities.
$a, e, i, o, u.$	used instead of the capitals by Harriot for the unknown quantities.
$b, c, d,$ &c.	for known quantities.
$a, b, c, d,$ &c.	used by Descartes for the known quantities.
$x, y, z,$ &c.	for the unknown quantities.
$\dot{x}, \dot{y}, \dot{z}.$	used by Newton to denote the first order of fluxions of the variable quantities.
$\ddot{x}, \ddot{y}, \ddot{z}.$	for the second order of fluxions.
$\dddot{x}, \dddot{y}, \dddot{z}.$	for the third order of fluxions.
$dx, dy, dz.$	used by Leibnitz for the differentials of the quantities to which the letter d is prefixed.
$\delta^r, x^r, \delta\delta^r, xx^r,$ &c.	initials used by Diophantus to denote the powers *dynamis cubus*, *dynamo-dynamis*, *cubo-cubus*, &c. i. e. the 2d, 3d, 4th, &c.
$2, 3, \mathfrak{q}, 33,$ &c.	used by Stifelius for *res*, or *cos*, *zensus*, *cubus*, *zenzezensus*, &c. i. e. the root, square cube, &c.
$\smile 1, \smile 2, \smile 3,$ &c.	used by Bombelli for the unknown quantity, and the 1st, 2d, 3d powers, &c.
⓪, ①, ②, ③, &c.	used by Stevinus for 0, 1, 2, 3, &c. powers of the unknown quantity 0.
⊕, ⊕, ⊕, &c.	used by Stevinus for the square root, cube root, 4th root, &c.
⊕, ⊕, &c.	for the cube root of the square and the square root of the cube, &c.
$a, aa, aaa, aaaa,$ &c.	used by Harriot to denote the quantity and its powers.
$a, a^2, a^3, a^4,$ &c.	numeral exponents substituted by Descartes in the place of the letters, and now in use.
℞	the sign of radicality, or the sign used to denote the root by Paciolus and others.
$\sqrt{}$	the sign of radicality substituted by Stifelius and Recorde; thus $\sqrt{x}$, or the square root of x.
$\sqrt{}, \sqrt{\sqrt{}}, \sqrt{\sqrt{\sqrt{}}}$,	the sign of the square cube and biquadratic roots used by Scheubel and others.
$\sqrt{q}, \sqrt{c},$ &c.	the sign of square, cube, &c. substituted by Recorde and others.

CHARACTER.

Characters		
$\sqrt{}$, $\sqrt[3]{}$, $\sqrt[4]{}$, &c.	the sign of the 2d, 3d, 4th, &c. root substituted by Girarde, and in present use.	
p	an abbreviation of *plus*, or *piu*, more, and the sign of addition used by Paciolus and others.	
$+$	the sign of addition, and also of a positive quantity, as $+a$, or $2+2$, i. e. 2 added to 2.	
m	an abbreviation of *minus*, less, and a sign of subtraction.	
$-$	a sign of subtraction, and also of a negative quantity, substituted by Stifelius and others, as $-a$, or $3-2$, i. e. 2 subtracted from three, or three less two.	
$\times$	a sign of multiplication, introduced by Oughtred.	
$\div$	a sign of division, introduced by Dr. Pell.	
$=$	the sign of equality, introduced by Recorde.	
$\propto$	a sign of equality, used by Descartes.	
$:$ $::$	a sign of proportionality, introduced by Oughtred.	
$\div$	a sign of continued proportion, by the same.	
$\therefore$	a sign signifying *ergo*.	
$>$	a sign of greater } used by Harriot.	
$<$	a sign of less	
⊐	signs of the same by Oughtred.	
	a sign of involution } by Dr. Pell.	
	a sign of evolution	
	a sign denoting a general difference between two quantities, used by Dr. Wallis.	
$(\ )$	the parenthesis, used as a vinculum by Girarde.	
——	the vinculum, used by Vieta.	

Geometrical Characters.

□	a Square,	< or ∠	an Angle,
△	a Triangle,	∟	a Right Angle,
▭	a Rectangle,	⊥	Perpendicular,
⊙ ○	a Circle,	=	Parallel.

Chemical Characters.

Chemical characters were formerly used to import some particular substance or process, and are as follow:

Ā	Abstrahere,	To abstract.
	Acetum,	Vinegar.
	Acetum distillatum,	Distilled Vinegar.
A	Aer,	Air.
⊕dd.	Ærugo distillata,	Distilled Verdigrease.
	Æs ustum,	Burnt Brass.
	Albumen,	The White of an Egg.
V̇A.	Alcahest vini,	{ Highly rectified Spirit of Wine.
	Alembicus,	Alembic.
	Alumen,	Alum.
	Alumen ustum,	Burnt Alum.
aaa.	Amalgama,	
a a	Ana,	Each.
	Antimonium,	Antimony.
	Aqua,	Water.
	Aquafortis,	
	Aqua regia,	
	Aqua vitæ,	Brandy.
	Arena,	Sand.
	Argentum limatum,	Filings of Silver.
	Argentum,	Silver.
	Argentum vivum,	Quicksilver.
	Arsenicum,	Arsenic.
	Atramentum,	Ink.
	Auripigmentum,	Orpiment.

Characters		
⊙	Aurum,	Gold.
	Aurum foliatum,	Leaf Gold.
	Aurum limatum,	Filings of Gold.
⊙ P.	Aurum potabile,	Vapour.
B.	Balneum,	A Bath.
MB.	Balneum mariæ,	The Heat of Boiling Water.
VB.	Balneum vaporis,	A Vapour Bath or Heat.
	Borax,	
Z	Cæmentare,	To cement.
C.	Calcinare,	To calcine.
	Calx,	Lime.
	Calx viva,	Quick Lime.
yr	Camphora,	Camphire.
	Caput mortuum,	
	Cera,	Wax.
	Cerussa,	Ceruss.
	Chalybs,	Steel or Iron.
	Cineres,	Ashes.
	Cineres clavellati,	Potash.
	Cinnabaris,	Cinnabar.
H.E.	Coagulare,	To coagulate.
C.C.	Cornu cervi,	Hartshorn.
	Creta,	Chalk.
	Crocus,	Saffron.
	Crocus Martis,	Crocus of Copper.
	Crucibulum,	Crucible.
	Crystallus,	Crystal.
	Cucurbitum,	A Cucurbite.
	Cuprum,	Copper.
d.	Distillare,	To distil.
	Dies,	The Day, or Light.
	Digerere,	To digest.
	Fæces vini,	Lees of Wine.
	Farina,	Meal.
	Farina laterum,	Brickdust.
	Ferrum,	Iron.
	Filtrare,	To filter.
	Fluere,	To flow.
	Fuligo,	Soot.
	Fumus,	Smoke.
	Gummi,	Gum.
	Hora,	An hour.
	Ignis,	Fire.
♃	Jupiter,	Tin.
	Lapis hæmatitis,	Blood-Stone.
	Lapis lazuli,	
	Later,	Brick.
	Lithargyrus,	Litharge.
D	Luna,	Silver.
N	Lutare,	To lute.
	Magnes,	The Magnet.
	Marcasita,	Marcasite.
	Mars,	Iron.
	Martis limatura,	Filings of Iron.
	Massa,	A Mass.
a a	Materia,	Matter.
	Mel,	Honey.
	Mensis,	A Month.
	Mercurius,	Mercury.
	Mercurius præcipitatus,	Mercury Precipitate.
	Mercurius sublimatus,	Mercury Sublimate.
	Nitrum,	Nitre.
	Nox,	Night.
	Oleum,	Oil.
	Oleum olivarum,	Oil of Olives.
	Orichalcum,	Brass.
	Phlegma,	Phelgm.
♄	Plumbum,	Lead.
	Præcipitare,	To precipitate.

CHARACTER.

	Pulvis,	Powder.
	Pumex,	Pumice Stone.
	Purificare,	To purify.
	Putrificare,	To putrify.
Q. E.	*Quinta essentia,*	Quintessence.
	Realgar,	
	Recipiens,	A receiver.
	Regulus,	
	Retorta,	Retort.
	Saccharum,	Sugar.
	Sal alcali,	Alkaline Salt.
	Sal ammoniacum,	Sal ammoniac.
	Sal commune,	Common Salt.
	Sal gemmæ,	
	Sal marinum,	Sea Salt.
	Sal nitrum,	Salt Petre, or Nitre.
	Sapo,	Soap.
	Saturnus,	Lead.
S. H.	*Sigillare hermetice,*	To seal hermetically
	Sol,	The Sun, or Gold.
	Solvere,	To dissolve.
	spiritus,	Spirit.
	Spiritus vini,	Spirit of wine.
	Stannum,	Tin.
S. S. S.	*Stratum, super stratum.*	
	Sublimare,	To sublime.
BB†	*Succinum,*	Amber.
	Sulphur,	Sulphur.
	Sulphur philosophorum,	The sulphur of philosophers.
	Sulphur vivum,	Mineral or Live Sulphur.
	Talcum,	Talc.
	Tartarus,	Tartar.
	Terra,	Earth.
	Tinctura,	Tincture.
	Tutia,	Tutty.
	Venus,	Copper.
	Vinum,	Wine.
	Viride æris,	Verdigrease.
	Vitellum ovi,	The Yolk of an Egg.
	Vitriolum,	Vitriol.
XX	*Vitrum,*	Glass.
	Urina,	Urine.
	Vitriolum album,	White Vitriol.

Botanical Characters.

The botanical characters were introduced by Linnæus, to distinguish annuals from biennials and perennials; and also fertile from barren flowers, &c. [vide *Botany*]

Grammatical Characters.

Grammatical Characters are either such as determine the pronunciation of words, and are called accents [vide *Accents*]; or they are such as distinguish words and sentences from each other, and are called points or stops. [vide *Punctuation*] To these may be added the following, which are employed for different purposes in writing and printing.

( ) Parenthesis	† ‡ & * Marks of reference
[ ] Crotchet	§ Section, Division, or Paragraph.
- Hyphen	
⁁ Caret	¶ Paragraph.
*** To denote something omitted.	" " A quotation.

Musical Characters.

Musical characters are employed to distinguish the notes from each other. [vide *Notes*]

Chronological Characters.

The only chronological characters which are not abbreviations, are the Dominical Letters, which mark the Sundays throughout the year. [vide *Chronology*]

Heraldic Characters.

The only heraldic characters, which are not abbreviations, are the letters which are employed to mark the different parts of the escutcheon. [vide *Heraldry*]

Assayer's Characters.

	1 dwt.		15 dwt.
	2		18
	5		19
	10	ob,	½ obulus.

CHARACTER (*Med.*) an hereditary disposition to some particular disease.

CHARACTER (*Poet.*) an assemblage of moral qualities combined by the fiction of the poet in one person, the excellence of which consists in its being a lively and just representation of the characters and manners of human life.

CHARACTER (*Nat.*) the property or quality which distinguishes natural objects, as plants, animals, &c. from each other. These are either generic or essential.—*Generic Characters* are those which distinguish many things of a kind, and constitute the genus.—*Essential Characters* are those which distinguish a small number of individuals.

CHARACTERI'STIC of a *Logarithm* (*Math.*) a term used first by Briggs for what is commonly called the index, or exponent; thus 0 is the characteristic of all numbers from 1 to 10, 1 the characteristic of all those from 10 to 100, 2 of those from 100 to 1000, &c.

CHARACTERISTIC *letter* (*Lit.*) in a Greek verb is that consonant which immediately precedes the varying termination.

CHARACTERISTIC *Triangle of a Curve* (*Geom.*) a rectilinear right-angled triangle, whose hypothenuse is a part of the curve, as the triangle Qqr, for if pq be parallel, and indefinitely near to the ordinate PQ and Qr parallel to the abscess AP, then Qr is the fluxion of the abscess AP, qr the fluxion of the ordinate PQ, and Qq the fluxion of the curve AQ; hence the elementary triangle Qqr is the characteristic triangle of the curve AQ, the three sides of which are $\dot{x}\dot{y}\dot{z}$.

CHARADE (*Lit.*) a sort of riddle, the subject of which is a word of one or two syllables.

CHARA'DRIUS (*Orn.*) χαράδριος, a bird, the sight of which cures a person of the jaundice, according to Ælian. *Aristot. Hist. Anim.* l. 9, c. 11; *Hist. Animal.* l. 17, c. 12.

CHARADRIUS, in *the Linnean system the Plover,* a genus of birds, Order *Animalia,* Class *Aves Grallæ.*
Generic Character. Bill straight, obtuse.—*Feet* formed for running.
Species. The principal species are the—*Charadrius hiaticula,* the ringed Plover.—*Charadrius Jamaicensis,* the collared Plover.—*Charadrius morinellus,* the Dotterel.

CHA'RAG (*Com.*) a tribute paid to the Grand Seignior by Christians and Jews, who either live or trade in the Turkish territories.

CHARAMA'IS (*Bot.*) the Turkish and Persian name for the *Ambela.*

CHARA'NTIA (*Bot.*) the *Momordica charantia* of Linnæus.

CHARBON (*Man.*) a little black spot which remains from a large one in the cavity of the corner teeth of a horse about seven or eight years old.

CHARCEDONIUS *lapis* (*Min.*) the same as *Chalcedonius.*

CHARCOAL (*Chem.*) the substance from wood half burnt.

CHA

—*Mineral charcoal*, a species of ore of the glance coal family, of a greyish black colour.

CHA'RDONE (*Bot.*) the same as *Cinara spinosa*.

CHARDO'NS *de fer* (*Mil.*) Cramp-irons used in scaling; also iron spikes on a gateway to prevent persons getting over.

CHARDS *of Artichokes* (*Hort.*) the leaves of fair artichoke plants bound in straw till they lose part of their bitterness and grow white.—*Chards of beet*, white beets which being transplanted into hot beds prepared for them produce the true *chard*.

CHARE (*Cus.*) from *care* or *charge*, a small piece of work; whence also charewoman, or charwoman, one who goes out by the day to job.

CHARE (*Ich.*) vide *Char*.

CHARE'A (*Archæol.*) a charr, carr, or cart.

CHARGE (*Law*) signifies that which binds a man to the performance of any thing, in distinction from *discharge*, which is the removal of such charge.—Land may be *charged* divers ways, as by grant of rent out of it, by statutes, judgments, and the like. *Lit.* § 648.—*Charge of horning*, in the Scotch law, the charging of persons to pay or perform certain debts, or duties, by warrants called *letters of horning*.—*Charge to enter heir*, a writing in the Scotch law passing under the signet, and obtained at the instance of the creditor, against the heir of his debtor, for fixing upon him the debt as representing his debtor, or against the debtor himself.

Charge is also used to signify the instructions given by the judge who presides on the bench to the grand jury, respecting the articles into which they have to make inquiry.

CHARGE (*Gun.*) in French *charge*; the quantity of powder and ball, &c. put into the gun at a time, for the purpose of producing a discharge. The charge of powder for proving guns is equal to the weight of the ball, but for service it may be ½, ⅓, and even less.

CHARGE (*Elect.*) the accumulation of electric matter on one surface of an electric, as the Leyden Phial, a pane of glass, &c. while an equal quantity passes off from the opposite surface. Electrics are in fact said to be *charged* when the equilibrium of electric matter on the opposite surface is destroyed, by communicating positive electricity to one side, and the negative kind to the opposite side; and on the other hand the electric is said to be *discharged*, when a communication can be made by means of conducting substances between the two opposite surfaces, so as to restore the equilibrium.

CHARGE (*Paint.*) or *over-charge*, an exaggerated representation of a person, in which the likeness is preserved, but in a form to be ridiculous.

CHARGE (*Vet.*) an external remedy applied to the body of a horse, or other beast.

CHARGE *of lead* (*Com.*) 36 pigs, each pig containing 6 stone wanting 2 lbs.

CHARGE (*Mar.*) a vessel when she draws much water, or swims deep in the sea, is called a ship of charge.

CHARGE (*Mil.*) taken absolutely signifies an attack of the cavalry; hence "To sound a charge," to give the signal by the sound of the trumpet for the cavalry to begin the attack. But *charge bayonet* is a word of command given to the infantry to rush on the enemy with the fixed bayonet. Also "To charge an enemy," signifies generally to attack, or fall upon him.

CHARGE (*Her.*) whatever occupies the field in an escutcheon, which is placed either throughout all the escutcheon, or only in some particular part. Charges are either proper, or common. *Proper charges*, so called because they peculiarly belong to the art of heraldry, are also called ordinaries, because they are in ordinary use in all coats of arms, and *honourable ordinaries*, because coat armour is much honoured thereby, being the gifts of emperors, kings, and princes. These are the Cross, Chief, Pale, Bend, Fesse, Escutcheon, Chevron, saltire and barre Orle, Gyron, Pile, Quarter, Quarter Sinister, Canton, Canton-Sinister Flask, Flanch and Voider. These are subdivided into the *more honourable* and the *less honourable*. [vide *Heraldry*]—Common charges are such as are composed of things natural and artificial, and so named because they are open and common to all other arts and sciences as well as this.

CHA'RGED (*Her.*) an epithet for any ordinary or figure which carries something else, as *azure a saltire, argent charged with another, gules.*" An escutcheon is also said to be charged with the figures represented on it.

CHARGED *cylinder* (*Gunn.*) the same as *Chamber*.

CHARGED (*Elect.*) vide *Charge*.

CHA'RGER (*Mil.*) in French *cheval de guerre*, a war-horse, or a horse used by officers, particularly in action or on parade.

CHARGER (*Mech.*) a large sort of dish.

CHA'RGES (*Her.*) vide *Charge*.

CHA'RIEN (*Bot.*) the name of a plant, the root of which, if applied to the navel but for a very short time, expels the dead fœtus.

CHARIENTI'SMUS (*Rhet.*) χαριεντισμός, a mode of speech which consists in an abundance of ornament and figure; also a sort of irony which consists in a pleasant piece of raillery, or a jest that bites with pleasantry, as Ruffinianus says. *Dionys. in Jud. Lys.* c. 13, &c.; *Rufin.*

CHA'RILA (*Ant.*) χαρίλα, a festival observed once in nine years by the Delphians, in honour of the virgin Charila, as described by Plutarch in his *Græcæ Quæstiones*.

CHA'RIOC (*Bot.*) a kind of herb.

CHARIOT (*Mil.*) a car in which armed men used to ride to battle. They were furnished with scythes, hooks, and other offensive weapons.—*Chariots*, in French, are military conveyances answering to what are called in English waggons, as—*Chariot à porter corps*, a four-wheeled waggon used for the carriage of a piece of ordnance that is not mounted.—*Chariot a ridelles*, a four-wheeled waggon with a rail around it for the carriage of bombs, shells, &c.—*Chariots d'une armée*, waggon-train. — *Chariots d'artilleries, des vivres, d'outils à pioniers*, &c. artillery-waggons, provision-waggons, waggons for the pioneers' tools, &c.

CHARIOT (*Mech.*) a sort of light coach with only back seats.

CHARI'SIA (*Ant.*) χαρισία, a festival celebrated in honour of the χάριτες, or Graces, with dancing which continued all night; he that was awake the longest was rewarded with a cake, called πυράμους. *Eustath. Odyss.* 6; *Meurs. de Fer. Græc. apud Gronov.*; *Thess. Antiq. Græc.* tom. 7.

CHARISTE'RIA (*Ant.*) χαριστήρια ελευθερίας, a thanksgiving-day at Athens upon the twelfth of Boedromion, which was the day whereon Thrasybulus expelled the Thirty Tyrants. *Plut. de Glor. Athen.*; *Meurs. de Fer. Græc. apud Gronov.*; *Thes. Antiq. Græc.* tom. 7.

CHARI'STIA (*Ant.*) a festival solemnized on the 11th calends of March, on which relatives by blood and marriage met, in order to preserve a good correspondence, and to accommodate all differences.

Ovid. Fast. l. 2, v. 617.

<blockquote>
Proxima cognati dixere Charistia patres,
Et venit ad socios turba propinqua Deos.
</blockquote>

Val. Max. l. 2, c. 1.

CHARI'STICARY (*Archæol.*) a sort of commendatory, or donatory, of one to whom the enjoyment of the revenues of a monastery was given.

CHARISTOLO'CHIA (*Bot.*) a name for the *Artemisia* of Linnæus.

CHARITE' (*Ecc.*) a French term employed as an epithet for some orders of religious, as—*Frères de la charité*, an order so called from St. Jean de Dieu.—*Charité Chretienne*, an order instituted by Henry III. King of France and Poland, for soldiers who had been disabled in the service of their country.—*Charité de Notre Dame*, an order for women corresponding to that of St. Jean de Dieu for men.

CHARITY (*Hierog.*) is represented in painting by a woman all in red, a flame on the crown of her head with an infant sucking on her left arm, and two others standing up, one of which is embraced with the right. The flame signifies that charity is never idle, but always active; the three children show the triple power of charity, for faith and hope without her signify nothing.

TO CHARK (*Mech.*) vide to *Charr*.

CHARKS (*Com.*) Pit-coal charred, or charked.

CHARLEMAGNE'S *Crown* (*Her.*) this crown, of which a representation is given in the annexed figure, is still preserved at Nuremberg. It is made of gold, and is divided into eight parts. The fore part is decorated with twelve jewels, all unpolished. On the second is our Saviour sitting between two cherubs with this motto, PER ME REGES REGNANT. On the fourth part is King Hezekiah sitting, holding his head with his right hand, and by his side Isaiah the prophet, with a scroll, ECCE ADJICIAM SUPER DIES TUOS 15 ANNOS: also over the heads of these figures ISAIAS PROPHETA, EZECHIAS REX. The sixth part has the effigy of a king crowned, and a scroll in his hand with these words, HONOR JUDICIUM DILIGIT; as also over his head REX DAVID. The eighth part has a king sitting with his crown upon his head, and on a scroll which he holds in both his hands is this motto: TIME DOMINUM ET REGEM AMATO; as likewise over his head REX SOLOMON. The other parts are occupied with pearls and gems, but the top of this crown is surmounted with a cross bearing this inscription, I. H. S. NAZARENUS REX JUDÆORUM; also in the arch, or semicircle, these words, CHVONRADUS DEI GRATIA ROMANORUM IMPERATOR AUG. which shows that this semircircle was added after Charles' time by the emperor Conrade.

CHARLES' *wain* (*Ast.*) a name commonly given to the constellation otherwise called *Ursa major*.

CHA'RLOCK (*Bot.*) a kind of herb with a yellow flower, which grows amongst corn. It is the *Sinapis arvensis* of Linnæus.

CHARME (*Med.*) or *charmis*, a cordial antidote. *Gal. de Antidot.* l. 1, c. 4.

CHARMS (*Myth.*) *carmina*, incantations or verses used by magicians and sorcerers to effect different purposes, but particularly that of exciting, or allaying the passion of love.

CHARNEL (*Cus.*) any place containing flesh or dead carcasses.—*Charnel-house*, a place under a church where the skull and bones of the dead are laid up.

CHARO'NIUS (*Ant.*) χαρωνιός, charonian; an epithet for caves, some of which are found in Italy, where the air is loaded with deleterious vapours.

CHARR (*Ich.*) or *Char*, a very small fish of the salmon kind, inhabiting the rivers of England and Switzerland, which feeds on the larva of the gnat tribe: it frequents, in spring and autumn, the shady borders, where it deposits its spawn. There are two sorts of charr, namely, the Silk Charr, *Salmo carpio* of Linnæus, having its sides and belly silvery, and the Red Charr, *Salmo alpinus*, having the belly orange.

CHA'RRE *of lead* (*Com.*) a weight of 30 pigs, each pig containing 70 pounds.

CHARRE (*Ich.*) vide *Charr*.

CHART (*Mech.*) in Latin *charta*, [vide *Charta*] is a representation or description of any place *in plano*, or the projection on a plane surface. Charts may be constructed on two principles, namely, by considering the earth as a large extended flat surface, or by considering it as a sphere. Charts of the first kind are called plain charts; those of the second kind are either Mercator's Charts, or globular charts. *Plain Charts* have the meridians, as well as the parallels of latitude, drawn parallel to each other, and the degrees of longitude and latitude every where equal to those at the equator.—*Mercator's Charts*, so called from the original designer, and otherwise called reduced or projected charts, have the meridians and parallels represented by straight lines like the plain charts; but the degrees on the meridian, or the degrees of latitude, are made to increase towards the poles in the same proportion that the parallel circles are made to decrease. *Globular chart* is a meridional projection, in which the parallels are equidistant circles, having the poles for their common centre, and the meridians are curvilinear, and converging so as to meet in the poles. Charts are also distinguished according to their use, into hydrographic, geographic, chorographic, topographic, heliographic, selenographic.—*Hydrographic chart*, a sheet of large paper, whereon several parts of the land and sea are described, with their respective coasts, harbours, &c. the points of the compass, and the latitudes and longitudes of the places. This is called also a *sea-chart*, because it is particularly constructed for the use of mariners.—*Geographic chart*, a draught of the whole globe of the earth on a plane surface, which is more commonly called a *map of the world*.—*Chorographic chart*, a description or representation of particular countries, or parts of the terrestrial globe.—*Topographic chart*, a description or representation of places or parts of any particular country.—*Heliographic chart*, a representation of the body of the sun, as also of the *maculæ, feculæ*, or spots, &c. observed in it.—*Selenographic chart*, a representation of the parts, mountains, valleys, &c. of the moon.

CHA'RTA (*Ant.*) a name for paper, or the material made of the Egyptian papyrus, was also used for whatever is written upon; whence *charta plumbea*, a sheet of lead. The name has been derived from χαίρω, to rejoice, or be useful, whence Martial calls it *charta salutatrix*; but with greater probability from χαράσσω, to engrave, and the Hebrew or Chaldee חמש, a graver or tool for writing. From this word comes the modern term chart, signifying generally a sheet or plain surface of paper, fitted for the representation of any object, or actually occupied with the representation. The charta among the Romans was distinguished into *charta Augusta*, fine paper; *charta Claudiana*, a thicker kind of paper, now known by the name of royal, or imperial paper; *charta fibula*, blotting paper; *charta hieratica*, the best sort of paper, used only for religious subjects. *Plin.* l. 13, c. 11, 13, &c.; *Voss. de Art. Grammat.* l. 1, c. 37; *Hug. de prim. scrib. Orig.* c. 2.

CHARTA (*Archæol.*) a charter or deed in writing, particularly such public deeds on the part of the King whereby any thing was granted or confirmed to the subject: of this description was *Magna Charta, charta pardationis*, &c. [vide *Charter*]

CHARTA *virginea* (*Anat.*) the same as *Amnion*.

CHARTA'GNE (*Mil.*) French for a strong entrenchment, most generally concealed from the enemy.

CHARTE'L (*Law*) in French *cartel*, a letter of defiance, or challenge to single combat. [vide *Cartel*]

CHA'RTER (*Law*) *charta*, in French *chartres*, a written evidence of things done between man and man. They are distinguished into charters of private persons and charters of the King.—*Charters of the King*, those by which any grant is passed by the King to any person, or any body politic, as a charter of exemption of privilege, &c. *Bract.* l. 2; *Britt.* c. 99.—*Charters of private Persons* are deeds and instruments for the conveyance of lands, &c. *Co. Lit.* 6.—*Charter of the Forest*, that wherein the laws of

CHA

the forest are comprised, as the charter of Canute, &c. *Flet.* l. 3, c. 14; *Kitch.* 314.—*Charter of pardon,* that by which a man is forgiven for any offence committed against the crown.—*Charter Land,* the same as *Bockland.*—Charter party, *charta partita,* in French *chartre partie,* i. e. a deed or writing divided; an indenture or agreement made between merchants and seafaring men concerning their merchandise, &c. It is frequently called "a pair of indentures." 2 *Inst.* 673.

CHA'RTERER (*Archæol.*) a freeholder so called in Cheshire.

CHARTER-LAND (*Law*) vide *Bockland.*

CHARTER-PARTY (*Law*) vide *Charter.*

CHA'RTIS *reddendis* (*Law*) an ancient writ lying against one who had charters of feoffment entrusted to him, and refused to deliver them. *Reg. Orig.* 159.

CHARTOPHYLA'CIUM (*Archæol.*) a place where books and writings are preserved, as the Rolls, &c.

CHARTO'PHYLAX (*Archæol.*) the Master of the Rolls.

CHARTERE'UX (*Ecc.*) Carthusian monk.

CHARTULARIUS-ROLL (*Law*) a chartulary of a register-roll, &c.

CHA'RVIL (*Bot.*) vide *Chervil.*

CHASE (*Print.*) an iron frame which serves to receive composed matter from the composing stick.

Chase (*Law*) vide *Chace.*

Chase (*Mar.*) vide *Chace.*

CHA'SER (*Mech.*) one who raises figures upon watch-cases, tweezers, lids of snuff-boxes, &c.

Chaser (*Mar.*) in French *vasseau en chasse,* any vessel pursuing another.—*Bow-chasers,* in French *canons de chasse,* the cannon situated in the forepart of the ship.—Stern-chasers, in French *canons de repaite,* those in the hind part of the ship. [vide *Chace*]

CHASI'DIANS (*Theol.*) another name for the Pharisees.

CHASING (*Mar.*) Fr. *chasser,* the act of pursuing a vessel or fleet.

CHA'SME (*Med.*) χάσμη, or χασμός, from χάω, to gape; oscitation, gaping: the same as *Oscitatio.*

CHASSE (*Mus.*) any instrumental composition written in imitation of hunting music.

Chasse (*Mil.*) French for a charge of coarse powder which is thrown into the bottom of the cartouche to facilitate the explosion of the firework which it contains.

Chasse (*Mech.*) French for the vibratory motion which puts a body in action.

CHA'SSELAS (*Bot.*) a species of grape.

CHASSER (*Carpent.*) a French term among workmen, signifying to fasten pieces of joinery by driving them home with a mallet, &c.

CHA'SSERY (*Bot.*) a kind of pear like the ambret, which ripens in December.

CHASSEURS (*Mil.*) French for a select body of light infantry men, which is formed on the left of a battalion in the same manner as our grenadiers are posted on the right. They are required to be particularly light, active, and courageous.—*Chasseurs à cheval,* a species of light horse in the French service.

CHASSI'S (*Mil.*) French for a square platform, made of wood, which is used in mining.—*Chassis de gallerie,* beams of different lengths which the miners use to support the earth in proportion as they advance into the gallery.— *Chassis à secret,* a particular method of drawing lines upon a sheet of folded paper, and folding it in such a manner that when the words which are written in the intervals are read, they appear unintelligible to all but the person who is provided with a correspondent sheet, folded in a similar manner, by the application of which he can decypher the contents of the writing.

CHASTE-TREE (*Bot.*) the *Vitex agnus castus* of Linnæus, a tree which derives its name from the antephrodisiac quality ascribed to it by the ancients: the moderns, however, so far from countenancing this opinion, ascribe to these trees on account of their aromatic pungency, the opposite quality.—*Chaste-wood,* the wood of the Chaste-Tree.

CHASTELA'IN (*Archæol.*) a governor of a castle.

CHASTELE'T (*Polit.*) a French term originally signifying a castle, or fortified place, but now applied to the common gaol at Paris.

CHASTELLAINE (*Her.*) a noble woman.

CHA'STISEMENT (*Hierog.*) is represented in painting by a furious looking man armed with an axe, in allusion to the Roman *fasces.*

CHASTISEMENTS (*Man.*) corrections by a severe application of the aids.

CHA'STITY (*Hierog.*) is represented in painting and sculpture by a woman of a modest aspect, holding in one hand a whip, as a mark of chastisement, clad in white, like a vestal, to show her purity and innocence. On her girdle is written, *Castigo corpus meum.* At her feet lies Cupid blinded and conquered, with his bow broken.

CHA'SUBLE (*Ecc.*) a priest's cope used at mass.

CHAT (*Mil.*) French for an instrument consisting of three sharp prongs, in the shape of claws, which is used for examining pieces of ordnance: it answers to the *searcher* used in the British service.—*Chat* is also a turreted castle. [vide *Cat*]

CHATE (*Bot.*) the *Cucumis chate* of Linnæus.

CHATELLA'NY (*Archæol.*) vide *Castellany.*

CHA'THAM (*Mar.*) a moiety of the duty payable by foreign built ships, and applied to the use of the chest at Chatham.—*Chest of Chatham* was established for the relief of English mariners who are either wounded or superannuated in their country's service.

CHA'TTELS (*Law*) or *Catals, Catalla,* all goods, moveable or immovable, except such as are in the nature of freehold, or parcel of it. They are either *personal,* as gold, silver, plate, household stuff, goods, wares in a shop, cattle, &c. &c.; or *real,* as terms for years of land, the next presentation to a church, &c. &c.

CHA'TTERER (*Orn.*) the *Ampelis* of Linnæus; a sort of birds that breed and pass their summer within the Arctic Circle. They are remarkable for their red horny appendages formed by the tips of several of the secondary feathers.

CHA'T-WOOD (*Husband.*) small sticks fit for fuel.

CHAUD-MEDLEY (*Law*) vide *Chance Medley.*

CHA'VENDER (*Ich.*) or *Chevin:* the same as *Chub.*

CHAUFFE (*Mech.*) French for that spot in a founder's furnace which is occupied with the wood; the heat of which, while it is burning, spreads over the whole inside of the furnace.

CHAULIODO'NTA (*Zool.*) from χαυλάω, to throw out, and ὀδύς, a tooth; an epithet applied to those animals whose teeth grow to a great length out of their mouths, as the Boar and Elephant.

CHAUMONTE'LLE (*Bot.*) a species of pear.

CHA'UMPERT (*Law*) a kind of tenure to the hospital of Bowes, in the isle of Guernsey. *Pa.* 1, 35 *Ed.* 3.

CHA'UNOS (*Med.*) tumours, χαυνός, soft, *lax;* an epithet applied by Hippocrates to the bones.

CHA'UNTRY *rents* (*Archæol.*) rents paid to the crown by the servants or purchasers of chauntry lands.

CHAUSSE (*Her.*) signifies literally shot, and in blazonry denotes a section in base, the line by which it is formed proceeding from the extremity of the base, and ascending to the side of the escutcheon, which it meets about the *fessepoint,* as if a chief had shoes, as in the annexed figure.

Chausse (*Fort.*) the level of the field, the plain ground.— *Chausse-traps,* vide *Caltrops.*

CHAUSSE-TRAPS (*Her.*) vide *Cheval-Traps.*

CHAUSSE'E (*Mech.*) French for a paved way, or causeway.

CHAW-STICK (*Bot.*) a shrub, the *Gounia Dominigensis* of Linnæus.

CHAYE (*Com.*) *Schai*, or *Chay*, the smallest silver coin current in Persia.

CHAYOTA (*Bot.*) the *Lecticum edule* of Linnæus.

CHE (*Mus.*) an Italian particle signifying *than*, as *Poco pui che allegretto*, a little quicker than allegretto.

CHEAP-GILD (*Law*) a restitution made by the hundred or county for any wrong done by one in *plegio*, or by one for whose good behaviour sureties were put in.

CHEATI'NQUAMINS (*Bot.*) or *Chechinquamins*, an Indian fruit resembling a chesnut.

CHECA'YA (*Mil.*) the second officer in command among the Janisaries—the aga's lieutenant.

CHECK-ROLL (*Law*) a roll or book containing the names of such as are attendants on, and in the pay of, the king or any other great personages; as their household servants, &c. *Stat.* 19 *Car.* 2, c. 1.

CHECK, *Clerk of the* (*Mar.*) an officer in his majesty's dock-yards, appointed to keep check and control the seamen and artificers in his majesty's service.

TO CHECK (*Mar.*) in French *choquer*, to ease off a little of the rope which is too stiffly extended.

CHECK (*Falcon.*) when rooks, pies, or other birds, come within view of a hawk, and she forsakes her natural flight to follow them.

CHECK-MATE (*Sport.*) when the king in the game of chess is so shut up that he cannot escape, by which means the game is ended: also, a movement that kills the opposite men, or hinders them from moving.

CHE'CKER-WORK (*Mech.*) checkered or set out with divers colours or materials.

TO CHECKER (*Mech.*) or *Chequer*, to diversify in the manner of a chess-board.

CHECKERE'LLI *Panni* (*Com.*) cloth checkered or diversified in weaving.

CHE'CKY (*Her.*) small squares of different tinctures alternately, made to represent a chess-board, as in the annexed figure, "He beareth checky *argent* and *sable*; a fess *gules*: name *Sir Thomas Acland, Bart.*"

CHE'DA (*Com.*) a pewter coin made and current in a kingdom of that name in the East Indies, of which there are two sorts; the first, of an octagon figure, weighing 1½ oz. value two sols Tournois; the second, of a round form, value four deniers.

CHE'DDER-CHEESE (*Husband.*) a sort of cheese, so called from Chedder in Somersetshire, the place where it is made.

CHE'DROPA (*Ant.*) χεδροπὰ, all sorts of corn, pulse, &c.

CHEEKS (*Mech.*) a general name among mechanics for those pieces of timber in any machine which are double, and perfectly corresponding to each other; as the—*Cheeks of a carriage*, the strong planks which form the sides.—*Cheeks of a mortise*, the two solid parts on the sides of a mortise.

CHEEKS (*Mar.*) pieces of timber fixed to the ship's bow and the knee of the head; as—*Cheeks of a block*, the two sides of its shell.—*Cheeks of the mast*, in French *joutereaux*, the parts projecting on each side of the masts to sustain the trestle-trees on which the frame of the top-mast immediately rests; also, the head of the masts which is above the steps.

CHEER (*Cus.*) a testimony of approbation somewhat resembling the *acclamatio* of the Romans.

CHEESE (*Husband.*) the curd of milk separated from the whey, then pressed and hardened, and afterwards left to dry.

CHEESE-CAKES (*Cook.*) a sort of cake made of curds, sugar, butter, and other ingredients.

CHEESE-RENNING (*Bot.*) or Rennet, the *Galium verum* of Linnæus, a perennial.

CHEESE-LIP (*Ent.*) a hog-louse.

CHEESE-LIP (*Nat.*) the stomach-bag of a sucking calf, from which rennet for cheese is obtained.

CHEESE-PRESS (*Mech.*) a press in which the curds are pressed for making cheese.—*Cheese-vat*, the case wherein the curds are pressed into the form of a cheese.

CHEF (*Her.*) the same as *Chief*.

CHEF (*Mil.*) in French, the chief or head of a party, troop, &c. as—*Chef d' Escadre*, a general officer who commands any part of an army or division of a fleet.—*Chef de Files*, the front rank of a battalion.—*Chef de File*, the man who stands on the right of a troop or company.

CHEILOCACE (*Med.*) χειλοκάκη, from χεῖλος, a lip, and κακὸν, an evil; the lip evil; a swelling of the lips.

CHEIMETTON (*Med.*) from χεῖμα, winter; a chilblain.

CHEIRA'NTHUS (*Bot.*) a genus of plants, Class 15 *Tetradynamia*, Order 2 *Siliquosa*.

Generic Characters. CAL. perianth four-leaved; *leaflets* lanceolate.— COR. four-petalled; *petals* roundish.— STAM. *filaments* six; *anthers* erect.—PIST. germ prismatic; *style* very short; *stigma* oblong.—PER. silique long; *seeds* very many.

Species. The species are biennials, perennials, or shrubs, and some few annuals; as—*Cheiranthus erysimoides, Erysimum*, seu *Leucoium*, Wild Wall-flower, or Stock, a biennial, native of Germany.—*Cheiranthus Helveticus, Boccone, Hesperis*, seu *Leucoium*, &c. Swiss Wall flower, or Stock, a biennial, native of Switzerland.—*Cheiranthus Alpinus, Hesperis, Erysimum*, seu *Eruca*, Alpine or Straw-coloured Wall-flower, or Stock, a perennial, native of Lapland.—*Cheiranthus cheiri, Leucoium, Viola*, seu *Keiri*, &c. Common Wall-flower, a biennial, perennial, or shrub, native of England, &c.—*Cheiranthus fruticosus*, &c. seu *Leucoium*, a shrub, native of Spain.—*Cheiranthus mutabilis*, Broad-leaved Stock-Gilliflower, a shrub, native of Madeira.—*Cheiranthus chius, Hesperis, Leucoium*, &c. an annual, native of Russia.—*Cheiranthus maritimus, Hesperis, Leucoium*, &c. Dwarf annual Stock-Gilliflower, an annual, native of the Mediterranean.—*Cheiranthus parviflorus*, an annual, native of Morocco.—*Cheiranthus incanus, Leucoium, Viola*, Stock-Gilliflower, a perennial or shrub, native of Spain.—*Cheiranthus fenestralis*, Cluster-leaved Stock-Gilliflower, a biennial.—*Cheiranthus annuus*, seu *Leucoium*, &c. Annual Stock-Gilliflower, or Ten-week Stock, an annual, native of Europe.—*Cheiranthus littoreus*, Sea Stock-Gilliflower, an annual, native of the shores of the Mediterranean sea.—*Cheiranthus pinnatifidus*, seu *foliis*, &c. native of Siberia.—*Cheiranthus tricuspidatus*, seu *foliis*, &c. Trifid Stock-Gilliflower, an annual, native of Tripoli.—*Cheiranthus odoratissimus*, a shrub, native of Persia.—*Cheiranthus cuspidatus*, seu *Turritis*, &c. a biennial, native of Tauria.—*Cheiranthus farsetia, Farsetia, Lunaria*, seu *Thlaspi*, &c. a shrub, native of Egypt.—*Cheiranthus tennuifolius*, Narrow-leaved Shrubby Stock-Gilliflower, a shrub, native of Madeira. *J. Bauh. Hist. Plant.; C. Bauh. Pin.; Ger. Herb.; Park. Theat. Botan.; Raii Hist. Plant.; Tournef. Instit.*

CHEIRANTHUS is also the *Heliophila integrifolia* and the *Hesperis lacera* of Linnæus.

CHEI'RI (*Bot.*) the *Cheiranthus cheiri* of Linnæus.

CHEIRIATER (*Med.*) χειριατρὸς, from χεὶρ, the hand, and ἰατρὸς, a physician, whose office it is to remove maladies by the operations of the hand; what is now properly understood by a surgeon.

CHEIRI'SMA (*Surg.*) χείρισμα, or χειρισμὸς, from χειρίζομαι, to labour with the hand; handling; or a manual operation.

S B

CHEIRI'XIS (*Surg.*) χειρίξις, surgery.
CHEIRODO'TA (*Ant.*) vide *Chirodota*.
CHEIRO'NIUM (*Med.*) the same as *Cacoethes*.
CHEIRO'NOMY (*Med.*) χειρονομία, an exercise mentioned by Hippocrates, which consisted in gesticulations with the hands. *Hippocrat. de Vict. Rat.* l. 2: *Foes. Œconom. Hippocrat.*
CHIRURGUS (*Surg.*) vide *Chirurgeon*.
CHEI'GI (*Chem.*) in the language of Paracelsus, signifies quicksilver, when speaking of minerals; and flowers, when speaking of vegetables.
CHE'LA (*Surg.*) χηλη, a forked probe, mentioned by Hippocrates, which was used in extracting a polypus of the nose.
CHE'LÆ (*Anat.*) χηλαί, the extremities of the *cilia*, which touch each other when the eyes are shut. *Ruff. Ephes. de Appell. Part. Corp. Hum.* l. 1, c. 4.
CHELÆ (*Nat.*) the claws of the crab.
CHELÆ (*Med.*) fissures in the heels, feet, or pudenda.
CHE'LIDON (*Anat.*) χελιδών, signifies, literally, a swallow; but is also applied to denote the hollow at the flexure of the arm.
CHELIDO'NIA (*Bot.*) a kind of purple fig. *Plin.* l. 15, c. 18; *Columel. de Re Rust.* l. 10.
CHELIDONIA is the *Ranunculus ficaria* of Linnæus.
CHELIDO'NIAS (*Ant.*) the West wind, so called because it comes with the swallows. *Plin.* l. 2, c. 47.
CHE'LIDONIUM (*Bot.*) χελιδόνιον, a plant, so called because it blossomed at the time of the swallows appearing. It was formerly called Pile-Wort, because it was supposed to be good for the piles. *Theoph. Hist. Plant.* l. 7, c. 14; *Dioscor.* l. 2, c. 211; *Plin.* l. 25, c. 8; *Schol. in Nicand. Theriac.*; *Schol. in Theocrit.* idyl. 13.
CHELIDONIUM, in the Linnean system, a genus of plants, Class 13, *Polyandria*, Order 1 *Monogynia*.
Generic Characters. CAL. *perianth* two-leaved; *leaflets* subovate.—COR. *petals* four.—STAM. *filaments* flat; *anthers* oblong.—PIST. *germ* cylindric; *style* none; *stigma* headed.—PER. *silique* cylindric; *seeds* ovate; *receptacle* linear.
Species. The species are perennials and annuals, as—*Chelidonium majus*, Common or Great Celandine, a perennial, native of Europe.—*Chelidonium Japonicum*, native of Japan.—*Chelidonium glaucium*, *Papaver*, &c. Sea Celandine, or Yellow Horned Poppy, a perennial, native of England.—*Chelidonium corniculatum*, &c. *Glaucium*, seu *Papaver*, &c. Red Celandine, or Horned Poppy, an annual native of Hungary.—*Chelidonium hybridum*, seu *Papaver*, Violet Celandine, or Horned Poppy, an annual, native of Europe. *Clus. Hist. Plant. Var.; Bauh. Hist. Plant.; C. Bauh. Pin.; Ger. Herb.; Park. Theat. Bot.; Raii Hist. Plant.; Tournef. Inst.*
CHELIDONIUM is also the *Bocconia frutescens*, the *Sanguinaria Canadensis*, and the *Ranunculus ficaria* of Linnæus.
CHELIDO'NIUS LAPIS (*Min.*) χελιδόνιος λίθος, a stone found, as it is said, in the craw of a young swallow. *Dioscor.* l. 2, c. 60; *Plin.* l. 11, c. 37.
CHELO'NE (*Bot.*) a genus of plants, Class 14 *Didynamia*, Order 2 *Angiospermia*.
Generic Characters. CAL. *perianth* one-leaved; *divisions* erect.—COR. monopetalous; *tube* cylindric; *throat* inflated; *border* closed; *upper lip* obtuse; *lower* almost equal to the upper.—STAM. *filaments* four; *anthers* incumbent.—PIST. *germ* ovate; *style* filiform; *stigma* obtuse.—PER. *capsule* ovate; *seeds* very many.
Species. The species are perennials, as—*Chelone glabra*, White Chelone, native of Virginia.—*Chelone obliqua*, Red Chelone, native of Virginia, &c.—*Chelone ruellioides*, seu *Ourifia*, native of the Straits of Magellan.—*Chelone barbata*, seu *Ruellioides*, &c. native of Mexico.—

Chelone hirsuta, seu *Digitalis*, Hairy Chelone, native of New England.—*Chelone pentstemon*, *Osarina*, *Dracocephalus*, *Digitalis*, *Pentstemon*, &c. seu *Cynorynchium*, native of North America.—*Chelone campanulata*, native of Mexico.
CHELONE (*Surg.*) χελώνη, a part of a chirurgical machine, mentioned by Oribasius, which was used for extending a limb. *Oribas. de Machin.* c. 4, 5.
CHELO'NIA (*Mech.*) the cheeks or side-parts of a windbeam or crane, for the lifting up great stones or timber. *Vitruv.* l. 10, c. 2.
CHELONIA (*Min.*) a stone like the eye of an Indian tortoise, which magicians used for divination. *Plin.* l. 37. c. 10.
CHELONI'TES LAPIS (*Min*) a name of the *Lapis Bufonites*.
CHELO'NIUM (*Nat.*) χελώνιον, a hump-back, so called from its resemblance to the shell of a tortoise.
CHE'LTENHAM-WATER (*Min.*) arises from a spring near Cheltenham in Gloucestershire, and is one of the most celebrated purging waters in the kingdom. Its heat is in summer 53° to 69°. It consists of a calcareous earth mixed with ochre and a purging salt.
CHE'LYS (*Mus.*) a stringed instrument resembling the harp.
CHELYS (*Anat.*) χέλυς, a shell; the breast; so called from its resemblance to the back of a tortoise.
CHELY'SCION (*Med.*) χελύσκιον, from χέλυς, a short dry cough.
CHE'ME (*Ant.*) or *Cheme*, a measure containing two small spoonfuls.
CHE'MICAL (*Chem.*) an epithet for what appertains to chemistry, as *chemical characters*. [vide *Characters*] *chemical processes*, and the like.
CHE'MICE (*Chem.*) the art of casting metals.
CHE'MICI (*Chem.*) chemists, or those who practised the art of chemistry.
CHEMI'N COUVERT (*Fort.*) vide *Covered way*.—*Chemin des Rondes*, a space between the rampart and the parapet under it, for the rounds to go about it.
CHEMI'SE (*Fort.*) an obsolete French term for the *revêtement*, made of brick-work.
CHEMISE *de coup de main* (*Mil.*) shirts which do not go below the waist, and are used in any *coup de main*, that soldiers may distinguish their comrades.
CHEMISE (*Mason.*) the solidity of a wall from the talus or slope to the stone row; also a lining or casing with stone.
CHEMISE *fire* (*Mar.*) a piece of cloth steeped in a composition, used to set fire to an enemy's vessel.
CHE'MISTRY (*Chemia*) is the science which treats of the properties of bodies, and the changes they undergo. The word has been derived from the Arabic word *Kyamon*, the substance or composition of bodies; but, with more probability, it comes from the Greek χέω, to melt; fusion having been originally the first and principal process employed in chemistry.
Chemistry may be considered under the two general heads of Theoretical Chemistry, and Experimental or Practical Chemistry.

THEORETICAL CHEMISTRY.

Theoretical chemistry, or the theory of chemistry, naturally divides itself into three distinct heads; namely, 1. Of chemical action in general. 2. Of chemical action in respect to particular bodies or substances. 3. Of the chemical analysis of natural bodies.

Of chemical action in general.

The principle by which bodies either tend towards each other, and come in contact, or remain united in one mass, is denominated in general *attraction*, which is of different kinds, according as this attraction acts, either

CHEMISTRY.

at sensible or insensible distances. Of the first kind is the *attraction of gravitation*, by which the planets are supposed to be kept within their orbits, the *magnetic attraction*, and the *attraction of electricity*. Of the second kind, there is the *attraction of aggregation*, commonly called *Cohesion*, and *chemical attraction*, commonly called *Affinity*.

Cohesion.

Cohesion is that principle by which the particles or atoms of matter, of the same kind, attract each other, so as to produce an aggregate body, called a mass. The cohesive force is most strongly exerted in solid bodies; in *liquids* it acts with considerably less energy; and in aeriform bodies it does not appear to exist at all, for their particles are mutually repulsive; and, if not held together by pressure, would separate to immeasurable distances. The force of this attraction in solids may be measured by the weight necessary to overcome it: thus, if a rod of wood, glass, or metal, be suspended in a perpendicular direction, and weights be attached to its lower extremity till the rod breaks, the weight attached to the rod just before it broke is the measure of the cohesive force of the rod. In the following table are given the results of experiments which have been made on different solids, showing the number of pounds which are just sufficient to tear asunder a rod of each.

1. Metals.

Steel bar	135,000	Cast tin	4,440
Iron bar	74,000	Bismuth	2,900
Cast iron	50,000	Zinc	2,600
Cast silver	41,000	Antimony	1,000
Cast copper	28,000	Cast lead	860
Cast gold	22,000		

II. Alloys.

Gold 2 parts, Silver 1 part	28,000	Brass	51,000
		Tin 2, lead 1	10,200
Gold 5, copper 1	50,000	Tin 8, zinc 1	10,000
Silver 5, copper 1	48,000	Tin 4, antimony 1	12,000
Silver 4, tin 1	41,000	Lead 8, zinc 1	4,000
Copper 6, tin 1	55,000	Tin 4, lead 1, zinc 1	13,000

III. Woods.

Locust tree	20,100	Pomegranate	9,750
Jujeb	18,500	Lemon	9,250
Beech and Oak	17,300	Tamarind	8,750
Orange	15,500	Fir	8,330
Alder	13,900	Walnut	8,130
Elm	13,200	Pitchpine	7,656
Mulberry	12,500	Quince	6,750
Willow	12,500	Cypress	6,000
Ash	12,000	Poplar	5,500
Plum	11,800	Cedar	4,880
Elder	10,000		

IV. Bones.

Ivory	16,270	Whalebone	7,500
Bone	15,250	Tooth of sea-calf	4,075
Horn	8,750		

Affinity.

Affinity is that principle by which particles of different kinds are disposed to unite with each other, and to remain in unison. Thus, for instance, an acid unites with a metal, an earth, or an alkaline salt, and with either of these the acid forms one body; which body does not consist of a combination of the properties of the acid, and the metal, &c.; but these losing their original properties on their union, a new body different from either is formed. This is forcibly exemplied in the case of potash and sulphuric acid. In their separate state each of these bodies is distinguished by striking peculiarities of taste, and other properties. The alkali changes the colour of blue vegetable infusions to green, and the acid turns them red; but when they are combined, the mixture will produce no effect on blue vegetables, and the taste is converted into a bitter.

This power in bodies is called *affinity*, not to denote the cause but the effect; for when an acid spontaneously quits a metal to unite with an alkali, it is said to have a greater affinity to the alkali than to the metal; or in other words, that it will unite with the alkali, in preference to the metal. On account of this seeming choice which certain bodies have to coalesce, by preference with others, affinity has been termed *elective*; and is also distinguished into different kinds, namely, simple, compound, double, disposing, quiescent, divellent, and reciprocal.—*Simple affinity* is when two substances unite merely in consequence of their mutual attraction: thus acetic acid combines with soda, and forms a salt called the acetate of soda.—*Compound affinity* is when three or more bodies, on account of their mutual affinity, unite and form one homogeneous body: thus, if to a solution of sugar and water be added spirits of wine, these three bodies will form an homogeneous liquid by compound affinity.—*Double affinity* is the action of two compound substances, which decompose each other, so as to produce two or more new compounds. If, for instance, nitric acid be added to the sulphate of ammonia, no decomposition takes place, because the sulphuric acid has a stronger affinity than nitric acid for ammonia; but, if nitrate of potash be added, two new bodies are formed, i. e. the potash attracts the sulphuric acid, while the nitric acid solicits the ammonia. This has been explained by the following diagram,

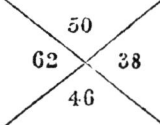

wherein the affinity of potash to sulphuric acid is supposed to be = 62, that of nitric acid to ammonia = 38, that between nitric acid and potash = 50, and that of the sulphuric acid and ammonia = 46. Now, if two lines or two rules be drawn, so as to cross each other, then it will appear that $62 + 38 = 100$, the sum of the affinities between potash, sulphuric acid, nitric acid, and ammonia will be superior to $46 + 50 = 96$, the sum of the affinities supposed to keep the sulphuric acid and ammonia; the potash and nitric acid together.—*Disposing affinity*, otherwise called *intermediate affinity*, or the affinity of an intermedium, is when two substances of different kinds, that show no affinity to each other, do, by the assistance of a third, combine, and unite into an homogeneous body; thus, if concentrated sulphuric acid be poured upon iron, no action will ensue; but, if a little water be added to dilute the sulphuric acid, an action will instantly ensue, and the iron will soon be dissolved. —*Quiescent affinity* is that when two or more bodies being presented to each other, their mutual attractions tend to preserve the original arrangement of their parts, as in the preceding example, the quiescent affinity between the sulphate of ammonia and the nitrate of potash, respectively, were equal to 96.—*Divellent affinity* is that which tends to destroy the old combination, as in the former case the affinities between the potash, sulphuric acid, nitric acid, and ammonia, being = 100, are the divellent affinities.—*Reciprocal affinity* is when a body, compounded of two others, is decomposed by a third, which forms with one of the two principles a new compound, that after some time undergoes decomposition by the means of the separated principle; thus, ammonia and magnesia will separate each other from muriatic acid. Tables of affinities have been drawn up by different writers, wherein the name of the substance, whose affinities are required, is placed at the head of the column, and the other substances underneath, in the order of their affinity to the first substance, as in the following example:

Sulphuric Acid.

Barytes,	Magnesia,
Strontites,	Ammonia,
Potash,	Alumina,
Soda,	Metallic oxides,
Lime,	Water.

where the sulphuric acid is the substance in question, to which barytes stands the nearest in the list, to show that it has the strongest affinity for sulphuric acid, and will detach it from any of the succeeding substances; strontites stands the next, because it will separate potash, &c. from sulphuric acid, and so on with the rest.

The following Table contains a general view of Affinities:

Acids.	Muriatic Acid.	Nitric Acid.	Sulphuric Acid.
Fixed alkalies, Volatile alkalies, Absorbent earth, Metals.	Tin, Antimony, Copper, Silver, Mercury, Gold.	Iron, Copper, Lead, Mercury, Silver.	Phlogiston, Fixed alkalies, Volatile alkalies, Absorbent earth Iron, Copper, Silver.

Absorbent Earth.	Fixed Alkalies.	Volatile Alkalies.
Sulphuric acid, Nitric acid, Muriatic acid.	Sulphuric acid, Nitric acid, Muriatic acid, Acetic acid, Sulphur.	Sulphuric acid, Nitric acid, Muriatic acid.

Metals.	Sulphur.	Mercury.	Lead.
Muriatic acid, Sulphuric acid, Nitric acid, Acetic acid.	Fixed alkalies, Iron, Copper, Lead, Silver, Antimony, Mercury, Gold.	Gold, Silver, Lead, Copper, Zinc, Antimony.	Silver, Copper.

Copper.	Silver.	Iron.	Antimony.	Water.
Mercury, Calamine.	Lead, Copper.	Antimony, Silver, Copper, Lead.	Iron, Silver, Copper, Lead.	Alcohol, Salt.

Here it is to be observed that the affinity between acids and fixed alkalies is greater than that between acids and volatile alkalies, and so on with the other substances.

Repulsion. The opposite principle to attraction is that of repulsion, by which the particles of matter are supposed to have a constant tendency to recede from each other. This operates like attraction either at sensible or insensible distances. Of the former kind are those of electricity and magnetism; as, for instance, suppose two small pith balls be suspended from an insulated body with a fine thread, so as to touch each other, and that body be charged with electricity, the pith balls will separate immediately; and, in regard to the magnet, there is a power of repulsion between two magnets which is directly opposed to the power they both possess, of attracting other objects to themselves.

On *affinity* depends all chemical action, which consists of decomposition and combination. When the constituent parts of bodies are separated from each other, the bodies are said to be *decomposed*, and the act of separating them is called *decomposition*. On the other hand, when bodies are so intimately united as to form new and distinct products, they are then said to be chemically combined, and the act by which this union takes place is termed *combination*, in distinction from *mechanical mixture*, which is the mere mixture of the bodies. By these two processes all bodies are chemically investigated in two forms, namely, by *analysis* and *synthesis*. Analysis is the separation of bodies by a series of decompositions and combinations, so as to come at the knowledge of their constituent parts. *Synthesis* is a similar process, for the purpose of forming new compounds. These two forms of investigation frequently accompany each other, and may be successively employed on the same substances, to prove the accuracy of the investigation: thus Epsom salt may be analyzed, and shown to consist of sulphuric acid and magnesia; or it may be synthetically compounded, by combining magnesia with sulphuric acid, when Epsom salt, in the form of crystals, will be the result.

Chemical investigations are mostly carried on by reducing bodies to a fluid state, which may be effected either by solution or by fusion.

Solution. When a solid disappears in a liquid, or when a solid or a liquid is taken up by an aëriform body, the act and the result are both called a *solution*: thus, when common salt is melted in water, its solution is said to have taken place, and the liquid thus obtained is called the *solution*. The liquid in which the solid disappears is termed the solvent, or *menstruum*; the body which is found capable of undergoing this change is called *soluble*, in distinction from the *insoluble* bodies, or such as are not susceptible of any such change: thus, common salt is a soluble body in water, and chalk is insoluble; but when muriatic acid is the menstruum, then chalk is also a soluble body. The capacity which bodies possess of uniting with and remaining dissolved in any liquid, is called their *solubility*, which is most frequently exemplified by the solution of saline bodies in water. The solubility, however, of salts is found to vary in degree in different substances. When any body has taken up as much of another body as it can dissolve, it is said to be *saturated* with it, and the point at which the liquid ceases to act upon the solid is termed the *point of saturation*, and the solution is termed a *saturated solution*.

Neutralization. When bodies, by reason of their affinity, combine in a solution in such manner that their peculiar properties disappear, they are then said to be *neutralized*: thus when muriatic acid ceases to act on lime, both the acid and the lime are said to be *neutralized.*

Precipitation. When bodies are dissolved, mixed, or suspended in a fluid, in such manner as to be separated from that fluid, and made to gravitate to the bottom of the vessel, they are said to be *precipitated;* the matter which is thus separated is called the *precipitate,* and the substance which thus separates another is called the *precipitant:* thus, if into a solution of nitrate of silver be dropped a quantity of liquid potash, a portion of the metallic oxide immediately separates from the solution and falls to the bottom; in this case the potash is the *precipitant,* and the oxide is the *precipitate.* The act of adding any particular substance in such manner as to produce any particular effect is called *treating;* thus the solution of nitrate of silver is *treated* with liquid potash.

Tests. Those substances which have the property of precipitating others are mostly used in detecting the ingredients which enter into any composition, and on that account are called *tests,* or *re-agents:* thus, suppose a single drop of a weak solution of carbonate of potash, and afterwards a few drops of a solution of sulphate of copper be added to a solution that contains arsenic, the presence of arsenic will be manifested by a yellowish-green precipitate. In this case the carbonate of potash and sulphate of copper are called the tests.

Volatilization and *Evaporation.* Substances which are in a fluid state sometimes fly off in the form of a gas, which is called volatilization, and sometimes in that of vapour, which is called *evaporation.* The *volatilizing* or *evaporating* of part of the water of fluids, in order to increase their strength, is termed *concentration.* This operation is performed on some acids, particularly the sulphuric and phosphoric; and also in solutions of alkalies and neutral salts.

Crystallization. If evaporation be carried on in some solutions so slowly as to afford an opportunity for the parts of the substance to unite regularly as they cool, the solution will be converted into crystals as perfect as those exhibited by nature. This process is known by the name of *crystallization,* which is one of the properties that characterizes the salts.

Water of crystallization. In the act of separating from the water, most of the salts carry away with them a portion of the fluid, which is essential to give them their crystalline form. This is termed their *water of crystallization,* and that which remains after the crystallization the *mother water.* The quantity of water of crystallization varies in different salts; being in some so abundant as to liquify them on the application of heat, which is called the *watery fusion.*

Efflorescence and *deliquescence.* Some crystals lose their watery ingredient by mere exposure to the atmosphere, when they are said to *effloresce;* others, on the contrary, attract more water, and on exposure to the atmosphere become liquid, which is called *deliquating,* or *deliquescing,* and the property is called *deliquescence.* The following table exhibits the action of atmospheric air on some of the most common salts.

Pure potash deliquesces.
—— soda, ditto.
Carbonate of potash, ditto.
Bi-carbonate of potash remains unchanged.
Carbonate of soda effloresces.
———————— ammonia, ditto.
———————— lime, unchanged.
———————— magnesia, ditto.
Sulphate of potash, ditto.
——————— soda effloresces.
Sulphate of lime, unchanged.
——————— magnesia, ditto.
Nitrate of potash, ditto.
———————— lime deliquesces.
———————— magnesia, ditto.
Muriate of potash, unchanged.
———————— lime deliquesces.
———————— magnesia, ditto.

Forms of crystals. Every solid that is susceptible of crystallization has a tendency to assume a peculiar shape; thus common salt forms regular cubes; nitre has the shape of a six-sided prism; and alum that of the octahedron. Crystals have been divided, according to their form, into primitive and secondary. The primitive form, otherwise called the *nucleus* of the crystal, has been found to be of six kinds, namely: The parallelopiped, which includes the cube, the rhomboid, and all solids terminated by six faces, parallel two and two. 2. The regular tetrahedron. 3. The octohedron with triangular faces. 4. The six-sided prism. 5. The dodecahedron terminated by rhombs. 6. The dodecahedron with isosceles triangular faces. [vide *Crystallurgy*]

Fusion. Many substances which are not soluble in water, or any other liquid, are notwithstanding reducible to a fluid state by an artificial application of heat, as in the case of metals, glass, and similar bodies. This process is called *fusion,* and when the substance is thus converted into glass, it is called *vitrification.* Those substances which admit of being fused are called *fusible;* but those which resist the action of fire, either altogether, or to a great degree, are called infusible, or *refractory.* Sometimes a substance, called a *flux,* is mixed with metallic ores, or other bodies, to promote fusion, as an alkali is mixed with silica to form glass. Ores are fused for the purpose of separating the metals from them, the process of which is termed *smelting;* if they are heated in crucibles to volatilize the sulphur, arsenic, &c. this is called *roasting.* When metals are separated from other metals, in order to obtain them in a state of greater purity, it is termed *refining;* if this be performed by means of another metal, the process is called *cupellation;* thus gold and silver are refined by fusing them with lead in pots called cupels. Sometimes the more fusible matter in a mass is caused to flow while the other remains infusible; this process is called *eliquation.* Metals are frequently refined, or otherwise changed, without fusion, by means of a composition called a cement, with which they are covered: thus iron, by being kept a long time in a certain degree of heat, surrounded by charcoal powder, is converted into steel. This process is called *cementation.*

Heat is applied not only to metals, but to other substances, and in different modes, of which the following are the principal.

Digestion. Digestion is the operation of exposing bodies to the action of a slow heat, that they may be the more gradually changed.

Calcination. Calcination is the reducing of any body to the state of a powder.

Distillation. Distillation is the process by which the volatile are separated from the fixed principles of any substance. When substances are re-distilled, in order to render them more pure, or concentrated, this process is called *rectification:* thus spirit of wine, æther, &c. are rectified by their separation from the less volatile, and foreign matter which debased their properties. That which is procured by distillation is frequently termed *essence,* as the *essential oils* distilled from odoriferous vegetable substances. That which remains in the pot, or retort, after the volatile part has been drawn off, is called the *residuum*, and sometimes the *caput mortuum*.

Sublimation. Sublimation is the process by which certain volatile substances are raised by heat, and then condensed by cold. If the subliming matter concretes into a solid mass, it is called a *sublimate*; if into a powdery form, it is called *flowers*, as the *flowers of arsenic*, the *flowers of antimony*, &c. Sublimation is, in regard to solid bodies, what distillation is to fluids. The principal subjects of this operation are volatile alkaline salts, neutral salts, as *sal ammoniac*, &c.

There are other minor processes connected with the analysis of bodies, as *lixiviation, reduction, edulcoration, dulcification, elutriation, detonation, fulmination,* &c. the explanation of which will be found in their respective places.

Compounds. The substances which are formed by means of chemical union are called compounds.

Base. That which forms the basis, as it were, or the principal part in the combination, is called the *base*. Bases are distinguished into—*Acidifiable base*, or that which may be formed into an acid by uniting with some other substance, as phosphorus is the *acidifiable base* in phosphoric acid.—*Acidifying base* is that which forms the acid, in the combination of which kind there is only one substance hitherto known, namely oxygen.—*Metallic bases* are the principal parts which enter into the composition of metals, and which, as far as they are known, and have been named, are distinguished by the termination *um*: thus *potassium*, the base of *potassa*, or potash; *sodium*, the base of soda; *calcium*, the base of *calx*, or lime, &c.—*Salifiable base* is that body with which an acid is combined to form a salt: thus, when we speak of the sulphate of potash, soda, &c. the potass, soda, &c. are the bases.

Nomenclature of compounds. Compounds which have acid properties are denominated *acids*, and are distinguished according to the proportion of oxygen which they contain by the terminations *ic* and *ous*, as nit*ric* acid and nitr*ous* acid; sulphu*ric* acid and sulphur*ous* acid, &c.; the former of which denotes the larger dose, or portion of oxygen, and the latter the smaller: when the syllable *hypo* is added to either of these it denotes a degree below it in point of oxidizement; thus, hypo*sulphuric* acid is intermediate between the sulphuric and sulphurous acid. When the compounds possess no sensible properties of an acid, they are distinguished by the termination *ide*, if they are supporters of combustion, or *et*, if they are combustibles, as the ox*ide*, chlor*ide*, or iod*ide* of arsenic, sulphur*et* of potassium, phosphur*et* of carbon, &c. The different combinations with oxygen, chlorine, and iodine, are distinguished by the prefix *pro*, to denote the first or smallest proportion, *deu* the second, *per* the largest quantity of oxygen, &c. with which the compound can be combined, as the pr*otoxide*, deu*toxide*, and p*eroxide*. Acids for the most part combine with alkalies, earths, and metallic oxides, and form compounds called *salts*; these are distinguished by the termination of *ate* when the acid contains the larger portion of oxygen, and that of *ite* when the acid contains the smaller; thus the combination of sulphuric acid and potassa is a sulph*ate* of potash, and that of sulphurous acid and potassa is a sulph*ite* of potash, &c. Salts are denominated *neutral* when the separate qualities of the component principles are not apparent; but when the acid predominates the prefix *super* is added; but when the base predominates, the prefix *sub*: thus the *sulphate of potash* denotes the salt in its perfect state of neutralization, without any excess of the sulphuric acid or the potash; super*sulphate of potash* is the same salt with an excess of acid; sub*sulphate of potash* is the same salt with an excess of base. Some acids are capable of combining with two bases at once, as tartaric acid, which combines at once with potash and soda, whence the salt is denominated *tartrate of potash and soda*; and this description of salts is called *triple salts*. All the combinations which metals form with one another are called *alloys*, except those formed by mercury with any other metals, which are named *amalgams*.

The substances which are the subjects and objects of chemical action.

Substances have been divided by modern chemists generally into simple and compound.

Simple Substances.

Simple substances were formerly called *elements*, because they were supposed to enter into the composition of all natural bodies, and were reduced by the ancients to the number of four, namely, air, earth, fire, and water. A simple substance is now defined to be one which has not hitherto been decompounded; a definition which, though liable to objections, is sufficiently correct for the purpose of a general treatise like the present. It will therefore be most convenient to treat first of the properties of simple substances, and afterwards of the compounds formed by the union of the simples. Simple substances are subdivided into imponderable and ponderable.—*Imponderable bodies* are such as are of too subtle a nature to be confined in any vessels that can be made. They are called imponderable because they do not sensibly affect the most delicate balance.—*Ponderable bodies* are those which admit of being confined in vessels, and exhibited in a separate state so as to determine their weight and other properties.

Imponderable bodies. The bodies, at present reckoned imponderable, are four; namely, light, heat, electricity, and magnetism, all of which, except the last, are chemical agents, by which the most important phænomena in the chemical science are produced.

Light. Light was considered by Aristotle, and most of the ancient philosophers, to be a property of matter, but the moderns suppose it to be a distinct fluid substance which passes off from luminous bodies, and, entering the eye, render objects visible: in either case the properties of light, as a chemical agent, are the same. The influence of light on different material bodies is evinced in a variety of ways. Plants lose their colour and become white if they are deprived of light, and the progress of vegetation, though not expressly stopped, is, in most cases, very sensibly impeded. The same plants when exposed again to the light recover their verdure and freshness. Hence it is that plants, when situated in rooms, or shady places, always turn their leaves to the light; and that many discous flowers follow the sun in his course, and keep themselves directed towards him from his rising to his setting. Animals in general droop and become unhealthy when they are deprived of light, and sometimes will even die. The complexions of men, in a state of close confinement, become sallow, and their bodies subject to eruptions, and different sorts of diseases: nor is the influence of light less visible on inanimate objects. Certain metallic bodies become combustible when exposed to light. The red oxide of mercury, and of lead become much lighter when exposed to the sun; and the white salts of silver, in the same situation, soon become black, and the oxide is reduced. Nitric acids are decomposed by coming in contact with the light, and other bodies experience similar changes. Almost all bodies have the property of absorbing light, and some few also of evolving it again unchanged; of this description are the bodies called phosphoric, also putrid animal substances, the glow-worm, and the like. The chemical effects of light, however, vary with the different rays of which light is composed; some of the rays excite heat and promote oxidation, as the red rays most, the green next, and so on, in a diminishing progression, to the violet. A second sort are termed *illuminating rays*, which follow a different order from that of the preceding; the red possessing the least degree; yellow and green the highest degree of this property. The third sort are the *deoxidizing rays*, which are in general the most refrangible of the rays, although this is not invariably the case in regard to all substances that admit of deoxidation.

Heat. The term *heat* is now restricted by chemists to the sensation of heat, and that of *caloric* has been substituted to express the cause of heat, which was formerly looked upon to be a property or affection of matter, but is now considered as a subtle fluid that is capable of insinuating itself into the densest bodies. Heat, considered as a distinct substance, is supposed to exist in two states; namely, in a state of combination, when it is not sensible to our organs; and, in a state of freedom, when it affects animals with the sensation of heat: in the first case, it is called *latent heat*; and, in the second, *sensible* or *free heat*, uncombined caloric, &c.

The motion of caloric, when it is not interrupted, is found to be equal in velocity to that of light. This motion is of two kinds, one in which it is transmitted from the surface of bodies, called its *radiation*; and the second, that by which it makes its way through bodies called *conduction*, and the power, which bodies possess of admitting the passage of heat, is called their *conducting power*. The bodies themselves are called *conductors*; if they allow the heat to pass freely they are denominated *good conductors*; and those through which the heat passes with difficulty *bad conductors*. Such as are supposed not capable of admitting the passage of heat at all are called *non-conductors*.

Both the radiating and conducting power have been found to vary in different bodies. The following table exhibits the differences of the radiating power; namely,

Lamp black	100	Isinglass	80
Writing paper	98	Plumbago	76
Rosin	96	Tarnished lead	45
Sealing wax	95	Mercury	20+
Crown glass	90	Clean lead	19
China ink	88	Iron polished	15
Ice	85	Tin plate	12
Minium	80	Gold, silver, copper	12

From this table it appears that the metals radiate much less than other substances; and, as the property of reflecting heat has been found to be by an inverse ratio to that of the radiating power, the surfaces of metals are more powerful reflectors than those of the other substances which are mentioned above.

Conducting power of solids. The conducting power of bodies is still more strikingly evinced than their radiating power, and arises from their affinity for caloric, and the property they have of combining indefinitely with additional doses of it. All solids are conductors of caloric, but they possess this property in very different degrees. All metallic substances are good conductors, but not all equally so. The following metals are set down in the order of their conducting power:

Silver,	Copper,	Platina,	Steel,
Gold,	Tin,	Iron,	Lead.

Stones are reckoned the next best conductors, but brick is a worse conductor than other sorts of stone. Glass differs but little from stones in its conducting power; but dried woods, which come next in succession, vary much with regard to each other, as may be observed from the following table, in which the conducting power of water is supposed $= 1$.

Water	1·00	Pear-tree	3·32
Ebony	2·17	Birch	3·41
Crab Apple	2·74	Oak	3·63
Ash	3·08	Pitch Pine	3·75
Beech	3·21	Alder	3·84
Hornbeam	3·23	Pine	3·86
Plum-tree	3·25	Fir	3·89
Female Oak	3·26	Lime-tree	3·90

Charcoal is a bad conductor, and all porous substances, as cork, and the like; but the worst conductors of all are feathers, silk, wool, and hair, which render them peculiarly fit for clothing, because they do not allow the heat of the body to be carried off by the cold external air. It has been found that the conducting power of these bodies is inversely as the fineness of their texture. The conducting power, however, of all solid bodies is so far limited as they are more or less exposed to a change in their state from the action of caloric. Bodies which, in the common temperature of the atmosphere, have the power of conducting *caloric*, lose that power when heated to the temperature at which they change their state; thus, at the temperature of 60°, sulphur is a conductor; but, when heated to 218°, or the point at which it melts, or is volatilized, it is no longer a conductor.

Conducting power of fluids. Liquids and gaseous bodies are conductors as well as solids, but in a less degree. The relative conducting powers of mercury, water, and linseed are as follow:

Equal Weights.		*Equal Bulks.*	
Water	1·	Water	1·
Mercury	2·	Mercury	4·8
Linseed oil	1·111	Linseed oil	1·085

As the cooling of hot bodies in gases is produced by a variety of causes, besides that of the conducting power of their fluids, it is difficult to form an estimate of their relative intensities as conductors.

Carrying power of liquids. Besides the conducting power, liquids have also a power which has been called their *carrying power*, by which the caloric is communicated, not from particle to particle, as in the case of conduction, but by the particles coming all individually in contact with the heating body. This, however, can only take place when the caloric is applied to the lower stratum of the fluid when it makes its way upwards independant of the conducting power; for, when the caloric is applied to the surface of the liquid, it can make its way downwards only, as in solids, by the conducting power of the fluid.

Distribution of caloric. As a consequence of the fore-mentioned properties in caloric, it has also been found to possess the tendency of distributing itself in such a manner, among all contiguous bodies, as that they should all acquire, in a certain time, the same temperature; thus, if one body be raised to the temperature of 200°, another to that of 100°, and a third to 60°; and if these three bodies be placed in the temperature of 80°, they all indicate in a short time the same temperature. The bodies which were at the temperature of 200° and 100° are reduced to 80°, and that of 60° rises to 80°. This is otherwise called the *equilibrium of caloric*.

CHEMISTRY.

The effects of caloric. The effects which caloric produces upon other bodies, either by entering into them, or by separating them, are reducible to three kinds of changes; namely, changes in bulk, changes in state, and changes in combination.

Expansion of caloric. One of the most general properties of caloric is, that by addition or abstraction in any degree it produces a corresponding change in the bulk of bodies; the addition of heat increasing their bulk, and the abstraction diminishing it. This property, however, which has been distinguished by the name of *expansion* to denote the positive effect of caloric, is not the same in all bodies. The expansion of gaseous bodies is the greatest of all, that of liquids is the next in degree, but that of solids is the smallest of all.

Expansion of gaseous bodies. By experiments it has been ascertained that all gaseous bodies whatever undergo the same expansion by the same additional heat, supposing them to be placed in the same circumstances: on this principle, therefore, the following table, which gives nearly the bulk of a given quantity of air at all temperatures, from $32°$ to $212°$, will suffice to illustrate that of other bodies:

Temp.	Bulk.	Temp.	Bulk.
32°	1,000,000	73°	1,085,416
33	1,002,083	74	1,087,499
34	1,004,166	75	1,089,383
35	1,006,249	76	1,091,666
36	1,008,333	77	1,093,749
37	1,010,416	78	1,095,832
38	1,012,499	79	1,097,916
39	1,014,583	80	1,099,999
40	1,016,666	81	1,102,083
41	1,018,749	82	1,104,166
42	1,020,833	83	1,106,249
43	1,022,916	84	1,108,333
44	1,024,759	85	1,110,416
45	1,027,083	86	1,112,499
46	1,029,166	87	1,114,583
47	1,031,249	88	1,116,666
48	1,033,333	89	1,118,749
49	1,035,416	90	1,120,833
50	1,037,499	91	1,122,916
51	1,039,583	92	1,124,999
52	1,041,666	93	1,127,083
53	1,043,749	94	1,129,166
54	1,045,833	95	1,131,249
55	1,047,916	96	1,133,333
56	1,049,999	97	1,135,416
57	1,052,083	98	1,137,493
58	1,054,166	99	1,139,583
59	1,056,249	100	1,141,666
60	1,058,333	110	1,162,499
61	1,060,416	120	1,183,333
62	1,062,499	130	1,204,166
63	1,064,583	140	1,224,999
64	1,066,666	150	1,245,833
65	1,068,749	160	1,266,666
66	1,070,833	170	1,287,499
67	1,072,916	180	1,308,333
68	1,074,999	190	1,329,166
69	1,077,083	200	1,349,999
70	1,079,166	210	1,370,833
71	1,081,249	212	1,374,999
72	1,083,333		

Expansion of liquids. The expansion of liquids is not equable like that of gaseous bodies. Liquids that are most readily brought to the state of vapour, are found to expand the most. With the same given temperature, the expansion of water is greater that that of mercury: and the expansion of alcohol is greater than that of water. The following table exhibits the ratio of expansion of several liquids, as they have been ascertained by different experiments.

Rate of Expansion of different Liquids in given Temperatures

Temp.	Mercury.	Linseed Oil.	Sulphuric Acid.	Nitric Acid.	Water.	Oil of Turpentine.	Alcohol.
32°	100,000	100,000	—	—	—	—	—
40	100,081	—	99,752	99,514	100,023	—	100,000
50	100,183	—	100,000	100,000	100,091	100,000	100,539
60	100,304	—	100,279	100,486	100,197	100,460	101,105
70	100,406	—	100,558	100,990	100,332	100,993	101,688
80	100,508	—	100,806	101,530	101,694	101,471	102,281
90	100,610	—	101,054	102,088	100,908	101,931	102,890
100	100,712	102,760	101,317	102,620	—	102,446	—
110	100,813	—	101,540	103,196	101,404	102,943	—
120	100,915	—	101,834	103,776	—	103,421	—
130	101,117	—	102,097	104,352	—	103,954	—
140	101,119	—	102,320	105,132	102,017	104,573	—
150	101,220	—	102,614	—	—	—	—
160	101,322	—	102,893	—	—	—	—
170	101,424	—	103,116	—	—	—	—
180	101,526	—	103,339	—	—	—	—
190	101,628	—	103,587	—	103,617	—	—
200	101,730	—	103,911	—	—	—	—
212	101,835	107,250	—	—	104,577	—	—

Expansion of Solids. The expansion of solid bodies is so small, as to render a nice apparatus necessary for the purpose of ascertaining it. The following table exhibits the results of different experiments upon this part of chemistry.

	Temp. 32°.	Temp. 212°.	White Heat.
Platina	120,000	120,104	—
Antimony	120,000	120,130	—
Steel	120,000	120,147	123,428
Iron	120,000	120,151	123,428
Iron	120,000	—	121,500
Cast Iron	120,000	—	122,571
Bismuth	120,000	120,167	—
Copper	120,000	120,204	—
Cast Brass	120,000	120,000	—
Brass Wire	120,000	120,232	—
Tin	120,000	120,298	—
Lead	120,000	120,344	—
Zinc	120,000	120,355	—
Hammered Zinc	120,000	120,373	—
Zinc ..8 } Tin....1 }	120,000	120,123	—
Lead ..2 } Tin....1 }	120,000	120,247	—
Brass ..2 } Tinc ..1 }	120,000	120,247	—
Pewter	120,000	120,274	—
Copper 3 } Tin....1 }	120,000	120,218	—

The expansion of glass has been more closely examined than that of other bodies, of which examination the following table exhibits the results.

Temp.		Temp.	
32°	100,000	150°	100,044
50	100,006	167	100,056
70	100,140	190	100,069
100	100,003	212	100,083
120	100,033		

CHEMISTRY.

The expansion of a gaseous body by the accumulation of caloric is shown by confining a quantity of air in a bottle, but not sufficient to fill it completely; after which, if the bladder be exposed to heat, the confined air expands, and the bladder becomes fully distended; but when it is cooled again, the air resumes its former bulk, and the bladder its original flaccid state. The expansion of liquids is exemplified by spirit of wine in a glass vessel having a slender neck. On the application of heat the liquid in the body of the vessel is expanded, and rises in the neck; and when the heat is abstracted, the liquid becomes contracted, and returns to its original bulk. The fixing of iron hoops on carriage wheels affords a familiar but striking example of the expansion of the solids. The hoop being made somewhat smaller than the wheel for which it is intended, is heated until it becomes of the suitable size, when it is fixed on; and afterwards, being cooled by the application of water, it contracts, and is thereby fast bound to the wood.

Thermometer. On the expansive property of bodies by the application of caloric depends the construction of the thermometer, which is employed for the measurement of the relative temperature of bodies. It consists of a hollow tube of glass, blown at one end in the shape of a hollow globe or bulb. This bulb, and part of the tube, are then filled with any liquid which has been first boiled to expel the air; after which, the open end of the tube being hermetically sealed, the rising of the liquid indicates an increase of heat, and its fall a diminution; the several proportions of which are marked by means of the degrees into which the tube is divided. The construction of the scale for this instrument was the result of long experience and observation; by which it was found, that as snow at all times melts at the same temperature, and water also boils at the same temperature, then by marking the two points at which the liquid stands in these two opposite cases, as for example, 0 for the freezing, and 100 for the boiling point; and by dividing the intermediate spaces into equal parts, a scale was procured which could be applied to all such thermometers, and also be extended to any distance above the boiling-point, and below the freezing point. The liquid most frequently used for the thermometer is mercury, because it is the most equable in its expansion.

Pyrometer. To measure the higher degrees of heat, to which the thermometer cannot be applied, another instrument has been invented, called the pyrometer, which consists of two pieces of brass fixed on a plate, so as to be 6-10ths of an inch asunder at one end, and 3-10ths at the other, which serves as a guage to measure certain pieces of baked clay before and after they have been heated; by which the difference in their dimensions is to be observed, and consequently the relative intensity of heat to which they were exposed may be ascertained. The pieces of clay must have been prepared in a red heat, and must be of given dimensions. A scale is marked on the pieces of brass, each of which is equal to 130° of Fahrenheit.

Exceptions to expansion by heat. Some apparent exceptions have been observed to this law of expansion by means of caloric, as in the case of water, which, when cooled down within about 7° of the freezing point, instead of contracting in consequence of the deprivation of heat, actually expands; alumine also contracts on being heated; and cast-iron, bismuth, &c. when fully fused, are more dense than when solid; for, as soon as they come into the latter state they decrease in density, and expand in the act of cooling; whence the sharpness of figures upon iron which has been cast in moulds, compared with that of others. But the expansion of these bodies is not considered as an exception to the general law, that bodies increase in bulk by the addition of heat, and decrease by its abstraction; for the expansion is here supposed to arise not from the diminution of the heat, but from the change of state which these bodies undergo in passing from liquids to solids.

Change of state in bodies by caloric. The three changes produced in the state of bodies by means of caloric are, the conversion of solids into fluids, that of fluids into solids, and, lastly, that of fluids into aeriform bodies.

Fusion, or fluidity. When solid bodies are submitted to the action of caloric to such a degree as to destroy their power of aggregation, they are reduced to a state of fluidity. The point of temperature at which a solid liquifies is called the *melting point*, which varies in different bodies, as may be seen from the following table:

Bodies.	Melting point.	Bodies.	Melting point.
Lead	612°	Ice	32°
Bismuth	476	Milk	30
Tin	442	Vinegar	28
Sulphur	218	Blood	25
Wax	142	Oil of bergamot	23
Bleached ditto	155	Wines	20
Spermacetti	112	Oil of turpentine	14
Phosphorus	106	Mercury	39
Tallow	92	Liquid ammonia	46
Oil of anise	50	Ether	46
Olive oil	36		

Fluidity is now generally supposed to be occasioned by the combination of a certain quantity of caloric with the solid bodies, which has been denominated, by some, *latent heat*, because its presence is not indicated by the thermometer; and by others, the *caloric of fluidity*.

Congelation, or freezing. When liquid bodies pass into the solid state by the abstraction of their caloric, this phenomenon is termed *congelation*, or *freezing;* and the point of the temperature at which this change takes place is called the *freezing point;* thus the freezing point of water is 32°, but it may be cooled down, in favourable circumstances, considerably below that temperature. When salts are dissolved in water, the freezing point of this solution is in most cases lowered; whence it is that sea-water does not freeze so readily as pure water. In the following table the names of the salts are given in the first column, the quantity of salt by weight dissolved in 100 parts of water in the second, and, in the third, the freezing point of the solution.

Salts.	Proportion.	Freez. point.
Common salt	25	4
Sal ammoniac	20	8
Rochelle salt	50	21
Sulphate of magnesia	41·6	25·5
Nitre	12·5	26
Sulphate of iron	41·6	28
Sulphate of zinc	53·3	28·6

From this table it appears that common salt is by far the most efficacious in lowering the freezing point of water. When acids diluted with water are exposed to cold, the weakest part freezes, while the stronger portion remains liquid; so that by the action of cold they are separated into two portions, differing very much in strength. This has been termed the *aqueous congelation* of acids.

Evaporation by caloric. All fluids may, by the application of heat, be converted into an aeriform elastic state, termed *vapour;* and the process by which it comes into that state is called *evaporation.* Some liquids assume the form of vapour at any temperature; as water, volatile oils, spirits of wine, and ether. This change is called

CHEMISTRY.

spontaneous evaporation; but there are others which remain unchanged till the temperature is raised to that point when the whole liquid comes into that state of intestine motion, which is called *boiling*, when the liquid becomes rapidly converted into vapour. That point of the temperature at which every liquid begins to boil is called the *boiling point*, which *cæteris paribus* is always the same in the same liquid; thus the boiling point of water is 212°, and never becomes hotter. The following table exhibits the boiling points of several liquids.

Ether	98°	Phosphorus	554°
Ammonia	140	Oil of turpentine	560
Alcohol	176	Sulphur	570
Water	212	Sulphuric acid	590
Muriate of lime	230	Linseed oil	600
Nitric acid	248	Mercury	660

But this boiling point is found to vary considerably; and this variation is caused by the different degrees of pressure on the surface of the liquid. When the pressure is diminished, liquids boil at a lower temperature; but when the pressure is increased, they require a higher temperature to produce boiling.

Elasticity of vapours. The elasticity of all the elastic fluids into which liquids are converted by heat increases with the temperature; and the vapour formed when the liquid boils in the open air possesses an elasticity just equal to that of air, or is capable, at a medium, of balancing a column of mercury 30 inches high. The following table exhibits the force of vapour from water in every temperature, from that of congelation of mercury, or 40° below zero of Fahrenheit, to 212°, as verified by experiments.

Temp.	Force of Vap. in Inch. of Mercury.	Temp.	Force of Vap. in Inch. of Mercury.	Temp.	Force of Vap. in Inch. of Mercury.
−40°	·013	29	·180	62	·560
−30	·020	30	·186	63	·578
−20	·030	31	·193	64	·597
−10	·043	32	·200	65	·616
0	·064	33	·207	66	·635
1	·066	34	·214	67	·655
2	·068	35	·221	68	·676
3	·071	36	·229	69	·698
4	·074	37	·237	70	·721
5	·076	38	·245	71	·745
6	·079	39	·254	72	·770
7	·082	40	·263	73	·796
8	·085	41	·273	74	·823
9	·087	42	·283	75	·851
10	·090	43	·294	76	·880
11	·093	44	·305	77	·910
12	·096	45	·316	78	·940
13	·100	46	·328	79	·971
14	·104	47	·339	80	1·00
15	·108	48	·351	81	1·04
16	·112	49	·363	82	1·07
17	·116	50	·375	83	1·10
18	·120	51	·388	84	1·14
19	·124	52	·401	85	1·17
20	·129	53	·415	86	1·21
21	·134	54	·429	87	1·24
22	·139	55	·443	88	1·28
23	·144	56	·458	89	1·32
24	·150	57	·474	90	1·36
25	·156	58	·490	91	1·40
26	·162	59	·507	92	1·44
27	·168	60	·524	93	1·48
28	·174	61	·542	94	1·53

Temp.	Force of Vap. in Inch. of Mercury.	Temp.	Force of Vap. in Inch. of Mercury.	Temp.	Force of Vap. in Inch. of Mercury.
95	1·58	135	5·00	174	13·32
96	1·63	136	5·14	175	13·62
97	1·68	137	5·29	176	13·92
98	1·74	138	5·44	177	14·22
99	1·80	139	5·59	178	14·52
100	1·86	140	5·74	179	14·83
101	1·92	141	5·90	180	15·15
102	1·98	142	6·05	181	15·50
103	2·04	143	6·21	182	15·86
104	2·11	144	6·37	183	16·23
105	2·18	145	6·53	184	16·61
106	2·25	146	6·70	185	17·00
107	2·32	147	6·87	186	17·40
108	2·39	148	7·05	187	17·80
109	2·46	149	7·23	188	18·20
110	2·53	150	7·42	189	18·60
111	2·60	151	7·61	190	19·00
112	2·68	152	7·81	191	19·42
113	2·76	153	8·01	192	19·86
114	2·84	154	8·20	193	20·32
115	2·92	155	8·40	194	20·77
116	3·00	156	8·66	195	21·22
117	3·08	157	8·81	196	21·68
118	3·16	158	9·02	197	22·13
119	3·25	159	9·24	198	22·69
120	3·33	160	9·46	199	23·16
121	3·42	161	9·68	200	23·64
122	3·50	162	9·91	201	24·12
123	3·59	163	10·15	202	24·61
124	3·69	164	10·41	203	25·10
125	3·79	165	10·68	204	25·61
126	3·89	166	10·96	205	26·13
127	4·00	167	11·25	206	26·66
128	4·11	168	11·54	207	27·20
129	4·22	169	11·83	208	27·74
130	4·34	170	12·13	209	28·29
131	4·47	171	12·43	210	28·84
132	4·60	172	12·73	211	29·41
133	4·73	173	13·02	212	30·00
134	4·86				

Decomposition by caloric. Another effect which caloric produces by its action on bodies is that of reducing them to their elements, or otherwise altering the nature of their combination: thus, when ammonia is heated to redness, it is resolved into azotic and hydrogen gases; and alcohol, by the same heat, is converted into carburetted hydrogen and water; and so on with many other substances.

Quantity of caloric. Equal weights of the same body, at the same temperature, contain the same quantities of caloric; and equal weights of the same body, at different temperatures, give on admixture the arithmetical mean; thus the temperature of a pint of hot water and a pint of cold is, when mixed, very nearly halfway between that of the two extremes. But this is not the case when equal quantities of different bodies, at different temperatures, are employed, for they will be found to contain unequal quantities. Wherefore the quantity of caloric has been divided into absolute and relative. The *absolute quantity* of caloric is the whole quantity contained in a body, the measurement of which is a problem in chemistry that is not yet solved. The *relative quantity* of caloric is that quantity which one body contains compared with that contained in another. This is called *specific caloric;* and the power or property which enables bodies to retain different quantities of caloric has been called *capacity for caloric.* Thus if a pint of quicksilver at 100° Fahrenheit be mixed with a pint of water at 40°, the resulting temperature will not be 70°, the arithmetical mean, but only 60°; wherefore the quicksilver loses 40° of heat, which nevertheless raises the temperature of the water only; consequently a larger quantity of caloric is required to raise the temperature of a pint of water than that of a pint of mercury through the same number of degrees. Hence it is inferred, that water has a greater capacity for caloric than is inherent in quicksilver.

Specific caloric. Although we do not know the absolute quantity of caloric requisite to produce a certain degree of heat in any body, yet if the unknown quantity that is requisite to heat the water be made = 1. we may determine by experiment how much more or how much less caloric other bodies require, to be heated the same number of degrees; thus suppose the quantity of caloric which heats water 1° heats the same weight of spermacetti oil 2°, it follows that the specific caloric of water is twice as much as that of oil, and consequently, that if the specific caloric of water be = 1. that of spermacetti oil must be = 0·5. The following is a table of the specific caloric of different bodies, which exhibits the results of different experiments.

The specific caloric of various bodies, that of water being 1·000.

Bodies.	Spec. caloric.
1. GASES.	
Hydrogen gas	21·4000
Oxygen gas	4·7490
Common air	1·7900
Carbonic acid gas	1·0459
Steam	1·5500
Azotic gas	3·7036
2. LIQUIDS.	
Water	1·0000
Carbonate of ammonia	1·8510
Arterial blood	1·0300
Cows' milk	0·9999
Sulphuret of ammonia	0·9940
Venous blood	0·8928
Solution of brown sugar	0·8600
Nitric acid	0·8440
Sulphate of magnesia 1 / Water 8	0·8440
Common salt 1 / Water 8	0·8320
Nitre 1 / Water 8	0·8167
Muriate of ammonia 1 / Water 1·5	0·7790
Tartar 1 / Water 237·3	0·7650
Solution of potash	0·7590
Sulphate of iron 1 / Water 2·5	0·7340
Sulphate of soda 1 / Water 22·9	0·7280
Oil of olives	0·7100
Ammonia	0·7080
Muriatic acid	0·6800
Sulphuric acid 1 / Water 5	0·6631
Alum 1 / Water 4·45	0·6490
Nitric acid 9¼ / Lime 1	0·6181
Nitre 1 / Water 3	0·6460
Alcohol	0·6021
Sulphuric acid	0·5968
Nitrous acid	0·5760
Linseed oil	0·5280
Spermacetti oil	0·5000
Oil of turpentine	0·4720
Vinegar	0·3870
Lime 9 / Water 16	0·3346
Mercury	0·3100
Distilled vinegar	0·1030
3. SOLIDS.	
Ice	0·9000
Ox-hide, with the hair	0·7870
Lungs of a sheep	0·7690
Lean of ox beef	0·7400
Pine	0·6500
Fir	0·6000
Lime	0·6200
Pitch-pine	0·5800
Apple-tree	0·5700
Alder	0·5300
Oak	0·5100
4. BODIES.	
Ash	0·5100
Crab-tree	0·5000
Rice	0·5050
Horse-beans	0·5020
Dust of the pine-tree	0·5000
Pease	0·4920
Beech	0·4900
Hornbeam	0·4800
Birch	0·4800
Wheat	0·4770
Elm	0·4700
Female oak	0·4500
Plum-tree	0·4400
Ebony	0·4300
Barley	0·4210
Oats	0·4160
Pitcoal	0·2777
Charcoal	0·2631
Chalk	0·2564
Rust of iron	0·2500
Quick-lime	0·2199
Stone-ware	0·1950
Agate	0·1950
Crystal	0·1929
Cinders	0·1923
Swedish glass	0·1870
Ashes of cinders	0·1885
Sulphur	0·1830
Flint-glass	0·1740
White oxide of antimony washed	0·2270
Oxide of copper nearly freed from air	0·2272
Rust of iron nearly freed from air	0·1666
White oxide of antimony do	0·1666
Ashes of the elm	0·1402
Oxide of zinc nearly freed from air	0·1369
Iron	0·1264
Brass	0·1141
Copper	0·1121
Sheet-iron	0·1099
Oxide of lead and tin	0·1020
Gun-metal	0·1100
White oxide of tin nearly freed from air	0·0990
Zinc	0·0981
Ashes of charcoal	0·0909
Silver	0·0820
Yellow oxide of lead nearly freed from air	0·0680
Tin	0·0661
Antimony	0·0637
Gold	0·0500
Lead	0·0424
Bismuth	0·0430

Cold. With the quantity of caloric is connected the phenomenon of cold, which, according to modern chemists, arises from the absence or abstraction of heat; so that when we say a substance is cold, we mean merely that it contains less caloric than usual, or that its temperature is lower than that of our bodies. Some have, however, supposed cold to be a distinct body, the subtle particles of which insinuate themselves into other substances; but this opinion has not had many supporters.

Artificial cold. The most remarkable phenomenon belonging to the theory of cold is, that it may be produced to a very great degree by the mixture of different solids, which suddenly become liquid. This mixture is called a *frigorific*, or *freezing mixture*, and the cold is called artificial. The different substances which admit of being employed for that purpose, and the degree of cold which each of them is capable of producing, are exhibited in the following tables:—

Table of freezing mixtures.

Mixtures.	Parts.	Thermometer sinks from
Muriate of ammonia	5	
Nitrate of potash	5	50° to 10°
Water	16	
Muriate of ammonia	5	
Nitrate of potash	5	50° to 4°
Sulphate of soda	8	
Water	16	
Sulphate of soda	3	50° to 3°
Diluted nitric acid	2	
Sulphate of soda	8	50° to 0°
Muriatic acid	5	
Snow	1	32° to 0°
Muriate of soda	1	
Snow, or pounded ice	2	0° to 5°
Muriate of soda	1	
Snow, or pounded ice	12	
Muriate of soda	5	5° to 18°
Muriate of ammonia and nitrate of potash	5	

CHEMISTRY.

Mixtures.	Parts.	Thermometer sinks from
Snow, or pounded ice	12	
Muriate of soda	5	18° to 25°
Nitrate of ammonia	5	
Snow	3	0° to 18°
Diluted nitric acid	2	
Muriate of lime	3	32° to 51°
Snow	2	
Snow	8	10° to 56°
Diluted sulphuric acid	3	
Diluted nitric acid	3	
Snow	1	20° to 60°
Diluted sulphuric acid	1	
Muriate of lime	2	0° to 66°
Snow	1	
Muriate of lime	3	40° to 73°
Snow	1	
Diluted sulphuric acid	10	68° to 91°
Snow	8	
Nitrate of ammonia	1	50° to 4°
Water	1	
Nitrate of ammonia	1	
Carbonate of soda	1	50° to 7°
Water	1	
Sulphate of soda	6	
Muriate of ammonia	4	50° to 10°
Nitrate of potash	2	
Diluted nitric acid	4	
Sulphate of soda	6	
Nitrate of ammonia	5	50° to 14°
Diluted nitric acid	4	
Phosphate of soda	9	50° to 12°
Diluted nitric acid	4	
Phosphate of soda	9	
Nitrate of ammonia	6	50° to 21°
Diluted nitric acid	4	
Sulphate of soda	5	50° to 3°
Diluted sulphuric acid	4	

Sources of caloric. The sources are six; namely, the sun, combustion, percussion, friction, chemical combination, and electricity.

The sun. Caloric comes to us from the sun, in the form of rays, at the rate of 200,000 miles in a second of time; but it has been found by experiment, as before observed, that the solar rays, which occasion heat, are distinct from those which illuminate and produce vision.

The effects of the solar rays on all bodies are not the same; the transparent bodies, through which they freely pass, are but little affected by them in their passage; whilst, on the other hand, opaque bodies are heated by them; and it has been ascertained by experiment, that the deeper the colour of the body the greater is the increase of temperature. It appears too, that those bodies which absorb most light acquire the greatest degree of temperature when exposed to the sun's rays.

The temperature produced in bodies by the direct action of the sun's rays seldom exceeds 120° but a much higher temperature may be obtained by collecting the rays on opaque bodies, which do not readily allow the caloric to be carried off by the surrounding bodies. It has, however, been found by experiment, that the heating power of the solar rays is not increased by concentrating them into a focus; but that the intensity of their action is occasioned by a greater number of them being brought to bear upon the same point.

Combustion. That process is so called by which substances undergo a total change in their nature, accompanied with the emission of light and heat. The manner in which this evolution takes place varies according to circumstances, and is distinguished into four kinds; namely, *ignition*, or glowing heat; *inflammation*, or ascension; and *detonation*, or explosion.

Many theories have been advanced to explain the process of combustion, which it would exceed the limits of this treatise to touch upon; it will, therefore, be sufficient, for the illustration of this subject, to divide bodies, as far as combustion is concerned, into *combustibles, supporters of combustion,* and *incombustibles.*

In every case of combustion there must be present a *combustible* body and a *supporter of combustion,* the former of which always unites with the latter during the process. It is this combination which occasions the apparent waste and alteration of the combustible. The new compound thus formed is called a *product of combustion,* and is either an acid or an oxide.

Percussion. The evolution of caloric by means of percussion is a well-known phænomenon; as in the case of iron, which may be hammered until it is red hot. This phenomenon is supposed to be the consequence of a *condensation* in the body struck, which, by the compression of the particles, forces out the caloric. Experiments have been made upon pieces of gold, silver, and copper, to ascertain the quantity of heat evolved when they are suddenly and forcibly struck; by which it has been ascertained that copper evolved most heat; silver was the next in degree; and gold evolved the least. The first blow evolved the most heat, which diminished on the second blow, and was hardly perceptible on the third.

Friction. The heat which is evolved by rubbing two pieces of dry stick smartly together until they take fire, is a familiar example of friction as a source of caloric; to which might be added numberless other examples from common life.

Chemical combination. As it is one of the characteristics of chemical action to produce a change of temperature, it has been established as a general law in the chemical science, that all bodies which pass from the solid to the fluid state absorb a quantity of caloric; and all bodies which pass from the fluid to the solid state give out caloric; hence it is, that when two substances in a gaseous state, as ammoniacal gas and muriatic acid gas, are mixed together, and combining form a solid salt, they at the same time evolve caloric; so, likewise, when two liquids, as alcohol and water, are mixed, caloric is evolved during the combination. A great quantity of caloric is also given out when a fluid body combines with a solid, as in the case of slacking lime; and, also, when two solids are mixed together which undergo fermentation, as horse-dung and tanners' bark, which are used in making hot-beds, because during the process of fermentation, a gradual and constant evolution of caloric takes place.

Electricity. The evolution of both light and heat in electricity is a phænomenon well known by familiar observation; for when an excited body is discharged through the air, there always appears a very bright flash of light, which is commonly called the spark; this is sometimes sufficiently strong to fuse the most refractory metals, and to set fire to gunpowder, alcohol, and other combustible bodies. [vide *Electricity*]

Ponderable Bodies.

A ponderable body is one whose weight admits of being ascertained. The weight of bodies gravitating in fluids is called *gravity;* which is, absolute and specific, or relative.—*Absolute* or *true* gravity is the whole force with which a body tends downwards.—*Specific* or *relative gravity* is the relative, comparative, or apparent gravity

CHEMISTRY.

in any body, as it respects that of an equal bulk or magnitude of another body.

The specific gravity of bodies is denoted in chemical writings by comparing it with that of pure water, which in decimal figures is always considered as 1·000.

Ponderable bodies, as to their general properties, may be divided into gases, alkalies, earths, and metals.

Gases. Gases are aeriform fluids that are transparent, elastic, for the most part invisible, and not condensible into a liquid or solid state by any degree of cold hitherto known. This last property distinguishes these substances from vapours. The elasticity of gases is increased by heat and diminished by cold, and they are all absorbed both by liquids and solids; but they vary in the measure of absorption, also in their specific gravity, and other properties, which will be noticed under the respective heads.

Alkalies. The word *alkali*, which is of Arabic origin, signifies, literally, the Kali, or plant so called, from the ashes of which a substance has been procured of peculiar properties. Three bodies have been generally ranked under this head; namely—potash, soda, and ammonia; to which have been added some others of a mixed character, and distinguished by the name of alkaline earths. The alkalies have an acrid and peculiar taste: they change vegetable blues, as an infusion of violets, to a green colour: they have a strong attraction for water, and combine with it in all proportions: they also combine with acids, and form salts; and they have a powerfully corroding quality that is sufficient to reduce woollen cloth to the state of a jelly.

The alkalies are divided into fixed and volatile. Potash, soda, and the newly-discovered earth lythnia, are denominated *fixed alkalies*, because they require a great degree of heat to dissipate or volatilize them. Ammonia, on the other hand, is termed a *volatile alkali*, because a very moderate degree of heat is sufficient to produce its volatilization.

Earths. The earths are substances which have neither taste nor smell; are nearly soluble in water, and have a specific gravity under 5. They are divided into *alkaline earths*, which partake of the character of both earths and alkalies, and *earths*, simply so called. The alkaline earths are barytes, strontites, lime, and magnesia. The earths are silex, alumina, zircon, glucina, thorina, and yttria.

Metals. The metals are distinguished by their brilliancy, called the *metallic lustre*; their colour, opacity, density, hardness, elasticity, ductility, malleability, tenacity, fusibility, and their power of conducting caloric and electricity. In addition to the recently-discovered bases of the alkalies and earths, the following are generally admitted to be metallic substances:—

1. Gold	11. Nickel	21. Manganese
2. Platinum	12. Tin	22. Chrome
3. Silver	13. Lead	23. Molybdena
4. Mercury	14. Zinc	24. Uranium
5. Rhodium	15. Bismuth	25. Tungsten
6. Palladium	16. Antimony	26. Titanium
7. Iridium	17. Tellurium	27. Columbium
8. Osmium	18. Selenium	28. Cerium
9. Copper	19. Arsenic	
10. Iron	20. Cobalt	

For the consideration of the simple substances in detail, they may be more conveniently arranged, on the principle of combustion, into combustibles, supporters of combustion, and incombustibles.—*Combustible* bodies are those which, in common language, are said to burn.—*Supporters of combustion* are bodies which of themselves, strictly speaking, are not capable of undergoing combustion, but which are absolutely necessary for the production of this effect in bodies; in so much that, whenever they are excluded, combustion ceases.—*Incombustibles* are bodies, which are incapable of undergoing combustion themselves, or of supporting combustion in other bodies; of which description azote is the only substance hitherto known. These several substances will be considered in the following order: supporters of combustion, incombustibles, and combustibles.

Supporters of combustion. The supporters of combustion, hitherto known, are three in number; namely, oxygen, chlorine, and iodine. The compounds which these bodies form with each other, are likewise supporters.

Oxygen. The properties of oxygen, which is the most important of all chemical substances, have hitherto been discovered only by its effects while in a state of combination, particularly when combined with light and heat in an aeriform state, called oxygen gas.

Oxygen gas. Oxygen gas is an invisible elastic fluid, which, like common air, is capable of indefinite expansion and compression. It has no perceptible taste; and when in a state of purity, is also destitute of smell. Its mean specific gravity, as determined by different experiments, is estimated to be 1·1088. It is not absorbed by water, but absorbable in the highest degree by combustible bodies, which, at the same time, disengage its heat and light. It hastens germination, is indispensable to respiration, and is the cause of animal heat; whence it has been denominated *vital air*. It is considered as the cause of acidity; and, from this last property, has derived its name of *oxygen*. The act of its combining with bodies is called *oxydisement* or *oxygenation;* and the bodies with which it is combined are called oxides or acids.

The following is the order of its affinity for the substances with which it enters into combination.

Oxygen.

Charcoal,
Titanium,
Manganese,
Zinc,
Iron,
Tin,
Uranium,
Molybdena,
Tungsten,
Cobalt,
Antimony,
Hydrogen,
Phosphorus,
Sulphur,
Azote,
Nickel,
Arsenic,
Chromium,
Bismuth,
Lead,
Copper,
Tellurium,
Platina,
Mercury,
Silver,
Oxide of arsenic,
Nitrous gas,
Gold,
Muriatic acid,
White oxide of manganese,
White oxide of lead.

CHEMISTRY.

Oxygen may be obtained from a great number of bodies; but in the largest quantities from the oxides of manganese, lead, or mercury, from the nitrate of potash, from the green leaves of vegetables, &c.

Chlorine. Chlorine is a gaseous body, so called from its greenish colour; it was at first denominated *oxymuriatic acid*, because it was supposed to be a compound of muriatic acid and oxygen. It possesses an uncommonly pungent and suffocating odour, is totally unfit for respiration; so that animals immersed in it die instantly. It is heavier than atmospheric air, the specific gravity being estimated at about 2·500. It destroys colours, supports combustion, and forms combinations with oxygen in four proportions, and with the combustibles in one proportion.

Chlorine gas may be exposed to a very high temperature, without experiencing any change, if it be passed through a white hot porcelain tube. The methods for obtaining it are various.

Iodine. This gas was first obtained in 1811, from kelp. It is a solid substance, in the form of scales, of a greenish black colour, with a metallic lustre. It destroys colour like chlorine, melts when heated to the temperature of $224\frac{1}{2}°$, and is volatilized under the common pressure of the air, when raised to the temperature of $351\frac{1}{4}°$. It is not very soluble in water, but more so in alcohol, and still more so in sulphuric acid. It combines with oxygen and chlorine, and also with the combustibles; and, as it appears, chlorine, oxygen, and iodine, separate each other from bases, at a red heat, in the following order; namely, chlorine, oxygen, and iodine; consequently chlorine has the greatest affinity for the bases, oxygen the next greatest, and iodine the weakest.

Fluorine. Fluorine is a gaseous body, otherwise called *fluoric acid*, or fluoric acid gas, because it is obtained from fluor spar, or Derbyshire spar. It is said by some not to possess the property of maintaining combustion, although by others it is reckoned among its supporters; but upon this, and other properties of fluorine, there is much room for further discovery.

Incombustibles. Azote, the only substance called incombustible, has also the name of nitrogen, and is a simple body, which is the radical principle of our atmospheric air, and forms a constituent part of many animal and vegetable substances. Its most important combination is with light and caloric, when it appears in a gaseous form, called azotic gas or nitrogen gas. It is possessed of no positive properties by which it can be characterized; but is principally distinguished by certain negative qualities; namely, that it is extremely hurtful to respiration, whence it is called *mephitic air*, and that no combustible will burn in it. This gas is not sensibly absorbed by water, nor is there any liquid which is known to be capable of condensing it. Its specific gravity is about 0·9722.

Azote has the property of combining with oxygen, and forming four compounds; and it also combines with chlorine and iodine.

Combustibles. The simple combustibles may be divided into three classes; namely, acidifiable combustibles, alkalifiable combustibles, and intermediate combustibles.—*Acidifiable combustibles* are those which have the property of forming acids.—*Alkalifiable combustibles* are such as form alkalies or bases, capable of composing neutral salts.—*Intermediate combustibles* are such as produce imperfect alkalies and acids.

Acidifiable combustibles. The acidifiable combustibles are eight in number; namely, hydrogen, carbon, borax, silica, phosphorus, sulphur, selenium, arsenic, and tellurium; the three last of which are reckoned among the metals.

Hydrogen. Hydrogen, as its name denotes, is one of the constituent elements of water, which is known only in a state of combination with caloric, which gives it the name of *hydrogen gas*: it was formerly called *inflammable air* or *phlogiston*. Besides the properties of invisibility, elasticity, &c. which it has in common with other gases, it is distinguished by being the lightest of all such bodies; its specific gravity, in respect to common air, being about 0·0694. It has a disagreeable smell, is incapable of supporting combustion, destructive to animal life, and not sensibly absorbed by water. In combination with oxygen it forms water, with chlorine gas it forms *muriatic acid*, with azote it forms the gaseous substance called *ammonia*. It also combines with iodine and fluorine.

Carbon. Carbon, from the Latin *carbo*, a coal, is frequently taken for *charcoal*; but in the chemical nomenclature it signifies the base of common charcoal, divested of all impurities, which is obtained in its purest state from the combustion of the diamond. Charcoal is generally black, sonorous, and brittle, very light, and destitute of smell. It is indestructible by age; a good conductor of electricity, but a bad conductor of heat; insoluble in water, yet it absorbs moisture in very considerable quantities. When freed from the air which it may contain, either by heat, or by being placed under an exhausted receiver, it has the property of absorbing gases in various proportions. The following table exhibits the bulk of the various gases absorbed by a volume of charcoal reckoned 1.

	Volumes.		Volumes.
Ammoniacal gas	90	Olefiant gas	35·
Muriatic acid	85	Carbonic oxide	9·2
Sulphurous acid	65·	Oxygen	9·25
Sulphuretted hydrogen	55	Azote	7·5
Nitrous oxide	40	Oxy-carburetted hydrogen	5·
Carbonic acid	35	Hydrogen	1·76

Carbon combines with oxygen and hydrogen in two proportions, and with azote in one proportion; by which is formed the compound called *cyanogen*.

Borax. Borax is a well known saline substance which yields an acid called *boracic acid*. The base of this acid, which is called *boron*, is a powder of a dark olive colour, that is not decomposed by heat, in a platina tube, though raised to whiteness, burns in oxygen gas, with a very brilliant light, and is not soluble in nitrous gas or hydrogen gas. It combines with chlorine, fluorine, and hydrogen; and seems to have a still greater affinity for oxygen, than either hydrogen or carbon.

Silica. Silica, or the siliceous earth, is obtained pure by fusing quartz or flint with twice its weight of potash, in a silver crucible. This earth is a white powder, without taste or smell, is infusible by the intense heat of the voltaic electricity, but has been melted by means of the blow-pipe. It is insoluble in water; yet, when it is fresh precipitated, water has the property of retaining in solution about one thousandth of its weight. It is not acted on by any of the acids, except fluoric; but is soluble in the alkalies, which solution has been called *silicated alkali*, or *liquor silicum*. When mixed with an equal weight of carbonate of potash, and exposed to a strong heat in a furnace, it forms a glass that is insoluble in water, and in other respects similar to common glass. Its specific gravity in quartz or flint is 2·6.

Silicon, or *Silicum*, the base of silica or siliceous earth, is

CHEMISTRY.

now most generally supposed to be a substance resembling borax, although previously it was supposed to be a metal, for which reason it had the name of silicium. Silicon seems capable of bearing a high temperature, without undergoing any change; it unites with oxygen, and forms silica, and combines also with fluorine to form *silicated acid* or *fluosilic acid*.

Phosphorus. Phosphorus, an inflammable substance, is generally of a flesh red colour, but in its purest state is colourless. It is so soft as to yield readily to the knife. It melts at about 90° Fahrenheit, and boils at 550°. It is insoluble in water, and dissolved, in a small degree, by alcohol, ether, and oils. When used internally it is poisonous. The mean specific gravity is 1·770.

Phosporus has the property of combining with oxygen in four proportions, with hydrogen in two, and with carbon in one proportion.

Sulphur. Sulphur, known by the vulgar name of *brimstone*, is a substance procured in the greatest abundance, by subjecting the mineral, called *pyrites*, to distillation. It is hard and brittle, commonly of a greenish yellow colour, without any smell: and is met with under two different forms: a compact solid, which has generally the shape of long rolls or sticks; or a light powder, called *flowers of sulphur*. Sulphur is readily fused and volatilized; and, when heated to the temperature of about 218° Fahrenheit, it melts and becomes as liquid as water; but when allowed to cool again, it crystallizes. At the temperature of about 290° Fahrenheit, it is converted into vapour; after which the volatilized sulphur may be collected in close vessels in a solid form. What remains has been called *sulphur vivum*. Sulphur combines with oxygen in two proportions, with iodine, hydrogen, and phosphorus in one proportion.

Arsenic. Arsenic, as it is to be met with in commerce, occurs in the state of a white oxide. It is of a bluish white colour, not unlike that of steel; has no sensible smell while it is cold, but when heated it emits a strong odour of garlic. It is the softest of all the metallic bodies; and is so brittle, that it may be easily reduced to a fine powder, by trituration in a mortar. Its specific gravity, when melted, is 5·7633. Its fusing point is not known, because it is the most volatile of all the metals; subliming, without melting, when exposed in close vessels to a heat of 356°; when sublimed slowly it crystallizes. Arsenic combines with two doses of oxygen, and with iodine, hydrogen, and sulphur in one proportion. It also forms alloys, by combining with the metals; and salts, by combining with acids. The order of its affinities is nearly as follows:

Arsenic.	Oxide of Arsenic.
Nickel	Lime
Cobalt	Muriatic acid
Copper	Oxalic
Iron	Sulphuric
Silver	Nitric
Tin	Tartaric
Gold	Phosphoric
Platinum	Fluoric
Zinc	Saclactic
Antimony	Succinic
Sulphur	Citric
Phosphorus	Lactic
	Arsenic
	Acetic
	Prussic

Selenium. Selenium is a substance of which, at present, little is known, except that it has the metallic lustre and other properties of a metal; becomes soft at 212°, and fuses at a little higher temperature; combines with most of the metals, and often with ignition. With the fixed alkalies it forms compounds of a cinnabar red colour; in fixed oils it forms reddish solutions; and dissolves in nitric acid, so as to produce a compound called selenic acid.

Tellurium. Tellurium, a metal of a bluish white colour, is very brittle, easily reducible to powder, melts when raised to a temperature somewhat higher than the fusing power of lead; and, when cooled slowly, crystallizes. Its specific gravity is said to be 6·115. Tellurium combines with oxygen, chlorine, hydrogen, and, as is supposed, with carbon.

The order of the affinities of the above mentioned bodies for oxygen, at a red heat, which seems necessary to promote their action, is as follow:

Oxygen.
Silica
Hydrogen
Carbon
Borax
Phosphorus
Sulphur
Arsenic
Tellurium

Alkalifiable combustibles. The alkalifiable substances are twenty-nine in number; namely; 1. Potash. 2. Soda. 3. Lime. 4. Barytes. 5. Strontian. 6. Magnesia. 7. Yttria. 8. Glucina. 9. Alumina. 10. Zircon. 11. Iron. 12. Nickel. 13. Cobalt. 14. Manganese. 15. Cerium. 16. Uranium. 17. Zinc. 18. Lead. 19. Tin. 20. Copper. 21. Bismuth. 22. Mercury. 23. Silver. 24. Gold. 25. Platinum. 26. Palladium. 27. Rhodium. 28. Iridium. 29.

Potash. Potash is a brittle substance, of a white colour, and of a smell similar to that which is perceived during the slacking of lime. Its taste is remarkably acrid; and it is so corrosive, as instantly to destroy any part of the body to which it is applied. It was formerly called *vegetable alkali*, because it is obtained in the greatest abundance from vegetable ashes; and when divested of many of its impurities by burning, it is called *pearl-ash*. Potash, in a perfectly dry state, is a non-conductor of electricity; but after exposure to the air for a few seconds, it acquires a moisture, which converts it into a conductor.

Potassium. By the decomposition of potash, a metallic substance has been separated from it in the form of small globules, which is considered as its base, and called potassium. This substance is white, and has completely the metallic lustre like silver or mercury. At the temperature of 50°, it is a soft and malleable solid; its fluidity becomes perfect at 136¼°, and at 32° it is hard and brittle. Potassium combines with oxygen in two proportions, so as to form *potash* and the peroxide of potassium. It also combines with chlorine, iodine, hydrogen, phosphorus, and arsenic.

Potash, or potassium, has so great an affinity for oxygen, that it separates this body from every one of the combustible substances before mentioned. The order of its affinities, for the supporters of combustion, is as follows:

Potash.
Chlorine
Iodine
Oxygen

It has the greatest affinity for sulphur of the acidifiable combustibles, and after that for phosphorus and hydrogen in succession. It combines readily with the acids; and the order of its affinities is nearly as follows:

Potash.

Sulphuric
Nitric
Muriatic
Phosphoric
Fluoric
Oxalic
Tartaric
Arsenic
Succinic
Citric
Lactic
Benzoic
Sulphurous
Acetic
Saclactic
Boracic
Carbonic
Prussic.

Soda. Soda was formerly called fossil, or *mineral alkali*; and, from the many properties which it has in common with potash, was confounded with it until the last century. The peculiar properties of soda are as follow:—It is the base of common salt; more fusible than potash; does not liquefy so rapidly when exposed to the air; is not altered by light; adheres less strongly to acids; attracts sulphur; and dissolves alumine more easily. Its specific gravity is 1·336.

Sodium. Sodium, the basis of soda, has been found to be a metallic substance, having an intermediate colour betwixt that of silver and lead. At the common temperature it is solid and very malleable, and melts when heated to the temperature of 194°. Its specific gravity is 0·97228. It combines with oxygen, so as to form two compounds, soda and the peroxide of sodium, in different proportions; also with chlorine, phosphorus, sulphur, arsenic.

The affinities of the simple supporters of combustion for soda, or sodium, are in the following order; namely,

Sodium.

Chlorine
Iodine
Oxygen.

Sulphur, of all the acidifiable combustibles, has the greatest affinity for soda; but the order of its affinities for the acids is the same nearly as that of potash.

Lime. Lime, *calx*, is an earth moderately hard, that is found in great abundance in nature, though never pure, or in an uncombined state. It is contained in the waters of the ocean, is found in vegetables, and forms the basis of bones, shells, and other hard animal substances. It is of a hot, acrid, urinous taste, produces nearly the same change on vegetable colours as the alkalies do, requires an intense heat for its fusion, and is not volatile. In its most caustic state it is called *quick lime*; but when by absorbing water it becomes an impalpable powder, it is called *slacked* lime, or *hydrate of lime*. Its specific gravity is 2·3.

Lime is very sparingly soluble in water, but has been found to dissolve more freely in cold than in hot water. The following table exhibits in the first column the temperature of the water; in the second the number of grains of water required to take up one grain of lime; and in the third the number required to dissolve one grain of hydrate of lime.

Temperature.	Grains of water to dissolve 1 grain of lime.	Grains of water to dissolve 1 gr. of hydrate of lime.
60°	778	584
130°	972	720
212°	1270	952

Lime, when thus dissolved, forms what has been termed lime-water.

Calcium. Calcium, the base of lime, is white like silver, solid, and considerably heavier than water. When heated in the open air it burns brilliantly, and quick lime is produced. It combines with oxygen in one proportion, so as to produce the compound called lime; also with chlorine and iodine.

The affinities of calcium, or lime, for the supporters of combustion, are in the following order:

Lime.

Chlorine
Oxygen
Iodine.

The order of its affinities for the acids is nearly as follows:

Lime.

Oxalic
Sulphuric
Tartaric
Succinic
Phosphoric
Saclactic
Nitric
Muriatic
Suberic
Fluoric
Arsenic
Lactic
Citric
Benzoic
Sulphurous
Acetic
Boracic
Carbonic
Prussic.

Barytes. Barytes is a heavy brittle mineral of a flesh-colour, and otherwise called *ponderous spar*. It is never found pure in nature, but always in combination with carbonic or sulphuric acid. It is obtained by the calcination of its carbonate or nitrate; and when pure it has a caustic state, changes vegetable colours to green, is poisonous, and entirely infusible by heat alone, but melts when mixed with various earths; changes quickly in the air, swells, becomes soft, and falls into a white powder. It has a more powerful attraction for water than lime, absorbing it with a hissing noise, and consolidating it strongly. It is soluble in twenty times its weight of cold, and twice its weight of boiling water. When the solution is allowed to cool slowly it shoots into regular crystals. The specific gravity of barytes is stated to be 4·000.

Barium. Barium, the metallic basis of barytes, is a solid metal of a silver colour, which melts at a temperature not below redness. It combines with oxygen in two proportions, forming the compounds barytes, and the peroxide of barium; also with chlorine and iodine.

Barytes, or *barium*, has an affinity for the simple supporters of combustion in the following order:

CHEMISTRY.

Barium.
Chlorine
Oxygen
Iodine.

The order of its affinities for the acids is nearly as follows:

Barytes.
Sulphuric
Oxalic
Succinic
Fluoric
Phosphoric
Saclactic
Nitric
Muriatic
Suberic
Citric
Tartaric
Arsenic
Lactic
Benzoic
Acetic
Boracic
Sulphurous
Carbonic
Prussic.

Strontian, or *Strontites.* Strontian is a mineral which bears a strong resemblance to barytes; but it is not poisonous, and does not act so powerfully on animal bodies.

Strontium, the base of strontian, or strontites, is white, solid, much heavier than water, and bears a close resemblance to barium in its properties. It combines with oxygen in only one proportion at present known, forming the compound strontian; and also with chlorine.

Strontites, or *strontium,* forms acids by combining with the acids for which it has an affinity, nearly in the following order:

Strontites.
Sulphuric
Phosphoric
Oxalic
Tartaric
Fluoric
Nitric
Muriatic
Succinic
Acetic
Arsenic
Boracic
Carbonic.

Magnesia. Magnesia is an earth in the form of a powder, not found pure in nature, but always obtained by art from some of its combinations. It is soft to the touch, and gives a smooth, unctuous feel to the bodies in which it is contained; such as talc, asbestus, and the like. It is very slightly soluble in water; and possesses the properties of an alcali, but in a less degree than the alkaline earths. Its specific gravity is between 2 and 3. It is infusible by the most intense heat, except when mixed with other earths. When heated strongly it becomes phosphorescent.

Magnesium. Magnesium, the base of magnesia, is a white solid metal, like silver, and heavier than water, which combines with oxygen in one proportion, and forms the substance well known by the name of magnesia.

Magnesia, or *magnesium,* also combines with chlorine, sulphur, and the acids; for which latter it has an affinity in nearly the following order:

Magnesia.
Oxalic acid
Phosphoric
Sulphuric
Fluoric
Arsenic
Saclactic
Succinic
Nitric
Muriatic
Tartaric
Citric
Lactic
Benzoic
Acetic
Boracic
Sulphurous
Carbonic
Prussic.

Yttria. Yttria is a perfectly white earth, devoid of either taste or smell, smooth to the touch like alumine, and infusible, except by an intense heat. It is very ponderous; its specific gravity is 4·842, and is insoluble in water, or the fixed alkalies; but it is readily dissolved by carbonated ammonia and sulphuric acid. *Yttrium,* the base of yttria, has not yet been exhibited in a separate form; but the presence of oxygen in yttria is established by its converting potassium into potash when ignited with that metal.

Glucina. Glucina, or Glucine, a new earth, which has been extracted from the *aqua marina,* or the beryl, is a fine soft powder that adheres to the tongue, and is insipid. Its specific gravity is 2·97. It is insoluble in water, but soluble in alkalies and their carbonates, and in all the acids except the carbonic and sulphuric acid. It forms sweet astringent salts with the different acids, and is fusible with borax, with which it forms a transparent glass. Of glucinum, the base of glucina, nothing is known at present; but the general fact of its existence is proved by igniting glucine with potassium, which is thus changed into potash.

The order of its affinities for the acids is nearly as follows:

Glucina.
Sulphuric acid
Nitric
Muriatic
Phosphoric
Fluoric
Boracic
Carbonic.

Alumina. Alumina, alumine, or the Earth of alum, so called because it is the base of the well-known salt called alum, is a white earth which enters into the natural composition of the schistus, of all stones, and of the earths called argillaceous. It is soft to the touch and insipid, adheres to the tongue, and occasions a dryness in the mouth. When moistened with water it forms a cohesive ductile mass, which, when dried to the temperature of the atmosphere, retains almost half its weight of water. When heated to redness it shrinks considerably in bulk, and at last becomes so hard as to strike fire with flint. It is dissolved by the liquid fixed alkalies, and is precipitated by acids unchanged. In ammonia it is very sparingly soluble, and is not soluble in alcaline carbonates. Alumina has no smell when pure; but if it contain oxide of iron it emits a peculiar smell when breathed upon, which is known by the name of the *earthy smell.* It is obtained by dissolving water in alum according to a given process; but it assumes two different appearances when thus obtained, according to the way in which the precipitation is conducted. If the earthy salt be dissolved in as little water as possible, it has a light and spongy appearance, whence it is called *spongy alumina*; if in a great quantity of water, it assumes the form of a brittle transparent mass, which is called *gelatinous alumina*. Barytes and strontites combine with alumine, both by fusion and in the humid way; it may also be united with the fixed alkalies, with most of the earths, and almost all the acids. The order of its affinities for the latter is nearly as follows:

Alumina.
Sulphuric acid
Nitric
Muriatic
Oxalic
Arsenic
Fluoric
Tartaric
Succinic
Saclactic
Citric
Phosphoric
Lactic
Benzoic
Acetic
Boracic
Sulphurous
Carbonic
Prussic.

Aluminum. Aluminum, or *alumium*, the base of alumina, is supposed to be a metallic substance like the preceding, but it has not yet been obtained in such a state as to make it a fit subject of investigation.

Zircon. Zircon is an earth drawn from a precious stone in Ceylon, called the zircon, or jargon. This earth has the form of a fine powder, entirely destitute of taste or smell, the specific gravity of which exceeds 4. It is insoluble in water; but yet it retains, after precipitation, one-third of its weight. It is also insoluble in pure liquid alcalies; nor does it even combine with them by fusion; but it is soluble in alkaline carbonates. When exposed to a strong heat it fuses, and assumes a grey colour. In this state it is very hard, its specific gravity is 3·5, and it is no longer soluble in acids. Of *zirconium*, the base of zircon, little is known except that it is of a metallic nature.

Its affinities for the acids are nearly in the following order:

Zircon.
Vegetable acids
Sulphuric
Muriatic
Nitric.

Thorina. Thorina is, when dried, a perfectly white earth, which absorbs carbonic acid, and dissolves with effervescence in acids. It differs from alumina by being insoluble in solution of potash; from yttria by its astringent taste without sweetness, and by its neutral solutions affording a precipitate when boiled; and from zirconia by its being precipitated by oxalate of ammonia, &c. The base of thorina is called *thorinum*.

Iron. Iron exceeds other metals in hardness, particularly when in the state of steel, and its specific gravity varies from 7·6 to 7·8. It has the singular property of possessing the magnetic virtue, or of being attracted by the magnet; but when it is perfectly pure, it is said not to retain this virtue very long. It is malleable in every temperature, and its malleability increases with the increase of the temperature; but its ductility is still more perfect, for it may be drawn out into wire as fine as a hair; and its tenacity is such, that a wire 0·078 of an inch in diameter is capable of supporting more than 500 lbs. avoirdupois without breaking. It is one of the most infusible of all metals, and is said to require a temperature of more than 150° of Wedgewood for its fusion. It becomes red long before it melts; and by the different shades of this redness are distinguished the different degrees of temperature: the first being called a *dull red*, the second *cherry red*, the third a *bright red*, and the fourth a *white heat*, or *incandescence*.

Iron has a strong affinity for oxygen; but, as far as is known at present, it combines with it in two proportions only. It combines also with sulphur in two proportions; with carbon in various proportions; but with phosphorus in one only. Iron forms salts in combination with the acids, and with the metals it forms alloys.

The affinities of iron for the supporters of combustion are nearly as follow:—

Iron.
Chloride
Oxygen
Iodine.

Its affinities for other metals, and those of its oxide for the acids, are nearly as follow:—

Iron.	*Oxide of Iron.*
Nickel	Oxalic acid
Cobalt	Tartaric
Manganese	Camphoric
Arsenic	Sulphuric
Copper	Saclactic
Gold	Muriatic
Silver	Nitric
Tin	Phosphoric
Antimony	Arsenic
Platinum	Fluoric
Bismuth	Succinic
Lead	Citric
Mercury.	Lactic
	Acetic
	Boracic
	Prussic
	Carbonic.

Nickel. Nickel, in a state of purity, is a metal of a fine white colour, resembling silver, rather softer than iron. Its specific gravity is between 8 and 9. It possesses the magnetic virtue of iron, and may, like steel, be converted into a magnet. It is malleable both hot and cold, and may be drawn into a very fine wire. It requires a temperature of above 160° of Wedgewood for fusion; but has never, hitherto, been crystallized. As a conductor of heat it is superior to zinc or copper.

Nickel combines with oxygen in two proportions; also with chlorine, carbon, phosphorus, and sulphur in one. It forms alloys in combination with the metals, and salts in combination with the acids.

The affinities of nickel for other metals, and those of its oxide for the acids, are nearly in the following order:—

Nickel.	*Oxide of Nickel.*
Iron	Oxalic acid
Cobalt	Muriatic
Arsenic	Sulphuric
Copper	Tartaric
Gold	Nitric

Nickel.	Oxide of Nickel.
Tin	Phosphoric
Antimony	Fluoric
Platinum	Saclactic
Bismuth	Succinic
Lead	Citric
Silver	Lactic
Zinc	Acetic
Sulphur	Arsenic
Phosphorus.	Boracic
	Prussic.
	Carbonic.

Cobalt. Cobalt, or Cobolt, is a mineral of a grey colour, having scarcely any taste or smell. It is rather soft, its specific gravity being from 8.5 to 8.7. It is brittle and easily reduced to powder; melts at the temperature of 130° Wedgewood, and is attracted by the magnet like iron.

Cobalt is never found in a state of purity, but always in the state either of an oxide, a sulphuret, an alloy, or a salt. It combines with oxygen in two proportions; with chlorine, phosphorus, and sulphur in one; and forms alloys by combining with metals, and salts by combining with acids. The order of its affinities is nearly as follows:—

Cobalt.	Oxide of Cobalt.
Iron	Oxalic acid
Nickel	Muriatic
Arsenic	Sulphuric
Copper	Tartaric
Gold	Nitric
Platinum	Phosphoric
Tin	Fluoric
Antimony	Saclactic
Zinc	Succinic
Phosphorus	Lactic
Sulphur	Acetic
	Arsenic
	Boracic
	Prussic
	Carbonic

Cobalt is used principally to give a blue colour to glass, porcelain, and the like. When it is mixed with earth, and appears in the form of a brown gritty powder, it is called *zaffre*; when melted with vitrifiable materials it is called *smalt*; and if this be formed into a very fine blue powder, it is called *azure*.

Manganese. Manganese never occurs in a metallic state, but always in that of an oxide. It is of a dusky white colour, and softer than iron. Its specific gravity is estimated from 6 to 8. It is very brittle, and requires for fusion the temperature of 160° Wedgewood. When in the state of a powder it is often attracted by the magnet, on account of the iron, from which it can be separated only with difficulty. It is the most combustible of all the metals. It very rapidly decomposes water by means of heat; as also most of the metallic oxides and sulphuric acid; but it is soluble in nitric acid.

Manganese attracts oxygen so powerfully, that exposure to the air is sufficient to render it brown, black, and friable in a short time; for that reason, it can only be kept in water, oil, or ardent spirits. It combines with oxygen in several proportions; also with chlorine, carbon, phosphorus, and with sulphur. It enters likewise into combination with the acids to form salts, and with the metals to form alloys.

Cerium. Cerium is a Swedish mineral that is white, very hard, brittle, and volatile. It combines with oxygen in two proportions; and the solutions of the oxides in acids are either yellow or red, and give precipitates of different shades of these colours. Cerium combines also with carbon and phosphorus.

Uranium. Uranium was discovered in 1789, in combination with sulphur, &c. It is a metal of a deep grey colour on the outside, and a pale brown on the inside. It is very porous, and so soft that it may be scraped with a knife. Its specific gravity is between 8 and 9, and its fusion is effected with great difficulty. It is soluble only in nitric acid; combines with oxygen in two proportions, and with sulphur. Of its alloys with other metals nothing is at present known; but it combines with the acids to produce salts.

Zinc. Zinc, otherwise known by the name of *Speltre*, is a metal of a brilliant white colour, never found pure, but in the state of an oxide, a sulphuret, sulphate, or carbonate. Its specific gravity varies from 6.86 to 7.1, and it is lightest when most pure. By particular treatment it is malleable. It melts at the temperature of 680 Fahrenheit, is volatilized at a higher temperature, but when allowed to cool slowly it forms crystals. By exposure to the air its lustre is tarnished, but it does not otherwise undergo any change. It is not acted on by water, but in a state of ignition it decomposes this fluid rapidly. It is oxydized and dissolved by the greater number of the acids. All the alkalies, when digested or boiled with zinc, blacken its surface and dissolve a minute portion of it. It decomposes muriate of ammonia, sulphate of potash, and various other neutral salts. Having a very strong attraction for oxygen, it precipitates the greater number of the metals from their acids and solutions. It likewise combines with iodine, phosphorus, sulphur; and forms alloys with some of the metals, as arsenic, potassium, sodium, &c.

The order of its affinities, for the metals and acids, is nearly as follows:—

Zinc.	Oxide of Zinc.
Copper	Oxalic acid
Antimony	Sulphuric
Tin	Muriatic
Mercury	Saclactic
Silver	Nitric
Gold	Tartaric
Cobalt	Phosphoric
Arsenic	Citric
Platinum	Succinic
Bismuth	Fluoric
Lead	Arsenic
Nickel	Lactic
Iron	Acetic
	Boracic
	Prussic
	Carbonic

Lead. Lead is one of the softest metals, and its specific gravity is above 11. It is malleable, but not very ductile, and less tenacious than any other metals. When cut it is very brilliant, but soon tarnishes by exposure to the air. It unites with oxygen in three proportions; with sulphur in two proportions; with chlorine, iodine, and phosphorus, in one. It is acted upon by the greater part of the acids, with which it forms salts. Lead may be alloyed with most of the other metals; but its alloys are not employed for any use.

Tin. Tin occurs in nature in three states; namely, in a native state, in the state of an oxide, and that of a sulphuretted oxide; it is one of the lightest of metals, and its specific gravity is between 7.291 and 7.299. It is very malleable, and may be beaten into thin plates, called *tin-foil*. Its ductility and malleability are inferior to most of the metals which have been long known. A tin wire 0.078 inch in diameter, is capable of supporting a weight of 34.7 pounds only without breaking. It is susceptible of considerable expansion by means of caloric, and is also one of the most fusible metals. It melts at the temperature of 442°, but does not evaporate without a very violent heat; and when allowed to cool slowly it forms rhomboidal crystals. It is a good conductor of electricity, and emits a peculiar odour, which is communicated to the hands by means of friction. It undergoes no other change from exposure to the air except that of being tarnished; but on being heated it combines with oxygen in two proportions; also with phosphorus and sulphur. It forms alloys with many of the metals, and also salts by combining with the acids.

The order of its affinities for the metals and acids is nearly as follows:—

Tin.	Oxide of Tin.
Zinc	Tartaric acid
Mercury	Muriatic
Copper	Sulphuric
Antimony	Oxalic
Gold	Arsenic
Silver	Phosphoric
Lead	Nitric
Iron	Succinic
Manganese	Fluoric
Nickel	Saclactic
Arsenic	Citric
Platinum	Lactic
Bismuth	Acetic
Cobalt	Boracic
Sulphur.	Prussic.

Copper. A metal of a fine red colour, is harder than silver, very malleable, and ductile. Its specific gravity is between 8 and 9, and its tenacity is such that a copper wire 0.078 inch in diameter is capable of supporting 302.26 pounds avoirdupois without breaking. It melts at the temperature of 27° Wedgewood, and evaporates in visible fumes at a higher temperature. When allowed to cool slowly it assumes a crystalline form.

Copper combines with oxygen, chlorine, and sulphur, in two proportions; with phosphorus in one. It forms alloys by combining with most of the other metals; and salts, by its union with the acids. The order of its affinities for the metals and acids is nearly as follows:—

Copper.	Oxide of Copper.
Antimony	Arsenic acid
Platinum	Phosphoric
Tin	Succinic
Lead	Fluoric
Nickel	Citric
Bismuth	Lactic
Cobalt	Acetic
Mercury	Boracic
Sulphur	Prussic
Phosphorus	Carbonic

Bismuth. Bismuth is a metal of a reddish white colour, almost without smell or taste, and composed of broad brilliant plates. It is rather softer than copper, and its specific gravity is 9.822. It is one of the most fusible metals, melts at about 476° Fahrenheit, and evaporates by a considerable increase of heat; but when allowed to cool slowly it readily forms distinct crystals.

Bismuth combines with oxygen in two proportions; with chlorine, iodine, sulphur, and phosphorus, in one proportion. It forms alloys by combining with some other metals; and salts, by its union with the acids. Its affinities for the metals and acids are nearly in the following order:—

Bismuth.	Oxide of Bismuth.
Lead	Oxalic acid
Silver	Arsenic
Gold	Tartaric
Mercury	Phosphoric
Antimony	Sulphuric
Tin	Muriatic
Copper	Nitric
Platinum	Fluoric
Nickel	Saclactic
Iron	Succinic
Sulphur.	Citric
	Lactic
	Acetic
	Prussic
	Carbonic.

Mercury. Mercury, commonly known by the name of Quicksilver, is found in nature in different states; namely, native, as an amalgam of silver, a sulphuret, and an oxide. It is of the colour of silver, very brilliant, and without taste or smell. Its specific gravity is about 13.568; but when in a solid state its density is increased. Mercury is the only one of the metals that retains a fluid state at the common temperature of the atmosphere. When the temperature is reduced to about 39° or 40° below zero of Fahrenheit, it becomes a solid, which happens, however, only in the northern climates. Solid mercury is both malleable and ductile; admits of extension, but to what degree has not yet been ascertained. When heated to about 656° it boils, and becomes changed into vapour. Hence it may be driven over by distillation, and be thus purified in some degree from the admixture of other metals. It is a good conductor of caloric, electricity, and galvanism; combines with oxygen, chlorine, and sulphur, in two proportions; forms amalgams with most of the metals, except iron; and salts, by combining with the acids. The order of its affinities for the metals and acids is nearly as follows:—

Mercury.	Oxide of Mercury.
Gold	Muriatic acid
Silver	Oxalic
Tin	Succinic
Lead	Arsenic
Bismuth	Phosphoric
Zinc	Sulphuric
Copper	Saclactic
Antimony	Tartaric
Arsenic	Citric
Iron.	Sulphurous
	Nitric
	Fluoric
	Acetic
	Boracic
	Prussic
	Carbonic.

Silver. Silver is softer than copper, but harder than gold. When melted its specific gravity is 10·474; but when hammered it is 10·510. In malleability it is inferior to none of the metals, not excepting gold, which it sometimes equals in this particular. It may be beat out into leaves not thicker than the hundred and sixty thousandth part of an inch, and drawn into wire the thousandth part of an inch thick. Its tenacity is such, that a wire of

CHEMISTRY.

silver 0·078 inch in diameter is capable of supporting a weight of 187·13 pounds avoirdupois without breaking. It melts at about 22° of Wedgewood's pyrometer, answering to 1000° of Fahrenheit, and at a higher temperature it becomes volatilized. When cooled slowly it forms rather large crystals. It combines with oxygen, chlorine, iodine, phosphorus, and sulphur; and forms alloys with most of the metals, and salts with most of the acids.

The order of its affinities for the combustibles and acids is nearly as follows:—

Silver.	Oxide of Silver.
Lead	Muriatic acid
Copper	Oxalic
Mercury	Sulphuric
Bismuth	Saclactic
Tin	Phosphoric
Gold	Sulphurous
Antimony	Nitric
Iron	Arsenic
Manganese	Fluoric
Zinc	Tartaric
Arsenic	Citric
Nickel	Lactic
Platinum	Acetic
Sulphur	Succinic
Phosphorus.	Prussic
	Carbonic.

Gold. Gold is a metal found in nature only in a metallic state. It is of an orange red colour, having no perceptible taste or smell. It is rather softer than silver; and its specific gravity, which varies according to the mechanical processes which it has undergone, may be stated, on an average, at 19·3. It exceeds all other metals in ductility and malleability, and may be beaten into leaves the $\frac{1}{280000}$th part of an inch in thickness. Its tenacity is also considerable, although less than that of iron, copper, platinum, or silver. It appears that a gold wire 0·078 inches in diameter is capable of supporting a weight of 170lbs. avoirdupois without breaking. It melts at a moderate red heat, i. e. at 32° of Wedgewood's pyrometer, but requires a very violent heat to volatilize it; wherefore it may be denominated exceedingly fixed. After fusion it is capable of assuming a crystalline form. Gold undergoes no alteration from the air, nor is it acted upon by water, but it combines by means of the intense heat of a burning glass with oxygen in two proportions, also with phosphorus and sulphur in one proportion. It forms alloys with most of the metals, and salts with some of the acids. The order of its affinities for the latter is nearly as follows:—

Gold.	Oxide of Gold.
Mercury	Muriatic acid
Copper	Nitric
Silver	Sulphuric
Lead	Arsenic
Bismuth	Fluoric
Tin	Tartaric
Antimony	Phosphoric
Iron	Prussic.
Platinum	
Zinc	
Nickel	
Arsenic	
Cobalt	
Manganese.	

Platinum. Platinum was first discovered in 1748, in South America, where it exists for the most part, although but little of it has hitherto been met with. It is a white metal which in point of hardness is intermediate between copper and iron. Its specific gravity has been estimated from 21·3 to 22·63. It is exceedingly ductile and malleable, so that it may be drawn into wires not exceeding $\frac{1}{1000}$ inch in diameter, and may be beaten into very thin plates. Its tenacity is such, that a wire of platinum 0·078 inch in diameter is capable of supporting a weight of 274·31 lbs. avoirdupois without breaking. It is the most infusible of all metals, and cannot be melted, in any quantity at least, without the aid of the blow-pipe. It combines with oxygen, chlorine, and phosphorus, in two proportions, but with sulphur in three. It forms alloys with most other metals, and salts with many acids.

Palladium and Rhodium. These two metals were discovered in 1803 and 1804, and were separated from the ore of platinum. Palladium is of a somewhat duller white than platinum, harder than wrought iron, its specific gravity varying from 10·972 to 11·871. Rhodium also resembles platinum in colour. Its specific gravity is stated to be 10·649. It is brittle, and requires a much higher temperature to fuse it than any other metal, unless iridium may be excepted. It has the remarkable property of being insoluble in all acids.

Iridium and Osmium. Iridium and Osmium are also newly discovered metals which have been separated from the ore of platinum. The former of these is distinguished by a very high degree of infusibility; but of the other properties of either little is known at present.

Intermediate Combustibles. The third class of combustibles is distinguished by the name of Intermediate Combustibles, because they differ from and agree with both the other classes in some particulars. Their compounds with oxygen do not, like the first class, neutralize acids; and they do not, like the second, enter into any gaseous combination. Their oxides possess acid properties in common with substances of the first class; but these acids, like those of the second class, are but imperfectly soluble in water, and act with but little energy upon animal and vegetable bodies. The substances are as follow: namely, Antimony, Chromium, Molybdenum, Tungsten, Columbium, and Titanium.

Antimony. Antimony, a compact brittle metal, exists in different states in nature, as native antimony, an oxide, a sulphuret, &c. It has a greyish white colour, with a good deal of brilliancy. Its hardness is nearly the same as that of gold, its specific gravity being above 6. It melts at 810° Fahrenheit, and may be volatilized at a higher temperature; but after cooling it assumes the form of oblong crystals. It undergoes no change by exposure to the air, nor by being kept under water; but when steam is made to pass over red hot antimony it is decomposed so rapidly that a violent detonation is the consequence. It combines with oxygen in several proportions, from 2 to 6, according to different statements. It combines also with chlorine, iodine, phosphorus, and sulphur, and forms alloys with other metals, and salts with the acids; the order of its affinities, for the combustibles and acids, is nearly as follows:

Antimony.	Oxide of Antimony.
Iron	Muriatic acid
Copper	Oxalic
Tin	Sulphuric
Lead	Nitric
Nickel	Tartaric
Silver	Saclactic
Bismuth	Phosphoric
Zinc	Citric
Gold	Succinic

CHEMISTRY.

Antimony.
Platinum
Mercury
Arsenic
Cobalt
Sulphur.

Oxide of Antimony.
Fluoric
Arsenic
Lactic
Acetic
Boracic
Prussic
Carbonic.

Chromium. Chromium, or Chrome, is a brittle, infusible, and fixed metal, found in an acidified state, combined with oxide of lead, in the red-lead ore of Siberia. Its specific gravity is 5·90. It combines with oxygen in three proportions, but is acted upon by acids with great difficulty.

Molybdenum. Molybdenum possesses so many properties in common with plumbago, or the oxide of lead, that it was till lately confounded with it. It is now, however, reckoned as a distinct metal. It is drawn from the mineral ore called the sulphuret of Molybdena, either in the form of an agglutinated friable mass, of little brilliancy, or of a black powder. Its specific gravity is about 8·611. It is one of the most infusible metals, but is capable of combining with a number of metals by means of fusion. It combines with oxygen in several proportions, and with sulphur in one proportion.

Tungsten. Tungsten is a metal procured from the mineral called tungsten or ponderous stone. It has a greyish white colour, like iron, is extremely hard and brittle, and its specific gravity is above 17·; so that it is surpassed in density only by gold, platinum, and iridium. It requires for fusion a temperature at least equal to 170°, and seems to have the property of crystallizing as it cools. It combines with oxygen in two proportions, forming an oxide and an acid, and also with sulphur; but of its action on the acids little is known at present.

Columbium, or Tantalum. Columbium, or tantalum, is a metal drawn from a mineral called tantalite, has a dark grey colour, and when scratched with a knife assumes the metallic lustre. Its specific gravity is 5·61. It combines with oxygen in one proportion; but of its other combinations little is known.

Titanium. Titanium, a metal obtained from the mineral called *titanite*, or *red schorl*, is found only in the state of an oxide. It seems to be one of the most infusible of the metals, combines with oxygen in three proportions, and with phosphorus in one proportion. It forms salts with some of the acids; but of its combinations with other metals little is known.

Compound substances.

Compound substances are those which are formed by the union either of simple substances with each other, or of compound substances with each other. They may be classed under the heads of oxides, chlorides, iodides, hydrogurets, ammonia, carburets, phosphurets, sulphurets, alloys, acids, compound combustibles, hydrates, and salts.

Compounds of oxygen. The compounds of oxygen are either oxides simply so called, or they are gases and acids. The oxides are as follow:—

Oxides of chlorine. The oxides of chlorine are *protoxide of chlorine* and *deutoxide of chlorine*, which are composed as follows:—

	Chlorine.	Oxygen.
1. Protoxide of chlorine	1 atom	+ 1 atom.
2. Deutoxide of chlorine	1 do.	+ 4 atoms.

Now supposing 1·00 to represent one atom of oxygen, and 4·5 one atom of chlorine, then the protoxide of chlorine is composed by weight of

Chlorine, 5·000 ...... 81·82 100
Oxygen, 1·111 ...... 18·18 ...... 22·22

The deutoxide is composed by weight of

Chlorine, 2·5 ...... 52·94 100
Oxygen, 2·222 ...... 47·06 ...... 88·88

The protoxide and the deutoxide are gases, both of which have a brighter yellow green than chlorine; the latter still more than the former.

Oxides of Azote or Nitrogen. The oxides of azote are the protoxide, or nitrous oxide gas, and the deutoxide or nitric oxide gas. The component parts of which are as follow:—

	Azote.	Oxygen.
Protoxide of azote, composed of	1 atom	+ 1 atom.
Deutoxide of azote	1 do.	+ 2 atoms.

These two gases have many properties in common, particularly that they are unfit for respiration, and that combustibles will not burn in them; but the nitrous gas is said to have a sweet taste, and the nitric gas to have none. The specific gravity of the first is estimated at 0·00197; that of the second at 0·001343.

Oxide of Carbon. Carbonic oxide gas is composed of 1 atom oxygen and 1 atom carbon: its specific gravity is about 0·972. It possesses the mechanical properties of air, burns with a blue flame, is totally unfit for respiration, and also for supporting combustion. When mixed with oxygen gas, and an electric spark passed through the mixture, it detonates.—*Oxide of Phosphorus.* The oxide of phosphorus is that compound in which oxygen combines with it in the smallest proportion. It is procured simply by the exposure of phosphorus to the atmosphere, when it emits a white smoke, which has the smell of garlic, and is luminous in the dark.—*Oxide of Silicon*, is silica which is supposed to contain about half its weight of oxygen, and the other half silicon.—*Oxide of Sulphur.* The oxide of sulphur is said to be a substance of a dark violet colour, fibrous fracture, and tough consistence; the specific gravity is 2·325, and it contains 2 $\tfrac{7}{10}$ of oxide in the hundred parts.—*Oxide of Tellurium.* The oxide of tellurium is volatilized in the form of a white powder.—*Oxides of Potash.* The oxides of potash are formed by the combination of its base, potassium, with oxygen, by which are formed *potash* and the *peroxide of potassium*, the former of which is composed of about 20 parts of oxygen to 100 of potassium; the latter of 60 parts of oxygen to 100. The peroxide is a solid body, of a yellow colour, which, when put into water, effervesces, and is reduced to the state of potash, giving out the excess of oxygen which it contained.—*Oxides of soda*, are soda, or the combination of oxygen with sodium, its base, and the *peroxide of soda;* the former is a compound of about 74·6 of sodium, and 25·4 oxygen per cent.; the latter of about 50 parts oxygen to the hundred of sodium. The peroxide of sodium, when quite pure, is of a dirty greenish yellow colour: by the action of water it evolves oxygen, and produces a solution of the protoxide.—*Oxide of lime* is lime which is a compound of about 19 parts of its metallic base, calcium, to a little more than seven parts oxygen.—*Oxide of barytes*, are *barytes* and the *peroxide of barium;* the barytes is a compound of about 10 parts oxygen, and 90 barium. The peroxide, of which the proportions are not known, is a substance of a grey colour.—*Oxide of strontian*, is strontian which is a compound of about 44 parts strontian, and 7 parts of oxygen.—*Oxide of magnesia*, is magnesia, a compound, which is supposed to consist of about 11 of its metallic base + 7 oxygen.—*Oxide of yttria*, is yttria, a compound, which is supposed to contain about 25 per cent. of oxygen.—*Oxide of glucina*, is glucina, which contains about 44 per cent. of oxygen.—*Oxide of alumina*, is alumina, a compound of about 100 parts of alum, its metallic base, + 28 parts of oxygen.—*Oxides of iron* are the *protoxide*, which is a black powder, known in medicine by the name of *martial ethiops*; and the *peroxide*, which is red, and was formerly called *saffron of Mars*. The proportion of oxygen which the protoxide contains, has been estimated from ·28 to ·29 parts of oxygen + 100 iron. The peroxide consists of 100 parts of iron + 42 nearly.—*Oxides of nickel* are the *protoxide*, which is blackish ash grey; and the *peroxide*, which is black. Their proportions are as follow:

	Nickel.	Oxygen.
Protoxide	100	29·68
Peroxide	100	44·445

The protoxide is tasteless, and soluble in the acids, forming with them a grass green solution.—*Oxides of cobalt*, are the *protoxide*, which is a blue powder, and the *peroxide*, which is black. Their proportions are nearly as follow:

	Cobalt.	Oxygen.
Protoxide	100	27·
Peroxide	100	36·77

The protoxide dissolves in acids, forming a green solution in muriatic acid, and a red one in sulphuric and nitric acids.—*Oxides of manganese* are the *protoxide*, which is green, and the *peroxide*, which is black, in nearly the following proportions:

	Manganese.	Oxygen.
Protoxide of manganese	100	28·75
Peroxide	100	56·213

The peroxide of manganese is found native in great abundance; and when pure, has a dark steel-grey colour. It is brittle, and very soft, soiling the fingers: the specific gravity is about four.—*Oxides of cerium* are the *protoxide*, which is black, and the *peroxide*, which is reddish brown, in nearly the following proportions:

	Cerium.	Oxygen.
Protoxide of cerium	100	17·41
Peroxide	100	26·115

Oxides of uranium are the *protoxide*, which is greyish black; and the *peroxide*, which is yellow, in nearly the following proportions:

	Uranium.	Oxygen.
Protoxide of uranium	100	6·4
Peroxide	100	9·6

Oxide of zinc, a white tasteless powder, insoluble in water, is composed of 100 parts of metal + 25· of oxygen nearly. It combines readily with acids, and forms neutral salts. It is used as a paint, and answers very well as a water colour.—*Oxides of lead* are the *protoxide*, which is yellow; the *peroxide*, which is brown; and the *red oxide*, which is considered as a compound of the two. Their proportions are nearly as follow:

	Lead.	Oxygen.
Protoxide of lead	100	7·692
Peroxide	100	15·384
Red oxide	100	11·08+

The protoxide is insoluble in water, but soluble in potash and acids. Carbonic acid, combined with this oxide, forms the powder, which is well known by the name of *white lead*. The peroxide is not acted on by sulphuric or nitric acid; and the red oxide, commonly called *red lead*, or *minium*, is a beautiful powder, used as a paint, but does not combine with any other substance without undergoing decomposition. All the oxides of lead are very easily converted into glass.—*Oxides of tin* are the *protoxide*, which is grey or black; and the *peroxide*, which is mostly yellow. Their proportions are nearly as follow:

	Tin.	Oxygen.
Protoxide of tin	100	13·5 or 13·55
Peroxide	100	27·2 or 27·64

The protoxide is a tasteless powder, soluble in both acids and alkalies; but the union of the peroxide with both is very weak, and may be separated by heat.—*Oxides of copper* are the *protoxide*, which, when native, is red, and when artificial is orange; and the *peroxide*, which is black, and of various shades. Their proportions are nearly as follow:

	Copper.	Oxygen.
Protoxide of copper	100	12·5
Peroxide	100	25·

The oxides of copper are easily reduced to a metallic, when heated with oils, &c.—*Oxide of bismuth* is a yellow powder, composed of 100 parts of metal, + 11 or 12 of oxygen. Bismuth dissolved in nitric acid produces a precipitate in the form of a powder, formerly called the *magistery of bismuth*, which is considered as a compound of this oxide and nitric acid.—*Oxides of mercury* are the *protoxide*, which is a black powder, otherwise called *æthiops per se*; and the *red oxide*, otherwise called the *red precipitate*. Their proportions are nearly as follow:

	Mercury.	Oxygen.
Protoxide of mercury	100	3·99
Red oxide	100	7·99

This latter oxide has an acrid disagreeable taste, possesses poisonous qualities, acts as an escharotic when applied to the skin, is insoluble in water, and acquires a black colour by heating, which it loses again as it cools.—*Oxide of silver* is considered to be a compound of 100 parts of the metals + 7·272 of oxygen, the average of different experiments.—*Oxides of gold* are the *protoxide*, which is green; and the *peroxide*, which is reddish brown. Their proportions are nearly as follow:

	Gold.	Oxygen.
Protoxide of gold	100	4·026
Peroxide	100	9·889 to 12·077

The peroxide is a tasteless powder, and insoluble in water, but soluble in muriatic acid.—*Oxides of platinum* are the *protoxide*, which is black; and the *peroxide*, which is dark brown or grey. Their proportions are nearly as follow:

	Platinum.	Oxygen.
Protoxide of platinum	100	4·423
Peroxide	100	11·86

The peroxide, a light powder, dissolves in the fixed alkalies, combines with lime, barytes, and strontian, and is the base of the salts of platinum.—*Oxide of palladium* is composed of 100 parts of the metal + 14·209 of oxygen.—*Oxides of rhodium* are the *protoxide*, which is black; the *deutoxide*, which is brown; and the *peroxide*, which is red. Their proportions are estimated to be nearly as follow:

	Rhodium.	Oxygen.
Protoxide of rhodium	100	6·71
Deutoxide	100	13·42
Peroxide	100	20·13

Oxides of chronium are the protoxide, which is green; and the deutoxide, which is brown. The protoxide is easily dissolved by acids; but if it be exposed to a heat rather below redness, it becomes insoluble.—*Oxides of titanium* are the *protoxide*, which is blue; the *deutoxide*, which is red; and the *peroxide*, which is white.

Chlorides. The principal substances worthy of notice, which are distinguished by the name of chlorides, are as follow:—*Chloride of azote*, a yellowish oily matter, is a compound of

Azote ...... 20 + Chlorine 80

Its smell is peculiar and strong, though not so disagreeable and injurious to the lungs as that of chlorine. It is very volatile, and soon dissipated when left in the open air. When heated to 212° it explodes with prodigious violence.—*Chlorides of phosphorus* are the *protochloride* and the *perchloride*; the former is a colourless liquid, having an acid caustic taste. The latter is a snow-white substance, which is exceedingly volatile. The specific gravity of the protochloride is 1·45.—*Chloride of sulphur* is a liquid of a brownish red colour, and of an acid, hot, and bitter taste: the specific gravity is about 1·7.—*Chloride of arsenic*, formerly known by the name of *butter of arsenic*, is a transparent substance of the consistence of oil, which is very soluble.—*Chloride of potassium*, formerly distinguished by the name of *febrifuge*, or *digestive salt of Silvius*, and by the French called *muriate of potash*, is a white saline mass, the specific gravity of which is 1·836. It is composed of about 100 parts of potassium + 90 of chlorine.—*Chloride of sodium* is another name for common salt, or sea salt, which is composed of

Chlorine .... 4·5 .... 60 150
Sodium............ 3· 40 100

Its specific gravity is 2·125.—*Chloride of lime* is another name for *muriate of lime*, formerly called *fixed ammonia*. It consists of 100 parts of chlorine + 58·3 of calcium. It is extremely soluble in water, and when exposed to the air it deliquesces. The specific gravity is 1·76.—*Chloride of barium*, otherwise called *muriate of barytes*, is formed by heating barytes in chlorine gas; and consists of 100 parts of barium + 51, nearly. It has a pungent taste, is poisonous, and requires 2·29 parts of water, of the temperature of 190°, to dissolve one of this salt. Its specific gravity is 2·8257.—*Chloride of strontium*, or *muriate of strontian*, is a salt of a peculiarly sharp and penetrating taste. It is composed of 100 strontium + 40 chlorine, nearly. The specific gravity is 1·4402.—*Chloride of magnesium*, or *muriate of magnesia*, an extremely bitter, hot, biting salt, which requires rather more than half its weight to dissolve it. Its constituents are about

Chlorine.... 74·2· + Magnesium 25·8 = 100

Chlorides of iron are the *protochloride*, which is grey; and the *perchloride*, which is brown. Their proportions are nearly as follow:

	Chlorine.	Iron.
Protochloride	100	87·16
Perchloride	100	54·08

Chloride of manganese, a substance procured by dissolving the black oxide of manganese in muriatic acid, is of a pure delicate light pink colour, which melts at a red heat without alteration in close vessels; when exposed to the air it deliquesces. It is composed of nearly the following proportions:

Chlorine .... 54 .... 100· .... 4·5
Manganese ...... 46 .... 85·18 .... 3·83

Chloride of zinc, originally called *butter of zinc*, is obtained by distilling a mixture of zinc filings and corrosive sublimate, and consists of nearly one-half chlorine, and one-half zinc. It deliquesces speedily when exposed to the air.—*Chloride of lead*, formerly distinguished by the name of *plumbeum corneum*, or horn-lead. It is a transparent greyish-white mass resembling horn in appearance, and consists of about

Chlorine .... 25·78 .... 100· .... 4·5
Lead........... 74·22 .... 287·88 .... 12·955
———
100·

Chlorides of tin are the *protochloride*, which is of a grey colour and resinous lustre; and the *perchloride*, long known by the name of the *fuming liquor of Libavius*, a colourless liquid which, when exposed to the air, smokes with great violence. Their constituents are nearly as follow:

	Tin.	Chlorine.
Protochloride of tin	100	60·7
Perchloride	100	122·02

Chlorides of copper are the *protochloride*, otherwise called *rosin of copper*, by the French *muriate of copper*, which is of an amber colour; and the *perchloride*, which is brownish-yellow. Their proportions are nearly as follow:

	Copper.	Chlorine.
Protochloride of copper	100	56·25
Perchloride	100	112·76

The protochloride is insoluble in water, but soluble in nitric and muriatic acids; when the perchloride is exposed to the air, it absorbs moisture, and changes its colour to white, and then green.—*Chloride of bismuth* is of a greyish white colour, and consists of

Chlorine .... 33·6 .... 4· 5 ⎫ nearly.
Bismuth............. 66·4 .... 8·89 ⎭

Chlorides of mercury are the *protochloride*, commonly called *calomel*; and the *perchloride*, known by the name of *corrosive sublimate*; they have likewise had the names of *submuriate of mercury* and *muriate of mercury*. Their constituent parts are nearly as follow:

	Mercury.	Chlorine.
Prochloride of mercury........	100	17·6
Perchloride	100	35·2

The protochloride of mercury is usually in the state of a dull white mass; but, when slowly sublimed, it crystallizes in four-sided prisms. It has very little taste, is not poisonous, and is employed in medicine as a purgative. The perchloride of mercury is generally in the form of a beautiful white transparent mass composed of very small prismatic needles. Its taste is excessively acrid and caustic, and its specific gravity is 5·1398; when swallowed it is one of the most virulent poisons known; it is soluble in half its weight of boiling water, and in about twenty parts of cold water.—*Chloride of silver*, otherwise called *horn silver*, and lately distinguished by the name of *muriate of silver*, is a curdy precipitate obtained by dissolving silver in nitric acid, and mixing the solution with a solution of common salt. Its constituent parts are nearly as follow:

Chlorine .... 75·5 .... 100· .... 4·5
Silver .... 24·5 .... 32·5 .... 13·75
———
100·

Chlorides of platinum are the protochloride, of which little is known, and the perchloride, which consists of

Platinum.......... 100· or nearly .... 12·125
Chlorine .... 37·93 .... 4·5

This chloride is of a dull olive brown or green, has a harsh feel, no taste or smell, and is insoluble in water.—*Chloride of antimony*, formerly called *butter of antimony*, is a fatty mass of a greyish white colour that is a compound of

Antimony,...... 54·88 .... 100·   .... 5·472
Chlorine........ 45·12 .... 82·22 .... 4·5
              ─────
              100·

This chloride melts at a moderate heat, is very volatile, and decomposed with water, when the white oxide of antimony and muriatic acid is formed.

Iodides.

The following table exhibits a view of the iodides, with all the most important particulars hitherto known respecting them:

Metals.	Iodides.	Colour.	Iodine combining with 100 metal.
Potassium	1	white	.... 312·5
Sodium	1	white	.... —
Calcium	1	white	.... —
Barium	1	white	.... —
Strontium	1	white	.... —
Iron	1	brown	.... —
Zinc	1	white	.... 390·6
Bismuth	1	orange	.... —
Lead	1	yellow	.... —
Tin	1	orange	.... —
Copper	1	brown	.... —
Mercury .... { 1	yellow	.... 62·5
{ 2	red	.... 125·
Silver	1	greenish-yellow....	—
Antimony....	1	dark red	.... —

Ammonia.

Ammonia is a gaseous compound of hydrogen and azote, which was formerly called *hartshorn*, because it was often distilled from the horn of the hart; also *spirit of urine*, and *spirit of sal ammoniac*. It is said to be composed of

Hydrogen .... 0·1947 .... 0·125 × 3
Azote............ 0·9722 .... 0·75

Ammonia is transparent and colourless, has a pungent smell, an acrid taste, immediately extinguishes flame, is fatal to animals, and is lighter than common air, its specific gravity being 0·590, that of common air being 1. When heated to the temperature of about 130° the ammonia separates under the form of a gas; at the temperature of 46°, it crystallizes; when cooled down to 68°, it assumes the appearance of a thick jelly, and has scarcely any smell. Ammonia combines rapidly with water; cold water absorbs this gas almost instantaneously, and at the same time heat is evolved; and the specific gravity of the water is diminished. A saturated solution of ammonia is said to be composed of 74·63 water + 25·37 ammonia = 100·000. Ammonia is acted upon with considerable energy by the supporters of combustion. It combines with sulphur and forms a sulphuret; also with the oxides of gold, silver, and platinum, from which are formed *fulminating gold*, *fulminating silver*, and *fulminating platinum*. The base of Ammonia is found to be a metal, to which the name of *ammonium* has been given.

Hydrogurets.

The principal substances thus named are as follow:—*Hydrogurets of carbon* are two; namely, *hydroguret of carbon*, otherwise called *olefiant gas*, which possesses the mechanical properties of common air, is destitute of taste and smell, burns with greater splendor than any other known gas, and detonates very loudly when mixed with thrice its bulk of oxygen, and an electrical spark is passed through it; its specific gravity is about 0·9745. Olefiant gas is composed by weight of

Carbon..... 0·832 .... 0·75 .... 6 .... 100·
Hydrogen .. 0·1388 .... 0·125 .... 1 .... 16·66

Water is said to absorb one-twelfth of its bulk of olefiant gas.—*Bihydroguret of carbon*, or *carburetted hydrogen*, is a gaseous substance which exhales in hot weather from stagnant waters. It is composed by weight of

Carbon......... 0· 416 .... 0·750 3
Hydrogen ...... 0·0694 .... 0·125 1

The gas which exhales in coal mines, known by the name of *fire-damp*, has been found to be carburetted hydrogen. Its specific gravity is 0·555.—*Hydrogurets of phosphorus* are the hydroguret and bihydroguret of phosphorus, two gaseous compounds. The hydroguret, otherwise called *phosphuretted hydrogen gas*, has the smell of onions, and a bitter taste, burns with great splendor when it comes in contact with the air; water dissolves rather more than 2 per cent. of this gas: it produces no alteration on vegetable blues, but precipitates silver, mercury, and copper. The bihydroguret, otherwise called *hydrosphoric gas*, does not burn like the former when it comes into common air or oxygen gas, but if it be mixed with oxygen, and heated to 300°, it explodes; when mixed with chlorine gas it burns spontaneously. Water is found to absorb one-eighth of its volume of this gas.—*Hydroguret of potassium*, a grey compound of hydrogen, is composed by weight of

Potassium .... 100·   .... 5·
Hydrogen .... 0·616 .... 0·0308

Carburets.

The principal compounds distinguished by this name are as follow:—*Carburet of nitrogen*, or *azote*, otherwise called *cyanogen*, a gaseous compound lately discovered, which is composed by weight of

Azote .... 0·9722
Carbon .... 0·832

It has a black colour, and the smell of bitter almonds, and it burns with a beautiful purple flame.—*Carburets of iron* are denominated, according to the different stages of the process, *natural steel*, or that which is obtained from the iron ore; *steel of cementation*, better known by the name of *blistered steel*; and *cast steel*, which is the most valuable of all.—*Carburet of manganese*, a compound occasionally to be met with in iron founderies, which is known by the name of *keesh*. It is composed of thin scales having the appearance and lustre of metal, but it is very brittle.

Phosphurets.

Of the phosphurets the following are the principal; namely —*Phosphuret of iodine*, a substance of a reddish brown colour; the solidity, fusibility, and volatility of which vary with the proportions of the ingredients.—Phosphu-

ret of carbon, a soft powder, of a dirty lemon colour, which is composed in nearly the following proportion of

   Phosphorus 1·5 200
   Carbon.... 0·75 100

It has neither smell nor taste, burns below a red heat, and when heated to redness gradually gives out its phosphorus, but does not melt.—*Phosphuret of sulphur* is a compound which bears a high temperature without decomposition.—*Phosphuret of arsenic* is a black compound, formed by distilling equal parts of its ingredients by a moderate heat. It ought to be preserved in water. *Phosphuret of potassium*, a compound of a chocolate colour, burns in the open air, and when thrown into water detonates.—*Phosphuret of soda* has the colour and appearance of lead. It is converted by water into phosphate of soda.—*Phosphuret of lime* is a compound of a deep brown colour, that falls to pieces in the air. It is insoluble in water, which it has, however, the property of decomposing.—*Phosphuret of barytes*, a compound of a dark brown colour, the constituents of which are supposed to be nearly in the following proportions:

   Barytes.... 9·75 100
   Phosphorus 1·5 .... 15·78

Phosphuret of strontian is a compound very similar to the preceding.—*Phosphuret of iron*, a metallic substance procured from that sort of iron which is called *cold short*. It is of a dark steel grey colour, exceedingly brittle, and not very soluble in acids.—*Phosphuret of nickel*, a metallic substance, composed, according to some, of 100 nickel + 15 phosphorus.—*Phosphuret of cobalt* contains about one-fifteenth of phosphorus, and is much more fusible than pure cobalt.—*Phosphuret of manganese* is of a white colour, and more fusible than manganese.—*Phosphuret of zinc* is of a white colour, has a metallic lustre, is somewhat malleable, and when exposed to a strong heat burns like zinc.—*Phosphuret of lead* is composed of about 12 parts phosphurus and 88 of lead. It may be cut with a knife, but separates into plates when hammered.—*Phosphuret of tin* is supposed to be composed of about 85 parts of tin and 15 of phosphorus.—*Phosphuret of copper* is a white substance composed of about 80 parts of copper and 20 of phosphorus. It is harder than iron, not ductile, and cannot easily be pulverized. Its specific gravity is 7·1220.—*Phosphuret of mercury* is of a black colour, and solid consistence.—*Phosphuret of silver* is composed of about 4 parts of silver and 1 of phosphorus. It breaks under the hammer, but may be cut with the knife.—*Phosphuret of gold* is composed of about 23 parts of gold and 1 of phosphorus. It is brittle, whiter than gold, and of a crystallized appearance.—*Phosphurets of platinum* are the *protophosphuret* and the *perphosphuret*, the constituent parts of which are nearly as follow:—

        Platinum. Phosphorus.
Protophosphuret of platinum .. 100 ...... 22·21
Perphosphuret .... 100 ...... 42·25

The specific gravity of the first is 6; that of the second 5·28. They are both destitute of taste and smell, and nonconductors of electricity.—*Phosphuret of antimony*, a white brittle substance, which emits a green flame when melted. It is composed of about 45 parts antimony and 11 phosphorus.

     Sulphurets.

The principal sulphurets are as follow:—*Sulphuret of iodine*, a black compound resembling sulphuret of antimony.—*Sulphuret of carbon*, a liquid as transparent and colourless as water; is composed of about 5·7 parts of carbon + 30 parts of sulphur. It has an acrid taste, a nauseous smell, and is one of the most volatile liquids known. Its specific gravity is about 1·272 or 1·263. Sulphuret of carbon is scarcely soluble in water, but readily so in alcohol and ether.—*Sulphuret of phosphorus*, a yellowish white compound, is composed in nearly the following proportions, by weight, of

  Sulphur ...... 2 ...... 4 100
  Phosphorus .. 1·5 ...... 3 75

Sulphur and phosphorus, by combining, have a strong tendency to liquidity.—*Sulphurets of arsenic* are two; namely, a scarlet coloured vitreous compound, called *realgar*, which is found native in different parts of Europe; and a yellow coloured powder, which is called *orpiment*, and may be artificially prepared by subliming arsenic and sulphur by a heat not sufficient to melt them. The specific gravity of the realgar is 3·3384; that of the orpiment 3·4522. It has been supposed by some, that these two substances differ merely in the proportions of sulphur which they contain; but this is denied by others. The sulphurets of arsenic consist of about 58 parts arsenic, and 42 sulphur.—*Sulphuret of potash* is of a brown colour, not unlike the liver of animals, whence it was called *hepar sulphuris*, or *liver of sulphur*. When exposed to the air, it becomes green, and even white. It has an acrid bitter taste, is deliquescent, and very soluble in water, forming a yellow solution of hydrosulphuret of potash.—*Sulphuret of lime* is an acrid reddish mass, which is formed by heating lime with sulphur. It is soluble in water, like the sulphuret of potash.—*Sulphuret of barytes* is a reddish yellow mass like the preceding.—*Sulphuret of magnesia* is a yellow powder, slightly agglutinated.—*Sulphurets of iron* are the *protosulphuret* and the *persulphuret*, which are called by mineralogists the *magnetic pyrites* and the *cubic pyrites*. The former is of a bronze colour, and the latter yellow, but both have the metallic lustre. The addition of sulphur to iron renders it permanently magnetic.—*Sulphuret of nickel* is a brittle yellow compound, that is not magnetic. It is composed of about 28 nickel + 15 sulphur.—*Sulphuret of cobalt* is a yellow compound that is scarcely decomposed by heat.—*Sulphuret of manganese*, a green compound, is composed in nearly the following proportions: of

  Manganese .... 74·5 ...... 100·
  Sulphur ...... 25·5 ...... 34·22

Sulphuret of zinc exists native in the ore called *blende*, and is composed of about 33 zinc + 15 sulphur.—*Sulphurets of lead* are the *sulphuret* and the *bisulphuret*. The sulphuret of lead is found native, and in that state is called *galena*, which is composed of about 100 lead + 15 sulphur. The bisulphuret is said to contain about 25 parts of sulphur.—*Sulphurets of tin* are the *protosulphuret* and the *persulphuret*. The first is composed of 100 tin + 25 to 27·234 sulphur, according to different experiments. The persulphuret, long known by the name of *aurum mosaicum*, or *musivum*, mosaic gold, is said to consist of 100 tin + 52·3 or 55·25 sulphur. Mosaic gold, which is in the form of light scales, is insoluble in water or alcohol, and not acted upon either by muriatic or nitric acid.—*Sulphurets of copper* are said to be the *sulphuret*, which is black, and composed of about 100 copper + 25 sulphur; and the *bisulphuret*, which is yellow, and composed of 100 copper + 30 sulphur. They are both found native, and the first may also be formed artificially.—*Sulphuret of bismuth* is of a blueish colour, and is composed of about 100 bismuth + 22·52 sulphur. It is sometimes found native.—*Sulphurets of mercury* are the *protosulphuret*, which is black, and the *persulphuret*, which is red. The first, which is in the form of a powder, and originally called *æthiops' mineral*, consists of 100 mercury + 8·2 sulphur. The persulphuret was formerly called *cinnabar*, and when reduced to a fine powder is known, in commerce, by the name of *vermillion*. It consists of 100 mercury + 16 sulphur. This sulphuret is decomposed by distillation with fixed alkalies, lime, and barytes; but it is insoluble in water and muriatic acid.—*Sulphuret of silver* is a black or deep violet compound, of about 100 silver + 14·9 or 14·59 sulphur. It is more fusible than silver; may be cut with a knife, and crystallizes in small needles. Its specific gravity is rather more than 7.—*Sulphuret of gold* is a black compound, of about 100 gold + 21·95 or 24·39 sulphur.—*Sulphurets of platinum* are the *protosulphuret*, which is blueish-grey; the *deutosulphuret*, which is blueish-black; and the *persulphuret*, which is a dark iron-grey. Their constituent parts are nearly in the following proportions:

	Platinum.	Sulphur.
Protosulphuret of platinum	100	19·04
Deutosulphuret	100	28·21
Persulphuret	100	38·8

The persulphuret is a conductor of electricity, and its specific gravity is 3·5.—*Sulphuret of palladium* is rather paler than the pure metal, and extremely brittle. It consists of about 100 palladium + 24 sulphur.—*Sulphuret of antimony* is a leaden-grey compound, of about 100 antimony + 29·870 or 37·000 sulphur, according to different experiments. Its specific gravity is about 4·368.—*Sulphuret of molybdenum* is found native in the metallic ore called *molybdena* in nearly the proportions of 100 molybdenum + 66·5 sulphur.—*Sulphuret of tungsten* is a greyish-black compound in nearly the proportions of 100 tungsten + 33·26 sulphur.

Alloys.

Metals undergo changes, by combination, in their ductility, malleability, hardness, &c. Their malleability and ductility are mostly impaired; thus gold forms brittle alloys with lead, tin, and other metals. Their hardness is frequently increased so, that iron, by a small addition of gold, is said to acquire a hardness superior to steel. Their colour is varied: thus the addition of a small quantity of arsenic to copper renders it white, and the alloy of antimony and copper is of a violet colour. The specific gravity of the alloy is seldom the mean of its component parts. In some cases it is superior, and in others inferior; as in the case of gold with zinc, tin, bismuth, antimony, and cobalt, where the specific gravity of the alloys is greater than the mean of their components; and in the case of gold with silver, iron, lead, copper, iridium, and nickel, their specific gravity is less; and so, likewise, in the case of other alloys. The fusibility of the alloys is in many instances increased; thus platinum is rendered easily fusible by arsenic; and the alloy of lead, tin, and bismuth, melts at a temperature below that of boiling water, although bismuth, the most fusible of the three, requires a much higher degree of heat. The alloy of iron and arsenic is found native, and is known among mineralogists by the name of *mispickel*; that of tin and iron is a useful alloy called *tin-plate*, and in Scotland white iron, which is formed by dipping thin plates of iron into melted tin. Tin and zinc are combined into the alloy, which is called *pewter*, which is much harder than zinc, and much stronger than tin.

The alloy of tin and lead is called *ley pewter*; and also *tin-foil*, which latter being more soluble than either of the other metals separately, is used by plumbers as a solder. The alloy of copper and arsenic is called *white copper* or *white tombac*; that of copper and zinc is known by the name of *brass*; and if zinc in the metallic state be melted with copper or brass, the alloy is known by the name of *pinchbeck*, Prince's metal, Prince Rupert's metal. The alloys of copper and tin are employed for a variety of purposes, under the names of *bell metal, cannon metal, bronze, tinned copper*, and the like. The alloy of silver and copper is employed in most countries for coinage. The standard or sterling silver of Britain is a compound of 12¼ silver, and 1 alloy, i. e. 1 copper. Its specific gravity, after simple fusion, is 10·200. Gold is alloyed with either silver or copper, or both for coinage. Sterling or standard gold consists of pure gold, with one-twelfth of alloy. The specific gravity of gold, alloyed with one twenty-fourth of silver and one twenty-fourth of copper, is 17·344. The bulk of the metals, before combination, is 2·700, after it 2·767. The alloy of antimony and copper was originally called by the alchymists the *regulus of Venus*.

The following table exhibits a view of the most important alloys, in the order of the different substances as they have been given.

Arsenic	and	Potassium	Copper and	Bismuth
		Sodium		Lead
		Iron		Tin
		Zinc	Mercury and	Arsenic
		Tin		Tellurium
		Copper		Potassium
		Lead		Iron
		Bismuth		Zinc
		Cobalt		Bismuth
Potassium and		Sodium		Lead
Iron	and	Arsenic		Tin
		Potassium		Copper
		Sodium	Silver and	Arsenic
		Tin		Iron
Nickel	and	Arsenic		Cobalt
		Iron		Zinc
		Cobalt		Bismuth
Cobalt	and	Iron		Lead
Manganese and		Iron		Copper
Zinc	and	Arsenic		Tin
		Potassium		Mercury
		Sodium	Gold and	Arsenic
		Iron		Potassium
Lead	and	Arsenic		Iron
		Potassium		Nickel
		Sodium		Cobalt
		Iron		Manganese
		Cobalt		Zinc
		Zinc		Bismuth
		Bismuth		Lead
Tin	and	Arsenic		Tin
		Potassium		Copper
		Sodium		Mercury
		Iron		Silver
		Zinc	Platinum and	Arsenic
		Bismuth		Sodium
		Lead		Iron
Copper	and	Arsenic		Zinc
		Potassium		Bismuth
		Iron		Lead
		Nickel		Tin
		Manganese		Copper
		Zinc	Copper and	Zinc

CHEMISTRY.

Platinum	and	Mercury	Antimony and	Mercury
		Silver		Silver
		Gold		Gold
Palladium	and	Gold	Molybdenum and	Arsenic
		Platinum		Iron
		Silver		Nickel
		Copper		Cobalt
		Lead		Manganese
		Tin		Zinc
		Bismuth		Bismuth
		Iron		Lead
Iridium	and	Lead		Tin
		Copper		Copper
		Silver		Silver
		Gold		Gold
Antimony	and	Arsenic		Platinum
		Potassium	Tungsten and	Silver
		Iron		Copper
		Zinc		Lead
		Bismuth		Antimony
		Lead		Bismuth
		Tin		Manganese
		Copper		

Acids.

The acids are now chemically distinguished by the following properties: they possess an acid taste, change the blue colours of vegetable substances to red; and if these blues have been previously converted to green by alkalies, the acids restore them again. They moreover unite with water in almost any proportion; and, by combining with alkalies, earths, and most of the metallic oxides, they form with them the compounds called *salts*.

The acids may be distinguished, according to their base, into those that contain oxygen, chlorine, iodine, fluorine, and cyanogen, in which order they may be most conveniently arranged as follows:

Acids containing oxygen. The acids having oxygen united to a combustible or combustibles are as follow:—*Nitric acid*, otherwise called *water of nitre* and *spirit of nitre*, but more commonly known by the name of *aqua fortis*, is a gaseous body obtained from nitre, which consists of 100 oxygen and 35 nitrogen or azote. The order of its affinities is nearly as follows:

Nitric acid.
Barytes
Potash
Soda
Strontites
Lime
Magnesia
Ammonia
Glucina
Alumina
Zirconia
Oxide of Zinc
Iron
Manganese
Cobalt
Nickel
Lead
Tin
Copper
Bismuth
Antimony
Arsenic
Mercury
Silver
Gold
Platinum.

Nitrous acid, another combination of nitrogen with a larger portion of oxygen, consists of 100 nitrogen and 230 oxygen.—*Carbonic acid*, a gaseous body, otherwise called *carbonic acid gas*, consists of 100 carbon and about 250 oxygen. Carbonic acid extinguishes a candle, and is unfit for respiration. Its specific gravity is 1·527. The order of its affinities is nearly as follows:

Carbonic acid.
Barytes
Strontites
Lime
Potash
Soda
Magnesia
Ammonia
Glucina
Zirconia
Metallic oxides.

Boracic acid is procured from borax in the form of a powder, which is sparingly soluble in water, but readily dissolves in alcohol. The order of its affinities is nearly as follows:

Boracic acid.
Lime
Barytes
Strontites
Potash
Soda
Magnesia
Ammonia
Glucina
Zirconia
Metallic oxides
Water
Alcohol.

Phosphoric acid is a compound of 100 phosphorus and about 114·6 oxygen, which dissolves readily in water, and is not volatile. The order of its affinities is nearly the same as that of the nitric acid.—*Phosphorous acid* is a compound of 100 phosphorus and about 76 oxygen. The order of its affinities is nearly as follows:

Phosphorous acid
Lime
Barytes
Strontites
Potash
Soda
Ammonia
Glucina
Alumina
Zirconia
Metallic oxides.

Hypophosphorous acid is a compound of 100 phosphorus and about 37·44 oxygen.—*Sulphuric acid*, formerly called *oil of vitriol*, is a compound of 100 sulphur and about 150 oxygen; it is colourless like water, somewhat of an oily consistency, without smell, but of an acrid taste. *Sulphuric acid* is nearly twice as heavy as water, the specific gravity being at least 1·850, and it boils at the temperature of 620°. Its affinities are nearly in the same order as those of the nitric acid.—*Sulphurous acid* is a compound of equal parts of sulphur and oxygen. The order of its affinities in forming sulphites is nearly as follows:

Sulphurous acid.

Barytes
Lime
Potash
Soda
Strontites
Magnesia
Ammonia
Glucina
Alumina
Zirconia.

Arsenic acid, a white solid compound of 100 arsenic and about 52·631 oxygen; its specific gravity is 3·391; when heated strongly it melts, and is converted into a glass; it dissolves slowly in cold, but readily in hot water, and is decomposed by the simple acidifiable combustibles. The order of its affinities is nearly as follows:

Arsenic acid.

Lime
Barytes
Strontites
Magnesia
Potash
Soda
Ammonia
Glucina
Alumina
Zirconia.

Arsenious acid, formerly called *white arsenic*, or simply *arsenic*, is a compound of 100 arsenic and from 32·979 to 34·930 of oxygen. Both these acids are noxious.—*Antimoniac acid*, a straw-coloured powder, consists of 100 antimony and about 35·536 oxygen.—*Antimonious acid*, or the *deutoxide of antimony*, consists of 100 antimony and from 23 to 29 oxygen.—*Chromic acid*, a compound of a deep red colour, and a sharp metallic taste, is composed of 100 chromium and about 87·72 oxygen; it gives different coloured precipitates with solutions of nitrate, of mercury, of silver and copper, &c.—*Molybdic acid* is a white powder which is soluble in 960 parts of boiling water. The solution is a pale-yellow. The specific gravity of the acid is 3·460.—*Tungstic acid* is a tasteless yellow powder insoluble in water. The order of its affinities is the same as that of arsenic acid.

Acids with two or more bases. These acids contain oxygen united to more than one substance as a base. They have been commonly called vegetable acids, because they are mostly derived from vegetable substances. They are as follow:—*Acetic acid* which exists in three states; namely, in that of *vinegar*, when it is first prepared; in that of *acetous acid*, when it is purified by distillation; and that of *acetic acid*, otherwise called *radical vinegar*, when it is concentrated by means of different processes. Vinegar is a liquor procured by bringing wine, beer, &c. into contact with the external air at a temperature of 80°. Its specific gravity varies from 1·0135 to 1·0251, according to the liquid from which it has been procured. It is very subject to decomposition.—*Acetous acid* is a colourless liquor, has an aromatic smell, and evaporates completely when exposed to a moderate heat.—*Acetic acid*, which was formerly distinguished by the name of *vinegar of Venus*, is colourless like the preceding, but has an empyreumatic smell. The specific gravity of distilled vinegar varies from 1·007 to 1·0095, that of acetic acid when at its highest is 1·080, but this varies according to the proportion of water which it contains. Acetic acid, in this state, is extremely acrid and pungent, reddens and corrodes the skin very quickly, is very volatile, and takes fire rapidly in the open air. It requires, however, a strong heat for its decomposition. The order of its affinities is nearly as follows:

Acetic acid.

Barytes
Potash
Soda
Strontites
Lime
Ammonia
Magnesia
Metallic oxides
Glucina
Alumina
Zirconia.

Benzoic acid, otherwise called *flowers of benzoin*, is a fine light powder procured from the gum benzoin, which is a compound of

Carbon 74·41 + Oxygen 20·43 + Hydrogen 5·16 = 100.

It is volatilized in white fumes by a moderate heat, requires for solution about twenty-four times its weight of boiling water, and is soluble in alcohol. The order of its affinities is nearly as follows:

Benzoic acid.

White oxide of arsenic
Potash
Soda
Ammonia
Barytes
Lime
Magnesia
Alumina.

Succinic acid, or the *acid procured from amber*, is a compound of

47·888 oxygen + 47·600 carbon + 4·512 hydrogen = 100.

It is obtained in the form of crystals, which are soluble in twenty-four times their weight of water. The order of its affinities is nearly as follows:

Succinic acid.

Barytes
Lime
Potash
Soda
Ammonia
Magnesia
Alumina
Metallic oxides.

Moroxalic acid is a compound obtained in the form of crystals from a salt, the production of the wood of the mulberry-tree, that is readily soluble in water and alcohol.—*Camphoric acid* is a compound obtained by distilling camphor, with four times its weight of nitric acid, till about twenty parts of acid have been employed; it has a slightly acid bitter taste, and a smell like saffron; it is soluble in 100 parts of cold water, and readily dissolved by boiling alcohol. The order of its affinities is nearly as follows:

Camphoric acid.

Lime
Potash
Soda
Barytes
Ammonia
Alumina
Magnesia.

Boletic acid consists of white crystals obtained from the juice of the *boletus pseudo-igniarius*; it resembles tartar in its taste, and requires 180 times its weight of water to dissolve it; when heated it rises in vapour.—*Suberic acid* is obtained in the form of a white powder by digesting one part of suber or cork in six parts of nitric acid. Water, at the temperature of 140°, dissolves one-thirty-eighth of its weight of this acid, and one-eightieth at the temperature of 55°; when heated it melts, and crystallizes on cooling; it precipitates the nitrate of silver, the muriate of tin, sulphate of iron, nitrate and acetate of lead. The order of its affinities is nearly as follows:

Suberic acid.
Barytes
Potash
Soda
Lime
Ammonia
Magnesia
Alumina
Metallic oxides.

Pyrotartaric acid is a sublimate obtained by distilling tartar with potash; it dissolves readily in water, and crystallizes again when subjected to evaporation.—*Oxalic acid*, an acid so called because it has been found to exist, native, in the *oxalis acetosella*, or wood sorrel, was originally called *saccharine acid*, or the *acid of sugar*, because it is obtained by the distillation of sugar with nitric acid in form of crystals, which dissolve in twice their weight of cold, and in an equal weight of hot water; they are also soluble in boiling water, and in ether, though sparingly; they effloresce in the air, and become covered with a white powder, but in a red heat they are entirely decomposed. These crystals, in a perfect state, are found to consist of real acid 77, water 23. The acid is composed of

Oxygen.. 64 + carbon.. 32 + hydrogen.. 4 = 100.

The order of its affinities is nearly as follows:

Oxalic acid.
Lime
Barytes
Strontites
Magnesia
Potash
Soda
Ammonia
Alumina.

Mellitic acid is obtained from a mineral called *mellite*, or the *honey-stone*, in the state of crystals, but is not very soluble in water. It is composed of

Oxygen 52·54 + carbon 47·11 + hydrogen 0·35 = 100.

Tartaric acid is obtained from the common cream of tartar, and forms regular crystals, which require for solution five or six parts of water at 60° Fahrenheit. These crystals are found to consist of real acid 88·75, and water 11·25. The acid is composed, according to different experiments, of

Carbon.   Oxygen.   Hydrogen.
21·050 or 35·98 .... 69·321 or 60·28 .... 6·629 or 3·79.

The order of its affinities is the same as that of oxalic acid.—*Citric acid* is obtained pure and in a crystallized form, by a particular process, from the expressed juice of lemons mixed with powdered chalk. The crystals consist of real acid 100 and water 26·58. The acid is decomposed at a high temperature, and found by different experiments to consist of

Oxygen.   Carbon.   Hydrogen.
59·859 or 54·831 .. 33·811 or 41·369 .. 6·330 or 4·800.

The order of its affinities is nearly the same as that of the oxalic acid. It is exceedingly soluble in water.—*Saclactic acid*, so called because it was first obtained from sugar of milk, is also procured in the form of a white powder by heating gum arabic, and other mucilaginous substances, with nitric acid. Heat decomposes this acid, and it is soluble in 60 parts of its weight of boiling water. It is composed, according to different experiments, of

Oxygen.   Carbon.   Hydrogen.
62·69 or 61·465 .... 33·69 or 33·430 .... 3·62 or 5·105.

The order of its affinities is nearly as follows:

Saclactic acid.
Lime
Barytes
Magnesia
Potash
Soda
Ammonia
Alumina
Metallic oxides.

Uric acid, a white powder obtained from the urinary calculi, is destitute of both taste and smell; it dissolves in 1720 parts of water, at the temperature of 60°, decomposes alkaline hydrosulphurets, and precipitates their sulphur. From the distillation of the uric acid is obtained a sublimate that is said to be analogous to succinic acid. The constituent parts of uric acid are nearly as follow:

Oxygen.   Carbon.   Hydrogen.   Azote.
22·857 + 34·286 + 2·857 + 40 = 100.

Malic acid, a liquid of a reddish colour, is obtained in the greatest abundance from the juice of apples, to which it owes its name; when evaporated it becomes thick and viscid; when heated in the open fire it exhales an acrid fume, and leaves behind it a voluminous coal. It is very soluble in water.—*Sorbic acid*, a transparent colourless fluid obtained from the *pyrus aucupatoria*, or Mountain Ash, which is soluble in alcohol or any portion of water.—*Formic acid*, a liquid procured from the *formica rufa*, or Red Ant; the specific gravity of which is 1·1168. Its constituent parts are found to be

Oxygen 64·223 + Hydrogen 2·807 + Carbon 32·970 = 100.

This acid when cooled becomes solid, but does not crystallize.—*Lactic acid*, procured from sour milk, is of a brownish-yellow colour, which has no smell while cold, but when heated acquires a sharp sour odour; it does not crystallize, but when evaporated to dryness forms a smooth varnish, which dissolves readily in alcohol. The order of its affinities is nearly as follows:

Lactic acid.
Barytes
Potash
Soda
Strontites
Lime
Ammonia
Magnesia
Metallic oxides
Glucina
Alumina
Zirconia.

Zumic acid, an acid liquor obtained from vegetable substances that have undergone an acetous fermentation.—*Gallic acid*, a compound substance in the form of transparent plates, or octahedrons, procured from nutgalls, is composed nearly in the following proportions: of

Oxygen 38·36 + Hydrogen 5·00 + Carbon 56·64 = 100.

When heated it has an aromatic and rather unpleasant smell, is soluble in 1½ parts of boiling water, and in 12 parts of cold water; and also in ether. It occasions a precipitate when poured into solutions of glucina, yttria, and zirconia in acids; and, upon metallic acids, it acts with considerable energy, changing the colour, and produces precipitates in many of them; on which account it has been frequently used as a reagent to detect the presence of metallic bodies.—*Tannin*, or the *tanning principle*, a substance of a reddish-brown colour, and an astringent taste, is to be procured from barks and many vegetable substances, but most readily, and in the greatest purity, from nutgalls and catechu. Tannin prepared from galls is found to consist of

Oxygen 54·654 + Hydrogen 4·186 + Carbon 41·186 = 100.

The bark of oak is generally preferred for the purpose of tanning; but other barks might be employed for the same purpose, as appears from the following table, which exhibits the quantity of tan afforded by 480 lbs. of different barks:

	lb.		lb.
Middle sized oak cut in spring.	29	Horse chesnut	9
		Sycamore	11
Spanish chesnut	21	Lombardy Poplar	15
Leicester willow, large size.	233	Birch	8
		Hazel	14
Elm	13	Black Thorn	16
Large common willow	11	Coppice Oak	32
Ash	16	Oak cut in autumn	21
Beech	10	Larch cut do.	8

The inner cortical layers of all barks are found to contain the greatest quantity of tan, that of oak bark being not less than seventy-two. Tannin forms precipitates with solution of starch, gluten, and albumen, and with many of the metallic oxides. Besides the natural tannin just spoken of, an artificial sort has been prepared from charcoal.

Acids containing chlorine. Chlorine forms acids by combining with oxygen or with a combustible. The principal of these acids are as follow:—*Chloric acid*, a colourless liquid, consists of 100 chlorine and about 111·11 oxygen. The order of its affinities is nearly as follows:

Chloric acid.

Potash
Soda
Barytes
Strontites
Lime
Ammonia
Magnesia
Alumina.

Perchloric acid is a compound of about 100 chlorine and 180 oxygen.—*Muriatic acid*, otherwise called *hydrochloric acid*, is a compound of chlorine and hydrogen in nearly the proportions of oxygen 100, muriatic acid 341·5. Muriatic acid gas, in its purest form, exists in the state of a gas which is permanent over mercury only. It has a very pungent smell, is sufficiently caustic to blister the skin, extinguishes a lighted candle, and detonates when exposed to the light of the voltaic discharge. It is greedily absorbed by water, which takes up 480 times its bulk, and has its specific gravity increased from 1 to 1·200. The order of its affinities is nearly as follows:

Muriatic acid.

Barytes
Potash
Strontites
Lime
Ammonia
Magnesia
Glucina
Alumina
Metallic oxides.

Chlorocarbonic acid, otherwise called *phosgene gas*, is a compound of chlorine 4·5, and carbonic oxide 1·75, or of chlorine 4·5, oxygen 1·0, and carbon 0·75. This gas is more disagreeable and suffocating than chlorine, and affects the eyes in a peculiar manner. When tin, zinc, antimony, or arsenic, are dissolved in it, they decompose it by absorbing the chlorine, and setting at liberty the carbonic oxide. It is also decomposed by water, and converted into muriatic acid and carbonic acid.

Acids containing iodine. Iodine combines with supporters and combustibles to produce the following acids:—*Iodic acid*, a white, semi-transparent solid, formed by the combination of iodine with oxygen in nearly the proportions of iodine 764 + oxygen 236 = 1000, or in the proportion of about 15 to 4. Its specific gravity is considerable, for it sinks rapidly in sulphuric acid.—*Chloriodic acid*, a volatile compound of 100 iodine and 57·6 chlorine. When exposed to the air it deliquesces, and its solution in water contains acid properties.—*Hydriodic acid*, a gaseous compound of about 8·6804 iodine, and 0·0694 hydrogen. Water absorbs this acid with avidity. When exposed to a heat below 262° the water is driven off, and the acid becomes concentrated. Hydriodic acid is colourless, and elastic like common air, having a smell similar to muriatic acid. The specific gravity is about 4·443.

Acids containing fluorine. Fluorine combines with combustibles, and produces the following acids.—*Fluoric acid*, which is obtained from fluor spar, is supposed to be a compound of fluorine and hydrogen. The order of its affinities is said to be nearly as follows:

Fluoric acid.

Lime
Barytes
Strontites
Magnesia
Potash
Soda
Ammonia
Glucina
Alumina
Zirconia
Silica.

Fluoboric acid, a powerful gaseous compound of fluorine and boron, the specific gravity of which is determined to be 2·3709. Water is said to absorb 700 times its volume of this gas. The specific gravity of the liquid thus obtained is 1·77, which is totally unfit for respiration. Its specific gravity is determined to be about 3·5735.

Acids containing cyanogen. Cyanogen combines with chlorine, and with combustibles, so as to form the following acids:—*Chlorocyanic acid*, or the compound of cyanogen and chlorine, is a colourless liquid with a strong smell that provokes tears. Its specific gravity, in the state of

CHEMISTRY.

a vapour, is about 2·152.—*Hydrocyanic acid*, or *Prussic acid*, in a pure state, is a limpid and colourless fluid, which was first obtained from the powder well known by the name of *Prussian blue*. It is capable of assuming a gaseous form, in which state it is absorbed by alcohol; is not inflammable, and when received into the lungs is speedily fatal. As a liquid its taste is at first cool, but soon becomes hot and acrid. Its specific gravity varies with the temperature. It is highly volatile, and boils at 79° Fahrenheit. A drop of it placed on paper becomes instantly solid.—*Sulphocyanic acid* is a colourless liquid compounded of sulphur 100 and cyanogen 53·3.—*Ferrocyanic acid* is a pale lemon-coloured compound of 100 cyanogen, and from 34 to 37 iron. It is destitute of smell, and decomposed by heat, or by exposure to a strong light. The order of its affinities is nearly as follows:

Ferro-cyanic acid.
Barytes
Strontites
Potash
Soda
Lime
Magnesia
Ammonia.

Compound Combustibles.

Compound combustibles comprehend alcohol, ether, oils, resins, and bitumens.—*Alcohol*, or the spirit of wine, is a transparent liquor, as colourless as water, of a pleasant smell, a strong agreeable taste, and an intoxicating power. It is procured from what is commonly called ardent spirits, as brandy, whiskey, rum, &c. and is properly nothing more than *rectified spirits* deprived of their water as far as is possible. The specific gravity of the alcohol, in its purest state, seems to be about ·820 at the temperature of 60°; but the alcohol of commerce, which is not better than rectified spirits, is seldom under ·8371. Alcohol has a strong affinity for water, with which it combines in every proportion, and caloric is evolved during the union. It is highly inflammable, remarkably expansible by heat, boils at 176°, but has never yet been congealed by any known method of producing artificial cold; and even when diluted with an equal weight of water it requires a cold of 6° below 0 to congeal it. Alcohol is also a powerful solvent, and acts upon many of the acids, volatile oils, resins, &c. It dissolves many of the salts copiously, others sparingly, and others not at all. The following exhibits the proportions at which some of the salts are taken up by 240 grains.

	Grains.		Grains.
Borate of ammonia ..	1	Nitrate of magnesia ..	694
Fluate of alumine ...	1	——— potash....	5
——— ammonia ..	1	——— soda	23
Muriate of ammonia..	17	Oxalate of alumine ..	7
——— lime.....	288	Tartrate of alumine..	7
——— magnesia	1313	——— ammonia	7
——— potash ...	5	——— potash...	7
Nitrate of alumine ...	240	Supertartrate of potash	7
——— ammonia..	214	———oxalate of potash	7
——— lime......	288		

Alcohol is composed of carbon, oxygen, and hydrogen; but in what proportions is not accurately known.

Ethers. Ethers are fragrant and volatile liquors procured by distillation from a mixture of alcohol with different acids, of which the following are the principal:—*Sulphuric ether*, a compound obtained from sulphuric acid and alcohol, was originally called *oleum vitrioli dulce*, and by the Germans at present *naphtha*. It is so volatile that it can scarcely be poured from one vessel into another before it is dissipated. It is composed of oxygen 17·62 + hydrogen 14·40 + carbon 67·98 = 100·00. —*Nitric ether*, which is obtained from nitric acid and alcohol, is a compound of about 34 oxygen, 16 azote, 9 hydrogen, and 39 carbon. It is specifically lighter than water, but heavier than alcohol, highly combustible, and much more volatile than the best sulphuric ether.—*Chloric ether* is a compound formed by the union of equal volumes of chlorine and olefiant gas.—*Muriatic ether* is obtained from muriatic acid and alcohol with some difficulty, and not without the aid of other substances, as manganese, muriate of soda, sulphuric acid, &c.—*Phosphoric ether*, obtained from phosphoric acid and alcohol, is specifically lighter than alcohol, and boils at 100°.—*Acetic ether*, obtained from concentrated acetic acid and alcohol, is a limpid colourless liquid, having a taste different from all other substances. Its specific gravity, at the temperature of 44½° is 0.866. It boils at the temperature of 160°. It burns with a yellowish, whitish flame; and acetic acid is evolved during the combustion.

Oils. Oils are unctuous liquids, which have been divided into two classes; namely, volatile and fixed.—*Volatile oils* are very combustible substances, which have an acrid taste and a strong fragrant smell; are volatilized by a gentle heat, and soluble in alcohol, but imperfectly so in water. They evaporate without leaving any stain on paper, and some of them detonate. These oils are obtained from every part of plants, except the cotyledons of the seed. Their specific gravity varies very considerably, as may be seen from the following table:

Oil of Sassafras...	1·094	Oil of Tansy	946
——— Cinnamon..	1·035	——— Carraway seeds..	940
——— Cloves.....	1·034	——— Origanum......	940
——— Fennel......	997	——— Spike	936
——— Dill........	994	——— Rosemary......	934
——— Pennyroyal.	978	——— Juniper berries..	911
——— Cummin ...	975	——— Oranges	888
——— Mint......	975	——— Turpentine.....	792
——— Nutmegs...	948		

These oils are otherwise called aromatic, from their fragrance; and essential, because they are supposed to contain the essence of the vegetable substances which furnish them.—*Fixed oils* are distinguished for the following properties; namely: they are liquid, or easily become so when exposed to a gentle heat, have an unctuous feel, and a mild taste, are very combustible, and perfectly insoluble in water, but partially soluble in alcohol. They leave a greasy stain on paper, and boil at nearly 600°. All fixed oils are greatly lighter than water, but they differ from each other considerably in their specific gravity. The following table contains the specific gravity of such as have been obtained:

Oil of Palm	968	Oil of Beech-nut	925
——— Hazle-nuts	941	——— Ben	917
——— Poppies	939	——— Olives	913
——— Linseed	932	——— Rape seed.....	913
——— Almonds	932	——— Cacao	892
——— Walnuts	928		

Fixed oils do not begin to evaporate till they be heated above the boiling point of water; and when in a state of vapour they take fire on the approach of an ignited body. It is upon this principle that candles and lamps burn. By exposure to the open air fixed oils become solid; but some retain their transparency in a solid state; while others become opaque, and assume the appearance of tallow or wax: the former are called *drying oils*, and the latter *fat oils*. By the combination of alkalies with the fixed oils are made the important compounds called soaps; by their combination with sulphur a compound is formed called the *ruby of sulphur*.

The order of the affinities of the fixed oils is nearly as follows:

Fixed Oils.

Lime
Barytes
Fixed alkalies
Magnesia
Ammonia
Oxide of mercury
Other metallic oxides
Alumina.

Resins. Resins are the inspissated juices of certain vegetable plants, which are generally of a yellow colour, dry, brittle, and inflammable, soluble in alcohol, ethers, and essential oils, but altogether insoluble in water. Both acids and alkalies act upon them, particularly the pure alkalies. The principal resinous substances are balsams and gum resins; of the latter kind are asafœtida, gum ammoniac, aloes, gamboge, myrrh, opium, &c.

Bitumens. Bitumens are highly inflammable fossil substances which have a certain resemblance to oily and resinous substances. The principal substances of this kind are naphtha, petroleum, mineral tar, mineral pitch, asphaltum jet, pit-coal, bituminous wood, turf, peat, &c.

Hydrates. Hydrates are those compounds which are formed by the combination of a body with water in such manner as for the water to lose its fluid form; of this description is the substance well known by the name of *slacked lime*, which is a hydrate of lime.

The following Table exhibits the composition of the principal hydrates which have been hitherto investigated:

	Atoms base.	Atoms water.	Weight of water.	Weight of base.
Hydrate of Potash	1	1	100	18·75
Soda	1	1	100	28·10
Lime	1	1	100	31·03
Barytes	1	1	100	67·69
Strontian	1	1	100	17·3
Magnesia	1	1	100	45·
Copper	1	1	100	11·25
Tin	1	2	100	24·
Boracic acid	1	2	100	78·26
Phosphorous acid	1	1	100	32·
Sulphuric acid	1	1	100	22·5
Nitric acid	1	1	100	13·23
Acetic acid	1	1	100	14·5
Crystallized oxalic acid	1	4	100	99·84
Crystallized tartaric acid	1	1	100	13·43
Crystallized citric acid	1	2	100	30·5

Many of the substances mentioned in this list combine with water in more than one proportion, whence they are distinguished into protohydrates, deutohydrates, tritohydrates, tetrahydrates, &c. of which only the protohydrate has been given.

Salts. Salts are now understood by chemists to be those compounds which are formed by the combination of acids with alkalies, earths, and metallic oxides, the most important of which, distinguished in the order of their bases, are as follow:—

Salts of ammonia. The salts of ammonia are all soluble in water, with very few exceptions; are dissipated in vapours by exposure to heat; let fall a white precipitate in a solution of salt of magnesia and phosphate of lime, and an orange precipitate in a solution of platinum.

The following Table exhibits the principal salts of ammonia which have been examined, together with their constituents and specific gravity, according to an average estimate:

Salts.	Acid.	Base.	Water.	Specif. grav.
Muriate of ammonia	100·	45·94		1·072
Nitrate	69·5	18·4	12·1	1·5785
Carbonate	55·	26·17	18·13	0·966
Bicarbonate	56·	19·	25·	
Borate	37·95	30·32	31·73	
Phosphate	100·	47·22		1·8051
Phosphite	100·	60·71		
Sulphate	54·66	14·24	31·10	
Sulphite	60·	29·	11·	
Arseniate	100·	29·31		
Acetate	62·45	37·55		
Oxalate	100·	47·11		1·0816
Citrate	100·	29·02		

Observations. The *muriate of ammonia* was formerly known by the name of *sal ammoniac*; the *nitrate*, by that of *nitrum semivolatile* and *nitrum flammans*; the *sulphate*, by that of *secret sal ammoniac*, or *vitriolated ammoniac*.

Salts of potash. The salts of potash are less soluble than those of ammonia. The following list contains the principal of these salts:

Salts.	Acid.	Base.	Water.	Specif. grav.
Nitrate of potash	44·	51·8	4·2	1·733
Muriate	58·3	39·2	2·5	1·836
Phosphate				2·8516
Carbonate	43·	41·	17·	2·012
Sulphate	45·2	54·8		2·928
Sulphite	40·	60·		1·586
Antimoniate	79·2	20·8		
Acetate	47·98	52·02		
Oxalate	100·	132·55		
Tartrate	58·	42·		1·5567
Citrate	55·	44·		

Observations. The *muriate of potash* was formerly distinguished by the names of *digestive salt, regenerated sea-salt*; the *nitrate*, commonly known by the name of *salt-petre*, was formerly called *nitre*, which is one of the principal ingredients in the composition of gunpowder. The *carbonate* was formerly called *fixed nitre, salt of tartar, vegetable alkali*, &c. The *silicate* was distinguished by the name of *liquor silicum*. The *sulphate*, by the names of *specificum purgans, arcanum duplicatum*, &c. still more commonly by that of *vitriolated tartar*. The *sulphite* by the name of *sulphurous salt of Stahl*. The *acetate*, by the names of *arcanum tartare, essential salt of wine, regenerated tartar, diuretic salt, digestive salt of Sylvius*. The *binoxalate*, by the name of *essential salt of lemons*. The *tartrate*, by the name of *tartar*; and *bitartrate*, by that of *cream of tartar*.

Salts of soda. The salts of soda are much more soluble in water than the salts of potash. The following Table contains the most important of these salts:

Salts.	Acid.	Base.	Water.	Specif. grav.
Nitrate of soda	43·	32·		2·0964
Carbonate	14·16	20·60	65·24	1·3591
Muriate	52·	42·	6·	2·120
Borate	34·	17·	49·	1·740
Phosphate	20·33	17·67	62·00	1·333
Ammoniophosphate	32·	43·	25·	1·509
Sulphate	23·52	18·48	58·00	2·246
Sulphite	24·5	24·5	51·	2·9566
Acetate	36·95	22·94	40·11	2·1
Tartrate				1·746
Citrate	60·7	39·3		

Observations. The *nitrate of soda* was formerly distinguished by the name of *cubic nitre*. The *carbonate of soda* is now known, in commerce, by the name of *barilla* or *soda*. The *muriate of soda* is no other than *common salt*. The *borate of soda* was formerly called *borax*, and an impure sort of it is distinguished by the name of *tinkal*. The *ammoniophosphate* was formerly known by the names of *microcosmic salt* and *fusible salt of urine*. The *sulphate* by that of *Glauber's salt*.

Salts of lime. The salts of lime are many of them insoluble in water, and some of them which are soluble cannot be crystallized. The soluble salts are thrown down in a white precipitate by potash or soda, and some of them are precipitated by mixing with them the infusion of nut-galls.

The following Table contains the most important of these salts:

Salts.	Acid.	Base.	Water.	Specif. grav.
Nitrate of lime	57·44	32·00	10·56	1·6207
Muriate	31·	44·	25·	1·76
Carbonate	34·	55·	11·	2·7
Phosphate	100·	84·53		
Sulphate	46·	32·	22·	2·1679
Sulphite	54·29	45·71		
Arseniate	67·	33·		
Tungstate	80·417	19·4		
Acetate	64·3	35·7		1·005
Camphorate	50·	43·	·7	
Oxalate	62·5	37·5		
Tartrate	50·55	27·8	27·81	
Citrate	62·66	37·34		
Kinate	83·	17·		

Observations. The *nitrate of lime* was formerly called *Baldwin's phosphorus*. The *muriate*, by the names of *fixed sal ammoniac*, *Homberg's phosphorus*, and *calcareous marine salt*. The *carbonate* is found in great abundance in nature, under the names of *chalk*, *lime-stone*, *marble*, &c. The *sulphate* is now known by the name of *gypsum*, and after it has been heated, and forms a powder, by that of *plaster of Paris*.

Salts of barytes. A still greater proportion of the salts of barytes are insoluble in water than of the salts of lime. They are white or transparent, and in general affect a crystalline form. Most of these salts are poisonous.

The following Table contains a general account of the most important of these salts:

Salts.	Acid.	Base.	Water.	Specif. grav.
Nitrate of barytes	38·	50·	12·	2·9149
Muriate	20·	64·	16·	2·8257
Carbonate	22·	78·		4·331
Phosphate	100·	214·46		
Phosphite	24·31	67·24	8·45	
Sulphate	33·96	66·04		4·4
Sulphite	100·	241·79	4·91	1·6938
Arseniate	34·	66·		
Chromate	40·16	59·84		
Acetate	39·98	60·02		1·828
Oxalate	31·62	68·38		
Citrate	50·	50·		
Formate	32·1	67·9		

Salts of strontian. The salts of strontian are generally more soluble than those of barytes, but less so than those of lime. They assume a crystallized form. Solutions of these salts are precipitated by the sulphates, phosphates, and oxalates. The most important salts of strontian are as follow:

Salts.	Acid.	Base.	Water.	Specif. grav.
Nitrate of strontian	48·8	47·6	4·	3·006
Muriate	23·6	36·4	40·	1·4402
Chlorate	46·	26·	28·	
Carbonate	30·	69·5	40·5	3·66
Phosphate	36·565	63·435		
Sulphate	43·	57·		
Acetate	52·69	47·31		
Oxalate	39·77	60·23		
Tartrate	47·12	52·88		

Salts of magnesia are mostly soluble in water, and capable of crystallizing. They are precipitated by the alkalies and carbonates, and form triple salts, particularly with ammonia. The most important of these salts are as follow:

Salts.	Acid.	Base.	Water.	Specif. grav.
Nitrate of Magnesia	43·	27·	30·	
Muriate	34·	41·	25·	1·601
of Magnesia and Ammonia		73· 27.		
Carbonate	50·	25·	25·	0·2941
Borate	73·5	14·6	11·9	2·566
Phosphate				1·548
of Ammonia and Magnesia		33·3 33·3	33·3	
Phosphite	44·	20·	36·	
Acetate	70·65	29·35		1·378
Oxalate	65·	35·		
Citrate	66·66	33·34		

Salts of yttria. There are but few of the salts of yttria which are as yet known. Of this description the most are insoluble in water; but its solutions in acids may be precipitated by phosphate and carbonate of soda, oxalate of ammonia, &c.

Salts of glucina. The salts of glucina are as imperfectly known as those of yttria, and although much more soluble in water, yet they rarely crystallize.

Salts of alumina. The salts of alumina are distinguished by a sweet and astringent taste, and are mostly soluble in water; some few are also capable of crystallizing. The most important of these salts is the *acidulous sulphate of alumina* and *potash*, which is commonly known by the name of *alum*, the component parts of which are 49 sulphate of alumina, 7 sulphate of potash, and 44 water. Alum crystallizes mostly in regular octahedrons, but when an unusual quantity of potash is added to alum liquor, the salt loses its usual form and crystallizes in cubes, in which case it is distinguished by the name of *cubic alum*.

It is soluble in 16 or 20 parts water, and when exposed to heat, melts in its water of crystallization; what remains after this process is called *burnt* or *calcined alum*. When alum is exposed to a strong heat, a black substance is formed by the alumina and the potash, which is called pyrophorus. The specific gravity of alum is 1·7109.

The nitrate of alumina was formerly known by the name of *nitre of argil* and *nitrous alum*. It has an austere acid taste, and its specific gravity is 1·645.

Salts of zirconia. The salts of zirconia have a harsh, astringent, and disagreeable taste; are mostly insoluble in water, but their solutions are precipitated by sulphuric acid, carbonate, oxalate of ammonia, an infusion of nut-galls, &c.

Salts of iron. Salts of iron were formerly called *martial*, because Mars was the title given by the alchymists to iron. They are for the most part soluble in water, and the solution has a greenish colour and an astringent taste. Ferrocyanate of potash occasions in them a blue precipitate; hydrosulphuret of potash, gallic acid, or the infusion of nut-galls, a black precipitate; phosphate of soda, a white precipitate; benzoate of ammonia, one of a yellow colour; and succinate of ammonia, one of a flesh colour.

The following Table exhibits a general view of the most important salts of iron:

Salts.	Acid.	Oxide.	Water.	Specif. grav.
Sulphate of iron	39·	23·	38·	1·8399
Carbonate	24·	76·		
Arseniate	38·	43·	19	
Red arseniate	42·4	37·2	20·4	
Phosphate	21·	45·	34·	2·6
Succinate	61·5	38·5		
Oxalate	55·	45·		
Citrate	69·62	30·38		

Observations. The *sulphate of iron* is known in commerce by the name of *green vitriol* or *copperas*. The *carbonate* is that which is commonly known by the name of *rust*. The *phosphate* is found native, and constitutes the colouring matter called *Prussian blue*. The *gallate* is that salt the solution of which forms what is now a writing-ink.

Salts of nickel. The salts of nickel are generally soluble in water, and the solution has a beautiful green colour. They are also precipitated by ferrocyanate of potash, and the hydrosulphuret. There are but few other particulars respecting these salts which have hitherto been ascertained.

Salts of cobalt. The salts of cobalt are distinguished by the property of changing their colour when heated, and thus forming what has received the name of *sympathetic ink*. They are for the most part soluble in water, and the solution has a reddish colour. They are also precipitated by the alkalies, the ferrocyanate of potash, the hydrosulphuret of potash, and the tincture of nut-galls. The precipitates are blue, black, and white.

Salts of manganese. The salts of manganese are mostly soluble in water, and the solution, when treated with fixed alkalies, deposits a whitish precipitate, which soon becomes black when exposed to the air. The most important of these acids are as follow:

Salts.	Acid.	Oxide.	Water.	Specif. grav.
Carbonate of manganese	37·93	62·07		
Sulphate	33·05	29·75	37·20	1·834
Acetate	41·46	29·33	29·21	
Benzoate	76·92	23·08		
Succinate	58·13	41·87		

Salts of cerium. The salts of cerium are either white or yellow, and of a sweet taste. Hydrosulphuret of potash, ferrocyanate of potash, oxalate of ammonia, and arseniate of potash, occasion precipitates mostly of a white colour.

Salts of uranium. The salts of uranium are for the most part soluble in water, and the solution has a yellow colour. The alkalies and alkaline carbonates, the ferrocyanate and hydrosulphuret of potash, and the infusion of nut galls, occasion precipitates of different colours.

Salts of zinc. The salts of zinc, for the most part, form a colourless solution in water, and are precipitated by the ferrocyanate, sulphocyanate, hydriodate, and hydrosulphuret of potash, sulphureted hydrogen gas, and the alkalies, the precipitates being mostly white. The most important of these salts are as follow:

Salts.	Acid.	Oxide.	Water.	Specif. grav.
Carbonate of zinc	28·	66·	6·	
Muriate				1·577
Nitrate				2·096
Sulphate	40·	20·	40·	1·912
Citrate	59·	41·		

Observations. The *carbonate of zinc* is found native under the name of *calamine*. The *sulphate* is the substance which in commerce is known by the name of *white vitriol*.

Salts of lead. The salts of lead were formerly distinguished by the name of *saturn*, the name by which lead itself was distinguished. They are scarcely soluble in water without an excess of acid, and the solution is colourless and of a sweetish taste. Gallic acid, infusion of nut-galls, &c. occasion white or black precipitates. The most important of these acids are as follow:

Salts.	Acid.	Oxide.	Water.	Specif. grav.
Nitrate of lead	33·	67·		4·068
Muriate	24·83	75·17		1·8226
Carbonate	16·15	83·85		
Phosphate	100·	300·		
Sulphate	26·5	73·5		1·8742
Sulphite	22·2	77·8		
Arseniate	33·	63·	4·	
Chromate	34·9	65·1		6·
Acetate	26·96	58·71	14·32	2·345
Benzoate	49·66	46·49	3·85	
Succinate	30·86	69·14		
Oxalate	24·54	75·46		
Citrate	34·18	65·82		
Tartrate	37·	63·		
Sublactate	17·	83·		
Tannate	36·5	63·5		

Observations. The *carbonate of lead* is known in commerce by the name of *white lead*. The *acetate* was formerly called *sugar of lead*, *sugar of Saturn*, *salt of Saturn*, &c.

Salts of tin. The salts of tin were formerly distinguished by the name of *Jovial*, because Jupiter was the title

CHEMISTRY.

given to tin. These salts are more or less soluble in water, and the solution is of a yellowish colour. Ferrocyanate and hydrosulphuret of potash, the corrosive sublimate and the muriate of gold, occasion different coloured precipitates.

Salts of copper. The salts of copper were formerly called *salts of Venus*, because Venus was the name given to copper. These salts mostly form a blue or green solution with, and are precipitated by, ferrocyanate and hydrosulphuret of potash, by gallic acid and a plate of iron, when plunged into a liquid salt. The precipitate in this last case is metallic. The most important salts of copper are as follow:

Salts.	Acid.	Oxide.	Water.	Spec. grav.
Nitrate of copper	16·	67·	17·	2·1710
Muriate	40·2	59·8		1·6776
Carbonate	100·	363·6		
Silicate	33·	55·	12·	
Phosphate	40·22	44·70	15·08	1·4158
Sulphate	33·	32·	35·	2·1943
Sulphite	32·18	56·82	11·	
Sulphate of potash and ammonia	36·075	21·425 18·00	24·5	
Obtuse octahedral arseniate	14·3	50·	35·7	2·881
Hexedral arseniate	43·	39·	18·	2·548
Acute octahedral arseniate	29·	50·	21·	4·280
Trihedral arseniate	30·	54·	16·	
Super arseniate	40·1	35·	24·4	
Acetate	25·12	39·41	35·47	1·779
Oxalate	31·08	68·92		
Oxalate of copper and ammonia	47·5	25· 10·	17·	

Observations. The native *carbonate of copper* is known among mineralogists by the name of *malachite* and *blue copper ore*. The *silicate*, by that of *emerald copper ore*. The *sulphate*, by that of *blue copperas*, and *blue vitriol* in commerce.

Salts of bismuth. The salts of bismuth form a colourless solution with acids; when water is poured into it, a white precipitate falls. Ferrocyanate and hydrosulphuret of potash, gallic acid, a plate of copper or tin, occasion precipitates. The most remarkable of these salts is the nitrate of bismuth, formerly called *magistery of bismuth*, which is a compound of 34·2 nitric acid, 48·8 oxide of bismuth, and 17· water. The paint called *pearl white* is supposed to be a precipitate from this salt by means of common salt or tartar.

Salts of Mercury. Mercurial salts are volatilized and dissipated by the application of a strong heat. Ferrocyanate and hydrosulphuret of potash, muriatic acid, gallic acid and a plate, occasion precipitates of different colours in their solution. There are two oxides of Mercury, and most acids seem capable of combining with them both, so as to produce two sorts of salts, namely, protosalts, many of which may be subdivided into sub and super salts. Of these the following are the principal:

Salts.	Acid.	Oxide.	Water.	Specif. grav.
Pernitrate of Mercury	12·	88·		
Carbonate	90·9	9·1		
Borate				2·266
Phosphate	28·5	71·5		4·9835
Sulphate	12·	83·	·5	
Persulphate	31·8	63·8	4·4	6·444

Observations. The *nitrate of Mercury* was formerly called *nitrous turpeth*, from which is procured a precipitate known by the name of the *red precipitate*. The *muriate* is now called a *chloride*. The *sulphate* was formerly named *turpeth*.

Salts of silver. The salts of silver when exposed to the action of the blow-pipe, are reduced; and precipitates of different colours are occasioned in their solution by sulphate of iron, a plate of copper, gallic acid, &c. The most remarkable salts of silver are as follow:

Salts.	Acid.	Oxide.	Water.	Specif. grav.
Nitrate of silver	30·	70·		
Muriate	18·	82·		
Carbonate	15·71	84·20		
Phosphate	17·025	82·975		
Sulphate	25·31	74·69		
Citrate	36·	64·		

Observations. The *nitrate of silver* has been called, on account of its exceedingly bitter taste, the *gall of the metals*; after fusion it cools into a black mass, when it is used by surgeons under the name of *lunar caustic, lapis infernalis*; and the precipitate which is procured from its solution, by means of ammonia, is called *fulminating silver*. The *muriate of silver* is otherwise called *luna cornea*, or corneous silver.

Salts of gold. The two salts of gold hitherto known are the muriate and the nitrate, which form a yellow solution in water. Precipitates of different colours are occasioned in the solution by gallic acid, muriate of tin, a plate of tin, &c.

Salts of platinum. The salts of platinum are nearly as little known as those of gold. The sulphate of platinum consists of 54·5 oxide, 45·5 acid and water, the nitrate of 89 yellow oxide, and 11 nitric acid and water.

Salts of palladium and iridium. The salts of palladium are almost insoluble in water, those of iridium form a red solution in water.

Salts of antimony. The salts of antimony usually form a brownish yellow solution, and in most cases a white precipitate falls when they are diluted in water. Precipitates of other colours are occasioned by gallic acid, a plate of iron or zinc, ferrocyanate and hydrosulphuret of potash, &c. The most remarkable of these salts is the tartrate of potash and antimony, which is known by the name of *tartar emetic*, and consists of 44·21 tartaric acid, 39·76 protoxide of antimony, and 16·03 potash.

Salts of titanium. The salts of titanium are in general colourless, and soluble in water. Alkaline carbonate, ferrocyanate and hydrosulphuret, of potash, a rod of tin, &c. occasion precipitates of different colours in the solutions.

Chemical analysis of natural bodies.

Natural bodies may be considered under the head of the atmosphere, waters, mineral, vegetable, and animal substances.

Atmosphere. The atmosphere, or atmospheric air, was till very lately considered to be a simple homogeneous substance, but it is now universally admitted to be a compound, consisting of the two ingredients oxygen and azotic gas, and in the proportions of from 23 to 30 oxygen gas in 100 parts of atmospheric air; to which have been added two other ingredients, namely, carbonic acid gas, and water, which are also supposed to enter principally into its constitution.

Water. Water, in its purest state, is now supposed to consist of two principal ingredients, namely, oxygen gas, and hydrogen gas; but as it is always impregnated more or less with other substances, it has been distinguished into

CHEMISTRY.

different kinds, as may be seen from the following table, which gives a general view of their ingredients.

Waters	consist of
Rain water,	Air, carbonic acid, carbonate of lime, &c.
Spring water,	Oxygen, carbonic acid, silica, salt, &c.
Well water,	Sulphate of lime, &c.
Sea water,	Common salt, sulphates of magnesia, &c.
Mineral waters,	Air, many acids, alkalies, earths, and salts. [vide *Water*]

Minerals. The chemical analysis of minerals may be found under the head of *Minerals*.

Vegetable substances. Plants are generally composed of the following ingredients; namely, gum, sugar, jelly, acids, starch, albumen, gluten, an extractive, a colouring, bitter, and narcotic matter, oils, wax, camphor, caoutchouc, resins, wood, tan, suber, alkalies, earths, metals; of which a more particular account may be found in their respective places, also under the head of *Plants*.

Animal substances. A general view of animal substances, and their principal ingredients, is exhibited in the following table:—

Substances	consist of
Blood,	water, febrina, albumen, gelatine, hydrosulphuret of ammonia, soda, phosphates of iron, soda, &c.
Bile,	water, albumen, resin, soda, sulphureted hydrogen, saccharine matter, muriate of soda, phosphates of lime and soda, and iron.
Urine,	water, phosphoric acid, phosphates of soda, ammonia, &c. carbonic acid, uric acid, &c. muriate of potash, sulphur, sulphates of lime, &c.
Milk,	water, oil, curd, gelatine, sugar, muriate of soda and potash, phosphate of lime, and sulphur.
Saliva,	water, mucilage, albumen, muriate of soda, phosphate of soda, &c.
Tears, and mucus,	water, mucilage, soda, muriate of soda, phosphates of lime and of soda.
Cerumen,	albumen, resin, colouring matter, soda, phosphate of lime.
Synovia,	fibrous matter, albumen, muriate of soda, phosphate of lime water.
Semen,	water, mucilage, soda, phosphate of lime.
Liquor of the amnios,	mucilage, fat.
Bones,	earthy salts, cartilage, gelatine, and fat.
Muscles,	fibrina, albumen, gelatine, extractive matter, phosphates of soda, ammonia, and lime, carbonate of lime.
Membranes,	gelatinous matter.
Brain,	water, white and red fatty matter, albumen, osmazome, phosphorus, acids, salts, sulphur.
Skin,	gelatine, mucus, &c.
Intestinal calculi,	magnesia, phosphoric acid, ammonia, water, animal matter.
Biliary calculi,	adipocire, &c.
Urinary calculi,	uric acid, urate of ammonia, phosphate of lime, magnesia, and ammonia, oxalate and carbonate of lime, silica, animal matter.
Hair and nails,	gelatine, oil, iron, phosphate and carbonate of lime, silica, sulphur.
Silk,	varnish, resin, wax, &c.
Ivory,	phosphate and carbonate of lime, gelatine, &c.
Hartshorn,	the same in different proportions.
Castor,	carbonate of potash, lime, and ammonia, iron, resin, mucilaginous matter, volatile oil.
Ambergris,	adipocire, resin, benzoic acid, charcoal.
Egg shells,	the same as bones, but in different proportions.
Yolk of eggs,	oil, albumen, &c.

EXPERIMENTAL OR PRACTICAL CHEMISTRY.

Under this head is comprehended a general account of the most important chemical processes, together with the apparatus by which they are performed.

Furnaces. As the application of heat is of the first importance in all chemical processes, the construction of a furnace is the first object of attention to one who wishes to have a laboratory. The furnaces of most general utility are, the *wind furnace*, in which an intense heat may be excited for fusing metals; a *reverberatory furnace*, which is used for the roasting and smelting of metals; a *muffle furnace*, for trying experiments on the habitudes of earths and stones, by long and violent heat: this is otherwise called a cupelling or enamelling furnace, and is exhibited in fig. 5, pl. 30, where *a* shews the fire-place, *b* the chimney, *c* the ash-pit, *d* the door of the ash-pit, *e* a register for regulating the quantity of air admitted to pass through the fuel. That part of the furnace called the muffle, from which it derives its name, is a hollow arched vessel with a flat bottom, as seen apart in fig. 7.

Crucibles. The crucible is employed to contain the materials which are to be submitted to the action of heat in a wind furnace, and is most commonly made of a mixture of clay and sand, consisting, as in fig. 6, of the cover *a*, the body *b*, and the stand *c*.

Cupels. A cupel is a solid paste of bone, moulded into a short cylindrical or truncated pyramidal form, with a shallow circular cavity at the top, as in fig. 10, which is used in the process of assaying metals.

Evaporating vessels. These vessels, which are formed of glass, earthen ware, and of various metals, require always to be of a flat shape, so as to expose them extensively to the action of heat.

Distilling apparatus. This apparatus is employed for a contrary purpose to that of the evaporating vessel; for as in the latter the object is to let the vapour escape, so by the former it is intended to collect the volatile part. This is called *distillation*, which is performed either by the common still or by a vessel called the alembic. This alembic is made of glass or earthen ware, and consists of two parts, namely, the cucurbit, or body, *a*, (fig. 4), for containing the materials, and the capital, or head, *b*, by which the vapour is condensed. Vessels termed *retorts* are likewise used for the same purpose. These are either of the common form, as *a* (fig. 1), or they are *tubulated*, or stoppered, as *a* (fig. 2). When a liquid is to be added at certain intervals, a retort, consisting of a bent tube, with a funnel at the end, may be conveniently added. To the retort a receiver is a necessary appendage, which may either be plain (fig. 1), *b*, or tubulated, as *d* (fig. 2.) To some receivers a pipe is added, as *e* (fig. 2), which may partly enter a bottle, *f*. This vessel, which serves principally for re-

1

moving the distilled liquid at different periods of the process, is termed a *quilled receiver*. The condensation of the vapour is much facilitated by lengthening the neck of the retort with a glass vessel, called an *adapter*, or *adopter*, as *b*, the upper end of which fits into the beak of the retort, and the lower end into the neck of the receiver. When the substance raised by distillation is partly a condensible liquid, and partly a gas, which is not condensed till it is brought into contact with water, a set of receivers is employed to effect this double purpose, called Woolfe's apparatus, as represented in fig. 3, where *a* is an iron stand, *b* a small Argand lamp, very convenient for chemical purposes, being flat and low, *c* a tubulated retort, *d* a tubulated receiver, resting on a tripod, *e*, *f* the conducting tube, with the melter's tube affixed. The receiver *d* is left empty in the beginning of the distillation, and the vapour which does not condense there passes through *f* into the bottle *g*, and through *h* into the bottle *i*. To make the apparatus complete for experiments of research, a bent tube may be fastened in the lateral opening of *i*, conducting to a pneumatic trough, as given in fig. 18. The *tube of safety*, as it is called, which is affixed to the tube *f*, is a single glass tube, bent as it is represented apart at *k*, having a bulb blown in that part of the tube that lies between the upper and lower flexure.

Apparatus for gases. Gases that are producible without a very strong heat may be procured by glass bottles furnished with ground stoppers and bent tubes, as in fig. 8; but for the procuring of gases without the possibility of their escaping into the room during the process, the apparatus represented at fig. 9 is the best adapted. In this manner sulphureted hydrogen gas is to be obtained from sulphuret of iron and diluted sulphuric acid. Suppose the sulphuret of iron, in coarse powder, or iron filings, be put into the body of the gas bottle, *c*, with a proper quantity of water, the acid holder *a* being filled with diluted acid, and the cock *b* shut, it is then fixed into the tubulure of the gas bottle, and acts on the sulphuret of iron. The bent tube *d* being made to terminate under a receiver filled with and inverted in water, the perforated cock *b* is gradually opened; in consesequence of which the acid descends into the gas bottle, and acts on the sulphuret of iron. The acid may be supplied at pleasure if the cock *b* be shut, and the stopper which closes the acid holder be removed.

Receiving glasses. For receiving the gases when obtained, glass jars of various sizes, as in figs. 11, 12, 13, are requisite, some of which are furnished with necks at the top, and fitted with ground stoppers, and others with brass caps and screws, for the reception of air-cocks, as at fig. 13.

Pneumatic trough. As in all the common operations of receiving and transferring gases the jars in which they are held must be inverted over water, it is necessary to have a water vessel, called a *pneumatic trough*, which may be made in different forms. One of the most convenient of its kind is that represented at fig. 18, where *a* is a deep oblong trough, made of thin tinned iron, well japanned, and having a shelf of the same material to extend entirely across the trough, and rather more than a third of its length, and fixed in its situation, when required, by two strong wires. This shelf has also two holes to receive two bottle supporters, as *b*. Then to the mouth of the glass jar *d*, inverted in water, is fitted the tube which connects the jar with the cock *c*.

Gazometer. The gazometer is a vessel of various shapes and contrivances, which serves as a reservoir for holding a considerable quantity of gas. It is made of thin tinned iron plate, and is mostly provided with some contrivance for measuring the quantity of gas which it contains. The one represented at fig. 16 is of the ordinary construction, where *a a* represents the outer pail, or circular vessel, with a spout at the top. Two tubes, *d* and *e*, are firmly soldered to the sides of the pail. The tube *d* penetrates at the bottom of the pail, and proceeds to the centre, where it joins the termination of the tube *e*, which enters the top of the pail, and proceeds downwards; and from the place of junction, the upright tube, *g*, rises through the middle of the pail a little above the level of its upper rim. The vessel *b* is open only at the bottom, and of less diameter than the pail, into which it is inverted. This cylinder has a solid stem, *c*, which passes through a hole in the wooden cross-bar of the frame round the top of the pail, and serves both to keep the cylinder in a perpendicular direction when moving up and down, and indicates the quantity of inclosed gas by the graduation on its surface. To use this gazometer, first let the cylinder fall to the bottom of the pail, and pour water into the spout of the latter till it is quite full. Then shut the cock *e*, and opening *d*, connect it with the tube which conveys the gas immediately from the retort. In this case the gas rises through the upright tube *g* to the top of the cylinder *b*, which it gradually lifts up, sufficient weight being allowed in the scale-dish to allow the cylinder to move with perfect freedom. When all the gas is obtained, shut the cock through which it passed, and it will remain in the cylinder ready for use. To take out a portion of it, connect with either of the stop-cocks a bent tube, dipping under the jar, or whatever vessel it is to be received in, inverted over water, and at the same time lift up the scale-dish, on which the cylinder will press down by its own weight, and force out the contained air.

Apparatus for obtaining potassium. The apparatus for procuring potash, as given in fig. 19, consists of *c*, a common gun-barrel, curved, and drawn out to rather a smaller diameter at one end. To the end *b* is adapted an iron tube, *a*, for containing the potash; and at the bottom of this tube is a hole, through which the potash gradually flows. To the opposite end of the gun-barrel a tube of safety, *e*, is to be cemented, and into this is poured a sufficient quantity either of mercury or naphtha. Into the gun-barrel are introduced 2¼ parts of clean iron turnings, which are pushed as far as the bent part, *c*. The tube, carefully luted, is then to be placed in a small furnace, and provided with a pair of double-blast bellows, the pipe from which is shewn at *f*. A strong heat being now excited in the furnace, the tube containing the potash, as well as the opposite end of the barrel, are in the mean time kept cool by ice; and when the barrel has attained a white heat, the potash in *a* being melted by a small portable furnace, will flow through the hole upon the iron turnings. A considerable quantity of hydrogen gas will be evolved by the decomposition of that portion of water which the potash retains even after fusion. When the furnace is quite cold, the safety tube *e* is to be removed; and if the end of the gun-barrel projecting from this side of the furnace has been kept carefully cooled during the experiment, the metal will be found adhering to it in the form of brilliant laminæ.

Apparatus for digestions. A small apparatus is given in fig. 14, which is employed for long digestions on a sand-bath, or other heat. This is now used in the place of the vessel called the *pelican*.

Precipitating glass. The precipitating glass is a very tall jar, with a narrower part at the bottom, in which any precipitate, when produced, may collect by subsidence, and allow the supernatant liquor to be decanted off with more ease, as in fig. 15.

2

Matrass. A matrass is a thin glass vessel, of the shape of a flask, which will bear a lamp-heat at bottom without breaking. It is useful for effecting the solution of bodies that require heat before they can be dissolved. It is either round at the bottom, or somewhat flattened, as in fig. 17.

CHEMO'SIS (*Med.*) χήμωσις, a swelling in the white coat of the eye, called the *Albuginea tunica*.

CHENALO'PEX (*Orn.*) χηναλωπηξ, from χὴν, a goose, and ἀλώπηξ, a fox; a bird, so called from its being of the goose kind, but crafty like the fox. It answers to what is now called the Shelldrake. *Plin.* l. 10, c. 22.

CHENE'LLE (*Her.*) French for streaming; an epithet for a comet which has a stream of light issuing from it. [vide *Comet*]

CHENI'SCUS (*Ant.*) χηνίσκος; that part of a ship whereby the anchor is fixed, so called because the figure of a goose is on the stern, as in the annexed cut. *Luc. de Navig.; Apul. de Asin.* l. 11; *Scheff. de Mil. Nav.* l. 2, c. 6.

CHENOCO'PRUS (*Med.*) χηνόκοπρος, goose-dung, which was formerly used as a powder, and reckoned resolvent and diuretic.

CHENOLE'A (*Bot.*) a genus of plants, Class 5 *Pentandria*, Order 1 *Monogynia*.
Generic Characters. CAL. *perianth* one-leaved.—COR. none.—STAM. *filaments* five; *anthers* minute.—PIST. *germ* superior; *style* filiform; *stigmas* two.—PER. *capsule* round; *seed* single.
Species. The only species is—*Chenolea diffusa*, seu *Salsola*, &c. native of the Cape of Good Hope.

CHENOPO'DIUM (*Bot.*) a genus of plants, Class 5 *Pentandria*, Order 2 *Digynia*.
Generic Characters. CAL. *perianth* five-leaved; *divisions* ovate.—COR. none.—STAM. *filaments* five; *anthers* roundish.—PIST. *germ* orbiculate; *style* two-parted; *stigmas* obtuse.—PER. none; *calyx* closed; *seed* single.
Species. Among the following species, the first is a perennial, the second and third shrubs, and the rest annuals, as—*Chenopodium Bonus Henricus, Mercurialis, Lapathum Bonus Henricus*, seu *Blitus*, &c. Angular-leaved Goosefoot, English mercury, or All-good, Good Henry, Good King Harry, or Wild Spinach, native of Europe.—*Chenopodium anthelminticum*, native of Pensylvania.—*Chenopodium multifidum*, Buenos Ayres Goosefoot.—*Chenopodium mucronatum*, native of the Cape of Good Hope.—*Chenopodium murale*, seu *Atriplex*, Wall or Nettle-leaved Goosefoot, native of Europe.—*Chenopodium serotinum*, &c. seu *Blitum*, &c. Fig-leaved Goosefoot, native of Spain.—*Chenopodium album*, seu *Atriplex*, &c. Common or White Goosefoot, native of Europe.—*Chenopodium hybridum*, seu *Stramonii, Pes Anserinus*, seu *Atriplex*, &c. Bastard Goosefoot, native of Europe.—*Chenopodium Botrys*, seu *Botrys*, &c. Butt-leaved Goosefoot, or Oak of Jerusalem.—*Chenopodium ambrosioides*, seu *Botrys*, &c. Mexican Goosefoot, or Oak of Cappadocia, native of Mexico.—*Chenopodium vulvaria, Atriplex, Vulvaria*, seu *Garosmus*, Stinking Goosefoot, native of Europe.—*Chenopodium polyspermum, Blitum*, seu *Polysperon*, &c. Round-leaved Goosefoot, Upright Blite, or Allseed, native of Europe.—*Chenopodium Scoparia, Linaria, Osyris*, seu *Scoparia*, &c. Flax-leaved Goosefoot, Belvidere, or Summer Cypress.—*Chenopodium maritimum*, seu *Kali*, &c. Sea Goosefoot, or White Glasswort, native of Europe.—*Chenopodium oppositifolium*, seu *Salsola*, &c. Opposite-leaved Goosefoot, native of Siberia.—*Chenopodium viride*, seu *Blitum*, &c. Green Goosefoot.—*Chenopodium punctulatum*, Dotted leaved Goosefoot.—*Chenopodium triandrum*, Three-stamened Goosefoot, native of New Zealand.—*Chenopodium laterale*, Branching oblong-leaved Goosefoot.

CHEOPI'NA (*Com.*) the same as *Chopino*.

CHEQUE'R (*Mech.*) a sort of stonework, in which stones in the facings of the walls have their joints continued in straight lines without interruption.

CHE'RAFIS (*Com.*) or *tela*, gold medals stamped in Persia.

CHERAME'LA (*Bot.*) a species of the *Averrhoa* of Linnæus.

CHE'RAMIS (*Conch.*) the hollow of a shell-fish called *myax*.

CHERAMI'TES (*Min.*) a kind of precious stone. *Plin.* l. 37, c. 10.

CHE'RAS (*Med.*) a name for a scrophulous humour in which kernels arise.

CHE'RAY (*Com.*) or *Chahy*, a Persian weight.

CHE'RIF (*Com.*) a small gold coin current in Egypt, equal in value to four shillings sterling.

CHERIF (*Polit.*) a title of dignity among the Saracens and Moors, next to a Khalif, or sovereign prince.

CHE'RIO (*Alchem.*) the heat or cold of things which leaves the substance in which it is contained, and passes into open space. *Paracel. de Grad. et Comp.* l. 2, c. 3.

CHERIO'NIUM (*Alchem.*) is that in which nature cannot be altered; thus a crystal hardened by nature cannot be melted.

CHERLE'RIA (*Bot.*) a genus of plants, Class 10 *Decandria*, Order 3 *Trigynia*.
Generic Characters. CAL. *perianth* five-leaved; *leaflets* lanceolate.—COR. *petals* none; *nectaries* five.—STAM. *filaments* ten; *anthers* simple.—PIST. *germ* ovate; *styles* three; *stigmas* simple.—PER. *capsule* ovate; *seeds* two or three.
Species. The only species is—*Cherleria sedoides, Knawel*, seu *Lychnis alpina, Sedum*, &c. Stone crop Cherleria, a perennial, native of Switzerland.

CHE'RMES (*Bot.*) from the Arabic *Charmah*, or *Karam*, Scarlet Grain, or Kermes Berries.

CHERMES (*Ent.*) a genus of animals, Class *Insecta*, Order *Hemiptera*.
Generic Characters. Snout placed in the breast; *antennæ* filiform; *thorax* gibbous; *hind legs* formed for leaping.
Species. The species are distinguished by the names of the plants or animals which they infest.

CHERNI'BION (*Med.*) χερνίβιον, a urinal. *Hipp. Epid.* l. 7.

CHERNI'TES (*Min.*) a stone like ivory that was used in preserving dead bodies.

CHERO'NIA (*Bot.*) another name for *Centaurium*.

CHE'RRY (*Bot.*) the fruit of the *Cerasus*, and also the tree itself. The cherry is distinguished into, the Common Red Cherry, the Red Heart, the Black Heart, White Heart, Bleeding Heart, Morello, May Duke, Kentish Cherry, and Cherry-Bay, a species of laurel.

CHE'RSA (*Med.*) the same as *Fæx*.

CHERSE'TUM (*Archæol.*) any customary offering made to the parish priest, or to the appropriators of a benefice.

CHERSI'NA (*Conch.*) a Land-snail. *Plin.* l. 9, c. 10.

CHERSY'DRON (*Zool.*) χερσύδρος, from χέρσος, earth, and ὕδωρ, water; an epithet for a serpent which inhabits both watery places and dry ground.

CHERT (*Min.*) a species of flint, the *Petrosilex* of Linnæus.

CHE'RUB (*Bibl.*) כרוב, in the plural, cherubim, an order of angels composed of various animals, as a man, an ox, an eagle, and a lion.

CHERUB (*Her.*) is represented in coats of arms with wings on a human head, as "He beareth Jupiter a cherub, having three pair of wings, whereof the uppermost and nethermost are counterly crossed, and the middlemost displayed luna." These were the arms of the cardinal Buocafoco, an Italian prelate.

CHERU'BICAL *hymn* (*Mus.*) a hymn in the form of "Holy, Holy, Holy Lord God of Hosts," &c.

CHESS.

CHERUB'S *head* (*Her.*) a human head between two wings displayed. [vide *Cherub*]

CHERUHU'NDA (*Bot.*) the *Solanum* of Linnæus.

CHE'RVIL (*Bot.*) the same as the *Cherophyllum* of Linnæus.

CHERVI'LLUM (*Bot.*) the *Scandix cerefolium* of Linnæus.

CHE'SLIP (*Ent.*) a kind of insect that lies under tiles and stones.

CHE'SNUT (*Bot.*) a well known tree; the *Fagus castanea et pumilla* of Linnæus.—Horse Chesnut, the *Æsculus* of Linnæus.

CHESS (*Sport.*) an ancient and scientific game; was long known in Hindostan by the name of *Chaturanga*, or the four members of an army; namely, elephants, horsemen, chariots, and foot soldiers; and afterwards styled in Persia *chatrang*, the game of king; and by the Arabians *shatranj*, the king's distress: from which words has been derived the English appellation of *chess*. This game is played on a board, consisting of sixty-four squares, alternately white and black, and with thirty-two pieces of different forms, denominations, and powers, divided into two colours or parties, namely, eight pieces each, black and white, consisting of a King, called by the orientals *schah* ; a Queen, called *pherz*; a general; two knights or horse soldiers; two Bishops, called *fil*; elephants, and two Rooks or Castles, called *rath*, chariots, or *rohk*, noblemen; and eight pawns, *pedones*, foot soldiers on each side. The king and his officers are ranged at the opposite ends, on the first lines of the board, a white corner of which, numbered 1 or 64, is to be placed towards the right hand of each player. The subjoined figures exhibit a view of a board numbered, and another with the pieces disposed in order.

Fig. 1. The board numbered.

Fig. 2. The men disposed in order.

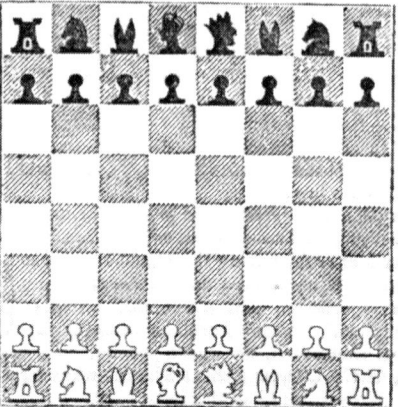

White. The white King must be upon the fourth, a black square, marked 61, at one end of the board, reckoning from the right. The Queen on the fifth, a white square, 60, on the left side of her king. The Bishops must be placed on each side their King and Queen, as 59, 62. The Knights on each side of the Bishops, 58, 63. The Rooks at the two corners of the boards, next to the Knights, as on 57, 64; and the Pawns, or common men, upon the eight squares of the second line, on 49, 50, 51, 52, 53, 54, 55, and 56.—*Black.* The black King must be placed on the fifth, a white square, marked 5, at the other end of the board. The black Queen on the fourth, 4, a black square, on the right of her king. The Bishops on 3 and 6; the Knights on 2 and 7; the Rooks on 1 and 8; and the Pawns on 9 to 16 inclusive. The chess-board is technically called the *exchequer*, because it is alternately chequered black and white: the squares are frequently styled *houses*, the ranges of which, in a straight line from left to right, are denominated *ranks*, as 1 to 8, 9 to 16, and 57 to 64; perpendicularly, from one player to another, are termed *files*, as from 1 to 57, 2 to 58, &c.; and the ranges, which are sloping, are termed *diagonals*, as from 8 to 57.

Names of the pieces, &c. The pieces and pawns on the side of each King take their names from him, as those on the side of the Queen do from her, namely, the white or black King's bishop, 62, 6; the King's knights 63, 7; the King's rooks, 64, 8; the King's pawns, 53, 13; the King's Bishop's pawns, 54, 14; the King's Knight's pawns, 55, 15; the King's Rook's pawns, 56, 16. The white or black Queen's bishops, 59, 3; the Queen's knights, 58, 2; the Queen's rooks, 57, 1; the Queen's pawns, 52, 12; the Queen's Bishop's pawns, 51, 11; the Queen's Knight's pawns, 50, 10; Queen's Rook's pawns, 49, 9. The squares are named from the places; i. e. where the King stands is called the *square of the King*; where his Pawn stands is called the *second square of the King*; that before the Pawn is called the *third square of the King*; that beyond it is called the *fourth square of the King*; and so of all the rest.

Moves of the pieces. The Kings move every way, but in general only one square at a time, and must always be at least one square distant from each other. Suppose the King placed on 37, he may be moved thence to 28, 29, 30, 36, 38, 44, 45, or 46. The King may leap once, and only once, in the game, either on his own side, or on the side of his Queen. In this case, the Rook is moved into the next square to the King, and the King moves to the square on the other side of him, which is called *castling*. The Black King castles on his own side, by moving from 5 to 7, and placing the Rook 8 on 6; on his Queen's side by moving to 3, and placing the Rook 1 on 4. The White King castles on his own side by moving from 61 to 63, and placing the Rook 64 on 62; on his Queen's side by moving to 59, and placing the Rook, 57, on 60. The King cannot castle after he has moved, nor after the Rook has moved, nor if there be any piece between him and the Rook, nor when the King is *in check*, nor when the square over which he means to leap is viewed by an adverse man, who would *check* him in his passage. The King is said to be *upon check*, or *in check*, when he is liable to be taken by one of the adversary's pieces or pawns, who warns him of his danger by crying *check*, or *check to the King*; in such case the King must defend himself, either by changing his place, covering himself with one of his own men, or taking the man who assaults; if he can do none of these things, he is said to be *check-matted*, or *chah-mat*, i. e. the King is dead, when the game is lost. The King cannot change his square, if by so doing he goes into check; and when he has no man to play, and

and is not in check, yet is so blocked up that he cannot move without going into check, this position is called a *stale mate*. In this case, the King who is stalemated wins the game in England, but in France this situation makes a drawn game. Thus, suppose the Black King on 33, with Pawns on 30 and 39, the White King on 44, a White Bishop on 34, with Pawns on 38 and 47; if the White King is moved to 35, Black wins the game by a stalemate, because the Black King cannot be moved to 25 or 41, on account of the White Bishop, nor to 26, 34, or 42, owing to the White King, as it is requisite that the Kings should always be at least one square distant from each other; neither can the Black Pawns be moved, their progress being stopped by the white.—The *Queen* can move in all directions the same as the King, but has the advantage of extending over any number of squares: thus, the Queen may be moved from 37 to 1, 5, 16, 33, 40, 58, 61, 64, or any intermediate squares in those directions. Many chess players give notice when the Queen is in danger, by crying *check to the Queen*.—A *Bishop* moves diagonally only, but over any number of squares; as from 36, the Bishop may be moved to 8, 9, 57, or 63, and from 37 to 1, 16, 58, 64, or any of the intervening squares.—A *Knight* moves obliquely backward or forward upon every third square, including that which he stands upon, from black to white, and from white to black, and also over the heads of the men, which no other piece is allowed to do: thus, a Knight may move from 36 to 19, 21, 26, 30, 42, 46, 51, 53, passing over any pieces on 28, 35, 37, 44; and from 37, the Knight can be moved to 20, 22, 27, 31, 43, 47, 52, 54, passing over any thing placed on 29, 36, 38, or 45.—A *Rook* moves in a right line, either forward, backwards, or sideways, through the whole file; can stop at any square, and take at any distance, when no other piece intervenes: thus, a rook placed on 37 may be moved to 5, 33, 40, 61, or any intermediate square.—A *Pawn* moves one square at a time, in a straight line forwards, and takes the enemy diagonally. He may be moved two squares the first move, but never backwards; and is prohibited from quitting his own file, except in case of making a capture, when he is moved into the place of the captive, and afterwards advances forward in that file: thus, suppose a White Pawn to be placed on 37, and a Black one on 28, either of them could take the other; but if the White Pawn be on 37, a Black Rook on 29, a Black Bishop on 28, and a Black Knight on 30, the Pawn then could not take the Rook, but might take either the Bishop or the Knight. A Pawn getting to the head of the board upon the first line of the enemy, is styled *going to Queen*, in which case it may be exchanged for any one of the pieces lost in the course of the game; and the piece chosen must be placed on the square at which the pawn had arrived. The pieces can take the adversaries who stand in their way, provided the road lies open; or they may decline, and must be placed in the same squares from which the contrary men are taken. Suppose the White Queen on 60, and a Black Knight on 46, the Queen can take the Knight, which then is moved off the board, and the Queen placed on 46; but if the Knight be on 45, then the Queen cannot take him, though he can take the Queen, which being removed, the Knight is placed on 60; or, suppose a White Rook on 61, and a Black Bishop on 13, the White Rook can take the Bishop, and afterwards is to be placed on 13. The power of taking is reciprocal; so that any adverse piece which you can take with one of the same kind, may take you. The goodness of play, therefore, consists in having the greatest number of pieces defending; so that in case of mutual exchanges, you may gain more than your adversary.

Power and value of the pieces. The relative value of the pieces and pawns is as follows:—

King	$6\frac{1}{2}$	Knight	$9\frac{1}{4}$
Queen	$23\frac{3}{4}$	Rook	15
Bishop	$9\frac{3}{4}$	Pawn	2

The power of the King for attack or defence is as above stated, though from the principle of the game he is invaluable. The power of the pawn is as 2; but, from its chance of promotion, the real value is calculated at $3\frac{3}{4}$. The knowledge of this relative value will enable a person to ascertain the propriety of sometimes sacrificing two inferior pieces for a superior one; as, for instance, a Bishop and Knight for a Queen, the joint value of the two former being 19, and that of the latter $23\frac{3}{4}$.

Different kinds of Check-mates. The following appellations have been given to a variety of mates.—*Queen's mate*, a gracious mate, as White King 27, Queen 26, Black King 25; or White King 22, Queen 15, Black King 8.—*Bishop's mate*, a gentle mate, White King 24, Bishops 22 and 21, Black King 8.—*Knight's mate*, a gallant mate, as White King 26, Knight 19; Black King 9, Bishop 1, Knight 10.—*The Rook's mate*, a forcible mate, as White King 27, Rook 41, Black King 25.—*The Pawn's mate*, a disgraceful mate, as White King 14, Pawn 15; Black King 8, Pawn 16.—*Mate by discovery*, an industrious mate, as White King 11, Rook 57, Bishop 49; Black King 9. Moving the Bishop gives mate by discovery.—*Smothered mate*, a shameful mate, as White King 61, Knight 14; Black King 8, Rook 7, Pawns 15, 16. The White Knight gives a smothered mate.—*Stale mate*, a dishonourable mate, as White King 21, Pawn 13, Black King 5; or White King 18, Queen 19, Black King 2.—*Mate in the middle of the board*, an unfortunate mate, White King 61, Queen 37, Pawn 44; Black King 29, Queen 22, Pawn 20.—*Mate at two moves*, a fool's mate, all the men in their first position.

	from	to
White King's Knight's Pawn	55	39
Black King's Pawn	13	21
White King's Bishop's Pawn	54	46
Black Queen gives check mate	4	40

Scholar's mate, the men in their first position.

	from	to
White King's Pawn	53	37
Black King's Pawn	13	29
White Bishop	62	35
Black Bishop	6	27
White Queen	60	32
Black Queen's Pawn	12	20
White Queen gives Check-mate	32	14

Difficult checkmates are a Knight and Bishop, or two Bishops, against a King; a Castle and Bishop against a Castle; and a Queen against a Bishop and Knight.

Laws of the Game.

1. If you touch your man you must play it, unless by so doing you should expose your King to check; in which case you are only, when possible, to move the king, and so long as you keep hold you may place the said man where you please; but, having once quitted, you then cannot recal the move. 2. If you touch one of your adversary's men, he may insist upon your taking it; and, when you cannot do so, then you are to move your king, provided that may be effected without putting him on check. 3. If, by mistake or otherwise, you make a false move, the opponent can oblige you to move the king, as in the second article; but, if he plays without noticing the said false move, neither of you can recal it.

CHESS.

4. If you misplace your men, and play two moves, it rests with your adversary to permit you to begin the game afresh or otherwise. 5. When your adversary gives check without warning, you are not obliged to ward it off; but if, on his next move, he warns you, then each must retract his last move, and you must remove your King off check. 6. Should your adversary warn you of check without however giving it, and you, in consequence, touch or move any piece, you are at liberty to retract, provided he has not completed his move. 7. You cannot give check to your adversary's King when, by so doing, you would discover check on your own King; thus, suppose the White King on 53, the Queen on 19, the Black King on 22, with a Knight on 21; then Black must not check the White King by moving the Knight to 36; as by that the Black King would be on check to the White Queen. 8. If you attempt to castle without having any right, your adversary may insist on your moving either your King or that Rook. 9. In each fresh game, the players have the first move alternately; but, where the advantage of a piece or pawn is given, the player giving that advantage is entitled to the first move.

Rules for playing the Game.

Of Opening the game. 1. Move the pawns before your pieces, and afterwards bring out the pieces for their support. 2. Avoid useless checks, because you may lose the move if your adversary can take or drive the piece away. 3. Never crowd your game by having too many pieces together; and, if it be crowded, endeavour to free it by exchanges of pieces or pawns; but when the adversary plays out his pieces before his pawns, attack them as soon as you can with your pawns; by which you may crowd his game, and make him lose moves.

Of Attacking. 4. Never attack the adversary's King without a sufficient force; and if he attack yours, and you cannot retaliate, offer exchanges, by which, if he retire, he may lose a move. 5. Play your men in guard of one another, but never guard an inferior piece or pawn with a better, because this piece may, in such case, be, as it were, out of play. 6. Never attack unless when well prepared to meet all the designs of your adversary, by which he may aim at defeating your project; but when your attack is in a prosperous way, never be diverted from it by any seeming advantage which he may throw in your way for a time. 7. When, in pursuing a well-laid attack, you find by a little fore-cast that you can sacrifice a piece or two to gain your end, never hesitate to make the bold attempt. 8. You should endeavour to have a move in *ambuscade*, that is, to place a pawn, or other piece, before a Bishop, Rook, or Queen, so that, by removing that Pawn or Piece, you discover a check upon your adversary's King; thus, suppose the Black King on 6, a White Bishop on 41, and a White Pawn on 34; by pushing forward the Pawn to 26 you discover a check upon the King by your Bishop. 9. As the Queen, Rook, and Bishop operate at a distance, it is generally better in your attack not to have them near your adversary's King, as they are not so likely to be driven away, and frequently prevent your giving a stalemate. 10. If you have one of your adversary's pieces in your power, which cannot escape, do not be in a hurry to take it; and, when two of your adversary's pieces are in your power, be determined in your choice of which you will take by the value each piece is of at that particular part of the game. 11. When your adversary has a Pawn on a square in front of your King, it is frequently adviseable not to take it, because it may chance to be a safeguard and protection to you; thus,

suppose a Black Rook placed on 5, a Black Pawn on 45, and the White King on 53, the Pawn protects the King from the attack of the Rook. 12. When your adversary seems to have left a piece in your power, as it were by oversight, consider whether he has not some important move in ambush.

Of Defence. 13. Never let your Queen stand so before the King as that your adversary, by bringing forwards a Rook or a Bishop, might check your King if she was not there, for you could hardly save her, or perhaps, at best, must sacrifice her for an inferior piece; thus, suppose the White King placed on 61, the White Queen on 53, the Black King on 4, and the Rook on 16, which last, if moved to 13, must be taken by the White Queen, who in return would be taken by the Black King, because the White Queen could not otherwise be moved without putting the King in check to the Black Rook. 14. Your adversary must not be permitted to *fork* two of your pieces, i. e. to advance one of his pawns on two of your pieces, as you would, of course, lose one of them for an inferior piece; so, in like manner, do not permit your adversary's Knight to fork your King and Queen, or King and Rook, or Queen and Rook, or your two Rooks, at the same time; for, in the two first cases, the King being forced to go out of check, the Queen must be lost at best for a worse piece; thus, suppose the White Queen placed on 5, the Rook on 7, and a Black Knight on 37; the latter piece, if moved to 22, will fork both the Queen and Rook, and, consequently, one of them must be lost for the Knight. 15. When your adversary attacks one of your pieces or pawns with two or three pieces at the same time, you should endeavour to have as many pieces to defend it; which, if practicable, should be of inferior value to those with which he attacks you. 16. In order to have as powerful pieces as you can in play, let those that are stationed to guard your other pieces or pawns be of no greater force than is necessary. 17. You must prevent your adversary, if possible, from getting prematurely amongst your pieces, because his Knights and Bishops, supported by his Pawns, and occasionally by his Queen, may decide the game while only half of your pieces are engaged. 18. When you play your King, endeavour, if possible, to place it on a square where one of your adversary's pawns will protect it from the attacks of his Rook; thus, suppose a Black Rook on 4, a Black Pawn on 36, and the White King on 53; by moving the King to 52, the Black Pawn prevents the Rook from giving check. 19. When you have a chain of pawns following one another in an oblique line endeavour to preserve the leading Pawn; thus, suppose four White Pawns on 29, 38, 47, and 56, that on 29 is the leading Pawn. 20. Do not hesitate to double a pawn; two in a direct line are not disadvantageous when surrounded by three or four others: three together are strong, as three White Pawns on 28, 35, and 37; but four, as 44 in addition, that make a square, with the help of other pieces well managed, form an invincible strength, and probably may produce you a queen; on the contrary, two pawns with an interval between, as on 35 and 37, are no better than one; and, if you should have three over each other in a line, as 26, 34, and 42, your game cannot be in a worse condition.

Of Exchanging. 21. Exchanges should not be made without reason; they often give the adversary an advantage, particularly if he be a good player. 22. Avoid, if possible, exchanging your King's Pawn, 13 or 53, for your adversary's Bishop's Pawn, 14 or 54; your Queen's Pawn, 52 or 12, for your adversary's Queen's Bishop's

1

Pawn, 51 or 11, because the former occupying the centre hinder your adversary from hurting you. 23. Do not be afraid of losing a rook for an inferior piece; for though the rook is next in value to the Queen, yet it seldom comes into play so as to operate until the end of the game; and it is generally better to have an inferior piece in play than a superior out. 24. Should your adversary attack your Queen, and another piece at the same time, and, by removing her, you must lose the piece, it may sometimes be adviseable to submit to the loss of her if you can get two pieces in exchange for her.

Of Giving or Covering check. 25. Refrain from useless checks, by which a move, or the piece you check with, may be lost; but, if you thereby deprive the King of his privilege of castling, or gain any other important advantage, it is advisable. 26. Be careful that, while you are intent on giving checkmate, you do not leave your King exposed to be checkmated by a single move of your adversary. 27. When you see the possibility of your adversary giving you checkmate be doubly careful of every move.

Of Castling. 28. After the King is castled, the pawns before it should be guarded as much as possible from the attacks of your adversary. 29. Sometimes it is better to play the King than to castle, as it may enable you best to attack with your pawns on that side. 30. If you purpose to castle on the King's side, you must not move your Knight's or King's Pawns without great necessity, because they form a protection to your King afterwards. 31. If your adversary should castle on the same side of the board as yourself, be cautious how you push forward your pawns, leaving your King unguarded; and rather make the attack with your pieces. 32. When the kings have castled on different sides of the board, you must attack your adversary with the pawns you have on the side on which he has castled, taking care to support them with your pieces.

Of the Conclusions of games. 33. At the close of a game your King must not be idle, as by him you generally gain the move and victory. 34. Each party having only three or four pawns on different sides of the board, and no pieces, the kings must endeavour to gain the move. Thus, suppose the White King on 54, and the Black King on 37, the White would gain the move by playing to 53, or the Black by playing to 38; and in either case the adverse King would be prevented from advancing. 35. A single pawn cannot win if the adverse King be placed in opposition to it: thus, suppose the White King placed on 30, a White Pawn on 22, and a Black King on 14, either side having the move, it must be a drawn game, or the Black wins by a stalemate. 36. A single pawn may win if the King be placed before his pawn. Thus, suppose the situations of the Kings reversed, placing the White on 14, and the Black on 30, the Black cannot prevent the Pawn from being pushed forward to *queen.* 37. Two pawns against one must win almost in all cases, but the player that has the two pawns must avoid changing one of them for his adversary's pawn. 38. A pawn, and any other piece, must win in all cases, except a pawn and a Bishop when the pawn is on a Rook's file, and the Bishop does not command the square on which the pawn will reach the royal line: thus, suppose the White King placed on 39, a White Bishop on 30, a White Pawn on 24, and the Black King on 6; the player of the Black can prevent the pawn pushing forward to Queen, which he could not do if the White Bishop was on 29. 39. Two Knights without any other piece, or pawn, cannot give check-mate. 40. Two Bishops may win. 41. A Knight and a Bishop may win. 42. A Rook against a Knight, or a Bishop, makes a drawn game. 43. A Rook and a Knight against a Rook make a drawn game. 44. A Rook and a Bishop against a Rook may win. 45. A Rook and a Bishop, or a Rook and a Knight, against a Queen, make a drawn game. 46. A Queen against a Bishop and a Knight may win, but a Queen against a Rook and two pawns makes a drawn game. 47. A Rook against a Bishop, or Knight, and two pawns, makes a drawn game, because the player who has the Rook cannot be prevented from sacrificing it for the two pawns. 48. At all conclusions of games, when a player does not seem to know how to give the difficult checkmates, fifty moves on each side must be appointed for the end of the game.

Different kinds of games.

There are either *close* games or *open* games, or games that are denominated *gambits*, which commence by pushing the King's and King's Bishop's Pawns, or those of the Queen and Queen's Bishop, two squares each, in lieu of employing one to defend the other.

Philidor's First Party.

This game begins with white, and is illustrated by observations on the most important moves.

1. W. The King's Pawn two squares; 53 to 37.
   Obs. The best and most usual opening move.
   B. The same, 13 to 29.
   Obs. The best counter-move.
2. W. The King's Bishop at his Queen Bishop's square; 62 to 35.
   B. The same; 6 to 27.
3. W. The Queen's Bishop's Pawn one move; 51 to 43.
   B. The King's Knight at his Bishop's third square; 7 to 22.
4. W. The Queen's Pawn two moves; 52 to 36.
   Obs. This move is intended to prevent your adversary's King's Bishop from playing upon your King's Bishop's Pawn; and also to bring the strength of your pawns into the centre of the board.
   B. The Pawn takes it; 29 to 36.
5. W. The Pawn retakes the Pawn; 43 to 36.
   Obs. When the game is in this situation, i.e. two pawns in a front line, you must take care not to push either of them before your adversary proposes to change a pawn with you. Pawns, when sustained in a front line, obstruct very much the adversary's pieces from entering in your game, or taking an advantageous part.
   B. The King's Bishop at his Queen's Knight's square; 27 to 18.
   Obs. If this Bishop, instead of retiring as he here does, should give check by moving to 34, you will cover the check by moving your Bishop 59 to 52; and in case he takes your Bishop, you must retake the Bishop with your Knight, who will then defend your King's Pawn.
6. W. Queen's Knight to his Bishop's third square; 58 to 43.
   B. King castles to 7.
7. W. King's Knight to his King's second square; 63 to 53.
   Obs. You must always avoid playing this Knight to 46, until after your Pawn 54 has moved, because the Knight would prove a hinderance to the Pawn.
   B. Queen's Bishop's Pawn one square; 11 to 19.
8. W. King's Bishop to his Queen's third square; 35 to 44.
   Obs. The Bishop retires to avoid being attacked by the Queen's Pawn, because you would be forced to take his pawn with yours, which would break the centre of your pawns.
   B. Queen's Pawn two squares; 12 to 28.

9. W. King's Pawn one square; 37 to 29.
   B. King's Knight to his King's square; 22 to 5.
10. W. Queen's Bishop to his King's third square; 59 to 45.
    B. King's Bishop's Pawn one square; 14 to 22.
    Obs. He plays this pawn to give an opening to his castle.
11. W. Queen to her second square; 60 to 52.
    Obs. If, instead of this, you had taken his Pawn 22, your Pawn 29 would have lost its column; by leaving it to be taken you can afterwards supply its place by your Pawn 36, which may then be supported by moving your Pawn 54 to 38.
    B. King's Bishop's Pawn takes the Pawn; 22 to 29.
    Obs. He takes the pawn to pursue his design of making an opening to his castle 6.
12. W. Queen's Pawn takes the Pawn; 36 to 29.
    B. Queen's Bishop to his King's third square; 3 to 21.
    Obs. He plays this Bishop to enable him to push afterwards his Queen's Bishop's Pawn 19.
13. W. King's Knight to his King's Bishop's fourth square; 53 to 38.
    Obs. Your Pawn 29 not being as yet in any danger, your Knight attacks his Bishop, in order to take him, or have him removed.
    B. Queen to her King's second square; 4 to 13.
14. W. Queen's Bishop takes the Bishop; 45 to 18.
    Obs. It is always dangerous to let the adversary's King's Bishop stand on the direct line which attacks your King's Bishop's Pawn.
    B. Pawn takes the Bishop; 9 to 18.
15. W. King castles on his side to 63.
    Obs. You castle on this side, in order to support your King's Bishop's Pawn, which you will advance two squares as soon as your King's Pawn is attacked.
    B. Queen's Knight to his Queen's second square; 2 to 12.
16. W. King's Knight takes the Bishop; 38 to 21.
    B. Queen takes the Knight; 13 to 21.
17. W. King's Bishop's Pawn two squares; 54 to 38.
    B. King's Knight to his Queen's Bishop's second square; 5 to 11.
18. W. Queen's Rook to its King's square; 57 to 61.
    B. King's Knight's Pawns one square; 15 to 23.
    Obs. He is forced to push this pawn to hinder you from playing your King's Bishop's Pawn 38 upon his Queen, which would give you two pawns in a front line upon his ground.
19. W. King's Rook's Pawn one square; 56 to 48.
    Obs. This move enables you afterwards to push forward your King's Knight's Pawn; 55 to 39.
    B. Queen's Pawn one square; 28 to 36.
20. W. Knight to his King's fourth square; 43 to 37.
    B. King's Rook's Pawn one square; 16 to 24.
    Obs. He plays this Pawn to hinder your Knight entering into his game and forcing his Queen to retire, which would immediately give an open field to your pawns.
21. W. Queen's Knight's Pawn one square; 50 to 42.
    B. Queen's Rook's Pawn one square; 18 to 26.
22. W. King's Knight's Pawn two squares; 55 to 39.
    B. King's Knight to his Queen's fourth square; 11 to 28.
23. W. Knight to his King's Knight's third square; 37 to 47.
    Obs. This move is to enable you to advance your King's Bishop's Pawn 38 to 30, which will then be supported by four pieces; namely the Rook 62, Bishop 44, Knight 47, and Pawn 39.
    B. King's Knight to adversary's King's third square; 28 to 45.
    Obs. He plays this Knight to cut off the communication between your pieces and break the strength of your pawns, which he would effect by pushing his King's Knight's pawn 23 to 31; but you prevent his design by sacrificing your castle.

24. W. Queen's Rook takes the Knight; 61 to 45.
    Obs. You are obliged to sacrifice this Rook to prevent your game being broken in upon.
    B. Pawn takes the Rook; 36 to 45.
25. W. Queen takes the Pawn; 52 to 45.
    B. Queen's Rook takes the Pawn of the opposite Rook; 1 to 49.
26. W. Rook to its King's square; 62 to 61.
    Obs. This move is to protect your King's Pawn 29, and to enable you to push forward your King's Bishop's Pawn 38 to 30.
    B. Queen takes the Queen's Knight's Pawn; 21 to 42.
27. W. Queen to her King's fourth square; 45 to 37.
    B. Queen to her King's third square; 42 to 21.
    Obs. The Queen returns to this square to prevent the checkmate which soon follows.
28. W. King's Bishop's Pawn one square; 38 to 30.
    B. Pawn takes the Pawn; 23 to 30.
29. W. Pawn takes the Pawn; 39 to 30.
    B. Queen to her fourth square; 21 to 28.
    Obs. The Queen offers to be exchanged for the other Queen, in order to break your scheme of giving checkmate with your Queen and Bishop.
30. W. Queen takes the Queen; 37 to 28.
    B. Pawn takes the Queen; 19 to 28.
31. W. Bishop takes the Pawn in his way; 44 to 26.
    B. Knight to his third square; 12 to 18.
32. W. King's Bishop's Pawn one square; 30 to 22.
    Obs. You must observe, that when your Bishop runs upon white squares, you must put your pawns upon black ones; or if your Bishop runs upon the black, you must have your pawns upon the white; because then your bishop may prevent the adversary's pieces getting between your pawns. This rule is hardly ever to be dispensed with, in case you attack and have some pawns advanced; but in case of a defence, the rule must be reversed, and the pawns set on squares of the Bishop's colour.
    B. Queen's Rook to adversary's Queen's Knight's second square; 49 to 50.
33. W. Bishop to his Queen's third square; 26 to 44.
    B. King to his Bishop's second square; 7 to 14.
34. W. Bishop to adversary's King's Bishop's fourth square; 44 to 30.
    Obs. Here is an example of the above-mentioned remark; if your Bishop had been on a black square, your adversary's King might now have moved to 21.
    B. Knight to adversary's Queen's Bishop's fourth square; 18 to 35.
35. W. Knight to adversary's King's Rook's fourth square; 47 to 32.
    B. King's Rook gives check; 6 to 7.
36. W. Bishop covers the check; 30 to 39.
    B. Knight to adversary's Queen's second square; 35 to 52.
37. W. King's Pawn gives check; 29 to 21.
    B. King to his Knight's third square; 14 to 23.
    Obs. Instead of this move the King might have gone into 6, but with as little chance of success.
38. W. King's Bishop's Pawn one square; 22 to 14.
    B. Rook to its King's Bishop's square; 7 to 6.
    Obs. This move is made to stop the progress of the white.
39. W. Knight gives check at his King's Bishop's fourth square; 32 to 38.
    B. King to his Knight's second square; 23 to 15.
40. W. Bishop to adversary's King's Rook's fourth square; 39 to 32.
    B. Plays any where; the White pushing to Queen.
    Obs. This game might be prolonged a few moves, but is inevitably lost at this point.

CHE′SS-APPLE (*Bot.*) a kind of Wild Service Tree.

CHESS-BOARD (*Sport.*) the board on which the game of chess is played, otherwise called the *exchequer*.

CHESS ROOK (*Sport.*) another name for the castles which stand at the outer corners of the chess-board, and serve as frontier-castles.

CHESS ROOK (*Her.*) is a bearing in some coats of arms, as in the annexed figure. "He beareth *azure*, a fess between three chess rooks *or*," by the name of *Bodenham* of Herefordshire.

CHESS TREES (*Mar.*) in French *poullots d'amure de grande voile*, two pieces of wood which confine the clews of the main sail, and are fixed perpendicularly on each side of the ship.

CHE'SSOM (*Min.*) a kind of earth, or mould, between clay and sand.

CHEST (*Com.*) an indefinite quantity of goods, so called from the chest in which they are contained.

CHEST of viols (*Mus.*) an old expression applied to a concert, or set of viols, consisting of six, which were generally two bases, two tenors, and two trebles, each with six strings.

CHEST (*Anat.*) the Breast, or Thorac, or that part of the human body which contains the heart and lungs.

CHE'ST-FOUNDERING (*Vet.*) a chronic inflammation in those parts of a horse which are situated immediately above the pleura.

CHE'ST-ROPE (*Mar.*) a rope added to the breast-rope when the boat is towed at the stern of the ship to keep her steady.

CHEST-TRAPS (*Mech.*) boxes, or traps for catching polecats, or other vermin.

CHE'STING (*Cust.*) the filling dead bodies with spices to preserve them.

CHE'STON (*Bot.*) a species of plum.

CHESTS, ammunition (*Mar.*) in French *Coffres d'ammunition*; chests placed at the top of ships of war, containing the ammunition of the swivels, &c.—*Arm chests*, in French, *coffres d'armes*, chests furnished with a ready supply of muskets, pistols, &c.—*Signal chests*, in French, *coffres de signaux*, chests for holding the signal flags.

CHEVA'GE (*Law*) *chevagium*, from the French *chef*, a head; a kind of poll-money formerly paid to the lord, in acknowledgement, by such as held lands, or tenements, in villenage. Bract. l. 1, c. 10; Britt. Fol. 79. Lambard writes this word *chivage*; but it should be written *chiefage*, and seems also to have signified a sum of money paid yearly to some chief, head, or leader, for his protection: and, according to Spelman, it also signified a duty paid in Wales *pro filiabus maritandis*. Co. Lit. § 140.

CHEVA'L-TRAPS (*Her.*) a military instrument, commonly called by the French *Chausse-traps*, and in English Caltrops, [vide *Caltrops*] is occasionally borne in coat-armour, as in the annexed figure: "He beareth *sable* on a pile *argent*, a cheval-trap of the first," — name *Kevridge*.

CHEVA'LEMENT (*Archit.*) French for a sort of prop made of one or two pieces of timber, with a head laid buttress-fashion on a rest. It serves to support jambs, &c.

CHEVALER (*Man.*) a French term for a horse, when, in passing upon a walk, or trot, his off fore-leg crosses the near fore-leg every second motion.

CHEVALET (*Mil.*) French for a raft to cross rivers upon. —*Chevalet d'armes*, or *faisceau d'armes*, a pile of arms.

CHEVALI'ER (*Her.*) signifies, in French, literally a horseman, or knight, answering to the English cavalier; but in coat armour it is taken for a horseman armed at all points, as in the annexed figure.

CHEVAN'TIA (*Law*) a loan of money.

CHEVA'STRE (*Surg.*) a double-headed roll.

CHE'VAUX DE FRI'ZE (*Fort.*) a large joist, or piece of timber, about 5 or 6 inches square, and 10 or 12 feet in length; into the sides whereof are driven a great number of wooden pins about 6 feet long and $1\frac{1}{2}$ inch diameter, crossing one another at right angles, and pointed with iron. They are used to stop up breaches, and on numberless other occasions. [vide *Fortification*]

CHEVAUX-LE'GERS (*Mil.*) French for a corps of cavalry, which, during the old monarchy, was composed of two hundred gentlemen, making part of the King of France's guard.

CHEVAUCHE'E (*Polit.*) a journey, or round, which is made on horseback by persons employed officially.

CHEVELEU'RS (*Bot.*) the fibres of plants or trees.

CHEVE'LLEE (*Her.*) the same as *Chenelle*.

CHE'VERIL *leather* (*Mech.*) from the French *chevereau*, a kid; kid-leather.

CHEVERI'LLUS (*Archæol.*) a cockling, or young cock.

CHEVE'T (*Archit.*) French for a quoin, or wedge; likewise that part of a wooden drawbridge to which the chains are fastened.

CHEVETAI'NE (*Mil.*) a term anciently used among the French to signify the leader, or company answering to the *capitaine*, or *connétable*, of more modern times; with this difference, that the commission lasted only during the time of hostilities.

CHEVILLE *d'affût* (*Gunn.*) French for an iron bolt which goes across the whole of a gun carriage.—*Cheville à oreilles*, a similar iron bolt having rings.—*Cheville ouvriere*, a large flat-headed nail, which confines the avant-train to the carriage of a piece of ordnance.

CHEVILLE (*Mus.*) the bridge of any instrument.

CHEVILS (*Mar.*) small pieces of timber fixed in the inside of a ship, to which the ropes called sheets or tacks are fastened.

CHEVISA'NCE (*Law*) from the French *chevir*, i. e. *venir à chef de quelque chose*, to come to the end of a business; an agreement or composition; sometimes taken for an unlawful bargain or contract.

CHEVI'TIÆ (*Archæol.*) or *chevise*, heads of ploughed land.

CHEVRE'TTE (*Mil.*) a kind of gin for raising guns or mortars into their carriages. It is made of two pieces, standing upright on a third, and pierced with holes opposite one another to hold a strong bolt of iron, which may be raised higher or lower at pleasure; and with the assistance of a hand spike raises the gun into the carriage.

CHE'VRON (*Her.*) or *cheveron*, is one of the eight honourable ordinaries, representing two rafters of a house joined together in chief, and descending like a pair of compasses to the extremities of the shield, as in fig. 1. The word *chevron* signifies ordinarily a couple, barge-couple, or rafter, answering to the *capreolus* of Vitruvius, and the *capriolo* or *caprioletto* of the Italians. It betokens the atchievement of some business of moment, or the finishing of some chargeable and memorable work; and is assigned by heralds to such as have served their king and country. A chevron is, according to some, a third; but according to others a fifth of the field. It is distinguished into the—*Chevron couped*, which does not reach the sides of the escutcheon, as in fig. 2. "He beareth *ermine*; a

Fig. 1. 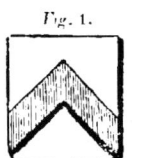 Fig. 2.  Fig. 3.  Fig. 4.

chevron, couped *sable*; by the name of Jones."—*Chevron engrailed*, as in fig. 3. "He beareth *azure*, a chevron, ingrailed."—*Chevron in chief* is a chevron which rises to the chief, or the top of the escutcheon, as in fig. 4. [vide *Chief*]—*Chevron abaised*, when its point does not approach the head of the chief, or reach farther than the middle of the coat.—*Chevron rompu*, i. e. broke, when one branch is separated into two pieces, as in fig. 5.—*Chevron cloven*, when the upper point is taken off, so that the two pieces touch only at one of the angles.—*Chevron couched*, when the point is turned downwards on one side of the escutcheon.—*Chevron divided*, or *counter chevron*, when the branches are of several metals, or when metal is opposed to colour.—*Chevron inverted*, when the point is towards the base of the coat, and it branches towards the chief.—*Chevron mutilated*, when it does not touch the extremes of the coat.—*Party per chevron*, is an epithet for the field, or a charge, when it is divided by single lines, in

Fig. 5.   Fig. 6.   Fig. 7.   Fig. 8.

the form of a chevron, as in fig. 6. The sub-divisions of the chevron, are the *chevronel*, as in fig. 7, which is half the chevron; and the *couple-close*, as in fig. 8, which is the fourth of the chevron.—*Chevron counterpoint*, vide *Counterpoint*.

CHE'VRONEL (*Her.*) a diminutive of the chevron, which is only half the chevron. Leigh says, that no more than three chevronels can be placed in a field.

CHEVRONNE' (*Her.*) an epithet for a shield laid out in several partitions chevron-wise, as in the annexed figure.

CHEVRONS (*Mil.*) a name for the distinguishing marks on the sleeves of non-commissioned officers.

CHEUSIS (*Med.*) χεῦσις, from χίω, χιόω, or χύω, to pour out; eliquation or fusion, i. e. an attenuation of the tears: opposed to τὸ πάχυς, crassitude. *Foes. in Hippocrat. Epid.* l. 6.

CHEWING-BALLS (*Vet.*) balls composed of several sorts of drugs, which are given to horses to recover a lost appetite.

CHE'ZANANCE (*Med.*) χιζανάγκη, from χίζω, to go to stool, and ἀνάγκη, necessity; any thing that creates a necessity of going to stool.

CHI'A (*Ant.*) the name of a sweet fig; and also of an earth found in Chios, an island of the Archipelago.

CHI'ACUM *collyrium* (*Med.*) a remedy for the eyes. *Paul. Æginet.* l. 7, c. 16.

CHI'ADUS (*Med.*) the same as *Furunculus*, according to Paracelsus.

CHIAN PEPPER (*Bot.*) the fruit of the *Capsicum* of Linnæus. [vide *Cayenne*]—*Chian turpentine*, a resin flowing from the *Pistacia terebinthe* of Linnæus.

CHIA'SMOS (*Med.*) χιασμός, the meeting of any two things in the form of a cross, or letter χ, from which it derives its name.

CHIASTOLITE (*Min.*) a precious stone of the feldspar family.

CHIA'STOS (*Surg.*) χιαστός, the name of a crucial bandage in Oribasius; so called because it has a cross, or the letter χ.

CHIA'STRE (*Surg.*) a bandage for the temporal artery, consisting of a double-headed roller.

CHIA'VE (*Mus.*) a cliff.

CHI'AUS (*Polit.*) an officer at the Turkish court who acts as usher; and is also an ambassador to foreign courts.

CHI'BOL (*Bot.*) a small sort of onion.

CHI'BOU (*Bot.*) a spurious species of gum elemi, little known in this country, though common in France.

CHI'BER (*Med.*) the same as *Sulphur*.

CHI'CHAR (*Ant.*) ככר, a talent, either of silver or gold; the first weighed 3,000 shekels, equal to 353*l*. 1*s*. 10*d*. sterling; and that of gold weighed the same, equal to 5,075*l*. 15*s*. 0*d*. sterling.

CHICHIAXO'COTL (*Bot.*) a species of the *Macaxacotlifera*.

CHI'CHINA (*Med.*) vide *Cinchona*.

CHICKEN-POX (*Med.*) an exanthematous distemper. [vide *Varicella*]

CHI'CK-PEA (*Bot.*) an annual; the *Cicer arietinum* of Linnæus.—Chick-Weed, an annual, the *Alsine Media*.—Water-Chick-Weed, an annual, the *Callitriche verna*.

CHICKLING-VETCH (*Bot.*) another name for the *Everlasting Pea*.

CHICO'S (*Ent.*) chigoes, chiegoes, or chigres, small worms which, in warm climates, frequently breed in the muscular parts of the flesh, particularly the feet; also the disease of having such worms in the flesh.

CHIEF (*Her.*) one of the eight honourable ordinaries, containing a third part of the field. As the head is the chief part of a man, so is the chief the head or principal part of the escutcheon. It is determined by one line, either straight, as in fig. 1; crenelle as in fig. 2. "He beareth *gules*; a chief crenelle *or*;" indented, &c. as in

Fig. 1.   Fig. 2.   Fig. 3.

fig. 5. Sometimes one chief is borne upon another, which is called surmounting, as in fig. 3. "He beareth *gules*; a chief, *argent*; surmounted of another, *or*." This is usually expressed by the line drawn across the uppermost part of the chief; but a similar line drawn along the lower part of the chief, is called a *fillet*, as in fig. 4. The French had also a *chief couvert*, which was, as it were, shadowed or covered the field with tapestry; and a *chief consu*, which was a chief sewed to the field. When a chief is charged with any thing, it is said to be on chief, as in fig. 5. "He beareth, *or*, on a chief indented, *sable*; three crescents, *argent*, by the name of *Harvey*;" but when any thing is

Fig. 4.   Fig. 5.   Fig. 6.

borne on the top of the escutcheon, it is said to be in chief, as in fig. 6. "He beareth, *argent*, a fess, and in chief, three lozenges, *sable*," by the name *Aston*. Chiefs are likewise distinguished into the *Chief chevroned, bended,* or *paled*: when it has a chevron, bend, or pale, contiguous to it, and of the same colour as itself.—*Chiefs supported*, are those which have two-thirds at the top, of the same colour as the field, and the third at the bottom of a different colour.

CHIEF *point* (*Her.*) is the uppermost point of an escutcheon, which is three-fold, dexter, middle, and sinister.

Chief *pledge* (*Law*) the same as *Headborough*.—*Chief rents*, the same as *Quit-rent*.—*Tenants in chief*, or *tenants in capite*, holding immediately under the king in right of his crown and dignity.

CHI'EGO (*Ent.*) vide *Chicos*.

CHIEN-DE'NT (*Bot.*) a French name for the *Gramen Caninum*.

CHIE'RE (*Bot.*) the *Leucoium luteum*, or Wall-flower.

CHIE'SA (*Mus.*) Italian for a church, is frequently employed as an epithet to signify that the music is in the church style.

CHI'FFER (*Alch.*) or *Chifir*, a name for the *Lapis animalis*, according to Libavius, in the preparation of the philosopher's stone. It is supposed to signify sulphur.

CHI'GOE (*Med.*) the disease otherwise called *chicos*.

CHI'GRES (*Med.*) vide *Chicos*.

CHI'LBLAIN (*Med.*) *pernio*, an inflammatory affection of the extreme parts of the body, occasioned by cold.

CHI'LDERMAS-DAY (*Ecc.*) a feast observed on the 28th of December, in commemoration of the murder of the children of Bethlehem by order of Herod.

CHI'LDING (*Bot.*) an epithet applied to plants when their offsets exceed their ordinary number.

CHI'LDWIT (*Law*) a fine or penalty imposed upon a bond-woman who was unlawfully gotten with child; this was 3s. 4d. in the manor of Writtle, in Essex.

CHI'LIADS (*Arith.*) from χιλιάς, the number 1000; a name given to tables of logarithms, because they were at first divided into thousands: in 1624, Mr. Briggs published a table of logarithms for 20 chiliads, and afterwards increased them to the number of 31.

CHI'LIAEDRON (*Geom.*) from χιλιάς, a thousand, and ἕδρα, base; a figure of a thousand sides.

CHILIA'GON (*Geom.*) from χιλιάς and γωνία, an angle; a plain figure having 100 sides and angles.

CHILIA'RCHUS (*Polit.*) χιλιαρχος, from χιλιάς a thousand, and ἄρχω, a governor; a colonel, or a commander of 1000 men.

CHI'LIASTÆ (*Ecc.*) or *Chiliasts*, a sect of Christians who maintained that before the last or general judgment Christ will come and reign, personally, 1000 years among his saints on earth. This opinion was broached in the early ages of Christianity, but condemned by Justin Martyr, and also by pope Damasus, in a council held against Apollinarius, in 373. *Just. ad Tryphon.; Euseb. Hist. Eccles.* l. 7, c. 24; *St. Aug. de Hæres.; Baron. Annal. Ann.* 373.—*Anti-Chiliasts* those who opposed the Chiliasts.

CHILIODYNA'MENE (*Bot.*) χιλιοδυναμένον, from χίλιοι, a thousand, and δύναμις, power; an epithet for the herb Polemonium, on account of its many virtues. *Dioscor.* l. 4, c. 8.

CHI'LIOPHYLLON (*Bot.*) the herb millefolium.

CHI'LLI (*Bot.*) a species of Indian pepper.

CHI'LOCACE (*Med.*) vide *Cheilocace*.

CHILON (*Ich.*) an epithet applied to some species of fishes of the Class *Capitones*, i. e. *Labeones*.

CHILO'NIAN (*Rhet.*) or *Chilonic*, a brief compendious style of writing, called the Chilonic style, from Chilo, one of the wise men of Greece, whose sentences were very short.

CHILPE'LAGUA (*Bot.*) a species of pepper which grows in Guinea.

CHI'LTERN-HUNDREDS (*Law*) a hilly district in Buckinghamshire, which has belonged from time immemorial to the crown, and to which is attached the nominal office of Steward of the Chiltern Hundreds. By the acceptance of this office every member of parliament vacates his seat; whence the phrase, " To accept the Chiltern Hundreds."

CHI'LTERPIN (*Bot.*) the same as the *Chilpelagua*.

CHIMÆRA (*Myth.*) χίμαιρα, a monster, feigned to be like a lion in the fore part, a dragon behind, and a goat in the middle.

CHIMÆRA (*Ich.*) a genus of animals, Class *Pisces*, Order *Chondropterigius*.
  Generic Character. Head pointed.—Spiracle single.— Tail ending in a slender thread.
  Species. The species are the—*Chimæra monstrosa*, Sea-Monster; and the—*Chimæra collorinchus*.

CHI'MALATH (*Bot.*) or *Chimalatl*, the same as *Corona Solis*.

CHIMA'RRHIS, (*Bot.*) genus of plants, Class 5 *Pentandria*, Order 1 *Monogynia*.
  Generic Characters. CAL. perianth margin entire.—COR. one-petalled; *tube* very short; *border* five-cleft; *segment* lanceolate.—STAM. *filaments* five; *anthers* oval.—PIST. *germ* roundish; *style* filiform; *stigma* bifid.—PER. *capsule* subovate; *seeds* solitary.
  Species. The only species is the *Chimarrhis cymosa*, a shrub, native of Martinica.

CHIMB (*Mech.*) or *Chine*, the end of a barrel, tub, &c.; thence *chine* hoop, that which is next the end.

CHIMES (*Mus.*) a kind of periodical music produced at equal intervals of time on clocks, or bells.

CHIMETHLON (*Med.*) the same as *Pernio*.

CHI'MIA (*Chem.*) vide *Chemia*.

CHIMIA'TER (*Med.*) from *chimia*, chemistry, and ἰατρί, a physician; physicians who make the science of chemistry subservient to the purposes of medicine.

CHIMIA'TRI (*Med.*) medicines prescribed by chemists.

CHIMI'N (*Law*) in French *chemin*, a way, of which there are two sorts; namely, *chiminus regius*, the king's highway, in which the king's subjects, and all under his protection, have free liberty to pass and repass.—*Chiminus privatus*, a private way, or the liberty which one or more have of passing through the grounds of another. This is either *chimin in gross*, where a person holds a way principally and solely in itself; or, *chimin appendant*, that way which a man hath as appurtenant to some other thing. *Kitch.* 117; *Co. Lit.* 56.

CHI'MINAGE (*Law*) *chiminagium*, a toll paid by those having a way through a forest. *Co. Lit.* 56.

CHIMMAR (*Ecc.*) or *Simar*, a kind of vestment formerly worn by bishops between their gown and rochets.

CHI'MNEY-PIECE (*Archit.*) the ornamental piece set over a fire-place.

CHI'MNEY-MONEY (*Law*) another name for hearth-money, a duty, imposed by the crown, of two shillings on every hearth.

CHIMOLE'A LAXA (*Med.*) the powders separated from the flowers of saline ores. *Paracel. de Morb. Gall.* l. 2, c. 4.

CHIMUR (*Min.*) the dross of the ore.

CHIN-SCAB (*Vet.*) a disease in sheep, called by shepherds *the darters*.

CHI'NA (*Bot.*) or China-Root, a dry tuberous nodous root, of an astringent quality, and an earthy taste, the *Smilax China* and *Indica* of Linnæus.—Bastard China, the *Senecio Madraspalorius*, &c.—China Chinæ, the same as the *Cortex Peruvianus*.—China-Pink, the *Dianthus Chinensis*.—China-Rose, the *Hibiscus Rosa Chinensis*.

CHINCH (*Ent.*) a bug.

CHINCHI'NA (*Bot.*) another name for the *cinchona*.

CHINE (*Mar.*) that part of the water-way left above the deck.

CHI'NE-COUGH (*Med.*) or *chin-cough*, a violent and convulsive cough incident to young children.

TO CHINE *a beast* (*Mech.*) to cut him down quite through the back bone.

CHINE'NSE (*Bot.*) or *Sinense pomum*, the China orange.

CHI'NESE *Smilax* (*Bot.*) the *Smilax China* of Linnæus.

CHINI'SCI (*Surg.*) pegs, such as are in a harp, serving instead of *fibulæ*, or braces to fasten axes, crossbeams, &c. *Orib. lib. de Machinam.* c. 4.

CHI'NKED (*Bot.*) *rimosus*, an epithet applied to the outer bark of trees, particularly when they are in a state of decay from age.

CHI'NQUAPINE (*Bot.*) the *Fagus pumella* of Linnæus.

TO CHINSE (*Mar.*) in French *remplir d'étoupe une coutine*, to thrust oakum into a seam or chink with a chisel or point of a knife.

CHINTZ (*Com.*) a fine Indian painted calico.

CHIO *turpentine* (*Bot.*) the resin of the *Pistacia terebinthus* of Linnæus.

CHIOCCOCCA (*Bot.*) the *Cestrum nocturnum*, and *Psychotria paniculata* of Linnæus.

CHIOCO'CCA (*Bot.*) a genus of plants, Class 5 *Pentandria*. Order 1 *Monogynia*.
   Generic Characters. CAL. *perianth* five-toothed. — COR. monopetalous; *tube* long; *border* five-parted; *divisions* equal.—STAM. *filaments* five; *anthers* oblong.—PIST. *germ* inferior; *style* filiform; *stigma* simple.—PER. *berry* roundish; *seeds* two.
   Species. The species are shrubs, as—*Chiococca racemosa, Lonicera, Periclymenum, Jasminum,* seu *Pandacaqui,* Climbing Snowberry-tree, or David's Root, native of Jamaica. — *Chiococca barbata,* native of the Society Island.

CHI'OLI (*Med.*) the same as *Kirunculus*.

CHIONA'NTHUS (*Bot.*) a genus of plants, Class 2 *Diandria*, Order 1 *Monogynia*.
   Generic Characters. CAL. *perianth* one-leaved. — COR. monopetalous; *tube* very short; *border* divisions linear. —STAM. *filaments* two; *anthers* cordate.—PIST. *germ* ovate; *style* simple; *stigma* obtuse.—PER. *drupe* round; *seed* nut striated.
   Species. The species are shrubs, as—*Chionanthus Virginica,* seu *Amelanchier,* &c. Virginia Fringe-tree, or Snowdrop-tree, native of America.—*Chionanthus colinifolia,* native of Ceylon.—*Chionanthus compacta,* native of the Carribbee islands.—*Chionanthus Zeylanica* seu *Thoninia,* &c. Ceylon Snowdrop-tree, native of Ceylon. —*Chionanthus incrassata, Mayepea,* seu *Schreberi,* native of Guiana.—*Chionanthus Mayepea,* seu *Mayepea,* &c. a tree, native of Guiana.—*Chionanthus axillaris,* native of the East Indies.

CHIO'PPINE (*Archæol.*) a high shoe formerly worn by ladies.

CHIQUE (*Com.*) a weight for weighing goats' wool in Smyrna, containing 500 drams or rokes, equal to 5 lbs. 10 oz. 7 dr.

CHIQUES (*Ent.*) French for worms called *chicos*.

CHIRA'GRA (*Med.*) χειραγρα, from χειρ, the hand, and αγρα, a capture or seizure; a name for the gout in the hands.

CHIRA'PSIA (*Med.*) χειραψια, from χειρ and αψις, a touching or handling; the rubbing a place affected with the itch.

CHI'RCHGEMOTE (*Law*) Chirchgemot, or Kirkmote, in Saxon Cincʒemot; a meeting in a church or vestry. Leg. Hen. 1, c. 8 apud Brompton; 4 Inst. 321.

CHIRIDO'TA (*Ant.*) χειριδωτα, an epithet for a garment, with long sleeves, which was not usual among the Romans. Aul. Gell. l. 7, c. 12.

CHIROGRAPHA'RIUS (*Ant.*) an epithet for a debtor who has given his note of hand for the sum due; so also *Pecunia chirographaria,* money due by bond.

CHIRO'GRAPHER *of fines* (*Law*) from χειρ, a hand, and γραφω, to write; an officer in the Common Pleas, who engrosses fines after they are examined and passed in the other office.

CHIRO'GRAPHIST (*Ant.*) the same as *Chirographer*.

CHIROGRA'PHUM (*Law*) Chirograph, any public instrument, or gift of conveyance, attested by the subscription and crosses of witnesses.

CHIRO'GRAPHY (*Law*) a writ under one's own hand.

CHIRO'LOGY (*Mech.*) χειρολογια, from χειρ, a hand, and λογος, a speech; a talking with the hands by signs.

CHI'ROMANCY (*My.*) *Chiromantia,* a prediction of a person's fortune and condition by the lines in his hands.

CHI'RONAX (*Ant.*) a manual artificer, or one who follows a mechanic trade.

CHIRO'NIA (*Bot.*) a genus of plants, Class 5 *Pentandria*, Order 1 *Monogynia*.
   Generic Characters. CAL. *perianth* one-leaved; *leaflets* oblong. — COR. monopetalous; *tube* narrower; *border* five-parted; *divisions* ovate.—STAM. *filaments* five; *anthers* oblong.—PIST. *germ* ovate; *style* filiform; *stigma* headed.—PER. ovate; *seeds* numerous.
   Species. The species are annuals or shrubs. Of the first kind are the following; namely, the *Chironia trinervia,* seu *Lysimachia,* native of Ceylon.—*Chironia Jasminoides,* native of the Cape of Good Hope.—*Chironia chilensis, Gentiana,* seu *Centaurium,* &c. native of Chili. —*Chironia centaurium, Gentiana, Centaurium,* seu *Erithræa,* native of Europe.—*Chironia inaperta, Vaillantii,* &c. seu *Centaurium,* native of Europe.—*Chironia maritima, Gentiana,* seu *Centaurium,* &c. native of Spain. Of the second kind are the following; namely—*Chironia linoides,* seu *Rapuntium,* Flax-leaved Chironia, native of the Cape of Good Hope.—*Chironia baccifera,* seu *Centaurium,* &c. native of Æthiopia.—*Chironia frutescens* seu *Centaurium,* &c. native of Æthiopia.—*Chironia tetragona,* native of the Cape of Good Hope.—*Chironia angustifolia,* native of the Cape of Good Hope.—*Chironia decussata,* native of the Cape of Good Hope.

CHIRONIA (*Bot.*) the same as *Gentiana*.

CHIRONION (*Bot.*) the herb Centaury.

CHIRO'NIUM (*Bot.*) the *Laserpitium chironium* of Linnæus.

CHIRONIUM (*Med.*) χειρωνιον, a malign ulcer difficult to heal, with a hard, callous, and tumid margin, so called from Chiron, by whom it is said to have been first cured.

CHIRO'NOMY (*Med.*) the same as *Cheironomia*.

CHRONOMY (*Rhet.*) a suitable action with the hand in speaking, from χειρ, the hand, and νομος, a law.

CHIRO'NOMON (*Ant.*) χειρονομων, a sort of dance, in which there was much gesticulation with the hands. *Juv. sat.* 6, v. 63; *Hesychius*.

CHIROTE'CHNES (*Med.*) the same as *Chironax*.

CHIROTHE'CA (*Anat.*) and *Podotheca,* from χειρ, and πους, a foot, and τιθημι, to put; a glove and shoe of the scarf skin, with the nails adhering, which are separated from the flesh in the preparation of anatomical subjects.

CHIROTRI'BIA (*Med.*) χειροτριβια, from χειρ and τριβω, to exercise; the being well versed in the practice of medicine. *Foes. Œconom. Hippocrat.*

CHIROTO'NIA (*Ecc.*) χειροτονια, from χειρ and τεινω, to extend; an imposition of hands in conferring priestly orders.

CHIRU'RGIA (*Surg.*) from χειρ and εργον, work; surgery, or that part of medicine which consists of manual operations.

CHISEL (*Carp.*) a tool for chipping and paring away wood.

CHIST (*Ant.*) the name of a measure. [vide *Sextarius*]

TO CHIT (*Bot.*) is said of seed when it first of all shoots its small root into the earth.

CHIT-LARK (*Orn.*) the same as *Titlark*.

CHI'TON (*Con.*) a genus of animals, Class *Vermes,* Order *Testacea*.
   Generic Character. Animal a Doris.—*Shell* consisting of several segments or valves disposed down the back.
   Species. The principal species are the *Chiton crinatus, punctatus, ruber,* &c.

CHITON (*Med.*) χιτων, a coat or membrane.

CHI'TTARA (*Mus.*) a *cithara,* a guitar.

CHI'VALRY (*Archæol.*) from the French *chevalier,* a tenure of lands by knight's service.

CHIUDE'NDO (*Mus.*) Italian for ending, is commonly used with some other word, as *chiudendo col aria,* ending with the air.

CHIVE (*Bot.*) 1. The name among ancient botanists for the anther. 2. A sort of small onion.

CHI'VEL *Sheveti* (*Bot.*) a cucurbitiferous tree, with a fruit as big as a large melon.

CHIVE'TS (*Bot.*) the small parts at the roots of plants, by which they are propagated.

CHIVILUILE'NZA (*Bot.*) a name for a species of *Catuputia Minor*.

CHI'UM *vinum* (*Med.*) χῖος οἶνος, Chian wine; a wine from the island Chios, now called Scio. *Dioscor.* l. 5, c. 10.

CHLAMY'DIA (*Bot.*) the *Phormium tenax* of Linnæus.

CHLA'MYS (*Ant.*) a tunic or loose coat worn over the vest or doublet.

CHLI'AROS (*Med.*) χλιαρός, tepid, lukewarm; an epithet for mild fevers, in opposition to the acute. *Gal. Com. Hippoc.* l. 4, aph. 37.

CHLIA'SMA (*Med.*) χλίασμα, from χλιαίνομαι, to grow tepid; a tepefactory or warming fomentation of the moist kind. *Hippocrat. de Rat. Vict. in Acut. Morb.; Foes. Œconom. Hippocrat.*

CHLO'E (*Bot.*) χλόη, an epithet for the herb or grass.

CHLO'RA (*Bot.*) a genus of plants, Class 8 *Octandria*, Order 1 *Monogynia*.
Generic Characters. CAL. *perianth* eight-leaved; *leaflets* linear. — COR. monopetalous; *tube* shorter than the calyx; *border* eight-parted; *divisions* lanceolate. — STAM. *filaments* eight; *anthers* linear. — PIST. *germ* ovate, oblong; *style* filiform; *stigmas* four. — PER. *capsule* ovate, oblong; *seeds* numerous.
Species. The species are annuals, as — *Chlora perfoliata, Gentiana, &c. Blackstonia, &c.* seu *Centaurium, &c.* Perfoliate Yellow-wort, or Yellow Centaury, an annual, native of Switzerland. — *Chlora quadrifolia*, seu *Gentiana, &c.* native of the S. of Europe, &c. &c.

CHLORA'NTHUS (*Bot.*) a genus of plants, Class 4 *Tetrandria*, Order 1 *Monogynia*.
Generic Characters. CAL. none. — COR. one convex *petal*. STAM. *filaments* none; *anthers* four. — PIST. *germ* obovate; *style* unequal; *stigmas* three. — PER. *drupe* oblong; *seed nut* oblong.
Species. The only species is, the — *Chloranthus inconspicuus Nigrana*, seu *Creodus, &c.* a shrub, native of China.

CHLORA'SMA (*Bot.*) from χλωρός, a palish green colour, shining with a sort of splendour inclining to watery. It is applied as an epithet to leguminous plants before they come to maturity.

CHLO'RATE (*Chem.*) the name of salts formed by the combination of chloric acid with different bases, as *chlorate of ammonia*, a salt formed by dissolving carbonate of ammonia in chloric acid; so *chlorate of soda*, *chlorate of lime*, &c. [vide *Chemistry*]

CHLORIC *acid* (*Chem.*) an acid compound of chlorine and oxygen, in the proportions of about 47 parts chlorine to 53 oxygen. It is destitute of smell, reddens vegetable blues without destroying them, and combines with different bases, so as to form the salts called chlorates. This acid is distinguished into *chloric acid* and *perchloric acid*, according to the proportion of oxygen. [vide *Chemistry*]

CHLORI'DE (*Chem.*) a compound of chlorine with a combustible substance, as the *chloride of azote*, the *chloride of manganese*, &c. The chlorides are distinguished into *protochloride* and *perchloride*, according to the proportion of chlorine. [vide *Chemistry*]

CHLO'RINE (*Chem.*) a gaseous body of a greenish yellow colour, and a suffocating smell, procured from the black oxide of manganese and muriatic acid. It was formerly called *dephlogisticated muriatic acid, oxymuriatic acid, or oxygenized muriatic acid*. The specific gravity is reckoned to be about 2·395. [vide *Chemistry*]

CHLORIO'DIC *acid* (*Chem.*) a compound of chlorine and iodine, consisting of about 64 parts iodine and 36 chlorine. [vide *Chemistry*]

CHLO'RITE (*Min.*) a mineral consisting of oxide of iron united to siliceous and aluminous earths.

CHLOROCARBO'NIC *acid* (*Chem.*) a compound of one atom carbon with two atoms of a supporter.

CHLOROCYA'NIC *acid* (*Chem.*) chlorine gas with a solution of hydrocyanic acid in water.

CHLORO'SIS (*Med.*) χλώρωσις, from χλωρός, green; the Green Sickness; a species of *Cachexy*.

CHLOROXYLON (*Bot.*) the *Laurus Chloroxylon* of Linnæus.

CHNUS (*Med.*) χνοῦς, fine soft wool.

CHO'A (*Ant.*) the same as *Chu*.

CHO'ACON (*Med.*) or *choacum*, a black plaister, made of spuma argenti, boiled oil, and resin.

CHOAKED (*Print.*) an epithet applied to the press when, for want of proper washing, the ink gets into the hollow of the face of the letter.

CHOA'NA (*Med.*) χοάνη, a cavity in the brain like a funnel.

CHO'ANOS (*Med.*) χοάνη, from χέω, to pour; a funnel or furnace for melting metals.

CHOASPI'TES (*Min.*) a precious stone, of a green colour, and glittering like gold.

CHOA'VA (*Bot.*) the same as *Caffea*.

CHOCK (*Mar.*) in French *cale acore*. 1. A sort of wedge used for confining a weighty body in a certain place. 2. Pieces for fastening some part of the vessel. — *Chock-a-block*, the same as *Block-a-block*. — *Chocks of a rudder*, large pieces of timber to stop the motion of the rudder in case of any accident.

CHOCOLA'TA (*Bot.*) or *cuccolata*, chocolate; a kind of cake prepared of cocoa nuts and other ingredients.

CHO'COLATE-TREE (*Bot.*) the *Theobroma cacao* of Linnæus.

CHO'EAC (*Chron.*) an Egyptian month which is the fourth from Thoth. [vide *Chronology*]

CHŒ'NICIS (*Surg.*) χοινικίς; another name for the trepan.

CHŒ'NIX (*Ant.*) χοῖνιξ, an Attic dry measure, containing 3 Cotyla, or Heminæ, i. e. one sectarius and a half. *Bud.*

CHŒRA'DES (*Med.*) χοιράδες, from χοῖρος, a swine; strumous swellings, painful to the touch, and exasperated by medicines.

CHŒRADOLE'THRON (*Bot.*) χοιραδόλεθρον, from χοῖρος, a swine, and ὄλεθρος, destruction; Hogbane, a name given by Ætius to the *Xanthum*, or louse-bur.

CHŒROGRY'LLUS (*Zool.*) an hedge-hog.

CHOIR in nunneries (*Mus.*) a large hall separated from the body of the church by a grate, where the nuns sing the office. — *Choir of a cathedral*, that part of the cathedral in which divine service is performed.

CHOIR-MAN (*Mus.*) any vocal officiate of a choir.

CHOI'RAS (*Med.*) χοιράς, from χοῖρος, a hog; the same as *Scrofula*.

CHOI'ROS (*Zool.*) χοῖρος, a very little hog, so called by the ancients.

CHOKE (*Bot.*) the filamentous or capillary part of an artichoke. — *Choke-pear*, a rough tasted pear.

CHOKE-DAMP (*Min.*) the name given by miners to the noxious air occasionally found in the bottoms of mines and pits.

CHO'KING *the luff* (*Mar.*) the placing the bight of the leading part or fall of a tackle close up between the nest part and jaw of the block.

CHOLA'DES (*Med.*) from χολή, bile; a name for the small intestines which contain bile.

CHOLA'GO (*Med.*) from χολή, the small intestines which contain bile.

CHO'LAGOGUES (*Med.*) χολαγωγά, from χολή, the bile, and ἄγω, to drive out or evacuate; medicines which expel or evacuate bilious fæces.

CHO'LAS (*Anat.*) χολάς, the cavity of the *Hypochondria*, or *Ilium*, so called because it contains the liver, as the strainer of the chole, or bile. *Arist. Hist. Animal.* l. 1, c. 13.

CHO'LAS (*Min.*) a precious stone of the emerald kind. *Plin.* l. 37, c. 3.

CHOLE (*Anat.*) the same as *Bile*.

CHOLE'DOCHUS (*Anat.*) χοληδόχος, from χολη, bile, and δέχομαι, to receive; a common epithet for the gall bladder, the biliary ducts, and the common gall duct, which communicates with the duodenum, called *Choledochus ducta*.

CHOLE'GON (*Med.*) χολαγον, χολαπω: the same as *Cholagoga*.

CHO'LERA *morbus* (*Med.*) χολερα, a disease consisting of an immoderate perturbation of the belly, attended with a discharge of the bile upwards and downwards, of which Hippocrates mentions two sorts, the humid and the dry. *Hippocrat. de Rat. Vict. in Acut. Morb. et Gal. Comm.*; *Aret. de Caus. et Signis Morb. acut.* l. 2, c. 5; *Cels.* l. 4, c. 11; *Paul. Æginet.* l. 3, c. 39.

CHOLERA, in the modern nomenclature, is a genus of diseases, Class *Nemoses*, Order *Spasmi*.

CHOLE'RICA (*Med.*) medicines which relieve the cholera.

CHOLE'RICUS (*Med.*) χολερικος, choleric; an epithet for one whose constitution abounds with bile.

CHOLIA'MBI (*Poet.*) a sort of Iambic verse, having a spondee in the 6th or last place.

CHOLICE'LA (*Med.*) a swelling on the right side, or rather near the pit of the stomach, from an accumulation of bile in the gall bladder.

CHOLOBA'PHINON (*Med.*) χολοβαφινον, from χολη, bile, and βαπτω, to immerge; a metal resembling gold, which appears as if dipped in gall.

CHOLO'MA (*Med.*) χολωμα, from χολος, lame, maimed; a distortion of a limb, according to Galen, in his Commentary on Hippocrates' περι αρθ, but in a particular sense a halting or lameness of the legs.

CHOLO'SIS (*Med.*) from χωλος, lame; a defect from one leg being shorter than the other.

CHO'MER (*Ant.*) or *Coron*, חומר, a measure containing 75 gallons, 5 pints, and 7 solid inches.

CHONDRI'LLA (*Bot.*) a genus of plants, Class 19 *Syngenesia*, Order 1 *Polygamia Æqualis*.
   Generic Characters. CAL. common cylindric.—COR. common imbricate; *corollets* equal; *proper* monopetalous. —STAM. *filaments* five; *anthers* cylindric.—PIST. *germ* subovate; *style* filiform; *stigmas* two.—PER. none; *calyx* cylindric; *seeds* solitary; *pappus* hairy; *receptacle* naked.
   Species. The species are—*Chondrilla juncea*, Rushy Gum Succory, a perennial, native of Germany.—*Chondrilla crepoides*, an annual, &c.

CHONDRILLA is also the *Apargia tuberosa* of Linnæus.

CHONDRILLÆGENUS (*Bot.*) the *Chicorium spinosum* of Linnæus.

CHO'NDRIS (*Bot.*) Bastard Dittany.

CHONDROGLO'SSUS (*Anat.*) from χονδρος, a cartilage, and γλωσσα, a tongue; a muscle inserted into the basis or cartilaginous part of the tongue.

CHONDROPHARYNGÆ'US (*Anat.*) from χονδρος, a cartilage, and φαρυγξ, the upper part of the fauces; a muscle which rises from the cartilaginous appendage of the os hyoides, and is inserted in the membrane of the fauces.

CHONDROPTERI'GIOUS (*Ich.*) an order of animals, Class *Pisces*, including those genera which have their gills cartilaginous; namely—*Accipenser*, the Sturgeon.—*Chimæra*, the Sea-Monster.—*Squalus*, the Shark; the Dog-Fish.—*Pristis*, the Saw-Fish.—*Raia*, the Ray; Torpedo; Thornback.—*Petromyzon*, the Lamprey.—*Gastrobranchus*, the Hag-Fish, or Glutinous Hag.

CHONDROSYNDE'SIMUS (*Anat.*) χονδροσυνδεσμος, from χονδρος, a cartilage, and συνδεσμος, a ligament; a cartilaginous ligament.

CHO'NE (*Med.*) χωνη, the same as *Choana*.

TO CHOP about (*Mar.*) in French *sauter*, is said of the wind when it varies frequently and suddenly.

CHOP-CHURCH (*Archæol.*) *Ecclesiarium permutatio*, probably a nickname for those who used to change benefices. 9 *Hen*. 6, c. 65.

CHO'PINEL (*Com.*) *Chopine*; a spirit measure at Paris, containing 15½ oz. or 16 oz.

CHO'PPINGS (*Com.*) a sort of Venetian shoes with very high heels.

CHO'RA (*Anat.*) χωρα, from χωρις, a place; is used by Galen for the cavities of the eyes. *De Usu. Part.* l. 8, c. 6.

CHORA'GIUM (*Ant.*) the tiring or dressing room in the theatres, for the players; also their dresses and furniture. *Cic. ad Heren.* l. 2, c. 48; *Vitruv.* l. 5, c. 9; *Fest. de Sig. Verb.*

CHORA'GUS (*Ant.*) a maker and keeper of dresses. *Sueton. in Aug.* c. 70.

CHO'RAL (*Mus.*) or *Choristic*, an epithet for what belongs to the choir, or is performed by a plurality of voices, as a choral anthem, a choral service, &c.

CHORA'ULES (*Ant.*) χοραυλης, a player on the flute. *Sueton. in Ner.* c. 54.

CHORD (*Geom.*) from the Greek χορδη, and the Latin *chorda*; signifies, literally, a string; but is applied in mathematics to the line which joins the extremities of any arc of a circle, such as the lines A B and D C. A line E O drawn from the centre to bisect a chord is perpendicular to it, and if it be perpendicular to the chord, it bisects both the chord and the arc.

CHORD (*Mus.*) signifies, literally, the line or string from which the vibration of the sensation of sound is excited; but it is also applied, in an extended sense, to a union of the sounds of several strings, pipes, or voices. In practical music there are several sorts of chords, namely—*Fundamental chord*, which consists of the three fundamental consonances, i. e. the 3d, 5th, and 8th, of the fundamental bass; or their inversions.—*Accidental chord*, that which is produced either by anticipation or retardation.—*Anomalous* or *equivocal chord*, in which some intervals are greater or less than those of the fundamental chord.—*Transient chord*, in which some intermediate notes are introduced not forming any component parts of the fundamental harmony.

CHORDA (*Anat.*) a term sometimes used for a tendon, as *chorda magnalis*.—*Chorda tympani*, the fifth pair of nerves from the brain.—*Chorda Willisii*, cords which cross the veins in the *dura mater*, so called from their discoverer.

CHORDA'PSUS (*Med.*) χορδαψος, from χορδη, a cord, and απτομαι, to touch; so called from the intestines appearing to be twisted into knots, like pieces of string, in a species of painful colic.

CHORDA'TA GONORRHOEA (*Med.*) a gonorrhoea attended with a painful tension of the penis.

CHORDE'E (*Med.*) or *Corde*, a painful involuntary erection of the penis.

CHORE'A (*Ant.*) a dance in which many take a part.

CHOREA SANCTI VITI (*Med.*) St. Vitus's dance, a convulsive motion of the limbs, which gives the person affected the appearance of dancing. It takes its name from St. Vitus, who is said to have cured sick persons by the force of his persuasions.

CHOREA, in the modern nomenclature, is a genus of diseases, Class *Neuroses*, Order *Spasmi*.

CHORE'GIA (*Med.*) χορηγια, from χορος, a company of dancers and singers, and αγω, to lead; all the apparatus necessary for a physician.

CHOREPI'SCOPUS (*Ecc.*) the same as *Suffragan*.

CHORE'US (*Poet.*) χορειος, a foot in Greek and Latin verse, consisting of two syllables, one short and the other long, the same as the trochee, according to Cicero and Quintilian; but according to others, it consists of three short syllables, like the tribacchus. *Cic. Or. ad Brut.* c. 63; *Quintil.* l. 4, c. 9; *Hæphest. Enchirid.*

CHORIA'MBUS (*Poet.*) χορίαμβος, or *Choriambic*, a foot of four syllables, one long at each end, and two short in the middle, − ◡ ◡ −, as *ēbriĕtās. Hæphest. Enchirid.*

CHORION (*Med.*) χορίον, χορίον: the external membrane of the fœtus.

CHORION (*Mus.*) a hymn sung in honour of Cybele, mother of the gods.

CHORI'STER (*Mus.*) one who officiates vocally in a choir.

CHOROBA'TES (*Ant.*) χοροβάτης, a level with a double square in the form of a T. *Vitruv.* l. 8, c. 6; *Bald. Lex. Vitruv.*

CHOROCITHARI'STA (*Ant.*) one who plays on the lute, or harp, to those who dance. *Sueton. in Domit.* c. 4.

CHORODIDA'SCULUS (*Mus.*) the master of the quire.

CHORO-FAVORI'TO (*Mus.*) an Italian epithet; a chorus in which the best voices and instruments are employed.

CHORO-RECITANTE, the little chorus.

CHORO'GRAPHER (*Geog.*) χωρογραφικος, from χωρος, a country, and γραφω, to describe; one who describes particular countries.

CHORO'GRAPHY (*Geog.*) χωρογραφια, from χωρος and γράφω; that part of geography which treats of the description of particular countries, provinces, &c. *Vitruv.* l. 8, c. 2; *Ptol. de Geog.* l. 1.

CHOROI'DES (*Med.*) χοροειδης, from χορίον, the chorion, and ειδος, likeness; an epithet for several membranes, which, on account of the multitude of their blood-vessels, resemble the chorion.—*Choroides plexus*, a plexus of blood-vessels situated in the lateral ventricles of the brain.

CHORO'METRY (*Geog.*) χωρομετρια, from χωρος, a country, and μετρεω, to measure; the art of measuring or surveying countries.

CHO'RUS (*Mus.*) 1. A kind of double trumpet. 2. A plurality of voices, or an assembly of vocal performers. *Serv. in Virg.*—*Chorus cidularis*, Barleybreak, a kind of dance in which the performers, taking hands, dance round.

CHOSE (*Law*) is used with various epithets, as —*Chose local*, any thing annexed to a place, as a mill, &c.—*Chose transitory*, any thing moveable that may be taken away and carried from place to place.—*Chose in action*, an incorporeal thing, and only a right, as an annuity, &c.

CHO'UAN (*Bot.*) French for a small seed of a yellowish-green colour, which grows on a low exotic plant brought from the Levant.

CHOU-DE-PALMI'STE (*Bot.*) French; the cabbage of the Palm-tree.

CHOUGH (*Orn.*) a bird like a jackdaw, but bigger, which frequents the rocks by the sea-side.

CHOULE (*Orn.*) the crop of a bird.

CHOW'DER (*Med.*) an antiscorbutic used on the New-foundland station.—*Chowder beer*, an infusion of spruce in water, from which beer is prepared in the common way.

CHOYNE (*Bot.*) an American cucurbitiferous plant, with leaves like Bay-leaves, and fruit the size of a moderate Citrul, of which the Indians make drinking-cups. *Raii Hist.*

CHRE'STOS (*Med.*) χρηστος, from χράομαι, to use; useful, good, wholesome, fit. A common epithet. *Hipp.*

CHRISM (*Ecc.*) χρῖσμα, or chrisom; an unction or anointing of children, as soon as they are born, with some aromatic drug.—*Chrisom-cloth*, the linen, or cloth, laid on the head of a child that is newly baptized.

CHRI'SMA (*Ecc.*) χρῖσμα, an unguent, from χρίω, to anoint. 1. Unction applied to sacred ceremonies. 2. A composition of oil and balsam consecrated by a bishop, and used in the ceremonies of baptism, confirmation, &c.

CHRISMA'LE (*Eccl.*) a chrisom cloth laid over the face of a child at baptism.

CHRI'SMATIS *denarii* (*Ecc.*) money paid by the parochial clergy to the diocesan of his suffragan for the chrisom consecrated by them about Easter for the uses of the ensuing year.

CHRI'SMATORY (*Ecc.*) a vessel in which the chrism is kept.

CHRI'STIAN D'OR (*Com.*) a gold coin current in Denmark for 16s. 6d. sterling. On the obverse of this coin is the head, name, and title of the reigning prince; and on the reverse, a sun and three crowns, with the legend as on the ducat current.

CHRISTIA'NA (*Com.*) a silver coin of Sweden, value 7d. sterling.

CHRISTIANA *radix* (*Bot.*) the *Astragalus Christiana* of Linnæus.

CHRISTIANITA'TIS *curia* (*Ecc.*) the spiritual or ecclesiastical Court, in which all ecclesiastical matters are determined.

CHRISTI *manus* (*Med.*) an epithet for depurated sugar boiled with rose-water, and cast into troches.

CHRI'STMAS (*Ecc.*) i. e. *Christi missa*, i. e. the mass of Christ; a festival observed in the Christian church on the 25th of December, in commemoration of our Saviour's nativity.

CHRISTMAS ROSE (*Bot.*) or Black Hellebore, the *Helleborus niger* of Linnæus; so called from the time of its flowering and the colour of its corolla.

CHRI'STOLITES (*Ecc.*) the name of some heretics in the sixth century, who maintained that Christ left both body and soul in Hell, and ascended to Heaven with his divinity only. *Johann. Damas. de Hæres.*; *Sander. de Hæres.*

CHRI'STOS (*Med.*) χριστος; applied by unction. *Castell. Lex. Med.*

CHRIST'S-THORN (*Bot.*) the *Rhamnus paliurus* of Linnæus.

CHRO'MA (*Mus.*) or *chromaticus melos*; a soft kind of music consisting of semitones and minor thirds. It was so called from χρῶμα, color, either because it was marked by various colours, or, as is mostly supposed, because it was, as it were, a colour between white and black. *Aristoxen. apud Meibom. Mus. Ant.*; *Vitruv.* l. 5, c. 4; *Plut. de Mus.*; *Ptol. Harmon.*; *Macrob. in Somn. Scip.* l. 2, c. 4; *Cæl. Rhodig. Lect.* l. 9, c. 3; *Bald. Lex. Vitruv.*; *Martian. Capell.*

CHROMA (*Rhet.*) a figure of speech which consists in speaking fairly, or giving such a colouring to one's speech as at least not to offend the hearer. *Dionys. Art. Rhet.* c. 8, &c.; *Quintil.* l. 4, c. 2; *Hermog. λεξ*; *Apsin. Art. Rhet.*

CHRO'MATE (*Chem.*) a salt formed by the union of earthy, metallic, and alkaline bases with chromic acid, as the *chromate of lead*, the *chromate of iron*, &c. which is the *Chromium* of Linnæus. [vide *Chemistry*]

CHROMA'TIC (*Mus.*) the modern name for the chroma of the ancients, [vide *Chroma*] it serves at present to distinguish the parts of melody by successive semitonic intervals.

CHROMA'TICS (*Opt.*) that part of optics which explains the several properties of the colours of light and of natural bodies. [vide *Optics*]

CHROMATI'SMUS (*Paint.*) a natural or artificial way of communicating colour.

CHRO'MBUS (*Ich.*) a kind of fish mentioned by Pliny. *Nat. Hist.* l. 32, c. 11.

CHROME (*Med.*) vide *Chromium*.

CHRO'MIC *acid* (*Chem.*) a sort of acid, of an orange red colour, which is obtained by decomposing the chromate of lead by potash, and treating the chromate of potash with nitric or muriatic acid.

CHRO'MIS (*Ich.*) a species of *sparus*, a fish, which is said by Pliny to make its nest in the water. *Plin.* l. 32, c. 11.

CHRONOLOGY.

CHRO′MIUM (*Min.*) *Chrome*, a sort of *white* mineral, drawn from an ore called the *red lead* of Siberia, which is used as a paint, and derives its name from χρῶμα, colour, because of its property to communicate colour. Its specific gravity is about 5·90; and it contains oxide of lead and iron, and chromic acid in different proportions.

CHRO′NICA (*Lit.*) Chronicles or books, containing an account of events which pass within certain times.

CHRO′NIC (*Med.*) or *Chronical*, a term applied to diseases which are of long duration, but mostly without fever, in distinction from those which are *acute*.

CHRO′NICUS (*Ant.*) a chronicler or writer of chronicles.

CHRO′NOGRAM (*Gram.*) a sort of verse, in which the figurative letters being joined together, make up the year of our Lord, or any other date.

CHRONOLO′GICAL (*Chron.*) an epithet for what belongs to the computations of time, as *chronological characters*, &c. [vide *Chronology*]

CHRONO′LOGY, from the Greek χρόνος, time, and λόγος, the doctrine, is the science which teaches the measure and division of times. It is either theoretical or practical. *Theoretical chronology* is chronology, properly so called, which is the subject of the present article.—*Practical chronology* is the application of this science to history, which will be considered under the head of history. [vide *History*]

Theory of Chronology.

Chronology treats, in the first place, of the nature and divisions of time; and, in the second place, of the characters by which they are distinguished.

Nature and Divisions of Time.

Time is that part of duration which is measured by the motions, or other phenomena of material objects, particularly by that of the heavenly bodies. It is either proleptic or historic. *Proleptic time* is that which is feigned to have preceded the creation, as the Julian Period, &c.—*Historic time* is that which is reckoned from the Mosaic account of the creation. The principal parts of time are the hour, day, week, month, and year.

Hours. An hour is a part of the day, mostly the twenty-fourth, and often the twelfth. It is either equal or unequal. *Equal hours* are the twenty-fourth parts of the civil day, which are so called because they are always of the same length, being neither greater or less. They are sometimes called *equinoctial*, because they divide the equator into twenty-four equal parts. The *unequal hour* is a twelfth part of the day, as distinguished from the night, which increases or decreases, together with the natural day. There are also *astronomical* hours, which are equal hours, numbered from noon, in a continued series of twenty-four. The hour is now sub-divided into *minutes*, *seconds*, and *thirds*; but formerly it was sub-divided into *scruples*, each of which was the one thousand and eightieth part of an hour. They were called *Chaldæan*, because they were used by the Chaldæans.

Day. The day is a natural division of time, which is deduced from the apparent revolution of the sun. It is distinguished into natural, artificial, and astronomical. —The *natural day* is the space of time which intervenes between sunset and sunrise, and is distinguished from the night.—The *civil day* is that space of time in which the sun performs a complete revolution; or that space of time in which the sun goes round from any given point to the same point again. This kind of day was called by the Greeks νυχθήμερον; by Sacro de Bosco, *artificial*. —The *astronomical day* is that space of time which is reckoned from noon to noon.

Beginning of the day. The civil day differed in different countries in respect to the point from which it was computed; being reckoned from sunset to sunset by the Jews, Greeks, and Arabians; from sunrise to sunrise by the Babylonians and modern Greeks; from noon to noon by astronomers; from midnight to midnight by the Egyptians, Romans, and the modern Europeans.

Divisions of the day. The division of the day has also varied in different countries. The ancient Hebrews divided the natural day into four proportions; namely, morning, high-day or noon, first evening, and last evening. The division of the night was into three parts, called *watches*; namely, night, midnight, and morning watches. The Romans, and after them the Jews, distinguished the day into four principal parts, which they called vigils or watches. The first began at sunrise, or six in the morning; the second at nine; the third at twelve; and the fourth at three in the afternoon. The night was in like manner divided into distinct portions, called *quarters*, the first of which began at six in the evening, the second at nine, &c. The Greeks, Romans, and Jews likewise divided the natural day into the twelve smaller portions, now known by the name of *hours*, which differed in length at the different seasons of the year, though still equal to each other. They were distinguished into first, second, &c. The first hour, especially at the equinoxes, answered to our seven, the second to our eight, the third to our nine, &c. till we come to twelve, which answered to our six in the evening, and concluded their day. The Jews had their hours of prayer distinguished by the names of the *third hour of prayer*, the *sixth hour of prayer*, &c. Each of these stated times contained the space of three hours; and each space was called by the name of that hour on which it began: thus the *third hour of prayer* was that which began at nine; the *sixth hour* that which began at twelve, &c. The civil day was divided by the Greeks, Romans, and Jews into four quarters, corresponding to the morning, noon, afternoon, and midnight, which are now in use. The first quarter with them contained the interval between sunset and midnight; the second, that between midnight and sunrise; the third, that between morning and noon; and the fourth, between noon and midnight. The Chinese and other oriental nations differ in some particulars from this division of the day and night.

Week. A week, called in the Greek ἑβδομας, and in Latin *Hebdomas*, or *septimana*, is a system of seven days that owes its origin to the creation of the world, which, according to the sacred historian, was performed within that space of time. The use of this division was borrowed from the Hebrews by the Egyptians, and from them transmitted to other nations generally; but the Persians, and some other Eastern nations, are said to be ignorant of this division of time; the Greeks had a division of ten days instead of seven; and the Romans appear to have had weeks of eight days. Among the Jews there were also weeks of years as well of days, as we learn from the sacred writings. The days of the week were formerly distinguished by the numbers first, second, third, &c. but afterwards they were named after the planets, as follow:—*Dies Solis*, the Sunday, or day of the Sun.—*Dies Lunæ*, Monday, or the day of the moon. —*Dies Martis*, Tuesday, or the day of Tun, the Mars of the Teutones.—*Dies Mercurii*, Wednesday, or the day of Woden, the Mercury of the Teutones.—*Dies Jovis*, Thursday, or the day of Thor, the Jupiter of the Teutones.—*Dies Veneris*, Friday, or the day of Friga, the Venus of the Teutones.—*Dies Saturni*, Saturday, or the day of Saturn. One day of the seven

CHRONOLOGY.

has always been held sacred among all nations. Among the Jews the seventh day, or Saturday, was set apart for the commemoration of the creation, which, on that account, was called a *Sabbath*, or day of rest from labour. Among the Christians the first day has been substituted in its place, to commemorate the resurrection of our Lord ; whence it has been denominated the Lord's Day.

Month. The month is a system of days, which is regulated by the motion of the moon ; it being properly the time in which the moon runs through the zodiac. The month is astronomical or civil.

Astronomical month. The astronomical or natural month is that which is measured by the motions of the heavenly bodies within any given period. The astronomical month is, therefore, distinguished into lunar or solar.

Lunar month. The lunar month is either periodical, synodical, or illuminative.—The *lunar periodical month* is that space of time in which the moon goes from one point of the zodiac to the same again. This is about $27^d\ 7^h\ 43''\ 8'''$.—The *lunar synodical month*, also called a *lunation*, is the time between two conjunctions of the moon with the sun, or between two new moons; the quantity of which is $29^d\ 12^h\ 44^m\ 3''\ 1'''$.—The *illuminative month* is the interval between the first appearance of one new moon and that of the next which follows. As the moon appears sooner after one change than after another ; the quantity of the illuminative month is not always the same. The Turks and Arabs reckon by this month, beginning from the first phasis.

Solar month. The solar month is the time in which the sun runs through one entire sign of the zodiac ; the mean quantity of which is $30^d\ 10^h\ 29^m\ 5^{sec}$, being the twelfth part of $365^d\ 5^h\ 49^m$.

Civil month. The civil month is any system of days which is specified and established by the laws of society, or of any particular nation. This is either lunar or solar. The *civil lunar month* consists of 29 and 30 days alternately ; the *civil solar month*, of 30 or 31 days, according to the use of which the form of the year was varied in different countries.

Jewish and Greek month. The division of the month among the Jews was into weeks, as is now in use ; the Greeks divided their months into three decades or parts, consisting of ten days, called δεκήμεροι; the first was called μηνὸς ἀρχομένου, or ἱσαμένου, i. e. the decade of the beginning of the month; the second, μηνὸς μεσοῦντος, i. e. the decade of the middle of the month ; the third was μηνὸς φθίνοντος, παυομένου, or λήγοντος, i. e. the decade of the end of the month. The first day of the first decade was termed νουμηνία, because the month began with the new moon ; the second, δευτέρα ἱσαμένου; the third, τρίτη ἱσαμένου, &c. : the first day of the second decade was πρώτη μεσοῦντος, or πρώτη ἐπὶ δέκα; the second, δευτέρα μεσοῦντος, or δευτέρα ἐπὶ δέκα, &c. : the first day of the third decade was δεκάτη φθίνοντος; the second, φθίνοντος ἐνάτη, φθίνοντος ὀγδόη, and so on in a reverse order until the last, which was called ἕνη καὶ νέα, i. e. old and new, because one part of that day belonged to the old, and the other to the new month ; this day was otherwise called δημοτρίας and τριακάς.

Roman month. The Roman months were divided into calends, nones, and ides, all of which were reckoned backward. The *calends* were the first day of the month; the nones fell on the seventh ; and the ides on the fifteenth of March, May, July, and October ; but, in all other months, the nones were on the fifth, and the ides on the thirteenth. [vide *Kalendarium*]

Year. The year is a system of months adjusted to the movements of the sun or moon. It is distinguished, as respects its commencement, into *fixed*, if its commencement be fixed to any given point of time ; but *erratic*, if it begin at different times ; and is moreover distinguished into astronomical and civil.

Astronomical year. The astronomical year is that which is determined by astronomical observation, and is either solar or lunar.—The *solar year* is that space of time in which the sun passes through the signs of the zodiac ; this is divided into the tropical or natural, and the sidereal or astral, year. The *tropical year* is that space of time in which the sun goes from any cardinal point and returns to the same again. This, which is the true solar or natural year, contains $365^d\ 5^h\ 48^m\ 48^{sec}$. The *sidereal year* is the space of time the sun takes in passing from any fixed star till his return to it again. This consists of $365^d\ 6^h\ 9^m\ 17^{sec}$, being $20^m\ 29^{sec}$ longer than the true solar year.—The *lunar year* is the space of 12 lunar months, which may be either periodical or synodical.

Civil year. The civil year is that which has been adopted for civil purposes, and which, by setting aside the odd hours and minutes, is supposed to consist of an even number of days ; hence the distinction of the solar year into *common*, consisting of 365 days, and *bissextile* or leap-year, which consists of 366 days, by the addition of a day every fourth year. The *civil lunar year* is also *common*, which consists of 12 months, and *embolismic* or *intercalary*, which consists of 13 months.

Forms of the civil year. The forms of the civil year have been very different in different countries. The most important of these forms are as follow ; namely—

Roman year. The year of the ancient Romans was lunar, and consisted of 10 months, according to the institution of Romulus, in the following order:

Months.	Days.	Months.	Days.
Martius	31	Sextilis	30
Aprilis	30	September	30
Maius	31	October	31
Junius	30	November	30
Quintilis	31	December	30

By the reformation of Numa Pompilius, two months were added to the year, which consisted of the following months and days :

Months.	Days.	Months.	Days.
Januarius	29	Quintilis	31
Februarius	28	Sextilis	29
Martius	31	September	29
Aprilis	29	October	31
Maius	31	November	29
Junius	29	December	29

making in the whole 355 days, which exceeded the civil lunar year by one whole day, and the natural lunar year by $15^h\ 11'\ 21''\ 48'''$. This year has undergone a still further reformation by Julius Cæsar, and in later times by pope Gregory XIII. which has given rise to the Julian and Gregorian years.

Julian year. The Julian year is a solar year, consisting of 365 days if it be the common year, and 366 if it be bissextile or leap year. The order of the months and number of days in each month are as follow :

Old Roman Months.	Julian Months.	Modern Months.	Days.
Januarius	Januarius	January	31
Februarius	Februarius	February	28
Martius	Martius	March	31
Aprilis	Aprilis	April	30
Maius	Maius	May	31
Junius	Junius	June	30
Quintilis	Julius	July	31
Sextilis	Augustus	August	31

CHRONOLOGY.

Old Roman Months.	Julian Months.	Modern Months.	Days.
September	September	September	30
October	October	October	31
November	November	November	30
December	December	December	31

In the bissextile or leap year, which happens every fourth year, an intercalary day is added to the month of February, making it 29 instead of 28. Julius Cæsar reformed the Roman calendar by the help of Sosigenes, a celebrated mathematician from Egypt, B. C. 45; and, in order to correct the errors that had crept into the computations of the Roman year, and to bring forward the months and festivals to their proper places, he first formed a year of 15 months, or 445 days, which, for its irregularity, has usually been styled the *year of confusion*. Thirty-six years after the introduction of the Julian year, it was found that errors had arisen from intercalating every third year instead of every fourth, as directed by Julius Cæsar; in consequence of which Augustus ordained, that the intercalations should be omitted in the 41st, 45th, and 49th of the Julian æra. This form of the year, which for its simplicity has been universally adopted, is, notwithstanding, imperfect; as the true solar year consists of $365^d\ 5^h\ 48^m\ 45''\ 30'''$; it follows that 131 years after the Julian correction, the sun must have arrived one day too soon at the equinoctial points. The following Table shows the number of days, &c. in the Julian, solar, and sidereal years, from 1 to 10,000.

	Solar					Julian	
Years.	Days.	H.	M.	S.	Th.	Days.	H.
1	365	5	48	45	30	365	6
2	730	11	37	31	0	730	12
3	1,095	17	26	16	30	1,095	18
4	1,460	23	15	2		1,461	
5	1,826	5	3	47	30	1,826	6
6	2,191	10	52	33	0	2,191	12
7	2,556	16	41	18	30	2,556	18
8	2,921	22	30	4		2,922	
9	3,287	4	18	49	30	3,287	6
10	3,652	10	7	35		3,652	12
20	7,304	20	15	10		7,305	
30	10,957	6	22	45		10,957	12
40	14,609	16	30	20		14,610	
50	18,262	2	37	55		18,262	12
60	21,914	12	45	30		21,915	
70	25,566	22	53	5		25,567	12
80	29,219	9	0	40		29,220	
90	32,871	19	8	15		32,872	12
100	36,524	5	15	50		36,525	
200	73,048	10	31	40		73,050	
300	109,572	15	47	30		109,575	
400	146,096	21	3	20		146,009	
500	182,621	2	19	10		182,625	
600	219,145	7	35	0		219,150	
700	255,669	12	50	50		255,675	
800	292,193	18	6	40		292,200	
900	328,717	23	22	30		328,725	
1,000	365,242	4	38	20		365,250	
2,000	730,484	9	16	40		730,500	
3,000	1,095,726	13	55	0		1,095,750	
4,000	1,460,968	18	33	20		1,461,000	
5,000	1,826,210	23	11	40		1,826,250	
6,000	2,191,453	3	50	0		2,191,500	
7,000	2,556,695	8	28	20		2,556,750	
8,000	2,921,937	13	6	40		2,922,000	
9,000	3,287,179	17	45	0		3,287,250	
10,000	3,652,421	22	23	20		3,652,500	

Gregorian year. The Gregorian year is the Julian year corrected, so as to prevent the seasons from receding for the future. To this end pope Gregory XIII. with the assistance of the most celebrated mathematicians of of his time, ordained, in 1582, that an intercalation of one day in February should be made every fourth year: and that the 1600th year of the Christian æra, and every fourth century thereafter, should be a bissextile or leap year. One day, consequently, is to be intercalated in the years 2000, 2400, 2800, &c.; but in the intervening centuries, 1700, 1800, 1900, 2100, &c. it is to be suppressed, and they are to be reckoned as common years. Moreover, as the equinoxes had fallen back ten days and the full moons four days, since the Nicene council, A. D. 325, he ordained, that 10 days should be cut off after the 4th of October, so that the 5th should be the 15th. This mode of computation, which was distinguished by the name of the *Gregorian or new style*, was gradually introduced into all the countries of Europe, except Russia. It is, however, still not perfectly correct; for as the excess of the Julian year, within the space of four centuries, is $3^d\ 1^h\ 20'$, that of the Gregorian is 1^h and $20'$ within the same period, or about a day in 7200 years. In order to find whether a Julian or a Gregorian year will be bissextile, let the given year be divided by 4, and if nothing remains it is bissextile; but if there be any remainder, the number shews the year since the last bissextile: thus, suppose the year 1822 be divided by 4, it leaves 2, i. e. the second year from the bissextile.

Jewish year. The ancient year of the Jews was solar, and consisted of twelve months of thirty days each; but on their departure from Egypt they adopted the lunar month, consisting of twenty-nine days and thirty alternately; in order to make it agree with the solar year, they sometimes added eleven or twelve days at the end of the year; and sometimes a whole month, which was called an *embolismic month*, whence the year in which this addition took place was called embolismic. The Jewish year was likewise divided into the civil and ecclesiastical, the former of which began at the autumnal equinox, and the latter at the vernal equinox. The following is the order of the months in these two kinds of years.

Ecclesiastical year.				Civil year.		
	Jew. M.	Rom. M.	D.	Jew. M.	Rom. M.	D.
1.	Nisan	March	30	Tisri	Sept.	30
2.	Jiar	April	29	Marchesvan	October	29
3.	Sivan	May	30	Casleu	Nov.	30
4.	Thammug	June	29	Thebet	Dec.	29
5.	Ab	July	30	Sebat	January	30
6.	Elul	August	29	Adar	February	29
7.	Tisri	Sept.	30	Nisan	March	30
8.	Marchesvan	October	29	Jiar	April	29
9.	Casleu	Nov.	30	Sivan	May	30
10.	Thebet	Dec.	29	Thammug	June	29
11.	Sebat	January	30	Ab	July	30
12.	Adar	February	29	Elul	August	29

Veadar the embolismic month.

The civil year is distinguished into the common, the abundant, and the deficient.—*The common year* consists of 354 days.—*The abundant year* is that in which the month *Marchesvan* is thirty days instead of twenty-nine, making the common year 355, and the intercalary 385 days.—*The deficient year* is that in which the month *Casleu* is twenty-nine instead of thirty, making the common year 353, and the intercalary 383.

Egyptian year. The Egyptian year, otherwise called the year of Nabonassar, because it is dated from the æra of

CHRONOLOGY.

Nabonassar, the first King of Babylon, is a solar year, consisting of twelve months, having thirty days each, and five days ἐπαγόμεναι, i. e. intercalary, or six in bissextile, making in the whole 365 or 366 days. As this year, by neglecting six hours, loses a day in every four years of the Roman year, its beginning runs through every part of that year in the space of 1460; whence it is denominated an erratic year. Ptolemy and the astronomers of his day used this form of the year in their calculations, for which reason it is of importance in comparing the observations of the ancients, with those of the moderns. The following tables exhibit the names and order of the months; and also a comparison between the Julian and Nabonassarean years.

Months and Days in the Egyptian Year.

Egyptian Months.		Julian Months.	No. of Days.
Θωθ	Thoth	August	30
Παωφὶ	Paophi	September	60
Ἀθυρ	Athyr	October	90
Χοιακ	Choeac	November	120
Τυβὶ	Tybi	December	150
Μιχὶρ	Mechir	January	180
Φαμενωθ	Phamenoth	February	210
Φαρμουθὶ	Pharmuthi	March	240
Παχὼν	Pachon	April	270
Παυνὶ	Pauni	May	300
Επιφὶ	Epiphi	June	330
Μισορὶ	Misori	July	360
		Pagin	
Ἐπαγόμεναι	intercalares	Epiphi	
πρώτη	prima	Mesophi	361
δευτέρα	secunda		362
τρίτη	tertia		363
τέταρτη	quarta		364
πέμπτη	quinta		365
ἕκτη	sexta		366 *bissex.*

Nabonassarean and Julian years compared.

Nab. Years.	Julian Years before Christ.	Nab. Years.	Julian Years before Christ.
1	26 Feb. 747	27	20 Feb. 721
2	26 746	28	19 720
3	26 745	29	19 719
4	25 744	30	19 718
5	25 743	31	19 717
6	25 742	32	18 716
7	25 741	33	18 715
8	24 740	34	18 714
9	24 739	35	18 713
10	24 738	36	17 712
11	24 737	37	17 711
12	23 736	38	17 710
13	23 735	39	17 709
14	23 734	40	16 708
15	23 733	41	16 707
16	22 732	42	16 706
17	22 731	43	16 705
18	22 730	44	15 704
19	22 729	45	15 703
20	21 728	46	15 702
21	21 727	47	15 701
22	21 726	48	14 700
23	21 725	49	14 699
24	20 724	50	14 698
25	20 723	51	14 697
26	20 722	52	13 696
53	13 Feb. 695	82	6 Feb. 666
54	13 694	83	6 665
55	13 693	84	5 664
56	12 692	85	5 663
57	12 691	86	5 662
58	12 690	87	5 661
59	12 689	88	4 660
60	11 688	89	4 659
61	11 687	90	4 658
62	11 686	91	4 657
63	11 685	92	3 656
64	10 684	93	3 655
65	10 683	94	3 654
66	10 682	95	3 653
67	10 681	96	2 652
68	9 680	97	2 651
69	9 679	98	2 650
70	9 678	99	2 649
71	9 677	100	1 648
72	8 676	200	7 Jan. 548
73	8 675	300	13 Dec. 448
74	8 674	400	18 Nov. 348
75	8 673	500	24 Oct. 248
76	7 672	600	29 Sept. 148
77	7 671	700	4 Sept. 48
78	7 670		A. D.
79	7 669	800	10 Aug. 52
80	6 668	888	19 July 140
81	6 667		

The foregoing table may be illustrated by a question. *Quest.* In what month, and in what day of the month, does the 230th Nabonassarean year begin?—*Ans.* Opposite to the Nabonassarean year, 200, is January 7, which was the day of the Thoth, or beginning of that year, and opposite to 30 is Feb. 19; then the difference between 19 and 26 being found to be 7, i. e. 7 days from Jan. 7, it is evident that the Thoth of 230 fell on December 31. The Thoth being found, it is easy to find the corresponding day of any other month. Thus, suppose it be asked with what day in the Julian year does Chœac 17, in the Nabonassarean year, 48, correspond; the answer is, that the Thoth of that year falls on Oct. 28, B. C. 262; and the 17th day of Chœac is 107 days from Thoth; but the sum of the days from the 4th Oct. to 31st Jan., being only 96, there is a difference of 11 days between 107 and 96, consequently the 11th Feb. B. C. 261, answers to the Chœac 17 of the Nabonassarean year 486.

On the conquest of Egypt by the Romans, the Egyptians adopted the Julian years, but retained the names of their months, after which this was denominated the *Actian year.* The beginning of this year, or the first day of the month, Thoth, answered to the 29th of August.

Ethiopian, Coptic, and Armenian year. The Ethiopian, Coptic, and Armenian years are the same as the Egyptian, except in the name of the months, which are as follow:

Ethiopian M.	Coptic.	Armenian.	Roman.
Mascaram	Tot or Tut	Navasardi	August
Ticmit	Baba or Bena	Huerri	September
Hader	Accur or Hatur	Sahmi	October
Tachsam	Chishac	Die	November
Thir	Tona or Tush	Khaguets	December
Jacathit	Anisheir	Arats	January
Magabit	Barmehat	Michieki	February
Miazia	Barmoudah	Arieki	March
Ginboth	Bashansh	Anki	April

CHRONOLOGY.

Ethiopian, M.	Coptic.	Armenian.	Roman.
Lene	Boua or Baune	Marieri	May
Hamlt	Abib or Abii	Maryats	June
Nahase	Massari	Huetits	July

The intercalation was made in the Egyptian, Coptic, and Ethiopic or Abyssinian years, on the 24th of August in common, and on the 25th in bissextile years. The Armenians added five days to the 5th or 6th of August. The beginning of these years was fixed to the 29th of August.

Syrian year. The Syrian was a solar year, which had a fixed beginning on the beginning of October in the Julian year. The months and days of this year are as follow:

Syrian M.	D.	Rom. M.	Syrian M.	D.	Rom. M.
Tisri I.	31	October	Nisan	30	April
Tisri II.	30	November	Icar	31	May
Canun I.	31	December	Haziran	30	June
Canun II.	31	January	Tamus	31	July
Sabat	28	February	Ab	31	August
Adar	31	March	Elul	30	September

Persian year. The Persian year is a solar year, consisting of 12 months, of 30 days each, with five intercalary days, called Museraca, which were added to the month *Aben.* The following are the names and order of the months to which the *Meh* is added, signifying month.

Pers. M.	Rom. M.	Pers. M.	Rom. M.
Afruden meh	September	Mehar meh	March
Ardchascht meh	October	Aben meh	April
Cardi meh	November	Adar meh	May
Thir meh	December	Di meh	June
Merded meh	January	Behen meh	July
Schaharir meh	February	Affirar meh	August

This year, which is erratic, like the Egyptian Nabonassarean, is also called the Yesdegerdic year, to distinguish it from the fixed solar year, called the Gelalean year, which the Persians began to use in 1079, and which was formed by an intercalation made six or seven times in four years, and then every fifth year. The Gelalean year keeps the solstices and equinoxes to the same day, and is adjusted with considerable accuracy to the motions of the sun, it being in fact a tropical year, which consists of 365 d. 4 h. 49' 15" 0"' 48"". The vernal equinox is fixed to the 14th of March in this year.

Grecian year. The Grecian year is Attic, Macedonian, Syro-Macedonian, Paphian, and Bithynian.

Attic year. The Attic year was a fixed lunar year, which was either common or embolismic.—*The Common Attic year* consists of 12 months of 30 and 29 days alternately, making in all 354. The months of 30 days were called πληρεις, full, and also δικαφθινοι, as ending upon the tenth day; they always preceded those of 29 days, which were called κοιλοι, hollow; and from their concluding on the ninth day, ναφθινοι. The following is the order and names of the months in the Attic year:

Attic Months.	Days.	Roman Months.
Εκατομβαιων	30	June and July
Μεταγειτνιων	59	July and August
Βοηδρομιων	88	August and September
Μαιμακτηριων	118	September and October
Πυανεψιων	147	October and November
Ποσιδηων	177	November and December
Γαμηλιων	206	December and January
Ανθεσηριων	236	January and February
Ελαφηβολιων	265	February and March
Μυνυχιων	295	March and April
Θαργηλιων	324	April and May
Σκιρροφοριων	354	May and June

Before the time of Solon the year consisted of 12 months, of 30 days each.—*The embolismic Attic year* consisted of 13 months, which was formed by the repetition of the month Posideon. These years fell on the 3d, 5th, 8th, 11th, 14th, 16th, and 19th of a cycle of 19 years.

The beginning of the Attic month is computed from that new moon, the full moon of which immediately followed the summer solstice. The ancient Greeks supposed that the summer solstice fell on the 8th of July, but it was afterwards brought back to the 27th of June.

Macedonian year. The Macedonian year was either lunar or solar. The lunar was the same in form as the Attic year, and the solar year as the Julian year.

These two kinds of years agreed with each other in the names of their months, but differed in their order. The first month, Διος, of the lunar Macedonian year answered to the Maimacterion of the Attic year, and its commencement was dated from the autumnal equinox. The names and order of the months are as follow:

Mac. Months.	Attic Months.	Roman Months.
Διος	Maimacterion	September & October
Απελλαιος	Pyanepsion	October & November
Αυδναιος	Posideon	November & December
Περιτιος	Gamelion	December & January
Δυστρος	Anthesterion	January & February
Ξανθικος	Elapheboliou	February & March
Αρτεμισιος	Munychion	March & April
Δαισιος	Thargelion	April & May
Πανημος	Scirrhophorion	May & June
Λωος	Hecatombœon	June & July
Γορπιαιος	Metageitnion	July & August
Υπερβερεταιος	Boedromion	August & September

Macedonian Solar Months.	Roman Months.
Αυδναιος	January
Περιτιος	February
Δυστρος	March
Ξανθικος	April
Αρτεμισιος	May
Δαισιος	June
Πανημος	July
Λωος	August
Γορπιαιος	September
Υπερβερεταιος	October
Διος	November
Απελλαιος	December

Syro-Macedonian year, &c. The Syro-Macedonian, Paphian, and Bythinian years differed from the Macedonian solar year only in the names of the months, which are given in the following table, together with the time of their commencement in the Julian year.

Syro-Mac. Months.	Paphian Months.	Byth. Months.	Time of commencement.
Υπερβερεταιος	Αφροδισιος	Ἡριος	Sept. 24.
Διος	Αφογονικος	Ἡρμιος	Oct. 24.
Απελλαιος	Αινιος	Μητρῷος	Nov. 23.
Αυδναιος	Ιυλος	Διωνυσιος	Dec. 24.
Περιτιος	Κισαριος	Ἡρακλειος	Jan. 23.
Δυστρος	Σιβαστος	Διος	Febr. 22.
Ξανθικος	Αυτοκρατορικος	Βενδιδαιος	Mar. 25.
Αρτεμισιος	Δημιαρχεξεσιος	Στρατγιος	April 25.
Δαισιος	Πλυθυπατος	Αριος	May 25.
Πανημος	Αρχιεριος	Περιτιος	June 25.
Λωος	Εστιος	Αφροδισιος	July 25.
Γορπιαιος	Ρωμαιος	Διμητριος	Aug. 25.

Arabian year. The civil year of the Arabians and Turks is lunar, and consists of 12 lunar months of alternately 30 and 29 days, i. e. 354 d. 8 h. 48'. Their civil year

CHRONOLOGY.

consists of 354 days for the common, and 355 for the intercalary, when a day is added to the end of the year. Hence the Arabian year is erratic, and its beginning passes through every day of the Julian year during a period of 30 years, when it returns to the same day. In this period there are 19 common and 11 intercalary years; namely, the 2d, 5th, 7th, 10th, 13th, 15th, 18th, 21st, 24th, 26th, 29th. These eleven days are formed by multiplying $8^h 48'$, the difference between the lunar and the civil years, by 30 the length of the period, at the conclusion of which the lunar and civil years of the Arabians are made to agree.

The following table exhibits the names and order of the months in the Arabian and Turkish year, together with the days in the Julian year, to which they answered in the first year of the *Hegira*, and the *feriæ* or days on which they commence.

Arabic Months.	Turkish Months.	Days. Single.	Days. Collected.	Julian Months.	Feriæ.
1. Muharram	Muharram	30	30	Jul. 16	6
2. Suphar	Sefer	29	59	Aug. 15	1
3. Rabie I.	Rabiul-euuel	30	89	Sept. 13	2
4. Rabie II.	Rabiul-achir	29	118	Oct. 13	4
5. Giumadi I.	Gimaasileuuel	30	148	Nov. 11	5
6. Giumadi II.	Gimaasilachir	29	177	Dec. 11	7
7. Regiab	Regeb	30	207	Jan. 9	1
8. Sahaben	Sahaaban	29	236	Feb. 8	3
9. Ramadhan	Ramazan	30	266	Mar. 9	4
10. Schevval	Schevrail	29	295	Ap. 8	6
11. Dulkaiadath	Zilkaade	30	325	May 7	7
12. Dulkagiadath	Zilkigge	29	354	Jun. 5	1
Intercalary	Intercalary	30	355		

These months are composed of weeks, each day of which begins in the evening after sun-set. Our Sunday is the first *feria*, and Saturday the seventh of the Arabic week.

Chronological Characters.

Chronological characters are the marks by which different portions or periods of time are distinguished from each other. These are either natural, artificial, or historical.—*Natural characters* are such as depend on the motions of the celestial bodies, such as eclipses, or the equinoxes, solstices, &c.—*Artificial characters* are such as have been framed for the civil purposes of human life, which are denominated cycles, or periods.—*Historical characters* are any historical facts, or circumstances resting on historical testimony, from which chronological computations may be made. These are denominated æras or epochas.

Cycles and periods. A cycle is a series of years which, being numbered in an orderly manner from first to last, return to the same point of reckoning from which they commenced. The period differs from the cycle only by comprehending a larger space of time, or a greater number of years. The principal cycles or periods invented by the ancients are as follow:—*The cycle of Cleostratus*, or the cycle framed by him 532 years before Christ, and consisting of eight years, or 2922 days, during the course of which, 96 lunations would elapse of 29 and 30 days alternately, together with three intercalary months. By this cycle he proposed to adjust the lunar year to the solar, so that at the conclusion of each cycle the moon should be renewed; but it failed in its object, for at the end of 16 years there was found to be an error of three days, which in the space of 160 years would amount to more than a whole month.—*The Metonic cycle*, a cycle so called from Meton, by whom it was invented at the commencement of the Peloponnesian war, consisted of 19 solar years, which were nearly equal to 19 lunar years, at the end of which the sun and moon are in the same quarter of the heavens. This cycle, though more accurate than the preceding, is still erroneous, and fails to the amount of eight or ten hours at the end of one period, and of three days in 133 years. It was, however, held in such high esteem by the Grecian states, that they gave it the name of the *golden number*, which is now transferred to the number of each year throughout the lunar cycle.—*The cycle of Eudoxus* was intended, according to Scaliger, to correct that of Cleostratus, by subtracting a month of 30 days from a period of 160 years, which was supposed to be equal to the difference that would subsist at the expiration of that period between the lunar and solar motions.—*The Calippic period* was a period contrived by Calippus at the new moon of the summer, B. C. 331, and was intended as an improvement on the cycle of Meton, which it multiplied by 4, so as to make a period of 76 years, or 27,759 days. As 940 lunations are equal to $97,758^d$ $9^h 5' 9'''$, which is only $40' 29'' 57'''$ less than 76 solar tropical years, it follows that the lunar motion, according to this calculation, did not vary more than $14^h 13' 22''$, wherefore this period has been chosen to form the basis of the more modern cycle of the moon.—*The cycle of Hipparchus* is a series or cycle of 304 years, obtained by the multiplication of the Calippic period by 4, at the end of which he rejected a whole day, with the view of restoring the new and full moons to the same day of the solar. But he did not succeed completely in his object, for as the quantity of this period is equal to $111,033^d 16^h 16'$, and 3760 lunations, at $29^d 12^h 44' 3'' 11'''$ each, are equal to $111,035^d 0^h 39' 29'' 20'''$, it follows that the new and full moons are anticipated at the expiration of this period by $1^d 8^h 23' 29'' 20'''$, and consequently not brought to the same day of the solar year. The cycles and periods which have been subsequently invented are as follow; namely—*The solar cycle*, a series of 28 years, at the completion of which the same order of bissextiles and dominical letters return. The *dominical*, or *Sunday letter*, is that letter which marks the Sunday throughout the year; for as the first seven letters of the alphabet have been chosen to distinguish the seven days of the week, it follows that whichever of these letters stands opposite to the first Sunday in the year, the same letter will of course fall throughout the whole year. But the Sunday letter is changed once every common year, and twice in every leap year; the reason for which is, that the common year does not consist of an exact number of weeks, but of 52 weeks and one day; so that if it begin with A set before New-year's day, it ends with A set before the last day; and the year beginning again at A, there will then be two A's falling together, namely, on Dec. 31, and Jan. 1: and if the former of them happen to be Sunday, the other in course must stand for Monday; and then reckoning onward, Sunday must fall upon G, and consequently G will be the dominical letter for the ensuing year. Thus the odd day shifts back the dominical letter every year by one letter; and this revolution would be completed in seven years, were there not the intervention of bissextile, or leap-year, when the dominical letter is again shifted by the addition of another day in February. In order, therefore, to come at a clear account of these changes, the cycle called the *cycle of the sun* was contrived, which should comprehend all the variations of the Sunday letter. By whom this cycle was invented is not known, but it came into use in the early ages of Christianity, to supply the place of the Roman

CHRONOLOGY.

Nundinæ, and it dated its commencement 9 years before the Christian æra. The following table exhibits the changes of the dominical letter for one solar cycle in Julian years, beginning with a leap-year.

1.	G F	5.	B A	9.	D C	13.	F E	17.	A G	21.	C B	25.	E D
2.	E	6.	G	10.	B	14.	D	18.	F	22.	A	26.	C
3.	D	7.	F	11.	A	15.	C	19.	E	23.	G	27.	B
4.	C	8.	E	12.	G	16.	B	20.	D	24.	F	28.	A

In order to find the solar cycle and the dominical letter for any given year of the Christian Æra add 9, the date of its commencement before the birth of our Saviour to the given year, and divide the sum by 28, the remainder is the solar cycle; and if there be no remainder, then 28 is the cycle itself. When the year of the cycle is found, the dominical letter opposite to it may be easily found in the foregoing table; suppose it be required to find the solar cycle in Julian years for the year 1715, then $1715 + 9 = 1724 \div 28 = 61$, and the remainder 16, which is the year of the solar cycle; and to which the dominical letter, B, in the foregoing table, answers. If there be two letters opposite to the cycle that is found, then the year is bissextile, or leap-year; thus, in the foregoing table, the double letters, G F, B A, D C, &c. opposite to the numbers 1, 5, 9, &c. denote the bissextiles, or leap-years. But, as this cycle is not perpetual, when computed in Gregorian years, it is necessary, in order to find the dominical letter in the Gregorian year, first to get that which answers to the Julian year in the solar cycle, and then counting three letters backwards you come at the dominical letter in the Gregorian year; thus, suppose the cycle of the sun in 1582, the year of the Gregorian reformation to be 23, and the dominical letter to be G, then counting three letters backward this becomes C; if then C be substituted in the Julian calendar for G, the rest of the letters will follow in a corresponding order. In this manner the dominical letters are regulated, in the Gregorian year, from 1582 to 1700; but as the three centesimal years are, according to this calculation, common, which, in the Julian years, would be bissextile, the same dominical letter runs through all these years, which, in the other case, would be double; whence the change of the cycle for a new century is made in the same manner as if it were a common year; thus, suppose the solar cycle for the year 1700 to be 1, the dominical letter would have been double: namely, B C, had the year been bissextile, but, this being passed over, the letter C runs through the whole year; and, in the second year, B is the dominical letter: on this principle the following perpetual table, for the dominical letters in Gregorian years, is constructed, which exhibits in seven orders all the variations which the series undergoes:

Solar cycle.	Order 1.	Order 2.	Order 3.	Order 4.	Order 5.	Order 6.	Order 7.
1	b, c	c, d	d, e	e, f	f, g	g, a	a, b
2	a	b	c	d	e	f	g
3	g	a	b	c	d	e	f
4	f	g	a	b	c	d	e
5	d, e	e, f	f, g	g, a	a, b	b, c	c, d
6	c	d	e	f	g	a	b
7	b	c	d	e	f	g	a
8	a	b	c	d	e	f	g
9	f, g	g, a	a, b	b, c	c, d	d, e	e, f
10	e	f	g	a	b	c	d
11	d	e	f	g	a	b	c
12	c	d	e	f	g	a	b
13	a, b	b, c	c, d	d, e	e, f	f, g	g, a
14	g	a	b	c	d	e	f
15	f	g	a	b	c	d	e
16	e	f	g	a	b	c	d
17	c, d	d, e	e, f	f, g	g, a	a, b	b, c
18	b	c	d	e	f	g	a
19	a	b	c	d	e	f	g
20	g	a	b	c	d	e	f
21	e, f	f, g	g, a	a, b	b, c	c, d	d, e
22	d	e	f	g	a	b	c
23	c	d	e	f	g	a	b
24	b	c	d	e	f	g	a
25	g, a	a, b	b, c	c, d	d, e	e, f	f, g
26	f	g	a	b	c	d	e
27	e	f	g	a	b	c	d
28	d	e	f	g	a	b	c
	1582 1600	1700	1800	1900 2000	2100	2200	2300 2400
	2500	2600	2700	2900 2800	3000	3100	3300 3200

In this manner the dominical letter, in Gregorian years, may be found for any year of the Christian æra, and no other order can occur; for, in the year 2500, the letters C and B would be the dominical letters according to the seventh order in the seventeenth year of the solar cycle; but as the leap-year is omitted in this century, the letter C runs through the whole year, and the letter B answers to the eighteenth year of the cycle in this century, which brings the letters back to the first order. *Lunar cycle*, or *cycle of the moon*, is a series of nineteen years, at the completion of which the new and full moons are restored to the same day of the Julian year; but as nineteen years exceed 235 lunations by $1^h\ 27'\ 31''\ 55'''$, it follows, that the new and full moons are not restored exactly to the same point of time; and that in 312 years the error will amount to one whole day. This cycle, which is more accurate than that of Meton, after which it has been constructed, is said to have commenced one year before the Christian year: if, therefore, we add 1 to any given year, and divide by 19, the quotient will give the cycle, and the remainder the golden number, or the number of years which have elapsed in a new cycle: thus, suppose it be required to find the golden number for the year 1822, then $1822 + 1 = 1823 \div 19 = 95$, the cycle, and 18 the remainder, which is the golden number.

Epact. An epact is the excess of any solar revolution above the lunar. The epacts are either menstrual, or annual.—The *menstrual epact* is the excess of the civil month above the lunar month: thus, suppose the New Moon to fall on the first of January, since the lunar month is $29^d\ 12^h\ 44'\ 3''$, and January is 31 days, the menstrual epact is $1^d\ 11^h\ 15'\ 37''$.— The *annual epact* is the excess of the solar year above the lunar year, for since the Julian year is $365^d\ 6^h$, and the lunar year is $354^d\ 8^h\ 48'\ 38''$, the annual epact is $10^d\ 21^h\ 11'\ 22''$, i. e. of 11 days; consequently, the epact of two years is 22 days, and of three years 33, or rather of 3, because 30 days complete the embolismic

CHRONOLOGY.

month: on this principle the following table is constructed, which shows the order of the epacts within a lunar cycle.

Order of years.	Epacts.	Order of years.	Epacts.
1	XI	11	I
2	XXII	12	XII
3	III	13	XXIII
4	XIV	14	IV
5	XXV	15	XV
6	VI	16	XXVI
7	XVII	17	VIII
8	XXVIII	18	XIX
9	IX	19	XXX
10	XX		

Since, in the nineteenth year, the epact is xxx, or 0, in the twentieth year the epact will be xi; therefore the cycle of civil epacts is completed with the revolution of the lunar cycle, and returns to the point from which the reckoning commenced. Therefore, to find the epact in a Julian year, multiply the lunar cycle by 11, and if the number be less than 30 it is an epact; but if greater, divide it by 30, and the remainder is the epact. Then the epact for the Gregorian year is easily to be found from the Julian year; for, if the Julian epact exceed 10, then subtract that number from it; but if less, add 30 to it, and subtract 10 from the sum. This rule holds good to the year 1700; but, from that year to the year 1900, 11 must be subtracted from the Julian year, and so on in succeeding centuries in an increasing ratio, as may be seen in the table of the equations of epacts which is given hereafter. The order of the epacts, as established in the Nicene Council, proceeded on the supposition that the lunar months consist of 29 and 30 days, and the civil year of 365 days, with a bissextile every fourth year; but this order is subject to irregularity from a twofold cause. In the space of nineteen years, or a complete lunar cycle, the excess of the Julian above that of the lunar year is reckoned to be 209 days, which is equal to six months at 30 days each, and one month at 29. To adjust, therefore, the motions of the sun and moon, at this period, exactly to each other, the last epact in the cycle, i.e. in the nineteenth year, must be reckoned as 12 instead of 11. In the next place, as the decemnovary cycle anticipates the New Moons one day in 312, this causes a diminution in the epact at the end of that period; and on the other hand, as the suppression of three bissextiles in the space of 400 years, according to the Gregorian computation, throws the new moons a day later, this causes an increase to the epact at the expiration of this period. For these reasons, therefore, the cycle of epacts varies in different centuries, and in order to obtain a full and correct account of the manner in which they correspond with the New Moons, it is necessary to give a series of epacts in thirty different classes, as exhibited in the following table:

TABLE OF THE EPACTS.

GOLDEN NUMBERS.

	3	4	5	6	7	8	9	10	11	12	13	14	15	16	17	18	19	1	2
							EPACTS.												
P	*	11	22	3	14	25	6	17	28	9	20	1	12	23	4	15	26	8	19
N	29	10	21	2	13	24	5	16	27	8	19	*	11	22	3	14	25	7	18
M	28	9	20	1	12	23	4	15	26	7	18	29	10	21	2	13	24	6	17
H	27	8	19	*	11	22	3	14	25	6	17	28	9	20	1	12	23	5	16
G	26	7	18	29	10	21	2	13	24	5	16	27	8	19	*	11	22	4	15
F	25	6	17	28	9	20	1	12	23	4	15	26	7	18	29	10	21	3	14
E	24	5	16	27	8	19	*	11	22	3	14	25	6	17	28	9	20	2	13
D	23	4	15	26	7	18	29	10	21	2	13	24	5	16	27	8	19	1	12
C	22	3	14	25	6	17	28	9	20	1	12	23	4	15	26	7	18	*	11
B	21	2	13	24	5	16	27	8	19	*	11	22	3	14	25	6	17	29	10
A	20	1	12	23	4	15	26	7	18	29	10	21	2	13	24	5	16	28	9
w	19	*	11	22	3	14	25	6	17	28	9	20	1	12	23	4	15	27	8
t	18	29	10	21	2	13	24	5	16	27	8	19	*	11	22	3	14	26	7
s	17	28	9	20	1	12	23	4	15	26	7	18	29	10	21	2	13	25	6
r	16	27	8	19	*	11	22	3	14	25	6	17	28	9	20	1	12	24	5
q	15	26	7	18	29	10	21	2	13	24	5	16	27	8	19	*	11	23	4
p	14	25	6	17	28	9	20	1	12	23	4	15	26	7	18	29	10	22	3
n	13	24	5	16	27	8	19	*	11	22	3	14	25	6	17	28	9	21	2
m	12	23	4	15	26	7	18	29	10	21	2	13	24	5	16	27	8	20	1
l	11	22	3	14	25	6	17	28	9	20	1	12	23	4	15	26	7	19	*
k	10	21	2	13	24	5	16	27	8	19	*	11	22	3	14	25	6	18	29
i	9	20	1	12	23	4	15	26	7	18	29	10	21	2	13	24	5	17	28
h	8	19	*	11	22	3	14	25	6	17	28	9	20	1	12	23	4	16	27
g	7	18	29	10	21	2	13	24	5	16	27	8	19	*	11	22	3	15	26
f	6	17	28	9	20	1	12	23	4	15	26	7	18	29	10	21	2	14	25
e	5	16	27	8	19	*	11	22	3	14	25	6	17	28	9	20	1	13	24
d	4	15	26	7	18	29	10	21	2	13	24	5	16	27	8	19	*	12	23
c	3	14	25	6	17	28	9	20	1	12	23	4	15	26	7	18	29	11	22
b	2	13	24	5	16	27	8	19	*	11	22	3	14	25	6	17	28	10	21
a	1	12	23	4	15	26	7	18	29	10	21	2	13	24	5	16	27	9	20

CHRONOLOGY.

The Golden Numbers, in the upper horizontal line, are made to commence with 3, because this was the Golden Number at the time of the Nicene Council, when the calendar was regulated. The lines which succeed are marked with the letters of the alphabet in retrograde order. The series marked P are the epacts of the sixth century, which, beginning with a or *, follow in uninterrupted succession, except with the addition of one day, when the Golden Number is 1, or when it passes from 19 to 1, because the last lunation, consisting of only 29 days, causes the New Moons to advance one day, as before observed. This rule of increase is therefore observed down the whole of the same column through the series of letters from N to a. As a further illustration of this subject, the following Table of the Equation of Epacts is added, to show to what centuries each of these cycles of epacts belong.

Days omitted besides the 10 for the correction of the calendar.		A.D.			A.D.	Days omitted.
	N	1		s	2900	10
	P	320	Biss.	s	3000	11
	a	800	Biss.	r	3100	12
	b	1100	Biss.	r	3200 Biss.	12
	c	1400	Biss.	r	3300	13
	D	1582	(10 days subtracted)	q	3400	14
				p	3500	15
	D	1600		q	3600	15
1	C	1700		p	3700	16
2	C	1800		n	3800	17
3	B	1900		n	3900	18
3	B	2000	Biss.	n	4000 Biss.	18
4	B	2100		m	4100	19
5	A	2200		l	4200	20
6	u	2300		l	4300	21
6	A	2400	Biss.	l	4400 Biss.	21
7	u	2500		k	4500	22
8	t	2600		k	4600	23
9	t	2700		i	4700	24
9	t	2800	Biss.	i	4800 Biss.	24

Suppose you wish to know the cycle of epacts for the year 320. you observe P to be the letter opposite to it in the above table, which, if found in the first table, gives the cycle of epacts *, 11, 22, 3, 14, 25, 6, 17, 28, 9, 20, 1, 12, 23, 4, 15, 26, 8, 19; if you look to the year 800 the letter a is opposite to it, and the corresponding letter in the first table gives the epacts 1, 12, 23, 4, 15, 26, 7, 18, &c. which are increased by one day owing to the lunar equation. In 1100, which is marked by the letter b, the cycle runs 2, 13, &c. because the moon anticipates in the same proportion as before. The year 1582, which is the year of the Gregorian correction, or the New Style, is marked D, and the cycle of epacts opposite to the same letter will be found to have gone backward ten days from the preceding century 1400, in order to adjust them to the correction of the calendar by the suppression of ten days. In the same manner the epacts for the year 1700, marked C, may be found to be 22, 3, 14, &c. and so on with any other succeeding years.

Use of the Epacts. The use of the epacts is to find the age of the moon, but particularly of the full moon, for the purpose of ascertaining the right time of celebrating the festival of Easter; of which more will be said when speaking of the calendar at the end of this article.

Cycle of Indiction. The cycle of Indiction is a series of fifteen years, which was introduced in the reign of Constantine, A. D. 312, and was used instead of the Olympiads for the purpose of keeping accounts, particularly such as related to the tributes, although but little is known respecting the introduction of this cycle, or the particular purpose for which it was introduced. It was of two kinds, Roman and Grecian. The Grecian Indictions commenced on the first of September, and were employed in the acts of councils, and the *novellio* of the emperors. The Roman Indictions, which commence on the first of January, are still used by the popes in signing their bulls and public acts. To find the cycle of the indiction add 3 to the year of the Christian æra, and divide by 15; the remainder, if there be any, will give the cycle of the year of indiction; but if there be no remainder, then 15 is the cycle itself. In this manner the year of indiction for 1822 is found to be 10.

Dionysian period. The Dionysian period, so called from Dionysius Exiguus, a Roman abbot, by whom it was contrived, was a series of 532 years, formed by multiplying the solar cycle 28 into the lunar 19, for the purpose of restoring the new and full moons to the same day; but it falls short in the computation by $1^d\ 16^h\ 58'\ 59''\ 40'''$. For the Dionysian period consists of $194,313$ days, but 6580 lunations make only $194,311^d\ 7^h\ 58'\ 6''\ 20'''$, leaving an excess in this period of $1^d\ 16^h$ &c. as before observed.

Julian period. The Julian period, invented by Scaliger, and so called because it is adapted to the Julian year, is a series of years formed by the multiplication of the solar and lunar cycles, and the cycle of indiction into one another, making the sum of 7980 Julian years. To find, in any given year of the Julian period, the cycles of the sun, moon, and indiction, divide by 19, by 28, and by 15; what remains in the first division is the cycle of the moon; what remains in the second is the cycle of the sun; and what remains in the third is the cycle of indiction. Let the given year be 2895, it is required to find the cycle of the moon, sun, and indiction; then, from the division of 2895 by 19, is left 7 the remainder, which is the cycle of the moon; from that of 2895 by 28 is left 11, the cycle of the sun; and from the division of 2895 by 15 is left 15, the cycle of indiction. On the other hand, the cycles being given to find the Julian period, multiply the cycle of the moon into 4200, that of the sun into 4845, and that of indiction into 6916, then the sum of all these products, divided by 7980, gives the Julian period: thus, suppose 7 the cycle of the moon, 11 that of the sun, and 15 that of indiction, then $4200 \times 7 = 29400$; $4845 \times 11 = 53295$; $6916 \times 15 = 103740$; and $29400 + 53295 + 103740 = 186435 \div 7980 = 23$, and a remainder 2895, which is the Julian period.

Historical characters. The historical characters are epochas, or æras, which are sometimes distinguished from each other, by supposing the epocha to be the head or beginning of any past time, and æra the series, or continuation of years, reckoned from some fixed point, and numbered onwards to an indefinite period. *Epocha* is, in fact, the Greek term for the point of time from which any reckoning commences, and is still applied to the accounts of years kept by particular cities of Greece, and marked on their medals. [vide *Epocha*] *Æra*, which is a term of later invention, is now generally applied to all historical accounts of time that run on in a continued series. These are all at present reducible in our chronological computations to the vulgar æra.— The *vulgar æra* is the computation made by Dionysius Exiguus from our Saviour's nativity, which is called *vulgar*, because it has been vulgarly, or commonly, adopted, since its introduction, in all Christian accounts of time, although it has been supposed by different writers to vary from the true time of our Saviour's birth by two, three, four, five, and even more years. To find the

CHRONOLOGY.

year of the Julian period that corresponds to the first year of Christ's birth, get the cycle of the sun, the moon, and the indiction, and then proceed as stated under the head of the Julian period; thus, the cycle of the sun for the first year of Christ's nativity being 10, that of the moon 2, and that of the indiction 4, the Julian period for that year will be found to be 4714. Any succeeding year of the Julian period may be found by adding 4713 to the given year of the vulgar æra: thus, if to the present æra, 1822, be added 4713, the sum of 6535 will be the Julian period; and, on the other hand, by subtracting 4713 from any given year of the Julian period, you may get the year of the vulgar æra: thus, if from 6396, the year of the Julian period, you subtract 4713, it leaves 1683, the year of the vulgar æra. The most important æras in history, before the vulgar æra, are the æra of the Creation, of the Olympiads, and of the building of Rome, and of Nabonassar; after the vulgar æra is that of the Hegira. There are others of less importance, of which an account will be found under the head of Æra. [vide *Æra*]

Æra of the Creation. Riccioli reckons up no less than seventy different computations which have been given of this æra, of which the principal that are used in chronological computations are as follow, namely,—*The historical æra of the Greeks* which is dated from the 787th year before the Julian period; consequently, by the addition of 787 to any given year of the Julian period, the year of this æra may be obtained; and, on the other hand, by subtracting 787 from any year of this æra, the year of the Julian period may be obtained: hence, by the addition of 787 to 4714, the year of the Julian period corresponding with the birth of our Saviour, 5500, is obtained, the year of this æra, which corresponds with the first year of the vulgar æra. In like manner any years of this æra may be reduced to the years of the vulgar æra, and *vice versa:* thus, if from 7215, a given year of this æra, 5500 be subtracted, the remainder, 1715, will be the year of Christ; and if to the year 1715, 5500, the sum 7215 is the year of this æra.—*The ecclesiastical æra of the Greeks* was dated 780 years before the Julian period, and consequently, by the addition of 4714 years, was 5494 years before the vulgar æra; this was otherwise called the Alexandrine æra, and was first employed by Panodorus, an Ægyptian monk, in calculating the Easter and other ecclesiastical matters. To reduce the years of this æra to those of the vulgar æra, add or subtract 5493: thus, if 5493 be added to 1822, it gives 7315, the year of the ecclesiastical æra; and if from 7208 be subtracted 5493, it leaves 1715, the year of the vulgar æra. To reduce, therefore, the years of this æra to those of the vulgar æra, and *vice versa,* add or subtract 5508: thus, if to the present year, 1822, be added 5508, it will give 7330, the year of this æra; and if from 7223, the given year of this æra, be taken 5508, it will leave 1715, the year of the vulgar æra.—*The civil æra of the Greeks,* which was used by the Emperors of the East in their public acts, and has since been used by the Russians, is dated 795 years before the Julian period, and 5509 years before the vulgar æra.—*The Jewish æra* of the world is the 953d year of the Julian period; and by subtracting 953 from 4714 leaves 3762, the number of years since the Creation to the vulgar æra; according to this mode of computation, which is still used by the Jews of the present day. To find, therefore, any year of the Jewish æra in a given year of the Julian period, subtract 952, and the number is the year required, which begins in autumn: thus, if from 6535, the present year of the Julian period, 952 be subtracted, 5583 remains, the year of the Jewish æra. Also, to reduce the years of this æra to those of the vulgar æra, and *vice versa,* add or subtract 3761: thus, 1822 + 3761 = 5583, the present year of the Jewish æra, and 5583 − 3761 = 1822, the present year of the vulgar æra.—The *Eusebian æra of the Creation* is the 486th year before the Julian period; to which, if 4714 be added, it will give 5200, the years of the Creation before the vulgar æra. If, therefore, the years of the world in the Eusebian chronicle, be less than 5200, subtract them from 5200, and the remainder will be the years before Christ; but if they exceed that number, subtract 5199 from them, and the remainder will be the years after Christ: thus, suppose 5158 of the Eusebian æra be subtracted from 5200, it will leave 42, the year before Christ; but if 5199 be subtracted from 5228, the year of the Eusebian, it will leave 29, the year after Christ. The knowledge of this æra is of use in reading the Chronicon of Eusebius and the Roman Martyrology. According to Scaliger, the world was created in the 764th year of the Julian period, and consequently 3949 years before Christ; but Usher dates the Creation from the 710th year of the Julian period, and 4004 before the vulgar æra; which computation is the most generally admitted among modern chronologers.

Æra of the Olympiads. The Olympiads are series of four years, each of which dates its commencement from the New Moon of the 3938th year of the Julian period, which was nearest to the summer solstice; and consequently 776 years before the vulgar æra. As the first year of this latter æra corresponds to the 194th Olympiad, all the years of any Olympiad which is less than 194 correspond to years before Christ; and all those of any Olympiad above the 194th are years after Christ. To reduce years of the Olympiads to those of the vulgar æra, take 1 from the given olympiads that you may have complete olympiads, multiply the remainder by 4, and to the product add the single years that are over and above the olympiads; then, if the whole sum be less than 776, subtract it from 776; but if it be less than it, or equal to it, then subtract 775 completed olympiads from it, and the remainder will be the year after Christ. Thus, let the first year of the 114th Olympiad be given to find the year before the vulgar æra, 114 − 1 × 4 = 452; then, 776 − 452 = 324, the year before Christ. Let the fourth year of the 113th Olympiad be given to find the year before Christ, 113 − 1 × 4 = 448, to which, if 3 be added for the single years of the Olympiad, the whole sum is 451; then 776 − 451 = 325, the year before Christ. Let the first year of the 195th Olympiad be given to find the year after Christ, then 195 − 1 × 4 = 776, and 776 − 775 = 1, the first year of the vulgar æra. Let the fourth year of the 202d Olympiad be given to find the year after Christ, then 202 − 1 × 4 = 804, + 3 = 807, − 775 = 32, the year after the vulgar æra. On the other hand, to reduce the years before and after the vulgar æra to the years of the Olympiads, let the year before Christ be subtracted from 776, and let 775 be added to the year after, divide the remainder or sum by 4, and that number increased by unity will give the Olympiad required. If there be any remainder, it will be the year of the Olympiad reckoned from the first year. Thus, let it be required to find the year of the Olympiad corresponding to 578 before Christ, then 776 − 578 + 1 + 4 = 50, the Olympiad, and a remainder 2, the third year of the Olympiad.

Æra of the building of Rome. The exact date of this æra is not to be ascertained with any degree of precision, as the chronology of the ancient Romans was very imperfectly preserved. According to the different computations of the Roman writers, the building of the city is

CHRONOLOGY.

said to have taken place at different periods between the 23d and 48th Olympiads; and, by modern chronologers, the earliest period, which is the computation of Varro, has been most generally adopted. The year of building the city, therefore, coincides with the 3,961st of the Julian period, the 23d Olympiad, and 753d the year before Christ. To reduce the years of this æra to those of the Julian period, and *vice versa*, add or subtract 753. If the number of years be less than 753, they must be subtracted from 753; if greater, they must be added, to obtain the year before Christ. On the other hand, if 753 be added to the year after Christ, it will give the year of the æra of the city.

Æra of Nabonassar. The æra of Nabonassar, which derives its name from Nabonassar, first King of Babylon, is dated from the 26th of February, of the year 3967 of the Julian, 747 years before Christ. The solar cycle was 19, the lunar 15, and the cycle of indiction 7. To reduce the years of this æra to those of the Julian period, add 3966, if the Nabonassarean does not exceed 227; 3965, if it do not exceed 1688; and 3964, if it be between 1688 and 3149: thus, the 139th year of the Nabonassarean æra begins in the year 4105 of the Julian period; and in like manner the 355th, of the Nabonassarean æra begins in the year 4320 of the Julian period. These rules depend on the nature of the Nabonassarean year, of which mention has already been made. Since the beginning of the Nabonassarean year recedes one day in four years, in the space of 228 years it is anticipated 68 days; but as between the 1st of January and the 26th of February, the day on which the Nabonassarean year commences, there are only 56 days, the beginning of this year does not go further than from February to December, as long as the Nabonassarean year does not exceed 227; consequently, in this case, 3966 years are to be added, in order to obtain the year of the Julian æra. But since, in the space of 1460 years, the beginning of the Nabonassarean year runs through all the days of the Julian year, and the sum of 1461 and 227 is 1688, and that of 1688 and 1461 is 3149, the reason for the addition of 3965 and 3964 is evident.

To find, therefore, the day on which the Nabonassarean year commences, divide by 4, and subtract the remainder from 57, if the number be less than 57; otherwise from 422; the remainder — 1, will be the day required, if reckoned from the 1st of January: thus, if it be required to find on what day of the Julian year the Thoth of the Nabonassarean year, 230, falls, divide 230 by 4, and the quotient will be 57, which, if subtracted from 422, leaves a remainder of 365; then 365 — 1 = 364, or the 364th day of the Julian year, i. e. the 30th day of December.

To find the day of any month in the Julian year, which answers to the given day and month in the Nabonassarean year: first let the day of the Julian year, on which the 1st of Thoth commences be found, then because all the months of the Nabonassarean years are 30 days each, let the number of complete months be multiplied by 30, and let the days, if there be any other, be added to the product; lastly, let the days of the Julian year, to the beginning of the complete Nabonassarean year, be added to the number already found; subtract 1 from the sum, and the remainder, if less than 365 in the common year, and 366 in the leap-year, will be the day sought; but, if it exceed either of these numbers, it must be subtracted from them, and the remainder is the day required: thus, what day of the Julian year answers to the 7th of Tibi of the Nabonassarean year 355, then 30, the number of days in the month, multiplied by 4, the number of months from Thoth, + 7 = 127, the collective number of days in the Nabonassarean year, to which, if 334, the number of days in the Julian year, be added, the remainder, — 1, is 460, and 460 — 365 = 95 days, or the fifth of April.

To convert any year of the Nabonassarean year to a year of the Vulgar æra. If the Nabonassarean year be less than 747, let 2 be taken from it, and the remainder subtracted from 747, which will give the year before Christ; but if it exceed 747, but be less than 1688, one only must be subtracted, and 747 be taken from the remainder; if the year exceed 1688, but be less than 3149, let 2 be subtracted from it, and 747 be taken from the remainder: thus, the 554th year of the Nabonassarean æra is found to coincide with the 195th before Christ, and the 859th of the Nabonassarean æra, with the 113th after Christ.

The following table exhibits a comparative view of the years of the above-mentioned æras in a continued series of Olympiads, or every four years:

A. M.	Jul. Per.	Olymp.	U. C.	Ær. Nab.	B. C.
3228	3938	1			776
3232	3942	2			772
3236	3946	3			768
3240	3950	4			764
3244	3954	5			760
3248	3958	6			756
3252	3961		1		753
3256	3962	7	2		752
3260	3966	8	6		748
3261	3967	8–2	7	1	747
3264	3970	9	10	4	744
3268	3974	10	14	8	740
3272	3978	11	18	12	736
3276	3982	12	22	16	732
3280	3986	13	26	20	728
3284	3990	14	30	24	724
3288	3994	15	34	28	720
3292	3998	16	38	32	716
3296	4002	17	42	36	712
3300	4006	18	46	40	708
3304	4010	19	50	44	704
3308	4014	20	54	48	700
3312	4018	21	58	52	696
3316	4022	22	62	56	692
3320	4026	23	66	60	688
3324	4030	24	70	64	684
3328	4034	25	74	68	680
3332	4038	26	78	72	676
3336	4042	27	82	76	672
3340	4046	28	86	80	668
3344	4050	29	90	84	664
3348	4054	30	94	88	660
3352	4058	31	98	92	656
3356	4062	32	102	96	652
3360	4066	33	106	100	648
3364	4070	34	110	104	644
3368	4074	35	114	108	640
3372	4078	36	118	112	636
3376	4082	37	122	116	632
3380	4086	38	126	120	628
3384	4090	39	130	124	624
3388	4094	40	134	128	620
3392	4098	41	138	132	616
3396	4102	42	142	136	612
3400	4106	43	146	140	608
3404	4110	44	150	144	604

CHRONOLOGY.

A. M.	Jul. Per.	Olymp.	U. C.	Ær. Nab.	B. C.	A. M.	Jul. Per.	Olymp.	U. C.	Ær. Nab.	B. C.
3408	4114	45	154	148	600	3674	4378	111	418	413	336
3412	4118	46	158	152	596	3678	4382	112	422	417	332
3416	4122	47	162	156	592	3682	4386	113	426	421	328
3420	4126	48	166	160	588	3686	4390	114	430	425	324
3424	4130	49	170	164	584	3690	4394	115	434	429	320
3428	4134	50	174	168	580	3694	4398	116	438	433	316
3432	4138	51	178	172	576	3698	4402	117	442	437	312
3436	4142	52	182	176	572	3702	4406	118	446	441	308
3440	4146	53	186	180	568	3706	4410	119	450	445	304
3444	4150	54	190	184	564	3710	4414	120	454	449	300
3448	4154	55	194	188	560	3714	4418	121	458	453	296
3452	4158	56	198	192	556	3718	4422	122	462	457	292
3456	4162	57	202	196	552	3722	4426	123	466	461	288
3460	4166	58	206	200	548	3726	4430	124	470	465	284
3464	4170	59	210	204	544	3730	4434	125	474	469	280
3468	4174	60	214	208	540	3734	4438	126	478	473	276
3472	4178	61	218	212	536	3738	4442	127	482	477	272
3476	4182	62	222	216	532	3742	4446	128	486	481	268
3480	4186	63	226	220	528	3746	4450	129	490	485	264
3484	4190	64	230	224	524	3750	4454	130	494	489	260
		64—4	233	227 & 228		3754	4458	131	498	493	256
3488	4194	65	234	229	520	3758	4462	132	502	497	252
3492	4198	66	238	233	516	3762	4466	133	506	501	248
3496	4202	67	242	237	512	3766	4470	134	510	505	244
3500	4206	68	246	241	508	3770	4474	135	514	509	240
3504	4210	69	250	245	504	3774	4478	136	518	513	236
3508	4214	70	254	249	500	3778	4482	137	522	517	232
3512	4218	71	258	253	496	3782	4486	138	526	521	228
3516	4222	72	262	257	492	3786	4490	139	530	525	224
3520	4226	73	266	261	488	3790	4494	140	534	529	220
3524	4230	74	270	265	484	3794	4498	141	538	533	216
3528	4234	75	274	269	480	3798	4502	142	542	537	212
3532	4238	76	278	273	476	3802	4506	143	546	541	208
3536	4242	77	282	277	472	3806	4510	144	550	545	204
3540	4246	78	286	281	468	3810	4514	145	554	549	200
3544	4250	79	290	285	464	3814	4518	146	558	553	196
3548	4254	80	294	289	460	3818	4522	147	562	557	192
3552	4258	81	298	293	456	3822	4526	148	566	561	188
3556	4262	82	302	297	452	3826	4530	149	570	565	184
3560	4266	83	306	301	448	3830	4534	150	574	569	180
3564	4270	84	310	305	444	3834	4538	151	578	573	176
3568	4274	85	314	309	440	3838	4542	152	582	577	172
3572	4278	86	318	313	436	3842	4546	153	586	581	168
3576	4282	87	322	317	432	3846	4550	154	590	585	164
3580	4286	88	326	321	428	3850	4554	155	594	589	160
3584	4290	89	330	325	424	3854	4558	156	598	593	156
3588	4294	90	334	329	420	3858	4562	157	602	597	152
3592	4298	91	338	333	416	3862	4566	158	606	601	148
3596	4302	92	342	337	412	3866	4570	159	610	605	144
3600	4306	93	346	341	408	3870	4574	160	614	609	140
3604	4310	94	350	345	404	3874	4578	161	618	613	136
3608	4314	95	354	349	400	3878	4582	162	622	617	132
3612	4318	96	358	353	396	3882	4586	163	626	621	128
3616	4322	97	362	357	392	3886	4590	164	630	625	124
3620	4326	98	366	361	388	3890	4594	165	634	629	120
3624	4330	99	370	365	384	3894	4598	166	638	633	116
3628	4334	100	374	369	380	3898	4602	167	642	637	112
3632	4338	101	378	373	376	3902	4606	168	646	641	108
3636	4342	102	382	377	372	3906	4610	169	650	645	104
3640	4346	103	386	381	368	3910	4614	170	654	649	100
3644	4350	104	390	385	364	3914	4618	171	658	653	96
3648	4354	105	394	389	360	3918	4622	172	662	657	92
3652	4358	106	398	393	356	3922	4626	173	666	661	88
3656	4362	107	402	397	352	3926	4630	174	670	665	84
3660	4366	108	406	401	348	3930	4634	175	674	669	80
3664	4370	109	410	405	344	3934	4638	176	678	673	76
3670	4374	110	414	409	340	3938	4642	177	682	677	72

CHRONOLOGY.

A. M.	Jul. Per.	Olymp.	U. C.	Ær. Nab.	B. C.
3942	4646	178	686	681	68
3946	4650	179	690	685	64
3950	4654	180	694	689	60
3954	4658	181	698	693	56
3958	4662	182	702	697	52
3962	4666	183	706	701	48
3966	4670	184	710	705	44
3970	4674	185	714	709	40
3974	4678	186	718	713	36
3978	4682	187	722	717	32
3982	4686	188	726	721	28
3986	4690	189	730	725	24
3990	4694	190	734	729	20
3994	4698	191	738	733	16
3998	4702	192	742	737	12
4002	4706	193	746	741	8
4006	4710	194	750	745	4
					A. D.
4010	4714	195	754	749	1
4014	4718	196	758	753	5
4018	4722	197	762	757	9
4022	4726	298	766	761	13
4026	4730	199	770	765	17
4030	4734	200	774	769	21
4034	4738	201	778	773	25
4038	4742	202	782	777	29
4042	4746	203	786	781	33
4046	4750	204	790	785	37
4050	4754	205	794	789	41
4054	4758	206	798	793	45
4058	4762	207	802	797	49
4062	4766	208	806	801	53
4066	4770	209	810	805	57
4070	4774	210	814	809	61
4074	4778	211	818	813	65
4078	4782	212	822	817	69
4082	4786	213	826	821	73
4086	4790	214	830	825	77
4090	4794	215	834	829	81
4094	4798	216	838	833	85
4098	4802	217	842	837	89
4102	4806	218	846	841	93
4106	4810	219	850	845	97
4110	4814	220	854	849	101
4114	4818	221	858	853	105
4118	4822	222	862	857	109
4122	4826	223	866	861	113
4126	4830	224	870	865	117
4130	4834	225	874	869	121
4134	4838	226	878	873	125
4138	4842	227	882	877	129
4142	4846	228	886	881	133
4146	4850	229	890	885	137
4150	4854	230	894	889	141
4154	4858	231	898	893	145
4158	4862	232	902	897	149
4162	4866	233	906	901	153
4166	4870	234	910	905	157
4170	4874	235	914	909	161
4174	4878	236	918	913	165
4178	4882	237	922	917	169
4182	4886	238	926	921	173
4186	4890	339	930	925	177
4190	4894	240	934	929	181
4194	4898	241	938	933	185
4198	4902	242	942	937	189
4202	4906	243	946	941	193

A. M.	Per. Jul.	Olymp.	U. C.	Ær. Nab.	A. D.
4206	4910	244	950	945	197
4210	4914	245	954	949	201
4214	4918	246	958	953	205
4218	4922	247	962	957	209
4222	4926	258	966	961	213
4226	4930	249	970	965	217
4230	4934	250	974	969	221
4234	4238	251	978	973	225
4238	4242	252	982	977	229
4242	4246	253	986	981	233
4246	4250	254	990	985	237
4250	4254	255	994	989	241
4254	4258	256	998	193	245
4258	4262	257	1002	197	249
4262	4266	258	1006	1001	253
4266	4270	259	1010	1005	257
4270	4274	260	1014	1009	261
4274	4278	261	1018	1013	265
4278	4282	262	1022	1017	269
4282	4286	263	1026	1021	273
4286	4990	264	1030	1025	277
4290	4994	265	1034	1029	281
4294	4998	266	1038	1033	285
4298	5002	267	1042	1037	289
4302	5006	268	1046	1041	293
4306	5010	269	1050	1045	297
4310	5014	270	1054	1049	301
4314	5018	271	1058	1053	305
4318	5022	272	1062	1057	309

Æra of the Hegira. The æra of the Hegira is that point of time which is dated by the Arabians from the Hegira, or flight of Mahomet from Mecca, which corresponds to the year of Christ 622. To find the year of the Hegira which corresponds to that of the vulgar æra, subtract 621 from the given year, divide the remainder by 33, and add the quotient to that remainder, the sum will be the year of the Hegira sought for: thus, suppose it be required to find the year of the Hegira corresponding to the present year 1822, 1822 − 621 = 1201 ÷ 33 = 36, then 36 + 1201 = 1237, the year of the Hegira required. As the Hegira commences on the 622d year of the vulgar æra, the subtraction of 621 complete years from the given year of Christ would show the number of Julian years which have elapsed since the commencement of that æra, if the Julian and Arabian years were equal; but the Julian year being 365^d 6^h, and that of the Hegira 354^d 8^h 48′, the former is anticipated by the latter 10^d 21^h 12′ in every year, making in the space of 33 years 359^d 3^h 36′, i. e. one year and 4^d 18^h 48′; hence the propriety of dividing by the number 33, which so long as the odd days do not amount to another year, will show the number of years of the Hegira which have passed beyond those of the Julian year. To find the feria or day of the week on which any given year of the Hegira commences, the following rule is necessary. First, let the given year be divided by 210, and the remainder by 30; then multiply the quotient by 5. Out of the remainder, from the second division, distinguish the intercalary from the common years, and multiply the former by 5, and the latter by 4; let both the products be added to the former product; add 6 to the sum of the whole, and divide by 7, the quotient of which is the number of the feria required: thus, let it be required to find the feria on which 1127 of the Hegira commences, 1127 ÷ 210 = 5, and a remainder 77; then, 77 ÷ 30 = 2 × 5 = 10; then 6, the number of inter-

CHRONOLOGY.

calary years, × 6 = 30, and 10, the number of common years, × 4 = 40, all which products, together with 6, must be added together: thus, 10 + 30 + 40 + 6 = 86 ÷ 7 = 12, the number. Here it is to be observed, that since the cycle of the years of the Hegira is 30, and the feriæ of the week are 7, the same order of the beginning of the year will return in 210 years; wherefore, if the given year be divided by 210, it shows how often that period has elapsed, and the remainder the year that is entered on in a new period. If this remainder be divided by 30, it will show the number of periods of 30 years that have elapsed, and the remainder the year of a new period. Now a period of 30 years contains 19 common years, and 11 intercalary years, making 10,631 days, or 1518 weeks, with 5 days over; wherefore, if you multiply the number of complete periods by 5, it will give the number of odd days within those periods. In like manner, since a common year contains 4 days above 50 weeks, and an intercalary day 5, if the number of the former above the complete period be multiplied by 4, and that of the latter by 5, the number of days is found that have passed above the weeks, within the years of the current period. Moreover, as the first year of the Hegira fell in the fifteenth cycle of the sun, when the dominical letter was C, its epocha or commencement, which is dated from the 16th of July, fell on the sixth feria, i. e. the Friday; if, therefore, to the odd days that are over and above in the weeks of the complete periods, and those of the current period, you add 6, and divide the sum by 7, you find the number of odd days above the weeks which have passed since the commencement of the Hegira. Thus, it will be found that the feria for the year 1127 was 6.

The following table of the years of the Hegira, compared with those of the Vulgar Æra, and also of the corresponding Feriæ, will serve to illustrate this subject still farther.

A. D.	Æra of the Hegira.	Fer.	A. D.	Æra of the Hegira.	Fer.
622	1 16 July	6	650	30 4 Sept.	7
623	2* 5 July	3	651	31 24 Aug.	4
624	3 24 June	1	652	32* 12 Aug.	1
625	4 13 June	5	653	33 2 Aug.	6
626	5* 2 June	2	654	34 22 July	3
627	6 23 May	7	655	35* 11 July	7
628	7* 11 May	4	656	36 30 June	5
629	8 1 May	2	657	37* 19 June	2
630	9 20 April	6	658	38 9 June	7
631	10* 9 April	3	659	39 29 May	4
632	11 29 March	1	660	40* 17 May	1
633	12 18 March	5	661	41 7 May	6
634	13* 7 March	2	662	42 26 April	3
635	14 25 Feb.	7	663	43* 15 April	7
636	15 14 Feb.	4	664	44 4 April	5
637	16* 2 Feb.	1	665	45 24 March	2
638	17 23 Jan.	6	666	46* 13 March	6
639	18* 12 Jan.	3	667	47 3 March	4
640 {	19 2 Jan.	1	668	48* 20 Feb.	1
	20 21 Dec.	5	669	49 9 Feb.	6
641	21* 10 Dec.	2	670	50 29 Feb.	3
642	22 30 Nov.	7	671	51* 18 Jan.	7
643	23 19 Nov.	4	672 {	52 8 Jan.	5
644	24* 7 Nov.	1		53 27 Dec.	2
645	25 28 Oct.	6	673	54* 16 Dec.	6
646	26* 17 Oct.	3	674	55 6 Dec.	6
647	27 7 Oct.	1	675	56* 25 Nov.	1
648	28 25 Sept.	5	676	57 14 Nov.	6
649	29* 14 Sept.	2	677	58 3 Nov.	3

A. D.	Æra of the Hegira.	Fer.	A. D.	Æra of the Hegira.	Fer.
678	59* 23 Oct.	7	743	126 25 Oct.	6
679	60 13 Oct.	5	744	127* 13 Oct.	3
680	61 1 Oct.	2	745	128 3 Oct.	1
681	62* 20 Sept.	6	746	129 22 Sept.	5
682	63 10 Sept.	4	747	130* 11 Sept.	2
683	64 30 Aug.	1	748	131 31 Aug.	7
684	65* 18 Aug.	5	749	132 20 Aug.	4
685	66 8 Aug.	3	750	133* 9 Aug.	1
686	67* 28 July	7	751	134 30 July	6
687	68 18 July	5	752	135 18 July	3
688	69 6 July	2	753	136* 7 July	7
689	70* 25 June	6	754	137 27 June	5
690	71 15 June	4	755	138* 16 June	2
691	72 4 June	1	756	139 5 June	7
692	73* 23 May	5	757	140 25 May	4
693	74 13 May	3	758	141* 14 May	1
694	75 2 May	7	759	142 4 May	6
695	76* 21 April	4	760	143 22 April	3
696	77 10 April	2	761	144 11 April	7
697	78* 30 March	6	762	145 1 April	5
698	79 20 March	4	763	146* 21 March	2
699	80 9 March	1	764	147 10 March	7
700	81* 26 Feb.	5	765	148 27 Feb.	4
701	82 15 Feb.	3	766	149* 16 Feb.	1
702	83 4 Feb.	7	767	150 6 Feb.	6
703	84* 24 Jan.	4	768	151 26 Jan.	3
704	85 14 Jan.	2	769	152* 14 Jan.	7
705 {	86 2 Jan.	6	770 {	153 4 Jan.	5
	87 23 Dec.	4		154 24 Dec.	2
706	88 12 Dec.	1	771	155* 13 Dec.	5
707	89* 1 Dec.	5	772	156 2 Dec.	4
708	90 20 Nov.	3	773	157* 21 Nov.	1
709	91 9 Nov.	7	774	158 11 Nov.	6
710	92* 29 Oct.	4	775	159 31 Oct.	3
711	93 19 Oct.	2	776	160* 19 Oct.	7
712	94 7 Oct.	6	777	161 9 Oct.	5
713	95* 26 Sept.	3	778	162 28 Sept.	2
714	96 16 Sept.	1	779	163* 17 Sept.	6
715	97 5 Sept.	5	780	164 6 Sept.	4
716	98 25 Aug.	3	781	165 26 Aug.	1
717	99 14 Aug.	7	782	166* 15 Aug.	5
718	100 3 Aug.	4	783	167 5 Aug.	3
719	101 24 July	2	784	168* 24 July	7
720	102 12 July	6	785	169 14 July	5
721	103* 1 July	3	786	170 3 July	2
722	104 20 June	1	787	171* 22 June	6
723	105 10 June	5	788	172 11 June	4
724	106* 29 May	2	789	173 31 May	1
725	107 19 May	7	790	174* 20 May	5
726	108* 8 May	4	791	175 10 May	3
727	109 28 April	2	792	176* 28 April	7
728	110 16 April	6	793	177 18 April	5
729	111* 5 April	3	794	178 7 April	2
730	112 26 March	1	795	179* 27 March	6
731	113 15 March	5	796	180 16 March	4
732	114* 2 March	2	797	181 5 March	1
733	115 21 Feb.	7	798	182* 22 Feb.	5
734	116* 10 Feb.	4	799	183 12 Feb.	3
735	117 31 Jan.	2	800	184 1 Feb.	7
736	118 20 Jan.	6	801	185* 20 Jan.	4
737 {	119* 8 Jan.	3	802 {	186 10 Jan.	2
	120 29 Dec.	1		187* 30 Dec.	6
738	121 18 Dec.	5	803	188 20 Dec.	4
739	122* 7 Dec.	2	804	189 8 Dec.	1
740	123 26 Nov.	7	805	190* 27 Nov.	5
741	124 15 Nov.	4	806	191 17 Nov.	3
742	125* 4 Nov.	1	807	192 6 Nov.	7

CHRONOLOGY.

A. D.	Æra of the Hegira.	Fer.	A. D.	Æra of the Hegira.	Fer.
808	193* 25 Oct.	4	960	349 3 March	7
809	194 15 Oct.	2	970	360 4 Nov.	6
810	195 4 Oct.	6	980	370* 17 July	7
811	196* 23 Sept.	3	990	380 31 March	2
812	197 12 Sept.	1	1000	391 1 Dec.	1
813	198* 1 Sept.	5	1010	401 15 Aug.	3
814	199 22 Aug.	3	1020	411* 27 April	4
815	200 11 Aug.	7	1030 {	421 9 Jan.	6
816	201* 30 July	4		422 29 Dec.	3
817	202 20 July	2	1040	432 11 Sept.	5
818	203 9 July	6	1050	442 26 May	7
819	204* 28 June	3	1060	452* 6 Feb.	1
820	205 17 June	1	1070	463 9 Oct.	7
821	206* 6 June	5	1080	473 22 June	2
822	207 27 May	3	1090	483 6 March	4
823	208 16 May	7	1100	494 6 Nov.	3
824	209* 4 May	4	1110	504* 20 July	4
825	210 24 April	2	1120	514 2 April	6
826	211 13 April	6	1130	525 4 Dec.	5
827	212* 2 April	3	1140	535 17 Aug.	7
828	213 22 March	1	1150	545* 30 April	1
829	214 11 March	5	1160 {	555 12 Jan.	3
830	215* 28 Feb.	2		556 31 Dec.	7
840	226* 31 Oct.	1	1170	566* 14 Sept.	2
850	236* 15 July	3	1180	576 28 May	4
860	246 28 March	5	1190	586 8 Feb.	5
870	257 29 Nov.	4	1200	597 12 Oct.	5
880	267 12 Aug.	6	1300	700* 16 Sept.	6
890	277* 15 April	7	1400	803 22 Aug.	1
900 {	287 7 Jan.	2	1500	906 28 July	3
	288 26 Dec.	6	1600	1009 3 July	5
910	298 9 Sept.	1	1700	1112* 7 June	6
920	308 23 May	3	1800 {	1215 13 May	5
930	318* 3 Feb.	4		5 June	1
940	329* 6 Oct.	3	1900 {	1318 18 April	1
950	339 20 June	5		1 May	3

The asterisk (*) is affixed to the intercalary year; and the two parellel dates of months in the two last centuries, answer to the Old and New Style. It may be farther remarked, in regard to the adjustment of the Arabian to the Julian year, that 43,830 of the former are exactly equal to 42,523 of the other; and that, when that portion of time has elapsed, the cycles will return to the same points in the Julian year as formerly.

Calendar. By the help of these divisions and characters, different nations have been enabled to take a due account of their civil and religious concerns, in the form of what is denominated a calendar, which has varied according to the constitutions of different countries, as the Roman calendar [vide *Kalendarium*]; and the Christian calendar, which has been adapted to the fasts and feasts observed in the Christian church. The Christian calendar is either Julian or Gregorian, according as it is formed on the Julian or Gregorian computation, otherwise called the *Old* and *New Style*.

Julian Calendar. The Julian Calendar is that in which the New and Full Moons, but particularly the Paschal Full Moon and the festival of Easter, are determined by the help of the Golden Numbers regularly disposed through the Julian year. The feasts observed in the Christian church are either immoveable or moveable. The *immoveable feasts* are those which are fixed to a given day, of which those that are observed in the church of England are as follow, namely:

Table of Immoveable Feasts and Fasts.

All the Sundays throughout the year
The Circumcision of our LORD JESUS CHRIST .... Jan. 1
The Epiphany 6
The Conversion of St. Paul 25
The Purification of the Blessed Virgin .... Feb. 2
St. Matthias the Apostle .... 24, or, in leap-year 25
Annunciation of the Blessed Virgin .... March 25
St. Mark the Evangelist .... April 25
St. Philip and St. Jacob the Apostles .... May 1
St. Barnabas the Apostles .... June 11
The Nativity of St. John the Baptist 24
St. Peter the Apostle 29
St. James the Apostle 25
St. Bartholomew the Apostle .... Aug. 24
St. Matthew the Apostle .... Sept. 21
St. Michael and all Angels 29
St. Luke the Evangelist .... Oct. 18
St. Simon and St. Jude the Apostles 28
All Saints .... Nov. 1
St. Andrew the Apostle 30
St. Thomas the Apostle .... Dec. 21
The Nativity of our LORD JESUS CHRIST 25
St. Stephen the Martyr 26
St. John the Evangelist 27
The Holy Innocents 28

The *Moveable Feasts* are those which are not fixed constantly to one and the same day. Of these Easter-day, on which the others depend, is, according to the decree of the council of Nice, always the first Sunday after the Full Moon, which happens upon or next after the 21st day of March; and if the Full Moon happen upon a Sunday, Easter-day is the Sunday after. According to this arrangement, the Easter-day can never fall earlier than the 22d of March, nor later than the 25th of April, which are denominated the *Paschal limits.*

Advent Sunday is always the nearest Sunday to the feast of St. Andrew, whether before or after.

Septuagesima Sunday, nine weeks before Easter.
Sexagesima   —   eight   —
Quinquagesima —   seven   —
Quadragesima   —   six   —
Rogation   —   five   — after Easter.
Ascension-day   forty days
Whit-Sunday   seven weeks
Trinity-Sunday   eight

Since, at the time of the Nicene council, the vernal equinox was fixed for the 21st of March, to which day it was supposed that it would remain invariably fixed, the Julian calendar was accordingly framed to make the Easter-day fall on the Full Moon that immediately followed the 21st of March; but it being found, as was before observed, that the Golden Number gave the Full Moons more than four days too late, a reformation was, in consequence, attempted in the Gregorian calendar, by which it was proposed to bring the Full Moon back to the season in which it was found at the time of the Nicene council.

Gregorian Calendar. The Gregorian calendar is that which, by the assistance of epacts rightly disposed through each month, is intended to show the New and Full Moons throughout the year, but in a particular manner the Paschal Moon; for by the help of the epacts the Moon's age is found for any given day of any month in this manner: add to the epact the day of the month and the number of the month, and the sum of these, casting away 30, or 29, as often as it arises, gives the age of the moon. The number of the month in this case

CHRONOLOGY.

implies that number which shows the moon's age at the beginning of each month when the solar and lunar years begin together, which are as follow:

Jan.	Feb.	March	April	May	June
0	2	1	2	3	4
July	Aug.	Sept.	Oct.	Nov.	Dec.
5	6	8	8	10	10

thus, suppose it be required to find the moon's age for the 3d of March, 1822, then 7 the epact + 3 the day of the month + 1 the number of the month = 11 the moon's age.

The following Table exhibits the order of these epacts in the Gregorian calendar throughout the year.

PERPETUAL GREGORIAN CALENDAR.

Jan.	D.L.	Epact	Feb.	D.L.	Epact	March	D.L.	Epact	April	D.L.	Epact	May	D.L.	Epact	June	D.L.	Epact	July	D.L.	Epact	Aug.	D.L.	Epact	Sept.	D.L.	Epact	Oct.	D.L.	Epact	Nov.	D.L.	Epact	Dec.	D.L.	Epact
1	A	*	1	d	29	1	d	*	1	g	29	1	b	28	1	e	27	1	g	26	1	c	xxv	1	f	23	1	A	22	1	d	21	1	f	20
2	b	29	2	e	28	2	e	29	2	A	28	2	c	27	2	f	26	2	A	25	2	d	23	2	g	22	2	b	21	2	e	20	2	g	19
3	c	28	3	f	27	3	f	28	3	b	27	3	d	26	3	g	xxv	3	b	24	3	e	22	3	A	21	3	c	20	3	f	19	3	A	18
4	d	27	4	g	26	4	g	27	4	c	26	4	e	25	4	A	23	4	c	23	4	f	21	4	b	20	4	d	19	4	g	18	4	b	17
5	e	26	5	A	xxv	5	A	26	5	d	xxv	5	f	24	5	b	22	5	d	22	5	g	20	5	c	19	5	e	18	5	A	17	5	c	16
6	f	25	6	b	23	6	b	25	6	e	23	6	g	23	6	c	21	6	e	21	6	A	19	6	d	18	6	f	17	6	b	16	6	d	15
7	g	24	7	c	22	7	c	24	7	f	22	7	A	22	7	d	20	7	f	20	7	b	18	7	e	17	7	g	16	7	c	15	7	e	14
8	A	23	8	d	21	8	d	23	8	g	21	8	b	21	8	e	19	8	g	19	8	c	17	8	f	16	8	A	15	8	d	14	8	f	13
9	b	22	9	e	20	9	e	22	9	A	20	9	c	20	9	f	18	9	A	18	9	d	16	9	g	15	9	b	14	9	e	13	9	g	12
10	c	21	10	f	19	10	f	21	10	b	19	10	d	19	10	g	17	10	b	17	10	e	15	10	A	14	10	c	13	10	f	12	10	A	11
11	d	20	11	g	18	11	g	20	11	c	18	11	e	18	11	A	16	11	c	16	11	f	14	11	b	13	11	d	12	11	g	11	11	b	10
12	e	19	12	A	17	12	A	19	12	d	17	12	f	17	12	b	15	12	d	15	12	g	13	12	c	12	12	e	11	12	A	10	12	c	9
13	f	18	13	b	16	13	b	18	13	e	16	13	g	16	13	c	14	13	e	14	13	A	12	13	d	11	13	f	10	13	b	9	13	d	8
14	g	17	14	c	15	14	c	17	14	f	15	14	A	15	14	d	13	14	f	13	14	b	11	14	e	10	14	g	9	14	c	8	14	e	7
15	A	16	15	d	14	15	d	16	15	g	14	15	b	14	15	e	12	15	g	12	15	c	10	15	f	9	15	A	8	15	d	7	15	f	6
16	b	15	16	e	13	16	e	15	16	A	13	16	c	13	16	f	11	16	A	11	16	d	9	16	g	8	16	b	7	16	e	6	16	g	5
17	c	14	17	f	12	17	f	14	17	b	12	17	d	12	17	g	10	17	b	10	17	e	8	17	A	7	17	c	6	17	f	5	17	A	4
18	d	13	18	g	11	18	g	13	18	c	11	18	e	11	18	A	9	18	c	9	18	f	7	18	b	6	18	d	5	18	g	4	18	b	3
19	e	12	19	A	10	19	A	12	19	d	10	19	f	10	19	b	8	19	d	8	19	g	6	19	c	5	19	e	4	19	A	3	19	c	2
20	f	11	20	b	9	20	b	11	20	e	9	20	g	9	20	c	7	20	e	7	20	A	5	20	d	4	20	f	3	20	b	2	20	d	1
21	g	10	21	c	8	21	c	10	21	f	8	21	A	8	21	d	6	21	f	6	21	b	4	21	e	3	21	g	2	21	c	1	21	e	*
22	A	9	22	d	7	22	d	9	22	g	7	22	b	7	22	e	5	22	g	5	22	c	3	22	f	2	22	A	1	22	d	*	22	f	29
23	b	8	23	e	6	23	e	8	23	A	6	23	c	6	23	f	4	23	A	4	23	d	2	23	g	1	23	b	*	23	e	29	23	g	28
24	c	7	24	f	5	24	f	7	24	b	5	24	d	5	24	g	3	24	b	3	24	e	1	24	A	*	24	c	29	24	f	28	24	A	27
25	d	6	25	g	4	25	g	6	25	c	4	25	e	4	25	A	2	25	c	2	25	f	*	25	b	29	25	d	28	25	g	27	25	b	26
26	e	5	26	A	3	26	A	5	26	d	3	26	f	3	26	b	1	26	d	1	26	g	29	26	c	28	26	e	27	26	A	26	26	c	25
27	f	4	27	b	2	27	b	4	27	e	2	27	g	2	27	c	*	27	e	*	27	A	28	27	d	27	27	f	26	27	b	xxv	27	d	24
28	g	3	28	c	1	28	c	3	28	f	1	28	A	1	28	d	29	28	f	29	28	b	27	28	e	26	28	g	25	28	c	23	28	e	23
29	A	2				29	d	2	29	g	*	29	b	*	29	e	28	29	g	28	29	c	26	29	f	xxv	29	A	24	29	d	22	29	f	22
30	b	1				30	e	1	30	A	29	30	c	29	30	f	27	30	A	27	30	d	25	30	g	23	30	b	23	30	e	21	30	g	21
31	c	*				31	f	*				31	d	28				31	b	25	31	e	24				31	c	22				31	A	20

The reader will observe in this calendar that the number 25 is sometimes printed in Roman numerals, to denote that in such places the calendar must have double epacts, namely, 24, 25; for, as twelve classes of epacts, consisting of 30 days each, make 360 days, which ought to make only 354, it necessarily follows, that double epacts must fall on the same day of alternate lunar months; whence the suppression of the epact 24 on the 5th of February, the 5th of April, the 3d of June, the 1st of August, the 29th of September, and the 27th of November.

Since, in the Gregorian calendar as well as the Julian, the vernal equinox is fixed for the 21st of March, and the day of the Full Moon is fourteen days after, if any given epact be found that falls immediately after the 21st of March, and eleven days be reckoned forward, the eleventh day will be the paschal limit, or the day on which the Full Moon falls. On this principle the following Table has been constructed, to show the paschal limits for the Gregorian calendar from 1700 to 1900.

Epacts.	Paschal Lim.		Epacts.	Paschal Lim.	
*	3 April	E	20	24 March	F
11	2 April	A	1	12 April	D
22	22 March	D	12	1 April	G
3	10 April	F	23	21 March	C
14	30 March	E	4	9 April	A
25	18 April	C	15	29 March	D
6	7 April	F	26	17 April	B
17	27 March	B	7	6 April	E
27	15 April	G	18	26 March	A
9	4 April	C			

To find, therefore, the Easter according to the Gregorian calendar, let the dominical letter and the Gregorian epact be found by the rule and table already given; and n the table of paschal limits, the limit corresponding to the epact with the letter denoting the day of the week; then, if this letter be compared with the dominical letter, it will show how many days must be added to come to Easter-day: thus, for the present year (1822) the Dominical letter is F, the epact is 7, corresponding to which epact is the 6th of April the paschal limit, and E the day of the week on which it falls, consequently the next day F, the 7th of April, is Easter-day.

The Easter may, however, be found by means of the number called the number of direction, which shows how many days after the 21st of March the Easter-day falls. As the paschal limits comprehend 35 days, and the 22d of March is the earliest day on which Easter-day can fall, the two following lines will show the succession of numbers; namely,

Easter-day .. 22, 23, 24, 25, 26, 27, 28, 29, 30, 31, 1, 2, &c.
No. of direct. 1, 2, 3, 4, 5, 6, 7, 8, 9, 10, 11, 12, &c.

and so on till the number of direction on the lower line be 35, which will answer to April 25, being the latest that Easter can happen. Therefore, if 21 be added to the number of direction, the sum will give the day in March for the Easter-day, if it do not exceed 31; otherwise it will give the day in April. To find the number of direction the following Table has been constructed according to the new style, with the dominical letter on the left hand, and the golden number at the top, so that where the column meets, the number of direction is to be found.

Dominical Letters. Gal. No.	1	2	3	4	5	6	7	8	9	10	11	12	13	14	15	16	17	18	19
A	29	19	5	26	12	33	19	12	26	19	5	26	12	5	26	12	33	19	12
B	27	13	6	27	13	34	20	13	34	20	13	27	20	6	27	13	34	20	6
C	8	14	7	21	14	35	21	7	28	21	7	28	21	7	28	14	28	21	7
D	19	15	8	22	15	29	22	8	29	15	8	29	15	1	22	15	29	22	8
E	30	16	2	23	16	20	23	9	23	16	2	23	9	30	23	9
F	24	17	3	24	10	31	24	10	31	17	10	24	17	3	24	10	31	17	10
G	25	18	4	25	11	32	18	11	32	18	4	25	18	4	24	11	35	18	11

Thus the Dominical Letter for 1822 being F, and the Golden Number 18, then 21 + 17 = 38 − 31 = 7 the Easter-day. *Scalig. Doct. Temp.; Petav. Rat. Temp.; Ricciol. Chronol.; Wolf. Chron.*

CHRONO'METER (*Hor.*) any instrument for the exact measuring of time, as clocks, watches, dials, &c. from χρόνος, time, and μέτρον, a measure.

CHRONOSCO'PE (*Hor.*) a name sometimes given to a pendulum or machine for measuring time, from χρόνος, time, and σκοπέω, to observe.

CHROS (*Anat.*) χρώς, the Ionians, according to Galen, understood by this word whatever is carnous in the body, as the skin, muscles, membranes, &c. in distinction from bones, cartilages, and ligaments. *Gal. Com. 2, in Lib. de Tract.*

CHROSTA'SIMA (*Min.*) a name for pellucid gems which appear of one simple and permanent colour in all shades of light, such as the diamond, carbuncle, ruby, garnet, amethyst, sapphire, beryl, emerald, and topaz.

CHRU'PSIA (*Med.*) a disease of the eyes in which a person perceives objects of a different colour from the reality.

CHRYPSO'RCHES (*Med.*) vide *Parorchidium*.

CHRY'SALIS (*Ent.*) χρυσαλίς, or nymph; the second apparent change of the maggot of any species of insects while it lies hid under a card pellicle, previous to its appearance as a butterfly. It is so called from its bright yellow or gold colour.

CHRYSALI'TES (*Min.*) a figured stone, of a glittering gold and iron colour.

CHRYSA'NTHEMOIDES (*Bot.*) the same as the *Osteospermum* of Linnæus.

CHRYSA'NTHEMUM (*Bot.*) a genus of plants, Class 19 *Syngenesia*, Order 2 *Polygamia Superflua*.
Generic Characters. CAL. common hemispherical; *scales* close incumbent.—COR. compound radiate *corollets* hermaphrodite; *proper* funnel-form.—STAM. *filaments* five; *anthers* cylindric.—PIST. *germ* ovate; *style* filiform; *stigmas* two.—PER. none; *calyx* unchanged; *seed* solitary; *receptacle* naked.
Species. The species are either annuals, perennials, or shrubs. Of the first kind are the following, namely—*Chrysanthemum segetum*, seu *Creticum*, Corn or Garden Marigold, native of Europe.—*Chrysanthemum Myconis*, native of Portugal. Of the second kind are the principal, namely—*Chrysanthemum atratum*, &c. seu *Bellis*, &c. Fleshy-leaved Chrysanthemum, native of Switzerland.—*Chrysanthemum leucanthemum*, *Matricaria*, &c. seu *Bellis*, &c. Common Ox-eye or Great Daisy, native of Europe.—*Chrysanthemum montanum*, *Leucanthemum*, Mountain Ox-eye, native of Silesia.—*Chrysanthemum graminifolium*, Grass-leaved Ox-eye, native of Montpellier.—*Chrysanthemum coccineum*, seu *foliis*, &c. seu *Buphthalmum*, &c. native of Iberia.—*Chrysanthemum Achilleæ*, seu *Parthenium*, &c. Milfoil-leaved Chrysanthemum, native of Italy.—*Chrysanthemum argenteum*, *Matricaria*, &c. seu *Chamæmelum*, &c. native of the East.—*Chrysanthemum areticum*, seu *Pyrethrum*, &c. native of North America. Of the third kind are the following, namely—*Chrysanthemum flosculosum*, *Tanacetum*, seu *Balsamita*, Bastard Chrysanthemum, an ever-

green, native of the Cape of Good Hope.—*Chrysanthemum incanum*, native of the Cape of Good Hope.—*Chrysanthemum sentinium aster*, seu *Bellis*, Creeping-rooted Chrysanthemum, &c.—*Chrysanthemum Indicum*, seu *Tis jetti-Pu*, native of the East Indies, &c. *Clus. Hist. Plant. rar.; Bauh. Hist. Plant.; C. Bauh. Pin.; Ger. Herb.; Park. Theat. Botan.; Raii Hist. Plant.; Tournef. Inst.; Pluk. Almag.*

CHRYSANTHEMUM is also the *Amellus lychnitis* in the Linnean system.

CHRYSA'SPIDES (*Ant.*) χρυσάσπιδες, soldiers armed with golden shields.

CHRYSE (*Med.*) the name of a plaster for recent wounds. *Paul. Æginet. l. 7, c. 17.*

CHRYSELE'CTRUM (*Min.*) amber of a golden yellow colour.

CHRYSIPPE'A (*Bot.*) a herb mentioned by Pliny. *Nat. Hist. l. 26, c. 8.*

CHRY'SIS (*Ent.*) Golden Fly, a genus of animals, Class *Insecta*, Order *Hymenoptera*.
Generic Character. Mouth horny.—*Feelers* unequal.—*Antennæ* short.—*Abdomen* arched.
Species. The principal species are, *Chrysis splendida*, *fulgida*, *ignita*, &c.

CHRYSIS (*Bot.*) the *Helianthus annuus* of Linnæus.

CHRYSISCE'PTRON (*Bot.*) White Chamæleon.

CHRYSI'TES (*Min.*) a kind of precious stone. *Plin. l. 37, c. 10.*

CHRYSI'TIS (*Min.*) the *Spuma argenti*, or Litharge, so called from its gold colour; recommended in ophthalmic cases. *Hippoc. de Mul. l. 1; Plin. l. 26, c. 6.*

CHRYSI'TRIX (*Bot.*) a genus of plants, Class 23 *Polygamia*, Order 3 *Dioecia*.
Generic Characters. CAL. *glumes* bivalve; *valvelets* close. COR. *chaffs* extremely numerous.—STAM. *filaments* solitary; *anthers* linear.—PIST. common; *germ* oblong; *style* filiform; *stigma* simple.—PER. .... *seed* ....
Species. The only species is the *Chrysitrix Capensis*, a perennial, native of the Cape of Good Hope.

CHRYSOBA'LANUS (*Bot.*) χρυσοβάλανος, a drug mentioned by Galen, supposed to be the nutmeg. *Gal. de Simpl. l. 8, c. 3.*

CHRYSOBALANUS, a genus of plants, Class 12 *Icosandria*, Order 1 *Monogynia*.
Generic Characters. CAL. *perianth* one-leaved; *divisions* expanding.—COR. *petals* five.—STAM. *stamens* very many; *anthers* small.—PIST. *germ* ovate; *style* of the shape and length of the stamens; *stigma* obtuse.—PER. *drupe* ovate; *seed* nut-ovate.
Species. The only species is the *Chrysobalanus Icaco*, seu *Guaiera*, Cocoa Plum, a shrub, native of South America. *Bauh. Pin.*

CHRYSOBERY'LLUS (*Min.*) a crystal stone, shining like gold. *Plin. l. 37, c. 5.*

CHRYSOCA'LLIA (*Bot.*) the same as *Chrysocome*.

CHRYSOCA'RPUM (*Bot.*) a sort of ivy. *Plin. l. 16, c. 34.*

CHRYSOCERA'UNIUS (*Min.*) vide *Cerauniochrysis*.

CHRYSOCHA'LCUM (*Min.*) vide *Aurichalcum*.

CHRYSOCO'LLA (*Min.*) χρυσόκολλα, from χρυσός, gold, and κόλλη, glue; the name among the ancients for gold solder, or Borax. [vide *Borax*]

CHRYSO'COMA (*Bot.*) vide *Chrysocome*.

CHRYSOCOMA, in the Linnean system, a genus of plants, Class 19 *Syngenesia*, Order 1 *Polygamia Æqualis*.
Generic Characters. CAL. common hemispherical; *scales* linear.—COR. compound tubular; *corollets* numerous; *proper* funnel-form; *border* five-cleft.—STAM. *filaments* five; *anthers* cylindric.—PIST. *germ* oblong; *style* filiform; *stigmas* two.—PER. none; *calyx* scarcely changed; *seeds* solitary; *pappus* hairy; *receptacle* naked.
Species. The species are shrubs or perennials.—*Chrysocoma comaurea*, *Conyza*, seu *Elichrysum*, &c. Great

shrubby Goldylocks, native of the Cape of Good Hope.—*Chrysocoma cernua, suffruticosa,* seu *Coma,* &c. Small shrubby Goldylocks, native of the Cape of Good Hope.—*Chrysocoma ciliaris, suffruticosa,* seu *Coma,* &c. native of the Cape of Good Hope.—*Chrysocoma, Aster,* seu *Conyza,* &c. a perennial, native of Siberia.—*Chrysocoma biflora,* Two-flowered Goldylocks, a perennial, native of Siberia.—*Chrysocoma linosyris Asyris,* seu *Linaria,* &c. German Goldylocks, a perennial, native of Europe.—*Chrysocoma oppositifolia, Eupatorium,* seu *Cyanus,* Opposite-leaved Goldylocks, native of the Cape of Good Hope, &c. *Clus. Hist. Plant. rar.; Bauh. Pin.; Ger. Herb.; Raii Hist. Plant.; Tournef. Inst.; Boerhaav. Ind.; Pluk. Almag.*

CHRYSOCO'ME (*Bot.*) χρυσόκομη, the herb Millefoil, or Yarrow; so called from χρυσός, gold, and κομή, hair because it has corymbs, or leaves, resembling golden locks. The root of the Chrysocome is heating and astringent. *Arist. de Plant. l. 2, c. 7; Dioscor. l. 4, c. 55; Plin. l. 21, c. 8.*

CHRYSOCOME, or *Chrysocoma, in the Linnean system,* is the *Conyza inuloides,* the Solidago Lanceolata.

CHRYSOGO'NIA (*Alchem.*) χρυσογονία, from χρυσός, gold, and γίνομαι, to be generated; the aurific or gold-making seed, most perfectly concocted from a solution of gold.

CHRYSO'GONUM (*Bot.*) χρυσόγονον, Red Turnep; a plant which was reckoned good against the bites of serpents. *Dioscor. l. 4, c. 56.*

CHRYSOGONUM, *in the Linnean system,* a genus of plants, Class 19 *Syngenesia,* Order 3 *Polygamia Necessaria.*

Generic Characters. CAL. common five-leaved; *leaflets* lanceolate.—COR. compound radiate; *corolets* very many; *proper* funnel-form.—STAM. *filaments* five; *anthers* cylindrical.—PIST. *germ* very small; *style* setaceous; *stigma* obscure.—PER. none; *calyx* unchanged; *seeds* none; *receptacle* chaffy.

Species. The only species is the *Chrysogonum Virginianum, pumilum,* seu *Chrysanthemum,* &c. native of Virginia.

CHRYSOGONUM is also the *Leontice chrysogonum* of Linnæus.

CHRYSOLA'CHANUM (*Bot.*) a herb, the same as *Atriplex.*

CHRYSOLA'MPIS (*Min.*) a precious stone, fiery by night, and pale by day. *Plin. l. 37, c. 10.*

CHRY'SOLITE (*Min.*) vide *Chrysolithus.*—*Chrysolite paste,* a kind of vitreous substance made in imitation of the natural.

CHRYSOLI'THUS (*Min.*) Chrysolite, a kind of jasper or green diaphonous gem, shining with a glittering splendour. It is endued with the virtue of stopping hæmorrhages, according to Pliny. *Plin. l. 37, c. 11.*

CHRYSOLITHUS, *in the Linnean system,* is classed under the genus *Gemma.* It is called Chrysolite, or Yellowish-green Topaz, and is found mostly in the East Indies, and sometimes in Europe.

CHRYSOME'LA (*Ent.*) a genus of insects of the Order *Coleoptera.*

Generic Character. Antennæ moniliform.—Feelers six, growing larger towards the end.—Thorax marginate.—Shells unmarginate.—Body mostly oval.

Species. This is a numerous and beautiful tribe of insects, that is found every where in woods and gardens, where they feed on leaves of trees. Their motion is slow, and sometimes when caught they emit an oily liquor of a disagreeable smell. The different species are distinguished generally by their colour.

CHRYSOME'LIA (*Bot.*) the *Citrus aurantium* of Linnæus.

CHRY'SOPAIS (*Bot.*) the Indian purging juice, called otherwise *Gummi-Gotta. Castell. Lex. Med.*

CHRYSOPA'SIUS (*Min.*) the Topaz. [vide *Chrysoprasus*]

CHRYSOPA'STUS (*Min.*) a precious stone, sprinkled as it were with a gold sand.

CHRYSO'PHRYS (*Min.*) a fish; so called from the gold colour it has over the eyes.

CHRYSOPHY'LLUM (*Bot.*) a genus of plants, Class 5 *Pentandria,* Order 1 *Monogynia.*

Generic Characters. CAL. *perianth* five-parted; *leaflets* roundish.—COR. monopetalous; *border* five-cleft; *segments* roundish.—STAM. *filaments* five; *anthers* roundish.—PIST. *germ* roundish; *style* very short; *stigmas* obtuse.—PER. *berry* globular; *seeds* solitary.

Species. The species are shrubs, as the—*Chrysophyllum cainito, Cainito,* &c. seu *Sideroxylon,* Broad-leaved Starapple, native of Martinica.—*Chrysophyllum monopyrenum,* native of Jamaica.—*Chrysophyllum microcarpum,* native of Hispaniola.—*Chrysophyllum argenteum,* Narrow-leaved Star-apple, native of Martinica.—*Chrysophyllum rugosum,* native of Jamaica.—*Chrysophyllum pyriforme,* seu *Macoucou,* &c. native of Guiana.—*Chrysophyllum glabrum,* native of Martinica.

CHRYSOPHYLLUM is also the *Jacquinia armillaris.*

CHRY'SOPIS (*Min.*) a precious stone, having the appearance of gold, from χρυσός, gold, and ὄψ, the aspect or appearance. *Plin. l. 37, c. 10; Isid. Orig. l. 16, c. 14.*

CHRYSOSPLE'NII FOLIIS (*Bot.*) the *Diandra Africana.*

CHRYSOSPLE'NIUM (*Bot.*) a genus of plants, Class 10 *Decandria,* Order 2 *Digynia.*

Generic Characters. CAL. *perianth* four or five parted; *divisions* ovate.—COR. none, unless the coloured calyx be so called.—STAM. *filaments* eight or ten; *anthers* simple.—PIST. *germ* inferior; *styles* the length of the stamens; *stigmas* obtuse.—PER. *capsule* two-parted; *seeds* very many.

Species. The two species are the—*Chrysosplenium alternifolium, Saxifraga,* seu *Sedum,* &c. Alternate-leaved Golden Saxifrage, a perennial, native of Sweden.—*Chrysosplenium oppositifolium, Saxifraga, Sedum,* seu *Aschimella,* Opposite-leaved Golden Saxifrage, a perennial, native of England. *Dodon. Pempt.; Lob. Hist. Plant.; Bauh. Hist. Plant.; Ger. Herb.; Park. Theat. Botan.; Raii Hist. Plant.; Tournef. Inst.*

CHRYSOPLI'CIUS PULVIS (*Med.*) a kind of powder mentioned by Helmont, which causes lead to harden. *Helm. Nat. contra Nesc. Tit.* 40.

CHRYSOPŒ'IA (*Alchem.*) χρυσοποιία, from χρυσός, gold, and ποιώ, to make; that part of the spagirical art which teaches the making of gold out of more imperfect metals.

CHRYSOPRA'SUS (*Min.*) a kind of green stone mixed with a bright gold colour. It is called by Isidore *Chrysopasius,* and by later mineralogists *Chrysolithus,* or the Topaz. To this stone were ascribed many superstitious virtues. *Plin. l. 37, c. 5; Solin. c. 52; Isid. Orig. l. 16, c. 7; Marbod. de Lapid. pret. c. 9.*

CHRYSO'PTERON (*Min.*) vide *Chrysoprasus.*

CHRY'SOS (*Ich.*) χρυσός, Gilt-head; a species of fish, of a gold colour, mentioned by Pliny on the authority of Ovid. *Plin. l. 32, c. 11.*

CHRY'STAL (*Her.*) is sometimes used in blazonry instead of *argent,* or silver, and most frequently pearl.

CHRY'STALLINE (*Min.*) vide *Crystalline.*

CHRYSTALLO'GRAPHY (*Min.*) vide *Crystallography.*

CHRYSU'LEA (*Met.*) Aqua-fortis, or the water with which gold-finers wash off gold when mixed with other metals.

CHRY'SUN (*Med.*) χρυσῶν, an epithet for two collyria for the eyes. *Aet.*

CHU (*Ant.*) choa or chus, χῦς; a liquid measure among the Athenians, answering to the congius of the Romans, and containing six sextarii, and twelve attic cotylæ, or nine pints. *Gal. de Mens.*

CHUB (*Ich.*) a river fish, of the carp kind; so called on account of its great head, from the Teutonic *konf,* a head; wherefore, also, it is denominated in Latin *capito;* Italian *capitone;* French *testard;* and in the Linnean system *Cy-*

5

prinus cephalus. The chub is a coarse fish, full of bones, frequents the deep holes of rivers, is very timid, and lives upon worms, caterpillars, and all insects of the coleopterous kind.

CHU'LAN (*Bot.*) a species of the *Chloranchus.*

CHUM (*Cus.*) a chamber-fellow to a student at the university.

CHUNDRI'LLA VERCURIA (*Bot.*) vide *Zacintha.*

CHU'NNO (*Bot.*) vide *Battatas.*

CHURCH (*Ecc.*) in Saxon cýnic, Teutonic *kirche*, is supposed to be abbreviated from κύριακη, i. e. οικία, a house, and κύριος, Lord, i. e. the Lord's House; is taken in its most general sense for the collective body of Christians, who, in respect to community of faith, are called the *catholic* or *universal church;* in respect to their Christian course here on earth, the *church militant;* in respect to their future condition, the *church triumphant*, or the body of faithful already in glory; and, according to the Romanists, the *church patient*, or the body of the faithful who are in purgatory. *Church*, in a limited sense, is taken for particular bodies of professing Christians, who are distinguished, geographically, into the *Latin* or *Western Church*, and the *Greek* or *Eastern Church*; the former comprehending the churches of Italy, France, Spain, Africa, and the northern countries; the latter, the churches of those countries which were formerly subject to the Greek or Eastern empires. The church is moreover distinguished, as respects its doctrine or discipline, into the *Romish Church*, the *Protestant Church*, the *Gallican Church*, the *Church of England*, &c.—*Church*, in the sense of a place of assembly for public worship, is ecclesiastically distinguished sometimes into the *grand church*, for the chief church of a place; and commonly into the *metropolitan church*, the *parochial church*, the *cathedral church*, *collegiate church*, and also by the names of the saints to which they are dedicated, as St. Paul's, St. Peter's, &c.

CHURCH (*Archit.*) an oblong building much in the form of a ship, which now commonly consists of a nave, or body, aisles, choir, chapel, belfry, &c. The Greek church, when complete, formerly consisted of two porches, namely, the πρόναος, or *vaunt-nave;* the νάρθηξ, or *ferula;* the ναξ, or *nave;* the *ambo*, or place where the deacons and priests read the gospels and preached; the *baptistery* or font; the χορὸς, or choir; and the *sanctuary*. The ancient churches were also distinguished, as to their form, into—*Simple Churches*, i. e. churches without aisles.—*Churches with aisles*, i. e. having a row of porticos in the form of vaulted galleries.—*Churches in a Greek cross*, where the length of the traverse part is equal to that of the nave.—*Churches in a Latin cross*, those which have the nave longer than the traverse part.—*Churches in rotundo*, the plan of which is perfectly circular, as the Pantheon at Rome.

CHURCH-A'LE (*Archæol.*) the same as *Whitsun-Ale.*

CHURCH-REE'VES (*Ecc.*) the same as *Church-Wardens.*

CHURCH-SCOT (*Law*) or *Churchesset*, a payment or contribution, frequently called *primitiæ seminum*, consisting of a certain measure of wheat paid to the priest on St. Martin's day, as the first fruits of the harvest. It afterwards became part of the tythe.

CHURCH-SE'RVICE (*Ecc.*) the public service performed according to the rites and ceremonies of the Church of England.

CHURCH-WA'RDENS (*Ecc.*) *ecclesiæ guardiani*, the guardians or keepers of the church, one of whom is most commonly appointed by the minister, and the other by the parish; wherefore the former is called the *rector's warden.* The office of the church-warden is to look to the repairs of the church; church-yard, &c. and to attend to all matters connected with the rights of the church and the decencies of public worship.

CHURCHING (*Ecc.*) the act of women who attend church for the first time after child-birth, to return special thanks for their delivery.

CHURL (*Archæol.*) in Saxon ca𝔯l, or ceo𝔯l, a clown; signified a tenant at will, of which there are two kinds; one who hired the lord's testamentary estate, like our farmers; and the other, that tilled and manured the demesnes, and were therefore called *Sockmen*, or *Ploughmen.*

CHUS (*Ant.*) vide *Chu.*

CHY'BUR (*Alchem.*) Sulphur.

CHYDÆ'US (*Ant.*) χυδαῖος, wine made of palms. *Plin.* l. 14, c. 16; *Pallad. de Re Rust.*

CHYLA'RIA (*Anat.*) from χυλὸς, chyle; a white mucous urine of the colour and consistence of chyle.

CHYLE (*Anat.*) a milky fluid, secreted from the aliments, in the lacteal vessels. It is separated by digestion from the chyme; and is that fluid substance from which the blood is formed. The constituent principles of chyle are water, oily cream, cheese, earth, and animal lymph. The uses of the chyle are to supply matter for the formation of the blood; to restrain, by its acessent nature, the putrescent tendency of the blood; to prevent the thickening of the fluids; and to supply milk for puerperal women.

CHYLI'FERA *vasa* (*Anat.*) vide *Lactea vasa.*

CHYLIFICA'TION (*Anat.*) the first process of digestion carried on in the small intestines, and principally in the duodenum, by which the aliment is converted into chyle.

CHYLI'SMA (*Med.*) from χυλὸς, an expressed juice.

CHYLI'STA (*Med.*) Glass of antimony obtunded by levigating it with mastich dissolved in rectified spirits of wine.

CHYLOPOIE'TIC (*Anat.*) from χυλὸς, chyle, and ποιέω, to make; an epithet for vessels which generate chyle.

CHYLO'SIS (*Anat.*) vide *Chylification.*

CHYLOSTA'GMA (*Chem.*) a fluid distilled from the *Theriaca andromachi.*

CHY'LOUS (*Anat.*) an epithet for what consists of chyle: thus, milk is the chylous part of an animal.

CHY'LUS (*Anat.*) vide *Chyle.*

CHYMA'TION (*Med.*) the name of a penetrating medicine in Marcellus Empiricus, c. 20.

CHYME (*Anat.*) in its most general sense, implies any humour incrassated by concoction; but, in its particular sense, that humour which is immediately prepared from the ingested food; and which, by farther concoction, becomes chyle.

CHY'MIA (*Chem.*) vide *Chemistry.*

CHYMIA'TER (*Med.*) vide *Chimiater.*

CHYMIA'TRIA (*Med.*) the art of curing diseases by the application of chemistry to medicine.

CHY'MICAL (*Chem.*) vide *Chemical.*

CHYMICOPHA'NTA (*Chem.*) a pretended chemist.

CHYMOLE'A (*Med.*) vide *Kymolea.*

CHYMO'SIS (*Med.*) vide *Chemosis.*

CHYMUS (*Chem.*) vide *Chyme.*

CHY'NLEN *radix* (*Bot.*) a cylindrical root, about the size of a goose quill, brought from China. It has a bitter taste, and is reckoned a stomachic when infused in wine.

CHY'SIS (*Med.*) χύσις, from χύω, to pour; fusion, or the reducing of solid bodies to a state of fluidity, by means of heat. *Foes. Œconom. Hippocrat.*

CHYTLON (*Med.*) χύτλον, a plentiful inunction with oil and water. *Erotian. Lex. Hippocrat.*

CHYTRA (*Ant.*) χύτρα, a pot or pipkin. *Foes. Œconom. Hippocrat.*

CHRYTRACU'LIA (*Bot.*) the *Calyptranthus* of Linnæus.

CIACO'NNE (*Mus.*) the same as *Chacone.*

CI'BAGE (*Bot.*) an eastern tree, much resembling the pine-tree. *C. Bauh. Pin.; Raii Hist. Plant.*

CIBA'RIA *Lex* (*Ant.*) a sort of sumptuary law respecting victuals and house-keeping expences. *Macrob.* l. 2, c. 13.

CIBA'RIUS *panis* (*Ant.*) Household bread, boulted, or coarse bread, which was given to the slaves. *Cic. Tusc.* l. 5, c. 34; *Isid. Orig.* l. 20, c. 2.

CIBARIUS *Sal* (*Chem.*) vide *Sal Marinus*.

CIBA'TION (*Med.*) the taking of food.

CIBATION (*Chem.*) an incorporation of bodies. *Castell. Lex. Med.*

CIBDELOPLA'CIA (*Min.*) an old term for a sort of spars, which are much debased by a large admixture of earth. They are opaque, formed of thin crusts, covering vegetables, and other bodies, by way of incrustation.

CIBDELOSTRA'CIA (*Min.*) an old term for such earthy spars as are formed into thin plates.

CIBO'RIUM (*Ant.*) κιβώριον, a sort of drinking cup used in Egypt, which was wide at the top, and gradually decreased towards the bottom.
Hor. l. 2, od. 7,

Oblivioso levia Massico
Ciboria exple.

Athen. l. 3, &c.

CIBORIUM (*Ecc.*) the covering of the altar in ancient churches, consisting of a dome, supported by four columns. *Ceremon. Episcop.* l. 1. c. 12; *Greg. Turon. de Mirab.*

CIBORIUM (*Bot.*) the pod of the Egyptian bean, which resembles the cup above mentioned; also the bean itself, and the whole plant is so called. *Diodor.* l. 1; *Dioscor.* l. 3, c. 148; *Nicand. in Georg. apud Athen.*; *Gal. Theriac ad Pamphil.*; *Aet. Tetrab.* l, serm. 1.

CIBOU'LS (*Bot.*) a sort of onions nearly allied to the scallions, which form no bulb at the roots; the *Allium fistulosum* of Linnæus.

CI'BUS *castrensis* (*Ant.*) the food which was used by the soldiers in camp. It consisted of bacon and cheese; and, for the drink, vinegar, mixed with water, which was called *posca*. *Spartian Adrian*, c. 10.

CIBUS *albus* (*Med.*) a sort of jelly; also the name of an American plant.

CICA'DA (*Ent.*) the *Baulm Cricket*, an insect, common in Italy, but unknown in England. It is very noisy, like the cricket, living on dew, and what it sucks from the dwarf ash. These insects are used, when dried, in colics. *Aldrov. de Insect.*

CICADA, *in the Linnean system*, a genus of animals, Class *Insecta*, Order *Hemiptera*.
Generic Characters. Snout inflected.—*Antennæ* setaceous.—Legs formed for leaping.
Species. Animals of this genus live on various plants: the *larva* is apterous; the *pupa* furnished with the mere rudiments of wings. The species are divided into the—*Membracis*, which have the antennæ subulate.—*Tettigonia*, or those which have legs not formed for leaping.—*Cercopis*, which have the antennæ filiform.—*Cicada*, which have the lip rounded.

CI'CATRICE (*Surg.*) a scar of a wound. [vide *Cicatrix*]

CICATRI'CULA (*Nat.*) a little white speck or vessel that appears in the coat of the yolk of an egg, wherein the first changes appear towards the formation of a chicken.

CICATRISA'NTIA (*Surg.*) such applications and medicines as dispose wounds to dry up and heal, so as to be covered with a new skin.

CICATRISA'TUS (*Bot.*) scarred; an epithet for a stem.—*Cicatrisatus caulis*, a stem, marked with the scars from leaves that have fallen off.

CI'CATRIX (*Surg.*) the seam or scar on the skin after the healing of a wound or ulcer.

CICCA (*Bot.*) a genus of plants, Class 21 *Monoecia*, Order 4 *Tetrandria*.
Generic Characters. CAL. *perianth* four-leaved; *leaflets* roundish.—COR. none.—STAM. *filaments* four; *anthers* subglobular.—PIST. *germ* roundish; *styles* four; *stigmas* acute.—PER. *capsule* subglobular; *seeds* solitary.
Species. The two species are the—*Cicca disticha*, *Averrhoo*, &c. *Phyllanthus*, &c. *Nelipoli*, seu *Cheramela*, a shrub, native of the East Indies.—*Cicca nudiflora*, a shrub, native of Java.

CI'CCUS (*Ent.*) κίκκος, a young grasshopper.

CI'CELY (*Bot.*) a perennial, the *Chærophyllum sylvestre* of Linnæus, which communicates a green and yellow dye to wool. According to some, it is a herb grateful to cows, and for that reason called *cow-weed*; but others have asserted that no animal will eat of it except the ass.

CI'CER (*Bot.*) a small pulse, less than peas; called in the Greek ἐρέβινθος; it is supposed to derive its name from κίκυς, strength. *Theophrast. Hist. Plant.* l. 8, c. 5; *Dioscor.* l. 2, c. 126; *Columel.* l. 2, c. 10; *Plin.* l. 18, c. 12.

CICER, *in the Linnean system*, a genus of plants, Class 17 *Diadelphia*, Order 4 *Decandria*.
Generic Characters. CAL. *perianth* five-parted; *segments* four.—COR. papilionaceous; *banner* flat; *wings* obtuse; *keel* sharpish.—STAM. *filaments* diadelphous; *anthers* simple.—PIST. *germ* ovate; *style* simple; *stigma* obtuse.—PER. *legume* rhomboid; *seeds* two.
Species. The species are—*Cicer arietinum*, seu *sativum*, Chick-pea, an annual, native of Spain.—*Cicer lens*, &c. *Ervum*, &c. seu *Lens*, &c. an annual, native of Germany.

CICER is also the *Astragalus cicer* of Linnæus.

CI'CERA (*Bot.*) ὄχρος, a kind of pulse like chichlings, good for fodder. *Columel. de Re Rust.* l. 2, c. 11.

CICERA is the *Lathyris* of Linnæus.

CICERA *Tartari* (*Med.*) small pills composed of tartar.

CICERBI'TA (*Bot.*) a species of *Sonchus*.

CICE'RCULA (*Bot.*) a diminutive of cicer, λάθυρος, chichlings, or little chiches. *Plin.* l. 18, c. 12; *Plut. de Quæst. Roman.*; *Columel. de Re Rust.* l. 2, c. 10; *Gal. de Simpl.* l. 1, c. 27.

CI'CERI *affinis* (*Bot.*) the *Astragalus* of Linnæus.

CICHO'RIS *affinis* (*Bot.*) the *Sigesbeskia orientalis*.

CICHO'RIUM (*Bot.*) κιχόριον, Cichory, Succory, or Wild Endive, a sallad herb; so called because it grows wild, διὰ τῶν χωρίων, i. e. in the fields. It is cooling and moistening, removes obstructions, and is good for the jaundice. *Theoph. Hist. Plant.* l. 7, c. 7; *Dioscor.* l. 2, c. 160; *Plin.* l. 20, c. 8; *Columel. de Re Rust.* l. 8, c. 14; *Gal. de Simpl.* l. 8, c. 8; *Schol. in Nicand Theriac.*; *Aet. Tetrab.* 1, serm. 1; *Paul. Æginet.* l. 3, c. 46; *Geopin. Auct.* l. 12, c. 1.

CICHORIUM, *in the Linnean system*, a genus of plants, Class 19 *Syngenesia*, Order 1 *Polygamia Æqualis*.
Generic Characters. CAL. *common* calycled cylindric; scales eight.—COR. *compound* flat; *corollules* hermaphrodite, twenty; *proper* monopetalous.—STAM. *filaments* five; *anther* cylindric-pentagon.—PIST. *germ* oblong; *style* filiform; *stigmas* two revolute.—PER. none; *calyx* cylindric; *seeds* solitary; *receptacle* somewhat chaffy.
Species. The species are of different kinds, as—*Cichorium intybus*, seu *Intybus*, Garden and Wild Succory, a perennial, native of Europe.—*Cichorium endivia*, *Endivia*, *Intybum*, seu *Intybus*, Broad-leaved Succory, or Common Endive, an annual or biennial, native of the East Indies.—*Cichorium divaricatum*, an annual, native of Morocco.—*Cichorium spinosum*, seu *Chondrillæ*, &c. Prickly Succory, a biennial, native of Crete.

CICHORIUM is also a name for the *Crepis Vesicaria*.

CI'CHORY (*Bot.*) or *Succory*, the plant classed under *Cichorium*, in the Linnean system, is a herb which, in its uncultivated state, called the *Cichorium intybus*, or Wild Cichory, abounds with a milky juice, of a penetrating bitterish taste. The roots are more bitter than the leaves or stalks, and these than the flowers. When cultivated in gardens it loses much of its bitterness. This herb is so, much like endive, that it was supposed to be the same plant in an uncultivated state; but the salad known by the name of Endive is an annual, and at most a biennial: for which reason they are both brought under one genus *Cichorium*.

CI'CI (*Bot.*) a shrub, in Latin called *Ricinus*, because the seeds of it are like the vermin called *teeks* or *ticks*. *Plin*. l. 15, c. 7.

CICILIA'NA (*Bot.*) vide *Androsæmum*.

CICINDE'LA (*Ent.*) Glow-Worm; was called by the Greeks λαμπυρίς, and by Aristotle πυγολαμπίς; but by the Roman peasants *stellans volatus*. *Aristot.* l. 5, c. 19; *Plin*. l. 18, c. 26.

CICINDELA, *in the Linnean system*, a genus of animals, Class *Insecta*, Order *Coleoptera*.

   Generic Character. *Antennæ* setaceous.—*Feelers* six filiform.—*Mandible* prominent; *eyes* prominent.—*Thorax* rounded.

   Species. Insects of this tribe are generally very beautiful, and very rapacious, seizing with great ferocity the other insects which fall in their way. The larva is soft, white, and long; and the species are distinguished into those which have the lip three-toothed, and those which have it entire.

CICI'SBEO (*Cus.*) a male attendant on ladies in Italy.

CI'CLA (*Bot.*) the *Beta cicla* of Linnæus.

CICO'NGIUS (*Ant.*) a measure containing twelve sextaries or pints.

CICO'NIA (*Ant.*) signified properly a stork; but was also used to denote an instrument used by husbandmen for making furrows even. *Isid. Orig.* l. 20, c. 15.

CICUS (*Bot.*) a name for the skin that divides the grains or kernels of the pomegranate.

CICUTA (*Ant.*) a hollow, intercepted between two knots of the stalks or reeds, of which the ancient shepherds used to make their pipes. *Serv. in Virg.*

CICUTA (*Bot.*) in Greek κώνιον, the herb which answers to our hemlock, of which, when bruised, the Athenians used to make a poisonous drink for their state criminals who were condemned to death.

CICUTA, *in the Linnean system*, a genus of plants, Class 5 *Pentandria*, Order 2 *Digynia*.

   Generic Characters. CAL. *umbel universal* roundish; *partial* roundish; *involucre universal* none; *partial* many-leaved; *leaflets* short; *perianth proper* scarcely visible. COR. *universal* uniform; *flosculus* all fertile; *proper* inflected.—STAM. *filaments* five; *anthers* simple.—PIST. *germ* inferior; *styles* two; *stigmas* headed.—PER. none; *fruit* subovate; *seeds* two.

   Species. The three species are the—*Cicuta virosa, suim, &c. Coriandrum, &c.* seu *Cicutaria*, Long-leaved Water Hemlock, a perennial, native of Europe.—*Cicuta bulbifera*, seu *Ammi*, native of Virginia.—*Cicuta maculata, Ægopodium, Angelica*, seu *Myrrha*, a perennial, native of Virginia.

CICUTA'RIA (*Bot.*) the *Chærophyllum sylvestre* of Linnæus.

CID (*Polit.*) an Arabic word, signifying chief commander or lord.

CI'DARIS (*Ant.*) from the Hebrew כתר, or the Chaldee כתרא, a crown; signifies 1. The high priest's mitre among the Jews. *Hier.* 2. A cap, turban, or sash, which the Persian kings and priests used to wear.

CI'DER (*Bot.*) שכר, in the Hebrew; σίκερα, Greek; and *sicera*, Latin; signify all manner of inebriating liquors except wine; and *sakar*, in the Arabic, signifies wine made of dates; whence comes the English word cider, to denote the juice of the apple expressed and fermented.

CI'DERKIN (*Bot.*) a diminutive of the word cider, signifying the liquor which is drawn from the cores and rinds of apples after the cider has been pressed out.

CIDO'NIUM *Malum* (*Bot.*) the quince, the fruit of the *Pyrus Cidonia*.

CIDONIUM *vinum* (*Bot.*) wine made of quinces.

CIDRA (*Bot.*) Cider.

CI'ELING (*Archit.*) vide *Ceiling*.

CIERGE (*Ecc.*) a wax taper, such as is carried about in processions.

CIERGE d'eau (*Archit.*) French for a water spout.

CIFRA (*Arith.*) a cypher.

CI'GNUS (*Ant.*) a measure of two drams.

CI'LERY (*Archit.*) a term for the drapery or foliage that is wrought upon the heads of pillars.

CI'LIA (*Anat.*) ταρσοί, the eye-lashes, or extreme parts of the *palpebræ*, or eye-lids, which are cartilaginous, and have the hairs inserted in them. *Ruff. Ephes. de Apell. Part. Corp. Hum.* l. 1; *Gal. de Usu. Part.* l. 10, c. 7; *Plin.* l. 11, c. 37.

CI'LIARY (*Anat.*) an epithet for several parts belonging to the *cilia*, or eye-lashes; as the—*Ciliary Glands*, i. e. excretory ducts in the inner edge of each eye-lids.—*Ciliary ligament*, the circular portion that divides the choroid membrane from the *iris*.—*Ciliary processes*, the white folds at the margin of the uvea of the eye.—*Ciliary Muscle*, that part of the *musculus*, or *bicularis palpebrarum*, which lies nearest to the *cilia*.

CI'LIATE (*Bot.*) an epithet for the leaf, *folium ciliatum*, a leaf, the edge of which is guarded by parallel bristles, longitudinally, that have the appearance of *cilia*, or eye-lashes, as in the *Drosera Crasula, Erica*, &c. This epithet is applied in the same sense to the *Stipule*, the *Spike*, and the *Corolla*, as in *Rue, Menyanthes, Tropæolum*, &c.

CILIBA'NTUM (*Ant.*) vide *Cillibantes*.

CI'LICES (*Ant.*) vide *Cilicia Velamenta*.

CILI'CIA *Velamenta* (*Ant.*) Garments made of goat's hair, with which the Arabians also made their tents. The ancients frequently used them in the service of the camp, and also at sea. *Vitruv.* l. 10, c. 22; *Varr. de Re Rust.* l. 2, c. 2; *Ascon. in Verr.* 1, c. 38; *Serv. in Virg. Georg.* l. 3, v. 311; *Veget.* l. 4, c. 6.

CILICIA *terra* (*Min.*) a bituminous substance which, when boiled, becomes viscous like birdlime, and was applied to the stocks of vines for the protection of the roots.

CI'LUM (*Anat.*) vide *Cilia*.

CI'LLIBÆ (*Ant.*) vide *Cillibantes*.

CILLIBA'NTES (*Ant.*) κιλλίβαντες, *cillibæ*, κιλλίβαι, rests or tables, with three legs, used by the ancients to lay their shields upon. *Fest. de Verb. Signif.; Hesychius; Suidas; Schol. in Aristoph.*

CI'LLO (*Med.*) one who is affected with a perpetual trembling of the upper eye-lids; a *cillendo*, i. e. *molitando*, from being in a continual agitation.

CILLO'NES (*Ant.*) Minstrels using filthy or obscene gestures.

CILLO'SIS (*Med.*) a spasmodic trembling of the eye-lids.

CILO (*Med.*) one who has a head with a sharp crown like a sugar loaf. *Fest. de Verb. Signif.*

CI'MA (*Bot.*) the top of an herb.

CIMA (*Archit.*) or *Sima*, a moulding something like an S; what is now called an O. G. *ogee*; and by the Greeks κυμάτιον, *cymatium*, a small wave, signifying a wave-like ornament.—*Cima recta*, or the *Cima reversa*. [vide *Architecture*]

CIMA'TIUM (*Archit.*) vide *Cima*.

CIME'LIARCH (*Ant.*) κειμηλιάρχης, the chief keeper of the plate, vestments, and κειμηλία, treasures of the church in general. *Cæl. Rhodig. Antiq. Lect.* l. 1, c. 9.

CIMELIARCHIUM (*Ant.*) κειμηλιάρχιον, the place where the treasures of the church were kept.

CIME'LIUM (*Archæol.*) from κειμηλίον, a treasure; and a treasury has been used to signify a cabinet of medals.

CIMETER (*Mil.*) vide *Scymeter*.

CI'MEX (*Ent.*) κόρις, Bug or Wall-louse; a fetid sort of

vermin which breeds in wood, paper, straw, &c. and infests the persons of those who are asleep. They are said to be good against the bites of serpents, and to cure the ague. *Dioscor.* l. 2, c. 36; *Aet. Tetrab.* 1, serm. 1; *Isid. Orig.* l. 12, c. 6.

CIMEX, *in the Linnean system*, Bug, a genus of animals, Class *Insecta*, Order *Hemiptera*.
 Generic Character. Snout inflected.—*Antennæ* longer than the thorax.—*Back* flat.—*Thorax* margined.
 Species. The species are distinguished into, 1. Those which have the *antennæ* inserted before the eyes. 2. Those which have the lip long and subulate. 3. Those which have the thorax spinous; and, 4. Those which have the thorax unarmed.

CIMICI'FUGA (*Bot.*) a genus of plants, Class 13 *Polyandria*, Order 4 *Tetragynia*.
 Generic Characters. CAL. *perianth* five-leaved; *leaflets* roundish.—COR. *nectaries* four.—STAM. *filaments* twenty; *anthers* twin.—PIST. *germs* four to seven; *styles* recurved; *stigmas* longitudinal on the style.—PER. *capsules* oblong; *seeds* very many.
 Species. The only species is the—*Cimicifuga fœtida, Actæa*, &c. seu *Thalictroides*, &c. a perennial, native of Siberia.

CI'MIER (*Mil.*) French for a heavy ornament, which the ancient knights, or chevaliers, were accustomed to wear upon their helmets.

CIMO'LIA Terra (*Min.*) κιμωλία γῆ, an earth; so called from Cimolus, an island in the Cretan sea, where it was found in great plenty. It was reckoned of great use in discussing tumours and repressing inflammations; and was also employed, like our Fuller's earth, for the cleaning of clothes. *Dioscor.* l. 5, c. 176; *Plin.* l. 35, c. 6.

CIMOLIA alba, *in the Linnean system, Argilla cimolia*, is now known by the names of Cimolite, Tobacco-Pipe Clay, and Fuller's earth. The *Cimolia purpurascens*, another species, is the same as what is now called Steatites, or Soap Rock.

CIMOLITE (*Min.*) the *Cimolia terra*. [vide *Cimolia*]
CINABA'RIS (*Bot.*) vide *Cinnabaris*.
CINABRE (*Her.*) vide *Gules*.
CINA-CI'NÆ (*Bot.*) the same as *Cinchona*.
CINÆ'DI (*Ant.*) Dancers and tumblers among the ancients.
CINÆ'DUS (*Orn.*) κίναιδος, the name of a sea-bird, the gall of which Galen recommends for rubbing the eyelids when the superfluous hairs in a trichiasis are pulled off. *Gal. de Comp. Med. sec. loc.* l. 4, c. 8.

CINAMO'MUM (*Bot.*) vide *Cinnamomum*.
CI'NARA (*Bot.*) the same as the *Cineraria*.
CINAROI'DES (*Bot.*) the *Protea cinaroides* of Linnæus.
CINCHO'NA (*Med.*) the name of the Peruvian bark, which is the bark of the tree called Cinchona.

CINCHONA (*Bot.*) the name of a tree growing in the hilly parts of Peru, which yields the bark called Peruvian bark.
CINCHONA, *in the Linnean System*, a genus of plants, Class 5 *Pentandria*, Order 1 *Monogynia*.
 Generic Characters. CAL. *perianth* one-leaved.—COR. monopetalous; *tube* long; *segments* lanceolate, or linear.—STAM. *filaments* five; *anthers* linear.—PIST. *germ* inferior; *style* the length of the stamens; *stigma* thick.—PER. *capsule* bipartite; *seeds* many.
 Species. The species are shrubs, as the *Cinchona officinalis*, seu *Quinquina*, Common Jesuit's-bark, or officinal Cinchona, native of Peru.—*Cinchona pubescens*, Pubescent Cinchona, native of Peru.—*Cinchona macrocarpa*, Long-fruited Cinchona, native of Santa Fé.—*Cinchona caribœa*, Caribœan Cinchona, native of the Caribbees.—*Cinchona corymbifera*, Corymbiferous Cinchona, native of the South Sea islands.—*Cinchona lineata*, native of St. Dominica.—*Cinchona floribunda, Quinquina*, &c. seu *Trachelium*, native of Jamaica.

CINCINNA'TI, Order of (*Her.*) an order formed in America after the revolution, by the officers who had borne a part in the contest.
CINCI'NNUS (*Anat.*) the hair on the temples.
CINCLI'SIS (*Med.*) or *Cinclismus*, κίγκλισις, or κιγκλισμός, a small and frequently repeated motion, as it is applied by Hippocrates. *Hippoc. de Art.*
CINCTI'CULUM (*Ant.*) a short garment that was girded about the waist, and went down to the middle of the leg. *Plaut. Bacch.* act. iii. sc. 3, v. 28.
CINCTU'RA (*Ant.*) a cincture; a girded tunic. *Quintil.* l. 11, c. S.
CI'NCTURE (*Arch.*) a list, or fillet, at the top or bottom of a column; that at the top is sometimes called *collier*, and sometimes *annulus*.
CI'NCTUS (*Ant.*) a kind of short coat girded a little below the breast.—*Cinctus Gabinus*, a sort of garment worn by the Gabii, who threw one part under their right arm, and the same lappet back again over the left shoulder. It is supposed to have been introduced into Rome on the occasion of a Gabinian excursion, when the enemy was repulsed. It was used by the priests who officiated at the sacrifices, as we learn from Lucan.
Lucan. l. 1, v. 595.

Pontifices, sacri quibus est permissa potestas,
Turba minor ritu sequitur succincta Gabino.

Also by the consul on opening the Temple of Janus, and declaring war, as Virgil informs us:
Virg. Æn. l. 7, v. 612.

Ipse Quirinali trabea, cinctuque Gabino
Insignis, reserat stridentia limina Consul.

It was likewise worn on other solemn occasions, as in the case of Decius, who devoted himself to death for his country: also by the generals when they burned the spoils of the enemy, and the like. *Liv.* l. 8, c. 9; *Appian. Mithrid. Bell.*; *Serv. in Virg.*
CINEFA'CTION (*Chem.*) the reducing any substance, but particularly vegetable substances, to the state of ashes, or powder.
CINERA'RIA (*Eccl.*) Ash-Wednesday, or the first day of Lent.
CINERARIA (*Bot.*) a genus of plants, Class 19 *Syngenesia*, Order 2 *Polygamia Superflua*.
 Generic Characters. CAL. common simple leaflets equal.—COR. compound, radiated; *corollets* hermaphrodite; *proper* funnelshaped.—STAM. *filaments* five; *anther* cylindric.—PIST. *germ* oblong; *style* filiform; *stigmas* two.—PER. none; *calyx* unchanged; *seeds* solitary; *pappus* hairy; *receptacle* naked.
 Species. The species are mostly shrubs, and natives of the Cape of Good Hope, as the *Cineraria nivea*, &c. seu *Doria*, &c.—*Cineraria incisa*, seu *Doria*.—*Cineraria pinnatifida*, seu *Doria*.—*Cineraria bipinnata*.—*Cineraria filifolia*.—*Cineraria geifolia, Solidago*, &c. *Othonga*, seu *Jacobæa*, &c. Kidney-leaved Cineraria.
 Of the second kind are the following, namely, the—*Cineraria malvæfolia*, native of the Canaries.—*Cineraria Sibirica, Othonna*, seu *Jacobæastrum, Jacobæoides*, seu *Solidago*, &c. native of Siberia.—*Cineraria palustris, Solidago, Jacobæa*, seu *Conyza*, Marsh Cineraria, native of Europe.—*Cineraria integrifolia*, seu *Jacobæa*, &c. Mountain Cineraria, or Fleawort, native of Austria.—*Cineraria Senecio, Solidago*, seu *Jacobæa*, &c. Heart-leaved Cineraria, &c. But the *Cineraria longifolia Othonna*, seu *Jacobæa*, native of Austria, is a biennial; and also—*Cineraria campestris*, seu *Othonna*, &c. native of Sweden. *C. Bauh. Pin.*; *Ger. Herb.*; *Park. Theat. Botan.*; *Raii Hist. Plant.*

CINERA'RIUM (*Chem.*) the ash-hole of a chemical instrument.

CINERA'RII (*Eccl.*) a name for those who venerated the ashes of the martyrs.

CINERA'RIUS (*Ant.*) a sort of tire-man who attended to the ashes which were used for the colouring the hair of the females.

CI'NERES *Russici* (*Med.*) vide *Clavellati cineres*.

CINERI'TIOUS (*Anat.*) ash-coloured; an epithet applied to the cortical substance of the brain, from its resemblance to the ash-colour; also to other substances resembling ashes in colour, or consistence.

CINERI'TIUM (*Chem.*) a cupel, or test; so called from its being commonly made of the ashes of vegetables.

CINE'RULAM (*Chem.*) a name for Spodium.

CINE'TUS (*Anat.*) a name for the diaphragm.

CINGULA'RIA (*Bot.*) another name for the *Lycopodium*.

CI'NGULUM *mercuriale* (*Med.*) or *Cingulum sapientiæ*; a sort of belt, or girdle, invented by Rulandus, which consisted of a woollen cloth sufficiently impregnated with mercury, and filled with hog's lard.

CINGULUM *veneris* (*Palmis.*) a semicircle drawn from the space between the middle and fore-finger to that between the little finger and the ring-finger.

CINIFICA'TUM (*Chem.*) vide *Calcinatum*.

CI'NIFLO (*Chem.*) a name for a vain boaster in chemistry.

CI'NIPHES (*Ent.*) a name for certain flies which sting severely, and are therefore supposed to have been one of the plagues of Egypt.

CI'NIS *lixivius* (*Chem.*) lye made of ashes.

CI'NNA (*Bot.*) a genus of plants, Class 1 *Monandria*, Order 2 *Digynia*.
Generic Characters. CAL. glume one flower.—COR. glume bivalve.—STAM. filament one; anther oblong.—PIST. germ turbinated; styles two; stigmas longer.—PER. none; glume involving; seed one.
Species. The only species is *Cinna arundinacea*, seu *Agrostis Cinna*, a perennial, native of Canada.

CI'NNABAR (*Min.*) *Cinnabaris*, κινάβαρι: 1. A mixture of the blood of the dragon and the elephant, which was called by the Indians *Minium*. *Plin.* l. 33, c. 7. 2. The gum of an Indian tree, called Dragon's blood. 3. A soft red stone, called also *Minium*, which it resembles in colour. According to Theophrastus and Dioscorides there are two sorts of cinnabar: the *native*, which is dug out of the mines in Spain, and the *factitious*. Cinnabar consists of a bright red sand, which was discovered by one Callias, an Athenian. *Theophrast. de Lapid.*; *Dioscor.* l. 5, c. 109; *Plin.* l. 33, c. 7. Cinnabar, in modern mineralogy, is likewise native and factitious.—The *native Cinnabar* is a ponderous, red, sulphureous ore of quicksilver found in Spain, Hungary, and the East Indies.—The *factitious Cinnabar* is a red sulphuret of mercury, or a preparation of antimony and corrosive sublimate of mercury, which, when reduced to a powder, is known in commerce by the name of *Vermilion*. *Aldrov. Mus. Metall.*

CINNABARI'NUM *Balsamum* (*Bot.*) a balsam very similar to the balsam of sulphur.

CINNAMO'MUM, *in the Linnean system*, is the *Laurus cinnamomum*.

CI'NNAMON (*Bot.*) the bark of the Cinnamon-tree, the *Laurus Cinnamomum* of Linnæus, which chiefly grows in Ceylon. This bark yields a fragrant volatile oil of a pungent taste, a water prepared by infusion, and a tincture which is prepared by digestion.—*Clove cinnamon* is the bark of a tree growing in Brazil, the fruit of which is often substituted for real cloves.—*Cinnamon water*, a water distilled from the bark of this tree.

CINNAMO'NUM (*Bot.*) κινάμωμον, Cinnamon-tree, the name of which is derived from the Hebrew קנם, or קנמן, a reed, and the Greek ἄμωμον. This tree was found by the ancients both in Arabia and India, and its bark, which was called *Cinnamomum*, or Cinnamon, was reckoned of a heating, emollient, and concocting quality. *Nicand. in Theriac.*; *Theophrast.* l. 9, c. 5; *Aristot. Hist. Anim.* l. 9, c. 20; *Herodot.* l. 3, c. 111; *Dioscor.* l. 1, c. 13; *Plin.* l. 12, c. 19; *Gal. de Simpl.* l. 6.

CI'NNARIS (*Bot.*) a herb which affords a remedy against poison to the stag and hart. *Plin.* l. 8, c. 7.

CINNIOGLOTTUS (*Alchem.*) and *cinnatus*, terms coined by Paracelsus to express the total destruction and corruption of mineral bodies. *Parac. Chirurg.* l. 5. c. 7.

CINQUA'IN (*Mil.*) an order of battle in former times, which consisted of five battalions drawn up so as to make three lines, i. e. a van, main body, and reserve.

CI'NQUEFOIL (*Bot.*) or five-leaved grass, a perennial, the *Potentilla reptans* of Linnæus. The root of this plant has a bitterish taste, and is used in medicine as a styptic.

CINQUEFOIL (*Archit.*) an ornament in the pointed style of architecture, consisting of five cuspidated divisions.

CINQUEFOIL (*Her.*) this plant, as a charge, answers to the five senses of man, and denotes that the bearer conquers his affections and appetites. Among the modern examples of this charge is that in the annexed figure, being the arms of the Marquis of Abercorn, " Quarterly, for Hamilton 1st and 4th *gules* three *cinquefoils* pierced *argent*. For Arran 2d and 3d *argent*, a ship with her sails furled."

CI'NQUE-PORTS (*Law*) a name for the five ports towards the coast of France, namely, Dover, Sandwich, Romney, Winchelsea, and Rye; which it was formerly thought expedient to watch with particular vigilance: for which reason a Lord Warden of the Cinque Ports was appointed, and other privileges were granted to them. 4 *Inst.* 222.

CINQUENI'LLES (*Mil.*) French for thick ropes used in the artillery service for throwing pontoons across a river.

CI'NTRE (*Archit.*) or *ceintre*, the figure of an arch, or any curved timber, which is used in roofs, &c.

CINY'RA (*Mus.*) in the Hebrew כנור, Greek κινύρα; a musical instrument of the harp kind used at funerals.

CINZI'LLA (*Med.*) vide *Zona*.

CI'ON (*Anat.*) κίων, the name of the *uvula*, from its pyrimidal shape. *Aret. de Caus. et Sig. Acut. Morb.* l. 1, c. 2. 2. A diseased enlargement of the uvula. 3. An excrescence of a similar shape in the *pudendum muliebre*. *Hippoc. de Mul.*

CIO'NIA (*Ich.*) κιωνία, the middle parts of the whelks and purple-fish near the centre of the *striæ*, which, when calcined, are more caustic than the rest. *Dioscor.* l. 2, c. 6.

CI'ONIS (*Med.*) a diseased enlargement and painful swelling of the *uvula*.

CI'PHER (*Arith.*) vide *Cypher*.

CI'PHRA (*Arith.*) vide *Cypher*.

CIPORE'MA (*Bot.*) a species of Garlic.

CI'PPUS (*Ant.*) a small, low column, with an inscription, serving as a memorial of any thing: when placed on a road it indicated the distances of places, and when erected over a grave it contained the epitaph, to which the poets allude.
Hor. l. 1, sat. 8, v. 12.
> *Mille pedes in fronte, trecentos cippus in agrum*
> *Hic dabat; haredes monumentum ne sequeretur.*

Per. Sat. v. 86.
> *Assensere viri, nunc non cinis ille poetæ*
> *Felix? Non levior cippus nunc imprimit ossa?*

As the Romans were buried on their own lands, it was customary to inscribe these letters on the *cippi*, H M H N S, i. e. *Hoc monumentum hæredes non sequitur*, to prevent the

CIR

heir from laying claim to the ground occupied by the monument; which explains the allusion in the quotation given from Horace. The *cippi* were also used as landmarks. *Bud. in Pand.* p. 16; *Lay. Comm. Reip. Rom.* l. 3, c. 18; *Bergier. de Viis Mil.* l. 2, § 38, &c.

Cippus was also the name of other things, as 1. A punishment among the Romans resembling the stocks. *Aul. Gell.* l. 16, c. 7; *Suidas*.—2. A sharp stake, or pallisado, in fortifications. *Cæs. de Bell. Gall.* l. 7, c. 73.

CIRCA'DA (*Ecc.*) a tribute anciently paid to the bishop, or arch-deacon, for visiting the church.

CIRCÆ'A (*Bot.*) a genus of plants, Class 2 *Diandria*, Order 1 *Monogynia*.

Generic Characters. CAL. *perianth* two-leaved; *leaflets* ovate.—COR. *petals* two.—STAM. *filaments* two; *anthers* roundish.—PIST. *germ* turbinate; *style* filiform; *stigma* obtuse.—PER. *capsule* turbinate, ovate; *seeds* solitary.

Species. The two species are—*Circæa lutetiana, Solanifolia*, &c. seu *Herba*, &c. Common Enchanter's Nightshade, a perennial, native of Europe.—*Circæa alpina*, Mountain Enchanter's Nightshade, a perennial, native of Europe.

CIRCELLIO'NES (*Eccl.*) vide *Circumcelliones*.

CIRCE'NSES Ludi (*Ant.*) Circensian games, Roman exercises so called because they were exhibited in the circus. They consisted of fighting with swords, staves, or pikes, wrestling, running, horse-racing, leaping, boxing, quoits, and the like. The first Circensian Games were exhibited on the occasion of seizing the Sabine virgins. *Virg. Æn.* l. 8, v. 635.

> *Nec procul hinc Romam, et raptas sine more Sabinas*
> *Consessu caveæ magnis Circensibus actis*
> *Addiderat.*

These games were either ordinary, or extraordinary. The ordinary, or grand games, lasted five days, and commenced on the 15th of September. The extraordinary games were exhibited either on the occasion of dedicating a temple, or at the pleasure of the consuls, and the like. *Liv.* l. 44, c. 9; *Tac. Annal.* l. 2, c. 83; *Suet. Aug.* c. 45; *Panvin. de Lud. Cir.*

CIRCENSIS (*Ant.*) of or belonging to the Circus, as *circense tomentum*, coarse flocks, or stuffing made of chaff, which were so called because they were sold in the Circus to poor people.

CI'RCGEMOT (*Archæol.*) vide *Chirchgemot*.

CIRCINA'LIS (*Bot.*) an epithet applied to leaves in foliation which are rolled in spirally downwards, the tip occupying the centre, as in the Ferns and some Palms.

CIRCINA'TION (*Archit.*) a marking or measuring with the compasses. *Vitruv.* l. 9, c. 8.

CI'RCINUS (*Geom.*) a pair of compasses. *Vitruv.* l. 9, c. 8.

CIRCITO'RES (*Mil.*) the soldiers who went the rounds at night. *Veget.* l. 3, c. 8.

CI'RCIUS (*Ant.*) a vehement southern wind blowing from France through Italy.

CI'RCLE (*Geom.*) a plane figure bounded by a curve line, called the *circumference*, every where equally distant from a point within it called the centre. The circumference of every circle is supposed to be divided into 360 equal parts, called degrees, marked °, each degree into 60 minutes, or primes, marked ', each minute into 60 seconds, marked ", and so on. A right line is said *to touch* a circle when meeting the same, and being produced, it does not cut it, as in fig. 1. Circles are said *to touch each other*, which meeting do not cut one another, as in fig. 1. Right lines in a circle are said to be equally distant from the centre when perpendiculars drawn from the centre to them are equal, as B A, A C, in fig. 2.—A *segment of a circle* is a figure contained under a right line and a part of the circumference of a circle, as in fig. 3. An angle is said to stand on the circumference of a circle when right lines which contain the angle receive any part of the circumference, as in fig. 4. [vide *Geometry*] Circles *of the higher orders* are curves, the properties of which are expressed by the following equations:

$$x^m : y^m :: y : \overline{a - x} \text{ or } y^m + 1 = x^m \overline{a - x}$$
$$x^m : y^m :: y^n : \overline{a - x^n} \text{ or } y^m +\ ^n = x^m \overline{a - x}^n :$$

where a is the axis, x is the absciss, and y the ordinate. Curves defined by this equation, will be ellipses when m is an odd number: but when m and n are each equal to 1 the equation becomes that of the common circle.—*Circle of curvature*, that circle which has the same curvature with any curve at a given point. It is otherwise called the *circle of equicurvature*; also the *osculating circle*, because the circle is said to osculate the curve at the point where it touches. The radius of this circle is called the *radius of curvature*, and its centre the *centre of curvature*.

CIRCLE *of the sphere* (*Astron.*) is any circle that cuts the mundane sphere, or has the circumference in its surface. These circles are either moveable or fixed.—*Moveable circles* are those whose circumferences revolve with the surface of the sphere, as the meridians, &c.—*The fixed circles* are those which have their circumferences in the immoveable surface, and consequently do not revolve with it, as the Equator and Ecliptic. These circles are also distinguished into great or lesser circles. *Great Circles* are those which divide the sphere into two equal parts, as the Horizon, the Meridian, the Equator or the Ecliptic, the Colures, Azimuth, Vertical Circles, Circles of Declination and of Latitudes.—*Lesser Circles* are those which divide the sphere into two unequal parts, having neither the same centre nor diameter as the sphere. These are the Tropics, the Polar Circles, Circles of Longitude, Circles of Perpetual Apparition and Occultation, Circles of Position, &c. [vide *Astronomy*]—*Circle of the equant* is a circle in the Ptolemaic system, described on the centre of the equant.—*Horary Circle*, or *Hour Circle*, a small brazen circle fixed to the north pole, and divided into twenty-four hours, with an index to point them out, and thereby to show the difference of the meridians in time.—*Circle of illumination* is an imaginary circle on the surface of the earth which separates the illuminated side, or hemisphere of the earth, from the dark side.—*Circles of excursion* are small circles parallel to the ecliptic, and at such a distance from it that the excursions of the planets towards the poles of the ecliptic may be included within them. They are usually fixed at 10°.—*Diurnal circles* are immovable circles, supposed to be described by the stars and other points of the Heavens in their diurnal rotation round the earth.

CIRCLE (*Log.*) the fault of an argument which supposes the principle which it should prove, and afterwards proves the principle by the thing which it seems to have proved.

CIRCLE (*Polit.*) a division of the German empire, which has a right of voting at the diet.

CIRCOCE'LE (*Med.*) from κημός, a dilatation of a vein, and κηλη, a rupture; a varicose distention and enlargement of the spermatic veins.

CI'RCUIT *electrical* (*Nat.*) the course of the electric fluid from the charged surface of an electric body to the opposite surface, into which the discharge is made.

CIRCUIT (*Mil.*) 1. The space immediately round any town, or place. 2. The circuitous march of soldiers, who do not go in a direct course.

Fig. 1. Fig. 2. Fig. 3. Fig. 4.

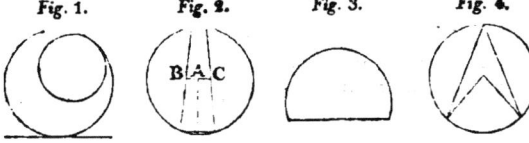

CIRCUI'TIO (*Ant.*) going the rounds as soldiers on guard do. [vide *Circitores*]

CIRCUI'TOR (*Ant.*) vide *Circitores*.

CI'RCUITS (*Law*) certain divisions of the kingdom which the judges are appointed to visit twice a year for the administration of justice. Of these circuits there are six, namely—*Midland*, including the counties of Northampton, Rutland, Lincoln, Nottingham, Derby, Leicester, Warwick.—*Norfolk*, including Bucks, Bedford, Huntingdon, Cambridge, Norfolk, Suffolk.—*Home circuit*, including Hertford, Essex, Kent, Sussex, Surrey.—*Oxford circuit*, including Berks, Oxford, Hereford, Salop, Gloucester, Monmouth, Stafford, Worcester.—*Western circuit*, including Southampton, Wilts, Dorset, Devon, Cornwall, Somerset.—*Northern*, including York, Durham, Northumberland, Cumberland, Westmoreland, Lancashire.

CIRCU'ITY OF ACTION (*Law*) *circuitus actionis*, a longer course of proceeding to recover a thing sued for than is needful.

CI'RCULAR (*Math.*) an epithet for any thing in the form of, or appertaining to, a circle; as—*Circular arcs*, any parts of the circumference of a circle.—*Circular instruments*, otherwise called *reflecting* or *multiplying circles*, instruments which, like Hadley's octant, and the marine sextant, serve for taking the altitudes, distances, &c. of the heavenly bodies, particularly by sea. They derive their name from their figure, which consists of a whole circle instead of a part, and are recommended for their accuracy in diminishing the errors of division and eccentricity at pleasure, by means of reflection.—*Circular lines*, are lines relating to the circle, as sines, tangents, &c.—*Circular numbers* are those numbers whose powers end in the same digits as the roots themselves, as 5, the square of which is 25, the cube 125, &c.—*Circular parts* are the five parts of a right-angled or a quadrantal spherical triangle; namely, the legs, the complement of the hypothenuse, and the two complements of the two oblique angles. They are also called *Napier's circular parts*, because he gave a rule in his logarithms respecting these parts, by which he proposed to comprehend within one theorem, all the rules for the solution of right-angled spherical triangles.—*Circular ring* is the measure or space included between two concentric circles, and the area of it is consequently equal to the difference of the areas of the two circles.—*Circular sailing* is the mode of navigation which is performed upon the arc of a great circle. — *Circular sectors* are the areas bounded by any arc of a circle and two radii.—*Circular segment* is the space bounded by any arc and its chord.

CIRCULAR (*Com.*) or *Circular letter*, a letter printed or written in the same form, which is sent round to any number of persons, to serve in the place of an advertisement.

CIRCULAR (*Bot.*) vide *Orbiculate*.

CIRCULAR VELOCITY (*Astron.*) a term denoting the velocity of a planet or a revolving body, which is measured by the arc of a circle.

CI'RCULATE (*Math.*) vide *Circulating*.

CI'RCULATING DECIMALS (*Math.*) also called *recurring* or *repeating decimals*, or simply *circulates*, are those decimal numbers in which a figure or figures are perpetually repeated, as ·646464, &c.—The circulates are simple, compound, or mixed.—A *simple circulate* is that which consists of one figure repeated, as ·222, &c. which is marked ·$\dot{2}$.—A *compound* or *multiple circulate* is that in which several figures are repeated, as ·232323, marked thus ·$\dot{2}\dot{3}$, and ·234234234, marked thus ·$\dot{2}3\dot{4}$.—A *mixed circulate* is that which consists of other figures that are not repeated, as 4·222, or 4·$\dot{2}$ and 45·$\dot{5}2\dot{4}$. That part of the circle which repeats is called the *repetend*, and the whole repetend, supposed infinitely continued, is equal to a vulgar fraction whose numerator is the repeating figure, and its denominator the same number of nines, as ·$\dot{2} = \frac{2}{9}$; $\dot{2}\dot{3} = \frac{23}{99}$; $\dot{5}2\dot{4} = \frac{524}{999}$.

CIRCULA'TION (*Anat.*) the circular or circulating action of the blood which passes from the heart through the arteries to every part of the body, and returns back to the heart through the veins. By means of this regular motion, the whole animal economy is kept in order.

CIRCULATION (*Chem.*) the particular motion which is raised in liquors by the application of fire, that causes the vapours to rise and fall.

CIRCULATION *of the sap* (*Bot.*) is a similar process that goes forward with the sap or juice in plants, as with the blood in the animal body.

CIRCULATION *of money* (*Com.*) is the passing of money from hand to hand according to some given value.

CIRCULATO'RES (*Ant.*) mountebanks and jugglers who went about amusing the people. *Mart.* l. 10, ep. 3.

Et fœda linguæ probra circulatricis.

Apul. Metam. l. 1; *Schol. Juv. sat.* 6, v. 582.

CIRCULATO'RIUM (*Chem.*) *Circulatory*, a chemical digesting vessel, in which the fluid performs a circulatory motion.

CI'RCULATORY LETTERS (*Ecc.*) or *Circular letters*, letters which are sent into different parts of a kingdom or a particular province by archbishops or bishops.

CIRCULA'TUM (*Chem.*) a preparation from sea salt, so called by Paracelsus, who gave the name of *Circulatum majus* to the preparation of the corrosive sublimate of mercury and sea salt, and that of *Circulatum minus* to the preparation of sea salt, water, the juice of the radish-root, and alcohol of wine. Some affirm that the former is no more than rectified spirits of wine, and the latter only spirit of vinegar.

CI'RCULI IGNEI (*Med.*) vide *Eclampsis*.

CI'RCULUS (*Anat.*) κύκλος, any round or annular part of the body, as the *circulus oculi*, the orb of the eye. *Hippoc. de Morb.* l. 2, &c.; *Gal. de Usu Part.*—*Circulus arteriosus*, the artery which runs round the *iris*, so as to form a circle.

CIRCULUS (*Surg.*) surgical instruments adapted to the different parts of the body. *Scultet. Armam. Chirurg.* tab. 22, 43, &c.—*Circulus quadruplex*, a kind of bandage having a fourfold circle.—*Gal. de Fasc.*

CIRCULUS (*Chem.*) a round iron instrument which is used for cutting off the neck of a glass, and which is otherwise called an *Abbreviatorium*.

CIRCUMAGE'NTES MUSCULI (*Anat.*) muscles that help to turn the eye about.

CIRCUMA'MBIENT (*Nat.*) an epithet for the air that immediately surrounds the earth.

CIRCUMCAULA'LIS (*Med.*) a name for the *tunica adnata* of the eye. *Aet. Tetrab.* 2, serm. 3, c. 1.

CIRCUMCELLIO'NES (*Ecc.*) a branch of the Donatists in Africa, in the fourth century, so called because they led a vagabond life, and committed so many irregularities that they called for the interference of the civil power, by which they were suppressed. *St. August. Hæres.* 69; *Baron. Annal. Ann.* 331, &c.; *Prateol. Doctrin. omn. Hæret.*

CIRCUMCIDANE'UM VINUM (*Ant.*) wine of the last pressing, after the grape-husks have been all mashed and cut to pieces to be brought to press again.

CIR

CIRCUMCI'SION (*Theol.*) περιτομή, or περικοπή, a rite or ceremony among the Jews, performed by cutting off the *præputium*, or foreskin. This ceremony was first annexed by God, as a seal to the covenant which He made with Abraham, and afterwards taken into the body of Mosaic institutions. Herodotus speaks of this custom as having prevailed among the ancient Egyptians and neighbouring people, who doubtless borrowed it from the Israelites.

CIRCUMCISION (*Ecc.*) or the feast of Circumcision, a festival celebrated in the Christian church on the first of January, in commemoration of our Saviour's circumcision.

CIRCUMDU'CTION (*Law*) is a term applied in the Scotch law to the time allowed for bringing proof of allegiances, which being elapsed, if either party sue for circumduction of the time of proving, it has the effect that no proof can afterwards be brought, and the cause must be determined as it stood when circumduction was obtained.

CIRCU'MFERENCE (*Math.*) περιφέρεια, the line or lines generally which bound any figure, but particularly the curve line which bounds the circle, and is every where equidistant from the point called the centre. *Euclid. Elem. Def.* l. 1, 3.

CIRCUM'FERENTOR (*Math.*) an instrument used in surveying, consisting of a large box and needle fastened on to the middle of a brass index, with sights at each end of the index, as in the subjoined figure. The quantity of

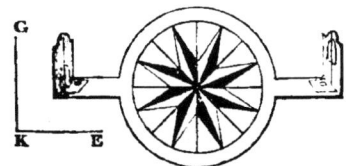

angles may be taken in the following manner: supposing the angle to be E K G, place the instrument at K, with the flower de luce of the card towards you; then direct the sights to E, and observe what degrees are cut by the south end of the needle, which suppose 295; then turning the instrument about on its stand, direct the sights to G, noting again what degrees are cut by the south end of the needle, which suppose to be 213; then subtracting the less from the greater, the remainder is the quantity of the angle sought; as 295 − 213 = 82 degrees, the quantity of the angle.

CIRCU'MFERUS (*Bot.*) an epithet signifying winding round, as the tendrils of the hop twist round the pole.

CI'RCUMFLEX (*Gram.*) an accent which when placed over a syllable makes it long, as this mark(ˆ), and this (ˆ) in Latin.

CIRCUMFLE'XUS (*Anat.*) an epithet for the muscle of the palate which serves to draw down the *velum pendulum palati*, and then to the side towards the pterygoid process.

CIRCUMFORA'NEI (*Ant.*) an epithet for mountebanks.

CIRCUMGYRA'TION (*Anat.*) the turning a limb round in the socket.

CIRCUMINCE'SSION (*Theol.*) a term used by divines for the reciprocal existence of the three persons in the Trinity in each other.

CIRCUMJO'VIALISTS (*Astron.*) an epithet applied to Jupiter's satellites.

CIRCUMI'TIS (*Med.*) a medicine used as a general unction or liniment to any part.

CIRCUMLOCU'TIO (*Rhet.*) circumlocution, a figure of speech answering to the periphrasis of the Greeks, which consists in expressing by many words what might be expressed by a few; which may sometimes be a beauty and at other times a fault. *Quint. Inst.* l. 8, c. 6.

CIRCUMOSSA'LIS (*Anat.*) an epithet for what surrounds a bone, as the *periosteum*; also an epithet for what is surrounded by a bone.

CIR

CIRCUMPO'LAR (*Astron.*) an epithet for such stars as being pretty near our North Pole, move round it. They never set or go below the horizon in our latitude.

CIRCUMPOTA'TIO (*Ant.*) a funeral entertainment which was given in honour of the deceased to the friends that attended, which being esteemed an absurd custom, is supposed to have been abolished by law. *Lex. Sept.* xii. *Tabb. apud. Cic. de Leg.* l. 2, c. 24; *Hottman. Antiq. Rom.* l. 3, c. 1.

CIRCUMSC'ISSUS (*Bot.*) cut round; an epithet for a capsule. —*Capsula circumscissa*, a capsule that opens, not longitudinally or vertically, as most capsules, but transversely and horizontally, like a snuff-box, usually about the middle, so as to fall nearly in two equal hemispheres, as in *Anagallis* and *Hyoscyamus*.

CI'RCUMSCRIBED (*Math.*) περιγραφομένος, an epithet for any figure so drawn about another as that each of its sides touch all the angles or planes of the inscribed figure. *Eucl. Elem. Def.* l. 4.—*Circumscribed hyperbola*, one of Newton's hyperbolas of the second order.

CIRCUMSCRI'PTION (*Phy.*) the certain bounds or limits of any natural body, which is either external or internal.—*External circumscription* is referred to the place in which any body is confined, and is termed local.—*Internal circumscription* is that which belongs to the essence and quality of any body whereby it has a determinate extension and figure.

CIRCUMSPE'CTE AGA'TIS (*Law*) the title of a statute made anno 13 Ed. I. stat. 4, relating to prohibitions, prescribing to the judges' cases in which the king's prohibition does not lie.

CIRCUMSTA'NTIBUS (*Law*) By-standers, a term signifying any number of jurors taken out of such persons as are present, to supply the deficiency after the number has been challenged. *Stat.* 35 Hen. 8, c. 6; 5 Eliz. c. 25.

CIRCUMVALLA'TION (*Fort.*) or *a line of circumvallation*, a trench bordered with a parapet thrown up around the besieger's camp, or round a town intended to be besieged.

CIRCUMVE'NTION (*Law*) in the Scotch law, any act of fraud whereby a person is reduced to a deed by decreet.

CIRCUMVOLU'TION (*Archit.*) the turns of the spiral line of the Ionic order.

CIRCUNCOLU'MNIUM (*Archit.*) περισύλιον, a place set round with pillars.

CIRCUNCU'RRENS (*Rhet.*) an epithet for the rhetorical art, because it is not limited to any certain matter.

CI'RCUS (*Ant.*) ιπποδρομος, a large circular building, particularly at Rome, where games were exhibited to the people. They were generally oblong, or nearly in the shape of a bow. In the middle was a bank or eminence, with obelisks, statues, and posts at each end, as in the annexed figure. This served them for the course of their *bigæ* and *quadrigæ*. *Ovid. Fast.* l. 4, v. 391.

Circus erit pompa celeber, numeroque Deorum:
Primaque ventosis palma petetur equis.

There were many of these buildings in Rome, but the most remarkable of the kind was the *Circus maximus*, built according to some by Romulus, according to others by Tarquinius Priscus, the length of which was 2187 feet, the breadth 960. It is said by some to have contained 300,000 spectators. *Dionys. Hal.* l. 3; *Liv.* l. 1, c. 35; *Plin.* l. 8, c. 42; *Aul. Gell.* l. 5, c. 14; *Tertull de Spectac.* c. 9; *Chrysost. Serm. de Human*; *Isidor. Orig.* l. 18, c. 27; *Panvin.de Lud. Circ.* l. 1, c.13; *Buleng.de Circ.* c. 9; *Ursat. de Not. Rom. apud Græv. Thes. Antiq. Rom.* tom. 11, &c.

CIRCUS (*Orn.*) κίρκος, a kind of hawk. [vide *Accipiter*]
CIRCUS (*Surg.*) a circular bandage; called also *laqueus plinthius*.
CIRE PREPARE'E (*Mil.*) French for a preparation of yellow wax, tallow, and pitch, for closing up the heads of fusees.
CIRNE'SES (*Med.*) a union of separate things.
CI'RRI (*Ich.*) the claws of the polypus fish. *Plin.* l. 9, c. 28.
CIRRI'FERUS (*Bot.*) tendril-bearing; an epithet for a leaf or a peduncle: *folium cirriferum*, a tendril-bearing leaf, as in *Fumaria*; *pedunculus cirriferus*, a tendril-bearing peduncle, as in *Cardiospermum* and *Vitis*.
CI'RRUS (*Bot.*) or *Cirrhus*, a tendril. [vide *Tendril*]
CI'RSION (*Bot.*) a species of the *Carduus* of Linnæus.
CI'RSIUM (*Bot.*) the *Aretium carduelis* of Linnæus.
CIRSO'CELE (*Med.*) vide *Circocele*.
CIRSO'IDES (*Med.*) from κιρσός, a varix, and ιιδος, the form; i. e. resembling a varix or distended vein; varicous, an epithet applied to the upper part of the brain. *Ruff. Ephes. de Appell Part Hum. Corp.* l. 1.
CI'RSOS (*Med.*) κιρσός, from κιρσόω, to dilate; a varix, or preternatural distension of a vein.
CI'SIUM (*Ant.*) a light sort of two-wheeled carriage. *Cic. Rosc. Am.* c. 7; *Scheff. de Re Vehic.* l. 2, c. 18.
CI'SLEU (*Chron.*) the ninth month of the Jewish ecclesiastical year, and third of their civil year, answering nearly to our November. When this month is 29 days instead of 30 the year is called *deficient*. [vide *Chronology*]
CISSA (*Nat.*) vide *Pica*.
CISSA'MPELOS (*Bot.*) a genus of plants, Class 22 *Dioecia*, Order 12 *Monodelphia*.
Generic Characters. CAL. none, unless the corolla be so called.—COR. *petals* four; *nectary* the membranaceous disk of the flower wheelshaped.—STAM. *filaments* four; *anthers* broad.—PIST. *germ* roundish; *styles* three; *stigmas* three.—PER. *berry* globular; *seed* solitary.
Species. The species are perennials or shrubs, as—*Cissampelos pareira*, *Clematis Convolvulus*, &c. *Caapeba*, seu *Abutylon*, native of South America.—*Cissampelos laurifolia*, a shrub, native of the island of St. Thomas.—*Cissampelos convolvulacea*, a shrub, native of the East Indies.—*Cissampelos caapeba*, seu *foliis*, &c. seu *Caapeba*, &c. a perennial, native of South America.
CISSAMPELOS is also the name of the *Pareira* of Linnæus.
CISSA'NTHEMOS (*Bot.*) κισσανθεμος, a species of *Cyclamen*. *Dioscor.* l. 2, c. 195.
CI'SSARUS (*Bot.*) the *Cistus Creticus* of Linnæus.
CI'SSINUM (*Med.*) κισσινον, a plaster for wounds of the nerves, &c. *P. Æginet.* l. 7, c. 17.
CISSI'TES (*Min.*) from κισσος, ivy; a precious stone, white and shining, with the figures of ivy leaves all over it. *Plin.* l. 37, c. 10.
CI'SSOID (*Geom.*) a curve of the second order, invented by Diocles, for the purpose of finding two continued mean proportionals between two other given lines, as the curve A M and A *m*, consisting of two infinite hyperbolic legs, having a right line A B for a diameter, and a right line C C its asymptote; so that calling A B, *a*; the absciss A P, *x*; and the correspondent semiordinate P M, or P *m*,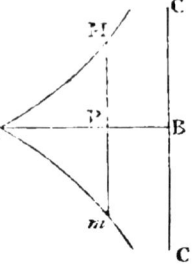
y; it will be $yy \times \overline{a - x} = x^3$. Sir Isaac Newton reckons this, in his *Enumeratio Linearum tertii ordinis*, amongst the defective hyperbolas.
CI'SSOS (*Bot.*) κισσος, a kind of ivy growing alone without stay. *Plin.* l. 16, c. 34.
CI'SSUS, in the Linnean System, a genus of plants, Class 4 *Tetrandria*, Order 1 *Monogynia*.

Generic Characters. CAL. *involucre* many-leaved; *perianth* one-leaved.—COR. *petals* four; *nectary* a rim surrounding the germ.—STAM. *filaments* four; *anthers* roundish.—PIST. *germ* roundish; *style* filiform; *stigma* simple.—PER. *berry* round; *seed* a roundish stone.
Species. The species are shrubs or perennials, as—*Cissus vitiginea*, &c. seu *Arbuscula*, &c. Vine-leaved Cissus, native of India.—*Cissus latifolia*, *Funis*, &c. seu *Schunambu*, &c. native of India.—*Cissus sicyoides*, *Vitis*, &c. *Irsiola*, &c. seu *Bryonia*, &c. a perennial, native of Jamaica.—*Cissus quadrangularis*, *Sælanthus*, *Funis*, seu *Planta*, &c. a perennial, native of Arabia.—*Cissus acida*, *Sicyos*, *Irsiola*, *Bryonia*, seu *Bryonioides*, &c. seu *Vitis*, &c. native of America.—*Cissus carnosa*, *Hedera*, seu *Tsjori-valli*, native of the East Indies.—*Cissus pedata*, *Sambucus*, seu *Belulla*, native of the East Indies.
CI'SSYMBIUM (*Ant.*) κισσυμβιον, a cup made of ivy, or bound about with ivy. *Cat. de Re Rust.* c. 110; *Macrob.* l. 5, c. 21.
CI'STA (*Archæol.*) a vessel of wine, containing two measures, or a measure and a half.
CISTA (*Ant.*) κιστη κιστις, a cupboard to hold provisions, or a trunk for clothes. *Poll.* l. 7, segm. 160.—*Cista mystica*, the mystic chest of Bacchus, which was used in celebrating his orgies. *Catull.* carm. 64, v. 260.

Celebrabant orgia cistis,
Orgia, quæ frustra cupiunt audire prophani.

Tibull. l. 1, eleg. 7, v. 48.

Et levis occultis conscia cista sacris.

Apul. Met. l. 6.

CISTA Gratiæ (*Archæol.*) a church coffer in which the alms for the poor were kept.
CISTA (*Med.*) a Cyst, or tumour in which the obstructed matter collects, as in a bag.
CISTA'RTIUM (*Archæol.*) a bread basket.
CISTE'LA (*Ent.*) a division of the genus *cryptocephalus*, consisting of those species that have the lip bifid, and the body oblong.
CISTE'LLA (*Archæol.*) a little chest.
CISTE'RCIAN (*Ecc.*) vide *Cistertian*.
CISTERN (*Mech.*) a vessel, in the form of a box, into which confectioners put their creams to ice them over.
CISTERN (*Archit.*) *Cisterna*, a subterraneous reservoir for water. *Vitruv.* l. 8, c. 7. It is now any reservoir for water.
CISTE'RNA (*Anat.*) a name for the fourth ventricle of the brain; and also for the concourse of the lacteal vessels in the breasts of women.
CISTE'RTIAN Monks (*Ecc.*) in French *Citeaux*, an order of Benedictine monks, instituted by Robert, abbot of Citeaux, in France, in 1098. *Hel. Hist. des Ord. Mon.* tom. v, &c.
CI'STIC oxide (*Chem.*) the name of an animal substance, found in a concrete form, in the human bladder, having the appearance of magnesian limestone.
CISTO'IDES (*Bot.*) the *Mahernia pinnata* of Linnæus.
CI'STUS (*Bot.*) κισθος, or κιθαρος, a herb, of an astringent quality, which was reckoned good to restrain spreading ulcers. *Theoph. de Hist. Plant.* l. 6, c. 2; *Dioscor.* l. 1, c. 126; *Hesychius*.
CISTUS, in the Linnean system, a genus of plants, Class 13 *Polyandria*, Order 1 *Monogynia*.
Generic Characters. CAL. *perianth* five-leaved; *leaflets* roundish.—COR. *petals* five—STAM. *filaments* numerous; *anthers* roundish.—PIST. *germ* roundish; *style* simple; *stigma* flat.—PER. *capsule* roundish; *seeds* numerous.
Species. The species are shrubs, as—*Cistus Capensis*, seu *arborescens*, &c. Cape Cistus.—*Cistus villosus*, Hairy Rock Rose, or Shrubby Cistus.—*Cistus populifolius*, *Ledon*, seu *Ledum*, &c. Poplar-leaved Cistus, or Rock

Rose.—*Cistus laurifolius*, *Ledon*, &c. seu *Ledum*, &c. Bay-leaved Gum Cistus, a shrub, native of Spain.—*Cistus ledon*, seu *Ladanifera*, *Ledum*, &c. seu *Ladanum*, native of the South of France.—*Cistus umbellatus*, *Ledon*, seu *Helianthum*, Umbelled Cistus, native of Spain.—*Cistus fumarius*, *Chæmecistus*, seu *Helianthemum*, Heath-leaved Cistus, native of France.—*Cistus Anglicus*, seu *Helianthemum*, &c. English Cistus.—*Cistus fruticosus*, *Helianthemum*, *Chamæcistus*, seu *Panax*, Dwarf Cistus, or Little Sun-Flower. But some of the species are annuals, as the—*Cistus plantagineus*, seu *herbaceus*, native of Crete.—*Cistus annuus*, Annual Spotted-Flowered Cistus, native of Italy. *Clus. Hist. Plant. rar.*; *Bauh. Hist. Plant.*; *C. Bauh. Pin.*; *Ger. Herb.*; *Park. Theat. Botan.*; *Raii Hist. Plant.*; *Tournef. Inst.*; *Linn. Spec. Plant.*

CISTUS is also the name of the *Diosma uniflora* and *Azalea Indica* of Linnæus.

CISTO'PHORUS (*Numis.*) κιστοφόρος, an Asiatic coin, in value somewhat more than a denarius, equal to three oboli and a half, or twopence farthing. It was so called, because it bore the impression of the *cista mystica*, or the mysterious chest of Bacchus, as in the annexed figure, which represents the reverse of a medal of Mark Anthony and Cleopatra. *Cic. ad Att.* l. 2, ep. 6; *Beg. Thes. Brand.*

CI'TADEL (*Mil.*) in French *citadelle*, and Italian *citadella*, a fort of four, five, or six bastions, built near a city, on the most advantageous ground for commanding the place and its vicinity.

CITATION (*Law*) a summons to appear, applied particularly to the proceedings in the spiritual court. *Stat.* 23 Hen. 8, c. 9.

CITERNEAU' (*Mech.*) French for a small reservoir, arched over so as to hold water.

CITHARA (*Ant.*) a musical instrument very similar to a lyre, although its exact form is not precisely known.

CITHARE'XYLUM (*Bot.*) a genus of plants, Class 14 *Didynamia*, Order 2 *Angiosperma*.
  Generic Characters. CAL. perianth one-leaved.— COR. one-petalled; *tube* twice as long as the perianth; *border* five-parted; *segments* above villose.— STAM. *filaments* four; *anthers* oblong.— PIST. *germ* roundish; *style* filiform; *stigma* obtuse-headed.— PER. *berry* roundish; *seeds* two.
  Species. The species are shrubs, as the—*Citharexylum cinereum*, seu *Jasminum*, &c. Ash-coloured Fiddle-wood, native of South America.—*Citharexylum caudatum*, seu *Berberis*, &c. Oval-leaved or Long-spiked Fiddle-wood, native of Jamaica, &c.

CITHARUS (*Anat.*) κίθαρος, the breast, as Galen explains in his Exegesis. *Erot. Lex. Hippocrat.*

CITHARUS (*Ich.*) a fish called Folio, whose teeth are like a saw. *Aristot. Hist. Anim.* l. 2, c. 17; *Plin.* l. 32, c. 10.

CI'TIZEN (*Law*) a freeman of a city.

CITOLE (*Mus.*) a musical instrument, which consisted of nothing but a small chest, *cistella*, with strings on the lid or top.

CI'TRA (*Bot.*) the Citron-tree; a reddish sweet scented wood, of an aromatic flavour, growing in the East Indies.

CI'TRAGO (*Bot.*) Balm-gentle.

CI'TRATE (*Chem.*) the name for salts formed by the union of citric acid with different bases, as the Citrate of Ammonia, Citrate of Potash, &c. [vide *Chemistry*]

CI'TREA malus (*Bot.*) the *Citrus medica* of Linnæus.

CI'TREUM (*Bot.*) or *Malum citreum*, is the Latin name for the *Citrus medica* of Linnæus, which is called by Theophrastus and Dioscorides μῆλον Μηδικόν. *Theoph. Hist. Plant.* l. 4, c. 4; *Dioscor.* l. 1, c. 166; *Plin.* l. 12, c. 3; *Athen.* l. 3, c. 7.

CI'TRIC acid (*Chem.*) the acid of lemons, which is obtained in concrete crystals, by saturating boiling lemon juice with pulverized chalk, and treating it with sulphuric acid.

CITRINA'TION (*Nat.*) complete digestion.

CI'TRINE (*Min.*) vide *Citrinus*.

CITRINE'LLA (*Orn.*) a bird about the size of a lark; so called from its yellow or lemon colour. *Gessn. de Av.*

CITRI'NULA (*Bot.*) spearwort, a herb much used by Paracelsus.

CITRI'NULUS (*Min.*) a stone between a crystal and a beryl.

CI'TRINUS (*Min.*) a peculiar species of sprig crystal, which is distinguished by its beautiful yellow colour. It is called by the jewellers *citrine*.

CI'TRON (*Bot.*) a pleasant fruit of the lemon kind, which is the fruit of the *Citrus medica* of Linnæus. The inside is white, fleshy, and thick, containing but a small quantity of pulp, in proportion to the size of the fruit.—*Citron water*, a strong water distilled from lemon-peel, orange-peel, and nutmegs in alcohol.—*Citron-tree*, another name for the Candle-wood-Tree.

CI'TRULUM (*Bot.*) or *Citrullus*, Citrul, a kind of pumpkin or gourd; the *Cucurbita citrullus* of Linnæus.

CI'TRUS (*Bot.*) the Citron, called by Theophrastus and Dioscorides μῆλον Μηδικόν. [vide *Citreum*]

CITRUS, in the Linnean system, a genus of plants, Class 18 *Polyadelphia*, Order 3 *Icosandria*.
  Generic Characters. CAL. perianth one-leaved.— COR. petals five.— STAM. filaments erect; anthers oblong.— PIST. germ superior; style cylindric; stigma globular.— PER. berry nine-celled; seeds in couples.
  Species. The species are—*Citrus medica*, Lemon, Lemonellus, seu *Malus limonia*, &c. a shrub, native of Asia. This species comprehends the Citron, the Lemon, and the Lime.—*Citrus aurantium*, *Aurantium*, seu *Malus*, &c. seu *Aurantia*, the Orange, a shrub, native of India.—*Citrus decumana*, &c. *Limo*, *Malus*, *Pumpelmus*, seu *Aurantium*, &c. Shaddock, a shrub, native of India.

CI'TTA (*Med.*) vide *Pica*.

CI'TTERN (*Mus.*) vide *Guitar*.

CITTO'SIS (*Bot.*) a disease in vines when grapes fall from the clusters and perish.

CI'TY (*Polit.*) contracted from the Latin *civitas*, formerly signified any large and populous place, which had, like its original, a particular reference to the inhabitants; but it is now applied solely to such corporate towns as have a bishop's see and a cathedral church. It was sometimes rendered by *civitas*, to denote its importance, sometimes by *oppidum*, the common term for any inhabited place or town; and sometimes by *urbs*, to denote that it was a walled town.

CI'VES (*Bot.*) a name for a sort of leeks; the *Allium schnoenoprassum* of Linnæus.

CI'VET (*Zool.*) an animal of the weasel kind, about the size of a cat; the *Viverra civetta* of Linnæus, which inhabits Æthiopia, Congo, and the Cape of Good Hope. The fat under its tail, near the anus, is the perfume called civet.

CIVET (*Com.*) a perfume which smells like musk, from a bag under the tail of the civet cat and the zibet, two species of the *Viverra* of Linnæus.

CIVET (*Cook.*) a particular way of dressing fowls, by first frying and afterwards stewing them.

CI'VICA corona (*Ant.*) the Civic Crown, a garland of oak, which was given to a Roman soldier who had saved the life of a citizen in battle, which was also commemorated on medals, as in the annexed figure, representing the crown, with the words OB. CIVIS. SERVATOS, to be found on the reverse of a medal, struck by Q. Ælius Flaminius.

CI'VIERE (*Mil.*) French for a small hand-barrow, carried by two men, and used much in the artillery.

CI'VIL Law (*Law*) is commonly defined to be that law which every particular nation or society of people has established for its own use, which is more commonly called *municipal law*; and the term *civil law* is now applied particularly to that law which was used by the Romans, and collected under the auspices of the emperor Justinian into a code or body of Law, consisting of, 1. Institutes, or first principles of Roman Law, which were so called because they served for instruction. 2. The *Digests* or *Pandects*, containing the opinions of eminent lawyers digested in methodical order. 3. Novels or Authentics, i. e. laws so called, because they were new, and authentically translated from the Greek into the Latin tongue. To these branches of the *Civil Law* may be added the *Book of Feuds*, containing the laws of the feudal system; and the *Constitutions of the Emperors*, which were either in the shape of rescripts or edicts. The *Civil Law* is used in England, under certain restrictions, in the Ecclesiastical Courts, Military Courts, or Courts of Chivalry, Courts of Admiralty, and the Courts of the two Universities —*Civil death*, any thing which cuts a man off from civil society, as outlawry, banishment, and the like.—*Civil List* is that which comprehends the whole of the King's revenue in his own distinct capacity, and serves to defray all expenses immediately connected with civil government, as the royal household, officers of state, judges, &c.

CIVIL war (*Polit.*) a war between subjects of the same state, or citizens of the same city.

CIVIL (*Chron.*) is applied as an epithet to different divisions of time, which are framed for the purposes of civil society, in distinction from those which correspond with the motions of the heavenly bodies, as the *civil day*, which is twenty-four hours, including day and night, in distinction from the solar day, which is twelve hours; and the *civil year*, which is 365 days, and in leap year 366, distinguished from the solar year, which is $365^d\ 6^h\ 48'\ 48''$. [vide *Chronology*]

CIVI'LIAN (*Law*) a doctor, professor, or student in the Civil Law.

CLACK of a Mill (*Mech.*) a bell that rings when more corn is required to be put into the mill.

TO CLACK wool (*Law*) to cut off the sheep's mark to make it weigh lighter, in distinction from *forcing wool*, which is to cut off the upper and hairy part; and *barding wool*, which is to cut off the head and neck from the rest of the fleece. *Stat.* 8, *Hen.* 6, c. 22.

CLA'DUS (*Archæol.*) a hurdle or wattle.

CLA'ER (*Chem.*) Bone-flour, or a powder prepared from the bones of the cranium of a calf.

CLAIE (*Mil.*) French for a hurdle which is used during a siege.

CLAIM (*Law*) a challenge of interest in any thing that is in the possession of another, or at least out of a man's own possession, as claim by charter, by descent, &c. A claim is either verbal, when it is made by words; or it is by an action brought, relating sometimes to lands, and sometimes to goods and chattels.—*Continual claim* is where a man has right and title to enter into any lands or tenements, whereof another is seized in fee or in fee-tail.—*Claim of liberty* is a suit or petition to the king to have liberties and franchises confirmed there by the King's Attorney-general.

CLAIR obscur (*Paint.*) vide *Claro obscuro*.

CLAIR-VOGE (*Carpent.*) French for too wide a space between beams and rafters.

CLAIRON (*Mil.*) French for a species of trumpet which is shriller in its sound than the ordinary trumpet.

CLAM (*Com.*) a small weight, and an imaginary coin at Siam.

CLA'MEA admittenda in Itinere per Attornatum (*Law*) an ancient writ by which the King commanded the justices in Eyre to admit a person's claim by attorney, who was employed in the king's service, and could not come in his own person. *Reg. Orig.* 19.

CLAMP (*Carpent.*) a little piece of wood in the fashion of a wheel used instead of a pulley in a mortice, as in the flaps of shutters, kitchen tables, and the like.—*Clamp-nails*, such as are used to fasten clamps in building and repairing ships.

CLAMP (*Mar.*) [vide *Cap-square*]—*Clamp* is also a piece of timber applied to a mast for strengthening it.

CLAMP of bricks (*Mech.*) a pile of bricks raised for burning, —*Clamp-irons* at the ends of hearths to keep up the fuel, called also *creepers* or *dogs*.

CLAN (*Polit.*) a term used among the Scotch for a number of families subject to one chief.

CLANDE'STINA (*Bot.*) the same as the *Lathræa* of Linnæus.

CLAP (*Med.*) the Gonorrhœa impura.

CLAP (*Sport.*) the nether part of a hawk's beak.—*Clap net*, a sort of net used in birding, which was contrived for catching larks by means of a looking-glass.

CLA'P-BOARD (*Carpent.*) a board ready cut for making casks.

CLA'PPER (*Sport.*) a place under ground where rabbits breed.

CLAPPER (*Mech.*) that part of a bell with which the sound is produced.

CLARENCIE'UX (*Her.*) the second king at arms, appointed by Edward IV. on the death of the duke of Clarence, from whom he received his name. His office is to marshal and dispose the funeral of all knights and esquires on the south of the river Trent.

CLARENDON, *Constitutions of* (*Law*) certain constitutions made in the reign of Henry II. in 1164, whereby the power of the pope and clergy was much curtailed. They were so called from Clarendon, in Wiltshire, the place where they were enacted.

CLA'RET (*Com.*) a general name for the red wines of France.

CLARE'TA (*Nat.*) the white of an egg.

CLARE'TUM (*Med.*) a wine impregnated with spices and sugar, otherwise called *vinum Hippocrateum*. There is also a *claretum purgativum*, which is mentioned by Schroeder in his Pharmacopia.

CLA'RICORDS (*Mus.*) a stringed instrument formerly in use, the strings of which were supported by five bridges. It much resembled a spinnet; but the strings were covered with a piece of cloth, so as to deaden the sound and render it softer.

CLARIFICA'TION (*Chem.*) the process of making any liquid, clear or free from heterogeneous matter. The substances usually employed for clarifying liquors are whites of eggs, blood, and isinglass.

CLARIGA'TIO (*Ant.*) 1. A demanding satisfaction for an injury, by an outcry, as it were, *claritate vocis*, which being done, war was proclaimed, as Livy informs us, by the Pater-patratus, who went for this purpose to the enemy's borders. *Liv.* l. 1. c. 32; *Plin.* l. 22, c. 2; *Serv. in Æn.* l. 9, v. 53. 2. An arrest or seizure of the person, which was called by the Greeks ἀνδροληψίαν. *Liv.* l. 8, c. 14; *Gloss. Lat. Græc. Philox.*; *Justinian. Novell.* 52; *Tumel. Adv.* l. 21, c. 1.

CLARINE'T (*Mus.*) a wind instrument of the reed kind, the scale of which includes every semitone; but it is heard to advantage only on the keys C and F.

CLARI'NO (*Mus.*) a kind of trumpet, consisting of a narrower tube than ordinary, and sending forth a very shrill note.

CLA'RION (*Mus.*) an octave trumpet.

CLARION (*Her.*) a bearing which represents an old fashioned trumpet used in war, as in the annexed figure. "He beareth *argent*, a chevron between three Clarions, *gules*, by the name of *Arthur*, of Clopton, in Somersetshire."

CLARMA'RTHEN (*Law*) a term in the Scotch law for warranting stolen goods.

CLA'RO *obscuro* (*Paint.*) or *Clair-obscure*, the art of distributing to advantage the lights and shades of a piece, so as to render it most pleasing to the eye, and give at the same time most effect to the whole piece.—*Claro-obscuro*, or *Chiaro-oscuro*, is sometimes employed to signify a design of two colours, as black and white, or black and yellow; also prints of two colours taken off at twice.

CLARY-WATER (*Med.*) a water composed of brandy, sugar, clary-flowers, and cinnamon, with a little ambergris dissolved in it.

CLA'SIS (*Med.*) κλάσις, from κλάω, to break; a fracture.

CLA'SMIUM (*Min.*) an old term for a certain description of gypsums, which are of a soft texture, and of a dull opaque look.

CLA'SPER (*Bot.*) another name for the *cirrus* or *tendril*. [vide *Tendril*]

CLASS (*Ant.*) vide *Classis* and *Census*.

CLASS (*Nat.*) a term applied to the most general subdivision into which the kingdom of nature is divided. The animal kingdom, *in the Linnean system*, is divided into 6 classes, the vegetable kingdom into 24, &c. Each class includes a certain number of orders, genera, species, &c. of which a description may be found under the respective heads.

CLASS (*Lit.*) is a scholastic term applied to any number of youth in a school who are of the same form, and learn the same thing.—*Class* in the University of Oxford is the division of the candidates who are examined for their degrees according to their rate of merit. Those who are entitled to this distinction are denominated *classmen*, answering to the *optimes* and *wranglers* in the University of Cambridge.

CLASSIA'RIUS *miles* (*Ant.*) a seaman, or one who served in the navy. *Cæs. de Bell. Civil.* l. 1, c. 58; *Hist. de Bell. Alex.* c. 11; *Tacit. Annal.* l. 15, c. 51; *Scheff. de Mil. Naval.* l. 2, c. 3.

CLA'SSICAL (*Lit.*) an epithet for authors and books which have acquired an established authority. [vide *Classicus*]

CLA'SSICEN (*Ant.*) or *Classicarius*, the trumpeter, or he who sounded the *classicum*.

CLA'SSICS (*Lit.*) a term applied in an especial manner to the writings of the ancients in the Latin and Greek.

CLA'SSICUM (*Ant.*) a flourish with the trumpet, which was sounded by the trumpeter either to assemble the army or to give the signal for battle.
Senec. Œdip. act 3, v. 733.

Sonuit reflexo classicum cornu.

Varr. de Lat. Ling. l. 5, c. 9; *Liv.* l. 7, c. 36, l. 38, c. 27; *Serv. in Æn.* l. 8, v. 637; *Veget.* l. 2, c. 22; *Isid. Orig.* l. 18, c. 4.

CLA'SSICUS (*Ant.*) 1. vide *Classicen*. 2. A denizen or freeman; one who is assessed and placed in a certain class of the citizens, but more particularly those who were of the first class, the aldermen or chief men of the city; whence the term *classicus scriptor* in Aulus Gellius for a classical writer, or an author of the first rank and authority.

CLASSIFICA'TION (*Phil.*) in its general sense, implies the disposing of any thing in a certain order, but in its particular sense is applied to the artificial arrangement of natural objects according to their external characters.

CLA'SSIS (*Ant.*) the class or division which was formed of the Roman people according to the estimate of their estate. Those of the first class, distinguished by the name of *classici*, were not to be worth less than 200*l*. [vide *Census*]

CLA'TES (*Fort.*) vide *Clayes*.

CLATHROI'DES (*Bot.*) and *Clathroidastum*, a species of the *Clathrus*.

CLA'THRUS (*Bot.*) a genus of *Fungi*.

CLA'VA *Herculis* (*Bot.*) the *Xanthoxylum clava Herculis* of Linnæus.—*Clava rugosa*. [vide *Calamus aromaticus*]

CLAVA (*Conch.*) a genus of animals, Class *Vermes*, Order *Mollusca*.
Generic Character. Body fleshy and clavate: *aperture* angle and vertical.

CLAVA'RIA (*Bot.*) a genus of *Fungi*.

CLAVA'RIUS (*Archæol.*) a verger or mace-bearer.

CLAVA'TIO (*Anat.*) a sort of articulation without motion, where the parts are as it were driven in with a hammer, like the teeth in a socket.

CLAVA'TUS (*Bot.*) an epithet for the Leaf, as in *Anabasis foliosa*; for the Petiole and the Peduncle; for the Calyx, as in *Iclene*; for the Style, as in *Leucoium vernum*; for the Capsule, as in *Papaver Argemone*.

CLAU'DERE (*Law*) to inclose land, and *claud*, a ditch, or inclosure. *Ken. Paroch. Antiq.*

CLAUDI'ACON (*Med.*) κλαυδιακον, a collyrium. *P. Æginet.* l. 7, c. 16.

CLAUDICA'TIO (*Med.*) lameness.

CLAVE (*Mar.*) a stool fourteen inches high, on which the shells are set up with wedges for making the sheave-holes.

CLAVE *Cymbala* (*Mus.*) vide *Clavicembalum*.

CLA'VECIN (*Mus.*) vide *Clavicembalum*.

CLAVELLA'TI *cineres* (*Chem.*) a name for potash, so called from the little billets into which the wood was cut in obtaining it.

CLA'VES *Insulæ* (*Law*) or keys of the island; a name given to the twelve weighty men who are chosen in the Isle of Man to determine difficult cases.

CLAVES *signatæ* (*Mus.*) a name for the coloured lines used by Guido, before the invention of cliffs, to determine the situation and power of notes.

CLA'VIA (*Archæol.*) per *serjeantiam claviæ*, i. e. by the serjeanty of the club or mace, is a sort of tenure in the counties of Essex and Hertford mentioned in the inquisition of serjeanties in the 12th and 13th of King John.

CLAVICE'MBALUM (*Mus.*) an ancient name for the harp.

CLAVICITHE'RIUM (*Mus.*) another name for the clarichord.

CLAVI'CULÆ (*Bot.*) vide *Tendril*.

CLAVICULÆ (*Anat.*) κλειδες, clavicles; the two channel-bones, or two small bones which fasten the shoulder-bones and breast-bone, being as it were keys situated at the basis or bottom of the neck, above the breast, each resembling a letter S in form. They are aptly enough described by Homer when he speaks of the part which Achilles aimed at in his contest with Hector.
Hom. Il. l. 22, v. 324.

Φαίνετο δ' ἦ κληΐδες ἀπ' ὤμων αὐχέν' ἔχουσι
Λευκανίης ὅθι τε ψυχῆς ὤκιστος ὄλεθρος.

CLAVI'CULUS (*Bot.*) vide *Tendril*.

CLA'VIGER (*Ant.*) Club-bearer; an epithet for Hercules, who is mostly represented on coins and medals carrying a club.

CLAVIGERA'TUS (*Archæol.*) a treasurer of a church. *Mon. Angl.* tom. 1, p. 184.

CLA'VIS (*Mus.*) cliff, or key. [vide *Cliff*]

CLAVIS (*Lit.*) a key, or whatever serves to decypher or explain.

CLAVIS *siliginis* (*Bot.*) a name for smutted rye.

CLAVIS (*Chem.*) any menstruum, particularly of minerals, which unlocks them as it were, and penetrates their inner substance.

CLAUSE (*Law*) an article, condition, or provision in a contract, deed, or other instrument.—*Clause rolls*, rolls containing records committed to close writs preserved in the Tower.—*Clause in the Scotch law* is of two kinds, *irritant* and *resolutive*.—*Clause irritant* is any provision which makes a penalty be incurred, and the obligation to be null for the future; or upon any other account makes the right to vacate or resolve.—*Clause resolutive*, a provision whereby the contract to which it is affixed is, for non-performance, declared to have been null from the beginning.

CLAU'SE-ROLLS (*Law*) vide *Close-Rolls*.

CLAU'SIKE (*Vet.*) the first rot in sheep.

CLAU'STRUM *gutturis* (*Med.*) the passage to the throat, which lies immediately under the root of the tongue and the tonsils.

CLAU'SUM *fregit* (*Law*) a writ in an action of trespass; so called because it demands the person summoned to answer *quare clausum fregit*, why he committed such a trespass.—*Clausum paschiæ*, the end of Easter, or Sunday after Easter-Day, so termed because it concludes that festival.

CLAUSU'RA (*Med.*) an imperforation of any canal or cavity of the body; thus *Clausura Uteri* is a preternatural imperforation of the uterus.

CLA'VUS (*Ant.*) signified, 1. A nail, as *clavus annalis*, the nail which was annually driven into the wall of Jupiter's temple by the Prætor, Consul, or Dictator, on the Ides of September, by which at first an account of the Roman years was kept. *Liv.* l. 7, c. 3; *Fest. de Verb. Signif.* 2. The rudder or helm of a ship. *Cic. ad Fam.* l. 9, ep. 15; *Serv. in Æn.* l. 5, v. 177. 3. A knap of purple, which was worn as a badge of distinction by Senators, whence the dignity itself was also called *clavus*; and *clavum tribuere aut adimere*, signified to raise one to the dignity of a senator, or to degrade him from it. The *clavus* was distinguished into the *latus clavus*, which belonged especially to senators, and the *clavus angustus*, which belonged to knights. The former of these is frequently mentioned or alluded to by the poets.
Ovid. Trist. l. 4, eleg. 10, v. 27.

> Induiturque humeris cum lato purpura clavo.

Mart. l. 4, ep. 46.

> Et lato variata mappa clavo.

This *clavus* was also worn by the priests of Saturn.
Sil. Ital. l. 3, c. 26.

> Discinctis mos thura dare, atque e lege parentum
> Sacrificam lato vestem distinguere clavo.

Sometimes the *clavus angustus* is likewise alluded to.
Mart. l. 5, ep. 17.

> Dum proavos atavosque refers, et nomina magna;
> Dum tibi noster Eques sordida conditio est;
> Dum te posse negas nisi lato, Gellia, clavo
> Nubere; nupsisti, Gellia, cistifero.

Ovid. Trist. l. 4, eleg. 9, v. 35.

> Curia restabat: clavi mensura coacta est:
> Majus erat nostris viribus illud opus.

Stat. Silv. l. 4.

> Contextus arcto lumine purpuræ.

Stat. Sylv. l. 5.

> ————— non sanguine cretus
> Turmali, trabeaque Remi, nec paupere clavo
> Augustam sedem, et Latii penetrale senatus
> Advena pulsasti.

Varr. de Ling. Lat. l. 1; *Hor. sat.* 6, v. 28; *Strab.* l. 3; *Petron. Arb.* c. 32; *Quintil.* l. 8, c. 5; *Tertull. de Pall.* c. 4; *Herodian.* l. 5, c. 5; *Sueton. Claud.* c. 24; *Ammian.* l. 16, c. 8; *Isidor. Orig.* l. 9, c. 4.

CLAVUS (*Med.*) 1. A name for tubercles in different parts of the body, as *clavus pedum*, hard skin on the toes or soles of the feet, corns; *clavus oculorum*, a staphyloma or tumour on the eye-lids; *clavus uteri*, an indurated tubercle in the uterus. *Cels.* l. 7, c. 7; *Plin.* l. 30, c. 10; *Plin. Valer.* l. 2, c. 5; *Marcell. Empir.* c. 34. 2. A fixed pain in one part of the forehead, not exceeding a thumb's breadth in extent. It much resembles the sensation which the driving a nail into the head might occasion, from which it derives its name. When connected with hysterics, as it is sometimes, it is called *Clavus hystericus*.

CLAWA (*Law*) a close, or small inclosure. *Mon. Angl.* tom. 2.

CLAWING (*Mar.*) or *clawing off*, in French *chicaner*, beating or turning to windward from a lee-shore.

CLAY (*Min.*) a fat clammy sort of earth, which is classed in the Linnean system under *Argilla*. It is distinguished into different kinds, as—Common Clay, or Brick-Clay, *Argilla communis*.—Potter's Clay, *Argilla lithomania*.—Pipe Clay, *Argilla leucargilla*.—Porcelain Clay, *Argilla porcellana*.

CLAYES (*Fort.*) or *Clates*, wattles made of stakes interwoven with osiers, &c. to cover lodgments, having earth heaped upon them; they are also used to lay in ditches that have been drained, and on marshy grounds, &c.

CLAYMORE (*Mil.*) vide *Clymore*.

CLAYTO'NIA (*Bot.*) a genus of plants, Class 5 *Pentandria*, Order 1 *Monogynia*.

Generic Characters. CAL. *perianth* bivalve.—COR. *petals* five.—STAM. *filaments* five; *anthers* oblong.—PIST. *germ* roundish; *style* simple; *stigma* trifid.—PER. *capsule* roundish; *seeds* three.

Species. The species are, the—*Claytonia virginica*, a perennial, native of Virginia.—*Claytonia sibirica*, seu *Limnia*, a perennial, native of Siberia.—*Claytonia perfoliata*, an annual, native of N. America.

CLEAN (*Mar.*) an epithet applied to the sharp part of a ship, both fore and aft.

CLEAN *proof* (*Print.*) a proof that has but few faults in it.

CLEAR (*Mar.*) an epithet applied to various objects, as a *clear coast*, which is free from rocks, sands, or any thing else to impede the navigation. A cable, &c. is *clear* when it is disentangled. Weather is *clear*, as opposed to the foggy or cloudy.

CLEAR (*Carpent.*) an epithet for joists that are at a proper distance apart from each other.—*Clear story windows* are those which have no transom in their height.

CLEAR *vision* (*Opt.*) is produced by a great quantity of rays in the same pencil, enlightening the correspondent points of the image strongly and vigorously.

TO CLEAR (*Mar.*) is applied to different objects, as "To clear the anchor," in French *degager l'ancre*, to get the cable off the flooks. "To clear the hawse," in French *defaire le croix*, to untwist the cables which are entangled. "To clear out," or "To clear out a ship," to obtain leave for filling the cargo and sailing out by paying the customs.

TO CLEAR *the trenches* (*Mil.*) to drive out those that guard them.

CLEARER (*Mech.*) a tool on which the hemp is always finished for making ropes, &c.

CLEATS (*Mar.*) in French *Taquets de manœuvres*; pieces of wood differently shaped, and occasionally used in a ship to fasten ropes upon. They are of different kinds, according to their form, as—*Belaying cleat*, which is formed with two arms.—*Comb cleat*, which is straight on the inner edge.—*Mast cleat*, which is made with a score to admit a seizing, and a hole in the centre for an under seizing.—*Shroud cleat*, formed like the belaying cleat, but with a grooved edge.—*Single cleat*, formed with one arm only.—*Stop cleat*, nailed on the bowsprit for gammoning collars, &c.—*Thumb cleat*, similar to a single cleat, but smaller.

CLE'AVER (*Mech.*) a butcher's axe for chopping the bones of meat.

CLE'AVERS (*Bot.*) the *Galium aperine*, an annual so called because it is a climbing plant that cleaves to other plants for its support.

CLECHE (*Her.*) or *cleiche*, an epithet for a cross, or any ordinary pierced throughout, so that nothing of it remains except the edges.

CLE'DONES (*Ant.*) κληδόνες, ominous words or presages drawn from voices or words. This sort of divination was most in use at Smyrna, where, according to Pausanias, they had κληδόνων ἱερὸν, a temple, in which answers were returned this way. *Paus.* l. 9; *Hesychius.*

CLEF (*Arch.*) French for the key-stone of an arch.

CLEF *de mousquet* (*Mil.*) an iron instrument with only one square hole and a handle, with which the piece is cocked.

CLEFF (*Mus.*) vide *Cliff.*

CLE'FT-GRAFTING (*Hort.*) a mode of ingrafting by cleaving a tree and inserting a branch.

CLEFTS (*Vet.*) cracks in the pasterns of a horse, supposed to be caused by a sharp humour.

CLEG *goose* (*Her.*) the same as *Barnacle.*

CLEI'DIES (*Anat.*) the same as *Claviculæ.*

CLEI'DION (*Med.*) κλειδίον, a pastil described by Galen and Paulus Ægineta. *Gal. de Comp. Med. sec. Loc.* l. 9, c. 5; *P. Æginet.* l. 7, c. 12.

CLEIDOMASTOI'DEUS (*Anat.*) a muscle. vide *Sternocleidomastoideus.*

CLEINE *alt possanne* (*Mus.*) another name for a Sacbut.

CLEISA'GRA (*Med.*) from κλεὶς, the clavicle, and ἄγρα, a prey; the gout in the articulation of the clavicles to the sternum.

CLEI'THRON (*Anat.*) vide *Claustrum.*

CLE'MA (*Bot.*) κλῆμα, the twig or tendril of a plant.

CLE'MATIS (*Bot.*) κληματίς, a plant so called because it has κλήματα, tendrils. *Dioscor.* l. 4, c. 7; *Plin.* l. 24, c. 15; *Gal. de Simpl.* l. 7.

CLEMATIS, in the Linnean System, a genus of plants, Class 13 *Polyandria*, Order 3 *Polygynia*.

Generic Characters. CAL. none. — COR. petals four. — STAM. filaments very many; anthers growing to the size of the filaments. — PIST. germs very many; styles longer than the stamens; stigmas simple. — PER. none; receptacle headed; seeds very many.

Species. The species are shrubs, as the *Clematis cirrhosa*, &c. Evergreen Virgin's Bower, native of Bœtica. — *Clematis florida*, &c. Large-flowered Virgin's Bower, native of Japan. — *Clematis viticella*, seu *Clematilis*, &c. Purple Virgin's Bower, native of Italy. — *Clematis viorna*, *Flaminula*, &c. *Scandens*, &c. Leathery-flowered Virgin's Bower, native of Virginia. — *Clematis vitalba*, Common Virgin's Bower, Wild Climbers, or Traveller's joy, native of the south of Europe.

CLEMATIS is also the *Atragene Zeylanica.*

CLEMA'TITIS (*Bot.*) κληματίτις, a plant so called because it climbs up trees by its claspers, or tendrils. *Dioscor.* l. 4, c. 182; *Plin.* l. 25, c. 8; *Clus. Hist. Rar. Plant.*; *Bauh. Pin.*; *Raii Hist. Plant.*

CLEMATITIS is now another name for *Clematis.*

CLE'MENTINES (*Eccl.*) a part of the canon law, consisting of decretals or constitutions of Pope Clement V., and enacted into laws by the council of Vienna.

CLE'NCH-BOLTS (*Carpent.*) iron pins in a ship clenched at the ends which are carried through. — *Clench-nails* are such as will drive through a board without splitting it.

CLE'OME (*Bot.*) a genus of plants, Class 15 *Tetradynamia*, Order 2 *Siliquosa*.

Generic Characters. CAL. perianth four-leaved. — COR. four-petalled. — STAM. filaments six; anthers lateral. — PIST. germ oblong; style simple; stigmas thickish. — PER. silique long; seeds very many.

Species. The species are shrubs, and annuals, as the *Cleome juncea*, &c. a shrub, native of the Cape of Good Hope. — *Cleome heptaphylla*, seu *Erucago*, *Sinapistrum*, &c. *Pentaphyllum*, &c. Seven-leaved Cleome, an annual, native of the Indies. — *Cleome pentaphylla*, *Sinapistrum*, &c., *Papaver*, &c. *Quinquefolium*, &c. seu *Capa*, &c. Five-leaved Cleome, an annual, native of the Indies. — *Cleome icosandra*, *Sinapistrum*, &c. seu *Lagansa*, &c. an annual, native of Ceylon.

CLEO'NIA (*Bot.*) a genus of plants, Class 14 *Didynamia*, Order 1 *Gymnospermia*.

Generic Characters. CAL. perianth one-leaved, upper lip flattish, lower two-parted. — COR. one-petalled, upper lip straight, lower bifid. — STAM. filaments four; anthers crossed in pairs. — PIST. germ four-parted; style filiform; stigmas four. — PER. none; calyx closed with hairs; seeds four.

Species. The only species is the *Cleonia lusitanica*, *Brunella*, &c. *Prunella*, &c. *Clinopodium*, &c. seu *Bugula*, &c. Sweet-scented Cleonia, an annual, native of Portugal.

CLEONI'CIUM (*Bot.*) the same as *Clinopodion.*

CLEO'NIS *collyrium* (*Med.*) a collyrium described by Celsus. *De Re Med.* l. 6, c. 6.

CLEONIS *gluten* (*Med.*) a medicine described by Orobasius. *Med. Coll.* l. 4.

CLEP (*Law*) a form of claim, libel, or petition, in the Scotch Law.

CLEPSAMMIDIUM (*Ant.*) an hour-glass which measured time by the running out of the sand.

CLEPSY'DRA (*Dial.*) κλεψύδρα, in French *clepsydre*, a waterclock, so called from κλέπτω, to steal, and ὕδωρ, water, because the water steals, as it were, out of the glass. An instrument of early invention for the purpose of measuring time in an hour-glass, by means of running water or sand. Orators, both among the Greeks and Romans, were regulated by this hour-glass, as to their time of speaking, which was called pleading, πρὸς κλεψύδραν, by the clepsydra, to which Martial refers. *Mart.* l. 6, epig. 35.

*Septem clepsydras, magna tibi voce petenti
Arbiter invitus Ceciliane dedit.*

Aristot. Poet.; *Demosthen. Orat.* περὶ παραπρεσβ. *Cic. Or.* l. 3, c. 34; *Vitruv.*

CLEPSYDRA (*Surg.*) an instrument mentioned by Paracelsus, for conveying suffumigations to the uterus.

CLE'RGY (*Eccl.*) *Clerici*, now signifies all persons who are in holy orders, and in ecclesiastical offices, as Archbishops, Bishops, Deans, and Chapters; Parsons, who are rectors or vicars, and curates. Formerly the clergy were divided into regulars and seculars. The *regulars* were such as lived under the rules of some order, as Abbots, Monks, &c. — The *seculars* were those who lived under no such rules, as Bishops, Deans, and Parsons. [vide *Clerk*] — *Benefit of clergy*, an ancient privilege whereby one in orders claimed to be delivered to his ordinary to purge himself of felony, which was also extended to the laity. [vide *Benefit*]

CLE'RICO *admittendo* (*Law*) vide *admittendo clerico.*—*Clerico infra sacros ordines constituto, non eligendo in officium*; a writ directed to those who have thrust a bailiwick, or other office, on one in holy orders, charging them to release him. *Reg. Orig.* 143. — *Clerico capto per statutum mercatorum*, &c. a writ for the delivery of a clerk out of prison, who is taken and imprisoned upon the breach of a statute merchant. *Reg. Orig.* 69.

CLERK (*Law*) *clericus*, a term peculiarly applied to a clergyman, or one who belongs to the Holy Ministry of the Church. The word is derived from *clerus*, a lot, signifying to be *de clero Domini*, of the Lord's lot, as the tribe of Levi was in Judea.

Clerk, in another sense, is taken for one who practises his pen in any court or office; so called because formerly these offices were executed principally by the clergy. Clerks are of different kinds, according to their office, viz. —*Clerk of the Acts*, an officer in the Navy Office, whose business it is to record all orders, contracts, bills, warrants, &c. transacted by the Lords Commissioners of the Admiralty.—*Clerk of affidavits*, an officer in the Court of Chancery who files all affidavits.—*Clerk of the assize*, he who writes all things down that are judicially done by the justices of assizes in their circuits. *Cromp. Juris.* 227.—*Clerk of the bails*, an officer who files the bail pieces taken in the Court of King's Bench.—*Clerks in Chancery*, six clerks under the twelve Masters. [vide *Chancery*]—*Clerk of the cheque*, an officer in the King's Court, so called because he has the check and controlment of the yeomen of the guard, and all other yeomen belonging to the King, Queen, or Prince of Wales. —*Clerk of the closet*, a clergyman, otherwise called *confessor to his Majesty*, whose office it is to attend the King at all religious services, and in all spiritual matters. —*Clerk controller of the King's House*, whose office it is to allow or disallow charges of Pursuivants, Messengers, &c. of the Green Cloth, &c.—*Clerk of the Crown*, an officer who frames, reads, and records all indictments against offenders arraigned or indicted of any public crime in the Court of King's Bench: he is otherwise called *Clerk of the Crown Office*, and exhibits informations.—*Clerk of the Crown in Chancery*, an officer in that court who continually attends the Lord Chancellor in person, or by deputy.—*Clerk of the declarations*, an officer that files all declarations in the Court of King's Bench.—*Clerk of the deliveries*, an officer in the Tower of London, whose office it is to take indentures for all stores, ammunition, &c. issued from thence.—*Clerk of the errors*, an officer in the Court of Common Pleas, who transcribes and certifies into the King's Bench the tenor of the records of the cause in action, upon which the writ of error made by the cursitor is brought there to be heard and determined.—*Clerk of the essoins*, an officer belonging to the Court of Common Pleas who keeps the *essoin rolls*.—*Clerk of the estreats*, an officer belonging to the Exchequer, who every term receives the estreats out of the Lord Treasurer's Remembrancer's office, and writes them out to be levied for the King.—*Clerk of the hanaper*, or *hamper*, an officer in chancery, whose office it is to receive all the money due to the King for the seals of charters, &c.; he is so called because the hanaper is an old term signifying *fiscum*, or treasury.—*Clerk of the inrollments*, an officer of the Common Pleas, who enrolls and exemplifies all fines, recoveries, returns, writs of entry, summons, and seisin, &c.—*Clerk of the juries*, an officer belonging to the Court of Common Pleas, who makes out writs of *habeas corpora* and *distringas* for the appearance of juries.—*Clerk of the market*, an officer of the King's house to whom it belongs to take charge of the King's measures, and keep the standards of them, which are the examples of all measures to be used throughout the kingdom. 13 *R*. 2, c. 4, &c.; *Flet*. l. 2, c. 8, 9.; 4 *Inst*. 274.—*Clerk Marshal of the King's Household*, an officer that attends the Marshal in his Court, and records all proceedings.—*Clerk of the nichils*, or *nihils*, an officer belonging to the Court of Exchequer, who makes a roll of all such sums as are nihiled by the sheriffs upon their estreats of green wax.—*Clerk of the ordnance*, an officer of the Tower, who registers all orders touching the King's ordnance.—*Clerks of the outlawries*, a servant, or deputy, to the Attorney General, who makes out writs of *capias ut lagatum*, after outlawry. —*Clerk of the Paper Office*, an officer in the Court of King's Bench who makes up the Paper-books of special pleadings and demurrers in that court.—*Clerk of the papers*, an officer of the Common Pleas, who has the custody of the papers of the warden of the Fleet; enters commitments and discharges of prisoners, &c.—*Parish Clerk*, vide *Parish*.—*Clerk of the Parliament Rolls*, an officer who records all things done in the high court of Parliament.—*Clerk of the patents*, or of the letters patent under the Great Seal of England.—*Clerk of the peace*, an officer belonging to the sessions of the peace, whose duty it is to read indictments, enrol proceedings, draw the process, &c.—*Clerk of the Pells*, a clerk belonging to the Exchequer, whose office it is to enter every teller's bill into a parchment roll, or skin, called *pellis receptorum*, and to make another roll of payments, called *pellis exituum*.—*Clerk of the petty bag*, an officer of the Court of Chancery, whose office it is to record the returns of all inquisitions out of every shire, to make out patents, &c.—There are three of these officers, of which the Master of the Rolls is the chief.—*Clerk of the Pipe*, an officer in the Exchequer who has the accounts of the debts due to the King, and charges them down in the great roll, called the *pipe*, from its shape, which resembles a pipe: he was formerly called *Ingrossator magni Rotuli*, Stat 33, *H*. 8, c. 22.—*Clerk of the Pleas*, an officer in the Court of Exchequer, in whose office all the officers of the court, upon special privilege belonging to them, ought to sue, or be sued in any action.— *Clerks of the Privy Seal*, four officers which attend the Lord Privy Seal, to write and make out all things that are sent by warrant from the Signet to the Privy Seal.— *Clerk of the Remembrance*, an officer who assists the Clerk of the Pipe.—*Clerk of the Rolls*, an officer who makes search for and copies, deeds, offices, &c. in the Court of Chancery.—*Clerk of the Rules*, he who draws up and enters all the rules and orders made in the Court of King's Bench.—*Clerk of the Sewers*, an officer belonging to the Commissioners of Sewers, who takes account of all their proceedings.—*Clerk of the Signet*, an officer continually attendant on his Majesty's Principal Secretary, who has the custody of the privy *signet*. There are four of these officers who attend in turn, and dine at the Secretary's table.—*Clerk of the King's Silver*, an officer in the Court of Common Pleas, who receives all fines that have passed the office of the *custos brevium*.—*Clerk of the supersedeas*, an officer in the Court of Common Pleas who makes out writs of *supersedeas* upon a defendant's appearing to the exigent on an outlawry, whereby the sheriff is forbidden to return the exigent.—*Clerk of the treasury*, an officer of the Common Pleas who has the records of the court in his charge, and is the servant of the Chief Justice. He is removeable at pleasure, in distinction from other clerks, who are for life. There is also a secondary, or *under clerk of the treasury*, who has one key of the treasury-door, and an *under-keeper*, who has another.—*Clerk of the King's great wardrobe*, one who keeps account of what belongs to the royal wardrobe. Stat. 1 *Edw*. 4, c. 1. —*Clerk of the warrants*, an officer of the Common Pleas who enters all warrants of attorney, deeds of indentures, of bargain and sale, &c.

Clerk is also applied in the sense of one who prays for benefit of clergy; thus the *clerk attaint* is one who prays for benefit of clergy after judgment has been given upon him for felony; *clerk convict*, one who prays for benefit before sentence is passed upon him.

CLERK (*Com.*) this term has been transferred from the law to commerce, in the same sense, to denote one who executes any office with his pen in a counting-house, or any other trading concern.

CLERK (*Ecc.*) *clericus sacerdotis*, a parish clerk, or an inferior assistant to the priest.

CLERKS (*Her.*) the company of clerks, called *parish clerks*, is ancient, being incorporated in the 17th of Henry III. Their arms are, "*Azure*, a fleur-de-luce, *or*, on a chief, *gules*, a leopard's head betwixt two books, *or*."

CLERODENDRUM (*Bot.*) a genus of plants, Class 14 *Didynamia*, Order 2 *Angiospermia*.
 Generic Characters. CAL. *perianth* one-leaved. — COR. one-petalled; *tube* slender; *border* five-parted. — STAM. *filaments* four; *anthers* simple. — PIST. *germ* roundish; *style* filiform; *stigma* simple. — PER. *drupe* roundish; *seed* one.
 Species. The species are shrubs, as the — *Clerodendrum infortunatum*, *Petasites*, &c. seu *Peragu*, native of India. — *Clerodendrum fortunatum*, Entire-leaved Clerodendron, native of India. — *Clerodendrum calamitosum*, &c. seu *Volkameria*, &c. native of Java. — *Clerodendrum phlomoides*, seu *Volkameria*, &c. native of the East Indies.

CLEROMANCY (*Ant.*) κληρομαντεία, a mode of divination, wherein they made conjectures by throwing κλῆροι, lots.

CLERONIMUS (*Archæol.*) an heir.

CLEROPEPLUM (*Ecc.*) the tippet or scarf worn by clergymen.

CLEROS (*Nat.*) κλῆρος, a miscarriage among the bees when, by reason of the hardness and bitterness of the wax, they do not bring forth their young, but both they and the comb rot together. Aristotle calls the *cleros* an insect which destroys the combs of the bees. *Aristot. Hist. Animal.* l. 8, c. 27; *Plin.* l. 1, c. 18.

CLERUS (*Ent.*) a division of the genus *Attelabus*, consisting of those species of insects which have the jaw one-toothed, the hind feelers hatchet-flashed.

CLERUS (*Ecc.*) a clerk or clergyman, one who is *de clero Domini*, i. e. of the Lord's lot or portion.

CLETCH (*Her.*) vide *Clecke*.

CLETHRA (*Bot.*) a genus of plants, Class 10 *Decandria*, Order 1 *Monogynia*.
 Generic Characters. CAL. *perianth* one-leaved; *leaflets* ovate. — COR. *petals* five. — STAM. *filaments* ten; *anthers* oblong-erect. — PIST. *germ* roundish; *style* filiform; *stigma* trifid. — PER. *capsule* roundish; *seeds* very many.
 Species. The species are shrubs, as the — *Clethra alnifolia*, seu *Alnifolia*, &c. Alder-leaved Clethra, native of Carolina. — *Clethra paniculata*, Panicled Clethra, native of North America. — *Clethra arborea*, Tree Clethra, native of Madeira. — *Clethra tinifolia*, *Tinus*, &c. *Volkmeria*, &c. seu *Baccifera*, &c. native of Jamaica.

CLEVERS (*Bot.*) the same as *Cleavers*.

CLEW (*Mar.*) in French *point d'une voile*, the lower corner of square sails, which reaches down to where the tackles and sheet ropes are fastened; whence the expressions " From *clew* to earing," signifying from the bottom to the top. "To *clew up*," in French *carguer une voile*, to haul up the clews of a sail to its yard by means of the clew-lines. To the *Clews* belong — *Clew-garnets*, in French *cargues-points de basses voiles*, a sort of tackle fastened to the clews of the main and foresail to truss them to the yard. — *Clew-Lines*, in French *cargue-points des voiles quarrées*, for the same purpose as the clew-garnets, only that the latter are solely appropriated to the courses; but the clew-lines are employed for all the square sails. — *Clews of a Hammock*, in French *points d'une hamac*, the combination of small lines, by which the hammock is suspended.

CLEYENA (*Bot.*) the same as the *Ternstrœmia*.

CLIBADIUM (*Bot.*) a genus of plants, Class 21 *Monoecia*, Order 5 *Pentandria*.
 Generic Characters. CAL. common imbricate; *scales* ovate. — COR. compound *corollules* of the disk many, of the ray three or four. — STAM. *filaments* five; *anthers* oblong. — PIST. *germ* very small; *style* filiform; *stigma* simple. — PER. common none; *calyx* ventricose; *seed* one.
 Species. The only species is *Clibadium Surinamense*, native of Surinam.

CLIBANARIUS (*Ant.*) καταφρακτος, a man or horse armed with complete armour, a cuirassier. *Ammian*. l. 16; *Nazar. in Panegyr. Constant.*

CLICH (*Mil.*) a sabre in use among the Turks, having a crooked broad blade.

CLICKETING (*Sport.*) a fox is said to go clicketing when he goes after the female.

CLICKS (*Mar.*) small pieces of iron falling into notched wheels attached to the winches in cutters, &c. and thereby serving the office of pawls.

CLIDIUM (*Ich.*) the throat of the tunny. *Plin.* l. 9, c. 15.

CLIENS (*Ant.*) a Roman citizen who was under the protection of some great man, who, in that relation, was called his patron, and assisted him with his counsel and support in all matters of dispute.
Hor. l. ii, ep. 1, v. 104.
 Romæ dulce diu fuit, et solenne reclusa
 Mane domo vigilare, clienti promere jura.

The client, on the other hand, was always devoted to the interests of his patron, and ready to pay every outward mark of respect. The poets allude to the morning salutations which the clients used to give to their patrons.
Mart. l. 2, epig. 18.
 Mane salutatum venio; tu diceris isse
 Ante salutatum; jam sumus ergo pares.

Juv. sat. 5, v. 19.
 ——— *Habet Trebius propter quod rumpere somnum*
 Debeat, et ligulas dimittere, sollicitus ne,
 Tota salutrix jam turba peregerit orbem
 Sideribus dubiis.

Senec. de Brev. Vit. c. 14.

CLIENT (*Law*) one who retains a lawyer or counsellor to manage or plead his cause.

CLIENTELARIS (*Law*) belonging to a vassal or tenant, *prædium clientelare*, a fee-farm.

CLIENTS (*Mil.*) noblemen who formerly served in the French armies under the pennant of a knight, the banner of a banneret, &c.

CLIFF (*Mus.*) or *clef*, a certain character or mark placed on one side of the lines, from which the proper places of all other notes in a piece of music are discovered; or it is a letter marked on any line which explains and points out the name of all the rest. It is called the *clef* or *key*, because thereby are known the names of all the other lines and spaces; and, consequently, the quantity of every interval. Formerly every line had a letter marked for a cliff, but now a letter on one line suffices; since by this all the rest are known reckoning up and down in the order of the gamut. The cliff which is thus marked is called the *signed cliff* or *clef*, of which there are three; namely, C, F, G. The cliff of the highest part in a song, called *treble* or *alt*, is G, as in *fig.* 5, set on the second stave or line, reckoning upwards. The cliff of the bass, or lowest part,

is F on the fourth line upwards, *fig.* 1. For the other mean parts, the cliff is C; namely, C, the *tenor cliff*, placed on the fourth line, as in *fig.* 2; C, *counter-tenor*, or *alto cliff,* placed on the third line, as in *fig.* 3; and C, *soprano,* or *canto cliff,* placed on the first line, as in *fig.* 4.

CLIFFO'RTIA (*Bot.*) a genus of plants, Class 22 *Dioecia,* Order 11 *Polyandria.*
  Generic Characters. CAL. *perianth* three-leaved; *leaflets* ovate.—COR. none.—STAM. *filaments* capillary; *anthers* twin.—PIST. *germ* oblong; *styles* two; *stigmas* simple.—PER. *capsule* oblong; *seeds* solitary.
  Species. The species are shrubs, and natives of the Cape of Good Hope, as the—*Cliffortia odorata.*—*Cliffortia serrata.*—*Cliffortia ferruginea.*—*Cliffortia cuneata.*—*Cliffortia ilicifolia,* seu *arbuscula,* &c. Ilex-leaved Cliffortia.—*Cliffortia tridentata.*—*Cliffortia ruscifolia,* seu *Frutex,* &c. Butchers' broom-leaved Cliffortia.—*Cliffortia strobilifera,* seu *Cedrus,* &c.

CLIFT (*Vet.*) a deficiency in the new, soft, rough, and uneven hoof that grows on horses' feet upon the hoof-cast.

CLIMA'CION (*Mech.*) κλιμακίον, the round or step of a ladder.

CLIMA'CTER (*Mech.*) vide *Climacion.*

CLIMA'CTERES (*Med.*) or *anni scansiles,* i. e. years ascending like steps, applied particularly to certain critical periods of a man's life.

CLIMACTE'RICAL *years* (*Med.*) certain years observable in a man's life, which are supposed to be attended with some great mutation. [vide *Climacterics*]

CLIMACTE'RICS (*Med.*) the climacter, climacterical, or critical periods in a man's life, which were the 7th, the 21st, made up of 3 times 7; the 27th, made up of 3 times 9; and the 81st, made up of 9 times 9; thus, every 7th or 9th year is said to be climacterical.—*Grand Climacteric,* the 63d and 81st, in which, if any sickness occur, it is accounted very dangerous.

CLI'MATE (*Geog.*) a part or portion of the earth between two circles parallel to the Equator, and of such a breadth that the longest day, in the parallel nearest to the equator, exceeds the longest day in that next the equator by some certain space, as half an hour, or an hour, or a month. The beginning of the climate is a parallel wherein the day is shortest; the end of the climate is that wherein the day is the longest; the climates, which are forty-eight in number, being reckoned from the equator to the poles. Each climate differs from its contiguous ones by being longer or shorter, by half an hour, in one place than in the other, as far as the polar circles, when the climates commence to be what is called hour-climates and month-climates. An *hour-climate* is a space comprised between two parallels of the equator, in the first of which the longest day exceeds that in the latter by an hour; a *month-climate* is a space between two circles parallel to the polar circles, whose longest day is longer or shorter than that of its contiguous one by a month, or thirty days.

CLIMA'TICS (*Nat.*) a sort of earth-quake, which, proceeding in an oblique direction, sweeps every thing down before it. *Ammian.* l. 17, c. 7.

CLI'MAX (*Med.*) a name given to some antidotes, which, in a regular scale of proportion, increased or diminished their ingredients.

CLIMAX (*Rhet.*) κλίμαξ, a figure of rhetoric called, by Cicero and Quintilian, *gradatio,* where the discourse proceeds by degrees from higher to higher subjects; as "Africano virtutem industria, virtus gloriam, gloria emulationem comparavit." *Cic. Academ.* l. 4, c. 16; *Demet. Eloc.* § 270; *Quint.* l. 9, c. 3; *Athen.* l. 2, c. 2; *Eustath.* Il. β; *Voss. Rhet. Inst.* l. 5, p. 294.

CLIMBERS (*Bot.*) another name for the *Clematis.*

CLI'MBING-BIRTHWORT (*Bot.*) the *Aristolochia Clematitis* of Linnæus.

CLI'MIA (*Min.*) the *Cadmia Fornacum.*

TO CLINCH (*Mar.*) in French *étalinguer un cable,* a particular method of fastening large ropes by a kind of knot, which is principally used in fastening the cable to the ring of the anchor.

CLI'NCHED (*Her.*) an epithet for the hand shut.

CLI'NCHER *built* (*Mar.*) an epithet for a vessel made with clincher-work.—*Clincher-Work,* that disposition of the planks in a boat or vessel, when the lower edge of every plank overlays the next under it like the slates on the roof of a house.

CLI'NCHING (*Mar.*) 1. The operation of fastening the point of a bolt or nail on a ring by hammering it so as to make it spread. 2. A kind of slight calking used about the ports when foul weather is expected about a harbour. This is done by driving oakum into the sides to keep out the water.

CLI'NICE (*Med.*) vide *Clinical.*

CLI'NICAL (*Med.*) κλινικὸς, an epithet relating to a bed, from κλίνη, a bed; as a *clinical physician,* one who attends on bed-rid people: *clinical medicine,* which treats of visiting patients who are confined to their beds: so likewise clinical lectures, notes, &c.

CLI'NICUS (*Med.*) a patient who is confined to his bed from sickness.

CLI'NIS (*Mus.*) a name given by the Greeks of the middle ages to one of their notes.

CLI'NKERS (*Mason.*) bricks impregnated with a considerable quantity of nitre or salt-petre, which, by the violence of the fire, run and are glazed over.

CLI'NK-STONE (*Min.*) a brittle mineral of the basalt kind, which is common in Scotland and Germany.

CLINO'IDES (*Anat.*) *Clinoid,* of the shape of a bed, from κλίνη, a bed, and ιδος, the form; an epithet for the processes surrounding the *sella turcica* of the sphenoid bone.

CLINOMASTO'IDEUS (*Anat.*) vide *Cleidomastoideus.*

CLINO'PETES (*Med.*) κλινοπέτης, one who is confined to his bed from sickness.

CLINOPO'DIUM (*Bot.*) κλινοπόδιον, a herb, so called from the resemblance which it bore to πὺς, the foot, and κλίνη, a bed. *Dioscor.* l. 3, c. 109; *Plin.* l. 24, c. 15.

CLINOPODIUM, *in the Linnean system,* a genus of plants, Class 14 *Didynamia,* Order 1 *Gymnospermia.*
  Generic Characters. CAL. *involucre* many bristled; *perianth* one-leaved. COR. one-petalled; *tube* short.—STAM. *filaments* four; *anthers* roundish.—PIST. *germ* four-parted; *style* filiform; *stigma* simple.—PER. none; *calyx* contracted round the neck; *seeds* four.
  Species. The species are perennials, as the—*Clinopodium vulgare,* Wild Basil, native of Europe.—*Clinopodium Ægyptiacum,* native of Egypt.—*Clinopodium incanum, Serpentaria,* seu *Origanum,* &c. Hairy Clinopodium, native of North America.—*Clinopodium rugosum,* Wrinkled Clinopodium, native of Carolina.—*Clinopodium capitatum,* seu *Hyptis,* &c. native of Jamaica.

CLI'O (*Conch.*) a genus of animals, Class *Vermes,* Order *Mollusca.*
  Generic Character. Body oblong, nayant.—*Arms* wing-like processes.—*Tentacula* three, besides two in the mouth.
  Species. The principal species are the *Clio caudata, pyramidata, retusa,* &c.

CLI'PPERS (*Law*) those who debase the coin of the realm by cutting or paring the edge of it. Clipping of coin was made treason by Stat. 3, Hen. 5, c. 1.

CLI'PPING *of wool* (*Agric.*) cutting off the coarse ends of the wool before it is washed.

CLI'SSUS (*Chem.*) a term denoting mineral compound spirits.

CLITO'NES (*Polit.*) a term used for all the sons of the King, but particularly the eldest, in the charter of King Æthelred. *Matth. Par.* p. 158; *Seld.* notes *on Œdmer.*

CLITO'RIA (*Bot.*) a genus of plants, Class 17 *Diadelphia,* Order 3 *Decandria.*

Generic Characters. CAL. *perianth* one-leaved.—COR. papilionaceous; *standard* very large; *wings* oblong; *keel* shorter than the wings.—STAM. in two brotherhoods; *anthers* simple.—PIST. *germ* oblong; *style* ascending; *stigma* obtuse.—PER. *legume* very long; *seeds* many.

Species. The species are perennials, as the — *Clitoria ternata, Flos*, &c. *Schlonga*, &c. *Lathyrus*, &c. seu *Phaseolus*, &c. Winged-leaved Clitoria, native of the East Indies.—*Clitoria multiflora*, native of St. Domingo.—*Clitoria Brasiliana*, Brasilian Clitoria, native of Brasil. *Clitoria Virginiana*, Small flowered Clitoria, native of Virginia.—*Clitoria mariana*, seu *Clitorius*, &c. Maryland Clitoria, native of North America.

CLITO′RIDIS-FLOS (*Bot.*) a beautiful flower in the island of Ternate.

CLITORIDIS *musculus* (*Anat.*) or *Erector Clitoridis*, a muscle arising from the *crus* of the *os ischium*, which serves to draw the *clitoris* downwards and backwards.

CLITORIS (*Anat.*) from κλείω, to inclose, or be hid, because in its natural state it is inclosed in the *vagina*, a small glandiform body situated above the nymphæ.

CLITORI′SMUS (*Med.*) a morbid or preternatural enlargement of *clitoris*, such as is visible in hermaphrodites.

CLI′VERS (*Bot.*) the same as *Cleavers*.

CLIVI′NA *avis* (*Ant.*) a bird that, in soothsaying, gave a sign that a thing was not to be done. *Plin.* l. 10, c. 14; *Fest. de Verb. Signif.*

CLOA′CA (*Ant.*) the jakes, or common sewer.

CLOACA (*Anat.*) the canal in birds, through which the egg descends from the ovary in its exit.

CLOACA′RIUM (*Ant.*) a tax or assessment for cleaning the common sewers. *Ulp.*

CLOCHES (*Mil.*) a military tax which was imposed upon bells.

CLOCK (*Hor.*) an instrument for measuring time and its sub-divisions with great exactness. [vide *Horology*]

CLOCK-BEETLE (*Ent.*) or *Don*, a beetle that flies about in an evening in a circular direction with a loud noise; the *Scarabæus stercorarius* of Linnæus.

CLOCK-WORK (*Mech.*) that part of the movement which strikes the hours, &c. on a bell, in distinction from that part called the *Watch-work*, which is designed to exhibit the time on a dial-plate.

CLO′DIA *Lex* (*Ant.*) a name for several laws enacted by the tribune Clodius, which tended to increase the power of the people.

CLODIA′NA *vasa* (*Ant.*) a kind of vessels, so called from their inventor. *Plin.* l. 33, c. 11.

CLOG (*Mech.*) a piece of wood fastened about the legs of beasts to keep them from running away.

CLOI′STER (*Archit.*) a place in a monastery with piazzas; also the monastery itself.

CLOMPANUS (*Bot.*) the *Sterculia balanghus* of Linnæus.

CLO′NIC *spasms* (*Vet.*) a morbid contraction of the muscles.

CLONO′DES (*Med.*) κλονώδης, an epithet for a sort of pulsation which is vehement, large, and, at the same time, unequal. *Castell. Lex. Med.*

CLOSE (*Mus.*) is either the end of a strain, which is called an *imperfect close*; or the end of a tune, which is a *perfect close*.

CLOSE (*Her.*) an epithet for any bird which is represented in coat armour with its wings close down upon it, i. e. not displayed, or in a standing position.

CLOSE (*Agric.*) a piece of ground fenced or hedged about for pasturage.

CLOSE ROLLS (*Law*) and *close writs* are letters from the king, sealed with his Great Seal, but closed up, and directed to particular persons, in distinction from letters patent, or open letters, which contain grants of land, &c. from the crown.

CLOSE-STRING (*Archit.*) a staircase in dog-legged stairs without an open newel.

CLOSE *fights* (*Mar.*) a name for bulk-heads erected fore and aft in the ship for the men to stand behind in close engagement, and to fire on the enemy; or if the ships be boarded to scour the enemy.

CLOSE-HAULED (*Mar.*) in French *au plus près*, the arrangement or trim of a ship's sails when she endeavours to make a progress in the nearest direction possible towards that point of the compass from which the wind blows.— *Close-quarters*, strong barriers of wood stretching across a merchant ship, to serve as a place of shelter in case the vessel is boarded, and from which the crew can fire their small arms on the enemy.

CLOSED *behind* (*Man.*) an imperfection in the hind-quarters of a horse.

CLO′SER (*Mason.*) the last stone laid in the horizontal length of a wall.

CLO′SET (*Her.*) the half of the bar, which latter ought to contain a fifth of the field. [vide *Bar*]

CLOSET (*Archit.*) a small retired apartment within another room.

CLOSH (*Vet.*) a distemper in the feet of cattle similar to the founders.

CLOSHE (*Sport.*) the game answering, as is supposed, to what is now called *nine pins*, which was forbidden by statute 18 Ed. 4.

CLOTH (*Com.*) signifies generally any kind of stuff that is woven or manufactured in the loom, whether it be composed of wool, hemp, or flax; but in a more particular sense it implies a web or tissue of woollen threads interwoven, whereof some, called the *warp*, are extended in length from one end of the piece to the other; and the rest, called the *woof*, disposed across the first, or breadthwise of the piece.

CLOTH-WORKERS (*Her.*) or *clothiers*, were incorporated the 22d of Henry VIII. in 1530, and form the 12th company in the City of London. Their arms are, as in the annexed figure, "sable a chevron ermine, in chief; two crabbets, argent, in beizel or beazel, or."

CLO′THED (*Mar.*) a mast is said to be clothed when the sail is so long as to reach down to the gratings of the hatches, so that no wind can blow below the sail.

CLO′THIER (*Com.*) one who manufactures woollen cloth. [vide *Clothworkers*]

CLO′THING *of the bolsters* (*Mar.*) laying several thicknesses of worn canvass well tarred over them, to make an easy bed for the shrouds.

CLOTHS *in a sail* (*Mar.*) are the breadths of canvass in its whole width.

CLO′TTINGS *of wool* (*Com.*) the hard and clotted wool on the breech of the sheep, which are otherwise called breechings.

CLOUDS (*Nat.*) a congeries of particles, chiefly watery, drawn or sent out of the earth in vapours into the middle region of the air. It is computed by some that they are never above one half or three-fourths of a mile above the earth.

CLOUD-BERRY (*Bot.*) a plant growing on Pendle Hills, in Lancashire, so called as if it came out of the clouds.

CLOVE (*Bot.*) a spice, the fruit of the clove-tree.—Clove-Tree, the *Caryophyllus aromaticus* of Linnæus, which grows in the Dutch Spice-islands.—Clove-Bark, the bark of the *Myrtus caryophyllata*, so called because it smells like cloves.— Clove-Gilliflower, or Clove-pink, the *Dianthus caryophillus*.

CLOVE (*Com.*) the two-and-thirtieth part of a weigh of cheese, equal to eight pounds. *Stat.* 9 H. 6, c. 8.

CLOVE-HITCH (*Mar.*) in French *deux demi-cles*, a knot or noose by which a rope is fastened.

CLOVER (*Bot.*) or Clover-Grass, the *Bufolium pratense* of Linnæus; an excellent feed for cattle.

CLOUGH (*Com.*) an allowance of two pounds to every three hundred weight, for the turn of the scale, that the commodity may hold out weight when sold by retail.

CLOUGH (*Mech.*) a sort of sluice for retaining or letting out the water of a canal, pond, &c.—*Clough-arches*, crooked arches in canals, through which the water is conveyed on drawing up the cloughs or paddles.

CLOUT *nails* (*Carpent.*) nails that are used in the nailing on of clouts to the axle-trees of carriages.—*Clouts*, the axle-tree clouts are iron plates nailed to the end of the axle-tree of a cart or waggon, to save it from wearing, and to the two cross-trees that hold the sides of a cart together.

CLOUTS (*Gunn.*) thin plates of iron nailed on that part of the axle-tree of a gun-carriage which comes through the nave.

CLOWN'S ALL-HEAL (*Bot.*) a perennial, the *Stachys palustris* of Linnæus.

CLOYED (*Gunn.*) an epithet for a piece of ordnance when any thing is got into the touch-hole.

CLOYED (*Vet.*) an epithet for a horse when he is pricked with a nail in shoeing.

CLUB *Law* (*Cus.*) a law by which every one is obliged to pay an equal share of the reckoning.

TO CLU'B-HAUL *a ship* (*Mar.*) a method of tacking by letting go the lee-anchor as soon as the wind is out of the sails, which brings her head to the wind.

CLUNCH (*Min.*) a blue substance found in coal-pits.

CLU'NES (*Anat.*) the buttocks, consisting of the skin, fat, and muscles, principally those called the *Glutæi*.

CLUNE'SIA (*Med.*) an inflammation of the buttocks.

CLU'NIAC *Monks* (*Ecc.*) an order of monks founded in the year 900, by Bernard, abbot of Cluny, in Burgundy.

CLU'PEA (*Ich.*) a genus of animals, Class *Pisces*, Order *Abdominales*.
  Generic Character. Head compressed; *mouth* rough within; *jaws* unequal; *tongue* short, rough, with inverted teeth; *gills* setaceous; *body* compressed, elongated; *tail* forked.
  Species. The principal species are—*Clupea harengus*, the Herring.—*Clupea pilcardus*, the Pilchard.—*Clupea alosa*, the Shad.—*Clupea sprattus*, the Sprat.—*Clupea encrasicolus*, the Anchovy, &c.

CLU'SIA (*Bot.*) a genus of plants, Class 23 *Polygamia*, Order 1 *Monoecia*.
  Generic Characters. CAL. *perianth* four; *leaflets* concave.—COR. *petals* four.—STAM. *filaments* many; *anthers* simple.—PIST. *germ* ovate, oblong; *style* none; *stigma* flat.—PER. *capsule* ovate; *seeds* numerous.
  Species. The species are shrubs, as, the—*Clusia rosea*, seu *Cenchramidia*, &c. Rose-coloured Balsam-tree, native of Carolina.—*Clusia alba*, White-flowered Balsam-tree, native of America.—*Clusia flava*, seu *Terebinthus*, &c. Yellow-flowered Balsam-tree, native of Jamaica.—*Clusia venosa*, Vein-leaved Balsam-tree, native of Martinica.

CLU'STERED (*Bot.*) or *crowded*. [vide *Confertus*]

CLUSTERED (*Archit.*) an epithet denoting the coalition of two or more members which penetrate each other: thus, a clustered column is one composed of two or more pillars, attached to each other, but having a distinct base and capital.

CLU'TABIUM (*Mech.*) a smithery forge where clouted shoes or horse shoes are forged.

CLU'TIA (*Bot.*) the *Clutio* and *Androgynia* of Linnæus.

CLU'YTIA (*Bot.*) a genus of plants, Class 22 *Dioecia*, Order 14 *Gynandria*.
  Generic Characters. CAL. *perianth* five-leaved; *leaflets* ovate.—COR. *petals* five; *claws* flat; *nectaries*, exterior five, interior five—STAM. *filaments* five; *anthers* roundish.—PIST. *germ* none; *style* cylindric.—PER. *capsule* globular; *seeds* solitary.
  Species. The species are shrubs, as—*Cluytia alaternoides*, *Croton*, &c. *Sithymulus*, seu *Chamælea*, seu *Alaternoides*, Narrow-leaved Clutia, native of the Cape of Good Hope.—*Cluytia polygonoides*, seu *Chamælea*, native of the Cape of Good Hope.—*Cluytia daphnoides*, *polygonoides*, &c. seu *Alaternoides*, &c. native of the Cape of Good Hope.—*Cluytia ericoides*, native of the Cape of Good Hope.—*Cluytia retusa*, *Corni*, &c. *Scherunam*, &c. *Arbor*, &c. native of the East Indies.—*Cluytia Eluteria*, *Croton*, *Ricinus*, seu *Maritima Clutia*, or Sea-side Balsam, a shrub, native of India.

CLY'DON (*Med.*) κλυδών, a flatulency or fluctuation in the stomach and intestines.

CLY'MA (*Min.*) the fæces of silver and gold.

CLY'MENOS *Dioscoridis* (*Bot.*) the *Scorpioides folio Bupleuri*. Boerh. Ind.

CLY'MENUM (*Bot.*) κλύμενον, a plant with a stalk like a bean, which is supposed to have received its name from King Clymenus, the discoverer. *Theoph. Hist. Plant.* l. 9, c. 19; *Dioscor.* l. 4, c. 13; *Plin.* l. 25, c. 7; *Gal. Oribas.*

CLYMENUM Chickling Vetch is now the *Lathyrus clymenum* of Linnæus. *Boerhaav. Ind.*

CLY'PEA (*Ich.*) vide *Clupea*.

CLY'-MORE (*Mil.*) or *Claymore*, a large two-handed sword, formerly in use among the Highlanders, two inches broad, and doubly edged.

CLYPER'LIS *cartilago* (*Anat.*) the *Theroid cartilage*.

CLYPEA'RIA (*Bot.*) the same as the *Adenanthera*.

CLYPEO'LA (*Bot.*) a genus of plants, Class 15 *Tetradymia*, Order 1 *Siliculosa*.
  Generic Characters. CAL. *perianth* four-leaved; *leaflets* ovate oblong.—COR. four-petalled; *petals* oblong.—STAM. *filaments* six; *anthers* simple.—PIST. *germ* roundish; *style* simple; *stigma* obtuse.—PER. *silicle* orbiculate; *valves* orbiculate; *seeds* orbiculate.
  Species. The three species are, the—*Clypeola Jonthlaspi*, *Thlaspi*, &c. *Jonthlaspi*, &c. Annual treacle mustard, or Buckler mustard, an annual, native of Italy.—*Clypeola tomentosa*, seu *Alyssum*, &c. Hoary treacle mustard, a perennial, native of the Levant—*Clypeola maritima*, *Alyssum*, seu *Thlaspi*, &c. Sea treacle mustard, or Churl's mustard, a perennial, native of the South of France.

CLY'PEUS (*Ant.*) a shield made of brass, which was less than the *scutum*, and was round instead of square.

CLYPEUS (*Ant.*) a sort of register belonging to the ancient baths, so called from its form. The use of it was to increase or diminish the heat, by excluding or letting in the air.

CLY'SMA (*Med.*) a glyster.

CLYSSIFO'RMIS *distillatio* (*Chem.*) a distillation of such substances as are subject to take fire and fulminate by a tubulated retort.

CLY'SSUS (*Chem.*) a term among the ancient chemists, importing a mixture formed by blending the essences of different substances, as oil, salt, and spirit.—*Clyssus antimonii*, a weak acid of sulphur.

CLY'STER (*Med.*) κλυστήρ, from κλύζω, to wash; a glyster, or instrument for the injection of any fluid.

CNEMODACTYLE'US (*Anat.*) a muscle; the *Extensor digitorum longus*.

CNEO'RUM (*Bot.*) κνέωρον, a plant which, according to Dioscorides, was the same as the *Gnestron* and *Thymelœa*, of which Hippocrates recommends a decoction as a purge for phlegm and bile. *Hippocrat. de Mul.* l. 1; *Dioscor.* l. 4, c. 173; *Plin.* l. 13, c. 21.

CNEORUM, in the Linnean system, a genus of plants, Class 3 *Triandria*, Order 1 *Monogynia*.

Generic Characters. CAL. perianth very small.—COR. petals three.—STAM. filaments three; anthers small.—PIST. germ obtuse; style erect; stigma trifid.—PER. berry dry; seeds solitary.

Species. The only species is, the—*Cneorum tricoccum*, seu *Chamælea*, &c. Widow-wail, or Spurge-olive, a shrub, native of Spain.

CNE′SIS (*Med.*) κνῆσις, a painful itching.

CNE′STRON (*Bot.*) vide *Cneorum.*

CO (*Geom.*) a contraction for complement, introduced by Gunter, as in the words co-secant, co-tangent, co-versed sine. [vide *Cosecant*, &c.]

CNICELÆ′ON (*Bot.*) κνικέλαιον, the oil of *Cnicus*, drawn from its seeds. *Dioscor.* l. 1, c. 44.

CNI′CION (*Bot.*) κνίκιον, Trifolium. *Dioscor.* l. 1, c. 123.

CNI′CUS (*Bot.*) κνίκος, or κνῆκος, a plant which, according to the description of the ancients, is supposed to be what is now called *Carthamus*. The whole plant is very bitter, except the root. *Theophrast. Hist. Plant.* l. 6, c. 4; *Aristot. Hist. Anim.* l. 5, c. 19; *Dioscor.* l. 1, c. 88; *Plin.* l. 21, c. 15.

CNICUS, in the Linnean system, a genus of plants, Class 19 *Syngenesia*, Order 1 *Polygamia Æqualis*.

Generic Characters. CAL. compound ovate; *scales* ovate.—COR. compound tubular; *corollets* equal; *proper* funnelform; *border* five-cleft.—STAM. *filaments* five; *anthers* cylindric.—PIST. *germ* short; *style* filiform; *stigma* oblong.—PER. none; *calyx* closed; *seed* solitary; *down* plumose; *receptacle* flat.

Species. The species are mostly perennials, as the—*Cnicus palustris*, Carduus, seu Cirsium, native of Europe.—*Cnicus helenioides*, Carduus, seu Cirsium, &c. native of Siberia.—*Cnicus serratuloides*, Carduus, &c. seu Cirsium, &c. native of Siberia.—*Cnicus medius*, seu Cirsium medium, native of Italy.—*Cnicus centauroides*, seu Centaurium, Artichoke-leaved Cnicus, native of the Pyrennees.—*Cnicus uniflorus*, seu Centaurea, native of Siberia.—*Cnicus pygmæus*, Carduus, Cirsium, seu Serratula, Pygmy Cnicus. But some are biennials, as the—*Cnicus lanceolatus*, native of Europe.—*Cnicus ferox*, native of Siberia.—*Cnicus eriophorus*, native of England; and the following are said to be annual—*Cnicus acarna*, Acarna, seu Chamæleon, Yellow Cnicus, native of France.—*Cnicus Syriacus*, native of Spain.—*Cnicus pinnatifidus*, Carduus, seu Jacea, native of Spain.

CNI′DE (*Bot.*) a name for the *Urtica*, or nettle. *Dioscor.* l. 4, c. 94.

CNIDELÆ′ON (*Chem.*) κνιδέλαιον, the oil prepared from the Grana cnidia. *Diosc.* l. 1, c. 43.

CNI′DIA grana (*Bot.*) Cnidian berries, recommended by Hippocrates as a purge. They are supposed to be the fruit of the *Thymelæda*. *Foes. Hippocr. Œconom.*

CNI′DOS (*Bot.*) vide *Cnidia Grana.*

CNIDO′SIS (*Med.*) κνίδωσις, an itching stimulating sensation, such as is excited by the *cnide*, or nettle. *Hippocrat. Prorrhet.* l. 2.

CNI′DUS (*Bot.*) vide *Cnidia Grana.*

CNI′PES (*Ent.*) a kind of small worms which infest vines.

CNI′PPOTES (*Med.*) κνιπότης, as expounded by Galen, signifies itching, but by Erotian it is taken for the dry opthalmy. *Gal. Exeges.; Erot. Vocab. Hippocrat.*

CNISSORE′GMIA (*Med.*) κνισσορεγμία, an acid eructation.

CNO′DAX (*Mech.*) κνώδαξ, the gudgeon in the spindle of a wheel, an iron spike. *Vitruv.* l. 10, c. 6; *Bald. Lex. Vitruv.*

CNY′MA (*Med.*) κνῦμα, from κνύω, to scrape, grate; a rasure, puncture, or vellication. *Gal. Exeges.*

CO′A *vestis* (*Ant.*) a garment of silk so thin that one might see the body.

COA (*Bot.*) a name given by Father Plumier to a plant in honour of Hippocrates. It is the same as the *Hippocratea* of Linnæus.

COACERVA′TION (*Phy.*) a heaping up together.

COACH (*Mar.*) or *Couch*, a chamber or apartment on board a ship, near the stern. It is generally occupied by the captain.

COACH-MAKERS (*Her.*) the coach-makers' company, which is of late incorporation, have for armorial ensigns, as in the annexed figure, " *azure* a chevron between three coaches *or*." The crest is Phœbus drawn in a chariot, and the supporters two horses argent armed; on their motto *Post nubila Phœbus*.

COACTI′LIS (*Ant.*) coarse and thick woollen cloths for packages. *Plin.* l. 8, c. 48; *Capitolin. in Pertin.* c. 8; *Ulpian. leg. argum.*

COA′CTIO (*Med.*) vide *Anance.*

COACTIO (*Vet.*) a disease in cattle when they are tired or over-wrought. *Veget.* l. 1, c. 37.

COA′CTOR (*Ant.*) a collector or receiver of taxes.—*Coactor agminis*, a bringer up of the rear.

COA′DJUTOR (*Ecc.*) one who during the life-time of the bishop was chosen to be his future successor, and assisted him in the discharge of his episcopal functions. *Pet. Marc. de Concord. Sacerd. et Imper.* c. 8.

COADUNA′TÆ (*Bot.*) a name for the fifty-second of Linnæus' Natural Orders.

COADUNA′TE (*Bot.*) *coadunatus*, an epithet signifying joined together, as *coadunata folia*, coadunate leaves, or leaves united at the base; so *condunati lobi*.

COAGMENTA′TION (*Chem.*) a melting any matter by casting in powders, and afterwards making it concrete or solid.

COAGME′NTUM (*Ant.*) the thickening of wool, and making felt of it.

COA′GULABLE *lymph* (*Anat.*) a component part of the blood, of glutinous consistence, obtained by stirring it about with a stick.

COAGULA′NTIA (*Med.*) such medicines as coagulate the blood, and juices flowing from it.

COAGULA′TION (*Chem.*) the *coagulatio* of the Latins, and πῆξις of the Greeks; the reducing any liquid to a thicker consistence, which is either *coagulatio per segregationem*, i. e. by the separation of the glutinous or viscid particles from the fluid or diluted particles, or *coagulatio per comprehensionem*, when the whole substance, without the loss of its parts, is reduced to such a consistence.

COA′GULUM (*Chem.*) any curded or coagulated substance, such as may be formed by putting acids into any fluid: thus *coagulum lactis*, the curds of milk. *Dioscor.* l. 3, c. 94; *Plin.* l. 22, c. 23.—*Coagulum aluminis*, a coagulated substance formed by beating up the white of an egg with a little alum, which is recommended as an application to the conjunctive membrane of the eye when in a relaxed state.

COAGULUM (*Med.*) the blood and other fluids when they assume a jelly-like consistency.

COAGULUM (*Nat.*) πιτύα, or τάμισος, the concreted milk found in the stomach of young quadrupeds, commonly called *Rennet*, which was prescribed by the ancient physicians, particularly on account of its astringent virtues. *Hippocrat. de Mul.* l. 2; *Aristot. Hist. Anim.* l. 3, c. 16; *Varr. de Re Rust.* l. 2, c. 4; *Dioscor.* l. 2, c. 85; *Plin.* l. 71, c. 41; *Columel. de Re Rus.* l. 7, c. 8; *Cæl. Aurel. de Tard. Pass.* l. 1, c. 4; *Gal. de Medic. Facult.* l. 10, c. 2; *Pallad. de Re Rust.* l. 6, Tit. 9; *Aver. apud Mercur. de Morb. Mul.* l. 3, c. 5.

COAGULUM (*Surg.*) a curdled substance growing in the hollow of a disjointed bone.

COAK (*Min.*) vide *Coke*.

COAKING (*Mar.*) the operation of uniting two or more pieces of wood together in the centre by means of small tabular projections, formed by cutting away the solid of one piece into a hollow, so as exactly to make a projection on the other, in such manner that they may exactly fit; whence the expression of "Coak and plane," to signify that a coak is formed, and a plane follows between.

COAKS (*Mar.*) 1. The metal holes in a sheave, through which the pin runs. 2. Certain oblong ridges left on the surfaces of main-masts by cutting away the wood round them. The intermediate part between them is called the plane. 3. *Chain coaks*, which are formed one on the end of the other, on the opposite sides of the centre line.

COAL (*Min.*) a solid inflammable substance, of a bituminous nature, which serves the purpose of fuel.—*Pit-coal*, or *Lithanthrax*, is distinguished by chemists into three kinds, namely—1. *Brown coal*, which contains a portion of the vegetable principle unaltered, from which they evidently derive their origin. Some, as the *Bovey-coal*, contains a resinous substance besides the bitumen and charcoal, which are its principal constituents: others are said to contain a vegetable extract. 2. *Black coal*, which contains no traces of vegetable principle, but is composed of bitumen, charcoal, and an earthy matter, in different proportions, as Cannel Coal, *ampelites*, of a dull black colour, which burns with a lively flame, and is said to consist of 75·2 charcoal, 21·7 bitumen, and 3·1 earth, in 100 parts; the specific gravity about 1·232. *Slate coal*, which contains a quantity of argillaceous earth, and burns slowly, with little flame. Its constituent parts are said to be nearly in the proportion of 47·6 charcoal, 32·5 bitumen, 19·9 earth; specific gravity 1·426. A variety of this coal is called *culm*. The Newcastle coal, which is among this class, contains less earth than all others, except Whitehaven and Wigan coal: the specific gravity of the first is nearly 1·271, of the second 1·257, of the third 1·268. 3. *Glance coal*, which comprehends those sorts of coal that contain only charcoal and earth, as the Kilkenny coal, consists of 97·3 charcoal and 3·7 earth; specific gravity 1·400. This sort of coal burns with less smoke and flame, and more intensely, than cannel coal; but it yields no volatile products, whereas those of the second class afford abundance of heavy inflammable air, a bituminous oil, at first fluid, then of the consistence of tar, and water impregnated with ammonia. The residue is *coke*, a sort of charcoal much used in manufactories.

COAL (*Com.*) is distinguished into *pit-coal*, in respect to the place where it is dug from, namely, the pit, or mine, and *sea-coal*, in respect to the manner in which it is conveyed, namely, by sea.

COAL-CRIMPS (*Com.*) a kind of factors, who sell shiploads of coals by commission to wholesale dealers.

COAL-METER (*Law*) an officer in London, whose duty it is to inspect the measuring of coals that go from the wharf.

COAL-MERCHANT (*Com.*) one who contracts for coals to be brought from the pit, which he sells out to private families and retail dealers, but never in less quantities than a chaldron.

COAL-FISH (*Ich.*) a sort of cod-fish: the *Gadus carbonarius* of Linnæus.

COALIER (*Mar.*) vide *Collier*.

COALESCENCE (*Phy.*) the cleaving or uniting together of the small fine parts which compose any natural body.

COALESCENCE (*Surg.*) the closing of a wound, or the growing together again of any parts which before were separated.

COALTERN (*Med.*) a term applied by Bellini to two fevers which come periodically, and as one attacks the patient the other recedes, and so alternately.

COAMINGS *of the hatches* (*Mar.*) certain raised borders about the edges of the hatches of a ship, to prevent the water on the deck from running down into the lower apartments.

COANE (*Chem.*) a name, as is said, for a sort of tutty among the Greeks.

COANENEPILLI (*Bot.*) the *Passiflora normalis* of Linnæus.

COAPOIBA (*Bot.*) vide *Caopoiba*.

COARCTATION (*Med.*) a strengthening or pressing together; rendering the canals narrow, or a contraction of the vessels.

COARCTATUS (*Bot.*) an epithet signifying squeezed or pressed together, as *coarctati rami*, condensed branches, opposed to *divergentes*; *coarctati pedunculi*, condensed peduncles, opposed to *patuli*; *coarctata panicula*, a close or contracted panicle, opposed to *diffusa*.

COARTICULATIO (*Anat.*) vide *Abarticulatio*.

COASSATIO (*Archit.*) the boarding or laying a floor. *Vitruv.* l. 7, c. 1.

COAST (*Geog.*) the country lying along the edge of the sea.

COASTER (*Mar.*) a vessel employed in going from one port to another on the same coast, and consequently seldom going out of sight of land.

COASTING (*Mar.*) in French *aller terre à terre*, the act of sailing within sight of land, or within the soundings of land.—*Coasting pilot*, in French *pilote cotier*, a pilot who conducts vessels from one port to another on the coasting trade.

COASTING (*Husband.*) is the transplanting a tree, and placing it towards the same point of the compass as before.

COAT (*Mech.*) in general whatever serves as a covering for any substance, as a coat of paint, or of plaster to a wall, &c.

COAT (*Anat.*) the membranous cover of any part of the body, as the coats of the eye, of the arteries, nerves, &c.

COAT (*Mar.*) a piece of tarred canvas put about the mast at the partners, and also about the pumps at the decks, that no water may go down there.

COAT *of Mail* (*Mil.*) a piece of armour made to fit the body, and wrought over with many rings of iron.

COAT-ARMOUR (*Her.*) or *Coats of arms*, armorial ensigns or bearings, which were originally painted on the coats of arms, and afterwards transferred to seals, which is said to have begun first in the reign of Richard I.

COATED (*Bot.*) an epithet for bulbs which are composed of concentrated layers, as the bulb of the onion; also for some stems which are clothed with membranes.

COATING (*Chem.*) or *Corication*. [vide *Cement*]

COATLER (*Bot.*) another name for *ben*.

COAXATIO (*Arch.*) vide *Coassatio*.

COAXOCHITL (*Bot.*) the Indian name for the Ta-jetes.

COB (*Com.*) a coin current in Gibraltar and the south of Spain, equal to 4s. 6d. English.

COBALT (*Min.*) a mineral of a grey colour, from which arsenic is obtained in the greatest quantities. When melted with glass, and pounded, it is termed *smalt*, and is much used in staining glass blue. In the Pharmacopœia it is called *cadmia metallica*; and in the Linnean system it is classed as a genus of metals, under the name of *cobaltum*. It has never been found pure in nature, but mostly in the state of an oxide, or alloyed with other metals. In the state of an oxide it forms the *black cobalt ore*; or combined with arsenic acid, the *red cobalt ore*; but in alloy with other metals, it forms the *white cobalt ore*. Its specific gravity is above 8. [vide *Chemistry*]

COBALUS (*Myth.*) the name of a spirit which in former times was supposed to haunt mines, whence it is supposed that the metal *cobalt* derives its name.

COBASTOLI (*Chem.*) Ashes.

CO'BBAN (*Bot.*) a small tree, resembling a peach-tree, that grows in Sumatra. *C. Bauh. Pin.*; *Raii Hist. Plant.*

CO'BBE (*Bot.*) another name for the *Rhus* of Linnæus.

CO'BBING. (*Mil.*) a mode of punishment for petty offences committed in barracks or elsewhere, which is inflicted on the offenders by soldiers among themselves, and consists principally in strapping with a belt, and the like.—*Cobbing, on board a vessel*, is also a sort of punishment, which consists in giving the offender a certain number of blows on the breech with a board called the *cobbing-board*.

COBE'LLA (*Zool.*) a species of Coluber.

CO'BILE (*Com.*) *Covid*, or *Coude*, a long measure used in several parts of India, which varies as the aune or ell does in Europe.

CO'BIO (*Ich.*) vide *Gobio*.

CO'BION (*Bot.*) a kind of spurge. *Plin.* l. 26, c. 8.

COBI'TIS (*Ich.*) a fresh-water fish mentioned by Pliny and Aldrovandus.

COBITIS, in the Linnean system, a genus of animals of the Class *Pisces*, Order *Abdominales*.
  Generic Character. Head small, oblong, naked.—*Eyes* in the upper part of the head.—*Vent* nearer the tail.

CO'BLE (*Mar.*) a boat used in the turbot fishery, twenty feet long and five feet broad, and about one ton burthen.

COBO'B (*Cook.*) a dish among the Moors, which is made of several pieces of mutton wrapped up and roasted in a cawl.

CO'BOOZE (*Mar.*) in French *fogon*, a sort of box or house to cover the chimney of some merchant ships.

CO'BRA DE CAPELLO (*Zool.*) the Rattle-Snake, or *Crotalus horridus* of Linnæus, the stone or bone of whose head was reckoned an antidote to some poisons.

CO'BRE VERO (*Zool.*) vide *Bojobi*.

COBRE'LLO (*Med.*) vide *Epilepsia*.

CO'BWEBBED (*Bot.*) *arachnoideus*, an epithet for a leaf, a peduncle, or a calyx, which is covered with a thick interwoven pubescence.

CO'BUS DE CIPO (*Zool.*) vide *Boitiapo*.

CO'CA (*Mar.*) or *Cocaccle*, a cog, or little boat, which is used in fishing.

CO'CAO (*Bot.*) vide *Cocoa*.

COCAZO'CHITL (*Bot.*) the Mexican name for the Tajetas.

CO'CCA CNIDIA (*Med.*) or *Gnidia*, vide *Cnidia*.

CO'CCA BAPTICA (*Ent.*) vide *Chermes*.

COCCA'RIUM (*Med.*) a very small pill. *Oribas. Synop.* l. 3.

COCCE'IRA INDICA (*Bot.*) the *Cocos coccifera* of Linnæus.

CO'CCI ORIENTA'LIS (*Bot.*) vide *Cocculus Indicus*.

COCCI'FEROUS (*Bot.*) an epithet for such plants or trees as bear berries.

CO'CCIGIS OS (*Anat.*) vide *Coccygis os*.

COCCINE'LLA (*Ent.*) a genus of animals, Class *Insecta*, Order *Coleoptera*.
  Generic Character. Antennæ clavate.—*Anterior feelers* hatchet-shaped.—*Thorax* and *Shells* margined.—*Abdomen* flat.
  Species. Animals of this tribe feed on plant-lice. They are distinguished principally by the colour of their shells.

COCCINELLO'IDES (*Ent.*) a species of Nitidala.

CO'CCION (*Med.*) κοκκιον, a weight mentioned by Myrepsus, the same as *siliqua*.

COCCOBA'LSAMUM (*Bot.*) the fruit of the true balsam.

COCCOCY'PSELUM (*Bot.*) a genus of plants, Class 4 *Tetrandria*, Order 1 *Monogynia*.
  Generic Characters. CAL. *perianth* one-leaved; *segments* acute.—COR. one-petalled; *tube* longer than the calyx. STAM. *filaments* four; *anthers* erect.—PIST. *germ* ovate; *style* the length of the stamens; *stigmas* simple.—PER. *berry* roundish; *seeds* numerous.
  Species. The species are—*Coccocypsilum repens*, seu *herbaceum*, &c. a perennial, native of Jamaica.—*Coccocypsilum uniflorum*, seu *Fernelia*, &c. a shrub, native of the island of the Mauritius.

COCCOLO'BA (*Bot.*) a genus of plants, Class 8 *Octandria*, Order 3 *Trigynia*.
  Generic Characters. CAL. *perianth* one-leaved; *divisions* oblong.—COR. none.—STAM. *filaments* eight; *anthers* roundish.—PIST. *germ* ovate; *styles* three; *stigmas* simple.—PER. none; *calyx* berried; *seed* nut ovate.
  Species. The species are shrubs.—*Coccoloba uvifera*, *Coccolobis*, *Polygonum*, *Uvifera*, *Guaiabara*, &c. seu *Prunus*, &c. Round-leaved Sea-side Grape, or Mungrove Grape-tree, native of America.—*Coccoloba pubescens*, seu *Scortea*, &c. Great-leaved Sea-side Grape, Native of America.—*Coccoloba excoriata*, *Coccolobis Guaiabara*, seu *Arbor*, &c. Oval-leaved Sea-side Grape, or Mountain Grape-tree, a shrub, native of America.—*Coccoloba punctata*, *Coronata*, *Coccolobis*, &c. seu *Uvifera*, &c. Spear-leaved Sea-side Grape, native of America.

COCCONI'LEA (*Bot.*) the *Rhus cotinus* of Linnæus.

COCCO'NES (*Bot.*) the *acini*, or grains of the Pomegranate.

COCCOTHRA'USTES (*Orn.*) a bird of the finch kind, so called because it feeds on the kernels of cherry-stones.

CO'CCULUS (*Bot.*) the *Menispermum cocculus* of Linnæus, which produces a poisonous berry, well known by the name of the *Cocculus Indicus*, which is one of the deleterious ingredients employed in the making of beer, the use of which is expressly prohibited by act of parliament.

CO'CCUM (*Ant.*) or *Coccus tinctoria*, κοκκος, βαφικη, the grain with which cloth was dyed; it had an astringent virtue, according to Dioscorides and Pliny. *Dioscor.* l. 4, c. 172; *Plin.* l. 24, c. 3; l. 27, c. 9.

COCCUM, taken by itself, signifies *Grana Cnidia* in Hippocrates.

CO'CCUS (*Bot.*) vide *Coccum*.—*Coccus* is also the *Cocos nucifera* of Linnæus.

Coccus (*Ent.*) Cochineal, a genus of insects of the *Hemipterous* Order.
  Generic Character. Snout seated in the breast.—*Antennæ* filiform.—*Abdomen* bristly behind.—*Wings* two, erect in the male, but without poisers.
  Species. These insects inhabit various parts of plants, and are extremely troublesome in hot-houses. The male is very active, having an oblong body, an ovate abdomen, and a tail furnished with bristles. The female is slow, and has a body nearly globular. Several of the species, when dried, produce a colouring matter, but the *Coccus cacti*, that inhabits the *Cactus opuntia*, is the best fitted for this purpose. The female of this insect is the true cochineal of the shops, which is well known for its great use in dyeing and painting.

CO'CCYGÆUS (*Anat.*) a muscle of the *Os coccygis*, by which it is moved forward.

CO'CCYGIS OS (*Anat.*) or *coccyx*, a cartilaginous kind of bone, joined to the extremity of the *os sacrum*; so called because it resembles the cuckoo's bill.

COCCY'GRIA (*Bot.*) or *Coccymalia*, the *Rhus cotinus* of Linnæus.

CO'CCYS (*Bot.*) the *Palma coccifera*.

CO'CCYX (*Anat.*) vide *Coccygis os*.

COCE'TUM (*Ant.*) hotch-potch, or a food made of honey and poppy seed.

COCH (*Med.*) an abbreviation for *cochleare*, a spoonful.

CO'CHIA (*Med.*) a sort of officinal pills, one variety of which consists of colycinth and aloes, &c.

COCHI'LIA COLUMNA (*Ant.*) a pillar with winding stairs for ascending.

COCHINE'AL (*Ent.*) an insect which in the Linnean system is called *Coccus* and *Coccinelli*, and in commerce is well known for its use in dyeing a rich scarlet. In their dried state these insects have the appearance of small grains. When dried, pounded, and prepared, the colour is sold in the shops under the name of carmine.—*Cochineal Grain*, the red berry which grows on an American tree, called the *Coccus cacti, Coccus Americanus*, or *Ficus Indianus*, is, on account of the beautiful scarlet dye that it yields, a great article of commerce. The insects which bear the same name, resemble these berries so much in appearance that they have been taken to be one and the same thing.

CO'CHLACÆ (*Nat.*) round stones in the rivers that look like snails.

CO'CHLEA (*Ant.*) 1. A pump for drawing up water, invented by Archimedes. *Diodor.* l. 5; *Vitruv.* l. 10, c. 11. 2. A kind of door belonging to the cavea of the Circus. *Varr. de Re Rust.* l. 3, c. 5. 3. The screw or spindle of a press. *Bud. in Pandect.* p. 172.

COCHLEA (*Anat.*) the internal cavity of the ear; so called from its resemblance to the spiral shape of a *cochlea*, or snail's shell. In it are observed the *modiolus*, or *nucleus*, extending from its basis to the *apex*, the *scala tympani*, *scala vestibuli*, and spiral *lamina*.

COCHLEA (*Mech.*) one of the five mechanical powers, otherwise called the *screw*.

COCHLEA'RE (*Med.*) a spoonful, which in prescriptions is abbreviated to *Coch.*

COCHLEA'RIA (*Bot.*) a genus of plants, Class 15 *Tetradynamia*, Order 1 *Siliculosa*.

Generic Characters. CAL. perianth four-leaved; *leaflets* ovate.—COR. four-petalled; *petals* obovate; *claws* narrow.—STAM. *filaments* six; *anthers* obtuse.—PIST. *germ* heart-shaped; *style* simple; *stigma* obtuse.—PER. *silicle* heart-shaped; *seeds* about four in each cell.

Species. The species are annuals, biennials, and some perennials, as the—*Cochlearia officinalis, Batava*, seu *Nasturtium*, &c. Common Scurvy-grass, an annual or biennial, native of Europe.—*Cochlearia Danica*, seu *Thlaspi*, &c. Danish Scurvy-grass, an annual or perennial, native of Denmark.—*Cochlearia Anglica*, seu *Britannica*, seu *vulgaris*, English or Sea Scurvy-grass, a biennial, native of England.—*Cochlearia Groenlandica*, seu *minima*, Greenland Scurvy-grass, an annual, native of Norway.—*Cochlearia coronopus, Lepidium, Coronopus, Nasturtium*, &c. seu *Ambrosia*, &c. seu *Pseudo-ambrosia*, Wild Scurvy-grass, or Swine's-cress, an annual, native of Europe.—*Cochlearia armoracia, Nasturtium*, &c. seu *Raphanus*, &c. Horse-radish, a perennial, native of Europe.—*Cochlearia macrocarpa*, seu *foliis, Glastifolia*, seu *Lepidium*, &c. Woad-leaved Scurvy-grass, a biennial, native of Rattisbon.—*Cochlearia draba*, seu *Lepidium*, &c. seu *Draba*, &c. a perennial, native of Austria.

COCHLEA'RIUM (*Ant.*) a very small measure among the Romans, which, according to Columella, was the fourth part of the cyathus. *Colum. de Re Rust.* l. 12, c. 21.

COCHLEATA (*Bot.*) the *Medicago lupulina*.

COCHLEA'TUS (*Bot.*) screw-shaped; an epithet for a pod. —*Legumen cochleatum*, a pod that is turned like a screw.

COCHLIA'XON (*Mech.*) κοχλιάξων, name for part of a machine described by Oribasius. *De Machinam.* c. 24.

COCHLI'DIUM (*Con.*) κοχλίδιον, and κοχλις, a small shell-snail.

COCHLI'TA (*Min.*) a stone of the shape and figure of a certain shell-snail.

COCHLI'TES (*Min.*) a precious stone. *Plin.* l. 37, c. 12.

COCHO'NE (*Anat.*) κοχώνη, according to Galen, the juncture of the *Ischium* near the seat or breech. *Hesychius.*

CO'CPLIO (*Med.*) the weight of eleven ounces.

COCK (*Or.*) the male of most birds, but particularly of the well-known domestic fowl in a farm yard.—Black Cock, the *Tetras* of Linnæus. [vide *Black*]

COCK (*Her.*) this bird, which Guillim calls the knight among birds, is blazoned in coats of arms by the epithets *armed, crested, jellopped*; sometimes also *wattled* and *membered*; as " he beareth *Azure*, three cocks, *argent*, armed, crested, and jellopped, *proper.*"

COCK (*Mech.*) the name for a part of several instruments, as 1. That part of the lock of a musket which sustains the jaws, or two small pieces of iron, between which the flint is put. 2. The pin of a dial or gun. 3. The needle of a balance. 4. The wrought piece which covers the balance in a clock or watch.

COCK (*Mar.*) vide *Cockboat*. — *Cocks* in a ship are small pieces of brass, with holes in them, which are put into the middle of large wooden shivers to prevent them from splitting or being galled by the pin or block of the pulley on which they turn.

COCK-CHAFFER (*Ent.*) or Tree-Beetle, a mischievous insect, the *Scarabæus melolontha* of Linnæus, which devours the leaves of trees, &c. The *grub* is soft and grey, with testaceous head and legs, remains in the earth for three years before it is transformed into the perfect insect, and devours the roots of vegetables.

COCK-FEATHER (*Archer.*) that feather of the shaft which stands upright in due notching.

CO'CK-HORSE (*Man.*) a tall kind of horse.

CO'CK-LOFT (*Husband.*) the highest loft or garret.

CO'CK-PIT (*Mar.*) vide *Cockpit.*

COCK-PIT (*Sport.*) a place where cocks fight.

COCK-ROACH (*Ent.*) the *Blatta* of Linnæus, which, with its larva, wanders about by night, and secretes itself by day. Insects of this tribe are fond of warmth, and haunt houses, where they devour meal and other provisions.

COCK-ROADS (*Fowl.*) a net chiefly used for catching woodcocks.

COCK-SWAIN (*Mar.*) vide *Cockswain.*

COCKTHRO'PLED horse (*Vet.*) one whose throple or windpipe is so long, that he cannot fetch his breath so easily as others do, which are loose thropled.

TO COCK a gun (*Mil.*) to fix the cock so as to have the piece ready for discharge.

COCKA'DE (*Mil.*) a ribbon worn by the soldiers in their hats.

COCKA'L-BONE (*Anat.*) vide *Astragalus.*

COCKARO'USE (*Polit.*) a name among the Virginian Indians for one who was of the king's privy council.

COCKATOO' (*Or.*) a species of the parrot or *Psittacus* of Linnæus, having a short tail, even at the end.

CO'CKBOAT (*Mar.*) a small boat used on rivers, or near the shore, which is of no service out at sea, because it is too small or feeble.

COCKCHAFFER (*Ent.*) vide *Cock.*

CO'CKEIN (*Com.*) an imaginary specie, used in Japan, like the pistole in many parts of Europe. It is equal to ten French livres.

CO'CKET (*Law*) *Cockettum*, the office at the custom-house, where the goods to be exported are entered; also the custom-house seal, or the parchment sealed and delivered by the officers of the customs to merchants, as a warrant that their goods are customed.

COCKET (*Law*) a measure made use of for the distinction of bread in the statute of bread and ale. 51 *H.* 3, stat. 1; *Flet.* l. 2, c. 9.

COCKETA'TA lana (*Law*) wool duly entered at the custom-house, and cocketed or allowed to be exported.

COCKE'TTUM (*Law*) 1. The custom-house seal. [vide *Cocket*] 2. The office belonging to the custom-house, where cockets are to be procured.

COCKFEATHER (*Archer.*) vide *Cock.*

COCKHORSE (*Man.*) vide *Cock.*

COC

CO'CKING *cloth* (*Sport.*) a frame made of coarse canvass, tanned, with two sticks set across to keep it extended, and a hole through which the muzzle of a gun may be put, to shoot pheasants, &c.

CO'CKING (*Carpent.*) a method of securing beams to wall-plates, by notching each beam at the end, and cutting reverse notches in the wall-plate.

CO'CKLE (*Bot.*) the *Agrostema githago* of Linnæus, an annual, and a weed that infests corn fields; it is otherwise called corn-rose.

COCKLE (*Conch.*) a sort of shell-fish; the *Cardium* of Linnæus.

CO'CKNEY (*Cus.*) a nickname given to one who is born and bred in the city of London, within the sound of Bow-bell.

COCKPIT *of a ship of war* (*Mar.*) a place where the wounded are dressed, on the lower floor or deck, lying between the platform or lower deck and the steward's room, where are partitions for the purser, the surgeon, and his mate.—*The Fore-Cockpit*, a place leading to the magazine passage, and the boatswain's, gunner's, and carpenter's store-rooms.

COCKPIT (*Polit.*) an apartment in the treasury where the king's speech is read before the meeting of Parliament, and also appeals in prize causes are heard.

COCKPIT (*Sport.*) vide *Cock*.

CO'CKREL (*Sport*) a young cock bred for fighting.

COCKS *for blocks* (*Mar.*) little square pieces of brass with holes in them, and put into wooden sheaves to keep them from splitting and galling by the blocks in which they move.

COCK'S-COMB (*Bot.*) an annual, the *Celsia* of Linnæus.—Cock's Foot-Grass, the *Dactylis*, a perennial.—Cock's Head, the *Hedysarum caput galli*, &c. a perennial.

COCKSWAIN (*Mar.*) vulgarly *Cockson*, in French *patron de chaloupe*, an officer of a ship who takes care of the cockboat, with all its furniture.

COCKS' WALK (*Sport.*) a place where cocks are bred for fighting.

CO'COA-NUT (*Bot.*) the nut or fruit of the *Cocos nucifera*. This fruit is properly a berried drupe, and the shell is of a bony substance, containing a kernel, and also a sweet refreshing liquor. The kernel is very nourishing, and much used as a substitute for almonds in cookery; and in medicine a pure sweet oil is extracted from it, which is also of great use. From the tree is drawn a sort of wine, called *toddy*, from which, when sour, is distilled the spirituous liquor called *arrack*. The husk of the shell is used for making chocolate; and the shell itself serves for many domestic purposes.—Cocoa Plum, the *Chrysobalanus* of Linnæus.

COCOLA'TA (*Bot.*) Chocolate.

COCO'MICA (*Med.*) a term used by Paracelsus, which seems to signify the effects produced upon the human body by blasts. *De Podag.* l. 2.

COCOS (*Bot.*) a genus of plants, Class 20 *Monœcia*, Order 6 *Hexandria*.
  Generic Characters. CAL. *spathe* universal; *spadix* branching; *perianth* three-parted; *divisions* concave.—COR. *petals* three.—STAM. *filaments* six; *anthers* sagittate.—PIST. *germ* scarcely manifest; *styles* three; *stigma* obsolete.—PER. abortient; *seed*, nut very large; *kernel* hollow.
  Species. The species are shrubs, as the—*Cocos nucifera*, seu *inermis*, seu *Coccus*, &c. seu *Palma*, &c. seu *Calappa*, &c. seu *Tenga*, seu *Inaja*, seu *Maron*, Cocoa-nut-tree, native of Asia.—*Cocos chilensis*, &c. native of Chili.—*Cocos butyracea*, seu *inermis*, seu *Pindova*, native of America.—*Cocos aculeata*, a shrub, native of Martinica.—*Cocos fusiformis*, seu *Palma*, &c. native of Jamaica.—*Cocos maldivica*, native of the Maldives.—*Cocos guineensis*, *Bactris*, &c. seu *Palma*, &c. Prickly Pole, native of South America.—*Cocos Nypa*, seu *Nypa*, native of the Philippines.
Cocos is also the *Palma coccifera*.

COD

COCOXIHIU'TL (*Bot.*) the *Bocconia frutescens* of Linnæus.

COCTI'LIA (*Ant.*) Charcoal, or wood burnt and dried, that it might not smoke.

CO'CTION (*Med.*) in Greek πίψις, and Latin *coctio*, boiling or digesting; signifies, 1. The reduction of the aliments to a sort of emulsion or chyle. 2. The reduction of morbific matter, or the matter which forms a disease to a natural and healthy state: this may be produced spontaneously, or by the force of medicine. The period of time in which the disease is undergoing that process is called its state of coction.

COCTU'RA (*Med.*) vide *Coctio*.

CO'CULA (*Archæol.*) a small drinking cup in the shape of a boat.

CO'CULUS *Indicus* (*Bot.*) vide *Cocculus*.

COCU'STA (*Bot.*) the tree which produces the *gum animé*.

COCY'TA (*Med.*) vide *Malis*.

COD (*Ich.*) a well known fish which inhabits the Northern seas; the *Gadus* of Linnæus.

CO'D-FISHER (*Mar.*) a vessel employed in the curing of cod; also the person so employed.

CO'D-PIECES (*Mil.*) iron appendages attached to ancient armour, to prevent the consequences of violent shocks in battle.

CO'DA (*Mus.*) Italian for a small number of bars at the end of a composition.

CO'DAGAM (*Bot.*) the *Hydrocotyle Asiatica* of Linnæus.

CO'DAGA *Pala* (*Bot.*) a tree growing in Malabar; the *Nerium antidysentericum* of Linnæus.—*Codaga pelavi*, the *Morinda citrifolia*.

CODDA-PU'LLIS (*Bot.*) vide *Carcapulli*.—*Codda-Panna*, the *Corypha umbraculifera*.

CO'DDED *Corn-violet* (*Bot.*) the *Campanula hybrida* of Linnæus.

CODE (*Law*) vide *Codex*.

CODESE'LLA (*Med.*) vide *Carbunculus*.

CODEX (*Law*) signifies literally a volume or roll; but is particularly applied to the volume of Civil Law, collected by the emperor Justinian from all the pleas and answers of the ancient lawyers, which were in loose scrolls or sheets of parchment; these he compiled into a book, which goes by the name of the codex.

CO'DIA (*Bot.*) a term formerly used for the top or head of any plant, but particularly that of the poppy.

CODIA, *in the Linnean system*, a genus of plants, Class 8 *Octandria*, Order 2 *Digynia*.
  Generic Characters. CAL. common four-leaved; proper four-leaved.—COR. *petals* four.—STAM. *filaments* eight; *anthers* ovate-angulate.—PIST. *germ* very small; *styles* two; *stigmas* simple; *receptacle* common villose.
  Species. The only species is the—*Codia montana*, a shrub, native of New Caledonia.

CODIÆ'UM (*Bot.*) a species of the *Croton* of Linnæus.

CODIA'MINON (*Bot.*) a herb which blossoms twice a year. *Plin.* l. 21, c. 21.

CODIA-VA'NACU (*Bot.*) an under-shrub growing in the East Indies; the juice of which, boiled in oil, is a restorative in case of weakness; the *Tragia chamela* of Linnæus. *Raii Hist. Plant.*

CODICA'RIÆ *naves* (*Ant.*) ships or barges made of thick planks. *Non. ex Varr.*

CO'DICIL (*Law*) *Codicillus*, a supplement to a will, by which the testator adds to, explains, or retracts what he has done.

CODI'NIAC (*Med.*) marmalade of Guinea.

CO'DLIN-TREE (*Bot.*) a variety of the *Pyrus malus*, or

Apple-Tree.—Codlins and Cream, a perennial, the *Epilobium hirsutum* of Linnæus.

CODOCE'LE (*Med.*) a bubo. *Fallopius.*

CODON (*Bot.*) a genus of plants, Class 10 *Decandria*, Order 1 *Monogynia*.
Generic Characters. CAL. perianth one-leaved; *leaflets* subulate.—COR. one-petalled; *border* equal; *nectary* ten-celled.—STAM. *filaments* ten; *anthers* thick.— PIST. *germ* superior; *style* simple; *stigmas* two.—PER. two-celled; *seeds* several.
Species. The only species is *Codon Royeni seu aculeatum*, an annual, native of the Cape of Good Hope.

CODO'NES (*Ant.*) κώδωνες, little bells. *Hesychius.*

CODONO'PHORI (*Ant.*) κωδωνοφόροι, those who at funerals go before, ringing bells. *Schol. in Aristoph.; Hesychius; Suidas.*

CODOSCE'LÆ (*Med.*) vide *Codocele.*

COE (*Min.*) a name which miners give to the little lodgement that they make underground for themselves as they work lower and lower.

CŒCA'LIS (*Anat.*) a vein so called, which is a branch of the concave side of the *vena mesaraica*.

CŒCUM (*Anat.*) vide *Cæcum.*

COEFFI'CIENTS (*Algeb.*) a term first employed by Vieta to denote any known quantity that is multiplied into any of the unknown terms of the equation; thus, in $3a + bx - cx^2$, 3, b and c are the coefficients which are thus multiplied into a, x, x^2. When no number is placed 1 is understood to be the coefficient, as x, which is equivalent to $1x$. *Viet. Isagog. c. 8.*—*Coefficients of the same order*, are such as are prefixed to the same unknown quantities in different equations, as in the equations $ax + by + cz = m$, $dx + ey + fz = n$, $gx + hy + kz = p$; $a, d, g,$ are coefficients of the same order, being coefficients of the letter x; $b, e, h,$ are coefficients of the same order, being coefficients of y; and so likewise $c, f, k,$ which are coefficients of z.—*Opposite coefficients*, are those which are taken each from a different equation, as $a, e, k,$ or $a, h, f,$ in the foregoing equations.—*Coefficients of any generating term in fluxions*, is the quantity arising from the division of that term by the generated quantity.

CŒ'LA (*Ant.*) κοῖλα, the cavities or hollows, as they are called, of the eyes: the one in the superior eyelid is properly the κοῖλον, in distinction from the other in the inferior eyelid, which is the ὑπόκοιλον: κοῖλα of the feet are those parts which are at the bottom of the feet adjacent to the heel.

CŒLES'TIAL (*Astron.*) vide *Celestial.*

CŒLESTI'NUS *Colour* (*Med.*) sky colour, a term used by Paracelsus to denote that a circle of this colour, in the urine of women, is a sign of leprosy in the matrix.

CŒ'LIA (*Anat.*) κοιλία, κοιλίη, a cavity in any part of the body, but particularly in the *viscera*. It was divided by the ancients into ἡ ἄνω κοιλίη, the stomach; ἡ κάτω κοιλίη, the belly.

CŒLIAC *artery* (*Anat.*) *arteria cæliaca*, the first branch given off from the *aorta* in the cavity of the abdomen, which sends branches to the diaphragm, stomach, liver, pylorus, duodenum omentum, and spleen.—*Cæliac vein*, that which runs into the *intestinum coecum*.

CŒ'LIAC *Passion* (*Med.*) *cœliaca passio*, κοιλιακή, a disorder of the stomach, which is so called from κοιλία, the part effected. This disorder is defined by the ancients to be a sort of *diarrhœa*, in which the aliment passes off in a dissolved but crude state. The disorder is not mentioned by Hippocrates; but those affected with it are called by Aretæus κοιλιακοί, and by Cælius Aurelianus *ventriculosi*: Celsus also speaks of a disorder under a similar name, which however differs materially, according to his description, from the one above-mentioned. *Aret. de Caus. et Sign. acut. Morb.* l. 2, c. 7; *Cæl. Morb. Chron.* l. 4, c. 3; *Cel.* l. 4, c. 12. The *Cœliac Passion* is defined variously by the moderns, but Cullen considers it to be a sort of *diarrhœa*.

CŒLI-FLOS (*Bot.*) or *Cœlifolium*, Starfall; the *Tremella nostoch* of Linnæus.

CŒLI-ROSA (*Bot.*) the *Agrostema* of Linnæus.

CŒLIT-LAWAN (*Bot.*) the *Laurus culilaban* of Linnæus.

CŒLO'MA (*Med.*) a hollow round ulcer in the horney tunic of the eye.

CŒLON (*Nat.*) a kind of sil, or painter's colour.

CŒLOSTO'MIA (*Med.*) κοιλοστομία, a defect in speaking; when a person's speech is obscured in such manner as to sound as if it came from a cavern.

CŒ'LUM (*Anat.*) a name for the cavity of the eye towards the corner.

CŒMENTA'TIO (*Mech.*) vide *Cement.*

CŒMETE'RIUM (*Ecc.*) Cemetery, a burying place.

COE'MPTIO (*Law*) a solemnity of the civil law whereby the man and wife (that were to be) did, as it were, buy one another, so, as by that means, they had a right to each other's goods. *Cic. Or.* l. 1. c. 56; *Ulp. Instant. apud. Boeth. top.* 3.

CŒ'NA (*Ant.*) the principal meal among the Greeks, Jews, and Romans, which was so called from κοινή, common, because it was the meal at which all the family met: it began at the ninth hour, or three in the afternoon, and corresponds, therefore, to the modern dinner, although the word is most frequently rendered by supper. This meal consisted of three courses; namely, the *First course*, διαστρωμίνον, *cœnæ præfatio vel gustatio*, consisting of eggs, oysters, fruit, &c.—The *second course*, δεῖπνον, *cœna*, or κεφαλὴ δείπνου, *caput cœnæ*, which was supplied with dainties of various sorts.—The *third course*, δευτέρα τράπεζα, *secunda mensa, mensa pomorum*, consisted of the desert, which was the richest part of the meal. The Romans distinguished it into different kinds, as the—*Cœna adjicialis*, an extraordinary entertainment, when something particular, *adjiciebatur*, was added to the elegance of the feast.—*Cœna adventitia*, a feast of welcome given to friends on their return home.—*Cœna auguralis*, an augural supper, and the like. *Plaut. Bacch.* act. 3, Scen. 6; *Cic. ad Fam.* l. 9, ep. 26; *Plin.* l. 10, c. 20; *Plin.* l. 3, epist. 1; *Tacit. Annal.* l. 2, c. 65.

CŒNACULA'RIUS (*Ant.*) a tenant living in a garret, or upper room of the house; also he who lets lodgings.

CŒNA'CULUM (*Anat.*) 1. The room set apart for supper. 2. A chamber or room in an upper part of the house. *Fest. de Verb. Signif.*

CŒNATIO (*Ant.*) a banquetting room.

CŒNIPE'TA (*Ant.*) a toad-eater, or smell-feast; one who hangs on another for a meal of victuals.

CŒNOBIA'RCHA (*Ecc.*) the superior of a convent, an abbot, or prior.

CŒNOBI'TA (*Ecc.*) Cœnobites, they who are of the society of a monastery, or college of priests. *Cæl. Rhodig.* l. 10, c. 4.

CŒNO'BIUM (*Anat.*) from κοινός, common, and βίος, life; a community of living, as in a monastery or convent. *Isid. Orig.* l. 15, c. 4.

CŒNOLO'GIA (*Med.*) κοινολογία, a consultation of physicians, from κοινός and λόγος, speech.

CŒNOTAPH (*Ant.*) vide *Cenotaph.*

CŒ'NOTES (*Med.*) κοινότης, signifies literally community, but was applied, by physicians of the methodic sect, to those disorders which arise both from relaxation and stricture, in distinction from those which arose from either one or the other singly.

CŒRULEUS *Lapis* (*Min.*) the sulphate of copper.

COETA'NEOUS (*Chron.*) an epithet for a person living

at the same time with another, or for any thing that happens in the same age.

COETE'RNAL (*Theol.*) an epithet applied to the three persons in the Holy Trinity.

CŒTUS (*Ant.*) though taken generally for any assembly, was more frequently used to denote an unlawful or seditious meeting.

CŒUR (*Her.*) or *party en coeur*, signifies a short line of partition in pale in the centre of the escutcheon, which extends but a little way, much short of the top and bottom, and is there met by other lines which form an irregular partition of escutcheon.

COE'VAL (*Chron.*) an epithet for any persons or things which are in the same age, or of the same duration.

CO'FFEA (*Bot.*) a genus of plants, Class 5 *Pentandria*, Order 1 *Monogynia*.
Generic Characters. CAL. *perianth* five-toothed.—COR. one-petalled; *tube* cylindric; *border* flat; *divisions* lance-shaped.—STAM. *filaments* five; *anthers* linear.—PIST. *germ* roundish; *style* simple; *stigmas* two.—PER. *berry* roundish; *seeds* one or two.
Species. The species are shrubs, as the—*Coffea sambucina, seu foliis*, &c. native of the Friendly Isles.—*Coffea opulina*, native of New Caledonia.—*Coffea odorata*, native of the Friendly Isles.—*Coffea arabica*, *Jasminum*, *Evonymo*, &c. seu *Bon*, Eastern Coffee-tree, native of Jamaica.—*Coffea triflora, seu foliis*, &c. native of Otaheite.—*Coffea occidentalis, Pavetta*, &c. seu *Jasminum*, &c. Western Coffee-Tree, native of America.

CO'FFEE (*Bot.*) the berry, or fruit of the Coffee-Tree; the *Coffea* of Linnæus, from which the well-known drink is prepared that goes by the same name.

CO'FFER (*Mech.*) a chest or trunk; also a long square box or trough, in which tin ore is broken to pieces in a stamping mill.

COFFER (*Fort.*) a hollow trench or lodgment cut in the bottom of a dry ditch.

COFFER (*Archit.*) a square depression or sinking in each interval between the modillions of the Corinthian cornice, and in other parts.

COFFER (*Mar.*) in inland navigation, a large wooden vessel with moveable ends to receive the barge or vessel. It answers the purpose of a lock.

COFFER-DAM (*Archit.*) or *Battardeaux, in bridge building*, a case of piling fixed in the bed of a river for the purpose of building a pier dry.

CO'FFERER (*Law*) the second officer in the King's household, next to the comptroller, who has the oversight of the other officers, and pays them their wages.

CO'FFILA (*Com.*) or *Bahar*, a weight used at Bencoolen, Malacca, and other parts of India, equal to 564 lbs. weight.

CO'FFIN (*Vet.*) the whole hoof of the horse's foot above the coronet, including the coffin-bone, the sole, and the frush.—*Coffin-bone*, that bone which lies within the hoof, as in a coffin.—*Coffin-Joint*, that which connects the pastern with the wheel.

COFFIN of Paper (*Com.*) a triangular piece, such as grocers put up pepper, &c. in form of a cone.

COFFIN (*Print.*) the framework of the printing-press, in which the stone is bedded.

COFFRE d'une batterie (*Fort.*) the solid work which covers the pieces of ordnance that are planted in a battery.—*Coffre à feu*, a machine filled with combustible materials for the purpose of doing mischief to a scaling party.—*Coffres des galeries de mine*, a sort of platform made of planks, which serve to support the galleries of a mine.

COG (*Mar.*) or *coggle*, a kind of little ship or vessel used in the river Ouse. Stat. 23 Hen. 8, c. 10.

COG (*Mech.*) vide *Cogs.*
CO'GGLE (*Mar.*) vide *Cog.*
COGNA'TI (*Law*) relations by the mother's side, in distinction from the *agnati*, who are on the father's side.

COGNA'TIONE (*Law*) a writ of cousenage, a writ that lies where the *tresail*, that is, the father of the *besail*, or great grandfather, dying, seized of lands and tenements, a stranger enters upon the heir and abates. Stat. 9 Hen. 4, c. 5; 8 Hen. 6, c. 26; Brit. c. 89; F. N. B. 221.

CO'GNISANCE (*Law*) signifies the hearing of a thing judicially; also the acknowledgement of a fine; and, in replevin, the answer given by a defendant who has acted as a bailiff, &c. to another in making a distress. But the term cognizance is particularly taken in the sense of *cognizance of pleas*, which is a privilege granted by the King to a city or town to hold the plea of all contracts, &c. within the liberty of the franchise.

COGNISE'E (*Law.*) vide *Cognisor.*

CO'GNISOR (*Law*) is one who passes or acknowledges a fine of lands or tenements to another, in distinction from the *cognisee*, to whom the fine of the said lands, &c. is acknowledged. Stat. 32 Hen. 8, c. 5.

COGNI'TIO (*Law*) the trial or hearing of a cause.

COGNI'TION (*Law*) in the Scotch Law, is the process whereby molestation is determined.

COGNITIO'NES (*Archæol.*) ensigns and arms.

COGNITIO'NIBUS *admittendis* (*Law*) a writ to a justice, or other person, who has power to take a fine, and having taken acknowledgement of a fine, delays to certify it in the court of Common Pleas, requiring him to do it.

CO'GNITOR (*Ant.*) one who managed the cause of another, or defended his cause. Ascon. in Cic. p. 17.—*Cognitor* is also the name of one who bore testimony that he knew a man to be a Roman citizen, who wanted to escape the ignominious punishment with which he was threatened. Cic. in Verr. l. 5, c. 65.

CO'GNIZANCE (*Her.*) a badge which subordinate officers, and even soldiers, bore on their shields, for distinction sake, in the place of the crest, which was worn only by superiors.

COGNO'MEN (*Ant.*) a surname, or a family name which a man has from his father, as Cæsar, the *cognomen;* in distinction from Julius, the *nomen.* Suet. Jul. c. 20; Diomed. l. 1; Priscian. l. 2, c. 578, Putsch. Ed.; Sigon. de Rom. Nom. c. 1.

COGNO'VIT *actionem* (*Law*) is when a defendant acknowledges and confesses the plaintiff's cause against him to be just and true; and, before and after issue, suffers judgment to be entered against him without trial. In this case confession extends no farther than to what is contained in the declaration.

COGS (*Mech.*) the teeth of a mill-wheel.

CO'GWARE (*Com.*) a sort of coarse cloths made in different parts of England, of which mention is made in Stat. 13 Rich. 2, c. 10.

COHÆRA'RIUS (*Ant.*) a coheir, or joint heir; and likewise a partner in any office.

COHE'SION (*Phy.*) that power or property by which the homogeneous particles of substances are kept attached to each other, in distinction from adhesion, which is a partial union between substances similar or dissimilar.

CO'HI (*Com.*) a large dry measure used in the kingdom of Siam for corn, &c. equal to five thousand pounds of European measure.

CO'HOB (*Chem.*) vide *Cohobation.*

COHOBA'TION (*Chem.*) or *cohob, cohobatio*, the returning of liquor distilled from any substance back again upon the same substance, and distilling it again.

CO'HOL (*Chem.*) vide *Alcohol.*

COHOL (*Med.*) a dry *collyrium* for the eyes. *Avicen. apud Castell. Lex. Med.*

CO'HORS (*Ant.*) a military body, which constituted the tenth part of a legion, and consisted in general of about 600 men. The first cohort exceeded all the rest in number and dignity, being chosen out of the *evocati*, and appointed to attend upon the Prætor; whence it was called *cohors Prætoria*. Its place, in the order of battle, was the right of the first line, and so of the rest in order. On medals and coins *cohors* is abbreviated COH. or COHORT. for *cohortis*, &c. *Varr. de Lat. Ling.* l. 4, c. 16; *Liv. passim.*; *Veget.* l. 2, c. 16; *Lips. de Milit. Rom.* l. 2, c. 4; *Salmas. de Mil. Rom.* c. 2; *Schel. in Polyb. apud Græv. Thes. Antiq. Roman.* tom. 10, &c.

COHORTA'LES (*Ant.*) a kind of commissaries, or masters of the horse, to Lieutenants or governors of Provinces; also, in general, any attendants or retainers to magistrates.

COHUA'GIUM (*Archæol.*) a tribute paid by those who met together promiscuously in a market or fair.

CO'HUM (*Ant.*) a thong wherewith the ox-bow and yoke were tied together.

COIANG (*Com.*) both a weight and measure of Cambaye in the East Indies.

COIF (*Anat.*) a name given by Winslow to the aponeurotic expansion which covers the head like a cap, and is spread round the neck, and on the shoulders like a riding-hood.

COIF (*Law*) a sort of hood, or cap for the head; whence *Serjeants of the Coif*, a title for the serjeants at law who formerly wore a coif of lawn on their heads under their caps. This is now worn upon the hinder part of their wigs.

COIL (*Mar.*) the ring or circle formed by a cable in coiling or winding it.—*Coil*, in French *cueiller*, the manner in which ropes are disposed in a vessel by winding them in the form of a ring, and making the circles to lie one upon another.

COILA'NTHIA (*Bot.*) the *Gentiana purpurea* of Linnæus.

COI'LING *of the stud* (*Man.*) the selecting of a colt or young horse for service.

COILOPHY'LLUM (*Bot.*) the *Sarracenea flavea et purpurea* of Linnæus.

COILOTA'PHALUS (*Bot.*) the *Cecropia peltata* of Linnæus.

COIN (*Ant.*) vide *Moneta*.

COIN (*Com.*) a piece of metal stamped with certain marks, and made current as money for a certain value. [vide *Coinage*]

COIN (*Archit.*) vide *Coins*.

COIN (*Print.*) vide *Coins*.

COIN (*Mar.*) vide *Coins*.

COINAGE (*Com.*) signifies either the act of coining, or the thing coined, of which it is a collective term equivalent to the word *coins*. The materials used for coinage are gold, silver, copper, brass, and sometimes even iron: the two first of which, from their high value, are denominated the precious metals, which, when in a state for converting into coin, are called *bullion*, and the pieces of bullion are called *bars* or *ingots*.

Standard. When any baser metal is mixed with gold or silver in coinage it is called an *alloy*, in distinction from the pure metal called *fine*. The fixed proportion in which this mixture is made is denominated the *standard of fineness*, and the weight of each piece or coin is the standard weight. The standard of silver coin has, with occasional variations, always been eleven ounces two pennyweights fine and eighteen pennyweights alloy; the weight twenty-four grains to each penny. This was also denominated *sterling*, a term which, from the high esteem in which this standard has always been held, is now made to signify the standard of excellence. Gold is estimated by carats and grains, each carat consisting of four grains. The Old Standard for gold consisted of 23 carats $3\frac{1}{2}$ grains fine and half a grain alloy; the New Standard of 22 carats fine and 2 carats alloy; both of which have been subject to occasional variation.

Mint. The place where the coinage of a country is carried on is called the *mint*, the officers of which, among the Saxons, were in general called *moneyers*, whose names are met with on the Saxon coins, together with that of the place where the coin was struck. - Plate No. I. (31.) The officers which have been since appointed are very various, as the Master, Wardens, and Comptroller of the Mint, Assay-Master, &c. [vide *Mint*]

Process of Coining. Coining was formerly carried on by means of the hammer, but now more expeditiously by means of a machine called a *mill*. [vide *Mill*] The piece of metal which is cut and prepared for the mill is called the *planchet* or *blank* before it is struck, and the steel masses on which the figures are marked are called the *dyes*, between which the planchet is pressed by the force of screws, so that at one pull the impression is made on both sides. Money coined by the hammer is called *hammered*, and that by means of the mill *milled*.

Assay. The act of ascertaining the purity of bullion gold, or the standard fineness of coins, is called the assay; and the pieces or coins selected for this purpose are called the *trial pieces*: of these two are selected, one for the private assay of the mint, and the other for the public trial by a jury of twelve goldsmiths, which is called the *trial of the pix*, from the pix, or box, in which the pieces are contained. The quantity or weight from which these two pieces are taken is called a *journey*, namely, of gold fifteen pounds, and of silver sixty-five; and the sum total of any monies coined within a given period, or out of any number of journies, is called *a delivery*, several of which are collected together for examination at the stated times of trial. At this trial the jury determine whether the monies so coined are of the standard fineness required by the *indenture*, or warrant, and return their verdict according as they find them within the *remedy*; i. e. within the legitimate allowance for deficiency or not.

Profits of the mint. The profits of the mint, which formerly constituted a considerable branch of the royal revenue, are known by the names of *seignorage*, which was a deduction from the bullion that was coined; *moneyage*, a triennial tax, which was imposed in the place of seignorage; and the *profit of the shere*, which was derived from the allowance for the *remedy*. But, in the lieu of these, a parliamentary allowance has been granted, to defray the expences of the coinage.

Coins. The several pieces of metal which are struck by the process of coining are denominated coins; having two sides, called the *obverse*, or face, on which the head or profile is put; and the *reverse*, which is the same as the back. The letters engraven in the field, or middle, are called the *inscription*; those on the *exergue*, or outer rim, the *legend*. Coins, according to their materials, are distinguished into *gold*, *silver*, *copper*, &c. to which may be added a sort of money formerly coined, called *black money*, which was copper washed with about one-fifth part of silver, in distinction from *white money*, which was standard silver. Coins are, moreover, distinguished according to the country in which they are current, into *Foreign* and *English*.

Foreign Coins. The following Tables comprehend a general account of the most important foreign coins in silver and gold that are now current; the first column contains the names of the coins in alphabetical order; the second, that of the country in which each is current; the third, the assay, or average standard of fineness: and the fourth, the average value, nearly, in sterling money.

Table of Foreign Gold Coins.

Coin.	Country.	Assay. car. gr.	Sterl. value. £ s. d.
Carl d'or	Brunswick	21 2¼	0 16 0
Carlino	Sardinia	21 1¼	1 19 0
Carolin	Bavaria	18 2	1 0 0
Christian d'or	Denmark	21 3	0 17 0
Copang, New	Japan	16 0	9 4 0
Coronnlla, or Golden Dollar	Spain	21 1½	1 5 0
Crusade, New, of 480 Rees	Portugal	21 3¾	0 2 6
Dobra of 24,000 Rees	Portugal	22 0	6 16 0
Doppia, or Pistole	Rome	22 0	0 14 6
Doubloon, or quadruple Pistole	Spain	21 2½	3 9 0
Ducat	Holland	23 2¼	0 9 6
Imperial of 1801	Russia	23 2¼	1 13 0
Joanese	Portugal	21 3¼	1 17 0
Louis d'or	France	21 2	0 19 0
Maximilian d'or	Bavaria	18 1¼	0 15 0
Milree	Portugal	22 0	0 3 6
Mohur, or gold Rupee of Shah Allum	India	23 2¼	1 15 0
Mohur, or Gold Sicca	India	23 3½	1 13 6
Moidore	Portugal	22 0	1 7 0
Pagoda	India	19 0	0 7 6
Pistole	Spain	21 3	0 16 0
——	Switzerland	21 2½	0 18 6
Ruble	Russia	22 0	0 3 6
Rupee	India	21 0¼	1 10 0
Ruspono	Tuscany	23 3¼	1 8 6
Ruyder	Holland	22 0	1 4 0
Sequin, or Zecchino	Turkey, Venice, &c.	19 1½	0 9 6
Scudo d'oro, or gold Crown	Venice	23 3½	5 14 0

Table of Foreign Silver Coins.

Coin.	Countrry.	Assay. oz. dwt.	Sterl. value. £. s. d.
10 Batzen Piece	Bavaria	93 18	0 1 0
5 Copeck Piece	Russia	10 6¼	0 0 2
Copfstuck, or 20 Crutzer Piece	Austria	6 17	0 0 8
New Crusade	Portugal	10 15	0 2 4
Crone, or old 4 Mark Piece	Denmark	7 19	0 2 9
Daalder, or Piece of 30 Stivers	Holland	10 10	0 2 6
Drittel, or Piece of 8 good Groschen	Prussia	8 19	0 1 0
Ducat	Naples, Parma	10 18	0 4 0
Ducatoon	Holland	11 5	0 5 6
Ecu, or Crown of six livres	France	10 13	0 4 9
Florin, or Gilder	Holland	10 17½	0 1 9
Francisconi, or Crown of Ferdinand III	Tuscany	10 17	0 4 6
Franc	France	10 15	0 0 10
8 Groschen Piece	Saxony	8 17	0 1 0
Gulden, or 24 Marien Gross Piece	Prussia	8 17	0 1 0
Lira	Venice	2 19	0 0 2½
Mark	Hamburgh, Lubeck, &c.	8 19	0 1 3
Paolo	Rome	10 16	0 0 6
Papetto	Rome	10 15½	0 0 2½
Patacão, or Sello	Brazil	10 12	0 2 9½
Pataca	Brazil	10 12	0 1 0
Patagon	Geneva	10 2	0 4 0
Peso duro, or Hard Dollar, or Dollar Piece of 20 Rials Vellon	Spain	10 15	0 4 6
Piastre	Turkey	5 16	0 1 1
Plott	Sweden	10 7½	0 3 0
Poltin Half Ruble, or 50 Copeck Piece	Russia	8 13	0 1 9
Real, or Rial	Spain	10 10	0 0 6
Rix-Dollar	Germany	10 19	0 4 0
Ruble	Russia	10 6	0 3 3
Rupee of Mahommed Shah	India	11 8½	0 1 11½
Rupee Sicca	East India Company	11 15	0 2 0½
Scudo della Croce	Genoa	11 7	0 6 6
Scudo	Rome	10 18	0 4 4
Scudo, Mezzo	Rome	10 18	0 2 2
8 Stiver Piece	Holland	10 19	0 0 8
Testoon	Portugal	10 15	0 0 6
Doee Vintems, or Piece of 240 Rees	Portugal	10 15	0 1 3

English Coins. The coins comprehended under this name are the British, or those which were current among the first inhabitants of Britain, of which a few specimens are given in Plate No. I. (31). The Saxon coins, the earliest of which are commonly distinguished by the name of *sceattæ* [vide Plate No. I. (31)]. The English coins, properly so called, comprehend those which have been coined from the time of the conquest to the present period, of which the following Table exhibits a general view: the first column containing the year of the reign, the king's name, and the year of our Lord in which the coins were struck; the second, the name of the species or pieces which were coined; the third, the standard fineness; the fourth, the standard weight; and the fifth, the value of the pound by tale.

Table of English Silver Coins.

Reign & Year.	Species.	Standard.	Weight. dwt. gr.	Value of the Pound by tale. £ s. d.
William I. 1066; —— II. 1087	Pennies	—	0 24	1 0 0
Henry I. 1100	Pennies, Halfpen. and Farthings	—	—	—
Stephen.. 1135	Pennies	—	—	—
Henry II. 1154	Pennies	11 oz. 12 dwts. fine, 18 dwts. alloy	—	—
Richard I. 1189	Pennies	—	—	—
John 1199	Pennies, Halfpen. and Farthings	—	—	—
Henry III. 1216	Pennies, Halfpen. and Farthings	—	—	—
Edward I. 1272	Pennies	—	—	—
3 —— —	Pennies			
	Halfpen. & Farth.	—	0 23½	1 0 3
18 —— —	Groats of various weights	—	from 94 to 139	—
Edw. II. 1307	Pennies	—	0 23½	1 0 3
Edw. III. 1327	Pennies, Halfpen. and Farthings	—	—	—
18 —— —	Pennies, Halfpen. and Farthings	—	0 21¼	1 2 6
25 —— —	Groats & Half-groats	—	3 4¾	1 5 0
43 —— —	Pennies & Halfpen. something lighter	—	—	—
46 —— —	The same as in the 25th year	—	—	—
Richard II. 1377	The same, with the addition of farth.	—	—	—
Hen. IV. 1399	The same	—	—	—
13 —— —	The same	—	2 16	1 10 0
Hen. V. 1412	The same	—	—	—
Hen. VI. 1422	The same	—	—	—
Edw. IV. 1460-1	The same	—	—	—
4 —— —	The same	—	2 3	1 17 6
49 Hen. VI. 1470	The same	—	—	—
10 Edw. IV. —	The same	—	—	—
Rich. III. 1483	The same	—	—	—
Hen. VII. 1485	The same	—	—	—
19 —— —	Shillings	—	—	—
Hen. VIII. 1509	Groats, Half-groats, pence, &c.	—	1 18½	2 5 0
18 —— —	Groats, &c.	—	—	—
25 —— —	Crown pieces, a few	—	—	—
34 —— —	Groats, half-groats, testoons, shill. &c.	10 oz. fine, 2 oz. alloy	1 16	2 8 0
36 —— —	The same	6 oz. fine, 6 oz. alloy	—	—
37 —— —	The same	4 oz. fine, 8 oz. alloy	—	
Ed. VI. 1546-7	Shillings, groats, &c.	—	—	—
3 —— —	Shillings	6 oz. fine, 6 oz. alloy	3 8	3 12 0
5 —— —	Shillings	3 oz. fine, 9 oz. alloy		
	Shillings, sixpences, threepennies, pennies, &c.	11 oz. 2 dwt. fine, 18 dwt. alloy	4 0	3 0 0

Reign and Year.	Species.	Standard.	Weight.	Value of the Pound by tale.
			dwt. gr.	£ s. d.
Mary I. 1553	Crowns, half-crowns, shillings, sixpences, groats, &c. rose-pennies & halfpen.	11 oz. fine 1 oz. alloy	0 12	2 0 0
Elizabeth 1558	Shillings & sixpences	—	4 0	3 0 0
2 —— —	Shillings & sixpences groats, half-groats, three-pences, three-halfpenny pieces, three-farthing piec. and farthings	11oz. 2dwts. fine, 18dwts. alloy	—	—
43 —— —	Shillings & sixpences two-pences, pence, halfpence, crowns, half-crowns, portcullis, crowns, half-dollars, rials or tester	—	3 21	3 2 0
James I. 1602-3	Shillings & sixpences two-pences, &c. crowns & half-crow.	—	3 21	3 2 0
Charles I. 1625	The same	—	—	—
2 —— —	The same	—	—	3 10 6
—— —	Shillings & sixpences groats, three-pences &c. crowns and half-crowns..........	—	3 21	3 2 0
17 —— —	Ten-shilling and 20-shilling pieces, besides many obsidional pieces of different weight......	—	—	—
Com. Wealth 1649	Shillings..........	—	—	—
Oliver.......1656	—	—	—	—

Table of English Gold Coins.

Reign and Year.	Species.	Standard.	Weight.	Value of the Pound by tale.
			dwt. grs.	£ s. d.
17 Edw. III. 1344	Florins at 6s. half and quarter-florins	23 car. 3½ gr. fine, and ½ gr. alloy	4 19½	15 0 0
18 —— —	Nobles 6s. 8d. half and quarter-nobles.	—	6 1¼	13 3 4
20 —— —	The same	—	5 17	14 0 0
25 —— —	The same	—	5 8	15 0 0
Rich. II. 1377	The same	—	—	—
Hen. IV 1399	The same	—	4 19½	16 13 4
Hen. V. 1412	The same	—	—	—
Hen. VI. 1422	The same	—	—	—
Edw. IV. 1461	The same	—	—	—
4 —— —	Nobles 8s. 4d. half and quarter-nobles	—	—	20 16 8
5 —— —	Nobles, or rials, 10s. half & quarter-rials	23 car. 3½ gr. fine, and ½ gr. alloy	5 8	22 10 0
	Angels at 6s. 8d. ...	—	—	—
	Angelets	—	—	—
49 Hen. VI. 1470	Angels & angelets, rials halves and quarters, as before	—	—	—
Rich. III. 1483	The same	—	—	—
Hen. VII. 1485	The same	—	—	—
	Sovereigns, or double rials, at 20s. half-sovereigns....	—	10 16	—
Hen. VIII. 1509	Sovereigns, half and quarter-rials, angels, &c.........	—	—	—
18 —— —	Sovereigns 22s. 6d..	—	10 0	27 0 0
	Rials at 11s. 3d. ...	—	—	—
	Angels at 7s. 6d. ...	—	3 8	—
	Half-angels, Georges & Nobles at 6s. 8d.	—	—	—
	Half-Georges, called 40-penny-pieces ..	—	—	—
	Crown of the double rose at 5s. and half-crowns	22 car. fine, and 2 alloy	2 9¼	25 0 0
34 Hen. VIII. 1509	Sovereigns at 20s. and half sovereigns	23 car. fine, and 1 alloy	8 8	28 16 0
	Angels at 8s. halves and quarters......	—	3 8	—
36 —— —	Sovereigns at 20s. and halves, Crowns at 5s. & half-crowns	22 car. fine, and 2 allo	2 9¼	—
37 —— —	The same	20 car. fine, and 4 alloy	—	—
1 Edw. VI. 1546-7	The same	—	—	—
3 —— —	Sovereigns, &c.....	—	7 1¼	34 0 0
4 —— —	Sovereigns at 24s. and halves, Angels at 8s. and halves, &c.	23 car. fine, and 1 alloy	—	—
5 —— —	Sovereigns at 30s..	—	10 0	36 0 0
	Angels at 10s. and halves	—	3 8	—
	Sovereigns at 20s. and halves........	22 car. fine, and 2 alloy	7 6½	33 0 0
	Crowns 5s. & halves.	—	1 18¼	—
Mary I. 1553	Sovereigns at 30s.. Rials at 15s. Angels at 10s. Angelets...	23 car. 3½ gr. fine, ½ gr. alloy	10 0	36 0 0
1 Elizabeth 1558	Sovereigns, &c.....	—	—	—
	Sovereigns at 20s. and halves........	22 car. fine, and 2 car. alloy	7 6½	33 0 0
2 —— —	The same as the first year, with the addition of rials at 15s.	23 car. 3½ gr. fine, and ½ gr. alloy	5 0	36 0 0
19 —— —	Angels, halves and quarters..........	—	—	—
26 —— —	Nobles at 15s. and double nobles.....	—	5 0	36 0 0
43 —— —	Angels at 10s. halves and quarters......	—	—	—
	Sovereigns at 20s. & half-sov. Crowns & half-crowns	23 car. fine, and 2 alloy	—	—
James I. 1602-3	The same	23 car. 3½ gr. fine, ½ gr. alloy	—	—
	—	22 car. fine, 2 car. alloy	—	—
2 —— —	—	22 car. fine, and 2 alloy	6 10¼	37 4 0
	Double crowns 10s..	—	3 5½	—
	Britain crowns 5s...	—	1 14¼	—
	Thistle crowns 4s...	—	1 7	—
	Half-crowns 2s. 6d..	—	—	—
3 —— —	Rose rials at 30s....	23 car. 3½ gr. fine, ½ gr. alloy	8 21¼	40 10 0
	Spur rials at 15s. ...	—	4 10½	—
	Angels at 10s.	—	2 23	—
9 —— —	All gold advanced 2s. in the pound by proclamation	—	—	—
10 —— —	Rose rials at 30s...	—	8 4¼	44 10 0
	Spur rials at 15s. ...	—	4 2	—
	Angels at 10s......	—	2 17½	—
	Units at 22s.......	22 car. fine, 2 car. alloy	6 10¾	40 18 4
	Double crowns 11s..	—	—	—
	Brit. crowns 5s. 6d..	—	—	—
17 —— —	Rose rials at 30s. ...	—	8 2	44 10 0
	Spur rials at 15s....	23 car. 3½ gr. fine, ½ gr. alloy	4 1	—
	Angels at 10s.	—	2 16¼	—
	Units at 20s.......	22 car. fine, 2 car. alloy	5 20½	41 0 0
	Double crowns 10s..	—	—	—
	Britain crowns 5s..	—	—	—
1 Cha. I....1625	The same	23 car. 3½ gr. fine, ½ gr. alloy	—	—
	—	22 car. fine, 2 car. alloy	—	—
2 —— —	The same	—	—	44 0 0

COINS.

Reign and Year.	Species.	Standard.	Weight.	Value of the Pound by tale.
			dwt. gr.	£ s. d.
2 Cha. I. 1625	Rose rials at 30s.	23 car. 3½ gr. fine, ½ gr. alloy	8 2	44 10 0
	Spur rials at 15s.	—	4 1	—
	Angels at 10s.	—	2 16¼	—
	Units of 20s. double crowns at 10s.	22 car. fine, 2 car. alloy	5 20	41 0 0
	Britain crowns 5s.	—	—	—
	Siege pieces of 10s. 20s. & three pounds, during the rebellion.	—	—	—
Com. Weal. 1649	Broad pieces of 20s. halves and quarters.	—	—	—
Oliver.... 1656	Pieces of 20s. & 50s.	—	—	—
12 Cha. II.	Units 20s. halves, and quarters.	—	—	—
15 — —	Guineas at 20s. halves, and doubles	—	5 9¼	44 10 0
	Five-pound pieces.	—	26 23½	—
1 James II. 1685	The same	—	—	—
Wm. & Ma. 1688	The same	—	—	—
Anne 1702	The same	—	—	—
1 Geo. II. 1614	The same	—	—	—
4 — —	Quarter-guineas.	—	—	—

Explanation of the Plates.

Plate, No. I. (31)

BRITISH COINS. *Fig.* 1. A brass coin; obverse a rude bust; reverse a Briton driving his chariot over a prostrate warrior.—*Fig.* 2. A tin coin; obverse an unknown head; reverse an eagle, apparently copied from a Roman standard.—*Fig.* 3. A tin coin; obverse two rudely drawn animals, resembling dogs erect, with a ring between them suspended by their fore paws; reverse two swine in the same posture.—*Fig.* 4. A gold coin of Cunobelinus; obverse the legend CAMV. for *Camulodunum*, Colchester; reverse two horses and a wheel; the legend CVNOBILI.—*Fig.* 5. A silver coin of Cunobelinus; obverse a bust, but whether of the monarch or not is doubtful; legend TASCIO VAN; reverse Apollo playing on a lyre, as he is represented on the Roman coins.—*Fig.* 6. A brass coin of Cunobelinus; obverse a bust which seems to be intended for the portrait of Augustus; legend CUNOBELINI; reverse a centaur winding a horn; legend TASCIO VANI.

SAXON COINS. *Fig.* 1. A sceatta, which is now known to contain on the obverse a rude representation of a bird; the characters on the reverse are unknown.—*Fig.* 2. Another sceatta bearing on the obverse the figure of a bird; and on the reverse the rude figures of Romulus and Remus, with the wolf.—*Fig.* 3. A coin of Egbert, bearing on the obverse a rude bust of the monarch; legend ECGBEARHT REX; reverse, the legend OBA MONETA, the cross, and a monogram, supposed to be Dorob. C.—*Fig.* 4. A coin of Alfred, bearing on the obverse a bust of the king, ornamented with a plain double fillet, and jewel in front; legend ELFRED REX; reverse, the name of the moneyer TILEVINE MONETA and LONDINIA, in a monogram.—*Fig.* 5. A coin of Edward I., bearing the bust of the king, with a plain double fillet, and legend EDWARD REX. Rev. the representation of a church, as is supposed, legend VVLFSIGE.—*Fig.* 6. A coin of Ethelred, bearing on the obverse the bust, adorned with a single fillet, having the ends pendent, and terminated with pearls, legend ÆTHELRED REX ANGLORUM. Rev. in the centre, *a* and *w*, with the hand of Providence, legend VALTFERTH. MOGIP. i. e. Ipswich.—*Fig.* 7. A coin of Canute, bearing on the obverse a bust of the king, with a kind of bonnet or helmet, surrounded by a fillet; both that and the bonnet have the ends pendent and ornamented with pearls; also a sceptre, surmounted with a *fleur de lis*, legend CNUT. REX. Rev. MOKULFON STAM. i. e. Stamford.

ENGLISH SILVER COINS. *Fig.* 1. A penny of William, which is ascribed to the Conqueror, from the circumstance of the double sceptre, to which his son Rufus had no pretension; the sceptre in his right hand is surmounted with a cross *paté*, or holy cross; that in his left is surmounted with three pellets or pearls crosswise at the point, legend WILLEM REX ANGLOR, the Saxon 𝖂 (W), being invariably used on these coins. Reverse, a cross, with four sceptres, *bottonné* or *pommetté* in the quarters, in form of an escarbuncle.—*Fig.* 2. An Irish halfpenny of King John; obv. full face, in a triangle, which is supposed to represent the Irish harp, legend JOHANNES REX. Rev. in a triangle, a crescent, and blazing star, with a small star in each angle of the triangle, legend WILLEM ON DI., i. e. Dub.—*Fig.* 3. An Irish farthing of King John, very similar to the former, except the blazing star in the triangle, and the legends on the obverse WILLEM ON: reverse JOHANES DW. i. e. Dublin.—*Fig.* 4. A groat of Edward I., II., or III.; obverse a head full faced, bearing an open crown, with three *fleur de lis*, and pearls between; hair much extended in a double tressure of four arches, with mullets and roses, legend EDWARDUS DI. GR. REX ANGL. Rev. a cross, fleury, extending to the outer edge of the piece, the pellets within the inner circle; legend in the outer circle DNS HIBNE DUX AQUT. inner circle CIVI. LONDONIA. Ireland and Aquitaine occur, for the first time, on the coins of this king, although the latter was inserted upon the Great Seals of Henry II. The crosses of different forms were laid aside in this reign, and a double or single cross with pellets, as in the figure, was introduced, and continued in use till the reign of Henry VII.; a crown of this form was also in use until his time.—*Fig.* 5. A shilling of Henry VII. Obv. Profile of the king to the left, with a crown of one arch only; mint mark a *fleur de lis* on both sides; legend HENRIC SEPTIM. DI. GRA. REX. ANGL. Z. FR. Rev. The arms of France and England quarterly, in a plain shield, surmounted by a cross fourchy. In the smaller coins is a key on each of the lower quarters of the cross below the base of the shield; legend POSUI DEU. ADIUTOREM MEU. The coins of this reign were distinguished from those of preceding reigns by several particulars: the arms of England and France took place of the pellets; numerals, as VII, were first used on some coins to distinguish the kings of the same name, besides the exchange of the side face for the full face: a practice which has continued ever since, with this difference only, that the heads are sometimes turned to the right, and sometimes to the left.—*Fig.* 6. A crown of Henry VIII, which is supposed to have been struck upon Henry's assuming the supremacy, and to have served more as a medal than a coin. Obv. Face nearly full, bust to the waist, crown of *fleurs de lis*, and plain crosses; in the right hand a sword, resting upon his shoulder, and in his left the orb, with the cross, denoting thereby that he was ready to defend his dominion and faith by the sword; legend HENRIC. 8. DEI. GRATIA. ANGLIE. FRANCI. Z HIBERN. REX. Rev. The royal arms crowned and supported by a lion and a dragon; legend ANGLICE Z HIBERNICE ECCLESIE SUPREMUM CAPUT, and beneath the shield, H. R.—*Fig.* 7. A crown of Edward VI. Obv. The king crowned, and in armour, with a naked sword, held upright close to his right side, mounted,

202

superbly caparisoned, and curvetting; mint mark the letter Y on both sides; legend EDWARD VI. D. G. AGL. FRA. Z HIBE. REX.; beneath the horse, 1551. Rev. Arms in a plain shield, surmounted by a cross fourchy.—*Fig.* 8, 9. Two testoons, or shillings, of Edward. Obverse, only the head of Edward; legend, EDWARD VI. D. G. AGL. FRA. Z. HIB. REX.; mint mark in fig. 8, a swan; in fig. 9, a rose, counter-marked, a portcullis in the one, and a greyhound in the other; these counter-marks were put on the base testoons, or shillings, which were reduced in value to six-pence; and in the reign of queen Elizabeth to four-pence, and even lower.—*Fig.* 10. A shilling of fine money of Edward VI. Obv. A bust of the king full-faced, crowned, and in Parliament-robes, with a chain of the order of the garter; on one side of the face a double rose, and on the other XII. to denote the value; mint mark a ton on each side; legend as before. Rev. The arms as before. This is supposed to be the first and only English coin or medal, whereon the collar of the order of the garter is to be seen; but, whether from the mistake of the engraver, or any other cause, this is different from the collar of the order appointed by the statutes of Henry VIII., which was to be composed of double roses encompassed with the garter; whereas this has single roses of four leaves only, without garters, and without knots between. The silver coins of this reign were the last on which the heads of any of our princes have been represented with a full face.—*Fig.* 11. A sixpence of Philip and Mary. Obv. A profile bust of the King and Queen facing each other, with the crown of England above, between the date 1554. The King bare-headed, with short hair, mustachios, and large beard, is in armour, with the order of the Golden Fleece, suspended by a ribbon on his breast. The queen is in her ordinary habit; legend PHILIP ET MARIA D. G. R. ANG. FR. NEAP. PR. HISP. Rev. A shield, crowned, and ornamented with the arms of Philip and Mary impaled. Above the shield, XII. for the value; legend POSUIMUS DEUM ADIUTOREM NOSTRUM.—*Fig.* 12. A half-crown of Queen Elizabeth. Obv. Bust of the queen, having the hair curled in two rows next the face, and turned up behind, ruff, and gown richly ornamented; sceptre fleury in the right hand, globe or mound in the left; mint mark on both sides the Arabic figure 1; legend ELIZABETH D. G. ANG. FRA. ET HIBER. REGINA. Rev. The arms and legend as before.—*Fig.* 13. A half-crown of Elizabeth, which is a specimen of the money, called Portcullis Money, which was struck for the conveniency of the East India Merchants. Obv. The royal shield between the letters E & R. all crowned; mint mark on both sides, a large annulet; legend as before. Rev. A large Portcullis crowned; legend POSUI, &c.—*Fig.* 14. A half-crown of James I. Obv. The King on horseback, in profile to the left, crowned, and in armour. In his right hand a drawn sword; the horse ambling; on the housing a rose crowned; mint mark on both sides a thistle: legend JACOBUS D. G. ANG. SCO. FRAN. ET HIB. REX. Rev. In an escutcheon, highly ornamented, the royal arms, quarterly —first and fourth, England and France, quartered; Scotland in the second; Ireland in the third. The arms of Ireland now appear for the first time upon the coins.—*Fig.* 15. A shilling of Charles I. Obv. Bust of the King turned to the right, crowned, and in armour, with long hair, the object of puritanical abhorrence; mint mark, on both sides, an anchor; legend CAROLUS D. G. MAG. BRI. FRA. HIB. REX. Rev. Arms of England, France, Ireland, and Scotland, on a plain square shield, and cross fleury; legend CHRISTO AUSPICE.—*Fig.* 16, 17. Obsidional, or siege pieces, of Charles I. during the rebellion. The first an irregular piece, stamped on each side with 3 dwts. 21 grs.; the second, an octagonal piece, a castle, with a streamer flying on the highest tower. Above the castle the letters P. C.; on the right side OBS, and a hand with a sword erect, issuing out of the left; beneath 1648. On the reverse, which is not here given, is a crown with C. R.; and the legend DUM SPIRO SPERO.—*Fig.* 18. A sixpence of the Common Wealth. Obv. St. George's Cross between a branch of palm and laurel; mint mark the Sun; legend THE COMMONWEALTH OF ENGLAND. Rev. Two escutcheons joined, the first charged with St. George's Cross, the other with the Irish harp; over the shield *v*.— *Fig.* 19. A shilling of Cromwell. Obv. Bust in profile to the right, laureat, with a Roman mantle; legend OLIVAR. D. G. R. P. ANG. SCO. HI. &c. PRO. Rev. In a shield, surmounted by an Imperial Crown, quarterly, first and fourth, St. George's Cross for England; second, St. Andrew's Cross for Scotland; third, the harp for Ireland. On an escutcheon of pretence a lion rampant; legend PAX. QUÆRITUR. BELLO. 1658.—*Fig.* 20. A crown of Queen Anne. Reverse only; in the top and bottom shields England and Scotland impaled, to denote the union of the two kingdoms; on the dexter side Ireland, and on the sinister France; a plume of feathers in each quarter. The position of France, in the sinister or third quarter, has prevailed to the present time, whenever the shields have been placed separately on the coins.

Plate, No. II.

ENGLISH GOLD COINS. *Fig.* 1. A quarter florin of Edward III. Obv. In a field *semè de lis* a helmet with lambrequins; crest a lion passant, gardant crowned; legend EDWR. R. ANGL. Z. FRANC. D. HIB. Rev. A cross fleury, with a rose in the centre; legend EXALT. ABITUR IN GLORIA. The lambrequin is a mantling formerly worn upon the helmet, as well for ornament as to keep off the sun. Edward III. is the first of our monarchs who bore this crest upon his helmet on the reverse of his great seal. Although the regular commencement of the gold coinage is dated from this reign, of which there are many specimens extant, yet Henry III. is said to have coined a gold penny that was in circulation for some time.—*Fig.* 2. A Noble of Edward III. Obv. The King, armed and crowned, standing in a ship, which has a streamer at the mast-head, with St. George's Cross, a naked sword in his right hand, and in his left a shield, bearing the arms of France (*semè de lis*) quartered with those of England. On the upper part of the side of the ship are lions passant gardant, towards the left, and fleurs de lis alternately, under these two tiers of ports, the lower of which has four projecting spikes placed alternately with the ports: legend EDWARD DEI GRA. REX. ANGL. Z. FRANC. D. HIB. Rev. In a double tressure of eight arches, with trefoils in the outward angles, a cross fleury voided. Over each limb of the cross a fleur de lis. In the quarters the Lion of England under a crown. In the centre a rose of four leaves, pointed with as many trefoils saltire-wise, including the letter E: legend IHC. (i. e. *Jesus*) AUTEM TRANSIENS PER MEDIUM. ILLORUM IBA (or *ibat*.) In some coins of this prince he is styled also DNS. AQUIT. i. e. Dominus Aquitaniæ. —*Fig.* 3. An Angel of Edward IV. Obv. The Archangel Michael standing with his left foot upon the dragon, and piercing him through the mouth with a spear, the upper end of which terminates in a cross crosslet: legend, EDWARD DEI. GRA. REX ANGL. Z. FRANC. Rev. A ship with a large cross for the mast, with the letter E on the right side, and a rose on the left; on the side of the ship the usual arms: legend, PER CRUCEM TUA' SALVA NOS XPE REDEMPT.—*Fig.* 4. A half rial of Edward IV. Obv. The type as before, with a full blown rose on the side of the ship, and a square flag at the stern, with the letter E, for *Edward:* legend, EDWARDI GRA. REX ANGL. Z FRANC. DNS. 'IB. Rev. In the usual tressure a sun of sixteen rays instead of the cross: in the centre a rose; mint mark, the sun: legend, DOMINE NE IN FURORE TUO ARGUAS ME. The sun is here put in commemoration of his victory at Mortimer's Cross.—*Fig.* 5. A Sovereign, or Double Rial, of Henry VII. Obv. The King sitting on his throne, in royal robes, crowned; in his right hand a sceptre, fleury, in his left the orb, the back ground diapered with fleurs de lis. This is said by Mr. Leake to be the first time that the orb and cross on the king's hand is to be met with on coins, though used on other occasions. Rev. In a double tressure of ten arches, with trefoils in the outer angles, the English Lion and Fleurs de Lis alternately, within a double rose. In the centre a plain escutcheon of France and England: legend, IHS. AUTEM TRANSIENS PER MEDIUM ILLORUM IBAT HE. The white rose is here united with the red, in respect to the union of the Houses of York and Lancaster.—*Fig.* 6, A double sovereign of Henry VIII. Obv. Within the inner circle, engrailed, and pointed with fleurs de lis, the King sits, crowned, in a chair of state, the back network; on each arm of it a cross patonce, as on the sceptre; at his feet the portcullis; mint mark on this side a fleur de lis, on the other a cross crosslet: legend, HENRICUS DEI GRATIA REX ANGLIE ET FRANC. DNS. HIB. The Portcullis is a badge which is said to have been assumed by Henry VII. in respect to his mother's descent from the Beauforts, signifying, as Leake says, that as the Portcullis was an additional security to the gate, so his descent from his mother strengthened his other titles. Hence this coin has been ascribed by some to this latter king.—*Fig.* 7. A Rial of Queen Elizabeth. Obv. The Queen in a large ruff, with her crown, sceptre in her right hand, and orb in her left, standing in a three-decked ship, turned to the right, with guns out, the usual rose on the side, and square flag at the head, on which is inscribed the letter E: legend, ELIZAB. D. G. ANG. FR. ET HIB. REGINA. Rev. IHS. &c. as in fig. 5. This legend was adopted by Edward III. on the occasion of his victory over the French fleet, and continued to be used on the coins of his successors until the reign of Elizabeth, after which it went out of use.—*Fig.* 8. A unit, or twenty shilling piece, of King James, whereby he laid aside the crown to take up with the laurel, which has ever since been in use. Obv. Bust in profile to the right, laureat; mustachios turned upward; mantle tied on the shoulder; xx. for the value, behind the head; mint mark on both sides a spur-rowel: legend, JACOBUS D. G. MAG. BRI. FRAN. ET HIB. REX. Rev. In the old cross fleury a plain escutcheon of the royal arms, crowned: legend, FACIAM EOS IN GENTEM UNAM.—*Fig.* 9. A Guinea of William and Mary. Obv. Heads of William and Mary in profile to the left; his laureat; necks bare: legend, GULIELMUS ET MARI DEI GRATIA. Rev. In an escutcheon garnished and crowned quarterly, first and fourth, France and England quarterly, second Scotland, third Ireland; on an escutcheon of pretence Nassau: legend, MAG. BR. FR. ET HIB. REX ET REGINA. It will be seen from the table of English coins that guineas were first struck in the reign of Charles II. and derive their name from Guinea, on the coast of Africa, whence the gold was brought, of which they were made.

COI'NCIDENS (*Math.*) an epithet for lines, points, or figures, which being placed one upon another exactly agree or cover one another.

COINDICA'NTIA (*Med.*) coindications or signs which do not indicate by themselves alone, but in connexion with other circumstances assist the physician to form a judgment of the disease.

COINS (*Archit.*) or *quoins*, from the French *coin*; signifies the angle formed by the two sides of any building, as the coin or corner of two walls.—*Rustic coins*, stones projecting out of a wall to which other buildings may be joined. They are so called because of their rustic appearance.—*Coin* signifies also a block cut obliquely, on which rests a column or pilaster.

COIN *de manœuvre militaire* (*Mil.*) a particular manner in which the ancients used to dispose their troops, in order the better to break the enemy's line, it resembling the figure of a wedge, the sharp extremity of which formed the front.

COINS (*Print.*) wedges used to fasten the composed matter into the form or chase.

COINS (*Gunn.*) large wedges of wood for the levelling, raising, or lowering a piece of ordnance.

COINS (*Mar.*) small wedges or pieces of wood to lay between casks, otherwise called *canting coins*, in distinction from *standing coins*, which are pipe-staves or billets to make casks fast.

COIRA (*Bot.*) vide *Acacia*.

COI'TION (*Nat.*) the mutual tendency of bodies one to another, for which the word *attraction* is more commonly substituted.

COITION *of the moon* (*Astron.*) is when the moon is in the same sign and degree of the zodiac with the sun.

COITS (*Sport.*) or *Quoits*, a kind of iron rings, resembling a horse-shoe, which is thrown to a certain distance at a certain point.

COIX (*Bot.*) a genus of plants, Class 21 *Monoecia*, Order 3 *Triandria*.

Generic Characters. CAL. *glume* two-flowered; *valves* oblong ovate.—COR. two-valved; *valves* ovate lanceolate.—STAM. *filaments* three; *anthers* oblong.—PIST. *germ* ovate; *styles* short; *stigmas* two.—PER. none; *seed* solitary.

Species. The species are shrubs and perennials, as the—*Coix lachryma*, *Lithospermum*, &c. *Lachryma*, &c. *Catriconda*, seu *Salee*, Job's tears, a shrub, native of the East Indies.—*Coix agrestis*, *Lithospermum*, &c. *Salee*, &c. seu *Lachryma*, &c. a perennial, native of Amboina.—*Coix arundinacea*, a perennial.

COKE (*Chem.*) a hard sonorous kind of charcoal which arises from the burning of black pit-coal.

COL. (*Ant.*) an abbreviation in medals and in inscriptions for *colonia*.

COLATION (*Chem.*) the passing any thing through a strainer.

TO COLATION *books* (*Print.*) vide *To Collate*.

COLATO'RIA-LACTEA (*Med.*) vide *Fluor Albus*.

COLATO'RIUM (*Ant.*) a vessel full of holes at the bottom.

COLATU'RE (*Chem.*) that which after being boiled is percolated or strained through a sieve.

COLCAQUAHU'ITE (*Bot.*) an American plant recommended in palsies and uterine disorders. *Raii Hist. Plant.*

CO'LCHICUM (*Bot.*) κολχικὸν, a name given by some of the ancients to the poisonous plant *Ephemerum*, because it grew in Colchis. *Dioscor.* l. 4, c. 84; *Plin.* l. 28, c. 9.

COLCHICUM, *in the Linnean system*, a genus of plants, Class 6 *Hexandria*, Order 3 *Trigynia*.

Generic Characters. Cal. none.—Cor. six-parted; *tube* angulated; *divisions of the border* erect.—Stam. *filaments* six; *anthers* oblong.—Pist. *germ* buried within the root; *styles* three; *stigmas* reflex.—Per. *capsule* three-lobed; *seeds* many.

Species. The species are perennials, as—*Colchicum autumnale*, Common Meadow Saffron, native of Europe.—*Colchicum montanum, seu foliis,* &c. native of Spain.—*Colchicum variegatum, seu foliis,* &c. seu *Chionense,* Variegated Meadow Saffron, native of Chios.—*Colchicum Byzantinum,* native of Constantinople.

Colchicum is also a name for the *Bulbocodium vernum.*

CO'LCHICUS (*Orn.*) or *Phasianus colchicus* of Linnæus, the Common Pheasant.

CO'LCOTHAL (*Chem.*) the dry substance which remains after the distillation of vitriol; it is now commonly called *caput mortuum.*

CO'LCOTHAR (*Chem.*) vitriol calcined over a strong fire. It is applied surgically to wounds, for stanching blood, &c.

COLD (*Nat.*) denotes not only the sensation of cold, but also the state of any body which causes the sensation.

COLDE'NIA (*Bot.*) a genus of plants, Class 4 *Tetrandria,* Order 3 *Trigynia.*

Generic Characters. Cal. *perianth* four-leaved; *leaflets* lanceolate.—Cor. one-petalled; *border* patulous.—Stam. *filaments* four; *anthers* roundish.— Pist. *germs* four; *styles* as many; *stigmas* simple.—Per. none; *fruit* ovate; *seeds* two.

Species. The only species is—*Coldenia procumbens,* seu *Teucrii,* an annual, native of India.

COLE (*Bot.*) Colewort, or Kale, a sort of winter cabbage, which is a variety of the *Brassica* of Linnæus.—Cole-Seed, the seed of the *Napus sativa,* or long-rooted narrow-leaved *rapa,* called in English Navew, which is reckoned by Linnæus as a variety of the *Brassica napus.* It is much cultivated on account of the oil which is expressed from it, as also for the feeding of cattle. It is sown about the middle of June, and the ground is prepared as for turneps.

COLE-MOUSE (*Orn.*) a species of the Titmouse, the *Parus ater* of Linnæus.

COLEOPTERA (*Ent.*) the first order of insects in the Linnean system, comprehending the genera which have four wings, the upper crustaceous, with a straight suture. The genera are furthermore distinguished into, 1. Those having the *antennæ* clavate, as *Scarabæus,* the Beetle; *Synodendron, Lucanus, Dermestes, Melysis,* the Leather-Eater; *Byrrhus, Silpha,* the Carrion-Beetle; *Tritoma, Hydrophilus,* one species of which is called the Water-Clock; *Tebratoma, Hister, Bostrichus, Anthrenus, Nitidula, Coccinella,* one species of which is the Lady-Bird; *Curculis, Pausus.* 2. Those having the *antennæ* moniliform, as, *Brentus, Attelabus, Erodius, Staphylinus, Zygia, Maloë, Tenebris, Cassida, Opatrum, Mordella, Chrysomela, Horia.* 3. Those having the *antennæ* filiform, as, *Apalus, Manticora, Pimelia, Gyrinus, Cucujus, Cryptocephalus, Bruchus, Ptinus, Hispa, Buprestis, Necydalis, Lampyris,* Fire-Fly, Glow-Worm, *Cantharis, Notoxus, Elater, Calopus, Alurnus, Carabus, Lytta.* 4. Those having the *antennæ* setaceous, as, *Serropalpus, Cerambyx, Leptura, Rhinomacer, Zonitis, Cucindela, Dytsicus, Forficula,* Earwig.

COLES (*Anat.*) or *colis.* [vide *Penis*]

CO'LE-SEED (*Bot.*) vide *Cole.*

CO'LET (*Mech.*) that part of a ring where the stone is set.

COLE'TTA VEE'TLA (*Bot.*) the *Barleria prionitis* of Linnæus.

CO'LEWORT (*Bot.*) a well-known variety of the Cabbage, or *Brassica* of Linnæus, which grows through the winter.

CO'LGIAT (*Mil.*) a large glove which the Turks wear in the field, covering the arm up to the elbow.

CO'LI *dextrum Ligamentum* (*Anat.*) the fold of that particular lamina which is turned to the right side, where the mesentery changes its name for that of mesocolon, near the extremity of the *ilium.*—*Coli sinistrum Ligamentum,* a contraction of the mesocolon a little below the left kidney.

CO'LIAS (*Ich.*) κολίας, Bastard-Tunny, supposed by some to be Mackarel. *Plin.* l. 32, c. 10; *Athen.* l. 3.

COLIBARTS (*Law*) tenants, or villeins, made free; persons of a middle condition, between servants and freemen.

COLIBUS (*Orn.*) another name for the Humming-bird.

COLI'CA (*Med.*) Colic, a pain in the abdomen, particularly in the intestine called the *colon,* from which it takes its name. This name, as well as the disorder itself, was first known, according to Pliny, in the reign of Tiberius; but Celsus is of opinion that it had been earlier described by the same name. *Cels.* l. 4, c. 9; *Plin.* l. 20, c. 12.

Colic is now distinguished according to the different causes and circumstances of the disorder, into the *bilious colic,* when accompanied with vomiting of bile; *flatulent* or *windy colic,* when attended with distension from flatulency; *inflammatory colic,* or *enteritis,* when attended with inflammation. When the disorder rises to a great height it is called the *Iliac passion.* It is placed by Dr. Cullen as a genus of diseases in the Class *Neuroses,* Order *Spasmi.*

COLICULUS (*Bot.*) a diminutive of *colis;* signifies the little stalk or tender branch of a plant, as the *coliculus fabæ,* the young stalk of a bean.

COLIFO'RME OS (*Anat.*) another name for the *os cribrosum.*

CO'LING (*Bot.*) a long pale apple.

CO'LINIL (*Bot.*) the *Convolvulus nil* of Linnæus; an American plant, the juice of which with a little honey, is said to be good for pustules in the mouth.

COLI'PHIUM (*Ant.*) a sort of coarse bread which wrestlers used to eat, in order to make them strong and firmfleshed; so called from κῶλα, limbs, and ἶφος, robust; or, according to some, from κέλλιξ, a sort of cake mentioned by Athenæus.

Plaut. Pers. act. 1, scen. 3, v. 12.

Collyria facite ut madeant, et coliphia
Ne mi hæc incocta detis.

Mart. l. 7, ep. 67, v. 12.

Cum coliphia sedecem comedit.
Post hæc omnia cum libidinatur,
Non fellat:

Juven. sat. 2, v. 53.

Luctantur paucæ; comedunt coliphia paucæ.

Athen. l. 3.

COLIUS (*Orn.*) Coly, a genus of animals, Class *Aves,* Order *Passeres.*

Generic Character. Bill convex above, and flat beneath; *nostrils* small, at the base of the bill, and nearly covered with feathers; *tongue* jagged at the tip; *tail* long.

Species. The birds of this tribe, which inhabit the Cape of Good Hope and Senegal, are principally distinguished by their colour.

COLLA (*Nat.*) any thing glutinous, or of the nature of glue.

COLLA'PSUS (*Med.*) a wasting or shrinking of the body or strength.

CO'LLAR (*Her.*) an ornament for the neck, worn by knights of any order, which serve as a badge of the order. [vide *Heraldry*]—*Collar days,* festival days, whereon the knights of the garter wear their collars.

Collar (*Mar.*) 1. In French *collier d'étai,* the lower part of any of the lower stays of the masts, or the part by which the stay is confined at its lower end. 2. A rope fastened about the beak-head of a ship, into which the pulley called dead-man's-eye is fixed, that holds her forestay; also one about the main-mast-head, called the collar or garland, which serves to prevent the shrouds from galling.

COLLAR (*Archit.*) a ring or cincture.—*Collar-beam*, a beam in the construction of a roof, placed above the lower ends of the rafters or base of the roof.

CO'LLARAGE (*Law*) a tax or fine formerly laid on the collars of horses that draw wine.

COLLA'RE (*Ant.*) a collar so called, from *collum*, the neck, because it was worn about the neck. It was a sort of chain put round the necks of runaway slaves, with an inscription stating their name and offence, with which, till the time of Constantine, they were branded on the forehead; but afterwards it was engraved upon the collar itself, of which several examples are given by antiquarians, as one quoted by Pignorius: TENE ME. QUIA. FUGI. ET. REVOCA ME. DOMINO. MEO BONIFACIO. LINARIO. *Turneb. Adv.* l. 29, c. 17; *Pignor. de Serv.* p. 31; *Spon. Misc. Erud. Act.* sect. 9, p. 300.

CO'LLARED (*Her.*) an epithet for any one having the collar of an order about his neck.

COLLARI'NO (*Archit.*) that part of a column which is included between the fillet and the astragal.

TO COLLA'TE books (*Print.*) to examine the whole number of sheets belonging to a book, in order to see if they are all gathered properly and placed in the order of their signatures. This is the business of the warehouseman, and has been vulgarly called *collationing*, and the person doing it the *collationer*. To *collate manuscripts*, is to arrange and compare them, so as to bring them into due order and connexion, &c.

COLLA'TERAL (*Law*) *collateralis*, from *latus*, a side; that is sideways, or not direct, as—*Collateral kinsmen*, those who descend from one and the same common ancestor, but not from one another, in distinction from *lineal kinsmen*; as if a man has two sons who have each issue; these issues are lineally descended from him as their common ancestor, but they are *collateral kinsmen* to one another; so collateral warranty, &c. [vide *Warranty*.]—*Collateral issue*, is where a criminal convict pleads any matter allowed by law, in bar of execution, as pregnancy, the king's pardon, and the like, which issue is to be tried by a jury instanter. —*Collateral assurance*, that which is made over and above the deed itself.—*Collateral security*, a bond that is attached to the deed itself for the due performance of covenants between man and man.

COLLATERA'LES (*Anat.*) a name for the *Erectores Penis*.

COLLA'TIO BONORUM (*Law*) is where a portion, or money advanced by the father to a son or daughter, is brought into hotch-pot, in order to have an equal distributory share of his personal estate.

COLLA'TION (*Cus.*) a treat, or entertainment, given between meals, or in the place of a meal; it mostly consists of cold dishes, when it is called a cold collation.

COLLATION *to a benefice* (*Law*) the bestowing of a benefice by the bishop or other ordinary when he hath right of patronage.—*Collation of seals*, was, in old deeds, when one seal was set upon the back of another upon the same libel.

COLLATIO'NE *facta uni post mortem alterius* (*Law*) a writ which enjoins the justices of the Common Pleas to send out their writ to a bishop to admit a clerk in the place of another presented by the king, who died during the suit between the king and the bishop's clerk.—*Collatione Hermitagii*, a writ whereby the king was wont to confer the keeping of a hermitage upon a clerk.

COLLATI'TIUM (*Archæol.*) a sort of food prepared of the flesh of a capon or pullet bruised and then mixed with mutton broth, and exhibited with verjuice or lemon juice.

COLLA'TIVE ADVOWSON (*Archæol.*) that which is lodged in the bishop. [vide *Advowson*]

CO'LLEAGUE (*Polit.*) a partner or sharer in any office.

CO'LLECT (*Ecc.*) a short prayer with the epistle and gospel, appropriated to any particular day or occasion in the Christian church. *Papias; Anastas. Hist. Eccles. Ann.* 21; *Hist. Tripart.* l. 1, c. 10.

COLLECTA'NEA (*Lit.*) things written or gathered out of many works; notes, collections, &c.

COLLE'CTION (*Lit.*) an assemblage of things collected together for some specific object; as, a collection of coins, of medals, of paintings, &c.

COLLECTION *of light* (*Astrol.*) a term applied to two principal significators which cast their aspect to a more dignified planet and do not behold each other.

COLLE'CTIVE (*Gram.*) an epithet for any noun which comprehends many persons or things in the singular number; as a *multitude*, *company*, *army*, &c.

COLLE'CTOR (*Elect.*) a small appendage to the prime conductor of the electrical machine, which serves to receive the electricity both positive and negative.

COLLEGATA'RIUS (*Law*) a partaker of a bequest or legacy with another.

CO'LLEGE (*Polit.*) *collegium*, from *colligo*, to collect or associate together; a particular corporation, company, or society of men, having certain privileges, founded by the king's licence; as, the *college of physicians*, which includes the body of physicians in London.

College is also a corporate body erected for the purpose of training up young men to any particular course of life, and provided with statutes for its maintenance; as, the *colleges* of the Universities, or the military *colleges*, &c.

COLLE'GIAN (*Lit.*) a fellow or member of a college.

COLLE'GIATE (*Ecc.*) an epithet for a church that is endowed, for a society, body corporate, a deanery, &c.

COLLE'GIUM (*Ant.*) a company or fraternity, of which there were many kinds among the Romans; as, the Collegium augurum, artificum, &c. *Cic. Orat. pro Sex.* c. 15; *Plin.* l. 8, c. 28; *Plut. in Num.*; *Flor. Hist. Roman.* l. 1, c. 6: *Sigon. de Ant. Roman. Jur.* l. 2, c. 12.

CO'LLET (*Gun.*) French for that part of a cannon which is between the astragal and the muzzle.

COLLE'TICA (*Med.*) conglutinating medicines.

COLLI'CIÆ (*Ant.*) ὀχετοὶ, ὑδροὶ, gutter-tiles; and also drains in the field. *Plin.* l. 18, c. 10.

COLLICIÆ (*Anat.*) the union of the ducts which convey the humours of the eyes from the *Puncta lachrymalia* to the cavity of the nose.

COLLI'CULÆ (*Anat.*) vide *Nymphæ*.

CO'LLIER (*Com.*) one who works in coals or at the coal mines.

COLLIER (*Mar.*) a ship that is loaded with coal.

CO'LLIERS (*Mech.*) French for iron or brass holdfasts, which are employed in flood-gates.

CO'LLIERY (*Com.*) the place where coals are worked and laid up.

CO'LLIFLOWER (*Bot.*) or Cauliflower, the finest sort of cabbage, a variety of the *Brassica oleracea* of Linnæus.

COLLIGAMEN (*Anat.*) a ligament.

COLLIGE'NDUM, *Bona defuncti ad*, (*Law*) letters granted to certain persons, who, in default of administrators and executors, are thereby authorized to collect the goods of the defunct, and to keep them in safe custody for the benefit of those who are entitled to the property of the deceased.

COLLIMA'TION, *Line of* (*Opt.*) the line, in a telescope, that passes through the intersection of those wires that are fixed in the focus of the object-glass and the centre of the same glass.

COLLINSO'NIA (*Bot.*) a genus of plants, Class 2 *Diandria*, Order 1 *Monogynia*.
Generic Characters. CAL. *perianth* one-leaved; *upper lip* three-cleft; *lower lip* two-parted.—COR. one-petalled; *tube* funnelform; *border* five-cleft; *upper divisions* obtuse; *lower lip* longer.—STAM. *filaments* two; *anthers* simple.—PIST. *germ* four-cleft; *style* bristleform; *stigma* bifid.—PER. none; *seed* single.
Species. The principal species are the—*Collinsonia Canadensis*, seu *serotina*, &c. Nettle-leaved Collinsonia, a perennial, native of Canada.—*Collinsonia scabriuscula*, seu *foliis, &c.* seu *præcox*, &c. Rough-stalked Collinsonia, a perennial, native of Florida.

COLLIQUAME'NTUM (*Nat.*) an extremely transparent fluid observable in an egg after two or three days incubation, which contains the rudiments of the chicken.

COLLIQUI'TIO (*Med.*) a term applied to the blood when it loses its *crasis*, or balsamic texture.

COLLI'QUATIVE (*Med.*) an epithet for any excessive evacuation which melts, as it were, the strength of the body, as a colliquative perspiration, a colliquative diarrhœa.—*Colliquative fever*, one attended with a diarrhœa, or profuse sweats from too lax a contexture of the fluids.

COLLIRI'DIANS (*Ecc.*) a sect of heretics in the fourth century, who worshipped the Virgin Mary as a goddess, and offered sacrifice to her. *S. Epiphan. Hæres.* 78, 79; *Baron. Annal.* ann. 373; *Sand. Hæres.* 92.

COLLI'SION (*Nat.*) the percussion or striking of bodies against each other.

COLLI'SIO (*Med.*) vide *Contusio*.

CO'LLIX (*Med.*) κόλλιξ, a sort of troche or pastil in a round flat form.

COLLOBO'MA (*Med.*) the growing together of the eyelids, from κολλάω, to glue together.

COLLOCA'TIO (*Ant.*) πρόθεσις, a ceremony at the funerals of the Greeks and Romans, which consisted in laying out the dead upon a bier, or on the ground. The place where the corpse was thus laid out was at the entrance of the house, near the threshold, in order that all might see whether the deceased had met his death by violence or not. *Poll. Onom.* l. 8, seg. 53.

COLLOCO'CCA (*Bot.*) the *Cordia collococca* of Linnæus.

CO'LLOP (*Cook.*) a slice of stewed meat.

COLLO'QUIUM (*Law*) the talking together, or affirming a thing laid in declarations for words in actions for slander, &c. *Mod. Cas.* 203.

COLLU'SION (*Law*) a fraudulent contrivance, or compact between two or more parties, to bring an action, one against the other, for some deceitful end, as the defrauding a third person of his right, &c. This collusion is apparent when it shows itself on the face of the act, or secret when it is covered with a show of honesty. *Stat. Westmin.* 13 Ed. 1, c. 33; *Co. Lit.* 109. 360; *Plow.* 54.

COLLUTHE'ANS (*Ecc.*) heretics in the fourth century, so called after their leader, one Colluthus, who held many of the doctrines of the Arians and Manicheans. *S. Athanas. Apol.* l. 1, c. 8; *S. August. Hæres.* c. 65; *S. Epiphan. Hæres.* c. 69; *Philast. Hæres.* c. 8; *Baron. Annal.* ann. 315.

COLLUTO'RTUM *oris* (*Med.*) vide *Gargarismus*.

CO'LLYBUS (*Ant.*) κόλλυβος, 1. A coin on which was engraven the image of an ox. *Hesychius*. 2. The exchanging of money, as a lesser coin for a greater, or the current money of the country for foreign coin, for which the exchanger had an allowance in consideration. *Cic. in Verr.* orat. 3, c. 78; *ad Attic.* l. 12, ep. 6; *Poll.* l. 3, c. 9; *Suet. in Aug.* c. 4; *Bud. in Pandect.* p. 134; *Sigon. de Ant. Jur. Liv. Roman.* l. 2, c. 11.

CO'LLY-FLOWER (*Bot.*) vide *Colliflower*.

CO'LLYRA (*Ant.*) κολλύρα, a sort of bread baked in the ashes. *Hesychius*. 2. A little round loaf.

COLLY'RIOM (*Or.*) another name for the *Blackbird*.

CO'LLYRITE (*Min.*) a sort of stone of the Lythomarge family.

COLLY'RIUM (*Med.*) κολλύριον, a medicinal composition, so called from κόλλα, glue, and ουρά, a tail, because these medicines were originally made up with something glutinous, and in the form of a rat's tail. The term is now only applied to a fluid application for the eyes, commonly called *eye-water*. *Cel.* l. 5, c. 28; *Oribas. Med. Coll.* l. 10, c. 28; *Scribon. Larg.* c. 69.

COLO'BIUM (*Ant.*) κολόβιον, a short garment without sleeves worn by monks and hermits. It is called by St. Jerom *tunica succinea et lineus saccus*. *Cassian. de Ægypt. Mon. Colob.* l. 1, c. 5; *Epiphan. Hæres.* c. 64; *Ammian.* l. 14, c. 9; *Isid. Orig.* l. 19, c. 22; *Serv. in Æn.* l. 9, v. 616; *Petav. in Them. Orat.* l. 14; *Doroth. Abbas. Doctrin.*; *Alcuin. de Divin. Offic.*; *Gregor. Tur. de Vit. Pat.* c. 8.

COLOBO'MA (*Med.*) vide *Colloboma*.

COLOBO'MATA (*Med.*) κολοβώματα, called by Celsus *Curta*, are deficiencies in any part of the body, particularly in the ears, lips, or alæ of the nostrils.

COLOCA'SIA (*Med.*) κολοκασία, from κόλος and κάσαι, to adorn; the *faba Ægyptiaca*, or Ægyptian-bean.

COLOCA'SIUM (*Bot.*) vide *Colocasia*.

COLOCHIE'RNI (*Bot.*) a plant differing but little from the *Atractylis*.

COLOCY'NTHIS (*Bot.*) κολυκυνθίς, a plant, so called from κῶλον, the colon, and κινέω, to move, on account of its purgative quality. Hippocrates speaks of this plant under the name of the κολοκυνθη αγρια, and Theophrastus gives it the name of κολυκύντη. *Hippocrat. Theoph.* l. 1, c. 22; *Dioscor.* l. 4, c. 178; *Plin.* l. 19, c. 19; *Gal. Exeges. Vocab. Hippocrat.*; *Athen.* l. 2, &c.

COLOCYNTHIS, *in the Linnean system*, is the same as the *Cucumis*, which is better known by the name of *Coloquintida*. [vide *Coloquintida*]

COLO'GNE *earth* (*Paint.*) a substance used by painters as a water colour approaching to umber in its structure, and of a deep brownish-tinge.

COLOME'STRUM (*Bot.*) Dogbane.

CO'LON (*Anat.*) κῶλον, contracted from κοῖλον, hollow, because of its great capacity; the greater portion of the large intestine which proceeds from the liver by a transverse arch to the other; and, descending into the *pelvis*, forms what is termed the *sigmoid flexure* when it becomes the intestine called the *rectum*. *Ruff. Ephes. de Appell. Part. Corp. Hum.* l. 1, c. 27.

COLON (*Gram.*) from κῶλον, a member, signifying the member of a sentence, but it is now applied to the point marked thus (:), which divides an entire member of a sentence from the rest. *Isid. Orig.* l. 1, c. 19.

COLONA'DE (*Archit.*) a range of pillars running quite round a building, and standing within the walls of it. The intervals between the columns measured by the inferior diameter of the column is called the *intercolumniation*, and the whole space between every two columns is an *intercolumn*. Intercolumniations are distinguished into the Pycnostyle, Systyle, Eustyle, &c.: also the colonade itself, according to the number of columns, into the Tetrastyle, Hexastyle, &c. [vide *Architecture*]

CO'LONEL (*Mil.*) the first in command of a regiment, whether of horse, foot, dragoons, or artillery, in England; but in France and Spain, and other southern nations, Colonels of horse are called *Maitres de camp*.—*Lieutenant-Colonel*, the second in command, who is the next to the colonel.

COLONE'LLI (*Archit.*) Italian for trussposts, or the posts of a trussframe.

CO'LONELLING (*Mil.*) a colloquial term which signifies beating about for troops, &c.

COLO'NNE (*Mil.*) French for a column. [vide *Column*]—*Colonne d'artillerie*, the march or movements of a corps of artillery in regular order.—*Colonne d'equipages*, the line of march which is observed by baggage waggons.

COLO'NIA (*Ant.*) ἀποικία, a colony; a company of people transplanted from one place to another with an allowance of land for their tillage, by which means the city was disburthened of its multitudes, the poor were provided for, and the borders of the empire, whither they were for the most part sent, were secured against the inroads of the enemy. The *colonia* is commonly marked in inscriptions and on medals by the abbreviations C. or COL.; and the common symbol is a husbandman driving oxen, as in the annexed figure of a medal of Gordianus III; on which, also, are to be observed military-standards, to denote that it was colonized by veteran soldiers. The inscription COL. CAES. ANTIOCH., with the letters S. R., i. e. *senatus Romanus*, signifying that the colony had been formed with the approbation of the senate. *Vaillant. Colon.*; *Beg. Thes. Brand.*

CO'LONY (*Polit.*) is applied, in the sense of the ancient colonia [vide *Colonia*], to signify any number of persons who go under the sanction of government to inhabit a distant country, and cultivate a place that has been before uncultivated.

COLO'NUS (*Law*) an husbandman, or villager, who was bound to pay yearly a certain tribute, and at certain times to plough some of the lord's land; whence comes our English word *clown*.

COLOPHO'NIA Resina (*Bot.*) κολοφωνία, Colophony; the resin which the pine-tree yields, so called from Colophon, a city of Ionia, whence it was first brought. *Dioscor.* l. 1, c. 92; *Plin.* l. 14, c. 20; *Gal. de Comp. Med. per Gen.* l. 7, c. 3.

COLOPHONIA signifies now the black resin which remains in the retort after distilling the common resin with a strong fire.

COLOPO'ON (*Bot.*) vide *Colpoon.*

COLOQUI'NTIDA (*Bot.*) or Bitter Apple, the fruit of the wild gourd; the *Cucumis colocynthis* of Linnæus; the pulp, or internal part, which is light, spongy, and white, is also remarkable for its intense bitterness.

CO'LOR (*Opt.*) or colour, was supposed by the ancients to be an inherent property of the colored substance, and was, therefore, defined to be the sensation produced by looking on any colored body, or the quality in bodies which produces this sensation; but, according to the doctrine of Sir Isaac Newton, which is now generally admitted, the difference of colour lies in the different rays of light, so that colour may be defined the property possessed by the elementary rays separated by any means whatever of exciting different sensations according to their different degrees of refrangibility. *Colors* are either primary or secondary. The *primary*, or *original colors*, are the colors of simple or homogeneal light, or produced by rays that have the same degree of refrangibility, and the same magnitude of their parts: of these colors there are seven; namely, violet, indigo, blue, green, yellow, orange, and red, which all admit of infinite gradations.—*Secondary*, or *heterogeneous colors*, are those which are compounded of the primary ones: of this kind of colors the most remarkable is that of whiteness, which requires all the primary colors to enter into its composition; whereas, on the contrary, black is produced by the absorption of all the rays of light, so that being suppressed in the black body they are not reflected outward. According to this theory the difference of colors in natural bodies is supposed to arise from the disposition which they possess to reflect rays of this or that color alone, or of this or that color more abundantly than any other, which disposition is ascribed to the different degrees of density which exist in different bodies.

COLOR (*Paint.*) is a term applied both to the drugs and to the tints produced by those drugs variously mixed and applied. Colors are divided by painters, in the first place, into opaque and transparent.—*Opaque colors* are such as, when laid over paper, wood, &c. cover them fully, so as to efface any other color or stain that may have been there before; such as white-lead, red-lead, vermilion, &c.—*Transparent colors* are those which leave the ground visible on which they are laid; of which kind are the colors used for *illuminating maps*. Colors are moreover divided, as respect their composition, into oil-colors or water-colors, simple or mineral.—*Oil-colors* are such as are prepared for painting in oil.—*Water-colors* are such as are mixed with water.—*Simple*, or *vegetable colors*, are those which are extracted from vegetables, and will not bear the fire, as the yellow made of saffron, lacca, &c.—*Mineral colors* are those which are extracted from metals, and from their property of standing fire are used by enamellers. Colors have also been distinguished into changeable or permanent, dark or light, true or false.—*Changeable colors* are such as depend on the situation of the objects with respect to the eye, as that of a pigeon's neck, taffetas, &c.—*Permanent colors* are not exhibited by refraction, but by reflection.—*Dark colors* are black, and all others that are obscure and earthy, as umbre, bistre, &c.—*Light colors* comprehend the white, and all that approach to it.—*True colors* are such as retain their color without fading, in distinction from *false colors*, which either lose their color, or change to some other.

Colors are prepared either by grinding, washing, or steeping; the following are the principal colors used in painting:—*White*; namely, white-lead, eggshells burnt, pearl-white, Spanish-white, spodium, ceruss, &c.—*Black*; namely, lamp-black, ivory-black, blue-black, Indian-ink, and verditer burnt.—*Red*; namely, carmine, lake, rose-pink, red-ochre, Venetian-red, vermilion, red-lead, scarlet-ochre, common Indian-red, burnt terra di sienna, &c.—*Green*, i. e. green-bice, green-pink, verdigrise, sap-green, pink mixed with bice, and Prussian-blue mixed with some other color, &c.—*Yellow*; namely, orpiment, masticot, deep and light saffron, pink-yellow, dark and light, gamboge, turpeth mineral, yellow-ochre, Roman-ochre, gall-stone, &c.—*Blue*; namely, ultramarine, indigo, Prussian-blue, smalt, blue-bice, blue-verditer, &c.—*Brown*; namely, umber, Spanish-brown, brown-bistre, Cologne-earth, rust of iron, mummy, &c.

The colors used in dyeing are five, called *primary* or *mother colors*; namely, blue, red, yellow, brown, and black, from the various mixture and combination of which other shades of color are produced.

COLOR (*Bot.*) the following is a table of the primary colors, with some of their shades, which are enumerated by botanists.

WHITE, *albus*.	Iron-color, *gilvus*.
Full-white, *candidus*.	RED, *ruber*.
Water-color, *hyalinus*.	Flesh-color, *incarnatus*.
Ash-colored, *cinereus*.	Blood-colored, *sanguineus*.
Milky, *lacteus*.	Scarlet, *coccineus*.
BLACK, *niger*.	PURPLE, *purpureus*.
Pitch-black, *ater*.	Hyacinth, *hyacinthinus*.
Sooty, *fulliginosus*.	Rosy, *roseus*.
BROWN, *fuscus*.	Violet-color, *cærulo-purpureus*.
YELLOW, *luteus*.	
Saffron, *croceus*.	BLUE, *cæruleus*.
Bright-yellow, or straw-color, *flavus*.	Sapphire, *sapphirinus*.
	Azure, *cyaneus*.
Flame-color, *fulvus*.	GREEN, *viridis*.

COLOR (*Man.*) the principal colors of horses are the Bay, the Chesnut, the Black, the Brown, the Grey, the Sorrel, and the Roan, which is a mixture of various colors.

COLOR (*Her.*) is the tincture with which the field, or any part of an escutcheon or a bearing, is distinguished; of these there are seven; namely, *Yellow*, blazoned by the French word *or*, represents *sol*, the Sun, among the planets; *aurum*, Gold among metals; the Topaz among stones; and Wisdom, Riches, and Magnanimity among virtues.—*White*, blazoned by the French word *argent*, represents *luna*, the Moon, among planets; *argentum*, Silver among metals, Pearl among precious stones, and Chastity among virtues. These two are generally called metals rather than colors.—*Red*, blazoned by *gules*, represents Mars among the planets, Ruby among the stones, and Boldness among virtues.—*Blue*, blazoned *azure*, represents the planet Jupiter, the Sapphire among the stones, and great Renown among the virtues.—*Black*, which is blazoned *sable*, represents the planet Saturn, the Diamond among stones, and Constancy among virtues.—*Green*, in blazon *vert*, represents Venus among the planets, the Emerald among stones, and Joyful Love among the virtues. —*Purple*, in blazon *purpure*, represents Mercury among the planets, the Amethyst among stones, and Temperance among the virtues. To these may be added—*Orange*, which is compounded of red and yellow, and blazoned *tenne*, representing the Dragon's Head, one of the nodes, and the Hyacinth among stones.—*Murrey*, in blazon, *sanguine*, i. e. blood-red, represents the other node, the Dragon's Tail, and the Sardonyx among the precious stones. Colors and metals, when engraved, are distinguished by points, hatched-lines, &c. as small dots or points for *or*, plain for *argent*, &c. [vide *Heraldry*]

COLOR (*Law*) signifies a plea that is probable, though really false, which is put in with an intent to draw the trial of the cause from the jury to the judges.—*Color of office*, an evil or unjust act committed by the countenance of an officer, or under the color of an office.

COLOR (*Mil.*) vide *Colors.*—*Color-Guard*, vide *Guard*.

TO COLOR *strangers' goods* (*Law*) is when a freeman permits a foreigner to enter goods in his name at the custom house to pay but single duty when he ought by law to pay double duty.

COLOR-MAN (*Com.*) one who prepares and sells colors.

COLORA'TION (*Metal.*) the brightening of gold or silver.

COLORA'TUS (*Bot.*) coloured, an epithet for a leaf that is of any other color than green, as the calyx in *Bartsia*.

CO'LORING (*Paint.*) the manner of applying colors to a picture, so that, by their apt union and blending, they may give a due proportion of light and shade, an agreeable contrast or opposition, a suitable degradation or management of their degrees, &c.

CO'LORS (*Mil.*) banners, flags, and ensigns used in the army. This word is used in the same sense in speaking of the navy.—*Camp-colors* are a small sort of colors placed on the right and left of the parade.—*A pair of colors* is a term in the British service denoting an ensigncy, or the first commissioned appointment in the army.

COLORS (*Ecc.*) in the Latin and Greek churches, serve to distinguish several mysteries or festivals, as white for the mysteries of our Saviour, the feast of the Virgin, &c.; red for the holy sacrament, &c. They were formerly more used than they are at present.

COLOSSI'NUS *color* (*Ant.*) a bright purple color, so called from Colossis, a city of Troas. *Plin.* l. 21, c. 9.

COLO'SSUS (*Ant.*) a large statue at Rhodes representing a giant, which was seventy cubits high, and between whose legs ships sailed; hence all very high or large figures are called colossal. *Plin.* l. 34, c. 7; *Fest. de Verb. Signif.*

COLOSTRA'TI (*Ant.*) children sucking the first milk after their birth. *Plin.* l. 28, c. 9.

COLOSTRA'TIO (*Nat.*) a disease incident to the young which suck the dam's milk two days after the birth. *Plin.* l. 11, c. 31.

COLO'STRUM (*Med.*) from κίλλα, glue; the first milk of any animal after bringing forth, which is commonly called *Beestings*. This milk is found to be a purgative, and serves both as an aliment and a medicine.

COLOTO'IDES (*Med.*) κωλωτοιδης, from κωλώτης, a spotted lizard, and ἰδος, the likeness, variegated like colotes; an epithet applied by Hippocrates to the excrements.

CO'LOUR (*Opt. &c.*) vide *Color.*

CO'LOURS (*Mil.*) vide *Colors*.

COLPOCE'LE (*Med.*) from κόλπος, the vagina, and κήλη, a tumor; a hernia forced into the vagina.

COLPO'DA (*Conch.*) a genus of animals, Class *Vermes*, Order *Infusoria*.

Generic Character. Worm invisible to the naked eye, very simple and pellucid.

Species. The principal species are the *Colpoda meleagris, cucullus, pyrum*, &c.

COLPO'ON (*Bot.*) a species of the *Euonymus* of Linnæus.

COLPOPTO'SIS (*Med.*) from κόλπος, vagina, and πίπτω, to fall; a bearing down of the vagina.

CO'LTER (*Husband.*) or *Coulter*, a piece of iron in a plough, which serves to cut up the ground.

COLT-E'VIL (*Vet.*) a preternatural swelling in the testes of horses.

COLTS-FOOT (*Bot.*) a perennial plant of a rough mucilaginous taste, much esteemed for its demulcent and pectoral virtues. It is the *Tussilago farfara*, &c. of Linnæus.

CO'LT'S-TOOTH (*Vet.*) an imperfect or superfluous tooth in young horses.

CO'LUBER (*Zool.*) Viper, a genus of animals, Class *Amphibia*, Order *Serpentes*.

Generic Character. Plates on the belly.—*Scales* under the tail.

Species. The species of this tribe are very numerous, but principally distinguished by the number of plates or scales on the body, or by their colour.

COLUBRI'NA (*Bot.*) Wild Briony.

COLUBRI'NUM *Lignum* (*Bot.*) Snakewood, a sort of wood brought from the Indies, which is so called from the snake-like contortions of its roots. It is solid, ponderous, acrid, extremely bitter, and inodorous.

CO'LUM (*Chem.*) a filtre.

COLU'MBA (*Bot.*) vide *Calumba*.

COLUMBA (*Orn.*) Pigeon, a genus of animals of the class *Aves*, order *Passeres*.

Generic Character. Bill straight.—*Nostrils* half-covered with a soft tumid membrane.

Species. The principal species are the—*Columba domestica*, the Dove and Pigeon, of which there are many varieties. [vide *Dove, Pigeon*]—*Columba montana*, Partridge Pigeon.—*Columba Caribbea*, Ring-tailed Pigeon.—*Columba coronata*, the Great-crowned Indian Pigeon.—*Columba cristata*, Lesser-crowned Pigeon. — *Columba oenas*, Stock Pigeon.—*Columba palumbus*, Ring Dove, having a white crescent on each side its neck.—*Columba Suratensis*, Surat Turtle.—*Columba viridis*, Green Turtle. *Columba melanocephala*, Black-capped Pigeon.—*Columba Turtur*, Turtle Dove.—*Columba risoria*, Collared Turtle. —*Columba migratoria*, Passenger Pigeon, &c.

COLU'MBAC *Noachi* (*Astron.*) Noah's Dove, a small constellation in the southern hemisphere consisting of ten stars.

COLU'MBAR (*Ant.*) 1. A sort of chain for the neck, so called from its resemblance to a pigeon hole, a pillory. *Plaut. Rud.* act. 3, scen. 6, v. 50.

— *Illic in columbum, credo, leno vertitur,*
Nam in columbari colium haud multo post erit.

Prisc. de Art. Gram. l. 5. 2. Holes in the sides of ships

resembling pigeon holes, through which the oars were put. *Fest. de Verb. Sig.; Isid. Orig.* l. 19, c. 2. 3. The mortoise holes wherein the ends of rafters were fastened; also holes and spaces whereout the water ran after it was taken up by the watermill-wheel. *Vitruv.* l. 10, c. 9; *Gyrald. Nav.* c. 11; *Cœl. Rhodig. Ant. Lect.* l. 21, c. 21; *Bald. Lex. Vitruv.*

COLUMBIC *acid (Chem.)* an acid supposed to be produced from *columbium*.

COLUMBINE *(Bot.)* a perennial, the *Aquilegia* of Linnæus.

COLUMBINE *(Her.)* this flower is borne in the arms of the company of cooks. [vide *Cooks*]

COLUMBITE *(Min.)* a mineral ore, a species of *Tantalum*.

COLUMBIUM *(Min.)* a mineral. [vide *Tantalum*]

COLUMBOLE *(Bot.)* vide *Calumba*.

COLUMELLA *(Bot.)* the central pillar in a capsule, which connects the inside with the seeds, and, taking its rise from the receptacle, has the seeds fixed to it all round.

COLUMELLA *(Med.)* an inflammation of the *uvula* and *clitoris*, when they are extended in length like a little column.

COLUMELLA *(Conch.)* the upright pillar in the centre of most of the univalve shells.

COLUMELLA'RES *(Anat.)* the dog-teeth. *Varr. de Re Rust.* l. 2, c. 7.

COLUMN *(Archit.)* in Latin *columna*, so called because it sustains columen, i. e. *culmen*, the top or upper part of a building; a cylindrical pillar formed for the support and ornament of a building. It is the principal part in an architectural order, and is composed of three parts, the *base*, the *shaft*, and the *capital*, each of which is subdivided into smaller members, called *mouldings*. [vide *Architecture*] The column is distinguished in respect to construction and form, materials, decoration, disposition, and destination.

Columns, as to their construction and form, are distinguished into the—*Doric column*, a delicate column of the Doric order, adorned with flutings, the height of which is between seven and eight diameters. The Grecian Doric, which is the original form of this order, has no base, and varies in many other respects from what now bears this name, which is only an imitation made by the Romans.—*Ionic column*, a still more delicate column than the preceding, being nine diameters long. It is distinguished from the rest by the volutes in its capital. —*Corinthian column*, the richest and most delicate of all, is ten diameters in height, and its capital is adorned with caulicles or rows of leaves.—*Composite column*, which is also ten diameters in height, is adorned with angular volutes like the Ionic, and with leaves like the Corinthian. — *Tuscan column* is the simplest and shortest of all, its height being 7 diameters, or 14 modules, and it diminishes ¼ of its diameter. Besides this distinction of orders, there are also—*Columns in bands*, or *tambours*, so called when the shaft is formed of courses of stone of a less height than the diameters of the column.—*Columns in trencheons*, when the shaft is formed in courses of greater height than the diameter of the column.—*Banded columns*, when the shafts of columns consist of plain or ornamented cinctures.—*Attic column*, an insulated pilaster, having four equal faces of the highest proportion.—*Conical column*, that which has the superior diameter of its shaft less than the inferior. —*Conoidal column*, that which has also the superior diameter of the shaft less than the inferior, but its exterior sides are convex.—*Cylindrical columns*, those which have the extreme diameters of the shafts of equal circles.— *Cylindroidal*, or *elliptic columns*, those whose sections are all similar, and equal ellipses alike situated.—*Gothic column*, one that is too short for its bulk, or too slender for its height.—*Polygonal columns*, those having the horizontal sections of their shafts similar, polygons alike situated.

Columns, as to their materials, are distinguished into— *Moulded columns*, those which are formed by cementing gravel and flints of different colours.—*Fusible columns*, those which are formed of fusible matter, as metals, glass, &c.—*Transparent column*, a column formed of transparent materials, as the columns in the church of St. Mark, formed of transparent alabaster.—*Scagliola columns*, those which are constructed with a kind of plaster, in such manner as to imitate marble both in the polish and the colour.—*Masonic columns*, columns built of rough stone or compass bricks, and cased with stucco. —*Incrustated columns* are formed of several ribs or thin shells of fine marble, or other rare stone, cemented upon a mould of stone or brick.—*Joinery column*, a column made of strong timbers, joined, glued, and pinned together. This is mostly hollow, and fluted.—*Water column*, one whose shaft is formed of a large jet d'eau, which being hollow, serves to send forth a column of water.

Columns, as to their decoration, are distinguished into— *Pastoral column*, one that represents the trunk of a tree, with the bark and knots.—*Diminished column*, one that diminishes from the base upwards, in imitation of trees. —*Carolitic columns*, those which are adorned with foliage. —*Cabled*, or *rudented columns*, which have the flutings of the shafts filled with astragals to about one-third of their height.—*Fluted columns*, those which have flutes cut in their sides, otherwise called *channelled*, or striated columns.—*Twisted columns*, those which make several circumvolutions in the height of the shaft.—*Serpentine column*, a column formed of three serpents twisted together, the heads of which form the capital.

Columns, as to their disposition, are distinguished into— *Angular columns*, those which are insulated in the corners of a portico, or any building.—*Cantoned columns*, those which are placed one at each corner of a square pier.— *Coupled columns*, those which are disposed in pairs in the same range or line, so as to touch at their bases. —*Doubled columns*, those which in any range of columns seem to have their two shafts penetrating each other.— *Engaged columns*, such as seem to penetrate the wall.— *Insulated columns*, those which are free, and detached on all sides.—*Flanked column*, one that has a semipilaster on each side of it.—*Grouped columns* stand in threes or fours on the same pedestal.—*Inserted column*, one that is let into a wall.—*Median columns*, two columns of a portico, which are placed in the middle of the range, at a wider interval than any other two in the same range.— *Niched column*, one placed in a nich.

Columns, as respect their destination, are distinguished into —*Agricultural columns*, which are raised for the purpose of agricultural information.—*Astronomical column*, an observatory consisting of a single column, with a winding staircase.—*Boundary* or *limitrophus column*, one that marks the frontiers of a country.—*Chronological* or *historic column*, one that bears an inscription of historical events in the order of time, or the account of any particular event. [vide *Columna*]—*Funeral column*, one that is placed over a tomb, bearing an inscription relative to the deceased.—*Gnomonic column*, a cylinder on which the hour of the day is represented by the shadow of the style.—*Triumphal column*, a column erected in honour of any distinguished person, as the columns of Trajan and Antonine. [vide *Columna*]—*Itinerary columns*, columns constructed with several faces, and placed at the intersection of two or more roads, to point out the different routes by suitable inscriptions.—*Legal column*, a column created in a public place among the Lacedemonians, on which were inscribed the fundamental laws of the state.—*Zoophoric column*, a kind of statuary column bearing the figure of some animal.

COLUMN (*Mil.*) a body of troops in deep files and narrow front, so disposed as to move in regular succession. Several bodies may move in columns who are intended to march successively in order of battle. A column is *close* which forms a compact body with little space between, and *open* when it has intervals between the divisions.

COLUMN (*Print.*) any printed matter in a page where the words are ranged vertically in an even order one after the other.

COLU'MNA (*Ant.*) the column was in frequent use among the Romans, of which the following are the principal entitled to notice, namely—*Columna lactaria*, or *lactary column*, a column erected in the herb market at Rome, where children were placed that had been abandoned by their unnatural parents. *Fest. de Signif. Verb.*—*Columna milliaris*, or *milliarium aureum*, a gilded pillar erected by Augustus in the forum where all the highways met in one common centre, and from which the miles to different parts were reckoned. This pillar is said to be still extant. [vide *Milliarium*]—*Columna rostrata*, a pillar erected in commemoration of a naval victory, and adorned with the beaks or prows of the ships which were taken, the first of which was erected on occasion of the naval victory gained by Duillius, of which the annexed figure, on the reverse of a medal of Titus, affords an illustration, bearing the inscription TRibunitiâ Potestate IX. IMPerator XV. COnSul VII. Pater Patriæ. *Quint.* l. 1, c. 7.—*Columna bellica*, a small pillar behind the circus, which was so called because the herald used to throw a spear from that point, as an act of defiance to the enemies of Rome, and as the prelude to a proclamation of war. *Ovid. Fest.* l. 6.—*Columna Trajani* and *Columna Antonini*, triumphal columns so called from the emperors whose exploits were commemorated thereon. Trajan's pillar, which was set up by the senate in honour of him, consists of 24 large pieces of marble, is 128 feet high, and ascended by a staircase of 185 steps, having 45 windows. The pillar of Antoninus is 176 feet high, having 56 windows, and a staircase of 106 steps. Both these columns are still standing, the former in Trajan's Forum, and the latter in the Campus Martius. *Plin.* l. 35, c. 5; *Nardin. Rom. Vet.; Marlian. Topogr. &c. apud Græv. Ant. Rom.* tom. 4.

COLUMNA (*Ant.*) a name given to several parts of the body resembling a column or pillar in shape, as—*Columna nasi*, the fleshy and lowest part of the nose.—*Columna oris*, the same as the *uvula*.—*Columna cordis*, or *columnæ carneæ*, small long fleshy productions in the ventricles of the heart.

COLU'MNAR (*Bot.*) an epithet signifying like the shaft of a column. [vide *Teres*]

COLUMNA'RIA (*Ant.*) vent-holes in aqueducts. *Vitruv.* l. 8, c. 7.

COLUMNA'RII (*Ant.*) bankrupts and spendthrifts, who being much in debt, were often sued and brought to the Columna-Mœnia, where actions for debt were tried. *Cic. ad Fam.* l. 8, ep. 9; *Manut. in Cic.; Turneb. Adv.* l. 17, c. 12.

COLUMNA'RIUM (*Ant.*) a tribute that was exacted for the pillars of private houses. *Cæs. de Bell. Civ.* l. 3, c. 32; *Cic. ad Attic.* l. 13, ep. 6.

COLUMNE'A (*Bot.*) a genus of plants, Class 14 *Didynamia*, Order 2 *Angiospermia*.
Generic Characters. CAL. *perianth* one-leafed; *divisions* erect.—COR. one-petalled; *tube* long; *border* two-lipped; *upper lip* straight; *lower lip* three-parted.—STAM. *filaments* four; *anthers* simple.—PIST. *germ* ovate; *style* filiform; *stigma* bifid.—PER. *capsule* two-celled; *seeds* numerous.
Species. The species are shrubs, as—*Columnea scandens*, Climbing Columnea, native of the Caribbees.—*Columnea hirsuta*, Achimenes, &c. seu *Rapunculus*, &c. Hairy Columnea, native of Jamaica.—*Columnea rutilans*, native of Jamaica.—*Columnea longifolia*, Achimenes, &c. *Babel*, &c. seu *Sesamum*, &c. Long-leaved Columnea.

COLUMNI'FERÆ (*Bot.*) the name of the thirty-fourth order in Linnæus' Fragments of a Natural Method, &c. including the *Malvaceous*, or *Mallow-like plants*, which are to be found in the class *Monodelphia*.

COLU'MNULA (*Bot.*) the same as *Columella*.

COLU'PPAL (*Bot.*) the *Illicebrum sessile* of Linnæus.

COLU'RA (*Ant.*) a name given to beasts without a tail, which it was not lawful to offer in sacrifice.

COLU'RES (*Astron.*) κόλυροι, two great imaginary circles which intersect one another at right angles. They are so called because to all, who are not living under the equinoctial, they appear κόλυροι, mutilated; i. e. as if with the tail cut off. The colures are called equinoctial and solstitial.—The *equinoctial colure* is that which passes through the Pole and the points *Aries* and *Libra*, making the seasons Spring and Autumn. The *solstitial colure* shows the solstitial points cutting *Cancer* and *Capricorn*, and making Summer and Winter. [vide *Astronomy*, and *Globe*] *Hipparch. ad Phænom. Eudox.* l. 1, c. 27; *Proc. de Sphær.; Cleomed. de Sphær.; Macrob. in Somn. Scip.* l. 1, c. 15.

COLU'RIUM (*Surg.*) a tent to thrust into a sore, to prevent a defluxion of humours.

CO'LUS JOVIS (*Bot.*) the same as *Sclarea*.

COLU'STRUM (*Nat.*) vide *Colostrum*.

COLU'TEA (*Bot.*) κολυτέα, Bladder-Senna, a plant described by Theophrastus. *Hist. Plant.* l. 3, c. 17.

COLUTEA, *in the Linnean system*, a genus of plants, Class 17 *Diadelphia*, Order 4 *Decandria*.
Generic Characters. CAL. *perianth* one-leaved—COR. *papilionaceous*.—STAM. *filaments*, diadelphous; *anthers* simple.—PIST. *germ* oblong; *style* ascending; *stigma* is a bearded line extended from the middle of the style to its tip.—PER. *legume* very large; *seeds* several.
Species. The species are shrubs, annuals, biennials, and perennials. The following are shrubs, namely—*Colutea arborescens*, &c. seu *Vesicaria*, Common Bladder-Senna, native of England.—*Colutea Pocockii*, seu *foliolis*, &c. seu *halepica*, &c. seu *istria*, &c. Pocock's Bladder-Senna, native of the East.—*Colutea frutescens*, Scarlet Bladder-Senna, native of the Cape of Good Hope. The following are annuals or perennials, namely—*Colutea herbacea*, seu *foliolis*, &c. seu *annua*, &c. seu *Africana*, &c. Annual Bladder-Senna, an annual or biennial, native of the Cape of Good Hope.—*Colutea perennis*, Perennial Bladder-Senna, a perennial, native of the Cape of Good Hope, &c. *Dod. Pempt.; Bauh. Hist. Plant.; Park. Theat. Botan.; Raii Hist. Plant.; Tournef. Instit. &c.*

CO'LY (*Orn.*) a bird that inhabits the Cape of Good Hope, the *Colius* of Linnæus.

COLY'DIUM (*Ent.*) a division of the genus *Dermestes*, including those insects which have four clavate feelers, the last joint longer than the other.

COLYMBA'DES (*Ant.*) pickled olives, so light that they swim in the pickle.

COLY'MBUS (*Orn.*) a genus of animals, of the Class *Aves*, Order *Anseres*.
Generic Character. Bill toothless, pointed.—Throat toothed.—Nostrils linear.—Legs fettered, and unfit for walking.
Species. This genus of animals is distinguished, in English, into the Guillemots, which have feet three-toed; the Divers, which have feet four-toed and palmate; and Grebes, which have their feet four-toed and lobed.

COLY'TEA (*Bot.*) vide *Colutea*.

CO'MA (*Bot.*) a sort of *Bracto*, which terminates in a tuft, or bush, as in Crown Imperial, &c. A spike of flowers terminated by a *coma* is called *comose*.

COMA (*Med.*) κῶμα, a preternatural propensity to sleep, according to the explanation of the term as given by Galen in his Exegesis, and elsewhere. It is now generally taken for a lethargic drowsiness.—*Coma Vigil*, a strong disposition to sleep without being able to do so, which Hippocrates denominates κῶμα ὐχ ὑπνῶδες ἢ ἄγρυπνον, and considers it as a usual symptom of a *phrenitis*. Hippocrat. Epid. l. 3; Foes. Œconom. Hippocrat.; Gal. Comm. in loc cit.—*Coma somnolentum*, when the patient continues in a profound sleep, and on waking finds himself unable to keep his eyes open.

COMA *Berenices* (*Astron.*) Berenice's Hair, a modern constellation, in the Northern Hemisphere, composed of unformed stars to the number of forty-three, between the Lion's Tail and Bootes.

COMAGE'NA (*Bot.*) a kind of herb, (so called from Comagene,) a country of Syria, from which was made an ointment called *Comagenum medicamentum*. Plin. l. 10, c. 22.

COMA'RCHUS (*Ant.*) the governor of a town or city.

COMARO'IDES (*Bot.*) a species of the *Potentilla*.

CO'MARUM (*Bot.*) the fruit of the Arbute-tree. [vide *Comarus*]

COMARUM, *in the Linnean system*, a genus of plants Class 12 *Icosandria*, Order 5 *Polygynia*.
  Generic Characters. CAL. *perianth* one-leaved; *alternate divisions* smaller.—COR. *petals* five.—STAM. *filaments* twenty; *anthers* lunular.—PIST. *germs* numerous; *styles* simple; *stigmas* simple.—PER. none; *common receptacle of the seeds* ovate; *seeds* numerous.
  Species. The only species is *Comarum palustre*, *Fragaria*, &c. *Potentilla*, &c. *Quinquefolium*, &c. seu *Pentaphyllum*, &c. Marsh Cinquefoil, a perennial, native of Europe.

CO'MARUS (*Bot.*) κόμαρος, the fruit of which, κόμαρον, is called in Latin *Unedo*, which, according to Pliny, signifies not to be eaten more than once at a time on account of its unpleasant taste. According to Theophrastus it is a species of the *arbutus*. Theophrast. l. 3, c. 16; Plin. l. 15, c. 24.

COMA'TA (*Med.*) an order of diseases in the class *Neuroses* in Cullen's system, consisting of those disorders in which the power of voluntary motion is suspended.

COMATO'SE (*Med.*) having a strong propensity to sleep.

COMB *of a ship* (*Mar.*) a small piece of timber set under the lowest part of the beak-head, which assists in bringing the tacks a-board.

COMBARO'NES (*Law*) formerly signified the fellow barons, or commonalty of the Cinque Ports; but, the title of baron being now given to their representatives in parliament, it implies a colleague, or fellow member, as the baron and his combaron. Placit. Temp. Ed. 1. & Ed. 2.

CO'MBAT (*Mil.*) a battle between individuals, in general not more than two.

CO'MBATANT (*Her.*) an epithet for two lions in a coat of arms, when they are borne rampant with their faces towards each other in a fighting posture.

CO'MBATANTS (*Mil.*) in French *Cumbattans*, troops engaged in action; in distinction from *Non-Combattans*, persons about an army, whose employments are purely civil.

CO'MBER (*Ich.*) a kind of fish, the *Labrus comber* of Linnæus.

COMBINA'TION (*Chem.*) a union of two or more substances in such a manner as to form a new compound, in distinction from a mere mechanical mixture, in which each substance retains its own properties.

COMBINATION (*Math.*) the alternations or variations of any number of quantities, letters, sounds, and the like in all possible ways: thus, the number of combinations which the twenty-four letters of the alphabet are said to amount to is 1,391,724,288,887,252,999,425,128,493,402,200. On the same principle two square pieces, each divided diagonally into two colours, may be arranged and combined sixty-four different ways.

COMBINATION (*Rhet.*) a figure of speech which consists in the immediate repetition of the same word.

COMBLEAU' (*Mil.*) French for a cord which is used in loading and unloading pieces of artillery, &c.

COMBRE'TUM (*Bot.*) a genus of plants, Class 8 *Octandria*, Order 1 *Monogynia*.
  Generic Characters. CAL. *perianth* one-leaved.—COR. *petals* four or five.—STAM. *filaments* eight or ten; *anthers* a little oblong.—PIST. *germ* inferior; *style* bristleform; *stigma* acute.—PER. none; *seed* single.
  Species. The species are perennials or shrubs, as the—*Combretum laxum*, seu *Gawia*, &c. a perennial, native of South America.—*Combretum secundum*, seu *laxum*, &c. a shrub, native of Carthagena.—*Combretum purpureum*, a shrub, native of Madagascar.—*Combretum decandrum*, seu *Cristaria*, &c. a shrub, native of the East Indies.—*Combretum alternifolium*, a shrub, native of Carthagena.

CO'MBUST (*Astrol.*) i. e. burnt; an epithet for a planet which is not above 8 degrees 30 minutes distant from the sun.

COMBU'STIBLES (*Mil.*) combustible materials used in offensive and defensive operations.

COMBUSTIBLES (*Chem.*) a term applied to all substances which have the property of uniting with the supporters of combustion. [vide *Combustion*] Combustibles are either simple, compound, or combustible oxides.—*Simple Combustibles* are sulphur, phosphorus, carbon, hydrogen, and all the metals except, as is supposed, gold, silver, and mercury.—*Compound Combustibles* are compounds formed by the simple combustibles uniting together two and two.—*Combustible Oxides* are simple combustibles combined with a dose of oxygen.

COMBU'STIO PECUNIÆ (*Law*) the ancient way of trying mixt and corrupt money, by melting it down upon payment into the Exchequer.

COMBU'STION (*Astron.*) vide *Combust*.

COMBUSTION (*Chem.*) the decomposition of certain substances by means of fire, or, as in modern language, decomposition accompanied with light and heat. Substances may be divided, as respects combustion, into combustibles, supporters of combustion, and incombustibles.—*Combustibles*. [vide *Combustibles*]—*Supporters*, or *Supporters of Combustion*, i. e. bodies not, strictly speaking, capable of undergoing combustion; but which must needs be present in other bodies that are to undergo this process.—*Incombustibles*, or bodies not capable of undergoing combustion, or supporting combustion, of which there is at present only one such body known, namely *Azote*. In the process of *combustion* every combustible body unites with its *supporter*, from which combination arises a new compound, called the *Product of Combustion*, which is always either an acid or an oxide. [vide *Chemistry*]

COME (*Mar.*) an order given on different occasions on board a vessel, as "Come not near!" in French, *pas au vent*, for the helmsman not to steer so near the wind. "Come up the capstan!" in French, *devire, ou cavire au cabestan*, to turn it the contrary way to which it was steering. "Come up the tackle-fall!" in French, *largue le palan*, to slacken it gently. "To come home," is said of the anchor when it loosens from the ground by the effort of the cable, and approaches the place where the ship floated at the length of her moorings. "To come up with," in French, *joindre*, is to overtake a vessel which is pursued.

TO COME (*Mil.*) is used in different phrases, as "To come in," speaking of soldiers who offer themselves as volunteers, recruits, &c. "To come over," said of those who join the enemy's forces. "To come into," i. e. to come to the help of a person, army, or body of men. "To come up," to overtake a force that is retreating.

COME (*Husband.*) a name given to the acrospire, or sprout, that comes out at the end of malt.

COME' (*Mus.*) Italian for *as*, is used sometimes in compositions or music books, as *come sopra*, as above, or as before, alluding to the style of some performance before mentioned. *Come sta*, as it stands, implying that the performer is not to embellish, but to take it as it stands.

COMEDO'NES (*Ent.*) a sort of worms which eat into the skin and devour the flesh.

CO'MES (*Mus.*) Latin for a companion or follower; a term formerly applied to the voices or instruments which followed the *dux*, or leading performer.

CO'MET (*Astron.*) κομήτης, a heavenly body appearing at uncertain periods, which has, during the time of its appearance, a motion very similar to those of the planets, except that its orbs are more eccentric. It derives its name from κομάω, to be hairy; because of its hairy appearance.

Comets are vulgarly called Blazing Stars, and distinguished into *tailed*, *bearded*, and *hairy*, according to the different appearances which they assume in different positions with the sun; but by astronomers it is divided into distinct parts, namely, the *Nucleus, Head, Coma*, and *Tail*.—The *Nucleus* is the dense part of the comet, supposed to be of a nature similar to that of other planetary bodies.—The *Head* is that part in which the *nucleus* is involved, which appears with a fainter light.—The *Coma* is a faint light surrounding the head; and the *Tail* is the long train of light with which these bodies are commonly attended.

The nature of comets has been a subject of much dispute among naturalists. Aristotle supposed them to be accidental meteors; but Seneca regarded them as permanent bodies, which is now become the general opinion.

COMET (*Her.*) This celestial body is occasionally borne in coat-armour, as in the annexed figure. "He beareth *azure* a blazing star or comet streaming in bend proper." Name *Cartwright*.

COMETA'RIUM (*Mech.*) a machine constructed to represent the revolution of a comet about the sun.

COME'TES (*Bot.*) a genus of plants, Class 4 *Tetrandria*, Order 1 *Monogynia*.

Generic Characters. CAL. involucre three-flowered; *leaflets* oblong.—COR. none.—STAM. *filaments* four; *anthers* roundish.—PIST. *germ* roundish; *style* filiform; *stigma* three-cleft.—PER. *capsule* tricoccous; *seed* solitary.

Species. The only species is the *Cometes alterniflora*, seu *Clinopodium*, an annual, native of Surat.

COMETO'GRAPHY (*Astron.*) from κομήτης, a comet, and γράφω, to describe; a description of, or a discourse upon, comets.

COMFREY (*Bot.*) a herb, the *Symphitum* of Linnæus, the root of which abounds in a pure tasteless mucilage, and is therefore useful as an emollient or demulcent.

COMIC (*Poet.*) an epithet for what belongs to comedy, as the comic muse, or a comic actor.

COMING-TO (*Mar.*) or *Coming-up*, in French *embarder au vent*, the place where the vessel stops in approaching the wind.

COMINGE (*Mil.*) French for a shell of extreme magnitude, which takes its name from the person who invented it.

COMITA'TU *commisso* (*Law*) a writ of commission, whereby the sheriff is authorized to take upon him the charge of the county.—*Comitatu et castro commisso*, a writ whereby the charge of the county, together with the keeping of a castle, is committed to the sheriff. *Reg. Orig.* 295.

COMITA'TUS (*Archæol.*) 1. A county. 2. A territory or jurisdiction of a particular place. *Matth. Parr. Ann.* 1234.

COMI'TIA (*Ant.*) an assembly of the people convened by proper authority, for the purpose of choosing magistrates and making laws. It was likewise called *comitia calata*, from the old Latin *calo*, to call or summon; because it was summoned by the public crier on special occasion. The comitia was first held in the Campus Martius, but afterwards, occasionally, in the Comitium. [vide *Comitium*] The people also, originally, gave their votes *vivâ voce*; but in process of time this was superseded by the use of *tabellæ*, or tablets.

The comitia was distinguished, according to the mode of voting, into the *Comitia curiata*, the *Comitia centuriata*, and the *Comitia tributa*.—*Comitia curiata*, so called because the people gave their votes by *curia*, or parishes, was instituted by Romulus, and most commonly held for the purpose of choosing the priests, or making particular laws.—*Comitia centuriata*, at which the people gave their suffrages by centuries, was instituted by Servius, not only for the appointment of the chief magistrates, but for making laws, deciding causes, and determining the most important concerns of state. As the consuls were specially chosen at this comitia, it was also called, on that occasion, the *Comitia consularia*, which was held at the end of July, or the beginning of August. At its first institution the kings alone had the power of calling the *comitia centuriata*, but afterwards this right was vested in the chief officers, and exercised most commonly by the consuls.—*Comitia tributa*, so called because the people gave their votes by tribes, is supposed to have been instituted in the year 263 U. C. when it was convened by Sp. Sicinius, the tribune, on the occasion of Coriolanus. This assembly was convened by the tribunes independently of the senate, for the purpose of enacting such laws as were proposed by the plebeian officers, which enactments were distinguished by the name of *plebis-cita*. *Dionys. Hal.* l. 4, &c.; *Liv.* l. 1, c. 44, 60, &c.; *Aul. Gel.* l. 13, c. 15; l. 15, c. 27; *Manut. de Com.*; *Sigon. de Antiq. Jur. Civ. Roman.* l. 1, c. 17 *apud Græv. Thes. Antiq. Rom.* tom. 1, &c.

COMITIA'LIS MORBUS (*Med.*) another name for the epilepsy, or falling sickness; so called, because if any person in the Roman comitia was attacked with it, the assembly was dissolved.

COMITI'SSÆ PULVIS (*Med.*) Peruvian Bark.

COMITI'VA (*Archæol.*) 1. A companion or fellow traveller. *Brompt. Regn. H.* 2. 2. A band of robbers. *Walsingh. Ann.* 1366.

COMI'TIUM (*Ant.*) a part of the Roman Forum where the *Comitiata curiata* used sometimes to assemble, and causes were heard.

Plaut. Poen. act. 3, scen. 6, v. 12.

Cras mane quæso in comitio estote obviam.

Plaut. Curc.

Qui perjurum convenire vult hominem mitto in comitium.

Varr. de Ling. Lat. l. 4, c. 32; *Cic. in Verr.* 3; *Liv.* l. 1, c. 36; *Plin.* l. 4, ep. 2; *Sigon de Jud. &c. apud Græv. Thes. Antiq. Rom.* tom. 1.

CO'MMA (*Gram.*) κόμμα, one of the points or stops used, marked thus (,) to denote the smallest pause, or rest, between words or sentences.

COMMA (*Mus.*) a name formerly given to the 9th part of a tone, or the interval whereby a semitone or a perfect tone exceeds the imperfect.

COMMAGE'NUM (*Med.*) vide *Comagena*.

COMMA'ND (*Mil.*) or *the word of Command*, a term used by the officers, in exercise or upon service; also, "To have in command," a form of expression used by any one writing with the authority or instruction of the Commander-in-

Chief.—*Command*, in French *commandement*, signifies also a particular situation in a fortification, which is differently distinguished, as —*A command in front*, when any eminence is directly facing the work which it commands.—*A command in rear*, when the same is behind the work.—*A command by enfilade*, when an eminence is situated along the line of any work.

COMMANDA'NT (*Mil.*) the officer who has the command of a garrison, fort, castle, &c. in distinction from the *commander*, which is commonly used for one who commands a body of men.

COMMANDANT (*Mar.*) that officer on whom the command devolves in absence of the commander-in-chief, to which it is usual to prefix his rank, as Lieutenant-Commandant, Captain-Commandant.

COMMA'NDE (*Mil.*) French for a rope made use of in pontoons.

COMMANDE' (*Mil.*) a French term signifying to be under orders.

COMMA'NDEMENT (*Mil.*) a French term signifying any spot that is higher than another; it is called *simple* when the difference between the two heights is 9 feet only; *double* when 18, and so on progressively. [vide *Command*] —*Commandement ordre de*, a right of command which formerly existed in the French service, between officers of infantry and cavalry. In fortified towns this right belonged to the infantry, and in the open country to the cavalry.

COMMA'NDER (*Mil.*) he who has the command of a body of men. — *Commander in chief*, in the British army, is he who has the supreme command over all his Majesty's land-forces in Great Britain, and acts immediately for the King.

COMMANDER *in chief* (*Mar.*) the chief admiral in any port, or on any station, appointed to hold command over all other admirals within that jurisdiction. — *Commander*, otherwise called the *Master*, is an officer next in rank to a post-captain, who has the command of a ship of war under 18 guns, a sloop of war, armed ship, or bomb-vessel.

COMMANDER, *Knight* (*Her.*) vide *Knight*.

COMMANDER (*Mech.*) a beetle or rammer used by paviours.

COMMA'NDERY (*Archæol.*) a certain benefice belonging to a military order; as the messuage and tenements of lands, which belonged to the priory of St. John of Jerusalem, which were given to Henry VIII. was called a commandery. *Stat.* 32, *Hen.* 8, c. 20.

COMMA'NDING *ground* (*Mil.*) a rising ground which overlooks any strong place: this may be either front, reverse, or enfilade. [vide *Command*]

COMMANDING *signs* (*Astron.*) the first signs of the zodiac are so called, namely, Aries, Taurus, Gemini, Cancer, Leo, and Virgo.

COMMA'NDMENT (*Law*) is when either the King or his justices commit a person to prison upon their authority.

COMMANDMENT (*Fort.*) is the height of nine feet which one place has above another.

COMMA'NSUM (*Med.*) vide *Apophlegmatismus*.

COMMA'RCHIO (*Archæol.*) confines of land.

COMMEA'TILIS *miles* (*Ant.*) a soldier who is allowed meat and commission bread for his pay.

COMMEATU'RA (*Archæol.*) another name for a commandery.

COMMELI'NA (*Bot.*) a genus of plants, Class 3 *Triandria*, Order 1 *Monogynia*.
Generic Characters. CAL. *spathe* cordate.—COR. *petals* six; *nectaries* three.—STAM. *filaments* three; *anthers* ovate.—PIST. *germ* superior; *style* subulate; *stigma* simple.—PER. *capsule* naked; *seeds* two.
Species. The species are perennials or annuals. The following are perennials, namely, the—*Commelina africana*, African Commelina, native of Æthiopia.—*Commelina benghalensis*, &c. seu *Ephemerum*, &c. East Indian Commelina, native of Bengal.—*Commelina erecta*, seu *corollis*, &c. seu *foliis*, &c. a native of Virginia.—*Commelina virginica*, seu *Ephemerum*, &c. native of Virginia.—*Commelina tuberosa*, seu *corollis*, &c. seu *foliis*, &c. seu *radice*, &c. Tuberous-rooted Commelina, native of Mexico.—*Commelina communis*, seu *procumbens*, Common American Commelina, native of America. —*Commelina vaginata*, native of the East Indies.—*Commelina nudiflora*, seu *Ephemerum*, &c. native of the East Indies.—*Commelina spirata*, Spear-leaved Commelina, an annual, native of the West Indies.—*Commelina Zanonia*, seu *Zanonia*, &c. seu *Tradescantia*, &c. Gentian-leaved Commelina, native of the West Indies.

COMMEMORA'TION (*Cus.*) the solemn remembrance of some remarkable event, particularly the public solemnity every year at Oxford, in honour of the founders and benefactors.

COMMEN'CEMENT (*Cus.*) an academical convention, or an annual public assembly of the University in Cambridge, answering to the *Act*, or more properly the *Commemoration* at Oxford. [vide *Commemoration*]

COMME'NDAM (*Law*) a void benefice *commended* to an able clerk till it be otherwise disposed of. In this case the living is said to be held in *Commendam*, and he who holds it is called the *commendatory*. There are different sorts of commendams, as—*Commendam semestris*, a provisional supplying of the benefice for six months only.—*Commendam retinere*, i. e. for a bishop to retain benefices on his preferment.—*Commendam recipere*, to take a benefice, *de Novo*, in the bishop's own gift, or in the gift of some other patron whose consent must be obtained. 25 H. 8, c. 21.

COMME'NDATARY (*Law*) one holding a church living *in Commendam*.

COMMENDA'TORS (*Law*) secular persons upon whom ecclesiastical benefices are bestowed; so called because the benefices were commended and intrusted to their oversight, not as proprietors, but as tutors.

COMMENDATO'RIUM (*Med.*) an epithet for the traumatic balsam, and other medicines, on account of their singular virtues and usefulness.

COMME'NDATORY *Letters* (*Law*) Letters sent from one bishop to another in behalf of any of the clergy, or others, of his diocese, in order to ensure them a good reception.

COMMENDA'TI *Homines* (*Archæol.*) Men living under the protection of, and doing homage to, some superior lord. Sometimes they depended on several lords, and did homage to each, when they were called *Commendati demidii*. They had likewise persons under them who were called *Sub-commendati*.

COMME'NSURABLE (*Math.*) σύμμετρος, an epithet for either magnitudes or numbers, which will measure one another, or which may both be measured by some third quantity, as in the annexed figure; if A B, two magnitudes, one 5 and the other 3, be measured exactly by C, a third magnitude, supposed to be 1, then the magnitudes A B are commensurable. Numbers, whether integers or fractions, are commensurable, when any other number will measure or divide them without a remainder; as 6 and 8, which may both be divided by 2, and $\frac{1}{7}$, or $\frac{1}{7}$, which may be divided by $\frac{1}{4}$ or $\frac{1}{17}$, are respectively *commensurable numbers*.—*Commensurable in Power*, δυνάμει σύμμετροι, is said, according to Euclid, of right lines, when their squares are measured by one and the same space or superficies. *Euc. Def. Elem.* l. 10.—*Commensurable surds* are such, as being reduced to their least terms, become true figurative quantities of the kind, and are therefore as a rational quantity to a rational.

COMME'NSUS (*Math.*) Commensuration, συμμετρία, the measure of one thing in proportion or comparison to another. *Vitruv.* l. 3, c. 1.

COMMENTA′CULUM (*Ant.*) a wand which those who were going to sacrifice held in their hand, to make people stand out of the way. *Fest. de Verb. Signif.*

COMMENTARIE′NSIS (*Archæol.*) a clerk, or one who kept a register of any thing, both in civil and military matters. *Ulp. leg. Div. § 1 ; ff. de Von. Damn. Paull.*

COMMENTA′RIUS (*Archæol.*) a brief register, or account of things as they occur.

COMMENTARY (*Lit.*) a note, or something added to the text by way of illustration.

CO′MMERCE (*Com.*) *Commercium*, i. e. *commutatio mercium*, or an exchange of commodities; signifies a trafficking or dealing with foreign countries, by means of exports and imports, according to specific laws, called the *Lex mercatoria*.—*Chambers of commerce*, assemblies of merchants and traders, established by virtue of letters patent from the sovereign, who are invested with certain privileges, particularly that of hearing and deciding causes, or matters of dispute, between individuals relative to trade. They are most numerous in France where every principal town has its chamber of commerce.

COMMERSO′NIA (*Bot.*) a genus of plants, Class 5 *Pentandria*, Order 5 *Pentagynia*.

Generic Characters. CAL. *perianth* one leaf; *divisions* ovate.—COR. five-petalled; *petals* linear; *nectary* five-parted; *divisions* lanceolate.—STAM. *filaments* five; *anthers* roundish.—PIST. *germ* globular; *styles* five; *stigmas* globular—PER. *capsule* globular; *cells* two, seeded; *seeds* ovate.

Species. The only species is the—*Commersonia echinata, Restiaria, &c.* seu *Dasypogon*, a tree, native of the Society Isles.

COMME′TICS (*Med.*) a name for certain things which give beauties not before in being; as paints to the face. They are said to differ from cosmetics, which are only useful in preserving beauties, of which one is already in possession.

CO′MMI (*Bot.*) κόμμι, gum, which, without any epithet, signifies Gum Arabic. The κόμμι λευκὸν, mentioned by Hippocrates, in his second book *de Mulieribus*, is the same. *Foes. Œconom. Hippocrat.*

COMMINA′TION (*Ecc.*) a ceremony in the Christian church, which consists in the recital of God's denunciations.

COMMINU′TION (*Mech.*) a breaking or bruising of things into very small parts.

CO′MMIS (*Com.*) French for a clerk, or inferior person, employed in any counting-house or office.

CO′MMISSARY (*Ecc.*) *Commissaire*, a church officer, who supplies the bishop's place in the exercise of ecclesiastical jurisdiction, in the remote parts of his diocese, or in such parishes as are peculiar to the bishop, and exempted from the archdeacon's visitation. 4 *Inst.* 338.—*Commissary court*, a court in Scotland, originally constituted for executing a certain jurisdiction in their name. It was modelled by Queen Mary, and has continued in being ever since.

COMMISSARY (*Mil.*) a civil officer, who was appointed to inspect musters, &c. They are distinguished by different names, according to their office, as—*Commissary-general of the Musters*, or Muster-Master-General, in French *Commissaires des guerres*, who takes account of the strength of every regiment.—*Commissary general of stores*, who has charge of the stores, and is accountable to the office of ordnance.—*Commissary of accounts*, who examines and controls all accounts in the army to which he is attached.—*Commissary-general of provisions*, in French *Commissaire des vivres*, has the charge of furnishing the army in the field with all sorts of provisions, forage, &c.—*Chief commissary*, in French *Commissaire ordonnateur*, the person to whom the chief management of the commissariat department is entrusted.

COMMI′SSION (*Law*) the warrant or letters patent, by which all persons exercising any jurisdiction, have authority to hear and determine causes, &c. Commissions are of different kinds, according to the nature of the duty to be discharged; namely,—*Commission of anticipation*, a commission, formerly under the great seal, to collect a tax or subsidy before the day.—*Commission of assize*. [vide *Assize*]—*Commission of association*, a commission to associate two or more learned persons with the justices, in the several circuits and counties of Wales, &c.—*Commission of bankruptcy*, a commission under the Great Seal to five or more commissioners, to inquire into the particular affairs and circumstances of the Bankrupt, and to act for the benefit of his creditors, according to the statute made for this purpose.—*Commission of charitable uses*, one issuing out of Chancery to the bishops, to inquire into any abuse or misapplication of lands given to charitable uses.—*Commission of delegates*, a commission, under the Great Seal, to certain persons, generally spiritual lords, to sit upon an appeal to the King in the Court of Chancery, in any ecclesiastical cause. 25 *H.* 8, c. 19.—*Commission of enquiry into faults against the law*, an ancient Commission, set forth on extraordinary occasions and corruptions.—*Commissions of the peace*, special commissions under the Great Seal to fit and proper persons appointed, in different parts of the kingdom, for the upholding the laws, and maintaining the public peace, who, on that account, are called Justices of the Peace.—*Commission of the Peace* is also one of the commissions of assize. [vide *Assize*]—*Commission of lunacy*, a commission out of Chancery, to inquire whether any person be a lunatic or not : so that, in the former case, the King may have the care of his estate, &c.—*Commission of Oyer and Terminer*, one of the five commissions of assize. [vide *Assize*]—*Commission of rebellion*, otherwise called a *writ of rebellion*, issued against a man, who, after proclamation, makes default in his appearance.—*Commission of sewers*, directed to certain persons, to see to the state of the drains, &c.—*Commission of treaty with foreign princes*, a commission granted to ambassadors and ministers, for the making of treaties, &c.—*Commission to take up men for war*, a commission for impressing men into the king's service in time of war.—*Commission of Teinds*, a court at Edinburgh, which came in the place of the committee of Parliament, for erecting new parishes, and valuing teinds for the support of the clergy.

COMMISSION (*Com.*) the order by which any person trafficks for another; also the per-centage given to factors and agents for transacting the business of others.—*Commission del credere*, an absolute engagement to the principal, from an insurance broker in effecting an insurance, which makes him liable in the first instance, and at all events, though the principal may resort to the underwriter as a collateral security.

COMMISSION (*Mil.*) the warrant or authority by which an individual holds any post in the army.—*Commission of array*, was a commission issued in the reign of Henry II. and his successors, to certain experienced officers, to draw out fit men for the service in each county. These commissions have been superseded by the statutes regarding the militia.—*Commission militaire*, French for a temporary court or tribunal, appointed to inquire into capital offences.

COMMI′SSIONED (*Mil.*) an epithet for an officer who has a warrant or commission, in distinction from the non-commissioned officers, or such as are immediately above the rank and file, as serjeants, &c.

COMMI′SSIONER (*Law*) one who has a commission to execute any public office, either by letters patent, the public seal, or any other way, as the Lords Commissioners of the Treasury, the Commissioners of Excise, the Com-

4

missioners of Customs, &c.—*Commissioners for the valuation of teinds*, those appointed by the Parliament for the valuation of the teinds or tithes in Scotland.—*The King's High Commissioner*, the person who represents the King in Scotland.

COMMISSU'RA (*Anat.*) any suture or juncture, particularly the corners of the lips where they meet together; and certain parts of the brain, which cross and join one hemisphere to the other, as the—*Commissura anterior cerebri*, the substance which crosses the anterior part of the third ventricle of the brain.—*Commissura magna cerebri*, the substance, otherwise called the *Corpus callosum.*—*Commissura posterior cerebri*, the substance which crosses the posterior part of the third ventricle.

COMMISSU'RE (*Mech.*) a close joining of planks, stones, &c.

COMMISSURE (*Anat.*) vide *Commissura.*

COMMISSU'RES (*Nat.*) a term used by some authors for the small pores of a natural body, or the little cavities or clefts that are between the particles of a body, especially when the particles are rather broad and flat, like thin lamellæ or plates.

COMMI'TMENT (*Law*) the sending to prison, by warrant or order, a person who stands charged with the commission of any crime.

COMMI'TTEE (*Law*) He or they to whom the ordering of any matter is referred by some court, or other persons concerned, as in the Parliament, where different committees are appointed for different purposes, as Committees of Privileges, Committees for private bills, Election Committees, &c.—*Committee of the King*, a widow of the King's tenant, so called as being committed by the ancient law of the land to the King's care and protection. *Kitch. fol.* 160.—*Committee of a lunatic*, &c. the person to whom the care and custody of such lunatic is committed by the Court of Chancery.

COMMI'XTION (*Law*) a method of acquiring property in the Scotch law, by mixing or blending substances belonging to different proprietors.

CO'MMODATE (*Law*) *commodatum*; the loan or free concession of any thing moveable, or immoveable, on condition of restoring again the same individual thing after a certain time. It is distinguished from a loan by being gratuitous, and not transferring the property; so that, in such case, the thing must be returned in essence, and without impairment.

COMMO'DITY (*Com.*) any ware, or merchandize, which a person deals or trades in.—*Staple commodities*, such wares and merchandizes as are the proper produce or manufacture of the country.

CO'MMODORE (*Mar.*) in French *Commandant provisoire d'un escadre*; a general officer in the British Navy invested with the command of a detachment of ships of war destined for any particular enterprise. His vessel is distinguished from the inferior ships in his squadron by a broad red pennant tapering towards the outer end.—*Commodore* is also a title given by courtesy to the senior captain where three or more ships are cruising in company.—*Commodore of a convoy* is the name given to the leading ship in a fleet of merchantmen, who carries a light in her top to direct the rest and keep them together.

COMMOIGNE (*Ecc.*) a brother monk residing in the same convent.

CO'MMON (*Gram.*) is an epithet which denotes belonging equally or alike, in which proper sense it is applied to nouns. A *common noun* is a name common to many things of the same kind, as man, horse, in distinction from a *proper noun*, or a name for a particular individual, as Alexander, Bucephalus. *Common* is also applied to the gender of nouns which are both masculine and feminine; and also to verbs which denote both action and passion.

COMMON (*Law*) as a noun, implies the right which one or more persons claim in another man's lands, waters, woods, &c. without having any property therein.—*Common of pasture*, or the right of pasture in common with others, is the most usual kind of common; but there is also *Common of piscary*, or *fishing*, and *Common of estovers*, *Common of turbary*, and the like. Common of pasture is divided into common in gross, common appendant, common appurtendant, and common *per cause de vicinage.*—*Common in gross* is a liberty to have common alone, without any lands or tenements granted by deed to a man and his heirs, &c. F. N. B. 37.—*Common appendant*, a right, appended or attached to a man's arable land, of putting beasts commonable into another man's ground. F. N. B. 180. —*Common appurtenant* differs from the preceding only in this, that it may be severed from the land whereto it appertains.—*Common per cause de vicinage*, or common by reason of neighbourhood, is a liberty that tenants of one lord have to common with the tenants of another lord.

Common is also attached as an epithet to many other things, namely—*Common Bench, bancus communis*, a name formerly given to the Court of Common Pleas.—*Common Council*, a court in the city of London, composed of the Lord Mayor, Aldermen, and a certain number of the citizens, called common-councilmen.—*Common* or *Town Clerk*, an officer in a city who keeps the original charters, &c. of the city.—*Common Cryer*, an officer in the City who, with the Serjeant at Arms, summons all executors and administrators of freemen to appear and to bring inventories of their estates, &c.—*Common day of a plea in land* signifies an ordinary day in court as *Octabis Hilarii Quindena Paschæ*, &c. mentioned in stat. 51 H. 3; stat. 2 and stat. 3.—*Common field land*, the same as *Common of Pasture.*—*Common fine*, a small sum of money which the resiants of some leets pay to the lord.—*Common hunt*, an officer in the City who has charge of the hounds belonging to the Lord Mayor and citizens, and attends them in hunting when they please.—*Common intendment*, the common meaning or understanding according to the subject matter, not strained to any unusual interpretation.—*Common Law*, the law of this kingdom, grounded on the general customs of the realm, as it was holden before any statute was enacted in Parliament to alter the same, whence the King's courts of justice are called Common Law Courts. —*Common Pleas*, or *Court of Common Pleas*, one of the King's courts now held in Westminster Hall, although formerly moveable. In this court all actions popular, and actions penal, of debt, &c. are tried before four judges, who are created by letters patent. The other officers of this court are the *Custos Brevium, Prothonotaries*, their *Secondaries, Chirographer*, fourteen *Filazers*, four *Exigenters, Clerk of the King's Silver, of the Treasury, of the Essoins, of the Warrants*, &c. [vide *Custos, Clerk*, &c.]—*Common Prayer*, the liturgy, or public form of prayer prescribed by the Church of England to be used in all churches and chapels at stated periods.—*Common Serjeant*, one of the City officers who attends the Lord Mayor and Court of Aldermen on court-days, and is in council with them on all occasions, within and without the precincts of the City.—*Common weal* is understood in our law to signify *publicum bonum*, which is the thing most consulted; and on that account monopolies, and whatever interferes with free trade, and the like, are void in law.

COMMON *centering* (*Carpent.*) a centering without trusses, having a tie-beam at the bottom.—*Common joists*, the beams in single, naked flooring, to which the joists are fixed.—*Common rafters*, those to which the boarding or lathing is fixed.

Common (*Math.*) an epithet for any angle, line, or measure, &c. that belongs to two or more figures, &c. of the same kind, as a common angle, a common side, a common base, &c.—*Common measure*, or *common divisor*, that number which measures or divides two others without a remainder: thus, of 8 and 12 the common measure is 2 or 4. The *greatest common measure* is the greatest number that can measure two other numbers: so of 8 and 12 the greatest common measure is 4.

Common (*Bot.*) an epithet applied, in the general sense of the word, to several parts of plants, as *communis gemma*, a bud containing both leaves and flowers; *pedunculus communis*, a peduncle bearing several flowers; *perianthium commune*, a perianth which is common to several flowers, or encloses several distinct fructifications, as in *Syngenesia*; *receptaculum commune*, a receptacle which connects several distinct fructifications, as in the *Syngenesia*.

Common-Council-Man (*Law*) a citizen of London who is a member of the Common-Council.

Common-Place-Book (*Lit.*) a book, or register, which a person keeps for himself, and in which he notes down all that he sees, hears, or reads of, that is worthy of observation.

Common Places (*Rhet.*) are the same as what are more generally called topics. [vide *Topics*]

Common ray (*Opt.*) a right line drawn from the point of concurrence of the two optical axes, through the middle of the right line passing through the centre of the pupil of the eye.

Common sensory (*Anat.*) is that part of the brain which is supposed to be the seat of all sensation, where the soul takes cognizance of the objects which present themselves to the senses.—*Common receptacle*, the name for a receptacle which is supposed to receive the chyle and the lymph, although its existence is not yet ascertained.

Common signs (*Astrol.*) a name given to *Gemini*, *Virgo*, *Sagittarius*, and *Pisces*.

Common Time (*Mus.*) is four or two crotchets in a bar.—*Common chord* is the combination of the third, fifth, and eighth of any note.

COMMONA'LTY (*Polit.*) the middle sort of the King's subjects, or such of the Commons as being raised above the peasantry are eligible to offices, and are only one degree inferior to burgesses.

CO'MMONER (*Polit.*) a member of the House of Commons.

Commoner (*Cust.*) a member of the university of Oxford who is on the usual footing, in distinction from the *gentleman commoner*, who enjoys certain privileges.

COMMON Pleas (*Law*) vide *Common*.

COMMONS (*Polit.*) in the general sense, the whole people of England, in distinction from the nobility; but, in the restricted and more usual acceptation, the body of Knights, Burgesses, &c. who represent the Commons in Parliament.—*House of Commons*, or *Commons House of Parliament*, the lower House of Parliament, so called because they represent the Commons of the realm.

Commons (*Cus.*) the provision which each member in a college takes at the common meal.

Commons (*Law*) or Doctors' Commons, sometimes termed the *college of Civilians*, a college founded by Dr. Harvey, dean of the Arches, for the professors of civil law residing in London, who live in a collegiate manner commoning together. To this college belong thirty-four proctors, who manage causes, &c.

COMMONWEA'LTH (*Polit.*) is that form of government in which the administration of public affairs is open, or common to all or many persons, without special regard to rank or property, as distinguished from monarchy or aristocracy. In this sense the government of England, after the death of Charles I, was distinguished by the name of the Commonwealth until the Protectorate of Oliver Cromwell.

CO'MMORANCY (*Law*) an abiding dwelling, or continuing as an inhabitant in any place. It consists properly in lying usually in any place.

CO'MMORTH (*Law*) from the British *Cymmorth*, i. e. *subsidium*; a contribution which was gathered at marriages, and when young priests said or sung their first masses, &c. *Stat.* 4 *Hen.* 4, c. 27; *Stat.* 26 *Hen.* 8, c. 6.

COMMO'SIS (*Nat.*) κόμμωσις, the first stratum of gummy matter with which bees line their hives.

Commosis (*Mech.*) vide *Cosmetics*.

CO'MMOTE (*Law*) 1. Half a *cantred*, or hundred, in Wales, containing fifty villages. *Stat. Wall.* 12 *Ed.* 1. 2. A great seignory, or lordship, including divers manors. *Co. Lit.* 5.

COMMU'NA (*Law*) the Common of pasture.

CO'MMUNANCE (*Law*) a title anciently given to the body of commoners, who had a right of commoning in open fields, &c.

COMMU'NE Concilium (*Law*) the common council of the king and people assembled in parliament.—*Communis Custodia*, a writ which anciently lay for the lord whose tenant, holding by knight's service, died and left a son under age, against a stranger who entered the land, and obtained ward of the body. *Fitz. Nat. Brev.* 89; *Reg. Orig.* 161.—*Communia Placita non tenenda in Scaccario*, an ancient writ directed to the treasurer and barons of the Exchequer forbidding them to hold plea between common persons, i. e. not debtors to the king, where neither of the parties belong to the same.

COMMU'NIBUS locis (*Lit.*) a term often used by writers for some medium, or mean relation between several places, as taking one place with another: thus, as Dr. Keil supposes the ocean is a quarter of a mile deep, *communibus locis*, i. e. at a medium, or taking one place with another.—*Communibus annis* is said, in respect to time, as the former phrase is in respect to place. The depth of rain, according to Mr. Derham, were it to stagnate on the earth, would amount, *communibus annis*, i. e. one year with another, to 42¼ inches in Lancashire, 19 at Paris, 32¼ at Zurich, &c.

COMMU'NICANT (*Ecc.*) one who partakes in the communion of the Lord's Supper.

COMMUNICA'NTES *febres* (*Med.*) a name for two fevers which afflict a person at one and the same time, the paroxysm of the one beginning as the paroxysm of the other ceases.

COMMU'NICATING doors (*Archit.*) doors which, when open, throw two apartments into one.

COMMUNICA'TION (*Law*) a discourse between several parties without coming to an agreement, upon which no action can be grounded.

COMMUNICATION, Line of (*Mil.*) a term in strategy, or modern tactics, to denote the line which communicates with the line of operation, and proceeds from the base point.

COMMUNICATION, Lines of (*Fort.*) trenches made to preserve a safe correspondence betwixt two posts or forts, or at a siege between two approaches.

COMMUNICATION of motion (*Mech.*) that act of a moving body, by which it gives motion, or transfers its motion to another body.

COMMUNICATION (*Rhet.*) ἀνακοίνωσις, a figure of speech, in which the orator holds a conference, as it were, with his audience. *Cic. Or.* l. 3, c. 53; and *Orat.* c. 39; *Quintilian. Instit.* l. 9, c. 2; *Jul. Rufinian.* p. 26.

COMMUNICATION of Idioms (*Theol.*) the communication of the attributes of one nature in our Saviour to those of another.

COMMU'NION (*Ecc.*) a name given to the Sacrament of the Lord's Supper, from the common participation of the faithful therein.—*Communion service*, the office for the administration of the Holy Sacrament in the church of England.—*Communion table*, the table erected at the east end of the church, round which the communicants kneel to partake of the Lord's Supper.

COMMU'NITY (*Law*) vide *Commonalty*.—*Community* signifies also sometimes the joint property in effects between husband and wife. It is either tacit or continued.—*Tacit Community* is that which is contracted between a man and woman by the mere mingling of their effects, provided they have lived together a year and a day.—*Continued Community* is that which subsists between two persons joined in marriage, and the minor children of that marriage, when the survivor has not made an inventory of the effects in possession during the marriage.

COMMUTA'TION, Angle of (*Astron.*) the distance between the sun's true place from the earth, and the place of a planet reduced to the ecliptic. [vide *Angle*]

COMMUTATION (*Rhet.*) ἀντιμεταβαλὴ, a figure of speech whereby a complete transposition of the words takes place; as "I do not live that I may eat, but I eat that I may live." *Cic. ad Heren.* l. 4, c. 48; *Quintil. Instit.* l. 9, c. 3.

COMMUTA'TIVE *Justice* (*Law*) that justice which ought to be observed in buying and selling, &c.

TO COMMUTE (*Law*) to substitute one punishment in the place of a greater.

COMOCLA'DIA (*Bot.*) a genus of plants, Class 3 *Triandria*, Order 1 *Monogynia*.
Generic Characters. CAL. *perianth* one-leaved.—COR. *petals* three. STAM. *filaments* three; *anthers* roundish.—PIST. *germ* ovate; *style* none; *stigma* obtuse.—PER. *drupe* oblong; *seed nut* membranaceous.
Species. The species are shrubs, as the—*Comocladia integrifolia*, seu *Paunus*, &c. native of America.—*Comocladia dentata*, native of South America.—*Comocladia ilicifolia*, *Ilex*, &c. seu *Dodonæa*, &c. native of the Caribbee Islands.

CO'MORTH (*Archæol.*) vide *Commorth*.

COMO'SÆ (*Bot.*) one of Linnæus's Natural Orders, consisting of plants with comose spikes.

COMO'SE (*Bot.*) an epithet for the spike of a flower which terminates with a *coma*, or tuft.

CO'MPACT (*Law*) an agreement or bargain.

COMPACT (*Bot.*) an epithet for a leaf having its pulp of a close firm texture.

COMPA'CTION (*Phy.*) the drawing together, or strengthening a body or substance by its having less parts, or by the closer adhesion of the parts; it is usually opposed to diffusion.

COMPA'GNE (*Mar.*) French for a room or cabin belonging to the chief of a galley.

CO'MPAN (*Com.*) a silver coin current in several parts of India, and worth about nine sols French money, but its value is subject to fluctuation.

CO'MPANAGE (*Archæol.*) any sort of victuals which is eaten with bread.

COMPA'NION (*Her.*) a term applied to knights of some orders, in distinction from commander, &c.; as C. B., Companion of the Bath; C. G., Companion of the Garter, &c.

COMPANION (*Print.*) the fellow press-man, or he who works with another at the press; also a fellow compositor, or one who is engaged with others on the same work.

COMPANION (*Mar.*) a sort of wooden porch placed over the entrance or stair-case of the master's cabin.—*Companion-Ladder*, in French *échelle de commandement*, the ladder in ships of war, by which the officers ascend to, and descend from, the quarter-deck.

COMPANY (*Law*) a society, or corporate body, such as the chartered companies of tradesmen in the city of London.

COMPANY (*Com.*) a trading association in which several merchants form a joint stock, with which they trade for the common interest of the stock-holders. The most important company of this kind is that known by the name of the East India Company.

COMPANY (*Mil.*) an indeterminate number of foot or artillery, varying from 50 to 120, commanded by a captain, lieutenant, and an ensign.—*Free Company*, an irregular corps acting like a detached army, either by itself, or in conjunction with some of its own kind.—*Independent Company*, a company which is not incorporated.

COMPANY (*Mar.*) the whole crew of a ship, including the officers.—*Company*, a fleet of merchantmen, who make a charter-party among themselves to sail together on certain conditions for mutual protection.

CO'MPARATES (*Log.*) things compared with one another, as "The life of a man with a leaf."

COMPA'RATIVE *degree* (*Gram.*) the second degree of comparison, as better, the middle degree between good and best.

COMPARATIVE *Anatomy* (*Anat.*) the anatomy of animals for the purpose of comparing the corresponding parts in different animal bodies.

COMPA'RISON *of Ideas* (*Log.*) the setting of two ideas together for the purpose of observing their agreement or difference.

COMPARISON (*Rhet.*) a figure of speech by which things are considered in relation to others for the purpose of heightening the effect of the representation.—*Parallel comparison* is the putting of two persons or things together in order to observe their agreement or difference.

COMPA'RTIMENT (*Archit.*) vide *Compartment*.

COMPARTI'TION (*Archit.*) the graceful distribution of the whole ground-plot of a building.

COMPA'RTMENT (*Archit.*) or *compartiment*, a proportionable division in a building; a particular square, or some device marked in an ornamental part of the building.—*Compartment of Tiles*, an arrangement of white or red tiles varnished for the decoration of a roof.—*Compartment* is also the symmetrical disposition of figures to adorn pannels.

COMPARTMENT (*Paint.*) a regular orderly disposition of figures about any picture, map, or draught, &c.

COMPARTMENT (*Hort.*) a bed, border, or knot, being a design composed of several different figures disposed with symmetry to adorn a parterre.

COMPARTMENTS (*Her.*) are partitions and quarterings of the escutcheon, according to the number of coats in it, when the arms of several families are borne in one and the same coat, in consequence of marriages, &c.

CO'MPASS (*Mar.*) or *Mariners' compass*, an instrument used by mariners to point out the course at sea, which is said to have been invented about the fourth century. It consists of a card or fly, a needle, and a box.—The *card* is a circle of stiff varnished paper representing the horizon, and divided into thirty-two parts, as in the annexed figure, by lines drawn from the centre to the circumference, called *points*, or *rhumbs*; [vide *Rhumbs*] the four principal of which are called *cardinal points*; namely, North, South, East, and West.—The *needle* is a small bar of steel made magnetical, which has the

property of pointing one of its ends to the North pole.—The *box*, which immediately contains the card and needle, is made of brass, and is hung within a wooden one by two concentric rings, called *gimbals*, so fixed by cross centres to the box, that the inner one, or compass box, retains its horizontal position in all motions of the ship. The top of the box is covered with glass to prevent the wind from disturbing the needle.—*Azimuth compass* differs from the common compass in that the circumference of the card or box is divided into degrees; and an index is likewise fitted to the box with two sights through which observations of the sun or stars may be taken.—*Variation of the compass* or *needle.* [vide *Variation*]—*Compass dials*, small dials fitted into boxes, for the pocket, to show the hour of the day by the needle that indicates how to place them right; for, by turning the dial about, the cock or style stands directly over the needle.

COMPASS-SAW (*Carpent.*) a saw with an edge so broad, and the back so thin, that it may easily follow the broad edge without having its teeth set. Its use is to cut a round, or any other compass kerf.

COMPASS-TIMBER (*Mar.*) timber incurvated or arched for the building of ships.

COMPASSES (*Math.*) or *pair of compasses*, a mathematical instrument which consists of two sharp-pointed branches or legs of brass, &c. for describing circles, measuring, and dividing lines, &c. They are distinguished according to their particular construction, form, use, &c. into—*Beam compasses*, which consist of a long straight beam or bar carrying two brass cursors, and are used for drawing large circles.—*Bow-compasses*, a small sort of compasses which serve to describe arcs or circumferences with a very small radius.—*Caliber compasses.* [vide *Caliber*]—*Clock-maker's compasses* are jointed like the common compasses, with a quadrant or bow, like the spring compasses, serving to keep the instrument firm at any opening.—*Cylindrical*, or *spherical compasses*, consist of four branches joined in a centre, two of them being circular, and two flat. Their use is to take the diameter of cylindrical bodies.—*Elliptical compasses*, or those which are used for drawing ellipses, are of a complicated structure.—*German compasses* have the legs bent out a little, so that when shut the points only meet.—*Hair-compasses*, a sort of compasses so contrived withinside, by a small adjusting screw to one of the legs, as to take an extent to a hair's breadth.—*Proportional compasses*, those whose joint lies not at the end of the legs, but between the points terminating each leg.—*Spring compasses*, or *dividers*, are made of hardened steel, with an arched head, which, by its spring, opens the legs.—*Triangular compasses*, the common compasses with the addition of a third leg or point, which has a motion every way. Their use is to take three points at once.—*Trisecting compasses*, for the trisecting angles mechanically.—*Turn-up compasses* differ from the common sort only by having two other points added towards the bottom of the legs; the object of which is to save the trouble of changing points.

COMPASSING (*Mar.*) the act of bending timber into a curve for the building of ships.

COMPELLATIVUS (*Archæol.*) an adversary, or accuser. *Leg. Athelstan.*

COMPENDIUM (*Ant.*) 1. Whatever is got by saving. 2. An abridgment.

COMPERENDINATIO (*Ant.*) a delay of the action or pleading until the third day following. *Ascon. in Cic.* p. 76; *Manut. de Leg.* c. 22; *Bud. in Pandect.* p. 32.

COMPERTORIUM (*Law*) a judicial inquest in the civil law, made by delegates or commissioners, to find out, and to relate the truth of a cause.

COMPETENCE *Militaire* (*Mil.*) French for military cognizance.

COMPETENCY (*Law*) the power of a judge, or of any court, to take cognizance of the matter in question.

COMPETITOR (*Polit.*) a rival candidate, or one who sues for the same office.

COMPITALIA (*Ant.*) *Compitalitia*, or *Ludi Compitales*, feasts in cross-ways solemnized by the friends of those who died in foreign parts. *Cat. de Re Rus.* c. 5; *Dionys. Halicarn.* l. 4; *Varr. de Lat. Ling.* l. 5; *Cic. ad Attic.* l. 7, c. 7; *Plin.* l. 36, c. 27; *A. Gell.* l. 10, c. 24; *Fest. de Verb. Signif; Ascon. in Cic.* p. 159; *Macrob. Sat.* l. 1, c. 7; *Gyrald. Syntag. Deor.* l. 17; *Laz. Comm. Reip. Rom.* l. 10, c. 4; *Turneb. Adv.* l. 21, c. 15.

COMPITUM (*Ant.*) a cross-way, or place where several roads met together, and at which the rustics used to keep their holidays, and celebrate their wakes. *Vet. Interp. Per. sat.* 4, v. 27.

COMPLAINANT (*Law*) one who prefers a complaint against another, a plaintiff at law.

COMPLEMENT (*Geom.*) παραπλήρωμα, a name for the two smaller parallelograms, A K and K C, formed by drawing the two right lines, H G and E F, through the point K in the diagonal. These are in every parallelogram equal to one another, as A K = K C. *Eucl. Elem.* prop. 43.—*Complement of an arc*, what an arc wants of 90°, or the quadrant of a circle.—*Complement of an angle*, what an acute angle wants of a right angle.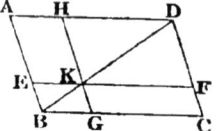

COMPLEMENT *of the Course* (*Mar.*) the number of points the course wants of 90°, or the fourth of the compass.

COMPLEMENT *of the Curtain* (*Fort.*) that part in the interior side of a fortification which makes the demi-gorge.—*Complement of the line of Defence*, the remainder of the line of defence after the flank-angle is taken away.

COMPLEMENT (*Mil.*) the full establishment of a regiment.

COMPLEMENT (*Mus.*) that quantity which is wanting to any interval to fill up the octave.

COMPLEMENT (*Her.*) signifies the full moon.

COMPLETE (*Mil.*) in French *complet*, a term applied to any regiment or company that has its established number.

COMPLETE (*Bot.*) an epithet for a flower; *flos completus*, a complete flower, or one that has the calyx, corolla, stamen, and pistil.

COMPLETION (*Med.*) another word for *plethora*.

COMPLETORIUM (*Ecc.*) the *complines*, or midnight devotions in the Romish church.

COMPLEX (*Log.*) an epithet applied either to the ideas or the faculty of the mind by which they are apprehended; thus, complex ideas are those which are composed of several simple ideas, and complex apprehension that which takes in several objects in their order, as " A reed in the hand."

COMPLEXIO (*Med.*) the constitution or temperament.

COMPLEXIO (*Log.*) the conclusion of a syllogism or argument. *Cic. de Invent.* l. 1, c. 31.

COMPLEXIO (*Rhet.*) a figure of speech which embraces both repetition and conversion, answering to the Greek *symploce*. [vide *Symploce*] *Quint. Inst.* l. 9, c. 3.—*Complexio verborum* signifies also a full period, taking in the context and series of a discourse. *Quintil.* l. 1, c. 5.

COMPLEXUS (*Anat.*) a muscle situated in the back part of the neck.

COMPLICATE (*Bot.*) *complicatus*, i. e. folded together, as the valves of the glume or chaff of some grapes.

COMPLICATIO *morbi* (*Med.*) a complication of diseases when several subsist in the same subject at the same time.

COMPLINES (*Ecc.*) the last prayers, or conclusion of the evening prayers in the Romish church.

COMPLUVIUM (*Archit.*) a pent-house, or eaves, down

which the water glides. *Varr. de Lat. Lin.* l. 4, c. 33; *Vitruv.* l. 6, c. 3.

COMPO'NY (*Her.*) or *counter compony*, when a border, pale, bend, or any other ordinary, is made up of two rows of squares, consisting of metals and colours.

TO COMPO'SE (*Mus.*) to invent music, or pieces of music, according to the rules of art.

COMPO'SED (*Fort.*) an epithet for a bastion, so called when the two sides of the inner polygon are very unequal, which makes the gorges unequal.

COMPO'SER (*Mus.*) one who composes pieces of music.

COMPO'SING (*Print.*) vide *Composition*.

COMPO'SING *stick* (*Print.*) a compositor's tool, made of iron plate, into which he gathers the letters, and thus composes the matter in printing. It consists of different parts, as in the subjoined figure; *a* the *Head*, *bb* the *Bottom*, *cc*

the *Back*, *d* the *lower sliding Measure*, or *cheek*, *e* the *upper sliding Measure*, or *cheek*, *ff* the *Male Screw*, *g* the *Female Screw*.—*Composing Rule*, a sort of brass rule used by compositors for regulating their lines.

COMPO'SITÆ (*Bot.*) the name of the twenty-first order in the Fragments of Linnæus' Natural Method, comprising the plants with compound flowers.

COMPO'SITE *order* (*Archit.*) one of the five orders of architecture, so called because it is composed of the Ionic and Corinthian orders. [vide *Architecture*]

COMPOSITE *numbers* (*Arith.*) such numbers as some other number besides unity can measure, as 12, which is measured by 2, 3, 4, and 6. *Composite numbers between themselves* are such as have some measure besides unity, as 12 and 15, which may both be measured by 3.

COMPOSI'TES (*Med.*) medicines made up of any simple ones as syrups, electuaries, &c.

COMPOSI'TIO *mensurarum* (*Archæol.*) the title of an ancient ordnance for measures.

COMPOSI'TION (*Mus.*) a piece of music composed according to the rules of art.

COMPOSITION (*Print.*) more commonly called *composing*, the act of disposing the type into a form fit for printing.

COMPOSITION (*Rhet.*) the act of arranging one's thoughts into a certain order, and clothing them with suitable words, aptly disposed.

COMPOSITION (*Math.*) or *synthetical method*, which is the reverse of the analysis, or analytical, is a mode of reasoning which proceeds upon principles self-evident, or otherwise demonstrated step by step, until it brings us to the knowledge of the thing sought for. [vide *Analysis*]—*Composition of forces or motion* is the union or assemblage of several forces or motions that are oblique to one another into an equivalent one in another direction.—*Composition of numbers*. [vide *Combination*]—*Composition of proportion*, is when of four proportionals the sum of the 1st and 2d is to the 2d as the sum of the 3d and 4th is to the 4th; as if $a:b::c:d$, then by composition $a+b:b::c+a:d$, or in numbers, if $2:4::9:18$, then by composition, $6:4::27:18$.—*Composition of ratios*, is the adding of ratios together, which is performed by multiplying their corresponding terms together, namely, the antecedents together and the consequents together, for the antecedent and consequent of the compounded ratio: thus the ratio of $2:4$, added to the ratio of $6:8$, makes the ratio of $12:32$, or the compound ratio compounded of the ratio of 2 to 4, and of 6 to 8.

COMPOSITION (*Paint.*) is the putting together the several parts of a picture so as to set off the whole to the best advantage.

COMPOSITION (*Law*) is when a debtor, not being able to discharge his whole debts, agrees with his creditors to pay them a part of what is due.

COMPOSITION (*Chem.*) the same as combination; but by some it has been taken for a simple mixture. [vide *Combination*]

COMPOSITION (*Med.*) the mixing of several ingredients together.

COMPO'SITOR (*Print.*) a workman in the printing-office who does the part of composing the matter for the press.

COMPO'SITUS (*Bot.*) compound. [vide *Compound*]

COMPOSIZIONE *da Tavolino* (*Mus.*) Italian for convivial melodies, or songs for the table.

CO'MPOST (*Hort.*) a compound mixture of dung and earths, &c. to serve as manure for the land, or as mould for the finer sort of plants.

CO'MPOTE (*Cook.*) fruit or meat stewed.

CO'MPOUND *quantities* (*Algeb.*) such as are connected together by the signs + and −, and expressed by different letters, or else by the same letters unequally repeated, as $a+b-c$, and $bb-b$.

COMPOUND *ratio* (*Geom.*) the ratio that the product of the antecedents of two or more ratios has to the product of their consequents, as 6 to 72 is in a ratio compounded of 2 to 8, and of 3 to 12.

COMPOUND *motion* (*Mech.*) that which is produced by several forces conspiring together, as when the radius of a circle moves about the centre, and at the same time a point be conceived to go forwards along with it.—*Compound pendulum*, one that consists of several weights, keeping the same distance both from each other and from the centre, about which they oscillate.

COMPOUND *interest* (*Arith.*) that interest which arises from the principal and interest put together; also the rule by which this interest is to be found on any given sum. [vide *Interest*]—*Compound Addition, Subtraction, Multiplication*, and *Division*. [vide *Addition*, &c.]—*Compound fraction*. [vide *Fraction*]—*Compound number*. [vide *Composite Number*]

COMPOUND *interval* (*Mus.*) any interval composed of two others; thus the 9th is composed of the second and the eighth.—*Compound measures* are marked by double characters.

COMPOUND *terms* (*Gram.*) those that are composed of two simple terms, as thankful, householder, &c.

COMPOUND (*Bot.*) *compositus* is an epithet for a petiole, flower, raceme, spike, corymb, umbel, fructification, &c.; *petiolus compositus* is a petiole supporting more than one leaf; *flos compositus*, a species of aggregate flower enclosed in a common perianth, and on a common receptacle, with the anthers connected in a cylinder, as in the class Syngenesia; *racemus compositus*, a raceme composed of several racemules, or smaller racemes; *spica composita*, a spike composed of several spicules, or spikelets; *corymbus compositus*, a corymb having all the flowers elevated upon pedicels, sitting upon the common peduncles; *umbella composita*, an umbel having all the rays or peduncles bearing umbellules, or small umbels, at the top; *fructificatio composita*, a fructification consisting of several confluent florets.

COMPO'UNDED (*Bot.*) vide *Compound*.

COMPO'UNDING *felony* (*Law*) or *Theft-bote*, where the party robbed not only knows the felon, but also takes his goods again, or any other amends, upon agreement not to prosecute, which formerly made a man an accessary, but is now punished with fine and imprisonment.

COMPREHE'NSIO *verborum* (*Rhet.*) the whole compass of a sentence included in a full period. *Cic. Brut.* c. 44.

COMPREHE'NSION (*Log.*) that act of the understanding whereby it takes a full view of the object presented to it, so as to have a thorough knowledge of all its parts and bearings.

COMPREHENSION (*Ecc.*) the name of a scheme which was once proposed for relaxing the terms of conformity in such manner as to admit of protestant dissenters into the communion of the church of England.

COMPREHENSION (*Rhet.*) a figure of speech whereby the name of a whole is put for a part, and that of a part for a whole.

COMPRE'SSÆ (*Surg.*) compresses or folded pieces of linen cloth contrived to make a gentle pressure upon any part.

COMPRESSED (*Bot.*) *compressus*, i. e. flatted; an epithet applied to a stem, a leaf, a silique, &c., as *caulis compressus*, a stem having its two opposite sides flat; *folium compressum*, a leaf which is pulpy, having its sides more flattened than the disk, in distinction from depressed: *siliqua compressa*, a silique which has the opposite sides approaching to each other.

COMPRESSIBI'LITY (*Phy.*) that property in a solid or fluid of yielding to the pressure of another body or force, so as to be brought into a smaller compass.

COMPRE'SSION (*Surg.*) a diseased state of the body arising from the pressure of something on the brain.

COMPRESSION, globe of (*Mil.*) an excavation of a globular form which is made in the earth, and is filled with gunpowder.

COMPRE'SSIVES (*Med.*) medicines which cause a dryness in an affected member.

COMPRE'SSOR *naris* (*Anat.*) a muscle of the nose that compresses the *alæ* towards the *septum nasi*.

COMPRE'SSUS (*Bot.*) vide *Compressed*.

TO COMPRI'NT (*Law*) to print by stealth a copy or book belonging to an other, to his prejudice.

CO'MPROMISE (*Law*) a promise of two or more parties at difference to refer their dispute to the decision of arbitrators.

COMPROMISSA'RIUS (*Ant.*) an arbiter or umpire chosen by compromise to deal indifferently betwixt both parties.

CO'MPTESSAS (*Mech.*) a French word from *compter les pas*, to count or measure steps; an instrument by which the ground a person has passed over is measured.

COMPTO'NIA (*Bot.*) a genus of plants, Class 21 *Monoecia*, Order 3 *Triandria*.
  Generic Characters. CAL. ament cylindric; *perianth* two-leaved; *leaflets* equal.—COR. none.—STAM. filaments three; anthers six.—PIST. germ roundish; *styles* two.—PER. none; seed *nut* oval.
  Species. The only species is the—*Comptonia asplenifolia*, *Liquidambar*, &c. *Myrica*, &c. *Gale*, &c. seu *Myrti*, &c. Fern-leaved Comptonia, a shrub, native of New England.

COMPTRO'LLER (*Law*) one who examines the accounts of collectors of public money.—*Comptroller of the Pipe*, an officer of the Exchequer that writes out summonses twice every year to the sheriffs to levy the farms and debts of the Pipe; he also keeps a contra-rollment of the Pipe.

COMPTROLLER *of the Artillery* (*Mil.*) a civil officer who formerly inspected the musters of artillery.—*Comptroller of the Navy*, one of the Commissioners of the Navy Board, at which he presides to direct the inferior and civil department of the marine service.

COMPULSO'RES (*Ant.*) those that forced people to quit or abandon a fort that had surrendered. *Ammian. Marcell.* l. 25, c. 9.

COMPU'NCTIO (*Med.*) a puncture.

COMPURGA'TOR (*Law*) one that by oath justifies another's innocence.

COMPUTA'TION (*Math.*) the manner of estimating time, weights, measures, &c.

COMPUTATION (*Law*) the true account and construction of time in which the law rejects all fractions and divisions of the day.

COMPU'TO *reddendo* (*Law*) a writ to compel a bailiff, receiver, or accountant, to yield up his accounts; founded on the statute of Westm. 2, c. 12. It also lies against guardians. *Reg. Orig.* 135.

CO'MRADE (*Mil.*) a fellow soldier in the same regiment or company.

CON (*Mus.*) an Italian preposition answering to the English *with*, which is used in music, as *con affetto*, to signify that the music must be performed in a moving, tender, and affecting manner, consequently rather slow than fast.

CONA'RIUM (*Anat.*) a name for the *pineal gland*, from its conical shape.

CONA'TUS *of motion* (*Phy.*) that disposition or aptitude in a body to go on, unless it be prevented by other causes; it is the same as attraction or gravitation in a body without motion.

CONCÆ'DES (*Ant.*) the cutting down trees to keep off the enemy's horse, either in a retreat or about a camp. *Tac. Annal.* l. 1, c. 50; *Ammian.* l. 16, c. 2; *Veget.* l. 3, c. 21.

CONCAMERA'TIO (*Archit.*) καμάρωσις, an arching or a vault. *Vitruv.* l. 2, c. 4.

CONCATENA'TION (*Phy.*) a term mostly applied to denote the dependance of second causes on each other.

CO'NCAVE (*Bot.*) an epithet for a leaf; *concavum folium*, a leaf having the margin more contracted than the disk, and the disk consequently depressed. This epithet is also applied to the calyx, the corolla, and the valves of the glume of grasses.

CONCAVE *glasses* (*Mech.*) such as are ground hollow on the inside, so as to reflect on the hollow side.—*Concavo-concave*, implies concave on both sides.—*Plano-concave*, concave on one side, and plane on the other side.—*Concavo-convex*, concave on one side, and convex on the other.

CONCAVE (*Gunn.*) the bore of a piece of ordnance.

CONCAU'SA (*Med.*) a cause which operates with another in the production of a disease.

CONCA'VUS (*Bot.*) vide *Concave*.

CONCEA'LERS (*Law*) *Concelatores*, from *concelando*, signifying, by antiphrasis, *revealers*; those who were used to find out concealed lands; i. e. such lands as are privily kept from the king by common persons having nothing to show for their title and estate therein. *Stat.* 39 *Eliz.* c. 22.

CONCE'NTO (*Mus.*) Italian for harmony resulting from many voices and instruments in concert.

CONCE'NTOR (*Mus.*) one who sings with another.

CONCENTRA'NTIA (*Med.*) concentrant medicines, those whose acids are so moderated by alkalies that neither of them predominate.

CONCENTRA'TION (*Chem.*) the volatilizing part of the water of fluids, in order to improve their strength.

CONCENTRICAL (*Astron.*) or *Concentric*, an epithet for circles that have the same centre.

CONCE'PTACLE (*Bot.*) or Follicle, *conceptaculum*, or *folliculus*, a pericarp of one valve opening longitudinally on one side, and having the seeds loose in it, as in *Apocynum*, *Asclepias*, *Stapelia*, &c.

CONCEPTA'CULUM (*Mech.*) any thing hollow that is fit to receive or contain any substances.

CONCE'PTIO *Formularum* (*Ant.*) the drawing up of bills and legal instruments.

CONCEPTIO (*Med.*) the impregnation of the *ovulum*, or *semen*, in the *ovarium*, or *uterus*, of the female.

CONCE'PTION (*Ecc.*) or the feast of the Immaculate Conception, is a feast in the Christian Church, celebrated on the 8th of December, in honour of the immaculate conception of the Blessed Virgin.

CONCEPTION (*Log.*) the simple apprehension which we have of a thing, without proceeding to affirm or deny any thing of it.

CONCEPTI'VÆ *feriæ* (*Ant.*) festivals not fixed to any certain day in the year, the celebration of which was determined by the magistrates.

CONCE'PTUS (*Anat.*) the very first rudiments of the fœtus in the uterus after conception.

CO'NCERT (*Mus.*) vide *Concerto*.

CONCERTA'NTE (*Mus.*) those parts of a piece that play throughout the whole, to distinguish them from those that play only in some parts.

CONCE'RTO (*Mus.*) Italian for a piece of music consisting of several parts that are all to be performed together.—*Concerto grosso*, the grand chorus of the concert, or those parts in which the whole is performed together at the same time.—*Concerto spirituale*, Italian for a miscellaneous concert, consisting of pieces selected from sacred music.

CONCE'SSI (*Law*) "I have granted," a phrase used frequently in conveyances creating a covenant; in distinction from *dedi*, which makes a warranty. *Co. Lit.* 334.

CONCE'SSIO (*Rhet.*) συγγνώμη, a certain form of defence adopted in pleading, where the defendant admits the charge, and pleads for indulgence. *Cic. de Invent.* l. 1, c. 11; 1 *Jul. Rufin.* p. 28.

CONCE'SSIT *solvere* (*Law*) an action of debt upon simple contract, and lies by custom in the courts of the cities of London and Westminster.

CO'NCHA (*Ant.*) a liquid measure among the Athenians, which contained two mystra, or half an ounce. *Gal. de Ponder.*; *Gorr. Def. Med.*; *Pæt. de Roman. & Græc. Mensur. apud Græv. Thes. Ant. Rom.* tom. ii. p. 1649.

CONCHA (*Con.*) κόγχη, a shell fish with two shells, as an oyster, an escallop, &c.

CONCHA (*Anat.*) a term applied to different parts of the body, as *Concha auris*, the hollow of the ear, or the cartilage of the outer ear; *Concha narium*, the inferior spongy bones of the nostrils, &c.

CONCHA (*Mus.*) a musical shell. [vide *Trumpet*]

CONCHIFO'LIA (*Bot.*) vide *Manga*.

CO'NCHIS (*Bot.*) an unshelled bean, or a bean in the husk, which, according to Apicius, was reckoned a delicacy among the Romans, when dressed with aromatic substances.

CO'NCHOID (*Math.*) the name given to the curve invented by Nicomedes, as in the annexed figure. Let the line Q Q be drawn, and A C perpendicular to it in the point E; then from the point C draw several right lines, C M cutting the right line in Q Q in Q, and make Q M = Q N, A E = E F; i. e. equal to an invariable line; then the curve wherein are the points M M, is the first conchoid; and the other, wherein are the points A C, is the second conchoid: the line Q Q is called the *Directrix*, and the point C the *Pole*.

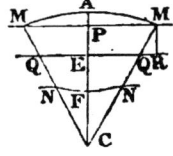

CONCHO'LOGY, from κόγχη, a shell, and λόγος, a discourse or doctrine; is that branch of natural history which treats of testaceous animals. These animals, which constitute the *testacea*, or third Order of the *Vermes* in the Linnean system, have a permanently testaceous covering, by which they are distinguished from the crustaceous animals, as lobsters, crabs, and the like, although they are both included under the name of *shell fish* in English.

Conchology may be considered under three heads, namely, the parts, figures, &c. of shells; the classification of shells; and the animals which inhabit shells.

Parts, Figure, &c. of Shells.

Parts of Shells. The principal parts of shells are, *valvula*, the Valve; *apex*, the Summit, or Tip; *basis*, the Base; *margo*, the Margin; *apertura*, the Aperture, or Mouth; *rostrum*, the Beak; *cardo*, the Hinge; *spira*, the Spire; *ligamentum*, the Ligament; *varices*, the Veins, &c.

Valve. The valve is the principal piece of which the shell is composed, and by which shells are distinguished into—*Univalves*, or those which consist of only one valve.—*Bivalves*, or those which are composed of two valves.—*Multivalves*, or those which consist of more than two valves. [Plate 33]

Valves are distinguished into—*Right valve*, or that which corresponds to the left of the observer, supposing the front or aperture of the shell to face him.—*Left valve*, that which corresponds to the right of the observer. When the right valve corresponds with the left in size, they are said to be equal.—*Superior valve*, is that valve which is not attached to solid bodies, in distinction from the inferior, or the one that is attached.—*Keelshaped valve*, *valvula carinata*, when one part of the convexity presents a sharp edge.—*Chambered valve*, *valvula concamerata*, when it exhibits testaceous plates in its cavity.—*Spinous valve*, a valve furnished with spinous processes.—*Banded valve*, *valvula fasciata*, exhibiting large transverse bands or stripes.—*Lamellated valve*, when the surface is furnished with plates.—*Radiated valve*, one exhibiting divergent or coloured rays.—*Sinuated valve*, *valvula lacunosa*, when one of the valves has a sensible depression at the middle of its margin, and a corresponding elevation of the opposite valve.—*Striated valve*, one that is marked with striæ.

To the valves belong the *Ligament*, or cartilage, the horny substance by which the valves of the shell are connected, c, fig. 8, 14. Some multivalve shells are connected by the parts of one valve fitting into another, as *l l*, fig. 1.—*Sides*, the right and left parts of the valves.—*Inside*, the concave part of a valve.—*Seam*, i. e. the line between the valves when they are closed.—*Disk*, the convex centre of the valves, as *d*, fig. 10.—*Margin* or *Limb*, the circumference of the valves from the disk to their edges, as *m*, fig. 6.

Apex. The Apex, or Summit, in a univalve shell, is the extreme point of the spire, as *a*, fig. 28: in bivalves it is the most elevated point of that part of the shell in which the hinge is placed. The pre-eminent part in the *Patella* is called the *vertex*.

Base. The base is the extremity or part opposite to the apex. In shells with a rostrum or beak, it implies the lowest part of the beak, as fig. 28, 29. In shells without a beak it is the lowest part, as *b*, fig. 1, or that part which is next the aperture, by which the multivalve shell in some cases is fixed to the rock, as *b*, fig. 1, 2.

Margin. The margin of the shell is the whole circumference or outline of the shell, as *m m*, fig. 6. This is either anterior, posterior, or superior.—The *anterior margin* is that which commences at the side of the ligament on the fore part of the beak, supposing the shell to be placed on its beak.—*Posterior margin* extends to one-third of the circumference from the beaks of the valves behind.—*Superior margin* includes the upper part of the circumference between the two preceding parts.—*Margin of the valves* is the whole interior circumference of the valves, and is distinguished into the furrowed, notched, toothed, folded, and striated margins.—*Crenulated margin*, a fine saw-like edge of most of the cockles, which correspond to the notch in the opposite valve. It is not uncommon in other shells, as the Donax, *m m*, fig. 15.

Rostrum or *Beak*. The beak is the extreme point in bivalves which turns downwards in the form of a beak, or to one side, as *r r*, fig. 10. The beak in univalve shells is the lengthened process or continuation of the canal, as *r*, fig. 29.

1

CONCHOLOGY.

To the beak in bivalves belong *auriculæ*, the ears, two processes on each side the beak, particularly in that division of the genus *Ostrea*, known by the name of Scallops, as *e e*, fig. 7. These ears are sometimes distinguished into superior and inferior.

Area, or *Slope*. The area, or slope, is either anterior or posterior. The *anterior slope* is that space in which the ligament is situated.—The *posterior slope*, or *areola*, is that part of the shell opposite to the anterior slope; in the viewing of which in the front the beaks point to you. The anterior slope is distinct, inflex, literate, &c.; the posterior, marginate, patulous, serrate, &c. In the Venus tribe is a spatulated mark formed by the union of the valves on the posterior and anterior slopes, which is called the *vulva*. There is also another mark or spot near the slopes, of a crescent-like form, called the *lunule*.

Hinge. The hinge is the solidest part of the circumference of the valve, and is the point by which bivalve shells are united, as *hh*, fig. 6, 8. It is on the peculiar construction of the hinge that the generic character of bivalve shells is principally founded. The hinge is either compressed, lateral, oblong, reflected, terminal, or truncated. Near the hinge, on the posterior side, is a depression called the *anus*. To the hinge belong the *teeth*, the projections in one valve which fit into the sockets or cavities of the opposite valve, by which the hinge is articulated. The teeth are of different forms and differently placed, as the *primary teeth*, which are placed about the centre, and are broad, large, and often elevated, as *p*, fig. 13, 14, 15, 16; *lateral teeth*, which diverge from the *umbo*, and are generally long and flat, as *l*, fig. 12, 13; *double teeth*, as *d*, fig. 12; *incurved teeth*, those which are bent round, as *i*, fig. 17. The teeth are likewise complicated, when they form an acute angle; duplicate, i. e. deeply cleft, or bifid; depressed, or turned inward; erect, i. e. perpendicular to the plane of the hinge; longitudinal, &c. Some hinges have no visible teeth, and are termed *inarticulate;* and some have numerous teeth, and are called *multarticulate*, as the hinges of the Arca, which are set in rows, as *n n*, fig. 20.—*Cavity of the hinge*, is the hollow depression in which the ligament of the ostrea is situated, which is generally of a triangular form, as *c*, fig. 18.

Operculum or Lid.—The operculum or lid in multivalves consists of four small valves in the *Lepas*, which is, however, in a certain degree, stationary, as *o*, fig. 2, and consequently distinguished from the operculum of the univalves, or that appendage to some of the turbinated shells which is affixed to the animal, and is sometimes a testaceous, and sometimes a cartilaginous substance. It is calculated for the protection of the animal when it retires within its dwelling, which it thus shuts up, as with a nicely fitted door. Of this description is the cartilaginous operculum of the *Turbo littoratus* of Linnæus, or the Common Periwinkle, which has a brown horny appearance, and must in general be removed before the animal can be taken out when boiled.

Aperture. The aperture or mouth is that opening in the univalves through which the animal protrudes itself, as fig. 27, 29. This is one of the principal distinctions of univalve shells, and differs very much in shape, some being bimarginate, i. e. having a lip with a double margin; bilabiate, i. e. with a double lip; gaping, the lower part of the lip distended; coarctate, i. e. straight; effuse, i. e. having the lips separated by a sinus or gutter; reflex, spreading, resupinate, &c. To the aperture belong the lip and the canal.—*Labium*, Lip, is the internal or columellar margin of the aperture, as *o, p, fig.* 31. This is, in respect to position, exterior, anterior, or posterior, in respect to form coarctate, digitate, disengaged, cloven, mucronate, &c.—*Canal* is the continuation or prolongation of the aperture along the beak, which forms a gutter from its commencement to the extremity, as *c*, fig. 29, 31.

Spire. The spire is all the whorls collectively, except the lower one, as *s*, fig. 30. The spire is a prominent feature of the univalve shell, and is either convex, crowned, capitate, or obtuse, exserted, or much attenuated, pointed, flattened, retuse, elevated, depressed, &c.—*The suture of the spire* is a fine spiral line, which separates the wreaths or whorls, as *s*, fig. 29.

Whorl. The whorl is one of the wreaths or convolutions of the shell, as *w*, fig. 34. The whorls are bifid, channelled, keeled, contiguous, crowned, leafy, imbricate, lamellate, lineate, striate, sulcated, &c. The contraction of the whorls, so as to correspond with the internal dissepiments or divisions, are called *geniculations*.

Body. The body is the first or lower whorl of the shell, which is in general longer than the remaining whorls, as *b b*, fig. 30. 32. To the body belong the venter and umbilicus. The *venter*, or Belly, is the most prominent part of the body, generally situated in the vicinity of the lip, and formed by the convexity of the aperture, as *v*, fig. 34.—The *umbilicus* is in general a circular perforation, in the base of the body of many univalves, and common to most of the *Trochi*, as *u*, fig. 27.

Columella or *Pillar*. The columella or pillar, *cccc*, fig. 32, is that process which runs through the centre of the shell in the inside, from the base to the apex in most univalve shells, and appears to be the support of the spire, or in fact to form that part of the shell. It is either abrupt, i. e. truncate at the base, elongated, i. e. so as to project beyond the body; flat, plaited, &c.

Chambers. Chambers are the divisions formed by partitions, at regular intervals, as in the Nautilus, *c c*, fig. 35. To the chamber belongs the *Siphunculus*, or *Sipho*, a small round perforation, which forms a communication between the chambers of the nautili, running through the whole spire of the shell, as *s*, fig. 35.

Ribs. The ribs are those longitudinal protuberances which are in many of the univalve shells, as *r*, fig. 36.

Furrows. Furrows are those impressions or interstices between the ribs, or rays on the surface of the valves, as *ff*, fig. 2, which are square, lamellated, &c.

Varices or *veins*. Varices are longitudinal or gibbous sutures, formed in the growth of the shell, at certain proportionable distances on the whorls. They are continuous, decussate, furrowed, &c.

Intestinal Ligature. The intestinum, or intestinal ligature, is a membranaceous tube, by which some species of the genus, *Anomia*, adhere to foreign substances.

Seam. The seam is the line between the valves when they are closed, as *s*, fig. 11.

Peduncle. The peduncle, or pedicle, is the support of the *Lepas anatifera*, and its corresponding species, by which they are attached to wood, &c. as *pp*, fig. 1. It is a kind of membranaceous substance, similar to a bladder, but materially thinner, and filled with a liquid, which affords nourishment to the animal.

Feelers. Feelers are the crenated arms evolved from the side of the *lepas anatifera*, and other shells of the genus *lepas*. While the animal is in the water, it continually moves its feelers for the purpose of entangling marine insects for food, as *ff*, fig. 1.

Byssus or *Beard*. The beard is an appendage composed of filaments, of a silky texture, by which some of the bivalves fasten themselves to their beds, such as the muscle, *b*, fig. 11.

4

CONCHOLOGY.

Figures or forms of Shells. Shells are distinguished, as to their form, into—*Antiquated*, i. e. longitudinally sulcate, or furrowed, but interrupted by transverse accretions, as if lesser valves were periodically added to the apex or beak.—*Bearded*, i.e. superficially covered with rigid hairs.—*Compressed*, when the valves are flattened.—*Dorsal*, when the back is obtusely keeled.—*Gaping*, when the valves close partially.—*Navicular*, being in the form of a boat.—*Pectinate*, i. e. longitudinally sulcate, or striate.—*Radiate*, i. e. with diverging rays flowing from the apex longitudinally to the circumference.—*Fastigiate*, leaving off transversely at the base. — *Saccate*, i. e. gibbous towards the summit.—*Rooted*, when it is attached to a solid, by a ligament proceeding from its base.—*Imbricated*, when the surface is covered with parallel scales, so arranged as to cover each other.—*Turbinated*, when the belly of the shell is large in proportion to the whorls, which seem to proceed from its centre.—*Bordered*, when the two sides of the aperture are broader and thicker than the rest of the diameter.—*Chambered*, when it is internally divided by dissipiments, chambers, or partitions.—*Convolute*, when the whorls turn round a lengthened coin, nearly vertical to each other.

Dimensions of shells. The *length* of the shell is taken from the ligament, or the beak, to the opposite margin, *e e*, fig. 9. The *breadth* of the shell is measured from the most extreme edge of the anterior and posterior slopes, being in a contrary direction from its length, *b b*, fig. 9. Many shells are broader than they are long, as the Myæ, Solen, Tellina, &c. Others are longer than they are broad, as the Mytilus, Ostrea, Pinna, &c.

Classification of Shells.

The classification of shells has been undertaken by different authors on different systems, of which the following are the principal:—*Lister's system.* The work of Dr. Lister, published in 1685, was divided into four Books; namely, Lib. I. *De Cochleis terrestribus*. Lib. II. *De Turbinibus et Bivalvibus aquæ dulcis*. Lib. III. *De Testaceis bivalvibus marinis*. Lib. IV. *De Buccinis marinis quibus etiam vermiculi dentalia et patellæ numerantur*.—*System of Langius*, published in 1722, was divided into three parts. Pars I. *Testacea marina univalvia non turbinata*. Pars II. *Cochleæ marinæ, seu testacea marina univalvia turbinata*. Pars III. *Conchæ marinæ, id est testacea marina bivalvia quæ duabus constant valvis in cardine*, &c.—*System of Breynius*. In this system, which was published in 1732, shells are divided into eight classes; namely, 1. *Tubulus*. 2. *Cochlidium*. 3. *Polythalamium*. 4. *Lepas*. 5. *Concha*. 6. *Conchoides*. 7. *Balanus*. 8. *Echinus*.—*Tournefort's system* divided shells into *Monotona*, *Ditoma*, and *Polytoma*.—*D'Argenville's system* comprehended shells within four divisions; namely, 1. Sea-shells. 2. Freshwater-shells. 3. Land-shells. 4. Fossil-shells.—*Klein's system.* Klein divided shells into six parts; namely, 1. *Cochlis*. 2. *Conchæ*. 3. *Polyconchæ*. 4. *Niduli testacei*. 5. *Echinus marinus*, seu *echinodermata*. 6. *Tubulus marinus*.—*Adamson's system.* This system, which was published in 1757, consists of three classes; namely, 1. *Limaçons*. 2. *Les Conques*. 3. *Les conques multivalves*.—*Geoffrey's system*, which was published in 1767, is very similar to that of Adamson.—*Muller's system*, which was published in 1776, arranges testaceous animals into three families; namely, 1. *Testacea animalia*. 2. *Testacea bivalvia*. 3. *Testacea multivalvia*.

In the preceding systems it is observable that in those of the earliest date, the characters are taken from the shells; but in the three last, the marks of discrimination are gathered from the animal as well as the shell. But this latter mode is not generally preferred, on account of the imperfect knowledge which has hitherto been obtained respecting the animals that inhabit shells. The *Linnean system*, which is the one now universally followed, notwithstanding the objections which have been started against it, is built entirely on the external character of the shell. It consists of the three usual divisions, or orders; namely, Univalves, Bivalves, and Multivalves, which are divided altogether into thirty-six genera, as follow:

MULTIVALVES.

1. *Chiton*.
2. *Lepas*, Acorn Shell.
3. *Pholas*, Piddock or Pierce Stone.

BIVALVES.

4. *Mya*, Gaper.
5. *Solen*, Razor or Sheath-Shell.
6. *Tellina*, Double Wedge-Shell.
7. *Cardium*, Cockle or Heart-Shell.
8. *Mactra*.
9. *Donax*, Wedge Shell.
10. *Venus*.
11. *Spondylus*, Spondyle.
12. *Chama*.
13. *Arca*, Ark-Shell.
14. *Ostrea*, Oyster.
15. *Anomia*, Bowl-shell.
16. *Mytilus*, Muscle.
17. *Pinna*, Nacre.

UNIVALVES.

18. *Argonauta*, Argonaut or Sailor.
19. *Nautilus*.
20. *Conus*, Cone Shell.
21. *Cypræa*, Gowry or Cowry.
22. *Bulla*, Dipper.
23. *Voluta*, Rhomb-Shell.
24. *Buccinum*, Whelk.
25. *Strombus*, the Screw.
26. *Murex*, the Caltrop, or Rock-Shell.
27. *Trochus*, Button-Shell.
28. *Turbo*, Whorl or Wreath.
29. *Helix*, Snail.
30. *Nerita*.
31. *Haliotis*, Sea Ear.
32. *Patella*, Limpet.
33. *Dentalium*, Tooth-Shell.
34. *Serpula*, Worm-Shell.
35. *Teredo*.
36. *Sabella*.

Animals inhabiting shells. The animals which inhabit shells are of the Order *Mollusca*, in the Linnean system, of which the following list contains a general account; namely,

Animal.	Inhabiting.
Doris,	*Chiton*.
Triton,	*Lepas*.
Ascidia,	*Pholas, Mya, Solen, Mytilus*.
Tethys,	*Tellina, Cardium, Mactra, Donax, Venus, Spondylus, Chama, Arca, Ostrea*.
Limax,	*Pinna, Conus, Cypræa, Bulla, Voluta, Buccinum, Strombus, Murex, Trochus, Turbo, Helix, Neritas, Haliotis, Patella*.
Terebella,	*Dentalium, Serpula, Teredo*.
Nereis,	*Sabella*.

To these may be added, the *Sepia* and *Clio*, if, as is supposed by some, they are the inhabitants of the *Argonauta*.

Explanation of the Plate (33).

Multivalves. Fig. 1. The *Lepas anatifera*, *b* the base, *p p* the peduncle, *f f* the feelers, *l l* the ligament, *w* a piece of wood to which the peduncle is affixed.—Fig. 2. The *Lepas rugosa*, *o* the *Operculum*, or lid, *b* the base, *f f* the furrows, *s* the stone to which the base of the shell is affixed.—Fig. 3. The *Chiton marginatus*.—Fig. 4. The *Lepas tintinnabulum*.—Fig. 5. The *Pholas crispatus*.

Bivalves. *Fig.* 6. The *Solen antiquatus*, *c* the cartilage, *m* the margin, or limb, *h* the hinge.—*Fig.* 7. The *Ostrea lævis*, *s* the longitudinal and transverse *striæ*, *e e* the ears, or auricles.—*Fig.* 8. The *Tellina fabula*, *c* the cartilage, or ligament, *h h* the hinge.—*Fig.* 9. The *Mytilus edulis*, *c* the cartilage, *l l* the length of the shell, *b b* the breadth of the shell.—*Fig.* 10. The *Chama cor*, *d* the disk, *r r* the rostrum, or beak.—*Fig.* 11. The *Mytilus edulis*, *b* the byssus, or beard, *s s* the seam.—*Fig.* 12. Hinge of the *Solen siliqua*, *l* the lateral teeth.—*Fig.* 13. Hinge of the *Mya pictorum*, *p* primary tooth, *d d* double teeth.—*Fig.* 14. Hinge of the *Tellina radula*, *p p* primary teeth, *c* cartilage.—*Fig.* 15. Inside of both valves of the *Donax trunculus*, *a* the left valve, *b* right valve, *l* lateral teeth, *p* primary complicated tooth, or cleft in the middle, *m m* crenulated margin.—*Fig.* 16. Hinge of *Venus gallina*, *p p* primary teeth, *l* lateral tooth.—*Fig.* 17. Hinge of *Spondylus Gæderopus*, *i i* incurved teeth.—*Fig.* 18. Hinge of *Ostrea varia*, *c* cavity of the hinge, *e* superior ear, *i* inferior ear.—*Fig.* 19. Hinge of the *Cardium aculeatum*, *l* lateral tooth, *m m* middle teeth, *s s* spines.—*Fig.* 20. Hinge of *Arca pilosa*, *n n* numerous small teeth the distinguishing characteristic of the genus *Arca.—Fig.* 21. The *Solen ensis.—Fig.* 22. The *Mya arenaria.—Fig.* 23. The *Mactra lutraria.—Fig.* 24. The *Arca Noæ.—Fig.* 25. The *Chama cor.—Fig.* 26. The *Mytilus incurvatus.*

Univalves. *Fig.* 27. The *Trochus umbilicatus*, *a* the aperture, *u* the *Umbilicus.—Fig.* 28. The *Helix vivipera*, *a* the apex, *b* the base, *w* a whorl, *f* *Fasci*, or bands.—*Fig.* 29. The *Murex muricatus*, *a* the aperture, *b* the base, *c* the canal, *r* the rostrum, *s s s* the sutures of the spire, or whorl.—*Fig.* 30. The *Helix subulata*, *s* the spire, *b* the body, *p* the pillar-lip.—*Fig.* 31. The *Strombus pugilis*, *s* the spire, *f* the front, *o o* the outer lip, *p* the pillar-lip, *c* the canal, or gutter.—*Fig.* 32. The *Turbo terebra*, *b* the shell rubbed through in the back, to show the pillar, or columella, *b* the body, *c c c* the columella.—*Fig.* 33. The *Argonauta argo* in the act of sailing, *m* the double membrane which it spreads and directs to answer the purpose of a sail, *a a a* the arms which it throws over the shell to answer the purpose of oars.—*Fig.* 34. The *Helix putris*, *b* the back, *v* the venter, *w* the whorl, or volution.—*Fig.* 35. The *Nautilus spirula*, *c c c c c* the chambers, *s* the siphunculus.—*Fig.* 36. The *Turbo costatus*, *r* the ribs.—*Fig.* 37. The *Turbo labiatus*, *s* reversed, or heterostrophe spire, *t* teeth of a univalve.—*Fig.* 38. The *Serpula triquetra.—Fig.* 39. The *Teredo navalis.—Fig.* 40. The *Dentalium entailis.—Fig.* 41. The *Sabella tubiformis.*

CONCHY'LIA *fossilia* (*Con.*) Fossile Shells.

CONCHY'LIUM (*Con.*) all sorts of shell-fish, particularly that from which the purple dye is procured, which is also called by the same name. *Plin.* l. 9, c. 35.

CONCHYRO'IDES (*Anat.*) vide *Coracoides Processus.*

CONCIDE'NTIA (*Med.*) a decrease of bulk in the whole or any part of the body; also the subsiding of a tumour.

CONCILIA'TOR *Furti* (*Ant.*) one who espied and watched whilst a theft was committed. *Ascon.*

CONCILIA'TORS (*Ecc.*) a title which has been given to writers of the Romish Church, who advocate the cause of their church in the fairest manner.

CONCI'NNOUS (*Mus*) an epithet for a performance in concerts, which is executed with delicacy, truth, and spirit.

CONCIONATO'RES (*Law*) Common-councilmen; freemen called to the hall, or the Common-council of the city of London as most worthy to be chosen.

CONCISO'RIUS (*Ant.*) a smith's tool with which horses' hoofs were pared; a butteris, or paring knife.

CONCLAMA'TIO (*Ant.*) a funeral cry over the body of a deceased person previous to its being burnt, by which it was expected to recall the departed soul, and to awaken the deceased, as it were, from his sleep. When this failed, he was given up for lost, which was expressed by the phrase *conclamatum est*. The poets allude to this custom. *Prop.* l. 4, eleg. 7, l. 23.

At mihi non oculos quisquam inclamavit euntes:
Unum impetrâssem, te revocante, diem.

Ovid. Trist. l. 3, eleg. 3, l. 43.

Nec mandata dabo; nec cum clamore supremo
Labentes oculos claudet amica manus.

Serv. in Virg. Æn. l. 6, v. 218.

CO'NCLAVE (*Ecc.*) *conclave*, a closet, or inner room, shut up under lock and key; more especially the room in the Vatican, where the cardinals meet to choose a pope; whence the assembly itself is commonly distinguished by this name.

CONCLU'SION (*Law*) is when a man, by his own act upon record, has charged himself with a duty.

CONCLUSION (*Log.*) the third proposition of a syllogism, so called after it has been proved, or drawn as a conclusion from the other two. Before it has been proved it is called the *Question.*

CONCOAGULA'TION (*Chem.*) the coagulation, concretion, or crystallization, of several different salts, first dissolved together in some fluid.

CONCO'CTION (*Med.*) is said to be such an operation of nature upon morbid matter, by the power of nature, and generally with the assistance of art, as renders it fit for separation from the healthy parts of our fluids, and to be thrown out of our bodies. Concoction, however, in its more obvious sense, is taken for digestion.

CON CO'MMODO (*Mus.*) Italian, signifying with an easy quickness.

CO'NCORD (*Gram*) that part of Syntax which treats of the agreement of words according to their several inflections. There are three principal concords, namely, between the Nominative and the Verb; the Adjective and the Substantive; and the Relative and the Antecedent.

CONCORD (*Law*) 1. An agreement made between two or more persons upon a trespass committed, by way of satisfaction for the damage done, &c. This concord is either executory or executed. *Plowd.* 5, 6. 8. 2. An agreement between parties who intend the levying a fine of lands one to the other, as to how and in what manner the land shall pass.

CONCORD (*Mus.*) in French *Accord*; the union of two or more sounds in such manner as to render them agreeable to the ear. *Concords* are either perfect or imperfect. *Perfect concords* consist of the fifth and eighth. *Imperfect concords* of the third and sixth, which are subdivided into the greater and less. Concords are moreover divided into *consonant* and *dissonant.—Consonant concords* consist of the *perfect concord*, and its *derivatives; Dissonant concords* of all other concords. Concord is applied also to the state of an instrument, as "The instrument is not in concord."

CONCO'RDANCE (*Lit.*) a general alphabetical index of all the words in the Bible.

CONCO'RDANT *verses* (*Poet.*) such as have in them several words in common, but by the addition of other words have a quite different meaning, as

Et {*canis* / *lupus*} *in silva* {*venatur* / *nutritur*} *et omnia* {*servat.* / *vastat.*}

CONCORDANT (*Mus.*) the French for what is commonly called *Tenor*. It is also an epithet for any thing harmonious, or agreeable in sounds.

CONCO'RDATE (*Ecc.*) a public act of agreement between the Pope and any prince.

CONCO'RDIA (*Ant.*) Concord was worshipped as a goddess among the Romans, and is most generally represented on medals by two hands joined, or by persons shaking hands. [vide *Manus*] *Concordia militum* was sometimes represented on coins, as on that of Didianus Julianus in the annexed figure, representing a female holding two military standards, the inscription CONCORD. MILIT. *Tristan. Comm. Histor.; Beg. Thes. Brand.*

CONCQUE (*Mil.*) French for a piece of ordnance wider about the mouth than at the breech. A kind of shell used formerly instead of a trumpet.

CONCREMA'TION (*Chem.*) the same as calcination.

CONCRE'TE (*Phy.*) a body, either *natural* or *factitious*, made up of different principles. Antimony is a *natural concrete* compounded in the bowels of the earth: soap, on the other hand, is a *factitious concrete* prepared by art.

CONCRETE (*Log.*) is an epithet for any quality considered with its subject, as snow is white, in distinction from the abstract when the quality is considered separately, as whiteness, which may belong to snow, paper, bones, &c. but is considered separate from them all.

CONCRETE (*Arith.*) is an epithet for numbers considered in connexion with some subject, as 3 men, 4 horses, 5 pounds, &c.; whereas, if nothing be joined to the number, it is taken abstractedly, as 5, which signifies simply an aggregate of five units, whether men, horses, pounds, or whatever else.

CONCRE'TION (*Phy.*) the growing together, or composition of several substances, or particles of substances, into one body.

CONCRETION (*Chem.*) the condensation of any fluid substance into a more solid state.

CONCRETION (*Surg.*) the growing together of parts which ought to be separate, as the concretion of the fingers.

CONCRETION (*Med.*) otherwise called morbid concretions, substances formed in the animal body, either by the condensation of things into a harder state than is natural, or by the growing together of different substances into one body. When the concretion approaches the nature of a bone it is termed an *ossification*, and when it resembles that of a stone it is called a *calculus*.

CONCUBA'RIA (*Archæol.*) a fold, or pen, where cattle lie.

CONCU'BEANT (*Law*) lying together. *Stat.* 1 H. 7, c. 6.

CONCU'BINAGE (*Law*) an exception against a woman that sues for her dower, on the ground that she is a concubine, and not a wife.

CONCUPI'SCIBLE *Faculty* (*Eth.*) the animal or irrational part of man, which is susceptible of inordinate concupiscence.

CONCU'RRING *Figures* (*Geom.*) those figures which, being applied to one another, will exactly concur, or coincide at all points.

CONCU'SSION (*Phy.*) a shock occasioned by two bodies moving in contrary directions.

CONCUSSION *of the brain* (*Med.*) a sudden violent motion of the brain and the adjacent parts from a fall or blow. Concussions are mostly unattended by any fractures, and followed by almost immediate death.

CONCUSSION (*Law*) the extortion of a public officer, who by threats, or pretence of authority, attempts to pillage the people.

To COND (*Mar.*) to conduct or guide a ship in a right course; to direct the steersman how to steer.

CONDA'LIUM (*Ant.*) or *condalus*, κόνδαλος, a kind of ring that slaves wore. *Plaut. Trin.* act 4, scen. 3, v. 7; *Fest. de Verb. Signif.*

CONDENSA'NTIA (*Med.*) medicines which condensate or inspissate the juices.

CONDENSA'TION (*Phy.*) the reducing of a body to a less bulk or space, by which it is rendered more dense and compact.

CONDENSATION (*Chem.*) generally signifies the stoppage and collection of vapours made by the top of an alembic, whereby it is returned in the form of a liquid, or as it is raised in the head or receiver, there to harden into a permanent and solid substance, as in sublimation of all kinds. *Condensation* and *Compression* are frequently used promiscuously, the one for the other; but they differ in this, that the compression of a body into a smaller bulk is the effect of external force, but condensation takes place without any external application, as in the inspissation of juices by cooling.

CONDENSATION (*Med.*) the contraction of the cutaneous pores by means of refrigerating, astringent, or drying medicines.

CONDE'NSED (*Bot.*) an epithet for branches *coarctati*, squeezed very close together.

CONDE'NSER (*Pneum.*) a pneumatic machine or syringe, by which an extraordinary quantity of air may be forced into a given space.

CO'NDERS (*Com.*) persons who stand upon high places near the sea-coast at the time of the herring fishery, to point out, with boughs or otherwise, which way the shoal passes.

CON DILIGE'NZA (*Mus.*) an Italian phrase, used in musical books, signifying with diligence or care.

CO'NDIMENT (*Cook.*) a pickle or preserve.

CON DISCRE'ZIONE (*Mus.*) an Italian phrase used in music books, signifying with judgment.

CONDITAMENT (*Med.*) a composition of conserves, powders, and spices, made up in the form of an electuary, with a proper quantity of syrup.

CONDI'TIO *sine qua non* (*Phy.*) a term used in speaking of some accident or circumstance which is not essential to the thing, but is yet necessary for the production of it.

CONDI'TION (*Law*) a bridle or restraint annexed to a thing, so that by the non-performance of it the party shall receive prejudice or loss, but by the performance benefit and advantage. Conditions are of different kinds, i. e. —*Conditions in a deed*, or *express*, when joined by express words to a feoffment, lease, or other grant.—*Conditions in law*, or *implied*, when, as in the case of granting any office, the law allows the grantor to dispossess the grantee of his office if he do not justly execute all things belonging to it.—*Condition precedent*, when a lease or an estate is granted to one for life, upon condition that if the lessee pay to the lessor a certain sum on such a day, then he shall have fee simple.—*Condition subsequent*, when a man grants to another his manor in fee, upon condition that the grantee shall pay him on a certain day such a sum, or his estate shall cease.—*Conditions inherent*, such as descend to the heir with the land granted.—*Condition collateral*, that which is annexed to any collateral act.—*Conditions affirmative*, which consist of doing something.—*Conditions negative*, which consist in not doing.—*Conditions copulative*, which require the doing several things.—*Condition disjunctive*, when one of several things is required to be done.

CONDITIONS, *Equation of* (*Flux.*) certain equations in the Integral Calculus, of this form, $\dfrac{\dot{A}}{\dot{y}} = \dfrac{\dot{B}}{\dot{x}}$, useful in ascertaining whether a proposed fluxion will admit of finite integration or a finite fluent.

CONDI'TIONS *of Peace* (*Polit.*) the terms upon which peace is concluded.

CONDITION (*Vet.*) a phrase of the turf, implying the particular good state of a horse, in point of strength, make, and general appearance, which renders him peculiarly fit for the purpose to which he is destined. The term is used either in a good or a bad sense, as a horse may be in good or bad *condition*.

CONDI'TIONAL *conjunctions* (*Gram.*) those which express some condition, as *if, unless, provided,* &c.

CONDITIONAL *Propositions* (*Log.*) are propositions consisting of parts connected by the conditional particle *if.*

CO'NDORIN (*Com.*) a small weight which the Chinese, particularly those at Canton, use in weighing the silver received and paid in trade.

CON *dolce maniera* (*Mus.*) an Italian phrase used in music books, signifying after a sweet and delicate manner.

CO'NDUCT (*Law*) is used in the phrase *safe conduct*, to signify the security given by a prince, under his Great Seal, to a stranger for his quiet coming into and passing out of the realm. A safe conduct is given to enemies, a passport to friends or subjects.

CONDUCT *safe* (*Mil.*) a guard of soldiers who serve to protect any individual or individuals from the attacks of a hostile force.

CONDUCTE'UR (*Mil.*) a person entrusted with the conveyance of military stores, &c. *Conducteur* signifies also one who acts as a guide to an army.

CONDU'CTIO (*Med.*) a spasm or convulsion, according to Cœlius Aurelianus.

CONDU'CTOR (*Mil.*) an assistant to a commissary of military stores, to conduct depôts or magazines from one place to another.

CONDUCTOR (*Mus.*) he who superintends and conducts the performances in a concert.

CONDUCTOR (*Surg.*) otherwise called a *Director*, a surgical instrument which serves to conduct or direct the course of the knife on several occasions.

CONDUCTOR (*Elect.*) a term first applied by Dr. Desaguliers to those substances which are capable of receiving and transmitting electricity, in distinction from *electrics*, in which the matter or virtue or electricity may be accumulated or retained.—*Prime Conductor* is an insulated conductor so connected with the electrical machine as to receive the electricity immediately from the excited electric.

CONDUCTOR *of Lightning* (*Elect.*) a pointed metallic rod which was contrived by Dr. Franklin to be fixed to the upper parts of buildings, to secure them from the effects of lightning.

CONDUCTOR, *marine* (*Mar.*) in French *paratonnerre*, a thick metal wire, generally of copper, extending from above the maintop-gallant-truck into the water, for the purpose of defending the ship from lightning.

CO'NDUIT (*Mech.*) a pump or water-course for the conveyance of water.

CONDUPLICA'TIO (*Rhet.*) a figure of speech in which, by reason of amplification and illustration, the same word or words are repeated.

CONDUPLICA'TIO (*Bot.*) doubling together, a term in vernation or foliation; *vernata conduplicata*, conduplicate leafing, is said of a bud when the two sides of a leaf are doubled over each other at the mid-rib, as in the Rose, Ash, Walnut, &c. This term is also applied to the sleep of plants; *conduplicans somnus* is when the leaves, during the night, fold together like the leaves of a book.

CO'NDUR (*Orn.*) a large kind of American vulture, the *Vultur gryphus* of Linnæus, measuring, with the wings extended, from tip to tip, 12 or 16 feet. It preys on birds, lambs, kids, and even children. Two are said to be able to kill and devour a cow. When passing near the ground they make a tremendous deafening noise.

CONDU'RDUN (*Bot.*) a plant which, when hung about the neck, represses strumous swellings. *Plin.* l. 26, c. 5.

CONDU'RI (*Com.*) a Malayan name for a small bean used in weighing gold and silver.

CO'NDYLE (*Anat.*) vide *Condylus*.

CONDYLO'IDÆ (*Anat.*) Apophyses, or what are called *Productions*, more commonly *processes*.

CONDYLO'MA (*Med.*) κονδυλώμα, from its resemblance to κόνδυλος, a joint; a tubercle or callous eminence which rises in the folds of the *anus*, or a hardening and swelling of the *rugæ*. These tumours also frequently happen about the orifice of the *uterus*, and other parts, and have different names, as that of *ficus, crystæ,* or *thymus*, according to their resemblance to the fig, &c. *Cels.* l. 16, c. 18.

CO'NDYLUS (*Anat.*) κόνδυλος, a knot in any of the joints, formed by the epiphysis of a bone; in the fingers it is called the knuckle.

CONE (*Geom.*) from the Greek κῶνος, is, according to Euclid, a solid figure, having a circle for a base, and being produced by the entire revolution of a right-angled triangle about its perpendicular leg, called the axis of the cone, as in *fig.* 1, where ABV is the cone, DV the axis, and ACB

Fig. 1.   *Fig.* 2.   *Fig.* 3.

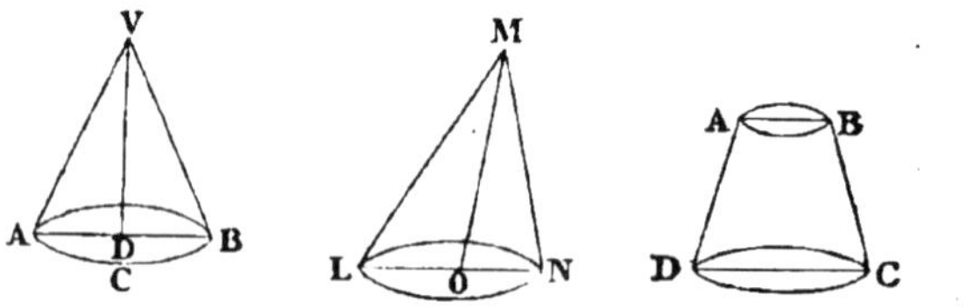

the circular base. When the axis is greater than the base of the triangle or the diameter of the circular base of the cone, namely, ADB, the cone is said to be *acute-angled, fig.* 4, i. e. the angle at the vertex AVB is acute; but if the axis is less than the diameter of the base, then AVB would be an obtuse angle, and the cone an *obtuse-angled cone, fig.* 5; if they be equal, then the angle AVB would be a right angle, and the cone *right-angled, fig.* 6. Cones are moreover divided into *right* and *scalene*, according to the position of the axis in respect to the base: if the axis be perpendicular, as in *fig.* 1, it is a *right cone*; but if the axis be not perpendicular, it is a *scalene* or *oblique cone*, as LMNO, *fig.* 2, where MO is oblique in respect to LN.—*Frustum of a cone* is that which is formed by cutting off the upper part of a cone by a plane parallel to the base, as ABCD in *fig.* 3.—*Cones of the higher kind* are those whose bases are circles of the higher kinds.

Fig. 4.   *Fig.* 5.   *Fig.* 6.

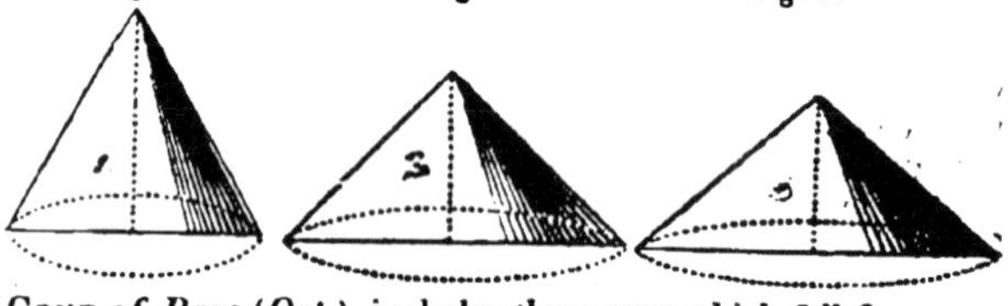

CONE *of Rays* (*Opt.*) includes those rays which fall from any point of a radiant on the surface of a glass, as in the annexed figure, where A is the point in any object, from which the rays fall on the surface of the glass BCD, then BCDA is the cone of rays.

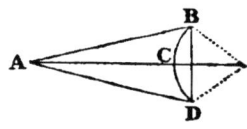

CONE (*Bot.*) the fruit of several evergreen trees, as of the Fir, Pine, Cedar, Cypress, &c. so called from its conical shape, being broad at the base, and tapering towards the end. It is composed of woody scales, that are usually open, each of which has a seed at the end. Linnæus has given to this fruit the name of *Strobilus*; but this term is of more extensive signification, comprehending several fruits, as that of the *Magnolia*, not commonly distinguished by the name of *cone*.

CONE (*Con.*) the *Conus* of Linnæus, a beautiful sort of shell, inhabited by the *Limax*, which is generally found on rocky shores. These shells mostly bear the highest price of any, one species being valued as high as a hundred pounds.

CONE'SSI (*Bot.*) a sort of bark which is reckoned a specific in diarrhœas. It is a production from the tree called in the Linnean system the *Nerium antidys entericum*.

CON *o senza violini* (*Mus.*) Italian, signifying either with or without violins.

CO'NEY-BURROWS (*Law*) places where conies breed and haunt. Commoners cannot lawfully dig up coney-burrows for a common.

CO'NFALON (*Ecc.*) a confraternity of seculars in the church of Rome, called Penitents.

CONFARREA'TIO (*Ant.*) a solemnization of marriage by the offering made with the bridal cake. *Plin.* l. 18, c. 2.

CONFE'CTA (*Med.*) confects, or seeds crusted over with dry sugar.

CONFE'CTION (*Med.*) a medicinal composition of gums, powders, syrups, &c. made up into one substance.

CONFE'CTIONER (*Cook.*) a maker and seller of confects and sweetmeats.

CONFE'DERACY (*Polit.*) an alliance between princes and states, for their defence against a common enemy.

CO'NFERENCE (*Polit.*) a discourse held between several persons on some matter of public interest.

CONFE'RTUS (*Bot.*) crowded, or clustered; an epithet for leaves, branches, or a whorl; *conferta folia*, are leaves so copious as to occupy the whole of the branches, scarcely leaving any space between, as in the *Antirrhinum, Lunaria*, &c.; *conferti rami*, are branches crowded close, in a similar manner; *confertus verticillus*, is a whorl, in which the peduncles, or flowers, stand as it were squeezed close together.

CONFE'RVA (*Bot.*) River-Weed, a genus of plants, Class *Cryptogamia*, Order *Algæ*.
Species. Withering has given upwards of one hundred and twenty species of the Conferva of British growth. The *Conferva corallina* is remarkable for its singular irritibility; for when quite fresh, and immersed into fresh water, several fibres have been observed to move in a horizontal direction, with a quick convulsive twitch, and then to stop suddenly, which they will continue to do for some time. The same effect is not observable in salt water.

CONFE'SSIO (*Ecc.*) 1. The confessionary. 2. The office of confession. *Card. Bon. Rer. Liturg.* l. 2, c. 5.

CONFE'SSION *of faith* (*Ecc.*) a public declaration of one's faith, or the faith of any particular community, as—*Confession of Augsburg*, or the articles of public faith which were drawn up by Luther, and presented to Charles V. at the diet of Augsburg.—*Auricular confession*, a private confession in the Romish church, which every man makes to his confessor; so called because it is made by whispering in his ear.

CONFESSION (*Rhet.*) vide *Concessio*.

CONFE'SSIONARY (*Ecc.*) or *Confessional*, the chair in which the priest sits to hear confessions. *Harnulf.* l. 4, c. 27.

CONFE'SSOR, *Father* (*Ecc.*) a priest of the Romish church who hears the confessions of penitents, and gives them absolution.

CONFE'SSORS (*Ecc.*) those who sealed the confession of their faith by their blood. *Anastas. Bibl. in S. Fab. Sidon. Apollin.* l. 7, ep. 17, &c.

CONFIGURA'TION (*Phy.*) the outward figure which bounds bodies, and gives them their exterior aspect or appearance, and by which bodies are principally distinguished from each other.

CONFIGURATION (*Astrol.*) the conjunction or mutual aspect of stars.

CONFIRMA'NTIA (*Med.*) strengthening medicines, or medicines which tend to confirm the strength of the body, or any part of it; also medicines which fasten the teeth in the gums.

CONFIRMA'TIO (*Rhet.*) βεβαίωσις, a figure of speech, which consists in giving strength or force to the things which have been advanced. *Cic. de Invent.* l. 1, c. 21; *Quintil.* l. 4, c. 3.

CONFIRMA'TION (*Polit.*) the rendering any title, claim, treaty, or public act, valid and indisputable.

CONFIRMATION (*Ecc.*) a holy rite or ceremony in the Christian church, whereby baptized persons are confirmed in a state of grace, and take upon themselves their baptismal vow. *Tertull. de Præscript.* c. 40; *de Baptis.* c. 7; *Cyprian. epist.* 70—73; *Cyrill. Catech.* l. 2, c. 3; *Ambros. de Initiand.* c. 6; *Dionys. de Eccles. Hierarch.* c. 2; *Alcuin. de Offic. divin.*—*Confirmation* is performed by the bishop, according to the rites of the Church of England, by laying of hands on all such as, on application, shall be found duly qualified, in point of age and Christian knowledge, to be admitted to this ceremony.

CONFI'SCATE (*Law*) forfeited to the public fisque, or king's treasury; as, the goods found in the possession of a felon, which he disavows.

CO'NFLUENT (*Bot.*) *confluens*, rendered by Withering *thronging*; is an epithet for leaves or lobes; *folia confluentia* are leaves united at the base, growing in tufts so as to leave the intermediate parts of the stem bare; *lobi confluentes*, lobes running one into another, in opposition to distinct.

CONFLUENT *Small-pox* (*Med.*) vide *Variola*.

CONFLUE'NTIA (*Med.*) a term used by Paracelsus, to express the conjunction or confederation of the microcosm with the stars; also of a disease with the remedies.

CONFORMA'TION (*Anat.*) a term applied to the parts which compose the human body; hence, *mal-conformation*, to denote some defect in the first rudiments, whereby a person comes into the world crooked, or with some of the viscera, &c. unduly proportioned; as when persons are subject to incurable asthmas from too small a capacity of the thorax, or the like.

CONFO'RMIS (*Bot.*) an epithet signifying, in the same form, or, in the same way; *folium conforme*, a leaf in all parts the same; *torsio conformis*, the twisting of a stem always the same way.

CONFO'RMIST (*Ecc.*) one that conforms to an establishment, or an established form of church discipline, particularly that of the Church of England; the seceders, or dissenters from whom, are known by the name of Nonconformists.

CONFORTA'NTIA (*Med.*) comforting medicines.

CONFRA'IRIE (*Ecc.*) or *Confrérie*, a fraternity, brotherhood, or society; as, the *Confrairie de St. George*, or *les chevaliers de la bleu gartier*, the honourable society of the Knights of the Garter.

CONFRA'TRES (*Ecc.*) or *Confrères*, brethren in a religious house; fellows of one and the same society. *Stat.* 32 *H.* 8, c. 24.

CONFRERES (*Ecc.*) vide *Confratres*.

CONFRICA'TIO (*Med.*) the reducing of any thing to powder by rubbing it with the hands.

CONFRONTE' (*Her.*) an epithet in blazoning, signifying facing one another, or full-faced.

CONFU'SÆ FEBRES (*Med.*) a sort of fevers mentioned by Bellini, which come together alternately in the same person, but do not keep their periods and alterations so exactly as to be easily distinguished from one another.

CONFUSA'NEUS PANIS (*Archæol.*) coarse brown bread.

CONFU'SIO (*Med.*) a disorder of the eyes, which happens when, upon a rupture of the internal membranes which include the humours, they are all confounded together.

CONFU'SION (*Chem.*) a mixture of liquid or fluid things.

CONFUSION (*Log.*) a term applied to the understanding when the idea of a thing is presented imperfectly, and mingled with that of other things.

CONFUSION (*Law*) *Property by confusion*, where the goods of two persons are so intermixed that the several portions cannot be distinguished.

CONFUTA'TIO (*Rhet.*) λύσις, a disproving of that which has been advanced; an answer to objections. *Cic. ad Heren.* l. 1. c. 3.

CONG. (*Med.*) an abbreviation for *Congius*.

CONGE' (*Mil.*) a term which formerly signified leave of absence.

CONGE (*Archit.*) a moulding which imitates the ring at the end of a wooden pillar.

CO'NGEABLE (*Law*) lawful, or lawfully done; done with permission; as entry congeable, &c.

CONGE' D'ACCORDER (*Law*) French for leave to accord or agree, mentioned in the statute of fines. *Lit.* Sect. 420.—*Congé d'élire*, French for leave to choose; the King's licence or permission to a Dean and Chapter to choose a bishop.

CONGELA'TI (*Med.*) persons afflicted with a catalepsy, so called because they seem to be deprived of all sensation.

CONGELA'TION (*Chem.*) a condensation of any fluid or liquid substance by means of cold.

CONGE'LATIVES (*Med.*) medicines which refrigerate and inspissate.

CONGE'NERES (*Anat.*) an epithet for muscles which are of the same kind or office.

CO'NGER (*Ich.*) κογγρίς, Conger-Eel, the *Muræna conger* of Linnæus, an eel of extraordinary size, and extremely voracious, which preys on carcases and on other fish. It is said that congers sometimes weigh a hundred pounds. *Aristot. Hist. Anim.* l. 8, c. 15.

CONGER (*Com.*) or *Congre*, probably from *congruo*, to meet together; a society of booksellers who join together in the publication of any work or works.

CO'NGES (*Archit*) vide *Conge*.

CONGE'STION (*Med.*) a collection of humours gradually formed.

CONGESTITIUS LOCUS (*Archit.*) false or loose ground, unfit for the foundation of a building.

CONGE'STUS (*Bot.*) an epithet signifying heaped together; *panicula congesta*, a panicle which has a great number of flowers, but not so squeezed or compressed as the *confertus*, or crowded.

CONGIA'RIUM (*Ant.*) a largess sometimes made to the people by the emperors, in order to gain their favour. It is distinguished from the *Donativum*, which was made only to the soldiers. *Liv.* l. 25, c. 2; *Sueton. in Aug.* c. 41; *Ursat. de Not. Roman. apud Græv. Thes. Antiq. Roman.* tom. 11, p. 638.

CO'NGIUS (*Ant.*) or *Congium*, from *congerendo*, i. e. increasing by augmentation; a liquid measure answering to the Chus of the Athenians, containing six sextaries, i. e. ten pints of wine, and nine of oil, equal to about our gallon; or at least somewhat more than our pottle. According to Pliny, Tully's son drank two of these at a draught. *Isid. Orig.* l. 14, c. 25.

CO'NGIUS (*Archæol.*) an ancient measure containing about a gallon and a pint.

CONGIUS (*Med*) a gallon or eight pints.

CONGLACIA'TIO (*Med.*) the same as *Coagulation*.

CONGLOBA'TA GLANDULA (*Anat.*) a conglobate gland, or a round gland formed by the contortion of the lymphatic vessels.

CO'NGLOBATE (*Bot.*) an epithet for cotyledons which are formed into a sphere.

CONGLOMERA'TA GLANDULA (*Anat.*) a conglomerate gland, or a gland composed of a number of glomerate glands, whose excretory ducts all unite in one common duct.

CONGLO'MERATE (*Bot.*) an epithet for the peduncle; *pedunculus conglomeratus*, a peduncle which bears flowers on a very short pedicle, closely heaped and compacted together without order, as in *Dactylis glomerata*.

CONGLUTINA'NTIA (*Med.*) healing medicines, or such as unite parts that are disjointed by accident.

CONGREGA'TION (*Phy.*) a term sometimes used to denote the least degree of mixture in which the parts of the mixed body do not touch each other more than in one point. This sort of mixture is said to be peculiar to water and other fluids.

CONGREGATION (*Ecc.*) an assembly of persons who meet together for purposes of divine worship.

CONGREGATIONALISTS (*Ecc.*) a sect of Protestants who reject all Church-government except that of a single congregation with a pastor at the head. They correspond to what are called Independants, in England.

CO'NGRESS (*Polit.*) an assembly of envoys, commissioners, deputies, &c. from different courts, meeting to agree on terms of political accommodation and pacification.—*Congress*, a general assembly of deputies from the different states in the republic of America.

CONGRESS (*Law*) a trial made by appointment of a judge, in the presence of surgeons and matrons, to determine whether a man be impotent or not, in order to dissolve a marriage.

CONGRU'ITY (*Rhet.*) signifies, in general, suitableness and propriety; but is applied, particularly, to any theme or composition which is clothed in apt and coherent language, free from any fault of grammar.

CONGRUITY (*Math.*) a term applied to figures, lines, &c. which exactly correspond when applied the one to the other.

CONGRUITY (*Eth.*) a certain fitness or apt relation between things, which determines their suitableness to form a coalition.

CONGRUS (*Ich.*) vide *Conger*.

CO'NGYLIS (*Bot.*) a rape root.

CO'NIC (*Math.*) an epithet for what appertains to a cone.

CONIC *Sections* (*Geom.*) imply the curve lines and plane figures which are produced by the intersection of a plane with a cone. A cone is a solid contained by a conical superficies and a circle; thus suppose, as in *fig.* 1, a straight line, A V D, be drawn through the point V, and extended indefinitely both ways, and this point remain fixed while the line A V D be moved round the whole circumference of the circle, two superficies will be generated by its motion, called a *conical superficies*; and these mentioned together are called *opposite superficies*. [vide *Cone*]

Sections. If a cone be cut by a plane, their common intersection is called a conic section, of which there are five different kinds; namely, the Triangle, Circle, Ellipse,

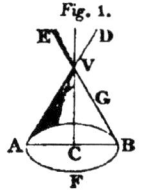
Fig. 1.

Fig. 2.

Fig. 3.

Parabola, and Hyperbola, although the three last only are peculiarly called Conic Sections.

Triangle. If the cutting plane pass through the vertex of the cone and any part of the base, the section will be a triangle, as V A B, *fig.* 2.

CONIC SECTIONS.

Circle. If the plane cut the cone parallel to the base, or make no angle with it, the section will be a circle, as B A D, *fig. 3*; but if the oblique cone, V A B, or V *a b*, *fig.* 4, having the circular base A E B, or *a. e b*, be so cut by a plane, D E C, that the angle D b*e* = ∠ B, or the ∠ C = ∠ A, then the cone is said to be cut by this plane in a *subcontrary position*, and the section in this case, D E C, which is always a circle, is called the *subcontrary section*.

Ellipse. The section is an ellipse which cuts the cone obliquely through both sides, or when the plane is inclined to the base in a less angle than the side of the cone, as D A B, *fig.* 5.

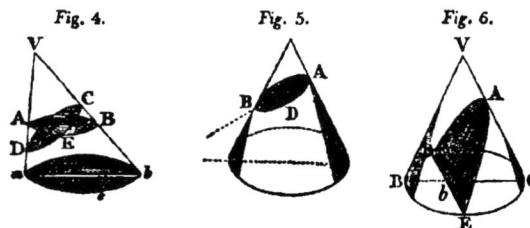

Parabola. The section is a parabola when the cone is cut by a plane, as A D E, *fig.* 6, parallel to the side V B, or when the cutting plane and the side of the cone make equal angles with the base.

Hyperbola. The section is an Hyperbola, as D A E, *fig.* 7, when the cutting plane makes a greater angle with the base than the side of the cone does; and if the plane be continued to cut the opposite cone, this latter section is called the *opposite Hyperbola* to the former, as B *b* E. Hyperbolas are said to be mutually conjugate where two pairs of opposite hyperbolas come together, as in *fig.* 15, where the curves D A E, F B G, and *d a e, f b g*, are mutually conjugate.

Parts of the Sections. The principal parts of the three sections, namely, the Ellipse, Parabola, and Hyperbola, are as follow:—

Vertex. The Vertices of any section are the points where the cutting plane meets the opposite sides of the cone, or the sides of the verticular triangular section, as A and B, *fig.* 5, 6, 7; hence the ellipse and opposite hyperbolas have each two vertices, but the parabola only one, unless the other be considered to be at an infinite distance.

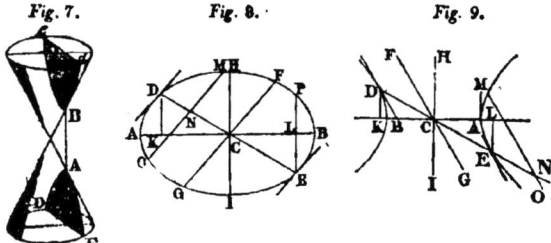

Centre. The Centre is that point in a figure in which every straight line passing through it, and terminated by the curve, or opposite curves, is bisected; as C in the ellipse, *fig.* 8, and C in the hyperbola, *fig.* 9; but the centre of a parabola is infinitely distant from the vertex.

Diameter. The Diameter is any straight line passing through the centre, and terminated by the curve, or opposite curves, as A B and D E, *fig.* 3. 5. 7. or *fig.* 8, 9. The Diameters of the parabola are infinite, because they are drawn through the centre point at an infinite distance, and they are also parallel to the side of the cone, as A *b, fig.* 6. The diameters are of two kinds; namely, transverse and conjugate. The *transverse diameter* is that which passes through the principal vertices, and is otherwise called the *axis*, as A B in the ellipse and hyperbola, *fig.* 8, 9, and A *b* in *fig.* 6 or 10. In the ellipse this is the longest diameter, but in the hyperbola it is the shortest. The *conjugate diameter* is the line drawn through the centre, and parallel to the tangent of the curve at the vertex; thus, H I is the conjugate of the axis A B in the ellipse and hyperbola, *fig.* 8, 9, and is parallel to the tangent A M at A; and F G, a conjugate to D E, is parallel to the tangent at D, *fig.* 8, 9. Hence the conjugate of the axis is perpendicular to the same, but the conjugates of all other diameters are oblique to them.

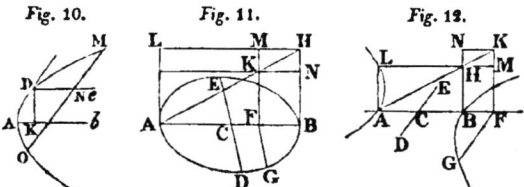

Ordinates. An Ordinate to any diameter is a line parallel to its conjugate, or to the tangent at its vertex, and terminated by the diameter and curve, as L E, which is parallel to A M, the tangent at the vertex A, in *fig.* 9; D K is also an ordinate to the axis A B and M N; N O are ordinates to the diameter D E. Hence the ordinates of the axis are also perpendicular to it, but the ordinates of other diameters are oblique to them. The line L P and L E, on each side of the diameter A B, in *fig.* 8, is called the *double ordinate*.

Absciss. An absciss is a segment of a diameter contained between its vertex, and an ordinate to it, as A K or B L, and D N or E N, *fig.* 8 and 10. Hence, in the ellipse and hyperbola, every ordinate has two abscisses, but in the parabola only one; the other vertex of the diameter being infinitely distant.

Parameter. The Parameter of any diameter, otherwise called the *Latus rectum*, is the third proportional to any two conjugate diameters in the ellipse or opposite hyperbolas, or to any absciss and its ordinate in the parabola. From this relation Apollonius deduced one of the primary properties, by which the ellipse, hyperbola, and parabola, are distinguished, and from which they derive their names; thus, suppose G F to be an ordinate to the diameter A B of the ellipse or hyperbola B G, *fig.* 11, 12, E D to be the conjugate diameter, and B H the parameter, or third proportional, between A B and E D. Moreover complete the rectangle L A B H, let L H meet F K in M, and let K N, the side of the rectangle K B opposite to B F, meet B H in N; then, in *fig.* 11, the square of the ordinate F G is less than the rectangle under the absciss F B, and the parameter B H, by the rectangle M N, similar to L B, and having one of its sides equal to B F: but, in *fig.* 12, the square of the ordinate F G is greater than the rectangle under the absciss B F, and the parameter B H, by the rectangle M N, similar to L B, and having one of its sides equal to B F. From this, ἔλλειψις, deficiency, comes the name of Ellipse, in the first case; and from the ὑπερβολή, or excess, that of Hyperbola. On the other hand, the Parabola derives its name from παραβολή, the equality which the square of H K, the ordinate, in *fig.* 13, bears to the rectangle under P and B K; supposing A B C to be a parabola, B K the diameter, A G and H K, the ordinates to it, and P the parameter, or third proportional to B G, the absciss, and A G its corresponding ordinate.

Focus. The Focus, or Umbilicus, is that point in the axis where the ordinate is equal to half the parameter, as K and L, *fig.* 8, 9, where D K or E L is equal to the semi-parameter. Hence the ellipse and hyperbola have each two *foci*, but the parabola only one.

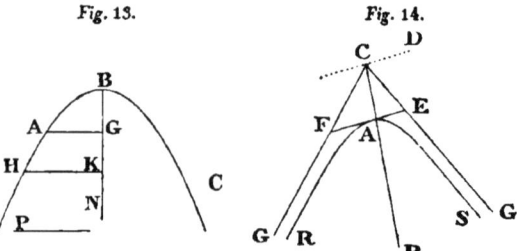

Fig. 13. Fig. 14.

Asymptote. The Asymptotes are two right lines which continually approach nearer and nearer to some curve, in such manner that, when they are both indefinitely produced, they are nearer together than by any assignable distance: suppose C P to be the diameter of the hyperbola R A S, and C D the semiconjugate to it, then, if F E be a tangent at the point A, and A E = A F = C D; then the lines C G, C G, drawn from the centre C, through the points E and F, will be the asymptotes to the hyperbola R A S, and may in like manner be produced so as to be the asymptotes to any opposite hyperbola. In the same manner the diagonals H C K and I C L, of the rectangle H I K L, are the asymptotes to the curves of the conjugate hyperbolas in *fig.* 15.

Fig. 15.

Directrix. The Directrix is a right light perpendicular to the axis of a conic section. [vide *Directrix*]

Conic (*Bot.*) or *conical*, an epithet for a receptacle which is round, broad at the base, and tapering to a point like a cone, as in *Bellis*, the Common Daisy.

CO′NICAL (*Math. & Bot.*) vide Conic.

CONJECTA′NEA (*Ant.*) books which contain the conjectures of writers.

CO′NIFERÆ (*Bot.*) the fifteenth Order in Linnæus's Fragments of a Natural Method, and the fifty-first of his Natural Orders, containing the cone-bearing trees, as the Fir, Pine, Cypress, &c.

CONINGE′RIA (*Law*) a coney-burrow, or a warren of conies. *Inquis.* anno 47, ii. 3.

CONJOINED *in Lure* (*Her.*) an epithet for two wings joined together with their tips downwards, as in the annexed figure. [vide *Conjunct.*]

CONJO′INT (*Mus.*) or *Conjunct Degrees*, two notes which immediately follow each other in the order of the scale, as Ut, Re. — *Conjoint tetrachords,* two tetrachords where the same chord is the highest of the one, and the lowest of the other.

CONJU′NCT (*Her.*) or *conjoined,* an epithet for charges which are joined together, as " *Gules,* two lions conjoined under one head, gardant, *argent ;* name *Kellum.*"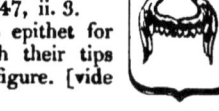

CONISSA′LÆ (*Min.*) an old term for a class of fossils which were not inflammable, nor soluble in water; of which number was sand, and other gritty substances.

CONISTE′RIUM (*Ant.*) the place where the wrestlers, after they had been anointed with oil, were besprinkled with dust, that they might take the surer hold of one another. *Vitruv.* l. 5, c. 10.

CO′NJUGAL *Rights, Restitution of* (*Law*) a species of matrimonial suit, which may be brought either by the husband or the wife against the party who is guilty of the injury of subtraction, or of living in a state of separation.

CONJUGA′TES (*Rhet.*) an epithet for what comes from one original, as when from one word we argue to another of the same original; as " Si risus gaudium est, ergo ridere est gaudere." *Cic. Top.* c. 9; *Quint.* l. 5, c. 10.

CO′NJUGATE (*Geom.*) an epithet to denote the junction of two lines, as a *Conjugate axis,* that which crosses another axis. [vide *Axis*]—*Conjugate Diameter,* the shortest axis in an ellipsis. [vide *Diameter*]—*Conjugate Hyperbolas,* hyperbolas having the same axes, but in contrary order. [vide *Hyperbola* and *Conic Sections*]

CONJUGATE (*Bot.*) *conjugatus,* an epithet for a leaf, or a raceme; *folium conjugatum,* a pinnate leaf which has only one pair of leaflets; *racemus conjugatus,* a raceme having two racemes only united by a common peduncle.

CO′NJUGATES (*Rhet.*) are such things as qualities, &c. which are derived from an original, as merciful, mercifully, from mercy.

CONJUGATES (*Log.*) is when from one word we argue to another, as " If weeping is to sorrow, then to weep is to sorrow."

CONJUGA′TING (*Gram.*) the act of going through the inflection of a verb according to its several moods, tenses, and persons.

CONJUGA′TION (*Gram.*) signifies generally the coupling or yoking of things together, but particularly the inflection of verbs; also the inflections themselves.

CONJUGATION (*Anat.*) a term for a pair of nerves, or for two nerves arising together, and serving for the same operation, sensation, or motion.

CONIUM (*Bot.*) a genus of plants, Class 5 *Pentandria,* Order 2 *Digynia.*

Generic Characters. CAL. *umbel* universal; *partial* similar; *involucre* universal many-leaved; *partial* halved; *perianth* proper.—COR. *universal* uniform; *proper* of five petals.—STAM. *filaments* five; *anthers* roundish.—PIST. *germ* inferior; *styles* two; *stigmas* obtuse.—PER. none; *fruit* nearly globose; *seeds* two.

Species. The species are of different sorts, as—*Conium maculatum, Cicuta, Cicutaria, Coriandrum,* &c. Common Hemlock, a biennial, native of Europe.—*Conium rigens,* &c. Fine-leaved Hemlock, a shrub, native of the Cape of Good Hope.—*Conium africanum,* seu *Caucalis,* &c. Rue-leaved Hemlock, an annual, native of Africa.—*Conium Royeni,* seu *Caucalis,* &c. native of Egypt.

CONJU′NCT (*Med.*) an epithet for the immediate cause of a disease; also for those signs of a disorder which are pathognomic.

CONJUNCT *Fiers* (*Law*) in Scotch Law when several people are conjunctly infelt, or otherwise have a joint fee.

CONJU′NCTI *morbi* (*Med.*) a name for two diseases which come together, and are distinguished into *connexi* and *consequentes,* the former subsisting at the same time, and the latter following one another.

CONJU′NCTION (*Astron.*) a termed applied to two planets which meet in the same degree of the zodiac, which is one of the principal aspects, marked thus [☌]. Conjunction is either apparent or true.—*Apparent conjunction* is when a right line, drawn through the centre of two planets, does not pass through the centre of the earth.—*True,* or *real conjunction,* is when a right line, passing through the centres of two planets, and being produced, passes also through the centre of the earth.

CONJUNCTION (*Gram.*) is a part of speech which joins words and sentences, and is distinguished, according to its use, into—*Copulative conjunctions,* because they join both the words and the sense, as *and, also,* &c.—*Disjunctive conjunctions,* are such as join the words, but disjoin things in the sense, as *neither, nor, either, or,* &c.—*Causal conjunctions,* which denote a reason, as *because, for,* &c.—*Conditional conjunctions,* which express a condition, as *if, unless,* &c.—*Enclitic conjunctions* are such, in Latin, as throw back the accent on the syllable going before, as *que, ne, ve,* &c.

CONJUNCTI'VA *tunica (Anat.)* vide **Adnata**.

CONJURA'TIO (*Law*) signifies, 1. An oath, and *conjuratus,* or *conjurator,* one who is bound by the same oath; and *conjurare* is where several affirm a thing on oath. *Mon. Ang.* tom. 1, p. 207. 2. A plot, or compact, made by several persons, who combine by oath to do some public harm; but it is particularly applied to the secret compact which persons were supposed to enter into with the evil spirit to work some mischief. It differs from witchcraft, inasmuch as conjurors endeavour by enchantments to raise the devil, but witches bargain with the evil spirit to do what they desire of him. Sorcerers, on the other hand, try, by force of incantations, to produce strange effects above the ordinary course of nature.

CON *Moto (Mus.)* an Italian phrase in Music-books, signifying with agitation.

CO'NNA (*Bot.*) the *Cassia fistula* of Linnæus.

CONNARUS (*Bot.*) a genus of plants, Class 16 *Monadelphia,* Order 5, *Decandria.*
Generic Characters. CAL. *perianth* one-leaved.—COR. *petals* five.—STAM. *filaments* ten; *anthers* roundish.—PIST. *germ* roundish; *style* cylindric; *stigma* obtuse.—PER. *capsule* oblong; *seed* single.
Species. The species are trees and shrubs, as—*Connarus monocarpos, Rhus, Phaseolus,* Ceylon Sumach, a tree, native of the island of Ceylon.—*Connarus Africanus,* a shrub, native of Sierra Leone. — *Connarus Asiaticus,* seu *monocarpos,* seu *Phaseolus,* a shrub, native of the East Indies.—*Connarus decumbens,* seu *Hermannia,* a shrub, native of the Cape of Good Hope.—*Connarus pinnatus,* seu *Perim,* a shrub, native of the East Indies. —*Connarus Santaloides, Santaloides,* &c. a shrub, native of the East Indies.—*Connarus mimosoides,* a shrub, native of the islands of Nicobar.

CO'NNATE (*Bot.*) *connatus;* an epithet for leaves, filaments, and anthers; *folium connatum* is said of two leaves, which are so united at their bases as to have the appearance of one leaf, as in the Garden Honeysuckle. Filaments and anthers are also called connate when united into one body, as in the Class *Monadelphia* and *Syngenesia.*

CONNETA'BLE de France (*Polit.*) Constable of France; an officer under the old regime, who succeeded the Grand Sénéchal de France. It was originally not a military place of trust, but merely an office belonging to the King's Household.
CONNETABLE *de France (Mil.)* was a particular corps immediately under the command and direction of the Marshal of France, composed of a provost-general, four lieutenants, four exempts, and forty-eight mounted guards, who wore a nouqueton for the King's service.

CONNEXION (*Anat.*) the same as *Symphysis;* a sort of articulation. [vide *Articulation*]

CO'NNING (*Mar.*) or Cunning, the art of directing the steersman to guide the ship in her proper course.

CONNI'VENS (*Bot.*) vide *Converging.*

CONNIVE'NTES GLANDULÆ (*Anat.*) those wrinkles which are found in the *Ilium* and *Jejunum* intestines.

CONNOISSE'UR (*Lit.*) a person well versed or thoroughly skilled in any science.

CONNUTRI'TIOUS (*Nat.*) that food which becomes habitual to a person from his particular diet.

CONOBE'A (*Bot.*) the *Conopea aquatica* of Linnæus.

CONOCARPODEN'DRON (*Bot.*) the same as *Protea.*

CONOCA'RPUS (*Bot.*) a genus of plants, Class 5 *Pentandria,* Order 1 *Monogynia.*
Generic Characters. CAL. *perianth* one-leaved; *divisions* subulate.—COR. *petals* five.—STAM. *filaments* either five or ten; *anthers* globose.—PIST. *germ* large; *style* single; *stigma* obtuse.—PER. none distinct from the seed; *seed* single.
Species. The species are shrubs, as the—*Conocarpus erecta,* seu *Manghana,* &c. seu *Foliis,* &c. seu *Alnus,* &c. seu *Alni,* &c. seu *Rudbeckia,* &c. seu *Innominata,* Jamaica Button-tree, native of Jamaica.—*Conocarpus procumbens,* seu *Rudbeckia,* native of Cuba.—*Conocarpus racemosa,* seu *Mangle,* native of the Caribbees.

CONOCRA'MBE (*Bot.*) the *Theligonum conocrambe* of Linnæus.

CONO'DIS (*Com.*) a small coin used at Goa, and in all the kingdom of Cochin.

CO'NOID (*Geom.*) a figure resembling a cone, except that its sides are curved instead of straight: it is generated by the revolution of a conic section about its axis, and is therefore denominated an elliptical, hyperbolic, and parabolic conoid.

CONOI'DES (*Med.*) an epithet for the Pineal gland, from its resemblance to a cone in figure.

CONOPE'A (*Bot.*) a genus of plants, Class 14 *Didynamia,* Order 2 *Angiospermia.*
Generic Characters. CAL. *perianth* one-leaved; *segments* erect.—COR. one-petaled; *tube* oblong; *upper lip* erect; *lower* trifid.—STAM. *filaments* four; *anthers* sagittate.— PIST. *germ* roundish; *style* filiform; *stigma* two-lobed. PER. *capsule* roundish; *seeds* very many.
Species. The only species is *Conopea aquatica,* seu *Conobea,* &c. native of Guiana.

CONO'PHORA (*Bot.*) the *Protea conocarpa* of Linnæus.

CO'NOPS (*Ent.*) a genus of animals, Class *Insecta,* Order *Diptera.*
Generic Character. Mouth with a proboscis; *antennæ* clavate.
Species. Insects of this tribe extract animal juices, and the species are distinguished into those that have a sucker geniculate at the base, and those that have a sucker geniculate at the base and the middle.

CONQUASSA'TION (*Med.*) a species of comminution, or an operation by which moist concrete substances, and the vegetables, fruits, &c. are by bruising in a mortar, as fresh affusion of some moist liquor, reduced to a soft pulp.

CO'NQUEST (*Law*) a feudal term for *purchase.*

CONRE'TA *pellis (Archæol.)* a skin, or hide dressed.

CONSANGUI'NEO (*Law*) a writ mentioned in the *Register Originalium Brevium.* [vide *Cosinage*]

CONSANGUI'NEUS *frater (Law)* a brother by the father's side.

CONSANGUI'NITY (*Law*) a kindred by blood and birth, in distinction from *affinity,* which is a kindred by marriage. [vide *Law*]

CO'NSCIENCE, *courts of (Law)* courts for the recovery of small debts.

CONSCRI'PTA *Veterum (Ant.)* the writings of the ancients.

CONSCRI'PTI (*Ant.*) or *Patres conscripti,* Conscript Fathers; an appellation for the Roman senators, who were so called because they were enrolled from the Equestrian order or the knights, for the purpose of completing the number of the senators. *Liv.* l. 2, c. 1.

CO'NSCRIPTS (*Mil.*) a revolutionary term applied to the recruits for the French army.

CONSECRA'TIO (*Ant.*) was a religious rite among the Romans, by which they set any person or thing apart for sacred purposes, as their high priests, &c.; or made it sacred, and a fit object of divine worship: as the emperors, their wives, or children, who, in this manner, were enrolled among the number of the gods. This was sometimes called *apotheosis,* but on medals it is distinguished by the name of CONSECRATIO, and is simbolically represented either by an altar, as in the subjoined figure 1;

Fig. 1.

Fig. 2.

or by the effigy of a person mounting to heaven on the back of an eagle, as fig. 2; and in other forms. The first of these figures represents the reverse of a medal of Claudius Gothicus, the second that of Saloninus, the son of Gallienus. *Dionys. Ant.* l. 2; *Liv.* l. 1, c. 16; *Sueton. Claud.* c. 2; *Herodian* l. 4, c. 2; *Firmic. de Error. Prof. Rel.*; *Lactant. de Fal. Rel.* l. 1, c. 15; *Gyrald. de Var. Sepel. Rit.* c. 16; *Panvin. Fastor.* l. 2; *Guther. de Jur. Man. apud Græv. Thes. Antiq. Rom.* vol. xii.

CONSECRA'TION (*Ecc.*) a ceremony in the Christian Church of hallowing, or making sacred, particular places, that are set apart for holy purposes.

CONSECTA'RIUM (*Rhet.*) consectary; a brief argument, wherein the conclusion necessarily follows the antecedent. *Cic. de Fin.* l. 3, c. 7.

CONSE'CTARY (*Geom.*) some consequent truth obtained from a demonstration.

CONSECU'TION month (*Chron.*) a name given to the lunar month, or the space between the conjunction of the moon with the sun.

CONSE'CUTIVE (*Mus.*) an epithet for two chords, one of which immediately succeeds the other.

CONSE'NT (*Eth.*) our simple approbation of means, as we judge them proper for our purpose when they are placed within our reach, or power; and those means, when they are placed within our reach and power, employ the two acts of the will, called *Eliciti* and *Imperati*.

CONSENT of Parts (*Anat.*) the mutual sympathy and correspondence between the several parts of the body; as when one nerve is affected with the hurt that is received by another; thus the head is mostly affected by what passes amiss in the stomach.

CONSE'NTIA (*Ant.*) sacrifices to the deities, called *Consentes*. [vide *Deity*] *Fest. de Verb. Signif.*

CO'NSEQUENCE (*Log.*) an inference, or conclusion.

CONSEQUENCE (*Astron.*) or *in Consequentia*. vide *Consequentia*.

CO'NSEQUENT (*Log.*) the last part of an argument, in distinction from the former part, called the *antecedent*.

CONSEQUENT (*Math.*) the latter of two terms of proportion, in distinction from the former, or antecedent, as in the ratio $a : b$, a is the antecedent, and b the consequent.

CONSEQUE'NTIA *Signa* (*Astron.*) the signs of the zodiac, as they follow in order from east to west; whence the direct motion of the planets is called a motion *in Consequentia*, in distinction from the motion *in Antecedentia*, or the contrary order. [vide *Antecedentia*]

CONSEQUE'NTIAL LOSSES (*Law*) or consequential damages: such losses or damages as arise out of a man's act, for which, according to a fundamental principle in law, he is answerable, in case he could have avoided them: as if a man should keep a savage beast, it is at his peril to keep him up; and he is answerable for all the consequences of his breaking loose.

CONSERVA'TIO (*Med.*) pickling, or preserving from putrefaction.

CONSERVATI'VA *medicina* (*Med.*) that part of medicine which relates to the preservation of health.

CONSE'RVATOR (*Law*) a standing arbitrator appointed to adjust differences that should arise between two parties.—*Conservator of the Peace*, an officer whose special charge it was to see that the king's peace was kept. This office is now performed by all judges and magistrates, but particularly by what are now called *Justices of the Peace*.—*Conservator of the Truce and Safe Conducts*, an officer appointed by the King's letters patent, to take charge of all offences done on the high seas out of the liberties of the Cinque Ports. *Stat.* 2 *H.* 5, st. 1, c. 6.—*Conservators*, in the Roman Catholic universities, are two persons, one of whom is the *conservator* of the royal privileges, or those granted by the King, taking cognizance of all causes between the regents, students, &c.; and the other the *conservator* of the apostolical privileges, or those granted by the pope.

CONSERVATO'RII (*Mus.*) Italian for the public music-schools in Italy.

CONSE'RVATORY (*Cus.*) a place to keep or lay up things that are to be preserved.

CONSERVATORY (*Hort.*) a place where plants are kept, which is commonly attached to the green-house.

CO'NSERVE (*Med.*) a medicine of the consistence of a pulp, prepared of flowers, herbs, and fruits.

CONSIDERA'TIO *Curiæ* (*Law*) the judgment of the Court.

CONSIDERA'TION (*Law*) the material cause of a bargain, or contract, either expressed or implied, without which the latter would not be effectual and binding.

TO CONSI'GN (*Com.*) vide *Consignment*.

CONSIGNA'TION (*Law*) the putting a sum of money into sure hands till the decision of a controversy, or lawsuit, of which it is the subject matter.

CONSI'GNE (*Mil.*) a French term for a person who is not permitted to go beyond certain limits, or to leave a house wherein he is detained by superior command.

CONSIGNE'E (*Com.*) he to whom goods are sent, or consigned, for the purpose of being disposed of by sale.

CONSI'GNMENT of *goods* (*Com.*) the sending over of goods to a correspondent, or factor, to have them disposed of at the best market.

CONSIGNMENT (*Law*) vide *Consignation*.

CONSI'GNOR (*Com.*) he who consigns goods to another for sale.

CONSI'LIGO (*Bot.*) Hellebore.

CONSI'LIUM (*Med.*) the advice given by one or more physicians relative to the state of a patient.

CONSILIUM (*Law*) or *Dies Consilii*, a time allowed for the accused to make his defence, and now more commonly used for a day appointed to argue a demurrer.

CONSI'MILI *casu* (*Law*) a writ of entry which, with the writ in *Casu proviso*, lay not at common law, but are given by statute, *Gloc.* 6 *Ed.* 1, c. 7. *Westm.* 2, 13 *Ed.* 1, c. 24, for the reversioner after alienation. *F. N. B.* 205, 206.

CONSI'STENT *bodies* (*Phy.*) bodies that hold together, and preserve their form, by their own solidity, in distinction from fluids, that must be kept within a certain boundary.

CONSISTE'NTIA (*Med.*) in respect to the state of a disease signifies its acme; but when applied to the humours, or excrements, it imports its consistence, or power of holding together.

CONSI'STOR (*Archæol.*) a magistrate.

CONSISTO'RIUM (*Ant.*) a council-house, or place of audience. *Sidon.* l. 2, ep. 2; *Ammian.* l. 14, c. 7; *Orderic. Vital.* l. 2.

CONSI'STORY (*Ecc.*) the principal court held by the Pope with much splendour and solemnity.—*Consistory* or *Consistory-court*, the session or assembly of ecclesiastical persons, held by the bishop, his chancellor, or his commissary, for the determination of ecclesiastical causes. *Stat.* 24, *H.* 8, c. 12; 4 *Inst.* 338.—*Consistory* signifies likewise the tribunal, or place of justice, where the consistory courts are held.

CONSOLA'TIO (*Rhet.*) one of the topics which consists in assuaging the grief of another. *Cic. Or.* l. 3, c. 35.

CO'NSOLE (*Archit.*) ancon; an ornament cut upon the key of an arch, in the form of a bracket or shoulder-piece, as in the annexed figure, having a projecture, and serving to support a cornice or busts, vases, &c. *Vitruv.* l. 3, c. 2; *Philand.* l. 8, c. 6; *Bald. Lex. Vitruv.*

CONSO'LIDA (*Bot.*) another name for *Gomfrey*.

CONSOLIDA'NTIA (*Med.*) Medicines calculated for promoting the cure of wounds, by removing the several impediments to their agglutination.

CONSOLIDA'TION (*Nat.*) the uniting or hardening of any substance into a solid mass.

CONSOLIDATION (*Surg.*) the uniting strongly together the parts of broken bones, or the lips of wounds.

CONSOLIDATION (*Law*) in Civil Law, the conjunction of the usufruct with the propriety of the thing. 2. In Common Law, the joining two benefices in one.

CO'NSOLS (*Com.*) a sort of transferable stocks. [vide *Funds*]

CO'NSONANCE (*Gram.*) is when two words have a similarity of sound at the end that causes them to rhime.

CONSONANCE (*Mus.*) an agreement of two sounds, one grave and one acute, which are combined together in such a manner as to produce harmony. A unison is the first consonance, an eighth is the second consonance, &c. When the interval of a consonance is invariable, it is called *perfect*; but when it may be either major or minor, it is *imperfect*.

CO'NSONANT (*Mus.*) an epithet for those intervals which produce consonant concords.

CONSONANT (*Gram.*) a letter which, having no sound by itself, requires the union of a vowel.

CONSONA'NTE (*Mus.*) an Italian epithet for all agreeable intervals.

CO'NSORT (*Mus.*) a piece of music, consisting of three or more parts, mostly written *concert*.

CONSORT (*Mar.*) any ship keeping company with another.

CONSPI'RACY (*Law*) originally signified an agreement of two or more persons to indict one, or procure him to be indicted; but it is now generally employed to denote an agreement of two or more persons to do any thing that may wrongfully prejudice a third person, either in the case of subjects conspiring against their prince, or workmen against their masters, &c.—*Conspirations*, or a writ of conspiracy, which a person has after his acquittal, against others who have conspired to indict him, or cause him to be indicted. 33 *Ed.* 1, stat. 2; 7 *H.* 5; 18 *H.* 6, c. 12.

CONSPI'RING Forces (*Mech.*) such forces as conspire or combine to act on bodies so as to impel them in a certain direction

CON SPI'RITO (*Mus.*) an Italian phrase in music books, signifying to be played with spirit.

CO'NSTABLE (*Law*) in French Connétable, from the Latin *comes stabuli*, signified a master of the horse, or a commander of the cavalry. It has since been employed to denote a civil officer, as—*Constables of the Hundred*, *Chief* or *High Constables*, in distinction from *Constables of the bills*, or *Petty Constables*, who act under the Head Constable, for the preservation of the peace. *Stat. of Winton and Winchester*; 13 *Ed.* 1, c. 6; 3 *Ed.* 4, c. 1; 5 *Eliz.* c. 4.—*Constable* is likewise a name of particular officers mentioned in our statutes and elsewhere, as—*Lord High Constable of England*, an officer of the highest dignity and importance in the realm, who took place of the Earl Marshal in the Marshal's court; and was also the leader of the king's armies. 13 *R.* 2, st. 1, c. 2; *Mad. Hist. of the Excheq.* p. 27.—*Constables of Castles*, Keepers or Governors of Castles, such as the *Constable of the Tower*, and the *Constable of London*, &c., some of which offices remain to this day. They are likewise called *Constables of the Fees. Mag. Chart.* cc. 17. 20; *Stat. West.* 1 (3. *Ed.* 1), c. 15; 5 *H.* 4, c. 10; 2 *Inst.* 31.—*Constable of the Exchequer*, mentioned in *Stat. de District. Scaccar.*; 51 *H.* 3, st. 5; *Flet.* l. 2, c. 31.—*Constable of the Staple*, mentioned in *Stat.* 27 *Ed.* 3, c. 8; 15 *R.* 2, c. 9; 23 *H.* 8, c. 6.

CO'NSTANT Quantities (*Math.*) such as remain the same, while others decrease or increase: thus, the semidiameter of a circle is a constant quantity, for while the abscissa and semiordinates increase, it remains the same.

CONSTANT *forces* (*Mech.*) such as remain and act continually the same for some determinate time.

CO'NSTAT (*Law*) a certificate given out of the court of exchequer of all there is upon record relating to any matter in question. *Stat.* 3 & 4 *Ed.* 6, c. 4; 13 *Eliz.* c. 6; *Co. Lit.* 225.

CONSTELLA'TION (*Astron.*) a company of fixed stars, which are imagined to represent the form of some creature, or thing, as a bear, a man, the ship *Argo*, &c. The constellations are divided into Northern, Southern, and Zodiacal, of which the ancients reckoned altogether 48; but this number has since been considerably increased. [vide *Astronomy*, and Plate 16, 17.]

CONSTELLA'TUM unguentum (*Med.*) an ointment made of earthworms, cleansed, dried, and powdered.

CONSTIPA'TION (*Med.*) a tightness or hardness in the alvus which prevents the necessary discharges.

CONSTIPATION (*Phy.*) a term used by naturalists for the union of a body which is closer than it was before.

CONSTI'TUENT (*Polit.*) one who constitutes, or by his vote elects, a member of parliament.

CONSTITU'TION (*Polit.*) implies literally the form of government constituted in any country; but is particularly applied to the popular part of our own government, as distinguished from the monarchy.

CONSTITUTIONS *of Clarendon* (*Law*) vide *Clarendon*.

CONSTITUTIONS (*Ecc.*) ordinances for the discipline of the church, particularly the Apostolical Constitutions, and a collection of regulations, attributed to the Apostles, and supposed to have been collected by St. Clement, whose name they bear.

CONSTRI'CTION (*Med.*) vide *Adstriction*.

CONSTRICTION (*Phy.*) the crowding of any parts close together for the purpose of producing condensation.

CONSTRI'CTOR (*Anat.*) an epithet for the muscles which contract any orifice of the body, as the—*Constrictor Labium*, that which purses up the mouth.—*Constrictor Alarum Nasi*, that which draws the alæ downwards—*Constrictor Ani*, vide *Sphincter Ani*.—*Constrictor Pharyngis*, a muscle which compresses the Pharynx.

CONSTRICTOR (*Zool.*) an epithet for the *Boa*, a fierce sort of serpent. [vide *Boa*]

CONSTRICTO'RII (*Med.*) diseases attended with constriction and spasmodic affections.

CONSTRINGE'NTIA (*Med.*) astringent medicines.

CONSTRU'CTION (*Geom.*) drawing figures, schemes, lines of a problem, &c.

CONSTRUCTION *of Equations* (*Algeb.*) the finding the unknown quantities or roots of an equation, either by straight lines, or by curves: thus, quadratic equations may be constructed by means of a right line and a circle. [vide *Algebra*]

CONSTRUCTION (*Gram.*) the natural and regular disposing of words in discourse, so as to make proper intelligible sense.

CONSTRU'CTIVE Treason (*Law*) Treason construed or implied from the statute, in distinction from that which is positively declared. This sort of construction is not admitted in the law of treason. 1 *Hawk. P. C.* 34.

CONSUA'LIA (*Ant.*) Feasts and games instituted by Romulus at the time when he stole the Sabine virgins, in honour of Neptune, whom, in consequence of the plot succeeding, he called Consus, or the God of Counsel. *Varr. de Lat. Lin.* l. 5, c. 3; *Dion. Hal.* l. 2; *Liv.* l. 1,

c. 9; *Plut. in Rom.*; *Gyrald. Syntag. Deor.* l. 5, p. 162, &c.; *Panvin. de Lud. Circ.* l. 1, c. 3.

CONSUBSTA'NTIAL (*Theol.*) an epithet signifying of the same substance; thus, in the second article of our church. Christ is declared consubstantial, or of one substance with the Father.

CONSUBSTANTIA'TION (*Theol.*) the doctrine of the Lutherans who maintain the substantial presence of the body and blood of Christ in the Lord's supper, together with the substance of the bread and wine.

CONSUETUDINA'RIUS (*Ecc.*) a ritual or book, containing the rites and forms of divine offices, or the customs of abbies and monasteries.

CONSUETUDI'NIBUS et SERVITIIS (*Law*) a writ of right lying against the tenant, that deforceth the lord of the rent or service due to him. *F. N. B.* 151.

CONSUETU'DO (*Med.*) a term sometimes used in respect to non-naturals.

CO'NSUL (*Ant.*) *a consulendo*, i. e. from giving counsel, a title given to the chief magistrates at Rome, of whom there were two, who continued in office for one year. Consuls were elected on the expulsion of Tarquin, U. C. 244, and continued, nominally, until the fall of the Roman empire. The names of those who filled this office have been handed down, with little interruption, from its institution to the year U.C. 1059, A.D. 306. Their power was regal during the year they were in office, and they were chosen from the Patricians only, till the year 387, U. C. when the people obtained the privilege of electing one from among themselves. The chief badges of their office were the *prætexta*, afterwards changed for the *toga picta*, or *palmata*; the *lictors*, the *fasces*, and *securis*, of which the annexed figure gives a representation, as it is found on the reverse of a medal, struck by Brutus after the assassination of Cæsar, and alluding to the first appointment of the consuls in the person of his ancestor Junius, and L. Tarquinius Collatinus, the two first consuls, who are supposed to be here represented, the one before and the other between the lictors. *Beg. Thes. Brand.* vol. ii.

Consul (*Law*) a name given to the chief governors of cities; and, according to Bracton, it signified an Earl, as *comes* signifies a count. *Bract.* l. 1, c. 8.

Consul (*Com.*) an officer appointed by virtue of a commission from any sovereign prince or government, to attend in a more especial manner to the commercial interests of the state from whom he receives his commission.

CONSU'LTA Ecclesia (*Archæol.*) a church full or provided for.

CONSULTA'TION (*Law*) a writ, whereby a cause having been removed by prohibition from the Ecclesiastical Court to the King's Court, is returned thither. *Statute of Writ of Consultations.* 24 Ed. 1.; *New Nat. Brev.* 119; *Reg. Orig.*

Consultation (*Med.*) the asking of advice from a physician or more commonly the taking of counsel, as is usual among physicians, who assemble in numbers to deliberate on particular cases, when they are said "To hold a *consultation.*"

CONSULTO'RIA *hostia* (*Ant.*) the victim which was slain in order to have its entrails examined by the Aruspices, in distinction from the *hostia animalis*, which was slain as an offering to the gods. *Fest. de Verb. Signif.*

CONSUMMA'TION (*Law*) the most intimate union of a married couple, which is essential to make a marriage binding.

CONSU'MPTION (*Med.*) vide *Phthisis.*

Consumption (*Mil.*) the waste or expenditure of stores.

CONSUMMATUM (*Med.*) a broth; so called because it was made of sufficient strength to concrete into a jelly.

CONTABESCE'NTIA (*Med.*) vide *Atrophia.*

CONTABULA'TION (*Ant.*) a joining of boards or planks together; the boarding of a floor.

CO'NTACT (*Math.*) ἀφή, the relative state of two things which touch each other; as a line, plane, or body touching another. The parts which thus touch are called the *points of contact*; as H; and the *angle of contact*, is that made by a curve line, and a tangent to it at the point of contact; as I H K, or K H L, formed by the line I H, with the curve H K M, or the circle of HKM with H L N.

CONTA'GION (*Med.*) the spreading or catching a disease.

CONTE'MPLATIVES (*Ecc.*) Friars of the order of Mary Magdalen, who wore black upper garments, and white ones underneath.

CONTEMPERA'NTIA (*Med.*) the same as *Temperantia.*

CONTE'MPORARY (*Chron.*) one living, or any thing happening at the same time, or in the same age.

CONTE'MPT (*Law*) a disobedience to the rules, orders, or process of a court: the word may likewise be applied in the same sense to the king's prerogative, by refusing to assist him for the public good, &c.; and also to an act of Parliament, by refusing to comply with it.

CONTE'NEMENT (*Law*) 1. Freehold land which lies near a man's dwelling-house. 2. A man's countenance, or credit, which he has by reason of his freehold. *Stat.* 1, *Ed.* 3. 3. That which is necessary for the support and maintenance of men according to their several qualities, conditions, or states of life. *Mag. Chart.* c. 14; *Glanvil.* l. 9, c. 6.

CONTE'NTA (*Med.*) a name given to the fluids which are contained in the solid parts of the body.

CONTE'NT (*Math.*) a term used for the measurement of bodies and surfaces, whether solid or superficial, the capacity of a vessel, and the area of a space, being the quantity either of matter or space included within certain bounds or limits.

CONTE'NTS (*Com.*) the wares contained in any cask, &c.

CONTESTA'TIO (*Ant.*) the trial of a cause, by putting in the plaintiff's declaration, and the defendant's answer. *Cic. Rosc. Com.* c. 11; *Ad Attic.* l. 16, ep. 15; *Fest. de Verb. Signif.*; *Macrob. Saturn.* l. 3, c. 9; *Hotom. de Form. apud Græv. Thes. Antiq. Rom.* tom. ii, p. 1912.

CO'NTEXT (*Lit.*) the general series of a discourse; the parts which precede and follow the sentence quoted.

CONTIGNA'TIO (*Archit.*) the laying of rafters together; also a flooring. *Vitruv.* l. 6, c 5.

CONTI'GUOUS (*Bot.*) *contiguus*; an epithet for cotyledons whose internal surfaces touch each other in every point.

Contiguous Angles (*Geom.*) Angles which have the same vertex, and one leg common to both. [vide *Angle*]

CO'NTINENS (*Rhet.*) τὸ συνέχον, is the name for that which is the foundation of a defence, and without which no further plea could be advanced. *Cic. de Invent.* l. 1, c. 26; *Quintil.* l. 3, c. 11.

Continens Febris (*Med.*) a continued fever, which proceeds regularly in the same tenor, without either remission or intermission.—*Continens causa*, that cause on which a disorder so much depends, that it continues as long as the cause continues, and no longer: thus, a stone sticking in the ureter is the continent cause of the stoppage of urine.

CO'NTINENT (*Geog.*) a great extent of land, which comprehends several kingdoms and regions not separated by a sea.

CONTINE'NTIA Verba (*Gram.*) words which are connected together by means of conjunctions.

CONTI'NGENCIES (*Mil.*) the items is an army account, consisting of casual expences.

CONTI'NGENT (*Mil.*) the quota of armed men, or pecuniary subsidy, which one state gives to another.

CONTINGENT *Line* (*Math.*) the same as *Tangent line.*
CONTINGENT *Legacy* (*Law*) vide *Legacy.*—*Contingent remainder,* where an estate in remainder is limited to take effect, either to a dubious or uncertain person, or upon a dubious and uncertain event.—*Contingent use,* a use limited in the conveyance of land, which may or may not happen, to vest or put into possession, according to the contingency expressed in the limitation of such use.
CONTI'NUA *Febris* (*Med.*) a continual fever; or one attended with light exacerbations and remissions, but no intermissions.
CONTI'NUAL *Claim* (*Law*) is a claim made from time to time within every year and day to land or other things, which cannot be attained without incurring some danger.
CONTINUAL *Fever* (*Med.*) vide *Continua.*
CONTINUAL (*Math.*) or *Continued Proportionals,* a series of three or more quantities compared, so that the ratio is the same between every two adjacent terms, i. e. between the 1st and 2d, the 2d and 3d, the 3d and 4th, &c.; as 1, 2, 4, 8, 16, &c.
CONTI'NUANCE (*Law*) is in Common Law the same as *prorogation* in the Civil Law, as " Continuance till the next assizes," i. e. putting off the trial.
CONTINUA'NDO (*Law*) a word used in a special declaration of trespass when the plaintiff would recover damages for several trespasses in the same action, where, to avoid a multiplicity of suits, a man may, in one action of trespass, recover damages for many trespasses, laying the first to be done with a *continuando* to the whole time in which the rest of the trespasses were committed. In this form *continuando,* i. e. by continuing the trespass aforesaid, &c. from the day aforesaid, &c. until such a day, including the last trespass.
CONTINUA'TO (*Mus.*) an Italian word signifying, in musical books, to continue a sound, or note, in an equal strength or manner; or to continue a movement in an equal degree of time all the way.
CONTI'NUED FEVER (*Med.*) vide *Continens.*
CONTINUED FRACTIONS (*Math.*) vide *Fractions.*—*Continued proportion,* that in which the consequent of the first ratio is the same as the antecedent of the second, as in these 3 : 6 :: 6 : 12 in distinction from *discrete Proportion.* [vide *Discrete*]—*Continued proportionals,* vide *Continual.*
CONTINUED *body* (*Phy.*) a body whose parts are no ways divided.
CONTINUED *quantity* (*Phy.*) that quantity whose parts are so joined and united together that you cannot tell where the one begins and the other ends, which is called *continuum.*
CONTINUED BASS (*Mus.*) is the same as *thorough bass,* because it goes quite through the composition.
CONTINU'ITY (*Surg.*) denotes that state in the parts of the body which are so united as to constitute an undivided whole.
CONTI'NUO (*Mus.*) Italian for thorough, or continued, as *basso continuo,* continued bass.
CONTO'RSIO (*Med.*) Contortion, or twisting, is taken in different senses to signify the iliac passion; a luxation of the vertebræ, &c.; an incomplete dislocation; a spasmodic contraction of the muscles in the head; a palsy of the antagonist muscles, &c.
CONTORSIO (*Bot.*) vide *Torsio.*
CONTO'RTÆ (*Bot.*) the twenty-ninth order of plants in Linnæus' Fragments of a Natural Method, and the thirtieth of the Natural Orders, in his Genera Plantarum.
CONTO'RTRIX (*Zool.*) a species of Boa.
CONTORTUPLICA'TUS (*Bot.*) vide *Writhed.*
CONTO'RTUS (*Bot.*) twisted; an epithet for a corolla and a pericarp; *contorta corolla,* a twisted corolla, having the edge of one petal lying over the next in an oblique direction, as in *Vinca*; *contortum pericarpium* is that which has the apex in a different line from the base.

CONTOU'R (*Paint.*) the outline, or that which determines and defines a figure, making what is called a draught or design.
CONTOUR (*Archit.*) the outline of any member, as that of a base, a cornice, &c.
CONTOURNE' (*Her.*) an epithet for a beast, standing or running with his face to the sinister side, as in the annexed figure, being always supposed to look to the right.
CONTOURNIA'TED (*Numis.*) an epithet for a sort of medals with a kind of hollowness all round leaving a rim on each side, the figures having scarcely any relievo compared with other medals.
CONTRA *Antiscion* (*Astrol.*) a term denoting the degree and minute in the ecliptic opposite to the antiscion.
CONTRA *Apertura* (*Med.*) a counter-opening, or an opening made opposite to the one that already exists, whether made by a bullet, a puncture, or otherwise.—*Contra Fissura,* a fissure in the skull opposite to the part in which the blow was given.—*Contra Indication,* a symptom attending a disease which forbids the exhibition of the remedy ordinarily employed.—*Contra-lunaris,* an epithet for a woman who conceives during menstruation.
CONTRA *harmonical proportion* (*Geom.*) that relation between three terms wherein the difference of the first and second is to the difference of the second and third as the third is to the first; thus, for example 3, 5, and 6, are numbers contra-harmonically proportional, for 2 : 1 :: 6 :: 3.
CONTRA *Formam Feoffmenti* (*Law*) a writ for a tenant who is feoffed by the lord's charter to make certain suit and service to his court, and is afterwards distrained for more than is contained therein.—*Contra formam collationis,* a writ lying where a man has given perpetual alms to any religious house, &c. and the governor has alienated the lands contrary to the donor's intent. *Stat. Westm.* 2, c. 1; *Vet. Nat. Brev.* 162; *Reg. Orig.* 176.—*Contra mandatio placiti,* a respiting, or giving a defendant further time to answer, i. e. properly a countermand of what was formerly ordered. *Leg. H.* 1. *apud Brompton.*—*Contra mandatum,* a lawful excuse, which a defendant in a suit by attorney allegeth for himself, to show that the plaintiff hath no cause of complaint.—*Contra positio,* a plea or answer. *Leg. H.* 1. *apud Brompton.*—*Contra Formam Statuti,* " Contrary to the form of the statute made and provided," the usual conclusion of every indictment, &c. laid on an offence created by statute.
CONTRA-BA'SSO (*Mus.*) Italian for counter-bass.—*Contra-Basso,* Italian for the instrument called Double Bass.—*Contrapunto,* the Italian word for counterpoint. [vide *Counterpoint*]—*Contra-tenor,* [vide *Counter-tenor*]
CONTRA-SE'MEN (*Bot.*) vide *Artemisia.*
CO'NTRABAND (*Com.*) an epithet for such goods as are forbidden by act of Parliament to be exported or imported.
CONTRACAUSA'TOR (*Law*) a criminal, or one charged with, and prosecuted for, a crime. *Leg. H.* 1, c. 61.
CO'NTRACT (*Law*) a covenant, or agreement between two or more persons, with a lawful consideration or cause. Contracts are called *good* when some consideration, however small, has been given, as when a sum of money is given for the lease of a manor. Contracts are *bad* and *nude* where no such consideration has been given.
CONTRACTA'TION HOUSE (*Com.*) a place where agreements or contracts are made for the furtherance of trade.
CONTRA'CTIBLE (*Anat.*) an epithet applied to the muscles, or such parts of the body as admit of contraction.
CONTRA'CTILE *Force* (*Mech.*) that inherent force by which a body, when extended, has the property of drawing itself up to its former dimensions.
CONTRACTI'LITY (*Phy.*) a power, inherent in some bodies, of contracting themselves into a shorter compass.

CONTRA'CTION (*Phy.*) the diminishing the extent, or dimensions of a body.
CONTRACTION (*Anat.*) a term applied particularly to the muscles, heart, and arteries.
CONTRACTION (*Log.*) a method in logic whereby the thing reducing abridges the thing reduced.
CONTRACTION (*Gram.*) the reducing two syllables into one, as *don't* for *do not*, *receiv'd* for *received*, &c. which is inadmissible in good writing or speaking.
CONTRACTION (*Arith.*) the shortening certain operations, or performing the rules by a shorter course, as in Multiplication, Division, and Extraction of the Square Root, &c.
CONTRACTU'RA (*Surg.*) a rigid contraction of the joints, which Cullen has placed as a genus of diseases, Class *Locules*, Order *Dyscinesiæ*.
CONTRADI'CTORY Opposition (*Log.*) is the contrariety of two propositions both in quantity and quality.—*Contradictory propositions*, such as consist of a universal and a particular, one affirmative and the other negative, both of which cannot be true, nor both false; as "All men are animals;" "Some men are not animals."
CONTRAFA'CTIO (*Law*) Counterfeiting.
CONTRA-FISSU'RA (*Surg.*) vide *Contra*.
CONTRA-FORMAM (*Law*) vide *Contra*.
CONTRA-HARMONICAL (*Geom.*) vide *Contra*.
CONTRAHE'NTIA (*Med.*) medicines which have the power of shortening the fibres, as in the case of astringents.
CONTRA-INDICA'TION (*Phy.*) vide *Contra*.
CONTRA'LTO (*Mus.*) Italian for Counter Tenor.
CONTRAMANDA'TIO *Placiti* (*Law*) vide *Contra*.—*Contramandatum*, vide *Contra*.
CONTRALUNA'RES (*Med.*) vide *Contra*.
CONTRAMURE (*Fort.*) a little outwall built before another partition wall, or about the main-wall of a city, &c. to strengthen it.
CONTRAPOSI'TION (*Law*) a plea or answer. *Leg. Hen.* 1, c. 34.
CONTRAPOSITION (*Log.*) that sort of conversion of propositions which consists, besides transposition also, in changing the terms from finite into infinite, as animal or man into not-animal not-man, which are called *infinite*; thus, "Something animal is not man, therefore something not man is an animal." [vide *Conversion*]
CONTRAPU'NTO (*Mus.*) vide *Counter-Point*.
CONTRAPU'NTIST (*Mus.*) a musician skilled in counterpoint.
CONTRA'RIENTS (*Polit.*) the name given to those Barons who took part with Thomas, Earl of Lancaster, against King Edward II.
CO'NTRARIES (*Log.*) a name for things directly opposed to each other, as light and darkness.
CONTRARY *Flexure* (*Geom.*) vide *Curve*.
CONTRARY *Propositions* (*Log.*) such as consist of two universal propositions, one affirming and the other denying; both of which may be false, but both cannot be true; as "All men are wise;" "No man is wise."
CONTRARY *Coned* (*Her.*) an ancient term for gironny.
CONTRARY *Motion* (*Mus.*) when one part ascends, and another descends simultaneously, they are said to be in contrary motion.
CO'NTRAST (*Paint.*) the due placing the different objects and parts of the figure.—*Well contrasted figures* are such as are lively and express the motion of the whole piece, or of any particular group.
CONTRAST (*Mus.*) the opposition and relief produced by the varieties of style in the several movements of a piece.
TO CONTRA'ST (*Archit.*) avoiding the repetition of the same thing in order to please by variety.
CONTRATE-WHE'EL (*Hor.*) the wheel in a watch, which is next to the crown-wheel; the teeth and hoop of which lie contrary to those of the other wheels.

CONTRATENE'RE (*Law*) to withhold. *Leg. Alfred, apud Bromph.* c. 9.
CONTRAVALLA'TION *line* (*Fort.*) a trench guarded with a parapet, and usually cut round a place by the besiegers to secure themselves, and stop the sallies of the garrison. It is generally a musket shot from the town, so that the whole army carrying on the siege lies between the lines of circumvallation and contravallation.
CONTRAVE'NTION (*Law*) the infringement of a contract.—*Contravention*, in the Scotch Law, is the action founded on the breach of Law-Burrows.
CONTRAYE'RVA (*Bot.*) a plant from the Spanish West Indies, the *Dorstenia contrayerva* of Linnæus, which is so called from *contra*, counter, and *yerva*, poison, because it is reckoned good against poisons. There is another Contrayerva, which is little inferior to the former, and is the root of the *Psoralea pentaphylla* of Linnæus.
CONTRE (*Her.*) French for Counter. [vide *Counter*]—*Contre escartéllé*, the same as Counter-quartered. [vide *Counter*]
CONTRE-COU'P (*Med.*) French for the fracture called *Contra-fissura*]
CONTRIBULES (*Archæol.*) or *Contribunales*, kindred or cousins. *Lamb.* p. 75.
CONTRIBUTION (*Law*) a joint giving of money towards any affair of importance.—*Contributione facienda*, a writ for those who are put to the burden of a thing to compel others equally obliged to bear an equal share.
CONTRIBUTION (*Mil.*) a tax paid by the inhabitants of any place to a hostile military force to save themselves from being plundered; whence the phrase "To put under contribution," in French *Mettre a contribution*.
CONTRIBUTIONE *facienda* (*Law*) vide *Contribution*.
CONTRI'TIO (*Phy.*) the same as *Comminution*.
CONTRO'LLER (*Law*) an overseer, or officer relating to public accounts; of which there are different kinds, as—*Controller of the King's household*, who has charge of the inferior officers.—*Controller of the Haniper*, an officer in Chancery who attends on the Lord Chancellor, and takes charge of things sealed and inclosed in a bag.—*Controller of the Poll*, an officer of the Exchequer, who keeps a controlment of Receipts and outgoings.—*Controller of the Pipe*, an officer in the exchequer who writes out summons to the sheriffs to collect the debts of the pipe.—*Controller General*, an officer in the artillery.—*Controller of the Navy*, the officer who sees to all payments.—*Controller of the Mint*, whose business it is to see that the money be made to the just assize, to overlook the officers, &c.
CONTROVE'RTED *Election* (*Polit.*) the same as *contested Election*.
CONTUO'LI (*Anat.*) an epithet for eyes looking narrowly. *Fest. de Verb. Signif.*
CONTU'SA (*Surg.*) bruises or wounds caused by contusion.
CONTUSION (*Surg.*) a bruise which destroys the continuity in the parts of the bones and the flesh, though the skin appears whole.—*Contusion of the skull* is such a hurt of the skull-bone that, although no fracture appears outwardly, yet the whole is separated in the inside.
CONVALE'SCENCE (*Med.*) that space from the departure of a disease to the recovery of the strength lost by it.
CONVALE'SCENT (*Med.*) one recovering or returning to a state of health.
CONVALE'SCENTS, *List of* (*Mil.*) a return made out by the surgeon of the battalion, hospital, &c. of such as may be shortly expected to do duty.
CONVALLA'RIA (*Bot.*) a genus of plants, Class 6 *Hexandria*, Order 1 *Monogynia*.
Generic Characters. CAL. none.—COR. monopetalous; border six-cleft.—STAM. *filaments six*; anthers oblong.—

Pist. germ globose; style filiform; stigma obtuse.—
Per. berry globose; seeds roundish.

Species. The species are perennials, as — *Convallaria maialis, Polygonatum, seu Lilium,* Sweet Scented Lily of the Valley. — *Convallaria japonica,* Grass-leaved Lily of the Valley, native of Japan. — *Convallaria spicata,* Spiked Lily of the Valley, native of Japan. — *Convallaria verticillata, seu Polygonatum,* &c. Narrow-leaved Solomon's seal, native of Europe. — *Convallaria polygonatum, seu Polygonatum,* &c. Single-flowered Solomon's Seal, native of Europe. — *Convallaria multiflora, seu Polygonatum,* &c. Many-flowered Solomon's Seal, native of Europe.—*Convallaria latifolia, seu Polygonatum,* &c. native of Austria.— *Convallaria racemosa,* Cluster-flowered Solomon's Seal, native of Virginia.—*Convallaria trifolia, seu Phalangium,* native of Siberia.— *Convallaria bifolia, Majanthemum, Unifolium, Lilium,* &c. seu *Monophyllon,* &c. Least Solomon's Seal, or One Blade, native of Europe.—*Convallaria latifolia,* Broad-leaved Solomon's Seal, native of Austria. *Dod. Pempt. Clus. Hist. rar. Plant.; Bauh. Hist. Plant.; Bauh. Pin.; Ger. Herb.; Park. Theat. Botan.; Raii Hist. Plant.*

CONVE'NABLE (*Law*) agreeable. *Stat. 27 Ed. 3, c. 21.*

CONVE'NIENCE (*Archit.*) the disposing the several parts of a building, so that they may not obstruct or interfere with one another.

CO'NVENT (*Ecc.*) *conventus,* signifies the fraternity of an abbey, or priory, as *societas* does the number of fellows in a college.

CONVE'NTICLE (*Law*) *Conventiculum,* signified properly a private meeting or assembly for the purposes of devotion, but was afterwards applied to the illegal meetings of the Non-conformists, mentioned in the statutes 2 *Hen.* 5, c. 15; 1 *Hen.* 6, c. 3; 16 *Car.* 2, c. 4.

CONVE'NTION (*Polit.*) any assembly of the states of the realm, particularly that which is held on particular occasions without the sanction of the sovereign, as the *Convention Parliament,* which restored king Charles II.

Convention (*Mil.*) an agreement entered into by troops that are opposed to one another for the evacuation of some post, the suspension of hostilities, &c.

CONVENTIO'NE (*Law*) a writ which lies for any covenant in writing that is unperformed.

CONVE'NTIONER (*Polit.*) the member of a convention.

CO'NVENTUAL *Church* (*Ecc.*) a church that consists of regular clerks professing some order of religion.

CONVENTUALS (*Ecc.*) religious men united together in a convent or religious house. *Matth. Par. ann.* 1233.

CONVE'NTUS (*Ecc.*) συνάξις, a meeting or coming together for devotional purposes, which, according to Eusebius, took place at the cemeteries of the primitive Christians; also a convent. *Euseb. Ecc. Hist.* l. 9, c. 2; *Concil. Tolit. ann.* 4, can. 35; *Order. Vital.* l. 4, p. 542.

CONVE'RGING *Series* (*Math.*) a method of approximating still nearer and nearer to the true root of any number or equation.

CONVERGING (*Geom.*) or *Convergent Lines,* those lines which continually approximate, or whose distance becomes continually less and less the farther they are continued; in distinction from divergent lines.—*Converging Hyperbola,* one whose concave legs bend in towards one another, and run both the same way.

Converging *Rays* (*Opt.*) those rays that issue from divers points of an object, and incline towards one another till at last they meet; and, if they cross each other, then they become *Diverging,* as in the annexed figure, where A B and C B converge towards the point B,

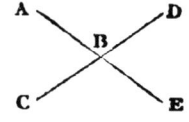

and thence diverge or run off from each other in the lines B D and B E.

Converging (*Bot.*) *connivens,* an epithet applied to the corolla, the anthers, and the sleep of plants; *corolla connivens,* a converging corolla that has the tops of the petals meeting so as to close the flower, as in *Trollius; antheræ conniventes,* converging anthers, or those which incline towards each other, as in the Class *Didynamia.* Plants are said to be converging in sleep when the leaves are so closely applied as to seem one leaf.

CO'NVERSE *Proposition* (*Math.*) one proposition is converse of another when, after drawing a conclusion from something first supposed, we return again by making a supposition of what had been before concluded, and draw as a conclusion what had been before a supposition; as if, from the supposed equality of two sides of a triangle, it be demonstrated that the angles opposite to the equal sides are equal; then the converse of this proposition is, from the supposed equality of the two angles, to prove the equality of the sides opposite to them.

Converse *Direction* (*Astrol.*) is when a significator is brought to the place of the promittors by the motion of the highest sphere, called *primum Mobile,* contrary to the succession of the signs.

CONVE'RSION (*Rhet.*) ἀντιστροφή, or ἐπιστροφή, a figure of speech by which we repeat continually the same word, as " Pœnos Populus Romanus justitia vicit, armis vicit, liberalitate vicit." *Cic. in Orator.* c. 39; *Quintil.* l. 9, c. 31.

Conversion *of Proposition* (*Log.*) changing the subject into the place of the predicate, and still retaining the quality of the proposition. Conversion *is* of different kinds, as— *Simple Conversion,* where the quantity remains the same; as " No man is a brute," therefore " No brute is a man."— *Conversion per Accidens,* when the quantity is diminished; as " Every man is an animal," therefore " Some animal is man."—*Conversion per Contra-positionem,* when the terms are changed from finite into infinite; as man or animal into not man, not animal, which are called infinite terms. [vide *Contra-Position*]

Conversion *of ratios* (*Geom.*) ἀναστροφὴ λόγου, is the comparing the antecedent with the difference of the antecedent and consequent; in other words, when of four quantities the first is to its excess above the second as the third is to its excess above the fourth, as suppose 8 : 6 :: 4 : 3, then *à convertendo,* or by conversion, 8 : 2 :: 4 : 1, or *a : b :: c : d,* then by conversion *a : a—b :: c : c—d.* *Eucl. Def. Elem.* l. 5.

Conversion *of equations* (*Algeb.*) the peculiar manner of altering an equation when either the quantity sought, or any member of it, is a fraction.

Conversion (*Mil.*) French for that movement which is called wheeling.

Conversion (*Theol.*) a turning to any profession of religion, in its most general sense, but in particular the turning to God, and to a sense of true religion.

Conversion (*Law*) is where a person finding or having in his possession the goods of another converts them to his own use without the consent of the owner, and for which the proprietor may maintain an action of *trover and conversion* against him.

CONVE'RSOS (*Law*) a name formerly given to the Jews who were converted to Christianity in England, for whom King Henry III. built a house in London. *Co. Lit.* 291, b.

CONVE'RTIBLE *terms* (*Log.*) terms which admit of being converted without altering the truth of the proposition, as " Every living creature is an animal," and " Every animal is a living creature."

CONVEX (*Math.*) an epithet signifying curved and protuberant outwards, as a convex lens, mirror, &c. [vide *Lens,* &c.]

CONVEXUS (*Bot.*) convex, an epithet for a leaf or a receptacle; *folium convexum* is that which rises in the centre, opposed either to the *depressus* or the *concavus*; *receptaculum convexum*, a receptacle which rises in the middle, as in *Chrysanthemum, Buphthalmum, Matricaria*, &c.

CONVEY'ANCE (*Law*) a deed or instrument by which lands, &c. are conveyed or made over to another. The most common conveyances now in use are, deeds of gift, bargain and sale, lease and release, fines and recoveries, settlements to uses, &c.

CONVEY'ANCER (*Law*) the person who follows that part of the legal profession which consists in drawing up conveyances.

CO'NVICT (*Law*) one who is found guilty of an offence by the verdict of a jury. *Staundf. P. C.* 186.—*Convict recusant*, one who has been indicted and convicted for refusing to come to church; a term formerly applied to persons of the Romish persuasion.

CONVI'CTION (*Law*) the finding a man guilty of an offence by the verdict of a jury, or when a man who is outlawed appears and confesses.

CONVICTION (*Theol.*) the first degree of repentance, or the assurance which a man has in his mind of the evil nature of sin, and his own guiltiness.

CONVI'VIUM (*Ant.*) a banquet or entertainment, which, as Cicero defines it, implied a conjunction of living among friends, and is therefore more expressive than the Greek *Symposium, Compotatio, concœnatio,* and the like. *Cic. de Senect.* c. 13.

CONVIVIUM (*Law*) the same thing among the laity as *procuratio* among the clergy, i. e. when the tenant, by reason of his tenure, is bound to provide meat and drink for his lord's table once or oftener in the year.

CONVOCA'TION (*Ecc.*) the assembly of the representatives of the clergy, which consists of an *Upper House*, where the archbishops and the bishops sit by themselves, and of the *Lower House*, where the inferior clergy sit. All the members have, for themselves and their officers, the same privileges as members of Parliament.—*Convocation House*, the place where the convocation is held.

CONVOLU'TA *ossa* (*Anat.*) the turbinated bones of the nose, which are superior and inferior.

CONVOLU'TUS (*Bot.*) *convolute*, an epithet in vernation or for a bud, petal, stigmas, and tendrils. *Gemma convoluta* is a bud, the nascent leaves of which are rolled together like a scroll, as in *Arum, Piper, Solidago, Brassica*, &c. It is applied to the petals and stigmas in the same sense as in *Crocus*; but *cirrus convolutus* is a tendril twisted into rings or spirals.

CONVO'LVULUS (*Ent.*) a little hairy worm which infests vines. *Cato de Re Rust.* c. 95; *Plin.* l. 17, c. 28.

CONVOLVULUS (*Bot.*) Bind-weed, a plant, the root of which yields a concreted juice called *scammony*. It is supposed to answer to the *Smilax* of the ancients. *Plin.* l. 21, c. 5.

CONVOLVULUS, in the Linnean system, a genus of plants, Class 5 *Pentandria*, Order 1 *Monogynia*.
Generic Characters. CAL. *perianth* five-parted. — COR. one-petalled. — STAM. *filaments* five; *anthers* ovate.— PIST. *germ* superior; *style* filiform; *stigmas* two.—PER. *capsule* roundish; *seeds* in pairs.
Species. The species are mostly perennials or shrubs; some few annuals. Of the first sort are the following—*Convolvulus arvensis, Smilax*, &c. seu *Helxine*, &c. Small or Field Bindweed, native of Europe.—*Convolvulus sepium, Smilax*, seu *Volubilis*, &c. Great or Hedge Bindweed, native of Europe.—*Convolvulus Wheleri*, &c. *Sagittaria*, seu *Ipomoea*, &c. native of Barbary.—*Convolvulus scammonia*, &c. *Syriacus scammonia*, seu *Scammonium*, &c. Syrian Bindweed, or Scammony, native of Syria.—*Convolvulus angustifolius*, seu *Ipomoea*, &c. native of the East Indies.—*Convolvulus japonicus*, seu *Kos*, native of Japan.—*Convolvulus panduratus*, seu *Megalorhizus*, Virginian Bindweed, native of Egypt.—*Convolvulus batatas, Batatas*, seu *Kappa Kelengu*, Tuberous-rooted Bindweed, or Spanish Potatoes, native of the Indies.—*Convolvulus maximus*, seu *Yiru-tali*, native of Ceylon.— *Convolvulus umbellatus*, seu *Polyanthos*, &c. Umbelled Bindweed, native of Martinica.—*Convolvulus turpethum, Zeylanicus*, seu *Turpethum*, Square-stalked Bindweed, or Turbith, native of Ceylon. — *Convolvulus verpens*, Dwarf Bindweed. — *Convolvulus saxatilis, Campanula Lychnis*, seu *Lychnidis*. Among the shrubs the following are the principal— *Convolvulus malabaricus*, seu *Kattu-Kelengu*, native of Malabar.—*Convolvulus canariensis*, seu *foliis*, &c. Canary Bindweed, native of the Canary Isles.—*Convolvulus grandiflorus*, seu *Munda-Valli*, native of India.—*Convolvulus speciosus*, &c. seu *Nervosus*, &c. Broad-leaved Bindweed, native of the East Indies. —*Convolvulus Jalapa*, seu *Bryonia*, Jalap Bindweed, native of Mexico. The following are annuals, namely *Convolvulus hederaceus*, Ivy-leaved Bindweed, native of India.—*Convolvulus nil*, seu *Ipomoea*, &c. Blue or Azure Bindweed, native of America.—*Convolvulus purpureus*, Purple Bindweed, native of America.—*Convolvulus tricolor*, Trailing Bindweed, native of Africa.—*Convolvulus soldanella*, seu *Soldanella*, &c. Sea Bindweed, native of England.—*Convolvulus pes capræ*, seu *Schouanna*, &c. Thick-leaved Bindweed, native of the East Indies.— *Convolvulus macrocarpus*, Long-fruited Bindweed.—*Convolvulus quinquefoliis*, Smooth five-leaved Bindweed, &c. *Clus. Hist. Plant. rar.*; *Bauh. Hist. Plant.*; *Bauh. Pin.*; *Ger. Herb.*; *Park. Theat. Botan.*; *Raii Hist. Plant.*; *Tournef. Instit.*; *Marcgr. Pis. Brasil. Hist.*

CO'NVOY (*Mar.*) a fleet of merchant ships protected by some vessels of war.

TO CONVOY is said of the vessels of war which attend merchant ships by way of protection in time of war.

CO'NUS *Fusorius* (*Chem.*) a vessel resembling an inverted cone, intended for separating *reguluses* from their respective *scoriæ*.

CONUS (*Conch.*) Cone, a genus of animals, Class *Vermes*, Order *Testacea*.
Generic Character. Animal a *limax*; *shell* univalve; *aperture* effuse, longitudinal; *pillar* smooth.
Species. The species are distinguished into, 1. Those which have their spire or turban truncate. 2. Those which have the spire pyriform, with a round base. 3. Those which have their spire elongated, or rounded at the base. 4. Those which are ventricose in the middle, and contracted at the end. The cones inhabit the ocean, and are generally found on rocky shores. Many of the shells are beautiful, and fetch a very high price.

CONUS (*Bot.*) vide *Cone* and *Strombilus*.

CO'NUSANCE *of Pleas* (*Law*) a privilege which a town or city hath to hold pleas.

CO'NUSANT (*Law*) knowing or understanding; as if the son be concusant, and agreeing to a feoffment. *Co. Lit.* 159.

CONVU'LSION (*Med.*) an involuntary contraction of the muscles.

CONVU'LSIVE *Motions* (*Med.*) are sudden and swift convulsions and shakings that cease and return again by turns.

CONY'ZA (*Bot.*) κονύζα, Fleabane; a plant so called because its leaves, when strewed and burned, kill gnats and fleas. It is commended much by the ancients for its medicinal virtues, and particularly for promoting the menses and curing the stranguary. *Hippocrat. de Morb. Mul.* l. 2; *Theoph. Hist. Plant.* l. 6, c. 2; *Dioscor.* l. 3, c. 136; *Plin.* l. 59, c. 8.

CONYZA, *in the Linnean system,* a genus of plants, Class 19 *Syngenesia,* Order 2 *Polygamia Superflua.*
Generic Characters. CAL. common imbricate; *scales* acute.—COR. compound tubulose; *corollets* numerous; *proper* funnel-form; *border* five-cleft.—STAM. *filaments* five; *anther* cylindric.—PIST. *germ* oblong; *style* filiform; *stigma* two-cleft.—PER. none; *calyx* converging; *seeds* solitary; *down* simple; *receptacle* naked.
Species. The species are of different kinds, as—*Conyza squarrosa,* seu *Baccharis,* &c. Great Fleabane, or Spikenard, a biennial, native of Germany.—*Conyza scabra,* Rough Fleabane, native of the East Indies.—*Conyza foliolosa,* native of the East Indies.—*Conyza patula,* seu *Serratula,* an annual, native of China.—*Conyza bifrons,* seu *Eupatoria,* &c. Oval-leaved Fleabane, a perennial, native of Canada.—*Conyza purpurascens,* seu *odorata,* &c. seu *major,* &c. an annual, native of Jamaica.—*Conyza Urinervis,* &c. native of the Brazils.—*Conyza serratula,* &c. native of the Brazils.—*Conyza madagascariensis,* &c. native of Madagascar.—*Conyza stricta,* &c. an annual, native of the East Indies.—*Conyza canescens,* &c. seu *pinifolia,* native of the Cape of Good Hope.—*Conyza oleæfolia,* seu *orientalis,* &c. a perennial, native of Armenia.—*Conyza candida,* seu *saxatilis,* &c. seu *Jacobæa,* &c. seu *Aster,* &c. Woolly Fleabane, a shrub, native of Crete.—*Conyza verbascifolia,* seu *Verbasci,* &c. seu *Aster,* a shrub, native of Sicily.—*Conyza cinerea,* seu *Senecioides,* seu *Senecio,* &c. seu *Olus,* &c. seu *Eupatorium,* &c. Ash-coloured Fleabane, an annual, native of the East Indies.—*Conyza Ægyptiaca, Erigeron,* seu *Jacobæa,* &c. Egyptian Fleabane, an annual, native of Sicily and Egypt.—*Conyza Gouani,* seu *Erigeron,* &c. an annual or perennial, native of the Canaries.—*Conyza Senegalensis,* seu *foliis,* &c. native of Senegal.—*Conyza dentata,* seu *foliis,* &c. native of Senegal.—*Conyza fœtida, Erigeron,* seu *Senecio,* &c. a perennial, native of Africa.—*Conyza sordida, Gnaphalium,* seu *Helichrysum, Stoechadi, Stoechas,* seu *Ageratum,* &c. Small-flowered Fleabane.—*Conyza saxatilis, Gnaphalium, Helichrysum,* seu *Stoechadi,* &c. Rock Fleabane, a shrub, native of Italy. *Bauh. Hist. Plant.; Park. Theat. Botan.; Raii Hist. Plant.*

CONYZA is also the *Baccharis ivifolia,* &c. of Linnæus.

CONYZE'LLA (*Bot.*) or *Conyzoides,* the same as the *Erigeron.*

COOK (*Ich.*) a small fish inhabiting the Cornish coasts; the *Clabrus coquus* of Linnæus.

COOK-ROOM (*Mar.*) the room in a ship where the cook and his mate dress the provisions.

COOKS, Company of (*Her.*) was incorporated in the year 1481, and confirmed by Queen Elizabeth, and afterwards by King James II. Their armorial ensigns are, as in the annexed figure, "*argent* a chevron engrailed *sable* between three columbines." The crest is a pheasant standing on a mount (upon a helmet and torse), the supporters a buck and doe, each vulned, with an arrow *all proper.* The motto, *vulnerati non victi.*

COO'LER (*Mech.*) a vessel used by brewers for cooling the beer after it is drawn off.

COO'LERS (*Med.*) medicines which produce an immediate sense of cold.

COOLING *the wool* (*Agric.*) spreading it out in the air after it has been sheared.

COOM (*Nat.*) soot which gathers over the mouth of an oven.

COOMB (*Com.*) a measure of corn containing four bushels.

COOP (*Mar.*) or *Fish-coop,* a vessel made of twigs, in which they catch fish in the Humber.

COO'PERS, Company of (*Her.*) was incorporated in 1530, by the name of Master and Wardens, or Keepers of the commonalty of the freemen of the mystery of coopers in London. Their armorial ensigns are, as in the annexed figure, "Party per pale *gules* and *or,* a chevron between three hoops in a chief *azure.*"

COO'PERY (*Mech.*) the art of making casks, barrels, &c. with boards bound by hoops. The boards of which casks are made are called in their rough state *clap-boards,* and when fit for use, *staves.*

CO-OPE'RTIO (*Anat.*) signifies properly a covering, in which sense it is applied to the membranes of the *fœtus,* the *uterus,* &c.

CO-OPERTIO (*Archæol.*) the head and branches of a tree cut down.

CO-OPERTO'RIUM (*Anat.*) the *Cartilago theroida.*

CO-OPERTU'RA (*Archæol.*) a thicket or covert of wood. *Chart de Forest.* c. 12.

CO-O'RDINATE *pillars* (*Archit.*) pillars standing in equal order.

CO-O'RDINATES (*Geom.*) a term applied to the *absciss* and *ordinates* when taken in connexion.

CO-ORDINA'TION *of causes* (*Phy.*) an order of causes wherein several of the same kind concur in the production of the same effect.

CO-O'STRUM (*Anat.*) the middle part of the *diaphragm.*

COOT (*Orn.*) a water-fowl, mostly of a black colour, called also a moor-hen, the *Fulica atra,* &c. of Linnæus. These birds frequent lakes and still rivers, where they make their nests among the rushes, &c. floating on the water, so as to rise and fall with it. They lay five or six eggs, of a dirty whitish hue, and sometimes they have been known to lay as many as fourteen.

COPA'IBA (*Bot.*) the balsam of Copaiva, a yellow resinous juice which flows from the *Copaifera officinalis* of Linnæus. It has an agreeable smell, and a bitterish biting taste. By distillation in water the oil is separated from the resin, in the former of which the taste and smell of the balsam are concentrated.

COPAI'FERA (*Bot.*) a genus of plants, Class 10 *Decandria,* Order 1 *Monogynia.*
Generic Characters. CAL. none.—COR. petals four.—STAM. *filaments* ten; *anthers* oblong.—PIST. *germ* round; *style* filiform; *stigma* obtuse.—PER. *legume* ovate; *seed* single.
Species. The only species is, the —*Copaifera officinalis,* seu *Copaira,* seu *Copaiba,* seu *Coapoiba,* Balsam of Capevi-tree, a shrub, native of the Brazils. *Marcgrav. Pis. Brasil. Hist.*

COPA'IVA (*Bot.*) vide *Copaiba.*

CO'PAL (*Nat.*) an American name for all odoriferous gums; it is particularly applied to a resinous substance imported from Guinea, where it is found in the sand. It is of a yellow colour, transparent, tasteless, and while cold inodorous. Its principal use is in laxities of the gums, but it is likewise accounted a cephalic.

COPA'LLI (*Bot.*) the *Rhus copallinum* of Linnæus.

COPA'LXACTL (*Bot.*) a tree like the cherry-tree, the fruit of which abounds much in a gelatinous juice. *Raii Hist. Plant.*

COPA'RCENERS (*Law*) those who have an equal share in the inheritance of an ancestor. *Bract.* l. 2, c. 30.

CO'PAU (*Bot.*) a sort of wood which grows in Brasil resembling that of the walnut-tree. *Raii Hist. Plant.*

COPE (*Archæol.*) signifies, in Domesday Book, a hill; but in the mines it was applied to the tribute of sixpence per load which was paid to the King, or the lord of the manor, out of the lead-mines in some parts of Derbyshire.

3 T

Cope (*Ecc.*) a priest's vestment fastened with a clasp before, and hanging down from the shoulder to the heels.

To Cope (*Archit.*) to jut out as a wall.

To Cope (*Falcon.*) to pare the beak or talons of a hawk.

Cope *Sale and Pins* (*Mech.*) irons that fasten the chains of one ox with other oxen to the end of the cope of a waggon.

CO'PECK (*Com.*) a small coin in Russia equal to about one farthing English.

COPE'LLA (*Chem.*) vide *Cupel*.

COPE'RNICAN *system* (*Astron.*) a particular system of the sphere proposed by Pythagoras, and revived by Copernicus, in which the sun is supposed to be placed in the centre, and all the other bodies to revolve round it in a particular order. [vide *Astronomy*]

COPER'NICUS (*Mech.*) an instrument invented by Whiston, to display the Copernican system of the planets.

COPE'S *mate* (*Com.*) a partner in merchandise.

COPEY'A (*Bot.*) a tree in the Spanish West India islands, which yields pitch like the pine. *Raii Hist. Plant.*

CO'PHER (*Chem.*) vide *Camphor*.

CO'PHOS (*Zool.*) κόφος, a sort of toad mentioned by Nicander.

COPHO'SIS (*Med.*) κόφωσις, deafness, dumbness, or dulness, in any of the senses.

CO'PIA *Libelli deliberandi* (*Law*) a writ that lies in a case where a man cannot get the copy of a libel at the hands of a judge ecclesiastical. *Reg. Orig.* 51.

COPIA'BA (*Bot.*) vide *Copaiba*.

CO'PING (*Mason.*) the stone covering on the top of a wall, which serves to strengthen and defend it from the injuries of the weather. It is of different kinds, as *Parallel Coping*, of equal thickness, used only on inclined surfaces.—*Feather-edged Coping*, thinner at one edge than the other for throwing off the water.—*Saddle-backed Coping*, which is thin at each edge, and thick in the middle.

CO'PING-IRON (*Falcon.*) an instrument for paring the beak or talons of a hawk.

CO'PIS (*Ant.*) κοπίς, a kind of falchion, or hooked sword, such as the Persians wore. *Xenoph. Cyropæd.* l. 1; *Quint. Curt.* l. 8, c. 14; *Plut. in Camill.*; *Suidas*; *Cæl. Rhodig. Antiq. Lect.* l. 8, c. 3; *Leun. clav. in Pandect Turcic.* c. 172.

COPI'SCUS (*Nat.*) κόπισκος, an inferior sort of frankincense. *Dioscor.* l. 1, c. 81.

CO'POS (*Med.*) κόπος, lassitude, or a morbid sensation of lassitude. *Gal. Comm. in Hippocrat.* l. 4, *Aph.* 31.

CO'POVICH-OCCASSOU (*Bot.*) a tree in the West Indies, the leaves and fruit of which resemble those of a pear-tree.

CO'PPA (*Archæol.*) a cop, cap, or cock of hay, or corn, which was originally a titheable portion. *Thorn in Chron.*

CO'PPEL (*Chem.*) vide *Cupel*.

COPPER (*Chem.*) one of the six primitive metals, and the lightest of all except iron and tin, and the hardest of all but iron. It mixes in fusion with both gold and silver, to both of which it serves as an alloy. It is the most liable to rust of all the metals; for all kinds of salts, and all unctuous bodies, and, in short, almost every thing in nature, is a solvent for it. It is remarkably sonorous, being the basis of all the compound metals in which that quality exists; and its divisibility is so great, that a grain dissolved in an alkali will give a sensible colour to 500,000 times its weight of water. The specific gravity of copper is from 7·788 to 8·584. It was formerly called Venus, and represented by the annexed character [♀].

CO'PPERAS (*Chem.*) a name given to blue, green, and white vitriol, or the factitious sulphate of iron.

CO'PPERED (*Mar.*) or *Copper-bottomed*, an epithet for a vessel sheathed with thin plates of copper to prevent the worms from eating into the planks.—*Copper-fastened*, fastened with bolts of copper instead of iron.

CO'PPICE (*Agric.*) a small wood consisting of underwood, which may be cut at the growth of twelve or fifteen years.

CO'PPIN (*Mech.*) the cone of thread which is formed on the spindle of the wheel by spinning.

COPRAGO'GUM (*Med.*) a gently cathartic electuary.

COPRIE'METOS (*Med.*) κοπρήμιτος, from κόπρος, excrement, and ἐμέω, to vomit; a person who vomits up his excrements, which happens in the last stage of the iliac passion.

COPROCRI'TICA *medicamenta* (*Med.*) gentle cathartics, from κόπρος, excrement, and κρίνω, to separate.

COPROPHO'RIA (*Med.*) from κόπρος, excrement, and φορέω, to bring away; a purgation.

COPRO'SMA (*Bot.*) a genus of plants, Class 23 *Polygamia*, Order 1 *Monoecia*.

Generic Characters. CAL. perianth one-leaved.—COR. one-petalled; *segments* acute.—STAM. *filaments* five; *anthers* oblong.—PIST. germ oblong; *styles* two; *stigmas* simple.—PER. berry ovate-globular; *seeds* two.

Species. The two species are the—*Coprosma fœtidissima, seu floribus*, &c. native of New Zealand.—*Coprosma lucida*, a shrub, native of New Zealand.

COPROSTA'SIA (*Med.*) from κόπρος, excrement, and ἵστημι, to stop; a constriction of the *alvus*.

COPTA'RION (*Med.*) κοπτάριον, a medicine formed in the shape of a very small cake.

CO'PTE (*Med.*) or *copton*, from κόπτω, to beat or pound a sort of cake made of vegetable substances, formed by beating the ingredients into a paste.

CO'PTIC (*Gram.*) vide *Alphabet*.

CO'PULA (*Anat.*) the name for a ligament.

Copula (*Log.*) the verb which joins any two terms in an affirmative or negative proposition, as "Man *is* an animal," in which case *is* is the copula.

CO'PULATIVE (*Gram.*) an epithet for conjunctions which join the sense as well as the words, as *and*, *also*, &c.

Copulative *propositions* (*Log.*) those which include several subjects, or several attributes joined together by an affirmative or negative conjunction, as *and*, *nor*, *neither*, &c.

CO'PY (*Law*) is the duplicate or transcript of an original writing.—*Copyhold*, a tenure for which the tenant has nothing to show but the copy of the rolls made by the Lords' Court, on such tenant being admitted to any parcel of land, or tenement, belonging to the manor; it is called *base tenure*, because held at the will of the lord, and also, as Fitzherbert says, *tenure in villenage*. The fundamental principles of a copyhold are, that it has been demised time out of mind by copy of court-roll, and that the tenements are part of, or within, the manor; for which reason no copyhold can be made at this day. [vide *Copyholder*]—*Copy-Right*, the exclusive right of printing and publishing copies of any literary performance.

Copy (*Print.*) the original after which the compositor sets his type. *Good copy* is that which is full of breaks and clearly written. *Bad copy* is that which has much close matter, with many interlineations, bad writing, &c. They are jocularly termed *fat* and *lean*.

COPYHO'LDER (*Law*) *tenant per copie*, according to Lyttleton, was called by statute 14 Hen. 4, c. 34, *tenant per le verge*; by 4 Ed. 3, c. 25, *tenant per roll*; by 4 Ed. 1, *customarius tenens*; and, according to Bracton, *villanus sockmannus*, not because he was a bondsman, but held by base tenure. *Bract.* l. 2, c. 8; *Brit. Fol.* 165; *Flet.* l. 1, c. 8; *Lit.* § 73.

COQ (*Med.*) an abbreviation for *coquo*, as *coq ad med consumpt.* boil it down to half the quantity; *coq in S Q Aq.* i.e. boil it in a sufficient quantity of water; *coq S A.* i.e. boil it according to art.

COQUE'NTIA *medicamenta* (*Med.*) medicines which promote digestion.

COQUI'LLES *à boulet* (*Mil.*) French for shells, or moulds, made of brass, that are used for casting cannon-balls.

COR (*Anat.*) the heart.

COR (*Bot.*) the inward, soft, pithy part of a plant.

COR CAROLI (*Astron.*) Charles's Heart; a name first given to a single star, but afterwards to a constellation consisting of three stars in the Northern hemisphere.—*Cor Hydræ*, a star of the second magnitude in the heart of the constellation Hydra.—*Cor Leonis*, the Lion's Heart, or Regulus, a star of the first magnitude in the heart of Leo.—*Cor Scorpii*, vide *Antares*.

COR (*Chem.*) another name for gold; also for an intense fire.

CO'RA (*Com.*) a sort of coin current at Athens.

CORA (*Anat.*) the apple of the eye.

CO'RAAGE (*Law*) *Coraagiu*, a sort of extraordinary imposition on particular occasions, probably consisting of corn. *Bract.* l. 2, c. 116.

CORA'CIAS (*Orn.*) the Roller, a genus of animals, Class *Aves*, Order *Picæ*.
Generic Character. Bill sharp-edged.—*Tongue* cartilaginous.—*Legs* short.—*Feet* formed for walking.
Species. The principal species are—*Coracias garrula*, Common Roller.—*Coracias varia*, Pied Roller.—*Coracias strepera*, Noisy Roller, &c.

CORACI'NE (*Med.*) κορακίνη, a sort of pastil. *Gal. de Comp. Med.* l. 5, c. 11.

CORACI'NI LAPIDES (*Ich.*) vide *Coracinus*.

CORACI'NUS (*Ich.*) κακῶος, Crow-fish, a sort of black fish, peculiar to the Nile. *Plin.* l. 9, c. 16; *Gal. de Simpl.*; *Oppian. Hal.* l. 1, v. 133; *Rondelet. de Pis.* l. 5, c. 8: *Aldrov. de Pisc.*

CO'RACLE (*Mar.*) a sort of small boat used by fishermen in the river Severn.

CORACOBO'TANE (*Bot.*) the *Laurus Alexandrina*.

CORACOBRACHIA'LIS (*Anat.*) from κόραξ, a crow, a muscle situated in the *humerus*; so called on account of its resemblance to a crow's beak. Its use is to raise the arm upward and forward.

CORACOHYOIDÆ'US (*Anat.*) a muscle arising from the upper end of the scapula, near the neck, and inserted into the *os hyoides*, which it pulls obliquely downwards.

CORACOI'DES (*Anat.*) an epithet for a process of the shoulder-blade; so called because it resembles a crow's beak in form.

CO'RACUM *Emplastrum* (*Med.*) a plaster which was used as a topic for spreading ulcers. *Paul. Æginet.* l. 7, c. 17.

CO'RAL (*Conch.*) a hard brittle calcareous substance, which is inhabited by the *Isis*, a genus of animals, Class *Vermes*, Order *Zoophyta*. [vide *Corallium*]

CO'RAL-TREE (*Bot.*) the *Erythrina* of Linnæus, a beautiful tree of America, bearing scarlet flowers, the seeds of which are red, like coral.—*Coral-Wort*, a bulbous root, otherwise called Tooth-Wort, the *Dentaria* of Linnæus.

CORA'LLIUM (*Bot.*) κοραλλίον, or κυραλίον, from κορη, a daughter, and ἅλς, the sea, because it is gathered out of the sea; a marine production which grows in the sea like a shrub, and when taken out waxes hard like a stone. While it is in the water it is of a greenish colour, but when it is dressed the best sort of it is red and smooth. *Ovid. Met.* l. 15, v. 415.

Sic et Coralium, quo primum contingit auras
Tempore durescit.

Dionys. Per. v. 1103.

Πάντες ἁ λίθος ἐςὶν ἐρυθρῦ κοραλίοιο.

The medicinal virtues of coral are those of a cordial, astringent, and sweetener of the blood. *Dioscor.* l. 5, c. 139; *Plin.* l. 32, c. 2; *Solin.* c. 2, p. 16; *Oribas. Med. Coll.* l. 13; *Geopon. Auct.* l. 15, c. 1; *Marbod. de Lapid. Pret.* c. 20.

CORALI'TICUS LAPIS (*Min.*) a white kind of marble, found near a river of Phrygia.

CORA'LIUM (*Bot.*) vide *Coral-tree*.

CORALLA'RIA (*Bot.*) the same as the *Adenanthera*.

CORALLI'NA (*Con.*) Sea Coralline, or Worm-seed, a marine production resembling a plant, which is a calcareous substance, and administered to children as an anthelmintic.

CORALLINA, *in the Linnean system*, a genus of animals, Class *Vermes*, Order *Zoophyta*.
Generic Character. Animal growing in the form of a plant.—*Stem* fixed, mostly jointed.
Species. The principal species are the *Corallina elongata officinalis*, *squamata*, &c.

CORALLOACHA'TES (*Min.*) a sort of agate resembling coral. *Plin.* l. 37, c. 10.

CORALLODE'NDRON (*Bot.*) from κοραλλίον, coral, and δένδρον, a tree; the Coral-tree of America, the *Erythrina* of Linnæus. *Bauh. Pin.*; *Raii Hist. Plant.*

CORALLO'IDES (*Bot.*) from κοραλλίον, coral, and εἶδος, appearance; coral-wort, a fungous substance, the *Clavaria coralloides* of Linnæus, so called from its resemblance to coral.

CORALLORHI'ZA (*Bot.*) the *Ophrys corallorhiza* of Linnæus.

CO'RAL-TREE (*Bot.*) vide *Coral*.

CO'RAL-WORT (*Bot.*) vide *Coral*.

CORAM *non judice* (*Law*) is when a cause is brought into a court out of the judge's jurisdiction.

CO'RANICH (*Cus.*) a name for the custom of singing and howling at funerals, which was formerly prevalent among the Scotch and Irish, and is still practised among the latter to this very day.

CORA'NTO (*Mus.*) Italian for a certain air, consisting of three crotchets in a bar.

CO'RBAN (*Theol.*) in Hebrew קרבן, a gift or offering made on the altar; is a term denoting the treasure that was kept for the use of the temple or the priests at Jerusalem.—*Corban* is also the ceremony among the Mahometans of performing solemn sacrifices, and also the day on which these sacrifices were made, which was the tenth of the last month in the year.

CORBA'TUM (*Min.*) Copper.

CORBEI'LLES (*Fort.*) French for large baskets which are filled with earth, and placed upon the parapet to serve as a protection for the besieged against the shot of the assailants.

CO'RBEILS (*Arch.*) a piece of carved work representing baskets filled with flowers or fruits to finish some ornament.

CO'RBEL (*Archit.*) 1. Corbel, Corbet, or Corbil, a shouldering-piece jutting out in walls to bear up a post, summer, beam, &c. 2. Corbel, or Corbetel, a nich in the wall of a church or other edifice in which an image is placed. 3. The vase in the Corinthian capital, which is in the form of a basket.—*Corbel-Steps*, steps in the gables of some old buildings which might serve either as an ornament, or the purpose of escape in case of fire.—*Corbel-Stones*, smooth polished stones in the front and outside of the Corbels and Niches.—*Corbel-Table*, a series of arches which project from the wall like brackets.

CORBELS (*Fort.*) vide *Corbeilles*.

CORBELS (*Archit.*) vide *Corbeils*.

CO'RBET (*Archit.*) vide *Corbel*.

CO'RBIE (*Her.*) or *corby*, a name for a raven.

CORBS (*Archit.*) ornaments for buildings.

CO'RCHORUS (*Bot.*) or *Corchoron*, κόρχορον, κόρχορος, or κόρχνρος, from κόρη, the pupil of the eye, and κορέω, to cleanse; a name for Pimpernel, or Chickweed, because it was thought to purge the eyes of rheum. Nicander also recommends it as a remedy against the poison of serpents. *Theophrast.*

Hist. Plant. l. 7, c. 7; *Nicand. in Theriac.*; *Dioscor*. l. 2, c. 209; *Plin*. l. 21, c. 22; *Schol. in Nicand.*; *Suidas*.

CORCHORUS, *in the Linnean system*, a genus of plants, Class 13 *Polyandria*, Order 1 *Monogynia*.
Generic Characters. CAL. *perianth* five-leaved; *leaflets* acute.—COR. *petals* five.—STAM. *filaments* numerous; *anthers* small.—PIST. *germ* oblong; *style* thick; *stigma* two-cleft.—PER. *capsule* oblong; *seeds* very many.
Species. The species are annuals, as—*Corchorus olitorius*, Bristly-leaved Corchorus, or Common Jews Mallow.—*Corchorus æstuans*, *Alcea*, seu *Triumfetta*, Horn-beamed Corchorus.—*Corchorus capsularis*, Heart-leaved Corchorus. But the *Corchorus, hirsutus, Japonicus*, &c. are shrubby plants.

CO'RCULUM (*Bot.*) a diminutive of *cor*, the heart: the Corcle or essence of the seed, the rudiment of the future plant, which is attached to, and involved in, the cotyledons. It consists of *plumula*, the Plume, or scaly ascending part; and *rostellum*, the Rostel, or Radicle, the simple descending part. [vide *Botany* and *Seed*]

CORD (*Mus. &c.*) vide Chord.

CORD (*Vet.*) Chord. 1. A strait sinew in the fore leg of a horse, which comes from the shackle-vein to the gristle of his nose. 2. That part by which the testicle of the male animal is suspended, and which passes through the abdominal ring in each groin.

CORD *of wood* (*Com.*) a parcel of firewood four feet broad, four feet high, and eight feet long.

CO'RDAGE (*Mar.*) a general term for all ropes, but particularly for those which belong to the rigging of ships.

CORDATU'RA (*Mus.*) a collective term for the open strings of any stringed instrument, as G, D, A, E, which form the cordatura of the violin. C, E, G, and their octaves, form the cordatura of the guitar.

CORDA'TUS (*Bot.*) cordate, or heartshaped: an epithet for a leaf; *folium cordatum*, a cordate leaf, or a leaf resembling a heart in its shape. [vide *Botany*] The term cordate is sometimes compounded with other epithets, as *cordate oblong*, signifying heartshaped and lengthened out; *cordate-lanceolate-sagittate*, &c. to signify that the leaf partakes of all these forms.

CO'RDEX (*Ant.*) κόρδαξ, a kind of rustic dance. *Hesychius*.

CORDEA'U (*Men.*) French for a cord used in measuring ground.

CORDED (*Her.*) an epithet for a cross which is wound about with cords, but yet so that the cords do not hide all the cross, as in the annexed figure.

CORDE'LIERS (*Ecc.*) or Grey Friars, monks of the Franciscan order, who wear a cord full of knots about their middle. *Heliot. des Ord. Mon.*

CORDIA (*Bot.*) a genus of plants, named, by Plumier, after Enricius Cordus, a German botanist in the sixteenth century; Class 5 *Pentandria*, Order 1 *Monogynia*.
Generic Characters. CAL. *perianth* one-leaved.—COR. one-petalled; *tube* petulous; *border* erect-spreading; *divisions* obtuse.—STAM. *filaments* five; *anthers* oblong.—PIST. *germ* roundish; *style* simple, with bifid divisions; *stigmas* obtuse.—PER. *drupe* globose; *seed* a furrowed nut.
Species. The species are trees, as—*Cordia myxa*, *Myxa*, *Nidi-Maram*, *Sebesten*, *Sebestena*, *Cornus sanguinea*, seu *Prunus Sebestena*, Smooth-leaved Cordia, or Assyrian Plum.—*Cordia Sebestena*, *Sebestena nigra*, *Caryophyllus*, seu *Novella*, Rough-leaved Cordia.—*Cordia macrophylla*, seu *Collococcus*, Broad-leaved Cordia.—*Cordia collococca*, *Collococcus*, seu *Cerasus*, Long-leaved Cordia.—*Cordia Patagonula*, seu *Patagonula*, &c. *Bauh. Hist. Plant.*; *Bauh. Pin.*; *Raii Hist. Plant.*; *Tournef. Inst.*

CORDIA is also the *Chretia bourreria*.

CO'RDIALS (*Med.*) cardiac medicines, to comfort the heart.

CO'RDIER (*Min.*) a sort of beryl.

CORDINE'MA (*Med.*) a head-ache attended with a vertigo.

CO'RDING-QUIRES (*Com.*) the outside quires in a ream of paper.

CORDO'LIUM (*Med.*) the heart-burn.

CORDO'N (*Archit.*) a plinth or edging of stone on the outside of a building.

CORDON (*Fort.*) a stone jutting out between the rampart and the base of the parapet, which goes quite round the fortification.

CORDON (*Mil.*) French for a chain of posts, or a line of separation between two armies, either in the field or in winter quarters.—*Cordon* also signifies ribbon, as the *cordon bleu*, the blue ribbon, the badge of the Order of the Holy Ghost.

CORDO'SUM *filum* (*Med.*) a contorted thread.

CO'RDOVAN (*Mech.*) a sort of leather made of goat-skins, at Cordova in Spain.

CORDU'BA (*Bot.*) the *Asparagus albus* of Linnæus.

CORDUBANA'RIUS (*Law*) the name given to a cordwainer in the statutes, as 3 *H*. 8, c. 10; 5 & 6 *Ed*. 6, c. 13; &c. &c.

CO'RDWAINER (*Mech.*) a shoemaker, so called from the Cordovan leather.

CO'RDYLA (*Ich.*) another name for the Thunny.

CO'RDYLINE (*Bot.*) the same as the *Yucca* of Linnæus.

CORES (*Archit.*) the interior part of any work in a building, as the main stones in a wall.

CORE'MATA (*Med.*) from κορέω, to cleanse, and κορήματα, brushes; is used to signify medicines for cleansing the skin. *Oribas. Med. Coll*. l. 7, c. 15.

COREO'PSIS (*Bot.*) a genus of plants, Class 19 *Syngenesia*, Order 3 *Polygamia frustanea*.
Generic Characters. CAL. doubled.—COR. *compound* rayed; *corollets* hermaphrodites, numerous in the disk; females, eight in the ray.—STAM. in the hermaphrodites, *filaments* five; *anthers* cylindric.—PIST. in the hermaphrodites, *germ* compressed; *style* filiform; *stigma* bifid, acute; in the females, *germ* like the hermaphrodites; *style* and *stigma* none.—PER. none; *calyx* scarcely altered; *seed*, in the hermaphrodite, solitary; in the female, none.
Species. The species are mostly perennials, as—*Coreopsis auriculata*, Ear-leaved Coreopsis.—*Coreopsis baccata*, Berried Coreopsis, &c.

COREOPSIS is also the *Rudbeckia angustifolia*.

CORE'TA (*Bot.*) the *Corchorus siliquosus* of Linnæus.

CORE'TES (*Archæol.*) pools or ponds.

CO'RIA (*Mason.*) the rows or courses of bricks as they are laid by the bricklayer. *Vitruv*. l. 7, c. 3; *Bald. Lex. Vitruv.*; *Salmas. Exercitat. Plin*. p. 1238.

CORIA'GO (*Vet.*) a disease in cattle, which consists in being hide-bound. *Columel. de Re Rust*. l. 6, c. 12.

CORIA'NDRUM (*Bot.*) κοριανδρον, κοριον, or κοριαννον, Coriander, which Nicander and Dioscorides reckon among the deleterious drugs.
Nicand. in Alexiph.

Ἡν γε μὲν ὑλομένον γε ποτὸν κορίοιο δυσαλθὲς
Ἀφραδέως δικαίοισιν ἀπεχθομένοισι πάσηται.

Hippocrat. de Intern. Affect.; *Theophrast. Hist. Plant*. l. 7, c. 3; *Dioscor*. l. 37; *Plin*. l. 20, c. 20; *Gal. de Simpl*. l. 7; *Schol. in Nicander*; *Hesychius*.

CORIANDRUM, *in the Linnean system*, a genus of plants, Class 5 *Pentandria*, Order 2 *Digynia*.
Generic Characters. CAL. *umbel universal* with few rays; *partial* with many rays; *involucre universal* scarce, one-leaved; *partial* three-leaved.—COR. *universal* difform;

floscules of the disk abortive; *proper of the disk* hermaphrodite; *petals* five; *proper of the ray* hermaphrodite.—STAM. *filaments* simple; *anthers* roundish.—PIST. *germ* inferior; *styles* two; *stigmas of the ray* headed.—PER. none; *fruit* spherical; *seeds* two, hemispheric.

Species. The two species are annuals, as the—*Coriandrum sativum*, seu *majus*, Common or Great Coriander.—*Coriandrum testiculatum*, seu *minus*, Small or Twin-fruited Coriander. *Bauh. Hist. Plant.*; *Bauh. Pin.*; *Ger. Herb*; *Park. Theat. Botan.*; *Raii Hist.*; *Tournef. Inst. &c.*

CORIA'NNON (*Bot.*) vide *Coriandrum*.

CORIA'RIA (*Bot.*) a genus of plants, Class 22 *Dioecia*, Order 10 *Decandria*.

Generic Characters. CAL. *perianth* five-leaved—COR. *petals* five.—STAM. *filaments* ten, the length of the corolla; *anthers* oblong; in the female, barren.—PIST. *germs* five, compressed; *styles* five, long bristleform; *stigmas* simple.—PER. none; *petals* five, covering the seed; *seeds* five, kidneyform.

Species. The species are shrubs, as—*Coriaria myrtifolia*, seu *Rhus myrtifolia*, Myrtle-leaved Sumach.—*Coriaria ruscifolia*, &c.

CORIBA'NTIA (*Nat.*) sleeping with open eyes like a hare. *Plin.* l. 11, c. 37.

CORICE'UM (*Archit.*) an exercising room belonging to the Gymnasium. *Vitruv.* l. 5, c. 2; *Bald. Lex. Vitruv.*

CO'RIDIS *folia* (*Bot.*) the *Linconia alopecuroidea*.

CO'RIDOR (*Fort.*) vide *Corridor*.

CORI'NDUM (*Bot.*) the same as the *Cardiospermum*.

CO'RINE (*Zool.*) a sort of antelope, the *Antilopa corinna* of Linnæus.

CORI'NTHAS (*Bot.*) a herb which, being sodden in water, heals the stinging of serpents. *Plin.* l. 24, c. 27.

CORI'NTHIAN *Brass* (*Ant.*) vide *Æs*.

CORINTHIAN *Order* (*Archit.*) the third and noblest of the five orders, invented by Callimachus. *Vitruv.* l. 4, c. 1. [vide *Architecture*]

CO'RION (*Bot.*) vide *Coriandrum*.

CORIOTRAGEMATODE'NDROS (*Bot.*) another name for the *Myrica*.

CO'RIS (*Bot.*) κόρις, a plant, the seeds of which were supposed to promote urine and menstruation, and to be good against the bite of serpents. It was otherwise called *Hypericum*. *Dioscor.* l. 3, c. 174; *Plin.* l. 26, c. 8; *Gal. de Simpl.* l. 7.

CORIS, *in the Linnean system*, a genus of plants, Class 5 *Pentandria*, Order 1 *Monogynia*.

Generic Characters. CAL. *perianth* one-leaved, bellied; COR. one-petalled; *tube* the length of the calyx; *border* five-parted; *divisions* oblong—STAM. *filaments* five, bristleform; *anthers* simple.—PIST. *germ* roundish; *style* filiform; *stigma* thickish.—PER. *capsule* globose; *seeds* very many.

Species. The only species is the *Coris Monspeliensis*, seu *Symphytum petræum*, Montpelier Coris.

CORIS is also the *Euphrasia linifolia*.

CORISPE'RMUM (*Bot.*) a genus of plants, Class 1 *Monandria*, Order 2 *Digynia*.

Generic Characters. CAL. none.—COR. *petals* two, compressed.—STAM. *filaments* one, shorter than the petals; *anthers* simple.—PIST. *germ* acute, compressed; *styles* two; *stigmas* acute.—PER. none; *seeds* single, oval.

Species. The two species are annuals, namely, the—*Corispermum hyssopifolium*, seu *Rhagostris*, Hyssop-leaved Tickseed.—*Corispermum squarrosum*, seu *Rhagostris foliis arundinaceis*, Rough-spiked Tickseed.

CO'RIUM (*Ant.*) any thing which serves as an integument or covering for a substance of which it forms a part; as the skin of man, the hide of an animal, the shell of an egg, &c. so called because it covers *caro*, the flesh. *Isid.* l. 11, c. 1.

CORIUM *foris facere* (*Law*) to undergo a whipping; and *corium perdere*, the same; but *corium redimere*, is to compound for a whipping.

CORK (*Bot.*) the bark of the *Quercus suber* of Linnæus, which was formerly employed as an astringent, and yields an acid.—Cork-tree, the *Quercus suber* of Linnæus, resembles the oak in every thing but its bark, and grows in several parts of Spain and Italy.

CORK-JA'CKET (*Mech.*) in French *chemise de liége*, a machine made in the form of a seaman's jacket, by the help of which the wearer may keep himself up in the water.

CO'RMORANT (*Orn.*) vulgarly used for *Corvorant*.

CORN (*Med.*) vide *Clavus*.

CORN (*Vet.*) a horny substance which grows on the sole of a horse's foot, arising from inflammation.

CORN (*Agric.*) the grain of wheat, barley, rye, &c.

CO'RN-RENTS (*Law*) rents paid in corn, as by statute 18 Eliz. c. 6, on college leases, one-third of the old rent shall be reserved in wheat, or malt, &c.

CO'RN-FLAG (*Bot.*) the *Gladiolus* of Linnæus, a perennial.—Corn-Flower, or Corn-Bottle, an annual, the *Centaurea cyanus* of Linnæus.—Corn-Marigold, the *Chrysanthemum segetum*, &c. mostly perennials.—Corn-Sallad, the *Valeriana dentata*, &c. a perennial, and a wholesome succulent plant, which is cultivated in gardens among the early salads.

CO'RNACHINI *pulvis* (*Med.*) a powder consisting of scammony, antimony, diagnidium, and cream of tartar, in equal quantities.

CO'RNAGE (*Law*) *Cornagium*, a tenure in grand sergeanty, the service of which was to blow a horn when any invasion of the Scots was perceived, by which tenure many persons held their estates northward of the wall called the Picts' wall. *Co.* 1 *Inst.*; *Cambd. Brit.*

CORNA'RE (*Archæol.*) to blow a horn. *Math. Par.* p. 181.

CORNE (*Fort.*) or *ouvrage à corne*, French for the bornwork in a fortification.

CO'RNEA LUNA (*Chem.*) a rough tasteless mass, almost like horn, made by pouring spirit of salt, or strong brine of salt and water, on prepared crystals.

CORNEA *Tunica* (*Anat.*) the second coat of the eye, otherwise called *Sclerotes*, and *Tunica dura*, which proceeds from a membrane or skin in the brain, called the *Dura meninx*. It is transparent in the fore part, to admit the rays of light to pass.

CORNEA'TA OPERA (*Archæol.*) work that was agreed on by the day, until candle-light.

CO'RNEL-TREE (*Bot.*) the *Cornus mascula* of Linnæus, a shrub. The wood of the Cornel is much recommended for its durability in wheel-work, pins, and wedges, where, according to Evelyn, it will last as long as the hardest iron.

CORNELIA (*Bot.*) the *Amniana baccifera* of Linnæus.

CORNE'LIAN-CHE'RRY (*Bot.*) the *Cornus mascula* of Linnæus.

CORNE'LIAN (*Min.*) or *carnelian*, in French *carnoline*, Italian *carnolino*, a precious stone of which rings are made, probably so called from *caro*, flesh, which it resembles.

CORNER (*Archit.*) is the common word for angle.

CO'RNER-TEETH (*Vet.*) the four teeth of a horse placed between the middle teeth and the tushes, two above and two below. They put forth when a horse is four years and a half old.

CORNERS (*Man.*) the angles of the volt, or the extremities of the four lines of the volt when working in a square.

CORNES *de Bélier* (*Fort.*) low flanks, in lieu of tenailles, for the defence of the ditch.

CORNESTA (*Chem.*) a retort.

CO'RNET (*Archæol.*) 1. A linen or laced head-dress of

women. 2. A scarf of black taffety, which doctors of law or physic used to wear on the collar of their robes.

CORNET (*Vet.*) an instrument used in letting blood, otherwise called a *Fleam*.

CORNET (*Chem.*) a paper head, in form of a cone, to cover a vessel.

CORNET *of paper* (*Com.*) a piece of paper wound about in the shape of a horn, such as grocers, &c. wrap up small wares in.

CORNET (*Mil.*) an instrument very similar to the trumpet. When the cornet was sounded alone, the ensigns were to march without the soldiers; but when the trumpet only sounded, the soldiers were to move forward without the ensigns.

Cornet is also the third commissioned officer in a troop of horse or dragoons, subordinate to the captain and lieutenant, and equivalent to the ensign among the foot.

CORNE'TTE (*Mil.*) French for the Cornet.—*Cornette* was also the term used to signify the standard peculiarly appropriated to the light cavalry.—*Cornette blanche*, an ornament of distinction for the superior officers in the French service, which used formerly to be worn on the top of the helmet.

CORN-FLAG (*Bot.*) vide *Corn* and *Corn-flower*.

CO'RNI SPECIES (*Bot.*) the *Cluytra* of Linnæus.

CO'RNICE (*Archit.*) *coronis*, any moulded projection which crowns or finishes the part to which it is affixed, as the cornice of a room, a door, &c.

Cornice signifies particularly the third and highest part of the Entablature, which is of different kinds, as the —*Architrave Cornice*, that immediately contiguous to the architrave.—*Coving Cornice*, which has a great casemate or hollow in it, commonly lathed and plastered upon compass sprockets or brackets.—*Cantaliver Cornice*, that has cantalivers underneath it.—*Modillion Cornice*, that has modillions underneath.—*Mutilated Cornice*, one whose projecture is cut or interrupted to the right of the larmier, or reduced into a platband with a cimaise.

CO'RNICE-RING (*Gunn.*) that which lies next the trunnion-ring in a piece of ordnance.

CO'RNICEN (*Ant.*) the trumpeter, or one who played the cornet, in the Roman army. *Veget.* l. 2, c. 12.

CORNI'CULA (*Surg.*) an instrument made of horn, almost in the form of a cupping-glass, except that at the more slender extremity there is a perforation.

CORNICULA'RIS (*Anat.*) the Coracoid process.

CORNI'CULATE (*Bot.*) or Cornute. [vide *Cornutus*]

CORNI'CULUM (*Ant.*) a military ornament attached to the crest of the helmet, which was given as a mark of distinction for good service. *Liv.* l. 10, c. 44; *Plin.* l. 10, c. 43.

CO'RNISH CHOUGH (*Her.*) a sort of crow, of a fine blue or purple-black colour, with red beak and legs, which was reckoned the finest of the species, and was therefore borne in coats of arms, as in the annexed figure. " He beareth *argent* three Cornish choughs *proper*: the name *Thomas*, M. A. of University College, Oxford."

CORNIX (*Orn.*) the Carrion Crow, the *Corvus cornix* of Linnæus.

CORN-MARIGOLD (*Bot.*) vide *Corn*.

CO'RNMUSE (*Mus.*) a sort of Cornish pipe, formerly much in use, and blown like the bagpipe.

CO'RNO (*Mus.*) Italian for the French horn.

CORN-SA'LLAD (*Bot.*) vide *Corn*.

CORNU-CE'RVI (*Med.*) hartshorn; or the horn of several species of the stag, from which are procured a liquor commonly called Hartshorn, an oil, and a salt; and, by calcination, a powder called *Calcined hartshorn*.

CO'RNU (*Bot.*) a horn or spur at the back of some flowers.

CO'RNUA *Exercitus* (*Ant.*) κέρατα, *alæ*, the Roman name for what are now called the wings of an army, which were assigned as the station for their auxiliaries. *Polyb. de Rom. Mil. Liv.* l. 27, c. 2, &c.; *Ælian. Tact.*; *Polyæn. Strateg.* l. 1.—*Cornua Antennarum*, ἀκροκέρατα, the yard-arms of the sails.

Virg. Æn. l. 3, v. 549.

Cornua velatarum obvertimus antennarum.

Vitruv. l. 10, c. 8; *Tertull. adv. Jud.* c. 10; *Gyrald. de Navigat.* c. 12; *Scheff. de Mil. Nav.* l. 2, c. 5.—*Cornua librorum*, the gilt bosses of the stick about which the ancients rolled their books as we do our maps.

Tibull. l. 3, eleg. 1, v. 13.

Atque inter geminas pingantur cornua frontes.

Auson. Profess. Burdigal. epig. 24, v. 1.

Quos legis a prima deductos menide libri
Doctores patriæ scito fuisse mee.

—*Cornua fluminum*, the turnings and windings of a river.

CORNUA (*Med.*) corns, or horny excrescences which usually form on the joints of the toes.

CORNUA *Uteri* (*Anat.*) the horns of the womb, or the four corners which are observable in the wombs of some quadrupeds resembling horns.

CORNUCO'PIA (*Ant.*) the horn which Hercules broke off from Achelous' head when he turned himself into a bull. This the nymphs filling with flowers and all manner of fruits, was afterwards applied to denote abundance. [vide *Abundantia*]

CORNUCO'PIÆ (*Bot.*) a genus of plants, Class 3 *Triandria*, Order 2 *Digynia*. It is so called from the manner in which the flowers grow in the involucre, like a *cornucopia*, or horn of plenty.

Generic Character. CAL. *perianth* commonly one-leaved, funnel-form.—COR. one-valved.—STAM. *filaments* three capillary; *anthers* oblong.—PIST. *germ* turbinate; *styles* two capillary; *stigmas* cirrose.—PER. none, the corolla including the seed; *seed* single.

Species. The two species are annuals, namely—*Cornucopiæ cucullatum*, Hooded Cornucopiæ, and the *Cornucopiæ alopecuroides*, both of which are nearly allied to the *Alopecurus*.

CORNUCOPIÆ is also the *Valeriana Cornucopiæ*.

CO'RNUM (*Bot.*) vide *Cornus*.

CORNUMU'SA (*Chem.*) a retort.

CO'RNUS (*Bot.*) in the Greek κρανία, the name of a tree, so called from κέρας, because its wood resembled the horn in its hardness and toughness, on which account the ancients made their arrows of this wood.

Virg. Æn. l. 10.

Conjecto sternit jaculo, velat Itala cornus.

Claud.

Apta fretis abies, bellis accommoda cornus.

Theophrast. Hist. Plant. l. 3, c. 12; *Hesychius*; *Suidas*.

CORNUS, in the Linnean system, a genus of plants, Class 4 *Tetrandria*, Order 1 *Monogynia*.

Generic Characters. CAL. *involucre* generally four-leaved; *perianth* very small.—COR. *petals* four, oblong.—STAM. *filaments* four, subulate; *anthers* roundish.—PIST. *germ* roundish, inferior; *style* filiform; *stigma* obtuse.—PER. *drupe* roundish; *seed* nut heartshaped.

Species. The species are trees, or shrubs, as—*Cornus mascula*, the Cornel-tree, or Cornelian Cherry, which, in a wild state, rises no higher than a shrub, but when cultivated it shoots up into a tree. It is a native of European countries.—*Cornus sanguinea*, Common Dogwood, seu *Virga sanguinea*, Female Cornel, Dogberry-trees, &c. a shrub.—*Cornus florida*, Great-flowered Dogwood.—*Cornus alba*, White-berried Dogwood.—*Cornus sericea*, Blue-berried Dogwood, or Dwarf Honeysuckle, native of Russia, &c.—*Cornus suecia*, *Periclymenum*, seu *Chamæ periclymenum*, Herbaceous Dogwood, native of Canada, &c. *Clus. Hist. rar. Plant.*; *Bauh. Hist. Plant.*; *Bauh. Pin.*; *Ger. Herb.*; *Park. Theat. Botan.*; *Raii Hist. Plant.*

CORNU'TA (*Ich.*) a sort of sea-fish, which, according to Pliny, derived its name from its horny appendages, which it used to rear out of the water; it is supposed to answer to what is now called the Gurnard. *Plin. l. 9, c. 27.*

CORNU'TIA (*Bot.*) a genus of plants, called, by Plumier, after Jacob Cornus, a botanist and physician of Paris, Class 14 *Didynamia*, Order 1 *Gymnospermia*.
  Species. The two species, namely, the *Cornutia pyramidata*, and the *Cornutia quinta*, are American trees.—*Cornutia* is also the *Premna integrifolia*.

CORNUTUM *argumentum* (*Log.*) a subtle or sophistical argument, which is, as it were, horned.

CORNU'TUS (*Bot.*) cornute, or hornshaped; an epithet for the anthers and some other parts of plants.

COROCO'TTA (*Zool.*) a kind of mongrel beast in Ethiopia, bred of a lion and a dog, or a wolf.

CORO'DIS *habendo* (*Law*) a writ for exacting a corody of an abbey or religious house. *Reg. Orig.* 264.

CO'RODY (*Law*) a sum of money, or au allowance of meat, drink, and clothing allowed by an abbot out of the monastery to the king for the maintenance of any one of his servants.

CORO'LLA (*Bot.*) from *corona*, a crown, the second of the seven parts of fructification, formed, according to Linnæus, of the *liber*, or inner bark, of the plant. It is commonly to be distinguished from the perianth by the fineness of its texture and the gayness of its colours; the perianth being rougher, thicker, and always green. The corolla is composed of one or more leaf-like pieces, named petals, according to the number of which it is distinguished into a one, two, three, or many-petalled corolla. When a corolla consists of one petal only, the lower contracted part is named the *tube*, as *a* in *fig.* 2, and the upper dilated part *limbus*, the limb; when a corolla is formed of two petals, the inferior narrow part of each is named the *claw*, as *fig.* 4, and the superior expanding part the *lamina*; in this case the whole of the dilated part, or border of the corolla, is named the *limb*. The corolla is moreover distinguished, according to the divisions, proportions, &c. into *bifida*, two-cleft, *trifida*, three-cleft, &c.; *regularis*, regular, when equal in the figure, magnitude, and proportion of the parts; *irregularis*, irregular, when the parts of the *limb* differ from each other; *inequalis*, unequal, when the parts do not correspond in size; *difformis*, difform, when the petals or their segments are of different forms. According to their figure, into *campanulata*, campanulate, or bell-shaped, as *fig.* 1, where *a* marks the perianth, and *b* the

Fig. 1. Fig. 2. Fig. 3. Fig. 4.

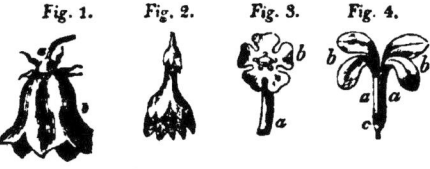

corolla; *infundibiliformis*, funnel-shaped, as in *fig.* 2; *hypocratiformis*, flat, and fixed upon a tube, as in *fig.* 3, where *a* is the tube, *b* the limb; *personata*, personate [vide *Personate*]; *ringens*, ringent; *papilionacea*, papilionaceous [vide *Papilionaceus*]; *rotata*, rotate; *cyathiformis*, glass-shaped; *urceolata*, pitcher-shaped; *cruciata*, cruciform, as in *fig.* 4, where *a a* are the claws, *b* the laminas of the petals, *c* the receptacle; *concava*, concave; *patens*, spreading; *rosacea*, rose-like; *undulata*, undulated; *plicata*, plaited; *revoluta*, revolute; *torta*, twisted. In respect to the margin, into *crenata*, crenate; *serrata*, serrate; *ciliata*, ciliate. In respect to the surface, into *villosa*, villous; *tomentosa*, tomentose; *sericea*, silky; *pilosa*, hairy; *barbata*, bearded.

CORO'LLULA (*Bot.*) Corollule, or *Corollet*, a small corolla is a term applied to the florets in aggregate flowers.

CO'ROLLARY (*Math.*) or *Consectary*, a consequence drawn from some proposition already proved or demonstrated; as if from the proposition, "That every triangle having two sides equal has two angles equal," this corollary be drawn that every equilateral triangle is also equiangular. These were called *porisms* by the ancients.

CORO'NA (*Ant.*) a crown or cap of dignity was worn as a badge of regal dignity by most of the Roman emperors; but crowns were bestowed upon military merit and success among the Romans on various occasions; wherefore it was a common emblem of victory on medals, sometimes in the mouth of the eagle, sometimes in the hand of the goddess of victory, and sometimes by itself, as in *fig.* 1, on the reverse of a monetal coin of L. Vinicius, representing four crowns, emblematical of four victories obtained by Augustus, namely, over Sextus Pompey, over the Pannonians, &c. at Actium, and lastly over Cleopatra, in Egypt.

Fig. 1. Fig. 2. Fig. 3.

The principal crowns bestowed on military men were as follow—*Corona civica*, a civic crown (as in the annexed figure) given to him who had rescued the life of a citizen, which was made of oak leaves. [vide

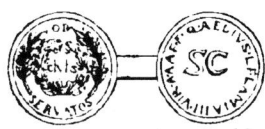

Civica]—*Corona navalis*, a naval crown given to him who first boarded an enemy's ship. It was made of gold, and beaked after the manner of ships, as in *fig.* 2, which represents the obverse of a coin of Agrippa; the legend AGRIPPA *Lucii Filius* COS*ul*. III.—*Corona muralis*, given to him who first scaled the walls of an enemy's garrison, representing the pinnacles of a wall, as in *fig.* 3, which is also the head of Agrippa thus adorned.—*Corona castrensis*, given to him who first entered the enemy's camp; it was made in the form of a trench. These three last were of gold.—*Corona obsidionalis*, an obsidional crown, given to the general who raised a siege. It was made of the grass of the place which had been besieged.—*Corona triumphalis*, given to a general on the day of triumph, was first made of laurel, and afterwards of gold.—*Corona ovalis*, which was of myrtle, and given to a general who was entitled to an ovation. To these might be added, the *corona pactilis*, made of rose leaves stitched together; *corona oleagina*, a crown of olive leaves; *corona plectilis*, a crown plaited with flowers, grass, ivy leaves, and the like. *Plin. l.* 22, c. 45; *Gell. l.* 5, c. 6; *Paschal. de Coron. l.* 2, c. 16, &c.; *Mader. de Coron. apud Græv. Thes. Antiq. Roman. tom. viii.*; *Buleng. de Triumph.* &c.

CORONA (*Archit.*) Crown, or Crowning, the flat and most advanced part of the cornice, so called because it crowns the cornice and entablature. It is called in the language of the workmen the *drip*, because it serves by its projecture to carry the rain off from the rest of the building. *Vitruv. l.* 2, c. 8; *Bald. Lex. Vitruv.*

CORONA (*Bot.*) vide *Crown.*—*Corona imperialis*, the same as the *Fritillaria.*—*Corona solis*, the *Bupthalmum frutescens* of Linnæus.

CORONA *imperialis* (*Conchol.*) a kind of *volvula*.

CORONA (*Opt.*) a luminous circle, otherwise called a *halo*, which is observable round the sun, moon, or largest planets, and usually coloured.

CORONA *Borealis* (*Astron.*) κρῶτος, ςίφανος. Northern Crown, one of the 48 old constellations in the northern hemisphere, containing 8 stars, according to Ptolemy, Tycho, and Hevelius, 20 according to Bayer, and 21 in the British Catalogue; one of which, namely, *Lucida Coronæ*, is of the second magnitude.—*Corona Australis*, or *Meridionalis*, κρκίσκος, the Southern Crown, a constellation of the southern hemisphere, which contains 13 stars, according to Ptolemy, and 12 in the British Catalogue. It is called by Proclus κηρυκίον. *Arat. Phænom.* v. 71; *Ptol. Almag.* l. 7, c. 5; *Manil. Astron. Poet.*; *Procl. de Sphær.*; *Ricciol. Almag. Nov.* l. 6.

CORONA'LIS *sutura* (*Anat.*) coronal suture, from *corona*, a crown or garland, so called because the ancients wore their garlands in that direction; the suture of the head, which extends from one temple to the other, uniting the two parietal bones with the frontal.

CORONA'RE *filium* (*Law*) to make one's son a priest, which the lords of manors anciently prohibited those of their tenants from doing who held by villenage, as ordination changed the condition of such persons, by making those free who might otherwise have been claimed as servants.

CORONA'RIA (*Bot.*) the *Agrostema coronaria* of Linnæus.

CORONARIA *vasa* (*Anat.*) coronary vessels, the arteries and veins of the heart, so called because they encircle it after the manner of a *corona*, or crown. The arteries of the stomach are also called by the same name.

CORONA'RIÆ (*Bot.*) the ninth Order in Linnæus' Fragments of a Natural Method, and the tenth of his Natural Orders, containing a part of the liliaceous plants, and such as, from their natural beauty, are adapted to the making of garlands.

CO'RONARY (*Bot.*) an epithet for plants that are adapted for making garlands.

CORONA'TION (*Polit.*) the ceremony of investing with the crown; a term particularly applied to kings. It is however employed to denote the ceremony of investing the pope with his sacerdotal dignity and character, of which a memorial has been left on the medals of Adrian VI. as in the subjoined figures, where, as in *fig.* 1, he has on the

Fig. 1.   Fig. 2.

sacerdotal robe called the *pluviale*, and in *fig.* 2 that called *planeta*.

CORONATO'RE *eligendo* (*Law*) a writ directed to the sheriff to call together the freeholders of the county in order to choose a new coroner. *F. N. B.* 163; *Reg. Orig.* 177.—*Coronatore Exonerando*, a writ for the discharge of a coroner for negligence or insufficiency in his duty. *F. N. B.* 164; *Reg. Orig.* 177; *2 Inst.* 32.

CORONA'TUS *Homo* (*Ecc.*) one who had received the first tonsure preparatory to superior orders; so called because the tonsure was in the form of a *corona*, or crown of thorns.

CORO'NE (*Anat.*) from κορώνη, a crow; the acute process of the lower jaw-bone, so called from its supposed resemblance to a crow's bill.

CORONE (*Law*) French for crown; under which head were formerly brought all matters of the crown, as treason, felony, &c.

CORONE'OLA (*Bot.*) a rose which flowered in autumn. *Plin.* l. 21, c. 4.

CO'RONER (*Law*) an officer so called from *corona*, a crown, because, with the assistance of a jury of twelve men, he makes inquisition into the untimely deaths of any of the king's subjects. *Bract.* l. 3, tract 2, c. 5, &c.; *Britt.* c. 1; *Flet.* l. 1, c. 18; *Mirror.* c. 1, § 3; *2 Inst.* 31, &c.—*Sovereign coroner*, the Lord Chief Justice of the King's Bench.—*Coroner of the verge*, an officer who has jurisdiction within the verge or compass of the King's Court. *Cromp. Jur.* 102.

CORONET (*Her.*) a small crown worn by the nobility, as a Duke's, Marquiss', Earl's, Viscount's, and Baron's crown. [vide *Duke*, &c.]

CORONET (*Vet.*) or *Cronet*, the upper part of a horse's hoof, where the hair grows down; or it is the lowest part of the pastern, which runs round the *coffin*.

CORONILLA (*Bot.*) a diminutive of *corona*, is the name of a genus of plants *in the Linnean system*, Class 17 *Diadelphia*, Order 4 *Decandria*.

Generic Characters. CAL. *umbellule* simple; *perianth* one-leaved, compressed.— COR. papilionaceous; *standard* heartshaped; *wings* ovate; *keel* acuminate, compressed.—STAM. *filaments* diadelphous; *anthers* simple.—PIST. *germ* columnar; *stigma* obtuse.—PER. *legume* very long, two-valved; *seeds* many.

Species. The species are mostly perennials, and natives of the South of Europe, as—*Coronilla emerus*, *Emerus*, seu *Colutea*, Scorpion Sena.—*Coronilla*, seu *Polygala*, Linear-leaved Coronilla.—*Coronilla glauca*, seu *Colutea*, Great shrubby Coronilla.—*Coronilla minima*, the Least Coronilla.—*Coronilla scandens*, Climbing Coronilla. But the *Coronilla securidaca*, Securidaca, seu *Hedysarum*, Hatchet Vetch, is an annual. *Clus. Hist. rar. Plant.*; *Bauh. Hist. Plant.*; *Bauh. Pin.*; *Ger. Herb.*; *Park. Theat. Botan.*; *Raii Hist. Plant.*; *Tournef. Inst.*

CORONILLA is also the *Galega villosa*.

CORO'NIS (*Archit.*) vide *Cornice*.

CORONI'SMA (*Ant.*) κορώνισμα, a begging sort of song among the Rhodians, sung by persons carrying about a crow or jackdaw, whence they were called *coronistæ*, from κορώνη, a crow. *Athen.* l. 8, c. 15.

CORONO'IDES (*Anat.*) from κορώνη, a crow, and ιδος, likeness; an epithet for different parts of the body bearing a resemblance to a crow's beak; as the *Coronoides Apophysis Ulnæ*; *Coronoides Apophysis maxillæ*, &c.

CORO'NOPUS (*Bot.*) κορωνόπους, a vulnerary plant; so called from the resemblance which its leaves bear to the foot of κορώνη, a crow. It is reckoned efficacious against the bites of venemous creatures. *Theophrast. Hist. Plant.* l. 7, c. 9; *Dioscor.* l. 2, c. 158; *Plin.* l. 22, c. 19.

CORO'PHIUM (*Ich.*) κορῶφιον, a kind of crab fish.

COROZO'RE (*Bot.*) another name for the *Sedum*.

CO'RPORA *Albicantia* (*Anat.*) Glands of a white colour in the brain.—*Corpora cavernosa*, two hollow crura forming the Penis.—*Corpora fimbriata*, the flattened terminations of the posterior crura of the fornix of the brain.—*Corpora lobosa*, the cortical part of the kidney.—*Corpora nervospongiosa*, or *nervosa*, the nervous spongeous bodies of the penis.—*Corpora olivaria*, the two external prominences of the medulla oblongata.—*Corpora pyramidalia*, the two internal prominences of the medulla oblongata.—*Corpora quadrigemina*, vide *Tubercula quadrigemina*. — *Corpora striata*, two prominences in the lateral ventricle of the brain.

CORPORAL (*Law*) an epithet for any thing belonging to the body, as corporal punishment.

CORPORAL (*Mil.*) a rank and file man, with superior pay to that of common soldiers, and with nominal rank under a serjeant.—*A Lance Corporal*, in French *corporal breveté*, one who acts as corporal, receiving pay as a private.

CORPORAL *Oath* (*Law*) is a name given to the ordinary oath administered in courts of law, because the party who takes it is obliged to lay his hand on the Bible.

CORPORAL *of a ship* (*Mar.*) an inferior officer, whose business it is to look after all the small shot, arms, &c.

CORPORALE (*Ecc.*) a communion cloth used in the Romish church, being a square piece of linen, on which the chalice and host are placed by the priest at mass. *Leg. Alphons. Reg. Castell.* part 1, tit. 4, leg. 57; *Amalar. de Eccles. Offic.* c. 19.

CORPORATION (*Law*) a body politic or incorporate, so called because the persons composing it are made into one body. *Corporations* are of different kinds as to the persons, as a—*Sole corporation*, when in one person, as in the King.—*Aggregate corporation*, when consisting of many, as a Dean and Chapter.—*Temporal corporation*, which is either *temporal by the King*, where there is a Mayor and Commonalty, as in many towns; or *temporal by the Common Law*, as the Parliament, consisting of the King as the head, and the two Houses which are the body. —*Spiritual corporation*, as consisting of Bishops, Deans, &c.—*Mixed corporation*, composed of persons spiritual and temporal, as the Heads of Colleges, Hospitals, &c.— *Corporations*, as to their object, are either *Ecclesiastical* or *Lay*. Lay Corporations are of two kinds, *civil* and *eleemosynary*. Of the former sort, are those erected for the good government of a town; of the latter, are colleges, hospitals, &c.

CORPOREAL *Inheritance* (*Law*) that which consists of houses, lands, &c.

CORPOREITY (*Phy.*) a term among the schoolmen for the nature of a body.

CORPORIFICATION (*Chem.*) the giving to a spirit the same, or a similar, body to what it had before.

CORPOSANT (*Nat.*) in Italian *Corpo santo*, another name for the volatile meteor, called the *Ignis fatuus*.

CORPS (*Archit.*) any part that projects or advances beyond the naked wall, and serves as a ground for some decoration.

CORPS (*Mil.*) French for any body of forces; of which there are different kinds, as—*Corps d'armée*, the whole army.— *Corps de Garde*, the Guards.—*Corps de Garde avancée*, advanced post of the cavalry.—*Petit corps de Garde*, the quarter guard, which is more in front.—*Corps de reserve*, the troops in reserve.—*Corps de Bataille*, the whole line of battle.—*Corps de Garde* signifies the place, i. e. guardhouse, as well as the men who occupy it.—*Corps de Casernes*, the barracks.

CORPUS (*Anat.*) a name given to several substances, or parts in the body, as *Corpus callosum, luteum*, &c.—*Corpus callosum*, the white medullary part joining the two hemispheres of the brain.—*Corpus glandulosum*, the prostate gland.—*Corpus luteum*, the granulous papilla which is found in that part of the ovarium of females from which an ovum has proceeded.—*Corpus mucosum*, or *reticulare*, vide *Rete mucosum.*—*Corpus pampiniforme*, or *corpus pyramidale*, a name given to the spermatic chord, and the thoracic duct.—*Corpus sesamoideum*, a little prominence at the entrance of the pulmonary artery.—*Corpus spongiosum urethræ*, the spongy substance of the Urethræ in male animals; the end of which, next to the prostate gland, is, on account of its bigness, called the *Bulb* of the Urethra.

CORPUS (*Lit.*) a term used to denote any matter of learning that is collected and digested into a regular and uniform whole, as *corpus canonum*, a body of canon law, &c.

CORPUS *Christi Day* (*Ecc.*) a moveable festival appointed by the church of Rome in honour of the sacrament of the Lord's supper. It is mentioned in the statute 32 *Hen.* 8, c. 21.

CORPUS *cum Causa* (*Law*) a writ issuing out of Chancery to remove both the body and record touching the cause of any man lying in execution upon a judgment for debt into the King's Bench, &c. there to lie till he has satisfied the judgment. *F. N. B.* 251.

CORPUSCLES (*Phy.*) the smallest parts or physical atoms of a body.

CORPUSCULAR *Attraction* (*Phy.*) that power by which the minute component parts of bodies are united and adhere to each other.—*Corpuscular Philosophy*, that scheme, or system of physics, in which the phenomena of bodies are accounted for from the motion, rest, position, &c. of the corpuscles or atoms of which bodies are composed.

CORR (*Ant.*) in the Hebrew כור, a Hebrew measure containing two quarts English. *Isid. Orig.* l. 14, c. 25.

CORRAGO (*Bot.*) the herb Bugloss.

CORRE (*Anat.*) from κειρω, to shave; that part of the jaws where the beard grows.

CORRECTIO (*Rhet.*) ἐπανορθωσις, a figure of speech by which the orator recalls what he has said, and substitutes something fitter in its place. *Cic. Or.* l. 3, c. 54; *Quintil.* l. 9, c. 2; *Rutil. Lup.* p. 5; *Georg. Trapezunt. Rhet.* l. 5, p. 79; *Jul. Rufinian.* p. 32.

CORRECTION (*Print.*) the correcting of proofs as they come from the compositors' hands, in order to free them from all faults, and fit them for the press. Corrections are placed on the margin as well as the text, and denoted by different marks, according to the nature of the fault; as ꝗ, i. e. dele, for any thing to be effaced; ʌ, caret. i. e. wanting, for what is to be added; ⌣, to denote that words, letters, &c. are too distant from each other; #, to show that they are too close, &c. [vide *Printing*]

CORRECTION (*Med.*) is when a salt, or any other thing, is added to a medicine to quicken it.

CORRECTING-STONE (*Print.*) a large slab of marble, or Purbeck-stone, placed on a stand, at which the compositor corrects the formes from the proofs that are returned to him.

CORRECTIVES (*Med.*) medicines which serve to correct the qualities of other medicines.

CORRECTOR *of the press* (*Print.*) one especially appointed in a printing office to correct the proofs as they come rough from the compositors' hands; in distinction from the *reader*, who looks over the revises, or after-proofs of the same sheet, and fits them finally for the press.

CORRECTOR *of the staple* (*Com.*) an officer of the staple, who records the bargains of merchants made there.

CORRECTORES (*Ant.*) provincial magistrates in Italy. *Pancirol. Not. Dignit. Imp. Orient.* c. 99.

CORREGIDOR (*Polit.*) a chief magistrate in a Spanish town.

CORRELATIVES (*Phy.*) things that bear a natural relation to each other, as a father to a son.

CORRELET (*Mil.*) vide *Corslet.*

CORRESPONDENCE (*Mil.*) a written or unwritten intercourse kept up between officers at the head of an army who communicate together in order to act in concert.— *Secrect correspondence* is secret communication, or intelligence, which subsists between the commander and some confidential agent acting in another quarter.

CORRESPONDENT (*Com.*) he who corresponds, or carries on a commercial intercourse by letter with another person at a distance.

CORRIDOR (*Fort.*) the covert-way lying round about the whole compass of the fortification of a place, between the outside of the moat and the pallisadoes.

CORRIDOR (*Archit.*) a long gallery leading to several chambers.
CORRI'GIOLA (*Bot.*) a genus of plants, Class 5 *Pentandria*, Order *Trigynia*.
   Generic Character. CAL. *perianth* five-leaved; *leaflets* ovate.—COR. *petals* five, ovate.—STAM. *filaments* five, subulate; *anthers* simple.—PIST. *germ* ovate; *style* none; *stigmas* three, obtuse.—PER. none; *seed* single.
   Species. The single species is the *Corrigiola litoralis*, *Polygonifolia*, *Polygonum littoreum*, seu *Alsine palustris*.
CORRIGIOLA is also the *Illecebrum verticillatum*.
CORRI'RA (*Orn.*) a genus of birds of the Order *Grallæ*.
   Generic Character. Bill short, without teeth.—*Thighs* longer than the body.—*Feet* four-toed, palmate.
   Species. The single species is the *Corrira Italica*.
CORROBORA'NTIA (*Med.*) corroborative or strengthening Medicines.
CORRODE'NTIA (*Med.*) medicines which consume, or eat away proud flesh.
CO'RRODY (*Law*) vide *Corody*.
CORRODY (*Mil.*) a defalcation from an allowance or salary for some other than the original purpose; thus, an officer, who retires on the full pay of a short company or troop holds a corrody.
CORRO'SION (*Chem.*) a dissolution of mixed bodies by *corrosive menstruums*.
CORRO'SIVE *Sublimate* (*Chem.*) or *Corrosive muriate of mercury*, is a perchloride of mercury, an extremely acrid and violently poisonous preparation.
CORRO'SIVES (*Chem.*) saline menstruums, which have the property of dissolving bodies.
CORRU'DA (*Bot.*) a herb called wild Asparagus. *Plin.* l. 20, c. 13.
CO'RRUGANT (*Anat.*) an epithet for muscles which help to knit the brows, or to draw the skin into wrinkles.
CORRUGA'TOR *Supercilii* (*Anat.*) the muscle which pulls down the skin of the forehead so as to make it wrinkle.
CORRUPTI'COLÆ (*Ecc.*) a sect of heretics in Egypt, in the sixth century, who maintained that the body of Jesus was corruptible.
CORRU'PTION (*Phy.*) the destruction of the form, or proper mode of existence of any natural body.
CORRUPTION *of blood* (*Law*) an infection growing to the blood, estate, and issue of a man attainted of treason.
CORRUSCA'TION (*Phy.*) a flash of lightning, or of light from a sudden spark of fire.
CO'RSAIR (*Mar.*) in French *pirate barbaresque*, a name for the piratical cruisers on the coast of Barbary, which plunder the merchant ships of European nations, with whom they are at peace.
CORSE-PRESENT (*Law*) from the French *corps present*, a mortuary; so called, probably, because where a mortuary became due on the death of any man, the best or second best beast was presented to the priest, and carried with the corps. *Stat.* 21 *Hen.* 8, c. 5.
CO'RSLET (*Mil.*) from the Latin *corpusculum*, a little body; the name of an ancient piece of armour, with which the body or trunk of a man was protected. It was used by the pikemen. 4 & 5 P. & M. c. 2.
CO'RSNED-BREAD (*Archæol.*) or ordeal-bread, a piece of bread consecrated by the priest for that purpose, which was eaten by the Saxons when they would clear themselves of any crime laid to their charge; in which case they wished it might be poison, and kill them if they were guilty.
CORSOI'DES (*Min.*) vide *Amianthus Lapis*.
CO'RTALON (*Bot.*) Groundsel.
CORTA'RIUM (*Archæol.*) vide *Cortularium*.
CORTE'GE (*Cus.*) French for the train, or retinue, that accompanies a person of distinction.
CORTES (*Polit.*) the states, or the assembly of the states of Spain and of Portugal.

CO'RTEX (*Bot.*) the outer bark of a plant, or the second integument of the *epidermis*, so called from *corium*, the hide or skin, and *tego*, to cover.
CORTEX (*Med.*) this word taken absolutely signifies Peruvian-bark, but it is applied with an epithet to many sorts of bark, which are used medicinally, as—*Cortex angelinæ*, the bark of a tree growing in Grenada.—*Cortex Chinchinæ*, the cinchona.—*Cortex tavola*, a bark supposed to belong to a tree which affords the *Anisum stellatum*, &c.
CORTEX *Cerebri* (*Anat.*) the cortical substance of the brain.
CO'RTICAL-BUD (*Bot.*) *gemma corticalis*, a bud having its origin from the scales of the bark.
CORTICA'LIS *substantia* (*Med.*) the external substance of the brain, which, being of a darker colour than the internal, is, on that account, called *cortical*.
CORTICA'TUS (*Bot.*) Corticate, an epithet for a capsule; *capsula corticata*, a capsule in which the outer hard part is lined by an inner soft layer, as in *Swietenia*, &c.; or when the outer spongy or cork-like part covers the proper crust of the capsule, as in *Triumfetta*, &c.
CO'RTIN (*Fort.*) or curtain, the wall or distance between the flanks of two bastions.
CORTI'NA (*Ant.*) 1. A cauldron, or kettle, in which wool was dyed. *Cat. de Re Rust.* c. 67. 2. The tripos sacred to Apollo, from which the oracles were delivered. *Plin.* l. 34, c. 3; *Suet. in August.* c. 5. 3. The bar, or that place in a court of law where the counsellors, the secretaries, &c. sate. *Tac. de Orat.* c. 19.—*Cortina Theatri*, the convex capacity of the theatre. *Virg. Ætn.* v. 294.—*Cortina cæli*, the hemisphere of the heavens. *Ennius, apud Varr. de Lat. Ling.* l. 6, c. 3.
CORTULA'RIUM (*Archæol.*) or *cortarium*, a yard adjoining to a farm.
CORTU'SA (*Bot.*) a genus of plants, Class 5 *Pentandria*, Order 1 *Monogynia*.
   Generic Character. CAL. *perianth* five-cleft; *divisions* lanceolate.—COR. one-petalled; *tube* scarce any; *border* flat, five-parted; *divisions* ovate; *throat* with an elevated ring.—STAM. *filaments* five, obtuse; *anthers* two-plated oblong.—PIST. *germ* ovate; *style* filiform; *stigma* almost headed.—PER. *capsule* ovate, acuminate; *seeds* numerous; *receptacle* columnar.
   Species. The two species are—*Cortusa Matthioli*, *Sanicula montana*, seu *Cortusa Matthioli*, a biennial, and native of Austria.—*Cortusa Gmelini*, very similar to the former. *Clus. Hist. rar. Plant.*; *Ger. Herb.*; *Park. Theat. Botan.*; *Raii Hist.*
CORU-CANA'RICA (*Bot.*) a quince-like tree of Malabar, which is antidysenteric.
CO'RVET (*Man.*) vide *Curvet*.
CORVETTE (*Mar.*) French for any vessel under twenty guns.
CORVI'NUS *lapis* (*Min.*) a stone, found in India, remarkable for making a noise like thunder when heated.
CORVI'TORES (*Ant.*) tumblers and merry-andrews. *Fest. de Verb. Signif.*
COBU'NDUM (*Min.*) a sort of adamantine earth.
CO'RVORANT (*Orn.*) vulgarly called *Cormorant*, an exceedingly voracious bird of the pelican tribe, the *Pelicanus carbo* of Linnæus. It builds on the highest cliffs hanging over the sea, and is tamed by the Chinese to catch fish.
CO'RVORANT'S *foot* (*Conch.*) a sort of testaceous animal, the *Strombus pes pelecani* of Linnæus.
CO'RUS (*Ant.*) vide *Caurus*.
CO'RVUS (*Ant.*) κόραξ, a kind of iron-hook or grapple in the form of a crow's beak, which was used in war, particularly in ships. *Polyb.* l. 1, c. 22; *Diodor.* l. 17; *Vitruv.* l. 10, c. 19; *Curt.* l. 4, c. 2; *Bald. Lex. Vitruv.*
CORVUS (*Orn.*) a genus of animals of the Class *Aves*, Order *Picæ*.

Generic Characters. Bill convex, sharp-edged.—*Nostrils* covered with setaceous recumbent feathers.—*Tongue* cartilaginous, bifid.—*Feet* fit for walking.

Species. The species of this tribe are distinguished in the English into the Raven, Crow, Rook, Jay, Nutcracker, and Magpie; as—*Corvus corax*, the Raven.—*Corvus corone*, the Carrion Crow.—*Corvus cornix*, the Hooded Crow.—*Corvus frugilegus*, the Rook.—*Corvus Monedula*, the Jackdaw.—*Corvus glandarius*, the Jay.—*Corvus cristatus*, the Blue Jay.—*Corvus caryocatactes*, the Nutcracker.—*Corvus pica*, the Magpie.

Corvus (*Astron.*) in the Greek κόραξ, in the Arabic *Algorab*; the Raven, one of the forty-eight old constellations in the Southern hemisphere, containing seven stars, according to Ptolemy, Tycho, and Bayer, and nine in the British catalogue. This bird is fabled to have been translated to heaven by Apollo, for discovering to him the infidelity of the nymph Coronis. *Arat. Phænom.* v. 444; *Eratosth. Characterism*; *Ptol. Almag.* l. 7, c. 5; *Hygin. Poet. Astron.*

CORYBA'NTES (*Ant.*) priests of Cybele. *Strab.* l. 10; *Plin.* l. 21, c. 37.

CORYBA'NTIAN (*Ant.*) κορυβαντιάω, to sleep with one's eyes open, after the manner of the Corybantes, when they watched over Jupiter in his infancy. *Plin.* l. 21, c. 37.

CO'RYCUS (*Med.*) κώρυκος, a sort of ball among the ancients, probably made of leather, and stuffed with the *acini* of the fig, or with bran, &c. for weak persons, but with sand for stronger persons; with which, when it was suspended from the ceiling, they used to exercise themselves in throwing it from them and catching it again.

CORYDA'LES (*Bot.*) the twenty eighth order of Linnæus' Fragments of a Natural Method, and the twenty-fourth of his natural orders.

CORY'DALIS (*Orn.*) the Lark.

CO'RYLUS (*Bot.*) the Hazle-Nut, a well-known tree, both among the ancients and moderns, is, in the Linnæan system, a genus of plants, Class 21 *Monoecia*, Order 8 *Polyandria*.

Generic Character. CAL. ament common imbricated; *scales* one-flowered.—Cor. none.—STAM. *filaments* eight; *anthers* ovate, oblong.—*Female flowers* remote from the males.—PIST. *germ* roundish.—PER. none; *seed* nut ovate.

Species. The species are trees, which bear the well-known nut, called the Hazle-Nut, or Filbert, which are varieties of the *Corylus avellana*.

CORY'MB (*Bot.*) *corymbus*, signifies literally a cluster of ivy berries, but is employed in modern Botany to denote a sort of inflorescence which is formed from a spike, each flower being furnished with a proper peduncle, and proportionally elevated. The *corymb*, the *cyme*, and the *umbel*, bear a strong resemblance to each other; but they may be distinguished as follow. In the *corymb*, fig. 1,

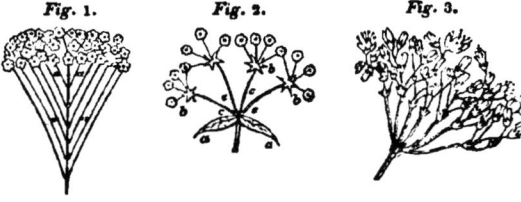

Fig. 1. *Fig. 2.* *Fig. 3.*

the peduncle or pedicels, *a a a a*, take their rise from different heights; but the lower ones being longer, they all form nearly an even surface at top. In the *umbel*, fig. 2, the peduncles *c c c c* take their rise from the same centre; and the whole is disposed with remarkable regularity. In the *cyme*, fig. 3, the peduncles, as in fig. 2, also take their rise from the same centre; but the sub-divisions are irregular. [vide *Botany*, *Inflorescence*]

CORY'MBIATE (*Ant.*) set about and garnished with clusters of ivy berries.

CORYMBI'FERÆ (*Bot.*) the name of one of Ray's classes; and of the third sub-division in the order of compound flowers in Linnæus's Natural Arrangement.

CORY'MBION (*Bot.*) the herb *Lychnis*.

CORYMBI'TES (*Bot.*) a kind of spurge with broad leaves.

CORY'MBIUM (*Bot.*) a genus of plants, Class 19 *Syngenesia*, Order 6 *Monogamia*.

Generic Character. CAL. *perianth* two-leaved; *leaflets* erect.—Cor. one-petalled.—STAM. *filaments* five; *anthers* oblong.—PIST. *germ* hirsute; *style* simple.—PER. none; *seed* single; *receptacle* naked.

Species. The species are mostly natives of the Cape of Good Hope, as—*Corymbium scabrum*, *glabrum*, *filiforme*, &c.

CORYNOCA'RPUS (*Bot.*) a genus of plants, Class 5 *Pentandria*, Order 1 *Monogynia*.

Generic Character. CAL. *perianth* five-leaved.—Cor. five-petalled; *nectary* with five leaflets.—STAM. *filaments* subulate; *anthers* oblong.—PIST. *germ* superior; *style* short; *stigma* obtuse.—PER. *nut* club-shaped; *seed* an oblong kernel.

Species. The single species is the *Corynocarpus lævigata*, native of New Zealand.

CO'RYPHA (*Bot.*) a genus of palms, of which the principal species is the *Corypha umbraculifera*, *Palma montana*, *Codda-panna*, seu *Laribus*, a native of Malabar, which scarcely flowers before it is thirty or forty years old.

CORYPHÆ'NA (*Ich.*) a genus of animals, of the Class *Pisces*, Order *Thoracica*.

Generic Character. Head sloping suddenly downwards. —*Gill-Membrane* five-rayed.—*Dorsal fin* as long as the back.

Species. The principal species are the—*Coryphæna hippuris*, *equisetalis*, *cærulea*, &c.

CORYPHÆ'US (*Ant.*) κορυφαῖος, from κορυφή, a top; the leader of the dance, or the band. *Suidas*.

CORYPHE (*Anat.*) κορυφή, the vertex or top of the head.

CORY'THIA (*Ich.*) a kind of purple fish. *Plin.* l. 32, c. 7.

CORY'ZA (*Med.*) κόρυζα, rendered by Celsus *gravedo*, by Cælius Aurelianus *catarrhus ad Nares*, signifies a defluxion from the head by reason of cold. *Cels.* l. 4, c. 2; *Cæl. Aurelian.*

COSCI'NOMANCY (*Ant.*) κοσκινομαντεία, from μαντεία, a divination, and κόσκινον, a sieve; a sort of divination by means of a sieve, used particularly in discovering suspected persons. The sieve was suspended in a room, and the diviner muttered a formula of words, repeating the name of the suspected person, when, if the sieve moved or shook, the suspicion was confirmed.

COSE'CANT (*Geom.*) the secant of an arc, which is the complement of another arc to 90 degrees.

CO'SENAGE (*Law*) a writ for the rightful heir against an intruder. *Brit.* c. 29; *F. N. B.* 221.

CO'SENING (*Law*) any thing done deceitfully, whether by contracts or not, which cannot be designated by any other name. *West. Symb.* p. 2, sect. 68.

CO'SHERING (*Law*) a prerogative which some lords of manors had, to sleep and feast with their retinue at the houses of their tenants.

CO'SIN (*Law*) or *cosen*, a cousin.

CO'SINE (*Geom.*) the right line of an arc, which is the complement of another to 90 degrees.

COSME'TA (*Ant.*) from κοσμέω, to adorn; a dresser or keeper of the wardrobe. *Schol. in Juv.* sat. 6, v. 476.

COSMETA (*Chem.*) Antimony.

COSME'TICS (*Med.*) κοσμητικά, from κοσμέω, to beautify; preparations which whiten and soften the skin, or in general any thing which tends to beautify the complexion.

COSMIA'NA *Antidotus* (*Med.*) an antidote mentioned by Marcellus Empiricus, c. 29.

COSMIA'NUM (*Med.*) a very sweet ointment; so called from one Cosmus, a perfumer.

COSMIA'TICUM (*Ant.*) from κοσμέω, to adorn; a tax on female ornaments.

CO'SMICAL (*Astron.*) a term denoting one of the poetical risings and settings of the stars. A star is said to rise *cosmically*, when it rises with the sun; and to set *cosmically*, when it sets at the same time as the sun rises. [vide *Astronomy*]

COSMO'GRAPHY (*Lit.*) κοσμογραφία, from κόσμος, the world, and γράφω, to describe; the science of describing the several parts of the visible world, delineating them according to their number, position, &c.

CO'SMOLABE (*Mech.*) from κόσμος, the world, and λαβεῖν, to take; an ancient mathematical instrument for measuring distances both in heaven and earth.

COSMO'LOGY (*Lit.*) from κόσμος, the world, and λόγος, discourse; the study of the world in general.

COSMO'METRY (*Math.*) from κόσμος, the world, and μετρέω, to measure; the measurement of the world by degrees and minutes.

COSMO'POLITE (*Polit.*) from κόσμος, the world, and πολίτης, a citizen; a citizen of the world.

CO'SMOS (*Med.*) κοσμὸς, a term used by Hippocrates for the order and series of critical days.

COSS, *Rule of* (*Algeb.*) another name for algebra, signifying the "Rule of the Thing," the unknown quantity being called the *Cosa*, or thing: whence also the term cossic numbers.

CO'SSACKS (*Mil.*) a sort of irregular troops attached to the Russian army, who followed originally a predatory system, for which their enterprizing temper and hardy habits peculiarly qualified them. They are at present distinguished principally by their dress and accoutrements.

CO'SSET (*Hus.*) a lamb, colt, calf, &c. brought up by the hand without the dam.

CO'SSIC *Numbers* (*Algeb.*) the powers of numbers, as the roots, the squares, the cubes, &c.

CO'SSUM (*Med.*) a virulent ulcer of the nose.

CO'SSYPHUS (*Ent.*) the name given by Fabricius to some species of insects of the genus *Lampyris*, having their feelers hatchet-shaped.

COST (*Her.*) or *Cottise*, an ordinary, which contains a fourth part of the bend or half. When only one is borne, it is called a *Cost*; but if they be borne by couples, as they mostly are between a bend, they are then called *Cottises*; as "He beareth *sable*, a bend, *argent*, between two cottises, dancette, *or*, by the name of Clopton of Suffolk."

CO'STÆ (*Anat.*) the ribs, which are in number 24, on each side of the vertebræ of the back. They are distinguished into *veræ*, true, and *falsæ*, false.—*Costæ veræ* are the seven uppermost ribs; so called because their cartilaginous ends are received into the sinus of the sternum.—*Costæ falsæ*, the five lowermost ribs; so called because they are shorter and softer, and not joined to the extremity of the sternum.

CO'STARD (*Bot.*) an early summer apple, so much esteemed formerly that the sellers of these apples were called Costard-mongers.

CO'STMARY (*Bot.*) the *Tanacetum balsamita* of Linnæus, a perennial, and odoriferous plant.

COSTO-HYO'IDES (*Anat.*) from *costæ*, a rib, and *hyoideus*, the hyoidal bone; a muscle so called from its origin and insertion.

COSTS (*Law*) *Expensæ litis*, those expenses which necessarily ensue from the prosecution of any suit in a court of law, consisting of stamps and duties to the government, fees to the officers of the court, &c. These are in some cases recoverable from the party who lose the causes.

CO'STUS (*Bot.*) κόστος, a kind of shrub growing in Syria and Arabia, the root of which has a most grateful spicy smell; it is a stomachic and deobstruent, being also of use in vertiginous disorders. *Theoph. Hist. Plant.* l. 9, c. 7; *Dioscor.* l. 1, c. 15; *Plin.* l. 12, c. 12; *Gal. de Simpl.*

COSTUS, in the Linnean system, a genus of plants, Class 1 Monandria, Order 1 Monogynia.

Generic Characters. CAL. *perianth* three-toothed—COR. *petals* three-lanceolate; *nectary* one-leaved; *lower lip* broader than the upper; *border* spreading.—STAM. *filament* supplied by the upper lip of the nectary, to which grows a twofold anther.—PIST. *germ* inferior; *style* filiform; *stigma* headed.—PER. *capsule* roundish; *seeds* many.

Species. The species are natives of the Indies, as the— *Costus Arabicus*, seu *Toganakua*.—*Costus glabratus*, &c.

CO'STIVE (*Med.*) a term denoting the constipation of the alvus.

COT-GARE (*Husband.*) refuse wool, so clotted together that it cannot be pulled asunder. It is mentioned in statute 13 R. 2.

COTA (*Bot.*) the *Anthemis cotula* of Linnæus.

COTANGENT (*Geom.*) the tangent of any complemental arc, or what the arc wants of a quadrant, or 90°.

COTA'RIA (*Min.*) a quarry or mine out of which whetstones are dug.

COTA'RIUS (*Archæol.*) a cottager, or one who held by a free socage tenure.

COTARO'NIUM (*Alch.*) a word coined by Paracelsus to denote the liquor into which all bodies and even their elements may be dissolved.

CO'TER (*Mensur.*) in French signifies to mark upon the plans and profiles of works of fortification, the exact measurement thereof divided into toises, feet, inches, and lines.

COTERE'LLI (*Archæol.*) a sort of straggling thieves or plunderers, like the moss-troopers on the borders of Scotland.

COTE'RELLUS (*Archæol.*) a servile tenant who held lands in mere villenage.

COTERI'E (*Cus.*) a French term signifying literally a trading partnership; is taken also for a club, or social party, formed for amusement.

COTE'SIAN *Theorem* (*Math.*) a particular property of the circle; so called from Mr. Cotes, by whom it was discovered.

CO'TESWALD (*Archæol.*) a place for sheep-cotes and sheep feeding on hills, from the Saxon *cote* and *pald*, a wood.

CO'THON (*Apt.*) a key or wharf. *Fest. de Verb. Sig.*

COTHU'RNUS (*Ant.*) κόθορνος, a sort of buskin and shoe, which was worn by tragedians and hunters of both sexes. *Virg. Æn.* l. 1, v. 336.

Virginibus Tyriis mos est gestare pharetram,
Purpureoque altè suras vincire cothurno.

Ovid. Amor. l. 3, el. 1, v. 14.

Lydius apta pedum vincla cothurnus erat.

Whence a man who sided with both parties was called a cothurnus. *Xenoph. Hist. Græc.* l. 2; and also the tragic muse was called by the same name. *Virg. Ecl.* 3, v. 10.

Solus Sophocleo tua carmina digna cothurno.

Horat. Art. Poet. v. 89; *Poll. Onym.* l. 6, sect. 16, &c.; *Serv. in Virg. Æn.*; *Hesychius.*; *Isid.* l. 19, c. 34.

CO'TICE (*Her.*) vide *Cost.*

CO'TICED (*Her.*) or *Cotised*, an epithet for any thing that is accosted, sided, or accompanied by another.

COTI'LLON (*Mus.*) a lively animated kind of dance.

CO'TINUS (*Bot.*) the same as the *Rhus.*

CO'TIS (*Anat.*) κοτίς, a term used by Hippocrates for the posterior part of the head, or the hollow of the neck.

COTLAND (*Law*) Land held by a cottager, whether in socage or villenage. *Paroch. Antiq.*

COTONE'A (*Bot.*) a herb smelling sweetly like thyme. *Plin.* l. 26, c. 7.

Cotonea, *in the Linnean System*, is another name for the *Cydonia*.

COTONEA'STER (*Bot.*) the *Mespilus chamæ*.

COTONE'UM (*Bot.*) a quince.

COTSCJOPI'N (*Bot.*) another name for the *Gardinea*.

COTSE'THLA (*Archæol.*) a little dwelling belonging to a small farm.

COTSE'THUS (*Law*) a cottager or cottage-holder, who, by servile tenure, was bound to work for the lord.

COTTA (*Com.*) a sort of measure, used for measuring of cauries or cowries, of which it holds 12,000.

COTTEM (*Bot.*) the *Mentha periculoides* of Linnæus.

COTTANUM (*Bot.*) a small kind of Syrian fig.

COTTISES (*Her.*) vide *Cost*.

COTTISED (*Her.*) vide *Cotticed*.

COTTOIDES (*Ich.*) a species of *Perea*.

COTTON (*Com.*) a sort of linen or cloth, which is manufactured from spun cotton.—*Cotton hank*, a skain of spun cotton done up ready for sale.

Cotton (*Bot.*) a sort of wool or flax which encompasses the seed of the tree, called, in the Linnean system, *Gossypium*, which is cultivated much in the East Indies, and yields materials for clothing to all parts of the habitable world.—Cotton-Grass, the *Enophorium*, a perennial of the Grass tribe; so called because its seeds have a downy substance attached to them which resemble cotton, and has been used in its stead.—*Silk cotton*, the downy substance produced from a tree, which, in the Linnean system, is called the *Bombax*, and much resembles the *Gossypium*.—Cotton-Thistle, *Onopordium*, an herbaceous plant, with a biennial root, which is so called because it has downy leaves.—Cotton-Weed, the *Athanasia maritima*, a perennial; so called on account of its downy leaves.

COTTOYER *une armée* (*Mil.*) a French term, denoting to keep a parallel line with the enemy, so as to prevent him from crossing a river.

COTTREL (*Mech.*) a trammel to hang or set a pot over the fire.

COTTUS (*Ich.*) Bull-head, a genus of animals, of the Class *Pisces*, Order *Thoracica*.
Generic Character. *Head* broader than the body.—*Eyes* vertical.—*Body* round without scales.
Species. The principal species are the—*Cottus cataphractus*, Pogge or armed Bull-head.—*Cottus scorpius*, Father Lasher.—*Cottus Gobio*, Miller's Thumb, or River Bullhead, &c.

COTUCHANS (*Archæol.*) boors or husbandmen.

COTULA (*Bot.*) a genus of plants, Class 19 *Syngenesia*, Order 2 *Polygamia Superflua*.
Generic Characters. CAL. *common* convex.—COR. *compound* the length of the calyx; *corollules* hermaphrodite; *proper* of the hermaphrodites tubular; of the females scarcely any.—STAM. *filaments* in the hermaphrodites four, very small; *anthers* tubular.—PIST. *germ* obovate; *style* filiform; *stigmas* two obtuse.—PER. none; *seeds* solitary.
Species. The species are mostly annuals, as—*Cotula anthemoides*, *Ananthocylus*, seu *Chrysanthemum*, Dwarf Cotula, native of the Southern parts of Europe.—*Cotula stricta*, *Lidbeckia*, seu *Lancisia*, Silvery Cotula, native of the Cape of Good Hope.—*Cotula coronopifolia*, *Anarthocyclus*, *Chrysanthemum*, *Bellis* Bucks-horn Cotula.—*Cotula turbinata*, *Chamamælum*, seu *Lancisia*, a Cape plant.—*Cotula Capensis*, *Lancisia*, *Matricaria*, seu *Chamamælum*, &c.

COTU'RNIX (*Or.*) the quail; the *Tetras Coturnix* of Linnæus. *Plin.* l. 10, c. 13.

COTYLE (*Ant.*) *cotyla*, or *cotula*, κοτύλη, signified not only a drinking cup of a deep capacity, but any thing having a cavity, as the hollow of the hand, &c. *Athen.* l. 11, c. 8.—*Cotyld* is also a measure about a pint or a pound. *Gal. de Pond. et Mensur.*; *Cenal. de Pond. et Mens. apud Græv. Thes. Antiq.* tom. ii. p. 1451.

COTYLE (*Anat.*) any deep cavity in a bone, in which another bone is articulated; but more particularly that cavity called otherwise the *acetabulum*, which receives the thighbone.

COTYLEDON (*Anat.*) certain glandular bodies adhering to the chorion of some animals; but no such substances are observable in the human chorion. The gapings, however, in the veins of the matrix of women are sometimes called *cotyledons*.

COTYLEDON (*Bot.*) κοτυληδὼν, from κοτύλη, a cavity, is the name of a plant mentioned by Dioscorides and Pliny, which, according to the former, was so called, because its leaf was of a hollow, orbicular form. The juice of this herb was recommended as an application to tumors and inflammations. *Dioscor.* l. 4, c. 92; *Pliny*, l. 28, c. 17.

COTYLEDON, *in the Linnean system*, is a genus of plants, Class 10 *Decandria*, Order 5 *Pentagynia*.
Generic Character. CAL. *perianth* one-leaved, five-cleft.—COR. *petal* bellshaped, five-cleft; *nectary* consisting of a concave scale.—STAM. *filaments* ten, subulate; *anthers* erect, four-furrowed.—PIST. *germs* five, oblong; *styles* subulate; *stigmas* simple.—PER. *capsules* five, oblong; *seeds* very many, small.
Species. The principal species are as follow, namely—*Cotyledon umbilicus*, *Sedum*, seu *Umbilicus Veneris*, Common Navelwort, Kidneywort, or Wall Pennywort, a perennial, and native of Great Britain, &c.—*Cotyledon Hispanica*, Spanish Navelwort, a biennial.—*Cotyledon orbiculata*, seu *Sedum*, Round-leaved Navelwort, a biennial, and native of the Cape of Good Hope.—*Cotyledon laciniata*, *Telephium*, seu *Planta Anatis*, cut-leaved Navelwort, a biennial.—*Cotyledon viscosa*, an annual. *Bauh. Hist. Plant.*; *Bauh. Pin.*; *Ger. Herb.*; *Park. Theat. Botan.*; *Raii Hist. Plant.*; *Tournef. Instit.* &c.

Cotyledon, as a species, is the *Crassula coccinea* and *aquatica*, the *Hydrocotyle vulgaris*.

Cotyledon, as the part of a plant, is the lobe or placenta of the seed destined to nourish the heart, and then to perish. It is, in the language of Linnæus, *Corpus laterale seminis*, *bibulum*, *caducum*, i. e. the lateral body of the seed, bibulous or imbibing moisture, and caducous or falling off quickly. The greater part of seeds have two of these cotyledons, or lobes, whence the distinction of all plants into *Acotyledones*, *Monocotyledones*, *Dicotyledones*, *Polycotyledones*, which forms the basis of Jussieu's Natural Arrangement.

COTYLEDONOIDES (*Bot.*) the *Crassula tetragona* of Linnæus.

COTYLE'DUM (*Bot.*) the same as *Cotyledon*.

COTYTTIA (*Ant.*) κοτυττία, a nocturnal festival in honour of Cotytto, the goddess of wantonness, which was celebrated by rites supposed to be most acceptable to such a goddess. Her priestesses were called *Baptæ*, because they painted themselves in a meretricious manner. *Schol. in Juv.* sat. 2, v. 92.

COVALUM (*Bot.*) a tall tree growing in Malabar and the island of Ceylon, the fruit of which resembles a round apple in shape.

COUCH (*Mech.*) a seat, or small moveable bed, to lie on.

Couch (*Husband.*) a layer, or heap of malt or barley, which is disposed for the purpose of drying it into malt.

Couch (*Paint.*) a term signifying the ground, bed, or basis on which the colour lies: thus, paintings are covered with a couch of varnish; and a canvass to be painted must first have two couches of size before the colour be laid on.

Couch (*Mech.*) is a term used in a similar sense in application to different arts: thus the leather-gilders lay a couch of water and whites of eggs on the leather before they apply the gold or silver leaf. Gilders apply a couch of gold or silver leaf in gilding or silvering of metals. The gold wire-drawers also apply a couch of gold or silver to the mass which is to be gilded or silvered, before they draw it through the iron that is to give it the proper thickness.

To Couch (*Surg.*) vide *Couching.*

To Couch (*Sport.*) to lie down or along, after the manner of a lion, a tiger, or a cat.

To Couch (*Mil.*) to set a lance on the rest.

CO'UCH-GRASS (*Bot.*) the *Triticum repens* of Linnæus, a perennial, and a troublesome weed in gardens and arable land, which runs very far into the ground. It is otherwise called Quick, Dog's grass, Creeping Wheat, &c.

COU'CHANT (*Her.*) an epithet denoting the posture of lions and other wild beasts lying on their belly with the head erect, as he beareth "*sable* three lioncels couchant, *argent*, by the name of Bateman of Essex."

COUCHE' (*Her.*) couched; an epithet for any thing lying along, as a *chevron couché*, a chevron lying sideways, having its top turned to the right or left side, as in the annexed figure, "He beareth, *or*, a chevron couched, *gules*, name Tourney."

COUCHE (*Carpen.*) French for a piece of timber which is laid flat under the foot of a prop, or stay.

COU'CHER (*Com.*) or Courcher, a factor that continued abroad in some place for traffic. The name is mentioned in statute 37 *Edw.* 3, c. 16.

Coucher (*Law*) the general book in which a corporation register their acts. 3, 4 *Edw.* 6, c. 10.

Coucher *en joue* (*Mil.*) French for to take aim with a firelock.

COU'CHES (*Archit.*) Courses, or layers of sand, which are spread about one foot deep over the boarding of a wooden bridge in order to place the stones upon it.

COU'CHING (*Surg.*) a surgical operation, which consists in removing the opake lens out of the axis of vision by means of a needle constructed for the purpose, and called a *couching needle.*

Couching (*Her.*) vide *Couchant.*

Couching (*Sport.*) the lodging of a wild boar.

COUDE' (*Fort.*) any line that turns back from the end of the trenches, and runs almost parallel with the place attacked.

COUDE'E (*Com.*) a measure taken from the elbow to the hand.

COVE (*Geog.*) a little harbour for boats, or small vessels.

CO'VENABLE (*Law.*) in French *convenable*; a term used for what is suitable or agreeable in, *Stat.* 31 *Edw.* 3, c. 2.

CO'VENANT (*Law*) *Conventio,* an agreement or consent of two or more by deed, or writing. Sealed Covenants are either in fact or in law.—*A covenant in fact,* is that which is expressly agreed upon between the parties.—*Covenant in law,* that which the law intends and implies.—*Covenants* are also real or personal, &c.—*Real covenant* is that whereby a man ties himself to pass a thing real.—*Personal covenant,* where the same is annexed to the person, as if a person covenants with another to build him a house.—*Inherent covenant* is that which tends to the support of the land or thing granted.—*Collateral covenant,* which is collateral to it.—*Affirmative covenant,* where something is to be performed.—*Negative covenant,* where any thing is to be left undone.—*Executed covenant,* as to what is already done.—*Executory covenant,* as to what is to be done.—*Covenant to stand seised to Uses* is when a man, having a wife, children, or kindred, doth, by covenant in writing under hand and seal, agree, that for their, or any of their provision, or preferment, he or his heirs will stand seised of land to their use. *Stat.* 27 *Hen.* 8. c. 10.—*Covenant,* or the *solemn League and Covenant,* a seditious conspiracy so called, which was set on foot in Scotland in the time of the Rebellion, and voted illegal by Parliament; against which provision is made by *Stat.* 14 *Car.* 2, c. 4.

CO'VENANTER (*Law*) one who makes a covenant.

Covenanter (*Hist.*) one who joined the Presbyterian Covenant in the time of the rebellion.

CO'VENTRY (*Mil.*) or *to send to Coventry;* a phrase applied to any officer who is excluded from the usual intercourse with his brother officers.

CO'VENTRY BELLS (*Bot.*) a sort of *Campanula.*

CO'VER (*Mil.*) in French *à couvert,* a term to express security, or protection, as to lay under cover of the guns.

To Cover (*Mil.*) such a nice disposition of the men in a company, or squad, as, that when each man looks exactly forward to the neck of the man who leads him he cannot see the second man from him. "To *cover* ground," to occupy a certain proportion of ground, either individually or collectively.

Cover (*Mech.*) that part of the slating in the slater's work which is covered, in distinction from the *margin,* or that part which is left visible.

CO'VERER (*Mil.*) the serjeant, corporal, or private, that is posted in the rear of the leader.

CO'VERLET (*Mech.*) a covering for a bed.

CO'VERED SINE (*Geom.*) the remaining part of the diameter of a circle after the versed sine is taken from it.

CO'VERT-*Way* (*Fort.*) a space of ground level with the field, on the edge of the ditch, three or four fathoms broad, ranging quite round the half-moons and other works towards the country. The *Second Covert-Way,* called by the French *Avant-chemin-couvert,* is the covert-way at the foot of the glacis.

Covert *baron* (*Law*) or *femme couverte,* a married woman, so called because she is covered by, or under the protection of, her husband.

Covert (*Sport.*) a thicket, or shady place for deer, or other animals.

CO'VERTURE (*Law*) the state of a married woman who is under the power and protection of her husband by law, and therefore disabled to contract with any person to the damage of herself or her husband. *Bract.* l. 1, c. 10, &c.

COUGH (*Med.*) *Tussis;* the well-known malady that frequently attends an affection from cold.

Cough (*Vet.*) otherwise called the *husk;* a disorder incident to young bullocks when their windpipes are choked with taper-worms.

COU'HAGE (*Bot.*) vide *Cowhage.*

CO'VIN (*Law*) a deceitful assent, or agreement, between two or more persons, to the prejudice of another.

CO'VING (*Archit.*) the projection in houses beyond the groundplot, which is lathed and plastered, so as to form a cover in wet weather.—*Coving cornice,* one that has a large *cavate,* or hollow in it.

COU'IT (*Com.*) a sort of ell-measure used at Mocha for measuring linens.

CO'UL (*Mech.*) a tub, or vessel with two ears.—*Coul-staff,* a pole on which the coul is carried.

To Coul (*Archer.*) to cut the feather of a shaft high or low.

CO'ULER *une pièce de canon* (*Mech.*) to melt down the metal for casting in a mould.

COULE'VERINE (*Mil.*) a culverin.

CO'ULIS (*Mason.*) French for plaster well mixed for the purpose of filling up the joints of stones, and keeping them together.

CO'ULTER (*Husband.*) vide *Colter.*

COUMAROU'NA (*Bot.*) the *Dipterix odorata* of Linnæus.

COUNCIL (*Ecc.*) a synod, or assembly of prelates and other ecclesiastical persons, for the purpose of regulating all matters of doctrine and discipline in the church. A *National Council* comprehends the prelates of a whole kingdom; a *Provincial Council*, of a particular province; and an *Œcumenial*, or *General Council*, of the prelates in all Christendom.

COUNCIL (*Polit.*) an assembly of the different members of any government, who meet to consult about affairs of state. It is called in England the *Privy Council*, or, by way of eminence, the Council wherein the King himself and his privy counsellors meet in the King's Court, or Palace, on matters of state.—*Cabinet Council* consists of those Ministers of State who are more immediately honoured with his Majesty's confidence, and are summoned to consult upon the important and arduous discharge of the executive authority.—*Common Council*, an assembly of a select number of citizens, chosen out of every ward to manage the public affairs of the city within their several precincts, and to act in concert with the Lord Mayor and Court of Aldermen. Council is also an assembly of the members of Lincoln's Inn.

COUNCIL *of War* (*Mil.*) an assembly of the chief officers in the army and navy, called by the general or admiral to concert measures on their conduct.

COUNCIL-MAN *common* (*Polit.*) a member of the Common Council.

COUNSEL (*Law*) or Council. vide *Counsellor*.

COUNSELLOR (*Law*) *Consellarius*, a person who is retained by a client to plead his cause in a court of law; a barrister.—*Privy Counsellor*, a member of the Privy Council.

COUNT (*Polit.*) in French *Comte*, probably from the Latin *comes*, is equivalent to the English earl.

COUNT (*Law*) a charge in an indictment; an original declaration of complaint in a real action. It is distinguished from a proper *declaration*, because the former applies to real causes, the latter to those which are personal. F. N. B. 16, 60.

COUNT (*Com.*) vide *Account*.

COUNT *wheel* (*Horol.*) a wheel in the striking part of a clock, which moves round in twelve or fourteen hours, by some called the *locking-wheel*.

COUNTEE' (*Archæol.*) an old term for a Count.

COUNTENANCE (*Law*) credit or estimation. Stat. 1 Ed. 3, c. 4; F. N. B. 111.

COUNTER (*Gram.*) is generally taken in composition for *contra*.

COUNTER (*Mar.*) in French *contre arcasse*, an arc or vault whose upper part is terminated by the bottom of the stern, and the lower part by the wing-transoms and buttock.

COUNTER (*Man.*) the breast of a horse, or that part of his forehand which lies between the shoulders and under the neck.—*Counter-marked*, when the teeth of a horse are artificially made hollow, that he may pass for under six years of age.—*Counter-time*, the defence or resistance of a horse that interrupts his cadence and the measure of his manege.

COUNTER (*Num.*) a piece of brass or any metal with a stamp, formerly used in counting, but now employed in playing at cards.

COUNTER-APPROACH (*Fort.*) works made by the besieged when they come out to hinder the approach of an enemy, and when they design to attack them in form.— *Counter-battery*, a battery raised to play upon another.

COUNTER-BOND (*Law*) a bond to save a person harmless who has given a bond for another.

COUNTER-BRACE (*Mar.*) the lee-brace of the fore topsail, so distinguished because at the time that the ship is tacking or going about, this brace is hauled in to flatten the sail against the leeside of the top-mast, and increase the effort of the wind in forcing her to turn round.

COUNTER-BREAST-WORK (*Fort.*) the same as a false bray.

COUNTER-CHARGED (*Her.*) or transmuted, an epithet for a bearing which consists of an intermixture of several metals, colours, or furs, both in field and charge, occasioned by the opposition of some one or more lines of partition; as he beareth "Party per pale *argent et gules*, a bend countercharged." These arms belonged to the celebrated poet Chaucer.

COUNTER-CHEVRONNED (*Her.*) a field chevronny, or parted by some line of partition.

COUNTER-COMPOUND (*Her.*) Counter-Compone or Compony; an epithet for a border which is compounded of two ranks of panes, or rows of checkers, of different colours, set checkerwise. [vide *Compound*]

COUNTER-DRAIN (*Archit.*) a ditch or channel parallel to a canal or embanked water-work, for collecting the soakage water.

COUNTER-DRAWING (*Paint.*) sketching a design through the medium of oil, paper, or any transparent substance laid on the drawing.

COUNTER-EMBATTLED (*Her.*) an epithet for an ordinary embattled or crenellé on both sides.

COUNTER-ERMINE (*Her.*) signifies the contrary to ermine, being a black field with white spots, as in the annexed figure.

COUNTERFEIT (*Com.*) an epithet for any thing so imitated as to be made to pass for what is genuine, as a counterfeit coin, or a counterfeit. Counterfeit taken absolutely, signifies a false coin, as a piece of brass silvered over to pass for a shilling.

TO COUNTERFEIT (*Law*) to imitate falsely, or to forge, as to counterfeit letters. To counterfeit the king's seal is high treason.

COUNTER-FISSURE (*Surg.*) vide *Contra-Fissura*.

COUNTERFLORY (*Her.*) an epithet denoting that the flowers with which an ordinary is adorned stand opposite to each other.

COUNTER-FOIL (*Law*) that part of a tally struck in the Exchequer which is kept by an officer of that court; the other being delivered to the person that has lent the king money upon the account. This is called either the foil or the stock.

COUNTER-FORTS (*Fort.*) certain pillars and parts of the walls of a place, about fifteen or twenty feet one from another, which are advanced as much as possible in the ground, and joined to the height of the cordon by walls.

COUNTER-FUGES (*Mus.*) fuges which proceed the one contrary to the other.

COUNTER-GUARDS (*Fort.*) large heaps of earth in form of a parapet, raised above the moat before the faces and points of the bastion, to preserve them.

COUNTER-GAUGE (*Carpent.*) a method of measuring the joints of timbers, by transferring the breadth of a mortise to the place where the tenon of the other timber is to be made, in order to make them fit each other.

COUNTER-HARMONICAL (*Math.*) vide *Contra-harmonical*.

COUNTER-LATH (*Carpent.*) a lath, in tiling, placed between every two gauged ones, so as to make equal intervals.

COUNTER-LIGHT (*Paint.*) a light striking from an opposite direction on a painting, which will make it appear to great disadvantage.

COUNTERMAND (*Law*) is where a thing formerly executed by some act or ceremony is made void by the party who did it, which is either actual when made void by some formal deed or writing, or implied in law, as when a man by his last will devises his land to A. B. and afterwards enfeoffs the same land to another, the enfeoffment is an implied countermand.

TO COUNTERMAND (*Com.*) to contradict a former order.

COU'NTER-MARCH (*Mil.*) a drawing up of soldiers so as to change the face of the wings of a battalion, whereby those who were on the right take up the ground originally occupied by the left, and *vice versâ*.

COU'NTERMARK (*Com*) a mark made to check or correspond with a mark made elsewhere.

COUNTERMARK *of a medal* (*Numis.*) is a mark made upon a medal some time after it has been struck.

COUNTERMARKED (*Vet.*) vide *Counter*.

COU'NTER-MINE (*Fort.*) the subterraneous passage made by the besieged in search of the enemy's mine, in order to give air to it, take away the powder, &c.

TO COUNTERMINE (*Fort.*) to make countermines for the purpose of defeating the enemy's projects.

COU'NTER-PAROLE (*Mil.*) a word which is given in time of any trouble or alarm, as a signal.

COU'NTER-PART (*Mus.*) a term denoting one part opposite to another, as the bass, which is the *Counter-part* of the tenor.

COUNTER-PART (*Law*) the duplicate or copy of any indenture or deed, so that one copy may be kept by one party and another by another.

COUNTER-PASSANT (*Her.*) an epithet for any two beasts on the same escutcheon, passing and going different ways, so as to look directly opposite ways, as in the annexed figure, representing two lions *counter-passant*.

COU'NTER-PERFLEW (*Her.*) vide *Perflew*.

COU'NTER-PLEA (*Law*) a cross or contrary plea, which may be either a *counter-plea* to the voucher, which is a replication to Aid Prier; or a *counter-plea* to the *warranty*, when the voucher is allowed, but the vouchee pleads any thing to void the warranty.

COUNTER-POINTE' (*Her.*) a term to denote that two chevrons meet with their points in an escutcheon, as in the annexed figure, where one rises as usual from the base, the other inverted, setting from the chief, so that they are counter or opposite one to another.

COU'NTER-POINT (*Mus.*) the old method of composing parts by setting pricks or points one against another to denote the several concords.

COUNTERPOISE (*Mech.*) whatever acts as a contrary weight to make the balance equal.

COUNTERPOISE (*Man.*) or *Balance of the body*, that liberty of action which a horseman acquires in his seat by practising in the manege.

COUNTER-POTENCE' (*Her.*) or *Potent-counter*, a term denoting pieces in an escutcheon which represent the tops of crutches, called in French *potences*, and in English *potents*, set opposite to each other, as in the annexed figure.

COU'NTER-ROLLS (*Law*) the rolls which sheriffs of counties have of their proceedings with the coroners. *Stat.* 3 *Ed.* 1, c. 10.

COU'NTERS (*Law*) vide *Countors*.

COU'NTER-SALIANT (*Her.*) leaping contrariwise; an epithet for two beasts leaping in contrary directions.

COU'NTERSCARP (*Fort.*) that side of the ditch which is next the camp, or the slope of the moat facing the body of the place; but when the enemy is said to have lodged themselves on the counterscarp, it is generally to be understood of the whole covert way.

COUNTER-SECURITY (*Law*) security given to a party who has entered into bonds for another.

COU'NTER-SIGN (*Mil.*) a sign which is exchanged between sentinels who are on guard and the persons appointed to go the rounds to visit the different posts.

TO COUNTER-SIGN (*Law*) to sign an order of a superior in quality of secretary.

COU'NTERSUNK (*Mar.*) a hollow, cut by a bit, round the edge of a hole.—*Countersunk-bit*, a bit having two cutting edges at the end, reversed to each other, which form an angle from the point.

COUNTER-TA'LLY (*Com.*) one of the two tallies on which any thing is scored.

COUNTER-TE'NOR (*Mus.*) one of the middle parts, so called because it is as it were opposed to the tenor.—*Counter-Tenor-Cliff*, the name given to the C cliff when placed on the third line.—*Counter-Tenor-Voice*, or *High-Tenor*, a term applied to the highest natural male voice.

COUNTER-TI'MBERS (*Mar.*) those short timbers in the stern, put in only for the purpose of strengthening the counter.

CO'UNTER-TIME (*Man.*) vide *Counter*.

COU'NTER-TRENCH (*Fort.*) a trench made against that of the besiegers, which of consequence has its parapet turned towards them.

COUNTER-TRI'PPING (*Her.*) an epithet for two beasts in an escutcheon tripping in opposite directions. [vide *Counter-Passant*]

COUNTER-VALLA'TION (*Fort.*) a counter-line or ditch made round a place that is besieged, to prevent the sallies and excursions of the besieged.

COU'NTER-VAIR (*Her.*) vide *Vair*.

COU'NTER-WORKS (*Mil.*) works raised in order to ruin or render useless those of the enemy.

COU'NTESS (*Her.*) the wife of a count or earl.

COUNTIES *corporate* (*Law*) are cities or ancient boroughs, as London, Bristol, Chester, &c. on which our ancient kings bestowed especial privileges. 2 *Inst.* 248.—*Counties Palatine*, so called, *a palatio*, because the owners thereof, namely, the Earl of Chester, Bishop of Durham, and Duke of Lancaster, formerly had in those counties *jura regalia* as fully as the king hath in his palace. *Bract.* l. 3, c. 8, § 4; 4 *Inst.* 204; *Seld. Tit. Hon.* l. 2, c. 5.

COU'NTING-HOUSE (*Com.*) an office in which a merchant transacts his business.

COUNTING-HOUSE *of the king's household* (*Law*) a former name for what is now called the Board of Green Cloth.

COU'NTORS (*Law*) a name for such serjeants at law as a man retains in a court to plead his cause.

COUNTRY-DANCE (*Mus.*) a lively pointed air calculated for dancing.

COUNTY (*Polit.*) in French *comté*, and Latin *comitatus*; a name which is equivalent to the Saxon word ꞅhiꞃe, and is employed to denote the several portions into which the kingdom is divided; namely, England into forty; Wales, twelve; Scotland, thirty-three; and Ireland, thirty-two. This mode of dividing England is said to have originated with Alfred. [vide *Counties*]

COUNTY-COURT (*Law*) *curia comitatus*, a court held every month by the sheriff or deputy; also a court held twice every year, which is called a *turn*. *Bracton passim*; *Glanvil.* l. 1, c. 2, &c.; *Britton passim*; *Fleta*, l. 2, c. 62; *F. N. B.* 152; *Cromp. Jur.* fol. 241. The power of this court was much reduced by Magna Charta, c. 17, and by 1 *Ed.* 4, c. 2.

COUNTY-RA'TES (*Law*) a rate which is assessed on every parish, &c. within the county, collected and paid by the high-constables of hundreds to treasurers appointed by the justices.

COUP (*Mil.*) a French term for stroke, or blow used on different occasions; as—*Coup de Canon*, a cannon shot.—*Coups de Corde*, blows given with a rope's end.—*Coup de Main*, a sudden and unpremeditated attack.—*Coup d'Epée*,

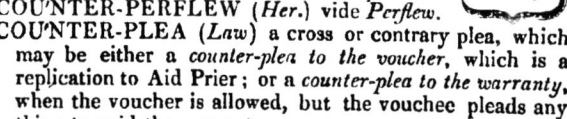

a thrust with the sword.—*Coup fourré*, a double thrust given in fencing.—*Coup de Jarnac*, an underhand blow, or one given unfairly.

Coup *de Partance* (*Mar.*) the signal of departure which a fleet, or a ship of war, makes by firing a canon.

Coup *d'œil* (*Nat.*) that first glance of the eye with which it surveys any object at large.

Coup *de Soleil* (*Med.*) erysipelas, apoplexy, or any disorder suddenly produced by the violence of a scorching sun.

COU'PANT (*Com.*) an oval piece of gold or silver of different sizes used in Japan; the biggest of the gold ones weighs an ounce and three-fourths, and of the silver seven penny-weights and a half.

COUPE (*Paint.*) French for the rough draught or design which represents the inside of a building, &c.

COU'PE-GORGE (*Cus.*) a cut-throat; also a dangerous spot or avenue where a man might be way-laid.

COU'PED (*Her.*) in French *coupé*, an epithet for the head or limb of any beast in an escutcheon, which is cut evenly and clear off, in distinction from *erased*, as in the annexed figure. When the head is cut off close it is blazoned 'coupled close.'—*Couped*, or *Humette*, is also an epithet for a cross that is shortened or cut so that the extremities do not reach the out lines of the escutcheon.—*Couped Pendants* are those pendants that are alternately divided, but in a vertical direction.

COUPE'E (*Mech.*) a motion in dancing wherein one leg is a little bent and suspended from the ground, and the other makes a motion forwards.

COUPE'LLE (*Mil.*) a kind of tin or copper shovel which is used in the artillery to fill the cartridges with gunpowder, &c.

COU'PLE (*Mech.*) two things of the same kind set together; also a band with which dogs are tied.

Couple *Close* (*Her.*) an ordinary so termed from its inclosing by couples the chevron. It contains the fourth part of the chevron, and is always borne in pairs, one on each side a chevron; as "*Sable*, a chevron between two couples-close, accompanied with three cinquefoils, or; name *Renton*."

COU'PLED *Columns* (*Archit.*) columns disposed in pairs so as to make a narrow and wide interval succeed each other alternately.

COU'PLES (*Carpent.*) rafters called *spars*, and framed together in pairs with a tie, which is generally fixed above the feet of the rafters.—*Main couples*, the same as trusses for roofs, which support the roof in different lays.

COU'PLET (*Poet.*) the division of a hymn, ode, or song, &c. wherein an equal number, or an equal measure of verses is found in each part.

COU'RANT (*Sport.*) French for a sort of dance.

Courant (*Com.*) French for current, as the *price courant*, the well-known, or current price.

Courant (*Her.*) an epithet for any beast represented in an escutcheon in a running attitude, as in the annexed figure of a buck courant.

COURANTI'N (*Mil.*) a French term for those fusees which carry the fireworks from one quarter to another by means of a cord.

COU'RAP (*Med.*) the Indian itch, a distemper very common in Java, and other parts of the East Indies, which is a herpes on the axilla, groin, breast, and face.

COURBARI'L (*Bot.*) the same as the *Hymenea*.

COURÇO'N (*Mil.*) a French term for a strong piece of iron, which serves to connect and secure the moulds for canon.

COURE'URS (*Mil.*) a French term for a sort of light armed troops that go on reconnoitring or flying parties.

COURGE (*Archit.*) French for the stone or iron crow which sustains the false mantle-tree of a chimney.

COURI'ER (*Polit.*) from the French *courir*, to run; a messenger sent express and in haste.—*Courier de Cabinet*, a state messenger.

COURIERS *de Vivres* (*Mil.*) messengers attached to the French army for the conveyance of packages, &c. to and fro.

COURO'N (*Com.*) a sum equivalent to 10 millions of rupees, or a hundred lacks, which is used in accounts at the court of the grand Mogul.

COURO'NDO (*Bot.*) a tall evergreen tree that grows in the East Indies, the juice of which, taken in warm whey, cures the dysentery. *Raii Hist. Plant.*

COURO'NNE (*Com.*) a gold coin in the reign of Philip de Valois, forty-eight of which went to the mark of gold. It was so called from the figure of the crown on the obverse.

Couronne *de Pieux* (*Mech.*) the head of a stake which is sometimes bound round with iron to prevent it from splitting when driven down by the rammer.

COURONNEME'NT (*Fort.*) French for the most exterior part of a work when besieged.

COUROU-MOE'LLI (*Bot.*) an Indian tree, the bark of which, taken in a decoction, is reckoned an antidote against the bites of serpents.

COURRA'CIER (*Archæol.*) a horse courser. 2 *Instit.* 719.

COURSE (*Archit.*) a continued range of bricks or stones of the same height throughout the length of the work.—*Course of the Face of an Arch*, the arch-stones, whose joints radiate to the centre.—*Course of Plinths*, the continuity of a plinth, in the face of a wall, to mark the separation of the stories. It is otherwise called *String-Course.—Course, Barge*, vide *Barge Course.—Course, Blocking*, vide *Blocking Course.—Banding course*, that which runs further into a wall than either of the adjacent courses for the purpose of binding the wall together.—*Heading course*, the same as *Bonding Course.—Springing course*, vide *Springing Course.—Course, Stretching*, vide *Stretching Course.—Course in Filing*, or *Slating*, a row of tiles or slates disposed with their lower ends in the same level.

Course (*Mar.*) in French *route*, that point of the horizon or compass which a ship steers on. The *Oblique Course* is that which crosses the meridian at equal and oblique angles.

Course (*Agric.*) a turn of hay, &c. laid on a cart.

Course *of Exchange* (*Com.*) vide *Exchange*.

Course *Civil* (*Law*) the collection of Roman laws made by Justinian.—*Course Ecclesiastical*, the collection of canon law made by Gratianus.

COURSER (*Man.*) a race-horse, or a horse for service.

COU'RSES (*Mar.*) in French *basses voiles*, a name by which the principal sails are usually distinguished; thus, when a ship sails under the main-sail and fore-sail only, without lacing on any bonnets, she is then said "To go under a pair of her *Courses*."

Courses (*Med.*) vide *Catamena*.

COU'RSEY (*Mar.*) a space or passage in a galley about a foot and a half broad, on both sides of which slaves are placed.

COU'RSING (*Sport.*) is the pursuing of any beast of chace, as the hare, fox, &c. with greyhounds.

COURT (*Law*) *curia*, the King's palace or mansion, but more especially the place where justice is judicially administered. These are generally distinguished into *superior courts* and *base courts*.—The *superior courts*, otherwise called *courts of record*, are those which have power to hold plea, according to the course of the Common Law, of real, personal, and mixed actions, where the debt or damages is forty shillings or above, as the King's Bench, Common Pleas, &c.—*Base courts*, or *courts not of record*, are such as have power to hold plea of any debt under forty shillings, such as Courts Baron, County Courts, &c. 1 *Inst.* 58. 117, &c. The following are the principal courts arranged under these two general heads.—*Admiralty,* vide *Admiralty.*—*Court of Arches,* vide *Arches.*—*Court-Baron,* a court which every lord of a manor has within his own precinct, being an inseparable incident to the manor that must be held by prescription, and cannot be created in this day. *F. N. B.* 18; 1 *Inst.* 584; 2 *Instit.* 268.—*Court of Chancery,* vide *Chancery.*—*Court of Chivalry,* otherwise called the *Marshal Court, curia militaris,* is said to be the fountain of martial law. It is held by the Earl Marshal, who has both a judicial and ministerial power; being not only one of the judges, but also seeing that execution is done. This court is grown almost into disuse, except for the purpose of keeping up the distinction of degrees and quality by correcting encroachments in matters of coat armour, precedency, &c.—*Court Christian,* in distinction from the *civil court,* or *lay-tribunal,* takes cognizance of matters relating to Christianity only; therefore the archbishops, bishops, archdeacons, &c. are the judges in such courts, which are also called *ecclesiastical courts.*—*Courts of Conscience* are courts for the recovery of small debts by summary process before commissioners appointed for that purpose. They are so called because the decisions are made according to equity and good conscience. The first court of this kind was erected in the City of London in the reign of Henry VIII.; since which time other courts of conscience have been established in different parts of the kingdom.—*Consistory court,* a sort of ecclesiastical court held by every diocesan bishop in his cathedral for the trial of ecclesiastical causes within his diocese.—*Court of Delegates,* or the *Great Court of Appeal,* appointed by the King's commission under his Great Seal, to represent his Royal Person, and hear all causes of appeal now made to him from the other ecclesiastical courts.—*Court of Equity,* any court, such as the Chancery, where decisions are grounded on equity, in distinction from courts of Common Law, such as the court of King's Bench.—*Courts of Guerra,* courts in Scotland holden upon neighbours' feuds and riots.—*Court of Hustings,* the highest Court of Record holden at Guildhall, for the City of London, before the Lord Mayor and Aldermen, the Sheriffs and Recorder, which determines all pleas, real, personal, and mixed.—*Court of Inquest,* vide *Inquest.*—*Court of Inquiry,* a meeting of officers who are empowered to inquire into the conduct of a commander of an expedition, &c.—*Court of the Dutchy of Lancaster,* vide *Dutchy of Lancaster.*—*Court Leet,* or *Leet,* a court belonging to the lord of a manor, in which all offences under high treason are inquired into. It seems to be derived from *leod plebis,* signifying *curia populi,* or folkmote, although the word is not used by any of our ancient law-writers, and does not occur in any statute prior to *Stat* 27 *Ed.* 3, c. 28.—*Court of Marshalsea,* a court of record to hear and determine causes between the servants of the King's household, and others within the verge.—*Court Martial,* a court for trying and punishing the military offences of officers, soldiers, or sailors.—*Court of Peculiars* is a branch of the court of Arches, to which it is annexed, having a jurisdiction over all the parishes dispersed through the province of Canterbury, &c.—*Court of Piepowder,* a court held in fairs for doing justice between buyers and sellers, so called, as is supposed, because it is usually held every summer, when the suitors to the court have dusty feet (*pied poudrés.*)—*Prerogative Court,* a court established for the trial of all testamentary causes, where the deceased has left *bona notabilia* within two different dioceses.—*Court of Requests,* a court of equity appointed for the help of such petitioners as wish, in conscionable cases, to deal with the King by supplication; but this court is now quite suppressed.—*Court of the Lord Steward of the King's House,* that in which the Lord Steward, or, in his absence, the Treasurer and Controller of the King's household, or the Steward of the Marshalsea, may inquire into and determine all treasons, murders, manslaughters, &c. committed in any of the King's palaces, residences, &c.—*Court of Star-Chamber,* an ancient court which took cognizance of all maintainers, rioters, and seditious persons, and punished them as if the offenders had been convicted at law by a jury, &c. This court was dissolved by *Stat.* 16 & 17 *Car.* 1, c. 10.—*University Courts* are the Chancellor's courts in the two Universities of England, Oxford, and Cambridge, wherein these two learned bodies enjoy the sole jurisdiction, in exclusion of the King's courts, over all civil actions and suits whatever, when a scholar, or privileged person, is one of the parties. 28 *Hen.* 3, A.D. 1244; 14 *Hen.* 8; 13 *Eliz.* c. 29.

COURT bouillon (*Cook.*) a particular way of boiling fish in wine, with spices, &c.

CO'URT-LANDS (*Law*) domains or lands kept in the lord's hands to serve his family.—*Court-Roll,* a roll containing an account of the number, &c. of lands which depend on the jurisdiction of the manor, and the nature of the tenants that are admitted to any parcel of land, &c.—*Court-days,* days in which courts of judicature are open, and pleas held.

COURTA'UD (*Man.*) a cropped horse.

COURTAUD (*Gunn.*) a short kind of ordnance used at sea.

COURTESY (*Law*) a tenure not by right, but by the favour of others.—*Courtesy of England,* a tenure whereby a man marrying an heiress possessed of lands in fee simple or fee tail, if he have a child by her, which comes alive into the world, although both she and the child die forthwith; yet, if he were in possession, he shall hold the land during life. *F. N. B.* 149; *Kitch.* 159; *Co. Lit.* 29, 30, &c.

COURTAIN (*Fort.*) vide *Curtin.*

COURT-LANDS (*Law*) vide *Court.*

COU'SCOUS (*Cook.*) the African name for a sort of paste made of the flour of millet with some flesh, &c.

COU'SIN (*Law*) a kinsman or kinswoman by blood or marriage.

COU'SINET (*Archit.*) or *cushion,* the stone which crowns a pier or piedroit, or that lies immediately over the capital of the impost, and under the sweep; also an ornament in the Ionic capital between the *Abacus,* and the *Echinus.*

COUSINET (*Mason.*) the first stone which commences a vault or arch.

COUSSI'N (*Gunn.*) in French a sort of wedge, or small piece of wood, which is placed under the breech of a cannon in order to point it properly, and to keep it steady in the proposed direction.

COUSSINE'T (*Mil.*) French for a wedge fixed between the carriage and the centre of a mortar.—*Coussinet à Mousquetaire,* a bag formerly worn by a French soldier on his left side beneath the cross-belt.

COUSU' (*Her.*) vide *Rempli.*

COUTEAU de Bois (*Mech.*) ou *Spatule,* French for a wooden instrument, in the shape of a short blunt blade, for pressing down earth, &c.

COUTHU'TLAUGH (*Law*) one who knowingly cherishes, entertains, or hides any outlawed person.

COUTO'N (*Bot.*) a tree growing in Candia, resembling the walnut-tree, which yields, by incision, a pleasant juice, resembling Orleans wine. *Bauh. Pin.*

COUTOUBE'A (*Bot.*) the same as the *Picrium* of Linnæus.

CO'UVERT (*Her.*) an epithet for the top of a chief, or other ordinary, over which something hangs as a covering.

COVY (*Fowl.*) an assemblage of wild fowls, particularly partridges.

COW (*Zool.*) the female of the species *Bos Taurus* in the Linnean system.

COW-POX (*Surg.*) vide *Vaccination*.

CO'WARD (*Her.*) or *cowed*, an epithet for a lion in an escutcheon, which in a timorous manner clappeth his tail between his legs, as animals do in case of extremity and fear; as he beareth " *Argent* a lion rampant coward, *purpure*, name *Rowe*."

CO'WHAGE (*Bot.*) or *Cow-Itch*, the *Dolichos urens* of Linnæus, an annual.—Cow-Parsley, or Cow-weed, the *Chærophyllum sylvestre*.—Cow-Quake, the *Briga media*, a perennial.—Cow-Wheat, a weed growing among corn.

COWL (*Ecc.*) a sort of hood, such as is worn by monks.

CO'WNER (*Mar.*) an arched part of a ship's stern.

CO'WPER'S *Glands* (*Anat.*) three large muciparous glands situated before the prostate gland of the male.

CO'WRING (*Falcon.*) the quivering of young hawks, which shake their wings in sign of obedience to the old ones.

CO'WRY (*Con.*) or *Gowry*, a testaceous animal, the *Cypræa* of Linnæus, the animal of which is a limax, which is said to have the power of leaving its shell, and forming a new one. The shells are univalve, and remarkable for their high polish. These animals live in sand at the bottom of the sea.

COWRY (*Com.*) is used as a coin in India.

CO'WSLIP (*Bot.*) the *Primula* of Linnæus, a perennial.

CO'XA (*Anat.*) another name for the *Ischium*.

CO'XCOMB (*Bot.*) vide *Cockscomb*.

COXE'NDIX (*Anat.*) the hip-joint.

COYNS (*Print.*) vide *Quoins*.

CRAB (*Ent.*) the *Cancer* of Linnæus; a sort of shell-fish which every year cast off their old shells with much pain and difficulty.

CRAB (*Mar.*) in French *petit cabestan*, a sort of wooden pillar which rests upon sockets, like a capstan; also an engine of wood with three claws, used at launching or heaving ships into dock.

CRAB (*Mech.*) a machine fixed in the ground at the lower end of rope-walks, and used in stretching the yarn; also a machine used by masons and others for raising large weights.

CRA'B-TREE (*Bot.*) the *Pyrus malus sylvestris* of Linnæus.

CRA'BBING (*Falcon.*) is said of hawks when they stand too near, and fight with one another.

CRA'B-LOUSE (*Ent.*) a species of *pediculus* which infests the *axilla* and *pudenda*.

CRA'BRO (*Ent.*) the hornet, a large kind of wasp, the *Vespa crabro* of Linnæus. According to Fabricius it includes a division of the genus *Vespa*, having the lips short and horny.

CRA'B'S *eyes* (*Nat.*) a stone in a crab-fish, resembling an eye, which is used medicinally.

CRA'B-YAWS (*Med.*) the name in Jamaica for a kind of ulcer on the soles of the feet, with callous lips, so hard that it is difficult to cut them.

CRA'CCA (*Bot.*) the *Ervum tetraspermum* of Linnæus.

CRA'CKER (*Mech.*) a kind of firework which cracks and flies about.

CRA'CKING (*Archit.*) a fissure in a building from some defect in the foundation, or in the materials.

CRA'CKNELS (*Cook.*) a sort of cakes baked hard, so as to crackle under the teeth.

CRACKS (*Vet.*) or *Chops* in the heels of horses, which are sores that are either constitutional or arise from uncleanliness.

CRADLE (*Mar.*) 1. A standing bedstead for wounded seamen, instead of a hammock. 2. A machine made of stout sail-cloth, for the purpose of shipping and unshipping horses. 3. A timber frame made along the outside of a ship, in order to conduct her smoothly and steadily into the water when she is to be launched.

CRADLE (*Archit.*) vide *Coffer*.

CRADLE (*Surg.*) a machine of wood to lay a broken leg in that is newly set, to hinder it being pressed by the bed clothes.

CRA'DLING (*Archit.*) the mass of timber-work disposed in arched or vaulted ceilings for sustaining the lath-and-plaster.

CRAFT (*Mar.*) all manner of lines, hooks, nets, &c. for fishing.—*Small craft* are vessels used in the fishing trade, as hoys, retches, lighters, smacks, &c.

CRAFT (*Mech.*) or handy-craft, any mechanical art or trade.

CRÆPALE (*Med.*) κραιπάλη, every disorder of the head produced by the excessive drinking of wine. *Gal. in Hippocrat.* sect. 5, aph. 5.

CRA'IERA (*Mar.*) a small vessel of lading; a hoy or smack mentioned in *Pat.* 2, *R.* 2; *Stat.* 14 *Car.* 2. c. 27.

CRAIL (*Mech.*) an instrument used in catching fish.

CRAKE (*Orn.*) a sort of Starling; the *sturnus cynclus* of Linnæus.

CRA'KE-BERRY (*Bot.*) the *Empetrum nigrum* of Linnæus.

CRA'MBE (*Gram.*) a repetition of words, or saying the same thing over again.

CRAMBE (*Bot.*) κράμβη, a name given by the ancients to the *Brassica*, or cabbage, from which it is however distinguished by modern botanists. When boiled or eaten a second time it was reckoned to create nausea; whence the proverb Δὶς κράμβη θάνατος, to which Juvenal alludes. *Juv. Sat.* 7. v. 154.

Occidit miseros crambe repetita magistros.

Cato de R. Rust. c. 157; *Dioscor.* l. 2, c. 147; *Plin.* l. 20, c. 10; *Athen.* l. 9, c. 2; *Geopon.* l. 12, c. 17.

CRAMBE, in the Linnean system, a genus of plants, Class 15 *Tetradynamia*, Order 2 *Siliquosa*.

Generic Characters. CAL. *perianth* four-leaved; *leaflets* ovate.—COR. four-petalled, cruciform; *petals* large, obtuse; *claws* erect, spreading.—STAM. *filaments* six; *anthers* simple; a *melliferous gland* between the corolla and the stamens.—PIST. *germ* oblong; *style* none; *stigma* thickish.—PER. *berry* dry, globose; *seed* simple, roundish.

Species. The species are perennials or shrubs, as—*Crambe maritima*, seu *Brassica maritima*, Sea Colewort, a perennial, and native of Europe.— *Crambe Hispanica*, Spanish Colewort, a perennial.—*Crambe Tartaria*, seu *Tartaria Ungarica*, a native of Hungary and Tartary. But the—*Crambe fruticosa*, Shrubby Colewort, and the—*Crambe strigosa*, seu *Megarum*, Rough-leaved Shrubby-leaved Colewort, are shrubs. *Clus. Hist. Plant. rar.*; *Bauh. Hist.*; *Bauh. Pin.*; *Ger. Herb.*; *Park. Theat. Botan.*; *Raii Hist. Plant.*; *Tournef. Inst.*

CRAMBE is also the *Bunias spinosa*.

CRAMBION (*Med.*) κραμβίον, a decoction of cabbage.

CRA'MBO (*Sport.*) a play in rhyming, in which he that repeats a word that was said before forfeits something.

CRA'MP (*Med.*) a spasmodic affection which causes a violent distortion of the nerves, muscles, &c.

CRAMP (*Falcon.*) a disease to which hawks are subject in their wings from cold, which affects them in their soaring.

CRA'MP-FISH (*Ich.*) another name for the *Torpedo*.

CRA'MP-IRONS (*Mason.*) irons which fasten stones in buildings; also grapling irons to lay hold of an enemy's ship.

CRAMP-IRONS (*Print.*) irons nailed to the carriage of the press to run it in and out.

CRAMPIT (*Mil.*) the chape at the bottom of the scabbard of a broad sword, called by the French *Botterolle*. [vide *Boterol*]

CRAMPONNE'E (*Her.*) an epithet for a cross in coat-armour. A cross cramponnee is so called because it has a cramp or crampoon at each end, as in the annexed figure.

CRAMPO'ON (*Mech.*) vide *Cramp.*

CRAMPO'ONS (*Mil.*) iron instruments fastened to the shoes of a storming party, to assist them in climbing a rampart.

CRANAGE (*Law*) *cranagium*, money paid for the use of a crane in landing and shipping wares at a wharf.

CRA'NBERRY (*Bot.*) a pale red berry, of a tart taste, which is the fruit of the *Vaccinium oxycoccus* of Linnæus. The berries are also called Mossberries, Moorberries, Fenberries, &c. because the plants grow in bogs and fens. The name of Cranberry, which belongs to the tree as well as the fruit, originates probably in the crookedness of the pedicles at the top, which resemble the head and neck of a crane.

CRANE (*Orn.*) a sort of heron, five feet in length, with a bald head, the *Ardea Grus* of Linnæus.

CRANE (*Astron.*) a southern constellation. [vide *Grus*]

CRA'NE-FLY (*Ent.*) a sort of insect, the *Tipula* of Linnæus, which much resembles the gnat.

CRANEQUIER (*Mil.*) French for an archer who served both on foot and horseback.

CRA'NE'S BILL (*Bot.*) an English name for the *Geranium* and *Erodium* of Linnæus.

CRANE'S BILL (*Surg.*) a pair of pincers.

CRA'NGOR (*Ich.*) the Prawn, a sort of *Squilla.*

CRA'NICHIS (*Bot.*) a genus of plants, Class 20 *Gynandria*, Order 1 *Diandria.*

Generic Characters. CAL. *spathes* wandering; *perianth* none.—COR. *petals* five, oblong; *nectary* vaulted.—STAM. *anthers* pedicelled.—PIST. *germ* obovate, oblique; *stigma* funnel-form.—PER. *capsule* oblong; *seeds* numerous.

Species. The species are all natives of Jamaica.

CRANIOLA'RIA (*Bot*) a genus of plants, Class 14 *Didynamia*, Order 2 *Angiospermia.*

Generic Characters. CAL. *perianth inferior* four-leaved; *leaflets* linear; *perianth superior* ovate, inflated.—COR. one-petalled; *tube* very long and narrow; *border* flat; *upper lip* entire; *lower lip* three-cleft.—STAM. *filaments* four, length of the tube of the corolla; *anthers* simple. —PIST. *germ* ovate; *style* filiform; *stigma* thickish, obtuse.—PER. coriaceous, two-valved; *seed* nut woody.

Species. The only species is, the—*Craniolaria annua*, seu *Martynia craniolaria.*

CRANIOLARIA is also the *Gessneria craniolaria.*

CRANIO·LOGY (*Eth.*) from κρᾱνιον, the skull, and λογος, doctrine; the discovering of men's characters and faculties from the external appearances of the skull, which is a subject of modern enquiry.

CRA'NIUM (*Anat.*) the skull, or superior part of the head, formed by the compages of all the bones of the head, which, like a helmet, defend the brain from external injuries.

CRANK (*Mar.*) or *Crank-sided*, an epithet for a vessel when she cannot bear her sail, or can bear only a small part, for fear of oversetting. A ship is also said to be *crank by the ground* when her floor is so narrow that she cannot be brought on the ground without danger.

CRANK (*Mech*) a machine resembling an elbow, except that it is in a square form, projecting out of an axis or spindle, which by its rotation serves to raise or lower the pistons of engines for raising water; also the draw-beam of a well.— *Crank-wheel*, a machine for rope-making, fixed on an iron spindle or axis, with a handle for turning it.—*Cranks* are also iron braces which support the lanterns on the poop-quarters.

CRA'NNOCK (*Archæol.*) an ancient measure of corn. *Castular. Abbot. Glaston.* MS. f. 39.

CRA'NTZIA (*Bot.*) the same as the *Tricera.*

CRA'NZIA (*Bot.*) a genus of plants called after Joachim Crantz, a German botanist, Class 5 *Pentandria*, Order 1 *Monogynia.*

Generic Characters. CAL. *perianth* five-parted.—COR. *petals* five, oblong, sessile.—STAM. *filaments* five, broad at the base; *anthers* roundish, incumbent.—PIST. *germ* subglobular; *style* cylindric; *stigma* three-lobed, obtuse. —PER. *berry* globose; *seeds* few.

Species. The only species is the—*Cranzia aculeata*, *Scopolia Paullinia Kaka-toddali*, a shrub of Malabar.

CRAPA'UD (*Gunn.*) French for a gun-carriage without wheels, on which a mortar is laid.

CRA'PAUDINE (*Vet.*) an ulcer on the coronet of a horse; called also a *tread upon the coronet.*

CRAPE (*Com.*) a light transparent stuff, resembling gauze, made of a raw silk gummed and twisted in the mill.

CRA'PULA (*Med.*) a surfeit.

CRA'SIS (*Med.*) κρᾶσις, from κεράννυμι, to mix; a proper constitution, or due temperament of the humours.

CRASIS (*Gram.*) a contraction of two syllables into one.

CRASPE'DIA (*Bot.*) a genus of plants, Class 19 *Syngenesia*, Order *Polygamia segregata.*

This plant is a native of New Zealand, and but little known at present.

CRA'SPEDON (*Med*) κρασπεδον, a disorder in the *uvula*, when it hangs down in the form of a thin oblong membrane. *Aret. de Caus. et Signif. Morb.* l. 1, c. 8.

CRA'SSA Arteria (*Anat.*) vide *Aorta.*—*Crassa Meninx.* [vide *Dura Mater*]

CRASSAME'NTUM (*Anat.*) the coagulated portion of blood when suffered to cool at rest.

CRASSE'NA (*Med.*) saline, putrefactive, and corrosive particles, which produce ulcers and tumours of various sorts.

CRA'SSINA (*Bot.*) the *Zennia pauciflora* of Linnæus.

CRA'SSULA (*Bot.*) a genus of plants so called from the thickness of its leaves, Class 5 *Pentandria*, Order 5 *Pentagynia.*

Generic Character. CAL. *perianth* one-leaved, five-cleft.— COR. *petals* five, long and linear; *nectaries* five.—STAM. *filaments* five, subulate; *anthers* simple.—PIST. *germs* five, oblong; *styles* the length of the stamens; *stigmas* obtuse. —PER. *capsules* five, oblong; *seeds* many.

Species. The species are natives of the Cape of Good Hope, mostly perennials or shrubs, some few annuals, and biennials, as — *Crassula coccinea*, seu *Cotyledon*, Scarlet-flowered Crassula.—*Crassula flava*, seu *Sedum*, Yellow-flowered Crassula.—*Crassula perfoliata*, seu *Aloe*. —*Crassula dichotoma*, Forked Crassula, &c.—But the *Crassula subulata*, Awl-leaved Crassula, is an annual, as also the—*Crassula verticillaris*, Whorl-flowered Crassula, &c.; and the—*Crassula barbata*, is a biennial.

CRASSULA is also the *Tillea aquatica*, &c. the *Othonna tenissima*, and a species of the *Claytonia.*

CRA'STINO (*Law*) *The morrow*, a word used with certain return days of writs in the beginning of terms, as *Crastino Animarum*, the Morrow of All Souls in Michaelmas Term; *Crastino Purificationis beatæ Mariæ Virginis* in Hilary Term; *Crastino Ascensionis Domini* in Easter Term; and *Crastino Sanctæ Trinitatis* in Trinity Term. *Stat.* 51 *Hen.* 3, st. 2 and 3; 32 *Hen.* 8, c. 21; 16 *Car.* 1, c. 6; 24 *Geo.* 2, c. 48.

CRATÆ'GONUM (*Bot.*) vide *Melampyrum.*

CRATÆ'GUS (*Bot.*) κράταιγος, the *Wild Service-Tree*, a plant, the fruit of which is astringent. *Theophrast. Hist. Plant.* l. 3, c. 15.

CRATÆGUS, in the Linnean system, a genus of plants, Class 12 *Icosandria*, Order 2 *Digynia.*

Generic Character. CAL. *perianth* one-leaved.—COR. *petals* five, roundish.—STAM. *filaments* twenty; *anthers* roundish.—PIST. *germ* inferior; *styles* two; *stigmas* headed.—PER. *berry* fleshy; *seeds* two.

Species. This genus consists chiefly of trees or shrubs, hardy and deciduous. as—*Cratægus aria, Mespilus, Aria,* seu *Sorbus,* White Beam Tree.—*Cratægus torminalis, Mespilus,* seu *Sorbus,* Wild Service, Sorb, or Maple-leaved Service.—*Cratægus cocci,* seu *Oxyacantha,* Great American Hawthorn —*Cratægus Oxyacantha,* Common Hawthorn, or White-thorn.—*Cratægus azarolus,* Azarolus, Azarolier, &c.—*Cratægus cordata,* Maple-leaved Hawthorn, &c. *Bauh. Hist. Plant.; Bauh. Pin. Ger. Herb.; Park. Theat. Bot.; Raii Hist. Plant.; Tournef. Instit.*

CRATÆOGONUM (*Bot.*) the *Bartsia Alpina* of Linnæus.

CRATCH (*Huib.*) a rack for hay or straw.

CRATCHES (*Vet.*) a stinking sore in a horse's heel.

CRATE (*Mech.*) a large wicker case in which earthenware is packed.

CRA'TER (*Ant.*) κρατηρ, either from κρατιω, to contain, or κιρανυμι, to mix; a very large wine-cup, a goblet, out of which the ancients poured their libations at feasts. *Poll. Onomast.* l. 4, § 16.

CRATER (*Nat.*) the hole or vent, as in Mount Ætna, which belches out fire. *Suet. in Cal.* c. 51.

CRATER (*Falcon.*) any line on which hawks are fastened when reclaimed.

CRATER (*Astron.*) κρατηρ, the cup; a southern constellation, the number of whose stars, according to Ptolemy, is 7; to Tycho 8; to Hevelius 10; and in the British catalogue 31. This is supposed by Hyginus to be the cup which Apollo gave to the Corvus, or Raven. *Hygin. Astron. Poet.; Ptol. Almag.* l. 7, c. 5.

CRA'TES (*Ant.*) 1. Engines of war used by the ancients to cover their workmen as they approached a besieged town. *Cæs. de Bell. Gall.* l. 7, c. 81; *Veget.* l. 4, c. 6; *Lips. Poliorc.* l. 1, c. 7. 2. An iron grate used before prisons.

CRATE'VA (*Bot.*) a genus of plants, Class 11 *Dodecandria,* Order 1 *Monogynia.*

Generic Character. CAL. *perianth* one-leaved, four-cleft.—COR. *petals* four; *claws* slender.—STAM. *filaments* sixteen or more, bristleform; *anthers* erect, oblong.—PIST. *germ* on a very long filiform pedicle; *style* none; *stigma* sessile, headed.—PER. *berry* fleshy.

Species. The species are trees, as—*Crateva gynandra,* seu *Anona,* Thin-leaved Crateva.—*Crateva tapia,* Tapia, seu *Anona, Apioscorodon,* seu *Malus Americana,* Smooth Crateva, or Garlic Pear, native of the West Indies, &c.—*Crateva Marmelos, Cydonia exotica, Bilanus,* seu *Covalam,* Prickly Crateva, native of India.—*Crateva religiosa,* called in Otaheite *Pura taruru,* which is planted in their burial places, and is supposed to be sacred to their idols. *Bauh. Hist.; Marcgr. Pis. Brasil.; Raii Hist. Plant.*

Crateva is also the same as the *Capparis.*

CRATI'CULA (*Chem.*) the bars, or grating, which cover the ash-hole in a furnace.

CRAVA'RE (*Archæol.*) to impeach.

CRA'VEN (*Law*) or Cravent, a term of reproach in the ancient trial by battle, which the vanquished party used when he yielded. If the appellant joined battle, and cried *cravent,* he was to lose *liberam legem*: if the appellee, he was to be hanged. 2 *Inst.* 248, &c.

CRAW (*Orn.*) the stomach of a bird.

CRAW-FISH (*Ent.*) vide *Cray-fish.*

CRAWL (*Mar.*) a sort of pen, or place of confinement, by the sea-side, formed by a barrier of stakes for the purpose of confining fish.

CRAX (*Orn.*) Curassow, a genus of animals, Class *Aves,* Order *Gallinæ.*

Generic Character. Bill strong, thick.—*Tail* large, straight, expansile.

Species. The principal species are, the—*Crax alector,* the Crested Curassow.—*Crax Pauxi,* Cushew Curassow.—*Crax vociferans,* Crying Curassow.

CRAY (*Falcon.*) a disease in hawks which hinders their muting; it is much like the pantass.

CRAY'ER (*Mar.*) a sort of small sea-vessel.

CRAY-FISH (*Ich.*) a small sort of lobster, the *Cancer astacus* of Linnæus.

CRA'YON (*Paint.*) a pencil of any sort of colouring stuff made into paste, and dried for drawing in dry colours on paper, &c.

CRE'A (*Anat.*) vide *Tibia.*

CREACE'NTRUM (*Ant.*) a hollow iron for interlarding meat.

CREAM (*Nat.*) the thickest, richest, and most substantial part of milk.—*Cream-water,* has a kind of oil upon it, which, when boiled, serves various medicinal purposes.

CREAM *of Tartar* (*Chem.*) or the *Bitartrate of Potash,* a salt prepared from the lees of wine.

CREANCE (*Falcon.*) or *Criance,* a fine, small, long line, fastened to a hawk's leash when she is first lured.

CREA'NSOR (*Law*) or *Creditor;* one who trusts another with any debt, money, or wares. *Stat.* 38 *Ed.* 3, c. 5; *F. N. B.* 66.

CREAST (*Her.*) vide *Crest.*

CREAT (*Man.*) an usher to a riding-master, or a gentleman educated in a riding-school for the purpose of teaching the art of horsemanship.

CREDENTIALS (*Polit.*) letters of credit, particularly those which are given to ambassadors and plenipotentiaries.

CRE'DIT (*Law*) a right which lords had over their vassals, to oblige them to lend money for a certain time.

CREDIT (*Com.*) a mutual loan of merchandises, &c. on the reputation for honesty and solvency of the parties negotiating.—*Letters of credit,* letters given by merchants to persons to whom they can trust to draw money from their correspondents.

Credit, or *Creditor,* is also the name for that side of a Merchant's Account book, which contains what is owing to him, or he has to receive in distinction from the *debit,* or *debtor* side, containing what he has to pay.

CREED (*Ecc.*) a summary of the principal articles of the Christian faith, of which three are allowed by the canons of the church, viz. The *Apostles' Creed,* the *Athanasian Creed,* and the *Nicene Creed.* [vide *Apostles,* &c.]

CREEK (*Com.*) that part of a haven where any thing is landed from the sea. It is also said to be a shore, or bank, whereon the water beats, running in any small channel from the sea.

CREE'PER (*Mech.*) an instrument of iron resembling a grapnel, for dragging along a river.

CREEPER (*Orn.*) a name for a sort of birds, the *Certhia* of Linnæus, which are dispersed through every country of the globe. They have an arched bill, and feet formed for walking.

CRE'MAILLE (*Fort.*) the inside line of a parapet, which is broken in a manner to resemble a saw.

CREMA'STER (*Anat.*) a muscle of the *testes,* by which they are suspended and drawn up.

CREME'NTUM *Comitatus* (*Law*) the name given by the sheriffs in their accounts to the improvement of the King's rents. *Hale Sher. Acc.* p. 36.

CRE'MER (*Med.*) a sort of *crapula.*

CRE'MNOI (*Med.*) κρημνοι, the lips of ulcers; also the *labia* of the female *Pudenda.*

CREMO'NA (*Mus.*) an appellation for the superior sort of violins, which were originally made at Cremona.

CRE'MOR (*Chem.*) Cream, or any substance floating on the top of a liquid, and skim med off.

CRE'NÆ (*Bot.*) Incisions in the edges of leaves.

CRENA'TUS (*Bot.*) crenate; an epithet for leaves that are jagged, or have the edges cut with angular or circular incisures, as in *Prunula farinosa.* When the edge of the leaf is cut into segments of small circles it is said to be *obtusely crenate*, and when the larger segments have smaller ones upon them, it is said to be *doubly crenate*. The same epithet is applied to the corolla in *Linum, Dianthus, Chinensis*, &c. and to the nectary in *Narcissus triandrus*. When the edge of a leaf is cut into very small notches, Linnæus applies the epithet *crenulate*.

CRENAU'X (*Fort.*) French for small openings, or loopholes, which are made through the walls of a fortified town.

CRE'NKLES (*Mar.*) or *crengles*; small ropes spliced into the bolt-ropes of the sails of the main-mast and fore-mast, and fastened to the bowling bridles to hold by when the bonnet-sail is taken off.

CRENELLA'TED PARAPET (*Fort.*) an embattled parapet with loop-holes to fire through.

CRENELLE' (*Her.*) or embattled; one of the lines by which ordinaries of all kinds may be diversified. It is made in form like the battlements of a castle, from which it takes its name, as in the annexed figure, "He beareth *azure*, a bend crenellé *or*," which were the arms of Scarron, the famous jester and comic writer, whose wife was mistress to Lewis XIV.

CRE'NULATE (*Bot.*) vide *Crenate*.

CRE'OLE (*Polit.*) a person born in the West Indies, but of European origin.

CRE'PANCE (*Vet.*) a chop, or scratch, in a horse's leg, given by the shoe of a hinder foot, which often degenerates into an ulcer.

CREPA'RE oculum (*Law*) to put out the eyes; the punishment for which was a fine of 60s. *Leg. H.* 1, *apud Brompton*.

CREPA'TIO (*Med.*) or *Crepatura*; the breaking or cracking of any seed in the boiling.

CREPATU'RA (*Med.*) an intestinal hernia, according to Paracelsus.

CRE'PIS (*Bot.*) a plant mentioned by Pliny. *Plin.* l. 21, c. 16.

CREPIS, in the Linnean system, Class 19 *Syngenesia*, Order 1 *Polygamia æqualis*.
  Generic Character. CAL. common double.—COR. compound imbricate; *corollets* hermaphrodite; *proper* one-petalled.—STAM. *filaments* five, capillary; *anther* cylindric.—PIST. *germ* somewhat ovate; *style* filiform; *stigmas* two, reflex.—PER. none; *calyx* roundish; *seed* solitary; *receptacle* naked, with cells.
  Species. The species are of different kinds, as—*Crepis barbata*, seu *Hieracium*, Spanish or bearded Crepis, or Purple-eyed Succory Hawkweed, a biennial.—*Crepis fœtida*, *Senecio*, seu *Erigeron*, Stinking Crepis, or Succory Hawkweed, a biennial, and native of Britain, &c.—*Crepis tectorium*, *Hedypnois*, seu *Cichorium*, Smooth Crepis, or Yellow Succory, an annual, &c. *Dod. Pempt.*; *Bauh. Hist. Plant.*; *Bauh. Pin.*; *Ger. Herb.*; *Park. Theat. Botan.*; *Raii Hist. Plant.*

CREPIS is also the *Apargia hirta*.

CREPITA'TION (*Chem.*) the crackling noise made by some salts during the process of calcination, otherwise called *detonation*.

CREPITATION (*Surg.*) the noise made by the bones when the surgeon moves a limb to assure himself by his ear of the existence of a fracture.

CRE'PITUS *lupi* (*Bot.*) vide *Lycoperdon*.

CREPU'NDIA (*Ant.*) signifies generally the swath-bands and other apparel proper for young children, but particularly those things which were exposed with young children, as rings, jewels, &c. by which they could be recognised, or which would serve as an inducement for others to take charge of them.
Plaut. Cist. act 3, scen. 1.

Nam hic crepundia insunt, quibuscum illa olim ad me detulit;
Quæ mihi dedit, parentes ts ut cognoscerent.

Terent. Heaut. act. 4, scen. 1.

—— *quum exponendam do illi. de digito annulum*
Detraho; et eum dico ut una cum puella exponeret,
Si moreretur, ne, expers partis esset de nostris bonis.

The crepundia were called γνωρίσματα by the Greeks. *Heliod. Æthiop.* l. 4; *Don. in Terent.*; *Long. Pastor.* 1; *Salmas. in Vopis. Aurel.* c. 4; *Scheff. de Torq.* c. 5, &c.

CREPU'SCULUM (*Astron.*) The Twilight, or the time from the first dawn, or appearance of the morning, to the rising of the sun; and in the evening the decline of the day, until the setting of the sun. This usually begins and ends about 18 degrees below the horizon.

CRESCE'NDO (*Mus.*) or abbreviated *cresc;* an Italian term in music-books, signifying that the notes of the passage over which it is placed are to be gradually swelled.

CRE'SCENT (*Astron.*) an appellation for the new moon, which, as it begins to recede from the sun, shows a small rim of light terminating in horns, or points. [vide *Astronomy*]

CRESCENT (*Archit.*) a range of buildings disposed in the form of a crescent, or half-moon.

CRESCENT (*Her.*) is the half-moon with the horns turned upwards, as in the annexed figure. It is used either as an honourable ordinary, or as a mark of distinction for the second sons of families, and those descended from him. It is said to be *montant* when the points look towards the top, as in the annexed figure; *inverted* when the points look towards the bottom; *turned* when they look to the dexter side of the shield; and *con-turned* when they look to the sinister side. Two crescents are said to be *adossed* which have their backs towards each other, and *affronted* when their points look towards each other.

CRESCENT, *Order of the* (*Her.*) an order instituted by Mahomet II. emperor of the Turks, who declared himself chief and head of it. The insignia consisted of a gold crescent, with sinople or green enamel, encircled by precious stones, or diamonds. The motto is, "*Donec totum impleat orbem.*"

CRESCENT (*Vet.*) a defect in the foot of a horse when the coffin-bone falls down, and presses the sole outwards.

CRESCENT-SHAPED (*Bot.*) vide *Lunate*.

CRESCENTED (*Her.*) an epithet for a cross having a crescent at each end.

CRESCE'NTIA (*Bot.*) a genus of plants, called after Pietro Crescentio, an Italian writer on agriculture, Class 14 *Didynamia*, Order 2 *Angiospermia*; in French *Calebassier, Couis*, in English Calabash-Tree.
  Generic Characters. CAL. *perianth* one-leaved, two-parted; *divisions* roundish.—COR. one-petalled; *tube* gibbous; *border* erect, five-cleft.—STAM. *filaments* four, subulate; *anthers* incumbent.—PIST. *germ* pedicelled, ovate; *style* filiform; *stigma* headed.—PER. *berry* oval; *seeds* very many.
  Species. The two species are the—*Crescentia cujete*, seu *Cujete*, Narrow-leaved Calabash-Tree.—*Crescentia cucurbitina*, Broad-leaved Calabash-Tree.

CRE'SPINUS (*Bot.*) another name for the *Berberis*.

CRE'SPULUM (*Bot.*) another name for the *Buphthalmum*.

CRESS (*Bot.*) or Ladies Smock, the *Cardamine*, some species of which are biennials, the rest perennials.— Bastard Cress, the *Thlaspi*, a biennial.—Garden Cress, the *Lepidium sativum*, an annual, which is cultivated as a salad.—Indian Cress, the *Tropæolum*, an annual.—Rock Cress, another name for a species of Candy-tuft, the *Iberis nudicaulis*.—Rocket Cress, the *Vella*, an annual.—Swines Cress, the *Cochlearia coronopus*.—Water and Winter Cress, the *Sisymbrium nasturtium*, a perennial, or, according to some, an annual.

CRE'SSA (*Bot.*) a genus of plants, Class 5 *Pentandria*, Order 2 *Digynia*.
  Generic Character. CAL. perianth five-leaved; *leaflets* ovate.—COR. one-petalled; *tube* bellied; *border* five-parted.—STAM. *filaments* five, capillary; *anthers* roundish.—PIST. *germ* ovate; *styles* ovate; *stigmas* simple.—PER. *capsule* ovate; *seeds* single.
  Species. The two species are the—*Cressa Cretica, Anthyllis, Quamoclit*, seu *Chamæpithys*, &c.—*Cressa Indica*. They are both shrubs and natives of Crete.
CRE'SSET (*Mil.*) any great light upon a beacon or watch tower.
CRE'SSIS (*Bot.*) vide *Cardamum*.
CREST (*Her.*) any figure placed upon a wreath, coronet, or cap of maintenance above the helmet or shield.
CREST (*Mil.*) a tuft of feathers; a plume or tassel generally worn on the helmet; the use of which is of great antiquity. [vide *Crista*]
CREST of a Parapet (*Fort.*) or *of the Glacis*, the superior surface, or top of the parapet, &c.
CREST (*Mech.*) an imagery or carved work to adorn the head, or top of any thing, like our cornice.
CREST (*Bot.*) vide *Crested*.
CREST (*Nat.*) the tuft of feathers on the head of a bird.
CREST Fallen (*Vet.*) is said of a horse when the upper part of the neck on which the mane grows, does not stand upright, but hangs either on one side or other.
CRE'ST-TILE (*Archit.*) a tile on the ridge of a house.
CRE'STED (*Her.*) an epithet for a cock, or any other bird, having its comb, in an escutcheon, of a different tincture from its body. The tincture, in that case, must be named; as a " cock, argent, crested, or, &c."
CRESTED (*Bot.*) *cristatus*, an epithet for some flowers and anthers that have an appendage, like a crest or tuft.
CRE'SWELL (*Mech.*) the broad edge or verge of the shoe sole.
CRE'TA (*Min.*) a genus of earths, of the Calcareous Order, which, by a chemical analysis, is found to consist of carbonate of lime, carbonic acid gas, with a few extraneous substances. It is friable; effervesces with, and is soluble in acids; calcines in the fire, but does not vitrify.
  Species. The principal species are as follow:—*Creta scriptoria*, seu *Calx creta*, Common Chalk.—*Creta pulverulenta*, Native Lime.—*Calx granulata*, seu *Calx testacea*, a calcareous substance, which serves as a nidus for the Testudo Midas to lay its eggs in. It is composed of shells and corals—*Creta squamosa*, Agaric Mineral, &c.
CRETA'CEOUS Acid (*Chem.*) vide *Carbonic acid*.
CRETE (*Fort*) the earth thrown out of the ditch in a fortification, trench, &c.—*Crête d'un chemin couvert*, the highest peak, or part of a covered way, or any other work.
CRE'THMON (*Bot.*) vide *Crithmum*.
CRE'TIS (*Ant.*) from *cerno*, to decide; a space of time which is given by a testator to an heir before he enters upon an estate. If he did not resolve, at least within one hundred days, he was to lose his estate. *Cic. ad Attic.* l. 11, ep. 12; *Varr. de Lat. Ling.* l. 5, c. 8; *Isid. Orig.* l. 5, c. 24.
CRE'VET (*Mech.*) a melting pot used by goldsmiths.
CRE'VICE (*Fort.*) a chasm or hollow in a piece of ordnance.
CREVI'SSE (*Ent.*) Cray-fish.
CREW (*Mar.*) the company of sailors belonging to a ship, boat, or any kind of vessel.
CRE'WEL (*Mech.*) fine worsted.
CRE'WET (*Mech.*) or *cruet*, a phial or narrow-mouthed glass to hold oil or vinegar.
CREUX (*Sculpt.*) a term signifying the reverse of relief; thus, to engrave, *en creux*, is to cut below the surface.
CRI (*Mil.*) French for the motto written upon colours.
CRI'ANCE (*Falcon.*) vide *Creance*.

CRI'BBAGE (*Sport.*) a sort of game played with cards.
CRI'B-BITING (*Man.*) a bad habit among horses, which is often occasioned by their uneasiness in breeding of teeth.
CRI'BBLE (*Husband.*) coarse meal, a little better than bran.
CRIBRA'TION (*Chem.*) the sifting of powder through a fine sieve.
CRIBRIFO'RME (*Anat.*) or *cribrosum*, a name for the ethmoid bone.
CRIC (*Gunn.*) or *Cricq*, French for a machine, which is used for dragging up a piece of ordnance. *Cric* is also the name of a poignard used by the Malayan people.
CRICELA'SIA (*Med.*) κρικηλασια, from κρικος, a ring, and ελαυνω, to drive; the name of an ancient exercise, very similar to the modern one, of driving a hoop. *Oribas. Med.* l. 6, c. 26.
CRICK (*Med.*) a sort of cramp or pain in the neck.
CRI'CKET (*Ent.*) a little insect haunting ovens, &c.
CRICKET (*Sport.*) a game with bat and ball, &c.
CRI'CO *arytænoides* (*Anat.*) from κρικος, a ring, αρυτης, a drinking cup, and ιδος, likeness; two muscles of the glotta, called *lateralis* and *posticus*, which open the *rima* by pulling the ligaments from one another.—*Crico-Pharyngeus*, vide *Constrictor-Pharyngis*.
CRICOI'DES (*Anat.*) from κρικος, a ring, and ιδος, likeness; a cartilage of the *Larynx*, or wind-pipe.
CRICO-THYROI'DES (*Anat.*) from κρικος, a ring, θυρεος, an helmet, and ιδος, likeness; an epithet for a pair of muscles, arising from the fore part of the *cricoides*, and ending in that called *scutiformis*.
CRI'MINAL (*Law*) relating to crimes, or having the character of a crime, as—*Criminal Law, Criminal Conversation*, &c.—*Crim. Con.*, abbreviation for criminal conversation.
CRIMNO'DE (*Med.*) κριμνωδης, from κριμνον, bran, and ιδος, likeness; branny, an epithet for urine which deposits a branny sediment.
CRI'MNON (*Med.*) κριμνον, a coarse sort of meal, made of zea and wheat, from which a drink was made, recommended often by Hippocrates. *Hippocrat. de Morb.* l. 3, &c.; *Gal. Exeges. Vocab. Hippocrat.*
CRIMP (*Com.*) an agent for Coal-Merchants.
CRIMPS (*Polit.*) persons who decoy others into the land or sea-service.
CRI'MSON (*Paint.*) a fine deep red colour.
CRIMSON GRASS-VETCH (*Bot.*) the *Lathyrus nissolia* of Linnæus.
CRINA'LE (*Ant.*) a hairpin.
CRINA'TA (*Bot.*) the *Pavetta caffra* of Linnæus.
CRINA'TED (*Bot.*) the same as *Crinite*. [vide *Crinitus*]
CRI'NED (*Her.*) an epithet for any animal having its beard of a different tincture from the rest of the body.
CRI'NELLS (*Falcon.*) vide *Crinites*.
CRINES VITIUM (*Nat.*) the tendrils of the vines.—*Crines Polypi*, the fins of the polypus.
CRI'NGLE (*Mar.*) in French *herseau de boulines*, a small hole formed in the bolt-rope of a sail, by intertwisting the strand of a rope alternately round itself and through the strands of the bolt-rope till it becomes threefold and assumes the shape of a ring.
CRINI'TES (*Falc.*) or *Crinells*, small black feathers in a hawk, like hair about the sere.
CRINI'TUS (*Bot.*) *crinite*, an epithet for some flowers having long hair, or beards resembling hair, as in *Phleum crinitum*; also an epithet for fronds.
CRINODE'NDRON (*Bot.*) from κρινον, a lily, and δενδρον, a tree; a genus of plants, Class 16 *Monodelphia*, Order 4 *Decandria*.
  Generic Characters. CAL. none.—COR. bellshaped; *petals* six, oblong.—STAM. *filaments* ten, erect; *anthers* ovate.—PIST. *germ* superior, ovate; *style* subulate.—PER. *capsule* coriaceous; *seeds* three, roundish.

Species. The single species is a superb evergreen branching tree, with a body of seven feet in diameter, a native of Chili.

CRINODES (*Med.*) from *crinis*, the hair; a name for collections of a fluid in the cutaneous follicles of the face and breast, which appear like black spots.

CRINO'MENON (*Ant.*) τὸ κρινόμενον, the issue in a suit of law, which Cicero calls the *Quæstio*. *Cic. Or.* l. 2, c. 10.

CRINOMY'RON (*Med.*) κρινόμυρον, from κρίνον, a lily, and μύρον, ointment; an ointment of lilies.

CRI'NON (*Bot.*) κρίνον, a red lily; so called by the Greeks, according to Pliny. Dioscorides also speaks of the crinon as a purple flower. *Plin.* l. 21, c. 5; *Discor.* l. 3, c. 116.

CRINO'NES (*Med.*) a sort of cutaneous worms which breed in the flesh of children.

CRI'NUM (*Bot.*) from κρίνον, a lily; a genus of plants, Class 6 *Hexandria*, Order 1 *Monogynia*.
Generic Characters. COR. one-petalled; *tube* oblong; *border* six-parted.—STAM. *filaments* six, subulate; *anthers* oblong, linear.—PIST. *germ* inferior; *style* filiform; *stigma* three-cleft—PER. *capsule* subovate.
Species. These species have bulbous roots, of which the two following are the principal:—*Crinum Asiaticum, Bulbine Asiatica, Amaryllis, Lilium Zeylanicum, Radix toxicaria, seu Bellutta-p·la-taly.*—*Crinum Americanum, seu Lilio-asphodelus*, Great American Crinum, &c.

CRINUM is also the name of the *Agapanthus*, the *Amaryllis falcata, latifolia purpurea et zeylanica*; *Cyrtanthus obliquus*, and the *Cyrtanthus angustifolia*.

CRIOBO'LIUM (*Ant.*) from κριός, a ram, and βάλλω, to knock down; the sacrifice of a ram by knocking it down with a hatchet. *Firmic. de Error. Prof. Relig.* p. 37; *Turneb. Adv.* l. 27, c. 21; *Salmas. in Lamprid. Heliogab.* c. 7.

CRIO'CERIS (*Ent.*) a division of the genus *cryptocephalus*, according to Fabricius, comprehending those insects of that genus that have the jaw bifid and the body oblong.

CRIO'GENES (*Med.*) κριογενής, an epithet for certain trochees recommended by Paulus Ægineta for cleansing sordid ulcers. *P. Aginet.* l. 7, c. 12.

CRIOMY'XUS (*Med.*) κριόμυξος, an epithet for persons abounding with mucus in the nose.

TO CRI'PPLE (*Mar.*) to damage a ship in her masts, rigging, yards, &c.

CRI'PPLINGS (*Carpent.*) short spars or piles of wood against the side of a house.

CRI'SIMOS (*Med.*) κρίσιμος, critical; an epithet applied to those days on which a crisis happens.

CRI'SIS (*Med.*) κρίσις, from κρίνω, to determine; most commonly signifies that sudden change in the symptoms of a disorder from which a judgment may be formed of its termination, whether it will be favourable or unfavourable. This is divided into an imperfect or perfect crisis; the former not clearly determining the disease; the latter that which terminates decisively either one way or another. *Hippocrat. de Affect. &c.*

CRISIS is likewise used by Hippocrates for the solution of a disorder which precedes recovery. *Hippocrat. Præcept.* Also for the secretion of any noxious humour. *Hippocrat. de Art.*; *Gal. Exeges.*

CRI'SOM (*Ecc.*) vide *Chrisom.*

CRISPATU'RA (*Med.*) a spasmodic contraction of the membranes and fibres.

CRI'SPED (*Bot.*) vide *Crispus.*

CRI'SPIN (*Cus.*) a name given to shoemakers, of whom St. Crispin was said to be the patron.

CRI'SPUS (*Bot.*) curled, an epithet for a leaf. [vide *Curled*]

CRI'STA (*Ant.*) λόφος, the crest; the upper part of the helmet, which served either for ornament or terror among the ancients.

Virg. Æn. l. 9, v. 365.

Tum galeam Messapi habilem, cristisque decoram Induit.

Æn. l. 8, v. 620.

Terribilem cristis galeam, flammasque vomentem.

The custom of wearing crests was introduced, according to Herodotus, by the Ethiopians, who used either horse-hair or the feathers of birds. *Herodot.* l. 7, c. 69, &c.; *Polyb.* l. 6, c. 21; *Strab.* l. 14; *Sil. Ital.* l. 10, v. 399; *Plin.* l. 7, c. 56; *Lamprid. in Heliogab.* c. 19; *Veget.* l. 1, c. 20, &c.; *Lips. de Milit. Roman.* l. 3, dial. 5.

CRISTA (*Bot.*) the *Cæsalpina pulcherrima et crista* of Linnæus.—*Crista Galli*, the *Rhinanthus crista galli*.—*Crista Pavonia*, the *Guilandina bonducella*.

CRISTA GALLI (*Anat.*) a process of the *Os Ethmoides.*

CRISTA'TUS (*Bot.*) crested. [vide *Crested*]

CRI'THE (*Med.*) κριθή, barley; a grain much recommended by Hippocrates.

CRI'THMUM (*Bot.*) κρίθμος, and κρίθμον, a plant which strengthens the stomach, provokes urine, and opens obstructions in the uterus. *Hippocrat. de Nat. Mul.*; *Dioscor.* l. 2, c. 157; *Plin.* l. 26, c. 8.

CRITHMUM, in the Linnean system, the *Echinophora spinosa.*

CRITHO'DES (*Anat.*) from κριθή, barley, and εἶδος, like; protuberances shaped like barley.

CRI'TICAL DAYS (*Med.*) are those days whereon there happens a sudden change of the disease, or on which it comes to the crisis.—*Critical signs*, signs taken from a crisis, either towards a recovery or otherwise.

CRI'TICI (*Med.*) critical fevers, which terminate with a lateritious sediment in the urine.

CRITO'NIA (*Bot.*) the same as *Kuhnia.*

CRIZZELLING (*Mech.*) a kind of roughness which arises on the surface of some kinds of glass, particularly that which is made of black flints, a crystallized sand, &c.

CRO'ATS (*Mil.*) a regiment of horse formerly in France; so called because at first they were of the country of Croatia.

CROATS (*Man.*) or *Cravats*, horses brought from Croatia, in Hungary, which for the most part beat upon the hand, and bear up to the wind; viz. bear their necks high, thrust out their noses, and shake their heads.

CRO'BYLUS (*Ant.*) κρωβύλος, a caul to wear on one's head, or a roll of hair braided, which belonged to the men, in distinction from the *corymbus*, which belonged to the females; and the *scorpius*, peculiar to boys. *Thucyd. Hist.* l. 1, c. 6; *Poll.* l. 2, § 3; *Petron.* 70; *Interpres in Thucyd.*; *Tertull. de Virg. Vel.* c. 10; *Salmas. Exercit. Plin* p. 536.

CRO'CARDS (*Com.*) a sort of money for some time current in England.

CRO'CHES (*Sport.*) the little buds about the top of a deer's horns.

CRO'CHET DE TRANCHEE' (*Fort.*) the further end of a trench or boyau, which is purposely carried to conceal the boyau, in order to prevent it from being enfiladed.

CRO'CI (*Bot.*) another name for the anthers.

CRO'CIA (*Archæol.*) the crozier or pastoral staff so called, *a similitudine crucis*, which bishops, &c. had the privilege of bearing.

CROCIA'RIUS (*Archæol.*) the cross-bearer, who, like our verger, went before the prelate, and bore his cross.

CRO'CIAS (*Min.*) a precious stone so called from its resemblance in colour to the crocus or saffron. *Plin.* l. 37, c. 11.

CRO'CIDE *Confectio* (*Med.*) a confection recommended by Myrepsus *de Antidot.*

CROCIDI'XIS (*Med.*) κροκιδίξις, a fatal symptom in some diseases, where the patient gathers up the bed-clothes, and seems to pick up substances from them.

CRO'CINUM (*Med.*) κρόκινον, the oil of saffron. *Dioscor.* l. 1, c. 64.

CRO'CIS (*Bot.*) κροκίς, a herb so called from its colour. *Plin. l. 27, c. 17.*

CRO'CKET (*Archit.*) from the French *croc*, a hook; an ornament placed at the angles of pediments, canopies, &c. resembling the buds of trees and the opening leaves in the spring season.

CRO'CODES (*Med.*) a name for trochees of a saffron colour.

CRO'CODILE (*Zool.*) an amphibious animal of the lizard tribe, the *Lacerta crocodilus* of Linnæus, which is an inhabitant of the Nile. It is covered with hard scales, which cannot easily be pierced, except under its belly. It has a wide throat, with several rows of teeth, sharp and separate, which run into one another. Though its four legs are very short, yet it runs with great swiftness, but cannot easily turn itself. It is very long-lived, has a very piercing sight, and buries its eggs in the sand, that the heat of the sun may hatch them. [vide *Crocodilus*]

CROCODILE'A (*Ant.*) κροκοδιλία, the sweet excrement of the land crocodile, from which women made an excellent wash for the face. *Plin. l. 28, c. 8.*

CROCODILOI'DES (*Bot.*) the same as the *Atractylis*.

CROCODI'LUS (*Num.*) the crocodile, which is a native of Egypt, was employed as a symbol of that country on medals, as in the annexed figure of a medal of Julius Cæsar. The inscription AEGYPTO CAPTA. *Goltz. Numis.*

CROCOMA'GMA (*Med.*) κροκόμαγμα, from κρόκος, saffron, and μάγμα, dregs; a trochee made of the dregs of oil of saffron, and other spices. *Plin. l. 21, c. 20.*

CROCO'TA (*Ant.*) a woman's garment of saffron colour, of which Aristophanes speaks under the name of κροκωτός. *Interpres in Aristoph. Ran.; Plaut. Aul. act. 3, scen. 5, v. 47; Cic. de Arusp. Resp. c. 20; Apul. Apol. p. 422; Salmas. ad Tertull. de Pall.*

CROCOTA'RII (*Ant.*) dyers of saffron-coloured garments. *Plaut. Aul. act. 3, scen. 5, v. 47.*

CROCO'TTA (*Zool.*) vide *Corocotta*.

CROCUS (*Bot.*) κρόκος, saffron or crocus, a bulbous plant celebrated by the poets of antiquity for the beauty of its colour and its fragrance.
Hom. Hymn. in Pan.

——— τόθι κρόκος ἠδ᾽ ὑάκινθος
Εὐώδης θαλέων καταμίσγεται ἄκριτα ποίη.

Theocrit. Idyl. 8.

Αἱ δ᾽ αὖτε ξανθοῖο κρόκου ἐνιοῦσα ἀλωιρῳ
Δρέπτον ἐιδμαίνυσαι.

Virgil. in Cir.

——— Aut suave rubens narcissus
Aut crocus alternâ conjungens lilia calthâ.

Stat. l. 3, sylv. 1.

Et tenui Arabum respirant gramine sylvæ
Sicaniisque crocis—

On account of its fragrance, an infusion in wine was sprinkled in the theatre, and on the spectators.
Mart. l. 5, epig. 25.

Hoc rogo non melius, quam rubro pulpita nimbo
Spargere, et effuso permaduisse croco.

Lucret. l. 2.

Et cum scena croco Cilici perfusa recens est,
Araque Panchæo exhalat propter odores.

It was supposed by some to derive its name παρὰ τὸ ἐν κρύει θάλλειν from blowing in the cold weather; but Ovid ascribes its name to the youth Crocus, who was changed into this flower.
Ovid. Metam. l. 4.

Et Crocum in parvos versum cum Smilace flores.

As to its medicinal virtues, saffron was reckoned a most noble cordial, a strengthener of the heart and vital spirits, a resister of putrefaction, and good in all kinds of malignant disorders. *Theophrast. Hist. Plant. l. 7, c. 3; Cic. de Orat. l. 3; Dioscor. l. 1, c. 25; Sen. Epist. 90, &c.; Plin. l. 21, c. 6; Sueton. in Ner. c. 25.*

CROCUS, *in the Linnean system*, a genus of plants, Class 3 *Triandria*, Order 1 *Monogynia*.
Generic Characters. CAL. spathe one-leaved.—COR. tube simple; border six-parted; divisions ovate.—STAM. filaments three, subulate; anthers sagittate.—PIST. germ inferior; style filiform; stigmas three, convolute.—PER. capsule three-celled, three-valved; seeds several, round.
Species. Two species of this well-known bulbous plant are distinguished, namely—*Crocus officinalis, sativus, seu autumnalis*, Officinal Crocus, or Saffron, and—*Crocus vernus*, Spring Crocus. The former of these has, according to Haller, a three-horned stigma that is odorous and aromatic, which the vernal crocus has not. It is not known of what country the crocus is indigenous.

CROCUS is also the name of the *Ixia bulbodicum*.

CROCUS (*Chem.*) a name given by the old chemists to several metalline preparations calcined to deep red or saffron colour, as—*Crocus Antimonii*, or *Metallorum*, sulphuretted oxide of antimony. *Crocus Martis*, green vitriol exposed to the fire till it becomes red, which was marked by the character *fig. 1.*—*Crocus Veneris*, copper calcined, marked with the character *fig. 2.*

CROFT (*Archæol.*) a little close adjoining to a dwelling-house, enclosed for pasture, arable, or any particular use.

CROISA'DE (*Mil.*) vide *Crusade*.

CROI'SES (*Ecc.*) pilgrims who wore a cross on their garments.

CROIX DE ST. LOUIS (*Mil.*) the Cross of St. Louis, a French military order instituted by Lewis the Great in 1693, of which the King is grand master. The cross consists of an enamelled golden fleur de lis, which is attached to the button-hole of the coat by means of a small ribbon, crimson-coloured and watered. On one side is the cross of St. Louis, with this inscription, *Ludovicus magnus instituit* 1693; on the reverse a blazing sword, with the words *Bellicæ virtutis præmium*.

CROME (*Husband.*) a fork with long prongs.

CROMMYXYRE'GMA (*Med.*) κρομμυξυργμία, acid and fetid eructations resembling the smell of onions.

CRONE (*Mech.*) French for a round low tower, covered at the top like a windmill, standing by the sea-side, or the river-side, and turning on a pivot, for the purpose of loading and unloading cargoes.

CRO'NET (*Vet.*) or coronet, the hair which grows over the top of a horse's hoof.

CRONET (*Mech.*) the iron at the end of a tilling spade.

CROOKS (*Mus.*) curved tubes occasionally applied to trumpets and horns, and made moveable, for the purpose of tuning them to different keys.

CROO'TES (*Min.*) a substance found about the ore in lead mines.

CROP (*Husband.*) the produce of any thing which is sown in a field.

CROP (*Orn.*) the craw of a bird.

CRO'PIO (*Bot.*) a small fruit like the Ethiopian pepper. *Clus. Hist. Rar. Plant.*

CRO'PPING (*Vet.*) an operation of cutting the ears or tails of horses short.

CRO'QUANTS (*Polit.*) a faction which committed great depredations in some parts of France during the sixteenth century.

CROQUE'TS (*Cook.*) a certain compound made of a delicious farœ.

CROSE'TTES (*Archit.*) the trusses or consoles on the flanks of the architrave under the cornice.

CRO'SIER (*Ecc.*) a bishop's staff made in the shape of a shepherd's crook, intimating that they are spiritual shepherds.

CRO'SLET (*Her.*) a name for a cross that is crossed at each end, as in the annexed figure. "He beareth *argent* a chevron, *gules* between three cross crosslets, fitchy *sable*, all within a double tressure flowered and counterflowered with fleurs de lis of the second *or*." These are the arms of the Kennedy family.

CROSS (*Ant.*) vide *Crux*.

CROSS (*Her.*) one of the most ancient and noble of all the honourable ordinaries, which contains one-fifth of the field, and is formed by the meeting of two perpendicular with two horizontal lines near the fess point, where they make four right angles: the lines are not continued throughout, but discontinued the breadth of the cross, as *fig.* 1, "He beareth *azure* a cross *or*, by the name of Shelton, Norfolk."

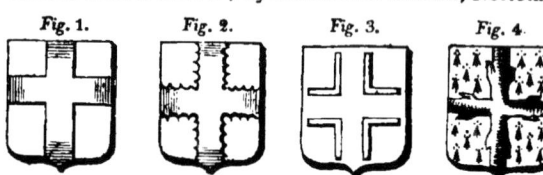

The cross is the most varied in its form of any ordinary. The *plain cross* is simply denominated the cross, as in *fig.* 1; but crosses are likewise diversified with crooked lines, namely,—*engrailed*, as *fig.* 2, "*Or* a cross engrailed *sable*;"—*voided* and *couped*, as *fig.* 3, "*Argent* a cross voided and couped *sable*;"—*raguled*, as *fig.* 4, "*Ermine* a cross raguled *gules*." To these may be added the cross *indented*, *wavy*, *pierced*, &c. There are other forms of crosses which are peculiar to them, of which the following are the principal—*Cross potent*, a cross terminating with the head of a crutch, called a potent, as *fig.* 5.—*Cross*

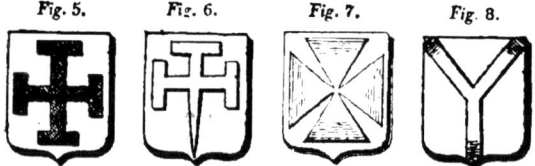

fitchy, i. e. sharp at the end, as *fig.* 6, "*Azure* a cross potent fitchy *or*," which was borne by Ethelred, King of the West Saxons, in 946.—*Cross pattee*, or *formy*, one that is sharp in the centre and broad at the ends, as in *fig.* 7.—*Cross pall*, which in Scotland is called a *Shake-fork*, as in *fig.* 8.—*Cross-milrine*, a cross like a mill link.—*Cross-flury*, the ends of which terminate with fleurs de lis.—*Cross-avelane*, the quarters of which resemble a filbert-nut.—*Cross pommée*, having a ball at each end.—*Cross botonnée*, the ends of which resemble trefoil.—*Cross-moline*, the ends of which turn both ways.—*Cross degraded*, with steps at each end.—*Cross Calvary*, with steps at the base.—*Cross patriarchal*, with two horizontal lines.—*Cross mascally*, composed of mascles.—*Cross bezanty*, composed of bezants.—*Cross of four ermines*,—*cross of four pheons*, &c.—*Order of the Cross*, an order of ladies instituted in 1668 by the Empress Eleonora de Gonzagna, wife of the Emperor Leopold, on the occasion of miraculously recovering a little golden cross from the flames, when the box which contained it was entirely consumed. In this little cross were said to be deposited two pieces of the true cross.—*Cross* is also the name of a knight wearing the cross as a part of the insignia of his order, as the Grand Cross is the first of the three classes into which knights of the order of the Bath are now divided.

CROSS (*Min.*) two nicks cut on the surface of the earth, + which the miners make when they take the ground to dig for ore. This cross gives them three days' liberty to make and set on stones; and for each of these crosses they may have a mear of ground in the vein, provided the stones be set on within the three days.

CROSS (*Num.*) a name given to the right side or face of a coin, the other being called the pile, or reverse: it was so called because the figure of a cross was represented on this side previous to the custom of stamping the head of a prince.

CROSS (*Law*) the figure of a cross made as a signature to a deed, &c. by those who cannot write. This custom originates, without doubt, in the sacredness of the thing represented, and the frequency of its use in all other cases.

CROSS, *invention of the* (*Ecc.*) a feast anciently solemnized on the third of May, to commemorate the discovery which St. Helena, the mother of Constantine, made of the cross, buried deep in the ground of Mount Calvary, on which spot she erected a cross.—*Exaltation of the cross* was another festival, kept on the 14th of September, in memory of the restoration by Heraclitus of the true cross to Mount Calvary, which had been taken away by Chosroes, King of Persia.

CROSS, ST. the ensign or grand standard borne by the crusaders, many of whom also bore the cross on that occasion as a part of their coat armour; whence the use of the cross has since become so frequent in coats of arms. [vide *Cross* under *Heraldry*] A *St. George's cross*, or the red cross in a field *argent*, is now the standard of England.

CROSS (*Mech.*) an instrument used in surveying for the purpose of raising perpendiculars. It consists merely of two pair of sights set at right angles to each other.

CROSS (*Archit.*) any building which is in the figure of a cross, as churches in a *Greek cross*; so likewise a *Market cross*, a pillar in this form erected in a market-place, &c.

CROSS (*Man.*) a term applied to the movements of a horse, as "To make a *cross* in ballotades," or "To make a *cross* in corvets," i. e. to make a sort of leaps or airs with one breath, forwards, backwards, and sideways, in the form of a cross.

CROSS in the hawse (*Mar.*) in French *croix dans les cables*; a phrase applied to a ship when, moored with two bars, she has turned the wrong way, so that the two cables lie across each other.

CROSS-BA'NDED (*Carpent.*) an epithet applied to handrailing when a veneer is laid upon the upper side of the rail, with the grain of the wood crossing that of the rail.

CRO'SS-BARS (*Carpent.*) bars laid across one another. The cross-bar in a carriage, sometimes called the *splinter*, or *master-bar*, is that part into which the shafts are fixed.

CROSS-BARS (*Mar.*) round pieces of iron, bent at each end, and used as levers to turn the shanks of the anchor.

CROSS-BAR-SHO'T (*Gunn.*) a round shot having a long iron spike cast as if it were let quite through the middle.

CROSS-BA'TTERY (*Mil.*) vide *Battery*.

CRO'SS-BEAM (*Carpent.*) any beam that goes across another.

CROSS-BEAM (*Mar.*) a great piece of timber which goes across two other pieces, called *bites*, to which the cable is fastened when it rides at anchor.

CRO'SS-BEARER (*Ecc.*) an officer in the Romish church who bears the cross before the pope, or any primate. A prelate bears a single cross, a patriarch a double cross, and the pope a triple cross, in his arms.

CRO'SS-BI'LL (*Law*) an original bill, by which the defendant prays relief against the plaintiff.

CROSS-BILL (*Orn.*) a sort of Grosbeak, the *Loxia curvirostra* of Linnæus, so called because the mandibles of its beak cross each other.

CRO'SS-BOW (*Mil.*) called by the Latins *arcus balistarius*, a military weapon of defence, in the use of which the English were formerly distinguished. [vide *Bow*]

CROSS-BRE'ED (*Husb.*) a term applied generally to animals, but particularly to horses, dogs, and sheep, where the male is one breed and the female of another.

CROSS-CHOCKS (*Mar.*) in French *espece d'accotars*, pieces of timber fayed across the dead-wood in midships, to make good the deficiency of the lower heels of the futtock.

CROSS-EXAMINA'TION (*Law*) a close and rigid examination on the part of the adversary, consisting of cross questions, in order to elicit the truth.

CROSS-GA'RNETS (*Carpent.*) a sort of hinges made in the form of the letter T.

CRO'SS-GRAINED (*Carpent.*) an epithet applied to building-stuff or timber with fibres in a contrary direction.

CRO'SS-JACK (*Mar.*) pronounced *cojeck*, in French *vergue sèche*, the lower yard on the mizen-mast, which is hence called the *cross-jack* yard, and the sail which is bent to that yard the *cross-jack* sail.

CROSS-MULTIPLICATION (*Arith.*) vide *Duodecimals*.

CRO'SS-PAWLS (*Mar.*) pieces of timber which keep the ship together whilst in her frame.

CRO'SS-PIECE (*Mar.*) in French *râteau*, *ratelier*, a rail of timber extended over the windlass of a merchant ship from the knight-heads to the belfry.

CRO'SS-SPALES (*Mar.*) pieces of timber placed across the ship, and nailed to the frames, securing both sides of the ship together till the knees are bolted.

CRO'SS-STAFF (*Mar.*) vide *Fore-staff*.

CROSS-TI'NING (*Husband.*) a method of harrowing crosswise.

CRO'SS-TREES (*Mar.*) in French *barres traversières des hunes*, pieces of oak timber supported by the cheeks and trestle-trees at the upper ends of the lower and top-masts, athwart which they are laid.

CRO'SS-TRIP (*Sport.*) a term used in wrestling when the legs are crossed within one another.

CRO'SS-WORT (*Bot.*) the *Valantia* of Linnæus, an annual.

CROSSOPE'TALUM (*Bot.*) another name for the *Rhocoma*.

CROSSO'STYLIS (*Bot.*) a genus of plants, Class 16 *Monadelphia*, Order 6 *Polyandria*; so called from κροσσός, a fringe, and ςυλις, a little pillar, because the stigma is fringed or jagged.
Generic Character. CAL. *perianth* turbinate; *segments* ovate.—COR. *petals* four, elliptic; *claw* narrow; *nectary* consisting of corpuscles.—STAM. *filaments* twenty, filiform; *anthers* small.—PIST. *germ* convex; *style* cylindric; *stigmas* four, trifid.—PER. hemispherical; *seeds* very many.
Species. The single species is the *Crossostylis biflora*, a native of the Society Isles.

CROTALA'RIA (*Bot.*) a genus of plants, Class 17 *Diadelphia*, Order 4 *Decandria*; so called from *crotalum*, a rattle, which the legume resembles.
Generic Character. CAL. *perianth* three-parted.—COR. papilionaceous; *standard* cordate; *wings* ovate; *keel* acuminate.—STAM. *filaments* ten, connate; *anthers* simple.—PIST. *germ* oblong; *style* simple; *stigma* obtuse.—PER. *legume* short; *seeds* one or globose.
Species. The plants of this genus are either annuals or shrubs, and mostly natives of the Cape of Good Hope.

CROTOLARIA is also the name of the *Sophora alba*.

CROTA'LIA (*Ant.*) κροτάλια, jewels so worn as to jingle by striking against one another. *Plin.* l. 9, c. 35.

CRO'TALUM (*Ant.*) the cymbal.

CRO'TALUS (*Zool.*) a Rattle-Snake, a genus of animals, Class *Amphibia*, Order *Serpentes*.
Generic Character. *Plates* on the belly.—*Plates* and *scales* under the tail.—*Tail* terminated by a rattle.
Species. The species, which are not numerous, are distinguished principally by the number of plates.

CROTAPHA'GA (*Orn.*) Ani, a genus of animals, Class *Aves*, Order *Picæ*.
Generic Character. *Bill* semioval—*Nostrils* pervious.
Species. The species are the—*Crotophaga Ani*, the Lesser Ani.—*Crotophaga major*, the Greater Ani.—*Crotophaga ambulatoria*, the Walking Ani.

CROTA'PHI (*Anat.*) κροταφοι, the temples; whence *Crotaphites*, the temporal muscles; *Crotaphium* and *crotaphos*, a pain in the head near the temples.

CRO'TCHES (*Mar.*) in French *fourcats*, Italian *croccia*, the crooked timbers placed upon the keel in the fore and hindparts of a ship, upon which the frame of her hull grows narrower below as it approaches the sternpost abaft.—*Crotches*, in French *cornes*, are also pieces of wood or iron, whose upper part opens into two horns or arms like a half-moon. They serve principally to support booms, &c.

CRO'TCHETS (*Print.*) are marks after this manner [ ] to separate what is not a necessary part of a sentence.

CROTCHET (*Surg.*) a curved instrument with a sharp hook for extracting the fœtus.

CROTCHET (*Mus.*) a note of time marked as in *fig.* 1, being of the sixth degree in length, equal in duration to one thirty-second part of a large, the sixteenth of a long, the eighth of a breve, the quarter of a semibreve, and half of a

Fig. 1.   *Fig.* 2.

minim.—*Crotchet rest*, marked as in *fig.* 2, is a character of silence equal in duration to the crotchet.

CRO'TCHETS (*Sport.*) the master teeth of a fox.

CROTE'LS (*Sport.*) the ordure, or dung of a hare.

CRO'TON (*Bot.*) κροτον or κικι, a shrub mentioned by Dioscorides; the seed of which resembles the insect called the *croton* or *tick*; whence it derives its name. From this shrub was extracted an oil that was used for food. *Dioscor.* l. 4, c. 164; *Plin.* l. 15, c. 7.

CROTON, in the Linnean system, a genus of plants, Class 21, *Monoecia*, Order 9 *Monadelphia*.
Generic Character. Female flowers remote from the males on the same plant.—CAL. *perianth* cylindric.—COR. *petals* oblong, obtuse.—STAMEN in the Males; *filaments* ten or fifteen; *anthers* twin.—PISTIL in the Females; *germ* roundish; *styles* three; *stigmas* reflex.—PERICARP in the Females; *capsule* roundish; *seeds* solitary.
Species. Plants of this genus are shrubs or annuals, and mostly aromatic, and natives of the Indies. Among the principal shrubs are the following; namely — *Croton lacciferum, Ricinoides, Ricinus, Halæcus*, seu *Lacca*, Lac Croton, a shrubby tree which exudes a very fine lac spontaneously, but this is distinct from what is called Gum Lac in Europe, which is the work of the red ants. *Croton lineare*, seu *Cascarilla*, Willow-leaved Croton, called in Jamaica Rosemary-tree, because it resembles the Rosemary in smell and appearance.—*Croton tiglium*, seu *Pinus Indica*, Purging Croton.—*Croton Rinocarpus*, seu *Rinocarpus*, Surinam Croton, &c. Among the annuals are the following :—*Croton tinctorium, Ricinoides*, seu *Heliotropium tricoccum*, Officinal Croton, which is the only native of Europe, and from which the dye called *turnsol* is extracted.—*Croton palustre, argenteum*, &c. *Bauh. Pin.*; *Ger. Herb.*; *Park. Theat. Botan.*; *Raii Hist. Plant.*; *Tournef. Instit.*

CROTO'NE (*Bot.*) κροτώνη, a fungous excrescence growing on trees. *Theophrast. Hist. Plant.* l. 1, c. 13.

CROTONE (*Med.*) a fungous tumour on the Periosteum.

CRO'UCH mass (*Ecc.*) or *Crouch-mass-day*, a festival observed by the Roman Catholics, in honour of the holy cross, on the 14th of September.

CRO'UMATA (*Mus.*) χρώματα, from χρόω, to beat; the musical tones resulting from the pulsation of instruments, which are mentioned by *Hippocrates de Vict.* l. 1; *Foes. Œconom. Hippocrat.*

CROUP (*Vet.*) the hindmost part of a horse, including the buttocks and tail, from the haunches to the dock.—*Racking Croup* is when a horse's fore-quarters go right, but his croup in walking swings from side to side. " To gain the *Croup* " is when one horseman makes a demi-tour upon another in order to take him upon the croup. " Without slipping the *Croup*," signifies without traversing, or letting the croup go out of the volt, or the tread of the gallop.

CROUPA'DE (*Man.*) a leap higher than a curvet, in which the horse keeps his fore and hind quarters of an equal height.

CROU'PER (*Man.*) a device put under the tail of a horse to keep the saddle more steady.

CROUTA'DE (*Cook.*) a peculiar manner of dressing a loin of mutton.

CROW (*Or.*) a prolific, social, and clamorous bird, which constitutes, a genus of birds, in the Linnean system, under the name of *Corvus*. The food of the crow is partly animal and partly vegetable.

CROW (*Mech.*) an iron instrument for raising heavy bodies. It is formed to act as a lever, and is employed particularly in moving of timber.

CROW (*Astron.*) vide *Corvus*.

CROW-BERRY (*Bot.*) the *Empetrum nigrum* of Linnæus.—Crow-Foot, the *Ranunculus gramineus, pyrænæus*, &c. a perennial.—Crow-Garlick, the *Allium vineale*, a bulbous root.

CRO'W-FOOT (*Mar.*) in French *arraignée*, a complication of small cords spreading out from a long block, like the small parts which extend from the back-bone of a herring.

CRO'W-NET (*Sport.*) an invention for catching wild fowls in the winter season.

TO CROWD (*Mar.*) to carry an extraordinary force of sail in a ship.

CROWLE (*Mus.*) an old English instrument, called by the French *chrotta*, which was supposed to resemble the flute.

CROWN (*Ant.*) vide *Corona*.

CROWN (*Her.*) a cap of state worn by sovereign princes. Crowns are divided generally into royal and imperial.—*Royal Crowns* were the ancient crowns, which were open and worn by Kings.—*Imperial crowns*, first worn by emperors, are the closed crowns, which have now generally taken place of the open ones. Crowns are moreover distinguished, according to the sovereigns or princes by whom, and the circumstances under which, they are worn, &c.—*Crown of England* is that with which the kings of England are crowned. It is called St. Edward's Crown, because it is made in imitation of the ancient crown supposed to have been worn by that monarch, which was kept in Westminster Abbey, for the use of his successors, till the rebellion, when it was sold with the rest of the Regalia. The one now in use was made after the pattern for the coronation of Charles II, and has remained unaltered for his successors ever since. This very rich imperial crown, as given in *fig.* 1, is embellished with pearls and precious stones of divers kinds, as diamonds, rubies, emeralds, and sapphires, having a mound of gold upon the top of it, which is surmounted by a cross of gold; both these are embellished with precious stones: the mound is also encircled with a band or fillet of gold; and the cross is enriched with three very large oval pearls. This crown is composed of four crosses, pattees, and as many fleurs-de-lis of gold placed on a rim or circlet of gold, all embellished with precious stones. From those crosses arise four circular bars or arches, which meet at the top in the form of a cross, at the intersection whereof is a pedestal, on which the mound is placed. The cap within this crown is of purple velvet lined with white taffeta, and turned up with ermine.—*Crown of State*, so called because it is always worn by the King when he goes in state to Parliament, is distinguished by a very large ruby set in the middle of the four crosses, and by the mound being of one entire stone of a seawater-green colour, known by the name of *aqua marine*. This is made for every succeeding king; and, of course, subject to variation. The one given in *fig.* 2. is the crown which was worn by his late Majesty, George III. A representation of the crowns worn by some of his predecessors may be seen on their coins. [vide *Plates* 31, 32]—*Queen's Crown*, or that worn by the Queen Consort at her coronation, was made for Catherine, Queen of Charles II, in commemoration of Egitha, the Queen Consort of King Edward. This is also a very rich imperial crown similar to King Edward's, but much lighter and smaller. The queens have also a cap called a *circlet of gold*, with which they proceed to the coronation; and also a particular crown, which they wear on other occasions. Among the foreign crowns, the following are the principal.—*Charlemagne's Crown*, vide *Charlemagne's Crown*.—*Papal Crown*, otherwise called the Triple Crown, *tiara papalis*, which is a high cap of silk environed with three crowns of gold, one above another. [vide *Papal Crown*] —*Imperial Crown*, vide *Imperial*.—*Iron Crown*, the crown with which the kings of Lombardy were anciently crowned, which was afterwards used by the Emperors of the West for the same purpose. The emperor Henry VII is said to have introduced the use of four crowns at his coronation in 1310; namely, the *iron crown*, by which it was intended to signify that the monarch would defend his dominions with the sword against all his enemies; a *crown of different metals* to imply that he would select men as his counsellors who were endowed with diverse talents; a *silver crown* to denote that he would be liberal and munificent; and a *gold crown* to denote his superiority over all other men. Buonaparte chose the iron crown for his coronation as King of Italy; and, upon that occasion, instituted the Order of the Iron Crown, which has not survived his fall.—*Turkish Crown*, vide *Turkish Crown*.

CROWN (*Ecc.*) a little circle of hair shaven from the crown of the head, which is the mark and character of the Romish ecclesiastics.

CROWN (*Anat.*) the vertex, top, or highest part of the head.

CROWN (*Mech.*) the upper work of the rose diamond among jewellers, which centers in a point at the top.

CROWN (*Geom.*) a ring comprehended between two concentric peripheries.

CROWN (*Astron.*) vide *Corona*.

CROWN (*Numis.*) a coin in value five shillings, which was first struck in the reign of Henry VIII. and so called from the figure of the crown upon it. [vide *Plate* 31]

CROWN (*Com.*) is a name given to the French *ecu*, and other foreign coins, nearly equal in value to five shillings.

CROWN (*Archit.*) the uppermost member of a cornice, comprehending the *corona* and its superior members.—*Crown of an arch*, the most elevated line or point that can be taken on its surface.

Fig. 1.

Fig. 2.

CROWN *of an anchor* (*Mar.*) in French *le collet d'une ancre*; the lowest end of the shank of an anchor where the arms are united.—*Crown of a cable*, the bights which are formed by the several turns.

CROWN-GLASS (*Mech.*) the finest sort of window-glass.

CROWN-IMPE'RIAL (*Bot.*) a well-known beautiful flower, the *Fritillaria imperialis* of Linnæus, a perennial.

CROWN-OFFICE (*Law*) an office belonging to the Court of King's Bench, of which the King's coroner or attorney there is commonly Master. The Attorney General, or the Clerk of the Crown, exhibits informations in this office for crimes and misdemeanors, the one *ex officio*, and the other by the order of the court.

CROWN-POST (*Carpent.*) the principal upright in truss-roofing, better known by the name of the King-Post.

CROWN-SCAB (*Vet.*) a mealy white scurf growing on the legs of horses.

CROWN-WHEEL (*Mech.*) the upper part of a watch next the balance that drives it by its motion.

CROWN-WORKS (*Fort.*) bulwarks advanced toward the field to gain some hill or rising ground; being composed of a large gorge and two wings, which fall on the counterscarp near the faces of the bastion.

CROWNED *hornwork* (*Fort.*) a hornwork with a crownwork before it.

CROWNED-TOP (*Sport.*) the first head of a deer, the crotchets and buds being raised in the form of a crown.

CROWNING (*Archit.*) the part that terminates any piece of architecture, generally in the form of a Crow's Bill, &c.

CROWNING (*Mar.*) in French *culde pore*; the finishing part of a knot made on the end of a rope. It is performed by interweaving the ends of the different strands artfully among each other, so that they may not become loosened or untwisted.

CROWS-BILL (*Surg.*) a kind of forceps for drawing bullets, &c. out of wounds.

CROWS-FEET (*Mil.*) another name for the *Caltraps*.

CROWS-STONES (*Min.*) a sort of petrefaction, the *Anomia gryphus* in the Linnean system.

CROY (*Archæol.*) Marsh-land. *Ingulph*.

CROY (*Law*) *in Scotch Law* a satisfaction that a judge, who does not administer justice as he ought, is to pay to the nearest of kin to the man that is killed.

To CROYN (*Sport.*) to cry as fallow deer do at rutting-time.

CRO'YSES (*Archæol.*) a term used by Britton for pilgrims, because they wear the sign of the cross on their garments.

CRUCHES *à feu* (*Mil.*) French for earthen pots with two handles filled with grenades, having the intervals between them filled with powder.

CRU'CIAL (*Anat.*) an epithet for some parts of the body which cross each other, as the crucial ligaments of the thigh.

CRUCIAL *Incision* (*Surg.*) an incision made in some fleshy part of the body in the form of a cross.

CRUCIA'LIS (*Bot.*) Mugweed, or Crosswort.

CRU'CIAN (*Ich.*) a fish of a dusky green colour of the carp kind, the *Cyprinus carassius* of Linnæus.

CRUCIANE'LLA (*Bot.*) a genus of plants, Class 4 *Tetrandria*, Order 1 *Monogynia*, so called from *crux*, a cross, because the leaves are placed crosswise.
Generic Character. CAL. *perianth* two-leaved; *leaflets* lanceolate.—COR. one-petalled, funnel-formed; *tube* cylindric; *border* four-cleft.—STAM. *filaments* four; *anthers* simple.—PIST. *germ* compressed; *style* two-cleft; *stigmas* two, obtuse.—PER. *capsule* two, connate; *seeds* solitary.
Species. Plants of this genus are herbaceous annuals, as —*Crucianella angustifolia*, seu *Rubra*, Narrow-leaved Crucianella.—*Crucianella latifolia*, Broad-leaved Crucianella, &c.

CRUCIA'TUS (*Bot.*) vide *Cruciform*.

CRUCIATUS (*Anat.*) a muscle of the thigh.

CRU'CIBLE (*Chem.*) a melting pot, made of earth, tempered so as to endure the strongest fire, for the melting metals and minerals. This was formerly represented by the annexed characters.

CRU'CIFIX (*Ecc.*) a figure representing our Saviour on the cross.

CRU'CIFORM (*Bot.*) or cross-shaped, *cruciformis*, or *cruciatus*; an epithet for a corolla, *corolla cruciformis*, a corolla consisting of four petals, that spread out in the form of a cross, as in the *Brassica oleracea*. These flowers constitute the fifth class in Tournefort's system, and are a principal character in the class *Tetradynamia*. A stigma is also said to be cruciform which is divided into four parts, standing opposite to each other.

CRUCI'TA (*Bot.*) another name for the *Cruzita*.

CRUDARIA (*Min.*) a vein of silver at the top of the mine. *Plin.* l. 33, c. 6.

CRU'DITY (*Med.*) a term applied not only to unripe fruits, but to undigested substances in the stomach, and unconcocted humours in the body.

CRUISE (*Mar.*) in French *compagnie de croisière*; a voyage, or expedition, in quest of an enemy's vessels; so called, because it consists chiefly in sailing to and fro, or crosswise.

CRU'ISER (*Mar.*) a vessel appointed for cruising.

CRU'MA (*Ant.*) κρῦμα, the timbrel, or tabor, and the music made by such instruments. *Mart.* l. 6, ep. 71.

CRUMENTATA (*Zool.*) an epithet for animals furnished with a pouch, or bag, wherein to receive their young in time of danger, as the Opossum.

CRU'NION (*Med.*) κρύνιον; a compound medicine described by Ætius, so called from its diuretic power.

CRU'OR (*Med.*) blood in general; or venous blood, and coagulated blood in particular.

CRUPELLA'RII (*Ant.*) Nobility among the Gauls, who were armed with a complete harness of steel. *Tacit.* l. 3, c. 43.

CRUPI'NA (*Bot.*) a species of the *Centaurea*.

CRU'PPER (*Man.*) vide *Crouper*.—*Crupper-Buckles*, large square buckles fixed to the saddle-tree behind for fastening the crupper.

CRU'RA (*Anat.*) the plural of *crus*, the leg, is applied to some parts of the body which resemble the leg in form, as —*Crura Cerebri*, two medullary columns proceeding from the basis of the brain.—*Crura Clitoridis*, the two spongeous substances which form the *Clitoris*.—*Crura Medullæ oblongatæ*, the two largest roots, or legs, of the *Medulla oblongata*.

CRURÆUS *musculus* (*Anat.*) or *Cruralis*; a muscle of the leg which serves to assist the *vasti* and *rectus musculus* to extend the leg.

CRU'RAL (*Anat. &c.*) belonging to the leg, as the *Crural Artery*, the artery of the thigh which spreads itself among the muscles.

CRURA'LIS (*Anat.*) vide *Cruræus*.

CRUREUS (*Anat.*) vide *Cruræus*.

CRUS (*Anat.*) otherwise called *magna Pes*, is all that part of the body which reaches from the Buttocks to the Toes, including the Thigh, Leg, and Foot.

Crus corvi (*Bot.*) the *Panicum crus corvi* of Linnæus. — *Crus galli*, the *Cratægus crus galli*.

CRUSA'DE (*Mil.*) in French *croisade*, from *crux*, the cross, is a well-known term for the expeditions undertaken by the princes of Christendom for the conquest of the Holy Land, in which every soldier bore a crucifix on his breast, as an emblem of spiritual warfare. The crusades were likewise denominated Holy Wars.

CRUSADE (*Com.*) vide *Cruzado*.

CRU'SMA (*Ant.*) vide *Cruma*.

CRUST (*Nat.*) vide *Crusta*.

CRU'STA (*Ant.*) wood or stone finely inlaid into vessels, so as to form various devices.

CRUSTA (*Med.*) the scurf and scab of a sore.—*Crusta lactea*, a disease to which young children at the breast are particularly subject, consisting of a scurf, or crusty scab, that breaks out on the face and other parts.

CRUSTA *vermicularis* (*Anat.*) the covering or skin of the intestines.—*Crusta villosa*, the inner coat of the stomach.

CRUSTA (*Nat.*) the shells of lobsters, &c.; also the cocar, crust, or cream, which forms on any liquor, as coagulated blood, urine, &c. or on fermentable liquors at a particular stage of the fermentation, as the crust of wine.

CRUSTA *ollæ* (*Bot.*) the *Œdenlandia repens* of Linnæus.

CRU'STULA (*Med.*) Ecchymosis, a discolouration of the flesh from a bruise, where the skin is entire, and covers it over like a shell.

Crustula among oculists is also a disease in the eye, occasioned by the falling of blood from the wounded arteries into the *tunica conjunctiva*.

CRUSTUM (*Archæol.*) a garment of purple mixed with many other colours. *Mon. Angl.* tom. i, p. 210.

CRUSTU'MIA *pyra* (*Ant.*) Pears, much admired by the Romans. *Columel. de Re Rust.* l. 5, c. 10.

CRUSTUMINA'TUM (*Med.*) κρυςυμίνατον, a sort of rob, made of the juice of apples and pears, boiled up with rain-water and honey. *Aet. Tetrab.* 2, serm. 1, c. 138.

CRU'SULY (*Her.*) an epithet for a field or charge strewed with crosses.

CRUTCH (*Mar.*) in French *corne de gui*, a support for the main boom of a brig, cutter, sloop, &c.

CRU'TCHES (*Mar.*) pieces of knee timber placed within side the ship, for the security of the heels of the cant-timbers abaft.

CRUX (*Ant.*) the cross or gibbet on which the Romans hanged their malefactors. It was an ignominious punishment inflicted on slaves, or the lowest sort of people. *Juv.*

Pone crucem servo.

And for its cruelty was denominated *summum*, or *supremum supplicium*; whence *cruciatus*, or suffering the death of the cross, also signified torment. And the cross or tree which was used for this purpose was denominated *arbor infelix*, *infame lignum, cruciatus servilis*, &c.; whence *Sil. Ital.* l. 1, v. 165.

Quem postquam diro suspensu roborem videt.

Scourging commonly preceded crucifixion, after which the offender was either nailed or tied with ropes to the tree, sometimes in an erect posture, and frequently with the head downwards. The figure of the cross also varied much. *Cic. pro Rab.* c. 4; *Dionys. Halic.* l. 5; *Senec ad Marc.* c. 20; *Val. Max.* l. 2, c. 12; *Tacit. Hist.* l. 4, c. 7; *Suet. in Galb.* c. 9; *Justin.* l. 18, c. 7; *Sigon. de Judic.* l. 3, c. 16, *apud Græv. Thes. Antiq. Roman.* vol. 4, &c.

CRUX-A'NDREÆ (*Bot.*) the *Ayxrum crux andreæ* of Linnæus.

CRUX-CERVI (*Anat.*) the bone of a stag's heart.

CRUZADO (*Com.*) a Portuguese gold coin, value about 2*l.* 9*s.* sterling. The cruzado of 400 rees was somewhat less in value. The new cruzado has on the obverse the name of the reigning sovereign, over it a crown, and under it two palms, with 400 at the bottom; on the reverse a cross, with the legend IN. HOC. SIGNO. VINCES.

CRUZITA (*Bot.*) a genus of plants, Class *Tetrandria*, Order *Digynia*.

Generic Character. CAL. *perianth* three-leaved.—COR. *petals* four, ovate.—STAM. *filaments* four, capillary; *anthers* small.—PIST. *germ* ovate, obtuse; *style* two, parted; *stigmas* simple.—PER. none; *corolla* converging; *seed* single.

Species. The single species is the—*Cruzita hispanica*, native of South America.

CRY de Pais (*Law*) the hue and cry which the country, in the absence of a constable, is obliged to set up after any offender, when a robbery or any felony has been committed. 2 Hales P. C.

CRYMO'DES (*Med.*) κρυμώδης, an epithet for a fever wherein the external parts are cold. *Aet. Tetrab.* 2, serm. 1, c. 138.

CRY'OLITE (*Min.*) a sort of aluminous salt.

CRY'PSIS (*Bot.*) a genus of plants, Class 2 *Diandria*, Order 2 *Monogynia*, of the Natural Order of Grapes; so called from κρύπτω, to hide, because the spike of the flowers is concealed within the sheath of the leaf.

Generic Character. CAL. *glume* one-flowered, two-valved *valves* oblong.—COR. *glume* two-valved.—STAM. *filaments* two, capillary; *anthers* oblong.—PIST. *germ* superior; *styles* two; *stigmas* hairy.—PER. none; *corolla* including the single seed.

Species. The single species, an annual, is the—*Crypsis aculeata*, Schœanus, Phleum, Anthoxanthum, Antitragus, seu *Phalaris*, Prickly Crypsis, native of Siberia.

CRYPSO'RCHIS (*Med.*) from κρύπτω, to conceal, and ὄρχις, a testicle; the state of the testicles when they lie hid in the belly.

CRYPT (*Ecc.*) vide *Cryptæ*.

CRY'PTA (*Archit.*) κρύπτη, from κρύπτω, to hide; Crypt, a hollow place or vault under ground. *Juven.* sat. 5, v. 106.

Et solitus mediæ cryptam penetrare Suburræ.

Vitruv. l 6, c. 8; *Sueton. in Cal.* c. 58; *Bald. Lex. Vitruv.* These crypts were afterwards used for religious purposes. [vide *Cryptæ*]

CRY'PTÆ (*Ecc.*) Crypts, subterraneous places, where the martyrs were buried, and the primitive Christians used to perform their devotions; whence the custom originated of building underground chapels, which were also called Crypts, as that of St. Faith's, under St. Paul's, London. *S. Hieron.* l. 12; in *Ezek.* XL.; *Gregor. Turon. Hist.* l. 1, c. 39.

CRYPTÆ (*Anat.*) from κρύπτω, to hide; the little rounded appearance at the end of the small arteries.

CRYPTOCE'PHALUS (*Ent.*) a genus of animals, Class *Insecta*, Order *Coleoptera*.

Generic Character. Antennæ filiform.—Feelers four.—Thorax margined.—Body cylindrical.

Species. The species are distinguished into those which have the feelers equal, those which have the feelers unequal, and those which have the hind ones hatchet-shaped.

CRYPTOGA'MIA (*Bot.*) the name of the twenty-fourth Class in Linnæus' artificial system, comprehending the vegetables whose fructification is concealed, or at least too minute to be observed by the naked eye: whence the origin of the term, which is derived from the Greek κρύπτος, hidden, and γάμος, nuptials. It is divided into four Orders; namely, 1. *Filices*, Ferns. 2. *Musci*, Mosses. 3. *Algæ*, Flags. 4. *Fungi*.

CRYPTO'GRAPHY (*Mech.*) the art of writing in cyphers, or with sympathetic ink, or in general in any concealed manner, from κρύπτος, hidden, and γράφω, to write.

CRYPTO-PO'RTICUS (*Archit.*) a gallery closed on all sides for coolness in summer; a sort of cloister. *Plin. Epist.* l. 5, ep. 6; *Sidon.* l. 2, ep. 2; *Bald. Lex. Vitruv.*

CRYPTOPY'ICA *Ischuria* (*Med.*) a suppression of urine, from a retraction of the penis within the body.

CRYPTO'STOMUM (*Bot.*) a genus of plants, Class 5 *Pentandria*, Order 1 *Monogynia*.

Generic Character. CAL. *perianth* one-leaved, funnel-formed.—COR. one-petalled; *tube* very short; *border* five-cleft; *nectary* broad, arched, and fastened to the base of the corolla.—STAM. *filaments* none; *anthers* five.—PIST. *germ* roundish; *style* cylindric; *stigma* capitate.—PER. *berry* globular, three-celled; *seeds* solitary. Species. The only species is the—*Cryptostomum Gujanense*, seu *Montabea*, a shrub of Guiana.

CRY'STAL (*Min.*) κρύσαλλος, a kind of glass or precious stone, frozen, as it was thought, into that bright substance. The crystal, otherwise called rock crystal, is a species of stone belonging to the quartz or siliceous genus. When the crystals are semi-transparent, or intermixed with opaque veins, they are called *milk crystals*; when in the form of pebbles, they are called *crystals*.

CRYSTAL (*Chem.*) that part of a salt which assumes a regular and solid form on the gradual cooling of its solution.

CRYSTA'LLI (*Med.*) eruptions about the size of a lupin, which sometimes break out over the whole body. They are also called *Crystallinæ*.

CRYSTALLI'NÆ Manus (*Med.*) κρυσάλλιναι χεῖρες, hard hands, so cold that they seem almost to be frozen. *Hippocrat. Epidem.* l. 7.

CRYSTALLINÆ (*Med.*) vide *Crystalli*.

CRY'STALLINE Heavens (*Astron.*) two spheres, conceived by the ancient astronomers, between the *primum Mobile* and the *firmament*, by the first of which they explained the slow motion of the fixed stars, which advance a degree in 70°; by the other, they accounted for the motion of *libration* or *trepidation*.

CRYSTALLINE Humour (*Anat.*) or the *Crystalline Lens*; so called from its transparency like crystal, the pellucid humour of the eye, which serves to transmit and refract the rays of light.

CRYSTALLI'NUM (*Chem.*) a name for white arsenic from its transparency.

CRYSTA'LLION (*Bot.*) vide *Psyllium*.

CRYSTALLIZA'TION (*Chem.*) the reducing of any salt into a regular solid form, by dissolving it in a menstruum, and allowing it to cool, until it shoots into the bodies called crystals. By far the greater number of salts assume the crystalline form; and it has been observed, both by chemists and mineralogists, that every substance has a particular form which it, for the most part, affects when it crystallizes. Thus, common salt is observed to assume the shape of a cube; alum that of an octohedron; saltpetre that of a six-sided prism; sulphate of magnesia that of a four-sided prism; and carbonate of lime is often found in the state of a rhomboid; but this is necessarily subject to great diversity.

CRYSTALLO'GRAPHY (*Lit.*) the description of crystals.

CRYSTALLOI'DES tunica (*Anat.*) the crystalline coat of the eye.

CRYSTA'LLUM *Minerale* (*Chem.*) the *Sal Prunellæ* purified by solution and crystallization.

CRYSTALLU'RGY (*Chem.*) vide *Crystallization*.

CRY'THE (*Med.*) a hard scirrhous immoveable stian in the interior part of the eyelid, containing a pellucid body.

CTE'DONES (*Anat.*) from κτηδών, a rake or comb; the name given to the fibres.

CTE'IS (*Anat.*) from κτείς, a rake; a name for the incisores, from their likeness to a rake.

CTESIPHO'NTIS *Malagma* (*Med.*) a plaster, described by Celsus, l. 5, c. 18.

CUB (*Nat.*) the young of particular beasts, as a fox or a bear.

CU'BA (*Ant.*) a horse-litter or bed.

CUBÆA (*Bot.*) a genus of plants, Class 10 *Decandria*, Order 1 *Monogynia*.
Generic Character. CAL. *perianth* one-leaved.—COR. *petals* five, oblong.—STAM. *filaments* ten; *anthers* oblong.—

PIST. *germ* oblong, pedicelled; *style* capillary; *stigma* acute.—PER. *legume* long, coriaceous; *seeds* several.
Species. The species are trees and natives of Guiana, as the—*Cubæa paniculata* and *Cubæa trigona*.

CU'BARIS (*Ent.*) vide *Aselli*.

CU'BATURE (*Math.*) the finding exactly the cubical solid content of any proposed body, in inches, feet, yards, &c.

CU'BBRIDGE *heads* (*Mar.*) the bulk heads of the forecastle and the half deck.

CUBE (*Math.*) a regular solid body, supposed to be generated by the motion of a square plane along a line equal and perpendicular to one of its sides. It is inclosed by six equal sides or faces, which are square, as in the annexed figure. A die is a small cube.—*Duplication of the cube*. [vide *Duplication*]

CUBE (*Arith.*) or *Cubic Number*, the third power of a number, which is formed by multiplying the number or quantity into itself, and then again into the product; as $3 \times 3 = 9 \times 3 = 27$, the cube $a \times a = a^2 \times a = a^3$.—*Cube root* is the side of a cube number; thus 3 is the root of 27.

CU'BEB (*Bot.*) cubebæ, a small round fruit, less than pepper, the fruit of the *Piper cubebæ*, or *Piper caudatum*. This fruit is aromatic, and good for strengthening the stomach.

CUBI'CULARIUS (*Archæol.*) a chamberlain or groom of the chamber.

CU'BIC EQUATION (*Algeb.*) that in which the unknown quantity rises to the third dimension, as $x^3 = a^3 - b^3$; or $x^3 + rxx = p^6$; or $x^3 + fxx - abx = mmn + pqr$, &c.—*Cubic Foot* is so much of any thing as is contained in a cube whose side is one foot.—*Cubic Hyperbola* is a figure expressed by the equation $xy^2 = a$, having two asymptotes, and consisting of two hyperbolas lying in the adjoining angles of the asymptotes.—*Cubic Number*, vide *Cube*.—*Cubic Parabola*, a curve, as B C D in the annexed figure, having two infinite legs, as C D, C B, tending contrary ways; and if the abscissæ A P, or *x*, touch the curve in C, the relation between A P (*x*) and P M (*y*) is expressed by the equation $y = ax^3, bx^2, cx, d$; or when A falls in C, by the equation $y = ax^3$, which is the most simple equation of the curve.

CUBI'DIA (*Min.*) a genus of spars.

CUBI'LE SALUTATORUM (*Ant.*) a little chapel or closet in a house, wherein the images of the household gods were placed. *Plin.* l. 15, c. 2; *Turneb. Adv.* l. 13, c. 28; *Casaub. in Suet.* p. 78.

CUBILE (*Archit.*) a ground work, or course of stones in building. *Vitruv.* l. 2, c. 8.

CU'BING a *Solid* (*Men.*) vide *Cubature*.

CU'BIT (*Ant.*) a measure frequently mentioned in Scripture, equal to one foot nine inches and 888 decimal parts, according to Arbuthnot.

CUBIT (*Anat.*) cubitus, from *cubo*, to lie or rest, because the ancients used to rest upon it at their meals; the Forearm, or that part between the elbow and the wrist.

CUBIT *Arm* (*Her.*) the hand and arm couped at the elbow, as in the annexed figure.

CUBITA'NS (*Anat.*) an epithet for two muscles of the wrist, one of which, called the *externus*, serves to extend the wrist; and the other, the *internus*, to bend it.

CU'BITAL (*Ant.*) a foresleeve for the arm to the elbow downwards.

CUBO-CU'BE (*Geom.*) the sixth power of any number, i. e. the cube cubed; thus, 64 is a cube cubed, being raised from the multiplication of the root 2 five times into itself.

CUBOI'DES (*Anat.*) a name for the seventh bone of the tarsus of the foot.

CU'CI (*Bot.*) the fruit of a species of the palm. *Bauh. Hist. Plant.*

CU'CKING-STOOL (*Archæol.*) i. e. a choaking-stool; because those who were put into it were almost choaked with the water; a punishment formerly inflicted on scolds and brawling women, who were placed in such a stool and immersed in water, sometimes in a muddy pond.

CUCKOLD-TREE (*Bot.*) the *Mimosa cornigera* of Linnæus.

CU'CKOW (*Orn.*) a well-known bird, the *Cuculus* of Linnæus, which is heard about the middle of April, and ceases to sing at the end of July. It deposits its eggs in the nests of other birds, generally that of the hedge-sparrow, and leaves the care of the young to foster-parents. The eggs are reddish-white, thickly-spotted with black brown spots.

CUCKOW-FLOWER (*Bot.*) a perennial and well-known flower of the field, the *Cardamine pratescens.*—Cuckow-Pint, or Pintle, the *Arum macula*, a tuberous root.

CU'CKOW SPITTLE (*Ent.*) the froth observable on plants, in which the larva of the *cicada spumaria* is found enveloped.

CUCU'BALUM (*Bot.*) or, *Cucubalus*, a herb whose leaves are good against the stinging of serpents. *Plin.* l. 27, c. 8.

CUCU'BALUS, in the Linnean system, a genus of plants, Class 10 *Decandria*, Order 3 *Tryginia*; Natural order of *Caryophyllei*.
Generic Characters. CAL. *perianth* one-leaved, tubular.—COR. *petals* five; *claws* the length of the calyx: *border* flat.—STAM. *filaments* ten, subulate; *anthers* oblong.—PIST. *germ.* oblong; *styles* three, longer than the stamens; *stigmas* pubescent.—PER. *capsule* acuminate; *seeds* very many.
Species. The species are mostly perennials, as—*Cucubalus bacciferus, Silene, Lychnis, Lychnanthus, Viscago, Cucubalum, seu Alsine*, Berry-bearing Campion, White Bottle, White Corn-Campion.—*Cucubalus behen, Viscago, Lychnis, Papaver, seu Behen*, Bladder Campion, or Spatling Poppy.—*Cucubalus Tartaricus*, Hyssop-leaved Campion.—*Cucubalus otites, Viscago, Lychnis otites, &c. samoides, Muscipula*, Spanish Campion, or Catch-Fly: but the following are biennials, namely—*Cucubalus fabarius.*—*Cucubalus viscosus*, and—*Cucubalus Italicus*. *Dod. Pempt.; Bauh. Hist. Plant.; Bauh. Pin.; Ger. Herb.; Park. Theat. Botan.; Raii Hist. Plant.; Tournef. Inst.; Boerh. Ind.*

CUCU'JUS (*Ent.*) a genus of animals, Class *Insecta*, Order *Coleoptera*.
Generic Character. *Antennæ* filiform.—*Feelers* four, equal.—*Lip* bifid.—*Body* depressed.
Species. The principal species are the *Cucujus depressus, sulcatus, rufipes, &c.*

CUCULA'TUM MAJUS (*Chem.*) Spirits of wine.

CUCU'LLA (*Anat.*) or *Cucullaris*, hoodshaped; the muscle otherwise called *Trapezius*.

CUCULLA'NUS (*Con.*) a genus of animals, Class *Vermes*, Order *Intestina*.
Generic Character. *Body* sharp.—*Mouth* orbicular.
Species. The species are mostly viviparous and intestinal, infesting the mammalia, birds, reptiles, and fish.

CUCULLA'RIA (*Bot.*) the *Valantia filiformis*.

CUCULLATUS (*Bot.*) cowled, or hoodlike; an epithet for a leaf, or the corona; *folium cucullatum*, a leaf which is wide at top, and drawn to a point below, in the form of a cone, as in *Geranium cucullatum*; *corona cucullata*, a crown which covers the pistil like a hood, as in *Asclepias*.

CUCU'LLUS (*Ant.*) a cowl or hood, which was anciently used as a covering for the head, to keep off the rain and cold. *Mart.* l. 10, ep. 76.

Pullo Mævius alget in cucullo.

It was likewise called *Cucullio*. *Colum. de Re Rust.* l. 1, c. 8; *Capitol. Ver.* c. 4; *Lamprid. Heliog.* c. 33; *Ferrar. de Re Vest.* l. 2, c. 1.

CUCULLUS was also a cornet of paper that apothecaries and grocers used to put their spices in. *Mart.* l. 3, ep. 2.

CUCULLUS (*Ecc.*) the cowl or hood; was adopted by the monks as a monastic habit. *Niceph. Hist.* l. 9, c. 14; *Cassian de Hab. Monach.* c. 4.

CU'CULUS (*Orn.*) Cuckow, a genus of animals, Class *Aves*, Order *Picæ*.
Generic Character. *Bill* smooth, a little curved.—*Nostrils* surrounded by a small rim.—*Tongue*, arrowed, short.—*Feet* formed for climbing.
Species. The principal species are the—*Cuculus canorus*, Common Cuckoo.—*Cuculus glandarius*, Great Spotted Cuckoo.—*Cuculus cristatus*, the Crested Black Cuckoo.—*Cuculus ridibundus*, Laughing Cuckoo.

CU'CUMBER (*Bot.*) a well-known garden vegetable, the common sort of which is the *Cucumis sativus* of Linnæus.

CU'CUMIS (*Bot.*) σίκυς, cucumer, i. e. *curvimer*, Cucumber; a plant, so called from its round form. The fruit of this plant was reckoned cooling to the stomach, quenches thirst, and provokes urine; but it is indigestible, and produces phlegmatic humours. *Hippocrat. de Diæt.* l. 2; *Theophrast. Hist. Plant.* l. 7, c. 4; *Varr. de Lat. Ling.* l. 4; *Dioscor.* l. 4, c. 154; *Plin.* l. 19, c. 5; *Columel.* l. 2, c. 3; *Gal. de Simpl.* l. 1; *Pallad. in Mart. Tit.* 9; *Geopon. Auct.* l. 12, c. 19.

CUCUMIS, in the Linnean system, a genus of plants, Class 21 *Monoecia*, Order 10 *Syngenesia*; Natural Order of *Cucurbulaceæ*.
Generic Character. CAL. one-leaved, bellshaped.—COR. five-parted; *divisions* ovate.—STAMEN in the males only; *filaments* three, converging; *anthers* lines creeping upwards and downwards; *filaments*, in the females without anthers.—PISTIL, in the females only, *germ* inferior, large; *style* cylindric; *stigmas* three, thick.—PERICARP, in the females only; *pome* three-celled; *seeds* numerous.
Species. This genus comprehends all annuals with herbaceous scandent stems, distinguished in English by the names of the Gourd, Cucumber, and Melon. The following are the principal, namely—*Cucumis colocynthis, seu colocynthis*, the Coloquintida, Bitter Gourd, or Cucumber.—*Cucumis sativus, seu Cucumer*, Common Cucumber.—*Cucumis milo, seu Melo*, Common or Musk Melon.—*Cucumis anguria, seu Anguria*, Round Prickly-fruited Cucumber, &c. *Dod. Pempt.; Bauh. Hist. Plant.; Bauh. Pin.; Ger. Herb.; Park. Theat. Botan.; Raii Hist. Plant.*

CUCUMIS is also a name for the *Anguria trifoliata*.

CUCU'PHA (*Med.*) a cover for the head, made of cephalic spices sown in a cap, and worn against catarrhs, &c.

CUCU'RBIT (*Chem.*) a chemical vessel of glass, for distillations and rectifications, which is made in the shape of a gourd, as in the annexed figures.

CUCU'RBITA (*Bot.*) a genus of plants, Class 21 *Monoecia*, Order 10 *Syngenesia*; Natural order of the *Cucurbitaceæ*.
Generic Characters. CAL. *perianth* one-leaved, bellshaped. COR. five-parted; *divisions* veiny, rugose.—STAMEN, in the males, *filaments* three, converging; *anthers* creeping upwards: STAMEN, in the females, *margin* surrounding.—PISTIL, in the females; *germ* large; *style* conic; *stigma* three-cleft.—PERICARP, in the females, *pome* three-celled; *seeds* very many.
Species. The plants of this genus resemble those of the *Cucumis* very much, being distinguished from them chiefly by the swelling rim of the seed. The principal species are as follow:—*Cucurbita lagenaria*, Bottle Gourd, or Long Gourd.—*Cucurbita pepo, seu Pepo vul-*

garis, Pompion, or Pumpkin Gourd.—*Cucurbita melopepo, seu Melopepo*, Squash Gourd.—*Cucurbita citrullus, Anguria, seu Citrullus*, Water Melon. *Bauh. Hist. Plant.; Bauh. Pin.; Ger. Herb.; Park. Theat. Botan.; Raii Hist. Plant.; Tournef. Inst.; &c.*

CUCURBITA is also the name for the *Tricosanthes anguina*.

CUCURBITA'CEÆ (*Bot.*) the forty-fifth order in Linnæus' Fragments of a Natural Method, and the thirty-fourth of his Natural orders.

CUCURBITI'FERA (*Bot.*) a species of the *Crateva*.

CUCURBITI'NI LUBRICI (*Ent.*) broad worms resembling the seeds of a gourd in shape, that breed in the human intestines, &c.

CUCURBI'TULA (*Med.*) or Cucurbita, σικύα, a cupping-glass, or hollow vessel, made of tin, horn, &c. which was frequently applied to the body in the bath, either with or without scarification. The cucurbita used without scarification was called *Cucurbita cæca*, or dry Cupping. *Hippocrat. Aphor. &c.; Aret. de Curat. Acut. Morb. l. 1, c. 10; Cels. l. 4, c. 2; Cæl. Aurelian. de Acut. Morb. l. 1, c. 11; Plin. l. 28, c. 1; Gal. Isagog. c. 15.*

CUD (*Vet.*) the first stomach of ruminating beasts; and also the food which it contains.

CUD-WEED (*Bot.*) the *Athanasia maritima*, a perennial.

CU'DDY (*Mar.*) a sort of cabin or cook-room in the fore-part, or near the stern, of a lighter, or barge of burden.

CU'DE Cloth (*Archæol.*) a face cloth formerly used in the baptizing of young children.

CUDUPARI'TI (*Bot.*) a tree of Malabar, the leaves of which, if bruised and boiled in milk, and applied to the head, relieve vertigoes.

CUE (*Lit.*) an intimation given to performers what or when they are to speak.

CUI *ante Divortium* (*Law*) i. e. to whom before divorce; a writ empowering a divorced woman to recover her lands from him to whom her husband did alienate them during the marriage, because she could not gainsay it. *F. N. B.* 240; *Reg. Orig.* 233; *New Nat. Brev.* 454.—*Cui in vita*, i. e. to whom in the life of (namely, her husband), a writ of entry for a widow upon her lands alienated by her husband in his life-time, which must contain in it, that during his life she could not withstand the alienation. *F. N. B.* 187, 193; *Reg. Orig.* 232.

CUJAI'RUS (*Bot.*) the *Psidium pyriferum* of Linnæus.

CUJE'TA (*Bot.*) the *Crescentia cujete* of Linnæus.

CUI'NAGE (*Mech.*) the making up of tin into pigs, &c. for carriage.

CUI'POUNA (*Bot.*) a tree growing in Brazil, from whose bark is expressed a juice good for cleansing ulcers. *Raii Hist. Plant.*

CUI'RASS (*Mil.*) a piece of defensive armour, made of iron plate, to cover the body from the neck to the girdle.

CUIRASSI'ERS (*Mil.*) a sort of heavy cavalry armed with cuirasses.

CUISI'NE (*Mil.*) in French signifies literally a kitchen, but is applied to the holes which soldiers dig in rear of the camp for the purpose of cooking their victuals.

CUI'SSES (*Mil.*) armour for the thighs.

CUI'TE (*Min.*) French for the preparation of the saltpetre which is used in making gunpowder.

CUL-DE-FOUR (*Archit.*) or *Cu-de-Four*, a sort of low vault, like an oven.—*Cul-de-Four* of a niche is the arched vault on a plan that is circular.—*Cul-de-Lamp*, a name for several decorations in vaults and ceilings.

CUL-DE-CHAUDRON (*Mil.*) the hollow or excavation left after the explosion of a mine.

CULA'GENIN (*Mar.*) *culage*, the laying up a ship in the dock to be repaired.

CULA'TUM (*Chem.*) calcined.

CULBI'CIO (*Med.*) a sort of strangury, or heat of urine.

CULDEE'S (*Ecc.*) a sect of monks in Scotland so called, *a colendo Deum*, i. e. from worshipping God, because they were much addicted to praying and devotional exercises.

CU'LEUS (*Ant.*) or *Culleus*, a leathern sack for wine or oil. *Fest.*

CULEUS is also a bag in which such as murdered their parents were sewed up and thrown into the sea. *Juv. sat.* 8, v. 214.

*Cujus supplicio non debuit una parari
Simia, nec serpens unus, nec culeus unus.*

Anian. Vet. Interpres de Parricid.; Zonar. Annal. l. 2; Isid. Orig. l. 5, c. 28.

CULEUS was also a measure containing twenty barrels, or forty urns, equal to 180 gallons. *Scæv. Cult. de Pignorat.; Columel. l. 3, c. 3; Cenal. de Ponder. ac Mensur. apud Græv. Thes. Antiq. tom.* 11, p. 1471.

CU'LEX (*Ent.*) the Gnat, a genus of animals, Class *Insecta*, Order *Diptera*.

Generic Character. Mouth with a single valved exserted flexile sheath; *feelers* of three articulations; *antennæ* approximate.

Species. The principal species are, the—*Culex pipicus*, the Common Gnat, called in the West Indies the Musquito Fly.—*Culex trifurcatus, pulicaris, reptans, morio, equinus*, &c.

CULILA'BAN (*Bot.*) the *Laurus culilaban* of Linnæus.

CULI'NA (*Ant.*) 1. A kitchen. *Varr. de Re Rust. l.* 1, c. 13. 2. That part of the funeral pile in which the banquet was consumed. *Fest. de Verb. Sig.* 3. *Culinæ*, in the plural, a public burying ground for the poor. *Frontin. de Contr. Agror.*

CU'LINARY Fire (*Nat.*) a portion of pure elementary or solar fire, attracted by the oily or sulphureous parts of the fuel with such velocity as to break and attenuate them until they are dispersed into air.

CU'LLENDER (*Mech.*) a sieve or large strainer used by cooks, &c.

CU'LLERS (*Husband.*) a name for the worst sort of sheep, or those which are left of a flock when the best are picked out.

CU'LLEUS (*Ant.*) vide *Culeus*.

CU'LLION (*Bot.*) a round root of any herb.

CULLION Head (*Fort.*) a sconce or blockhouse; the same as a bastion.

CU'LLIS (*Cook.*) a strained liquor made of meat boiled.

CULM (*Bot.*) *culmus*, the stalk or stem of corn or grasses, which is usually jointed and hollow. In speaking of the dry stalk of corn it is commonly called *straw*.

CULM (*Min.*) a sort of coal in Wales, very brittle, and burning with little or no flame; the *Bitumen oxygenatus* in the Linnean system.

CU'LMEN (*Archit.*) the Latin word answering to the ridge piece of a roof. *Vitruv. l.* 5, c. 1.

CULMEN *cœli* (*Astron.*) the highest part in the heavens to which a star can rise in any given latitude; whence a star is said to *culminate* when it comes to that point.

CULMI'FERÆ (*Bot.*) the same as *Calamariæ*.

To CU'LMINATE (*Astron.*) is said of a star when it comes to the meridian, or the highest point in the heaven.

CULMI'NIÆ (*Bot.*) the twenty-sixth order in Linnæus' Fragments of a Natural Method.

CU'LMUS (*Bot.*) the culm or stalk of grasses, &c.

CU'LPRIT (*Law*) a word of form used by the clerk of arraignments in trials to a person indicted for a criminal matter when he has registered the prisoner's plea, *Not Guilty*. It is in all probability composed of the words *culpa*, fault, or crime, and *prit*, French for *prehensus*, taken, i. e. taken in the fact, or as some will have it, *prit*, for *prêt*, ready, i. e. ready to prove the fact.

CU'LREACH (*Law*) a caution in the Scotch law given by a lord of regality to punish a malefactor whom he has replevied from the sheriff.

CULTELLA'TION (*Mensur.*) a measuring of heights by parts, and not all at one operation.

CU'LTER (*Ant.*) from *colo*, to till, *cultus*, tilled, a kind of short plough, from which our word *coulter* is derived. *Plin.* l. 18, c. 18.

CULTER was also the knife used in the sacrificing of victims. *Ovid. Metam.* l. 15, v. 134.

——— *Percussaque sanguine cultros*
Inficit.

Senec. Thyest. act 4, scen. 1, v. 688.

Tangensve salsa victimam culter mola.

CULTER *venatorius*, a wood-knife, or small sword, shorter than the *venabulum*, or boar-spear. *Plaut. Aul.* act 3, scen. 2, v. 2; *Tac. Annal.* l. 3, c. 43; *Suet. in Aug.* c. 19; *Turneb. Adv.* l. 9, c. 23; *Barth. Adv.* l. 10, c. 20.

CULTER (*Anat.*) the third lobe of the liver, so called from its resemblance to a knife.

CU'LVERIN (*Mil.*) a piece of ordnance which, *of the least size*, is five inches diameter at the bore, carrying a ball of fourteen pounds weight; *of the ordinary size*, is five inches and 1 quarter diameter at the bore, carrying a ball of 17 pounds weight; *of the extraordinary size*, five inches and a half diameter at the bore, carrying a ball of 20 pounds weight.

CU'LVERTAGE (*Law*) the escheat or forfeiture of the vassal's lands to the lord of the fee.

CU'LVERTAIL (*Carpent.*) or dovetail, the particular manner of fastening boards, by letting one piece into another.

CULVERTAIL (*Mar.*) the fastening the ship's carlings into the beam.

CUMA'NA (*Bot.*) an Indian tree resembling the mulberry, both in its appearance and fruit; the latter of which, when boiled and made into a cataplasm, cures the colic.

CUMANDA-GUA'CA (*Bot.*) a large sort of Indian Kidney-beans.

CU'MBULU (*Bot.*) a tall tree growing in Malabar, the root of which, in a decoction with a little rice, is said to be of service in a symptomatic fever attending the gout.

CU'MERUM (*Ant.*) a kind of large basket used at weddings for carrying the bride's goods and household stuff covered.

CU'MIN (*Bot.*) the *Cuminum cyminum* of Linnæus, an annual.

CUMI'NI (*Bot.*) the *Myrtus cumini* of Linnæus.

CUMINOI'DES (*Bot.*) the same as the *Dagoe*.

CUMI'NUM (*Bot.*) κύμινον, cumin, a plant, the seeds of which are hot, and if drank in wine were thought to produce paleness; whence Horace calls it *exsangue*, bloodless, and Juvenal *pallens*, pale.

Hor. l. 1, ep. 19, v. 17.

——— *Quod si*
Pallerem casu, biberent exsangue cuminum.

Juv. Sat. 5, v. 55.

——— *Pallentis grana cumini.*

Dioscor. l. 3, c. 68; *Plin.* l. 20, c. 14.

CUMINUM, in the Linnean system, a genus of plants, Class 5 *Pentandria*, Order 2 *Digynia*, Natural Order of *Umbellatæ*, or *Umbelliferæ*.

   Generic Character. CAL. *umbel universal*, and *partial* four-parted; *perianth* proper, scarcely visible.—COR. *universal* uniform; *proper* five-petalled.—STAM. *filaments* five; *anthers* simple.—PIST. *germ* ovate; *styles* two; *stigmas* simple.—PER. none; *fruit* ovate; *seeds* two, ovate.

   Species. The only species is the—*Cuminum cyminum*, seu *sativum*, Cumin, an annual, native of Egypt.

CUMINUM is also the name for the *Cuminum hypecoum* of Linnæus.

CU'MMIN-SEED (*Bot.*) the seed of the *Cuminum* of Linnæus, is a long slender seed, not so thick as anise-seed, but much longer, of a rough texture, not easily powdered, unctuous when bruised, of a strong smell, and an acrid pungent taste.

CUMMIN-SEED (*Chem.*) in a chemical analysis is found to yield a quantity of essential oil, an austere phlegm, containing an acid, and a urinous salt.

CUNACA'NTHE (*Bot.*) a shrub bearing grapes like a vine.

CUNA-CERVISIÆ (*Archæol.*) a tub of ale, as mentioned in Domesday-Book.

CUNA'NE (*Bot.*) the large fruit of an Indian tree, which is dried, roasted, and eaten as a remedy against the headache. *Raii Hist. Plant.*

CUNEA'LIS *sutura* (*Anat.*) the suture by which the *os sphenoides* is joined to the *os frontis*.

CU'NEI (*Archit.*) the coins of walls in buildings. *Vitruv.* l. 7, c. 4.

CU'NEIFORM (*Bot.*) or wedgeshaped, an epithet for a leaf.

CUNEIFO'RMIA *ossa* (*Anat.*) the three bones of the *tarsus*.

CUNE'OLUS (*Surg.*) a crooked tent to put into a fistula.

CUNE'TTE (*Fort.*) a deep trench, about three or four fathoms wide, sunk along the middle of a dry moat, to make the passage more difficult.

CU'NEUS (*Ant.*) signifies literally a wedge, but is applied to the seats and benches on which the spectators sat in a theatre, which were narrow near the stage, and broad behind.

Juv. sat. 6, v. 61.

——— *Cuneis an habent spectacula totis*
Quod securus ames?

Wherefore Ausonias speaks of *theatrum cuneatum*.
Auson. de Urb. c. 4, v. 5.

Circus et inclusi moles cuneata theatri.

Vitruv. l. 5, c. 6; *Sueton. in Aug.* c. 44; *Apul. Flor.* p. 799; *Bald. Lex. Vitruv.*; *Salmas. Exercitat. Plin.* p. 645.

CUNEUS (*Mil.*) a company of foot drawn up wedgewise, or like a triangle, in this form [△] the better to break the ranks of the enemy. *Liv.* l. 8, c. 10, l. 22, c. 47, l. 32, c. 17; *A. Gell.* l. 10, c. 9; *Veget.* l. 3, c. 19; *Agath. Hist.* l. 2: *Suidas*.

CUNEUS (*Archæol.*) a mint or place to coin money; whence *cuneum Monetum*, the king's stamp for coining money.

CUNI'CULUS (*Ant.*) a coney-burrow, or a mine under the earth. *Cæs. de Bell. Gall.* l. 7, c. 22; *Joseph. de Bell. Ind.* l. 3, c. 12; *Veget.* l. 4, c. 24.

CU'NILA (*Bot.*) κυνίλη, the name for the *Origanum*, according to Dioscorides. *Dioscor.* l. 3, c. 32.

CUNILA, in the Linnean system, a genus of plants, Class 2 *Diandria*, Order 1 *Monogynia*.

   Generic Character. CAL. *perianth* one-leaved.—COR. one-petalled.—STAM. *filaments* two, filiform; *anthers* twin.—PIST. *germ* four-parted; *style* filiform; *stigma* two-cleft.—PER. none; *seeds* four.

   Species. The principal species are—*Cunila mariana*, seu *satureia*, Mint-leaved Cunila, a perennial, native of the North of Europe.—*Cunila pulegioides*, seu *Melissa*, Penny-Royal-leaved Cunila, an annual, native of the South of France, &c.

CUNILA'GO. (*Bot.*) Fleabane, a kind of savory.

CU'NNING a ship (*Mar.*) directing the person at the helm how to steer her.

CUNNINGHA'MIA (*Bot.*) a genus of plants, Class 4 *Tetandria*, Order 1 *Monogynia*.

   Generic Character. CAL. *perianth* one-leaved.—COR. one-

petalled; *tube* short.—Stam. *filaments* four; *anthers* roundish.—Pist. *germ* roundish; *style* filiform, bifid; *stigmas* obtuse.—Per. *berry* ovate; *seed* single.
Species. The single species is, the—*Cunninghamia carmentosa*, a shrub.

CUNO′NIA (*Bot.*) a genus of plants, Class 10 *Decandria*, Order 2 *Digynia*, called after J. C. Cuno, a Dutch botanist and poet.
Generic Character. Cal. *perianth* five-leaved.—Cor. *petals* five, obovate.—Stam. *filaments* ten, subulate; *anthers* roundish, twin.—Pist. *germ* conic, *styles* two; *stigmas* obtuse.—Per. *capsule* oblong; *seeds* very many.
Species. The only species is, the—*Cunonia Capensis*, a shrub, and a Cape plant.

Cunonia is also a trivial name for a species of *Antholyza*.

CUNTEY-CUNTEY (*Law*) a kind of trial mentioned by Bracton, which seems to signify a trial by the ordinary jury. *Bract. l. 4, tract. 3, c. 18.*

CU′NTOR (*Orn.*) an American Eagle. [vide *Condur*]

CUP (*Mech.*) a vessel of various forms, and for various domestic purposes. but particularly for drinking out of.

CUPA (*Ant.*) a large round vessel which was used for holding wine. Vessels of the same name, when empty, were also used for bearing up the hulls of ships when they were careened.
Luc. l. 4, v. 420.

Namque ratem vacuæ sustentant undique supæ.

Varr. apud Nonn. l. 2, c. 113; Herodian. l. 4, c. 8; Capitol. Maximin. c. 22; Veget. l. 3, c. 7; Casaub. Salmas. in Capitol.; Scheff. de Mil. Nav. Addend. p. 320.

CUPA′MINI (*Bot.*) the *Azalea Indica* of Linneus.

CUPA′NIA (*Bot.*) a genus of plants, Class 8 *Octandria*, Order 1 *Monogynia*.
Generic Character. Cal. *perianth* five-leaved.—Cor. *petals* five-cowled.—Stam. *filaments* eight; *anthers* incumbent.—Pist. *germ* ovate; *style* short; *stigma* obtuse.—Per. *capsule* coriaceous; *seed* solitary.
Species. The species are trees, as the—*Cupania tomentosa*, seu *Trigonis.*—*Cupania glabra saponarides*, &c.

CUPE′LLA (*Chem.*) a chemical vessel made of earth, ashes, or burnt bones, and in which assay-masters try metals. It suffers all baser ores, when fused and mixed with lead, to pass off, and retains only gold and silver. [vide *Chemistry*]

CUPELLA′TIO (*Chem.*) the process of purifying the perfect metals by the addition of lead, which, at a due heat, becomes vitrified, and in that state carries off all other vitrified metals of the baser sort, leaving those of the perfect kind in a state of purity.

CUPERO′SA (*Min.*) Copperas.

CUPHE′A (*Bot.*) the *Lythrum cuphea* of Linnæus.

CU′PHOS (*Med.*) κύφος, an epithet signifying properly light; but when applied to aliments it imports easily digestible; and to humours mild and gentle.

CUPI (*Bot.*) a species of the *Condeletia* of Linnæus.

CU′POLA (*Archit.*) a roof, or vault, rising in a circular or elliptic form, otherwise called the *Tholus*, or *Dome*.

CU′PPING-GLASS (*Surg.*) a sort of glass vessel applied to the fleshy part of the body, for the drawing away corrupt blood and humours.

CUPRE′SSO-PINULUS (*Bot.*) a species of the *Brunea* of Linnæus.

CUPRE′SSUS (*Bot.*) κυπάρισσος, Cypress; a tree that grew to a remarkable height, particularly in Crete, the wood of which being very durable was used for the building of ships, as we learn from the prophet Ezekiel, xxiii. 5. Among the Greeks and Romans it was planted at the doors of the great when they *died*, and served as an emblem of death.

Lucan. l. 3, v. 442.

Et non plebeios luctus testata cupressus.

Wherefore it is called by Virgil *atra* and *feralis*, by Horace *invisa*, &c. by Statius *mæsta*, &c.
Virg. Æn. l. 3.

Aggentur tumulo tellus, stant manibus aræ
Cæruleis mæstæ vittis, atrâque cupresso.

Virg. Æn. l. 6.

Ingentem struxere pyram cui frondibus atris
Intexerunt latera, et ferales ante cupressos
Constituunt.

Hor. Carm. l. 2, od. 14, v. 22.

— Neque harum, quas colis, arborum
Te, præter invisas cupressos,
Ulla brevem dominum sequetur.

Stat. Sylv. l. 4.

— tempus nunc ponere frondes
Phœbe tuas, mæstaque comam damnare cupresso.

According to Ovid the cypress derives its name from Cyparissus, the son of Amicleus, who was changed into this tree. *Plat. de Leg. l. 3; Thucyd. l. 2, c. 34; Theophrast. Hist. Plant.; Cato de Re Rust.*

Cupressus, *in the Linnean system*, a genus of plants, Class 21 *Monoecia*, Order 9 *Monadelphia*, Natural Order *coniferæ*.
Generic Character. Male flowers disposed in an ament, female flowers heaped into a roundish cone on the same plant.—Cal. *ament* common in the male; *strobile* common; in the females roundish.—Cor. none.—Stam. in the males; *filaments* none; *anthers* four, borne on the calycine scale.—Pist. in the female; *germ* scarcely evident.—Per. none; *seeds* in the females several, oblong.
Species. The principal species are the—*Cupressus sempervirens*, seu *Cupressus*, the Evergreen Cypress.—*Cupressus disticha*, Deciduous Cypress-Tree.—*Cupressus thyoides*, White Cedar, or Arbor Vitæ.—*Cupressus pendula*, Portugal Cypress.—*Bauh. Pin.; Raii Hist. Plant.*

Cupressus is also the name of the *Thuja articulata*.

CU′RA *avenacea* (*Med.*) a decoction of oats and succory roots.

CU′RASSON (*Orn.*) a bird of South America, the *Crax* of Linnæus, three feet long, which inhabits the mountains and woods, feeding on fruits and roosting on trees.

CU′RATE (*Ecc.*) *Curator*; he who represents the incumbent of a parson, or vicar, and takes care of divine service in his stead.

CURATE′LA (*Law*) the office of an administrator to an infant, or lunatic.

CURATE′LLA (*Bot.*) a genus of plants, Class 13 *Polyandria*, Order 2 *Digynia*.
Generic Character. Cal. *perianth* five-leaved.—Cor. *petals* three or four, roundish.—Stam. *filaments* very many; *anthers* roundish.—Pist. *germ* two-parted; *styles* two; *stigmas* headed.—Per. *capsule* two-celled; *seeds* in pairs.
Species. The single species is the *Curatella Americana*.

CURA′TOR (*Ant.*) signified generally an overseer, surveyor, or commissioner, to which some other word was affixed to designate his office as—*Curator Aquarum*, surveyor of the water-works; *Curator Anonæ*, overseer of the public granary, or clerk of the market; *Curator Calendarii*, he who controlled the public accounts of each city, and put out the public monies to interest; *Curator Ludorum*, master of the public games; *Curatores Viarum*, commissioners of the high ways, &c. to which frequent allusions are made in the inscriptions as well as writings of the Romans. *Cic. ad Attic. l. 1; Varr. de Lat. Lin. l. 7, c. 13; Tacit. Annal. l. 11, c. 35; Plin. l. 5, ep. 15; Plut. in Cæs.; Lamprid. Alex. Sever. c. 33; Cassiod. Var. l. 7, c. 13; Panciroll. Nolit. Dign. Imper.; Occident. de Magistr. Mu-*

nicip. et Descript. Urb. Rom. apud Græv. Thes. Antiq. Roman. tom. 3.

CURB (*Man.*) a chain of iron made fast to the upper part of the branches of the bridle; whence the phrase, "To give a leap upon the curb," i. e. to shorten the curb by laying one of the mails, or S like joints of the chain, over the rest.

CURB (*Vet.*) a tumour situated on the back part of the hinder leg of a horse immediately below the hock.

CURB (*Archit.*) signifies generally whatever serves as a check or restraint, and is applied to different parts of a building, as a—*Curb for Brick steps*, a timber-nosing to prevent them from wearing.—*Curb Plate*, a wall-plate in a circularly ribbed dome, &c.—*Curb Rafters*, the upper rafters on both sides in a curb roof.—*Curb Roof*, a particular kind of roof consisting of four sides.—*Curb-stones*, the stones which separate the carriage-way from the foot-path.

CU'RCAS (*Bot.*) the Barbadoes nut; a drastic purge. It is the *Iatropha curcas*, in the Linnean system.

CURCULI'GO (*Bot.*) a genus of plants, Class 23 *Polygamia*, Order 1 *Monoecia*; so called because its seed has a process resembling the *rostrum*, or beak of the *Curculio*.
Generic Character. Hermaphrodite flowers few, male flowers many.—CAL. none.—COR. petals six, oblong.—STAM. filaments six; anthers linear.—PIST. in the hermaphrodite flowers; germ sessile; style very short; stigma large, tapering.—PER. capsule three-celled; seeds one to four.
Species. The only species is the *Curculigo orchioides*, a tuberous root.

CURCU'LIO (*Ent.*) a genus of animals, Class *Insecta*, Order *Coleoptera*.
Generic Character. Antennæ clavate; feelers 4, filiform.
Species. The larvæ of this tribe have six scaly legs, and a scaly head. They infest granaries, and live upon the grain. The species are distinguished into those which have the jaw cylindrical toothed, called by Fabricius the *Curculio*; and into those having the lip bifid and the jaw bifid, called the *Anthribus*.

CURCU'MA (*Bot.*) Turmeric, an Indian plant, which was formerly called *cyperus*.
CURCUMA, in the Linnean system, a genus of plants, Class 1 *Monandria*, Order 1 *Monogynia*.
Generic Character. CAL. *perianth* superior.—COR. one-petalled; *nectary* one-leaved. — STAM. *filaments* five; *anthers* adnate.—PIST. *germ* roundish; *style* length of the stamens; *stigma* simple.—PER. *capsule* roundish, three-celled; *seeds* very many.
Species. The species are mostly perennials, as—*Curcuma rotunda*, Round-rooted Turmeric.—*Curcuma longa*, seu *Amomum Curcuma*, Long-rooted Turmeric; but the—*Curcuma pallida* is an annual.

CURD (*Nat.*) the coagulum of milk.

CURE (*Falcon.*) a medicine given to hawks in form of little balls, or pellets of hemp, cotton, or feathers, to imbibe or drink up their phlegm.

CU'RFEW (*Law*) contracted from the French *couvre-feu*, i. e. cover or put out the fire; a law made by William the Conqueror that all persons should put out their fires and lights, and go to bed at eight o'clock on the ringing of a bell.—*Curfew* signified also the bell, and the ringing of this bell, which announced the hour for putting out fire and candle.

CU'RIA (*Ant.*) the place where they conducted *curas publicas*, the public concerns, the council-house, or state-house. According to Varro, the *Curiæ* were of two kinds; those which were set apart for the priests to settle the religious concerns of the state, and those which were devoted to civil matters, as the senate-house, and the hall, or moot-house of every tribe, or ward. The *Curia* was also the assembly or ward itself. *Varr. de Lat. Ling.* l. 4; *Aul. Gell.* l. 14, c. 7; *Sigon. de Ant. Jur. Roman.* l. 1, c. 3; *Manut. in Cic. Ep. ad Famil.* l. 4.

CURIA (*Law*) signifies generally a court, but it was taken particularly for the assemblies of bishops, peers, and great men of the realm, whom the kings of England used to call together at the chief festivals, which were named *solemnis curia, Augustalis curia, curia publica*, &c. It is also used sometimes for the feudatory, or other customary tenants, who did their suit and service at the court of their lord.—*Curia advisare vult*, the deliberation which a court of judicature sometimes takes where there is any point of difficulty before they give judgment in a cause.—*Curia Cursus Aquæ*, a court held by the lord of the manor of Gravesend for the better management of barges and boats using the river Thames.—*Curia claudenda*, a writ to compel another to make a fence or wall which he ought to make between his land and the plaintiff's. *Reg. Orig.* 155; *New. Nat. Brev.* 282, &c.—*Curia Domini*, the lord's hall or court, where all the tenants attend at the time of keeping courts.—*Curia penticiarum*, a court held, by the sheriff of Chester, in a place there called Pendice or Pentice.

CURIA'LES (*Ant.*) 1. Those who were of the same curia, ward, or tribe. *Dionys. Hal.* tom. ii. p. 124; *Cic. de Offic.* l. 2, c. 18. 2. The chiefs in every city answering to the head-boroughs, or tithing-men of modern times. *Isidor. Orig.* l. 9, c. 4; *Turneb. Adv.* l. 30, c. 31; *Salmas. in Vopisc. Aurel.* c. 33.

CURIA'TA (*Ant.*) vide *Comitia*.

CURIME'NTOS (*Med.*) a Portuguese name for pains in the limbs, which are relieved by a warm bath.

CURLED (*Bot.*) *crispus*, an epithet for a leaf or nectary; *folium crispum* is a leaf, the periphery of which is larger than the disk admits, wherefore it becomes waved, as in Curled Parsley; *nectarium crispum*, a nectary having the cups waved or curled, as in *Narcissus pseudo-narcissus et minor*.

CU'RLEW (*Orn.*) a waterfowl with blue legs and black wings, the *Scolopax aquatica* of Linnæus, which inhabits moist and fenny places, feeds on worms and marsh insects, and lays four eggs of an olive-brown colour. The same name is also given to several species of the *Scolopax*.

CU'RLING (*Carpent.*) an epithet for timber, the grain of which turns or curls about so as to make it less manageable by the tool.—*Curling-stuff* is near akin to what is termed cross-grained.

CU'RLINGS (*Sport.*) the little spotted curls with which the burr of a deer's head is powdered.

CU'RMI (*Med.*) κύρμι, a drink made of barley answering to our common ale. *Dioscor.* l. 2, c. 110.

CU'RNOCK (*Archæol.*) a measure containing four bushels, or half a quarter. *Flet.* l. 2, c. 12.

CU'RRANT (*Com.*) vide *Current*.

CURRANT (*Bot.*) the well-known fruit of a shrub, classed under the *Ribes* in the Linnean system.

CURRA'NTO (*Mus.*) or *currant*, a running French dance; also a musical air consisting of triple time.

CU'RRENCY (*Com.*) the paper, stamped in the English colonies, which passed current for money: the term has since been employed for paper-money in general issued by authority.

CU'RRENT (*Nat.*) the slope of any ground which serves to discharge the water.

CU'RRENT-MONEY (*Com.*) that which passes at a fixed value.

CU'RRENTS (*Mar.*) impetuous streams of water, which, in certain latitudes, run and set on particular points of the compass.

CURRI'CULUS (*Archæol.*) the year, or the course of a year.

CU'RRIER (*Mil.*) a kind of piece, formerly used in sieges,

of the same calibre and strength as a harquabuss, but having a longer barrel.

CU'RRIERS, Company of (Her.) were incorporated in 1438, in the 12th of King Henry I, and bear, for their armorial ensigns, "Sable, a cross engrailed, or, between four pair of shears in saltire, argent." The crest two arms, the hands holding a share. The supporters a buck, or, and a goat, argent. The motto Spes nostra Deus.

TO CURRY a horse (Man.) to rub him down with the curry-comb.

CURRY-COMB (Husband.) an iron tool for the dressing of horses.

CURSITOR (Law) an officer belonging to the Chancery, who makes out original writs for any particular county or shire.

CURSO'NES terræ (Archæol.) ridges of land.

CU'RSOR (Mech.) a little brass ruler representing the horizon.

CU'RSORES (Ant.) 1. Σταδιοδρομοι, runners at a race. Poll. Onom. l. 3, segm. 146. 2. The vancouriers of an army. Ammian. Marcell.

CURSU'MA (Bot.) vide Chelidonium.

CURSU'TA (Bot.) vide Gentiana.

CU'RTAIL (Man.) the name given to a horse's tail after it has been docked.

CURTAIL double (Mus.) an instrument, formerly so called, that played the bass.

CU'RTAIN (Fort.) the front of a wall, or fortified place between two bastions.

CURTA'NA (Archæol.) or curteyn, a name for King Edward the Confessor's sword without a point, an emblem of mercy, which is carried before the Kings and Queens of England at their coronation.

CU'RTATE distance (Astron.) the distance of a planet's place from the sun reduced to the ecliptic. [vide Astronomy]

CURTA'TION of a planet (Astron.) the difference between the distance of a planet from the sun and curtate distance.

CU'RTESY (Law) vide Courtesy.

CU'RTEYN (Archæol.) vide Curtana.

CURTI cone (Geom.) a cone whose top is cut off by the plane parallel to its basis.

CU'RTILAGE (Archæol.) a piece of ground lying near a dwelling house. Stat. 4 Ed. 1, c. 1; 35 Hen. 8, c. 4; 39 Eliz. c. 10.

CU'RTILES terræ (Law) court-lands, or lands properly belonging to the court or house of a lord of the manor. Spelm. of Feuds. c. 5.

CURTI'SIA (Bot.) a genus of plants, Class 4 Tetrandria, Order 1 Monogynia, called after Curtis, the botanist, and author of the Flora Londinensis.
Generic Character. CAL. perianth one-leaved four-parted.—COR. four-petalled.—STAM. filaments four; anthers ovate.—PIST. germ superior; style subulate; stigma four or five-cleft.—PER. drupe subglobular; seed nut roundish.
Species. The single species is Curtisia faginia, seu Sideroxylon, Beech-leaved Curtisia, or Hassaquay-Tree, native of the Cape of Good Hope.

CU'RVATURE of a line (Geom.) is that bending or flexure by which it becomes of any particular form, &c. as the curvature of a circle, the property of which is that every point in the circumference is equidistant from a point in the interior called the centre.—Circle of Curvature, or circle of the same curvature, is a circle which touches a curve in a point so that no other circle, touching it in the same point, can pass between it and the curve. This is otherwise called the osculating circle, because it is the most intimately connected with the curve.—Radius of curvature is the radius of the circle of curvature.—Double Curvature is a term applied to the curvature of a line which twists so that all the parts of it do not lie in the same plane as the rhumb-line, or the loxodromic curve.

CURVE (Geom.) a line whose parts incline different ways, in distinction from a straight line, which lie in the same direction. The principal parts of every curve are the Diameter, the Vertex, the Axis, the Ordinates, or Applicates, Absciss, and the Centre; thus, in the annexed figure, the line A D, which bisects all the parallel lines, M N, is called a Diameter; the point A, where the diameter meets the curve, is the Vertex; when the line A D bisects all the parallels at right angles it is called the Axis; the parallel lines M N, M N, M N, &c. are the Ordinates, P M or P N the Semiordinate; or, as is more usual, the latter is the ordinate, and the former the double ordinate: any portion of the diameter, as A P between the vertex and another fixed point, is called the absciss, and that point in which all the diameters meet is called the Centre. This definition of a diameter, however, respects the Conic Sections only. [vide Conic Sections, Ordinates, Diameter]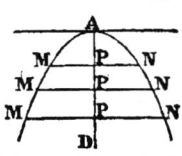

Curves are distinguished into Algebraical or Geometrical, and Transcendental or Mechanical.—Algebraical or geometrical curves are those in which the relation of the absciss A P to the ordinates P M can be expressed by a common algebraic equation; thus, suppose the curve to be a circle, and the radius $AC = r$, the absciss $AP = x$, the ordinate $PM = y$; then, according to the nature of the circle, the rectangle $AP \times PB$ being always $= PM^2$, therefore the equation is $x \cdot (2r - x) = y^2$, or $2rx - x^2 = y^2$, which is the equation that defines this algebraical curve. Curves have been distinguished into different orders, according to the number of the equation expressing the relation between its ordinates and abscisses. Curves of the First Order comprehend the circle and conic sections. Those of the second order, according to the enumeration of Sir Isaac Newton, are reducible to the four following cases of equations, expressing the relation between the ordinate and absciss; namely,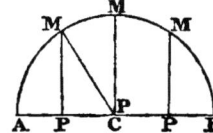

In the 1st case, $xy^2 + cy = ax^3 + bx^2 + cx + d$
2d $xy = ax^3 + bx^2 + cx + d$
3d $y^2 = ax^3 + bx^2 + cx + d$
4th $y = ax^3 + bx^2 + cx + d$

Under these cases are included curves of different forms, which he distinguishes, as follows, into—Inscribed hyperbola, which lies wholly within the angle of the asymptotes.—Circumscribed hyperbola, which cuts the asymptotes, and contains the parts cut off within its own periphery.—Ambigenal hyperbola, having one of its infinite legs inscribed, and the other circumscribed.—Converging hyperbola, one whose legs tend towards each other.—Diverging hyperbola, when the legs tend different ways.—Cross-legged hyperbola, which has its legs convex different ways.—Conchoidal hyperbola, when the asymptote has a concave vertex and diverging legs.—Anguineal hyperbola, that which cuts asymptote with contrary flexures.—Cruciform hyperbola, which cuts its conjugate across.—Nodated hyperbola, which, returning around, cuts itself.—Cuspidated hyperbola, one whose parts concur in the angle of contact, and there terminate.—Pointed hyperbola, one whose conjugate is oval

1

and infinitely small.—*Redundant hyperbola*, is that whose number of legs exceeds that of the conic hyperbola.—*Deficient hyperbola* has but one asymptote, and only two hyperbolic legs, &c. *Newton. Enumerat. Lintesh. Ord.* &c.

Parabolas are in like manner denominated *converging, diverging, cruciform,* &c.

Transcendental or *mechanical curves* are such as cannot be so easily defined or expressed by an algebraical equation. —*Rectification, Inflection, Quadrature of Curves.* [vide *Rectification,* &c.]—*Curves of double curvature,* a curve, all the parts of which are not in the same plane.—*Family of curves,* an assemblage of several curves, of different kinds, all defined by the same equation, of an indeterminate degree, but differently, according to the diversity of their kind: thus, suppose an equation of an indeterminate degree, $a^{m-1} x = y^m$, if $m = 2$, then will $a x = y^2$; if $m = 3$, then will $a^2 x = y^3$; if $m = 4$, then will $a^3 x = y^4$, &c.; all which curves are said to be of the same family or tribe.—*Catacaustic* and *diacaustic curves.* [vide *Catacaustic,* &c.]—*Exponential curve,* that which is defined by an exponential equation, as $a x^x = y$.—*Logarithmic curve.* [vide *Logarithmic*]—*Curve reflectoire,* is so called because it is the appearance of the plane bottom of a basin covered with water, to an eye perpendicularly over it.—*Radical curves,* a name given by some authors to curves of the spiral kind.—*Regular curves* are such as have their curvature turning regularly and continually the same way, in distinction from the *irregular curves,* or those which have points of contrary flexure.

CU′RVED (*Bot.*) *incurvus*, bowed or bent inwards; an epithet applied to legumes and prickles; curved or bowed outwards, *recurvus*, an epithet for leaves and prickles.

CU′RVET (*Man.*) an air in which the horses legs are more raised than in the demivolts, being a kind of leap up and a little forwards.

CURU′RU-APE (*Bot.*) a scandent tree growing in Brazil, bearing pods, which contain seeds like beans. The green leaves bruised and applied to recent wounds are said to cure them by the first intention.

CURU′TA-PALA (*Bot.*) a shrub growing in Malabar, the bark of whose root, when bruised and drank with warm water, cures the diarrhœa.

CURU′LIS (*Ant.*) Curule, from *currus*, a chariot; an epithet for what appertained to a chariot, was applied to magistrates, their dignity, &c.—*Curules magistratus,* were consuls, censors, prætors, and ædiles, who were so called, as some suppose, because they were carried in a chariot. On this account the ædiles were, in an especial manner, called *Curule*.—*Curulis sella,* the curule chair, a chair of estate, which was made of ivory, and placed in a chariot, wherein the head officers of Rome were carried to the council.

Lucan. l. 5.

Lentulus è celsa sublimis sede profatur.

Hor. l. 1, ep. 6, v. 53.

Cuilibet hic fasces dabit, eripietque curule
Cui volet, importunus, ebur.

Juv. sat. 5, v. 91.

——— illi sellas donare curules
Illum exercitibus præponere, &c.

Ovid. Pont. l. 4, el. 5, v. 18.

Signa quoque in sella nostem formata curuli.

It was also taken for the tribunal or seat of justice.
Mart. l. 11, ep. 99, v. 17.

Sedeas in alto tu licet tribunali
Et è curuli jura gentibus reddas.

Silius Italicus deduces its origin from the town of Vetulonis, now Viterbo.
Ital. l. 8, v. 147, speaking of this town,

Hæc altas eboris decoravit honore curules.

CURUR′LET (*Orn*) a sort of plover, the *charadrius* of Linnæus.

CUSCU′TA (*Bot.*) a genus of plants, Class 4 *Tetrandria,* Order 2 *Digynia*.
Generic Character. CAL. *perianth* one-leaved, cup-formed. —COR. one-petalled, ovate; *nectary* of four scales.— STAM. *filaments* four, subulate; *anthers* roundish.— PIST. *germ* roundish; *styles* two, erect; *stigmas* simple. —PER. fleshy; *seeds* in pairs.
Species. Plants of this genus are parasitical and annual; as —*Cuscuta Europœa,* seu *Cuscuta, Cassitha,* seu *Cassutha,* Common Dodder.—*Cuscuta epithymum,* seu *Epithymum,* Small Dodder, &c.

CUSCUTA is also the name of the *Basella rubra.*

CUSP (*Geom.*) the point or corner formed by two parts of a curve meeting, and there terminating.

CUSP (*Astron.*) a term denoting the points or horns of the moon.

CUSP (*Astrol.*) the first point of the twelve houses in a figure or scheme of the heavens.

CUSP (*Archit.*) a term introduced by Sir James Hall in his essay on Gothic architecture to express any one of the pendants of a pointed arch. Two cusps form a trefoil, three a quatrefoil, &c.

CUSPI′DIA (*Bot.*) a species of *Gorteria*.

CU′SPIDATE (*Bot.*) *cuspidatus*, an epithet for a leaf; *folium cuspidatum*, a cuspidate leaf, having the end sharp like the point of a spear, or terminating in a bristly point.

CU′SPIDATED *hyperbola* (*Math.*) an hyperbola whose two parts concur, and terminate in the angle of contact.

CU′SPIS (*Anat.*) which properly signifies the point of a spear, is applied as an epithet to the glans penis.

CUSSO′NIA (*Bot.*) a genus of plants, Class 5 *Pentandria,* Order 2 *Digynia;* so called after the botanist Cusson.
Generic Character. CAL. *perianth* one-leaved, truncate. COR. *petals* five, acute.—STAM. *filaments* five; *anthers* ovate.—PIST. *germ* inferior; *styles* filiform; *stigmas* obtuse.—PER. *twin* compressed; *seeds* solitary.
Species. Plants of this genus are shrubby, and natives of the Cape of Good Hope.

CU′STARD apple (*Bot.*) the *Annona* of Linnæus.

CUSTODE *admittendo* (*Law*) a writ for admitting a guardian; and *Custode amovendo,* a writ for removing a guardian. *Reg. Orig.*

CUSTO′DES *Libertatis, &c.* (*Law*) the title assumed by Oliver Cromwell and his party, during the grand rebellion, in the making out writs and processes. It was declared traiterous by the statute of 12 *Car.* 2, c. 3.

CUSTO′DIA *Militaris* (*Ant.*) the name for that sort of custody practised by the Romans, where the keeper and his prisoner were bound together by the same chain, that they might not be asunder. *Sen. de Tranquill.* l. 1, c. 10; *Athen.* l. 5, c. 11; *Suet. Domit.* c. 14.

CU′STOM (*Law*) an unwritten law, or that which has been established by a long use, and the consent of our ancestors, *ultra tritavum,* i. e. beyond the third generation, commonly accounted about 100 years; which is deemed as a right in law.

CUSTOM (*Com.*) a duty paid by the subject to the king upon the importation or exportation of commodities; so called because tonnage and poundage were only granted by Parliament for certain years, till the time of Henry VI.; but then constantly and for a perpetuity; thence called *customs,* or customary payments.—*Custom-house* is a warehouse or building in sea-port towns, where the King's customs are received.

CU'STOMARY tenants (*Law*) such as hold, by the custom of the manor, the same as copyholders. [vide *Copyholders*]

CU'STOMER (*Com.*) one who buys any thing of another.

CUSTOMS and *services* (*Law*) belong to the tenure of lands, and are such as tenants owe unto their lords, which, being withheld, he may have a writ of customs and services.

CU'STOS (*Ant.*) 1. One who was set to watch the plaintiff, that he might not tamper with the defendant. *Ascon. in Cic.* 2. One who was employed, during the elections, to see that no fraud was committed with the urns that held the votes. *Cic. Sen. post Red.* c. 11; *Varr. de Rust.* l. 3, c. 5. 3. One who was set to watch at feasts that the jewels were not taken out of the cups. *Juv. sat.* 5, c. 37. —Custos armorum, an officer who had the tackle and all the appurtenances of the ships in his charge. *Schæff. de Mil. Nav. Adden.* p. 333.

Custos *Brevium* (*Law*) the principal clerk belonging to the Common Pleas.—*Custos Rotulorum*, Keeper of the Rolls, he that has the keeping of the records of the Sessions of the Peace; he is always Justice of the Peace, and of the *Quorum*, in the county where appointed. *Lamb. Eiren.* l. 4, c. 3.—*Custos Placitorum Coronæ*, an officer similar to what is now called a *Custos Rutulorum*. *Bract.* l. 2, c. 5. —*Custos of the spiritualities*, he that exercises jurisdiction during the vacancy of a see.

Custos *Oculi* (*Surg.*) an instrument for preserving the eye from being hurt in some operations.

CU'STREL (*Archæol.*) a servant to a man of arms, or a prince's life-guard.

CUT (*Mil.*) an action in the broad-sword exercise, or in fencing, which consists in using the edge of an instrument, in distinction from the thrust, which consists in using the point. There are six cuts established for the use of the cavalry, to be made with the broad-sword or sabre: from this action arise several military phrases, as " To cut up," to destroy promiscuously: " To cut through, sword in hand," to make a passage through an enemy's ranks by means of the sword.

Cut (*Mar.*) another name for a canal, or the branch of a canal, which is artificially cut for the purpose of inland navigation.

Cut (*Carpent.*) the cut which is made in the thickness of a deal, with a saw, for the purpose of dividing it into parts called leaves; thus a five-cut deal is divided into six leaves.

CUT-BRA'CKETS (*Archit.*) those which are moulded on the edge.—*Cut-Roof*, a truncated roof.—*Cut-Standards*, a name for shelves, the front edge of which is cut into mouldings.

CUT-BA'STION (*Fort.*) vide *Bastion*.

CUT-PURSE (*Law*) a sort of thieves who rob by means of cutting the purses of the people.—*Cut-Throat*, a murderer.

CUT-WATER (*Mar.*) an epithet for a ship, to denote the sharp edge with which it cuts or divides the water as it makes way. This word *cut* is also employed in other phrases, as, " To cut a feather," is said of a well-bowed ship, which passes so swiftly through the water that it foams before her, and in a dark night seems to sparkle like fire: " To cut and run," to cut the cable and sail immediately: " To cut the sail," to unfurl it and let it fall down.

To Cut *the Round* (*Man.*) or *To cut the Volt*, i. e. to change the hand when a horse volts upon one tread, so that dividing the volt in two, he turns and parts upon a right line to recommence another volt.

CUTA'MBULI (*Med.*) certain worms, either in the skin or under it, which cause an uneasy sensation by their creeping: also, wandering scorbutic pains, which resemble the sensation of crawling worms.

CUTA'NEOUS *muscles* (*Anat.*) the muscles by which animals are enabled to shake their skins, so as to throw off dust or whatever adheres to it.

CUTANEOUS *diseases* (*Med.*) those diseases which affect the skin, as the itch, leprosy, &c.

CUTICLE (*Anat.*) *Cuticula, Epidermis*, or Scarfskin; a thin pellucid membrane, which is the outermost covering of the animal, which defends the true skin, and is connected with it by means of the hairs, the exhaling and inhaling vessels, and the *reta mucosum*.—*Cuticularis membrana*, the same as the *Dura mater*.

CUTICULO'SUS (*Anat.*) vide *Sphincter ani*.

CUTI'LIÆ (*Med.*) cold fountains in Italy, which were used as baths.

CU'TIO (*Ent.*) an insect with many feet.

CU'TIS (*Anat.*) the *derma*, or inner skin, which lies under the cuticle or scarfskin; it is full of pores, and consists of the filaments or veins, arteries, nerves, fibres interwoven with each other and with glandules, lymphatic ducts, &c. It is called the *Cutis vera*, or true skin, in distinction from the cuticle.—*Cutis anserina*, the rough state into which the skin is thrown by the action of the cold, which makes it resemble the skin of a goose in appearance.

CU'TLER (*Mech.*) a maker and seller of knives and all cutting instruments.

CU'TLERS, *Company of* (*Her.*) This company was first incorporated in 1413, and bear for armorial ensigns, " Gules six daggers in three saltire crosses, *argent* handled and hilted, *or* pointing towards the chief." The *supporters* two elephants *argent*. The *crest*, a third elephant with a castle on his back.

CUT'LET (*Cook.*) any slice of veal in the fleshy part.

CUTPURSE (*Law*) vide *Cut*.

CUTT (*Mar.*) a sort of flat-bottomed boat, formerly used in the channel for transporting horses.

CUTTER *of the Tallies* (*Law*) an officer in the Exchequer, to whom it belonged to provide wood for the tallies, and to cut on them the sums paid, &c.

CUTTER (*Mar.*) a small vessel commonly navigated in the Channel of England, furnished with one mast and a straight running bowsprit that can run in on the deck occasionally. It is used in the illicit trade, and also by Government in seizing the smuggling vessels.

CUTTER is also a small boat attached to a man of war.

CUT-THROAT (*Law*) vide *Cut*.

CU'TTING (*Vet.*) vide *To interfere*.

CUTTING (*Paint.*) the laying one strong lively colour on another without any shade or softening.

CUTTING-DOWN-LINE (*Mar.*) a curved line used by shipwrights in the delineation of ships, by which they determine the thickness of all the floor-timbers, and likewise the height of the dead-wood afore and abaft.

CUTTING *the Neck* (*Husband.*) the cutting the last handful of standing corn, which being done, the reapers give a shout and go to merry-making.

CUTTINGS (*Bot.*) branches or sprigs of plants cut to set again.

CU'TTLE-FISH (*Ich.*) a sort of sea fish, the *Sepia* of Linnæus, which is armed with a dreadful apparatus of holders and suckers, wherewith it secures most effectually its prey, and conveys it to its mouth. It has the property of emitting from itself a black fluid, which is said to form an ingredient in the composition of Indian ink, and from its back is procured a bone which is converted into pounce. The eggs of the female resemble a bunch of grapes, and are of a white colour until they are impregnated by the male, when they turn black.

CUTTS (*Mar.*) vide *Cutt*.

CUTTEE' (*Mech.*) the box to hold the quills in a weaver's loom.

CU'TWATER (*Mar.*) vide *Cut*.

CU'VA (*Archæol.*) a vessel for brewing.

CUVETTE (*Fort.*) or *Cunette*, a trench sunk in the middle of a great dry ditch.

CUYNAGE (*Com.*) vide *Cuinage*.

CUZ (*Print.*) a jocular title for one who is admitted to the fraternity of a printing-office.

CYA'MEA (*Min.*) a kind of precious stone resembling a bean when it is broken. *Plin.* l. 37, c. 11.

CY'AMOS (*Bot.*) the Egyptian bean.

CY'AMUS (*Ent.*) a woodlouse rolled up in the form of a bean, into which form these insects put themselves upon the apprehension of any danger.

CY'ANA (*Bot.*) a species of the *Gentian*.

CYANE'LLA (*Bot.*) a genus of plants, Class 6 *Hexandria*, Order 1 *Monogynia*.
: *Generic Characters.* CAL. none.—COR. *petals* six, oblong.—STAM. *filaments* six; *anthers* oblong.—PIST. *germ* three-corned; *style* filiform; *stigma* somewhat sharp.—PER. capsule superior, roundish; *seeds* many.
: *Species.* Plants of this genus are perennials, and natives of the Cape.

CY'ANITE (*Min.*) an argillaceous sort of stone, which is a species of the *Zeolithus* in the Linnean system.

CYANO'GEN (*Chem.*) a name for carbon combined with azote.

CYANOI'DES (*Bot.*) a species of the *Centaurea*.

CY'ANUS (*Bot.*) Blue Bottle; a plant so called, according to Pliny, from its colour. *Plin.* l. 21, c. 8, &c.

CYANUS, in the Linnean system, the same as the *Centaurea*.

CYANUS (*Min.*) a kind of jasper of an azure colour, answering to what is now called *Lapis lazuli*. *Plin.* l. 37, c. 9.

CY'AR (*Anat.*) the orifice of the internal ear.

CYATHIFO'RMIS (*Bot.*) glass-shaped or cupshaped; an epithet for the calyx and corolla; *calyx cyathiformis*, a calyx widening a little at the top, as in *Mauritia*; *corolla cyathiformis*, as in *Peziza cyathoides*.

CYATHI'SCUS (*Surg.*) the hollow part of a probe, formed in the shape of a small spoon.

CYATHOI'DES (*Bot.*) a species of the *Peziza*.

CY'ATHUS (*Ant.*) κύαθος, a cup, or drinking vessel; of which the Romans used to drink as many as there were Muses, or letters in the name of their patron, or mistress. It was also a measure both of the liquid and dry kind, equal to about an ounce, or the twelfth part of a pint, or, according to Pliny and Galen, to 10 drachmas. *Plin.* l. 21, c. 33; *Gal. de Mensur. et Ponder.*; *Isidor. Orig.* l. 14, c. 25; *Bud. de Ass.*; *Pæt. de Pond. apud Græv.*; *Thes. Antiq. Rom.* tom. 3, &c.

CY'BELES *pomum* (*Bot.*) a pine-apple.

CY'BITOS (*Anat.*) vide *Cubitus*.

CY'BIUM (*Ant.*) 1. A piece of salt fish cut into a square form. 2. A sort of fish. *Mart.* l. 5, ep. 79, v. 5; *Plin.* l. 9, c. 15, &c.; *Athen.* l. 3.

CYBOI'DES (*Bot.*) vide *Cuboides*.

CY'CAS (*Bot.*) a genus of plants, which was classed by Linnæus first among the Palms, and afterwards among the Ferns.

CY'CEON (*Med.*) κυκεών, a sort of pap made of flour and water, sometimes mixed with honey and wine.

CY'CIMA (*Min.*) Litharge.

CY'CHRAMA (*Orn.*) a bird which accompanies the quails on their leaving any country. *Plin.* l. 10, c. 23.

CY'CLAMEN (*Bot.*) κυκλάμινος, a plant so called ἀπὸ τοῦ κύκλου, from the circular form of its leaf, or the orbicular form of its root. It is otherwise called *tuber terræ*. *Theophrast. Hist. Plant.* l. 11, c. 10; *Dioscor.* l. 2, c. 184; *Plin.* l. 25, c. 9.

CYCLAMEN, in the Linnean system, a genus of plants, Class 5 *Pentandria*, Order 1 *Monogynia*.
: *Generic Character.* CAL. *perianth* half, five-cleft.—COR. one-petalled; *tube* globose.—STAM. *filaments* five; *anthers* straight.—PIST. *germ* roundish; *style* filiform; *stigma* sharp.—PER. berry globose; *seeds* very many.
: *Species.* The species are tuberous, of which the following are the principal.—*Cyclamen corum*, Round-leaved Cyclamen, or Sow-Bread.—*Cyclamen Europæum*, Common Cyclamen, &c.

CYCLA'MINUS (*Bot.*) vide *Cyclamen*.

CY'CLAS (*Ant.*) a sort of gown for females, with a long train. *Propert.* l. 4, ep. 7, v. 36.

Hæc nunc aurata cyclade signat humum.

It was so called because it had a border which the Greeks called κυκλάς. *Joseph. Antiq. Jud.* l. 19, c. 1; *Sueton. in Cal.* c. 52; *Vopisc. Saturn.* c. 9; *Alex. Gen.* l. 5, c. 18.

CYCLAS (*Bot.*) a genus of plants, Class 10 *Decandria*, Order 1 *Monogynia*.
: *Generic Character.* CAL. *perianth* one-leaved; *tube* short. COR. none.—STAM. *filaments* ten, capillary; *anthers* ovate.—PIST. germ ovate-oblong; *stigma* obtuse.—PER. roundish; *seeds* single.
: *Species.* The two species are trees and natives of the Caribbee Islands, as—*Cyclas spicata*, seu *Apalatoa spicata* and *Cyclas aromatica*, seu *Touchiwa*.

CY'CLE (*Chron.*) *cyclus*, from κύκλος, a circle; a continual revolution of numbers as applied to a series of years which go on without any interruption from first to last, and then return to the same order as before. Such cycles have been invented for the purpose of measuring the periodical motions of the heavenly bodies, and of obtaining a more exact computation of time. These cycles are either periods, [vide *Period*] or cycles properly so called; the principal of these latter are the Cycle of the Sun, the Cycle of the Moon, and the Cycle of Indiction.—*Cycle of the Sun*, or *solar cycle*, is a period or revolution of 28 years, beginning with 1, and ending with 28, at the end of which the Dominical or Sunday Letters, and those that express the other feasts, &c. return nearly the same as before.—*Cycle of the Moon*, or *lunar cycle*, a period of 19 years, in which time the new and full moons return nearly to the same day of the Julian year.—*Cycle of Indiction*, a series of 15 years. [vide *Chronology*]

CYCLI'DIUM (*Ent.*) a genus of animals, Class *Vermes*, Order *Infusoria*.
: *Generic Character.* Worm invisible to the naked eye, simple, pellucid, and orbicular.
: *Species.* The principal species are the *Cyclidium, bulla, radians, nucleus, pediculus,* &c.

CYCLI'SCUS (*Surg.*) from κύκλος, a circle; an instrument in the shape of a half-moon, formerly used for scraping rotten bones.

CY'CLOGRAPH (*Mech.*) from κύκλος, a circle, and γράφω, to describe; an instrument used for describing the arcs of circles.

CY'CLOID (*Geom.*) a kind of mechanical curve, as A D B generated by the rotation of the circle A E along a line A B. The circle A E is called 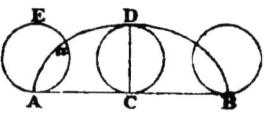 the *Generating Circle*, the line A B the *Base*, and the perpendicular D C the *Axis*.

Cycloids are either curtate, prolate, or common.—The *curtate* or *contracted Cycloid* is the path described by some point without the circle.—The *prolate* or *inflected Cycloid* is the path described by some point within the circle.—The *common Cycloid* is the path described by some point in the circumference of the circle, as *a* in the above figure.

CYCLO'IDAL (*Geom.*) the space contained between the curve, or crooked line, and the subtense of the figure.

CYCLO'METRY (*Math.*) the art of measuring cycles.

CYCLOPÆ'DIA (*Lit.*) κυκλοπαιδία, from κύκλος, a circle, and παιδεία, discipline; the circle of sciences, or universal knowledge; also the book which treats on the whole circle of sciences. This is commonly arranged in alphabetical order.

CYCLOPHO'RIA *sanguinis* (*Anat.*) the circulation of the blood.

CYCLO'PION (*Anat.*) κυκλώπιον, the white of the eye.

CYCLO'PTERUS (*Ich.*) Sucker; a genus of animals, Class *Pisces*, Order *Branchiostegei*.
Generic Character. Head obtuse.—Tongue short, thick.—Body short, thick, without scales.—Ventral Fins united into an oval concavity.
Species. The species are the *Cyclopterus lumpus, minutus, nudus, ventricosus,* &c.

CY'CLOS (*Anat.*) κύκλος, a circle, is applied by Hippocrates to the orbits of the eye.

CY'CLUS (*Chron.*) vide *Cycle*.

CYCNA'RION (*Med.*) κυκνάριον, a collyrium, mentioned by Galen and Paulus Ægineta. *Gal. P. Æginet.* l. 7, c. 11.

CY'DAR (*Min.*) Tin.

CY'DER (*Husb.*) vide *Cider*.

CYDONA'TUM (*Med.*) κυδωνάτον, a preparation of quinces mixed with aromatics. *Paul. Æginet.* l. 7, c. 11.

CYDO'NIA (*Bot.*) the *Crateva Marmelos*.

CY'GNET (*Nat.*) a young swan.

CYGNET *royal* (*Her.*) a term in blazoning given to swans when they are collared about the neck with an open crown, and a chain affixed thereto, as in the annexed figure. "He beareth *azure*, a bend engrailed between two cygnets royal *argent*, gorged with ducal crowns with strings reflexed over their backs *or*; name *Pitfield*." It is otherwise blazoned. "A swan *argent*, ducally gorged and chained *or*."

CY'GNUS (*Astron.*) κύκνος, or ὄρνις, the Swan; an old constellation of the Northern hemisphere, containing, according to Ptolemy, 19 stars, to Tycho 18, to Bayer 36, to Hevelius 47, British Catalogue 81. This is fabled to be the Swan into which Jupiter transformed himself in order to deceive Leda. *Arat. Phænom.* v. 274; *Eratosth. Charact.*; *Ptol. Almag.* l. 7, c. 5; *Ricciol. Almag. nov.* l. 6, c. 4.

CYI'TES (*Min.*) vide *Ætites*.

CYLI'CHNE (*Med.*) κυλίχνη; a small vessel, or galley-pot, for holding medicines.

CY'LINDER (*Geom.*) κυλίνδρος, from κυλίνδω, to revolve; a figure conceived to be generated by the rotation of a rectangle about one of its sides, as the figure A B C D, which is generated by the revolution of the rectangle P B D Q about the side B Q. This side is called the axis, which connects together the centres of the two circular ends.

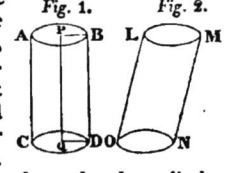

When the line is perpendicular to the ends, the cylinder is called a *right cylinder*, as in fig. 1; and if otherwise *oblique* as in fig. 2, L M N O, which is an oblique cylinder, conceived to be generated by carrying a right line parallel to itself about the circumference of two equal and parallel circles. *Euc. Def. Elem.* l. 11.

CYLINDER (*Gunn.*) or *concave cylinder*, all the hollow length of the piece, or bore.—*Charged cylinder*, the chamber of a great gun, or that part which receives the powder and ball.—*Vacant cylinder*, that part of the hollow, or bore, which remains empty when the piece is loaded.

CYLI'NDRIC *Ring* (*Geom.*) a solid which may be conceived by supposing a cylinder to be bent round into a circular form.—*Cylindric Ungula*, a solid formed by a plane passing obliquely through the side and base of a cylinder, as E D G, in the annexed figure, passing through the base A B G of the cylinder.

CYLI'NDRICAL *Ceiling* (*Archit.*) a ceiling which is either a semicylinder, or a segment less than a semicylinder.

CYLINDRICAL (*Bot.*) another name for *Columnar*.

CYLI'NDROID (*Geom.*) a solid resembling the common cylinder, except having elliptical instead of circular ends.

CYLI'NDRUS (*Ant.*) 1. A stone roller for levelling paths, &c. *Vitruv.* l. 10, c. 6; *Virg. Georg.* l. 1, v. 178. 2. The trunk of a tree, several of which were laid out in the way to impede the progress of an enemy on their march. *Veget.* l. 4, c. 8; *Ammian.* l. 31, c. 15. 3. A precious stone of a round form that was worn in the ear. *Plin.* l. 37, c. 5; *Tertull. de Hab. Mul.* c. 7.

CYLI'STA (*Bot.*) a genus of plants, Class 17 *Diadelphia*, Order 4 *Decandria*.
Generic Character. CAL. perianth one-leaved, four-parted. —COR. papilionaceous.—STAM. filaments diadelphous; anthers roundish.—PIST. germ superior; style subulate; stigma subcapitate.—PER. legume ovate, oblong; seeds two, oval.
Species. The single species, the *Cylista villosa*, is a shrub.

CY'LLOS (*Med.*) κυλλός, one affected with a kind of luxation which bends outwards, and is incurvated or hollow inwards. *Hippocrat. et Gal. Comm. in Hippocrat. de Art.*

CY'MA (*Archit.*) *Sima*, or *Cymatium*, κυμάτιον, vulgarly called *ogee*; a member or moulding of the cornice, whose profile is waved, i. e. concave at top and convex at the bottom. It is so called from κυμαίνω, to undulate, because of its undulated form. When the concave part of the moulding projects beyond the convex part, the *cymatium* is denominated a *Sima-recta*; but when the convex part forms the greatest projection, it is a *Sima reversa*. Vitruvius speaks of the *Tuscan Cymatium*, supposed by Philander to be an ovolo, or quarter round; the *Doric Cymatium*, probably a cavetto; and the *Lesbian Cymatium*, which has its projecture subduple of its height. *Vitruv.* l. 5, c. 7; *Philand. in Vitruv.*; *Bald. Lex. Vitruv.*

CYMA (*Bot.*) vide *Cyme*.

CYMATO'DES (*Med.*) κυματώδης, from κῦμα, a wave, undulating; an epithet for the pulse.

CY'MBA (*Ant.*) a skiff or fishing-boat. *Cic. de Offic.* l. 3, c. 14; *Plin.* l. 7, c. 56; *Non.* l. 13, c. 14.

CYMBA (*Anat.*) a bone of the wrist, so called from its supposed likeness to a skiff or fishing-smack.

CYMBA'CHNE (*Bot.*) a genus of plants, Class 23 *Polygamia*, Order 1 *Monoecia*, Natural Order *Grasses*.
Generic Characters. CAL. two-valved in hermaphrodite and one-valved in female flowers.—COR. two-glumed; in female flowers none.—STAM. in hermaphrodite flowers, filaments three; anthers black.—PIST. germ minute; style simple; stigmas two.
Species. The single species is the *Cymbachne ciliata*.

CYMBALA'RIA (*Bot.*) the *Antirrhinum cymbalaria et pilosa* of Linnæus.

CYMBALA'RIS *cartilago* (*Anat.*) a name for the *Cricoid cartilage*.

CY'MBALUM (*Mus.*) κύμβαλον, a cymbal, so called from κύμβος, a cavity; a musical instrument in use among the ancients, as in the annexed figure.
Catull. Carm. 63, v. 29.

Leve tympanum remugit, cava cymbala recrepant.

Liv. l. 39, c. 8; *Plut. Sympos.* 8; *Quest. Propert.* l. 3, cl. 16; *Clemens. Alexand. Protrept.* p. 11; *Arnob.* l. 7, p. 237; *August. in Psalm.* 130; *Gregor. Nyssen. in Psalm.* c. 9.

CYMBA'RIA (*Bot.*) a genus of plants, Class 14 *Didynamia*, Order 2 *Angiospermia*, so called from its boat-shaped fruit. It is distinguished from all other plants by its ten-toothed calyx. The whole plant is hoary, and nearly allied to the *Antirrhinum*.

CYMBIFO'RME os (*Anat.*) the name of a bone in the heel.

CYMBIFO'RMIS (*Bot.*) vide *Boat-shaped*.

CYME (*Bot.*) signifies properly a sprout or shoot, but is used by Linnæus to denote a species of *inflorescence*, in which the florets do not all rise from the same point. [vide *Corymb*]

CY'MIA (*Mech.*) vide *Carora*.

CY'MINUM (*Bot.*) the *Cuminum cyminum* of Linnæus.

CYMO'SÆ (*Bot.*) the sixty-third of Linnæus' Natural Orders, consisting of such flowers as are disposed in the form of a cyme.

CYMO'THOS (*Ent.*) a division of the genus *Oniscus*, according to Fabricius, consisting of those species of insects of this tribe which have no feelers, and four antennæ.

CY'NA (*Bot.*) a tree in Arabia, resembling the palm-tree in its leaf, of which garments are made.

CYNAMO'LGUS (*Orn.*) a bird in Arabia, so called from its building its nest on the cinnamon tree. *Plin.* l. 33, c. 10.

CYNA'NCHE (*Med.*) κυνάγχη, a species of quinsy, so called from κύων, a dog, and ἄγχω, to suffocate.

CYNANCHE, in the modern nomenclature, is classed by Cullen as a genus of diseases, under the Class *Pyrexiæ*, Order *Phlegmatiæ*.

CYNA'NCHICA (*Med.*) a name for medicines that are good for the quinsey.

CYNA'NCHUM (*Bot.*) a genus of plants which are all shrubs or undershrubs, and mostly twining; but the structure of its parts is so minute that botanists are not agreed on its character.
Species. The principal species are as follow—*Cynanchum viminale*, *Euphorbia*, *Apocynum*, seu *Fel Tavil*, Naked Cynanchum.—*Cynanchum hirtum*, *Periploca*, seu *Apocynum*, Hairy Cynanchum, &c.

CYNA'NTHEMIS (*Bot.*) the *Cotula fœtida*.

CYNANTHRO'PIA (*Med.*) madness occasioned by the bite of a mad dog, from κύων, a dog, and ἄνθρωπος, a man.

CYNA'PIUM (*Bot.*) the *Æthusa Cynapium*.

CY'NARA (*Bot.*) κύναρα, ἄκακβα, or κίναρα, a plant which answers nearest to the description of the artichoke. *Poll.* l. 6, c. 9; *Dioscor.* l. 3, c. 10; *Gal. de Alim. Fac.* l. 2, c. 51.

CYNARA, in the Linnean system, a genus of plants, Class 19 *Syngenesia*, Order 1 *Polygamia Æqualis*.
Generic Character. CAL. ventricose.—COR. compound tubulous; proper one-petalled.—STAM. filaments five; anthers cylindric, double.—PIST. germ ovate; style filiform; stigma simple.—PER. none; seeds solitary; receptacle bristly.
Species. This plant, which is well known by the name of the Artichoke, was classed by the ancient botanists under the head of the *Carduus*, and is called *Cinara* by Tournefort. *Bauh. Hist. Plant.*; *Bauh. Pin.*; *Ger. Herb.*; *Park. Theat. Botan.*; *Raii Hist. Plant.*; *Tournef. Instit.*

CY'NCHNIS (*Med.*) κυγχνίς, a small box for holding medicines.

CYNE'BOTE (*Law*) a mulct formerly paid by one who killed another, to the kindred of the deceased.

CYNEGE'TICS (*Lit.*) κυνηγητικά, from κύων, a dog, and ἡγέομαι, to lead, books or treatises on hunting.

CY'NICKS (*Ant.*) κυνικοί, a sect of philosophers first instituted by Antisthenes, who were so called from κύων, a dog, on account of their currish and churlish behaviour.

CY'NIPS (*Ent.*) Gall-Fly, a genus of animals, Class *Insecta*, Order *Hymenoptera*.
Generic Character. Mouth with a short-toothed membranaceous jaw.—Feelers four, unequal.—Antennæ moniliform.—Sting spiral.
Species. Animals of this tribe are distinguished principally by the trees which they infest.

CY'NNIA (*Mech.*) vide *Carora*.

CYNOBO'TANE (*Bot.*) the *Cotula fœtida* of Linnæus.

CYNOCEPHALE'A (*Bot.*) a herb called by the Egyptians *Osirilis*, after their god Osiris. *Apul. de Herb.* c. 86; *Plin.* l. 13, c. 2.

CYNOCE'PHALIS (*Zool.*) a sort of ape with a head like a dog, from κύων, a dog, and κεφαλή, a head. *Plin.* l. 6, c. 29.

CYNOCO'CTANUM (*Bot.*) a name for the *Aconite*.

CYNOCO'PRUS (*Med.*) from κύων, a dog, and κόπρος, dung; the dung of a dog.

CYNOCRA'MBE (*Bot.*) Dog's Mercury.

CYNOCRAMBE, in the Linnean system, the *Mercurialis perennis*.

CYNOCY'TISIS (*Bot.*) vide *Cynosbaton*.

CYNODE'CTOS (*Med.*) κυνόδηκτος, an epithet for a person bitten by a mad dog.

CYNODE'SMION (*Med.*) κυνοδέσμιον, from κύων, which imports sometimes the lower part of the prepuce, and δέω, to bind; a ligature by which the prepuce is bound to the glans. *Gorr. Def. Med.*

CYNODO'NTES (*Anat.*) from κύων, a dog, and ὀδούς, a tooth; dog-teeth betwixt the fore-teeth and the grinders, in each jaw two, one on one side and the other on the other. *Plin.* l. 11, c. 37.

CYNOGLO'SSA (*Bot.*) the *Cynoglossum Apenninum* of Linnæus.

CYNOGLOSSOI'DES (*Bot.*) the *Borago Indica* of Linnæus.

CYNOGLO'SSUM (*Bot.*) κυνόγλωσσον, from κύων, a dog, and γλῶσσα, a tongue, Hound's-tongue; a plant so called from the similarity in the form of its leaves to that of a dog's tongue. The leaves are vulnerary and detersive. *Dioscor.* l. 4, c. 129; *Plin.* l. 25, c. 8.

CYNOGLOSSUM, in the Linnean system, a genus of plants, Class 5 *Pentandria*, Order 1 *Monogynia*.
Generic Character. CAL. perianth five-parted.—COR. one-petalled, funnel-form.—STAM. filaments five; anthers roundish.—PIST. germs four; style subulate; stigma emarginate.—PER. none; seeds included in four arils.
Species. The principal species are as follow—*Cynoglossum officinale*, Common Hound's Tongue, a biennial, and native of Europe.—*Cynoglossum cheirofolium*, Silvery-leaved Hound's Tongue, a perennial.—*Cynoglossum linifolium*, Flax-leaved Hound's Tongue, or Venus' Navel-wort.—*Cynoglossum omphalodes*, *Borrago*, seu *Symphytum*, Comfrey-leaved Hound's Tongue, &c. *Clus. Hist. Rar. Plant.*; *Bauh. Hist. Plant.*; *Bauh. Pin.*; *Ger. Herb.*; *Park. Theat. Botan.*; *Raii Hist. Plant. Tournef. Instit.*

CYNOLO'PHA (*Anat.*) κυνόλοφα, the asperities in the dorsal vertebræ. *Poll. Onom.* l. 2, seg. 180.

CYNOLY'SSA (*Med.*) vide *Lyssa*.

CYNO'MAZON (*Bot.*) κυνόμαζον; a herb so called from κύων, a dog, and μᾶζα, bread, because when put into a piece of bread it kills dogs.

CYNOME'TRA (*Bot.*) a genus of plants, Class 10 *Decandria*, Order 1 *Monogynia*.
Generic Character. CAL. perianth four-leaved, oblong.—COR. petals five, lanceolate.—STAM. filaments ten; anthers oval.—PIST. germ boatform; style filiform; stigma simple.—PER. legume crescent-shaped; seed single.
Species. The species are trees, and natives of the East Indies.

CYNOMO'RIUM (*Bot.*) a genus of plants, Class 21 *Monœ-*

cia, Order 1 *Monandria*, Natural Order *Amentaceæ*. The male flowers of which are disposed in an imbricated ament with the female flowers.

CYNOMORIUM is also the name of the *Cynometra cauliflora*.

CYNO'MYA (*Bot.*) vide *Psyllium*.

CYNOPHALLO'PHOROS (*Bot.*) the *Capparus Cynophallophorus* of Linnæus.

CY'NOPS (*Bot.*) the *Plantago Cynops* of Linnæus.

CYNO'PTICON (*Med.*) vide *Dacneron*.

CYNORE'XIA (*Med.*) a canine appetite. [vide *Bulima*]

CYNORRHO'DON (*Bot.*) from κυων, a dog, and ῥοδον, a rose; the dog-rose, or wild rose; also the flower of the red lily. *Plin.* l. 25, c. 2.

CYNORRY'NCHIUM (*Bot.*) the *Chelone pentistemon* of Linnæus.

CYNO'SBATON (*Bot.*) vel *Cynosbatos*, the Eglantine or Sweet-Briar; also the Caper-Bush. *Theophrast. Hist. Plant.* l. 3, c. 18; *Plin.* l. 16, c. 37.

CYNOSO'RCHIS (*Bot.*) the herb Dog-Stones. *Plin.* l. 27, c. 8. [vide *Orchis*]

CYNOSORCHIS, *in the Linnean system*, is the *Orchis globosa et pyramidalis*.

CYNOSPA'STON (*Bot.*) vide *Cynosbaton*.

CYNOSU'RA (*Astron.*) from κυνος ὑρα, dog's tail; the lesser bear-star, or the star in the tail of the lesser bear.

CYNOSURA (*Nat.*) κυνοσυρα, dog's-tail; an epithet for addled eggs, especially in the dog days. *Plin.* l. 10, c. 60.

CYNOSU'RUS (*Bot.*) a genus of plants, Class 3 *Triandria*, Order 2 *Digynia*, Natural Order *Gramina*, or Grasses.
Generic Character. CAL. glume many-flowered, two-valved.—COR. two-valved, awnless; *nectary* two-leaved.—STAM. *filaments* three; *anthers* oblong.—PIST. *germ* turbinate; *styles* two, villose; *stigmas* simple.—PER. none; *seed* single in the corolla.
Species. The species are mostly perennials, as—*Cynosurus cristatus*, seu *Phleum*, Crested Dog's-Tail Grass, or Bent-Grass.—*Cynosurus durus*, *Lolium*, seu *Poa duras*, Rigid Dog's-Tail Grass.—*Cynosurus corocanus*, *Panicum*, seu *Eleusine*, Thick Spiked Dog's-Tail Grass. But the—*Cynosurus Indicus*, Indian Dog's-Tail Grass, is an annual. *Bauh. Hist.*; *Bauh. Pin*; *Ger. Herb.*; *Park. Theat. Botan.*; *Raii Hist.*

CYNOSURUS is also the name of a species of the *Alopecurus*.

CYNO'XYLON (*Bot.*) the *Nyssa integrifolia* of Linnæus.

CY'NZOLON (*Bot.*) a stinking weed of the thistle kind. *Plin.* l. 22, c. 18.

CY'ON (*Anat.*) κυων, a dog; signifies also the inferior part of the prepuce.

CYOPHO'RIA (*Med.*) κυοφορια, from κυημα, the fœtus, and φερω, to bear; gestation, or the time of gestation, applied to pregnant women.

CYPARI'SSÆ (*Ant.*) Fiery meteors, or appearances in the air at night.

CYPARI'SSIAS (*Bot.*) the largest kind of spurge. *Plin.* l. 26, c. 8.

CYPARISSIAS, *in the Linnean system*, is the *Euphorbia cyparissias*.

CYPARI'SSUS (*Bot.*) vide *Cupressus*.

CYPERE'LLA (*Bot.*) the same as the *Schoenus*.

CYPE'RI *genus* (*Bot.*) a species of the *Sciapus* of Linnæus.

CY'PERIS (*Bot.*) an Indian herb like ginger.

CYPEROI'DES (*Bot.*) the same as the *Carex*.

CYPE'RUS (*Bot.*) or *Cyperum*, κυπειρος or κυπειρος, a kind of angular rush, white at bottom, and black at top. *Theophrast. Hist. Plant.* l. 4, c. 11; *Varr. de Re Rust.* l. 3, c. 16; *Cels.* l. 3, c. 16; *Dioscor.* l. 4, c. 22.

CYPERUS, *in the Linnean system*, a genus of plants, Class 3 *Triandria*, Order 1 *Monogynia*, Natural Order *Calamariæ*.
Generic Character. CAL. *spike* imbricate; *scales* ovate.—COR. none.—STAM. *filaments* three; *anthers* oblong.—PIST. *germ* very small; *style* filiform; *stigmas* three, capillary.—PER. none; *seed* single.
Species. Most of the species have three-cornered culms or stems, are perennials, and natives of the Indies, having a grateful smell. The root is bulbous or tuberous. The most important species of this plant is the—*Cyperus papyrus*, or the Egyptian Papyrus, of which paper was originally made.

CY'PHI (*Med.*) κυφι, a composition of honey, wine, cyperus, rosin, and many other ingredients, which was much used in Egypt. *Gal. de Antidot.*; *Suidas*.

CY'PHIA (*Bot.*) the *Lobelia bulbosa* of Linnæus.

CYPHI'LLA (*Bot.*) a little cup, or a peltated concavity, with a raised rim, which is found on the underside of some *Algæ*, as *Lychnis sylvaticus*.

CYPHO'MA (*Med.*) κυφωμα, from κυφοω, to bend; a preternatural incurvature of the dorsal vertebræ outwards.

CYPI'RA (*Bot.*) vide *Curcuma*.

CYPRÆ'A (*Conch.*) Cowry, or Gowrie, a genus of animals, Class *Vermes*, Order *Testacea*.
Generic Character. Animal a slug.—*Shell* univalve, involute.—*Aperture* effuse at each end.
Species. The principal species are the—*Cypræa pediculus*, *bullata*, *exanthema*, &c.

CY'PRESS (*Bot.*) a tree celebrated in antiquity. [vide *Cupressus*]

CY'PRINUM *oleum* (*Med.*) κυπρινον ἐλαιον, the flowers of cypress, calamus, cardamus, &c. boiled in olive oil. *Dioscor.* l. 1, c. 65.

CY'PRINUS (*Ich.*) a genus of animals, Class *Pisces*, Order *Abdominales*.
Generic Character. Mouth small.—Body smooth, generally whitish.
Species. The species are distinguished into, 1. Those that are bearded, as the—*Cyprinus carpio*, the Carp.—*Cyprinus barbus*, the Barbel.—*Cyprinus gobio*, the Gudgeon.—*Cyprinus tinca*, the Tench. 2. Those with the tail nearly even at the end, as—*Cyprinus curassius*, the Crucian.—*Cyprinus cephalus*, the Chub, &c. 3. Those having the tail three-parted, as—*Cyprinus amatus*, the Gold-Fish.—*Cyprinus ophthalmus*, the Telescope Carp, &c. 4. Those having the tail bifid, as—*Cyprinus leuciscus*, the Dace.—*Cyprinus rutilus*, the Roach.—*Cyprinus orfus*, the Finscale or Rud.—*Cyprinus erythrophthalmus*, the Red-Eye.—*Cyprinus alburnus*, the Bleak.—*Cyprinus brama*, the Bream, &c.

CYPRIPE'DIUM (*Bot.*) a genus of plants, Class 20 *Gynandria*, Order 1 *Diandria*.
Generic Character. CAL. *spathes* vague; *spadix* simple.—COR. *petals* four or five, lanceolate; *nectary* slipper-form.—STAM. *filaments* two, very short; *anthers* erect.—PIST. *germ* long; *style* very short; *stigma* obscure.—PER. *capsule* obovate; *seeds* numerous; *receptacle* linear.
Species. Plants of this genus have bulbous roots. The principal species are the—*Cypripedium calceolus*, Calceolus, seu *Helleborine*, Common Ladies' Slipper.—*Cypripedium bulbosum*, Bulbous Ladies' Slipper, &c. *Dod. Pempt.*; *Bauh. Hist.*; *Bauh. Pin.*; *Ger. Herb.*; *Park Theat. Bot.*; *Raii Hist. Plant.*; *Tournef. Inst.*

CYPRIPEDIUM is also the *Arethusa ophioglossoides*.

CY'PRUS (*Bot.*) the *Lawsonia spinosa* of Linnæus.

CY'PSELE (*Med.*) κυψελη, the wax in the ear.

CY'PSELUS (*Orn.*) a martin, which builds its nest like, κυψελη, a capsule, a little box. *Plin.* l. 10, c. 39.

CYRÆ'NIA (*Chem.*) the fœces of saffron infused in oil.

CYRBA'SIA (*Med.*) κυρβασια, properly a tiara, or a cap for Persian monarchs, is applied by Hippocrates to a covering for the breasts of women. *Hippocrat. de Morb. Mul.*

CYRE'BIA (*Bot.*) κυρηβια, the husks of barley or other corn.

CYRE'NAICUS *sal* (*Chem.*) Sal Ammoniac, produced in Cyrene.

CYRI'CBRICE (*Law*) a breaking into the church, which was sacrilege, according to the laws of Canute.

CYRICKSCEAT (*Archæol.*) a tribute or duty anciently paid to the church among the Saxons.

CYRI'LLA (*Bot.*) a genus of plants, Class 14 *Didynamia*, Order 2 *Angiospermia*; so called from Dominico Cyrillo, a botanist of Naples.
Generic Character. CAL. *perianth* superior; five-leaved. COR. one-petalled.—STAM. *filaments* four; *anthers* ovate.—PIST. *germ* villose; *style* filiform; *stigma* two-lobed.—PER. two-celled; *seeds* numerous.
Species. The single species is the—*Cyrilla pulchella*, seu *Achemines*, a beautiful plant, native of Jamaica.

CYRSE'ON (*Anat.*) the podex or anus.

CYRTA'NDRA (*Bot.*) the *Besleria biflora* of Linnæus.

CYRTA'NTHUS (*Bot.*) a genus of plants, Class 6 *Hexandria*, Order 1 *Monogynia*.
Generic Character. CAL. none.—COR. one-petalled.—STAM. *filaments* six; *anthers* oblong.—PIST. *germ* inferior, ovate; *style* filiform; *stigma* trifid.
Species. The two species are bulbous roots, from the Cape of Good Hope, as—*Cyrtanthus angustifolius*, seu *Crinum*, Narrow-leaved Cyrtanthus.—*Cyrtanthus obliquus*, seu *Amaryllis*, Oblique-leaved Cyrtanthus.

CYRTO'MA (*Med.*) κύρτωμα, a humour in any part of the body.

CY'SSARIS (*Anat.*) the podex or anus.

CYSSI'TES (*Min.*) the *Lapis Ætites*.

CYSSOID (*Geom.*) vide *Cissoid*.

CYSSO'TIS (*Med.*) vide *Proctalgia*.

CYSTEOLI'THOS (*Med.*) from κύστις, the bladder, and λίθος, a stone; a stone in the bladder.

CYSTHEPATICI *Ductus* (*Anat.*) Cysthepatic ducts, which convey the bile from the liver to the gall-bladder.

CY'STICÆ *Arteriæ* (*Anat.*) the cystic arteries, the two principal branches of the hepatic artery.

CYSTICA'PNOS (*Bot.*) the same as the *Fumaria*.

CY'STIDES (*Med.*) Encysted tumours, or such as have their substance included in a membrane.

CY'STINX (*Anat.*) κύστιγξ, a small bladder.

CYSTIPHLO'GIA (*Med.*) from κύστις, the bladder, and φλέγω, to burn; an inflammation in the bladder.

CYSTIRRHA'GIA (*Med.*) from κύστις, the bladder, and ῥήγνυμι, to break forth; a discharge of blood from the bladder.

CY'STIS (*Anat.*) from κύστις, a bag, the bladder; any receptacle of morbid humours.—*Cistis choledocha* or *fellea* is the gall-bladder.

CY'STITIS (*Med.*) from κύστις, the bladder; an inflammation in the bladder; a genus of diseases, according to Cullen, in the Class *Pyrexiæ*, Order *Phlegmasia*.

CY'STOCELE (*Med.*) from κύστις, the bladder, and κήλη, a rupture.

CYSTOLI'THICA *Ischuria* (*Med.*) a suppression of urine from κύστις λίθος, a stone in the bladder.

CYSTOPHLE'GICA (*Med.*) from κύστις, the bladder, and φλέγω, to burn; an epithet for an *ischuria*, or a suppression of urine from an inflammation in the bladder.

CYSTOPHLEGMA'TICA (*Med.*) from κύστις, the bladder, and φλέγμα, phlegm; an epithet for an *ischuria*, or suppression of urine, from too much matter or mucus in the bladder.

CYSTOPROC'TICA (*Med.*) from κύστις, the bladder, and πρωκτός, anus; an epithet for an *ischuria*, or a suppression of urine, caused by wind, inflammation of the rectum, &c.

CYSTOPTO'SIS (*Med.*) from κύστις, the bladder, and πτῶσις, a fall; a protusion of the inner membrane of the bladder through the urethra.

CYSTOSPA'STICA (*Med.*) from κύστις, the bladder, and σπάσμα, a spasm; an epithet for an *ischuria*, or suppression of urine, from a spasm in the sphincter of the bladder.

CYSTOSPY'ICA (*Med.*) from κύστις, the bladder, and πύον, pus; an epithet for an *ischuria*, or suppression of the urine, from purulent matter in the bladder.

CYSTOTHROMBOI'DES (*Med.*) from κύστις, the bladder, and θρόμβος, coagulated blood; an epithet for an *ischuria*, or suppression of urine, from a concretion of grumous blood in the bladder.

CYSTOTO'MIA (*Med.*) from κύστις, the bladder, and τέμνω, to cut; the operation of cutting, or piercing the bladder.

CYTHA'RUS (*Ich.*) a sea-fish of the turbot kind.

CY'THION (*Med.*) a collyrium mentioned by Celsus.

CY'TINUS (*Bot.*) κύτινος, the fruit of the pomegranate.—*Cytinus hypocistis*, the plant from whose fruit the *succus hypocistis* is procured. *Theoph. Hist. Plant.* l. 1, c. 22; *Nicand. Alex.*; *Dioscor.* l. 1, c. 102; *Plin.* l. 23, c. 6.

CYTINUS, in the Linnean system, a genus of plants, Class 20 *Gynandria*, Order 7 *Octandria*.
Generic Character. CAL. *perianth* one-leaved, tubular.—COR. none.—STAM. sixteen; *filaments* none; *anthers* oblong, growing on the style under the stigma.—PIST. *germ* inferior; *style* cylindric; *stigma* eight cleft.—PER. berry crowned; *seeds* numerous.
Species. The single species is the—*Cytinus hypocistus*, *Hipocistus orobanche*, seu *Asarum*, Rape of Cistus, is a parasitical plant, growing at the roots of the Cistus. *Bauh. Pin.*; *Ger. Herb.*; *Raii Hist. Plant.*

CY'TISUS (*Bot.*) κύτισος. Bean Trefoil-tree, a plant which was much liked by cattle, and reckoned good for their milk. *Virg. Ecl.* 2, v. 64.

Torva leæna lupum sequitur, lupus ipse capellam
Florentem cytisum sequitur lasciva capella.

It is supposed to have taken its name from *Cythnus*, an island of the Cyclades, where it was first found. *Theophrast. Hist. Plant.* l. 4, c. 20; *Dioscor.* l. 4, c. 113; *Columel.* l. 9, c. 4; *Plin.* l. 13, c. 24; *Gal. de Antid.* l. 1, c. 4.

CYTISUS, in the Linnean system, a genus of plants, Class 17 *Diadelphia*, Order 4 *Decandria*.
Generic Character. CAL. *perianth* one-leaved, bell-form. COR. papilionaceous; *standard* ovate; *keel* acuminate.—STAM. *filaments* diadelphous; *anthers* simple.—PIST. *germ* oblong; *style* simple; *stigma* obtuse.—PER. *legume* oblong; *seeds* few.
Species. Plants of this genus are shrubs, without spines, the principal of which are—*Cytisus Laburnum*, Laburnum, seu *Anagyris*, Laburnum, formerly called Bean-Trefoil-Tree.—*Cytisus sessilifolius*, Common Cytisus.—*Cytisus Cajan*, seu *Phaseolus*, Pigeon Cytisus, or Pigeon Pea.—*Cytisus supinus*, Trailing Cytisus, &c. *Clus. Hist. Plant. rar*; *Bauh. Hist.*; *Bauh. Pin.*; *Ger. Herb.*; *Raii Hist. Plant.*; *Tournef. Instit.*, &c.

CYZICE'NUS *Stater* (*Ant.*) a sum the value of sixteen shillings and four-pence.

CYZICENUS (*Med.*) the name of a plaster mentioned by Galen. *Gal. de Comp. Med. per Gen.*

CZAR (*Polit.*) a title of honor assumed by the emperors of Russia, contracted no doubt from Cæsar.

CZA'RINE (*Polit.*) title of the empress of Russia.

CZA'ROWITZ (*Polit.*) title of the eldest son of the Czar or Czarine.

D.

D. (*Ant.*) as an abbreviation, stands for *Divus, Decius, Decimus*, &c. [vide *Abbreviations*] As a numeral it denotes 500.

D. (*Lit.*) stands for Doctor. [vide *Abbreviations*]

D. (*Her.*) as a sign, stands for the Honour point in the escutcheon. [vide *Escutcheon*]

D. (*Chron.*) as a sign, is one of the seven letters which, in its order, is the Dominical or Sunday Letter. [vide *Chronology*] As an abbreviation, it stands for *Domini*. [vide *Abbreviations*]

D. C. (*Mus.*) as an abbreviation, stands for *da capo*, i. e. to the head. [vide *Da*] As a sign, it is the nominal of the second note in the natural diatonic scale, to which Guido applied the monosyllable *re*.—*D flat*, the flat seventh of E flat.—*D in alt*, the fifth note in alt.—*D in altissimo*, the fifth note in altissimo.

DA (*Law*) a word equivalent to yes.

DA (*Mus.*) an Italian preposition used in music books, as—*Da Camera*, music for the chamber.—*Da Capella*, music for the chapel.—*Da Capo*, to the head or beginning; an expression written at the end of a movement, to direct the performer to return to, and end with, the first strain.

DA'ALDER (*Com.*) a Dutch coin, worth thirty sols, a guilder and a half, or about 2s. 7d. sterling.

DAB (*Ich.*) a flat fish, thinner and less than the flounder; the *Pleuronectes Limander* of Linnæus.

DABE'STIC (*Zool.*) a tortoise.

DA'BURI (*Bot.*) vide *Achiotl*.

DACE (*Ich.*) a river fish of the carp kind; the *Cyprinus leuciscus* of Linnæus.

DACE'TON (*Med.*) δακητὸν, from δάκω, to bite; an epithet for such animals as bite.

DA'CHEL (*Bot.*) the Palma major.

DA'CNADES (*Orn.*) a sort of bird mentioned by Festus.

DACNE'RON (*Med.*) δακνηρὸν, biting, from δάκω, to bite.

DACROI'DES (*Med.*) vide *Dacryodes*.

DACRY'DION (*Bot.*) vide *Scammonium*.

DACRYGELO'SIS (*Med.*) from δακρύω, to weep, and γελάω, to laugh; a species of insanity, which consists in laughing and weeping at the same time.

DACRYO'DES (*Med.*) δακρυώδης, an epithet for an ulcer that runs.

DACRYO'MA (*Med.*) from δακρύω, to weep; a closing of one or more of the *puncta lachrymalia*, so as to cause a weeping.

DACRYON (*Med.*) δάκρυον, a tear.

DACRYOPŒOS (*Med.*) δακρυοποιὸς, an epithet for things which excite tears by their acrimony, as onions, horseraddish, &c.

DA'CTYLE (*Poet.*) a foot or measure, in Greek or Latin verse, consisting of three feet, the first long, and the two last short, as *dŏmĭnŭs*.

DACTYLE'THRÆ (*Med.*) δακτυλήθραι, from δάκτυλος, a finger; a topical medicine intruded into the stomach to create vomiting. *Oribas. Med. Coll.* l. 8, c. 6.

DACTYLE'TUS (*Bot.*) the *Hermodactylus*.

DACTY'LIC (*Gram.*) an epithet for verses which end with a dactyle instead of a spondee, as in the following instance from Virgil.

Æn. l. 6, v. 33.

Bis patriæ cecidere manus; quin prōtĭnūs ūnnĭū.

DACTYLIOMA'NCY (*Ant.*) δακτυλιομαντεία, a divination by enchanted rings made according to some position of the celestial bodies. The ring was held suspended by a fine thread over a round table, on the edge of which were made divers marks with the twenty-four letters of the alphabet; and, the ring stopping at certain letters, they composed out of these the answer they sought for.

DACTY'LIOS (*Med.*) from δάκτυλος, a ring; a trochee in the shape of a ring mentioned by *Hippoc. de Mul*.

DACTYLIOTHE'CA (*Ant.*) from δάκτυλος, a ring, and θήκη, a box; a box to hold rings.

DA'CTYLIS (*Bot.*) δακτυλὶς, a long grape like a finger; a date raisin. *Plin.* l. 14, c. 3; *Colum.* l. 3, c. 2.

DACTYLIS, in the Linnean system, a genus of plants, Class 3 Triandria, Order 2 Digynia. Natural order of Grasses.

Generic Character. CAL. *glume* many flowered two-valved.—Cor. two-valved, the *lower valve* larger, the *inner* lanceolate; *nectaries* two lanceolate.—STAM. *filaments* three capillary; *anthers* oblong.—PIST. *germ* ovate; *styles* two spreading; *stigmas* feathered.—PER. none; *seed* single oblong.

Species. The species are perennials, as—*Dactylis cynosuroides*, American Cocks-foot Grass, native of Virginia.—*Dactylis glomerata, Bromus, seu Gramen spicatum*, &c. Rough Cocks-foot Grass, native of England and Portugal.—*Dactylis stricta, seu Spartum essexianum*, &c. Sea Cocks-foot Grass, native of Portugal.

DACTYLIS is also the name of the *Phœnix dactylifera*.

DACTY'LOGY (*Mech.*) a discoursing by signs made with the fingers from δάκτυλος, the finger, and λέγω, speech.

DA'CTYLON (*Bot.*) is the *Panicum dactylon* of Linnæus.

DACTYLO'NOMY (*Arith.*) from δάκτυλος, a finger, and νόμος, a law or measure; the art of numbering on the fingers.

DA'CTYLOS (*Ant.*) δάκτυλος, the shortest measure among the Greeks, being the fourth part of a palm, and the sixteenth part of a foot, the same as *digitus* among the Latins.

DACTYLOS (*Gram.*) vide *Dactyle*.

DACTYLOTHE'CE (*Surg.*) from δάκτυλος, a finger, and θήκη, a case; the name for an instrument for raising a finger or a thumb when pendulous from some hurt received.

DA'CTYLUS (*Bot.*) vide *Dactylis*.

DA'DDOCK (*Bot.*) the heart or body of a tree thoroughly rotten.

DA'DO (*Archit.*) a common name for the dye, which is the part in the middle of the pedestal of the column betwixt its base and cornice; also for the lower part of a wall.

DADU'CHI (*Ant.*) δᾳδοῦχοι, from δᾲς, a torch, and ἔχω, to hold, priests of Cybele so called because they ran about the temple with lighted torches in their hands. *Poll. Onom.* l. 1, c. 1, seg. 31.

DÆ'DALA (*Ant.*) δαίδαλα, festivals celebrated in Greece, particularly at Platæa, when the inhabitants, assembling in a large grove, and exposing in the open air pieces of sodden meat, carefully observed whither the crows that came to prey upon them directed their flight, when they hewed down all the trees on which the birds alighted, and made them into statues called δαίδαλα, after the ingenious artificer Dædalus. A similar festival was observed in other parts of Bœotia, by carrying about the statue of a woman which they called δαίδαλα.

DÆDA'LEUS (*Bot.*) dædaleous, an epithet of a leaf, *folium*.

DÆ'DIS (*Ant.*) δᾳδὶς, a solemnity in Greece which lasted three days, during all which time torches, δᾷδες, were burned, which gave occasion to the name. *Lucian. Pseudomant*.

DÆ'MONES (*Med.*) such distempers as cannot be assigned to a natural cause, and supposed to arise from the influence of some evil spirit.

DÆMONOMA'NIA (*Ant.*) a madness which was supposed to arise from the possession of some dæmons.

DA'FFODIL (*Bot.*) a species of the Narcissus, the *Narcissus Pseudo Narcissus* of Linnæus.—Sea Daffodil, the *Pancratium* of Linnæus.

DAG (*Mil.*) an obsolete word for a hand-gun, so called from its serving the purpose of a dagger.

DA'GGER (*Mil.*) a short sword or poignard about twelve or thirteen inches long.

DAGGER (*Mar.*) a piece of timber that crosses all the puppets of the bilgeways to keep them together; the plank that secures the heads of the puppets is called the *dagger plank*; and the pieces, whose sides are cast down and bolted through the cramp, are called *dagger-knees*, or *lodging-knees*.

DAGGER-POINTED (*Bot.*) mucronatus, an epithet for a leaf; *folium mucronatum*, a leaf ending in a point like that of a dagger, as in *Bromelia ananas*; so also in application to the calyx.

DAGGES (*Husband.*) the skirts of a fleece when cut off.

DAHLBE'RGIA (*Bot.*) vide *Dalbergia*.

DAI'DALA (*Ant.*) vide *Dædala*.

DAIL (*Mar.*) a trough in which the water runs from the pump over the deck.

DAI'LY (*Astron.*) vide *Diurnal*.

DAI'RY (*Husband.*) *Dayeria*, signified originally the daily yield of milch cows, or the profit made by them; whence its present signification of a place, and accommodation, for keeping cows and milk.

DAIS (*Med.*) δαἲς, a sort of pine-tree, and also the substance of that tree recommended by Hippocrates for the expulsion of the fœtus, &c. *Hippocrat. de Morb.*

DAIS, in the Linnean system, a genus of plants, Class 10 *Decandria*, Order 1 *Monogynia*.
 Generic Character. CAL. involucre four-leaved; *leaflets* scariose; *perianth* none.—CAL. one-petalled funnel form; *tube* filiform.—STAM. *filaments* ten; *anthers* simple.—PIST. *germ* somewhat oblong; *style* filiform; *stigma* globose ascending.—PER. *berry* ovate; *seed* single ovate.
 Species. The species are shrubs of the deciduous kind, as—*Dais cotinifolia*, Cotinus-leaved Dais, native of the Cape of Good Hope.—*Dais octandria*, native of India.—*Dais disperma*, native of Tongatabu.

DAISY (*Bot.*) the *Bellis* of Linnæus.—Great Daisy, or Ox-eye, the *Chrysanthemum Leucanthemum* of Linnæus.—Blue Daisy, the *Globularia vulgaris* of Linnæus.

DAI'TIDES (*Bot.*) δαΐτιδες, signify literally "great torches," but are metaphorically applied to heads of garlic. *Gal. Exeges. Vocab. Hippocrat.*

DA'KER (*Archæol.*) a number of ten hides.

DAL (*Mus.*) Italian for *for* or *by* in music books.

DALBE'RGIA (*Bot.*) a genus of plants, Class 17 *Diadelphia*, Order 4 *Decandria*.
 Generic Character. CAL. *perianth* one-leaved.—COR. papilionaceous; *standard* large; *wings* oblong.—STAM. *filaments* ten; *anthers* roundish.—PIST. *germ* oblong; *style* subulate; *stigma* simple.—PER. *legume* oblong; *seed* single or few.
 Species. The two species are—*Dalbergia lanceolaria*, a tree, native of Malabar and Ceylon.—*Dalbergia monetaria*, a shrub, native of Surinam.

DA'LEA (*Bot.*) the *Eupatorium dalea*, the *Lippia ovata*, and the *Psoralea dalea* of Linnæus.

DALECHAMPIA (*Bot.*) a genus of plants, Class 21 *Monoecia*, Order 9 *Monodelphia*, called after Jacobus Dalechampius.
 Generic Character. CAL. *involucel* two-leaved; *scales* numerous; *perianth* proper.—COR. none.—STAM. *filaments* many; *anthers* roundish.—PIST. *germ* roundish; *style* filiform; *stigma* perforated.—PER. *capsule* roundish; *seed* solitary.
 Species. The two species are biennials, as—*Dalechampia colorata*, Coloured-Dalechampia, native of the West Indies.—*Dalechampia scandens*, seu *Lupulus*, native of New Granada.

DALIBA'RDA (*Bot.*) the *Rubus dalibarda* of Linnæus.

DA'LLOPS (*Agric.*) patches of grass, or weeds among corn.

DALMA'TICA (*Ecc.*) an exterior vest of a priest or bishop, with sleeves, in distinction from the *Colobium*. [vide *Colobium*]

DA'LUS (*Archæol.*) a certain measure of land; whence *Dali Prati*, narrow slips of pasture land.

DAM (*Law*) a boundary or confinement, as to dam up, or to dam out; *infra damnum suum*, within the bounds or limits of his own property or jurisdiction. *Bract.* l. 2, c. 37.

DA'MA (*Zool.*) Fallow-Deer, the *Cervus Dama* of Linnæus.

DAMAGE *cleer* (*Law*) a duty formerly paid to the prothonotaries and other clerks, being a third, sixth, or ninth part of the damages recovered upon a trial in any court of justice. This duty was taken away by *Stat.* 17 *Car.* 2, c. 16.—*Damage faisant*, i. e. doing hurt or mischief; a term used when the beast of a stranger gets into another man's ground and feeds, there spoiling grass or corn; in which case the occupier of the ground may distrain or impound them as well in the night as in the day. *Stat.* 51 *Hen.* 3; *Stat.* 4, 1 *Inst.* 142; 2 *Danv. Ab.* 364.

DA'MAGES (*Law*) *damnum*, any hurt or hindrance which a man receives in his estate, particularly what the jurors are to inquire of, or bring in, when an action passeth for the plaintiff. *Co. Lit.* 257.

DA'MAS (*Mil.*) a sabre made of Damascus steel. [vide *Damascus*]

DA'MASCENE (*Bot.*) *Prunus damascena*, the Damask Plum or Damson, a variety of the *Prunus domestica* of Linnæus.

DAMA'SCUS STEEL (*Com.*) a very fine kind of steel made at Damascus, remarkable for its excellent temper.

DA'MASK (*Com.*) a silk stuff with a raised pattern, consisting of figures and flowers. The *caffart damask* is an imitation, made in France, of the true Indian damask.

DA'MASK ROSE (*Bot.*) a rose of a red colour, the *Rosa centifolia* of Linnæus.

TO DAMASK *wine* (*Cook.*) to warm it a little, in order to take off the edge of the cold.

DAMASKEE'NING (*Com.*) a kind of Mosaic work, which consists in ornamenting iron, steel, &c. by making incisions therein, and filling them up with gold or silver wire.

DA'MASON (*Bot.*) vide *Damascene*.

DAMASO'NIUM (*Bot.*) a genus of plants, Class 6 *Hexandria*, Order 5 *Hexagynia*.
 Generic Character. CAL. *spathe* one-leaved; *perianth* one-leaved.—COR. *petals* three.—STAM. *filaments* three; *anthers* linear.—PIST. *germ* oblong; *styles* six; *stigmas* villose—PER. *berry* oblong; *seeds* many.
 Species. The single species is the *Damsonium alismoides*, *Seratiotes*, *Alismoides*, seu *Ottel-ambel*, native of the East Indies, Malabar, and Ceylon.

DAMASONIUM is also the name of the *Alisma flava*, *damasonium*, &c.

DAMA'SSE (*Com.*) or *petite venise*, a kind of wrought linen, made in Flanders; so called from the fashion of its large flowers, something like those of damasks.

DAMELO'PRE (*Mar.*) a kind of vessel used in Holland, for conveying merchandise from one canal to another.

DAME-SIMONE (*Hort.*) a particular way of forcing cabbage lettuce.

DA'MES-VIOLET (*Bot.*) another name for the Rocket.

DA'MIANISTS (*Ecc.*) a branch of the Acephali. [vide *Acephali*]

DAMISE'LLA (*Law*) a light damosell, or miss. *Stat.* 12 *Ed.* 1.

DA'MIUM (*Ant.*) a kind of sacrifice; so called from δάμιω,

dorice pro, δᾶμιω, the people; because it was made for the people in honour of *Bona Dea*.

DAMNA'TA TERRA (*Chem.*) *Caput mortuum*.

DA'MNUM (*Law*) Damages. [vide *Damages*]

DA'MPERS (*Mus.*) certain moveable parts in the internal construction of the piano-forte, which are covered with cloth in order to deaden the vibration.

DAMPS (*Min.*) noxious exhalations in mines which sometimes suffocate those that work in them. They are distinguished into different kinds, as—the *Peas-bloom Damp*, in the mines of the Peak of Derbyshire, which are supposed to proceed from the multitude of red trefoil flowers, called honeysuckles, with which the meadows there abound.—*Fulminating Damps*, common in coal mines, which explode when they catch fire.—*Common Damps*, which affect persons with shortness of breath and difficulty of respiration.—*Globe Damps*, supposed to arise from the effluvia of the candles and the bodies. These ascend into the highest part of the vault, and condensing into an incrustation, corrupt and become pestilential.

DA'MSIN (*Bot.*) vide *Damascene*.

DAN (*Archæol.*) formerly a title of honour for the better sort of men in this kingdom, answering to the Spanish *Don*.

DA'NCERIES (*Mus.*) French for collections of galliards, allemandes, ballad-tunes, and other lively tunes.

DA'NCES (*Mus.*) tunes composed for or used in dancing, as the minuet, reel, hornpipe, &c.

DANCE'TTE (*Her.*) an epithet signifying indented in a particular manner. The lines *dancette* and *indented* differ not in form but in quantity, the acute angle in the former being much larger and deeper than in those of the latter. The difference may be further observed by the two subjoined figures, as *fig.* 1: " He beareth *azure* a fesse *dancette, or*, between three cherubims heads *argent*, crined of the second; name *Adye*:" *fig.* 2, " He beareth *azure* two bars indented *or*, a chief *argent*; name *Storr*."—*Double dancette* is an epithet applied particularly to the bend, as *fig.* 3, " He beareth *azure* a bend double dancette *argent*, by the name of *Lorks*."

Fig. 1.   Fig. 2.   Fig. 3.

DANDELI'ON (*Bot.*) the *Leontodon* of Linnæus.

DANDE-PRAT (*Num.*) or *Dande-Part*, a small coin said to have been coined in the reign of Henry VII.

DANDRIFF (*Med.*) a scurfy sort of disorder in the heads of young children. [vide *Pityriasis*]

DA'NEGELT (*Archæol.*) a tax of one shilling, and afterwards of two shillings, for every hide of land, imposed by king Ethelred on his subjects, in order to clear the seas of Danish pirates, and to purchase a temporary peace with that people. *Hovedon. par post. Annal. Ann.* 344; *Seld. Marc. Claus.*

DA'NELAGE (*Archæol.*) the laws which were in force in England during the time of the Danish government.

DA'NE-WORT (*Bot.*) another name for the Dwarf Elder.

DANGE'RIA (*Law*) or *Dangerium*, a payment of money anciently made by the forest tenants to their lords, that they might have leave to plough and sow in the time of pannage or mast-feeding. *Main. For. Law*.

DANK (*Com.*) a small silver coin current in Persia and Arabia, weighing one-sixth of a drachm, and of correspondent value: also a small weight for precious stones in Arabia.

DA'NTIA (*Bot.*) the *Isnardia palustris*.

DAOU'RITE (*Min.*) a kind of schorl-stone.

DA'PHNE (*Bot.*) δάφνη, the Laurel or Bay Tree, a plant; so called from the nymph Daphne, who was fabled by the poets to have been changed into a laurel. [vide *Laurel*] *Theophrast.* l. 3, c. 11; *Ovid Metamorph.* l. 1; *Dioscor.* l. 1, c. 106.

DAPHNE, in the Linnean system, a genus of plants, Class 8 *Octandria*, Order 1 *Monogynia*.

Generic Character. CAL. none.—COR. one, one-petalled.—STAM. *filaments* eight; *anthers* roundish.—PIST. *germ* ovate; *style* very short; *stigma* headed.—PER. *berry* roundish; *seed* single.

Species. The species are shrubs, as—*Daphne mezereon, Thymelea, Laureola, Daphnoides*, seu *Chamelea*, native of the north of England.—*Daphne thymelæa*, seu *Sanamunda*, native of Spain, Italy, and the South of France.—*Daphne tartomaria*, seu *Tarton raire*, Silvery-leaved Daphne, or *Tartoniana*.—*Daphne laureola*, seu *Laureola*, Spurge-Laurel, native of Britain, France, Switzerland, &c. &c.—*Daphne tinifolia*, seu *Laurus*, native of Jamaica.—*Daphne Gnidium*, seu *Gnidium*, Flax-leaved Daphne, native of the South of France, &c.—*Daphne cneoum*, seu *Cneoum*, Trailing Daphne, native of France, &c.

DAPHNE is also the name of the *Strumsia maritima*.

DAPHNELÆ'ON (*Nat.*) δαφνέλαιον, from δάφνη, the bay-tree, and ἔλαιον, oil; oil of Bay.

DAPHNE'PHAGI (*Ant.*) δαφνηφάγοι, from δάφνη, the laurel, and φάγω, to eat; diviners and prophets, who after eating the laurel or bay-leaves, became inspired.

Ὡς ἔφασαν κούραι μεγάλα Διὸς ἀρτιέπειαι
Καί μοι σκῆπτρον ἴδον, δάφνης ἐριθηλέας ὄζον
Δρέψασαι θηητόν ἐνέπνευσαν δέ μοι αὐδὴν
Θείην, ὥς κλείοιμι τά τ' ἐσσόμενα πρό τ' ἐόντα.

Lycoph. v. 6; *Eustath.*; *Cassian. Bass. in Virg. Georg.* l. 2, c. 3.

DAPHNEPHO'RIA (*Ant.*) δαφνηφόρια, a novennial festival celebrated by the Bœotians in honour of Apollo, to whom boughs of laurel were offered. The priest who performed the ceremony was called the δαφνηφόρος, i. e. laurel-bearer. *Pausan. Bœot.*

DA'PHNIA (*Min.*) a precious stone, said to cure the epilepsy. *Plin.* l. 37, c. 10.

DA'PHNIN (*Chem.*) the Bitters, or the bitter principle extracted from the *Daphne Alpina* of Linnæus.

DAPHNOIDES (*Bot.*) the *Daphne mezereon*.

DA'PIFER (*Polit.*) *a dapes ferendo*, i. e. from serving the feast on the table; a domestic officer like to our Steward of the Household, or rather *Clerk of the Kitchen*; but it was afterwards used for the chief steward or bailiff of an honor or manor.

DA'PPLE (*Vet.*) an epithet for the colour of a horse, which is of a light grey shaded with spots of a deeper grey.

DARA'PTI (*Log.*) an arbitrary term expressing the first mood of the third figure of syllogisms, where the two first propositions are universal affirmatives, and the last a particular affirmative; as,

D a   All believers are loved by God;
R a P All believers are afflicted; therefore,
T i   Some afflicted are beloved by God.

DA'RATOS (*Med.*) an epithet for bread that is unfermented.

DARD à *feu* (*Mil.*) a javelin trimmed with fireworks to be sent against ships or any places intended to be set on fire.

DARE ad *Remanentiam* (*Law*) to give away in fee or for ever. *Glanv.* l. 7, c. 1.

DA'REA (*Bot.*) the *Trechomanes membranaceum crispum hirsutum, &c. &c.* of Linnæus.

DA'RIC (*Ant.*) δαρικός, a gold coin, so called from Darius, by whom it was struck. It is said to have been made of very fine gold, and is supposed to have been equal to 25s. of our money. In Scripture the darics are called *Adarkonim*.

DA'RII (*Log.*) an arbitrary term for a mode of syllogisms of the first figure, wherein the major proposition is a universal affirmative, and the minor and conclusion particular affirmatives; thus,

   d A All men are endued with reason;
    r I Some animals are men; *ergo*,
      I Some animals are endued with reason.

DARK CHAMBER (*Mech.*) vide *Camera obscura.*—*Dark Tent*, a portable *Camera Obscura*, made somewhat like a desk, and fitted with optic glasses, &c.

DARKING-COCK (*Orn.*) a variety of the *Phasianus Gallus* of Linnæus.

DARNEL-GRASS (*Bot.*) the *Lolium*; most of the species are perennials, but the *Lolium temulentum* is annual.

DA'RREIN (*Law*) a corruption of *dernier*, last; as, the *darrien presentment*, the last presentment, an assize or writ against a stranger who preferreth to a church, the advowson whereof belongs to another. F. N. B. 31; 2 Inst. 355.—*Darrein Continuance* is when, after the continuance of the plea, the defendant pleads a new matter.

DARSE (*Mar.*) French for the interior of a port which is shut with a chain, where galleys and other small craft are sheltered.

DA'RSIS (*Med.*) δάρσις, an exulceration of the skin.

DA'RTARS (*Vet.*) a kind of scab or ulceration on the skin, to which lambs are subject.

DA'RTER (*Orn.*) a bird with a small head and long slender neck, the *Plotus* of Linnæus. It lives principally upon fish, which it catches by darting forward the head whilst the neck is contracted like the body of a serpent.

DA'RTOS (*Anat.*) δαρτός, the coat which immediately covers the testes.

DA'SYPUS (*Zool.*) δασύπους, from δασύς, rough, and πούς, the foot; an epithet for a hare or rabbit. Gal. de Simpl. l. 5, c. 9.

DASYPUS, in the Linnean system, Armadillo, a genus of animals, Class *Mammalia*, Order *Bruta*.

  Generic Character. Tusks none; grinders short, cylindrical, seven or eight in each jaw.—Body covered with a bony shell, intersected by zones or bands.

  Species. Animals of this tribe feed on roots, melons, insects, worms, &c.; are gentle; rest by day and wander in the night; burrow in the ground, and roll themselves into a globular form when they apprehend any danger; females bring forth every month; flesh eatable. The species mostly inhabit South America, and are distinguished by the number of their bands.

DA'SYS (*Med.*) δασύς, rough; is a term applied by Hippocrates to the tongue condensed and exasperated with heat and dryness. Cal. Comm. in Hippocrat.; Prorrhet & Coac.

DASYSTE'PHANA (*Bot.*) the *Gentiana asclepaides*.

DA'TA (*Math.*) such things or quantities as are supposed to be given or known, in order to find out thereby that which is unknown or sought for.

DATARY (*Ecc.*) the chief officer in the chancery of Rome, through whose hands most vacant benefices pass.

DATE (*Chron.*) the number which marks the day of the month when any writing, coin, &c. was made.

DATE (*Bot.*) the fruit of the Date Tree.—Date Plum, the *Diospyros* of Linnæus.

DATE TREE (*Bot.*) the *Phœnix dactylifera*.

DATHI'ATHUM (*Bot.*) a coarser kind of frankincense of the second gathering. Plin. l. 2, c. 14.

DA'THOLITE (*Min.*) a sort of spar stone.

DATI'SCA (*Bot.*) a genus of plants, Class 22 *Dioecia*, Order 10 *Dodecandria*.

  Generic Character. CAL. *perianth* five-leaved.—COR. none.—STAM. *filaments* scarcely any.—PIST. *germ* oblong.—*styles* three; *stigmas* simple.—PER. *capsule* oblong; *seeds* numerous.

  Species. The species are perennials, as—*Datisca cannabina*, Cannabis, seu *Luteola*, native of Candia, or Crete—*Datisca hirtea*, Rough-stalked Bastard Hemp, native of Pennsylvania.

DA'TISI (*Log.*) an arbitrary term for a mode of syllogisms in the third figure, wherein the major proposition is a universal affirmative, and the minor and conclusion are particular affirmatives; as,

   d A All believers are dear to God;
    t I Some believers are afflicted; *ergo*,
     s I Some afflicted are dear to God.

DA'TIVE (*Law*) signifies that which may be given or disposed of at will and pleasure. Stat. 9, R. 2, c. 2.—*Dative Tutelage*, in Civil Law, the tutelage of a minor appointed by a magistrate.

DATIVE (*Gram.*) from *do*, to give; is the third case of nouns; so called because thereby we show that something is given or taken away. Priscian. et alii. Vet. Gram. Putsch. Ed.; Isidor. Orig. l. 1, c. 6.

DATU'RA (*Bot.*) a genus of plants, Class 5 *Pentandria*, Order 1 *Monogynia*.

  Generic Character. CAL. *perianth* one-leaved.—COR. one-petalled.—STAM. *filaments* five; *anthers* oblong.—PIST. *germ* ovate; *style* filiform; *stigma* thickish.—PER. *capsule* ovate; *seeds* numerous.

  Species. The species are annual, as—*Datura ferox*, seu *Stramonium*, Rough Thorn-Apple, native of China.—*Datura stramonium*, seu *Solanum*, Common Thorn Apple. Bauh. Hist.; Bauh. Pin.; Park. Theat.; Raii Hist.; Tourn. Inst.

DAVA'TA *terra* (*Law*) a portion of land so called in Scotland.

DAUBE' (*Cook.*) or *à la daube*, a particular way of dressing a leg of veal, &c.

DA'UCUS (*Bot.*) δαῦκος, Carrot, the well-known garden vegetable, is said to derive its name, ἀπὸ τῦ δαίειν, from its hot quality. It was also called *Dircæus*, according to Dioscorides. Theoph. l. 2, c. 5; Diosc. l. 3, c. 83.

DAUCUS (*Bot.*) a genus of plants, Class 5 *Pentandria*, Order 2 *Digynia*. Natural order of *Umbellatæ* or *Umbellifera*.

  Generic Character. CAL. *umbel* universal.—COR. *universal* difform.—STAM. *filaments* five; *anthers* simple.—PIST. *germ* inferior; *styles* two; *stigmas* obtuse.—PER. none; *seeds* two.

  Species. The species are biennials and annuals. Of the first kind the following are the principal:—*Daucus barota*, Caucalis, seu *Staphilinus*, Wild Carrot, or Bird's Nest.—*Daucus mauritanicus*, seu *Pastinaca*, Fine-leaved Carrot, native of Italy, Spain, Barbary, &c. Of the second kind are the following; namely—*Daucus visnaga*, seu *Visnaga*, Spanish Carrot, or Pick-Tooth, native of the South of Europe, Barbary, and Mount Libanus.—*Daucus gingidium*, seu *Gingidium*, Shining-leaved Carrot, native of the South of France, &c. Clus. Hist.; Bauh. Hist.; Bauh. Pin.; Ger. Herb.; Park. Theat.; Raii Hist.; Tourn. Inst.

DAUCUS is also the name of several species, as the *Æthusa cynapium*, the *Ammi glaucifolium*, the *Athamanta libanotes sicula, et Cretensis*; the *Caucalis grandiflora*, the *Phellandrium mutillina*, the *Pimpinella peregrina*, the *Seseli glaucum, et elatum*; the *Sium verticillatum, et siculum*.

DA'VIDISTS (*Ecc.*) a sect of fanatics in the 16th century, so called after their leader one George David, a glazier, of Ghent, who pretended to be the Messiah.

ST. DAVID'S DAY (*Cus.*) the first of March, kept by the

Welsh in honour of St. David, bishop of Miney, in Wales, at which time they wear leeks in their hats, in commemoration of a singular victory obtained by them, under the conduct of St. David, over the Saxons.

DAVID'S STAFF (*Mar.*) an instrument made use of in navigation.—*David's quadrant*, the common back quadrant.

DA'VIT (*Mar.*) a short piece of timber used on board a ship, to hale up the flook of an anchor and fasten it to the bow of the ship.

DAULONTAS FRUTEX (*Bot.*) an American shrub, which has the properties and virtues of chamomile.

DA'UMUR (*Zool.*) a species of serpent.

DAUPHIN (*Ant.*) an ancient military instrument. [vide *Delphinus*]

DAUPHIN (*Polit.*) the title of the next heir to the crown of France, which is supposed to have originated with the Dauphins of Viennois, who were sovereigns of the province of Dauphiny, and bore a dolphin for their arms. The last of those princes having no issue gave his dominions to the crown of France, upon condition that the heir to the crown should be called Dauphin, and ever after bear a dolphin for his arms.

DAUPHIN'S CROWN (*Her.*) a circle of gold set round with eight fleur-de-lis, closed at the top with four dolphins whose tails conjoin under a fleur-de-lis, as in the annexed figure.

DAUPHINS de Canons (*Mil.*) French for the dolphins which are made in relief on the trunnions of field pieces.

DA'URA (*Bot.*) vide *Helleborum*.

DAW (*Orn.*) vide *Jackdaw*.

DAWN (*Astron.*) the commencement of the day when the twilight appears.

DAY (*Ant.*) vide *Dies*.

DAY (*Chron.*) a space of time reckoned from the apparent motion of the sun. It has been divided into the *day*, properly so called, in distinction from the night, which Sacro de Bosco calls the *artificial day*; and into the *natural day*, as he calls it, including both day and night, which by others is called the *artificial day*. [vide *Chronology*] The day is moreover distinguished into civil and astronomical. —The *civil day* is a space of twenty-four hours, which has been reckoned from different points, by different nations; namely, from sunset to sunset, or from sunrise to sunrise, &c.—*Astronomical day* is also a space of twenty-four hours, reckoned from twelve o'clock at noon till the next succeeding noon, i. e. beginning when the sun's centre is in the meridian of any given place. This day is divided accordingly into two parts; namely, A.M. *ante meridiem*, i. e. before noon; and P.M. *post meridiem*, i. e. after noon. [vide *Chronology*]

DAY (*Law*) is taken, 1. For the civil day, or the space of twenty-four hours, including day and night; so that if the fact be done in the night, it must be stated in law proceedings in the night of the same day. 2. Day is also taken for the *day of appearance* of the parties, or the continuance of the suit, where a day is given, &c. whence the phrases "To be dismissed *without day*," to be finally dismissed the court. "To be put *without day*," i. e. when the justices, before whom causes are depending, do not come on the day to which they have been continued. A day of appearance in court is, by the writ, the roll; *by writ*, when the sheriff returns the writ; *by roll*, when the sheriff not returning the writ, the defendant, to save his freehold, loss of time, imprisonment, &c. may appear by the day he hath by the roll. *Co. Lit.* 134, 135.—*Common days*. [vide *Dies*]—*Special days*. [vide *Dies*]—*Days of grace*. [vide *Dies*]—*Return days*, certain days in term for the return of writs, which, if they happen on a Sunday, or any festival, as Ascension Day, St. John Baptist, and the like, the day following is taken instead of it.—*Days in Bank*. [vide *Dies*]

DA'Y-FLY (*Ent.*) the *Ephemera* of Linnæus, an insect; so called from the shortness of its existence, which rarely exceeds a day, and sometimes not an hour. The larva lives under water, is six-footed, and active; the pupa is similar to the larva, but it has also the rudiments of future wings.

DA'Y-LILY (*Bot.*) the *Hemerocallis* of Linnæus; a plant so called because the beauty of its flower is of short duration, seldom exceeding a day.

DA'Y-NET (*Sport.*) a particular sort of net for catching larks, martins, hobbies, &c.

DA'Y-RULE (*Law*) vide *Day-Writ*.

DA'Y-WERE of land (*Archæol.*) *diurnalis diuturna*, as much land as could be ploughed up in one day's work, or in one journey, as it is called.

DA'Y-WRIT (*Law*) or *Day-Rule*, a rule or order of court permitting a prisoner in custody, in the King's Bench prison, &c. to go without the bounds of the prison for one day.

D'AYE'NIA (*Bot.*) the *Ayenia pusilla* of Linnæus.

DA'YER (*Archæol.*) an old word in Lorrain and Champagne for the meeting of the day-labourers, to give an account of their daily work.

DAYE'RIA (*Archæol.*) a dairy. [vide *Dairy*]

DA'Y-LILY (*Bot.*) vide *Day*.

DAYS ember (*Ecc.*) vide *Ember*.

DAYS intercalary (*Chron.*) vide *Chronology* and *Intercalary*.

DAYS of grace (*Com.*) are a customary number of days allowed for the payment of a bill of exchange, &c. after the same becomes due. Three days of grace are allowed in Britain, where they are given and taken as a matter of course; but in other countries, where the time allowed is much longer, it would be reckoned dishonourable for a merchant to avail himself of it. Bills are, therefore, paid on the very day they fall due.

DA'Y'S-MAN (*Archæol.*) a term for an arbitrator, or mediator, in any matter of dispute.

DAYS of grace (*Law*) vide *Dies*.

DAY's Work (*Mar.*) the reckoning, or account of a ship's course, and distance run, during twenty-four hours, or from noon to noon.

DAZE (*Min.*) a kind of glittering stones, found in the tin and lead mines.

DE (*Law*) a preposition used in many law phrases, as—*De bene esse*, as, to take a thing *de bene esse*, i. e. to allow or accept of it for the present, till the matter shall come to be more fully debated.—*De non decimando Modus*, a writ to be discharged of tithes.—*De non Residentia clerici Regis, &c.* an ancient writ, to excuse a person employed in the King's service, &c. and to discharge him of non-residence.— *De Novo damus*, the clause of a charter, which, in fact, renders it a new charter.—*De Onerando pro Rata Portionis*, an ancient writ, where a person was distrained for rent that ought to be paid proportionably by others. *F. N. B.* 234; *New. Nat. Brev.* 586; 2 *Inst.* 624.

DE'ACON (*Ecc.*) διάκονος, *diaconus*, from διακονέω, to minister to; a minister or servant in the church, whose office it is to assist the priest in divine service, &c. *S. Jonat. Epist. ad Trallian.*; *Clemens. Constit. Apost.* c. 4; *Justin. Apolog.* l. 2.; *S. Cyprian. de Laps.*; *August. Quæst.* 101; *Isidor. de Eccles. Offic.* l. 2, c. 28; *Alcuin de Divin. Offic.* l. 2, c. 8, &c.

DEAD (*Mar.*) a term used in many sea-phrases, as—*Dead-doors*, doors fitted to the outside of the quarter gallery doors, in case the quarter gallery should be carried away. —*Dead-eye*, a sort of flat block, encircled with a rope, and

4 B

pierced with three holes through the flat part, to receive the rope called the lanyard.—*Dead-flat*, a name for the midship bend.—*Dead-lights*, strong wooden posts fitted to the cabin windows, in which they are fixed in case of a storm.—*Dead-men's-eyes*, little blocks and pullies, with many holes, wherein the lanniers run.—*Dead-neap*, a low tide.—*Dead reckoning*, the estimation which the seamen make of the place where the ship is, by keeping an account of her course without any observation of the heavenly bodies. This is found, by keeping an account of the distance she has run by the log, and of her course steered by the compass, and then rectifying these data by the usual allowances for drift, lee-way, &c. according to the ship's known trim.—*Dead-rising*, or rising line of the floor, in French *la large des façons*, those parts of a ship's floor or bottom throughout her whole length, where the floor timber is terminated upon the lower futtock.—*Dead-ropes*, those which do not run in any block.—*Dead-water*, in French *remoux de sillage*, the eddy of water, which appears like little whirlpools, closing in with the ship's stern as she sails through it.—*Dead-wind*, in French *vent de bout*, the wind right against the ship, or that blowing from the very point to which she wants to go.—*Dead-wood*, in French *courbes de remplissage*, certain blocks of timber laid upon the keel, particularly at the extremities, afore and abaft. This dead-wood is equal in depth to two-thirds that of the keel, and as broad as can be procured, so as not to exceed the bread of the keel.—*Dead-works*, in French *œuvres mortes*, a name given to all that part of a ship which is above the water when she is laden.

To DE'ADEN *a ship's way* (*Mar.*) to impede her velocity through the water.

DEAD-EYE (*Mar.*) vide *Dead*.

DEAD-LA'NGUAGES (*Gram.*) those languages which have ceased to be spoken by any nation or community of people. Under this name are commonly included the Latin, Greek, and Hebrew, to distinguish them from the living languages that are now in regular use.

DEADLY *Carrot* (*Bot.*) the *Thapsia villosa* of Linnæus.—*Deadly nightshade*, the *Atropa* of Linnæus.

DEA'D-MEN'S-EYES (*Mar.*) vide *Dead*.

DEAD-NETTLE (*Bot.*) the *Lamium* of Linnæus, a plant of the nettle tribe; which is so called because it is without stings.

DEA'D-PLEDGE (*Law*) vide *Mortgage*.

DEAD-RE'CKONING (*Mar.*) vide *Dead*.

DEAD-RI'SING (*Mar.*) vide *Dead*.

DEA'D-ROPES (*Mar.*) vide *Dead*.

DEA'D-WATER, &c. (*Mar.*) vide *Dead*.

DEA'D'S-PART (*Law*) the remainder of the defunct's moveables, besides what is due to the wife and children.

DE-AFFO'RESTED (*Law*) *deafforestata*, discharged from being a forest, exempt from the forest laws. 17 Car. 1, c. 16.

DEAL (*Carpent.*) the wood of the fir-tree cut up for the purpose of building. It is cut again into various thicknesses, which are called *boards* or *leaves*, and the deal so divided is called two, three, four, five, &c. *cut stuff*.—*Whole Deals*, are one inch and a half thick.—*Slit Deals* are the half of that.

DE-ALBA'TION (*Mech.*) the process of whitening any thing.

DEAN (*Ecc.*) a dignified clergyman, who has power over ten or more canons.—*Dean and Chapter*, a corporate body, composed of the dean and his prebendaries.

DE-ARTICULA'TIO (*Anat.*) vide *Abarticulation*.

DE-ASCIA'TIO (*Surg.*) the same as *Aposceparnismus*.

DEATH, *civil* (*Law*) is where a man, though not actually dead, is adjudged so by law; as if any person, for whose life any estate hath been granted, remain beyond sea, or is otherwise absent seven years, no proof being made of his being alive, he shall be accounted dead. Stat. 19, l. 2, c. 6; 6 Ann. c. 18.

DEATH-WATCH (*Ent.*) the *Ptinus pulsator* of Linnæus; a little insect which inhabits old wooden furniture, and is distinguished by a peculiar ticking which it makes with the fore part of its head, something like the beating with a nail upon a table. This it does in seven, nine, or eleven distinct strokes, which were formerly looked upon as ominous to the family where they were heard; and gave rise to its vulgar name. It has since been ascertained that this ticking is only a call of one sex to the other. [vide *Plate* 35]

DEBA'NDEMENT (*Mil.*) a French term expressing the act of being out of the line.

DEBA'UCHER (*Mil.*) French for enticing a soldier from the service of his king and country.

DEBELLA'TION (*Mil.*) the subduing a people by military force.

DEBENTURE (*Law*) an instrument in the nature of a bond or bill to charge government, &c. There are different kinds of debentures; as, *custom-house debentures*, certificates by which a person is entitled to receive a drawback; *debentures in the King's household*, by which the King's servants can claim their wages.

DE'BET (*Law*) he owes; the form of a writ of debt, which is more frequently put *debet et detinet*, or *detinet* alone, i. e. he owes and detains, or keeps back from paying the debt. F. N. B. 119, &c.—*Debet et solet*, a writ of right, as if a man sue for any thing which is now denied, having been enjoyed before by himself, and his ancestors before him. F. N. B. 98; Reg. Orig. 140.

DEBI'LITIES (*Astrol.*) certain affections of the planets, by which they are weakened, and their influences become less vigorous.

DEBI'LLER (*Mar.*) French for taking the horses off, that are employed in dragging boats up a river.

DE'BIT (*Com.*) a term used in Book-keeping to express the left-hand page of the ledger, to which are carried all articles supplied or paid on the subject of an account, or that are charged to that account.

DEBIT (*Law*) vide *Debet*.

DE'BITUM (*Law*) vide *Debt*.

DEBLA'YER (*Mil.*) signifies, commonly, to make holes or excavations in the earth; but *deblayer un camp*, to evacuate a camp, for the purpose of clearing and purifying the ground; *deblayer les terres d'un fossé*, to clear away the superfluous earth from the parapet.

DEBOUCHE' (*Mil.*) French for an outlet of a wood, or narrow pass; *Debouché de tranchée*, the opening made at the extremity of a trench, in order to carry the work forwarder.

DEBO'UCHEMENT (*Mil.*) French for the marching of an army from a narrow place into one that is more open.

DEBO'UCHER (*Mil.*) French for to march out of a defile or narrow pass, &c.; also to begin a trench or *boyau* in fortification: *Deboucher une grosse bouche à feu*, to take the wadding out of a heavy piece of ordnance.

DEBO'UT (*Mil.*) Up! a word of command in the French when troops kneel upon one knee in the presence of the consecrated host.

DEBRI'S (*Mil.*) French for the remains or wreck of an army that has been routed.

DEBRUI'SED (*Her.*) an epithet for a bend, or other ordinary, placed over some animal, as in the annexed figure. He beareth "*Gules* a lion rampant *or*, debruised by a bend *argent*, charged with three crosses formy *sable*."

DEBT (*Law*) *Debitum*, in common parlance is a sum of money due from one person to another; in a legal sense it is an action which lieth where a man oweth another a certain sum of money, either by a debt of record, by specialty, or by simple contract. *F. N. B.* 120, &c.; *New Nat. Brev.*

DEBTS *and Credits* (*Mil.*) a title given to the monthly accounts given in by the captain of every troop, or company, in the British service.

DEBU'SQUER (*Mil.*) French for to drive an enemy's party from an ambuscade, or advantageous position.

DECACHO'RDUM (*Ant.*) an instrument of ten strings.

DECACLI'NION (*Ant.*) a dining-chamber with couches for ten persons.

DECA'DE (*Chron.*) the number, or space, of ten days, which formed the third part of the Attic month. [vide *Chronology*]

DECADE (*Lit.*) the number of ten books which was formerly the division of some volumes, particularly on historical subjects, as the decades of Livy.

DE'CAGON (*Geom.*) δικάγωνος, from δίκα, ten, and γωνία, a corner; a plane geometrical figure, consisting of ten sides and ten angles. If all the sides and angles are equal, it is a regular decagon, otherwise not.

DECAGY'NIA (*Bot.*) from δίκα, ten, and γυνή, a wife; the name of one of the orders in Linnæus' Artificial System, comprehending those flowers which have ten styles, as in the Class *Decandria*. [vide *Decandria*]

DE'CALOGUE (*Ecc.*) δικάλογος, from δίκα, ten, and λόγος, a discourse; a name for the Ten Commandments.

DECA'MERON (*Lit.*) a name given to a division of a volume into ten books, as the Decameron of Boccacio.

TO DECA'MP (*Mil.*) to march an army from the ground where it lay encamped; also to quit any place in an unexpected manner.

DECA'MYRON (*Med.*) from δίκα and μύρον, ointment; a malagma mentioned by Oribasius, containing ten ingredients. *Oribas. Med. Collect.*

DECANDRIA (*Bot.*) from δίκα, ten, and ἀνήρ, a man; ten-stamened; a name for the tenth class of Linnæus' Artificial system, comprehending those plants which have ten stamens. It consists of six orders, namely—*Monogynia, Digynia, Trigynia, Tetragynia, Pentagynia, Decagynia.* The following are the principal genera under the several orders, namely—Monogynia, *Cercis,* Judas Tree; *Bauhinia,* Mountain Ebony; *Hymenæa,* LocustTree; *Cæsalpinia,* Brasiletta; *Guilandina,* Bonduc, or Nicker Tree; *Dictamnus,* Fraxinella; *Hæmatoxylon,* Logwood; *Melia,* Bead Tree; *Swietenia,* Mahogany; *Guaiacum,* Lignum Vitæ; *Ruta,* Rue; *Tribulus,* Caltrops; *Zygophyllum,* Bean Caper; *Monotropa,* Yellow Bird's Nest; *Pyrola,* Winter Green; *Dionæa,* Venus' Fly-trap, &c. — Digynia, as *Scleranthus,* Knawel; *Chrysosplereian,* Golden Saxifrage; *Selene,* Catchfly; *Soponaria,* Soapwort; *Dianthus,* Pink, &c. — Trigynia, as *Arenaria,* Sandwort; *Stellaria,* Stichwort; *Cucubalus,* Campion, &c.—Pentagynia, as *Cotyledon,* Navelwort; *Sedum,* Stonecrop; *Spergula,* Spurrey; *Cerastium,* Mouse-Ear Chickweed; *Agrostemma,* Cockle; *Oxalis,* Wood-Sorrel; *Spondias,* Hog Plum, &c.

DECANDRIA is also the name of an order in the classes *Monadelphia, Diadelphia, Gynadria,* and *Diœcia.*

DECANTA'TION (*Chem.*) the pouring off the clear part of any liquor by inclination, so that it may be without any sediment.

DE'CANTER (*Mech.*) a glass bottle made so as to hold the wine which is for immediate use.

DE'CANUS (*Ant.*) the leader or foreman of a file of soldiers, which was ten deep. *Veget.* l. 2, c. 8; *Panciroll. Notit.; Dignit. Imp. Orient.* c. 20.

DECANUS also signified formerly a juggler, according to Galen. *De Simpl.* l. 6.

DECANUS (*Ecc.*) a dean. [vide *Dean*]

DECA'NUTE (*Astrol.*) or Decury, is ten degrees, attributed to some planet within which it is said to have one dignity.

DECAPHY'LLOUS (*Bot.*) *decaphyllus,* ten-leaved; an epithet for a calyx, as in *Hibiscus.*

DECAPITA'TION (*Law*) the punishment of putting a person to death by taking off his head.

DE'CAPROTI (*Archæol.*) δικάπρωτοι, i. e. *decem primi,* the ten chief officers of the empire.

DECA'RCHUS (*Ant.*) a tithing-man, or headborough.

DECASPE'RMUM (*Bot.*) the *Psidium Decaspermum* of Linnæus.

DECA'STICH (*Poet.*) an epigram, or stanza consisting of ten verses.

DECA'STYLE (*Archit.*) or *decastylos,* from δίκα, ten, and στῦλος, a column; a colonnade, consisting of ten columns. *Vitruv.* l. 3, c. 1.

DECATO'RES (*Ant.*) δικατολόγοι, tithe-gatherers.

DECATORTHO'MA (*Med.*) a medicine made of ten ingredients.

DECEI'T, *writ of* (*Law*) a writ that lies for one that receives damage or injury from him that doth any thing deceitfully in the name of another person.

DECEI'VED (*Man.*) a horse is said to be deceived upon a demivolt of one or two treads: when working, as for instance, to the right, and not having furnished above half the demivolt, he is pressed one time or motion forwards with the inner leg, and then is put to a reprize upon the left, in the same cadence.

DECE'MBER (*Chron.*) *Decembris,* i. e. *decimus mensis,* the tenth month; the last month in the year, when the sun enters the tropic of Capricorn, making the winter solstice. This month was a season of festivity among the ancients, in which all games were allowed that were otherwise prohibited by the laws.
Mart. l. 4, ep. 14, v. 7.

*Dum blanda vagus alea December
Incertus sonat hinc et hinc fritillis.*

Juv. Sat. 7, v. 96.

*Tunc par ingenio pretium: tunc utile multis
Pallere, et vinum toto nescire Decembri.*

Ovid. Fast. l. 3, v. 50.

Acceptus geniis illa December habet.

Senec. Epist. 18; *Plutarch. Quæst. Roman.* 34; *Macrob. Saturn.* l. 1, c. 7; *Stuck. Ant. Conv.* l. 1, c. 33, &c.

DECE'MFIDUS (*Bot.*) ten-cleft; an epithet for a calyx that is cut into ten parts. — *Decemlocularis,* ten-celled; an epithet for a pericarp that is divided into ten cells.

DECE'MPEDA (*Ant.*) δικάπους, a perch or pole ten foot long to measure land with.
Hor. Carm. l. 2, od. 15, v. 14.

*Nulla decempedis
Metata privatis opacum
Porticus excipiebat Arcton.*

Augustus assigned the decempeda as a weapon to a deserter, or runaway, instead of a spear. *Cic. Phil.* 14, c. 4; *Suet. in Aug.* c. 25; *Veget.* l. 3, c. 8.

DE'CEM *tales* (*Law*) a writ which gives to the sheriff *apponere decem tales,* i. e. to appoint ten such men, for the supply of jurymen when a sufficient number do not appear to make up a full jury.

DECEM *primi* (*Ant.*) the ten chief men, or senators, of every city or borough, called by Livy *Decem principes. Cic. Rosc. Am.* c. 9; *Liv.* l. 29, c. 15; *Sigon. de Ant. Jur. Ital.* l. 2, c. 8.—*Decemviri,* extraordinary magistrates created A. U. C. 302, for the particular purpose of collecting the laws of the twelve tables, which they gathered out of the writings of Solon. They were also entrusted with the government of the city in the stead of consuls; but this lasted only a short time. *Dionys. Hal.* l. 4, p. 260; *Liv.* l. 3, c. 33.

Decemviri were also particular magistrates appointed by the decrees of the senate to determine particular causes. *Cic. Orat.* c. 46; *Pompon. in Orig. Juris.*; *Siccam. de Jud. Centumvir.* c. 9, 10.

DECENNA'LIA (*Ant.*) or Decennia; a festival every ten years instituted by Augustus, on the occasion of his resuming the imperial authority at the end of that term. The same festival was observed by his successors. *Dio.* l. 53.

DECE'NNARY (*Law*) a town, or tithing, consisting originally of ten families of freeholders. Ten of these Decennaries constituted a *Hundred*, the origin of which is ascribed to Alfred.

DECE'PTIO (*Law*) vide *Deceit*.

DECER'MINA (*Ant.*) boughs and leaves that *decerpebantur*, were plucked for the purpose of being used at lustrations. *Fest. de Verb. Sig.*

DECHARGE'URS (*Mil.*) French for men who were appointed to attend the park of artillery, and assist the non-commissioned officers.

DECHOU'ER (*Mar.*) French for getting afloat a ship that has been stranded.

DE'CIDENCE (*Med.*) a decay, or tendency to any distemper.

DECI'DUUS (*Bot.*) deciduous; an epithet for a leaf, calyx, corolla, stipules, bractes, and legumes; *folium deciduum*, a leaf that falls off in autumn; whence also plants which lose their leaves in autumn are called deciduous; *perianthium deciduum*, a perianth that falls after the corolla opens, as in *Berberis*, and the class *Tetradynamia*; *corolla decidua*, a corolla that falls off with the rest of the flower; *stipula decidua*, a deciduous stipule, as in *Padus*, *Cerasus*, *Populus*, *Tilia*, *Ulmus*, *Quercus*, and many other trees.

DE'CIES *tantum* (*Law*) i. e. ten times as much; a writ which lies against a juror (who had been bribed to give his verdict) for the recovery of ten times as much as he took. *Stat.* 38 Ed. 3, c. 12; *Reg. Orig.* 188; *F. N. B.* 171.

DE'CILE (*Astron.*) a new aspect invented by Kepler, when two planets are distant 36 degrees.

DE'CIMÆ (*Archæol.*) Tenths or Tithes.

DE'CIMAL (*Math.*) an epithet for any thing proceeding by tens, as Decimal Arithmetic, decimal Fractions, decimal Scale, &c.—*Decimal Arithmetic* signifies, in a general sense, that arithmetic, or mode of computation, which proceeds on the scale of ten figures. [vide *Notation*] but in a particular sense it implies simply—*Decimal fractions*, which are such as have 10, 100, 1000, 10,000, &c. for their denominator, as $\frac{1}{10}$, $\frac{1}{100}$, $\frac{1}{1000}$, $\frac{1}{10000}$, &c. which, for brevity sake, are expressed with a point thus ·5 for $\frac{5}{10}$.—*Decimal chain*, a chain for measuring of lands, divided decimally, or into an hundred equal parts, marks being placed at every ten.—*Decimal scales*, flat rules, or scales divided decimally. —*Circulating Decimals*. [vide *Circulating*]

DECIMA'TION (*Ant.*) a military punishment among the Romans, inflicted upon such as behaved themselves ill in the field, by selecting from among the number every tenth man who was to be put to death. *Polyb.* l. 6, c. 36; *Dionys. Hal.* l. 9; *Cic. Cluent.* c. 46; *Liv.* l. 2, c. 59; *Plutarch in Crass.*; *Veget.* l. 3, c. 4; *Sigon. de Ant. Jur. Civ. Rom.* l. 1, c. 15; *apud. Grav. Thes. Antiq.* tom. 3.

DECIMATION (*Archæol.*) a tithing, or paying a tenth part.

DE'CIMIS *solvendis*, &c. (*Law*) a writ against those who had farmed the prior-alien's lands of a king, for the rector of the parish, to recover his tithe from them.

DE'CINERS (*Law*) *Decenniers*, or *Dosiners*, such as had the jurisdiction over ten friburghs for keeping the King's peace.

To DECI'PHER (*Lit.*) to find out the meaning of any manuscript, which is written with ciphers.

DECK (*Mar.*) a planked floor on which the guns lie, and the men walk. *Decks* are of different kinds, as—*Gathering Deck*, which rises higher in the middle than at each end.— *Flush Deck*, fore and aft, which lies upon a right line without any fall.—*Half-Deck*, which reaches from the mainmast to the stern.—*Lower-Gun-Deck*, which is the first deck in first and second rate ships.—*Middle Deck*, which is the second deck.—*Upper*, or *Main-Deck*, which is much slighter than the two preceding.—*Quarter-Deck*, which is above the upper deck.—*Gun-Deck*, in frigates and sloops, is the main or upper deck.—*Spar-Deck*, that which is continued in a straight line from the quarter-deck to the forecastle, and appropriated for the reception of spars, cables, &c. It is otherwise called the Orlop. " To raise a *deck*," is to put it up higher, and " To sink a *deck*," to lay it lower. [vide *Navigation*]

DE'CKER (*Mar.*) a term implying the rate of force in a ship of war, as " A two or three *Decker*," i. e. a vessel with two or three entire tiers, or ranges of cannon.

DECLAMA'TION (*Rhet.*) a set speech, made for the sake of exercise upon a given subject.

DECLARA'TION *of war* (*Polit.*) the public proclamation of a state, by which it declares itself to be at war with any foreign power, and forbids all and every one to aid and assist the common enemy, at their peril.

DECLARATION (*Law*) *Declaratio*, *Narratio*, a legal specification on record of the cause of action by a plaintiff against a defendant. *Declarations* are of two kinds, namely— *Declaration de bene esse*, or *By-the-by*, which is made on the return-day, conditionally until special or common bail be filed.—*Declaration in chief*, which is after the filing of bail.

DECLARA'TOR (*Law*) an action in the Scotch law whereby we pray something to be declared in our favour.—*Declarator of property*, is when the complainer, declaring his right to lands, desires he should be declared sole proprietor. —*Declarator of redemption* is when, after a process before the Lords against a wadsetter who refuses to renounce after the order of redemption is used, the Lords force him to renounce, and by decree declare the lands redeemed.

DECLA'RATORY *Actions* (*Law*) are those actions in the Scotch law, wherein the right of the pursuer is craved to be declared; but nothing claimed to be done by the defender.

DECLE'NSION (*Gram.*) the inflection of cases to which nouns are subject; also the act of going through these inflections.

DECLENSION *of a disease* (*Med.*) that abatement in a distemper which follows when it is come to its height.

DECLINA'TION (*Astron.*) the distance of any star, or point of the Heavens, from the Equator. The greatest declination of the sun is 23° 30′. The declination is either North or South, as it is North or South of the Equator. It is also apparent or true.—*Apparent declination*, the distance of the apparent place of a planet from the Equator. —*True declination*, the distance of the true place from the Equator.

DECLINATION *of the mariner's compass* (*Mar.*) its variation from the true meridian of any place.

DECLINATION *of a wall* (*Hor.*) or a plane for dials; an arc of the horizon comprehended either between the plane and the prime vertical circle, if it be reckoned from the East or West, or else between the meridian and the plane, if from North or South.

DECLINA'TOR (*Mech.*) a mathematical instrument to take the declination of the stars.

DECLI'NATORY (*Mech.*) a box fitted with a compass and needle, to take the declination of walls for dialling.

DECLINA'TUS (*Bot.*) declined or declining, that is, bending towards the earth; an epithet for a stem, peduncle, stamen, style; but *folium declinatum* is a leaf bent downwards like the keel of a boat.

DECLI'NERS (*Math.*) or *Declining Dials*, are those which cut obliquely either the plane of the prime vertical, or the plane of the horizon.

DECLI'VIS (*Med.*) declining; an epithet for the abdominal muscle, so called on account of its posture.

DECO'CT (*Med.*) a name for water once boiled, or heated, which was afterwards cooled in the snow to make it a more grateful drink, which, according to Pliny, was the emperor Nero's invention. *Plin. l.* 31, c. 3; *Gal. de Meth. Med.* l. 7.

DECO'CTION (*Med.*) a medicinal liquor, or diet-drink made of roots, herbs, &c. boiled.

DECO'CTUM (*Med.*) vide *Decoct*.

DECOI'FFER *une fusée* (*Mil.*) French for to take off the wax, or mastic composition, by which the inflammable matter in a fusée is confined.

DECOLLA'TIO (*Surg.*) the loss of a part of the skull, so called from *decollo*, to behead.

DECOLLA'TION (*Ecc.*) signifies literally beheading, but is seldom applied except to the beheading of John the Baptist.

DECOLORA'TION (*Mech.*) the staining or marring a colour.

DECOMBRES (*Mil.*) French for the rubbish which is made by any breach that is effected in the works of a fortification.

DECOMPO'SITE (*Gram.*) vide *Decompound*.

DECOMPOSITE (*Chem.*) an epithet for a metallic or other body composed of the metal and a menstruum, &c.

DECOMPOSITE (*Med.*) vide *Decompositum*.

DECOMPOSI'TION (*Chem.*) the reduction of a body into the parts of which it is composed.

DECOMPO'SITUM (*Med.*) a term which augments the signification of *compositum*. *Composita* are things which suffer corruption, and are compounded. *Decomposita* are things united in composition by means of corruption and generation.

DE'COMPOUND (*Gram.*) an epithet for a word which is compounded of two or more words, as Ware-house-man.

DECOMPOUND (*Bot.*) *decompositus*, an epithet for a leaf, an umbel, and a flower; *folium decompositum*, a leaf which has its primary leaf so divided that each part forms a compound leaf. These leaves are distinguished into the *bigeminate*, *biternate*, and *bipennate* [vide *Bigeminate*, &c.]; *umbella decomposita* is the same as *prolifera*; *flos decompositus*, a flower compounded of compound flowers, or containing within a common calyx smaller calyces, as in the Order *Segregata*, Class *Syngenesia*.

DECO'MPTE (*Mil.*) a liquidation, or balance, which from time to time was made in the old French service between the captain and every private soldier for monies advanced or in hand.

DECORA'TIONS (*Archit.*) the ornaments in churches, or other public buildings, that tend to increase its beauty.

DECORTICA'TION (*Bot.*) from *de*, and *cortex*, bark; the pulling off the outward bark of a tree.

DECO'RUM (*Archit.*) or *decor*, the suiting all the parts of a building so that they may best become the situation. *Vitruv. l.* 1, c. 2.

DECOU'PLE (*Her.*) the same as *uncouple*.

DECO'Y (*Sport.*) an enclosed aviary; a place fitted for catching of wild fowl.—*Decoy duck*, a duck which goes abroad and decoys others into the place, where they become a prey.

DECOY (*Mar.*) a stratagem employed by a small ship of war to draw a vessel of inferior force into an incautious pursuit, until she is come within the range of her cannon, or, as it is called, within gun-shot.

DECOY (*Mil.*) a stratagem to carry off the enemy's horses in a foraging party.

DECRE'ASE *of the Moon* (*Astron.*) another name for the wane.

DECRE'E (*Law*) a judgment in a court of equity on a bill preferred, as a decree in Chancery, &c.

DECREES (*Lit.*) vide *Decretals*.

DECRE'ET *cognitionis causa* (*Law*) is, in the Scotch law, when the *apparent heir* is called to hear the debt constitute, it not being already clearly constitute by writ; and the appearing *heir* renounces, being charged to enter Heir.—*Decreet cognitionis causa against Executors* is when the nearest of kin are pursued by the Executor Creditor, who hath no writ to instruct his Debtor to hear the debt constitute.—*Decreet of comprising* is when, at the day appointed in the letters, the Debitor being called, the messenger offers him his lands for the money, which, if he have not ready, the Inquest declares the lands to belong to the creditor for his payment.—*Decreet of exoneration*, a decreet of the Commissars against the Creditors, or nearest of kin, wherein it is proved that the executor hath executed the whole testament, and that all is exhausted by lawful sentences.—*Decreet of locality*, a decreet modifying a stipend to a minister, dividing and proportioning the same among the heritors.—*Decreet of modification* is modifying a stipend to a minister, but not dividing it.—*Decreet of valuation*, a sentence of the Lords, determining the extent and value of teinds.

DE'CREMENT (*Her.*) the wane of the moon, which in this state is said to be a *moon decrescent*. [vide *Decrescent*]

DECREMENT *equal of life* (*Math.*) a term in the doctrine of annuities, signifying that out of a certain number of lives there should be an equal annual decrease within a given period of years; as suppose that out of 56 persons at the age of 30 one die every year, so that in fifty-six years they should all be dead.

DE'CREMENTS (*Phy.*) are the small parts by which a variable and decreasing quantity becomes less and less.

DECREMENTS (*Cus.*) fees paid by the students at the Universities for the damage of things which are in their use.

DECREPITA'TION (*Chem.*) the crackling noise which arises from salt being thrown into an unglazed earthen pot.

DECRESCE'NDO (*Mus.*) Italian for decreasing or sinking, as opposed to *crescendo*.

DECRE'SCENT (*Her.*) a term in blazoning to denote the state of the moon when she declines from her full to her last quarter, when she has her horns turned to the sinister side of the escutcheon, as he beareth "Azure a moon decrescent *proper*, by the name of De la Lune."

DECRETALS (*Law*) or *Decrees*, a collection of the canon law made by Gratian, a monk of the Order of St. Benedict.

DECRETALS (*Ecc.*) are rescripts and letters of a Pope, whereby some point or question in the ecclesiastical law is solved or determined. *Nicol. I. Ep.* 6.

DECRE'TORY (*Law*) a definitive sentence.

DECRE'TUM (*Law*) vide *Decree*.

DECRUSTA'TION (*Mech.*) an uncrusting or taking away the uppermost crust or rind of any thing.

DE'CUMÆ (*Ant.*) the tenth or tithes of all goods which were given as an offering to any of the gods, or paid as a tribute to the state. *Plaut. Stich.* act. 1, scen. 3, v. 81; *Cic. in Verr. Orat.* 3, c. 7; *Plutarch. in Syll.*; *Dio.* c. 78; *Appian. de Bell. Civ. l.* 1.

DECUMA'NUS (*Ant.*) belonging to the tenth, as *Decumani*, i. e. *milites*, soldiers of the tenth cohort; also collectors of the tenths, or tithes.—*Decumanus limes*, a line or meer dividing the field from East to West, in distinction from the *cardo*, which divided it from North to South.—*Decumanus* *ager*, a field that pays tithe. -*Plin.* l. 17, c. 22; *Columel. de Re Rust.* l. 4, c. 18.

DECUMA'RIA (*Bot.*) a genus of plants, Class 11 *Dodecandria*, Order 1 *Monogynia*.
Generic Character. CAL. *perianth* superior.—COR. *petals* ten.—STAM. *filaments* from sixteen to twenty-five; *anthers* twin.—PIST. *germ* top-shaped; *style* cylindric; *stigma* gibbose.—PER. *capsule* eight-celled; *seeds* solitary.
Species. The single species is a tree, as the—*Decumaria barbara* Forsythia, seu *Clausia*, Climbing Decumaria, native of Carolina.

DECU'MBENS (*Bot.*) decumbent, an epithet for a flower on a stem; *flos decumbent*, a flower having its stamens and pistils declined, or bending down to the lower side of it, as in *Cassia*; *caulis decumbens*, a stem lying on the ground, with the base higher than the other parts.

DECU'MBITURE (*Astrol.*) a scheme erected for the moment that the disease invades or confines one to his bed or his chamber.

DECUMBITURE (*Med.*) a lying down in consequence of sickness.

DE'CUPLE (*Arith.*) a term of proportion implying tenfold, or ten times as much as another.

DECU'RIA (*Ant.*) a band or company of ten men, whether soldiers or judges. *Cic. pro Dom.* c. 5; *Ascon. in Cic.*; *Plin.* l. 33, c. 1.

DECU'RIO (*Ant.*) δεκάδαρχος, a captain over ten horse or foot. *Polyb. Varro. de Lat. Ling.* l. 4, c. 1; *Veget.* l. 2, c. 24.—Decurio was also an alderman in a corporation, answering to a senator at Rome.—*Cic. pro Sext.* c. 5.—*Decurio Pontificum* presided over the *decuriæ curiatæ*, according to an inscription. D. M. C. MALERI. PETRONIANI. DECUR. PONTIF. SACERD. JUVEN. MED. CAUSID.—*Decurio Ostiariorum*, steward of the household, an officer mentioned in an inscription, T. FLAVIUS. AUG. DECURIO. OSTIARIORUM. FECIT. SIBI. ET. HADRIÆ. OCRIBILLÆ.

DECU'RRENS (*Bot.*) an epithet for a leaf, a petiole, and a stipule; *folium decurrens*, a sessile leaf, having its base extending downwards along the stem, as in *Symphytum*, *Verbesina*, *Carduus*, &c.

DECURSIO (*Ant.*) a ceremony, called in Greek περιδρομη, of going three times in solemn procession round the funeral pile of any one to whom they wished to show respect. In this decursion the motion was to the left, to indicate sorrow. *Hom. Il.* l. 23, v. 13; *Virg. Æn.* l. 11, v. 188; *Luc.* l. 8, v. 734; *Stat. Theb.* l. 6, v. 213; *Tac. Annal.* l. 2, c. 7; *Dio.* l. 56; *Suet. in Claud.* c. 1; *Appian. de Bell. Civ.* l. 1.

DECURSIO, a military exercise, consisting of a running march. *Sen. ep.* 18; *Suet. Ner.* c. 7, &c.; *Veget.* l. 1, c. 9, &c.

DECU'RSIVELY-PINNATE (*Bot.*) *decursivo-pinnatum*, an epithet for a leaf having its leaflets decurrent, or running along the petiole.

DECU'SSATE (*Bot.*) *decussatus*, an epithet for leaves and branches which, growing in pairs, alternately cross each other at right angles; so that if the stem be viewed vertically, or the eye be directed right down it, the leaves or branches will appear to be in fours.

DECUSSA'TION (*Opt.*) the crossing of any two rays, &c. when they meet in a point, and then go on, parting from one another.

DECUSSIS (*Ant.*) a coin or piece of money of the value of the Roman penny, ten asses, and ten pounds weight. *Vitruv.* l. 3, c. 1.—*Decussis* is also the figure of the letter X, which being parted in the middle makes another figure of V. *Plin.* l. 18, c. 34.

DECU'SSIVE (*Bot.*) vide *Decussate*.

DECUSSO'RIUM (*Surg.*) a surgeon's instrument for pressing the *Dura mater* in the case of a fractured skull.

DE'DACHORD (*Mus.*) a harp or lyre with ten strings.

DEDBA'NA (*Archæol.*) a man slayer.

DE'DI (*Law*) i. e. I have given; a term in a warranty in law to a Feoffee and his heirs. *Co. Lit.* 304.

DEDICA'TION, Feast of (*Theol.*) a feast among the Jews which was kept in memory of Judas Maccabæus, by whom the temple and altar had been dedicated anew after its profanation by Antiochus Epiphanes.

DEDICA'TION-DAY (*Ecc.*) *Festum dedicationis*, a festival in honour of the saint and patron of a church, which was celebrated on the day of its dedication, or the anniversary of that day.

DE'DIMUS *potestatem* (*Law*) a writ whereby commission is given to a private man for the speeding of some act appertaining to a judge; by the Civilians it is called *delegation*.—*Dedimus Potestatem de Attornato faciendo*, a writ or power by which the defendant could make an attorney in any action or suit. *New. Nat. Brev.* 55, 56.

DEED (*Law*) an instrument written on parchment or paper, consisting of three things, signing, sealing, and delivery, and comprehending a contract between two or more parties. There are two sorts of deeds, indented and polled, according to their form or fashion.—A *deed indented*, or an *indenture*, is that which is cut in and out at the top, or in the side, consisting of two or more parts, for there are deeds tripartite, quadripartite, and septempartite; in which it is expressed that the parties thereto have, to every part thereof, set their several seals.—A *deed poll*, or *polled*, is a plain deed without indenting, which is used when the vendor, for example, only seals, and there is no need of the vendee's sealing a counter-part. *Co. Litt.* 171, &c.

DE'EMSTERS (*Law*) a kind of judges in the Isle of Man, chosen from among, and by, themselves, who, without process, writing, or charge, decide controversies there. *Camd. Brit.*

DEEP-SEA-LE'AD (*Mar.*) a lead, at the bottom of which is a coat of white tallow to bring up stones, shells, &c. in order to learn the difference of the ground.—*Deep-Sea-Line*, a small line tied to the sea line, with which seamen sound in deep waters.—*Deep-Sea-Line-Block*, a small wooden snatch-block, from nine to eleven inches long.—*Deep-waisted*, in French *haut accostillé*, the distinguishing fabric of a ship's decks, when the quarter deck and the fore-castle are elevated from four to six feet above the level of the upper or maindeck, so as to leave a space called the *waist on the middle deck*.

DEEP (*Mil.*) a term applied to the disposition and arrangement of soldiers, as two deep, or three deep, i. e. two, ranks one before the other, &c.

DEER (*Zool.*) a well-known animal classed by Linnæus under the genus *Cervus*. The two principal species so called are the Rein-Deer, *Cervus tarandus*; and the Fallow-Deer, *Cervus dama*. [vide *Cervus*, &c.]

DEER (*Sport.*) one of the wild beasts of the forest.—*Deerhayes*, inclosed places for the preservation of deer.

DEE'SIS (*Rhet.*) δέησις, *obsecratio*; a figure of speech in which the orator beseeches or implores the Gods. *Jul. Rufinian.* fig. 16.

DE *essendo punctum de Telonio* (*Law*) a writ that lies for those who are by privilege freed from the payment of toll.—*De Expensis Civium et Burgensium*, a writ for levying two shillings per diem for every citizen and burgess.—*De expensis militum*, a writ which requires the sheriffs to levy so much per diem for the expenses of the knight of the shire serving in Parliament. 12 *Rich.* 2, c. 12; 23 *Hen.* 6, c. 10; 4 *Inst.* 46.

DE FACTO (*Law*) i. e. in deed; a term used to denote a thing actually done; a King *de Facto* is a King who is in actual possession of the crown, in distinction from a King *de jure.*

DEFA'IT (*Her.*) an epithet for a beast whose head is cut off smooth.

DEFALCA'TION (*Polit.*) a failure or falling off in any public accounts.

DEFAMA'TION (*Law*) the speaking slanderous words of a person so as, *de bona fama aliquid detrahere,* to hurt his good fame.

DEFA'MED (*Her.*) an epithet for any beast that has lost its tail, which is a mark of infamy.

DEFAULT (*Law*) a non-appearance in court without sufficient cause made out, although it extends to any omission of that which we ought to do. *Bract.* l. 5, tract. 3 ; *Co. Lit.* 259.

DEFAULTER (*Mil.*) the same as a *Deserter.*

DEFAULTER (*Com.*) one who is deficient in his accounts, or fails in making his accounts correct.

DEFE'ASANCE (*Law*) a condition relating to a deed, which, being performed, the act is made void.

DEFECA'TION (*Chem.*) a purging from dregs.

DEFE'CTION (*Polit.*) a falling off either from church or state.

DEFE'CTIVE *nouns* (*Gram.*) such nouns as want the ordinary cases or numbers.—*Defective verbs,* verbs which have not all their moods and tenses.

DEFE'NCE (*Law*) the reply which the defendant makes after the declaration is produced, and then proceeds either in his plea or to imparlance.—*Defence of the Realm,* any legislative provision which is made in time of war for the better securing the kingdom against the attacks of an enemy.

DEFENCE (*Fort.*) any work that covers or defends the opposite posts, as flanks, parapets, &c.—*Active Defences,* consist of every offensive operation to annoy the besiegers, as the discharge of artillery, &c.—*Passive Defence* is chiefly confined to inundations.—*Distant Defence* consists in being able to interrupt the enemy's movements by circuitous inundations.—*Line of Defence,* that which flanks a bastion; it is either *fichant* or *razant* ; the *fichant* is that which is drawn from the angle of the curtain to the flanked angle ; the *razant* is that which is drawn from a point in the curtain razing the face of the bastion.—*Defence of Rivers* is the effort made to prevent an enemy from passing. —*To be in a posture of Defence* is to be prepared to resist an enemy with all the means of defence in our power.

TO DEFEND (*Law*) signified formerly to forbid, from the French *defendre*; it is used in this sense in a statute entitled *De defensione portandi arma.* 7 *Ed.* 1. " God defend " is still used in some parts for " God forbid."

DEFE'NDANT (*Law*) is one who is sued in an action personal, as a *tenant* is one who is sued in an action real.

DEFENDENDE'MUS (*Law*) a word in a feoffment which bindeth the donor and his heirs to defend the donee. *Bract.* l. 2, c. 16.

SE DEFENDE'NDO (*Law*) is a plea used by one who kills another in his own defence, which justifies the fact.

DEFE'NDER *of the Faith* (*Ecc.*) a title given by Pope Leo X. to King Henry VIII. for writing against Luther. *Lord Herbert. Hist. Hen.* 8.

SE DEFE'NDERE (*Law*) a term in Doomsday-book signifying to be taxed for a certain quantity of land.—*Se defendere per suum corpus* was to offer combat or Duel as an appeal or trial at law. Similar to this was the expression *Defendere unica manu.* *Bract.* l. 3, c. 26.

DEFE'NDERS (*Ecc.*) vide *Defensores.*

DEFENSA (*Archæol.*) a park, or place fenced in.

DEFE'NSATIVES (*Med.*) medicines which divert humour from a part affected.

DEFE'NSES (*Fort.*) vide *Defence.*

DEFE'NSITIVE (*Surg.*) a plaister or bandage to keep on a dressing, and secure the wounds from the air.

DEFENSI'VA (*Archæol.*) the Lords or Earls of the Marches, the defenders or wards of the county.

DEFENSIVA (*Med.*) Defensives, medicines which resist infection.

DEFE'NSIVES (*Med.*) vide *Defensiva.*

DEFE'NSO (*Law*) or *in defenso,* a term applied to that part of an open field upon which there was no commoning.

DEFENSO'RES (*Polit.*) officers of state, or dignitaries in the church, who undertook to guard or protect the privileges of particular towns or churches.—*Defensores Civitatum* were the same as Syndics; the *Defensores Ecclesiarum* were otherwise called *Advocates.* *Chrysost. et Œcam. in Act. Apost.* X.; *Ammian.* l. 20, c. 7, &c.; *Justin. Nov.* 15, d, &c.

DEFE'NSUM (*Archæol.*) any inclosure, or fenced ground. *Mon. Angl.* tom. ii. p. 114.

DE'FERENT (*Astron.*) an imaginary circle or orb, in the Ptolemaic system, that is supposed, as it were, to carry about the body of the planet, being the same as the eccentric.

DEFERE'NTIA *vasa* (*Anat.*) two white solid flatted tubes arising from the *Epididymis,* which are so called from *defero,* to carry down, because they convey the semen to the *vasiculæ seminales.*

DEFI'CIENT *Hyperbola* (*Geom.*) a name given by Newton to a curve having only one asymptote, and two hyperbolical legs running out infinitely towards the sides of the asymptote, but the contrary ways. *Newt. numerat. Lin. tert. Ordin.*

DEFICIENT *Numbers* (*Arith.*) are such whose aliquot parts added together make less than the integer whereof they are the parts; as 8, whose parts, being 1, 2, 4, make but 7; and 16, whose aliquot parts are 1, 2, 4, 8, make but 15.

DEFICIENT *year* (*Chron.*) the Jewish year, so called when the month Cisleu is twenty-nine days instead of thirty.

DE'FILE (*Mil.*) a narrow lane or passage, through which a company of soldiers can pass only in file.

TO DEFILE (*Mil.*) to reduce divisions or platoons into a small front so as to march through a defile, or any narrow place.

DEFI'LEMENT (*Fort.*) the art of disposing all the works in a place that they may be commanded by the body of the fortress.

DEFINI'TION (*Log.*) the explaining the signification of a word, or determining the nature of things by words, which serve as limits or boundaries to distinguish them from other things. A *definition* is *nominal* when it explains one word by another; *real* when it explains the nature of the thing. A *real definition* is again *accidental,* or a description of the accidents, as causes, properties, effects, &c.; or *essential,* which explains the constituent parts of the essence. An *essential definition* is moreover *metaphysical* or *logical,* defining the genus and difference; or *physical,* which distinguishes the physical parts of the essence: thus, for example, " A man " is defined *nominally* by the derivation of *homo* from *humo,* the ground; *accidentally,* " A biped without wings;" *metaphysically,* " A rational animal;" *physically,* " A natural being consisting of body and soul."

DEFI'NITIVE (*Polit.*) positive and express, as a definitive treaty.

DEFI'NITOR (*Ecc.*) an assessor, or counsellor to a general, or superior in religious orders.

DEFLAGRA'TION (*Chem.*) the kindling, or burning off in a crucible, a mixture of salt, or some mineral body, with a sulphurous one in order to purify it.—*Deflagration,* a gradual sparkling combustion of any substance without violent explosion; a term particularly applied to combustion produced by nitre.

DEFLE'XION (*Phy.*) the turning of any thing out of its true course.

DEFLEXION (*Mar.*) the tendency of a ship from her true course by reason of currents, &c.

DEFLEXION *of the Rays of Light* (*Opt.*) a property distinct from reflection and refraction, being made perpendicularly towards the opake body. It is called by Newton *Inflection*.

DEFLE'XUS (*Bot.*) bowed, or bent down archwise, an epithet for a leaf.

DEFLORA'TUS (*Bot.*) an epithet for a flower which has discharged its pollen.

DEFLU'VIUM (*Bot.*) a disease in trees whereby they lose their bark.

DEFLUVIUM *capillorum* (*Med.*) a preternatural falling off of the hair.

DEFLU'XIO (*Med.*) from *fluo*, to flow, and *de*, down; the falling of a humour from a superior upon an inferior part.

DEFOLIA'TIO (*Bot.*) defoliation, or shedding the leaves.

DEFO'RCEMENT (*Law*) a withholding lands or tenements by force from the rightful owner.

DEFO'RCEOR (*Law*) *Deforciator*, one that overcometh and casteth out by force. *Stat. 23 Eliz. c. 23.*

DEFORCIA'TO (*Law*) a distress or holding goods for satisfaction of a debt. *Paroch. Antiq.* 239.

DEFO'SSIO (*Ant.*) burying alive; a punishment inflicted by the Romans on the vestal virgins who were found guilty of incontinence.

DEFRU'TUM (*Husband.*) from *defervendo*, must; or a decoction of new wine made by boiling away one-third. *Plin.* l. 14, c. 9; *Columel.* l. 12, c. 20; *Isid. Orig.* l. 19, c. 3.

DEFU'NCT (*Law*) a term used for one that is deceased, or dead.

DEFU'NCTION (*Law*) the final performance of any office.

DEGA'GEMENT (*Archit.*) French for a private passage, or small back staircase.

DEGA'RNER *une Fortresse, &c.* (*Fort.*) French for to dismantle a fortress.

DEGA'ST (*Mil.*) French for laying waste an enemy's country.

DEGLUTI'TIO (*Med.*) from *deglutio*, to swallow; deglutition, or the act of swallowing.

DE'GMOS (*Med.*) δηγμός, from δάκνω, to bite; a biting pain at the orifice of the stomach.

DEGO'RGEOIR (*Mil.*) French for a steel pricker used in examining the touch-hole of a cannon.

DEGO'RGER *une embrassure* (*Fort.*) to lower the earth of an embrasure so as to afford a view of any object against which a gun is planted.

DEGOUTE' (*Vet.*) a French epithet for a horse that goes off his feed.

DEGRADA'TION (*Ecc.*) an ecclesiastical censure, whereby a clergyman is divested of his holy orders: it is distinguished from *deposition*, which is simply a displacing or suspension from his office. *Seld. Tit. of Hon.*

DEGRADATION (*Law*) at Common Law, is the depriving a lord, knight, &c. of his rank, title, and honor.

DEGRADATION (*Mil.*) the depriving an officer for ever of his commission, rank, and degree of honour; also, the reducing of non-commissioned officers to the rank and station of private soldiers, which is necessary before they can receive corporal punishment.

DEGRADATION (*Paint.*) is the lessening and rendering confused the appearance of distant objects in a landscape, so that they may appear there as they would to an eye placed at that distance from them.

DEGRA'DED (*Her.*) an epithet in blazoning for a cross that has steps at each end, as in the annexed figure. "He beareth *argent* a cross degraded, *sable*. Name *Wyntworth*."

DEGRE'E (*Math.*) the three-hundred-and-sixtieth part of the circumference of a circle. It is subdivided into sixty parts called *minutes*, and each of those again into sixty parts more, called *seconds*.—*Degree of Latitude*, a portion of land between two parallels of latitude, equal to 60 miles.—*Degree of Longitude*, a portion of land between two meridians, equal to 60 miles.

DEGREE (*Algeb.*) the power of the unknown quantity in an equation: if the index be 2, the equation is of the second degree; if 3, of the third degree; thus, $x^3 = p$ is an equation of the third degree.—*Parodic*, or *parodical degrees* are the indices of the powers when they ascend or descend orderly in an arithmetical progression in the equation: thus, $x^3 + m x^2 + n x = p$. The parodical degrees are 3, 2, 1, 0, the indices of the terms regularly descending.

DEGREE (*Law*) an interval in kinship, by which proximity and remoteness of blood are computed.

DEGREES *of comparison* (*Gram.*) are the inflections of adjectives which express different degrees of the same quality: these are three, namely, *positive*, which is the first degree, or the adjective itself, as *good*; *comparative*, the second degree, as *better*; *superlative*, the highest degree, as *best*.

DEGREES *of heat* (*Chem.*) are four, the first of which is the gentlest of all; the second sufficient to warm a vessel sensibly; the third sufficient to boil five or six quarts of water in a vessel; the fourth is the highest degree that can be procured by a furnace.

DEGREES (*Lit.*) titles of honour conferred by a University on any person for his merit in the arts and sciences.

DEGREES, *theoretical* (*Mus.*) are the differences of position or elevation between two notes. Degrees are either conjunct or disjunct.—*Conjunct Degrees* are those which are so situated as to form the interval of a second.—*Disjunct Degrees* are those which form a third.

DEHISCE'NTIA (*Bot.*) the gaping or opening of capsules, also the season in which this takes place.

DEHO'RS (*Law*) a term used in ancient pleading for *without*; as *dehors* the land, or *dehors* the point in question, &c.

DEJE'CTIO (*Med.*) from *dejicio*, to cast out; the discharge of excrement by stool.

DEJE'CTION (*Astrol.*) is said of the planets when they are in their detriment, i. e. when they have lost their force or influence, by reason of being in opposition to some others which check and counteract them.

DEJECTO'RIA (*Med.*) from *dejicio*, to cast out; purging medicines.

DEINCLI'NERS (*Dial.*) or *Deinclining Dials*, such as both decline, incline, or recline, at the same time.

DE *injuria sua propria absque tali causâ* (*Law*) words used in replications in actions of trespass.

DEI JUDI'CIUM (*Law*) the old Saxon trial by ordeal, so called because it was supposed to be an appeal to God.

DEINO'SIS (*Med.*) δείνωσις, from δεινόω, to exaggerate; an enlargement of the supercilia. *Hippocrat. de Rat. Vict. in Acut.*

DEIPNO'SOPHISTS (*Ant.*) from δεῖπνον, a supper, and σοφιστής, a sophist; a company of wise men who discoursed on philosophical matters at supper; whence the title of Athenæus' book, which recounts such discourses.

DE'IRA (*Anat.*) vide *Cervix*.

DEIS (*Archæol.*) the high table of a monastery.

DE'ISM (*Theol.*) the belief in the existence of a God as deduced from reason. This is called Natural Religion, in distinction from Revealed Religion, or the belief that is drawn from Inspired Writings.

DE JURE (*Law*) by right. [vide *De Facto*]

DEL (*Mus.*) Italian for *by*, as *del Corelli*, by Corelli.

DEL (*Paint.*) an abbreviation for *delineavit*, placed in copperplates, by the name of the draughtsman, to denote by whom it was designed.

DELACRYMATI'VA (*Med.*) from *de* and *lachryma*, a tear; medicines which dry the eyes, first purging them of tears.

DELA'PSIO (*Med.*) from *delabor*, to slip down; a falling down of the anus, uterus, intestines, &c.

DELA'TIO (*Ant.*) the informing against another; a secret accusation. [vide *Delatores*]

DELATIO (*Med.*) vide *Indicatio*.

DELATO'RES (*Ant.*) common informers; a description of persons much encouraged by Domitian and the worst of the Roman emperors. *Tacit. Annal.* l. 4, c. 30; *Suet. in Domit.* c. 12. The *delateurs* of the French were equally busy in the time of the French Revolution.

DELATU'RA (*Law*) an accusation, and sometimes taken for the reward of an informer.

DEL CREDERE (*Com.*) Italian for the word *guarantee* or *warranty*, as applicable to factors, who, for an additional premium, become bound when they sell goods upon credit to warrant the solvency of the parties. This is called a *Commission del credere*.

DE'LEGATES (*Law*) commissioners of appeal, appointed by the king under the Great Seal, in cases of appeal from the ecclesiastical court. *Stat.* 25 *H.* 8, c. 19.

DELEGA'TION (*Law*) is a term in the Civil Law when a debtor appoints one who is a debtor to him, to answer a creditor in his place.

DELETE'RIOUS (*Med.*) δηλητήριος, from δηλέω, to injure; an epithet importing pernicious, injurious, or poisonous, as applied to drugs or medicines.

DELETI'TIOUS (*Ant.*) an epithet for paper on which one may write things and blot them out again, to make room for new matter.

DELF (*Archæol.*) a quarry or mine where stone or coal is dug. *Stat.* 31 *Eliz.* 7.

DELF (*Her.*) the first of the nine abatements. [vide *Abatement*]

DE'LIA (*Ant.*) Δήλια, a quinquennial festival in the island of Delos, instituted by Theseus at his return from Crete, in honour of Venus, by whose assistance he had met with success in his expedition. *Thucyd.* l. 3, c. 104; *Callim. Hym. in Del.*; *Plut. in Thes.*

DELICATE'ZZA (*Mus.*) Italian for delicacy, as *con delicatezza*, with delicacy of expression.

DELIGA'TIO (*Surg.*) from *de*, and *ligo*, to tie; the application of bandages for the binding up of wounds, ulcers, &c.

DE'LIMA (*Bot.*) a genus of plants, Class 12 *Polyandria*, Order 1 *Monogynia*.
Generic Character. CAL. *perianth* five-leaved.—COR. none.—STAM. *filaments* numerous; *anthers* roundish.—PIST. *germ* superior; *style* cylindric; *stigma* simple.—PER. *berry* larger; *seeds* two.
Species. The single species is a tree, as the *Delima sarmentosa*, seu *Peripu*, native of Ceylon.

DELIQUA'TION (*Chem.*) from *deliqueo*, to melt. [vide *Solution*]

DELI'QUIUM (*Chem.*) or *deliquescence*, implies a spontaneous solution which some salts experience by exposure to the air. [vide *Chemistry*]

DELIQUIUM (*Med.*) vide *Syncope*.

DELI'RIUM (*Med.*) from *deliro*, to rave or talk idly; a febrile symptom, consisting in a person's acting or talking unreasonably.

DELI'VERANCE (*Law*) a term used by the clerk in court to every prisoner who puts himself on his trial by pleading *not guilty*, to whom he wishes a good *deliverance*.—*To wage deliverance*, to give security that a thing shall be delivered up.

DELI'VERY (*Law*) or *Gaol-Delivery*, a term applied to the sessions at the Old Bailey, by which the gaol is delivered or cleared of the prisoners.—*Clerk of the deliveries*, an officer who draws up orders for the delivering stores or provisions.—*Delivery*, a term in the mint implying the moneys which have been coined within a certain period.

DE'LLIS (*Mil.*) French for a select body of men from Albania, who volunteer to serve in the Grand Seignior's army.

DELOCA'TIO (*Surg.*) from *de* and *locus*, a place; a dislocation, or putting any part out of its proper place, particularly applied to the bones that are put out of joint.

DE'LPHICA (*Ant.*) a kind of table or cupboard with three legs, like that at Delphos, at which the priestess sat, who gave the oracle.
Mart. l. 12, ep. 67.
Argentum atque aurum non simplex Delphica portat.
Vet. Interp. Juv. Sat.; *Procop. de Bell. Vandal.* c. 21.

DELPHI'NIA (*Ant.*) διλφίνια, a festival at Egina in honour of the Delphinian oracle. *Pind. Schol. Olymp.* 8.

DELPHI'NIUM (*Bot.*) διλφίνιον, a plant; so called, according to Dioscorides, because the flower before it opens was supposed to bear some resemblance to a dolphin. *Dioscor.* l. 3, c. 83, 84.

DELPHINIUM, *in the Linnean System*, a genus of plants, Class 12 *Polyandria*, Order 3 *Trigynia*.
Generic Character. CAL. none.—COR. *petals* five.—STAM. *filaments* many; *anthers* erect.—PIST. *germs* three; *stigmas* simple.—PER. *capsules* three; *seeds* very many.
Species. The species are perennials or annuals. The following are the principal perennials, as the—*Delphinium intermedium*, seu *americanum*, Palmated Bee Larkspur, supposed to be a native of Siberia or Tartary—*Delphinium elatum*, seu *aconitum*, Common Bee Larkspur, native of Switzerland.—*Delphinium exaltatum*, seu *elatum*, American Larkspur. The following are the principal annuals:—*Delphinium consolida*, seu *Consolida*, Branching Larkspur.—*Delphinium ambiguum*, Doubtful Larkspur, native of Barbary. *Clus. Hist.*; *Dod. Pempt.*; *Bauh. Hist.*; *Bauh. Pin.*; *Ger. Herb.*; *Park. Theat.*; *Raii Hist.*; *Tourn. Inst.*

DELPHI'NUS (*Ant.*) or *Delphinos*, an ornament on vases, couches, &c. in the likeness of a dolphin. The same name was also given to certain pillars in the middle of the circus, which bore the figure of the dolphin, in honour of Neptune. *Plin.* l. 33, c. 11; *Dio.* l. 49; *Tertull. de Spectac.* c. 8.

DELPHINUS, δελφίς, a leaden machine of immense weight, which was thrown on board the enemy's ship, during an engagement, for the purpose of sinking it. It was so called probably because it was made in the form of a dolphin, and the ship which carried it was called δελφινίφορος. *Thucyd.* l. 7; *Aristoph. Schol. Equit.* act. 2, scen. 3; *Vitruv.* l. 10, c. 13; *Poll. Onom.* l. 1, c. 9; *Suidas*; *Gyrald. de Navig.* c. 12; *Scheff. de Mil. Nav.* l. 2, c. 5; *Salmas. Solin.* p. 570, &c.

DELPHINUS (*Zool.*) the Dolphin, is described by the ancients as the swiftest of all animals, either by land or sea; and, according to Aristotle, so agile in leaping, that it will clear ships. Their love of music, and attachment to the human species, is mentioned by Herodotus and other writers. According to Juvenal, it was less than the Balæna.
Juv. sat. 10, v. 14.
Quantò delphinis balæna Britannica major.
The dolphin of the Nile was reckoned no less an enemy to the crocodile than the ichneumon. *Herodot.* l. 1, c. 24; *Aristot. Hist. Animal.* l. 1, c. 11, &c.; *Senec. Nat. Quæst.* l. 4, c. 2; *Plin.* l. 8, c. 25; *Ælian. Hist. Animal.* l. 6, c. 15; *Salmas Solin.* p. 445.

DELPHINUS, a genus of animals, Class *Mammalia*, Order *Cete*, having teeth in each jaw.
Species. The species are—*Delphinus phocæna*, the Porpoise.—*Delphinus delphis*, the Dolphin.—*Delphinus Orca*, the Sword Grampus, the dorsal fin of which resembles a scymetar.

DELPHINUS (*Astron.*) δλφίς or δλφίν, a constellation of the northern hemisphere, having, in Ptolemy's catalogue, 10 stars, in Tycho's 10, Hevelius' 14, and in Flamstead's 18. The Dolphin is fabled to have been translated to heaven by Neptune. *Arat. Phænom.* v. 316; *Eratosthen. Characterismi*; *Hygin. Poet. Astron.*; *Manil. Poet. Astron.*; *Ptolem. Almag.* Nov. l. 7, c. 5; *Ricciol. Almagest* Nov. l. 6.

DE'LPHYS (*Med.*) διλφύς, the *uterus*, or *pudendum muliebre*.

DE'LTA (*Ant.*) δλτα, the Greek letter Δ.

DELTOI'DES (*Mid.*) δλτοιδης, from δλτα, the Greek letter Δ, and ιδος, likeness; the name of a very thick triangular muscle covering the upper part of the arm, and forming what is termed the stump of the shoulder.

DELTOIDES (*Bot.*) or *Deltoideus*, deltoid; an epithet for a leaf which has something of the figure of a delta.

DELVE (*Com.*) a quantity of coals dug at the mine or pit.

DEM (*Med.*) Human blood.

DE'MAGOGUE (*Polit.*) from δῆμος, the populace, and ἄγω, to lead; a leader of the people, i. e. the head of a faction.

DEMA'IN (*Law*) or *demesne*, an inheritance; a term employed to distinguish those lands which the lord of a manor has in his own hands, or in the hands of his lessee; from other lands of the said manor which belong to freehold or copy-hold.—*Ancient-demain*, a tenure by which crown lands were held in the time of William the Conqueror.

DEMA'RCHUS (*Ant.*) δήμαρχος, from δῆμος, a township or village, and ἄρχος, a ruler; the name of a magistrate in a borough, particularly of Neapolis in Greece. *Spartian. in Adrian.* c. 19; *Turneb. Adv.* l. 29, c. 12.

DEMA'ND (*Law*) a calling upon a man for any thing due. There are three sorts of demands:—one in writing without speaking, as in every *Precipe*; one without writing, being a verbal *demand* of the person who is to do or perform the duty. These two are called *Demands in deed*. The third is a *Demand in law*, as in cases of entries on lands, &c.

DEMA'NDANT (*Law*) the pursuer in real actions, in distinction from the plaintiff. *Co. Lit.* 127.

DEME'ASE (*Law*) vide *Demise*.

DEME'NTIA (*Med.*) from *de* and *mens*, mind, i. e. without mind; madness, delirium, absence of intellect.

DEME'RSUS (*Bot.*) from *demergo*, to sink down; an epithet applied to the leaves of aquatic plants, which are sunk or grow below the surface of the water.

DEME'SNE (*Law*) or *demeine*, vide *Demain*.

DEME'TRIA (*Ant.*) otherwise called *Cerealia*, a festival in honour of Ceres, who was called by the Greeks Δημήτηρ. *Poll. Onom.* l. 1, c. 1; *Hesychius*.

DE'MI (*Ant.*) δῆμοι, a term particularly applied to the townships into which all Attica was divided.

DEMI (*Gram.*) a term which, used in composition, signifies half, as demi-god, &c.

DEMI' (*Cus.*) a half-fellow at Magdalen College, Oxford.

DE'MI (*Her.*) vide *Demy*.

DEMI-AI'R (*Man.*) vide *Demivolt*.

DEMI-CA'NNON (*Gunn.*) a sort of great gun carrying a ball of about six inches in diameter.

DEMI-CHA'SE-BOOTS (*Cus.*) a sort of riding boots for summer.

DEMI-CRO'SS (*Mar.*) an instrument for taking the height of the sun and stars.

DEMI-CU'LVERINE (*Gunn.*) a piece of ordnance, varying in length from nine to ten feet, and in the diameter of the bore from four inches and a half to four inches and three-quarters. It requires a charge from six to seven pounds of powder, and a ball of three or four inches in diameter.

DEMI-DI'STANCE (*Fort.*) the distance between the outward polygons and the flank.

DEMI-DI'TONE (*Mus.*) the same as *Tierce minor*.

DEMI-GA'NTLET (*Surg.*) a bandage used in setting disjointed fingers.

DE'MI-GOD (*Myth.*) heroes who were accounted of human nature, but enrolled among the gods.

DEMI-GO'RGE (*Fort.*) half the gorge or entrance into the bastion, but not taken from angle to angle where the bastion joins the courtin, but from the angle at the flank to the centre of the bastion.

DEMI-HAGUE (*Gunn.*) vide *Hague*.

DEMI-QUA'VER (*Mus.*) the same as *Semi-quaver*.

DEMI-SA'NG (*Law*) the same as *Half-blood*.

DEMI'SE (*Law*) *Demissio*, a letting or make of lands, tenements, &c. by lease or will. 2 *Inst.* 483.—*Demise and Re-demise*, a conveyance where mutual leases are made from one to another on each side.—*Demise of the King*, implies a demise or transfer of his crown, dignity, &c. to his royal successor on his death. It is therefore equivalent to his death.

DEMIVOLT (*Man.*) one of the seven artificial motions of a horse when his foreparts are more raised than in the *terra a terra*, but the motion of his legs is not so quick.

DEMIU'RGI (*Ant.*) or *Damiurgi*, officers among the Achæans, who proposed to the assembly the matter on which they were to deliberate, equivalent to the speaker in our Parliament. *Liv.* l. 32, c. 22.

DEMO'CRACY (*Polit.*) δημοκρατία, from δῆμος, the people, and κρατέω, to exercise power; a form of government in which the supreme power is lodged in the people at large, or persons chosen from among them. *Aristot.* l. 3, c. 8.

DEMOCRATIS *theriaca* (*Med.*) a theriaca, described by Ætius. *Tetrab.* l, serm. l, c. 3.

DEMOISE'LLE (*Mech.*) French for a pavier's instrument.

DEMONO'CRACY (*Theol.*) from δαίμων, a demon, and κρατεία, government; the government or influence of devils.

DEMONSTRA'TIO (*Rhet.*) ἐνδειξις, called also *Ostensio*, a mode of pronunciation, or figure of speech, so clear and evident, as to set the thing, as it were, before the eyes of the hearers. *Cic. ad Herenn.* l. 3, c. 13; *Quintil.* l. 2, c. 10, &c.; *Georg. Trapez. Rhet.* l. 4; *Aquila. Rom. de Fig.* p. 186.

DEMONSTRA'TION (*Math.*) a proof, or chain of argument, founded on self-evident or admitted principles. Demonstrations are *geometrical*, which are proved from the elements of Euclid; or *mechanical*, when proved from the rules of mechanics.

DEMONSTRATION (*Log.*) a chain of deduction, so powerful as to produce an invincible proof of the truth of a proposition. Demonstrations are either positive or negative, à priori, or à posteriori.—*A positive Demonstration* is one which, proceeding by positive or affirmative propositions, ends in the thing to be demonstrated.—*A negative Demonstration* is that whereby a thing is shown to be true, by proving the absurdity of a contrary supposition.—*Demonstration à priori* is that whereby an effect is proved from a cause, or a conclusion is drawn from something, previously proved, whether a cause or an antecedent.—*Demonstration à posteriori*, is one whereby either a cause is proved from an effect, or a conclusion by something posterior, either an effect or a consequent.

DEMO'NSTRATIVE (*Rhet.*) one of the genera or kinds of eloquence used in panegyrics, invectives, &c. *Quintil.* l. 3, c. 7.

DEMO'NTER (*Mil.*) French for laming a horse, or otherwise rendering it unfit for service.

DEMOTI'VUS *elapsus* (*Med.*) sudden death.

DEMPSTER (*Law*) vide *Deemster*.—*Dempster of court*, another name in Scotland for the common hangman.

DEMULCE'NTIA *Medicamenta* (*Med.*) are medicines which render the acrimonious humours mild.

DEMU'RRAGE (*Com*) an allowance to a master of a ship for staying in a port longer than the time first appointed.

DEMU'RRER (*Law*) a pause or stop upon a point of difficulty, which must be determined by the court before any farther proceedings can be had in any action. *Demurrers* are *general* where no particular cause is shown, or *special* where the particular causes of demurrer are set forth.

DE'MY (*Her.*) an epithet for any charge that is borne, half, as a demy-lion, in the annexed figure. "He beareth, *or*, a demy-lion, rampant, *gules*. Name Mallory."

DEM'Y (*Cus.*) vd e Demi.

DEMY' (*Com.*) the name of paper, of particular dimensions, as it comes from the manufacturer. It is so called because it is half the size of a sheet of columbier.

DEN and Strond (*Archæol.*) liberty for a ship to run aground, or come ashore.

DE'NA (*Archæol.*) a term in Doomsday-Book for a hollow place between two hills.

DENARIA'TA *terræ* (*Archæol.*) the fourth part of an acre of land.

DENA'RII *de Caritate* (*Ecc.*) customary oblations made by parochial churches to the cathedral or mother church.

DENA'RIUS (*Ant.*) an epithet for any thing pertaining to the number of ten, as *Denariæ fistulæ*, conduit pipes ten feet long; and *Denariæ ceremoniæ*, ceremonies which were observed for ten days. *Fest. de Verb. Signif.* Denarius signified particularly a Roman coin, equal in value to eightpence in our money, marked with the leter X, to signify ten asses. It was of the same weight with the attick drachm or groat, and was reckoned for some time at four Sesterces.

DENARIUS (*Archæol.*) an old name for the English penny, in French *denier*.—*Denarius Dei*, God's Penny, or Earnest Money given and received by the parties to contracts.—*Denarius S. Petri*, Peter-Pence, an annual payment from every family of one penny to the pope.—*Denarius tertius comitatus*, a third part or penny, reserved for the Earl of the county, from fines and other profits of the County-Courts.

DE'NBERA (*Archæol.*) a place for the runnings of hogs.

DE'NCHED (*Her.*) the same as *Indented*.

DE'NDE (*Bot.*) the oriental name for a species of Ricinus, called also *Abelmoluch*.

DENDRACHA'TES (*Min.*) δενδραχάτης, a precious stone of the agate kind, with streaks like the branches of a tree in it. *Orph. de Lapid.; Plin.* 1. 37, c. 10.

DENDRI'TIS (*Min.*) δενδρῖτις, a precious stone mentioned by Pliny. *Nat. Hist.* l. 17, c. 10.

DENDROCI'SSOS (*Bot.*) a kind of ivy growing by itself, like other trees.

DENDROI'DES (*Bot.*) from δένδρον, a tree, and εἶδος, a likeness; a name for plants which grow like trees.

DENDROLI'BANUS (*Bot.*) from δένδρον, a tree, and λίβανος, frankincense; the herb Rosemary.

DENDRO'LOGY (*Bot.*) from δένδρον, a tree, and λόγος, a discourse; a treatise or discourse on trees.

DENDROMA'LACHE (*Bot.*) from δένδρον and μαλάχη, the mallow; a name for the *Malva arborescens*.

DENDRO'METER (*Mech.*) from δένδρον, a tree, and μέτρον, a measure; an instrument for measuring trees.

DENDRO'PHORI (*Ant.*) from δένδρον, a tree, and φέρω, to carry; those who carried branches of trees in the solemn processions which were made in honour of Bacchus, Sylvanus, Cybele, or any other god. They were also employed in cutting down and collecting wood, and are mentioned in several inscriptions on basso relievos, marbles, &c. *Cod. Theodos. de Pagan. et Templ.* l. 14, tit. 8; *Voss. de Idolol.* l. 1, c. 20; *Turneb. Adv.* l. 29, c. 16; *Ursat. de Not.*

Roman. apud Græv. Thes. Antiq. tom. 11, p. 632; *Spon. Misc. Erudit. Ant.* sect. 2, art. 11, p. 56.

DE'NEB (*Astron.*) an Arabic word, signifying tail, is the name of the bright star in the Lion's tail.

DENICA'LES *feriæ* (*Ant.*) a kind of solemnity on the tenth day in the house where a person had died, for the purpose of cleansing it.

DENIE'R (*Numis.*) one of the earliest French coins, so called from the Latin *denarius*, answering nearest to our penny. They were first made of silver, but afterwards with an alloy of copper, or altogether of copper, until they finally fell into disuse. The denier was the twelfth part of a sol, and was either *Parisois*, i. e. Parisian, or made at Paris, or *Tournois*, i. e. made at Tournaye, the former of which was worth a quarter more than the latter. The annexed figure is a representation of a Denier in the time of Pepin; on the obverse the inscription PEPINUS, and on the reverse R. F. i. e. *Rex Francorum*; the import of the marks on these coins is not known. *Blanch. Trait. Hist.*

DE'NIZEN (*Law*) i. e. *donaison*; an alien born who has obtained, *ex donatione regis*, letters patent to make him an English subject.

DENODA'TIO (*Med.*) from *denodo*, to loosen; dissolution.

DENOMINA'NS (*Log.*) vide *Denominativum*.

DENOMINATI'VUM (*Log.*) the name for any term that is derived from another, as prudent from prudence, which is called *Denominans*; and the word for the thing or person denominated prudent, as a man, &c. is termed *Denominatum*.

DENO'MINATOR *of a fraction* (*Arith.*) that part of a fraction which stands below the line of separation, and denominates or denotes the number of parts into which the integer is divided, as in $\frac{7}{10}$ 10 is the denominator.—*Denominator of any proportion* is the quotient arising from any division of such a ratio by its consequent.

DENOMINA'TUM (*Log.*) vide *Denominativum*.

DE *non decimando* (*Law*) a modus to be discharged of tithes. —*De non residentia*, vide *De*.—*De novo damus*, vide *De*.

DENS (*Anat.*) quasi *edens*, from *edo*, to eat, or from ὀδούς, ὀδόντος, a tooth, &c.

DENS *caninus* (*Bot.*) the *Panicum* of Linnæus.—*Dens canis*, the *Erythronium* of Linnæus.—*Dens Leonis*, the *Arnica crocea*; the *Apargia hispida, hirta, et canubialis*, &c.; the *Hyoseris fœtida, radiata, et lucida*, and the *Hypocheris helvetica*.

DENSE (*Bot.*) *densus*; an epithet for a panicle having an abundance of flowers very close.

DE'NSHIRING (*Husband.*) the practice of cutting off the turf of land, and, when it is dry, laying it on heaps and burning it to ashes, which is so called from Devonshire, the place where this was first done.

DE'NSITAS (*Med.*) πυκνότης, from *densus*, thick. Denseness is sometimes opposed to *raritas*, thinness, and then signifies closeness, or compactness. *Hippoc.* l. 5, aph. 62.

DE'NSITY (*Phy.*) that property in bodies by which they contain a certain quantity of matter under a certain bulk or magnitude.

DE'NTAGRA (*Surg.*) ὀδοντάγρα, from ὀδούς, a tooth, and ἄγρα, a capture; a surgeon's instrument, or forceps for extracting teeth.

DENTA'LIS *Lapis* (*Med.*) the tartareous and tophaceous matter, which, being formed of a coagulation of vitreous particles, adheres to the teeth, and is consolidated into almost a stony hardness.

DENTA'LIUM (*Con.*) the Dog-like Tooth Shell, a genus of animals, Class *Vermes*, Order *Testacea*.

Generic Character. Animal a Terebella.—*Shell* univalve, tubular, and open at both ends.

Species. The principal species are the—*Dentalium entalis, imperforatum, glabrum,* &c.

DENTA′RIA (*Bot.*) from *dens,* a tooth, so called because its root is denticulated; Septfoil toothwort and Coralwort.

DENTARIA, *in the Linnean system,* a genus of plants, Class 15 *Tetradynamia,* Order 2 *Siliquosa,* Natural Order of *Siliquosæ.*

Generic Character. CAL. *perianth* four-leaved. — COR. four-petalled.—STAM. *filaments* six; *anthers* cordate.— —PIST. *germ* oblong; *style* very short; *stigma* obtuse. —PER. *silique* long; *seeds* many.

Species. The species are perennials, as the—*Dentaria enneaphylla,* Nine-leaved Toothwort; *coralloides, seu ceratia.*—*Dentaria Bulbifera,* Bulbiferous Toothwort, or Coralwort.—*Dentaria pinnata,* Seven-leaved Toothwort. —*Dentaria pentaphylla,* Five-leaved Toothwort.

DENTARIA is also the *Lathrea squamaria* and *Tozzia alpina.*

DENTA′RIUS (*Surg.*) ὀδοντικός, a physician or surgeon who professes the art of drawing and curing the teeth. *Gal. ad Thrasyb.* c. 24.

DENTARPA′GA (*Surg.*) from ὀδούς, a tooth, and ἁρπάζω, to fasten upon; an instrument for drawing teeth.

DENTA′TUS (*Bot.*) toothed, an epithet for a root; *radix dentata,* a root consisting of a concatenation of joints resembling a necklace; *dentatum folium,* a toothed leaf, having horizontal points, with a space between each.

DENTATUS (*Med.*) from *dens,* a tooth, the second vertebra of the neck; so called from its having a tooth-like process at its upper part.

DENTE′LLA *Bot.*) a genus of plants, Class 5 *Pentandria,* Order 1 *Monogynia.*

Generic Character. CAL. *perianth* five-parted.—COR. one-petalled.—STAM. *filaments* five; *anthers* oblong.—PIST. *germ* roundish; *style* cylindrical; *stigmas* two.—PER. *capsule* globular; *seeds* many.

Species. The single species is the—*Dentella repens,* native of Carolina.

DENTELLA′RIA (*Bot.*) from *dentella,* a little tooth; the herb Toothwort, the *Knoxia zelanica* and *Plumbago europea* of Linnæus.

DE′NTES (*Anat.*) vide *Teeth.*—*Dentes sapientiæ,* a term applied to the two double teeth behind the rest; so called because they come when persons are arrived at years of maturity.

DE′NTICLE (*Archit.*) vide *Dentil.*

DENTICULA′TUS (*Bot.*) toothletted, i. e. having small teeth or notches; an epithet for a leaf, as in the *Hyperis.*

DE′NTIL (*Archit.*) *Denticulus,* which signifies literally a little tooth, is applied to a member of a cornice, square, and cut out at convenient distances, so as to give it the form of a set of teeth. *Vitruv.* l. 1, c. 2; *Bald. Lex. Vitruv.*

DENTI′DUCUM (*Med.*) from *dens,* a tooth, and *duco,* to draw; an instrument for drawing of teeth.

DENTIFRI′CIUM (*Med.*) ὀδοντότριμμα, dentrifice; a medicine for rubbing the teeth, and purging them from sordes.

DENTILLA′RIA (*Bot.*) from *denticula,* a little tooth; a name for the *Plumbago quorundam,* Leadwort.

DENTISCA′LPIUM (*Surg.*) ὀδοντόγλυφον, from *dens,* a tooth, and *scalpo,* to scrape; a surgeon's instrument for cleansing the teeth.

DENTI′TIO (*Med.*) ὀδοντοφυΐα, from *dentio,* to breed teeth, Dentition; the breeding of the teeth in children.

DE′NTO (*Med.*) from *dens,* a tooth; one whose teeth are raised and prominent to an extraordinary degree.

DENTODU′CUM (*Med.*) vide *Dentiducum.*

DENUDA′TÆ (*Bot.*) the seventh of Linnæus' Natural Orders, comprehending some genera of flowers that appear at a different time from their leaves, and therefore have a naked appearance, as the *Colchicum.*

DENUDA′TIO (*Med.*) γύμνωσις, from *denudo,* to make bare; a term applied to parts that are laid bare by the flesh being torn from them.

DEO′BSTRUENTIA (*Med.*) from *de* and *obstruo,* to obstruct; medicines that are exhibited with a view of removing any obstructions.

DE′ODAND (*Law*) i. e. *Deo dandum;* any thing forfeited to the king, to be applied to pious uses, and distributed in alms by his high almoner, is the forfeiture commonly levied on the personal chattel of any person that has been the immediate occasion of the death of any reasonable creature. *Fleta,* l. 1, c. 25; *Bract.* l. 3, c. 5; 1 *H. P. C.* 419; 3 *Inst.* 57.

DE *onerando pro rata portione* (*Law*) a writ which lies for one that is distrained for a rent that ought to be paid by others proportionably with him.

DEOPPILA′NTIA (*Med.*) from *de* and *oppilo,* to stop up; medicines which serve to open obstructions.

DEO′XIDIZING *rays* (*Chem.*) rays of light which were supposed to deprive metals of their oxides.

DEPALA′TIO (*Ant.*) a term used by Vitruvius to express the increments or increases in the length of the day.

TO DEPA′RT (*Chem.*) a particular operation, whereby the particles of silver are made to depart or separate from gold, when being before melted in the same mass they could be separated no other way.

DEPART (*Law*) vide *Departure.*

DEPA′RTERS (*Chem.*) artists who part and purify the precious metals from the coarser sort.

DEPA′RTURE (*Law*) or *depart from the plea,* is when a man pleads in bar of action, and reply being thereto made, he shows another matter, contrary to his first plea.—*Departure in spite of the court,* is when the defendant appears to the action brought against him, and makes a default afterwards.

DEPARTURE (*Mar.*) the easting or westing of a ship with respect to the meridian it departed or sailed from.

DEPARTURE *of gold and silver* (*Metal.*) the parting or dividing of those metals from others that are coarser.

DEPA′SCENS (*Med.*) νομώδης, from *depasco,* to eat down: is an epithet for a putrid ulcer corroding and spreading itself over the adjacent parts. *Gal. in Hipp.* l. 6, aph. 45.

DEPE′NDENS (*Bot.*) from *dependo,* to hang from, dependent, hanging down, pointing towards the ground: an epithet for a leaf, and also applied to the sleep of plants, when the leaves which are erect in the day hang down in the night.

DEPERDI′TIO (*Med.*) ἀποφθορά. [vide *Abortus*]

DEPE′RIR (*Mil.*) a French term applied to an army wasting away by disease, or any other accident.

DEPE′STA (*Ant.*) δίπαφον, wine vessels which the Sabines in their sacrifices used to set upon the tables of their gods. *Varr. de Ling. Lat.* l. 4, c. 26; *Athen.* l. 11, c. 5; *Alex. Gen. Dier.* l. 3, c. 10; *Stuck. Antiq. Conviv.* l. 2, c. 27.

DEPETI′GO (*Med.*) from *de* and *petigo,* a running scab; a ring worm or tetter.

DEPHLEGMA′TIO (*Med.*) from *de* and *phlegma,* phlegm; the operation of rectifying or freeing spirits from their watery parts.

DEPHLEGMA′TION (*Chem.*) the depriving any liquid of the superfluous water it may contain, which has the effect of concentration; in this manner sulphuric acid is dephlegmated by boiling, when, for a time, it loses nothing but water.

DEPHLOGI′STICATED *air* (*Chem.*) another name for Oxygen.

DEPILA′TIO (*Med.*) ψίλωσις, a falling off, or defluxion of the hair.

DEPILATO′RIUM (*Med.*) ψίλωθρον, from *de* and *pilus,* hair; a medicine which destroys the hair.

1

DEPI'LIS (*Med.*) ἀψις, vide *Alopoecia.*
DEPLO'YMENT (*Mil.*) in French *deploiement,* the act of unfolding or expanding any given body of men so as to extend its front.
DEPLUMA'TIO (*Med.*) πτίλωσις, from *de* and *pluma,* a feather; a disease of the eyelids, which causes the hair to fall off. *Aet. Tetrab.* 2, serm. 3, c. 78.
DEPO'NENT (*Law*) one who gives information on oath before a magistrate.
DEPONENT *verb* (*Gram.*) a verb which has an active signification, but a passive termination. It is so called because *deponit* it, lays aside its passive participle future in *dus.* *Isid. Orig.* l. 1, c. 8.
DEPONTA'NI (*Ant.*) old men past threescore years of age, and no longer fit for public service. They were so called from the *pontes,* or narrow boards, over which the people passed into the *septa* or *ovilia,* when they went to give their votes; so that persons who were disqualified were said to be *de ponte dejecti. Fest. in Sexigenariis. Non.* l. 12, c. 22; *Manut. de Leg.* c. 7; *Sigon. de Ant. Jur. Civ. Rom.* l. 1, c. 17.
DEPOPULATO'RES *agrorum* (*Archæol.*) a term applied to great offenders, who, as it were, unpeopled, and laid waste the lands.
DEPORTA'TION (*Ant.*) a severe sort of banishment among the Romans, which consisted in sending the offender to a distant island, confiscating all his property, and depriving him of all his rank and dignity. It was distinguished from *Relegatio,* in which the estate of the exile was not touched. *Dio.* l. 57; *Ulp.* l. 1, § *deportatos ff. de legat.* 3; *Rhodig. Ant. Lect.* l. 27, c. 15; *Manut. de Leg.* c. 23.
DEPO'SIT (*Com.*) any thing given by way of security, as the deposit-money on the purchase of a house.
DEPOSI'TION (*Law*) the testimony of a witness, who, on that account, is called the *deponent,* which is taken down, and, after being read over, and signed by him, is admitted as evidence. *Deposition* is also the information given on oath before a magistrate. *Deposition* is likewise taken in the sense of depriving of a dignity [vide *Degradation*]; and also for a man's death; *Dies depositionis,* the day of one's death.
DEPO'T (*Mil.*) in French *depôt,* any particular place in which military stores are deposited; also a place of reception for recruits, or detached parties belonging to different regiments; and, in a fortification, a particular place at the tail of the trenches out of the reach of the canon where the besiegers assemble.
DEPOUI'LLE (*Mil.*) or *mettre en depouille,* French for stripping a cannon, when it has been cast, of its matting, clay, &c.
DEPREHE'NSIO (*Med.*) from *deprehendo,* to catch unawares; the epilepsy is so called from the suddenness with which persons are seized with it.
DEPRE'SSED *Gun* (*Gunn.*) any piece of ordnance having its mouth depressed below the horizontal line.
DEPRE'SSIO (*Med.*) ἰσφλασις, from *deprimo,* to press down, depression: when the bones of the skull are forced inwards by fracture, they are said to be depressed.
DEPRE'SSION (*Mil.*) the placing of a piece of ordnance so that its shot be thrown under the point blank line.
DEPRESSION *of an Equation* (*Algeb.*) the reducing an equation to lower degrees, as a biquadratic to a cubic equation, or a cubic to a quadratic; as if, in the equation $x^3 - 6x^2 + 11x - 6 = 0$, it be discovered that x is equal to 2, then $x - 2$ will be the divisor, with which, if the equation be divided, it is depressed to the quadratic $x^2 - 4x + 3 = 0$; the two roots of which are 1 and 3.
DEPRESSION *of a star* (*Astron.*) or *of the Sun, &c. below the horizon,* is the distance of a star from the horizon below, and is measured by an arc of the vertical circle or azimuth passing through the star, intercepted between the star and the horizon.
DEPRESSION *of the Pole* (*Mar.*) is said of a person sailing or travelling from the Pole to the Equator, because so many degrees as he approaches nearer the Equator so many degrees will the Pole be nearer the Horizon.—*Depression of the visible Horizon,* or *dip of the Horizon,* its sinking or dipping below the true horizontal plane by the observer's eye being above the surface of the sea, as in the annexed figure; suppose the eye to be at E, then is A E the height above the surface of the earth whose centre is C, E A is the true horizon, E *h* the visible horizon lower than the former by the angle H E *h* by reason of the elevation of the eye.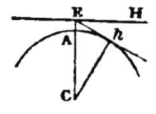
DEPRESSION *of a planet* (*Astrol.*) is when the planet is in a sign opposite to its exaltation.
DEPRE'SSOR (*Anat.*) from *deprimo,* to pull or draw down; a term applied to several muscles, because they depress the parts to which they are fastened; as *Depressor alæ Nasi,* that draws the upper lip and the *alæ Nasi* down.—*Depressor Anguli Oris,* that pulls the angle of the mouth downward.—*Depressor Oculi,* the same as the *Rectus inferior oculi,* &c.
DEPRESSO'RIUM (*Surg.*) the name of an instrument used for depressing the *Dura Mater* after the operation for the Trepan.
DEPRE'SSUS (*Bot.*) *depressus,* an epithet for a leaf which is hollow in the middle, or having the disk more depressed than the sides, in distinction from *conversus* and *compressus.* It is applied to succulent plants only.
DE'PRIMENS (*Med.*) from *deprimo,* to depress; the name of a muscle which depresses the external Ear.
DEPRIVA'TION (*Law*) a depriving, or taking away, as when a parson, vicar, &c. is deposed from his preferment. Deprivations are of two kinds; namely, *Deprivatio a beneficio,* when the person is wholly deprived of his living; and *Deprivatio ab officio,* where he is for ever deprived of his orders, which is also called *Deposition* and *Degradation.* [vide *Degradation*]
DEPTH (*Mil.*) is the number of men that are in a file; which of a squadron is three, and of a battalion six.
DEPTH *of a sail* (*Mar.*) the extent of the square sails from the head-rope to the foot-rope.
DEPURA'TION (*Chem.*) from *depuro,* to purify; is the purging a body of all the lees, fæces, &c.
DEPURATION (*Surg.*) the cleansing of a wound of all foul matter.
DEPURATO'RIA *Febris* (*Med.*) from *de* and *purus,* pure; a name given by Sydenham to a fever which prevailed during the years 1661 and 1664.
DEPUTATI (*Ant.*) 1. Armourers, or makers of arms. *Novel.* 85; *Basil. Ec.* l. 57. 2. Active persons who were appointed to attend the army, particularly on the field of battle, when they carried away the wounded, and waited upon them. *Leo. Constitut.* 3; *Panciroll. Notit. Dignit. Imp. Orient.* c. 65. *apud Græv. Thes. Antiq.* tom. iii. 7.
DE'PUTY (*Mil.*) a person appointed by commission to act for another, as Deputy-Barrack-Master, Deputy-Commissaries, Deputy Judge Advocate, &c.
DE *quibus sur disseisin* (*Law*) a writ of Entry. *F. N. B.* 191.
To DERAIGN (*Law*) from the French *deraigner,* signifies, 1. To confound, or put out of its course, as *dèraignment,* or departure from religion. *Stat.* 33 Hen. 8, c. 6. 2. To prove, as " To *deraign,* a right, a warranty, &c." 3. Britton applies the term to a summons challenged as defective, and Skene uses it in the sense of waging, or making of law.
DE'RAS (*Alchem.*) δρας, a sheep skin; is the title of a book in Alchemy treating of the art of making gold of baser metals.

DERBIA (*Med.*) a name given by some surgeons to the impetigo.

DE'RELICT (*Law*) *derelictus*, forsaken, or left; *derelict lands*, lands which the sea has suddenly left; *derelict goods*, as spirits and tobacco, which are liable to duties as if legally imported; *derelict ships*, vessels forsaken at sea.

DERIVA'TIO (*Med.*) παρεχίτωσις, from *derivo*, to draw from; is when a humour, which cannot be conveniently evacuated at the part affected, is attracted thence and discharged at some more proper place in its vicinity.

DERI'VATIVE (*Gram.*) any word which takes its origin from another called the *primitive*, as manhood, deity, &c. The word derivative is also an example, being derived from the Latin *rivus*, a channel or source.

DE'RIVE (*Mar.*) French for the driving of a ship.

DE'RMA (*Med.*) δέρμα, the skin.

DERMATO'DES (*Med.*) δερματώδης, from δέρμα, skin, and είδος, likeness, resembling skin or leather; an epithet applied to the *dura mater*.

DERMATOLO'GIA (*Med.*) from δέρμα, the skin, and λόγος, a discourse; a treatise on the skin.

DERME'STES (*Ent.*) the Leather Eater, a genus of Insects of the Hemipterous Order.
 Generic Character. *Antennæ* clavate, the club perfoliate.—*Thorax* convex.—*Head* inflected and hid under the Thorax.
 Species. Insects of this tribe are distinguished into those which have jaws bifid, and those which have the jaw one-toothed, called by Fabricius *apate*. The *larva*, or grubs, of this tribe, devour dead bodies, skins, leather, and almost any animal substance, being exceedingly destructive in museums and libraries. They are of a lengthened oval shape, with more or less hair on the body. The most familiar species are the *Dermestes lardarius* and *pellis*.

DE'ROUTE (*Mil.*) French for the total overthrow of an army.

DE'RRICK (*Mech.*) a contrivance to serve the temporary purpose of a crane for hoisting up goods.—*Derrick*, in French *martinet d'artimon*, a tackle used at the outer quarter of a mizen-yard, consisting of a double and single block.

DE'RRIS (*Ent.*) a genus of worms of the Order *Mollusca*, having a cylindrical body, a terminal mouth, and two feelers: it inhabits the coast of Pembrokeshire.

DE'RSE (*Med.*) an occult fume or vapour of the earth, from whence all ligneous substances have their rise and growth. *Paracel. Philos. ad Athenian.* l. 3, text. 4.

DE'RTRON (*Med.*) δέρτρον, from δέρας, the skin; the omentum, or peritonæum, so named from its skinlike consistence.

DE'RVISE (*Theol.*) an order of religious persons among the Turks who practise great austerities on themselves.

DESA'RMER (*Gun.*) a French term which signifies literally to disarm, but when applied to a piece of ordnance it imports to draw the charge out, or altogether to dismount it.

DE'SCANT (*Mus.*) a term used by old musical writers to denote the art of composing in several parts. It is plain, figurative, and double.—*Plain descant* is the groundwork of a musical composition which consists in the orderly placing of many concords.—*Figurative*, or *florid descant*, is that wherein discords as well as concords are concerned. —*Double descant* is when the parts are so contrived that the treble may be made the bass, and, on the contrary, the bass the treble.

To DESCANT (*Mus.*) is to run a division, or variety, with the voice upon a musical ground in true measure, and metaphorically signifies to paraphrase ingeniously upon any subject.

DESCE'NDENS (*Bot.*) vide *Descending*.

DESCE'NDER, *writ of Formedon in* (*Law*) a writ which lieth where a gift in tail is made, and the tenant in tail aliens the land entailed and dies; then the heir in tail shall have this writ against him who is then the actual tenant of the freehold. *F. N. B.* 211, &c.

DESCE'NDING (*Astron.*) an epithet opposed to ascending, as descending degrees, signs, stars, &c.—*Descending node* is that where the planet descends from the north to the south side of the Equator.—*Descending latitude* is the latitude of a planet in its return from the nodes to the Equator.

DESCENDING (*Bot.*) *descendens*; an epithet for the *caudex*, or that part of a plant which goes down into the earth: *caudex descendens* is the same as the root.

DESCE'NDRE (*Mil.*) a French term for, to quit on being relieved, as *descendre la garde*, to come off guard; *descendre la tranchée*, to quit the trench.

DESCE'NSIO (*Med.*) κατάβασις, from *descendo*, to move downwards, is properly spoken of the moderate or gentle motion of the body or humour downwards.

DESCE'NSION (*Chem.*) is the falling downwards of the essential juice, dissolved from the distilled matter.

DESCENSION (*Astron.*) an arc of the equator which descends or sets with any sign or point in the zodiac. It is either right or oblique, according as it takes place in a right or oblique sphere.—*Right descension* is the arc of the equator which descends with a point of the zodiac in a right sphere.—*Oblique descension* is an arc of the equator which descends with a point of the zodiac in an oblique sphere. —*Refraction of Descension*, vide *Refraction*.

DESCE'NSIONAL *Difference* (*Astron.*) the difference between the right and oblique descension of a star, or any point in the heavens.

DESCENSO'RIUM (*Chem.*) from *descendo*, to move downwards; a vessel in which the distillation *by descent* is performed.

DESCE'NSUS (*Chem.*) Distillation is said to be *per descensum*, by descent, when the fire is applied at the top and round the vessel whose orifice is at the bottom, whereby the vapours are caused to distil downwards.

DESCE'NT (*Chem.*) vide *Descensus*.

DESCENT (*Phy.*) is the tendency of heavy bodies towards the earth.

DESCENT *into a moat*, &c. (*Fort.*) is a digging deep into the earth.—*Descents* are the holes and hollows made by undermining the ground.

DESCENT (*Mil.*) or to make a descent upon a country, is to land on it with a hostile force, for the purpose of invasion.

DESCENT (*Her.*) a term in blazonry used to signify coming down. "A lion *in descent*" is a lion coming down, i. e. with his heels up towards one of the points, as though he were leaping down from some high place.

DESCENT (*Law*) *Descensus*, hereditary succession; the title whereby a man, at the death of his ancestor, obtains his freehold by right of representation as his heir at law. Descent is of two kinds, lineal and collateral.—*Lineal Descent* is that which is conveyed down in a right line from the grandfather to the father, and from the father to the son.—*Collateral Descent* is that which springs out of the side of the line, or blood, as from a man to his brother, nephew, &c. [vide *Law*]

DESCE'NTS (*Fort.*) vide *Descent*.

DESCRI'BENT (*Geom.*) a line, or superficies, by the motion of which a superficies, or solid, is described. [vide *Dirigent*]

DESCRI'PTION (*Log.*) an imperfect kind of definition, which includes some accidents, or circumstances, peculiar to it, so as to distinguish it from others, generally without defining its nature precisely.

DESCRIPTION (*Law*) in deeds and grants of lands must contain an exact account of the lands, the place where they lie, and of the persons to whom they are granted.

DESCU'REA (*Bot.*) another name for the *Sisymbrium*.

DESE'MPARER *un camp* (*Mil.*) French, to break up the camp, to strike the tents.

DESENCLOU'ER (*Mil.*) French for to take the nail out of a gun that has been spiked, or out of a horse's foot, &c.

DESE'RTER (*Mil.*) one that runs away from his colours, or goes over to the enemy.

DESHA'CHE (*Her.*) a term in French blazonry for a beast that has his limbs separated from his body.

DESICCA'TIO (*Med.*) from *desicco*, to dry up, ξήρωσις, drying; a term used by the chemists formerly in the sense of calcination.

DESI'CCATIVES (*Med.*) drying medicines.

DESICCATI'VUM (*Med.*) an epithet for an ointment, or plaister, for drying up thin humours flowing from an ulcer.

DESIDERA'TUM (*Lit.*) from *desidero*, to desire, or want, is used for whatever is an object of particular desire, or want; in this sense a book is denominated a desideratum, if it be of a nature to fill up a chasm in literature, or to supply the wants of any number of readers.

DESI'GN (*Paint.*) the first draught or sketch of any picture, which serves to give the general idea which the artist has formed in his mind of his subject; in a particular sense, the drawing of a building to be executed; comprehending the invention and disposition of the whole. The design of a building consists of three parts; namely, the *plan*, or ground-plan, which shows the distribution of the parts; the *elevation*, which shows the exterior; and the *section*, which exhibits the interior.

DESI'GNATOR (*Ant.*) an officer who assigned seats to the spectators at the games called by the Greeks ἰσοδίκτης. *Plaut. Poen. Prol.* v. 19.

Neu designator, præter os obambulet
Neu tessum ducat, dum histrio in scend siet.

He also marshalled the order of funeral processions, and had lictors assigned to him. *Hor.* l. 1, epist. 7, v. 6.

———— *cum ficus primus calorque*
Designatorem decorat lictoribus atris.

There were also *designatores decumæ* in the provinces. *Senec. de Benefic.* l. 6, c. 38; *Dio.* l. 56; *Quintil. Declam.* 6; *Donat. Adelph.* act. 1, scen. 1, v. 7; *Tertull. de Spectac.* c. 10; *Panciroll. de Magistrat. Municip.* c. 25; *Ursat. de Not. Roman. apud Græv. Thes. Ant. Rom.* tom. 11, p. 670.

DESIPIE'NTIA (*Med.*) παραφροσύνη, from *desipio*, to dote; a defect of reason, a symptomatic phrenzy.

DE'SME (*Med.*) δισμη, from διω, to bind; a bandage, or ligature.

DESMI'DION (*Surg.*) δισμίδιον, from δισμη, a handful; a small bundle, or little bandage.

DE'SMOS (*Surg.*) δισμός, is an affection of the joints after luxation in manner of a tie, or ligature. *Hippoc. Lib. de Fract.*

DE *son tort demesne* (*Law*) vide *De injuriâ suâ propriâ*.

DE'SPERATE (*Med.*) ἀνέλπιστος, is an epithet applied to incurable diseases.

DE'SPOTISM (*Polit.*) from the Greek δεσπότης, a lord, or master; a form of government where the monarch rules by his sole and sovereign authority.

DESPUMA'TION (*Chem.*) from *despumo*, to clarify; is the clarification of a liquor by elevating its impurities in a spume or froth, and then taking them off.

DESQUAMA'TION (*Surg.*) from *de*, privative, and *squama*, the scale of a fish, generally means the same as *Abrasio*.

DESQUAMATO'RIUM (*Surg.*) from *desquamo*, to scale off; an epithet for a trepan.

DESUDA'TIO (*Med.*) ἰφίδρωσις, from *desudo*, to sweat down; an unnatural and morbid sweating.

DESULTO'RII (*Ant.*) or *Desultores*; persons of great agility, who used to leap from one horse to another at the Circensian games. *Liv.* l. 23, c. 29: *Hygin. Fab.* 80; *Artemidor.* l. 1, c. 58; *Cassiodor.* l. 3, c. 51; *Veget.* l. 1, c. 18.

TO DETA'CH (*Mil.*) to send a party of soldiers upon any particular expedition.

DETA'CHED *pieces* (*Fort.*) are demi-lunes, hornworks, or crownworks, and even bastions, when separated from the body of the place.

DETACHIA'RE (*Law*) to seize, or take into custody a man's goods, or person.

DETA'CHMENT (*Mil.*) a certain number of men, drawn out from several regiments, or companies, for particular employments, or expeditions.

DETAI'NDER (*Law*) a writ for holding any one in custody.

DETAI'NER (*Law*) is commonly coupled with *forcible Entry*, as *Forcible Entry and Detainer*, signifying violently taking and keeping possession of lands and tenements; but a *Detainer* may be forcible whether the entry were forcible or not; as when a tenant keeps possession of the land at the end of his term against the landlord, it is a forcible detainer. *Co. Lit.* 256, &c.; 1 *Hawk. P. C.* c. 64.

DETE'NTIO (*Med.*) from *detineo*, to stop, or hinder; a name for the epilepsy, from the suddenness with which it seizes the patient.

DE'TENTS (*Hor.*) are those stops which, being lifted up, or let fall down, do lock or unlock a clock in striking.

DETE'NT-WHEEL (*Hor.*) called also the *hoop-wheel*, which has a hoop all around it, except in one part, where the clock locks.

DETE'RGENTS (*Med.*) ῥύπτων, deterging, from *detergeo*, to wipe off; medicines which cleanse and remove such viscid humours as adhere to and obstruct the vessels.

DETE'RMINATE (*Math.*) an epithet for a number, and a problem. A *determinate Number* is that which is referred to a given unity, as three, in distinction from the indeterminate, which refers to some imaginary or variable unity, called *Quantity*.—A *determinate Problem*, a problem that has but one solution, or limited number of solutions, in distinction from indeterminate problems, which admit of infinite solutions.

DETERMINA'TION (*Phy.*) the disposition or tendency of a body towards one way; also the action by which the cause is restrained to act, or not to act, in this or that manner.

DETE'RMINED *problem* (*Geom.*) a problem which has either but one, or but one certain number of solutions.

DETERRA'TION (*Phy.*) the removal of sand, earth, &c. from higher grounds to lower.

DETERSO'RIUM (*Ant.*) an apartment at the baths, where the sweat was deterged and the body anointed.

DETERSO'RIUS (*Med.*) ῥυπτικός, detersive; a common epithet of medicines endued with a cleansing quality, whether inward or outward.

DE'TINET (*Law*) i. e. he detains; a writ which lies where a man owes an annuity to another, and refuses it; or, in general, where he withholds from another what is due. *F. N. B.* 119.

DE'TINUE (*Law*) a writ which lies against him who refuses to deliver goods or chattels which are delivered him to keep. 1 *Inst.* 295.

DETONA'TION (*Chem.*) from *detono*, to make a noise; that noise and explosion which some substances make on the application of fire or heat.

DETRACTA'RI (*Archæol.*) to be torn in pieces by horses. *Flet.* l. 1, c. 37.

DETRA'CTIO (*Med.*) vide *Catharesis*.

DETRA'CTOR (*Med.*) from *detraho*, to draw down; an epithet for a muscle whose office it is to draw down the part to which it is attached.

DETRAHENS QUADRATUS (*Anat.*) vide *Platysma Myoides.*

DETRA'NCHED (*Her.*) an epithet in blazonry for a line that falls bend-wise.

DE'TRIMENT (*Astrol.*) the greatest of the essential debilities of a planet, i. e. the sign directly opposite to that which is its house; as the detriment of the Sun in Aquarius, because it is opposite to Leo.

DETRIMENT (*Her.*) a term applied to the moon in her eclipse.

DE'TRIMENTS (*Cus.*) a term used at the Universities and the Inns of Court, for the charge made to each member to defray loss and damage.

DETRI'PLER (*Mil.*) French for, to take some files out of a battalion, troop, or company, when the men are drawn up three deep.

DETRI'TIO (*Med.*) vide *Rhacosis.*

DETRU'SOR (*Anat.*) from *detrudo*, to thrust out; the name of a muscle belonging to the bladder, which serves to discharge the urine.

DEVADIA'TUS (*Law*) an epithet for an offender without sureties or pledges.

DEVA'NCER *une armée* (*Mil.*) French for, to get an advantageous position in front of an army by means of a forced march.

DEVASTA'VIT (*Law*) or *Devastaverunt bona Testa*, a writ lying against an executor or executors for paying legacies and debts, without speciality, before the debt upon the said specialities be due.

DEUCE (*Sport.*) in French *deux*, the number two at cards or dice.

DEVELOPPE'E (*Geom.*) French for, a curve formed by the opening or unfolding of another curve.

DEVENE'RUNT (*Law*) a writ to the King's escheator on the death of any one of the King's tenants holding *in capite*, commanding him to enquire what lands or tenements came to the King by his death.

DEVE'ST (*Law*) vide *Divest.*

DEVIA'TION (*Astron.*) a term in the ancient astronomy for a motion of the deferent either towards or from the ecliptic.—*Deviation of a falling Body*, that deviation from the perpendicular which falling bodies experience in their descent, in consequence of the rotation of the earth on its axis.

DEVI'CE (*Paint.*) a representation of some object with a motto serving as an emblem of some virtue or good quality in a person or thing.

DEVIL IN A BUSH (*Bot.*) another name for the *Nigelia.*

DEVIL'S-BIT (*Bot.*) an epithet for the *Scabiosa præmorsa*, because it has its root premorse, i. e. bitten off as it were at the end.—Devil's-Guts, the *Cuscuta epithymum* of Linnæus.

DEVI'SE (*Law*) a gift of lands, &c. by a last will and testament. The giver is called the *Devisor*, and the person to whom it is given the *Devisee.*

DEVISE'E (*Law*) he to whom the devise or bequest is made.

DEVI'SOR (*Law*) he who makes the devise.

DE'UNX (*Ant.*) a weight of eleven ounces, or eleven-twelfths of a pound, or of any entire quantity.

DEVO'IRES of *Calais* (*Law*) the customs due to the King for merchandise brought to or carried out from Calais when our staple was there. *Stat. 34 Ed.* 1, c. 18; *2 Rich.* 2, st. 1, c. 3.

DEVOU'RING (*Her.*) vide *Vorant.*

DEUS (*Ant.*) Θεὸς, the name among the Greeks and Romans for their deities, to whom they paid divine honours. These were divided generally into—*Dii Majorum gentium*, or *Dii Magni*, which are enumerated in these lines of Ennius:

Juno, Vesta, Minerva, Ceres, Diana, Venus, Mars,
Mercurius, Jovis, Neptunus, Vulcanus, Apollo.

—*Dii Minorum gentium*, which were otherwise called *Dii Breves*, included all the rest except the—*Selecti Dii*, which were in number eight, and were added to the *Dii Magni*, these were Sol, Luna, Tellus, Genius, Janus, Saturnus, Liber, Pluto. These gods were moreover distinguished by different appellations, as—*Dii Ascriptitii*, those who were, παρεγγραμμένοι, enrolled among the number of the gods, and were of course among the number of the inferior deities.—*Dii averrunci*, among the Greeks ἀλεξίκακοι, ἀπομπαῖοι, those who were supposed able to avert evils.—*Dii cælestes*, another name for the *Dii Magni*.—*Dii communes*, the gods who were worshipped in common by several nations.—*Dii consentes* were *Dii Magni*, the superior gods, so called because they composed the grand assembly of the gods. When mentioned in inscriptions the name of Jupiter is placed before all, as

IO.M.
CETERISQ
DIS·CONSENTIBUS.

—*Dii geniales*, namely, water, earth, fire, and air, which were the elements of all things.—*Dii genitales*, an epithet applied to the *Dii Magni*, as is supposed, because they were looked upon as the authors of all things.—*Dii ignoti*, Θεοὶ ἄγνωστοι, the unknown gods, had altars erected to them both by the Greeks and Romans.—*Dii littorales*, the gods who were worshipped on the sea-shore, as Glaucus, Panopea, &c.—*Dii Marini*, θαλάσσιοι Θεοὶ, marine gods, were very numerous, of which Neptunus, Nereus, and Oceanus, were the principal.—*Dii natalitii*, the gods who presided at births, of which Jupiter and Juno were the principal.—*Dii nuptiales*, the gods who presided at marriages, as Jupiter, Juno, Venus, Suada or Suadela, and Diana or Lucina.—*Dii patrii*, πατρῷοι Θεοὶ, gods of one's own country, i. e. such gods as are honoured particularly in one's own country.—*Dii Penates*, ἐφέστιοι Θεοὶ, household gods, or such as were worshipped at home.—*Dii privati*, those which were worshipped by particular families or communities.—*Dii publici* were those gods which were worshipped in the public temples.—*Dii regales*, Θεοὶ βασίλειοι, those who were the special guardians of kings.—*Dii rustici*, or *rusticani*, rustic deities, those who presided over the fields, as Pan, Silenus, the Satyrs, Fauns, Nymphs, and Dryads.—*Dii terminales*, were those who marked the boundaries of fields, and were known by the *lapides termini*, or boundary stones, which were made to represent a certain image.—*Dii viales*, those deities which presided over the highways, as Mercury, Apollo, Bacchus, Hercules, Ceres, Diana, Priapus, Vius, and Fortuna.—*Dii urbani*, another name for the *Dii consentes*, so called because they had their temples and altars in the city. *Cato. de Re Rust.* c. 140; *Varr. de Ling. Lat.* l. 6, c. 5; *de Re Rust.* l.1, c. 1; *Liv.* l. 5, c. 52; *Vitruv.* l. 1, c. 2; *Manil. Astron. Poet.* l. 2, v. 433, &c.; *Catull.* l.4, *Carm.* 22; *Hygin. Fab.*; *Plin.* l. 33, c. 7; *Plut. Alex. Justin.* l. 11, c. 15; *Tertull. Apolog.* c. 13, &c.; *Serv. in Æneid.*; *Macrob. Sat.*; *Gyrald. Syntag. Deor.*; *Turneb. Adv.* l. 5.

DEUTE'RIA (*Husb.*) δευτερία, from δεύτερος, second; a poor kind of wine which the Latins call *lora.*

DEUTER'ION (*Med.*) τὸ δευτέριον, τὰ δευτέρια, from δεύτερος, secundus; the secundines.

DEUTERO'GAMY (*Law*) δευτερογαμία, from δεύτερος, the second, and γάμος, marriage; a second marriage.

DEUTERO'NOMY (*Bibl.*) δευτερονόμος, from δεύτερος, the second, and νόμος, law; the fourth book of Moses, so called by the Greeks because the law is repeated in it.

DEUTEROPA'THIA (*Med.*) δευτεροπάθεια, from δεύτερος, the second, and πάθος, an affection; an affection which proceeds from another disease.

DEUTEROPO'TMI (*Ant.*) δευτερόποτμοι, those who being thought dead unexpectedly recovered after the celebration of their funeral rites; or who returned safe home after a long absence in foreign countries where they were believed to have died. It was unlawful for such persons to enter the temple of the Eumenides until they were purified by passing through the lap of a woman's gown that they might seem to be born again.

DEU'TZIA (*Bot.*) a genus of plants, Class 10 *Decandria*, Order 3 *Trigynia*.

Generic Characters. CAL. perianth one-leaved.—COR. petals five.—STAM. filaments ten; anthers globular.—PIST. germ superior; styles three; stigmas simple.—PER. capsule globular; seeds several in each cell.

Species. The single species is a tree, as the *Deutzia scabra*, native of Japan.

DEVI'NDER (*Man.*) French for, the movement of a horse who works upon volts, making his shoulders go too fast for the croupe to follow easily.

DEW (*Nat.*) the moisture which, being exhaled from the earth by means of the sun, and in the form of a vapour, falls down again upon the earth in drops.

Dew *of vitriol* (*Chem.*) a phlegm or water drawn from that mineral salt.

DE'W-BERRY (*Bot.*) the *Rubus cæsius* of Linnæus.

DE'W-CLAWS (*Sport.*) the bones or little nails behind a deer's foot.

DE'W-LAP (*Zool.*) that part which hangs down under the throat of an ox or cow.

DE'W-WORM (*Ent.*) the *Lumbricus terrestris* of Linnæus, a sort of worm which inhabits the earth and decayed wood, feeds on the cotyledons of plants, and is the food of moles, &c.

DE'WAN (*Polit.*) a receiver-general and governor of a province in the dominions of the Grand Mogul.

DEWS (*Sport.*) vide *Deuce*.

DE'XTANS (*Ant.*) the weight of ten ounces Troy, or ten-twelfths of an integer. *Varr. de Lat. Lin.* l. 5.

DE'XTER aspect (*Astrol.*) an aspect which is contrary to the natural order and succession of the signs.

DEXTER *epiploic vein* (*Anat.*) the second branch of the splenetic vein that passes to the caul or epiploon.

DEXTER *point* (*Her.*) signifies the right-hand side of the escutcheon; whence—*Dexter-Base*, the right side of the base, represented by the letter G.—*Dexter-Chief*, the angle on the right-hand side of the chief, represented by the letter A. [vide *Escutcheon*]

Dexter is also an epithet for any thing on the right-hand side, as " *a dexter hand*," or " *a dexter wing;*" and likewise for the male side in an impaled coat of arms.

DE'XTRÆ (*Ant.*) the name given to those flutes which the Romans played upon with their right hand, in distinction from those which they played with their left, called the *sinistræ*.

DEXTRA'RIUS (*Archæol.*) one at the right hand of another. Sometimes this word is used for the light horse.

DEY (*Polit.*) the title of the supreme governor in Tunis, Algiers, and the other states of Barbary.

DI'A (*Gram.*) a Greek preposition, signifying *of, by, through, with*, which is often joined to the names of physical compositions, as *Diascordium*, &c.

DIABA'CANU (*Med.*) διὰ βακάνυ; an hepatic remedy. *Trallian.* l. 8, c. 2.

DIABA'THRA (*Ant.*) a kind of shoes used in Greece. *Fest. de Verb. Signif.*

DIA'BEBOS (*Med.*) διαβεβώς, an epithet for the *Malleoli*, or ancle bones, not kept asunder but closed together, speaking of a mechanical operation for reducing a gibbosity. *Hippocrat. de Art.*

DIABESA'SA (*Med.*) from διὰ and βισασὰ, Wild Rue; the name of a preparation in which rue forms a part.

DIABE'TES (*Med.*) from διαβαίνω, to pass off; an excessive discharge of crude urine, exceeding the quantity of liquid drank. In the system of Cullen it is a genus of diseases, Class *Neuroses*, Order *Spasmi*.

DIA'BOLUS METALLO'RUM (*Min.*) Tin.

DIABO'TANON (*Med.*) διαβότανον, from βοτάνη, a herb; a plaister prepared of herbs. *Gal. de Com. Med. P. G.* l. 6, c. 2.

DIABRO'SIS (*Med.*) διάβρωσις, vide *Anabrosis*.

DIACA'DMIAS (*Med.*) διακαδμίας, from διὰ and καδμία, Cadmia, the name of a plaister whose basis is cadmia.

DIACALAMI'NTHES (*Med.*) διὰ καλαμίνθης, from διὰ and καλαμίνθη, Calamint; the name of an antidote whose basis is calamint.

DIACA'RCINON (*Med.*) διακαρκίνων, from καρκίνος, a crab or cray-fish; the name of an antidote prepared of those fish, as an antidote against the bite of a mad dog.

DIACAR'YON (*Med.*) διακαρύων, from κάρυον, a walnut; a rob made of walnuts.

DIACA'SSIA (*Bot.*) vide *Cassia*.

DIACASTO'RIUM (*Med.*) from διὰ and κάστωρ, castor; an antidote whose basis is castor.

DIACATHO'LICON (*Med.*) from διὰ and καθολικός, universal; an epithet for a universal purge.

DIACAU'STIC *curve* (*Math.*) a kind of caustic curve generated by the refraction of rays in a particular direction, so as to form a given ratio with other lines meeting them; thus, suppose an infinite number of rays, B A, B M, B D, &c. issuing from the same luminous point B refracted to or from the perpendicular M C by the given curve A M D, so that C E, the sines of the angles of incidence C M E, be always in a given ratio to C G, the sines of the refracted angles C M G; then the curve H F N, that touches all the refracted rays A H, M F, D N, &c. is called the *diacaustic*.

DIACELTATE'SSON (*Med.*) a term in Paracelsus relating to the cure of fevers. *Parac. de vita long.* l. 2, c. 5.

DIA'CENOS (*Med.*) διάκενος, from διὰ and κενός, empty, void; an epithet for porous bodies, such as sponge or pumice-stone.

DIACENTAU'RION (*Med.*) from διὰ and κενταύριον, centaury; the Duke of Portland's powder is so called because its chief ingredient is centaury.

DIACENTE'TON (*Med.*) from διὰ and κεντέω, to prick; the name of a stimulating collyrium. *Aet. Tetrab.* 2, serm. 4, c. 110.

DIACE'RATON (*Med.*) from διὰ and κέρας, a collyrium in which hartshorn is the principal ingredient. *Cels.* l. 6, c. 6.

DIACHALA'SIS (*Med.*) διαχάλασις, from διαχαλάω, to relax; a relaxation of the suture of the cranium.

DIACHALCI'TIS (*Med.*) from διὰ and χαλκῖτις, chalcitis; a plaister whose chief ingredient is *chalcitis*.

DIACHEIRI'SMOS (*Med.*) διαχειρισμός, from διὰ and χείρ, the hand; any manual operation.

DIACHELIDO'NIUM (*Med.*) διαχελιδόνιον, from χελιδών, a swallow; a preparation of swallows.

DIACHORE'MA (*Med.*) διαχώρημα, any excretion or excrement, but chiefly that by stool.

DIACHRI'STA (*Med.*) διάχριστα, from χρίω, to anoint; are medicines applied to the fauces, uvula, palate, and tongue for the abstertion of phlegm. *P. Aginetа.* l. 1, c. 46.

DIACHRY'SU (*Med.*) διὰ χρυσοῦ, from χρυσός, gold; the name of a plaister for fractures. *Gal. de Dynamid.*

DIA'CHYLON (*Med.*) διάχυλον, from χυλός, a juice; is an emollient digestive plaister composed of juices. *Gal. de Com. Med. per Gen.* l. 7, c. 9.

DIA'CHYSIS (*Med.*) διάχυσις, from χέω, to fuse or melt; liquefaction or fusion.

DIA'CHYTOS (*Med.*) διάχυτος, an epithet for wine prepared of grapes dried seven days in the sun. *Plin. l.* 14, *c.* 9.

DIACINE'MA (*Med.*) διακίνημα, from κινέω, to move or agitate in a slight manner; a slight dislocation. *Galen. de Fract.*

DIACLY'SMA (*Med.*) διάκλυσμα, from κλύζω, to wash out or rinse; a collution of the mouth, held therein for a time, and then discharged.

DIACOCCYME'LON (*Med.*) διακοκκυμήλον, from διά and κοκκυμήλον, a plum; an electuary made of prunes.

DIACO'CHLACON (*Med.*) διακοχλάκων, from διά and κόχλαξις, flints; an epithet for milk in which red hot flints have been extinguished.

DIACO'DIUM (*Med.*) from διά and κώδια, a poppy head; a composition made of the heads of poppies.

DIACOLOCY'NTHIDON (*Med.*) διά κολοκυνθίδων, from διά and κολοκυνθίς, colocynth; a remedy, of which colocynth is a principal ingredient.

DIACO'MERON (*Med.*) the name of an antidote. *Myrep. de Antid. c.* 39.

DIA'CONUS (*Ecc.*) vide *Deacon*.

DIA'COPE (*Med.*) διακοπή, from κόπτω, to cut; signifies a deep cut or wound. *Hippocrat. l.* 7, *aph.* 24.

DIACOPRÆ'GIA (*Med.*) διακοπραιγία, from διά, κόπρος, dung, and αἴξ, a goat; a remedy prepared of goat's dung against disorders of the spleen.

DIA'COPUS (*Ant.*) a breach in the bank of a river.

DIACOU'STICS (*Nat.*) or *Diaphonics*, the science which teaches the property of refracted sound as it passes through different mediums.

DIA'CRISIS (*Med.*) διάκρισις, from διακρίνω, to distinguish; the distinguishing diseases one from another by their symptoms.

DIACRO'CIUM (*Med.*) from διά and κρόκος, saffron; a collyrium containing saffron.

DIACRO'CU (*Med.*) διά κρόκου, from κρόκος, saffron; the name of a dry Collyrium, whose basis is saffron. *P. Ægin. l.* 7, *c.* 16.

DIACRO'MMYON (*Med.*) from κρόμμυον, an onion; a medicine made with onions.

DIACURCU'MA (*Med.*) from διά and κυρκῶμα, turmeric; an antidote in which turmeric or saffron is a principal ingredient.

DIACYDO'NIUM (*Med.*) διά κυδωνίων (μήλων), from κυδώνιον (μῆλον), a quince; a remedy prepared of the juice of quinces.

DIADA'PHNIDON (*Med.*) διά δαφνίδων, from δαφνίς, the bay-tree, or bay-berry; the name of a drawing plaister prepared of bay-berries and other ingredients. *Celsus. l.* 5, *c.* 19.

DIADE'LPHIA (*Bot.*) from δίς, twice, and ἀδελφός, a brother, twin brotherhood; the name of the seventeenth class in Linnæus' artificial system, comprehending those plants which bear hermaphrodite flowers with two sets of united stamens. This is a natural class with papilionaceous flowers and leguminous fruits, answering nearly to the *Leguminosæ* of Ray, and the *Papilionacei* of Tournefort. The orders are founded on the number of stamens, and ten being the predominating number in this class, the order *Decandria* is much the largest. [vide Plate 28]

The following are the principal genera, namely—Hexandria, as *Fumaria*, fumatory, &c.—Octandria, *Polygalia*, Milkwort, &c.—Decandria, *Amorpha*, Bastard Indigo; *Erythrina*, Coral-tree; *Spartium*, Broom; *Genista*, Broom; *Lupinus*, Lupin; *Anthyllis*, Kidney Vetch; *Piscidia*, Jamaica Dogwood; *Ulex*, Furze Whins, or Gorse; *Arachis*, Earth-nut; *Ononis*, Rest Harrow; *Colutea*, Bladder Senna; *Phaseolus*, Kidney Vetch; *Lathyrus*, Everlasting Pea; *Vicia*, Vetch, or Tares; *Astragalus*, Milk Vetch; *Phaca*, Bastard Vetch; *Trifolium*, Trefoil; *Glycyrhiza*, Liquorice; *Hedysarum*, Sainfoin; *Ornithopus*, Bird's Foot; *Scorpiurus*, Caterpillar; *Hippocrepis*, Horseshoe Vetch; *Trigonella*, Fenugreek; *Robinia*, Acacia; *Indigofera*, Indigo; *Cicer*, Chick Pea; *Ericum*, Lentil; *Galega*, Goats' Rue; *Lotus*, Bird's Foot Trefoil; *Medicago*, Medick.

DIADE'LPHOUS STAMENS (*Bot.*) stamina diadelpha; stamens forming two brotherhoods, as in the Class *Diadelphia*.

DIADE'MA (*Med.*) διάδημα, from διά, to bind; in the strict sense signifies a bandage for the head.

'DIADEMA (*Polit.*) from διαδέω, to bind round; was a fillet wherewith kings anciently encircled their foreheads, whence it became the emblem of dignity. *Tac. Annal. l.* 42, *c.* 6; 43, *c.* 2, &c.; *Plut. in Crass.; Curopalat. de Off. Aul. Constantinop.*

DIADE'XIS (*Med.*) διάδεξις, from διαδέχομαι, to succeed; a transposition of humours from one place to another.

DIA'DOCOS (*Min.*) a stone like a beryl. *Plin. l.* 34, *c.* 10.

DIA'DOSIS (*Med.*) διάδοσις, from διαδίδωμι, to distribute; the distribution of the aliment over all the body.

DIADRO'ME (*Mech.*) διαδρομή; the vibration or swing of a pendulum.

DIÆ'RESIS (*Med.*) διαίρεσις, from διαιρέω, to divide or separate; a division or separation of the vessels.

DIÆRESIS (*Surg.*) the dividing or separating of those parts which by their union hinder the cure of wounds, as of the continuity of the skin in impostumes.

DIÆRESIS (*Rhet.*) the partition of the subjects to be treated of.

DIÆRESIS (*Gram.*) a figure by which one syllable is divided into two, which is usually noted by two points, as *evoluisse* for *evolvisse*.

DIÆRE'TICA (*Med.*) from διαιρέω, to divide; corrosive medicines.

DIÆ'TA (*Med.*) δίαιτα, διαίτη, from διαιτάω, to nourish; a way and method of living, comprehending what we call diet.

DIETA'RII (*Ant.*) slaves who attended at meals. *Ulp. l.* 2, ff. *nautæ.*—*Dietarii Fures*, thieves who watched their opportunity of going into dining-rooms to steal things.

DIÆTE'TICS (*Med.*) from *diæta*; that part of the science of medicine which prescribes a due regimen with regard to the use of the Non-naturals.

DIAGLAU'CION (*Bot.*) διαγλαυκίον, from διά and γλαυκίον; the blue juice of a herb; an eye-water made of the purging thistle.

DIAGLY'PHICA (*Sculp.*) διαγλυφική; the art of cutting or making hollow figures in metals.

DIAGNO'SIS (*Med.*) διάγνωσις, from διαγνώσκω, to discern; the science which teaches the signs by which a disease may be distinguished from another.

DIAGNOSIS (*Bot.*) the discrimination of plants by their external characters.

DIAGNO'STIC SIGNS (*Med.*) the signs by which diseases are distinguished from each other.

DIAGNOSTIC SIGNS (*Bot.*) the signs or characters by which plants are distinguished from each other.

DIA'GONAL (*Geom.*) a straight line drawn across a figure from one angle to another, which by some is called a diameter. Diagonals principally belong to quadrilateral figures, and divide them into two equal parts, as A C, which divides the parallelogram into the two equal parts B C D and B A D. Two diagonals, as A C, B D, mutually bisect each other, as in the point E.—*Diagonal Scale*. [vide *Scale*]

DI'AGRAM (*Geom.*) a scheme drawn for the demonstrating or proving any thing, as the above figure.

DIAGRAM (*Mus.*) a proportion of measures distinguished by certain notes.

DIAGRA'PHICAL (*Mech.*) an epithet for what belongs to painting or engraving.

DIAGRY'DIUM (*Bot.*) vide *Scammonium*.

DI'AH (*Polit.*) or *diat*; a name among the Arabians for the punishment of retaliation inflicted according to the Mahometan law on a murderer by the relatives of the deceased.

DIAHERMODA'CTYLU (*Med.*) δι' ἑρμοδακτύλυ, from διὰ and ἑρμοδάκτυλος, a purging remedy in which the Hermodactyl is a principal ingredient. *Trallian*. l. 2.

DIAHEXA'PLA (*Vet.*) or Diahexaple; a drink for horses, so called from its six ingredients.

DIA'ION (*Med.*) from διὰ and ἴον, a violet; the name of a pastil, in which the violet is a principal ingredient.

DIAI'REOS (*Med.*) from διὰ and ἴρις, the Iris; the name of an antidote in which the Iris is a principal ingredient. *Myrep.* sect. 1, c. 103.

DI'AL (*Hor.*) from *dies*, the day; any plane upon which are drawn several lines and figures, and a gnomon, or style, so fixed as to show the hours of the day by the shadow of the sun, whence it is called a *sun-dial*. Dials are of different form, construction, and situation, namely—*Erect or direct dials*, which directly face any one of the cardinal points, North, South, East, or West.—*Inclining dials*, whose planes incline or bow forward toward the horizon.—*Reclining dials*, whose planes bend backward toward the horizon.—*Parallel dials*, otherwise called *horizontal dials*, lie parallel with the horizon.—*Perpendicular dials*, such as stand perpendicular to the horizon.—*Equinoctial dials* such as are described on the equinoctial plane.—*Vertical dials*, such as are drawn on the plane of a vertical circle.— *Polar dials*, those which are described on a plane passing through the poles of the world, and the East and West points of the horizon.—*Moon dials*, such as show the hour of the night by the light of the moon.—*Mural dials*, such as are placed against a wall.—*Universal dials*, those which serve for all latitudes.

DIALA'CCA (*Med.*) from διὰ and λάκκα, the name of an antidote in which Lacca is a principal ingredient.

DIA'LAGOU (*Med.*) from διὰ and λαγός; a medicine in which the dung of a hare is an ingredient. *Alex. Trallian*. l. 8. c. 2.

DI'ALECT (*Gram.*) διάλεκτος; a manner of speech peculiar to some part of a country, and differing from that of other parts, all of which use the same radical language. Such dialects, in modern times, are accounted vulgar corruptions; but among the Greeks there were five dialects, namely, the Attic, Ionic, Poetic, Æolic, and Doric, which were used by the best writers, either singly or intermixed. Homer wrote in all the dialects.

DIA'LECTICS (*Log.*) διαλεκτικὴ; the art of logic, which teaches to discourse and reason in mood and figure, and of which the ancient writers on rhetoric made much account. *Aristot. Rhet.* l. 1, c. 10; *Cic. de Or.* l. 1, c. 15, &c.; *Senec. Epist.* 39; *Quintil. Proem*. l. 1, &c.

DIALE'PSIS (*Med.*) διάληψις, from διαλαμβάνω, to interpose, or intermit; an intermission, also a space left between a bandage.

DIALI'BANON (*Med.*) from διὰ and λίβανος, frankincense; a name of several medicines in which frankincense is an ingredient.

DIA'LIUM (*Bot.*) a genus of plants, Class 2 *Diandria*, Order 1 *Monogynia*.
 Generic Character. CAL. none.—COR. petals five.—STAM. *filaments* two; *anthers* oblong.—PIST. *germ* superior; *style* subulate; *stigma* simple.—PER. *legume*; *seed* none.
 Species. The single species is a tree, as the—*Dialium indicum*, native of the East Indies.

DI'ALLAGE (*Rhet.*) διαλλαγὴ; a figure of speech which consists in bringing all arguments to bear towards one point, called in Latin *consummatio*. *Rutil. Lup*.

DIA'LLEL (*Math.*) such lines as run across, or cut one another.

DI'ALLING (*Hor.*) the art of drawing dials on any given surface. [vide *Horologiography*]—*Dialling globe*, an instrument contrived for drawing all sorts of dials, and to give a clear demonstration of the art.—*Dialling sphere*, an instrument contrived to demonstrate the doctrine of spherical triangles, and to give a true idea of drawing dials on all manner of planes.

DIA'LOES (*Med.*) δι' ἀλόης; the name of several medicines whose basis is Aloes.

DIALOGI'SMUS (*Rhet.*) διαλογισμὸς, called in Latin *sermocinatio*; a figure of speech whereby a man reasons and discourses with himself as though it were with another. *Jul. Rufin.* fig. 20.

DIALO'GO (*Mus.*) an Italian word used in music-books to denote a piece of music for two or more voices, or instruments, which answer one to another.

DI'ALOGUE (*Rhet.*) διάλογος; a conference or discourse between two or more parties; or a written discourse in which two or more parties are talking together.

DIALTHÆ'A (*Med.*) διαλθαία, from διὰ and ἀλθαία, the mallow; an ointment composed chiefly of mallows.

DIA'LYSIS (*Med.*) διάλυσις, from διαλύω, to dissolve; a dissolution of the strength, or a weakness of the limbs.

DIALYSIS (*Print.*) a mark or character consisting of two points, thus ¨ placed over two vowels, to show that they must be sounded distinctly, as Mosäic, &c.

DIALYSIS (*Rhet.*) διάλυσις, or διαλελυμένη λέξις, i. e. asyndeton; a figure of speech in which several words are put together without being connected together by a conjunction, as *veni, vidi, vici*. *Aristot. Rhet.* l. 3, c. 19; *Demet. Elocut.* § 61, &c.; *Dionys. Jud. Isæi*, c. 31; *Menand.* περὶ σχημ.; *Herodian.* περὶ σχημ.; *Phot. Bibl. Cod.* 79.

DIALY'TICA (*Med.*) from διαλύω, to dissolve; medicines which heal wounds and fractures.

DIAMARENA'TUM (*Med.*) from διὰ and *amarenæ*, acid cherries; a confection of acid cherries.

DIAMARGARI'TON (*Med.*) διαμαργαρίτων, from διὰ and μαργαρίτης, a pearl; an antidote in which pearls are the chief ingredients. *Myrep.* sect. 1, c. 37.

DIAMA'SCIEN (*Min.*) vide *Æris Flos*.

DIAMASTIGO'SIS (*Ant.*) διαμαστίγωσις; a solemnity at Sparta in honour of Diana Orthia, so named ἀπὸ τῦ μαστιγοῦν, i. e. from whipping, because boys used to be whipped upon her altars until the blood gushed out. The boys selected for this purpose were called Βωμονίκαι, from βωμὸς, an altar, and νίκη, contention, because the boys contended for the honour of enduring the stripes with the greatest fortitude. *Cic. Tusc. Quæst.* l. 2; *Hygin. Fab.* 261; *Plut. Lacon. Instit.*; *Themist. Orat.*; *Tertull. ad Martyr.* c. 4.

DIA'MBRÆ (*Med.*) the name of two medicines in the London Dispensatory.

DIAME'LON (*Med.*) the name of two compositions in which quinces are a principal ingredient. *Trall.* l. 7, c. 7.

DIA'METER (*Math.*) διάμετρος; a line which passes through the centre of any curvilinear figure from one point of its circumference to another.—*Diameter of a circle* is a line which passes through the centre of a circle, and is bounded by the circumference on each side, dividing the circle into two equal parts.—*Diameter of a conic section*, a right line drawn through the centre of a figure, and dividing all the ordinates into two equal parts. These are either conjugate or transverse. [vide *Circle, Conic Sections*]

DIAMETER (*Astron.*) is the measure of any celestial body, which is either real or apparent.—*Real diameter of the planets*, &c. is their absolute measurement in miles, &c.— *Apparent diameter* is the angles under which they appear to spectators on the earth, which are different under different circumstances, i. e. according as they are nearer to, or more remote from, the earth.

DIA'MNES (*Med.*) an involuntary discharge of urine.

DIA'MOND (*Min.*) the hardest and most valuable of all the precious stones. Diamonds are distinguished by lapidaries into *oriental* and *occidental*.—*Cornish diamond*, a name given to the rock crystals found in the tin mines of Cornwall.—*Rough diamond*, a diamond in the state as it is dug out of the earth.—*Rose diamond*, one that is quite flat underneath with its upper part cut in divers little faces, usually triangles.—*Factitious diamonds*, or *Paste*, those which are produced by artificial means.

DIAMOND (*Her.*) a name for the sable colour in the arms of the nobility.

DIAMOND letter (*Print.*) one of the smallest printing letters.

DIAMOND (*Mech.*) an instrument among glaziers for cutting glass, and in the glass trade for squaring large plates or pieces.

DIAMOND BEETLE (*Ent.*) an exceedingly beautiful insect, the *Curculio imperialis* of Linnæus, so called from the marks on its wing-sheaths, which, when properly magnified, have the dazzling splendour of the most brilliant gems.

DIAMONDS (*Sport.*) one of the four suits of cards.

DIA'MORON (*Med.*) διὰ μόρων; the name of a Preparation of Mulberries and Honey.

DIAMO'SCHU (*Med.*) from διὰ and μόσχος, musk; an antidote in which musk is a chief ingredient. *Mirep.* sect. 1, c. 37.

DIAMOTO'SIS (*Med.*) διαμότωσις, from μοτός, lint; the introduction of lint into a wound or ulcer.

DIA'NA (*Chem.*) the silver of Philosophers.

DIANANCA'SMUS (*Med.*) διαναγκασμός, from ἀνάγκη, necessity; the forcible restitution of a dislocated part into its proper place.

DIA'NDRIA (*Bot.*) from διὰ and ἀνήρ; the second class of Linnæus' artificial system, comprehending all hermaphrodite flowers which have two stamens, consisting of three orders, according to the number of the styles, namely—*Monogynia*, *digynia*, and *trigynia*. The following are the principal genera, namely—Monogynia, as *Olea*, Olive; *Ligustrum*, Privet; *Syringa*, Lilac; *Veronica*, Speedwell; *Pinguicula*, Butterwort; *Utricularia*, Bladderwort; *Verbena*, Vervain; *Lycopus*, Water Horehound; *Rosmarinus*, Rosemary; *Circæa*, Enchanter's Nightshade.—Digynia, as *Anthoxanthum*, Vernal Grass, &c.—Trigynia, as *Piper*, Pepper, &c.

DIANE'LLA (*Bot.*) is the Dracæna of Linnæus.

DIANŒ'A (*Rhet.*) διανοια; a figure of speech by which an apt sense and interpretation is given to a subject suitable to the occasion.

DIANTHE'RA (*Bot.*) a genus of plants differing somewhat from *Justicea*.

DIA'NTHON (*Med.*) δι' ἀνθῶν; the name of an Antidote taken from Galen. *Myrep.* sect. 1, c. 454.

DIA'NTHUS (*Bot.*) a genus of plants, Class 10 *Decandria*, Order 2 *Dygynia*, Natural Order *Caryophylleri*.
Generic Character. CAL. *perianth* cylindric.—COR. *petals* five.—STAM. *filaments* ten; *anthers* oblong.—PIST. *germ* oval; *styles* two; *stigmas* bent back.—PER. *capsule* cylindric; *seeds* very many.
Species. The species are perennials or annuals. The following are the principal perennials, as the—*Dianthus barbata*, *Tunica caryophyllus*, seu *Armeria*, Sweet William.—*Dianthus carthusianorum*, seu *Betonica*, Carthusian Pink, native of Germany.—*Dianthus caryophyllus*, Clove Pink.—*Dianthus deltoides*, Maiden Pink, native of Sweden.—*Dianthus cæsius*, Mountain Pink. The following are the principal annuals :—*Dianthus armeria*, seu *Viola*, Deptford Pink.—*Dianthus prolifer*, seu *Viscaria*, *Dianthus diminutus*, &c. Proliferous Pink.

DIANTHUS is also a name for the *Gysophila saxafraga*.

DIAOPO'RON (*Med.*) διὰ ὀπωρῶν, a composition of autumnal fruits, as quinces, medlars, &c. *Trallian.* l. 7, c. 7.

DIAPA'SMA (*Med.*) from διαπάσσω, to sprinkle; a medicine reduced to powder and sprinkled over the body. Also a perfume.

DIAPA'SON (*Mus.*) διαπασῶν, a term in ancient music, signifying an internal of the octave, is now used among instrument makers for a kind of rule, by which they determine the measures of the pipes, and other parts of their instruments. Bell-founders have likewise a diapason for the regulation of the size, weight, &c. of bells. This term is also the appellation of certain stops in an organ; so called because they extend through the whole scale of the instrument.—*Diapason diapente* is an interval, compounded of an octave and a fifth conjoined, i. e. a twelfth.—*Diapason diatesseron*, an interval, compounded of an octave and a fourth conjoined, i. e. an eleventh.

DIAPEDE'SIS (*Anat.*) διαπήδησις, from διαπηδάω, to leap through; a transudation of the fluids through the sides of their containing vessels.

DIAPE'NSIA (*Bot.*) a genus of plants, Class 5 *Pentandria*, Order 1 *Monogynia*.
Generic Character. CAL. *perianth* eight-leaved.—COR. one-petalled.—STAM. *filaments* five; *anthers* simple.—PIST. *germ* roundish; *style* cylindric; *stigma* obtuse.—PER. *capsule* roundish; *seeds* roundish.
Species. The single species, the—*Diapensia Laponica*, is a perennial, and native of Lapland and Norway.

DIAPENSIA is also the name of the *Aretia helvetica* and the *Saniculum Europœa*.

DIAPE'NTE (*Mus.*) διαπέντε, the name by which the Greeks distinguished the interval of the fifth, being the second of the concords.

DIAPENTE (*Med.*) from διὰ and πέντε, five; a medicine composed of five ingredients.

DI'APER (*Com.*) linen cloth wrought with flowers and figures.

DI'APERED (*Her.*) a bordure, fretted all over with such things as bordures are commonly charged with, appearing between the frets, as in the annexed figure.

DI'APERING (*Paint.*) is when a piece, after the back-ground is quite finished, is overrun with branches or other works.

DIAPHŒ'NICON (*Med.*) from διὰ and φοῖνιξ, a date; a medicine made of dates.

DIA'PHANOUS (*Opt.*) διαφανής, transparent like glass.

DIAPHLY'XIS (*Med.*) διάφλυξις, from διαφλύσσω, to moisten; an effusion or ebullition.

DIAPHO'NIA (*Mus.*) a term employed by Guido and others, to denote the precepts formerly taught for the use of the organ.

DIAPHO'NICS (*Phy.*) vide *Diacoustics*.

DIA'PHONI (*Mus.*) διάφωνοι, discords, in distinction from the symphony.

DIA'PHORA (*Med.*) διαφορά, from διαφέρω, to differ; comprehends the characteristic marks or signs that distinguish one disease from another.

DIAPHORA (*Rhet.*) a figure of speech, in which a word repeated is taken in a signification different from what it was at first understood. *Rutil. Lup.* l. 1, c. 12.

DIAPHORE'SIS (*Med.*) διαφόρησις, from διαφορέω, to carry through; perspiration or increased cutaneous secretion.

DIAPHORE'TICA (*Med.*) diaphoretics, or medicines which promote perspiration.

DIAPHO'RICA (*Mus.*) διαφορικά, an epithet for every dissonant interval.

DIAPHRA'GMA (*Anat.*) διάφραγμα, from διαφράσσω, to make a partition, the midriff or diaphragm; a muscle which divides the thorax from the abdomen. This is frequently called, by Cœlius Aurelianus *Discrimen, Thoracis.*

DIAPHRAGMATICÆ (*Anat.*) Arteries belonging to, or connected with the diaphragm.

DIAPHRATTO'NTES (*Anat.*) another name for the pleura, or membranes which cover the inside of the thorax.

DIA'PHTHORA (*Med.*) διαφθορά, from φθείρω, to corrupt; an abortion where the fœtus is corrupted in the womb.

DIAPHYLA'CTICUS (*Med.*) διαφυλακτικός, from φυλάσσω, to keep; medicines which resist putrefaction or prevent infection.

DIA'PHYSIS (*Med.*) διάφυσις, from διαφύω, to divide; an interstice or partition between the joints.

DIAPISSELÆ'ON (*Med.*) from διά and πισσέλαιον, the oil of pitch; a composition in which liquid pitch was a principal ingredient. *Marcell. Empir.* c. 35.

DIAPLA'SIS (*Med.*) διάπλασις, from πλάσσω, to form; the replacing a luxated or fractured bone in its proper situation.

DIAPLA'SMA (*Med.*) διάπλασμα, from διαπλάσσω, to anoint; an unction or fomentation applied all over the body.

DIAPLA'STICS (*Med.*) medicines proper for a limb that is out of joint.

DIA'PNE (*Med.*) from διαπνέω, to perspire; an involuntary discharge of urine.

DIAPNO'E (*Med.*) διαπνοή, from διαπνέω, to perspire; transpiration of vapour through the pores of the skin.

DIAPORE'MA (*Med.*) διαπόρημα, from διαπορέω, to be in doubt; nervous anxiety.

DIAPORE'SIS (*Rhet.*) διαπόρησις, a figure in rhetoric, when the subjects to be handled being of equal worth, the orator seems in doubt which he shall begin with.

DIAPRA'SIUM (*Med.*) διαπράσιον, from πράσιον, horehound; a composition in which horehound is one of the ingredients. *Trallian.* l. 5, c. 4.

DIAPRU'NUM (*Med.*) from διά and *prunum*, a prune; the name of two compositions which contain prunes.

DIAPSA'LMA (*Ant.*) διάψαλμα, a pause or change of note in singing.

DIAPTE'RNES (*Med.*) from πτέρνα, the heel; a medicine made of the heels of animals and cheese.

DIAPTERO'SIS (*Med.*) διαπτέρωσις, from πτερόν, a feather; the cleaning the ears with a feather.

DIAPYE'MA (*Surg.*) from πύον, pus; an abscess or suppuration.

DIAPYE'MATA (*Surg.*) from διαπύημα, a suppuration; suppurating medicines.

DIA'RIA *febris* (*Med.*) from *dies*, a day; a term applied to fevers which last but one day.

DIA'RIUM (*Archæol.*) Daily food, or as much as will last one day.

DIAROMA'TICUM (*Med.*) a medicine compounded of aromatics.

DIA'RRHAGE (*Surg.*) διάρρηγα, from διαρρήγνυμι, to break asunder; a fracture, particularly of the temporal bones.

DIARRHODO'MELI (*Med.*) from διά, ῥόδον, a rose, and μέλι, honey; the name of a composition of scammony, juice of roses, &c.

DIA'RRHODON (*Med.*) from διά and ῥόδον, a rose; a name for a great many compositions in which roses are the principal ingredients.

DIARRHŒ'A (*Med.*) διάρροια, from διαρρέω, to flow through; a disorder which consists in a frequent and plentiful discharge of a thin watery mucous, bilious, or blackish matter from the intestines.

DIARRE'XÆ (*Surg.*) from διαρρήγνυμι, to break asunder; interstices betwixt the circumvolutions of bandages.

DIARTHRO'SIS (*Anat.*) from διαρθρόω, to articulate; a moveable connexion of bones.

DI'ARY (*Lit.*) *diarium*, from *dies*, a day; an account of what passes within the day.

DIASAPO'NIUM (*Med.*) from διά and σάπων, soap; an ointment in which soap is a principal ingredient. *Nicol. Myreps.* sect. 3, c. 88.

DIASA'TURION (*Med.*) from διά and σατύριον, satyrion; an electuary in which satyrion is a principal ingredient.

DIASCHI'SMA (*Mus.*) an interval in ancient music, forming the half of a minor semitone.

DIASCI'LLION (*Med.*) from διά and σκίλλα, a squill; oxymel and vinegar of squills.

DIA'SIA (*Ant.*) διασία, a festival at Athens in honour of Jupiter, who was surnamed Διὸς μειλίχιος, i. e. the propitious Jupiter. It was celebrated about the latter end of Anthesterion. *Thucyd.* l. 1, c. 126; *Aristoph. Schol. in Nub.; Suidas.*

DIASCI'NSI (*Med.*) from διά and σκίγκος, skink; a name for Mithridate which originally contained this kind of lizard.

DIASCO'RDIUM (*Med.*) from διά and σκόρδιον, the water germander; electuary of scordium.

DIASE'NA (*Med.*) from διά and σένα, an antidote consisting of sena. *Nicol. Myreps.* sect. 1, c. 112.

DIAS'ERICOS (*Med.*) διά and σηρικός, silk; a composition in which silk is an ingredient. *Trallian.* l. 3, c. 7.

DIA'SMYRNON (*Med.*) διάσμυρνον, from σμύρνα, a myrrh; the several collyria in which myrrh is an ingredient.

DIASO'STICA (*Med.*) from σώζω, to preserve; that part of medicine which relates to the preservation of health.

DIASPERMATON (*Med.*) διὰ σπερμάτων, the name of two Malagmas compounded of seeds. *Gal. de Comp. Med. per Gen.* l. 7; *P. Ægineta.* l. 7, c. 18.

DIA'SPHAGE (*Med.*) διασφαγή, from διασφάζω, to separate; an interstice or interval between two branches of a vein. *Foes. Hippoc. Œconom.*

DIASPHY'XIS (*Med.*) διὰ φύξις, from σφύζω, to strike; the pulsation of an artery.

DIASTA'LTIC (*Mus.*) from διαστέλλω, to dilate; an epithet for the major third, major sixth, and major seventh, because they are extended or dilated at intervals; also for the grand part of the Melopœia.

DIA'STASIS (*Med.*) διάστασις, from διίστημι, to separate; a separation frequently used with respect to bones which recede from each other.

DIASTE'ATON (*Med.*) from στέαρ, fat; the name of an ointment in Marcellus Empiricus, in which the fat of the stag, swine, goose, and hen, is united.

DIA'STEMA (*Med.*) vide *Diastasis.*

DIASTEMA (*Rhet.*) a modulation of the tones of the voice, by observing due intervals between its elevation and depression.

DIASTEMA (*Mus.*) διάστημα, an interval or space; sometimes a simple incomposite degree, in distinction from a compound interval.

DIASTOLE (*Anat.*) διαστολή, from διαστέλλω, to stretch or dilate; the dilatation of the heart, auricles, and arteries, in distinction from *Systole*, or contraction.

DIASTOLE (*Gram.*) a figure whereby a syllable, short by nature, becomes long.

DIASTOMO'TRIS (*Med.*) διαστομωτρίς, is usually joined with μήλη, a probe, and implies any dilating instrument.

DIASTRE'MMA (*Med.*) διάστρεμμα, from διαστρέφω, to distort; a distortion of the limbs.

DIA'STYLE (*Archit.*) διάστυλος, from διά, between, and στῦλος, a column; a sort of sacred edifice, in which the columns stand at a distance of three diameters from each other. *Vitruv.* l. 3, c. 2; *Bald. Lex. Vitruv.*

DIASU'LPHURIS (*Med.*) from διά and *sulphur*, brimstone; a prescription containing sulphur, with wax, &c.

DIASY'RMOS (*Rhet.*) διασυρμός, a figure of rhetoric, which consists in exaggerating the praises of a person by way of derision. *Longin. Alexand.*

DIATA'MARON (*Med.*) the name of an antidote. *Nicol. Myrep.* sect. 1, c. 25.

DIATA'SIS (*Med.*) διάτασις, from διατείνω, to distend; the extension of a fractured limb with a view to its reduction.

DIATECO'LITHOS (*Med.*) διατηκόλιθος, from διά and τηκόλιθος, the Jew's stone; an antidote which contains the *lapis Judaicus*.

DIATERE'TICA (*Med.*) from διά and τηρέω, to preserve; medicines which preserve health, and prevent disease.

DIATE'SSERON (*Med.*) διατισσάρων, the name of a composition, so called from the four ingredients it comprehends.

DIATESSERON (*Mus.*) διατισσαρων, an interval composed of a greater and a less tone, the ratio of which is that of four to three.

DIATESSERON (*Bibl.*) a term applied to the four Gospels.

DIATESSERONA'RE (*Mus.*) a term denoting to sing in fourths.

DIATETTIGON (*Med.*) διατεττίγων, from τέττιξ, a grasshopper: the name of an antidote in which grasshoppers are an ingredient. *Paulus Ægineta*, l. 7, c. 11.

DIA'THESIS (*Med.*) διάθεσις, from διατίθημι, to dispose; an affection or disposition expressive of a particular state of the constitution.

DIA'THYRA (*Arch.*) διάθυρα, a screen or fence to keep out the wind; a rail or fence before a door. *Vitruv.* l. 6, c. 10; *Bald. Lex. Vitruv.*

DIA'TONI (*Archit.*) διάτονοι, diatoni, or *frontati lapides*, Corner-stones, Band-stones, or Parpen-stones, such as, in building of a wall, reach over the whole breadth.

DIATO'NIC (*Mus.*) διάτονος, diatonicum, an epithet denoting the most ordinary sort of music, proceeding by different tones either in ascending or descending.

DIA'TONOS *hypaton* (*Mus.*) διάτονος ὑπάτων, the musical note among the ancients answering to that now called *D-sol-re*.—*Diatonus meson*, διάτονος μέσων, another ancient note, answering to what is now called *G-sol-re-ut*.

DIATRAGACA'NTHI *species* (*Med.*) medicines composed of *tragacanth*. *Myrep.* sect. 1, c. 98.

DI'ATRIBE (*Rhet.*) διατριβή, a dwelling or insisting on a particular point, an excursion or episode by way of amplification on a point. *Aristot. Rhet.* l. 3, c. 17; *Cic. ad Heren.* l. 4, c. 45; *Menand. διαιρ. ἐκιδ*, p. 596; *Lucian. de Cons. Hist.* c. 27; *Hermog. περὶ διωοτητ.* p. 8; *Gregor. ad h. l.* c. 5.

DIATRINSA'NTALON (*Med.*) a confect, in which is the *santalum*.

DI'ATRION *Pipereon species* (*Med.*) from διά and τρεῖς, three; a powder prescribed by Galen, which chiefly consists of three peppers.

DIATRITA'RII (*Med.*) an epithet for the Methodics, who recommended the *Diatritos*.

DIATRI'TOS (*Med.*) διάτριτος, from διά and τρίτος, the third; an abstinence of three days enjoined by physicians of the Methodic sect upon their patients, one of the most considerable points in practice, by which they distinguished themselves from other physicians.

DIATU'RBITH (*Med.*) an electuary of *turbith*.

DIATU'REI (*Ant.*) ἀπὸ τῆς διαίτης i. e. from the living, or board, and ὕρευς, a keeper; men who were hired for their board to keep or watch the vessels.

DIATYPO'SIS (*Rhet.*) διατύπωσις, descriptio; a figure of rhetoric, which consists in the lively delineation of a thing, so as to set the object before our eyes. *Longin. de Sublimit.* c. 20.

DIA'ULUS (*Ant.*) δίαυλος, from δίς, twice, and αὐλή, a station, signifies a course backwards and forwards, i. e. from the starting place to the goal and back again. *Aristot. de General.* l. 2; *Schol. in Aristoph. Av.*; *Suidas.*

DIAULUS is also a measure of ground, containing two stadii, or furlongs. *Vitruv.* l. 5, c. 2; *Bald. Lex. Vitruv.*

DIAZEU'XIS (*Mus.*) διάζευξις, separation, from διαζευγνύμι, to separate; the name given by the ancients to the tone which separates two disjunct tetrachords.

DIAZO'MA (*Anat.*) διάζωμα, the *Diaphragm*.

DIAZO'STER (*Anat.*) διαζωστήρ, a name for the twelfth vertebra of the back, so called because the ζωστήρ, belt, lies upon it.

DI'BBLE (*Husband.*) a tool wherewith seeds are sown.

DI'CA (*Archæol.*) a tally for accounts; also an ancient name for a process or action at law.

DICÆO'LOGY (*Rhet.*) δικαιολογία, a figure of speech wherein the orator, by way of episode, attempts to move the affections of the audience in his favour. *Rutil. Lup.* l. 2, c. 3; *Quint.* l. 9, c. 3; *Eustath. ad Hom. Il.* 14, p. 1050.

DICE (*Sport.*) pieces of bone or ivory, of a cubical form, marked with dots on each of their faces, from one to six, according to the number of the faces.

DICENTE'TON (*Med.*) δικέντητον, the name of a hot and acrid *Collyrium* described by P. Ægineta, l. 3, c. 13.

DI'CERA (*Bot.*) a genus of plants, Class 13 *Polyandria*, Order 1 *Monogynia*,
Generic Character. CAL. *perianth* four or five-parted.—COR. *petals* four or five.—STAM. *filaments* twelve to twenty; *anthers* linear.—PIST. *germ* roundish; *style* awl-shaped; *stigma* simple.—PER. *berry* ovate; *seeds* very many.
Species. The species are trees, as the—*Dicera dentata*, seu *Elæocarpus serratus*, native of Zealand.—*Dicera serrata*, native of Zealand.

DICHA'LCON (*Ant.*) δίχαλκον, a weight equal to two *æreola*, or one-third of an *obolus*.

DICHA'STERES (*Anat.*) the *Dentes incisores*.

DICHO'NDRA (*Bot.*) a genus of plants, Class 5 *Pentandria*, Order 2 *Monogynia*.
Generic Character. CAL. five-leaved.—COR. five-cleft.—STAM. *filaments* five; *anthers* roundish.—PIST. *germs* two; *styles* two; *stigmas* capitate.—PER. *capsules* two; *seeds* globular.
Species. The single species is the—*Dechondria repens*, seu *sibthorpia*, native of Jamaica.

DICHOPHYIA (*Med.*) διχοφυΐα, a distemper of the hairs, which consists in their growing forked. *Galen.*

DICHORE'US (*Poet.*) διχόρειος, a foot consisting of two trochees, as *audiāmus*.

DICHO'TOMO-CORYMBOSUS (*Bot.*) an epithet for any flower having *corymbs*, the *pedicles* of which divide and subdivide in pairs.

DICHOTOM'US (*Bot.*) from δίχα, double, and τέμνω, to cut; an epithet for a stem; *caulis dichotomus*, a forked or dichotomous stem, which continually and regularly divides by pairs from top to bottom, as in *viscum*, or Missleto, &c. It is also an epithet for a *peduncle*.

DICHO'TOMY (*Astron.*) a term denoting an aspect of the moon when she is in her quadrature, or shows just half her disk.

DICHOTOPHYLLUM (*Bot.*) from δίχα, double, and φύλλον, a leaf. [vide *Ceratophyllum*]

DI'CKER (*Archæol.*) a quantity of leather, consisting of ten hides.

DICKSONIA (*Bot.*) a genus of plants, Class 24 *Cryptogamia*, Order 1 *Felices*, Natural order of *Ferns*.
Generic Character. Fructifications kidney-shaped.
Species. The species are perennials, as the—*Dicksonia arborescens*, Tree Dicksonia, native of St. Helena.—*Dicksonia culcita*, seu *Polypodium*, native of Madeira.

DICO'CCOUS (*Bot.*) dicoccus, an epithet for a capsule, which consists of two cohering grains or cells, with one seed in each.

DICO'CTA (*Med.*) δίκοκτα, water first heated and then refrigerated with snow. *Galen. de Meth. Med.* l. 7, c. 4.

DICONA'NGIA (*Bot.*) another name for the *Itra* of Linnæus.

DICOTYLE'DONES (*Bot.*) an epithet for such plants as split into two lobes in germinating.

DI'CRA *ferri* (*Archæol.*) a quantity of iron, consisting of ten bars.

DICRA'NUM (*Bot.*) a genus of Mosses.

DI'CROTUS (*Anat.*) δίκροτος, from δὶς, twice, and κρύω, to beat, an epithet for a certain pulse, in which the artery beats, as it were, double.

DICTAMNITES (*Med.*) δικταμνίτης οἶνος, a wine medicated with Dittany, described by Dioscor. l. 5, c. 57.

DICTA'MNUM (*Bot.*) the *Origanum dictamnus* of Linnæus.

DICTA'MNUS (*Bot.*) δίκταμνος, or δίκταμος, Penny-Royal; a plant so called either from the Dictæan mountain, in Crete, where it was first found, or ἀπὸ τῦ τίκτειν, from its bringing forth the young of animals, or expelling the fœtus. It is said that the goats and stags of Crete, when they were wounded with arrows, expelled them by eating of this herb. *Virg. Æn.* l. 12, v. 412.

> Dictamnum genetrix Cretæa carpit ab Idâ,
> Puberibus caulem foliis et flore comantem
> Purpureo: non illa feris incognita capris
> Gramina, cum tergo volucres hæsere sagittæ.

It is generally reckoned an excellent vulnerary and powerful cordial. *Aristot. Hist. An.* l. 9, c. 8; *Theoph. Hist. Plant.* l. 9, c. 16; *Cic. de Nat. Deor.* l. 2; *Dioscor.* l. 3, c. 38; *Plin.* l. 25, c. 8; *Apul.* c. 72; *Plut. de Solert. Animal.*

DICTAMNUS, *in the Linnean system,* a genus of plants, Class 10 *Decandria*, Order 1 *Monogynia*.

Generic Character. CAL. perianth five-leaved.—COR. petals five.—STAM. filaments ten; anthers four-sided.—PIST. germ five-cornered; style simple; stigmas sharp.—PER. capsules five; seeds in pairs.

Species. The two species are perennials, as the—*Dictamnus albus*, seu *Fraxinella alba*, Fraxinella.—*Dictamnus capensis*, seu *Pallasia capensis*, native of the Cape of Good Hope.

DICTAMNUS is also a name for the *Origanum dictamnus* of Linnæus.

DICTATOR (*Ant.*) a Roman magistrate, who was invested with sovereign authority during the period of his administration. He was always chosen by the Consul in the night-time, and on some emergency, and laid down his office again as soon as the occasion ceased for which he had been appointed. The first dictator was Titus Largius Flavius, U. C. 253. *Polyb.* l. 3, c. 87; *Dionys.* l. 11; *Cic. de Leg.* l. 3, c. 3; *Liv.* l. 4, c. 13; *Plut. Marcell.*

DI'CTIONARY (*Gram.*) dictionarium, from *dictum*, a word; a collection of the words of a language explained in alphabetical order.

DI'CTUM *de Kennelworth* (*Law*) an act, award, or edict made for composing differences between King Henry III. and his barons, who had been in arms against him, anno 51, 52. *Hen.* 3.

DICTYOI'DES (*Med.*) δικτυοειδὴς, from δίκτυον, a net, and εἶδος, fern; a name for the *Rete mirabile*.

DICTYOTON (*Archit.*) δικτυωτὸν, *reticulata structura*; a sort of structure which consists principally of grating. *Vitruv.* l. 2, c. 8; *Plin.* l. 36, c. 22; *Philander. in Vitruv.*

DIDAPPER (*Orn.*) or Dipper, an aquatic bird, the *Colymbus minor* of Linnæus, which inhabits the fresh waters of Europe.

DIDE'LPHIS (*Zool.*) a genus of animals, Class *Mammalia*, Order *Feræ*.

Generic Character. Foreteeth rounded.—Tusks long.—Grinders crenate.—Tongue fringed.—Pouch abdominal.

Species. Animals of this tribe, which are well-known in English by the names of Opossum and Kangaroo, are inhabitants of America, where they live in holes, and climb trees by means of their prehensile tails. The females are distinguished by having several pouches in which they conceal their young in time of danger. The principal species are as follow, namely—*Didelphis opossum*, the Virginian Opossum.—*Didelphis marsupialis*, the Amboyna Opossum.—*Didelphis cayopollin*, the Mexican Opossum.—*Didelphis volans*, the Flying Opossum.—*Didelphis sciurea*, the Squirrel Opossum.—*Didelphis orientalis*, the Phalangi.—*Didelphis gigantea*, the Kangaroo.—*Didelphis tridactyla*, the Kangaroo Rat.

DIDE'LTA (*Bot.*) a genus of plants, Class 19 *Syngenesia*, Order 3 *Polygamia Frustanea*, so called from δὶς and the Greek letter Δ. Natural order of compound flowers.

Generic Character. CAL. common double.—COR. compound radiated.—STAM. filaments five; anthers cylindric. PIST. germ inferior; style slender; stigma subulate.—PER. nuts three; seeds small kernels.

Species. The single species is annual, as the *Didelta carnosa*, seu *Polymnia*, native of the Cape of Good Hope.

DI'DUS (*Orn.*) the Dodo, a genus of birds, of the Order *Grallinæ*, having a narrow bill, oblique nostrils, wings unfit for flight, and no tail. These birds mostly inhabit the Isle of France and Bourbon.

DI'DYME (*Bot.*) δίδυμη, a name for the root of the *Orchis*. *Galen Exeg.*

DIDYMÆA (*Med.*) διδυμαία, the name of a malagma or cataplasm.

DI'DYMI (*Anat.*) δίδυμοι, twin; an epithet for the testes, and also for the two eminences in the brain.

DIDYMO'DON (*Bot.*) a genus of mosses, according to Hedwig.

DI'DYMUS (*Bot.*) vide *Twin*.

DIDYNA'MIA (*Bot.*) from δὶς, twice, and δύναμις, power; a name given by Linnæus to the Fourteenth Class in his Artificial System, comprehending those plants which have hermaphrodite flowers with four stamens in two pairs of different lengths, the outer pair being the longest and the middle pair converging. It is a natural class, containing the *Labiati* and *Personati* of Tournefort; and is divided by Linnæus into two orders, namely, the *Gymnospermia*, or such as have naked seeds; and the *Angiospermia*, or such as have the seeds enclosed in a vessel. The following are the principal genera in the first Order, namely—*Ajuga*, the Bugle or Ground Pine.—*Teucrium*, the Germander.—*Satureia*, the Savory.—*Hyssopus*, the Hyssop.—*Nepeta*, the Catmint.—*Lavendula*, the Lavender.—*Sideritis*, Iron-Wort.—*Mentha*, Mint.—*Lamium*, Archangel.—*Stachys*, Wound-Wort.—*Ballota*, Black Horehound.—*Leonoris*, Mother-Wort.—*Clinopodium*, Wild Basil.—*Origanum*, Marjoram.—*Melissa*, Balm.—*Dracocephalum*, Dragon's Head.—*Melitis*, Bastard Balm.—*Ocimum*, Basil.—*Scutellaria*, Scull-Cap.—*Prunella*, Self-Heal, &c. The genera in the second Order will be found under *Angiospermia*.

DIE (*Archit.*) or Dado, the middle of a pedestal, i. e. the part lying between the basis and the cornice.

DIECBO'LION (*Med.*) διεκβόλιον, a medicine causing abortion.

DE DIE IN DIEM (*Law*) from day to day, in a continued succession.

DIELE'CTRON (*Med.*) διήλεκτρον, a troche; so called from amber, a principal ingredient in it. *Marcel. Empir.* c. 16.

DIEM *clausit extremum* (*Law*) a writ which lies when the heir of one, who holds land of the king, dies, for the escheator to inquire of what estate he was possessed. *F. N. B.* 251.

DIER'S-BROOM (*Bot.*) the *Genista tinctoria* of Linnæus, a shrub; so called from its flowers, from which is prepared a colour used by dyers in dyeing wool green.—*Dier's-weed*, the *Riseda luteola* of Linnæus, annual or biennial: so called because from its flowers is prepared a yellow dye.

DIERVI'LLA (*Bot.*) another name for the *Lonicera* of Linnæus.

DI'ES (*Ant.*) days among the Romans were distinguished in a variety of ways, the principal of which are as follow:—*Dies agonales*, those days in which the *rex sacrorum* sacrificed a ram, called Agone. *Varr. de Ling. Lat. l.* 5, c. 34.—*Dies Alliensis*, a day of mourning, in commemoration of the defeat of the Romans at the battle of Allia. *Fest. de Verb. Signif.*—*Dies atri*, the same as the *dies nefasti.*—*Dies civilis*, the space of time which is comprehended within one revolution of the sun, which the Roman priests reckoned from midnight to midnight. *Plin. l.* 2, c. 77; *Censor. de Die Nat.* c. 10.—*Dies comitiales*, days in which the comitia were held. *Macrob. Lat. l.* 1, c. 16.—*Dies comperendini*, days of adjournment to the number of twenty, on which the defendant could give bail. *Macrob. l.* 1, c. 16.—*Dies exempli* were days on which no public business was done.—*Dies fasti* were the same as the *dies juridici*, or court-days of modern times, in which it was lawful for the prætor to sit in judgment and, *fari tria verba*, pronounce these three solemn words, *do, dico, addico*. *Liv. l.* 1, c. 19; *Macrob. Sat. l.* 1, c. 16.—*Dies feriati*, or *dies non juridici*, days on which the courts were shut.—*Dies festi*, holidays, or days on which sacrifices, lustrations, and the like, were performed. *Macrob. l.* 1, c. 16.—*Dies intercisi*, a sort of half holidays, one half of which was devoted to the ordinary business, and the other half to religious exercise.—*Dies justi* were those days in which *jus*, or the execution of any sentence on a defendant was suspended, which, according to the laws of the twelve tables, was thirty days. *Gel. l.* 15, c. 13.—*Dies lustrici*, days of purification for children. *Plut. Quæst. Rom.*; *Fest. de Verb. Signif.*; *Macrob. Sat. l.* 1, c. 16.—*Dies nefasti* were the opposite to the *fasti*, for on them it was, *nefas*, unlawful to do any public business. *Var. de Ling. Sat. l.* 5, c. 4, &c.—*Dies præliares* were days on which the Romans held it favourable to engage an enemy. *Fest. de Verb. Signif.*; *Macrob. l.* 1, c. 16.—*Dies pro festi* were, in general, all days which were allotted to the civil concerns of men, such as the *fasti, comitiales*, &c.—*Dies religiosi* were fast-days, similar to the *dies atri.*—*Dies sanguinis*, the day on which the priests of Bellona used to cut themselves with knives. *Trebel. Claud.* c. 4; *Tertull. Carm. ad Senat.*; *Gyrald. de Ann. et Mens. Dieb.* c. 1; *Sigon de Judic. l.* 1, c. 27; *Augustin. ad Leg. XII.* § 35; *Ursin. ad Leg. et Seta. apud Græv. Thes. Antiq. Rom.* tom. ii. p. 1354, &c.

DIES (*Archæol.*) a term in doomsday-book, signifying the charge of one day's entertainment for the king.—*Dies marchiæ*, the day of meeting formerly held on the marshes or borders between the English and Scotch.

DIES (*Law*) is distinguished into—*Dies datus* a respite given by the court to the defendant.—*Dies juridici*, court-days, or days on which the law is administered.—*Dies non juridici* are days on which no pleas are held in any court of justice.—*Dies in Banco*, Days in Bank, i. e. stated days of appearance in the Court of King's Bench during every term.

DIES *critici* (*Med.*) critical days in which some fevers are supposed to arrive at a crisis; they are otherwise called *dies indicantes*, because they indicate the state of the disease.—*Dies internuncii*, such days as intervene between the increase of a disorder and its decrease.

DIES *caniculares* (*Astron.*) the Dog-days.

DIES *intercalares* (*Chron.*) intercalary days. [vide *Chronology*]

DIE'SIS (*Print.*) the mark ‡; called also a double dagger.

DIESIS (*Mus.*) δίεσις, a division, signified the smallest interval in the music of the ancients; but is now taken for a tone below a semitone, or a sharp.—*Diesis enharmonical*, the difference between the greater and the lesser semitone.

DI'ET (*Polit.*) a convention of the states or princes of a kingdom or empire; the same thing, in Germany, as a parliament in England.

DIET (*Med.*) δίαιτα, food regulated by the rules of medicine, on which Hippocrates and the ancients wrote much. *Hippocrat. de Vict. in Acut. Morb.*; &c. &c.—*Diet-drink*, a drink made of medicinal ingredients.

DI'ETA (*Archæol.*) a day's work or journey.

DIETE'TICS (*Med.*) that part of medicine which considers the way of living with regard to food or diet suitable to any particular case.

DIEU *et mon droit* (*Her.*) i. e. God and my Right, the motto on the arms of the Kings of England.

DIEU *et son acte* (*Law*) a maxim in law, that the act of God shall not be a prejudice to any man; thus, if a house be thrown down by a tempest, the lessee shall be free from an action of waste, and shall also have liberty to take timber to rebuild it.

DIE'XODOS (*Med.*) διέξοδος, from διά and ἔξοδος, a way by which any thing passes; is taken by Hippocrates for the descent or passage of the excrement by the anus.

DIE'XODUS (*Rhet.*) a figure of speech by which any thing is diffusely treated, in distinction from brevity of discourse.

DIFFAEM' (*Her.*) vide *Defamed*.

DIFFARREA'TIO (*Ant.*) a sort of sacrifice which was made by a man and a woman on the dissolution of their marriage. *Fest. de Verb. Signif.*

DI'FFERENCE (*Log.*) διαφορά, one of the five predicables which serves to distinguish different species of the same kind one from another. *Porphyr. Instit.* c. 11.

DIFFERENCE (*Math.*) the excess of one quantity above another.

DIFFERENCE (*Mil.*) the sum paid by an officer in the British service when he changes from half to full pay.

DIFFERENCE *of Latitude* (*Geog.*) is an arc of the meridian included between the parallels of latitude, in which any two places lie; when the latitudes are both North or both South, the less latitude taken from the greater gives the difference; but when the one is North and the other South, they must then be added together to give the difference.—*Difference of Longitude*, an arc of the equator comprehended between the meridians of two places. When the longitudes are both East or West, the one taken from the other gives the difference; but when the one is East and the other West, they are then to be added together to show the difference.

DI'FFERENCES (*Her.*) such things in coats of arms as distinguish one family from another, or members of the same family from each other. Guillim divides differences into ancient and modern.—*Ancient differences* were bordures of all kind.—*Modern differences* are the file, crescent, label, mullet, &c. [vide *Heraldry*]

DIFFERE'NTIAL *calculus* (*Arith.*) a method of differencing quantities, that is, of finding a differential, or that infinitely small quantity which, taken an infinite number of times, is equal to a given quantity.—*Differential of the first power or degree*, is that of an ordinary quantity, as dx.—*Differential of the second power*, is an infinitesimal of a differential quantity of the first degree, as ddx, or $dx dx$, or dx^2.—*Differential of the third power*, an infinitesimal of a differential quantity of the second power, as $dddx$, or dx^3.—*Differentio-differential calculus* is a method of differencing differential quantities, as the sign of a differential is, that of a differential of dx is ddx, and the differential of ddx is $dddx$, or d^2x, d^3x, &c., similar to the fluxions $\dot{x}, \ddot{x}, \dddot{x}$, &c. —*Differential equation*, an equation involving or containing differential quantities, as the equation $3 x^2 dx - 2 a x dx + a y dx + a x dy = 0$. The differential equation has been explained by some to signify that which defines the nature of a series.—*Differential method*, a method of finding quantities by means of their successive differences.—*Differential scale*, a name for the scale of relation subtracted from unity.

DIFFLA'TIO (*Med.*) the same as *Transpiration*.

DIFFLA'TION (*Chem.*) is when spirits which are raised by heat are blown into the opposite arch of the furnace with a sort of bellows.

DIFFLU'VIUM (*Bot.*) a distemper in trees, by which they lose their bark.

DIFFORCIA'RE RECTUM (*Archæol.*) to take away or deny justice. *Mat. Par. Ann.* 1164.

DIFFO'RMIS (*Bot.*) Difformed, irregular, or anomalous; an epithet for a flower, the parts of which do not correspond in size or proportion.—*Difformis torsio* is a twisting first one way and then the other; *difformia folia* are leaves of different shapes, on the same plant.

DIFFRA'CTION (*Opt.*) another word for *Inflection*.

DIFFU'SION (*Phy.*) the dispersing the subtle effluvia of bodies into a kind of atmosphere all round them.

DIFFU'SUS (*Bot.*) Diffuse, i. e. spreading wide; an epithet for a stem or a panicle; *caulis diffusus*, a stem which has spreading branches, as in the *Teucrium*; *panicula diffusa*, a panicle with pedicles spreading about loosely.

To DIG a Badger (*Sport.*) to raise or dislodge a badger.

DIGA'MMA (*Gram.*) δίγαμμα, an old Greek letter, as F, answering to the letter Γ, which was so called because it was supposed to represent a double Gamma.

DIGA'STRICUS (*Anat.*) from δὶς, importing double, and γαστὴρ, a belly; a muscle of the lower jaw.

To DIGEST (*Chem.*) vide *Digestion*.

DIGE'STA (*Law*) the Digests, or books of civil law.

DIGESTER (*Chem.*) an apparatus for reducing animal and vegetable substances to a pulp or jelly.

DIGE'STION (*Surg.*) the disposing an ulcer or wound to suppurate, or discharge good *pus*, by the application of proper medicines.

DIGE'STIVES (*Med.*) medicines which help digestion.—*External digestives*, such as dissolve a swelling or breed good matter in a wound.

DIGE'STS (*Law*) *digesta*, the first tome or volume of the Civil Law, so called because the author digested every book and title into a regular form.

DIGESTOR (*Chem.*) vide *Digester*.

DI'GIT (*Arith.*) *digitus*, a measure equal to three quarters of an inch.—*Digit* is also a character which denotes a figure; as 1 for one, 2 for two, &c.

DIGIT (*Astron.*) the twelfth part of a diameter of the sun or moon, used to denote the quantity of an eclipse.

DIGITA'LIS (*Bot.*) the name of a genus of plants, *in the Linnean system, Class* 14 *Didynamia*, Order 2 *Angiospermia*. Generic Character. CAL. *perianth* five-parted.—COR. one-petalled.—STAM. *filaments* four; *anthers* two-parted.—PIST. *germ* acuminate; *style* simple; *stigma* sharp.—PER. *capsule* ovate; *seeds* very many.
Species. The species are perennials. The following are the principal, as the—*Digitalis lutea*, Small Yellow Foxglove, native of the South of Europe.—*Digitalis ferruginea*, Iron-leaved Fox-glove, native of the Canary Islands.—*Digitalis sceptrum*, Madeira Shrubby Fox-glove; but the following is a biennial.—*Digitalis purpurea*, Purple Fox-glove, native of Denmark, Germany, Switzerland, and Britain. *Bauh. Hist.*; *Bauh. Pin.*; *Ger. Herb.*; *Raii Hist.*; *Tourn. Inst.*

DIGITALIS is also the *Chelone penstemon*, the *Gerardia purpurea*, the *Mimulus regens*, and the *Sesamum orientale*.

DIGITA'RIA (*Bot.*) another name for the *Panicum* of Linnæus.

DIGITA'TION (*Mech.*) a pointing with the finger; also the form of the same finger in both hands joined together; or the manner of their joining.

DIGITA'TUS (*Bot.*) from *digitus*, a finger; *digitate*, an epithet for a leaf; *folium digitatum*, a digitate leaf, or one the leaflets of which spread out after the manner of fingers, as in the case of the binate, ternate, and quinate leaves, &c.

DIGITE'LLUS (*Bot.*) a name for several fungusses.

DIGI'TIUM (*Med.*) from *digitus*, a finger; a contraction of the joint of a finger, and also a whitlow or sore upon the same part.

DIGITO'RUM TENSOR (*Anat.*) vide *Extensor Digitorum communis*.

DI'GITUS (*Ant.*) finger's breadth, a finger, or digit—*Digiti*, the fingers, were designated by different epithets, as—*Digitus annularis*, the ring-finger, also called *medicus*.—*Digitus index*, διακτικός, from δικνύμι, to show or point the forefinger. It was also called *salutaris, a salutando*, from saluting.—*Digitus medius*, the middle finger, being used as a mark of supreme contempt, was on that account called *infamis, vespus, impudicus*, &c. *Cic. ad Heren.* l. 3, c. 20; *Aul. Gell.* l. 10, c. 10; *Macrob. Sat.* l. 7, c. 13; *Isid. Orig.* l. 11, c. 1.

DIGITUS *Manus et Pedis* (*Anat.*) the finger and toe. The fingers and thumb in each hand consist of fourteen bones, which are distributed into three orders called *Phalanxes*. The same applies to the toes of each foot.

DIGLIPH (*Archit.*) an ornament on friezes resembling the triglyph, except that it has only two channels instead of three.

DIGLO'SSON (*Bot.*) δίγλωσσον, from δὶς, double, and γλῶσσα, a tongue; a name for the *Laurus Alexandrina*.

DI'GNITARY (*Ecc.*) one who has authority and jurisdiction in the church, as a dean, a prebend, &c.

DI'GNITY (*Law*) honour and authority. Dignities may be divided into superior and inferior, as the titles of Duke, Earl, and Baron, &c. are the highest names of dignity, so those of Baronet, Knight, Sergeant at Law, &c. are the lowest.—*Ecclesiastical Dignity* is defined by canonists to be an administration joined with some power and jurisdiction.

DIGNITIES (*Astrol.*) the advantages which a planet has upon account of its being in a particular place of the zodiac, or in a particular station with regard to other planets.

DIGNO'TIO (*Med.*) vide *Diagnosis*.

DI GRADO (*Mus.*) an Italian word signifying that the passage to which it refers moves by conjoint intervals.

DIGY'NIA (*Bot.*) from δὶς, double, and γυνὴ, a female; an order in Linnæus' artificial system, comprehending those plants which have two pistils. This order is the second in the first thirteen classes, except the ninth.

DIHÆ'MATON (*Med.*) διὰ τῶν αἱμάτων, from αἷμα, blood; an antidote composed of the blood of many animals. *Galen de Antid.* l. 2, c. 8; *Paul. Ægineta*, l. 7, c. 11.

DIHA'LON (*Med.*) διὰ ἁλῶν, from ἅλς, salt; a plaster prepared chiefly of common salt and nitre. *Ægineta*, l. 7, c. 17.

DIHE'LIUS (*Astron.*) that ordinate in the ellipsis, which passes through the focus in which the sun is supposed to be placed.

DII (*Ant.*) vide *Deus*.

DIJA'MBUS (*Poet.*) διίαμβος, a diambic, from δὶς and ἴαμβος, an Iambic, a foot in verse, consisting of four syllables, or two Iambics, i. e. the first and third short, the second and fourth long: as Ἀταρπιον. *Hæphest. Enchirid.*

DII'PETES (*Med.*) διιπετής; an epithet applied to γόνος, *semen*, and imports a sudden or immediate Defluxion.

DIIPOLI'A (*Ant.*) Διιπόλια; a festival celebrated at Athens on the fourteenth of Scirrophorion, so named because it was sacred τῷ Διὶ Πολιεῖ, i. e. to Jupiter, surnamed Polieus, or protector of the city. At this festival it was customary to place sacrifice-cakes on a brazen table, and to drive round them a number of oxen, of which the one that eat any of the cakes was immediately slaughtered. The person killing the ox was called βύτης, or βυφόνος, and the sacrifice itself sometimes βυφόνια, i. e. the ox-slaughter. The origin of this custom is differently accounted for by Pausanias and Ælian. *Ælian. Var. Hist.* l. 8, c. 3; *Porphyr. de Abstinent. ab Anim.*; *Hesychius*; *Suidas*.

DILAPIDATION (*Law*) is either the letting a building go to ruin, or the ruin and damage which accrues to a building in consequence of such neglect.

DILATATION (*Med.*) ἱνρυσμός, ἀπορμωδός; an affection of the vessels of the human body when they have their dimensions enlarged.

DILATATO'RES (*Anat.*) muscles which dilate the *alæ* of the nose.

DILATATO'RIUM (*Surg.*) a surgical instrument for dilating the mouth; also for pulling barbed irons out of a wound.

DI'LATORY (*Surg.*) vide *Dilatorium*.

DILA'TRIS (*Bot.*) a genus of plants, Class 3 *Triandria*, Order 1 *Monogynia*.
  Generic Character. CAL. none.—COR. six-petalled.—STAM. *filaments* three; *anthers* ovate.—PIST. *germ* inferior; *style* filiform; *stigma* simple.—PER. *capsule* globular; *seeds* solitary.
  Species. The species are—*Dilatris umbellata, viscera*, and *paniculata*.

DILE'MMA (*Log.*) an argument consisting of two or more propositions, so disposed that neither of them can be well denied without involving the party denying in equal difficulties.

DILEMMA (*Rhet.*) a figure of speech in which two interrogations being put to the adversary, we are ready to refute him in both; or a double hypothetical proposition, which Cicero calls *complexio*. *Cic. de Invent.* l. 1, c. 29; *Hermag. περὶ δυνάτ.*; *Aspin. Rhet.* p. 703; *Ulpian. in Demosth. Olynth.* 3, p. 25.

DILL (*Bot.*) the *Anethum graveolens* of Linnæus; an annual, having a strong aromatic smell.

DILLE'NIA (*Bot.*) a genus of plants called after Dillenius, a professor of Botany at Oxford, Class 13 *Polyandria*, Order 7 *Polygynia*.
  Generic Character. CAL. *perianth* five-leaved.—COR. *petals* five.—STAM. *filaments* scarce any; *anthers* very numerous.—PIST. *germ* ovate; *styles* several; *stigmas* simple.—PER. roundish; *seeds* numerous.
  Species. The species are trees, as the *Dillenia speciosa*, seu *Syalita*, native of Malabar.—*Dillenia elliptica*, seu *Songium*, native of Amboyna, Celebes, and Macassar.—*Dillenia serrata*, seu *Sangius*, native of the Celebes, Macassar, and Java.—*Dillenia dentata*, seu *Wormia*, native of Ceylon.

DILO'GIA (*Rhet.*) a figure of speech which consists in using equivocal terms that mean two things.

DI'LUENTS (*Med.*) are such things as cause or increase fluidity in substances.

TO DILU'TE (*Chem.*) to dissolve the parts of a solid body in a fluid.

DILU'TUM (*Med.*) diluted, is spoken of what has passed under the action of Diluents.

DILYTÆ'A (*Med.*) διλυταία in *Myrepsus*, sect. 3, cap. 12, is, as Fuchsius says, the fat of some animal unknown.

DIMACHÆ (*Ant.*) διμάχαι; a kind of soldiers who served both on foot and on horseback, answering to the dragoons of the moderns. *Poll. Onom.* l. 1, sec. 132; *Ælian. Tact.* p. 156; *Curt.* l. 5, c. 13; *Hesychius*; *Turneb. Adv.* l. 19, c. 32, &c.

DIME'NSION (*Geom.*) a term denoting the affections of a line, surface, or figure, as respect its extension in breadth and thickness: a line has one dimension, namely length; a surface two, namely length and breadth; a solid three, namely length, breadth, and thickness.

DIMENSION (*Algeb.*) is a term applied to the powers of any root in any equation: thus, in a biquadrate equation the highest dimension of the root is 4.

DIMIDIA'TUS (*Bot.*) from *dimidium*, half, halved; an epithet for a spathe, a capitulum, and an involucre.

DIMIDIETAS (*Law*) is used in records for one half.

DIMI'NISHED Angle (*Fort.*) vide *Angle*.

DIMINI'SHED (*Mus.*) an epithet for an interval, when, by the application of a sharp or natural to the lower tone, or of a flat or natural to an upper one, it becomes contracted within its natural compass.

DIMI'NISHING *the Coin* (*Law*) the reducing of the coin to less quantity or value by clipping, cutting, filing, &c.

DIMINUENDO (*Mus.*) abbreviated *dim.*; an Italian word in music-books, implying that the loudness of the passage over which it is placed is to be gradually lessened.

DIMINU'TION (*Mus.*) the abating something of the full quantity of a full note.

DIMINUTION (*Her.*) the defacing of some particular point in the escutcheon.

DIMINUTION (*Archit.*) the lessening a pillar by little and little.

DIMINUTION (*Law*) an omission in the record, or in some part of the proceedings, which is certified in a writ of error on the part of either plaintiff or defendant. *Co. Ent.* 232.

DIMI'NUTIVE (*Gram.*) a word that lessens the meaning of the original term from which it is derived, as *culter*, a knife, *cultellus*, a little knife.

DIMI'SSORY (*Ecc.*) an epithet for a letter sent by a bishop; *dimissory letters* are sent from one bishop to another in favour of one who stands candidate for Holy Orders in another diocese.

DI molto (*Mus.*) an augmentative expression in the Italian, as *allegro di molto*, very quick.

D *in alt* (*Mus.*) the fifth note in alt.—*D in altissimo*, the fifth note in altissimo.

DIMO'RPHA (*Bot.*) a genus of plants, Class 17 *Diadelphia*, Order 4 *Decandria*.
  Generic Character. CAL. *perianth* one-leaved.—COR. *petals* very wide.—STAM. *filaments* diadelphous; *anthers* incumbent.—PIST. *germ* short; *style* longer than the stamens; *stigma* simple.—PER. *legume* large; *seeds* few.
  Species. The species are trees, as the—*Dimorpha falcata*, seu *Eperua*, native of Guiana.—*Dimorpha grandiflora*, seu *Parivoa*, native of Guiana.

DIMORPHOTHE'CA (*Bot.*) another name for the *Calendula* of Linnæus.

DINICA (*Med.*) from δινέω, to turn round; medicines against a vertigo.

DI'NOS (*Med.*) δίνος; the vertigo.

DIOBO'GON (*Med.*) vide *Scrupulus*.

DIO'BOLUS (*Ant.*) a coin equivalent to two oboli.

DIO'CESAN (*Ecc.*) a name for a bishop who has the charge of a diocese committed unto him; also one living within the jurisdiction of the diocesan.

DI'OCESE (*Ecc.*) the circuit or bounds of a bishop's jurisdiction: of these there are twenty-one in England, and four in Wales. *Co. Lit.* 94; *Wood's Inst.* 2.

DIOCLI'A (*Ant.*) Διόκλεια; a spring festival at Megara, in honour of the Athenian Hero, Diocles. *Theocrit.* idyl. 12, v. 27.

DIO'DEA (*Bot.*) a genus of plants, Class 4 *Tetrandria*, Order 1 *Monogynia*.
  Generic Character. CAL. *perianth* two-leaved.—COR. one-petalled.—STAM. *filaments* four; *anthers* versatile.—PIST. *germ* roundish; *style* filiform; *stigma* two-cleft.—PER. *capsule* oval; *seeds* solitary.
  Species. The species are natives of the West Indies.

DI'ODON (*Ich.*) a genus of fishes, Order *Branchiostegous*, having bony jaws, a body covered with spines, and no ventral fins. Fishes of this tribe mostly inhabit the Indian seas.

DI'ODOS (*Med.*) διόδος, from διὰ, through, and ὁδός, the way; evacuation by stool.

DIŒ'CIA (*Bot.*) from δὶς, *bis*, and οἶκος, a house; the name of the twenty-second Class in Linnæus' Artificial System, comprehending those plants which have no hermaphrodite flowers, but the males and females on distinct individuals. The principal genera are as follow, namely, in—Monandria, as *Pandanus*, Screw Pine; *Brosimum*, Milk-wood.—Diandria, *Cecropia*, Snake-wood; *Salix*, Osier, Willow.—Triandria, *Empetrum*, Crowberry, Crakeberry; *Ruscus*, Butcher Broom; *Osyris*, Poet's Cassia; *Myristica*, Nutmeg-Tree; *Phoenix*, Date Plum.—Tetrandria, *Viscum*, Misseltoe; *Myrica*, Candle Berry; *Anthospermum*, Amber-Tree.—Pentandria, *Pistacia*, Fistic or Pistachio Nut-Tree; *Xanthoxylon*, Toothach-Tree; *Spinacia*, Spinach; *Acnida*, Virginian Hemp; *Cannabis*, Hemp; *Humulus*, Hop.—Hexandria, *Tamus*, Black Bryony; *Bocassus*, Fan Palm.—Octandria, *Populus*, Poplar, Aspen, Tacamahas.—Enneandria, *Mercuriales*, Mercury; *Hydrocharis*, Frog-bit.—Decandria, *Coriaria*, Sumach.—Decandria, *Datisca*, Bastard Hemp; *Stratiotes*, Water-Soldier.—Monadelphia, *Juniperus*, Juniper; *Taxus*, Yew-Tree; *Ephreda*, Sea-Grass.

DIO'ECOUS (*Bot.*) an epithet for plants that have the male and female flowers on distinct individuals, from which comes the Class *Diœcia*.

DIŒNANTHES (*Med.*) διὰ ἀνάθης, the name of an epithem against the *Cholora Morbus*, in Trallian, l. 7, c. 44.

DIO'GMOS (*Med.*) from διώκω, to persecute; distressing palpitation of the heart.

DIOMEDE'A (*Orn.*) the Heron or Hern, so called from Diomedes, whose companions, as the fable says, were converted into Herons.

Diomedea, *in the Linnean system*, a genus of birds of the order *Anseres*.

Generic Character. *Bill* straight.—*Nostrils* oval, wide.—*Tongue* very small.—*Feet* four-toed.

Species. Birds of this tribe are aquatic, and mostly inhabit the Indian ocean. The principal species are as follow; namely,—*Diomedea exulans*, the Wandering Albatross, or Man of War Bird.—*Diomedea spadicea*, Chocolate Albatross.—*Diomedea Chlororhynchos*, Yellow-nosed Albatross, &c.

DIOMI'A (*Ant.*) Διομεία, a festival at Athens in honour of Jupiter Diomeus. *Eustath. Il. l.* 4.

DI'ON (*Ant.*) δίον, the name of a month in which the autumnal equinox happened: it was in use only among the Macedonians. *Gal. com.* 1. *in Hippocrat. Epid.* l. 1.

DIONCO'SIS (*Med.*) διόγκωσις, from ὄγκος, a tumor; tumefaction, ampliation.

DIONÆ'A (*Bot.*) a genus of plants, Class 10 *Decandria*, Order 1 *Monogynia*.

Generic Character. CAL. *perianth* five-leaved.—COR. *petals* five.—STAM. *filaments* ten; *anthers* roundish.—PIST. *germ* roundish; *style* filiform; *stigma* spreading.—PER. *capsule* one-celled; *seeds* very many.

Species. The species, the *Dionæa Muscipula*, Venus' Fly-trap, is a perennial or biennial, native of Carolina.

DI'ONIS (*Med.*) the name of a *Colyrium*. Oribas. Synops. l. 3.

DIONY'SIA (*Ant.*) Διονύσια, solemnities in honour of Διόνυσος, or Bacchus, which were celebrated at Athens in greater splendour than in any other part of Greece. In most cases they were attended with much riot and revelling, particularly on the part of those who officiated as his immediate votaries, who ran about uttering hideous yells, and distorting themselves by every sort of frantic grimace and gesticulation. The festivals of Bacchus were almost innumerable, and distinguished by the names of the Διονύσια ἀρχαιότερα, νεώτερα, &c. *Thucyd.* l. 2; *Demosth. Orat. in Neæram. et Neptin.*; *Poll. Onom.* l. 8; *Harpocration.*; *Hesychius.*

DIONYSIA (*Surg.*) a sort of plaister for abscesses.

DIONY'SIAS (*Bot.*) vide *Androsæmum*.

DIONYSI'SCI (*Anat.*) διονυσίσκοι, from Διόνυσος, Bacchus, who was represented with Horns; certain bony eminences near the temples.

DIONY'SONYMPHAS (*Bot.*) from Διόνυσος, Bacchus, and νύμφα, a nymph; a herb which if bruised smells of wine, and yet resists drunkenness.

DIONY'SOS (*Med.*) διόνυσος, the name of a collyrium containing myrrh. *Aet. Tetrab.* 2, serm. 3.

DIOPO'RON (*Med.*) a medicine for the quinsy. *Cæl. Aurelian. de Acut. Morb.* l. 3, c. 3.

DIO'PSIS (*Ent.*) a genus of Insects of the Dipterous Order, having two inarticulate filiform *antennæ* much longer than the head, at the tip of which are placed the eyes. The body is reddish, and the abdomen clavate.

DIO'PTER (*Mech.*) vide *Dioptra*.

DIO'PTRA (*Mech.*) or *Diopter*, διόπτρα, διόπτης, from διοπτεύειν, to take a level or aim; an instrument among the ancients for taking altitudes, levelling water-courses, &c. *Vitruv.* l. 8, c. 6; *Plin.* l. 2, c. 69; *Martian. Capell.* l. 6, c. de posit. terr.

Dioptra is now the name for the index or alhidade of an astrolabe.

DIO'PTRA (*Surg.*) an instrument to enlarge the womb for the extraction of the fœtus.

DIO'PTRICS (*Opt.*) from διόπτομαι, to see through; that part of optics which treats of refracted rays, and their union with one another, according as they are received by glasses of this or that figure.

DIOPTRISMOS (*Surg.*) the operation which consists in dilating the natural passages with a *dioptra* or *speculum*.

DI'OROBON (*Med.*) δι' ὀρόβων, a medicine having vetches as a principal ingredient.

DIORRHO'SIS (*Med.*) διόῤῥωσις or διόρωσις, from ὀρός or ὀρρός, *serum*; a conversion of the humours into water or *serum*.

DIORTHO'SIS (*Med.*) διόρθωσις, from διορθόω, to make straight; operations where crooked and distorted members are made straight, and restored to their due shape.

DIOSCO'REA (*Bot.*) a genus of plants called after Dioscorides, Class 22 *Dioecia*, Order 6 *Hexandria*.

Generic Character. CAL. *perianth* one-leaved.—COR. none.—STAM. *filaments* six; *anthers* simple.—PIST. in the female; *germ* very small; *styles* three; *stigmas* simple.—PER. *capsule* large; *seeds* in pairs.

Species. The species are perennials, as the—*Dioscorea alata*, *Volubilis*, seu *Ricophora*, Winged-stalked Dioscorea, native of the West Indies.—*Dioscorea Bulbifera*, seu *Rhizophora*, native of the Indies.—*Dioscorea villosa*, *Polygonum*, Hairy Dioscorea, native of Florida, &c.

DIO'SCURI (*Anat.*) διόσκουροι, Castor and Pollux; was the name given to the parotids on account of their twin-like shape and appearance.

DIOSCU'RIA (*Ant.*) διοσκύρια, a festival in honour of Castor and Pollux, particularly observed by the Spartans. *Pausan.* l. 4; *Pindar. Schol. Pyth.* od. 5.

DIO'SMA (*Bot.*) a genus of plants, Class 5 *Pentandria*, Order 1 *Monogynia*.

Generic Character. CAL. *perianth* five-leaved.—COR. *petals* five.—STAM. *filaments* five; *anthers* erect.—PIST. *germ* crowned with the nectary; *style* simple; *stigmas* obscure.—PER. *capsules* five; *seeds* solitary.

Species. The species are all shrubs, and natives of the Cape of Good Hope, as the—*Diosma oppositifolia spiræa*, seu *Hypericum*, Opposite-leaved Diosma.—*Diosma rubra*, seu *Erica*, Red Flowered Diosma.—

Diosma cupressina, seu *Brunia uniflora.*—*Diosma uniflora, Cistus*, seu *Hartogia uniflora*, One-flowered Diosma.—*Diosma pulchella*, seu *Hartogia pulchella*, Oval-leaved Diosma.

DIOSPOLI'TICON (*Med.*) διοσπολιτικὸν, a compound carminative. *Gal. de sanit. tuend.* l. 4, c. 5.

DIOSPYROS (*Bot.*) διοσπύρος, a fruit like a cherry mentioned by Theophrastus and Galen; the latter of whom reckons it among the aliments of small nutrition. *Theophrast. Hist. Plant.* l. 3, c. 13; *Gal. de Alim. Fac.* l. 2, c. 38.

DIO'SPYROS (*Bot.*) a genus of plants, Class 23 *Polygamia Diœcia*, Order 2 *Octandria Monogynia*.
 Generic Character. CAL. *perianth* one-leaved.—COR. one-petalled.—STAM. *filaments* eight; *anthers* oblong.—PIST. in the female; *germ* roundish.—PER. *berry* globose; *seeds* solitary.
 Species. The species are Trees, as the—*Diospyros Lotus*, European Date-plum, *Lotus Africana, Pseudo-lotus, Guaiacum, Guajacana*, seu *Zizyphus.*—*Diospyros Virginiana*, American Plum Tree, *Lotus Virginiana.*—*Diospyros Kaki*, seu *Kis Kaki.*—*Diospyros Ebenaster*, seu *Hebenaster*, native of Ceylon.

DIO'TA (*Ant.*) a jar for wine with two handles.

DIOTA (*Chem.*) a circulating or double vessel.

DIOTOTHE'CA (*Bot.*) another name for the *Morina* of Linnæus.

DIOXELÆ'UM (*Med.*) from διὰ, through, ὀξύς, acid, and ἔλαιον, oil; a malagma of oil and vinegar, for the gout. *Cœl. Aurelian. Chron.* l. 5, c. 2.

DIO'XUS (*Med.*) from ὀξύς, acid; a collyrium in which vinegar is the chief ingredient. *Marcell. Empyric.* c. 8.

DIP *of the Horizon* (*Astron.*) vide *Depression*.

DIP *of the magnetic Needle* (*Mar.*) a property which all needles possess, when rubbed with the loadstone, of inclining the north end below the level of the horizon.

DI'PCADI (*Bot.*) vide *Muscari*.

DIPE'TALUS (*Bot.*) dipetalous, an epithet for a corolla having two petals only, as in *Circæa, Commelina*, &c.

DIPHORETICUS *Sudor* (*Med.*) a faint, excessive sweat.

DI'PHRIS (*Min.*) vide *Diphys*.

DI'PHRUX (*Min.*) from δὶς, twice, and φρύγω, to burn, because it is twice burnt; a name for the dregs of brass which remain in the furnace after melting; it is reckoned astringent and a potent cleanser. *Dioscor.* l. 5, c. 120; *Plin.* l. 34, c. 13.

DIPHTHERA (*Nat.*) διφθέρα, an entire goat's skin, which was the habit of a slave. *Aristoph. Vesp.*; *Schol. in Nub.* act. 1, scen. v. 73; *Lucian. Timon.*; *Poll. Onom.* l. 7, seg. 70; *Rhodig. Ant. Lect.* l. 16, c. 10.

DIPHTHONG (*Gram.*) δίφθογγος, from δὶς and φθέγγομαι, to sound; two vowel sounds united into one.

DIPHY'LLUS (*Bot.*) diphyllous, an epithet for a calyx having two leaves, as the *Papaver* and *Fumaria*. It is also applied to the *cirrus*, or tendril, as in *Lathyris*; and to the peduncle, as in *Gomphrena*.

DI'PHYS (*Min.*) διφυὴς, from δὶς and φύω, to generate; a precious stone of a double kind, or gender, black and white, male and female. *Plin.* l. 37, c. 10.

DIPHY'SA (*Bot.*) a genus of plants, Class 17 *Diadelphia*, Order 4 *Decandria*.
 Generic Character. CAL. *perianth* one-leaved.—COR. *papilionaceus.*—STAM. *filaments* ten; *anthers* ovate.—PIST. *germ* pedicelled; *style* rising; *stigma* simple.—PER. *legume* linear; *seeds* oblong.
 Species. The single species is *Diphysa carthaginensis*, native of Carthagena.

DIPLASIA'SMUS (*Med.*) διπλασιασμὸς, from διπλόω, to double; a reduplication of diseases.

DI'PLE (*Ant.*) a mark formerly used in the margin of books by way of reference to authorities. *Cic. ad Attic.* l. 8, ep. 2; *Isid. Orig.* l. 1, c. 22.

DIPLI'NTHIUS (*Archit.*) from δὶς and πλίνθος, a brick; an epithet for a wall two bricks thick.

DI'PLOE (*Anat.*) διπλόη, the soft meditullum which lies between the laminæ of the bones of the cranium.

DIPLOE (*Chem.*) a double vessel. [vide *Diploma*]

DIPLO'MA (*Ant.*) διπλῶμα, from διπλόος, double; a letter, patent, or a charter from the prince; so called because it was folded or doubled. *Cic. in Pison.* l. 37; *Plin.* l. 10, ep. 121; *Suet on. Ner.* c. 12, &c.; *Plut. in Galba*; *Macrob. Sat.* l. 1, c. 23; *Sigon. de Ant. Jur. Prov.* l. 2, c. 5; *Bud. Pandect.* p. 231; *Panciroll. Notit. dignit. imp. Orient.* c. 6; *Laz. Comment. Reip. Rom.* l. 2, c. 4.

DIPLOMA (*Polit.*) a licence for exercising certain functions; as a physician's diploma, &c.

DIPLOMA (*Chem.*) a double vessel. Thus, "To boil in *diploma*," is to put the vessel which contains the ingredients into a second vessel, to which the fire is applied.

DIPLO'PIA (*Med.*) from διπλόος, double, and ὄπτομαι, to see; a disease in the eye in which the person sees an object double or triple.

DIPO'NDIUM (*Ant.*) a weight of two pounds. *Isid. Orig.* l. 16, c. 24.

DI'PNOUS (*Surg.*) δίπνοος, from δὶς, double, and πνέω, to breathe; an epithet for wounds which have two spiracula or orifices.

DI'PPEL'S *animal oil* (*Chem.*) a volatile oil, formed during the distillation of different animal substances; so called from the chemist who first observed it.

DI'PPING *Needle* (*Mar.*) an epithet for the magnetical needle, which, when duly poised about an horizontal axis, will have a direction of altitude in an horizontal position above the horizon, besides its direction towards the North.

DI'PSACUS (*Bot.*) δίψακ, or δίψακος, Teasel; a prickly plant so called from δίψα, thirst, because it provokes thirst. *Theoph. Hist. Plant.* l. 4, c. 8; *Dioscor.* l. 3, c. 13; *Plin.* l. 27, c. 9; *Gal. de Simpl.* l. 6; *Act. Tetrab.* 1, serm. 1.

DIPSACUS, *in the Linnean system*, a genus of plants, Class 4 *Tetrandria*, Order 1 *Monogynia*.
 Generic Character. CAL. *perianth* common.—COR. *proper universal.*—STAM. *filaments* four; *anthers* incumbent.—PIST. *germ* inferior; *style* filiform; *stigmas* simple.—PER. none; *seeds* solitary.
 Species. The species are biennial, as the—*Dipsacus sylvestris*, seu *Carduus*, Cultivated Teasel.—*Dipsacus sylvestris*, seu *Labium*, Wild Teasel.—*Dipsacus laciniatus*, Cut-leaved Teasel.—*Dipsacus pilosus*, seu *Virga pastoris*, Small Teasel.

DIPSACUS is also the *Scabiosa alpina*.

DI'PSAS (*Zool.*) a sort of serpent; so called because it provokes great thirst in the person who is bitten by it. *Isid.* l. 12, c. 4.

DI'PTERA (*Ent.*) the sixth order of insects in the Linnean system, comprehending the genera which have two wings, with a poiser on each side. The genera are distinguished into, 1. Those which have a proboscis and sucker; namely, *diopsis*; *tipula*, the Crane-Fly; *musca*, the Fly; *tabanus*; *empis*; *conops*. 2. Those which have a sucker and no proboscis, as *oestrus*, the Gad-Fly and the Breeze; *asilus*; *stomoxys*; *culex*, the Gnat; *bombylius*, the Humble-Bee; and *hippobosca*.

DI'PTERON (*Archit.*) δίπτερον, a building which has a double wing or isle. *Vitruv.* l. 3, c. 1.

DIPTERYX (*Bot.*) a genus of plants, Class 17 *Diadelphia*, Order 4 *Decandria*.
 Generic Character. CAL. *perianth* one-leaved.—COR. *papilionaceus.*—STAM. *filaments* eight to ten; *anthers* small.

7

—Pist. *germ* oblong; *style* awl-shaped; *stigma* acute.—Per. *legume* large; *seeds* ovate.

Species. The two species are—*Dipteryx odorata et oppositifolia*, which are trees.

DIPTO'TES (*Gram.*) διπτωτα, a name for those nouns which have only two cases. *Isid. Orig.* l. 1, c. 6.

DIPTYCHA (*Archæol.*) διπτυχα, from δις, twice, and πτυχη, a leaf or fold; a register so called because it consisted of two leaves, on one of which were written the names of the living, and on the other those of the dead, who were honoured with the distinction of having their names recited in the liturgy.

DI'PTYCHUM (*Ecc.*) διπτυχον, a table in which the Greek church enrolled the names of persons baptized; also a register of eminent persons deceased, whose names were rehearsed at the altar.

DIPYRE'NON (*Surg.*) διπυρηνον, from δις, twice, and πυρην, a kernel; a probe having two buttons at one end. *Cæl. Aurel. de Morb. Acut.* l. 3, c. 3; *Gal.*

DIPY'ROS (*Ant.*) from δις, twice, and πυρ, fire; an epithet for bread twice baked.

DIRADIA'TION (*Med.*) an invigoration of the muscles by the animal spirits.

DI'RÆ (*Ant.*) another name for the *Furies*.

DI'RCA (*Bot.*) a genus of plants, Class 8 *Octandria*, Order 1 *Monogynia*.

Generic Character. Cal. none.—Cor. one-petalled.—Stam. *filaments* eight; *anthers* roundish.—Pist. *germ* ovate; *style* filiform; *stigma* simple.—Per. *berry* one-celled; *seeds* single.

Species. The single species is a shrub, as the—*Dirca palustris*, seu *Strymella*, Marsh Leather Wood.

DIRE'CT (*Arith.*) an epithet for a rule; namely, " The Rule of Three Direct," when the proportion of any terms or quantities is in the natural or direct order in which they stand, in distinction from " The Rule of Three Inverse." [vide *Rule of Three*]

Direct (*Astron.*) is when a planet, by its proper motion, goes forward in the zodiac according to the natural order and succession of the signs, in distinction from the retrograde.—*Direct sphere,* is the same as *Right sphere*.—*Direct dials,* vide *Dials.*

Direct ray (*Opt.*) a ray which is carried from a point of the visible object directly to the eye, without being turned out of its rectilinear direction by any intervening body, opaque or pellucid.—*Direct vision,* that vision which is performed by means of direct rays.

Direct (*Mus.*) a certain character placed at the end of a stave, to apprize the performer of the situation of the first note in the succeeding stave.

Direct (*Law*) an epithet for the line of ascendants and descendants in genealogical succession.

DIRECTION, *line of* (*Gunn.*) the direct line in which a piece is pointed.

Direction (*Astron.*) the motion and other phænomena of a planet when direct.

Direction (*Astrol.*) a motion by which any star, or part of the celestial sphere, that is supposed to have any influence on mundane affairs, is carried to another star, or another part of the heaven, which has also a signification in reference thereto.

Direction, *line of* (*Mech.*) the line of motion which any natural body observes, according to the force impressed upon it.—*Angle of direction,* the angle comprehended between the lines of direction of two conspiring powers.—*Quantity of direction,* the quantity which arises from the multiplying the velocity of the common centre of gravity by the sum of their masses.

Direction, *number of* (*Chron.*) one of the thirty-five numbers between the Paschal Limits, or between the earliest and latest day on which Easter can fall, namely, between March 22 and April 25, comprehending a space of thirty-five days. [vide *Chronology*]

Direction Word (*Print.*) the word which begins the next page, that is set at the bottom of the page preceding.

DIRE'CTOR (*Surg.*) a hollow instrument for guiding an incisor knife.

Director (*Mus.*) the person who undertakes the management of a concert.

DIRECTO'RES (*Anat.*) another name for the *Erectores penis*.

DIRE'CTORY (*Polit.*) a form of public prayer, &c. used in the time of the rebellion instead of the Book of Common Prayer.

DIRE'CTRIX (*Math.*) a right line, perpendicular to the axis of a conic section, as A B, in the annexed figure, which is so placed, that if any point, F, be assumed without it, and while the line, F D, revolves about F as a centre, 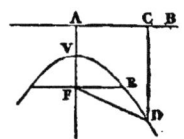 a point, D, moves in such a manner, that its distance from F shall always be to C D its distance from the line A B, in a constant ratio: then V D, described by the point D, is a conic section, which is either an ellipse, a parabola, or an hyperbola, according as F D is less than, equal to, or greater than, C D, or F V than V A.

DIRGE (*Mus.*) a song of lamentation sung at funerals.

DIRIBITO'RES (*Ant.*) 1. Officers at the Roman elections who distributed the tables among the electors who were to give their vote. *Cic. post. Red. in Sen.* c. 11. 2. Servants who distributed the different portions to the respective guests at entertainments. *Apul. Met.* l. 2, p. 53; *Buleng. de Conviv.* l. 2, c. 1.

DI'RIGENT (*Geom.*) a term expressing the line of motion along which a describent line or surface is carried in the genesis of any plane or solid figure. Thus, if the line A B move parallel to itself, and along 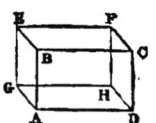 the line A D, so that the point A always keeps in the line A D, and the point B, in the line B C, a parallelogram, A B C D will be formed, of which the line A B is the describent, and the line A D the dirigent.

DIRENGA (*Bot.*) a name for the sweet-scented flag.

DIRK (*Mil.*) a kind of dagger used by the Highlanders, which they generally wear stuck in their belts.

DI'SA (*Bot.*) genus of plants, Class 10 *Gynandria*, Order 1 *Diandria*, Natural Order of *Orchideæ*. The species are natives of the Cape of Good Hope.

DISA'BLED (*Mar.*) an epithet for a seaman who is by wounds rendered unfit for service; and also for a vessel which, by the loss of her masts, sails, yards, &c. is unable to prosecute her voyage.

DISABI'LITY (*Law*) an incapacity in a man to inherit lands, or enjoy the possession of them, &c. which may happen by the act of the ancestor, who is attainted of treason, &c.; by the act of the party who has disabled himself by entering into a previous obligation; by the act of God, where a person is of non-sane memory, &c.; by an act of the law, as an alien born.

DISALLO'WANCES (*Mil.*) deductions made from military estimates, when the charges against the public do not appear.

DISA'NDRA (*Bot.*) a genus of plants, Class 7 *Heptandria*, Order 1 *Monogynia*.

Generic Character. Cal. *perianth* one-leaved.—Cor. one-petalled.—Stam. *filaments* five to eight; *anthers* sagitate.—Pist. *germ* ovate; *style* filiform; *stigma* simple.—Per. *capsule* ovate; *seeds* ovate.

Species. The species are perennials, as the—*Disandra prostata,* Trailing Disandra, seu *Sibthorpia,* native of

Madeira.—*Disandra africana*, seu *Chrysosplenii*, native of Africa.

DISBA'NDED (*Mil.*) an epithet for a regiment who, in a body, are discharged from the conditions of military service.

DISC (*Astron.*) or *disk*, the body or face of the sun or moon, as it appears to us. The *illumined disc* of the Earth is that which is otherwise called the *Circle of Illumination*. [vide *Circle of Illumination*]

Disc (*Opt.*) the magnitude of a telescope glass, or the width of its aperture, whether plane, convex, or of any other form.

DISCARCA'TIO (*Archæol.*) the unloading of a ship.

DISCE'NT (*Law*) vide *Descent*.

DISCE'SSUS (*Chem.*) in general the separation of any two bodies before united; but in particular the separation of gold from silver by *aqua fortis*. *Ovid. Met.* l. 10, v. 176; *Poll. Onom.* l. 3, segm. 151, &c.; *Eustath. Hom. Il.* l. 23, v. 774; *Mercur. Gymnast.* l. 2, c. 12; *Stuck. Ant. Conv.* l. 3, c. 12; *Panvin. de Lud. Circ.* l. 2, c. 1.

DISCHA'RGE (*Law*) a release from confinement, or the restraints of any legal process, when a man who is arrested shall have done what he is required to do.

Discharge (*Mil.*) a remission of the service for the remainder of the time that a man has been engaged.

DISCHA'RGER (*Elec.*) or *Discharging Rod*, an instrument made of glass, or baked wool, by the help of which an electric jar is discharged.

DISCIPLINA'RIANS (*Ecc.*) sectaries who pretend to a stricter discipline than those of the established church.

DISCLAI'MER (*Law*) a plea, containing an express denial or refusal.

DI'SCIPLINE (*Mil.*) signifies generally the instruction and government of soldiers; but *marine discipline* the training up of soldiers for sea service.

DISCLO'SED (*Falcon.*) a term applied to young hawks newly hatched, and, as it were, put forth from their shells.

DISCO'BOLOS (*Ant.*) from δίσκος, a disk, and βάλλω, to cast; one who was skilled in throwing the disk or quoit. *Plin.* l. 35, c. 2; *Quintil.* l. 2, c. 13.

DISCO'MMON (*Cus.*) a term in the universities for depriving the trades-people of their privileges who offend against the statutes.

DISCONTI'NUANCE *of a plea or process* (*Law*) is when the opportunity of prosecution is lost, and is not recoverable but by the recommencement of the suit.

DISCONTINUA'TION *of possession* (*Law*) is when a man may not enter upon his own land and tenement alienated, whatsoever his right be, but must bring his writ, and seek to recover possession by law.

DI'SCORD (*Mus.*) a dissonant or inharmonious combination of sounds, in distinction from a concord. There are various *Discords*, as those which arise from the union of the fifth with the sixth, the fourth with the fifth, the seventh with the eighth, and the third with the ninth and seventh.

DISCO'VER (*Law*) a term for a woman unmarried, or a widow, i. e. one not within the bonds of matrimony.

DISCO'VERY (*Law*) the act of disclosing or revealing by a defendant, in his answer to a bill filed against him in a court of equity.

DI'SCOUNT (*Com.*) or *Rebate*, an allowance made on a bill, or any other debt not yet become due, in consideration of making immediate payment of the bill or debt.

Discount (*Arith.*) a rule for making calculations of discount.

DISCRE'TA *purgativa* (*Med.*) a sort of purgatives, by which a certain determinate humour is evacuated.

DISCRE'TE *proportion* (*Arith.*) is when the proportion disjoins in the middle, or when the ratio of the first term to the second is not the same as that of the third to the fourth.—*Discrete quantity*, is such as is continued and joined together.

DI'SCRETIVE *proposition* (*Log.*) such propositions as have discretive or disjunctive particles; as, *but*, *notwithstanding*, &c.; whereby the sense is disjoined.

DISCRE'TO (*Mus.*) an Italian word, signifying to play or sing with care; moderation or judgment.

DISCRETO'RIUM (*Anat.*) another name for the *Diaphragm* or *Midriff*.

DISCRI'MEN (*Surg.*) a bandage used in bleeding on the forehead and temples.

DISCU'RSUS (*Log.*) the third part of logic, which consists in ratiocination: it is otherwise called *Argumentation*.

DI'SCUS (*Ant.*) δίσκος, from δίκειν, for ἱέναι, to cast, a disc or quoit; any round substance of stone, lead, or iron, with a hole in the middle, which was used by way of a game, to see which could throw it farthest. *Pind. Isth.* 1.

Οἷά τε χερσὶν ἀκοντίζοντες αἰχμαῖς
Καὶ λίθινος ὁπότε δίσκος, ἵν.

Mart. l. 14, ep. 164.

Splendida cum volitant Spartani pondera disci
Esto procul pueri: sit semel ille nocens.

Propert. l. 3, el. 12, v. 10.

Missile nunc disci pondus in orbe rotæ.

DI'SCUS (*Astron.*) vide *Disk*.

Discus (*Bot.*) the Disk, or whole surface of a leaf, which is either *supinus*, the upper, or *pronus*, the under surface. The disk of a flower is the central part in radiate compound flowers, consisting generally of regular corollules or florets. It is also applied to other aggregate flowers, the florets of which, towards the middle, differ from those in the circumference.

DISCU'SSION (*Surg.*) a dispersing the matter of any swelling, i. e. a discharge of some thin matter which is collected in any part by insensible evaporation.

DISCU'TIENT (*Med.*) or *Discussory medicines*, those which dissolve impacted matter.

DISE'ASE (*Med.*) any settled affection in the body which throws it out of its natural course.

To DISEMBA'RK (*Mil.*) to land troops from any vessel.

To DISEMBO'GUE (*Geog.*) from the old French *disemboucher*, or *des* and *bouche*, a mouth; a term applied to rivers which discharge themselves into the sea.

To Disembogue (*Mar.*) also a term applied to vessels which pass from the mouth of a strait into the sea.

To DISENGA'GE (*Mil.*) to clear a column or line which may have lost its front by the overlapping of any particular division, company, or file.

To Disengage (*Fenc.*) to quit that side of your adversary's blade on which you are opposed by his guard, in order to effect a cut or thrust where an opportunity may present.

DISER'MAS (*Bot.*) a species of the *Salvia*.

To DISFRANCHI'SE (*Law*) to take away the franchise or freedom of any individual, or of any town.

To DISGARNISH (*Fort.*) to take away guns from a fortress.

DISHE'RISON (*Law*) disinheriting.

DISHE'RITOR (*Law*) one who puts another out of his inheritance.

DI'SJUNCT (*Mus.*) διεζυγμένων, an epithet for those tetrachords which were so disposed with respect to each other that the gravest note of any tetrachord was a note higher than the acutest note of the tetrachord immediately beneath it.

Disjunct *proportion* (*Math.*) vide *Discrete Proportion*.

DISJU'NCTIVE (*Gram.*) an epithet for any particle, such

as *or*, *nor*, &c. which separates the sense, in distinction from the *conjunctive* particles.

DISJUNCTIVE *proposition* (*Log.*) διαζευγμένω, *disjunctum*, a proposition in which two or more simple propositions are connected by a disjunctive conjunction. *Aul. Gell.* l. 5, c. 11.

DISK (*Astron.*) *discus*, the round face of the sun or moon as it appears to the eye.

DISK (*Bot.*) vide *Discus*.

DISLOCA'TION (*Surg.*) from *disloco*, to put out of its place; the putting of a bone out of its place, or the removal of the moveable extremity of a bone from the hollow or socket in which it is naturally moved, otherwise called *Luxation*.

DISLOCATION *of an army* (*Mil.*) is equivalent to its distribution into cantonments.

TO DISLO'DGE (*Mil.*) to drive an enemy from any post or station.—*To dislodge a camp* is to strike the tents, &c. and to march away.

TO DISLODGE (*Sport.*) to rouse beasts of the chase from their lodging, or harbour.

TO DISMA'NTLE (*Fort.*) in French *demanteler*, to take off the cloak; to beat or pull down the walls or fortifications of a city.

TO DISMANTLE (*Mar.*) to unrig a ship, and take out all her stores, guns, &c.

DISMA'STED (*Mar.*) an epithet for a ship which is deprived of her masts.

DISME'MBERED (*Her.*) an epithet for an animal, a cross, or any thing else which is, as it were, cut in pieces, but not so as to destroy the form, as "*Or* a lion rampant, *gules* dismembered," &c.

DISMES (*Law*) the tithes.

TO DISMI'SS (*Mil.*) to take an officer's commission or warrant from him.

TO DISMISS *a cause* (*Law*) a term in the court of chancery for removing it out of court without any farther hearing.

TO DI'SMOUNT (*Mil.*) to unhorse. "To *dismount* the cavalry," to make them alight.

TO DISMOUNT *a piece of ordnance* (*Gunn.*) to throw or take it down from the carriage.

DISPA'RAGEMENT (*Law*) the disposing of an heir or heiress in marriage under his or her degree, or against decency. *Magn. Chart.* c. 6; *Co. Lit.* 107.

DISPARA'GO (*Bot.*) a species of the *Stoebe*.

DI'SPARATES (*Log.*) opposites, or things altogether unlike one another.

DI'SPART (*Gunn.*) the thickness of the metal on the mouth and breech of the piece.

TO DISPART *a cannon* (*Gunn.*) to set a mark at or near the muzzel-ring of a gun, that a sight-line taken upon the top of the base-ring, against the touch-hole, may thereby be parallel to the concave cylinder of the piece, by which the gunner takes his aim.

DISPA'TCHES (*Polit.*) letters sent abroad upon public affairs.

DISPA'UPERED (*Law*) put out of the capacity of suing *in forma pauperis*; as if a person, before his suit is ended, have any lands, &c. fall to him, he is then dispaupered, or put out of the capacity of suing in that form.

DISPE'NSARY (*Med.*) a place where medicines are retailed, or delivered out.

DISPENSA'TION (*Ecc.*) an indulgence or licence from the pope to do what is otherwise prohibited, as the marriage of first cousins, &c.

DISPENSATION (*Law*) an exclusive privilege to do any thing that is otherwise contrary to law, which is granted by the king in council.

DISPENSATION (*Ecc.*) an indulgence or permission from the pope to do that which is otherwise prohibited by the church.

DISPENSATION (*Med.*) is when the simples of a composition are set in order, lest any of the ingredients should be forgotten.

DISPENSATION (*Theol.*) the gift of divine revelation to man, namely, of the Levitical Law to the Jews, and of the Gospel to Christians.

DISPENSA'TOR (*Ant.*) a steward, or one who managed the expenses of a family. *Cic. Hort. apud Non.* l. 3, c. 18; *Plin.* l. 33, c. 2; *Suet. Aug.* c. 67.

DISPENSATOR (*Med.*) a name for an apothecary, because he is a dispenser of medicines.

DISPE'NSATORY (*Med.*) a book which directs apothecaries in the compounding of medicine, defining the ingredient and the quantity, &c.

DISPE'RMUS (*Bot.*) *dispermous*, or two-seeded, an epithet for fruit which contains only two seeds, as in *umbellate* and *stellate* plants.

DISPE'RSION (*Opt.*) the divergency of the rays of light.— *Dispersion of light* is occasioned by the refrangibility of the rays, or the nature of the refracting medium.—*Point of dispersion* is a point from which refracted rays begin to diverge, when their refraction renders them divergent.

DISPERSONA'RE (*Archæol.*) to scandalize or disparage.

TO DISPLA'Y (*Mil.*) in French *deployer*, to extend the front of a column.

DISPLA'YED (*Her.*) an epithet for birds having their wings expanded, as he bears "*Azure* an eagle displayed, *argent* armed *gules*; on a canton of the second a sinister hand couped as a third." These were the arms of Sir Robert Cotton, founder of the Cotton Library.

DISPOSI'TION (*Mil.*) the placing an army in such manner as may be most suitable for a vigorous attack or defence. *Faire des dispositions* signifies to make the necessary arrangements for a battle.

DISPOSITION (*Archit.*) the just placing all the several parts of a building. *Vitruv.* l. 1, c. 2.

DISPO'SITOR (*Astrol.*) the planet which is lord of the sign where another planet chances to be.

DISRU'PTIO (*Med.*) a violent rupture, penetrating the skin to the flesh.

DISSE'CTION (*Anat.*) the cutting asunder of animal bodies, in order to come at the knowledge of their parts. [vide *Anatomy*]

DISSIDIUM *dissectio* (*Bot.*) gashed; an epithet for a leaf, as *folium dissectum*, a gashed leaf, which is distinguished from the *laciniate leaf* by the sections being more determinate.

DISSEISE'E (*Law*) vide *Disseisin*.

DISSEI'SIN (*Law*) an unlawful dispossessing a man of his lands, tenements, or other immoveable or incorporeal rights. The person dispossessing is called the *disseisor*, and the person dispossessed the *disseisee*.—*Disseisin upon disseisin* is where the disseisor is put out of possession by another.

DISSEI'SOR (*Law*) vide *Disseisin*.

DISSE'NTER (*Ecc.*) one who dissents or departs from the communion of the Christian church, particularly from that part of it established in England.

DISSE'PIMENTUM (*Bot.*) a partition, or wall, by which the pericarp is separated into cells; this is *parallelum* when it approaches in breadth, and its transverse diameter to the valves; *contrarium* when it is narrower than the valves.

DISSI'LIENS (*Bot.*) bursting, or elastic; an epithet for the pericarp, or fruit, which opens with a spring, as in *Hura*, *Dentaria*, *Cardamine*, &c.

DISSIPA'TION (*Phy.*) a gradual, slow, insensible loss or consumption of the minute parts of a body.

DISSIPATION, *Circle of* (*Opt.*) or *Circle of Aberration*, that circular space on the retina of the eye which is occupied by the rays of each pencil in indistinct vision.—*Radius of Dissipation*, the radius of the circle of dissipation.

DISSO'LVENT (*Med.*) a medicine fitted to disperse collected humours.

Dissolvent (*Chem.*) a liquor proper for dissolving a mixed body.

DISSOLVENTIA (*Med.*) dissolvents.   [vide *Dissolvent*]

DISSOLU'TION (*Med.*) the mingling of mixed electuaries or powders in waters.

Dissolution (*Chem.*) that action by which fluids loosen the texture of immersed bodies, and reduce them into very small parts, as water dissolves sugar, aqua fortis dissolves brass, &c.

DISSOLUTUS morbus (*Med.*) another name for the *Dysentery*.

DI'SSONANCE (*Mus.*) a discordant interval between two sounds, which being continued together offend the ear.

DISTAFF-THISTLE (*Bot.*) a species of the *Atractylis* of Linnæus.

DISTANCE (*Geom.*) the shortest line between any two points or objects.—*Accessible distances* are measured with a chain, &c.—*Inaccessible distances* are found by taking bearings to them from the two extremities of a line whose length is given.

Distance (*Astron.*) as applied to the planets, and other heavenly bodies, is either apparent, real, or relative.—*Apparent distances* are such as are judged of by the eye.—*Relative distances* are deduced from the theory of gravity.—*Real distances* from the parallax, relative distances, &c.—*Distance of the sun from the moon's node*, or *apogee*, an arc of the ecliptic, intercepted between the sun's true place and the moon's node, or apogee.—*Curtate distance.* [vide *Curtate*]

Distance *of the bastions* (*Fort.*) the side of the exterior polygon.

Distance (*Geog.*) the arc of a great circle intercepted between two places.

Distance (*Mar.*) the number of miles or leagues which a ship has sailed from any point or place.

Distance, *line of* (*Perspect.*) a right line drawn from the eye to the principal point.—*Point of distance*, a point on the horizontal line at the same distance from the principal point as the eye is from the same. [vide *Perspective*]

DISTANS (*Bot.*) or *remotus*, distant; an epithet for a whorl, *verticillus distans*, a distant whorl, when the flowers which compose it are few in number.

DISTEMPER (*Vet.*) a well-known disease incident to dogs, horses, and other domestic animals.

Distemper (*Paint.*) a term applied to colours not mixed with oil or water, but with size, whites of eggs, &c.; whence to do a piece in distemper is to paint in such colours.

DISTENSION (*Med.*) a term applied to any parts of the body which are loosened or widened.

DISTICH (*Poet.*) δίστιχον, from δὶς, twice, and στίχος, a verse; a couplet.

DISTICHIA (*Med.*) διστιχία, a double row of hairs upon the eye-lids.

DISTICHUS (*Bot.*) two-ranked, an epithet for a stem or stalk; *caulis distichus*, a two-ranked stem or stalk, putting forth branches not decussated, but in a horizontal position, as in the Fir. This term is applied in the same sense to a spike; *spica disticha*, a spike with flowers all pointing two ways.

DISTILLATION (*Chem.*) an extraction of the humid parts of things by virtue of heat: it is performed either *per ascensum* or *per descensum*. To distil *per ascensum*, is performed by placing the vessel over the fire in which the matter is contained; to distil *per descensum* is to place the fire above the vessel in which the matter is contained.

DISTILLATIONS (*Phy.*) watery vapours drawn up by the sun into the air, which fall down to the earth again when the sun is set.

DISTI'LLATORY (*Her.*) a part of the arms of the distillers' company.

DISTILLERS, *Company of* (*Her.*) This company was incorporated in the reign of Queen Elizabeth. Their armorial ensigns are, " *Azure* a fess wavy, *argent* between a sun drawing up a cloud, distilling drops of rain; and a distillatory double armed *or*, with two worms and a bolt-head receiver *argent*.

DISTI'NCT BASE (*Opt.*) that distance from the pole of a convex glass at which objects beheld through it appear distinct, and well-defined.—*Distinct vision.* [vide *Vision*]

DISTI'NCTUS (*Bot.*) distinct; an epithet for leaves or anthers that are quite separate from each other, in distinction from the *connate*: *folia distincta*, distinct leaves, are to be found in several of the *Mysembryanthema*: *foliola distincta*, distinct leaflets, as in *Jasminum officinale*, as contrasted with the confluent: *antheræ distinctæ*, distinct anthers, are to be found in most flowers.

DISTO'RTION (*Surg.*) a term denoting that the parts of an animal body are ill placed or ill figured.

DISTO'RTOR *oris* (*Anat.*) a muscle, whose office is to draw the mouth aside.

DISTRA'CTION (*Chem.*) a forcible separation of substances from one another which were before united, as by calcination, &c.

Distraction (*Surg.*) the act of pulling a fibre or membrane, &c. from its natural extent; and what is so pulled or extended is said to be distracted.

To DISTRA'IN (*Law*) to seize upon a person's goods for the payment of rent or taxes.

DISTRE'SS (*Law*) 1. The taking of a personal chattel out of the possession of the wrong-doer into the custody of the party injured, to procure a satisfaction for the wrong committed. *Distresses* are *personal*, which are on a man's moveable goods, and *real*, which are on the immoveable goods. They are also *finite*, when limited by law as to how often it shall be made to bring the party to trial of action, and *infinite* when without limitation, until the party appears.

DISTRE'SSES (*Law*) *districtiones*, pledges taken by the sheriff from those who came to fairs, for their good behaviour; which, at the end of the fair, or mercat, were delivered back, if no harm was done.

DISTRIBU'TION (*Log.*) a resolving the whole into its parts.

Distribution (*Rhet.*) an applying to every thing its peculiar property.

Distribution (*Med.*) a term applied to the chyle when, after due preparation in the ventricle and intestines, it passes through the lacteal veins, and falling into the subclavian vein, it circulates with the blood.

DISTRI'BUTIVE *justice* (*Law*) that justice which is administered by a judge, arbitrator, or umpire, who, in executing his office, may be said to distribute or give to every man his own.

Distributive *noun* (*Gram.*) a noun which betokens the reducing of things into several orders or distinctions.

DISTRICHIA'SIS (*Med.*) vide *Distichia*.

DI'STRICT (*Law*) the circuit within which a man may be bound to appear: also, the place where one hath the power of distraining. *Brit.* c. 120.

DISTRICTU'RES (*Law*) vide *Distresses*.

DISTRI'NGAS (*Law*) a writ directed to the sheriff or any other officer, commanding him to distrain a person for a debt to the king; or for his appearance on a certain day. *F. N. B.* 138.—*Distringas juratores*, a writ directed to the sheriff, to distrain upon a jury to appear.—*Distringas nuper vice-cometem,* [vide *Venditione exponas*]

DISTRIX (*Med.*) from δις, twice, and θριξ, the hair; a disease of the hair, when it splits and divides at the ends.

DISVE'LOPED (*Her.*) another name for *displayed.*

TO DISUNI'TE (*Man.*) is said of a horse that drags his haunches, and gallops false or upon a wrong foot.

DITCH (*Fort.*) vide *Foss* or *Moat.*

DITHYRA'MBUS (*Ant.*) a song anciently sung in honour of Bacchus; or, in general, any poem composed with wildness or enthusiasm. Horace designates the odes of Pindar *dithyrambi.*

DITO'CA (*Bot.*) another name for the *Mniarum* of Linnæus.

DI'TONOS (*Mus.*) διτονος, a ditone; a double tone, or the greater third.

DITRI'CHIUM (*Bot.*) a genus of mosses.

DITROCHÆ'US (*Poet.*) διτροχαιος, a foot, consisting of two trochees, as *cāntĭlēnă.* Hephest. Enchirid.

DITTA'NDER (*Bot.*) the *Lepidum latifolium* of Linnæus, a perennial.

DI'TTANY of Crete (*Bot.*) the *Origanum dictamnum* of Linnæus, a perennial.—White Dittany, the *Dictamnus albus,* a perennial.

DITTO (*Com.*) or, abbreviated, *Do.* an Italian word derived from the Latin *dictum,* said, i. e. literally, the aforesaid; is used in statements and accounts to signify the same, in order to avoid the too frequent repetition of the same word or words.

DITTO'LOGY (*Lit.*) διττολογια, a double reading, as in most ancient authors sacred and profane.

DI'TTY (*Mus.*) a song that has the words set to music.

DI'VAL (*Her.*) a term, in blazoning, for nightshade.

DIVA'LIA (*Ant.*) another name for the Roman festival called Angeronalia.

DI'VAN (*Polit.*) the great council or court of justice in Turkey and Persia.

DIVAPORA'TION (*Chem.*) the driving out of vapours by means of fire.

DIVARICA'TUS (*Bot.*) divaricate, or straddling, according to Withering; standing out wide, an epithet for branches, a panicle, petiole, and peduncle.—*Rami divaricati,* divaricate branches, i. e. making an obtuse angle with the stem, opposed to *coarctati; panicula divaricata,* a divaricate panicle, when the pedicles form an obtuse angle with the main peduncle; so, in the same sense, *pedunculum divaricatum,* a divaricate peduncle; *petiolus divaricatus,* a divaricate petiole.

DI'VER (*Orn.*) a water-fowl that frequents lakes, and goes with difficulty on land; the *Colymbus septentrionalis* of Linnæus.

DIVE'RGENS (*Bot.*) diverging, an epithet for branches; *rami divergentes,* branches diverging or making a right angle with the stem. It is applied also to the sleep of plants; *somnus divergens* is when the leaflets, in their state of repose, approach each other at the base, but spread at the tops.

DIVERGENT (*Math.*) or *Diverging,* an epithet for several things which have the property of diverging.—*Divergent or diverging rays,* those rays which issuing from a radiant point do continually recede from each other.—*Divergent lines,* those lines which continually remove to a greater distance from each other.—*Diverging hyperbola,* one whose legs turn their convexities to each other.—*Diverging parabola,* vide *Parabola.*—*Diverging series,* a series the terms of which always become larger the farther they are continued.

DIVERSION (*Mil.*) a movement which is made towards a point that is weak and undefended, in order to draw an enemy off from continuing his operations in another quarter.

DIVERSION (*Med.*) the turning of the course or flux of humours from one part to another by medicinal applications.

DIVERSO'RIUM (*Ant.*) an inn or place of entertainment for strangers. *Cic. ad Fam.* l. 6, ep. 19.

DIVERSORIUM (*Anat.*) the *Receptaculum chyli.*

DIVERTI'CULUM (*Anat.*) a mal-formation, or a diseased appearance of any part, owing to its deviation from the usual course.

DIVERTICULUM *fluminis* (*Ant.*) the turning or arm of a river.

DIVERTIME'NTO (*Mus.*) Italian for a light composition, written in a familiar style.

DIVERTISSEME'NT (*Mus.*) a French term for certain airs and dances formerly introduced between their operas.

TO DIVEST (*Law*) to take away the possession of a thing from another as opposed to *invest.*

DIVIDEND (*Arith.*) the number to be divided. [vide *Division*]

DIVIDEND (*Com.*) the share of the profits in a joint stock which is to be divided among the shareholders: also that part of a debtor's effects which is to be divided among the creditors.

DIVIDEND (*Cus.*) the share which falls to the fellows of any college, out of the annual income of the foundation.

DIVIDENDS (*Law*) a name for the parts of an indenture.

DIVI'DERS (*Math.*) a particular sort of compasses.

DIVI'DUALS (*Arith.*) numbers in the rule of Division, being parts of the dividend distinguished by points, &c.

DIVINA'TIO (*Ant.*) *Divination* was of two kinds; *natural,* that which the bird itself declared by its flight, cry, &c.; the other *artificial,* which consisted in the interpretation of the augur. *Cic. Bell. de Divin.* l. 1, c. 6.

Divination signified likewise a sort of sentence for the purpose of deciding who should be the accuser in cases where two or more persons bring forward the same charge wherefore Cicero's first oration against Verres is entitled *Divinatio,* because he pleaded to be the prosecutor of Verres.

DI'VING-BELL (*Mech.*) a contrivance by which persons may descend below the water and remain for some time without serious inconvenience.—*Diving-Bladder* was a contrivance, made by Borelli, to answer the same purpose.

DIVI'NITY (*Ecc.*) the study which treats of God and Divine Revelation, particularly in regard to the Gospel.

DIVI'SA (*Archæol.*) goods devised by will.

DIVI'SI (*Mus.*) an Italian word signifying divided into two parts.

DIVISIBI'LITY (*Phy.*) the property of being able to be divided to an infinite or indefinite extent.

DIVI'SION (*Arith.*) one of the four principal rules or operations in Arithmetic, by which we find how often one quantity is contained in another. There are three numbers concerned in this operation, namely, the *dividend,* or that which is to be divided; the *divisor,* or that by which one divides; and the *quotient,* or that number which shows how often the second is contained in the first; thus, suppose 10 to be divided by 5. 10 is the dividend, 5 the divisor, and 2 the quotient, or the result of the division. Division is distinguished into division of integers, division of fractions, division of decimals, algebra, &c.—*Division of integers* is either simple or compound.—*Simple division* is the division of integers of one denomination.—*Compound division* is the division of numbers of different denominations, as pounds, shillings, pence, &c.—*Division of Fractions* is performed by inverting the terms of the divisor, and then multiplying the two numerators together for a new numerator, and two denominators for a new denominator; thus, $\frac{1}{4} \div \frac{1}{2}$ is the same as $\frac{1}{4} \times \frac{2}{1} = \frac{2}{4}$.—*Division of Decimals* is performed the same as in whole numbers, except, that regard must be had to the number of decimals; viz. making as many in the quotient as those of the dividend exceed those in the divisor.—*Division of Powers* is performed by subtracting their exponents, as, $a^6 \div a^4 = a^{6-4} = a^2$.—*Division of Proportion* is comparing the difference between the antecedent and the consequent with either of them; as if $a:b::c:d$, then by division $a-b:b::c-d:d$.

DIVISION (*Mus.*) dividing the interval of an octave into a number of lesser intervals, as quavers, semiquavers, &c.

DIVISION (*Mil.*) is a body of men commanded by a particular officer; thus brigades are *divisions* of an army; platoons are *divisions* of a troop or company; also any number of men detached from the main body on military duty is denominated a *division*.

DIVISION (*Log.*) is an oration which explains any thing part by part.

DIVISION (*Print.*) a small line which serves to divide compound words, as "Man-hood."

DIVISION *of mathematical instruments* (*Mech.*) the dividing them off into degrees, and minutes, &c.

DIVISIONES (*Ant.*) doles, or donations which persons left in their wills to be made annually to the people, to colleges, &c. on the anniversary of their birth-day. *Paul. l. Civitatibus ff. de Legat.* 1.

DIVISOR (*Arith.*) the dividing number. [vide *Division*]—*Divisors of a number*, those numbers by which it is exactly divisible.

DIVISORES (*Ant.*) persons employed at elections by the candidates to distribute money among the poor citizens, to buy up their votes. *Cic. in Verr. Proem.* c. 8; *Ascon. in Cic.*

DIVO'RCE (*Law*) *divortium a divertendo*, a separation of man and wife, which is of two kinds, namely—*Divortium a mensâ et thoro*, which does not dissolve a marriage, and consequently does not debar a woman her dower or bastardize the issue; the second and complete divorce is the *divortium a vinculo matrimonii*, which absolutely dissolves the marriage. *Co. Lit.* 235, &c.—*Bill of divorce*, a writing formerly given to a woman, by which the husband renounced all claim upon her.

DIVO'TO (*Mus.*) an Italian word signifying a serious manner of playing or singing so as to excite devotion.

DIURE'SIS (*Med.*) from διά and οὖρος, the discharge of the urine through the bladder.

DIURE'TICS (*Med.*) medicines which by dissolving and fusing the blood, precipitate the serum, and promote the urinary discharge.

DIU'RNAL (*Astrol.*) an epithet for those planets which contain more active than passive qualities.

DIURNAL (*Astron.*) an epithet for whatever relates to the day, as—*Diurnal arc*, the arc described by the sun, moon, or stars, between their rising and setting.—*Diurnal circle*, the apparent circle described by the sun, moon, or stars, in consequence of the supposed rotation of the earth.—*Diurnal motion of a planet*, so many degrees and minutes as any planet moves in a hour. *Diurnal* is also used in speaking of the natural day; thus, the diurnal revolution of the earth or sun is its revolution on its own axis in 24 hours.

DIURNA'LIS (*Archæol.*) a book for registering things down every day, which has since been called a *journal*.

DIVU'LSIO URINÆ (*Med.*) urine with a ragged uneven sediment.

DIYLI'SMOS (*Chem.*) διυλισμός, from διυλίζω, to strain; the percolation or straining of a liquor, for the purpose of its depuration.

D. L. S. (*Com.*) an abbreviation for double-refined loaf sugar.

D. LA, SOL, RE (*Mus.*) the fifth note in each of the three septenaries of the gamut.

DO (*Mus.*) a monosyllable which has been substituted for *ut* that was applied by Guido to the first note of the natural major.

Do Law (*Law*) the same as to make a law.

DOCHME (*Ant.*) δοχμή, a measure of length among the Greeks, equal to the breadth of four fingers.

DO'CHMIUS (*Poet.*) δοχμίος, a foot of five syllables, a short and two long, a short and long, as ἀμικός τένης. *Cic. Orat.* c. 6. 4.

DOCIMA'SIA (*Ant.*) δοκιμασία, the probation of magistrates previous to their admission into any public office at Athens. *Harpocrat. in Lys.*

DOCIMA'STICE (*Min.*) the art of examining fossils, in order to ascertain what metals or minerals they contain.

DO'CIS (*Nat.*) δοκίς, a fiery impression or meteor, like a beam.

DOCK (*Man.*) a large case of leather, as long as the horse's tail, which serves it for a cover, and is made fast by the straps to the crupper.

DOCK (*Bot.*) the *Rumex* of Linnæus, a weed that infests corn fields.

DOCK (*Mar.*) a broad deep trench formed on the side of a harbour fitted for the building or repairing of ships. It is either dry or wet.—*Dry Dock*, in French *Bassin de radoub*, is provided with flood-gates for keeping out the water while a ship is either building or repairing. These gates are opened to let in the water when the vessel is to be floated or launched.—*Wet Dock*, in French *Bassin du port*, is a place out of the way of the tide, into which a ship may be hauled so that she may dock herself, or sink herself a place to lie in.—*Dock-yards*, magazines containing timber and all sorts of stores for ship-building.

TO DOCK (*Vet.*) to cut off a horse's tail.

TO DOCK *herself* (*Mar.*) is said of a ship when brought into oozy ground she makes herself a place to lie in.

DOCK-CRE'SSES (*Bot.*) a plant, otherwise called Nipple-Wort, or the *Lapsana* of Linnæus.

DO'CKET (*Com.*) a bill with a direction tied to goods, and directed to the person and place whither they are to be sent.

DOCKET (*Law*) a small piece of paper or parchment, containing the head of a large writing: also, a subscription at the foot of letters patent, by the clerk of the dockets. "To strike a docket," is said of a creditor who gives bond to the Lord Chancellor, proving his debtor to be a bankrupt; in consequence of which a commission of bankruptcy is taken out against him.

TO DOCKET (*Law*) to enter upon the dockets; in this manner judgments in the court of King's Bench, decrees in Chancery, commissions of Bankruptcy, and the like, are docketted.

DOCTILE'TUS (*Med.*) a medicine which Paracelsus recommends for the cure of the gout.

DO'CTOR (*Ant.*) διδάσκαλος, a teacher or preceptor whose office in particular arts is mentioned in inscriptions; as—*Doctor librarius*, one who is supposed to have taught the art of making up books.—*Doctor sagittarius*, one who taught the soldiers the art of shooting. *Reines. Inscript.* class 11, n. 123; *Spon. Mis. Erud. Ant.* sect. 7, p. 256.

DOCTOR (*Lit.*) the highest degree in any particular faculty in a university, as D. D. Doctor of Divinity; M. D. Doctor of Physic; D. M. Doctor of Music; LL. D. Doctor of Laws.

DO'CTOR'S *Commons* (*Law*) a college of civilians. [vide *Commons*]

DO'CUMENT (*Mil.*) or a *Death-bed Document*, a term for the resignation which an officer sends in who supposes himself to be on his death-bed.

DO'CUS (*Nat.*) δοκός, a meteor like a beam.

DODA'RTIA (*Bot.*) so called from M. Dodart, a genus of plants, Class 14 *Didynamia*, Order 2 *Angiospermia*.

Generic Character. CAL. *perianth* one-leaved.—COR. one-petalled.—STAM. *filaments* four; *anthers* small.—PIST. *germ* roundish; *style* subulate; *stigma* oblong.—PER. *capsule* globose; *seeds* very small.

Species. The two species are perennials, and natives of India.

DODARTIA is also the name of the *Antirrhinum bellidifolium.*

DO'DDER (*Bot.*) the *Cuscuta* of Linnæus, a parasitical plant, fastening itself to, and drawing nourishment from, other plants. Its root is said to die as soon as it has fastened itself to another plant.

DODECADA'CTYLON (*Anat.*) another name for the first of the small intestines.

DODE'CAGON (*Geom.*) from δώδεκα, twelve, and γωνια, an angle; a regular polygon, consisting of twelve equal sides and angles.

DODECAGON (*Fort.*) a place with twelve bastions.

DODECA'HEDRON (*Geom.*) δωδεκα ἑδρα, a geometrical solid bounded by twelve equal and equilateral pentagons. It is one of the Platonic or regular bodies. [vide *Body*]

DODECA'NDRIA (*Bot.*) from δώδεκα, twelve, and ἀνηρ a man or husband; twelve-stamened; a name for the eleventh class in Linnæus' artificial system, comprehending all those plants which have hermaphrodite flowers, with from twelve to nineteen stamens inclusive. It consists of six orders, namely, *Monogynia, Digynia, Tryginia, Tetragynia, Pentagynia, Dodecagynia.* The principal genera are as follow: Monogynia, *Asarum,* Asarabacca; *Garcinia,* Mangostan; *Portulaca,* Purslane; *Lythrum,* Loosestrife.—Digynia, *Agrimonia,* Agrimony.— Trigynia, *Reseda,* Dyer's-Weed, &c.—Dodecagynia, *Sempervivum,* Houseleek.

DODECAPHA'RMACUM (*Med.*) from δώδεκα, twelve, and φαρμακον, an ingredient; a composition consisting of twelve ingredients.

DO'DECAS (*Bot.*) a genus of plants, Class 11 *Dodecandria,* Order 1 *Monogynia.*
  Generic Character. CAL. *perianth* one-leaved.—COR. *petals* roundish.—STAM. *filaments* twelve.—PIST. *germ* half superior; *style* filiform; *stigma* simple.—PER. *capsule* ovate; *seeds* oblong.
  Species. The single species is a shrub, as the—*Dodecas Surinamensis,* native of Surinam.

DODECATEMO'RION (*Astron.*) δωδεκατημοριον, the twelve signs of the zodiac, and also the twelfth part of every sign. Manil. l. 2, v. 670.

    Perspice nunc tenuem visu rem, pondere magnum,
    Quæ tantum Graio signari nomine possit,
    Dodecatemorion, titulus signatio causæ.

DODECA'THEON (*Bot.*) a kind of herb with leaves like a lettuce, which was so called from δώδεκα, twelve, and θεος, a god; because it was supposed to possess the virtues of the twelve superior gods. Plin. l. 25, c. 4.

DODECATHEON, in the Linnean system, a genus of plants, Class 5 *Pentandria,* Order 1 *Monogynia.*
  Generic Character. CAL. *involucre* many-leaved.—COR. one-petalled.—STAM. *filaments* five; *anthers* sagittate.—PIST. *germ* conic; *style* filiform; *stigma* obtuse.—PER. *capsule* oblong; *seeds* small.
  Species. The single species is the *Dodecatheon Media, Media,* seu *Auricula,* Virginian Cowslip, a perennial.

DO'DO (*Orn.*) a bird larger than a swan, otherwise called the Monk's Swan, which inhabits the Isles of Bourbon and France. It is the *Didus* of Linnæus.

DODONŒ'A (*Bot.*) a genus of plants, so called from Rembert Dodonœus, a botanist, Class 8 *Octandria,* Order 1 *Monogynia.*
  Generic Character. CAL. *perianth* four-leaved.—COR. none.—STAM. *filaments* eight; *anthers* oblong.—PIST. *germ* three-sided; *style* cylindric; *stigma* a little acute.—PER. *capsule* three-furrowed; *seeds* in couples.
  Species. The species are shrubs, as the—*Dodonœa viscosa, Thlapsoides,* seu *Carpinus,* Broad-leaved Dodonœa, native of the Society Islands.—*Dodonœa angustifolia,* Narrow-leaved Dodonœa, native of the Cape of Good Hope, &c.

DO'DRA (*Ant.*) a kind of drink among the Romans, made of nine different ingredients. Auson. Epigram. 86.

DO'DRANS (*Ant.*) nine ounces, nine inches, or nine parts out of twelve; so called because *deest quadrans,* a fourth part is wanting, to make up the *as.*

DO'EDYX (*Med.*) vide *Cochleare.*

DOG (*Astron.*) a constellation. [vide *Canis*]—Dog-days, the vulgar name for the canicular days. [vide *Canicular*]

DO'G-FISH (*Ich.*) a fish of the shark kind, of which there are two sorts, the Spotted Dog-fish, and Lesser Spotted Dog-fish, the *Squalus canicula* and *catulus* of Linnæus.

DO'G-LEGGED-STAIRS (*Archit.*) stairs which are solid between the upper flights, having no well-hole.

TO DOG-DRAW (*Law*) a term employed in the forest laws for the drawing after a deer by the scent of a dog; of which a man stands chargeable if he be found leading a dog in his hand. [vide *Backberind*]

DO'GA (*Ant.*) from δεχομαι, to receive; a large wine vessel, and also a pipe for conveying water. Vopis. Aurelian. c. 48; Greg. Turon.

DO'GBERRY-TREE (*Bot.*) another name for the *Cornus* of Linnæus.

TO DO'GDRAW (*Law*) vide *Dog.*

DOGE (*Polit.*) the chief magistrate of either Venice or Genoa.

DO'GGER (*Mar.*) a small vessel, provided with a well, for the conveyance of fish alive to shore.—*Dogger-men,* fishermen who use such vessels.

DO'GGREL *rhyme* (*Poet.*) an irregular kind of versification.

DOGMA'TIC *sect* (*Med.*) an ancient sect of physicians, at the head of which is placed Hippocrates. They supposed principles, and from them drew conclusions which they applied to particular cases, whence they were also called *logici,* as distinguished from the *empirici,* or *methodici.* They answer to what are now called scientific physicians, as opposed to quacks.

DOGMATIC *philosophy* (*Eth.*) a philosophy which is founded on stable fixed principles, as opposed to the *sceptic philosophy.*

DO'G-ROSE (*Bot.*) the *Rosa Canina.*

DO'G'S-BANE (*Bot.*) the *Apocynum* of Linnæus.—Dog's-Grass, the *Triticum repens,* a perennial.—Dog's-Mercury, the *Mercurialis Perennis.*—Dog's-Tail-Grass, the *Cynosurus.*—Dog's-Tooth, the *Erythronium dens Canis.*

DO'GWOOD (*Bot.*) another name for the *Cornus.*

DO'ITKIN (*Com.*) from the Dutch *duytkin,* a small coin in Holland, in value less than one farthing.

DOLABRIFO'RMIS (*Bot.*) hatchet-shaped, an epithet for a leaf; *folium dolabriforme,* a hatchet-shaped leaf, as in *Mesembryanthemum dolibriforme.*

DO'LCE (*Mus.*) an Italian epithet signifying sweet, as *con dolce maniera,* i. e. in a soft agreeable manner, a phrase applied to passages in music books.

DO'LCEMENTE (*Mus.*) Italian; the same as *Dolce.*

DOLE (*Min.*) a pile of ore for sale.

DOLE (*Law*) signifies in the Scotch law a malevolent intention, which is essential to constitute a crime.

DO'LE-FISH (*Com.*) from *dole, deal,* or the Teutonic *theil,* a part, signifies that portion of the fish caught in the North Seas which the fishermen receive for their allowance.

DOLE-MEADOW (*Archæol.*) one wherein divers persons have a share.

DOLES (*Archæol.*) slips of pasture left between furrows of ploughed lands.

DOLG-BOTE (*Archæol.*) in the Saxon. bolᵹ, a wound; a fine for inflicting a wound.

DO'LICHOS (*Bot.*) a genus of plants, Class 17 *Diadelphia*, Order 4 *Decandria*.

Generic Character. CAL. *perianth* one-leaved.—COR. papilionaceous.—STAM. *filaments* diadelphous; *anthers* simple.—PIST. *germ* linear; *style* ascending; *stigma* bearded.—PER. *legume* acuminate; *seeds* oblong.

Species. The species are mostly annuals, and natives of the East and West Indies, as the—*Dolichos Lablab*, seu *Phaseolus*, Black-seeded Dolichos.—*Dolichos sinensis*, Chinese Dolichos.—*Dolichos altissimus*, seu *Kakuvalli*, Tall Dolichos.—*Dolichos pruriens*, seu *Phaseolus*, seu *Stizolobium*, Horse eye Bean.—*Dolichos urens*, *zoophthalamum*, seu *Mucuna*, Cow itch Dolichos. But the —*Dolichos Bulbosus*, seu *Cacara*, Bulbous Dolichos, and a few others, are perennials. *Clus. Hist.*; *Bauh. Hist.*; *Bauh. Raii Hist.*

DOLICHOS is also the *Glycine tubola* of Linnæus.

DO'LIMAN (*Polit.*) vide *Dolman*.

DOLICHU'RUS (*Poet.*) δολιχύρος a long-tailed verse, having a foot or syllable too much.

DO'LICHUS (*Ant.*) δόλιχος, a space of ground, containing twelve furlongs.

DOLIOCA'RPUS (*Bot.*) a genus of plants, Class 13 *Polyandria*, Order 1 *Monogynia*.

Generic Character. CAL. *perianth* five-leaved.—COR. *petals* three.—STAM. *filaments* many; *anthers* compressed.—PIST. *germ* globular; *style* long; *stigma* flat.—PER. *berry* globular; *seeds* two.

Species. The species are shrubs, native of Guiana, as the —*Doliocarpus rolandri, major, et calinea.*

DO'LLAR (*Com.*) a foreign coin, of different values, from four shillings to four and sixpence, according to the country or place in which it is current.—*Rix Dollar*, from the German *Reichsthaler*, is a money of account as well as a silver coin in Germany, Holland, Sweden, &c.—*Spanish Dollar* is a piece coined either at Mexico or in Spain. The former are called *pillar dollars*, because they bear on the reverse the arms of Spain between two pillars, with the inscription on them NEC PLUS ULTRA. Those coined in Spain have on the obverse the head of the reigning prince, with his name, and the legend DEI GRATIA; on the reverse it has no pillars, and the legend is only HISPANIARUM REX, instead of HISPAN. ET IND. REX, as on the other. The value of this dollar is computed to be 4s. 8¼d. in sterling money.

DO'LMAN (*Polit.*) a robe, of which the Grand Signor makes a present to the Janizaries on the first day of their *Ramadan*, or Lent.

DO'LOMITE (*Min.*) a sort of stone which is ranked among the calcareous salts.

DO'LON (*Ant.*) 1. A great staff or pole, with a small head of iron, and a sword within it. *Suet. Claud.* c. 13; *Hesychius Serv. Æneid.* l. 7, v. 664; *Alex. Gen. Dier.* l. 4, c. 5. 2. A small sail in a ship, called the *trinket*. *Liv.* l. 36, c. 44; *Gyrald. de Navig.* c. 14; *Scheffer de Re Nav.* l. 2, c. 5.

DO'LOR (*Med.*) vide *Pain*.

DOLORO'SO (*Mus.*) Italian for a soft pathetic style of music.

DO'LPHIN (*Astron.*) a constellation. [vide *Delphinus*]

DOLPHIN (*Zool.*) though reckoned among the fishes, from its habit of life, is classed by Linnæus under the *Mammalia*, as a genus by the ancient name of the *Delphinus*. [vide *Delphinus*] It has an oblong body, a narrow sharp snout, swims with great velocity, preys upon fishes, and adheres to whales as they leap out of the water.

DOLPHIN (*Her.*) this animal is mostly represented in an escutcheon in a curved form, when it is termed *imbowed*; but sometimes it is borne straight, and then it is named *extended*, as "He beareth three dolphins extended, *naiant*," as in the annexed figure. When it is placed perpendicular, with its body in the form of a letter S, as it is commonly represented on ancient medals, then it is termed "A dolphin springing and torqued hauriant," or "A dolphin hauriant."

DOLPHIN *of the mast* (*Mar.*) a kind of wreath, formed of plaited cordage, to be fastened round the masts, as a support to the puddening.

DO'LPHINS (*Gunn.*) handles to pieces of ordnance made in the form of a dolphin.

DOLPHINS (*Ent.*) a name given by gardeners to the small black insects that infest beans, &c.

DOM. (*Polit.*) an abbreviation of *dominus*, for which Don is used as a title in Spain.

DOMA'IN (*Law*) vide *Demesne*.

DO'MBEC (*Archæol.*) or *Domboc*, a statute of the ancient Saxons, containing the laws of preceding kings.

DOMBE'YA (*Bot.*) a genus of plants, Class 22 *Diœcia*, Order 13 *Monodelphia*.

Generic Character. CAL. *perianth* none.—COR. none.—STAM. *filaments* none.—PIST. *germ* oblong; *style* none; *stigmas* bivalve.—PER. none; *seeds* many.

Species. The only species is a tree, as the *Dombeya Chilensis*, native of Chili.

DOMBEYA is also the *Tourrettia Cappaca* of Linnæus.

DOME (*Archit.*) a spherical roof raised over the middle of a building, as a church, hall, &c. When it rises higher than the radius of the base it is a *surmounted Dome*; if lower than the radius, it is a *diminished*, or *surbassed Dome*; and if it have a circular base it is a *cupola*. It answers to the *tholus* of Vitruvius. *Vitruv.* l. 4, c. 7; *Isidor. Orig.* l. 19; *Suidas*.

DOME (*Chem.*) an arched cover for a reverberatory furnace.

DO'ME-BOOK (*Archæol.*) *liber judicialis*; a book composed under the direction of Alfred, for the general use of the whole kingdom, containing the local customs of the several provinces.

DO'MESDAY-BOOK (*Archæol.*) *liber judiciarius vel Censualis Angliæ*, an ancient record, made in the reign of William the Conqueror, which is now remaining in the Exchequer, fair and legible, in two volumes: to which belong three other volumes, that consist of abridgments or extracts from the former. The addition of the word *day* is supposed to have been made only for the purpose of giving confirmation and authority to a record which was to be referred to at all times in dooming judgment and justice.

DO'MES-MAN (*Archæol.*) a judge appointed to hear and determine law-suits.

DOME'STICI (*Archæol.*) assistants at the court of Constantinople either to the judges on the bench or to the officers in the palace, of which there were different descriptions, as the *domestici Mensæ, scholarum Domestici, murorum vel regionum Domestici*, &c. *Cassiod. Var.* l. 9, c. 13; *Buleng. de Imp. Roman.* l. 4, c. 38, &c.

DOMICE'LLUS (*Archæol.*) a title formerly given to the king's natural sons in France, of which we have also examples in the natural sons of John of Gaunt, Duke of Lancaster, in the statute of legitimation. 20 R. 2.

DOMICI'LIUM (*Archæol.*) a domicil or habitation.

DO'MIFYING (*Astrol.*) the dividing or distributing the houses into twelve parts.

DOMIGE'RUM (*Archæol.*) signified formerly danger, but was more frequently taken for power over another. "Sub domigero alicujus vel manu esse." *Bract.* l. 4, tract 1, c. 10.

DO'MINA (*Archæol.*) a title given to honourable women

who anciently, in their own right, held a barony. *Paroch. Antiq.*

DO'MINANT (*Mus.*) the dominant of any mode is that sound which makes a fifth to a final.

DOMINANT *Tenement* (*Law*) a term in the Scotch feudal law, signifying the tenement or subject in favour of which the service is constituted.

DO'MINI, ANNO (*Chron.*) abbreviated A. D, in the year of our Lord.

DOMI'NICA *Dies* (*Ecc.*) The Lord's Day.—*Dominica in Ramis Palmarum*, Palm-Sunday.

DOMI'NICAL (*Chron.*) one of the first seven letters of the alphabet, wherewith the Sundays are marked throughout the year in the almanack. It changes every year, and after the term of twenty-eight years, the letters return to the same order as before; whence this period is called the cycle of the Sunday or Dominical Letter. [vide *Chronology*]

DOMI'NICANS (*Ecc.*) an order of friars, founded in the year 1216, by one Dominicus, of Toulouse. They were otherwise called the *preaching friars*. *Hel. Hist. des Ord. Mon.* tom. iii, c. 24.

DOMI'NICUM (*Archæol.*) 1. The sacrament of the Lord's Supper. 2. A demain or demesne.

DOMI'NIUM (*Law*) right or power, of which there are two kinds in the Scotch feudal law: the *Dominium directum*, i. e. the right of the superior or lord; and *Dominium utile*, the right of the vassal, by which he enjoys the whole fruits and produce of the estate.

DO'MINO (*Ecc.*) a sort of hood worn by canons of a cathedral church; also a mourning vest for women.

DOMINO (*Sport.*) a game played by two or four persons with twenty-four pieces of oblong ivory, called cards, plain at the back, but on the face divided by a black line in the middle, and indented with spots from one to a double six. These pieces are distinguished by the names of *double-blank, ace, deuce, trois, four,* &c.; or *ace-blank, double-ace, deuce-blank, deuce-ace, double-deuce,* &c.

DOMINUS (*Law*) a word which, when prefixed to a man's name, formerly denoted him to be a knight or gentleman. —*Dominus Litis,* an advocate in the civil law, who, after his client's death, prosecuted a suit to sentence for his client's use.

DOMIPO'RTA (*Con.*) from *domus*, a house, and *porto*, to carry; an epithet for a snail because she carries her house on her back.

DOMITE'LLUS (*Archæol.*) the same as *Domicellus*.

DOMO *reparando* (*Law*) a writ lying against one whose house going to decay, may endanger his neighbour's by its fall. *Reg. Orig.* 153.

DO'MUS *conservorum* (*Archæol.*) the ancient name for the house where the Rolls are kept in Chancery-Lane.

DON (*Polit.*) a title of honour in Spain, put for *dom* or *dominus*, Sir or Lord.

DONA'CEA (*Ent.*) a division of the genus *Leptura*, comprehending those insects which have the lip entire.

DONA'RIA (*Archæol.*) things set apart for sacred use, answering to the anathemata of the Greeks. *Justin. Instit.* § 8 *de Reb. Divin.*

DONA'TIA (*Bot.*) a genus of plants; so called after Vitaliano Donati, Class 3 *Triandria*, Order 2 *Trigynia*.
Generic Character. CAL. *perianth* three-leaved.—COR. *petals* nine.—STAM. *filaments* three; *anthers* twin.—PIST. *germ* inferior; *styles* three; *stigmas* bluntish.—PER. *none; seeds* none.
Species. The single species is the—*Donatia fascicularis.*
DONATIA is also the *Avicennia tomentosa.*

DO'NATISTS (*Ecc.*) a sect of heretics who greatly disturbed the church in the third and fourth centuries. They held, among other tenets, that the Son in the Holy Trinity was less than the Father, and the Holy Ghost less than the Son. *Optat. Milvat. de Schismal.; Donatist. Epiphan. Hæres.; August. Oper.* tom. ix; *Theodoret. de Heres.; Hen. Vales. de Sect.*

DO'NATIVE (*Law*) a benefice given to a clerk by the patron without presentation to the bishop, or institution or induction by his order. *F. N. B.* 35; *Co. Lit.* 344.

DONATI'VUM (*Ant.*) a largess or benevolence bestowed upon the soldiers by the Roman emperors. *Lamprid. Heliogab.; Cassiod. Var.* l. 4, c. 14; *Bud. in Pandect.* p. 258; *Turneb. Adv.* l. 19, c. 21.

DONATIVUM (*Archæol.*) a dole or gift made by a nobleman.

DONATORY (*Law*) that person, in the Scotch law, on whom the King bestows his right to any forfeiture that has fallen to the crown.

DO'NAX (*Bot.*) the *Arundo Donax* of Linnæus.

DONAX (*Conch.*) a genus of testaceous animals, having a bivalve shell and a crenulate margin. The animal is a *tethys*.

DO'NEE (*Law*) he or she to whom lands, &c. are given.

DO'NJON (*Fort.*) or *dongeon*, a large tower or redoubt where the garrison may retreat in case of necessity, and capitulate with greater advantage.

DONJON (*Archit.*) a small wooden pavilion raised above the roof of the house, where any one may command a fine view.

DO'NIS DE (*Law*) a statute so named, *de donis conditionalibus*, which revived the ancient feudal restraints originally laid on alienations.

DO'NOR (*Law*) one who gives lands, &c. to another.

DOO'LIES (*Mech.*) an Indian word for palanqueens, of a particularly easy construction, for the conveyance of the sick.

DOO'MSDAY-BOOK (*Archæol.*) vide *Domesday-Book.*

DO'PPIA (*Com.*) an Italian coin, consisting either of a single, double, or quadruple pistole, &c. the pistole being equal to about 16s. 6d.

DOR (*Ent.*) or Clock-Beetle, the *Scarabæus stercorarius* of Linnæus, which flies buzzing about of an evening, and is said to foretel a fine day.

DORA'DO (*Astron.*) a southern constellation not visible in our latitude. It is otherwise called *Xiphias*, or the Sword-Fish, and is reckoned to have six stars.

DORÆ'NA (*Bot.*) a genus of plants, Class 5 *Pentandria*, Order 1 *Monogynia*.
Generic Character. CAL. *perianth* one-leaved.—COR. one-petalled.—STAM. *filaments* very short; *anthers* oblong.—PIST. *germ* conic; *style* filiform; *stigma* truncate.—PER. *capsule* ovate; *seeds* many.
Species. The single species is a tree, as the—*Doræna japonica*, native of Japan.

DO'REA (*Med.*) a person who can see by day but not by night.

DO'REE, (*Ich.*) or John Dory, a fish so called because its sides, varied with light blue and white, have the appearance of being gilt. It is the *Zeus faber* of Linnæus.

DO'RIA (*Bot.*) the *Athonna arborescens* of Linnæus.

DO'RIAN *Mode* (*Mus.*) δωριςὶ ἁρμονία, one of the most ancient modes among the Greeks, which was so called from the Dorians, by whom it was introduced. The character of this mode is serious and grave, but of a gravity so tempered as to render it fit for martial or sacred subjects, on which account Plato deemed it worthy a place in his republic. *Plat. Polit.* l. 3.

DO'RIC *Order* (*Archit.*) the most ancient of the Grecian orders, is said to have been made in imitation of the hovels which were erected by the original inhabitants of Greece, consisting of roofs, supported by the trunks of trees. The order, which is at present most generally known by this name, is an imitation of the Grecian Doric made by the Romans. [vide *Architecture*]

DORIC Dialect (*Gram.*) a particular form of the Greek language, which was so called from the Dorians, by whom it was first used. It was afterwards the language of the Lacedæmonians, Argives, and the inhabitants of Epirus, Lybia, Sicily, Rhodes, and Cyprus. The principal writers in this dialect were Archimedes and Theocritus.

DORIS (*Ent.*) a genus of animals, Class *Vermes*, Order *Mollusca*.
 Generic Character. Body creeping, oblong.—Mouth placed below.—Feelers from two to four, situated on the upper part of the body, and bent behind on the back.
 Species. The species are generally distinguished into those which have two, and those which have four feelers.

DO'RMANT (*Her.*) an epithet in blazonry for a lion or other beasts sleeping, as in the annexed figure. He beareth "*Gules*, a Lion dormant, or. Name *Aylesworth of Essex*."

DO'RMANT-TREE (*Carpent.*) a great beam which lies across a house. [vide *Dormer*]

DORMANT WRITING (*Law*) a deed which has a blank to put in the name of a person.

DORMER (*Archit.*) or *Dormant*, a window made in the roof of a building, or above the entablature, being raised upon the rafters.

DO'RMITORY (*Archit.*) a gallery in convents or religious houses, divided into several cells, in which the monks sleep or lodge.

DO'RMOUSE (*Zool.*) an animal of the mouse kind, which remains torpid during winter, walks or rather leaps on its hind legs, feeds only on vegetables, burrows under ground, sleeps by day, and watches by night. It is the *Myoxus* of Linnæus.

DORO'NICUM (*Bot.*) a genus of plants, Class 19 *Syngenesia Polygamia*, Order 2 *Superflua*.
 Generic Character. CAL. common, with leaflets.—COR. compound rayed.—STAM. filaments five; anthers cylindric—PIST. germ oblong; style filiform; stigmas two.—PER. none; receptacle naked.
 Species. The species are perennials, as the—*Doronicum Pardaleanches*, Great Leopards Bane. — *Doronicum Plantagineum*, Plantain-leaved Leopards Bane.—*Doronicum Bellidiastrum*, *Bellidiastrum*, seu *Bellesmedia*, Daisy-leaved Leopards Bane. *Clus. Hist.*; *Bauh. Hist.*; *Bauh. Pin.*; *Ger. Herb.*; *Park. Theat. Bot.*; *Raii Hist.*; *Tourn. Inst.*

DORONICUM is also the *Arnica montana*, *Scorpoides crocea*, &c. &c.

DO'RSAL (*Med.*) an epithet applied to those distempers the seat of which lies in the back.

DORSA'LES *nervi* (*Anat.*) the nerves which pass out from the vertebræ of the back.

DORSA'LIS (*Bot.*) an epithet for an awn; *arista dorsalis*, an awn fixed to the back or outer side of the glume, not springing from the end, as in *Bromus* and *Avena*.

DORSI *longissimus* (*Anat.*) a great muscle inserted into the transverse processes of the vertebræ of the loins.

DORSIFEROUS (*Bot.*) an epithet formerly applied to plants of a capillary kind, without stalk, that bear the seeds on the back of the leaf.

DORSTE'NIA (*Bot.*) a genus of plants, so called from Theodorus Dorstenius, Class 4 *Tetrandria*, Order 1 *Monogynia*.
 Generic Character. CAL. receptacle common.—COR. none.—STAM. filaments four; anthers roundish.—PIST. germ roundish; style simple; stigma obtuse.—PER. none; seeds roundish.
 Species. The species are perennials, as the—*Dorstenia Contrayerva*, *Drakena radix*, seu *Cyprus*, native of South America.—*Dorstenia lucida*, seu *Elalostema*, native of the Society Islands.

DO'RSUM (*Anat.*) the Back.

DORTMANNA (*Bot.*) the *Lobelia* of Linnæus.

DORTURE (*Cus.*) dorter, or *dortoir*, the common room where all the friars of one convent sleep at nights.

DORY'CNIUM (*Bot.*) the *Lotus Dorycnium*.

DORYPHO'RI (*Ant.*) δορυφόροι, from δόρυ, a spear, and φέρω, to carry; a sort of Persian soldiers, who acted as a body-guard to the monarch. The body-guard of the Roman emperors were called by the same name. *Plin. l.* 34; *Curt.* l. 3, c. 3.

DOSE (*Med.*) from the Greek δόσις, a giving; the quantity of any medicine prescribed by the physician to be taken by the patient at one time.

DOSSA'LE (*Mech.*) hangings of tapestry, or curtains for a choir.

DO'SSER (*Fort.*) a sort of basket used by the men in fortified towns to carry earth from one place to another.

DO'SSES (*Archit.*) French for the thick beams which are laid to secure a foundation.

DO'SSIL (*Surg.*) lint made into a cylindric form resembling the shape of dates or olives.

DO'TE ASSIGNANDO (*Law*) a writ for the escheator to assign a dowry to the widow of the King's tenant, swearing in chancery not to marry without the King's leave; these are called the *King's widows*. Stat. 15 Ed. 4, c. 4; *F. N. B.* 26; *Reg. Orig.* 297.—*Dote unde nihil habet*, a writ of dower for the widow against the tenant who bought land of her husband, whereof he was solely seised in fee-simple or fee-tail, and of which she is dowable. *F. N. B.* 147.

DO'THIEN (*Med.*) a hard and painful swelling, as large as a pigeon's egg, which proceeds from thickness of blood.

DO'TIS ADMENSURATIONE (*Law*) vide *Admeasurement of Dower*.

DO'TKIN (*Com.*) vide *Doitkin*.

DOTTED (*Bot.*) *punctatus*; an epithet for a leaf and a receptacle; *folium punctatum*, a leaf besprinkled or pounced with hollow dots, or points, as in *Anthemis maritima*; *receptaculum punctatum*, a dotted receptacle, as in *Leontodon*, *Cacalia*, &c.

DO'TTEREL (*Orn.*) a foolish bird found in different parts of England, the *Charadrius morinellus* of Linnæus. It is said that it will mimick the actions of the fowler, regardless of the net which he is spreading for it.

DO'UBLE (*Bot.*) *geminus*; an epithet for a leaf, stipule, peduncle, &c; *folium geminum*, a double leaf connected by one petiole; *stipula gemina*, double stipule, or two and two by pairs; *pedunculus geminus*, double peduncle, or two peduncles from the same point.

DOUBLE *avail of marriage* (*Law*) the double of the value of the vassal's wife's tocher due to the superior, because he refused a wife equal to him when offered by the superior.—*Double plea*, a plea consisting of several things that are independent of each other, either whereof is sufficient in bar of plaintiff's action. *Kitch.* 223.—*Double quarrel*, *duplex querela*, a complaint made by a clerk to the archbishop against any inferior ordinary for delaying to do justice in some ecclesiastical matter. It seems to be so denominated because it is most commonly made both against the judge and him at whose suit justice is denied. *Double* is also the same as the duplicate of letters patent.

DOUBLE *vessel* (*Chem.*) a name for two mattrasses, when the neck of one is well luted into the neck of the other.

DOUBLE *horizontal dial* (*Math.*) one with a double gnomon, the one pointing out the hour on the outer circle, the other on the stereographic projection drawn upon it. This dial finds the meridian, the hour, the sun's place, &c.—*Double point*, a point in the higher geometry which is common to two parts or legs, or branches of some curve of the second or higher order, such as an infinitely small ellipse, or a cusp, or the cruciform intersection of such curves. [vide *Curve*]

DOUBLE STARS (*Astron.*) are those luminous bodies which, though they appear single to the naked eye, are found by the help of the telescope to be composed of two stars.

DOUBLE *building* (*Archit.*) one in which the walls are carried up double.—*Double doors*, two doors made in the same aperture of a wall to keep an apartment warm.—*Double floor*, one constructed of binding or bridging joists.—*Double-hung sashes*, a window consisting of two sashes, each of which is moveable by means of weights.—*Double margin door*, that which represents two doors in the same breadth, but is in fact only one door.

TO DOUBLE (*Sport.*) is said of a hare when she winds about to deceive the hounds.

TO DOUBLE *a cape* (*Mar.*) in French *doubler un cap*, the act of sailing round or passing beyond it, so that the point of land separates the ship from her former situation, and intercepts the view of any distant object. " To *double* upon a fleet," the act of enclosing between two fires any part of a hostile fleet in a naval engagement, or of cannonading it on both sides.

TO DOUBLE (*Man.*) a horse is said *to double* the reins, when he leaps several times together to throw the rider.

DOUBLEAU (*Archit.*) French for a joist, or the chief arch which reaches from one pile to another.

DOU'BLED *together* (*Bot.*) vide *Conduplicate*.

DOUBLE'R *un Battalion* (*Mil.*) to extend the front of a battalion for it to cover twice the ground that it did before.

DOUBLER (*Elec.*) an instrument capable of augmenting a very small electricity, so as to render it more than sufficiently manifest by means of an electrometer.

DOU'BLET (*Cus.*) an old-fashioned garment made after the fashion of a waistcoat.

DOUBLET (*Min.*) a false jewel, or stone, being two pieces joined together.

DOUBLETS (*Num.*) two medals of the same sort.

DOUBLETS (*Sport.*) a game with dice inserted in tables.

DOU'BLING (*Mil.*) is the placing two or more ranks or files into one. " To *double round*," is to march by an inversion of a second line on the extremity of a first line, thereby to outflank an enemy.

DOUBLING (*Carpent.*) a term in Scotland for eaves-boards.

DOU'BLING-NAILS (*Mar.*) the nails which are commonly used in fastening the linings of the gun-ports, &c.

DOU'BLINGS (*Sport.*) the turnings of a hare. [vide *To double*]

DOUBLINGS (*Her.*) the linings of robes or mantles of state.

DOUBLOO'N (*Com.*) a Spanish coin, the quadruple of the pistole, coined in 1772, equal to 3*l*. 6*s*. sterling. The same name has also been given to the modern pistole, worth about 16*s*. On the obverse of this coin is the head of the reigning king, with the name and the title, " *Dei Gratia* HISP*aniarum* ET IN*Diarum* REX;" reverse, arms of Spain with the collar of the golden fleece; the legends various; at the bottom the letter M with a crown over it, to signify Madrid; or M with an O over it, to signify Mexico, the place where it was coined.

DOUBLY *compound* (*Bot.*) vide *Decompound*.—*Doubly crenate*, an epithet for a leaf that has smaller notches on the larger.—*Doubly pinnate*. vide *Bipinnate*.—*Doubly serrate*, an epithet for a leaf having smaller teeth on the larger.—*Doubly ternate*, or biternate, an epithet for a petiole that has two ternate leaflets, as in *Epimedium*.

DOU'CETS (*Sport.*) the *testes* of the deer or stag.

DOUCI'NE (*Archit.*) French for an ornament of the highest part of a cornice, or a moulding cut in form of a wave, half concave and half convex, answering to the *sima recta*.

DOUDOU' (*Com.*) a copper coin current in many parts of the East Indies, particularly at Pondicherry; it is equal to two French liards.

DOVE (*Orn.*) one of the varieties of the *Columba domestica* of Linnæus. There are three sorts of pigeons known by this name, viz.—The *Ring Dove*, which is the largest of the pigeon tribe, and has a semicircular line of white on the hind part of the neck. It is so wild that it cannot be domesticated.—*Stock Dove*, having a fine bluish gray head, neck, and part of the back. This species is migratory, and roosts in trees.—*Turtle Dove*, a shy and retired bird that lives in the woods. The irides of its eyes are of a fine yellow, the neck is black, back ash-coloured, feathers brown; breast red, and belly white.

Dove (*Her.*) is borne as a charge in many escutcheons; sometimes, as in the annexed figure, " Field argent, a chevron between three crescents sable, on a canton of the second a dove with an olive branch in her bill, all *proper*; name *Walker*." Sometimes it is blazoned a *dove volant* upright, beaked and membered; sometimes *a dove* rising, &c.

DOVE'S FOOT CRANE'S BILL (*Bot.*) the *Geranium molle* of Linnæus, a perennial.

DO'VE-TAIL (*Carpent.*) a piece of wood formed like the tail of a dove.

DO'VE-TAILING (*Carpent.*) a method of joining one board into another by projecting pins cut in the form of dove-tails in one piece, and let it into hollows of the same form in another. Dove-tailing is either *exposed* or *concealed*; concealed dove-tailing is either *lapped* or *mitred*.

DOUGLA'SSIA (*Bot.*) a genus of plants, so called from James Douglas, Class 18 *Polyadelphia*, Order 4 *Polyandria*.

Generic Character. CAL. perianth one-leaved.—COR. none. STAM. *filaments* none; *anthers* many.—PIST. germ ovate; stigma six-cleft.—PER. berry ovate; seeds single.

Species. The single species, the *Douglassia Guianensis*, Guiana Douglassia, is a tree.

DOUILLE (*Mil.*) French for a small iron socket at the heel of the bayonet; and also a cavity at the end of the ramrod.

DOUVIJILLE'T (*Cook.*) a particular manner of dressing a pig, called *au père douyillet*.

TO DOUSE (*Mar.*) in French *molir*, to lower or slacken suddenly, in application to a sail in a squall of wind, &c.

DOUSING-CHOCKS (*Mar.*) pieces fayed across the apron, and lapped on the knight-heads, or inside stuff above the upper-deck.

DOUX (*Mus.*) a term, in music books, for soft, sweet.

DO'WAGER (*Polit.*) signifies literally a widow who enjoys her dower; but is commonly applied as a title to the widows of princes and nobility.—*Queen Dowager* is the widow of the King, who enjoys most of the privileges that belong to the Queen Consort.

DOWE'LLING (*Mar.*) a method of coaking among shipwrights by letting pieces into the solid, or by uniting two pieces together by tenons.

DOWER (*Law*) *dotarium*, the portion which a widow has of her husband's lands at his decease, for the sustenance of herself, and the education of her children. Dower is of several kinds; namely,—*Dower of the Common Law*, which is a third part of the lands, &c. whereof he is seized.—*Dower by Custom*, i. e. by the custom of any place, which is, of course, various, being in some cases a half.—*Dower ad ostium ecclesiæ*, a dower made at the Church door immediately after marriage, which could not exceed the third part, though it might be less.—*Dower ex assensu patris* was a species of *dower ad ostium ecclesiæ*.—*Dower*.

de la pluie belle, a dower of the fairest part of a husband's estate.

DOWL *and Deal* (*Archæol.*) signify a division; whence boundary-stones, which parted off lands, were called *Dowlestones*.

DO'WLAS (*Com.*) a sort of linen cloth.

DOWN (*Mar.*) a term employed in many sea phrases, as " *Down* all chests," an order for the deck to be cleared of all chests preparatory to an engagement. " *Down* haul," for letting down a rope of the stay-sail in order to shorten sail. " *Down* foresail," &c.

DOWN (*Bot.*) signifies properly any sort of pubescence, but it is used for the *pappus*, or little crown fixed on the top of some seeds, by which they fly, as *Dandelion*, &c.

DOWNS (*Mar.*) a bank, or elevation of sand, which the sea gathers and forms along its shores.

DO'WNY (*Bot.*) vide *Tomentosus*.

DO'WRY (*Law*) vide *Dower*.

DOXO'LOGY (*Ecc.*) δοξολογία, a song, or short hymn of praise said or sung in divine service, as the *Gloria Patri*, i. e. glory be to the Father, &c.

DOZE'IN (*Archæol.*) a territory or jurisdiction. *Stat.* 18, *Ed.* 2.

DRAB (*Com.*) vide *Drap*.

DRA'BA (*Bot.*) a genus of plants, Class 15 *Tetradynamia*, Order 1 *Siliculosa*.
Generic Character. CAL. *perianth* four-leaved.—COR. *petals* oblong.—STAM. *filaments* six; *anthers* simple.—PIST. *germ* ovate; *style* scarce any; *stigma* headed.—PER. *silicle* oblong.
Species. The species are mostly perennials, as the—*Draba aizoides*, seu *Alyssum*, Hoary-leaved Alpine Whitlow Grass, native of the South of Europe.—*Draba pyrenaica*, seu *Alyssum*, native of Provence.—*Draba hirta*, seu *Bursa pastoris*, native of Lapland: but the *Draba verna*, seu *Alsine*, Common or Spring Whitlow-Grass, is an annual; and the *Draba incana*, seu *Leucoicum*, Hoary Whitlow-Grass, is a biennial.

DRA'BANTS (*Mil.*) a select body of men, who were commanded in person by Charles IX, King of Sweden.

DRABLER (*Mar.*) an additional part of a sail laced to the bottom of the bonnet on a square sail.

DRABS (*Mech.*) a kind of wooden boxes, in the salt works, for holding the salt when taken out of the boiling pan: they are made shelving that the brine may run off.

DRAC (*Myth.*) an imaginary being, who was formerly much dreaded by the country people.

DRACÆ'NA (*Bot.*) a genus of plants, Class 6 *Hexandria*, Order 1 *Monogynia*.
Generic Character. CAL. none.—COR. *petals* six.—STAM. *filaments* six; *anthers* oblong.—PIST. *germ* ovate; *style* filiform; *stigma* obtuse.—PER. *berry* ovate; *seeds* solitary.
Species. The species are perennials, as the — *Dracæna draco*, *Asparagus*, *Palma draco*, seu *Draco arbor*, Dragon Tree, native of Cape Verd Islands.—*Dracæna ferrea*, seu *Terminalis rubra*, Purple Dracæna, native of China. *Dracæna ensifolia*, *Dianella*, seu *Gladiolus*, Sword-leaved Dracæna, native of the East Indies.—*Dracæna marginata*, seu *Aloe purpurea*, Aloe-leaved Dracæna.

DRACHM (*Com.*) a weight used particularly by apothecaries containing just sixty grains. It is now the eighth part of an ounce, though formerly reckoned only the seventh. [vide *Drachma*]

DRA'CHMA (*Ant.*) δραχμή, a coin current at Athens, and other parts of Greece, which was equal in value to 7½*d*. English money. It was very similar to the Roman *denarius*. *Plin*. l. 21, c. 34; *Plut. Fab.*; *Bud. de Ass.*; *Camerar. de Re numm. apud Gronov. Thes. Antiq. Græc.* tom. 9, &c.

DRACHMA (*Med.*) the drachm, or dram, was also formerly a weight used among physicians, which was the seventh part of an ounce, at the rate of eighty-four to the pound. *Scrib. Larg*.

DRA'CMON (*Num.*) vide *Darcon*.

DRA'CO (*Ant.*) δράκων, a dragon; a sort of flying serpent, so called, ἀπὸ τοῦ δέρκειν, from seeing, on account of its quick sight.
Draco was also the name of the ensign which bore the figure of a dragon, and belonged to the several companies in the Roman army, as did the *Aquila*, Eagle, to the whole legion; whence the *Draconarius* was the bearer of such an ensign. *Claud. Rufin.* l. 2, v. 365; *Amm.* l. 16, c. 10; *Veget.* l. 1, c. 23; *Isid. Orig.* l. 18, c. 3; *Suidas.*; *Curopal. de Offic. Constant.*

DRACO (*Astron.*) the Dragon, a constellation in the northern hemisphere, which was so called because it was supposed to represent the Dragon that guarded the Hesperian fruit, and was killed by Hercules, after which Juno took it up to heaven, and placed it among the constellations. It contained according to Ptolemy, 31 stars; according to Tycho, 32; Hevelius, 40; Bayer, 33; Flamstead, 80. *Arat. Phænom.* v. 46; *Eratosth. Charact.*; *Hygin. Astron. poet.*; *Ptol. Almag.* l. 7, c. 5; *Ricciol. Almag. nov.* l. 6, c. 4.

DRACO (*Zool.*) Dragon, a genus of animals of the Class *Reptilia*, Order *Amphibia*; of which there is but one species, the *Draco volans*. It resembles the lizard, except that it has a lateral membrane by which it supports itself in the air for a short time.

DRACO *Arbor* (*Bot.*) the *Dracæna draco* of Linnæus.—*Draco Herba*, the *Artemisia dracunculus* of Linnæus.

DRACOCE'PHALOS (*Bot.*) the *Chelone Penstemon*.

DRACOCE'PHALUM (*Bot.*) a genus of plants, Class 14 *Didynamia*, Order 1 *Gymnospermia*.
Generic Character. CAL. *perianth* one-leaved.—COR. *petals* one.—STAM. *filaments* four; *anthers* cordate.—PIST. *germ* four-parted; *style* filiform; *stigmas* sharp.—PER. none; *seeds* four.
Species. The species are perennials, as the—*Dracocephalum Virginianum*, *Pseudo digitalis*, seu *Lysemachia*, Virginian Dragon's Head.—*Dracocephalum canariense*, *Camphorosma*, seu *Melissa*, Canary Dragon's Head, or Balm of Gilead.—*Dracocephalum Austriacum*, *Hyssopus*, *Ruyschiana*, seu *Chamæpethys*, Austrian Dragon's Head, native of Hungary.—*Dracocephalum canescens*, *Moldavica*, seu *Sideritis*, Hoary Dragons' Head, native of the Levant.

DRACOCEPHALUS (*Bot.*) another name for the *Dracocephalum*.

DRACONARIUS (*Ant.*) vide *Draco*.

DRACONI'TES (*Min.*) a precious stone taken out of the brain of a dragon whilst alive. *Plin.* l. 33, c. 10.

DRACO'NTIAS (*Min.*) vide *Draconites*.

DRACO'NTIC *Month* (*Astron.*) the time of the moon's revolution, from her ascending node to her return thither, so called from the name of the node, *caput draconis*.

DRACO'NTIDES (*Anat.*) δρακοντίδες, a name for some veins proceeding directly from the heart. *Ruff. Ephes. de Appell. Part. Hum. Corp.* l. 1, c. 33.

DRACO'NTIUM (*Bot.*) δρακόντιον, a plant so called because its stalk resembles the dragon in its form. It is otherwise called *arum*. *Theophrast.* l. 7, c. 11; *Dioscor.* l. 2, c. 196. *Plin.* l. 24, c. 16; *Gal. de Alim. Fac.* l. 2, c. 69; *Erot. Lex. Hippocrat.*

DRACONTIUM (*Bot.*) a genus of plants, Class 20 *Gynandria*, Order 8 *Polyandria*.
Generic Character. CAL. *spathe* boat-form.—COR. *petals* ovate.—STAM. *filaments* seven; *anthers* oblong.—PIST. *germ* ovate; *style* straight; *stigma* obscure.—PER. *berry* roundish; *seeds* many.

Species. The species are perennials, as the—*Dracontium fœtidum*, Field Scunkweed, seu *Arum*, native of America.—*Dracontium pertusum*, seu *Arum*, Perforate-leaved Dragon, native of the West Indies.

DRACONTIUM is also the *Arum Dracunculus* of Linnæus.

DRACU'NCULI (*Med.*) small worms called *Guinea worms*, which breed in the muscular parts of the arms and legs. *Plut. Sympos.* l. 8, c. 9; *Aet. Tetrab.* l. 4, serm. 2, c. 8; *P. Ægineti.* l. 4, c. 59.

DRACUNCULOI'DES (*Bot.*) another name for the *Hemanthus*.

DRACU'NCULUS (*Bot.*) the *Arum Calea* of Linnæus.

DRAFT (*Husband.*) a name sometimes given to swill or hogwash.

DRAFT (*Com.*) a bill or check by which one person draws upon another for a certain sum of money.

DRAFT (*Mar.*) vide *Draught*.

DRAG (*Mar.*) in French *drague*, a machine consisting of a sharp square frame of iron encircled with a net, and commonly used to rake the mud off from the platform, or bottom of the docks. "To drag the Anchor," in French *chasser sur son ancre*, to trail the anchor along the bottom after it is loosened from the ground, by the effort of the wind or current upon the ship.

DRAGANT gum (*Bot.*) the same as the *Tragacanth*.

DRAGACA'NTHA (*Bot.*) the gum of the *Astragalus*, the same as the *Tragacanth*.

DRA'GOMAN (*Polit.*) in modern Greek δραγομανος, from תרגמן; an interpreter in the Eastern countries.

DRA'GON (*Zool.*) the *Draco* of Linnæus, a four-footed beast of the lizard tribe, tailed and winged, a native of India and Africa, which wanders about among the trees; it is able, by means of its lateral membrane, to support itself for a short time in the air. [vide *Draco*]

DRAGON (*Bot.*) the *Dracontium fœtidum* of Linnæus.

DRAGON (*Mil.*) a short piece or firelock formerly in use, having a barrel sixteen inches in length, and a full musket bore.—*Dragon*, or *Dragon volant*, a French name for an old piece of artillery which was a forty pounder.

DRAGON (*Her.*) though generally supposed to be a fabulous monster, is borne both in coats, crests, and supporters, as in the annexed figure; he beareth, "*Gules*, three Dragons passant in pale *ermine*; by the name of *Bloss*, in Suffolk."—*Knights of the Order of the Dragon*, an order instituted by the emperor Sigismond in 1417.

DRAGON Beams (*Carpent.*) two strong braces which stand under a bressummer, and meet in an angle on the shoulder of the King-piece.

DRAGON, *flying* (*Zool.*) vide *Draco*.

DRAGON, *flying* (*Nat.*) a fat heterogeneous meteor in the shape of a flying Dragon.

DRA'GON-FLY (*Ent.*) a particularly ravenous insect which hovers over stagnant waters. It is the *Libellula* of Linnæus.

DRAGON-TREE (*Bot.*) the *Dracæna dracocephalum* of Linnæus.

DRAGONE'T (*Ich.*) Dragon-Fish, the *Callionymus* of Linnæus.

DRAGO'NNE (*Mil.*) French for a sword knot at the extremity of which hangs a tassel, which was originally worn by the Germans as a mark of distinction for an officer when in plain clothes.

DRAGONNE' (*Her.*) an epithet for any beast, the lower part of which is in the form of a dragon, as a lion dragonné.

DRA'GON'S-BLOOD (*Bot.*) a gum or resin from a tree called *Arbor Draco*, the *Astragalus* of Linnæus. It is a very powerful astringent, incrassant, and drier, which is given with great efficacy in diarrhœas, &c.

DRAGON'S-HEAD (*Her.*) the tawny colour in the escutcheon of sovereign princes.

DRAGON'S-HEAD (*Astron.*) and *Dragon's-Tail*, the nodes of the planets, or those points in which the orbit of any planet, particularly the moon, intersects the orbit of the sun, or the ecliptic in an angle of about 5° 18'; the former, marked thus ☊, is the northward point as she ascends from the South to the North; the latter, marked thus ☋, is the southward point as she descends from the North to the South.

DRAGON'S-HEAD (*Bot.*) the *Dracocephalum* of Linnæus.

DRAGON TREE (*Bot.*) vide *Dragon*.

DRAGO'ON (*Mil.*) a soldier who fights sometimes on foot and sometimes on horseback; he is so called from *dragon*, because he was supposed to fight like a dragon.

TO DRAGOON (*Mil.*) in French *dragonner*, signifies commonly to bring a person to reason by blows, who cannot be persuaded by fair words; but, in application to a town, it implies to deliver up to plunder.

DRAGS (*Mech.*) floating pieces of timber so joined together that, by swimming on the water, they may carry any load down the river.

DRAIN (*Husband.*) a water-course sunk in a field for the purpose of carrying off the water from the surface of the land.

DRAIN (*Fort.*) a trench cut to clear a moat or ditch of the water.

DRA'INING (*Husband.*) or *land-draining*, the process of making drains in the land for the purpose of carrying off the water.

DRAKE'NA (*Bot.*) the *Dorstenia contrayerva* of Linnæus.

DRAM (*Com.*) or *drachm*, a weight of sixty grains; the one-eighth of an ounce Apothecary's Weight; the one-sixteenth of an ounce Avoirdupoise.

DRA'MA (*Poet.*) a play consisting either of tragedy or comedy.

DRAMA'TIC (*Poet.*) an epithet for what belongs to the drama.

DRANK (*Husband.*) a name for the wild oats which infest corn.

DRA'PER'S Company (*Her.*) were incorporated in the reign of King Henry VI. Their armorial ensigns are, as in the annexed figure, "*Azure*, three clouds radiated *proper*, each adorned with a treble-crown."

DRAP de Berry (*Com.*) a sort of frieze, or thick cloth, first made in Berry.

DRA'PERY (*Paint.*) the clothing of a human figure represented on the canvass. It is applied, in the same sense, to the representations in stone. Drapery is also used for hangings, tapestry, curtains, and most other things that are not carnations or landscapes.

DRA'STICS (*Med.*) remedies which work speedily and effectually.

DRAUGHT (*Paint.*) the plan or delineation of any object, particularly in application to things of which the outlines only are represented, as the plans of buildings, fortifications, &c.

DRAUGHT (*Mar.*) the quantity of water a ship draws when afloat, or the number of feet under water when laden.

DRAUGHT (*Mil.*) a certain number of men drawn from a regiment, or larger body.

DRAUGHT (*Com.*) an allowance in weighing commodities.

DRAUGHT Compasses (*Mech.*) compasses which are provided with several moveable points to make fine draughts in architecture, &c.

DRA'UGHT-HOOKS (*Gunn.*) large iron hooks fixed on the cheeks of a gun-carriage, two on each side.

DRAUGHT-HORSE (*Man.*) a coarser breed of horses, which are employed only in waggons, drays, carts, &c.

DRAUGHTS (*Sport.*) a game played on a checkered board like the Chess-Board, with twenty-four pieces, which, by angular movements, are enabled to take each other, according to certain rules, until one of the parties has lost all his men, or is placed in a situation to lose them all, when the game is at an end.

DRAUGHTSMEN (*Paint.*) those who are bred to the art of regularly taking plans and sketches of buildings and places.

TO DRAW (*Com.*) or *to draw on a person*, is to write a bill, sign it, and deliver it to the person to whom it is addressed for payment.

DRAW-BACK (*Com.*) a return of some part of the duties paid for goods on importation, which are drawn back on exportation.

DRAW-BRIDGE (*Archit.*) a bridge made, after the manner of a floor, to be drawn up, or let down, at pleasure.

DRAW-GEAR (*Husband.*) any furniture or harness of cart-horses.

DRAW-LATCHES (*Archæol.*) a name for thieves. Stat. 5 Ed. 3, c. 14; 7 Rich. 2, c. 5.

DRAW-NET (*Sport.*) a net for catching the larger sort of birds.

DRAWING (*Paint.*) is the art of representing objects upon a plane surface by means of lines, shades, and shadows, formed either with a pen or a pencil. It is also taken for the representation so made, as drawings in India-Ink, pencil-drawings, &c.

DRAWING (*Sport.*) is beating the bushes, &c. after a fox. "*Drawing* amiss" is when the hounds hit the scent of their chase contrary, i. e. up the wind instead of down. "*Drawing* in the slot" is when the hounds, having touched the scent, draw till they hit on the same again.

DRAWN-BATTLE (*Mil.*) a battle in which both parties claim the victory, or retire upon equal terms as before.

DRAY (*Mech.*) a sort of low cart without sides, on which brewers carry their casks of beer.

DRAY (*Sport.*) a name for squirrels' nests on the tops of trees.

DREDGE (*Com.*) in French *drague pour prendre des huitres*, a kind of drag used with a long rope to catch oysters.

DREDGEMEN (*Com.*) or *Dredgers*, those who fish for oysters.

DREDGING (*Com.*) a process of removing or dragging the mud in the beds of rivers, &c. in order to catch oysters.

DREIT-DREIT (*Law*) a double right, i. e. of possession and dominion.

TO DRENCH (*Vet.*) to give a medicinal drink to a horse, cow, &c.

DRENCHES (*Law*) or *drenges*, a name for such tenants as, being put out of their estates at the conquest, were afterwards restored by King William, because they were not against him in person, or by their counsels. *Mon. Angl.* tom. ii. fol. 298.

DRENGAGE (*Law*) the tenure by which the drenches held their lands.

DREPANIS (*Orn.*) δρεπανίς, a sea-swallow. *Aristot. Hist. Anim.* l. 1, c. 2; *Plin.* l. 11, c. 47.

TO DRESS *a line* (*Mil.*) to arrange any given number of men so as to stand perfectly correct with regard to the several points of alignment that have been taken up; whence the soldiers are said to "*Dress* by one another" in ranks in order to form a continuity of line. "To *Dress* a battalion," to bring all its relative parts in a line with the object or point, towards which it was directed to move. And "*Dress*," as a word of command, is equivalent to halt when the men arrive at a particular point of the alignment.

TO DRESS *a ship* (*Mar.*) to ornament her with a variety of colours, as ensigns, flags, pendants, &c.

TO DRESS *a Chase* (*Print.*) or *a Form*, to fit the pages and the chase, or form, of the matter that has been composed.

DRESSED (*Mason.*) the preparation of a stone, for the mason's work, by the mallet and chisel.

DRESSERS (*Mil.*) those men who take up direct or relative points, by which a corps is enabled to preserve a regular continuity of front.

DRESSING (*Man.*) the cleaning and trimming which a horse undergoes by means of brushes, curry-combs, cloths, &c.

DRESSING *letters* (*Mech.*) a process among letter founders, by which they fit the letters that have been cast for the immediate use of the compositor, by scraping, bearding, &c.

DRESSING (*Husband.*) a term applied to the cleaning of hemp, flax, &c. so as to prepare it for spinning.

DRESSINGS (*Archit.*) all kinds of mouldings projecting beyond the naked wall.

DRIFT (*Mar.*) signifies generally any thing that floats upon the water; a boat is said to drift, or to go a-drift, when it hath nobody in it to row or steer it.—*Drift-sail*, a sail used only under water, which is veered out right a-head upon the sea in a storm to keep the head of the ship right upon the sea.—*Drift-way*, or *Drift*, is the course which a ship makes when she is driven by a storm.—*Drift of a current*, its angle and velocity.

Drift also signifies the difference between the size of a bolt and the hole into which it is to be driven. *Drifts*, in the sheer-draught, are those pieces where the rails are cut off.

DRIFT *of a Forest* (*Law*) a view or examination of the cattle that are in a forest in order to know whether it be surcharged or not, or whether the beasts be commonable, &c. Stat. 32 Hen. 8, c. 13.

DRIFT (*Archit.*) the force which an arch exerts from the pressure of the stones.

DRIFT (*Min.*) a passage cut out under the earth betwixt shaft and shaft, or turn and turn.

DRILL (*Mech.*) a small instrument for boring holes which cannot be made conveniently with punches.

TO DRILL (*Mil.*) to teach young recruits the first principles of military movements; whence "To be sent to *Drill*," to be placed under the command of the Drill-officer. "Knapsack-Drill," a sort of punishment for minor offences, which consists in marching soldiers round the barrack-yard, &c. for a certain time, with 6 or 12 lb. shot tied to their knapsacks.

DRILLING (*Mech.*) boring with the drill.

DRILLING (*Husband.*) the process of sewing with a machine, called a *drilling machine*, by which the seed is disposed in regular order, and at an equal depth of earth.

DRIMYPHAGIA (*Med.*) from δριμύς, acrid, and φάγω, to eat; the eating of acrid substances.

DRINK (*Vet.*) a liquid form of medicine occasionally administered to horses, or other cattle.

DRINKLEAN (*Archæol.*) a certain quantity of drink provided by tenants for the lord and his steward.

DRIP (*Archit.*) the most advanced part of the cornice, otherwise called the *larmier*, or *eaves*.

DRIPPING (*Falc.*) a term for a hawk that mutes directly downwards in several drops.

TO DRIVE (*Mar.*) is said of a ship when she cannot be held fast by the anchor.

TO DRIVE (*Print.*) a term used frequently among printers and letter founders. A compositor is said to *drive out* when he sets wide; the matter in the chace is said to *drive out* when, by the addition of fresh matter, it is obliged to be moved forwards into the next page; a letter *drives out* when it is cast too thick in the shank, &c.

DRIVER (*Mech.*) vide *Pile-Driver*.

DRIVER (*Mar.*) in French *tappe-cul*, a large sail occasionally set upon the mizen-yard or gaff; also the foremast spur in the bulge-ways.—*Driver-Boom*, the boom on which the driver is extended.

DRI'VERS (*Mil.*) pieces of bone or wood made in the shape of a flint.

DRO'FDENE (*Archæol.*) a thicket.

DRO'FLAND (*Law*) anciently a quit-rent, or yearly payment, made, by some tenants, to the King, or their landlords, for the liberty of driving their cattle through the manor to fairs and markets.

DROIT (*Law*) the highest writ of all other real writs whatsoever, and that which has the greatest respect, and the most assured and final judgment, therefore it is called a *Writ of Right*, and in the old books *Droit*. Co. Lit. 158.—*Droit de entrie*, Right of Entry, or a writ for one seised of land in fee, against the one who has disseised him of it.

DRO'MA (*Med.*) a plaster so called. *Myrep.* sect. 10, c. 26.

DRO'MEDARY (*Zool.*) a sort of camel, having two bunches on the back, which is the *Camelus Bactrianus* of Linnæus; and differs from the Arabian Camel principally in being larger.

DROMO (*Ant.*) δρόμων, a sort of caravel or swift bark that scoured the seas. It is called by Sidonius *navis cursoria*. *Sidon.* l. 1, ep. 5; *Cassiodor. Var.* l. 4, c. 15; *Isid.* l. 19, c. 1.

DROMONA'RII (*Ant.*) the rowers of the dromones.

DRONE (*Ent.*) a large kind of bee or wasp which is without a sting. It is the male of this tribe of insects which takes no part in the labours of the hive or nest, and is therefore killed or expelled by the labourers on the approach of winter.

DROO'PING (*Bot.*) *cernuus*, having the top or end pointing to the ground; an epithet for the peduncle or flower, as in *Bidens cernua*.

DROP (*Archit.*) an ornament in pillars of the Doric Order, representing drops or little bells under the triglyphs.

DRO'P-WORT (*Bot.*) the *Spiræa filipendula* of Linnæus, a perennial; so called because it consists of oval tubes, or solid lumps, hanging from the main body by threads.

To DROP (*Mar.*) a term used in several sea-phrases, as to *drop astern*, to denote the retrograde motion of a ship; to *drop anchor*, i. e. to anchor; the sail *drops* so many yards, i. e. it is so many yards long.

DRO'PAX (*Med.*) *Dropacismus*, a stimulant plaster of pitch, wax, &c. for taking off hair.

DRO'PPING (*Vet.*) a name given to that disease in a cow, which is analogous to the puerperal fever in women.

DROPS (*Med.*) any liquid medicine which is taken by the measure of drops.

DRO'PSY (*Med.*) a collection of serous fluid in the cellular membrane, viscera, and the circumscribed cavities of the body; as the—*Dropsy* of the Belly, [vide *Ascites*]—*Dropsy* of the Brain, [vide *Hydrocephalus*]—*Dropsy* of the Cellular Membrane, [vide *Anasarca*]—*Dropsy* of the Chest, [vide *Hydrothorax*]—*Dropsy* of the Testicle, [vide *Hydrocele*]

DRO'P-WORT (*Bot.*) vide *Drop*.

DROSATUM (*Med.*) vide *Rosatum*.

DRO'SERA (*Bot.*) a genus of plants, Class 5 *Pentandria*, Order 5 *Pentagynia*.
Generic Character. CAL. *perianth* one-leaved.—COR. *petals* five.—STAM. *filaments* five; *anthers* small.—PIST. *germ* superior; *styles* five; *stigmas* simple.—PER. *capsule* ovate; *seeds* many.
Species. The species are natives of the Cape of Good Hope, as the—*Drosera rotundifolia*, Rorella, seu Rossolis, Round-leaved Sun Dew, a perennial.—*Drosera longifolia*, seu Salsirora, Long-leaved Sun-Dew, &c.

DRO'SERON (*Med.*) an ointment so called. *Myrep.* sect. 3, c. 93.

DROSO'MELI (*Nat.*) δροσόμελι, from δρόσος, dew, and μέλι, honey; manna.

DRO'VED (*Mason.*) a term in Scotland for chiselled, in application to a stone.

DRO'VERS (*Com.*) men who are employed to drive cattle for hire or for sale.

DRUGGE'RIA (*Archæol.*) a druggist's shop.

DRU'GGET (*Com.*) a kind of woollen stuff.

DRUGS (*Med.*) all kinds of simples, which are for the most part dry, and form a part of medicinal compositions.

DRU'IDS (*Archæol.*) probably from the Greek δρῦς, an oak; a sort of priests among the ancient Gauls and Britons; so called because they celebrated their rites under the oak. *Cæs. de Bell. Gall.* l. 6, c. 13; *Strab.* l. 4; *Plin.* l. 30, c. 1; *Tacit. Agric.* c. 11; *Lamprid. in Sever.* c. 60; *Vopis. in Aurel.* c. 1, &c.

DRUM (*Anat.*) *tympanum*; a membrane of the cavity of the ear.

DRUM (*Mil.*) a well known musical instrument, which is much used in the army, to give notice to the troops of what they are to do, according to the different beats. [vide *Beat*]—*Kettle-drums*, a sort of basin-formed drums, made of brass or copper, which are used by the cavalry.—The *Drum-Major*, he who has the command over the other drummers.—*Drum-Major-General*, an officer formerly in the King's household, without whose licence no one, except the King's troops, could beat a drum.

DRU'NGUS (*Ant.*) a body of troops among the Romans, consisting of one thousand and upwards. *Vopisc. in Prob.* c. 19; *Veget.* l. 3, c. 19.

DRUPÆ (*Ant.*) δρυπεπεῖς, olives ready to fall off from excessive ripeness, from πίπτειν, to fall, and δρῦς, an oak, or any tree in general. *Poll. Onom.* l. 6, c. 8; *Plin.* l. 15, c. 1; *Gal. de Alim. Fac.* l. 2, c. 27; *Athen.* l. 2, p. 56; *Hesychius*.

DRUPA (*Bot.*) a Drupe, i. e. a pulpy pericarp or fruit, without valves, containing a nut or stone with a kernel. It is usually a moist succulent fruit like the plum; but sometimes dry like the almond.

DRUPA'CEÆ (*Bot.*) the thirty-eighth order in Linnæus' Fragments of a Natural Method.

DR'Y Blow (*Med.*) a blow that neither wounds nor sheds blood.—*Dry-Belly-Ache*, the same as the *Colic*.

DRY Rent (*Law*) a rent reserved without clause of distress.—*Dry Multures*, quantities of corn, in the Scotch law, paid to a mill, whether the payers grind or not.

DRY Rot (*Archit.*) a disease incident to timber in floorings, joists, wainscot, &c. which is a sort of putrefaction caused by moisture.

DRYA'NDRA (*Bot.*) a genus of plants, Class 16 *Dioecia*, Order 4 *Monodelphia*.
Generic Character. CAL. *perianth* two-leaved.—COR. *petals* oblong.—STAM. *filaments* nine; *anthers* minute.—PER. tricoccous; *seeds* oblong.
Species. The single species is the—*Dryas cordata*, Oil-Tree.

DRYAS (*Bot.*) a genus of plants, Class 12 *Icosandria*, Order 5 *Polygynia*.
Generic Character. CAL. *perianth* one-leaved.—COR. *petals* eight.—STAM. *filaments* numerous; *anthers* small.—PIST. *germs* many; *styles* capillary; *stigmas* simple.—PER. none; *seeds* many.
Species. The two species are perennials, as the—*Dryas anemoides*, anemone, seu *Carophyllata*.—*Dryas octopetala*, seu *Teucruim*.

DRYAS is also the *Geum potentilloides*.

DRYI'TES (*Min.*) a precious stone found at the roots of trees, from δρῦς, an oak, or tree in general. *Plin.* l. 37, c. 11.

DRYO'PETIS (*Zool.*) a small green frog which lies in thickets.
DRYOPHO'NON (*Bot.*) a herb like oak-fern. *Plin.* l. 27, c. 9.
DRY'OPHYTE (*Zool.*) a kind of frog.
DRYO'PTERIS (*Bot.*) vide *Dryophonon*.
DRYOPTERIS, *in the Linnean system*, the *Polypodium fragrans*.
DRY'OS (*Bot.*) a kind of misletoe.
DRY'PA (*Bot.*) vide *Drupa*.
DRYPS (*Bot.*) a genus of plants, Class 5 *Pentandria*, Order 3 *Trigynia*.
Generic Character. CAL. perianth one-leaved.—COR. petals five.—STAM. filaments five; anthers oblong.—PIST. germ obovate; styles three; stigma simple.—PER. capsule roundish; seeds single.
Species. The single species is a biennial, as the—*Drypis spinosa*, seu *Carduus*, native of Barbary.
DRYPIS is also the *Cucubalus stellatus*.
DU'AL (*Gram.*) dualis, from *duo*, two; the name of a number which signifies only two persons or things, of which the Greek language furnishes examples.
DUAL (*Mil.*) a weapon used by the New-Hollanders.
DUA'RIUM (*Law*) a wife's jointure. [vide *Dower*]
TO DUB (*Carpent.*) to reduce a piece of timber by means of the adze.
TO DUB *a knight* (*Her.*) probably from the Saxon buban, to gird; to confer the honour of knighthood on any one.
DU'BBING *of a cock* (*Vet.*) the cutting off a cock's comb and wattles.
DU'BEL-CO-LEPH (*Med.*) a composition of coral and amber.
DU'BELECH (*Med.*) the cavity of an imposthume.
DUBHE (*Astron.*) a bright star of the second magnitude in the back of Ursa Major. Right Ascension, for 1812, 162° 36′ 25″; Annual variation in Right Ascension 57″; Declination 62° 45′ 57″ N.; annual variation in the same 19″.
DUBLE'TUS (*Med.*) an incysted tumour.
DU'CAL Coronet (*Her.*) a circle of gold, with eight strawberry or parsley leaves, of equal height, above the rim. None of inferior rank can have flowers raised above the circle.
DUCAL *Mantle* (*Ent.*) a testaceous animal, the *Ostrea Pallium* of Linnæus.
DUCAPE (*Com.*) a sort of silk formerly used for women's garments.
DU'CAT (*Com.*) probably so called because it was coined in the territories of a duke; a foreign coin of different values, according to the places where current. The Dutch ducats, which are reckoned the purest gold, are about 9s. 6d. sterling.
DUCATOO'N (*Com.*) a silver coin in Holland worth about 5s. 6d.
DUCENA'RIUS (*Ant.*) a captain of two hundred. *Veget.* l. 2, c. 8.
DU'CES *tecum* (*Law*) i. e. bring with thee; a writ commanding a person to appear on a certain day in the Court of Chancery, and to bring with him some writings, evidences, or other things, which the court would view.
DUCK (*Orn.*) a well-known water fowl, the different species of which are classed under the *Anas* of Linnæus. [vide *Anas*]
DUCK (*Com.*) or *Russia Duck*, a name for the best sort of canvas.
DUCK *up* (*Mar.*) a term used by the steersman, signifying to haul up, as "*Duck up the clew lines of those sails.*"
DU'CK-WEED (*Bot.*) the *Lemna* of Linnæus, an annual, growing in ditches and stagnant waters; so called because it is freely eaten by ducks.
DU'CKING Stool (*Law*) vide *Cucking Stool.*

DU'CK'S *foot* (*Bot.*) the *Pedophyllum pellatum* of Linnæus.
—*Duck's Meat,* another name for the *Duck-Weed.*—*Duck-Weed.* [vide *Duck*]
DUCK *up* (*Mar.*) vide *Duck.*
DUCTA'RIUS *funis* (*Ant.*) the rope that runs in a pulley. *Vitruv.* l. 10, c. 3.
DUCTI'LITY (*Metal.*) the property which bodies possess of yielding to any pressure by which their parts are expanded. This property is particularly observable in metals in which it is found in different degrees. [vide *Chemistry*]
DU'CTUS *adiposi* (*Anat.*) certain bladders of fat about the skin.—*Ductus alimentalis,* the alimentary duct, consisting of the throat, stomach, and bowels.—*Ductus arteriosus,* a duct found in the fœtus, or in very young children, betwixt the pulmonary artery and the aorta, which is closed in adults.—*Ductus ad Nasum,* vide *Canalis nasalis.*—*Ductus auris palatinus,* the Eustachian tube.—*Ductus biliaris,* vide *Choledochus ductus.*—*Ductus hepaticus,* vide *Hepatic Duct.*—*Ductus lachrymalis,* vide *Lachrymal ducts.*—*Ductus lactiferi,* the excretory ducts of the glandular substance composing the female breast.—*Ductus pancreaticus,* a little channel arising from the *pancreas,* and inserted into the Duodenum.—*Ductus salivales,* the excretory duct of the salival glands.—*Ductus Stenonis,* the duct so called after its discoverer Steno, arises from the excretory ducts of the parotid gland.—*Ductus thoracicus,* the thoracic duct.—*Ductus venalis,* a channel that runs off from the *vena cava,* when it passes the liver in the fœtus.—*Ductus umbilicalis,* the naval passage of a child in the womb.—*Ductus urinarius,* the urinary passage; the same as the Ureter.
DU'DAIM (*Bot.*) the *Cucumis dudaim* of Linnæus.
DUE'LLA (*Ant.*) the third part of an ounce, containing eight scruples, or two drams and two scruples. *Bud. de Ass.* p. 10.
DU'EL (*Law*) Duellum, originally signified a combat between two persons for the trial of the truth. It now signifies a battle between two persons upon a quarrel precedent; in the which if death ensue, both the principal and seconds are guilty of murder. *H. P.* c. 47.
DUES, *ecclesiastical* (*Law*) dues or monies due to the clergy, under the names of offerings, oblations, &c. which are cognizable in the spiritual court.
DUETT (*Mus.*) in Italian *duetto,* a name for little songs or airs in two parts.
DUGLA'SSIA (*Bot.*) another name for the *Douglassia* of Linnæus.
DUKE (*Polit.*) from *dux,* is the title of many princes in different parts of Europe, who possess sovereign authority within their principality.
DUKE (*Her.*) the highest title of honour in England next to the Prince of Wales. He is created by patent, girded with a sword, a mantle of state, a cap and coronet of gold on his head [vide *Ducal*], and a rod of gold in his hand. [vide *Heraldry*]
DUKI'GI-BACHI (*Mil.*) the second officer of the Turkish artillery.
DULCACI'DIUM (*Med.*) a medicine prepared of acid and sweet ingredients.
DULCAMA'RA (*Bot.*) the *Solanum dulcamara* of Linnæus.
TO DU'LCIFY (*Chem.*) to wash the salt off from any mixed body which was calcined with it.
DU'LCIMER (*Mus.*) a musical instrument.
DU'LCINISTS (*Ecc.*) a sect of heretics; so called from one Dulcin, their ringleader, who asserted that the Father having reigned from the beginning of the world until the coming of the son; then the reign of the latter began, and lasted till the year 1300, when that of the Holy Ghost began. *Genabrard. in Clemen. V.; Prateol. de Doct. Omn.; Sander. de Hæres.* c. 159; *Brov. Hist. Eccles. Ann.* 1330; *Spond. Annal. Ann.* 1307.

2

DULCIS RA'DIX (*Bot.*) the *Glycyrrhiza echinata* of Linnæus.

DU'LEDGE (*Mech.*) a peg of wood which joins the ends of six felloes that form the round of a wheel of a gun carriage.

DULECH (*Med.*) a sort of tartar or spongy stone, according to Paracelsus, which, generated in the body, causes great pain. *Parac. de Tartar.*

DU'LEST (*Bot.*) a sort of Alga. *Raii Hist. Plant.*

DULL (*Mar.*) an epithet for a horse that has white spots round the eye, &c.

DULO'CRACY (*Polit.*) from δοῦλος, a slave, and κρατία, government; a government in which slaves and base people possess the power.

DU'M *fuit intra ætatem* (*Law*) a writ to recover lands that had been sold during a minority. *F. N. B.* 477; *New. Nat. Brev.* 426.—*Dum non fuit compos mentis*, a writ to recover lands made over by one not of sound mind. *F. N. B.* 202; *New. Nat. Brev.* 449.

DU'MB-BELLS (*Mil.*) weights which are used in drilling a soldier, who holds one in each hand, which he swings backwards and forwards.

DUMO'SÆ (*Bot.*) from *dumus*, a bush; the nineteenth order in Linnæus' Fragments, and the forty-third of the Natural Orders. *Linn. Phil. Bot.*

DUN (*Nat.*) a colour something like brown.

DUN (*Archæol.*) a down.

DU'NA (*Archæol.*) a bank of earth cast on the side of a ditch.

DU'N-BIRD (*Orn.*) another name for the Pochard-Duck, or the *Anas ferina* of Linnæus.—*Dun-diver*, the female of the Goosander, the *Mergus Castor* of Linnæus.

DU'NG-MEERS (*Husband.*) pits where dung, weeds, &c. are mixed, to lie and rot together.

DUNGEON (*Polit.*) from *donjon;* the darkest, closest, and most secluded part of a prison.

DU'NNAGE (*Mar.*) in French *fardage*, a quantity of faggots, boughs, &c. laid at the bottom of the hold, to keep the goods dry in a leaky vessel.

DU'O (*Med.*) a name for some compositions, consisting of two ingredients.

DUODE'CIMALS (*Arith.*) a kind of multiplication, otherwise called *Cross Multiplication*, which is used by artificers.

DUODE'CIMO (*Print.*) in the twelfth, or in twelves; a name for a particular sized book, each leaf of which is the twelfth part of a sheet.

DUODE'NA (*Law*) a jury of twelve men anciently so called. *Walsing.* 256.—*Duodena manu*, twelve witnesses to purge a criminal of an offence.

DUODENA'LIS *arteria* (*Anat.*) an artery belonging to the duodenum.

DUODE'NUM (*Anat.*) the first of the intestines, in length about 12 fingers' breadth.

DUPLA'RES (*Ant.*) or *Duplicarii*, soldiers who received double pay. *Varr. de Lat. Ling.* l. 4, c. 16; *Liv.* l. 2, c. 59; *Poll. Onom.* l. 4, c. 23; *Veget.* l. 2, c. 7.

DU'PLE (*Math.*) or *double Ratio*, that in which the antecedent is double the consequent, or where the exponent of the ratio is 2; thus 6 to 3 is in a duple ratio. The *subduple Ratio* is that in which the consequent is the double of the antecedent, or in which the exponent of the ratio is $\frac{1}{2}$, as 3 to 6, which is in a subduple ratio.

DUPLEX (*Bot.*) the same as compound, when applied to the parts of plants.

DUPLICA'RII (*Ant.*) vide *Duplares*.

DU'PLICATE (*Lit.*) any manuscript copied after another, i. e. the same matter written a second time; it is particularly applied to deeds, and other legal instruments.

DUPLICATE *ratio* (*Geom.*) the product of a ratio multiplied into itself, i. e. the square of a ratio, or the ratio of the squares of two quantities; thus the duplicate ratio of *a* to *b* is the ratio of a^2 to b^2, or of the square of *a* to the square of *b*. And in a series of geometrical proportionals the first term to the third is said to be in a duplicate ratio of the first to the second, or as the square of the first to the square of the second; thus in the geometricals 2, 4, 8, 16, the ratio of 2 to 8 is duplicate of that of 2 to 4, or as the square of 2 to the square of 4; wherefore duplicate ratio is the proportion of squares, as the triplicate ratio is the proportion of cubes, &c.

DUPLICA'TIO (*Law*) is in the Civil Law what the rejoinder is in the Common Law.

DUPLICA'TION (*Rhet.*) the same as *Anadiplosis*.

DUPLICATION (*Arith.*) the multiplying any number by two.—*Duplication of the cube* is when the side of the cube is found which shall be the double of the cube given.

DU'PLICATURE (*Anat.*) the doubling of any membranes when they go off to some distance and return again.

DUPLICA'TUS (*Bot.*) is used frequently in composition, in the sense of doubly, as *duplicato,—crenatum,—pinnatum,—serratum,—ternatum,* &c.

DUPLI'CITY *in pleading* (*Law*) offering a double plea, which ought to be avoided.

DUPO'NDIUM (*Ant.*) a weight equal to four drams. *Gal. de Pond.*

DURA MA'TER (*Anat.*) a thick and somewhat opake membrane which enwraps the brain: it is called *dura* on account of its hardness, when compared with the *Pia mater;* and it is called *mater* because it is supposed to be the mother of all other membranes.

DURA'NTE (*Law*) a term equivalent to during, which is used in some law phrases, as *Durante absentia*, during absence; *Durante minore ætate*, during minority.

DURA'NTIA (*Bot.*) a genus of plants, Class 5 *Pentandria*, Order 3 *Trigynia*.
Generic Character. CAL. *perianth* one-leaved.—COR. *petals* five.—STAM. *filaments* four; *anthers* roundish.—PIST. *germ* inferior; *style* filiform; *stigma* thickish.—PER. *berry* roundish; *seeds* kernels, four.
Species. The species are shrubs, as the—*Durantia Plumieri*, Smooth Durantia, seu *Castorea repens*, native of South America.—*Durantia Ellisia*, *Ellisia*, seu *Jasminum*, native of Jamaica.

DURA'TE (*Mus.*) an epithet for a hard sound, which naturally offends the ear.

DURA'TION (*Met.*) the continuance of the existence of things abstractedly considered, which is the same as *absolute time*.

DURATION *of an eclipse* (*Astron.*) the time that the sun or moon, or any part of them, remains eclipsed or darkened.

DU'RDEN (*Archæol.*) a coppice or thicket in a valley.

DU'RESS (*Law*) an unjust imprisonment, in which a person is restrained of his liberty contrary to law. 2 *Inst.* 483.

DU'RIO (*Bot.*) a large tree growing in Malabar, which bears a fruit as big as a melon. *Raii Hist. Plant.* A genus of plants, Class 18 *Polydelphia*, Order 4 *Polyandria*.
Generic Character. CAL. *perianth* one-leaved.—COR. *petals* five.—STAM. *filaments* subulate; *anthers* twisted.—PIST. *germ* roundish; *style* bristle form.—PER. *pome* roundish; *seeds* large.
Species. The single species is a tree, as the—*Durio zibethinus*, native of the East Indies.

DURO'IA (*Bot.*) a genus of plants, so called from Phil. Du Roi, Class 6 *Hexandria*, Order 1 *Monogynia*.
Generic Character. CAL. *perianth* one-leaved.—COR. monopetalous.—STAM. *filaments* none; *anthers* six.—PIST. *germ* inferior; *style* filiform; *stigmas* two.—PER. *pome* globular; *seeds* many.
Species. The single species is a tree, as the—*Duroia Ercopila*, native of Surinam.

DU'RSLEY (*Archæol.*) an old word for dry blows, or blows without wounding or bloodshed.

DYS

DUSTY *foot* (*Com.*) a name for a foreign trader or pedlar, or one who has no settled habitation.

DU'TCHY (*Polit.*) a seignory or lordship established in Great Britain by the King under that title, with several privileges, honours, &c.

DUTCHY *court* (*Law*) a court wherein all matters belonging to the Dutchy of Lancaster are decided by the decree of the Chancellor of that court.

DU'TY (*Com.*) that which is paid by way of custom or due on merchandise in general.

DUTY (*Mil.*) that which enters into the functions of a soldier to do.

DUU'MVIRI (*Ant.*) extraordinary officers in the Roman republic, so called from their number *duo*, two; they were chosen for different purposes, as, *Duumviri Perduellonis judicandi causa*; *Duumviri navales*; *Duumviri ad ædem Junoni Monetæ faciundam*, &c. *Liv.* l. 1, c. 26; l. 9, c. 30; l. 7, c. 28, &c.

DUUMVIRI were also magistrates in the colonies, the same as the consuls at Rome: they were sometimes chosen every five years, with censorial power, when they were called *Quinquennales*; and when chosen a second time, *Quinquennales iterum*, as in the annexed figure, which represents the reverse of a medal struck by one of the family of the Æbutii, bearing the inscription, *Publio* AEBUTIO *Caio* JULIO HERA*Clide* II VIR*is* QUI*nquennalibus* ITER*um*.

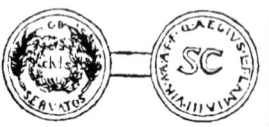

DWALE (*Bot.*) the *Atropa Belladonna* of Linnæus.

DWARF (*Bot.*) an epithet for any plants that are below the ordinary size of those of the same genus.

DYE (*Sport.*) or *Die*, a small cube of bone or ivory with six faces, marked from 1 to 6.

DYE (*Archit.*) 1. The middle of the pedestal, or that part which lies between the base and the cornice, frequently made in the form of a cube, or dye. 2. A stone of a cubical form, placed under the feet of a statue, and under its pedestal, to raise it the higher.

DYERS, *Company of* (*Her.*) was incorporated in the reign of Henry VI. Their arms are, as in the annexed figure, "*Sable* a chevron engrailed, three madder bags *argent*, banded and corded *or*."

DYER's *weed* (*Bot.*) vide Dier's Weed.

DY'KE-REED (*Law*) or *Dyke Reeve*, an officer that hath the care and oversight of the dykes and drains in fenny countries: he is mentioned in statute 16. 17 *Car.* 2, c. 11.

DYNA'MICS (*Mech.*) the science of moving powers, particularly of the motion of bodies that mutually act on one another.

DY'NAMIS (*Med.*) δύναμις, force, or power, is defined by Galen an efficient cause or substance.

DYNA'STES (*Ant.*) δυνάστης, a governor or ruler, next to a tetrarch of any place. *Cic. Phil.* 2, c. 12; *Suet. in Tib.* c. 26; *Athen.* l. 4, p. 174.

DY'NASTY (*Chron.*) δυναστεία, from δυνάστης, a ruler; a series of princes who have reigned successively in any particular line or family, especially applied to the Egyptian kings.

DYNO'METER (*Mech.*) an instrument for measuring the power of animal bodies.

DYO'TA (*Chem.*) a circulating vessel with two ears, resembling in shape a man standing with his arms a kembo.

DYSÆSTHE'SIA (*Med.*) δυσαισθησία, from δυς, difficult, and αίσθάνομαι to feel; an impaired feeling.

DYSÆSTHESIA, in *Cullen's system*, is an order of diseases, in the Class *Locales*.

DYSANAGO'GOS (*Med.*) from δυς and ἀνάγω, to remove; an epithet for viscous matter, which it is difficult to expectorate.

DYSCATAPO'TIA (*Med.*) from δυς and καταπίνω, to swallow; a difficulty of swallowing, which particularly attends canine madness.

DYSCINE'SIA (*Med.*) from δυς, difficult, and κινέω, to move; imperfect motion.

DYSCINE'SIÆ, an order of diseases in *Cullen's Nosology*, under the Class *Locales*.

DYSCRASIA (*Med.*) δυσκρασία, from δυς, difficult, and κεράννυμι to mix; intemperance; an undue mixture of the fluids that is inconsistent with health.

DY'SCRITOS (*Med.*) δυσκριτος, from δυς, difficult, and κρίσις, crisis; difficult to be brought to a crisis, or brought to an imperfect crisis.

DY'SECOIA (*Med.*) δυσηκοία, from δυς, difficult, and ἀκούω, to hear; difficulty of hearing.

DYSE'LCES (*Med.*) δυσέλκης, from δυς, difficult, and ἕλκος, an ulcer; an epithet for such ulcers as are difficult to cure.

DYSEME'TUS (*Med.*) from δυς, difficult, and ἐμέω, to vomit; an epithet for a person who is with difficulty made to vomit.

DYSENTE'RIA (*Med.*) δυσεντερία, from δυς, difficult, and ἔντερα, the intestines; Dysentery, a difficulty or disturbance in the intestines, which impedes their functions, and is attended with exulceration. *Hippocrat. περὶ παθ. Aret. de Caus. et Sign. Morb. diuturn.* l. 2, c. 9; *Cels.* l. 4, c. 15; *Cæl. Aurel. de Morb. Chronic.* l. 4, c. 6; *Gal. Def. Med. Foes.*

DYSENTERIA, in *Cullen's Nosology*, is a genus of diseases, Class *Pyrexiæ*, Order *Profluvia*.

DYSEPULO'TOS (*Med.*) δυσεπούλωτος, from δυς, difficult, and οὐλή, a scar; an epithet for an ulcer which is difficult to be healed.

DYSHÆMO'RRHOIS (*Med.*) from δυς, difficult, and αἱμορροΐς, the bloody piles; suppression of the bleeding piles.

DYSHE'LCES (*Med.*) vide *Duselces*.

DYSIA'TOS (*Med.*) δυσίατος, from δυς, difficult, and ἰάομαι, to cure; an epithet for a disorder that is difficult to be cured.

DYSMENORRHŒ'A (*Med.*) from δυς and μηνορροία, the menses; a difficult or painful menstruation.

DYSO'DES (*Med.*) δυσώδης, from δυς, bad, and ὄζω, to smell; an epithet signifying fetid. It is also applied by Galen and Paulus Ægineta to a particular malagma. *Hippoc. Prorrhet.* l. 1; *Gal. de Com. Med. per Gen.* l. 7, c. 12; *Æginet.* l. 7, c. 18.

DYSO'PIA (*Med.*) from δυς, difficult, and ὤψ, an eye, difficulty of sight; a genus of diseases in *Cullen's Nosology*, Class *Locales*, Order *Dysæsthenæ*.

DYSORE'XIA (*Med.*) δυσορεξία, from δυς, bad, and ὄρεξις, appetite; a bad or depraved appetite.

DYSOREXIÆ, an order of diseases in *Cullen's Nosology*, Class *Locales*.

DYSPE'PSIA (*Med.*) δυσπεψία, from δυς, difficult, and πέττω, to concoct; indigestion.

DYSPEPSIA is a genus of diseases in *Cullen's Nosology*, Class *Neuroses*, Order *Adynamiæ*.

DYSPERMATI'SMOS (*Med.*) from δυς, difficult, and σπέρμα, semen; a difficult emission of the semen; a genus of diseases in *Cullen's Nosology*, Class *Locales*, Order *Epicheses*.

DYSPHA'GIA (*Med.*) from δυς, difficult, and φάγω, to eat; a difficulty of deglutition.

DYSPHO'NIA (*Med.*) from δυς, difficult, and φωνή, the voice; a difficulty of speech.

DYSPNŒ'A (*Med.*) δύσπνοια, from δυς, difficult, and πνέω, to breathe; difficult respiration. *Hippocrat.* l. 3, aph. 26; *Gal. Com. in Hippocrat. et Def. Med.*

DYSPNŒA is a genus of diseases in *Cullen's Nosology*, Class *Neuroses*, Order *Spasmi*.

DY'SPNOON (*Med.*) vide *Dyspnœa*.

DYSRACHI'TIS (*Med.*) δυσραχίτις a plaister. *Gal. de Com. Med. per Gen.* l. 5, c. 3.

DYSTHERAPE'NTOS (*Med.*) δυσθεράπευτος, from δυς and θεραπεύω, to heal; difficult to heal.

1

DYSTO'CIHA (*Med.*) from δυς, difficult, and τικτω, to bring forth; difficult labour, or child-birth.
DYSTŒ'CHIASIS (*Med.*) δυστοιχιασις, from δυς, difficult, and στιχος, order; an irregular disposition of the hairs in the eyelids.
DYSU'RIA (*Med.*) δυσυρια, from δυς, difficult or painful, and υρον, urine; a painful discharge of urine, by reason of the sharpness of the water, and the inflammation or exulceration of the neck of the bladder.
DYSURIA is a genus of diseases in *Cullen's Nosology*, Class *Locales*, Order *Epischeses*.
DYTI'SCUS (*Ent.*) a genus of insects of the *coleopterous* order, having setaceous *antennæ*, six feelers, and the hind legs *natatorii*, or formed for swimming.

E.

E. (*Ant.*) as an abbreviation stands for *est*, &c. [vide *Abbreviations*] As a numeral stood for 250.
E. (*Law*) vide *Abbreviations*.
E. (*Her.*) the Fess Point in an escutcheon.
E. (*Mus.*) a name for particular notes in the gamut, as E *flat*, the minor seventh of F, and the second flat introduced in modulating by fourths from the natural diatonic mode.
E. (*Log.*) stands for propositions which are universal negatives. [vide *Logic*]
E. G. (*Abb.*) *Exempli gratiâ*, i. e. for example.
EA'GLE (*Orn.*) a well-known bird of prey, which has been described under the ancient name of *aquila*. [vide *Aquila*] Linnæus has classed this bird under the genus *Falco*. [vide *Falco*]
EAGLE (*Her.*) as a bearing is reckoned as honourable among the birds as the lion is among the beasts. It is commonly represented displayed as in the annexed example. "He beareth *per fesse* in chief *or*, an eagle displayed, *sable*, beaked and legged, *gules*, charged on the breast with two chevronels *argent*; in base paly of six, erminois and azure." These are the arms of the A'Court family.—*White Eagle*, a Polish order of knighthood, instituted in 1325 by Uladislaus V. The knights of this order were distinguished by a gold chain with a silver eagle crowned. —*Black Eagle*, a similar order instituted in 1701 by the King of Prussia on his being crowned in 1701. The knights of this order wore a black eagle suspended from an orange-coloured ribbon.
EAGLE (*Astron.*) a northern constellation.
EA'GLES (*Com.*) a base coin formerly current in Ireland.
EAGLE-STONE (*Nat.*) vide *Ætites*.
EA'GLET (*Her.*) a young eagle; the name by which the eagle is blazoned when there is more than one in the escutcheon.
EALDERMAN (*Archæol.*) vide *Alderman*.
EALE (*Zool.*) a beast in India the size of a horse with moveable horns. *Plin.* l. 8, c. 21.
EALHO'RDA (*Law*) the privilege of selling ale and beer.
EAR (*Anat.*) *auris*, the organ of hearing, is divided into external and internal.—The *External ear*, otherwise called *Auricula*, comprehends all that lies without the external orifice of the *meatus auditorius*; and the *Internal* all that within the cavity of the *Os Temporis*.

> The *External Ear* has two portions, the upper one large and solid, called *Pinna*, or wing, and the lower one small and soft, called the *Tibia*, or lobe. The parts of the *Pinna* are—The *Helix*, the large folded border.—The *Antehelix*, a large oblong eminence.—The *Tragus*, the small anterior protuberance below the anterior extremity of the *Helix*, and—The *Antitragus* below the inferior extremity of the *Antihelix*. The cavity formed by the extremities of the *Helix* and *Antihelix* is called *concha*: the hollow in the middle is the *Alvearium*.

The *Internal Ear* is divided into the *Meatus Auditorius*, a conduit about an inch in length.—*Membrana Tympani*, at the farther end of the *Meatus*.—*Tympanum*, a drum or barrel, a cavity behind the *Membrana Tympani*, formed by the four bones *Malleus, Incus, Stapes*, and *Os Orbiculare*.—*Eustachian tube*, which goes from the *Tympanum*.—*Labyrinth*, which terminates the *Tympanum*, and consists of the three parts; the anterior called the *Cochlea*, the middle called the *Vestibulum*, and the posterior, which are semicircular canals. The muscles of the ear are either common or proper; the common muscles are the—*Attollens Aurem, Anterior Auris*, and *Retrahentes auris*, which move the whole ear. The proper are the *Helicis Major* and *Minor, Tragicus*, and *Antitragicus*, and *Transversus Auris*, besides those of the internal ear the *Laxator Tympani, Pensor Tympani*, and *Stapedius*. The nerves of the external ear are branches of the *Nervus auditorius durus*, those of the internal branches of the *Nervus auditorius mollis*.
EAR (*Man.*) a horse is said to have a brisk hardy ear when he carries it pointed forwards in travelling.
EA'R-WIG (*Ent.*) a well-known insect, the *Forficula* of Linnæus.
EA'R-WORT (*Bot.*) the *Hedyotis auricularia* of Linnæus, so called because it is supposed to be good for deafness.
EA'RED (*Bot.*) *auritus, auriculatus*; an epithet for a leaf, leaflet, and frond having an appendage.
EA'RINGS (*Mar.*) small ropes to fasten the corners of a sail to its respective yard. *Reef Earings* differ from the common *Earings*, inasmuch as the latter are spliced to the cringle, but the former are rove through the cringle.
EARI'TES (*Min.*) the blood-stone.
EARL (*Her.*) a title of nobility between a marquis and a viscount.—*Earl Marshal*, an officer who has the care and direction of funeral solemnities. This office belongs, by hereditary right, to the Duke of Norfolk.
EARL'S *Coronet* (*Her.*) has no flowers raised above the circle like that of a duke and marquis, but only points rising, and a pearl on each of them as in the annexed figure.
EA'RNEST (*Law*) money advanced to bind the parties to the performance of a verbal bargain.
EARTH (*Chem.*) was formerly considered to be one of the four elements of which the whole system of the material world was composed. Earth is now the name for such substances as have neither taste nor smell; that are incombustible and nearly insoluble in water, the specific gravity being under 5, as lime, barytes, &c. [vide *Chemistry*]
Earths are distinguished according to the ingredient which enters into their composition, into aluminous, argillaceous, calcareous, &c.

EARTH *sealed* (*Med.*) a name for little cakes of bolar earth, which are stamped with impressions. They were formerly esteemed as absorbents, but are now fallen into disuse.

EARTH (*Geog.*) the habitable globe, the general divisions of which are land and water. [vide *Geography*]

EARTH (*Astron.*) one of the primary planets, marked by the astronomical character ⊕, which, according to the Ptolemaic system, is immoveable in the centre of the system; but, according to that of Copernicus, moves from West to East, so as to occasion the succession of day and night, and also annually with its whole mass round the sun, so as to cause the vicissitudes of the seasons. [vide *Astronomy*]

EA'RTH-NUT (*Bot.*) the *Arachis* of Linnæus, so called from its pods, or nuts, which ripen under ground. These nuts yield a considerable quantity of oil.—*Earth-pea*, the *Lathyrus amphicarpos* of Linnæus, an annual, so called because it bears its fruit under ground.

EA'RTH-WORM (*Ent.*) a well-known animal, which is commonly denominated an insect, but in the Linnean system is the genus of a distinct class, namely, the *Lumbricus*, a genus in the Class *Vermes*, Order *Intestina*.

EA'RTH-BAGS (*Fort.*) vide *Bags*.

EASE (*Mar.*) a term used in some sea-phrases, as "*Ease the ship*," i. e. put the helm close to the lee-side. "*Ease off*," slacken any rope that is formed into a tackle.

EASE (*Mil.*) a term used in military phrases, as "Stand at *Ease*," a command to draw the right foot back, and bring the weight of the body upon it. "*Ease arms*," a command to drop the right hand to the full extent of the arm.

EA'SEL (*Paint.*) a wooden frame on which a painter sets the cloth, &c. to be painted.—*Easel-pieces*, such small pieces as are painted on the easel.

EA'SEMENT (*Law*) a service which one neighbour has of another; as a way through his ground, a sink, &c.

EAST (*Astron.*) one of the four cardinal points of the horizon situated between North and South on the side where the sun rises.

EA'STER (*Chron.*) a solemn festival, in commemoration of our Saviour's resurrection from the dead; in all probability derived from the East, the point of the sun rising, as emblematic of our Saviour's resurrection. [vide *Chronology*]

EA'STER-OFFERINGS (*Ecc.*) or *Easter Dues*, money paid to the parson of a parish at Easter.

EASTERLING (*Num.*) a money coined by Richard II. in the East, which is supposed by some to have given rise to the present name of Sterling.

EA'T *inde sine die* (*Law*) "Let him go without day or trial;" words used on the acquittal, &c. of a defendant, signifying to be dismissed.

EAU *de luce* (*Chem.*) Spiritus Ammoniæ succinatus.

EAU (*Mil.*) or *Buvage d' Eau*, a punishment in France answering to the *bread and water* system pursued in the English service.

EAVES (*Archit.*) the edges of the roof of a house which overhangs the wall, for the purpose of throwing off the water.—*Eaves-lath*, or *eaves-board*, a thick feather-edged board, placed at the eaves of a roof, for raising the bottom of the first course of slates above the sloping plane of the roof.

EAVES-DRO'PPER (*Law*) one who stands under the eaves of houses, for the purpose of listening to what passes within. Such persons are called evil members of the commonwealth, in Statute of Westminster 1, c. 33.

EAUX *meres* (*Chem.*) the water which remains after the first boiling of saltpetre, in distinction from the *petites Eaux*, the water which remains after the boiling of the saltpetre to a still greater degree.

EBB (*Nat.*) the retirement or going away of the tide.

EBDOMADA'RIUS (*Ecc.*) a weeksman; an officer in cathedral churches, appointed weekly, to overlook the performance of divine service.

EBENA'STER (*Bot.*) or *Ebenum*, the Ebony-Tree; the *Diospyros eben-aster* and *ebenum* of Linnæus.

E'BENUM (*Bot.*) vide *Eben-aster*.

EBENUS (*Bot.*) a genus of plants, Class 17 *Diadelphia*, Order 4 *Decandria*.
  Generic Character. CAL. *perianth* one-leaved.—COR. papilionaceous.—STAM. *filaments* diadelphous; *anthers* roundish.—PIST. *germ* roundish; *style* capillary; *stigma* acuminate.—PER. *legume* ovate; seeds single.
  Species. The two species are the *Ebenus Cretica*, Cretan Ebony, a perennial; and the *Ebenus pinnata*, Pinnated Ebony, a biennial, native of Barbary and The Levant.

EBENUS is also the name of the *Amerimnum Ebenus* of Linnæus.

E'BEREMOTH (*Archæol.*) in Saxon ebeꞃemoꞃƀ, downright murder.

E'BIONITES (*Ecc.*) a sect of heretics in the second century, who, among other things, denied the Divinity of our Saviour. *Iren.* l. 3; *Tertull. de Præscript.* c. 34; *Origen. contra Cels.* l. 2; *Epiphan. Hæres.* 30; *Euseb. Hist. Eccles.* l. 3, c. 31; *Optat. Milvat.* l. 4; *S. August. de Hæres.; Hieron. in Lucifer. Philast.* c. 37; *Theodor. Hæret. Fabular.* l. 2.

EBI'SCUS (*Bot.*) vide *Hibiscus*.

E'BONY (*Bot.*) in Latin *ebenum*, from the Hebrew חבנים; a sort of black wood, from the Ebony-tree, or the *Ebenus* of Linnæus.

EBOU'LEMENT (*Fort.*) the crumbling or falling away of a wall or rampart.

EBRACTEA'TUS (*Bot.*) an epithet for any peduncle or raceme that is without a bracte.

EBRA'NLER (*Mil.*) French for to shake or make an impression upon an enemy's forces.

EBRIECA'TUM (*Med.*) a term used by Paracelsus to denote a partial privation of reason, such as is caused by drunkenness, or by the infusion of any supernatural spirit. *Paracel. Philos. Sagac.* l. 1.

EBULLI'TION (*Chem.*) the effervescence which arises from the mixture of an acid and alkaline liquor.

E'BULUS (*Bot.*) the *Sambucus ebulus* of Linnæus.

ECALCARA'TUS (*Bot.*) an epithet for a corolla without a spur.

ECAPA'TLI (*Bot.*) the *Senna orientalis*.

ECASTAPHY'LLUM (*Bot.*) another name for the *Dalbergia* of Linnæus.

ECBASIS (*Rhet.*) ἔκβασις, from ἐκβαίνω, to go out; signifies literally the event; and is applied to those parts of the proœmium in which the orator treats of things according to their events or consequences. *Quintil.* l. 5, c. 10; *Apsin. Art. Rhet. apud. Ald.* p. 682.

E'CBOLE (*Rhet.*) ἐκβολὴ, a digression, or a figure of speech wherein the narrator introduces some other person speaking in his own words. *Longin.* l. 3, c. 20; *Hermog. Progymn.* c. 9.

ECBOLE (*Mus.*) a change in the enharmonic genus of the Greek music, when a chord was accidentally elevated five Diesis above its ordinary pitch.

ECBOLICA (*Med.*) Medicines which procure abortion.

ECBO'LIUM (*Bot.*) the *Justicia ecbolium*.

ECBRA'SMATA (*Med.*) ἐκβράσματα, from ἐκβράσσω, to cast out as the sea does; fiery pustules breaking out on the surface of the body. *Gal. Exeges. Vocab. Hippocrat.; Myrep. de Emplast.* sect. 10, c. 64; *Gorr. Defin. Med.; Foes. Œconom. Hippocrat.*

ECBRA'SMUS (*Med.*) ἐκβράζω, to be very hot; fermentation.

ECBYRSO'MATA (*Med.*) ἐκβυρσώματα, from βύρσα, a skin;

protuberances of the bones at the joints. *Gal. Com. in Hippocrat. de Art.*; *Foes. Œconom. Hippocrat.*

ECCATHA'RTICA (*Med.*) from καθαίρω, to cleanse; medicines applied to the skin to open its pores. *Gorr. Def. Med.*

ECCE HOMO (*Paint.*) the name of any painting which represents our Saviour given up to the people by Pilate.

ECCE'NTRIC (*Astron.*) vide *Excentricity*.

ECHINOMELOCA'CTUS (*Bot.*) the *Cactus molinaris* of Linnæus.

ECCHYLO'MA (*Med.*) ἐκχύλωμα, from χυλὸς, a juice; an extraction.

ECCHY'MATA (*Med.*) vide *Ecbrasmata*.

ECCHYMO'MA (*Med.*) or *Ecchymosis*, ἐκχύμωμα, ἐκχύμωσις, from ἐκχέω, to pour out; a bruise, or a disorder in the superficial parts of the body, when, by a contusion, the capillary vessels are broken, the fluids therein contained are extravasated; and the colour of the part becomes livid or brown. *Hippocrat.* κατ'. ἰατρ; *Gal. Exeges.*; *Oribas. de Morb. Curat.* l. 3. c. 29; *Act. de Meth. Med.* l. 2, c. 11; *Foes. Œconom. Hippocrat.*

ECCHYMO'SIS (*Med.*) vide *Ecchymoma*.

ECCLE'SIA (*Law*) literally signifies a church, but is used by Fitzherbert in the sense of a parsonage.

ECCLE'SIÆ SCULPTU'RA (*Archæol.*) the image of a church cut out or cast, which used formerly to be kept as a relic. *Morg. Angl.* tom. 3, p. 309.

ECCLE'SIANS (*Ecc.*) an epithet formerly given to those who stood up for the spiritual authority of the church in opposition to the civil power.

ECCLESIA'STES (*Bibl.*) a book in the Scriptures. [vide *Canon*]

ECCLESIA'STICAL, an epithet for whatever belongs to the discipline and rites, &c. of the Christian Church.—*Ecclesiastical* or *Spiritual Courts* are various, namely, the Archdeacons' Court, the Court of Arches, the Peculiars, the Prerogative, and the Court of Delegates. [vide *Court*, &c.]—*Ecclesiastical corporation*, a corporation consisting of spiritual persons.

ECCLESIA'STIC (*Ecc.*) a clergyman or minister in the Christian Church.

ECCLESIA'STICUS (*Bibl.*) an apocryphal book of Scripture. [vide *Canon*]

ECCLI'SIS (*Med.*) ἔκκλισις, from ἐκκλίνω, to bend; a luxation or a recession of a bone from its proper place.

E'CCO (*Mus.*) an Italian word signifying, in music books, the repetition of any part of a song in a low or soft manner, in imitation of a real or natural echo.

E'CCOPE (*Med.*) the same as *Excision*.

ECCO'PEUS (*Surg.*) from ἐκκόπτω, to cut out; a knife used by the ancients for cutting out bones, particularly of the head. *Cel.* l. 4, c. 8; *Gal. Isagog. Fin. Med.*; *Paul. Æginet.*; l. 6, c. 90; *Foes. Œconom. Hippocrat.*

ECCOPRO'TICA (*Med.*) from κόπρος, dung; mild cathartics which reach no farther than the intestines. *Act. de Meth. Med.* l. 2, c. 8.

ECCRINOLO'GICA (*Med.*) from ἐκκρίνω, to secrete; that part of medicine which treats on the doctrine of excretions.

E'CCRISIS (*Med.*) ἔκκρισις, from ἐκκρίνω, to secrete; the secretion of excrementitious matter.

E'CDICUS (*Ant.*) a proctor or attorney for a corporation, who protects the interests of the body.

E'CDORA (*Med.*) ἐκδορά, from δέρω, to excoriate; excoriation in general, but particularly of the urethra.

ECHANTILLO'N (*Mil.*) French for the plank which is covered on one side with iron, and serves to finish the mouldings, &c. of a piece of ordnance.

ECHAPE' (*Man.*) the name of a horse bred from a stallion and a mare of different breeds and different countries.

ECHARPE' (*Gunn.*) as *battre en echarpe*, i. e. to fire obliquely.

ECHECO'LLON (*Med.*) ἐχέκολλον, a glutinous medicine.

ECHEI'A (*Mus.*) ἠχεῖα, vases used among the Greeks and Romans in their theatres, for the purpose of augmenting the sound of the voices. *Vitruv.* l. 1, c. 1.

E'CHELON (*Mil.*) signifies, literally, a ladder; but in application to military tactics, it signifies the movement in which each division follows the other, like the steps of a ladder.

ECHEMY'THIA (*Ant.*) ἐχεμυθία, the five years' silence imposed by Pythagoras on his scholars. *Aul. Gell.* l. 1, c. 9.

ECHENE'IS (*Ich.*) the Sea-Lamprey, a fish that sticks to the keels of ships.

ECHE'TÆ (*Ent.*) Grasshoppers.

ECHETRO'SIS (*Bot.*) White Briony.

ECHEVI'N (*Polit.*) French for a magistrate elected by the inhabitants of a city or town to take care of their common concerns.

ECHI'DNY (*Zool.*) the Viper.

E'CHINATE (*Bot.*) an epithet for the seeds of plants that are rough and prickly; also for the pericarp, as in *Datura stramonium*.

E'CHINEIS (*Ich.*) the Sucking Fish, a genus of fishes of the Thoracic Order, having a fat naked head and a naked body. This fish inhabits the Mediterranean seas, and adheres by its head so fast to other fish, and to the sides of vessels, that it is often removed with difficulty.

ECHINOME'TRA (*Ich.*) ἐχινομήτρα, a larger sort of Sea-urchin. *Arist. Hist. Anim.* l. 4, c. 5; *Plin.* l. 9, c. 31.

ECHINO'PHORA (*Ich.*) a sort of shell-fish.

ECHINOPHORA (*Bot.*) a genus of plants, Class 5 *Pentandria*, Order 2 *Digynia*.
Generic Character. CAL. *umbel* universal.—COR. *universal* difform.—STAM. *filaments* five; *anthers* roundish.—PIST. *germ* oblong; *stigmas* simple.—PER. none; *seeds* oblong.
Species. The species are perennials, as the—*Echinophora spinosa*, Prickly Sea-Parsnip, seu *Erithmum*, native of Europe.—*Echinophora tenuifolia*, seu *Pastinaca*, Fine-leaved Sea-Parsnip, native of Apulia.

ECHINOPHORA is also the *Caucalis daucoides* of Linnæus.

E'CHINOPS (*Bot.*) a genus of plants, Class 19 *Syngenesia*, Order 5 *Polygamia-Segregata*.
Generic Character. CAL. common.—COR. one-petalled.—STAM. *filaments* five; *anthers* cylindric.—PIST. *germ* oblong; *style* filiform; *stigmas* double.—PER. none; *seeds* single; *receptacle* common.
Species. The species are perennials, as the—*Echinops sphærocephalus*, Carduus, Chalcepos, seu *Chamæleon*, Great Globe Thistle, native of the South of Europe.—*Echinops spinosus*, seu *Carduus*, Thorny-headed Globe Thistle, native of Egypt.—*Echinops ritro*, Ritro, seu *Crocodylium*, Small Globe Thistle; but the *Echinops strigosus*, Scabiosa, seu *Spina*, Annual Globe Thistle, is an annual, and native of Spain. *Dod. Pempt.*; *Bauh. Pin.*; *Park. Theat.*; *Tourn. Inst.*

ECHINOPS is also a species of the *Carthamnus* and the *Rolandia*, &c.

ECHINOPTHA'LMIA (*Med.*) from ἐχῖνος, a hedgehog, and ὀφθαλμία, an inflammation of the eyelids.

ECHI'NOPUS (*Bot.*) ἐχινόπους, a prickly plant; so called because it resembles the feet of the hedge-hog, from ἐχῖνος, a hedge-hog, and πούς, a foot. *Plin.* l. 11, c. 8.

ECHINOPUS, in the Linnean system, the *Echinops sphærocephalus*, &c.

ECHINORY'NCHUS (*Ent.*) a genus of animals, of the Class *Vermes*, Order *Intestina*, having a round body and a cylindrical retractile proboscis. Worms of this tribe are found fixed very firmly to the viscera of other animals.

ECHI'NUS (*Conch.*) ἐχῖνος, a kind of crab-fish, having prickles instead of feet; so called, παρὰ τὸ ἔχειν, or συνέχειν, because it contracts itself when it is touched. *Aristot. Hist. Anim.* l. 4, c. 45, &c.; *Varro. de Lat. Ling.* l. 4; *Plin.* l. 9, c. 31; *Ælian. Hist. Anim.* l. 7, c. 33; *Plut. de Solert. Anim.*; *Oppian. Halieut.* l. 2, v. 225; *Cassiodor. Varr.* l. 3, ep. 48.

ECHINUS, *in the Linnean system*, a genus of animals, Class *Vermes*, Order *Mollusca*, having a roundish body covered with a bony sutured crust. It is called, in English, Sea-urchin; is an inhabitant of most seas, and has been found frequently in a fossil state.

ECHINUS (*Bot.*) the *Allamanda cathartica* of Linnæus.

ECHINUS (*Archit.*) a member or ornament placed on the top of the Ionic capital. *Vitruv.* l. 3, c. 3; *Bald. Lex. Vitruv.*

E'CHII FACIE (*Bot.*) the *Anchusa angustifolia* of Linnæus.

ECHIOI'DES (*Bot.*) another name for the *Lycopsis* of Linnæus.

ECHION (*Bot.*) vide *Echium*.

ECHI'TES (*Bot.*) a genus of plants, Class 5 *Pentandria*, Order 1 *Monogynia*.
  Generic Character. CAL. perianth five-parted.—COR. one-petalled.—STAM. *filaments* five; *anthers* oblong.—PIST. *germs* two; *style* filiform; *stigma* oblong.—PER. *follicles* two; *seeds* many.
  Species. The species are shrubs, as the—*Echites biflora*, seu *Apocynum*, native of the Caribee Islands.—*Echites suberecta*, seu *Nerium Echites scholaris*, seu *Lignum*, Oval-leaved Echites, or Savannah Flower, native of the East Indies.—*Echites costatex*, seu *Kametti-valli*, native of the Society Islands.

ECHITES is also the *Carissa calendas* of Linnæus.

ECHIUM, *in the Linnean system*, a genus of plants, Class 5 *Pentandria*, Order 1 *Monogynia*.
  Generic Character. CAL. perianth five-parted.—COR. one-petalled.—STAM. *filaments* five; *anthers* oblong.—PIST. *germs* four; *style* filiform; *stigmas* obtuse.—PER. *seeds* four.
  Species. The species are shrubs, as the—*Echium fruticosum*, seu *Buglossum*, Shrubby Viper Bugloss, native of the Cape of Good Hope.—*Echium Italicum*, seu *Lycopsis*, Wall-Vipers' Bugloss, native of Italy.—*Echium gigantium*, Gigantic Vipers' Bugloss. But the *Echium vulgare*, Common Vipers' Bugloss, and the *Echium strictum*, Upright Vipers' Bugloss, are biennials.

ECHIUM is also the *Lycopsis echium* of Linnæus.

ECHO (*Myth.*) is fabled by the poets to have been an airy nymph, who returned an answer in the sounds that were repeated.

ECHO (*Archit.*) a term applied to vaults, most commonly of the elliptic and parabolic kind, which used to redouble the sounds.

ECHO (*Poet.*) a name for a sort of verse which returns the sound of the last syllable, like an echo, as *gratia malis lis*.

ECHOMETER (*Mus.*) a rule with a scale divided on it, which serves to measure the duration and length of sounds.

E'CHOS (*Med.*) ἦχος, a sound; is taken by Hippocrates for the *tinnitus aurium*, a ringing in the ears.

ECLA'MPSIA (*Med.*) vide *Eclampsis*.

ECLA'MPSIS (*Med.*) ἐκλαμψις, signifies, literally, effulgence; but is taken for the *Scintillarum Micæ*, i. e. scintillations or flashings which dart from the eyes of epileptic patients. *Hippocrat. Epid.* l. 6, &c.; *Cæl. Aurelian. Tard. Pass.* l. I, c. 4.

ECLE'CTIC (*Med.*) from ἐκλέγω, to select; an epithet for a sect of physicians who, after Archigenes, their leader, selected what was best and most rational; hence their medicine was called *Eclectic Medicine*. *Dioscor.* l. 4, c. 30; *Plin.* l. 29, c. 6; *Gal. de Comp. Med. sec. Loc.* l. 8, c. 8; *Or. Med. Coll.* l. 11; *Paul. Ægin. de Re Med.* l. 7, c. 3.

ECLE'CTICI (*Phil.*) ἐκλικτικοι, a sect of philosophers who professed to be guided by no particular sect or system, but to embrace whatever appeared to themselves as best. *Voss. de Sect. Philos.* l. 3, c. ult.

ECLI'CTOS (*Med.*) ἐκλικτός, from λείχω, to lick; a linctus, or soft form of composing a medicine. *Gal. de Comp. Med. sec. Loc.* l. 7; *Aet. Tetrab.* 2, serm. 4, c. 51; *Paul. Ægin. de Re Med.* l. 7, c. 11.

ECLI'GMA (*Med.*) vide *Eclictos*.

ECLIPSA'REON (*Mech.*) an instrument invented by Mr. Ferguson, for showing the phænomena of eclipses.

ECLI'PSE (*Astron.*) in Greek ἔκλειψις, from ἐκλείπω, to fail; an obscuration of the sun, moon, or any of the heavenly bodies. An eclipse is either total or partial.—*Partial eclipse* is when the body is darkened only in part.—*Total eclipse* is when it is wholly darkened. An eclipse is distinguished, as respects the body, into lunar and solar.—*Lunar eclipse* is the depriving the moon of the sun's light by the interposition of the earth between the sun and moon. —*Solar eclipse* is the privation of light which the sun suffers in regard to us by the interposition of the moon between the sun and the earth. [vide *Astronomy*]

ECLI'PSIS (*Gram.*) ἔκλειψις, is when a word is wanting in a sentence.

ECLI'PTA (*Bot.*) a genus of plants, Class 19 *Syngenesia*, Order 2 *Polygamia-Superflua*.
  Generic Character. CAL. common.—COR. *compound* rayed. —STAM. *filaments* four; *anthers* cylindric.—PIST. *germ* oblong; *style* middling; *stigmas* two-cleft.—PER. *seeds* oblong; *receptacle* flattish.
  Species. The species are annuals, as the—*Eclipta punctata*, seu *Bellis*, Dotted Stalked Eclipta, native of Domingo.—*Eclipta prostata*, Trailing Eclipta, *Verbesina*, *Micrelium*, seu *Chrysanthemum*; but the *Eclipta erecta*, seu *Eupatoriophalacron*, Upright Eclipta, a biennial, is a native of the West Indies.

ECLI'PTIC (*Astron.*) a great circle of the sphere, in which the sun performs his apparent annual motion. It is supposed to be drawn through the middle of the zodiac, making an angle with the Equinoctial of 23 degrees 30 minutes. It is called ἐκλειπτικόν, the Ecliptic, because the eclipses of the sun and moon always happen under it. In modern astronomy the Ecliptic is the path which the Earth is supposed to describe amidst the fixed stars in performing its annual motion round the sun.

E'CLOGUE (*Poet.*) ἐκλογη, from ἐκλέγω, to select; a choice piece, particularly the Bucolics of Virgil, which are called by that name.

ECLOGA'RIUS (*Ant.*) from ἐκλέγω, to select; a gatherer of scraps from different writers. *Cic. ad Attic.* l. 16, ep. 2.

E'CLOPES (*Bot.*) another name for the *Relhania* of Linnæus.

E'CLYSIS (*Med.*) ἔκλυσις, from ἐκλύομαι, to be loosened; a general faintness and feebleness in the frame; also a loosening of the belly by a free and copious discharge by stool. *Hippocrat. Coac.*

ECMA'GMA (*Med.*) ἔκμαγμα, a kneaded or worked mass. *Gal. Exeges. Vocab. Hippocrat.*

E'COI (*Mus.*) the tropes or modes sung in the modern Greek churches during Passion-Week.

ECOUVILLO'N (*Gun.*) French for a spunge made use of to clean and cool the inside of a cannon after it has been discharged.

ECPEPIE'SMENOS (*Med.*) ἐκπεπιεσμένος, from ἐκπιέζω, to depress outward; an epithet for an ulcer with protuberating lips.

ECPHONE'MA (*Rhet.*) ἐκφώνημα, a breaking out of the voice with some interjectional particle.

ECPHONE'SIS (*Rhet.*) ἐκφώνησις, in Latin *exclamatio*; a figure of speech whereby the orator gives utterance to the warmth of his feelings. *Cic. Or.* l. 3, c. 54; *Quintil.* l. 9, c. 3; *Macrob. Saturn.* l. 4, c. 6.

ECPHRA'CTICA (*Med.*) ἐκφρακτικά, from ἐκ, privative, and φράσσω, to obstruct: deobstruent medicines, or those which remove obstructions. *Gal. de Comp. Med. sec. Loc.* l. 4, c. 1; *Gorr. Defin. Med.*

E'CPHYAS (*Med.*) ἐκφυάς, from ἐκφύω, to grow out: an excrescence particularly applied to the *Appendicula vermiformis*. *Gal. de Usu Part.* l. 5, c. 2; *Gorr. Defin. Med.*

ECPHYSE'SIS (*Med.*) ἐκφύσησις, a quick breathing. *Gal. de Mot. Muscul.* l. 2.

ECPHY'SIS (*Med.*) vide *Ecphyas*.

ECPIE'SMA (*Med.*) ἐκπίεσμα, from ἐκ and πιέζω, to press: 1. A fracture of the *Cranium* when the bones press inwardly on the membranes of the brain. *Gal. Def. Med. Isagog.*; *Paul. Ægin. de Re Med.* l. 6, c. 90. 2. The mass remaining after the juices of vegetables have been pressed out: also the juice itself. *Dioscor.* l. 4, c. 160; *Cels.* l. 6, c. 5; *Gorr. Def. Med.*; *Foes. Œconom. Hippocrat.*

ECPIE'SMOS (*Med.*) ἐκπιεσμός, from ἐκ and πιέζω, to press; a disease in the eye when the ball is as it were thrust out of the orbit by reason of humours. [vide *Proptosis*]

ECPLERO'MA (*Med.*) ἐκπλήρωμα, from πληρόω, to fill up; a small hard ball of leather to fill up the cavity of the armpit in reducing a luxated *Os Humeri* to its place. *Hippocrat.* περὶ ἄρθ.

ECPLE'XIS (*Med.*) ἔκπληξις, from ἐκπλήσσω, to terrify or astonish; stupor, stupefaction, as when the patient lies without motion with his eyes open like one in a trance. *Gal. in Hippocrat.* l. 7, aph. 14.

ECPNEUMATO'SIS (*Med.*) vide *Ecpnoe*.

ECPNOE (*Med.*) ἔκπνοη, from ἐκ and πνέω, to breathe; that of respiration which consists in expelling the breath.

ECPTO'MA (*Med.*) ἔκπτωμα, from ἐκπίπτω, to fall out; the luxation of a bone; also exclusion of the *secundines*; a falling down of the womb, descent of the omentum, &c. *Hippocrat. de Fractur.* and l. 5, aphor. 49, &c.; *Gorr. Def. Med.*; *Foes. Oeconom. Hippocrat.*

ECPTOSIS (*Med.*) vide *Ecptoma*.

ECPYE'MA (*Med.*) or *Ecpiesis*, from ἐκ and πύον, pus; a collection of pus in a tumour. *Gorr. Def. Med.*

ECRE'XIS (*Med.*) ἔκρηξις, from ῥήγνυμι, to break; a laceration of the womb, as applied by Hippocrates. *Gorr. Def. Med.*; *Foes. Oeconom.*

E'CROE (*Med.*) ἐκροή, from ἐκρέω, to flow; any duct or passage by which the humours are evacuated. *Hippocrat. Epid.* l. 2.

ECRY'SIS (*Med.*) ἔκρυσις, from ἐκρέω, to flow out; an efflux of the semen not mature enough to be called an abortion. *Hippocrat.* περὶ ἐκταμ. *Arist. Hist. Anim.* l. 7, c. 3.

ECRY'THMUS (*Med.*) ἐκρύθμος, from ἐκ privative, and ῥυθμός, rythm; a term applied to pulses which are disorderly, or entirely out of order. *Gal. de Different. Puls.* l. 1, c. 9; *Paul. Æginet. de Re Med.* l. 2, c. 11; *Gorr. Def. Med.*; *Foes. Oeconom. Hippocrat.*

ECSARCO'MA (*Med.*) from ἐκ and σάρξ; an excrescence of flesh. *Gorr. Def. Med.*

E'CSTASIS (*Med.*) ἔκστασις, from ἐξίσταμαι, to be out of one's senses; Ecstasy, a vehement emotion of the mind, or a delirium, according to Hippocrates. *Gal. Com. 2 in Hippocrat. Prorrhet.* l. 1; *Gorr. Def. Med.*; *Foes. Oeconom. Hippocrat.*

Ecstasis (*Gram.*) a figure in grammar, whereby a short syllable is made long.

ECSTRO'PHIUS (*Med.*) ἐκστρόφιος, from ἐκστρέφω, to invert, or turn out; an epithet for a medicine which causes the blind piles to appear externally.

ECTA'SIS (*Med.*) ἔκτασις, from ἐκτείνω, to extend; a tension of the skin. *Hippocrat. Epid.* l. 6; *Foes. Oeconom. Hippocrat.*

ECTE'XIS (*Med.*) ἔκτηξις from τήκω, to liquefy; a colliquation of the solids.

ECTHELY'NSIS (*Med.*) ἐκθελύνσις from ἐκθηλύνω, to render effeminate; a term applied to the skin when lax and soft, and also to a bandage not sufficiently tight. *Hippocrat. Epid.* l. 1; *Gal. Comm.*; *Foes. Oeconom. Hippocrat.*

ECTHLI'MMA (*Med.*) ἔκθλιμμα, from ἐκθλίβω, to dash or press out; an exulceration on the surface of the skin made by collision or compression. *Hippocrat. de Fract.*

ECTHLI'PSIS (*Med.*) ἔκθλιψις, from ἐκθλίβω, to dash out; a term applied to swollen eyes, which dart forth corruscations of light. *Hippocrat. de Fract.*; *Gal. Comm.* 2; *Gorr. Def. Med.*; *Foes. Oeconom. Hippocrat.*

ECTHLIPSIS (*Gram.*) the cutting off a vowel or consonant, especially the letter *m* with its vowel, or the letter *h* at the end of a word in Greek and Latin verse, as *βυλομ' ἐγώ* for *βυλόμαι ἐγώ*; *monstr' horrend' informe* for *monstrum horrendum informe*.

ECTHY'MA (*Med.*) ἔκθυμα, from ἐκθύω, to break out; a pustule, or cutaneous eruption. *Hippocrat. Epidem.* l. 2; *Gal. Com.* 3; *Gorr. Def. Med.*; *Foes. Oeconom. Hippocrat.*

ECTILLO'TICA (*Med.*) from ἐκτίλλω, to pull out; medicines which consume callous tubercles. *Gorr. Def. Med.*

E'CTOME (*Med.*) from ἐκτέμνω, to cut out; excision.

E'CTOMON (*Bot.*) Black Hellebore.

ECTO'PIÆ (*Med.*) from ἐκ and τόπος, a place; parts displaced; an order of diseases in the Class *Locales* of Cullen's Nosology.

ECTOPOCI'STICA Ischuria (*Med.*) a suppression of urine from a rupture, or hernia.

ECTRI'MMA (*Med.*) ἔκτριμμα, from ἐκτρίβω, to rub off, rubbing or galling; a term for exulcerations of the skin about the *os sacrum*.

E'CTROPE (*Med.*) ἐκτροπή, from ἐκτρέπω, to divert; a duct or passage by which the humours are diverted. *Hippocrat. Epid.* l. 2.—*Ectrope*, a disease in the eyelid. [vide *Ectropium*]

ECTRO'PIUM (*Med.*) or *Ectrope*; a disease in the eyelids when they are so inverted, or retracted, that the eyes cannot be sufficiently covered by them. *Cels.* l. 7, c. 7; *Gal. Defin. Med. Isagog.*; *Aet. Tetrab.* 2, serm. 3, c. 2; *Paul. Æginet.* l. 3, c. 22, &c.; *Act. de Meth. Med.* l. 2, c. 7; *Gorr. Def. Med.*; *Foes. Oeconom. Hippocrat.*

ECTRO'SIS (*Med.*) ἔκτρωσις, from ἐκτιτρώσκω, to miscarry; a miscarriage.

ECTRO'TICA (*Med.*) medicines which produce a miscarriage.

ECTYLO'TICA (*Med.*) from τύλος, a callosity; remedies for consuming a callosity.

ECTYPE (*Ant.*) *Ectypum*, from the Greek τύπος, a type or model; a copy taken from an original. *Senec. de Benef.* l. 3, c. 26; *Plin.* l. 35, c. 12.

Ectype (*Paint.*) or craticular ectype; the space marked out for an anamorphosis. [vide *Anamorphosis*]

ECZE'MA (*Med.*) from ζέω, to boil; a hot, fiery pustule. *Aet. Tetrab.* serm. 1, c. 128.

E'DDY (*Nat.*) the running back of the water at any place contrary to the main tide, or stream.

EDDY-WATER (*Mar.*) the water that falls back as it were on the rudder of a ship under sail.—*Eddy-wind*, a wind checked by the sail, by a mountain reach, or any other thing that makes it recoil or return back.

EDE'CHIA (*Bot.*) the *Laugeria odorata* of Linnæus.

EDE'LPHUS (*Med.*) a person who makes prognostics from the nature of the elements. *Paracel. de Tartar.* l. 2; *Tractat.* 2, c. 3.

EDE'NTULUS (*Med.*) without teeth.

EDE'RA (*Bot.*) the *Rhus Toxicodendron* of Linnæus.

EDESSE'NUM (*Med.*) an eyewater of Tragacanth.

To EDGE (*Mar.*) a term in the sea phraseology for a gradual movement, as "To *edge away* from a coast," to decline gradually. "To *edge in* with a ship," to advance gradually towards the shore.

E'DGINGS (*Hort.*) a border of grass for a flower-bed.

E'DICT (*Polit.*) a public ordinance, or decree, issued by supreme command.

EDI'CTAL CITATION (*Law*) in Scotch law is the citation of a foreigner who is not in Scotland, but has a landed estate there.

E'DILE (*Ant.*) vide *Ædilis*.

EDI'TION (*Print.*) the publication of a book, and also its republication.

EDITIO'NES (*Ant.*) exhibitions of games. *Tacit. Annal.* l. 3, c. 37.

E'DITOR (*Print.*) he who undertakes the revisal and republication of any work.

E'DRA (*Med.*) a fracture; also the lower part of the *rectum*.

EDULCORA'TION (*Chem.*) the washing of things that have been calcined in order to purify them from their salts.

EDULCORATION (*Med.*) the sweetening of any medicinal composition.

E'EL (*Ich.*) a voracious fish, the *Muræna* of Linnæus, which resembles the lizard both in appearance and habit. The bite of this fish is dangerous. [vide *Muræna*]

EEL (*Her.*) the eel is borne in the escutcheon either hauriant or naiant, as in the annexed figure. He beareth " *Argent* three eels naiant, in pale barways *sable*, name *Ellis*."

EEL-FARES (*Archæol.*) or Eel-vares, a fry or brood of eels.

EEL-POUT (*Com.*) a young eel.—*Eel Spear*, a forked instrument with which eels are caught.

EEL SPEAR (*Her.*) this instrument is also a charge in an escutcheon, as in the annexed figure. " He beareth *sable* a chevron between three eel-spears by the name of *Strandell*."

E Flat (*Mus.*) vide E.

EFFE'CTION (*Geom.*) the geometrical construction of a proposition; also such problems and practices as are deducible from general propositions are called *effections* of them.

EFFE'CTIVE (*Mil.*) an epithet for any body of men that are fit for service, as " 30,000 *effective* men;" also a word to denote the actual presence of an officer or soldier.

EFFE'CTS (*Com.*) the moveables or goods of any merchant, tradesman, &c.

EFFECTS *of the Hand* (*Man.*) the aids or motions of the hand which serve to conduct the horse. There are four, i. e. four ways of using the bridle; namely, to push the horse forward; to give him head or hold him in; and to turn the hand either to the right or the left.

EFFE'CTUAL *abjudication* (*Law*) a legal security for a debt on the estate of the creditor in Scotland.

EFFEE'RERS (*Law*) vide *Affeerers*.

EFFELLO'NIE (*Her.*) vide *Rampant*.

EFFENDI (*Polit.*) a title of distinction in Turkey.

EFFERVE'SCENCE (*Chem.*) a violent commotion in the parts of any liquor, accompanied with some degree of heat. It differs from a fermentation only in the violence of the motion. This term is particularly applied to the effect produced by the mixture of an acid with an alkali.

EFFI'CIENT *cause* (*Phy.*) any cause that actually produces the effect.

E'FFIGY (*Paint.*) any representation whatever which gives the figure of the person, whether in whole or in part. On coins the effigy consists mostly of the head of the prince.

E'FFILA (*Med.*) Freckles.

EFFLORA'TIO (*Med.*) vide *Exanthema*.

EFFLORE'SCENCE (*Bot.*) *efflorescentia*; the flowering season, or the time of the month in which different sorts of plants first show their flowers.

EFFLORESCENCE (*Med.*) a preternatural redness of the skin.

EFFLU'VIA (*Nat.*) such small particles as are continually flowing out of almost all mixed bodies.

EFFLU'VIUM (*Med.*) is taken in an especial manner for the vapours which pass through the pores or insensible holes of the skin.

EFFRACTU'RA (*Med.*) a species of fracture of the cranium when the bone is broken and much depressed.

EFFRO'NTES (*Ecc.*) a sect of heretics in the sixteenth century who scraped their foreheads till they brought blood, which they substituted for the ceremony of baptism.

EFFU'SIO *Sanguinis* (*Law*) a fine or penalty imposed by the ancient English laws for bloodshed and murder, which the King granted to many lords of manors.

EFFU'SION (*Chem.*) the pouring out a liquor by the inclination of the vessel, in such manner that the sediment may remain behind.

EFFUSION (*Surg.*) the escape of any fluid out of the vessel, or viscus naturally containing it; also the natural secretion of fluids from the vessels.

EFT (*Zool.*) a sort of lizard, the *Lacerta seps* of Linnæus, which has a body covered with truncate scales and a verticillate tail. It is reckoned venomous.

E. G. (*Gram.*) an abbreviation for *exempli gratia*, i. e. for example. [vide *Abbreviations*]

EGE'STIO (*Med.*) Excretion; applied generally to evacuations by stool.

EGG (*Nat.*) the fœtus or production of feathered creatures; also the spawn and sperm of other animals.

EGG-PLANT (*Bot.*) the *Solanum Melongena* of Linnæus; so called because the fruit is like an egg.

EGG-SHAPED (*Bot.*) vide *Ovate*.

EGISTMENTS (*Law*) vide *Agistments*.

EGLANDULO'SUS (*Bot.*) an epithet for a petiole that is without glands.

EGLANDTERIA (*Bot.*) another name for the *Rosa lutea* of Linnæus.

EGLANTINE (*Bot.*) the Wild Rose.

E'GRET (*Zool.*) an animal of the monkey tribe; the *Simia aygula* of Linnæus.

EGRET (*Orn.*) a bird of the heron kind, of which there is the *Great Egret*, that is about two feet long, and the *Little Egret*, which is a foot long.

EGUI'SCE (*Her.*) vide *Aiguisce*.

EHRE'TIA (*Bot.*) a genus of plants; so called after G. D. Ehret, a famous botanist, Class 5 *Pentandria*, Order 1 *Monogynia*.

Generic Character. CAL. *perianth* one-leaved.—COR. one-petalled.—STAM. *filaments* five; *anthers* roundish.—PIST. *germ* roundish; *style* filiform; *stigma* obtuse.—PER. *berry* roundish; *seeds* four.

Species. The species are trees or shrubs, as the—*Ehretia unifolia*, seu *Cerasso affinis*, Tinus-leaved Ehretia.——*Ehretia Bourreria*, *Cordia*, *Bourreria*, *Pittoniæ*, seu *Jasminum*, Oval-leaved Ehretia, native of the West Indies.——*Ehretia exsucca*, seu *Rhamnus*, Dry-fruited Ehretia, native of Carthagena.

EHRETIA is also the name of the *Lycium Boerhaaviæfolium*.

EHRHA'RTIA (*Bot.*) a genus of plants; so called from Frederick Ehrhart, Class 6 *Hexandria*, Order 2 *Digynia*.

Generic Character. CAL. *glume* one-flowered.—COR. double.—STAM. *filaments* six; *anthers* upright.—PIST. *germ* ovate; *style* compressed; *stigma* simple.—PER. none; *seeds* ovate.

Species. The species are perennials, as the—*Ehrhartia cartilaginea*, seu *Mnemateia*, native of the Cape of Good Hope.—*Ehrhartia bulbosa*, seu *Trochera*, native of the Cape of Good Hope.—*Ehrhartia calycina*, seu *Aira capensis*, native of the Cape of Good Hope.

EJACULA'NTIA (*Anat.*) or *Ejaculatoria Vasa*, the vessels which receive the seminal fluid, elaborated in the testes, and convey it to the penis: these are the *Epididymis*, the *Vasa Deferentia*, *Vesiculæ Seminales*, and *Prostatæ*.

EI'DER-DUCK (*Orn.*) a species of the Anas tribe, which is remarkable for the softness of its down. This is gathered in the breeding season, when the bird strips its breast for the purpose of making its nest.

EIDOURANION (*Astron.*) from ουρανος, heaven, and ιδος, the form or appearance; an exhibition of the heavens and the heavenly bodies, with their motions, &c.

EJE'CTIO (*Med.*) the same as *Excretio*.

EJECTI'ONE *custodiæ* (*Law*) a writ lying against one who casts a guardian out from any lands whilst the heir is under age. *F. N. B.* 139; *Reg. Orig.* 162.—*Ejectione firmæ*, Ejectment, a writ which lies for a term of years, for the lessee who is cast out before the expiration of the term. *F. N. B.* 220.

EJE'CTMENT (*Law*) a writ by which any tenant or inhabitant of an estate or house, is commanded to depart.

EJE'CTUM (*Archæol.*) jetsom, or wreck of goods thrown overboard in a storm.

EIGHTH (*Mus.*) an interval comprehending seven conjunct degrees, or eight diatonic sounds.

EIGHTE'ENTH (*Mus.*) an interval comprehending two octaves and a fourth.

EIGHT-FOIL (*Her.*) or *double quatre foil*, eight-leaved grass, given by Morgan as a difference of the ninth branch of a family.

EI'KING (*Mar.*) a piece in ship building, fitted to make good a deficiency in length, as the lower part of the supporter under the cat-head.

EILA'MIDES (*Anat.*) ιλαμιδες, from ιλεω, to involve; an epithet for the Meninges, or membranes of the brain.

EILE'MA (*Anat.*) ιλημα, from ιλεω, to involve; a painful circumvolution of the intestines.

EI'LEON (*Anat.*) the *Ilium*.

EIRE (*Law*) the name for the court of justice, itinerant and Eyre; the justices *in Eyre*, are called by Bracton *justiciarios itinerantes*; and the *Eyre* of the Forest is the seat of justice. *Bract.* l. 3, c. 11; *Horn's Mir.*; *Manw. For. Laws Par.* l. 1, p. 121.

EI'SBOLE (*Med.*) εισβολη, from εισβαλλω, to inject; is taken for an access or attack of a particular distemper; and also for an irruption.

EI'SPNOE (*Med.*) εισπνοη, from εις, and πνεω, to breathe; inspiration.

EKEBE'RGIA (*Bot.*) a genus of plants, Class 10 *Decandria*, Order 1 *Monogynia*.
Generic Character. CAL. *perianth* one-leaved.—COR. *petals* four.—STAM. *filaments* ten; *anthers* ovate.—PIST. *germ* superior; *style* cylindric; *stigma* capitate.—PER. *berry* globular; *seeds* five.
Species. The species is a tree, as the *Ekebergia capensis*.

E'KLYSIS (*Mus.*) εκλυσις, a particular kind of tuning among the ancients, in which, from a certain sound, the performer dropped by an interval of three quarter tones.

E'LA (*Mus.*) a name formerly given to the highest note in the scale of Guido.

ELA-CA'LLI (*Bot.*) the name of a shrub which grows in sandy soils in the East Indies. The *Euphorbia nervifolia* of Linnæus. *Raii Hist. Plant.*

ELÆA'CHNUS (*Nat.*) another name for the *Elæagnus* of Linnæus.

ELÆA'GNUS (*Bot.*) a genus of plants, Class 4 *Tetrandria*, Order 1 *Monogynia*.
Generic Character. CAL. *perianth* one-leaved.—COR. none. —STAM. *filaments* four; *anthers* oblong.—PIST. *germ* roundish; *style* simple; *stigma* simple.—PER. *drupe* ovate; *seeds* nut oblong.
Species. The species are trees, as the *Elæagnus angustifolia*, seu *Oleaster*, Narrow-leaved Oleaster.—*Elæagnus orientalis*, seu *Zizyphus*, Oriental Oleaster, native of Persia.—*Elæagnus crispa*, Curled-leaved Oleaster.

ELÆ'GRUS (*Bot.*) the *Elæagnus orientalis* of Linnæus.

ELÆ'IS (*Bot.*) a genus of plants, Natural Order of Palms.
Generic Character. CAL. *perianth* six-leaved.—COR. one-petalled.—STAM. *filaments* six; *anthers* oblong.—PIST. *germ* ovate; *style* thickish; *stigmas* three.—PER. *drupe* fibrous; *seed* nut ovate.
Species. The species is a tree, as the—*Elæis guineensis*, *Nucula*, seu *Palma oleosa*, native of the West Indies.

ELÆOCA'RPUS (*Bot.*) a genus of plants, Class 13 *Polyandria*, Order 1 *Monogynia*.
Generic Character. CAL. *perianth* one-leaved.—COR. *petals* five.—STAM. *filaments* twenty to thirty; *anthers* linear. PIST. *germ* globular; *style* filiform; *stigma* sharp.—PER. *drupe* oblong; *seed* nut oblong.
Species. The species are trees, as the—*Elæocarpus dentatus*, seu *Dicera serrata*.—*Elæocarpus copalliferus*, seu *Vateria*, native of the East Indies.

ELÆODENDRUM (*Bot.*) a genus of plants, Class 5 *Pentandria*, Order 1 *Monogynia*.
Generic Character. CAL. *perianth* five-leaved. — COR. *petals* five.—STAM. *filaments* five; *anthers* erect.—PIST. *germ* roundish; *style* conical; *stigma* obtuse.—PER. *drupe* ovate; *seed* nut ovate.
Species. The two species are trees, as the *Elæodendrum orientale* et *argan*.

ELÆO'MELI (*Nat.*) ελαιομελι, from ελαιον, oil, and μελι, honey; a gum thinner than resin, and thicker than honey, which is of an oily nature, and drops from the olive trees in Syria. *Dioscor.* l. 1, c. 37; *Plin.* l. 23, c. 4.

ELÆOPHY'LLON (*Bot.*) the herb Mercury.

ELÆOSA'CCHARUM (*Chem.*) from ελαιον, oil, and σακχαρον, sugar; a mixture of essential oil with sugar.

ELÆOSELI'NUM (*Bot.*) Water-Parsley.

ELÆOTHE'SIUM (*Ant.*) ελαιοθεσιον, a place where the ancients used to anoint their bodies after bathing. *Vitruv.* l. 5, c. 2; *Philand. in Vitruv.*; *Bald. Lex. Vitruv.*

ELAIOCA'RPOS (*Bot.*) another name for the *Elæocarpus* of Linnæus.

E'LAIN (*Chem.*) a fine oil obtained from tallow and fat.

E'LAIS (*Bot.*) another name for the *Elæis* of Linnæus.

ELA'NULA (*Chem.*) an old name for alum.

ELA'OLITE (*Min.*) a species of Felspar.

ELAPHEBO'LIA (*Ant.*) a festival in honour of Diana Elaphebolus, celebrated by the Phocensians. *Athen.* l. 14.

ELAPHEBOLION (*Chron.*) ελαφηβολιων, a Greek month; so called from ελαφηβολος, an epithet of Diana, because she hunts stags. It answers to our December, or, according to Gaza, to our February.

ELA'PHICON (*Med.*) vide *Elaphoboscon*.

ELAPHOBO'SCON (*Bot.*) ελαφοβοσκον, a herb commonly called Wild Parsnep. *Plin.* l. 22, c. 22.

ELAPHOSCO'RODON (*Bot.*) vide *Ophioscorodon*.

ELA'PHRIUM (*Bot.*) the *Fagara octandra* of Linnæus.

E'LAPHRUS (*Ent.*) a division of the genus *Cicindela*, comprehending those insects which have the lip rounded and entire.

E'LAPS (*Zool.*) a sort of serpent mentioned by Aetius, the bite of which induces something like the Iliac Passion. *Act. Tetrab.* 4, serm. 1, c. 32.

E'LAS (*Chem.*) Burnt Lead.

E'LASIS (*Nat.*) Elasticity.

ELA'SMA (*Med.*) ελασμα, from ελαυνω, to drive; properly signifies a lamina, or plate of any kind: but is taken for a Clyster-Pipe.

ELA'STIC CURVE (*Geom.*) vide *Catenaria*.

ELA'STIC (*Phy.*) an epithet for all bodies endowed with the property of elasticity, or springiness; so also the force of

7

a spring is called its elastic force. Gases are distinguished by the name of *elastic fluids*, because of the property which they possess in a peculiar manner of returning to their former place.

ELA'STIC GUM (*Bot.*) the same as *Caoutchouc*.

ELASTI'CITY (*Phy.*) that property in bodies by which they restore themselves to their former figure. Hence it is that naturalists speak of the *Elasticity of Fluids*, or *of the Air*, which may be compressed into a smaller space, but revert to their former extent when the external force is removed.

E'LATE (*Bot.*) the Fir-Tree.

ELATE, *in the Linnean system*, a genus of plants, of the Natural Order of Palmæ.
  Generic Character. CAL. spathe two-valved.—COR. *petals* three.—STAM. *filaments* three; *anthers* adnate.—PIST. *germ* roundish; *style* subulate; *stigma* sharp. — PER. *drupe* ovate; *seed* nut ovate.
  Species. The single species is a tree, as the *Elate sylvestris*, seu *Palma*, Prickly-leaved Elate, native of the East Indies.

E'LATER (*Ent.*) a genus of Insects of the Coleopterous order, so called because its thorax terminates in an elastic spine placed in the abdomen, by means of which the insect, when placed on its back, springs up, and recovers its natural posture.

ELATE'RIUM (*Bot.*) ἐλατήριον, from ἐλαύνω, to agitate; a plant so called from its purgative qualities. *Cels.* l. 5, c. 12; *Dioscor.* l. 4, c. 155; *Plin.* l. 20, c. 1; *Gal. Exeges. Vocab. Hippocrat.*; *Oribas. Med. Collect.* l. 12; *Aet. Tetrab.* l, serm. 1; *Paul. Æginet.* l. 7, c. 3.

ELATERIUM, *in the Linnean system*, a genus of plants, Class 21 Monoecia, Order 2 Monandria.
  Generic Character. CAL. none.—COR. one-petalled.—STAM. *filament* single; *anthers* linear.—PIST. *germ* inferior; *style* columnar; *stigma* capitate.—PER. *capsule* inferior; *seeds* several.
  Species. The species are annuals, as the—*Elaterium carthaginense.*—*Elaterium trifoliatum*, seu *Sicyos*, native of Virginia.

ELATERIUM, the same as the *Momordica*.

ELATERIUM (*Phy.*) the elastic property peculiar to the air.

ELATERIUM (*Med.*) the juice of wild cucumbers made up into a thick consistence in fragments of flat or thin cakes.

ELATHE'RIA (*Bot.*) a name for the Cascarilla Bark.

E'LATINE (*Bot.*) ἐλατίνη, from ἐλάσσω, the less; a herb so called because it is a smaller species of the *Helxine*. *Dioscor.* l. 4, c. 40; *Plin.* l. 27, c. 9.

ELATINE, *in the Linnean system*, a genus of plants, Class 8 Octandria, Order 4 Tetragynia.
  Generic Character. CAL. *perianth* four-leaved.—COR. *petals* four.—STAM. *filaments* eight; *anthers* simple.—PIST. *germ* large; *styles* four; *stigmas* simple.—PER. *capsule* orbicular; *seeds* several.
  Species. The species are annuals, as the—*Elatine Hydropiper*, Opposite-leaved Water-wort, seu *Alsinastrum*, native of Denmark.—*Elatine Alsinastrum*, seu *Equisetum*, Whorl-leaved Water-wort, native of Aboa.

ELATINE is also the *Antirrhinum elatine* of Linnæus.

ELA'TIO (*Ant.*) ἐκκομιδή, the ceremony of carrying out the corpse on the day of the funeral.

ELATO'STEMA (*Bot.*) the *Dorstenia lucida* of Linnæus.

E'LBOW (*Anat.*) the outer angle made by the flexure or bend of the arm.

ELBOW (*Archit*) the obtuse angle of a wall or building.

ELBOW *in the hawse* (*Mar.*) a particular twist in the cables, by which a ship rides at anchor.

ELCESAITÆ (*Ecc.*) ἐλκεσαΐται, a sect of heretics in the first century, so called from their ringleader Elcasæus, who maintained that denying Christ to escape persecution was an indifferent matter. *Orig. in Homel.*; *Euseb.*

Eccl. Hist. l. 6, c. 48; *Epiphan. de Hæres.* 19. 53, &c.; *August. de Hæres.* c. 32; *Niceph.* l. 5, c. 24; *Baron. Annal.* ann. 105.

ELCO'SIS (*Med.*) from ἕλκος, an ulcer; a disease attended with fetid ulcers.

E'LDER (*Mil.*) an epithet for officers whose commissions bear the earliest date; and also for battalions that have been first raised.

ELDER (*Ecc.*) is another name for the presbyter; an officer in the Christian Church mentioned in the New Testament.

ELDER (*Bot.*) a well-known shrub, the *Sambucus* of Linnæus; the two principal species of which are the *Sambucus nigra*, Common Elder; and the *Sambucus ebulus*, the Dwarf Elder.—Marsh Elder, the *Viburnum apulus* of Linnæus, is a shrub, so called from its growing in watery places.

ELECAMPA'NE (*Bot.*) the *Inula Helinium* of Linnæus.

ELE'CT (*Polit.*) signifies the same as elected, as the Lord Mayor Elect, i. e. he who is appointed to succeed in the mayoralty.

ELECT (*Theol.*) a Calvinistic term for such as are supposed by this sect to be chosen for salvation by the special grace of God, irrespective of their good or bad deeds.

ELECTA'RIUM (*Med.*) vide *Electuarium*.

ELE'CTION (*Polit.*) which signifies properly choice, is particularly applied to a popular choice by vote of a person for any office.

ELECTION *of a Clerk of Statutes-Merchant* (*Law*) a writ that lies for the choice of a clerk assigned to take bonds called *Statutes-Merchant*.—Election *of a Verder of the Forest*, a writ that lies for the choice of a Verderor in case of a vacancy by death or otherwise.

ELECTION (*Arith.*) the several ways of taking any numbers of quantities given, without having respect to their places.

ELE'CTIONS (*Astrol.*) certain times pitched upon as fittest for undertaking a particular business.

ELE'CTIVE *Attraction* (*Chem.*) another name for the chemical affinities of bodies.

ELE'CTOR (*Polit.*) a title belonging to certain princes of the German empire, who, according to the institution of Charles IV, have a right to choose the emperors.

ELECTOR (*Law*) signifies generally any one who elects, but is particularly applied to those who have a voice in the election of a member of Parliament.

ELE'CTORAL *Crown* (*Her.*) a scarlet cap faced with ermine, diademed with half a circle of gold set with pearls supporting a globe with a cross of gold on the top, as in the annexed figure.

ELE'CTRIC (*Phy.*) from ἤλεκτρον, amber; a term for any substance in which the electric fluid can be excited; so called because this property was first observed by the ancients in amber. *Electrics* are otherwise called *Non-Conductors*, because they accumulate the fluid without transmitting it. To the class of *Electrics*, or *Non-Conductors*, belong resins, bituminous substances, glass, and all vitrifications; dry animal substances, as feathers; paper, white sugar; air, oils, chocolates, calces of metals, &c.

Electric, or *electrical*, is an epithet applied to different things connected with electricity, as — *Electrical air Thermometer*, an instrument for determining the effects of the electrical explosion upon air.—*Electrical Atmosphere*, a stream or mass of the electric fluid which surrounds an electrified body at a certain distance.—*Electrical Balls*, vide *Balls*.—*Electrical Battery*, consisting of a number of coated jars connected with each other, which, being charged or electrified, are then exploded or discharged with prodigious effect.—*Electrical Bells*, a set of bells mounted in a peculiar manner so as to be rung by means of the action of the electric fluid.—*Electrical Machine*, the apparatus so called, in which electric bodies are subjected to friction so as to excite in them an electrical power. The machine is of various forms, of which the most common is, as given in the annexed figure, where A B C D represents the frame of the machine; E, F, two round pillars which support the cylinder; G, by the axles of the brass or wooden cups; H, turned sometimes by a simple winch, as I in this figure, and sometimes by a pulley and wheel. The rubber is fixed to a glass pillar, K, which is fastened to a wooden basis, L, at the bottom. The conductor, N, is usually made of brass, or tin japanned, and is insulated by a glass pillar, O, screwed into a wooden basis or foot most conveniently placed parallel to the cylinder.—*Electrical Phial*, vide *Leyden Phial*.—*Electrical Rubber*, a part of the electrical apparatus which is made of black oiled silk with an amalgam, &c. —*Electrical Shock*, the sudden explosion between the opposite sides of a charged electric.—*Electrical Star*, vide *Star*.

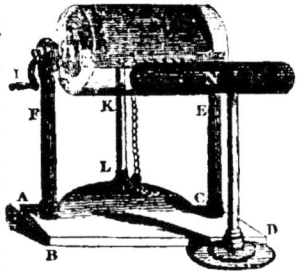

ELE'CTRICAL *Eel* (*Ich.*) the *Gymnotus electricus* of Linnæus, a particular sort of fish so called from its power of producing an electrical shock whenever it is touched. By this power it stupifies, and then seizes, such animals as venture to approach it.

ELECTRICITY (*Nat.*) or *Electric force*, that power or property, first observed in amber, of attracting light bodies when excited by heat or friction, which is also capable of being communicated in particular circumstances.

Electricity is also taken for the theory or science which treats on the nature and effects of the electric power. *Electricity*, according to the modern system, is distinguished into *positive* and *negative*, according to the ways in which bodies are excited. When to bodies a superabundant quantity of electricity is added they are said to be electrified *positively*; but, when they are deprived of a portion of what they naturally contain, they are electrified *negatively*, or *minus*; they were originally called *vitreous* and *resinous* Electricity. When bodies contain the usual quantity of the fluid, and exhibit no signs of electricity, they are said to be *neutral*. Those which are capable of being excited by friction are called *Electrics*, the others *Non-Electrics*; and those which become electric by being placed in the neighbourhood of an excited body, are called *Conductors*, and those which do not undergo such change are called *Non-Conductors*. [vide *Electric*]

ELECTRO'DES (*Med.*) ἠλεκτρώδης, an epithet for stools that shine like amber.

ELECTRO'METER (*Mech.*) an instrument for measuring the quantity, and determining the quality, of electricity in any electrified body.

ELE'CTRUM (*Nat.*) ἤλεκτρον, amber.

ELECTRUM *minerale* (*Med.*) the tincture of metals.

ELECTUA'RIUM (*Med.*) an Electuary.

ELEEMO'SYNA (*Archæol.*) alms; but *Eleemosyna Regis* was the penny which King Ethelred ordered to be paid for ever towards the support of the poor. *Leg. Ethelred.* c.1.—*Eleemosynæ*, the possessions belonging to the church.

ELEEMOSYNA'RIA (*Archæol.*) Eleemosynary.

ELEEMOSINA'RIUS (*Archæol.*) the Almoner.

ELEEMO'SYNARY *Corporations* (*Law*) corporate bodies constituted for the perpetual distributions of free alms, and bounty of the founder.

ELEGI'A (*Bot.*) a genus of plants, Class 22 *Dioecia*, Order 3 *Triandria*.
Generic Character. CAL. spathes within spathes.—COR. none.—STAM. *filaments* three; *anthers* oval.—PIST. *germ* oblong; *styles* three; *stigmas* simple.—PER. .... *seed* ......
Species. The single species is the *Elegia juncea*, native of the Cape of Good Hope.

ELE'GIAC *Verse* (*Poet.*) ἐλεγιακός, a sort of verse used in elegies, which is always pentameter.

ELEGIA'MBIC *Verse* (*Poet.*) a sort of verse used by Horace in his poems called *Epodes*.

ELE'GIT (*Law*) a writ that lies for him who has recovered debt, or damage, in the King's Court against one not able in his goods to satisfy his creditors.

ELE'GMA (*Med.*) a Linctus.

ELELI'SPHACOS (*Med.*) a sort of sage.

ELE'MBAT (*Chem.*) Alkaline Salts.

ELEME'NTARIES (*Myth.*) a sort of fairy beings who were supposed to inhabit the elements.

E'LEMENTS (*Chem.*) the first principles of which bodies are composed. Among the ancients there were reckoned four elements or elementary principles, namely, fire, air, earth, and water; which, as they supposed, entered into the composition of all other bodies, but themselves admitted of no decomposition. In modern chemistry no such elementary principles are admitted, it being supposed that all bodies either are or may be decomposed; thus water is said to consist of hydrogen and oxygen.

ELEMENTS (*Geom.*) the infinitely small parts or differentials of a right line, curve, surface, or solid.

ELEMENTS (*Lit.*) the first principles of any art or science.

E'LEMI (*Bot.*) a sort of gum flowing from the *Amyris elemifera* of Linnæus.

ELEMI'FERA (*Bot.*) the *Amyris elemifera* of Linnæus.

ELE'NCHUS (*Log.*) ἔλεγχος, from ἐλέγχω, to confute; a sophistical sort of argument.

ELE'NGI (*Bot.*) a tree of Malabar, the *Mimusops elengi* of Linnæus.

ELE'NIA (*Ant.*) ἑλένια, a festival celebrated by the Laconians in honour of Helena. *Hesychius.*

ELENOPHO'RIA (*Ant.*) ἑλενοφορία, an Athenian festival, so called from the ἑλέναι, i. e. vessels made of bulrushes, which were carried about at that time.

ELEOCHRYSUM (*Bot.*) vide *Gnaphalium*.

ELEOSELI'NUM (*Bot.*) the *Apium graveolens* of Linnæus.

E'LEPHANT (*Her.*) is borne as a charge in coat armour, either whole or in parts, as in the annexed figure. He beareth " *Gules* an elephant passant *argent*, tusked *or*; by the name of *Elphinston*."—*Order of the Elephant*, or *Order of St. Mary*, an order of knighthood instituted by Canute in 1184. Knights of this order wear a blue ribband, with a towered elephant pendant, and an image of the Holy Virgin encircled with rays.

ELEPHA'NTIA (*Med.*) vide *Elephantiasis.*

ELEPHANTI'ASIS (*Med.*) or *Elephantia*, ἐλεφαντίασις, from ἐλέφας, an elephant; a species of leprosy; so called because it makes the legs of the person affected appear like those of an elephant. *Aret. de Sig. & Caus Diut. Morb.* l. 2, c. 13; *Cels.* l. 3, c. 25; *Gal. Defin. Med.; Cæl. Aurel. Morb. Chron.* l. 4, c. 1; *Aet. Tetrab.* 4, serm. 1, c. 120; *Paul. Æginet.* l. 4, c. 1; *Act. de Meth. Med.* l. 2, c. 11; *Avicenn.* l. 22, *Fen.* 3, tract 1, c. 16, &c.; *Foes. Œconom. Hippocrat.*

ELEPHANTIASIS is a genus of diseases, Class *Cachexiæ*, Order *Impetigines*, in Cullen's Nosology.

ELEPHANTINI LIBRI (*Ant.*) books among the Romans, in which their public acts were registered. They were so called, as is supposed, because they were made of ivory.

Vopis. in Tacit.; *Ulp.* l. 52, *D. de Legat.*; *Oisel. in Aul. Gell.* l. 2, c. 17.

ELEPHANTI'NUM EMPLASTRUM (*Med.*) a plaster described by Celsus, and another by Oribasius. *Cels.* l. 5, c. 19; *Oribas. Synop.* l. 3.

ELEPHANTO'PUS (*Bot.*) a genus of plants, Class 19 *Syngenesia*, Order 5 *Polygamia-Segregata*.

Generic Character. CAL. *involucre* of three broad petals.—COR. *compound* tubular.—STAM. *filaments* five; *anthers* tubular.—PIST. *germ* ovate; *style* filiform; *stigmas* two.—PER. none; *seeds* solitary; *receptacle* naked.

Species. The species are as follow—*Elephantopus scaber*, *Scabiosæ affinis*, *Bidens*, seu *Echinophora*, Rough-leaved Elephant's Foot, a perennial.—*Elephantopus spicatus*, seu *Conyza*, &c.

E'LEPHANT'S-FOOT (*Bot.*) the *Elephantopus* of Linnæus, a plant so called, from the form of its lower leaves.

ELEPHANTS' HEADS (*Her.*) are mostly borne *erased*.

E'LEPHAS (*Zool.*) Elephant; a genus of animals, Class *Mammalia*, Order *Bruta*, having foreteeth in either jaw, and no lower tusks; upper tusks elongate, and a long prehensile proboscis.

E'LEPHUS (*Bot.*) another name for the *Rhinanthus* of Linnæus.

ELEPHEBO'LIA (*Ant.*) vide *Elaphebolia*.

ELETTA'RI (*Bot.*) the *Amomium Granum paradisia* of Linnæus.

E'LEVATED (*Astrol.*) a planet is said to be elevated above another when, being stronger, it weakens the influence of the other.

ELEVATED (*Her.*) an epithet for wings, signifying the same as *Erect*.

ELEVA'TION (*Surg.*) a name for a tumour, because it is an elevation of the part affected.

ELEVATION (*Chem.*) the rising up of any matter in the manner of fume and vapour.

ELEVATION (*Gunn.*) the angle which the chace of a cannon or mortar, or the axis of the hollow cylinder, makes with the place of the horizon.

ELEVATION (*Astron.*) a term applied to the Equator, Pole, Star, &c. to denote its height above the horizon.—*Elevation of the pole* is the height of the pole above the horizon, or the number of degrees the pole is raised above the horizon.

ELEVATION *of the pole* (*Dial.*) the angle which the style makes with the substilar line.

ELEVATION (*Archit.*) a draught and description of the face or principal side of a building, which in common language is called the *upright*. The word is sometimes taken for the perspective representation of the whole body of a building.

ELEVATION *of the Host* (*Ecc.*) that part of the ceremony of the mass which consists in the priest's raising the host above his head for the adoration of the people.

ELEVATION (*Chem.*) the causing any matter to rise in fume or vapours by means of heat.

ELEVA'TOR (*Anat.*) an epithet for several muscles which serve to draw the parts of the body upwards, as—*Elevator labii superioris et inferioris*, those which serve to draw up the upper and lower lips.—*Elevator oculi*, the muscle of the eye, arising near the place where the optic nerves enter the orbit.

ELEVATO'RIUM (*Surg.*) a surgeon's instrument, wherewith depressed skulls are raised up again.

ELE'VENTH (*Mus.*) an interval consisting of ten conjunct degrees, or eleven diatonic sounds.

ELEU'SINE (*Bot.*) another name for the *Cynosurus* of Linnæus.

ELEUSI'NIA (*Ant.*) ἐλευσίνια, one of the most mysterious solemnities of any in Greece, which, on that account was called, by way of distinction, μυστήρια, i. e. the mysteries. It was celebrated in honour of Eleusis, or Proserpine, the daughter of Ceres. *Aristoph. Plut.*; *Isocrat. in Panegyric.*; *Diodor. Sicul.* l. 6; *Poll. Onom.* l. 1, segm. 37; *Strab.* l. 9; *Pausan.* l. 10, c. 31; *Plut. in Demet.*; *Tertull. adver. Valerian.*; *Clem. Alexand. Stromat.* l. 5; *August. de Civ. Dei.* l. 7, c. 20; *Gregor. Nazian. Orat.* περὶ ἁγίων φώτων; *Harpocration*; *Suidas Tetz. ad Lycoph.*; *Meurs. de Eleus. &c.*; *Castellus, &c apud Gronov.* tom. 7.

ELEUTHE'RIA (*Ant.*) ἐλευθέρια, a festival celebrated at Platæa, in honour of Jupiter Eleutherius, i. e. the assertor of liberty; by delegates from all parts of Greece. This festival was celebrated in commemoration of the signal defeat of the Persians under Mardonius. *Pind. Olymp.* l. 7; *Strab.* l. 9; *Plut. Aristid.*; *Pausan.* l. 9, c. 2; *Athen.* l. 3; *Eustath. in Il.* l. 2; *Schol. Anthol. Epigram. Græc.* l. 2, tit. 1, &c.

ELF-A'RROWS (*Archæol.*) flint-stones sharpened and jagged like arrow-heads, which were weapons of offence among the ancient Britons.

ELICHRY'SUM (*Bot.*) the *Gnaphalium Stœchas* of Linnæus.

ELI'CITI (*Eth.*) an epithet applied to the more immediate acts of the will, as loving, hating, &c.

ELIGMA (*Med.*) a Linctus.

ELIMINA'TION (*Algeb.*) an operation by which any number n of equations containing n unknown quantities being given, we find one equation, which involves only one unknown quantity. [vide *Algebra*]

ELIOCA'RPOS (*Bot.*) the *Ornithogalum umbellatum* of Linnæus.

ELI'QUAMENT (*Chem.*) a fat juice squeezed out of fat or fish.

ELI'SION (*Gram.*) the cutting off a vowel at the end of a word in a verse.

ELI'SORS (*Law*) two persons named by the court, and sworn to indifferently choose a jury in cases of challenge to the sheriff and coroners for partiality, &c.

ELI'XIR (*Med.*) a medicine made by strong infusion, where the ingredients are almost dissolved in the *menstruum*, and give it a thicker consistence than a tincture. This was formerly held in such high esteem, that the word has since been used to imply any very powerful tincture; and the *grand elixir* is another word for an all-powerful medicine.

ELIXIVA'TIO (*Chem.*) from *elixo*, to boil; the extraction of a fixed salt from vegetables by an affusion of water.

ELK (*Zool.*) the *Cervus alces* of Linnæus, a beast of the stag kind, equal to a horse in size, which inhabits all the four quarters of the world except Africa. It has a skin hard enough almost to resist a musket-ball, goes on its hoof with a shambling gait about 50 miles a day, and feeds on the branches of trees and marsh plants.

E'LKE (*Bot.*) a kind of yew formerly employed in the making of bows.

ELL (*Com.*) a measure containing three feet nine inches.

ELLEBORI'NE (*Bot.*) the *Ashantia epipactus* of Linnæus.

ELLEBO'RUM (*Bot.*) the *Helleborus viridis et fœtidus*. *Oribas. Med. Coll.* l. 15; *Act. Tetrab.* l, serm. 1; *Paul. Ægin.*

ELLI'PSIS (*Geom.*) ἔλλειψις, a defect, is taken for a conic section, vulgarly known by the name of an oval, which was so called by Apollonius, because in this figure the squares of the ordinates are less than, or defective of, the rectangle under the parameters and abscissæe. [vide *Conic Sections*]

ELLIPSIS (*Rhet.*) a figure whereby some part of a discourse is left.

ELLI'PSOID (*Geom.*) an elliptical spheroid, being the solid generated by the revolution of an ellipse about either axis.

ELLI'PTIC (*Bot.*) an epithet for a leaf that is in the form of an ellipse.

ELLI'PTICAL (*Math.*) an epithet for any thing in the form of or appertaining to an ellipsis.

ELLIPTI'CITY (*Geom.*) of the terrestrial spheroid is the ratio or the difference between the two semiaxes.

ELLI'PTOID (*Geom.*) an infinite or indefinite ellipse defined by the indefinite equation, as $y^{m+n} = bx^m (a-x)^n$, where m and n are greater than 1.

ELLI'SIA (*Bot.*) a genus of plants so called in memory of John Ellis, F. R. S., Class 5 *Pentandria*, Order 1 *Monogynia*.
- Generic Character. CAL. perianth one-leaved.—COR. one-petalled.—STAM. *filaments* five; *anthers* roundish.—PIST. *germ* roundish; *style* filiform; *stigma* oblong.—PER. *capsule* bag-form; *seeds* globose.
- Species. The species is an annual, as the—*Ellisia Nyctelea, Polemonium, Planta,* seu *Scorpiurus*, Cut-leaved Ellisia, native of Virginia.

ELLISIA is also the *Durantia ellisia* of Linnæus.

E'LLOBOS (*Bot.*) ἐλλοβος, an epithet for such seeds or fruits as are contained in pods or lobes.

ELM (*Bot.*) the *Ulmus* of Linnæus; a sort of tree which grows to a very great height, is raised either by seeds, suckers, or layers, and thrives best in a rich black earth. The sorts most fit for cultivation are, the common Elm, the Witch-Elm, and Witch-Hazle. The timber of elm is next to that of oak for value, being particularly useful for mills, and all other works which are exposed to wet.

ELMI'NTHES (*Ent.*) worms.

ELO'DES (*Med.*) an epithet for a fever which is attended with a profuse sweat.

ELOI'NE (*Law*) from the French *éloigner*, signifies to send to a distance. Stat. 13 Ed. 1, c. 15.

ELONGA'TA (*Law*) a return of the sheriff that cattle are not to be found, or are removed so far that he cannot make deliverance.

ELONGA'TION (*Surg.*) a kind of imperfect disjointing, when the ligament of a joint is stretched and extended, but not so that the bone is quite out of joint.

ELONGATION (*Astron.*) the removal of a planet to the farthest distance it can be from the sun, as it appears to an observer on the earth.—*Angle of Elongation* is an angle contained under lines supposed to be drawn from the centres of the sun and planet to the centre of the earth. [vide *Astronomy*]

ELO'PEMENT (*Law*) the going away from a husband; for which, without voluntary reconcilement to her husband, a wife shall lose her dower; nor is he obliged to allow her any maintenance.

E'LOPS (*Ich.*) a genus of Fishes of the *Abdominal* Order, having a smooth head, and a palate rough with teeth.

ELO'PHORUS (*Ent.*) a division of the genus *Nitidula*, comprehending the insects which have the lip square.

E'LVELA (*Bot.*) another name for the *Helvella* of Linnæus.

E'LVERS (*Ich.*) a sort of small gregs or eels.

E'LUL (*Chron.*) אלול, a Jewish month answering to part of August.

ELUTE'RIA (*Bot.*) the *Cluytia eluteria* of Linnæus.

ELUTRIA'TIO (*Chem.*) the pouring a liquor out of one vessel into another, in order to separate the subsiding matter from the clear and fluid part.

ELU'VIES (*Med.*) the humour discharged in a *Fluor Albus*; also the effluvium from a swampy place.

ELYCHRY'SUM (*Bot.*) the *Stæhelina dubia* of Linnæus.

E'LYMUS (*Bot.*) a genus of plants, Class 3 *Triandria*, Order 2 *Digynia*.
- Generic Character. CAL. *receptacle* common.—COR. two-valved.—STAM. *filaments* three; *anthers* oblong.—PIST. *germ* top-shaped; *styles* two; *stigmas* simple.—PER. none; *seeds* covered.
- Species. The species are perennials, as the—*Elymus arenarius, Triticum,* seu *Gramen caninum,* Sea Lyme-grass, native of Europe.—*Elymus Virginicus,* seu *Hordeum,* Virginian Lyme-grass.—*Elymus europeus,* Wood Lyme-grass, or Barley-grass; but—*Elymus Caput medusæ,* seu *Avena,* Portugal Lyme-grass, and *Elymus histrix,* Lyme-grass, native of the Levant, are annuals.

ELYMUS is also the *Hordeum jubatum* of Linnæus.

ELY'SIAN *fields* (*Myth.*) a paradise of delightful groves and meadows, into which the heathens imagined that the souls of good men passed after death.

ELYTHRO'IDES (*Anat.*) the *tunica vaginalis* of the testes.

ELY'TRA (*Ent.*) from the Greek ἔλυτρον, a sheath; a name for the wing-sheaths, or upper crustaceous membranes, which cover the wings of the insects of the beetle tribe.

ELYTROCE'LE (*Anat.*) from ἔλυτρον, a vagina or sheath, and κήλη, a tumour; a hernia in the vagina.

ELY'TRON (*Anat.*) ἔλυτρον, a sheath, from ἐλύω, to involve, is applied by Hippocrates to the membranes which involve the spinal marrow. *Hippocrat. de Artic.; Gall. Comm.* 3; *Gorr. Def. Med.; Foes. Œconom. Hippocrat.*

EMACIA'NTES (*Med.*) diseases which occasion a wasting of the body.

EMANCIPA'TIO (*Ant.*) the setting of children free from the power of their fathers. *Sigon. de Judic.* l. 1, c. 2.

EMA'NSIO (*Med.*) cohibition of the menses.

EMANUE'NSIS (*Lit.*) one who writes what another dictates.

EMARGINA'TIO (*Surg.*) taking away the scurf about the brims of wounds and sores. *Plin.* l. 28, c. 9.

EMARGINA'TUS (*Bot.*) an epithet for a leaf that is notched at the end; also for a corolla, as in the *Agrostemma coronaria,* &c.; and for the stigma, as in the Class *Didynamia*.

EMBA'MMA (*Med.*) ἔμβαμμα, from ἐμβάπτω, to immerge or dip in; a medicated pickle, or sauce for the food. *Marcell. de Med.* c. 30; *Aet. Tetrab.* 3, serm. 1, c. 24.

EMBA'PHION (*Med.*) vide *Acetabulum*.

EMBARCADE'RE (*Com.*) the name for places on the coasts of America that serve for the landing of goods.

EMBA'RGO (*Mar.*) a prohibition upon all shipping not to leave any port, which is commonly issued by public authority on the breaking out of a war, &c.

EMBARKA'TION (*Mar.*) the act of going, or putting things on board a vessel for the purpose of sailing.

E'MBASIS (*Med.*) ἔμβασις, from ἐμβαίνω, to go in; a bathing-tub or vessel filled with warm water.

EMBA'SSADOR (*Polit.*) one appointed to act for and represent the person of a prince, or state, in a foreign country.

EMBA'TER (*Ant.*) the hole or sight of a cross-bow. *Vitruv.* l. 1, c. 2.

EMBATEU'TICON *jus* (*Law*) a law by which people might keep things pawned to them, in their own possession.

EMBA'TTELED (*Her.*) in the form of a battlement. [vide *Crenelle.*]

E'MBER-DAYS (*Ecc.*) particular days of humiliation in the Ember-Weeks, namely, Wednesdays, Fridays, and Saturdays, so called from the custom of putting ashes on the head.—*Ember-Weeks,* four seasons in the year more particularly set apart for prayer and fasting, i. e. the first week in Lent, and the next after Whitsunday, the 14th of September, and the 13th of December.

EMBERI'ZA (*Orn.*) a genus of Birds, Order *Passeres,* having a conical bill, and mandibles receding from each other.
- Species. Birds of this genus are principally known in English by the name of the Bunting, except the *Emberiza hortulana,* which is called the Ortolan, feeds principally on panic grass, and grows prodigiously fat, when it is esteemed a great delicacy. The Emberiza is a migratory bird, which appears in England before the setting in of frost and snow.

EMBLE'MA (*Ant.*) ἔμβλημα, from ἐμβάλλω, to insert; picture-work of wood, stone, or metal, finely set in divers colours, as in seals, chess-boards, tables, and the like: also ornaments embossed which may be taken off or put on at pleasure. *Cic. in Verr.* 4, c. 17; *Or.* l. 3, c. 43; *Varr. de Re Rust.* l. 3, c. 2; *Suet. in Tib.* c. 71; *Dio*, l. 57; *Bud. in Pandect.* p. 120; *Jun. de Pict.* l. 3, c. 1; *Salmas in Solin.* 736.

E'MBLEMENTS (*Archæol.*) the profits of lands which have been sowed. *Co. Lit.* 55.

E'MBLERS *de Gentz* (*Law*) carrying off people.

EMBLICA (*Bot.*) the *Phyllanthus emblica* of Linnæus.

EMBOI'TEMENT (*Mil.*) French for the closing up a number of men for the purpose of securing the front ranks from injury.

EMBOI'TURE (*Mech.*) French for an iron box screwed over the nave of a wheel, and which covers the axle-tree.

E'MBOLE (*Surg.*) ἐμβολὴ, from ἐμβάλλω, to put in; the reduction or setting of a dislocated bone.

EMBOLIMÆ'US (*Chron.*) ἐμβολιμαῖς, i. e. intercalary; an epithet for what is commonly called Leap-year.

EMBOLI'SMUS (*Chron.*) ἐμβολισμὸς, the adding to or putting in a day in any year, as in Leap-year.

EMBO'LIUM (*Ant.*) an interlude.

EMBO'LUM (*Ant.*) ἐμβολον, the beak, head, or stern of a ship. *Poll. Onom.* l. 1, c. 9; *Petron.* c. 30; *Suidas.*

EMBORI'SMA (*Med.*) Aneurism. *Cic. pro Sext.* c. 4.

EMBO'SSING (*Sculpt.*) a sort of sculpture, or carving, where the figure is protuberant and projects from the plane in which it is cut; it is called by the Italians *basso mezzo*, and *basso relievo*, according as it projects more or less.

EMBO'ST (*Sport.*) an epithet for a deer that foams at the mouth when he is hard chased.

EMBO'THRIUM (*Bot.*) a genus of plants, Class 4 *Tetrandria*, Order 1 *Monogynia*.
Generic Character. CAL. none.—COR. petals four.—STAM. filaments four; anthers oblong.—PIST. germ linear; style none; stigma roundish.—PER. follicle round; seeds ovate.
Species. The species are shrubs, as the *Embothrium umbellatum*, native of New Caledonia.—*Embothrium coccineum*, native of Terra del Fuego.

E'MBOTUM (*Surg.*) a funnel which serves to convey fumes into any orifice of the body.

EMBOUCHU'RE (*Mus.*) French for the aperture of a flute, or other wind instrument.

EMBO'WED (*Her.*) an epithet for any thing bent like a bow, as the dolphin; also a sinister arm, couped at the elbow, is said to be embowed.

EMBRACE'OUR (*Law*) or *embrasour*, he who, when a matter is in trial between party and party, comes to the bar with one of the parties, and being bribed thereto, endeavours to corrupt the judge. *Stat.* 19 *H.* 7, c. 15; *Co. Lit.* 369.

EMBRA'CERY (*Law*) the offence of an *embraceour*.

EMBRA'CING (*Bot.*) or stem-clasping; an epithet for a leaf.

EMBRASU'RE (*Archit.*) an enlargement made in the wall to give more light or convenience to the windows, &c.

EMBRASURE (*Gun.*) French for a piece of iron which grasps the trunnions of a piece of ordnance when it is raised upon the boring machine.

EMBRASU'RES (*Fort.*) the holes in a parapet through which the cannons are laid to fire into the moat, or field.

EMBRE'GMA (*Med.*) ἔμβρεγμα, from ἐμβρέχω, to irrigate; an embrocation, or external kind of remedy, which consists in irrigating the part affected; it is commonly called a fomentation.

E'MBRING-DAYS (*Ecc.*) the same as *Ember-Days*.

EMBROCATION (*Med.*) vide *Embregma*.

EMBRO'CHE (*Med.*) vide *Embregma*.

EMBROI'DERY (*Mech.*) figured work wrought on silk or cloth with gold or silver thread.

EMBRU'ED (*Her.*) an epithet for a weapon, &c. that is bloody.

E'MBRYO (*Anat.*) ἔμβρυον, the child, or fœtus, in the womb, so called because, βρύω, it pullulates and grows within the womb. Galen divides the time of gestation into four periods, of which the embryo is the third period, when the fœtus begins to develope itself. According to Marcellus the embryo is what a pregnant woman carries in her womb until the period of her delivery. *Hippocrat.* l. 5, aphor. 31, &c.; *Gal. de Caus. Symptom.* l. 1; *Gorr. Def. Med.*

EMBRYONA'TUM *Sulphur* (*Chem.*) Sulphur united with minerals and metals.

EMBRYORE'CTES (*Med.*) ἐμβρυορήκτης, from ἔμβρυον and ῥήττω, to break; an instrument with which a dead child is drawn out of the mother's womb.

EMBYOTHLA'STES (*Surg.*) an instrument wherewith they break the bones of a dead child, that it may be more conveniently taken out of the womb.

EMBRYO'TOMY (*Med.*) from ἔμβρυον, a fœtus, and τέμνω, to cut; an exsection of the child out of the mother's womb. *Paul. Æginet.* l. 6, c. 74; *Gorr. Def. Med.*

EMBRYU'LCUS (*Med.*) vide *Embryorectes*.

EMBULA'RCHI SUFFUMIGIUM (*Med.*) a suffumigation described by Aetius. *Tetrab.* 4, serm. 4, c. 122.

EMBUSCA'TUM *marmor* (*Min.*) the name of a particular kind of marble dug out of Mount Sinai.

EME'NDALS (*Archæol.*) an old word used in the Inner Temple for what remains in bank, or in the Stock of the House.

EMENDA'RE (*Law*) to make amends for any trespass or crime committed. *Leg. Edw. Confess.* c. 35. Hence a capital crime not to be atoned for by a fine was called "inemendabile." *Leg. Canut.*

EMENDA'TION (*Law*) an amending or correcting of abuses, as *Emendatio Panni*, the power of looking to the assize of cloth.—*Emendatio Panis et Cervisiæ*, the power of supervising the weights and measures of bread and beer.

E'MERALD (*Min.*) a precious stone of a green colour.

EMERALD (*Her.*) another name for *vert*, or the green tincture in coat armour.

TO EME'RGE (*Nat.*) is said of any body specifically lighter than water, which, after being pressed down, forcibly rises again to view.

EME'RGENT (*Astron.*) an epithet for a star at the moment that it goes out of the sun's beams, so as to become visible.

EMERGENT *year* (*Chron.*) the year, or epoch, from which any computation of time is made, as in Christian countries from the time of our Saviour's birth.

E'MERIL (*Min.*) or emery, a sort of stone used in burnishing metals, &c.; also a glazier's diamond to cut glass.

EME'RITUS (*Ant.*) an epithet for a soldier that has served his time, a veteran. *Veget.* l. 2, c. 3; *Isid. Orig.* l. 9, c. 3.

EME'RSION (*Astron.*) an epithet for the sun and moon, which become visible just after they have undergone an eclipse; it is also applied to a star that becomes visible after it has been hidden by the rays of the sun.

EME'RSUS (*Bot.*) is the *Coronilla camerus* of Linnæus.

E'MERUS (*Med.*) a laxative.

E'MERY (*Min.*) Ground iron ore. [vide *Emeril*]

EME'SIA (*Med.*) or *Emetos*, ἔμετος, from ἐμέω, to vomit; the act of vomiting, particularly applied by Hippocrates to a discharge of the blood from the stomach by the mouth. *Hippocrat. de Morb.* l. 1; *Foes. Oeconom. Hippocrat.*

EME'TICS (*Med.*) from ἐμέω, to vomit; medicines which provoke vomiting. The word is used in this sense by Cicero in speaking of Cæsar, who, he said, ἐμετικὴν agebat, i. e. took an emetic. *Cic. ad Attic.* l. 3, ep. ult.

EMETOCATHA'RTICUM (*Med.*) a medicine which both vomits and purges.

EME'U (*Her.*) a sort of bird, otherwise called the Cassowary, which goes by this name among the Heralds.

EMIGRA'TION (*Polit.*) the leaving one's native country to reside in foreign parts.

E'MINENCE (*Polit.*) a title of honour given to cardinals.

EMINENCE (*Fort.*) a height which overlooks and commands a place.

EMINENCE (*Med.*) any protuberance or preternatural tumour.

EMINE'NTIAL *Equation* (*Algeb.*) an artificial kind of equation, which contains another eminently.

EMIR (*Polit.*) a Turkish prince, or lord, particularly one that is descended from Mahomet.

EMIRA'LEM (*Mil.*) the general of the Turks, or the keeper of all their colours.

EMISSA'RIUM (*Med.*) any orifice in the body, either natural or morbid, by which any thing is emitted.

E'MISSARY (*Polit.*) a person sent on a secret mission among the people, or into a foreign country, to sound their minds and tempers.

E'MISSARY *of a gland* (*Anat.*) its duct or canal, by which it emits its contents.

EMMENAGO'GA (*Med.*) ἐμμεναγωγὰ, from ἐμμένια, the menses, and ἄγω, to bring; medicines which promote the menses in women.

EMME'NIA (*Med.*) vide *Emmenagoga*.

E'MMET (*Ent.*) another name for the ant.

EMMO'TOS (*Med.*) from μοτός, lint; an epithet for parts of the body, or any thing which requires the application of lint. *Hippocrat. de Art.*; *Gal. de Comp. Med. per Gen.* l. 2, c. 2; *Gorr. Defin. Med.*; *Foes. Oeconom. Hippocrat.*

EMO'DIA (*Med.*) a stupor of the teeth.

EMO'LLIENTS (*Med.*) μαλθακτήρια, softening; medicines which soften the asperities of the humours, and render the solids at the same time supple. *Hippocrat. de Mul.* l. 1; *Aret. de Curat. Acut. Morb.* l. 2, c. 7; *Gal. de Simpl.* l. 1, c. 26; *Act. de Meth. Med.* l. 6, c. 9.

EMOU'SSER (*Mil.*) a French term signifying to cut off; the four corners of a battalion which has formed a square so as to give it an octagon figure.

EMPA'LEMENT (*Bot.*) a former name for the calyx of flowers.

EMPA'NEL (*Law*) vide *Inpanel*.

EMPA'RLANCE (*Law*) vide *Imparlance*.

EMPA'SMS (*Med.*) medicines composed of sweet powders to take away sweat, and allay inflammation. *Oribas. Med. Collect.*; l. 10, c. 31; *Gorr. Def. Med.*

E'MPETRUM (*Bot.*) a genus of plants, Class 22 *Diodecia*, Order 2 *Triandria*.
Generic Character. CAL. *perianth* three-leaved.—COR. *petals* three.—STAM. *filaments* three; *anthers* upright.—PIST. *germ* superior; *style* scarce any; *stigmas* nine.—PER. *berry* orbiculate; *seeds* nine.
Species. The species are shrubs, as the—*Empetrum album*, seu *Erica*, White-berried Heath, native of Portugal.—*Empetrum nigrum*, seu *Erica*, Black-berried Heath, native of Europe.

EMPETRUM is also another name for the *Begonia* of Linnæus.

EMPHATICAL *Colours* (*Nat.*) colours so called, which are often seen in clouds before the rising of the sun, and after its setting.

EMPHRA'CTICA (*Med.*) ἐμφρακτικὰ, from φράττω, to obstruct; medicines which have a tendency to stop up any passage. *Gorr. Def. Med.*

EMPHYSE'MA (*Med.*) ἐμφύσημα, from φυσάω, to inflate; signifies generally any flatulent humour; but is particularly applied to the air confined in the cellular membrane. *Hippocrat. Epid.* l. 3; *Gal. de Meth. Med.* l. 14; *Act. de Meth. Med.* l. 2, c. 12.

EMPHYTEU'SIS (*Law*) a renting of land, in the Civil Law, on condition of planting it.

EMPI'RIC *Sect* (*Med.*) from πεῖρα, to experience; a sect of physicians who practised medicine from experience, and not from theory. *Cels.* l. 1, c. 1; *Gal. de Sect.*
Empirics are now such as deviate from the rules of science and regular practice to follow nostrums and private opinions; they are better known by the name of *quacks*.

E'MPIS (*Ent.*) a genus of Insects of the Dipterous Order, having a *mouth* with an inflected sucker and proboscis; *antennæ* setaceous; and *feelers* short.
Species. These minute insects live by sucking the blood and juices of other animals.

EMPLA'STICS (*Med.*) medicines which constipate and shut up the pores of the body so that sulphureous vapours cannot pass. *Gorr. Def. Med.*

EMPLA'STRUM (*Med.*) a plaister.

EMPLE'CTO *opus* (*Archit.*) a work knit and couched together, when the stones are so laid as to join one in the other.

EMPLATTO'MENA (*Med.*) vide *Emplastics*.

EMPLE'UTUM (*Bot.*) a genus of plants, Class 21 *Monoecia*, Order 4 *Triandria*.
Generic Character. CAL. *perianth* one-leaved.—COR. none.—STAM. *filaments* four; *anthers* oblong.—PIST. *germ* superior; *style* none; *stigma* cylindric.—PER. *capsule* oblong; *seed* solitary.
Species. The single species is a shrub, as the *Empleurum serrulatum*, seu *Diosma*, Cape Empleurum, native of the Cape of Good Hope.

EMPNEUMATO'SIS (*Med.*) ἐμπνευματώσις, from ἐμπνέω, to inflate; an inflation of the stomach, or the womb. *Gal. Def. Med.*; *Marcell. de Med.* c. 20; *Paul. Æginet.* l. 3, c. 70; *Act. de Meth. Med.* l. 2, c. 21.

EMPO'RIUM (*Anat.*) the common sensory of the brain.

EMPRION (*Med.*) ἐμπρίων, from πρίω, to saw; an epithet for a pulse when the artery is serrated or indented like a saw. *Gal. de Puls.*

EMPROSTHO'TONOS (*Med.*) ἐμπροσθότονος, from ἔμπροσθεν, forward, and τείνω, to bend; a sort of convulsions of the neck, when the chin is immoveably fixed on the breast; in distinction from the ὀπισθότονος, when the head is bent backwards; and the τέτανος, when it is immoveably upright. *Aret. de Caus. et Sign. Acut. Morb.*; *Cels.* l. 4, c. 3; *Oribas. Synop.* l. 9, c. 16.

EMPTY'SIS (*Med.*) ἔμπτυσις, from πτύω, to spit; a spitting of blood, which is limited by Aretæus to such a discharge only as comes from the mouth, and adjacent parts. *Aret. de Acut. Morb.* l. 2, c. 2.

EMPYE'MA (*Med.*) ἐμπύημα, from πύον, pus; a collection of pus, or matter, in any part of the body, particularly in the cavity of the chest. *Hippocrat.* l. 7, aphor. 38; *Aret. de Caus. et Sign. Morb. Acut.* l. 1, c. 8, 9; *Gal. Comm. in Hippocrat. Progn.* l. 3; *Cæl. Aurelian. de Morb. Chron.* l. 5, c. 10; *Marc. de Med.* c. 7; *Gorr. Def. Med.*; *Foes. Œconom. Hippocrat.*

EMPYE'MATA (*Med.*) suppurating medicines. [vide *Empyema*]

E'MPYI (*Med.*) ἔμπυοι, an epithet for such persons as have purulent abscesses internally. [vide *Empyema*]

EMPYRÆUM *cælum* (*Astron.*) the highest of the celestial spheres.

EMPY'REAL *air* (*Phy.*) the fiery element above the ethereal.

EMPYREU'MA (*Chem.*) ἐμπύρευμα of ἐμπυράω, to burn; that taste or smell of the fire which, in distillations, happens to some oils, &c.

EMPYREU'MATA (*Med.*) the remains of a fever after the critical time of a disease.

E'MPYROS (*Med.*) ἔμπυρος, one labouring under a fever. *Hippocrat. de Morb.* l. 2.

E'MRODS (*Med.*) vide *Hæmorroids*.

EMU'LGENT (*Anat.*) an epithet for the vessels of the kidneys, so called from *emulgeo*, to milk, because they were supposed to strain, and, as it were, to milk the serum through the kidneys. The emulgent artery is a branch of the *Aorta*, and the emulgent vein of the *Vena Cava*.

EMU'LSION (*Med.*) a medicinal drink made of the kernels of seeds infused in a convenient liquor.

EMU'NCTORY (*Anat.*) an epithet for the passage by which any thing vitiated or useless is passed off; thus, the skin is the *emunctory* of the body, the nose the *emunctory* of the brain, and the glands are also *emunctories* of different parts.

EMU'NDANS (*Med.*) an epithet for an external detersive medicine.

ENÆ'MOS (*Med.*) ἔναιμος, from αἷμα, blood, a medicine for stopping blood. *Hippocrat. de Art.*; *Cel. l. 5, c. 19*; *Cæl. Aurelian. de Morb. Chron. l. 2, c. 1*; *Gal. Com. in Hippocrat.*; *Foes. Œconom. Hippocrat.*

ENÆORE'MA (*Med.*) ἐναιώρημα, from αἰωρέω, to exalt; a name for the pendulous substance in the urine, otherwise called *sublimamentum*, or according to Celsus *suspensæ nebeculæ*. *Hippocrat. Epid. l. 1, &c.*; *Gal. Comm.*; *Gorr. Defin. Med.*; *Foes. Œconom. Hippocrat.*

E'NALLAGE (*Gram.*) a figure in grammar where there is a change of one case or mood for another.

ENALU'RON (*Her.*) an epithet for a bordure charged with birds. [vide *Bordure*]

ENA'MEL (*Anat.*) the cortex, or fine exterior covering of the teeth, which is a vitreous substance.

ENAMEL (*Paint.*) to paint with various mineral colours. *Enamel* is also a kind of coloured glass used in painting in enamel.

ENANTE'SIS (*Anat.*) ἀντησις, from ἀντάω, to meet; a meeting, or near approach of the ascending and descending vessels. *Gal.*

ENANTIO'SIS (*Rhet.*) ἐναντίωσις, a rhetorical figure where, that which is spoken negatively, is to be understood affirmatively.

ENARGE'A (*Bot.*) a genus of plants, Class 6 *Hexandria*, Order 1 *Monogynia*.
Generic Character. CAL. none.—COR. *petals* six.—STAM. *filaments* six.—PIST. *germ* roundish; *style* three.—PER. *berry* three-celled; *seeds* four.
Species. The single species is the *Enargia marginata*, native of Terra del Fuego.

ENARI'CYMON (*Med.*) vide *Aricymon*.

ENARTHRO'SIS (*Med.*) from ἄρθρον, a joint; the ball and socket joint; a species of *diarthrosis*, or moveable connexion of bones.

ENBRE'VER (*Archæol.*) to write down in short. *Brit. 56*.

ENCÆ'NIA (*Ant.*) anniversary feasts to commemorate the building a city, the completing or consecrating of any new and public work, &c. St. Augustin interprets the feast of the dedication of the temple by the same word; and the consecration days, in the Christian church, have also been so called. *Quintil. l. 7, c. 2*; *S. August. in Johann. xlviii. 1*; *Suidas.*; *Paul. Diacon. in Justinian. l. 16*; *Gyrald. Syntag. Deor. l. 17, p. 502*; *Rhodig. Ant. Lect. l. 22, c. 14*; *Stuck. de Ant. Conviv. l. 1, c. 33*.
Encænia is used, in modern times, in application to the commemorative festival, at Oxford, at the close of the session, &c.

ENCA'NTHIS (*Med.*) ἐγκανθίς, from κανθός, the angle of the eye; a disease in the *caruncula lachrymalis*, of which there are two kinds; namely, the *Encanthis benigna*, and the *Encanthis maligna*, seu *inveterata*. *Cels. l. 7, c. 7*; *Gal. Defin. Med.*; *Oribas. Synop. l. 8, c. 54*; *Paul. Æginet. l. 3, c. 22*; *Act. de Meth. Med. l. 4, c. 11*.

ENCA'RDIA (*Min.*) a precious stone bearing the figure of a heart. *Plin. l. 37, c. 10*.

ENCA'RDION (*Med.*) ἐγκάρδιον, the heart, or pith of vegetables.

ENCA'RPIA (*Archit.*) flowerwork or fruitwork on the corner of pillars. *Vitruv. l. 4, c. 1*; *Philand. in Vitruv.*; *Bald. Lex Vit.*

ENCATALE'PSIS (*Med.*) vide *Catalepsis*.

ENCATHI'SMA (*Med.*) ἐγκάθισμα, from ἐγκαθῆσθαι, to sit in; a semicupium, or bath for half the body.

ENCA'UMA (*Med.*) ἔγκαυμα, from καίω, to burn; a pustule contracted by a burn; or the mark left by a burn. *Act. Tetrab. 2, serm. 3, c. 25*.

ENCA'USIS (*Med.*) the same as *Encauma*.

ENCA'USTIC (*Paint.*) the art of enamelling or painting with fire, which was in use among the ancients; but is now unknown. *Plin. l. 35, c. 2*; *Salmas. Exercit. Plinian. p. 164*.

ENCEI'NTE (*Fort.*) the whole compass of a fortification, or of the ground fortified.

ENCE'PHALOS (*Anat.*) ἐγκέφαλος, the brain.

ENCE'RIS (*Med.*) ἐγκηρίς, from κηρός, wax; small concretions of wax sometimes found in plaisters as they cool. *Gal. de Com. Med. per Gen.*

ENCHA'NTER'S NIGHTSHADE (*Bot.*) the *Circæa* of Linnæus, a perennial.

ENCHARA'XIS (*Surg.*) ἐγχάραξις, from χαράσσω, to scarify.

ENCHIRI'DIUM (*Ant.*) ἐγχειρίδιον, from χείρ, the hand; a manual, or a portable volume.

ENCHELIS (*Ent.*) a kind of worms so small as not to be visible to the naked eye. They are very simple, and have a cylindrical body.

ENCHRI'STA (*Med.*) ἔγχριστα, from χρίω, to anoint; unguents or medicines with which to anoint.

ENCHU'SA (*Bot.*) vide *Anchusa*.

ENCHYLO'MA (*Med.*) from χυλός, chyle; an inspissated juice or elixir.

E'NCHYMA (*Med.*) ἔγχυμα, from ἐγχέω, to infuse; an infusion, or liquid medicine to be infused into the eyes, ears, or injected into the thorax: it also implies a fulness of the vessels in regard to themselves, as πλῆθος κατὰ τὰ ἔγχυμα, a fulness from infusions. *Gal. de Mul. c. 6*; *Gorr. Def. Med.*

ENCHYMO'MA (*Med.*) or *Enchymosis*, ἐγχύμωμα, ἐγχύμωσις, a sudden effusion of blood into the cutaneous vessels, such as takes place in blushing. *Hippocrat. Epid. l. 2*; *Gorr. Def. Med.*; *Foes. Œconom. Hippocrat.*

ENCHYMOSIS (*Med.*) vide *Enchymoma*.

ENCHY'TA (*Med.*) from ἐγχέω, to infuse; a funnel by which any thing is instilled into the eyes, &c.

ENCHYTOS (*Med.*) ἔγχυτος, from ἐγχέω, to infuse; a funnel by which any thing is infused or instilled into any cavity of the body.

ENCLY'SMA (*Med.*) ἔγκλυσμα, from κλύζω, to wash; a clyster.

ENCLI'TIC (*Gram.*) certain particles joined to the end of a word, as *que*, *ne*, *ve*; so called because they cast back the accent to the syllable preceding.

ENCOE'LIA (*Anat.*) ἐγκοιλία, from κοιλία, the belly; the abdominal viscera.

ENCOLA'PTICA (*Mech.*) ἐγκολαπτικὴ, the art of making brass plates, and cutting in letters.

ENCO'LPIAS (*Ant.*) ἐγκολπίας, from κόλπος, a creek; winds arising out of creeks and nooks.

ENCO'MIUM (*Rhet.*) ἐγκώμιον, from κώμη, a tribe, or assembly; an oration or song in praise of a person.

E'NCOPE (*Med.*) ἐγκοπή, from κόπτω, to cut; an incision or impediment.

ENCO'RE (*Mus.*) French for, again, once more; a well-known expression at the theatre, when the audience wish for a performance to be repeated.

ENCO'RED (*Mus.*) an epithet for the performance or piece which has been called for a second time by the audience.

ENCRA'NION (*Anat.*) vide *Cerebellum*.

ENCRAIN (*Vet.*) a horse either wrung or spoiled in the withers.

ENCRATITÆ (*Ecc.*) a sect of heretics who forbad marriage and affected continence.

E'NCRIS (*Med.*) ἐγκρίς, a sort of cake made of fine meal and oil.

ENCROACHMENT (*Law*) an unlawful gaining upon the rights and possessions of another; as if, for example, two men's grounds lying together, the one presses too far upon another; or if a tenant owes two shillings rent-service to the lord, and the lord takes three.

ENCYCLOPÆDIA (*Lit.*) ἐγκυκλοπαιδία, from ἐν, in, κύκλος, a circle, and παιδεία, learning, i. e. the whole circle or compass of learning; a term now particularly applied to dictionaries which profess to explain the whole circle of sciences.

ENCY'SIS (*Med.*) from ἐγκύω, to bring forth; parturition.

ENCYS'TED (*Med.*) an epithet for humours which consist of a fluid or other matter enclosed in a sac or cyst.

END FOR END (*Mar.*) a term for a rope that runs all out of the pulley, or off the block.

E'NDBITTEN (*Bot.*) vide *Præmorsus*.

ENDE'CAGON (*Geom.*) ἑνδεκάγωνος, a plain figure of eleven sides and angles.

ENDEI'XIS (*Med.*) ἔνδειξις, an indication of diseases showing what is to be done.

ENDE'MIAL (*Med.*) or *Endemical*, an epithet for disorders which infect a great many people in the same country, or is common to the inhabitants of the same country. *Gal. Comm.* 1, *in Hippocrat. Epid.* l. 1; *Foes. Œconom. Hippocrat.*

E'NDESIS (*Med.*) ἔνδεσις, from δέω, to bind; a ligature, or connexion by means of a ligature. *Hippocrat. de Oss.*

E'NDICA (*Med.*) the Fæces.

E'NDIVE (*Bot.*) an herbaceous plant, and a species of the succory, the *Chicorium endivia* of Linnæus, a biennial.

ENDO'RSE (*Her.*) the fourth part of a pale, which is seldom borne but when a pale is between them. [vide *Pale*]

ENDO'RSED (*Her.*) an epithet signifying back to back, the same as *addorsed*.

ENDO'WMENT (*Law*) the giving or assuring a dower to a woman.

ENDO'RMI (*Mil.*) or *un soldat endormi*, a soldier asleep on guard.

ENELLAG'MENOS (*Anat.*) ἐνηλλαγμένος, from ἐνηλλάττω, to interchange; an epithet for the vertebræ, because of their alternate and mutual insertion.

E'NEMA (*Med.*) a Clyster. *Act. Meth. Med.* l. 5, c. 10.

E'NEMY (*Law*) signifies properly an alien or foreigner, who in a public capacity, and with a hostile intention, invades any kingdom.

ENERGE'TICAL BODIES (*Phy.*) such bodies or particles as are eminently active, and produce manifest operations of different natures, according to the various circumstances or motions of those bodies.

ENERGU'MENS (*Ant.*) persons supposed to be possessed with an evil spirit.

E'NERGY (*Med.*) an active motion of the animal spirits.

ENERGY (*Rhet.*) a figure of speech which consists in great expression.

ENERVA'TIO (*Med.*) a weakness in the nerves and tendons.

ENE'RVIUM (*Bot.*) nerveless; an epithet for a leaf.

E'NFANS *perdues* (*Mil.*) i. e. lost children; a term applied in French to those soldiers who, at the head of a detachment, begin an attack, or an assault, &c.

ENFEOFFMENT (*Law*) vide *Infeoffment*.

ENFILA'DE (*Mil.*) the situation of a post that may be scoured all the length of a straight line.

ENFILADE (*Archit.*) a series or continuation of several things disposed, as it were, in the same thread or line.

ENFI'LED (*Her.*) an epithet in blazoning, implying that the head of a man, beast, or any other charge, is placed on the blade of a sword.

TO ENFRANCHI'SE (*Law*) to make a person a denizen, or free citizen.

ENGASTRIMYTHI (*Ant.*) ἐγγαστρίμυθοι, a name given to the Pythias, or priestesses of Apollo, because they were accustomed to deliver their oracles from within, without moving their lips, or even their tongues. *Plut. de defect. Orat.; Schol. in Aristoph. Vesp.* To this mode of prophesying the prophet Isaiah alludes in chapter the eighth, verse the nineteenth, &c.

E'NGINE (*Mech.*) from the French *engin*, and the Latin *ingenium*, signifying wit, or contrivance; any mechanical instrument in which various parts and movements concur to produce some considerable effect.

ENGINEER (*Mil.*) in French *engineur*, signifying literally an ingenious person, is now applied to the person who is well skilled in that branch of the military art which consists in the attack and defence of forts.

E'NGISCOPE (*Mech.*) from ἐγγύς, near, and σκοπέω, to view; an instrument for viewing small bodies more distinctly; the same as the microscope.

ENGISO'MA (*Med.*) ἐγγίσωμα, or ἐγγύσωμα, a fissure of the cranium; so called from ἐγγύς, near, because the bone lies near the membrane which is under it. *Gal. Def. Med; Gorr. Def. Med.*

ENGISOMA (*Surg.*) a surgical instrument used in fractures of the cranium.

ENGLE'CERY (*Law*) or *Englechire*, the being an Englishman, which it was necessary to prove a man to be in the reign of Canute, in case he was murdered, that the hundred might be exempt from an amercement that was otherwise laid upon it. This law was made to protect the Danes, who were frequently waylaid by the English, and killed.

E'NGLISH *Mercury* (*Bot.*) the *Chenopodum bonus Henricus* of Linnæus, an annual.

ENGOMPHO'SIS (*Anat.*) vide *Gomphosis*.

ENGONA'SI (*Astron.*) ἐγγόνασι, i. e. *in genibus*, an epithet for the constellation Hercules, because he is represented resting on his right knee.

ENGO'NIOS (*Anat.*) ἐγγώνιος, from γωνία, an angle; an epithet applied to the flexure of the cubit.

ENGOULE'E (*Her.*) an epithet for crosses, saltires, &c. when their extremities enter the mouths of lions, leopards, &c.

ENGRA'ILED (*Her.*) vide *Ingrailed*.

ENGRAVING, the art of cutting figures, or the representations of objects on metals, stones, or wood. Engraving is performed in different manners, namely— in strokes with an instrument called the *graver*; and the design having been first traced with a sharp tool called the *dry-point*; in strokes cut with the dry-point, and afterwards eaten in with aqua fortis, which is called *etching*; in *mezzotinto*, which is performed by a dark *barb* or *ground*, being raised uniformly upon the plate with a toothed tool, &c.; in *aqua tinta*, a newly invented method of etching.

TO ENGRO'SS (*Law*) to write the rude draught of a thing fair over in a large hand.

ENGRO'SSING-BLOCK (*Mech.*) a tool made use of by the wire-drawers.

ENGUA'MBA URUVAPENSIUM (*Bot.*) a tree of moderate size, from the fruit of which an oil is expressed that is good for wounds. *Raii Hist. Plant.*

ENHÆ'MON (*Med.*) ἔναιμον, the name of a plaster in Myrepsus.

ENHA'NCED (*Her.*) an epithet for an ordinary that is placed above its usual situation, which principally happens to the bend and its diminutives. [vide *Bendlet*]

ENHARMO'NIC (*Mus.*) a term implying a particular manner of tuning the voice, and disposing the intervals in such manner as to render the music more moving.

ENHY'DRIS (*Zool.*) ἔνυδρις, an adder, or water snake. *Plin.* l. 30, c. 3.

ENHY'DROS (*Min.*) a round stone containing a liquid in the inside. *Plin.* l. 37, c. 11.

ENHY'DRUS is now the name of a genus of incrustated ferruginous bodies, which contain a certain quantity of fluid.

ENI'XA (*Surg.*) the same as *Puerpera*.

ENI'XUM *sal* (*Chem.*) a salt which partakes of the nature of an acid and an alkali, as common salt, nitre, &c.

TO ENLA'RGE (*Man.*) to make a horse go large, that is, to make him embrace a larger space of ground.

ENLA'RGEMENT (*Mil.*) the act of going, or of being allowed to go, beyond the prescribed bounds, as in the case of an officer under arrest.

ENMA'NCHE (*Her.*) vide *Manche*.

ENNEADECA'TERIS (*Chron.*) a period of nineteen years, which is known by the name of the *Metonic Cycle*, or the *Lunar Cycle*.

E'NNEAGON (*Geom.*) from ἐννέα, nine, and γωνία, a corner; a regular geometrical figure of nine sides and angles.

ENNEA'NDRIA (*Bot.*) from ἐννέα, nine, and ἀνήρ, a man, or husband, nine-stamened; the name of the ninth Class in Linnæus' Artificial Arrangement, comprehending those plants which bear hermaphrodite flowers with nine stamens. It is divided into orders, according to the number of the pistils, namely, *Monogynia*, *Trigynia*, and *Hexagynia*: the principal genera are as follow, Monogynia, *Laurus*, Bay, *Anacardium*, Cashew Nut, &c.—Trigynia, *Rheum*, Rhubarb, &c.—Hexagynia, *Butomus*, Flowering Rush, &c.

ENNEAPE'TALUS (*Bot.*) i. e. nine-petalled; an epithet for a corolla having nine petals, as in *Thea viridis*, *Magnolia*, and *Lirisdendron*.

ENNEAPHA'RMACOS (*Med.*) ἐννεαφάρμακος, from ἐννέα, nine, and φάρμακον, a medicine; a medicinal composition of nine ingredients. *Cels.* l. 5, c. 19; *Gal. de Comp. Med. secund. Loc.* l. 9, c. 6; *Act. Paul. Ægin.* l. 7, c. 24.

ENNEAPHY'LLUM (*Bot.*) the *Helleboraster*.

ENNEATICAL (*Med.*) an epithet for what appertains to the period of nine days, as every ninth day of sickness, which is called an enneatical day.

ENNEE'MIMERIS (*Gram.*) from ἐννέα, nine, ἥμι, half, and μέρις, a part; the cæsura after the fourth foot, i. e. on the ninth half foot, as in this example.

Illē lā | tūs nivē | ūm mūl | tī fūltūs hȳā | ciūthō.

E'NOCHS *pillars* (*Ant.*) two pillars said to have been erected by Enoch, the son of Seth, the one of brick and the other of stone, upon which the whole science of astronomy is said to have been engraven.

ENO'DIS (*Bot.*) knotless, i. e. without knots; an epithet for a culm.

ENQUIRY, *Writ of* (*Law*) vide *Inquiry*.

ENS (*Med.*) the essence or most efficacious part of any substance.

ENS (*Met.*) signifies literally being; but is taken for that which is conceived in its most abstract form. The schoolmen have divided it into the *ens reale*, or *positivum*, i. e. the real being; and the *ens rationis*, which is an imaginary being.

ENSA'TÆ (*Bot.*) the fifth Order in Linnæus' Fragments, and the sixth in the Natural Orders, containing some of the liliaceous plants.

ENSEE'LED (*Falcon.*) an epithet applied to a hawk which has a thread drawn through his upper eye-lids, and fastened under the beak to take away his sight.

E'NSIENT (*Law*) the being with child, which, in case of a woman condemned for any crime, is no ground to stay judgment; but may afterwards be alleged against execution.

ENSIFO'RMIS (*Bot.*) ensiform or sword-shaped; an epithet for some leaves, which are two edged, and have the shape of a sword, as the *Gladiole*, *Iris*, &c.

ENSIFORMIS (*Anat.*) an epithet for the lowest part of the sternum.

EN'SIGN (*Mil.*) the banner under which the soldiers are ranged, according to the different regiments they belong. —*Ensign*, or *Ensign Bearer*, is the officer who carries the colours; the lowest commissioned officer in a company of foot, being subordinate to the captain and lieutenant.

E'NSIGNED (*Her.*) an epithet equivalent to ornamented, as in the annexed figure, which represents a man's heart ensigned with a crown, " *Argent*, a man's heart, *gules*, ensigned with an imperial crown, *or*, on a chief, *azure*, three mullets of the field." The bearer of these singular arms was a man of the name of Douglass, and the occasion of his bearing them was his being sent on a pilgrimage to the Holy Land, with the heart of Robert of Bruce.

ENSTA'CTON (*Med.*) ἔνστακτον, from στάζω, to distil a liquid collyrium, called stacticon by Paulus Ægineta. *Gal. de Comp. Med. sec Loc.* l. 4, c. 7; *Paul. Æginet.* l. 7, c. 16.

E'NSTASIS (*Med.*) ἔνστασις, from ἐνίστημι, to stand in or adhere to, i. e. a lodgment or inhesion. *Cass. Problem.* 79; *Gorr. Med. Def.*

ENTA'BLATURE (*Archit.*) that part of a column which is over the capital, comprehending the architrave, frize, and cornice. Sometimes the entablature is taken for the last row of stones on the top of a building, on which the timber and covering rest. [vide *Architecture*]

ENTA'BLER (*Man.*) the fault of a horse whose croupe goes before his shoulders in working upon volts.

ENTA'DA (*Bot.*) the *Mimosa entada* of Linnæus.

ENTAI'L (*Law*) a fee-tail, or fee-entailed, i. e. the estate settled, scanted, or shortened, by which the heir is limited or tied up to certain conditions with regard to the descent.

ENTA'LI (*Min.*) Fossil Alum.

ENTALIA (*Nat.*) called by the Italians *Entaglia*, are shells or coverings for sea-worms.

E'NTASIS (*Med.*) ἔντασις, from τείνω, to stretch; a distension of any part. *Hippocrat. de Rat. Vict. in Morb. Acut.*; *Foes. Œconom. Hippocrat.*

ENTA'TICA (*Med.*) ἐντατικά, medicines which provoke venery. *Cœl. Aurelian. de Acut. Morb.* l. 3, c. 18; *Paul. Æginet.* l. 7, c. 17; *Gorr. Def. Med.*

E'NTE (*Her.*) an epithet signifying grafted or ingrafted, which is used in the fourth grand quarter of his majesty's arms, as Brunswick and Lunenburgh impaled, with Saxony, *ente en pointe*, i. e. grafted in point.

ENTELECHI'A (*Phy.*) ἐντελέχεια, a term applied by Aristotle to the soul, the perfections as it were of nature, which he supposed to be distinct from matter. *Aristot. de Anim.* c. 3; *Cic. Tusc.* l. 1, c. 10.

TO E'NTER (*Carpent.*) to insert the end of a tenon in the mouth or beginning of a mortoise.

TO ENTER (*Falcon.*) is said of a hawk when she first begins to kill.

E'NTERA (*Anat.*) vide *Enteron*.

ENTERADA'NES (*Anat.*) ἐντεραδένες, from ἔντερον, an intestine, and ἀδήν, a gland; the Intestinal Glands.

ENTERENCHY'TÆ (*Surg.*) ἐντερεγχύται, from ἔντερον, the viscera, and ἐγχέω, to infuse; surgical instruments for administering clysters.

ENTERI'TIS (*Med.*) from ἔντερον, viscera; an inflammation of the viscera; a genus of diseases, Class *Pyrexiæ*, Order *Phlegmasiæ*, in Cullen's Nosology.

ENTEROCE'LE (*Med.*) ἐντεροκήλη, from ἔντερον, an intestine, and κήλη, a hernia; a protrusion of any portion of the intestines, either into the navel or the groin, which is known commonly by the name of a rupture. *Gal. Def. Med.; Oribas. de Morb. Curat.* l. 3, c. 52; *Paul. Æginet.* l. 3, c. 54; *Act. de Meth. Med.* l. 1, c. 22; *Gorr. Def. Med.*

ENTERO-EPIPLOCELE (*Med.*) from ἔντερον, an intestine, ἐπίπλοον, the epiploon, and κήλη, a tumor; a rupture in which a part of the intestine, with a part of the epiploon, likewise is protruded. *Gal. Def. Med.; Gorr. Def. Med.*

ENTERO-HYDROCELE (*Med.*) from ἔντερον, an intestine, ὕδωρ, water, and κήλη, a tumor; a watery rupture.

ENTERO'MPHALOS (*Med.*) from ἔντερον, an intestine, and ὀμφαλὸς, the naval; an umbilical hernia or rupture, formed by the protrusion of the intestines at the navel.

E'NTERON (*Med.*) ἔντερον, from ἐντὸς, within; a term applied by Hippocrates to the colon only. *Hippocrat.* l. 4, aphor. 3, &c.; *Foes. Œconom. Hippocrat. Entera*, ἔντερα, in the plural, is also taken for sacks or bags into which fomentations were put. *Hippocrat. de Morb.* l. 3.

ENTEROPHY'TON *vulgare* (*Bot.*) the sea chitterling; a plant which grows in the form of ἔντερον, an intestine. *Raii Hist. Plant.*

ENTERO'RAPHE (*Anat.*) from ἔντερον, an intestine, and ῥαφή, a suture; a suture of the intestines, or the sewing together the divided edges of an intestine.

ENTEROSCHEOCE'LE (*Anat.*) ἐντεροσχεοκήλη, from ἔντερον, an intestine, ὄσχεον, the scrotum, and κήλη, a tumor; the *Hernia scrotalis*, or rupture of the intestines when they descend into the scrotum.

To ENTERPE'N (*Falcon.*) a term applied to a hawk which has his feathers snarled or entangled.

To ENTERPLEA'D (*Law*) to discuss a point incidentally falling out before the principal cause can have an end.

ENTERTAI'NMENT (*Mus.*) a little afterpiece, either musical or dramatic.

ENTERVI'EW (*Falcon.*) the second year of a hawk's age.

ENTHÆ'MON (*Med.*) a medicine made of the tears that drop from olive-trees in Arabia.

ENTHE'MATA (*Husband.*) grafts fixed into the clifts of trees.

ENTHEMATA (*Med.*) medicines applied to green wounds to stop the blood and course of the humours.

E'NTHETOS (*Med.*) ἔνθετος, from ἐντίθημι, to put in; an epithet for medicines applied to the nose to stop an hæmorrhage.

ENTHLA'SIS (*Med.*) ἔνθλασις, from ἐν and θλάω, to break; a bruise or illision which leaves marks in the place where it has been made. *Hippocrat. de Intern. Affect.; Gal. Exeges. Hippocrat. Vocab.*

ENTHUSIA'SMUS (*Med.*) ἐνθουσιασμὸς, from θεὸς, god; a fanatic perculsion or divine inspiration, as when a person, performing holy rites, loses his reason, and falling into an ecstacy, sees strange sights, and hears strange sounds. *Gal. Def. Med.*

ENTHYMEM (*Log.*) ἐνθύμημα, an imperfect syllogism, where either the Major or the Minor is wanting, as being easily to be supplied by the understanding; as "Virtue is a good thing, because no one can abuse it." As a complete syllogism it would be, "That is a good thing, which no one can abuse:" "No one can abuse virtue;" therefore, "Virtue is a good thing." This sort of syllogism was called the *Rhetorical Syllogism*, because it was much in use among rhetoricians. *Arist. Rhet.* l. 1, c. 1; *Cic. Top.* c. 13; *Dionys. in Jud. Lys.* c. 15; *Hermog. de Inven.* l. 3; *Plin.* l. 2, ep. 3; *Demet. de Eloc.* c. 30; *Aul. Gell.* l. 6, c. 13; *Quint.* l. 14, c. 14; *Schol. Hermog. apud Ald. Rhet.* tom. ii; *Cur. Fortunat.* l. 2; *Apsin. Rhetor. apud Ald. Rhet.* p. 703.

ENTIERTE (*Law*) Entireness, as distinguished from moiety.

ENTIRE *Tenancy* (*Law*) sole possession in one man, as distinguished from several tenancy.

ENTIRE *pertransient* (*Her.*) a line which crosses the middle of the shield.—*Entire pertingent*, is the longest line in the partition of the shield, which does not pass through the centre.

ENTIRE (*Mil.*) or *Rank entire*, a line of men side by side.

ENTO'GANUM (*Bot.*) another name for the *Melicope* of Linnæus.

ENTOMOLI'THUS (*Min.*) the body or other part of an insect changed into a fossile substance, of which many examples have been found.

ENTOMOLOGY, from ἔντομος, an insect, and λόγος, the doctrine; is that part of general zoology which treats of insects. An insect, as defined by Linnæus, is a small animal breathing through lateral spiracles, furnished with moveable antennæ and many feet, and covered either with a crustaceous or a hairy skin. He has, however, separated the worms from the class of insects; but throughout this work, except in the present article, they are brought under the head of Entomology, agreeably to the ordinary meaning of the term. Insects may be considered in respect to their anatomy, their metamorphoses, and their classification.

Anatomy of Insects.

The organization of Insects comprehends their external and internal parts.

External Parts.

The body of an insect consists of four principal parts, namely, *caput*, the Head; *truncus*, the Trunk; *abdomen*, the Abdomen; and *artus*, the Limbs or Extremities.

The Head. The Head, which is a distinguished part in most insects, is furnished with *oculi*, Eyes; *antennæ*, Horns; and *os*, a Mouth.

The Eyes. The Eyes are commonly situated on each side the head, and for the most part two in number, destitute of eyelids, and immoveable. In some insects, as spiders, they are eight in number; and, in respect to their structure, they are frequently compound, i. e. consisting of small hexagonal protuberances, placed with the utmost regularity and exactness in lines crossing each other, after the manner of lattice-work. In the two eyes of the *Libellula*, or Dragon-Fly, there have been reckoned not less than 25,000 such protuberances, which are supposed to be so many lenses, or object-glasses.

The *eyes* are, moreover, distinguished into *oculi approximati*, when placed close together; *colorati*, when of a different colour from that of the head; *concolores*, of the same colour with the head; *contigui*, touching one another; *fasciati*, marked with stripes of a different colour; *fenestrati*, having the pupil glassy and transparent; *hemispherici*, convex, like the section of a globe; *inferi*, placed on the under side of the head; *interrupti*, broken, but continued either above or below; *lunati*, resembling a crescent or new moon; *obliterati*, having the pupil scarcely distinguishable; *pedunculati*, or *stipitati*, elevated on a stalk or peduncle; *ovales*, eggshaped; *simplices*, furnished with only one lens; *verticales*, placed on the crown of the head.

Ocelli or *Stemmata*. Besides the larger eyes many insects have three small spherical bodies placed triangularly on the crown of the head, called *ocelli*, or *stemmata*. They are simple, and made for viewing large and distant objects.

Antennæ. The Antennæ are two articulated moveable processes placed on the head, which are subject to great variety and form, the principal distinction between the genera in the Linnean system: they are called *setaceæ*, setaceous, or bristle-shaped, when they gradually taper towards their extremity; *filiformes*, or threadshaped, when they are of equal diameter throughout, not visibly smaller at the tip than at any other part; *moniliformes*, moniliform, when the joints are shaped like the beads of a necklace, each joint being globular, or nearly so; *cla*-

vatæ, clavate, or clubshaped, which thicken at the tip into a knob or small club, as in the major part of the butterflies; *fissiles*, fissile, those which are split or divided at the tip into several lamellæ or flat divisions, as in the *Scarabæi*, or Beetle tribe; *pectinatæ*, pectinated, those which are divided into numerous processes resembling the teeth of a comb; *barbatæ*, bearded, those which are slightly feathered either on one or both sides with fine lateral fibres or hairs; *perfoliatæ*, perfoliate, those which have the joints of a flattened and circular shape, with the stem or body of the antennæ passing through them, after the manner of a perfoliate leaf, as exemplified in some of the beetle tribe: to these may be added *breves*, those shorter than the body; *approximatæ*, approximate; *coadunatæ*, connected at the base; *plumosæ; rigidæ; ramosæ*, &c.

The Mouth. The Mouth is commonly situated in the under part of the head, and varies much in different tribes of insects. The parts observable in the mouth of insects are as follow; namely—*Labia*, the Lips, upper and lower. The Upper Lip is a transverse, moveable, soft piece, of a coriaceous or membranaceous nature, known from its situation at the anterior part of the mouth, and very distinctly visible in many of the Coleopterous tribe, as the *Gryllus, Apis*, &c. The Lower Lip is situated immediately under the maxillæ; this is frequently lengthened so as to form the process which is called the *ligula*, consisting of a single piece, of a soft texture, and often bifid.—*Mandibulæ*, the Mandibles, are two horny substances placed one at each side of the mouth, below the upper lip. They have a lateral motion, by which they are distinguished from the lips which move up and down as in other animals. In rapacious insects the mandibles are stronger than in those that perforate woods; and these latter have stronger mandibles than the herbivorous insects.—*Maxillæ*, the Jaws, two membranaceous substances, differing in figure from the mandibles, under which they are situated, and above the lower lip. They have a lateral motion, and are distinguished, as to their form, into *dentatæ*, i. e. set with sharp-pointed processes; *forcipatæ*, pincer-shaped; *furcatæ*, forked; *lunulatæ*, thick in the middle and smaller towards the base and the apex; *prominentes*, placed straight before the head.—*Lingua*, the Tongue, an involuted tubular organ, which constitutes the whole mouth in lepidopterous insects: this is of a setaceous form, and frequently very long, as *fig.* 8, Plate No. II. (35). Through this tube the insect draws the nectarious juices of the flowers on which it subsists. When it takes its food the tongue is exserted; but at other times it is rolled up spirally between the palpi.—*Rostrum*, the Beak or Snout, a moveable articulated member, which forms the mouth in many of the Hemipterous Order, as the *Cicada, Cimex, Aphis, fig.* 4, 5, 6, where the inflected snout is visible. This beak is hollow, and contains, as in a sheath, several very fine bristles, with which these insects perforate the substances from which they extract their nutriment.—*Proboscis*, the Trunk, serves the purpose of a mouth in most of the Dipterous Order. It is fleshy, retractile, and often cylindrical, terminating with two lips, which are supposed to possess the sense of taste in a high degree. The House-Fly and the Bee afford familiar examples of the proboscis.—*Palpi*, Feelers, small moveable filiform organs, placed mostly at each side the jaw, which resemble the antennæ, but are smaller, and more distinctly articulated, as *f*, Plate No. I. (34), fig. 2, 3. They vary in number from two to six in different insects. The *palpi* are distinguished into *clavati*, clubshaped; *elongati*, longer than the mouth; *exserti*, projecting out; *filiformes*, of the same thickness throughout; *incurvi*, turning straight upwards at the ends; *recti*, straight; *recurvi*, turned back; *setacei*, setaceous; &c.—*Clypeus*, the Shield of the head in coleopterous insects, which corresponds with the front of the head in other insects.—*Vertex*, the Summit or Crown of the head.—*Gula*, the Throat, that part which is opposed to the front of the head.

The Trunk. The Trunk, the second principal division of which an insect consists, comprehends that portion which is situated between the head and the abdomen. The trunk includes *thorax*, the Chest; *pectus*, the Breast; *sternum*, the Breast-bone; and *scutellum* the Scutel or Escutcheon.—*Thorax* is the upper part of the body to which the first pair of legs is attached, as *p*, fig. 2, 3. It varies much in form and structure, and is therefore denominated *convexus*, convex; *cordatus*, cordate; *gibbus*, gibbous; *inæqualis*, having the surface not flat; *lineatus*, marked longitudinally; *oblongus*, oblong; *punctatus*, marked with points; *villosus*, hairy, &c.—*Pectus*, the Breast, is the under part of the Thorax, to which the four posterior feet are attached, and from which the wings in lepidopterous insects have their origin. This part is capable of being compressed and dilated, as is observable in insects of the butterfly and moth tribe.—*Sternum*, or Breastbone, a ridge running under the breast, which is conspicuous in some insects.—*Scutellum*, the Escutcheon, is a lobelike process situated at the posterior part of the thorax, as *s*, fig. 1, Pl. No. I. (34). Its form is generally triangular, although in the coleopterous tribes it approaches to the heartshape.

Abdomen. The Abdomen, the third principal division, is the posterior part of an insect's body, which is composed of annular joints, or segments, as *o*, fig. 2, 3. These rings vary in number in different insects, and the form of the abdomen is also distinguished into *æquale*, when it is of the same breadth with the thorax; *barbatum*, having tufts of hair at the sides or extremity; *falcatum*, shaped like a sickle; *petiolatum*, attached to the thorax by means of a slender elongated tube; *planum*, flat in the under part; *sessile*, attached to the thorax in its whole breadth, &c. The upper part of the abdomen is called *tergum*, the Back; the inferior, *venter*, the Belly; and the opening at the posterior part, the *vent*; and in most insects the extremity is occupied with the organs of generation. The motion of the abdomen is most visible in those insects of the hymenopterous tribe in particular which have that portion of the body pediculated. This motion is effected by means of muscles inserted in the rings. To the abdomen belong *cauda*, the Tail, and *aculeus*, the sting. The tail is any appendage which terminates the extremity of the abdomen, which is *aristata*, when it terminates in a slender thread; *foliaceous*, spreading out like a leaf, as in the *Blatta*; *forcipata*, shaped like a forceps; *setacea*, bristle-shaped, as in the *Podura*; *biseta*, having two slender attenuated setæ, &c. The sting, a well-known instrument of offence in some insects, is denominated *simplex*, having one dart; *compositus*, having two or more darts; *exsertus*, projecting, not lying within the body; *retractilis*, capable of being drawn in, as in the bees and wasps; *reconditus*, always hid in the body, or seldom thrust out; *vaginatus*, enclosed in a bivalve sheath. In some tribes of insects it exists in the male, in others the females only are provided with it; but it is seldom met with in both sexes of the same kind.

The *Members*. The Members, or Extremities, are, *pedes*, the legs; *alæ*, the wings.

Legs. The legs of insects are six in number, but never more; but the larvæ of insects have many others, which are denominated *spurious* feet. The *pedes* are distinguished, according to their form and use, into—*cursorii*, formed for running; *mutici*, without claws or spines; *natatorii*, compressed and formed for swimming; *saltatorii*, with thick thighs fitted for leaping; *serrati*, toothed like a saw; *spinosi*, set with large spines. The leapers are principally found among the Curculio tribe; the genera *Hydrophylus* and *Dytiscus* are examples of the swimmers. The parts of the legs are *femur*, the Thigh; *tibia*, the Shank; and *tarsus*, the Foot, as fig. 4, pl. No. I. (34.) *Femur* is the first or upper joint, which is *arcuatum*, bent like a circular arch; *dentatum*, having a margin with indentations; *hispidum*, set with short rigid bristles; *incrassatum*, growing thicker in the middle; *spinosum*, set with spines; *muticum*, without spines; *saltatorium*, thick and formed for leaping, as in the Locust tribe. That part which connects the thigh to the body is called its *basis*.—*Tibia*, or Shank, the second joint, is that part of the leg which varies its form most, according to the use which is made of the *pedes*, as *t*, fig. 4.—*Tarsus*, the Foot, or last joint, consists of several articulations, which vary in number according to the insect's mode of life. To the apex of the tarsus are attached *ungues*, the claws.

The Wings. The Wings, the well-known organs of flight, are either two or four in number, and consist of—*basis*, a base, or that part by which it is attached to the *thorax*; *apex*, the part opposite to the base; *costa*, the margin between the base and the apex; *discus*, the space between the base, the apex, the margin, and the suture; *pterigostia*, wing-bones, the streaked parts of the wings which are placed between two thin membranes, and constitute the true wings of insects. Wings are placed on each side of the insect so as that each pair should correspond in situation and form, &c.; but where there is more than one pair, the first are mostly larger than those behind. The wings are distinguished according to their form, figure, texture, construction, &c. into *acuminatæ*, terminating in a subulated apex; *caudatæ*, when the hinder wings are extended into processes; *crenatæ*, having the margin notched; *angulatæ*, having the margin angular; *denticulatæ*, set with teeth; *digitatæ*, divided to the base nearly like fingers; *integræ*, without indentations; *incurvatæ*, the anterior margin bent like an arch; *nervosæ*, full of nerves or vessels; *reticulatæ*, the nerves disposed like network, as in the *Libellula*; *maculatæ*, or *pictæ*, spotted or marked with coloured spots, bands, &c.; *variegatæ*, of different colours; *radiatæ*, the nerves diverging like rays; *ocellatæ*, marked with one or more ocelli, or eyelike spots, of which the central is termed the *pupil*, the exterior one the *iris*; *planæ*, which cannot be folded up; *plicatiles*, that admit of being folded up at pleasure; *patentes*, extended horizontally; *erectæ*, such as stand erect when the insect is at rest; *incumbentes*, which rest on the upper part of the abdomen; *deflexæ*, such as are partly incumbent, or simply bent down, &c. To the wings belong also *elytra*, the Wing-Cases, and *halteres*, the Poisers or Balancers.—*Elytra* are two coriaceous wings, which are expanded in flight; but when at rest serve to cover the abdomen, and to enclose the membranaceous wings. The parts of the elytra are the *base*, the *apex*, the *margo* or outer rim next the belly, and the *sutura*, the part where the elytra meet and form a line in the middle of the back from the base to the apex. They belong to the coleopterous tribe of insects, and are distinguished according to their variety in colour, marks, form, &c. into—*lineata*, marked with depressed lines; *punctata*, marked with very small dots; *pubescentia*, covered with hair; *rugosa*, wrinkled; *hispida*, set with short bristles; *scabra*, rough, with hard raised points; *spinosa*, the margins set with spines; *dentata*, set with toothlike processes; *præmorsa*, the apex terminating obtusely; *sinuata*, hollowed as if scooped out; *subulata* linear at the base, and pointed at the apex; *integra*, completely covering the back; *dimidiata*, covering but half the back; *inæqualia*, the surface not flat; *immarginata*, without a margin, or distinct rim; *muricata*, rough with rigid spines; *striata*, slightly channelled; *convexa*, convex, &c.—*Halteres*, Poisers, two globular bodies in insects of the Order *Diptera*, which are placed on slender stalks behind the wings, and seated on the thorax: they are so called because they are supposed to keep the insect steady in its flight.

Internal Organization of Insects.

The internal parts of insects are much less perfect and distinct than those of larger animals, and of that which is visible is very little known.

Brain, &c. The brain of insects is altogether different from the substance which commonly goes by that name, being little more than ganglions of nerves, which are two in number, as observed in the crab, lobster, &c. Each of these is supposed to serve the office of the brain. Their muscles consist of fibres formed of *fasciculi*, and seldom produce more than *two* sorts of motion, namely, that of an *extensor* and a *flexor*. There are no salivary glands to be met with in the mouths of insects, but they have a set of floating vessels which secrete a fluid varying in colour in different insects, which is very similar to saliva. The *œsophagus*, or organ of deglutition, is a straight short tube, which consists of annular muscular fibres, of which the trunk of the butterfly, the proboscis of the common fly, and the snout of hemipterous insects, forms a principal part.

Stomach, &c. The organs of digestion consist of the stomach and intestinal canal, which, however, vary materially in different insects. For the most part they have a single stomach, but it is sometimes double, and sometimes manifold. The stomach also varies according to the nature of the food which the insect takes; in some, which subsist on vegetable juices, it is membranaceous, as the Bees, which suck the nectar of flowers, &c.: some, which feed on animal substances, as the Bug, Boatfly, &c. have a muscular stomach; in others this stomach is nothing but a continuation of the œsophagus, such as the Cockchaffer, and all Beetles, &c. which feed on leaves and the roots of vegetables. The *double stomach* is found in the coleopterous tribe, which feed on other insects, as the *Cicindela, Carabus*, &c.; the first of the two stomachs is muscular, after the manner of a gizzard; the second is a long membranaceous canal. The insects, such as the Cricket and Grasshopper, which have many stomachs, seem to employ them much after the manner of the ruminating animals; some for the reception and digestion of the food, and others for its farther mastication.

Organs of respiration. Although insects have not lungs like other animals, yet it has been ascertained that they have vessels called *spiracula*, which run along each side of the body, and serve for the reception of air; and other vessels proceeding from these pores by the sides, which are called *tracheæ* and *bronchiæ*, because they serve for the exspiration of the air.

Circulation and *Secretion in Insects.* Of the process of circulation in insects little more is at present known, than that a contraction and dilatation of the vessels is observable in some kinds, particularly caterpillars; but the fluid which is supposed to supply the place of blood is not of the same colour; for which reason insects were reckoned, by the ancients, to be *animalia exsanguia*, bloodless animals. It is, however, now generally admitted, that not only circulation, but also secretion, is common to insects with other animals. The latter process is supposed to be performed by means of a number of long slender vessels which float in the internal cavities of the body, and serve to secrete the different fluids which are peculiar to different insects. Thus the Bee, the Wasp, Sphex, &c. have two vessels situated at the bottom of the sting, through which they discharge an acrid fluid. The silk of the common Silkworm is said by some to be a fluid. The Carabus and Dytiscus contain an acid which reddens the infusion of litmus. From the ant is extracted an acid well known to chemists, and the like is observable in other insects.

Distinction of sex in insects. Insects are divided, in respect to sex, into the males, or those which have the male organs of generation visible; females, or those furnished with female organs; and the neuters, or those which have no such organs of either kind visible, and are therefore supposed to be of neither sex: although others have imagined that they are females with the organs undeveloped. The neuters are found mostly among insects of the Hymenopterous Order, as bees and ants, where they act the part of labourers for the whole community. The organs of generation are mostly situated near the extremity of the abdomen; except in the Spider, which has them in the feelers; and the Dragon-Fly, the male organ of which is situated in the breast, and that of the female in the abdomen. But besides the organs of generation, insects have also other marks by which the sexes are distinguished, as difference of size, brightness of colours, form of the antennæ, &c. The male is always smaller than the female, and in some cases, as in that of the Termes, the female is two or three hundred times larger than the male; but the latter have the advantage of the former in the bright colours of their wings, and the largeness of their antennæ. In many cases the females have no wings; and in some instances, as that of the bee, the female has a sting, but the male none. The male insects are marked in entomological writings by the character ♂, the same as for Mars; and the female by ♀, the sign of Venus.

Metamorphoses of Insects.

Insects appear in four states, namely, the *Ovum*, or Egg; the Larva, the Pupa, and the *Imago*, or perfect insect.

The *Egg*. The first state in which insects mostly appear is that of an *ovum*, or egg; but there are some examples of viviparous insects, as in the genus Aphis, Musca, &c.

Larva. From the egg is hatched the insect in its second or Caterpillar state, which is now generally denominated the *larva*, on the authority of Linnæus; although before his time it was commonly called the *eruca*. The *Larvæ*, or Caterpillars of insects, differ very much from each other, according to the tribe to which they belong. Those of the Butterfly and Moth tribe are emphatically known by the name of Caterpillars; those of flies, bees, &c. are generally known by the name of Maggots. The *Larvæ* of the beetle tribe are generally of a thick, clumsy form; those of the Locust and Grasshopper differ but little in appearance from the complete insect, except in being destitute of wings; but those of the Dragon-Fly, and other insects, are of a peculiar form. Vide Plates No. I. II. (34, 35.) It is in the Larva, or Caterpillar state, that insects are observed to be most voracious; for in their complete state, as in the instance of the Butterfly, they are satisfied with the lightest and most delicate nutriment.

Pupa, or *Chrysalis*. The Pupa, or Chrysalis, is the third state into which insects transform themselves. In order to go through this process they cease to feed, and placing themselves in a quiet situation, they by a laborious effort, frequently repeated, divest themselves of their external skin, or larva coat, and immediately appear in their chrysalis form, which varies in different insects as much as that of the larva. In most of the beetle tribe it is furnished with short legs, but the Pupa of the butterfly tribe is entirely destitute of legs. In most of the fly tribe it is perfectly oval, but in those of the bee tribe it is very shapeless. The term Pupa has been mostly adopted from Linnæus, in lieu of the more ancient term Chrysalis.

Imago. The last and perfect state into which the insect is transformed has been denominated, by Linnæus, *Imago*; in which state it continues until the period of its extinction. This commonly takes place within the period of a year, although some insects, as bees and spiders for example, are supposed to live a considerable time; and many whose existence in the perfect state is not protracted beyond a year, and in some instances not above many hours, will live in the state of larvæ for a considerable time previous to their transformation. This is particularly observable of water-insects, which are found to be of much longer duration than land-insects.

Classification of Insects.

Entomology, in common with every other branch of Natural History, has in an especial manner engaged the attention of writers within the last two centuries, previous to which it was only treated of occasionally, and incidentally. One of the earliest works, in which entomology was considered scientifically, was published by Agricola in 1549, in which he divided insects into 1. Creeping Insects, 2. Flying Insects, and 3. Swimming Insects. Aldrovandus distinguished Insects into *terrestria et aquatica*, which he subdivided into orders, according to the number, nature, position, &c. of their wings. Ray published in 1710 his Historia Insectorum, which was the joint labour of himself and Willoughby. In this history, insects are divided into *transmutabilia* and *intransmutabilia*, which were subdivided according to the number of their legs, their place of habitation, size, &c. The *transmutabilia* are divided into four orders: 1. *Vaginipennes*, those which have wings covered with a sheath. 2. *Papiliones*, lepidopterous insects. 3. *Quadripennes*, four-winged insects. 4. *Bipennes*, two-winged insects. These are again subdivided into families.

Linnean System. In 1735 the system of Linnæus was published, which has since been universally adopted, with little or no alteration, except such as he himself thought proper. At first it consisted of only four orders, which he afterwards increased to the number of seven, namely, *Coleoptera, Hemiptera, Lepidoptera, Neuroptera, Hymenoptera, Diptera*, and *Aptera*, which are founded on the number and construction of the wings.—*Coleoptera*, the first order, contains all those insects whose wings are guarded by horny sheaths or cases, called the *elytra*; among the principal genera of this order are the Beetles. —*Hemiptera*, i. e. half-winged, the second order, comprehends those insects which have the upper half of their wing-sheaths tough and leathery, and the lower part membranaceous. The principal insects of this tribe are the Locusts, Grasshoppers, *Cicadæ*, &c.—*Lepidoptera*, i. e. scaly-winged, the third order, consist of the insects commonly known by the names of the Moth and Butterfly. This Order derives its name from the powder observable on their wings, which is supposed to consist of minute scales, although this has been by some disputed.—*Neuroptera*, i. e. nerve-winged, is the fourth order, which is distinguished by the reticular form of the wing in the insects of which it is composed. The Dragon Fly is the most remarkable among the genera.—

Hymenoptera, the fifth order, comprehends those insects which have four wings, all of them furnished with a sting, or some process similar thereto, of which the Bee and Wasp afford the best examples.—*Diptera*, the sixth order, includes the two-winged insects, as the Fly and the Gnat.—*Aptera*, i. e. wingless, the seventh order, comprehends those insects which are totally destitute of wings, as Spiders, Centipedes, Scolopendræ, &c. under which class Linnæus has also comprehended the Crab and the Lobster, that are generally excluded from the number of insects.

Since his time the number of writers on Entomology has increased incalculably; and some of them, as Degeer, Reitzius, and Fabricius, have attempted to improve the Linnean system by increasing the number of orders, but their alterations have not been generally adopted.

Explanation of the Plates.

Plate No. I. (34.)

The Parts of Insects.—Fig. 1. The *Lucanus cervus*, having *a a*, the *clavate antennæ* clubpectinate; *p p*, the *maxillary palpi*; *l l*, the *labial palpi*; *m m*, the *mandibles*; *t*, the thorax; *s*, the *scutellum*; *e*, the *elytra*; *ff*, the *femora*; *g g*, the *tibiæ*; *h h*, the *tarsi*; *u u*, the *ungues*. 2. 3. The *Ditiscus*, having *a a*, the *setaceous antennæ*, or Horns; *fff*, the feelers; *e e*, the Eyes; *p*, the Thorax; *b*, the breast; *o*, the Abdomen; *m m*, the membranaceous Under-Wings; *t*, the tail; *l l*, the ciliate Legs, formed for swimming. 4. The *Pes* of an insect, consisting of, *f*, the *Femur*; *s*, the Shank, or Leg; *t*, the *Tibia*; *u*, the *Ungues*, or Claws. 5. An insect of the papilionaceous tribe, having, *a a*, the *clavate antennæ*; *u*, the interior part of the wing; *d*, the disk of the wing; *p*, the posterior part of the wing; *e*, the exterior; *o*, the *ocellate*, or eye-like spot, having the Pupil in the centre, and the ring round, called the *Iris*; *t*, the Tail, or process at the end of the wing.—States of the Insect. Fig. 6. *e*, the Eggs; *l*, the Larva; *p*, the Pupa.—Orders of Insects. Order I. *Coleoptera*. Fig. 7. The *Scarabæus Hercules*, or Hercules Beetle. 8. The *Ptinus fatidicus*, or Death-Watch, in its natural size, and magnified. 9. The *Lampyris*, or Glow-Worm, female and male; *o*, the *Ova*, or Eggs; *l*, the Larva; *p*, the Pupa. 10. The *Curculio palmarum*, the Palm-Worm and its Larva.

Plate No. II. (35.)

Order II. *Hemiptera*. Fig. 1. The *Mantis oratoria*, or Camel-Cricket. 2. The *Mantis siccifolia*, or Walking leaf. 3. The *Gryllus monstrosus*. 4. The *Cicada lanata*. 5. *Cimex stagnorum*. 6. The *Aphis Rosæ*, or Plant Louse. 7. *Coccus cacti*, or the Cochineal, in the Male; *f*, the Female.—Order III. *Lepidoptera*. Fig. 8. The Sphinx; *l*, the Larva; *p*, the Pupa. 9. *Phalæna mori*, or the Silk Worm; *l*, the Larva; *p*, the Pupa.—Order IV. *Neuroptera*. Fig. 10. *Libellula variegata*, the Dragon-Fly; *l*, the Larva; *p*, the Pupa. 11. *Ephemera*, or the Day-Fly. 12. The *Raphidia Ophiopsis*. 13. The *Hemorobius*.—Order V. *Hymenoptera*. Fig. 14. The *Ichneumon puparum*. 15. *Ichneumon larvarum*.—Order VI. *Diptera*. Fig. 16. *Oestrus*, the Gad-Fly.—Order VII. *Aptera*. Fig. 17. The *Scolopendra morsitans*.

ENTOYER (*Her.*) an epithet for a bordure charged with dead or artificial things, as in the annexed figure; he beareth " *Argent* a bordure *or*, entoyer of rests or clarions *azure*."

E'NTRAVO'NS (*Man.*) French for horses' pasterns, being pieces of leather, two inches broad, turned up, and stuffed on the inside, to prevent hurting the pastern.

ENTREE' (*Law*) or *entre*. [vide *Entry*]
ENTRE'MES (*Mus.*) a short musical interlude much used in Spain.
ENTRE-ME'TS (*Mus.*) French for the inferior and lesser movements inserted in a composition between those of more importance.
ENTREPA'S (*Man.*) the broken pace of a horse that is neither a walk nor a trot, but most resembles an amble.
ENTRESO'LE (*Archit.*) a kind of little story contrived occasionally at the top of the first story, for the conveniency of a wardrobe, &c.
ENTREPO'T (*Com.*) a public magazine appointed by the state for the reception of merchandize from foreign countries.
ENTRICHO'MA (*Anat.*) the utmost extremity or edge of the eyelid.
ENTRI'MMA (*Med.*) vide *Intritum*.
EN'TRIES (*Mus.*) the acts of operas, burlettas, &c.
ENTRIES (*Sport.*) thickets or places through which deer are found to have lately passed.
ENTRING (*Mar.*) the same as *boarding*.
EN'TROCHUS (*Min.*) a sort of extraneous fossils, made up of round joints.
ENTRU'SION (*Law*) vide *Intrusion*.
E'NTRY (*Law*) in French *entrée*, in Latin *introitus*, or *ingressus*, signifies the taking possession of lands or tenements where a man hath title of *entry*; it is also used for a writ of possession, as—*Entry ad communem legem*, a writ lying, where a tenant for life alienes lands, and dies, for the party in reversion against the person who is in possession.—*Entry ad terminum qui præteriit*, a writ which lies for a lessor in case lands being let to a man for the life of another, and he for whose life the lands are leased dies, and the lessee or tenant holds over his term.—*Entry causa matrimonii prælocuti*, a writ lying where lands or tenements are given to a man upon condition that he take the donor to wife, and he marries another, or refuses to fulfil the condition.—*Entry in casu proviso*. [vide *Casu*]—*Entry sine assensu capituli*, a writ lying when an abbot or prior, &c. aliens lands, &c. without the assent of the convent, and dies, &c.
ENTRY *of goods* (*Law*) at the Custom House is the passing the bills through the hands of the proper officers.
ENTRY (*Com.*) the act of setting down the particulars in a merchant's books; this is done either by *single* or *double entry*, which are two distinct modes of book-keeping. [vide *Book-keeping*]
ENVE'LOPE (*Fort.*) a work of earth, sometimes in the form of a breastwork, or parapet, which is sometimes called a *conservé*, a *lunette*, &c.
ENVE'LOPED (*Her.*) vide *Enwrapped*.
E'NULA (*Bot.*) another name for the *Inula* of Linnæus.
E'NULON (*Anat.*) ἴουλον, from ἴλων, the gums; the internal flesh of the gums. *Poll. Onom*. l. 2, segm. 94.
ENUMERA'TION (*Rhet.*) a part of the peroration, in which the orator collects the scattered heads of his speech.
E'NVOYS (*Mus.*) the old English ballads, as they were formerly called.
ENU'RE (*Law*) to be available, or of force.
ENURE'SIS (*Med.*) from ἐνουρέω, to make water; an incontinency, or involuntary flow of urine, a genus of diseases, Class *Locales*, Order *Opocenoses*, in Cullen's Nosology.
ENU'RNEY (*Her.*) an epithet for a bordure charged with wild beasts, as in the annexed figure, as " He beareth *argent* a bordure quarterly, i. e. ruby, enurny of three lions passant guardant *or*. The second *azure*, verdoy of as many fleurs de lis *or*. The third is as the second; the fourth as the first."

ENWRA'PPED (*Her.*) an epithet for a child's head couped

below the shoulder, enwrapped about the neck with a snake.

ENY'STRON (*Anat.*) ἤνυστρον, the second ventricle of the stomach in ruminating beasts. *Arist. de Part. Anim.* l. 3, c. 14.

EODO'RBRICE (*Archæol.*) Hedge-breaking, mentioned in the laws of King Alfred. *Leg. Alfred,* c. 35.

E'OLIAN (*Mus.*) vide *Æolian.*

EOLO'PILE (*Hyd.*) vide *Æolopile.*

EO'RA (*Ant.*) vide *Æora.*

E'ORLE (*Polit.*) vide *Earl.*

EPA'CHTHES (*Ant.*) ἐπαχθής, a festival celebrated by the Bœotians in honour of Ceres. *Plut. de Isid. et Osir.*

EPACMA'STICOS (*Med.*) an epithet for a sort of fever that increases in strength. [vide *Anabasis*]

EPA'CRIS (*Bot.*) a genus of plants, Class 5 *Pentandria*, Order 1 *Monogynia*.
  Generic Character. CAL. *perianth* five-leaved.—COR. one-petalled.—STAM. *filaments* five; *anthers* incumbent.—PIST. *germ* roundish; *style* short; *stigma* capitate.—PER. *capsule* globular; *seeds* numerous.
  Species. The species are all natives of New Zealand, as the *Epacris longifolia*, seu *Ardisia.*—*Epacris juniperina,* seu *Stephelina,* &c.

E'PACT (*Chron.*) a term denoting the excess of the solar month above the lunar synodical month, or of the solar year above the lunar year of twelve synodical months. [vide *Chronology*]

EPAGO'GE (*Rhet.*) ἐπαγωγή, from ἐπάγω, to induce, oratorical induction; a figure of speech which consists in demonstrating and proving universal propositions by particulars. *Arist. Rhet.* l. 1, c. 2; *Cic. de Invent.* l. 1, c. 31; *Dionys. Hal. Comp.* 4; *Rufinian.* fig. 26; *Quintil.* l. 5, c. 10; *Plut.* sect. 53; *Suidas.*

EPAGO'GION (*Med.*) ἐπαγώγιον, from ἐπάγω, to induce, or cover over; the prepuce. *Diosc.* l. 3, c. 25.

E'PAGON (*Mech.*) ἐπάγων, from ἐπάγω, to induce; a truckle in a crane, or such like engine.

EPAINE'TIC (*Poet.*) from ἐπαινέω, to praise; an epithet for a poem that is spoken in praise of any eminent person.

EPANADIDO'NTES Pureti (*Med.*) ἐπαναδιδόντες πυρετοί, an epithet for fevers which increase in the degree of heat. *Hippocrat. Epid.* l. 6, aphor. 17.

EPANADIPLO'SIS (*Rhet.*) a figure of speech, in which the sentence begins and ends with the same words. [vide *Palilogia*]

EPANADIPLOSIS (*Med.*) a reduplication. [vide *Anadiplosis*]

EPANALE'PSIS (*Med.*) ἐπανάληψις, a restoration to life.

EPANALEPSIS (*Rhet.*) a figure of speech, in which the same word is repeated by way of emphasis. *Hermog.* περὶ ἰδ. apud. *Ald. Rhet.* p. 50; *Demet. de Eloc.* p. 196.

EPANA'PHORA (*Rhet.*) vide *Anaphora.*

EPANA'STASIS (*Med.*) ἐπανάστασις, from ἐπανίστημι, to raise; a tumor, or tubercle. *Hippocrat. de Coac.*; *Act. de Meth. Med. Præf.* l. 6.

EPANCYLO'TUS (*Med.*) ἐπαγκυλωτός, a sort of bandage described by Galen and Oribasius. *Gal. de Fasc.; Oribas. de Laq.*

EPA'NODOS (*Rhet.*) a figure in which the same or similar words are used in two or more sentences, as "Neither the light without the sun, nor yet the sun without its light."

EPANORTHO'SIS (*Rhet.*) the act of an orator, who, thinking his expressions too faint and weak, corrects his discourse by adding others that are stronger. *Jul. Rufinian.*

EPAPHÆ'RESIS (*Med.*) ἐπαφαίρεσις, from ἀφαιρέω, to take away; a removal, or taking away; applied particularly to repeated phlebotomy. *Gal. de Curand. Rat. per Sang. Miss.* c. 1.

EPA'RER (*Man.*) a French term for the flinging and yerking of a horse.

EPA'RGEMOS (*Med.*) ἐπάργεμος, an epithet for a person affected with the argema. [vide *Argema*]

EPARI'TA (*Min.*) a sort of argillaceous earth of the colour of the liver.

EPA'RMATA (*Med.*) the swellings of the glandules, or kernels behind the ears, called *parotides.*

EPA'RSIS (*Med.*) or *eparma*, ἔπαρσις, ἔπαρμα, from αἴρω, to raise; any sort of tumor, but particularly of the parotid glands.

EPA'ULE (*Fort.*) the shoulder of the bastion, or the angle of the face and flank; whence that angle is often called the *angle of the epaule.*

EPA'ULER (*Fort.*) a French term for raising any work, as *epauler une Batterie,* to raise a battery.

EPAULE'TTES (*Mil.*) Shoulder-Knots worn as marks of distinction, by the commissioned and warrant officers, on one or both shoulders; those for serjeants are of the colour of the facing; those for the officers are made of gold or silver lace.

EPAU'LEMENT (*Fort.*) a sidework made of earth thrown up, gabions, &c.; it is also used for a *demibastion.*

EPA'ULIER (*Mil.*) the shoulder plate of armour.

EPAUXE'SIS (*Rhet.*) a rhetorical figure which serves to increase the energy of the discourse.

EPENCRA'NIS (*Anat.*) ἐπεγκρανίς, the cerebellum. *Gal. de Usu. Part.*

EPE'NTHESIS (*Gram.*) the putting of a letter or syllable in the middle of a word, as *induperator* for *imperator.*

EPE'RLANUS (*Ich.*) the Smelt.

EPE'RVA (*Bot.*) the *Dimorpha falcata* of Linnæus.

EPHA (*Ant.*) or *ephah,* איפה, a measure among the Hebrews, both for liquid and dry things; as a liquid measure, it contained the same as the bath; as a dry measure, it was equal to three pecks, three pints, twelve solid inches, and four decimal parts.

EPHÆ'STIA (*Ant.*) vide *Hephestia.*

EPHE'BIA (*Ant.*) ἐφηβία, puberty, or the age of fifteen.

EPHEBI'UM (*Ant.*) ἐφήβιον, the place where young men wrestled and exercised themselves. *Vitruv.* l. 5, c. 2; *Philand. in Vitruv.*; *Bald. Lex. Vitruv.*

EPHE'DRA (*Bot.*) or *Ephedron,* ἔφεδρα, ἔφεδρον, is another name for the *Hippuris,* or horse-tail. *Dioscor.* l. 4, c. 46; *Plin.* l. 26, c. 7.

EPHEDRA, *in the Linnean system*, a genus of plants, Class 22 *Diœcia*, Order 12 *Monodelphia*.
  Generic Character. CAL. *perianth* proper.—COR. none.—STAM. *filaments* seven; *anthers* roundish.—PIST. *germs* two; *styles* simple; *stigmas* simple.—PER. none; *seeds* two.
  Species. The species are shrubs, as *Ephedra distichya,* seu *Ova Polygonum,* Great Shrubby Horse-tail, or Sea Grape.—*Ephedra monostichya,* Great Shrubby Horse-Tail, &c.

EPHEDRA (*Surg.*) an instrument for the reduction of luxated bones.

EPHEDRON (*Bot.*) vide *Ephedra.*

EPHE'LCIS (*Med.*) ἐφελκίς, from ἕλκος, an ulcer; an abrasion from an ulcer; also something bloody brought up by coughing in an Hæmoptysis. *Gal. de Loc. Affect.* l. 1, c. 1; *Gorr. Def. Med.*

E'PHELIS (*Med.*) from ἐπί and ἥλιος, the sun; sun-burning, a disorder from exposure to the sun. *Cel.* l. 6, c. 5; *Oribas. de Loc. Affect.* l. 4, c. 52.

EPHE'MERA (*Med.*) ἐφημέρα, from ἐπί and ἡμέρα, a day; an epithet for a fever which lasts through the whole course of the day. *Gal. de Cris.* l. 2, c. 9; *Act. de Meth. Med.* l. 2, c. 1.

EPHEMERA (*Ent.*) the Day-Fly, a genus of insects of the Neuropterous Order.
  Generic Character. Mouth without mandibles; *feelers* four

very short; *antennæ* filiform; *stemmata* three large; *wings* erect; *tail* terminating in bristles.

Species. This insect derives its name from the shortness of its existence, which seldom exceeds the space of a day, and sometimes not that of an hour. It is seen every where about waters in the summer.

EPHEME'RIDES (*Med.*) an epithet for diseases which attack patients at particular times of the moon.

EPHE'MERIS (*Astron.*) ιφημιρις, from ἡμέρα, a day; a journal, or a calendar, that contains a register of the daily motions or changes of the position of the planets.

EPHE'MERUM (*Bot.*) ιφημιρον, a plant which is reckoned deleterious by Theophrastus, and some other writers, and is supposed to be so called because it was said to kill, in one day, any one who ate of it. It is otherwise called *Colchicum*, because it grew in Colchis.
Nicand. in Alexiph.

> ὦ δὲ τὸ Μηδικῆς Κολχχίδος ἰχθόμινον πῦρ
> κάυω ποτὸν δέχεται ἐφημιρον, ὃ παραχεῖλη
> δισοβριην δυσάλυκτος ἱάπτεται ἐνδοθι κηδμός.

According to Galen there was another plant of this name, which was not poisonous. *Theophrast.* l. 9, c. 16; *Dioscor.* l. 4, c. 88; *Plin.* l. 25, c. 18; *Gal. de Simp.* l. 6; *Oribas. Med. Collect.* l. 11; *Aet. Tetrab.* 1, serm. 2; *Paul. Æginet.* l. 7, c. 3.

EPHEMERUM, in the Linnean system, is the *Commelina Bengeltrensis*.

EPHE'SIA (*Ant.*) ιφισία, a festival, celebrated in Arcadia, in honour of Diana. *Thucyd.* l. 3, c. 104; *Strab.* l. 14; *Poll. Onom.* l. 1, c. 1; *Pausan.* l. 8, c. 13.

EPHE'SIUM (*Med.*) a plaister described by Celsus. *De Re Med.* l. 4, c. 85.

E'PHETÆ (*Ant.*) ιφέται, from ιφίημι, to appeal; judges at Athens who tried cases of manslaughter. They were probably so called because appeals were made in an especial manner to them for the decision of causes. They were either instituted originally, or reduced to the number of fifty by Draco, and afterwards had their power considerably reduced by Solon. *Poll.* l. 8, c. 10; *Plutarch. in Solon; Harpocration; Suidas; Sigon. de Rep. Athen.* l. 3, c. 3.

EPHIA'LTES (*Med.*) vide *Incubus*.

EPHIDRO'SIS (*Med.*) ιφίδρωσις, from ιφιδρίω, to break out into a sweat: a symptomatical sweat which breaks out either over the whole body, or is confined to the face, head, and neck. *Hippocrat. Prorrhet.* l. 1; *Gal. Comm.* 2.

EPHIE'LIS (*Bot.*) a genus of plants, Class 8 *Octandria*, Order 1 *Monogynia*.
Generic Character. CAL. *perianth* one-leaved. — COR. *petals* five.—STAM. *filaments* eight; *anthers* roundish.— PIST. *germ* ovate; *style* none; *stigma* blunt.—PER. *capsule* oblong; *seeds* two.
Species. The single species is a tree, as the *Ephielis guianensis*, seu *Mataiba*, native of Guiana.

EPHI'PPIUM (*Anat.*) part of the *os sphenoides*, in which the pituitary gland is placed.

EPHIPPIUM (*Ant.*) ἐφίππιον, from ἐπὶ, upon, and ἵππος, a horse; the trappings or coverings for a horse, whence the saying of Horace, *Optat bos ephippia*, proverbial for a person discontented with his condition. *Xenoph. Cyropæd.* l. 8; *Varr. apud Non.* l. 2; *Cæs. de Bell. Gall.* l. 4, c. 2; *Poll. Onom.* l. 1, segm. 185; *Dio.* l. 57.

EPHI'PPUS (*Ant.*) a gymnastic exercise among the Lacedæmonians. *Suidas; Hesychius.*

EPHOD (*Theol.*) אֵפוֹד, a linen garment worn by the Jewish high priest and the other inferior priests.

E'PHODOS (*Med.*) ἔφοδος, from ἐπὶ, and ὁδός, a way; signifies in Hippocrates, 1. The duct or passage by which the excrements are evacuated. *Epid.* l. 6, sect. 2, aph. 25.

2. The periodical attack of a fever. *De Prognos.* 3. The accession of things, similar or dissimilar, which may benefit or hurt the body. *De Diæt.; Gal. Comm. in Hippocrat.*

E'PHORUS (*Ant.*) ἔφορος, from ἐφοράω, to inspect, an officer of great power among the Lacedæmonians; so called because he was admitted to an inspection of the greater mysteries of Ceres. The Ephori were five in number, and possessed a power that was more than regal, for they took upon them to punish the Spartan Kings, as in the case of Pausanias and others. *Aristot. Polit.* l. 2, c. 9; *Plut. in Cleom. Pausan.; Pausan.* l. 3.

E'PIALOS (*Med.*) ἠπίαλος, from ἤπιος, gentle, and ἀλεαίνω, to heat; an epithet for a fever attended with a sensation of heat and cold in the same part, and at the same time. *Hippocrat. περὶ ἐπιάλης. Gal. de Diff. Feb.* l. 2, c. 6; *Paul. Ægin.* l. 2, c. 25.

EPIAU'LA (*Ant.*) the name of a popular song among the Greeks, answering to what might now be called the *song of the Millers*.

EPI'BADES (*Ant.*) ἐπιβάδες, Passage-boats, or ships to carry burdens.

EPIBATE'RION (*Ant.*) ἐπιβατήριον, verses made on the occasion of a person's return to his country. *Scalig. Poet.* l. 1, c. 50.

EPIBATE'RIUM (*Bot.*) a genus of plants, Class 21 *Monoecia*, Order 6 *Hexandria*.
Generic Character. CAL. *perianth* double.—COR. *petals* six.—STAM. *filaments* six; *anthers* roundish.—PIST. *germs* three; *styles* three; *stigmas* compressed.—PER. *drupes* three; *seeds* nut kidney form.
Species. The single species is the *Epibaterium pendulum*.

EPI'BOLE (*Med.*) vide *Incubus*.

E'PIC (*Poet.*) ἐπικὸς, from ἔπος, a verse; an epithet for hexameter verse, because it is always used in epic poetry.— *Epic Poem*, a poem, the subject of which is always some hero or distinguished person.

EPICA'NTHIDES (*Anat.*) ἐπικανθίδες, the two angles of the eye.

EPICA'RPIUM (*Med.*) ἐπικάρπιον, a medicine applied to the wrist to drive away intermitting fevers.

EPICA'UMA (*Med.*) ἐπίκαυμα, a crusty ulceration on the surface of the pupil of the eye, in distinction from the encauma, which is situated either on the pupil or the white of the eye, and the caligo, which covers the greater part of the pupil. *Gal. Defin. Med.; Aet. Tetrab.* 2, serm. 2, c. 2; *Paul. Æginet.* l. 3, c. 22; *Act. de Meth. Med.* l. 2, c. 7.

EPICE'DIUM (*Ant.*) ἐπικήδιον, a funeral song, or copy of verses in praise of a person deceased. The *Epicedium* is made previous to burial; the Epitaph after the burial. *Serv. in Virg.*

EPICE'NE (*Gram.*) ἐπίκοινος, i. e. common; an epithet for the gender of such words as are common to both sexes; as *hic, et hæc parens*; a parent, father, or mother.

EPICERA'STICA (*Med.*) ἐπικεραστικὰ, medicines which moderate sharp humours. *Gorr. Def. Med.*

EPICHIRE'MATA (*Rhet.*) ἐπιχειρήματα, rhetorical artifices which the orator uses either in proving or persuading, called by Aristotle *πίστεις*, and by Cicero *argumenta*. *Aristot. Rhet.* l. 2, c. 20; *Cic. de Juv.* l. 1, c. 34; *Dionys. Hal. Jud. in Lys.* c. 15; *Hermog. περὶ εὑρέσ.; Apsin. Art. Rhet. περὶ ἐνθυμημ.; Quintil.* l. 5, c. 14; *Minucian. περὶ ἐπιχειρ. apud Ald.* p. 731; *Menander. Rhet. περὶ ἐπιδεικτ. δαιμ.* l. 3, c. 2.

EPICHIRE'SIS (*Med.*) vide *Enchiresis.*

EPICHIROTO'NIA (*Ant.*) ἐπιχειροτονία, the annual ceremony of revising the laws, which was instituted by Solon; it was so called from the manner of giving their suffrages by holding up their hands.

EPICHO'LOS (*Med.*) ἐπίχολος, from χολὴ, the bile; bilious.

2

EPICHO'RDIS (*Med.*) ἐπιχορδίς, from χορδή, an intestine; the mesentery. *Aret. de Caus. et Sign. Acut. Morb.* l. 2, c. 6.

EPICHO'RIOS (*Med.*) vide *Epidemius*.

EPICHY'SIS (*Ant.*) a brass vessel like an ewer to pour wine out of.

EPICITHARIS'MA (*Ant.*) ἐπικιθάρισμα, the last part of the interlude, or a flourish of music after the play was done.

EPICLI'DIA (*Ant.*) ἐπικλίδια, an Athenian festival in honour of Ceres. *Hesychius.*

EPICO'ELIS (*Med.*) ἐπικοιλίς, the upper eye-lid.

EPICŒ'NUS (*Gram.*) vide *Epicene*.

EPICO'LICÆ regiones (*Anat.*) the lateral or lumbar regions adjacent to the colon.

EPICOPHO'SIS (*Med.*) vide *Cophosis*.

EPICRA'NIUM (*Anat.*) the common integuments, apaneurosis, and muscular expansion which lie upon the cranium.

EPICRA'SIS (*Med.*) ἐπίκρασις, an attemperation of the humours; a cure performed in the alterative way by degrees, and, with attempering medicines, is called a cure *per Epicrasin*. *Gal. de Meth. Med.* l. 12, c. 8.

EPICRE'NÆ (*Ant.*) ἐπίκρηναι, a Lacedemonian festival in honour of Ceres. *Hesychius.*

EPICTE'NION (*Anat.*) ἐπικτένιον, the pubes and adjacent parts. It is also used by Hippocrates to signify fine lint. *Gal. Exeges. Hippocrat. Vocab.*; *Gorr. Def. Med.*; *Foes. Œconom. Hippocrat.*

EPICURE'AN *Philosophy* (*Phil.*) a system of philosophy; so called from its author Epicurus, who maintained that the world was composed of atoms, of various forms and magnitudes, which were united and separated at random, without the intervention of a superior power.

EPICY'CLE (*Astron.*) a little circle whose centre is in the circumference of a greater, which, being fixed in the deferent of a planet, according to the Ptolemaic hypothesis, is carried along with it, and yet with its own peculiar motion, carries the body of the planet fastened to it round its proper centre. *Ptol. Almag.* l. 3, c. 3; *Copern.* l. 3, c. 15.

EPYCY'CLOID (*Geom.*) a curve generated by a point in one circle, which revolves about its convex or concave circumference; the former is called the *exterior or upper Epicycloid*; the latter the *interior or lower Epicycloid*, as in the annexed figure, where G E H F represents an exterior Epicycloid. The revolving or generating circle is called the *generant*, as E, and the arc of that circle along which it revolves is called the *base*, as G B F.

EPICYE'SIS (*Med.*) ἐπικύησις, from ἐπί and κύω, to conceive; superfœtation, or the conception of one fœtus upon another before conceived; on which subject Hippocrates wrote a book.

EPIDE'MIA (*Ant.*) ἐπιδημία, private festivals celebrated in honour of friends returned from a journey. *Meurs. Græc. Fer.*

EPIDE'MICAL (*Med.*) ἐπιδημικός, from ἐπί and δῆμος, the people; a disease which, proceeding from some common cause, spreads itself among the inhabitants of a country.

EPIDE'MIUM (*Med.*) an epidemic disorder.

EPIDE'NDRUM (*Bot.*) a genus of plants, Class 20 *Gynandria*, Order 1 *Diandria*.
 Generic Character. CAL. *spathes* vague.—COR. *petals* five.—STAM. *filaments* two; *anthers* covered by the upper lip of the nectary.—PIST. *germ* slender; *style* very short; *stigmas* obscure.—PER. *silique* long; *seeds* numerous.
 Species. The species are perennials, as the—*Epidendrum vanilla*, seu *Lotus*, Vanilla.—*Epidendrum spatulatum*, seu *Helleborine*, native of the East Indies.—*Epidendrum fervum*, seu *Thalia*, native of the East Indies.
 Epidendrum is also the name of a species of *Lycoperdon*.

EPIDE'RMIS (*Anat.*) ἐπιδερμίς, from ἐπί and δέρμα, the skin; the cuticle or scarf-skin. [vide *Cutis*] *Ruff. Ephes. de Appell. Part. Corp. Human.*

EPIDE'RMOS (*Bot.*) the outer, dry, and very thin covering of a plant corresponding with the scarf skin of the animal body.

EPIDE'SMOS (*Surg.*) ἐπίδεσμος, from δέω, to bind; a bandage by which bolsters, splinters, and the like are secured.

EPIDICA'SIA (*Ant.*) ἐπιδικασία, a suit instituted between persons who pretended to be nearest allied to an heiress, who, according to the laws of Athens, was obliged to marry her nearest relation. The virgin who was the object of contest, was called ἐπίδικος.

EPIDI'CTICUS (*Rhet.*) another name for *Demonstrative*.

EPIDI'DYMIS (*Anat.*) ἐπιδιδυμίς, from ἐπί and δίδυμος, a testicle; a production of the testicle, or a hard vascular oblong substance that lies upon the testicle. *Gal. de Usu Part.* l. 14, c. 14; *Gorr. Def. Med.*

EPIDO'SIS (*Med.*) ἐπίδοσις, from ἐπιδίδωμι, to add to; a term applied to the enlargement of any part of the body, but more particularly to the growth of a disease. *Gal. de Morb. Temp.* c. 2.

EPIDRO'MI (*Med.*) ἐπιδρομή, from ἐπί and δρέμω, to run; an afflux of humours, as happens when a ligature is made on any part. *Hippocrat. κατ' ἰητρ.*

EPIDRO'MIS (*Ant.*) the arming of a net, namely, the ropes, by which it is opened and drawn together. *Plin.* l. 19, c. 1.

EPIDRO'MUS (*Ant.*) ἐπίδρομος, the poop or mizen sail in a ship spread backwards. *Isid. Orig.* l. 19, c. 3; *Hesychius.*; *Gyrald. de Navigat.* c. 14; *Scheff. de Mil. Nav.* l. 2, c. 5.

EPIGÆ'A (*Bot.*) a genus of plants, Class 10 *Decandria*, Order 1 *Monogynia*.
 Generic Character. CAL. *perianth* double.—COR. one-petalled.—STAM. *filaments* ten; *anthers* oblong.—PIST. *germ* globose; *style* filiform; *stigma* obtuse.—PER. *capsule* globose; *seeds* many.
 Species. The two species are shrubs, as the—*Epigæa repens*, seu *Arbutus*, Creeping Epigæa, or Trailing Arbutus.—*Epigæa cordifolia*, Heart-leaved Epigæa, native of Gaudaloupe.

EPI'GEE (*Astron.*) vide *Perigee*.

EPIGA'STRIC (*Anat.*) an epithet for what belongs to the epigastrium; the—*Epigastric region*, the same as the *epigastrium*.—*Epigastric artery*, a branch of the Iliac artery that distributes itself among the muscles of the *epigastrium*.

EPIGA'STRIUM (*Anat.*) ἐπιγάστριον, from ἐπί, upon, and γαστήρ, the belly; the epigastric region, i. e. the forepart of the abdomen or Lower Belly. *Ruff. Ephes. de Apell. Part. Corp. Hum.* l. 1, c. 11; *Gal. Com. in Hippocrat.* l. 7, aphor. 56, &c.

EPIGI'A (*Ant.*) ἐπίγυια, or πείσματα, the cords wherewith ships were tied to the shore. *Poll. Onom.* l. 10, segm. 134.

EPIGENE'MA (*Med.*) ἐπιγένημα, from ἐπιγινάω, to grow to or be added to; something grown or closely adhering to another, as applied by Hippocrates to the saliva adhering to the tongue; also an accessory symptom according to Galen. *Hippoc. Coac. Prænot.*; *Gal. de Diff. Symp.* tom. iii; *Foes. Œconom. Hippocrat.*

EPIGINO'MENA (*Med.*) ἐπιγινόμενα, from ἐπιγίνομαι, to succeed, or be an accession; accessory symptoms.

EPIGLO'SSUM (*Bot.*) the *Laurus Alexandrinum*.

EPIGLO'TTIS (*Anat.*) ἐπιγλωττίς, of ἐπί, above, and γλῶττα, the tongue; the fifth cartilage of the larynx, which serves to cover the opening of the windpipe. *Ruff. Ephes. de Appell. Part. Corp. Hum.* l. 2, c. 4; *Plin.* l. 21, c. 27; *Gal. Def. Med.*; *Oribas. Med. Collect.* l. 25, c. 1; *Gorr. Def. Med.*; *Foes. Œconom. Hippocrat.*

EPIGLOTTIS (*Bot.*) a species of the *Astragalus* of Linnæus.

EPIGLU'TIS (*Anat.*) ἐπιγλυτίς, the superior part of the buttocks.

EPIGO'NATIS (*Anat.*) ἐπιγονατίς, the patella or knee-pan.

Ruff. Ephes. de Appell. Part. Corp. Hum. l. 1, c. 16; *Gal. de Comp. Med. per Gen.* l. 1.

EPIGO'NIDES (*Anat.*) vide *Epigunides.*

EPIGONI'UM (*Mus.*) ἐπιγόνιον, an ancient instrument which was said to be composed of forty strings. It was called after Epigonius its inventor. *Poll. Onom.* l. 4, segm. 59.

EPIGO'NON (*Med.*) *Epicyesis.*

E'PIGRAM (*Lit.*) ἐπίγραμμα, is usually understood to signify a short witty poem, playing upon such fancies as arise from any particular subject, of which the poems of Martial afford good specimens.

EPIGRA'PHE (*Ant.*) a term among antiquaries for an inscription on a building, statue, &c.

EPIGRA'PHEIS (*Ant.*) ἐπιγραφεῖς, from ἐπιγράφω, to inscribe; officers who assessed every one according to his ability, of whom taxes were required. *Poll. Onom.* l. 8, segm. 103.

EPIGU'NIDES (*Anat.*) ἐπιγυνίδες, muscles inserted into the knee. *Ruff. Ephes. de Appell. Part. Corp. Hum.* l. 1, c. 16.

EPILE'NIA (*Mus.*) ἐπιλήνια, a name for the song of the Grape-gatherers among the ancient Greeks. *Poll. Onom.* l. 4, segm. 53.

EPILE'NTIA (*Med.*) a corruption of Epilepsy.

E'PILEPSY (*Med.*) ἐπιληψία, from ἐπιλαμβάνω, to seize; the *Falling Sickness*, so called because persons affected with it fall down on a sudden. It is otherwise called *Morbus Comitialis.* *Hippocrat. Coac. Prænot.*; *Scribon. Larg. Compos. Med.* c. 2; *Gdl. de Different. Morb.* c. 5; *Trallian.* l. 1, c. 15; *Act. de Meth. Med.* l. 1, c. 16; *Foes. Œconom. Hippocrat.*; *Gorr. Def. Med.*

EPILEPSY, in Cullen's Nosology, is a genus of diseases, Class *Neuroses*, Order *Spasmi.*

EPILE'PTICS (*Med.*) ἐπιληπτικά, medicines good against the epilepsy.

EPILO'BIUM (*Bot.*) a genus of plants, Class 8 *Octandria*, Order 1 *Monogynia.*
  Generic Character. CAL. *perianth* one-leaved. — COR. *petals* four. — STAM. *filaments* eight; *anthers* oval. — PIST. *germ* cylindric; *style* filiform; *stigma* obtuse. — PER. *capsule* oblong; *seeds* oblong.
  Species. The species are perennials, as the — *Epilobium angustifolium*, *Chamænerion*, seu *Lysimachia*, Narrow-leaved or Rose-bay Willow-Herb. — *Epilobium angustissimum*, seu *Pseudolysimachium purpureum*, Linear-leaved Willow-Herb, native of Provence. — *Epilobium hirsutum*, Large-flowered Willow-Herb, native of Europe.

EPILO'GUS (*Rhet.*) ἐπίλογος, Epilogue, the conclusion of a speech; so called because, ἐπιλέγεται, it is added to what has been already said.

EPIME'DIUM (*Bot.*) ἐπιμήδιον, a plant with leaves something like the ivy, which was reckoned good for cataplasms. *Dioscor.* l. 4, c. 22; *Plin.* l. 27, c. 9; *Gal. de Simpl.* l. 6; *Oribas. Med. Collect.* l. 11; *Paul. Æginet.* l. 7, c. 3.

EPIMEDIUM, a genus of plants, Class 4 *Tetrandria*, Order 1 *Monogynia.*
  Generic Character. CAL. *perianth* four-leaved. — COR. *petals* four. — STAM. *filaments* four; *anthers* oblong. — PIST. *germ* oblong; *style* shorter than the germ; *stigma* simple. — PER. *silique* oblong; *seeds* oblong.
  Species. The single species, the *Epimedium alpinum*, Alpine Barrenwort, is a perennial.

EPIME'LAS (*Min.*) a white precious stone, having a blackish colour over it.

EPIME'LIS (*Bot.*) a sort of wild apple. *Paul. Ægin.* l. 7, c. 3.

EPIME'NIA (*Ant.*) ἐπιμήνια, a monthly tribute sent from Africa to Rome. *Juv. Sat.* 7, v. 120; *Casaub. in Athen.* l. 2, c. 22.

EPIMONE (*Rhet.*) ἐπιμονή, a figure of speech by which any thing is magnified above measure. [vide *Auxesis*]

EPIMO'RIOS (*Med.*) ἐπιμόριος, superficial; an epithet denoting the inequality of time or rhythm in the beating of the pulse. *Gal. De Diff. Pul.* l. 1, c. 9.

EPI'MYLIS (*Med.*) ἐπιμυλίς, the patella of the knee, or the kneepan. *Gal. Exeges. Hippocrat. Vocab.*; *Foes. Œconom. Hippocrat.*

EPINENEU'COS (*Med.*) ἐπινενευκώς, from νεύω, to nod or incline; an epithet for a pulse that beats unequally in different parts of the artery. *Gal. Isagog. de Puls.*; *Gorr. Def. Med.*

EPINE'PHELES (*Med.*) ἐπινεφελής, from νεφέλη, a cloud, cloudy; an epithet applied to an enæorema, which appears in the urine. *Hippocrat. Epid.* l. 3; *Foes. Œconom. Hippocrat.*

EPINI'CIA (*Ant.*) ἐπινίκια, triumphal songs on the occasion of a victory; also feasts and rejoicings at the same time. *Poll. Onom.* l. 4, segm. 53; *Suet. Ner.* c. 43; *Meurs. Græc. Feriat.* l. 3, apud *Gronov. Thes. Antiq.* tom. 7, p. 769.

EPINY'CTIDES (*Med.*) ἐπινυκτίδες, sores which make the corners of the eyes water; so called because they are particularly painful in the night. *Cels.* l. 5, c. 28; *Plin.* l. 20, c. 8; *Gal. de Meth. Med.* l. 2, c. 2; *Oribas. de Morb. Curat.* l. 3, c. 54; *Aet. Tetrab.* 4, serm. 2, c. 61; *Act. de Meth. Med.* l. 2, c. 11.

EPINO'TIUM (*Anat.*) ἐπινώτιον, from ἐπί, and νῶτος, the back; a name for the shoulder-blade.

EPIPA'CTIS (*Bot.*) ἐπιπακτίς, a small shrub with very small leaves, a decoction of which is good against poisons. Boerhaave takes it to be a species of the *Helloborine*. *Dioscor.* l. 4, c. 109.; *Oribas. Med. Collect.* l. 11; *Paul. Æginet.* l. 7, c. 3.

EPIPACTIS, in the Linnean system, is the *Astrantia epipactis.*

EPIPAROXY'SMUS (*Med.*) ἐπιπαροξυσμός, from ἐπί, and παροξυσμός, a paroxysm; a febrile exacerbation which happens more frequently than usual.

EPIPA'STON (*Med.*) ἐπίπαστον, from ἐπί, and πάσσω, to sprinkle; any powdered drugs sprinkled on the body.

EPIPE'CHYS (*Med.*) ἐπίπηχυς, from ἐπί, and πῆχυς, the cubit; that part of the arm above the cubit.

EPIPE'PHYCOS (*Med.*) the same as *Adnata.*

EPIPHÆNO'MENA (*Med.*) ἐπιφαινόμενα, from ἐπί, and φαινόμενον, a phenomenon; adventitious symptoms, which do not appear before the disease is actually formed. *Hippocrat. Epidem.* l. 6; *Gal. Com.* 2, in *Hippocrat. de Rat. Vict. in Acut. Morb.*

EPI'PHANY (*Ecc.*) ἐπιφάνεια, signifies, literally, an appearance of light, a manifestation; whence it has been applied to signify a festival celebrated on the twelfth day after Christmas, or our Saviour's nativity, wherein he was manifested to the Gentiles by the miraculous appearance of a blazing star, conducting the Magi to the place of his abode. *Isidor. Orig.* l. 6, c. 18.

EPIPHLE'BOS (*Med.*) ἐπίφλεβος, from ἐπί, and φλέψ, a vein; an epithet for one whose veins appear prominent.

EPIPHLOGI'SMA (*Med.*) ἐπιφλόγισμα, from ἐπί, and φλογίζω, to inflame; a violent inflammation, attended with a pain and a tumour.

EPIPHONE'MA (*Rhet.*) ἐπιφώνημα, exclamation; a figure of rhetoric, consisting of a smart sentence at the close of the speech. *Hermog.* περὶ ἰδ. l. 4, apud *Ald. Rhet.* p. 202; *Schol. in Hermog.* p. 392; *Dionys. Art. Rhet.* c. 10; *Quintil.* l. 8, c. 5; *Eustath. ad Hom.* v. p. 1038.

EPI'PHORA (*Rhet.*) ἐπιφορά, or ἐπιφορικός λόγος, a figure of speech, in which the orator inveighs with vehemence. *Sopatr. δαιρ.*

EPIPHORA (*Log.*) a conclusion or consequence drawn from the assumption in a syllogism.

EPIPHORA (*Med.*) from ἐπιφέρω, to carry with force; an impetuous flux of the humours. *Cel.* l. 6, c. 6; *Scribon. Larg.* c. 19; *Columel.* l. 7, c. 17; *Plin.* l. 20, c. 13; *Gal. de Comp. Med. sec. Loc.* l. 4, c. 7; *Marsell. de Med.* c. 8;

Trallian. l. 2, c. 1; *Myrep. de Antidot.* sect. 1, c. 383; *Gorr. Def. Med.*

EPIPHYLLA'NTHUS (*Bot.*) is the *Xylophylla angustifolia* of Linnæus.

EPIPHYLLOSPE'RMÆ (*Bot.*) an epithet for plants which bear seeds on the leaf.

EPIPHY'SIS (*Med.*) ἐπίφυσις, from ἐπιφύω, to grow to; a sort of articulation of the bones when they grow to one another by simple and immediate contiguity. *Hippocrat. de Tract.*; *Gal. de Usu Part.* l. 11, c. 18; *Oribas. Med. Collect.* l. 24, c. 1; *Gorr. Def. Med.*; *Foes. Œconom. Hippocrat.*

EPIPLA'SMA (*Med.*) ἐπίπλασμα, the same as *Cataplasma*.

EPIPLERO'SIS (*Med.*) ἐπιπλήρωσις, from ἐπί, and πλήρωσις, repletion; super-repletion, or an excess of repletion.

EPIPLE'XIS (*Rhet.*) ἐπίπληξις, from ἐπιπλήσσω, a figure in rhetoric, which, by an elegant kind of upbraiding, endeavours to convince. Hippocrates thinks this a desirable talent in a physician. *Hippocrat. Jul. Rufinian.* p. 15, c. 21; *Philostrat. Vit. Apollon.*; *Phot. Cod.* 165.

EPI'PLOCE (*Rhet.*) ἐπιπλοκή, a rhetorical figure; a gradual rising of one clause of a sentence out of another. *Hermog. apud Ald. Rhet.* p. 29; *Quintil.* l. 7, c. 1.

EPIPLOCE (*Med.*) vide *Symploce*.

EPI'PLOCELE (*Med.*) ἐπιπλοκήλη, from ἐπίπλοον, the omentum, and κήλη, a tumour; a hernia in which the omentum is fallen down. *Cel.* l. 1, c. 18; *Gal. Def. Med.*

EPIPLO'ICÆ *Appendiculæ* (*Med.*) small appendages to the colon and rectum.

EPIPLO'IS (*Med.*) a branch of the cœliac artery, springing out of the lower end of the *Splenica*, which is either the *Epiplois postica*, that runs to the back of the omentum, or *Epiplois sinistra* that runs to the left side of the omentum.

EPIPLO'ITIS (*Med.*) from ἐπίπλοον, omentum; an inflammation of the process of the peritoneum, which forms the omentum.

EPIPLOOCOMI'STES (*Med.*) ἐπιπλοοκομιστής, an epithet for a man having a very large omentum. *Gal. Adm. Anat.* l. 6, c. 5.

EPIPLOOM'PHALON (*Med.*) from ἐπίπλοον, and ὀμφαλός, a navel rupture. *Gal. Def. Med.*

EPIPLO'ON (*Med.*) ἐπίπλοον, from ἐπιπλέω, to sail upon; the Greek name for the omentum, or caul; so called because it is mostly found floating as it were on the intestines. *Ruff. Ephes. de Appellat. Part. Corp. Hum.* l. 1, c. 28; *Gal. de Adm. Anat.* l. 6, c. 5; *Oribas. Med. Collect.* l. 24, c. 21.

EPIPLOSCHEOCE'LE (*Med.*) from ἐπίπλοον, the omentum, ὄσχιον, the scrotum, and κήλη, a hernia; a rupture of the omentum when it descends into the scrotum.

EPIPOGE'UM (*Bot.*) is the *Satyrium epipogeum*.

EPIPOLA'SIS (*Med.*) ἐπιπόλασις, a redundance or fluctuation. *Hippocrat. de Nat. Human.* l. 1.

EPIPORO'MA (*Med.*) ἐπιπώρωμα, a callous concretion. *Hippocrat. Prorrhet.* l. 2.

EPISARCO'DIUM (*Med.*) vide *Anasarca*.

EPISCE'NIUM (*Archit.*) ἐπισκήνιον, the columniation or rows of beams above the scene. *Vitruv.* l. 5, c. 7; *Philand. in Vitruv.*; *Bald. Lex. Vitruv.*

EPISCHE'SIS (*Med.*) ἐπίσχεσις, from ἔχω, to stop; a suppression of due excretions. *Gal. Com.* 2, *in Hippocrat. Epid.* l. 3.

EPISCHI'DION (*Mech.*) from σχίζω, to cleave; a wedge to cleave wood with. *Vitruv.* l. 10, c. 17; *Bald. Lex. Vitruv.*

EPI'SCHION (*Anat.*) ἐπίσχιον, from ἐπί, and ἰσχίον, the ischium; the pecten, or *os pubis*.

EPI'SCOPACY (*Ecc.*) ἐπισκοπή, in Latin *episcopatus*; a form of church government by bishops.

EPISCOPA'LES VALVULÆ (*Anat.*) the same as the *Valvulæ mitrales*.

EPISCOPA'LIA (*Ecc.*) synodals, pente-costals, and other customary payments from the clergy.

EPISCOPA'LIANS (*Ecc.*) those who support episcopacy.

EPI'SCOPUS (*Ant.*) ἐπίσκοπος, from ἐπισκέπτομαι, to superintend; an Athenian magistrate, particularly one who had the superintendance of the markets.

EPISCOPUS *Puerorum* (*Sport.*) an old custom in former times, for a lay person, at a certain season, to plait his hair; and, putting on the garb of a bishop, to exercise his functions to the entertainment of the rest. *Mon. Angl.* tom. 3, p. 69.

EPISCY'NIUM (*Anat.*) ἐπισκύνιον, the extreme wrinkle of the eyebrow; also the eyebrow itself. *Ruff. Ephes. de Appell. Part. Corp. Human.* l. 1, c. 1; *Gorr. Def. Med.*

EPISEI'ON (*Anat.*) ἐπίσειον, the pubes. *Ruff. Ephes. de Appell. Part. Corp. Human.* l. 1, c. 11.

EPISEMA'SIA (*Med.*) the same as *Annotatio*.

E'PISODE (*Poet.*) ἐπεισόδιον, from ἐπεισόδιος, adventitious; a separate story, or action, which a poet connects with the main plot of his poem, in order to give it diversity; as the story of Dido, in Virgil. *Aristot. de Art. Poet.* c. 12.

EPISPA'SMOS (*Med.*) ἐπίσπασμος, from ἐπισπάω, to attract; a quick inspiration of the breath. *Hippocrat. Epidem.* l. 6.

EPISPA'STICS (*Med.*) ἐπισπαστικά, from ἐπισπάω, to draw; medicines which draw blisters. *Cel.* l. 5, c. 18; *Gal. de Comp. Med. per gen.* l. 6.

EPI'SPHÆRIA (*Med.*) the turnings and windings of the exterior substance of the brain.

EPISTA'LMA (*Ant.*) a prince's commission under his hand and seal.

EPI'STASIS (*Med.*) ἐπίστασις, from ἐφίστημι, to place upon; the substance swimming on the surface of the urine. *Hippoc.* l. 7, aphor. 34.

EPI'STATES (*Ant.*) ἐπιστάτης, the president of the proedri, who had in his charge the keys of the public exchequer, which was thought to be a trust of such magnitude that no one was permitted to hold it more than once. *Aristot. Polit.* l. 6, c. 8; *Demosth. Timocrat.*; *Poll. Onom.* l. 8, serm. 96.

EPISTA'XIS (*Med.*) ἐπίσταξις, from ἐπί, and στάζω, to distil; a repeated distillation of blood from the nose. *Hippocrat. apud Gorr. Def. Med.*

EPISTO'MION (*Mech.*) ἐπιστόμιον, a cock, tap, spiggot, stopper, &c.; also the stop in an organ, to make the sound high or low. *Vitruv.* l. 10, c. 13; *Philand. in Vitruv.*; *Bud. in Pandect.* p. 164.

EPI'STROPHE (*Rhet.*) a figure in rhetoric, by which sentences end in the same word, called by Hermogenes *antistrophe*, by Rutilius *epiphora*, by Aquila *anastrophe*. *Jul. Rufinian.*

EPISTROPHÆ'US (*Anat.*) an epithet for the second vertebræ of the back.

EPISTY'LE (*Archit.*) ἐπιστύλιον, a mass of stone, &c. laid upon the capital of a pillar. *Vitruv.* l. 3, c. 3; *Bald. Lex Vitruv.*

EPITA'SIS (*Med.*) ἐπιτείνομαι, to be heightened; an increase of the paroxysm of a fever. *Hippocrat. Prorrhet.* l. 2; *Cæl. Aurelian. de Morb. Chron.* l. 4, c. 3; *Gorr. Def. Med.*; *Foes. Œconom. Hippocrat.*

EPITASIS (*Rhet.*) that part of an oration in which the orator addresses himself most forcibly to the passions. *Dionys. Jud. in Isocr.* c. 13; *Longin.* c. 38; *Alexand. περὶ σχημ.*; *Æl. Herod.* tom. ii. p. 90.

EPITHALA'MIUM (*Ant.*) ἐπιθαλάμιον, a nuptial song, or a song sung at weddings. *Poll. Onom.* l. 4, segm. 53.

EPITHE'LIUM (*Med.*) the cuticle on the red part of the lips.

EPITHE'MA (*Med.*) ἐπίθεμα, a lotion, or any external application. *Gal. Com. in Hippoc.* l. 7, aphor. 55; *Oribas. Synop.* l. 3; *Aet. Tetrab.* 3, serm. 1, c. 50, &c.

EPI'THESIS (*Surg.*) ἐπίθεσις, the rectification of crooked limbs by means of instruments and machines.

E'PITHET (*Rhet.*) ἐπίθετον, a word which is joined to another to qualify or explain its signification.

EPITHYMUM (*Bot.*) is the *Cascuta epithymum* of Linnæus.

EPITIME'SIS (*Rhet.*) ἐπιτίμησις, a figure in rhetoric, by which a rebuke or reproach is conveyed. *Aristot. Poet.* c. 26; *Tiber. Rhetor.* c. 4; *Hermog. περὶ διανοί.*; *Rufin.* fig. 21; *Alexand. περὶ σχημ.*; *Ulp. ad Demosth. Olynth.* 1, p. 6.

EPI'TOME (*Rhet.*) ἐπιτομή, an abridgement, abstract, or short draught of a book.

E'PITRITE (*Poet.*) ἐπίτριτος, a foot consisting of four syllables, one of which is short and the rest long ‿ ‒ ‒ ‒, as Āristīdēs. *Hæphest. Enchirid.*

EPITRI'TOS (*Arith.*) a proportion containing some number, and the third part added; thus, eight is an epitrite number in regard to six, for two, which is added to six to make the number eight, is the third of six. *Vitruv.* l. 3, c. 1; *Bald. Lex Vitruv.*

EPITROCHA'SMUS (*Rhet.*) ἐπιτροχασμός, a figure in rhetoric wherein we hastily run over several things. *Hermog. περὶ ἰδ.* l. 1, *apud Ald. Rhet.* p. 150.

EPI'TROPE (*Rhet.*) ἐπιτροπή, a figure in rhetoric, in which the orator grants what he may freely deny in order to obtain what he demands. *Quintil.* l. 9, c. 3; *Rutil. Lup.* l. 2, c. 16.

EPIZEU'XIS (*Rhet.*) the same as *Anadiplosis.*

EPIZY'GIS (*Mech.*) ἐπιζυγίς, the hole wherein the nut of a steel-bow lies. *Vitruv.* l. 10, c. 16; *Turneb. Adv.* l. 2, c. 5.

EPO'CHÆ (*Ant.*) ἐποχαί, a term signifying literally stops, was applied to those resting points or dates from which many of the Grecian cities commenced their computations of time. Some of them dated their Epochas from the building of their cities; but the greater part of those whose epochas are numbered on their coins or medals are reckoned from the restoration of their liberty by the Romans, the remission of their tributes by the emperors, the gaining an independent government, or the liberty of being governed by their own magistrates and laws, &c. *Vaill. Num. Græc.*

EPO'DE (*Med.*) ἐπῳδή, a method of curing diseases by incantations.

EPODE (*Mus.*) ἐπῳδός, the name given to the third stanza of the Greek ode. [vide *Ode*]

EPO'DES (*Ich.*) ἐπῳδίς, a kind of fish. *Plin.* l. 32, c. 11.

EPO'MIS (*Anat.*) ἐπωμίς, from ἐπί and ὦμος, the shoulder; the upper part of the shoulder. *Ruff. Ephes. de Appell. Part. Corp. hum.* l. 1, c. 9; *Gal. Comm.* 1 *in Hippocrat. de Art.*

EPOMIS (*Archæol.*) a hood such as graduates, and liverymen, used to wear.

EPOMPHA'LION (*Med.*) ἐπομφάλιον, from ἐπί and ὀμφαλός, the navel; a medicine which purges by being applied to the navel. *Aet. Tetrab.* 1, serm. 3, c. 135; *Paul. Æginet.* l. 7, c. 9.

EPROUVE'TTE (*Gunn.*) a machine for showing the strength and quality of gunpowder.

EP'SOM *salts* (*Med.*) a purging salt formerly procured by boiling down the mineral water of the spring at Epsom; but now prepared from sea-water. They are in the form of crystals, and consist chiefly of sulphate of magnesia.

EPULA'RES (*Ant.*) were those who took part in a religious rite, which was celebrated at night, when they feasted together. *Fest. de Verb. Signif.*

E'PULIS (*Med.*) ἐπουλίς, from ἐπί and ἴλη, the gums; a sort of tubercle growing on the gums. *Gal. Introd.*; *Oribas. de Loc. Affect. Curat.* l. 4, c. 66; *Aet. Tetrab.* 4, serm. 2, c. 50; *Paul. Æginet.* l. 6, c. 27.

EPULO'NES (*Ant.*) the three public officers in the time of Julius Cæsar, whose duty it was to conduct the banquets in honour of Jupiter, and the rest of the Gods, at their public sports. *Cic. de Orat.* l. 3, c. 19; *Liv.* l. 33, c. 42; *Fest. de Signif. Verb.*; *Aul. Gell.* l. 1, c. 12.

EPULO'TICS (*Med.*) ἐπουλωτικά, from ἴλη, a cicatrix; topical medicines applied to wounds or ulcers for drying up superfluous humidity, and repressing fungous flesh. *Gal. de Simpl. Med. Fac.* l. 5, c. 15, 16; *Gorr. Def. Med.*

E'QUABLE (*Phy.*) an epithet for motion, celerity, velocity, &c. which is uniform, or without alteration, by which equal spaces are passed over in equal times; whence also *equably, accelerated*, or *retarded*, when motion is increased or decreased in equal quantities or degrees in equal times.

E'QUAL (*Math.*) an epithet expressing the relation between things that agree in kind, magnitude, quantity, or quality; as *equal circles*, those which have their diameters equal; *equal angles*, whose sides are equally inclined; *equal lines*, lines of the same length; *equal plane figures*, whose areas are equal; *equal solids*, that are of the same space, capacity, or solid content; *equal curvatures*, that have equal radii of curvatures; *equal geometrical ratios*, those whose least terms are similar to some aliquot or aliquant parts of the greater; *equal arithmetical ratios*, those wherein the difference of the two less terms is equal to the difference of the greater.

EQUAL (*Opt.*) an epithet for things seen under the same angle.

EQUA'LITY (*Math.*) the exact agreement of two things in respect to their quantity. [vide *Equal*]

EQUALITY (*Algeb.*) the comparison between two quantities which are really or effectually equal. The sign of equality, which was introduced by Recorde, and which is now in universal use, consists of two parallel lines, as $=$; thus, $a - x = d$. [vide *Algebra*] — *Ratio*, or *proportion of Equality*. [vide *Æqualitas*]

EQUALITY, *circle of* (*Astron.*) vide *Equant.*

E'QUANT (*Astron.*) a circle formerly conceived by astronomers to be in the plane of the deferent or eccentric, for regulating certain motions of the planets, and reducing them more easily to a calculus: but, in modern astronomy, this circle is not employed.

EQUA'TED *anomaly* (*Astron.*) vide *Anomaly.*

EQUATED *bodies* (*Math.*) a name on Gunter's Scale for two lines which relate to the comparison of the sphere and the regular bodies.

EQUA'TION (*Algeb.*) any expression in which two quantities differently represented are put equal to each other by means of the sign of equality, as $7ax + 3x = b$. The quantities composing the equation are called the *terms of the equation*; the terms on each side the sign of equality compose the *sides* of the equation; the *root* is the value of the unknown quantity. *Equations* are, in respect to their construction, *simple, affected* or *compound, quadratic, cubic, biquadratic, binomial, determinate, reciprocal, transcendental, exponential*, &c. [vide *Simple, &c.* and *Algebra*] The operations with equations are Generation, Reduction, Solution or Resolution, Depression, Extermination, Elimination, Transformation, and Construction. [vide *Generation*, &c. and *Algebra*]

EQUATION *of payments* (*Arith.*) the finding a time, when, if a sum be paid, which is equal to the sum of several others due at different times, no loss will be sustained by either party; according to the rule commonly given, this is found, if each payment be multiplied by the time at which it is due, and then the sum of the products be divided by the sum of the payments for the equatic time.

EQUATION (*Astron.*) a term used to express the correction, i. e. the quantity added to, or subtracted from, the mean position of a heavenly body to obtain the true position: the term may likewise be applied to the correction that arises from any erroneous supposition whatever.—*Equation of the centre* is that which is otherwise called *prosthapheresis.*—*Equation of time* is the difference between mean

4 L

and apparent time, or the reduction of the apparent unequal time or motion of the sun, or a planet, to equable and mean time or motion.—*Equation to corresponding altitudes* is a correction which must be applied to the apparent time of noon in order to ascertain the true time.

EQUA'TOR (*Astron.*) a great circle which is described on the terrestrial sphere, and equidistant from the poles of the world. It is called the Equator because, when the sun is in this circle, the days and nights are equal all over the world; whence it is also called the *Æquinoctial*, *Æquinoctial line*, and, among mariners, simply the *line*.

EQUATO'RIAL (*Astron.*) or *Portable Observatory*, an instrument which serves for the solution of most problems in practical astronomy.

EQUE'RRY (*Polit.*) an officer who has the care and management of the horses of a king, or any prince.

E'QUES (*Her.*) a horseman, or man at arms.—*Eques auratus*, or simply *eques*, a knight so called because he was allowed to wear gilt spurs.

EQUE'STRIA (*Ant.*) seats in the theatre for those of the Equestrian order at Rome. Senec. de Benef. l. 7, c. 12; Suet. Cal. c. 26; Turneb. Adv. l. 4, c. 19, &c.

EQUIA'NGULAR (*Geom.*) an epithet for any figures that have equal angles, as *equiangular triangles*, &c.

EQUICRU'RAL (*Geom.*) an epithet for a triangle that has two of its sides equal.

EQUIDI'FFERENT (*Math.*) an epithet for such things as have equal differences, or are arithmetically proportional.

EQUILA'TERAL (*Geom.*) an epithet for any figure that has all its sides equal. An *equilateral Hyperbola* is that which has the two axes equal to each other, and every pair of conjugate diameters equal to each other.

EQUILI'BRIUM (*Mech.*) an equality of weight or poise. The two ends of a balance are said to be *in equilibrio* when they hang exactly even, neither of them ascending or descending.

EQUIMU'LTIPLE (*Geom.*) ἰσάκις πολλαπλάσιον, any number or quantity which may be multiplied by the same number, as 3 *a* and 3 *b*, which are equimultiples of *a* and *b*. Euc. Elem. Def. l. 5.

EQUINO'CTIAL (*Astron.*) *æquinoctialis*, a name for the great circle of the sphere on the celestial globe, which corresponds to the equator on the terrestrial globe.
Equinoctial is also an epithet for whatever belongs to the equinoctial; as the—*Equinoctial Points*, the two points, Aries and Libra, where the Equinoctial and Ecliptic cross each other.—*Equinoctial Colure*, the great circle passing through the Poles of the World, and the Equinoctial points.—*Equinoctial Dial*, one whose plane is parallel to the equinoctial.

E'QUINOXES (*Astron.*) the times wherein the sun enters the first points of Aries and Libra, so called from *æquus*, equal, and *nox*, night, because the days and nights are equal at those times. The equinox is called *vernal* when it falls in the spring, about the 21st of March; and *autumnal* when it falls in autumn, about the 21st of September.

EQUI'NUS *barbatus* (*Astron.*) a kind of comet. [vide *Hippeus*]

E'QUIPAGE (*Cus.*) in French *equipage*, the provision of all things necessary for a voyage or journey; as attire, furniture, horses, attendance, &c. It is frequently used for a coach and a number of footmen.

EQUIPAGE (*Mil.*) all kinds of furniture which are made use of by an army; *Camp-Equipage*, or *Field-Equipage*, comprehends tents, kitchen furniture, saddle-horses, baggagewaggons, &c.

EQUIPO'LLENCE (*Log.*) from the Latin *æquipollentia*, which signifies equal force or value; a term applied to two or more propositions which signifies one and the same thing, though expressed after a different manner; as " Some man is learned," and " Not every man is learned," which are equipollent propositions.

EQUI'RIA (*Ant.*) games which consisted in horse-racing, that were instituted by Romulus in honour of Mars, and were celebrated on the third of the Calends of March, i. e. the 27th of February.
Ovid. Fast. l. 2, v. 857.

Jamque duæ restant noctes de mense secundo,
Maraque citos junctis turribus urget equos.
Et vero positum permansit Equiria nomen,
Quæ deus in campo prospicit ipsa sua.

Varr. de Lat. Ling. l. 5, c. 3; Marlian. Topograph. Urb. Rom. &c. apud Græv. Ant. Rom. tom. 3, &c.

EQUISE'TUM (*Bot.*) ἱππυρις, Horse-tail; a plant so called from the resemblance which it bears to a horse's tail. It is generally admitted to be very vulnerary and astringent. Aet. Tetrab. 1, serm. 1.

EQUISETUM, *in the Linnean system*, a genus of plants, Class 24, *Cryptogamia*, Order 1 *Felices*. Natural order of ferns.
Species. The species are perennials, as the—*Equisetum sylvaticum*, seu *Hippuris*, Wood Horse-Tail.—*Equisetum arvense*, Corn Horse-Tail.—*Equisetum palustre*, Marsh Horse-Tail.—*Equisetum fluviatile*, River Horse-Tail.—*Equisetum giganteum*, Giant Horse-Tail, &c.

EQUISETUM is also the *Ceratophyllum dimersa* of Linnæus.

EQUITANGE'NTIAL *curve* (*Geom.*) a curve so denominated because the tangent of it is always equal to a constant line.

E'QUITANT (*Bot.*) a term used in the foliation of plants; *folia equitantia*, leaves that ride, as it were, over one another, i. e. when the inner leaves of a bud are inclosed by the outer ones.

EQUITATU'RA (*Archæol.*) the liberty of riding on horseback; also of carrying grist, &c. from the mill on horseback.

E'QUITY (*Law*) the correction of the Common Law in cases wherein it is deficient.—*Court of Equity*, a title given, by way of distinction, to the Court of Chancery, because the rigour of the Common Law, and the severity of other courts, is there moderated.

EQUIVENTER (*Anat.*) vide *Venter*.

EQUI'VOCAL (*Log.*) an epithet for words which have a double meaning, and may be applied equally to both.

EQUIVOCAL *generation* (*Nat.*) a term formerly applied to the generation of plants without seeds, and of animals without any sexual intercourse, which is now believed never to happen; but that all bodies are univocally produced.

EQUIVOCAL *signs* (*Surg.*) certain accidents, or signs of the fracture of the skull, which confirm other signs called *universal*.

EQUU'LEUS (*Astron.*) *Equiculus*, or *Equus Minor*, one of the 48 old constellations, having, according to Ptolemy, only four stars, according to Tycho four, to Hevelius six, Flamstead. It is called by Proclus προτομὴ τῦ ἵππυ, a section of the horse. Ptol. Almag. l. 7, c. 5; Procl. de Sphær.

E'QUUS (*Zool.*) a genus of animals of the Class *Mammalia*, Order *Belluæ*.
Generic Character. Foreteeth, upper six, erect; lower six, more prominent; *tusks* solitary, included; *teats* two, inguinal.
Species. This tribe of animals comprehends the domestic quadrupeds well known by the names of the Horse, the Ass, and the Mule.

EQUUS *coopertus* (*Archæol.*) a horse set out with a saddle, and other furniture.

EQUUS *Major* (*Astron.*) vide *Pegasus*.—*Equus Minor*. [vide *Equuleus*]

ERACLI'SSA (*Bot.*) the *Adrachne telephoides* of Linnæus.

ERAGRO'STIS (*Bot.*) the *Briza eragrostis* of Linnæus.

ERA'DICATED (*Her.*) an epithet for a tree or plant torn up by the root, as in the annexed figure. " He beareth *gules* the trunk of a tree eradicated and couped in *pale*, sprouting out two branches *argent*, name Borough."

ERA'DICATIVES (*Med.*) medicines that work powerfully, and, as it were, root out the disorder.

ERANGE'LIA (*Bot.*) another name for the *Galanthus* of Linnæus.

ERA'NTHEMUM (*Bot.*) a genus of plants, Class 2 *Diandria*, Order 1 *Monogynia*.
 Generic Character. CAL. perianth five-cleft.—COR. one-petalled.—STAM. filaments two; anthers subovate.—PIST. germ ovate; style filiform; stigma simple.—PER. none; seeds none.
 Species. The species are undershrubs, as the—*Eranthemum capense*, *Ephemerum*, seu *Centaureum*.—*Eranthemum angustifolium Thymelæa*, seu *Valerianoides*, &c.

ERA'SED (*Her.*) an epithet for the head or limb of any creature violently torn from the body, so as to appear jagged, as in the annexed figure. He beareth " *Argent* a lion's head, erased *gules*, name Govis." When Boars', Bears', Wolves', Whales', and Otters' Heads are erased close to the head, it is termed *erased close*.

ERA'STIANS (*Ecc.*) a sect of heretics, who maintained, among other things, that the right of excommunication belonged to the civil magistrate.

EREBI'NTHUS (*Bot.*) the same as *Cicer*.

ERE'CT (*Bot.*) *erectus;* an epithet for a stem, leaf, flower, anther, &c.; *erectus caulis*, a stem standing perpendicularly from the ground, in opposition to *volubilis*; *folium erectum* is a leaf which makes an angle with the stem, so acute as to be close to it; *flos erectus*, an erect flower, has its aperture directed upwards, as in *Trillium sessile*, opposed to the *nutans*, the nodding; *anthera erecta*, an anther fixed by one end to the top of the filament, in opposition to *incumbens*. This epithet is applied in the same sense to the petiole, peduncle, and stipule.

ERECT (*Her.*) an epithet for any thing upright, or perpendicularly elevated, as wings *erect*, &c.

TO ERECT *a figure* (*Astrol.*) to divide the twelve houses of the heavens aright, putting down the signs, degrees, &c. in their right places, according to the position of the heavenly bodies at the moment of time that the scheme is erected.

ERECTIU'SCULUS (*Bot.*) an epithet signifying nearly upright.

ERECTO'RES (*Anat.*) an epithet for muscles of the *clitoris* and the *penis*. The *Erector Clitoridis* draws it downwards and backwards; the *Erector Penis* drives the urine and semen forwards.

ERE'GMOS (*Bot.*) ἔρεγμος, from ῥήγνυμι, to break; an epithet for a bean that is decorticated.

ERE'SIA (*Bot.*) the *Theophrasta americana* of Linnæus.

ERETHI'SMOS (*Med.*) ἐρεθισμός from ἐρεθίζω, to excite; increased sensibility and irritability. Hippoc. de Rat. Vict. in Morb. Acut. et Gal. Comm. 2; Foes. Œconom. Hippocrat.

ERE'TRIA *terra* (*Med.*) ἐρετριάς γῆ, Eretrian earth, the best sort of which is ash-coloured. It is reckoned astringent and refrigerating. Hippocrat. de Morb. l. 3; Dioscor. l. 5, c. 171; Plin. l. 35, c. 6; Gal. de Simpl. l. 9; Oribas. Med. Coll. l. 15; Gorr. Def. Med.; Foes. Œconom. Hippocrat.

EREU'MENA (*Med.*) ἐρεύμενα; an epithet for urine that looks cloudy. Hippocrat. Coac.

ERGA'SIMA (*Med.*) ἐργάσιμον, a bad sort of myrrh. Dioscor. l. 1, c. 77; Oribas. Med. Coll. l. 12.

ERGASTE'RIUM (*Chem.*) ἐργαστήριον, from ἐργάζομαι, to work; a laboratory, or that part of a furnace in which is contained the matter to be acted upon.

ERGA'STULUM (*Ant.*) ἐργαστήριον δεσμωτήριον, from ἐργάζομαι, a house of correction; a bridewell, which Juvenal calls a rustic prison.
 Juv. l. 14, v. 24.
  Quam mire afficiunt inscripta ergastula, carcer
  Rusticus?
 Liv. l. 7, c. 4; Plin. l. 18, c. 6; Plut. in Grach.; Salmas. Spart. in Hadrian. l. 18.

E'RGOT (*Vet.*) a stub, like a piece of soft horn, about the size of a chesnut, placed behind and below the pastern joint of a horse, which is commonly under the tufts of the fetlock.

E'RIACH (*Law*) a recompense or compensation for the murder of a person made, by the Brehon law in Ireland, to the relations of the deceased.

ERI'CA (*Bot.*) ἐρίκη, a plant very similar to the tamarisk-tree, which is much liked by bees. A fomentation of the flowers is good against the bites of serpents. Dioscor. l. 1, c. 119; Plin. l. 11, c. 16; Gal. de Simpl. l. 6; Oribas. Med. Coll. l. 11; Paul. Æginet. l. 7, c. 3.

ERICA, *in the Linnean system*, a genus of plants, Class 8 *Octandria*, Order 1 *Monogynia*.
 Generic Character. CAL. perianth four-leaved. — COR. one-petalled.—STAM. *filaments* eight; *anthers* two-cleft. —PIST. *germ* roundish; *style* filiform; *stigma* crowned. —PER. *capsule* roundish; *seeds* numerous.
 Species. The species are undershrubs, as the—*Erica vulgaris*, Common Heath.—*Erica lutea*, Yellow Heath, native of the Cape of Good Hope.—*Erica halicacaba*, Purple-stalked Heath, native of the Cape of Good Hope. —*Erica Monsoniana*, Bladder-flowered Heath, native of the Cape.—*Erica arborea*, Tree Heath, native of the Cape.

ERICA is also the name of the *Andromeda daboecia*, and the *Frankenia lævis*.

ERICÆFO'RMIS (*Bot.*) the *Diosma ericoides*.

ERICÆ'US (*Nat.*) ἐρικαῖος, a kind of honey collected from the Erica. Dioscor. l. 1, c. 117; Plin. l. 11, c. 16.

ERICE'RUM (*Med.*) ἐρίκηρον, the name of several collyria. Art. Tetrab. 2. serm. 3, c. 102.

ERI'CEUS (*Ant.*) a warlike instrument, full of sharp-pointed nails, resembling a portcullis. Cæs. Bell. Gall. l. 3, c. 67; Turneb. Adv. l. 4, c. 8.

ERICO'IDES (*Bot.*) a species of the *Elatine*.

ERICO'ILA (*Bot.*) the *Gentiana verna* of Linnæus.

E'RICU (*Bot.*) the *Asclepias Gigantia* of Linnæus.

ERI'DANUS (*Astron.*) Ἠριδανός, or ποταμός, one of the 48 old constellations in the southern hemisphere, in which Ptolemy reckons 34 stars, Tycho 10, and the British Catalogue 84. The principal star of the first magnitude at the extremity of the river is Achernar. Erat. Phænom.; Eratosthen. Charact.; Ptol. Almag. l. 7, c. 5; Ricciol. Almag. nov. l. 6, c. 5.

ERI'GERON (*Bot.*) vide *Erigeron*.

ERIGERON, *in the Linnean system*, a genus of plants, Class 19 *Syngenesia*, Order 2 *Polygamia Superflua*.
 Generic Character. CAL. common oblong. — COR. compound rayed.—STAM. filaments five; anthers cylindric.— PIST. germ small; style filiform; stigmas two.—PER. none; seeds oblong.
 Species. The species are perennials and annuals: of the first kind the following are the principal, as the—*Erigeron viscosum*, seu *Conyza*, Clammy Erigeron, native of Portugal.—*Erigeron glutinosum*, Glutinous Erigeron.— *Erigeron philadelphium*, Spreading Erigeron.—*Erigeron purpureum*, Purple Erigeron. Of the second kind the following are the principal—*Erigeron graveolens*, Strong-smelling Erigeron.—*Erigeron siculum*, Red-stalked Eri-

geron.—*Erigeron carolinananum*, Carolina Erigeron.—*Erigeron canadense*, Canadian Erigeron, native of North America.

ERIGERON is also the *Conyza Ægyptiaca*.

ERI'GERUM (*Bot.*) ἠριγέρων, a plant called by the Latins *Senecio*, because, γηράσκει, it grows old, ἦρι, very soon. It was reckoned vulnerary. *Theophrast. Hist. Plant.* l. 7, c. 8; *Dioscor.* l. 4, c. 98; *Oribas. Med. Coll.* l. 11; *Aet. Tetrab.* l, serm. 1; *Paul. Æginet.* l. 7, c. 3.

ERIGERUM, in the Linnean system, is the *Senecio vulgaris*.

ERINA'CEA (*Bot.*) another name for the *Anthyllis* of Linnæus.

ERINA'CEUS (*Bot.*) another name for the *Hydnum* of Linnæus.

ERINACEUS (*Zool.*) another name for the Urchin.

ERINACEUS, in the Linnean system, a genus of animals of the Class *Mammalia*, Order *Feræ*.

Generic Character. Foreteeth, upper, two, distant; lower, two, approximate; *tusks*, upper, five; lower, three; *grinders*, four on each side in each jaw; *back* and *sides* covered with spines.

Species. This animal is well known by the name of the Hedge-Hog. [vide *Hedge-Hog*]

ERI'NGO (*Bot.*) the *Eryngium* of Linnæus.

ERI'NUS (*Bot.*) ἔρινος, or ἔρινον, a plant, the leaves of which resemble those of the *Ocymum*. It grows near fountains and rivers, and, mixed with sulphur, was used to relieve pains in the ears. *Theophrast. Hist. Plant.* l. 3, c. 6; *Nicand. in Theriac.*; *Dioscor.* l. 4, c. 29; *Plin.* l. 23, c. 7; *Oribas. Med. Coll.* l. 11; *Paul. Ægin.* l. 7, c. 3.

ERINUS, in the Linnean system, a genus of plants, Class 14 *Didynamia*, Order 2 *Angiospermia*.

Generic Character. CAL. *perianth* five-leaved.—COR. one-petalled.—STAM. *filaments* four; *anthers* small.—PIST. *germ* ovate; *style* very short; *stigma* headed.—PER. *capsule* ovate; *seeds* small.

Species. The species are perennials and annuals: the following are the principal perennials, namely, the—*Erinus alpinus*, seu *aquaticus*, Alpine Erinus, native of the Alps.—*Erinus Africanus*, seu *Buchnera*, native of Africa.—*Erinus capensis*, native of the Cape of Good Hope.—*Erinus frutescens.* The following are the principal annuals, namely, the—*Erinus fragrans*, seu *Selago*, native of the Cape of Good Hope.—*Erinus peruvianus*, seu *Lychnidea*, native of Peru.

ERINUS is also the *Campanula erinus*.

ERIOCAU'LON (*Bot.*) a genus of plants, Class 3 *Triandria*, Order 3 *Trigynia*.

Generic Character. CAL. *perianth* common.—COR. *universal* convex.—STAM. *filaments* three; *anthers* oblong.—PIST. *germ* slender; *styles* three; *stigmas* simple.—PER. none; *seeds* solitary.

Species. The species are annuals, as the—*Eriocaulon setaceum*,' Randalia, seu Gramen Eriocaulon quadrangulare, native of Cochinchina, &c.

ERIOCE'PHALUS (*Bot.*) a genus of plants, Class 19 *Syngenesia*, Order 4 *Polygamia Necessaria*.

Generic Character. CAL. common upright.—COR. compound rayed.—STAM. *filaments* five; *anthers* cylindric.—PIST. *germ* small; *style* simple; *stigma* sharp.—PER. none; *seeds* in the females, solitary.

Species. The species are shrubs, as the—*Eriocephalus Africanus*, seu *Abrotanum*, Cluster-leaved Eriocephalus, native of the Cape.—*Eriocephalus racemosus*, Silvery-leaved Eriocephalus.

ERIO'PHOROS (*Bot.*) ἐριοφόρος, a sort of bulb mentioned by Theophrastus, l. 7, c. 13.

ERIOPHOROS, in the Linnean system, is the *Bombax petandrium*.

ERIO'PHORUM (*Bot.*) a genus of plants, Class 3 *Triandria*, Order 1 *Monogynia*.

Generic Character. CAL. *spike* on all sides imbricate.—COR. none.—STAM. *filaments* three; *anthers* oblong.—PIST. *germ* small; *style* filiform; *stigmas* three.—PER. none; *seeds* acuminate.

Species. The species are perennials, as the—*Eriophorum vaginatum*, Zinagrostis, Juncus, seu Gramen, Mountain or Single-spiked Cotton-Grass, native of Europe.—*Eriophorum polystachion*, seu *Gnaphalium*, Many-spiked Cotton-Grass.—*Eriophorum angustifolium*, Narrow-leaved Cotton-Grass.

ERIO'PILA (*Bot.*) the *Duroia eriopila* of Linnæus.

ERISI'THALES (*Bot.*) the *Cnicus erisithales* of Linnæus.

ERI'SMA (*Archit.*) ἔρισμα, an arch-buttress, or shore-prop. *Vitruv.* l. 6, c. 11; *Philand. in Vitruv.*; *Salmas. in Solin.* p. 1216.

ERITHA'CE (*Nat.*) ἐριθάκη, a kind of wax, honey, or red juice in the honey-combs. *Arist.* l. 5, c. 22; *Varr. de Re Rust.* l. 3, c. 16; *Plin.* l. 11, c. 7.

ERITHALIS (*Bot.*) a genus of plants, Class 5 *Pentandria*, Order 1 *Monogynia*.

Generic Character. CAL. *perianth* one-leaved.—COR. one-petalled.—STAM. *filaments* five; *anthers* oblong.—PIST. *germ* inferior; *style* filiform; *stigma* sharp.—PER. *berry* globose; *seeds* small.

Species. The species are trees, as the—*Erithalis fruticosa*, seu *Iambicus*, native of Jamaica.—*Erithalis polygamia*, seu *Timoneus*, native of the Society Isles.

ERITHRÆ' (*Bot.*) the *Gentiana Centaureum* of Linnæus.

E'RIX (*Anat.*) ἔριξ, the superior part of the liver.

E'RMINE (*Her.*) one of the two furs used in coat-armour, which is composed of two or more tinctures, and is supposed to represent the linings and doublings of mantles and robes, the ermine being so called from the skin of the little beast which bears that name. Ermine is represented by a white field powdered or *semé* with black spots. When the ground is black, and the spots white, it is called *ermines*, &c. [vide *Heraldry*]

ERMINE (*Zool.*) the *Mustela erminea* of Linnæus, a little animal about the size of a squirrel, which is well known for its valuable fur, and is supposed to derive its name from Armenia, where it was found in the greatest numbers. In Northern climates this animal is white all over, except the tip of the tail, which is black. It lives on the banks of rivers, and in hollow trees, and preys on mice and other small animals. Ermine is also the name of the fur of the *ermine*.

ERMINE'E (*Her.*) or a *cross-ermine*, is a cross composed of four *ermine* spots placed crosswise, as in the annexed figure.

ERMINI'TES (*Her.*) is a kind of ermine in which the field is white, and the spots are red and black.

ERMINOI'S (*Her.*) an epithet for a sort of ermine in which the field is *or* with black spots.

ERMINES (*Her.*) a sort of ermine in which the field is black with white spots.

ERNES (*Archæol.*) the loose scattered ears of corn which are gleaned from the field, so called from the German *erndten*, to reap.

ERNO'DEA (*Bot.*) a genus of plants, Class 4 *Tetrandria*, Order 1 *Monogynia*.

Generic Character. CAL. *perianth* four-parted.—COR. one-petalled.—STAM. *filaments* four; *anthers* erect.—PIST. *germ* inferior; *style* filiform; *stigma* obtuse.—PER. *berry* roundish; *seeds* solitary.

Species. The single species is the *Ernodia littoralis*, Knoxia, seu Hymelæa, native of Jamaica.

ERODE'NTIA (*Med.*) ἐσθιόμενα, Erosiva Medicamenta, eroding or corroding medicines, Hippocrat. Epid. L 4;

Cels. Gal. de Comp. Med. sec. Loc. l. 4, c. 1; *Aet. Tetrab.* 4, serm. 2, c. 52; *Paul. Æginet.* l. 4, c. 34.

ERODI'NIUM (*Med.*) a prognostic.

ERO'DIUM (*Orn.*) ἐρώδιος, a bird of the hawk tribe, so called because in time of treading, ἱας ἱδροῖ, it sweats blood. *Suidas.*

ERODIUM, *in the Linnean system*, a genus of plants, Class 16 *Monadelphia*, Order 2 *Pentandria*.
   Generic Character. CAL. *perianth* five-leaved.—COR. *petals* five.—STAM. *filaments* five; *anthers* oblong.—PIST. *germ* five-cornered; *style* awlshaped; *stigmas* five; *seed* solitary.
   Species. The species are perennials and annuals: the following are the principal perennials, as the—*Erodium Romanum*, seu *Geranium*, Roman Crane's bill, native of Italy.—*Erodium incarnatum*, Flesh-coloured Crane's bill.—*Erodium absinthoides*, Wormwood-leaved Crane's bill.—*Erodium chrysanthemum*, Golden-flowered Crane's bill. The following are the principal annuals, as the—*Erodium cicutarium*, Hemlock-leaved Crane's bill.—*Erodium moschatum*, Musk Crane's bill.—*Erodium grunium*, Broad-leaved Annual Crane's bill. *Bauh. Hist.; Bauh. Pin.; Park. Theat.; Raii Hist.; Tourn. Inst.*

ERO'DIUS (*Ent.*) a genus of insects of the coleopterous order, having the *antennæ* moniliform; *feelers* 4 filiform; *body* roundish; *thorax* transverse; *shells* closely united; *jaw* horny, bifid.

EROMA'NIA (*Med.*) ἐρωμανία, from ἔρως, love, and μανία, madness; melancholy madness occasioned by love.

ERO'SUS (*Bot.*) gnawed, an epithet for a leaf; *folium erosum*, a leaf having obtuse sinuses on its edge that give it the appearance of having been gnawed, or eaten by insects.

EROSION (*Med.*) the same as ulceration.

ERO'TIC (*Lit.*) an epithet equivalent to amatory.

EROTE'MA (*Rhet.*) ἐρώτημα, *interrogatio*; a figure of speech which consists in putting questions, in order to aggravate the adverse case. *Cic. de Orat.* l. 3, c. 52; *Quintil.* l. 9, c. 2.

EROTE'UM (*Bot.*) a genus of plants, Class 13 *Polyandria*, Order 1 *Monogynia*.
   Generic Character. CAL. *perianth* five-leaved.—COR. *petals* five.—STAM. *filaments* numerous; *anthers* roundish.—PIST. *germ* ovate; *style* erect; *stigma* obtuse.—PER. *berry* roundish; *seeds* oblong.
   Species. The two species are the *Eroteum theoides* et *undulatum*, natives of Jamaica.

ERO'TION (*Bot.*) the *Apiastrum*.

ERO'TYLOS (*Min.*) a precious stone like a flint used in divination. *Plin.* l. 37, c. 10.

ERO'TYLUS (*Ent.*) the name given by Fabricius to a division of the genus *Cryptocephalus*, comprehending those insects which have their feelers unequal, and the fore ones hatchet-shaped.

E'RRANT (*Law*) an epithet applied to justices who go the circuit; also to bailiffs travelling at large.

ERRANT. (*Her.*) an epithet for knights who were formerly supposed to wander in search of adventures.

ERRA'TA (*Print.*) a list of typographical errors which have escaped correction at press.

ERRA'TIC (*Astron.*) i. e. wanderers; an epithet for the planets, as distinguished from the fixed stars.

ERRA'TICUM (*Archæol.*) a waif or stray beast.

ERRA'TUM (*Print.*) a single error left in a work after it is printed.

ERRHI'NA (*Med.*) ἐρρίνα, from ῥίν, the nose; medicines which, when snuffed up the nose, promote a discharge of mucus. *Gal. de Simpl.* l. 7; *Trallian*, l. 1, c. 11; *Paul. Æginet.* l. 3, c. 5; *Act. de Meth. Med.* l. 3, c. 6; *Myrep.* sect. 15.

ERRI'PSIS (*Med.*) ἔρριψις, from ῥίπτω, to precipitate; a sinking in the strength of the whole body, or of any particular part. *Hippocrat. de Humor.* l. 1, & *Gal. Comm.* 24; *Erot. Lex. Hippocrat.; Gorr. Def. Med.; Foes. Œconom. Hippocrat.*

E'RROR (*Law*) a fault in pleading, or in the process, whence the writ brought for the remedy of this oversight is termed a writ of error.—*Writ of error*, a writ which lies to redress a false judgment in any court of record.—*Clerk of the errors*, a clerk whose business it is to copy out the tenor of the records of a cause upon which a writ of error is brought.

ERROR *Loci* (*Anat.*) a term introduced by Boerhaave to denote the deviation which he supposes to take place sometimes in the circulation of the different parts of the blood, as when the larger sized globules force themselves into the lesser vessels not destined for them. This idea is founded on the supposition that there are different-sized globules for the blood, lymph, and serum.

ERTHMIO'TUM (*Archæol.*) a meeting of the neighbourhood to settle differences among themselves. *Leg. Hen.* 1, c. 57.

E'RUCA (*Ent.*) a name given to insects in the caterpillar state, now more commonly called the *larva*.

ERUCA (*Bot.*) the *Arabis canadensis* of Linnæus.

ERUCA'GO (*Bot.*) the *Bunias erucago* of Linnæus.

ERUCA'STRUM (*Bot.*) the *Brassica erucastrum* of Linnæus.

ERUCTA'TION (*Med.*) the discharge of wind from the stomach through the mouth.

ERU'PTION (*Med.*) an issuing or breaking forth in a morbid or preternatural manner, as spots, &c. on the skin.

E'RVUM (*Bot.*) a genus of plants, Class 17 *Diadelphia*, Order 4 *Decandria*.
   Generic Character. CAL. *perianth* five-parted.—COR. papilionaceous.—STAM. *filaments* rising; *anthers* simple.—PIST. *germ* oblong; *style* simple; *stigmas* obtuse.—PER. *legume* oblong; *seeds* four.
   Species. The species are annuals, as the—*Ervum Lens*, seu *Lens*, Flat-seeded Tare, or common Lentil.—*Ervum tetraspermum*, seu *Vicea*, Smooth Tare.—*Ervum hirsutum*, seu *Cracca*, Hairy Tare.—*Ervum ervilla*, seu *Orobus*, native of France. *Dod. Pempt.; Bauh. Hist.; Bauh. Pin.; Park. Theat.; Raii Hist.; Tourn. Inst.*

ERUTHE'MATA (*Med.*) from ἐρυθέω, to make red; red fiery pustules on the skin.

ERY'NGIUM (*Bot.*) ἠρύγγιον, a prickly plant of an aromatic taste. It is so called from ἐρύγω, to vomit, because when goats eat of it they were stupified, and stood perfectly still until they had vomited it up. *Aristot. Hist. Animal.* l. 9, c. 4; *Theoph.* l. 6, c. 1; *Dioscor.* l. 3, c. 24; *Plin.* l. 22, c. 7, &c.; *Plut. Sympos.* l. 7, quest. 2; *Schol. Nicand. in Theriac.; Gal. de Alim. Fac.* l. 2, c. 39: *Oribas. Med. Collect.* l. 11.

ERYNGIUM, *in the Linnean system*, a genus of plants, Class 5 *Pentandria*, Order 2 *Digynia*.
   Generic Character. CAL. *receptacle* common.—COR. *petals* oblong.—STAM. *filaments* five; *anthers* oblong.—PIST. *germ* hispid; *styles* two; *stigmas* simple.—PER. *fruit* ovate; *seeds* oblong.
   Species. The species are perennials, as the—*Eryngium aquaticum*, Marsh Eryngo, native of Virginia.—*Eryngium planum*, Flat-leaved Eryngo, native of Austria.—*Eryngium pusillum*, Dwarf Eryngo, native of Spain.—*Eryngium maritum*, Sea-Holly; but the *Eryngium fœtidum*, Stinking Eryngium, and the *Eryngium tricuspidatum*, Trifid Eryngium, are biennials. *Dod. Pempt.; Bauh. Pin.; Bauh. Hist.; Ger. Herb.; Park. Theat.; Raii Hist.; Tourn. Inst.*

ERYNGIUM is also the *Atractylis cancillata*.

ERY'SIMI *varietas* (*Bot.*) the *Sinapis lævigata* of Linnæus.—*Erysimo similis*, the *Turritis hirsuta*.

ERY'SIMUM (*Bot.*) ἐρύσιμον, a plant so called from ἐρύω, to draw, because of its astringent virtue. It was reckoned an antidote against poison. *Theophrast. Hist. Plant.* l. 8, c. 7; *Dioscor.* l. 2, c. 188; *Plin.* l. 18, c. 10; *Gal. de Alim. Fac.* l. 1, c. 30; *Oribas. Med. Collect.* l. 11; *Aet. Tetrab.* 1, serm. 1; *Paul. Æginet.* l. 7, c. 3.

ERYSIMUM, *in the Linnean system*, a genus of plants, Class 14 *Tetradynamia*, Order 2 *Siliquosa*.
 Generic Character. CAL. *perianth* four-leaved.—COR. *petals* oblong.—STAM. *filaments* six; *anthers* simple.—PIST. *germ* linear; *style* short; *stigma* headed.—PER. *silique* oblong; *seeds* many.
 Species. The species are mostly annuals, as the—*Erysimum officinale*, seu *Sisymbrum*, Common Hedge Mustard.—*Erysimum repandum*, Small-flowered Hedge Mustard. *Erysimum cheiranthoides*, seu *Myagrum*, Treacle Hedge Mustard; but the—*Erysimum barbara*, seu *Eruca*, Winter Hedge Mustard, is perennial, and the *Erysimum albaria*, Garlick Hedge Mustard, is a biennial. *Clus. Hist.*; *Dod. Pempt*; *Bauh. Hist.*; *Bauh. Pin.*; *Ger. Herb.*; *Park. Theat. Bot.*; *Raii Hist.*

ERYSI'PELAS (*Med.*) ἐρυσίπελας, a disorder in the skin, vulgarly called St. Anthony's Fire, which consists in a preternatural swelling, accompanied with redness, heat, and pain. The name is supposed by some to be derived from ἐρυθρός, red, and πελός, livid. *Hippocrat.* l. 5, aphor. 23; *Cels.* l. 5, c. 26; *Gal. Def. Med. &c.*; *Oribas. de Morb. Curat.* l. 3, c. 47; *Aet. Tetrab.* 4, serm. 2, c. 59; *Paul. Æginet.* l. 4, c. 17; *Act. de Meth. Med.* l. 2, c. 12; *Gorr. Def. Med.*; *Foes. Œconom. Hippocrat.*

ERYSIPELAS, *in Cullen's Nosology*, is a genus of diseases, Class *Pyrexiæ*, Order *Exanthemata*.

ERYSIPELATO'IDES (*Med.*) a humour resembling the Erysipelas.

ERYSISCE'PTRUM (*Bot.*) a name for the *Aspalathus*.

ERYTHE'MA (*Med.*) ἐρύθημα, from ἐρυθρός, red; a morbid redness in the skin, as is observed to accompany a violent inflammatory fever.

ERYTHRI'NA (*Bot.*) a genus of plants, Class 17 *Diadelphia*, Order 4 *Decandria*.
 Generic Character. CAL. *perianth* one-leaved.—COR. *petals* five.—STAM. *filaments* ten; *anthers* ten.—PIST. *germ* subulate; *style* the length of the stamens; *stigma* simple.—PER. *legume* long; *seeds* kidneyform.
 Species. The species are trees, as the—*Erythrina herbacea*, seu *Corallodendron*, Herbaceous Coral-tree.—*Erythrina Corallodendron, Siliqua, Mouricou, Boa Erathrina*, seu *Gelala aquatica*, &c. *Bauh. Pin.*; *Tourn. Inst.*

ERYTHRINA is also the *Piscedia erythrina*.

ERYTHRI'NUS (*Ich.*) ἐρυθρῖνος, a sea-fish all red but the belly, which is white; it is now called Rochet. *Apic.*

ERY'THRION (*Med.*) ἐρύθριον, a malagina. *Paul. Æginet.* l. 7, c. 18.

ERYTHROBU'LBUS (*Bot.*) the *Wachendorsia paniculata* of Linnæus.

ERYTHRO'DANUM (*Bot.*) the plant now called Madder, which dyers use. It is so called from the redness of its root.

ERYTHROEI'DES (*Anat.*) from ἐρυθρός, red, and εἶδος, likeness; an epithet for the innermost coat of the testes. *Ruff. Ephes. de Appell. Part. Corp. Hum.* l. 1, c. 32.

ERYTHRO'NIUM (*Bot.*) a species of *Satyrion*. *Dioscor.* l. 3, c. 144.

ERYTHRONIUM, *in the Linnean system*, a genus of plants, Class 6 *Hexandria*, Order 1 *Monogynia*.
 Generic Character. CAL. none.—COR. *petals* six.—STAM. *filaments* six; *anthers* oblong.—PIST. *germ* turbinate; *style* simple.—PER. *capsule* globose; *seeds* ovate.
 Species. The single species is a perennial, as the *Erithronium dens canis*, Dens canis, seu *Satyrium*.

ERYTHRO'PYLON (*Bot.*) a genus of plants, Class 10 *Decandria*, Order 3 *Trigynia*.
 Generic Character. CAL. *perianth* one-leaved.—COR. *petals* five.—STAM. *filaments* ten; *anthers* heartshaped.—PIST. *germ* ovate; *styles* three; *stigmas* obtuse.—PER. *drupe* ovate; *seed* nut oblong.
 Species. The species are shrubs, and natives of the West Indies, as the—*Erythoxylon areolatum*, seu *Carthagenense*.—*Erythoxylon havense*, &c. *Clus. Hist.*; *Dod. Pempt.*; *Bauh. Hist.*; *Bauh. Pin.*; *Ger. Herb.*; *Park. Theat. Bot.*; *Raii Hist.*; *Tourn. Inst.*

E'SAPHE (*Med.*) ἐσάφη, from ἐσαφάω, to feel with the fingers; a term particularly applied to feeling the mouth of the uterus, so as to discover its state. *Hippocrat. de Mul.*

ESBRANCATU'RA (*Archæol.*) the cutting off branches or boughs in forests, &c.

ESCALA'DE (*Mil.*) a vigorous assault made upon a wall or rampart, by means of ladders, upon which the besiegers mount for the purpose of taking a place by storm.

ESCALDA'RE (*Law*) an ancient tenure in serjeanty.

ESCALLO'NIA (*Bot.*) a genus of plants, Class 5 *Pentandria*, Order 1 *Monogynia*.
 Generic Character. CAL. one-leaved.—COR. *petals* five.—STAM. *filaments* five; *anthers* incumbent.—PIST. *germ* oblate; *style* upright; *stigma* capitate.—PER. *berry* roundish; *seeds* many.
 Species. The species are shrubs, as—*Escallonia myrtilloides* et *seriata*, &c.

ESCALLOP-SHELL (*Her.*) a frequent bearing in the escutcheon, it having been the pilgrims' ensign in their expeditions to holy places, as in the annexed figure. " He beareth *argent*, on a bend *azure*, three escallop-shells *or*; name *Browne*."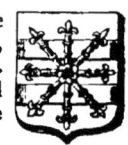

ESCA'MBIO (*Law*) from *cambier*, to exchange; a licence granted to make over Bills *of Exchange* to another beyond sea. *Stat.* 5, R. 2, c. 2; *Reg. Orig.* 194.

ESCAPA'TLI (*Bot.*) a species of Sena.

ESCA'PE (*Law*) a violent or privy evasion out of some lawful restraint; as where a man is arrested or imprisoned and gets away before he is delivered in due course of law. *Staundf. P. C.* c. 26, &c.

ESCA'PIO QUIETUS (*Law*) he who is delivered from the punishment which, by the laws of the forest, lieth upon those whose beasts are found within the land where forbidden.

ESCA'RBUNCLE (*Her.*) the heraldic name for the precious stone called the Carbuncle, which is represented as in the annexed figure. " He beareth *argent* two bars *azure*, over all an escarbuncle of eight rays *gules*; pomettee and florettee *or*."

ESCA'UN (*Com.*) a Dutch and Flemish silver coin, value sixpence sterling.

ESCE'PPA (*Archæol.*) a scepp, or measure of corn. *Mon. Angl.* tom. 1, p. 382.

ESCHANDE'RIA (*Archæol.*) the chandry, or office where candles were reposited and delivered out for daily use.

ESCHA'RA (*Med.*) ἐσχάρα, an incrustation from an ulcer, according to Aretæus; or from a caustic medicine and a red hot iron, according to Celsus and Galen. *Aret. de Acut. Morb.* l. 1, c. 9; *Cels.* l. 6, c. 26; *Gal. de Simpl.* l. 1, c. 18; *Scrib. Larg. de Compos. Med.* c. 25; *Marcell.* c. 8.

ESCHAROPE'PA (*Med.*) ἐσχαρόπηττα, coarse barley-meal, of which Hippocrates speaks. *Hippocrat. Epid.* l. 4.

ESCHAROTICS (*Med.*) ἐσχαρωτικα, from ἐσχαρόω, medicines which promote the incrustation of a wound or sore.

ESCHA'RPE (*Mil.*) French for the scarf which formerly served to distinguish the military from other persons.

ESCHE'AT (*Law*) in French *eschette*, from *escheoir*, or *eschevir*, to fall; any lands or profits that fall to a lord within his manor, either by forfeiture, the death of the tenant, &c.; also the name of a writ for the recovery of escheats, and of the circuit within which the King, or any other lord, has escheats of his tenants. *Flet.* 1. 6; 2 *Instit.* 36, &c.; *Hawk. P. C.* c. 49.

ESCHE'ATOR (*Law*) an officer formerly appointed by the Lord Treasurer, &c. in every county, to make inquests of titles by escheats. They are called, by Fitzherbert, officers of record; but having their chief dependance on the *court of wards*, which is done away by Act of Parliament, they are now almost entirely out of date. 14 *Ed.* 3, c. 8, &c.; 8 *H.* 8, c. 16, &c.; *F. N. B.* 100; 2 *Inst.* 206; 4 *Inst.* 225, &c.

ESCHE'CCUM (*Archæol.*) a jury or inquisition. *Matth. Par. Ann.* 1240.

ESCHEVI'N (*Polit.*) a magistrate in France and Holland, very similar to our sheriff.

ESCHYNO'MENE (*Bot.*) the *Mimosa pudica* of Linnæus.

ESCLATTE' (*Her.*) an epithet among the French for a bend, or any other ordinary that is as it were torn away.

ESCLOPPE' (*Her.*) an epithet among the French for a bend, that has an indenture or cut in it.

ESCOPE'CHES (*Mech.*) French for large pieces of wood used in scaffolding.

ESCORT (*Mil.*) a company of armed men attending upon any person or thing, by way of guard, or distinction.

ESCORTA'TIO MORÆ (*Archæol.*) the paring of the turf of moorish or sedgy ground for burning.

E'SCOT (*Law*) vide *Scot*.

ESCOUA'DE (*Mil.*) a French term for the third part of a foot company, so divided for the more convenient mounting of guard.

ESCRO'LL (*Her.*) one of the exterior ornaments of the escutcheon, representing a slip of parchment or paper, on which is generally put the motto. [vide *Heraldry*]

ESCRO'W (*Law*) a deed delivered to a third person, to be the deed of the party making it, upon a future condition when a certain thing is performed, and then it is to be delivered to the party to whom it is made. *Co. Lit.* 31.

ESCU'AGE (*Law*) in French *ecuage*, a kind of knight's service, called holding the shield, which was a sort of tenure that obliged the tenant to follow his lord to the wars at his own charge. Escuage was *uncertain* when it consisted of uncertain services, which the tenant was bound to perform according to circumstance; *certain* when the tenant was set at a certain sum of money to be paid in lieu of such services.

E'SCULENT (*Bot.*) an epithet for plants, &c. that may be eaten.

E'SCULUS (*Bot.*) the *Quercus esculus* of Linnæus.

ESCU'TCHEON (*Her.*) or *Shield*, is the representation of the ancient shields used in war, on which were borne the ensigns of the individual or his family. It serves now to contain the armorial bearings which are painted on its surface, called the field. [vide *Heraldry*]

The *Escutcheon* is also one of the Honourable Ordinaries, which, according to Leigh, should contain the fifth part of the field. It is made to represent the shape of the outer escutcheon or shield, as in the annexed figure. "He beareth *ermine*, an escutcheon *gules*, by the name of *Hulgrave*."

E'SDRÆ ANTIDOTUS (*Med.*) an antidote described by Paulus Ægineta, 1. 7, c. 2.

E'SEBON (*Chem.*) Common Salt.

ESKETO'RES (*Archæol.*) robbers or destroyers of other men's estates. *Plac. Parl.* 20, *Ed.* 1.

ESKI'PPESON (*Archæol.*) shipping or passage by sea.

ESKY'-BAS (*Mil.*) a Turkish soldier who carries the colours; in general he is the senior man in the company.

ESLI'SORS (*Law*) vide *Esslisors*.

E'SNECY (*Law*) in French *aisnesse*, the right of choosing first in coparcenary, or a divided inheritance on the ground of priority of age.

ESO'CHE (*Med.*) ἰσωχη, from ἰξέχω, to protuberate; a protuberance about the anus.

E'SOX (*Ich.*) the Pike, a genus of fishes, of the abdominal Order, having a flat head, a large mouth, jaws toothed, body elongated, dorsal and anal fins very short.

E'SPADON (*Mil.*) a kind of two-handed sword, having two edges of great length and breadth.

ESPA'LIER (*Hort.*) a sort of branching fruit trees that grow on a frame and spread laterally.

ESPEALTA'RE (*Archæol.*) the expeditating of dogs.

ESPERVA'RIUS (*Archæol.*) a Sparrow-hawk.

E'SPHLASIS (*Med.*) ἰσφλασις, from ἰσφλάομαι, an intropulsion, or recession of a part inwards from some external violence. *Hippocrat. de Vulnerib.*

ESPIGURNA'NTIA (*Law*) the office of Spigurnel, or Sealer of the king's writs.

ESPI'ONAGE (*Mil.*) the act of obtaining and giving secret intelligence of what is passing in the camp or army, &c. of the enemy.

ESPLANA'DE (*Fort.*) a declivity or slope of earth commencing from the top of the counterscarp, and losing itself in the level of the campaign, which serves as a parapet for the counterscarp or covered way. The esplanade is now chiefly taken for the void space between the glacis of a citadel and the first houses of a town.

ESPLEE'S (*Law*) the full profit that ground yields, as the feeding of pastures, the hay of meadows, &c.; sometimes the word is applied to the lands themselves, as in *Plac. Parl.* 30 *Ed.* 1.

ESPOU'SALS (*Law*) a contract or mutual promise between a man and woman. Marriage is said to be an *espousal de præsenti*. *Wood's Inst.* 57.

ESPRE'SSIONE (*Mus.*) Italian for expression, or that quality in a composition which consists in an appeal to the feelings.

ESPRI'NGOLD (*Mil.*) a warlike engine anciently used for the casting of great stones.

ESPRIT DE CORPS (*Mil.*) that species of attachment with which military men are particularly animated to the corps, company, or service, to which they belong.

E'SPRIT, Ordre d' (*Her.*) vide *Holy Ghost*.

ESQUI'RE (*Her.*) in French *escuyer*, in Italian *scudiero*, Spanish *escudero*, Latin *armiger*, signifies literally an armour-bearer; but has since been employed as a title of honour to the sons of Knights, and to those who serve the King in any worshipful calling, &c.

ESSAI des armes à feu (*Mil.*) French for proving fire-arms.

ESSA'TUM (*Med.*) the medicinal virtue which is in vegetables and minerals.

ESSA'Y (*Metal*) vide *Assay*.

ESSAY hatch (*Min.*) a little trench which miners dig when they are in search of ore.

ESSAY of a Deer (*Sport.*) the breast or brisket of a deer.

ESSEDA'RII (*Ant.*) a sort of gladiators who fought *Esseda*, in a chariot. *Cic. ad Fam.* l. 7, ep. 6; *Petron. Fragm.* p. 8; *Senec. Epist.* 29; *Suet. Cal.* 35.

ESSE'DUM (*Ant.*) the chariot armed with scythes which was used by the Gauls and Britons.

Virg. Georg. l. 3, v. 204.

Belgica vel molli melius fert esseda collo.

Propert. l. 2, el. 1, v. 86.

Esseda cœlatis siste Britanna jugis.

These chariots were known in Rome before Cæsar's expedition into Britain, but still more afterwards. *Cic. ad Attic.* l. 6, ep. 1; *Cæs. de Bell. Gall.* l. 4, c. 33; *Serv. in Virg.; Jornand. Rer. Goth.* c. 2.

E'SSENCE (*Met.*) the same as *Being.*

ESSENCE (*Chem.*) the purest and most subtle part of any body, or the spirit drawn out of certain substances.

ESSENCE (*Med.*) the chief properties or virtues of any simple, collected into a small compass.

ESSE'NDI *quietum de telonio* (*Law*) a writ which lies for the citizens and burgesses of any town or city that has any charter or prescription to free them from toll, in case toll be demanded of them wrongfully. *Reg. Orig.* 258.

ESSE'NES (*Theol.*) a sect among the ancient Jews who separated themselves from the people, and led a kind of monastic life.

ESSE'NTIAL *debilities* (*Astrol.*) are when the planets are in their fall, detriment, or peregrine.—*Essential dignities,* certain real advantages belonging to planets, by which they are strengthened and fortified, as when they are in proper houses, or in their exaltation.

ESSENTIAL *oils* (*Chem.*) are acrid volatile oils, having a strong aromatic smell, which are drawn from plants by distillation, in distinction from native oils, that are procured by coction. *Boerhaav. Elem.*

ESSENTIAL *properties* (*Log.*) such as necessarily depend upon, and are connected with, the nature and essence of a thing, in distinction from the *accidental.*

ESSENTIAL *salts* (*Chem.*) salts which are procured from plants, and which have the property of crystallizing.

ESSENTIAL *character* (*Bot.*) a term applied to the particular properties or characteristics which distinguish one species of plants from another.

E'SSERS (*Med.*) eruptions that are rather hard and red, and cause a violent itching as if from the sting of a bee or a nettle.

ESSIE'U (*Mech.*) French for a solid piece of timber which runs across the carriage, enters the wheel at both ends, and is fastened by means of an iron.

ESSLI'SORS (*Law*) persons appointed by a court to impannel a jury on challenge to a jury and coroner.

ESSO'DINUM (*Med.*) a certain presage of a future event from the signs that indicate it.

ESSO'IN (*Law*) an excuse for one that is summoned to appear and answer to an action, &c. by reason of sickness, or any other just cause, &c. *Bract.* l. 5; *Britt.* c. 122; *Flet.* l. 6; *2 Inst.* 125, &c.—*Clerk of the Essoins,* an officer in the court of Common Pleas, who keeps the essoin rolls.—*Essoin day of the Term,* the first return in every term, i. e. the first day in every term whereon the court sits to take Essoins.—*Essoins* and *Proffers,* words used in the statutes 38 H. 8, c. 21.

E'SSORANT (*Her.*) a French epithet for a bird standing on the ground with its wings expanded, as if they were wet, and it was drying them.

ESSU'YER *le premier Feu* (*Mil.*) French for to receive the first fire without attempting to fire first.—*Essuyez la Pierre,* is a word of command in the platoon exercise, signifying to try the flint.

ESTA'BLAGE (*Mech.*) French for the harness which is between the two shafts of a cart.

ESTA'BLISHMENT *of Dower* (*Law*) the assurance of dower given to a wife or her friends, by the husband or his friends, previous to the marriage. *Britt.* c. 102, &c.

ESTABLISHMENT (*Mil.*) the quota of officers and men in an army, regiment, troop, or company, which, being much greater during war than peace, has given rise to the distinction of a *War-Establishment* and a *Peace-Establishment.* A *Military Establishment* is an establishment in India so called, comprehending the allowances for tents, camels, and drivers.

ESTACA'DE (*Mil.*) French for a dyke constructed with piles in the sea, a river, or morass to oppose the entry of troops.

ESTAFE'TTE (*Mil.*) French for a military courier sent from one part of an army to another.

ESTA'NDARD (*Mil.*) vide *Standard.*

ESTA'TE (*Law*) the title or interest a man has in lands or tenements.—*Conditional estate,* one that has a condition annexed to it though it be not in writing.

ESTA'TES *of the realm* (*Polit.*) are in England the distinct parts of the government or constitution; namely, Kings, Lords, and Commons.

ESTE'LE (*Her.*) French for the term erased.

ESTHIO'MENOS (*Med.*) ἰσθιομένος, corroding; an epithet for a spreading ulcer.

ESTIVAL (*Astron.*) another name for summer.

ESTO'ILE (*Her.*) French for a star; a charge in the escutcheon, which differs from the mullet, by having six waved points, the former having only five points. [vide *Star*]

ESTO'PPEL (*Law*) an impediment or bar to an action which a man has by his own act and deed.

ESTOUFA'DE (*Cook.*) a particular way of cooking meat.

ESTO'VER (*Law*) from the French *étoffe,* signifies that subsistence which a man, accused of felony, is to have out of his lands or goods during his imprisonment; also an allowance of wood to be taken out of another man's woods.

ESTOVE'RIIS *habendis, Writ de* (*Law*) a writ for a woman divorced from her husband, *à mensâ et thoro,* to recover her alimony.

ESTRA'C (*Vet.*) an epithet for a horse that is light bodied and lank-bellied.

ESTRADIO'TTES (*Mil.*) a set of hardy warriors in Italy, who were formerly very expert in managing their horses.

ESTRA'DER, *batteurs d'* (*Mil.*) scouts of horse sent out to get intelligence of the position of the enemy.

ESTRA'DE (*Archit.*) the one half of an alcove or chamber raised above the level of the floor, and richly furnished for the reception of great persons.

ESTRA'NGLE (*Gram.*) a name for the alphabet of the ancient Persian. [vide *Alphabet*]

ESTRA'NGERS (*Law*) foreigners or persons born beyond sea.

ESTRAPA'DE (*Man.*) the action of a restive horse who, by plunging, kicking, and rearing, strives to resist his rider.

ESTRA'Y (*Law*) a tame beast found, without any owner known, which if it be not reclaimed within a year and a day, falls to the Lord of the manor.

ESTRE'AT (*Law*) from the Latin *extractum,* the copy of an original writing; but especially of fines set down in the rolls of a court, to be levied of any man for his offence. *F. N. B.* 57.—*Clerk of the estreats,* a clerk that receives the estreats out of the Lord Treasurers' office, and writes them to be levied of any man for his offence.

ESTRECIA'TUS (*Archæol.*) an epithet for roads, signifying streightened. *Hoved.* p. 783.

ESTREG-BOARDS (*Carpent.*) boards of deal, fir, &c. brought out of the East.

ESTRÉPEMENT (*Law*) spoil made in lands and woods by a tenant, for term of life, to the damage of the reversioner.

E'STRO (*Mus.*) an Italian word, signifying gracefulness and elegance in application to movements.

E'STUARY (*Geog.*) any ditch or pit where the tide comes, or which is overflowed by the sea at high-water.

E'SULA (*Bot.*) the *Apocynum venetum* of Linnæus.

E'SURINE *Salts* (*Chem.*) salts of a fretting or eating quality, which abound in the air of places situated near the sea coast, and where great quantities of coal are burnt.

ETA'BLIES (*Mil.*) a word formerly used in France for what are now called garrisons.

ETA'GES *de Fourneaux ou de Mines* (*Min.*) French for the chambers in a mine.

ETA'MPER (*Vet.*) French for to pierce a horse-shoe in eight places.

ETA'NCONS (*Min.*) French for the stays or supporters that are set up in mines to support the weight of the earth that is laid upon the galleries.

ETA'PIER (*Mil.*) French for a purveyor to the army.

ETA'T-MAJOR (*Mil.*) French for a specific number of officers belonging to the same corps.

ETCHING (*Mech.*) a method of engraving on copper, whereby the lines or strokes are eaten in with aquafortis, instead of being cut with a tool or graver.

ET'ESIÆ (*Nat.*) ἐτησίαι, cool winds that blow constantly every year for forty days together in the dog-days. They are so called from ἔτος, a year, because they return every year. *Hippocrat. Epid.* l. 1, &c.; *Plin.* l. 18, c. 34; *Gal. de Temp.* l. 1.

E'THER (*Nat.*) vide *Æther*.

ETHE'REAL *oil* (*Chem.*) a very fine or exalted oil, or rather spirit of an oily nature which instantly takes fire.

E'THICS, the science of moral philosophy, which teaches the springs and principles of human conduct.

ETHIO'PIAN *sour gourd* (*Bot.*) *Adansonia digitalis* of Linnæus.

ETHMOI'DES (*Anat.*) ἠθμοειδής, from ἠθμός, a sieve, and εἶδος, the form; a bone in the inner part of the nose resembling a sieve in form. *Ruff. Ephes. de Appell. Part. Corp. hum.* l. 3, c. 1.

ETHO'LOGY (*Rhet.*) a figure of speech which consists in the drawing of characters. *Quintil. Inst.* l. 6, c. 6.

ETHU'LIA (*Bot.*) a genus of plants, Class *Syngenesia*, Order 1 *Polygamia Æquales*.
Generic Character. CAL. common.—COR. compound tubular.—STAM. *filaments* five; *anthers* cylindric.—PIST. *germ* prismatic; *style* filiform; *stigmas* two.—PER. none; *seeds* solitary; *receptacle* naked.
Species. The species are annuals, as the—*Ethulia conyzoides*, seu *Kahira*, Panicled Ethulia, native of the East Indies.—*Ethulia sparganophora*, seu *Sparganophora*, native of the East Indies.—*Ethulia divaricata*, seu *Chrysanthemum*, native of Malabar.

ETIQUETTE (*Polit.*) signified originally in French a ticket affixed to a bundle of papers expressing its contents. It is now commonly used for a certain rule observed at courts, and in the higher circles.

ETO'ILE (*Fort.*) French for a star-redoubt, or a small work, consisting of four, five, or more points.

ETRAPA'DE (*Archæol.*) a crane and pulley, which was formerly used in France by way of a torture.

ETYMO'LOGY (*Gram.*) ἐτυμολογία, from ἔτυμος, the true origin, and λόγος, to speak; a part of grammar which teaches the original of words, in order to fix their true meaning.

ETYTHO'XYLUM (*Bot.*) the *Brasilium lignum*.

EVA'CUANTS (*Med.*) medicines proper to expel, or carry off any peccant or redundant humours in the animal body by the proper way of the emunctories.

EVACUATION (*Med.*) any discharge of superfluous humours or excrements out of the body, either by the course of nature, or the force of art.

EUÆ'MIA (*Med.*) from εὖ, well, and αἷμα, blood; goodness of blood.

EUALTHES (*Med.*) εὐαλθής, from εὖ, well, and ἀλθέω, to heal; easy to be healed. *Hippocrat. de Artic.*

EUANALE'PTOS (*Med.*) εὐανάληπτος, from εὖ, well, and ἀναλαμβάνω, to recover; easy to be recovered.

EUANASPHA'LTOS (*Med.*) εὐανάσφαλτος, from εὖ, well, and ἀνασφάλλω, to recover strength; an epithet for a medicine which serves to recover strength.

EVANGE'LIA (*Ecc.*) a term formerly applied to processions and prayers of joy for good tidings, from εὐαγγέλιον, a joyful message, or glad tidings. *Anastas. Biblioth. in Pelag.; Mon. Angl.* tom. iii. p. 192.

EVA'NGELIST (*Bibl.*) εὐαγγελιστής, signifies literally a messenger of glad tidings; but is commonly applied to the writers of the Gospel History.

EVA'NIA (*Ent.*) a name given by Fabricius to a division of the genus *Sphex*, comprehending those insects which have the *antennæ* setaceous, the lip entire, and no tongue.

EUA'NTHEMON (*Bot.*) another name for *Chamamælum*.

EUA'NTHES (*Bot.*) εὐανθής, from εὖ, well, and ἄνθος, a flower, highly florid, or highly coloured; an epithet applied by Hippocrates to the blood and the urine. *Hippocrat. in Coac.*

EUA'PHION (*Med.*) a medicine so named for its gentleness, from εὖ, well, and ἀφή, the touch. *Gal. de Com. Med. sec. Loc.* l. 9, c. 7.

TO EVA'PORATE *to a Pellicle* (*Chem.*) to consume a liquor by a gentle heat till a thin skin is perceived to swim on the top of it.

EVAPORATION (*Chem.*) a process in which the superfluous moisture of any liquid substance is dispersed by means of fire.

EVA'SION (*Law*) a subtle device to set aside truth, or to escape the punishment of the law, as if a man should tempt another to strike him first, in order that he may have an opportunity of returning it with impunity. In this case, if the person first striking be killed, it is not murder. *H. P. C.* c. 81.

EVA'TES (*Myth.*) a branch of the Druids who were reckoned the priests and naturalists.

EUCALY'PTUS (*Bot.*) a genus of plants, Class 12 *Icosandria*, Order 1 *Monogynia*.
Generic Character. CAL. *perianth* superior.—COR. none.—STAM. *filaments* numerous.—PIST. *germ* inferior; *style* single.—PER. *capsule* four-celled; *seeds* many.
Species. The species are trees, as the—*Eucalyptus obliqua*, Oblique-leaved Eucalyptus, or Red Gum Tree, &c.

EUCA'RDIOS (*Med.*) εὐκάρδιος, cordial; an epithet for what is grateful to the stomach.

EUCATASCE'PTON (*Med.*) εὐκατάσκηπτος, from εὖ, well, and κατασκήπτω, to be incumbent; an epithet for a wound which is properly supported, or rests on something soft.

EU'CERA (*Ent.*) a name given by Fabricius to a division of the genus *Apis*, comprehending those insects which have the tongue seven-cleft, and the lip five-cleft.

EU'CHARIST (*Ecc.*) εὐχαριστία, from εὖ, well, and χάρις, grace; signifies literally a thanksgiving; whence it has been in a particular manner applied to the sacrament of the Lord's supper.

EUCHARI'STOS (*Med.*) an epithet for an antidote in Nicolaus Myrepsus. sect. 1, c. 178.

EUCHA'STIC (*Mus.*) an epithet for that part of the Melopœa which constituted the calm and assuaging.

EUCHOLO'GIUM (*Ecc.*) a name for the Greek ritual, or Book of Common Prayer.

EUCHRŒ'A (*Med.*) εὔχροια, from εὖ, well, and χρόα, colour, of a good colour; a plaister so named by Scribonius Largus. *De Comp. Med.* c. 71.

EUCHY'MIA (*Med.*) εὐχυμία, from εὖ, well, and χυμός, a humour; goodness of the humours or juices, as well in aliments as in the animal frame. *Gal. Com. de Hippocrat.*

Aphor. l. 5; *Act. de Meth. Med.* l. 9, c. 12; *Gorr. Def. Med.*

EU'CLEA (*Bot.*) a genus of plants, Class 22 *Dioecia*, Order 10 *Dodecandria*.
  Generic Character. CAL. *perianth* one-leaved.—COR. one-petalled.—STAM. *filaments* thirteen; *anthers* erect.—PIST. *germ* ovate; *styles* two; *stigmas* obtuse.—PER. *berry* globular; *seeds* single.
  Species. The single species is a tree, as the *Euclea racemosa,* seu *Padus,* Round-leaved Euclea, native of the Cape of Good Hope.

EUCOI'LIA (*Med.*) εὐκοιλία, from ἐυ, well, and κοιλία, the belly; an epithet for cherries, as good for the belly. *Dioscor.* l. 1, c. 1.

EU'COMIS (*Bot.*) a genus of plants, Class 6 *Hexandria*, Order 1 *Monogynia*.
  Generic Character. CAL. none.—COR. inferior.—STAM. *filaments* subulate.—PIST. *germ* superior; *stigma* simple. PER. *capsule* three-celled; *seeds* many.
  Species. The species are bulbous, as the—*Eucomis nana, fritellaria,* seu *Orcridia,* Dwarf Eucomis, &c.

EU'CRASY (*Med.*) an agreeable temperament, a suitable mixture of qualities in the body, that tend to keep it in good order.

EUDIO'METER (*Mech.*) an instrument by which the quantity of oxygen and nitrogen in atmospherical air can be ascertained.

EUDO'XIANS (*Ecc.*) heretics so called from Eudoxus, their ringleader, who held impious notions respecting the Son. *Epiphan. Hær.* 76; *Prateol. Dog. Omn. Hæret.*

EVE'CTICA (*Med.*) evectics, that part of physic which teaches how to acquire a good habit of body.

EVE'CTION *of the moon* (*Astron.*) one of her most considerable irregularities, caused by the action of the sun upon her. Its general effect is to diminish the equation of the centre at the syzyies, and to increase it in the quadrature.

E'VEN *number* (*Arith.*) a number which may be divided into two equal parts, without a fraction.—*Evenly even number.* [vide *Evenly*]

E'VENINGS (*Archæol.*) the delivery at even or night of a certain portion of grass, corn, &c. given to a customary tenant, who performs the service of cutting, mowing, &c. for his lord gratuitously, by way of reward.

E'VENLY *even number* (*Arith.*) that which may be divided by 4 without a remainder.—*Evenly odd number,* that which may be divided by 2, but not by 4, without a remainder.

EVE'NT (*Mil.*) French for the vent or cavity which is left in cannon, or other fire-arms, after they have been proved and found defective.

EVE'RGETES (*Polit.*) εὐεργέτης, from ἐυ and ἐργω, a work; a title signifying as much as benefactor, which was given to several of the Syrian kings.

E'VERGREEN (*Bot.*) an epithet for such plants as retain their verdure throughout the year.—Evergreen Thorn, the *Mespilus pipacantha* of Linnæus.

EVERLA'STING (*Bot.*) the *Gnaphalium* of Linnæus, a shrub.—Everlasting Pea, the *Lathyrus sylvestris.*

EVERRI'CULUM (*Mech.*) a fishing-net, similar to what is now called the drag-net.

EUE'XIA (*Med.*) εὐεξία, from ἐυ, well, and ἕξις, habit; a good habit of body, in distinction from *Cachexia*. *Aret. de Deut. Morb.* l. 1, c. 16.

EU'GEOS (*Med.*) an epithet applied sometimes to the uterus and sometimes to the hymen.

EUHARMO'NIA (*Mus.*) an epithet signifying perfectly harmonious.

EVI'CTION (*Law*) a recovery of lands, &c. by form of law.

E'VIDENCE (*Law*) any proof by the testimony of men, or by writings. The former is called *parole evidence.* It is called *evidence* because thereby the point in issue in a cause to be tried is to be made evident to the jury. *Co. Lit.* 283.

EU'LE (*Med.*) εὐλή, a particular sort of worm that is bred in ulcers.

EU'LOGY (*Ecc.*) from the Greek εὐλογία, which signifies benediction; is a term used in the Greek church either for the Eucharist itself or for the consecrated bread which was sent to those that were absent.

EUNO'MIANS (*Ecc.*) a sect of heretics in the fourth century, so called from one Eunomius, their ringleader, who maintained that faith alone was sufficient for salvation without good works. *Epiphan. Hær.* 75; *Theodoret. Hær. Fab.* l. 4; *Hieron. Adver.; Ruffin.* l. 2, c. 67; *Baron. Annal. Ann.* 356, &c.

EVOCA'TI (*Ant.*) veteran soldiers, who after having served their time entered as volunteers; they were otherwise called *Emeriti.* *Veget.* l. 2, c. 3; *Isidor. Orig.* l. 9, c. 3.

EVOCA'TIO (*Ant.*) a religious ceremony observed by the Romans at the commencement of a siege, when they invoked the tutelary deity of the place to come over to them; for which reason the Romans would not allow their tutelary deities to be invoked by name, that they might not be known. *Plin.* l. 28, c. 2; *Macrob. Sat.* l. 3, c. 9.

EVOCA'TION (*Gram.*) a figure of construction, which consists in changing the third person into the first or second.

EUO'DIA (*Bot.*) the *Agathophyllum* of Linnæus.

EVO'LVENT (*Geom.*) a name for the involute or curve resulting from the evolution of a curve, in distinction from the evolute or curve supposed to be open or evolved.

E'VOLUTE *curve* (*Geom.*) a curve described from evolution, as Mr. Huygens, the inventor, calls it; if a thread F C M be wrapped or wound round the curve B C F, and then unwound again, the point M will describe the curve A M M, which is the *involute;* the curve B C F is the *evolute,* the part M C of the thread being called the *radius of the evolute.*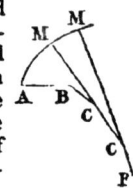

EVOLU'TION (*Arith.*) the extraction of the roots of any power as opposed to involution.

EVOLUTION (*Mil.*) any circuitous or complicated movement, by which a body of men change their position in the field.

EVOLUTION (*Geom.*) the unfolding or opening of a curve. [vide *Evolute*]

EVO'LVULUS (*Bot.*) a genus of plants, Class 5 *Pentandria*, Order 4 *Tetragynia*.
  Generic Character. CAL. *perianth* five-leaved.—COR. one-petalled.—STAM. *filaments* five; *anthers* oblong.—PIST. *germ* globose; *styles* four; *stigmas* simple.—PER. *capsule* globose; *seeds* solitary.
  Species. The species are annuals, as the—*Evolvulus nummularius,* seu *convolvulus,* native of Jamaica.—*Evolvulus alcinoides,* Chickweed-leaved Evolvulus, native of the East Indies, &c.

EUONYMOI'DES (*Bot.*) another name for the *Celastrus* of Linnæus.

EUO'NYMO *similis* (*Bot.*) the *Caffea arabica.*

EUONYMUS (*Bot.*) εὐώνυμος, i. e. unlucky; a tree so called because it kills cattle. *Theoph. Hist. Plant.* l. 3, c. 18; *Plin.* l. 33, c. 22.

EUONYMUS, *in the Linnean system,* a genus of plants, Class 5 *Pentandria*, Order 1 *Monogynia*.
  Generic Character. CAL. *perianth* five-parted.—COR. *petals* five.—STAM. *filaments* five; *anthers* twin.—PIST. *germ* acuminate; *style* short; *stigma* acute.—PER. *capsule* succulent; *seeds* ovate.
  Species. The species are trees, as the—*Euonymus Europeus,* Common Spindle Tree.—*Euonymus latifolius,* Broad-leaved Spindle Tree, native of Austria.—*Euonymus verrucosus,* Warted Spindle Tree, native of the

Carniola.—*Euonymus atropurpureus*, Purple-flowered Spindle Tree. *Clus. Hist.*; *Dod. Pempt.*; *Bauh. Hist.*; *Bauh. Pin.*; *Ger. Herb.*; *Park. Theat.*; *Raii Hist.*; *Tourn. Instit.*

EUONYMUS is also the *Ceanothus americanus* of Linnæus.

EUPA'REA (*Bot.*) a genus of plants, Class 5 *Pentandria*, Order 1 *Monogynia*.
 Generic Character. CAL. perianth five-leaved.—COR. *petals* five.—STAM. *filaments* five.—PIST. *germ* roundish; *style* long; *stigma* simple.—PER. *berry* globular; *seeds* many.
 Species. The single species is the—*Euparea amoena*, native of New Holland.

EUPATO'RIA (*Bot.*) the *Agrimonia eupatoria* of Linnæus.

EUPATOROI'DES (*Bot.*) another name for the *Gnaphalium* of Linnæus.

EUPATORIOPHA'LACRON (*Bot.*) the *Eclipta erecta*.

EUPATO'RIUM (*Bot.*) ιὐπατώριον, a plant so called from Mithridates, surnamed Eupator, by whom it was discovered. It was otherwise called Agrimonia, and was reckoned good for complaints in the liver. *Dioscor.* l. 4, c. 4; *Plin.* l. 25, c. 6; *Gal. de Simplic.* l. 6; *Oribas. Med. Collect.* l. 11; *Aet. Tetrab.* c. 1, serm. 1; *Paul Æginet.* l. 7, c. 3.

EUPATORIUM, *in the Linnean system*, a genus of plants, Class 19 *Syngenesia*, Order 1 *Polygamia Æqualis*.
 Generic Character. CAL. *common* oblong.—COR. *compound*.—STAM. *filaments* five; *anthers* oblong.—PIST. *germ* small; *style* filiform; *stigmas* slender.—PER. none; *seeds* oblong.
 Species. The species are perennials, as the—*Eupatorium dalea*, seu *Dalea*, Shrubby Hemp Agrimony.—*Eupatorium scandens*, seu *Conyza*, Climbing Hemp Agrimony, native of Jamaica.—*Eupatorium album*, White Hemp Agrimony.—*Eupatorium purpureum*, Purple Hemp Agrimony. *Bauh. Hist.*; *Bauh. Pin.*; *Ger. Herb.*; *Park. Theat.*; *Raii Hist.*; *Tourn. Inst.*

EUPATORIUM is also the name of the *Baccharis ivæfolia*.

EUPE'PSIA (*Med.*) ιὐπεψία, from ιὐ, well, and πέπτω, to digest; good digestion.

EUPE'TALOS (*Min.*) a precious stone of four colours, fiery, blue, vermillion, and green. *Plin.* l. 15, c. 30.

EUPHEMI'SMUS (*Rhet.*) ιὐφημισμος, a figure of speech whereby a harsh word is exchanged for one that is unoffending, as Eumenides for the Furies. *Quintil.* l. 9, c. 2; *Demet. Eloc.* § 281.

EUPHO'NIA (*Rhet.*) ιὐφωνία, from ιὐ, good, and φωνη, sound euphony, otherwise called ιὐφημία, a graceful sound, or smooth flow of words. *Quintil.* l. 1, c. 5; *Aristid. περὶ λόγ. πελλ.*; *Eustath. ad Hom. Il.* l. 11, p. 852.

EUPHO'RBIA (*Bot.*) a genus of plants, Class 11 *Dodecandria*, Order 3 *Trigynia*.
 Generic Character. CAL. *perianth* one-leaved.—COR. *petals* four.—STAM. *filaments* filiform; *anthers* twin.—PIST. *germ* roundish; *styles* three; *stigma* obtuse.—PER. *capsule* roundish; *seeds* solitary.
 Species. The species are mostly annuals, as—*Euphorbia antiquorum*, seu *Tithymalus*, Triangular Spurge, native of the East Indies.—*Euphorbia nervifolia*, *Ligularia*, seu *Elacalle*, Olander-leaved Spurge, native of the East Indies, &c.—*Euphorbia hirta*, seu *Esula*, Creeping Hairy Spurge, native of both Indies.—*Euphorbia chamæsyce*, seu *Chamæsyce*, Crenated Annual Spurge, native of the South of Europe.—*Euphorbia peplis*, seu *Peplis*, Purple Spurge, native of the South of France. But the—*Euphorbia triaculeata*, Three-spiked Spurge, native of Arabia, and the—*Euphorbia anacantha*, Scaly Spurge, native of the Cape of Good Hope, are shrubs. *Clus. Hist.*; *Dod. Pempt.*; *Bauh. Hist.*; *Bauh. Pin.*; *Ger. Herb.*; *Park. Theat. Bot.*; *Raii Hist.*; *Tourn. Inst.*

EUPHORBIA is also the *Cynanchum viminale*.

EUPHORBII *arbor* (*Bot.*) the *Cactus Peruvianus*.

EUPHO'RBIUM (*Bot.*) another name for the *Euphorbia*.

EUPHO'RIA (*Bot.*) another name for the *Scytalia*.

EUPHRA'TIA (*Bot.*) a genus of plants, Class 14 *Didynamia*, Order 2 *Angiospermia*.
 Generic Character. CAL. *perianth* one-leaved.—COR. *one-petalled*.—STAM. *filaments* four; *anthers* two-lobed.—PIST. *germ* ovate; *style* filiform; *stigma* obtuse.—PER. *capsule* ovate-oblong; *seeds* numerous.
 Species. The species are annuals, as the—*Euphrasia Odonites*, *Bartsia*, seu *Odonites*, Red Eyebright.—*Euphrasia linifolia*, seu *Coris*, Flax-leaved Eyebright, native of France.—*Euphrasia viscosa*, seu *Pedicularis*, Clammy Eyebright, native of Provence.—*Euphrasia officinalis*, Common Eyebright. *Dod. Pempt.*; *Bauh. Hist.*; *Bauh. Pin.*; *Ger. Herb.*; *Park. Theat. Bot.*; *Raii Hist.*; *Tourn. Inst.*

EUPHRATIA is also the *Bartsia viscosa* of Linnæus.

EUPHRO'SYNUM (*Bot.*) another name for the herb Bugloss.

EUPNŒ'A (*Med.*) ιὐπνοια, from ιὐ, well, and πνέω, to breathe; an easy respiration.

EUPORI'STA (*Med.*) medicines easily prepared.

EUROPE'E (*Bot.*) vide *Veronica*.

EURO'TIAS (*Min.*) a precious stone, black, as with a kind of mould upon it. *Plin.* l. 37, c. 10.

EURY'A (*Bot.*) a genus of plants, Class 11 *Dodecandria*, Order 1 *Monogynia*.
 Generic Character. CAL. *perianth* five-leaved. — COR. *petals* five.—STAM. *filaments* thirteen; *anthers* upright.—PIST. *germ* superior; *style* subulate; *stigmas* three.—PER. *capsule* globular; *seeds* many.
 Species. The single species is the—*Eurya Japonica*, seu *Fisakaki*, native of Japan.

EURYA'NDRIA (*Bot.*) a genus of plants, Class 13 *Polyandria*, Order 3 *Trigynia*.
 Generic Character. CAL. *perianth* five-leaved. — COR. *petals* three.—STAM. *filaments* many; *anthers* twin.—PIST. *germ* ovate; *styles* three; *stigmas* two.—PER. *follicles* three; *seeds* some.
 Species. The single species is the—*Euryandria scandens*, native of New Caledonia.

EURY'THMIA (*Rhet.*) a graceful proportion and carriage of the body, particularly in application to an orator. *Quintil.* l. 1, c. 10.

EURITHMY (*Archit.*) the exact proportion between all the parts of a building. *Vitruv.* l. 1, c. 2.

EURITHMY (*Med.*) a good disposition of the pulse. *Gal. de Diff. Puls.* l. 1, c. 9; *Gorr. Defin. Med.*

EUSTA'THES (*Med.*) ιὐσταθης, from ιὐ, well, and ἵστημι, to stand, constant and regular; an epithet applied to the seasons and to diseases.

EUSTA'THIANS (*Ecc.*) a sect of heretics in the fourth century, so called after one Eustathius, a bishop in Armenia, who, under pretence of greater purity and severity, introduced many irregularities. *Epiphan. Her.* 40.

EUSTO'MACHUS (*Med.*) ιὐστόμαχος, an epithet for a good state of the stomach; also for the food that is proper for it.

EU'STYLE (*Archit.*) ιὐστυλος, from ιὐ, well, and στυλος, a pillar; a term for a building wherein the pillars are placed at a convenient distance. *Vitruv.* l. 3, c. 2.

EUTHA'NASY (*Med.*) ιὐθανασία, a soft and quiet death.

EU'THIA (*Mus.*) a term in the Greek music.

EUTY'CHIANS (*Ecc.*) a sect of heretics in the fifth century, called after their ringleader, one Eutychus, who maintained, among other things, that the flesh of Christ was not like ours. *Baron. Annal. Ann.* 448.

EWA'GIUM (*Archæol.*) toll paid for water carriage.

EWE (*Husband.*) the female of the sheep.

EX *post* (*Law*) a Latin preposition used on several occasions, as—*Ex post facto*, i. e. from something done afterwards; as, an *ex post facto* law, or a law which operates upon a subject not liable to it at the time the law was made.—*Ex mero motu*, words used in a charter, signifying that the prince does it of his good will and pleasure.—*Ex officio*, i. e. by virtue of one's office; signifying the power a person possesses of doing certain things by virtue of his office; as the *ex officio* informations of the Attorney-General, which he files *ex officio*, i. e. by virtue of his office, without applying to the court for permission.—*Ex parte*, i. e. partial, or of one party; as an *ex parte* commission in Chancery taken out and executed by one party only.—*Ex parte talis*, a writ that lies for a bailiff or receiver, who having auditors assigned to take his account, cannot obtain of them reasonable allowance, but is cast into prison. F. N. B, 129.

EXACERBA'NTES (*Med.*) remitting fevers.

EXA'CTION (*Law*) wrong done by an officer, or by one who under colour of office takes more than what the law allows. Between *Extortion* and *Exaction* there is this difference: that in the former case the officer extorts more than his due, when something is due to him; and in the latter case he exacts what is not his due, when nothing is due to him. Co. Lit. 368.

EXA'CTOR *Regis* (*Law*) the King's exactor, or collector of taxes; also, sometimes taken for the sheriff. *Liber Niger Scacc.* par. 1, c. ult.

E'XACUM (*Bot.*) a genus of plants, Class 4 *Tetrandria*, Order 1 *Monogynia*.
Generic Character. CAL. *perianth* four-leaved.—COR. one-petalled.—STAM. *filaments* four; *anthers* roundish.—PIST. *germ* roundish; *style* filiform; *stigma* headed.—PER. *capsule* roundish; *seeds* numerous.
Species. The species are mostly annual, as the—*Exacum Albens*, seu *Centaureum*, native of the Cape of Good Hope.—*Exacum viscosum*, seu *Gentiana*, native of the Canary Islands, &c.
EXACUM is also the *Gentiana filiformis*.

EXA'GIUM (*Ant.*) ἐξάγιον, a kind of standard weight. *Suidas.*

EXAGO'GA (*Ant.*) ἐξαγωγή, the exportation or carrying of goods outward-bound. *Fest. de Verb. Sign.*

EXÆ'RESIS (*Surg.*) ἐξαίρεσις, the act of taking away or drawing out of the body things hurtful to it.

EXAGGERA'TION (*Rhet.*) a figure whereby the orator enlarges or heightens things, making them appear more than they really are.

EXA'LMA (*Med.*) ἔξαλμα, a starting out, from ἐξάλλω, to leap out; a term applied by Hippocrates to the starting of the vertebræ out of their places. *Hippocrat. de Artic.*

EXALTA'TION (*Astrol.*) an essential dignity of a planet, next in virtue to being in its own house.

EXALTATION (*Chem.*) an operation by which a thing is raised to a higher degree of virtue, or an increase of the principal property in any body.

EXALTATION *of the Cross* (*Ecc.*) vide *Cross*.

EXAMBLO'MA (*Med.*) and *Examblosis*, ἐξάμβλωμα, ἐξάμβλωσις, from ἀμβλόω, to miscarry; an abortion.

EXA'MINERS (*Law*) two officers in the Court of Chancery, who are appointed, on oath, to examine witnesses on either side.

EXAMPLE (*Rhet.*) an imperfect kind of induction or argumentation, whereby it is proved that a thing which has happened on some other occasions, will happen on the present one.

EXANASTOMO'SIS (*Anat.*) vide *Anastomosis*.

EXA'NGUIOUS (*Anat.*) from *exanguis*; or *ex*, privative, and *sanguis*, blood; bloodless, an epithet for the bones and cartilages which are the white parts of the body.

EXA'NNUAL ROLL (*Law*) a roll, in which fines that could not be levied, and bad debts, were formerly entered, that they might be annually read over to the sheriff, to see if any thing could not be recovered. Hale. *Sheriff. Acc.* 67.

EXANTHE'MATA (*Med.*) pustules that break out on different parts of the body. *Hippocrat. Epid.* 1. 6, & *Gal. Comm.* 2, &c.; *Cels.* 1. 5, c. 28; *Marcell. de Medicam.* c. 18; *Oribas. de Morb. Curat.* 1. 3, c. 21; *Act. de Meth. Med.* 1. 1, c. 20; *Gorr. Def. Med.*; *Foes. Œconom. Hippocrat.*

EXANTHRO'PIA (*Med.*) from ἐξ and ἄνθρωπος, a man, i. e. without the faculties of a man; a species of melancholy madness, in which the patient fancies himself a brute.

EXARA'GMA (*Surg.*) from ἐξαράττω, to break; a fracture. *Gal. Exeg. Hippoc. Vocab.*; *Pancirol. Notit. Dig. Imp. Occident.* c. 1.

EXA'RMA (*Med.*) from ἐξαίρω, to lift up; an elevated tumour. *Hippocrat. Epid.* l. 4; *Foes. Œconom. Hippocrat.*

EXA'RSIO (*Med.*) an intemperature from heat, attended with dryness.

EXARTHRE'MA (*Med.*) from ἐξαρτάω, to suspend; an amulet or charm hung round the neck.

EXARTHRO'SIS (*Surg.*) from ἐξαρθρόω, to put out of joint; a dislocation or luxation.

EXARTICULA'TION (*Surg.*) the disjointing or putting out of joint.

EXAUCTORA'TIO (*Ant.*) a partial discharge from military service in the Roman army, in distinction from the *missio*, which was a full discharge. *Tacit. Annal.* l. 1, c. 36; *Lamprid. in Alex. Sever.* c. 52; *Tertullian. de Coron. Milit.* c. 1; *Veget.* l. 2, c. 3; *Ulp. ff. de eis qui not. in fam.* tit. 2, l. 2.

EXCAMBIATO'RES (*Archæol.*) exchangers of land, who are supposed to have been what we now call brokers.

EXCA'MBIUM (*Com.*) Exchange.

EXCATHI'SMA (*Med.*) vide *Semicupium*.

E'XCELLENCY (*Polit.*) a title now given to embassadors, commanders, and to other persons not entitled to that of highness.

EXCE'NTRIC (*Geom.*) an epithet for such figures as circles, spheres, &c. not having the same centre.

EXCENTRIC *Circle* (*Astron.*) or the *excentric*, otherwise called the *deferent*, a circle in the Ptolemaic system, which was the orbit itself that the planets were supposed to describe round the earth. It is now supposed that the planets describe elliptic orbits round the sun.—*Excentric Circle*, in modern astronomy, is the circle described from the centre of the orbit of a planet, with half the greatest axis as a radius; or it is the circle that circumscribes the elliptic orbit of the planet.—*Excentric Anomaly*, or *Anomaly of the Centre*, vide *Astronomy*.—*Excentric place of a Planet* in its orbit is the heliocentric place, or that place in which it appears as seen from the sun.—*Excentric Place in the Ecliptic* is the point of the ecliptic to which the planet is referred as viewed from the sun. This coincides with the heliocentric longitude.—*Excentric Equation*, in ancient astronomy, is an angle made by a line drawn from the centre of the earth with another line drawn from the centre of the excentric. This is the same with the Prosthaphæresis. [vide *Equation of the Centre*]

EXCENTRICITY (*Geom.*) the distance between the centres of two circles or spheres not having the same centre.

EXCENTRICITY (*Astron.*) in the Ptolemaic system is that part of the line of the Apsides lying between the centre of the earth and of the Excentric, i. e. the distance between the centre of a planet and the centre of the earth.—*Excentricity*, in modern astronomy, is the distance between the centre of the Ellipse, i. e. between the sun and the centre of the Excentric. [vide *Astronomy*] This is called Single or Simple Excentricity, in distinction from the Double

Excentricity, which is the distance between the two Foci of the Ellipse, and is equal to twice the Excentricity.

EXCE'PTIO (*Ant.*) Exception, a bar, or prevention, by which the defendant stops the action from going directly to a sentence or condemnation. *Cic. de Inv. Rhet.* l. 2, c. 20; *Paull. tit. de Except.*; *Sigon. de Indic.* l. 1, c. 21.

EXCE'PTION (*Law*) a stop or stay to an action, consisting either of a denial of the matter alleged in bar to the action; or, in Chancery, of what is alleged against the sufficiency of an answer, &c. Exceptions are distinguished into *dilatory* and *peremptory*. *Bract.* l. 5, tract 5; *Co. Lit.* 47; 1 *Lev.* 287; *Cro. Eli.* 244.

Exception, in Scotch law, is equivalent to *Defence*. *Exceptio Rei judicatæ* is an Exception or defence that the matter has been adjudged in another court or country, and the judgment carried into effect.

EXCEPTION (*Med.*) the embodying or mixing of dry powders with any sort of moisture.

EXCE'PTIVE PROPOSITION (*Log.*) any proposition which contains some particle of exception; as *but*, *unless*, &c.

EXCE'SS, Spherical (*Trigon.*) is the excess of the sum of the three angles of any spherical triangle above two right angles.

EXCHA'NGE (*Law*) *Excambium*. 1. The *King's Exchange*, or the place appointed by the King for the exchange of plate or bullion for the King's coin, &c. There were formerly divers such places, but now there is only one, namely, the Mint, in the Tower. 2. Any contract or agreement whereby persons or things are exchanged one for another; as—*Exchange of Lands or Tenements*, a mutual grant of equal interest in lands, the one in consideration of the other, which is used peculiarly in our common law for that compensation which the warrantor must make to the warrantee, value for value, if the land warranted be recovered from the warrantee. The word *Exchange*, when taken by itself, applies appropriately to this case in law: it is, however, applied to other things, as *Exchange of Church Livings*, &c.

EXCHANGE (*Com.*) 1. The trucking or bartering one thing for another. 2. The giving a sum of money in one place to be repaid in another, *par pro pari*, value for value, according to the sundry species of coins current. This was called *Cambio commune*, or Common Exchange, when coin was exchanged for coin, in distinction from *Cambio reale*, or Real Exchange, when moneys were paid to the exchanger, and bills were drawn without naming the species, but according to the value of the several coins. [vide *Bill of Exchange*]—*Exchange Brokers* are men who act between one merchant and another in the business of Exchange. 3. *Exchange* also stands for the rate at which one coin is exchanged for another, which depends upon the balance of trade and the political relations which subsist between two countries. 4. The place where merchants meet to negotiate bills and transact all other business.

EXCHANGE (*Arith.*) is the finding what quantity of the money of one place is equal to a given sum of another, according to a certain course of exchange.—*Course of Exchanges* is the current price betwixt two places, which is always fluctuating and unsettled.—*Arbitration of Exchange* is a calculation of the exchanges of different places, to discover which is the most profitable. [vide *Arbitration*]

EXCHANGE (*Mil.*) 1. *Exchange of Prisoners*, the act of giving up men on both sides, upon certain conditions agreed to by the contending parties. 2. *Exchange between Officers*, who remove from one regiment to another, or from full to half pay, for which a consideration is usually given, called the *Difference*.

EXCHA'NGERS (*Com.*) those who transmit money to foreign parts by bills of exchange, &c.

EXCHE'QUER (*Law*) in Latin *scaccarium*, in old French *l'eschouier*; the place or office where the King's cash is kept and paid, properly called the receipt of the Exchequer.—*Exchequer Court*, a court of record, in which all causes relating to the crown revenue are determined. It is governed by the Chancellor of the Exchequer, the Lord Chief Baron, and three other Barons, who are the sovereign auditors of England, and the judges of the court. The prerogative court of the Archbishop of York also goes by this name.—*Black-Book of the Exchequer*, a book composed in the reign of Henry II, containing a full account of this court, its officers, &c.

EXCHE'QUERED (*Law*) a colloquial term for one who is summoned before the court of Exchequer to answer any charge.

EXCI'PULUM (*Chem.*) a chemical receiver.

EXCI'SE (*Law*) an inland imposition paid sometimes on the consumption of the commodity, or frequently upon its retail sale which immediately precedes the consumption.

EXCI'SION (*Bibl.*) in the scripture sense, is the cutting off a person from the number of his community, as a punishment for his sins.

EXCITABI'LITY (*Med.*) and *Excitement*, terms of modern use; the first, to denote the capacity of the body to admit of an increased action; the latter the state of increased action. The causes which produce this increase of action are called *exciting causes*.

EXCLAMA'TION (*Rhet.*) a figure of speech by which any passion of the mind is expressed. [vide *Ecphonesis*]

EXCLUSA (*Law*) or *Exclusagium*, a sluice for water; and the payment to the lord for the use of such a sluice. *Mon. Angl.* tom. 1, p. 398, &c.

EXCLU'SIONERS (*Polit.*) a name given to those members of parliament, who, in the reign of King Charles II, were for excluding the Duke of York from the succession to the throne.

EXCLUSO'RIUM (*Med.*) a medicine which causes abortion.

EXCŒCA'RIA (*Bot.*) a genus of plants, Class 22 *Dioecia*, Order 3 *Triandria*.

Generic Character. CAL. ament cylindric.—COR. none.— STAM. *filaments* three; *anthers* roundish.—PIST. *germ* roundish; *styles* three; *stigma* simple.— PER. *berry* smooth; *seeds* solitary.

Species. The species is a shrub, as the—*Excoecaria Agallocha*, seu *Arbor excoecaris*, native of Tongatabu.

EXCOMMUNICA'TION (*Law*) *Excommunicatio*, an ecclesiastical censure, which is divided into the greater and the less; the former excluding a person from the communion of the church, and the company of the faithful altogether; the latter excluding him only from the communion of the church.

EXCOMMUNICA'TO *capiendo* (*Law*) a writ directed to the sheriff for the apprehension of one who stands obstinately excommunicated forty days.—*Excommunicato deliberando*, a writ to the under sheriff for the delivery of an excommunicated person out of prison.—*Excommunicato recipiendo*, a writ whereby excommunicated persons, who have been unlawfully delivered from prison before they have given caution to obey the authority of the church, are commanded to be sought after and retaken. *F. N. B.* 62; *Reg. Orig.* 37.

EXCORIA'TION (*Surg.*) the rubbing off or fretting away the skin from any part of the body.

EXCORTICA'TION (*Bot.*) the stripping a tree of its bark.

EXCREME'NTA (*Anat.*) whatever is evacuated from the animal body after digestion. *Ruff. Ephes. de Appellat. Part. Corp. hum.* l. 1, c. 36; *Act. de Urin.* c. 5.

EXCRE'SCENCE (*Surg.*) from *ex*, and *cresco*, to grow; any preternatural formation of flesh on any part of the body, as a wart, wen, &c.

EXCRE'TA (*Med.*) and *Retenta*, fluids thrown out or retained in the body.

EXCRE'TION (*Med.*) the act of separating and voiding excrementitious humours from the aliments and mass of blood.

EXCU'BIÆ (*Ant.*) the watches and guards kept in the day by the Romans, in distinction from *vigiliæ*, which were kept by night. *Isidor. Orig.* l. 9, c. 3; *Serv. in Virg. Æn.* l. 9, v. 159; *Schel. in Polyb. apud Græv. Thes. Antiq. Rom.* tom. 10.

EXCULPA'TION, Letters of (*Law*) a warrant in the Scotch law to an offender indicted for citing witnesses in his own defence.

EXCU'RSION (*Astron.*) another word for Elongation. [vide *Elongation*]—*A circle of Excursion* is a lesser circle parallel to the ecliptic, and at such a distance from it that the excursions of the planets towards the poles of the ecliptic may be included within them, being usually fixed at 10 degrees.

EXCUSA'TI (*Ant.*) an epithet for slaves who, having taken refuge in a church, obtained pardon from their masters, who bound themselves by an oath to pass over their offence. *Greg. Turon. Hist.* l. 5, c. 3.

E'XEAT (*Ecc.*) a term employed in the permission which a bishop grants to a priest to go out of his diocese.

EXECHEBRO'NCHOS (*Med.*) ἐξεχίβρογχος, an epithet for one having a prominent βρόγχος, or throat. *Hippocrat. de Art. & Gal. Com.*

EXECHEGLU'TOS (*Med.*) ἐξεχίγλυτος, an epithet for one having prominent buttocks.

EXECU'TION (*Law*) signifies generally the last performance of an act by a judicial writ, grounded on the judgment of the court from which it issues; particularly the obtaining possession of any thing recovered by judgment of law.—*Prerogative Execution* is an execution for the king's debt, which is always preferred before any other execution.

Execution (*Mil.*) the plunder and waste of a country where the inhabitants refuse to submit to the terms imposed upon them.

EXECU'TIONE *facienda in Withernamium* (*Law*) vide *Replevin*.—*Executione Judicii*, a writ directed to the judge in an inferior court to do execution upon a judgment therein. *F. N. B.* 20; *New Nat. Brev.* 43.

EXE'CUTIVE (*Polit.*) an epithet signifying capable of executing, is particularly applied to that branch of the government which is invested with the power of executing the functions of governing the state. In all monarchical states this power, called by distinction the *Executive power*, rests in the prince.

EXE'CUTOR (*Law*) a person nominated by a testator to take care and see his will and testament executed.—*Executor de son Tort*, &c. of or to his own wrong; an executor who takes upon him the office of an executor by intrusion, not being constituted thereto by the testator.

EXE'CUTORY (*Law*) an epithet for what belongs to an execution. An *executory estate* is, where an estate created by deed, or fine, is to be afterwards executed by entry, livery, writ, &c.; leases for years, rents, annuities, &c. are called *inheritances executory*; an *executory devise* is the devise of a future interest.

EXEGE'SIS (*Lit.*) ἐξήγησις, an explication of words, or an elucidation of sentences.

Exegesis *numerosa et linealis* (*Math.*) a term used by Vieta for the numeral or lineal solution of the extraction of roots out of adfected equations.

EXEGE'TES (*Ant.*) ἐξηγηταί, from ἐξηγέομαι, to explain; an interpreter of the laws and religious rites among the Athenians. *Plat. de Leg.* l. 6; *Demosth. cont. Everg.*; *Theophrast. Charact.* c. 17; *Poll. Onom.* l. 8, segm. 124, &c.

EXELCO'SIS (*Med.*) vide *Exulceratio*.

EXELCY'SMOS (*Med.*) ἐξελκυσμός, from ἕλκω, to draw; a depressure of the bones. *Gal. Def. Med.*

EXEMPLIFICA'TION (*Law*) a duplicate, or copy of letters patent, taken from the enrolled originals.

EXEMPLIFICATIO'NE (*Law*) a writ granted for the exemplifying an original. *Reg. Orig.* 290.

EXE'MPT (*Mil.*) a French term for an officer in the guards, who commands in the absence of the captain and lieutenant.

EXE'MPTION (*Law*) a privilege to be free from service or appearance, as knights, clergymen, &c. are exempt from appearing at county court by statute, &c.

EXE'MPTS (*Polit.*) persons originally so called from being exempted from certain services, or entitled to particular privileges. The Exons of St. James derive their name from the exempts. In France there were three classes—*Exempts des gardes du corps*, belonging to the body guard.—*Exempts du ban et arrière ban*, persons exempt from that service, and—*Exempts des Maréchaussées*, those belonging to the Marshalsea, who were exempt from all taxes, &c.

EXE'NNIUM (*Archæol.*) or Exhenium, a gift or present; more properly a new year's gift.

E'XERCISE (*Mil.*) the practice of all military movements and use of arms, by which a soldier is instructed how to carry himself in the field, and on duty.

EXERGA'SIA (*Rhet.*) a figure of speech, by which the same thing is repeated in different terms.

EXE'RGUE (*Numis.*) a term among medalists denoting the little space around and without the work or figures of a medal for an inscription, &c.

EXFOLIA'TION (*Surg.*) from *exfolio*, to shed the leaf; the scaling off, or separation of a dead piece of bone in the form of a leaf or scale.

EXFOLIATI'VUM (*Surg.*) from *exfolio*, to shed the leaf; an instrument for rasping a bone, so as to clean it from all exfoliations.

EXFREDIA'RE (*Archæol.*) to break the peace.

EX *gravi querela* (*Law*) a writ which lies for one who is kept from the possession of his lands and tenements by the devisor's heirs, who enters and detains them from him.

EXHALA'TION (*Nat.*) a fume, or vapour, which rises out of the earth.

EXHAU'STED Receiver (*Pneum.*) a glass, or other vessel, applied on the plate of an air pump, to extract the air out of it by the action of the pump.

EXHAU'STIONS (*Math.*) or *the method of Exhaustions*, a mode of demonstration founded on the principle of exhausting a quantity by continually taking away certain parts of it.

EXHI'BIT (*Law*) a term used in a suit of Chancery, when a deed or other writing is exhibited to be proved by witnesses, and the examiners or commissioners certify on the back, that it was shown to such or such persons at their examination, which is called an *exhibit*.

EXHIBI'TION (*Law*) in the Scotch law is an action for compelling the production of writings.

Exhibition (*Ecc.*) an allowance for meat and drink which was customary among the religious appropriators of churches, who usually made it to the depending vicar; whence the benefactions now settled for the maintaining of scholars at the Universities, not depending on the foundation, are called exhibitions.

EXHIBITIONER (*Lit.*) one who enjoys an exhibition at the Universities. [vide *Exhibition*]

EXHUMA'TION (*Law*) the act of digging up a body that has been interred in holy ground, by the authority of a judge.

EXIGE'NDARIES (*Law*) vide *Exigenter*.

EX'IGENT (*Law*) or *Exigi facias*, a writ lying where the defendant in a personal action cannot be found, nor any thing of his within that county to be distrained: it is directed to the sheriff to call the party five county days successively to appear under pain of outlawry. *Stat.* 18 *Ed.* 3, c. 1; 6 *Hen.* 8, c. 4; 31 *Eliz.* c. 3; 3 *Inst.* 31, &c.

EXIGE'NTER (*Law*) or exigendary, an officer of the court of Common Pleas who makes out exigents and proclamations in all actions in which process of outlawry lies.

E'XIGI *facias* (*Law*) vide *Exigent*.

EXI'LIUM (*Archæol.*) a spoiling; also an injury done to tenants by altering their tenure, ejecting them, and the like. *Stat. Marlb.* c. 25; *Flet.* l. 1, c. 11.

EXIPO'TICOS (*Med.*) ἐκπωτικὸς, from ἐκπόομαι, to press out; an epithet for digesting or detersive medicines.

EXI'SCHIOS (*Anat.*) an epithet signifying jutting out.

EXITU'RA (*Med.*) a running abscess.

E'XITUS (*Law*) the issues or profits from lands.

EXITUS (*Med.*) a prolapsus, or falling of the anus.

EXLEGA'LITUS (*Law*) he who is prosecuted as an outlaw. *Leg. Ed. Confes.* c. 38.

EX MERO MOTU (*Law*) vide *Ex*.

EXOACA'NTHA (*Bot.*) a genus of plants, Class 5 *Pentandria*, Order 2 *Digynia*.
  Generic Character. CAL. *umbel* universal.—COR. universal.— STAM. *filaments* five; *anthers* roundish. — PIST. *germ* inferior; *styles* two; *stigmas* two.—PER. *fruit* subovate; *seeds* two.
  Species. The single species is a biennial, as the—*Exoacantha heterophylla*, a native of Nazareth.

E'XOCHAS (*Med.*) from ἐξ and ἔχω, to have; a tubercle of the anus. *Paul. Æginet.* l. 3, c. 59; *Gorr. Def. Med.*

EXOCŒTUS (*Ich.*) the Flying-Fish; a genus of fishes of the Abdominal Order, having the *head* scaly, a *mouth* without teeth, and long pectoral fins that enable the fish to suspend itself for a time in the air.

EXOCY'STUS (*Med.*) from ἐξ and κύστις, the bladder; a prolapsus of the inner membrane of the bladder.

EXODIARIUS (*Ant.*) the performer of the exodium.

EXO'DIUM (*Ant.*) an interlude, or farce, at the end of a play.
  Juven. sat. 6. v. 7.

  Urbicus exodio risum movet Atellanæ.

The actor who performed the exodium was called the *exodiarius*. *Liv.* l. 7, c. 2; *Schol. in Juv.* sat. 3, v. 175.

EX *officio* (*Law*) vide *Ex*.

EXO'MPHALOS (*Med.*) ἐξόμφαλος, a prominence of the ὀμφαλὸς, or navel; likewise the person having such a prominence, particularly when caused by a rupture, which Paulus calls the ἐξ ὀμφαλοπαθὴς. *Gal. Def. Med.; Paul. Æginet.* l. 6, c. 51; *Gorr. Def. Med.; Foes. Œconom. Hippocrat.*

EXO'NCHOMA (*Med.*) from ἐξ and ὄγκος, a tumour; a very large tumour.

EXONEIRO'SIS (*Med.*) ἐξονείρωσις, a species of gonorrhœa, commonly called *pollutio nocturna*, when the semen flows involuntarily in sleep. *Hippocrat. Epidem.* l. 5; *Foes. Œconom. Hippocrat.*

EXONERATIONE *Sectæ* (*Law*) a writ lying for the king's ward to be disburdened of all suit, &c. during the time of the wardship.—*Exoneratione Sectæ ad Curiam Baroniæ*, a writ of the same nature sued by the guardian of the king's ward, and directed to the sheriffs, that they distrain him, &c. for not doing suit of court. *F. N. B.* 158, 394; *New Nat. Brev.* 352.

EXONS (*Mil.*) vide *Exempts*.

EXOPHTHA'LMIA (*Med.*) from ἐξ and ὀφθαλμὸς, an eye; a protuberance of the eye out of its natural position.

EXO'RCISM (*Theol.*) ἐξορκισμὸς, the laying or casting out spirits.

EXO'RDIUM (*Rhet.*) the commencement of a speech, by which the orator prepares the minds of the auditors for what is to follow. *Cic. de Inv.* l. 1, c. 5; *Quintil.* l. 4, c. 1.

EXORESCE'NTIA (*Med.*) Exacerbation.

EXOSTO'SIS (*Anat.*) ἐξόστωσις, from ἐξ and ὀστέα, a bone; a preternatural excrescence of a bone, or a hard tumor. *Gal. de Tumor.* c. 14; *Foes. Œconom. Hippocrat.*

EXOSTOSIS is a genus of diseases, in the class *Locales*, order *Tumores*, in Cullen's Nosology.

EXO'STRA (*Ant.*) a bridge thrust out of a turret by pullies on the walls, by which the besiegers gained an entrance into the town. *Veget.* l. 4, c. 21; *Turneb. Adv.* l. 20, c. 21.

EXOTERICÆ (*Rhet.*) ἐξωτερικαὶ, a term applied to such of Aristotle's lectures as were open to all persons.

EXO'TIC (*Bot.*) a term applied to plants which are of foreign origin.

EXPA'NSION (*Nat.*) the swelling, or increase in the bulk of fluids when agitated by heat.

EXPA'NSUS (*Bot.*) spread out; an epithet for the calyx, as in *Helianthus*.

EX *Parte* (*Law*) vide *Ex*.

EXPE'CTANCY, *Estates in* (*Law*) are those which are created by the act of the parties, called *Remainder*, or those, by the act of law, called a *Reversion*.

EXPE'CTANT (*Law*) an epithet for whatever has a relation to, or dependance upon, another; in this manner there may be a *fee expectant* after a feetail.

EXPECTATI'VÆ *gratiæ* (*Ecc.*) certain bulls given by popes or princes for future benefices before they become void.

EXPE'CTORANTS (*Med.*) medicines which promote expectoration.

EXPECTORA'TION (*Med.*) the discharge of mucus from the breast.

EXPEDITA'TÆ *arbores* (*Law*) trees rooted up, or cut up by the roots. *Flet.* l. 2. c. 41.

TO EXPE'DITATE (*Law*) *expeditare*, to cut out the ball of a dog's fore-foot for the preservation of the King's game; and whoever, living near the forest, kept a dog which was not *expeditated* forfeited to the King 3s. 4d. *Crompt. Jur.* 152; *Manw. For. Laws.* part 1, c. 16; 4 *Inst.* 308.

EXPE'LLENTS (*Med.*) medicines supposed to expel morbid humours from the body.

EXPE'NDITORS (*Law*) persons appointed by the Commissioners of Sewers to disburse the money collected for the repairs of sewers: also the steward who supervises the repairs of the banks, &c. in Romney Marsh is called an *expenditor*.

EXPENSÆ *litis* (*Law*) costs of suit.

EXPE'NSIS *militum non levandis* (*Law*) an ancient writ to prohibit the sheriff from levying any allowance for knights of the shire, upon those that hold lands in ancient demesne. *Reg. Orig.* 261, &c. Also a writ for levying expences for Knights of the Parliament, &c. *Reg. Orig.* 191.

EXPE'RIMENT (*Phil.*) a trial of the effect or result of certain applications and motions of natural bodies in order to discover something of their laws, nature, &c.

EXPERIMENTAL *Philosophy* is that philosophy which proceeds on experiments.

EXPERIME'NTUM *crucis* (*Phil.*) such an experiment as leads to the true knowledge of things sought after, in the same manner as the cross on the highway directs the traveller in his course.

EXPIRA'TION (*Anat.*) from *ex* and *spiro*, to breathe; that part of respiration which consists in expelling the air out of the lungs.

EXPLORATO'RES (*Ant.*) scouts, or soldiers, who explored the designs of the enemy. *Appian. de Bell. Punic.; Herod.*

l. 8, c. 1; *Procop. de Bell. Persic.* l. 1; *Veget.* l. 3, c. 5; *Menand. l. omne. ff. de Re Milit.*; *Panciroll. Notit. Dignit. Imp. Orient.* c. 154.

EXPLORATO'RIUM (*Surg.*) a surgical instrument better known by the name of a probe.

EXPLO'SION (*Nat.*) a violent expansion of an aerial or elastic fluid accompanied with a sudden noise, as in the case of gunpowder and some gases.

EXPO'NENT *of a Power* (*Algeb.*) the number or quantity expressing the degree or elevation of the power; thus, in x^2, 2 is the exponent or index of the square numbers; in x^3, 3 is the exponent or index denoting the cube of x; and so on with higher powers. These exponents were expressed by Diophantes in words, as μονάς, ἀριθμός, δυναμις, κύβος, δυναμοδυναμις, &c. equivalent to 1 a, a^2, a^3, a^4, &c. Lucas Paciolus, or Lucas de Burgo uses the terms *Cosa, Censo, Cubo, Relato primo, secundo, tertio,* &c. for root, square, cube, &c.; or the abbreviations *co, ce, cu,* and ℞ for root or radicality. Stifelius and his cotemporaries used the following contractions of these words, ℂ, 2, 3. But, besides the above contractions, Stifelius, who introduced the word exponent, also made use of the figures now employed.—*Exponent of a Ratio* is the quotient arising when the antecedent is divided by the consequent.

EXPONE'NTIAL *Calculus* (*Flux.*) the method of differencing or finding the fluxions of exponential quantities, and of summoning up their fluents.—*Exponential Curve* is that whose nature is defined or expressed by an exponential Equation.—*Exponential Equation* is one in which is contained an exponential quantity, as the equation $a^x = b$, or $x^x = a\,a$, &c.—*Exponential Quantity* is that whose power is a variable quantity, as the expression a^x, or x^x. Exponential quantities are of several degrees, a^x of the first order, a^{x^x} of the second order, $a^{x^{x^x}}$ of the third order, and so on.

EXPO'SITOR (*Lit.*) one who explains the writings of others; it is applied particularly to those who profess to expound the scriptures.

EX *Post Facto* (*Law*) vide *Ex*.

EXPRE'SS (*Polit.*) a messenger sent with direct and specific instructions.

EXPRE'SSED *Oils* (*Chem.*) such as are procured from any substance by simple pressure, as the oil of olives, &c.

EXPRE'SSION (*Algeb.*) any quantity expressed in an Algebraical form, as 3 a, 2 a b, $\sqrt{(a^2 \pm c^2)}$. It is sometimes called a *function*.

EXPRESSION (*Chem.*) the pressing or squeezing any oil or juice out of vegetables, &c.

EXPRESSION (*Mus.*) that part of composition, or performance, which makes its appeal to the feelings.

EXPRESSI'VO (*Mus.*) an Italian epithet signifying with expression.

EX PROFESSO (*Law*) by profession.

EXPU'RGATORY *Index* (*Ecc.*) a book sent forth by the pope, containing a catalogue of those authors and writings which were thought censurable, and forbidden to be read by the priests.

E'XEQUIAL (*Mus.*) or *funereal*, an epithet applied to music which is used at the funeral ceremony.

EXSE'RTUS (*Bot.*) protruded, an epithet for stamens, or anthers, that stand out of the corolla, or appear above it, as in some species of the *Erica*.

EXSTIPULA'TUS (*Bot.*) without stipules, an epithet for many plants.

E'XSTASIS (*Med.*) a species of *Catalepsis*.

EXSU'CCATION (*Med.*) vide *Ecchymosis*.

EXSU'CCUS (*Bot.*) juiceless, an epithet for leaves, as opposed to the *succulent*.

TO EXTE'ND (*Law*) to value the lands or tenements of one bound by a statute, who has forfeited his bond, at such an indifferent rate, as, by the yearly rent, the creditor may in time be paid his debt. [vide *Extendi*]

EXTE'NDI *Facias* (*Law*) or *Extent*, a writ of execution, or commission to the sheriff, for the valuing of lands or tenements, and sometimes the act of the sheriff, or other commissioner upon this writ.—*Extent in Aid* is a seizure made by the crown when a public accountant becomes a defaulter, and prays for relief against his creditors.

EXTE'NSOR (*Anat.*) an epithet applied to muscles whose office it is to extend any part, in opposition to the *flexor*; as *extensor brevis digitorum pedis*, the muscle that extends the toes; *extensor digitorum communis*, that which extends all the joints of the fingers, &c.

EXTE'NT (*Mus.*) the compass of a voice, or instrument.

EXTENT (*Law*) vide *Extendi facias*.

EXTENUA'TION (*Med.*) the leanness of the whole body.

EXTENUATION (*Rhet.*) a figure of speech by which the things are diminished, or made less than they really are.

EXTE'RIOR *polygon* (*Fort.*) the outlines of the works drawn from one outer angle; or the distance of one outer bastion to the point of another reckoned quite round the works. —*Exterior talus*, the slope allowed the work on the outside from the place towards the champaign, or field.

EXTERMINA'TION (*Algeb.*) or *Exterminating*, the taking away certain unknown quantities from depending equations, so as finally to have only one equation containing one unknown quantity.

EXTERNAL (*Math.*) an epithet for those angles which are formed without a figure by producing its sides externally. [vide *Angle*]

EXTERNAL *digestives* (*Surg.*) applications which ripen a swelling, and breed good and laudable matter in a wound, so as to prepare it for cleansing.

EXTE'RNUS *Auris* (*Anat.*) a muscle, the same as the *laxator tympani*.

EXTI'NGUISHMENT (*Law*) the extinction or annihilation of a right, estate, &c. by means of its being merged or consolidated with another, generally a greater, or more extensive right.—*Extinguishment* is applied to different rights, as Commons, Estates, Copyholds, Debts, Liberties, Services, and Ways.—*Extinguishment of Common* is by purchasing land wherein a person hath Common appendant. —*Extinguishment of Estates* is when a man hath a yearly rent out of lands, and afterwards purchases the lands whereout it ariseth.—*Extinguishment of Copyhold* is by any act of the copyholder's, which denotes his intention not to hold any longer of his lord.—*Extinguishment of debt* is when a *feme sole* takes the debtor to husband.—*Extinguishment of Liberties* is when the liberties or franchises, granted by the king, come to the crown again.—*Extinguishment of Services* is when the lord purchases or accepts parcel of the tenancy, out of which an entire service is to be paid.—*Extinguishment of Ways* is if a man hath a highway as appendant, and afterwards purchases the land wherein the way is.

EXTIRPA'TION (*Surg.*) the complete removal or destruction of any part, either by excision, or by means of caustics.

EXTIRPA'TIONE (*Law*) a writ which lies against one who, after a verdict found against him for land, &c. does despitefully overthrow any house upon it. *Reg. Jud.* 19, 56.

EXTO'RTION (*Law*) the unlawful act of any public officer who, by colour of his office, takes any money, or valuable thing, where none at all is due. [vide *Exaction*]

EXTRA *Constellary Stars* (*Astron.*) such as are not properly included in any space.—*Extra Mundane Space*, the infinite void space which is supposed to be extended beyond the bound of the universe.

EXTRA-JUDI'CIAL (*Law*) is when judgment is had in a

cause not depending in that court where it is given, or wherein the judge has not jurisdiction.—*Extra-parochial*, i. e. out of the parish, an epithet for any thing privileged or exempt from the duties of a parish, as extra-parochial land, &c.

E'XTRACT (*Law*) a copy or draught of any writing, or part of a writing.

EXTRACT (*Chem.*) the purer parts of any substance extracted from its grosser parts.

EXTRACT (*Med.*) a solution of the purer parts of a mixed body inspissated by distillation, or evaporation, nearly to the consistence of honey.

EXTRA'CTA *curiæ* (*Archæol.*) the issues or profits of holding a court, which arise from customary fines, fees, &c.

EXTRA'CTION (*Surg.*) the taking extraneous substances out of the body.

EXTRACTION *of roots* (*Math.*) the finding out of any number or quantity, which, being multiplied by itself once, twice, or three times, &c. gives the respective power, out of which the given root is to be extracted; as the extraction of the square root, the cube root, &c.

EXTRA'CTOR (*Surg.*) a surgical instrument used in the operation of cutting for the stone.

EXTRA-FOLIA'CEÆ (*Bot.*) an epithet for stipules growing on the outside of leaves, or below them; as in *Betula*, *Tilia*, &c.

EXTRA'DOS (*Archit.*) the outside of an arch, or vault. [vide *Building*]

EXTRAJUDI'CIAL (*Law*) vide *Extra*.

EXTRAMU'NDANE (*Astron.*) vide *Extra*.

EXTRAORDINA'RII (*Ant.*) a chosen body of men in the Roman army picked from the auxiliary forces of their allies, consisting of a third part of the cavalry, and a fifth of the foot. *Polyb.* l. 6, c. 24; *Liv.* l. 34, c. 47, &c.

EXTRAO'RDINARY (*Polit.*) an epithet for whatever is out of the common course, as an—*Extraordinary ambassador*, one sent to negotiate on some special affair.—*Extraordinary courier*, one sent express on an urgent occasion.—*Extraordinary gazette*, a gazette published on purpose to announce some particular event.

EXTRA-PARO'CHIAL (*Law*) vide *Extra*.

EXTRA-TE'MPORA (*Ecc.*) a licence from the pope to take holy orders at any time.

EXTRAVAGA'NTES (*Ecc.*) decretal epistles published after the Clementines by Pope John XXII. and other popes, and added to the canon law. They were so called because they were not ranged in any order.

EXTRAVAGA'NZA (*Mus.*) Italian for a sort of composition remarkable for its wildness and incoherence.

EXTRAVASA'TION (*Surg.*) from *extra*, without, and *vas*, a vessel; a term applied to the fluids which are out of their proper vessels or receptacles; as when the blood is effused on the surface, or in the ventricles of the brain, there is said to be an *extravasation*; or when the urine, in consequence of a wound, makes its way into the cellular substance among the abdominal viscera, it is said to be *extravasated*.

EXTRE'ME *and mean proportion* (*Geom.*) is when a line is so divided that the whole line is to the greater segment, as that segment is to the less.

EXTREME *unction* (*Ecc.*) a solemn anointing of any person who is at the point of death; which is one of the seven sacraments in the Romish church.

EXTRE'MES (*Log.*) the two extreme terms of the conclusion of a syllogism, namely, the predicate and subject.

EXTREMES (*Mus.*) those parts in a composition or piece of harmony which are at the greatest distance from each other in point of gravity or acuteness.

EXTREMES *conjunct* (*Trigon.*) the two circular parts that lie next the middle part, in distinction from the *disjunct extremes*, which lie remote from the middle.

EXTRE'MITY (*Mus.*) the last note in any compass of sounds, reckoning from grave to acute, or from acute to grave.

EXTRI'NSECUS (*Anat.*) an epithet for the external parts of the body, particularly the limbs.

EXU'BERES (*Med.*) an epithet for children that are weaned.

EXULCERA'TION (*Surg.*) an ulceration, or turning to an ulcer.

EXUMBILICA'TION (*Surg.*) a starting of the navel.

EXUNGULA'TION (*Chem.*) the cutting off the white part from the leaves of roses.

EXUPERA'RE (*Archæol.*) to apprehend or seize, as " Exuperare vivum aut mortuum." *Leg. Edm.* c. 2.

EXU'VIÆ (*Nat.*) the sloughs of serpents, i. e. the skins which they cast off in the spring.

EYE (*Anat.*) *oculus*, the organ of vision, is divided into external and internal parts. The external parts are the Eyebrows, or *supercilia*; the Eyelashes, *cilia*; the Eyelids, *palpebræ*, to which belong the external *canthus*, the internal *canthus*, and the *tarsus*, or margin of the eyelid; the Lachrymal Glands; the Lachrymal Caruncle; the *puncta lachrymalia*; the Lachrymal Ducts; the Lachrymal Sac; the Nasal Duct; and the *membrana conjunctiva*, called also the white of the eye. The internal parts of the eye compose what is called the Bulb or Globe of the eye, and consist of membranes, chambers, and humours. Among the membranes of the eye are — the *membrana sclerotica*, a horny membrane, which forms the spherical cavity of the eye, the more convex part of which is called the *cornea*; and the *membrana choroidea*, which forms the middle tunic of the bulb. The circular continuation of the choroidea in the anterior surface is called the *iris*; in the posterior surface the *uvea*. The round opening in the centre is called *pupilla*, the Pupil, which can be dilated or contracted at pleasure. The *membrana retina* is the innermost tunic, of a white colour, being an expansion of the medullary part of the optic nerve. The chambers of the eye are the *anterior* and the *posterior*, which are filled with aqueous humour. The humours of the eye are the Aqueous Humour which fills both the chambers; the Crystalline Lens, or pellucid body, included in an exceedingly fine membrane, or *capsula*; the Vitreous Humour, which is a beautifully transparent substance that fills the whole bulb of the eye behind the crystalline lens. The muscles, by which the eye is moved in the orbit, are six in number. They are surrounded with much adeps that fills up the cavities in which the eyes are seated. The arteries are the internal orbital, the central, and the ciliary arteries. The veins empty themselves into the external jugulars. The nerves are the optic, and branches from the third, fourth, fifth, and sixth pair. The bones which form the orbits of the eye are the frontal, maxillary, jugal, lachrymal, ethmoid, palatine, and sphenoid.

EYE (*Bot.*) vide *Hylum*.

EYE (*Archit.*) the middle of the volute of the Ionic capital, cut in the form of a little rose, &c.

EYE (*Print.*) the thickness of the type used in printing, or more properly the top or face of the letter.

EYE (*Archer.*) vide *Bull's-Eye*.

EYE (*Mar.*) vide *Bull's-Eye*.

EYE (*Min.*) vide *Cat's-Eye*.

EYE (*Astron.*) or *Bull's-Eye*, another name for *Aldebaran*.

EYEBRIGHT (*Bot.*) the *Euphrasia*, an annual, so called from its supposed efficacy in disorders of the eyes.

E'YE-GLASS (*Mech.*) the glass that is put close to the eye, whether used apart or in any optical instrument.

EYRE (*Law*) vide *Eire*.

F.

FAC

F. (*Ant.*) an abbreviation for Filius, &c. [vide *Abbreviations*]

F. (*Archæol.*) as a numeral letter, stood for forty, and with a dash over it thus, F̄, for 40,000.

F. (*Law*) vide *Abbreviations*.

F. (*Gram.*) vide *Abbreviations*.

F. (*Her.*) stands for the nombril or navel point in an escutcheon. [vide *Heraldry*]

F. (*Mus.*) the fourth note of the natural diatonic scale. [vide *Cliff*]—F above the Base-Cliff Note, is that F which occupies the first space of the treble stave.

F. stands as an abbreviation for *Forte*.

F. (*Law*) the letter with which felons are branded on receiving benefit of clergy.

F. (*Chron.*) one of the seven dominical letters. [vide *Chronology*]

F. (*Med.*) or *ft*, an abbreviation in prescriptions for fiat or fiant, as *F. s. a, fiat secundum artem*, let it be done according to art.

FA (*Mus.*) the name given by Guido to the fourth note of his hexachord, answering to the letter F in the natural hexachord.—*Fa la* was the name of a short song set to music, having the syllables *Fa la* at certain intervals.—*Fa-Burden*, an old term for a sort of counterpoint.

FA'BA (*Bot.*) the *Vicia narbonensis* of Linnæus.

FA'BA-DULCIS (*Bot.*) a species of the *Cassia*, the *Mimosa scandens* of Linnæus.

FABAGI'NEA (*Bot.*) the *Zygophyllum fabago* of Linnæus.

FABA'LE (*Bot.*) a bean straw or stalk on which the cod hangs.

FABA'GO (*Bot*) the *Zygophyllum fabago et coccineum* of Linnæus.

FABA'RIA (*Bot.*) the *Sedum telephium* of Linnæus.

FABARIA *Calendæ* (*Ant.*) the first of June, sacred to the goddess Carna, to whom beans were then offered. *Macrob. Saturn.* l. 1, c. 12.

FA'BER (*Ich.*) a kind of fish mentioned by Columella.

FA'BRIC (*Com.*) a term used to distinguish the different species of the same article, as the *fabric* of St. Quintin, the *fabric* of Valenciennes, &c.

FABRI'CIA (*Bot.*) a species of the *Melaleuca* of Linnæus.

FA'BRICK Lands (*Law*) lands given towards the re-building or repairing of cathedrals, churches, &c.

FACE (*Anat.*) πρόσωπον, facies, the lower and anterior part of the skull, or *cranium*. *Ruff. Ephes. de Appell. Part. Corp. hum.* l. 1, c. 7; *Cels.* l. 8, c. 1; *Gal. Isagog.* c. 10.

FACE (*Mech.*) signifies generally any thing that lies before the eye, in distinction from the back; as the *face* of a stone, an anvil, &c.

FACE (*Archit.*) a member of the Architrave. [vide *Fascia*]

FACE (*Astrol.*) the third part of a sign, each side being supposed to be divided into faces, each face consisting of ten degrees.

FACE (*Fort.*) a term applied to many parts of a fortification, as the—*Face of a Bastion*, the two sides, reaching from the flanks to the salient angle, which is the most advanced part towards the field.—*Face prolonged*, or *extended*, that part of the line of defence, *razant*, which is betwixt the angle of the shoulder and the curtain.—*Face of a Place*, the front, comprehended between the flanked angles of the two neighbouring bastions, composed of a curtain, two flanks, and two faces.

FACE of a gun (*Gunn.*) the superficies of the metal at the extremity of the muzzle.

FACE of a square (*Mil.*) the side of a battalion, &c. when

FAC

formed into a square, as "The right *face*," "The left *face*," "The front *face*," and "The rear *face*."

TO FACE (*Mil.*) to look towards an object: in which sense it is employed in many military phrases, as "*To face* about, to the right, left," &c. a word of command in military exercising. "*To face* the enemy," to oppose a front to him. "In *face* of the enemy," under the line of his fire.

FACE-PAINTING (*Paint.*) the art of taking portraits.

FA'CET (*Mech.*) the small side of a diamond, &c. which is cut with a great number of angles.

FACH (*Med.*) a Turkish medicine, of use as an antidote against poisons.

FA'CIA (*Archit.*) vide *Fascia*.

FACIAL (*Anat.*) belonging to the face, as the *facial* nerve, a part of the auditory nerve.

FA'CIES *Hippocratea* (*Med.*) that particular disposition of the features which immediately precedes the stroke of death; so called from Hippocrates, by whom it has been so justly described in his prognostics. *Cels.* l. 2, c. 6.

FA'CINGS (*Mil.*) the different movements of the men to the right, left, &c. in order to face an object. Also the lappels, cuffs, and collar of a military uniform, which are generally of a different colour from the rest.

FA'CTA *armorum* (*Archæol.*) feats of arms, justs, tournaments, &c.

FA'CTIO (*Ant.*) a name primarily given to the different parties of combatants or charioteers, who were distinguished by different colours, as green, blue, red, and white. *Juven. Sat.* 11, v. 195.

——— *et fragor aurem*
Percutit, eventum viridis quo colligo panni.

Mart. l. 14, ep. 131.

Si veneto, prasinove faves, qui coccina sumis,
Ne fias istá transfuga veste vide.

Sidon. Apollin. carm. 23.

——— *Mirant colores*
Albus vel venetus, virens, rubensque.

To these colours Domitian added two others. *Petron.* c. 28; *Plin.* l. 8, c. 47; *Plin.* l. 9, ep. 6; *Suet. in Domit.* c. 7, &c.; *Fest. de Verb. Signif.*; *Tertull. de Spectac.* c. 9; *Panvin. de Lud. Cir.* l. 1, c. 10; *Panciroll. Descrip. Urb. Rom. apud Græv. Thes. Antiq. Rom.* tom. iii, p. 357, &c.

FA'CTION (*Mil.*) French for the duty done by a soldier when he stands sentry, &c. as "*Entrer en Faction*," &c. to come upon duty.

FACTIONNA'IRE (*Mil.*) French for the soldier that does all sorts of duty.

FACTI'TIOUS (*Chem.*) any epithet for what is made by art, in distinction from what is natural. Soap is a factitious substance; fuller's earth is a natural one.

FA'CTO (*Law*) in fact; a term applied to what is actually done. [vide *De Facto*]

FA'CTOR (*Com.*) the agent for a merchant abroad, who is authorized by a letter of attorney, with a salary or allowance for his care, called *Factorage*.

FACTOR (*Arith.*) a name given to the two numbers or quantities that are multiplied together; so called because they, *faciunt productum*, make the product.

FACTOR (*Algeb.*) the quantities so called which constitute an algebraical expression, answering to the *Divisor* in Arithmetic, as $a + b$, and $a - b$, which are the factors of $a^2 - b^2$; also a, b, c, d, are the factors of the quantity $abcd$.

FA'CTORAGE (*Com.*) vide *Factor*.

FA'CTORY (*Com.*) a place in a distant country, where a considerable number of factors reside for the convenience of trade; also the traders themselves collectively.

FAC-TO'TUM (*Com.*) one who manages all the concerns of another, domestic or mercantile, &c.

FAC-TOTUM (*Print.*) a border within which printers inclose an initial letter.

FA'CTUM (*Law*) a man's own act and deed, particularly in the civil law, for any thing stated and made certain.

FACTUM (*Arith.*) the product of two quantities multiplied together, as the factum of 3 and 4 is 12; 3 and 4 being the *factors*.

FA'CULÆ (*Astron.*) a name given to certain bright spots in the sun.

FA'CULTY (*Phy.*) that power by which a living creature moves and acts: if this power be exerted by the animal body alone, it is called a corporeal or animal faculty; as that by which a man walks, or moves his limbs, &c.: if it belong to the mind or soul of a rational agent, it is called the rational faculty. The faculty may also be distinguished into the *natural*, if it be that by which the body is nourished and increased; and the *vital*, if it be that by which life is preserved, &c.

FACULTY (*Law*) is equivalent, in Scotch law, to power.

FÆ'CES (*Chem.*) the gross substance, dregs, settlings, or impurities, which settle after fermentation, or remain after the purer, more volatile, and fluid parts have been separated by distillation, evaporation, &c.

FÆ'CULA (*Chem.*) small dregs or lees.

FAGA'GO (*Bot.*) a species of the *Zygophyllum* of Linnæus.

FAGA'RA (*Bot.*) a genus of plants, Class 4 *Tetrandria*, Order 1 *Monogynia*.
Generic Character. CAL. *perianth* four-cleft.—COR. *petals* four.—STAM. *filaments* four; *anthers* ovate.—PIST. *germ* ovate; *style* filiform; *stigmas* two-lobed.—PER. *capsule* globular; *seed* single.
Species. The species are shrubs, as the—*Fagara euodia*, seu *Euodia*, Sweet-scented Fagara, native of the Friendly Islands.—*Fagara pterota, Schenus,* seu *Pterota,* seu *Lentiscus,* Wing-leaved Fagara, or Bastard Iron-Wood, native of Jamaica.—*Fagara Tragodes,* seu *Rhus,* Prickly-leaved Fagara, native of Domingo, &c.

FAGARA is also the *Xanthoxylon Clava Herculis*.

FAGONIA (*Bot.*) a genus of plants, Class 10 *Decandria*, Order 1 *Monogynia*.
Generic Character. CAL. *perianth* five-leaved.—COR. *petals* five.—STAM. *filaments* ten; *anthers* roundish.—PIST. *germ* five; *style* awl-shaped; *stigma* simple.—PER. *capsule* round; *seeds* ovate.
Species. The species are perennials, as the *Fagonia Cretica*, seu *Trifolium*, the Cretan Fagonia, native of Candia.—*Fagonia Arabica*, Arabian Fagonia.—*Fagonia Hispanica*, Spanish Fagonia. *Clus. Hist.; Bauh. Hist.; Bauh. Pin.; Ger. Herb.; Park. Theat; Raii Hist. Plant.; Tourn. Inst.*

FAGOPY'RUM, the *Polygonium divaricatum* of Linnæus.

FA'GOT (*Ecc.*) a badge which was formerly worn on the sleeve of the upper garments by such persons in the Romish church as had recanted and abjured heresy.

FAGOTS (*Mil.*) French for the men who were hired by the officers to muster, in order to make a false return of companies that were not completed.

FAGOTTI'NO (*Mus.*) or *Fagotto*, Italian for the bassoon.

FAGRÆ'A (*Bot.*) a genus of plants, Class 5 *Pentandria*, Order 1 *Monogynia*.
Generic Character. CAL. *perianth* one-leaved.—COR. one-petalled.—STAM. *filaments* five; *anthers* ovate.—PIST. *germ* superior; *style* filiform; *stigma* peltate.—PER. *berry* ovate; *seeds* smooth.
Species. The single species is a shrub, as the *Fagræa zeylanica*, native of Ceylon.

FA'GUS (*Bot.*) a genus of plants, Class 21 *Monoecia*, Order 8 *Polyandria*.
Generic Character. CAL. *perianth* one-leaved.—COR. none.—STAM. *filaments* many; *anthers* oblong.—PIST. *germ* covered with the calyx; *styles* three; *stigmas* simple.—PER. *capsule* large; *seed* nuts, one or two.
Species. The species are trees, as—*Fagus Castanea*, seu *Castanea*, Common Chesnut Tree,—*Fagus sylvatica*, Common Beech Tree.—*Fagus ferruginea*, American Beech Tree. *Bauh. Hist.; Bauh. Pin.; Ger. Herb.; Park. Theat. Botan.*

FAGUS is also the *Fagus betulus* of Linnæus.

FAIDA (*Law*) malice or deadly feud. *Leg. H. 1. c. 88.*

FAI'LING *of Record* (*Law*) is when the defendant having a day to prove a matter by record, he fails, or else brings in such an one as is no bar to action.

FA'ILLIS (*Her.*) a term used to denote some failure or fraction in an ordinary, as if it were broken or a splinter taken from it.

FA'ILLON (*Mil.*) a kind of standard formerly made use of in the army for assembling the baggage.

FA'ILURE (*Com.*) an unsuccessful termination of a man's mercantile dealings.

FAINT *action* (*Law*) is such an one, as, that though the words of the writ are true, yet, for certain causes, there is no title to recover thereby. *Co. Lit.* 361.

FAINT *vision* (*Opt.*) is when a few rays make up one pencil, which, though it may be distinct, yet is obscure.

FAINTS (*Chem.*) the weak spirituous liquor that runs off from the still after the proof spirit is taken away.

FAIR (*Mar.*) an epithet applied to different things, as "A fair wind," in opposition to "A foul wind."—Ropes are said to "lea *fair*," when they suffer little friction in a pulley.—A *Fair-Curve*, in delineating ships, is a winding line whose shape is varied according to the part of the ship it is intended to describe.—*Fair way of a Channel* is the path of a narrow bay, river, or harbour, in which ships usually go in their passage up and down.

FAIR MAID OF FRANCE (*Bot.*) the *Ranunculus aconitifolius* of Linnæus, a perennial.

FAIT (*Law*) a deed or writing lawfully executed, to bind the parties thereto.—*Fait enrolle* is a deed of bargain and sale.

FA'ITOURS (*Law*) a name for vagabonds or idle livers, mentioned in statute 7 *R.* 2, c. 5.

FAKE (*Mar.*) one roll of a cable or rope which is coiled round.

FA'KIR (*Theol.*) or *Faqueer*, a sort of dervises or Mahometan monks.

FA'LA (*Ant.*) a high tower made of wood. *Fest. de Verb. Signif.*

FA'LANG (*Archæol.*) a jacket or close coat.

FALA'RICA (*Ant.*) a spear bound with wild fire, to shoot out against a tower or any other object. *Non. l.* 18, c. 18; *Ser. in Virg. Æn. l.* 9; *Veget. l.* 4, c. 18.

FALCA'DE (*Man.*) a horse is said to make *falcades* when he throws himself upon his haunches two or three times, as in very quick curvets.

FALCA'RIA (*Bot.*) the *Sium falcaria* of Linnæus.

FALCA'TA (*Bot.*) the *Medicago annata* of Linnæus.

FA'LCATED (*Astron.*) one of the phases of the moon, vulgarly called horned, when she appears in the form of a crescent, like a *falx*, sickle, or reaping hook.

FALCATU'RA (*Archæol.*) one day's mowing performed by an inferior tenant, as a custom for any service due to his lord.

FA'LCHION (*Mil.*) a kind of sword turned up somewhat like a hook.

FA'LCIFORM PROCESS (*Anat.*) a process of the *dura*

mater, in the form of a *falx,* or sickle, that arises from the *crista galli,* and separates the two hemispheres of the brain.

FALCINE'LLUS (*Orn.*) a sort of heron, so called from the crookedness of its beak.

FA'LCO (*Orn.*) a genus of birds of the Order *Accipitres.*
Generic Character. Bill hooked, the base covered with a cere; *head* covered with close-set feathers; *tongue* bifid.
Species. This genus comprehends the Eagle, Osprey, Kite, Falcon, Buzzard, Hawk, &c. as the—*Falco chrysactos,* the Golden Eagle.—*Falco fulvus,* the Ring-tailed Eagle.—*Falco ferox,* the Fierce Eagle.—*Falco Harpyga,* the Crested Eagle, which inhabits South America, and is said to be able to cleave a man's skull at a stroke.—*Falco ossifragus,* the Osprey.—*Falco milvus,* the Kite.—*Falco communis,* the Common Falcon.—*Falco nisus,* the Sparrow Hawk.—*Falco palumbarius,* the Goshawk.—*Falco buteo,* the Buzzard.—*Falco gyrfalco,* the Gyrfalcon.—*Falco candidus,* the White Gyrfalcon.—*Falco cyaneus,* the Hen Harrier.—*Falco lanarius,* the Lanner.—*Falco tinnunculus,* the Kestril.—*Falco subbuteo,* the Hobby.—*Falco esalon,* the Merlin.

FA'LCON (*Orn.*) a bird, nearly allied to the hawk, which is about the size of a raven, and is capable of being trained for sport, in which it was formerly much employed. The species are classed under the genus *Falco,* in the Linnean system, together with the Eagle, the Hawk, &c. [vide *Falco*]

FALCON (*Gunn.*) a small piece of cannon formerly so called.

FALCON (*Her.*) These birds are usually represented with bells on their legs, and when decorated with hood, bells, virols, or rings, and leishes, they are said in blazon to be hooded, belled, jessed, and leished, as in the annexed figure. He beareth "*Azure,* a falcon volant *argent,* armed, jessed, and belled *or,* within a bordure *ermine;* name Fairbourne."

FA'LCONER (*Falcon.*) one who looks after and trains hawks.

FA'LCONET (*Gunn.*) a small sort of falcon or gun so called.

FA'LCONRY, the art of keeping and training hawks.

FA'LDA (*Archæol.*) a sheep-fold.

FA'LDÆ CURSUS (*Archæol.*) a sheep-walk, or feed for sheep.

FA'LDAGE (*Archæol.*) the privilege which, anciently, lords reserved to themselves, of setting up folds in any fields of their manors, for the better manuring them; and this not only with their own but their tenants' sheep.

FA'LDE-FEY (*Law*) or *Faldfee,* a fee or rent paid for the privilege of folding.

FA'LDWORTH (*Archæol.*) a person of such an age that he may be reckoned of some decennary.

FA'LERA (*Falcon.*) a disease in hawks.

FA'LERÆ (*Archæol.*) the tackle or furniture of a cart or wain. *Mon. Angl.* tom. 2, p. 256.

FALE'SIA (*Archæol.*) a great rock, bank, or hill, by the sea side.

FA'LKIA (*Bot.*) a genus of plants, Class 5 *Pentandria,* Order 2 *Digynia.*
Generic Character. CAL. *perianth* one-leaved.—COR. one-petalled.—STAM. *filaments* five; *anthers* ovate.—PIST. *germs* four; *styles* two; *stigma* capitate.—PER. none; *seeds* four.
Species. The single species is the *Falkia repens,* Creeping Falkia, a perennial, native of the Cape of Good Hope.

FALL (*Phy*) the descent or natural motion of bodies towards the centre of the earth.

FALL (*Mil.*) a term equivalent to a surrender when a town ceases to be able to hold out any longer.

FALL (*Mar.*) this term is used in some sea phrases, as—"The *fall* of a tackle," the loose end of a tackle.—" To *fall* a-stern," to be driven backwards.—" To *fall* down," to sail down a river or towards its opening.—" To *fall* in,"
to meet with a ship.—" To *fall* off," i. e. not to keep so near the wind as she should do.—" *Fall* not off!" a command to the steersman to keep the ship near the wind.—*Land-Fall,* when the ship makes or sees land.—*Fall,* among ship-builders, is when one part of the ship has risings above the others.

FA'LLING-SICKNESS (*Med.*) vide *Epilepsia.*

FA'LLING OFF (*Mar.*) the movement or direction of the ship to leeward of the point whither it was lately directed. [vide *Fall*] Also the angle contained between her nearest approach to the direction of the wind and her farthest distance from it.

FALLO'PIAN TUBES (*Anat.*) two ducts, so named from Fallopius, their discoverer, arising on each side the fundus of the uterus, and extended to the ovaries. They are of great use in the process of conception.

FA'LLOW (*Husband.*) a piece of land laid up or left to remain untilled for a time; the act of so leaving land is called *fallowing.*

FALLOW *Deer* (*Zool.*) a species of deer, the *Cervus dama* of Linnæus, having horns branched, recurved, and compressed. This species is the most common in Europe, particularly in England, where it forms one of the ornaments of the park.

FALLOW-FINCH (*Orn.*) or *White-Ear,* a sort of bird, the *Motacilla œnanthe* of Linnæus.

FALLS (*Mar.*) vide *Fall.*

FALSE *Quarter* (*Vet.*) a rift, or crack in the hoof of a horse, which is an unsound quarter, seeming as if it were a piece put in, and not entire.

FALSE *conception* (*Med.*) the formation of a shapeless mass of flesh, &c. in the *uterus.*

FALSE *flower* (*Bot.*) a flower which does not seem to produce any fruit.

FALSE *diamond* (*Min.*) a diamond counterfeited with glass.

FALSE *arms* (*Her.*) those wherein the fundamental rules of heraldry are violated, as if metal be put upon metal, colour upon colour.

FALSE *imprisonment* (*Law*) the trespass of imprisoning a man without lawful cause; also the name of the writ brought upon the commission of such a trespass. *False claim* is when a man claims more than his due.

FALSE (*Mil.*) an epithet employed on many occasions; as *False alarm,* an alarm given either through ignorance, or with the view of trying the vigilance of the men.—*False attack,* a feigned attack made for the purpose of diverting the enemy from the real point of attack.—*False muster,* that in which men, not actually enlisted, pass for soldiers.

FALSE *roof* (*Carpent.*) that part of a house which is between the roof and the covering.

FALSE *bray* (*Fort.*) a small mound of earth, four fathoms wide, erected on a level round the foot of the rampart on the side which is towards the field, bordered with a parapet to defend the moat.

FALSE (*Mar.*) an epithet in sea phrases; as a *False keel,* a second keel sometimes put under the first to make it deeper.—*False stem,* a second stem fastened to one that is too flat.—*False post,* a piece of timber fixed on the aft part of the stern post to make good a deficiency therein.

FALSI *crimen* (*Law*) fraudulent concealment, in the Civil Law, or subornation with design to darken or hide the truth, so as to make things appear otherwise than what they really are.

FA'LSIFY (*Law*) to prove a thing to be false; as " To *falsify* a record," " To *falsify* a verdict," " To *falsify* recovery."

TO FALSIFY *a thrust* (*Fenc.*) to make a feigned pass.

FA'LSING *of Dooms* (*Law*) an old term, in the Scotch Law, for an appeal.

FA'LSO *judicio* (*Law*) a writ which lies for false judgment given in the county, hundred, court baron, or other courts that are not of record.—*Falso returno Brevium*, a writ which lies against a sheriff for making false returns of writs. *Reg. Jud.* 43.

FA'MA *clamosa* (*Law*) a judicial procedure of the church of Scotland, wherein a ground of action is laid before a presbytery, against one of its members, independently of any regular complaint by a particular accuser.

FAMI'LIA (*Law*) signified all the servants that were under one master, or that portion of land which was sufficient to support one family.

FAMI'LIARS (*Ecc.*) officers of the Inquisition, who assist in the apprehension of such as are accused. They are so called because they assist the inquisitor, and belong to his family.

FA'MILY (*Archæol.*) a hide of ploughed land.

FAMILY of Curves (*Math.*) a congeries of several curves of different orders or kinds, all which are defined by the same equation, but in a different manner, according to their different orders.

FAMILY (*Bot.*) a term applied by Linnæus to plants naturally allied to each other; he divides the vegetable kingdom into seven families; namely, 1. *Fungi*; 2. *Algæ*; 3. *Musci*, or Mosses; 4. *Filices*, or Ferns; 5. *Gramina*, or Grasses; 6. *Palmæ*, or Palms; 7. *Plantæ*, or plants, including all that are not in the foregoing families.

FAN (*Her.*) vide *Winnowing Basket*.

FA'NAM (*Com.*) a small coin in India, both of gold and silver; the former of which is valued at about 6d., and the latter at 4½d.

FANA'TICI (*Ant.*) a sort of enthusiasts among the Romans, so called because they spent most of their time, *fanis*, in the temples. They pretended to revelations and inspirations, and, in their frantic fits, they committed many extravagances.

FANAU'X (*Mil.*) French for lights at the top of a high tower at the entrance of a sea-port.

FA'NCIES (*Mus.*) lively little airs.

FANDA'NGO (*Mus.*) a dance much used in Spain, the air of which is lively, and much resembling the hornpipe.

FA'NG-TOOTH (*Her.*) has been sometimes borne as a charge in the escutcheon.

FA'NGOT (*Com.*) a quantity of wares, as raw silk, &c. containing from one to two hundred weight, three quarters.

FA'NION (*Mil.*) in the Italian *Ganfonne*, a particular standard, which was carried formerly in front of the ordinary belonging to a brigade in the French service.

FANNA'TIO (*Archæol.*) a term used, in the forest laws, for the fawning, or bringing forth young hinds.

FA'NNEL (*Ecc.*) a sort of ornament like a scarf, worn by a mass priest on the left arm when he officiates.

FA'NNERS (*Husband.*) a machine for winnowing corn.

FA'NO (*Com.*) a small weight used at Goa, and other places in the East Indies, equal to two Venetian carats.

FA'NON (*Com.*) a coin, current on the coast of Malabar, worth about five-pence English money.

FAN-PALM (*Bot.*) the *Chamærops humilis* of Linnæus.

FANTA'SIA (*Mus.*) a kind of air in which the composer is not confined to such strict rules as in ordinary cases.

FAONA'TIO (*Archæol.*) vide *Fannatio*.

FAPE'SMO (*Log.*) the fourth imperfect mood of the first figure of a categorical syllogism.

FARA'ND-MAN (*Archæol.*) a merchant stranger, to whom, according to the practice of Scotland, justice ought to be done with all expedition, that his business and journey be not hindered.

FARATE'LLE (*Com.*) a weight, made use of in some parts of India, equal to two pounds Lisbon.

FARCE (*Lit.*) a sort of mock comedy, which contains much of grimace and buffoonery.

FA'RCES (*Cook.*) meat chopped small and well spiced, &c. fit for a stuffing.

FARCIMINA'LIS *tunica* (*Anat.*) a coat pertaining to a child in the womb, which receives the urine from the womb; it is so called because, in many animals, it resembles a gut pudding. The existence of this membrane in the human subject has been denied.

FA'RCIN (*Vet.*) a sort of mange among horses and oxen.

FARCTU'RA (*Med.*) the stuffing any exenterated animal or fruit with medicinal ingredients.

FA'RCTUS (*Bot.*) stuffed, an epithet for a leaf; *folium farctum* is a leaf of pith, or pulp, in opposition to *tubulosum*, tubular or hollow; it is also applied to a stem and a pericarp.

FA'RCY (*Vet.*) a disease in horses something similar to a leprosy.

FA'RDEL *of land* (*Archæol.*) the fourth part of a yard of land.

FA'RDINGALE (*Cus.*) a hoop made of whalebone, by which females formerly used to spread out their petticoats.

FA'RDING *Deal* (*Archæol.*) the fourth part of an acre of land.

FARE (*Com.*) money paid for the passage of a person in any vehicle, either by land or water.

FA'RFARA (*Bot.*) the *Fusselago farfara* of Linnæus.

FARI'NA (*Nat.*) signifies literally meal or flour; but is also applied to the pulverulent and glutinous part of wheat, and other seeds, before it is ground as well as after.

FARINA'GIUM (*Archæol.*) toll of meal or flour. *Ordin. Insul. de Jersey.* 17 *Edw.* 2.

FA'RLEU (*Archæol.*) a duty of sixpence paid to the lord of the manor of West Slapton, in Devonshire, in the western parts; *farleu* being the best thing generally, as *heriot* is the best beast.

FARLINGA'RII (*Archæol.*) whoremongers and adulterers.

FARM (*Law*) a large messuage of land taken by lease under a certain yearly rent payable by the tenant.

FA'RMER (*Law*) he who holds a farm, and is a tenant or lessee thereof.

FARRA'GO (*Husband.*) a mixture of several sorts of grain sown in the same plot of ground, or afterwards mingled together.

FA'RREA *Nubes* (*Med.*) vide *Ptyriasis*.

FA'RRIER (*Vet.*) signifies literally one who professes to shoe horses, but is also used for a horse doctor, now called *veterinary surgeon*.

FARRIER'S *Company* (*Her.*) consists of a master, three wardens, twenty-four assistants, and thirty-nine on the livery. Their armorial ensigns are, as in the annexed figure, *argent*, three horseshoes, *sable*. The Farriers trace their origin to one Henry de Ferrarius, or Ferrers, who was farrier, or master of the horse, to William the Conqueror, from whom he received the Honour of Tutbury, in Staffordshire.

TO FA'RROW (*Husband.*) to bring forth pigs.

FARSETIA (*Bot.*) the *Cheiranthus farsetia* of Linnæus.

FA'RTHELLING *lines* (*Mar.*) small lines made fast to all the top-sails, top-gallant sails, and the mizzen-yard arm.

FA'RTHING (*Com.*) in Saxon ꝼeoꞃðlinᵹ, or ꝼeoꞃðinᵹ, i. e. ꝼouꞃðlinᵹ; the fourth part of a Saxon penny; there were also farthings of gold, which were the fourth part of a noble, or twenty-pence of silver.

FA'SCES (*Ant.*) bundles of rods bound round the helve of a hatchet, which were carried before the consuls as the *insignia* of their office. [vide *Consuls*]

FA'SCETS (*Mech.*) irons, used in a glass manufactory, which are thrust into the necks of bottles to convey them to the annealing tower.

FA'SCIA (*Surg.*) a swathe, or long bandage.

FASCIA (*Anat.*) the name of any aponeurotic expansion

of muscles which binds parts together.—*Fascia lata*, a thick and strong tendinous expansion sent off from the back, and from the tendons of the *glutei*, and adjacent muscles, to surround the muscles of the thigh.

Fascia (*Archit.*) a flat member, of which there are three in the architrave, having a great breadth and small projecture. *Vitruv.* l. 3, c. 3; *Bald. Lex. Vitruv.*

FA'SCIÆ (*Astron.*) vide *Belts*, and *Astronomy*.

FASCIA'LIS (*Anat.*) an epithet for a muscle which moves the leg.

FASCIA'TION (*Surg.*) a binding up with swaddling bands.

FASCICULA'RIS (*Bot.*) fascicular, an epithet for a sort of tuberous roots with knobs collected in bundles, as in *Pæonia*.

FASCICULA'TUS (*Bot.*) fascicled, an epithet for leaves growing in bundles or bunches from the same point.

FASCI'CULUS (*Bot.*) fascicle, a diminutive of *fascis*, a bundle; a species of inflorescence in which several upright, parallel, fastigiate, approximating flowers, are collected together. [vide *Botany*]

FA'SCINES (*Fort.*) small branches, trees, or bavins bound up in bundles, which, mixed with earth, serve to fill up ditches.

FA'SCIOLA (*Ent.*) the Gourd-Worm, or Fluke, a sort of worms, of the order *Intestina*, having a flattish body, with an aperture, or pore at the head, and generally another at a distance beneath. These are hermaphrodite and oviparous animals, which are generally found in the intestines of other animals.

FA'SHION pieces (*Mar.*) in French *cornières*; the aftmost or hindmost pieces of timber which terminate the breadth and form the shape of the stern.

FAST (*Ecc.*) an abstinence from food upon a religious account.

FA'STI (*Ant.*) the Roman calendar, in which were set down all days of feasts, pleadings, games, ceremonies, the names of their officers, and all other public concerns throughout the year.

Auson. l. 1, epig. 1.

> *Ignota ne sint tibi tempora Romæ*
> *Regibus, et patrum ducta sub imperiis,*
> *Digessi Fastos, et nomina præpetis ævi*
> *Sparsa jacent Latiam siqua per historiam.*

Cic. pro Sext. c. 14, &c.; *Val. Max.* l. 7, c. 2; *Liv.* l. 9, c. 18, &c.; *Tacit. Annal.* l. 1, c. 15; *Isid. Orig.* l. 5, c. 18; *Panvin. Fast.* l. 1.—*Fasti Dies*, days on which pleadings were carried on. [vide *Dies*]

FASTIGIA'TUS (*Bot.*) from *fastigium*, the pointed roof of a house; an epithet for a stem, peduncles, umbel, &c.; as *caulis fastigiatus*, *pedunculi fastigiati*, and *umbella fastigiata*.

FASTI'GIUM (*Archit.*) vide *Pediment*.

FA'STING Men (*Archæol.*) bondsmen, or pledges, who answered for the peaceable demeanor of their companions.

FA'STNESS (*Fort.*) a strong hold naturally fortified by the bogs, &c. of the surrounding country.

FAT (*Anat.*) *Adeps*, a concrete oily matter contained in the cellular membrane of animals, of a white or yellowish colour, with little or no smell nor taste.

FAT (*Mar.*) an epithet which is equivalent to broad; thus, if the trussing in or tuck of a ship's quarter under water be deep, they say she has a fat quarter.

FAT (*Mech.*) vide *Vat*.

FATHEMITES (*Polit.*) the descendants of Mahomet, in the female line, from his daughter Fatima.

FA'THER (*Ecc.*) a title given to bishops, as the Right Reverend Father in God; also to the principal writers among the primitive Christians. This epithet is likewise applied to priests in the Romish Church, as a Father Confessor.

FATHER (*Theol.*) the first Person in the Holy Trinity.

FATHER-LA'SHER (*Ich.*) a voracious fish, the *Cottus Scorpius* of Linnæus, inhabiting the shores of Greenland and Newfoundland, and having spines on its tail, with which it lashes the sharks, and other predacious fish that offer it any molestation.

FATHER-LO'NG-LEGS (*Ent.*) a well-known insect, the *Tipula pectinicornis* of Linnæus, which is remarkable for the length of its legs.

FA'THOM (*Com.*) in Saxon *fathom*, a measure of six feet.

FA'UCES (*Anat.*) Isthmion, or Amphibronchia, a cavity behind the tongue, arch, uvula, and tonsils, from which the pharynx and larynx proceed. It is commonly termed in Greek φάρυγξ. [vide *Pharynx*]

FA'UCHION (*Mil.*) vide *Falchion*.

FAU'CON (*Orn.*) vide *Falcon*.

FAULX (*Mil.*) French for an instrument very similar to a scythe, which was used in fortifications to prevent an enemy from scaling the walls of a besieged town.

FAUNA'LIA (*Ant.*) festivals celebrated, in honour of Faunus, on the Ides of February, and on the Nones of December, of which Horace gives a description in his ode to Faunus. *Hor.* l. 3, od. 18, v. 10.

> *Cum tibi nonæ redeunt Decembres.*

Ovid. Fast. l. 2, v. 193.

> *Idibus agrestis fumant altaria Fauni*
> *Hic ubi discretas insula rumpit aquas.*

Gyrald. Syntag. Deor. l. 18; *Jun. Fast. apud Græv. Thes. Ant. Rom.* tom. viii. &c.

FAVO'NIUS (*Ant.*) the western breeze, or zephyr, which, according to Pliny, blew from Crete. *Plin.* l. 4, c. 12.

FAUSETUM (*Archæol.*) a faucet or flute.

FAUSSE *braye* (*Fort.*) a low rampart. [vide *False*]

FAUSSE EQUERRE (*Mech.*) an instrument in the shape of a square or rule, which describes angles that are not straight.—*Fausse-lance*, a wooden piece of ordnance, vulgarly called a sham-gun.

FAUSSE-MARCHE (*Mil.*) a feigned march.—*Fausse attaque*, a false attack.

FAUTEA'U (*Mil.*) French for a sort of battering ram formerly used.

FAU'TOR (*Law*) a favourer or abettor.

FA'VUS (*Med.*) a sort of achor, or ulcer, resembling the favus, or honeycomb.

FAUX (*Bot.*) jaws, or throat; the opening of the tube of the corolla.

FAWN (*Zool.*) a young deer; a buck or doe of the first year.

To FAY (*Mech.*) to fit any two pieces of wood, so as to join close together.

FAYA'LL (*Com.*) an imaginary coin, valued by some as the pistole of France, or ten livres.

FAYE'NCE (*Com.*) a name in France for all sorts of crockery ware which come from China.

FA'YTOURS (*Law*) vide *Faitours*.

FE' (*Ecc.*) Spanish for faith, whence the *Auto de Fé*, or act of faith, i. e. the execution of heretics by the Spanish inquisition.

FE'AL (*Archæol.*) i. e. trusty; an epithet for the tenants who were said to be feal and leal, i. e. faithful and loyal to their lord. *Spelm. de Parliament*. 59.—*Feal and Divot*, a right in Scotland similar to the right of Tarbury in England for fuel, &c.

FEAL-*dyke* (*Husband.*) a cheap sort of fence in Scotland made of feal, or sod.

FE'ALTY (*Law*) changed from *fidelitas*; an oath taken at the admittance of a tenant, by which he binds himself to be faithful to his lord.

FEAR-NOUGHT (*Mar.*) in French *frise*, a particular sort

of thick woollen stuff much used in ships for lining port-holes, &c.

FEAST (*Ecc.*) anniversary times of feasting and thanksgiving, such as Christmas, Easter, Whitsuntide, &c. Feasts are either moveable or immoveable. — The *immoveable Feasts* are those which are celebrated on the same day of the year, as *Christmas-Day*, the *Circumcision*, *Epiphany*, *Candlemas*, *Lady-Day*, *All Saints*, the several days of the *Apostles*, &c.—The *moveable Feasts* are those that are not confined to the same day of the year, as *Easter*, and all that are governed by it, as *Palm Sunday*, *Good Friday*, *Ash-Wednesday*, *Sexagesima*, *Ascension-Day*, *Pentecost*, and *Trinity Sunday*.

FEATHER (*Chem.*) the constituent parts of feathers are similar to those of hair, consisting chiefly of albumen, but with little or no gelatin.

FEATHER (*Mil.*) an ornamental mark worn by officers and soldiers on their caps and hats; the *hackle feather*, which is the round feather taken from the fowl in its natural state, is worn by subalterns; the *flush feather*, a straight smooth feather worn by officers on the staff.

FEATHER (*Mar.*) *To cut a feather* is said of a ship when she makes the water foam before her.

FEATHER-*edged Boards* (*Carpent.*) boards that have one edge thinner than the other.

FEATHER (*Man.*) a row of hair turned back and raised on the neck of a horse, which forms a mark just like the blade of a sword.

FEATHER (*Bot.*) a name given to some plants, as the — Prince's Feather, the *Amaranthus hypochondriacus* of Linnæus.—Feathered Columbine, the *Thalictrum aquilegifolium*; the Stipa, a sort of perennial grass.

FEATHER is also another name for the *pappus*, or down. [vide *Pappus*]

FEATHERED (*Bot.*) the same as plumose. [vide *Plumosus*]

FEATHERS (*Her.*) or Prince's Feathers, the name given to the ostrich feathers which adorn the cognizance of the Prince of Wales.

FEBRI'CULA (*Med.*) a diminutive of *febris*, a fever, implying a slight degree of symptomatic fever.

FE'BRIFUGA (*Bot.*) the plant Fever-few, or lesser centaury.

FE'BRIFUGE (*Med.*) from *febris*, a fever, and *fugo*, to drive away; a name for medicines which possess the property of abating the violence of a fever.

FE'BRUA (*Ant.*) an expiatory sacrifice for the ghosts of the dead; a sort of purification.
Ovid. Fast. l. 2, v. 19.

Februa Romani dixere piamina patres
Nunc quoque dant verbo plurima signa fidem.

That which was purified by this sacrifice was called *februatum*, and the month in which this purification took place was called *Februarius*. *Cic. de Leg.* l. 2, c. 21; *Varr. de Lat. Ling.* l. 5; *Plut. in Num.*; *Aurel. Vict. de Vir. illust.* c. 3; *Auson.* eid. 8; *Macrob. Sat.* l. 1, c. 13; *Sidon.* l. 2, ep. 14; *Ursat. de Not. Roman. apud Græv. Thes. Antiq. Rom.* tom. 2, p. 714.

FE'BRUARY (*Chron.*) *Februarius*, the second month in the year, so called from the expiatory sacrifices, *Februa*. [vide *Februa*]

FECIA'LES (*Ant.*) certain Roman priests instituted by Numa Pompilius, who were selected from the best families for the purpose of assisting in all treaties of peace and declarations of war. *Varr. de Ling. Lat.* l. 4, c. 15; *Liv.* l. 1, c. 24; *Plin.* l. 22, c. 2; *Aurel. Vict. de Vir. illust.* c. 5.

FE'CULA (*Med.*) a white mealy powder, which subsides and gathers at the bottom of the juices or liquors of divers roots.

FE'CULÆ (*Astron.*) certain spots which are occasionally observable in the disk of the sun.

FEE (*Law*) in Saxon feoh, modern Latin *feudum*, is in all probability derived from, or allied to the German *Vieh*, cattle, because the principal right of property was vested originally in cattle. The word fee is used in several senses, namely, for the compass or circuit of a lordship or manor, as "The lord of the fee," &c.; for a perpetual right incorporeal, as to have the keeping of prisons, &c. *in fee*; also a rent and annuity granted to one, and his heirs, which is a *fee personal*: but the ordinary use of the term is to denote the right which a man has in land, or some immoveable thing, to use the same, and take the profits of it for himself and his heirs for ever. This is called the *fee-simple*, in distinction from the *fee-tail*, which is a limited sort of fee, or an inheritance whereof a man is seised to him and the heirs of his body limited at the will of the donor. A fee-tail is *general* where land is given to a man and the heirs of his body, and *special* where a man and his wife are seised of land to them and the heirs of their two bodies. This latter is also called a *fee expectant*. *Bract.* l. 2, c. 5; *Kitch.* 153; *Co. Lit.* c. 1, &c.; *Old Nat. Brev.* 41.—*Fee-farm*, *feodi firma*, or fee-farm rent, is when the lord, upon creation of the tenancy, reserves to himself and his heirs the rent, or something equivalent.

FEED (*Mil.*) a certain proportion of corn and hay given to the cavalry. A *short feed* is a portion less than the regulated quantity.— *Heavy-horse-feed*, a larger proportion given to the heavy dragoons, in distinction from —*Light-horse-feed*, which is given to the hussars and the light horse.

FEE'DER (*Mech.*) a cut or channel, sometimes called a carriage or catch drain, by which a stream or supply of water is brought into a canal.

TO FEEL (*Man.*) is said in certain cases of the movements of a horse, as "To *feel* a horse on the hand," i. e. to observe that the will of the horse is, in one's hand. "To *feel* a horse upon the haunches," to observe that he plies or bends them.

FEE'LERS (*Ent.*) organs fixed to the mouth of insects, generally less than the *antennæ*, and often jointed.

FEES (*Law*) certain perquisites allowed to officers in the administration of justice, as a recompence for their labour and trouble.

FEIGNED ACTION (*Law*) an action which is brought to try the merits of any question. It is otherwise called a *feigned issue*.

FEINT (*Mus.*) a semi-tone, the same as the *Diesis*.

FEINT (*Fenc.*) a show of making a thrust at one part that you may make it at another with more facility.

FEINT (*Mil.*) a mock attack, generally made to conceal the true one.

FEL (*Med.*) Bile.

FE'LAGUS (*Archæol.*) a friend or companion; one who was bound in the decennary for the good behaviour of another, i. e. *quasi fide cum eo ligatus*.

FELA'PTON (*Log.*) a technical term for one of the modes in the third figure of syllogisms, which consists of a universal negative, a universal affirmative, and a particular negative, as

Fe No brutes have a sense of religion:
Lap All brutes are animals: *ergo*,
Ton Some animals have no sense of religion.

FE'LFELTAUIL (*Bot.*) the *Cynachium viminale* of Linnæus.
FELE *homagers* (*Law*) or *Feal Homagers*; faithful subjects.
FE'LIS (*Zool.*) a genus of animals of the order *Feræ*.
Generic Character. Fore-teeth intermediate ones equal; grinders three; tongue prickly backwards; claws retractive.

Species. This tribe of animals, comprehended under the names of the Lion, Tiger, Panther, Ounce, Leopard, Tiger-cat, Cat, and Lynx; are temperate in their habits, climb easily, see best at night, alight on their feet when they fall, and suddenly spring on their prey: the females bring forth many young, having eight teats.

FELLI'FLUA *passio* (*Med.*) a name given to the *Cholera morbus.*

FE'LLING *of timber* (*Husband.*) the cutting down trees close by the roots for the purpose of building.

FE'LLOES (*Mech.*) or Fellows, the pieces of wood which joined together by duledges, form the circumference, or circular part of a wheel, which is altogether called the felloes of the wheel.

FELLOW (*Mech.*) vide *Felloes.*

FELLOW (*Cus.*) the member of a college in universities who forms one of the corporate body.

FE'LLOWSHIP (*Arith.*) a rule by which, in divers accounts of divers persons, their several stocks, together with the whole loss and gain being propounded, the loss or gain of each particular person may be discovered. Fellowship is either single or double. *Single Fellowship,* or *Fellowship without time,* is the case in which the times of continuance of the shares of partners are not considered, they being all the same.—*Double Fellowship,* or *Fellowship with time,* is that in which the times of the stocks' continuing are considered, because they are not all the same. In this case the shares of the gain or loss must be proportional, both to the several shares of the stock, and to the times of their continuance, and consequently proportional to the products of the two.

FE'LO DE SE (*Law*) one who commits a felony by the act of self-murder.

FE'LONY (*Law*) any offence that is in degree next to petty treason, such as murder, burglary, rape, &c.

FE'LSPAR (*Min.*) a siliceous mineral found mostly in mountains, in solid masses or crystallized.

FELT-GRAIN (*Carpent.*) the grain of cut timber that runs transversely to the annular rings or plates.

FE'LTING (*Carpent.*) the splitting of timber by the *felt-grain.*

FE'LTRE (*Mil.*) a piece of defensive armour, which was a kind of cuirass made of wool well pressed and dipped in vinegar to resist cuts from weapons.

FELU'CCA (*Mar.*) a little open vessel with six oars that is much used in the Mediterranean.

FE'LWORT (*Bot.*) a species of the *Gentiana* of Linnæus.

FE'MALE *screw* (*Mech.*) a screw, the spiral thread of which is cut in the cavity of a cylinder; it is frequently called the *nut.*

FEMALE *flower* (*Bot.*) *femineus flos,* a flower having pistils or stigmas without stamens, or at least anthers.—Female Plant, *Femina planta,* a plant which has female flowers only.—Female Fern, the *Pteris aquilina* of Linnæus.

FEME (*Law*) a woman, as *Feme couvert,* a married woman; *Feme sole,* an unmarried or single woman.

FE'MININE *planets* (*Astrol.*) such as surpass in the passive qualities, i. e. in moisture and dryness.

FEMININE *Gender* (*Gram.*) a term applied to such nouns as, by their termination, or other sign, denote the female sex.

FEMI'NINUS (*Bot.*) vide *Female.*

FEMORA'LIS *Arteria* (*Anat.*) a continuation of the external iliac along the thigh.

FE'MORIS *os* (*Anat.*) vide *Femur.*

FE'MUR (*Anat.*) the thigh, or thigh-bone, a long cylindrical bone situated between the Pelvis and Tibia. *Ruff. Ephes. de Appell. Part. Corp. hum.* l. 3, c. 5; *Cels.* l. 8, c. 1.

FENCE (*Carpent.*) the guard of a plane, which obliges it to work to a certain horizontal breadth from the arris.

FENCE (*Bot.*) a term used by Dr. Withering for the involucre.

FENCE (*Mil.*) any guard, security, or outwork.

FENCE (*Husband.*) a hedge, or inclosure.

FENCE *month* (*Law*) a month in which, according to the forest laws, it is unlawful to hunt in the forest, because in that month the female deer fawn: this is fifteen days before and after Old Midsummer. *Manw. For. Laws* part. 2, c. 13; *Fleetwood. For. Laws,* 5 *Stat.* 20, *Car.* 2, c. 3.

FE'NCIBLE (*Mil.*) an epithet for regiments which are raised for temporary purposes of defence.

FE'NCING (*Mil.*) the art of using the sword in the attack of an enemy, or the defence of oneself. To this art belong several movements and positions, which are distinguished as follow; namely,—*Appel,* the sudden beat of your blade on the contrary side to that on which you join your adversary, and a quick disengagement to that side again.—*Beating,* parrying with a sudden short beat.—*Battering,* i. e. striking the feeble of your adversary's blade, &c.—*Back-quarte,* a round quarte over the arm. —*Cave,* a tierce on the quarte side, &c.—*Darting,* defending a blow, and darting a thrust forward.—*Feint-forward,* i. e. advancing your point a little from your line and coming to it again.—*Guard,* the posture proper to defend the body from the sword of the antagonist. [vide *Guard*] *Lurching,* i. e. making an opening to invite your adversary to thrust at you, so that you may find an opportunity of getting a *risposte* at him.—*Locking* is to seize your adversary's sword arm by twining your left arm round it after you close your parade, shell to shell, &c. in order to disarm him.—*Flanconade,* the action of dropping the point of your sword under your adversary's hilt, in seizing with force the feeble of his blade, &c.

To FEND (*Mar.*) is the same as defend, or keep off; as "Fend the boat," prevent its striking against any thing; "Fend off," prevent a boat or vessel from running foul of another.

FE'NDERS (*Mar.*) pieces of old cable, ropes, or wooden billets, hung over the sides of a ship, to keep other ships from rubbing against her.

FENE'STRA (*Anat.*) a name for two holes in the barrel of the ear, next the drum; one of which is called *ovalis,* and the other *rotunda.*

FENE'STRATE (*Ent.*) an epithet for the naked transparent spots on the wings of butterflies.

FE'NGELD (*Archæol.*) a tax or imposition for the defence of the realm.

FE'NNEL (*Bot.*) the *Anethum fœniculum;* Fennel Flower, the *Nigella;* Giant's Fennel, the *Fecula,* an annual; Hog's Fennel, the *Peucidanum,* a perennial.

FE'NUGREEK (*Bot.*) the *Trigonella* of Linnæus.

FE'OD (*Law*) or *feud,* i. e. feed, or in fee, the right which the vassal had in land, or some immoveable things of his lord's, to use the same, and take the profits thereof, rendering unto his lord such fee, duties, and services, as belonged to military tenure. *Spem. of Feuds and Tenures.*

FE'ODAL (*Law*) an epithet for what appertains to a fee.

FE'ODARY (*Law*) or *feudatory,* a tenant who holds his lands by feodal service.

FE'ODUM (*Law*) a feod, or fee.—*Feodum militis,* a knight's fee.—*Feodum laicum,* a lay-fee, or land held in fee of a lay-lord.

FEOFFE'E (*Law*) he that is infeoffed, or to whom a feoffment is made.

FE'OFFER (*Law*) the person who puts another in possession.

FE'OFFMENT (*Law*) the gift or grant of honours, castles, manors, messuages, lands, or other corporeal or immoveable things, to another in fee-simple, i. e. to him and his heirs for ever, by the delivery of seisin, and the possession of the thing given. When it is in writing it is called a *deed of feoffment;* and in every feoffment the giver is called the *feoffer,* or *feoffator,* and he that receives by virtue thereof the *feoffee.* The difference between a *feoffer* and a donor is, that the *feoffer* gives in fee-simple, the *donor* in fee-tail. *Litt.* l. 1, c. 6.

FE'OFFOR (*Law*) the same as *Feoffer.*

FE'ORM (*Law*) a certain portion of victuals, and other necessaries, which tenants formerly gave to their thanes, or lords.

FE'RÆ (*Zool.*) the third Order of animals, in the Class *Mammalia,* in the Linnean system, which have from six to ten conic fore-teeth, and one tusk. They comprehend the following genera, namely—*Phoca,* the Seal.—*Canis,* the Dog, the Wolf, the Fox, the Hyæna, and the Jackal.—*Felis,* the Lion, the Tyger, the Panther, the Leopard, the Ounce, the Lynx, and the Cat.—*Viverra,* the Weasel.—*Mustela,* the Otter, the Weasel, the Martin, the Stoat, the Ferret, the Polecat, the Sable, and the Ermine.—*Ursus,* the Bear, the Badger, the Racoon, &c.—*Didelphis,* &c. [vide *Animal Kingdom*]

FERÆ *Naturæ* (*Law*) beasts and birds that are wild, in distinction from those that are tame.

FE'RAL *Signs* (*Astrol.*) an epithet for *Leo* and *Sagittarius,* because they were supposed to have a certain degree of savage influence.

FERA'LIA (*Ant.*) solemnities which were celebrated in February and May, and dedicated to the manes.
Ovid. Fast. l. 2, v. 567.

> *Non tamen hoc ultra, quam quot de mense supersunt*
> *Lucifer, quot habent carmina nostra pedes,*
> *Hanc, quia justa ferunt, dixere Feralia lucem,*
> *Ultima placandis Manibus illa dies.*

They were so called *a ferendo,* i. e. from carrying, because the ancients carried victuals to the sepulchres of their deceased relatives. *Varr. de Lat. Ling.* l. 5, c. 3; *Fest. de Signif. Verb.; Ursat. de Nat. Roman. apud Græv. Thes. Antiq. Rom.* tom. 11, p. 715.

FER (*Her.*) another name for a cross, as *fer de fouchette,* or *croix à fer de fouchette,* i. e. a cross with forked irons at each end.

FER *de Moline* (*Her.*) vide *Moline.*

FE'RCULUM (*Ant.*) a pageant carried about in triumph, representing victories, &c. *Liv.* l. 1, c. 10; *Suet. in Jul.; Plut. in Rom.*

FERDE'LLA *terræ* (*Archæol.*) a fardel of land, or a portion of ten acres.

FE'RDWIT (*Law*) a formulary by which the king pardoned manslaughter in the army. *Fleta.* l. 1.

FERENTA'RII (*Ant.*) a sort of light armed soldiers. *Varr. de Lat. Ling.* l. 6, c. 3; *Fest. de Verb. Signif.; Lips. de Mil. Roman.* p. 271.

FE'RIÆ (*Ant.*) i. e. ἱεραί, sacred; holidays, or certain days that were vacant from labour or business. The *feriæ* were distinguished into different kinds, namely—*Feriæ stativæ,* stated festivals, fixed to certain days of the month.—*Feriæ conceptivæ,* moveable feasts appointed by the magistrates and priests for particular occasions.—*Feriæ imperitivæ,* occasional festivals enjoined by the command of the consuls or other magistrates on the breaking out of a war, or any other public occasion.—*Feriæ denicales,* private festivals kept by families on particular occasions, as the death of a relative, &c.—*Feriæ Latinæ,* festivals kept by the fifty Latin towns on Mount Albanus.—*Feriæ nundinæ,* or *novemdiales,* festivals kept for nine days on the appearance of any prodigy. *Cic. de Leg.* l. 2, c. 22; *Fest. de Verb. Signif.; Liv.* l. 1, c. 31; *Dionys.* l. 4.; *Macrob. Sat.* l. 1, c. 16; *Plut. in Camill.; Aul. Gell.* l. 2, c. 28; *Serv. in Virg. Georg.* l. 1, v. 268; *Ursat. de Not. Rom. apud Græv. Thes. Ant. Rom.* tom. xi. &c. &c.

FE'RIAL *days* (*Law*) vide *Feriæ.*

FE'RINE (*Med.*) ἱερώδης; an epithet properly signifying savage, but when applied to disorders it signifies malignant.

FE'RIO (*Log.*) a mode in the first figure of syllogisms, consisting of a universal negative, a particular affirmative, and a particular negative, as

f E " No men are destitute of reason.
r I Some animals are men; *ergo,*
O Some animals are not destitute of reason."

FE'RISON (*Log.*) a mood of syllogisms in the third figure, consisting of a universal negative, a particular affirmative, and a particular negative, as

f E " No brutes have a sense of religion.
r I Some brutes are animals; *ergo,*
s O n Some animals have not a sense of religion."

FERLINGA'TA *terræ* (*Archæol.*) a quarter or fourth part of a yard of land.

FERM (*Archæol.*) a house and land let by lease.

FE'RMARY (*Archæol.*) the same as *Infirmary.*

FERME *a ferme* (*Man.*) a term used to signify in the same place, without stirring or parting.

FE'RMENT (*Chem.*) any substance which has the property of causing a fermentation in any other body with which it is mixed, as the acid in leaven.

FERMENTA'TION (*Chem.*) the intestine commotion in the small insensible particles of a mixed body without any apparent mechanical cause, usually from the operation of some active acid matter. Chemists after Boerhaave have divided fermentation into the *spirituous fermentation,* which affords ardent spirits; *acetous fermentation,* which produces vinegar or acetic acid; and the *putrid fermentation,* which produces volatile alkali. All fermentation requires a certain degree of fluidity, with the aid of heat and of air.

FERMISO'NA (*Law*) the winter season of killing deer, as *Tempus Pinguedinis* is the summer season.

FERN (*Husband.*) a weed very common in dry and barren places, which is very injurious to the land in which it has once taken root.

FERN (*Bot.*) vide *Filices.*—Male Fern, the *Polypodium filix mas* of Linnæus.—Female Fern, the *Polypodium filix fœmina,* and the *Pteris aquilina.*—Flowering Fern, the *Osmunda.*—Mule Fern, the *Hæmionitis.*—Stone Fern, the *Osmunda crispa.*—Sweet Fern, the *Scandia odorata.*

FE'RNIGO (*Archæol.*) a heath, or waste place.

FERRAME'NTA (*Mech.*) all instruments of iron, particularly those used in surgery.

FERRA'NDUS (*Archæol.*) an iron colour, particularly applied to horses which are now called iron grey.

FERRA'RIA (*Bot.*) a genus of plants, Class 20 *Gynandria,* Order 2 *Diandria.*
Generic Character. CAL. *spathes* two.—COR. *petals* six.—STAM. *filaments* three; *anthers* roundish.—PIST. *germ* inferior; *style* simple; *stigmas* three.—PER. *capsule* oblong; *seeds* roundish.
Species. The species are bulbous, as the—*Ferraria undulata, Iris, Narcissus,* seu *Gladiolus,* Cape Ferraria, native of the Cape of Good Hope.—*Ferraria pavonia,* seu *Flos Tigris,* Mexican Ferraria.

FE'RREOLA (*Bot.*) a genus of plants, Class 22 *Dioecia,* Order 6 *Hexandria.*
Generic Character. CAL. *perianth* one-leaved.—COR. one-petalled.—STAM. *filaments* six; *anthers* oblong.—PIST. *germ* oval; *style* short; *stigma* flat.—PER. *berry* round; *seeds* two.
Species. The single species is a tree, as the *Ferreola buxifolia, Ehretia, Pisonia, Pishanna,* seu *Irumbilli,* native of Coromandel.

FE'RRET (*Zool.*) an animal of the weasel tribe, with red eyes, and a long snout, the *Mustela furo* of Linnæus. This animal is much used in catching rabbits: it procreates twice a year, is gravid six weeks, and brings forth from six to seven young.

FE'RRETS (*Mech.*) the irons with which glass-makers try the melted metal.

FE'RRIAGE (*Com.*) the hire of a ferry-boat, or money paid for a passage over a river, &c.

FERRO-CY'ANATE (*Chem.*) a salt formed by the union of ferrocyanic acid with a salifiable base, as the ferro-cyanate of ammonia, of potash, of soda, &c.

FERROCYA'NIC *acid* (*Chem.*) an acid composed of protoxide of iron and hydrocyanic acid.

FERRUGI'NEUS (*Bot.*) ferruginous; an epithet for a colour of rusty iron.

FE'RRULE (*Mar.*) a small iron hook fixed on the extremities of the yards, booms, &c.

FE'RRUM (*Min.*) iron; a genus of minerals of the Order of Metals, of a bluish grey colour, easily rusting in the air, very hard, tenacious, elastic, sonorous, exceedingly malleable and ductile, &c. [vide *Chemistry*]
  Species. The principal species are, the—*Ferrum nativum*, seu *Nudum*, Native Iron.—*Ferrum selectum*, Magnetic Iron-Stone, or Common Iron Ore.—*Ferrum magnes*, the Magnet-Stone.—*Ferrum hæmatites*, a sort of iron that is not magnetic.—*Ferrum micaceum*, Micaceous Iron Ore not magnetic.

FE'RRY (*Law*) the liberty to have a boat for passage on a frith or river.

FERRY (*Mar.*) a vessel employed for conveying persons and goods over narrow pieces of water; also the place in a river, &c. where persons are carried over.

FE'RRY-MAN (*Com.*) one who keeps a ferry-boat for the conveyance of passengers, &c.

FE'RRÆ (*Med.*) the measles.

FE'RSCHET (*Archæol.*) in Saxon ꝼæɲe-ꝼcoꞇ, the ferriage, or customary payment for being ferried over.

FE'RULA (*Mech.*) an instrument of correction formerly used in schools for striking on the hand.

FERULA (*Bot.*) a genus of plants, Class 5 *Pentandria*, Order 2 *Digynia*.
  Generic Character. CAL. *umbel* universal.—COR. universal.—STAM. *filaments* five; *anthers* simple.—PIST. *germ* inferior; *styles* two; *stigmas* obtuse.—PER. *fruit* oval; *seeds* two.
  Species. The species are perennials, as the—*Ferula communis*, Common Fennel Giant.—*Ferula ferulago*, seu *Ferulago*, Broad-leaved Fennel Giant, native of Sicily. *Ferula nodiflora*, seu *Libanotes*, Knotted Fennel Giant, native of Austria. *Dod. Pempt.*; *Bauh. Hist.*; *Bauh. Pin.*; *Ger. Herb.*; *Park. Theat. Bot.*; *Raii Hist.*; *Tourn. Inst.*

FERULA (*Bot.*) is also the *Bubon Galbanum* of Linnæus.

FERULA'CES (*Bot.*) the *Ferula Galbanifera* of Linnæus.

FE'RULÆ (*Surg.*) splints used about the binding up of a broken leg.

FERULA'GO (*Bot.*) the *Ferula ferulago*.

FERULA'NA (*Bot.*) a species of the *Ferula*.

FE'RVOR *of the Matrix* (*Med.*) a preternatural heat in the womb.

FESCE'NNINA (*Mus.*) a sort of nuptial song, so called from Fescenninum, a town of Campania, where it originated. *Serv. Virg. Æn.* l. 7, v. 695.

FE'SCUE-GRASS (*Bot.*) the *Festuca*, a perennial sort of grass cultivated for cattle.

FESSE (*Her.*) an honourable ordinary which possesses the third and middle part of the field horizontally, as *fig.* 1, "*Argent* a fesse *gules.*" A Fesse is borne under various accidental forms, namely, *Transposed*, i. e. placed higher than the centre, as *fig.* 2, "*Argent* on a fesse transposed a *crescent* between two *stars* of the first." *Couped*, i. e. as it were cut off from the sides, as *fig.* 3, "*Or* a fesse couped azure." *Wreathed* of different tinctures, in French *tortille* as *fig.* 4, "*Argent* a fesse tortille, *azure* and *gules.*"

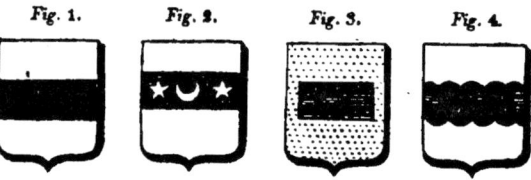

Fig. 1.   Fig. 2.   Fig. 3.   Fig. 4.

The fesse is likewise engrailed, invecked, wavy, indented, dancette, embattled, voided. [vide *Ingrailed*, &c.] When figures are contained within the breadth of the fesse it is said to be charged, or they are said to be *on fesse*, as *fig.* 2. When any figures occupy the place of the fesse they are said to be *in fesse*. [vide *Heraldry*]—*Fesse Point*, the middle point of the escutcheon.—*Party per Fesse*, i. e. parted across the middle of the shield, through the fesse point. [vide *Heraldry*]

FE'STING *Men* (*Archæol.*) vide *Fastingmen*. — *Festing-Penny*, the same as *Earnest-money*.

FESTI'NO (*Log.*) a mood of syllogisms in the second figure, in which the first proposition is a universal negative, the second a particular affirmative, and the third a particular negative, as

 f E s No unbeliever can have salvation through Christ.
 t I   Some Jews are saved through Christ, ergo.
 n O   Some Jews are not unbelievers.

FESTOO'N (*Archit.*) an ornament of carved wood, in manner of wreaths or garlands hanging down, which was anciently used at the gates of temples, &c. [vide *Architecture*, Plate, No. III, (11).

FESTU'CA (*Bot.*) a genus of plants, Class 3 *Triandria*, Order 2 *Digynia*.
  Generic Character. CAL. *glume* upright.—COR. two-valved.—STAM. *filaments* three; *anthers* oblong.—PIST. *germ* turbinate; *styles* two; *stigmas* simple.—PER. none; *seeds* single.
  Species. The species are perennials, as the—*Festuca ovina*, seu *Bromus*, Sheep's-Fescue Grass.—*Festuca rubra*, seu *Gramen*, Red-Fescue Grass.—*Festuca spadicea*, *Anthoxanthum*, seu *Poa*.—*Festuca uniglumis*, seu *Lolium*, Sea-Fescue Grass. *Bauh. Hist.*; *Bauh. Pin.*; *Ger. Herb.*; *Park. Theat. Bot.*; *Tourn. Inst.*

FESTUCA is also the *Agrostis serotina*.

FE'STUCINE (*Min.*) an epithet for a shivery or splintery fracture.

TO FETCH (*Mar.*) a term employed in some sea-phrases, as " To *fetch* to windward of an object," to reach it. " To *fetch* away," to be shaken, or rocked backwards and forwards, as casks, boxes, and the like in a storm. " To *fetch* the pump," to pour a cann of water into the upper part of it, in order to expel the air which is contained between the lower box and the piston.

FE'TLOCK (*Vet.*) a tuft of hair, as large as the hair of the mane in some horses, that grows behind the pastern-joint.—*Fetlock-joint*, the joint at a horse's fetlock, the ankle-joint.

FE'TTERS (*Law*) a sort of irons put on the legs of malefactors.

FETTERED (*Zool.*) an epithet applied to the feet of animals when they are stretched backward, and appear unfit for the purpose of walking, or when they are concealed in the integuments of the abdomen.

FEU (*Law*) a free and gratuitous right to lands, in the Scotch Law, made to one for service performed by him.—*Feu*, or *Feu-holding*, a holding or tenure, whereby the vassal is obliged to pay to the superior a sum of money annually.

—*Feu*, or *Feu annual*, the rent which was due by the *reddendo* of the property of the ground, before the house was built within burgh.—*Feu-duty*, an annual rent or duty paid by the tenant.

FEUD, *deadly* (*Archæol.*) a combination of kindred in former times to revenge the death of any of their blood, on the slayer or his posterity.—*Feud-Bote*, a recompense for engaging in a feud or faction.

FEUD (*Law*) vide *Feod*.

FEUDS (*Law*) a volume of the Civil Law; so called because it contains the customs and services done by a vassal to a superior lord.

FE'VER (*Med.*) *febris*, from *ferveo*, to burn; a disease characterized by an increase of heat, an accelerated pulse, a foul tongue, and an impaired state of several functions of the body. Fevers, as respect their duration, are distinguished into—*Continual fevers*, which have no intermission, but exacerbations that usually come on twice a day, as the synocha, the typhus, &c.—*Intermittent fevers*, which are known by the *cold*, the *hot*, and the *sweating* stages, in succession, attending each paroxysm, and followed by an intermission or remission.—*Intermitting fevers* are subdivided into—*Quotidian fevers*, or agues, the paroxysms of which return in the morning at the interval of twenty-four hours.—*Tertian fevers*, or agues, the paroxysms of which commonly come on at mid-day, at an interval of forty-eight hours.—*Quartan fevers*, the paroxysms of which come on in the afternoon, with an interval of about seventy-two hours. These have also their varieties, into *semi-tertian*, *double-tertian*, or *quartan*, *triple-quartan*, &c. Fevers are moreover distinguished, according to their symptoms, into—*Inflammatory fever*, which is known by an increased heat.—*Typhus fever*, which has a putrid tendency, and but moderate heat.—*Putrid fever*, which arises from the discharge of some putrid purulent matter from some morbid part, as an ulcer in the lungs.—*Hectic fever*, which is slow, durable, extenuating, and emaciating the body by insensible degrees.—*Scarlet fever*, which is attended with an eruption very similar to that of the measles.—*Miliary fever*, one in which rough pustules appear about the whole body.—*Symptomatic fever*, is that which arises, as an accident, or symptom of some disorder, that is antecedent to them.

FE'VER-FEW (*Bot.*) the *Matricaria* of Linnæus.—*Fever-root*, the *Triostium*, a perennial.

FEUILLE'A (*Bot.*) a genus of plants, Class 22 *Dioecia*, Order 5 *Pentandria*.
  Generic Character. CAL. *perianth* bell-shaped.—COR. one-petalled.—STAM. *filaments* five; *anthers* twin.—PIST. *germ* inferior; *styles* three; *stigmas* heart-shaped.—PER. *berry* large; *seeds* compressed.
  Species. The two species are the—*Feuillea trilobata*, seu *Trichosanthes*, native of the East Indies.—*Feuillea cordifolia*, native of Jamaica.

FI'AR (*Law*) in opposition to the renter, in the Scotch law; the person in whom the property of an estate is vested, subject to the life-renter's estate.

FI'AT (*Law*) a short order or warrant of some judge for making out and allowing certain processes.—*Fiat justitia* are the words written by the king on his warrant to bring a writ of error in judgement, &c. *Stamf. Prærog. Reg.* 24.

FI'BER (*Zool.*) the *Castor fiber* of Linnæus. [vide *Beaver*]

FI'BRA *auris* (*Anat.*) the lower part of the ear.

FIBRA'RIÆ (*Min.*) a class of minerals of a fibrous structure.

FI'BRE (*Anat.*) ἶνα, *fibra*, a simple filament which is supposed to consist of earthy particles, connected together by an intermediate gluten. Fibres are distinguished, according to their position and course, into direct, transverse, oblique; and by their different arrangement are formed the membranes, muscles, vessels, nerves, &c. Those fibres which compose muscles are called muscular; those which form nerves, nervous; the rest are distinguished into *carneous* or fleshy, and *osseous* or bony. *Ruff. Ephes. de Appell. Part. Corp. hum.* l. 2, c. 3; *Gal. de Usu. Part.* l. 9, c. 2.

FIBRE (*Bot.*) a name for the minute threads of a root which imbibe moisture from the earth. These fibres properly constitute the roots of plants.

FIBRIL'LA (*Bot.*) the branch or division of a radical fibre.

FIBRI'LLÆ (*Anat.*) fibrils or small fibres.

FI'BRIN (*Chem.*) the name given by chemists to that particular substance which constitutes the fibres of animals.

FI'BROLITE (*Min.*) a sort of stone of the schorl family.

FIBRO'SUS (*Bot.*) fibrous; an epithet for a root that consists wholly of fibres, as in many vines.

FI'BULA (*Anat.*) a long bone of the leg situated on the outer side of the tibia, and forming, at its lower end, the outer ankle. [vide *Anatomy*, Plate No. I. (9.)]

FIBULA (*Surg.*) a needle with which wounds are sewed together. *Cels.* l. 7, c. 25.

FIBULA (*Archit.*) an iron cramp with which square stones are held together. *Vitruv.* l. 10, c. 2.

FIBULÆ'US (*Anat.*) another name for the *Peroneus*.

FICA'RIA (*Bot.*) the *Ranunculus ficaria* of Linnæus.

FICA'TIO (*Med.*) from *ficus*, a fig; tubercles near the *anus* and *pudenda*.

FICA'TUM (*Ant.*) a sort of food made with figs.

FICOI'DEA (*Bot.*) the *Aizoon hispanicum* of Linnæus.

FICOI'DES (*Bot.*) the *Aizoon canariense* of Linnæus.

FI'CTION (*Law*) a supposition of law that a thing is true, without inquiring whether it is or not, that it may have the effect of truth, so far as is consistent with equity: thus, the Seisin of Conusee is a *Fiction in law*, being only an invented form of conveyance.

FI'CUS *Ruminalis* (*Numis.*) the tree under which the wolf gave suck to Romulus and Remus, of which the memory is preserved on many medals. [vide *Lupus*] It was so called, according to Pliny, because the wolf gave *rumen*, her teat, to the children. *Liv.* l. 10, c. 23; *Plin.* l. 15, c. 18; *Tacit. Annal.* l. 13, c. 58.

FICUS (*Med.*) a tumour, particularly in the *anus* or *pudenda*.

FICUS (*Bot.*) a genus of plants, Class 23 *Polygamia*, Order 3 *Trioecia*.
  Generic Character. CAL. *perianth* proper.—COR. none.—STAM. in the male, *filaments* three; *anthers* twin.—PIST. in the female, *germ* oval; *style* subulate; *stigmas* two.—PER. in the female, none; *seed* single.
  Species. The species are shrubs or trees, as the—*Ficus carica*, *Caprificus*, seu *Chameficus*, Common Fig-Tree.—*Ficus sycomorus*, seu *Sycomorus*, Egyptian Fig or Sycomore.—*Ficus pumila*, seu *Itabu*, native of China.—*Ficus religiosa*, Poplar-leaved Fig-Tree.—*Ficus Bengalentiensis*, Bengal Fig-Tree.—*Ficus Indica*, Indian Fig-Tree. *Dod. Pempt.*; *Bauh. Hist.*; *Bauh. Pin.*; *Ger. Herb.*; *Park. Theat.*; *Tourn. Inst.*

FICUS is also the *Cecropia peltata*—*Ficus indica*, the *Cactus ficus indica*.

FID (*Mar.*) or *Mast-Fid*, a square bar of wood or iron, with a shoulder at one end, which used to support the weight of the top-mast. The *Splicing-Fid*, a large pin of *lignum vitæ*, tapering to a point, which is used for splicing of cables.

FIDD (*Gunn.*) or *fuse*, a little oakum shaped like a nail, to put into the touch hole of a gun, which being covered with a plate of lead, keeps the powder dry in the gun.

FI'DDLE-DOCK (*Bot.*) the *Rumex pulcher* of Linnæus, a perennial.—Fiddle-Wood, the *Citharexylum* of Linnæus. This wood in French is called *fidelle*, which has been corrupted in English into *fiddle,* as if it were fit for musical instruments, which is a mistake.

FIDEICOMMI′SSUM (*Law*) a feoffment of trust, when a thing is put by will into one's hand upon his honesty, to dispose of to some certain use. *Justin. Instit.* l. 2, c. 23.—*Fidei jussor,* in the Civil Law, a surety.

FIDEM *mentiri* (*Law*) is said of a tenant who does not keep the fealty which he has sworn to his lord.

FIDI′CINAL (*Mus.*) an epithet for all stringed instruments.

FIDICINA′LES (*Anat.*) the *combricales,* or muscles of the fingers; so called from their use to musicians.

FIEF (*Law*) the same as *Fee.*

FIELD (*Paint.*) the ground or blank space on which figures are or may be drawn.

FIELD (*Agric.*) arable land, or any portion of land parted off for cultivation.

FIELD (*Her.*) the whole surface of the shield or escutcheon; so called, probably, because it bore the atchievements which were borne in the field of battle.

FIELD (*Mil.*) the ground chosen for any battle.—*Field-colours,* small flags carried along with the quarter-master-general in marking out the ground for the squadrons and battalions of an army.—*Field-Bed,* a folding bed used by officers in their tents.—*Field-Officers,* officers who command a whole regiment, as the colonel, lieutenant-colonel, and major.—*Field-Marshal,* a commander in chief, or one who has the command of the whole army.—*Field-Pieces,* a sort of cannon, consisting of eighteen pounders and less.—*Field-staff,* a weapon carried by the gunners about the length of a halberd, having a spear at one end.—*Field-Works,* those that are thrown up by an army in besieging a fortress.

FIELD *of Vision* (*Opt.*) or *Field of View,* the whole space or extent within which objects can be seen through an optical machine at one view, without turning the eye.

FIELD *Ale* (*Archæol.*) or *Filk-Dale,* a kind of drinking bout among bailiffs of the hundreds, for which they gathered money of the inhabitants. It has long been out of use. *Bract.*

FIELD-BA′SIL (*Bot.*) the *Thymus acinos* of Linnæus.—*Field-Madder,* the *Sherardia Arvensis,* an annual.

FI′ELD-BED (*Mil.*) vide *Field.*

FI′ELD-BOOK (*Survey.*) a book used for setting down angles, distances, &c. as they arise in the field practice.

FI′ELD-COLOURS (*Mil.*) vide *Field.*

FI′ELD-FARE (*Orn.*) the *Turdus pilaris* of Linnæus, a migratory bird that visits England about Michaelmas in vast flocks, and leaves it about March.

FIELD-MA′DDER (*Bot.*) vide *Field-basil.*

FI′ELD-PIECE (*Mil.*) vide *Field.*

FI′ELD-STAFF (*Mil.*) vide *Field.*

FIERAME′NTE (*Mus.*) an Italian term, signifying that the movement before which it is placed, is to be performed in a bold, firm, energetic style.

FI′ERI *facias* (*Law*) a writ which lies for him who has recovered in an action of debt or damages, against him from whom the recovery is to be had, commanding the sheriff to levy the debt or damages on his goods.

FI′ERY *triplicity* (*Astrol.*) those three signs, namely, Leo, Aries, and Sagittarius, which surpass the rest in fiery qualities.

FIFE (*Mus.*) a shrill wind instrument used in military music, particularly as an accompaniment to the drum.

FIFE *Rails* (*Mar.*) such as are placed on the bannisters, on each side the top of the poops, &c.

FI′FFARS (*Mus.*) a small pipe, flute, or flageolet, used by the Germans in their army.

FIFTE′ENTH (*Mus.*) an interval consisting of two octaves.

FIFTE′ENTHS (*Law*) a tribute or imposition, anciently laid on cities, boroughs, &c.; so called because it consisted of a fifteenth of which each place was valued at.

FIFTH (*Mus.*) a distance comprising four diatonic intervals, i. e. three tones and a half. The *Sharp Fifth* is an interval consisting of eight semitones.

FIG (*Bot.*) the well known fruit of the *Ficus.*

FIG (*Vet.*) a spongy excrescence which grows out on the feet of some horses.

TO FIG (*Man.*) a trick among horse dealers of applying ginger to the fundament of a horse, to make him hold his tail erect.

FIGE′NTIA (*Chem.*) such things as have the property of fixing volatile and concentric acids.

FIGHT (*Mil.*) a combat or battle. A *running Fight* is that in which the enemy is continually chased.

FI′GHTING-MEN (*Mil.*) such as are effective and able to bear arms.

FIGHTS (*Mar.*) waste clothes which hang round a ship in a fight, to prevent the men from being seen by the enemy.—*Close Fights* are bulk heads, set up for men to stand secure behind, and thence fire on the enemy in case of boarding.

FI′GURATE *Numbers* (*Math.*) such numbers as are formed from the addition of all the leading terms of successive series.

FIGURATE *Descant* (*Mus.*) otherwise called *florid descant,* is that descant which, instead of moving note by note with the base, consists of a free and florid melody.—*Figurate counterpoint,* that which consists of a mixture of discords with the concords.

FI′GURATIVE (*Rhet.*) an epithet for words which convey a figurative or typical meaning; also for a style which abounds in figures of speech.

FI′GURE (*Geom.*) a surface or space enclosed on all sides, which is *superficial* when it is enclosed by lines, and *solid* when it is enclosed by surfaces. Figures are either straight, curved, or mixed, equal, equiangular, equilateral, circumscribed, inscribed, plane, regular, irregular, or similar, &c. [vide *Straight,* &c.] The exterior bounds of a figure are called its *sides,* the lowest side its *base,* and the angular point opposite the base is the *vertex.*—*Figure of the diameter* is the rectangle under any diameter and its proper parameter, in an ellipse and hyperbola.—*Figures of the sines, cosines,* &c. figures made by conceiving the circumference of a circle, extended out in a right line, upon every point of which are erected perpendicular ordinates equal to the sines, cosines, &c. of the corresponding arcs; and then drawing the curve line through the extremities of all the ordinates, which is called the *figure* of the sines, cosines, &c.

FIGURE (*Arith.*) the numeral characters by which numbers are expressed in writing, as the ten digits, 1, 2, 3, 4, 5, 6, 7, 8, 9, 0: they are called Arabic, because they are supposed to owe their introduction into Europe to the Arabians.

FIGURE (*Astrol.*) a description or scheme of the heavens at a certain hour, representing the places of the planets and stars marked down in a figure of twelve triangles.

FIGURE *of an Eclipse* (*Astron.*) a representation on paper, &c. of the path of the sun or moon during the time of an eclipse, &c.

FIGURE (*Sculpt. &c.*) any representation of things made in wood, stone, &c.

FIGURE *apparent* (*Opt.*) that figure or shape under which an object appears when viewed at a distance.

FIGURE (*Fort.*) the plan of a fortified place, or the interior polygon.

FIGURE (*Gram.*) any mode of speaking in which words are employed in a form or sense different from that in which they are ordinarily used. Figures are either grammatical or rhetorical. Under *grammatical figures* are comprehended the ellipse, the hyperbola, the zeugma, the enallage, ecthlipsis, synalepha, synæresis, &c. [vide *Grammar*]—*Rhetorical figures* are either changes of words from their natural signification, which are otherwise called *tropes*, or they are varied forms of expression, suited to the purposes of the orator. [vide *Rhetoric*]

FIGURE (*Danc.*) the several steps made by the dancers, in order and cadence, which mark divers figures on the floor.

FIGURE (*Log.*) the manner of disposing the middle term in a syllogism. [vide *Logic*]

FI'GURED (*Mus.*) vide *Figurate*.

FIGURED (*Mech.*) an epithet applied to stuffs on which figures are worked.

FI'LACER (*Law*) from *filum*, a thread; an officer in the court of Common Pleas; so called because he files those writs on which he makes process.

FILA'CIUM (*Law*) a term for the thread or wire on which deeds or writs, &c. are filed.

FILA'GO (*Bot.*) a genus of plants, Class 19 *Syngenesia*, Order 4 *Polygamia Necessaria*.

Generic Character. CAL. common.—COR. hermaphrodite, funnel form; female scarcely visible.—STAM. filaments four; anthers cylindric.—PIST. germ scarce any; style simple; stigma acute.—PER. none; seeds none.

Species. The species are mostly annuals, as the—*Filago acaulis, Eva, seu Gnaphalium.*—*Filago germanica* Common Cudweed, native of Europe.—*Filago pyramidata,* Flowering Cudweed, native of Spain.—*Filago arvensis,* Corn Cudweed. But the—*Filago Leontopodium, seu Leontopodium,* Lion's Foot Cud-weed, is a perennial. *Clus. Hist.; Bauh. Hist.; Bauh. Pin.; Ger. Herb.; Park. Theat. Botan.; Raii Hist.; Tourn. Inst.*

FILAGO is also the *Athanasia maritima*.

FI'LAMENT (*Bot.*) *filamentum*, the thread-like part of the stamen, supporting the anther, and connecting it with the flower. Filaments in the same flower are *equal*, i. e. all of the same length; *unequal*, i. e. of different lengths; *connate*, or united, alternate, &c. Most filaments are simple; some few are bifid; other tricuspidate or broad, and trifid at the end.

FI'LAMENTS (*Med.*) little slender rays like threads that appear in urine.

FILAMENTS (*Anat.*) the small fibres or threads which compose the texture of the muscles.

FILA'NDERS (*Falcon.*) small thread-like worms which infest the intestines of a hawk.

FILA'NDRES (*Vet.*) French for white streaks like threads in the wounds of horses.

FILA'RIA (*Ent.*) a genus of animals, Class *Vermes*, Order *Intestina*, which have a round filiform body, and a dilated mouth. They infest the intestines of different animals.

FI'LBERT (*Bot.*) another name for the *Corylus* of Linnæus, a shrub.

FILE (*Mech.*) 1. An iron tool used by smiths for smoothing of iron, &c. 2. A wire or thread on which papers are strung.

FILE (*Fenc.*) or Foil, a sword without edges, with a button at the point.

FILE (*Her.*) the strait line in a label, from which the several points issue.

FILE (*Mil.*) any number of men drawn up in a straight line behind each other. Files are distinguished into *close, open, double,* &c.—*Flank file,* the extreme file on the right or left of a squadron, troop, &c.—*File-leader,* the soldier placed in the front of any file.

TO FILE (*Mil.*) to advance to, or from, any point by files, as to *file off,* to *file* to the front, to *file* to the rear, &c.

FILE'LLUM (*Anat.*) the *frænum*, or bridle, by which the prepuce is connected to the glans of the penis.

FILE'TS (*Cook.*) meat, fowl, or fish, sliced and dressed in a ragout.

FILE'TUM (*Anat.*) the nervous ligament under the tongue, which midwives usually divide with their nail immediately after the birth.

FILIA'TION (*Law*) the descent from father to son.

FILICA'STRUM (*Bot.*) the *Osmurida struthropteris* of Linnæus.

FILI'CES (*Bot.*) ferns, the first Order of the Class *Cryptogamia*, in Linnæus' artificial system, and the Fourth Family in his General Distribution of Vegetables.

FILICIFO'LIA (*Bot.*) the *Xyloptylla sulcata* of Linnæus.

FILI'CULA (*Bot.*) a species of the *Acrostichum* of Linnæus.

FI'LIFORM (*Nat.*) thread-shaped, or slender like a thread; an epithet applied to different parts of insects and plants.

FI'LIGREE (*Mech.*) vide *Filligrane*.

FILIPE'NDULA (*Bot.*) the *Pedicularis flaminea* of Linnæus.

FI'LIUS *ante patrem* (*Bot.*) a term formerly applied by botanists to plants whose flowers come out before their leaves.

TO FILL (*Mar.*) in French *faire servir*, to brace the sails in such a manner, as that the wind entering their cavities from behind, dilates them to their full extent.—*To fill a ship's bottom*, to drive a number of nails with broad heads into her, so as to give her a sheathing of iron, to prevent the worms from getting into the wood.

FILLAGREE (*Mech.*) vide *Filligrane*.

FI'LLET (*Archit.*) a little member that connects the larger members in a column: it is otherwise called a listel. [vide *Listel*]

FILLET (*Anat.*) the extremities of the membranaceous ligament under the tongue, more commonly called the *frænum*, or bridle.

FILLET (*Her.*) an ordinary, which, according to Guillim, contains the fourth part of a chief.

FILLET (*Paint.*) a little rule, or ringlet of leaf gold, drawn over certain mouldings, or on the edge of frames, panels, &c.

FILLETS (*Vet.*) the fore parts of the shoulder next the breast.

FI'LLIGRANE (*Mech.*) a kind of enrichment on gold and silver, delicately wrought in the manner of little threads or grains, or both intermixed.

FI'LLINGS (*Mar.*) small pieces of timber, used for the purpose of making the curve fair for the mouldings, between the edges of the fish-front and the sides of the mast.

FI'LLY (*Vet.*) a young mare.

FILM (*Bot.*) the thin woody skin that separates the seeds in the pods.

FI'LOSE (*Nat.*) ending in a thread-like process; an epithet applied to insects and plants.

FI'LTERING-STONE (*Min.*) vide *Filtrum*.

FILTRATION (*Med.*) a straining of liquor through paper, which, by reason of the smallness of the pores, admits only the finer parts through, and keeps the rest behind. It was formerly marked by this character ℈.

FI'LTRUM (*Min.*) a Mexican stone, which has the virtue of filtering or purifying waters, by making them deposit a certain quantity of insensible fæces. It is commonly known by the name of the Filtering Stone.

FILTRUM (*Mech.*) a filtrer or straining instrument.

FI'LUM *Aquæ* (*Archæol.*) the thread or middle of the stream where a river parts two lordships. *Rot. Parl.* 11 H. 4; *Mon. Angl.* tom. i, p. 390.

FILUM (*Mus.*) the name formerly given to the line drawn from the head of a note downwards, now called the *tail* or *stem*.

FILUM *arsenicale* (*Chem.*) corrosive sublimate.

FI'MBRIÆ (*Anat.*) the extremities or borders of the *Tubæ*

Fallopianæ, formerly so called because they resemble a fringed border.

FI'MBRIATED (*Her.*) an epithet for an ordinary that is edged round with another of a different tincture, as in the annexed figure.

FIN (*Ich.*) the organ in fishes by which they perform all their movements in the water.

FIN (*Mus.*) vide *Finale*.

TO FIN *a chevin* (*Cook.*) to cut up or carve a chevin or chub-fish.

FI'NAL (*Mus.*) the last sound of a verse in a chant, which, if complete, is on the key note of the chant; if incomplete, on some other note in the scale of that key.

FINAL *letters* (*Gram.*) any letters which are used solely at the end of words, as in the Hebrew and other oriental languages. [vide *Alphabet*]

FINAL (*Sculpt.*) an emblem of the end of life, being an enrichment placed on monuments; namely, a boy without wings, holding in his hands an extinguished torch, with the flame end fixed on a death's-head at his feet.

FINA'LE (*Mus.*) the last piece performed in any act of an opera, or that which closes a concert, &c.

FINA'NCE (*Polit.*) a French term, signifying a fine, or sum of money, paid formerly to the French king for the enjoyment of any privileges; whence the word *finances* has since been generally employed to denote the treasures or revenue of the king.

FINA'NCIER (*Polit.*) an officer who manages the finances.

FINCH (*Orn.*) a bird well known in Europe. The two principal species are the—Chaffinch, the *Fringilla cœlebs* of Linnæus; and the Goldfinch, the *Fringilla carduelis*.

FI'NCKLE (*Bot.*) the same as *Fennel*.

TO FIND *the Ship's trim* (*Mar.*) to discover how she will sail best.

TO FIND *a Bill* (*Law*) in French *recevoir l'accusation*, to establish grounds of accusation, which is done by a Grand Jury of the county. *Finding*, in Court's-Martial, is equivalent to finding guilty.

FI'NDERS (*Law*) officers of the customs, now called searchers.

FINE (*Law*) 1. A penalty, or amends made in money for an offence. 2. A formal conveyance of lands by acknowledging a perfect agreement before a judge. 3. A sum of money paid for lands and tenements let by lease; also for alienations of copyholds paid to the lord, &c.— *Fine adnullando levato de tenemento*, a writ directed to the C. B. for making void a fine levied on lands holden in ancient demesne. *Reg. Orig.* 15.— *Fine levando de tenemento*, &c. a writ empowering the justices to admit of a fine for sale of lands holden in *capite*, &c.

FINE (*Mus.*) or *Fin*, Italian for the end, as *Fine del Atto*, end of the act; *Fine del Aria*, end of the air.

FI'NE-DRAWING (*Mech.*) the art of sewing up the rents of woollen cloth in so fine a manner, that the place where it was torn should not be perceived.

FI'NERY (*Metal.*) the furnace in which the operation of refining metals is performed.

FI'N-FISH (*Ich.*) a smaller sort of whale, the *Cete physalus* of Linnæus.

FI'NGER (*Anat.*) vide *Digitus*.

FINGER (*Ent.*) a cartilaginous slender appendage sometimes observable in fishes between the pectoral and ventral fins.

FINGER (*Mus.*) a figurative term to imply skill in execution, particularly on keyed instruments.—*Finger-Board*, a thin black covering of wood laid over the neck of a violin, violincello, &c. and on which, in performance, the strings are pressed by the fingers.

FI'NGERED (*Mus.*) a term applied to piano-forte exercises over or under the notes of which figures are placed to signify the finger with which each corresponding key is to be struck.

FI'NGERING (*Mus.*) disposing of the fingers in a convenient, natural, and apt manner, in the performance of any instrument, but more especially the organ and pianoforte.

FINGER'S BREA'DTH (*Arith.*) a measure equal to the length of a barley-corn, or four barley-corns laid side by side.

FI'NGRIGO (*Bot.*) the *Pisonia aculeata* of Linnæus.

FINI'RE (*Archæol.*) to fine, or pay a fine upon composition, making satisfaction, &c. equivalent to *finem facere*, mentioned *leg. H.* 1, c. 53, *apud Brompt*.

FINIS (*Mus.*) the same as *finale*.

FI'NISHING (*Archit.*) the same as a crowning, &c.

FINISHING (*Mar.*) a term used in ship-building for the ornaments to the upper gallery.

FI'NITE (*Math.*) an epithet for a series, line, &c. which is bounded or limited in extent, duration, &c. in distinction from the infinite.

FINI'TO (*Mus.*) Italian for finished.

FINI'TOR (*Man.*) an Italian term for the end of a career, or course.

FINITOR (*Astron.*) the same as the horizon.

FINO'CHIO (*Bot.*) the *Anethum fœniculum* of Linnæus.

FI'NORS (*Min.*) or *finers*; those who purify gold, silver, &c. from dross.

FI'NSCALE (*Ich.*) a fish of the carp kind, the *Cyprinus orfus* of Linnæus.

FI'RTREE (*Bot.*) the *Pinus* of Linnæus, a tree valuable for the timber, pitch, tar, &c. which it yields in abundance. The resinous roots of the Scotch Fir, the *Pinus sylvestris*, are used instead of tallow candles by the Highlanders. The fishermen make ropes of the inner bark, which the Laplanders even convert into bread. The Silver Fir, *Pinus picea*, is a noble, upright tree, so called from the under side of its leaves being white. The other kinds of fir best known are the Canada Fir, or Balm-of-Gilead Fir, *Pinus balsamæa*, and the Norway Spruce Fir, *Pinus picea*. All sorts of firs are raised best by seeds, which must be sown in April or May.

FI'RDEFARE (*Archæol.*) vide *Ferdwit*.

FIRDERI'NGA (*Archæol.*) a preparation to go into the army. *Leg. H.* 1.

FIRE ! (*Mil.*) a word of command to soldiers to discharge their fire-arms, &c. *Fire* is also used to denote the discharge itself, as—*Fire of the curtain*, or *second Flank*, which is from that part of the curtain comprehended between the face of the bastion prolonged and the angle of the flank.—*Fire razant* is produced by firing the artillery and small arms in a line parallel with the horizon.—*Running Fire* is when a rank of men drawn up fire one after another, &c.—*Fire-arrow*, a small iron dart furnished with a match that is impregnated with sulphur and powder. It is principally used for firing the sails of an enemy's ship.—*Fire-balls*, vide *Ball*.—*Fire-brand*, a piece of wood kindled.—*Fire-Cross*, an ancient signal in Scotland for the nation to take up arms.—*Fire-ship*, a ship filled with combustibles to set fire to the vessels of the enemy. —*Fire-arms*, all kinds of arms charged with powder and balls, as guns, pistols, &c.—*Fire-lock*, the gun, piece, or arms, carried by foot soldiers, which is so called because it produces fire by the action of the flint and steel. *Firelocks*, in the plural, signify men or soldiers equipped and actually under arms.—*Fire-master*, an officer who directs all the compositions of fire-works. The Fire-master's mate, or assistant Fire-master, acts under the direction of the Fire-master.—*Fire-pan*, the receptacle for the priming powder.—*Fire-pot*, a small earthen pot into which is put a charged grenade, and covered with powder, for the purpose of making an explosion.—*Fireworks*, particular compositions made of sulphur, saltpetre, and charcoal, which exhibit a handsome appearance when fired off.

FIRE (*Chem.*) was formerly esteemed one of the four elements; but among the moderns it has been the subject of a dispute, whether fire is a distinct substance, or whether it arises solely from the intestine and violent motion of the parts of bodies. It is now most generally supposed to be a subtle invisible fluid.—*Circulatory* or *reverberatory fire*, vide *Reverberatory*.

FIRE (*Vet.*) a term employed in regard to a horse, as "To give the *fire* to a horse," i. e. to apply the firing iron red-hot to some preternatural swelling, in order to discuss it.

FI'RE-ARMS (*Mil.*) vide *Fire*.
FI'RE-ARROW (*Mil.*) vide *Fire*.
FI'RE-BALL (*Mil.*) vide *Fire*.
FI'RE-BALLS (*Meteorol.*) a kind of luminous bodies usually appearing at a great height above the earth with a splendour surpassing that of the moon.
FI'RE-BRAND (*Mil.*) vide *Fire*.
FI'RE-CROSS (*Mil.*) vide *Fire*.
FI'RE-LOCK (*Mil.*) vide *Fire*.
FI'RE-MAN (*Cus.*) one who is employed in extinguishing fires.
FI'RE-MASTER (*Mil.*) vide *Fire*.
FIRE-POT (*Mil.*) vide *Fire*.
FI'RE-PAN (*Mil.*) vide *Fire*.
FI'RE-SHIP (*Mar.*) vide *Fire*.
FI'RE-STONE (*Min.*) the vulgar name for the *pyrites*.
FI'RE-WORKERS (*Mil.*) officers subordinate to the fire-masters.
FI'REWORKS (*Mech.*) vide *Fire*.
FI'RKIN (*Com.*) a measure containing eight gallons of ale, and nine of beer.—*Firkin-man*, one who buys small or table beer of the brewer to sell it again.
FI'RLOT (*Com.*) a dry measure used in Scotland.
FI'RMA (*Law*) victuals, provision, &c.—*Firma alba*, rent of lands paid in silver, not in provision, to the lord's house.—*Firma Noctis*, a custom or tribute anciently paid towards the entertainment of the king for one night, according to Domesday Book.
FI'RMA REGIS (*Archæol.*) the same as *villa regia*.
FI'RMAMENT (*Astron.*) the sphere of the fixed stars.
FIRMAME'NTUM (*Rhet.*) the chief stay and support of any cause. *Cic. de Inv.* l. 1, c. 14, &c.
FI'RMAN (*Com.*) a passport granted in Turkey and India for the liberty of trade.
FIRMARA'TIO (*Archæol.*) or *firmatio*, the doe season, as distinguished from the buck season: also a supplying with food. *Leg. In.* c. 34, *apud* Brompt.
FIRME (*Her.*) a term for a cross pattee throughout.
FI'RMED (*Falcon.*) or full firmed, i. e. well fledged; an epithet for a hawk when all the feathers of his wings are entire.
FIRST *fruits* (*Law*) the profits of every spiritual living for one year, given to the king.
FIRST (*Mus.*) the upper part of a duett, trio, &c.
FI'RSTLING (*Husband.*) the young of cattle which are first brought forth.
FI'SCAL (*Polit.*) from *fiscus*, the treasury; an office of the exchequer.
FISH *Royal* (*Law*) the Whale and Sturgeon are so denominated, because the king is entitled to them whenever they are thrown on shore, or caught near the coasts.
FISH (*Mar.*) in French *candelette*; a machine employed to hoist and draw up the flooks of ships' anchors towards the top of the bow.—*Fish-Front*, or *Paunch*, in French *jumelle*, a long piece of oak, or fir, convex on one side, and concave on the other, used to strengthen the lower masts or yards.—*Fish-Gig*, in French *foëne*, an instrument used to strike fish at sea.—*Fish-Room*, the place between the after-hold and the spirit-room.—*Fishes-Side*, two long pieces of fir coaked on the opposite side of a made mast, to give it the diameter required.

FI'SHERY (*Com.*) the place where fish are caught for the purpose of trade; and also the trade of thus catching fish.
FI'SHES (*Zool.*) vide *Animal Kingdom* and *Icthyology*.
FISHES (*Her.*) are borne after divers manners, as *hauriant*, i. e. directly upright; *naiant*, i. e. transverse the escutcheon; *imbowed*, i. e. with the back bent; *extended*, i. e. stretched lengthwise; *endorsed*, i. e. back to back; *devouring*, i. e. feeding, &c.
FI'SH-GARTH (*Com.*) a dam or wear in a river for the taking of fish.
FI'SH-GIG (*Mar.*) vide *Fish*.
FI'SH-GLUE (*Nat.*) the same as Isinglass.
FI'SHING-FLY (*Sport.*) a bait used for catching divers kind of fish, which is either the natural insect, or an imitation of it, called the *artificial fly*.
FI'SHING-HOOK (*Mech.*) a small instrument, of steel wire, of a proper form to catch and retain fish.
FI'SHING-LINE (*Mech.*) a line made of twisted hair, silk, &c. which is fixed to a rod for the purpose of angling.
FI'SHING-ROD (*Mech.*) a long slender rod or wand, to which the line is fastened for angling.
FI'SHMONGERS, *Company of* (*Her.*) were formerly two companies; namely, the Stock-fish and Salt-Fish-mongers, which were united in 1536. Their armorial ensigns are "*Azure*, three dolphins naiant in pale between two pair of lucies saltirewise proper crowned, *or*, on a chief, *gules*, six keys in three saltires, the ward ends upwards as the crowns *or*."
FISSURA *magna Sylvii* (*Anat.*) the name for a deep narrow sulcus between the lobes of the brain.
FISSURE (*Surg.*) that species of fracture in which the bone is slit, but not completely divided.
FI'STIC *Nut* (*Bot.*) the *Pistachacia vera* of Linnæus.
FI'STULA (*Anat.*) 1. σύριγξ, a musical instrument, a flageolet, made of a reed, or other stuff. *Virg. Ecl.* 2, v. 36. 2. A pipe for the conveyance of water. *Ulp.* l. 47; *ff. de contrah. empt.*
FISTULA (*Surg.*) σύριγξ, a term applied to any long and sinuous ulcer that has a narrow opening sometimes leading to a larger cavity.—*Fistula lachrymalis* is when the little hole in the bone of the nose is grown hard and callous, so that there is a continual defluxion of tears.—*Fistula sacra*, that part of the backbone which is perforated.
FISTULA *Pulmonis* (*Anat.*) the Wind-Pipe.
FISTULA (*Bot.*) the *Cassia fistula* of Linnæus.
FISTULA'RIA (*Bot.*) the *Pedicularis sylvatica*.
FISTULARIA (*Ich.*) Tobacco-Pipe-Fish, a genus of fishes of the Abdominal Order, having a cylindrical snout and a round body.
FISTULO'SUS (*Bot.*) hollow like a pipe or reed, an epithet for a stem, or a leaf.
FIT *for service* (*Mil.*) an epithet for healthy men capable of undergoing the fatigues of service.
TO FIT *out a ship* (*Mar.*) in French *armer un vaisseau*, to provide a vessel with a sufficient number of men, to navigate and arm her for attack or defence.
FITCHE'E (*Her.*) an epithet for a cross that ends in a sharp point, as in the annexed figure. It is supposed to have taken its rise from the practice of Christians formerly carrying the cross with them wherever they went, which they fixed in the ground as they stopped.
FITCHET (*Zool.*) an animal of the weasel or ferret kind that is classed, in the Linnean system, under the *Viverra*.
FI'TCHY (*Her.*) vide *Fitchee*.

FI'THWITE (*Law*) a fine imposed upon a person for breaking the peace.

FITT-WEED (*Bot.*) the *Eryngium fatidium*, so called because it is reckoned a very powerful antihysteric.

FIVE (*Bot.*) is an epithet used frequently in composition, as five-cleft, *quinquefidus*; five-fold, *quinus*; five-lobed, *quinquelobatus*; five-parted, *quinquepartitus*; five-toothed, *quinquedentatus*.

FIVE-LEAVED Grass (*Bot.*) the *Potentilla reptans* of Linnæus.

FIXA'TION (*Chem.*) the making any volatile spirituous body endure the fire, and not fly away either by repeated distillations or sublimations.

FI'XED *Bodies* (*Chem.*) are such as neither fire nor any corrosive menstruum have the power of reducing or resolving into their component elements, as ammonia, and other alkalies. Bodies are likewise called fixed which are not easily reducible to a fluid state; the term is, in both cases, opposed to volatile.

Fixed *Air* (*Chem.*) a name formerly given to the air which is extricated from lime, magnesia, and alkalies; it is now commonly called *Carbonic acid gas*.

Fixed *Signs* (*Astrol.*) are *Taurus, Leo, Scorpio,* and *Aquarius*.

Fixed *Stars* (*Astron.*) are such as do not, like the planets, or erratic stars, change their positions and distances in respect to one another. [vide *Astronomy*]

Fixed *line of defence* (*Fort.*) a line drawn along the face of a bastion, and terminated in the curtain.

FI'ZGIG (*Mar.*) or fishgig, a dart wherewith mariners strike fish while they swim.

FLACO'URTIA (*Bot.*) a genus of plants, Class 22 *Dioecia*, Order 7 *Polyandria*.
Generic Character. CAL. *perianth* one-leaved.—COR. none.—STAM. *filaments* numerous; *anthers* roundish.—PIST. in the female *germ* ovate; *style* none; *stigma* flat.—PER. *berry* ovate; *seeds* in pairs.
Species. The species is a small tree or shrub, as the— *Flacourtia Ramontchi, Alamoutou,* seu *Flacourtia*.

FLAG (*Bot.*) or *sedge*, a sort of rush.—Common Flag, or Water Iris, the *Iris Pseudacorius* of Linnæus.—Corn Flag, the *Gladiolus*, a bulbous plant.—Sweet Flag, the *Acorus*, a perennial.

FLAG (*Mar.*) an ensign or banner usually set out on the tops of masts, at the heads of ships, &c. When flags are displayed from the top of the mainmast they are the distinguishing marks of Admirals; when from the foremast, of Vice-Admirals; and when from the mizenmast, of Rear-Admirals. They are likewise distinguished by their colour into *red* for the first, *white* for the second, and *blue* for the third. The first flag in Great Britain is the *Standard*, only to be hoisted when the King or Queen is on board; the second is the *Anchor of Hope*, which is hoisted for the Lord High Admiral, or Lords of the Admiralty; and the third is the *Union*, which is appropriated to the Admiral of the Fleet.
Flag is a term employed in the above sense in many sea phrases, as "To hang out the *white flag*," i. e. to call for quarter. "To hang out the *red flag*," to give the signal of defiance and battle. "To lower or strike the *flag*," to pull it down upon the cap, or to take it in, as a token of respect or submission to a superior power. "To lower or strike the *flag*" in an engagement, is a sign of yielding, or submission.—*Flag-officer*, an officer commanding a squadron.—*Flag-ship*, a ship commanded by a general or flag-officer.—*Flag-staff*, a continuation of the top-gallant mast above the top-gallant rigging.

FLA'GELLANTS (*Ecc.*) a sect of heretics in the 13th century who reckoned flagellation as essential in order to obtain remission of sins. Sigon. *de Regn. Ital.* l. 19; Prateol. *de Doct. Omn. Hæret.*; Spondan. *Annal. Ann.* 1260, &c.

FLAGELLA'RIA (*Bot.*) a genus of plants, Class 6 *Hexandria*, Order 3 *Trigynia*.
Generic Character. CAL. *perianth* six-leaved.—COR. none.—STAM. *filaments* six; *anthers* oblong.—PIST. *germ* ovate; *style* length of the stamens; *stigmas* three.—PER. *drupe* roundish; *seed* a round stone.
Species. The two species are perennials, as the—*Flagellaria indica et repens*, natives of Cochinchina.

FLA'GEOLET (*Mus.*) a sort of pipe.

FLAG-O'FFICER (*Mar.*) vide *Flag*.

FLA'GON (*Mech.*) a large drinking vessel.

FLAGS (*Falcon.*) the feathers in a hawk's wing next to the principal one.

FLA'G-SHIP (*Mar.*) vide *Flag*.

FLA'G-STAFF (*Mar.*) vide *Flag*.

FLA'G-STONE (*Mason.*) or *Flag*, in French *fleche*, a species of stone used for smooth pavement.

FLAIL (*Husband.*) the instrument used for threshing corn.

TO FLAIR (*Mar.*) a term applied to a ship the upper part of which, when housed near the water, hangs over too much.

FLAKE (*Hor.*) a name given by florists to a sort of carnations which are of two colours only, and have very large stripes.

Flake (*Paint.*) or white *Flake*, a colour formed by the corroding of lead with the acid of grapes.

Flake (*Mar.*) a sort of platform made of hurdles, and supported by stancheons. It is used for drying codfish in Newfoundland.

FLAM (*Mil.*) a signal given with the drum, formerly used in military exercise instead of the word of command.

FLAME (*Nat.*) the most subtle part of fire.

Flame (*Her.*) is a bearing occasionally in coat armour to denote, as is supposed, fervency of zeal, as in the annexed figure. "He beareth *argent* a chevron voided *azure* between three flames of fire *proper*; name Wells."

FLA'MENS (*Ant.*) priests so called from the hat they wore, which was of a flame colour. There were three appointed by Numa, who were patricians, to which were added twelve others afterwards, who were plebeians. The Flamens bore the name of the God to whom they were consecrated, as—The *Flamen Dialis*, the priest consecrated to Jupiter, who was chief over all.—The *Flamen Martialis*, the priest of Mars.—The *Flamen Quirinalis*, the priest of Romulus, &c. &c. Varr. *de Lat. Ling.* l. 4; Dionys. *Hal.* l. 2; Liv. l. 1, c. 20; Aul. Gell. l. 15, c. 27.

FLAMI'NGO (*Orn.*) a sort of bird in Africa and South America, the *Phœnicopteros* of Linnæus, which has long legs and neck, is four feet four inches long from the tip of the bill to the end of the tail, feeds on aquatic insects and fishes, and makes its nest on hillocks in shallow water.

FLA'MMULA (*Bot.*) the *Clematis viorna* of Linnæus.

FLANCH (*Her.*) one of the honourable ordinaries formed by an arch line, which begins at the corners of the chiefs, and ends in the base of the escutcheon, as in the annexed figure.

FLANCONA'DE (*Fenc.*) a thrust in the flank or side.

FLANK (*Mil.*) the side of an army or battalion from the front to the rear, of which there are different kinds, as the—*Inward Flank*, in manœuvring the first file on the left of a division, subdivision, or section.—*Outward Flank*, the extreme file on the right or left of a division.—*Leading Flank*, the first battalion, division, &c. which conducts to the attack.—*Flank Files*, the two first men on the right and the two last men on the left.—*Flank Company*, a certain number of men drawn up on the right or left of a battalion.—*Flank en potence*, any part of the right or left wing formed at a right angle with the line.

FLANK (*Fort.*) any part of a work that defends another work along the outside of its parapet, of which there are different kinds, as the—*Flank of the Bastion*, that part which joins the face to the curtain.—*Oblique* or *second Flank*, that part of the curtain from which the face of the opposite bastion may be discovered.—*Retired Flank, low Flank*, or *covered Flank*, the platform of the casemate, which lies hid in the bastion.—*Flank prolonged*, the extending of the flank from the angle of the epaulement to the exterior side. —*Flank fichant*, the flank from which the cannon playing fires directly on the opposite bastion.—*Flank razant*, the point from which the line of defence commences.—*Flanks of a frontier*, the different salient points of a large extent of territory.

TO FLANK (*Fort.*) to erect a battery which may play on an enemy's works on the right or the left without being exposed to his fire.

TO FLANK (*Mil.*) to take such a position as to be enabled to attack the enemy's flanks without being exposed to all his fire.—*To outflank*, to outstretch the enemy's forces, so as to get upon his flanks.

FLANKARDS (*Sport.*) the knobs or nuts in the flank of a deer.

FLANKED angle (*Fort.*) vide *Angle*.

FLANKER (*Fort.*) a fortification jutting out so as to command the side or flank of an enemy marching to the assault.

TO FLANKER (*Fort.*) to fortify the walls of a city with bulwarks or countermines.

FLANKERS (*Mil.*) the most active men and horses in cavalry manœuvres, who are selected to do the duty of flankers. [vide *Flanking Party*]

FLANKING (*Fort.*) the same as defending.—*Flanking angle*, the angle composed of the two lines of defence, and pointing towards the curtain.

FLANKING party (*Mil.*) any body of men detached from the main army to get upon the flanks of an enemy, so as to secure a line of march. The men and horses selected to do this duty are called *Flankers*.

FLANKS (*Vet.*) a wrench or any other harm to the back of a horse.

TO FLARE (*Mar.*) or to *flare over*, to hang over, i. e. when a vessel is let out broader aloft than the due proportion will allow. *Flaring*, in distinction from falling home, is when a ship's side forward falls out from a perpendicular; then she is said to have a flaring bow.

FLASK (*Mech.*) a measure for holding gunpowder, and measuring it out when the piece is loaded.

FLASK (*Her.*) or *flasque*, an ordinary which resembles the flanch in form, but is smaller. Gibbon makes the flask and flanch to be the same thing.

FLASQUES (*Gunn.*) the two cheeks of the carriage of a great gun.

FLAT (*Mar.*) in French *bas-fond*, or *batture*, a level ground lying at a small depth under the surface of the sea, otherwise called a shoal, or shallow.—*Flat aft*, is the situation of the sails when their surfaces are pressed aft against the mast.—*Flat bottomed*, an epithet for boats built to swim in shallow water.

FLAT (*Mus.*) a character marked thus [♭] depresses the note before which it is placed one semitone lower. The *double Flat* depresses a note already flattened another semitone lower.

FLAT (*Bot.*) planus; an epithet for a leaf; *folium planum*, a leaf having an even surface.

TO FLAT in the sail (*Mar.*) in French *traverser la voile*, is to draw in the aftmost clew of a sail towards the middle of the ship.—*Flat in forward!* an order to draw in the jib and fore-topmast-stay-sail sheets towards the middle of the ship.

TO FLATTEN (*Paint.*) in house-painting, is to give a newly painted wall such a coat of colour as takes off its glossy appearance.

FLATS, in *ship-building*, the name given to all the timbers in midships.

FLATUS (*Med.*) flatulencies; air contained in the cavity of the body.

FLAUTINO (*Mus.*) Italian for a small flute.

FLAW (*Gunn.*) any crack or small opening in a gun.

FLAW (*Min.*) a defect in precious stones, metals, &c.

FLAW (*Mar.*) a sudden breeze or gust of wind.

FLAX (*Bot.*) a well-known plant classed by Linnæus under the genus *Linum*. The Common Flax, *Linum usitatissimum*, is an annual, but the other sorts are mostly perennial. The seeds of flax, called linseed, yield, by expression, an oil well known by the name of *linseed oil*.—Toad Flax, the *Antirrhinum* of Linnæus.

FLAX (*Min.*) Earth or Mountain Flax, the *Asbestos* of Linnæus.

FLEA (*Ent.*) a well-known insect, the *Pulex* of Linnæus.

FLEABANE (*Bot.*) the *Conyza* of Linnæus.—Flea Grass, the *Carex pulicaris*, a perennial.—Flea Wort, the *Plantago psellium*.

FLEAM (*Surg.*) an instrument for lancing the gums.

FLEAM (*Vet.*) an instrument for bleeding a horse.

FLEAU (*Mech.*) French for a beam or balance of a pair of scales.—*Fleau de porte*, the strong iron or wooden bar which falls across the inside of the gates of a town.

FLEBILE (*Mus.*) an epithet signifying soft and doleful, applied to a style of performance.

FLECTA (*Archæol.*) a feathered arrow.

FLEDWITH (*Law*) from the Saxon ꝑlyȝht, flight, and ƿite, a fine; a discharge from fines where an outlawed fugitive comes to the place of his own accord.

FLEECE (*Her.*) the *golden fleece*, or *toyson d'or*, has been borne in the escutcheon in some instances, as in the annexed figure; he beareth " azure a toyson d'or, by the name of Jason."

FLEET (*Mar.*) a number of ships together in company, or under one commander.

TO FLEET (*Mar.*) in French *affaler*, to change the situation of a tackle when the blocks are drawn together.

FLEGME (*Her.*) or *fleam*, is borne in the arms of the company of surgeons.

FLEM (*Law*) an outlaw; whence *flemaflare*, to claim a felon's goods, as may be gathered from a *quo warranto*. Temp. Ed. 3.

FLEMAFLARE (*Law*) from the Saxon ꝑlyma, an outlaw, and ꝑlean, to slay; a claim of a felon's goods.

FLEMEN (*Med.*) a tumour about the ancles.

FLEMENEFRIT (*Ant.*) or *Flemenesfrinthe*, from the Saxon ꝑlyma, an outlaw, and ꝑinmean, to afford victuals; the receiving or relieving a fugitive or outlaw. *Leg. In.* c. 29; *LL. H.* 1, c. 10.

FLEMESWITE (*Law*) from the Saxon ꝑlyma, a fugitive, and ƿite, a fine; the liberty of challenging the chattels or fines of one's servant who is an outlaw. *Flet.* l. 1, c. 47.

FLERESIN (*Med.*) a name for the gout.

FLESH (*Anat.*) the similar and fibrous parts of the body, which is soft and thick. It is distinguished into the *muscular*, or *fibrous*, as of the heart and other muscles; *perenchymous*, as that of the lungs; *viscerous*, as that of the stomach and intestines; *glandulous*, as that of the tonsils; and *spurious*, as the flesh of the gums, lips, &c.

Flesh is also particularly applied to the red part of a muscle.

FLESH (*Bot.*) the soft pulpy substance of any fruit.

TO FLESH a sword (*Mil.*) to draw blood by means of a sword.

4 F

FLE'SH-POT (*Her.*) was borne formerly in some escutcheons.

FLE'SHY (*Bot.*) an epithet for a leaf that is full of pulp within, as the *sedum*.

FLEUR-DE-LI'S (*Her.*) i. e. Flower-de-Luce, a bearing in the arms of France, which consist, as in *fig.* 1, of three fleurs-de-lis, *or*, in a field, *azure*.—*Fleur-de-lis*, a general

Fig. 1.   *Fig. 2.*

bearing, signifies, as authors observe, service in France. It occurs very frequently in escutcheons, as in *fig.* 2. He beareth, " *Or*, a Fleur-de-Lis, *azure*." The *Fleur-de-Lis* is also the distinguishing mark for the sixth son of a family.

FLEURE'TTE (*Her.*) vide *Fleury*.

FLEU'RONS (*Cook.*) fine puffs of pastry work for garnishing.

FLEU'RY (*Her.*) an epithet for a cross which is similar to the *Cross-flory*.

FLE'XILIS (*Bot.*) flexible, an epithet applied to the stem and the raceme of a plant.

FLE'XOR (*Anat.*) an epithet for several muscles whose office it is to bend the parts into which they are inserted, as *flexor carpi radialis*, a muscle of the wrist ; *flexor tertii internodii*, a muscle of the thumb ; *flexor pollicis brevis*, a muscle of the great toe, &c.

FLE'XURE (*Geom.*) or *Flexion*, the bending or curving of a line or figure ; thus, when a line first bends one way and then another, the point where the bend changes to the other side is called the *point of contrary flexure*.

FLEXUO'SUS (*Bot.*) flexuose, or, according to Withering, zig-zag ; an epithet for a stem that changes its flexure, or bending direction, from bud to bud, as in the *Ptelea*, *Smilax*, &c. ; also an epithet for a peduncle.

FLI'GHERS (*Archæol.*) masts for ships. *Mon. Angl.* tom. i. p. 799.

FLIGHT (*Mil.*) a term applicable to missile weapons signifying a shot, as "A *flight* of arrows," "A *flight* of bombs," &c.—*Flight-shot*, the motion of an arrow shot from a bow.

FLIGHT (*Mech.*) a substance so called, which flies away in the smoke in the melting of lead.

FLINT (*Mil.*) the stone which is fixed into the *jaws* or pieces of iron belonging to the cock of a gun, by which fire is elicited for the purpose of discharging the piece.

FLITCH (*Mar.*) the name of a piece of small timber applied to ships for the purpose of sawing up into boat-timber ; so called perhaps from the resemblance which its smaller parts bear to a flitch of bacon.

FLITCHWITE (*Law*) from the Saxon flit, a contention, and pite, a fine ; a fine on account of broils and quarrels.

FLI'TTERING (*Husband.*) the act of a horse which, fastened to a stake, eats up all the grass within his reach.

FLI'TTERMOUSE (*Zool.*) another name for the bat.

FLIX-WEED (*Bot.*) the *Sisymbrium sophia* of Linnæus.

FLOAT (*Her.*) an instrument used by the bowyers, which is borne in their arms.

FLOAT (*Mar.*) a raft, or a number of pieces of timber fastened together with rafters athwart, to be driven along a river with the tide or current. "To *float*," to be borne, or wafted along with the tide on the surface of the water.

To FLOAT (*Mil.*) is said of a column when it loses its perpendicular line in its march, and becomes unsteady.

FLO'ATAGES (*Law*) vide *Flotages*.

FLOAT-BOARDS (*Mech.*) the boards fixed to the outer rim of undershot water wheels.

FLOAT-BOARDS (*Mech.*) boards fixed to the water wheels of undershot mills, serving to receive the impulse of the stream.

FLO'ATING (*Husband.*) the watering or overflowing of meadows.

FLOATING *battery* (*Mar.*) vessels used as batteries to cover troops in landing on an enemy's coast.

FLOATING (*Bot.*) *natans*, an epithet for a leaf that floats on the surface of the water.

FLOATING *bridge* (*Mil.*) a bridge made in the form of a redoubt, consisting of two boats covered with planks.

FLOATING *light* (*Mar.*) a hollow vessel of tinned ironplate made in the form of a boat, &c. with a reflector or lanthorn, for the purpose of saving those who may have the misfortune to fall overboard in the night.

FLOATS (*Mar.*) vide *Float*.

FLOCK (*Husband.*) a number of sheep in company ; also a lock of wool.

FLOOD (*Nat.*) in French *le flot*, the flux of the tide, or the time that the water continues rising. When it commences it is called a *young Flood*, after which it is *quarter Flood*, *half Flood*, and *high Flood*.

FLOOD-GATE (*Mech.*) a gate or sluice which may be opened or shut at pleasure for the admission or exclusion of the water.

FLO'OD-MARK (*Mar.*) the mark which the sea makes on the shore at the highest tide, otherwise called *high-water-mark*.

FLOOK (*Mar.*) vide *Flouk*.

FLOOR (*Carpent.*) the area, or horizontal surface of a room ; if made of brick, it is called a *pavement* ; if of plaster, a *lime floor* ; if of wood, a *boarded* or *timber floor*. The term *floor* is also applied to that part of a building which is on the same level, as the *basement floor*, the *ground floor*, the *first floor*, *second floor*, &c.

FLOOR *of a ship* (*Mar.*) so much of a ship as rests on the ground.

FLO'ORING (*Carpent.*) the act of laying a floor ; also the workmanship in a floor, and the boards which compose the floor. The timbers which support the boarding are called *naked flooring*.

FLO'RAL *bud* (*Bot.*) an epithet for a bud and a leaf ; *gemma floralis*, a bud that contains the flowers ; *folium florale*, a leaf that immediately attends the flower.

FLORAL *games* (*Archæol.*) a ceremony anciently performed in France on May-Day, when poems were rehearsed, and prizes adjudged to the best performances.

FLORA'LIA (*Ant.*) a Roman festival in honour of the goddess Flora, which was celebrated by all sorts of obscenities. *Ovid. Fast.* l. 5 ; *Senec.* epist. 97 ; *Val. Max.* l. 2, c. 10 ; *Lactant.* l. 1, c. 12 ; *Panciroll. Descript. Urb. Roman. apud Græv. Thes. Antiq. Roman.* tom. iii. p. 344.

FLO'REN (*Numis.*) vide *Florin*.

FLO'RENCE (*Numis.*) vide *Florin*.

FLO'RENTINE *marble* (*Min.*) otherwise called *Landskip marble* ; a sort of marble in which the figures of buildings, &c. are naturally represented.

FLO'RES (*Chem.*) vide *Flowers*.

FLORESCENCE (*Bot.*) *florescentia*, the flowering season.

FLO'RET (*Bot.*) *flosculus*, the partial or little flower of an aggregate flower, chiefly in the Class *Syngenesia*, of compound flowers properly so called.

FLO'RID *Style* (*Archit.*) or *Florid Gothic*, a sort of Gothic architecture which is filled with points, ramifications, mullions, &c.

FLORID (*Mus.*) an epithet for any composition or performance which is of a fanciful, rich, and embellished style.

FLORID (*Rhet.*) any epithet for a discourse which is full of figures and tropes.

FLO'RIN (*Numis.*) or *Florence*, a gold coin so called because it was struck first in Florence, and became afterwards the general name for all gold coin throughout

Europe. The first English Florins were coined in the reign of Edward III. [vide *Coinage*]

FLORIN (*Com.*) is now either a coin of different values, or a money of account in different countries.

FLORI'NIANS (*Ecc.*) a sect of heretics in the second century, so called after their ring-leader, one Florinus, who maintained, among other impieties, that God not only permitted, but also did evil. *Iren* l. 5; *Euseb.* l. 5, c. 14; *S. August. de Hær.* c. 69; *Theodoret. Hær. Fab.* l. 1; *Philast.* c. 58.

FLO'RIST (*Bot.*) one who is skilled in the art of cultivating flowers.

FLO'RY (*Her.*) an epithet signifying flowered with the Fleurs-de-Lis. — *A cross flory* has flowers at the ends circumflex and turning down, as in the annexed figure; so likewise a *Bend flory*, &c.

FLOS (*Bot.*) is a general name for the flower. [vide *Flower*]

FLOS is also the name of several species of plants, as— *Flos adonis* the same as the *Adonis* of Linnæus.—*Flos æris,* the *Epidendrum flos æris.*— *Flos africanus,* the *Tagetes patula.*—*Flos cœruleus,* the *Clitoria ternatea.*—*Flos cardinalis,* the *Ipomœa quamœlit.*—*Flos clitoridis,* the *Clitoria ternatea.*—*Flos cuculi,* a species of the *Cardamum.*—*Flos globosus,* the *Gomphrena globosa.* — *Flos Passionis,* the *Passiflora perfoliata.* — *Flos pergularius,* the *Purgularia glabra.*—*Flos rigens,* another name for the *Delphinium.*— *Flos solis,* another name for the *Cistus.*—*Flos Susannæ,* the *Orchis Susannæ.*—*Flos trinitalis,* another name for the *Viola.*—*Flos vestivalis,* another name for the *Hibiscus.*

FLOS (*Chem.*) vide *Flowers.*

FLO'TA (*Archæol.*) a fleet.

FLO'TAGES (*Law*) things that float on the sea, or in great rivers.

FLOTANT (*Her.*) an epithet for a banner, or any thing flying.

FLOTSAM (*Law*) a name for the goods which float upon the sea when a ship is sunk, in distinction from *Jetsam*, i. e. the goods thrown out to lighten the ship in case of danger; *Lagan,* or *ligan,* heavy goods cast into the sea in case of danger; *Wreck,* i. e. the ship or goods cast upon land by the sea. In law these terms are mostly used together. *Bract.* l. 2, c. 5.

FLOUK (*Mar.*) or *Flook,* that part of the anchor which takes hold of the ground. [vide *Anchor*]

FLOU'NDER (*Ich.*) a sort of flat-fish, and a species of the *Pleuronectes* of Linnæus. It inhabits the European seas, and enters the rivers; seldom exceeds six pounds in weight, and has short spines on the right side of the fins.

FLOU'RET (*Bot.*) vide *Floret.*

FLO'URISH (*Mus.*) a prelude, or preparatory air, without any settled rule: also the decorative notes which a singer, or instrumental performer, adds sometimes to a passage.

FLOURISH (*Mil.*) is the sounding of the trumpet on receiving any officer or person of distinction.

TO FLOW (*Mar.*) is used in some sea-phrases, as "It *flows* south," it is high water when the sun is at that point at New or Full Moon. "It *flows* tide and half tide," i. e. it will be half flood by the shore before it begins to flow in the channel. "*Flown* sheets," i. e. when the sheets are not haled home, or close to the block.

FLO'WER (*Bot.*) *flos,* that part of a plant which contains the organs of generation with their covering. A flower, when complete, consists of a *calyx, corolla, stamen,* and *pistil;* but the essential parts to constitute a flower are the *anther* and the *stigma,* either together, or in separate flowers.

FLOWER is also the name of several species of plants, as— Flower-de-Luce, the *Iris pseudacorus* of Linnæus.—Flower Fence, a species of the *Adenanthera.*—Flower Gentle, the *Amaranhus spinosus.*—Flower Fern, the *Osmunda regalis.*— Everlasting Flower, the *Gnaphalium.* — Sun-Flower, the *Helianthus.* — Sultan-Flower, the *Cyanus.* — Trumpet-Flower, the *Bignonia.*

FLO'WERING-RUSH (*Bot.*) the *Butomus umbellatus* of Linnæus.

FLO'WERS (*Chem.*) the fine mealy matter which, in sublimation, is carried up into the head and aludels, and adheres to them in the form of a powder, as the Flowers of Benjamin, zink, sulphur, &c.

FLOWER-STALK (*Bot.*) the same as the peduncle. [vide *Pedunculus*]

FLO'WING (*Mar.*) or *flowing sheets,* the position of the sails when they are loosened to the wind.

FLU'ATES (*Chem.*) a salt formed by the combination of fluoric acid with different bases, as the *fluate* of ammonia, potash, lime, &c.

FLUCTUA'TION (*Surg.*) the undulatory motion of any fluid, as *pus* in an abscess, &c.

FLUE (*Archit.*) the long tube of a chimney, from the fire place to the top of the shaft.

FLUE (*Husband.*) the soft down from feathers, and the skins from rabbits, &c.

FLUE'LLIN (*Bot.*) the *Antirrhinum elatine* of Linnæus, an annual.

FLU'ENT (*Flux.*) or *flowing quantity,* the variable quantity which is considered as increasing or decreasing. *Newt. Introd. Quadrat. Curv.*

FLU'GEL-MAN (*Mil.*) a well-drilled soldier, who is advanced in front to give the time in the manual and platoon exercises.

FLU'ID (*Nat.*) or *fluid Body,* is that whose parts, according to Newton, yield to the smallest force impressed, and by yielding are easily moved among each other. Fluids are either *elastic,* as the air, or *non-elastic,* as water, mercury, &c.

FLU'IDS, *of the Body* (*Anat.*) the fluid parts of the body distinguished from the solids, as the blood, chyle, saliva, &c. [vide *Anatomy*]

FLUKE (*Ent.*) or *Gourd-Worm,* an hermaphrodite oviparous animal of the worm tribe, the *Fasciola* of Linnæus.

FLUKE (*Mar.*) vide *Flouke.*

FLU'OR *albus* (*Med.*) ῥοῦς λευκός, a cachectic disorder, to which females are subject at all ages, but particularly in the prime of life, consisting of an irregular discharge of impure mucid humour. *Hippocrat. de Morb. Mul.* l. 2; *Aret. diut. Morb.* l. 2, c. 10; *Gal. Def. Med.; Oribas. Med. Collect.* l. 6; *Paul. Æginet.* l. 3, c. 13.

FLUOR (*Min.*) or *Fluor Spar,* a species of salt which abounds in nature, and is found to consist of fluoric acid and lime. It is called *Fluor* because it melts readily: it is called *Spar* because it has a sparry form and fracture: and it is called *vitreous Spar* because it has the appearance of glass.

FLUO'RIC *Acid* (*Chem.*) an acid which is extracted from the mineral called *fluor.*

FLUOSI'LIC ACID (*Chem.*) a composition of fluoric acid and silica.

FLU'RRY *of Wind* (*Mar.*) a light breeze of wind shifting to different places.

FLUSH (*Carpent.*) a term among workmen, signifying that two bodies joined together make an even surface.

FLUSH *fore and aft* (*Mar.*) a term applied to a ship when the decks are laid level from head to stern.

FLUSH (*Sport.*) a term in a game at cards where they are all of a suit.

FLU'STRA (*Ent.*) a genus of animals, Class *Vermes,* Order *Zoophyta.*

Generic Character. *Animal* a polype, proceeding from porous cells; *stem* fixed and foliaceous, consisting of numerous rows of cells.

Species. Animals of this tribe, called in English Horn-wrack, inhabit the seas and oceans, adhering to rocks and shells.

FLUTE (*Mus.*) a wind instrument, consisting of a boxen or ivory tube, furnished with holes at the sides for varying the sounds. The *common flute* was formerly called *Flute à bec*, because one end resembled the beak of a bird. The German flute consists of a tube formed of several joints screwed into each other.

FLU'TED (*Archit.*) an epithet for a column which has flutes. [vide *Flutes*]

FLUTED (*Mus.*) an epithet for the upper and extra notes of a soprano voice.

FLUTES (*Archit.*) or *Flutings*, are the hollow channels formed along the surface of a column, which is then said to be fluted. The Doric, Ionic, Corinthian, and Composite columns, are usually fluted all along the body of the pillar from the base to the capital. Each column has 24 flutes, and each flute is hollowed in exactly a quarter of a circle, when a portion of the surface is left between the flutes, this is called the *fillet*.

FLUVIA'LIS (*Bot.*) the *Najas marina* of Linnæus.

FLUX (*Med.*) another word for Dysentery.

FLUX *and Reflux* (*Nat.*) the regular and periodical motion of the sea, which happens twice in 24 hours, 48 minutes. The *flux* is one motion of the tide, by which the water rises; and the *reflux*, or ebb, is the other motion, by which it sinks. Between the Flux and Reflux there is a kind of rest when the water is at its highest point, called *High-water*.

FLUX *Powders* (*Chem.*) or, as the French call them, *fondants*, are powders prepared to facilitate the fusion of the harder metals. Powder of antimony is a very good flux in many cases.

FLU'XION (*Chem.*) the running of metals into a fluid.

FLUXION (*Med.*) a flowing of humours or rheum.

FLUXION (*Surg.*) that which raises a swelling by the fluidity of its matter.

FLUXION (*Math.*) in the Newtonian Analysis, implies the magnitude by which any flowing quantity would be increased in a given time with a certain invariable velocity, in distinction from the *fluent* or flowing quantity, which is constantly and indefinitely increasing.—*Fluxions*, or the *method of Fluxions*, is the analysis of fluxions and flowing quantities. The notation, as introduced by Sir Isaac Newton, is as follows: the letters v, x, y, z, stand for the variable or flowing quantity; the same letters, with a dot over them, for the fluxions, as $\dot{v}, \dot{x}, \dot{y}, \dot{z}$; and if the fluxions themselves are variable quantities, their fluxions are denoted by two dots, as $\ddot{x}, \ddot{y}, \ddot{z}$; in the same manner the fluxions of the last fluxions may be continually denoted by the addition of a dot, as $\dddot{y}, \dddot{x}, \dddot{z}$, for the third fluxion; $\ddddot{y}, \ddddot{x}, \ddddot{z}$, for the fourth, &c. If the flowing quantity be a surd, as $\sqrt{x-y}$, its fluxion is denoted by $(\sqrt{x-y})\dot{}$; if a fraction as $\frac{xx}{d-y}$ by $\left(\frac{xx}{d-y}\right)\dot{}$; but sometimes the fluxions are denoted by the letter F, and the fluent by f, as $F. \sqrt{(x-y)}$, the fluxion of $\sqrt{(x-y)}$; and $f. \dot{x} \sqrt{(+a x^2)}$, the fluent of $\dot{x} \sqrt{(x-a x^2)}$. Invariable quantities are denoted by the letters a, b, c, d, &c.

FLY (*Ent.*) an insect of different kinds, which is classed under different names and genera. The *common Fly* is the *Musca* of Linnæus. The other kinds, as the Boat-fly, Butter-fly, Day-fly, Dragon-fly, Gad-fly, Golden-fly, Horse-fly, Lanthorn-fly, and Saw-fly, will be found in their respective places.

FLY (*Mech.*) a heavy weight applied to certain machines, to regulate their motions, as in a jack; or to increase their effect, as in the coining engine.

FLY *of the Compass* (*Mech.*) that part of the compass on which the thirty-two points or winds are drawn, and to which the needle is fastened underneath.

FLY *of an Ensign, Pendant,* &c. (*Mar.*) in French *battant d'un pavillon,* &c. the breadth or extent from the staff to the extreme edge or end that flutters loose in the wind.—*Fly-Boat,* a large vessel with a broad bow, used in the coasting trade.

Fly is also used in the sea phrase: "To let *fly* the sheets," i. e. to let the sails go out a-main.

TO FLY (*Falcon.*) is used in some phrases, as "To *fly* gross," said of a hawk when she flies at great birds. "To *fly* on head," i. e. when a hawk, missing her quarry, betakes herself to her next check.

FLY'-BOAT (*Mar.*) vide *Fly*.

FLY-CATCHER (*Orn.*) a sort of bird, inhabiting Asia, Africa, and America, which is so denominated because it feeds on insects, chiefly flies. It is the *Muscicapa* of Linnæus.

FLY-HONEYSUCKLE (*Bot.*) the *Halleria lucida* of Linnæus, a shrub.—Fly-Orchis, the *Orchis mucifera*, a plant, so called from the resemblance it bears in figure to that of a fly.—Venus' Fly-Trap, a kind of sensitive plant, the leaves of which consist of two lobes that close when they are irritated within, and consequently entrap any insect that lights upon them; from which circumstance it derives its name. It is the *Dionæa muscipula* of Linnæus.

FLY'ERS (*Archit.*) a series of steps in a flight of stairs which go straight forward, without winding round, and are made equally broad at both ends.

FLYING-BRI'DGE (*Archit.*) a bridge composed of two moveable parts, which may be transferred from place to place.

FLYING-DRA'GON (*Zool.*) a fourfooted reptile, inhabiting Africa and India, which is tailed and winged. It differs from the lizard tribe only by having a lateral membrane, which serves as a wing.

FLYING-FISH (*Ich.*) a sort of fish which inhabits the European and American seas: it is so called because it is enabled, by means of its long pectoral fins, to raise itself out of the water and remain suspended in the air for some time, which it does for the purpose of escaping from the jaws of predatory fish. It is the *Exocætus* of Linnæus.

FLYING-FISH (*Her.*) is occasionally borne as a charge in coat-armour.

FLYING-PI'NION (*Mech.*) that part of a clock which has a fly or fan wherewith to gather the air, and so to check the rapidity of the clock's motion when the weight descends in the striking part.

FLY'ING-TYGER (*Ent.*) an insect in America, spotted like the tyger.

FOAL (*Vet.*) a young colt.

FO'CAGE (*Archæol.*) Hearth-money.

FO'CAL DISTANCE (*Conic.*) the distance of the focus, which, in the parabola, is understood to be its distance from the vertex; and in the ellipse, or hyperbola, from the centre.

FOCA'LE (*Cus.*) a sort of kerchief or mufler, formerly worn about the neck, to guard the fauces from the cold.

FO'CILE *majus* (*Anat.*) the greater bone of the arm, called *ulna*; or the greater bone of the leg, called *tibia*. The lesser bone of the arm or leg is called *focile minus*.

FO'CUS (*Metal.*) another name for a smelting-house.

Focus *morbi* (*Med.*) ἰσία, the part in which a disease was supposed to keep its principal residence, as the *focus* of a fever, of which Galen speaks. *De Marasm.* c. 7.

Focus (*Anat.*) was formerly the name given to the first lobe of the liver, from a persuasion that it contributed to concoction.

Focus (*Geom.*) certain points in the transverse axis of the ellipse, hyperbola, and parabola, from which two lines drawn to any point in the curve will bear a certain proportion; namely, their sum in the ellipse or parabola, and their difference in the hyperbola is equal to the transverse axis. [vide *Conic Sections*] They are so called because the rays reflected from all parts of these curves concur or meet, i. e. rays issuing from a luminous point in one focus, and falling on all points of the curves, are reflected into the focus or the line directed to the other focus, viz. into the other focus in the ellipse and parabola, and directly from it in the hyperbola.

Focus (*Opt.*) the point of convergence or concourse in which several rays meet or are collected, after being either reflected or refracted. It is so called because the rays being here united, their force is increased; but it is worthy of observation, that although denominated a point, it is not strictly so, because it occupies a space of some small breadth.

FO'DDER (*Law*) a prerogative which the king has, to be provided with corn, &c. for his horses in warlike expeditions.

Fodder *of lead* (*Com.*) a weight consisting of 19½ hundred weight.

Fodder (*Husband.*) any kind of food for cattle, which is either green or dry. *Green Fodder* consists of grass, tares, hay, vetches, &c. *Dry Fodder* of corn, oats, barley, and beans.

FODERTO'RIUM (*Law*) provision of fodder, or forage, made to the King's purveyors.

FODI'NA (*Anat.*) the labyrinth, or lesser pit in the bone of the ear.

FŒMI'NEUS (*Bot.*) vide *Female*.

FŒNI'CULUM (*Bot.*) the *Anethum fœniculum* of Linnæus.

FŒNUM BURGUNDICUM (*Bot.*) the *Medicago sativa* of Linnæus.—*Fœnum Græcum*, the *Ononis ornithopodioides*.—*Fœnum Græcum* is also Fenu-Greek. [vide *Fenugreek*]

FOETA'BULUM (*Med.*) an incysted abscess, or foul ulcer.

FŒ'TUS (*Anat.*) *epicyema*, the child enclosed in the uterus of its mother, so called from the fifth month after pregnancy until the time of its birth. The internal parts peculiar to the fœtus are, *thymus gland*, *canalis venosus*, *canalis arteriosus*, *foramen ovale*, and the *membrana pupillaris*.

FOG (*Nat.*) a mist or meteor, consisting of condensed vapours floating near the surface of the earth or sea.

FO'G-BANK (*Mar.*) an appearance in hazy weather, which frequently resembles land at a distance, but which vanishes as you approach it.

FOIL (*Fenc.*) an elastic piece of steel, mounted like a sword, which is used in fencing for exercise.

Foil (*Sport.*) a fall in wrestling not cleverly given.

Foil (*Mech.*) a sheet of thin tin to be laid on the back side of looking-glasses.

FOI'LING (*Sport.*) the footing or treading of deer that are on the grass.

TO FOIN (*Fenc.*) to make a pass, or thrust, in fencing.

FOINES (*Com.*) from the French *foine*, a weasel; a sort of fur of that animal.

FOI'SON (*Husband.*) a term sometimes used to denote the natural juice or moisture of the grass, &c.

FOI'TERERS (*Archæol.*) vide *Faitours*.

FO'LCLANDS (*Archæol.*) copyhold lands so called in the time of the Saxons, in distinction from the Boclands. *Spelm. Feuds.* c. 5.

FO'LC-MOTE (*Archæol.*) or *Folkmote*, in Saxon folcgemot, from folc, the people, and gemot, or mot, a meeting or assembly; two courts, one now called the County Court, and the other the Sheriff's Turn.

FOLD (*Husband.*) an inclosed place in the fields in which sheep are confined.

FO'LDAGE (*Archæol.*) a liberty to fold sheep.

FO'LD-NET (*Sport.*) a sort of net for taking small birds in the night.

FOLE (*Vet.*) vide *Foal*.

FOLGAR'II (*Archæol.*) menial servants or followers, in distinction from Husfastene, or housekeepers. *LL. H.* 1, c. 9; *Bract.* 1. 3, tract. 2, c. 10.

FOLIA'CEUS (*Bot.*) foliaceous or leafy; an epithet for a leaf, or the glands: *spica foliacea* is a spike having leaves intermixed with the flowers; *glandulæ foliaceæ*, glands situated on the leaves.

FO'LIAGE (*Archit.*) a kind of ornament in cornices, friezes, &c. representing the leaves of plants. [vide *Architecture*, Plate No. III.]

Foliage (*Paint. &c.*) branched work in painting, tapestry, &c.

FOLIA'RIS (*Bot.*) an epithet for a tendril and a bud: *cirrus foliaris*, a tendril placed on a stalk; *gemma foliaris*, a leaf bud containing leaves, not flowers.

FO'LIATE (*Geom.*) an epithet for a curve of the second order, expressed by the equation $x^3 + y^3 = a x y$, which is one of the defective hyperbolas.

TO FOLIATE *a looking-glass* (*Mech.*) to lay the foil on so as to make it reflect the image.

FOLIA'TIO (*Bot.*) vernation, or leafing; one stage of vegetation, in which the nascent leaves are disposed in a particular manner in the form of a bud. The different modes of foliation are by Involution, Revolution, Obvolution, Convolution, Imbrication, Equitation, Conduplication, Plaiting, Reclination, Circinal or Spiral direction. [vide *Involution*, &c.]

FOLIA'TUS (*Bot.*) foliate, or leafy; an epithet for a stalk.

FO'LIO (*Com.*) the page, or rather the right and left hand page, in a merchant's ledger, which are numbered by the same figure corresponding to each other; whence, to folio is to put numbers on the pages.—*Folio* signifies the largest form of paper such as it comes from the manufactory; whence, also, books made in this form are called *folio*.

FOLIOLUM (*Bot.*) a partial or small leaf; a leaflet.

FOLIO'SUS (*Bot.*) leafy, an epithet for a *capitulum*, or head, having leaves intermixed with the flowers.

FO'LIUM (*Bot.*) vide *Leaf*.

FOLLI'CULUS (*Bot.*) the diminutive of *follis*, a bag, signifying a follicle or little bag; a univalvular pericarp, opening on one side longitudinally, and having the seeds loose in it.—*Folliculus* is also the name of little vessels or bags filled with air, called, by Withering, *air bags*, as at the root of the *Utricularia*.

Folliculus (*Surg.*) the bag or cystis, resembling a membrane, which contains the matter of anomalous abscesses.

Folliculus *fellis* (*Anat.*) the gall-bladder.

FO'MAHAUT (*Astron.*) a fixed star, of the first magnitude, in the constellation Aquarius, whose mean longitude at the beginning of 1760 was 11° 0° 28′ 55″; latitude 21° 6′ 28″ South.

FOMENTA'TION (*Med.*) the bathing any part of the body with a decoction of herbs, &c.—*Dry fomentation* is an application to the body, consisting of bags stuffed with herbs and other ingredients.

FO'MES *Ventriculi* (*Med.*) Hypochondriacism.

FO'MITES (*Med.*) a name given mostly to such things as are imbued with contagion.

FONS PULSA'TILIS (*Anat.*) vide *Fontanella*.

FONT (*Ecc.*) a basin or place in a church, for baptizing.

Font (*Print.*) a cast or complete set of letters for printing.

FONTANE'LLA (*Anat.*) the membranous part found in new-born infants at the coronal and sagittal commissures, which, in length of time, hardens into bone. It is either anterior or posterior.

FONTANELLA (*Surg.*) another name for an issue.
FONTANE'SIA (*Bot.*) a genus of plants, Class 2 *Diandria*, Order 1 *Monogynia*.
Generic Character. CAL. four-parted.—COR. *petals* ovate. STAM. *filaments* two; *anthers* oblong.—PIST. *germ* ovate; *style* compressed; *stigmas* two.—PER. *capsule* subovate; *seeds* oblong.
Species. The single species is the—*Fontanesia phyllyreoides*, native of Syria.
FONTILA'PATHUM (*Bot.*) the *Potamogeton crispum* of Linnæus.
FONTINA'LIA (*Ant.*) a Roman festival at which wells were crowned with garlands. It was celebrated on the Ides of October. *Varr. de Ling. Lat.* l. 5, c. 3; *Fest. de Verb. Signif.*; *Gyrald. Syntag. Deor.* l. 17, p. 496; *Ursat. de Not. Roman. apud Græv. Thes. Rom. Antiq.* tom. 11, p. 724.
FONTINA'LIS (*Bot.*) a genus of Mosses.
FONTINALIS is also a species of the *Byrum*.
FOOLS-PARSLEY (*Bot.*) the *Æthusa cynapium* of Linnæus.
FOOT (*Arith.*) a measure of length which in England consists of 12 inches: in Holland and other countries it is less than 12; and at Venice above 13 inches.—A *square Foot* is the same measure both in length and breadth, containing 12 × 12 = 144 square or superficial inches.—A *cubic Foot* is the same measure in all the three dimensions (length, breadth, and thickness), containing 12 × 12 = 144 × 12 = 1728 cubic inches.
FOOT (*Poet.*) a certain number of syllables which serve for the measuring of verses. The Greek and Roman poets employed feet of two syllables, as the Spondee, Trochee, Iambic, &c.; of three syllables, as the Dactyl, Anapæst, Molussus, &c.; of four syllables, as the Choriambus, Epitritus, Antispastus, &c. [vide *Grammar*]
FOOT *of a vertical line* (*Perspec.*) that point in the intersecting line which is made by a vertical plane passing through the eye and the centre of the picture.—*Foot of the Eye-Director*, the same point in the directing line.
FOOT (*Mil.*) soldiers who serve on foot, otherwise called *infantry*.
FO'OT-BANK (*Fort.*) or *foot-step*, a step about a foot and a half high and three feet wide, raised of earth under a breast-work, upon which men ascend to fire over.
FO'OT-FAT (*Vet.*) a term applied to a horse whose hoof is thin and weak so as to be unfit for shoeing.
FO'OT-GELD (*Law*) an amerciament for not expeditating a dog in the forest.
FO'OT-HALT (*Vet.*) a disorder peculiar to sheep, occasioned by an insect that infests the foot.
FO'OT-HOOK (*Mar.*) vulgarly pronounced *futtocks*, the compassing timbers, which give the breadth and bearing to the ship.
FOOT-I'RONS (*Mech.*) pieces of iron plate fixed to the soles of the shoes of those who dig canals, &c.
FO'OT-PACE (*Archit.*) the broad part of a stairs, on which a person may rest after taking four or six steps.
FO'OT-ROPE (*Mar.*) the rope to which the lower edge of the sail is sewed.—*Foot-waling*, the whole inside planks or lining of a ship.
FO'OT-STALK (*Bot.*) a term used either for the peduncle or the petiole.
FO'RAGE (*Mil.*) provender for horses in an army.—*Forage-Master-General*, formerly an officer under the marshal, who saw to the forage for the army, which duty is now performed by the Quarter-Master-General.
FORA'GIUM (*Archæol.*) straw or stubble after the corn is thrashed out.
FORA'GON (*Ant.*) a thread by which spinners mark so much as they spin in a day. *Fest. de Verb. Signif.*
FORA'MEN (*Anat.*) a perforation or opening, as—*Foramen cæcum*, an opening at the basis of the cranium; and also in the middle of the tongue.—*Foramen opticum*, the hole transmitting the optic nerve.—*Foramen ovale*, the opening between the two auricles of the heart of the fœtus.—*Foramen ischium*, a large hole in the hip-bone.
FORAMINULE'NTUM *os* (*Anat.*) the Ethmoid bone.
FORBA'LCA (*Archæol.*) a forebalk, or balk lying next the highway.
FORBA'RRE (*Law*) to bar or deprive one of a thing for ever. *Stat.* 9, *R.* 2, c. 2; 6 Hen. 6, c. 4.
FORBATU'DUS (*Archæol.*) one slain in a combat.
FORCE (*Phy.*) otherwise called *Power*, is whatever is or may be made the primary cause of motion in bodies. Force is exerted either on a body at rest, or a body in motion, the former is called *Vis mortua*, *Conatus movendi*, *Conamen*, &c. the latter *Vis motrix*, or *Vis viva*. Forces are likewise accelerative or retarditive, constant or variable, centripetal or centrifugal.—*Accelerative* or *retarditive Force* is that which respects the velocity of the motion only, accelerating or retarding it.—*Constant Force* is that which remains and acts continually the same for some determinate time, in distinction from—*Variable Force*, which is perpetually varying its effect and intensity.—*Centripetal Force* is that by which a body is perpetually urged towards a centre, in distinction from—*Centrifugal Force*, by which it is made to recede. *Newt. Princip.*
FORCE (*Law*) unlawful violence, which is either simple, compound, or mixed.—*Simple force* is that which is so committed that it is not complicated with any other crime.—*Compound*, or *mixed force*, is the violence committed in doing a thing otherwise unlawful.
FORCE (*Mil.*) any body of men collected together for a warlike enterprize. The *effective Force* of an army or a country, is that part which may be brought into action.
TO FORCE (*Mil.*) to take or effect by main force, as "To *force* a place," i. e. to take it by storm. "To *force* a passage," to oblige an enemy to retire. "To *force* an adversary's guard or blade," in the broadsword exercise, to strike away the adversary's sword, so as to be enabled to give a cut at the part which he aims to secure.
TO FORCE *Wool* (*Husband.*) to cut off the upper and most hairy part of it.
FO'RCENE (*Her.*) an epithet for a horse rearing or standing on its hinder legs.
FO'RCEPS (*Surg.*) a surgeon's tongs, pincers, &c. wherewith dead or corrupt parts may be removed.
FORCER (*Mech.*) a piston without a valve.
FO'RCERS (*Surg.*) an instrument with which teeth are drawn.
FORCES (*Mil.*) vide *Force*.
FORCES, *Equilibrium of*, (*Mech.*) i. e. the Composition or Resolution of Forces, is the conspiring or opposing of forces, so as to balance one another, or keep a body in equilibrio.
FO'RCIBLE (*Law*) an epithet implying with force, or by means, as a—*Forcible Entry*, i. e. violently taking possession of lands or tenements.—*Forcible Possession*, i. e. violently keeping possession, otherwise called a *Detainer*.
FO'RCIER (*Archæol.*) a water mill.
FO'RCING (*Hort.*) a method of obtaining flowers or fruits before their season by artificial means, particularly by the application of heat.
FORCING (*Com.*) a method of fining down wines, so as to render them fit for immediate draught.
FORCING *Pump* (*Mech.*) a pump that acts by a forcer, or a forcing piston.
FO'RDA (*Archæol.*) a cow with calf, or a milch-cow.
FO'RDIKA (*Archæol.*) herbage, or grass that grows on the edges of dikes or ditches.
FO'RDOL (*Archæol.*) a but or head-land abutting on other lands.
FORE (*Mar.*) the distinguishing character of all that part of a

ship's frame and machinery which lies near the stem; whence "*Fore and Aft*" signifying from stem to stern: so likewise—*Fore-bowline*, the Bowline of the foresail.—*Fore-braces*, belonging to the fore-yardarms.—*Fore-castle*, a short deck in the forepart of the ship.—*Fore-castle-Men*, men stationed at the fore-castle.—*Fore-cat-harpings*, a complication of ropes for the fore shrouds.—*Fore-foot*, a piece of timber terminating the keel at the fore-end.—*Fore-foot* is also said of one ship lying or sailing in another's way.—*Fore-ganger*, a rope to fix on a harpoon when it is intended to strike a whale.—*Fore-hooks*, the same as *Breast-hooks*.—*Fore-Knight*, a piece of timber, carved in the figure of a man's head, and fixed to the deck.—*Fore-land*, a cape or promontory projecting into the sea.—*Fore-lock*, a flat-pointed wedge of iron to drive through a hole at the end of a bolt.—*Fore-mast*, a mast in the fore-castle, or fore part of a ship.—*To Fore-reach upon a ship*, to advance upon, or gain ground of, a ship.—*Fore-runners* of the Log-line, a small piece of red buntin laid into that line at a certain distance from the log.—*Fore-staff*, an instrument formerly used at sea for taking the altitudes of bodies.—*Fore-tackle*, a tackle on the fore-mast.

FO'RE-CLOSED (*Law*) an epithet signifying barred beforehand, quite excluded.

FORE-FANG (*Law*) the taking up of provisions in fairs and markets before the King's purveyors are served.

FO'RE-FOOT (*Mar.*) vide *Fore*.

FO'RE-GA'NGER (*Mar.*) vide *Fore*.

FORE-GO'ERS (*Law*) purveyors who go before the king and queen when in progress, to make suitable provision for them.

FORE-HARPINGS (*Mar.*) vide *Fore*.

FO'RE-HOOKS (*Mar.*) vide *Fore*.

FO'REIGN (*Law*) out-landish, of another country; an epithet for several things, as—*Foreign answer*, an answer not triable in the county where it was made.—*Foreign attachment*, an attachment of foreigners' goods found within a liberty or city.—*Foreign matter*, is a matter triable in another county.—*Foreign apposer*, or *opposer*, an officer, in the Exchequer, to whom all sheriffs, after they are opposed of their sums out of the pipe-office, repair to be apposed or charged by him of their green wax.—*Foreign plea* is the rejecting of a judge as incompetent, because the matter in hand was not in his precinct.—*Foreign-service* is that whereby a mean lord holds over another, without the compass of his own fee.

FOREIGN *service* (*Mil.*) in a general sense, signifies every service not British; but, in a limited sense, any service out of the British Isles.

FO'RE-JUDGED *the Court* (*Law*) is when an officer of any court is expelled the same for some offence; as, for not appearing to an action by bill filed against him.

FO'RE-JUDGER (*Law*) a judgement whereby a person is deprived of, or put by, the thing in question.

FO'RE-KNIGHT (*Mar.*) vide *Fore*.

FO'RE-LAND (*Mar.*) vide *Fore*.

FORE-LAND (*Fort.*) a confined space of ground between the rampart and the moat.

FORE-LOCK (*Mar.*) vide *Fore*.

TO FO'RE-LOYN (*Sport.*) is when a hound, going before the rest of the cry, meets chase and goes away with it.

FO'RE-PRIZED (*Law*) a term in conveyancing, which signifies excepting.

FO'RE-SCHOKE (*Law*) the same as *Forsaken*.

TO FO'RE-SHORTEN (*Paint.*) is to make a head or face in a drawing appear shorter before.

FO'REST (*Law*) a large wood, privileged to hold the king's game of all kinds; so called, as some suppose, *quasi ferarum statio*, the abode of game or wild beasts.

FO'RESTER (*Law*) a keeper of a forest. A *forester in fee* is one who has that office to him and his heirs.

FO'RE-STAFF (*Mar.*) vide *Fore*.

TO FORE-STALL (*Com.*) to buy or bargain for corn, &c. as it is coming to market.

FO'RE-STALLER (*Law*) one who lies in wait to stop deer that have broken out of the forest.

FORE-STALLER (*Com.*) a monopolizer, or one who forestalls the market.

FORE'T (*Gunn.*) French for a steel instrument to bore the touch hole of a piece of cannon.

FORETHOUGHT-FELONY (*Law*) premeditated killing, in the Scotch Law.

FO'RFEITURE (*Law*) the effect or penalty of transgressing some penal law.—*Forfeiture of marriage*, a writ formerly lying for a lord against his ward, or tenant under age, who refused a convenient marriage offered him by his lord. F. N. B. 141; Reg. Orig. 163.

FORFI'CULA (*Ent.*) the Earwig; a genus of insects, of the *Coleopterous* Order, having setaceous *antennæ*, unequal filiform *feelers*, *shells* half as long as the abdomen, *wings* folded up under the shells, and *tail* armed with a forceps.

FORGA'BULUM (*Law*) or *forgavel*, a small rent reserved in rent, a quit-rent.

FORGE (*Mech.*) a place where a smith heats his irons, or a large furnace where iron ore is melted.

TO FORGE *over* (*Mar.*) to force a ship violently over a shoal by the effort of a great quantity of sail.

FORGER *of false deeds* (*Law*) one who makes and publishes false writings.

FO'RGERY (*Law*) the fraudulent making or altering any record, deed, writing, instrument, register, stamp, &c. to the prejudice of another man's right.

FORI'NSECUM *manerium* (*Law*) a manor which is not included within the liberties of a town.

FORIS-BANNI'TUS (*Archæol.*) banished. Mat. Par. Ann. 1245.

FORISFAMILIA'RI (*Law*) to be discharged from a family; which is said of a son who accepts lands in his father's life time, and being content therewith can claim no more.

FORK (*Bot.*) *furca*, a divided prickle, called bifid or trifid, according to the number of divisions, as in *Berberis*, *Ribes*, &c.

FO'RKED (*Sport.*) an epithet for the heads of deer which bear two croches on the top, or have their croches doubled.

FORKED (*Bot.*) *furcatus*, branched or subdivided; an epithet for anthers, bristles, fronds, and stems.

FORLA'NA (*Mus.*) Italian for a slow kind of jig.

FORLO'RN-HOPE (*Mil.*) a name given to a body of men put upon the most desperate service.

FORLO'YN (*Sport.*) a retreat when the dogs are called off from a wrong scent.

FORM (*Phil.*) the essential and distinguishing modification of the matter of which any substance is composed.

FORM (*Mech.*) a kind of mould in which any thing is wrought.

FORM (*Print.*) a name given to the chase when it is filled with type, or letter: when it is empty it is properly called a chase.

FORM (*Sport.*) the seat of a hare; whence the phrase "The hare *forms*," for she squats.

FORM (*Law*) certain established rules to be observed in processes or judicial proceedings.

TO FORM (*Mil.*) to assume any figure in military movements, according to prescribed rules, as "To *form* line," to wheel to the right or left, so as to present one continued line. "To *form* rank entire," to extend the front by reducing the depth as much as possible. "To *form* echelon," to move so as to produce a diagonal direction in a line. "To *form* two deep, three deep, &c."

FO'RMA *Pauperis* (*Law*) a mode of bringing a suit in the character of a pauper, when a man will swear that he is not worth five pounds; in such cases he is released from costs of suit, &c.

FORME' (*Her.*) vide *Pattee.*
FO'RMED (*Nat.*) an epithet for any bodies, such as stones, spars, &c. which are found in the earth so formed, that their outward shape very nearly resembles muscles, &c.
FORME'DON (*Law*) i. e. *forma donationis*, a writ which lies for one who has a right to lands or tenements by virtue of an entail. *F. N. B.* 255, &c.; *New Nat. Brev.* 476, &c.
FO'RMERS (*Gunn.*) round pieces of wood fitted to the bore of a great gun, which hold the carriages for the powder.
FO'RMIATE (*Chem.*) a salt produced by the union of the formic acid with different bases, as *formiate* of ammonia.
FO'RMIC ACID (*Chem.*) the acid of ants, which is obtained chiefly from the red ant, the *Formica rufa* of Linnæus.
FORMI'CA (*Ent.*) the Ant, or Emmet, a genus of insects of the Hymenopterous Order, having four unequal feelers; *antennæ* filiform; females and neuters armed with a sting; males and females with wings.
  Species. This gregarious and industrious tribe of insects consists, like bees, of males, females, and neuters, which last are the labourers, who construct the nests, or ant-hills, and guard the *larvæ*, commonly known by the name of *ants' eggs.*
Formica (*Surg.*) the name of a black callous wart, that is broad at the bottom.
Formica (*Falcon.*) a distemper in a hawk's beak which eats it away.
FORMULA (*Math.*) a general theorem, or literal expression for resolving any part of a problem: thus $x = a \pm \sqrt{(a^2 + b)}$ is an algebraical formula; hyp. log. $(1 + y) = y - \frac{1}{2}y^2 + \frac{1}{3}y^3$; a logarithmic formula and sin. $(a + b) = $ sin. a, cos. $b + $ sin. b, cos. a, a trigonometrical formula.
Formula (*Med.*) a little form or prescription, such as physicians give in extemporaneous practice in distinction from a regular prescription.
FO'RMULARY (*Law*) a book of forms, or precedents, for law matters; also the written form of an oath to be taken on certain occasions.
Formulary (*Mus.*) the name formerly given to the prescribed number and disposition of the ecclesiastical notes.
FORNACA'LIA (*Ant.*) a festival instituted by Numa Pompilius, at which all the people baked cakes *ad fornacem*, i. e. at the oven. *Fest. Signif. Verb.*
FORNA'GIUM (*Law*) from *fornax*, a furnace; a fee taken by a lord of his tenants who were bound to bake in his oven, or for the liberty of using their own.
FO'RNAX (*Chem.*) a furnace.
FORNICA'TUS (*Bot.*) vide *Vaulted.*
FO'RNIX (*Anat.*) a part of the *corpus callosum* of the brain, so called because of its resemblance in form to the arch of a vault.
Fornix (*Bot.*) vide *Arch.*
FORPRI'SED (*Law*) vide *Foreprized.*
FO'RRAGE (*Mil.*) vide *Forage.*
FO'RSECHOKE (*Law*) vide *Foreschoke.*
FORSKOHLE'A (*Bot.*) a genus of plants, so called from Forskohl, a Swedish botanist, Class 8 *Octandria*, Order 4 *Tetragynia*, or Class 10 *Decandria*, Order 5 *Pentagynia*.
  Generic Character. CAL. *perianth* four or five-leaved.—COR. *petals* eight.—STAM. *filaments* eight or ten; *anthers* twin.—PIST. *germs* four or five; *styles* bristle-shaped; *stigmas* simple.—PER. none; *seeds* four, five.
  Species. The species are mostly annuals, as the—*Forskohlea tenacissima, Caidbeja, seu Chamædrifolia*, Clammy Forskohlea.—*Forskohlea angustifolia*, Narrow-leaved Forskohlea, native of the Cape of Good Hope; but the *Forskohlea candida*, Rough Forskohlea, is a shrub and native of Teneriffe.
FO'RSPEAKER (*Law*) one who pleads for another.

FO'RSTAL (*Law*) vide *Forestal.*
FORSTE'RA (*Bot.*) a genus so called from J. and G. Forster, father and son, Botanists, Class 20 *Gynandria*, Order 2 *Diandria*.
  Generic Character. CAL. *perianth* double.—COR. one-petalled.—STAM. *filaments* two.—PIST. *germ* oval; *style* erect; *stigmas* two.—PER. *capsule* oval; *seeds* many.
  Species. The single species is the *Forstera sedifolia*, native of New Zealand.
FORSYTHIA (*Bot.*) the *Decumaria barbara* of Linnæus.
FORT (*Fort.*) a castle, or strong hold of small extent; a work encompassed with a moat, rampart, and parapet, to secure some high ground, or passage of a river, to make good an advantageous post, to fortify the lines and quarters of a siege, &c.—*Royal-fort* is a fortification having at least 26 fathoms for the line of defence.—*Star-fort*, a redoubt which is made of re-entering and saliant angles.—*Field-fort*, otherwise called *fortin* or *fortlet*, and sometimes a *sconce* a small fort built in haste to defend a pass or post.
FORTA'LIEL (*Archæol.*) a fortress or place of strength.
FO'RTE (*Mus.*) an Italian word signifying strong, is frequently applied in music books to parts that are to be performed in a strong manner; *piu forte* signifies still stronger; *forte forte* very strong.
FO'RTHCOMING action of (*Law*) an action in the Scotch law in the nature of an attachment.
FORTIA (*Law*) power or dominion.
FORTIFICA'TION, otherwise called *military architecture*, the art of strengthening and fortifying a place by encircling it with certain works to secure and defend it from the attacks of enemies. Fortification is either theoretical or practical, defensive or offensive.—*Theoretical fortification* consists in tracing plans and profiles on paper with scales, &c.—*Practical fortification* consists in forming the project of a work according to the nature of the ground and other existing circumstances, &c.—*Defensive fortification* is that by which a town is defended in case of a siege.—*Offensive fortification* consists in making and conducting all the works requisite for the attack or siege of a town, &c.—Fortification, in the sense of a fortified place, is either durable or temporary, regular or irregular.—*Durable fortification*, that which is built with a view to remain for a permanency.—*Temporary fortification*, that which is raised on some particular emergency, and only to last for the time required, as field-works, &c.—*Regular fortification*, that in which the bastions are all equal, or which is built in a regular polygon.—*Irregular fortification* is that in which the sides and angles are not uniform, equidistant, or equal, owing to the inequalities in the situation from hills, valleys, rivers, &c.
To a fortification belong lines, angles, solid works, and appurtenances.
Lines of a fortification. The following are the principal lines, namely—*Capital line*, an imaginary right line that divides any work into two equal and similar parts.—*Line of circumvallation*, the line drawn by a fortification of earth round a town intended to be besieged.—*Line of communication*, the space of ground which joins the citadel to the town.—*Line of contravallation*, a line similar to the line of circumvallation. [vide *Contravallation*]—*Line of counter-approach*. [vide *Approaches*] —*Line of defence*, the distance between the saliant angle and the opposite flank. Lines of defence are either *fichant*, *razant*, or *prolonged*. [vide *Fichant*, &c.]
Angles. The principal angles in a fortification are the Angle of the Flank, of the Bastion, of the Epaule, of the Tenaille, of the Face, of the Base, &c. [vide *Angle*]
Works of a fortification. The works of a place are the fortifications about the place, in distinction from the outworks, or such as are detached from the walls of the

FORTIFICATION.

fortification. The principal works are as follow: namely, —*Appareille*, the slope, or easy ascent, which leads to the platform of the bastion. — *Approaches*, roads or passages sunk in the ground by the besiegers, whereby they approach the place.—*Area*, the superficial content of a rampart, or other work.—*Arrow*, a work placed at the salient angle of the glacis.—*Banquette*, a kind of step made on the rampart near the parapet.—*Barriers*, pointed stakes to prevent the horse or foot from rushing in upon the besieged with violence.—*Bastion*, a part of the inner inclosure of a fortification, making an angle towards the field. Bastions are full, flat, solid, hollow, detached, cut, &c. [vide *Bastion*]—*Berme*, a little space or path between the ditch and the talus of the parapet.—*Bonnet*, a work consisting of two faces placed before the salient angle of the bastion to cover it. —*Breach*, an opening or gap made in a wall or rampart to cover it.—*Caponnière*, a passage made in a dry ditch from one work to another.—*Cascanes*, a kind of cellars made under the capital of a fortification.—*Casemate*, a work made under the rampart with loopholes for the guns. — *Cavaliers*, works raised, generally within the place, ten or twelve feet higher than the rest.—*Cordon*, a semicircular projection made of stone, which goes round the wall.—*Covert-way*, a space, five or six toises broad, that extends round the counterscarp.—*Counterforts*, a sort of buttresses behind the walls.—*Counterguard*, a work placed before the bastions to cover the opposite flanks. — *Counterscarp*, the exterior talus of the ditch, or that slope which terminates its breadth.— *Crown-work*, a work resembling a crown in form, having two fronts and two branches.—*Curtain*, that part of the body of a place which joins the flank of one bastion to that of another.—*Cuvette*, a small ditch in the middle of a dry ditch.—*Defilement*, the disposing the works of a fortress in such a manner, that they may be commanded by the body of the place.—*Descents*, vaults and hollow places.—*Ditch*, the trench made round each work, which may be wet or dry.—*Drawbridge*, vide *Bridge*.—*Embrasures*, vide *Embrasure*.—*Envelope*, any work that envelops or surrounds another work, a spot of ground, &c.—*Enceinte*, the interior wall or rampart. *Epaulement*, vide *Epaulement*.—*Epaule*, the shoulder of the bastion.—*Faces* of any work, those parts where the rampart is made which produce an angle pointing outwards. [vide *Face*]—*Fascines*, vide *Fascines*. — *Flank*, any part of a work which defends another along the outsides of the parapets. Flanks are of different kinds. [vide *Flank*]—*Flèche*, a work of two faces, often constructed before the glacis.—*Gallery*, a passage made under ground, leading to the mines.—*Glacis*, the part beyond the covert way, to which it serves as a parapet. —*Gorge* of any work is that part next to the body of the place where there is no rampart or parapet.— *Half-moon*, an outwork that has two faces which form a salient angle, the gorge of which resembles a crescent.— *Horn-work* is composed of a front and two branches, and is mostly used to take possession of some rising ground.— *Horse-shoe*, a small oval outwork with a parapet, generally made in a ditch.—*Loop-holes*, square or oblong holes in the walls.—*Lunettes*, works made on both sides of a ravelin.—*Merlon* is that part of the breastwork of the battery which is between the embrasures.—*Orilon*, that part of the bastion near the shoulder which serves to cover the retired flank from being seen obliquely.—*Palisades*, stakes fixed in the ground within the covert way to secure it from surprise.—*Parapet*, that part of a rampart which serves to cover the troops placed there to defend it. — *Portcullis*, a falling gate, or door, resembling a harrow in shape. —

Place of arms, a part of the covert way.—*Rampart*, an elevation of earth raised along the faces of any work to cover the inner part.—*Ram's-horns*, low works of a circular form made in a ditch.—*Ravelin*, a work placed before the curtain to cover it.—*Redans*, indented works consisting of lines and facings that form salient or re-entering angles flanking one another.—*Redoubt*, a work placed beyond the glacis, of various forms.—*Retrenchment*, any work raised to cover a post, and fortify it against an enemy.—*Revêtement*, a strong wall built on the outside of the rampart and parapet. — *Rideau*, a small elevation of earth extending along a plain to cover a camp, &c. — *Sapping*, vide *Siege*. — *Sillon*, a work raised in the middle of a ditch to defend it when too broad.—*Swallow's-tail*, an outwork resembling a *tenaille*. —*Talus*, a slope made either on the outside or the inside of a work.—*Tenailles*, low works made in the ditch before the curtains.—*Tenaillons*, works made on each side of the ravelin, much like the lunettes. — *Terrepleine*, the horizontal superficies of the rampart. — *Tower-bastions*, small towers made in the form of bastions.—*Traditore* signifies the concealed or hidden guns in a fortification.—*Traverses* are parapets made across the covert-way opposite to the salient angles of the works. —*Trous de loups*, Wolf-Holes, round holes generally made round a redoubt to obstruct the enemy's approach. According to the disposition of these several parts various systems have been formed by different writers, as Pagan, Vauban, Cohorn, Belidor, Blondel, &c. In the annexed plate (36) is given a general view of those parts as they may be disposed according to circumstances. To the attack and defence of a fortification belong cannons, petards, mortars, bombs, chandeliers, chevaux de frises, caltrops, gabions, fascions, chevrettes, caissons, &c. [vide *Cannon*, &c. and Plate 36]

Explanation of the Plate 36.

Fig. 1. Plan of a Fortification. A. A single Bastion. B. A double Bastion, or Cavalier, to overlook the enemy's bastions, and scour their trenches. C. A flat Bastion which is made where the line of defence is too long. It is here placed in the middle of the curtain. D. A Half-bastion placed on the side of a river. E. A Bastion tenailed when the angle of the bastion is less than 70 degrees. F. A Ravelin which covers the gates, bridges, and curtains. G. The Glacis. H. A Half-Moon made to cover the flanked angle of the bastion. I. A Counterguard raised instead of a half-moon. K. A Single Tenaille. L. A Swallow's Tail. M. A Bonnet à *Prestre*. N. A Hornwork whose head is fortified with two demi-bastions, or epaulements, joined by a curtain, and closed by parallel sides ending at the gorge of the work. N n. A Hornwork whose sides are not parallel. O. A Crownwork to cover a large spot of ground. P. Tenailles to defend the ditch. Q. A Half-Moon covered with R R, Two Counterguards to make it the stronger. S S. Places of Arms on the counterscarp. 3. The Ditch. T T. The Counterscarp, or Covered-way. V. A Retrenchment within or behind. X. A Breach. W. A place for a Magazine. *a a*. Redoubts. *b b b*. Batteries. *c c*. Lines of Communication. *d d*. Trenches by which the approaches are carried on. *e*. A Mine under the glacis and covered-way of the horn-work. *f*. A lodgement at the foot of the glacis.

Fig. 2. The parts of a piece of ordnance. A B. The length of the cannon. *a z*. The bore or caliber. A E. The first reinforce. E F. The second reinforce. F B. The chace. H B. The muzzle. A O. The cascabel, or pomelion. A C. The breech. A I. The breechment. C D. The vent-field. T T. The trunnions.

F I. The chace-girdle. C c. The bare-ring. d. The vent, astragal, and fillets. e, f. The first reinforce-ring and ogee. g, h. The second reinforce-ring and ogee. k. The chace, astragal, and fillets. l. The muzzle, astragal, and fillets. m. The swelling of the muzzle. n. The muzzle mouldings.

Fig. 3. The inside of a piece of ordnance. a. The chace. b. The chamber for the powder.

Fig. 4. A petard.—Fig. 5. A mortar. Fig. 6. Bombs. a a. The fusees.—Fig. 7. Chevaux-de-Frises.—Fig. 8. Caltrops.—Fig. 9. Chandeleers.

FORTI'LITY (*Archæol.*) a fortified place.

FO'RTIN (*Fort.*) a fortlet, sconce, or little fort.

FORTIO'RI (*Log.*) or *à fortiori*, an epithet for any conclusion, or inference, which is much stronger than another.

FORTI'SSIMO (*Mus.*) an Italian epithet signifying very loud. [vide *Forte*]

FO'RTITUDES (*Astrol.*) certain advantages which planets are supposed to have to make their influences stronger.

FO'RTLET (*Fort.*) a little fort.

FO'RTRESS (*Fort.*) a general name for all places that are fortified either by nature or art.

FO'RTUNES (*Astrol.*) a name for the two benevolent planets, Jupiter and Venus.

FORTU'NIUM (*Archæol.*) a tournament, or fighting with spears. *Math. Par. Ann.* 1241.

FO'RTY-DAYS'-COURT (*Law*) the court of attachment in forests, or the *Woodmote Court*.

FO'RUM (*Ant.*) a public place in Rome where causes were tried and business transacted. The fora are consequently divided into the *civilia* and the *venalia*.—*Fora civilia* were public courts of justice in which causes were tried and orations delivered to the people. There were six of these, namely, 1. *Forum Romanum*. 2. *Julianum*. 3. *Augustum*. 4. *Palladium*. 5. *Forum Trajani*. 6. *Forum Sallustii*. The *Forum Romanum*, the most noted of all, was in general denominated, by way of eminence, simply the *Forum;* in which was the Rostrum, the Comitium, the Sanctuary of Saturn, &c.—*Fora venalia*, or places of traffic, answered to our market-places. The chief of them were the *forum boarium, suarium, pistorium, cupedinarium, olitorium,* &c. according as they were used for oxen, swine, bread, dainties, vegetables, &c. The Grecian ἀγορά corresponded altogether with the Roman Forum. *Dionys.* l. 2; *Cic. in Ver.* 2, c. 20, &c.; *Ovid. Fast.* l. 3, v. 704; *Liv.* l. 26, c. 2; *Senec. de Ira*, l. 2, c. 9; *Panciroll. Descript. Urb. Rom. &c. apud Græv. Thes. Ant. Rom.* tom. 3, &c.

FO'RWARD (*Mil.*) a word of command for soldiers to proceed on their march, having halted.

FOSS-WAY (*Mil.*) one of the great Roman roads in England, so called from the ditches on both sides.

FOSSA (*Law*) a ditch full of water, in which women who committed felony were drowned.

FOSSA (*Anat.*) the interior of the *pudendum muliebre*.

FO'SSAGE (*Law*) a composition paid to be exempt from the repairing or maintaining the ditches round a town.

FOSSATO'RUM OPERA'TIO (*Law*) foss work, or service formerly done by inhabitants for repairing and maintaining the ditches round a town.

FOSSA'TUM (*Archæol.*) a ditch or a place fenced within a ditch or trench.

FO'SSILES (*Min.*) *fossilia*, from *fodio*, to dig: a general name for whatever is dug out of the earth, whether it be native, as metals, stones, &c.; or extraneous, i. e. that which has been accidentally buried in the earth, as trees, plants, parts of animals, &c.

FO'SSILUS (*Anat.*) the bone of the leg.

FO'STER-FATHER (*Cus.*) one who brings up another man's child.

FOSTER-LE'AN (*Law*) a wife's jointure.

FO'STER-LAND (*Law*) land allotted for the provision of any persons.

TO FO'THER (*Mar.*) or *Fodder*, in French *aveugler une voie d'eau;* to endeavour to stop a leak in the bottom of a ship while she is afloat, either under sail or at anchor.

FOTHERGI'LLA (*Bot.*) a genus of plants, Class 13 *Polyandria*, Order 2 *Digynia*.

Generic Character. CAL. *perianth* one-leaved.—COR. none.—STAM. *filaments* many; *anthers* erect.—PIST. *germ* ovate; *styles* two.—PER. *capsule* hardened; *seeds* solitary.

Species. The single species is a tree, as the *Fothergilla alnifolia*, native of Carolina.

FOTHERGILLA is also another name for the *Melastoma*.

FO'TUS (*Med.*) vide *Fomentation*.

FO'VEA (*Med.*) a sudatory or sweating bath.

FOVEA (*Anat.*) a sinus of the *Pudendum muliebre*.

FOUGA'DE (*Fort.*) French for a sort of mine in which are fireworks to blow any thing up.

FOVI'LLA (*Bot.*) a fine substance, imperceptible to the naked eye, exploded by the pollen in the anthers of flowers.

FOUL (*Mar.*) an epithet applied mostly in opposition to clean or clear; as, "a *foul* anchor," when the cable is twisted round the stock, &c.—"A *foul* bottom," the bottom of a ship which is very dirty.—"*Foul* ground of a road, bay, &c." ground that is rocky and full of shallows, &c.—"*Foul* hawse" cables twisted round each other.— "*Foul* rope," an entangled rope.—"*Foul* water," shallow water made foul by a vessel under sail which throws up mud from the bottom.—"*Foul* wind," a contrary wind.— "To run *foul* of a ship," to get entangled in her rigging.

FOUNDA'TION (*Archit.*) that part of a building which is under ground, and serves to support the superincumbent mass.

FO'UNDAY (*Archæol.*) the space of six days, formerly so called in the ironworks.

FO'UNDER (*Ecc.*) one who builds and endows a college, church, &c.

TO FOUNDER (*Mar.*) is said of a ship when, by reason of a great leak, &c. or heavy sea breaking in upon her, she takes in so much water that she cannot be freed from it, and eventually sinks.

TO FOUNDER a Horse (*Vet.*) vide *Foundring*.

FOUNDERS, Company of (*Her.*) was incorporated in 1614. Their armorial ensigns are, as in the annexed figure, *azure*, an ewer between two pillars *or*.

FOU'NDLING (*Cus.*) a child exposed to chance, and found without any parent or owner.

FOU'NDRING (*Vet.*) a defluxion of humours upon the sinews of the legs, occasioned by hard riding, &c. which causes an unusual stiffness in them, so that they lose their usual motion.—*Chest-foundring*, a disease in the chest of horses, very similar to that which affects the feet.

FOUNT (*Print.*) vide *Font*.

FOU'NTAIN (*Geog.*) a natural source or spring of water rising out of the ground.

FOUNTAIN (*Hydraul.*) a machine by which water is spouted out; it is also called a *jet d'eau*.

FOUNTAIN (*Her.*) is drawn as a roundle, barry wavy of six, as he beareth "*sable*, a bend, *or*, between six fountains *proper*." These are the arms of Lord Stourton, which were borne in signification of the six springs which give rise to the river Stour, in Wiltshire.

FOUNTAIN-PE'N (*Mech.*) a pen contrived to hold a quantity of ink, and to let it flow gently, so as to supply the writer for a long time without the necessity of taking fresh ink.

FOUR (*Bot.*) a term used frequently in composition as four-cleft or quadrufid, four-cornered, four-leaved, &c.

FO'URCHER (*Law*) in Latin *furcare*, and in French *fourcher*; the delaying or putting off an action which might be determined in a short space of time. *Stat. West.* 1, (3 Ed. 1) c. 43; 2 *Inst.* 250.

FO'URCHY (*Her.*) or *Fourchee*, an epithet for a cross. A cross fourchee is one which, as in the annexed figure, is forked at the ends, having its forks composed of straight lines and ends as if cut off.

FOU'MEAU (*Min.*) the chamber of a mine.

FOURTEE'NTH (*Mus.*) the octave or replicate of the seventh; a distance comprehending thirteen diatonic intervals.

FOURTH (*Mus.*) a distance comprehending three diatonic intervals, i. e. two tones and a half. The *minor or lesser fourth* consists of five semitones; but the *fourth sharp*, or *greater*, consists of six semitones. The Fourth is the third of the consonances.

FO'WLER (*Gun.*) the name formerly of a piece of ordnance.

FOWLER (*Sport.*) one who practises fowling, or the art of hunting birds.

FOX (*Zool.*) a crafty, lively, libidinous animal, the *Canis vulpes* of Linnæus, which sleeps much in the day, but seeks its prey at night among the poultry, rabbits, hares, and feathered game. It breeds only once a year, and brings forth commonly in April four or five young, which, like puppies, are born blind. It has a remarkably bushy tail, called by sportsmen the *brush*, and its smell is very strong, particularly that of the urine, which is so fetid that the dogs have sometimes been deterred by it from approaching the animal. There is another kind of Fox, called the Brant Fox, the *Canis alopex* of Linnæus, which inhabits Asia, is somewhat less, and much darker. The Arctic Fox, *Canis lagopus* of Linnæus, which lives near the Frozen Sea, is remarkable for its hairy feet.

Fox (*Her.*) as a charge, is supposed to denote a subtle wit, by which a man has served his country. It is borne either whole or in part, as he beareth "Argent two foxes counter-saliant in bend, the dexter surmounted of the sinister saltire wise, gules, by the name of Kadxod Hard, of Wales." There are also examples of Foxes' Heads as a bearing.

Fox (*Mar.*) in French *tresse de vieux cordages*, a sort of strand formed by twisting several rope-yarns together, and used as a seizin. The *Spanish Fox* is a single rope-yarn untwisted and twisted up the contrary way.

FOX-GLOVE (*Bot.*) the *Digitalis* of Linnæus, the species of which are mostly perennials.—Fox-Grape, the *Vitis vulpina*, so called because it resembles the scent of a fox.—Fox-Tail Grass, the *Alopecurus*.

FOY (*Cus.*) from the French *voie*, a way; a treat given to their friends by those who are going a journey.

To FOYL (*Husband.*) to fallow land in the summer or autumn.

FO'YLING (*Hunt.*) the footsteps of a stag upon the grass.

FRA'CTION (*Math.*) a broken number which consists of a part or parts of any quantity considered as unity or a whole; thus, suppose any number to be divided into 5 parts, then 1, 2, 3, &c. of those parts form what is termed the fraction; as $\frac{1}{5}, \frac{2}{5}, \frac{3}{5}$, &c. The number below the line, namely 5, is the *Denominator*, because it denominates the number of parts into which the unit or quantity is supposed to be divided; and the number above the line, as 1, 2, or 3, is the *Numerator*, because it enumerates how many of those parts are taken.

Fractions are of different kinds, namely—*Vulgar Fractions*, i. e. the common fractions, in distinction from *Decimal Fractions*. [vide *Decimals*]

Proper Fractions have the numerator less than the denominator, as $\frac{1}{3}, \frac{2}{3}, \frac{3}{4}$.—*Improper Fractions* have the numerator either equal to, or greater than, the denominator, as $\frac{3}{3}$, or $\frac{4}{3}$.—*Simple Fractions* consist of a single numerator or denominator.—*Compound Fractions* consist of several fractions connected by the word of, as $\frac{1}{4}$ of $\frac{1}{4}$ of $\frac{1}{17}$, &c.—*Complex Fractions*, those whose numerator and denominator consist of fractions, as $\frac{\frac{1}{3}}{7\frac{1}{4}}$.—*Mixed Fractions*, or Mixed Numbers, where an integer and a fraction is joined together, as $7\frac{1}{4}, 9\frac{1}{17}$, &c.—*Continued Fractions* are fractional quantities running in a series, as $\frac{1}{2} + \frac{1}{3} + \frac{1}{4} + \frac{1}{5}$, &c.

Fractions are worked by the rules of Addition, Subtraction, Multiplication, Division, Reduction, &c. in a manner similar to whole numbers, of which more may be seen under the respective words.

FRA'CTIONAL (*Arith.*) an epithet for what is in the form of a fraction, as fractional quantities, exponents, &c.

FRA'CTURE (*Surg.*) κάταγμα, the separation of a bone, by means of violence, into two or more fragments. A *simple Fracture* is that where a bone is broken only in one part.—A *compound Fracture* is when two large bones, contiguous to each other, as the *Ulna* and the *Radius*, are both broken.—A *complicated Fracture* is that which is attended with a train of symptoms, as a wound or ulcer.

The ancients divided Fractures according to their different directions, into *raphanedon*, transverse; *cauledon*, stalkwise; *sicyedon*, *schedacedon*, *alphitedon*, *apothrausis*, *apocope*, &c. of which a further account may be found under the respective words.

FRÆNA'TOR (*Anat.*) a name for several muscles which serve to move the head.

FRÆ'NULUM (*Anat.*) a membraneous string under the tongue.

FRÆ'NUM (*Anat.*) the ligament by which the prepuce is bound to the *glans penis*.

FRAGA'RIA (*Bot.*) a genus of plants, Class 12 *Icosandria*, Order 3 *Polygynia*.

Generic Character. CAL. *perianth* one-leaved.—COR. *petals* five.—STAM. *filaments* twenty; *anthers* lunular.—PIST. *germs* numerous; *styles* simple; *stigmas* simple.—PER. none; *seeds* numerous.

Species. The species are perennials, as the—*Fragaria vesca*, seu *Potentilla*, Esculent Strawberry.—*Fragaria Monophylla*, seu *Le Frasier*, Simple-leaved Strawberry.—*Fragaria sterilis*, Barren Strawberry. *Dod. Pempt.*; *Bauh. Hist.*; *Bauh. Pin.*; *Ger. Herb.*; *Park. Theat.*; *Raii Hist.*; *Tourn. Inst.*

FRAGARIA is also the *Comarum palustre* of Linnæus.

FRAGA'RIÆ AFFI'NIS (*Bot.*) the *Sibbaldia procumbens* of Linnæus.

FRAGA'RIUS (*Bot.*) the *Melastoma melabathrica* of Linnæus.

FRAGILI'TAS OSSIUM (*Anat.*) brittleness of the bones.

FRAISE (*Fort.*) stakes fixed in bulwarks made of earth on the one side of the rampart below the parapet.

To FRAIZE a *battalion* (*Mil.*) to line it every way with pikes.

FRAMBÆ'SIA (*Med.*) the yaws; a disease in Africa, somewhat similar to the *lues venerea*: it is arranged by Cullen as a genus of diseases in the Class *Cachexiæ*, Order *Impetigines*.

FRAME (*Paint.*) a kind of square, composed of pieces of wood joined together, that serves for reducing figures.

FRA'MEWORK-KNITTERS, *Company of* (*Her.*) were incorporated about the year 1664. Their arms are "*Or*, a chevron between two combs, and as many leads of needles in chief, and an iron jack-sinker in base; a main spring between two small springs;" all which parts belong to a frame.

FRA'MPOLE FENCES (*Law*) fences set up by the tenants in the manor of Writtle, who are entitled to the wood that grows on them.

FRANC (*Com.*) vide *Frank*.

FRA'NGA (*Bot.*) the *Frankenia lævis* et *hirsuta* of Linnæus.

FRANCHILA'NUS (*Law*) a freeman.

FRANCHI'SE (*Law*) a privilege or exemption from ordinary jurisdiction; as for a corporation to hold pleas to such a value, &c.; this is otherwise called a Royal franchise.

FRANCIGE'NÆ (*Archæol.*) a name formerly for all foreigners.

FRANCI'SCANS (*Ecc.*) an order of friars, founded by St. Francis, in Italy, in 1198.

FRA'NCLAIN (*Archæol.*) a freeman or gentleman.

FRA'NCOLING (*Falcon.*) the name of a bird employed in hawking.

FRA'NGIPANE (*Mech.*) an exquisite kind of perfume formerly used in perfuming leather.

FRA'NGULA (*Bot.*) the *Cassine maurocena* of Linnæus.

FRANK (*Archæol.*) a place to feed boars in.

FRANK (*Com.*) a French coin worth 20 sols, 1 livre, or 10½*d.* English money.

FRANK (*Law*) free, an epithet applied to many things in old law-books, as—*Frank-almoign*, a tenure of lands or tenements bestowed for perpetual arms. *Co. Lit.* c. 94, &c.—*Frank-bank*, vide *Free-Bench*.—*Frank-chase*, a liberty of free chase in a circuit adjoining to a forest. *Cromp. Jur.* 187.—*Frank-fee*, that which is in the hands of the king, or lord of the manor, being *ancient demesne of the crown*; whereas that which is in the hands of the tenant is *ancient demesne* only. *F. N. B.* 161; *Reg. Orig.* 12.— *Frank ferme*, lands or tenements in which the nature of the fee is changed by feoffment, &c. *Britt.* c. 66.—*Frank-fold*, the liberty which the lord has of folding his tenant's sheep on his manor for the sake of manuring his land.—*Frank-Law* is the free enjoyment of all those privileges, which the law allows to a man not found guilty of any heinous offence. *Lib. Assis.* 59; *Crompt. Juris.* 156.— *Frank marriage*, a tenure in land special, whereby a man has land with a woman, to him and the heirs of his body, without doing any service but fealty to the donor. *Bract.* l. 2, c. 7; *Glanv.* l. 7, c. 18; *Flet.* l. 3, c. 11; *West. Symb.* pars 1, l. 2.—*Frank pledge*, an ancient custom for the freemen of England, at fourteen years of age, to find surety for their fidelity to their king, and good behaviour to their fellow subjects.

TO FRANK *letters* (*Law*) a privilege of sending letters free of postage, which belongs to Members of Parliament.

FRANKE'NIA (*Bot.*) a genus of plants, Class 6 *Hexandria*, Order 1 *Monogynia*.
 Generic Character. CAL. *perianth* one-leaved.—COR. *petals* five.— STAM. *filaments* six; *anthers* twin.—PIST. *germ* oblong; *style* simple; *stigmas* three.—PER. *capsule* oval; *seeds* many.
 Species. The species are mostly perennials, as—*Frankenia lævis*, Franca, Lychnis, Erica, seu *Polygonum*, Smooth Frankenia.—*Frankenia hirsuta*, seu *Nothria*, native of the South of France; but the—*Frankenia pulverulenta*, seu *Anthyllis*, Sea Heath, is an annual. *Clus. Hist.*; *Bauh. Hist.*; *Bauh. Pin.*; *Ger. Herb.*; *Park. Theat.*; *Raii Hist.*; *Tourn. Inst.*

FRA'NKINCENSE (*Nat.*) the gum resin, which is the juice of the *Juniperus lycia* of Linnæus. [vide *Thus*]

FRANKINCENSE (*Theol.*) or *free incense*, the incense burnt freely upon the altar.

FRANKLI'NIA (*Bot.*) the *Gordonia franklinia* of Linnæus.

TO FRAP *a ship* (*Mar.*) to pass a large cable-laid rope four or five times round the hull or frame of a ship. "*To frap the tackle*," to cross and draw together the several complications of the ropes so as to increase the tension.

FRAZIER (*Her.*) another name for a strawberry plant.

FRASSE'TUM (*Archæol.*) corrupted, from *fraxinetum*; a wood, or woody ground, where ashes grow. *Co. Lit.* 4.

FRA'TER (*Law*) a brother; *Frater consanguineus*, a brother by the father's side; *Frater nutricius*, a bastard brother; *Frater uterinus*, a brother by the mother's side.

FRATE'RIA (*Law*) a brotherhood, or society, or religious persons and others.

FRATE'RNITY *of arms* (*Mil.*) an alliance, or association of arms, concluded between two knights, who thereby agreed to go together, share their fortunes, and mutually assist each other.

FRA'TRAGE (*Law*) a partition among brothers or coheirs coming to the same inheritance or succession; also that part of the inheritance that comes to the youngest brothers.

FRA'TRES *conjugati* (*Archæol.*) sworn companions, i. e. those who were sworn to defend the King against his enemies. *Leg. W.* 1; *Leg. Ed.* 1, c. 35; *Hoved.* p. 44.— *Fratres pyes*, pied friars, or friars wearing black and white garments. *Walsing.* p. 124.

FRATRIA'GIUM (*Law*) a younger brother's inheritance. *Bract.* l. 2, c. 35.

FRA'TRICIDE (*Law*) the killing of a brother; also one who commits the act.

FRATRICE'LLI (*Ecc.*) a sect of heretics in the fourteenth century, who held that there ought to be a community of goods and of women. *Prateol. Doct. omn. Hæret.*

FRAUD (*Law*) deceit in grants and conveyances of lands, bargains and sales of goods, &c. to the damage of another person.

TO FRAY (*Sport.*) is said of a deer that rubs her head.

FRAXINE'LLA (*Bot.*) the *Dictamnus albus* of Linnæus, a perennial.

FRAXINE'TUM (*Archæol.*) an ash-grove. *Domesd.*

FRA'XINUS (*Bot.*) a genus of plants, Class 23 *Polygamia*, Order 2 *Dioecia*.
 Generic Character. CAL. none.—COR. none.—STAM. *filaments* two; *anthers* oblong.—PIST. *germ* ovate; *style* cylindric; *stigma* thick.—PER. none; *seed* lanceolate.
 Species. The species are trees, as the—*Fraxinus excelsior*, Common Ash-tree. — *Fraxinus rotundifolia*, Manna, Ash-tree. — *Fraxinus Ornus*, Flowering Ash-tree.— *Fraxinus Americana*, American Ash-tree. *Dod. Pempt.*; *Bauh. Hist.*; *Bauh. Pin.*; *Ger. Herb.*; *Park. Theat.*; *Raii Hist.*; *Tourn. Inst.*

FREAM (*Husband.*) arable land worn out of heart.

TO FREAM (*Sport.*) is said of a boar who makes a noise at rutting time.

FRE'CKLES (*Nat.*) a kind of reddish dusky spots on the face or hands.

FRE'E-BENCH (*Law*) *Francus Bancus*, a custom whereby, in certain cities, the wife shall have the whole lands of her husband for dower, &c. in case she live sole and continent. *F. N. B.* 150; *Kitch.* 102.

FRE'EBOOTER (*Mil.*) a soldier that serves for plunder without pay.

FREEBO'RD (*Law*) *francbordus*, ground claimed in some places beyond or without the fence. *Mon. Angl.* tom. ii. p. 141.

FREE-BO'ROUGH-MEN (*Law*) such great men as did not engage, like the Frank-pledge-men, for their decennary.

FRE'E-CHAPEL (*Law*) *libera capella*, one that is exempt from the jurisdiction of the diocesan. *Stat.* 3 *Ed.* 4, c. 4.

FREED-STOLE (*Archæol.*) vide *Fridstole*.

FREEDOM *of a city* (*Law*) the right of exercising a trade or employment in a city or town corporate.

FREE'HOLD (*Law*) *liberum tenementum*, that land or tenement which a man holds in fee-simple, fee-tail, or for term of life. Freeholds are of two sorts, *Freehold in deed*, which is the real possession of the lands for life; or *Freehold in law*, which is the right a tenant has to such lands or tenements before his entry or seizure. *Bract.* l. 2, c. 9; *Lit.* 57; *Co. Lit.* 6; *Reg. Judic.* 68, &c.

FREE'HOLDERS (*Law*) possessors of a freehold estate.

FREE'MAN (*Law*) *liber homo*, was distinguished from a vassal under the feudal policy; the former denoting an allodial proprietor; and the latter, one who held of a superior.

FREEMAN is now one who enjoys the freedom of a city, or corporate town.

FREE'-SCHOOL (*Cus.*) an endowed school where a certain number of children are taught free of expense.

FREE'-STONE (*Min.*) a sort of stone much used in building, which is dug up in many parts of England.

FREETHINKER (*Theol.*) one who professes to think lightly and contemptuously on religion.

FREE-WA'RREN (*Law*) the power of granting any one the licence of hunting on any given lands.

FREEZE (*Com.*) a sort of coarse woollen cloth, so called because it was probably first made in Friezland.

FREEZE (*Gunn.*) the same as the muzzle-ring of a cannon.

FREEZE (*Archit.*) *Frize*, or *Frieze*, from the Italian *Fregio*, and French *Frise*, is called in the Greek ζωφόρος, *a ferendis imaginibus*, because it has many figures sculptured on it; that part of the entablature of columns which is between the architrave and the cornice. It is distinguished, according to the orders, into the Tuscan, Doric, Ionic, Corinthian, and Composite freezes, which vary in their height and ornaments. The *Tuscan freeze*, according to Vitruvius, is flat and plain; the *Doric* carved with metopes and triglyphs; the *Ionic* with acanthus leaves, lions, &c.; the *Corinthian* like the Ionic; and the *Composite* with cartouses. Subsequent writers have varied, in certain particulars, from these forms. *Vitruv.* l. 3, c. 3.

Freezes are likewise distinguished into *convex*, or *pulvinated*, having the profile a curve; *flourished*, enriched with fantastical flowers; *historical*, adorned with Basso Relievos; *marine*, representing Tritons, sea-monsters, &c.; *rustic*, having the courses rusticated; *symbolical*, adorned with symbols.

FRE'EZING *Mixture* (*Chem.*) a composition of ingredients, which, when mixed with other bodies, cause them to congeal.

FREIGHT (*Com.*) the sum agreed on for the hire of a ship, or the carriage of goods, which must be paid in preference to all other debts, for whose payment the goods stand engaged. *Freight* also implies the burden or lading of the ship, the cargo of goods, &c.

FRENCH *Crown* (*Her.*) a circle decorated with stones, and heightened up with eight arched diadems, arising from as many fleurs-de-lis, that conjoin at the top under a fleur-de-lis, all of gold.

FRENCH-HONEYSUCKLE (*Bot.*) the *Hedysarum coronarium.*—French-Marygold, the *Tagetes patula* of Linnæus, an annual.

FRE'NDA (*Anat.*) a name for the sockets of the teeth.

FRE'NDWITE (*Law*) from the Saxon ꝼꞃeonꝺ, a friend, and pite, a mulct; a mulct or fine enacted of him who harboured his outlawed friend. *Flet.* l. 1, c. 7.

FREQUE'NTATIVES (*Gram.*) an epithet for a sort of verbs which express the repetition of an action.

FRE'SCA (*Archæol.*) fresh water, rain, or a land flood.

FRESCA'DES (*Hort.*) Italian for shady cool walks.

FRE'SCO (*Paint.*) an Italian word which signifies literally fresh; but to *paint in fresco* is to paint upon bare walls, &c. newly done, that the colours may sink in and become more durable.

FRESH-WATER-SOLDIER (*Bot.*) the *Stratiotes aloides* of Linnæus.

FRESH (*Law*) *frisca*, in French *frais*; an epithet applied to several things, as—*Fresh Disseisin*, that disseisin which a man might formerly seek to defeat of himself, and by his own power, without resorting to the King or the law. *Bract.* l. 4, c. 5; *Britt.* c. 5.—*Fresh Fine*, a fine, levied within a year past, mentioned in the statute of Westm. 2, 13 Ed. 1, st. 2, c. 45.—*Fresh Force*, a force newly done in any city or borough, for which the party aggrieved may bring Assize, or bill of Fresh Force, within forty days after the force is committed, and recover the lands, &c. of which he is disseized. *F. N. B.* 7; *Old. Nat. Brev.* 4; *New. Nat. Brev.* 15.—*Fresh Suit*, otherwise called *recens insecutio*, such a present and earnest following of an offender, where a robbery is committed, as never ceases, from the time of the offence done or discovered, until he be apprehended. *Staundf. Pl. Cor.* l. 3, c. 10, &c.; 2 *Hawk. P. C.* c. 29.

FRESH (*Mar.*) an epithet used in many sea-phrases, as—*Fresh Water*, in French *eau douce*, water fit to drink, in distinction from salt water.—*Fresh-water-sailor*, a raw inexperienced sailor.—*Fresh-way*, the increased velocity of a ship, which is said to get *fresh-way* when she sails more swiftly.—*Fresh-gale*, a wind that blows immediately after a calm.—*Fresh-spell*, a fresh gang of rowers to relieve those who are fatigued.—*Fresh-shot*, the falling down of any great river into the sea, by means whereof the sea has fresh water.

FRE'SH-MAN (*Cus.*) a novice, or young student in a university.

TO FRESHEN (*Mar.*) the wind is said to *freshen* when it increases in strength. "To *freshen* the hawse," in French *raffraicher le cable*, to relieve that part of the cable which has, for some time, been exposed to friction in one of the hawe-holes.

FRE'SHES (*Mar.*) in French *eaux sauvages*, the impetuosity of an ebb-tide increased by heavy rains.

FRET (*Her.*) one of the subordinaries which is composed of a saltire and a mascle, as in the annexed figure; it is supposed to be a badge of fastness and fidelity like a knot or tie of ribbons; whence by some it has been called a *true lover's knot*.

FRET (*Archit.*) an ornament that consists of two lists, or small fillets, variously interlaced or interwoven, as in the annexed figure. Frets were used by the ancients on flat members, as the faces of the corona, or eaves of cornices, under the roofs, soffits, &c.

FRET (*Mus.*) a particular stop on a musical instrument.

FRETS (*Min.*) a term, used among mariners, for openings made in the banks of rivers by land floods.

FRETTED (*Her.*) an epithet for a cross, or any other bearing, which is in the form of a fret, as in the figure above. [vide *Fret*]

FRE'TTS (*Min.*) a term used by miners to express the worn side of the banks of rivers in mine countries.

FRE'TTY (*Her.*) an epithet for a bordure consisting of eight, ten, or more pieces, each passing to the extremity of the shield, interlacing each other figure after the manner of a fret. [vide *Fret*]

FRE'T-WORK (*Archit.*) timber or plaster-work in imitation of fret.

FRIAR (*Ecc.*) vide *Frier*.

FRI'BURGH (*Law*) or *frithburg*, from the Saxon frith, peace, and borze, a security; a surety for one's good behaviour.

FRICASE'E (*Cook.*) a dish of fried meat, as rabbits, chickens, &c.

FRI'CIUM (*Med.*) a medicine appointed for the friction or rubbing of the body.

FRI'DAY (*Chron.*) in the Latin *Dies Veneris*, in the Saxon Frize-baez, i. e. the day of *Friga*, the Venus of the Saxons and other Northern nations, so called from *frigan*, to love; the sixth day of the week.—*Good Friday*, the Friday immediately preceding Easter, which is kept holy in commemoration of our Saviour's crucifixion.

FRI'DSTOLE (*Archæol.*) from the Saxon frith, peace, and ſtole, a stool; a sanctuary, or place of refuge for malefactors.

FRI'ENDLESS MAN (*Law*) a name given to an outlaw, because upon, being expelled the king's protection, he was, after a certain number of days, denied the help of friends. "Nam forisfecit amicos." *Bract.* l. 3, tract 2, c. 12.

FRI'ENDLY SOCIETIES (*Cus.*) associations, chiefly among the lower class of tradespeople, for affording relief to each other in sickness, or to the widows and children at their death.

FRI'ER (*Ecc.*) or *Friar*, from the French *frère*, Latin *frater*, the name for an order of religious persons, of which there were four principal branches, namely—1. The Minors, Grey Friers, or Franciscans. 2. The Augustines. 3. The Dominicans, or Black Friers. 4. White Friers, or Carmelites; from which all the rest descend. *Stat.* 21 H. 7, c. 17; *Lyndew. de Relig. Dom.* c. 1.—*Friers observant*, a branch of the Franciscan friers who observed their rules more strictly than the conventuals. 25 H. 8, c. 12; *Zach. de Rep. Eccles. de Regular.* c. 12.

FRIER'S COWL (*Bot.*) the *Arum arisarum* of Linnæus, a perennial.

FRI'GATE (*Mar.*) a light nimble ship, built for the purpose of swift sailing. English frigates mount from 20 to 50 guns. *Frigate-built* is an epithet for merchant vessels which have a descent of four or five steps from the quarterdeck and forecastle into the waist, in distinction from the galley-built, whose decks are in a continued line.

FRIGATO'ON (*Mar.*) a Venetian vessel built with a square stern, without any foremast; it is used in the Adriatic.

FRIGERA'NA (*Med.*) a putrid fever.

FRI'GID (*Rhet.*) an epithet for a style which is wanting in force, ornament, and elegance.

FRIGIDA'RIUM (*Ant.*) a place in the Roman baths where people used to cool themselves.

FRIGORI'FIC *particles* (*Phil.*) such particles of matter as are supposed, by entering into other bodies, to produce the quality of cold.

To FRILL (*Falcon.*) is said of a hawk when she trembles.

FRINGED (*Bot.*) *fimbriatus*, an epithet for a corolla, as in the *Menyanthes trifoliata*.

FRI'NGE-TREE (*Bot.*) the *Chionanthus Virginica* of Linnæus.

FRINGI'LLA (*Orn.*) the Finch, a genus of birds, of the Order *Passeres*, which have a conic and straight bill. The principal species are, the—*Fringilla carduelis*, the Goldfinch.—*Fringilla cœlebs*, the Chaffinch.—*Fringilla montefringilla*, the Brambling.—*Fringilla Canaria*, the Canary Bird.—*Fringilla spinus*, the Siskin.—*Fringilla linota*, the Linnet.—*Fringilla cannabina*, the Greater Red-Poll.—*Fringilla linaria*, the Lesser Red-Poll.—*Fringilla domestica*, the House Sparrow. — *Fringilla montana*, the Hedge Sparrow, &c.

FRI'PERER (*Com.*) one who new vamps old clothes to sell again.

FRI'SCUS (*Archæol.*) fresh uncultivated ground. *Mon. Angl.* tom. 2, p. 56.

FRI'SEA (*Bot.*) the *Thesium frisea* of Linnæus.

To FRIST (*Com.*) to sell goods at time, or upon trust.

FRIT (*Chem.*) ashes and salt baked and tried together in sand.

FRITH (*Archæol.*) from the Saxon frith, signifies a wood, woods having been held sacred among the Saxons. *Co. Lit.* 5.

FRITH (*Geog.*) from the Latin *fretum*, is now used in Scotland for an arm of the sea.

FRITH-BRECH (*Archæol.*) from the Saxon frith, peace; a breaking of the peace. *Ld. Æthelred.* c. 6.

FRI'THGEAR (*Archæol.*) from the Saxon frith, peace, and ʒeap, year, a year of jubilee.

FRI'THGILD (*Archæol.*) a guildhall; also a company or fraternity.

FRI'THMAN (*Archæol.*) one belonging to a frith, or fraternity.

FRITHSO'KEN (*Law*) from the Saxon frith, peace, and ſocn, liberty; a liberty of having frankpledge, or suretyof defence.

FRI'THSTOLE (*Archæol.*) vide *Fridstole*.

FRITILLA'RIA (*Bot.*) a genus of plants, Class 6 *Hexandria*, Order 1 *Monogynia*.
Generic Character. CAL. none.— COR. six-petalled.— STAM. *filaments* six; *anthers* erect.—PIST. *germ* oblong; *style* simple; *stigma* triple.—PER. *capsule* oblong; *seeds* many.
Species. The species are bulbous, as the—*Fritillaria imperialis, Corona, seu Tusai*, Imperial Fritillary, or Crown Imperial.—*Fritillaria persica, seu Lilium*, Persian Fritillary, or Persian Lily.—*Fritillaria pyrenaica, seu Meleagris*, Black Fritillary, native of France.—*Fritillaria meleagris*, Common Fritillary, or Chequered Lily, native of the South of Europe. *Clus. Hist.; Dod. Pempt.; Bauh. Hist.; Bauh. Pin.; Ger. Herb.; Raii Hist.; Tourn. Inst.*

FRITILLARIA is also the *Stapelia variegata* of Linnæus.

FRI'TTA (*Chem.*) vide *Frit*.

FRODMO'RTEL (*Law*) or *freomortel*, from the Saxon freo, free, and mort-bæd, man-killing; an immunity or freedom for manslaughter or murder. *Mon. Angl.* tom. 1, p. 173.

FROG (*Zool.*) an amphibious animal which has a smooth body, and longer legs than the toad. There are several species of it, which are classed by Linnæus under the genus *Rana*. [vide *Rana*]

FRO'G-BIT (*Bot.*) the *Hydrocharis Morsus ranæ* of Linnæus.

FRO'G-FISH (*Ich.*) Fishing-Frog, or Angler, the *Lophius* of Linnæus; a sort of fish so called because its shape resembles that of the frog in its tadpole state. It is called the *fishing-frog* because it puts forth the slender horns it has under its eyes, by which it entices the little fish to play around it, when it darts upon them as soon as they come within its reach. It is called by Aristotle βάτραχος; by Pliny *Rana piscatrix*; by Cicero *Rana marina*. *Aristot. Hist. Anim.* l. 5, c. 37; *Cic. de Nat. Deor.* l. 2; *Plin.* l. 9, c. 24; *Oppian. Halieut.* l. 2, v. 86.

FROND (*Bot.*) from the Latin *frons*, a leaf, is applied by Linnæus to the peculiar leafing of palms and ferns. He defines it to be a kind of trunk or stem which has the branch united with the leaf, and frequently with the fructification.

FRONDA'TION (*Husband.*) the removal of luxuriant branches.

FRONDESCE'NTIA (*Bot.*) the leafing season, or the time of the year when plants first unfold their leaves.

FRONDO'SUS (*Bot.*) *frondose*, an epithet for the stem; also sometimes for a flower; *frondosus prolifer flos*, a leafy proliferous flower, as is occasionally to be met with in the Rose Anemone, &c.

FRONS (*Anat.*) μέτωπον, that part of the face between the eyebrows and the hairy scalp. *Ruff. Ephes. de Appell. Part. Corp. Hum.* l. 1, c. 4; *Gal. Introd.* c. 10; *Oribas. Med. Collect.* l. 25, c. 27.

FRONT (*Archit.*) the principal face or side of a building, that which presents itself chiefly to the aspect or view.

FRONT (*Perspec.*) the orthographical prospect of an object upon a parallel plane.

FRONT (*Mil.*) the foremost rank of a battalion, squadron, or other body of men.

FRONT (*Fort.*) the face of a work.

FRO'NTAL (*Man.*) the bridle of a horse.

FRONTAL (*Anat.*) an epithet for what belongs to the forehead, as the *frontal* bone and the *frontal* sinus.

FRONTAL (*Archit.*) vide *Fronton*.

FRONTA'LE (*Med.*) any external medicine applied to the forehead.

FRONTA'LIS (*Anat.*) an epithet for a muscle of the forehead which serves to contract the eyebrows.

FRONTIE'RS (*Geog.*) the limits or borders of a country.

FRONTI'NIAC (*Com.*) or Frontignac, a sort of rich luscious French wine, so called from the place where it is made.

FRO'NTIS OS (*Anat.*) one of the bones of the scull which joins the bones of the sinciput and temples by the coronal suture.

FRO'NTISPIECE (*Paint.*) *frontis spicium*, i. e. *frontis hominis inspectio*, the figure or effigy of a man; the ornament or picture which fronts the book, or forms the first page in a book.

FRONTISPIECE (*Archit.*) the forefront of a building.

FRO'NTLET (*Cus.*) an attire for the forehead.

FRONTO'N (*Archit.*) a member which serves as an ornament over doors, windows, &c.

FRO'ST-NAIL (*Mech.*) a nail with a prominent head, driven into the horse's shoes, that it may pierce the ice.

FROUNCE (*Falcon.*) a disease in the mouth of a hawk.

FRU'CTED (*Her.*) an epithet for trees bearing fruit of a different tincture.

FRUCTIFICA'TION (*Bot.*) the temporary part of vegetables appropriated to propagation, which terminates the old and commences the new vegetable. It consists of flower and fruit, comprehending seven parts, namely—1. Calyx. 2. Corolla. 3. Stamen. 4. Pistil. 5. Pericarp. 6. Seed. 7. Receptacle. Of these the four first belong to the flower; the two next to the fruit; and the last is common to both. [vide *Botany*]

FRU'GGIN (*Mech.*) a fork to stir about the fuel in an oven.

FRUIT (*Bot.*) *fructus*, is the seed with its pericarp; or if there be no pericarp, the seed itself is the fruit.—*Fruit-stalk*. [vide *Pedunculus*]

FRU'ITERER (*Com.*) one who deals in fruits.

FRU'ITERERS, *Company of* (*Her.*) was first incorporated in 1604. Their armorial ensigns are, as in the annexed figure, " *Azure* the tree of Paradise between Adam and Eve, all proper."

FRU'ITFUL *signs* (*Astrol.*) are the signs Gemini, Cancer, and Pisces.

FRUITS (*Law*) are in the Canon Law every thing whereof the revenue of a benefice consists, as glebe, tithes, rents, offerings, &c.

FRU'MEN (*Anat.*) the upper part of the throat.

FRUMENTA'CEUS (*Bot.*) an epithet for plants that have their stalks pointed, and their leaves like reeds, bearing their seeds in ears, like corn.

FRU'MENTY (*Cook.*) a kind of potage, made of wheat, milk, and sugar.

FRU'MGILD (*Law*) the first payment made to the kindred of a slain man, in recompence for the murder. *L. L. Edmund.*

FRU'MSTALL (*Archæol.*) the chief seat, or mansion-house. *Leg. Inc.* c. 38.

PRU'SCA *Terræ* (*Archæol.*) waste or desert lands. *Mon. Angl.* tom. 3, p. 22.

FRUSH (*Vet.*) the tender part of a horse's heel, next the hoof.

FRUSSU'RA *domorum* (*Archæol.*) housebreaking.—*Frussura terræ*, land newly broken or ploughed up.

FRUSTA'NEA *Polygamia* (*Bot.*) the name of the third Order in the Class *Syngenesia* of Linnæus' Artificial System, comprehending such of the Compound Flowers as have perfect florets in the disk, producing but imperfect florets in the ray, which, for want of a stigma, are barren. [vide *Botany*, Plates No. V, &c.]

FRU'STUM (*Geom.*) the part of a solid next the base, left by cutting off the top or segment by a plane parallel to the base.—*Frustum of a cone.* [vide *Cone*]

FRUTE'CTUM (*Archæol.*) a place where shrubs or tall herbs grow. *Mon. Angl.* tom. 3, p. 22.

FRUTE'SCENS (*Bot.*) frutescent, an epithet for a stem; *caulis frutescens*, a stem growing shrubby.

FRU'TICES (*Bot.*) shrubs, a branch of the seventh family of plants, which, according to Linnæus, are distinguished from trees by having no buds.

FRUTICO'SUS (*Bot.*) shrubby; an epithet for a stem.

FU'AGE (*Law*) from *feu*, fire; hearth-money, or a tax of 1s. laid upon every hearth in the dutchy of Aquitaine by the Black Prince. *Rot. Parl.* 25 *Ed.* 3. A similar tax was imposed in the reign of Charles II. [vide *Fumage*]

FU'CHSIA (*Bot.*) a genus of plants, Class 8 *Octandria*, Order 1 *Monogynia*.
Generic Character. CAL. *perianth* one-leaved.—COR. *petals* four.—STAM. *filaments* four; *anthers* twin.—PIST. *germ* inferior; *style* simple; *stigma* obtuse.—PER. *berry* ovate; *seeds* many.
Species. The species are trees, as the—*Fuchsia triphylla*, three-leaved Fuchsia.—*Fuchsia coccinea*, seu *Thilea*, Scarlet-flowered Fuchsia, native of Chili.—*Fuchsia excorticata*, seu *Skinnera*, native of New Zealand.

FUCOI'DES (*Bot.*) a species of the *Fucus*.

FU'CUS (*Bot.*) a genus of plants, Class 24 *Cryptogamia*, Order 3 *Algæ*.
Generic Character. Male, *vesicles* smooth, hollow, with villose hairs within.—Female, *vesicles* smooth, filled with gelly sprinkled with immersed grains; *seeds* solitary.
This genus comprehends most of those plants which are commonly called Sea-Weed. They may all be used to manure land, or may be burnt to make kelp, which is an impure fossil alkali. Some of the species are eaten fresh out of the sea, or boiled tender, as the *Fucus saccharinus, digitatus, palmatus*, &c.

FU'ER (*Law*) flight, or flying, is used substantively in law phrases, and is of two kinds, namely—*Fuer en fait*, when a man doth actually fly; and *Fuer en ley*, when a man being called into the county does not appear till he be outlawed. *Standf. Plac. Cor.* l. 3, c. 22.

FU'GA *catellorum* (*Law*) a drove of cattle; whence *fugatores carrucarum*, waggoners who drive oxen without beating or goading. *Flet.* l. 2, c. 78.

FUGA *vacui* (*Phy.*) an abhorrence of a vacuum, which the peripatetics and other ancient philosophers ascribed to nature, and by which they explained many of the effects which we daily witness.

FUGA (*Mus.*) Italian for a Fugue. [vide *Fugue*]

FUGA'CIA (*Archæol.*) a chace; whence *fugatio*, hunting.

FU'GAM *fecit* (*Law*) the words denoting a *flight in law*, which if found against a convicted felon he shall forfeit his goods. Hawk. P. C. c. 49.

FUGA'TA (*Mus.*) an Italian epithet for compositions written in the style of fugues.

FUGA'TIO (*Archæol.*) vide *Fugacia*.

FU'GAX (*Bot.*) fleeting; an epithet for a corolla which lasts but a short time.

FU'GITIVE *pieces* (*Lit.*) little compositions, so called because they are printed on loose sheets, and may be easily lost.

FU'GITIVE'S *goods* (*Law*) the goods of him that flies upon felony. [vide *Fugam fecit*]—*Fugitives over sea*, those who departed the realm without the king's licence, which was forbidden to all persons except great men, merchants, and soldiers, by the statutes 9 *E.* 3, c. 10; 5 *R.* 2, st. 2, c. 2.

FUGUE (*Mus.*) in Italian *Fuga*, a species of composition in which the different parts follow each other, each repeating in order what the first had performed. There are three distinct kinds of fugues; namely, the simple, double, and counter. The *simple Fugue* contains but one subject; the *Double* two, and the *counter Fugue* is that in which the subjects move in a direction contrary to each other.

FU'GUIST (*Mus.*) one who composes fugues.

FUI'RENA (*Bot.*) a genus of plants, Class 3 *Triandria*, Order 1 *Monogynia*.
Generic Character. CAL. ament oblong; awn cylindric; *flowers* between the scales solitary.—COR. glume three-valved; *valves* petal-shaped.—STAM. *filaments* three linear; *anthers* linear, erect.—PIST. *germ* large; *style* filiform; *stigmas* two, revolute.—PER. none; *seed* three-cornered.
Species. The single species is the—*Fuirena paniculata*, a lofty Grass, native of Surinam.

FU'LCIMENT (*Mech.*) the same as the point of suspension, or that point upon which a *libra* or *vectis* plays, or is suspended.

FU'LCRUM (*Bot.*) from *fulcio*, to prop, a fulcre, prop or support; a name for those parts of plants which serve for their due sustentation. They are reckoned to be as follow: the Stipule, Bracte, Spine or Thorn, Prickle, Cirrus Clasper or Tendril, Gland, and Pubescence. [vide *Botany* and *Stipule*, &c.]

FULCRA'TUS (*Bot.*) an epithet for a stem having fulcres.

FULGO'RA (*Ent.*) Lanthorn-Fly, a genus of insects, of the Hemipterous Order, having the *head* hollow and inflated; *antennæ* short; *snout* elongated; *legs* formed for walking.
Species. Insects of this tribe are inhabitants of South America and Africa; and are so called from the strong phosphoric light which they emit.

FU'LGURATING *Phosphorus* (*Chem.*) a sort of phosphorus, so called because it not only shone in the dark, but communicated its light to any thing it was rubbed on.

FU'LICA (*Orn.*) a genus of birds, of the Order *Grallæ*, having the *bill* convex; *upper mandible* arched over the lower; *front* bald; *feet* four-toed.
Species. Birds of this tribe frequent waters; and are distinguished in English into the Gallinules, which have their feet cleft, and the upper mandible membranaceous at the base; and the Coots which have the toes surrounded by a scalloped membrane, the mandibles equal, nostrils oval, narrow, and short.

FULI'GINOUS (*Nat.*) an epithet applied to thick smoke, or vapour replete with soot or other crass matter. The fusion of lead causes a great exhalation of fuliginous vapour.

FULL (*Mus.*) an epithet for the *organ* when all its stops are out; for the *score*, the several parts of which are complete; and for a *band*, when all the voices and instruments are employed.

FU'LLER (*Com.*) one who cleanses cloth from the grease.

FULLER'S-EA'RTH (*Min.*) a sort of clay, the *Argilla fullonica* of Linnæus, which has the remarkable property of absorbing oil, wherefore it is used by fullers in taking grease spots out of cloth.

FU'LLUM *Aquæ* (*Archæol.*) a fleam or stream of water which comes from a mill.

FULMART (*Zool.*) another name for a pole-cat.

FU'LMINANS (*Nat.*) Fulminant, fulminating or thundering; an epithet for any thing that makes a noise like thunder, as *Aurum fulminans*, a preparation of gold, which explodes with a thundering noise.—*Pulvis fulminans*, a preparation of nitre, salt, and sulphur. There is also fulminating silver, quick-silver, &c.

FU'LMINATING *damp* (*Min.*) vide *Damp*.

FULMINA'TION (*Chem.*) a term applied to the noise which metals make when heated in a crucible.

FUMADEE'S (*Com.*) a name in Italy and Spain for pilchards, garbaged, salted, and dried in the smoke.

FUMA'GIUM (*Archæol.*) dung for soil, or manuring with dung.

FUMAGIUM (*Law*) Fumage, or smoke-money, a tax upon every house that had a chimney.

FUMA'NA (*Bot.*) the *Cistus fumana* of Linnæus.

FUMA'RIA (*Bot.*) a genus of plants, Class 17 *Diadelphia*, Order 2 *Hexandria*.
Generic Character. CAL. *perianth* two-leaved.—COR. oblong.—STAM. *filaments* two; *anthers* three.—PIST. *germ* oblong; *style* short; *stigma* erect.—PER. silicle one-celled; *seeds* roundish.
Species. The species are annuals and perennials. The following are the principal annuals.—*Fumaria officinalis*, seu *Capnos*, Common Fumitory.—*Fumaria vesicaria*, seu *Cysticapnos*, Bladdered Fumitory, native of the Cape of Good Hope.—*Fumaria fungosa*, Spongy-flowered Fumitory, native of North America.—*Fumaria semper virens*, Glaucous Fumitory, native of North America.—*Fumaria Siberica*, Siberian Fumitory, native of Siberia. The following are the principal perennials, as the—*Fumaria cucullaria*, seu *Caponorchis*, Naked-Stalked Fumitory, native of Virginia.—*Fumaria nobilis*, Great-Flowered Fumitory, native of Siberia, &c. *Clus. Hist.*; *Dod. Pempt.*; *Bauh. Hist.*; *Bauh. Pin.*; *Ger. Herb.*; *Park. Theat.*; *Raii Hist.*; *Tourn. Inst.*

FUMARIA is also the *Adoxa moschatellina*.

FUME'TS (*Sport.*) the ordure or dung of a hare, &c.

FUMIGA'TION (*Med.*) the clearing or purifying the air of any infected place by means of smoke, or vapours, &c.

FUMIGATION (*Chem.*) an erosion or eating away of metals by smoke or vapour.

FUMIGATION (*Surg.*) the raising a salivation by the smoke, or fumes of mercury.

FUMIGA'TION-LAMPS (*Mech.*) a sort of lamps constructed for the purpose of expelling foul air from close places, particularly the holds of ships.

FU'MITORY (*Bot.*) another name for the *Fumaria* of Linnæus.—Bulbous Fumitory, the *Adoxa moschatellina*.

FUNA'RIA (*Bot.*) a genus of Mosses.

FU'NCTION (*Med.*) vide *Action*.

FUNCTION (*Algeb.*) an algebraical expression of a certain letter or quantity any how compounded: thus, $a - 4x - ax + 3x^2$, or $2x - (a^2 - x^2)$, is each of them a function of the letter x.—*The Functions of a Calculus*, a branch of analysis which treats of the doctrine of functions.

FUND (*Com.*) from *fundus*, land, or a bottom; the capital or stock of a public company or corporation, particularly applied to the stock which consists of the public money. [vide *Funds*]

FUND *of the eye* (*Anat.*) the part possessed by the choroides and retina.

FUNDAME'NTAL (*Mus.*) an epithet for whatever serves as a base or foundation for something else, as a—*Funda-*

mental note, the lowest note of the chord.—*Fundamental chord*, that from which the lowest note is derived.—*Fundamental bass*, that formed by the fundamental notes of every chord.

FUNDAMENTAL *diagram* (*Math.*) the projection of a sphere upon a plane.

FUNDS (*Polit.*) Public Funds or Stocks, is the national debt formed into different capitals, upon which interest is payable. Those who have any share in the funds are called *fund-holders*, or *stock-holders*; those who buy a share are said *to buy in*; and those who sell their share, *to sell out*. The act of transferring a share from the seller to the buyer is termed the *transfer*; and the days appointed for this transaction are the *transfer-days*. The interest which is received at the stated times of payment is the *dividend*. The largest of the public funds is known by the name of the *consols*, i. e. funds formed by the consolidation of different annuities, which had been severally formed into a capital. When a loan is composed of different funds, they are, collectively, called *omnium*. What remains of any loan unpaid by the subscribers, is noted down under the name of *scrip*.

FUNDUS (*Anat.*) signifies properly a bottom, in which sense it is applied to some parts of the body; as the—*Fundus ventriculi*, the bottom of the stomach—*Fundus uteri*, the bottom of the womb.

FUNDUS *plantæ* (*Bot.*) that part of a plant where the stalk meets and joins the root.

FU'NGI (*Bot.*) Funguses or Mushrooms; the first of the great Families into which Linnæus distributed the whole vegetable kingdom, and the Fourth Order, of the Class *Cryptogamia*, in his Artificial System. [vide *Botany*, Plates No. V, &c.]

FU'NGIBLES (*Law*) a name in the Scotch Law for moveable goods, which may be estimated by weight, number, or measure.

FUNGI'LLI (*Bot.*) the *Lichen ericetorum* of Linnæus.

FUNGO'IDES (*Bot.*) a species of the *Clavaria* of Linnæus.

FU'NGUS (*Surg.*) a fleshy tumour or excrescence that arises on the membranous and soft parts of the body.

FUNI'CULUS *umbilicalis* (*Anat.*) the Navel-string.

FUNI'CULAR (*Math.*) an epithet for a curve, which is the same as the Catenary; and also for a polygon hanging freely by its extremities.

FU'NIS (*Bot.*) the *Cissus latifolia* of Linnæus.—*Funis murænarum*, a species of the *Melastoma*.—*Funis musarius*, the *Uvaria zelanica*.—*Funis quadrangularis*, a species of the *Menispermum*.

FU'NNEL (*Mech.*) contracted from *fundible* and *infundibulum*, a tube of a particular shape for pouring liquor into a vessel.

FU'NNEL-SHAPED (*Bot.*) *infundibuliformis*, an epithet for a corolla, as in *Lithospermum*, *Cynoglossum*, *Pulmonaria*, &c.

FUNZIO'NI (*Mus.*) Italian for oratorios, and other pieces of sacred music, occasionally performed in the Romish church.

FU'-RAN (*Bot.*) a species of the *Epidendrum*.

FUR'BELOW (*Cus.*) from *fur*, formerly served as an ornament to garments.

FU'RCA *et Fossa* (*Law*) i. e. the Gallows and the Pit; a jurisdiction formerly granted by the king of punishing felons, the men by hanging, the women by drowning. According to Coke the *fossa* is abolished, although the *furca* remains. 3 *Inst.* 58.

FURCA'LE *os* (*Anat.*) vide *Furcella*.

FU'RCAM *et Flagellum* (*Law*) the meanest kind of tenure, when the bondman was at the disposal of his lord for life and limb. *Placit. Term. Mich.*; 2 *Joh. Rot. Parl.*

FURCA'RE *ad Tassum* (*Archæol.*) to pitch corn with a fork in loading a waggon, or in making a rick or mow.

FURCE'LLÆ *os* (*Anat.*) the upper bone of the *sternum*, otherwise called the *jugulum*.

FURCHY (*Her.*) vide *Fourchée*.

FU'RFURES (*Med.*) from *furfur*, bran; a disease of the skin, when the cuticle or scarf-skin separates from the cutis or real skin in small scales like bran.

FU'RIA (*Mus.*) Italian for fury or violence, as applied to the rapidity of the performance.

FURIA (*Ent.*) a genus of animals, of the Class *Vermes*, Order *Intestina*, which have a linear body, furnished with reflected prickles. These animals inhabit the marshy plains of Bothnia and Finland, and infest both men and horses, by burying themselves under the skin, where they cause excruciating pains, inflammation, gangrene, and sometimes death.

FURIÆ (*Myth.*) Furies; a name given to the infernal deities, who were supposed to enter and possess men, for the purpose of punishing and tormenting them.

FURIBO'NDO (*Mus.*) an Italian epithet applied to parts of compositions which are to be performed with vehemence.

FU'RIGELD (*Law*) a mulct paid for theft. LL. *Æthelred*.

FURIO'SITY (*Med.*) Madness, as distinguished from Fatuity or Idiocy.

FURIO'SO (*Mus.*) or *con furia*, Italian, signifying furiously, or with vehemence.

TO FURL (*Mar.*) is to wrap or roll the ship's sails close to the yard, stay, or mast, to which they respectively belong.

FURLING *in a body* (*Mar.*) is a particular method of rolling up a topsail, which is practised only in harbours.—*Furling-lines*, the ropes employed in the operation of furling.

FU'RLONG (*Arith.*) in Saxon furlang; a measure of length, consisting of forty poles, and equal to the eighth part of a mile.

FU'RLOUGH (*Mil.*) leave granted to a soldier, or non-commissioned officer, to be absent for a given time from his regiment or company, in which case he is said to be on furlough.

FU'RNACE (*Chem.*) a fire-place employed for melting, distilling, and all other chemical processes. Furnaces are of different kinds, as *moveable furnaces*, *wind furnaces*, &c. [vide *Chemistry*]

FURNA'GIUM (*Law*) a tribute formerly paid to the lord for baking bread in his oven.

FURNA'RIUS (*Archæol.*) a baker who kept an oven, whence *furniare*, to bake, or put any thing into an oven. *Matth Par. Ann.* 1258.

FU'RNISHED (*Her.*) an epithet for a horse when bridled, saddled, and completely caparisoned.

FU'RNITURE (*Diall.*) a name given to the lines drawn on a dial; as the parallels of declination, length of the day, azimuth, almacantars, &c.

FUROLE' (*Nat.*) the name for a little blaze of fire which has been observed by night on the tops of the sentinels' lances, or the sailyards of ships, which dances from place to place, and soon disappears.

FUROR UTERI'NUS (*Med.*) vide *Nymphomania*.

FURR (*Com.*) the coat or covering of a beast, which is used either for ornament or warmth. Of these there are different kinds, named after the beasts from which they are taken, as Sables, Beavers, Lucerns, Genets, Foins, Martens, Fitchets or Polecats, Cababars, Squirrels, &c.

FURRS (*Her.*) are a sort of tinctures which are supposed to represent the furrs of animals. The principal furrs which occur in coat armour are, the—*Ermine*, which has black spots on a white field.—*Ermines*, or *counter ermine*, white spots on a black field.—*Erminois*, black spots on a field or.—*Vair*, in which *argent* and *azure* are represented by figures of small escutcheons ranged in a line, so that the *base argent* is opposite to the *base azure*.—*Counter-vair*, when the bells or cups of the same colour are placed base against base and point against point.—*Potent-counter-potent*, a field covered with figures like the heads of crutches, called potents. [vide *Heraldry, Ermine*, &c.]

FU'RRENS (*Mar.*) pieces in ship-building to supply the deficiency of the timber in the moulding way.

FU'RRING *a ship* (*Mar.*) laying on double planks on the sides of a ship after she is built, called plank upon plank, for the purpose of making her stronger.

FURRING (*Carpent.*) the fixing of thin scantlings or laths on the edges of timbers, to bring them to the even surface they were intended to form. Thus the timbers of a floor, though level at first, are often obliged to be furred; also the rafters and joists of old roofs require a furring.

FURRINGS (*Carpent.*) the pieces of timber employed in bringing any pieces of carpentry to an even surface.

FU'RROW (*Husband.*) a trench cast up by a plough.

FU'RROWED (*Bot.*) *sulcatus*, fluted or grooved; an epithet for a stem.

FURU'NCULUS (*Surg.*) δοθιήν, a boil, or hard tumour rising in the fat under the skin, accompanied with inflammation, redness, and pain. *Gal. de Tum.* c. 15; *Cel.* l. 5, c. 28; *Oribas. Med. Coll.* l. 3, c. 3; *Paul. Æginet.* l. 4, c. 23.

FURZE (*Bot.*) another name for the *Ulex* of Linnæus.

FUSA'NUS (*Bot.*) a genus of plants, Class 23 *Polygamia*, Order 1 *Monoecia*.
 Generic Character. CAL. *perianth* one-leaved.—COR. none.—STAM. *filaments* four; *anthers* roundish.—PIST. *germ* large; *style* thick; *stigmas* four.—PER. a drupe.
 Species. The single species is a tree, as the *Fusanus compressus*, seu *Colpoon*, Flat-stalked Fusanus, native of the Cape of Good Hope.

FUSARO'LE (*Archit.*) a moulding or ornament placed immediately under the echinus in the Doric, Ionic, and Composite capitals.

FUSE'E (*Gunn.*) *fuse*, or *fuze*, the tube fixed into a bomb or granade shell, which is filled with combustible materials, and furnished with a quick-match on the top of it. It is cut to a length proportional to the distance the bomb is to be thrown, that it may continue burning all the time the shell is in its range, and afterwards set fire to the powder as soon as it touches the ground, which causes the shell to burst.

FUSEE (*Hor.*) the conical part drawn by the spring of a watch, and about which the chain or string is wound.

FUSIFORMIS (*Bot.*) fusiform, or spindle-shaped; an epithet for a root, as in the case of the Radish, Parsnip, &c.

FU'SIL (*Mil.*) a small light musquet.

FUSIL (*Her.*) is a sort of artificial charge, which is taken for spindles of yarn, millpecks, or weaver-shuttles, as in *fig.* 1; it differs from the lozenge by being longer. The spindle is likewise blazoned as a fusil in coat armour, as in *fig.* 2. "He beareth *argent* three fusils upon slippers, *gules*, by the name of Hoby." When a field is covered with fusils it is said to be *fusilly*, as in fig. 3.

Fig. 1.   *Fig. 2.*   *Fig. 3.*

FU'SILLY (*Her.*) vide *Fusil*.

FU'SION (*Metall.*) the act of founding, melting, or running metals by means of heat.

FUST (*Archit.*) the shaft of a column from the astragal to the capital, or that part comprehended between the base and capital, called also the *naked*.

FU'STIAN (*Com.*) a sort of nappy cotton cloth, so called from Fustan, a place in Spain where it was first made.

FU'STICK WOOD (*Bot.*) the *Morus tinctoria* of Linnæus, a tree growing in the West India islands, the wood of which yields a yellow die.

FU'TTOCKS (*Mar.*) the middle division of a ship's timbers. Those next the keel are called *ground futtocks*, the rest *upper futtocks*.—*Futtock-plates*, iron plates, the upper part of which is open, like a ring.—*Futtock-staves*, or *foothook-staves*, a short piece of rope served over with spun yarn, to which the shrouds are confined at the cat-harpings.

FUTURE (*Gram.*) the name of a tense in verbs, by means of which the futurity of an action is expressed.

FYRDERI'NGA (*Archæol.*) *fyrthing*, or *fyrding*, from the Saxon Fynðerunᵹ, a going out to war, or on a military expedition, the omission to do which when summoned was punished by fine at the king's pleasure. *Leg. H.* 1, c. 10.

END OF VOL. I.

C. Baldwin, Printer,
New Bridge-street, London.

TABLE I

ORIENTAL ALPHABETS

1 Hebrew Modern	3 Phœnician (from Coins &c) Name	Pow.	No.	4 Syriac Ancient or Strangelo Name	Syriac Modern Name	Pow.
א	Aleph	A	1	Olaf	Alepha	A
ב	Bheth	Bh	2	Beth	Beth	B
ג	Ghimel	Gh	3	Gomal	Gamla	G
ד	Dhaleth	Dh	4	Dolath	Delta	D
ה	He	H	5	He	He	Hh
ו	Vau	V	6	Waw	Waw	W
ז	Zain	Z	7	Zain	Zetha	Z
ח	Cheth	Ch	8	Hheth		
ט	Teth	T	9	Teth	Tetha	T
י	Jod	J	10	Yud	Jota	Y
כ ך	Chaph	Ch	20	Cof	Kappa	K
ל	Lamed	L	30	Lomad	Lambda	L
מ ם	Mem	M	40	Mim	Me	M
נ ן	Nun	N	50	Nun	Nun	N
ס	Samech		60	Semcath	Semcha	S
ע	Gnain	AA O	70	E	Oe	O AA
פ ף	Phe	Ph	80	Pe	Phe	Ph
צ ץ	Tzadi	Ts	90	Tsode	Tzode	Ts
ק	Koph	K	100	Kof	Kophe	K
ר	Resh	R	200	Rish	Roe	R
ש	Schin Sin	Sch	300	Shin	Schin	Sch
ת	Thau	Th	400	Tau	Thau	Th

5

EGYPTIAN HIEROGLYPHICS

6

CHINESE CHARACTERS

黹 tchì	黽 min	鼎 tìng	鼓 koù
馬 mà	骨 kŏ	高 caō	髟 piēou
隶 táï	隹 tchōui	雨 yù	青 tsing
赤 tchĕ	走 tçèou	足 tçŏ	身 chīn
色 sĕ	艸 tçào	虍 hoù	虫 tchông
网 vàng	羊 yang	羽 yoù	老 laò

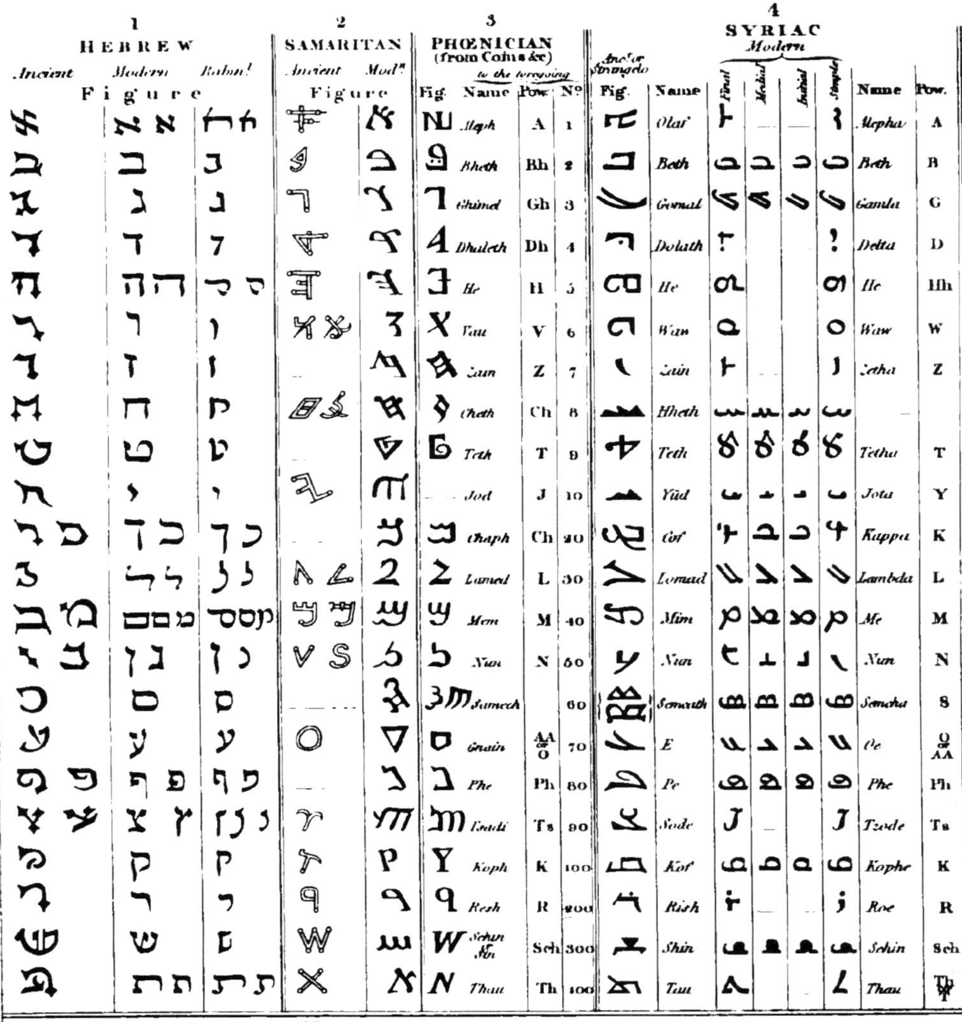

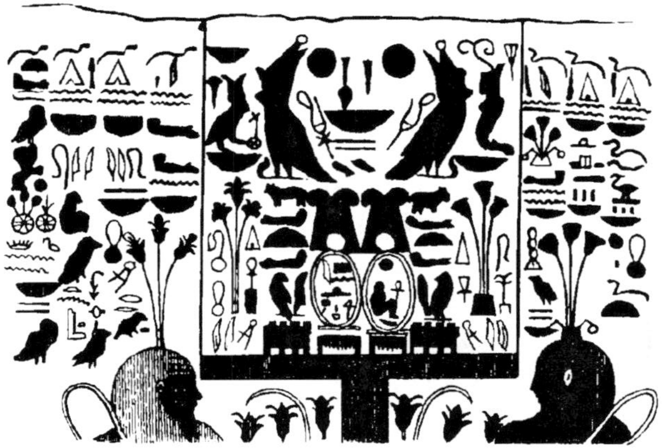

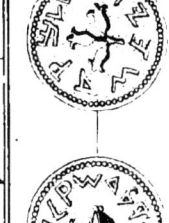

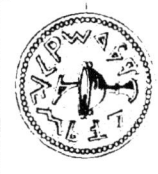

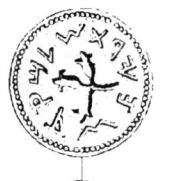

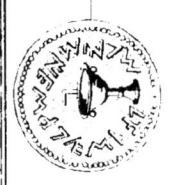

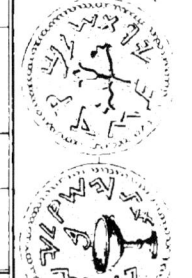

Pl. 2.

TABLE III
LATIN ALPHABETS
of different ages.

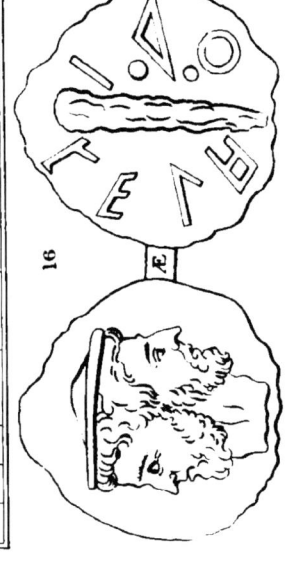

ETRUSCAN			B.C. 114	A.D. 1	A.D. 306 A.D. 15	A.D. 400	A.D. 500
Fig.	Power				Figure		
Π	a	a	Ala	ʌʌʌ	ʌʌʌʌ	ʌʌʌʌ	ʌ𝛡aa
B	b	b	Bb6	B	Bb	Bbb	Bbb
	c	d	Cc	Cc	Ccc	Ccc	Ccc
	d		Dd	D	Ddd	Dddd	Dddd
	e		Ee	EεE	Ee	eee	eee
	f		Ff	Fff	Ff	FFF	FaF
	g		Cg	Gg	Gg	Ggg	Ggg
	h		Hh	ıɪH	H·h	Hħh	hħh
	i		ıı	ıɪ	ıɪ	ıɪtɪ	ıɪɪ
	k		Kk	Kkk	Kk	Kk	Kk
	l		LL	LLL	LL	L·LL	L·LL
	m		MD	ʌʌM	MM·m	Mmoo	∞m
	n		NO	N	N	NNNN	NN
	p		O	O	O	OO	O
	q		Qq	PPP	PPP	PPP	PPP
	r		Rr	RRR	RRR	qqq	qqq
	s		Sr	RRR	RRR	RRR	Rr
	t		St	SSS	SSS	SSS	SsS
			Tt	TTI	TI	TTT	TTT
	ph	V	Vy	v	vuɪɪvɪ	vnuvɪ	uuɪ
	ps		X	X	x	XX	XX
			Ty	rr	zz	zz	zz
	z		Zz	zz	zz		

16

TABLE II *(continued)*
GREEK ALPHABETS

11

ΦΑΛΟΔΙΚΟ:ΕΙΜΙ:ΤΟΝ
ΟΚΟΥΤΟΥ:ΖΟΤΑϘΝΟΥϘΕ
ΛΕΖΙΟ:ΚΑΛΟ:ΚΡΑΤΕΡΑ
ΨΘΕΗΙΑΚΜΟΤΑΤΣΙΠΑΚ
ΟΜΕΖΠΨΤΑΜΕΙΟΝ:Κ
ΤΑΛΙΡ:ΛΜΕΨΜ:ΑΚΟΛ
ΕΙΖΙ:ΕΑΡΔΕΤΙΡΑΣ✢
ΟΣ■:ΨΕΜΙΑΔΕΝΕΜΟ
ΖΙΛΕΙΕΖ:ΚΑΙΜΕΠΟ
ΙΑΥΖΟΠΟΣΙΥΗΞΜΕΖΙΣ
ΗΑΡΕΥϘΟΙ

12

ΠερΗΜωΝοεΝΤΟΙCΟΥΝΟΙC
ΑΠΙCΘΗΤωΤΟΟΝΟΜΑCΟΥ·
εχεθετωΗΒΑCΙΧΕΙΑCΟΥ·ΓεΝΗ
ΘΗΤΟΤΟΘΗΛΗΜΑCΟΥωC
εΝΟΥΝωΚΑΙεΠΙΓΗC·ΤΟΝ
ΑΡΤΟΝΗΜωΝΤΟΝεΠΙΟΥCΙΟ
ΔΙΑCΥΗΜεΙΝΤΟΙCAΛΗΜερΑ
ΚΑΙΑΦεCΗΜΙΝΤΑCΑΜΡΤΙΑC
ΗΜωΝ·ΚΑΙΓΑΡΑΥΤΟΙΑΦΙΟΜε

13

Ὅταμ ἀκούῃ διος θυμοῦ καὶ ὀργῆλυ..
Ὅταν ακησης θυμον και οργην,
μηδεὶς ἀφ᾽ ὁ ψυρου ὑπο αἰσθήσει
μηδεν ανθρωπιν υποπτευσης
συγκατανιωστωσ γράφει τῷ ρ
συγκαταβασεως γαρ εστι τα ε

14

ALPHABETS DERIVED FROM, OR ALLIED TO, THE ORIENTAL ALPHABETS.

ALPHABETS DERIVED FROM THE ORIENTAL OR GREEK ALPHABETS

TABLE VI.

ALPHABETS DERIVED FROM THE GREEK OR LATIN.

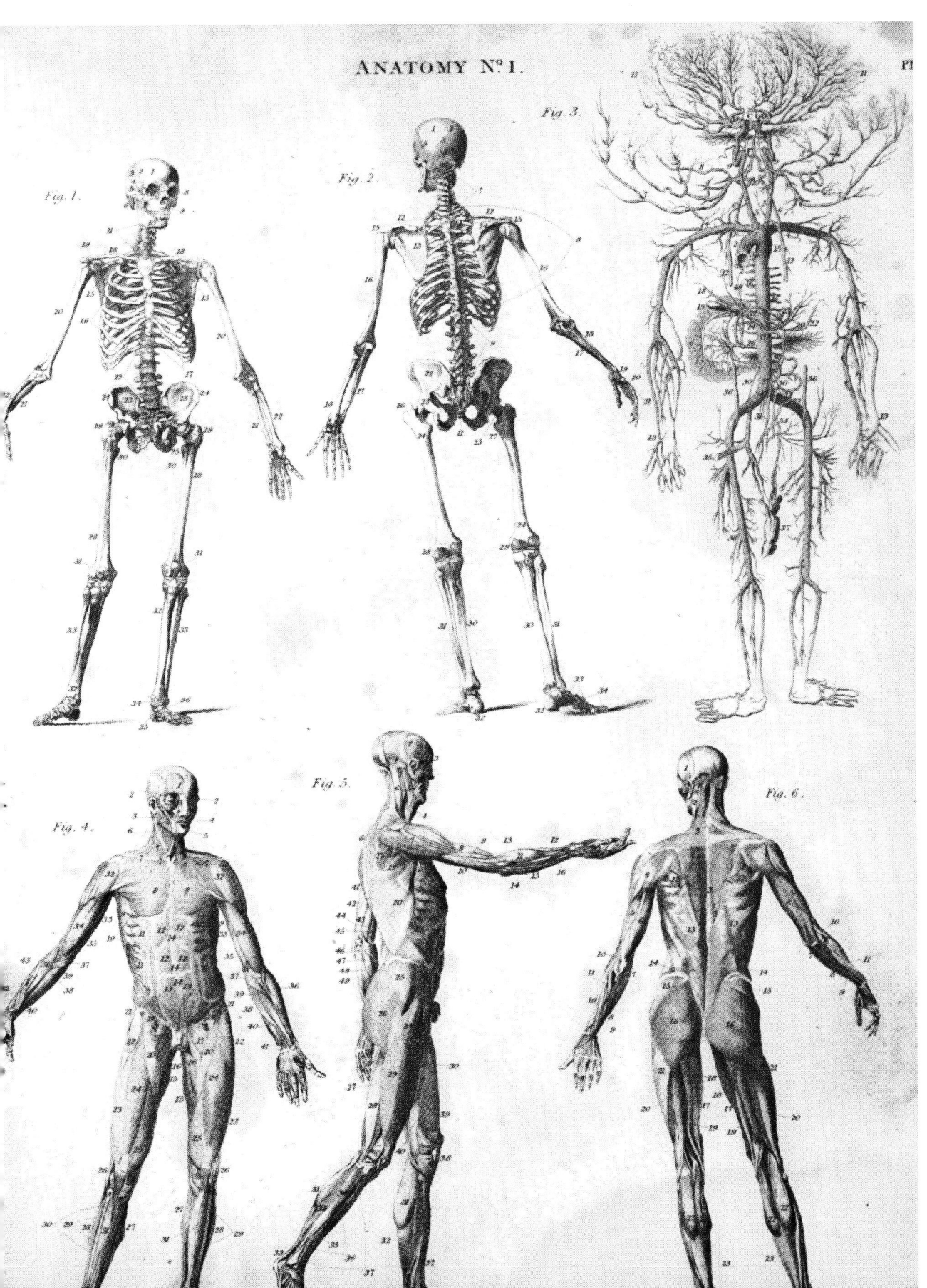

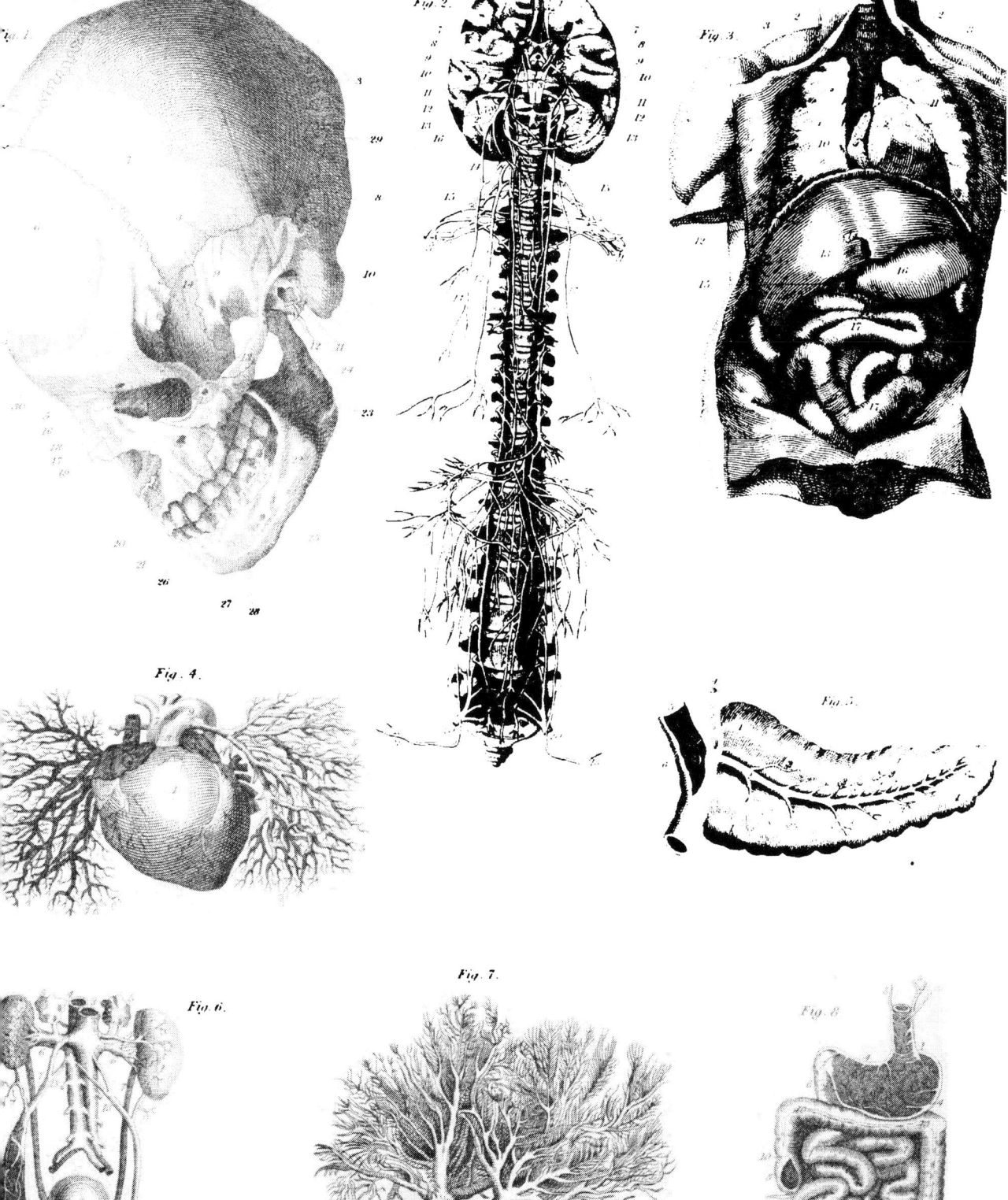

ARCHITECTURE Nº 1.

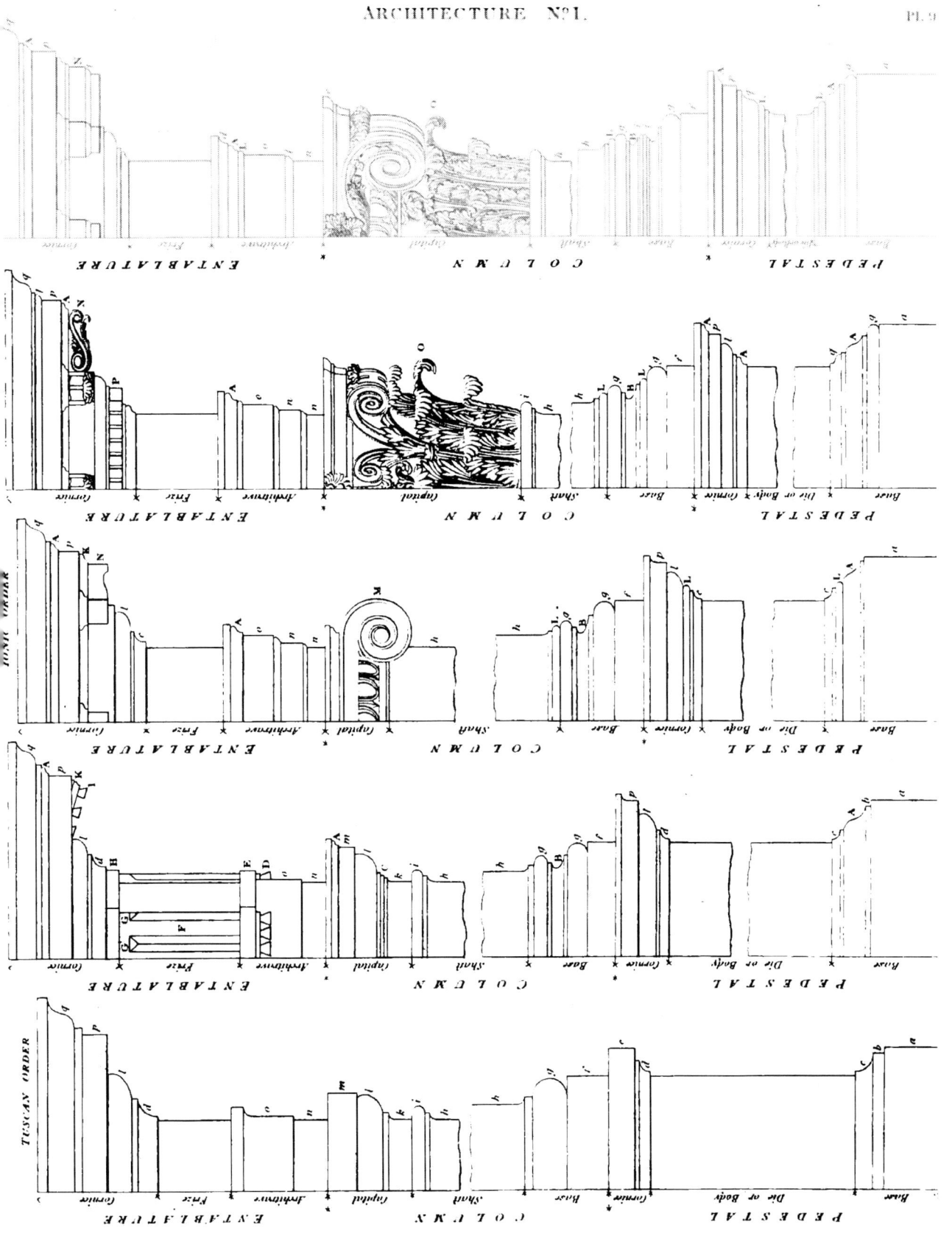

ARCHITECTURE Nº II.

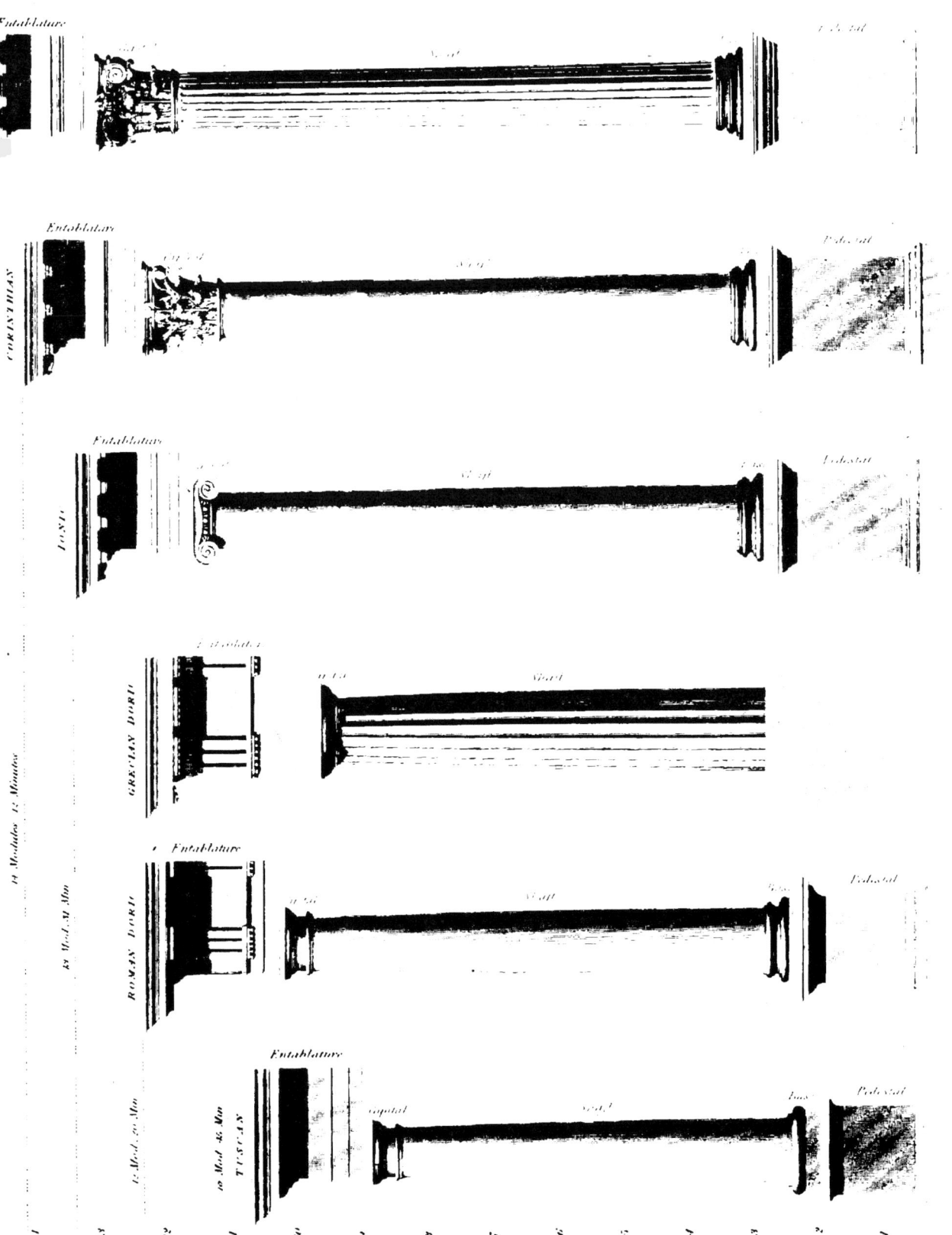

ARCHITECTURE N?III.

NUMERALS

A. PHŒNICIAN NUMERALS ANCIENTLY USED AT SIDON

/	I	//////⁻	XVI	⁻NNN	LXX
//	II	///////⁻	XVII	NNNN	LXXX
///	III	////////⁻	XVIII	⁻NNNN	XC
////	IV	/////////⁻	XIX		
/////	V	NNNN)	XX	(Phoenician script)	C
//////	VI	N ⁀ ⁀)			
///////	VII	/N	XXI	ρII	CC
////////	VIII	//N	XXII	ρIII	CCC
/////////	IX	///N	XXIII	ρIIII	CCCC
ρ ⁀ ρ⁻	X	////N	XXIV	ΓIIIII	D
/⁻	XI	/////N	XXV	ρIIIIII	DC
//⁻	XII	⁻N	XXX	ρIIIIIII	DCC
///⁻	XIII	NN	XL	ρIIIIIIII	DCCC
////⁻	XIV	⁻NN	L	ρIIIIIIIII	DCCCC
/////⁻	XV	NNN	LX	/////////⁻NNNNρIIIIIIIII	DCCCCXCIX

	B GREEK		C IRISH Ancient / Modern	D PALMYRENE	E EGYPTIAN	F INDIAN Ancient / Modern	G ARABIAN	H PLANUDES	I BOETHIUS	K ARABIAN PERSIAN & INDIAN	L SPANISH	M SACRO DE BOSCO
	1	△△△	30	/ /	I	⊏	1 /	1 q	1	ι	I	1	1	1
I	2	△△△△	40	// 2	II	⊏	υ z	μ	ρ	σ	μ	Z.7	ζ
II	3	⌐	50	/// 3	III	⊏	ω ε	μ	μ	ш	μ	3	3
III	4	⌐△	60	//// ⋌	IIII	⊏	⊏ γ	⊏	⊏	Ψ	⊏	⋌	⋌
⌐	5	⌐△△	70	γ 4	⋋Y	⊏	o8 Y	O	ϑ	G	ϑ8	1.4	4
I	6	⌐△△△	80	IV 6	IY	⊏	Y7 3	4	4	J	4	6	6
⌐II	7	⌐△△△△	90	IIIγ 7	IIY	⊏	V 9	V	V	Λ	V	7	Λ
⌐III	8	H	100	IIIV 8	IIIY	⊏	⋌ ζ	Λ	Λ	8	Λ	8	8
⌐IIII	9	HH	200	IIIIV 9	IIIIY	⊏	9 ℓ	9	9	9	9	9	9
△	10	HHH	300	X 1.10	⊐.⊃	⊏	0 q	1.	10	1.10	110	10
△△	20	HHHH	400									

N

 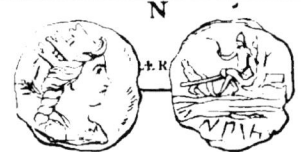 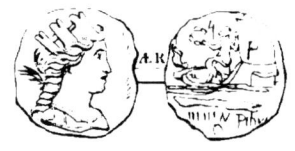

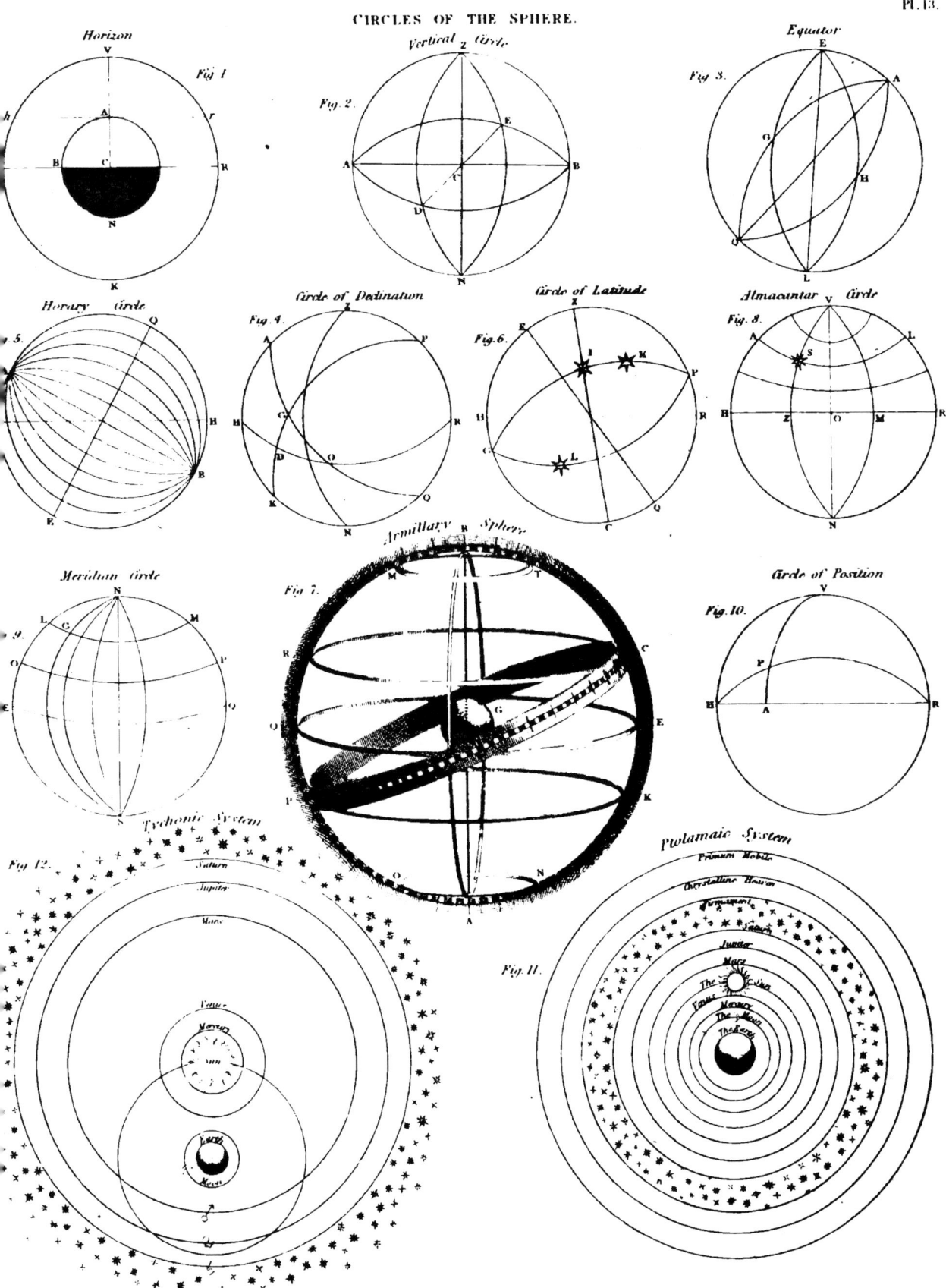

Fig 13. ASTRONOMY Nº II. Pl. 14.
COPERNICAN SYSTEM.

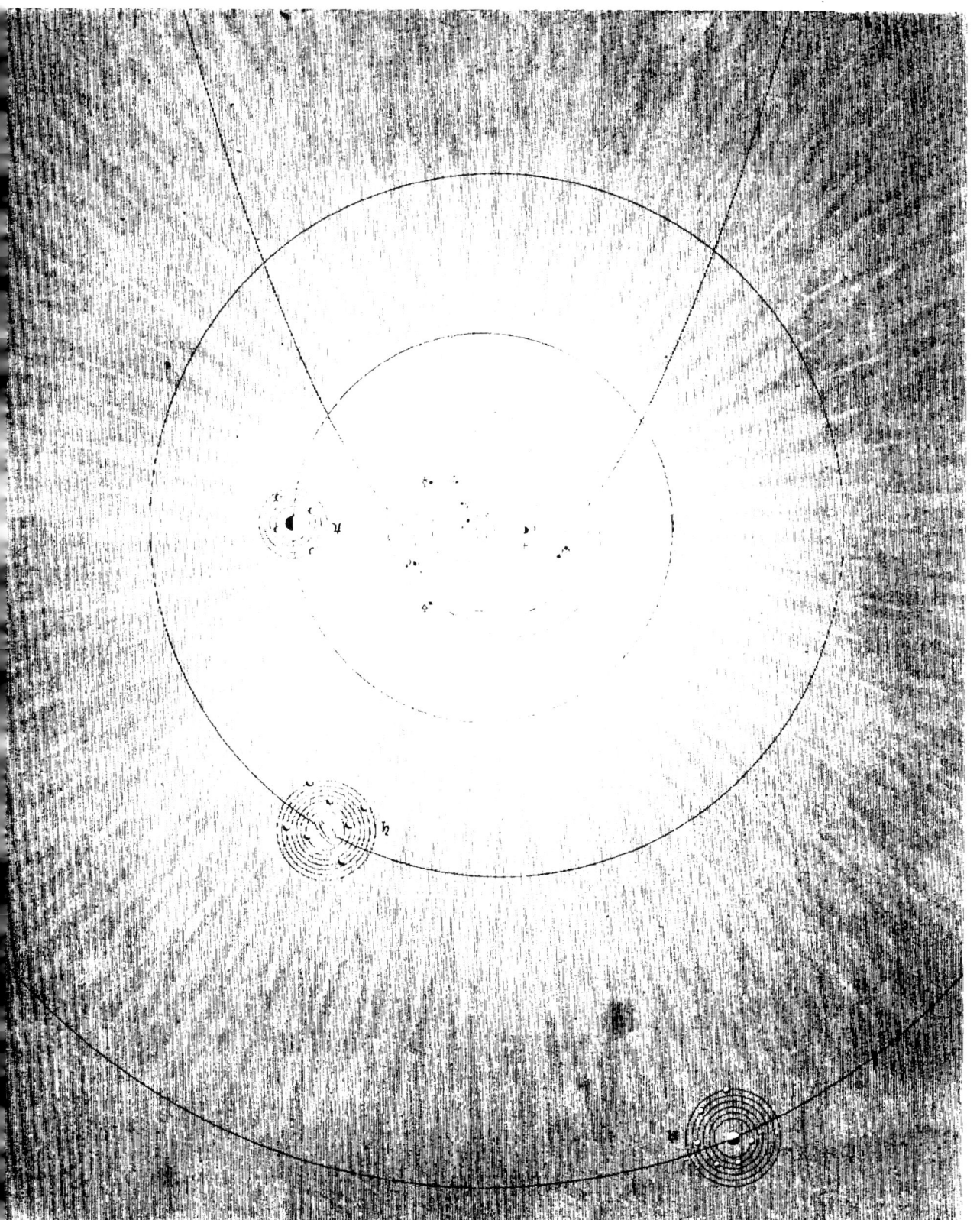

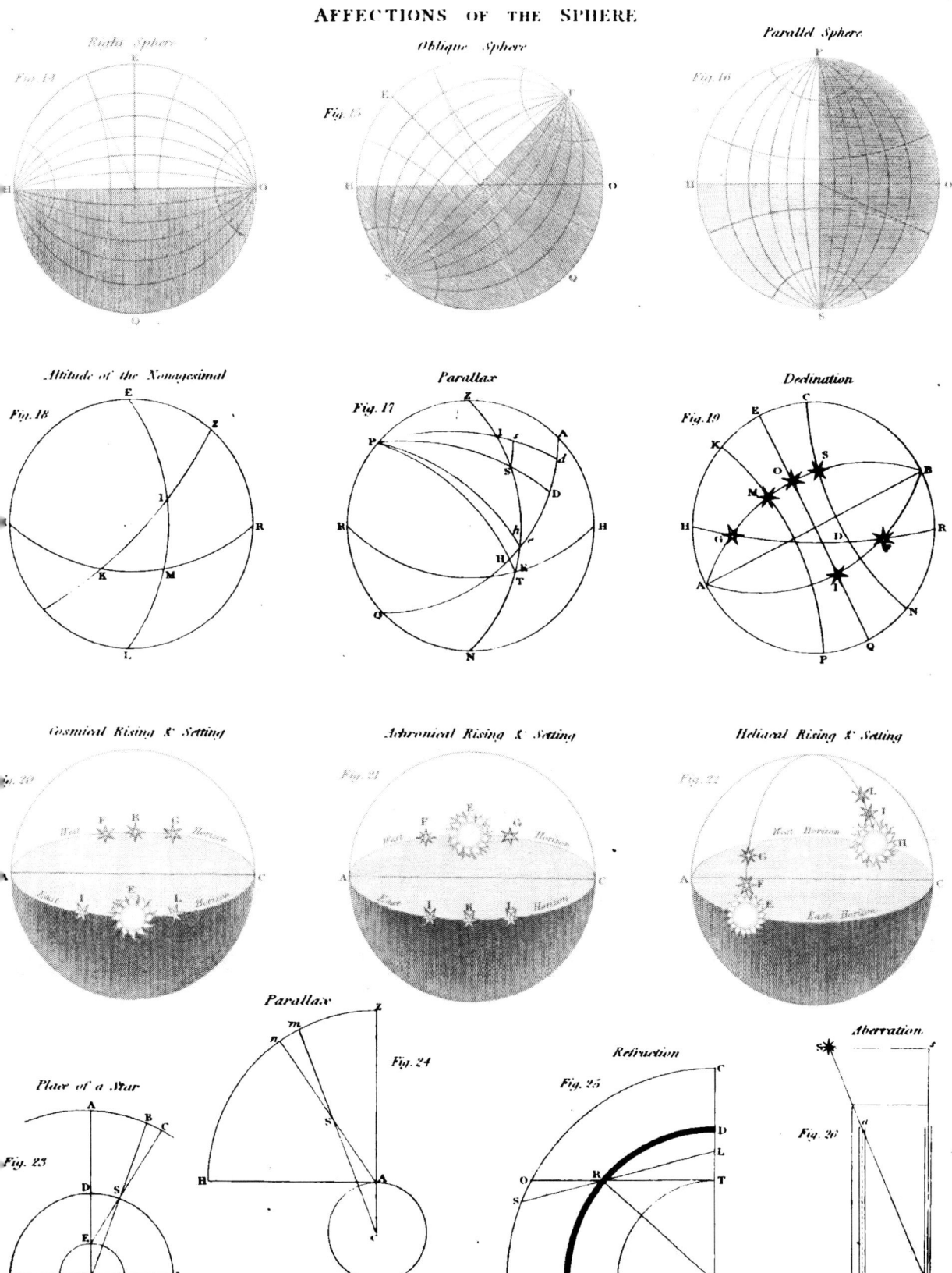

ASTRONOMY N.º V.

NORTHERN HEMISPHERE.

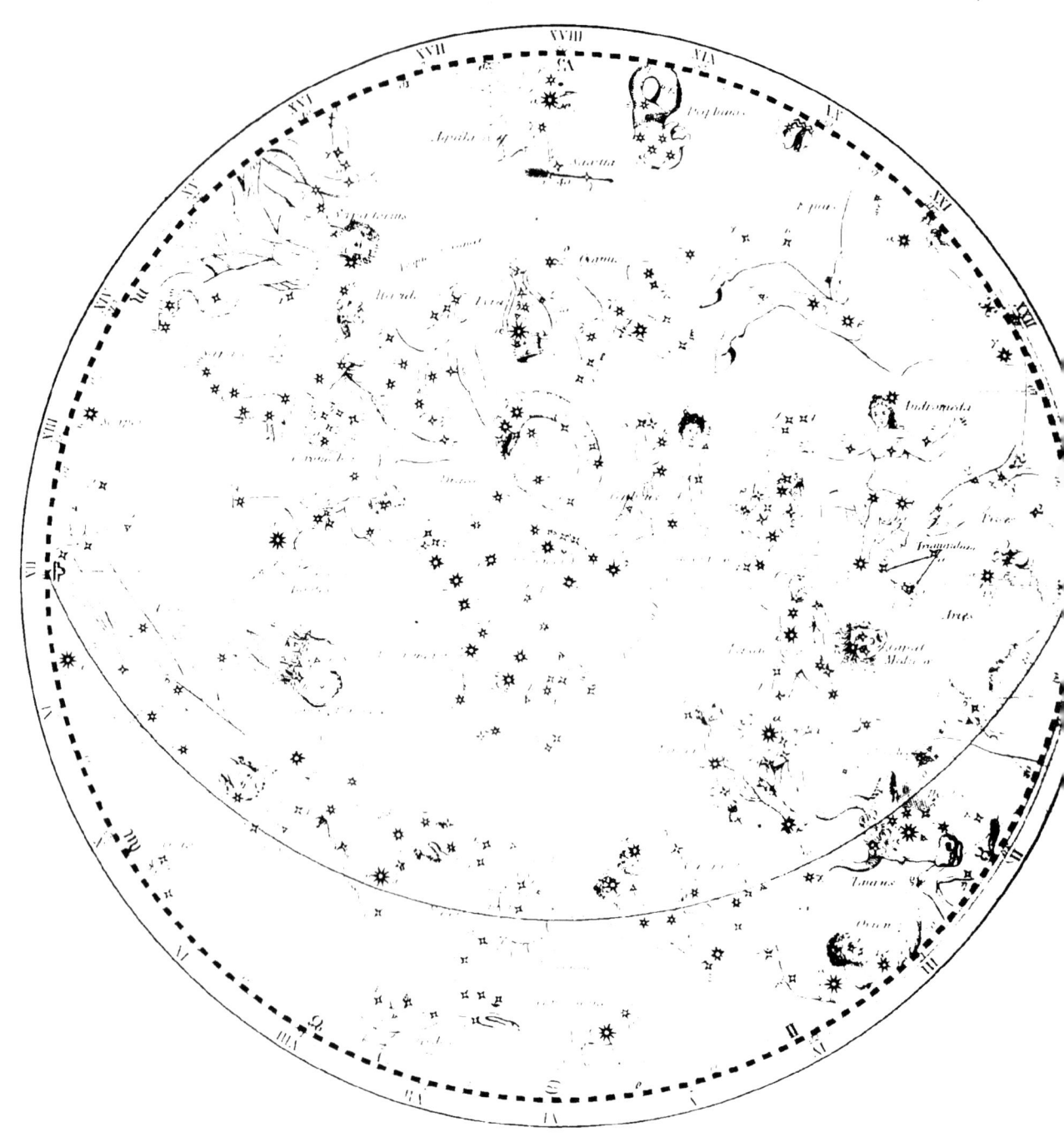

ASTRONOMY Nº VI.

Pl. 17.

SOUTHERN HEMISPHERE.

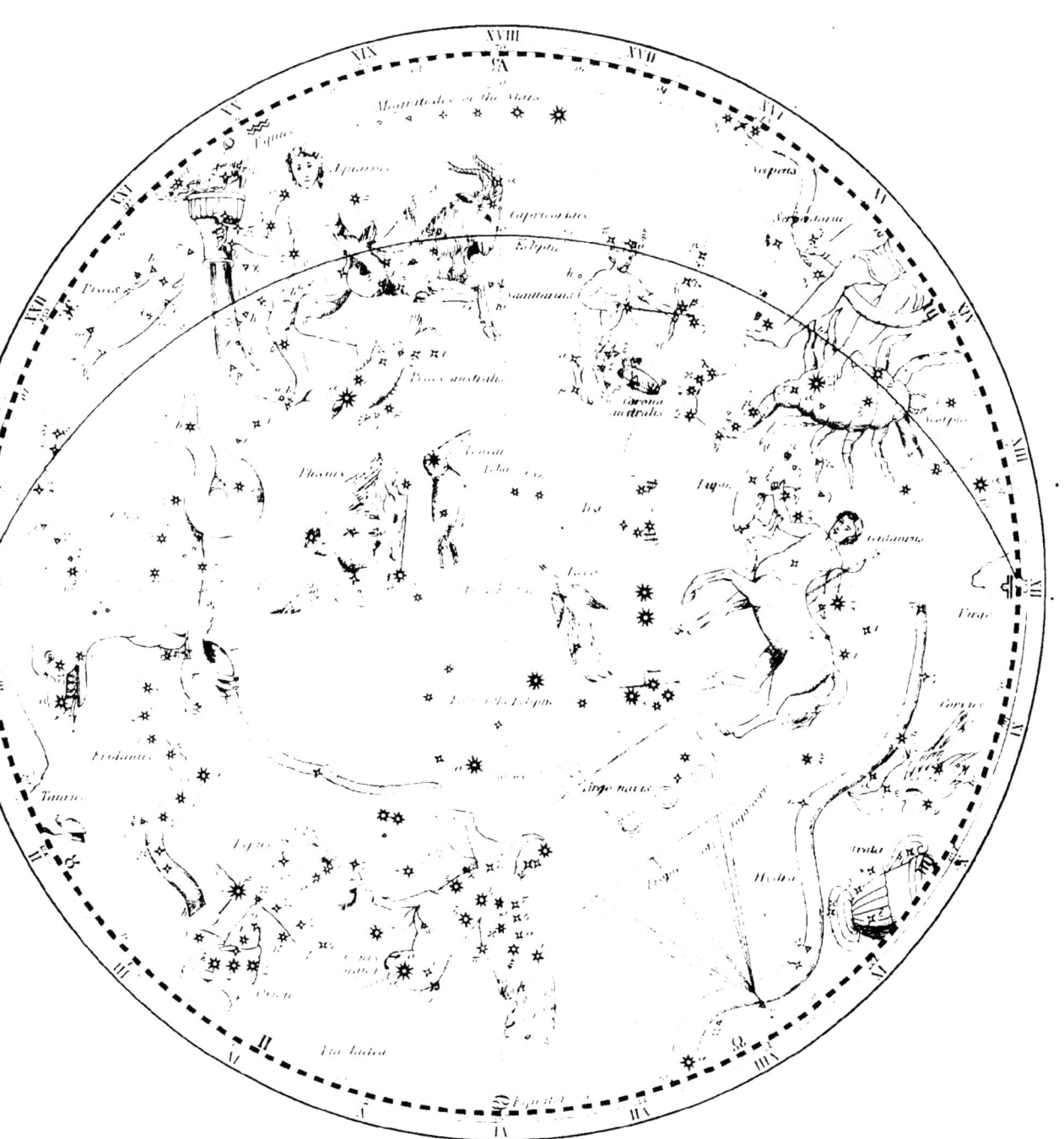

ASTRONOMY Nº VI.

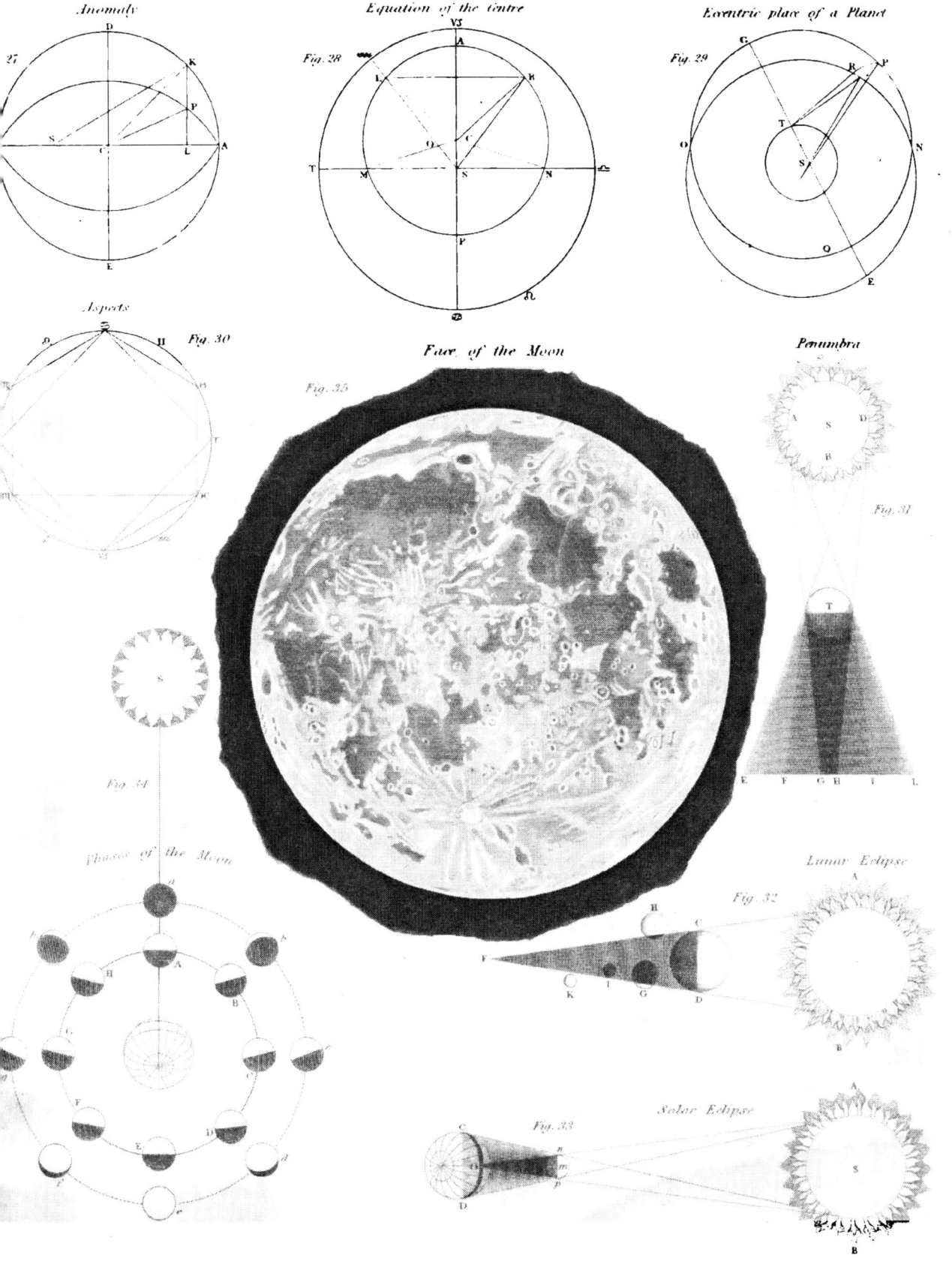

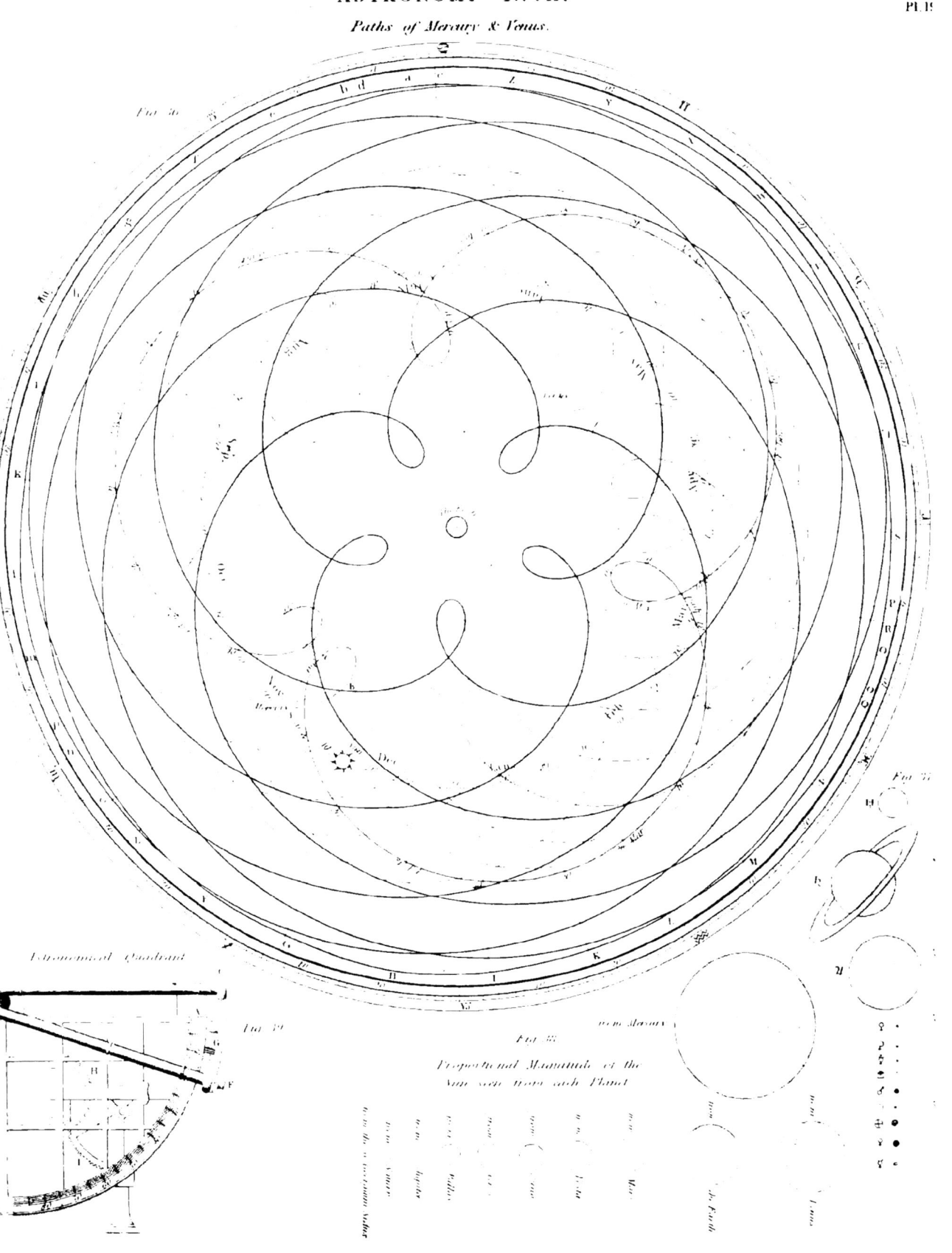

ASTRONOMY Nº VIII.

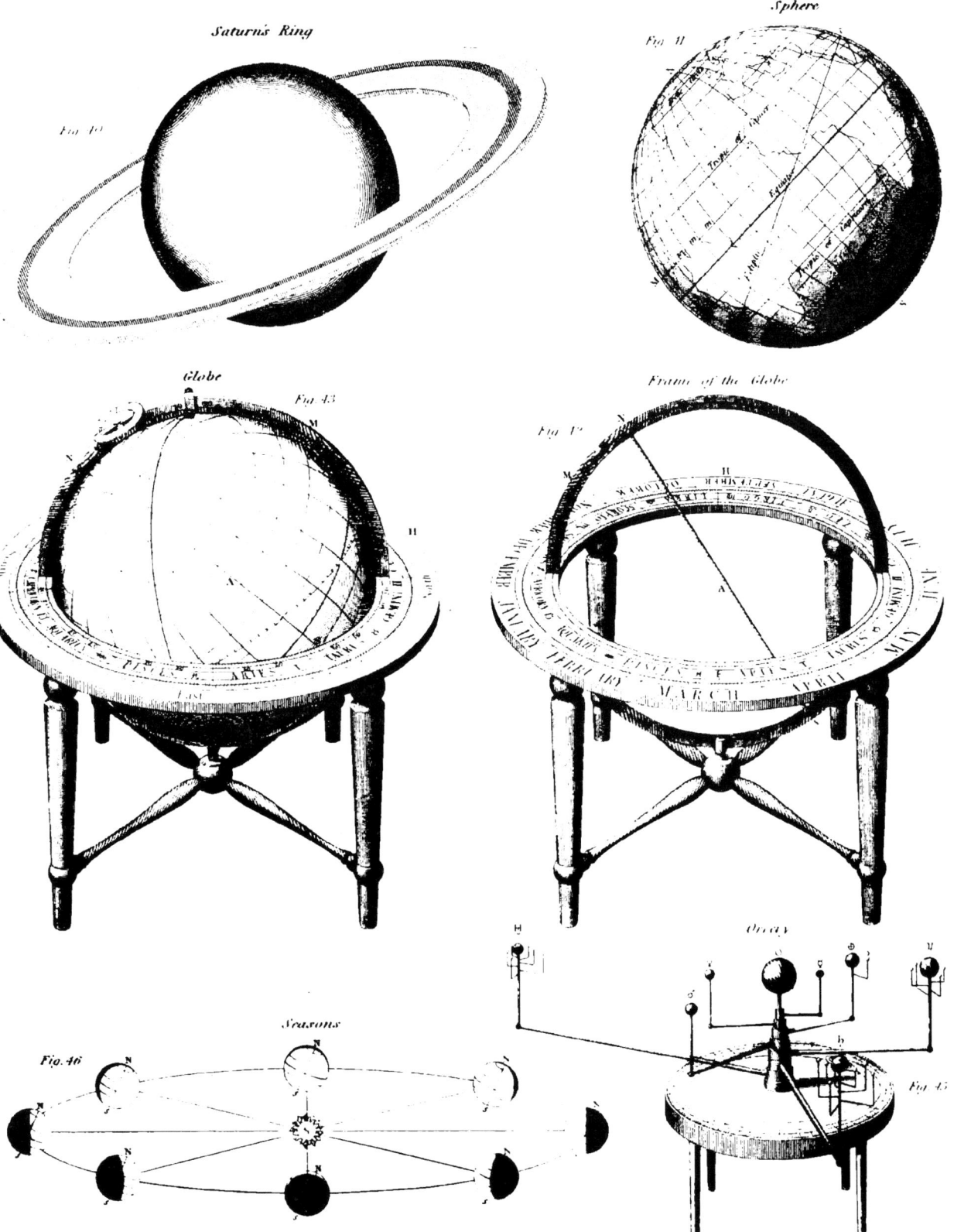

BOTANY No. 1.

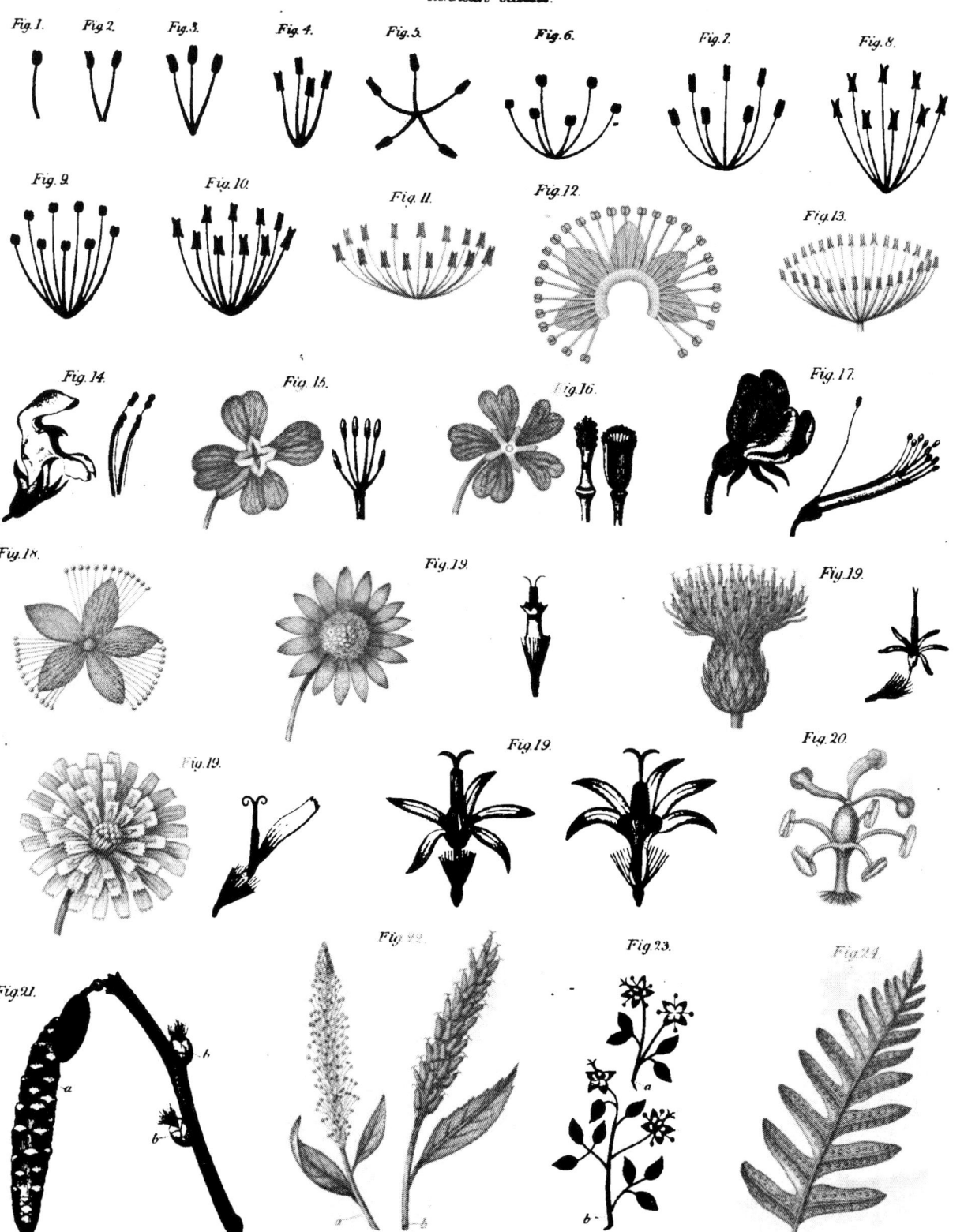

BOTANY. N.º V.
Linnean Classes.

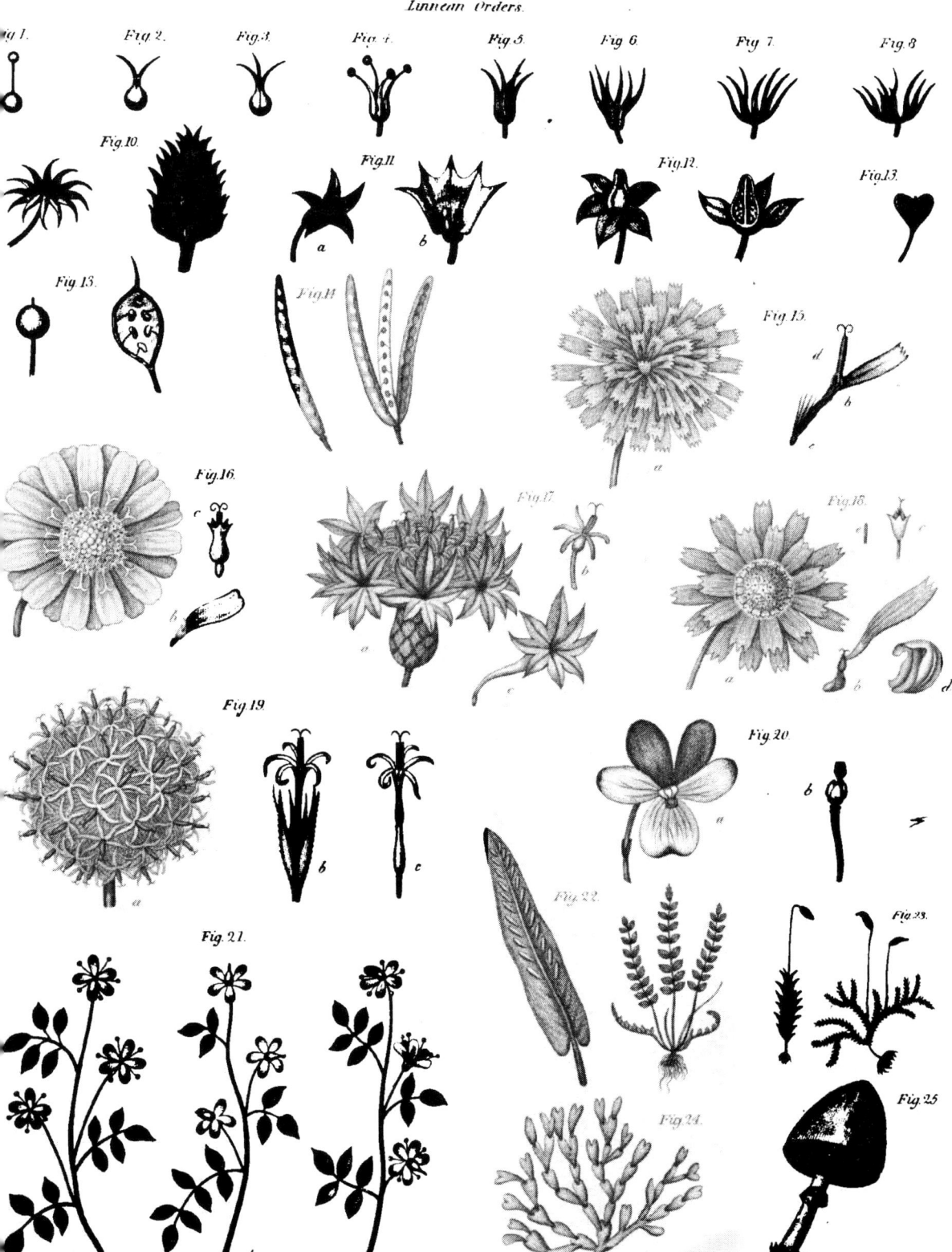

BOTANY. Nº VIII.

Linnean Classes & Orders.

Pl. 28.

BUILDING

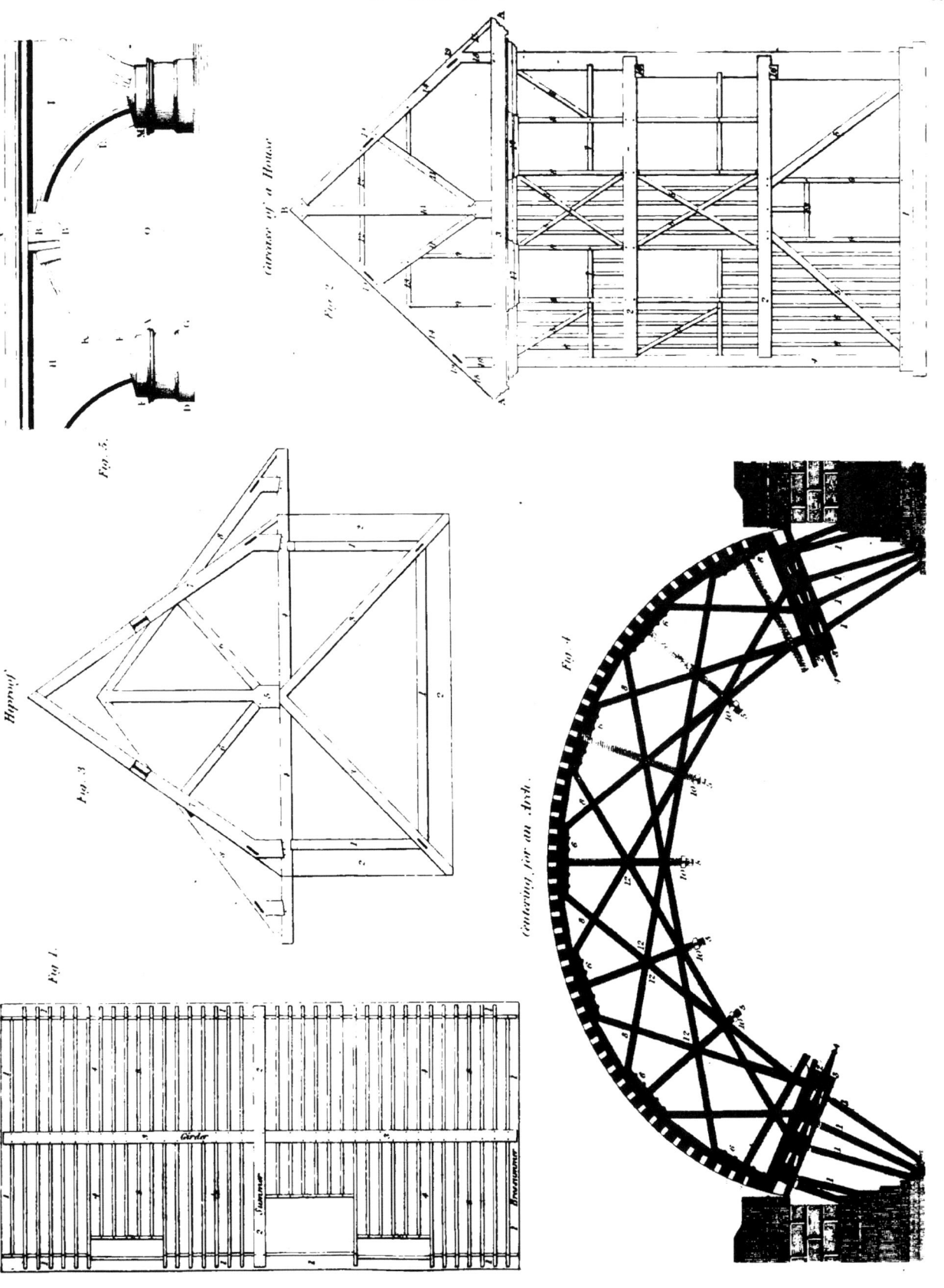

CHEMISTRY.
CHEMICAL APPARATUS.

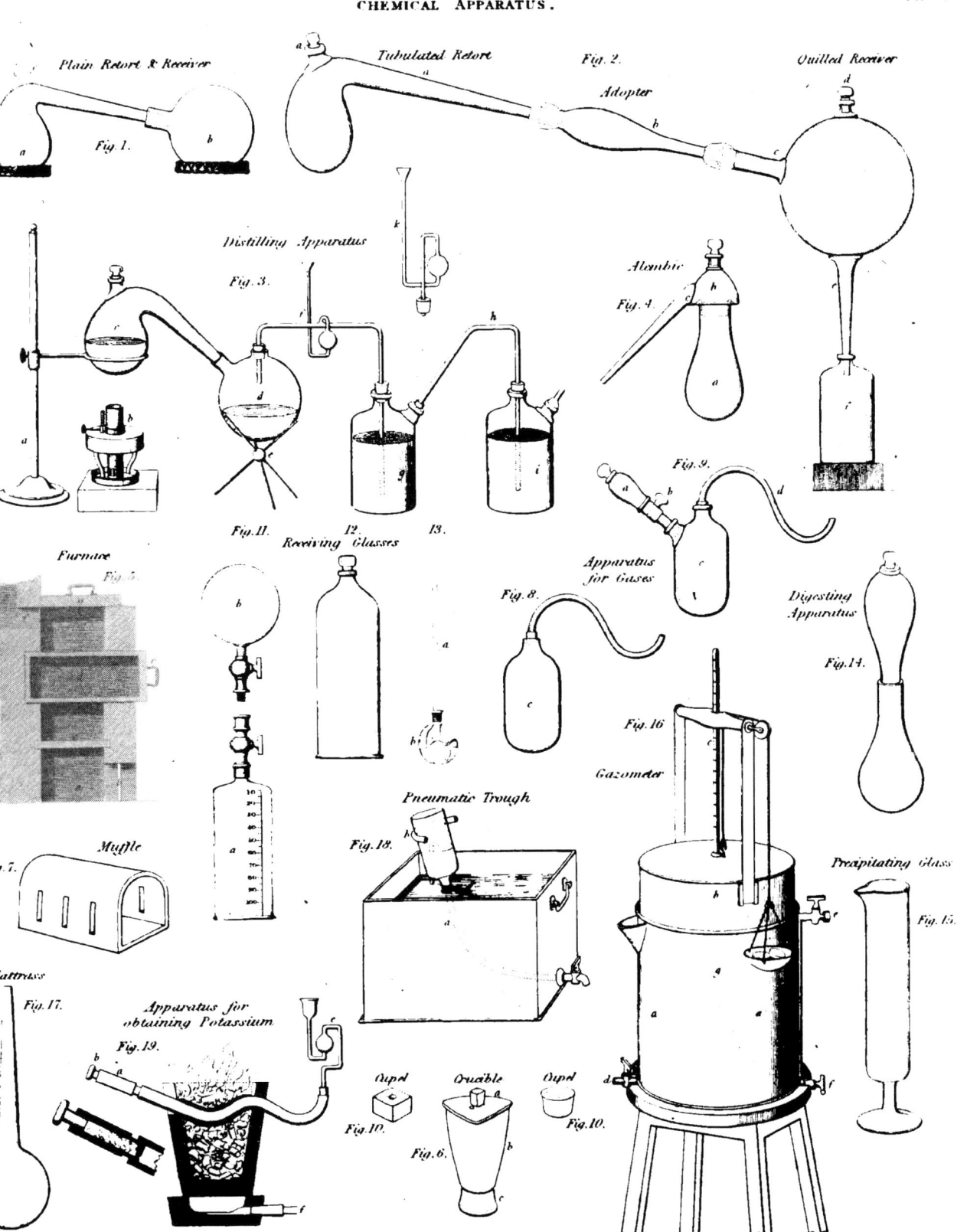

COINS Nº I.

Pl. 31.

BRITISH COINS

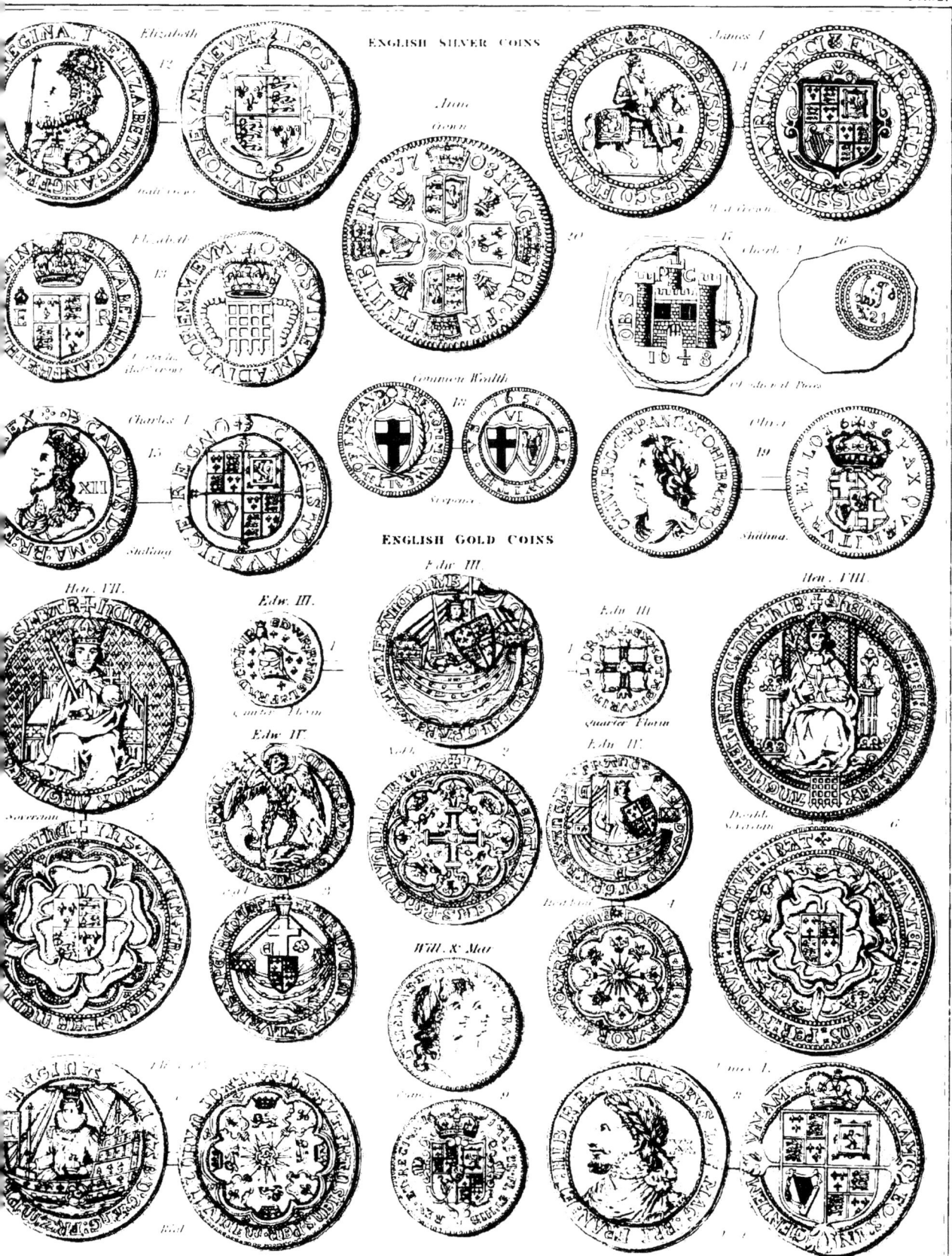

CONCHOLOGY.

Multivalves.
Bivalves.
Univalves.

ENTOMOLOGY, Nº 1.

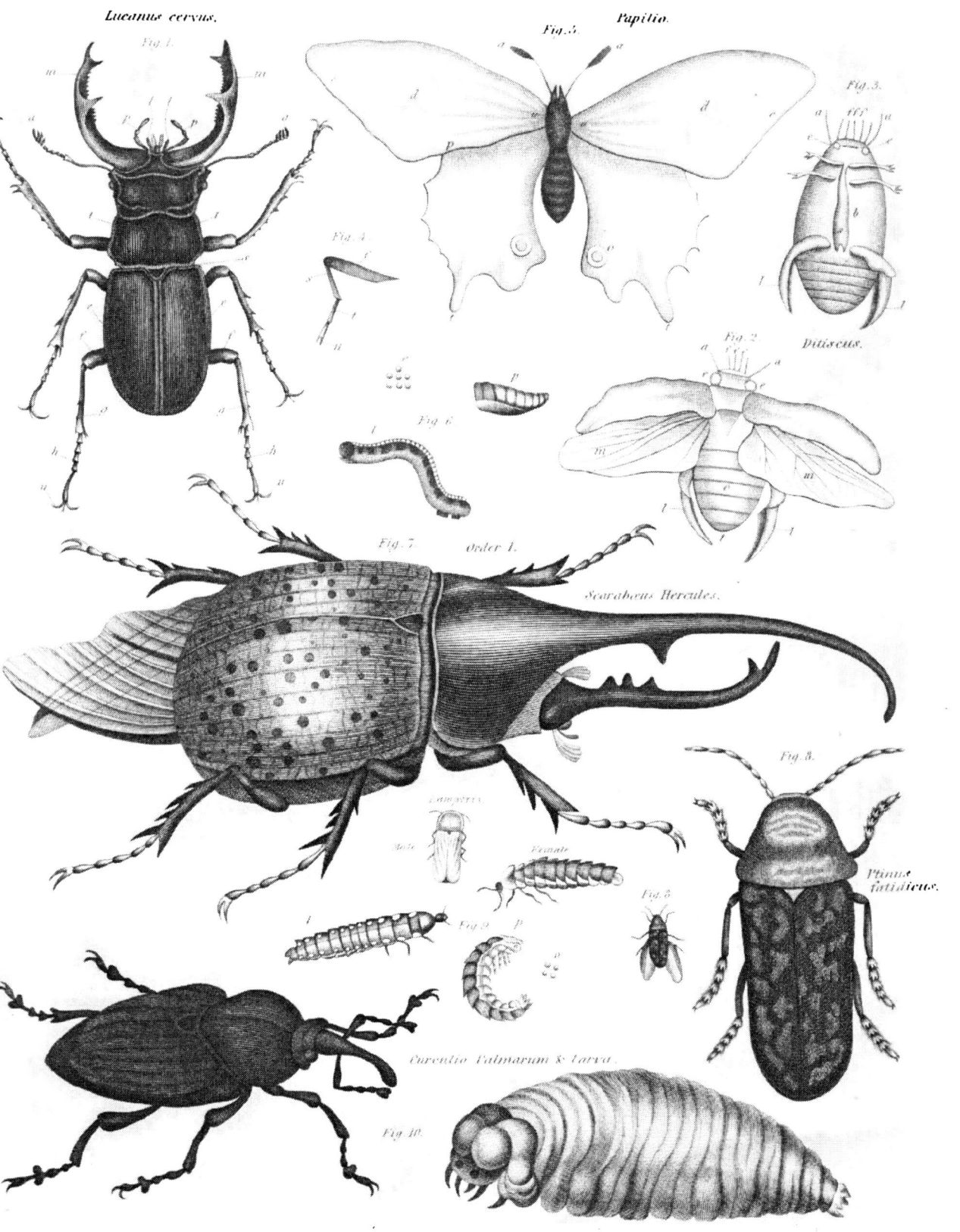

ENTOMOLOGY. N.º II.

FORTIFICATION

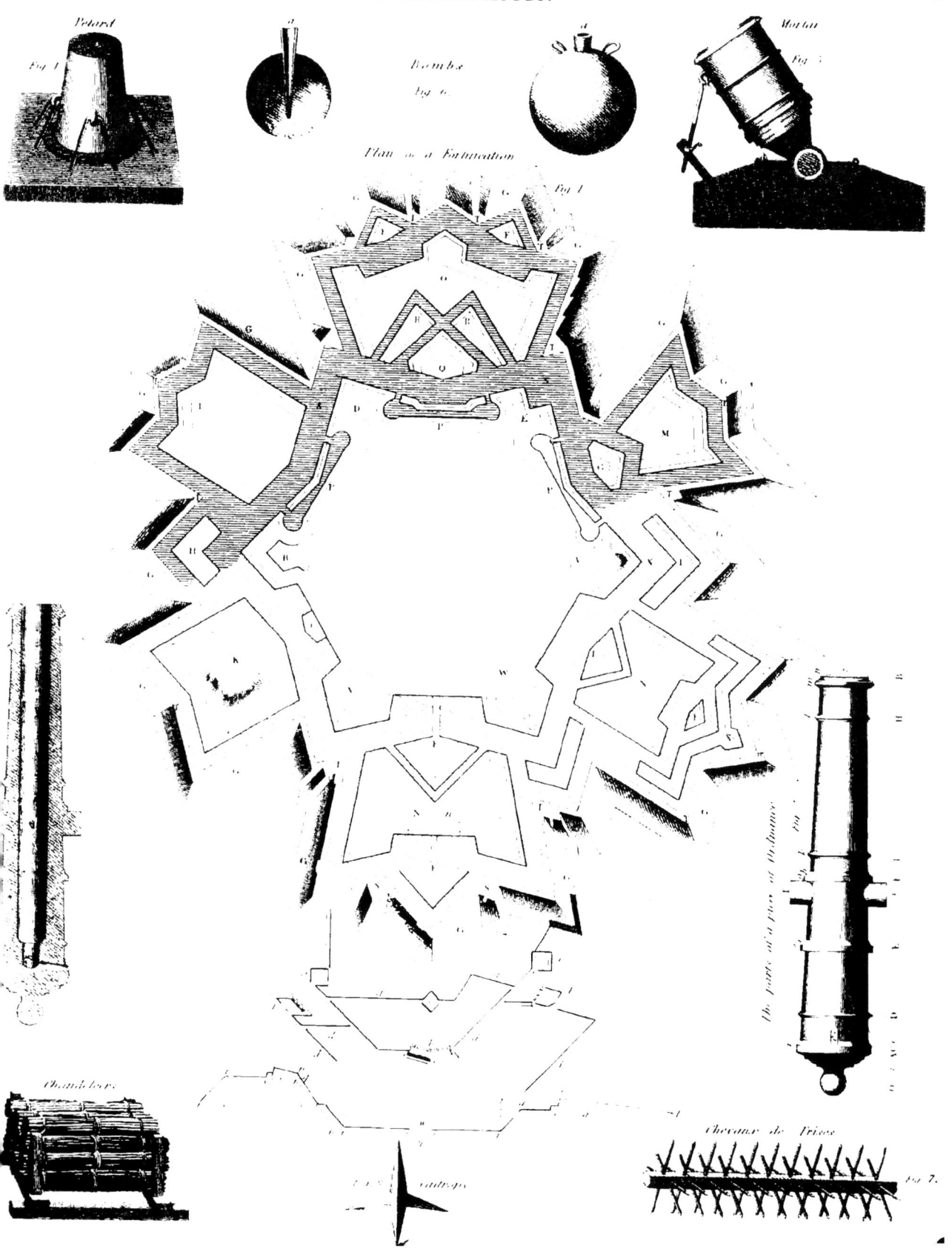

THE NEW YORK PUBLIC LIBRARY
REFERENCE DEPARTMENT

This book is under no circumstances to be taken from the Building

APR 8 - 1918